ROCK 'n' ROLL

GOLD RUSH

ROCK 'n' ROLL

GOLD RUSH

A Singles Un-cyclopedia

Maury Dean

Algora Publishing
New York

Library of Congress Cataloging-in-Publication Data

Dean, Maury.
  Rock and roll : Gold rush / by Maury Dean.
      p. cm.
Includes bibliographical references (p.   ) and index.
  ISBN 0-87586-208-X (alk. paper) — ISBN 0-87586-207-1 (pbk.: alk. paper)
  1. Rock music—History and criticism. I. Title: Gold rush. II. Title.

  ML3534.D42 2003
  781.66'09—dc21
                                    2003009634

Proofreader, Copy Editor — Molly Altizer
Text formatting — Mary Ann Still
Picture selection and layout — Jeremy Dean

TABLE of CONTENTS

"Hearing Elvis for the first time was like busting out of jail."

– Bob Dylan –

"If you remember the 60s, you weren't there."

– Rock & Roll Hall of Fame bumper sticker –

"If it's too loud, you're too old."

– Ted Nugent [of Amboy Dukes] –

"The function of Rock and Roll is to annoy parents."

– Bob Merlis, Record Executive –

"Not even boot camp is as tough as being in Rock and Roll."

– Patty Smith –

"Without Elvis, none of us could have made it."

– Buddy Holly, 1958 –

"Rock and Roll will be gone by June."

– Music trade magazine *Variety*, 1955 –

"I like Rock and Roll, and I don't like much else."

– John Lennon –

"We got into music to avoid a job, and get lots of girls."

– Paul McCartney –

Quotes above from video clips, New York Metropolitan Museum of Art,
Rock Hall of Fame Costume Collection, 1-8-2000 [Elvis's would-be 65th birthday]

"We all just want to be heard ..."

– Oprah Winfrey, inadvertently expressing the chief reasons for every Rock and Roll song,
Emmy Awards, NBC, 9-22-2002

Introduction

Many R&R texts abound. Most of them write about the groups, sketch out the eras, and try to bring you a quick peek at the Rock Revolution. What's different about *Gold Rush?* We zero in on the most important nugget in the music you love – the **single song.** We give you the facts – *Billboard* chart numbers, personnel, music analysis, geographical factoids – but more important, we strive to bring you the Heart and Soul of Rock and Roll. We also identify a few formulas for that magic hit record that your fledgling garage band seeks.

Gold Rush is designed for use as a college-level Rock and Roll History text, a Mass Media text, or a handy guide just to learn more about your favorite songs. More than a playlist, *Gold Rush* gives you the music, the personalities, and the stories behind all that glory that is Rock and Roll. There's a good chance that 38 of your Top 40 tunes are snugly harbored here in *Gold Rush*. And maxwellhunter@aol.com is looking forward to hearing from you about those other two tunes, as our next edition takes shape. Whether it's Vintage Country Rock, Heartland Rock, Motown or Philly Soul, Rap, Heavy or Light Metal, or Manitoban Polka Zydeco Chalypso Rock, all this stuff interconnects.

Gold Rush celebrates the great Rock and Roll hits of three centuries. We do **Foreground Music** here, searching from 1897 Yukon/Klondike/Alaska saloons to 1950s sock hops to this week's stadium concerts to find all the songs that have been important to Rock.

Though we love the top-notch albums and box-set compilations, we focus primarily upon the single solitary super song of the Rock Era and beyond, concentrating on the 1950s to the present. Our biggest criteria for including single songs are success, genius, romance, or just great throbbing rhythm or dynamic chord changes. We don't believe in chart segregation. The Motown chapter might feature a surprising Country tune, and the Country section might highlight some vintage Ray Charles Soul music.

We are fair to the entertainers, both the good and not-so-good – leaving the character assassinations to mean-spirited tabloids. We find the stars, try to make them live again, and explain their musical passions, their behind-the-scenes adventures, and the loves of their lives. We even throw in a few of our own shenanigans back in our Garage Band & Beyond days.

If we could cite only ONE major performer, this book would be dedicated to the inspiration, the life, and the music of Buddy Holly. As Michael Campbell and James Brody say (*Rock and Roll,* Schirmer, 1999), "Male teens may have wanted to be another Elvis, but they could put themselves in Buddy Holly's shoes more easily." Personally, I first heard Buddy's monster hit "That'll Be the Day" in July 1957, wafting over Lake Erie from the birthplace of the term 'Rock and Roll' (DJ Alan Freed, '52, Cleveland, Ohio). As soon as its mesmerizing *shuffle* beat captured our 14-year-old hearts, Rosemary Thorlaksson bought the Cricket-tune with its burgundy-labeled Brunswick 45 rpm platter. She brought "That'll Be the Day" and four other hits (like Jimmie Rodgers II's "Honeycomb") to a makeshift dance floor, a stardust romantic plateau that we 12 semi-cool new teenagers created atop her dad's boathouse (with a zillion-foot extension cord). Buddy's edgy lead vocal surfed our summer with power and promise. Just hearing Buddy Holly for the first time grew me up – almost instantly. The **Beatles** agreed. They named themselves after Holly's band – the **Crickets.**

Back in 1957, a single record was expensive – 99 cents. Albums cost $4.99. In those days, many kids couldn't afford many albums, so we bought singles. Today, kids can't afford $20 albums, and the Big Six record/CD companies don't make singles available – so downloading and Napster and MP-3 and CD burners arrived. Now rock stars get all the glory and very little, if any, royalties. No matter how long singles are jailed in expensive albums, the singles will escape, even at great cost, still becoming the songs we will love and cherish. The lockdown album system can't touch this . . .

Though you can't measure the success of a great song, we do anyhow, via the *Billboard* Hot 100 chart numbers that tell the objective sales and popularity facts; meanwhile, we tell you the song's unique story. Thanks to *Joel Whitburn's Record Research* team, which enabled us to give each song's first chart number – the HOT 100 peak position and the month of chart entry. We also use two other main chart number systems, also chronicled by Whitburn's expert family team: 1) What began in 1942 as the 'Harlem Hit Parade' and is now the *Rhythm and Blues (or R & B)* chart; and 2) The former 'Hillbilly Hit Parade,' now the *Country (or 'C')* charts [in the 50s, they were the Country & Western or C & W charts]. All the charts share the date of *first entry,* and the *top position* achieved. Our British/U.K. charts give *Melody Maker* magazine's peak position and date of peak position, unlike *Billboard's* date of first entry. *Gold Rush* also furnishes you with occasional information on other *Billboard* charts: Adult Contemporary, Airplay, Modern Rock, Latino, Jazz, or even Bluegrass, Gospel, or Classical charts.

Gold Rush makes no claim to be totally objective. We're not robots. We include occasional familiar Rock Classics which amazingly never hit the Singles charts on the HOT 100: George Thorogood & the [Delaware] Destroyers' "Move It on Over," the Ramones' "I Wanna Be Sedated," and the song chosen #1 EVER on many nostalgia surveys: Led Zeppelin's Celtic Renaissance crescendo masterpiece – "Stairway to Heaven." For these superlative songs, which bizarrely never crunched into the HOT 100, we must reach beyond our singles format.

Paul McCartney & Wings' #1(5) 1976 classic "Silly Love Songs" hints that there might not be any *silly* songs of love – ALL love songs are cherished somewhere. *Gold Rush agrees,* and whether it's Hard Rock, Easy Rock, Alt Rock, Art Rock, Rap Rock, or Rock Around the Clock, we'll probably Capitalize it, because this great stuff really matters to you, and to us.

Author Maury Dean has been teaching college-level Rock History Appreciation for over three decades. While earning his doctorate, he penned the first-ever Rock history book, *The Rock Revolution* – a tiny 160-page volume –in 1967, before most of the Rock and Roll story had unfolded. Here is the rest of the story – to date.

In 1957, when Danny & the Juniors followed up their #1(7) blockbuster "At the Hop" with #19 **"Rock and Roll Is Here to Stay,"** few dreamed just how prophetic that line would be. And indeed, what 1956 adults would never believe – that Rock and Roll would highlight the new millennium – has clearly come true.

Acknowledgements

First, I'd like to thank my wife Toni. Her support and her inspiration have been the guiding force of this project. My son Jeremy and his wife Kristen gave for encouragement and immense help with the photos, graphics, and scanning. Our younger daughter Rambha, too, was helpful on R&R areas, particularly the Macarena. Lauri Dean Barnes and her husband Larry have helped us see this project through, and I dedicate the book to grandson Maxwell, and our whole family.

Since our subject is great songs of the Rock Era and beyond, I'd like to thank all the super-stars, stars, and almost-made-it wannabes that *Gold Rush* celebrates.

Besides the back-page photo credits, I especially must thank *Rockin'50s* publisher, and Buddy Holly Memorial Society President, Bill Griggs of Lubbock, Texas, and my other long-time Buddy Pal, and BHMS Vice-President, George Nettleton, of Bellport, NY and Kansas City. Photo thanks, too, to Lo-Anne Rios Kong of Sony/Epic/Columbia Records' archives; and Howard Mandelbaum and his tremendous staff over at Photofest. Thanks also to Stuart Rock, Elizabeth DeLeonardo, and the Quick Print speedo printing team who made Quick work out of an endless opus; and of course to the Algora Publishing team for professional editing advice and book design and publishing expertise.

Mary Ann Still brought her graphics expertise, patience and organizational skills to solidify this rock and roll dream. Among helpful editors, I must thank Joyce Blum, Brooke Piper, Ari Wexler, and Paul Carty of Kendall/Hunt, and Don Gulbrandsen of *Goldmine* and Krause Publications.

Molly Altizer of Suffolk College deserves a round or three of applause, and Maria of the AV Department. So do my colleagues Craig Boyd, Ed Joyce, Gerry O'Connor, Sandra Sprows, and Michele Aquino. I remember, too, the sound advice given to me by my late colleagues and friends Charles Scheef and Paul Satzman – and I appreciate the input of so many of my colleagues at Suffolk College.

Thanks, too, to my old bandmates "Boogie' Bob Baldori and Danny Beaubien, and to Lewis Julian, Bill Metros and Jeff Baldori, and all the other individuals who have helped me make music, and to Jack and Devora Brown of Detroit's Fortune Records, and Ed McCoy, President of Detroit's Big Mack Records.

I'd like to thank Buddy Holly's Crickets, and especially Sonny Curtis for writing "The Real Buddy Holly Story," the first great antidote to the cosmic gloom of Don McLean's brilliant, brooding masterpiece "American Pie" (dedicated to Buddy's memory). Jeremy and I recently wrote the tune "American Sky" on a similar theme, available at *maxwellhunter@aol.com* [oops – in Rock and Roll, hype springs eternal]. Buddy Holly's mother encouraged me, in 1969, to write this book. Sorry, Mrs. Holly, it's a little late, but late sure beats never.

Mostly, I'd like to thank 99,999 other 'friends' – all the great single songs which have sparked our audio soundscape. They are enduring proof that the real gold of *Gold Rush* is plain old *love*.

Acknowledging all who have contributed to my effort in creating this book is even harder than cataloguing the cherished songs themselves. But the book is long, and life is short. My gratitude goes to my friends and relatives, colleagues past and present, and students too, too many to mention by name but treasured, like these songs, every single one.

About the Author

Maury Dean was lucky enough to hit his teenage years in Detroit just at the defining moment when Rock and Roll busted loose. At Michigan State, Dean sang and strummed for the Night Shift, which as the Woolies hit #95 with Delta Blues legend Bo Diddley's "Who Do You Love?"

Dean wrote the first Rock history book — *The Rock Revolution* (1966 — now in the Rock Hall of Fame) while in graduate school. His doctorate, from University of Michigan, was among the first to incorporate Popular Music with more traditional studies.

Dean had a short stint in 1966 as a Motown songwriter; for most of the lifetime that has sped by since then, he has been teaching the History of Rock and Roll at the college level.

He loves all kinds of Rock and Roll and refuses to choose sides.

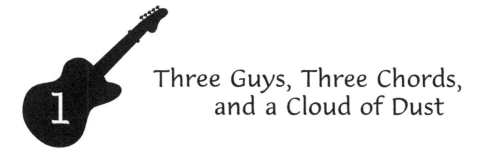

Three Guys, Three Chords, and a Cloud of Dust

Hot, sultry day. Mid-July. Your car air conditioner is on permanent vacation. The steamy pavement oozes frustration. You check out the dignified guy in the $22,000 dinky Sardinemobile (gray), and he's going bananas. Rhythmically pounding his little dashboard. Suit jacket flapping, fluttering, flying. He's into some groovy tune from the Mobile Goldie Yesteryear Vaults. Despite his A.C. at 68°, you hear him wailing through the driver's window:

"Baby, woo-hoo, baby, I really love you!"

He thinks he's alone.

With rock and roll no one is ever alone. It surges over the globe. Rock and Roll cascades in up-tempo majesty over all the world's airwaves, reeling in postmodern pandemonium…or time-warp classic chaos. Rock and Roll makes you happy, it makes you sad, it defines your life, it embraces your day.

Rock and Roll hugs you with its starswirl promises of evermore love. It teases you with false hopes of glory. It takes you away from humdrum flyswatters, cannibal card-chomping ATM's, home equity debtors' prison, grubby coffee grounds, catbarf, and National Bad Hair Day.

It will never leave you alone. You wouldn't want it to.

Rock and Roll did not begin in some Happy-Days Eden in the semi-fabulous fifties. In some ways, it has always been with us.

Rock and Roll's archetypal superstars from Elvis to Fats Domino to Jerry Lee Lewis to James Brown to the Everly Brothers did not emerge, fully created, from their own brand of harmonic and rhythmic genius – they honed their craft on the music of many mentors. African field hands hollering, congregations calling back to their preacher, electric-wizard cord-pluggers plugging chords, and accordion-wheezing Swiss yodelers all preceded the 50s flowering of the big new beat. Midcentury America produced a backwash of turbulent conditions that launched Rock and Roll:

1. Pop Standards' drummers seem to have all died – or at least surrendered to permanent coffee break. Melodic songs like Rosemary Clooney's (#1[6], 7-54) "Hey There" staggered along beatless, unanchored by the rhythmic pulse that breathes life into music. American rebellion always steps in to fill such a vacuum.

2. In *Rebel Without a Cause*, heartland actor **James Dean** defined the teenager. Despite a cool Jazz, rock-less soundtrack, you felt the big beat looming on the horizon; no musical generation gap would never be so stark as it was for our 50s teenybopper generation and our easybeat 30s parents.

3. The Gibson, Gretsch, and Fender guitar companies, already spearheading bands via country ('Hillbilly') music like Roy Acuff's (#12, 12-38) "Wabash Cannonball," were turning to basement guitar gurus like **Les Paul**. Paul pioneered double-tracking (overdubbing): you can mix a voice over a voice or guitar or drums, and then blend them for a superb sound. Melded with his wife Mary Ford's velvet contralto, the Les Paul sound revolutionized the key position of the solid-body electric guitar, which Les Paul invented for Leo Fender. LES PAUL paved the way for a swoon of Eric Claptons and Jimi Hendrixes and Eddie Van Halens and Stevie Ray Vaughans.

4. Record players went portable. Even transistorized. You could twiddle a stack of hot 45 wax on your thumb, and blast a beach-blanket-bingo dance party in the warm California sun. No more clumsy 78s. Your Rock and Roll could follow you anywhere, even to the backseat of a '55 Chevy.

5. The 1950s brought us Dr. Martin Luther King Jr., the Cold War, Rock and Roll, and TV. Wow, talk about culture shock. Like true practical American pragmatists, we tackled these reality sandwiches one by one: we integrated the lunch counters; we beat the Russians to Memphis and Nashville; we launched an amazing All-American musical genre that was distinctively ours; we sculpted and crafted and preened our manifold musical styles, like Rockabilly and Soul and Delta Blues and Surf Rock and Streetcorner and Soft Rock and Philly Pop; and we became a nation of TV buffs, turning over AM radio to a host of platter-pushers like DJ **Alan Freed**, who coined the term 'Rock and Roll' on his Cleveland Moondawgie show in 1952. Television added faces to the great voices we heard on AM radio – pre-*MTV* 'Rock Videos" from *Your Hit Parade*, Dick Clark's *American Bandstand*, and Ricky Nelson on *Ozzie and Harriet.*

6. People got too much money. We dumped the depression, limped home from John Wayne's biggest war, and plunked down a grand on our own suburban home to be filled with kids, joy, love, baseball, and Rock and Roll records. In 1955, you could buy the Platters' single "The Great Pretender" (#1, 12-55) for 99 cents, and **Elvis**, the album, would set you back $4.99. By my 1961 high school graduation, I had amassed a king's collection of over forty-five 45's, and over seven (wow) albums. People heard their single favorites on AM radio, and played them a thousand times.

So WOOMP, there it was.

No-beat music created a vacuum and R&R thundered in. James Dean invented teenagerism, and we glommed our wallets to buy Gibson guitars and records. With a hit record, you didn't need to be a 6'4", 220# varsity football hero to get with the girl; all you needed were a twang, a holler, and a dream. Suddenly, Rock and Roll was talkin' 'bout our generation.

Though Rock and Roll may amplify your own religion, hopefully it will never become one. But it does have a trinity.

Elvis, **Buddy**, and **Chuck**. The Big Three. The Triumvirate of Troubadors. Were it not for the musical contributions of these 50s conquistadores of Rock and Roll, we might all be awash in a grim gray sea of elevator Muzak.

Rock and Roll's formative years, of course, zinged and twanged with the tremendous tones of other major artists: Little Richard, Eddie Cochran, LaVern Baker, Clyde McPhatter and the Drifters, Hank Ballard & Midnighters, Bill Haley & Comets, Gene Vincent, and Buddy Knox & Rhythm Orchids. If you had to pick three major pioneers, however, to tie it all together, you'd have to choose **Elvis Presley**, **Buddy Holly**, and **Chuck Berry**.

Elvis Presley

Elvis – the most famous and successful singer of all-time. Born in a two-room shotgun shack in Tupelo, Mississippi, Elvis (1-8-35 – 8-16-77) rose from lower-middle class anonymity to become the world's most identifiable icon with just one name. Indeed, out beyond the icon stage is the only more identifiable first name: Jesus. Elvis was discovered by record producer Sam Phillips at Sun Records on Memphis's Union Boulevard (of skyrocket-stardom dreams). As a 19-year-old trucker for Crown Electric, the Humes High grad with princely pompadour rocked to fame, fortune, and "That's All Right" [Mama] in April 1954. Sam and his friend, disc jockey Dewey Phillips, realized that if you "give me a white kid with a flair for rhythm and blues, I can make a million dollars." Had Sam waited a tad longer, he might've. Young Elvis just got too hot, too soon.

After a string of Country-chart crunchers like "Mystery Train" (#11, 12-55 Country [C]), "I Forgot to Remember to Forget," and dynamite debut charter "Baby, Let's Play House (#5, 7-55 C), Elvis's contract was swapped to RCA Victor for $35,000 – a deal which compares to buying Alaska for $7,200,000 or Manhattan Island for $24 worth of beads and baubles and bangles.

It didn't take very long. Hoyt Axton's mom Mae had written an eerie lachrymose ditty about a sad limbo, where lovers dwell: "Heartbreak Hotel" (#1 [8], 3-56, but #1 [17] Country charts and even #3 R&B). It was Elvis's first of 18 #1 songs on the big Top or Hot 100 chart in *Billboard*.

Nobody goes it alone.

Our favorite Rock stumper? "Which Gospel group sold a billion records?"

The semi-sneaky answer surfaces – the **Jordanaires**, Elvis's back-up group. Elvis's fine lead guitarist **Scotty Moore** made the Rock and Roll Hall of Fame (Cleveland) in 1999 – though it was too late for his super stand-up bassist **Bill Black** (1926-65). Bill's 'slap bass' on the big upright bull fiddle complements Elvis/Sam's echo-chamber expertise. Drummer D.J. Fontana was among the very first drummers to play country music, though Bob Wills' Western Swing Band, the Texas Playboys, featured percussion. With his innovative band, and his rock-of-ages-solid vocal quartet, named for the Jordan River in the Holy Land, Elvis sought the crown as the King of Rock and Roll, and for many years he reigned.

*"Buddy Holly didn't LOOK dangerous –
but his music was VERY dangerous."*
Erik Lund, Punk/Rockabilly musician, 2001.

Even in the long-time aftermath of the Day that the Music supposedly died, **Buddy Holly** may still be the best kept musical secret in America. Buddy's talent was by far the most versatile. Fifteen years before the term 'Singer-Songwriter' hit the R&R books, Buddy penned a cornucopia of Rock Classics and sang Screaming Blues or Soft Rock with equal amazing dexterity. Buddy Holly never met a musical genre he didn't like. With his downswoop rhythm guitar blur, and a heavenly host of Holly hiccups, the lean Texan could twist the Texas tornadoes that lambasted hometown Lubbock – and fling them back to Oz. Beyond his Clark Kent specs and super smile, Buddy and his Crickets thundered an American rhythm which dashed the departing destinies of no-beat Yester-music.

Buddy was the youngest kid among brothers Larry and Travis and sister Pat. Born September 7, 1936 to Ella and Lawrence Holley, Buddy flirted with piano and violin before discovering his real love, the guitar. Co-hosting a radio show on KDAV Lubbock – first-ever all country radio station – at the tender age of 15, Buddy and pal Bob Montgomery cut some hillbilly tracks. It came down to a Nashville recording contract with Decca in 1956. By now, all the biggee labels were searching for a new Elvis. Bob was amicably bumped from the slate, and Buddy went solo. Owen Bradley's Nashville barn, however, got Buddy a mini-hit (18,000 copies for "Blue Days, Black Nights"), but his "That'll Be the Day" rough draft labored over a too-high key of 'C' and a dim date with temporary obscurity. Discouraged, Buddy beat it back to Lubbock on the high dusty Texas panhandle plains.

Enter the **Crickets**. Like piano boogie-meister **Johnnie Johnson**, who tickled ivories all through Chuck Berry's escapades, Buddy's drummer **Jerry Allison** was the hidden superstar in this rock and roll combo: friendly, fun-loving, and simply the best American drummer in the history of rock and roll. *Rolling Stone*'s 1977 poll rated **Keith Moon** of the **Who** #1, **John Bonham** of **Led Zeppelin** #2, and in third place the only one alive in 2002+ – Jerry Allison, Cricket and sole Yankee. No one can ever forget Jerry Allison's famous 16th note paradiddle drum blur in Buddy's "Peggy Sue" (#3, 10-57). Neither will Jerry – he married the real Peggy Sue in the song. Bassman **Joe B. Mauldin** rounds out the Crickets' super sound. Buttressed in 1957 by Niki Sullivan on rhythm guitar, the group dwindled to just three in 1958 and split in late '58 over Buddy's marriage to pretty Maria Elena Santiago of New York and Puerto Rico. Super baritone singer/guitarist/banjoist **Sonny Curtis** anchored the Cricket countdown, playing lead for Buddy at the Nashville session, and becoming an integral part of the long-term band after the aftermath. Only three Crickets, however, bedazzled Australia and England with the loudest three-guy band in the 1958 universe. And three major invading bands would have some later link to the Crickets: the **Hollies** (obvious borrowing of name, and third-biggest Brit group in the 60s); the **Rolling Stones**, whose first hit was Buddy's "Not Fade Away"; they took their name from **Muddy Waters** (1950 "Rolling Stone," and #5, '55 R & B "Mannish Boy"), and Buddy's Ben Franklin 'rollin' stone gathers no moss' line in "Early in the Mornin'" (#32 for Buddy in 1958); and also the **Beatles**, who named themselves after the **Crickets**.

Buddy Holly (top), and Crickets'
Jerry Allison (L) and Joe B. Mauldin (R)

Besides singing, writing, and doing his hits on the **Ed Sullivan**, **Steve Allen**, **Arthur Murray**, and *American Bandstand* shows, Buddy Holly blanketed all phases of the business. He played a mean lead guitar behind those horn-rimmed glasses, and he helped producers Norman and Vi Petty of Clovis, New Mexico, sculpt classy new innovations in Rock and Roll. Buddy and Norman experimented, via Dick Jacobs' studio in Manhattan, with strings – to pioneer the orchestral rock of the later Moody Blues or Emerson, Lake, and Palmer. In addition, Holly did his own hyping at first. Hype is a term which means to plug or push a record. Hyping is generally the bailiwick of the A & R (Artists & Repertoire) folk who descend upon disc jockeys and program direc-

tors at radio stations. Buddy Holly was not averse to stocking the Crickets' tunes on local jukeboxes, hitting the local stations for airplay, and calling in muffled requests for his own records (you know, like all of us bands have done). With his likable personality, his polite demeanor, and his winning smile, Holly was a tremendous salesman of song. Like Richie Cunningham (Ronny Howard) of *Happy Days* fame, Buddy Holly was one well-liked guy. DJ's could relate to Buddy. He was like a nice kid from your woodshop class or cross-country team. Buddy Holly, you knew, was at the top by dint of his multiple musical talents.

When Buddy Holly, **Ritchie Valens**, and the Big Bopper ascended to their destiny on February 3, 1959, it cut the heart out of America's innocence and adolescent naiveté. We all had to grow up, fast.

Chuck Berry helped. He was cool. He wrote songs about hoppin' and boppin' down at the high school shindig, and dancin' on *Bandstand*, and sloshing down malts while you ogled the swirling poodle skirts and rosy cheeks of Sweet Little Sixteen and her dazzling cheerleader pals. Yep. Chuck Berry was the poet of Rock and Roll. His left hand, too, poeticized the emerging world of lead guitar. Wordman and extraordinary musician, Berry was born (perhaps) 10-18-26. His middle-class St. Louis upbringing caused him, via his musical mentors, to create an almost-Rockabilly rock style out of a cradle of Chicago Blues and New Orleans Soul.

Sleek, suave, and cool, Chuck Berry fashioned stompin' classics which celebrated James Dean's teenagerism. Berry epitomized the crossover style (one tune blankets many genres of rock popularity). His first hit was "Maybellene"; it was not only originally named "Ida Red," but was named for a cow. The song juggled between #1 on the Rhythm n' Blues (R & B) chart and #5 on the mainstream pop-rock charts. Chuck's speedo lead guitar riff in "Sweet Little Sixteen" (#2, 2-58) was nearly xeroxed, as was the tune, for the Beach Boys' surf anthem "Surfin' U.S.A." (#3, 3-63). Throughout Chuck Berry's 50s romp, he celebrates the American experience: neon nightscapes, rock and roll romance, speed-guitar thunder, hot dogs, confetti, and skyscrapers.

World-class showman, too, Chuck. Armed with his secret weapon dusting the mile-a-minute ivories – Johnnie Johnson – Chuck bedazzled and enchanted the gaga gala teenybopper throngs with his behind-his-back lead riffs and his bizarre supercool Duckwalk. The poetic landscape of Mid-American master blaster Berry throbs to his unique verbal concoctions: 'Coolerators' stuffed with fizzy ginger ale and TV dinners; sizzling burgers on smoky grilles; fuse-blowing jukeboxes; rags-to-riches ever-green dreams; making out despite squeezy seatbelts; and white-line fever of '55 fan-tailed Caddies sucking up the raw hot sundown American night.

Elvis and Buddy and Berry, like the executive-legislative-judicial branches of the U.S. democracy, fill in any gaps in each Rock and Roll area. They each produce a distinctively American contribution to the sound track of human history. **Elvis** turned over his songwriting to Tin Pan Alley Afro-American songster **Otis Blackwell** (1931-2002), whereas **Buddy** and **Chuck** wrote most of their own music. Chuck's musical versatility was complemented by Buddy's uncanny vocal leaps from hard traditional Rockabilly to dreamy ballads, hiccuping vocal experimentations, and thunderdrum teenage laments. Chuck's dynamic Roll-Over-Beethoven poetry could paint the pulsating canvas of America in the 50s for a world to enjoy today – a world to whom *Baywatch*, a movie-star bikini-bunny TV show, is America. Without Chuck Berry, the whole surf scene would be cultish and perhaps ignored. If Elvis was too manipulated by manager Colonel Tom Parker, Chuck carted his band and cash wad around on his own. Buddy Holly was the first do-it-yourself teenage idol via his genius at music and sincere nice-guy salesmanship.

Buddy Holly is the favorite singer of President George W. Bush, and Vice-President Al Gore (1992-2000) is a big fan, too, of the modest Texan legend [*USA Today*, 1-19-01].

For one brief-candle year and beyond, October 1957-February 1959, Elvis, Buddy and Chuck strode the stages of the world. Their musical destinies may be forever allied.

Everybody knows that **Elvis, Buddy** and **Chuck** were not the first to rock and roll; they simply anchored, with their three timeless styles, the main foundation of the most important musical movement in history.

Your favorites will be here too. If you're deeply into the 50s, you'll discover Dion's Belmonts, Mr. Versatility Bobby Darin, those blue-eyed brothers

Everly with the cherubic Scotch-Irish mountain tenors, saucy Brenda Lee, or curvaceously-crooning Connie Francis; you'll revel in the down-home Delta and uptown blues of Jimmy Reed, Muddy Waters, John Lee Hooker, and others who launched Chuck Berry at Chicago's Chess Records. You'll check out the Elvis echoers, from first punk-rocker tenor Gene Vincent and quaking-suede blue Rockabilly Carl Perkins to Canadian-Italian rustbelt rocker Jack (Scafone) Scott. You'll learn of the hyped Philly Bandstand teenage-idol lads like Bobby Rydell and Chubby Checker and Fabian, and you'll rock and roll with the more secret superstars: New Orleans' Jimmy Clanton, Texan Buddy Knox and the Rhythm Orchids, Ronnie Hawkins and Hawks, country balladeer Conway Twitty, the amazing female Rockabilly Wanda Jackson, and Clarence 'Frogman' Henry.

If you're a sixties or Brit buff, you'll trace the R & R connections between the Beatles and Buddy and Chuck and Little Richard; the Rolling Stones and Eric Clapton's debt to the American bluesmasters and Jerry Lee Lewis; the Morrison-Joplin-Hendrix connection to writer **Jack Kerouac** and the Beat Generation of 50s coffee houses, plus their musical mentors Elvis and country balladeer **Marty Robbins**, of "White Sport Coat" and pink carnation fame (#2, 4-57). Marty accidently discovered Heavy Metal, via the fuzz-tone bass and feedback guitar techniques in a long-gone recording session ("Don't Worry", #3, 1-61). Marty's amp tube blew up, and he chose not to replace it but leave it in the weird new extraterrestrial sound. All music is interconnected. Sometimes that great 'new' record is just a nifty hodge-podge of the rags and tatters and scraps of Classic Rock.

Rock and Roll can be either a solitary or a shared experience. You may prefer the solo sounds of Beach Boy Brian Wilson's "In My Room" (#23, 11-63) or the rafter-raising gusto of "At The Hop" (Danny Rapp and the Juniors, #1[7], 1957 – first 'Rapp' song?).

Rock throbs on the backbeat, usually accenting the second and fourth beats of the 4/4 songs. All you need are drums, bass, guitar, and a dream.

Gold was struck up on the Klondike and Yukon Rivers in Canada's arctic Yukon territory in 1897. Gold Fever marshalled millions of Gold Rushers to conquer the treacherous Chilkoot Pass over the blue icy mountains northeast of Skagway, Alaska, in their quest for fortune and fame. On the heels of this Gold Rush pandemonium, a little army of Ragtime piano players packed up their bowler hats and suspenders, and pounded the seething ivory keys. Into a new century, a new beat was born.

Somewhere in deep Delta Louisiana, lost among the evergreens bearded with Spanish moss, a little cool dude twanged his dime-store guitar. From a backwoods cabin swathed in mud and dreams, he dragged his treasure down by the railroad tracks. He brandished Boogie Blues and Vintage Soul, serenading with his Rock and Roll Rhapsody of the American Dream. His name? **Chuck Berry**'s **"Johnny B. Goode."**

Chuck Berry

Rocket riffs and marquee destiny.

Chasing a dream. Rock and Roll rainbows streamed to lost leprechaun gold.

Three chords and a cloud of dust.

HOW TO USE *GOLD RUSH*

The System . . . is simple:

R & B = Rhythm & Blues Chart
C = Country Chart

We use *Billboard* chart numbers in *Gold Rush* in three major categories: 1) the HOT 100; 2) Rhythm & Blues charts [designated as "R & B"] and 3) Country charts, designated as "C." We follow the high charting standards instituted by **JOEL WHITBURN** in their Record Research books like *Top Pop Singles* -- the most comprehensive such information in the world. For songs previous to 1955, the 'Rock Era,' we refer to either the R & B, the Country, or the *Pop Memories* top 30 or so -- chronicled by Joel Whitburn, **Kim Bloxdorf**, Frances Whitburn, Jeanne Olynick, Bill Hathaway, Paul Haney, and the rest of the Record Research team. We occasionally refer to hits on the Classical or Adult Contemporary Charts from *Billboard*. For United Kingdom information, we use the charts from *Melody Maker*, and the acronym "U.K."

Example?

"Blue Suede Shoes" – Carl Perkins, #2(4), 3-56; #2(4), R & B; #1(3), 2-56 C; #10, 5-56 U.K.

Rockabilly idol Carl Perkins sang the song "Blue Suede Shoes." It was #2 for four (4) consecutive weeks, and it entered the top 100 chart in 3-56, or the third month of 1956 – March. "Blue Suede Shoes" also hit #2 for four weeks on the Rhythm & Blues charts with the same entry date. It entered the Country chart a month earlier, and crossed over. Then it hit #1 for three (3) weeks on the Country charts. It peaked at #10 in May 1956 in Great Britain.

Gold Rush, due to providential poetic license, is apt to capitalize names of types of music frequently, like Rock and Roll, Jazz, Blues, or Old Wave North Dakota Surf Rock Bop-Hop.

And AL? "Al." = Album. We *italicize* albums; singles are in "quotes."

Stardust Yesteryear
Pioneers

Did Rock and Roll really begin in Alaska? Did the bold, brazen beat cascade out of the Gold Rush honkytonks like the Red Dog Saloon in Juneau, Alaska, and the Riverboat Casino Honkytonk in Dawson, way up in the midnight-sun Yukon? One thing's certain – you can call Rock and Roll a musical phenomenon of the 90s: the **18**90s. When the Jack Londons and Robert Services heard their call of the wild, and tromped north to Alaska stoned on gold fever, they yokked and yakked it up in the raucous and ribald saloons of redlight tundra. Their music? RAGTIME.

On floors bespangled with peanut shells, gartered gals strutted under the arctic moon. The Malamute Saloon in Alaska's Anchorage (a two-bit hamlet in 1899) hosted a bold new breed of piano player. He played fast and furious music, booming with ragtag rhythm. His left hand thumped a tattoo of something new, chords and swing bass. When my wife Toni and I did my R & R sabbatical to Graceland and Motown and the Holly statue in Lubbock, Texas's Tornado Alley, we had no idea the tempest would swirl us so far north. I recalled Johnny Horton's "North to Alaska" (#4, 9-60, #1 C). The great northern wilderness first heated up the big beat.

Thanks to my uncle, Lowndes (Lou) Maury (1911-75), who banged out dynamite Ragtime piano in the saloons and speakeasies and blind pigs (illegal bars) of Prohibition Butte, Montana, in 1926, I had some inkling of the Birth of Rock and Roll. My uncle was a serious musician who had classical symphonies recorded. Uncle Lou also did movie scores (even Mr. Magoo cartoons) when he moved to Hollywood. He really loved Rock when David Clayton-Thomas of Blood, Sweat, and Tears convinced him it could blend with great Jazz. When I was nine, I watched my California uncle swing that rampaging left hand blazingly across the deep keys,

rocking a raunchy rhythm that rolled all the way back to the century-turning razzmatazz of Scott Joplin and **Eubie Blake**.

Bing Crosby, #1 singer from 1900-1950.

Biographers Rudi Blesh and Harriet Janis cite Blake as the 'patriarch of Harlem stride ragtime.' You might remember Eubie. Born in 1883, this African-American piano dynamo lived 100 years and five days. He trumped an entire century, like songwriter's songwriter, **Irving Berlin** (1888-1989, 101), whose "White Christmas" of 1942 once outsold everything, ever. And, alas, **Bing Crosby's** Christmas carol is not even Rock and Roll. Bing's #19, 8-41 "You Are My Sunshine" (#23 by cowboy Gene Autry) was written by an EVEN OLDER songwriter than either Eubie Blake or Irving Berlin:

Governor Jimmie Davis (1899-2000), whose life straddled three centuries. Rock and Roll, too, roared past Millennium III into its THIRD CENTURY.

Bronx buffs and Bomber fans to the contrary, it was not beloved Mickey Mantle – but EUBIE BLAKE – who first cornered this cute comment: "If I know'd I was gonna live so long, I woulda took better care of myself…" While speaking, Eubie smiled at the curly swirls of his cigarette smoke, as pressfolks asked the 98-year-old ragtimer about his secrets of health and longevity.

Ragtime thrives on syncopation (alla zoppa in Italian, for 'lame' or 'limping'). Ragtime romps along on these misplaced or delayed accents. Piano ragtime, says Blesh, was developed from Afro-American melodies and from the "syncopation of the plantation banjos" (a distinctively American instrument). Banjos almost found their way into Rock and Roll via folk purists like Weavers' Pete Seeger (Rock Hall inductee, 1996), folk stars the **Kingston Trio**, or the Brothers Four. By the time Folk-Rock blossomed, banjos had plunked away on down the dusty road (except on a few classics like **Neil Young**'s #1, '72 "Old Man").

Ragtime got birthed in Sedalia, Missouri, where the gaslight glow suffused its romantic reverie on the roseate cheeks of the evening ladies and their sundown gamblers and high rollers and studs, and yok-it-up party people seeking a 'rock and roll' in the hay or featherbed. Rock and Ragtime didn't do pedigrees. They were street-wise blue-collar rhythmic styles.

Eubie Blake composed piano roll rags (for player pianos, the first machine to put the working musician out of business) including the #1, 1924 "Charleston." In the Alaska/Yukon Gold Rush, Texarkana, Texas's **Scott Joplin** was pushing thirty. Dapper and serious, Joplin embarked on his Ragtime career in 1896; nearly two years went by before anyone ever really named this new music.

Many other names spark the 1899 Ragtime gaslight glow: Arthur Marshall, **Buddy Bolden,** Fred S. Stone, Scott Hayden, and charismatic comedian of the Lower East Side and Coney Island a few years later, piano man **Jimmy Durante**.

If you're looking for the first Rock and Roll song to anchor your list, you may select Scott Joplin's "Maple Leaf Rag."

"Maple Leaf Rag" – U.S. Marine Band, #2 (1), 3-1907. This tune so predates modern Rock and Roll that too many music fans have forgotten it – nor may we linger over the lyrics. There aren't any. It's a straight-up Tempo di marcia (marching pace) instrumental in the key of "Ab". It has not yet been blessed with the ease of chords, for Jazz Rock improvisors. Joplin sports an octave-straddling bass line. His lightning right hand dusts the 16th-note octave mini-chords. Most music fans are familiar with Marvin Hamlisch's 1974 #3 rendition of Joplin's 1902 classic, "The Entertainer," a Ragtime instrumental from Paul Newman and Robert Redford's film *The Sting* [NOT Billy Joel's #34, 11-74 vocal].

Chuck Berry's St. Louis, midway on the muddy Mississippi, bisects America. The 1904 St. Louis World's Fair brought us hit records like **Billy Murray**'s #1(9), 7-1904 "Meet Me in St. Louie, Louie," which rollicked a bit, but chose the traditional Waltz form in 3/4 time, a largely unrockable beat. Here at the fair, Gibson Girls with whalebone bustles and bouffant hairdos rocked to another new beat on the American musical horizon.

Though 3/4 is unrockable, don't bet the ranch against 2/4 time. **John Philip Sousa**, Portuguese-American violinist, had had enough of symphonies and his violin. It was time to take the show on the road with a big brass band (and murdelize the silence). Born in 1854 in our nation's capital, Sousa led the U. S. Marine Corps Band from 1880-92, and he soon blasted out, on vigorous tours, songs like #3, 4-1902 "Semper Fidelis," the Marine Corps Hymn written in 1890 for President Chester P. Arthur (think humungous sideburns lost in a monstrous Fu Manchu moustache). Sousa's 2/4 thunderbeat marches almost rocked!

Modern-day rock combos grubbing for gigs might well consider John Philip Sousa. Somehow, he managed to pay (well) **64** different traveling musicians. Besides the standard bandsmen galumphing around with saxes and trumpets and trombones, Sousa featured a reed crew of oboes, bassoons, and of course clarinets. Among the brassier brass, Sousa embarked on such exotic items as euphoniums, flügelhorns, and, naturally, his new faux tuba, the Sousaphone. Blesh points out Sousa's cakewalk syncopation. No egghead snob, Sousa gladly and pragmatically featured many of the new musical styles as the century dawned, including Ragtime and its wild new kid, Jazz.

Ragtime, like wildire, spread fast and furiously. It is our first hack at Rock and Roll. Without the boogie beat of Joplin's bass octaves, **Antoine "Fats" Domino** might never have gone to "Blueberry Hill" (#2, '56). Elvis's "Hound Dog" might have lullabied itself to sleep as a sweet, syrupy waltz.

If you backtrack to the pre-bop pre-boogie 19th century, you'll find a lot of sweet ballads. Few Rock. Among the prettiest melodists of our era are Lennon-McCartney ("Yesterday," "The Long and Winding Road"), Felice and Boudleaux Bryant (Everlys' "All I Have to Do Is Dream," "Devoted to You," "Wake Up, Little Susie"), and Simon and Garfunkel ("Sounds of Silence"). Also, Dan Fogelberg ("Longer"), David Gates ("If"), and Richard Marx ("Now and Forever" and #6, 9-2000 N'Sync's song "This I Promise You"). Just because rockers rock, it does not mean they can't conjure sweet melodies plumped up with lush major chords blending divinely. Master melodist of the nineteenth century?

Stephen Foster wrote the book on melody. Without his gorgeous Southern plaintive ballads, we'd have to wait until "The Twelfth of Never" (#9, 10-57, Johnny Mathis) for beautiful melodies to arrive. Foster (1826-64) presented a vision of Southern antebellum life resplendent with fragrant magnolias, twittering birds, and breathtaking Swanee Rivers, plus happy old slaves crooning in the moonlight. Lyrically, it was deeply sentimental, totally lacking in presenting slavery's inherent evils, and chock full of deep sincere emotion: dear old jolly slaves with benevolent masters ("Old Folks at Home," "Uncle Ned"); sunny homesteads of familial bliss ("Old Kentucky Home"), precious romantic sweethearts of up-on-a-pedestal worship ("I Dream of Jeannie with the Light Brown Hair"), beloved animal pals ("Old Dog Tray"). It's a Gone-with-the-Wind glory land that outshone the sun. In his 37 years, he was fraught with financial hardship (everybody ripped off the primitive royalties on Foster's sheet music). His plain rustic house now reposes in Henry Ford's Greenfield Village in Dearborn, Michigan, my own boyhood home [DHS, Jan. '61]. Like Sir Walter Scott of Scotland, Foster described a never-was romantic kingdom of a world gushing with castles and knights and Holy Grails. But, wow, could Foster write melodies! And hey, aside from the horrible slavery part, Foster did splash down some pretty Disneyesque colors of summery bliss on his lyrical canvas.

FOSTER'S FAVORITE 3 CHORDS

The older, sadder, wiser, and more rosy with wine that Foster became, the better those golden melodies rolled. His musical paintbrush dealt, like mainstream Rock and Roll, with the Big Three Chords: the Tonic (I), the Dominant (V), and the Sub-Dominant (IV). In other words, if you play your piano in the key of "C", your tonic chord is C major, using a root C note, a thirds note E, and a fifth note G. To rise to your sub-dominant four chord (IV), you go up four steps to an F major (F & A & C are your three notes for this chord); your dominant V chord is G major (G-B-D notes). With the C, F, and G chords, creating together a majestic and harmonic pattern, you can do most of Foster's classics and 25 percent of early Rock and Roll. You don't need to get to the minors (**Cm**), sevenths (**G7**), diminished ninths (**F dim 9**), and other complex constellations of notes for Jazz maestros, in booming lightning arpeggios of speed and power. With Foster, and Rock and Roll, three gorgeous chords may be all you need.

Stephen Foster rode a wave of teary-eyed sentiment in his cherished-by-America hit tunes. Due to a stark lack of recording technology, we shall never know how the first great American songwriter sounded back in the 50s (1850s). Foster's sheet music, though, found its way to nearly every parlor piano on the planet. Foster belonged to a hometown Singing Club – neighbors with good song and good cheer. The average alcohol consumption in Lincoln's USA – and Foster's – was three times what it is now. Fortunately, the HORSE found its way home from the bar better than the CAR. Among his top hits (stolen by everyone before Napster), are: "Camptown Races" (1850), "Oh, Susanna" (1848, with surrealistic comedy lyric), the first Gold Rush (California) chart-topper; "Old Black Joe" (1860), and "Old Folks at Home" a/k/a "Swanee River" (1851). The latter two certainly compromise slavery, but deliver a genuine affection for the songs' subjects. The 1851 tune was originally "Way Down

Upon the [South Carolinian] Little Peedee River"; even Foster couldn't warble that line with a straight face, so his fingers jogged over a map until he found a totally uninhabited (at that time) river in Florida, the Suwanee, whereby he simply zapped a letter and a syllable to ease the rhyme. Supreme sentimentalist, melodist of gorgeous timeless tunes, and #1 songster of the mid-19th century, Stephen Foster died as sadly as the Great Ghost Trio of the early 70s: Jim Morrison, Jimi Hendrix, and Janis Joplin – the wine ran out, and they all died old in their youth.

Popular music of the 19th century was not yet ready to Rock and Roll. Foster's waltzes and ballads, plus his zingier time signatures (9/8), wove a sweet/sad tapestry of American folk life: "Louisiana Belle," "Massa's in De Cold, Cold Ground," "Nelly Was a Lady," or "Angelina Baker." His song heroes always had a nice blend of angel/demon, not unlike the Rolling Stones or Jerry Lee Lewis. Angelina, indeed. But Foster was not the sole soul sentimentalist. Among fellow hitmakers? Rexford and Danks' lyric and music to "Silver Threads Among the Gold," #1 tune of 1873 about the reality of aging (gray hair); "Grandfather's Clock," Henry Clay Work's 1876 classic about a clock that stopped when the old man died at 90 (redone c. 1960 on a rare Everly Brothers cut); "Dixie's Land," the original "Dixie," song written by Long Islander Dan Emmett, 1860; and some multicultural offerings like African-American James Bland's minstrelsy "In the Evening by the Moonlight" (1880, AND #3, 1907, Harry MacDonough). This song helped launch the Bowery's Barber Shop Quartet 1890s craze, and in turn "doo-whop" 50s Rock and 2003+ N'Sync-style 'Boy Bands.' Zinging heartstrings zoomed to 1818s "Old Oaken Bucket," by Samuel Woodworth, where S.W. rhapsodizes over a grubby, mossy, slimy bucket everyone must drink out of.

Most of us can readily relate to songs of our own childhood and adolescent romantic odysseys. Rock and Roll is bent upon one generation (the younger) grossing out the older. In the 50s, raucous rockabillies zapped no-beat crooners with a dose of teenage terror. Currently generations grapple with Death Metal, no-holds-barred Rap and Gothic, Grunge, and 'Rage Rock' (see Album #1[2] 11-2000 by Limp Bizkit, which LED OFF on the *Billboard* 200 at #1 its first week – *Chocolate Starfish and Hot Dog Flavored Water* [whew – amazing title]).

Before we get back to the semi-shocking sound of NOW, we have a few more surprising 1800 hits to mention: how about the first save-the-environment song? It's "Woodman, Spare That Tree," from 1837, by lyricist George Pope Morris and musicman Henry Russell. Lyric-music duos were the norm until the rise of R & B.

Antiwar songs? From the 60s? OK, which 60s? George Frederick Root's "Just Before the Battle, Mother" underscored the deadly combat on the bloody horizon in 1864's bitter Civil War.

You want Death Metal? Perhaps no more maudlin pop song exists than Nelson Kneass's "Ben Bolt"; the mourner and his 1846 pal are discussing their late dead flame 'Alice'. The two living beaus of departed Alice swallow their sanity, and ponder the poor ex-lass mouldering under the gravestone. I don't know which century is weirder.

Elvis never could have shifted from Rock and Blues and Rockabilly to ballads without William Whiteman Fosdick's masterpiece tune, "Aura Lea," an 1861 Civil War song that had the Everlys or Simon and Garfunkel written all over it, for angelic glimmering sweet thirds harmonies. This golden-haired maiden was a wisp or two too ethereal for Elvis's handlers in sophisticated 1956, so they simply reworked 'Aura Lea' as "Love Me Tender" and called it #1.

Both "O Come All Ye Faithful" ("Adeste Fidelis") and "Amazing Grace" come to us from faraway 1803. The first beloved hymn is probably the work of John Francis Wade; the latter, done up vocally admirably by Judy Collins (#15, 1971), and instrumentally by the Royal Scots Dragoon Guards (#11, 1972) in the Rock Era, was penned by **John Newton**. According to troubadour Banjo Jack Williams of Long Island, Newton was a slaverunner between Africa and the U.S.A. Nabbed by a British Man-O'-War (Brits hated slavery, and jailed slaverunners, freeing the slaves who weren't tossed overboard by cruel overseers), Newton fell victim to a vicious storm at sea. Realizing his sins, he bargained with God to repent his slaveswindle ways and devote his last days to freeing slaves and preaching the Gospel. When Little Richard's 1958 plane to Australia spluttered in midair, the outrageous rocker wheedled the same bargain, vowing to be a preacher forever (forever, for Richard, lasted a few years). Newton repented, wrote "Amazing Grace," and died a devoted Christian. Rock and Roll, we all know, celebrates the carnal side of human nature, a side we try to tame. Over the years, many an errant rocker has found Jesus, "Amazing Grace," and magnificent melody. With a beat. The hymn underscored funerals for New York's 9-11-01 heroes.

Handkerchiefs galore flagged down tears for: African-American composer James Bland's 1878 "Carry Me Back to Old Virginny"; Julia Ward Howe's "Battle Hymn of the Republic" (1862, to counter "Dixie"); Tom Bayly's timeless (no date) "Long, Long Ago," one of few song titles, like **Stones'** "Paint It, Black," with punctuation; John Howard Payne's (peripatetic worldwide nomadic rambler, sometimes of Easthampton, NY) homespun weepy classic "Home! Sweet Home!"; the miner's-kid drowning saga "Clementine" (1884); "When You and I Were Young, Maggie" (1866); and the one that brings us around to R & R's Barber-Shop Streetcorner phase, "Sweet Genevieve," George Cooper's 1869 forerunner of everything.

On the sidewalks of New York, brimming and booming with 1890s Irish tenors and folks who wished they were Irish, Sweet Genevieve metamorphosed into "Sweet Adeline." There was a "Hot Time in the Old Town" in the 1880s, and the young bucks on the corner, back from watching Casey at the Bat striking out, decided to hit pop-tune home runs with pretty Colleens. And Marys. And Nellies. A Tree Grew in Brooklyn, and Birds chortled in Gilded Cages as the new century started to swoon.

Here's a bittersweet and tragicomic duo of Harrys, written by **Harry Von Tilzer**, and crooned by Irish Tenor Harry Tally long, long ago:

"Wait Till The Sun Shines, Nellie" – Harry Tally, #1, 2-1906. Born Harry Gumm in Detroit in 1872, Harry Von Tilzer hightailed for the Big Apple with a dollar (actually $1.65) and a dream – to write the hits. "Nellie" fomented around in his mind until he teamed with Andrew Sterling to pen the finished tune. It's a perfect Irish or Barber Shop or Streetcorner R & R ballad that separates the romantic fluff from the sucker-punch of reality. Maybe the sun will shine soon, Nellie. Maybe the clouds will all drift by. Maybe we'll wander down blissful Lover's Lane. Maybe, honey, in the Sweet Bye-and-Bye. Wow. How furtive. How tentative. How lovingly hopeful. You'll hear from this plaintive ditty again, as Buddy Holly serenades his beloved Maria Elena just before he flies off to his darkling destiny. "Nellie," like life, is a mixed bag of joy and pain.

Harry Von Tilzer knew the ropes. He taught **Irving Berlin** everything he knew about the Tin Pan Alley music biz. Von Tilzer's cheapo furnished-room luck changed as the century dawned, with a dynamic little ditty he wrote about a ginchy gold-digging gal:

"Only A Bird In A Gilded Cage" – Jere Mahoney, #1(5), 4-1900. Bird? We also get the raunchy roots of rock. Harry took a lyric from Art Lamb about a heroine living "in sin" with a rich dude just for his money. Von Tilzer convinced Lamb to prissy up the lyric so the girl was at least married to the sugardaddy geezer. Enchanted by the lyric, Von Tilzer and pals whooped it up at a wild party that ended up with him plunking out the emerging tune at a brothel piano, while his boogie-down buddies smooched the gals. It netted the faux-Dutchman a groovy million-seller. [Back then, you could also do a million in sheet music.] Piano buffs bought sheet music with colors more artsy and colorful than the height of album cover art in the psychedelic 60s. "Bird" chirped to the top, and Von Tilzer's hit convinced his non-baseball-fan brother **Albert** that it was high-nigh time to create his own #1 classic: "Take Me Out to the Ball Game," in 1908. [Looney Tunes' Tweety tweets this fluttery "Bird" ditty to kitty Sylvester].

"Take Me Out To The Ball Game" – Haydn Quartet, #1(7), 10-1908. Brother Albert tapped into our new national pastime with this glorious tribute to the gold rush of our diamonds. Apparently Albert never attended a pro baseball game for 25 years after his winsome waltz rocked the rafters of long-ago glory fields that predated Yankee Stadium, Tiger Stadium, or Fenway Park. Barber Shop Quartets ruled the Waltz King Era of the 1890s and 1900s (see our "Sports Rock/Waltz King chapter). Along with the **Peerless Quartet** and the **American Quartet**, the **Haydn Quartet** was among the most famous. Often high 1st tenor ['Irish' tenor], 2nd tenor ['Italian' tenor], baritone, and bass were interchangeable solo superstars, like **Billy Murray** or **Harry MacDonough**. Barber Shop Quartets featured four voices in these ranges.

You can draw a straight musical line from the 'Sweet Adeline' Barber Shop Quartets of the 1890s and the Boy Band phenomenon of the 2000s, like the **Backstreet Boys** or **N'Sync**, with harmonic threads weaving through Rock and Soul: **Frankie Lymon & the Teenagers**, the **Temptations** and **Miracles of Motown (Boyz II Men, II)**, and even the **Beatles**. **The Haydn Quartet's** #1(10), 10-1904 "Sweet Adeline (You're the Flower of My Heart)" named the barber-shop genre. Just as Rock stars like **Dion and the Belmonts** hung out on their [Belmont Ave.] corner in the Bronx and serenaded streetlights and maybe cute girls, so did their great-

grandfathers in the gas-lamp glow of their own titanic times.

Dion (top) and the Belmonts

The Haydn Quartet scored with their "Put on
Your Old Grey Bonnet" at #1(11) in 12-1909, and
proved that their market share wasn't aimed solely
at the teenage trade. The song celebrated this beloved couple's Golden Wedding anniversary, a 1909
rarity. The **Peerless Quartet**, often anchored by
Billy Murray and Albert Campbell, topped the fledgling charts with schmaltzy waltz "Let Me Call You
Sweetheart" at #1(7), 11-1911.

Most of the tunes in this brief 1890-1950 section can be found in the Rock Era via Columbia
Records' Singalong series legacy; Columbia Music
Director **Mitch Miller** (b. 4th of July 1911) was aged
five months when this "sweetheart" ditty dominated
the pop chart. In **Lawrence Welk** fashion, Miller
rounded up barber-shoppers galore for a mega-choir
that rendered the classic campfire canon in harmonic
profusion. Three #1 *Singalong* albums in the 1958-
61 zone, like #1(8) Al. 7-58 *Sing Along With Mitch*,
kept these classic songs alive, although their faraway
lead singers' voices have long been stilled.

The biggest barber-shop crew of the other new
century was the **American Quartet**: #1(11), 6-1910
train ballad "Casey Jones"; #1(8) minstrel-inspired

harmonic 3-1908 "Moonlight Bay'; World War I anthems #1(9). 9-1917 "Over There," and #1(7), 11-
1914 favorite of **Charlie Brown's** superdog **Snoopy,**
"It's a Long, Long Way to Tipperary'; and the song
Jack Dawson croons to his lady love atop the prow
of the plunging H.M.S. *Titanic* prior to the tragedy:
#1(3), 5-1911 "Come, Josephine, in My Flying Ma-
chine." The American Quartet first featured John
Bieling as lead tenor (till 1914), with baritone Steve
Porter and bass William Hooley. The best-known
lead singer of the American Quartet, AND all
America, from 1890-1920, according to master
chronicler **Joel Whitburn** in his classic *Top Pop
Memories* 1890-1954, was **Billy Murray** (1877-
1954).

"Take Me Out to the Ball Game" could just as
easily be listed as Billy Murray's biggest hit [Billy
Murray & the Haydn Quartet]. Popular music is
rarely far from commercialization, and the song ad-
vertises a new sugary popcorn treat called **Cracker-
Jack**. After many Rock concerts, fans often don't
care whether they ever come back. Whitburn says
Murray was first known as the 'Denver Nightingale,'
for his clear tenor. Henry Ford did not do the first
continuous production car; Murray immortalized my
favorite brand in his #1(7), 10-1905 "In My Merry
Oldsmobile," where Billy and his gal Lucille putt-
putt to a tete-a-tete of snuggly smoocherama in his
rockin' rocket Olds. Those who think Rock and Roll
invented rebellion need only check out the Lost
Generation of the 20s. They practically invented
short skirts, cigarettes, hip flasks of booze, and back
seats of merry mobile motels.

Billy Murray rendered the patriotic songs of
George M. Cohan into World War I fervor: #1(10)
"You're a Grand Old Flag a/k/a Grand Old Rag";
#1(5), 6-1905 "Give My Regards to Broadway"; and
#1(8), 2-1905 "Yankee Doodle Boy." Murray lived
until the dawn of Rock and Roll, just as **Bill Haley**
cut "Rock Around the Clock" and **Elvis Presley**'s
first song "That's All Right" stunned Sun Records
in Memphis. Many of Murray's most famous collaborations featured **Ada Jones** (1873-1922), perhaps the #1 female singer of the Pre-Jazz Age (1890-
1917); they did #1 (5), 5-1909 "Shine On, Harvest
Moon," #1(5), 10-1912 "Be My Little Bumble Bee,"
and #1(6), 11-1907 "Let's Take an Old-Fashioned
Walk." Their harvest ditty was trumped by Ontario's
Scottish balladeer **Harry MacDonough** (1871-

1931). His own Canadian "Shine On, Harvest Moon" clutched the #1 spot for nine weeks in 1-1909, and his #1(7), 12-1911 "Down by the Old Mill Stream" and Irish #1(6), 2-1910 "Where the River Shannon Flows" endeared him to a young record-buying public hunched around the big brass morning-glory bells of their Victor record players. At this time, not everyone had electricity. No matter. You could crank up your own record player and watch it wind down. Records were pricey, though: five bucks for a one-sided ¼-inch-thick 78 rpm by the King of the Waltz Kings, **Dan Quinn**, and his #1(7), 12-1896 "A Hot Time in the Old Town."

In Dan Quinn's era, if Dad made $15/week he was doing well. Dan Quinn had one of the greatest straight #1-song streaks in recorded history (see Mariah Carey/Whitney Houston). The premier of three 1890s **Waltz Kings** (see **George J. Gaskin** and **Len Spencer**), Dan Quinn (1859-1939) recorded 2500+ tunes in his 20-year career (Whitburn), and his #1 1890s streak was highlighted by: #1(5), 1-1893 "The Bowery," #1(9), 9-1893 "Daisy Bell/'Bicycle Built for Two'," #1(9), 2-1895 "Sidewalks of New York," and #1 (10), 8-1895 "The Band Played On." **George Gaskin** ('the Silver-Voiced Irish Tenor') was actually born in Belfast, Ireland, and triumphed with his own fleet of #1s: #1(10), 4-1893 "After the Ball," #1(8), 11-1893 "The Fatal Wedding," and #1(10), 12-1898 "My Old New Hampshire Home." Sentimentality was still as big as it was in Stephen Foster's day. Comedy often arrived as minstrelsy, a racist form of entertainment where white men put on 'blackface' and masqueraded as African-Americans. Much minstrelsy was whimsical and even harmless (watch the 'Comedy Channel' lately?), but much of it lampooned former slaves with ghost and watermelon skits. **Len Spencer** (1867-1914) became our first national star on the new medium of RECORDS via his minstrelsy in #1(4), 3-1891 "Little Liza Loves You." Under the guise of comedy, he specialized in a fortunately-extinct genre of discriminatory tunes called 'coon songs.' Until white/Jewish **Benny Goodman**, clarinet virtuoso, hooked up with Afro-American piano guru **Teddy Wilson** in the 1930s, segregated popular music stalked the American scene in many forms. Rock and Soul, from the **Dell Vikings** and **Lloyd Price** to **KC & the Sunshine Band** to **Tony Orlando & Dawn** to **Hootie & the Blowfish** to the **Dave Matthews Band**, have shown that integrated music produces some magnificent sounds. Spencer's big hits (whose titles we would mention) include Foster's classic "Old Folks at Home" #1(6), 8-1892; #1(5), 4-1895 "Dat New Bully'; and #1(6), 4-1899 "Hello! Ma Baby," which celebrated both the advent of telephones and Ragtime.

Lower-voiced singers had hits, too, but the Rock & Ragtime Eras tout the tenor tones of the tiptop tunesters. Baritone **J.W. Myers'** #1(7), 10-1902 "In the Good Ol' Summertime" waltzed to the same message as Reggae's debut tune #3, 7-70 "In the Summertime," by Mungo Jerry. Bass **Frank Stanley** (1869-1910) scored with #1(4), 5-1904 "Blue Bell." Drinking songs ran rife in the Oughts (1900-09): **Arthur Collins** (1864-1933) teamed up with **Byron Harlan** (1861-1936), and #1(10), 2-1907 "My Gal Sal"), and the impish result emblazons a river of beer, suds bubbling "Down Where the Würzburger Flows" [#1(5), 3-1911]. Check out the **Andrews Sisters'** #1(10), 40s smash "Rum and Coca Cola." Did you recollect that our national anthem "The Star-Spangled Banner," #1(3), 5-1917 by the great **John McCormack**, was once a German drinking tune called "To Anacreon in Heaven"? Harlan's 'greatest' hit, however, is a revamp of an ode to corporal punishment and pedagogical sadism, where reading and writing are taught by whipping kids with a lash of hickory: "School Days (When We Were a Couple of Kids)," #1(11), 5-1907. 'Child abuse' was undefined then, and shamefully almost universal.

Henry Burr (1882-1941) of New Brunswick, Canada, often did duets with **Albert Campbell** (1873-1947), like their #1(3), 6-1913 "The Trail of the Lonesome Pine," of Boy Scout nostalgia. The RECORD and the MICROPHONE (a/k/a 'Mike' or 'Mic') made it no longer necessary to need a big booming voice to fill a hall with sound. Legend and Whitburn have Burr singing over 12,000 recordings, with his niftiest nuggets nudging Number One: #1(7), 4-1905 "In the Shade of the Old Apple Tree"; #1(8), 9-1909 "I Wonder Who's Kissing Her Now"; and #1(7), 5-1914 "The Song That Stole My Heart Away." That last song may not be the magic song that captured your heart, but hang on, we'll get there soon.

The 19th century's biggest beat? **John Philip Sousa** (1854-1932), 'March King,' provided the brassy oom-pah, the thundering 2/4 beat, and a volcano of vital popular music which still blasts boldly over the football destinies of America at eternal half time: #1(3), 8-1895 "Washington Post March"; #1(7), 6-1895 "El Capitan March"; and his eternal "Stars and Stripes Forever" at #1(8), 7-1897 and #1(3), 2-1901, plus #4, 7-1917 as "The Stars and Stripes March."

Though it's hard to sustain the bursting budgets of maybe five guys in a Rock band, plus their entourage of managers, roadies, drivers, groupies, and A & R (Artists & Repertoire record-pushers) personnel, somehow John Philip Sousa and his U.S. Marine Band found a way to pay over 60 musicians. They toured the world with vigor and a big foot-stomping beat that signaled a new century – a century awaiting the ribald rise of Rock and Roll.

It was almost time for **Louis 'Satchmo' Armstrong** (1900-1971) to crank up his cornet, define Jazz, and herald the infancy of America's great musical offerings from Dixieland Jazz in New Orleans, the Blues in Memphis, and Rock and Roll from everywhere all at once.

Quiet acoustic guitars were flirting with dobro-style metal resonators. The Blues now cascaded under a marshmallow Delta Memphis moon. Up in the "Arsenal of Democracy," Detroit – later Motown

– Henry Ford was tinkering with both **Country** music in its infancy, and a way to tote it around – the **tour bus**.

It was almost time for Mr. Beaubien to plug in his guitar.

Louis 'Satchmo' Armstrong

Carl Perkins, Ringo Starr (drums), *George Harrison* (guitar), *Eric Clapton* (guitar), and *Stray Cats' Lee Rocker* (bass)

Dixieland Cowboys -- Moonlight Serenade

When the Beatles blasted "Come Together" (#1, 10-69) to a fragmented, strung-out world, perhaps it symbolized the many vagabond forms of Rock and Roll. Launched from ragtag Ragtime and all its seamy and steamy roadhouses in House of Blue Lights America, Rock and Roll combined many rhythmic kinds of music into the big beat in the mid-50s. Yep: Ragtime, Dixieland Jazz, Blues, Swing Jazz, Simple Childhood Rhymes, Military Marches, Polkas, Big Bands, Bluegrass/Hillbilly, Hawaiian, Caribbean, African, Native American, and even (via Buddy Holly's introduction of strings) Symphonic Music, that 18th-century 'Rebel Without a Cause' Wolfgang Amadeus Mozart could have dug. Rock's two major forebears, for the record, are Jazz and Blues. Both come from Ragtime.

The two-room shotgun shack that housed young **W. C. Handy** (1873-1958) was plucked like Dorothy's Kansas/Oz house, and Handy's home landed smack dab in the middle of Memphis, just a block down Beale Street from **B.B. King's Club.** **King's** duo album with **Eric Clapton**, *Riding with the King* (Al. #1, 3-2000), features the great British Blues guitar guru chauffeuring B.B. King in a vintage circa 1962 Cadillac convertible. W.C. Handy got both of them their jobs as Blues superstars. With his "Yellow Dog Blues" of 1912, his "Memphis Blues," and his classic 1917 "St. Louis Blues," Handy is known as the "Father of the Blues." An African-American gentleman with a British bowler hat, and a polychordal savvy far beyond the three basic Blues chords, Handy launched the sound of the Blues in the Ragtime afterglow.

Soon we'll do a hefty chapter on Blues stars from Bessie Smith to Ma Rainey to Jimmy Reed to Janis Joplin, but W.C. Handy's "Memphis Blues" defined the genre. The Blues thrives on the 12-Bar progression (see Chord Theory). The Blues also thrives on minors and seventh notes, a whole lot of seventh notes. The Blues are a reflection of mood (see **Duke Ellington's** marvelous #3, 2-31 "Mood Indigo"). Both Blues and Jazz stem from New Orleans, mixing an exotic French/African musical combo which also later helped launch Rock and Roll.

Jazz cannot be simply classified; it is too large, too all-encompassing, too profound. Great Jazz coruscates with improvisation, and Jazz continues reinventing itself. From its sentimental Swing of the **Benny Goodman** era to its most esoteric and way-out excursions of the **Dave Brubeck** (piano) or **Charlie 'Bird' Parker** (sax) ilk, Jazz can be all things to all musicians. It took 100 years for Jazz courses to permeate the hallowed halls of Classical Music academe. Now Jazz must deal with its upstart offshoot Rock and Roll, as the big beat storms the ramparts of the ivy-tufted towers of college knowledge. In *Gold Rush*, we revere Jazz as one of the sanctuaries of musical virtuosity. If we had time, we'd study Jazz at great length beyond our Jazz Rock chapter. If we seem to defer to great innovative Jazz Rock over simpler 'Bubble-Gummy' styles, it's not that we don't love the sweet simple songs – it's just that we chase musical excellence in all its varied forms and beats and polychordal masterpieces. In *Gold Rush* we examine the biggest hits, from **Al Jolson** to **Bing Crosby** to **Artie Shaw** to **Tommy Dorsey** to **Frank Sinatra** to **Billy Joel**, and Jazz accompanies them all.

Of course **Louis 'Satchmo' Armstrong** (1900-71) is the musical link between Jazz, Blues, and even Rock and Roll. We'll chart his triumphant life and career from the beginning of *Gold Rush* until the last page. Though born into tawdry poverty in New Orleans, Louis learned trumpet in the Waifs' Home where he stayed. After a few years apprenticing in the Dixieland Jazz Bands at the New Orleans Mardi

Gras, at wild wakes, and at steamy Houses of the Rising Sun, Armstrong sallied north to discover Chicago Blues. Armstrong headlined his young century with *joie de vivre*, gusto, and musical splendor. From Blues to Jazz, he was the benchmark for musical excellence.

Though many early 20th-century stars may get the sad short shrift of a sentence or a tune or two, please remember they were the **N'Syncs**, **Metallicas**, **Mariah Careys**, **Nirvanas**, **Bon Jovis**, **Bruce Springsteens**, **Elton Johns**, **Bee Gees**, **Ashantis**, **Doors**, and **Beatles** of their respective eras.

Paul Whiteman (1890-1967) rendered the African-American young Jazz music into a smooth 'Caucasian persuasion' style of universal pop music: #1(6), 7-21 "Cherie"; #1(5), 8-21 "Song of India" [notice his international romantic intrigue theme]; #1(11), 6-26 "Valencia"; #2(4), 11-26 "Moonlight on the Ganges," and his get-down-and-boogie tune "Hot Lips" – #1(6), 9-22. I recall the big 300# friendly bandleader still conducting into the Rock era on many a 50s variety show.

Gene Austin (1900-72) nearly matches Louis's lifeline, and in the Jazz Age – at the height of the Flapper craze and the Charleston – Austin's popularity may have slightly eclipsed Louis's own: #1(7), 8-25 "Yes Sir? That's My Baby"; #1(1), 3-26 "Five Foot Two, Eyes of Blue"; and #1(8), 5-28 "Ramona" (reprised by Indonesian/Dutch Blue Diamonds to #72, 11-60). Gene's biggest hit was my third 45 rpm record (for **Antoine 'Fats' Domino**, it was #16, 4-56) – "My Blue Heaven," at #1(13), 12-27 for Austin. It describes honeymoon bliss in a picket-fence cottage with cozy fireplace, a nestling nuzzling nest with roses galore.

Great Jazz/Classical composer **George Gershwin** (1898-1937) hit the charts with his piano masterpiece "Rhapsody in Blue" – scoring twice at #3, 10-24 and #7, 9-27. Its ultra-complex score is a hallmark of Jazz profundity and power and glory. Along the more pop-style line, **Ben Bernie** (1881-1943) schmoozed a Flapper sweetheart or two with #1(4), 4-27 "Ain't She Sweet" and #1(5), 6-25 "Sweet Georgia Brown." The latter tune became the theme of the Harlem Globetrotters, and played no small role in the eventual emergence of Michael Jordan and the National Basketball Association.

Rudy Vallee (1901-88) hailed from Vermont, went to Yale, wore spiffy raccoon coats, and warbled drinking songs into a megaphone ["Stein Song (University of Maine)," #1(10), 3-30]. A couple years later America's stock market went belly-up, and woebegone investors lost their shirts. The forlorn landscape was littered with soup kitchens, bedraggled tent families, and hobo jungles. Vallee's heady heigh-de-ho turned morose, and he scored again with #1(2), 11-32 "Brother, Can You Spare a Dime?" Nonsense and whimsy often ruled the roost. **Ben Selvin** (1898-1960) asked the Zen musical statement "Yes, We Have No Bananas" in 9-23 [#1]. Selvin lambasted the tuneful competition, too, with his mega-monster "Dardanella" at #1(13) in January 1920. From Chicago's Selvin, we traipse to **Fred Waring and His Pennsylvanians**, as they hightail it down "Memory Lane" (#1[5], 8-24), and ponder the #10, 9-24 "Down Home Blues."

The real deep Blues were delivered by Blues diva **Bessie Smith** (1895-1937, see Blues chapter), whose original "Down Home Blues" at #1(4), 6-23 was her biggest charted hit. Among the fledgling Blues geniuses, **Fletcher Henderson** (1898-1952) was a pianist/arranger extraordinaire, working with Bessie Smith, as well as in the forefront of integrated jazz bands via Benny Goodman. Henderson's #8, 10-25 "Sugar Foot Stomp" may not have commandeered the top charts for half a year, but his Blues savvy and vision would spread all the way down to Rock and Soul.

Al Jolson was born Asa Yoelson in St. Petersburg, Russia, in 1886. His cantor father thought it shameful he should sing popular music (see Ty Cobb's father on the follies of pro baseball). Borrowing a dollop of sentimental schmaltz, some twinkly-eyed minstrelsy, a few vaudeville-hoofer steps Fred Astaire could dig, and a towering resonant baritone, Jolson became one of the most popular and beloved entertainers of all time. Among his memorable top tunes, you'll find #1(6), 8-1919 "I'll Say She Does"; #1(6), 5-24 "California, Here I Come" (which heralded a westward nomadic wave); and his Southern nostalgic extravaganza – #1(9), 5-20 "Swanee." Among Al's most popular tunes was his tender #1(12), 10-28 "Sonny Boy." Jolson was among the top artists of the 1910-30 era, and enjoyed hits up until his death in 1950, just before the rise of Rock (see later Jolson songs).

Isham Jones (1894-1962) not only had a #1(1), 9-30 debut version of the 1900-50 era's most popular song "Star Dust" [songwriter Hoagy Carmichael], but he also pioneered the Blues with his catchy #1(6), 12-21 "Wabash Blues."

One of the top Jazz performers in the 1930-50 zone was saxman **Jimmie Lunceford** (1902-47). Ken Burns's spectacular PBS series *Jazz* (1-2001) shows black and white video clips of the animated Afro-American Jazz superstar and his captivating choreography. Motown's Temptations might have learned a lot from Lunceford; his horn section played, danced, and spun their horns like flaming batons in the neon dazzle of his #1(1), 5-35 "Rhythm Is Our Business." For a guy whose gig job was a business, Jimmie (and his electrifying band) seemed to be having a lot of fun!

Joel Whitburn, no less, calls **Edward Kennedy 'Duke' Ellington** (1899-74) 'perhaps the single most important creative talent in American popular music history!' Born into an upper-class background in Washington D.C., the fair-skinned African-American piano man fronted a band that was the epitome of class, elegance, and cerebral Jazz – with a hint of deep purple moonmist and stardust mood indigo.

A musician's musician, Duke Ellington's lofty Jazz career sparked the tribute of the man once rated #3 of all time (after the Beatles and Elvis) – **Stevie Wonder**, and his monumental Jazz-Soul Fusion classic, #1(3), 4-77 "Sir Duke." Ellington's hits include #1(3), 10-30 "Three Little Words, " #3, 2-31 "Mood Indigo," #2(1), 10-34 "Solitude," #2(2), 10-34 "Moon Glow," #1(5), 5-34 "Cocktails for Two," and his mainstay swan song, #11, 7-41 "Take the 'A' Train" (about riding the New York City Subway). Though not a practitioner of the Big Beat, Ellington nevertheless forecast the latter-century direction of music with his clairvoyant classic — #19, 3-31 "Rockin' in Rhythm."

William 'Count' Basie (1904-84) carries Duke's American-royalty title motif (also see Gene Chandler's #1 '62 "Duke of Earl"). The suave Basie's theme tune is his #15, 9-37 "One O'Clock Jump."

If you've ever seen *The Blues Brothers* (1980****, Belushi/Aykroyd), you'll recall the #1(1), 3-31 hit "Minnie the Moocher" by **Cab Calloway** (1907-94). The Rochester, NY stage dynamo regaled his rapt audiences with taboo tunes of sidelong Jazz punch and power: #2(4), 7-39 "(Hep-Hep!) The Jungle Jive," and (yes, Virginia, reefer madness), his pot-besotted #11, 7-32 "Reefer Man." Marijuana was illegalized and demonized in Detroit in 1928, in the aftermath of Prohibition gone amok; when it didn't work to take away the booze, the law went after this rare weed – which suddenly burst into popularity as soon as it became illegal.

Fats Waller gave the nickname to one of the Rock and Soul's original 1986 Inductees into the Cleveland Rock Hall of Fame – New Orleans' Antoine 'Fats' Domino. Waller himself (1904-43) was not blessed with the amiable Domino's burly lifespan, but scored key Jazz/Soul tunes: like #1(4), 6-36 "It's a Sin to Tell a Lie."

Pianist **Eddy Duchin** (1910-51) spun piano moods with **Leo Reisman's Orchestra** (#1[10], 12-32 "Night and Day"). Duchin hit with #1(5), 2-34 "Let's Fall in Love," #1(3), 1-36 "Moon Over Miami," and #1(3), 3-35 "I Won't Dance."

Billie Holiday (1915-59) you'll encounter later in *Gold Rush's* extensive Blues chapter, where we also tout **Ma Rainey, Blind Lemon Jefferson, Memphis Slim, Nat King Cole, LaVern Baker, Elmore James, Louis Jordan, Charlie Christian, Jimmie Rodgers I**, and **Robert Johnson**. Born Eleanor Gough in Baltimore, Billie sang 'behind the beat' and murmured her Blue-note lullabies of angst and sorrow: #3, 1-37 "Pennies from Heaven"; #1(3), 4-37 "Carelessly"; #25, 10-41 "God Bless the Child"; and her blockbuster *a cappella* chiller "Strange Fruit" (about the obscene horror of lynching) at #25, 10-41 despite a ban on air play. Many consider "Lady Day" of Baltimore the finest Blues singer of all time. One thing's for sure: Billie Holiday lived her Blues to the hilt – suffering from agonizing substance abuse for much of her tortured and abbreviated life.

Ella Fitzgerald (1918-96) has been called (by Whitburn) the most honored Jazz singer of all time. From her Virginia dockside debut, she utilized Holiday's behind-the-beat technique to score with #1(2), 11-44 "I'm Making Believe" and her biggee "1(10), 6-38 "A-Tisket, A Tasket." More Ella later. **Sarah Vaughan** (1924-90), with her rich contralto phrasings, is in the same league, but was born too late for the jazz heyday she celebrates in #10, 9-50 "I Love the Guy," and Rock Era masterpiece "Brokenhearted Melody," #7, 7-59.

The **Mills Brothers** scored many a Jazz-tinged Barber-Shop hit, with their mellow harmonics and gentle, whimsical lyrics (more Millses later, too):

#1(5), 6-44 "You Always Hurt the One You Love."
Lead tenor Billy Kenny sparked the Ink Spots to high
hitdom with #1(13), 5-46 "The Gypsy" and other
melodic songs. **Ruth Etting** sang "Love Me or
Leave Me" to #2(2), 2-29, and Etting (1907-78) was
a forerunner of the notable singers to emerge from
the aegis of notable Jazz bands.

Enter the Crooner Era and **Bing Crosby** (1903-
77). Crosby may well have been 'the most important singer of the entire 1900-1950 era.' With his
mellifluous soothing baritone, his Mister Rogers
sweater and tie, and his cozy, homey resonance,
Crosby mesmerized a nation yearning for sleep, for
certitude, for prosperity, for peace. *Gold Rush* will
feature many Crosby songs later (not just Crosby,
Stills, Nash, and Young), particularly the #1 song
of all time, until usurped by Elton John's Princess
Di tribute "Candle in the Wind." The song? Irving
Berlin's immortal Christmas carol "White Christmas" – #1(12), 12-42 . . . and even forevermore.
Among Crosby's other legacies are: #1(6), 10-32
"Please," where he emerged from Paul Whiteman's
band as featured vocalist; #1(7), 11-34 "June in January"; and #1(10), 11-36 "Pennies from Heaven." The
Irish-American California baritone created an aura
of assurance and solidity that kept the homefires
burning throughout World War II. Into the millennium, Crosby's 'yippie-yo-kie-ay' is heard in Nelly's
#14, 2000 "Country Grammar" Rap song; the non-
sense syllables stem from Bing's cowboy satire
#2(4), 8-36 "I'm an Old Cowhand."

Perry Como (1912-2001) sparked **Ted Weems'
Orchestra** (Ted's latter-day hit is #1[13], 8-47
"Heartaches" – at age 50). The amiable and delightful Perry will be featured later on, as he happily co-
existed with the Rock Era. He even tossed in a little
Ultra-Soft Rock ["Hot Diggity," #1, '56] among his
croon tunes, like #1(10), 8-45 "Till the End of Time."

Into the 40s, **Big Bands** ruled. Buttressed by
Jazz techniques, they featured a profusion of horns.
Woodwinds wailed at the Savoy or Paradise or
Avalon Ballrooms of America. Some bandleaders
nearly rocked. Others provided music so sleepy that
they gave Rock and Roll something to rebel against.

Harry James (1916-83) played the golden
sound on his trumpet, and his #1(13), 1-43 "I've
Heard That Song Before" chomped the wartime
charts, as did his #1(4), 4-42 "Sleepy Lagoon."
James was among the biggest Big Band stars of all

time, but he is best known for launching the career
of a Hoboken kid who idolized Bing Crosby —
Frank Sinatra (1915-1998). Even into the rock era,
Sinatra is still recognized as the penultimate #2 artist of all time in the *Billboard* album rankings.
Though we'll slather Sinatra songs into *Gold Rush*
later on, let's just mention his #1(2), 6-43 "All Or
Nothing at All." Frank Sinatra wrote the book on
enunciation and phrasing. Under COOLTH or Ultimate Coolth in the dictionary, you'll find Frank bedecked with his pompadour that inspired Elvis, and
his screaming fans that inspired the Beatles . . .
Woody Herman's (b. 1913) #21, 7-43 "At the
Woodchopper's Ball" inspired Boogie-Woogie and
Blues and Rock with its 12-Bar Blues drive and hot
power. The **Andrews Sisters**, a harmonic trio who
often sang with Bing, had a few megahits of their
own in the Boogie-Woogie Style (see "The Boogie-
Woogie Bugle Boy") like #2(3), 11-40 "Beat Me
Daddy, Eight to the Bar."

Glenn Miller (1904-44) took the romantic pulse
of America and boomed it back with his ultra-mel-
low trombone. **Tommy Dorsey** (1905-56) also
played trombone (#1[12], "I'll Never Smile Again,"
6-40). Their two towering trombones held back the
terror of European gunfire and the deaths of 300,000
American soldiers in the bloodiest war of all time.

Brother **Jimmy Dorsey** (1904-57) played a virtuoso alto sax, reeling off splendid mellow moods
into the Rock Era: In Whitburn's Artist Rankings
from 1890-1954, Tommy Dorsey is 4th with 30,439
points, with Jimmy notching 17th with 10,552.
Jimmy's hits include #1(10), 3-41 "Amapola" (about
a poppy), and a colorful array on his alto sax or clarinet: #1(6), 4-42 "Tangerine"; #1(1), 7-41 "Blue
Champagne"; and #1(4), 6-41 "Green Eyes." As
Tommy Dorsey's "Tea for Two Cha Cha" hit #7 in
9-58 (Buddy Holly or Chuck Berry's big R & R
year), so Jimmy's "So Rare" was climbing the charts
to its #2(4), 2-57 gold record as Jimmy passed away
from the #1 scourge of America's people – heart
disease at age 53. Brother Tommy never heard his
own Cha Cha hit, since he lost to the same disease
at age 51. Rock and Roll has never been conducive
to longevity, and for that matter neither has Swing
Jazz or the Blues.

Among the most talented up-and-coming trumpet or piano stars of the jazz age was **Bix
Beiderbecke** (1903-31, #15, 2-28 "At the Jazz Band

Ball"), whose mentor **Frankie Trumbauer** (1900-56, a comparative Methusaleh) scored with an early version of **Ray Charles/Michael Bolton**'s classic "Georgia On My Mind" (#1, '60 for Charles, #36, '90 for Bolton, and #10, 8-31 for saxman Trumbauer). Beiderbecke's magic horn was prematurely stilled, as was the pumping piano of **Clarence 'Pine Top' Smith**, a Boogie-Woogie keyboard man (1905-29) with some claim as the discoverer of Rock and Roll via his February **1929** #20 "Pine Top's Boogie Woogie," later covered as "Boogie Woogie" to #3 in 1938 by Tommy Dorsey (and #4, '44 and #5 '45). Pine Top Smith was shot to death in a blind-pig bar, proving **Notorious B.I.G.** and **Tu-pac Shakur** did not corner the market on violence. Indeed, Blues guru **Leadbelly (Huddie Ledbetter)**, somehow survived 60 years (1888-1949), and served 6½ years on a murder charge (today's impartial juries might have doled out manslaughter). Both **Eddy Duchin** and **George Gershwin** succumbed at around forty to dreaded long illnesses. Life on the road for the Blues or Jazz musician, huddled in frozen bus stops, and eating raw greaseburgers washed down with stale beer, is not the ideal health regimen. For some, easy drug access, and myriads of two-pack cigarette days don't make for the ultramarathon lifespan. In **Glenn Miller**'s case, his plane went down over the stormy English Channel as he flew to entertain the troops like trooper **Bob Hope** (b. 1903, and #15, 1-39 "Two Sleepy People," with Shirley Ross). Hope, on the other hand, gives long-life hope to those whose On the Road to . . . adventures take them to faraway places and exotic shores. Four centenarians prove our short-lifespan musician theory wrong.

Irving Berlin (1888-1989) wrote "White Christmas," and had only one charted hit as a singer: #10, 6-1910 "Oh, How That German Could Love." His tunesmith blockbusters are legion, like "Blue Skies" (#1 '27 Ben Selvin and #2 '27 George Olsen), and "Alexander's Ragtime Band" (#1 1911 Arthur Collins/Byron Harlan, #2 1911 Billy Murray, #3 1912 Prince's Orchestra). This latter song helped inspire **Paul McCartney**'s father Jim, and is one genesis of the concept album *Sgt. Pepper's Lonely Hearts Club Band* Al. #1(15), 1967.

Eubie Blake (1883-1983) smoked up until age 99½, and the wiry Afro-American Ragtime piano plunker dished out #8, 11-21 "Bandana Days" and #10, 1-22 "Arkansas Blues." **Governor Jimmie Davis** of Louisiana (1899-2000) was a Country star in his elusive spare time, writing campfire classic "You Are My Sunshine" (#19, '41 Bing Crosby, #23, '43 cowboy singer Gene Autry). Spanning three centuries – 19th to 21st – Davis also hit lucky #13 in 12-38 with "Meet Me Tonight in Dreamland." Our final centenarian, **George Burns** (1896-1996) hit hitdom as a 'Rapper' with his amiable wife **Gracie Allen**. Born Nathan Birnbaum in the roiling Italian-Jewish Lower East Side of Greenwich Village, Burns grew up on the Vaudeville Circuit, doing spritzes of song, garnished with comedy shtick from behind a puffy cigar-smoke cloud. He and Gracie hit with #6, 6-33 RAP item *Burns and Allen Dialog, Parts One and Two* (the 'Pt. I' stuff sounds like a **James Brown** title, eh?). At age 84, Burns started singing: #49, 1-80 "I Wish I Was Eighteen Again" (or, perhaps, eighty again). With his burbling baritone, Groucho Marx straight lines, and Gracie's adorable 'Edith Bunker' voice and zany dialogue, George was a vaudeville legend for nearly 100 years. He starred with **John Denver** in the whimsical flick *Oh, God* (***½, 1977). Among the most profound Vaudeville talents Burns shared the billing with are **Eddie Cantor** [#2(2), 2-29 "Makin' Whoopee"], **Milton Berle** (b. 1908), **George Jessel, Eddie Jackson, Jack Benny**, and **Sophie Tucker**, 'Last of the Red Hot Mamas.' Tucker (1885-1961) was born Sonia Kalish in Russia, and strutted the stages of America into the 50s (#2[3], 7-11 and #1[5], 2-27 "Some of These Days") on the *Jimmy Durante Show*.

Jimmy Durante (1893-1980, [#6, 2-34 "Inka Dinka Doo"]) was a Vaudeville comic, former Coney Island piano banger and early TV star. Universally beloved, Durante grew up in Burns's neighborhood and touted his self-deprecating humor via ultra-cool mispronunciations and jokes about his big nose ('Da Schnozz,' which sported its own 'nose-muffs' – like earmuffs – on cold days). His good-natured **Spike Jones** styles of occasionally wrecking the band (he'd yell "STOP DA MUSIC!") spilled over into the band-smashing showmanship of **Jerry Lee Lewis** (torched his piano), **Jimi Hendrix** (torched his guitar), or the **Who** (smashed and torched the whole band). Whether Durante did Blues or Boogie or Jazz it is not determined, but he was the consummate comedian, showman, and skilled musician.

Jimmy Durante

As a kid, I remember solemnly plunking away on my Uncle Lou's castaway piano, untuned for aeons, at a nifty little ditty called "Ragtime Cowboy Joe." This 1912 #1 Bob Roberts classic featured a cool horse that clopped along to the syncopated shots of Joe's pistol. Mixed-beat. Forerunner of the Blues. The cowhand's six-shooter sputtered the Ragtime beat. Though the beat lumbered and stumbled over Gila monsters and cactus, "Ragtime Cowboy Joe's" swing bass kept the fledgling big beat easily rocking. Filtered through the jolly lyric, you had chunks of blue notes (sevenths, like **C7** – C-E-G-Bb; others are diminished notes, like when you flat the second and third note of your big major chord C-E-G to C-Eb-Gb). Tunes like "Ragtime Cowboy Joe" highlighted the colorful revues of Vaudeville, which combined jumpy numbers with sizzling pie-in-the-face comedy.

Ragtime featured funky Blues notes, and the shimmering beginning of Jazz chord theory streamed out of honkytonks and speakeasies (illegal bars) and Coney Islands. Jazz explored wild new mood-altering chords, like augmented chords (on the standard Tonic **C-major** chord C-E-G, you'd sharp the fifth note to C-E-G# or C-E-Ab). Or like major sevenths: instead of standard seventh chord C-E-G-Bb, you'd do C-E-G-B (see our Chord Theory Section). Delv-

ing into the muted complexities and esoteric backwash chords of deep Jazz, you have to consider two maestros of the genre: **Benny Goodman**, and the most important musician to straddle the entire century of popular music – **LOUIS 'SATCHMO' ARMSTRONG.**

Benny Goodman (1909-86) grew up in Chicago, and was among the first to fuse the great Jewish and Afro-American musical contributions to music. In a way, popular music has always been color-blind, but Benny and his Swing band carried the Emancipation Proclamation of President Lincoln on its way to Dr. Martin Luther King. His prime Swing quartet featured two African-American stars: **Teddy Wilson** on piano and **Lionel Hampton** on vibes, with superstar white drummer **Gene Krupa**. Besides a cultural and musical icon, Benny was perhaps the greatest clarinetist of all time. His Benny Goodman Orchestra furnished the modern-day model for kids WATCHING bands as an AUDIENCE – not just as dancers on the sidelong scene. When Benny played the Savoy or the Paramount in New York City – maybe even Carnegie Hall – people went to WATCH him play.

Louis Jordan and His Tympani Five*[plus one]*
*Left to right: J. Kirkwood, B. Mitchell, B. Payne, C. Laine, **L. Jordan**, S. Jay, C. Hastings*

Benny and his band brought blessed relief from a dim Depression. Down and out people dwelt in unpainted shacks, stooped at soup lines, and hawked sad rotten apples, yearning for a wisp of fluffy romance and reverie. Goodman's clarinet soared over the tribulations of millions of deprived would-be consumers, whose only bleak future involved a faraway war to end the world or save it. No wonder Benny & Band blasted the blue view away into soft blue skies of hope and promise. No wonder Benny and his Afro piano maestro **Teddy Wilson** (#2, 5-37 "There's a Lull in My Life") wove a musical tapestry of golden tomorrows and deep purple nights of splendor and glory, and good times galumphing out of the marathon gloom. In ballrooms throughout America, the sound of Swing Jazz cascaded. Its pied piper fervor led us from despair to hope.

In 1938 alone Benny Goodman had 26 hits in the Top 20. Among his mega-monsters, you'll find #1(1), 6-34 "Moon Glow," a reflection of the sweet stardust his band delivered; "2(2), 1-35 "Blue Moon," which set up Rock's 'Streetcorner' chord pattern [**C-Am-F-G7**], and proved a huge hit for Elvis and a #1 for the 1961 Marcels; 2-36 #1(6) "Goody Goody," which inspired Frankie Lymon and the Teenagers (#20, 7-57); #1(6), 5-36 "The Glory of Love"; #1(5), 4-39 "And the Angels Sing"; and one that pervaded a *Donald Duck/Ducktales* comic when I was a kid in Detroit – #7, 6-38 "The Flat Foot Floogie." Other Goodman goodies? #1(4), 1-37 "Goodnight My Love, " which inspired Sha Na Na's TV show of the 70s about the 50s; #1(5), 3-38 "Don't Be That Way"; #1(4), 3-41 "There'll Be Some Changes Made"; #1(4), 3-42 "Jersey Bounce"; and #1(3), 4-43 "Taking a Chance on Love." During the Cold War, Benny was the first American Jazz artist to play in Moscow. It took another generation for the old Soviet Union to accept Rock and Roll artists, because they were afraid it might undermine communism, which, perhaps, it did (see Beatles' supercool Beach Boy tribute "Back in the U.S.S.R."). Goodman's INTEGRATED BAND combined pianist virtuoso Wilson, vibes superstar **Lionel Hampton** (b. 1908, #6, 11-37 "After You've Gone") and #1 drummer **Gene Krupa** (#7, 10-45 "Along the Navajo Trail"). These serious musicians took several cues from their Vaudeville compadres in terms of showmanship, and always brought down the house.

Without Durante and Burns, there might never have been a slapstick comedy-style video movie like *Help*, and its logical American TV spin-off *The Monkees*, which effectively videoized Rock and Roll for the generations to come. **Mike Nesmith**, Monkee singer and guitarist, is responsible for setting up, commandeering and inventing Music Television (*MTV*) for 24-hour videocast on the 80s phenomenon – Cable

TV. Rock and Roll, sailing on a few laughs, had gone from just the music to Music + Video. A mixed blessing.

Perhaps the #1 showman of all? **Louis Armstrong** – perhaps the most endearing artist of all time. With a trumpet and a dream, Louis melded comedy and glory into his 'Wonderful World' of American popular music. The oldest artist ever to have a number one record just might be the Father of Rock and Roll: Louis 'Satchmo' Armstrong (8-4-01 – 7-6-71). Like Durante and Burns he wore that showbiz laurel wreath of 'BELOVED'. Few singers or politicians today enjoy that same awesome adoration. Armstrong barnstormed the gaslight midnight Jazz joints and riverboats of New Orleans. For years Louie has been revered as the greatest soloist (cornet-trumpet) in Jazz, but I'd like to borrow him here for Rock and Roll temporarily. Apprenticing with Kid Oliver, the smiling trumpeter soon built up a reputation for inventing many musical concepts that lay the groundwork for Jazz and Rock and Roll. He especially created improvising, a typically American one-person up-front idea. With backing band, the maestro (Louie) blew wild supersonic riffs; **Eric Clapton, Stevie Rae Vaughan** and **Muddy Waters** applied this to the guitar. Louis Armstrong later moved to New York, living in a small modest house for a multimillionaire — because he humbly liked his neighbors in Corona, Queens, now in the shadow of the Mets and Shea Stadium.

Armstrong invented Dixieland Jazz, to some degree. Listen to Louis sometime doing the gospel-tinged happy-funeral tune #10, 4-35 "When the Saints Go Marchin' In." With a brassy bellowing batch of happy horns (trumpet, trombones) and woodwinds (saxes, clarinets) and big thumping bass drums, you can hear him start mildly and then build. In many ways, Armstrong invented the big-beat Crescendo (Tschaikovsky's *1812 Overture* not withstanding), which would later power singer's singer **Roy Orbison** (Running Scared," "Crying,") to vault to eerie extra-terrestrial tenor heights on his bolero-crescendo classics.

Best known today for his spellbinding Carol of Life, #32, 2-88 "What a Wonderful World" (see book's finale), Louis 'Satchmo' Armstrong is among early Rock and Roll's main movers and shakers. Louis parleyed his raspy whisky baritone to stardom.

Satchmo strutted the low notes, signing his singalongs with Scat, a vocal style he invented (singer makes up nonsense-syllables over complex beat, crystallizing in 60s jazzfolk Lambert, Hendricks, and Ross). Louie's Dixieland-Ragtime-Ballad-Pre-Rock-and-Roll classics feature: #12, 12-27 "Potato Head Blues," #1, 2-30 "St. Louis Blues," and even Hoagy Carmichael's super-complex-chorded "Stardust" [Louie #16, 12-31], the 1930-31 classic that was the #1 American favorite song – until Rock and Roll hit.

Satchmo was adaptable. He liked everybody, and everybody liked him. R & R admitted the sexagenarian (60+) triple-stop stomper (trumpet technique) to its teenage kingdom with many top tunes: Louie covered Fats Domino's #2 1956 "Blueberry Hill" (original Kay Kyser #11, 9-40) to a #29 1956 triumph. Louie did the "Moritat/Three-Penny Opera"prototype vocal (#20, 2-56) to "Mack the Knife," three years before Bobby Darin's Jazz Rock classic Vegas version.

The great music tabulator, Joel Whitburn, calls charismatic Satchmo "one of the towering giants in twentieth-century American music." Born in the hottest neighborhood in the Fertile Crescent (City) of Rock and Roll and Jazz – New Orleans – Louie Armstrong hitched his fortunes to the train they'd later dub "The City of New Orleans." He stormed north with his horn of plenty, joining the band of the mentor, **Kid Oliver**. Wife Lil persuaded him around 1926 to concoct a band of his own (she disdained his playing SECOND trumpet), and Louis became an international superstar. **Ken Burns**'s marvelous PBS epic *Jazz* (1-2001) cites Louis as being influenced by the man who may have invented Rock and Roll's direct ancestor Jazz in 1905 – **Buddy Bolden**. The name BUDDY will loom large in sculpting Rock and Roll, too. Louis Armstrong first crunched the top ten with #8, 7-26 "Muskrat Ramble," headlining his magnificent band: **Kid Ory** on trombone, Johnny Dodds (clarinet), Johnny St. Cyr on banjo, and rounding out his Hot Five, wife **Lil** Armstrong on piano. She once wryly remarked that Louie's international fame caused some women to throw themselves at him. Louie, she lamented, didn't always get out of the way.

Burns marvels at the 12-bar Blues progression (R & R forerunner) and virtuoso riffs and *cadenzas* of Louie's #8, 9-28 "West End Blues." His other masterpieces include #7, 9-29 "Ain't Misbehavin',"

#11, 2-30 "St. Louis Blues," his first #1 "All of Me" [#1(2), 2-32], #14, 8-32 "Rockin' Chair," and #1, 1964 "Hello Dolly."

Louis Armstrong's vision embraced the whole century. Ostensibly born on the 4th of July, 1900, Louis sculpted Jazz via Dixieland, and helped launch Rock and Roll on the spirit of his booming beat. Perhaps no one ever loved popular music and performed it with more vigor and enthusiasm and charisma than Satchmo. Fortunately for America, we were blessed with Louis Armstrong from 1900 to 1971 . . . and his music dazzles our future with hope and glory and love. Oh, yes, the oldest person ever to get a #1 hit?

"Hello, Dolly!" – Louis Armstrong. #1(1), 2-64; No Chart R & B. Note date. Flying higher than the moptop barrage of happy Beatle tunes, 63-year-old Louie's song hit the height on the absolute crest of Beatlemania. Just two months later, the Fab Four placed nine out of the top ten on the Miami charts. "Hello, Dolly!" is a gentle Dixieland crescendo tune, loosely based on 1949 song "Sunflower." Louie's homespun lyric is a hearth and fireside testimonial to the wonder and glory of Dolly's return home. Whereas Louis Armstrong was pumping out classics with thumping 2/4 downbeats way back in 1917 just like "Hello, Dolly!," he was about forty years ahead of his time. Teenagers today recall Louie "Satchmo" Armstrong for his haunting posthumous ballad (by 17 years), "What a Wonderful World" (#32, 2-88). Had the Hendrix-Morrison-Kurt Cobain crew of rock nihilists and downside dreamers, who had some of Louie's musical genius, picked up on the UP side of his philosophy (funny-cig-puffing Louie was no saint or health fanatic), they might still be around today, cranking out classics.

Popular music can be pretty simple. Louis would begin with a pop melody like "Saints," which launched Tony Sheridan and the **Beatles** in 1961, and then pad and embellish it to stamp his brand of genius upon it for the ages. Much early rock and roll took ultra-simple themes: Nursery Rhymes. Mom Goose. Remember Vito Piccone and the Elegants' streetcorner classic "Little Star" (#1, 7-58)? It rolls with a sweet Chalypso beat: combo of Rock and Roll, Calypso, and Cha-Cha-Cha.

"Little Star" – The Elegants. #1(1), 7-58; #1(4), R & B. Boy wonder "Wolfy" Mozart wrote this classic tune, "Twinkle, Twinkle, Little Star," when he was only five years old, prompting esoteric musicians to label rock as too-simple music. The Elegants project the Streetcorner Chord Pattern upon their rolling 'wo-uh-ho' Hollyesque intro. Then they twist the sparkling toddler's star into a wishing star for lovers. Clever remake. Staten Island semi-soul sounds. Good beat. You can dance to it. Dick Clark and *American Bandstand* dug it. Give it a 99. Whoopee. Rock and Roll can be simple. And fun. And here to stay. Will it never die? Beat goes on.

Vito + Elegants were not alone on their hilly Isle of Staten. Nursery Rhyme themes dominate the panorama of Rock and Roll. Buddy Holly's Crickets puffed out their *That'll Be the Day* album with a hard-rock tune called "Rock Me My Baby," (No Chart [or N.C.], 1957) which was semi-loosely woven around "Hickory, Dickory Dock." Sammy Turner hornswoggled critics with his #3 rock nursery ballad "Lavender Blue" in 1959. On the Byrds' *Mr. Tambourine Man* #6 1965 album, "The Bells of Rhymney" nursery rhyme interweaves their haunting harmonies. Chubby Checker's first pre-Twist hit, "The Class" (#38, 5-59), features crackerjack imitations of Elvis, the Coasters, Fats Domino, and the Chipmunks (some other comedy rock in the hodge-podge). The tune Chubby uses? "Mary Had a Little Lamb"!

THE NUMBERS GAMES:
Right On? Or . . . Smoke & Mirrors?

I'd like to say every number in this book is absolutely, totally accurate. *Billboard* magazine's accuracy is profound, Joel Whitburn's books on the *Billboard* charts are as accurate as humanly possible. You might wonder, though, if some record store owner in Keokuk or Kalamazoo or Kauai maybe fudges his own 'sales chart' a tad, for his own favorite song. You wonder if all those bleary neon jukeboxes can really tabulate number-of-plays so fast it hits the big *Billboard* charts.

No, I DON'T believe the charts are like the HUMBUG Wizard of Oz, faking his omnipotence in an emerald haze of smoke and mirrors. Yes, I do believe the Recording Industry strives for total chart accuracy. The charts may not be PERFECTLY cast in [Rolling] Stones, but they are ANCHORED in ROCK. Mostly, I believe.

As Buddy Holly modestly remarked, "Without Elvis, none of us would have made it." Without Buddy, **Bobby Vee** ("Take Good Care of My Baby," #1, 8-61) and **Tommy Roe** ("Sheila", #1, 9-62) might never have made it. Nor would the **Beatles.**

When searching for the roots of Rock and Roll, nobody ever seems to cite the Polka. Many rock fans enjoy Weird Al Yankovic's parody of Michael Jackson's #1 "Beat It" ("Eat It," #12, 3-84) or "Gump" (#18, 5-96), parody of rocker "Lump." Few know Al is related to the Polka King Frankie Yankovic.

"Just Because" – Frankie Yankovic & His Yanks, #9, 5-48. Cleveland's Frankie Yankovic wowed the factory towns like Detroit, Milwaukee, Youngstown, and Pittsburgh in the 40s and 50s. His lusty downbeat 2/4-time polkas streamed out of longgone radios and stompin' Saturday nights of joy, kielbasa, and smog. Frankie's supersonic accordion rolled out the ol' barrel for 'brewski' camaraderie under gaslight glow and fiery forges. For 1948, Frankie and the boys followed up his top tenner with #12, 3-49 "Blue Skirt Waltz," featuring the Marlin Sisters' vocal. Frankie really ROCKED!

To prove the Polka pedigree in early rock music, check out Elvis's SUN Records demo of "Just Because" which never charted. From Warsaw, Poland, and from Czechoslovakia, Switzerland, Lithuania, or Austria, Polka Power was the harbinger of something with a much bigger beat to come: from the duple meter 2/4 to the back beat 4/4 (accentuate the 2 & 4 beats) of Rock and Roll.

What is the most important instrument in Rock and Roll? THE HUMAN VOICE

During the cavalcade of zillions of Rock anthems which have twanged, bleeped, squawked, shrieked, boomed, blasted, or murmured the Rock Revolution, the overarching lead instrument is almost always the human voice.

Rock and Roll has been dominated by belltone 'Irish' tenors. [Bear in mind some of the greatest 'Irish tenors' are Afro-American, or Swedish, or Japanese.] Immediately, Smokey Robinson and Ritchie Valens and Aaron Neville and Vince Gill and Tommy Roe and Art Garfunkel and N'Sync's Justin Timberlake and Phil Everly come to mind. If you go any higher, you'll hit the falsetto guys:

Frankie Valli, Disco-phase Bee Gee Barry Gibb, Russell Thompkins. The Temptations' Eddie Kendricks floated celestially between Irish tenor and falsetto. The early 60s trio of semi-recognized superstars, **Del Shannon**, **Roy Orbison**, and Gene Pitney, could sing pretty much anywhere from bass to falsetto.

Let's take it back to the beginning. Various faux-Dutchmen like Harry Von Tilzer were writing various faux 'auld sod' Irish ditties for the Tin Pan Alley market. **Tin Pan Alley**, of course, was that New York City coterie of music publishers who wrote the folks what they wanted. What they wanted were green green Irish homeland tunes of Galway Bay and Killarney and Tralee or Scottish Brigadoon, replete with gray-green mountain vistas and sheep and nevermore misty reverie. What they didn't want was anything to remind them of their squashed cold-water flats on Bleecker Street, with noisy pushcarts and poverty, and gray snowbanks grimed with the recycled food of horses and wild pigs. They found an actual Irishman to be their tenor – **John McCormack** (6-16-1884 – 8-16-1945 [same August death date as Elvis]). His crystalline *bel canto* voice could fill opera houses and make hardbitten cops cry:

"Where the River Shannon Flows" – John McCormack, #3, 3-1913. Pop music chronicler extraordinaire Joel Whitburn calls my grandmother [Nana's] ELVIS the best-known Irish tenor of all time. McCormack also did #1(5), 7-1911 "Mother Machree," #1(8), 1-1915 "It's A Long, Long Way to Tipperary," and #1(7), 6-1911 "I'm Falling in Love with Someone." This River Shannon was near and dear to Irish-American hearts, but McCormack's swan song is his #1(3), U.S.A. tribute "The Star-Spangled Banner" of 5-17 World War I, before it became the National Anthem (McCormack was from Athlone, Ireland).

McCormack did not discover operatic recording. **Enrico Caruso** (1873-1921) became the first recording star millionaire. He was gifted with a deeper Italian Dramatic Tenor, like **Luciano Pavarotti** (b. 1935, Modena, Italy, Album #4, 9-94 *The 3 Tenors in Concert)*. Caruso's scratchy recordings, which sold hundreds of thousands to crank-'em-up Victrolas in WWI parlors, symbolized America's quest for High Culture in a prosperous Pre-Depression era. Scratches were due, obviously, to emerging technology, and no fault of Caruso's magnificent voice. Operatic rock singers of the rock

era include the versatile Roy Orbison, Jackie Wilson (#4, '60s *Samson & Delilah* aria "Night"), Jay Black of the Americans, Elvis in "It's Now or Never" (#1, '60), Gary Puckett, Joe Perry, Tom Jones, Meat Loaf, and female stars Aretha Franklin, Timi Yuro, Della Reese, Odetta, Mariah Carey, Whitney Houston, and Patti LaBelle. They run the gamut of tones from deep contralto (Odetta) to high coloratura soprano (Carey).

"Le Donne e Mobile (Woman Is Fickle)" – Enrico Caruso, #5, 7-1908. Among oldest RECORDS – not just sheet music. From opera *Rigoletto*. Caruso classic. Audio tapes didn't emerge till the late 40s. Via Nazi battlefield engineering skills, we absorbed their scientists like Einstein and Von Braun, and discovered the atomic bomb and a trip to the moon. With no taping or overdubbing, every 'take' for McCormack or Caruso was a 'keeper.' Using a gaggle of horns, big-beat rhythm via bass and snare at times, and sweet strings, Caruso lofts his mammoth resonant voice over the entire band. He's super-resonant. Very booming in timbre. To hear a great Caruso imitation, catch Mario Lanza's "Loveliest Night of the Year" (#3, 4-51) This waltz gets played on carny carousels throughout the known universe. Caruso actually made a couple of million in the Oughts and Teens (1900-20) from RECORDS, which would dominate the airwaves until tapes and CD's and maybe someday DAT's would brush on by.

Big Bands formed a pre-rock backdrop. Perhaps the most famous Big Bandsman is **Glenn Miller** (1904-44), who quite sadly started the cavalcade of great music makers who fell victim to small planes on bad flying nights. Big bands began to coalesce in the 20s under **Paul Whiteman**, who topped the bandstand with his enormous presence until well into the 50s TV era. Often they featured vocalists; Rudy Vallee and **Frank Sinatra** and Dinah Shore and Sarah Vaughan and Ella Fitzgerald emerged from the musical umbrella of the Big Bands. Glenn Miller, with his bespectacled (Holly wasn't first) dignified demeanor, proved to a nation of moonlight-sonata romance fans that love was just a 'Tuxedo Junction' around the corner in 'Kalamazoo' to get 'In the Mood' for love (a 'String of Pearls' of Miller's hit-song titles, capitalized for your glee). Glenn's biggest hit, however, via trombone, trumpet, or bandstand, is this golden goodie:

"Moonlight Serenade" – Glenn Miller (& Orchestra), #3, 7-39. Huge debut and theme song for beloved Clarinda, Iowa, band star. Easy flowing melodic masterpiece – a sweet counterpoint to the mad flashing cannons in Europe and Pearl Harbor. "Moonlight Serenade" reels shimmeringly with the star-streaming huddle and cuddle fandango fantasia of all the deep purple stardust ballrooms of longlost America. Lovers whispered sweet forever promises, and shared insta-passions under a palm-frond moonlight wash of sweet Miller music, filling hearts with hope that might not shatter on the smoke-on-the-water, skyfire sands of Iwo Jima. Or Bataan. Or Anzio Beach head. Surf, flak, and destiny were up. Our 50s idols bounced off the Big Bands; sometimes their seeming rebellion was an actual salute. Elvis recorded early ballads like "My Happiness," [#2(2), 5-48 John & Sandra Steele]. Buddy enjoyed Country and Jazz standards, and Chuck was a Jazz/Big Band aficionado, actually joining Johnnie Johnson's band – rather than vice-versa. Miller's easy style of music was great to cure a chaotic and war-torn era. Miller Time. As we settled down into the sweet malt shop 50s, however, and gazed at twirling swirling poodle skirts and cheerleaders, something a little more frantic bolted forth – the Age of Rock and Roll.

Enter **Mr. Beaubien**. Harry James and Count Basie and Duke Ellington and Tommy & Jimmy Dorsey and veteran Paul Whiteman were batting about the U.S.A. and U.S.O., making fine music for the troops and Americans of all ages. Teenagers, however, were looking to the Blues. Danny Beaubien's master electrician father, whose name to me was always Mister Beaubien, was playing in a Big Band in the 20s. His son Danny (keyboards) and I (guitar, vocals, bass sometimes) played in a rock combo called the Trade Winds at $\Delta\Sigma\Phi$ and ΣAM and ZBT fraternity parties in 1962 at Detroit's Wayne State University. We also did the Tuesday night gig at the Alcove Pub, where songwriter **Joni Mitchell** (and longgone hubby Chuck) had the Saturday night gig. Anyhow, way back in, I believe, 1926, Mr. Beaubien (Danny was 19 and his dad 66 in 1962) wanted to get his rhythm dobro (big hollow-body, with resonator) guitar a bit louder. He rigged up a jiffy pick-up to amplify the sound. Mr. Beaubien invented the hollow-body electric guitar?

Many rock critics have sought the fountain-of-youth date when someone actually invented the most important instrument of Rock and Roll. You can study the early era of Les Paul and the pioneering efforts of **Leo Fender**, whose Les Paul-inspired solid-body Stratocaster Buddy Holly made famous. Nowhere, however, have we detected any earlier claim than Mister Beaubien's 1926 do-it-yourself ELECTRIC GUITAR. Who can forget Mister Beaubien's choppy, crunching style, as he hammered out something rather new on the ukulele-blooming

horizon – JAZZ CHORDS, gleaned from his spanking-new 1926 chord book and thundering down to 1962, as Danny and I chortled in wonder.

Muddy Waters, *Mississippi Delta bluesman*

Then came the Country/Bluegrass/Folk deluge. The microphone replaced the megaphone of **Rudy Vallee**. Archivist Allan Lomax and poet Carl Sandburg followed folk singer **Woody Guthrie** around on his Dust-Bowl odyssey. They also recorded then-cotton-picking field hand **Muddy Waters** of Mississippi on his Delta Blues back in 1941 for the Library of Congress. The **Carter Family** sang sweet Scotch-Irish Appalachian thirds harmonies on #3, 8-1928 "Wildwood Flower" and gospel-inspired #17, 8-35 "Can the Circle Be Unbroken?" (redone by son-in-law **Johnny Cash**). Folk/Country music was getting very big, like #4, 5-25 "The Wreck of the Old 97" of Vernon Dalhart, later parodized in a subway snafu ("M.T.A.", #15, '59) by the Kingston Trio. Dalhart's #1(5), 3-25 AND #1(7), 12-25 "Prisoner's Song" notched seven million sales – the #1 non-Christmas tune of the entire pre-Rock (to 1955) era (Whitburn).

Somewhere back there, under an Allegheny Moon in the misty mountain moonlight madness, somebody noticed that the miked singers were getting too much louder than the semi-silent guitar. Enter again Mr. Beaubien. The electric guitar twanged at first in traditional Bluegrass, flashily featuring a swift picking style, nasal thirds harmony, and folk lyrics often 500 years old from Scotland. Finally, **Roy Acuff** (1903-92) and his Acuff-Rose Publishing empire took over Nashville. Acuff's steel/electric guitar song celebrates American geography:

"The Wabash Cannonball" – Roy Acuff, #12, 12-38. Fiddler by trade, Acuff cruises the 'hobo jungles' of trackside pre-R & R America. His melody plods magnificently along with the whistling train. Acuff celebrates the roar and the rumble, as the chugging locomotive glides regally past lakes and woodlands and hobo haunts. Acuff's dreamy vignettes gloss pleasantly the bedrock reality of frozen Depression drizzles, and a can of cold homeless hobo beans split among five nomadic drifters on the iffy road of life. In this song, you've got to love the crying steel guitar (Hawaiian guitar) as it overlays triplet arpeggios (notes of the chord played one at a time). He dusts the romantic whistle stops, chugging along with hope and harmony and several good homespun reasons to win the war and bring the boys home.

Can't forget the Caribbean. **Mitchell Torok**'s #26, 8-53 unclassifiable "Caribbean" (and #27, 8-59) predates Reggae, Calypso, or even regular Rock and Roll before his more traditional standard rock ballad "Pledge of Love" (#25, 4-57). His frenzied second verse covers this supercute *Curious George*-style monkey, high in a tree, pondering why people actually mimic HIM; finally, the party-animal simian forsakes his arboreal perch, jumps down, and joins the people's Conga Line. The Louisiana Hayride's Torok flirts with Cajun music in "Caribbean." Torok, in this one, jumps upon the early-50s dance crazes from the sunny, balmy, palm-frondy, girls-in-grass-skirt dreamlands of the American male: the Mambo, Rhumba, Samba, the Conga, the Cha-Cha. Somehow he mixes in all their frantic, feisty beats – anticipating Gloria Estefan's English/Spanish & 'Spanglish' hits of the 80s and 90s like "Conga" (#10, 10-85) or "Live for Loving You" (#22, 10-91), or Lou Bega's #3, 8-99 "Mambo No. 5 (A Little Bit Of . . . .)."

Torok is no ganja-grooving Rastafarian. He is no supercool UB-40 Elvis interpreter, nor a Claptonish **Bob Marley** type. Caribbean beats, also antithetical to no-beat music, were the forefront of Rock and Roll. The first big Rock and Roll Caribbean song came from Liverpool, Nova Scotia, Canada – home of the original **Cajuns [Acadians]:**

"Rhumba Boogie" – Hank Snow, N.C. 1951; #1(8) 3-51 Country. Hank Snow, (1914-99) aptly named for his local weather, scorched a hot Country career in the early 50s playing flat-out Rock and Roll long before Haley and Holly. In 1955, his fiscally-unimpaired manager, **Colonel Tom Parker**, ran off to manage a sideburned movie-star-faced kid called The Hillbilly Cat from Sun Records in Memphis. Elvis or something.

Rock and Rockabilly are kissin' cousins. Snow's "Rhumba Boogie" glommed onto his two train hits, both Country #1's: #1(21), 7-50 C "I'm Movin' On" (#40 for soul-crossover genius Ray Charles in 1959) and "The Golden Rocket (#1[2], 11-50 C.) Snow's booming country baritone sings about Madame Mazonga, who teaches the conga. Down in Havana, she's got a groovy cabana.

Snow plumps the Pre-Castro Cuban paradisical good times, with fun to spare. "Rhumba Boogie" is a Hillbilly hammerin' rhumba.

Jazz, like Rock, had a tough start. Rejected as gross midnight music from speakeasies and Houses of the Rising Sun, Jazz took Paul Whiteman's road to respectability. By the time **Benny Goodman** got hold of it, it was bound for glory. Rock and Roll was waiting in the wings. Goodman, who played his sweet, sophisticated "licorice stick" clarinet to a bamboozling enchantment of his giant audiences, started the whole concept of an audience. Huh? Before Goodman, musicians played to dancers. Bands provided a musical backdrop for dance and romance.

With Goodman and his clarinet, Jazz aficionados just listened to Benny and marveled at his speedo expertise. It was a very big deal, to the symphonic minions of NYC's upper crust, when the modest lad from Chicago brought down the house at Carnegie Hall. Mesmerized super stupors of adoration.

The audience sat transfixed. Goodman was held in great awe by the music-watchers, who were termed ALLIGATORS by the jazz-buff press. Hence, "See You Later, Alligator" (#5, '56) was a smash phrase/song for Bill Haley. These Alligators of the late thirties provided the later audiences for Carlos Santana, Eric Clapton, or Jimmy Page, as their sizzling solos wailed across the high-arctic icy topmost squealing frets of their Fenders and Gibsons. Without Benny Goodman, Eddie Van Halen might have plunked and twanged some twiddly little note and sat down glumly.

"Stompin' at the Savoy" – Benny Goodman, #11,7-36. Swing essence. The 30s brought us Swing Jazz, with Goodman's crackerjack musicians playing the utmost in musical technique. Like Armstrong on the trumpet, Goodman's solos improvised magnificent solos called cadenzas. In the late 50s, goodwill ambassador

Goodman toured the Soviet Union, melting Cold War ice with Cool Jazz. The Savoy was a storied dance hall.

"God Bless America" – Kate Smith, #10, 4-39; #5, 7-40; #23, 1-42. As the Nazi menace deepened, "God Bless America" returned. Kate's American anthem, warbled sweetly by the zaftig mezzo soprano, is a paragon of patriotism. When "God Bless America," by Jewish Irving Berlin, rattled the dance halls and airwaves of America, we were 100% behind the dump-Hitler war effort. As "God Bless America" shook the U.S.A., *Der Führer* was rattling sabres and invading Poland (see Spike Jones's great-but-gaseous #3, 10-42 "Der Fuehrer's Face"). Kate's rallying unified Americans to stand on guard for the oncoming onslaught. Nearly 300.000 Americans were killed in this ghastly Armageddon (Vietnam? 50,000): let no one doubt the power of popular music to change the ultimate destiny of history. "God Bless America" is so much more than our new 7th-inning stretch song at major-league ball parks.

Just as Pearl Harbor (12-7-41) rallied America to action via Smith/Berlin's silver-medal anthem, so did it rally the American people on 9-11-2001. The World Trade Center attack, imputed to Osama Bin Laden of Saudi Arabia, galvanized America to respond strongly to terrorism. Christians, Jews, Muslims, Hindus, Buddhists, and all religious people of good will envision America as a land sanctified by freedom and democracy and justice.

Osama Bin Laden and his Taliban associates in Afghanistan opted to forbid music – especially Rock and Roll. Here in America, citizens of all faiths praise God with music, and we make a joyful noise!

Now let's praise the obvious roots of rock – the ones everybody cites: Jazz and Blues. Jazz overlaps many musical forms. We'll skirt Jazz and return later.

Let's check out downtown Memphis. Revel in its renaissance at **B.B. King**'s club on Beale Street. King is often called the Father of the Blues, via his guitar 'Lucille' ("The Thrill Is Gone," #15, 1-70). If you head east, you'll pass the public park with the authentic street Blues band and the 6-year-old prodigy banging his lilliputian mini-drum set along with them. Then look left. There's a tiny "shotgun shack" (two-room house where you could shoot a shotgun from the front and out the back door) that will come in handy:

W. C. Handy. **William Christopher Handy** escaped a minstrel show, and founded his own music publishing company in Memphis in 1908; it was a bold entrepreneurial move in that day, for an African-American songwriter and cornet player. Ironically, the first real blues song he ever did got its start as "Mr. Crump," a song for a candidate for Memphis mayor. By 1912, three years later, it had

evolved into "Memphis Blues." "St. Louis Blues" (#9, 11-23) is Handy's dandy. Many Blues scholars, like their rock counterpart scholars who cite Bill Haley's 1954's "Rock Around the Clock," have decided that Handy's "St. Louis Blues" of 1923 was the first real Blues tune. They count the Blues era from here.

If you saw the Robert Macchio movie *Crossroads* (1986), you may be familiar with **Robert Johnson**, the world's most mysterious and elusive Blues legend. Born, perhaps, on May 8, 1911, Johnson succumbed on August 16, 1938, by either getting stabbed by a jealous husband, or a woman, or perhaps he was poisoned . . . Johnson, with an electric countertenor voice, fondled wild supersonic Blues riffs on his acoustic guitar. Johnson cut a mere 45 sides in his stubby career. "Crossroads Blues" and "Terraplane Blues" achieved modest hitdom (NC, 11-36) in a tentative Depression record market. Reared in Greenwood, Mississippi, Johnson became one of those revered American Delta Blues guitarists who jolted the Brit-invaders with his staccato machine-gun guitar pyrotechnics and unforgettable songs. Check out his 'cover bands': the **Rolling Stones** redid "Love in Vain" and "Stop Breaking' Down." The first English super-group, **Cream**, featured Johnson's "Crossroads" (#28, 1-69) in their Fillmore East live show, with guitar guru **Eric Clapton** at full-tilt boogie.

Deeper than Johnson or Handy are the roots of Rock and Roll. Musicologist **Craig Boyd** cites field chants of Africans, plus the engagingly complex conga-drum message movers of tribal rainforest rhythm couriers. Alan Lomax and Carl Sandburg (in his *American Songbag*) rustled up Bluesman tunes by Muddy Waters (1941) on the cusp of Rock and Roll. Robert Palmer cites the Graves Brothers' "Barbecue Bust" with "fully formed Rock and Roll guitar riffs and a stomping rock and roll beat" in Hattiesburg, Mississippi between (like, wow) 1929 and 1936.

Jimmie Rodgerses I & II helped define rock music. **Jimmie Rodgers I** (1897-1933, died of tuberculosis), among the first white Blues artists, was nicknamed the "Mississippi Blue Yodeler." Hoboing on midnight rails over the breadth of the U.S.A., Rodgers I wailed 12-Bar Blues on his sonorous twelve-string, combining high, wide, and handsome yodels with a glottal stop suggesting a Buddy

Holly hiccup. Recording 13 'Blue Yodels,' he's most famous for "Blue Yodel #9," with Louis Armstrong; the first "T for Texas" (#2[1], 3-28) sold a million in a penny-pinching era.

Jimmie Rodgers II (born 1933), no relation, pioneered Folk Rock seven years before Bob Dylan or the Byrds: "Honeycomb" (#1, 9-57), and Weavers' 1951 anthem "Kisses Sweeter Than Wine" (#3, 11-57), about a multi-generational love affair with his own wife.

Jimmie Rodgers's 12-string in the 30s was soon accompanied by the Hawaiian guitar, effectively invented in 1931 by **Joseph Kekeku**, who first toyed with open tuning. Joseph Kekeku invented slide guitar, which sloshes to heady heights via 80s Caucasian-persuasion Blues legends George Thorogood and the Delaware Destroyers. During the 2000's, Joe Kekeku's 1931 SLACK-KEY guitar style currently dominates the Hawaiian hit parade via stars like Leabert Lindsey and the Ka'au Crater Boys.

Rodgers' yodeling is a Swiss technique; the 30s singer shifts instantly between an ordinary tenor or baritone and then falsetto, via soaring octaves and quick shifts back to normal range. A mainstay of cowboy singers like **Gene Autry**, **Roy Rogers**, or cowboy-oriented **Bob Wills and his Texas Playboys**, yodeling hits its Swiss peak of zest and zowie and zoom in the eclectic 1972 vocal exercise "Coopersville Yodel" of **Del Shannon**, cut live on the English Isle of Wight, and named after his Michigan home town. As kindergarten 50s cowboys, we were all Roy Rogers' "Little Buckaroos":

"Happy Trails" – Roy Rogers and Dale Evans, the 40s, NC. This melodic home-on-the-range classic told all of us postwar kids that good was good and bad was bad. Rogers, "King of the Cowboys" and bronco buster extraordinaire, patrolled the Wild West with his adorable real-life wife Dale Evans, his noble palomino Trigger (hers was Buttermilk), and his trusty six-shooters. To many today, Roy is a fast-food joint. To me, he was a hero worth believing in. As a singer, he's a fine yodeling maestro who thrives on Western music, and the 2nd-best yodeler I've ever heard (see Shannon, above).

"Back in the Saddle Again" – Gene Autry, 1943 NC. New sound, sort of. Both songs are now campy city-slicker soundtrack stuff. Autry, unadorned with Riders of the Purple Sage for harmony, had to hoof it alone. With a truly kindly tenor, Autry's anthem here is labeled Western Swing. Autry croons mellowly of the glories of sundown gold and long lost lone Colorado trails. His Western Swing style, like Bob Wills's, dovetails into Country Rock, using Boogie-Woogie 12-Bar Blues and the

big beat. Oddly, neither of these two Western signature anthems charted.

Best-known devotee of the Western Swing style, and forerunner of Rock and Roll, was **Bob Wills**. Bob's "San Antonio Rose" (#15, 6-39) " energized a generation. Bob's #8 Country-only 11-50 "Faded Love" may be among the top 20 Country songs of all time, in terms of defining Country music.

Cajun music, too, developed in the Crescent City. New Orleans, apex of the Mississippi Delta, imparted its unique Mardi Gras French flavor on its Acadian emigres from Nova Scotia ('Acadia' = 'Cajun'). Tunes jumped like "Big Mamou" in 1953 (#19, Pete Hanley), and accordion-laced rockin' Cajuns like Clifton Chenier (1925-87) throbbed "Louisiana Stomp" and "Squeeze Box Boogie." Chenier sang in French patois, Creole, and English, inspiring the 1980s Zydeco fad. #1 Hillbilly legend Hank Williams' famous Cajun song (#20, 9-52 & #1[14], 8-52 C) "Jambalaya," rife with crawfish pie, yummy gumbo, and bayou romance, inspired Creedence Clearwater Revival's superstar John Fogerty to a 1972 #16 remake.

Rock and Roll is a heavenly hodge-podge. Rock and Roll is a lot of different kinds of music. It's a multicultural cornucopia of big-beat music. Rock and Roll ties together shreds of Ragtime, Melodic Ballads, Big-Band Standards, Dixieland, Swing, Cool Jazz, Western Swing, Hillbilly/Country-Western, Cajun, Polka, Marches, Opera, Hawaiian, African, Down-Home Delta Blues, and a score of other diverse musical strains. Most of the time, Rock and Roll fronts a dynamic singer and an electric guitar. By the late 50s, the electric bass, popularized by Cricket **Joe B. Mauldin**, dumped the old bull fiddles, and **Elvis's D. J. Fontana** made the drummer a permanent fixture in every Rock and Roll band. You can coalesce the whole thing into the singer, the guitar, bass, and drums. Rock and Roll. Simple, yet profound.

The straightest line to Rock and Roll runs directly from Ragtime to Rhythm and Blues and Boogie-Woogie – we get the 12-bar Blues chord progression. It's time to stop pussyfooting around the Kool Kats of Rock and Roll. It's nearly time to Rock Around the Clock. So where did Rock's Greatest Instruments come from? And which ones found Memory Lane a dead-end alley?

Just a Song at Twilight, with (Guitar) Strings Attached

4

Basic Rock boils down to tremendous songs improved by the guitar and its rhythmic pals – the drums, bass (guitar), and often the piano/keyboard and/or sax. Although great rock songs are occasionally enhanced by unique instrumentation from ukuleles to tubas to flügelhorns and oboes, the mystique of Rock and Roll glory swirls around the singer and his/her guitar.

This next totally unanswerable question will get you 800 discordant answers. Awhile back, we touched upon it, but it needs some elaboration:

"WHAT IS THE MOST IMPORTANT INSTRUMENT IN A ROCK BAND?"

From superstars like **Eric Clapton, Jimi Hendrix, Les Paul, Jimmy Page,** or **Carlos Santana,** you'd get a resounding chorus of "GUITAR!" From similar superstars like **John Bonham, Keith Moon, Charlie Watts** or **Neil Peart,** you'd hear a thumping tattoo of "DRUMS!" Beyond the spotlight, and hammering the bottomtone thick cables that could hold up the Brooklyn Bridge, booming bass maestros like **Paul McCartney, 'Sting,' James Jamerson, John Entwistle,** or **John Paul Jones** might thunder from the deeps, "the BASS!" Better not ask **Jerry Lee Lewis** or **Little Richard** or **Elton John** or **Billy Joel,** because they might sing out with a loud "PIANO!" Then again, they might wait up for the answer this paragraph is pussyfooting around; and if you asked **Junior Walker** or **King Curtis** or **Kenny G** (or **Daddy G** or **Clarence Clemons**), they just might holler "SAXOPHONE!" All these great answers, however, can at best garner the silver medal. How so?

If you polled all the Rock and Roll fans since the dawn of rhythm, only one answer would blast bombastically forth: "the HUMAN VOICE!"

For proof, simply rack up the number of instrumentals on the charts. Now, blend in sung songs. Case closed? Obviously, a cappella biggees are rare, too. Rock vocals marry rock guitars and live semi-happily ever after.

As Rock blasted past a smooth wave of Perry Como crooners, who lavished slow love songs, a wild wave of belters emerged. **Little Richard** [Penniman] led the crew with wild whoops and yodel-kicks on "Tutti Frutti" and "Rip It Up." His Specialty brand of Rock and Soul was tempered by the pioneering R & B Belter Blues of **Lloyd Price**, Big Joe Turner, or Louis Jordan. Soon he would be joined by **James Brown** with all of his electrifying energy – and whose first hits featured crooner Como's #1 1946 classic "Prisoner of Love." From easygoing crooners like **Buddy Clark** ["Linda," a 1947 ode to Paul McCartney's future wife] or **Al Martino** ["Here in My Heart"] or **Kitty Kallen** ["Little Things Mean a Lot"], Rock and Soul electrified the quietude with **Little Richard's** proteges: **Wanda** "Let's Have a Party" **Jackson; Willie Mae 'Big Mama' Thornton** and the #1 R & B 1953 original "You Ain't Nothin' but a Hound Dog"; **Screamin' Jay Hawkins** (1930-2000, who lugged a skull in his wild stage act) with "I Put a Spell on You"; **Jackie Wilson,** super Opera-Soul belter from **Bill Haley's** Highland Park, Michigan, and his "Reet Petite" and "Lonely Teardrops."

In a way, CROONING and R & R vocal BELTING combined. Records featured fast and slow sides, and vocal styles converged.

As Rock and Roll stampeded the quiet crooning caravan with a wailing wall of strident sound – and a few merry melodies – the era's superstars juggled on a jiggly tightrope the very best of each sound. Sometimes they could blast the best crooner/belter licks into the same song. **Buddy Holly** had the most versatile 50s voice, though **Elvis** and **Bobby Darin** were no slouches at speed-shifting musical moods. On "Rave On" and "I'm Gonna Love You Too" and "Not Fade Away" and "Rock Around with Ollie Vee," Holly's louder credentials charge into the musical fray. Yet on "True Love Ways" and "Everyday" and "Moondreams" and "What do Do," Holly matches the softest and sweetest and moodiest of the timeless stardust crooners. Buddy bounces brazenly into middle ground on many of his classics, charging from booming tunes into easygoing balladry and then comfortably into that no-man's land in the middle with an engaging grin and an unforgettable melody: the happy hiccuping of "Peggy Sue," the playful yodel-kicks of "Maybe Baby," the shifting existential moods of his swan song "It Doesn't Matter Anymore." Buddy Holly's amazing versatility took him to the top, and translated Rock and Roll into reality for a sleepy, croony America plodding along with phantom drummers and non-rhythmic pretty melodies. Who else helped?

Elvis, you say. Of course. The King belts out "Money Honey" and **Thornton**'s "Hound Dog" and "Wear My Ring Around Your Neck" and his ultimate Hard Rock video anthem, **Leiber/Stoller**'s masterful "Jailhouse Rock." El stomps the mellifluous middle ground just as expertly, and croon-belts his biggest hit "Don't Be Cruel," plus "Too Much," "A Fool Such As I," "Suspicious Minds," and "Return to Sender." His mesmerizing crooning overlays his profoundest smoochy ballads: both "Love Me" and "Love Me Tender" (#2 and #1 simultaneously), "Don't," "Are You Lonesome Tonight," and his most requested hit ever – "Can't Help Falling in Love." And **Bobby Darin**? Yes. "Splish Splash" is his R & R belter debut that hit #3; "Dream Lover" is his 'Light Metal' croonily-belted #2 hit, and his #1(9) Kurt Weill classic "Mack the Knife" plunks Darin into an esoteric musical style warp, melding the best Jazz vocals of **Frank Sinatra** with the exciting crescendo power of crooner **Frankie Laine** or the operatic rock majesty of **Roy Orbison**. Other 50s VOCAL HYBRIDS? **Buddy Knox**'s smooth-crooned Rockabilly #1 belter "Party Doll" – #1, 2-47; **Fats Domino's** classic #2 1956 "Blueberry Hill," with hammering rock triplet notes and smooth-as-silk vocal; **Ricky Nelson**'s "Believe What You Say"; **Sam Cooke**'s "Chain Gang" at the decade's finale, and **Dee Clark**'s supercharged "Hey Little Girl"; or **Brenda Lee**'s "Sweet Nothin's" or the **Chantels'**

plaintive ballad "Maybe."

Can we compare more modern artists to the crooner/belter clash of the mid 50s? Why not? Try **Sting**'s moltenly mellow #23, 6-93 classic "Every Breath You Take." Or, N'Sync's **Justin Timberlake** on Richard Marx-penned #6, 8-2000 "This I Promise You." Or, try **Pearl Jam**'s #2(1), 5-99 reprise of **J. Frank Wilson**'s also-#2 1964 Graveyard Rock "Last Kiss." Although Heavy Metal's **Kiss** is known for screamers like "Detroit Rock City," their biggest hit was the croony jammin'-with-the-band-alibi song "Beth" (#7, 9-76). And if anyone ever had the gall to believe that crooning croaked at the half-century mark, they need only listen to the biggest hit of the second half – **Mariah Carey** and **Boyz II Men**'s incredible elegiac #1(16), "One Sweet Day." Whereas **James Brown** and the **Otis Redding/Wilson Pickett/Stax/Volt** crew besieged the sounds of silence with belting blasters, the softer side of Soul was crooned and platooned by the sensuous **Supremes** of Motown. A smooth cavalcade of **Temptations** and **Miracles** and **Pips** surges into Millennium III with **Boyz II Men**, and is heard in a million echoes from croon-rock idols the **Backstreet Boys** to other Barber Shop/harmonic crews like #1, 4-2000 "Bye Bye Bye" of 'N Sync **All-4-One**. YOU CAN TRACE A DIRECT LINE BETWEEN THE 2000+ "BOY BANDS" and their BARBER-SHOP PREDECESSORS from Dion's Belmonts and Little Anthony's Imperials to the Temps, the Miracles, and the Spinners.

Case in point? Whether it's Soft or Hard Rock, the most important and versatile instrument is the HUMAN VOICE. Little proof is needed to nail down this ultimate truth. We need only listen to a few songs commandeered by the passionate pipes of singers like **Celine Dion, Don Henley, John Fogerty, Barry Gibb (Bee Gees), Shania Twain, Paul McCartney, James Brown, Janis Joplin, Bobby Vee, Darren Hayes** ["I Knew I Loved You" **Savage Garden** #1, 1-2000], **Ricky Martin, Ritchie Valens, Roy Orbison, Del Shannon, LeAnn Rimes, Stevie Nicks, Bob Seger, Bruce Springsteen, Marc Anthony** (#2, 3-00 "You Sang to Me"), **Bobby** "Righteous Brother" **Hatfield, Elton John,** or **Tina Turner.** Whether it's the bewitching "Irish Tenor" style of Motown's **Smokey Robinson** or the rafter-shuddering bass of **Barry White**, the VOCALIST is the CAPTAIN of the song's ship as it glides on the Sea of Popularity.

But hold on. Here come the instruments, twanging and tuning up. And which one could nearly wipe out Rock and Roll if it took a sick day? The **GUITAR**, naturally . . .

When Buddy Holly strode out on stage with his red Fender Stratocaster at the Lubbock, Texas, roller rink in 1956, he never claimed to be the virtuoso that Les Paul was. Les dragged his solid-body guitar to the Gibson Guitar Company back in 1946, and was ostensibly laughed out of the place, but **Leo Fender** knew a bonanza when he saw one. Buddy never said he was a riff-romping raconteur of the upper-fret pyrotechnics, like "Maybellene's" Chuck Berry or Bill Haley's "Rock Around the Clock" lead guitar whiz **Danny Cedrone**, or a musical maestro like Les Paul himself on the flying frets, or **Chet Atkins** or **Charlie Christian**. Nope, the kid from Lubbock was primarily a singer/songwriter, who used his savvy on the Strat to augment and embellish his already tremendous tunes. With **Joe B. Mauldin** on acoustic bass (bull fiddle), **Jerry Allison** on drums, and third-cousin **Niki Sullivan** on rhythm guitar, Holly hammered out the Bo Diddley leads and the rhythmic blur of "Peggy Sue." Their **Crickets** were the first big modern Rock and Roll combo: lead and rhythm guitar, bass, and drums, with a lead singer and harmony from the background vocalists, who also played their instruments. Without the Crickets, there could have been no **Beatles!**

Relic acoustic guitars had four or five courses (1-2-3 gut strings together) according to Tony Bacon's super *Electric Guitars - The Illustrated Encyclopedia* (Thunder Bay Press, 2000). By 1560, five was the norm, with ten strings of five double courses, like a mandolin (four double courses) or today's 12-string guitar. By 1810, the A-D-G-B-E-tuned guitar added a sixth string – low E – to create today's 6-string.

Orville **Gibson** experimented with steel strings around 1880 in Kalamazoo, Michigan – to amplify his guitars. National guitars offered Dobro resonators in 1931, while **George Beauchamp** and **Paul Barth** offered a 1931 magnetic guitar pickup.

The actual invention of the electric guitar is lost in the swirling mists of antiquity. For lack of a better source, let's say **Mr. Beaubien** of Detroit, electrician by day and rhythm guitarist by night, was playing electric guitar actively in bands in the mid-20's. Other pioneers include **Django Reinhardt, Charlie Christian**, **Leo Fender**, and amp experimenter **Doc Kauffman**. **Joe Kekeku** of Hawaii modified it to become the steel or Hawaiian guitar in 1931, and it revolutionized emerging Country music, kissin' cousin of Rock and its hybrid, Rockabilly. By the time Leo Fender arrived at the Stratocaster in 1954 (via the Telecaster and Broadcaster), **Les Paul** and Gibson had already reunited with the Gibson Les Paul guitar model in early 1952. In the middle 60s, the Rickenbacker 12-string electric mellowized the sound of the Byrds via **Roger McGuinn**, and the wireless electric has created new freedom of motion since the 80s. Besides **Gene Vincent's Cliff Gallup** of the Blue Caps, and Ricky Nelson's lead-guitar superstar **James Burton**, three other 50s and 60s guitar stars were Corning NY/Phoenix Arizona's **Duane Eddy (& His Twangy Guitar)**, the **Ventures' Bob Bogle**, and **Dave Yorko** of **Johnny & the Hurricanes** from Toledo, Ohio – a town with few hurricanes, but a lot of ice and snow and wild night clubs (ah, my misspent youth). In the 60s, session superstars like **Joe Messina** and **Steve Cropper** sparked the sound of Soul. Upfront guitar giants like the Stones' **Keith Richard(s)**, the **Yardbirds' Eric Clapton and Jeff Beck and Jimmy Page**, or Seattle's fuzztone kahuna **Jimi Hendrix** turned the guitar from filler on the song's bridge to an instrument to nearly usurp the power of the singer. Among Heavy Metal bands, fiery fingers on the frets still make short shrift of the singer, dooming him/her to second-string stardom.

The fuzztone feedback sound was accidentally discovered by Country rocker **Marty Robbins** in 1961's #3 "Don't Worry" on the bass amp, and sparked a profusion of wah-wah pedals, tonal changes, distortions, and eventually synthesizer technology in the 80s. Guitars, like keyboards, may now echo the tonal timbre of a steam calliope, a flügelhorn, an oboe, or a bassoon. From **Stevie Ray Vaughan** to **Steve Vai** to **Yngwie Malmsteen** to **Akira Takasaki** (Tokyo's **Loudness**), dynamic lead guitar is the vanguard of Rock and Roll.

So what's the bronze medalist, after the VOICE and Guitar get voted in at GOLD and Silver? In **Gloria Estefan**'s words, "Rhythm's Gonna Get You."

In some lost Congo musical fiesta, the thobbing thump of the tempestuous tom-toms powered the people to heights of rhythmic glory. Ecstasy, maybe.

The roots of Rock and Roll might not even be in the Old Millennium (1000-1999, or maybe 1001-2000); they may dart back to primordial primeval time. From Congas to Bongoes to the onset of the snappitty snare, **DRUMS** furnish the pulse and power and heartbeat of Rock and Roll. Among the few instruments to be played with feet as well as hands, drums furnish the basic Rock rhythm and some of the Blues. You'll find a foot-driven bass drum, a central snare, a tenor and a tom-tom drum, a cowbell, a wood block, and four cymbals in a full set of traps. Plus two hi-hat cymbals, a ride cymbal, crash cymbal, and a sock cymbal. Drums are played with regular sticks, brushes, and soft tom-tom mallets.

The greatest American drummer of the Rock era is Crickets' other superstar, **Jerry Allison**. *Rolling Stone*'s 1980+ survey of the Greatest Rock Drummers showed the following three in order: 1) **Keith Moon** of the **Who;** 2) **John 'Bonzo' Bonham** of **Led Zeppelin;** and 3) **Jerry Allison** of the **Crickets.** The stark question of "Which one is still alive?" gives us a surprising answer for the World's Greatest Drummer tally. Sadly, as well, very few are aware of Jerry's accomplishments in the rhythmic multitude. Buddy Holly's first-year induction into the Hall of Fame ['86] did not include his great band the Crickets [yet], but we're working on the problem as we speak. Among other great R & R drummers are the Stones' **Charlie Watts**, the Beatles' **Ringo Starr** [Richard Starkey], Rush's **Neil Peart**, Motown session man **Benny Benjamin,** Billy Joel's **Liberty DeVito**, and Bruce Springsteen's **Max Weinberg.** So what really ticks drummers off? MIDI-sequenced electronic drum machines, part of the sneaky musician-replacement process. So what's next on the rock list of indispensable instruments? Another guitar?

The ELECTRIC BASS finally caught up to the guitar, string-wise, in 1986 when **Paul Simon** played 6-string electric bass on #3 album *Graceland*'s "You Can Call Me Al." The bass guitar started as a 4-string bass fiddle caressed by a big violin bow; somewhere along the Rock and Roll road, it got downsized and upsounded. Huh? Like the guitar, the bass was fitted with basic electromagnetic pickup devices and amplified (the Fender Bass amp was an early arrival). Early on, the big, quiet, fretless bass fiddle crystallized into a smaller, much louder instrument with the same four bottom strings as a guitar (the ones with steel wound around them – thicker and deeper than the high 'B' and 'E' string, so they're an octave lower). The Crickets' **Joe B. Mauldin** started by thumping the big bull fiddle with the Slap Bass method used by his predecessor – Elvis's **Bill Black**. Early in 1958, Mauldin opted for modern technology and revolutionized rock music. Joe selected an Electric bass guitar.

OK – so where did Simon get one with six strings? Back when the **Byrds** tuned their low E-string down to a 'D' for their #1 "Mr. Tambourine Man" (#1, '65), rock bassfolk always yearned for even LOWER notes to vibrate the rafters. Somewhere in the 80s, bass guitars developed the new lower strings (sez Nine Days' bassguy **Nick DiMichino**), and it wasn't long before five and six-string (even 8 & 10 string) basses proliferated [7-string guitar options marked 2001]. After you hit the higher strings, each string rises four notes, so it differs from guitar. In late 90s and early 2000s Rap music, the bass is of paramount importance. Swaggering car trunks thunder with the deep bass rumbles of Rap stars – and the drivers who are kind enough to share their favorite songs with you as you saunter down once-quiet boulevards.

John Paul Jones of Led Zeppelin, **John Entwistle** of the Who, **James Jamerson** of Motown, and **Donald 'Duck' Dunn** of Muscle Shoals, Alabama, and **Booker T. & the M.G.'s**, are often regarded among the top bass players of all time. The biggest difference between bass and guitar is that bass players very rarely chord – and play single notes most of the time. Also, although early bass players almost always used a pick, many modern bassists never do, utilizing the thumb in a finger-picking manner used long ago by Folk singers.

The bass guitar itself does yeoman service and double duty. Maybe triple duty: 1) it carries the bottom rhythms with the bass drum; 2) it carries the chords on the guitar's bottom four strings, via its arpeggio single-note; and 3) it carries the lower notes of the piano/keyboards. This brings up the next rhythmic synthesis, the piano/bass player:

Beware of the following trick question: "Who plays bass for the Doors?" The non-answer is musical genius **Ray Manzarek**, who plays KEY-BOARD – but the 'bass' is really his piano/keyboard.

In our three-piece combo the Night Shift (1963-65), Bob Baldori did the same, as does **Billy Joel** on many of his recording extravaganzas. This technique is nothing new, and emerges from Ragtime piano in 1899 or so. You know, the Klondike and the *Gold Rush*. Listen to Manzarek's rare album *The Golden Scarab*, solo from 1974. On it, he sounds spookily like longlost Doors' baritone rock-crooner **Jim Morrison**, vocally and instrumentally (though this time he hires Jerry Scheff to play bass).

Ragtime uprights were as portable as your refrigerator. When **Ray Charles** introduced the electric piano to R & R in his #6, 1959 "What'd I Say," he changed the sound of Rock and Soul forever. All the great 50s piano rockers – **Jerry Lee Lewis, Fats Domino, Ronnie Hawkins, Huey 'Piano Smith** – were encumbered by lumbering, elephantine, 88-keyed upright and baby grands equipped with only rudimentary microphonics. In 1962, I recall lugging Danny Beaubien's 100# 'portable' electric piano to a Michigan biker bar. Leaden-tubed monster.

By 1961, 'Johnny & the Hurricanes' **Paul Tesluk** (Hammond B-3 organ, invented 1939 by Lauren Hammond) gave **Del Shannon**'s organist/piano guy **Max(imilian) Crook** a million-dollar sound for their 1961 #1 "Runaway." It was the MUSITRON, a pre-Solovox that delivered a shrill voluptuous overarching shriek of passion. Later the Moog synthesizer (invented by Moog) revolutionized Rock and Roll by way of the pioneering Musitron and Mellotron. Without Shannon, Crook, Tesluk, Charles, and Hammond, no MIDI sequencing would be possible during Millennium Three. If you want to hear the epitome of esoteric Rock and Roll via keyboards on vinyl or disc, simply locate **Keith Emerson**'s [Emerson, Lake, and Palmer] album *Brain Salad Surgery*, featuring the darkly magnificent "Karn Evil 9." Joe Stuessy (*Rock and Roll*, 1990) says they had racks of instruments which looked like the cockpit of a 747. Indeed, the keyboard player often does the sequencing of synthesizers, and must have extraordinary knowledge of programming and math – to create new polyrhythms in a flash and flair of percussive fire.

Right after Elvis and James Brown, many of the top hit makers of all time are primarily piano men: **Billy Joel**, **Elton John**, and **Stevie Wonder**. Beatle guitarists/bassists John Lennon and Paul McCartney each played acoustic (non-electric) piano on their signature songs: #3, 1971 "Imagine," and #1, 1970 "Let It Be." The piano melds well into the magic synthesis of voice and instrument that weaves an enchanting tapestry of music. It's much easier to play in the Keys of "C" and "F" on the piano, and much easier on the guitar and bass to do "E" or "A". Middle ground is the Key of "G" for both pianos and guitars. Since it fits well into the vocal range of many R & R singers, it's a frequently used key. Rock and Roll revels in its sounds of horns. Sax is the key horn.

So where do Rock's Greatest Instruments come from? Good question. Without the **Clavicytherium** and **Sarrusophone**, and maybe the **Ophicleides**, Rock and Roll might just have been drums and vocals. Your trip to the New York Metropolitan Museum of Art (& Music) might have yielded the following crucial info: "Guitar prototypes appeared in Spain before the 15th century." OK, yep, Spain and the guitar. No new news. Of course. Now a clavicytherium is a kind of primitive clavichord, forerunner of the harpsichord and the pumping pianos of **Jerry Lee Lewis** and **Chuck Berry**'s ivory maestro **Johnnie Johnson**. Joseph Sax (hmm) invented the saxophone in 1840 with a little help from his papa. His main competitor was a Frenchman named Sarrus, whose own Sarrusophone rivaled the Sax men in belltone splendor. So friendly competition sparked the sensuous rise of the super snarly sax as the lead singer's pinch hitter on the song's bridge.

Five saxes now exist, though the (alas) sarrusophone stumbled off with the extinct dodo bird or passenger pigeon or tyrannosaurus. The saxes correspond to vocal categories, with the soprano sax (Kenny G) the highest, and often looking more like a clarinet; it also often looks like its bigger brothers, featured here from highest to lowest in order of pitch: [soprano], alto, tenor, baritone, and bass. A contrabass sax exists at 'Baltimore's' shop in Manhattan. This behemoth is about eight feet long (or seems eight feet long). Many great sax players of the **Charlie 'Bird' Parker** ilk come out of Jazz, but great R & R sax players include Springsteen's **Clarence Clemons**, Buddy Holly's great sessionman **King Curtis, Johnny Pociak** (Johnny Paris of Johnny & the Hurricanes), **Joey d'Ambrosia** (Bill Haley's Comets), and Motown's

Junior Walker. The post-millennial sax phalanx is led by young stars like the Dave Matthews Band's **Leroi Jones.** Though **Bobby Darin** played everything, sax was his main thing. It's the main horn for the main music.

So what's an Ophicleides? A "Serpent Horn" or bass horn that dead-ended into the Met Museum.

Now and then, R & R features something completely different. **Dan Fogelberg's** flügelhorn on ballad "Longer"; the electric viola of **Count Peter Pilafian** on "California Dreamin" (#4, Mamas & Papas, 1966); a kazoo on **Ringo Starr**'s "You're Sixteen," or a celeste on Buddy Holly's "Everyday." Upfront airplay, however, is not the general province of the oboe, the French horn, the Sousaphone, the bassoon, the piccolo. Banjo maestro **Eddie Peabody**

invented the banjoline, with a mellow Hawaiian banjo/mandolin/guitar sound. On our album *Far From Everyday* (Wombat Studios, 2001), son Jeremy played a potato (well actually a maracca disguised as a potato). So let the rutabagas rock on.

Africa gave us the drums. Spain gave us the guitar. Mr. Beaubien and Joe Kekeku and Les Paul plugged it in, and the Clavicytherium launched the careers of **Little Richard** and **Ludwig von Beethoven.**

Soon the time crept up. It was time to tell ol' Tchaikovsky all the great news. And, thanks to Chuck Berry's riffs and chops and savvy and chutzpah, to "Roll Over, Beethoven."

VOCAL RANGE

Interpolated from a similar list of OPERA classification,
as offered by Martha Campanile and Josephine Gallarello:

Male

Falsetto:
Frankie Valli, Lou Christie, Andy Gibb, Michael Jackson, Russell Thompkins, Smokey Robinson, Aaron Neville.

Lyric "Irish" Tenor, Countertenor, or 1st Tenor:
John McCormack, Robert Plant, Stevie Wonder, Dan Fogelberg, Darrin Hayes, Gene Pitney, Justin Timberlake, Michael Bolton, Paul McCartney, Bryan Adams, Tom Petty, Rod Stewart, Don Henley, John Hampson, Luciano Pavarotti.

"Italian" Dramatic Tenor or 2nd Tenor:
Buddy Holly, Ricky Martin, John Lennon, Meat Loaf, Bob Seger, Billy Joel, Elton John, Del Shannon, Bruce Springsteen, Elvis Presley, Jackie Wilson, Jim Croce, Otis Redding, Kid Rock.

Baritone:
Frank Sinatra, Neil Diamond, Conway Twitty, Mick Jagger, Kenny Rogers, David Bowie, Bing Crosby, Bob Shane, Jack Scott, Pat Boone.

Bass:
Johnny Cash, Barry White, Harold Reid.

Female

Coloratura Soprano:
Yma Sumac, Mariah Carey, Arlene Smith.

Lyric Soprano:
Diana Ross, Dolly Parton, Jewel.

Mezzo Soprano:
Aretha Franklin, Whitney Houston, Sarah McLachlan, Madonna, Connie Francis, Janet Jackson, Celine Dion, Amy Grant.

Alto:
Sheryl Crow, Janis Joplin, Patti Page, Shania Twain, Britney Spears, Brenda Lee, Melissa Etheridge, Anne Murray, Mary Travers, Bonnie Tyler, Tracy Chapman, Cher, Karen Carpenter

Contralto:
Timi Yuro, LaVern Baker, Toni Braxton, Mary Ford, Samantha Mumba, Odetta, Stevie Nicks.

Our chart sadly ignores the great range of a
Roy Orbison or **Mariah Carey**,
who can cover the entirety – but it does
zero in on the Vocal Comfort Zone
of these singers.

Roll Over the Boogie: Dig That Rhythm and Blues

Technique time. For your R & R understanding pleasure, here's a page of Rock Chord Theory. If you prefer just reading about songs and singers, simply flip a page or two, OK?

Boogie Woogie? It's a chunky thump-bass piano style addicted to hot rhythm. Rolling raucously out of Ragtime, Boogie Woogie attached itself to the 12-Bar Blues Progression of chords. Older croon tunes lived and died in a 32-measure package:

1st Verse, 8 bars
2nd Verse, 8 bars,
Bridge, 8 bars, and
Last verse, 8 bars.

Your basic three chords would include the TONIC I, SUB-DOMINANT IV, and DOMINANT V7. In the piano-friendly key of 'C' major, your major big three chords would be Tonic I (C), Sub-Dominant IV (F), and Dominant V7 (G7). Boogie Woogie blasted out of the 32-measure croon tune rut with its own 12-bar pattern – usually without a Bridge which varies the chord pattern. Boogie Woogie pattern? Often 12-Bar Blues.

12-Bar Boogie Pattern

TONIC I, **C,** 4 bars
SUB-DOMINANT IV, **F**, 2 bars,
TONIC I, C, 2 bars,
DOMINANT V7, **G7**, 1 bar,
SUB-DOMINANT IV, **F**, 1 bar,
TONIC I, **C**, 1 bar,
DOMINANT V7, **G7,** 1 bar
(turnaround, and repeat).

On your 12th bar, you turn around your Tonic I 'C' chord to your Dominant V7, 'G7' – and you begin again. It also enables you to play the Blues and Boogie Woogie. Beyond the demystification, you get to become a Rock and Roll star for fun and profit in your spare time. "No Money Down," [Chuck Berry, NC 1956; #8, 2-56, R & B].

12-BAR BLUES Chord Progression [Boogie-Woogie]

	Tonic Chord	Sub-Dominant	Tonic	Dominant	Sub-Dominant	Tonic	Dominant
Keys friendly to Piano/Organ	I	IV	I	V	IV	I	V7
	C	F	C	G7	F	C	G7
	F	Bb	F	C7	Bb	F	C7
BOTH Piano/Guitar	G	C	G	D7	C	G	D7
Keys friendly to Guitar/Bass	E	A	E	B7	A	E	B7
	A	D	A	E7	D	A	E7
	-- 4 bars --	-- 2 bars --	-- 2 bars --	-- 1 bar --	-- 1 bar --	-- 1 bar --	-- 1 bar --

In a way, you could argue that Rock and Roll was never really invented. Through Boogie-Woogie/Blues, it was already throbbing in the thirties, the twenties, even before. **Pine Top Smith**'s "Pine Top's Boogie Woogie" (#20, 2-1929) is often listed as R & R's 12-Bar Blues birthplace in popularity [Big Band revamp is Tommy Dorsey's #3, '38 "Boogie Woogie"], but even Smith's classic is nowhere near the fountainhead of the 12-Bar form.

Crossover means that one song crosses over into other musical areas. How so? Take Madonna (Ciccone's) rock ballad "True Blue" (#3, 1986). With a Streetcorner chord pattern (**C-Am-F-G7**), you could classify it something like this: Doo-Whop Streetcorner, Breathy Croony Soft-Rock Romantic Ballad. Or take the Pointer Sisters' animated "Jump" (#3, 4-84): Hard Rock-Disco-Soul Up-Tempo Harmony Gospel-Call-and-Response Hit Classic. Rock and Roll crosses over into all other musical forms with reckless desperado abandon. Rock and Roll just loves the big beat. But the melody lingers on.

Let's get back to basics. In August 1947 (#4 Country), legend **Hank Williams** – the singing legend Nashville built a Hall of Fame for – cut a pure, unadulterated Rock and Roll song, "Move It on Over." Bill Haley's "Rock Around the Clock" sounds uncannily and craftily like Hank's first hit. Though Williams is best-noted for his agonizingly blue dirges of musical magnificence (with lonesome whippoorwills, midnight train whistles, and gleaming beer bubbles of golden isolation), "Move It on Over" shows a droll and wry sense of humor. Basic 12-Bar Blues. Essence of pure 50s Rock and Roll. "Move It on Over" typifies the crossover flavor of Rock music. Though we can't bring you Hank's exact lyric, if you've heard the song you can sleuth it out:

Our sorry **E** (I) hero drags guiltfully home at
  10:30,
His baby **E** (I) just wouldn't let **E7** (I) him in
"Move Over" **A** (IV) he says, **E** (I) to his
  confused hound dog
Move over, **B7** (V) tiny little dog, because
A huge dog is now **A** (IV) movin' in **E** (I)
  B7 (V)

Few rock critics have ever cited **Hank Williams**, Country's own, as an archetypal Rock guru. He shows the power of crossover in wresting Rock and Roll from tangled skeins of Delta Blues, Country, and booming Boogie Woogie.

"Move It on Over" – George Thorogood and the [Delaware] Destroyers. Single, NC, but album #33, 3-79. George is a top-notch white Blues singer, a raspy gung-ho baritone who doubles with fast ax-slash guitarist Steve Christmar on slide guitar. No-holds barred frantic Blues. Rumbles with power and glory with a Delaware drive the size of Texas – on Hank's archetypal song.

"Move It on Over" – Hank Williams, NC, 1947: #4, 8-47, Country. Hank laments the doghouse role of a tipsy hubby or boyfriend. Williams's version diverts the typical chord pattern a bit from standard 12-Bar Blues. In spots, IV follows the V chord in resolving back to a Tonic I chord. Blues is diatonic, for it sticks within the seven pitches of the scale for the I, IV, and V chords. Soon, however, the real Blues notes arrive – sevenths. The V7 is common (G-B-D-F), as is the flatted third note (Im, or I minor, or C-Eb-G **C-minor** chord). Basic Blues doesn't go as far as Jazz in seeking way-out esoteric chords like diminished 11ths and augmented ninths. Blues may start simply, but the Muddy Waterses and Eric Claptons and Carlos Santanas take it to the heights. Hank took it to the doghouse, and nearly invented pure Rock and Roll.

The Fifties dawned, sleepily and somnambulently swaying to the Sandman. Few who heard the croontune music of postwar Levittown America could have believed what was coming. The first half of the decade was astoundingly quiet. Music whispered. IT didn't dare shout. Or stomp. One of the sweet pastel chart-nudgers belonged to **Rosemary Clooney**. Rosie sang ballads, with excellent expression and bell-like alto enunciation. Her drummer, tragically, must have been stuck in Timbuktu or Katmandu or Kalamazoo (looking for Elvis); or maybe he fell asleep looking for his lost coffee fix:

"Hey There" – Rosemary Clooney, #1(6), 7-54. Nice, sweet, rhythm-impaired melody. This whimsical beatless tune offers advice to a loveless lovelorn friend who isn't listening anyhow. In this pre-Rock era, one good song might have 3-5 hit versions by a whole crowd of crooners. The singer wasn't as important as the song. Records were shifting from old bustable scratched 78s to the more durable frisbee 45s. "Hey There" has absolutely no beat at all. Zilch. Rosie, and other crooners like Johnnie Ray and Frank Sinatra and Tony Bennett, carry lilting lovelorn Landers ditties like this on their good voices alone – Easygoing, friendly, well-enunciated voices that make you yearn for white bread and strawberry jam. Rock and Roll, stealthily, was fomenting on the horizon, a mammoth mammato-cumulus tornado cloud down at Humes High in Memphis. A football-team 135# reject was combing his pompadour and plotting his shooting-star rise, as Marlon Brando and James Dean flickered on midnight screens, awash in a soundtrack of vapid faux-jazz muzak. Like a panther, Elvis waited to pounce upon sleepytime pop music.

"Mambo Italiano" – Rosemary Clooney, #10, 11-54. It's not quite Rock and Roll, but this time Rosie has a real drummer and a real beat. Many Mambo kings and queens roared romantically over the 1953-54 Pre-Rock air waves – a firestorm of big-beat prelude. This one "sprinkles Italiano jargon, like oregano," says Christine Martino, over the whole Moonstruck song. **George Clooney's** aunt did a Siciliano Italian-accent that jumps with rhythmic power and comic musical fun.

In the Pre-Rock Mambo prelude, we also had Perry Como's #4, 10-54 "Papa Loves Mambo" and Vaughn Monroe's #7, 8-54 "They Were Doin' the Mambo" to celebrate the new dance fad; however, the first incarnation of Bill Haley's "Rock Around the Clock" was perched to pounce at #23, 5-54 – but REALLY exploded in #1(8) May 1955. **Tito Puente** was the ultimate Mambo King (see Latin Rock chapter). Rosie also did pop standards, but her biggest hit is the Italianate #1(8), 7-51 "Come On A My House" which got its 'explicit lyrics' banned on *Your Hit Parade* – seems the singer's persona offered the guy first a peach, then a pear, and then (gasp) 'everything.' Into the millennium, they don't sweat dinky double entendres anymore.

Clooney's most unique chart-chomper? #1(3), 8-54 "This Old House," about a tumble-down house, and a poor decrepit man who's too old to fix anything on it; he moans he's getting prepared to meet those saints – and they bring it off as a comedy. My sixth-grade class sang it in the 'Morning Program' with Miss Schuenemann, and it's the first time contemporary music was ever performed at Joshua Howard Elementary School – our collective goading and coaxing and nagging convinced her to do Rosie's homey ode to a ramshackle reverie – and "This Ole House" rocked Dearborn, Michigan! (Psst – you and your popular music can change the world – no matter how many years young you are.)

"White Christmas" – Bing Crosby, #1(11), 10-42, and perhaps forevermore . . . Also #7, 12-55. #34, 12-57, #26, 12-60, #12, 12-61 and on and on. The most popular song of all time (till Elton John's 1997) – sung by the most popular singer (sez the authority Joel Whitburn) of the 1st half of the 20th century! First featured in technicolor-splashed *Holiday Inn*, Irving Berlin's enduring Christmas classic teamed with the sonorous velvet baritone of Bing Crosby – most popular crooner of all time, until, perhaps, Frank Sinatra. "White Christmas," despite the rumblings and rapid thunder of the Rock Era, was for the 20th century the most popular song of all time,

in record sales (Guinness Book), until edged out in 9-97 with Elton John's Princess Di tribute "Candle in the Wind II" [#1(14 weeks, 33-million+ sales)].]. Nothing else ever rocked "White Christmas" from its lofty perch; Bing's is an anti-rock Christmas anthem. "Der Bingle's" smooth Irish baritone voice wafted over the dim Depression and the terror-blazing Second World War with a soothing dose of home and family and teddy bears and Santa. Written by great Jewish composer Irving Berlin for a man who only dreamed of sea-level snow in Southern California, "White Christmas" is hopeful, unlike Bing's scary wartime "I'll Be Home for Christmas" (#3, 12-43), almost sarcastic in its doubt and despair and never-get-home desolate resignation.

"White Christmas" is straightforward and optimistic. Bing/Berlin's masterpiece juggles jingle bells, silvery evergreen tops, Currier & Ives colorful cards to loved ones, nostalgia for childhood Santa encounters, and well-wishes to all for health, prosperity, and joy throughout the coming years. We really needed some technicolor. In *Saving Private Ryan's* (1998****) terrible World War II, you can view the bleak "most realistic . . . harrowing battle footage ever committed to a fiction film" [Leonard Maltin]. In the atomic cocoon of horror and brimstone, everybody needed a Christmas with mom's apple pie and Winnie the Pooh. Maybe "White Christmas" didn't make all the pain go away, but Bing's reassuring, lulling lilting baritone kept the Worry Monster at bay for a few anesthetized moments, between bombshells. Mostly, however, "White Christmas" is a wish song, a fervent desire to be reunited with friends and family. In a world torn by Hitler's Second World War, "White Christmas" is a soothing leap of faith to a bright tomorrow. Tom Brokaw was right in *The Greatest Generation* (1998). After all the Hell our daddies (and mommies) went through, they came home and brought us a heavenly Christmas, somehow. God bless them, every one . . .

What could be more multicultural than America's popular music? Irving Berlin writes the #1 song of all time – a Christmas carol. He paved the way for the dust-bowl Blues of another great Jewish composer: Hibbing, Minnesota's **Bob (Zimmerman) Dylan**, named after poet Dylan Thomas, and blasting neo-Kerouackian subterranean bop prosody blues anthems, like "Subterranean Homesick Blues" (#34, 1965) and "Stuck Inside of Mobile with These Memphis Blues Again/Rita May" (#110, 1-77). Only **Bob Dylan** had the courage to jump from acoustic to electric hit music.

What could Rock and Roll have become, though, without a little help from its friend – the electric guitar? Polish-American Lester Polfus (Les Paul) first snatched up the all-American instrument, the banjo, and soon gravitated to guitar and harmonica. Born in 1915 in Wisconsin, Paul's resume looks like the ultimate American pragmatist – hitting the height of hitdom: in 30s, he performed as Rhubarb and Hot Rod Red in a country band; the **Les Paul Trio** '36 played with **Fred Waring** (1900-84) and His Pennsylvanians; later he performed way in the background for Bing Crosby; he worked with **Charlie Christian** – legendary guitarist, who, like Muddy Waters, was the main influence on Rock and Roll's best-known guitar man of the 50's Chuck Berry.

When Les Paul invented the solid-body guitar in 1946, he took it to the tycoons of Gibson Guitars. They refused him and called this Rock and Roll revelation a "broomstick." **Leo Fender** was not so inhospitable, and their names adorn countless world-wide guitar battalions today. When he met the sprightly contralto **Mary Ford** (Colleen Summer, 1928-77), he married both her and big-time success. They created a breathtakingly fluttering symphony of guitar magic (all Les, in his basement recording studio – Les invented the home-studio concept, too, for R & R aspirants). His "Vaya Con Dios," #1(11), 6-53 with Mary's soft, low mystique, commandeered the #1 spot in 1953 as long as Elvis's biggest hit "Hound Dog"/"Don't Be Cruel." Their "How High the Moon" hit #1(9) as well, while "Tiger Rag" and "Mockin' Bird Hill" were #2 for Les and Mary. Also #2, a 20s Charleston-Era hit:

"The World is Waiting for the Sunrise" – Les Paul and Mary Ford. #2(2), 8-51. Isham Jones, tenor sax dance band troubador, took this tune to #2 too, on 11-11-22; Jones later had the #1 hit on the favorite un-Christmas song of 1900-50: "Stardust" (#1[1], 9-30). Les Paul's version, though, takes the good ol' Spanish guitar – amplified – to a new intergalactic dimension of shimmering sound – a vortex of vibrato stardust soundscape.

In a recent TV ad, 85-year-old **Les Paul** admired a kid's flashy fret-flying fingers on a new guitar. The lad asked Les whether he could play guitar. Modestly, Les said 'Yes.' The youth asked what his name was. Les said, "It's on your guitar . . ."

The Gibson-Les Paul is a prestige guitar, for serious axesmiths. Three-chord garage-band duffers don't get their embossed signatures on guitars. Sometimes, it takes 50 years to become an overnight sensation. No one is more responsible for the modern sound of the electric guitar than Les Paul. Les pioneered pickups, overdubbing, echo chambers, and lightning-lead-guitar fireworks on the SOLID BODY GUITAR THAT HE INVENTED. You can't get any closer to the Heart of Rock and Roll than that. Les didn't have to sing a note, This tune uses dynamic harmonies and chord progressions. It poetically delivers the romantic rush of a lover's dawn.

"Mockin' Bird Hill" – Les Paul and Mary Ford, #2(6), 2-51; #7, 3-51 C. Also concurrent #2(1), 2-51 hit by Patti Page, who uses Les's own overdubbing. (See Page's "Tennessee Waltz," #1[13], '50). Paul and Ford's version flaunts the soft velvet tones of Ford's cooing contralto. As rural Americans drifted north to smoky razzmatazz cities, they longed for the old outback quietude. Pretty mocking birds sang, echoing Septimus Winner's 1855 hit "Listen to the Mocking Bird." Life in the country was a little slower and maybe easier. This Rural Expatriation theme is emblazoned in the Country Rock era with John Denver's goodwill theme songs: "Take Me Home, Country Roads" (#2, 4-71) or "Back Home Again" (#5, 9-74). Listening to "Mockin' Bird Hill," you get to revel in one of the prettiest, purest melodies ever penned.

Pete Seeger was (ironically) voted into the Rock and Roll Hall of Fame in Cleveland in 1996. He's the guy who pulled the plug, so they say, on **Bob Dylan**, when the young folk singer tried to electrify his folk music for the first time at the Newport Folk Festival in 1965. Purists insist Seeger merely covered his ears in disgust at the strident sounds. Born 5-3-19 in New York City, Seeger, along with Lee Hays, Fred Hellerman, and contralto **Ronnie Gilbert**, founded the **Weavers.** The Weavers are crucial to American Folk music – to its purity, authenticity, and popularization. Their influence over the Folk Flowering of 1958-63 (**Kingston Trio**, Brothers Four, Highwaymen, Rooftop Singers, New Christy Minstrels and Peter, Paul & Mary) is profound. Seeger had one solo hit in the Rock Era, Malvina Reynolds' anti-conformity song about "ticky-tacky" houses . . . (that) all look exactly the same, except for coming in pink, yellow, green, or whatever: "Little Boxes" (#70, 1-64). In 1951, Seeger and the Weavers, who popularized the Singalong where everybody gets into the act, had a monster megasmash with "On Top of Old Smoky":

"On Top of Old Smoky" – Weavers, #2(8), 3-51; #8, 6-51 C. Quintessential song-of-the-people. "Smoky" was not one of their protest songs, or was it? It's a good ol' Folk song about what they say all guys really want, and it tells young innocent girls to beware, a decade before Carole King and the Shirelles implored the rapscallion rake: "Will You Love Me Tomorrow?" (#1, 11-60). "Smoky" muses – that boys are irascible; 99 out of 100 can't be trusted; beyond their smoochy hugs and kisses, they'll tell more lies than the number of crossties on an entire railroad, or even stars in the heavens. The Weavers, like Ray Charles, use the Gospel Call and Response pattern. Seeger calls, Weavers and singalong audience respond. Super song.

"Mockin' Bird Hill" and "On Top of Old Smoky," for reasons of folk melody, overdubbing, and/or a throbbing beat, help set the stage for the Rock Revolution. Both are waltzes. Very few waltzes of 3/4 splendor have hit big in the Rock Era. Among the few: Faux-Elvis Jack Scott's "My True Love" (#3, 6-58); Billy Joel's "Piano Man" (#25, 2-74) and Seal's #1(1), 6-95 tune, "Kiss From a Rose."

"Begin the Beguine" – Artie Shaw, #1(6), 9-38. Big Band clarinet star Shaw scorched the charts with his remake of songscribe **Cole Porter**'s classic Latin tune. You'd classify it Easy Listening today, or perhaps Millennial Latino Explosion. The song coaxes lovers to dance and sway to the shimmering palms and moonglow. All the while it builds a magnificent crescendo of unique chords, culminating in a swooping finale. In the 70s the inimitable Johnny Mathis did a superb cover of the song featuring a dash of Disco.

"Glow Worm" – Mills Brothers, #1(3), 9-52; NC, R & B). The Crooner Era featured nifty ditties like this. If Easy Listening is your bag, you can't beat the soulful barber-shop song stylistics of the Mills Brothers. The pristine promenade casts a spell of violet sundown gloaming. Two lovers stroll and smooch amidst blinking lights from a glistening sea of LIGHTNING BUGS? FIRE-FLIES? This buggy little tune snatched the phosphorescent #1 position on the Hit Parade. From the opera *Lysistrata* the song first hit #1 (5) in May 1908 by the Victor Orchestra (later RCA Victor); even the Oldies are Oldies.

Perry Como was the most important crooner of the early Rock Era. Like Bobby Vee or Ronny Howard (*Happy Days'* Richie Cunningham), Como proves that nice guys can finish first. The Canonsburg, Pennsylvania, ex-barber not only dominated the late 40s with his monster hits, but he plunked 47 hits into the Top 100 charts in the Rock Era. Unencumbered by any noticeable beats at all, Como soared to the top on the strength of his velvet baritone with "Prisoner of Love" (#1[3], 1946), and his timeless OVERtime chartbuster, #1(10), 8-45 "Till the End of Time." Gentle romance is the main ingredient.

Como was cool. He heard the rumblings of Rock and Roll on the horizon, and he adapted. Many of his tunes covered cute lyrics with jolly intent: his 2/4 nearly-rock #1(5), 1952 "Don't Let the Stars Get in Your Eyes" hammered a delicious rampaging rhythm. Como placed three tunes at #1 during the Rock Era. The first one, #1(1), 3-56 "Hot Diggity," was adapted

from an 1883 Espana Rhapsody tune by Chabrier. "Hot Diggity" signaled a clash of musical cultures. It was bounced, in March 1956, by the first rampant pressing by RCA for young Elvis Presley, Mae Axton's haunting "Heartbreak Hotel" #1(8), 3-56. In a sense, the Rockin' Fifties really began on the St. Patrick's Day in 1956 – and continued into the Beatle Era in 1964.

Brenda Lee *and* ***Perry Como***, *1961*

Como clicked with his counterpoint tune (two simultaneous melodies) "Round and Round" (#1, 2-57) and his "Catch a Falling Star" (#1, 1-58). Perry's songs are fireside chats, cozied up with cardigan sweaters and hot apple cider with cinnamon and family and optimism. Born in 1912, and cruising beyond the Millennium, Como emerged periodically for Christmas TV galas.

Much Crooner Era music dabbles in astronomy: falling stars, deep purple starry nights, moonglow, moonbeams, moonshine, stardust, swinging on stars, and rampaging sunsets and sunrises. This fluffy ethereal stuff, with heavenly celestial bodies bopping around the purple sky, made postwar 'party animals' forget the taxman, smelly garbage, snake tattoos, and charred meatloaf.

A true missing link between the Rock Era and the distant past belonged to **Kay Starr**'s #1(6), 12-55 triumph, "Rock and Roll Waltz." The "Rock and Roll Waltz" actually alters its meter several times during the song – it lurches from a 3/4 waltz beat to a thrusting 4/4 Blues. Kay's brassy alto also earned her top honors of #1(10), 2-52 with "Wheel of Fortune," a semi-soft rock ditty which later inspired the TV mainstay quiz show (what is Vanna wearing?).

Kay Starr's style was inspired somewhat by **Teresa Brewer** (b. 1931) of Toledo, Ohio. Twenty-two top 100 tunes in the rock era were earned by 'carrot-topped' Teresa, whose bouncy style found the Big Beat before the sleepy world noticed. She debuted with #1(4) "Music, Music, Music," (1950), which struts a honkytonk piano as Teresa confesses her addiction to jukeboxes. The rollicking "Music" beat was shadowed the next year by female Ragtime/honky-tonk/boogiemeister **Del Wood**, in her dynamite tune "Down Yonder" (#4, 9-51). "Down Yonder" harks back to the Al Jolson #1(9), 5-1920 "Swanee" mood, and the tune ROCKS. Catch the R & R remake by Toledo's **Johnny (Paris) and the Hurricanes** (#48, 5-60) – thrill-riding a tootling Hammond organ, "Down Yonder" jumps and tumbles and pirouettes over the pirogues and bayous and Okeefenokee swamps of the Deep South – conjuring Creedence.

Teresa Brewer also scored with #2(2), 10-53 "Ricochet," a big-beat goodie with two distinct meters. The lyric cleverly zaps the romantic wanderings of her rapscallion beau, who ricochets from girl to girl like a speeding bullet. Like Starr, she teases the R & R craze with #7, 6-56 "A Sweet Old Fashioned Girl." In the innocent ingenue verse, Teresa is that sweet old-fashioned girl; in the dazzler verse that follows, she's a red-hot rock and roller. Her nonsense line of "Scooby-oop-ee-doo" in this hit helped suggest the hit cartoon show *Scooby Doo*, America's canine hero (and therefore 2001 megastar Reggae Rapper **Shaggy**). Brewer also covered, in the style of her crooner compatriots, other torch singers and rock stars: Joan Weber's 4-week #1 (12-54) "Let Me Go, Lover" hit #6 for Toledo Tessie in 1955. Fledgling superstar **Sam Cooke**'s soft-rock classic #1 "You Send Me" was #8, '57 for Teresa.

"Till I Waltz Again with You" – Teresa Brewer, #1(7), 12-52. Teresa plaintively cajoles the hunk to dreamy promises in her biggest hit. In the aftershadow of **Patti Page**'s monumental hit "Tennessee Waltz" (#1[13], 11-50), Brewer, too, dances with her lover; she, however, is not forsaken via best friend's sneaky flirting. Bizarrely, this #1 is not a Waltz; it plies throbbing triplets (12 per measure) like **Fats Domino**'s "Blueberry Hill" to glide the couple to true troth, fabulous fealty, and hot pink happily-ever after.

The vivacious Toledo redhead's cutest-titled song – and bit of a bizarre rocker – is #22, 7-54 "Skinny Minnie (Fish Tail)," while she also scored Pre-Rock hits with #6, 4-54 "Jilted," and the wild whirligig #17, 9-52 "You'll Never Get Away." She also did a dynamite cover of **Ivory Joe Hunter**'s #15, 3-56 R & B hit (who covered whom?) to #5, 2-56 with "A Tear Fell." Hunter's #43 "Empty Arms" (#2, 4-57) produced a lucky #13, 4-57 hit for Teresa, who in no way was bulldozed by Rock and Roll. The beautiful Toledoan adapted beautifully. Her last charted hit, #74, 5-61 "Milord," was produced by Buddy Holly's last producer Dick Jacobs (as were most of her tunes on the Coral label, the one Buddy used for his solo career).

Teresa Brewer

Family connections bloom in pop music: Nat and Natalie Cole; Hank Williams Sr. and Jr.; Pat and Debby Boone; Jerry and Gary Lewis; John and Julian Lennon; the Jackson Six [OK, Janet . . .]; Dionne Warwick and cuz Whitney Houston; the Judds; Johnny and Roseanne Cash; the Bee Gees.

Can't forget **Nat King Cole** [Rock Hall 2000]. Some say he was the best of the crooner era; with 59 hits in the rock era, and countless biggees before, Cole dominated the airwaves with his smooth, suave vocals hovering between tenor and baritone. You know Nat's 1991 hit "Unforgettable," audially superimposed with daughter Natalie:

"Unforgettable" – Nat and Natalie Cole. #14, 7-91; #10, 6-91 R & B. Also #12, 11-51; NC, R & B for Nat solo. This ultraeasy tune epitomizes the best of the crooners' efforts. Cole (1917-65) started as a piano player. One midnight dreary, some plug-ugly thug in a piano bar ordered Nat to attempt to sing a song. Result? Instant celebrity status. Nat Cole, like Satchmo Armstrong, was universally revered. Cole even hosted his own TV-variety show in the 50s; despite peaking at #10 on the Nielsen Ratings, the *Nat King Cole Show* was dropped because of wimpy sponsors who bowed to certain Southern hate groups in the racial firestorm that made not all days in the 50s 'happy days.' In this unforgettable recording, audio splice wizards resurrected the marvelous crooner's reverie-riven original. Sound engineers attached the sweet soprano of almond-eyed daughter Natalie ("Pink Cadillac," #5, 3-88) to blend a breathtaking duo part.

Nat King Cole was very versatile. His malleable style covered Ragtime: Al Jolson's 1913 #1 tune "You Made Me Love You" (#45, 5-59). He did Slow Ballads: "A Blossom Fell", #2, 5-55; "Ramblin' Rose", #2, 8-62. Cole cruised through Soft Rock: "When Rock and Roll Come to Trinidad," previewing Reggae, #48, 4-57; and his bouncy anthem of partytime glee, "Those Lazy-Hazy-Crazy Days of Summer," #6, 1963. "Lazy Days" sang out the whoop-it-up clarion call of male bonding – BEER – a sentiment which would certainly not have made it to the radio if sung by some younger teenage idols.

Musicians were not the ones who set up rivalries between styles of music. The really-big stars, like Como and Cole and Brewer, and naturally, Starr, assimilated the new music and bounced back a softer brand of it. The major middle-ground ombudsman is **Pat Boone** (born 1934); though his Rock Hall of Fame aspirations have been spurned by the Cleveland shrine, in 1955-56 only one artist outsold the clean-cut Floridian with the white bucks and Boone Christian message – **Elvis**. Boone placed 60 songs on the singles charts, including six #1's and 18 in the top ten. His biggest song of all time is a reprise of Ted Black's Orchestra's #6, 1931 "Love Letters in the Sand" (#1[7] for the mellifluous Boone baritone). Of all the crooners, Pat Boone cash-boxed his talents to Rock and Roll most successfully. So did Easy-R & B's **Tommy Edwards** (1922-69): #1(6), 8-58 "It's All in the Game."

Billy Ward fronted a missing-link orchestra between Rock and Big Bands that showcased Rock & Soul's top tenors of the age: **Clyde McPhatter, Jackie Wilson,** and **Eugene Mumford**. My reverence for 30s romantic music was wrought by these twin tunes:

"Stardust" – Billy Ward & the Dominoes. #12, 6-57; #5, 7-57 R & B. Nineteen other versions of this 1930-31 Hoagy Carmichael song charted. Artie Shaw, especially. With Italian tenor soaring skyward, "Stardust" blossoms into an astronomical journey, a bittersweet refrain. "Stardust" splashed jazz chords galore. It is not a kiddie song. I like the move to the 5½ chord, or what has often been called the Polynesian Chord Progression: in other words, your tonic **C** chord reels, not to the simpler sub-dominant IV **F** chord or dominant seventh V **G7** chord, but to the intermediary **Ab** chord (**bVI**). Big band music of the 30s and 40s caters to the musically literate. More than complex chords and melodic magnificence, however, "Stardust" pulsates with romantic feeling, via the Mitchell Parish lyric. The song just ain't down and dirty; it places romance way up on a pedestal, with his lady love smiling over shimmering chiffon. The vocal climax to the song reels skyward into an Irish tenor/falsetto combo note. "Stardust" stuns you.

"Deep Purple" – Billy Ward & the Dominoes. #20, 9-57; NC, R & B. The logical follow-up. Both of these hits feature the billowy tenor of Eugene Mumford. Same feel as "Stardust," via Mitchell Parish. Original is Larry Clinton's #1(9), 2-39 smash. "Purple" is the gleaming gloaming, the irresistible lovers' twilight. Sleepy flower-flecked walls, mists of memory, and moonlight beams bring us the ultimate streetcorner R & R lyric. The title for "In the Still of the Night," Fred Parris and the Five Satins' #1-doo-whop-favorite-song-of-all-time hit (only #24) of 1956, comes directly out of "Deep Purple." [#1, '63 Tempo/Stevens].

Johnnie Ray (1927-90), of the Dalles, Oregon, was a unique singer with a unique problem he shared with Ludwig von Beethoven: deafness. Perhaps the only major singer of two generations to use a hearing aid, Johnnie Ray made it OK to cry a little bit. Rock and Roll singers, via the emotive, sultry style of the movie icon who almost solitarily created the T-shirt/jeans TEENAGER, actor **James Dean**, discovered that is was all right to express emotion. Many early crooners, however, were too dapper and cool to let it all hang out. Enter Ray.

"Cry" – Johnnie Ray, #1(11), 11-51; #1(1), 12-51 R & B. Backed with #2(2), 11-51 "The Little White Cloud That Cried," "Cry" is about a weepy cloud undergoing a Generation X crisis. Ray's human-like cloud suffered from being lonesome. Wow. In "Cry," Ray actually got down on his knees on stage and bawled. An ambassador between crooning and Rock and Roll, Ray could emote. He flashed 16th-note melismas; he crunched syllables to a super slur blur. He cried REAL TEARS. Some woozy crooners could almost fall asleep on stage, performing their no-beat numbers. Not so Ray. He tenored on his kneecaps, wringing his hands and soul with a real bluesworthy lowdown agony. Johnnie Ray pioneered what would later be called "Blue-Eyed Soul" (like 'Bobby Hatfield/Righteous Brothers' "Unchained Melody," #4 in 1965 and #13 in 1990).

Absolutely essential in the evolution of Rock and Roll is **Hank Williams, Senior** (1924-53) the lonesome troubadour from Montgomery, Alabama. His country-rock son **Hank, Junior**, implores us Monday-Night sports buffs to instantly get ready for some football. Hank Senior's touchdown tune?

"Your Cheatin' Heart" – Hank Williams, #25, 3-53; #1(6), 2-53 C. The term Hillbilly is a non-derogatory term actually coined way up in the Porcupine Mountains of Michigan's Upper Peninsula. "Your Cheatin' Heart" was recorded September 23, 1952. This doleful ballad is the archetype for all the neon roadhouse nightscapes and nevermore love affairs of yesteryear. Thrown from a horse, Hank battled back pain with pills and bottled courage. This one is Hank's signature song and his last lifetime hit. He died on New Year's Day, 1953, of old age (29) and *Weltschmerz* (the Pain of the World). With a lonesome gloomy despair, Williams underscored the live-fast die-young rock and roll lifestyle that would bring the Grim Reaper's scythe early to Hendrix, Moon, Joplin, Bonham, Andy Gibb, Cobain, Tupac, Notorious B.I.G., Big Pun and Alice In Chains' Layne Staley. [See Alan Jackson's #3, 4-92 C "Midnight in Montgomery"].

While searching the musical efforts of **Frank Sinatra** (b. 12-12-15, Hoboken, NJ), you recall the giant cast of crooners who wanted to be Sinatra: Tommy Sands, Dick Haymes, Russell Arms, Al Martino, Ed Ames, Sammy Davis Jr., Dean Martin, Frank Sinatra Jr., Eddie Fisher, Harry Connick Jr., and Vic Damone. Or Georgia Gibbs, Joni James, Kitty Kallen, Jo Stafford, Doris Day, Rosemary Clooney, and Jaye P. Morgan. No one, however, quite captured the essence of Sinatra except Sinatra. Many know Sinatra today for the theme song to Al Bundy's *Married – With Children* sitcom – "Love and Marriage" (#5, 11-55). With 66 hits in the Rock Era, Sinatra was the 'Chairman of the Board.' He fired off a #1 hit as rock exploded, "Learning the Blues" (#1, 5-55); it has nothing to do with Rock and hardly anything to do with Blues. It radiates a jazzy midnight moping mood that every star-crossed lover knows when he's "Learnin' the Blues" – a hey-there-pal chunk of advice to the lovelorn. Sinatra hit the top ten in "All the Way" (#2, 10-57 and a double-entendré title), "Witchcraft" (#6, 1-58), and his #1's "Strangers in the Night" (5-66) and duet-with-daughter-Nancy "Something Stupid" (3-67). You always

think of Sinatra at Yankee Stadium ("Theme from New York, New York" #32, 5-80), and at party-ending-kick-lines. Frank's best-known anthem, however, is Paul Anka's "My Way" (#27, 3-69). Sinatra sings it convincingly; he survived beyond his 82nd birthday to June 1998, contrasting to Elvis's very sad rendition. As #2 Album Artist of All Time (Whitburn), Frank Sinatra was no singles slouch, either. Legend is an understatement.

Rounding out the Crooner Crew is **Tony Bennett** (b. 1918, Queens, the Big Apple). Horatio Alger #1(8) hit? "Rags to Riches" in 9-53 for Bennett. His biggest Rock Era hit isn't the croon-anthem "I Left My Heart in San Francisco" (#19, 8-62), but his Caribbean-chalypso "In the Middle of an Island" (#9, 8-57). Bennett signed with Columbia Records, and debuted with "Boulevard of Broken Dreams" in 1950. In 2002, you could still see Tony Bennett woo and wow Grammy crowds with his silver-haired regal presence. If anyone has ever been accused of topping the vaunted Sinatra at his own super-enunciation game, it is Anthony Benedetto [Tony B.] of Queens.

Great Broadway Show tunes paralleled the Crooners, like first album ever (and flip the eight 78rpm sides yourself) #9, 1943 *Oklahoma* revived on 2002 Broadway. *South Pacific* and *Carousel* were also blockbusters. *Brigadoon* sings about an enchanted Scottish village that only materializes every 100 years. Though they didn't chart, the 'Irish' tenor of Lee Sullivan paces the breathtaking "Come to Me, Bend to Me," and "The Heather on the Hill" of *Brigadoon*.

The year 1950 brought us a #2 R & B-only tune called "The Fat Man," from New Orleans, by a slightly hefty Afro-French ivory-tickler who named himself after jazz great "Fats" Waller – **Antoine "Fats" Domino**. And the rest is Rock and Roll.

Nat 'King' Cole (l) and Mel Torme

Rock Around the Block

On Rock and Roll's Wheel of Fortune, you may begin almost anywhere.

"The Fat Man" – Fats Domino, NC, 1950; #2(1), 2-50 R & B. Before Bill Haley's clock got rocked around, **Antoine Domino** and songwriter Dave Bartholomew were rockin' New Orleans' Vieux Carre French Quarter with their Boogie-Woogie stylistics. Fats waits to do the vocal until his two-verse instrumental is complete. He does a whole verse of falsetto ('woo-woo'), too, beating Del Shannon, Jimmy Jones, and Frankie Valli's Four Seasons to the punch by a decade. This "Fat Man'" item usually gets the prize for spearheading the rise of Rock and Roll.

Or you could backtrack to **Louis Jordan** (1908-75). Known on 90s Broadway for the show *Five Guys Named Moe*, saxman Jordan literally sparked Rock and Roll; some of his band's mid-40s numbers featured videos where they're lit up with (egad – how?) neon suits and saxophones. His material is R & R oriented, too: #3 R & B-only 10-42 "I'm Gonna Leave You on the Outskirts of Town." TOP 30 chart #2(3) "Is You Is or Is You Ain't (My Baby)" hit in 1944, a raspy bluesy ditty with Shadow Wilson on drums, Arnold Thomas on piano, and Eddie Roane on trumpet. Needless to say, an electric guitar is conspicuous in its absence. Let's check out Jordan's pioneering patter on –

"Open the Door Richard" – Louis Jordan, #6, 3-47; #2(4), R & B. Talk about tiny-tot memories. I was 4 and some big kids kicked my little football up in an extinct elm tree (my own nightmare on Elm Street – it came down a month later). They LOVED "Open the Door Richard." It's not only Rock but RAP. Much of the song bounces off the dozens, with groovy ghetto guys scoring off one another, and slamming the jerk landlord. By this time, the Pre-Rock mood is enhanced by Carl Hogan on electric guitar.

Jordan's other rock-rhythm tunes feature "Boogie Woogie Blue Plate," mainstreamer ('Top 30') #21, 9-47, but R & B #1(14); Gangsta Rap preview #21, 7-47 "Jack, You're Dead"; risque 1947 "Pettin' and Pokin': (1947), and Louis's anticipation of Punk Rock, and Cyndi Lauper:

"You Dyed Your Hair Chartreuse" (1950). Or his falsetto comedy song"Caledonia Boogie" (#6, 6-45; #1[7] R & B). Is Louis Jordan Rock and Roll's real papa? Maybe. Or **T-Bone Walker** (1910-75, NC '47 & #3, 1-47 R & B "Bobby Sox Blues"), or **Charlie Christian**. Or perhaps it's **Wynonie Harris**. Or the real Chess Chicago bluesmen, like **Jimmy Reed** or **Muddy Waters**. Like the car, invented by Benz or Daimler or Ford, nobody knows quite where Rock and Roll sprang from. Boogie hotbeds heated from coast to coast: Memphis, New Orleans, Detroit, Chicago, Los Angeles, San Francisco, New York City.

Elvis's magnificent crossover genius? You've got to deal first with the odd musical connection between **Little Richard** and **Pat Boone**. Married at 19 to Shirley Boone, daughter of country-hymn star Red Foley ("Peace in the Valley"), Boone (b. '34, Jacksonville, Florida) won *Ted Mack's Amateur Hour* contest. Soon Boone's rolling baritone hit the charts with "Two Hearts" (#16, 4-55), and cover of Fats Domino's #10 (#1[11], R & B) "Ain't It a Shame," at #1(2) for Pat in 7-55, and even #14, 9-55 on the then integrated-well R & B charts. Boone had five national smash hits before Elvis even got out of the blocks. Via a turned-up collar, white bucks, and (ulp) milk, Pat Boone parleyed his clean-cut college swimming-team image into heartthrob heaven. One of his best covers is the Flamingos' (Rock Hall 2001) #5 R & B classic, "I'll Be Home" (#4, 2-56). Pat purrs, even raps about his lady love. Flipside rocker celebrates all flavors of ice cream: "Tutti Frutti" (#12, Boone, #17 for Little Richard).

Born **Richard Wayne Penniman** (b. 1932, Macon, Georgia), Little Richard was actually signed to RCA Victor, five years before Elvis, but they weren't too concerned with launching a rock revolution early. Shadowing the stage routine of a drag queen named Esquerita, Richard's outrageous moves and giant hair kept the swooning teenyboppers frantic and wild. **Little Richard** joined a long chain of rock stars who never had a #1 hit (Dylan, Creedence, Chuck Berry until the 70s); his top-charting biggest seller was his second hit, "Long Tall Sally":

"Long Tall Sally" – Little Richard, #6, 4-56; #1(8), R & B. Uncle John's been steppin' out with saucy sizzling Sally. He bolts back into the trash-can alley at Aunt Mary's approach. Furtive extracurricular speedo love. When Richard's band zings into the R & R conglomeration, you hear a blast of triple saxes and Richard's mile-a-minute piano riffs. His sax men, anticipating the fraternity coolth of multicultural idols Hootie and the Blowfish, were first to wear Bermuda shorts on stage. **Jimi Hendrix** was fired by Little Richard as lead guitarist. Why? Hendrix once dressed very flashily, and stole Richard's thunder. In case anybody wondered whether Richard had any ambiguous erotic intent in the Sally song, they wondered no longer with "Good Golly Miss Molly" (#10, 2-58), where he bellows one scoundrel line.

Little Richard [Penniman], 1957

"Long Tall Sally" – Pat Boone, #8, 4-56. Wonder Bread version of Richard's Screaming Blues epic. Pat down-pedals tone into his lulling easy style. Whatever soulful stirrings erupted with Little Richard, were toned down to a crooniferous murmur, by smooth and silky baritone Boone (great-great-great-great-great-great-great grandkid of Daniel Boone). Pat ambassadored R & R to the stuffiest of the Parental Units; he showed with-it unsquare mommies/daddies that even "rockers" could be good guys who might raise religious kids who went to college. 'COVER VERSION' is the rock critics' euphemism for an Afro-American masterpiece of authenticity, blandly diluted by some non-soulful kid who enunciates too well, and can't flip a melisma grace-note arpeggio. His only real suffering Blues is having to take out the trash and freeze his knees. Boone a cover artist? He took Domino-Richard rockers and reconstructed them in his moderate style. Boone outsold everyone in the mid-50s but Elvis. The Boone vs. Presley furor suggested the Beatles vs. Stones frenzy for Showdown of the Decade. Boone crooned top-notch Soft Rock.

Boone's a bit of a be-bop Bing and R & R ambassador to the yesteryear generations. Protesting nothing, he stood up for American family values, smiled sincerely, and turned my generation into a bipolar multitude: one day we malleable teenagers would wear our pure white buck shoes and good-natured smiles; the next day we pranced like Presley, sulking with soulful sneers, mumbling and mulling our cosmic angst like James Dean, and leering at Marilyn Monroe calendars, puzzled by dynamic desire.

Boone brought us back to earth. He sang home, family, religion, relationships. Serving others. When the Me-Generation Boat weighed anchor and set sail on the Sea of Sensuous Forbidden Delights, Pat missed the boat.

However, Pat Boone's 1997 Heavy Metal/Jazz album In a Metal Mood still has everyone guessing in disbelief. Rock and Roll is stranger than fiction.

Not that Pat was the Last Crooner. Pat was a Rocker/Crooner. That's a wild hybrid. The last crooner was **Eddie Fisher**?

"Oh! My Papa" – Eddie Fisher, #1(8), 12-53. Tremendous sentimental dad tribute. His 'funny, adorable' pop is gone; he misses him disconsolately. A stunning gush of pure emotion. Compare it to Mike and the Mechanics' #1(1), 1-89 masterpiece "The Living Years." In each song, treasured memories of a late father are shared. Mike internalizes guilt of parting; Mike sees his dad's spirit in his young son who will never really know his grandpa. Fisher's Papa is an immigrant with a marvelous sense of humor. "The Living Years" is cool and Stoical; "Oh! My Papa" is schmaltzy and homespun. "Living Years" is understated; "Oh! My Papa" cries out at the finale how much he misses his gone-forever papa. Fisher, some say, married the two most beautiful women in the world: Debbie Reynolds [see daughter Carrie Fisher in Blues Brothers or Star Wars (Princess Leia)], and violet-eyed Elizabeth Taylor.

So long, Crooners. Hello, Rockabillies.

The 5th-longest #1 song 1955-95 was a Latin instrumental, (Perez Prado's) "Cherry Pink and Apple Blossom White" (#1[10], 3-55). In September 1999, **Lou Bega** uses a Perez Prado tune for his #3 "Mambo #5." Prado's rolling Cha-cha-cha Chalypso beat unfurled the red carpet on Rock and Roll's doorstep. Quick – which song commanded the #1 position in the United Kingdom (U.K.) longest in the 1955-90 R & R Age? Good question. Glad you asked:

"Rose-Marie" – Slim Whitman, #22, 5-54; #1(11), 7-55 U.K. Denizens of late-night TV telemarketers and adblasters (QUICK! BUY SLIM WHITMAN'S GREATEST HITS NOW!) know the Tampa, Florida, yodeler well; Slim's #93 1957 reprise of 1912 Will Oakland hit "I'll Take You Home Again, Kathleen" is early Death Rock. The grim song hints that it's her body he's returning to their homeland and the Auld Sod. "Rose-Marie" hopefully is more hopeful, declaring this dainty lass a queen. Australia, too, lists "Rose-Marie" as their best-seller ever Down Under, according to Pete Drake (until 1998's Savage Garden's #1 "Truly, Madly, Deeply"). Not Elvis, and not the Fab Four, ever lasted at the pinnacle this long (in 90s, see Bryan Adams, Elton John). Nowadays Whitman compilations, hawked in tacky fashion by Cable-TV screamers, belie Slim's (b. 1923) incredible sound. This tough-looking Floridian cowboy balladeer delivers seraphic tenor sounds just about as far from Heavy Metal as possible. In the Pre-Rock Era, Slim scored with a yodeliferous #9, 7-52 Native American extravaganza, "Indian Love Call."

"Rocket 88" – Jackie Brenston, NC 1951; #1(50, 5-51 R & B. When looking for the Fountain of R & R, don't overlook **Tina Turner**'s ex – **Ike**. The vocalist is Jackie Brenston, but listen to Ike Turner pumping the piano keys. The song is named for a swift model of Oldsmobile V-8 that rampaged through the drag-racing 50s, wiping out Ford V-8's, Caddies, and Hopped-up Hudsons in its path. The lyrics can also have a more sexy connotation, depending on where your mind is:

Catch the hot riffs of pioneer **T-Bone Walker**'s influence. This is **Sam Phillips'** first real hit record at the Memphis Sun Studios, and something much bigger was on the royal horizon for him. Robert Palmer cites the genesis of Ike's amp sound: the amp fell off the car on the way, and Sam stuffed some paper in the ruptured speaker cone. Result? A "fuzzed-out, overamplified electric guitar." 1951. It's akin to **Marty Robbins'** accidental discovery of Heavy Metal ten years later.

In three years since "Rocket 88," **Sam Phillips** hadn't yet concocted a kingly empire at 706 Union Boulevard, Memphis. It's a nice small studio. You can visit it today. Sun Records straddles an oblique street and sits astride a super souvenir café and T-shirt emporium. You can snag Billy Lee Riley's extraterrestrial 1957 uncharted vinyl 45rpm swan song: "Flying Saucers Rock and Roll." The neighborhood is urban. Steamier in mid-May than Detroit in July, Union Boulevard sports a tired tawny brick building. Rock and Roll Dawn was ushered in by the Sun.

"That's All Right" – Elvis Presley, NC, 1954. From a shotgun shack in Tupelo, Mississippi, a poor white kid, whose father Vernon did a year in the slammer for a bad check ($4, to buy a hog), moved to Memphis in 1948. When he showed up for a bumbling attempt at ballads at

Sam's Sun studio, paying his own way, he was just a kid who drove a truck for Crown Electric Company at $40 a week. His excellent biographer Peter Guralnick mentions him going over and over "Harbor Lights" and "I Love You Because" with session guitarist Scotty Moore. Something needed more OOOMPH. After a desultory go-around with weary songs, suddenly the kid switched gears. He launched into a Blues number by Arthur "Big Boy" Crudup – "That's All Right [Mama]." Sam Phillips, snurfling around the control room, was considering catching some Z's. Suddenly, he stuck his head outside, and yelled:

"ELVIS – what are you doing?"

"We don't know," confessed the kid with a pink shirt and black pants and duck-tail haircut.

"Well, back up, try to find a place to start, and do it again."

The result is Rockabilly. It took just 1½ years for the Elvismania pandemonium to bring down the lullaby walls. **Elvis Presley** (1935-77) simply became the most important singer in the history of the world.

Bill Black wrestled with the bull fiddle. **Scotty Moore** splashed hot licks on the electric guitar. Elvis handled the acoustic guitar and sang. Like no one ever before! Sun Records, Memphis, would soon explode with fame. This three-chord Blues number blended a Rockabilly tenor lead with two marvelous musicians' strumming and plucking expertise. While Elvis thrummed the rhythm chords, Sam Phillips twirled the dials, creating the Slap Bass sound for Bill Black, plus an incredible new sound with his Echo Chamber. Sales? A modest 18,000 or so. But wow. Calls galore lit up the radio station phone lines at WHBQ, Memphis. DJ Dewey Phillips (no relation to Sam) shouldered Elvis's first nervous interview. Elvis, like you and me, was a strange combination of confidence and shyness.

"Blue Moon of Kentucky" – Elvis Presley, NC, 1954. Flip side. Bluegrass standard via Grand Ole Opry's **Bill Monroe**. This Rockabilly anthem affirms R & R's Country roots. Elvis did just the opposite of the Bee Gees, whose voices lurched form 60s tenor to 70s falsetto. "Blue Moon of Kentucky" shows Elvis's command of quavering, trembling tenor. As his career raced into his most revered song, "Can't Help Falling in Love" (#2, 12-61), Elvis descends from booming Italian tenor to resonant baritone.

"Mystery Train" – Elvis Presley, NC, 1955; #11, 12-55 C. Peter Guralnick previews this Presley prelude to "Heartbreak Hotel." "There was a floating sense of inner harmony mixed with a ferocious hunger, a desperate striving linked to a pure outpouring of joy, that just seemed to tumble out of the music. It was the very attainment of art and passion." Yes, sir. "Mystery Train" floats along rapturously, a Ghost Train plummeting through the inky purple bayou swamp night – suspended between life and death in a limbo of lost-soul majesty. Anyhow, it's a very deep song. Deep enough to hock Atlantic Records' $25,000 brain-trust fortune to buy his contract – which RCA moguls parleyed for 35 grand and a semi-dinky $5,000 bonus. Elvis – for forty grand. Wow to that.

Isn't it about time we mentioned the song everybody and his brothers and sisters think is the First Rock and Roll Song in the Universe?

"Rock Around the Clock" – Bill Haley & the Comets, #23, 5-54; #1(8), 5-55; #3, 6-55 R & B. Haley cut this classic on April 12, 1954, but it didn't buzz on the high charts until Hollywood spun it. Then it topped the charts for eight weeks from May 1955. **Haley** was born July 6, 1925 in Highland Park, Michigan, a mile from me over the Detroit border. Fronting a C & W crew called the Downhomers out of Indiana, Haley yodeled his way to lukewarm local success. The big break came when he chucked the cowboy hat and yoked the C & W style to the urban thump of Rhythm and Blues. Rhythm and Blues (R & B) pulsated in the smoky factory town of Henry Ford's first monster factory and the monumental five-dollar day for auto workers (1917). Transplanted Mississippi Delta Blues gurus **Muddy Waters, Jimmy Reed,** or **John Lee Hooker** apprenticed their craft via vaudevillean Blues belters (Ma Rainey, Blind Lemon Jefferson, Amos Milburn, Bessie Smith). Bill Haley wailed an R & B sound. To augment his rare Caucasian Bluesman situation, Haley synthesized the twangy up-tempo beat of **Hank Snow**. Via a metamorphosis of bands (the Aces, the Saddlemen), Haley charted with 100% genuine bona-fide Rock and Roll hits via a wild wax threepeat: #12, 5-53 "Crazy, Man, Crazy"; #24, 8-53 "Fractured"; and #25, 10-53 "Live It Up." In 1954 Haley and the Comets signed with **Decca,** the posh label that later (1956) gave Buddy Holly a taste of glory.

Bill Haley

Haley's monster clock-rocking hit was first cut by **Sonny Dae and His Knights** (Subtle pun, eh?). Inked by James Myers, "Rock Around the Clock" was droopy in its first go-round, 1954. Tagged into *Blackboard Jungle,* starring teacher Glenn Ford and student/roughneck Sidney Poitier, the tune roared skyward, dumping the competition in James Dean's *Rebel* Summer of '55. Significant sidemen include Joey D'Ambrosia on tenor sax and a dynamite fast-fingered lead guitarist – **Danny Cedrone**.

Among Rock's first fast-lane martyrs, Cedrone succumbed to a fatal heart attack in June 1954, before his Speed Metal frenzy was fully appreciated. One rumor says he fell down the stairs first, after a party, which certainly couldn't have aided any recovery process. Haley's brief *a cappella* tacets burst at you. Basic 12-Bar Blues, with hang-fire tacets (short vocal-only parts with no instrumentation). Haley launched his own Oldies Industry? Elton John's #1(3), 1972 smash "Crocodile Rock," alludes to this next Haley hit:

"See You Later, Alligator" – Bill Haley and the Comets, #6, 1-56; #7, 2-56 R & B. Bill (1925-81) opens on a falsetto tacet of "See You Later, Alligator." Haley's appeal was musical. Unblessed with Elvis's Hollywood looks, Haley was a tad burly, thirty-something, a spit-curl dangling over his ample forehead. If you're a Haley buff, dig "Razzle Dazzle" (#15, 7-55), "Birth of the Boogie" (#17, 3-55), or his spiffy Little Richard cover, Haley's soulful "Rip It Up" (#25 for Haley, 8-56, #17 for L.R., 7-56).

Female rock stars in the beginning? Yes. **Ruth Brown**'s "Lucky Lips" landed her a '57 #25 hit. Superstars?

"Jim Dandy" – LaVern Baker, #17, 12-56; #1(1) R & B. Unsung Detroit heroine of Rock and Roll's rendezvous with Rhythm and Blues. Solid rocker. No wishy-washy wimp rock. Born Delores Williams, in Chicago. **Ahmet Ertegun** of Atlantic Records, who handled **Aretha Franklin**'s career, helped the **LaVern Baker & the Gliders'** sound. LaVern Baker is R & R's first diva. Her career was virtually launched with the whimsical "Tweedlee Dee." This #14, 1-55 hit shows LaVern's influence upon Buddy Holly – the timbre of her voice changes from a thin, playful alto to a husky, almost-growling voice. Baker (1929-97) sang great gusto. Her biggest is a ballad – #6, 1-58 "I Cried a Tear." Her most basic Boogie Blues tune is #34, 12-62 "See See Rider" [See MITCH Ryder]. The Jim Dandy lyric: Dandy is Superman, arriving to the rescue of the damsel in distress on mountaintops, in airplanes, and amid the various dragons of life's thorny road. Zesty song and singer.

Underground Blues music fought to get on the air. Risque lyrics, combined with a mid-century-Victorian afterglow of prudery, kept the Blues underground. Lo and Behold, a few radio stations started to spin the new stuff: WCHB and WJLB in Detroit, among the first Afro-owned stations in the U.S.A., debuted some of the ribald ANNIE songs on their air waves.

Georgia Gibbs of Worcester, Massachusetts, was the female Pat Boone, covering LaVern Baker's "Tweedlee Dee" to #2(1), 1-55; then she vanilla-ized Detroit's Afro 'Irish tenor' **Hank Ballard** and his Midnighters with her #1(3), 3-55 "Dance with Me, Henry (Wallflower)." In this G-rated ditty, Miss Gibbs doubled her coverage: first she switched young Etta James's (R & R Hall of Fame 1996) "Wallflower," and then she altered Hank's racy "Work with Me, Annie."

"Work with Me, Annie" – Hank Ballard and the Midnighters, NC, 1954; #1(7), 4-54 R&B. Vaulting to the R & B pinnacle, this double-meaning Blues tune, "Work," seemingly, wasn't work at all (but very sexy fooling around). Erotic play, even. Hank's incredible quavering Irish tenor floats to falsetto plateaus – as the thrusting 12-bar blues melody pumps the two and four beats with rhythmic dynamite. Hank's #1 follow-up yields the inevitable result of all that hard "work":

"Annie Had A Baby" – Hank Ballard and the Midnighters, NC, 1954; #1(2), 9-54 R & B. Back in 1954, abortion was illegal (and dangerously back-alley) and birth control was hammered by regular church doctrine and custom. So what did Insta-Love create? Yup. Kids. And a #1 R & B hit for Hank which bamboozled America. This tune sports a lyrical phenomenon never seen before (or since?) in Rock and Roll lyrics – Paternal Jealousy over: 1) All the attention the cute little bundle of joy is getting [and not Papa]; 2) Those six weeks or whatever when they can't make love. Next hit? #10 R & B-only 12-54 "Annie's Aunt Fannie." Alas, poor Hank?

"The Twist" – Hank Ballard and the Midnighters, #28, 7-60; #6, R & B. Hank Ballard had two mainstream monster hits, the 'Hall Party Rockers' "Finger Poppin' Time" (#7, 5-60) and "Let's Go, Let's Go, Let's Go." These powerhouse tunes paced the Motowner to a wider white-bread suburban audience. My old Auto Shop teacher Mr. Nelson even allowed "Let's Go3" on his radio, as we greasy-fingernailed groovers hopped and bopped senior year at Dearborn High – awash in J-2 six-barrel carburetors, high-compression heads, and overdrive. And Rockin' Soul.

Hidden on the flip side of Ballard's first mainstream chart-song, #87 "Teardrops on Your Letter" of March 1959 (#4 R & B), Hank plunked a torrid torque tune for aspiring pretzels: "The Twist" (N.C. '59; #16, 4-59 R & B). It faded to oblivion, briefly. On the brawny shoulders of "Finger Poppin' Time," King Records let "The Twist" out of the bag again for the Summer of 1960. By mid-July it was a smash #28 dance craze (#6, 7-60 R & B) for HANK.

Enter **Dick Clark** and *American Bandstand*, the #1 R & R show of all time. Started in 1957, the Philadelphia-based after-school TV champion flooded airwaves everywhere. Youthful Dick Clark was the perfect host. Amidst the frantic, frenzied Rock and Roll panorama that besieged his studio, Clark maintained his epitome-of-coolth persona. Clark was suave, debonair, a little conservative, yet totally cool. He cobbled together every star just a jot lower than Elvis onto his show, and that included all the big

stars of the fifties: Chuck Berry, Buddy Holly, Jerry Lee Lewis, Fats Domino, Little Richard, Freddy Cannon, Dion and the Belmonts, the Everly Brothers, Connie Francis, Brenda Lee, Bill Haley, Pat Boone, the Platters, and many lesser luminaries in the Rock and Roll galaxy.

Clark especially encouraged local talent. South Philadelphia High School, a huge working-class integrated urban school, mirrored the multicultural Dr. Martin Luther King spirit that united segregated parts of 50s America. At the risk of ethnic stereotyping, let us say there has always been a lot of musical talent in the Italian community. Crooners like Sinatra, Bennett, and Dean Martin (Dino Crocetti) blanketed the early fifties with #1 hits. Dick Clark brought us: **Frankie Avalon** (Avallone), of "Venus" fame (#[5], 2-59); **Connie Francis** (Concetta Franconero), with her tremendous trombonish "My Happiness" (#2, 12-58), or "Everybody's Somebody's Fool" (#1, 5-60); **Bobby Rydell** (Ridarelli), whose resonant low Italian tenor trumped teenage troubles with his fun songs ("Forget Him", #4, 11-63). Kid star on **Paul Whiteman's Show** 1951-54, Bobby relied less on Clark's influence than the others, like **Fabian** (Forte), whose song "Tiger" (#3, 6-59) rivalled Elvis only in the category of good-looking singer. Buying records, young girls care more about looks than we musicians would like to admit. (Also see good-looking singers Jimmy Clanton, Ricky Nelson, Dion [DiMucci]).

Back to the lost Twist. Dick Clark's Italian rock stars were complemented by a few Afro-American stars, too: **Dee Dee Sharp** ("Mashed Potato Time," #2, 3-62, whose follow-up "Gravy" became the prototype for **Bobby 'Boris' Pickett**'s #1 "Monster Mash"); and **Little Eva** (Eva Narcissus Boyd). Eva also babysat two songwriters from the Big Apple who worked in that legacy of Tin Pan Alley, the Brill Building of Times Square – **Carole King** and Gerry Goffin. Eva's #1 "The Locomotion" (6-62) re-surfaced in the Big Hair Band Era as an Aussie Techno-Disco triumph for Melbourne's Kylie Minogue (#3, 8-88). Ernest **"Chubby Checker"** Evans (b. '41) began his career doing impersonations of famous stars, like **Fats Domino**:

"Blueberry Hill" – Fats Domino, #2(3), 10-56; #1(11), R & B. Antoine Domino (b. 2-26-28, New Orleans) sold more singles than anyone in the 50s but Elvis, but this super #2 tune had the same problem that Carl Perkins and everybody else suffered in the Elvis Era: no matter how great your tune was, there was some Elvis song in the way at #1 (for Fats here, "Jailhouse Rock," #1[7]). Even Elvis had this self-inflicted problem; never actually released as a single, "Love Me" soared to #2 – off an album, *Elvis*. It was stuffed by his own #1(5), 10-56 "Love Me Tender," with an extra word in the title.

Like **Buddy Holly** (until they revamped the charts in the 70s), **Bob Dylan, Jerry Lee Lewis, Bruce Springsteen,** or **Little Richard, Antoine Domino** suffered from that chart-womping stigma that hit many superstar victims of the Elvis phenomenon and beyond – he never had a #1 hit on the HOT 100. For Little Richard and Fats, however, the R & B charts are another story entirely. Fats was a legend in Rhythm and Blues, even Reggae.

With his friendly smile, his Ringo style of rings on his

flying fingers on his red-hot piano, and his delightful New Orleans accent, Fats Domino enjoyed a multi-generational and multicultural charisma. Besides early triumph "The Fat Man" (NC, 1950, but #2[1], 2-60 R & B), Domino is listed as #7 in Joel Whitburn's Rock Era number of Top 100 hits (66). He also hits 11th-ever in Top 40 hits. With his polite and jovial demeanor, **Antoine Domino** carried the charismatic stature reserved for **Jimmy Durante** or **Bob Hope** or **Louis 'Satchmo' Armstrong**. The amiable New Orleans piano guru steered the burgeoning ship of Rock and Roll along the muddy Mississippi meander bends of the early 50s. Playing on sessions for rock pioneer **Lloyd Price** ("Lawdy Miss Clawdy" N.C. '52 but #1[7], 5-52 R & B), Fats Domino was one of the most important pioneers of Rock; Fats (5'4", 225#) was voted into the Rock and Roll Hall of Fame on the first ballot – Class of 1986 – with such crucial luminaries as **Buddy Holly, Elvis Presley, the Everly Brothers, Little Richard, Sam Cooke, Chuck Berry, James Brown, Ray Charles,** and **Jerry Lee Lewis**. Fats made it the year before **The Beatles, Aretha Franklin, Bill Haley**, or **Roy Orbison**, so you know he's got to be good. VERY good.

Antoine Domino's funtime stompin' Soul Rock is a mirror and a reflection of the Mardi Gras way of life, in the cozy Crescent City at the mouth of the big Mississippi Delta. New Orleans has a Let-the-Good-Times-Roll French Connection [*"Laissez le bon temps rouillez"*]; Antoine Domino, like Chuck Berry, is something like one-quarter French. "Let the Good Times Roll" was a biggee for **Shirley and Lee** [#20, 8-56, and #1(3), 7-56 R & B]. Their song title represents the best spirit of everybody's favorite early Rock and Roll personality, the universally revered Fats Domino. [A personal note: not only was "Blueberry Hill' one of the first seven 45-rpm singles I ever owned (at age 13), but it was my wife Toni's first and favorite record, too, and she didn't even own a record player yet!] Fats might have enjoyed even MORE hits on the list if you could count pre-1955 tunes. In the R & B category, Domino is fifth in most weeks at #1, and seventh in **Crossover** hits [i.e., hits on other charts, too, like HOT 100, or Country or Adult Contemporary]. Fats is seventh R & B in Top 10 hits, too.

The Fats chart phenomenon began with #30, 6-52 "Goin' Home" (#1[1], 4-52) and #24, 6-53 "Goin' to the River" (#2[4], 4-53 R & B). New Orleans, five feet above sea level TOPS, is never too far from the river. After the semi-joyous wakes and funerals Crescent City people celebrate lives with, the departed are buried in above-ground mausoleums for fear of floods.

Fats's two-sided second-biggest hit is #3 "I'm in Love Again" (#1[9] R & B) of April 1956. It's backed with #19 "My Blue Heaven" (#5 R & B) which Whitburn cites as hitting #1 in 1927 for Gene Austin and Paul Whiteman. Baritone Rockabilly **Ricky Nelson** (Rock Hall 1987) launched his recording career on the strength of his Fats Domino cover "I'm Walkin'" (#4, 3-97 Fats & #1[6], R & B), #4, 5-57 for Ricky.

Fats's workaday lament, #5, 1-57 "Blue Monday," (#1[8], 12-56 R & B) follows-up "Blueberry Hill." Fats spells out

a common workingman's problem. After trudging through the dragging drudgery in the chunky part of the workweek, he edges closer to his magic Friday payday. Then, in joyous celebration of his beloved paycheck, he goes out Saturday night with friends/girlfriends/whoever, and has too much of a blast. Sunday morning the poor celebrant awakens with a bad head. He says his Alka-Seltzer experience was worth it for the euphoric super time he had that glorious night before. He drags his buffetted bod through slogging Sunday – and Monday he must return to the humdrum blah job. "Blue Monday" sums up the ennui and boredom and angst and bad vibes of everyone whoever worked anywhere for a day's pay. In perhaps the least dangerous and most subtle protest ever registered, Fats concludes the MONDAY is an absolute MESS!

Fats's "Blue Monday" is perhaps the best-known Monday Blues song of all time, but perhaps it's only the bronze medalist. Remember the Mamas and Papas' "Monday, Monday" at #1(3), 4-66? Or how about #2(1), 1-86 the Bangles' "Manic Monday"? At any rate, we all must work to put food on the table and Fats's Greatest hits on the CD players.

Buddy Holly covered (chartlessly) Fats's classic weepy "Valley of Tears," at #8, 5-57 (#2[1] R & B) tune in the geographical vicinity of Heartbreak Hotel, on Lonely Street, in Lonesome Town. It uses Domino's famous triplet technique; he pounds three quick notes on each beat of his 4/4 song, accenting the big TWO and FOUR beats (or the 4th and 10th beats of the 12). Fats Domino often used a fab 50s technique, a fast side and a slow side. Hacking away at triplet 12-beat Boogie-Woogie or throbbing balladry, he created dance sensations at all speeds for all lovers and friends. Everybody loved Fats Domino. Regardless of an iffy racial climate in the segregated 50s, Fats Domino was universally revered. Mothers didn't consider him dangerous. Like the **Mills Brothers** of the 40s, Fats Domino was considered one of the nicest guys in the business. They say Fats Domino sold more records in the 50s than any other artists except Elvis (yep, passing Pat Boone, more than Buddy, Chuck, Little Richard, Jerry Lee, blah, blah, blah). Fats had so many big hits that many of them rarely get airplay on the Oldies Overkill networks, who bash poor "Blueberry Hill" into a blueberry blob of overplayed incessant triplets trailing to infinity.

DOMINO CAMEOS? OK.

How about this #6, 5-57 "It's You I Love," (#2 R & B), as the "Valley of Tears" flipside? Who remembers his #6, 11-58 (#2 R & B) "Whole Lotta Lovin'," where he makes a funny sound for kissing the girl? Or his giant Top Ten "Be My Guest" – #8, 10-59 (#2, 11-59 R & B)? Among other Domino mini-monster hits, we feature: #8, 8-59 "I Want to Walk You Home" (#1 R & B), followed by a more marathon pedestrian item where he wears out two pairs of shoes on a world-class hike, #6, 6-60 (#2, 7-60 R & B) "Walking to New Orleans." Among other Domino triumphs? #17 class-conscious 7-59 "I'm Gonna Be a Wheel Someday"; #16, 5-59 "I'm Ready"; his big leadoff #10, 7-55 "Ain't It a Shame" [#1(11) R & B]; his merry mariner ditty #14, 7-56 "When My Dreamboat Comes Home" (#2

R & B); and his all-time New Orleans anthem that struggled on the lower charts despite its profound greatness, the 1897 Rock and Roll/Soul/Gospel classic by Katharine and James Black "When the Saints Go Marching In" (#50, 2-59, NC, R & B).

Antoine 'Fats' Domino

Fats enjoyed a string of R & B-only classics in the pre-Rock era. They didn't hit what passed for the HOT 100 in the old days – a Top 30 that loosely combined Juke Box Charts, Best Selling Records, and Disc Jockey Charts (Joel Whitburn's tremendous *Pop Memories 1890-1954*). Fats hit the R & B charts with his aforementioned #2(1), 2-50 leadoff blockbuster "The Fat Man," a rollicking 12-bar Blues classic. "Every Night About This Time" (#5 R & B, 11-50) Fats would seek his ol' (#9 R & B, 12-51) "Rockin' Chair," because he was "Goin' Home" (#1) to his first #1 hit R & B record in April 1952. His #3 R & B, 7-53 "Please Don't Leave Me" preceded #10 R & B, 10-53 "Rose Mary" and his prelude to the huge "Ain't It a Shame, " #7 R & B, 3-55 "Don't You Know." For over half a century, Fats Domino has been revered as one of the greatest Rock and Rollers of all time. Everyone who was anyone would trust Fats as a tour guide up on "Blueberry Hill." He is one of the premier AMBASSADORS of Rock and Roll to the world. Despite health scares that have rippled for forty years, Fats kept rockin'. To be successful, beloved, and coolest of the cool, well, hey, it doesn't get much better than that, does it? Long may Fats rampage on the Rock and Roll Stage.

On Fats's remake of **Glenn Miller**'s #1 hit of 1940, "Blueberry Hill," you can hear the pulse of New Orleans. Catch the throbbing bassline on the deep keys. Fats lavishes the treble trill. The bottom, though, rumbles the rafters. Fats and his rockin' piano were as beloved as Louis Armstrong in his day.

To parents, Fats was non-threatening. They saw him as smiley, friendly, and fun. Like Pat Boone and Buddy Holly, Fats Antoine Domino took the rough and tough edge off the rebellious sound of Rock and Roll. What was that 'thrill' on Blueberry Hill? Who cared? If Fats sang it, it must be rated PG. Who cared that blueberries grow at low level – bogs, even – and that the wind in the willow also doesn't make sense, since willows seek streams, not hilltops. Songs have never been noted for their scientific accuracy (neither has love). "Blueberry Hill" has a super beat. You can dance to it. Let's give it a 99. Rock on.

"Let the Good Times Roll" – Shirley and Lee, #20, 9-56; #1(3), 7-56 R & B; #48, 9-60. Shirley (Goodman) and Leonard Lee feature sensuously-purring Shirley's invitation to shut the door and rock, baby, some more. Their Mardi Gras fiesta throbs with double-entendre passion. Shirley's tigress growl touts innocence as a no-fun limbo to chuck away with the frisbee of desire. New Orleans is a cradle of both good times and Rock and Roll: Fats Domino, Shirley and Lee, Clarence 'Frogman' Henry, and the whole Cajun-Swamp Rock-Zydeco conglomeration.

Elvis, anyone?

"Heartbreak Hotel" – Elvis Presley, #1(8), 3-56; #3 R & B; #1(17) C. This one changed the world! Launch pad from Sun Records to giant RCA Victor. Hitched to the Jordanaires' gospel back-up group, plus Scotty and Bill and D. J. Fontana, Elvis vaulted from Louisiana Hayride venues, with a few screaming hundreds, to the *Ed Sullivan Show* and an international audience of millions. Maybe a billion or so. This Mae Axton song prowls eerily along dark Lonely Street. Dazzled by getting ditched by his ex-babe, grieving Elvis groans in tremulous tenor. Free-form instrumental mirrors lonely mood; Axton was inspired by someone's suicide note: "I walk a lonely street." Since *Rebel Without a Cause*, James Dean showed that adolescent angst, trauma, and travail were rampagingly marketable: it was the stuff of power and glory and legend. And it sold gold. Bedecked with weepy bellhops, and funerally-garbed desk clerks, this haunted Hotel Purgatorio is awash alongside a trail of tears. Elvis cried all the way to the bank.

"Hound Dog"/"Don't Be Cruel" – Elvis Presley, #1(11), 8-56; #1(6), 8-56, #1(6) R & B; #1(10) C. Elvis's biggest hit(s) ever. The "A" side, represented by a weepy Bassett Hound on *The Steve Allen Show*, is an Elvis update of a 1953 Screaming Blues number by Willie Mae "Big Mama" Thornton. Trumping sleepy Crooners, Elvis gives an early explanation to the term "Blue-Eyed Soul." Elvis's syllable-chopping, funky *melismas*, and murmured mumblings are half the fun. El never claimed to be a super-pronouncer like Sinatra. Elvis's *Total Sound* is a snazzy three-ring circus of raspy gutsy tenor, 6th & 7th & 3rds blues-note Scotty Moore guitar, and the machine-gun-flurry drumming of D.J. Fontana. And Bill Black's big bull fiddle burbled along beauteously.

"Don't Be Cruel" is the reason **Buddy Holly** became a star. This soft-rock masterpiece is by Afro Tin Pan Alley song craftsman Otis Blackwell (1931-2002). He wrote Jerry Lee Lewis's "Great Balls of Fire" (#2, 11-57), but his greatest hit "Don't Be Cruel" hurdles teenage moods of lovelorn blue funk and wistful happily-ever-after. Elvis brandishes the glottal stop, a quick vocal trick later modified into the Holly 'hiccup.' Elvis implores the gal not to stop 'a-hinkin" of him. The 'hinkin', for thinkin', energized a whole Rockabilly arsenal of "Wo-uh-hos," "Woo-hoos," hiccups, bass rasps, glide notes, and 16th-note *melismas* splattered ubiquitously enough to impress Mariah Carey or Whitney Houston or Boyz II Men. And **Buddy Holly**'s trademark hiccup sound.

"Don't Be Cruel," "Hound Dog" flipside, kept the dual single #1. Elvis showed he was part "Teddy Bear" (#1[7], 6-57). A culture drowning in macho cowboy stoicism made Elvis so vulnerable, so endearing, so loved by millions of fans. Here was a teenage idol with a hard side and a soft side – like his hero **James Dean.**

"Jailhouse Rock" – Elvis Presley, #1(7), 10-57; #1(5), R & B; #1(1) C. The hard side of Elvis. If anyone doubted the King's potential to sing Hard Rock (nearly Heavy Metal), this First Video zaps their cynicism. In the movie, a choreographed scene of jumping-jack prisoners in stripes lambasts the viewer [in living black-and-white.] Elvis leaps over barriers, slides down poles, and hurdles into pre-MTV destiny with his gutsy, swaggering portrayal of the slammer set. Leiber-Stoller's "Jailhouse Rock" held #1 on ALL THREE BIG CHARTS. In the segregated 50s, Rock and Roll was a lot more integrated than it is today. Rock and Roll smashed the musical barriers. It flew frantically forward. Elvis's follow-up, "Hard-Headed Woman" (#1, 6-58), passed Little Richard's 192-beat/minute "Long Tall Sally" as the fastest song of the 50s, says Stuessy, with 195 beats/minute (Boyz II Men's "End of the Road" plods along at the sub-60 tempo). Elvis became the Instant King of Rock and Roll. It took ten years, said troubadour Don McLean in his prophetic Buddy Holly tribute, "American Pie" (#1[4], 11-71, for "the Jester" (Bob Dylan) to steal Elvis's thorn-torn crown.

Like the painful Crown of Thorns Jesus was forced to wear as he ascended with the Cross to Calvary, the throne of the King of Rock and Roll proved to be a Hot Seat. Electric guitar to electric chair? The spotlight burns, and Elvis was incarcerated within the "Jailhouse Rock" of his own fame and fortune and superstardom. The ELVIS SPOTLIGHT, the JESTER hinted, pressed upon his feverish brow as a thorny crown, indeed.

Fortunately for the rest of us who dabbled in Johnny B. Goode's rock and roll dream, the Big Spotlight eluded us.

"Love and Marriage" – Frank Sinatra, #5, 11-55. A big hit for the Hoboken and Teaneck, New Jersey, Chairman of the Board. With 19th-century horses and carriages and Currier and Ives homespun LOVE, the song was an Establishment delight. After all, isn't all pop music about LOVE? This sing-song melody symbolizes the misadventures of unhappily-married Al and Peg Bundy; in this blunt sitcom, Al is a shoe-selling 'financial flop' who somehow earned a 5-bedroom, 2-story colonial mini-mansion in *Married, With Children.*

This Sinatra smash of the mid-50s, on the cusp of the Rock Revolution, takes on a sarcastic aura in this ultrasophisticated sitcom. Tin Pan Alley songwhiz Sammy Cahn sculpted this dream-factory song to zoom back to horse and buggy bliss.

Francis Albert Sinatra (1915-98) is the most enduring of crooners. Joel Whitburn's *Top Pop Albums 1956-96* lists him as the #2 Artist ahead of the BEATLES, and just behind Elvis Presley. Sinatra even beats silver-medalist Elvis with 49 Top 40 albums during the whole rock era of 1955-90, in the Most Top 40 category.

Of our BIG THREE, Elvis, Buddy, and Chuck, it may be surprising to discover that Chuck Berry hit the big time first.

"Maybellene" – Chuck Berry, #5, 8-55; #1(11) R & B. When Chuck Berry joined Johnnie Johnson's combo in steamy St. Louis at mid-century, neither had any idea their #8, 5-58 tune "Johnny B. Goode" would be literally launched into space as a living symbol of our hopeful culture. Chuck just wanted a hit. A smooth Jazz buff on lead guitar, Chuck emulated Charlie Christian and T-Bone Walker. **Muddy Waters** got him his start with Leonard Chess at Chicago's mini-palace of blues, Chess Records.

Chuck Berry invented Rock Lead Guitar, Rock and Roll Singer/Songwriter Poetics, and Surf Music. How so? Chuck's guitar filled the spaces between his vocal lines; an in-breath meant a zippy lead riff. **Elvis** and **Jerry Lee** and **Ricky Nelson** let others write the songs, so Chuck Berry splashed a verbal American canvas that mirrored our postwar affluence: zooming Cadillacs with "passing lanes" (extinct and dangerous 3-lane highways, often with 'monkeys in the middle', crashing head-on); school days ameliorated with jumping jukeboxes, sizzling burgers, and yummy slurpy malts; and the pursuit of the rags-to-riches Horatio Alger American Dream, channeled through the lusty lead guitar licks of the immortal Johnny B. Goode, future teenage idol. Surf Music's flipsides often depended on the beefy beasts of the highways, streaming from Motown's factories. "Maybellene's" motorside escapades (110 mph on rickety three-lane 50 mph highways), shadowed by Marlon Brando's *Wild One* motorcycle marauders, and James Dean's '51 Merc *Chickee Run* daredevils, didn't do much for us American teenagers' safe-driving urges. Berry's #2 "Sweet Little Sixteen" blasts a clever plug for Dick Clark's *American Bandstand* – and it certainly helped air-play as Chuck celebrates American geography from his 'Saint Louie', plus New Orleans, Boston, Pittsburgh, and Bandstand's Philly. "Maybellene" can't be true. Chuck chases her and some rival 100mph down 3-lane Horror Highway, pleading his romantic case.

If you're doggedly searching for the best pure singer to unite the 40s and 50s generation through soft-rock balladry, search no more: **Tony Williams**. Williams (1932-92), with his mercurial countertenor and belltone enunciation, piloted the **Platters** to a string of 50s smash hits that sealed their #1 group status in sales:

"The Great Pretender" – The Platters, #1(2), 12-55; #1(11) R & B. Tagging the old Pagliacci theme (the sad clown), Tony Williams vaults to dizzying heights. Buck Ram's bittersweet song tells us all about the masks we wear (see "Eleanor Rigby" or Billy Joel's "The Stranger"). The poor jilted jester hunkers down into pretense and play-acting. He can't conceal the misery in his heart, and he's overwhelmed by make-believe. The beat chugs along at slow dance tempo, with bursts of triple-beat rhythm between each of the measure's four regular beats. That way you get 12 beats per measure – and though the bottom blasts fast, the top lumbers along at a squeeze-your-date pace [see Beatles' "All My Loving" (#45, 3-64) and "Eight Days a Week" (#1[2], 2-65)]. My cool cuz Joan Dean gave me the 45 rpm record, but I left the poor Platter platter above the back seat on a swell 85° honey of a summer day. "The Great Pretender" looked like "The Great Licorice Potato Chip." I mourned for months, finally scraping the 99 hard-earned cents to re-buy it.

To those of us battling zits and wallflowerism at the crepe-streamer cafeteria dolled up like Hawaii at our Bryant Junior High Friday Night Dance, this song was gospel. You got to whirl in the arms of the cutest girl in class for 2½ glorious minutes. We were ALL great pretenders, trying on lines, stepping on feet, cracking jokes, and stumbling on our happy dreams. The Platters philosophized, and our world whirled.

"Only You" – Platters, #5, 10-55; #1(7), 7-55 R & B. Allow me to introduce the concept of OLDIES OVERKILL. This poor tune is so overplayed that even we "Only You" lovers get tired of it. Oldies Overkill means they take a great oldie, and alas, nearly spin the poor platter to death. Orbison's wonderful "Oh, Pretty Woman" (#1, '64) and Dion's superstud anthem "The Wanderer" (#2, '62) fall into the same category. Some songs blanket the Oldies Goldies Airwaves [like WCBS-FM, New York, or WBZO, Bay Shore, Long Island]. Some soar to fame, flop to earth, and croak. Take **Lloyd Price**'s super song "I'm Gonna Get Married" (#3, 8-59). When was the last time you heard that? It outbid "Only You" by two positions. A mammoth hit, the poor annulled song has been consigned to the coal bin, the scrap heap, the Muzak mausoleum. Alas, the super songs slide off down Lonely Street to Heartbreak Hotel and Oblivion Dumps!

Tony Williams' rippling lyric tenor floats majestically over 2nd-tenor David Lynch; soprano Zola Taylor, bass guy Herb Reed, and baritone Paul Robi. A Barber Shop Quartet plus one fine female voice, the **Platters** preview a prelude to the 'Boy Band' wave: **Boyz II Men, the Backstreet Boys, N' Sync.** "Only You," however, cascades on its own dreamy wavelength. Winging heavenward on a mediant III (Like an **E-major** in Key of 'C') major chord, Williams swoops to belltone glory. He defines the way his lady love brightens his otherwise-drab universe. His semi-wept stutter tacet ('Uh-uh-only you') anchors his fervent emotions into True Love – the hallmark of great popular music. Though most of his group have passed of old age (Tony was 60), the song will live on as long as Rock and Roll is played. Ringo Starr took "Only You" to #6, 11-74, with a little help from his friends.

"Harbor Lights" – The Platters, #8, 1-60; #15, 2-60 R & B. Five top ten versions of this tune stalked the 1950 Hit Parade, like #1 Sammy Kaye. I recall Snooky Lanson crooning it on our first Sears Silvertone TV when I was seven; in the glowing façade of the little set, tiny lights twinkled, far out in a misty harbor – you don't forget these kidhood images. "Harbor Lights" is the ultimate romantic ballad; Tony Williams' soaring tenor magnetizes you. Though you're a mini-kid nestled into the smoky copper-colored night of a waterless harborless Heartland industrial colossus (Detroit), you can feel the soft sea breeze. You even sense the lovers' passion as he glides over silvery notes – you vicariously visualize a whole golden sunset harbor, with twinkling technicolor lights blinking in romantic afterglow. "Harbor Lights" is LOVE stuff – not the faded, jaded "C'mere, witch . . . get down and boogie now" crude lewd mood that changes lifetime relationships into one-night sleepovers, or feeble fractured grope-and-hope sessions with lifelong Love Hangovers. Harbor lights – they twinkle and glow. They promise everlasting love.

"(You've Got the) Magic Touch" – Platters, #4, 3-56; #4, 4-56 R & B. Presaging the Holly hiccup, **Tony Williams** begins with a trapeze tenor tacet. He skates the sky. He chops the word "you've" into THREE syllables at the outset – followed by four harmonic Platters spinning their dream-machine '56 Cadillac Coupe de Ville of sweet romantic promise. He compares the lass's charms to a four-alarm fire. He glows with sweet desire. She sends him reeling into a Tasmanian Devil whirl of tender love.

This 'Magic Touch' waxes religious in their biggest hit "My Prayer" [#1(5), 7-56 & #1(2) R & B], a buoyant ballad seething with the glow of true love. He prays she'll answer his fervent prayer. "My Prayer" shimmers through a soul-searing array of emotions, and wistful, imaginative, vocal chords and cords. As Rock and Soul hymns go, it's long gone on its glory trail of gorgeous melodies and vinyl gold.

Even the Platters' second-string songs glow with the Magic Touch of Twilight Time, Enchanted Heaven on Earth. Huh? Beyond their smokescreen of #1(3), 11-58, "Smoke Gets in Your Eyes," they scored one #12, 3-59 with "Enchanted," a wispy ballad of heavenly harmony. "My Prayer's" neighborly flipside is #39 "Heaven on Earth" of 7-56. "You'll Never Never Know" hit #11, 9-56, as "I'm Sorry" won lucky #11 in 3-57. Tony Williams reprised the **Inkspots'** #2, 1939 "If I Didn't Care" to #30 in 1-61, and **Platters** hit #21 with "To Each His Own" in 10-60.

Superchronicler Joel Whitburn lists the Platters as the #1 Group of 1955-59, and #50 in his 1997 Top 500 Artists category. The Platters didn't just sweetly serenade the fifties; they overwhelmed the ultracool decade with melody and majesty and class and charm.

"Twilight Time" – Platters, #1(1), 4-58; #1(3) R & B. Manager/songwriter Buck Ram ("The Great Pretender") saw to it his premiere group splashed Old Standards to woo the 30+ record buyers with chubby wallets. Ram echoed this #14 hit by the Three Suns from 1944. One of the most romantic songs of all time. Swirling with purple curtains of twilight, and lovers groping giddily in the hushed mists, "Twilight Time" rules the romance roost. Similar sugary lyrics powered many a haggard and bushed dude, dusty from his frantic Indy-500 day on a forklift, to return home to rose-red gloaming, the Victoria's Secret catalog, and WonderWifey, dressed in a smile.

Romance lives, as the Platters live on.

Columbia and Capitol Records sent out a Want-Ad. WANTED: AN ELVIS. After #1(8), 3-56 "Heartbreak Hotel," Elvis was the hottest shooting star in entertainment. Columbia, with staid Mitch Miller ("We'll never do Rock and Roll") at the helm, waited all the way till 1959 to pussyfoot around to Crash Craddock's ballad, #94, 11-59 "Don't Destroy Me." Stock-car racer Billy Craddock was one of a fine line of Faux Elvises (later #16, 6-74 & #1 C "Rub It In"). Elvis's Greatest Impersonator? Maybe:

"Be-Bop-A-Lula" – Gene Vincent & His Blue Caps, #7, 6-56; #8, 7-56 R & B; #5, 7-56 C. This kid, with the bad leg from the motorcycle, was good. Quintessential Irish countertenor. Born Vincent Eugene Craddock, in Norfolk, VA. Songwriter Sheriff Tex Davis's "Be-Bop-A-Lula" flew to fame with blue Gene in between "Heartbreak Hotel" and "Hound Dog." Capitol Records bonanzaed a gold mine. Coruscating echo chambers and throbbing slap-bass antics boosted Gene's amazing quivery vocal. His #13, 8-57 "Lotta Lovin'" thrummed a twangy guitar, and Gene's mountaintop tenor subdued itself to a booming low-tenor shimmy. Vincent is almost the only singer I've ever heard ("Words," Bee Gees #15, 1-68) who could lock in his vocal tremolo to the beat: VOCAL PERCUSSION. In other words, his voice volume pulses along with the beat. Tuff stuff. In Fall 1999, Paul McCartney recorded his "Blue Jean Bop".

As the hits faded, Gene, the First Punk Rocker, took his leather suit to London. For twelve years, he did six-night/week gigs in cheesy, chintzy beer bars. Vincent survived the terrible taxi crash that stole the life and aspiring career of **Eddie** "Summertime Blues" **Cochran** (#8, 7-58). **Gene Vincent** influenced the **Beatles** and the **Stones** and the **Who** and **Clapton**. Vincent is perhaps the first Punk Rock icon. Most of the time, Gene eased the pain from his leg brace. For a preview of the demise of Morrison,

Joplin, Hendrix, and even Elvis himself, you could look at Gene Vincent's last soggy, sodden year. He died of old age suddenly, from a self-imposed bottle attack, at 35, when one of his wives split. The spotlight burns.

Elvis's other great imitator, **Carl Perkins**, found that his "Blue Suede Shoes" shuffled him down the yellow-brick road to Oz. When he got there, the Wizard was only half a humbug. Tiptonville, Tennessee's troubadour is the essence of Rockabilly. With his family band and Flip Records (1st record "Movie Magg," '54), Carl motated to Sun Records in Memphis. Sam Phillips, lamenting Elvis's bolting to RCA, created Carl and vice versa; between them, they nearly toppled Elvis.

"Blue Suede Shoes" – Carl Perkins, #2(4), 3-56; #2(4) R & B; #1(3), 2-56 C. Essence of Rock and Roll. First Carl's classic tacet. Then his steamy lead guitar, ringing in after-beat splendor. Basic 12-bar Blues Progression. Carl, the coolest of the kool kats, was hot and cool at the same time. Everyone loved the song – even Elvis (#20 for El). Unfortunately, shortly after the record went national, Perkins, too, was in a tragic auto wreck. Though seriously injured, he managed to convalesce slowly. No record he ever did matched the intensity of "Blue Suede Shoes" though the Beatles recorded his "Matchbox"; Carl semi-scored on "Boppin' the Blues" (#70, 7-56) and "Pink Pedal Pushers" (#91, 5-58, a half-calf girls' pants outfit). Then the hits dribbled away and Carl nobly attempted to body-slam some personal demons. Staggering dangerously close to Gene Vincent's fate, Carl found his career resurrected by his old Sun Records friend **Johnny Cash**. Carl latched onto Johnny's touring troupe, and his TV show from 1965-75. Carl headlined Oldies Extravaganzas galore. In 1996, before his long illness conquered, Carl launched one of the best Rockabilly compilations of all time, *Go Cat Go*, witih **John Fogerty [CCR], Bono, George Harrison, Tom Petty, Johnny Cash, Ringo Starr, Paul Simon, Willie Nelson**, and featuring "Blue Suede Shoes" versions by **Jimi Hendrix** and **John Lennon**. Perkins (1932-98) was among the great gentlemen of Rockabilly legend. Never too busy to grant an autograph to a devoted fan, the 1987 Rock Hall inductee lived his later life as an exemplary ambassador for Rock and Roll.

Elvismania headlined the mid-50s. In the aftermath, Rock and Roll decided it had a lot of new directions to travel. The sky was robin's-egg blue, the dreamy sidewalks shone double-white, and Danny and the Juniors sang 'Rock and Roll Was Here to Stay' – It Would Never Die.

Happy Daze

Rock and Roll is the story of visionary giants, but it is also the story of the people. From grungy garages come the bands which may someday rule the world. Rock and Roll is a dynamic and democratic type of popular music that thrives under free-enterprise hustle and hype and hubbub.

Any kid band down the street, with three chords and a dream, just might nab the upper rungs of success's long ladder with their new R & R triumph. The Crooner Era involved a lot of dues-paying. You had to audition with a big working band. You had to get a contract with a big label. You had to have a network of Artists and Repertoire A & R men and women to push your song. Other artists would steal your song anyhow, and maybe Sinatra would end up goldenizing the record that sold you 38 copies.

In the fab fifties, big labels faded. **ASCAP** (American Society of Composers and Publishers) loosened its power over royalties, and **BMI** (Broadcast Music Incorporated) lurched into the breach. Rock and Rollers went with BMI, and overnight fly-by-night midnight recording studios sprang up in every garage and extinct storefront in Chicago and Buffalo.

Big labels like Capitol and Columbia and Decca and RCA were challenged by mini-outfits on the rise: King and Federal and DooTone and Nasco and Coed and Abner and Smash – much like Rappers today. It was the first flowering of INDIE-label independents. The topsy-turvy success scene made overnight sensations of **Berry Gordy, Jr.**, of Carlton/Jobete/Anna, and finally Motown. Or **Sam Phillips** and Sun Records in Memphis, audial launch pad for Roy Orbison, Jerry Lee Lewis, Johnny Cash, and Elvis. Everybody but Elvis never became Elvis. Or "The Fonz." Perhaps it is better that way.

Let's check out a few other excellent entertainers who caressed the Rock Revolution with their spirited sounds:

"At the Hop" – Danny [Rapp] and the Juniors, #1(7), 12-57; #1(5) R & B. First #1 RAPP song! In the 50s, dances and hops and parties were everywhere. "At the Hop" sparks gusto with its double R & R chord pattern; starting in Philly as the Juvenairs in 1955, and plumping Harry Von Tilzer's 1890s barbershop style, the Juniors blasted out both 12-Bar Blues and Streetcorner chord progressions in this teenage R & R tribute to the Stroll and Bop.

12-Bar Blues vs. Streetcorner Progression

12-Bar Blues

Key of E	E	A	E	B7	A	E	B7
	I	IV	I	V7	IV	I	V7
	1	4	1	5	4	1	5
Key of C	C	F	C	G7	F	C	G7
Key of G	G	C	G	D7	C	G	D7

Keys are reversed. Why? 'C' is the piano-friendly key; 'E' is the guitar or bass-friendly key. The Blues are often played on guitar, in 'E' or 'A'; for the old barbershop streetcorner songs, the piano is the central instrument, and 'C' is the easy key. Maybe 'F.' When compromising between piano and guitar, you can do the key of 'G':

Streetcorner

Key of C	C	Am	F	G7
	I	VIm	IV	V
	1	6m	4	5
Key of E	E	C#m	A	B7
Key of G	G	Em	C	D7

"Rock and Roll Is Here to Stay" – Danny and the Juniors, #19, 3-58; #16 R & B. The follow-up. Sounds like the original, as does "Back to the Hop" (#80, 9-61). With nine top 100 tunes, Danny & Crew can't be dubbed one-hit wonders. Only these two and #27, 9-60 "Twistin' U.S.A." hit Top 30. After too many oldies concerts in 1983, Danny Rapp abruptly ended his own life, and it reminded all of us that Grunge or Generation X have no monopoly on despair. Danny's happy song will live on, however, and his rockster message. Only a few R & R aficionados will know his sad end – unlike the **Jim Morrison** Legend of macabré cult fervor. Rapp music tickled the horizon.

Streetcorner groups like **Dion and the Belmonts** are the bulwark and backbone of the sidewalks of New York. Their logical protegés, the **Backstreet Boys**, named themselves for their Orlando, Florida, Backstreet Market. Millennially, 'Boy Bands' like N'Sync, 98 Degrees, and these Backstreet Boys serenade this R & R tradition with multi-platinum CDs.

"Come Go with Me" – Dell Vikings, #4, 4-57; #2(1), 3-57 R & B. Multiracial R & B streetcorner crew who met at Pittsburgh Air Force Base. Gus Backus and Dave Lerchey, two white guys, teamed up with Krips Johnson, Clarence Quick, and Norman Wright. They follow the pattern, except for the zesty vocal bridge, which climaxes in a wild war whoop of shrieking glee. The regular Streetcorner Chord Pattern formula, derived from Hoagy Carmichael's "Heart and Soul" (#1, 1938, Larry Clinton), is as simple as Carmichael's "Stardust" is complex:

    I   IVminor   IV (or II minor)   V7

In 'C', as **Danny and the Juniors** showed, you'd do:

    C   Am   F   G7   (or **C**   Am   Dm   G7)

Streetcorner Pattern in other keys:			
F	Dm	Bb	C7
G	Em	C	D7
E	C#m	A	B7
A	F#m	D	E7
Eb	Cm	Ab	Bb7
D	Bm	G	A7
F#	Ebm	B	C#7

Barreling along beyond this basic pattern, the Dell Vikings vault to that high-energy bridge. Everything builds a gung-ho scream of utter joy and ecstasy at the heart of Rock and Roll. Compare this to Buddy Holly/Bill Pickering magnificent yay-hooray whoop in "Oh Boy" – #10, 1-58. The velvet baritone of **Chuck Jackson** ("Any Day Now", #23, 4-62) was featured with the Dell-Vikings for awhile. The debonair Dell Vikings had another Top Ten Tune with "Whispering Bells" (#9, 7-57). Frantic revelers kept the

bells shaking and quaking at bust-the-sound-barrier speed: #12, 7-57 "Cool Shake."

Another famous multiracial/ethnic 50s crew? Check out the **Impalas**, named for 1) an antelope; and 2) a flawless '58 (and 2000) Chevy convertible named for an antelope:

"Sorry (I Ran All the Way Home)" – the Impalas, #2(2), 3-59; #14, 5-59 R & B. Like Hootie and the Blowfish, fronted by Afro lead singer – this time Joe "Speedo" Frazier. The Impalas' hopeful follow-up? "Oh, What a Fool" (#86, 6-59). Speedo?

"Speedo" [a/k/a "Speedoo"] – Cadillacs, #17, 12-55; #3, 1-56 R & B. When Larry Glazer, 13, first picked up his pawnshop axe in 1956, his two-song repertoire included: the Cadillacs' super "Speedo" and some jingle for a Midwest supermarket called "Let's Go Krogering." And Speedo? **Earl** (that's **Mister Earl**) **'Speedo' Carroll** sang the supercool baritone lead: they call him Speedo, he offers, but his true name? Mister Earl. Since Caveman Ughlook, guys have boasted uproariously about their studly lovemaking prowess. 'Speedo' was a complimentary moniker in 'The Wanderer's' love-'em-and- leave-'em 50s and 60s. For a female counterpoint view, try the Pointer Sisters' 1981 #2 "Slow Hand," which celebrates the easy lover who builds their mutual ecstasy. Speedo Carroll, after leaving his Cadillacs (named after Detroit's 1701 founder and classiest car), joined those zany streetcorner laff-a-minute **Coasters**:

"Yakety Yak" – Coasters, #1, 6-58; #1(7) R & B. Carl Gardner booms out his scratchy L.A. lead tenor in **Jerry Leiber** and **Mike Stoller**'s lyric to toss the dog out, bring the cat in, ditch the garbage, and dump those hoodlum friends. Cool generation-gap lyric from with-it parental angle. Seems chores galore are killing the poor kid. Hardly a tragedy. Normal teenage wear and tear. Super snarly sax. Kicky groove.

"Searchin'"/"Young Blood" – Coasters, #3 & #8, 5-57, #1(12) and #1(1) R & B. Street-savvy humor. Predates Rap. Like the Penguins #8, 12-54 "Earth Angel" or Sonny Til and the Orioles #11,8-53, "Cryin' in the Chapel," early R & B barbershop quartets often named themselves after BIRDS – from whence sprang the **Robins**, the Coasters' earliest group-name. Clown Princes of in-yer-face Streetsoul Rock, the Coasters lambasted the pop charts with hit upon hit, each revving the Leiber/Stoller Laugh Meter higher and higher. "Searchin'" milks the private-eye motif. Tenor lead Carl Gardner spins the tale of romantic escapades, cross-checked by baritone sideswipes by Billy Guy and BOOMING basso profundo explosions from Bobby Nunn. Bluesy guitar riffs are c/o Adolph [Adolph?] Jacobs. An odyssey of radio-days detectives helps out our Love Pilgrim – Charlie Chan, Boston Blackie, Sergeant Preston of the Yukon and Young Unchained Libido. Guys on zoot-suit streetcorners ogle and wolf-whistle at shapely 'young blood' chicks bobbing by.

"Along Came Jones" – Coasters, #9, 5-59; #14 R & B. Bobby Nunn split and was replaced by BOOOOOMING bassman Will 'Dub' Jones. The lyric is a stop-action melodrama from the 1909 silver screen. Some poor damsel is tied to the railroad track, cinched to the buzz-saw, and screaming for heavenly mercy. Just as the lass approaches her dastardly doom, suddenly we hear the welcome sound of a loud "EH-EH!" And so "Along Came" lanky hero Jones . . ." Coasters also scored on #7, 8-59 "Poison Ivy," #2(3), 2-59 "Charlie Brown," and #23, 4-61 fan-dancer fandango "Little Egypt." King Curtis sax.

Paul Evans of New York City also did comedy. Like Camas, Washington's Jimmie Rodgers [II], he was also a previewer of Folk Rock.

"Midnite Special" – Paul Evans, #16, 1-60. A #12 R & B hit for Tiny Grimes in 1948, this ancient Leadbelly prison song dates back much farther. Roberta in the old folk song is visiting her glum man in jail; no one is happy. Toting an umbrella and a hopeful document, she hopes to sweet-talk the governor to set her main man free. Johnny Rivers (Ramistella) sure liked the song in 1965 (#20). Evans tagged his first top-tenner with two Sues, the 'Curls' (Sue Singleton and Sue Terry). This silly stooge sheepishly chauffeured seven beautiful girls around while they all smooched with some Casanova named Fred – "Seven Little Girls, Sittin' in the Back Seat" (#9, 9-59).

Folk Rock begins with Jimmie Rodgers II. Or Lonnie Donegan and his Skiffle Group.

Jimmie Rodgers [II] and **Connie Francis**

"Honeycomb" – Jimmie Rodgers, #1(4), 8-57; #1(2), 9-57; #7, 10-57 C. One wondrously sweet song. Soft-rock Chalypso. Newcomers Buddy Holly and Jimmie Rodgers saw their first charted hits simultaneously hit (and tie) the #1 position. Armed with Elvis's good looks and Bill Haley's spit-curl, the Washington State Scottish tenor lofted to the high notes and resonantly sang the low. Comparing his girl's lips to honey wasn't new: Charlie Gracie's nifty Rockabilly "Butterfly," (#1, 2-57) did it, xeroxed by latter-day crooner Andy Williams (#1, 3-57). Rodgers just pulled it off beautifully. His hits had an almost-religious fever about them, swooping heavenward in celestial crescendo. "Honeycomb" speaks of the Lord making a bird, and a bee. The song is pleasantly chaste and G-rated. "Honeycomb" is an aural pleasure, blooming like lilacs and azaleas and rhododenrons in a splashy sun-suffused May morning. It never stings like a bee.

"Kisses Sweeter Than Wine" – Jimmie Rodgers, #3, 11-57; #8, 12-57 R & B. Rodgers relies on Pete Seeger and the Weavers' #19, 1951 Irish folk song. The song covers a man's whole life of raising kids and grandkids. With rising minor-key intensity, Rodgers hits heights of cosmic happiness. Semi-suddenly, he's the doting grandpop of eight. As he ponders eternity in his old age, he muses: Honey, we had lots of kids, some trials and troubles, but we'd live it all over again. Why? Because she's got 'kisses sweeter than wine'. Rodgers' trademark is ending on a majestic high note and holding the note into a climactic flourish via vibrato guitars and lightning drum riffs. For the clean-cut, Air-Force vet, smooth singer Rodgers, life was a wonderful lark. HAPPY:

"Party Doll" – Buddy Knox and the Rhythm Orchids, #1, 2-57; #3, 3-57 R & B. Buddy Knox hailed from Happy, Texas, and attended West Texas State on an athletic scholarship where he met one of today's major music moguls, Jimmy Bowen. Bowen played bull fiddle in his band, the Rhythm Orchids.

"Party Doll" is Rockabilly heaven. Knox gushes his fine tenor, so curled in Texas drawl that "hair" sounds like "har." Bowen's baritone smash hit surfaced the same month with the multi-echo Slap Bass classic "I'm Stickin' with You" (#14, 2-57). Bowen's be-bop-baby tune brandishes a little rare-for-rock sarcasm reminiscent of Huey Lewis and the News' similar sentiments (#1, 3-86) three decades later – after sticking with her loyally all along, his punch line pounces and he says he's STUCK with her. Tossing out the term 'make love,' which could mean simple smooching in the 50s, Knox seeks sweet ecstasy. Anyhow, Buddy Knox, with his twinkly blue eyes, curly red hair, broad shoulders and cut muscles, plus that Kirk Douglas dimple, wouldn't really be thinking thoughts like that, would he? He would. All guys did, do, and will. "Party Doll" was Knox's solitary #1, despite #9 "Hula Love" later that year. Knox passed on at 65 in 1999, and he left a lot of happy Texas fans very sad.

"Hula Love" – Buddy Knox and the Rhythm Orchids, #9, 9-57; #13, 10-57 R & B. It's this Polynesian-Caribbean thing. Fifties Americans were hung up on the tropical dreams of Gilligan's romantic palm-frond paradise.

"Hula Love" jumps with Caribbean rhythms over Polynesian waves. It has been linked closely to Kay

Medford's" 1911 "My Hula Hula Love." It stars a ferocious Balu chieftain from the nasty Zinga-Zulaland versus the good guys from the peace-loving Bella-Lillaland. Back and forth they race in their war canoes, scrapping for the love of a beautiful maiden. It reads like Herman Melville's pre-*Moby Dick* epics: *Typee, Omoo,* or *Mardi.* In 50s fashion, Knox twists out a happy ending for the gorgeous grass-skirt maiden and her lover.

"Running Bear" – Johnny Preston [By the Big Bopper (J.P. Richardson)], #1(3), 10-59; #3, 1-60 R & B. This tragic tale of native American woe presages Graveyard Rock. It stars two ill-starred Romeo and Juliet lovers: Running Bear and his lady love, Little White Dove. Their warring tribes quarrel amidst a strident chorus of "AH-OO-GA's"; remember **Blue Swede**'s daffy-but-lucrative "OO-GA-CHUCKA," in their #1, 1974 remake of **B.J. Thomas**'s "Hooked on a Feeling" (#5, 11-68)? The "Running Bear" story saga pits two lovers against their warring tribes. Preston/Bopper's song struts two different rhythms: the war-drum smitten verses – versus the snarling-sax triplet-splashed chorus which stuffs twelve beats into each frantic four-beat measure.

Sad ending. Running Bear proves he's a better sprinter than swimmer. From opposing sides of the gurgling stream, Running Bear and Little White Dove swim to their tragic destiny. Their hands touch, lips meet, but the rampaging rIver drags them downward. The Big Bopper's composition reminds us they'll be forever together in that cosmic "Happy Hunting Ground." By the time the song hit big, the Bopper's little snowplane had already fallen out of the sky, and Don McLean lamented the Day the Music Died. Native American cosmology. Graveyard Rock – crude beginning of Death Metal? Let's get happier.

"Banana Boat Song" – Harry Belafonte, #5, 1-57; #7, 2-57 R & B. Also known as "Day-O." Harlem's Harry, like **Lionel Richie** on "All Night Long" (#1, 1983) mastered authentic Jamaican dialect. This song represents the flowering of Calypso. The bongo-drum-powered rhythms of the Caribbean evoke a Call-and-Response Gospel style. Harry chronicles the tough sweaty life of beefy stevedores working the banana boats – they labored all night on a glug of rum. Daylight comes? They just want to plod home. Belafonte's album *Calypso* corraled the #1 spot for 31 weeks, devouring the last half of 1956 in the Year of Elvis. "Banana Boat" was also a hit for the **Tarriers** (#4), whose white Irish tenor **Vince Martin** was also not a longshoreman (Navy guy, though). Tarriers' lead singer Erik Darling pioneered Folk Rock in 1963 with the **Rooftop Singers**' #1(2) "Walk Right In."

"Cindy, Oh Cindy" – Vince Martin and the Tarriers, #9, 10-56. Martin's haunting voice overarches this muted, gorgeous Chalypso melody. Stuck on a Navy ship and gazing at galaxies of lonesome stars, he strolls the desolate deck, wrapped in reverie for the pure pedestal memory of his sweet, adorable lovely Cindy back home. He's no dummy. He dreads the Dear John letters. As he sings to the rolling navy-blue waves, he pleads with fate for sweet

Cindy never to let him down. As peacetime rolled into the Vietnam quagmire, how many spurned lovers made the ultimate sacrifice for their country?

Jackie Wilson

"Lonely Teardrops" – Jackie Wilson, #7, 23-58; #1(7) R & B. Also #1, U.K., 1994. **Jackie Wilson**, of Bill Haley's Motown enclave Highland Park, was shot and seriously wounded by his jealous girlfriend/groupie while performing on stage. A somewhat similar fate befell Latina star **Selena** (#22, 10-95 "Dreaming of You"), when she was killed on 3-31-95 by her fan club founder. Wilson, with his big booming Italian tenor (though Afro-American) not only defined Soul in the Pre-Motown era – but he was a tremendous opera singer as well, like **Mario Lanza** (#1[1], 12-50 "Be My Love"). With a mammoth, stadium-busting voice, Jackie Wilson carried that booming tradition over into Rock and Soul. Like Buddy Holly, Wilson's voice had a dual timbre; he could range from a quavery Irish tenor on the chugging Chalypso "Lonely Teardrops" (with falsetto swoops and glissandos), to a Carusan-Lanzan-Pavarottian bombastic profundo in "Night." On a Dick Clark Oldies Show, ironically while singing the lyrical line about how his heart was crying from 'Lonely Teardrops,' 40-year-old Jackie slumped to the stage, clutching his heart. A combination heart attack/stroke left him in a vegetative state for his last nine years in a Detroit institution. When he finally died, no one could afford a funeral. How many artist/geniuses, confined to threadbare garrets, have suffered such a miserable fate? Meanwhile, chuckling tycoons, who silently rake off musical fortunes, slink off to shuffleboard Florida and gazillion-dollar estates.

"Night" – Jackie Wilson, #4, 4-60; #3, 4-60 R & B. Jackie's highest chart position ever, for the singer listed at #52 in the *Top 500 Artists 1955-99.* Aria from the opera *Samson and Delilah.* An amateur boxer in his youth, like welterweight Berry Gordy, Jr., Wilson scored 54 Top 100 hits in his 15-year (1957-72) career heyday. Cameos:

"Reet Petite" (#62, 11-57), "Baby Workout" (#5, 3-63) and "(Your Love Keeps Lifting Me) Higher and Higher" (#6, 8-67 for Jackie and #2 Rita Coolidge, 5-77).

Some experts say **Jackie Wilson**, godfather of Jody Watley ("Real Love," #2, 3-89), may have been the greatest Rock and/or Soul singer of them all. Incredibly malleable crossover sound: Grand Opera, Soul, Chalypso, Rock and Roll, Ballad-Crooning, and even Irish tenor "Danny Boy" (#94, 2-65). **Lionel Richie** and the Commodores' elegy to Jackie (6-9-34 to 1-29-89), #3, 1-85 "Nightshift," is an amazing tribute.

The 'Happy Daze' of 1955-60 featured a flowering of Rock and Roll and its many sub-styles: Calypso, Rockabilly, Slow Rock, Wimp Rock, Soul, Blues, Streetcorner/Doo-Whop Rock, Comedy Rock, Country Rock, Old Standards-Re-rocked Rock, and Jump-Up-and-Down-on-Your-Piano Rock.

"Keep-a Knockin'" – Little Richard, #8, 9-57; #2(1) R & B. With a frantic phalanx of saxmasters, in Bermuda shorts, blasting bari, tenor, and alto in major-key harmony, Little Richard would strut out, dwarfed by a baggy suit, and topped by a five-inch hairdo that would make 'Little' Richard about 6'5'. Gliding up the three keys to his major key (say, G-A-Bb-then C) he'd launch his screaming Rock and Roll barrage. More laid-back **Fats Domino** launched his mainstream pop-rock career with "Goin Home" at #30, 6-52 [#1(1), 4-52 R & B]. In the Rock Era, Fats's #10, 7-55 "Ain't It a Shame" led off, and hit #1(11), 5-55 R & B. Fats played nifty triplet rhythm in soft-rock splendor; Richard's audial attack on the establishment busted speakers everywhere. Knock all you want, Richard bellowed defiantly, but you'll never get in! Frantic, frenzied, hell-bent-for leather Screaming Blues. Nary a stop was pulled out. Little Richard (and the **Tempo Toppers**) rocked the rafters, blew the speakers, and brought down the house. The lyrical theme is domestic dispute: girl is ticked off at guy; girl tries to batter down door.

"I'll Be Home" – Pat Boone, #4, 2-56. Pat Boone's true vocal power? He's a rock balladeer. The Flamingos released the first version. Boone's devoted rendition follows mainstream Americana. Pat's rolling golden baritone reverberates in a convincing message that – True Love Is Service. Boone's trophies? Sixty hits in *Billboard's Top 100, 1955-99*; and 10th ever in Joel Whitburn's *Top 500 Artists of the Rock Era.*

1) Elvis Presley – 9641 pts.   6) Madonna – 4071
2) Beatles – 5360   7) Rolling Stones – 3819
3) Elton John – 5176   8) Aretha Franklin – 3782
4) Stevie Wonder – 4455   9) Michael Jackson – 3775
5) James Brown – 4152   **10) Pat Boone** – 3692

For the 50s decade, *Billboard's* 1977 success chart puts Pat just behind Elvis: 3694 points to Pat's 2836 (Whitburn).

"Moonlight Gambler" – Frankie Laine, #3, 12-56. Born Frank LoVecchio in windy 1913 Chicago, Laine was the booming crooner (oxymoron?) of *High Noon*. "Moonlight Gambler" throttles the full range of odd chord changes, mysterious modulations of key, and spoken pre-Rap poetry. Romeo tosses romantic dice for fun and profit.

Rock and Roll welcomed the crooners, as long as they welcomed Rock and Roll. Frankie sure did. Laine's gambling ends hopefully, as all gambling must: he'll gamble for many miles, until Lady Luck smiles. Then Frankie's truly Italian tenor trails off into the cactus West with his haunting repeated refrain: they call him, he booms, the Moonlight Gambler . . .

Aren't we all moonlight gamblers?

"Ain't Got No Home" – Clarence 'Frogman' Henry, #20, 1-57; #3 R & B. Fats Domino's greatest protégé brought his piano and trombone to Cajun Soul & Roll – and sky-highed this comedy classic. 'Frogman' lofts his normal cool smooth tenor, then fires off a falsetto verse (like Domino's '50 "The Fat Man'). He croaks/burbles a jiffy verse as Muppet Kermit-the-Frog's grandfather Jeremiah **Bass**-Frog. I loved this song (of course, I was 13). Into the sizzling sixties, Henry's biggest chartbuster "But I Do" rolls along on a swash of throbbing triplets (#4, 2-61, pressed with alternate title "I Don't Know Why" ... why? I don't know why). Henry's trombone-laced R & B cruisers also nabbed fame via the **Mills Brothers** #1[5], 6-44 "You Always Hurt the One Your Love" (#12, 5-61 Henry). Among his best? #57, 8-61 "Lonely Street". Henry previews and mainstreams the stratospheric sound of the sixties, falsetto: Del Shannon, Jimmy Jones, Four Seasons.

"Guess Things Happen That Way" – Johnny Cash, #11, 6-58; #1(8) C. Note that this is Top 100, not just COUNTRY. It's the same sound Big John brought with him to Sam Phillips in the aftermath of Elvis to RCA. Sun Records, after Elvis flew the coop, made stars out of **Jerry Lee Lewis, Carl Perkins, Roy Orbison**, and this big Arkansas bass/baritone. He takes the semi-religious view that the Lord gave him the girl to prop him up, but now the Lord has put him on his own. He prays for the manly strength to "stand alone." Sage stuff.

In the premiere wave of the British Invasion, Rock, Folk, and Country blended into the plunkitty American BANJO of Glaswegian Scottish tenor **Lonnie Donegan**. In the early 50s, Scottish jug and banjo bands got together, fussing around with American Folk/Blues/Country classics in the **Weavers'** afterglow. **Leadbelly (Huddie) Ledbetter**, 1889-1949, father at 15, wrote classics "The Midnite Special" plus "Cotton Fields" (#13, 11-61, the Highwaymen) and "The Boll Weevil" (#2, 5-61, Brook Benton). Plus this mongreliferous mix of styles:

"Rock Island Line" – Lonnie Donegan and his Skiffle Group, #8, 3-56; #8 U.K. Banjo-crunching Scotsman Lonnie, doing Country Bluegrass Folk Rock Comedy, told his whimsical story: a trainman, headed for New Orleans on the Rock Island (Illinois) line, claims to the tollgate warden that he's simply hauling pigs, cows, horses, sheep. He's really smuggling pig iron. As Donegan & Skifflers' train accelerates, so does the song's tempo. In his finale chorus, Donegan's slick vocal whirls at the speed of light, over the fugitive Mississippi Delta.

How did Rock and Roll take over in the fifties? ROCK JOCKS! TV liberated the air waves for Top 40 radio. Wes Smith's excellent study, *The Pied Pipers of Rock and Roll*, cites the 3,100,000 portable radios sold annually and quadrupling by 1965. Among key jocks of early rock, according to Smith, **Alan Freed** coined the term Rock and Roll, Cleveland, 1952. Biographer **John Jackson** chronicles his turbulent life, fraught with fame, scandal, and dynamo energy. See *Big Beat Heat*.

Dick Clark – the first major VeeJay (V.J. – video jock), parleyed his *American Bandstand* into Rock and Roll's biggest showcase, and power base, ever. More about Clark throughout. And, oh . . . check your mailbox. John Jackson's definitive *American Bandstand* (Oxford, 1997) links Clark as gatekeeper to nearly all the R & R stars of three decades. Other Rock Jocks?

Bob Horn – Philly rockjock who invented term Bandstand; **Todd Storz** – inventor of Top 40 radio, later used by **Bill Drake**; (AM R & R jocks were role models for us tiny teenage terrors, as we rampaged the neighborhoods, puberty-stricken, tossing eggs and pandemonium); **Bill 'Hoss' Allen** – Nashville's jive-talkin' WLAC Soul jock, who slung the hepcat lingo. Wes Smith notes DJ's called 'Jet Pilot of Jive,' 'Dogface,' 'Lord Fauntleroy,' 'Professor Bop,' and 'Daddy-O Hot Rod.' Also, **Martha Jean, the Queen** – Detroit institution. Her regal pronouncements were revered in the Afro-American community; **Bill Lowery** – Atlanta jock/entrepreneur; **Dewey Phillips** – Sam Phillips' pal and rockjock connection for Sun Records.

Jack Cooper did first disc jockey programming from the early 30s to the 50s in Chicago. In 1919, **Frank Conrad** fashioned a rudimentary radio studio atop his Pittsburgh garage. Hooking a mike in front of a Victrola phonograph, he serenaded a few neighbors that he'd equipped with receivers (Richard Campbell); **Gladys Hill** – Houston's "Dizzy

Lizzy" of KYOK (stations east of Mississippi generally start with W, like WAVC. West they're led off by K like KYOK; Canada has 'C' [CKLW], and Mexico 'X' [XERB]).

Jocko Henderson, **Tom Joyner**, and **Dick Biondi** – just about Chicago's most important gregarious DJs of all time. (Joyner and Henderson often commuted DAILY to Dallas).

Joel Sebastian – ultracool rock jock of Detroit's WXYZ and Chicago, WBBM, with vest and smile. Or the NYC WINS/WCBS-FM crew of **Cousin Brucie Morrow, Don K. Reid, Harry Harrison, Dan Ingram, Bob Shannon** and **Bobby Jay.**

Other jocks? Yep, Buffalo's **George Lorenz** ('Mad Man Mancuso' in *The Buddy Holly Story*), Chicago's **Dex Card** and **Ron Riley,** and **Murry the K** (Kaufman), the 'Fifth Beatle.' **George Nettleton**, rock-jock critic of *Rockin' 50s*, has a definitive book soon covering these hepcat catalysts of Coolth.

Cream of the crop, say many, is **Wolfman Jack** (actually Bob Smith) of Brooklyn and *American Graffiti***** (1973) fame. Perched on a frenzied rumbling baritone, the Wolfman circumnavigated the rock and roll globe, from Brooklyn's Paramount Theatre in L.A. to Chicago, to a border semi-private clear-channel 100,000-watt monster, XERF of Mexico. Wolfman Jack circumscribes their microcosmic moonglow cruising universe (see Rockflix).

In the 50s, DJ's had the power to make or break music. In the 60s, after the payola scandals dried up and blew away, the big decisions were made by backroom Program Directors, and maybe Rock and Roll wasn't quite as young and fun anymore.

Over the long years, America's most beloved radio DJ is ubiquitous **Casey Kasem**, whose *American Top 40* has been heard weekly for generations of Americans. Thanks, Casey – we're ALL listening to *American Top 40*.

"Diana" – Paul Anka, #1, 7-57; #1(2), 9-57 R & B. The girl he loves is so OLD, and he is so YOUNG, lamented 15-year-old Paul of Ottawa, Ontario, about his lady love. Despite a great bouncy song it is perhaps the worst pick-up line in history. The real Diana was 15-year-old Paul's younger siblings' babysitter, Diana Ayoub, according to *Uncle John's Bathroom Reader* (St. Martin's). Good luck showered, however, the Lebanese/Canadian lad. His first songwriting extravaganza made him a millionaire at barely 15. The cool teenage idol crooned Soft Rock "Puppy Love" (#2, 2-60) and he wept "Lonely Boy" (#1[4], 6-59) crocodile-rock tears all the way to his

Scrooge McDuck three cubic acres of money vault. Super Chalypso beat.

"Rebel Rouser" – Duane Eddy, #6, 6-58; #8, 7-58 R & B. With his Gretsch, made along the Williamsburg Bridge, Brooklyn, and his machine-gun staccato sax trip headlined by Steve Douglas, the Upstate Eddy (Corning, New York) embarked on his twangy odyssey. Crackling with basstone lead guitar, muted piano riffs, and double driving drums, Duane and his Rebels tossed a new meaning into the ho-hum term "instrumental." [Eddy twanged lead guitar on 80s superstar group **Foreigner**'s #42, 3-95 "Until the End of Time."] Tennessee's **Chet Atkins**' (1924-2001) #49, 9-59, "Boo-Boo Stick Beat" entertained 50s guitar fans with his finger-picking expertise.

"The All American Boy" – Bobby Bare ('Bill Parsons'), #2(1), 12-58. Toss-up with Bo Diddley for First Rap Song status, but this is certainly first Country Rock Rap (harking back to older Talking Blues style of Leadbelly). Rock Rap Ohioan Bare penned a Johnny B. Goode-Elvis classic here, spoofing teenage-idol-hood.

"Say Man" – Bo Diddley, #20, 9-59; #3, 9-59 R & B. Born Otha Elias McDaniel, and named after a one-stringed African guitar. First Rap song? No way – but it's the first major Soul tune to feature a total spoken patter of pal put-downs to a rockin' beat. The Bo Diddley beat thumped and boomed and crunched the semi-sleepy 50s with guitar-driven energy. Also motor-scooter-driven: one album cover featuring Bo on a scooter. Diddley nabbed R & B honors before his #20 "Say Man" HOT 100 gambit: his #1(2) R & B flipside "I'm a Man" (see Muddy Waters) and the A-side self-titled "Bo Diddley" topped the R & B charts. This big #1 tune is based on a folk song called "Hambone," rockingly crooned by top stars **Jo Stafford** and **Frankie Laine** to #6 in 3-52. Buddy Holly posthumously took "Bo Diddley" to #8 in the United Kingdom 4-63 (only #116 here two months later, pre-British Invasion). Bo scored R & B-only with #11, 7-55 follow-up "Diddley Daddy," #4, 1-56 "Pretty Thing," and 1-67 #17 "Ooh Baby." The McComb, Mississippi Delta Bluesman (b. 12-30-28) rocks on, basking in his amiable living-legend status.

"Say Man' features two guys dissing each other on Any Urban Streetcorner, U.S.A. Bo and his 'pal' are both Bo's voices – a tenor and a baritone rapper. The baritone alter ego scores on the tenor one via 'the dozens' (dozens of put-downs) as they bounce down the skybright street. Tromping the trudging dude with chuckly barbs, he scores on the 'uglitude' of the other guy's girlfriend – her flying wig, her weird figure, her gorgonic face. As the rhythm-meisters fracture the silence along with Bo's screaming odd-shaped guitar, Bo's lightning right hand chops chords like sugar cane. The incessant beat throbs into the hot American evening nocturne of streetwise savvy. Rap – with a side of ghetto-blast humor. Elvis made their dads cringe.

Music since eternity has offered a choice: love me now or never.

"One Night" – Elvis Presley, #4, 11-58; #10 R & B; #24, 12-58 C. "One Night" represents the Elvis Danger Zone. In this lush Blues ballad, Army Private Presley commands his Rock and Roll baritone rasp with flamboyant moaning gusto. His passionate yearning is powerful and fleeting. He offers no rings, no tomorrows, no picket fences. Bouncing babies, however, just could arrive, not so welcomely, if "One Night" breeds reality.

"One Night" is the essence of all El's seduction saga. ONE NIGHT – not the rest of her life. Such dreamy dog-gerel prompts wary women like Carole King and Shirelle Shirley Alston to beseech: Tonight, honey, lovelight may be sparkling your soft brown eyes, but hey – you gonna love me tomorrow, too? ["Will You Love Me Tomorrow? #1, 11-60].

In "One Night" Elvis puts together all the instantaneous male desire that ever shuddered groovily to the curvy girl boppin' by. Elvis booms the baritone rasp, with Jordanaires free-falling through lusty layers of harmony. Many innocent lasses, however, are still snowed on smoke rings of desire. Elvis made their dads cringe.

Among super singing groups of the Rock Revolution, you'll find the **Drifters** with many great lead singers: **Clyde McPhatter** (and nearly **Jackie Wilson** via Billy Ward's Dominoes), **Ben E. King** ("Stand by Me," #4, '61 & #9, '86), **Rudy Lewis** ("On Broadway", #9, '63), and **Johnny Moore**. They're like the **Yardbirds** with guitarists: **Jimmy Page**, **Eric Clapton** and **Jeff Beck**. McPhatter, whose life and career were consumed at 39 by a bad liver plus a broken heart, was inducted solo into Rock's Hall of Fame in 1987:

"Treasure of Love" – Clyde McPhatter, #16, 6-56; #1(1) R & B). As Clyde's piano man tromped the triplet *arpeggios*, Clyde belted out one of Slow Dancing's finest. Gospel Soul. Despite Durham, North Carolina, Afro heritage, Clyde could sling an Irish "Danny Boy" with the best of the shamrock shouters. From Dominoes, Drifters, and solo shot, McPhatter's star exploded into the supernova scene with #1(11) R & B (N.C. Top 30) "Money Honey." Elvis echoed it to #76, 5-56.

McPhatter's dynamic follow-up is #21 '54 "Honey Love" [#1(8), 6-54 R & B]. With that buzzy bee honeycomb sweet-lips bit, it sent censors reeling. Clyde's oohs and ahhs were too sexy to rate PG. "Treasure of Love" represents the slow dance, just as crucial to the rock revolution as the fast dance. McPhatter's ballads coaxed and implored and cooed listeners to intimacy. He puffed up love to ethereal heights. He also scored with #6 "A Lover's Question" in 1958 and his swan song, "Lover Please" (#7, 3-62). McPhatter debuted the Drifters with a rare platter (#80, 12-55, recorded 1953, with bass Bill Pinckney) of **Bing Crosby**'s #1 classic "White Christmas." The hot Drifters' version influenced Elvis to use the same arrangement on #1(4), 12-57 *Elvis' Christmas Album*, (worth $500 in 2000).

"Save the Last Dance for Me" – Drifters, #1(3), 9-60; #1(10), 10-60 R & B. Buddy Holly's last producer **Dick Jacobs** introduced strings to Rock and Roll ("It Doesn't Matter Anymore," #1 U.K., 3-59). Drifters' **Ben E. King**'s syrupy second tenor skates skillfully over Chalypso guitars. He grants his date her right to have a good time and dance with other guys. At the gala finale, though, he chides her to be back in his arms, because sharing is great — for things other than girlfriends.

Overarching the sprightly Drifters' theme song are golden ringing violins. Rock and Roll was expanding, reaching out, hybridizing to encompass new styles and orchestral arrangements. "Save the Last Dance for Me" is a harbinger of the musical complexity that would spearhead the superstars on the way to the ultimate Beatles: **Del Shannon**, Gene Pitney, **Bobby Vee**, Johnny and the Hurricanes. King's #2(1) vocal on Drifters' "There Goes My Baby" serenaded a romantic era.

"Rock Around with Ollie Vee" – Buddy Holly, NC, 1956. Recorded November 15, 1956, in Owen Bradley's Barn, Nashville. Young Holly signed with Decca and they tried to make a pure Country Rockabilly of him. Of Bradley's four sides of Buddy, including a 1956 rough draft of his 1957 smash #1 "That'll Be the Day," Ollie Vee is the best. Whiz saxman **Boots Randolph** and lead guitar ace Grady Martin drive Holly's first great (though unsuccessful) record. It's a Rockabilly statement the world needed another year to get ready for.

"The Fool" – Sanford Clark, #7, 8-56; #5, 9-56 R & B; #14, 10-56 C. Lee Hazelwood and Phoenix's Sanford Clark gambled $215 on a recording session. Clark's bass-baritone Rockabilly talent hit the one-shot jackpot. Rockabillies are often Irish tenors. Clark and **Johnny Cash** and **Ricky Nelson** and **Eddie Cochran** are in the minority in their bass/baritone bailiwick. The slap bass sound is extraordinary, the echo of Clark's deadpan delivery haunting. The lyric, too, was revolutionary for teenage music in 1956: guy drinking to 'some fool' with pals at Miller-Bud Time in bar . . . in 'O. Henry' surprise ending, he turns out to be the fool who told his girlfriend goodbye. The song was written by Naomi Ford, Hazelwood's wife; Clark's sound impressed young Phil Spector, arguably America's most famous record producer. He hightailed it to Phoenix to apprentice. This was long before young Spector transferred his father's tombstone epitaph into a #1 song, "To Know Him, Is to Love Him" (#1, 9-58, with Phil murmuring baritone do-do-do-do-do-do's and Carol Connors mellowizing the sweet soprano lead).

Sanford Clark looked the Rockabilly part: brooding ebony eyes, black ivy-league shirt, corrugated wool tie. His Hollywood Roll to his 50s pompadour suggested the pipeline rolling into *Baywatch* Beach, swirly surf smashing Malibu shores. "The Fool" was just too good; Clark could never buy another hit.

Without Mississippi **Delta Blues**, Rock and Roll might never have rocked. Legendary **Jimmy Reed** of Dunleith, Mississippi, and Chess Records of Chicago had more Blues hits than any other artist except **B.B. King**. Reed entered the Rock Hall of Fame in 1991. With twelve Top 100 songs between 1957-63, Jimmy had about eleven more hits than most cult or backwash Blues legends:

"Honest I Do" – Jimmy Reed, #32, 9-57; #4, 10-57 R & B. Reed's nomadic entourage skipped all over the U.S.A. in pursuit of 12-bar perfection. This chugging bluesmeister taught the world the running rhythm bass line on guitar. His funky nasal Blues twang – slow and drawly – energized Rock and Soul. One of the original Mississippi Delta Bluesmen – Reed rambles over Bo Diddley "Talking Blues" (the first Rap), and lives the mystery life epitomized by **Robert Johnson**'s ghost in *Crossroads.*

"Baby, What You Want Me to Do" – Jimmy Reed, #37, 2-60; #10, 3-60 R & B. This classic Blues number creeps and slinks, as the poor man ponders everything he has done for his yet-unsatisfied gal. He's up, down, in, out . . . runnin', hidin', peepin', whatever.

Reed dumped his ironworking job in the Jackson Five's Gary, Indiana, in 1950, and plied his hard-pumping Blues sound in smoky 'Paradise Alley' bars on Detroit's Hastings Street (now a red-hot misty memory) – or in Chicago's neon glow, below a marshmallow moon.

Jimmy Reed, bluesman. When **Bob Dylan** was haunting the coffee-houses and Beat-Generation hangouts of Jack Kerouac's Greenwich Village in the early 60s, he picked up a simultaneous harmonica-guitar technique. It landed the young poet with the craggy voice a Columbia Records contract. His mentor, of course? **Jimmy Reed**.

"Baby, What You Want Me to Do" is a 12-bar classic. It splashes Jimmy's favorite little triplet riff just as you come down to the turnaround (landing on your tonic **E**, you flip back to the dominant **B7**, all the while scooping this hot frantic little floorp of notes off the G and high E strings). As "Peepin' and Hidin'," the same song hit the Canadian charts for Ontario's Count Victors, and made the Keener Countdown top 30 (WKNR-Detroit) for local Jamie Coe (George Colovas) and the Gigolos, who also had a nice version of Sanford Clark's #6, '56 "The Fool" in 1963. They performed it live when Del Shannon showed up and almost became a Beatle. More later. It all connects . . .

Teen idols dominated 50s charts. We'll cover some of those stars (**Ricky Nelson, Jerry Lee Lewis**, and their mutual ill-fated airplane) soon.

It's time to move on to the most popular innovator in the history of Rock and Roll. Nice kid. Became a teenage idol on talent. He had only a year and a half to make his mark.

Since the day the music supposedly died, the legend of the next lad and his music found two billion new worldwide fans.

Rock and Roll is here to stay.

Holly Days --
Nevermore to Evermore

Broiling dog-day Summer 1955. A grubby bus lumbered through Texas boomtown Lubbock to Rock and Roll's most fateful crossroads: 2½ miles out the Slaton Highway to the Highway 84 Cotton Club. This was no mystic midnight rendezvous between some longgone bluesman and some diabolical speed-guitar pact with the Devil. It was just a major meeting between two young good ol' boys who went to church and strummed their guitars and prayed for a hit record someday.

Young **Elvis Presley** was billed as "The Hillbilly Cat." He headlined the Louisiana Hayride and now the Elvis Presley Jamboree. A new kid on the Lubbock block dumped his dollar to see his hero Elvis. Flanked by guitar wizard **Scotty Moore** (Rock Hall of Fame '99) and stand-up bass magician **Bill Black**, young Elvis barnstormed the sweltering South, seeking a 1956 gold mine – "Heartbreak Hotel." As the bus diesel snorted outside, the footlights fired up, the spotlight exploded with promise, and Elvis cut loose. Rock and Roll was banging on sleepy Lubbock's door.

Yippees and yays and yahoos rocked the rafters. Elvis grinned, encored, and exited. As the Elvismania afterglow subsided, the recent Lubbock High School grad stood starstruck. He hadn't just gazed at just any hillbilly cat – Elvis was a bonafide TIGER. The starstruck kid stood transfixed. He wiped off his hot horn-rimmed glasses and whisked away his childhood.

Buddy Holly headed for his trusty old guitar. "Without Elvis," he reverently and modestly murmured, "none of us could have made it." [Ren Grevatt's liner notes, *The Buddy Holly Story*, Al. #11, 4-59].

Nice guy, Buddy. With his lariat of Lubbock lads, the **Crickets**, Buddy Holly would soon corral the hearts of America with his bold new breed of Rock and Roll. Grinning behind aw-shucks specs and an unleashed musical genius, Buddy Holly rose to become the single most important rocker in the 50s in the aftermath of Elvis.

Buddy Holly's story is Everyman's: Born Charles Hardin Holley, Lubbock, Texas, September 7, 1936. Folks might just as easily have called him "Good Ol' Charlie" Holley. Brothers Larry and Travis, sister Pat, and Buddy's mom somehow ended up with the endearing "BUDDY." Brunswick and Coral and Decca Records accidentally chucked the "E" from Holley; the result made Buddy more a Christmas present [Holly] than a member of his kissing-cousin extended family – related to the Holley Carburetor Company. Buddy's dad, Lawrence Holley, and his older brothers labored at the family tile business.

"Family values" were strong in the Holly household. Middle-class in mere money, they were millionaires in family love and togetherness. Buddy's mother, **Mrs. Ella Holley**, was the positive force behind Buddy's superstardom. She even helped Buddy write his big #17 hit "Maybe Baby." In the Oscar-nominated film *The Buddy Holly Story*, well-meaning Innervisions producers portray Buddy's folks as fuddy-duddyish and annoyed at Rock and Roll. Not so. Buddy's mom was his inspiration. Although Buddy grudgingly toted a tiny fiddle off to fourth grade, his musical gusto really took off when he discovered the guitar and piano.

Unlike many 50s teen idols puppeteered by tycoons only for their "cute teddy-bear-cuddly looks," Buddy Holly brought one additional trump credential to the Rock and Roll Arena: he was the best musician of the whole batch.

Buddy Holly and his Crickets symbolize the "Happy Days" Rock and Roll Good-time Era of the late 50s. America was strong and growing more prosperous. Rock music had just shattered Too-Easy Listening charts forever. After apprenticing to Elvis and the Elvismania Phenomenon, Buddy Holly flipped on his Clark Kent glasses and penned "That'll Be the Day." He peddled it unsuccessfully from Nashville for a year until his big break came – with producer **Norman Petty**, who spearheaded Buddy Knox and Jimmy Bowen and the Rhythm Orchids from Clovis, New Mexico (just an hour down the Texas road 100 miles away).

In Buddy's squashed 1¼ -year career as a rock star, he changed music forever. Most innovative performer of the 50s, Buddy Holly was a Do-It-Yourself Teen Idol in an era of stars manipulated and puppeteered by backstage deals and big-bucks payola. The Crickets' "Oh Boy" and "Maybe Baby," and Buddy's "Peggy Sue," commandeered the American air waves on the strength of their pure musical excellence.

Buddy Holly shaped the next decade: The **Beatles** took their name from Buddy's **Crickets**, and **Bob Dylan** might have become just a nonmusical decent poet without Holly's melodic influence.

Buddy wasn't a seven-year-old prodigy like Wolfgang Amadeus **Mozart** and his twinkly little star. Holly and Hutchinson Junior High School pal Bob Montgomery debuted at an elderly ten or twelve on 'Hillbilly' and Bluegrass music: **Flatt & Scruggs, Bill Monroe,** plus **Hank Williams**. Before long – in those un-canned, non-national, VERY local radio days – the lads soon hosted their own live *Buddy and Bob Show* on KDAV Lubbock, first station in the nation to program a solid Country music format. KDAV jock **Hi-Pockets Duncan** was their early mentor and first manager. All the while, Buddy's pliable musical mind absorbed all the varied pop music of the Late Crooner Era and beyond. Buddy could croon along with **Frankie Laine**'s silk-smooth "That's My Desire," wail a wild and woolly **Fats Domino** "Blue Monday," sling a molasses-slow **Little Richard** Blues ("Slippin' & Slidin'," #33, 4-56), and rock out on a dashing **Carl Perkins** "Blue Suede Shoes" (#2[4], 3-56).

The essence of rock and roll genius is synthesis. Before young Buddy could sculpt his own melodies and style, he apprenticed and assimilated all the best of the rest. Aw-shucks modesty, Buddy Holly.

Dissatisfied with mere imitation, Buddy and Bob wrote a few western-style songs; one of them,

"Flower of My Heart," may be a metaphorical oddity, but the tuneful melody, spurred by close thirds harmony, became the official Lubbock High School theme song in 1954.

Soon some Crickets chirped their musical way into the scene. Buddy hired 16-year-old **Jerry (J.I.) Allison** to thump drums. The kid was good. Very good. Buddy, in fact, was not the sole superstar among the Crickets. A late 70s *Rolling Stone* magazine poll nominated Jerry and voted him 3rd-greatest rock drummer of all time. Bronze medal, not bad. Numbers One and Two? The **Who's Keith Moon** and **Led Zeppelin's John Bonham**. Sadly, Moon O.D.'d at the premiere of *The Buddy Holly Story*, while Bonham died similarly two years later. Hmmm. Do the math. Could Jerry Allision, Cricket, be rock's greatest drummer?

In the same *Rolling Stone* fan poll, Cricket bass man **Joe B. Mauldin** (who introduced the electric bass when his bulky bull fiddle bugged him one night) got himself voted #20 or so. Very talented crew, Crickets.

Among other Crickets who weren't there when Buddy hit the big time were **Sonny Curtis, Waylon Jennings**, Larry Welborn, and David Box (the only singer who did a dynamite imitation of both Buddy Holly and incomparable Roy Orbison). **Niki Sullivan**, Buddy's cousin, starred with the Crickets during their boomdays of late 1957; Sullivan played rhythm guitar, looked a bit like Buddy, and sang background vocals on the big 1957 hits.

Later Crickets' lead singers after 1959 included the splendid singer Box (killed in a Dallas commuter plane crash, 1964); Glenn Hardin, who later backed Elvis; Jerry Naylor, ("But for Love", #69, 3-70); **Sonny Curtis** again, who sang lead when we talked on Long Island in 1995; Earl Sinks (1960-61), and 80s-90s lead singer Gordon Payne. The post-Holly Crickets cut some of the most astonishingly cool rock tunes of the early 60s. Only their **Bobby Vee** collaboration, #42 Al. 7-62 *Bobby Vee Meets the Crickets*, helped launch an American Top 100 tune that echoes Buddy's #1, '57 "That'll Be the Day" – "Someday" (#99, 9-62 Vee and the Crickets). The Crickets' "Don't Ever Change" hit #5 in the U.K. during the post-Holly years, and the **Beatles** recorded it for the BBC. In the aftermath of the 1959 aerial snowsquall tragedy, the left-back Crickets did session work with R & R's hottest duo – the **Everly**

Brothers, Don and Phil: ("'Till I Kissed You," #4, 8-59). Holly's most famous sideman, however, isn't his music-maestro lead guitarist **Tommy Allsup** from the 1958 latter Crickets ("It's So Easy," #17 U.K.), nor is it his drummer Charlie Bunch – who perhaps hit a bonanza by suffering frostbitten feet in a Winter Tour hospital, and missed the plane. Ironically, however, Allsup won the first Cricket Grammy Award (2000), despite hearing on February 3, 1959 that HE had been killed in the plane crash. He wasn't, of course. More later.

Nope. It's Buddy's second-bassman: **Waylon Jennings** (1937-2002). Second bass (base?). The 18-year-old Holly protégé, now country star, had his first record, "Jole Blon ," produced by Buddy, who at 22 was expanding his musical universe in every direction. Jennings ("Theme from Dukes of Hazzard" [#21, 9-80] and #25 with **Willie Nelson**, "Good Hearted Woman" [2-76])) became a legendary country star with many #1 songs. Buddy had advised the Texan lad to do his own music his own way (sez Holly Memorial Society Prez **Bill Griggs**). Waylon chopped his way from carping criticism to stunning stardom with his 'Texas Outlaw' sound..

Now that we've loaded the stage with extraordinary talent, let's bring back the young man who revolutionized Rock and Roll – **Buddy Holly**. Holly's versatile voice spearheaded the Crickets' meteoric rise to the #1 song of August 12, 1957. But he couldn't have done it without the Duke. Like Texan lads of the 50s who weren't cruising chicks, flinging footballs, running for Prez (George W. Bush, 2000), or rampaging to Rock and Roll, Buddy and his buddies Jerry and Joe B. snuggled into the smoky seats with their dates, like Echo and 'Cindy Lou' or Peggy Sue Gerron. On the Bijou bill? **John Wayne**'s masterpiece, *The Searchers****. 'The Duke' bellowed this catchy phrase, responding to some smarmy blaggard's snide crack about Wayne perhaps quitting his quest: "THAT'LL BE THE DAY!" – roared the Big Cowpoke.

Screen credits faded, stale popcorn crusted the Pepsi floor, and the purple-uniformed usher's push-broom tailed the young Crickets into the garish 101° furnace of summerstreet Lubbock. The guys ended up at Buddy's. In half and hour, Holly and Allison had a song and a dream.

It was a dream deferred. Buddy's pals hung out in high-plains-drifter Lubbock, flubbed around with jobs and girls and hot-rods, and rocked the roadhouse scene. Then Buddy checked out Elvis. The Kid from Lubbock went from groupie to preparing to become a rock and roll star. Like 'Johnny B. Goode,' minus the railroad track. Though no Holleys were ultra-rich, Buddy's generous brother Larry Holley loaned Buddy the cash to buy what would become his legendary red Fender Stratocaster guitar. (**Jimi Hendrix** would follow Buddy's guitar lead on Fender Strat lead guitar).

When Elvis rolled the big bus into Lubbock the second time, poised with local fame for international superstardom, the Kid was waiting in the wings – Buddy Holly and his nameless combo were the opening act.

Imagine being there. Ponder this: you paid (ulp) $1.75 to see them both! **Elvis** and **Buddy**. How many megazillions would your friendly Ticketmaster monopoly charge today, if cosmically possible? [Probably the Gross National Product – GNP – of Sierra Leone, Andorra, or Bhutan].

Buddy's own road to destiny forked off somewhere between **Norman Petty**'s Nor-Va-Jak Studios in Clovis, new Mexico, 100 speedorama miles away – and **Owen Bradley**'s Barn in Nashville, Tennessee. Petty's contacts with Elvis's manager, 'Colonel' Tom Parker, both helped and hindered Buddy's stardust pursuits with the Nashville Decca contract. Decca Records were big, and they could vitally help Buddy's career, but they pigeonholed the rebel-rousing Rockabilly into a traditional Country/Bluegrass bag. Buddy's itty-bitty band (Buddy and **Bob Montgomery**) was chopped in half in a nasty 50s version of 'downsizing.'

Country kingpins in Nashville loved Buddy's voice. Not Bob's. They canned the other good-voiced lad, who nobly insisted his friend sign solo, despite his personal disappointment. Ironically, Buddy's fired friend became a millionaire record producer/tycoon/mogul.

When Buddy first cut "That'll Be the Day" in Bradley's Barn, it flopped. Why? Bradley, a whiz at standard country music production, was unprepared to unleash a unique singer like Holly. Bradley tried to change Buddy into a nasal hillbilly tiptop tenor. Didn't work. Buddy's other Nashville release was a mild success, zooming to the exact same 18,000 sales that Elvis's debut nabbed. Buddy's first minor hit? "Blue Days, Black Nights," backed with

"Love Me" (a different "Love Me" from Elvis's #2 hit of 1956).

Meanwhile, back in Clovis, **Norman** and his talented wife **Vi Petty** kept the door open for the Crickets and kept the faith. Petty had just scored his first gold million-seller with the first rock group with two lead singers – **Buddy Knox** (with Jimmy Bowen) and his **Rhythm Orchids**' "Party Doll" (#1, 3-57). This cranked up Petty's New Mexico hit machine for Buddy Holly's Rock Revolution:

"Think It Over" – Buddy Holly & the Crickets, #27, 7-58. Buddy's 6th biggest hit is his least known. Powered by Vi Petty's Boogie-Woogie piano, and Allison's thunderous rhythmic pulse, "Think It Over" is one of Buddy's top three rockers. **John Goldrosen**'s outstanding *Remembering Buddy* lists a Valentine's Day 1958 session with Joe B. Mauldin on bass. Vi overdubbed it with backing vocals by the Roses (Bob Linville, Ray Rush, David Bigham). Holly's background singers on "That'll Be the Day" are Gary and Ramona Tolletf. On "Oh, Boy," he's backed by the **Picks**: Bill and John Pickering, and Bob Lapham. "Think It Over" is a rockin' macho 12-Bar Blues of Tex-Mex splendor, with a bass acoustic piano lead.

Like the **Beatles** revolutionized haircuts with their Prince Valiant bangs, Buddy Holly and the Crickets almost became the first band to wear white t-shirts, and Levis on stage, but Vi Petty stuffed them into gangly gray suits for their initial album. Buddy Holly, at six feet and 145 pounds, looked more like an insurance agent or star miler or cross-country star, maybe a future computer whiz, than a teenage idol – said his astounded fans. **Paul McCartney** idolized Buddy: "[When we first heard Buddy on the radio], we didn't know if he was white or black – we just had this mystic image of this great music."

Paul couldn't have said it better. I fondly recall hoppin' and boppin' to "That'll Be the Day" at age 14 on top of Rosemary Thorlaksson's boathouse at Oxley, Ontario. July 1957. Boathouse roof dance floor. Buddy's brand-new Clovis version of "That'll Be the Day' was discovering stardom over Lake Erie from Hall-of-Fame Cleveland. From DJ 'Mad Man Mancuso' over the big inland sea to Buffalo, we were discovering Buddy Holly and teenagerism. With no TV and no pictures and just a fusty clunky pink record player on a three-mile extension cord, we slopped and stomped along. We attempted the Lindy and Jitterbug and 50s Chicken and the middle-aged-fogey Fox Trot. I guess when we first heard the supercool "That'll Be the Day," long before MTV, we all imagined Buddy looked like Elvis. We heard the song and got hooked, like those globby sheepshead fish down at the seagull Colchester jetty. Rosemary and her sister Joanie owned only five 45-rpm platters; we owned none. If you took "Honeycomb," "Bonaparte's Retreat," and "The Alabama Jubilee" (the other one I forget), they never got as much combined boathouse airplay as Buddy's first classic. We all had a rip-roaring blast far, far into the tropical star-spangled Canadian summer night. Buddy's happy-go-lucky teen anthems were a crucial chunk of growing up for everyone in the waning 50s. Buddy Holly was one of us, and we believed in him.

> The songs that were great hits when you were 11-16 years old you will never forget. What are yours?

When Buddy came to Clovis, Petty let him experiment. He gave the boys unlimited studio time to complete what the visionary producer knew would make it. The NEW and IMPROVED "That'll Be the Day," 1956 Nashville floppo, illustrated the value of a rough draft. In summer's sizzling peak of August 1957, the revamped, revised gangbusters Holly tune, stamped CRICKETS this time, championed the charts: #1.

Major coup for the Everyday Kid. Buddy Holly, that average kid from Lubbock . . . Buddy Holly, who looked like that not-so-wild zany jokeslinger from Study Hall . . . Buddy Holly, who probably just outkicked you over the Finish Line in your flawless 4:49 mile at the State Regionals . . . that Buddy Holly, toting horn-rim specs and a lean and mean red blazing guitar . . . that Buddy Holly toppled Elvis the King from his throne. For one shining moment.

Why is Buddy Holly the most important rock musician during rock's early years? He was the first rock star to create the entire superstar package virtually on his own.

Buddy wrote the songs (Elvis never did). Buddy created unique chord patterns and new progressions to spice up the timeworn 12-bar Blues style. Buddy's melodies and harmonic sense were breathtaking; he shared this gorgeous-melody gift with a handful of other 50s writers (like the Everly Brothers' remarkable husband-wife songwriting team: **Boudleaux** and **Felice Bryant**). No other 50s teen idol could write music so well, though **Chuck Berry** fashioned some stupendous lyrics.

Buddy played fine lead guitar, too. When Elvis was juggling three chords early-on, Buddy was the first rock star to flash the Fender Stratocaster, the guitar that slam-dunked quietude and conquered the audial universe.

Most importantly in the do-it-yourself department, Buddy Holly actually produced and arranged and directed his Crickets' entire throbbing sound. No rock star had ever wrestled that much POWER before from patronizing paternal producers (Petty excluded). For most powerless would-be teenage idols, starmakers commanded the naïve kid to simply squawk into the mike while they magically spun the control-room dials. And deals. Some teen idols were paid 100% of all the glory they could eat.

Holly fronted the first modern rock and roll band, thanks to Norm and Vi's Petty's expertise, tutelage, and genuine kindness. Many fellow 50s combos sprouted weird and bizarre instruments with hangovers from big band days — accordions, clarinets, bass fiddles, even gospel choirs with trumpets or French horns, or a washtub-washboard or steam calliope.

The Crickets introduced the Modern Rock and Roll Band. How? Here's the prototype, the template for Rock and Roll forever. The basics. **Buddy Holly** (lead vocals and lead guitar); **Niki Sullivan** (vocal back-up and rhythm guitar); **Joe B. Mauldin** (electric bass and back-up vocals); and **Jerry Allison** (drums and vocal background). You know – the basic **4-Guy** Rock and Roll Band. Did it work? Check out the **Beatles'** arrangement. On "Think It Over," three guys were enough.

Building on Knox's Rhythm-Orchid duo lead, Buddy enjoyed **Jerry Allison's** novelty vocal "Real Wild Child" (#68, 9-58). "J.I." Allison burbled into the echoing mike, laughing all the way. Result? A cute hit plus Holly's tie-in to future Punk Rock: the song was covered by rail-thin **Iggy Pop** [Al. #75, 10-86 *Blah Blah Blah*]. Iggy spearheaded the 1969 Detroit Punk uprising (MC5, early **Bob Seger**, Southbound Freeway, Underdogs) at Grand River Avenue's Grande Ballroom, eight years before **Sid Vicious**, and **Johnny Rotten**. Buddy Holly? Punk Rock? The Lubbock Kid, in inventing rock music as we know it, covered all the bases, even baseball, in his only **Chuck Berry** song, "Brown Eyed Handsome Man" (#113, 10-63). It's later alluded to in **John Fogerty** of **CCR**'s ballpark anthem "Centerfield" (only #44, 5-85, off #1, 2-85 album). In November 1999, **Paul McCartney**, who once owned all Buddy's music, cut this Berry song [*Run Devil Run* album, #26 1st week out] with Holly Cajun flair from his memories of Buddy's #3, 3-63 U.K. monster hit of the Berry tune.

Buddy Holly brought to young Rock and Roll the most versatile voice of the 50s. Elvis's voice, via his commanding stage charisma, panther strut, and burning expression, was more popular than Buddy's in record sales. Buddy Holly's pipes, however, played the entire pop-rock panorama. Buddy could ram Hard Rock, coo croony ballads, sing with symphonies, sling driving Blues, wax Weird-Al-type comedy tunes, overdub himself into Everlyish or Simon & Garfunkel woven angelic harmonies, invent tricky-hiccup vocal punctuation, and slash a fiery Fender vibrato guitar. At age 19.

Check out Buddy's gutsy Little Richard flashback on "Reddy Teddy," or Holly's tendertoned love blossom, "Moondreams," buoyed skyward by New York Philharmonic violins. WOW to Holly's craggy volcanic "Rave On" (80s cover **John Cougar Mellencamp**). Waft blithely along on his easy-rock majestic melodies, rolling riverly like Creedence's #2, '69 "Proud Mary." Cascade strange new mediant three (III) chords (like Key of 'C' to **E major**) while defining true feelings of love and loss: "That's What They Say," "Take Your Time," and the haunting "What to Do," a bittersweet lament of yesteryear sock hops, nostalgic soda shops, and bygone long lost love.

Just as Holly lullabies you into Slumberland, he jumps into "I'm-a Gonna Love You Too" [#38, 3-64, in Australia during Beatlemania]. Two Holly-voices storm in *a cappella* effervescence into the heart of Rock and Roll. Bop to his kicky Blues stomper (covered on Beatle bootleg), "Mailman – Bring Me No More Blues," or his slick molasses-slow Penniman prowler "Slippin' & Slidin'." Or marvel at this triumphant tenor gospel groove in **Bobby Darin** and

the Rinky-Dinks' "Early in the Mornin'" (#32 for Buddy, #24 for the original, 7-58). Or grasp the titillating tones of "Fool's Paradise" (#58, 8-58); Holly spirals an ancient cliché into a jitterbug. In the Summer of 1958, Holly mimicked the Beatles – he had six songs, plus or minus Crickets, bouncing around on the *Billboard* Top 100 list (Bloxdorf).

Here is the Holly essence: he synthesized the best of all 50s Rock and Roll styles, to coalesce his personal blend of chart success. Of all the 50s rock superstars, Holly not only confusingly imitated his colleagues more, but also employed much more originality and versatility than his fellow idols: **Jerry Lee Lewis** played a great rock piano, but didn't write or do ballads; **Little Richard** was a frantic showman and a super song-screamer, but his musical range circumscribed a smaller orbit; **Ricky Nelson** looked great and enchanted teenybop teenage girls, but didn't write or star on his guitar, and his fine resonant baritone couldn't ratchet up to FRANTIC range; **Fats Domino** had a long piano career, and a nice predictable style; **Chuck Berry** flashed a razzle-dazzle red or blonde Gibson ES 335-TD, and poeticized 50s teenage America, but his chord structures and progressions and melodic harmonics lacked Holly's classical sophistication; **Bill Haley** could rock around the clock, but the next Haley occasionally sounded like the last one; the **Everly Brothers** were cool, and had the songster Bryants backing them, but their million-dollar contract with neophyte Warner Brothers pulled the songwriters' rug out from under them, and their 60s chart numbers skidded; **Brenda Lee** and **Wanda Jackson**, great rockers, were hampered by the 50s penchant for male rock stars; the melodic **Platters** disdained heavy rock music; faux Elvises like **Jack Scott** and **Conway Twitty** couldn't wander too far from their mentor; preppy folk gurus like the **Kingston Trio** (who created the ALBUM, saleswise) wouldn't plug in; **Johnny Cash** is a country legend, while **Jackie Wilson** and **Roy Orbison**, blessed with magnificent operatic voices, had to await the 60s to get their burgeoning fame; **Jimmy Clanton, Duane Eddy, Eddie Cochran, Paul Anka, Dion** [DiMucci], and **Ritchie Valens** were great teenage idols, but their total package didn't quite add up to the Holly versatility.

There was just one guy in Buddy's Versatility League – **Bobby Darin**. Manhattan's suave splish-splash rockster parleyed a penchant for Jazz into a nine-week #1 run with his ode to a hit man, "Mack the Knife," in 1959. Darin's easy-ballad and Hard Rock and cool Jazz efforts rate him a close second to Holly in versatile talent. Fans of the Travolta-Newton-John *Grease* will be impressed to know Bobby married the REAL **Sandra Dee**, sweet ingenue blonde actress (*Gidget*, ***½ stars if you like fluff flicks). One reason for the Holly vote? Buddy Holly was totally committed to pure Rock and Roll, Darin to his Vegas dreams. Holly's total musicianship was multi-faceted, multi-talented, and universally endless in its appeal.

Buddy's career here covered just 1¼ years. That's all the time he had to lay down all his songs for all the ages. The Crickets, loudest band in early Rock and Roll, busted through with their Big Three in just five wild whirlwind months. Each blockbuster reverberates with the heart of the Holly-Cricket Sound: modest, magnificent second tenor who spins JOY, garnished by the good ol' glottal-stop Holly hiccup. Behind him? The World's Greatest 50s Rock and Roll Band. Who is Rock's biggest 50s innovator? "Think It Over."

"That'll Be the Day" – Buddy Holly/Crickets, #1(1), 8-57; #2(1), 9-57 R & B; #1, 9-57 U.K.; #2 Australia; #85, 9-86 U.K. Super stats. Using falsetto, cool harmonics, and a thunder of bass and drums, Holly roared, crooned, stomped, and played cool lead guitar – hitting #2 R & B. A feisty street-savvy jump Blues tune, "Day's" opening riff reprises Hank Ballard's "Annie" saga from 1954. Lyrically, it's a guy squabbling with his girlfriend about a complacent relationship. She teases she'll up and leave him, and he retorts, ominously playfully, the title. Irony looms later. The Crickets sound was so soulful that they were 'accidently' booked as the first white group to play Harlem's storied Apollo Theatre.

"Peggy Sue" – Buddy Holly/Crickets, #3, 10-57; #2(1), 12-57 R & B; #6, 1-58 & #32, 4-68 U.K.; #2, 2-58 & #34, 8-64 Australia. Buddy's ode to sweet blonde Lubbock High cheerleader Peggy Sue Gerron. She had a crush on Buddy at Lubbock High, but later married drummer Jerry Allison. Inauspiciously birthing as a choppy Chalypso "Cindy Lou," "Peggy Sue" did a sizeable switcheroo in Petty's studio. Wise and laid-back, Petty just twirled dials and watched the one-of-a-kind melody aerobically sweat its way into hit-record shape. Banished to the studio vestibule for his O.D. on volume, Jerry sculpted a 16th note paradiddle roll on his tom-toms, shifting to a new drum every quarter-beat. To cinch the right beat, Petty patiently phased levels and steered the pulsing VU Meter. Buddy spanked a boffo Guitar Blur on his Fender solid-body. Revolutionary new sound. All **Niki Sullivan** did was work the dials and bar on Buddy's guitar, since Holly's lightning-fast right wrist (locked straight) raced Jerry's tumultuous tom-toms. Since Buddy had no time to shift gears from bass to treble for his legendary rhythm-lead solo, Niki functioned like the concert pianist's page-turner.

"Peggy Sue" shows Buddy's genius in altering regular Rock and Roll to cult status. A basic 12-bar Blues with a power-shift "I" to "IV" chord and back on each verse, "Peggy Sue" glides in the guitar-friendly key of "**A** major." On the third verse – Buddy suddenly steeplechases into a wild weird blow-your-mind Polynesian "**F**" major chord. His vocal bag of tricks, too, reveals a hiccup deluge and wo-uh-ho jubilee unrivalled in pop music. Was he kidding, lashed the crass critics? Well – yes and no. A terrific business man, Buddy Holly was not above a little gimmickry to boost sales. So the wild wo-uh-hos flowed like wine. But no, Holly spoke to his girlfriends in the tender playful tone the locker-room lads would never hear. His choppy glottal stop stuff passed the romantic sincerity test. Peggy zoomed to Olympic million-seller gold on Coral Records. Coral released Holly solos, with tender songs like "Peggy Sue," the overdub-pioneering "Listen

to Me" (#16, 3-58 U.K.), and the Hollytune the Beatles copied, "Words of Love" (#13, 6-57 Holly composition cover by **Diamonds**). All hard-edged ribald Rock and Roll they released on Brunswick's labels got credited 'the Crickets.' Indeed, when we first heard "That'll Be the Day," no one really even knew the name BUDDY HOLLY for a month or so.

"Peggy Sue" redefines male roles. **James Dean** started this new sensitive awareness in 1955's classic *Rebel Without a Cause*****and *East of Eden*****. Teen idol actor Dean of Fairmount, Indiana, showed that real men and reel men can be gentle and tender, too – not just blustering yahoo cowboys. In Verses One and Two, Buddy sort of first raps with the guys about how he's blue – due to Peggy Sue. Just as Folk-Rock pioneer **Jimmie Rodgers** [#1, 8-57 "Honeycomb"] finished on HIGH notes, Buddy unexpectedly nails a LOW note ['A'] at Peggy Sue's hard-driving finish, showing his baritone power. A savvy marketing ploy by a phalanx of Coral-Brunswick execs. By Verses Three and Four, Buddy addresses Peggy Sue herself in a swath of sweet-nothin's and lovers' small talk. In surrendering his vulnerability underneath a macho cloak, Buddy joins James Dean; they revolutionize and rework the male mass media persona: tough was OK, but tender is better.

Suddenly, guys were capable of gentle love as well as touchdowns and home runs and 100-yard-dash-flash fever. Holly's staccato hiccup barrage shows the easygoing, fun-loving, goof-off side of impish Buddy Holly. He wasn't too inhibited to innovate. The song proved to teenage guys that you needn't always be gruff and growly. Buddy's "I love you" lines to Peggy ponder true and rare love; it captures the sweet quintessence of affection from a regular high school guy to a gorgeous blonde Texas cheerleader. It's a rock classic. It admits vulnerability. It is the antithesis to **Simon and Garfunkel**'s icy, estranged, urban-despair "I Am a Rock" (#3, 5-66), where the lone lorn speaker, enisled in bleak skyscraper isolation, considers himself a rock, an island. Love sleeps in his memory, but he's built an impenetrable fortress, a citadel, to shield himself existentially from all human emotion.

"Peggy Sue" is the essence of emotion. It represents Buddy's most passionate "Heartbeat" (which at #82, 12-58 was his last living hit record). When you wholeheartedly confess your love, you're suddenly very out there, man. Ugly, possibly disastrous situation – if SHE doesn't share your love. You can't quite grab your mushy words and stuff them back into your gaping mouth. You must now live them.

"Oh Boy" – Buddy Holly/Crickets, #10, 11-57; #13, 12-57 R & B; #3, 12-57 U.K.; #2, 2-58 Australia. As tender and sweet and blurry with guitar power as "Peggy Sue' is, "Oh Boy" is HAPPY. "Oh Boy" just might be the happiest Oldie that ever lived. And thrives today. And tomorrow, as Buddy promises all his fervent kissin' and lovin'. The song swaggers with the delightful sure-fire tone of a Texan having a great time. It's a brilliant blend of shyness and swagger, spiced with 100% JOY to the world. A happy-go-lucky hooray anthem, "Oh Boy" is the musical antidote to down-in-the-dumps-despair. It zaps all the whiny beer-bubbles-in-my-stubble dirges of dark mood chaos and sorrow. "Oh Boy" is a musical vitamin pill for the sagging spirit: stars arrive out of the deep purple, while shadows fall romantically. For Buddy and the boys, nighttime was the right time to celebrate and dance to the music with their covey of cheerleader cuties in the hot mystic American teenage night. [All Holly's 'Big 3' hit #2 'Down Under'].

Like Chuck Berry's rags-to-riches "Johnny B. Goode" – launched recently into outer space on radar, so aliens can groove to the eager ebullient Earthling spirit – "Oh Boy" flashes and sparks and smirks with mid-century American optimism. "Oh Boy" also throttles with a rampaging speedy drum blur from Jerry Allison.

"Oh Boy" leads off on a traditional 12-bar Blues double verse. Innovatively, Buddy stomps off into a bombastic booming bridge on the downbeat dominant seventh chord **E7**. He flirts with a hiccup at the bridge's volcanic climax, chimes a glorious rebel yell, and grins his joy-faced way into rock and roll destiny.

Buddy's famous "Oh Boy" on the *Ed Sullivan Show*, in living black and white, is his major media moment. Astoundingly, no color video exists from Buddy's TV stints on *Steve Allen* and *Arthur Murray*'s shows either, and only a few voiceless primitive home-movie film clips. On *Sullivan*, who did the top half of Elvis and all of the Fab Four, the happy oh-boy 1957 Christmas season brings the crowning media success cup to the lanky starbound Texan. Buddy smiles very sincerely when Sullivan calls him "Tex," hustles off the burning-spotlight stage, and is gone.

Buddy even hyped his own records. Many teen-puppet idols had no clue how to push a record. Mere striplings on stage, they knew not the convoluted web of distributors, A & R (Artists and Repertoire), song hustlers, or program directors vis-à-vis rock jocks (DJs and the newer VJs like Dick Clark & *Bandstand*). That whole rigamarole was Holly's turf – record hop freebies, local radio stations, and even the semi-sneaky thing all we bands puttered with, later: calling the local station Request Line, and posing as somebody's cute moppet little sister, in fake falsetto, requesting your own song. Buddy Holly knew Rock and Roll was a complicated success game, and he played the game and loved it.

Cricket Niki Sullivan told me in 1978 that Buddy actually patronized Lubbock burger-catfish-malted roadhouses, squeezed his nickels into rippling-rainbow Wurlitzer jukeboxes, and then anonymously bellowed to burger munchers, "WOW, that's a GREAT new record playing, now isn't it?" Of course he had just stuffed the Wurlitzer nickelodeon with his red-hot platters. Similar jolly hyping ploys buzzed up a few sales, and started the plunky Crickets snowballing to Fame and Four-Tunes. Holly sparked his own success: Rock and Roll's first do-it-yourself teenage idol.

In Fall 1966 I received an uplifting letter from Buddy's mother, **Mrs. Ella Holley** (1902-90), a sweet and gracious Christian lady. As Buddy Holly was my favorite singer, I wrote Mrs. Holley a couple of letters about his inspiration and futuristic R & R ideas. A burgeoning manuscript was dribbling from my relic typewriter. An intrepid First History of Rock and Roll was lurching and wallowing in the queasy quagmire of Terminal Writer's Block. Mrs. Ella Holley encouraged me to finish *The Rock Revolution* (1966), which found its way into about 1/5 of the major public libraries in the U.S.A. The distributor told me it was the most ripped-off paperback (95¢) they ever stocked. Anyhow, Cleveland's Rock and Roll Hall of Fame asked me for a copy in 1995 – *The Rock Revolution* has become a wee bit of a collector's item, since it's the first Rock and Roll history book.

Mrs. Holley encouraged me to get back to my unemployed typewriter and finish. Anyhow, she loved the stuff I wrote about her son. I am no acerbic sarcastic poison-pen slanderer anyhow, and the Buddy Holly sketch was naturally chock full of praise.

Since Mrs. Holley inspired me, I wrote the Lubbock Chamber of Commerce in 1968. I asked them to please consider a Buddy Holly statue.

I was flabbergasted at their non-answer.

"Buddy WHO?" was their essential reply.

In the fragmented 50s, Rock and Roll was still a one-generational phenomenon. Many parents and Chamber of Commerce businessfolk had scant idea what the big beat was all about. The music was simply too loud. Maybe too sexy. 'Elvis the Pelvis' and that 'Killer' **Jerry Lee Lewis** weren't helping, some folks squawked. It took born-again **Pat Boone** and that nice Mr. **Antoine 'Fats' Domino** to shepherd this strident teenage music into the older folks' trust and respectability. When lineman Fats passed the punchy pigskin to wide-receiver Buddy, he scampered for a touchdown. By 1959, Rock and Roll tottered upwards toward mainstream respectability, thanks to Buddy Holly. And to that nice smiling Philly entertainer – **Chubby Checker** and his "Twist," cut by Hank Ballard in March 1959.

By 1978, Hollywood finally discovered Lubbock. Before *Buddy Holly Story* film crews could embarrass the 200,000 folks in town, the Chamber of Commerce finally fired up a 2500-pound, eight-foot bronze statue of Buddy and his Fender Stratocaster. They also renamed a park full of prairie dogs, pristine ponds, and hardly any rattlesnakes.

In 1994, my wife and I, along with Buddy Holly Memorial Society President **Bill Griggs**, were interviewed on Lubbock's Channel 12 for the induction of **Virgil Johnson** to the West Texas Walk of Fame. The better-late-than-never Chamber highlights the Holly statue shrine with bronze stars for Waylon Jennings, the other Crickets, Mac Davis, and other star entertainers. Virgil was lead tenor of the Odessa, TX, Rhythm and Blues streetcorner group the Velvets ("Tonight Could Be the Night," #26, 1961). Virgil is the first African-American to be voted into the West Texas Walk of Fame (few Afro-Americans live in West Texas). Anyhow, Buddy would have been proud, since he married Puerto Rican Maria Elena Santiago in the Summer of 1958. Let's jump back to 1958.

"Raining in My Heart" – Buddy Holly, #88, 3-59. Buddy told his brother Larry (1985 *PBS* bio) that this Felice and Boudleaux Bryant's song was the prettiest melody he ever sang. An inverted triad chord plays the 5th note as bottom note. It rises to the sharped 5th (say, A+ in Key of A), and then to the 6th and 7th. This beautiful melody was Holly's last charted hit.

In a whirlwind tour year of monster hits and second-string songs, the Crickets' year waxed and waned. Holly's crew scored big on #17 "Maybe Baby," #27 "Think It Over," and Peggy's flipside "Everyday," but bickering band squabbles thumped morale. Brotherlike rivalry all bands must face caught the Crickets off guard. Buddy fell in love with New York, not just Maria Elena. Joe B. and J.I. wanted to ride their motorcycles around the outskirts of prairie Lubbock. Big Apple, big pressure, big time.

Buddy was multicultural when multicultural wasn't cool. Buddy met Maria Elena Santiago at Coral Records, dated her twice, and on the same day proposed! Lovestruck. Two giddy weeks later they were married. The blissful couple enjoyed a five-month happily-ever-after before Buddy boarded the Beechcraft Bonanza.

Joe B. and J.I. were less than enthralled with Buddy's Manhattan metamorphosis. Or his Fifth Avenue Apt 4H overlooking Washington Square. Finally, the three old friends split up. Buddy, devastated by their refusal to agree, reluctantly acquired drummer Charlie Bunch, guitarman Tommy Allsup, and 18-year-old DJ baritone bassman **Waylon Jennings** to re-Cricketize his waffling career. Some minor hits burst forth: "Early in the Morn-

ing" and "Heartbeat," but Buddy, besieged by posh city bills, opted to do the Winter Dance Party tour of 1959. Frozen cornfield destiny.

Buddy headlined the tour for two other big stars: Pocoima, California's wonder-kid Latino **Ritchie Valens** and Beaumont, Texas's own basso boogie-down blaster, the **Big Bopper**. Born J(iles) P. Richardson, just a 26.2 mile marathon away from Janis Joplin's Port Arthur, the Beaumont DJ sported leopard-skin sport coats.

The three stars boarded another grubby, snorting relic bus. On the Winter Tour were **Dion and the Belmonts**, plus wannabe teen idol Frankie Sardo; they all suffered on the squeaky freezing mammoth jalopy. The heater busted, and the groaning behemoth ferried the frostbitten rockers over the −20° arctic icebox of high plains January America. Deep dark Dakota.

Dakota is the name of the hotel on Central Park where John Lennon was killed. It was snowing in everybody's hearts.

Young Bobby Zimmerman (later Dylan) gazed transfixed at Buddy's fifth-to-last show in Duluth, Minnesota. Barring this experience, **Bob Dylan** might have sparked poetry readings to 38-teacup academic venues, rather than selling out stadiums with the Band. Holly taught Dylan everything he ever needed to know about melody.

Two rapt Liverpudlians, **John Lennon** and **Paul McCartney**, sat in red-velvet splendor, on March 20, 1958, at the Liverpool Philharmonic Hall, stoned on Rock and Roll. Blew a month's pay? Yep. Was it worth it? Yep. Lifetime opportunity – they got to check out BUDDY HOLLY AND THE CRICKETS. After the Winter Dance Party, Buddy might be back. Kid Mick Jagger watched the live Crickets too (March 1 – Trocadero, London).

Out of all the Winter Tour vets like Paul Anka, Dion's Belmonts, and LaVern Baker, at least a score of stars and semi-stars have laid claim to selling their seat on the ill-fated little plane to Ritchie Valens. Dion's father Pasquale DiMucci had to pay $40/month rent in the Bronx. The plane ticket? $40. Dion balked, for a good Scottish financial reason. He has been asking, along with Waylon Jennings, for nearly 40 years, the cosmic riddle, "Why me, Lord?"

"Rainin' in My Heart" stalls in blue-sky, big sky country. Buddy's song romance is sad. Brokenhearted, he wishes for rain to wash away his misery – like **Everlys**' #6, 1-62 "Crying in the Rain." Like a true Texan, Buddy steels himself to stoicism, but he knows tears will come soon. What he didn't know is that they'd be OURS.

Why fly? The furshlugginer heater busted on the rattletrap bus in sub-zero Minnesota. Out there, you don't sweat getting mugged; you worry about freezing to death. Pragmatic Bronx Belmont Carlo Mastrangelo set fire to a pile of newspapers on the bus floor to keep cozy. Cricket Charlie Bunch was rewarded with a toasty 70° hospital room for his frostbitten toes.

Buddy decided to hire a tiny plane to the next gig in Fargo, North Dakota, and Moorhead, Minnesota, from the last one in Clear Lake, Iowa. Fargo's 16-year-old **Bobby Vee** didn't yet know his Shadows [not Cliff Richard's] would have to fill in for Buddy, his idol. Date with dusky destiny.

Polyester might have saved Buddy. And his two-passengers – Ritchie and Richardson. Yep, polyester. Wrinkled cotton was one reason they took to the eerie skies. Polyester hadn't been perfected yet, and ironing was a drag. The reason for the "Day the Music Died?' Laundry. It's as bitterly ironic as Martin Luther King getting killed working a garbageman's strike in Memphis, home of the Blues. Why did they fly? To get their clothes laundered.

Rookie pilot Roger Peterson took off from Mason City airport after the triumphant 2000-fans-strong Surf Ballroom gig at Clear Lake. Regardless of 2001 Internet rumor (B. Holly Memorial Society Veep George Nettleton assures me), the name of Peterson's Beechcraft was NOT "American Pie." It was one a.m., eighteen degrees, and a light flurry was dusting the gossamer wings. Apparently a darker snow squall came up, and Peterson lost his bearings. Licensed for day flying only, the young pilot valiantly tried to find his way, but the little plane disappeared into the inky icy night.

In **Don McLean**'s #1(5), 12-71 "American Pie" (voted #2 rock song EVER in 2000 VH-1 poll), Don was delivering his paper route at age 13 in New Rochelle, New York, up the Hudson River. He heard the bad news and couldn't recall whether he'd cried or not – when he read about Buddy's widow Maria. Something, though, hit Don very deeply, as it hit me at sixteen in a snowdrift Michigan world of blue stars and lost teenage dreams.

Don and I both lost a friend in places 700 miles apart where our mutual friend had never been. Even on the darkest night, music helps us all reach the stars. Don dedicated "American Pie" to Buddy Holly.

Amen, Don. A part of all of our childhoods went down with that little plane.

Buddy Holly's passing brought the carefree Rock and Roll bikini beach party to a screeching halt. Due to one bungling episode of pilot versus blizzard, classic Rock and Roll lost its top troubadour, plus a great Latino tenor and Texan baritone. Obviously, Buddy could never be replaced, though a thousand talented Bobby Vees and Tommy Roes and George Harrisons and Ric Ocaseks and Billy Joels might leap to take part of his place on the panoramic canvas of Rock and Roll History.

Cricket Sonny Curtis's retort to "American Pie," and the 1978 *Buddy Holly Story* movie, didn't enjoy so much press. Basically, he said the levee never really dried, the music never really died, and that Buddy Holly simply lives whenever we all play good 'ol Rock and Roll. [*The Real Buddy Holly Story*, Sonny Curtis, 1980; #38, 3-80, Country chart. Also dedicated to Buddy Holly, by his lead guitarist and back-up singer in 1956.]

"Maybe Baby" – **Buddy Holly & Crickets, #17, 5-58; #4 R & B; #4, 3-58; and #53, 6-66 U.K.; #15, 3-58 Australia.** First cut at Petty's Nor-Va-Jak Studio in Clovis, New Mexico, with chirpier beat and Niki Sullivan background baritone, "Maybe Baby" was temporarily abandoned. Six months later, as "That'll Be the Day" blasted smaller songs bottomward on the Top Forty, Buddy and chirpers re-cut "Maybe Baby" at Tinker Air Force Base in a cavernous labyrinth of a sound studio.

Staccato slashes branded the song with rhythmic fire. No song had ever had a beat quite like "Maybe Baby." And who helped write it? Surprise. Despite Innervisions' mistaken impression that Buddy's folks disliked Rock and Roll, Buddy penned this song with his main musical inspiration – his mom, **Mrs. Ella Holley**. Later she wrote a sprightly cut for *Bobby Vee Meets the Crickets*. It slices, dices, and splices a batch of Hollytune titles into a snazzy interwoven lyric in "Buddy's Song" (covered by Fleetwood Mac). Buddy's great protégé **Bobby Vee** echoes that wholly Holly tone. Mrs. Ella Holley's hit "Maybe Baby" skips jollily on the big three chords (I, IV, V), but she shuffles their deck into new combos of notes. Buddy's songwriting expertise was obviously genetic.

In June of 1958, Buddy soloed on Bobby Darin's gospel-groove shouter "Early in the Morning" (#32, 8-58; #17 U.K.). The summer of '58 brought a crop of *Baywatch*-ish teen idols. One was 'cuter' than the next, and some couldn't carry a tune in a bucket. None toted specs. Holly's skyrocket career plateaued. His masterful recording projects and productions drifted, in an onslaught of super-cute teen idols who had the special talent of being able to sing, too, not just look terrific: **Jimmy Clanton, Ricky Nelson** and Honolulu's **Robin Luke** ("Susie Darlin'," #5, 8-58). Buddy got married, too, to the demure and beautiful Maria Elena, and his press corps kept denying it. If that wasn't enough career trouble, a bunch of Bobby's, the **Everly Brothers**, and **Elvis** were still hammering out hits.

On August 15, 1958, Buddy and Maria got married in Buddy's folks' Baptist home in Lubbock. Meeting at Decca where she worked as a secretary in A & R (Maria was five years older), they strolled the Big Apple buying guitar picks and knick-knacks.. Then he took her to P.J. Clarke's Pub for dinner and proposed on virtually the FIRST DAY THEY DATED! No one can trump Buddy Holly on whirlwind courtship. Buddy never looked back.

"Not Fade Away" – **Buddy Holly and the Crickets, NC, 1958.** #48 for Rolling Stones in 5-64, their first American chart hit (#3, 3-64, U.K.). Bold Blues thumps insistently over Allison's raging tom-toms. With Bo Diddley-style fervor, Buddy booms his love is bigger than some finny 50s Cadillac. Vocally he zooms to the hot, muggy Mississippi Delta Bluesland just a hop, skip, and jump east of Panhandle Lubbock. Buddy, like Elvis, never forgot his roots. His Tex-Mex Rockabilly riffs were grounded in the Blues. His Cadillac metaphors got forged and stamped and pressed in the rolling mills of Detroit (where Bluesbuster **Jimmy Reed** and Country Rock legend **Johnny Cash** toiled). Buddy Holly was a natural Blues belter. He never was a croony throwback to moderate big-banders, "covering" superstars. Buddy revered the foot-stompin', stuff-kickin' wild WAIL of the true Blues – and Buddy synthesized his best Bo Diddley beat to fashion "Not Fade Away." **Bo Diddley** (Elias McDaniel) had a song named after a primordial African one-string guitar, and himself, called "Bo Diddley" (N.C. #55; #1 R & B). Buddy loved his confident strum, his rooster-macho style, and his total sound; so Buddy wrote his own wild breed of Diddley-beat song. Jerry Allison tattooed the tom-toms with Bo's swaggering African thunderbeat. In 1975, Diddley covered Buddy's Diddley-beat "Not Fade Away."

An exciting Holly tribute album debuted at #119 in 1996: *Not Fade Away!* The Mavericks use **Raul Malo**'s haunting tenor for Holly's symphonic "True Love Ways"; *La Bamba's Los Lobos* Latinize Buddy's Annie-saga "Midnight Shift"; Bob Dylan's old band, the **Band** (Levon Helm) teams up with the current Crickets – Jerry, Joe B., and Sonny – on "Not Fade Away," powered by three crackerjack drummers; "Mr. Bojangles'" (#9, 11-70) **Nitty Gritty Dirt Band** deals "Maybe Baby"; **Marty Stuart** and **Steve Earle** rock out on "Crying, Waiting, Hoping." The real thrill, however, is a newly-mixed combo of Buddy Holly and the third-biggest group of the 60s British Invasion – the **HOLLIES**, as they perform "Peggy Sue Got Married."

Buddy was in the 1986 First Wave into the Rock Hall of Fame. "Not Fade Away" eventually notched a million sales for the Crickets. Ironically, it was the happy-go-lucky flip side, "Oh Boy," which thundered to the top ten for 1957 Christmas. Whereas the **Beatles** sought the smooth style and pristine harmonic genius of Buddy Holly, the **Rolling Stones** dug his scruffy, slashing blues rhythms in "Not Fade Away." Isn't it fitting that the band many call the World's Greatest Rock and Roll Band should nab their first Yankee chart success (#48, 5-64) from a bold, brash lanky Texan, whose Blues expertise was but one minor chunk of his astonishingly versatile career? Hits of the Holly Summers?

"Summertime, Summertime" – Jamies, #26, 8-58 & #28, 6-62. Tom and sister Serena Jamison, of Dorchester, Massachusetts, fired up this perennial summery song: swimming, thrills, heading for hills, anti-work, fun extravaganza. It's Bugs Bunny, baby – dat wascally Wabbit thwarts the American Gospel of Work, and so do the party-animal Jamies. Song struck Top 100 twice, heralding two swingin' summer jamborees. Close harmony and nasal tone on this speedo huff and puff classic.

"Summertime Blues" – Eddie Cochran, #8, 6-58; #11, 9-58 R & B. Brandishing his fret-fire Gretsch axe,

Eddie Cochran was armed and a bit dangerous. His hijinx lament seethes with Southern promise-the-moon politicos, scrappy straw bosses, flimsy excuses, and sultry summertime lack of love, money, and respect. The Oklahoma City blond Rockabilly belter blasted some of the best Screaming Blues of the Buddy Holly Era. They shared the stage (watch *Buddy Holly Story*). Some say cool Cochran magnetized more groupie girls than anyone but Elvis with his hard-edged, hammering songs: the smoochy "Sittin' in the Balcony" (#18, 3-57) and the risky-business song about the folks-away-and-the-kool-cats-will-play: "C'mon Everybody" (#35, 11-58). This one just may be the opening salvo in the newly-discovered War of the Generation Gap. Beneath a veneer of bravado humor, "C'mon Everybody" manhandles any trust between folks and kid. Parents split. Kid and friends blow up the world. Heavy Metal harbinger. Punk Rock, too.

Protest Music was a ways off in the 60s, but Cochran's charismatic lament sings his workaholic blues. His carefree teen summer has exploded into a hot nightmare of grudging drudgery. Can't get car, can't leave work, no date, no dice. Biggest anti-work song until Blink 182's #4, 2-2000 "All the Small Things." Dreamy potential heaven drools into barfly hell. Sniffles of sympathy from workaholic rock fans. Protest and problems. Great beat.

"Problems" – Everly Brothers, #2(1), 11-58; #17, 12-58 C. On Cochran's bandwagon, tenor Don and Irish tenor Phil can't get car, marks dropping at school, girlfriend and teacher mad, parents too. Angst can be fun . . .

"Take Your Time" – Buddy Holly, NC, 1958. Cut Valentine's Day, 1958. Norman Petty on organ. Pristine melody. Has sweet musicbox "Everyday" quality. Norman Petty's overdubbed swirling riffs catapult this magnificent melody to heavenly status. **Buddy Holly** pretty much invented Soft Rock; "Take Your Time" flows timelessly, dovetailing sweetly and sleepily into the realm of Easy Listening's Greatest Near-Hits.

"Queen of the Hop" – Bobby Darin, #9, 10-58; #6 R & B. Pays homage to the mystic image of Peggy Sue. Manhattan's supercool Bobby Darin was inspired by Peggy and the other queens of early Rock and Roll. He cleverly packaged them into his lyrics. "Oh Julie" (#5, 1-58 for the **Crescendos**'), "Good Golly Miss Molly", and "Peggy Sue" reigned supremely (five years before the Supremes hit) at Bobby's Hop.

"I'm Lookin' for Someone to Love" – Buddy Holly and Crickets, #1, 8-57 (flip side of "That'll Be the Day"). The plugged side, this one, "Lookin'" is a fine blues tune on its own: choppy, jivey, supercharged.

"Sheila" – Tommy Roe, #1(2), 8-62; #6, 8-62 R & B. More Roe later. Holly is basically a straight second tenor. His two alter-ego echoes, **Bobby Vee** and **Tommy Roe**, take his baritone side and Irish tenor side, respectively. Roe's "Sheila" is so xeroxy of "Peggy Sue" that she could be the Lubbock cheerleader's kid sister. Actually, she started as "Frieda," ["Peggy Sue" was first "Cindy Lou"] Tommy's high school sweetheart in Atlanta. Sheila/Freida launched the handsome football star into R & R stardom (22 Top 100 hits, two #1's): "Sweet Pea" (#8, 6-66), "Dizzy" (#1 a month, 2-69), and supersweet risque #8 "Jam Up and Jelly Tight" (11-69).

"Rave On" – Buddy Holly and Crickets, #37, 6-58; #5 U.K. Buddy hammers Hard Rock. Long feted as #1 composer, singer, arranger, lead guitarist, and hypestar/ hyperstar of hot hits, Holly is rarely appreciated as a Hard Rocker. "Rave On" is Buddy's second closest approach to Heavy Metal. The touring time frame of "Rave On" corresponds to Holly & Crickets' whirlwind British tour. Their wildly successful campaign lassoed the Liverpool Philharmonic Hall. Buddy prompted a new crew of Liverpool lads to consider adding a Fab Fourth, and name themselves after some other insect.

"Rave On" stirs your flagging gusto. With wahoo yahoo Texan abandon, Buddy revs up the "Oh Boy" happytone treble. As the Crickets rampage off Verse Two into the stomping RAVE ON and/or 'CRAZY-FEELING' chorus, his staccato guitar flirts with noiseless *tacets*, and then booms bombastically back on the big downbeat. "Rave On" is a rocking carefree tune. It gushes forth a sea of saddle shoes, poodle skirts, khakis, and smiley young love. It bombs the nervous silence with jumping joy. "Rave On' is the stomping ground of the Fonz.

"Big Bopper's Wedding" – Big Bopper (Jiles Perry Richardson), #38, 12-58. Not-too-huge Bopper (5'9½", 230#) is best noted for the #6 tune when Buddy hit #1 with "That'll Be the Day" – "Chantilly Lace." OLDIES OVERKILL declares that every 50s fan know the lace-clad lass's pony tail, wiggling walk, and how she got him real, real loose. How loose? Loose as a goose. Few know sequel. Too much window-fogging kissyface leads to, uh-oh, that bane of pre-birth-control in the Old South – the Shotgun Wedding. Big Daddy drags scamp to altar, kicking and screaming.

It is one very eerily seriocomic finale and swan song. Richardson was a great DJ, and R & R comedian (Weird Al's mentor?), tremendous songwriter, fine baritone, devoted Beaumont, Texas real-life husband and father.

"Ooh! My Head" – Ritchie Valens, N.C., 1958. Did Ritchie Valens pen this novelty number for his hard-drinking brother Bob (*La Bamba*, 1987****)? N.C., 1959? This bushwhacking blaster shows two tenets of Valens' talent few knew: Ritchie's supersonic right-wrist guitar speed, and his Screaming Blues superstar status. In this love-hangover celebration, he almost makes Little Richard sound like Pat Boone. It's a frothing frantic conglomeration of Eddie Cochran, Little Richard, Larry Williams ("Bony Moronie" #14, 11-57), Bobby Darin, and Screaming Jay Hawkins (1930-2000), the uncharted Screaming Blues guru ("I Put a Spell on You").

"Little Girl" – Ritchie Valens, #92, 7-59. Before Roy Orbison ever attempted those stratospheric non-falsetto

tiptop high notes, teenage Ritchie (Rock Hall of Fame 2001) was lofting them with ease and coolth. The first Hispanic-American Rock and Roll star clutches soul-searing high notes here you'd never believe. Great song.

"Donna" – Ritchie Valens, #2(2), 11-58; #11, 2-59 R & B. "He could have been the next Elvis," mourned manager Bob Keane, Del-Fi Records Prez. Pocoima, California's Ritchie Valenzuela (b. 5-13-41), related to Los Angeles Dodgers ace Fernando Valenzuela, captivated his high school with his singer/songwriter blessings. Of Mexican heritage, his Spanish was rudimentary, but his music surged throughout the San Fernando Valley. Despite a numbing fear of flying, Ritchie, battling a fever and cold, 'won' the flip of either Waylon Jennings' or guitarist Tommy Allsup's seat on the fated 2-3-59 Beechcraft. Spun to destiny on that sad plane, Valens' piercing 'Irish' tenor shines today wherever they play Rock and Roll.

Performed for his girl Donna Ludwig, "Donna" is one of the prettiest slow ballads ever written. "Donna" is a gorgeous ballad, an edifice, a foundation of love for his sweet Donna, up there on that pedestal of romantic worship.

Ritchie Valens (left) with Bob Keane, President of Del-Fi Records

"La Bamba" – Ritchie Valens, #22, 12-58; N.C., R & B. Once you hear the crackle, snap, and pop of Ritchie's bedazzling lead guitar, you know you're in for the biggest Spanish R & R song of the decade. As a flipside afterthought of his breathtaking love ballad, "La Bamba's" popularity over three generations shows Ritchie's immortal influence as the young (17) father of Latino Rock and Roll. Manager Bob Keane produced and helped select this dynamic 200+-year-old folk song about a sailor. As the fountainhead of Spanish-language Rock in the U.S.A., Ritchie Valens opened up the melodic floodgates for **Ricky Martin, Gloria Estefan, Enrigue Inglesias, Marc Anthony, Jennifer Lopez, Selena, Christina Aguilera**, and in the earlier years **Trini Lopez, Chris Montez, [Carlos] Santana,** and **? and the Mysterians.** The sensational biopic *La Bamba* (1987***¾), starring Lou Diamond Phillips as Ritchie, launched **Los Lobos**' peak performance – "La Bamba" #1(3), 6-87. Sparkling with Cesar Rosas' gonzo guitar, singer **David Hidalgo** also blasted Ritchie's debut #42, 9-58 "Come On, Let's Go" to #21, 9-87 in an almost audial xerox of Ritchie's great voice.

Ritchie was just 17 – and had four months to call it a career. Hidalgo and Rosas combine excellently on Ritchie's incredible sound, via vocals and guitar, but Ritchie – like **Buddy Holly** – did it all. He sang, he wrote his own hits, and played his own [expert] lead guitar. With a little help from Bob Keane's keen management, Ritchie, too, became a do-it-yourself superstar. With four months to dance in Elvis's shaky spotlight!

"Suzie Baby" – Bobby Vee and the Shadows, #77, 6-59. Young **Bobby Velline (Vee)** filled in for Holly at the Fargo, North Dakota, Winter Tour Show of February 3, 1959. Grief-stricken, 15-year-old Vee had lost his rock mentor a few hours before, and now he was called upon to BE BUDDY on stage. One show-biz commandment glowered at him from the burning footlights: the Show Must Go On! Vee's Hollyesque singing dovetailed into songwriting. A Chalypso groover, this "Suzie Baby" debut is among Bobby's uncut, unpolished, unsmooth best. Guitars and stuff. No strings and things for his later teen idol role that sparked the 60s Opening Day. Although the Teen Idol dominions were sparked by a whole lot of handsome Bobbys for starstruck teens to buy records from, **Bobby Vee** was one with super talent, too.

Vee's 1995 *The Early Rockin' Years*, with the Shadows, is a major nugget as vintage rockabilly seekers pan for audial gold. Not only is "Suzie Baby" infused with tremendous talent from the Finnish-Swedish North Dakotan. Bobby's big brother **Bill Velline** called the first practice in Spring 1958, Bobby told me at the 1999 Novi [Michigan] 50s Festival. He got together in Dick Dunkirk's basement for a jam session, which included drummer **Bob Korum**, already a pro with the Paul Hanson Dance Band, and with bassman **Jim Stillman** later.

"I was the lead singer," Bobby chuckled, "of Fargo's first nameless garage band." Great guy, Bobby. Self-deprecating humor.

On February 3, 1959, the 'day the music died' in Don McLean's "American Pie," Bobby Vee, brother Bill, plus Jim and Bob (the **Shadows**), played a fill-in appearance at the Moorhead Armory. From this gig just across the big river in Minnesota from arctic February Fargo, they soon traveled to their first paid band job. The Armory job? They didn't even have an official band name; the M.C. literally named them on stage. Their first $ gig was on Valentine's Day, 1959, in Breckenridge, Minnesota. [I remember traveling in piano guy **Bob Baldori**'s heaterless 1938 Buick named the 'Mad Bomber' to a Night Shift/Woolies job in Charlotte, Michigan, at –17°, as Bobby Vee swapped stories about his brother Bill's woebegone heaterless Rocket 88 1951 Olds].

No band ever forgets cutting its first record. Keybank Studios in Minneapolis charged the Shadows $500 for a nine-to-noon session. Cheap that wasn't. In 1963, union

factory workers at Ford where I worked between semesters at Wayne State made $3.00/hour, or roughly $5000/year without overtime. Half a grand was over a month's pay – good pay. Fortunately, via brother Bill's **Mark Knopfler**-style thumb and fingernail plucking, according to Bobby, they got the sound they were searching for on "Suzie Baby."

"Suzie Baby" is not just a good record – it is a great record. A virtuoso performance by Bill. Bobby, 16, demonstrated that mature 22-year-old Holly technique of melding a tender-style vocal with a certain macho sensational growl. From the wo-oh-hos to the guy-next-door friendly vocal style, Bobby Vee was obviously following in the big Texan footsteps, ready to launch his own style at Liberty Records. The Chalypso chop on "Suzie Baby," and Bobby/Bill's breathtaking rush from the tonic '**C**' chord up to the III major '**E**' chord, show they'd assimilated Holly's incredible songwriting abilities. Plus his unique approach. The scintillating combo of Bill's swirling guitar rhythm and Bobby's terrific teenage voice spelled a bright future for the Fargo Kid and the Shadows.

The June 1, 1959 Keybank sessions netted two other cut songs – the groovy garage-style instrumental "Flyin' High" and the incredible "Lonely Love." Drummer Bob Korum shows in "Lonely Love" that he can sound like Jerry Allison on the "Peggy Sue" paradiddle, only Korum adds his own accents on the four big beats in the 16-sixteenth-note measure. Korum smacks the ONE and TWO beats hard, echoing back the dimmer THREE and FOUR thumps. (Technically, he thumps the 1 & 5 notes hard, downpedaling the 9 & 13). Another Keybank session followed in September 1959 with standout tracks like "Laurie" and "Love Must Have Passed Me By." By March 1960, Bobby's Shadows recorded at Holly's own studio – *Norman & Vi Petty's Nor-Va-Jak Studios* in Clovis, New Mexico. Bobby did an uncanny "That'll Be the Day" echo, plus Charlie Gracie's "Butterfly," Buddy Knox's "Party Doll," and a version of Don Rondo's "White Silver Sands" with more Holly hiccups per measure than there are stars in the skies. **Vi Petty** played keyboards as recording wizard Norman spun the right dials. With **Dick Dunkirk** on bass and Buddy Holly's former vocal group (like Elvis's Jordanaires) the **Roses** on vocals, the result is an amazing Holly echo. It wasn't long for Bobby's transition to the real big time. Combining TEEN IDOL looks and a baritone Holly sound, **Bobby Vee** became one of the key players in the Rock Revolution.

Snuff Garrett, Liberty Records' Hollywood producer, knew the value of a potential teen idol who combined handsome moppet appeal, a friendly demeanor, musical virtuosity, and incredible talent to go with looks like Elvis or Ricky Nelson. To their limelight charisma, Bobby added songwriting talent, in the Buddy Holly tradition. Sadly, just as Fargo's Fab Foursome approached the big time, Bobby's own songs got sidetracked by a plethora of glitzy Hollywood material. The year 1960 plunked Bobby into the national spotlight, via his pair of #6 hits: "Devil or Angel" and "Rubber Ball" in August and November. Garrett, true to Bobby's roots, linked him with the surviving Crickets (including new lead singer Jerry Naylor) for Al. #42, 7-

62 *Bobby Vee Meets the Crickets.* One single, #99, 9-62 "Someday (When I'm Gone from You)," is a symmetrical kissin'-cousin of the **Crickets**' #1(1), 8-57 "That'll Be the Day." Had it arrived in early 1958, when Tex-Mex Rockabilly fervor was in full power, the song might easily have gone Top Ten.

The Bobby Vee Era is an ongoing phenomenon. Although his chart blockbusters bunched buoyantly into the 1960-68 zone, making Bobby a Beatle contemporary, his good-natured melodic teen anthems and all-age supertunes are still just as much fun whether Bobby performs them live in 1960 or 2000+.

"I never actually met Buddy Holly," Bobby told me at the Novi 50s festival. "But he's one of the main reasons my brother Bill and I formed the Shadows. Buddy was a great inspiration – even a role model – and we all fantasized about getting a do-it-yourself hit record with our sound based on Buddy's basic sound, but with our own musical flavor." While millions of hopeful garage bands just dreamed, Bobby Vee succeeded.

For awhile the young teen idol jammed with a kid from the ZBT fraternity house at the University of Minnesota. The kid also played guitar and harmonica at the same time. They dug both Buddy Holly and Folk music. The kid came from Hibbing, Minnesota, about the only place this side of Alaska in the U.S.A. that's as cold or colder than Fargo (only North Dakota, just north of Fargo, has an average January low temp below zero [-18° C]). The kid had gone to the fifth-to-last show on Buddy-Ritchie-Big Bopper's Winter Dance Party, up in Duluth, thereby trumping Bobby. Bobby and Bill and Jim Bob Korum and Dick Dunkirk tried and tried to work the kid into the act – as a piano player, but since the unportable piano was about the size of a puny rhinoceros, the Shadows parted with the other Bob, Bob Zimmerman. And the Rest of the Story [Paul Harvey]? Zimmerman took his ultraportable guitar and harmonica to Greenwich Village and the Bitter End – and became **Bob Dylan**.

"Well, All Right" – Bobby Vee, NC, 1977. Also reprised by **Eric Clapton** and **Santana** (Carlos Santana's zesty version hit #69, 11-78, and was partially inspired by Bobby Vee's effort. In March 2000, Santana won eight Grammy Awards for #1 "Smooth" and album *Supernatural*.)

Bobby Vee's version of Holly's "Well, All Right" (*Buddy Holly Story, Vol. II* album) is blessed with commanding rhythmic firepower in the Jerry Allison tradition. Vee's rumbly baritone singes the stratosphere with the haunting audial echo of Buddy Holly. A lost jewel.

This magnificent song (*Buddy Holly Story, Vol. II,* 1960) didn't chart for Buddy either, somehow, and Bobby sounds a bit like someone who emulated Bobby – the #13 album artist of all time, **Neil Diamond**. Had Dylan's dad sprung for a NEW electric piano, young Bob might have first toured as a SHADOW of BOBBY VEE.

Bob Dylan's rookie piano era yielded a later Columbia Records grand-slam home run. Holly/Vee sent Bob Dylan off in a greater direction: Guitar, harmonica, songwriting, and craggy arctic and Woody Guthrie Dust Bowl voice. Off to Greenwich Village and glory.

"Peggy Sue" – Beach Boys, #59, 9-78. Missed this version, eh? **Al Jardine**, lead. Imagine how great "Peggy Sue" would sound if nurtured with the Brian Wilson multilayer Cosmic Surf Rock touch. Now you've got it. Great rendition.

"Peggy Sue" – John Lennon, N.C., off album *Rock and Roll*, #6, 3-75. The wayward Beatle offers us perhaps the best imitation of Buddy Holly's top solo song. John's throbbing rhythm guitar rips the gutsy chords, blasting the **A major** modified Twelve-Bar Blues. He goes into the augmented fifth-based Polynesian **F** chord. Drums thunder. Lennon's vocal is almost a Clovis carbon copy.

The February 13, 1995, *People* devotes a section to tracking down rock and roll teen queens: from the real Peggy Sue Gerron to the real Donna Ludwig to singer Judy Collins of "Suite: Judy Blue Eyes" (#21, 10-69) to the real "My Sharona" (Sharona Alperin, #1[6], the Knack, 7-79). Peggy Sue first flipped for Buddy as a sophomore in the longest high school corridor in Texas at Lubbock High. ("He was not a nerd; he was very attractive"), but finally fell for drummer Allison. Remember Buddy wrote "Cindy Lou" as an erstwhile Chalypso, like Anka's "Diana," But Jerry blasted it with a flying paradiddle for Buddy's guitar blur. Jerry also asked Buddy if he'd name the song after Peggy Sue. No problem. After recent retirement from her plumbing contractor's business, and divorce from her Roto-Rooter husband after Jerry, she exclaimed at 54 in 1995: "The best part about those days was being a part of something we believed in. The establishment didn't want to hear about it, but we knew Rock and Roll would never die."

Do you or Peggy Sue, or I really understand all the revolutionary musical ramifications her swinging little tune stirred up? A pop song means vastly different things to each precious pair of ears that hears it. No one else ever had quite the same feeling about a certain song. Peggy Sue herself just loved the music. She didn't try to tear apart the song and put it back together. Sometimes you can over-dissect a song. What about frogs? Your song can come out smelling like a dead formaldehyde frog in sophomore biology class. When you lie back, listen, and love the song, that's what really matters.

Lennon did just one more living album, *Shaved Fish* (Al. #12, 11-75), with #3 "Instant Karma," in 1975. Then he semi-retired to househusbanding for Yoko Ono and baby Sean Lennon at the grand old gloomy gothic Dakota hotel – at the top of the long grueling hill to the NYC Marathon finish line.

Flying out into Dakotan oblivion, the little Beechcraft bailed into a cornfield less than 10 miles from the airport, dashing the dreams of 50s teenagers. On December 8, 1980, a self-professed 'fan,' Mark David Chapman, an overprivileged psychopath from Colorado, murdered John with a gun any lunatic could easily buy. The word AS-SASSINATION amplified the dignity of Rock and Roll to the role of kings and presidents. And the world mourned.

Peggy Sue is alive and retired and happy. And the beat goes on.

"Susie Darlin'" – Robin Luke, #5, 8-58; #6, 9-58 R & B. Did anyone successfully mirror Buddy's style during his own lifetime? Yep. Sixteen-year-old Robin Luke cut this super song in manager Bob Bertram's basement. The mammothly magnifique Chalypso beat is just Bob smashing a key in his pants pocket with his drumsticks. After several guitar and ukelele 'cuts' on this song, dedicated to Robin's toddler sister Susie, who was temporarily misplaced, Bob Bertram's whipped leg is said to have healed.

Luke's one hit showed all of us that Buddy Holly's sound was possible. Luke parleyed a tremendous chord shift: dominant **E7** to subdominant **D** on the tacet "Wo-oh-ho Sueie Darlin'" through the mediant III chord **C#** major. Sounds tuff enuff. Really, all you do is twang the **E7** and slide up a fret from the **C#** to the **D**. The effect is electrifying. The blond, blue-eyed Honolulu, Hawaiian, lad barnstormed *Ed Sullivan* and *Bandstand*.

I was 15. This song was a big deal to me. Since 22% of the girls I went out with were named Sue or Suzie/Suzie or Peggy Sue or SueEllen, it was a one-size-fits-all hit record and gold million-seller. Most of all, I could visualize him standing on some wild windswept bluff gazing out over perfumed tropical seas at the sky-fire flamingo sunset. I could hear the waves crashing in my Michigan snowswirl mind. These sweet visions of swaying Suzies in grass skirts by piña colada shifting sands kept ambushing my thoughts. It was hard to think about algebra, snow shovels, Alpo for our boxer Sox, or even mom's great wheat germ cookies for me. I had too many "Susies" streaming and undulating and smiling through the dank corridors of my impish adolescent mind. Robin Luke's Hawaii Holly-tone anthem was my escape to tropical paradise. With similar glossy tunes, Bobby Vee was luckier – he had Snuff Garrett to produce a profusion of pop posterity.

Rockin' Robin swirled away on intergalactic fluff, like the Star of Bethlehem faded slowly away after its one magic Christmas Eve.

Buddy Holly, 1959.
c/o Mrs. Ella Holley, 1966.

That'll Be the Day came far too soon for rock pioneer Buddy, as Cricket Sonny Curtis mused. Holly infused all of Rock and Roll with his songwriting, his versatile singing, his happy goodguy personality, and his total msical inspiraton. The recent past bodes no slip-up in the Holly charisma – "Buddy Holly", Weezer, #34, 2-95. Of all the three 50s giants, **Elvis, Buddy** and **Chuck Berry**, Buddy was the most selfless, the most talented, the most likeabl. You got theimpression he was in your woodshop class, or that you used to soap windows or tip over outhouses with him. His enthusiastic laugh reverberated around the globe, but he never got too important to give out autographs. He loved his folks and he loved his music and he loved his wife and he loved his fans.

Buddy Holly's proteges are legion, like Robin Luke and Bobby Vee and Tommy Roe, the Beatles and Hollies and Stones, the Cars and Linda Ronstadt, Debbie Harry's Blondie and Cyndi Lauper and the Jackson Five, or Shania Twain or young LeAnn Rimes – who recorded her first HOT 11 hit, "Blue," (#26, 6-96) at Buddy's Nor-Va-Jak Studios in New Mexico – just before her penultimate prize, #2(4), 6-97 "How Do I Live?" Speaking of living, Buddy Holly earned a #1 album in the Untied Kingdom in 1978; titled *20 Golden Greats* in the U.S.A., its subtitle is a little more supernatural: *Buddy Holly Lives!* The Buddy Holly legacy triumphed over the seeming demise of the sleepy old 20th century. Beyond the millennium, the rock forecast echoes the sentiments of Cricket Sonny Curtis (lead guitar, 1956-57, 1960-present): Buddy Holly lives, Sonny says, each time anyone plays rock and roll.

The Buddy Holly legacy triumphed . . .

We'll Sail on
That Sloop 'John B'

"When our song 'Tom Dooley' hit #1 in September 1958," baritone and 4-string guitarist **Nick Reynolds** told me, "they didn't know HOW to categorize us." He slowly slurped a Red Dog ale between sets at a 400-seat Long Island venue in 1992, "So they called us the #1 COUNTRY Band in the U.S.A. and gave us one of the very first Grammy Awards. Since we were 'unplugged,' they couldn't call us Rock Stars. Finally, they found the term FOLK they'd applied to the **Weavers.** Whatever we were, we had some fun and sold some records."

Modest talk from Nick, one of the legendary **Kingston Trio,** who singlehandedly created the ALBUM (Harry Belafonte and/or Frank Sinatra fans may differ here). The Trio is listed as fourth ever in album weeks at Number One. **Nick Reynolds, Bob Shane**, and **Dave Guard,** and Guard's later replacement **John Stewart**, powered the $4.99 album collectors to new nadirs of holey-pocket poverty. Bizarrely, the Trio never charted on the Country charts; somehow, this semi-country band sold the 5th-most albums in both the 50s and 60s.

"Tom Dooley" – Kingston Trio, #1(1), 9-58; #9, 12-58, R & B. Many teen idols went collegiate, like Honolulu's **Dave Guard** (banjo) and **Bob Shane** (guitar), and University of Arizona's **Nick Reynolds** (four-string guitar). From San Francisco's Stanford and nearby Menlo Park College, the three tremendous baritones wove an enchanting melody into a Folk fame dream. Record sales ran amok, as the Trio stormed the college campus circuit – in a day when Rock bands were often consigned to less pricey backstreet venues of stale beer and tattered amps.

If *Seinfeld* and *Friends* had been yuppie-track teenagers in 1958, they would have 'flipped' over the with-it, pun-slinging, fun-loving **Kingston Trio.**

"Tom Dooley" is a gloomy folk tale of an actual 1868 Blue Ridge Mountain hangee, Tom Dula. Dula murdered a girl, and a kangaroo court sent him instantly swinging from a gnarled oak tree. The Trio renders this true story from the grisly vantage point of Dula – pondering his own imminent mortality.

*The **Kingston Trio** (top to bottom: **Dave Guard, Nick Reynolds, Bob Shane**), 1959*

From their college hootenannies and chalk-talk midnight bull sessions, the Trio named for Jamaica's capital Kingston (**Bob Marley**'s Reggae home base) began to play at the **Purple Onion,** San Francisco's Beat Generation coffee house and hangout. Capitol Records hornswoggled a deal usually reserved in 1958 for R & R Teen Idols with three #1 hits – they released an entire album. "Using one mike for ALL our unplugged voices," Nick told me, "we completed our *The Kingston Trio* album [Al. #1(1), 11-58] in just TWO amazing days."

The trio never looked back. Their first record zoomed to

#1. "Tom Dooley" floats a counterpoint (two tunes at once) into the seemingly simple two-chord song. This polyphonic chorus of doomed Tom, hanging his head for his evil deed, and the other two Trio tunesmiths, pumps up to a climactic crescendo. After pitiful creepo Dula swings from his death oak (in 1958 capital punishment did not exist), the ballad shuffles back into a somber dirge of decrescendo. Tom plods, sadly and slowly, to his dark destiny.

The Kingston Trio, during Rock's Golden Age **Holly Heyday,** performed hard-rockin' acoustic music. The **Everly Brothers** played acoustic guitar, too, but had **Chet Atkins** on electric to cinch their 1986 induction into the FIRST class (1986) of the new Rock and Roll Hall of Fame.

Since we thrive on Rock and Roll, let's bop on up to a group who could rock with the best, despite their stubbornly acoustic 1963 approach:

"Greenback Dollar" – The Kingston Trio, #21, 2-63. "This was the first censored song," Bob Shane told me, "because they blotted out the word damn with a handclap. So I guess we're also the forerunners of some pretty spicy Rap music." "Greenback Dollar" is straight-up Rock and Roll. **Bob Shane**, with some drum thunder and an electric twang, might have been one of the top 20 singers in rock music. Previewing **Bob Dylan** and the **Byrds,** rhythm guitars crash (acoustically) into their anti-money lyric about a carefree vagabond and his beloved guitar. **Hoyt Axton** (1937-99) penned this ode to the nomad's footloose wanderings. Money just doesn't matter, and gets instantly squandered – but a 'wailin' song' and a fine guitar are the only things our pilgrim troubadour understands. [For an opposite approach, catch #2, '85 money-clutching "Material Girl," by **Madonna**]. Championing the freewheeling life, the Trio knocks the regular job, the bills, the hassles, the constrictions.

Mostly, the song rocks. **Simon & Garfunkel** began as Folk singers. If Capitol had overdubbed "Greenback Dollar" with heavy bass and drums and electric leads, as they did Simon & Gar's #1 '65 "Sounds of Silence" at Columbia, the Trio could have commandeered both the Folk AND Rock venues a full three years before the big boom hit. Greenbacks galore might have materialized.

The preppy mode cornered the U.S.A. in the 1960 zone: sleepy early Kennedy Era, or late-stage Ike years. If you were a kid in the 50s, you suffered the sneaking suspicion that the Rock and Roll you secretly loved could make you a social peon or pariah at the fraternity or sorority house. Many people – get this – actually believed that faddish Rock and Roll was something you must one day *outgrow* to thrive in a collegiate setting. It was chic to dig something more cerebral and eggheadish and intellectual. Maybe great Jazz: Charlie 'Bird' Parker, Wes Montgomery, Al Hirt, Miles Davis. Maybe Classical:

Leonard Bernstein, Pops Fiedler, Van Cliburn. Or maybe FOLK: the Trio, the Brothers Four, the Highwaymen, the Limelighters, the New Christy Minstrels, or **John Denver's** debut crew – the Chad Mitchell Trio. Or that new spectacular trio, **Peter, Paul, & Mary,** named for two apostles and a very divine Mother. Besides "Tom Dooley," however, very few FOLK songs juggled superstardom to the #1 spot on *Billboard's* Hot 100. This 19th-century Folk hymn and 20th-century campfire anthem did:

"Michael" – Highwaymen, #1(2), 7-61. Weslyan University (Middletown, CT) sported the Highwaymen: Chan Daniels, Bob Burnett, Dave Fisher, and two Steves – Trott and Butts. Easy in the Key of 'C', the song rises to a sweet **F** chord, then modulates through the minors: **Em, Dm,** and resolves to the dominant **G7** and finally back to good ol' **C.** Michael rows his proverbial boat ashore, questing after milk & honey, and trims some sails with either a sibling or a nun ["Sister"]. The soothing melody bedazzled many a campfire church retreat with its lullaby aura and harmonic hallelujahs. The Highwaymen's follow-up "Cotton Fields" (#13, 11-61) stemmed from **Stephen Foster's** 1850 era. It's a subtle protest *Folk Holler* once called a 'Negro Spiritual,' and protests rotten cotton bolls and iffy plantation days of yore (it's also sung by **Odetta**).

"MTA" – Kingston Trio, #15, 6-59. Or was THIS comic lampoon the first PROTEST SONG? This tongue-in-cheek Mock Epic tells the wild tale of woe of one displaced prisoner on the Boston Subway, "Charlie." The tune is 100% "Wreck of the Old 97" (Vernon Dalhart, #4, 5-25), a million-selling train-wreck tragedy.

On the MTA (Metro Transit Authority), Charlie is left on a whirring subway somewhere between the Kendall Square Station and Downtown Oblivion. Doomed to ride eternally because of a fare increase while he was on the train, Charlie may ride forever (unless we vote for some politico named George O'Brien). This banjo-powered ditty rocks, too. One super parody.

The **Brothers Four** sported 2003+ crew-cuts in 1960. Phi Gamma Delta fraternity brothers at University of Washington, Dick Foley, Mike Kirkland, John Paine, and Bob Flick's #2(4), 10-60 harmonic ballad blockbuster was "Greenfields," a melancholy yestertune of romantic reverie.

"The Green Leaves of Summer" – Brothers Four, #65, 10-60. John Wayne's *The Alamo******½** theme forges chords and harmonies of dynamic sweep and breadth. The Chalypso tune uses a minor-key baritone sound to mesh four giant notes into one golden chord A cyclic circular song, like the seasons and life itself . With a faraway and fey feel, this Alamo tribute and pre-Death Rock ode to resignation may remind you of:

"Seasons in the Sun" – Kingston Trio, NC, 1963 (lyrics Rod McKuen, music Jacques Brel) Like the doleful mood of Evan Williams's Scottish "Loch Lomond," the dying singer laments his last days with his true love. We have had joy and we've shared fun, and enjoyed the sunny seasons, but now our glorious seasons are gone and the time for love and even life have run out. Folk songs weren't all frolic, festivity, and/or fun.

"Seasons in the Sun" – Terry Jacks, #1(3), 1-74. Dormant ten years, the baleful ballad punctured the Disco strobe light with its sad refrain; Jacks's plaintive Winnipeg Canadian tenor caresses his mortality with heart-rending, guitar-throb poignancy. One of the biggest Death Rock tunes of all time (see Pearl Jam's 2 5-99 remake of J. Frank Wilson/Cavaliers' auto-wreck "Last Kiss").

"El Matador" – Kingston Trio, #32, 2-60. Fluent in Spanish, the Trio tromps Hemingway's turf – the bullfight. Moreover, it tackles a R & R chord change that would later spearhead a whole new R & R direction: **Johnny & the Hurricanes'** 'Greensleeves'-inspired "Molly-O" (N.C. '60) and 1999 Rock Hall of Famer **DEL SHANNON's** amazing #1(4) 3-61 "Runaway":

Am —— G —— F —— E7

When Western Michigan's Shannon runs this down twice early, he shifts up to the Key of **'A' major.** An electrifying shift. "El Matador" is a wild waltz that makes good-natured fun of bullfighting extravaganzas and the vainglory of bloodsport.

"Tijuana Jail" – Kingston Trio, #12, 3-59. Pals get bombed in border-town Tijuana, Mexico (see rowdy scene in *La Bamba* 1987***¾). They end up in gambling den, bubbling with befuddling booze, hot dice, and equally hot chicks. No one, alas, seems to have five hundred bucks to bail them out of Tijuana Jail. In 1958, much R & R music had serious themes; Trio mixed HUMOR, too, enchanting college audiences.

"Green, Green" – New Christy Minstrels, #14, 6-63. The OLD Christy Minstrels batted about the post-Civil War stages in blackface and banjos, plucking and crooning Stephen Foster's sentimental songs. Led by Randy Sparks, the NEW Christy Minstrels were a hipper lot, steeped in **President John F. Kennedy's** Camelot idealism. BIGGEST singing group! FOURTEEN singers – mostly white guys – hopped a freight train (30s hobo vagabond spirit) for a humungous Polaroid album-cover photo. A far cry from **Woody Guthrie**-style Dust Bowl troubadours and **Robert Johnson**-type Delta Bluesmen in shirtsleeves and ramblin' feet, the New Christy Minstrels were among the harbingers of true Folk-Rock.

Lead singer **Barry McGuire**, with his gruff, gravelly baritone (a '10' on the Macho Meter), told the world about sleeping on his grubby rocky road. McGuire's #1, 8-65 "Eve of Destruction" sang the coming military Armageddon, and then he moved into Contemporary Christian music. Also using the Minstrels as a superstardom spring-board was another gravelly baritone, **Kenny Rogers**, whose pre-Country-music ROCK group the Fifth Edition scored big with #5, 2-68 "Just Dropped In (To See What Condition My Condition Was In)." The distaff vocal gravel was supplied in the Minstrels by **Kim Carnes. Kim** is blessed with a silver medal for most weeks at #1 for a R & R song (after **Olivia Newton-John's** #1[10] '81 "Physical") with her cinematic #1(9), 3-81 "Bette Davis Eyes." Few groups have launched so many solo superstars as the NC Minstrels, whose 2nd-biggest hit was the lovely ballad #17, 4-64 "Today."

"Lucille" – Little Richard, #21, 3-57; #1(2) R & B. Absolute opposite of Folk music. Little Richard booms out, with gung-ho groovy gusto, his gripe about Lucille's cheating binge; she runs off and marries, but he still loves her. She ditches him when he wakes up, and all his so-called pals clam up when he asks about the wayward lass. Richard fires off yodel-kicks and assorted falsetto flourishes to establish his supreme displeasure about Lucille, and his inability to ditch her during her unfaithful spree. The **Everly Brothers** reprised "Lucille" to #21, 3-60, and did a folk-acoustic album at the heart of their Rock and Roll popularity – *Songs Our Daddy Taught Us* (NC, '58). Many Folk Rock stars sprang out of pure Folk groups, but very few rockers parleyed the Folk craze to the top. Buddy Holly's talented manager **Norman Petty** made sure his rock group the Fireballs was headed for #1 via their Juilliard-educated tenor singer Jimmy Gilmer:

"Sugar Shack" – Jimmy Gilmer & the Fireballs, #1(5), 9-63; #1(1), R & B. As **Duane Eddy**-style guitar-driven instrumentalists, the Fireballs hammered the Hot 100 with #39, 9-59 "Torquay" [a beach in Cornwall, England] and #24, 1-60 "Bulldog." Norm and Vi Petty connected Gilmer and the Duane Eddy/Ventures-echo Fireballs, and amazingly ended up with a Holly-style vocal that eclipsed even all of Holly's biggest ("That'll Be the Day" was #1 only ONE week). "Sugar Shack's" plot concerns a lovers' rendezvous at this Beat-Generation coffee house on the outskirts beyond those railroad tracks. The Greenwich Village culture of **Jack Kerouac** (1922-69) odysseyed to Raton, New Mexico; Gilmer and gal get legally and serendipitously stoned on the last legal drug with no age limit – caffeine. Gilmer's monster hit set the stage for : 1) Folk Rock, and 2) The Beatles, via Gilmer's Hollytone echo and Tex-Mex driving rhythm. It's a fun song about young love and black turtle-neck sweaters (see **Paul McCartney's** #1, '76 "Silly Love Songs"). As Gilmer tippy-toes the top notes with belltone clarity and Sinatra-standard enunciation, he is followed by the crisp sound of a flute on filler *cadenzas* echoing the melody. In his fadeout finale, Jimmy nails a 'wo-uh-ho' to make his mentor Buddy proud. In one swell foop of bubble-gum bliss, Gilmer gets the girl for happily-ever-after, and foretells Folk Rock. The Beatles harness his sound and capture first England, then America, as a prelude to the entire universe.

After the Kingston Trio, the quartets arrived. Then the quintets, and octets. and Serendipity Singers used NINE, on their way to the New Christy Minstrels' multitude of fourteen:

"Don't Let the Rain Come Down" – Serendipity Singers, #6, 2-64. Some folkists pushed nursery rhymes – which are often beehives of nonsense, wigged-out illogic, and Zen Buddhist chaos. This one stars a crooked tiny man with a matching house. Seven University of Colorado guys and two ultra-cute smiley girls, four guitars, a banjo, and a string bass the size of Delaware seek *Serendipity* (making lucky discoveries by accident). This diminutive dude tries to fix a hole in his roof, fretting about DROWNING from the Swiss-cheese roof. Meanwhile, he prays to some amorphous cosmic presence: "Don't Let the Rain Come Down!" You'll hear this lyrical echo in "Absolutely (Story of a Girl)", #6, 4-2000, **Nine Days,** where lead singer **John Hampson** sings of a girl who cries this river which drowns the entire world – but absolutely does he love her, whenever she smiles.

If nine Serendipity Singers weren't enough, or fourteen New Christy Minstrels, how about Up with People? Affiliated with Moral Rearmament on Michigan's breathtaking Mackinac Island, their leader Frank Buchman had them create the biggest Folk Group of all (trumping the gospel Mormon Tabernacle Choir). Up with People boasted 417 singers, a gaggle of guitars, a bevy of banjos, and a buzzing swarm of bouffant hairdos with flip-de-doo flips and perky page-boys. The Up with People kids were super-scrubbed and interminably white, though a few token minority singers blended smilingly. These mega-groups often protested nothing at all.

"Draft Dodger Rag" – Phil Ochs, NC, 1964. Though **Folk-Rock** star **John Denver** rebelled very little against his Army dad, such was not the case for Admiral Morrison's son **Jim Morrison** of the **Doors**, or **Phil Ochs.** Many Army kids, raised in quonset huts and gray barracks, travel the terrestrial globe seeking a bunk, a bath, or some beans. Phil Ochs was less than enchanted with the military life. A young firebrand, Ochs bounces two bullets off the Army bunker. Bullet One, this tune, is a bit of a joke. "Draft Dodger Rag" explores Ochs's 'humor in a jugular vein' via this bouncy Ragtime-style folk song. An acerbic black-comedy songwriter, Ochs goofs on all the daffy ways to beat the draft (Vietnam in 1964 was a skirmish with a few American 'advisors'). Ochs's excuses? Vision like a bat, flat feet, ruptured spleen, his invalid aunt, wrapped back, allergies to bombshells, multi-drug addiction, sneezing when the enemy arrives, and even carrying a purse (despite his 'straight' orientation). At the finale, he wishes the hardscrabble nails-chomping Sarge good luck, and tells him if he gets a war with no blood or gore, he'll be its

first volunteer. Ochs's stunning sarcasm and dark humor belie his serious antiwar message. Ochs was the inspiration for **Bob Dylan's** "Masters of War," and also for Barry McGuire's "Eve of Destruction." And Country Joe & the Fish's "Fixin' to Die Rag." And even **John Lennon**/Yoko Ono's "Give Peace a Chance."

"I Ain't Marchin' Anymore" – Phil Ochs, NC, 1964. As the Vietnam War heated up, miring us down into a ten-year quagmire of questionable offensives and unwinnable jungle guerrilla warfare, Phil Ochs wrote this dead serious song. Long before punji sticks and shoeshine kit grenades, Ochs sounded the un-battle cry.

Working out of the East Village with young Dylan, Ochs wanted to declare a victory and bring the boys home. His steely baritone drones grimly. He condemns ALL of military history, parrying and thrusting with sweeping verbal swashes of his own. He blames everyone in charge, from generals to foot soldiers. The FBI was not overjoyed with Ochs's rabble-rousing lyrics. Air play was squashed and squelched to college dorms, and Ochs spent his career checking for microphones in his soup.

Popular music is underwritten by advertisers. If a song is TOO controversial, and enough folks scream into their phones about it, its hit potential gets instantly curtailed. Witness Napoleon XIV's #3, 7-66 "They're Coming to Take Me Away, Ha-Haaa." 'Napoleon' Jerry Samuels of New York claimed a million-seller, but after two days stations reeled from a fiery flurry of negative calls saying the song made vicious fun of the emotionally ill – which it *did*.

Phil Ochs shuffled into the 70s with nary a Hot 100 hit, but a protest rep and some blacklisting. After deep depression and despair, he took his own life – one of a long line of lonely entertainment stars for whom life grew too sad and confusing: Danny Rapp (Danny & the Juniors, #1 '57 "At the Hop"); **Kurt Cobain** of **Nirvana,** Donnie Hathaway, Michael Hutchence of INXS, Sid Vicious of the Sex Pistols. In the grander scope, Ochs pulled his finger out of the proverbial Holland dike, and the onrush of a sea of protestors filled the U.S. and Europe. Ochs was the harbinger of a gushing torrent of troop-train stoppers, draft-card torchers, parade marchers, and more moderate letter-writers.

Vietnam and Phil helped an entire nation get in touch with our political processes.

"Blue Water Line" – Brothers Four, #68, 1-62. Protest song? Talk about no-danger topics . . . save the ol' hometown train and RR depot! A very pretty song that *modulates* up one-half step to new keys on each melodic verse. A new breed of Folk music resounded out of Hibbing, Minnesota, from a genius bard who once played keyboards for **Bobby Vee, Buddy Holly's** best-known protégé:

"Girl from the North Country" – Bob Dylan, NC, 1963. "The most important figure in white rock music," my fellow encyclopedist Donald Clarke calls Dylan. Bobby Zimmerman's dad steered an appliance shop at the top of America, where Bob [Zimmerman] Dylan wrote this great unheralded song about shrieking North winds hanging heavily upon the blue-northern Canadian borderline. Before Bobby transformed into Bob Dylan (for Welsh poet Dylan Thomas), he absorbed the divergent styles of Hank Williams, Little Richard, Johnnie Ray, and heroes Woody Guthrie and Buddy Holly. Dropping out of University of Minnesota, Dylan never let stuffy ivy gentility come between him and the Blues. Or Rock and Roll. To him, there was no distinction between great Folk and Rock music.

"Girl from the North Country" is about love and climate. Love is the warmest thing we crave. Dylan dabbles in muted irony, his burnt-out love stabbing like a falling icicle. The tune weaves and twists, like the swooping –40° Yukon winds. Its bitter, evocative, poignant vision floats out far beyond the dinky metaphors of old song hacks. You can depend on Dylan for fresh images, buoyed by deep reading of Beat Literature, like Jack Kerouac and Gary Snyder and Lawrence Ferlinghetti and Allen Ginsberg. Dylan wrote this nostalgic love song in 1959. It finally appeared on his second Columbia offering, *The Freewheelin' Bob Dylan* (Al #2, 9-63), his first big commercial success. "Girl from the North Country" is a masterpiece of solitude and gloom and resignation and nostalgia.

Bob Dylan, armed with just a guitar, a Jimmy Reed harmonica, a raspy Dust Bowl voice, and a dream, somehow whisked away the gigundo groups of sparkly, super-scrubbed preppy princes and princesses, clad in jiffy suits and natty ties, or flouncy crinoline skirts and bubbly hairdos the size of kitchens. Dylan didn't just echo the establishment status quo. He attacked evil and injustice, hard-edging Kennedy's New Frontier, to pick up the sword and slay dragons of despair and discrimination and desolation. Dylan never shrank from taboo ["Girl from the North Country" contains the uh-oh word 'breast,' which obviously zapped its AM radio airplay potential in 1964]. In the next song, also recorded by **Joan Baez** and by **Janis Joplin's** hero, Afro-American folksinger **Odetta, Dylan** deals with a young girl's plight and misery in a New Orleans brothel. It's the kind of place where our hero **Louis Armstrong** got his subteen start as the #1 trumpet player in 17 solar systems. Dylan heard it from Folk singer **Dave Van Ronk** (and mentions him on his Talking Blues intro), and Dylan passed it on to British Invasion destiny:

"House of the Rising Sun" – Animals, #1(3), 8-64. Eric Burdon hails from smoky British coaltown Newcastle – a 5'1" singer with a seven-foot voice. British Invasion promo kingpins caged the Animals off the airplane for their American tour. **Joan Baez** (Al. *Joan Baez*, #15, 3-62) cut the song in 1960, and sings about the sorry situation of a female sold into sin and degradation, whereas the Animals and Dylan deal with the GUY'S guilt pangs. The Animals fire into the musical mix Alan Price and bass guy Chas Chandler, plus John Steel on drums and Hilton Valentine's crisp guitar *arpeggios* – chords played one note at a time, in this case, triplets. "House" is a unique chordal flow, too, beginning with the minor:

Am — C — D — F — Am — C — E7

As Burdon laments the ruination of many unfortunate maidens, "House" touts a chord progression from its normal **Am – E7** range up into the Key of 'C' with **C, F,** and the **II chord D. Burdon's** booming smoky baritone, reeling with raspy passion, carves out the first two stanzas. When he pole-vaults up an octave to the third stanza , like **Billy Joel's** "Piano Man" or **Kid Rock's** "Only God Knows Why," Burdon wrings out his passionate confession of bawdy tawdry dalliances amid the faded flowers of this New Orleans Vieux Carre house of prostitution. You could call this tune Folk Rock, long before Dylan's #39, 4-65 "Subterranean Homesick Blues" supposedly launched the genre.

"House of the Rising Sun" – Weavers, NC, 1951. Not long ago, we explored **Pete Seeger** and the Weavers' #2(7) '51 "On Top of Old Smoky." Somehow, they got writing credits to their hootenanny (Folk singalong) version. Bass Lee Hays, tenor Fred Hellerman, and contralto Ronnie Gilbert first sing about this New Orleans hot spot, near the birthplace of Jazz, Dixieland, and maybe Rock and Roll. The name "House of the Risin' Sun" is deliciously ambiguous; even the prudier early 50s could songsterize a prostitute's lament – as long as it was smothered in RISING SUN euphemisms, which could just as easily have been a saloon, a deli, a Fabric Fiesta store, a yogurt emporium, or a penny arcade.

The Folk movement energized Americans with a social vision. We bore the crosses of injustice, discrimination, poverty, and the Cold War with the Soviet Union. Bob Dylan touched all the bases on his New Frontier anthem of President **John F. Kennedy's** vision of Camelot:

Bob Dylan

"Blowin' in the Wind" – Bob Dylan, NC, 1963.
Bob's Freewheelin' liner notes emblazon his prophecies: "I'm only 21 years old, and I know there's been too many wars . . . you people over 21 should know better." Dylan sang the craggy soul-searing songs of my own generation of idealistic pilgrims. "Blowin' in the Wind" became a secular hymn (see Religious Rock chapter). Dylan questions how many oceans a lone white dove must sail aloft over , and over the battlefield, before she sleeps safely down in the soft sands. He asks about abolishing cannonballs, and segregationist standards of manhood, and he chastises those who would play ostrich and pretend not to see evil and injustice. Bob zaps the lumbering do-nothing hordes with his tough-minded political and philosophical questions. He comes to an odd combo of existential acceptance and New Frontier optimism, via an equal blend of John F. Kennedy and Beat Generation writers **Jack Kerouac** and **Allen Ginsberg** (1926-97). Bob's NYC Village odyssey of Kerouac's coffeehouse world was a neon nocturnal life. From cold-water walk-up brownstone flats to cig-butt gutters of crusty gray old snows, young Dylan sang for drinks and tips and cosmic enlightenment. Jewish songwriter Dylan was inspired by Ginsberg, apocalyptic Whitmanesque poet of *Spontaneous Bop Prosody*, and Jewish-American genius from Paterson, NJ. Ginsburg took much of his philosophy from Hindu gurus, starting the whole Maharishi Mahesh Yogi movement that would inspire the **Beatles** – particularly **George Harrison.** **Jack Kerouac** began as a Catholic in Lowell, Massachusetts, but turned Buddhist ("all life is dukkha, suffering") before returning to Catholicism on his deathbed. Kerouac and Ginsberg taught Dylan how to tear apart the old American language and put it back together in new, dynamic images.

Buddy Holly (1936-59) taught Dylan virtually everything he knew about melody, though Dylan was equally inspired by Dust-Bowl troubadour **Woody Guthrie** and Delta Blues legends. Young Bob attended Holly's fifth-to-last-ever concert at the Duluth Armory, and later played keyboards for the cool teen idol who filled in for Buddy with the Shadows after 'the Day the Music Died' – **Bobby Vee,** of nearby arctic Fargo, North Dakota (where the icicle winds swoop beyond the Yukon-Manitoba borderlines). Holly's musical genius, love-directed poetry, happy outlook, and melodic magnificence ironically helped Dylan survive to 60+ with Holly's sunny Texan outlook on love, song, and love songs. "Blowin' in the Wind" was a futuristic clarion call for the vanguard of the New Frontier to change the old grumpy world. They might have, had not Vietnam gotten in the way. Enter the apostles and the Mother of Christianity:

"Blowin' in the Wind" – Peter, Paul, and Mary, #2(1), 7-63. Louisville, Kentucky's **Mary Travers** (b. '37) became one of the first female superstars of the Rock Era. Brandishing a husky Folk contralto of operatic power, and taking the torch from the Weavers' Ronnie Gilbert, the nearly six-foot Mary tossed her long sweeping blonde hair, as her full lips caressed anthems of protest, power, and fiery

aspiration. In our dorm at Michigan State University (McDonel Hall), girls used to actually *iron their HAIR* to imitate this Folk idol. Baltimore's **Paul Stookey** just might sing at your wedding [#24, 7-71 "The Wedding Song (There Is Love)"].

Though Peter, Paul, and Mary leaped to Insta-Fame on the college Folk circuit, Dylan was as yet an underground up-and-coming act. This cover tune helped put him on the superstar map. **Peter Yarrow** (b. '38, a year after Paul & Mary) went to P.S. 6 on 81st Street. When weary winter 10K runners, wiped out from a 19-degree dash around Central Park (6.2 miles), gather in the P.S. 6 auditorium for bagels, hot chocolate, and maybe trophies, we're greeted by a giant green cardboard "Puff, the Magic Dragon" (song #2[1], 3-63). From cozy burgundy velvet chairs to gazing at this big green Barney-style dragon is one wild trip.

Dylan's song uses white doves, crooked roads to manhood, unemployed cannonballs, and anti-hypocrisy rhetoric to tell the blunt truth: all people need FREEDOM, and the time is now.

It is a song of profound idealism and secular faith – rivaling John Lennon's #3, '71 "Imagine" in scope and optimistic aspiration.

On Dylan's secular hymn, Peter, Paul, and Mary fondle crescendoes; each line adds more dramatic intensity and intricate low harmony (the guys are baritones), and the song's impact is powerful and profound: we CAN change the world for the better. Vanguard of idealism.

Peter, Paul, and Mary enjoyed many hits, nudging but missing Number One, until their final tune:

Peter, Paul & Mary 1964
(L-R) Paul Stookey, Mary Travers &
Peter Yarrow

"Leaving on a Jet Plane" – Peter, Paul, & Mary, #1(1), 10-69. Oddity here – their last charted hit (of 20) just happened to hit #1, thanks to up & coming songsmith **John Denver**'s song about the bittersweet adventure of parting. He kisses his lover goodbye, and doesn't know exactly when they'll meet again. The interwoven splendid harmonies render this Ultra-Soft Rock ballad a classic. The Folk trio also scored with debut #35 , 5-62 "Lemon

Tree," #9 Dylan sayonara escapade "Don't Think Twice, It's All Right," the breathtaking father-son #21, 4-69 "Day Is Done," and a tongue-in-cheek Soft Rock look at R & R censorship – #9, 8-67 "I Dig Rock and Roll Music." Their Pete Seeger "Hammer Song" as "If I Had a Hammer" glommed #10, 8-62, and certainly rocked for an acoustic-guitar tune; it was covered as another candidate for First Folk Rock Hit to #3, 7-63 by Dallas's Latino sensation **Trini Lopez. Peter, Paul, and Mary's** second millennium continues apace on PBS, with various benefit concerts and reunion extravaganzas.

A few stuffy purist folksters disdained Rock and Roll as too loud or strident or sexy. Many rock critics, too, ignore Folk contributions to Rock. The Folk Boom is also the rise of 'UNPLUGGED' Rock and Roll. It was zesty, gung-ho, even boisterous and loud. And fun. The Kingston Trio faded away for awhile, but **John Stewart** hooked up with **Fleetwood Mac's** enchanting **Stevie Nicks** and gonzo guitar guy Lindsey Buckingham for his record industry classic #5, 5-79 "Gold" and this classic:

"Midnight Wind" – John Stewart [with Stevie Nicks & Lindsey Buckingham], #28, 8-79. After transforming music into pure GOLD with a Big Mac attack (Nicks, Buckingham), the Trio's resonant baritone Stewart cleaves the roaring Midnight Wind in search of destiny and adventure. Stewart replaced **Dave Guard** (1935-91), who moved to Australia in 1961 with his Whiskey Hill Singers; John carried on the Trio tradition of sandpapery molten baritones with commanding voices. Via Stewart, original Folk and original Rock came together in a rush of power. Booming out his macho tones, Stewart glides as Nicks coos her bewitching background vocal. On their obscure *Kiln House* (Al. #69, 7-70), **Fleetwood Mac** sings a song penned by **Buddy Holly's** mother Ella Holley – "Buddy's Song" [a great 'lost track']. Long ago, many Folk singers eschewed commerciality for the purity of their craft, but later even the hard-bitten purist Phil Ochs performed a Holly medley. For a tidal wave of greenback dollars, many true purists have been known to hype deodorant or toothpaste or cat food or Jiffy 8-Minute Abs/Buns Tape. See similar Rock parodists like #48 Al. 1-68 *The Who Sell Out*, with Pete Townshend gleefully rolling on deodorant, or Frank Zappa's 50s greasyband parody #110 Al. *Cruising with Ruben & the Jets*, 12-68. Or Dire Straits' "Money for Nothing" (#1[3], 7-85).

Folk music didn't disappear as we drifted into the mid-60s. It simply assimilated into Rock or R & B. All three flourished from the transfusion of tremendous talent. Rock and Roll furnished the driving beat, dynamic new chord changes, and wild new studio experimentation with multi-tracking. Folk music provided meaningful lyrics, heavy poetic metaphors,

and social consciousness and caring attitudes toward changing the world. R & B provided the funky hammering beat, the throbbing bass riffs, and the Soul and gusto. Motown chugged along and its thrashing beat energized the world. The mid-60s were a time of profound musical integration.

On the seamier side, and as the Vietnam War heated up in Southeast Asia, many disenfranchised Folk-Rock fans turned away form their old drugs – nicotine, caffeine, and alcohol – and discovered a blazing new furnace of fiery anesthesia to mask their gloom and angst and ennui and existential despair. Iffy 'feelgood' substances had long buoyed and sunk the Jazz world, with many of the Modern Jazz greats – Miles Davis, Charlie Parker, Wes Montgomery – riddled with self-inflicted health hassles. In the early 60s, pop music saw a flowering of Jazz among other Jazz greats to whom drugs did not play a role – Dave Brubeck or Stan Kenton. Some folk songs swaggered through many a decade with universality:

"Wreck of the John B" – Weavers, NC, 1951.
Wild tale of woe and joy of one Sloop John B. A SLOOP? For you Nebraskans and Wyoming wombats, a sloop is a single-masted sailboat rigged fore and aft (2 sails).

An intrepid sailor, complete with his bottle and his grandfather, attempts to woo the ginchy gals of Nassau, Bahamas. The poor old boat's derelict carcass, in this true story from 1927, still protrudes off aquamarine shores of Nassau's Governor's Harbor. The sailor gets smashed and sleeps in slammer (see Trio's "Tijuana Jail" or "Bimini," or anything like **Jimmy Buffett's** "Margaritaville"). He laments loud and long. He wants to go home. Ah, yes, a tale of hangover hassles— a sad sorry sickness, with no sympathy.

"Wreck of the John B" – Jimmie Rodgers II, #64, 8-60. Jimmie's bold Scottish tenor overarches this tale about a blast, a boat, a donneybrook, and a night in the clink. Great piercing last note. Rodgers has a legitimate claim to First Folk-Rocker, too, with his Soft Rock Chalypso classic "Honeycomb" (#1, '57). As we mentioned in a previous chapter, **Jimmie Rodgers II** is the father of Folk Rock – eight years before Dylan went electric and the Byrds flew high on harmony and Roger McGuinn's 12-string Rickenbacker guitar. Remember Jimmie's #1(4), 8-57 "Honeycomb" and his #3, 11-57 version of the Folk-star **Weavers'** #19, 8-51 "Kisses Sweeter Than Wine"? The Washington State Scottish tenor broke into Folk singing in the Air Force, and parleyed his looks and talent into superstardom.

Jimmie's "Wreck of the John B" is perhaps the sleeper of these versions, floating ethereally with a pristine *pizzicato* guitar plucked dreamily. With low-amp splendor, Rodgers' soaring tenor commands the song, rolling rockfully in a mellow Chalypso mood. Jimmie enjoyed many Folk-based hits, eight years before Bob Dylan, with his big amplified orchestral guitar that resembled the Gibson ES-335: #7, 2-58 "Oh-Oh, I'm Falling in Love Again," #11, 11-58 "Bimbombay," #32's "Ring-A-Ling-A-Lario" (6-59) and "Tucumcari" (9-59), and later the Kingston Trio's "2:10, 6:18 (Doesn't Anybody Know My Name?" to #78, 10-63. Rodgers even predated the Folk-Craze Kingston Trio by over a year. Rodgers was a major balladeer, too: #3, 5-58 "Secretly," #10, 8-58 "Are You Really Mine," and later #37 (5-66) "It's Over." Like Buddy Holly, Rodgers' appeal was nice-guy but cool. With the waterfall-haircut pompadour of Elvis and even, on his album cover, a cigarette (aargh), Rodgers' image was never Goody Two shoes – just a very with-it Folk singer whose 'John B' ode prompted the Beach Boys and Bob Marley. In 2002, Rodgers was packing nostalgia venues in Branson, Missouri.

"The JOHN B Sails" – compiled on sheet music by Carl Sandburg, 1927. The kindly white-haired "Chicago" stacker-of-wheat poet ("Fog" – "The fog come in on little cat feet . . .") first championed the sorry saga of the John B in his 1927 American Songbag with Allen Lomax. His preface offers a stunning apology for the great songs he meant to include, but overzealous editing crunched his scope; his apology is a prayer. I know how he felt, but the 'bottom line' of publishing decides which songs shall thrive and which shall wither unseen or unheard. As I unintentionally gloss over YOUR favorite song, or the bottom line zaps it, I share Sandburg's humility.

"Sloop John B" – Kingston Trio, NC, 1958. Debut album #1, '58 **The Kingston Trio** featured the threesome, bedecked in ivy-league collars and black exec pants, throatily harmonizing newly-titled "Sloop John B" to a boffo bongo blur. The same ol' song, this one was a nice easy-going version. Let's do another universal song, and return to the sloop:

Kingston Trio, mid-60s
(L-R) Bob Shane, Nick Reynolds,
semi-ferocious wild animal, & John Stewart

"Wimoweh" – Weavers, #14, 2-52. Zulu South African folk song (like Johnnie's Ray's back-ups, the Four Lads, on their #7 "Skokiaan" Zulu hit tune). This Weavers' singalong features a counterpoint of intriguing harmonies, and employs a towering falsetto plus 'Wimoweh' chant. It was covered well by the Kingston Trio first, with more bongos and baritones. Tokens added lyrics.

"The Lion Sleeps Tonight" – Tokens, #1(3), 11-61; #7, 1-62, R & B, also #51, 8-94. Folk Rock, four years early. Hank Medress and the Brooklyn Lincoln High group once featured master Brill Building songsmith **Neil Sedaka.** "Streetcorner"-style Tokens take the "Wimoweh" lion hunt to Coney Island. The Tokens are named after grubby leaden subway 'slugs.' The song blossoms into a Folk Rock fantasy. A gazillion things happen at once. With wild overswooping soprano/falsetto "Eee-yo-mum-away" atop the tune, the "Wimoweh" chorus grunts along groovily. Finally the verse intrudes with its tale of a [hopefully]sleepy lion. At the fine tune's finale, we're treated to a triple-counterpoint bombasto fortissimo crescendo of harmonic glee and supersound that's as quiet as an eruption of Hawaii's Mt. Kiluaea.

Let's bop back to that floundering sloop and the jolly jailbirds:

"Sloop John B" – Beach Boys, #3, 2-66. Party Animal Anthem. The Beach Boys' tight and precise harmonies downpedal to their informal wild-party-casual mood, like their "Barbara Ann" (#2, 1-66 Beach Boys, #13, 5-61, for East Coast **Regents,** who echo Tokens). Brian Wilson's Beach Boys fashion their honey-toned harmonies from the **Lettermen** (#7, 11-61, "When I Fall in Love") and the Four Freshmen. Cousin Mike Love and Hawthorne High pal Al Jardine add a new Easy Rock twist to this grand old Folk song. Their party-tune triumph is really about a bad trip: the cook ate the guy's grits, he and his in-shape GRANDFATHER got into some fight with a few other rapscallions, Sheriff John Stone flung him (and Gramps) into the ratty slammer, and now he's nursing a fat lip and nasty noggin from taking second prize in a two-man scrap. The Beach Boys' bouncy rendition, however, sounds like a madcap fun-filled gala jamboree, with all the crew and gals and pals having the Ultimate Blast of Their Lives. In their gleeful sandbox *Baywatch* free-for-all, even GRAMPS is in great shape for a tropical brawl. In their hang-on sloopy adventure, the Beach Boys – America's Band – discover the essence of Dylan's mentor Jack Kerouac's lifetime quest – the Center of Saturday Night in America.

Rock and Roll. Friends. Good times. Isn't that what life's about?

Though Folk spent some sad moments segregated from Rock and Roll in the 50s, the 60s Civil Rights Era ushered in a great coming together of upscale collegiate harmonies, and guitars of throbbing thunder.

Johnny B. Badde, Bandstand Teen Dreams, and the Sizzling Sixties

If you ever had a band, you shared the dream of fame and fortune of **Chuck Berry's** alter-ego **Johnny B. Goode.** You know – rags-to-riches kid w/ guitar. Rock and Roll – the American Dream. During the Buddy Holly Era, 1957-59, Chuck Berry enjoyed the pinnacle of pop power. We all recall Chuck as America's Poet Laureate of Rock and Roll. He sang of sensuous summer fun and the hoppin', boppin', goodtime tunes of *American Bandstand.*

* * * * * * *

Allow me to introduce to you our Siamese fighting fish Bloof. My wife brought home this blue fish [Bloof] in a tiny spherical fishbowl. With his gorgeous fins of lapis lazuli blue, Bloof has something in common with Chuck Berry. My wife plopped down a shimmering translucent glass ball next to Bloof's modest fishbowl. When Bloof gazes north four inches, from the refracted light on his bowl, he scopes in the OTHER fishbowl thing next to him. He must figure he's looking at a Parallel Universe. Now this is deep stuff. Plato's Cave has nothing on Bloof. Or Chuck Berry. Say what?

In 1960, two parallel universes existed: one with Bandstand and Rock and Roll and pompadoured Teen Idols; and the preppy Folk collegiate world, of sea chanteys and Zulu sleepy-lion songs. It took real rock musicians, like Buddy Holly and Chuck Berry, to forge these two universes together and unite Rock and Roll. By 1960, Dr. Martin Luther King and TV and Rock and Roll united our diverse multicultural society. Chuck and Bloof to the rescue.

* * * * * * *

Like Buddy Holly, Chuck Berry WROTE, PLAYED, and SANG his own songs. Unlike Holly,

Chuck's band and even his birth date are mysteriously obscure. Estimates [October 18, 1926?] surrender a decade to Elvis (1935) and Buddy (1936). Aside from his loyal keyboard colleague, **Johnnie Johnson,** Berry's combo differed starkly in each region he toured. He'd hire local bands (like my old crew the Night Shift/Woolies), pay them a modest fee, and let them share his spotlight.

Johnson is Berry's ivory maestro. Arms akimbo, the burly piano vet tickles the treble keys in speed-of-light splendor. Splashing out glissandos, arpeggios, and trills, Johnson is the greatest unheralded piano man of the 50s. In his 1997 Berry-less tour, he referred to himself as JOHNNY B. BADDE, and insisted that he hired CHUCK first, back in the rinkytink honkytonks of mid-century St. Louis. Bill Backe cites Johnson's N.C. album Step in Whut?? for super piano riffs. My son Jeremy, keyboard man for **Nine Days** ["Absolutely (Story of a Girl)" – #6 4-2000] first hit the R & R big time for 2000 Detroit fans when drummer Bill 'Bee' Metros, and Woolies brothers Jeff (guitar) and Bob (Boogie Bob, piano) had Jeremy and me on stage with Chuck at Renaissance Plaza; Jeremy was 13 at this 1987 open-air concert. Chuck passed the torch to my generation, and my generation to our sons.

All for a song.

"School Day" – Chuck Berry, #3, 4-57; #1(5), R & B. Chuck told us Teentowners (St. Anselm's Church, Dearborn, MI, where I hung out when attacked by puberty) we had to HAIL the new Rock and Roll. It would deliver us from the olden days of boring, no-beat, thumb-twiddling music. In his teen anthem, hapless school inmates stagger through one tough academic day that drools with drudgery: stonefaced teachers, cardboard lunch, terminal homework. Finally – three o'clock ESCAPE to FREEDOM. Paradise? Almost . The JUKE JOINT. These *Happy Days* malt shops of good friends, good times, and nickel jukebox dances with sweethearts padded the 50s glossy image of fun, fun, fun. You know – munching fries, slurping strawberry shakes, digging teenage groovitude. Living and loving it all. And the name of the magic? ROCK and ROLL. Chuck Berry sounded the clarion call, and pied-pipered a nation of sleepy teens to get up and boogie down.

"Rock and Roll Music" – Chuck Berry, #8, 11-57; #6, R & B. Chuck chides Modern Jazz, blue Tangos, Mambos, and other early 50s dance fads. Though Berry's music talents lay in ANY music genre (including these three), he was pragmatic enough to go where the big greenbacks sang to him. **Chuck Berry** of St. Louis is the master wordsmith of early rock music. When modern parents bewail current kids' staggering miseducation about American geography, they should lament that they no longer have Chuck Berry – a musical *Rand-McNally Atlas* of American places and cool scenes.

Chuck Berry's archetypal guitar techniques were mentored by the virtuoso chops and riffs of **Charlie Christian, Benny Goodman**'s Afro-American electric guitarist from 1939-41 (Whitburn), who tragically succumbed to pneumonia at only 22. Besides Swing Jazz, Christian was proficient in the rudiments of Boogie-Woogie and Blues. His big amplified hollow-body guitar pioneered Rock and Roll in the Pre-World War II Era. Berry also owed his brilliance on lead guitar to Elmore James and **Muddy Waters**, among dozens of other Pre-Rock pioneers. The Beatles did "Rock and Roll Music" NC, 1965, from #1(9) 1-65 *Beatles '65*. George does lead-guitar firepower. The **Beach Boys** hit #5, 7-76 with the tune in the midst of Discomania.

"Sweet Little Sixteen" – Chuck Berry, #2(3), 2-58; #1(3), R & B. In the 50s, sweet 16 is the snuggliest Chuck ever schmoozed to a #1 song (he had MANY R & B #1s). Finally, in 1972, some Ding-A-Ling thing hit #1 for him (see Madonna's #3, 10-94 "Secret," or touching self-portrait, #3, 10-92 "Erotica"). Chuck's teen anthem is the 32-year-old's ode to a fickle teen queen. In Rand-McNally profusion, he bounces from his cozy home "St Louie" to America's R & R cradle, the Crescent City, New Orleans. Though he alludes to the 2nd-biggest English speaking city in the world in **1750**, Philadelphia, along with Pittsburgh, PA, his Philly reference is a bold plug for air play; he mentions *Bandstand*, thereby hyping Vee-Jay **Dick Clark** to spin this catchy 'platter' for his teenage troupe – and all of us nationwide tuned in to his 4:30-6:00 p.m. daily dance fiesta.

Clark's own South Philadelphia High Teen Idols commandeered a lot of air time on *Bandstand*. The **Backstreet Boys & N'Sync** owe some popularity to Clark's **Frankie Avalon** (#8, 5-59 "Bobby-Sox to Stockings," plus "Beauty School Drop-Out" in cult classic Grease***). Or to **Bobby Rydell,** for whom Rydell High is named in *Grease* (#11, 6-59 "Kissin' Time"). The major 50s 'hunk' was **Fabian** [Forte], and his #9, 11-59 "Hound Dog Man." Their waterfall haircuts and handsome Italian-American faces splattered teen mags and moppet fanzines like Britney Spears or Ricky Martin.

Chuck Berry celebrates the quintessential bouncy sweet kid who DANCED on Clark's show. *Bandstand* had a whole array of local regulars (like 'Bob & Justine'), many of whom sported more nationwide fans than the singers. "Sweet Little Sixteen" is the hyperactive curvaceous cutie who flounces her charms onto the glowering Cathode Cyclops of TV across mainstream America. She's a whirling-dervish phantom of delight. Chuck Berry, Rembrandt of Rock, captured the spirit and vision of Sweet-Little-Sixteen Dancing-Queen Justine. With Johnnie Johnson cascading bouquets of piano gracenotes and *glissandos,* Berry reminds us of rock's basic reason for being – DANCING and HAVING A BLAST.

Oops, another Surf & Berry combo:

"Surfin' U.S.A." – Beach Boys, #3, 3-63. Stage dad Murry Wilson decked out his quarterback son **Brian**, and brothers **Carl** and **Dennis**, in clean-cut Kingston Trio ivy-league striped shirts. After Brian's project "Surfin'" botched his music teacher's favor, he got a second opinion via Candix Records. The 12-Bar Blues song started the Surf Rock movement, and it zoomed to local stardom and #75, 2-62 nationally. After blasting the top 20 via nearby Capitol Records with #14, 8-62, "Surfin' Safari," their monster breakout hit became "Surfin' U.S.A." Tune sounded faintly familiar . . . When Chuck/Brian's swashbuckling summer surf swan song rolled out on tidal waves of sun and fun, Chuck Berry's lawyer showed up and spoiled the surf jubilee. Chuck had been gouged out of "Maybellene" (#5, '55) royalties by his sponsoring DJ, **Alan Freed,** who sweetened writers' credits to resemble this – (Berry-Freed). Freed offered Chuck some record promo, and deals like this [even (Holly-Petty)] were not uncommon in rock's infancy.

"Surfin' U.S.A." celebrates American geography like "Sweet Little 16," but it's OFFSHORE, rather than interior America. Their surf odyssey blooms in La Jolla and Manhattan Beaches, California, or among the thundering heavies smashing Oahu's Hawaiian North Shore at Waimea Bay. Unlike the Beach Boys, Chuck didn't use a *falsetto* finale. Carl Wilson's ginchy guitar riffs mirror Chuck's own bizarrely Rockabilly style. The clever Beach Boy lyric is inclusive: EVERYBODY, even in Kansas, can surf, and he visualizes all of America with baggies, vintage 12-foot longboards, huarachi sandals.

Rock and Roll, Chuck and the Beach Boys discovered, is a $haring experience.

We've spun three of Chuck's Big Five. The next one a fading Elvis pumped back to #14 in 1974 on his 428th comeback:

"Promised Land" – Chuck Berry, #41, 12-64. Johnny B. Goode grows up. Reality intrudes. Berry's cross-continent sojourn is only slightly tamer than Moses' Exodus and parting of the Red Sea. An African-American, Chuck sees his California pilgrimage as an escape to freedom from years of oppression for his people. The song is a bicoastal quest for adventure, meaning, and happiness. In Chuck's westward-bound trek, Los Angeles is the end of the road, the kitschy epicenter of ever-quaking, ever-shaking American culture. "Promised Land" juggles every type of transportation except rickshaw and pogo stick – trains, planes, and the good ol' Greyhound bus.

Chuck's musical mission? To hightail it from his modest Norfolk, Virginia, home to his golden California paradise. Not a new theme [Al Jolson, #1(6) 5-24, "California, Here I Come!"]. Chuck can feel the *Mississippi's Burning* (1988***) tension of an Afro man trying nervously to avoid cop encounters of the worst kind, with Southern KKK-fan sheriffs, kings of their segregationist magnolia domain. Berry hits the tough turf. His struggles get worse when the Greyhound punts its motor. Stranded in Birmingham, Alabama, where Dr. King marched, he frets 50s Deep South racial tribulations. The subtlest of satirists, Berry's grin in this song shows a lot of tenacious teeth.

In Borderline Bitter Gear – not the smiling duckwalk showman blowing kisses to his adoring audience – Berry sings out his political protest in fluent Rock and Roll. Revered and respected, Chuck Berry is no one to be trifled with. Why didn't this song hit the top ten, in the wake of other Berry comeback hits, like his ragin' Cajun super tune "You Never Can Tell" (#14, 8-64)? Perhaps it's the I-IV-V7 block chords, over and over, and the lack of a bridge. Chuck goes back farther even than the 12-Bar Blues with "Promised Land." Like "Frankie and Johnny," Chuck follows the repetitive Pure Blues tradition. He darts back to the old Eight-Bar Blues Progression ("Stagger Lee").

You can feel Chuck's palpable joy and relief as he finally cops a jet and ascends aloft. He's beyond the Texas cactus and airborne out of Albuquerque, New Mexico. Celebrating, he eats T-bone steak and other gastronomic goodies that rich Americans thought were good and healthy back in 1964 (you know, eggs, butter, whole milk, maybe lard). Chuck's triumphant long-distance call to the Norfolk folks back east proudly announces that the 'po' boy' has made it to the California Promised Land..

Yes indeed. Rock and Roll (and life) are often pilgrimages of an almost-religious fervor and zeal. Just two years later Motown's magnificent blind superstar, **Stevie Wonder,** followed up Chuck's West Coast quest with "A Place in the Sun" (#9, 11-66). The Wonder Kid wunderkind touts the warm glow of hope for everyone, somewhere below December Detroit arctic blasts. Someday before he's gone, he vows, he'll find that magic spot.

Berry finds his Promised Land. The strong retirement urge to a balmier climate hits many of us Northerners and Canadians at all ages. It hit Stevie at 16, me at 23, and we've both spent the last 35 years or more working in the snowswept North – dreaming of swaying palm trees. Aloha.

Looking for one that says it all? The American Dream, Fame and Fortune, the Power and the Glory that is Rock and Roll – here it is!

"Johnny B. Goode" – Chuck Berry, #8, 8-58; #2(2) R & B. To the ardent rock critics who claim that "Johnny B. Goode" is the greatest Rock and Roll story of all time –

many more gung-ho rock critics might argue that that is an understatement. The plucky gunny-sack guitar kid strums his railside dreams to a mile-a-minute engineer, and then to a floodlight universe.

Johnny B. Goode. Epitome of Rags-to-Riches Superstar. Story of America,

Berry's "Johnny B. Goode" is now blasting down the Captain Crunch-Trix-Count Chocula-Cheerio aisle at Piggly-Wiggly hypermarket. It follows you from Aerobics Funzo Bunzo No-Flabs-Abs Workout #7 to the Muffller Monster. With super-duper rotation saturation, it is everywhere, always. It is the Omnipotent Oz of Oldies Overkill. It defines Rock and Roll. With blazing **profundo 12-Bar Blues,** "Johnny B. Goode" blasts the lesser songs to Obscurity Limbo. "Johnny B. Goode" defines Rock and Roll. Perhaps no other character in American song better epitomizes Rock and Roll than the feisty Johnny B. Goode, armed with a guitar, a song, and a dream.

This Horatio Alger success vision pumps the heart and soul of any rock study, and Johnny's vision is quintessentially American. Anyone who ever found this land of promise has lived Johnny's aspirations. When our N.A.S.A. Space Program selected typical American items for its outer-space probe, it beamed "Johnny B. Goode" into extraterrestrial space, hoping for communication with otherworldly beings. Chuck's piano man Bob Baldori (ours, too, in the 1963 Night Shift) tells the story of how the aliens have answered us back with the first message from outer space. The message? "Send more CHUCK BERRY!"

Chuck Berry, *around 1979.*

Johnny B. Goode IS America. He is the fountainhead of our optimistic splendor. Streets paved with gold. All that jazz. Every schoolkid for three generations can tell you Johnny's victory tale of triumph over obscurity and hopelessness. A little country boy grows up back in the evergreens (Southern yellow pine), He strums his gunnysack guitar on the low, sultry Mississippi Delta. Down by – what else? Rock's birthplace **New Orleans**.

On Chuck's #124, 12-64 St. Louis to Liverpool album, he wears a spiffy French beret. Chuck is ¼ French. His hot French guitar licks pervade his renaissance romper, #10, 6-64 "No Particular Place to Go," featured in 1995's kill-everybody bloodbath *Pulp Fiction* (¼ star, for iconoclasm). Chuck's music blossomed like the fragrant hibiscus and bougainvillea on the subtropical Delta. He celebrates America with this "Let the Good Times Roll" French connection.

Johnny's name? Chuck grew up on **Goode Street** in St. Louis, Missouri, so no really mysterious allusion exists in naming his superest swan song (see Beatles' "Strawberry Fields Forever").

Chuck has the thickest sideburns I have ever seen. In 1971, when mutton-chop whiskers swallowed guys' faces, Chuck's French ancestor was hirsutely apparent, as his bushy sideburns careened down to two scimitar-sharp points. Berry's past has been checkered with early and late encounters with the law, and he has done hard time for his transgressions. Every time he was down, however, he got back up stronger.

When Chuck plays a gig, he doffs the dreary gray threads he wore to pass unnoticed, and then dons duds as colorful as Van Gogh's palette. In these grand and glorious moments on stage, Berry stands tall, (6'2"), looking nearly two decades younger than his 3/4 century would have you believe. Yet in some mysterious way, he still IS young Johnny B. Goode – and Johnny is Chuck.

Could be one of a million moms calling to her kid: "Johnny – BE GOOD!" Sounds like Mom, over apple pie, admonishing her lad to become a paragon of virtue. But the story of Johnny B. **Goode** is also the most cherished of American biographies: it is the story of our great emancipator **Abraham Lincoln** (1809-65). Johnny rises from log-cabin humble beginnings. Dirt floor. No electricity or running water. Poverty Flakes for breakfast. Johnny loves to strum his raggedy guitar by the po-folks tracks near his ramshackle, hardscrabble cabin. He hopes to impress Engineer Mike on the Midnight or Orange Blossom Special or 'The City of New Orleans.' Maybe it's the legendary Wabash Cannonball. Train songs ARE American Folk and Country and R & B music. We have often been a nation of nomads, going new places for new beginnings and new dreams, after the old ones vanished into downtrodden despair. We roll on down that lonesome road, hoping to hitch our dreams to a blazing star. And our names to a blazing marquis of stardom.

We don't want to know that the engineer can't hear a thing Johnny is strumming (unless Johnny has an amp to blast away the **Who** at Wembley). "Johnny B. Goode" is no mournful weepy tear-jerking ballad, wailing wild woes to wayfaring whippoorwills. "Johnny B. Goode" is a YAY-saying YES-I-CAN song.

Chuck knew exactly what he was doing, putting kid Johnny in the sleepy noon shade just strumming his mol-

ten axe. Little Johnny has no MTV, no DVDs or CD player, no cassettes. Maybe no wind-up Victrola record player or radio or TV. Johnny keeps time to the rolling rocking rhythm of the rail pulse of America. The engineer hails him ALMOST like the Wise Men hailed the Baby in the manger.

Obviously, John B [Goode] is neither a savior nor a sloop. He's just a Rock and Roll star.

Bob Seger, in Rock anthem "Rock and Roll Never Forgets" (#41, 7-77), says that 'Chuck's [R & R] children' (meaning his millions of musical followers and proteges) are now out playing Chuck's riffs and best licks as a tribute to Berry. Seger's #28 4-79 "Old Time Rock and Roll" is the 2nd-most-played jukebox song of all time.

Chuck's greatest almost-gigantic song is his #5 '55 "Maybellene" follow-up, "Roll Over Beethoven" (#26, 6-56; #68 George Harrison & Beatles, 3-64; #42 ELO 4-73). Chuck chides his sister, classically piano-trained, in this Classical knockabout lyric. The juke box busts a fuse, down by the rockin' rhythmic review. Chuck gets the 'Rockin' Pneumonia,' a phrase Huey Smith's Clowns turned into #52, 8-57 "Rockin' Pneumonia & the Boogie Woogie Flu" (#5, 7-57 R & B, plus Johnny Rivers' great #6, 10-72 reprise). Chuck's guitar licks and All-American lyrics are a seedbed for future stars to review and rehash and revamp. Rock and Roll, via Beethoven's tune here, slaps an in-yer-face style against whatever gets too smug and comfy and stuffy. Rock smashes icons, and 'Johnny B. Goode' rules!

Though there weren't enough women in early rock music, the R & B ranks began the movement:

"Maybe" – Chantels, #15, 1-58; #2(1), R & B. In 1996, no solo male singer hit #1 for months. Conversely, in 1957, the only FEMALE #1 song was the marshmallow movie-star ballad "Tammy" by ultracute dancer Debbie Reynolds . Her whispery song made a lot of us Debbie fans wonder why Last-of-the-Crooners Eddie Fisher ditched her for Elizabeth Taylor (Husband #3?). For similar blather, please check the *Enquirer* or *Weekly World News*, at the deli. "Maybe's" **Arlene Smith** pumps up the lyric soprano range. She could give **Mariah Carey** ("Fantasy," #1[8], 9-95) a run for her money, dusting off the tippytop notes of the female vocal spectrum. With Bronx schoolmates Sonia Goring, Rene Minus, Jackie Landry, and Lois Harris, the Chantels throb to the slow-dance beat, cajoling millions of make-out sessions on zillions of squeaky basement couches by the kitty litter.

The Chantels are the first major Afro-American 'Girl Group' (see 2000+ 'Boy Bands'). **Arlene Smith** was a rather ancient 15 when she caressed this classic with sensational soprano gusto. The Chantels' only major competition, the Bobbettes (at first Harlem Queens) were only 11 to 13 when their Hot-for-Teacher #6 "Mr. Lee" barnstormed *Bandstand* ["Hot for Teacher"? **Van Halen**, #56, 10-84]. The Chantels introduced Rock-Idol longing to a new half of the audience – the GUYS. Since we were barely 13-14 ourselves, the concept of 'Robbing the

Cradle' didn't compute. "Maybe" reverberates with teen-age passion. Smith's towering soprano is the highest in early Rock and Soul. If piercing isn't your thing, twirl the treble.

The enchanting Chantels debuted with #71, 9-57 "He's Gone." "Maybe" snagged #2(1), 1-58 on the R & B chart, and they became the vanguard of the Girls Group Era. They're the first African-American female group in the Rock Era to sustain a string of big hits – paving the way for the **Shirelles, Supremes, Pointer Sisters, TLC,** and **Destiny's Child** ("Independent Women, Pt. I" #1[10+], 11-2000). The Chantels' sophomore selection, "Every Night," hit #39, 3-58 (#16 R & B). Their biggest success was #14 "Look in My Eyes" of 8-61 (#6 R & B). Like the Everlys' #1 '60 "Cathy's Clown," the Chantels boom out the unison tune at first, as Smith grips the note and the others dip downward into harmonic swirls of delight and pleasure.

In a March 1, 2000 PBS special, the ingenue-emeritus Chantels re-united in a Streetcorner Doo-Whop Panorama with host **Jerry Butler** and stars **Jimmy Beaumont & Skyliners, Herbie Cox & Cleftones, the Jive Five** (starring Eugene Pitt, #3, 5-61 "My True Story"), **Gene 'Duke of Earl' Chandler,** the "Speedoo"**Cadillacs,** some surviving **Platters,** and **Johnny Maestro (Crests/Brooklyn Bridge)** amidst a dynamic cast. Arlene Smith dedicated their tunes to Jackie Landry, wishing her well in Heaven, and jubilantly believing she is shining down like the line in **Mariah Carey/Boyz II Men's** #1 hit (#1[16]) of the half-century, "One Sweet Day." The Chantels' last hit answered Genius **Ray Charles'** #1(2), 9-61 "Hit the Road, Jack" with "Well, I Told You" (#29, 11-61, NC R & B).

"What'd I Say? " – Ray Charles, #6, 7-59; #1(1) R & B. 12-Bar Blues *Call & Response* Rock and Soul Classic. Ray and his banned band cut a wide swath on this lengthy rocker, and Side B got banned in unprudish DETROIT – for alleged heavy breathing by Ray's sultry back-up boosters the **Raelettes.** Ray plays zesty riffs on the basic diatonic triads; in the Key of **C,** Ray's **I, IV,** and **V** chords are **C** (C—E—G), **F** (F-A-C), and **G**(G-B-D). Then he fires off a seventh: **G7** (G—B—D—F).

Call & Response is used often by African-American ministers. Minister calls, congregation/choir responds. "What'd I Say's" risque lyric invokes the Raelette congregation to coo and purr sensuously back to passionate preacher Ray. Part I is Ray, solo. In banned Pt. II, the Raelettes croon and festoon and balloon their tune with steamy sighs and mellifluous murmurs.

Ray introduced the electric piano to top ten music on this tune. Like Bill Doggett's two-part #2, '56 "Honky Tonk," Charles split the six-minute song to beat the 4½-minute length record by Marty Robbins' #1, 4-59 "El Paso." In 1959, the lightest portable keyboards weighed 100+ pounds, so you hired the Hulk to lug and plug your piano. In 1959, Ray's monumental "What'd I Say" was a blazing hit. It still is.

"The Class" – Chubby Checker, #38, 5-59, NC, R & B. South Philly High's Ernie Evans {Chubby] added an Afro multiculturalism to Dick Clark's *Bandstand* Italian idols

(Fabian, and a bunch of Bobbys). Chubby's cover of **Hank Ballard's** #28, 7-60 "The Twist" bizarrely hit #1 twice (8-60 & 11-61), and revolutionized our national perception of Rock and Roll to include ADULTS for the first time (like **Jackie Kennedy & the Prez** at NYC's Studio 54 or Peppermint Lounge).

Chubby's debut 'platter' shows his uncanny imitative vocal ability. He apprentices his Rock & Soul craft with echoes of: his namesake **Antoine 'Fats' Domino;** class clowns the **Coasters;** drummer Cozy Cole (#3, 8-58 "Topsy," follow-up "Turvy #36, 12-58); and even **Elvis.** This rare disc represents (in full spoof) Rock and Roll's first attempt to teach its own history (see "American Pie," #1, '71 Don McLean). Checker merely sang the ancient nursery rhyme "Mary Had a Little Lamb" for mentor Dick Clark. This may be the first 'class' ever in Rock history. Ever, or Evans. Chubby uses a faux 'class' and serenades Mary's lamb to a buzzy crew of daffy little dudes and dudettes. Somehow, the little record reminds you of *Tiny Toons,* those infant Bugs Bunnys and teeny-tiny Tweetys and stubby grubby Tasmanian Devils. Teen idol Checker's cool nursery rhyme plays off a super snarly sax.

The turn of the 60s decade sparked the rise of cuddlesome teen idols for guys, too, like **Connie Stevens, Shelley Fabares**, or **Ann-Margret** (#17, 7-61 "I Just Don't Understand"). It paralleled the 2000+ Mouseketeer Disney barrage with **Britney Spears** and **Christina Aguilera** (or Boy Bands for girls like Son by Four, BBMack, or **N'Sync**). The ratio was all wrong for us guys in the 50s (surplus of male Teen Idols), but at least we had the celestially lovely **Annette:**

"Pineapple Princess" – Annette [Funicello], **#11, 9-60.** This darling Utica, NY, Mouseketeer was not only the answer to our teenage prayers, but she also **launched Surf Music** with this Hawaiian novelty tune. She could have sung it underwater. Who heard it? We were too busy ogling the shapely chaste lass with our gaga googly eyes. The knockout Disney Mickey Mouse Club Mouseketeer perfectly bulged her demure bathing suit. She sang this syrupy surf's-up song two years before the Beach Boys spearheaded Surf Rock.

"Pineapple Princess" championed the sunny Waikiki sands and blue romantic waves and endless summer. It was a mysterious thing, our 25-million-guy worship of the Italian-American pop princess. She was marriage material, not like va-va-voom Marilyn Monroe, a calendar full of jiggly joy. You did not look at Annette like, say, *Beavis & Butthead* might drool over Toni Braxton's #1(11), 10-96 video "Un-Break My Heart" – Braxton brandishes twirling tongue, flawless bod, blue-eyed Afro gorgeous feline-slinky moves. She purrs bedroom Blues as she eagerly eyes a dozen musclemen and a few kooks, dorks, and nerds. Annette featured no bikinis, no hanky-panky. Her ingenue *Beach Blanket Bingo* cinema adventures made her a sweet teen idol—not exactly every guy's "Genie in a

Bottle" (**Christina Aguilera**, #1[5], 7-99).

Annette didn't write, produce, play an instrument, or hype the song, but who cared? Her sunny surfside tune trumpets many R & R innovations: 1) a Hawaiian guitar spikes the Bridge; in the aftermath of Santo & Johnny's #1 '59 "Sleepwalk," "Pineapple Princess" previewed Surf gurus **Jan & Dean**'s Hawaiian-steel slide show on #11 '63 "Honolulu Lulu"; 2) Annette's come-hither alto is a welcome FEMALE lead, like Joanie Sommers, Robin Ward, Kathy Young, or the Paris Sisters, in a male-dominated rock sphere; and 3) as mentioned, "Pineapple Princess" led off the Surf Era, trumping **Dick Dale & the Deltones, Jan & Dean**, and the **Beach Guy**s by at least a year.

"Broken-Hearted Melody" – Sarah Vaughan, #7, 7-59; #5, 8-59 R & B. Sarah Vaughan of Newark, NJ, carried on the behind-the-beat audial aura of classic Jazz divas **Ella Fitzgerald or Billie Holiday.** Fitzgerald (1918-96, #1 '44 "I'm Making Believe") began with the great bandleader **Chick Webb** (1909-39, TB, and #8, 3-39 "Undecided"). Vaughan slurs and bends notes like Ella or Billie, and her skillful Jazz hesitation and Blues *melismas* indicate she's one of the greatest Jazz singers of all time. All over the alto range, "Sassy Sarah" glided with ease and expertise; she lulled, while the Big Beat banged. Tickling and tantalizing the high notes, she teases the Streetcorner Chord Progression in her breathtaking "Broken-Hearted Melody" (like **C — Am — F[or Dm] — G7**) with IIIm chords and glides and slurs, paralleling great Jazz guitarist **Wes Montgomery**. Her Blues riffs lament her lost love, and her almost-downbeat Jazz improv vocal riffs highlight Vaughan's (1924-90) unique and spectacular style. Great synthesis of Jazz, Rock, and Soul.

"Lipstick on Your Collar" – Connie Francis, #5, 5-59; #10, 6-59, R & B. With 56 HOT 100 hits, perky Concetta Franconero (Connie) graced *Bandstand* with this telltale story about boyfriend 'Frankie' [Avalon?] and his smoochy exploits with some floozaloo. Connie, ditto from Newark, sang sweet trombone-toned ballads. With funtime booming bass drum, Connie's rare R & R rip-roarer bops groovily along. She also scored #1(2), 6-60 "My Heart Has a Mind of Its Own" and #7, 11-59 three-kleenex 1928 reprise weeper "Among My Souvenirs."

"Who's Sorry Now?" – Connie Francis, #4, 2-58; #4, 3-58 R & B. Connie's seemingly sweet demeanor rampages into Revenge Gear here, a motif also explored in: **Del Shannon**'s #28, '61 "So Long Baby" and his #126 version of the **Rolling Stones**' "Under My Thumb," which never charted for Jagger's band; or in #36, 2-2000 & #1 Country "How Do You Like Me Now?" by Toby Keith. From 1923, "Who's Sorry Now?" hit #3 for Isham Jones and #5 for Marion Harris ('23) and #18 for Harry James ('46). Connie's cunning conclusion to the doleful ditty: she's HAPPY the inconsiderate clod is finally SORRY now. In 1996, Connie was not sorry she cut a Buddy Holly tribute album. Like Annette, Connie was Italian, sweet, and very

curvy. The #1 female singer of the 50s Rock Era, Francis was an irregular on *American Bandstand*, and her frequent appearances kept the gold records gleaming. Another Francis Classic is #2(2), 12-58 "My Happiness" (#6, '48, *Ella Fitzgerald)*, where her Connie + Connie overdubs show her admiration of the Everly Brothers.

Toledo's **Teresa Brewer**, like Sarah Vaughan, carried over from the Pop Standards early 50s. Her #7, 6-56 "A Sweet Old Fashioned Girl" plods the lumbering verse – then (like #10, '76 Vicki Sue Robinson) 'Turns the Beat Around' and rocks out. Her #5, 2-56 "A Tear Fell" and #13, 4-57 "Empty Arms" place Teresa among top 50s female stars.

"Sweet Nothin's" – Brenda Lee, #4, 12-59; #12, 3-60 R & B. Brenda Lee Tarpley, 4'9" teen alto princess, purrs a creaky porch swing scenario. Guy & gal playing midnight kissyface. Mommy intrudes. Brenda is best known for perennial "Rockin' Around the Christmas Tree" (#14, 12-60, and #4-most-played-carol ever). "Sweet Nothin's" is her hallmark hit – for the whispery sweet nothin's she murmurs into her porch partner's smoldering ear. From her #1(3), 5-60 "I'm Sorry" to her #11, 10-66 "Comin' on Strong," Brenda Lee's hits kept coming on strong: #1(1), 9-60 "I Want to Be Wanted"; #7, 12-60 "Emotions"; #3, 10-61 "Fool #1"; or #3, 9-62 "All Alone Am I." Her plaintive ballads garnered her 52 Hot 100 hits – rockers #4 "Dum Dum," and #6, 6-60 "That's All You Gotta Do." They both showed Brenda could echo the most volcanic, fiery female Rocker of her era, an Oklahoma tornado named **Wanda Jackson** whose promo execs tried to shape her sound to echo **Brenda Lee . . .**

"Let's Have a Party" – Wanda Jackson, #37, 8-60. Rockabilly was gender-integrated by Wanda Jackson, whose guitar-fire band could blast most male Rockabillies off the stage. Touring with Elvis in his 1954-55 'Hillbilly Cat' stage, Wanda was in on the ground floor. Bold, brawny, buxom, and unabashed, Wanda womped the frantic male Rockabillies (like Ersel Hickey, #75, 4-58 "Bluebirds over the Mountain") at their own shimmying shake-a-tailfeather game. Wanda covered this Elvis Hard Rock classic from his Al #1(10) *Loving You*, 7-57. If anyone had the raw, shrieking chutzpah of **Little Richard** on his own turf, it was wildly wailing Wanda. A super singer-songwriter, her stuff was never ho-hum or dull. One Japanese-volcano-inspired belter, "Fujiyama Mama," became a Village CBGB's Punk Rock cult classic in the 90s. The uptight record establishment couldn't hack Wanda's Screaming Blues vulcanism, so they squelched her style into tame teardrop ballads (#29, 7-61 "Right Or Wrong," # 9, C). This Jayne Mansfield-type JACKSON didn't quite match the Gloved One's sister for pop success (Janet Jackson (9 #1's to 2000, like 6-2000 "Really Doesn't Matter") But it didn't matter. The 50s were tough sledding for women rockers, who had to wait until Mariah and Madonna and Toni and Janet and Alanis and Britney and Celine and Ashanti (#1[8+], 1-2002 "Foolish") and Shakira conquered the world.

"The Lord loves a sinner man." Televangelist Jimmy Swaggart, before his fall (in the company of a lusty lady he didn't even touch), actually cried for forgiveness – for his cousin the Killer.

If you seek a wimpy, wishy-washy Muzak idol, do not call **Jerry Lee Lewis** (b. 9-29-35). Ol' Jerry Lee of Ferriday, Louisiana, went to Bible School, got kicked out for mangling the hymns with Boogie-Woogie Rock and Roll fire and brimstone, and boasted two marriages under his belt when he met the lovely Myra Brown. Myra, Jerry Lee's bubble-gum wife, was the cute 13-year-old kid of his bass man. Not only that, she was his second cousin.

"Breathless" – Jerry Lee Lewis, #7, 3-58; #3 R & B; #4, C. With a golden lion's mane, sensuous smirk, and piano lightning like Johnnie Johnson's flashing from his pale right hand (Honkytonk Moontan), the Killer stormed into the Holly Daze arena. Jerry had all the pussyfooting quietude of Lions vs. Christians, with Lions ahead at half-time in the Super Gladiator Bowl. Since Sam Phillips of Sun Records lost his cushy **Elvis** contract, and with **Johnny Cash** going Country, **Roy Orbison** going nowhere (till 1960-65), and with **Carl Perkins** and his #2, '56 "Blue Suede Shoes" badly scuffed and battered from a bad auto wreck, Phillips set his sights on a new Golden Boy. Enter Jerrrrry Lee Lewis!

Tickets to stardom are financed by blood, sweat, and tears. The Killer had a different angle. The spunky back-water Delta Boogie Man **sold 33 dozen EGGS**, with his raunchy pop Elmo Lewis, and they commandeered Memphis by storm with Humpty Dumpty as their battering ram. With his own father egging him on, Jerry Lee gunned the big Olds with white line fever on the wild 120-mph three-lane thoroughfare to Sam's Sun Memphis empire.

Once Jerry hit national TV, he was an Insta-Star. Jerry's amiable ambassador to fame was renaissance genius **Steve Allen** (12-26-21 - 10-31-2000). Comedian, songwriter (Al. 5-55 *Music for Tonight*), and host of both *The Steve Allen Show* AND The *Tonight Show* (pre-Leno, pre-Carson), Allen hosted Jerry Lee Lewis to jiffy fame in a network-dominated world devoid of 55 Cable channels, VH-1, and MTV. Though the *Ed Sullivan Show* gets most of the rock critic glory for launching Elvis, Buddy, and the Beatles, Steve Allen deserves a very close Silver Medal. Multi-faceted genius Allen also boosted Buddy and Elvis in their early careers.

Jerry Lee scored only THREE top ten hits in his tabloid-torn meteoric career, but his raging rebel reputation pumps him to near-Elvis stature for his golden year of 6-57 to 6-58. The Big Three? "Whole Lot of Shakin' Going On" (#3, 6-57), "Great Balls of Fire" (#2[4], 11-57), and "Breathless" (#7, 6-57, no relation to great same-name song by the Corrs of Ireland, #8, 1-2001 on Adult Top 40 & #1 in Europe). "Breathless" is rated "R." It's the best booming Lewis Boogie of all. Jerry Lee's sizzling chops go back to Ragtime or at least Clarence 'Pine Top' Smith's 1929

"Boogie Woogie." Pouncing on pianos, Jerry had the zest of Little Richard. Jerry specialized in long swooping *glissandos* – speedy thumb-glides up or down the keys.

A 1958 British tour magnetized media mavens and paparazzi to query Jerry: "Who is this child in your entourage?" In 1957 Southern kids (see Loretta Lynn) often got hitched at 13-14-15 (see Dolly Parton). Brit tabloid info-sharks pounced on this juicy scoop. They ambushed the Rock and Roll lion with his huge curly blond mane, and his career was shorn like Samson.

After Jerry's rock-idol career exploded into oblivion, he staggered into the woozy honkytonk scene, bobbing beneath the surface, buoyed up by his liquid armor (at a June 2000 gig, it was *Sprite,* straight).

Country music, 60s refuge of a few roadhouse rapscallions, took in a thirtysomething Rock and Roll ramblers like the Killer (#94, 7-68, but #2, 6-68 C "What's Made Milwaukee Famous [Has Made a Loser Out of Me]"). Milwaukee makes BEER. Once more the neon dazzle and jukebox midnight world welcomed the Killer from his deep-swamp Louisiana Deltaland. After some dark tales of his personal quagmire, the wasted and wounded Mississippi Delta Marauder groped his way into Millennium III. Still looks halfway decent, too. Full head of hair. Twinkling impish grin. Mother-of-pearl complexion glow in the roadhouse glare. When I interviewed him in June 2000, 65-year-old Jerry had stopped dancing atop his swaggering piano, but his frantic fingers still bashed the soaring glissandos – and his righteous starfire smirk danced over the rapt throng. Refugee from Disasterland, Original Rock Hall of Fame Inductee (1986) **Jerry Lee Lewis** still ROCKED on into his glowing midnight swirl of pulsating piano, throbbing guitar, and heavenly devilish drum thunder. Kool Kats get nine lives.

"Breathless" is Jerry's greatest hit. The Wiggling Wonder of Ferriday grew up in the magic land of Swamp Rock, Delta Blues, and funky New Orleans Soul. As a tiny piano-pounding tot, Little Jerry slurped up a rich taste of Boogie-Woogie Soup. Cousin to fallen televangelist Jimmy Swaggart but country star Mickey Gilley too (#1, C, Buddy Holly's "True Love Ways," 7-80), Jerry Lee wallowed in get-down-and-boogie Blues from the day he first stuffed a bullfrog down sweet Suzie's dress.

Lewis's wacky life continues on the off-track "Highway to Hell" (#47, 10-79, AC/DC Classic Hard Rock) in a handbasket, according to paparazzi prognosticators, and revered rock critics like Harry Sumrall. Sumrall chortles that in 1973 alone, Lewis shot his bass player (accidentally, of course), skidded his Rolls Royce into a ditch (the car was drinking, not Jerry), and got arrested for brandishing a smoking Derringer pistol at Graceland in Memphis (while Jerry blearily demanded to see his pal, sleeping Elvis, at 4:32 a.m.). The way Jerry Lee Lewis leers and drools, chuckles rock critic guru Dave Marsh, is a strong argument from prudes that they really DID have something to fear from Rock and Roll. Great Rock music is often a little dangerous, and it leaves you breathless.

"Breathless" is a Boogie-Woogie masterpiece. Jerry rarely wrote songs; his best were often created by

Manhattan's Tin Pan Alley genius—the stogie-chomping, elfin Afro-American **Otis Blackwell**, who penned Elvis's biggest bombshell, #1(11), '56 "Don't Be Cruel." We all recall Blackwell's Lewis triumph #2(4), "Great Balls of Fire," where a surfeit of sensuality can drive a man bananas.

"Breathless" seethes with unbridled passion/lust. Please don't tease me, Jerry pleads, just squeeze. The chick, leaves him . . . . . "AAAAAHHHHHHH, Breathless-AAHHHH!"

In his leonine heyday, the Killer shuffled suavely to the grand piano, started with languor and dignity and semi-silence . . . and then EXPLODED the hapless auditorium in a paroxysm of Rock and Roll power and glory. Blondeened mane ablaze with light and hell-bent-for-leather frenzy, Jerry Lee Lewis warned non-vigilant parents that danger lurked in every gazelle glissando, every quivering, quavering tenor line, every sly smirky come-hither-honey smile. Suddenly, Elvis's hips belonged to a choirboy. Jerry Lee ascending. Lewis never befuddled fans with mere HINTS of desire. He GUZZLED it! Jerry's Pumping Piano spewed out Chug-A-Lug Love.

Blackwell's Boogies provided the brash bridges, too, for Lewis's soaring antics on treble piano: thumbs raking ivory, honkytonk rat-a-tats, clanging R & R walking bass lines, hanging Blues sevenths crashing into sensuous sub-dominant IV chords – and 12-Bar Blues paranoia puddling into the power of Jerry's feeding frenzy on the flashing keys (his music gets fans arrested for alliteration). In the waning months of 1957, Jerry duked it out with Buddy and Chuck and Elvis for the King of Rock and Roll crown. Tolerating the spec-toting lanky Lubbock lad, and mildly griping about the King, Jerry Lee showed less than love for his super confident rival – Chuck Berry. When rock jock legend ALAN FREED asked Jerry to OPEN a rock revue for Berry, because Berry's hit was higher on the charts, the non-Ego-Impaired Lewis was furious. Drooling lighter fluid all over his grand piano on stage, Lewis closed his own act by torching the poor hapless piano. In the pandemonium and swirling smoke, Jerry ostensibly yelled: "I'd like to see any son of a b — follow THAT!"

"Whole Lot of Shakin' Going On" – **Jerry Lee Lewis, #3, 6-57; #1(2), 8-57 R & B; #1(2) Country; #8, 10-57 U.K.** Jerry's wriggly rocker snuffs all the Mr. Nice Guy stereotypes Pat Boone and Buddy Holly had been slowly and painstakingly bringing to Rock and Roll. Coarse, lusty, and crass, Lewis pumps his piano and unravels. He'd stride out in a crisp suit, his longest-hair-of-the-50s slicked nattily back. As he leaped into his frantic number, he'd flip a quick strip tease of coat and tie, jump atop his battered piano, wiggle and dance upright on top with his footlong curls swirling down into the piano's steely, stringy guts, and wrap up the song in his torrid scorching climax. Despite Little Richard, Lewis may have burst forth with the most dynamic act in the 50s (though **James Brown** [#48, 12-58, "Try Me"] waited in the wings). Whole lotta barnyard shimmying in this tune, with horned bulls, barn stomps, and squawking chickens. Jerry Lee pumps vin-

tage 12-Bar Blues, moving from soft to very loud. He throttles octaves, and gearshifts from slowly snarling to fast and frantic. Riding high over the smashing sound is Jerry Lee's floating seductive tenor – one of the great voices of Rock and Roll. Jerry Lee Lewis, his melody unchained, conquers the planet.

Jerry Lee Lewis, 1957

"Great Balls of Fire" – **Jerry Lee Lewis, #2(4), 11-57; #3, 12-57 R & B; #1(2), C. GOSPEL**-inspired? Jerry claims it's an old Biblical expression about flashing comets. From panting tacets to thunder-booming backbeat rushes (via 'goodness' & 'gracious'), the Killer cranks up his most memorable melody, with no mention of poor stooge Elmer Fudd, who usually uses that "Gwacious, you wascally wabbit" lingo with our hero Bugs Bunny. Jerry's throbbing off-beat piano hits the troughs of the notes' waves, pumping his virtuoso piano up to fever pitch in the dark heart of unleashed White Delta Boogie Soul. This Otis Blackwell Boogie is what Rock and Roll is all about. A swaggering strut, a rebel yell, and music that is full speed ahead, come hell or high water.

"High School Confidential" – **Jerry Lee Lewis, #21, 6-58; #5, R & B; #9, C.** Jerry's fourth straight hit got side-tracked on its charge up the charts by Jerry's controversial marriage. Movie theme. Tremendous tacet intro. Jerry's last biggee was bashed, bopped, and thunderstruck by a merciless press. Had Myra been, say, FIFTEEN, ol' Jerry Lee might have become the King of Rock and Roll when Elvis was drafted and Buddy split with the Crickets on a dark date with airborne destiny. Aside from Jerry's super cover (#30, 4-61) of **Ray Charles**' masterpiece "What'd I Say?", "High School Confidential" was his last big hit.

Rock's early era thrived not only on LEGEND-ARY SUPERSTARS. Some guys had to settle with being simply STARS:

"Tonite, Tonite, " – **Mello-Kings, #77, 8-57, and #95, 1-61.** 'Coulda' fooled US! We Motor City teens all thought it was #1 in the universe. Regionalism causes some songs to be #1 in one market, Number Zilch in the Outback. The way I figure it, if the record makes YOUR heartstrings zing, that's what REALLY counts. "Tonite" stars 'White Soul' Streetcorner virtuosos Bud Scholl (d. 1975), lead tenor; brother Jerry Scholl plus Ed Quinn (also tenors, no relation to Dr. Scholl or the Mighty Quinn); Larry Esposito (bass), and Neil Arena (baritone). Their magic harmonies still float like blue stars.

"Rosie Lee" – **Mello-Tones, #24, 5-57.** Legal hassle: Mello-KINGS lost name Mello-Tones to THIS crew. "Rosie" has a bear's shape, a tadpole's face, but great loving. Somehow, this streetcorner crew whistles as she wobbles down the faraway 50s avenue. Rosie's lover's rendez-vous, we imagine, involved a lot of darkness. "Rosie Lee" rings with sugary metallic major chords, and tonic harmonies on the last high-octave rave-up verse. Magnificent frantic finale. This rosy tune makes you feel glad all over.

"You Got What It Takes" – **Marv Johnson, #10, 11-59; #2(2), 10-59, R & B.** Marv Johnson (1938-93) helped spring the Motown Empire on the fledgling world of Rock and Soul. His Afro 'Irish tenor' enchanted millions when the **Temptations, Supremes, Vandellas, and Jackson Five** were still merely a puff of possibilities. Like tadpole Rosie's story above, the girl in Johnson's too-honest narrative is wooed in wishy-washy fashion; though she has no money, beauty, or fashion sense, she's mildly presentable, so he digs her anyhow. Marv's first Motown Top Ten tune bounces to a swirling background of Detroit Symphony strings. Motown owner **Berry Gordy** fires up the Motown formula on his modest 4-track at Hitsville, U.S.A., on Detroit's Near West Side on West Grand Boulevard: snarling bari sax, trio of go-go girls to chime 'yeah yeahs,' and a funky drum and bass throb that typifies the Rock and Soul underbeat:

BASIC ROCK: THE BEAT

	>			>
Right Hand:	♪	♩		♩
	1	2	3	4
Left Hand:	♩	♩	♩	♩
	1	2	3	4

The crucial role of Motown's main session drummer would be filled by **Benny Benjamin,** while the other pulse – electric bass – would fall to the nimble fingers of 1999 Rock Hall of Famer **James Jamerson.** [Same first/last name musicians include Jimi Hendrix's drummer **Mitch Mitchell,** and **Robyn Robbins – Bob Seger**'s keyboard guy]. Gordy conquered the world with Soul – and tight symphonic orchestrations to complement Benny and James and **Earl Van Dyke**'s and **Joe Messina**'s world-class session band. Marv's hit had what it took: chutzpah, romantic reality, comic vigor. A frolicking bouncy beat foretold the big debut of Detroit's second-biggest export beyond the wheeling of the world – the silvertoned silver-medal Sound of Soul – Motown.

For anyone suffering many musicians' dreaded fear – paralyzing stage fright – Marv's is not the story you want to read before ascending to the 'Elvis Spotlight' at your local Karaoke bar. After suffering pangs of early stage fright, the sensitive Johnson 'retired' into behind-the-scenes record production, songwriting, financial comfort, and posterity. The urge to perform somehow drove him back to the siren stage. Sadly, he collapsed and died at his comeback concert in South Carolina (see Jackie Wilson). Too old to die young, at 54, Marv Johnson's courage to face his stage fright, and to bravely perform as a young Soul star, may be the main reason for the stunning meteoric rise of the Motown Empire. Without Johnson, Motown might have churned out some humble halfway ho-hum hit, and vanished into the oldies ozone.

"Shout" – **Isley Brothers, #47, 6-59,** [amazingly] **NC, R & B.** You've romped to this Soul ultra-classic classic at parties all your life. Flabbergasted it charted so low? Me, too. Our Michigan State rock band the Night Shift once played some outback barn party out in rural Shiawassee County with headliner **Rudolph Isley.** This is Michigan Militia turf (home of mad bomber Timothy McVeigh, who blew up the Oklahoma City office building). We wore our levis and flannel shirts to the fraternity barn dance, but Isley was resplendent in Motown's dress-for-success threads: a tony tuxedo. Just when we cranked up the roaring din of "Shout," the barn was raided by some Boss Hogg "Dukes of Hazzard"-type sheriff and his dashing deputies. Under-21 co-eds and dudes leaped out into the dark summer night. This major gig for us was instantly zapped by the Beer Patrol, and the cops rounded up the non-escapees in a caravan of cars threading grumpily to a free night's lodging at the Shiawassee County Jail – for big-bucks bail revenue from disgruntled dads springing their sweet ingenue daughters from behind bars.

Only the BAND, for cryin' out loud, we crept along in the caravan in the middle of the 100+ captured pack of cars. Our shaking, quaking Isley Brother, after shouting half of "Shout" and bringing down the house/barn, was fearful of rural Michigan KKK kooks. **Tom Helderman,** our quick-witted drummer (and signed to pitch in the Chicago White Sox FARM system), fomented our escape. Scrunched into the middle of a jailbird caravan slinking off to kangaroo court [our 'crime' was being the BAND], Tom doused our lights and hit the gravel road to the right. Then he chopped a quick left into a cornfield tractor row trail. The Jail Parade of hapless underage coeds, full of four beers and bookended by police cruisers, snaked away to a yummy dinner of bread and water. And until recently, THAT is the "Absolutely" [#6, 4-2000] closest I ever got to a blockbuster hit record that reverberates down the echoing corridors of time. When YOU hear "Shout," with its varying volume like Jerry Lee's "Shakin'," and its frantic fiery bursts of volcanic vocal power, you might conjure some nostalgic prom or wedding. Me – I still recall **Rudolph Isley**'s spiffy, snazzy tuxedo at that old barn, and us doing our Martin Luther King thing for equal justice and racial dignity – by Tom Helderman creeping safely away into the soft warm Michigan cornfield night on the 1964 Freedom Trail.

"Mr. Blue" – Fleetwoods, #1(1), 9-59; #3, 10-59, R & B. With icy-blue soft sadness, the lullaby Fleetwoods lament a lost love. How this hit R & B Number Three I'll never figure. Crisp interwoven harmonies from Seattle's non-Grunge trio: Gary Troxel, Barbara Ellis, Gretchen Christopher. These timeless make-out music makers (a la **Johnny Mathis**, times three) sang the sweet refrain, pushing romance at passionate lovers who needed no push. "Mr. Blue" employs minor-key harmonic splendor and patriotic color imagery (he's blue while she paints the town red with other guy) to weave a forlorn tale of insincere apologies and faithless sprees.

Never underestimate the passion of your parents. Or grandparents. With Johnny Mathis, the Fleetwoods, Everlys, Journey, Streisand, Sinatra, Diamond, or Boyz II Men, love can lurch into mortgages and computers and bird feeders and Little League barbecues.

And what is worse/better—it could happen to you.

"Come Softly to Me" – Fleetwoods, #1(4), 3-59; #5 R & B. Seattle! To 90s buffs, cool cloudy Seattle means Grunge Rock or perhaps **Jimi Hendrix,** one great reason the guitar exists. *Nirvana* fans (#6, 12-91 "Smells Like Teen Spirit") ponder the tragic suicide of lead singer **Kurt Cobain,** 27. His widow **Courtney Love,** of blunt rant band Hole (#58, 10-94 "Doll Parts") was left with a very bewildered little child. Seattle, Washington, in its gray-green forested majesty, suggests Soundgarden, **Nirvana,**Alice in Chains, Pearl Jam, Screaming Trees, and Neo-Grunge supergroups like Scott Stapp's **Creed** ("With Arms Wide Open," #1, 9-2000). Many Grunge bands pounced on minor-key strident cacophony. They raspily declared their annoyed Generation X messages with the verve and fervor of **Ray Manzarek**'s dark cavernous labyrinthine moods (the **Doors'** keyboard genius). Protesting the Spandex, big hair, and make-up of many great older Heavy Metal stars (Kiss, Poison, Bon Jovi, Van Halen) that their music sprang from, Seattle Grungers punted the buttoned-up topcoat & tie inanity of the fax and fashion phantasmagoria. They opted for the Lumberjack Chic look (see Isley barn dance raid above): flannel shirts, ripped levis, Doc Maarten boots, black wool gangsta pullover hats, longjohn undershirts too bulky). They go back to another Seattle nonconformist, **Jimi Hendrix,** who took his paratrooper act on the road to England to attain Rock and Roll destiny. Grunge groups crunched Hendrix speed-riffs, and delivered deliberate atonal angst over Robert Plant-style vocal high-wire dances. Much of their claim to fame is Alternative Rock and Roll.

But hey – hasn't Rock and Roll ALWAYS been 'Alternative'?

If the status-quo uptight Establishment digs it, it's time to move on.

The **Fleetwoods'** make-out anthem doesn't rasp or boom or buzz or shriek or growl. Their torrid trio's sweet counterpoint is alluring and lulling and sleepy and intoxicating. Gary weaves his background baritone nonsense syllables: "don-don, dom-bee-doo-wom-bee-doo-bee-doo." Gretchen and Barbara blend a swath of honeytoned harmony in the shimmering alto range. Result? Gary's spare lyric suffuses the make-out mood with a quick hint of possible passion. The 50s seductive songs were muted and reserved, but in no way can that title get labeled 'PG,' especially in those sockhop & burger & fries Happy Days.

"Kansas City" – Wilbert Harrison, #1(2), 4-59; #1(7) R & B. Fishing-for-chicks song. Original was 1952 "KC Loving." Harrison's hammering band track was never duplicated. Guitar lingers on offbeat grace note. Catchy tune chugs a Midnight Special groove of pulse-pounding passion. Songwriter superstars? **Jerry Leiber/Mike Stoller.** A decade later, Harrison re-hit with #32, 12-69 "Let's Work Together" (dynamite reprise by Canned Heat to #26, 10-70), but "Kansas City" is the one swan song Harrison (1929-94) is best remembered for.

"Ruby Baby" – Ronnie Hawkins and the Hawks [later the *Band*], NC, 1958. Dion [DiMucci] did a sensational cover (#2, 1-63) of Hawkins' cover of the **Drifters'** "Ruby Baby" (NC, '56, #10, 5-56 R & B). Dion's "Ruby Baby" is a direct line of Streetcorner/Snarly Sax White Soul, coming off his monster hits #1, 9-61 "Runaround Sue" and #2 12-61 "The Wanderer."

Ronnie Hawkins, though, might just have the best of the three versions. With his vintage Rockabilly tenor growl, he suggests early **Elvis, or Gene Vincent,** at their best. The Arkansas and Toronto traveler later assembled his Canadian Hawks into Robbie Robertson's famous the **Band, Bob Dylan**'s back-up band. The Band starred Levon Helm and bassist Rick Danko (1943-2000). In this rollicking Rockabilly stomper, Hawkins' on-fire piano prances and zooms at Nascar speed, rivaling Jerry Lee Lewis or Little Richard or Johnnie Johnson.

"Lovers Never Say Goodbye" – Flamingos, #52, 1-59; #25, 3-59, R & B. Number five or so in Detroit. Many Motown teens felt this molasses-slow ballad to be the greatest love song ever vocally fondled. Sparse national chart action doomed its classic destiny, unlike Flamingoes' Oldies Overkill champ – #11, 6-59 "I Only Have Eyes for You" (#3 R & B). Bestrewn with Jazz minors and ringing 5-part harmonic majesty, "Lovers" features lead tenor **Nate Nelson** with Zeke Carey, Tommy Hunt, and Terry Johnson. Flamingos are among best R & B balladeers of all time. My 1960 pals and I almost saw them live in Toledo, Ohio, but the bouncers wouldn't let my friend Al Taylor in because he was African-American (so were the Flamingos); my friend Denny Jaggers, buttressed by brewskis, fired an ironing board through a window in defiance of their segregationist hypocrisies [I'm not recommending civil rights vandalism here, just telling another wild true story of my good ol' misspent youth and my love for Rock and Roll]. Anyhow, the Flamingos were an amazing Soul ballad troupe.

"Everyday" – Buddy Holly, NC, 1957, flip side of #3 "Peggy Sue." This delightful music-box tune was covered by **John Denver** (#81, 3-72), **James Taylor** (#61, 11-85), and **Don McLean** (NC, but #1[7], 11-71 Al. *American Pie*), three guys who truly sparked the singer-songwriter trend that **Buddy Holly** started. "Everyday" pleasantly bubbles just below your consciousness, murmuring like the Fleetwoods into elevators and receptionists' vestibules and into your deepest soul. "Everyday" features one of the prettiest PURE melodies in the history of music. "Everyday" always springs up suddenly, and you enjoy one happy musical moment in your dippy day, fraught with seedy laundromats, frozen ketchup, bird-poop picnic tables, and mosquitoes the size of Rhode Island.

Nothing simple in Norman Petty's and Holly's music-box melody. Vi Petty tickles the celeste for the instrumental bridge. "Everyday" bubbles and dips and spins in an upbeat bouncy melody you can't shake. Lyrically, songwriter Buddy cruises over lost-love memories. He psyches himself up, padding his wounded self-image, and cites the healing power of TIME, which rolls speedier than a big rollercoaster. Healing TIME subsides the aftermath of romantic disaster.

Nancy Norwich, in "Faster Than a Rollercoaster" in March 2000's *Car & Travel* (NY State AAA mag), writes about getting Buddy's autograph when she was a starry-eyed 13-year-old in Grand Rapids, Michigan at a Buddy Holly concert. Surfing the millennial back roads and twisty lanes of Easthampton, New York, she listens to Buddy on the CD player of her 1990 Mazda Miata, while 'tears of joy are being blown off [her] cheeks by the wind." After nabbing most of the 50s superstars for autographs [Jerry Lee Lewis, Chuck Berry, Frankie Lymon] Nancy finally encountered her idol: "He was sweet and patient, inking both my record and my program, making a nervous little twerp of a girl wearing glasses with rhinestone trim feel very grown-up." It was a gift Nancy might forever treasure . . .

After Buddy subsided to memory, and Nancy encountered a career, marriage, and bills, she recently unearthed these lost autograph treasures. Punting sentimentality for cold hard fiscal reality, Nancy discovered **eBay,** listing the record for 7-day sale. In a flash, she also dumped the program and ticket stub – and bought the Mazda Miata with the astounding profits – via us true Holly collectors.

Every day, in our roller coaster lives, we all make changes [I have forsaken my beloved Brother electric typewriter for this – harrrumph – computer monitor temporarily]. As Buddy squelched his romantic pain in "Everyday," Norwich too takes the pragmatic approach to sentimentality. Buddy himself was the ultimate pragmatist: were the versatile 50s star alive, HE might be getting eight Grammy Awards with **Carlos Santana** or **Creed** after vanquishing the arenas of Latino Rock, Neo-Grunge like **Creed** (from his Christian outlook), or British Invasion Rock, Southern

Rock, Disco, Hip-Hop, Psychedelia, Heartland Rock, Hip Hop, Techno/Industrial, World Music/New Age, Adult Top 40, Country, Blues, or Tex-Mex Thunder Rock.

We'll never know, though, whether he would have sold his own ticket for a Mazda. Maybe a Chevy, for the levee.

"Everyday" is about coping with loss. Pick yourself up and plunge back into life's race (Sinatra's "That's Life" – #4, 11-66). Dealt lemons? Make lemonade (Banjo Jack Williams, '85). "Everyday" shifts from grief to hope.

Vintage Holly. His good-natured musical mom Ella Holley helped buoy up her boy's self-image. Buddy always knew he was loved at home. Seemingly shy, Holly could write the book on positive self-awareness. No braggart, Holly knew he was a good singer/guitarist/songsmith with a great band, the **Crickets.** Buddy's unique style and melodies and revolutionary chord progressions in "Everyday" bolster this idea (see Glossary – Chord Theory).

Buddy Holly and the Crickets, remember created the modern rock band lineup: drums, bass guitar, rhythm and lead guitar. The lead singer uses background voices, and the band does original songs. Elvis and Jerry Lee Lewis rarely wrote music. Buddy Holly, however, like Chuck Berry and Little Richard, pioneered the singer-songwriter concept. Holly's boy-next-door tenor, sincere lyrics, and world-class melodies became the Rock and Roll model for stars from the Beatles and Beach Boys, to the Rolling Stones, Bob Dylan, Elton John, the Eagles, the Cars, Debbie Harry/Blondie, Linda Ronstadt, Cyndi Lauper, Eric Clapton, Led Zeppelin, and even early Motown (Berry Gordy Jr./Bob Kayli). **John Lennon** and **Paul McCartney**'s 1st-ever demo record was the Crickets' #1, '57 "That'll Be the Day." The Stones' first American hit was Holly & the Crickets' flipside "Not Fade Away."

Crickets' drummer **Jerry Allison**, remember, was voted the #3 drummer of all time in the late-70s *Rolling Stone* R & R poll. First was the Who's great drummer **Keith Moon**, whose last act on earth was to view the premiere of *The Buddy Holly Story*, starring Academy Award nominee Gary Busey. Voted second-best was Led Zeppelin's amazing **John 'Bonzo' Bonham**, who was influenced by Allison. Crickets' bassman **Joe B. Mauldin** also grazed the Top Twenty Bassists category, on the NEW electric bass that HE popularized. Allison, however, remained the OTHER Cricket SUPERSTAR. Though you might get arguments from Rush fans of Neal Peart, or Metallica's Lars Ulrich, or Nine Days' Vince Tattanelli, the big question remained beyond the millennium: WHO IS THE GREATEST ROCK DRUMMER OF ALL TIME? Next question – which one was still alive beyond the millennium [Hint: Jerry Allison turned 63 in 2002]? Though Buddy Holly was a first-year Rock Hall Inductee from 1986, the **Crickets** were not selected by 2002 . . .

"It Doesn't Matter Anymore" – Buddy Holly, #13, 3-59. #1(3), 3-61 UK, #1(8), Australia. Paul Anka, songwriter, penned this eerily desolate last hit for the upbeat smiling Buddy Holly. Almost a premonition of impending disaster, the song floats a forlorn and somber mood over the cold blue skies of Clear Lake, Iowa. Buddy, the Big Bopper, and 17-year-old Latino sensation **Ritchie Valens** (Rock Hall 2001) chugged in an icy bus to their last gig at Carroll Anderson's big, friendly Surf Ballroom—on the windswept north shore of the frozen February lake. Anka, who wrote "My Way" for Elvis and Sinatra, penned this wistful song that wallows in existential despair, almost futility. "It Doesn't Matter Anymore," by its title alone, dabbles in nihilism, belief in NOTHING. It might make the grungiest Grunge Rock leathertoggers and spiky head-banging metalheads and green-Mohawk Punk Rockers listen spellbound. Why? The eerie tone.

The song pioneers orchestral strings in Rock and Roll. Another Holly first. Sadly, a last as well. After settling down on Fifth Avenue with his bride **Maria Elena Santiago Holly**, and parting with the Crickets, Buddy met new producer Dick Jacobs, who added *pizzicato* plucked violins to bolster the dark mood of the song. The message is cryptic, desolate, futile. Holly lavishes his best bipolar voice. On the sing-songy verse, he leads with his thin, vulnerable tenor tones. When he rises to the bridge, he points out the uselessness of crying, and how he's tried everything to no avail. You can sense his tonal GEARSHIFT – a ring of macho command overtakes the melody, and growls his gloom. Sliding into the VI minor chord, his husky new baritone revamps his puzzled tenor mood. Stomping into the finale, where he vows to meet a new girl, the song runs the emotional gamut. And gauntlet. The *dramatic irony* we share is that Buddy will never find his happily-ever-after, and never rise from this blue-funk mood. Despite many hours of sketchy Holly tapes 'sweetened' by the polished Norman Petty studio, nothing would ever bring us a perfect studio-quality Buddy Holly record again. This was it.

The flip side, #88, 3-59 "Rainin' in My Heart," by the Everlys' super songsmiths Felice and Boudleaux Bryant, is technically Holly's last charted hit. Buddy's brother Larry, pondering the magnificent melody's excursion into Jazz major sevenths [**Gmaj7 =** G – B – D – F# Jazz chord], said the fiddle-fluttering song was the prettiest Buddy thought he'd ever recorded; Jacobs also did Buddy's famous love song "True Love Ways" (#14, 4-65 Peter & Gordon) at Manhattan's Knights of Pythias Hall; "True Love Ways" and the otherworldly Jacobs-powered "Moondreams" were both for Buddy's bride Maria. Among Buddy's posthumous releases are several home tape recorder cover tunes that sailed in England: "Bo Diddley" (#116, 4-63, & #8 UK & #5 Australia); *Chuck Berry's* "Brown-Eyed Handsome Man" (#113, 10-63, #3 UK), and #105, 4-69 "Love Is Strange."

Buddy was the first rock and roller to overdub his own vocals—he admired the Everly Brothers and wanted to sound like them both. So he DID. Catch this sound on his 1957 "Words of Love," a Mickey/Sylvia "Love Is Strange" echo recorded by the Beatles (and Diamonds). Or try Buddy's magnificent (he even RAPS a tad) "Listen to Me" (#16, 3-58 U.K.). Buddy's American popularity was always high. In the United Kingdom and Australia, he is revered as a Rock and Roll Archangel.

So "It Doesn't Matter Anymore" is no usual happy Holly

tune. How many new musical directions would Holly have pioneered – had Karma granted him more than his paltry big-time career allotment of 1½ years? As he rollercoastered to the abrupt finish line, we can only wonder as we listen to his Beatle echoes. And beyond.

* * * * * * *

Elvis, Buddy, and Chuck – Rockin' heart of the 50s. And a kind word for the penumbra-shadow stars who create the superstars. Without 2000 Hall of Fame guitarist **Scotty Moore or the Jordanaires,** would Elvis have outsold them all? Without Johnny B. **Badde, Johnnie Johnson** on lightning keyboards, would Chuck Berry's solo guitar and rent-a-drummer-machine have taken his act to the Paramount? Without #1-ever drummer **Jerry Allison,** could Buddy have thumped the thunder out of the Texan prairie Panhandle skies? In every Elvis Spotlight, a loyal troupe of bandmates, roadies, and session musicians toils on the sidelines. And what about the FANS that buy the records and hold the superstar careers aloft? We're all a part of this Rock and Roll adventure.

* * * * * * *

In 1995, Chuck Berry was called upon to play the opening of the Rock and Roll Hall of Fame in Cleveland, where a half-century ago or more DJ Alan Freed coined the term Rock and Roll. In 1971, he cut *San Francisco Dues* at Night Shift/Woolies' piano man Bob Baldori's Lansing (MI) Sound Studios. Since Johnnie Johnson was on temp furlough in '95, Bob backed Chuck at the gig.

Berry's R & R longevity secrets? Guzzle orange juice, and mainline (in season) peaches. The 6'2" 180# well-muscled Berry had the guts to pose TOPLESS at age 61 for his autobiography photo. Chuck always loved the fast lane, wolfing speedfood, puffing a Camel-pack per day, and zooming along in huge Detroit land yachts of indiscreet hue. First big star rocker to challenge the 3/4 century barrier, his survival skills include picking good parents (85 & 91 or so). He NEVER touches alcohol; once young Chuck watched in horror as a hapless drunk became a punching bag and butt of violent jokes, so he vowed to stay in fighting shape. Berry is the quintessential Rock survivor, patriarch of the pulsating panorama of American Rock and Roll.

Elvis. Buddy. Chuck. They WERE the 50s.

The forefathers of rock are three . . .

In the Shadow of Elvis

From the word GO, the goal of Rock and Roll was to BE ELVIS! You had to get up on the sparkling stage, negotiate a whirling blur of lights and glory, and BECOME THE KING. Since President George Washington dumped the concept of a monarch or emperor for America, we've had to earn our applause and kudos and perks with big deeds, big money, or big singing talents. With Johnny B. Goode and Horatio Alger Rags-to-Riches stories, and **Thomas Carlyle**'s (1795-1881) Scottish Anglo-American Gospel of WORK, Teen Idols sprang out of shotgun shacks like April daffodils. The term NEXT ELVIS took on a haunted and supernatural connotation, in the aftermath of Don McLean's 'Day the Music Died.' Presley himself, scorched by the hissing 'Elvis Spotlight,' was no paragon of longevity himself, like Chuck Berry or Irving Berlin. Elvis spent the next 20 years doing what everybody else in rock music was doing – trying to BE ELVIS.

For one brief shining moment, however, those golden yesteryore 50s, Elvis Presley was the most important entertainer on the planet! In some ways, perhaps he still is. Voted Entertainer of the Century in 1999, Presley is the embodiment of Vintage Rock and Roll. Besides shaking up the staid and stuffy establishment with his James Dean good looks and magnetic appeal, Elvis and his *Guitar Army* electrified the world with the clanging, jangling, booming shock waves of newly-minted, hurricane-force Rock and Roll. After half a century of amplified thunder, a few sturdy bastions of the Old Way fell by the wayside: rhythmless music, fussy gentility, and the Iron Curtain. Back in the 60s, somebody said you can convert more people to democracy with Rock and Roll than bombs or guns. "In the Long Run" (**Eagles**, *America*), maybe it worked.

Elvis, however, was no protestor. Yanked by Uncle Sam for the Yankee Army from the garish spotlight, and attired in camouflage combat fatigues with a 1959 (or current) crewcut, Elvis fit the good ol' boy soldier ideal. Although his hit-record tidal wave was 'sorta' snuffed out by the wipeout over his draft notice, the King would return to woo America and the world. Would he ever be the same? Nope. Is anything ever the same?

Round One for Elvis was the most swashbuckling fusillade of gold-hit blockbusters in the history of popular music. From his SUN Records apprenticeship and his barnstorming 1954-55 *Louisiana Hayride*, Elvis did a hitch at "Heartbreak Hotel" (#1[8], 3-56). Following his wooferiferous "Hound Dog" with double-sided #1(11), 5-56 "Don't Be Cruel," Elvis rode a #1 hit train that chugged through the 50s in champ form: "Too Much," #1(9) "All Shook Up," "Jailhouse Rock," "Love Me Tender," "Teddy Bear," "Don't," "Hard Headed Woman," "A Big Hunk O' Love," "Stuck on You," "It's Now Or Never," and "Are You Lonesome Tonight?" All big #1 songs. The only thing anywhere like it ever topped the charts at Christmastide 2000 – the **Beatles'** 27 #1 tunes finally were assembled like Elvis's Golden Records (Al. #3, 4-58); the Beatles' collection held the top album position for something like 10 weeks plus, a full three decades after their semi-amiable splitsville. For Elvis in the 50s, the Silver Medal went to everybody else. With Elvis riding the charts, the #2 spot was scrapped for by the great audial efforts of Buddy, Chuck, Jerry Lee, and the other superstars. Elvis Presley?

> ELVIS **IS** ROCK AND ROLL.

Joel Whitburn's astounding *Billboard* chart compilation *Top Pop Singles* gives the King credit. No other artist had 100+ hits on the Top 100 over the years. The 'Godfather of Soul' **James Brown,** silver medalist, chalked up an even 99 (1958-86), How about Top 40 hits? Silver medalist scores 57 (1999 Edition) – **Elton John** – with Elvis at 104! For Top Ten hits, it's a tad closer, with the **Beatles** charting 34 to Elvis's #1 36; indeed, they edge him out (20 to 18) for #1 U.S. hits, and the Most Weeks at #1 shows Elvis at 80, **Mariah Carey** (b. 3-27-70) with 61, and the Beatles at bronze with 59 weeks.

Other categories bludgeon the King's utter chart domination: Most Consecutive #1 Hits, 10 (Whitney Houston, silver with 7); Most Consecutive Top Ten Hits, 30 (Beatles 24); Most Two-Sided Hits – 52 (Beatles 2nd with half – 26); Most Gold and Platinum Hits – 53 to Fab Four's 23. No one else is even close to Sam Phillips's Memphis ex-truck-driver blockbuster King of Rock and Roll. No one dominated the charts like Elvis Presley (1935-77).

From a hardscrabble whitewashed two-room shotgun shack in Tupelo, Mississippi, Elvis soared meteorically to become the GREATEST ENTERTAINER OF ALL TIME.

In everyone's quest to become some fraction of ELVIS, many other crossroads led to destiny. Take the time Buddy Holly met Elvis at Lubbock's Cotton Club in 1955. Or the haunted Crossroads where bluesman **Robert Johnson** supposedly sold his soul to the Devil. You know, that faustian bargain down on Highway 61, snuggled down deep on the snaky midnight Delta bottomland. Home of Delta Blues.

How about other crossroads? Maybe the Big Apple's hit factory—the Brill Building? Or CBGB's Punk/New Wave birthplace down on the drizzle-dazzle neon Bowery, deep in the Village? Or maybe West Grand Boulevard and 14th Street in Detroit, where Hitsville USA/Motown burgeoned and blossomed from a garage studio and a factory forge? Or SUN Records' Memphis mecca on Union Boulevard? Or Leonard Chess's Chicago Blues spot? Or the Psychedelic springboard, Haight-Ashbury in San Francisco?

Beale Street in Memphis is just such a crossroads. Beale Street, the fertile home of the Blues, ragging craggily back to the zoot-suit saloons. On roaring Beale Street, the hot sweat singes your shoes along the beery gutter where **B.B.** [Blues Boy] **King** (b. 9-16-25) fondled the first of his many guitars named 'Lucille' into the swooning soulful bleary midnight.

Beale Street. Where Elvis walked.

The greatest Rock and Roll crossroads is out on the Slaton Highway in Lubbock, Texas. The Cotton Club. Buddy and Elvis. You pick the order.

When **Ed Sullivan** zapped Elvis's lower half on his family TV show, Elvis was already taming down; **Steve Allen** took his usual comedic way out – he had Elvis sing to a forlorn Bassett Hound on the release of his Willie Mae Thornton cover (NC, '53, but #1[7], 3-53 R & B) "Hound Dog." By 1957 (June), Elvis's #1(11) "Hound Dog" had tamed to a #1(7) "Teddy Bear." His Hard Rock "Jailhouse Rock" style subsided to Vaughn DeLeath's #4, '27 torch tune, #1(6), 11-60 "Are You Lonesome Tonight."

Though Elvis never toured abroad until drafted (March 1958-March 1960), he easily conquered the international music world, which scarfed up American Rock and Roll records as fast as the air waves could broadcast. Elvis's early Rockabilly quavering tenor deepened to operatic baritone (see Great Singers chapter) as he sailed into the 60s. El was influenced by soulster Jackie Wilson, and by labelmate Roy Orbison, whose shift to Fred Foster's Monument Records was a monumental leap of faith (#2, '60 "Only the Lonely"). Elvis emulated our FIRST big recording star – **Enrico Caruso** (1873-1921) – and released two Italian-opera bombshells in his newfound soaring Italian tenor (with spritzes of resonant baritone – a *territone?*): *"O Sole Mio"* (#3, 1908, Emilio DeGogorza) became #1(5), '60 "It's Now Or Never," and "Torna a Sorriento (Come Back to Sorrento)" became #1, 2-61 "Surrender." Disco king **Barry White** heard Elvis's 'It's Now Or Never" at a particular crossroads of his own life, deciding upon Robert Frost's 'Road Not Taken' when many of his friends had taken the thrill-ride fast-lane roads to drugs and maybe early death. When White (#18, 10-94 "Practice What You Preach") heard Elvis crank up the electrifying Italian tenor, he decided to take the best path and practice what Elvis preached – to become his own singer, a bass-baritone Disco and R & B legend. Barry chose NOW!

"It's Now Or Never" – **Elvis Presley, #1(5), 7-60.** Elvis echoes the great Operatic tenors with this Italian love song – *"O Sole Mio'* means 'O, My Sun." The song throbs to a Chalypso beat, paced with Elvis's booming *tacets* on the breaks. He is very convincing and romantic.

When Elvis served America in Germany, his mother Gladys couldn't handle the pressure, and died in Memphis at age 42 (maybe 45). The crestfallen King never recovered from the emotional onslaught. Army Elvis hadn't blanched at press mavens scribbling, or becoming Crewcut #376,759. He easily became just another soldier, a mere blip number in the greatest fighting force in all world history. He was no protestor. Of course, there was no war.

Before his induction, El commanded center stage, but his snazzy sidemen really formulated his sound. While guitarist **Scotty Moore** punched out sizzling licks on his trusty axe, **D.J. Fontana** debuted drums into Country Rock in 1954-55 Sun sessions. **Bill Black** (1926-65) invented the Slap Bass technique for his ancient stand-up bass fiddle (a/k/a 'bull fiddle' at that time). Band's comic Black danced and wrestled and argued with his lumbering double bass on stage, till Sam Phillips forbade it for the center-stage glory of Elvis. Using state-of-the-art recording innovations like Phillips' Echo Chamber, Bill Black's Combo had SIX top-20 instrumentals, like Don Rondo tune "White Silver Sands" (#9, 3-60) or his/Elvis's own "Don't Be Cruel" – #1(11) with the the King, #11, 9-60 for Black.

El's sensational songs rock on to include: #1(7), 10-57 "Jailhouse Rock," his plaintive #1(5), 1-58 "Don't"; the fastest- Rock song of all at 195 beats/minute, #1, 6-58 "Hard-Headed Woman"; #1, 7-59 "A Big Hunk O' Love," and #1(4), 4-60 comeback "Stuck on You." Among his saddest ballads is #47, 12-56 "Old Shep"; where a poor Southern kid has to shoot his dear old dying dog for want of money for the vet. Have you ever heard Elvis's loneliest dirge of all? It's #32, 2-61 "Lonely Man," a sure 1961 sign that both HOLLY DAYS and HAPPY DAZE had been terminated. Now, or never.

Hank Snow's song must be great, because Bob Dylan didn't do a lot of COVER songs (#55, 12-73 for Bob on this next Elvis item):

"(Now and Then There's) A Fool Such As I" – **Elvis Presley, #2(1), 3-59; #16, 4-59 R & B.** Hank Snow (1914-99) covered all the bases in his long life. He's alternatively listed as getting born in LIVERPOOL and BROOKLYN – but they're BOTH in Nova Scotia, Canada, north of Maine. Elvis's manager, Colonel Tom Parker, ditched managing Snow when Elvis's career hit superstardom. The song fires off a Mediant III major chord (like Key of **C**, hitting an **E major chord**), which inspired Phil Phillips' #2 '59 classic "Sea of Love." Catch the deep bass growl of the bottommost Jordanaire on the title line. A great Elvisong, tragically missing from Oldies Overkill on Oldies stations (#3, 12-52, C-only for Snow).

Hovering nearby Elvis's premier spotlight were a bunch of singers – some who sounded like Elvis (Ral Donner, **Terry Stafford** [#3, 2-64 "Suspicion" and #25, 5-64, "I'll Touch a Star"]). Some had their own sounds (Everly Brothers, Jack Scott, Little Ri-chard, Fats Domino, Johnny Cash, Conway Twitty). ALL of them rode the rep of Elvis to help them catch their shooting stars and hang on for dear career.

One group escaped the solo spotlight that Elvis and Elvis protégés had to handle all alone – the **Everly Brothers, Don** (b. 2-1-37, Brownie, Kentucky) and **Phil** (b. 1-19-39, Chicago). These two lean handsome brothers sang like the top half of an angelic Barber Shop Quartet, and blazed a gold-record trail to teen idol destiny. Of the 100+ photos I've seen of them, Don is always the one on our left as we face the photo. They are the only DUO elected on the first ballot (1st Class of '86) into the Rock Hall of Fame. With Buddy, Chuck, and Elvis. "Without Elvis," **Buddy Holly** modestly murmured in his self-effacing way, "none of us could have made it."

If anyone had the claim to being Elvis even before Elvis was Elvis, it was **Bill Haley,** backed by his Comets. The Scottish-American rocker from Jackie Wilson's Highland Park, Michigan, fractured the former quietude with his Rock anthem "Rock Around the Clock," #23 in 1954, but #1(8) a year later; Haley had already struck gold with his #7 version of Big Joe Turner's "Shake, Rattle, and Roll" (#22, 8-54 for R & B Turner, and #1[3], 5-54 R & B) in Summer 1954, and Haley hammered the fledgling Top 100 with #11, 11-54 "Dim, Dim the Lights" and #17, 3-55 "Birth of the Boogie." Without Bill fronting the Caucasian sound of roaring R & B, Elvis would have had a tougher time of it.

Like Elvis, the Everlys basically started in 1956. They rocked right into a highway-fever Scotch-Irish Bluegrass family, fronted by daddy Ike Everly – who chased LIVE Country radio and **Bill Monroe**'s Bluegrass dreams coast to coast. Kids in tow. Family show. Like "Little Miss Dynamite" Brenda Lee, or the **Jackson Five**'s pint-size cute prodigy **Michael Jackson** (b. 1958) back in 1970, or adorable moppet Gladys Knight (8) on *Ted Mack's Amateur Hour*, **Don and Phil Everly** rode the grade school gravy train. When adolescence spun their sopranos down to satin-smooth tenor (Don) and 'Irish tenor' (Phil), it was Teen Idol time.

"Keep-A Lovin' Me" debuted on February 6, 1956 by giant label Columbia Records. The big company recorded them, but downpedaled the promo for more established acts like **Guy Mitchell** or new easy-listening icons like Johnny Mathis. Cadence

Records to the rescue. Archie Bleyer, bandleader and top-shelf producer, and **Chet Atkins,** #1 Nashville session guitarist, unleashed a package of Rock and Roll energy for the Everlys – who played ACOUSTIC guitars.

They were either the vanguard of the Unplugged Generation, or two Folk singers angelically harmonizing, and displaced atop the R & R charts. Young **Simon & Garfunkel** were definitely listening, and echoing (#49, 12-57 "Hey, Schoolgirl," as 'Tom & Jerry'). Gospel harmonies blended beautifully into mainstream music. Folk melodies were blooming (see Jimmie Rodgers II's #1, '57 '57 "Honeycomb"). Parents liked the Everlys. They didn't bump and grind, they didn't look like they'd punch an innocent guy in the nose, and they faintly resembled the Boy Next Door (but were better-looking). Hits loomed, via three consecutive #1s (with huge hit flipsides):

"Bye Bye Love" – Everly Brothers, **#2(4), 5-57; #5, 6-57 R & B; #1(7), 5-57, C.** "Bye Bye Love" was victimized by Elvis's #1(9) "All Shook Up." In the with-it **Felice** and **Boudleaux Bryant** lyric, the jilted and jinxed guy claims he's all through with lovin', and with counting stars, and now he's free. Why? His girl split, and the Everly harmony cascaded into almost one glorious angelic voice at equal volume on two separate notes. Don ditches romance semi-permanently, with Phil weaving Irish tenor leprechaun magic on high '*Appalachian Thirds*' harmonies of willowy enchantment. Strumming their acoustic guitars, Don surveys stars above, but with his debut song's success (and all the concomitant new *Groupies*), he won't have to search for love on Venus or Neptune or Pluto or Goofy. Instead of so-long & sayonara happiness, his gold record guarantees some sweet willing lass to float over the Rock and Rainbow with him here on earth.

Hope she brings a friend for Phil.

"Wake Up, Little Susie" – Everly Brothers, **#1(4), 9-57; #1(1) R & B; #1(8) C.** Yep, that's right – #1 on on ALL THREE big charts. Into our supposedly enlightened era, we're a far cry from such music-genre integration – with Hip-Hop and Latino and Modern Rock Tracks and Gospel all fragmenting into melancholy solitude. IMP describes the song that smashed their 'one-hit-wonder' worries forever – "Wake Up, Little Susie," #1(4), 9-57. Not blatantly seductive like Elvis's daring #4 "One Night (with You)," nevertheless Little Susie got her cute little bod banned in Boston. Naturally, sales ricocheted off the Milky Way. Susie's ultracute song is a cameo of that (alas) wondrous 50s institution – the 'Passion Pit.' At the 1957 drive-in movie, Susie and this Everly guy totter in cinema excitement from WHOOPEE to STALE POPCORN BORING. Susie and beau snooze. Or schmooze. Or smooch. Waking up at 4 a.m., snoozy Susie and smoochy date

shudder over pal's innuendoes and her pa's temper.

Producer Archie Bleyer constructed his whole Susie classic around a cool jangling rhythm guitar riff. It's a jiffy speedmetallic jump up 1½ notes to the major and then the *Sub-Dominant IV chord*. In their guitar-friendly Key of '**A**', it's

$$A — C — A — D — C — A$$

Nifty fifties riff. The same moxie chord progression powers the Birth of Motown: **Barrett Strong**'s mammoth manifesto of materialism – "Money" (#23, 2-60, & #2(6), 1-60 R & B). In the Key of '**E**' – Bluesfolks' favorite key – you'd play:

$$E — G — E — A — G — E$$

We call this 1½-step shift a Chromatic chord change – and indicate it by a '**bIII**' designation (see Chord Theory, and/or listen to Beach Boys'#23, 4-63 drag-race fight song "Shut Down").

Meanwhile, back at Susie, Boston banned the record – insuring ultra-mega sales. Why? Either the rendezvous, the rumor, or the upcoming baby in this smoochy 4 a.m. drive-in passion scenario. Seemingly innocent, the song cleverly stirred up libidos and sales.

"All I Have to Do Is Dream" – Everly Brothers, **#1(5), 4-58; #1(5) R & B; #1(3) C.** Everly apex on the charts. This smooth romantic ballad somehow topped the RHYTHM & BLUES charts for over a month, too. Due to its supreme excellence as a Bryant/Bryant melody, "All I Have to Do Is Dream" has surrendered some of its glory in becoming so Oldies-Overkill overplayed that the dreaded '**M**'-word – Muzak – has rendered the poor beautiful melody a "Guilt by Oversaturation' verdict. Nevertheless, this song spins on its gorgeous simple aforementioned Chordal Descent of V — IV — IIIm — IIm — I.

In Key of 'C', that would be:

$$G7 — F — Em — Dm — C$$

One of the most pristine and angelic melodies ever lovingly sculpted, "All I Have to Do Is Dream" is a wish-fulfillment fantasy song, rated PG. Seems the guy may not get the girl – but he can sure DREAM about her. Her perfect image is indistinct; she haunts his blue midnights. He needs her so much he says it nearly kills him. Yet the DREAMING will satisfy him for now. Amazing mental turnabout of resignation to satisfaction! **Glen Campbell** and Bobbie Gentry took the tremendous tune to #27 in 2-70.

"Devoted to You" – Everly Brothers, **#19, 8-58; #7, 9-58 C.** **Astonishing** magical melody. Profound. Reverent. **Riveting**. "Devoted to You" is one of the sweetest pure melodies ever discovered. As music theorists grumble about the shameful loss of MELODY (**all** generations believe this, as they age), we need only to turn to "Devoted to You" to set the standard for an eternal love song with a spellbinding tune. Or, in the Everly's case – TWO melodies. Interwoven. Inextricable. Gorgeous.

Third of this trilogy of Everly ballad masterpieces is #40, 11-58, "Love of My Life." Cherubic vocals mesh with ringing guitars, and the tremolo trails off into dreams of hope and glory and evermore love.

"Bird Dog" – Everly Brothers, #1(1), 8-58; #196)
C. Don & Phil did comedy, too. A "Bird Dog" is a so-called 'friend' who horns in on his pal's girlfriend. Culprit 'Johnny' kisses up to the teacher to fudge the seating chart so Johnny can sit next to our hero's girl. Verbal pokes, jabs, & sucker punches. The Everlys term Johnny as a 'joker,' but grouse that this BIRD DOG might be a birdbrain who flies too close to the classroom cutie. Sometimes comedy songs had answer songs or offshoots. Folk music generally ignored the Rock scene, but this next tale is a direct echo and a spiffy allusion to the Everly-style melodic charm:

"Everglades" – Kingston Trio, 10-60. "Everglades" (semi-direct EVERLY reference) is a lampoon of the Everly sound – rendered in acoustic baritone and buttressed by banjos. Bob Shane, Nick Reynolds, and Dave Guard sing of a fugitive consigned to Floridian life imprisonment for killing a man in a fight. He boldly escapes jail. He bumbles into the snake-slimy, skeeter-strewn swamp the EVERGLADES. Somehow, he survives YEARS of frantic flight. A second jury determines (no Capital Punishment, 1958) he was semi-innocent via self-defense.

On the Everly-echo fadeout, the Trio even mentions them by name, rhyming 'trees' with 'Everlys' in another vivid example of a candidate for First Folk-Rock hit record.

The Everly Brothers charted 38 hits. Good friends with Buddy Holly, they welcomed the remaining **Crickets** (Jerry Allison, Joe B. Mauldin, and Sonny Curtis) for their 1959 sessions in the aerial aftermath of Holly's untimely departure. Their #4, 8-59 "('Til) I Kissed You" featured the percussive magic of Allison. Songsmith Sonny wrote their next monster hit they all cut (yep, the Everly Brothers PLUS the Crickets), Sonny never got time to write a second verse because they loved the first so much and cut it twice. "Walk Right Back" hit #7, 2-61. Other Everly cameos? Songwriter and budding superstar **Roy Orbison's** song about his wife "Claudette"(#30, 5-58); #7, 1-60 "Let It Be Me" (#5 cover in 9-64 by 'Iceman' Jerry Butler and Betty Everett); and pleading #16, 3-59 "Take a Message to Mary."

Million-dollar recording contracts may be a dime a dozen today, but the Everlys were the first, signing with Warner Brothers in 1960, and practically CREATING their record division. [Michael Jackson may have signed a BILLION-dollar contract]. The Everlys now had to WRITE their own hits, as their Bryant songwriting connection was tied into their old label Cadence. Though their chart numbers were still wildly successful, chart domination subsided.

Ironically, their first Warner salvo tied their "Dream" tune at #1 five weeks. "Cathy's Clown" [#1(5), 4-60] relies on vocalic expertise rather than pristine melody or ultra-catchy lyrics. Their Hook is that each Everly hits the 'word' LOVE on the same note, but Phil holds the note, while Don descends in a clever curl of melismas. This ginchy gimmick sold gold. The Warner hit train chugged: #8, 5-60 "When Will I Be Loved? (#2[2], 4-75 **Linda Ronstadt**); #7, 9-60 forlorn-mood ballad "So Sad'; 'Graveyard Rock' plane-crash tragedy "Ebony Eyes" (#8, 1-61), and #6, 1-62 "Crying in the Rain." Their final top-ten experience

was #9, 5-62 "That's Old Fashioned."

By 1984, their Albert Hall comeback concert offered #50, 9-84 "On the Wings of a Nightingale," written by their admirer **Paul McCartney**.

In 1957, Everly appeal was instant. With their wholesome mugs adorning purses and poodle skirts, make-up cases and wallets, they brought long hair and hearty smiles into American hearts. Everlys smiled from balloons and ballrooms and bumperstickers. No one would expect one of their kids from their R & R dynasty would marry **Axl Rose** of **Guns 'N Roses**, himself one of the best tenors in the Heavy Metal genre. Erin Everly and Axl discovered bittersweet bliss and blisters, and Insta-Divorce.

To this day, however, the Everly Brothers represent the very best of melodic magnificence, and the only 'Double-Elvis' act in this Elvis Shadow chapter. They challenged the King on his own hit turf, and briefly almost won. From a personal standpoint, though I never met an Everly, they taught me everything I ever learned about HARMONY (when as a 14-year-old I did the dishes every other night by my teen-tiny turntable). Before rampant multi-tracking techniques turned four-track studios into 256-track monsters with shimmering neon dials spun by nobody-home dimwits, the Everly Brothers wrote the book on basic tenor harmony. [For a rare Everly BARITONE item, check out Don's solo 1972 Kris Kristofferson "Somebody Nobody Knows" – Don hits the 'Ab' deep into the Bass Clef, 1 1/3 octaves below Middle 'C']. Like **Johnny Mathis's** breathtaking love song "The Twelfth of Never," (#9, 10-57), Everly songs throb with the most important thing in music – LOVE.

Their forever promises of "Devoted to You" are not for love wimps. He vows never to hurt her, or lie, or cheat, or do anything to make her sad (cynics here might consult Dionne Warwick's #19, 11-68 "Promises, Promises"). In this sunnyfest of Everly empathy, however, he declares he'd be unhappy if she felt blue. Wow. It doesn't get much deeper than that. Love will endure, for a song.

Everly imitators? We haven't really done the Elvis imitators yet. **Simon & Garfunkel** we mentioned, and they get a big section later. As 'Tom and Jerry,' the Queens teens (north of Brooklyn) hit with #49, 12-57 'Hey Schoolgirl,' a 'platter' as rare as green-haired Headbangers at a 1949 Polkafest. Two dual duos coming up:

"It Was I" – Skip & Flip, #11, 6-59. Clyde 'Skip' Battin and Gary 'Flip' Paxton harmonized Everlyesque rock from their University of Arizona. Skip later hit #1(1), 5-60 with quasi-RAP tune about caveman comic strip, "Alley Oop."

"Tell Him No" – Travis & Bob, #9, 3-59; #21, 4-59 R & B. Travis Pritchett and Bob Weaver (Jackson, Alabama), harmonize Country Rock sound of the Everlys.

Little Richard Penniman's (b. 12-5-32) late-60s non-hit "I'm the King of Rock and Roll" may sound like wild braggadocio, but hey – his career preceded Elvis and Buddy and Jerry Lee. Maybe he really DOES have a claim to royalty. In the 50s, almost everyone was trying to BE ELVIS. One exception: sometimes Elvis, musically, was trying to be Little Richard; anyhow, one of the greatest Little Richard echoes of all time is **Paul McCartney.** Richard attacked the piano, the stage, and the limelight with 300-megaton atomic paroxysms of pure Rock and Soul. Quivering with the 12-Bar Blues Fever and Boogie Woogie Obsession, Richard defined the Screaming Blues style. A fired-up phalanx of four saxguys blatted the rasp razzmatazz, clad in baggy Bermuda shorts. Little Richard caught his breath and bounded back onto his Rock and Roll battlefield in full command of his troops. **Jimi Hendrix** once played lead guitar for Richard, but was let go because of his flashy threads – Richard wanted to be the ONLY guy to stand out. Richard preened and pranced and pounced. In a suit baggy as Gangsta Rap pants, the Raspmaster Extraordinaire flaunted a processed hairdo five inches high (and at six feet, the name LITTLE hardly computed). Little Richard's vocal arsenal contained state-of-the-art fireworks. He does Yodel Kicks**,** where the last tiny chunk of a singer's syllable hits an instant falsetto high note that quickly disappears. Rasp Screams are high gravelly growlish shrieks of uninhibited magnitude, and Richard rampages, raspily. He is a master of the MELISMA, beating **Mariah Carey** to the 16th-note or grace note punch by 35 years (in all fairness, true 'Irish Tenor' **John McCormack** [1883-1945] employed this technique magnificently, as do many Grand Opera singers). Little Richard spins and circles and skirts notes, nailing as many as seven on one quickie syllable.

Born in 1932 in Macon, Georgia, Richard nabbed an RCA contract in 1951 via his hyperactive imitations of New Orleans' RuPaul-style singer Esquerita. In 1951, the sleepy postwar planet wasn't ready for atomic Richard just yet. After signing with Specialty Records, he crunched the Big Time a month before Elvis, debuting with #17, 1-56 "Tutti-Frutti" (#2[6] R & B, covered to #12, 1-56 by Rock Crooner **Pat Boone** [b. 6-34]). It's an energetic ode to Italian ice cream that mixes all the flavors, like Rock and Roll was about to do. Richard's highest Top 100 hit followed – #6, 4-56 "Long Tall Sally" (but #1[8] R & B), about a shifty gal with the hots

for 'Uncle John' (#8, Boone, w/PG-lyrics). Backalley rendezvous. When 'Aunt Mary' arrived, this 'John' ducked surreptitiously back into his secret alley. "Keep A-Knockin'" (#8, 9-57, #2 R & B) hammered the Richard rapscallion rep, and covers two pugilistic ex-lovers separated from fisticuffs by a locked door (that she won't open).

Mitch Ryder (b. '45, Detroit) **and the Detroit Wheels** gave 60s fans a shot of vintage Richard with their double-barrelled Heartland Rockers: Richard's #10, 2-58 "Good Golly Miss Molly" combined for Mitch & Wheels with "Devil with a Blue Dress On" to #4, 10-66. Richard's original Miss Molly does wild things to elude the 50s Censor Army.

Check it out. Richard's #10, 6-57 "Jenny, Jenny" (#2 R & B) metamorphosed as #10, too, in Mitch's 12-65 "Jenny Take a Ride"; it also cameos (like Rappers sampling other songs) **Chuck Willis**'s #12 4-57 "C.C. Rider," an old Blues classic. Ryder's fire-frothing forge White Soul interpreted Richard in a Screaming Blues style Pat Boone never attempted. Ryder battled the gray snowcrust saltscum gutters of crusty ice in Motown. In the 50s, however, anybody who was anybody honed their Rock and Roll pipes on the hallelujah Hollers of vintage **Little Richard**: Elvis (Richard's #17, 7-56 "Rip It Up"), Pat Boone, Buddy Holly ("Reddy Teddy"), the Everlys (#21, 3-57 "Lucille"), and later the Beatles ("Long Tall Sally"), via Paul's amazing second-gear Screaming Blues high tenor.

"Miss Ann" – Little Richard, #56, 7-57; #6, 6-57 R & B. ANN was an actual sweet matronly white lady who helped raise Little Richard. She taught many of us munchkin boppers all we ever needed to know about the Blues.

A Classic 12-Bar Blues Progression

Al Taylor taught us all the 12-Bar Blues on the church piano. He was the only African-American of our piano group: Larry Glazer, Jeff Forrest, Karl Perrin, and Ross Radke. We Five would glom an ancient creaky upright with a goofus outatune sound. We'd all make the **C chord** on separate octaves, hitting the Triad Tonic I chord of 'C – – E – G', chopping dotted-eighths and sixteenth notes in our integrated "Miss Ann" enterprise. We never sounded like Little Richard's tune very much, but it taught us all Basic Blues Progression:

From the 'C' we'd jump to the Sub-Dominant IV or 'Four Chord' (Tonic 'C' is the 'One' chord). Then we'd return to the 'C', then do a quick trip up to the Five chord, the Dominant 'G' back to the Four ['F'], and return to the One 'C', Then we'd do the 'Turnaround' 'G' and start a new verse on the same pattern. Here it is, for your piano-pounding pleasure:

C	F	C	G	F	C	G
I	IV	I	V	IV	I	V
(One)	(Four)	(One)	(Five)	(Four)	(One)	Five)
4 Measures	2 Meas.	2 Meas.	1 Meas.	1 Meas.	1Meas.	1Meas.

Now and then, we'd get fancy: hit one note of the **F#** chord as we came down from the **G to the F**, and two notes of the **Dm (D-minor) chord, or IIm (Two-minor)** between the second **F** and last **C** chords of the verse.

Like some beer ad gloated, you never forget your very first girl. Let me add – you never forget your first songs. Or your old friends.

Little Richard's "Miss Ann" pounds the same dotted-eighth/16th-note beat on his 12-Bar Blues. His magic melismas float majestically off the swaggering slow rocker. His Miss Ann calls him sweetly, she does things nobody else can, and he doesn't want to free her, because he loves her and that's that. Dynamic song.

After his 1958 chart fadeaway, Richard retired to a tripartite trio of personalities: original oldies rocker, conservative evangelical preacher, and flamboyant talk-show guest on *Oprah* or Conan O'Brien's shows. His preaching? Seems the wing wavered on a flight to Australia. Hanging gloomily over the drop edge of yonder, Richard prayed and vowed to preach the Gospel if the plane safely landed. It did. He did. Despite some alternative backsliding, Richard rocks on – one of the original 1986 Rock Hall of Fame Inductees. At 63 in 1995, he looked 42; his 3-86 "Great Gosh A'Mighty" hit #42 – and he's still rocking!

"Mannish Boy" [a/k/a "I'm a Man"] – Muddy Waters, NC, 55; #5, 7-55, R & B. Though he never had a hit on the HOT 100, Muddy Waters (born McKinley Morganfield, 1915-83) made the Rock Hall of Fame in its 2nd year ('87), due to his Blues pioneering. No Elvis imitator, Waters is simply one of the main founders of Rock and Roll – via his Chicago Blues style. Were it not for Muddy, there could have been no **Eric Clapton** as we know him. This is the MAN who named the 'World's Greatest Rock and Roll Band' – the **Rolling Stones** – from a line in THIS song AND his earlier '50 song "Rolling Stone." Born in Rolling Fork, Mississippi, on the marge of the muddy Delta, he named himself after the sodden silt of the bottomland cotton fields where he worked with forklorist **Alan Lomax** (via poet Carl Sandburg, see "Sloop John B"). Lomax found Muddy working cotton by Highway 61.

Muddy was born April 4, 1915 [ironically the date Dr. King was slain in Memphis exactly 53 years later]. Muddy nailed down his nickname with a $10 acoustic guitar he flashed at fish fries. In 1943 he ventured north – like **Louis Armstrong** – to Chicago to seek his musical fortune. He met **Leonard Chess**, and formed his famous Blues band. Even during the 50s, when Waters serenaded the smoke and steel and dark gray snow of howling February Chi-

cago, his slew of Top Ten R & B cult classics barely put juice in his amp – so Muddy sunlighted (opposite of *moonlighted*) at a clanking paper mill.

"I'm a Man" was also songwriter-credited to fellow Delta Blues icon **Bo Diddley**, who hit #1(2) on the R & B charts (only) in 5-55 with it. Muddy's best recording of this seminal Blues classic (also see **Eric Clapton/Jeff Beck's Yardbirds**, #17, 10-65 "I'm a Man") is off his #143 Al. 2-77 *Hard Again*. It stars some of the best multicultural bluesmen in 72 galaxies: albino virtuoso **Johnny Winter** and Bob Margolin on guitars, plus the inimitable **Pine Top Perkins** on piano.

Margolin helped the 80+ Perkins to the stage, and told me of his days with Muddy as he now backed Muddy's son Bill Morganfield. A whole generation of British and American Rock and Blues pioneers owe their lifeblood to the macho swagger of Muddy's masterpiece here. The Chicago Blues superstar blasts his leaping libido to a multitude of women waiting in line for his amorous attentions. "Mannish Boy" is the fountainhead of kick-butt Blues and rockin' Soul. In the Shadow of Elvis, Muddy Waters defined his own destiny, and himself became the Father of Electric Blues.

"The Twelfth of Never" – Johnny Mathis, #9, 10-57, NC R & B. Speaking of Un-Elvis, we have singer's singer **Johnny Mathis** (b. 9-30-35, San Francisco). From his early Gospel hymns ("Ave Maria," "Deep River" in #10, 4-58 Al. *Good Night, Dear Lord*) to his smooth, romantic ballads ("12th of Never's" #1 flipside "Chances Are"), Johnny Mathis is a musical GENRE unto himself. From his scholar-athlete origins (basketball and Olympian-potential California high-jump champion) in high school, Mathis shaped his most extraordinary gift – his celestial voice, to become one of the most incredible entertainers of all time. Though his style reflects the 40s Crooning era, he adds a further dimension of intricate melismas, effortless baritone-to-falsetto shifts, tremulous tremolo, and operatic tenor power. "The Twelfth of Never" is a long shot for the prettiest song of all time. But it's got a prayer.

The piano dances on Tonic arpeggios, toying with the Streetcorner Chord Pattern seemingly at first. Johnny shuffles roses and the snows of April (like Bette Midler's #3, 3-80 "The Rose"). He brings in poets with writer's block, and unscented flowers, to show that his LOVE transcends anything so fleeting as these earthly items. Love is eternal. His love will stand, literally, until the twelfth of never. On the Bridge, he shoots into Irish tenor range, booming his undying love into summers of immortality.

This is not a song. It is a romantic adventure. Don't miss it. It is to be cherished.

Albums. Yes. **Johnny Mathis.** Over forty years, his albums have dominated the charts. We do singles mostly here, but we can't ignore the Mathis magic touch at 33 1/3 rpm. Among the Top 500 Artists in Joel Whitburn's *Top Pop Albums 1955-96*:

1)	Elvis Presley	15,538
2)	Frank Sinatra	12,766
3)	The Beatles	10,918
4)	**JOHNNY MATHIS**	**10,072**

5) Barbra Streisand   9,207

Johnny Mathis, we see, barely missed the bronze Olympic medal for albums, getting edged out by the Fab Four. His 5-96 Al. *All About Love* highlights 40% of a century cruising the Album charts. A consummate professional singer, Johnny Mathis helped CREATE an entire generation with his ultraromantic mood music. Johnny's 45 charted 45s and his two #1s ("Chances Are" and 4-78's DeNiece Williams duo "Too Much, Too Little, Too Late") show that the Mathis magic dominates decades of popular romantic song.

Though "The Twelfth of Never" may be his prettiest melody, you could make a case for many of his other rare, poignant gems sculpted by top Tin Pan Alley Afterglow songsmiths. Lush Jazz arrangements, muted minors, 11th or 9th or Diminished Chords, and silky strings highlight the Mathis magic. We don't just look for three chords and a cloud of guitarfire dust.

How about his beach-strolling odyssey, debut "Wonderful Wonderful" (#14, 2-57), in the magic year that brought us **Buddy Holly, the Everly Brothers, Jerry Lee Lewis, Sam Cooke,** the Dell Vikings, Jimmie Rodgers II, or Buddy Knox & the Rhythm Orchids? Also, it was **Elvis's** second monster year for sales. Intricate mellow-mood "It's Not for Me to Say" (#5, 5-57, NC R & B), a delicate ballad, toys with a lilting crescendo and wafts to sonorous glory. Johnny's "All the Time" (#21, 4-58) flirts with *Polynesian and Chromatic Chord Patterns* that Rock barely comprehended (see Buddy Holly/Norman Petty's "What to Do" or "Moondreams") in 1958. Here Mathis showcases the pulsating power of his baritone range. Years before **Del Shannon** and **Frankie Valli** and **Jimmy Jones** fractured the silence with their soaring FALSETTOS, **Mathis** cruised the high notes – effortlessly gliding between soft Irish tenor and wispy falsetto, with never a vocal speed-bump. Had Mathis decided to cut Rock and Soul of the more common ilk, he could have done so magnificently. Later, *Gold Rush* does a Great Singers chapter with a focus on the early 60s. Consider Johnny Mathis a member of that chapter, even though we place him here, for the calendar's sake, since his superstardom surfaced in 1957. Later we'll do his closest thing to Rock: Cole Porter/Artie Shaw's "Begin the Beguine," from 2-79, #122 Al. *The Best Days of My Life*) – which previews the 1999-2001 Latino Explosion. Premier balladeer of the 50s, 60s, and 70s, Johnny still plays gargantuan sold-out arenas worldwide. Gliding beyond 65, the former prep track star could easily pass for 45, his number of charted singles. And SINGLES were his second-string career for this ALBUM KING.

Through the moonlit magic of Mathis's murmuring make-out music, millions of future Rock and Roll (or Easy Listening/Adult Contemporary) fans may have been created. Moments of real togetherness accompanied Johnny's spirited lullabying of #22 's 12-57 "Wild Is the Wind" and 2-58 "Come to Me," or #21's 4-58 "All the Time" and 9-58 "Call Me." Or the impeccable musical majesty of #12, 10-59 "Misty" or #9, 1-63 "What Will Mary Say." Or his silver-medal for beauty to "The Twelfth of Never" – #30, 5-63 "Every Step of the Way". On squeaky porch

swings, or dumped into coalsmoke yester-basements beneath the smoldering furnace of desire, and beneath Aunt Maud's Victoria's-Secret rejects dangling damply from the frayed clotheslines, new life began. Thanks to Johnny Mathis and his magnificent Mr. Mellow murmurings! When half a century of American smoochers heard the clock strike Lucky Thirteen O'Clock on the Twelfth of Never, the passionate call came out for 'Herrrrre's Johnny!!! ...

Why Jimmy around with success?

"Just a Dream" – Jimmy Clanton, #4, 7-58; #1(1) R & B. Jimmy Clanton (b. 9-2-40, Baton Rouge, Louisiana) is a Teen Idol who thundered out of the swirling forge of Cosimo Matassa's New Orleans hit-machine studio. Clanton's *Blue-Eyed Soul* teamed with fellow Caucasian **Frankie Ford's** (b. '39) thunder-beat "Sea Cruise" (#14, 2-59, #11 R & B). It sports more Yodel-Kicks than any other hit of the era. Jimmy's brother Ike Clanton played bass with **Duane Eddy's** (#6, 6-58 "Rebel-'Rouser") Rockin' Rebels. Jimmy paced a mostly Soul contingent at Matassa's along star-studded skyways: Huey 'Piano' Smith & the Clowns' ("Rockin' Pneumonia & Boogie-Woogie Flu" – #52, 8-57, #5 R & B); Clarence 'Frogman' Henry (#4, 2-61 "But I Do"); and **Lloyd Price** ("Stagger Lee" – #1[4], 12-58).

Jimmy epitomized the Teenage Idol: perfect ultrathick waterfall hair, cascading down to Windex blue eyes, dimpled shy smile, throbbing tenor voice – and just 17. Great bandmates sculpted Jimmy's sound, with Afro-American Soul and Roll. Heart of Mississippi Delta Blues. Clanton's trumpet-toned tenor whooshed up the fickle charts with Summer 1958's #4 "Just a Dream" (#1 R & B, too). Clanton pleads plaintively with the ex-girlfriend to flee his feverish memory and tortured dreams in this debut hit. "Go Jimmy Go""(#5, 12-59, #19, 1-60 R & B) and "Venus in Blue Jeans" (#7, 8-62) highlighted Jimmy's career: His Aegean dungaree doll's tune is festooned with saxes, and was penned by the Tokens' own Teen Idol, Brill Building melody builder **Neil Sedaka** (b. '39, Brooklyn). Sedaka scored multiple big hits himself: #4 12-60 "Calendar Girl," #11, 5-61 "Little Devil," and #1(2) "Breaking Up Is Hard to Do" of 6-62 (and slow version to #8, 12-75). A melody maestro, and wordsmith of metaphorical savvy, bouncy-Rock Sedaka also clicked with #9, 10-59 "Oh, Carol," for his Brill Building friend **Carole King,** plus #6, 11-61 "Happy Birthday, Sweet Sixteen" and #5, 10-62 "Next Door to an Angel."

Jimmy's "Just a Dream" symbolizes adolescent longing and furtive fantasy: Cosimo Matassa picked the right method—blend a clean-cut Teen Idol with dynamite multicultural session stars. Clanton's cherubic smile and Matassa's Birth of Rock epicenter united to skyrocket the lad to power and glory. Propelling the bridge with a wondrous wail, Jimmy drives the internal tacet with pure thunder. Earl King's flourish on lead guitar, and Huey 'Piano' Smith's hammering triplets on piano, complement the booming bass drum that drones poor Jimmy's romantic Disaster Area – and record-selling triumph. The climax of the Bridge finds Jimmy free-falling ["Free Falling," #7, 11-

89, Tom Petty/Heartbreakers]. He plummets back to the third verse, sadder, wiser, and richer.

"Just a Dream" throbs with the usual romantic teen torment. Despite their hot fling's afterglow, he can't dump her iridescent image from his 'mournful' reverie. He carts her photo everywhere (bikini?), doomed to eternal misery if she won't come back. To teens everywhere and anytime, such burning obsessions don't make growing up any easier. Clanton paves the way for the 3-minute angst adventures of Great Singer **Roy Orbison** (1936-88), whose #2, '61 "Crying" and #2 '60 "Only the Lonely" defined the forlorn Isolato, singing his Blues to the sky, and thereby sharing the true meaning of music – an expression of deepest, most sincere, emotions. And, hopefully, love.

"Just a Dream" epitomizes everybody's Rock and Roll aspirations. Clanton was a very real teen idol. With a wash of seaswept New Orleans White Soul, Jimmy's tenor hugged the high notes and pulsated the hot center of unrequited teenage love. All of us rookie guitar-slingers (without varsity letters) jumped onto Jimmy's "Just a Dream" bandwagon. We tried our level best to hit his high notes without cracking voices and crumbling egos.

Lee Allen plays tenor sax, leading a horn section to blow the sox off anybody's doomed quietude and former serenity. Jimmy Clanton ROCKED. He pioneered multicultural Rock and Soul – like the Marcels, the Dell Vikings, Hootie and the Blowfish, or the **Dave Matthews Band**.

Clanton's forte was ballads. With crying saxes and aching bass drums, Jimmy tossed and turned through #22, 4-60 "Another Sleepless Night." Squeezed between twilight and dawn, this hit inspired the #1 song of 1961, **Bobby Lewis**'s #1(7), 4-61 [#1(10), R & B] "Tossin' and Turnin'." Jimmy's #33, 8-59 "My Own True Love" – melodic theme from *Gone with the Wind* (1937***½) – wafts magnolia memories and golden horns. It inspired the super Staten Island sound of **Joey Vann & the Duprees**' #89, 3-63 "Gone with the Wind." Jimmy's first big rocker was #5, 12-59 (#19 R & B) "Go Jimmy Go" – a song very hard to cover if your name isn't JAMES. I chased Jimmy's torch tune #63 "Come Back" for 35 years, and it finally came back on a Clanton compilation. In the 70s, Clanton did a disc jockey stint in Amish-country Lancaster, Pennsylvania. In *Gold Rush*, many great artists dwell – as yet untapped for the Rock Hall of Fame into 2002 or so. Along with **Bobby Vee, Neil Diamond, Bob Seger, the Crickets (w/o Buddy Holly)**, or **Connie Francis, Jimmy Clanton** is a great candidate.

Competing with Elvis and Ricky Nelson in the movie-star LOOKS department wasn't easy, but Clanton challenged. Jimmy was a very big star. Not quite Elvis – but he had half as many charted hits as Chuck Berry. After his DJ stage, he became a Texas rancher, not unlike President George W. Bush's 90s career. After a long hiatus, Jimmy Clanton returned to the big-arena stage for a 12-1-96 benefit for Hall of Fame Rock diva **LaVern Baker** in a Richard Nader Productions extravaganza at Nassau Coliseum on Long Island. Topped with thick silvering hair, Clanton looks and sings better than ever.

Jimmy Clanton, 1959

Everybody from 2000+ Punk Rockers to Arkansas truck drivers knows **Johnny Cash** is a country legend. He's a national treasure, too. Few know Cash was a Teen Idol who marched in the footsteps of Elvis at their own break-out record outfit – Sun Records of Memphis, Tennessee. Johnny's trademark "I Walk the Line" (#7, 9-56, #1[6] C), is STILL a cult classic. His biggest 50s hit "Guess Things Happen That Way" (#11, 5-58, #1[8] C) puts anybody's humpty-dumpty self-image back together fast.

Beyond the ashes of crash and burn romance, Johnny just sings his lean, spare songs. No melismas, yodeling, or falsetto. Nothing fancy. His big-echo bass and/or low baritone skims over details and cuts to the chase. It's a John Wayne macho approach to a song, garnished with Wayne's wry sardonic humor. Johnny vacillates from gruff and macho to teddy-bear funny (#2, '69, "A Boy Named Sue"). Grunge and Punk Rockers and Headbanger Metal crews worship Johnny Cash as an early archetype, garbed in midnight ebony, and fanning the fervent flames of pure vintage Rockabilly from the bass-clef perspective. Cash commandeers our Country chapter. Early Rock and Country music weren't that far apart. They still aren't.

"Ballad of a Teenage Queen" – Johnny Cash, #14, 2-58; #1(10), 1-58 C. Big John (6'2, 210#) tells bittersweet saga of teenage girl dreaming of becoming a movie star. **Johnny B. Goode's** America has always cherished the Rags-to-Riches dreams. And dreamers. Sometimes, starwishers find their dreams actually do come true.

"Home of the Blues" – Johnny Cash, #88, 10-57; #3, 9-57 C. Masterpiece of Cash and his Tennessee Two (Luther Perkins, guitar, Marshall Grant, 'slap' bass). Reprises Elvis's "Heartbreak Hotel" mournful lyric, but big beat drives like a locomotive (maybe Johnny's #80, 2-65 & 3 C. "Orange Blossom Special)." The bass thunders, and Cash's deep echo plies the Stygian lyrical waters of love-gone-bad gloom and desolation. **Bobby Vee**'s brother Bill Velline (d. 1997) did a great 9-60 vocal echo of Johnny Cash on Bobby/Bill & the Shadows' "Leave Me Alone."

This "Home of the Blues" is dastardly damp. Cash hyperbolizes that pals will have to WADE in because of the teardrops. The place is so dark it's always NIGHT despite the grubby windows. He concludes on a basic truth about love, and one good reason for bartenders beyond the drinks served – 'misery loves company,' so sufferers assuage their collective pain.

Bobby Darin (1936-73), born Walden Robert Cassotto in Manhattan, stormed the ladder of Rock and Jazz, becoming Elvis AND Frank Sinatra all at once for one brief shining moment. Ambassador of all Rock styles: Folk, Hard Rock, Ballads, Adult Contemporary, Jazz, Popular Standards. To dive into the fray, Bobby said he wrote this item in 12 minutes:

"Splish Splash" – Bobby Darin, #3, 6-58; #1(2), 7-58 R & B. Guy in bathtub hears nearby wild party. Interrupted like comic-strip Dagwood, he dons towel, checks out scene, and puts on dancing shoes (hopefully t-shirt & pants, too).

"Dream Lover" — Bobby Darin, #2(1), 4-59; #4, 5-59 R & B. Chalypso breezer halfway up Bobby's 3-2-1 ascent to the top spot. Don't miss the perfectly plucked *pizzicato* guitar and its muted rhythm blanket that surrounds this fantasy tune. Bobby wooed and won sweet Gidget-star Sandra Dee (see *Grease*) by conjuring up this pedestal princess. Or by adding sweet sounds like this next one to their romantic soundscape:

"Sail Along Silvery Moon" – Billy Vaughn & Orchestra, #5, 12-57. One of the prettiest trombone tunes of all time. The red-crewcutted bandleader (says Whitburn) had more charted hits than any other orchestra leader in the entire Rock Era. Like Johnny Mathis, his suave smooth tunes were a prelude to romance. Vaughn also waltzed to #2(1) with 12-54 "Melody of Love." Also did gorgeous #20, 8-58 "La Paloma."

"Mack the Knife" – Bobby Darin, #1(9), 8-59; #6, 9-59 R & B. Contractual cover-up forced Bobby's second hit "Early in the Morning" (#24, 7-58, and #32 for **Buddy Holly)** to be credited to 'Rinkydinks.' Darin covered **Louis 'Satchmo' Armstrong's** #20, 2-56 cover of "Mack." Tune is pianist/bandleader's Dick Hyman's #8 instrumental "Theme from the Three-Penny Opera (Moritat)," written in 1928. By 1959, the multiple-titled song became all Bobby Darin.

If anybody could out-Sinatra **Frank Sinatra** at his Ultimate Coolth best, young Bobby did it here. Let's take a quick look at just whom Darin et al are celebrating.

For those folks disgruntled over blood & guts violence from video games to Gangsta Rap, let's check out this wannabe hero 'Mack the Knife' – he's a **hit man** who needs no National Rifle Association to bless his sharp weapon. In crescendo Jazz Rock fashion, Darin points out Mack's miserable murder methods: cement shoes, outslashing sharks, and scarlet billows oozing down stinking gutters. Mack is no saint indeed. His victims? Louis Miller, Jenny Diver, Lotte Lenya, Suky Tawdry. And elderly Lucy Brown. LOTTE LENYA, bizarrely, was the actual wife of songwriter Kurt Weill.

Billy Vaughn took "Mack the Knife"/"Moritat" to #37 in 1956, with North Dakota bandleader **Lawrence Welk** notching #17. Even solid-body guitar inventor **Les Paul** hit #49 with it in 1956, and Richard Heyman (not Hyman) snared the #11 spot. **Hyman** played a gorgeous piano that sounded very much like the Clavichord of Johann Sebastian Bach. Fascinatingly, the only other version to cover "Mack the Knife" in Darin's latter-day 1959 was the gracious lady Joel Whitburn tabs the "greatest Jazz singer of all time" – **Ella Fitzgerald** (#27, 5-60) – a year after Darin's version womped the competition for over two months, tied for 18th-longest #1 in the Rock Era). Bobby's ultra-cool version also builds from Dixieland Jazz (see Kenny Ball) in its rise to a towering crescendo. Darin's spectacular vocal swoop of Territone (wedged between tenor and baritone) seems perfectly built for a chic Las Vegas orchestral arrangement. Though tempered with Rock and Roll rhythms, Bobby's "Mack" seems inextricably wedged into the Jazz heritage of Tommy/Jimmy Dorsey, Benny Goodman, Harry James, Ted Weems, Artie Shaw, or Les Brown and His Band of Reknown {#1[9] 3-45 "Sentimental Journey"). Bobby's "Mack" builds with a Satchmo rasp in Bobby's narrative. He conjures key Jazz inflections with just a hint of Gangsta growl. The antihero hitman MACK skulks all over Gotham, offing innocent victims. Miller takes out his bankroll and disappears. Others pursue various fated routes to their dastardly doom. No matter how he cuts it, Slasher Mack cannot be misconstrued as a nice guy.

Darin's signature song was so flawless, so tight, so climactic, that it had to take only the virtuosity of **Ella Fitzgerald** to dare cover his tune in the Rock Era. No one else, perhaps, had the expertise. Amazingly, Mr. Versatility Darin could record just as expertly in the sidelong fields of: Folk (#8, 9-66 Tim Hardin's "If I Were a Carpenter"); 100% Rock (#9, 10-58 "Queen of the Hop"); International Jazz (#45, 5-64 Edith Piaf's "Milord"), Gospel or

Seasonal (#24, '58 "Early in the Morning," #51, 12-60 "Christmas Auld Lang Syne"); and Latin-based Chalypso:

Bobby Darin
Rock/Jazz/Standards/Folk Star

"18 Yellow Roses" – Bobby Darin, #10, 5-63; #28, 7-63 R & B. This harmonic ballad plots the plight of a seemingly stood-up guy wondering just why 1½ dozen roses arrived for the girl in his home. You ponder their relationship. Darin sounds 58 years old in the song. A boy arrives at his door, and Bobby's speechless. In his nifty O. Henry surprise ending, you discover the roses are for his daughter. You knew HE loved her, and you wonder about a tragic love triangle. When you find out she's his KID, you breathe a sigh of relief, and juggle whether or not the young beau has plans to get a ring for her.

In Steve Martin's(or Spencer Tracy's) *Father of the Bride* (1991***½, and way back in the 50s) poor Pop was the last to know. Our daughter Lauri recently married Larry, and yep, I bought her 18 yellow roses and sang her the Chalypso Darin song. Darin's heart-tugging coda? A dad's love, like Buddy Holly's Blues belter, will "Not Fade Away."

Darin's lucky star was brief, like Buddy's. Both born in 1936, Holly's tragic aerial accident was a portentous prelude to Darin's own untimely calling – of natural causes [fatal cardiac mis-beat, on operating table, age 37 (1973)]. The two were the most versatile artists in the 50s – and for Bobby, thirteen fateful years beyond (see Bobby's stunning Jazz ballad "Beyond the Sea" – #6, 1-60, later in *Gold Rush*).

New York City was never rinkydink on Rock and Soul talents. A myriad of Barber Shop Streetcorner Quartets serenaded the sundown streetlights from the cobblestones of the Bronx and Brooklyn and Queens and Staten Island and naturally Manhattan. Or Jersey, Westchester, and Long Island.

"One Summer Night" – Danleers, #7, 6-58; #4, 7-58 R & B. Jimmy Weston (d. '93) and his Brooklyn R & B streetcorner serenaders sweetly spun this slow-dance magic teen anthem to a nation of romantic couples. For one magic summer, the Danleers' sole Soul hit took over all the AM radio waves of America.

"Could This Be Magic?" – Dubs, #23, 11-57; NC R & B. Big Apple transcendent experience, starring Richard Blandon (d. '91). Subway-echo glories, that **Larry Chance & Earls** celebrate in #24, 12-62 "Remember Then." "Magic" is among most cherished of Sock Hop Splendor songs. Silvertone tenor floating on high . . . sterling vocal blend.

"A Thousand Miles Away" – Heartbeats, #53, 12-56; #96, 11-60; #5, 11-56 R & B. James 'Shep' Sheppard's (murdered '70, on LIE Expressway) slow-dance masterpiece. Lovers from concrete-canyoned Manhattan, who hadn't ever journeyed five subway stations away, now dreamed of lone and limitless distances of starry mountain vastness and painful separation. A thousand miles vanished, and Sheppard (with Clarence Bassett & Charles Baskerville) enjoyed a triumphant homecoming:

"Daddy's Home" – Shep & the Limelites. #2(1), 3-61; #4, 4-61 R & B. Daddy returns to stay? As in Darin's "18 Yellow Roses," the concept of DADDY is puzzling. Is he dear old Dad? Big Daddy? Sugar Daddy? Anyhow, she welcomes him back from his 1000 or 2000-mile sojourn. Limelite harmonies interweave nostalgically. A renaissance of sweet romance blooms on a gray/brownstone smudged street of timeworn stoops and mangy-dog gutters. Shep's NYC sidewalks could be **Dan Quinn's** #1(9), 2-1895 "Sidewalks of New York," or any Barber-Shop Streetcorner anywhere and anywhen, from **N'Sync, the Stylistics, Four Tops, Mills Brothers, Four Seasons, Beatles, Beach Boys, or Boyz II Men.**

"In the Still of the Nite" – Five Satins, #24, 9-56; #3 R & B. Also #81, 1-60, and #99, 1-61. Despite its sketchy Top 100 chart adventure, "In the Still of the Nite" is #1 in the hearts of Doo-Whop Streetcorner music fans everywhere. Number 24? Sometimes it takes us all awhile to truly realize a song is as great as it is. Lead singer **Fred Parris** was doing an Army stint when the song first charted, and was replaced by **Bill Baker** – who sings their even-MORE-melodic and gorgeous wedding hymn "To the Aisle" – #25, 7-57 & #5 R & B. The Streetcorner Chord Pattern dominates most of these Slow Rock/Soul classics, with or without a **Bridge.** They use **Four Chords – the I – VIm – IV – V7 pattern (or the I – VIm – IIm – V7**

pattern). Streetcorner groups are **piano-oriented—not guitar-driven—**and often followed the Keys of **C, F, or G,** rarely guitar keys like **E or A.** Typical Streetcorner keys and progressions?

		I – VIm – IV (or IIm) – V7
Key:	C	C – Am – F (or Dm) – G7
	F	F – Dm – Bb(or Gm) – C7
	G	G – Em – C (or Am) – D7
	D	D – Bm – G (or Em) – A7
	E	E – C#m – A (or F#m) – B7
	A	A – F#m – D (or Bm) – E7

Streetcorner classics like "In the Still of the Nite" differ, too, in that YOU DON'T HAVE TO BE ELVIS, all ALONE in the blazing spotlight. If our streetcorner quartets are as bad as we're hoping they aren't, we can get laughed off the stage with THREE FRIENDS who absorb 75% of the nasty yoks and guffaws aimed our way. SOLO SINGERS don't get that luxury.

"In the Still of the Nite" is the most popular doo-whop tune of all time. It promises passion, privacy, and eternity. Its smooth flow and angelic harmonies still cascade off the lost corners of bygone streetlights and broken dreams. This song is one of our collective best friends.

"Out of Sight, Out of Mind" – Five Keys, #23, 9-56; #12, 10-56 R & B. Rudy West and his Newport News (Virginia) quintet bring us a poignant Streetcorner classic, plus their Pagliacci sad-clown #35, 12-56 "Wisdom of a Fool." Perfect enunciation, lyric tenor, super songs. Sometimes great Streetcorner groups come from Texas deserts:

"Tonight (Could Be the Night)" – Velvets, #26, 5-61, N.C. R & B. High school PRINCIPAL Virgil Johnson sings lead with his STUDENTS of Odessa, Texas, in this doo-whop tune voted #11 greatest Streetcorner tune of all time in New York CITY. Though they could just as easily be Italian-American, since most great doo-whop groups are Italian or Afro, this African-American quartet spins Classic Streetcorner with the gusto of Vito:

"Unchained Melody" – Vito & the Salutations, #66, 10-63. Brooklyn's Vito Balsamo, lead falsetto, is a huge, gruff-looking guy with a heart of gold and a rooftop vibrato. Rest of quintet is all over the scale with background blanket of superfine harmonies. Far from Al Hibbler/Righteous Brothers' slow version.

"You Belong to Me" – Duprees, #7, 8-62. Jersey City presented the great Italian-American harmonies of the Duprees. They did reprises of Pop Standards like this Patti Page/Dean Martin/Jo Stafford 1952 #1 ditty. **Joni James** hits were their forte: "Have You Heard" (#18, 11-63; #4 JJ '53) and "Why Don't You Believe Me?" (#37, 8-63, #1 JJ '52). **Joey Vann** (1944-84) had a big volcanic Italian tenor like **Jerry Vale** (#14, '56, "You Don't Know Me"). Joey swashbuckled his dramatic Elvis opera tenor for a sensational two-year heyday.

Two other Italo-American Teen Idols had an even stronger claim to nearly BECOMING ELVIS (the King metamorphosed his medium brown hair to black to LOOK ITALIAN). **Dion [DiMucci]** did Elvis the Bronx way, with streetcorner serenaders the **Belmonts** and **Del-Satins. Jack [Scafone] Scott** took on the whole Elvis persona directly – from suburban Detroit – bench-pressing Buicks to boom his big baritone voice to the top of the charts with a chart oddity – a thundering WALTZ.

Dion & Belmonts borrowed their street's name (Belmont Avenue). Like **the Platters, Five Satins, Temptations, Backstreet Boys,** or **Boyz II Men,** the Belmonts are essentially a Barber-Shop Quartet/Quintet. These quartets feature a First or Irish Lyrical Tenor, a Second or Italian Dramatic Tenor, a Baritone, and a Bass – in descending order of pitch. Dion & Belmonts create morphemic masterpieces, c/o of Carlo Mastrangelo, bass, Fred Milano (Dramatic Tenor), and Angelo D'Aleo (Lyric Tenor), pioneer new areas of harmony.

"I Wonder Why" – Dion and the Belmonts, #22, 5-58. With the amazing Carlo Mastrangelo – a bass who did sensational baritone, too – Dion parleyed his resonant Italian tenor to hot hit heights, even dabbling in *falsetto* on this tune with D'Aleo four years before Frankie Valli (Castelluccio) & his Four Seasons made falsetto the name of the game. On their doo-whop tunes, they sprinkled "Did-did-did-dihs' and 'bop-be-bops' as Dion overlofted his cool-clique tenor in budding superstar form. This first hit shows them at their best. They followed up with some ultra-slow items like star-wishing Disney item #30, 4-60 "When You Wish Upon a Star" (#10, 2-40, Cliff Edwards, a/k/a 'Ukulele Ike'). Or #19, 8-58 "No One Knows" and #40, 12-58 "Don't Pity Me." On "I Wonder Why," the vocals spar and pounce, drift and soar, mesh and spin; it's a stunning example of Streetcorner Splendor.

On "I Can't Go On (Rosalie)," bass boss Carlo Mastrangelo takes over so much of the song from lead man Dion that it's nearly a *Bass Lead* (see Marcels, Devotions). Carlo's rat-a-tat-tat line of Gatling Gun staccato speed on the ol' "BAA-BUP-BUP-BAA-BAA" line leaves no time to inhale. Super sleeper song where nobody sleeps. Dion crunched big success with #4, 4-59 teen lament "Teenager in Love," and hit #3, 12-59 on Hal Kemp's #1 '37 "Where Or When."—written by master songwriters **Rodgers** and **Hart.**

By 1960, Dion split with the **Belmonts** due to D'Aleo's Navy career. The **Del Satins** accompanied him on a totally different melody of "In the Still of the Night" (#38, 7-60), a Cole Porter standard that hit #3 for Tommy Dorsey in 1937 [Whitburn]. Other Dion tunes include #12, 10-60 "Lonely Teenager" and #3, 4-62 "Lovers Who Wander." Belmonts' between-the-lines cool nonsense-syllables caused a satire by Brill Building songscribe Barry Mann:

"Who Put the Bomp?" – Barry Mann, #7, 8-61. Spinoff spoof by songscribe Cynthia Weil's hubby Barry – who lampoons the great bassmen like **Marcels**' Fred Johnson. With a shifty Streetcorner pattern and deft melismas, Mann's melody thanks songwriters (i.e., himself) who got his girlfriend and him together via extra-lyrical gimmicks and groovy 'bop-be-bop-bidda-bops.' One cool line echoes **Edsels** (named for extinct Ford car), and their #21, 5-61 "Rama Lama Ding Dong."

"A Teenager in Love" – Dion and the Belmonts, #5, 4-58. "A Teenager in Love" is tamer than "I Wonder Why," where the tintinnabulations of their tonsils race with red-line fever to the majestic max. Defining the frustrations of our zit & cheeseburger years, Dion told a universal teen-age story on his Laurie label (moving to giant Columbia in 1963). Echoing his hero and tourmate Buddy Holly's Soft Rock expertise, Dion & Belmonts stride through a harmonic Streetcorner Chord Pattern, and describe tribulations of love gone bad. Dion implores the few wan stars protruding through the garish Bronx midnight to cure his moping misery and find him some super-true 'Peggy Sue.'

When Dion started 'wandering,' the elusive chart-toppers arrived. He got the wrong Sue – #1(2) "Runaround Sue," in a bad romantic deal in 9-61. [Dion's wife is named Sue, but she's sweet and true, and helped him out of substance miseries in the 60s, chronicled in his tremendous autobiography *The Wanderer*].

"The Wanderer" – Dion [with unadvertised Del Satins], **#2(1), 12-61.** Dion's signature song. Teenage ode to wanderlust and omni-studly worldwide romantic escapades. The happily footloose dude, perhaps burned from a jilted affair, tackles a world of frantic freeways. Seeking beautiful girls (see Ricky Nelson's #1, '61 "Travelin' Man"), he tattoos their sensuous memories upon his immortal pounding heart. Dion's eternal Chick-Flick Wish List gleams with romantic havoc wreaked upon 'Rosie' and 'Jeannie' and 'Mary' and 'Flo.' Dashing Dion travels globe-wide, making out with Mary and Jeannie, a 'Rosie' tattoo adorning his chest (tattoos were rarer then). **Leif Garrett** (#49, '78) reprised Dion's global-stud song, and you can hear its multi-girl echo in **Lou Bega's** #3, 8-99 "Mambo No. 5 (A Little Bit Of …)" or its predecessor Kenny Ball & His Jazzmen's #18 U.K.-only 4-61 "I Still Love You All." Dion's raspy low tenor plays off a bari sax gravellizing the bottom raunchy notes. Footloose Dion hops into his car, 'cruises chicks' worldwide, and lives every pent-up guy's dream life internationally.[We tried Dion's suggestion to drive all around the whole world, in 1994, but we ran out of Alaska, and never could find the Bridge to Hawaii . . .].

Dion's pal Ernie Maresca (#6, 3-62 same-sound "Shout, Shout [Knock Yourself Out]" with Dion's Del Satins) wrote "The Wanderer" about this Moonlight Gambler. It's a guy thing – this hit song. Why a guy thing? In the history of the world, no guy has ever gotten pregnant. For a girl-oriented antidote, see **Shirelles' Carole King** #1 '60 song, "Will You Love Me Tomorrow?"

Meanwhile, back at Dion's Make-out-mobile, his romantic rampage continues apace and unabated—gas keeps flowing, car keeps going. He escapes, hell bent for leather, easing on down the road, and cured of the hassle of commitment. Does life imitate art?

Silly question. Real-life Dion, blindsided by falling *Billboard* chart numbers and Beatlemania [his #48, 6-63 Dell-Vikings' "Come Go with Me," #71, 8-64 Chuck Berry's "Johnny B. Goode"], also wandered amok. For a sad while, he ditched the comfy home provided by his true Sue. Dion nosedived into shenanigans and worse, zapping his health in a high-life endless party before the crash of morning. He bottomed out in the late 60s, before his sensational comeback hymn (see later #4, 10-68 "Abraham, Martin, & John"), Due to a childhood rift with his perennially poor puppeteer papa Pasquale DiMucci, Dion's *It's a Wonderful Life* 'Guardian Angel Clarence' (or *Touched by an Angel* Della Reese) turned out to be his father-in-law, who pointed him to born-again evangelical Christianity. He offers advice to similar wayward pilgrims in The Wanderer, and confesses how the love of his wife helped him kick many bad habits. His Al. #130, 5-89 comeback album *Yo Frankie* serves notice that slim, buoyant, young-looking Dion can still Rock and Roll.

The Elvis Spotlight scorched Dion temporarily. Yes, he spiraled to obscurity, oblivion, and back – #75, 8-89 "And the Night Stood Still," with Dave Edmunds and Patty Smyth. In 2000, Dion wrote a song about tourmate Buddy Holly, "Everyday with You." It shiveringly recalls Dion's vision of the spectacled superstar as the big brother he never quite had. And his 'guardian angel' living example showed how to be a rock star and not compromise your integrity.

Thousands of stars lingered in the shadow of Elvis. Among the better Elvis echoes, we had Billy **"Crash" Craddock** (#94, 11-59 "Don't Destroy Me"); **Ersel Hickey** (#75, 4-58, "Bluebirds over the Mountain"); **Tony Bellus** (Bellusci, b. Chicago '36, and #25, 4-59 "Robbin' the Cradle"); **Ray Smith** (1934-79, suicide, #22, 1-60, "Rockin' Little Angel"); Britain's **Cliff Richard** (b. '40, a zillion UK hits, and later #6, 6-76 "Devil Woman"); **Charlie Gracie** (#1[2], 2-57 "Butterfly" & #16, 5-57 "Fabulous", b. '36 Philly) ; **Dorsey Burnette** (1932-79, "(There Was a) Tall Oak Tree," #22, 2-60) and his brother **Johnny Burnette** (1934-64, killed swimming by speedboat), #8, 10-60 "You're Sixteen" – see JB's section later); and the amazing 'Silver Fox' [premature gray hair], **Charlie Rich** (1932-95), #22, 3-60 "Lonely Weekends" and #21, 8-65 "Mohair Sam"). Before we finish our Elvis Shadow chapter with the Hollywood Teen Idol who challenged the King in the looks department – **Ricky Nelson** – we must look at three big stars with a direct pipeline to Elvis's sound.

Former minor-league baseball player **Conway Twitty** (Harold Jenkins, 1933-93) had twice as many #1 songs as Elvis, and reprised both the King's prowl AND his growl. Teen idols, as a rule, avoided Elvis's macho stance. Many were harmlessly cute, cuddly, shy, polite, tiny. Not so Conway. As he rambled through the bush-league baseball buses barnstorming for home runs, he realized he could hit musical home runs on a better bus all his own. Until Country giants Alabama steamed past Conway's 41 #1's in the late 90s, Twitty had more #1 songs than any artist, anytime, anywhere.

One dinky catch. Only ONE topped the HOT 100, and the rest crowned the COUNTRY charts. The first big Rock musical was *Bye Bye Birdie* (1963***), playing incessantly at your local high school. Twitty's alter-ego character became the prototype for the hedonistic teen idol as 'Conrad Birdie' (Twitty was nothing like this egomaniac, and treated his fans in a kind and attentive manner).

"It's Only Make Believe" – Conway Twitty, #1(2), 9-58; #12, 10-58 R & B; NC, C. Triple crescendoes pave way for Roy Orbison's surreal and otherworldly three-minute crescendo dramas. Twitty's outstanding GROWL, seemingly inhaled in low baritone, permeates the rising lines as he ascends from Power Baritone to 'Whiskey' Italian Tenor. He climaxes each volcanic verse (there's NO chorus) with quivering 'Blue-Eyed Soul.' He debuted with #93, 5-57 "I Need Your Lovin'," so this one isn't quite a debut #1, but it's close. Follow-up "The Story of My Love" (#28, 1-59) ploughs same crescendo pattern, and it's 92.7% as good as this nifty fifties' bombshell belter for Twitty, who sounded uncannily like Elvis. "Danny Boy" (#10, 9-59 and #18, 11-59 R & B) was labeled an Englishman's/Orangeman's revenge. In raging rock and roll, Twitty scotches this unofficial Irish anthem in a rush of rasp and snarl and crunch. Leprechaun's pot of gold for Conway.

"Lonely Blue Boy" – Conway Twitty, #6, 12-59; #27, 3-60 R & B. Conway switches from Kelly Green to Royal Blue. Whitburn says this was originally 'Danny', from Elvis's King Creole. It's a throbbing ballad shimmering with tremolo guitar, and it's a rock rhapsody. Our lonely hero scribbles a letter, and mails it to the four winds; if any beautiful girl finds it, he gambles, maybe we can live bluelessly ever after. Astoundingly, the Country charts never noticed Conway until #18 C 3-66 "Guess My Eyes Were Bigger Than My Heart." His #26, 3-60 "What Am I Livin' For?" is also a great ballad. We'll see Conway a lot in the Country chapter . . .

In 1958, a baritone/bass Elvis-style kid from Hazel Park, Michigan, bench-pressed 300 pounds. In those pre-steroid days, nobody ever did that. His album's liner notes call him the American Dream – an 'Italian-Canadian-American Hillbilly.' We kids growing up on the suburban outskirts of Motown knew he was our own ELVIS. Born Jack Scafone (1-28-36, Windsor, Ontario, Shania Twain's home town, and my dad John Dean's – 1-28-1910 to 2-24-70), Jack and his dad worked the blazing blast furnaces and wrestled the eternally clanging, jangling, crashing assembly lines in the shadow of the big Dodge Main Plant on Nine Mile Road, by **Eminem**'s 2002 *Eight Mile*.

"My True Love" – Jack Scott [and the Chantones, pronounced 'Shantones'], **#3, 7-58, #5, R & B.** Quick – how many great Elvis-echo singers can you name who were
1) Italian.
2) Canadian, and –
3) Gospel/Country singers and auto workers from Detroit?

Wait a minute! [OK, you peeked]. There was one – Jack Scafone of Hazel Park, hugging Detroit's sulfur-smoke smudged boundary. With no Parks or Hazel-nut trees, Hazel Park (b. 1-28-36), had a lot of tough lunchbox teenage hoods (short for 'hoodlum'). Trouble found them everywhere. They drove Ghosts of the Old Road along the Woodward/Eight Mile corridors of cruising 50s America. They floated like Dukes of Earl in James Dean chopped & channeled '51 Mercs, fire-breathing Rocket 88 Oldsmobiles, or kick-butt Pontiac Star-Chiefs with Straight Eight warp speed.

Slinking in shackled levis, black leather jackets, and (yep) pink shirts with turned-up collars, they changed the oil weekly (10-40) on their Detroit flat-tops-with-fenders or D.A. or waterfall haircuts. Their favorite sport was marauding my cuz Darrell Amlin's Denby High turf, looking for crewcut preps to manhandle, maul, stomp, and spit out. For those of us waffling between hooditude hair and college-bound khakis, like Curt (Richard Dreyfuss) in *American Graffiti* (1973****), Hazel Park cruising was a white-knuckle trip.

We went anyhow. The urge for girls drives guys to fantastic daredevil delights. Also, we had to catch Jack's act. We had to check out Detroit's coolest of the cool – our own ELVIS, when even MOTOWN wasn't invented yet. Jack's **Chantones** looked like they owned the gym Jack bench-pressed Buicks in. These guys picked up their cool Cadillacs with one hand, and their biceps exploded their T-shirts. The Chantones led off "My True Love," a rare Soft Rock WALTZ in 3/4 time. They crooned a bottomtone baritone blanket of deep harmony, and Jack's low baritone cruised on in. Jack began to preach his hit.

The crepe-paper-streamer old sweatsock gym reeled, rolled, and vibrated volcanically with Jack's hall-filling sound that shook the bars on the school's windows, Flirting with full BASS, Jack is among the lowest singers of the Rock Revolution. Since the genuine Elvis hung out around Memphis or someplace on the moon far from us, this was our first taste (at tender age 15) of the smashing sound of rock and roll royalty. Chantones Jack Grenier, Jim Nantais, Roy Lesperance, and Larry Desgarlais added their French connection of French-Canadian Gospel Soul (Scott & Chantones did a Gospel album called *The Spirit Moves Me* in 1959-60, doing Louis Armstrong's "When the Saints Go Marchin' In"). "My True Love" rumbles a long, low, endless bass tone that continues seemingly to their #28, 9-58 follow-up "With Your Love," another passionate plodding waltz. Like Elvis's **Jordanaires,** only much lower, the Chantones undergirded Scott's deep Rockabilly waltzes.

In "My True Love," Jack even RAPS a little. He says the Lord sent him an angel out of Heaven, and the gravely-serious-looking Chantones seemingly agreed, sneering with rumblous intent at the hoody crowd while flexing triceps and Adam's-apples. Jack is Mr. Sincerity. Mr. Serious, too. With his princely pompadour, large Italian brown eyes, and hulking physique in a fries & Pepsi world of 149# weaklings, you could watch the dewy-eyed girls wilt, swoon, and tremble. As they quivered in the faux-Elvis center-stage glow, it was really ridiculous. They should have been swooning for us. Well, me, actually.

Jack's flipside "Leroy," #11, 6-58, covers the misadventures of Scott's chum Leroy Johnson of Hazel Park High. Sometimes-jailbird Leroy dwells in Cell-Block II in this "Jailhouse Rock" tune written by singer-songwriter Scott. Elvis didn't write – nor play Speed Metal lead guitar like Jack.

Though his star dimmed via the forget-about-'em fickle chroniclers, Jack Scott was a star. Almost a superstar, with 19 charted hits, and four Top Tens. Despite great R & R contributions by Neil Young, Mamas/Papas' Denny Doherty, Bryan Adams, Burton Cummings, Randy Bachman, and recent distaffers Alanis Morissette and Shania Twain, gonzo rock critic Dave Marsh simply calls Jack Scott the "greatest Canadian rock singer of all time." Not bad, eh?

Jack Scott

"Goodbye Baby" – Jack Scott, #8, 12-58. Jack means it. Jack's fervent song romances seem to spiral down in flames ("Burning Bridges" #3, 4-60). Scott forges "Goodbye Baby" down in the bass basement, and the Chantones dig down even deeper. When he ups the octave like Billy Joel's #25, 70s "Piano Man," and farewells his long-lost lady love, guys look at his 16" shaggy arms and decide it might not be a prudent idea to ask 'Baby' on a date for a long while.

Scott clicked on #35, 6-59 "The Way I Walk," and #5, 1-60 "What in the World's Come Over You?" His 1961 move to Capitol Records didn't pan out on the high charts, so he retired to Country music (#92 C, 7-74 "You're Just Getting Better") and his arms workout at the gym in Hazel Park. He was in great shape at the 1999 Bobby Vee concert in Novi, Michigan, bench-pressing Harleys at 63.

"You Don't Know What You've Got" – Ral Donner & the Starfires, #4, 7-61. Besides sounding the most like Elvis of ANY of these great Elvis echoes, Ral Donner had this group name you had to love: the STARFIRES. Like Bill Haley's COMETS, they shrieked fire around the Heavens and trailed audial glory down to earth. More mundanely, Chicago's Ralph Donner named his Jordanires/Chantones-style back-up vocalists (and bandmates) for an OLDSMOBILE model. Donner offered nearly an ELVIS XEROX. In the King's lifetime, no one could copy his vocal style better. Though this baritone Chalypso ode to sorry hindsight was Ral's biggest, his best was possibly an Elvis demo gone awry – to #19, 4-61 "Girl of My Best Friend" (El '60). It touts the dilemma of being attracted to a pal's gal (see #35, 10-78 Cars' "My Best Friend's Girl").

Donner (1943-84) also clicked with #18, 12-61 "She's Everything (I Wanted You to Be)" to round out his only big year crunching the charts. **Terry Stafford**'s #3, 2-64 cover "Suspicion" of Elvis's 1962 demo wins 2nd Soundalike prize.

The SOUTH produced most of the Elvis-echo multitude, and most were tremulous TENORS. Sure, the Italian-American Elvis challengers – Jack Scott, Bobby Darin, and Dion DiMucci – grew up amid smoke and steel and concrete canyons. Some sold 33 dozen eggs (Jerry Lee Lewis) to finance a rainbow trip to the stars. Some hassled with $10 guitars in shotgun shacks (Elvis himself), or by the side of Johnny B. Goode hummocks by the bayou, as engineers sped their hustling trains down to magic New Orleans. Many Rockabillies grew up on the Delta or Mississippi riverboat towns, with antebellum mansions and magnolia memories. Some thrived in Texas boomtowns (Buddy Holly, upcoming Roy Orbison), towns that shimmied out to roadhouse prayer tent revivals – on the fading frontier edge of dust and desert and chaos beyond.

Not a one was a rich kid from Hollywood. The badge of membership to the Teen Idol fraternity (#7, '58 "You Are My Destiny's" Canadian **Paul Anka** aside) seemed to be Southern poverty and a 'Johnny B. Goode' dream.

Ricky Nelson (1940-85, aerial disaster) rocked Hollywood. His was not the typical Freeway to Fame – Southern raggedy teen snags $9 trashcan guitar, sells snake-milking stools door-to-door till discovered by cigar-eating circus barker with jiggly jowls, and takes high road to *Ed Sullivan, Bandstand,* and relentless arms of a gazillion groovy groupies

"Poor Little Fool" – **Ricky Nelson, #1(1), 7-58; #3, 6-58 R & B; #3, 7-58 C.** On August 4, 1958, "Poor Little Fool" became the FIRST #1 EVER on the revamped Billboard HOT 100—with a better tabulating system and more accuracy and objectivity. Ricky's first #1 features no chorus and no bridge, but a great lullaby voice. He laments his Casanova days, and sings that he has to pay for similar romantic games he once played. The song Streetcorners:

I – Vi-minor – IV – V7 or **C – Am – F – G7**
No fluff, no chorus, no hot-lick instrumental. Just a great song of good teenage love gone bad.

Though born by Kirsten and Jennifer Forrest's George St. in Teaneck, New Jersey, Ricky grew up near Beverly Hills 90210. Not simply a nice little rich kid – Ricky was the first Teen Idol nurtured on television, growing up in the national spotlight on the "Ozzie & Harriet" show. In many ways, he forecast the eventual arrival of Michael Nesmith's **Monkees** – and eventual '24-7-365' institutions: MTV and VH-1. Nope, the overprivileged nice kid's daddy's own weekly sitcom gave him national exposure BEFORE he ever opened up his singing career with a showcase every Lodi band, every lounge cover band, and every garage band can only dream of – a DEBUT on NATIONAL PRIME-TIME TV. Then there were only 3-5 channels to choose from. Can't beat that, eh?

Bandleader papa **Ozzie Nelson** lived in Teaneck, a delightful town of solid-brick foursquare homes, 100-ft. sycamores and tulip trees, massive white oaks and Little League frenzy. Bedrock America. Currier & Ives. From hometown, U.S.A., Ricky was hustled off to Hollywood with mom Harriet and brother David Nelson.

Ricky never played asphalt roadhouses with soggy beer-stained amps, beyond the darkness on the grizzled edge of town.

Ricky at 16 played varsity tennis at Hollywood High, and cruised Sunset Strip in his OWN new '57 Chevy in 1956. Suddenly, his girlfriend got googoo gaga over ELVIS. Rick bristled. "Hmmph," he idly bragged, "I'm going to cut a record someday." After his girl's Elvis swoon, he *had* to back up his comment. His famous bandleader dad Ozzie Nelson fired up a gaggle of A-1 session musicians, and Ricky covered the fine song of Elvis's heretofore biggest sales competitor – **Fats Domino**'s #4, 3-57 "I'm Walkin'"; Ricky's TV-debut two-sided smash matched Fats at #4, 5-57, and his flipside, "A Teenager's Romance," kept rising to #2. Overnight, Ricky (see **Ricky Martin**, 2000) became the hottest Rockabilly crooner in the world.

Ricky Nelson had to work at being a Rockabilly. 'Frantic' wasn't a part of his vocabulary. Maybe R & R stardom has always favored the overprivileged. We Johnny B. Goode fans hate to think that. We pay lip service to humble beginnings, but many a rich kid has lolled and lazed a breezy, easy road to rock fame and fortune. Jerry Lewis's son Gary? Lesley Gore? Carly Simon? Even Mick Jagger? Maybe, maybe not. No matter what your income, there's nothing EASY about the ELVIS SPOTLIGHT. All of those talented artists donate their blood, sweat and tears.

Critics critiqued Ricky's easygoing Hollywood style as sleepy and tame. The same carping critics knocked Rock and Roll two years before for its noisy pandemonium. Now they knocked the Hollywood Kid for his relaxed Perry Como-style Soft Rock. Ricky was two smidgeons jumpier on stage than Pat Boone, but rockin' rebels like **Eddie Cochran, Buddy Holly,** or **Jerry Lee Lewis** made laid-back Ricky look like a comparative One-Man Energy Crisis.

What could the poor nice kid do? With turquoise eyes, perfect hair and teeth, and a come-hither smile, Ricky was among the few Teen Idols in the 50s to rival the King (Fabian, Jimmy Clanton, Frankie Avalon) in the looks department. Could Ricky sing? Yep. Perfect pitch, resonant baritone notes, croony behind-the-beat slurring grace-notes. Best of all, he impressed everybody by being so sincere.

The fifties dug SINCERITY. Ricky made it on his looks, his fan base, and his good voice. Also on the gonzo guitar riffs of Hall of Fame Guitarist (2000)

James Burton. Burton pumped out his flying-fret treble power, ably backing Ricky's soft romantic baritone. Ricky's girlfriend grew to regret her Elvismania, as railroad cars of fan mail sidetracked to the Nelson hacienda. Ricky Nelson outsold Chuck Berry, Buddy Holly, Jerry Lee Lewis, and Little Richard combined (don't ask about Elvis – Ricky wasn't even close):

"Lonesome Town" – Ricky Nelson, #7, 10-58; #15, 11-58 R & B. You want slow? Ricky's answer to Elvis's forlorn "Heartbreak Hotel" rides a rise to IIIm chord (like 'C' to 'Em') and a town littered with broken hearts that somehow produce tears galore. Ricky's sincerity makes this hyperbolic metaphorical absurdity very plausible, very believable, very real. With this basic baritone ballad, Ricky highlights the low lights of life. Profound, stark, hauntingly beautiful. Funereally fabulous, even. Catch **Paul McCartney**'s speedier tenor treatment on Al. #26, 11-99 *Run, Devil, Run.* Elected the 2nd year ('87) to the Rock Hall of Fame, Rick is arguably still the only "Teen Idol" voted into it.

"Travelin' Man" – Ricky Nelson, #1(2), 4-61. Ricky's "Travelin' Man" followed our zany van all over Europe – Monaco, San Marino, Liechtenstein, and naturally Britain, France, Germany, and even the Arctic Circle up in Norway and the Midnight Sun. With piano man Bob Baldori, [Dr.] Jan Radke, front-man for Two President Bushes – Ed Cowling, and later pacemaker salesman Jim Cook, I lived all over the Continent for three months when we were all 18-year-old 'travelin' men' (see Dion's 'The Wanderer"). Ricky salutes his worldwide sweethearts: a demure Mexican senorita, cute Alaskan Eskimo, Berlin hot fraulein, and a Hong Kong 'China Doll.'

How do popular songs change the world? How did American Rock and Roll play a major part in bringing down the Berlin Wall and communism? Norwegian-American Ricky starts modestly here. Of all his amours, he picks out two Asian ladies (Alaska, Hong Kong). In 1961, this was revolutionary. The 'M' word – miscegenation – still stalked the minds of many. As late as March 2000, Bob Jones University in the South forbade interracial dating. In the 50s (not so much California or Hawaii), actual laws against intermarriage boded hard jail time for Americans committing the 'crime' of falling in love with and marrying someone of a slightly duskier hue. Or even ADOPTING a kid interracially.

The 50s were a weirder world than you might think? Superman Ricky Nelson changed the day – for a SONG.

Society's great changes are not always dominated by rabble-rousing rebels lighting their feet on fire in furious protest. They are done gradually—by W.A.S.P.-Scandinavian suburban kids like Ricky Nelson, too. Normal, mainstream kids. He had yet to attend his Garden Party.

"Hello Mary Lou" – Ricky Nelson, #9, 5-61. Ostensibly written by Gene Pitney's MOTHER (Gene had some contract hassle, and farmed out credit to his maternal parental unit), "Hello Mary Lou" explodes with Rock and Roll energy. Rumor has it Gene's mom also 'wrote' **Teen Idol Bobby Vee's** smash #6 ultrabouncy "Rubber Ball" '60.) Statler Brothers hit #3, '85 C. with a similar arrangement. James Burton's frantic cadenzas wobble a whirlagig of dramatic fill. Mary Lou is an irresistible beauty. Ricky falls hard for her charms. The III-major mediant chord highlights the verse, and the magnificent melody overarches the whole great song.

"Teen Age Idol" – Ricky Nelson, #5, 8-62. Pensive ballad delivers the down side to the T.A.I.'s road-weary nomadic life. The singer gripes about how lonesome he is, despite what people think. Yeah, sure, we all grumbled back in '62. Ricky Nelson with problems. Uh-huh. We munched factory smoke for lunch, drove ratty rustbuckets, and celebrated Michigan's two seasons – Winter and July (National Mosquito Month).

You get older, hopefully. As you do, you realize Ricky was right. Never envy the other guy, mused Bert Barnes, because you "never know what's on the other side of the big front door." "Teenage Idol" is starkly profound. Idols are shooting stars (Dollar, #74, 1-80 "Shooting Star", also on Bad Company album, or see Foreigner's "Juke Box Hero" or Bob Seger's "Turn the Page"). These R & R superstars meteorically blast their electric guitars to the glory-glutted heavens. For a short time. As **Cat Stevens** put it (#10, 3-74 "Oh, Very Young"), our dance upon this earth takes a very short while.

Paths of glory are short scraggly paths.

As nice kid-next-door Ricky Nelson burned in Elvis's hot klieg lights, the sizzling 60s frazzled his composure.

Ricky Nelson

Unlike many fellow idols, frozen into Fiftiesmania, Nelson transformed. He sprouted long hair, troubadoured with his Country-based Stone Canyon Band, and ditched all the puppeteers on his ex-entourage. In Rock and Roll, Teen Idols were bruised by Starmakers. If it weren't for Colonel Tom Parker firing Hank Snow to manage Elvis, the King might have been the Prince. When Elvis died in 1977, Parker mourned briefly, and signed a management contract with Ricky Nelson.

Ricky, by now, was his own man. He made just one grievous mistake.

Would you buy a rickety used airplane from Jerry Lee Lewis?

"Garden Party" – Ricky Nelson and the Stone Canyon Band, #6, 7-72; #44, 9-72, C. Nelson started writing his own stuff, via Dylan's influence (#33, 10-69, Ricky did Dylan's "She Belongs to Me"). "Garden Party" covers his gig at Madison Square Garden. It's about disillusionment. His regular Oldies audience shuffles in, expecting Flashback 1958: poodle skirts, cherry cokes, bobby-sox. By 1972, 'coke' had a new meaning, and shaggy unshorn rockers ascended the New York stage with Ricky – whose barber, too, was Missing In Inaction.

After ho-hum applause and obvious audience disappointment, a ticked-off Ricky (FURY never darkened Rick's vocabulary) penned this 2nd-comeback smash. It alludes to **John** and **Yoko Lennon, Bob Dylan**'s R & R deification, reclusive zillionaire Howard Hughes, and whether to play Ricky's Greatest Hits/Oldies to stunned 50s-Forever fanatics, frozen in time and unwilling to change. One super song. Why?

The punch line. It shuffles musically along the chugging verses, powered by a megabass, easy drum thump, and catchy singalong chorus. Nelson corners the market on self-image on his philosophical zinger – there's no way to please everybody. Ultimately, you have to do what? Please yourself. Bizarrely, that's not actually a very selfish statement. Why not? You have to love yourself enough FIRST, before you can truly love others.

Sadly, Ricky Nelson, always the considerate family kid, was victim of the steely lonesome road (see Simon & Gar's #5, '66 "Homeward Bound"). His daughter Tracy became a popular actress (*Father Dowling Mysteries*), and his twin blond sons Gunnar and Matthew followed Dad's tri-generational dynasty to musical fame: **Nelson,** #1, 7-90 "Love and Affection," and #6, 11-90 "After the Rain." Ricky returned to one-nighters in mid-size venues.

Ricky was the first Teen Idol inducted into the Rock Hall of Fame (1987), but it was too late. New

Year's Eve is the Scottish National Holiday – Hogmanay. Celebrations galore. Ricky and friends were celebrating Rick's 3rd comeback, on Hogmanay 1985. Forty-five-year old Rick still had all of his leonine mane, though rifled with wisps of gray. They'd brought down the house headlining their last show. The final song? Ironically, **Buddy Holly**'s joyous rocker "Rave On."

Jerry Lee Lewis's claptrap ex-plane clattered off the tarmac into the wobbly sky. Nelson's entourage partied into the night, smoking and singing and guzzling and joking. When Holly's plane crashed on the 'Day the Music Died' (2-3-59), it was mercifully 'Instant Eternity' for them all. Since the little Beechcraft slammed into the Iowa cornfield, there was no lingering agony. On Ricky's plane, the fuselage caught fire. Suffice it to say that Ricky Nelson nearly actualized his teen dream to BE ELVIS. While singing on his bittersweet earth for a short while, he shimmered in the hissing spotlight and caught a glimpse of the lonesome stars above.

People called Ricky a teenage idol.

*Don & Phil - **Everly Brothers***

Surf's Up . . .
Sixties Surf and
Road Warrior Rock

Sunny surf music began long before 6'3", 200# quarterback **Brian Wilson** of California's Hawthorne High lobbed passes at wide receivers on the gridiron – and at bikini honeys at magical Malibu Beach. You can chase Surf Rock to **Joe Kekeku**'s 1931 open-tuned Hawaiian guitar invention, to spark Annette's #11, 1960 "Pineapple Princess." Or megabook author **James Michener**. His soundtrack movie score album *South Pacific* hit #1 for 31 weeks, in 1958; *South Pacific* gave most American guys grass-skirt hammock fantasies – and bathing-beauty dreams.

Here's the Surf Recipe:
  2 parts Chuck Berry guitar riffs.
  1 part Del Shannon – Frankie Valli –
      Jimmy Jones falsetto.
  1 part drummer/bassist at speed of light.
  1 part Dick Dale & Del-tones Speedmetal
      rhythm riffs.
  2 parts Cool Lyrics, 80% beaches and 20%
      cruising/racing.

As President Ronald Reagan put it, the "Beach Boys are America's band."

"Surfin'" – **Beach Boys, #75, 2-62.** Head Beach Boy Brian's opening volley. Hint of later Beach Boys' stupendous Jazz savvy: simple streetcorner harmonies, basic 12-Bar Blues. Father Murry Wilson was just getting the kids' harmonies and riffs waxed and ready for the golden crest of the next great wave.

"Surfin' Safari" – **Beach Boys, #14, 8-62.** Endless summer intro. This one drags bored kid out of class, like Berry's "School Day," and hotfoots him onto massive 60s surfboard, before fiberglass revolutions. Of Brian's brother **Carl** (lead guitar) and **Dennis** (drums), Dennis was only regular surfer. Cousin **Mike Love** (baritone and lead vocals, saxophone, guitar) and pal **Al Jardine** (Al-of-all-trades) rounded out the Beach Guys, who deftly memorized ultra-complex Lettermen or Four Freshmen harmonies. "Surfin' Safari" snarfs them around on their first beach adventure. #1 TV show in the mid-90s world, *Baywatch*, began here on safari. Every summer, Surf Music blooms.

"Shut Down" backed with "Surfin' U.S.A." – Beach Boys, #23, 4-63; #3, 3-63; #20, 4-63 R & B. Drag race? DETROIT is one of the major surfing sites. Huh? When the Beach Boys weren't surfing, they were doing what adolescent males maybe shouldn't be doing – drag racing their dads' enormous Detroit powerhouse V-8s. This Drag-Race Rock classic pits two 'shorts': this fuel-injected (Corvette) Sting Ray versus a 413 (cubic-inch engine). They tach 'em up (rev the tachometer), with male winning pride: To shut a racer down means to beat him on the asphalt strip, whether official course or midnight avenue. After a 12-Bar Blues tune or two, the Beach Boys dumped the chord progression and established their own: "Shut Down" revs up the rhythm guitar into a dynamic chromatic sequence (the MIDEASTERN bIII chord). The song chortles along; say you're doing it in the Key of 'E' – suddenly you vault 1½ notes up to **G**, and then slide one-half step at a time back to your root key: **G – F# – F – E.** No big deal. But it changed the world of Rock and Roll.

"Little Deuce Coupe" – Beach Boys, #15, 8-63; #28 R & B. Little Deuce Coupe? A 1932 Ford Coupe. A coupe is an old one-seater car, sometimes sporting a rumble seat boinging out of the back of the trunk. Their speedo Mo-chine boasts a flathead mill (type of engine from early 50s profusion of V-8s). Watch my smoke, Turkey.

Drag racing involved either suburbanites who spent a lot of money fixing up their cars, or people who had too much money anyhow – and lavished it on swift chariots with shrieking tires. Rolling down the line as the stoplight turns green? This drag race lingo involves the Christmas tree. When you officially or unofficially drag race, the light blinks and you're off. His Deuce Coupe blows out water as he's roaring, and he peels off rubber in four gears. Tempestuous torque braggadocio. You power-shift the stick shift, snapping the raging clutch back as you slam from first to second gear. When the 1st-to-2nd shift is done right, it thrusts like a knockout punch from your power-packed right arm, and your mill lurches into the lead (not that we ever did anything like this, of course).

"Little Deuce Coupe" is one of many outlets for male competitive fire. Whether brandishing a pigskin, surfboard, or Deuce Coupe packing a flathead mill, we're out to win.

Silver medal? No thanks. Therein lies one dinky problem with the American character. Sore losing. If you can't stomach your defeats, it churns inside and zaps your health. Drag Race Music and Surf Music are scrappy siblings. Surf and Drag Music are the Heart of America, from Coast to Coast and everywhere in between.

Chuck Berry's "Promised Land" is the sunny California Coast. 'Tis a rare Yankee who never ponders punting the snowdrifts and hightailing it for gold and glory and sunshine in the San Fernando Valley. Papa Murry Wilson peddled Tin Pan Alley-reject songs, and fired up his workadaddy and showbiz frustrations on his three boys. Stephen Gaines's *Heroes and Villains* take a dim view of Murry, writing him off as a hot-tempered firebrand who battered his boys about in drunken rages. Perhaps this is documented, but he also loved and guided his battery of Beach Boys to hit the height of achievement in athletics, scholarship, and eventually music. A ruddy bipolar man, Murry died of a heart attack at 58, and remains an enigma – he did great good, he did some bad.

Anchoring the Wilson family with love, stability, and unswerving support was their mom Audree Wilson (d. '97). The Beach Boys were nowhere near alone in piping the surf pipeline to even greater fame and riches. SURF INSTRUMENTALS ROCKED!

"Let's Go Trippin'" – Dick Dale and the Del-Tones, #60, 11-61. Rippling rhythm guitar leads. Covering Buddy Holly's fast-fired flourish on "Peggy Sue," Dick Dale (b. '37, Boston) of Southern California and also Beirut, Lebanon, rocketed his lightning right hand to guitar virtuoso cadence. He still tours as newfound Surf Rock cult hero. #1 supreme surf guitarist, DD, active in 2001+.

"Mule Skinner Blues" – Fendermen, #5, 5-60; #16, 7-60 C. Dick Dale's surf-guru guitar riffs? Phil Humphrey and Jim Sundquist dwelt about as far from surf as the Motor City – Wisconsin (though Lake Michigan has a few surfable days/year). This rippling **Jimmie Rodgers I** Blues classic from 1929 romps with reverb, as the lead guitar sparkles on dueling Fender guitar octaves in the bridge at supersonic Punk Rock speed. One of the best Hard Rock yodelling songs ever. Last lung-busting note is a miracle of stamina.

"The Lonely One" – Duane Eddy, #23, 1-59. Vamped with vibrato, the Radio Luxembourg theme song blanketed Britain in a surf-style Chalypso instrumental. Eddy and the 'Twangy Guitar' came from both Phoenix, Arizona, and Corning, New York. His chops and hooks and riffs powered a whole gaggle of Surf guitars into the sizzling 60s.

"Enchanted Sea" – Islanders, #15, 9-59. NOT the Long Island hockey team. Guitarist **Randy Starr** and accordionist **Frank Metis** delivered one of the most haunting Polynesian beach tunes of all time. Messing with the **Am** to **G** shift, the lead whistler ascends to a dramatic **Bb** major,

and counts purple sunsets of romantic Bali Ha'i bliss. I was flabbergasted to discover that the faux Hawaiian Starr was actually my friend George Nettleton's New York dentist later in life [*Rockin 50s*, March 2000].

"Aloha Oe" – Harry Ka'apuni & His Royal Polynesians, NC, c.1958. Song penned in 1880s by Hawaii's Queen Liliokalani – magnificent sensuous melody. The three official languages of the United States? English, Spanish, and Hawaiian, an ancient language with very few letters but very mellifluous sounds.

This record is one of those gems you unearth in the $1.99 bargain bin at the Hyper-Mega-Monster Market while toiling in vain to find Crunchio Munchios. Hawaiian music is also the granddaddy of Rock and Roll. *Check* out great 1965 BANJOLINE version by Eddie Peabody on this metallic self-invented instrument. Big hit by Frank Ferera, #10, 2-24. Surf's up.

"Walk – Don't Run" – Ventures, #2(1), 7-60 [also #8, 7-64, as "Walk – Don't Run '64"]. Premier Surf Rock vanguard, the **Ventures**. No Grunge or Flaming Psychedelia from these early Seattle/Tacoma instrumental rockers: **Don Wilson** (1937-96, rhythm guitar); **Howard Johnson** (1939-88), drummer; **Nokie Edwards** (b. '39, bass), and lead guitar star **Bob Bogle** (b. '37). Along with **Annette** [Funicello, #11, '60 "Pineapple Princess"], the Ventures may have begun Surf Rock, along with **Dick Dale,** the **Fendermen,** or New York dentist Randy Starr (#15, '59 "Enchanted Sea"), and Hawaiian/Polynesian cavalcade from Frank Ferara to Martin Denny.

Next to **Duane Eddy**, the Ventures were the #1 instrumental group as the decade turned, surpassing Toledo's semi-surf organ-fired **Johnny & the Hurricanes** (#5, 8-59, "Red River Rock" and #15, 2-60 "Beatnik Fly"). Riding the wavecrest of "Walk – Don't Run," the Ventures lofted 37 charting ALBUMS into the fray, sculpting the Surf Sound Track forevermore: Al. #11, 12-60 *Walk Don't Run*; #24, 1-62 East/West Coast hybrid Al. *Twist with the Ventures*; #8, 1-63 pop-powered Al. *The Ventures a-go-go*. Though more singles proliferated (#4, 3-69 "Hawaii Five-O" [TV show theme], the Ventures' vein of rockin' gold involved twangy instrumental album versions of current hits. Though hot Seattle surf might hit 55° in frying July, the Ventures eschewed the surfboards, but set up the sound system for the Surf Rock Explosion.

Musically, "Walk – Don't Run" is wild and adventuresome: BEFORE Del Shannon's #1, '61 "Runaway," the Ventures used the **Am–G–F–E7** chord progression – plus many new chord experiments into Rock music that would help create the magic happy sound of America's Band – the **Beach Boys** (1961 – Forever).

Graveyard Rock actually preceded Surf Rock, starting in the surf. The whole Death Metal headbanging horde has **Jody Reynolds** to thank for popularizing VIBRATO guitar and his Suicide Hot Line. Seems his lover is creeping off into the deep:

"Endless Sleep" – Jody Reynolds, #5, 5-58; #5, 6-58 R & B. Slipping dangerously into the swirling midnight ocean deeps, Jody's girl grapples with the abyss and the void. And the sharks. We never discover why she's so despondent, but Jody's commanding Rockabilly baritone convinces her life is worth living. Waves crash viciously around as Jody pulls her safely to shore. Jody's "Fire of Love" (#66, 8-58), throbs with same pulsing vibrato amp, but lacks urgency of pending disaster. Just hot desire.

Surf Music isn't tied to Death Metal? Or Graveyard Rock? Ever been smashed by a 10-foot 'Heavy' wave, or been knocked off the road by some useless drunk slug whose '56 Chevy just lost a drag race? Sadly for many pursuing longevity, really FUN activities often involve punting safety and shmoozing with danger. Boyz II Ghoulz dirges?

"Teen Angel" – Mark Dinning, #1(2), 1-60; # 5 R & B. Ultimate Graveyard Rock song. Dinning's belltone tenor quavers over the abysmal canyon. Teenage lad buys girl high school ring. Improbable story line? Car stalls on railroad track. He pulls her out as monster train approaches, but she goes running back for ring and is squashed by the Midnight Flyer. Even in 1960, some cried, some giggled at improbability. Dinning, of Drury, Oklahoma, recorded with his sisters. He had one black eyebrow that met in the middle. Few even know his name. He died on stage recently (52); one queries the quaking cosmos – was he reunited with his teen angel?

"Tell Laura I Love Her" – Ray Peterson, #7, 6-60. Swedish tenor **Ray Peterson**, of Denton, Texas, sings of Tommy's quest to buy sweetheart Laura a wedding ring. 'Tommy' chooses a stock-car race. Prize $1000. Judas sold secrets about Jesus for 30 pieces of silver. You know the dastardly outcome of Tommy's star-crossed race before it begins; he suffers a fiery crash. As they valiantly pull him out of the smoldering wreck, his brave last words are, of course, "Tell Laura I Love Her" – the title, refrain, and eerie echo. It gets creepier. Alone in this chapel at his wake, she still hears his imploring, beseeching, ghostly echo – "Tell Laura I Love Her." The disembodied echo adds eternal hope, that Tommy's true love for Laura will never die. Ray, however, moved from Laura to #9, 11-60 "Corinna, Corinna."

"Last Kiss" – J. Frank Wilson & the Cavaliers, #2, 9-64 and #92, 12-73. Lufkin, Texan, with Orbison/Holly echo voice, tells true-life-death tale of smashup on rainy Texas night. Car is stalled ahead. Collision unavoidable. Seatbeltless lover thrown out. Bleeding, he crawls to his girl in time for last words, last kiss. She dies in his arms. Nothing unrealistic about this ghastly story. **Eddie Vedder** and **Pearl Jam**, releasing it as a long shot on the 1999 *No Boundaries* Kosovo catastrophe album, watched astoundedly as the anachronistic Graveyard goodie crept

to J. Frank Wilson's #2 *Billboard* position – among the few singles of the album-oriented 90s to make it without a parent album. Vedder's fluke, yes, but what band wouldn't want a gold-record fluke? A Lite Metal Chalypso with the flavor of Buddy Holly's masterpiece melody "Everyday," Wilson/Vedder's song laments a multiple annual American tragedy. Fifty thousand Americans die in similar accidents yearly, like Pastor Milt Heitzman and wife Rosalind (5-15-97), two of God's greatest people.

"Patches" – Dickey Lee, #6, 8-62. Before we slog back into the sunny surf, let's do the zaniest plot-line of all. And the grimmest tale. **Ozzy Osbourne** and Metallica have been severely chided by the press, for suggesting suicide solutions to teens' terror. Tabloids to the contrary, you can't heh-heh-heh this stuff away. Death sells. Dickey's ditty stormed Detroit and was promptly banned. Patches and this aging teen do a suicide pact because they're forbidden to date. She drowns in dirty river. He vows to join her that night. Up in arms. The PTA. The Church League. The City Fathers. A song advocating suicide – long before Michigan's Dr. Kevorkian. So how did thunderstruck Detroit stop the suicide censorship and return Dickey's lost graveyard hit to the top ten? Some kid called up WKNR, Detroit's rock-jock station, and said they were reading a tear-jerky play in English about 15-year-olds' double suicide: "Romeo and Juliet." Case closed.

From the sunny, bubbly happy surf and the bikini beach to the groaning graveyard? Sometimes, it's a short hop. Let's do just one more grisly grizzly ghoulie goodie.

"Monster Mash" – Bobby 'Boris' Pickett, #1, 9-62 and #10, 6-73, plus a jiffy stint at #91, 8-70; #9, 10-62 R & B. #1 Halloween Carol. The Devils' minions and dominions run roughshod over order, law, and outhouses? Pickett parodied the Philadelphia Sound of **Dick Clark** with his own macabre Halloween phantasmagorical lyric. Remember Igor? Remember his back-up groups the Baying Hounds and the Crypt Kickers? Recall the dance his Mash displaced – the Transylvania Twist? Why 1962? Ask **Dee Dee Sharp** whose "Gravy" (#9, 6-62) furnished the melody. Philly's Dione LeRue (Dee Dee's) "Gravy" followed her #2(2), 3-62 (#1[4] R & B) dance craze "Mashed Potato Time."

Fledgling Surf Rock turned to the second-biggest Surfin' Singers – **Jan & Dean**. They waltzed with Graveyard Rock, too, so we'll combine the two kindred genres. **Jan Berry** and **Dean Torrence** (born '41 and '40) previewed the Beach Boys by four years [#8, 5-58 "Jennie Lee"].

"Baby Talk" – Jan & Dean, #10, 8-59; #28, 9-59 R & B. YOUNG Love. Our song hero is only FIVE years old and his "baby," yep, is only THREE. They gleefully prattle and babble on with cooing nonsense 'baby talk.' The song sparks the early credo – Rock and Roll should be FUN music. Jan and Dean were neither Italian nor Afro-American, but they echoed the best of Philly or Bronx Streetcorner Rock and Roll. Via the **Beach Boys**, East Coast Doo-Whop shifted to West Coast Surf Rock.

Jan and Dean are blond. Not even the Beach Boys (except Al and Mike) could claim total natural Surf Rock blonditude. If surfers weren't blond, sometimes they dyed their hair blond – therefore, they previewed the Sid Vicious-Johnny Rotten-**Clash** axis which spilled from 1977 on-the-dole British scene to NYC's Neo-Surf sound **Ramones** and Glam Rock spillovers the New York Dolls. Or 2000's **Sisqo** or **Eminem**. Anyhow, any green or pink or purple hair you see jangling down the Village streets, possibly accompanied by spikelet wrists and leather **Jim Morrison** pants, might just be a Surfer's Spinoff. It all relates.

Every song harmonizes. Handsome meant big record sales in 1962. Grotesque hadn't hit the scene big yet. We opened for **Jan & Dean** at the Walled Lake Casino (Michigan) in 1964 [nobody noticed us].

"Surf City" – Jan & Dean, #1(2), 6-63; #3, 7-63 R & B. Beach Boy progenitor papa Murry Wilson was furious with son Brian for giving away his song "Surf City" to Jan & Dean. Why? #1(2), 6-63. It would have been the Beach Boys' first #1 if they'd recorded it. The Beach Boys were already kings of Surf Rock. Jan and Dean were still fooling around with old East Coast standards. They also toyed with Buddy Holly's hobby overdubbing, making the two L.A. voices sound like a quartet, a quintet, a sextet.

Jan and Dean charged to #28 in 2-63 with Buddy Clark's (Ray Noble Orchestra) #1 1947 hit "Linda." Amazingly, the little cute blonde toddler in the tune turned out to be, in real life, **Linda McCartney**, Beatle Paul's wife. Instead of Clark's blander straight version, they added festoons and gonfalons of "Luh-luh-la-la-Lindas."

"Surf City' is in California, but I think of the one in New Jersey on the golden Bert & Donna Barnes strand. In Jan & Dean's utopian hot spot (from Brian Wilson's poetic libido), there are a magic two girls for every boy. Fun Fun Fun Paradise of Tina Good, Sandra Sprows, and Kim Southard. Surf Music lives and dies on the strength of its snarly, gnarly rhythm guitar. Jan and Dean power "Surf City" with the thunderous Del-Tone style in their rockin' rhythm surf guitar. Then they bring in Motor City beasts to crank up the firepower. Result? Utopia. Jan and Dean preen their '34 Woody station wagon. An uncut surf gem?

"Ride the Wild Surf" – Jan & Dean, #16, 9-64, The #1 Surf Rock song. Obsessed by 'Surf Fever,' the best surfers hang out on the beach and wait for mammoth waves to vault them Heavenward. Death Metal? Nah, but the strumming is staccato and fierce. Waimea Bay 12-foot surf keeps this varsity sport wimpless, and seafloor sand impact kills more than sharks – but the Surf Lure impels us on. The lone surfer darts into the mammoth swirling pipeline, and he walks on toothy waters in the golden glow of sundown Hawaiian triumph.

"The Little Old Lady from Pasadena" – Jan and Dean, #3, 6-64. She's pictured on *Golden Hits Volume II* album (#107, 10-65). Has gardenia flowerbed. Also has cherry-red super-stock Dodge in ramshackle old garage. Jan & Dean's "Little Old Lady" is a nifty stereotypes spoof. You think the grandmotherly dowager is turtling along at 20mph in a 40 zone. Actually, she suckers stooges to choose her superstock Dodge at the next light. Hemi, headers, Holley carbs – blasting into orbit. Supergrandma . . .

Jan (Berry) & Dean (Torrence), 1964
'Extreme Sports' inventors?

"Dead Man's Curve" – Jan & Dean, #8, 3-64. Life imitates art? A 1978 TV movie was based on duo's autobiography. "Dead Man's Curve" tells a true story that happened two years later. In the song, a Jaguar XKE pulls up next to Jan's 'Vette Sting Ray. They're dueling it out for the 'pink slip' (registration): some drag gamblers actually gave their cars away if they lost.

Case in point. *American Graffiti* (1973****) magnificently chronicles this Cal car culture. Seeded for many champ actors (Richard Dreyfuss, Ronny Howard). **Paul LeMat** is John Milner, the cool guy whose whole persona and whole life is wrapped up in having the fastest car in the valley. When bad lad **Harrison Ford** beats his classic yellow deuce coupe, Milner is crestfallen.

Jan heads for DEADMAN'S CURVE. THE XKE and Sting Ray whisk away at supersonic speeds, flinging their screaming tires quiveringly close to self-destruction. They slide into the curve, start to swerve. When Jan comes to, the doctor tells him what happened. Then grim life-imitates-art scenario: On April 19, 1966, high-flying Jan Berry crashed into a truck in his Vette at some intense speed.

Critically injured, he was comatose for months. He finally came out of the coma, losing a lot of motor coordination. Despite ardent comebacks after the accident, their carefree California mood was long gone:

"Sidewalk Surfin" – Jan & Dean, #25, 10-64; #107, 7-76. Same band track as pals the Beach Boys' song "Catch a Wave" (about surfing). Jan and Dean promoted new, fun-in-the-sun activities with desperado devil-may-care irreverent humor. In this zany romp, they introduce a newly invented sport which is all about 'sidewalk surfing' – SKATEBOARDING, now the darling of cable TV via the spleen-splitting daredevil panorama known euphemistically as **Extreme Sports.** This Rump Rock chartbuster also impishly mentions that the skateboarder will also suffer busted 'buns' (semi-taboo word in '64).

"This Land is Your Land" – Kingston Trio, NC, 1961. Off *Goin' Places* album, #3, 7-61. Bob Dylan's mentor, scratchy-voiced Folk bard **Woody Guthrie**, penned "This Land." Cig dangling from five-o'clock-shadow jowl, Oklahoman Guthrie drifted across dustbowl 1930s America, writing songs for disenfranchised people. This is his most optimistic and his greatest. The **Trio's** striped shirts were command-performance attire for surfer **Beach Boys** (orders from pa). With two of three **Trio** members from Hawaii, too, they certainly tie into Folk Surf bandwagon. "This Land" celebrates the mystery and majesty of faraway America's mystique – a generation before Chuck Berry's teenage anthems. Beach Boys' "Sloop John B" adventure is c/o the Kingston Trio's 1958 rendition.

"New York's A Lonely Town" – Trade Winds, #32, 2-65. Pete Andreoli and Vinnie Poncia prove that not all surfers were affluent West Coast W.A.S.P.s. Manhattan dudes surfed Long Island beaches. When the heavies roll in at Jones Beach or Long Beach or Smith Point or the Hamptons, you can get stoked and rolled and wiped out just as well as California clobberations by tsunami tidal waves. The Trade Winds' poignant image? A sad 'woody' parked outside in a quasi-arctic New York City snowdrift.

"Pipeline" – Chantay's, #4, 3-63; #11, 4-63 R & B. The pipeline, you know, is the curl of the surf wave – the great riding part. Dick and Dale & Del-Tones-inspired instrumental classics: **Bob Spickard**, lead guitar; **Brian Carman**, lightning bumblebee rhythm guitar, which outspeeds the lead guy. Also "Penetration," by shaved-head **Pyramids**, hit #18, 2-64 for Long Beach, California Surf quintet.

"Wipe Out" – Surfaris, #2(1), 7-63; #16, 8-66: #110, 8-70; #10, 7-63 R & B. Surf anthem, written by Morton Downey, Jr. Perennial chart bouncer. Sun and Fun Paradise. Surf Rock #1 instrumental ever. Buddy Holly lives! How? Rippling rampaging 16th-note paradiddle drum blur is a reprise of Jerry Allison's "Peggy Sue" rhythm power. Eternal favorite at parties and dances. Glendora, California, Surfaris feature drummer **Ron Wilson** (D. 1989, aneurysm), no relation to Beach Boys or Ann. **Jimmy Fuller** on lead guitar. Flipside #62, 8-63

"Surfer Joe" asks where does Rap begin? Spoken verse defines beach bleach 'blondie' Surfer Joe of Huntington Beach; he 'hangs ten' (toes), walks the nose (of board and wave), and captures Surf Trophy. Gets shanghaiied into Marines at Camp Pendleton. Cult classic song with Holly hiccups galore, "Joe."

"Little Honda" – Hondells, #9, 9-64. Early ad jingle for motor bike. **Brian Wilson**, vocal. **Glen Campbell**, lead guitar. Surf sound extraordinaire. First intrusion of commercial advertising into pure Rock and Roll. Before HONDA was a Civic or Prelude, it was a scooter. No Harley. Little 150cc. Made-for-ad name for group.

"Hey Little Cobra" – Rip Chords, #4, 12-63. Key super-group personnel. Movie-star Doris Day's son Terry Melcher and future Beach Boy **Bruce Johnston** duo. Other Beach 'Boys' over the years include **Glen Campbell** and **Toni Tennille**, contralto for **Captain & Tennille** ("Love Will Keep Us Together" #1, 4-75). "Cobra" stars a speedy sports car hauled by a Cadillac. East Coast Streetcorner songs often feature poor guy serenading maiden – promising paradise and a 2-bedroom ranch by Roosevelt Mall in Massepequa (*Seinfeld*'s actual home town.) West Coast mega-money amazes – with Jags, Porsches, Vettes, Caddie Escalades, and buxom blonde *Baywatch* below the Cash Canyon.

Ripchords croon to Cobra to spring and strike – and the speedburner BLASTS AWAY THE COMPETITION IN A PUFF OF GLORY and smoke. Beyond the smiley blond Nice Guy persona lurks a tense, brittle combatant, ready to strike. Testosterone oozing, the bad dude fires up his car into the gladatorial arena, hell bent for leather.

"Listen to Me" – Buddy Holly, NC, 1958; #16, 2-58 U.K. Essence of the Sound of Surf Rock. Buddy pioneers overdubs. Hawaiian Robin Luke's #5, 8-58 Proto-Surf classic "Susie Darlin'" follows Holly's swashbuckling rhythm.

"Buzz, Buzz, Buzz" – Hollywood Flames, #11, 11-57; #5 R & B. Missing link, like Regents' #13, 5-61 (recorded '58) "Barbara Ann," between Surf and Streetcorner Rock. **Flames** spearheaded Jan & Dean's early East Coast sound on "Baby Talk" (#10, 8-59).

"Bluebirds over the Mountain" – Beach Boys, #61, 12-68. James Watt, misguided Secretary of the Interior in the (California Governor) Reagan Presidential administration, dumped on America's beloved favorite band. He said they couldn't play on the Fourth of July on Washington Mall in the 80s. Why? Their wild ideas, or something equally inane. So who charged to their rescue?

His **President Ronald Reagan** himself (whose wife Nancy adored the Hawthorne High Surf Team); "Why, the BEACH BOYS ARE AMERICA'S BAND," aw-shucksed the Prez. 'Nuff said. Once again, the Wilsons, with Love (and Jardine), wowed 'em in Washington. Watt fumed.

"Bluebirds over the Mountain"? A vintage Rockabilly extravaganza from one of Rock and Roll's cult classic stars – **Ersel Hickey** (#75, 4-58). Hickey's obscure

Rockabilly rouser bubbled back via **Dick** (St. John) and **Dee Dee** (Sperling), a terrific Santa Monica semi-surfy duo whose 2nd biggest hit got named after a Commandment: #13, 11-64 "Thou Shalt Not Steal." The Beach Boys anchored the 60s, rivaling the **Beatles** in their output and musical profundity. As the Surf stuff simmered down, the Boys of the Beach just cranked up the hit machine. With 6,613 points in Whitburn's champ album area, the Beach Boys are the 12th most successful album artists.

The Beach Boys:
*Left to right **Bruce Johnstone, Carl Wilson, Mike Love, Brian Wilson, Al Jardine, Dennis Wilson***

"When I Grow Up to Be a Man" – Beach Boys, **#9, 9-64.** And here's the great news about the Beach Boys. They never really had to grow up. And here's the great news for you and me – neither do we! The Beach Boys bring us starry-eyed deep-purple paradise songs, culminating in their Shangri-La "Kokomo" (#1, 9-88). One good reason the world loves the boyish American spirit is because the Beach Boys have brought us our "Forever Young" (#12, 8-88 **Rod Stewart**) national consciousness. In our California Land of Ponce de Leon and the Fountain of Youth, the sun always shines, and guys call each other by their first names. Nobody wears a tie, or an uppity air of snobbish gentility. Though our cool British cousins brought us the concept of **Peter Pan**, it's the Beach Boys who pump up the idea of ETERNAL ADOLESCENCE. Isn't that what Rock and Roll is all about?

"When I Grow Up" is a Wish Song. The Beach Boys' youthful voices of **Carl** and Brian Wilson conjure what it's be like to be adults. Background voices chime in the fast-flying years: 'Sixteen, Seventeen, Eighteen, Nineteen,' and beyond Never-Never Land into a world of jobs and mortgages and responsibility. Will the kids be proud of Pop? Or peg him as a square? They dabble in Generational Musical Chairs and muted harmonies. To really understand the Beach Boys' intricate harmonic genius, it's best to listen to their cover (or the original) of the **Four Freshmen**'s #17, 5-56 "Graduation Day." Add Chuck Berry sparkling guitar riffs, and you've got the essence of "When I Grow Up to Be a Man." Or its thematic follow up:

"Wouldn't It Be Nice?" – Beach Boys, **#8, 7-66 & #103, 8-75.** Wish Tune II. This pleasant melody imagines the guy in bed snuggling cozily with his girl. So what's different? This one envisions Ye Olde Wedding Ring on her finger. Begone One-Night Stand. These two are dream-castle odes of brothers Brian and Carl's respective honeys, serenaded in tenor triumph. A bunch of surfer guys look for super surfer girls to marry and live happily ever after with. Indeed, Brian's wife Marilyn's rock group was even called the **Honeys**. In real life, their romantic interludes and lifetime interlocks didn't always work out. Brother **Carl Wilson**, 51, passed away in 1998 after a long illness. He had been the gentle spark of these tender tunes. But wouldn't it be nice, millions of Beach Boy fans agreed, if when we all grew up, we could slice off a chunk of California paradise? Howzat? Well, a gorgeous wife with a dynamite figure; a really important job where you don't have to wear a tie, and you only need to work three easy hours a day; a fab pad to cavort between trips to the beach or drag strip; and a cozy, rosy future. Idyllic dreams. We Americans were not alone in such utopian fantasies. **John Lennon** brought us "Imagine."

"The Way You Look Tonight" – Lettermen, **#13, 9-61.** Much critical hoopla touts the Beach Boys' aural shadow of the **Hi-Los, the Four Freshmen**, and **Chuck Berry**'s lead guitar (via Carl Wilson). The absolutely most powerful harmonic influence on the Beach Boys (beyond the Everlys) is fellow Los Angeles jocks' singing group the **Lettermen**. **Tony Butala** (b. '40), **Jim Pike** ('38), and **Bob Engemann** (b. '36) were fresh out of college (not teenagers), and bloomed as the #1 Adult Contemporary group of the 60s (Whitburn/Bloxdorf). Incredulously omitted from press puffery, the Easy Listening serenaders met in college – earning varsity letters in various sports – and laid down a rainbow ribbon of sound that crossed all genres: Streetcorner harmony; falsetto before Frankie Valli's **Four Seasons**; night-club Jazz to pace the Sinatra/Bennett/N.K. Cole establishment superstars; Lite Rock/covers (#7, 12-67 "Going' Out of My Head"/Can't Take My Eyes off You"); and lush orchestral productions of massive power and profundity.

"The Way You Look Tonight" hit #1(6) 8-36 for World's-Greatest-Male-Dancer **Fred Astaire.** When the Lettermen brought it back, the sweet song was awash in three-part harmony of seraphic significance. Like the Everlys, no one voice stands out. The blend is tremendous.

The Lettermen, who didn't play instruments like the Beach Boys, are the forerunners of the **Backstreet Boys, N'Sync, BBMak, 98°,** and the 2000+ 'BOY BANDS.' The way the Lettermen looked tonight was pretty good. Their biggest chartbuster was #7, 11-61 follow-up "When I Fall in Love," a blend so beatific you didn't really need a rhythm section. They sustained a lucrative 70s Vegas career and SPEARHEADED the BEACH BOYS' high-tenor tunes touting Brian and Carl Wilson, two extraordinary Irish-tenor siblings – like "Surfer Girl," "I Get Around," and "In My Room." Other cameo Lettermen hits include: #17, 2-62

"Come Back Silly Girl"; **Little Anthony's** #10 '65 "Hurts So Bad" to #12, 5-69; and the vocal version "Theme from A Summer Place" (#12, 5-69 Lettermen); and **John Lennon**-penned #42, 10-71 "Love." With its triple-thread breathtaking harmonic tapestry, "They Way You Look Tonight" is one of the 100 prettiest songs of the Rock Era.

Without California's **Lettermen**, spellbinding Beach Boys harmonies might never have coalesced, and they'd be left rockin' Chuck Berry car-tunes only, plus some surfer stomps with Carl's great lead guitar.

"In My Room" – Brian Wilson & the Beach Boys, #23, 11-63. This one is 99% Brian. America's Surf Genius wrote a fervent song about retreating back to your own cozy room to hibernate from all the world's disasters. "In My Room," Brian shares with us all, I can cry and sigh and I can flash back to a sweeter, happier past of Glory Days on the gridiron. With Hi-Lo harmonies, Brian Wilson sings his sincere Hymn to Solitude. We all have some stage fright, unless we're terminally unaware of anybody else in our orbit. Sometimes we just feel like staying inside in our rooms. And pondering. And isn't it a lot more fun to brood now that we have cable? And our own albums and CD's?

Musically, the Beach Boys' "In My Room" is a harmonic masterpiece. It's a Jazz chordal tapestry. They juggle ninths and major sevenths and all that deep stuff that the three-chord Garage Band down the block will never begin to understand. "In My Room" is true to the 50s fad of Fast + Slow Side on 45rpm records.

The flip is their RAH-RAH #6, 11-63 pigskin-power "Be True to Your School" (see Jock Rock chapter).

"Barbara-Ann" – Regents, #13, 5-61. First this Bronx crew cut this Party Animal Anthem in 1958 and disbanded. Then what? Then their song alighted from the Lost Ozone, hit the hit trail, and they reunited for fun and profit. **Guy Billari** sings the original lead, backed by Belmont-style Streetcorner stars Sal Cuomo, Tony 'Hot Rod' Gravagna, Don Jacabucci, and the only Un-Italian Regent, Chuck Fassert – whose cute sister was the original "Barbara-Ann" (complete with hyphen).

One thing that makes the **Beach Boys'** "Barbara-Ann," of #2(2), 1-66 fame, so splendid is that it's an amalgam of the best of American Rock and Roll. These guys can really synthesize. They take the best of the **Lettermen**'s [#13, 9-61 "The Way You Look Tonight"] Jazz harmonies. They take the best of **Chuck Berry**'s speedo riffs and his love of American geography and pop culture. They take the boyish innocence of **Buddy Holly** and his pure American tunes. Then they synthesize the best of East Coast falsetto of the **Four Seasons** variety. The result is a tight and together sound, spliced from Murry Wilson's Tin Pan Alley dreams to their skyrocket of success with their own can't-miss combination of super sounds.

The **Regents** of the Bronx sang of everybody's quintessential dream girl, Peggy Sue (who else?). They interact with Betty Lou who comes to us from **Bobby Freeman**'s #37, 8-58 "Betty Lou Got a New Pair of Shoes." His classic is #5 "Do You Want to Dance," where the San Fran-cisco soul-star overlays a snazzy organ, as he climbs the tonic notes to the zippy seventh. His #5 song was dynamically covered by **Del Shannon** (#43, 9-64). "Do You Wanna Dance?" hit #8 in 8-64 with a rare vocal lead by **Dennis Wilson** of the Beach Boys.

The **Regents** sing "Barbara Ann" pretty straight. Their swirling harmonies cascade over Yankee Stadium as Mickey Mantle and Yogi Berra blast homers galore into the violet neon streets of chili-dogs, egg creams, and confetti – long, long ago. Their hopeful demo failed to materialize as a hit – and they all went back to their day jobs. Lo and behold, three years later, stardom struck. They were blessed with one other hit – #28, 7-61's "Runaround," (no relation to #8, 3-95 Blues Traveler).

The Beach Boy difference is in their song's party-animal mood. For once in their precision-tuned musical lives, they allowed themselves to let their blond surfy hair down and do a musically raggedy song. Nope, not Ragtime. Their "Barbara Ann" gold rush is powered by woozy boozy harmony spiked with yoks and giggles and guffaws.

"Barbara Ann" at #2 is their solitary silver medalist. "Surfin' USA" took #3 bronze in 3-64 (also #36, 8-74); so did #3's "California Girls" in 7-65 and "Sloop John B" in 4-66. "Barbara Ann" showed that they didn't need to shower their fans with Jazz thirteenths and augmented experiments. All you need are three chords, a bottle of fun, and a Rock and Roll dream.

"Sail on Sailor" – Beach Boys, #79, 2-73; #49, 4-75. Double whammy. Among least played of Beach Men's classic tunes. How come? Dunno. A straight-ahead rush of vocal power. This one glides like a skimming sloop over a stormy sea. Full speed ahead.

"California Girls" – Beach Boys, #3, 7-55. Beach Boys declare that California girls are best looking on entire planet. Are they right? California isn't just a state. It's a state of mind. With 30,000,000+ Californians, it's not just our biggest state, but it's bigger than most countries. The West Coast has that sunshine, yep. The Beach Lads are conciliatory to other American girls: They dig the way Southern girls drawl, and the sweet charms of Midwestern daughters of farmers. Anyhow, California beach bunnies are bandied about as best in 72 universes.

Musically, "California Girls" is an adventure in chromatics; any Garage Band trying to follow their bizarre bVII tidal wave of dipping and swooping chromatic major chords will have to buy the sheet music, or hire Sherlock Holmes to find the missing chords.

David Lee Roth covered the tune to #3, too (1985), when he escaped from **Van Halen**. It's an enduring multi-generational hit. With magnanimous charm, the Beach Boys fervently wish that every girl could be a California Girl. Hmm.

"Good Vibrations" – Beach Boys, #1(1), 10-66. Somewhere in the middle of Beatlemania, Brian Wilson's competitive gridiron fire, processed through Murry Wilson, told him to Beat the Beatles at their own game. **Al Jardine** took "Help Me Rhonda" to #1(2) in 4-65, with baritone **Mike Love** supplying the cool "BOW-BOW-POW" bass line. Al gave up dental school for superstardom.

It all started with a theremin, an ultra-weird instrument that does the haunting "WEEE-OOOOOOH" shriek at the finale. The Beach Boys were sweating over a concept album to match #1(15), '67 *Sergeant Pepper* by Liverpool's Fab Four. Brian booked umpteen hours at the studio. Rumor has it that "Good Vibrations" cost 25 or 50 grand to cut. And splice. An unheard-of sum in those days. The song was so complex that they had to record it eight bars at a time, and paste the chunks together. Brian wanted to call his mega-album *Smiley Smile*, but it only halfway materialized into half of that (*Wild Honey*, Al #24, 1-68; title cut #31, 11-67.) Despite his #1 success with "Good Vibrations," Brian Wilson sadly pronounced it a FLOP, and retreated into his lonely room, despondent and gloomy. His #12 follow-up, which to any of us aspiring bands with less genius would have been a monumental success, was even more dismal to him:

"Heroes and Villains" – Beach Boys, #12, 8-67. Whoa! Number twelve – a flop? No way. Same sweeping musical experimentation. Brian's vocal overlays float like satellites in the stratospheric half-light of glimmering starshine. A marvelous chunk of work. Brian decided "Wild Honey" and project "Smiley Smile" were a little too way out. They floated back to earth with more standard Rock songs like #19, 12-67 "Darlin'" and "Do It Again" at #20, 7-68. **Roy Orbison**'s back-up group the Candymen ("Georgia Pines" #81, 11-67), covered "Good Vibrations" supremely, as did (#34, 6-76) **Todd Rundgren**.

Rock and Roll changed as the Beatles and Beach Boys spearheaded a new level of music complexity. Once Rock and Roll, like genius Jazz, went esoteric and obtuse and brilliant (see Bob James – Fusion keyboardist, #23, 11-79 Al. *One on One*), it lost its basic audience who liked to chime in on "Barbara Ann." According to Joe Van Denburg (12-31-96): The change in Rock and Roll came: when the music went beyond the ability of the layman to sing and play along.

"Fun, Fun, Fun" – Beach Boys, #5, 2-64. Hey, like wow. FUN3 . . . isn't that what Rock and Roll's supposed to be all about? Simultaneous favorite of my old Michigan State rock band's two greatest drummers ever – **Tom Helderman** and **Dan Ellinger**. The "FUN3" song is loaded with cruising fever. It's a wacky wonderful Wayne/Garth nightscape, or 1964's Beach Blasters burning down the thunder roads of nevermore Santa Monica Boulevard.

It's a cute song about deception: Pleasant Valley Princess punts the library-idea-she-told-her-dad (to get the car). Now, unabashed, she cruises, seeking ultimate California party. Yep, how many of us, as teenagers, ever wangled some similar off-the-wall story in order to get the girl or car (a snazzy T-Bird) for the evening? Teenage hijinx. Justice inevitably triumphs. The stodgy older gen-

eration takes her festive T-bird away, and now she's forced to go out with the guy singing the song, who also promises FUN FUN FUN. It's a slice of vintage Americana.

You can almost go cosmic with this, and preview the Religious Rock chapter. This fluffy T-Bird joyride represents our carefree youth. We barrel about the summery streets seeking the Ultimate Blast. You know, Kerouac's Center of Saturday Night in America.

We are knights errant, searching for a Holy Grail of Ultimate Fun and Good Times. Then, alas, the Rug of Responsibility is pulled out from under our footloose feet. We must grow up. We can't be Beach Boys anymore. We've got to go to work in the salt mines, the drab Dilbert cubicle, the Dagwood office, the Elmer Fudd carrot patch, or, says Mary Ann Still, Fred Flintstone's quarry.

"I Get Around" – Beach Boys, #1(2), 5-64. Beach Boys' biggest hit ever (2 weeks at #1). The lyric stifles the specter of boredom. Getting 'bugged' driving the exact same mall strip, they seek out new teenage haunts where all the kids are, naturally, cool. That couplet summarizes the Spirit of Restlessness and Wanderlust that drives the world. It's a song about respect. These guys are hip and everybody knows it. All the peripheral Baddd Dues know their jock rep, and leave them alone. In a way, they all seek to be King of the Hollywood Midnight. Romantic quest. It's not a song that pushes modesty and humility. It's not airy braggadocio, either. "I Get Around" packs a power punch of self-confidence. It sells a safe social place in the hierarchy of street rods and midnight cruisers on the Broadway strips of the day-glo American night. Weekends are divided up: one night tomcatting with your friends, and Saturday night with your best girl.

"I Get Around" is a positive chunk of energy flowing from California to the universe. Wimps need not apply. They yearn for the Boss **Bruce Springsteen**'s 'Born to Run' Jersey Highway Nine – the hot asphalt. The Beach Boys cruise for the ultimate drag race. [Like my cousin Kent Maury versus Ricky Nelson's hot '57 Chevy.] "I Get Around," however, is not a 'deadman's curve' of motorized gladiatorial combat. It's a song of knowing one's lofty place in the teenage American night. It's a nugget of Gold Rush confidence – a musical booster that says Rock and Roll will save us from boredom and meaninglessness.

Michigan makes cars, and Rock dreams. In 1999, the Rock Hall finally recognized one of Rock and Roll's Ten Greatest Artists of All Time:

*Birthplace of **Del Shannon**, Coopersville, MI*

The Really Great Singers And a Few 'A-' Ones

13

Splotch! As surfers wiped out, and blonde California dudes hurtled in zillion-dollar sports cars to tire-squealing greasepaint destiny, a bold new breed of singer trailed Elvis and his "Now or Never" operatic odyssey. New York's Brunswick Records' **Jackie Wilson** of Detroit, Soul singer extraordinaire, inspired his friend **Berry Gordy** with early Motown, but also crucially influenced the careers of the Big Three Great 60s Pre-Beatle Singers: **Del Shannon, Gene Pitney**, and **Roy Orbison**.

They skied mountaintops of vocal adventure. **Shannon** hailed from snowy West Michigan; **Pitney** ("the Rockville Flash") came from the Pitney-Bowes fortune in Rockville, Connecticut; **Orbison** ('greatest singer of all' – said **Elvis**) emerged from hot, dusty, near-ghost town Wink, Texas, a long 100-mile shadow away from Buddy Holly's Lubbock.

"My Empty Arms" – Jackie Wilson, #9, 1-61; #25, 2-61 R & B. From sad-clown opera *Pagliacci*, Wilson lifted aria *"Vesti La Giubba,"* and fired off Dramatic Italian-Tenor majesty with his Afro-American Detroit Casanova style. Opera Rock arrived, with the UN-Beach Boy Wilson.

"Baby Workout" – Jackie Wilson, #5, 3-63. Ex-boxer Wilson strutted the stage, jumped gymnastic gyrations, and crashed to his knees with passionate imploring for his lady love(s). Strangely, two of these great singers came from Michigan. It's also amazing that tiny Highland Park, literally swallowed by Detroit, would produce both **Jackie Wilson** and rock-papa **Bill Haley**. Jock Rock.

O.K., so who's the 1999 Rock Hall of Fame high-school football star from up North? The one with the Big Voice and recent Rock hall inclusion? **Charles Westover!!!** Charles WHO? Well, he changed his name to DEL (somehow from Cadillac's Coupe de Ville). Also to SHANNON – after a river in that rainbow leprechaun land of Irish tenors, the Emerald Isle. THE Irish tenor, **John McCormack**, hit #3, 3-1913 with his lilting "Where the River Shannon Flows." Ask Elvis: how good was Del Shannon? Well, there's just one song Elvis wished he'd done first:

"Runaway" – Del Shannon, #1(4), 3-61; #3, 4-61 R & B; #112, 1967 live version. Elvis said this singer/songwriter Shannon debut was simply the greatest rock and roll song ever written! Afro-American Ann Arbor producer Ollie McLaughlin, of Tera-Shirma Records, sculpted Del's meteoric career. Del Shannon was born in Coopersville, Michigan, by Grand Rapids, in 1934. After a U.S. Army stint in Germany where he discovered his considerable guitar skills, he toiled back in Kellogg's cereal mecca Battle Creek, selling linoleum, carpet, and Rock and Roll destiny.

Del plunked his cheapo guitar and honed his pipes on the *Hank Williams Songbook*. His high school football coach, Del said, only kept him on the team for his coach's favorite "Your Cheatin' Heart" medley. Unlike 6'3" 210# Hawthorne High quarterback, Beach Boy Brian Wilson, Del was a running back ('fullback'), 5'8" but 180 muscular pounds. Del lumbered over little Class 'D' high school lines like a Buick over a beer can.

Like other teen idols, Del shaved five years off the calendar, claiming a 1939 birth date. His original VFW-Hall band photo (*Vintage Years* album, N.C., 1975) shows Del with some 55-year-old bass fiddle plunker and a flannel-shirted crew-cut sheriffish 250# guitarist with a mini-amp from Gibson in Kalamazoo. Other Michigan towns made cars. Michigan not only transported the world, but gave it a song to sing. The Gibson Guitar Company is centered in Kalamazoo; of all the big rock stars, **Del Shannon** is closest to the musical fountainhead.

"Runaway." In the sloshing rain, Del ponders the sad demise of his love affair. He walks alone, in the rain, feelin' some pain. Del's lyric bleeds gray, gusty, rainswept brooding night. Cloudy Grand Rapids is one of the snowiest spots in America, like Buffalo, New York. Morose, stoical sorrow is much easier in slush-ooze Northern Cloud Towns than in San Diego. "Runaway" turns on a crucial chord change rarely used in R & R before:

> **Am — G — F — E7**

Remember the **Kingston Trio**'s "El Matador" (#32, 2-60)? And **Ventures**' #2, 7-60 "Walk – Don't Run"? It's an ancient chord change. We must spin off briefly to the oldest Rock and Roll song in the history of the world, the 500-year-old madrigal "Greensleeves":

So Del Shannon's "Runaway" begins on this chordal run: **Am – G – F – E7**. Then it rumbles into all its other innovations: 1) Falsetto; 2) **Max Crook**'s otherworldly Musitron; 3) The lyrical motif of flight or escape; and 4) Shannon's magnificent powerful Swiss tenor, over-arching the whole musical revelation.

"Runaway" is NOT **Janet Jackson**'s #3, 9-94 tune, nor Soul Asylum's **Tom Petty** echo (#5, 6-93) "Runaway Train." On #23, 70-89 "Running Down a Dream," Jacksonville's Petty conjures a mystic kinship with his mentor Del Shannon, Petty sings of singing along with Del on the "Runaway" refrain. For a song with so much lyrical forlorn sadness, how could Del's MUSIC be having so much FUN?

When 8-year-old Tom first heard Del in Jacksonville, Florida, we five American vagabonds (aged 18) were chortling down Mr. Vesuvius, and gallivanting around Europe in a shoestring VW Microbus. Sinuous Italian razorback road. Sundown orange, aquamarine Bay of Napoli below. "Runaway" pounced on Radio Luxembourg and all of Europe with volcanic effervescence. Del Shannon came booming off the smoldering volcano, with a kick-stomp beat and dynamic wild new instruments (musitron), falsetto flashes, and revolutionary chords.

Falsetto? It's a male singer's leap into high soprano range. Nope, of course Del didn't invent it. (See Jan & Dean, Jimmy Jones, Clarence 'Frogman" Henry, Fats Domino, Louis Jordan.) Shannon simply perfected it, energizing his bullwhip falsetto flourishes with surging power. No one had ever shifted vocal gears so well before.

Sitting on top of the big-beat bonanza was a small-town goof-off football and Army kid, good ol' Charlie Westover. Somehow he became DEL SHANNON. Great name for a rock star.

As Charlie, he could hang out at the soda shop, hawk tile, do the Army gig, toss a pigskin. Plunk Hank Williams on guitar. Be normal. Share Miller Time with poker pals at gas station. Good ol' Charlie Westover. Both **Buddy Holly** and **Del Shannon** sold tile. Stationed in Germany in the U.S. Army, Del apprenticed in the "Get Up and Go" radio show, rocking with his dextrous lead guitar riffs, and mountainous Swiss-American tenor.

Becoming Del, he shucked 25 pounds to squeeze into his tight teenage idol pants. Then he unleashed that incredible VOICE – that voice that could swoop into a yodel, or dance over towering notes **Frankie Valli** and the other Three Seasons could only dream about. Del had to storm the stage, bounce bombastically amongst the shrieking moppets, and fill Fillmores and Albert Halls and Isles of Wight with the raw unleashed power of his super Hard Rock tenor. A tough act to follow? His own.

After eluding Ollie McLaughlin's kindly managerial reins, Del cranked out a few vintage masters at Twirl Records and Big Top on seedy Alexandrine Street of Detroit's Lower West Side. Del netted a paltry $12,000 in "Runaway" royalties – the big bucks got poltroonly squirreled away for 'recording time,' 'DJ copies," 'mastering expenses,'

or some other euphemism for lost cash. Today, not much has improved. Richard Campbell says "fewer then 5% of musicians to earn advances on royalties EVER recoup them on record sales."

Del Shannon didn't invent the falsetto technique. Mediaeval torture monsters discovered hideous tortures to insure lads' rooftop sopranos to be 'permanent.' For post-pubescent singers to accomplish some skyscraper notes, however, it took a lot of talent and practice.

Falsetto followed Barber-Shop Quartets from Ragtime days. First tenors often shifted to faux soprano. In the streetcorner era of the early 50s, falsetto flair flashed. Del Shannon was propped by the gimmicky supernatural sound of keyboard man Max(imilian) Crook and his clattery contraption. Greg Shaw sez Crook's musitron was "an odd sort of modified organ like an electric ocarina." Shannon and Crook were cover-band gigging for some fifty lackluster beerswogglers at Battle Creek's Hi-Lo Club in 1960, covering hits by Roy Orbison, Elvis, and Conway Twitty. Good bar band.

"Hold it!" commanded Del, halfway through a song, as he heard Max Crook drift from **Am** to **G** on the squeaky musitron. "Hit those chords again." Crook did. Del and Max struggled for the next 15 minutes in musical confusion, forging a song that would permit Del to BE ELVIS. A song that would for a brief moment rule the world.

This otherworldly MUSITRON solo explodes out of the blue. It drifts in from full-moon cumulonimbus skies. It thunders mammothly. Call it a gimmick. Call it a smash success.

Singer/songwriter Shannon, ten years before the Elton John-James Taylor-Jim Croce-Don McLean onrush, sets up his own lyrical tension; "Runaway" plods gloomily, the British or West Michigan omnipresent drizzle lacing his face with grim resignation. Del's romantic tears co-mingle with the downswoop rainstorm. He ponders: what went wrong? He ponders why the girl went away. If some mysterious third person would return, it would finish off his misery. Del plods on in the sodden roadside gloom.

As tears fall, Del grapples with some mysterious nasty pain paralyzing his will to cope. Whether it's a wounded ego or muscle pull, we never know. For Del Shannon a/k/a Charlie Westover, life held a lot of pain. Maybe Charlie might have been happy and lived a long time swizzling the odd beer with his poker cronies down at the Sunoco station. Not Del.

Del and Max splashed down "Runaway" onto the 1/2-inch tape in less than three hours. Rife with Rock and Roll gimmicks, "Runaway" contains multiple lines everybody remembers. Particularly that wild falsetto POUNCE: "Why-why-why-why-why . . ?" Why did she run away? Hindsight. In his bitter hindsight, he longs for the loving little lass who's eluded him, his long lost runaway.

Throughout 1961-63, Del often toured with the Fab Four, and DEL HEADLINED THE SHOW. Del Shannon electrified the **Beatles** with his high-voltage energy and Rock and Roll dynamism that verged on the dangerous. Like Buddy Holly and Gene Vincent, his Yankee popularity was eclipsed by the British reaction of absolute adoration. Del Shannon became a rock icon in the British Isles. Del pioneered let-it-all-hang-out THUNDER ROCK.

Del Shannon

Del Shannon not only introduced the Beatles' music to the United States – Del Shannon BECAME A BEATLE! Sort of.

Wow. Bold assertions. The Beatles' "From Me to You' was climbing the British charts after their initial "Love Me Do" debut success (#17, U.K., '62). Del heard John Lennon's version of the new Beatle tune. My old pink-label Big Top single of Del's "From Me to You" has a very curious songwriting credit; it reads, backwards – (McCartney-Lennon).

One hot July 1963 night at Dearborn's Haven Club, we snuck in on iffy fake I.D. Del Shannon, megastar, just happened to be partying with pals in the audience. They good-naturedly dragged him up on stage. When he crashed forth into "Runaway," the rowdy bar just shut up and listened in awe. He announced that on his British tour, he'd met some kids from Liverpool. Nice guys. Gonna be stars. Uh-huh, we muttered. He busted forth with "From Me to You," and it shortly became a minor hit for him (#77, 6-63), the first HOT 100 charted **Beatle** tune ever in the U.S. – six months before the official British Invasion. Swamped by awe of Shannon's magical musical pipes pealing with power and rockin' resonance, the audience just sat there dumbstruck.

On the Beatles' first American tour, **George Harrison** got sick. Rather than risk a roller coaster stomach on stage, George hired a replacement Beatle. One night only: DEL SHANNON. At the turn of the Millennium, George Harrison was stabbed by a London intruder; providentially, he recovered quickly. Shannon's later fate would not be so lucky at the same age (55). Del played a glorious Beatle concert. His guitar-playing and vocals were, as usual, world class. It almost went farther. Or furthest. The alleged conversation, it is rumored, went something like this:

"Del's a better guitarist than George, isn't he, John?"
"Yup."
"Del's a better singer than George, isn't he?"
"Yup."
"D'ya think we ought to consider firin' George – like we did Pete Best for Ringo – and hire Del to replace George?"
"Naaaahh!"
"Why not?"
"George is our old friend!"

Funny thing about bands. They love each other like brothers. They also fight like brothers.

"Runaway" ran away with all the honors. Shannon became an overnight international star. From Del's modest white clapboard house on the Eastern outskirts of Coopersville – just a quarter-mile from flashing freeway I-96 – he never realized he'd go from just one of the guys in the backfield or gas station to international superstar overnight. It's a tough road. Paradise, it ain't. Or **Nirvana**.

"Molly-O"/"You Are My Sunshine" – Johnny & the Hurricanes. "Molly-O" N.C., 1960; "Sunshine" #91, 12-60. "You Are My Sunshine" is a country classic #1 hit (#23, 1941 for Gene Autry), written in 1940 by Louisiana Governor Jimmie Davis (1898-2000), "Molly-O" is simply "Greensleeves" or "What Child Is This?". "Greensleeves" hit #25 in 3-52 for the silky strings of **Mantovani**, 8th most popular Album Artist of All Time, in *Top Pop Albums* points. Johnny & Hurricanes' "Molly-O" was cut at Detroit's Twirl Records, Del Shannon's Big Top label. It used the **Am-G-F-E7** chord revolution from "Runaway" three months earlier. The Hurricanes often backed Del at Twirl/Big Top Records in Detroit. Coincidence?

"Red River Rock" – Johnny & the Hurricanes, #5, 8-59; #5 R & B. No futuristic ditty itself, this original 1800s grade-school cowboy lost-love lament. This is the ROCKIN' instrumental version of "Red River Valley." The RED is the only American river which flows to the Arctic Ocean via the MacKenzie River system – the Red River of Minnesota and Manitoba. The OTHER Red River borders Texas and Oklahoma, and flows 40 miles from Buddy Holly's Lubbock, up in the Texas Panhandle.

Johnny's Toledo, Ohio, is a miniscule Detroit. This Polish-Czech-Ukrainian-American semi-surf rock band features lead sax man **Johnny Paris** (Pociak); **Paul Tesluk** on fab Farfisa organ (1959 R & R novelty); **Butch Mattice** (bass); **Tony Kaye** (dynamite drummer), and **Bo Savitch** (an even better one). Johnny & Crew rip into the ol' "Red River Valley" with a firebrand Farfisa, **Dave Yorko's** sizzling guitar, and Johnny's jackhammer sax.

"Earth Angel" – Penguins, #8, 12-54: #1(3) R & B. Cleveland Duncan piloted a masterful R & B 'Irish tenor' lead. Just when you think it'll be only rumbling baritone Bruce Tate, or deeper bass Curtis Williams, over three verses and one vocal bridge, suddenly a wondrous wide swath of falsetto magic (Dexter Tisby and crew) comes cascading through. Dancing through straight streetcorner chords (I – VI min. – IV – V7), it hits this ethereal bridge; (I⁷ – IV – I – V7 – I – I7 – IV – VI min – II min – V7). By the time you strike that magic dominant seventh at the finale of the second vocal bridge, then Tisby hits a super climactic rush of R & B euphoria.

"Earth Angel," however, is a lot more than just a magic interwoven chord pattern by a great Barber Shop Quartet. It's a Rock and Soul ballad landmark. Every guy at every cheesy sock hop in America had some girl he perceived as an Earth Angel. She is the Chiffon Madonna of every kid's dreams. Del was listening.

The **Penguins** got their name from a cutesy cartoon character on Kool cigarettes – Willie the Penguin. To this day, I can visualize the hoppitty boppitty little penguin, dragging on a big cig, and crowing in mountaintop falsetto: "Willie the Penguin sez smoke KOOLS." They banned Joe Camel in 1998 for pushing smoke to kids, but Willie in 1954 was twice as cute. Swathed in Sierra Club Green on the cig pack, and be-bopping off icebergs into his bracing Antarctic swimming pool, Willie the Pusher Penguin appealed to pint-size dudes like me (age 11 in 1954).

Though "Earth Angel" was the Los Angelino Penguins' only Top 100 tune, it's like Margaret Mitchell's only novel – *Gone With the Wind*. "Earth Angel" is in everybody's Doo-Whop Top Three. Back in the 50s, we did pedestals. Teen Queens perched on pedestals of adoration. Guys worshiped them. Swooning Duncan beseeches, implores, begs, coaxes, and cajoles the superfine sweetie to be his own. The 'vision' of (her) 'loveliness' obsesses him and inspires his every waking breath. Del's obsession was Rock and Roll destiny.

Del Shannon didn't miss any hot licks in sculpting his falsetto magic. He grooved to Clarence 'Frogman' Henry's #20, '56 "Ain't Got No Home," and wowed to the falsetto flair and flash of R & B wonder **Jimmy Jones:**

"Handy Man" – Jimmy Jones, #2(1), 12-59; #3, 2-60 R & B. The initial "COMMA COMMA COMMA COMMA COM COM" was neither a punctuational lesson, a political statement, nor a computer program – it was Jimmy's reaction to a radio station call-letter jingle for Oklahoman KOMA-AM radio. Huge hit, too, firing falsetto with glee and finesse [covers by #22, 7-64 **Del Shannon**, and #4, 6-77 **James Taylor**.]

"There's a Moon Out Tonight" – Capris, #3, 12-60; #11, 2-61 R & B. **Nick Santamaria** of Queens led these guys named for a gorgeous Italian Isle off Napoli. First tenor **Mike Mincelli** marvelizes their high falsetto.

"Lover's Island" – Blue Jays, #31, 8-61. L.A. R & B singer **Leon Peels** fronted this fab falsetto group. Incredible assemblage of R & B, Soul, Surf-Island, Balladeer, Rock and Roll, Streetcorner Blues maestros? Super song.

"Don't You Just Know It?" – Huey 'Piano' Smith and the Clowns, #9, 3-58: #4 R & B. Cosimo Matassa's Crescent City cutups crafted this Call and Response Boogie Woogie tune from deep Delta Gospel Blues. Smith bangs an old Ragtime upright which magically reverberates. Singer **Bobby Marchan**'s finale bounces "KOOBA-KOOBA" off rafters and brings down the house.

"Blue Moon" – Elvis Presley, #55, 9-56. #1 hit for Glen Gray Orchestra in 1935, this other streetcorner fountainhead (I – VI min – IV – V7) features Elvis mournful and sad. Elvis wails his grief and gloom to a cosmos not used to assuaging cosmic grief. Unearthly falsetto. In astronomy, a 'blue moon' is the 2nd full moon during the same month (say, one on the 1st and again on 31st of that month). Of course, Elvis is among the greatest Great Singers!

"Two Silhouettes" – Del Shannon, NC, '63; #23, U.K. Flipside of Beatle song, #77, 6-68 "From Me to You." Del reprises O-Henry ending of Rays' #3, 10-57 "Silhouettes." Better than 'A'-side. Probably **Ronettes** on background. Del never made a 'B'-side. Each side of the hot pink 45 record is "A+" Rock and Roll.

"Hats Off to Larry" – Del Shannon, #5, 6-61; #9 U.K., 9-61. No weepy sayonaras for Del. Shannon locked into a never-before-attempted new lyrical concept – you pat the romantic rival on the back, because you're glad your annoying ex is gone. Shannon leads off with the **Am-G-F-E7** run again. He shifts to the Key of 'A' major when the lines are complete, running down a modified streetcorner pattern on "Hats off the Larry" who broke her heart. He pumps the IV chord minor to torque up the drama, and ratchets the falsetto flourish. Del's twisty lyrical actually congratulates rival Larry for breaking her heart after she'd hurt Del. Del's third hit in a row takes it a step farther, perhaps launching the mixed-bag genre of Revenge Rock:

"So Long Baby" – Del Shannon, #28, 9-61; #10, 12-61 U.K. A slurring, snarling electric viola (like "California Dreamin'," Mamas & Papas, #4, 1-66) sound cuts through Del's embittered lyric. Del pioneers REVENGE ROCK. His quest for romantic competition sizzles to fever pitch. Shannon's musical motif is minor; he hammers the jangly, strident **Am** Grunge-style chord, driving it incessantly to denote his dismay. At football, romance, or checkers/chess, Del Shannon NEEDED to win. He's GLAD she's gone. In their romantic checker game, she got one jump on him – but he jumped TWICE. His next song returns him to his well-adjusted Love Handyman theme:

"Hey! Little Girl" – Del Shannon, #38, 11-61; #2, 3-62 U.K. Super sleeper. Good ol' Del. He runs a broken heart fix-it shop like Jimmy Jones's "Handy Man." For this sweet little girl he comforts, and cuddles.

"Cry Myself to Sleep" – Del Shannon, #99, 6-62; #29 U.K. Despite a ton of tears, this is the song that launched the #1 song for the #1 artist of All Time, (Whitburn's): Elton John's "Crocodile Rock" #1(3), 12-72.

"Little Town Flirt" – Del Shannon, #12, 12-62; #4, 1-63 U.K. For 'Flirt,' Del introduced a chorus of girls; Del warns his chum to shun the notorious flirt. Inspired by Dion's mega-chartbuster #1, '61 "Runaround Sue," "Flirt" uses 'Girls' Group' – perhaps the **Ronettes**.

"The Swiss Maid" – Del Shannon, #64, 9-62; #2, 10-62 U.K. Writer Roger Miller was poised for stardom via his campy spoofs, like "Chug-A-Lug" (#9, 9-64). One of few Shannon hits not written by Del, the Swiss maid tune is more idyllic, arcadian. She lives on a beautiful Heidi *Sound of Music* Swiss mountaintop – an ocean of pristine green with strawberry ice-cream-cone snowy peaks. Shannon's heritage is Swiss-American. The song features two great gimmicks: his only Buddy Holly wo-uh-ho hiccup, and his own trademark yodel. Del was simply the best yodeler (see "Coopersville Yodel") in the history of the world.

"Keep Searchin'" – Del Shannon, #9, 11-64; #3, 1-65 U.K. Deep in the midst of his fervent search, Del married a girl from Custer, Michigan; they had three kids, and moved to a big blue house in the San Fernando Valley of California. "Keep Searchin'" is a falsetto work of art, however. Del hits one of the highest notes ever heard ["A"] in his shrieking fade-out by a male singer. Stratosphere stuff.

"Stranger in Town" – Del Shannon, #30, 2-65. Del's sister-song follow-up to "Keep Searchin'" is this eerie runaway drama. Alarming minor chords ambush the rhythm guitar. Bashing drums and bass hammer. Del carries the grim story to a darker dimension. Dave Marsh brooks no diplomacy, psychoanalyzing the duality between the Shannon vs. Westover personalities:

"It's one long bleat of terror, the singer and his lover [are] pursued by some unnamable person for a reason just beyond the fringe of rational understanding" [Marsh feels Shannon has ducked out with some too-young groupie, and the parents are royally ticked off]. Personally, I think Marsh exaggerates Del's fugitive drama, which stars two lovers. Marsh explains the song's formal structure is based on fear: "the beatless recitation of gloom and doom in Del's parched intro; the spare bass guitar note, starved and blotchy." Del's fade-out is a wild banshee wail of falsetto "woooo's" of a man "so tortured by his own thoughts that all he can do is scream his fear out into the night sky."

Maybe so. Pigskin star Charles Westover was tortured by the spotlight, by the obsession to BE ELVIS on the hissing stage. He was tortured by the fame of someone that was a piece of him called 'Del Shannon.' Fortunately for his next decades, Prozac had not yet been given him to 'relax.'

"Stranger in Town" takes me back to my third Shannon encounter. Bay Shore, Long Island, second was Dearborn's Haven Club in 1963. In 1961 we were almost trampled and squashed with 8000 other Shannon fanaddicts by Detroit's Lightguard Armory, where we realized that Del had something weird to do with doom. We almost got crushed, so we split, and didn't get to hear him live until the Haven two years later. My second success-

ful fandom proved more productive. In 1976 Bay Shore, on the Oldies circuit with goodtime pal **Gary U.S. Bonds** ("Quarter to Three" #1, 5-61), Shannon seemed genuine. He was gabby, jolly. He recalled my Woolies era, and how my band after I left opened a concert or two of his.

Rock and Roll is no place for people hunting for 'benefits,' the regular paycheck, the gold watch, the pension, the shy life. When he performed "Keep Searchin'" in Bay Shore, Del seemed to be truly having fun.

Tom Petty, big 80s and 90s fan, produced Del's last successful comeback single, Phil Phillips' #2, 1959 "Sea of Love" (#33, 1-82). Elvis once sang along with Del; Del cut the original version of El's "His Latest Flame" (#4, '61, for Elvis) on Del's debut album.

As the sixties boomed psychedelic, Del was caught in a crossfire (as usual) between musical generations. Del's spectacular "Break Up" hit only #95, 5-65. His "Sister Isabelle" has such a sad finalé that his ex-girlfriend Isabelle joins a convent and becomes a nun. Del cut the **Box Tops'** #1(4) "The Letter" with a plethora of phasers and state-of-the-art **Hendrix** concepts. Del's big sound explodes, too, with his revamp of **Miss Toni Fisher's** #3, 11-59 "The Big Hurt" (#94, 5-66). Del's own producing career produced the only certified million-seller for Brian Hyland, already of "Sealed with a Kiss," (#3, 6-62) fame. Del turned the NYC fanzine Teen Idol into a suave purveyor of Blue-Eyed Soul; Hyland's "Gypsy Woman" is awash with the soul stylistics of **Curtis Mayfield** and the **Impressions'** original (#20, 11-61).

"The Coopersville Yodel" – Del Shannon, NC, 1973. Amazing song! Shannon emerged briefly from a woozy blue funk to command a myriad-fan concert on England's 'tropical isle,' Wight. Palm tress actually sway in the chilly 69° summer breeze. Remember Paul McCartney's cottage on that selfsame Isle of Wight ["When I'm 64"] on the Beatles' breakthrough concept album *Sergeant Pepper* (#1[15], 6-67)? Hair unkempt, and a silly sardonic smile wreathing his downtrodden face, Del performed the YODEL TO END ALL YODELS. You dig Speed Metal? Try the Speed Yodel? Province of cowboy yodel-crooners Roy Rogers and Gene Autry, and "Rose Marie's" (#1[11], U.K. Floridian Slim Whitman, yodeling is one of the most skilled and least appreciated singing skills in the world. To yodel, you shift gears.

Bill Monroe is the master yodeler. Although largely ignored on the pop charts, the Rosine, Kentucky, (1911-95) mandolin maestro established an entire GENRE of music – BLUEGRASS – which combines Bill's characteristic "high lonesome" sound with the contemporary yodel-suffused style of Western Swing. Cowboys like Gene Autry and Roy Rogers pioneered and sculpted this gear-shifting vocal technique. It was used quite effectively by Jimmie Rodgers I, (1897-1933), known as the Mississippi Blue Yodeler (Whitburn calls him the Father of Country Music). Perhaps the first yodelers stood atop lofty crags on the Alpenhorns of alpine Switzerland, ancestral home of Del Shannon's people. The Scottish-American Monroe ["Scotland" N.C., '58 & #27 Country] was adept at incredibly-proficient speedo yodels. Yodeling casts off the male natural vocal range – and vaults skyward into the Soprano Zone. It's a quick trip, however, and doesn't hover in TOTAL falsetto like the Newbeats or some **Frankie Valli** or David Lasley or the Disco **Bee Gees**. With the silver medal to Hawaiian paniolo cowboy singer Leabert Lindsey, the best yodeler I have ever heard is Del Shannon. On the unlikely Isle of Wight.

Obviously , yodeling is not for everyone – hence its rarity. First off, it's VERY tough to master. Second, once you do, it may not be sufficiently appreciated (by your sister, who calls out the EMS when she hears your yodeling in the shower),

In order to truly yodel, you must shift gears. Its tenor-to-falsetto power-shift concept was developed by Del's Swiss ancestors on Zermatt or the Matterhorn or lofty green cliffs and daisy-dotted *Sound of Music* mountain meadows. You can hear tremendous Yodel Kicks, rapid ascents to quick yodel notes at the end of song lines, as in Johnny Horton's #4, 9-60, "North to Alaska." Diverse yodel-kick experts are Horton, Shannon, **Little Richard** and **Cyndi Lauper**. "Swiss Maid" is Shannon's only pre-Beatle yodeler, throbbing with cotton-candy true love.

Del's melody foghorns and leaps to the top of Mt. Jungfrau like a jet-propelled mountain goat. In accelerando yodeling profusion, he shifts gears and ditches the leggiero pace. He doubles his speed from baritone to falsetto. His lyricless high and lonesome song flashes flourishes of spun gold: from moderato to presto, Shannon vaults the vocal range and the Italian Alps, power-shifting with supersonic speed. On his last fortissimo crescendo, with guitars and drums at the speed of light, Shannon's precise tenor never quavers, nailing each note like a perfect Swiss watch. After this dance macabre of frantic gasping gusto, the one-of-a-kind song ends in a deafening discombobulation of fluttery cymbals and amps turned up to eleven. World-class yodel . . .

Real life brought him a couple of comebacks. Del's real life story is not as sad as James Dean's reel life story; for a guy who died young, Del made it to be comparatively old. The Del Shannon tragedy is in the method. First, and saddest, Shannon came back. He beat the substances. He settled in a modest California mansion with his wife, and his daughter Kim Westover. Unfortunately, Del danced with his demons. Seems he never really got over the dual personality of superstar DEL SHANNON versus good ol' boy Charlie Westover. When push came to shove, the duality drove him to drastic consequences, like the grotesque inmates of the Eagles' #1(1), 2-77 "Hotel California." Too bad Del couldn't hear the Eagles' sage "Learn to Be Still", off *Hell Freezes Over* (Al. #5, 2-95). An older, wiser Don Henley points out the sheepishness of the human herd, and how everybody follows satanic 'Messiahs' of violence over cliffs of doom.

Late in Del's life he re-emerged, blasting hopped-up "Runaway" lyrics and "Stranger in Town" to a new crime-sotted audience of late 80s TV viewers as theme song to *Crime Story*. Clad in a scruffy brown suit, Del showed little of the raging renaissance of health he'd enjoyed in his #123, 12-81 Al. *Drop Down and Get Me*. Had he learned to be serenely still, and accept himself with a satisfied mind, Del might be cranking out the odd newie modest hit.

"Come As You Are"– Nirvana, #32, 3-92. **Kurt Cobain** (1967-94) was the Byronic Rock martyr for the 90s. His Seattle Grunge crew, **Nirvana**, anchored by super drummer **Dave Grohl** and guitarist **Jason Everman**, wished Kurt the best in '92 when he married **Courtney Love** of **Hole** (#58, 12-94 "Doll Parts") and they had a baby. Somehow, Kurt came unglued. Dogged by headaches, medicines, and dark depression, Kurt took the fast dark path.

Del Shannon was, for a time, the Heart of Rock and Roll (1961-65). Something went desperately wrong. Late in the American Century, much has been made about the tragic suicide of talented Nirvana lead singer **Kurt Cobain** – found dead by wife Courtney love of a self-inflicted shotgun blast in drizzly Seattle in 1994. The spotlight burns the wriggling star, and the starlight snuffs out.

Similar fates stole the talents of troubador Phil Ochs, Danny Rapp of "At the Hop" #1 fame, plus Johnny Ace and Sid Vicious and Tommy "I Wonder What She's Doing Tonight" Boyce (#8, 1-68). Also Terry Kath of Jazz-Rock kingpins Chicago. Scores of other superstars have O.D'd on booze, pills, love, life or just plain self-destruction. Look at Donny Hathaway, the Skyliners' Janet Vogel, or Michael Hutchence of INXS, whose #2(2), 2-88 is all too prophetic: "Devil Inside" . . .

You might say Del Shannon was the first Grunge Rock singer. His Grand Rapids cloud is as dark as Seattle's -- and his happy music is dragged down to sodden gloom by his grim, anguished romantic catastrophes in so many world-class songs.

Del Shannon, born January 30. 1934, died of a self-inflicted gunshot wound on February 8, 1990. It would have been the 59th birthday of James Dean. Del was probably 56. Michigan has a passionate belief in deer hunting. Good ol' boy Charlie took his guns to his lonely, isolated, dancing-demon Hotel California. He'd just been put on Prozac to relax.

After Roy Orbison left us in 1988, Del's protégé Tom Petty and his Traveling Wilburys (Bob Dylan, George Harrison, Jeff Lynne) were looking for a replacement. Their first supergroup album *Volume One* hit #3 in 1988. They picked Del Shannon. It was not to be. It was too late.

In 1999, after incessant lobbying by us fans, Del Shannon finally made the Hall of Fame.

* * * * * * *

Ever wonder where one-man Minneapolis band **Prince Nelson** ("When Doves Cry" #1[5], 6-84) got his production ideas? Thank **Gene Pitney**, 2002 [whew! – finally] Rock Hall of Fame Inductee, born in Hartford, Connecticut, in 1941.

"(I Wanna) Love My Life Away" – Gene Pitney, #39, 1-61. ALL Gene Pitney. This spliced basement chunk of drummer Gene, guitarist Gene, and singers Gene & Gene, is the first R & R song featuring the whole shebang done by one very gifted musician and tekkie whiz.

Before consolidating his talents with THE producer **Phil Spector**, Gene did a great solo shot here. He lavishes yodel-kicks, Holly hiccups, and honeyed harmonies on his Jiffy-Soprano Self-Propelled Girls Group Kit. He bangs the drums in perfect pulse. No MIDI/synthesizer technology yet existed. His guitar surges along with his insistent bass – foreshadowing the Motown Jamerson-Benjamin-Van Dyke session bonanza.

Pitney's voice was the most malleable one in early 60s Rock and Roll. He could sling a commanding gunfighter baritone in "The Man Who Shot Liberty Valance" (#4, 4-62). Pitney could cascade and crescendo and overdub with the best. Catch his "Every Breath I Take" (#42, 8-61). It is "Love My Life Away," however, which highlights Pitney's extraterrestrial vocal power and versatility.

All of the Big Three early 60s Great Singers come from small American towns. Pitney did his share of jagged, on-the-edge lyrics:

"Twenty-Four Hours from Tulsa" – Gene Pitney, #17, 10-63; #5, 12-63 U.K. Road-running protagonist heads for his own wedding in oil town Tulsa. His matrimonial dreams explode in an Oz tornado of passion for a honkytonk angel. Pitney also scored on: movie theme #13, 10-61 "Town Without Pity"; #4, 4-62 "(The Man Who Shot) Liberty Valance"; #12, 12-62 "Half Heaven – Half Heartache"; #9, 10-64 "I'm Gonna Be Strong," and #12, 6-63 "Mecca." Great CRESCENDO boomers all.

"Only Love Can Break a Heart" – Gene Pitney, #2(2), 9-62. Pitney's biggest hit. Masters Conway Twitty's rasp. Rococo rendition, shining with celestial strings. Like Pat Boone's whistling in #1(7), '57 "Love Letters in the Sand," Pitney whistles his way to his topmost charted tune.

"It Hurts to Be in Love" – Gene Pitney, #7, 7-64. Whereas Del Shannon's crescendos are often reduced to frantic fadeouts (the high 'A' on "Keep Searchin'), for Pitney crescendos are a way of life. "It Hurts," however, reverts to his first do-it-yourself hit. It throbs along on a guitar-drum blur reminiscent of Buddy Holly's "Peggy Sue." Souped-up poetic lyrics were waiting for Bob Dylan's spontaneous-bop Kerouackian touch.

One of the true miracles of 50s music is that it hobbled along on lyrics. Trying to charm 13-year-old girls, the basic record market did not require Shakespeare. **Smokey Robinson** once told us at Motown: "We write songs for 13 and 15 year-old girls – not English professors." **Bob Dylan** juiced up the lyrics. **Del Shannon** and **Gene Pitney** opened up the chord structure. With ultra-complex producer **Phil Spector**, Gene also introduced musical gimmicks never before seen. The crescendo is the special domain of Gene Pitney.

Pitney (often crediting his Mom) also made it as a spectacular songwriter: #8, '61 "Hello Mary Lou" for Ricky Nelson; "Rubber Ball" (#6, 12-60) for Bobby Vee. Gene's greatest songwriting triumph occurred, though, with Darlene Love and the Crystals' Girls Group goldmine – "He's A Rebel" (#1[2], 9-62). It's a great rock and roll song for the Brooklyn **Barbara Alston**, **Mary Thomas**, and **Mary Kennibrew,** and a massive political statement. America thrives on Individual Liberty. Pitney preaches this girl's ardent love for a guy not running with the common herd. He's a dude with the courage of his own convictions. "He's a Rebel," chide the gal's pals.

"He's a Rebel" – Crystals, #1(2), 9-62; #2(1), 10-62 R & B. James Dean said it first – it's cool to be different, especially when you stand up for your beliefs. A Cold War seeped like a sluggish glacier; the communist world said that the individual was subservient to the State. The Crystals said NO WAY. Do your own thing.

"That Girl Belongs to Yesterday" – Gene Pitney, #49, 1-64: #8, 3-64, U.K. Gene launched the songwriting talents in America of two Stone legends (**Jagger-Richard**). Pitney looked like Ed Cowling, with sincere blue eyes and thick black hair, flecked with a few strands of gray in his mid-20s.

Mick Jagger and Keith Richard wrote this dramatic Pitney mega-hit. Pitney's star was launched via this song in Europe, where he almost became Elvis in Italy and Sweden, and several other Pitneymania republics. Absolutely antithetical to anything the Rolling Stones ever sang, Jagger and Richard(s)'s Pitney classic is a monument to the ages. Play it at full volume.

Elvis belongs as an Honorary Member of this Big Three, for he launched them all. Among 60s Elvis songs are these: His always-a-bridesmaid "Return to Sender" at #2(5), 10-62; his Del demo tune "(Marie's the Name) of His Latest Flame" (#4, 8-61), simply a super song; and his two favorite baritone ballads of all time – "Are You Lonesome Tonight?" (#1[6], 11-60) and "Can't Help Falling in Love" (#2, 12-61).

In his last Vegas-jumpsuit haggard performances, stoned on 1500-calorie peanut-butter-and-butter-jelly-banana sandwiches and 14 prescription drugs from Dr. 'Feelgood' Nick . . . after bleary-eyed gasping "My Way" performances, the King had not lost his super sense of humor. In the wings with his adoring entourage, the fading King would laugh and blurt: "Somebody bring me the Greatest Singer in the World to hit the high note for me … ROY ORBISON!"

Roy Orbison was born April 23, 1936 and Elvis said he was the greatest singer of them all.

"Mean Woman Blues" – Roy Orbison, #5, 9-63. Elvis hit #11 in both Country and R & B with this 12-Bar Blues Rockabilly anthem in 1957– but missed the HOT 100. Not so Roy. The VOICE. Roy played football at Wink High. Football is the Texan national sport. Young Orbie wasn't real strong, like Del Shannon. Also, he wasn't very fast. To top it off, he wasn't too coordinated, either, and he didn't see too well. Fortunately for Roy, he wasn't tiny (5'11", 180#), and more fortunately for Roy, he had the tough spirit and tenacity of a bulldog. Roy was never blind – just myopic, but he played his best. The gridiron taught him how to compete in the big arena.

The Wink High School Glee Club shows Roy as a featured soloist. He formed a little combo powered by gung-ho gusto and Roy's crystalline voice. He was on his way to Rock and Roll destiny. And Elvis's Memphis. I had the pleasure of interviewing Roy Orbison in Victoria, British Columbia, in 1967, for the first rock history book, my *Rock Revolution.*

"The Big O" took 15 minutes after the show to relax and tell a few ribald stories of the road. Current tragedies plagued the poor troubadour: his wife's fatal motorcycle crash after Roy and she had reconciled; Roy's brother rolling off a switchback mountain-road curve; and his ultimate desolation strike-out – the loss of two of his three children in a fire in that fated Hendersonville, Tennessee home. Due to an overabundance of security devices (like urban window bars), his family was unable to get out.

At Roy's 1987 Rock Hall of Fame induction, presenter **Bruce Springsteen** was starstruck. Springsteen, among the most powerful performers ever to tear up a stage, bowed in turgid reverence to the mysterious Orbisonic phenomenon. In 1995, 'the Boss' said of 'The Big O'" "Beyond his physical frailty, there was something otherworldly – about that VOICE." Starstruck. Orbison, like Elvis, started in Memphis at Sun Records:

"Ooby Dooby" – Roy Orbison, and the Teen Kings, #59, 5-56. The Great One's R & R heyday blistered the early 60s charts, but his winsome debut tune was shrouded in unrealized potential. Haunting 12-bar Blues, starring Roy's super-natural tenor.

Roy would return. He came home to Wink, married a pretty girl named Claudette, and fended off verbal barbs from her crotchety Paw, who thought Roy wasn't good enough for his gorgeous gardenia. Their turbulent marriage was fraught by early poverty (one year after "Ooby Dooby," Roy only made #1500). Then Roy's Nashville junket landed him some big bucks as songwriter for the teen queens' darlingest duo:

"Claudette" – Everly Brothers, #30, 5-58. Roy's royalties did a double whammy here. Not only were his profits jacked up handsomely when the Everlys sang about Roy's shapely wife, but Roy collected, as writers do, on the gold-record fab flipside: #1(5) "All I Have to Do Is Dream," by songwriter superstars Felice and hubby Boudleaux Bryant. Ellis Amburn's *Dark Star* plumbs the

seediest depths of Roy's stormy relationship, ending gruesomely in the motorcycle accident. We avoid gruesome here. Roy penned hits for the Everlys and Buddy and Jerry Lee Lewis ("Down the Line," gold flipside) which kept the coffers clinking. Like the firebird Phoenix, his career rose from the ashes of defeat.

Roy's voice could compete with anyone, anytime. Monument producer Fred Foster treated Roy to #72, 12-59 "Up Town." It started the ball rolling.

"Only the Lonely" – Roy Orbison, #2, 6-60; #14, 8-60 R & B. The shuddering cannon of Roy's bolero-crescendo classics reads like a prayer book for the lonely. Beginning in Norm & Vi Petty's Clovis, New Mexico, Nor-Va-Jak studios in 1956, Roy soon scored with Sun and Sam Phillips in Memphis. Stuffed with the burgeoning careers of superstars Elvis and Johnny Cash and Jerry Lee Lewis, Sam had to cut some slack and alas, it was Roy. An overcrowded house caused Roy to sleep in his car one night, where he wrote "Only the Lonely." Scribbling nifty ditties late into the Happy Daze decade, Roy dragged into **Phil Everly**'s office.

"Roy, that's a great one . . . why don't you sing it yourself?" Not eager to shun the advice of an Everly Brother, Roy soon had Foster's Monument Records release it. (Fated Roy's label was, ulp, named after a tombstone). Just as music-writer **Elton John** has a 'silent' songwriting partner who furnishes half the FABULI sounds (lyricist **Bernie Taupin**), or David Bartholomew with Fats Domino, Roy Orbison had another singer/songwriter penning half his tunes. No silent one, either.

Joe Melson. "Only the Lonely"? Duet? Yep. Check it out. Melson never crosses over into Half & Half Everly Territory, but his vocal part is very substantial. Joe's in charge of the blander, softer vocal intro: "Dum dum dum dum-be-doo-wah / Oo yay ya yay yah / O wo wo wo doo-wah-ah / Only the Lonely." Then the VOICE. Roy corners the market on heartbreak. He speaks to billions of broken-hearted lovers weeping in the purple gloom . . .

"Blue Angel" – Roy Orbison (& Joe Melson), #9, 9-60; #23, 10-60 R & B. Joe Melson chimes in with another super UN-lyric: "Oo, sha la la, dooby wah, dum dum dum, yay yay." To rock and rollers, steeped in the soothing mellow Chalyspo – Orbison was King . . . until Elvis returned to the spotlight. Each got seared by the blinding kleig lights and dazzling dark destiny. "Blue Angel" calms a crying young girl. He guides us through a desolate and moody wasteland of lost loves, unrequited affections, and nevermore dreams.

His songs are three-minute one-act plays, complex and interweaving tapestries of golden soulful reverie. Roy's Blue Angel message still lives: Don't cry, I'll be your friend when you need me. "I'm Hurtin'," (#27, 12-60) anchors his lonely trilogy.

"Running Scared" – Roy Orbison, #1(1), 4-61. When Ravel's semi-classical *Bolero* first jolted the symphony world decades ago, audiences were shocked at the rising orchestral meter. It erupted in a stirring spark-of-passion climax at the sinfully sensuous finale. Not so Roy O.

"Running Scared" kept the tempo at a steady regular rate, but the orchestra added instruments dramatically. "Runnin' scared," Roy blurts, suddenly surrounded by a tympanic overflow of DRUM thunder. Seems his girl's old boyfriend is due back in town. Roy shudders at his potential loss. Bass drums boom bombastically. Ominously. With fearful foreboding, tympanic drums drone on, picking up guitars and basses in their rampaging wake. In "Running Scared," Roy quavers in operatic magnificence. He admits he's afraid to lose her.

As soon as the preening, pompous rival shows up (Mr. Self-Assurance, nose in the air), Roy jimmies the climax; at this point, a gaggle of violins galumphs into the fray. Conceit evaporates into stunned consternation. Though hundreds of party people don't know it, a Major Cosmic Drama just took place with a swoop of strings and classic surprise ending: Roy's girlfriend surprises everyone, especially the legend-in-his-own-mind ex-boyfriend. She walks out of the dance-floor scenario not with the conceited ex, but with our hero; Roy is not-so-sheepishly surprised, and all of us live happily ever after. The ex stomps off in a raging crimson sulk.

Roy pulled off the impossible here. Enmeshed within a *Bandstand* universe of "Great beat – give the song a 95, you can dance to it," Roy went all the way to #1 with a totally undanceable bolero. His last note hits a towering "Ab" – WITHOUT falsetto. Thunderstruck. All would-be dancers just STOOD and listened to Roy . . .

"Take Five" – Dave Brubeck Quartet, #25, 9-61. Obviously, not Rock and Roll. Progressive Jazz guru Brubeck (b. David Warren, '20, Concord, California) played a way-out West Coast Cool Jazz piano with alto sax maestro Paul Desmond, drum kingpin Joe Morello, and bass boss Eugene Wright. Cerebral sound in unique 5/4 time signature; never before achieved on charts. Four virtuosos on jazz paths never before explored. Pioneers of time and meter. Technical perfection from Al. #2(1), 11-60 *Time Out*.

"I Still Love You All" – Kenny Ball & His Jazzmen, NC 1961; #18, 5-61 U.K. Dixieland song hit heights in the Orbison Great Singer era with this multi-girl fantasy reminiscent of Lou Bega's #3, '99 "Mambo #5". Ball scored a #2 on "Midnight in Moscow" for his "Trad Jazz" combo in March 1962, like New York City **Village Stompers** "#2, '63 "Washington Square". Its pinnacle? **Louis 'Satchmo' Armstrong's** #1, 1964 "Hello Dolly" (with the 62-year-old New Orleans legend the oldest person ever to hit #1). Ball performs crescendo classic.

"The Girl from Ipanema" – Stan Getz, Astrid Gilberto, #5, 6-64. Tenor sax Jazz star **Stan** (Gayetzsky) **Getz** (1927-91) hosted the *Bossa Nova* Slow Rock/Jazz craze of the 60s, after apprenticing with big bandleaders Woody Herman, Stan Kenton, Jimmy Dorsey, and Benny Goodman. Getz teams with João Gilberto's guitar glides, mirroring the wondrous Jazz guitar riffs of **Wes Montgomery** ("Windy", #44, '67). Getz's other

bossa nova hit? "Desafinado" (#15, 9-62). Other great Jazz stars? Art Blakey (1919-90, drums), Ornette Coleman (1930, sax), and able saxman Don Howard's (b. 1934) favorite Erroll Garner (1921-77, piano).

"Crying" – Roy Orbison, #2(1), 8-61. Roy's ultimate crescendo song. The secret to this song's magnificence is a Jazz chord, the + chord. You sharp the fifth note. In the Kay of 'D', it's your **D+** chord – a much prettier chord than it is a grade on a math quiz: **D+** is a D-F#-A# triad.

So Roy Orbison's +5 jazz chord in "Crying" merely reflects a new complexity by Buddy Holly and producers the Pettys and Dick Jacobs, and the ruddier Thunder Rock of Del Shannon.

After Orbison's romantic conflict in "Crying" builds, his resonant baritone phase fades into towering tenor. The lyric is smaller than the song: she returns after breaking his heart, she squeezes his hand to say hello and wishes him well, and she never realizes the stoical Hell his tortured soul is suffering.

The climax is the thing. The miracle of Roy's towering finales on "Running Scared" and "Crying" is that he is NOT doing falsetto. He's hitting that incredible note at the apex of his NORMAL tenor range.

Closest I've ever heard to an Orbison imitator is **David Box**, though there have been nice "Crying" imitations by Roy's friend **Del Shannon**, and **Don McLean** (#5, 1-81), **Ray Peterson** (1997), **Glen Campbell, Jack Scott**, and **Jay Black** of Jay and the Americans (#25, 5-66). Box flaunts his Orbisonic expertise on the Acuff-Rose standard "No One Will Ever Know," flip of Box's perfect "Peggy Sue" imitation "Little Lonely Summer Girl" (#11, Detroit, '64). On this song, Box is Orbison.

The Lubbock, Texas, Box filled in with the post-Holly Crickets, doing a dynamite "Peggy Sue Got Married" in 1950. Then David Box split for a solo stint. Headed for stardom at last, tragedy awaited. On a small commuter flight out of Dallas in late 1964, Box was killed.

In essence, "Crying" is the story of Orbison's abbreviated life. No matter how many stunning tragedies life handed him, he bravely returned again and again to this music. Like guitar guru **Les Paul** (whose beloved wife Mary Ford died of a heart attack at 49) and countless Bluesmen/women, Orbison used music to ease the sorrow and pain of life. **Les** and **B.B. King** saw their guitars as pals – "The best pal a guy could have," mused Les. King got even more intimate, naming his guitar LUCILLE, after a girl two men scrapped other over at a 1949 gig. His guitar was knocked over, the place caught on fire, and B.B. ran back and rescued his beloved guitar, which he named for the inadvertent firebug.

"Crying, Waiting, Hoping" – Beatles, NC, 1961-62. Beatle bootleg albums galore highlight their Holly and Orbison debt. **George Harrison** sings vintage Holly – and the polychordal seedbed for Orbison-Melson's "Crying." Their August 6, 1963 BBC tapes (released 1994-95, #1 CD) contain this *Buddy Holly Story Volume II* sleeper.

"Candy Man" – Roy Orbison, #25, 8-61. "Crying's" flipside. And Beatle wellspring? On the British tour Roy headlined, Lubbock lad Delbert McClinton (#8, 12-80, "Giving It Up for Your Love") showed the Beatles how to play Blues harmonica from this bluesy Orbisong. Their first Brit hit? Michelle Pirraglia cites John Lennon's euphoric harmonica explosion on Fab 4 debut "Love Me Do," #17, 1962 U.K. In "Candy Man," Roy reprises Dunleith Delta style of his fave bluesman **Jimmy Reed**. [This is NOT Sammy Davis, Jr. song (#1, '72) of same name.]

Roy Orbison

"Oh, Pretty Woman" – **Roy Orbison, #1(3), 8-64.** Roy's Del Shannon-style THUNDER ROCK. Bouncing the Beatles at their zenith, Orbison's chance encounter hinges on a romantic rhetorical question? Is she really walking back toward me? For once, Roy's rhythm guitar/bass-unison riff almost outstrips his soaring tenor in gusto. **Van Halen** covered "Oh, Pretty Woman" (#12, 2-82). The Dutch Heavy Metal Hunk **Eddie Van Halen**, who wedded Valerie Bertinelli, hopscotches some rapid riffs here, echoing Orbison's major big-beat contribution.

For Roy Orbison, singing was the meaning of life. He brought so much joy, and friendly commiseration, to millions of people with "(Oh) Pretty Woman." He also played a cool throbbing lead or rhythm guitar, a black Gibson XS-335TD, with floppity uncut strings shimmying at the pegs. This one song clinches the 1987 Rock Hall inductee's place in music history. His other, sadder three-minute vocal adventures brought solace and empathy to all of us groping humans somewhere in the night – fighting silent stoic tears over lost loves, nevermore romances, and the ravages of demon time.

Almost tragically, "Oh, Pretty Woman" is about the only

Orbison song most recent kids ever get to hear anymore, thanks to Oldies Overkill. It's a mere slight slice of his vocal genius. Roy plunders the surreal dreamscape with his enchanting crescendo classics: "In Dreams" (#7, 2-63), "It's Over" (#9, 4-64). Or his Christmas compassion waltz, #15, 12-63 "Pretty Paper." Roy Orbison's peak is 1960-66. His last top 40 in his lifetime was "Twinkle Toes" (#39, 1-66). Roy stood stock still on stage garbed in funereal black, but his VOICE moved mountains.

"Cry Softly Lonely One" – Roy Orbison, #52, 7-67. Roy Orbison's Greatest Song? His splendid chord structure slaloms from major to minor, blasting the subdominant IV and then the exotic chromatic bVII – (Key of 'C,' it's a **Bb**). The drifting, shuffling guitar mirrors the hopeful mood. It is a song about grappling with sorrow, and comforting a sad jilted girl.

Had this Chalypso crescendo masterpiece have been released 1960-63, Top Ten is a given and #1 a probability. In 1967, with Jimi Hendrix, the Who, and Psychedelia, "Cry Softly" became a quaint slice of aural beauty wafting above the desert. Beatlemania waved goodbye to Roy and dusty Wink, Texas: As kitschy and souvenir-saturated as Graceland in Memphis is, Roy's Texas homeland is stark, windswept, lonely, and mostly gone. Real gone.

Wink flourished, a Roaring 20s 50,000-strong boomtown. When we got there in May 1994, it was mostly vanished. On our Rock and Roll Sabbatical, we took a trip from Motown to Chicago Blues to Graceland to the Delta in New Orleans to Lubbock, Wink, and ALASKA: seven weeks, 18,000 miles on our ancient Chevy wagon. Among eclectic shrines: **Janis Joplin**'s junior high, **Robert Johnson**'s Crossroads, **B.B. King**'s Memphis Beale Street, **Johnny Horton**'s Seward, Alaska Hardware Store, the Lubbock **Holly** statue and tiny home where Peggy Sue got married. And Wink. You just go a hundred miles down the pike – over the shifting, whispering, tawny-bright sands of a Yankee Sahara.

Wink, Boomtown. In the 20s, Wink had Black Gold Fever – like the Skagway-to-Dawson gold rush Chilkoot Trail of 1898 Nugget Fever. Shuddering just south of the Arctic Circle 66½° N), the Yukon's Dawson City snared snaggletooth miners lusting for gold, or a whizbang gambling casino (Gravel Tooth Gertie's) by Klondike Kate's Saloon. Dawson, home of Rock and Roll, 1899 Ragtime Rock and Roll.

In Dawson, now on a pick-me-up tourist boom, there is a sad hint of the desolation that struck when the gold was gone. Texan town Wink sits, quiet and bone-white and alone, waiting for the pick-me-up re-boom boomerang to slice them off a chunk of joy. Roy Orbison and I both grew up in towns that faded away as we grew. We had come to see Roy Orbison's Graceland. We expected an iridescent blue tour bus and the Flying Elvises. We gazed at the bushy-tailed banner astride the deserted main street of Metro Wink – busted from 50,000 lost souls to 1000, grabbing anything they can hang onto before all of Wink disappears in a Wink of jet-propelled *Brigadoon* time:

ROY ORBISON DAY – June 11ᵗʰ

So said the lonely banner, flapping with forlorn pigeons in the dusty Texas 90°May heat.

Roy Orbison's own museum, relates my wife Toni's journal: "is open only on request; people alternate days to be on call." We were quickly surrounded by Pauline Kline, who looks about 39, and her eager grandkids, who ushered us around the tiny little storefront. They unfolded the six-foot cardboard Roy Orbison statue and portable façade, and stood him up in spectacled sentinel glory to guard the silent summer town. We had showed up, alas, two weeks early; we missed **Carl Perkins** and his "Blue Suede Shoes" (#2, 3-56). Sometimes as you watch your old R & R idols age, or die young, or wither ingloriously early, or simply fade away, you are reminded of your own mortality. It is not a pleasant thought.

Super little museum, though. Bargains galore: Roy Orbison T-shirts $5, caps $3; no wonder Wink is not thriving financially – they're Santa Clausing Roy's storied past. Wink is practically a ghost town, and the hopes of a Roy Resurrection of Cash Flow are thumped by economic reality. "They are planning the 4th Annual Roy Orbison Festival," Toni writes, "but it is going slowly . . . This is a project of love and a dream. They're saving for a real Orbison statue like Lubbock's Buddy Holly one, and a brick walk, each brick sponsored by a donor at $30 apiece; they're not piling up donors fast . . ."

If you're disappointed when you see the REAL Graceland that it's just a dinky $3,000,000 home, bought by Elvis in 1957 for $100,000, you "ain't seen nothin' yet." Go to Wink. After perusing Roy's high school pix with the Wink Westerners in his encased high school yearbook, we attempted Dave Walker's *American Rock and Roll Tour* Find-It-Yourself tour of Roy's boyhood haunts and hangouts: the drug store where he'd strum and yodel on the chicory and cornflower corner; the last catfish and eggs diner in town ("Peggy Sue's"), which closed forever two years ago; and finally, Roy's ivied birthplace.

Both the diner and the drug store being defunct, we lazily cruised by his home site. Sad part of the Orbi-Pilgrimage. You get to his ex-address. It's a Nancy and Sluggo neighborhood like Detroit now, where a few last sad ancient houses duke it out with wildflowers and bulldozed dreams.

Roy's ex-house stood at the tremblingly hand-lettered sign's place – amber waves of skinny-grass grain. Brown in May. Nothing lives there anymore . . . except field mice, grasshoppers, floppitty jackrabbits, and you don't even want to consider reptiles. Whatever Roy had there is gone. SO is Roy. Sadly, none of us is a permanent inhabitant on this tragicomic planet.

"It was not a 'Gifted and Talented' class that helped develop his talent," sez Toni's Journal. "It wasn't money – what was it? Apparently as a child he sang for people, and in school he played in a band. As a high school senior his goal was to be a successful Western singer."

"He had a gift," Toni mused, "and he couldn't be kept in Wink. The world would appreciate his talent. Success is a fascinating thing to ponder." Or, like Liz Dean (my mom) said in 1949, 1953, 1957, 1961, 1965, etc., "You can be anything you want to be." Wonder if Mom Orbison had

the same advice to Roy? (And I'll bet chances are 93% your mother said that to YOU).

The Wink Post Office is overrated. To satiate the postcard-hunger of our pals strewn about the terrestrial globe, we stopped in to procure a few stamps. This may be hard to grasp, but the Post Office was out of stamps! Poor ol' Wink was almost out of gas, too. Roy was long gone. Pauline Kline and other good folks still sing his praises at the little museum. Please buy a brick (Roy Orbison Museum, Wink, Texas, Zip code?).

Roy's musical dream, however, wafts on, rippling the airwaves of the world with his towering tenor, his Tex-Mex Soul, his once-in-a-millennium voice, and his Rock and Roll vision.

"That Lovin' You Feelin' Again" – Roy Orbison & Emmylou Harris, #55, 6-80; # 6 C. The silver-haired country star songstress renewed Roy's fading career. Nifty duo sound, for Roy's last hit in his lifetime.

By 1988, Roy enjoyed a lofty resurrection. He joined Bob Dylan-George Harrison-Tom Petty-Jeffy Lynne's **Traveling Wilburys.** Their ill-starred bronze-medal #3 album seemed bound for glory. Roy had also been inducted in the second-ever Class of '87 to Cleveland's Rock Hall of Fame by nervous Bruce Springsteen.

On December 6, 1988, Roy had been shopping for model airplanes. He had homey hobbies like that. He returned to Mom Orbison's. At 44, Roy underwent bypass surgery for his frail heart. To BE ELVIS also meant that he'd have to feel his life flickering out, falling against the bathroom door. Death mocks glory.

Roy Orbison died suddenly, of the terrible scourge that harvests millions more than plane crashes and drugs and meteorites will ever do – a heart attack at semi-young age 52. There will be no replacements for Roy Orbison.

"You Got It" – Roy Orbison (also written by **Jeff Lynne** and **Tom Petty** of the **Traveling Wilburys,** #9, 1-89; #7, 2-89 C.** Roy's posthumous farewell. His marvelous pipes almost sound up to 1962 form. Great song. Singer's singer. **Bonnie Raitt** (Rock Hall 2000) took "You Got It" to #33, 2-95.

In the 70s, **Kiss**'s glam Hard Rock was the driving edge of the R & R panorama of tenor **Gene Simmons** and guitar slingers **Ace Frehley** and **Paul Stanley** – with **Peter Criss** powering the skins. Kiss was over 50% video-oriented. It ballooned their success: "Beth" / "Detroit Rock City" hit #7, 9-76. "I Was Made for Lovin' You" hit #11, 5-79. Good video rock group, Kiss. Vivid vital video, Kiss.

Now contrast **Roy Orbison.** The Big O was blatantly anti-visual. He stood starkly rigid, garbed in Johnny Cash black, armed with an ebony guitar and deadeye voice. Roy's stage movements were nil, like a 'wind' at dead calm. The Wink cardboard Orbison danced in the frisky little summer breeze more than Roy ever did on stage. When Roy sang, people just sat there bewitched. Transfixed. Mesmerized. Instant charisma.

Myopic Roy lived his later life in dark shades. His small eyes smarted from the ruddy glow of beefy Texan life. Though Roy hailed from molten golden sunburned West

Texas, Dracula had a better tan. When his weak body gave out, his strong voice sang on beyond the world's airwaves. And on.

Singer gone? Song lives on. Rock and Roll pads its immortality. It's too bad the only Orbisong many know today is 'Pretty Woman,' a nice imitation of Van Halen's 1982 #12 tune.

Thunder Rock.

Del Shannon was Michigan macho. Roy was Texas Tough. There is nothing more frail than a great rock star in the hot spotlight of Elvis.

Three major great singers grace this chapter. Here are a few others, doomed to less press. Nevertheless – they are fine contributors to the Rock and Roll Revolution:

"Since I Don't Have You" – Skyliners, #12, 2-59. Among the best of this Italian-Afro genre of Doo-Whop Streetcorner songsters is this curly bronze-haired French-American from Pittsburgh, lead tenor **Jimmy Beaumont**. In this teenage classic, Jimmy (b. 1940) practically reinvents the *melisma*, Truly HIGH soprano Vogel [d. 1980, similarly to Del's untimely departure] soars 38 clouds above Del Shannon on final note.

"If You Wanna Be Happy" – Jimmy Soul, #1(2), 3-63; #1(1), 4-63 R & B. Jimmy Soul lightened our national mood with this semi-chauvinistic ditty about a damsel divine. Seems her rampaging beauty rampaged out the door and ducked back into the alley. 'Soul' (NYC's **James McCleese**, billed as "Wonder Boy") fires off this comic lyric on an iffy premise: Marry an ugly woman (author's note: there are no ugly women), and you'll share a lifetime of happiness. Soul dotes on her delicious cooking, touts her sweet faithfulness, and praises her willingness to please him and satisfy his every whim.

Fun song. Offends everybody – regardless of race (marathon), color (green), or creed (Rock and Roll is Here to Stay). Super-high stratospheric final Soul's Soul note!

"Bony Moronie" – Larry Williams, #14, 11-57; #4, R & B. Born 1935, New Orleans, died violently in L.A. 1980. Little Richard-style Screaming Blues songwriter bedazzled the Beatles, who lofted his super-fast "Slow Down" to #25, 9-64. Biggest hit is PG-13 "Short Fat Fannie," #5, 6-57 (#1 R & B), but "Bony" is unforgettable via simile rhyme: she is as 'skinny as' – one stick of macaroni. Super songwriter. Gift? Internal rhyme: "Dizzy, Miss Lizzy," #69, 4-58 was recorded by the Beatles, too. In 11-99, Paul McCartney's *Run Devil Run* album featured yet another Larry Williams hopeful hit: "She Said Yeah."

"Why Do I Love You So?" – Johnny Tillotson, #42, 1-60. Flipping from singer/songwriter Teen Idoldom to a Country Ballad trapeze, the Jacksonville smiling tenor

(b. 1939) fired falsetto into the rock star firmament a year before Del Shannon's #1 "Runaway." Like the Brill Building's master melodist **Neil Sedaka**, Tillotson-penned orchestral songs exuded the essence of dreamy teenage sincerity, with a side of cherry marshmallow honey-toned harmonies. We should logically pick Tillotson's chartbusters: #2(1), 10-60 "Poetry in Motion," "Without You" (#7, 8-61), or #3, 5-62 "It Keeps Right on A-Hurtin'," for their power and impact upon American popular music. But nope, this #42 song with an entire supermelodic falsetto chorus, is by far the most tender, the most poignant. How so? In "Why Do I Love You So?", teen idol Johnny sings a painfully lilting and lachrymose line about his girlfriend's tears when her tiny puppy dies. It's perhaps the saddest, most tender lyrical line uttered as the new decade reeled in Cold War icy tension and palpable terror.

Tillotson got bumped as child-prodigy opening act for "Heartbreak Hotel's" writer Mae Axton's show – to a new kid in town they paid fifty dollars to play. His name? **Elvis Presley.** Though unblessed, like the rest of us, with a #1 song, **Johnny Tillotson** soared some salvos into the tall charts in the Orbison Era: "Send Me the Pillow That You Dream On" #17, 8-62 and #11 C. [#77, 6-58 Hank Locklin, #5 C]; Hank Williams' N.C. '51 and #2, 6-51 C "I Can't Help It" to #24, 10-62; and #7, 11-63 "Talk Back Tremblin' Lips." Johnny's soothing tenor wasn't as theatrically reverberating as Shannon or Orbison, but his boy-next-door style blended with his perfect pitch to groom him as eligible teen idol – a friendly and compassionate kind of kid who holds the world together. His double-year hit "Dreamy Eyes" (#63, 11-58 & #42, 1-60), previews on its final glide-swoop 16th-note melismas, the whole Mariah Carey multi-note creation. For Johnny, it was just the strawberry frosting on the angel-food cake. Another Teen Idol icon of Nice Guy Rock resounded his six-pack of top ten tunes out of snowswirl Fargo's North Dakota:

"Run to Him" – Bobby Vee, #2(1), 11-61. Cashing in on the Orbisonic crashing crescendo craze, the greatest Teen Idol singer, **Bobby Vee**, follows his pals Del, Gene, and Roy. Pumping up his fulsome Finnish baritone, Vee overdubs double. Gerry Goffin penned this equal-gender opportunity song in the NYC Brill Building, where the jilted guy ducks out politely. It follows Bobby's #33, 2-61 raspier rocker, "Stayin' In," where the hotheaded firebrand kid stews in the principal's office. Crime? Slugged ex-pal for nasty remarks about girlfriend. Seems the so-called chum was blabbing rumors about the sweetie pie in question, so Bobby decked him. Song was BANNED for violence.

GREAT is a subjective word. From the early 60s, Del Shannon, Gene Pitney, Roy Orbison, and Elvis were a few vocal giants we could all appreciate. Now, let's move to some of the great, near-great, and semi-remarkable singers of the North Coast. And the East Coast.

North Coast, East Coast, and No Coast Rock

14

In the *Gold Rush* spirit of joining together Rock and Soul styles, this "North Coast" chapter mixes a mammoth mish-mosh of unforgettable hits that climbed the *Billboard* battlements in the diverse and amazing early sixties.

"A Thousand Stars" – Kathy Young and the Innocents, #3, 10-60. Kathy calls out with purring petulance to the guys of America to find that she's the answer to a teenage prayer. Nothing esoteric or profound or eggheadish here. Just a typical **C—Am—F—G7** streetcorner ballad of a more innocent age. A thousand luscious stars shining on her romance.

"Happy, Happy Birthday Baby" – Tune Weavers, #5, 9-57; #4 R & B. R & B classic with **Margo Sylvia** (d. '91) on dreamy blue lead. Also hubby **John Sylvia** (bass), plus her brother Gilbert Lopez, tenor. She weaves a tale of a sad candled cake, and wishes him a happy birthday even though the rakish rogue has run off with Floozy #3 behind Door #2. Also hit #1(1), 3-86 for Country Soul (that's right) blind piano player **Ronnie Milsap** on the Country charts (NC HOT 100). Same theme? Young's follow-up with Kathy Young/Innocents, "Happy Birthday Blues" (#30, 2-61). Want a cheerier contrasting opinion?

"26 Miles" – Four Preps, #2(3), 1-58; #6, 3-58 R & B. How far? 26 miles – like a marathon – off the California Coast. It's about a preppy boat trip. Idyll at Santa Catalina Island. Girls. Streetcorner chords. Melodic enunciation of Bruce Bellard and three overprivileged Hollywood High grads (*Beverly Hills 90210*?). Bali Ha'l of palm fronds, grass skirts, mint juleps, timeless tropical fun in sun. Bad surf. Their right-on imitations of Belmonts, Kingston Trio, Fleetwoods, Platters in #17, 8-61 "More Money for You and Me" is a ditzy $poof of the $eamy $ide of R & R $hows.

"Battle of New Orleans" – Johnny Horton, #1(6), 4-59; 1(10), 4-59 C. Master of yodel-kick gimmick. One of most important Country Rock singers of all time. Married to Hank Williams' widow Billie Jean (no relation to Michael ackson's R & B "Billie Jean.") In the War of 1812, Americans defeated the British in New Orleans. Andrew "Old Hickory" Jackson won a major battle here. Horton commemorates the achievement. The song didn't fly too high in the U.K. (#16 – they were good sports . . .)

"North to Alaska" – Johnny Horton, #4, 9-60; #1(5), 11-60 C. Making amends to his British friends, Horton (1925-60) scored a #3 hit on the British heroes of the Hood, who vainly tried to dismantle the WWII German submarine the Bismarck: "Sink the Bismarck" (3-60). To Horton, with his gruff tenor rasp and his electrifyin' rebel yell, military adventurism was exciting and grand. His spirited songs are the musical equivalent of John Wayne. Horton, a geology major from Tyler, Texas (and California) and an Alaska fisherman, was a Country Rock colossus. He was much too old to pass himself off as a teen idol. "North to Alaska" pits gold against love in a white-gold arctic valley below an Alaska mountain near Nome (hey, there's no place like Nome for the holidays).

"I Can't Stop Loving You" – Ray Charles, #1(5), 5-62; #1(10) R & B. Flip of "Born to Lose." Slow Raelettes chorus, soothes Charles' soulful ballad of deep obsession and love denial. He'll stoically endure his life cloaked in yesterday's dreams. Monumental monster hit. This **Don Gibson** classic (#81, 2-58, #7, 3-58 C) anchors Charles' revolutionary *Modern Sounds in Country and Western Music*, Al. #1(14), 5-62; flip "Born to Lose" hit #41, 5-62. Ray scored Jock Rock hit with "Hit the Road, Jack" (#1[2], 9-61). Song used when starting pitcher is ditched and switched for a relief pitcher. Alas, loving a sports team is like loving a woman . . . it'll break your heart. Jock Rock Anthem. Sing it, Ray.

"Sleepwalk" – Santo & Johnny (Farina), #1(2), 8-59; #4, R & B. Born in steaming Brooklyn, Santo and Johnny created the most sinuously sensuous of all 50s instrumentals. Song weaves web of eerie sounds in air crash nightmare of Ritchie Valens in *La Bamba* (1987****). Older brother Santo (b. 1937) caressed the first rock and roll steel guitar (odd Brooklyn item), while the young lad (1941) handled rhythm guitar.

"A White Sport Coat (And a Pink Carnation)" – Marty Robbins, #2(1), 4-57; #1(5), C. Sock-hop sadness. Sweet and melodic, the ringing ballad tells of the forlorn lad all dressed up with his summery white sport coat – but his dippy date dumps him. Bells ring raucously, nastily in the big-beat background. In dude get-up, sorry rejected suitor is left with pallid coat, withering pink flower, and broken heart. Note pure melody. Also "Doo-wah" thirds country harmonies of meadowlark background singer. Insistent beat throbs with jilted juvenile's hurtin' heart. Flower mentioned in "American Pie."

"El Paso" – Marty Robbins, #1(20, 11-59; #1(7), C. From *Gunfighter Ballads and Trail Songs*, #6, 12-28-59. Perhaps the first CONCEPT ALBUM. Truly Western saga (not just Country). Robbins' bad luck posits morality play: cowboy messes with 'wicked Felena.' Bad hombre arrives. Cut to thrilling chilling chase. Scooting past saguaro cacti and Joshua trees and mesquite and canyons and mesas, our hero, drowning in Western realism, is gunned down. Protagonist sings dying lament (in Robbins' rich resonant 2nd tenor). At his last groan, Felena swoops to his bleeding side, pillowing his weary lovestruck head on her ample bosom. The cowboy breathes his last gasp.

As favorite records whirl into our consciousness, they become FRIENDS. Your favorite songs are like FRIENDS; it's a happy handshake to unexpectedly hear them again. Howdy, pal. Too bad the 'good guy' died.

An unlikely R & R rebel, Robbins commandeered the veneered hardwood at the Grand Ol' Opry's Ryman Auditorium in Nashville for many years. Little did anyone suspect this good ol' boy would INVENT HEAVY METAL music.

"Don't Worry" – Marty Robbins, #3, 2-61; #1(10) C. Marty Robbins had 24 HOT 100 entries, but his only Top Ten tunes just happened to lasso #'s 1, 2, & 3. The bronze medalist made the most noise – down the long echoing corridors of Rock and Roll. Marty's lately obscure "Don't Worry" charts the absolute moment of birth for the Heavy Metal sound. Mistaken purists trace it back to **Steppenwolf**'s John Kay (Joachim Krauledat of East Germany) and his prophetic phrase "HEAVY-METAL THUNDER' in "Born to Be Wild" (#2, 7-68). **LeAnn Rimes**' covered "Don't Worry" on '99 Al. *Faded Love*.

During Marty's recording session, his stoic ballad was grooving along smoothly. ('I hurt, but you'll never know it; watch me swallow my pain'). Marty's rock ballad seemed destined for a nice #19 or so.

Suddenly, Marty's bassman's amp buzzed out. Back then, you had to replace amp tubes. Transistors were new and light and unavailable for Marty. The tube store (drugstore) was closed. Why? Because everybody in the history of the universe has recorded his best stuff at 2:30 a.m. Sunday night. No tube? Dilemma!

"We'll have to come back in the morning, " groused the aggravated engineer and the bleary musicians.

"Hang on," offered Marty, "let's give this a try."

Like Del Shannon's flutish Musitron, recorded virtually at the same time, Marty's busted bass amp furnished a new dimension in Rock and Roll. GIMMICK! Marty blasted the Fuzztone Feedback on the instrumental bridge (sending some treble guitarist grumpily packing). With the booming bass as the lead, Marty included it on the last earth-shattering verse. Mr. Unrebel Opry Robbins became the smooth First Voice of Heavy Metal back in 1961. By accident!

Marty also scored big with Temptress tale "Devil Woman" (#16, 6-62), no relation to British idol **Cliff Richard**'s American hit of the same name and different tune (#6, 7-76). Catch Marty in the Country chapter, too.

Berry Gordy's Hitsville enterprise was nestled into three 4-square Post-Victorian homes on Detroit's West Grand Boulevard. A surging sixties phenomenon. Let's move mysteriously back to the Missing Link between Motown and Lubbock, Texas: **Bob Kayli**.

"Shop Around" – (William) "Smokey" Robinson and the Miracles, #2(1), 12-60; #1(8) R & B. First Motown gold record. Smokey (b. '40, Detroit) is named for smoky blue-gray eyes. Via a hundred hot hits on R & B or the HOT 100, he notched a second-year Rock Hall invite ('87), and rose to Veep in the Motown Empire. Like Cliff Richard and beyond, Smokey's songs spread-eagle five decades. Miracle **Bobby Rogers** lived a block away on Cloverlawn in Detroit when I was a child groom (22), and we used to discuss lawn mowers. His brother Emerson was replaced by Claudette Rogers (Smokey's wife – not Roy Orbison's or Roy Rogers'). MOTOWN IS A FAMILY TRADITION.

"Shop Around," yes. Mom warns kid (Smokey is one of 10 kids) to shop around for perfect Soulmate. Play the field. Pick the best. Smokey Robinson impressed me when I worked as a Motown songwriter (1966), as cordial, friendly, helpful, kind, and all those Boy-Scout traits of personality power. Smokey radiates this special aura of positive energy. So does Motown. Never averse to profit, Motown also cut its own Answer Song for Smokey's mom's advice: Debbie [no relation] Dean's #92, 2-61 "Don't Let Him Shop Around." Amply backed by bass Pete Moore and baritone Ronnie White (d. 1995), Smokey smacks towering notes with suave dynamism.

Bob Kayli hit #96, 11-58 with Holly-hiccup Soul song "Everyone Was There." Kayli, actually, is Berry Gordy's brother Bob (Robert Gordy, b. '31). Bob features lyrically all the 50s teen queens – Peggy Sue, Patricia, Bony Moronie, Jennie Lee.

The **Crickets** chugged along wistfully in the early 60s. Buddy Holly's band toured with Earl Sinks trying Hollyclone vocals. Joe Mauldin and Allison had, of course, split with Buddy in 1958. Holly's Cricket II Crew included **Waylon Jennings** and **Tommy Allsup** on the final tour. Bizarrely, when they found the battered plane, there were five wallets to go with four lost fliers. Session superstsar guitarist Allsup, with over 10,000 recording sessions, first Cricket ever (including Buddy) to win a Grammy award (2000), shuddered to hear his own 1959 death report on the radio. He'd planned to fly, but given Holly his wallet for some Fargo, North Dakota hotel reservation – and sold his ticket to the 'winner' of the coin toss, **Ritchie Valens**.

"I Fought the Law" – Bobby Fuller Four, #9, 1-66. The Lubbock sound at its best. Drums and rhythm guitars thunder Sonny Curtis's great R & R hit. Detroit Red Wings' hockey penalty box theme song. Fuller followed with Holly-written "Love's Made a Fool of You' (#26, 6-66). 100% pure Rock and Roll!

The Cricket captaincy rotated between Allison, Sinks, Mauldin, Curtis, Jerry Naylor, and Glen Hardin, who later plunked piano for Elvis on tour.

"My Little Girl" – Crickets, #134, 3-63; #17, 2-63 U.K. For this pre-Beatle chart-nudger, Jerry sings lead. He covers Buddy's tonal timbre with alarming precision, rendering Holly's doubletone gruff/tender contrast. Closest song ever to original "Peggy Sue," this Cricketune has the basic sound of the basic Post-Holly Cricket nucleus: singer/songwriter, guitarist/banjoist **Sonny Curtis** (mellow baritone), drummer/singer **Jerry Allison** (tenor); and **Joe B. Mauldin** on bass and vocal background (tenor). Their fresh harmonic sound sailed to semi-sunny England, and the Beatles. As much as "My Little Girl" echoes Buddy's super "Peggy Sue," its great melodic flipside, "Teardrops Fall Like Rain," mirrors the music-box magic of Buddy's tender flipside tune "Everyday."

"Don't Ever Change" – Crickets, NC, 1962; #5, 7-62 U.K. Penned for **Bobby Vee** by Brill Building's **Carole King**, "Don't Ever Change" rose to their biggest success over the Big Pond. Sedaka-style sweet melody. On their BBC lost tapes (Al. #3, 12-94), the **Beatles** covered their namesakes' sentimental ballad.

Squat by Times Square, the venerable Brill Building was the wellspring of R & R hits in Richard Aquila's *Real Fifties*, 1954-63. Brill songwhizzes penned hundreds of hits which bounced on *Bandstand*. If budding 'Johnny B. Goodes' couldn't write, but had TEEN IDOL written all over their dimples or muscles or boyish/girlish charm, the R & R Melody Poets of Times Square would cinch their songs with: GOOD BEAT – DANCE TO IT – GIVE IT A 92! Some legendary tunesmiths who clustered their charismatic R & R talents at 1619 Broadway included **Gerry Goffin** (Carole King's husband), plus **Cynthia Weil, Bobby Darin, Howie Greenfield, Toni Wine, Neil Sedaka, Jeff Barry, Neil Diamond, Doc Pomus**, and **Mort Shuman**.

This cotton-candy fluff stuff was big business. It also overarched the teenage dreams of an entire nation yearning and burning for that sweet true love, to march them down the dreamy aisle to picket-fence

paradise and Happily-Ever-Afterland. REJOICE! Now we're tromping upon Teen Idol territory.

"Oh! Carol" – Neil Sedaka, #9, 10-59; #27, 11-59 R & B. Juilliard classic piano players like Jimmy Gilmer and Neil Sedaka now infused the rock and roll range, adding musical complexity and technique to pop labors of love in songwriting. **Sedaka** is the key Brill melodist. Loosely going along **Paul Anka**'s teen idol flow, Sedaka sculpted a choppy Chalypso ode to Goffin's wife **Carole King** (nee Klein). He sings Romantic Tough Times in a Happy Daze cheeseburger-malt-fries world of adolescent blue funk and golden glory. Twirly little melody. Carole King emerges teen queenly.

Though the #1-voted song of all time, **Led Zeppelin**'s "Stairway to Heaven," was shackled into an album, and incredibly NEVER CHARTED, **Neil Sedaka** did! His totally-different song, the melodic "Stairway to Heaven" (from TV show *Stairway to the Stars*), hit #9 in 3-60 for the Brooklyn tenor songsmith.

"Lonely Boy" – Paul Anka, #1(4), 6-59; #1(2), 9-57 R & B. Jumps from I tonic chord down a major peg to VII major (like 'C' to 'Bb' – bVII). Paul's poor-little-rich-boy lyric convinces unattached bobbysoxers that he really needs a sweet little girl just like all of them. Anka penned Elvis/Sinatra smash "My Way."

Many of the Brill Building classics were sculpted for the Girls' Groups of the early star-spangled sixties, but a few found their way to teen idols, like this **Carole King** classic:

"Take Good Care of My Baby" – Bobby Vee, #1(3), 8-61. Rapscallionish lyric. Starts with guy untrue to his girl. Like his friend Del Shannon's #5, 1961 "Hats Off to Larry" sentiment showed, it was now possible to address the romantic rival. Bobby's song-guy unwittingly fooled around, lost the girl, and exercises a contrite remorse. If the rival, too, messes up as he did, footloose Bobby will bounce back like his "Rubber Ball" (#6, '60).

Romantic politics, in the backwash of King-Weil-Wine's feminine viewpoints, now had a sounding board from the distaff perpective. For five years R & R had been the macho streetcorner province of Dukes of Earl and dancing dervishes – Have Guitar, Will Travel. **Don Kirshner** and **Al Nevins** formed Aldon Music in the late 50s, commandeered a lofty chunk of 1619 Broadway, and plastered their pianos about. They hired the cream of the NYC songwriting crop, and the Song Showdown began: GUITAR vs. PIANO.

Page 144 of *The Rolling Stone Illustrated History of Rock and Roll* flashes a fantastic Brill photo. Wearing black sox, shiny fab herringbone pants, exec white shirt, and a Mona Lisa smile is **Barry Mann** (#7, 81 "Who Put the Bomp?"). His serviceable Steinway baby grand is flanked by a sprightly grinning **Carole King**. A mini-bouffant flip adorns her debutante smile. She's donned a vertically-pinstriped white co-ed dress and 1½" Baker Qualicraft gray shoes. Rising above them both in Kilimanjaro majesty is **Cynthia Weil**. Her four-inch high blonde flip surveys Mann's hasty new notes on the musical page. That's the vignette! The Brill Building is a PI-ANO-dominated songwriting scenario, just like Harry Von Tilzer's cold-water walk-up in 1899 on the fringes of Tin Pan Alley history.

Garage bands (see Grunge, much, much, later) usually had no pianos at all. They plugged into Dad's battery-charger plug in the ricketty old garage – sharing their creative billion-decibel bliss with something resembling half of a '49 Ford (whose V-8 engine was in the bedroom). It was the GUITAR vs. PIANO SHOWDOWN. You had your Tin Pan Alley geniuses (C. King et al) athwart the Steinway pianos, and your Lenny & the Thundertones combos hacking away at millions of ringing rhythm guitars. All had the same good ol' Revenge Rock (see Del Shannon) Dream:

REVENGE OF THE GARAGE

Score a monster hit record, sell five million, buy a Cadillac and a summer cottage and a mansion, and never, ever have to work in that slimy, crummy @#$%^& factory again! Drive past the grubby house of that dorky bimbo who dumped me, and just back down the mellow pipes of our [other] Corvette a little, until she turns green with envy and purple with passion, lusting over the flawless teen-idol bod of the great guy she stupidly lost to superduperstardom. Ah, Sweet Rock and Roll Revenge!

One dinky difference. Big Apple rockers played the piano in the easier keys of 'C', 'F', and 'G'. Guitar guys? They sided with the Blues masters of the Mississippi Delta, like Jimmy Reed, Rock Hall Class of 1991. Their keys were 'E' or 'A'. **Bobby Vee and the Shadows** were guitar guys. Their #77, 8-59 "Suzie Baby" flip is a guitar instrumental called (heh heh) "Flyin' High." Peering out their snowdrift windows at a North Dakota frozen steppe just below the tundra, they got the whole neighborhood together to fool around with guitars. Like the Crickets they worshipped, they started with drums, bass, lead and rhythm guitar. Bobby's super lead-guitarist brother **Bill Velline** energized the Shadows, with Bob Korum's Jerry-Allison-style drums, and Jim Stillman on guitar/bass; 15-year-old Bobby sang (now that his baritone shift was complete). They did songs of Holly, Holly, and Holly, plus a few second-string superstars.

Rock and Roll was still fun. It was really, truly possible

then for a Johnny B. Goode gaggle of guitarists to go down to Frump's Studio – and eke out the next #49 in the whole U.S.A. on an airwave and a prayer. With great songs like "Suzie Baby" and "Lonely Love," Bobby's Shadows burst out beyond the bounds of the Joe Average Garage Band.

Here's the Rock and Roll Rundown for One Million Garage Bands (NOT Bobby Vee & Shadows) with Five Million Guitars and NO PIANOS.

GROOVY GARAGE BAND RECIPE

One Drooling Drummer with white socks and 'Kramer' shirts;
One Bass Plucker, Chesterfield flitting by his chunky lip;
One Lead Guitarist (guy who knew four chords);
48 'Rhythm Guitarists,' gnarled knuckles clutching to find just one chord, and stay on it until the Lead Guitarist got furious and unplugged their amps.

Every band on the planet started this way in 1961. I oughta know. I was the 14th rhythm guitarist on the left side when the big guy with the real Gibson unplugged my Supro Sahara (faux Fender Strat) back at some beery dive in Toledo.

Once a piano player showed up from the University of Minnesota. Vee, attuned to the 'Key of 'E' and 'A'' world, tried to find a spot for keyboard whiz Bobby Zimmerman, but destiny sent Bobby packing off to New York City where he decided – if you can't beat em, join 'em. The piano was just too un-portable. Somewhere on his way to the Big Apple, Piano Bob Zimmerman transformed to **BOB DYLAN**. He switched from piano to guitar 'C' chords to the macho catwalk of trebletone 'E' guitars. It's just a Minnesota snowflake's drift from **Bobby Vee** to Bobby Zee/Bobby Dee . . .

"Masters of War" – Bob Dylan, NC, 1963. Lyrical flagship of Columbia Bob's cruise into stardom. This antiwar song predates Vietnam by two years. **Bob Dylan** (from poet Dylan Thomas) ditched the Zimmerman: he seethes anger and bitterness never seen in a world of drive-ins, malts, barbershop quartets, and political ostriches who buried their heads in the sand. When they emerged, these apolitical mugwumps were blindsided by Vietnam. Most of the rest of us saw it gradually creeping up, but we were too busy making a living to think about it. Not Bob. He lambasts munitions moguls who build bombs and death planes. The executioner stays well-hidden.

"The Wayward Wind" – **Gogi Grant, #1(8), 4-56.** Long before the 'Girls' Group' era, Gogi's restless, wind-blown, Wild-West Wayward Windsong describes movie star James Dean. The sweet alto tells of tumbleweeds, border towns, broken vows, and nevermore love. Gogi salutes ramblin' man with violin paced Orchestral Rock.

"Castles in the Sand" – Stevie Wonder, #52, 2-64; #52 R & B. Stevie, in the throaty throes of gliding down from sky-high soprano to Irish tenor (age 14), delivered this bongo-powered Motown masterpiece.

Whereas his hero **Ray Charles** lost his sight at age ten, Stevie Wonder was born blind. His experiences with castles of sand, like castles of dreams, are tactile rather than visual. Born in Saginaw, Michigan, Steveland Morris attended the Lansing School for the Blind; the only Michigan water standing nearby is little Lake Lansing – the sea is 800 miles away, and the only waves are three inches high in raging gales. Sand castles are safe in Mid-Michigan.

"Love Letters in the Sand" – Pat Boone, #1(7), 5-57; #12, 7-57 R & B. A beautiful ballad, the Pop Standard (#6, 9-31 for **Ted Black & Orchestra**) doubles between Pat's resonant rolling baritone and the triple subdivision beats between each beat of the slow-dance anthem (you get 12 beats for the price of four). Like Wonder's song, "Love Letters" covers the sad metaphor of the sea washing away the letters in the sand (or the dream castles).

Ketty Lester's #5, 2-62 "Love Letters" was sung in a bathroom (Wayne Jancik's *One-Hit Wonders*) due to lack of studio space. Gorgeous Roberta Flack song, though, despite the odd background gurgle.

"Duke of Earl" – Gene 'Duke of Earl' Chandler, #1(3), 1-62; #1(5) R & B. Two questions: what's this song really about and who is this guy, anyhow? Born Eugene Dixon in Chicago in 1937, the Duke of Earl's nothing-can-stop-me *chutzpah* is also evident in his other two Top 20 tunes, "Just Be True" (#19, 7-64), and (gulp) "Nothing Can Stop Me" (#18, 4-65). Twenty-five Duke ditties twirled in the HOT 100. He strutted his cape and top hat to the zenith of popularity in his first Vee-Jay release.

Beyond gritty humor in a jugular vein, "Duke of Earl" is an incendiary political statement. As John Cougar Mellencamp says, "Ain't this America?" ("Pink Houses", #8, 12-83). Rejecting grammar, peerage, social stratification, and ritzy hotsy-totsy tradition, America still champions the inherent right of the individual to rise to his/her own level of success. Even in Dukedom. But in CHICAGO? Why not? Washington's **Duke Ellington** (1899-1974), was the Emperor of Jazz piano.

By declaring himself to be one, in an international blockbuster hit record, Gene Chandler (in soaring falsetto) BECOMES THIS RICH HOTSHOT DUKE. No longer just Gene from the Chicago streets, he simply states his social superiority, and becomes this Duke that Britons cannot ever become, unless born into it (even the Beatles had to settle for Knighthood and the M.B.E.). Beatle **Paul McCartney** had a special ceremony in December 1996 with Her Majesty Queen Elizabeth II. It took American John Wayne 50 horse operas to get dubbed THE DUKE – all Gene Chandler needed was one hit record! Under these upwardly-mobile conditions, how tough is it (in stuffy klieg lights) BE ELVIS and get crowned King?

"You're the Apple of My Eye" – Four Lovers, #62, 5-56. Re-recorded as Four Seasons, #106, 1964. Frankie Castelluccio (Valli) started with Variatones with Tommy DeVito in Newark, New Jersey. Streetcorner groups. **Bob Gaudio** showed up from Fort Lee (Royal Teens' "Short Shorts," #3, 1-58). Songsters shifted to the name of their regular-gig bowling alley – the **Four Seasons**.

"Sherry" – Four Seasons, #1(5), 8-62; #1(1), 9-62 R & B. Back in the Motor City, "Sherry" and "Sheila" (T. Roe, #1) were spatting over pole position at #1. Bob Gaudio, coached by crackerjack producer **Bob Crewe** at Vee-Jay with the Duke of Earl, put together winning combos: **Frankie Valli, Nick Massi,** and **Tommy DeVito** (d. 2001, 71). They added handclappers galore. It sweetened the hulking production, giving dancekids a bashing beat they could hang onto (compare thunder drum sound of **Irene Cara**'s "Flashdance" #1[6], 4-83).

One of the great freewheeling moments of soup-it-up White Soul occurs as Valli lofts to his first 'CRY-Yigh-Yigh-Yigh'. It's one of R & R's magical mystifying moments. "Sherry" has become a part of American pop folklore, thanks to the Four Seasons' inherent musical excellence.

"Big Girls Don't Cry" – Frankie Valli & the Four Seasons, #1(5), 10-62; #1(3), 11-62 R & B. When goaded to top "Sherry," Frankie's doo-whop contingent tied the score at five glorious weeks atop the Gold Pipeline. They took the "What's Your Name" 2-62 **Don & Juan** style and exploded its power with **Bob Crewe**'s stompin' beat.

"Dawn" – Four Seasons, #3, 7-63. Here we go with the Seasons' poverty shtick. First she's rich – too good for him. Then they somersault to "Rag Doll," with her "Patches" poverty theme again – but no graveyard. "Dawn" has a marvelous mélange of drum-blur fadeouts.

"Rag Doll" – Four Seasons, #1(2), 6-64. Cinderella saga in the flesh. Complete opposite theme from "Rag Doll": HE's rich, she's poor. She's a "rag doll," and his folks won't let him see her because they say that she's common. **Frankie Valli**, unlike the poor dolt in "Patches," doesn't do the nihilistic life-doesn't-matter thing. In #1(3), 1-63 "Walk Like a Man," his trusted father gave him sage advice to bolster his courage, and saunter away with brave resignation. He still cares what his dad thinks in "Rag Doll." But he's a man himself. His romances are his business. The vocal finale swoons to a high crag, far atop the Mt. Falsetto. Valli hovers there in the splendor reserved for American eagles – surveying with his chosen lady love the Dukedom he has forged. Catch the "OOOOOO" falsetto lyric-less harmonies toward the finale; the Four Seasons' shift from the Tonic "I" chord to the Sub-Dominant "IV" chord is among the most angelically harmonic moments in Rock and Roll.

"Uptown Girl" – Billy Joel, #3, 9-83; #1(5), 11-83 U.K. Question? Why is Billy Joel here so soon? Answer. The Oyster Bay, Long Island versatile virtuoso not only does a nifty Frankie Valli vocal mirror, all by himself *a cappella*, with just a bass – he writes a vastly personal love song to his former wife, 'Supermodel' Christie Brinkley.

From the Echoes to the Lost Souls to the Hassles, Billy Joel definitely came at R & R via the East Coast Brill Building PIANO route. His "Uptown Girl" is a super carbon copy of the Seasons' best. All the voices are overdubbed Billy, anchored by a muted bass guitar.

"December, 1963 (Oh, What a Night)" – Four Seasons, #1(3), 12-75 & #14, 8-94. Valli duels lead vocal. This one thrived in swish of Discomania, and enjoyed a virile revival in the mid-90s via Techno/Dance/Neo-Disco. With '94 resurgence, "1963" is among longest-running *Billboard* hits of all time.

"Ginny Come Lately" – Brian Hyland, #21, 3-62; #5, U.K. Despite ultra-light Oldies rotation on air waves, "Ginny" is a sweet melody of boy-meets-new-girl – who captivates him with her demure innocence and celestial personality. She's also a knockout for the love-strewn lad. Delightful marshmallow teenage romance, with a garnish of cool chromatic chords.

"Mind Over Matter" – Nolan Strong & Diablos, #112, 11-62; NC R & B. How in the world can you score a #1 in Detroit and still clunk down to #112 nationally? Distribution, distribution, distribution! Devora and Jack Brown's Fortune Records is a small operation on Third Street in Detroit. Small outfits, when faced with surging national sales potential, often sell the master tape to a major national label for distribution and/or promotion. Devora didn't.

Once she did, though, with a #1 Detroit smash, **Nathaniel Mayer**'s #22, 4-62 (#16 R & B) "Village of Love." Nate was the loudest guy in the world. Epitome of Soul. His cape swirling draculinely about him, black-belt karate-chopper Mayer could have taught James Brown something about fired-up Soul singing.

"Money" – Barrett Strong, #23, 2-60; #2(6), 1-60 R & B. Motown is a 60s phenomenon. Honest lyric about guy's love of long green petty cash. Everly "Susie" echo in wild chord shift **E-G-A-G-E-G-A-G-E**. Echoes world of fiscal reality in lyric. Strong craves CASH on the barrelhead. Anthem of Rock-flick *Animal House*.

"Spanish Harlem" – Ben E. King, #10, 12-60; #15, 1-61 R & B. Smooth tenor for Drifters' 1st solo shot. Despite blight of economic hopes, a lovely rose blooms in mean streets replete with silky-strings bridge and gorgeous melody. Nifty Latin/Soul beat. Also #2(2), 7-71 for Sister Soul **Aretha Franklin**. Prelude to universally known "Stand by Me" (#4, 5-61, #9, 10-86). [See Santana & #1(10), 3-2000 "Maria Maria"].

"100 Pounds of Clay" – Gene McDaniels, #3, 3-61; #11, 5-61 R & B. Covered in U.K. (#8) by Craig Douglas. Quasi-religious Chalypso song about the Lord sculpting his beautiful lady love out of 100# of earthy raw material. Reminds all us self-puffing humans that we're still just a tad higher out of the earth than beasts, and a whole lot lower than the Angels (or the White Sox or Rockies or Dodgers). Great song.

The Drifters

"On Broadway" – Drifters, #9, 3-63; #7 R & B. 'Johnny B. Goode's' rags-to riches dream. Name in lights. King of the Big Apple. **Rudy Lewis** takes over Drifters from superstar lead singers **Clyde McPhatter** (Rock Hall 1987) and **Ben E. King** (#4, '61 "Stand by Me"). **Drifters** (Rock Hall '88) had 36 charted hits, like #2, 6-59 "There Goes My Baby," #16, 2-60 "This Magic Moment," #1(3), 9-60 "Save the Last Dance for Me," #5, 11-62 "Up On the Roof," and #4, 6-64 "Under the Boardwalk." Tragically, Lewis [1937-64] died of a heart attack after scoring his Broadway dream.

"Tribute to Buddy Holly" – Mike Berry and the Outlaws, NC, 1961,; #18, 10-61 U.K. Three years after the fact, the haunting baritone of Scottish star Mike Berry rebounded throughout the British Isles and Canada, not the U.S.A. Berry underscores the musical impact of Holly in England, and sets the stage for the British Invasion. Berry's "Tribute" takes the high road for good taste in eulogizing Buddy – with no tacky Graveyard Rock grotesquerie. In 1961, we hadn't heard much real British Rock and Roll. **Joe Cocker** began with Berry.

Before the British rockers could prepare their own American Invasion, the stage was overtaken by a multitude of magnificent FEMALE rockers – for the first time in the Rock Revolution.

Kim Dandy to the Rescue ⁑ Women Who Rock & Roll

15

Trixie Smith shocked the joint with "My Daddy Rocks Me (With One Steady Roll)" back at the dawn of time. The Big Band **Andrews Sisters** bounced the no-beat WWII world with #2(3), "Beat Me Daddy, Eight to the Bar," plus the bibulous "Beer Barrel Polka" (#4, 5-39, Czech folk song), and their hoppy Swing version of "The Boogie Woogie Bugle Boy" #6, 3-41 (**Bette Midler**'s cover #8, 1973). Ruth, Etta, and LaVern set the stage:

"This Little Girl's Gone Rockin" — **Ruth Brown, #24, 9-58; #7, 10-58 R & B.** Ruth's follow-up to steamy #25 "Lucky Lips" ballad. Ruth (1993 Rock Hall Inductee) shows her husky contralto range and power here, blending brusquely with sax man **King Curtis**. Brown is a consummate R & R performer with gusto and firepower.

"All I Could Do Was Cry" — **Etta James, #33, 5-60; #2(1) R & B.** Etta too gained the Hall in 1993 for her crisp "Miss Peaches" renditions of torch songs and hard soulful rockers. Ruth Brown's R & B career was launched five years before "Rock Around the Clock" in 1949 with "So Long"/ "It's Raining" (#4, R & B) on Turkish emigrant **Ahmet Ertegun**'s up-and-coming Atlantic label – later home for 1st female inductee **Aretha Franklin** ('87).

Remember Hank Ballard's risqué Annie saga? "Willie and the Hand Jive" (#9, 6-58) bandleader **Johnny Otis** and **Etta James** recorded answer to "Work with Me, Annie": "Roll with Me, Henry," later retitled "The Wallflower" for censors (NC '53; #1[4], 2-55 R & B). Raunchy, raspy, and rockin', this tune etched Etta's name forever. Of course it was 'covered:' **Georgia Gibbs** (Fredda Gibbons of Worcester, Massachusetts), also paced LaVern Baker's smash "Tweedlee Dee" to #2 above LaVern's #14. Etta's Wallflower ripsnorter became a subdued "Dance with Me Henry" (#1[3], 3-55) for Gibbs.

"See See Rider" – **LaVern Baker, #34, 12-62; # 9 R & B.** First Rock Diva? Or, Rock and Soul Diva? Maybe **LaVern Baker** (1929-97). From her frantic raspy "Tweedlee Dee" to her Jim Dandy Saga (also "Jim Dandy Got Married"). LaVern Baker was the Queen of R & B, Rock and Soul. Detroit's LaVern captured a big national audience with her expressive breed of Soul, which she and **Ray Charles**

(b. 1930) defined. After barnstorming with Jim Dandy and Buddy Holly and the Big Bopper, LaVern jolted the HOT 100 with this scorchy tribute to #14, 1-25 **Ma Rainey** original. LaVern signed with Ahmet Ertegun on Atlantic, #2 Soul label to Motown over the years (see ARETHA). Baker's all-knowing take-charge contralto and with-it stage presence sent this tune toward the top.

Gillian Garr's *He's A Rebel* (Yoko Ono intro) goes into vivid detail about **Bo Diddley**'s female guitarist, "Lady Bo," **Peggy Jones**, in 1957.

"Fujiyama Mama" – **Wanda Jackson, NC, Rec. 9-11-57.** Mt. Fuji lofts its snow-covered regalness over Japan. An eagerly erupting volcano, it hisses and glowers, waiting to get ticked off enough to blow its top. Wanda Jackson offers us the ultimate Virile Female metaphor here. **Wanda Jackson** (b. '37) did volcanic Rockabilly. Only a few female rock and rollers like **Janis Joplin, Joan Jett, Tina Turner, Melissa Etheridge,** or **Gracie Slick**, have ever blasted Wanda's incredible energy. She rocked Elvis's "Let's Have a Party" (#37, 8-60). Wanda wailed, until the system tamed her down. It happened to Elvis, too, with his post-military Princeton haircut.

"Right or Wrong" – **Wanda Jackson, #29, 6-61; #9, 7-61 C.** With this torch tune, she became a **Brenda Lee** echo. The atomic Jackson contralto buzzed down to a purring murmur. Wanda wrote her own unique stuff in the 50s: "You Bug Me Bad," "Mean Mean Man," or "Savin' My Love." Jackson looked like a brunette Jayne Mansfield, and she sang like Elvis.

"You Ain't Nothin' But a Hound Dog" – **Willie Mae 'Big Mama' Thornton, NC, 1953; #1(7), 3-53 R & B.** Gaar sympathetically describes the burly 350# Blues belter's hard life. Willie Mae's Hound Dog is a lot scruffier than Elvis's. It's one mangy mutt, a fleabag of gigundo grungoid proportion – a Flea Condo, maybe, of snappitty teeth so sharp it would terrify Jim Croce's "Leroy Brown" Junkyard Dog (#1, 4-73).

"I'm Sorry" – **Brenda Lee, #1(3), 5-60; $4, 6-60 R & B.** When we called Wanda a Brenda echo, that was a compliment, for most singers. The 4'9" "Little Miss Dynamite", **Brenda Lee** [Tarpley (b. 1944, Georgia)] may be the best-known female Rock and Roll star of the fifties and early sixties. In all, she placed 55 HOT 100 hits on the charts, tying for 19th-ever and 4th best-selling female artist. With a baby-doll smile, a come-hither twinkle in her big brown eyes, and a vampish contralto, Brenda charmed the entire world. Brenda's debut top ten was #4, '59 "Sweet Nothin's," a porch-swing sultry 'rocker.'

She sounds so sincere and selfless and believable in this Ronnie Self song (not **Platters'** #11, 3-57 "I'm Sorry"). You can't help but believe every word out of her mini-Barbie lips. Brenda hit #1 (9-60) with Italian folk tune "I Want to Be Wanted." She also triumphed on #6, 6-60, "That's All You Gotta Do" and #7, 12-60 "Emotions."

Brenda Lee & Bobby Vee

"All Alone Am I" – **Brenda Lee, #3, 9-62.** Bass drum heavily thumping in BIG 2 & 4 beats of R & R, Brenda snurfles into her best blue mood. Her rendezvous with reverie is always emotive, forlorn, and slurpily sad. "All Alone Am I" surrounds the Roy Orbison bubble of isolation. Buoyed valiantly by tremolo guitars, and the ringing of a new electronic 1961 discovery – REVERBERATION – Brenda's songs of loneliness throb with her sad refrains. Cousin tunes to this lament? "Losing You" (#6, 4-63), "As Usual" (#12, 12-63), and #3, 10-61 "Fool #1."

Harbinger of the Girls' Group Era? The **Chantels** and the **Bobbettes** (#6, 6-57, "Mr. Lee"). 1890s male Barber Shop Quartet style was echoed by the Wisconsin female quartet the **Chordettes:**

"Born to Be With You" – **Chordettes, #5, 6-56.** One of the prettiest melodies ever woven, by 'bass' Janet Buschman, 'baritone' sister-in-law Carol Buschman, 'tenor' Margie Needham, and lead 'tenor' **Dorothy Schwartz**. Already top entertainment on *Arthur Godfrey Show* 1949-53, according to Whitburn, Janet Ertel Buschman married Archie Bleyer the bandleader – and their daughter married **Phil Everly**.

"Lollipop" – **Chordettes, #2(2), 3-58; #3 R & B.** To attain one sound, a Chordette placed her finger in her mouth and BLIP – the hollow popping "Lollipop" gimmick that characterizes this tune. Jimmie Rodgers II's #1, 8-57 "Honeycomb" girl had honey-sweet lips. It was only fitting that the Chordettes would compare the guy's kisses to a lollipop. This is grand exaggeration of the utmost utter degree. Many people's lips in the fifties probably tasted more like a raggedy combo of liverwurst, Virginia Slims cigarettes, garlic, intertooth parsley wads, and Pepsi-burp.

Chordettes clicked with #8, 9-57 "Just Between You and Me"; cover of **Teen Queens'** #14, 3-56 "Eddie My Love" (#14, 3-56, ditto); #16, 9-56 "Lay Down Your Arms"; and the theme from TV theme "Zorro" (#17, 5-56). Any Chordette MONSTER HITS? One: #1(7), 1-54 "Mr. Sandman." She asks Sandman for "dreamy" guy.

"Mr. Lee" – **Bobbettes, #6, 8-57; #1(4), 9-57 R & B.** Emma and Janice Pought led Doo-whop quintet from the Big Apple. Mr. Lee was either their junior-high teacher or their principal . . . or perhaps some minor cog in a vast educational bureaucracy. All five seemed to have a major crush on him. With nursery-rhyme numbers and cute predictable rhymes, the ode to Mr. Lee is a cotton-candy confection of bubbly teenybop sugar. Sub-bopper (11 to 13) harmonies were profound. The beat rollicked along in a funky little groove. Everybody had a lot of fun. The follow-up contains a vicious terminator plot too gruesome to mention, so we won't. It makes Gangsta Rap sound like Nursery Rhymes about the Funky Little Bunny.

"Baby It's You" – **Shirelles, #8, 12-61.** 26 HOT 100 hits, on tap, **Shirley Owens** began stardom in Passaic, New Jersey. Like **Frank Sinatra** in Hoboken and Jersey City, they could gaze eastward over the Hudson River, and catch the soaring buildings and bright Broadway lights of their magical musical destinies. She and her schoolmates started singing together for fun. After all, isn't that what rock music is supposed to be all about? The quartet congealed, Shirley fronting a fine lineup of **Addie 'Micki' Harris, Beverly Lee,** and **Doris Kenner.** Much of the most memorable Rock and Soul has been energized by an African-American and Jewish collaboration, such as the **Ronettes. Ronnie Spector** (part Afro, part Native American) married producer **Phil Spector** (1968-74).

Shirley and Crew got off the ground as the POQUELLOS (Whitburn) or the PEQUELLOS (*Penguin Encyclopedia of Popular Music*), and then the **Honeytones.** Finally, they hit upon the SHIRELLES, from Shirley. At the group's school debut, their friend Mary Jane Greenberg signed them to her own tiny Tiara label, and they cut this classic:

"I Met Him on a Sunday" – Shirelles, #49, 4-58; NC R & B. Note one key innovation – handclapping. It's paramount here to the evolution of this great sound. A little finger-popping works wonders with the Starmakers, too . . . Who wrote it? The Shirlelles did. Buddy Holly, Chuck Berry, and the Shirelles were cracking up the old Tin Pan Alley system of "songwriters do demos, stars sing them."

The song took off locally, and **Florence Greenberg** had too much record to handle. She farmed it out to Decca for national distribution. Decca didn't exactly botch the deal, like they did in their misfortunate handling of both Buddy Holly and the Beatles. They downpedaled it with faint praise, and dinky hype. Hey, #49 is pretty good.

"Dedicated to the One I Love" – Shirelles, #83, 7-59; #3, 1-61; #2(2), 2-61 R & B. If ever there were an Exclamation Point Convention (!!!!!!) for IF AT FIRST YOU DON'T SUCCEED, this was it. Dissatisfied with the A & R people at Decca not jumping on the Shirelles' #83 hit at DJ conventions, or when they drank their lunch together, Florence Greenberg actually FORMED HER OWN RECORD COMPANY, Scepter, two years before Del Shannon, to go up against the big guns at Decca. Legally, we must suppose, Shirley's Shirelles hadn't signed their lives away. "Dedicated" begins on a sensuous, come-hither tacet, starring the title. Suddenly, you're besieged by a big bass, a throbbing tremolo guitar, and a drummer slashing the snare, low on the big two and four. The lyric revolves around parting. She's far away. She asks him to say a little prayer for her. To Shakespeare's 50s teenagers, "the darkest hour" just before dawn was a philosophical truth. Unrequited romance burns down. From the smoldering ashes of yesterday comes a flickering new flame. Maybe a new love. This song had no darkest hour.

"Will You Love Me Tomorrow" – Shirelles, #1(2), 11-60; #2(4); 12-60 R & B. When my Folk-fan sister Blair bought this album, I knew it must be important.

"Will You Love Me Tomorrow" throws musical curves that would strike out Ty Cobb or Babe Ruth. It was written by brilliant Brill Building Big Apple composer **Carole (Klein) King**. Not only a song – but a Gender Anthem.

PIANO – it comes to us from the world of Brill Pianos – not GUITARS. The tune begins in 'C', pumped by the most basic of R & R drum beats:

BASIC ROCK & ROLL RHYTHM

Left Hand: ♩ ♩ ♩ ♩
1 2 3 4

Right Hand: ‿ ♩ ♩ ‿ ♩
1 2 2½ 3 4

Her torch tune dances from Tonic I chord **C** to wild Mediant Major III chord **E**, lurching to more normal Streetcorner Sub-Mediant VI minor **Am**, Dominant Seventh V7 **G7**, and gorgeous Sub-Dominant IV **F**.

After all this chord passion, will he still love and RE-SPECT her by dawn's early light? What's a poor kool kat to do? He's poised for sweet affection. For magnetic action. For the instant gratification inherent to his gender breed. Suddenly she asks a very tough question: what'll it be, guy? The dim grim reality finally gets emblazoned upon a lyrical canvas. She is up against WILD THING (Troggs, #1, 6-66). WILD THING is the male ego. Or libido. Or just plain lust in the dust. For some reason, I often envision WILD THING as the Tasmanian Devil. Mr. W. Thing craves affection, then darts away in a whirlwind, looking for a new conquest. His romantic line is nothing new. It's the ol' PROVE-YOUR-LOVE line: to know whether he loves her, she must first hold him tightly; THEN he might love her. Maybe, baby. As every lass should know, a man occasionally speaks of love when he has something more basic (sex) on his mind.

Carole King and the Shirelles knew a basic truth that many teens, unexpectedly expecting, choose to forget – THROUGHOUT HISTORY, NO MAN HAS EVER GOTTEN PREGNANT (except Arnold Schwarzenegger, in a funny 1993 flick, *Junior* ***½).

The song talks about Consequences of Actions. It's a very powerful song. Its message stings. The girl gets left with the Bundle of Love, while her supercool Casanova (the Wanderer) wanders off with new tattoos, muscles, Corvettes, and bragging rights about his easy seduction.

The Shirelles embellish the serious message with silvery strings into Verse II. On the hyperactive bridge, violins spin and fly frantically in the upper skies. Pulsating stars are passionate beacons of love. The girl, caught up in the moment's passion, mightily and valiantly strives to whisk him away. But she wants him, too. Tantalizingly the Shirelles' #1 song leaves us all still waffling:

Did she or didn't she? Cotton-candy confection of love. If nothing else, the song is a little Jiminy Cricket conscience. It tells her to beware of Insta-Love and Goodbye Romeo. Then the ebbing night greets the morning sun.

In the *Field Guide to Rock and Roll*, "Will You Love Me Tomorrow" is the robin. A MUST in any R & R collection. Female song? Nope. **Bobby Vee** sang it on an album, and the **Four Seasons** had a substantial hit (#24, 2-68).

"Soldier Boy" – Shirelles, #1(3), 3-62; #3, 4-62 R & B. Shirelles' biggest hit. Relates to the Cold War before Vietnam. No protest song. The Shirelles' 'Little Soldier Boy' vows to be true. He is her first and last love. This one is idyllic and perfect. She finishes on a snare roll, pledging her eternal love.

"Mr. Lonely" – Bobby Vinton, #1(1), 10-64. Since gender discrimination is not our thing, let's insert a guy tune or two. This one fits here anyhow, segueing off the Shirelles' curtain call. Bobby Vinton's boy-next-door tunes whisked spun-sugar melodies. The Polish-American Pennsylvanian (b. '35) backed **Dick Clark**'s Caravan of Stars, and scored with #1(4), 6-62 "Roses Are Red," #1(3), 8-63 "Blue Velvet" (#16, '51 **Tony Bennett**), and "There I've Said It Again." This nice-guy's #1(4), 11-63 ballad

was "There! I've Said it Again." His Pop Standards totaled 47 HOT 100 hits over 18 years. Among nicest melodies: #3, 9-74 "My Melody of Love" and #6, 9-67 "Please
Love Me Forever."

Vinton croons about his foxhole displeasure. Pulling
guard duty, Mr. Lonely surveys Lonesome Land. He
yearns for mail call. Nope, no letter today. Not even
$10,000,000 You-may-already-be-a-winner news from Ed
McMahon or Bandstand's Dick Clark. So what does Bobby
do? He yodels. A sad soldier all alone. It could be worse.
He could be in a war. In 1964, Vietnam was rumbling,
and R & R fury fanned the flames.

Other early female recording stars? The **Carter
Family** did #14, 5-30 "Worried Man's Blues" and
#3, 8-28 "Wildwood Flower."

**"Chains" – Cookies, #17, 11-62; #6, 12-62 R &
B. Ethel 'Earl Jean' McCrea** and the Cookies ran a
tight Barber-Shop Quartet. "Chains" slurs its masochistic
line about how his lady has him all locked into chains of
love. A 12-Bar Blues song, it sounds a bit like the
Chordettes. One sings 'bass', plunging the depths of her
mega-contralto down into the male baritone range – one
of the lowest female singers of all time, like Toni Braxton
in #1(11), 10-96 "Un-Break My Heart." Cookies rotated
NYC personnel like musical chairs. Their "Don't Say
Nothin' Bad (About My Baby)" [#7, 3-68] actually tells the
romantic rival to shut her mouth! Sometimes, cookies are
sweet?

**"Angel Baby" – Rosie & the Originals, #5, 12-60;
#5, 1-61 R & B.** Suddenly, a female falsetto phenom-
enon: San Diego's **Rosalie Hamlin** yodeled her own
way high above her normal alto style. "Angel Baby" throbs
along to the 60-beat/minute pulse. Streetcorner chord
pattern.

**"Ain't Gonna Kiss Ya" – Ribbons, #81, 2-63; NC
R & B.** Best of the bunch? In Detroit, R & B mecca, this
song hit at least the top seven. Super Girls' Group from
L.A. On the rolling finale, their anonymous expert drummer rips it up into a "Peggy Sue" tom-tom blur of 16th-
note paradiddles – tuff enuff stuff. SHE must have been
an excellent drummer. This #81 Girl Anthem 'coulda' been
#1 somewhere, but got victimized by Light Hypes (and
maybe an overzealous Vigilante Posse of Terminally-
Miffed Grammarians). The Ribbons pull back the affection. The shlumpish slug deserves it. The Beatles' pals
the **Searchers** covered the Ribbons' sound on *Meet the
Searchers/Needles & Pins*, Al. #22, 8-64. Soul spinoff.

"Crazy" – Patsy Cline, #9, 10-61; #2(2), 11-61 C.
"Crazy" is THE #1 record spun on all the jukeboxes in
America over the decade of the 1990s. (Bob Seger is
second with his #28, 4-79 "Old Time Rock and Roll").
Before bandanna or beard, **Willie Nelson** crafted this
classic for Patsy. Patsy's "Crazy" serenades whirly
bubbles of old red-blue-yellow-gold-green Wurlitzers of
bygone jukebox midnight hot America. Slow sensuous
beat. Floyd Cramer style piano. Patsy and Willie ponder

the total insanity of falling in love: it is irrational, you lose
money, you're crazy just to try or cry. Love may be irrational and quixotic and fraught with joy and/or pain, but this
love song is the favorite song of over 1% of the American
people. Ed Lent heard Willie wrote it in 20 minutes in a
bus station.

Why is it, in the long Dew Drop Inn jukebox eternities of
flying generations, that Patsy's one song "Crazy" has captured everyone's hearts so intensely? Patsy sounds very
sincere. Everyone has felt foolish going off the deep end
for love; the melody is crisp and pure; it is a perfect Country hit with a blue-funk piano.

Produced by Owen Bradley in his Nashville Barn.
"Crazy" is marbled with honkytonk splendor. Patsy delivers plaintive little yodel-kicks that power the plodding
band track. Guitars cry. The song is a vision of loneliness
and sorrow. Patsy Cline discovers the very hard rock
bottom of the well of isolation. Most folks figure Patsy's a
contemporary of Hank Williams. She isn't. She's a musical contemporary of the **Cookies**, and the **Crystals**,
and the **Shirelles**, and a young cheerleading swimmer
from the Cass Tech High School for Detroit's Gifted Students – the **Supremes' Diana Ross**. Cline classics?
#12, 5-61 "I Fall to Pieces"; #14, 1-62 "She's Got You"; and
Bob Wills' Texas classic "Faded Love" (#96, 8-63; #7 C).

**"Walkin' After Midnight" – Patsy Cline, #12, 2-57; #108,
3-63; #2(2), 3-57 C.** Virginian's best tune? Patsy was the
first female Country singer to regularly cross over into the
HOT 100. She bleeps in these little chunks of skyscraper-
soprano yodel-kicks on top of her assertive alto phrasing
in the verse. Victim of a lost love, she goes out walking
after midnight – not a safe habit in anybody's neighborhood even in the relative safety of 1957. In the astounding lyric, a WILLOW cries on a PILLOW.

Guy time. Gender gapping rots. In no way does
this chapter discriminate against men, a very fine
gender I happily represent:

**"Louie Louie" – Kingsmen, #2(6), 11-63; #97, 5-
66.** In this serious Vietnam dawn, with a beloved President assassinated, what was Congress up to? Trying to
decipher lyrics of **Jack Ely**'s 'X'-rated rock classic
"Louie2", Dave Marsh wrote an entire book on this song's
sociological and comic ramifications. Suffice it to say
here that the marvelous slurring of words inherent in R &
R managed to splice a faux dirty song out of some innocent sea shanty. Check out Beach Boys' squeaky-clean
NC version. What's tremendous is the unique beat of
drummer **Lynn Easton**, and the staccato machine-gun
volley of **Mike Mitchell**'s fiery guitar.

Tale of woe. **Richard Berry** (1927-97) wrote "Louie
Louie" in 1956. Like so many songwriters, Berry (alas)
sold the entire rights to his song for a FLAT FEE, $750. In
the 80s, he won a big lawsuit for royalties.

We'll do a section later on Ska and Reggae and Calypso and Chalypso. They all tie into the enchanted isle
of Jamaica – particularly Kingston, the town the internationally famous **Kingston Trio** chose for half their name.

"Louie[2]" is essentially a Jamaican-flavored song. Berry wrote it about a Jamaican bartender (named, ahem LOUIE), and some bar patron looking for love in all the wrong Jamaican places.

"Louie Two-ey" had its first go-round by Rockin' Robin Roberts and the Wailers ("Tall Cool One," #36, 5-59). (NOT related to **Bob Marley**'s Wailers; they were a Pacific Northwest group like the Portland Oregonian Kingsmen.)

Jack Ely's version by the Kingsmen is the famous one. Ely was quickly replaced by **Lynn Easton**, The 'obscene' lyrics? Berry took the Wailers' straight-ahead song and presented a woozy act. As Elvis deliberately murmured – even mumbled syllables, so did Jack Ely. Some actual words? They MIGHT be: "I sailed dat ship all alone" or "Me catch dat ship across big sea." Then again, they might not. Nobody figured them out. The Jamaican patois dialect shimmers through, albeit couched in a mumbletypeg vocal swirl of "She snevver a girl (gerbil?) I'd (#$%&) at Nome" or something.

Despite Punk versions of deliberately obscene origin, and a pristinely PG-rated version by the silver-toned Beach Boys, "Louie" said PHOOEY to those who would dare strive to unlock its mystical lyrical secrets. Naturally, it was banned on many radio stations and even investigated by the FCC (Federal Communications Commission) who shook their heads and finally blurted: "We found the record to be unintelligible at any speed we played it."

The Kingsmen always said the words were not obscene. The musical excitement comes from **Mike Mitchell**'s incredible lead guitar attack. Buttressed by a unique Bob Marley/Reggae/Islands beat 20 years ahead of its time (like "Bo Diddley" in 1955), Mitchell fired off a bazooka bombshell of blistering treble-fret profundity. He hits the beat head-on, then he skirts it and pussyfoots around it in a consternation of spooktacular supernatural sound. Though it is not Hendrix or Clapton, or Santana's #1, 11-99 supergroup album *Supernatural*, it is one of the archetypal lead guitar solos in Rock and Roll history. Mitchell K.O.'s the opposition with his rockets' red glare.

"Louie Louie" lives on. It will continue to blast its magic party-on vibes wherever people get together for good times, raunchy rapscallion romps, and bleary beery bopping into the molten Midnight Hour.

And to this day, nobody quite has any idea just what it's about. If YOU find out, please let us know.

"The Jolly Green Giant" – Kingsmen, #4, 1-65. Unique BEET! R & R topics of the 50s were staidly serious. Burly **Lynn Easton**, beefy blond lead Kingsman, looked like your high school's jovial left tackle. He told me at Detroit's Masonic Temple in 1966 that he likes this rollicking tune about veggies best. "We're, like, this buncha guys from Portland [Oregon], and we're out to have a blast – know what I mean? You know, meet chicks, have a good time, make a few bucks." "Jolly Green Giant" reverberates with veggies; they lace the end-of-line guitar bloops with deliberately out-of-tune and out-of-time whoops and hollers: BEETS, BROCCOLI, BRUSSELS' SPROUTS, CORN, PEAS. With great glee and garage-sale gusto, the band has a rollicking rockin' time dancing with rutabagas, turnips, spuds, and artichoke hearts. No one will ever write an esoteric academic dissertation on "Jolly Green Giant," but the Kingsmen and their gaga dancers were having a lot of fun. The Kingsmen were performing GOODTIME music. Since Marsh wrote one entire book on "Louie2" "Jolly Green Giant" warrants a few bars of purple prose amidst its cavalcade of green peppers, Vidalia onions, celery stalks, Dracula-begone garlic bulbs, and okra.

The Kingsmen

In Garage Band tradition, the Kingsmen reached a pinnacle of their Frat Rock genre with "Jolly Green Giant." A mythical green giant smiling verdantly from supermarket shelves, the big non-alien green guy reminds all us growing kids to eat our veggies – as Bugs Bunny chomps carrots and Popeye chugs his spinach to get strong. In the song, his normal friendly A & P demeanor is stifled by the fact that he can't find any Jolly Green Giantesses for loving purposes. Finally, the big emerald dude crosses paths with a lusciously lovely and atrociously attractive Amazon. Nestled among friendly ears of corn and battalions of scallions, the gargantuan couple smooches under a green cheese Blue Moon.

Fading into their Heyday Sunset behind the golden-oldies cornfield, the Kingsmen reprised Barrett Strong's Motown "Money," #16 in 3-64, followed by a dynamite Righteous Brother cover of "Little Latin Lupe Lu" (#46, 7-64). "Death of an Angel" is their Graveyard Rock Ghoulie Goodie (#42, 9-64), and then this GIANT #4 veggie blockbuster that nearly outstreaked "Louie" on the charts. Their #47, 8-65 "Annie Fanny" champions a shapely *Playboy* cartoon girl, with the tune of #1, '60 **Hollywood Argyles'** "Alley Oop." "Killer Joe" at #77, 4-66 suggests the Manila, Philippines' biggest hit – (Pop & 4 sons) the **Rocky**

Fellers. The Frat/Garage/Party Kingsmen opened the floodgates to the party-animal Psychedelic Rock Era. Their working band previews those 70s and 90s superstars from Madison, Wisconsin, the **Steve Miller Band**.

"The House of the Rising Sun" – Joan Baez, NC, 1961. More convincing version of the Animals & Bob Dylan classic New Orleans brothel folk song. No matter how Animals' lead singer **Eric Burdon** growls about his song guy's own sin and misery, he's still the "John," taking care of carnal business – whereas a woman singing such a song can better highlight the day-to-day miseries of a young street girl's tribulations . . . for men's prurient release. Her fate is of a non-glamorous public utility. **Odetta**, too, sang the song strikingly.

Emerging from the Folk milieu was a crystalline soprano whose finger-picking frenzy on the acoustic guitar earned her a generous Folk purist following – **Joan Baez**. Her peripatetic wanderings and 'silvery voiced, unfussy treatment of trad ballads' (*Penguin*) combined for a rich pure sound of woman and guitar, unadorned with frumpy frills. Baez is really crucial to the same unplugged guitar stylistics of her good friend **Bob Dylan** of Minnesota. Their dual stardom snowballed in tandem. Baez first:

Baez, of course, lofted herself, via that innocent soprano, over the seedy sleazy fray. [#15, 3-62 (recorded 1960) album *Joan Baez*]. Sometimes appearing barefoot, she showed Appalachian authenticity in her Folk/Bluegrass/Country/Tradition repertoire. The raven-haired chanteuse became a force for political action. Baez founded the Institute for the Study of Non-Violence, and became an early activist against the Vietnam War. Many WWII vets were less than enamored with her idealistic stance. She is best known for bringing tears to a million eyes:

Joan Baez

"We Shall Overcome" – Joan Baez, #90, 11-63. Civil Rights Anthem. 'Live' recording from Miles College in Dr. Martin Luther King's Birmingham, Alabama. Daughter of a Mexican professor and Scottish mother, Staten Island's Baez (b. '41) was educated at Boston University. She championed liberal causes from an early age, weaving her traditional Folk songs around peace and freedom. Anthem of the Civil Rights movement, her song lit up the 800,000-strong march on Washington – where Dr. King gave his impassioned "I Have A Dream" speech in 1963. Her *Joan Baez in Concert, Part 2* album hit #7.

Along with the **Kingston Trio** and close friend **Bob Dylan**, Baez helped establish the ALBUM as mainstay of record sales. She was a banner wildfire force in progressive politics. This one great song answers the violent KKK fanatics and the bashers who burn, burn, burn – it filters the nonviolent love of Jesus from flames of hate.

Her sweet soprano cleaves the long faraway years, and America wafts back to a harmonic racial vision. The essence of Martin Luther King's Dream. With acoustic majesty, and flying fingers caressing her guitar, Baez reflects the multicultural power of Dr. King's dream; half Hispanic, half W.A.S.P., she represents the polyglot composition of the noble American democratic ideal. Back in Kennedy's 1963 Camelot of golden idealistic dreams, education meant a lot more than just a few bucks. It was a supercharged season of commitment and sacrifice.

The haunting refrain of white and black together, marching for freedom and justice, powered America's starry-eyed New Frontierswomen and Men to the King promise . . . long before our kidhood dreams were shattered by the icy bullet of Lee Harvey Oswald on November 22, 1963 – the Day Our Childhood Died. Our President, very suddenly, was gone. Reluctantly, we became instant adults.

The torch had been passed. Baez, like **Peter, Paul and Mary**, was among the last Folk purists to adorn the R & R bandwagon. On #3, 8-71s "The Night They Drove Old Dixie Down," she takes on the persona of a Civil War soldier. It had been the B-side of Dylan's band's (the **Band**) #25, 1969 "Up on Cripple Creek." Canadian Robbie Robertson's song features a nebulous antiwar slant about the Civil War – until Lincoln could take the humpty-dumpty pieces and glue them back together with civil rights over slavery. Paul McCartney's Rock hymn "Let It Be" scored #49, 11-71 for Joan, with #35, 9-75 "Diamonds and Rust" rounding out her Top 50 collection of single songs.

"You Were on My Mind" – We Five, #3, 8-65. Hoopla arises when pop profs attempt to pinpoint the Birth of Folk Rock. Is it the Byrds' Dylan tune "Mr. Tambourine Man" (#1, 5-65)? Or the Rooftop Singers/Erik Darling's #1(2), 1-63 "Walk Right In"? Or Dylan's own #39, 4-65 Kerouac-inspired "Subterranean Homesick Blues"? Perhaps the **Searchers**' Malvina Reynolds nuclear-fallout-protest rallying song against nuclear fallout threatening unborn kids: "What Have They Done to the Rain?" (#29, 1-65; #13, 12-64 U.K.) Among first female Folk Rock honors goes to California's Orange Coast Junior College's **Beverly Bivens**. We Five Bivens' growly contralto powers this crescendo classic. A muted rhythm guitar accompanies her spare intro instrumentation.

Bivens' wonderful voice dips and swoops, spins and soars. When she wakes up, this hunk guy is on her mind. She states the sorry symptoms of her love hangover – tribulations, worries, wounds she must bind. Then her bassman Mike Stewart harmonizes, along with Peter Fullerton, Jerry Burgan, and Bob 'What's His Real Name' Jones. Their credits on their #32 album list a bunch of acoustic 12-string guitars and one all-American banjo amongst the R & R/Folk fray. We Five II? #31, 11-65 "Let's Get Together."

"I Only Want to Be with You" – Dusty Springfield, #12, 1-64. First British Folk Rock influenced female star to chase the Beatles up the charts? DUSTY SPRINGFIELD. She began as a London folkster with brother Tom and another guy whose name looks like a misspelling – Tom Feild. Their Bluegrass-styled classic "Silver Threads and Golden Needles," hit #20 in 1962. Tragically, Dusty's too-long postponed inclusion in Cleveland's Rock Hall of Fame ('99) came two weeks too late. Dusty had just passed away from a long illness.

"Have I the Right?" – Honeycombs, #5, 9-64. Jumping the Brit Invasion gun, we have pioneer **Ann 'Honey' Lantree** on drums and lead singer **Dennis d'Ell** on the most TREBLE record in R & R history. Lantree is the first major R & R female drummer. Her pants outfit (obvious reasons) started a Carnaby Street trend in the flashy midst of a figureful forest of lithe miniskirted limbs. Their follow-up was "I Can't Stop" #48, 12-64.

"Tell Him" –Exciters, #4, 12-62; #5 R & B. This Jamaica, New York, R & B group included a token male, **Herb Rooney**, hubby of **Brenda Reid**. Pittypat drum chunks on filler between vocals. Also double-gender #1(2), 6-63 [#1(2) R & B] "Easier Said Than Done," by the **Essex**, featured a harmonic quintet (3 guys & 2 girls) from the Marine base at Camp LeJeune, North Carolina.

The shimmery Chiffons lullabyed the welkin with their (Goffin-King) teenage fun tune:

"He's So Fine" – Chiffons, #1(4), 2-63; #1(4), 3-63 R & B. Bronx boogie belters **Judy Craig, Barbara Lee Jones** (d. 1992, 48), **Patty Bennett**, and **Sylvia Peterson** weren't overjoyed with #76 debut on BIG DEAL label. They shifted R & R gears to Dion's Bronx-bombshell label Laurie. The happy result? A new national nonsense jingle " 'Doo Lang Doo Lang Doo Lang' – and a #1 record. (See George Harrison and #1, '71 "My Sweet Lord"). Their #10, 5-68 "Sweet Talkin' Guy" warns pal to ditch dude who doles marshmallow promises where love should be.

"Remember (Walkin' in the Sand)" – Shangri-Las, #5, 8-64; # 5 R & B. Ultimate bittersweet beach romance song. How they got all those squealy seagulls into the studio I'll never know. Queens' Jackson High launched the Shangri-Las' queenly double dynamic duo: sisters **Mary** (lead singer) and **Betty Weiss**, and twins **Marge** and **Mary Ann Ganser**. Shangri-La, as we all know, is another name for paradise. Like many a summer romance under Coney Island's Boardwalk, the fires of sand-walking Shangri-La passion simmered down into autumnal coolth. Then, poof, out. Another faded summer love. One unforgettable yesterlove tune. For Kansas and Montana and Arizona and Tennessee teens without beaches to shuffle along, hand in hand, this lost-love song was still of paramount significance. Dynamite #67, 1-80 cover version by **Aerosmith**. Shangri-Las' "Leader of the Pack" (#1, 10-64) is their best known hit.

"Shangri-La" – Four Coins, #11, 5-57. Barbershop quartet of mellifluent Greek-American songsters from Bobby Vinton and **Perry Como**'s hometown Canonsburg, Pennsylvania. Their biggest hit. Song of Utopia. Paradise. Bali Ha'i. Nice #64 Xerox reprise by talented 10-69 **Lettermen**. Molten honeyed harmonies of two Georges: Mahramas and Mantalis.

"I Can Never Go Home Anymore" – Shangri-Las, #6, 11-65; NC R & B. This deathless teen anthem plays upon our own deepest fears and anxieties. Some rules of a happy home must never be broken [Like their #1, 10-64 "Leader of the Pack"]. With powerful major chords, the Shangri-Las offer a stunning wail of woe, repeating the bleating title over and over in tragic echo. For 98 cents, you not only got a record of your own tears and fears, but as a bonus it would psychoanalyze you. If any group matched the resonance of the Beach Boys' heart-tugging harmonies among female groups, it was the **Shangri-Las**; "I Can Never Go Home Anymore" will give Brian Wilson a run for his money on introspection for his #23, 11-64 "In My Room." In its spare time, this is also a tremendous song (OK, OK, it's a tad weepy, but isn't life?) Many Rock & Soul female groups followed their example of peer-group patter and hot topics: TCL, Blaque (#18, 3-2000 "Bring It All to Me"), or the Spice Girls. **Shangri-Las**' #18, '64 "Give Him a Great Big Kiss" has all the gusto-glutted groovitude of Buddy Holly busting loose on "Oh Boy." The Shangri-Las give us this sweet smackeroo – a huggy, cuddly, cozy fireside swan song.

"I'm Available" – Margie Rayburn, #9, 10-57. You want cute? You want female Holly hiccups in Holly's Heyday? Don't omit Madera, California's Margie (1924-2000) and her medley of hit. Margie's wondrous waterfall of 'wo-uh-hos' left us thirsting for her nevermore follow-up.

"Sugartime" – McGuire Sisters, #1(4), 12-57. **Phyllis, Christine,** and **Dorothy McGuire** were sort of a Beauty Shop Trio (not Barber Shop Quartet) who straddled the Big Band to Rock Era. Their Wonder Bread harmonies wafted sweetly from Middletown, Ohio (where else?). "Sugartime" is an uptempo blast of pure melody and harmony about a blissful kissful relationship. Happily-ever-after mode. No gloomy tunes. The McGuires had an early biggee to swamp even a hot-fudge #1 champ, their #1(1), 1-55 "Sincerely." The mellow McGuires stomped the competition with their candycane version of Harvey Fuqua & the Moonglows' Rock and Soul hymn:

"Sincerely" – Moonglows with Harvey Fuqua, #20, 3-55; #1(2), 12-54 R & B. **Harvey Fuqua**'s Louisville, Kentucky group hailed from Muhammad Ali's home town, and rostered Bobby Lester, Pete Graves, Prentiss Barnes, and Billy Johnson. Their tight tapestry of harmonic expertise sets the pace for the entire multitude that followed: the Belmonts, Four Seasons, Temptations, Miracles, Spinners, Jackson Five, Alabama, Boyz II Men, N'Sync, Backstreet Boys, and the Beatles. And yep, Destiny's Child (#2[2+], 3-2001, "Survivor").

Rock and Roll Royalty. Harvey was the nephew of Ink Spots' Charlie Fuqua, and **Marvin Gaye** did an apprenticeship with the New Moonglows. Harvey's mastery of the *melisma* puts his right-on 1954 style right back in style. Influenced the **Shangri-Las** and **Chiffons**, too.

"One Fine Day" – Chiffons, #6, 6-63; #6 R & B. Fanning the FINE flames of 1st lyric, this FINE song was originally geared for **Little Eva** (Boyd), but an incumbent #1 group (Chiffons) got first dibs of this top-notch melody and lilting arrangement. "One Fine Day" combines the throbbing, rolling pulse of vintage Girl Group R & R with distaff harmonies mirroring "Sweet Adeline" barber-shop quartets of long ago. She WAITS incessantly for the cool dude to return. She mirrors the ol' **Lou Christie-Timi Yuro** dilemma of his falsetto flashback:

"Lightning Strikes" – Lou Christie, #1, 12-65. Lugee Sacco of Glen Willard, Pennsylvania (b. '42) is a unique hybrid singer. With catlike green eyes and Elvis's best pompadour and jumpsuits, Christie played at the BE ELVIS game in two dimensions – tremendous Italian tenor and high falsetto. Once he built his conflict, he leaped to the lofty crags and swooped. "Lightning Strikes" concerns some electrification in his upper atmosphere. Macho Lou's song-guy's lyric tells the girl "Wait for me to fool around a lot and score on a lot of girls. Be chaste and virginal. When I'm done with my conquests and my cattin'-around love hangover, maybe I'll return, we can get married, and you can pick up my socks forever" (those weren't precisely the lyrics, but the gist, yes). Musically great song, with guitar slashes and funky rhythm track. From a feminist standpoint, a lyrical monster.

Lou's wife **Timi Yuro** huddles in the wings as we return to our pedestal girl waiting demurely for Mr. Prince Right to return from his nocturnal howl. Christie is the only Teen Idol I recall, other then Elvis, to have a TV show photograph him only from the waist UP.

"Hurt" – Timi Yuro, #4, 7-61; #22, 8-61 R & B. Timi Yuro (b. '40, Chicago) is the female artist of the early 60s who best belongs with Del Shannon, Gene Pitney, Roy Orbison, Jackie Wilson, Jimmy Beaumont, and Elvis in the GREAT SINGER category. Her uncanny operatic contralto is a lesson in vocal firepower. She reflects the vocal power of Detroit's pre-Motown 'angel' (and angel on 1994-2000+ TV drama *Touched By an Angel*) **Della Reese** (#2, 9-59, "Don't You Know"). At times, Timi's scruffy lower notes can sound just as macho as her hubby Christie's falsetto doesn't. Yet their sensual orientation was notoriously mainstream, and they built careers on such contrasting gimmickry. On her #12, 7-62 and #16 R & B hit "What's A Matter Baby?" Yuro suggests "And That Reminds Me's" [#12, 8-57] Della Reese of Detroit, or Heart's **Ann Wilson**, or **Janis Joplin, Grace Slick**, or **Joan Jett**. Timi's an operatic super-rocker with a dash of Blues.

"My Boyfriend's Back" – Angels, #1(3), 8-63; #2(1) R & B. Hot handclaps pave the way for similar Beatle beats in "I Want to Hold Your Hand" (#1, 1-64). Ironically, they backed Lou Christie's aforementioned hit, and covered a Roger Williams hit, their #14, 10-61 "Til." Sweet harmonies, tough talk. Boyfriend returns to kick meddler's butt.

"The Shoop Shoop Song (It's In His Kiss)" – Betty Everett, #6, 2-64; #6 R & B. Vee-Jay Records. The Greenwood, MS, gospel singer tried to put out a tune with a NORMAL name, about his kiss. The SHOOP SHOOP background boomed so much they re-titled the tune. The Shoop Extravaganza by Betty Everett reflects the funtime years of Rock and Roll. You didn't have to dissect it. You didn't have to understand its interior monologues or epistemological ramifications. You just got out on the dance floor and boogied down.

"Uptown" – Crystals, #13, 3-62; #18, 6-62 R & B. Barbara Alston actually sang lead for the Crystals, one of America's most successful girl groups. Producer **Phil Spector** tweaked the roster, junking Barbara's voice for **Darlene Love's** in their biggest hit "He's a Rebel" (#1, 9-62, by G. Pitney). "Uptown," however, projects a realistic cityscape. Alston's husky alto carries the lyric admirably. The guy is a big zero in his daytime downtown world. When he returns home to her blossoming apartment (and her arms), he is spiritually and sensually renewed. Stars and moons were fading from rock lyrics, and reality ruled. Motown, too, was teeming with Girl Group activity.

"Dancin' in the Street" – Martha and the Vandellas, #2(2), 8-64; #2(2) R & B. Detroit streets in 1964 pulsed with positive energy. A smoky twilight flamingo glow gleamed from the Ford Rouge Auto Assembly juggernaut to massive McLouth Steel in riverside Wyandotte. The sweet Vandella Sound throbbed from sultry Woodward Avenues of Big D Motor City. A marshmallow moon beamed over tarpaper alleyways. Hotshots cruised the Metro Motown arterial freeways of backstreet bedroom bliss in Dearborn, Royal Oak, Ann Arbor, Bloomfield Hills, or Union Lake. The blazing flame of the Monster Beat was held aloft by a whole constellation of paler kids who swayed to their own white-hot brand of Michigan Blue-Eyed Soul: **Bob Seger, Mitch Ryder and the Detroit Wheels**, the **MC5**, the **Eagles' Glenn Frey, Question Mark** and the **Mysterians, Ted Nugent** and the **Amboy Dukes**, and even mini-kid **Madonna** (Ciccone) of Pontiac, Michigan, aged five. Metro Motown, Mojo Rising.

Martha's Vandellas are **Annette Beard, Rosalind Ashford**, and of course the incomparable **Martha Reeves**. Despite 38,428 'Umbrella' jokes, they stuck with their combo name: Detroit's inner-city artery Van Dyke Avenue (and Motown sessionband chief), plus part of Della Reese's name. Reese's star re-shone in the 90s with the *Touched by an Angel* TV role, beyond the supersinger stage lights. Nudging out **Mary Wells**, the Marvelettes and the **Velvelettes** (#45 "Needle in a Haystack" Western Michigan University college soul quintet), Martha was supposedly headed for the top of the Motown heap, until supreme intervention.

During the year 1957 the ONLY female #1 song was **Debbie Reynolds'** #1(5), 7-57 vanilla-malt ditty "Tammy," from her starring role in the movie of the same name. In March 2000, just about HALF the Top 20 artists were female, so we could hardly divvy it up any better. She's so fine.

Ringo's Rockers
On an International Role

February 9, 1964 – the British conducted their first successful invasion of the United States of America. Their clever scout, Brian Epstein, convinced Capitol Records to release "I Want to Hold Your Hand" a tad early – in time for Christmas, 1963. America, dragging through the Kennedy aftermath, sorely needed a Christmas present. When the Beatles hit the *Ed Sullivan Show*, 70 million Americans gazed in awe at the first British vocal group to hit #1 on the American charts.

Naturally, this scribe was among those couch potatoes. Down in the labyrinthine basement of Michigan State University's McDonel Hall, I watched the B & W show with my future bride Toni. The next day at Lansing Record Stop, I got the first *Meet the Beatles* [#1(11), 2-64] album in our quarter-million metropolis, and our band the Night Shift committed about four great songs to memory.

"I Saw Her Standing There" – Beatles, NC, 1964; flip #1(7), 1-64. Known to ΣAE brothers as ONE TWO THREE FOUR, this one cranks out Power Rock and Roll with the genius of **Buddy Holly**, the charisma of **Elvis**, and the thumping thunderation of **Little Richard**. Paul takes the high Irish tenor (his folks were a bit Irish), with John tending the raspier second tenor; George fills in anywhere his wide-ranging vocals are wanted, and the lads give baritone Ringo a later tune or two. The song busts the exquietude. No longer at the Brill Building, where PIANOS RULE, "I Saw Her Standing There" is basically a GUITAR Blues sound, and so it's naturally in the Key of 'E' major. On the part where she refuses to dance with any other one, the Beatles perch like eagles on their lofty crag of the GIANT **E7** chord. When they finally resolve into the sub-dominant IV '**A major**' chord, it's a majestic release. They sit on the crag a second, hanging fire. Then they swoop up and down interchangeably on the IV minor '**Am**' on the next note. Paul hits his blazing falsetto, John grabs his gritty lower note, and George sandwiches the whole vocal moment together with mustardly magnificence. For music novices? Great beat. Give it a 99. After all, it is the Flipside of this Beatle classic that conquered the WORLD:

"I Want to Hold Your Hand" – Beatles, #1(7), 1-64. Wow, this is it, Rock fan-addicts. The Big One. Suddenly Elvis's kingly crown whisked across the Big Pond and fragmented into a Fab Foursome. Rock and Roll, an American concept and institution, splintered internationally. With the Beatles' big bombastic #1 song, Rock and Roll became fun again. You could dance to it! These Liverpool guys were actually smiling at their own goodtime romp. BINGO, RINGO!

Back here in the droopy U.S.A., we needed a quick pick-me-up. Dealing with the horrific death of a beloved President, we needed something bobbing and buoyant and downright FUN, FUN, FUN – to whisk the gloom away.

We were besieged by four airborne guys with Prince Valiant haircuts, honeyed harmonies, and a snappy band track to blow your socks off. They gave us back our childhood, our innocence, our enthusiasm, our American boyish charm.

"I Want to Hold Your Hand," lyrically, blossoms with the flowering of teenage dreams. All the lovestruck dude in the tune has to do is touch his girlfriend's hand. A rush of pure 100% genuine LOVE. And isn't that what Rock and Roll is all about? Best, their music attracted girls.

I sat there, in this dinky TV room, gazing at the future of Rock and Roll. America had grown tired of formula groups, hyping the same old beat, the same old chords, the same old schlock rock. As our own American **Beach Boy** troubadours put it in #1(2), 5-64 "I Get Around," they were seeking some new strip with hip kids – not the same ol' crew. Who would have guessed the place would be England? Suddenly, we were all confronted by the idea that our own American musical innovation was now undergoing a Continental metamorphosis of stunning proportions. Now, for one shuddering yet glorious moment in time, Rock and Roll was now ENGLAND.

To my fellow (and girl) Michigan State students, the Beatles were a lot more than four cool guys in Edwardian suits on a teeny colorless TV. That *Ed Sullivan Show* was a transcendent experience. Instant euphoria. Nary a skeptic in the agog multitude.

Was "I Want to Hold Your Hand" an entirely new concept? Had the Beatles swiped the 'King of Rock and Roll' crown from America? Had the Fab Four created something entirely NEW under the sun? Nope.

What's so great about "I Want to Hold Your Hand"? A hundred things. Songs don't clutch the #1 banner for seven weeks without something magical going on. Matter of fact, it would have commandeered the apex of the charts a lot longer had it not been pushed away by other great Beatle songs. The song is a super combo package. First you get the great music. Then you get the fresh, sparkling new image. Beatles' earlier drummer **Pete Best**, supposedly the best looking of the Fab Four in the Pre-Ringo era, shied away from their radical haircut. A hundred million Americans watched four great musicians playing something new and exciting and fun. It would revitalize and resurrect Rock and Roll. They almost brought back the innocent joy we all lost in the American Sky when a little Beechcraft Bonanza went down in a lonely snow-swept Iowa cornfield in frozen 1959.

"I Want to Hold Your Hand" pulls no musical rabbits out of a hat. It simply synthesizes the best of everything in American Rock and Roll in **Buddy Holly**'s enthusiastic tradition. The Beatles offer us their mega-hit in the easy Key of 'G', the compromise key for pianos and guitars. Catch the heavy handclapping, which they picked up from American Soul institutions like Motown. Note the zingy **Buddy Holly** beat and gung-ho gusto in the **Everly**-harmony vocals of Fab Duo John and Paul. Sometimes even Beatle experts can't tell them apart.

Check out Paul's super soaring high notes he snagged from the best Screaming Blues of **Little Richard**, the supernatural crescendos of **Roy Orbison**, and the Rolling Thunder Rock and Roll of **Del Shannon**. Notice Ringo's smashing Surf Rock beat from the "Let's Go" (#18, 11-62 Routers – later echoed by the #14 "Let's Go" '79 Cars). Groove to the Doo-Whop Barber Shop Streetcorner splendor of the Beatles' best harmonies in vintage **Dion and the Belmonts** Bronx tradition. Mix it all together and you have the Fab Four Sound that conquered the universe.

The British Beatles are the most successful group in history to accomplish the impossible – to BE ELVIS for one golden moment in time. Quadri-Elvis?

But wasn't the Beatles' Sound 100% British? Oops. Yep, that's a spot of dramatic irony in the tea and under the crumpet. In the evolution of Rock and Roll, originality never really exists. We're all in this big Rock and Roll experiment together. We all borrow a tad here, a snippet there, to sculpt our own unique sound. The 1964 Beatles were four guys invading the U.S.A., having fun, and synthesizing the upper echelons of American Rock and Roll music. Surrounded by the natty influence of manager Brian Epstein, they did the same thing as their namesake Lubbock heroes, the **Crickets** – for Norman Petty – they chucked the T-shirt and levi-type scruffy duds for the snazzo suits of the era. They downsized Pete Best and snatched a unique thumper of tomtoms from Rory Storm and the Hurricanes – **Richard 'Ringo' Starkey**.

The really radical thing was the Prince Valiant haircut, AN X-FACTOR all along. An elaborately rococo comic strip pitted the mediaeval Prince Valiant against dragons and dungeons galore, carting off the voluptuous Alana or someone else similarly vivacious and buxom. Epstein's haircut idea certainly worked. Their first British chart tune, #17, "Love Me Do" 12-62 was sparked by Roy Orbison's harmonic sideman **Delbert McClinton**. McClinton hefted the hot harp riffs from Bluesmeister **Jimmy Reed**. A

tangled musical web [not yet a web SITE].

In "Hand's" vocal bridge, amidst mild handclap fever, the Fab Four make an astounding leap – they shoot the key from 'G' to 'C', so that when they hit the supposed II chord, it's the old dominant seventh V7, the **D7** chord. It sounds a bit basic; it's not. It's a revolutionary musical exploration. Joe Stuessy explains:

"The rhythmic underpinning of mainstream rock was its insistent 4/4 meter, the moderate to fast tempos, the heavy backbeat, and the duple division of each beat."

***The Beatles** (l-r George, Ringo, Paul & John)*

This kind of revolutionary change is apparent in their first album as well. Too many musicologists never attached themselves to early rock music because of Complexity Inferiority Complex (if it isn't highly technical, it's not worth academic interest). Check out the pre-*Sgt. Pepper* innovative surprises of a real sleeper from *Meet the Beatles*.

"It Won't Be Long" – Beatles, NC, off #1(11), 2-64 Al. *Meet the Beatles.* This one plasters that ol' Hawaiian-Polynesian chord jolt all over the first lines: It's your 5½ step major chord (in Key of 'C', bVI would be **Ab**; in 'A', **F**; in 'G', **Eb**). All the YEAH YEAH YEAH screaming they peddle in "She Loves You" comes rampaging forth in this one. Furthermore, they delve into tight chromatic shifts, rolling glibly from **E** to **Eb** to **D** to **C#** on the early bridge, before dervishly whirling back to more normal subdominant chord paths of **A** and back to **E**.

Esoteric and deep as it all sounds, these Beatle nuances are really nothing never before seen on the planet. Bach or Beethoven or Brahms never quite put this chordal concept together (though Mozart must've), yet perhaps that was not their arpeggio intent. *Arpeggios* are the notes of a chord played separately. Maybe some clavichord kook discovered the entire theory of chord structure in 1692 – but the time wasn't ripe. And he or she forgot to write it down in nifty letters: **Ab, G7, E6**. OK, beyond the technical superiority of the Beatles, let's return to the very real Liverpudlian blokes behind those dancing phosphors on *Ed Sullivan*'s variety show. Who are the Beatles?

John Lennon's (1940-80) ship-steward father farmed the little lad out immediately to Aunt Mimi (his mother Julia's sister) and Uncle George. George died in 1955, John got into a lot of trouble in school, Julia taught him to play banjo, and then she was killed by a bus. You can see how John Lennon never had it easy. John's pipeline to R & R music was a pirate station – Radio Luxembourg. The BBC (British Broadcasting Company) was still on an archaic culture-vulture tack. Their Classical/Big Band format caused 'pirate' broadcasters to beam from four miles out on English Channel barges. John dug **Lonnie Donegan**'s (1931-2002) American "Rock Island Line" (#8, 3-56).

Paul McCartney's (b. 1942) dad apprenticed with his Jim Mac Jazz Band. Paul was as clever and irreverent as John, but his family situation was buttressed with a caring crew of music fans. Living a mile from John in Liverpool's smoky British shipbuilding town of gray-gloom drizzle and golden dreams, Paul grew up a happy lad with high grades, many friends, and popularity. At 14, however, he experienced the death of his beloved mother Mary McCartney from a long illness. On a brighter note, their mutual grief is what brought the two boys together into John's band the Quarrymen. A kid named Ivan Vaughan in John's neophytic rock band introduced Paul to John at a crossroads garden party in nearby Woolton. John just couldn't believe how well the conservative-looking Paul could handle those flying falsetto flashes of Little Richard-style Screaming Blues. From their impish first R & R tunes, the Fab Four were destined for superstardom. Paul, the Beatles' main ELVIS, has been the most stable over the years, winging it after 1970 with wife Linda Eastman and his band **Wings** with **Denny Laine**.

George Harrison (1943-2001) grew up on #1, '67 "Penny Lane" (unrelated to Denny Laine), and was heavily into Hindu philosophy and Khrishna consciousness in the late 60s. A lot of top Beatle hits are just local Liverpool street signs, like Chuck Berry's Goode Street and "Johnny B. Goode." George did Buddy Holly's "Reminiscing," and "Crying, Waiting, Hoping." George was Paul's pal initially, the younger third party, but a necessary part of the Beat magic. George is one-quarter of the reason why 170,000,000 Americans, starved for good news at a bleak Christmas of distant drums in faraway Vietnam, freaked out with 4th of July Beatlemania frenzy.

Before we pick up **Ringo**, we have **Pete Best** and **Stu Sutcliffe**. Best was among the best drummers around, and he possessed the catlike Elvis charisma which could upstage even Paul. His wavy Elvis hairdo, jock masculature, and suave uncomic Beatle manner suggested American teen idols like **Len Barry** (Borisoff, America's only Macedonian/Russian rock idol) whose **Dovells** hit #2, 1961 with the "Bristol Stomp" and supersonic "You Can't Sit Down" at #3, 4-63. [Barry's solo "1-2-3" hit #2 in 1965.] No one had ever seen anything resembling bangs. Or Prince Valiant. Impetuously, Barry verbally zapped the masculinity of long-haired groups to a fanzine. Then Barry disappeared from the charts. The Beatles did not. Could **Pete Best** have been shafted by Beatle destiny for something as dinky as wanting to keep his Elvis hair style? Stranger things have happened in Rock and Roll. *MTV* ditches all the music AND doles out merely-visual 'Fashion Awards.'

Stu Sutcliffe's demise is shrouded in mystery to this day. Original bass player for the group, the talented artist toured with the Beatles in Germany but died mysteriously at 22 (Cerebral hemorrhage? Brain tumor? Beating from a fight in an alley? All of the above?)

The Beatles' very first recording, cut in a record booth at a local carnival in 1958, is a terminally scratched and primitive (but good) rendition of Buddy Holly's "That'll Be the Day." After playing seven-hour gigs, where their vocal cords resembled raw hamburger in Hamburg, they were bound for glory. By this time, Paul, originally a left-handed guitarist who handled keyboards too, appropriated Stu's bass spot. Think of it. How many big superstars in the R R world can you name whose main instrument is the bass guitar? [OK, **Sting**, (Gordon Sumner), #8, 8-85 "Fortress Round Your Heart."] John Paul Jones (Led

Zep) and John Entwistle (Who) are virtuoso rock bassists, but it's unlikely anyone will be as FAMOUS a bassist as Paul.

"The Saints" – Tony Sheridan & the Beatles, NC, 1961. Air play in Germany for this (#10, 4-39) **Louis 'Satchmo' Armstrong** remake. Nice Elvis/Jerry Lee Lewis imitation in Sheridan's hip vocal. Only George's lead guitar work tips off later Fab Four greatness. The flip, "My Bonnie," an old Scots folk song, glommed #26, 2-64 for the Fab Four in the U.S.A.

The 'Backbeat' years were filled with glory and frustration for the Beatles, commuting between Liverpool's Cavern Club and the Hamburg, Germany, Reeperbahn, the wide-open sin district. In the Hamburg neon flicker, scantily-attired lasses sold kisses and what-not from adjustable windows (like, ulp, the Dairy Queen or Taystee Freeze). The Beatles launched raunchy Rock and Roll from the Indra and the Kaiserkeller Clubs. Propped up on Hofbrau, they unabashedly screamed their nonstop hot rock to the summer skies.

In 1961 a rickety old balloon of a VW Microbus wheezed into the wilds of Hamburg. Five bedraggled guys from Michigan (Jim Cook, Bob Baldori, Ed Cowling, Jan Radke, and I) were haggling and struggling around the day-glo neon streets in search of a lost laundromat, or something. Burgerless in Hamburg, we settled on a brew or two. Garish wild neon animals flashed chartreuse royal blue-hot pink-vermilion-violet as we stalked the wild backbeat street.

Crossroads. Big one that got away.

First off, a deutschmark at that time was worth a measly quarter. Rich we weren't. We prowled the Reeperbahn, Cook chuckling at the wild women and song that filled the daylight gloaming windows with mystique and exotic fascination. As we ambled, we listened to snarfy little snatches of live rock. Starved for Rock and Roll on the whole trip, our faithful Blaupunkt AM gave us the noble pirates at Radio Luxembourg when the cloudy airwaves allowed. 'Live band' action in 1961 Europe was a quagmire of Lederhosen accordion jamborees, strolling violinists, or Italian tenors surprising the whitewashed streets with the odd Sunday morning line of *Rigoletto*.

Dressed in our own road-haggard duds – black levis, pointed black shoes, leather jackets, straggly hair – we could have passed for the Fab Four's roadies. We were all about the same age.

"Hey, guys," I yelled, "let's check out this place – there's some guy fooling around with Buddy Holly's 'Maybe Baby.' They sound like they're from Scotland or England."

George, perhaps, was wailing away on "Maybe Baby," with Pete. It was dark in there. Two guys were lighting cigarettes and grappling with wires and guitars. A beautiful blonde flanked the guy with the sunglasses. Eddie took a look at the girl and was all set to enter the cavernous biergarten.

"How much?" Eddie demanded.

"Four marks." A dollar.

"Let's check it out, guys," I chimed in.

Bob Baldori, eventual piano backup for **Chuck Berry**

and later lifelong rocker, stood strangely silent; he was still a classical pianist.

"NAAAAHH!" yelled future Vietnam Marine Lt. James Cairns Cook, more Scottish than I am, "Across this [flippin'] alley here you see that sign? Three marks!"

In a nutshell, we blundered over, shuffled in, and watched Joe Potatoes and His Rummy Dummy Dipstick Dorks, and Jim ended up with a lass who resembled an ostrich (at evening's end, he was no Tom Cruise himself).

We all saved a flipping quarter.

And that is how we 'saw' the **Beatles**.

Tuning up. For two minutes.

Returning to the Beatle-Cricket connection, you need only to listen to "Little Child."

"Little Child" – Beatles, NC, off #1(11), 2-64 Al. *Meet the Beatles.* Paul's passionate tribute to Texan Cricket Soul. The lyric echoes tribulations of teenage crepe-gym sock hops, young naïve love, and rocking romance.

"I'll Be on My Way" – Beatles, NC, *BBC Collection*, 1994. Cut originally as a demo for pals **Billy J. Kramer** and the **Dakotas** – Billy was 'England's' Ricky Nelson from the Mersey River area of Liverpool – this Lennon-McCartney-(Hollyesque) tune reverberates sweet major chords and 'Peggy Sue' Tex-Mex thunder.

The Beatles' superstardom road was a comedy of errors. **Brian Epstein** ran his father's NEMS record store in a larger Liverpudlian enterprise. When kids scrambled in, begging for the Beatles' "My Bonnie," he said he'd never heard of them. Flabbergasted he was, to find out they were playing just down his street at the Cavern, a fireman's nightmare. A cavernous basement, it was stuffed to busting with lunchtime R & R fans after getting converted from the Jazz Club it had been since 1957. The Beatles now skipped between the Cavern in Liverpool and the Top Ten Club on the raunchiferous Reeperbahn. The Cavern gigs were not as sleepless as a band's normal 8 p.m. to 2 a.m. marathon – they got to play noon shows, for local office workers and middle management chaps, in smoky stuffy suits.

Brian checked out the Beatle scene. He held a certain fascination for the four scruffy lads with derring-do, chutzpah, and the greatest potential R & R sound in the history of popular music. Knowing not one iota about the business, he stammered "Can I be your manager?" Eureka, they accepted. The fastidious 30ish businessman scoured the British recording world, blurting into top-level offices at EMI, Philips, Decca, and **Kenny Ball**'s big British label, Pye. Naturally, they all rebuffed Brian and his incipient Fab Four. Liverpool wasn't exactly London, sophistication center of the Anglo-American universe.

The 1962 Decca sessions ring with déjà vu, again. Remember Buddy Holly and Owen Bradley's barn in 1956? Zilch. The same sorry story blasted the nervous Beatles; they set up, hastened through 15 decent tunes – and got zapped by some Decca nowhere men who insisted they play standards like "Red Sails in the Sunset." After muddling and mucking through "The Sheik of Araby," and Anita Bryant's (Miss Oklahoma, 1958) #30, 6-59 "Till There Was You," they slogged through "Besame Mucho" (at #70, 5-60 **Coasters**, and #1[8], 1-44, **Jimmy Dorsey Orchestra**).

"Thanks, but no thanks." The Unfab 4 skedaddled out the door, blindsided by lukewarm Pop Standards. Ticked off. Brian was their target. He'd insisted on the stupid standards. From here, their stormy relationship swooped down to its bottommost nadir.

Brian rebounded. He confronted the British Decca corporate commandos. He realized his guys were good. They'd sold out Liverpool, had great press in Melody Maker, and were destined for a big contract, somewhere. He stormed into **Dick Rowe**'s office (London A & R chief) but the music mogul was, of course, in a meeting. Brian raved he'd withhold all NEMS orders (his father's big Liverpool operation), then recanted and offered to buy 3000 copies of any Deccan Beatle single.

"What is it about the word NO you don't understand?" was the dry reply.

Furious, Epstein stamped out, rebounding with one very prophetic comment:

"You'll regret this. Someday the Beatles will be bigger than Elvis!"

A sly smile ballooned on the tycoon's face. He'd heard that song before . . .

* * * * * * *

Ritchie Starkey's life began as the Luftwaffe strafed Liverpool in 1940. Ringo grew up slightly poor. The British grade-grinding system chucked the spunky lad out on the gray cobble streets at 15. He'd already spent a year in bed due to peritonitis when his appendix burst at six. On his 7th birthday, Ritchie fell out of bed. That great fall humpty-

dumptied his kidhood into misery and convalescent misfortune. Fortunately, Ritchie had pluck, true grit, and drumsticks.

At 16, he left the Dingle, a drizzly dockside raft of tacky tenements in the smoky Nowhereland of Cast Iron Shore. Liverpool is the edge of England's industrial Heartland, and shares with Detroit a smoggy aura of smoke and steel (more misty fog than crusty gray snow, though). Ringo dug Country music and Motown – cool crossover combo. His pop, Richard Starkey Sr., paved his Deadbeat Dad road with good intentions when he deserted his wife Elsie and three-year-old Ritchie. He sent 30 shillings a week child support until inertia and distance stole the money and Ringo's dad, whom he would see only thrice in his life. Mom Elsie tended bar to eke out rent, and Ritchie joined the Slow Learner Bluebirds reading group at school. After a week stint in the hospital ward banging the drums, Ritchie skiffled until the fad faded. He waffled from a British Railways job to an apprentice joiner position, all the while practicing his drums.

By age 19, Ritchie had acquired two handsful of opulent rings and a new stage name – **RINGO STARR**. Better yet, he had a steady gig with **Rory Storm and the Hurricanes** (nee Raving Texans, who, of course, as Liverpudlians, weren't). Storm's fury of popularity had subsided to a brisk breeze at their Butlin's Holiday Camp summer gig. Then Ringo got an offer of £25/week ($125). Good pay. Best of all, it was from George and the cresting **Beatles**.

It took about ten minutes for Ringo to shave his 'beatnik' beard and sculpt a new Beatle haircut from his shaggy 50s waterfall.

* * * * * * *

No slouch, Epstein tramped Albion's entire Sceptered Isle searching for a decent record contract. The sacking of Pete Best was met with raging placards from female fans. On September 12, 1962, the Beatles arrived at super-producer **George Martin**'s Parlophone studio. Brian wangled a promising deal with a major label. Like **Phil Spector**, Martin was among the very top in his field – a master producer – and the key to their success.

One glitch. Conservative Martin was baffled at Ringo's appearance. Their first record features Ringo grumpily banging tambourine only, while studio drummer Andy White handled the drums on their first big hit, the #17 U.K. Holly & Jimmy Reed-inspired "Love Me Do"; its flip tune had the title of a #12, 1934 Rudy Vallee (#4, '53 Hilltoppers) song, "P.S. I Love You"; Paul's song was nothing like the original, the acronym 'PS' dedicated to Peggy Sue:

"P.S., I Love You" – Beatles, #10, 5-64 (rec. 9-62). Paul's ultra-cool epistle to Lubbock's teenqueen Peggy Sue. Andy White thrums a Jerry Allison beat.

How many great bands have been victimized by scanty advertising? How many have had to resort to the DO-IT-YOURSELF hit record? Brian and the Fab Four did.

Brian padded the charts, so he thought, by buying 10,000 copies himself for NEMS. He fired off a fan club letter campaign to BBC and Radio Luxembourg. Finally, pirate R & R Radio Luxembourg picked it up.

When our record "Catch You Later" was released on obscure R & B Blues label Fortune from Detroit in 1965, we marshaled phone call pals to swamp WKNR and CKLW and WXYZ and whatever. We scribbled postcards in various handwriting styles, blowing my entire nine-dollar promotion budget. This was Brian Epstein's modus operandi to zoom his busy-haired Beatles to stardom. Sadly, you need a little seed money (Zowie! 10,000 copies) to hit big. Does it 'take money to make money'? For every success story like the Beatles, you get a myriad (10,000+ from the common R & R horde like our "Catch You Later" saga – our hopeful tune plunged into the Michigan market, made a little splash on tiny-town charts, and then drowned).

Pumped up with the one-million strong Liverpool market, "Love Me Do" made U.K. #17. When they finished their second song, "Please Please Me," George Martin confidently barked over the staticky intercom – "Gentlemen, you have just recorded your first number one." His prophecy rang true. The Hollyesque upbeat song sparks Everly harmonies and "Oh Boy" gusto. Let's show the speedy rise, not just "Please Please Me's" U.K. chart zenith: **#47, #39, #21, #9, #1.** Forget its downslide and drop-off. That's no fun.

Let's hustle back to burgeoning Beatlemania. And that **Del Shannon** crossroads. When I sat in the Haven bar in Summer 1963, and listened to Del sing a giddy new tune he'd happily hoisted from 'McCartney-Lennon', I had no idea I was among a handful of Americans nibbling at musical destiny:

"From Me to You" – Del Shannon, #77, 6-63. Instantly you know this is a Del Shannon song; the Fab Four could have frisbeed a demo to him. Vintage Shannon style. It was so good that the 'Moptop Movers' (Melody Maker) kept it for themselves. Del's version served as the unwitting vanguard of the British Invasion.

"From Me to You" – Beatles, #116, 8-63; #1, 4-63 U.K. On Jimmy Reed's Vee Jay label; then #41, 3-64 on Vee-Jay in Beatle wake from new Capitol contract. Crisp, sharp interplay between John's husky tenor and Paul's concordant falsetto flashes. Their energetic and euphonious mix is one of the all-time blessings of Rock and Roll.

Having conquered England, something Adolf Hitler and his Luftwaffe blitzkrieg could never do, the Beatles decided it was time to vanquish the United States and Canada too. Brian Epstein had certainly tried. Righteous patriotic xenophobes cast a Vinyl Curtain around the U.S. pop charts – only Americans, need apply. [Catch the 2002+ 'British EVASION similar problem on the Yankee charts.]

The Beatles, however, were too good not to make it. Once they broke the bonds of insularity on their magnificent North Sea Island, they sponsored a whole R & R émigré rush of **Rolling Stones, Hollies, Hermits, Clarks Dave** and **Petula**, and a lead balloon (**Led Zeppelin**) full of international R & R legend.

* * * * * * *

England was already getting tough for Paul, who impishly taunted stampedes of lovestruck moppets chasing his Liverpool limo, "Run, girls, run!" The Beatles played a Royal Command Performance following their 15-million-strong "Sunday Night at the Palladium" audience. John was asked about possible ad libs he might use during their performance for Princess Margaret, the Queen Mother (1901-2002), and a bejeweled cast of knights, earls (the 'Duke of Earl'?), and sequined royalty. John spluttered: "OK, Everyone, rattle your (insert your favorite gross obscenity here) jewelry!"

The Beatles were as rebellious and iconoclastic as we Americans. That's why we love them! Irreverent. Anti-authoritarian. Willing to poke the bloated bubbles of ritzy snobs. When asked by a withering-sneer reporter what they called their haircut, John [later George] snapped "Arthur." Rock critic Greil Marcus says: "The Beatles delivered with all the grace of [Smokey Robinson and the] Miracles, the physicality of 'Louie, Louie', and the absurd enthusiasm of **Gary U.S. Bonds**." HOLD IT! STOP THE MUSIC! ENTHUSIASM IS ABSURD??

"Quarter to Three" – Gary U.S. Bonds, #1(2), 5-61; #3 R & B. Norfolk, Virginia's **Gary Bonds** (b. Jacksonville, Florida 1939) gets an A+ for enthusiasm! Gary's 2:45 a.m. anthem whoops its happy hullabaloo to anyone except catchers of Z's. Bonds's rave-up, supercharged, Screaming Blues paced a whooshing tidal wave of unleashed Rock and Soul. Bonds bellows about how he danced till Quarter to Three at this wild party. With saxman **Daddy G.**, Bonds also scored with "New Orleans" (#6, 10-60). His Del Shannon-Bruce Springsteen-inspired comeback song, "This Little Girl" (#11, 4-81), featured **Bruce Springsteen**'s own Daddy G, **Clarence Clemons**. Bonds's bombshells of blaster Blues include twin twister tornadoes, #9, 11-61 "Dear Lady Twist" and #9, 3-62 "Twist Twist Senora." The Bonds formula was five-alarm hot sauce and full-race Frantic Gear. Compare the joyous aura of Bonds's "School is Out" (#5, 7-61) with equally voluminous but angrier "School's Out" (#7, 6-72) of Detroit's Vincent Fournier (**Alice Cooper**). A light-skinned Soul stomper, Bonds was among the first Afro artists to succeed in Country songwriting ("She's All I Got," #91, 12-71; #2 C, by Johnny Paycheck [of "Take This Job and Shove It" fame]). The raggedy raw Bonds sound is due to Frank Guida's deliberately muddy, overmodulated sound, and a 'live' audience (actually, Norfolk studio denizens and hangouters, clapping and shouting vociferously). Bonds's mammoth voice (times two) powered the Beatles to believe in an upcoming resurrection of Basic Rock.

February 9, 1964 just might be the most important day in Rock and Roll history. Might not. It's the first Beatle appearance on the *Ed Sullivan Show*. Despite three number one records and "She Loves You" threatening to eclipse the other three in Britain, Epstein had to take a bath on the picayune $3500 per show Sullivan promised. The Beatles were not yet Elvis (i.e., 50 Grand), but still existed as an iffy British act when Sully's lawyers cinched the contract. Epstein knew American exposure was worth the $50,000 gamble he was taking from the petty cash. The population of the U.S.A. and Canada meant a fourfold jump in Beatle record sales if they boomed big on North America's bonanza charts. Most important as a Sullivan preview, Epstein had finally wangled a cushy posh deal with Capitol Records, the Beach Boys' big label.

"She Loves You" – Beatles, #1(2), 1-64 [on Swan]. Also German version *"Sie Liebt Dich,"* #97, 6-64. The royal incarnation of all the euphoric Fab Four frenzy. "She Loves You", trailed by "YEAH" three times, is the refrain every schoolchild in the world knows by now. Where did the Beatles get that saucy word YEAH for yes? Americans, of course. When we toured England, I slept once on the 1961 beach at Blackpool, Liverpool's 'beach resort', in my ol' sleeping bag. One comely local lass kept asking me to say 'Yeah,' because she thought it was the coolest thing. It was, she laughed, so American.

We pedaled bikes from the White Cliffs of Dover (#118, 10-66, Righteous Brothers) to foggy London town. Our quads ached so much the next day (80 hilly miles) we wimped out, sold the bikes, and hitchhiked to Glasgow and the 'bonnie banks' shores of Loch [lake] Lomond in Scotland – where my father was born in Kilwinning, and moved to Windsor, Ontario, Canada, when he was 13. After touring the about-to-be Liverpool birthplace of "She Loves You," Jim Cook and I hitchhiked in a grungy drizzle through the smoky industrial birthplace of the world – Sheffield, Wolverhapton, Birmingham. The future Vietvet U.S. Marine and I got into some squabble. He slept in the rain in some lady's hydrangeas and roses in Wolverhampton. I pushed on alone to midnight Birmingham – everything looked just like Detroit, with the old redbrick sadnesses of lost sundown drizzle and lonesome midnight, 5000 weary miles from home. I fell asleep in an enclosed red phone booth, scrunching embryonically into the venerable sleeping bag beyond the smoky 52° midnight drizzle.

Why is "She Loves You," with its sad/glad bittersweet lyric and joyous trio harmonics, a quintessential Beatle tune loved and revered by their American fans? Because the Beatles mirror and reflect who we are in America. They showed this upstart yahoo feisty nation of ours that something we did musically beyond Jazz was finally getting the respect, the appreciation, and the LOVE worldwide it deserved. "She Loves You's" lyric is a pal-advice theme, like Del Shannon's 12-62 "Little Town Flirt" via Dion's #1, 9-61 "Runaround Sue." Beatles' guitars pulsate with Buddy Holly's "Peggy Sue" fervor and energy. Their vocals combine 150% of the Everly Brothers' cherubic harmonies [THREE great voices] with the marvelous catchy 'absurd enthusiasm' of Rock and Soul basher/crasher/smasher blaster Gary U.S. Bonds. Great fab mix.

How, then, could semi-small Swan steal this Beatle blockbuster? Brian Epstein negotiated contracts for American releases with several small American labels hoping some would flourish. Swan, before the Beatles, had **Freddy 'Boom Boom' Cannon** – part of the throbbing heart of Rock and Roll himself.

"Tallahassee Lassie" – Freddy Cannon, #6, 5-59; #13, 6-59 R & B; #15 U.K. Freddy Picariello (b. '39) had a musical mom who wrote this uptempo Rock and Roll boomer for her Lynn, Massachusetts son whom she did not baptize as Freddy 'BOOM BOOM' Cannon. Charlie Gillett says: "'Tallahassee Lassie' does have some claim to be the worst rock n' roll record ever made." Bob Woffinden of British *New Musical Express* calls that a wild error of judgment. I side with British Bob.

Since my 1966 *The Rock Revolution* is among the very few R & R books to predate Gillett's 1969 classic Sound of the City, let me say that Freddy never claimed to be Elvis or Buddy or Del. He offered simply an explosive enthusiasm, a nonstop hurrah, and wild roaring goodtime Rock and Roll.

Swan and Freddy thrived. "Tallahassee Lassie" rip-roars with saxes and guitars dueling. The drum beat could nail the Moon to the wall. After his first hit flashed upon *Bandstand* (and Dick Clark loved Freddy's Everyman enthusiasms and coolth), Freddy swooped back to a 1922 Peerless Quartet hit, #3, 11-59 "Way Down Yonder in New Orleans" (#4 U.K.). Bronze medallist Cannon pumped up his 1959-65 heyday to hit four decades: "Let's Put the Fun Back in Rock and Roll" – #81 in 1981, performed with Dion's Belmonts. Freddy and Swan did the theme for the big 60s R & R TV show *Where the Action Is* ("Action," #13, 8-65). Boom Boom's biggest hit ever (#3, 5-62) was a bombastic nostalgia ode to an old amusement park they were ripping down on the Hudson River Palisades (cliffs) in New Jersey: "Palisades Park." They munch out on hot dogs (Nathan's), dance amok to a rockin' band, and smooch in the 'Tunnel of Love' (Springsteen). At the tip-top of the ferris wheel's arch (where many barf), Freddy takes this opportunity to fall in love with the cool chick. Such a zany carnival romp was aptly penned by **Chuck Barris**, 70s TV writer/mogul/producer/songwriter – best known for his campy *Gong Show* (remember "Gene, Gene, the Dancing Machine?)

While the Cold War oozed into icy showdowns with the Cuban Missile Crisis ('62), and syrupy singers crooned the hopeful death of Rock, **Gary U.S. Bonds** and **Freddy Cannon** – on little Legrand and midsize Swan – were letting the whole world know they still bore the flaming torch for those who love REAL ROCK AND ROLL! They passed their rockin' rhythmic torch on to Liverpool.

"Palisades Park" hit #20 in England for Freddy. In November 2000, Tallahassee went back on the big map via the Al Gore/George W. Bush presidential showdown, with 300 votes deciding who would lead the free world, out of nearly 300,000,000 Americans.

Suddenly hits boomed out of the Beatle canon, too. Everything they touched turned to gold. Via the American-sound audial mirror of the Beatles, America's musical gift had now become Worldwide Rock and Roll. Third-world nations now owned megatons of transistor radios instead of nuclear arsenals. Radio Free Europe, and several new pirate stations, were setting up shop – pumping up the world's airwaves with AMERICAN R & R music. Rock and Roll now played on Iron-Curtain short-wave radios in Novaya Zemlya, Lithuania, Leningrad, Saigon, and Outer Mongolia. Eskimos from Siberia's arctic Kamchatka Peninsula in the Sea of Okhotsk now tuned in to the Beatles, who echoed **Buddy Holly, Chuck Berry, Elvis**, and **Little Richard**.

Rock and Roll in 1964 was no longer an exclusive American phenomenon. It blanketed the world. And the sound was fun.

"Can't Buy Me Love" – Beatles, #1(5), 3-64. This one, the Beatles' bronze medallist at clinging to #1 longest, flies in the philosophical face of **Madonna**'s "Material Girl" (#2, 2-85). What can't buy me love? Money. No matter how rich you are, money can't buy you true love.

"Love Me Do" – Beatles, #1(1), 4-64; #17, 12-62 U.K. Beatles' first-ever hometown hit, with Hollyesque vocal by Paul McCartney. Harmonica by John.

"A Hard Day's Night" – Beatles, #1(2), 7-64. Jazz booms in. The Beatles started fooling around with ninth chords about this time ('**C9**' is a C-E-G-D), plus a whole lot of feedback, used earlier in Marty Robbins' #3, '61 "Don't Worry."

In the grand gung-ho gusto that energized **Buddy Holly**'s #10, '57 "Oh Boy, " or the **Dave Clark Five**'s joyful #6, '64 "Glad All Over," The Fab Four (chiefly John Lennon) rampage through "A Hard Day's Night." Firing off a feedback express jolt from Marty Robbins at the outset, the Beatles glide into a roaring, rollicking song that celebrates the good ol' Anglo-American penchant for working too hard, in order to enjoy Play Day (and Pay Day) twice as much.

The Beatles choose a romantic interlude. After he gets home from a tough gridlock day, SHE is there to relax him into a coy, double-entendre mood of pleasure and passion. Up-tempo fireworks boom happy major chords and chromatics, and they rock on with ringing guitars and Ringo's pounding percussion. The Beatles prove to a world of grey stratus-cloud suits, and dim, grim drones, that a blue/gold tropical island of blissful smooching (and more) turns the drizzle into a rainbow trail of instant happiness.

"A Hard Day's Night" rings with jangling, clanging chords at the outset. John and Paul regularly dangle ninth chords like **G9** next to our ears used to tonic triad treasures like **C major** (C-E-G). The strident results are a mixed bag of appreciation and confusion to the listener schooled on total chordal simplicity.

The lyric in "Hard Day" is east of the sun, west of the moon. It's a middle-ground malaise about hard work all day long in the hustle-bustle workaday world – and the need for some relaxation and affection at home. After workin' like a dog, he finds that when he bops on home to her, all the things she does ['That Thing You Do' – Wonders, #41, 12-96] make him feel super.

With British reserve and aplomb, that's a heady hint at forthcoming passion. The Beatles here express pure unbounded ungrounded JOY, ballooning up into the happy purple sky with excited exaltation and euphoria (under a wrap of British reserve). Rock on, Fab Four.

Musicologists marveled at their Polynesian chord changes. Only Buddy Holly ever did this stuff before. Fans didn't dissect the unique chords – they just loved the song. A Polynesian shift is like **C – Ab – C** (see Chord Theory in Glossary), and was also used by Del Shannon and Gene Pitney

"Half Heaven – Half Heartache" – Gene Pitney, #12, 1-63. Skyrocketing on these Pre-Beatle Polynesian chord swirls, Pitney and his amazing four-octave-range voice perform a rising Cressendo ballad that soars to an amazing Orchestral Rock climax. A singer's singer, Pitney overtopped entire symphonies of string sections. Pitney's sound suggested to Paul McCartney his Beatle masterpieces of "Yesterday" and "Eleanor Rigby."

"Help" – Beatles, #1(3), 8-65. Let's fact it – music is THERAPY! John Lennon delivers an impassioned plea for Help from another someone (or anyone). As a kid, he says, I was more self-sufficient. Now this wild puzzling world is stifling and smothering, and it's dragging him down. With a little help from his Beatle friends, and some McCartney/Harrison counterpoint sympathy, Lennon finds his was back to whatever the real world is; John Mayer's #13, 5-2002 "No Such Thing" took a fantasy flight back to yesteryear's old high school corridors – and Mayers discovers nothing at all like the real world ever existed. **John Hampson/Nine Days**' "Good Friend" (#9, New York City, #24, Hot Adult Contemporary, 8-2002) reflects the Beatle wisdom that friendship matters. Hampson says, "Every good thing that I do is you." (c/o John H., 10-23-2002). For John Lennon, his relationship with Yoko Ono solved many of his problems (and created a few more for Beatle togetherness). Like "I Feel Fine" or "A Hard Day's Night," "Help" stands among the Beatles' greatest YAY-saying hit classics.

"Slow Down" – Beatles, #25, 9-64. Off the Beatles' *Something* (#2[9], because it was stuck behind their #1[14] *Hard Day's Night*). Not only are Lennon-McCartney often deemed the World's Greatest Songwriters, but the Beatles might also be the World's Greatest Cover Band. How so? Holly "Words of Love"; Berry's "Rock and Roll Music"; Isley Brothers' "Twist and Shout" (#17, 6-62, #2[4] Beatles); Miracles' "You've Really Got a Hold on Me"; Country star Buck Owens' "Act Naturally" (#47 Ringo, 9-65, #1 Country for Buck '63); pioneer Rockabilly Carl Perkins "Matchbox" (#17, 9-64); and Los Angeles' Little Richardish **Larry Williams** (1935-80). "Slow Down" is Larry's B-side of #69, 4-58 "Dizzy, Miss Lizzy." Many English lads, muckin' about for quid, found American albums relatively unaffordable. Like we did in mid-50s Motown, they listened to a lot of good B sides, like "Slow Down." Matter of fact, Holly's "That'll Be the Day" began its second tour as a B-side to the jumpy Blues number, **"I'm Lookin' for Someone to Love."** Buddy kicks off his verse with a drunk man, a streetcar, plus a foot slip to rampage vocally on the title. Now he's back. "Slow Down" is a rare 12-Bar Blues tune for the Beatles.

"I Feel Fine" – Beatles, #1(3), 12-64. Jingles and jangling chords again of "Hard Day's Night." Hair flopping like Mary Travers on "Puff (The Magic Dragon)" (#2, 3-63), the Beatles fired off this uptempo cavalry charge. After flipping fabulously the I to bVII (**G** to **F** in Key of 'G') for awhile, they carouse up to the mediant minor (IIIm) **B-minor** on being glad. One happy Beatle anthem, in

Buddy Holly's "Oh Boy" mood. Who first bounced the Beatles from their lofty British #1 throne?

"Yellow Submarine" – Beatles, #2(1), 8-66. Artist **Peter Max** provided the full-length cartoon artistry for the *Yellow Submarine* movie. With Ringo at the vocal helm, he found his biggest Beatle hit at #2 in America. Like his N.C. "Octopus's Garden," it's a bit of undersea whimsy, sprinkled with mildly scary critters and dashing denizens of the deep (in glowing vibrating Technicolor, and Psychedelic splendor). Ringo's good-natured baritone (the lowest Beatle) features three of the greatest BACK-UP singers in history: John, Paul, and George. At the height of Beatlemania and Beatle charisma, the Fab Four show their world-class talents from the top of Mt. Everest, at the end of their #1(2), 5-70 "Long and Winding Road," tot he bottom of the swirling day-glo Psychedelic Sea.

"Glad All Over" – Dave Clark Five, #6, 2-15-64; #1, 11-63 U.K. "Glad's" uptempo overjoyed lyric is another sentiment of the Holly "OH BOY" ilk – a genre fast fading beyond minor-key Nirvana-Pearl Jam Nine-Inch-Nails nihilistic frustration and Gangsta Angst. The closest recent feeling to this? The Rembrandts' #1, 1995 "I'll Be There for You." Or **Hanson**'s #1(3), 5-97 "Mmmbop." Or Nine Days' "Absolutely (Story of a Girl)" [#6, 4-2000]. The Dave Clark Five sought to pay for Dave's youth club soccer team to fly to Holland to play. Clark is the drummer and second vocalist. Gruff vocal leads go to piano-keyboard man **Mike Smith**. The Five round out to saxman Denny Payton, guitarist Lenny Davidson, and jack-of-all-axes Rick Huxley on bass, guitar, and harmonica.

"Because" – Dave Clark Five, #3, 8-64; NC, U.K. Despite graveltone gusto, Smith fires off a devoted romantic gem that very closely approximates 100% PURE MELODY. *Gold Rush* seeks those few nearly perfect tunes that make the Rock Era sparkle and flash. "Because" meets all the melodic criteria of coolth. With a dreamy Chalypso rhythm track, and organ riffing along on high, baritone Smith woos the sweet lass with his utter devotion. He doesn't ask for the Moon: Just one tiny kiss and he'll be very happy. With the mediant major III chord – the sweet song has an aura of **Phil Phillips'** timeless #2, '59 "Sea of Love." No more a rampaging and raucous Rock and Roll crew of stompin' soccer stormers, the DCV serve up 'Moonlight and Roses' instead.

"You Must Have Been A Beautiful Baby" – Dave Clark Five, #35, 6-67. Unlike many Brit bands of the Invasion, the DCV had at least half of their stuff in the guise of American cover songs:

"You Must Have Been A Beautiful Baby" – Bobby Darin, #5, 9-61. Bobby Darin was among the most versatile artists in the American pop panorama. Also a major cover: "You Must Have Been a Beautiful Baby" – **Bing Crosby**, #1(2), 12-38. To American music fans who love his "White Christmas," it's nice to know Bing did other tunes. The suave Tacoma, Washington baritone (California, too) has been called the most important singer of the first half of the 20th century. [Billy Butterfield trumpet]. In this beautiful baby tune, Mike Smith and Bobby Darin and Bing all agree: the gorgeous gal must have been one great-looking kid, because look at her NOW!

Beatles' Miami Tour, 1964
(l-r John, Paul, George & Ringo)

"Eight Days a Week" – Beatles, #1(2), 2-65. Like **Johnny Mathis**'s "The Twelfth of Never" (#9, '57), the Fab Four parleyed calendar impossibilities into international megamillion record sales. In just six short American impact years, the Beatles stormed to the top in many categories (tabulated by Joel Whitburn): 5th in charted hits (72); 3rd in Top 40 hits – 51; 2nd in Top Ten hits – 34; and #1 in Most #1 Hits (20). This one is just another ultra-cool #1 typical Beatle song. "Eight Days a Week" is powered by triplets, rendering twelve little beats into the standard 4/4 measure. On February 3, 2001, *Billboard* listed the Christmas 2000 Beatles' album *1 [One]* at #1(8) on the American charts. It features 27 #1 Beatles' songs (Anglo-American charts – since they 'only' copped 20 #1's here).

We'll get to their utter chart domination throughout *Gold Rush*, but here are a few standouts: unearthed John Lennon demo #6, 12-95 "Free As a Bird"; double platinum single #1(1), 10-69 "Come Together"; Arizona epic Paul-powered [#1(5), 5-69] "Get Back"; oxymoron-titled #1(3), 12-67 "Hello Goodbye"; local Liverpool spots #8, 2-67 "Strawberry Fields Forever" and #1(1), 2-67 "Penny Lane." Or how about their passionate plea "Help" (#1[3],

8-65)? Also #1(1) "Ticket to Ride"; #17, 9-64 Carl Perkins' "Matchbox" and "Yellow Submarine" (#2, '66) via Ringo; or their amazing musical adventure #96, 3-68 "The Inner Light"; and their irrepressible #1(1), 7-67 "All You Need Is Love." With these big #1 hits rendered comparatively ho-hum by their mammoth blockbusters like #1(9), 9-68 "Hey Jude" or #1(5), 3-64 "Can't Buy Me Love," it's easy to see how they're often modestly termed the greatest band in the history of the world. And it's comforting to know, for those of us who cherish the New Orleans/Memphis/L.A./Detroit/Chicago/Philly/New York origins of Rock and Roll, that the Beatles play a Super Synthesis of Great American Rock Music.

"You Got What It Takes" – Dave Clark Five, #7, 4-67. This Clark classic segues us into the Motown Dominion. Mike Smith hammers **Marv Johnson**'s #10, 11-59 soulful Motown monster. Clark's crew shipped over many other hot hits: #4, 6-64 "Can't You See that She's Mine" in their first 1964 blitz, with four top tenners in six months: #14, 11-64 "Anyway You Want It," which could pulverize the average lead singer's vocal chords into raw hamburger; Hermits-style #4 "Catch Us If You Can" of 8-65; plaintive #2 U.K. 1967 reissue (#15, 10-64 U.S.) "Everybody Knows"; and their solo stateside #1 Bobby Day's #41, 8-58 "Over and Over," at #1(1), 11-65.

"You Got What It Takes" demonstrates Smith's marathon stamina, and Clark's hyperactive drum thumping extraordinaire. They share the raw enthusiasm of **Freddy Cannon**, the Screaming Blues style of **Little Richard**, and the best of the American Rock and Roll beat. The DCV was the vanguard of the British Invasion beyond the Beatles.

Other invaders would follow; the Caravelles, the Searchers, and Billy J. Kramer's Dakotas surfed over to the States on the same British Tidal Wave.

Motown? Time for Dancing in the Street.

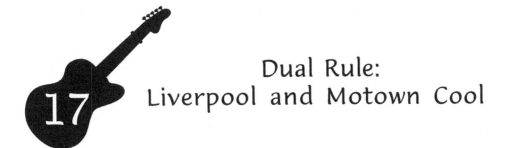

Dual Rule:
Liverpool and Motown Cool

We left them dancing on the Detroit thoroughfares. The rise of Motown Records is a testimonial to the rugged American spirit of **Johnny B. Goode**. Little Johnny we left strumming by the railroad track. He impressed the engineer, said goodbye to his evergreen-shrouded woodsy shack, and hotfooted it north. **Berry Gordy Jr.** (the III's) grandfather was an astute businessman farmer, killed by lightning while his terrified son (24) watched. The son married teacher Bertha Fuller, and the Afro-Indian couple made $2600 selling stumps on the Gordy plantation in 1922. Fearing the Ku Klux Klan, Berry II and Bertha cashed in their chips, literally, and boarded that 'Midnight Train from Georgia' (Gladys Knight, Pips, #1, 9-73).

North. To the Big D. In 1920, Detroit, Michigan, surged as the sawdusty hub of industry. Clanging epicenter of the factory colossus – Arsenal of Democracy. In the peaceful valley between World Wars I and II, Detroit became the birthplace of everybody's Dream Machine. Nelson George cites the elder Gordy's pilgrimage in *Where Did Our Love Go?*

Detroit was a major drop-off point on Harriet Tubman and *Uncle Tom's Cabin's* Underground Railroad to freedom in Canada. [Harriet B. Stowe's novel sold one million in 1860s England].

"Follow the Drinkin' Gourd" – New Christy Minstrels, NC, off *Ramblin'* (#15, 9-63). Subtitled *The Muddy Road to Freedom.* Harriet Beecher Stowe's flight with her baby across the Detroit River to Amherstberg, Ontario, Canada, and freedom flight, has its own Folk song – a song of a runaway fugitive slave's quest for freedom. 'The Drinkin' Gourd' is the British name for the Big Dipper. Runaway slaves followed the supernova Star of Bethlehem to the Manger of Jesus. Folk/Soul version by **Odetta** [Holmes], 1963, NC.

Detroit nurtured the biggest Afro economic triumph of the twentieth century, Berry Gordy III's Motown Records Empire. He grew up in the Detroit milieu of his father's various enterprises: construction, printing, and even selling Christmas trees. Berry boxed, sparring with Great Singer **Jackie Wilson**, too, Brunswick recording star and Golden Gloves champ. They both admired **Joe Louis**, Detroit's world heavyweight champ. As a 126# featherweight, Gordy won $650 at Olympia Stadium, turned pro, went 6-2, and disappeared into pugilistic oblivion.

After an Army hitch, Berry III borrowed $700 from 'Pops' Gordy and opened the 3-D Record Mart. Berry figured every record buyer would dig hepcat Beat Jazz, but the men "who toiled in hot, dirty factories all week . . . wanted a beat to dance away the Blues to." Who'd they call?

"Boom Boom" – John Lee Hooker, #60, 5-62; #16, 6-62 R & B. THE authentic Delta Bluesmaster (1917-2001) was actually born at legend **Robert Johnson**'s Highway 61 Crossroads: Clarksdale, Mississippi. Hooker's purling, coarse baritone zinged along with his foot-stomping gutsy blues beat. Hooker was so cool he recorded on any label he wanted. He didn't do regular cheat-the-artist contracts. In 1953 the BLUES were the predominant Afro music in Detroit. The real Delta Blues have always backseated themselves to mainstream music. Real authentic Blues withers away on musty-dusty labels in the back of the store. Berry preferred **Nat King Cole** or **Della Reese**'s suave Pop styles. At Motown, only the **Contours** ("Do You Love Me" #3, 8-62) did the kind of Little Richard-style frantic Screaming Blues loved and emulated by so many British groups from the early DCV to Led Zeppelin.

Gordy's 3-D Record Mart? Went bust in 1955. Gordy squirmed behind the 8-Ball – no job, no store, a second-string G.E.D. equivalency diploma with reading disabilities, and a surging family (wife Thelma, kid Hazel, and Terry on the way). In April 1955 Gordy went to work at the mammoth Ford Rouge Plant at $86.40 a week, nailing upholstery to Lincolns slithering by on the ceaseless assembly line. In 1957, Gordy teamed with **Jackie Wilson**, working on his debut "Reet Petite" (#62, 11-57, top ten Detroit). Here Gordy got his flair for horns, as Big Bands & Soul & Rock & Roll hybridized a bold new breed of Big Beat.

Gordy branched into songwriting for Wilson, with "That's Why (I Love You So)' [#13, 3-59] and "I'll Be Satisfied," (#20, 6-59). In 1957, too, he met **Smokey Robinson** (b. 2-19-40) and the **Miracles** (nee Matadors). "Got a Job," answered the Silhouettes' blockbuster tune about Afro unemployment:

"Get a Job" – **Silhouettes, #1(2), 1-58; #1(6), R & B.** Tenor **Rick Lewis** apprenticed as road manager for the **Drifters'** best Xerox soundalikes the Turbans ("When You Dance" #33, 12-55). Silhouettes' **Bass Raymond Edwards'** "YIP YIP YIP BOOM BOOM BOOM" cascaded down through the decades, sparking revival group **Sha Na Na** "(Just Like) Romeo and Juliet" #55, 4-75.

"Heat Wave" – **Martha and the Vandellas, #4, 8-63; #1(4), 8-63 R & B.** Never hurts to get your foot in the door. **Martha Reeves** started as an A & R secretary at Motown, sliding along with a few back-up Marvin Gaye tunes. Combining her talents in 1963 with **Annette Beard** and **Rosalind Ashford**, Martha describes the stifling hot flares she gets when she's with the guy of her dreams. Her follow-up "Quicksand" (#8, 11-63) quakes with quivering, quavering squigglies of purple passion power – despite rhythmic fire, she's stuck in the Mud of Love.

"Please, Mr. Postman" – **Marvelettes, #1(1), 9-61; #1(7) R & B.** This Inkster High School quintet included: lead singer **Gladys Horton** and **Wanda Young** (Miracle Bobby Rogers' wife); **Georgenna Gordon, Juanita Cowart**, and **Katherine Anderson.** Inkster, Michigan (pop. 38,000) began as a cruel joke by auto baron Henry Ford, and turned into a nice Afro suburb.

Black sharecroppers from the South, ripped off from their meager post-Civil War landholdings by shrewd carpetbaggers, made the hopeful trek to Motor City golden-paved streets, joining Polish and Italian and Croatian immigrants on the clanging assembly lines.

"Please Mr. Postman" anchored their Soul. Seems the 'postman' has yet to deliver a very romantic letter, and she fidgets nervously. Obviously, phones were too expensive then, cell phones and e-mail not invented yet, and writing skills were sharp. You can decipher a lot about an entire culture by the faded letters of long ago. Reprised by Beatles.

"Playboy" – **Marvelettes, #7, 5-62; #4 R & B.** Nifty little ditty about a Dion-ish Wanderer, smooching girls with a scorecard. This Marvelette ain't buyin' that jive. Motown's Jamerson/Benjamin band track is half the fun.

Along with United Sound Studios on Second and Antoinette, Motown Studios had the only 4-track recording machine in town in the early 60s (United did commercials). Among the biggest and greatest teams in Motown songwriting history are (Holland-Dozier-Holland). On a record/tape/CD, you'll always find songwriting credits caressed by parentheses (   ). **Lamont Dozier** teamed up with brothers **Brian** and **Eddie Holland** to produce mega-hits for **Marvin Gaye** and a host of others, like Marvin's Greatest Hit:

"Can I Get a Witness?" – Marvin Gaye, **#22, 10-63; #15, 11-63 R & B.** "Witness" brandishes a kicky beat, uptempo groove, and a super background vocal in his Call and Response classic. "Witness" trumpets the burgeoning Kennedy optimism, the romantic swagger, the persuasive formula for treating women, to woo and win their unleashed affections. Background singers? The SUPREMES (before big fame).

Cool 12-Bar Blues epic, too. Breezy musical hooks. Gaye's golden "Grapevine" (#1[7], 11-68) was 60s 6th-biggest hit, but Motown's biggest EVER, "Witness" is so much more fun. Gaye's title comes from Afro preachers' imploring congregation to witness what he/she's just said – invoking a chorus of Amens.

"Jamie" – **Eddie Holland, #30, 1-62; #6 R & B.** Singer/songwriter inducted into R & R Hall in 1990. Doing demos in **Jackie Wilson's** style, Holland's tenor was – some say – best of the batch.   He sings of this long-haired girl with divine kisses and starshiny eyes. Vibrating violins from the Detroit Symphony Orchestra caress the vocal riffs. "Jamie" concludes with a big happy cool "Ha!" Rock and Soul are all about LOVE. Brother **Brian** scored a #52, 12-73 "Don't Leave Me Starving for Your Love" (#13, R & B); Lamont Dozier hit #15 on "Trying to Hold on to My Woman" in the Disco dawn #4, R & B (12-73).

Telephones had lettered 'EXCHANGES,' (LOgan 1-3627, for instance):

"BEechwood 4-5789" – **The Marvelettes, #17, 9-62; #7, 8-62 R & B.** Writers: (William Stevenson, Marvin Gaye, George Gordy [Berry's older brother]). BEECHWOOD – A TRUE Inkster phone exchange like LUzon and LOgan nearby. She's given the cute guy her phone number, and she wants him to call her up any time, literally. The bubbly song reverberates with Benny Benjamin-style snare and tom-tom flourishes. And Molly Altizer's favorite?

Remember "864-5309/Jenny" by **Tommy Tutone** (#4, 1-82)? Tommy's Motown echo. Motown royalty?

Motown's Sound was powered by the heralded MOTOWN RHYTHM SECTION. **Benny Benjamin**, drums; **James Jamerson**, bass (Rock Hall, 1999); **Earl Van Dyke**, keyboards; **Joe Messina**, guitar; **James Giddons**, percussion; and **Robert White** on guitar. Session superstars all. This multicultural Motown session crew nicknamed themselves the **Funk Brothers**, to Gordy's dismay. Too risque, he grumbled. Take, for example, any bass line, any Motown hit of that era – **James Jamerson** adds a unique funkiferous touch never before attained in the old R & R world of basses plodding the tonic *arpeggios* (split chords with individual notes) of 12-Bar Blues. JJ flaunted wild dotted-eighth, 16th grace note constructions, and octave swings and runs and riffs.

"When the Lovelight Starts Shining Through His Eyes" **– Supremes, #23, 11-63; #23 R & B.** Diana Ross (b. 3-26-44) lived a mile from me over in Detroit's Brewster Project. We went to different schools together. Money never grew on the scraggly, spindly dying elms and blotchy sycamores that Project dogs saluted (or polluted). Diana was among the gifted and talented very early in life. Cass Tech. Two excellent reasons for Diana's coronation into R & R & Soul Royalty? **Mary Wilson** (1944-) and **Flo Ballard** (1943-76), the **Supremes**.

They began as the **Primettes**, backing group for the Primes, later the **Temptations**. They used tight choreography, polished harmonies, sophisticated and suave songwriters, and a dyno-mite rhythm section. Diana's come-hither soprano launched tracers before their atomic hits: #95 in 8-62, "You Heart Belongs to Me" and one with a title the size of the planet Pluto: ("A Breath Taking, First Sight Soul Shaking, One Night Love Making, Next Day Heartbreaking Guy"). Naturally, snipped to: "A Breath Taking Guy" (#75, 7-63).

"Lovelight" was their national breakthrough! All Holland-Dozier-Holland, both production and song credits. Three R & R debutantes to near-instant stardom. The 5'5" 105# Diana was used to practicing on the Cass Tech Swimming Team. Their next song, "Run, Run, Run" ran the other way on the charts (#94, 3-64). Something very bonanzic glowed on the far horizon . . .

"Where Did Our Love Go?" – Supremes, #1(2), 7-64; same # R & B. Ten years before its heyday, the Supremes were essentially doing DISCO. Regular run-of-the-mill Rock and Roll thrashes the backbeat with major accents on the 2 & 4 beats of a 4/4 time signature, like so:

ROCK BEAT

The Supremes' rhythm rockers, however, just stamped out their insistent everybeat-accented meter, with the thudding precision of a metronome banging and booming the beat:

DISCO BEAT

Keyboarder **Earl Van Dyke** carved out his keyboard career in the apprenticed expertise of Jazz legends Yusef Lateef, Kenny Burrell, Cammy Brown, Ahmad Jamal, Thelonius Monk, or Mose Allison. The Funk Brothers put together this bare, spare, handclap-action song "Where Did Our Love Go?". It was simple yet confoundedly complex – one beat, one pulse, one groove. Disco Dawn Dynomite. Number one. Beat the Beatles.

The sizzling summer of 1964 earned the beginning of a dizzying string of 12 #1 hits. Here's where it all began. Check out the down beat. It's all downbeat. This is the essence of DISCO music, with a slightly different rhythmic pulse from run-of-the-mill R & R. Chords are major. Harmonies are angelic. Diana's sultry soprano coos and woos with stunning magnetism.

"Baby Love" – Supremes, #1(4), 10-64. See above. Same thudding hammering nail-to-the-wall DISCO beat. Same groove. Same ethereal soprano voice, purring teen-queenly with throb of Funk Brothers' stomping band track. Supreme **Mary Wilson** adds a great dimension, with Flo Ballard, to the super sound. In squeezy sequined gowns and mile-high bouffant hairdos, they followed up with #1(2), 2-65 "Stop! In the Name of Love."

"She's a Woman" – Beatles, #4, 12-64. Dual Rule. Jump the pond. Hearing the Supremes' equal-beat phenomenon, **George Martin** did just the opposite. He kicked the heavy beat into the backswing eighth notes on the beat's return. Chopping bluesy Jazz sixths, sevenths, and ninths, the Beatles create a heavy beat structure that essentially blasts four loud beats, but they're inner eighths, like this:

| 1 | 1½ | 2 | 2½ | 3 | 3½ | 4 | 4½ |

With Paul screaming Little Richard style on high, the Beatles produced a funky new sound. They always admired Motown, and assimilated and synthesized the best of a whole slew of music genres. ("You've Really Got a Hold on Me" by Smokey is on their 2nd album.) In 1964, the Fab Four and friends made sure that not quite everything was coming up stamped MOTOWN.

"From a Window" – Billy J. Kramer and the Dakotas, #23, 8-64. Collectors of Lennon-McCartneyabilia really must have a decent Billy J. Kramer collection. Born William Ashton ['43], and no relation to *Seinfeld*'s zany COSMO Kramer, Billy of Liverpool (and now Long Island) booms a baritone Beatle sound on his own, using their early reject material like this one. His amazing chord changes are dynamic and refreshing. In "Little Children" (#7, 4-64), Kramer has to pay off spunky annoying little snoopy kids. Golden-voiced Kramer is busily trying to make out with kids' shapely older sister on a sofa. The little giggly bluggards keep popping up on the stairs, peeking at the Kramer smoocherama.

Few Afro-American female acts made the *Ed Sullivan Show* in the early 60s, despite #1 songs, while has-been paleface hacks might squeeze between the Armenian firewalkers and the Alaskan dancing bears. As beautiful as Diana and Mary Wilson (b. 3-6-44) were, their actual pictures still do not grace their #1(5) *Greatest Hits* album in 1967. Glamorous artist's sketches (Robert Taylor) adorn the album – with their skin hue so blazingly golden that they could have been Coppertone ad models, not Soul singers of the Sixties. A strange era.

"I Hear a Symphony" – Supremes, #1(2), 10-65; #2(2), 11-65 R & B. Buddy Holly's #1 U.K., 3-59 "It Doesn't Matter Anymore" introduced strings to Rock and Roll. "I Hear a Symphony" lavishes the breezy struts of violins from the prestigious Detroit Symphony Orchestra. After years of huffy disdain for the musical machinations of Rock and Soul practitioners, many modestly-paid classical musicians suddenly raked in high coin in the employ of the Gordy Empire. They scratched their heads, tweaked their bows, and chuckled at life's bittersweet tragicomedy. Strings float and chirrup and wheedle in a hurdy-gurdy combo of blithe instrumentation. Berry Gordy miraculously melded just enough Jazz, Blues, Soul, Rock, and Classical Music. Gordy fired them all in together, producing a mulligatawny stew, a magnificent mish-mosh of music. Supreme American pragmatist, like Chuck Berry. Also catch #5, 1-66 "My World is Empty Without You," and James Jamerson's bass:

That last sixteenth note is plucked so quietly as to be nearly indiscernible.

"You Can't Hurry Love" – Supremes, #1(2), 8-66; #1(2) R & B. Maternal Advice Department. Shadows of "Shop Around" by Miracles and Shirelles' "Mama Said." The Supremes' supreme hit string seemed untouchable for 35 years. **Destiny's Child**, another beautiful Afro-American 'Girls Group,' hit #1(11+), 2000 with "Independent Women" after a few salvo #1s scratched the stratosphere.

"You Can't Hurry Love" – Phil Collins, #10, 11-82; NC, R & B. Collins of Jazz-Rock **Genesis** follows Mom Ross's advice 15 years later. Love must be a slow, easygoing process. No flash flood.

Genesis formed in 1967 with a nucleus of singer **Peter Gabriel** and drummer **Phil Collins**. Genesis gets often clumped into the Art Rock category, due to their superior instrumental technique. In the late 80s Collins emerged as a superstar. Gabriel's "Sledgehammer" hit #1 in 1986, with "Big Time" jouncing to #8 in early 1987. Phil Collins, with his carefully metered tenor voice, and his dynamite

drum riffs, created classics: #1(2), 9-88 "Groovy Kind of Love"; #1(2), 11-86 "Two Hearts"; #1(1), 10-85 "Separate Lives"; #1(1), 5-85 "Sussudio"; #1(2), 2-85 "One More Night"; ;and his homeless wry ode, #1(4), 11-89 "Another Day in Paradise," a caring, committed song. The latter cites the lack of help for the poor homeless street folks in our midst. Popular songs can trump, in two minutes, all the bureaucratic reams of unread paper on the sad same issue.

Jeremy Dean plays keyboards, sax, and sings with **Nine Days** ("Absolutely [Story of a Girl]" #6, 4-2000). Jeremy drew this Jamerson bass line for you and *Gold Rush*; Genesis' Michael Rutherford plays it on this Collins cover of a Supreme monster hit. Touring Nine Days is coming to your town maybe next week [hype springs eternal].

With Jamerson on bass, Benjamin on drums, Van Dyke on keyboards, and Sicilian Joe Messina multiculturalizing the guitar section, the Funk Brothers' spearheaded the 60s Motown Sound.

Ironically, Detroit is the only major American city totally captured by a foreign army – British/Canadians (War of 1812) after the Revolutionary War. The mid-60s were a golden era for the Motor City. Detroit made almost all the important cars in the world; Motown and the Beatles now made many of the world's most important records. We marched with Dr. Martin Luther King in 1964, and our burgeoning, booming city north of Canada (Windsor) represented the best of hope in the pre-Vietnam Camelot that was America. We had come a long way from Eliza and baby crossing the Detroit River ice to freedom on the Underground Railway in 1850s *Uncle Tom's Cabin* (Stowe).

Rock and Roll always reverberated with Boy Wonders – **Frankie Lymon**, 'Little' **Stevie Wonder, Michael Jackson**. Back in the 50s, two young singers – one British, one American – scorched the American charts with their sensational song stylistics:

"He's Got the Whole World in His Hands" – Laurie London, #1(4), 3-58: #3, 4-58 R & B. The British invaded, secretly, and purloined the American #1 crown for a month. Six years before the Beatles. Laurie London, aged 13, recorded his only Top 100 tune, this moderate-paced Gospel standard. Like '58 folk song "Tom Dooley,"

London's #1 song uses only two chords (I and V7), or 'C' and 'G7'. The British Gospel Invasion arrived long before the secular one.

"Why Do Fools Fall in Love?" – Frankie Lymon and the Teenagers, #6, 2-56; #1(5) R & B. A more direct link to the [Michael] Jackson Five Motown song stylistics came from the Bronx. **Frankie Lymon** (1942-68) leaped into the Rock and Soul fray with his prepubescent falsetto on "Why Do Fools Fall in Love." With his group the Teenagers he charted a Dynasty of Sound. Jimmy Merchant and Herman Santiago sang tenor, with the deeper Sidewalks-of-New-York barber shop quintet tones booming from baritone Joe Negroni (d. 1978) and bass Herman Garnes (d. 1977). Without **Frankie Lymon**, who passed of a drug overdose in 1968, there might never have been a **Stevie Wonder**, or **Michael Jackson**. Or **Janet Jackson**. Or **Boyz II Men**. Or **N'Sync**.

Frankie's Teens beat ELVIS to the searing soulful spotlight by a month. Five happy-go-lucky-looking Afro and Latino Bronx guys, pomade pompadours slicked back, snapped their fingers in joyous celebration of the Rock that was about to Roll. On #19, 1-57 album *The Teenagers*, they wore white varsity letter sweaters, like cartoon Archie and Jughead carousing for Betty and Veronica.

Frankie had the perfect kid voice; his snappy soprano spelled the epitome of cute. First hit was biggest. Also reprised Benny Goodman's #1, 1936 "Goody Goody" to #20, 7-57. "I Want You to Be My Girl" arced to #13 in 4-56. "I Promise to Remember" (#57, 7-56) is Frankie's Streetcorner anthem. The Teenagers still perform with brother Lewis Lymon on Oldies Circuit with Dubs and Heartbeats and **Skyliners**.

"Uptight (Everything's Alright)" – 'Little' Stevie Wonder, #3, 1-66; #1(5) R & B. Motown marshalled the troops to recycle Stevie from cute boy wonder with his little harmonica to rocking cool teen idol. Stevie (b. 5-13-50, Saginaw, Michigan) penned the tune, utilizing a contemporary cliché, and got his song polished by producer **Henry Cosby**. Motown? NEPOTISM?

On a 1988 poster at Patchogue-Medford High School, Long Island, blind Stevie smiled out in his sunglasses at all high schoolers connected with M.A.D.D. or S.A.D.D., the teenage campaigns to keep drunks far away from steering wheels. With a wry sense of humor about his unsighted fate, Stevie said: "You're probably safer with ME driving than some drunk – Designate a sober driver."

"Little Old Man" – Bill Cosby, #4, 9-67; #18 R & B. Temple University's resident comedy genius steered the indulgent 80s through #1 family sitcom *Cosby*. He already had five million-selling comedy shtick albums under his belt, like #2(1), 5-67 *Revenge*. Charismatic Cosby's "Little Old Man" pioneers Rap music. Using Stevie's near-verbatim band track from "Uptight," Cosby follows Rap progenitor **Louis Jordan** [#6, 1947 "Open the Door, Richard"] and **Bo Diddley** [#20, 1959 "Say Man"]. One cool tune/chant.

"Blowin' in the Wind" – Stevie Wonder, #9, 7-66; #1(1), 7-66, R & B. Motown does Dylan. Early in his career, Wonder hopped on the social activism bandwagon. You can thank Stevie for one vacation day a year: Dr. Martin Luther King's birthday in January! Stevie and Afro-American activist Detroit Congressman **John Conyers** worked together to shepherd a bill through Congress guaranteeing Americans this major holiday to honor Dr. King's lifetime achievements. You'd be hard pressed to find a spokesman more eloquent than Stevie Wonder as the living embodiment of Dr. King's Dream.

Michael Jackson's album *Thriller* (#1[37], 1982) is the #1 album of the Rock Era. Only 1961 sound-track *West Side Story* (#1[54]), topped Jackson's achievement. Hardly anything in it qualifies as remotely related to Rock and Soul. Michael is ranked fourth of all time at #1 albums behind the Beatles, Elvis and the Kingston Trio.

"Why Do Fools Fall in Love? – Diana Ross, #7, 10-81; #6, R & B. Though Diana never knew her contemporary, Frankie Lymon, she always looked upon Michael Jackson as her little brother. Diana's version reprises the Lymon spontaneity. She shares, In Frankie's early vocal range, the lilt and lift and buoyant bounce of the original. A truly tremendous cover version, it captures the best of Frankie Lymon and his 50s malt shop egg-cream innocence. Lymon's squeaky-clean soprano mirrors Michael Jackson's on the very early days of the Jackson Five:

"ABC" – Jackson Five, #1(2), 3-70; #1(4) R & B. Just when Motown was aging (one decade), the simplest remedy popped up – an 11-year-old incarnation of a NEW Stevie. The Jackson Five prospered into the Motown Disco 70s: Sigmund, Jackie, Marion, Tito, Jermaine (3-80, #9 "Let's Get Serious") and Michael. Randy arrived later, swapped for Jermaine, and kid sister **Janet**'s records devoured NOW and beyond. September 2000 gave Janet a #1 hit "Doesn't Really Matter." In March 2001, her "All For You" new single featured the most glamorous and semi-nude picture I've ever seen in *Billboard*. "All For You" hit #1[3+] during April/May 2001.

Frankie Lymon and I were the same age. At thirteen he had a million-seller; I had a paper route – I made $7.59 a week, plus tips. I blew the big moolah on Camel cigarettes, which James Dean helped me to smoke, by personal example. At 13, I quit the habit, thanks to a girl named Peggy Sue who stomped on my crushproof pack and squished the cigs. Around 13, Frankie Lymon started doing heavy substances. By 25 (2-68), the child star was dead of old age. Dr. King's 4-68 fated Memphis rendezvous with death was two miles from Sam Phillips' Sun Studio and **Elvis**'s hot spotlight. Frankie was Elvis, for a little while. Frankie beat **Jim Morrison**, **Jimi Hendrix**, and **Janis Joplin** by three years in his breakthrough to that mystical "other side" (See Red Hot Chili Peppers.)

Arising from the ashes of both the Lymon and King tragedies, Michael and his talented family act started at the top and worked laterally sideways. Taught choreography by their father and family, and cradled by Motown prompters, **Michael** and **Janet Jackson** sparkled in the Elvis or Judy Garland glow. OZ was their limit – bound for glory on the RAINBOW, not the tornado, thank you.

Harvey "Moonglow" Fuqua ran Artist Development, and his wife Gwen and sister Anna prepped primping hints from their knowledge on cosmetology. **Maxine Powell**'s Powell Finishing and Modeling School taught young Detroit debs and would-be Motown divas how to act. Powell was her name, and poise was her game. Maxine Powell, George says, would tell the Temps, the Supremes, the Four Tops, Mary Wells, or the Jacksons that "they were being trained to perform in only two places: Buckingham Palace and the White House." She effused Dale Carnegie shoptalk on success, and convinced Gordy that real longevity in music involved blending into white crossover venues – like Windsor's Elmwood Casino. **Frank Sinatra** played the Elmwood Casino. It was big time. Fame always comes with strings attached. Slingshot karma.

When Michael Jackson arrived, sporting jiffy bell-bottoms, a tanned Brady Bunch smile, and the cutest chirpy falsetto voice, were there real dues to pay? The cute kid grabbed the top spot and hung on with tenacious talent for an entire generation.

"I'll Be There" – **Jackson Five, #1(5), 9-70; #1(6) R & B.** J5's biggest blockbuster. Champions power of friendship. Falsetto escapades. Magical message. Written by BERRY GORDY, JR. "I'll Be There" is one of the greatest love and friendship songs ever written. Great range, melodic chords. Jackson rides the soaring "I'll Be There" melody line, sweeping up emotion and sincerity as he dusts off the golden dreams. He fervently reaches out his hands (one gloved) to her. The song peddles friendship, trust, understanding, and empathy. How can you lose? **Mariah Carey** and **Trey Lorenz** took the tune to #1(2), 5-92 (#11 R & B).

"The Way You Do the Things You Do" (Eddie Kendricks and the) Temptations, #11, 2-64; #11 R & B. EDDIE KENDRICKS is the 1st tenor of the Motown Temptations, arguably the greatest Barber-Shop Quintet of all time. Their first song, "Dream Come Home," was penned by Berry Gordy and attained #22 on the R & B charts in 5-62 (NC HOT 100). This #11 debut is a Smokey Robinson reject. Like Stevie Wonder, **Smokey Robinson** of the Miracles is also one of Motown's primary singer-songwriters, and the 60s Veep to boot. Kendricks caresses "The Way You Do the Things You Do" with steamy energy and dynamic tension. The song flexes its audial firepower in its number of cover versions. Successful covers? BIGGEES are Rita Coolidge (#20, 1978), Hall & Oates (with Kendricks and David Ruffin) – #20 in 1985, and the Reggae-inspired UB40 of 1990 (for the Birmingham, England bureaucratic form 'Unemployment Benefits 40'): For interracial quartet UB40, it hit #6, 9-90 (NC, R & B). From dim offices with crusty clerks and fusty linoleum in patterns of despair.

The thrilling Temps plunked #33 "I'll Be in Trouble" and "Girl (Why You Wanna Make Me Blue)" to #26 in the Year of the Beatle 1964. Most great groups would be satisfied. Not the Temps. They acquired **Otis Williams II** (midrange), and marvelous **Melvin Franklin** (d. 1995) on deep bass. Their professional producer **Ronnie White** (baritone), was one of the nicest in the organization – diminutive, dapper, supercool. His resonant baritone in the **Miracles** perfectly complemented **Pete Moore**'s ruddy bass – together they laid down a featherbed of soft sounds overarched by the legendary sky-high tenor of **Smokey Robinson**.

At Motown, one artist wore many hats: songwriter, producer, singer, friend, and counselor in time of emotional need. Ronnie White (d. 1995, age 57) was one of those privileged souls to whom everybody down on her luck would gravitate. His calm, rational advice was as a lodestar in the starry galaxy, a flagship for a floundering foundering fleet – or just a spare shoulder for a temporarily drifting Vandella, Supreme, or Velvelette to cry on.

"My Girl" – **Temptations, #1(1), 1-65; #1(6) R B.** Sunshine on this cloudy day. When **David Ruffin** took over on this stratus-drizzle classic, the tepid record industry scored a MONSTER hit! Far beyond just a one-week #1 grabber, the song tugged everyone's heartstrings, with double decades of air play in every office, supermarket, elevator, lunch room, and gas station in the land. A hit like "My Girl" is the dreamstuff of every group's success fantasies.

How did Motown build this unforgettable love song? First, they took **Ronnie White's Greatest Hit**. Ronnie and Smokey produced it in the little Hitsville U.S.A. four-track studio on West Grand Boulevard. One riff on a twangy Duane Eddy guitar combines with a little fingerpopping. With strings in the wings, David Ruffin scrambles his emotions. The dramatic first-rate second tenor croons about Motown weather. It's essentially a song about echoes: when Ruffin's hard-edged smooth-rasp voice rhapsodically careens into his soulful canticle, the world perks up its attention and the rare spring sun SHINES. Franklin, Williams, Kendricks, and the other Williams Paul chime in. David Ruffin was the heart and soul of the Temptations.

"My Girl," for the Temps, is more than a weather report about sodden, gray, gloomy drizzle. Or sad moods. In December 1966 NINE hours of sunshine caused Detroit's all-time cloudiest month ever. It's a song about the hope and pleasure and seething ecstasy that love can bring. "My Girl" toasts the ardent love of a man for a woman, and the brightening effect it has on his whole workaday universe. His girl is not just a patch of azure blue in a steely sad sky; she is a godsend.

In the best Roy Orbison tradition, "My Girl" flaunts several sweet crescendos. Each one rises and dips to chronicle the joy and euphoria he feels just being with her. She is a breath of fresh air in the soft fleecy clouds; they rise beyond the inner-city turmoil, the rats, roaches, crusty gray snow, the shootouts and gutterbarf and backfiring clang of the 24-hour mankiller factories and despair. Great songs like "My Girl" loft us up skyward beyond the gray gloom. "My Girl" Sings DELIVERANCE TO THE PROMISED LAND through romantic love. Sunshine – on some ghastly, grubby day. Yay.

One of my greatest R & R memories was when my band finked out and I had to play Detroit's big fab Soul/R & B venue, the Twenty Grand on 14th Street by Warren Avenue in early 1965. (Detroit equivalent of Harlem's fabled Apollo Theatre). Anyhow, our tune "Catch You Later" was blubbering around on local DJ's and Program Directors' desks. We had to do some freebies for local jocks. When my band heard about the perilous location in the soulful heart of Detroit, somebody's father panicked for his kid's health. Bottom line? Aside from pal Jeff Forrest, I was the only white guy in the place – and had to lip-sync our tune alone like Buddy Holly at the Apollo, to about 2000 Afro-American fans (more fans than we had ever played for). I was a mite nervous. Lip-sync? Pantomime? Solo. 20 Grand flashback. Maybe 25 "record-hopper" recording artists just like us. All nervously twitching backstage. Fidgeting with curtains and routines. Chewing gum. Guzzling strong stuff.

By some fantastic quirk of fate, I actually had to follow the Temps on stage after wrestling our '47 Buick out of a snowbank the size of Delaware. Coming to the sad realization that I'd have to solo (just me and my lonely iridescent green suit) for the biggest crowd of my life, I blundered into the back dressing rooms twiddling my courage. Suddenly I saw the **Temps**, seemingly six and a half feet tall, and goofin' on each other. They had just left the stage after performing their up-and-coming smash "My Girl", which would spiral to national #1 in a month.

We "record-hopped" without ever plugging in one guitar or bass. It was all pantomime lip-syncing along with your record. [See Backstreet Boys, N'Snyc, Britney Spears.] Those awaiting recording contracts were a garage or basement band, driving your kid sister up the wall with never-ending pandemonium, or grandfather to start an Earmuff and Earplug Emporium. Unlike **Milli Vannilli**, singer-imposter hoax of 1989, we all truly recorded our own lip-sync tunes first. Then we mimed them.

Just as I was about to fry for a 3-minute shot in ELVIS's SPOTLIGHT, **David Ruffin** proffered some super advice to a greenhorn suburban kid with Johnny B. Goode dreams: "Hey, don't sweat it, Kid. They're gonna love ya . . . after all, you're followin' US!" He had a good point. Ruffin continued: "Just jump around in that cool green suit, and they'll go, like, wild, man . . ." So I did. My vocal showed I sure wasn't Elvis or Orbison, or Holly or a Beatle. Gymnastic experience, and Jackie Wilson or James Brown, had taught me how to jump up and twirl 360° in the air. The appearance sold a whole buncha "Catch You Later" records. I'll have to admit the 20 Grand fans' frantic acceptance of a lone jumpy green-garbed white rocker wasn't really due to me at all. It was the magic Temps' afterglow. Maybe they didn't even hear our record in their screams and wails and whoops from the multitude. It was simply the greatest audience we ever played for in enthusiasm. We surfed a Temptations Wave.

A gray misty rain slices my day in half as I write about these long-ago Temps. David Ruffin succumbed to toxic substances in 1991, while Eddie Kendricks' cigarette addiction killed him in 1992 at 52. Lewis Grizzard, top humorist who wrote Elvis Is Dead and I Don't Feel So Good Either, passed away not long ago. When Paul Williams died in 1973, it was not a shock. When Melvin Franklin died in 1995, though, I began to realize that my contemporaries in this very regal superstar groups are all dying of old age. At my age. As your role models fade away, you begin to regard time as a vastly more precious gift:

"September Song" – Jimmy Durante, #51, 9-63. How many stars caress the biblical three-score-and-ten 70 years – and then get a Top 50 record? The beloved comic with rumpled hat, large "Schnozzola" nose, and charismatic "STOP DA MUSIC" command celebrated his last hit here, about the September of life. Durante was a maestro: one part comic genius, one part sentimental schmaltz, and one part Heart of Gold. Bittersweet, beautiful, sad song. Timeless message? We are fragile and precious. Let's love one another: (See Louis Armstrong's "What a Wonderful World.").

"A Place in the Sun" – Stevie Wonder, #9, 11-66; #3 R & B. How ironic! Here's a budding Motown star, bereft of sight, yearning for some paradise beach of leisure and renewal and joy. Despite his lack of ocular vision, he can hear the lapping waves, feel the sunny breeze, and smell the hibiscus and bougainvillea wafting in the tropical air – as voluptuous maidens cavort. Stevie scoots along with the frisky breeze, beginning on the tonic (say **C** or **I**) and sliding to the SUPER TONIC minor (say **Dm** or **IIm**) chord; he oscillates between the happy major mood and the questionable minor. Songwriters see the earth as weary and tired, like #7, 6-28 "Ol' Man River," by Afro basso-profundo **Paul Robeson**. Slow rock tempo. Shouldn't R & R writers be Meteorology majors? Maybe. Compare:

"I Wish It Would Rain" – Temptations, #4, 1-68: #1(3) R & B. Great gloom tune to herald our national Disaster Year, 1968, nadir of bottomless-pit abyss of the American Spirit. You name it – Dr. King's assassination, Bobby Kennedy killed (June), and a quagmire of war in Vietnam. The Temps' lament requests the sunshine and blue sky to please go away. They want some stormy rolling skies to simulate their surly moods. The girl has gone, and they want weepy weather to match. [Contrast to "My Girl" super weather].

From Berry Gordy Jr.'s Hitsville, U.S.A. hit factory in Detroit come a few cameo items:

"My Guy" – Mary Wells, #1(2), 4-64; #1(2) R & B. Motown's former #1 diva rode a whirlwind of hot Soul Rock tunes. It's all **Smokey**'s fault. **Nolan Strong** was his singing hero, and Nolan once cut an obtuse undiplomatic item entitled "She's Not Good Looking, But She's Presentable" by Fortune's Devora Brown. Smokey recalled its essence, and sculpted this #1 tune for Mary (1943-92); she tells her girlfriends that her guy's no movie-star, no Muscle Beach fop, no pro athlete. He's a normal regular guy (like

Stevie in the "Uptight" lyric) who loves her. She vows to stick with him because he's true and good-hearted – not a superstar. Love can be very, very faithful like that. The song swoops in minor-key purring profundity, steered by Mary's throaty alto. In **Wells**'s #7, 12-62 (#1 R & B) "Two Lovers," Smokey concocted an odd ode to a "bi-polar" dude. Seems Mary has two lovers. One's sadistic, nasty, selfish, fierce. The other's kind, considerate, loving, tender, all those good vibes. We come to find out he's the same guy. Howzabout some psychoanalysis with your hit record? This manic-depressive two-lovers guy, with his physical abuse, is borderline creepy.

"Shotgun" – Junior Walker and the All-Stars, #4, 2-65; #1(4) R & B. Firebrand-sax guru Walker (b. Audry DeWalt, 1942-96) of Blythesville, Arkansas, rocketed to #1 on R & B. The saxophone never really left Rock and Soul in the Beatle era, after its 50s Streetcorner heyday. Profound and mellow today (**Kenny G** and **David Sanborn**), real big contributions (**Charlie Parker**, alto **Joe Morello**) come from Progressive, Be-Bop Hot Jazz. Junior Walker's sax spat and snarled and snapped with raw pure Soul.

"I Got You (I Feel Good)" – James Brown, #3, 11-65; #1(6) R & B. Non-Motown **James Brown** (99) leads everyone but ELVIS (151) in charted HOT 100 hits, yet never had a #1 song there [Ray Charles 76; Aretha Franklin 76; the Beatles 72; Frank Sinatra 68; Fats Domino 66] (info – Joel Whitburn's tremendous *Top Pop Singles to 1999*). Georgia (& Barnwell, SC) Soul/Blues/Rap guru Brown launched bombshells into the HOT 100 arena: #7,7-67 "Cold Sweat"; #8, 4-66 "It's a Man's Man's World"; #8, 7-65 "Papa's Got a Brand New Bag"; #15, 7-71 "Hot Pants"; #11, 6-69 "Mother Popcorn"; #13, 10-70 "Super Bad" [most JB tunes feature 'Part I, Part II']; modesty-Impaired #15, 7-70 "Get Up (I Feel Like Being a Sex Machine)"; and his community pride and awareness anthem, #10, 9-68 "Say It Loud – I'm Black and I'm Proud." Brown's bold new breed of Soul is rawer than Motown's suave softer sound (Brown's been on the King and Polydor labels).

Saxman **Maceo Parker** steers the song through all its raw, punchy bleats of bleary Blues. Touted as the 'Godfather of Rap,' Brown shifts the music mode from melody and dreamy lyric to solid rhythm and dynamic vocal filler.

"It's the Same Old Song" – Four Tops, #5, 7-65; #2(4), 6-65 R & B. Last member of Motown's super quartet of groups – **Supremes**, **Temptations**, **Miracles**. These Tops formed a long time before Motown, lassoing the year 1953 for **Levi Stubbs**'s first go-round with the **"4 Aims"** (other 3? **Duke Fakir, Lawrence Payton, Obie Benson**). The Four Tops' basic line-up stayed virtually the same for 43 years until Lawrence Payton, 59, passed away (6-97). In honor of their fallen friend, the Three Tops go on as the **Tops**, and pay Payton's salary to his family.

The "Same Old Song" isn't. Dynamic NEW treatment, with just a hint of Benny Benjamin's thundering drums echoing their #1(2) signature 5-65 "I Can't Help Myself,"

with ultracutest pet names 'Sugar-Pie' and "Honey-Bunch."

"Standing in the Shadows of Love" – Four Tops, #6, 12-66; #2(2) R & B. The Tops debuted with #11, 8-64 "Baby I Need Your Loving." Their sound was macho and mellow. Then they decided to ROCK: "Shake Me, Wake Me (When It's Over)," #18, 2-66, and big #1 tune "Reach Out I'll Be There" (9-66). "Shadows . . ." revolves around this shadowy metaphor – SHE is about to dump him, he figures. He's waiting for the Wile E. Coyote anvil to drop on his fervent love, and he'll be history. He psyches himself up motivationally to handle the surging romantic onslaught of grief. He stoically works on acceptance, resignation – and getting fired up for a new flame. Their "7 Rooms of Gloom" delivered a similar R & R theme (#14, 7-67). In "Bernadette" (#4, 3-67), suddenly, Levi and 3 Tops explode with a beseeching, imploring cry: "BERNADETTE!!!!!" Maybe SHE didn't hear him, but the rest of us sat up thunder-struck at his volcanic command – and bought the record.

"Sukiyaki" – Kyu Sakamoto, #1(3), 5-63: #18, 6-63 R & B. Quick! Which ethnic group has been royally ripped off by the R & R powers that be? Certainly not the average clump of white kids bopping and grooving with Ampeg amps in their garage. Certainly not the Soul Streetcorner crew. Who, then?

Asian rock and rollers. Kyu was Japanese. His pristine melody glommed the plum position, yet it's sung entirely in Japanese. **Four P.M.** (#8, 9-94) covered "Sukiyakii" elegantly in English. [4 **P.M.** stands for **Positive Music**: Buzz Cason, Tom Leslie, **Hachidai Nakamura**, and **El Rokusuke**.] It's totally incredible how few Asian songs pierce the American Top Thirty.

Japan is the world's second-largest record market. Japan instituted the karaoke concept through their electronic genius. Current computer-recording MIDI technology functions on Japanese innovations. Still, where are the Japanese-American recording stars?

"Sukiyaki's" real title is "Ue O Muite Aruko." Fred Bronson says it translates into the craftily cryptic "I Look Up When I Walk." First given to British Trad jazz trumpeter Kenny Ball and His Jazzmen, "Sukiyaki" became the first Rock-Era foreign-language #1 song in the U.S.A. Kyu's lukewarm follow-up? #58 "China Nights (Shina No Yoru)," 8-63. Sakamoto died in 1985 at 43 when a big Japan 747 airliner crashed into the Shinto shrine, Mt. Fujiyama.

"This Magic Moment" – Jay and the Americans, #6, 12-68. Jay Black's soaring dramatic 'Italian tenor' suggests the Great Singers' Zone. His excellent Chalypso echoes the magic moments of Ben E. King and the fabulous **Drifters** (#16, 2-60). Jay, Caucasian New Yorker, brought a soulful Jackie Wilson sound to Rock.

"Mickey's Monkey" – Miracles, #8, 8-63; #3, 8-63 R & B. Dance fare of Girls Group Era. Dance, obviously, was the Monkey, one of most uninhibited of Mashed Potato, Frug, Philly Dog, Shake, Boogaloo, Madison, Twist, Hully Gully years.

"I Second That Emotion" – Miracles, #4, 11-67: #1(1) R & B. Smokey's cool expertise with pun and pen. Take a cliché. Flip it around inside out, and come up with an exploding title. "Emotion" granted the Miracles their second-biggest HOT 100 prize until second Pagliacci masterpiece (1st is #16, 7-65 "The Tracks of My Tears"):

"The Tears of a Clown" – Smokey Robinson and the Miracles, #1(2), 10-70; #1(3) R & B. The Irish-tenor Motown Veep Miracle celebrated hits in five decades with 2-81, #2(3) "Being with You" and #91 in '91 "Double Good Everything" (#23 R & B). The original SAD CLOWN was #1(4) in 1907 by Italian opera legend **Enrico Caruso**: "Pagliacci – Vesti La Giubba (On with the Show)." In the Rock Era, the first Pagliacci theme smash was the **Platters'** "Great Pretender" (#1[2], 12-55 and #1[11] R & B). Others bobbed along, like **Billy Myles'** (#25, 11-57; #13, 1-58 R & B) "The Joker." "The Joker" glows with dazzling neon dragons and streetlight or oil slick rainbows. A Myles stone. Clown **Jerry Lewis** had a great partner, crooner **Dean Martin**:

"Memories Are Made of This" – Dean Martin, #1(6), 12-55. ELVIS adored his sound, and wanted to someday be just like Frank Sinatra's pal Dean (when the R & R fad passed). This tune sifts bliss and happiness into a sweet paradigm for a great marriage. It thrives on counterpoint (2 tunes at once). One of the sweetest, suavest, coolest songs ever performed. Bridges the Big Band Enunciators (Bing Crosby, Frank Sinatra, Buddy Clark), with Rock Generation Majestic Mumblers, and Super Slurrers. Dean Martin's huge #1 hit spells out goodtime romance. With cushiony murmurs and sweet nothin's of wedded and bedded bliss, the Steubenville Ohio ex-boxer (1917-95) croons kisses and hugs and cuddlesome coziness. [Though I was an avid subteen rocker at 12, I bought this super song, and it supplied everything for me except a girlfriend]. Jerry's kid **Gary Lewis** has a wry clown tale:

"Everybody Loves a Clown" – Gary Lewis and the Playboys, #4, 9-65. Outstanding sad-clown bouncy dirge. Dynamite drum riffs, top-notch lead guitars, Al Ramsay and Johnny West. Gary's baritone vocal carries a mangled message – if everybody loves a clown, why can't she? Life of the party? Goat of the jokes. Super beat. Gary's sprightliest hit is his sunny #8, 5-66 "Green Grass"; like #1(2), 1-65 weeper "This Diamond Ring," "Grass" sports a tremendous rhythm track by ardent drummer Gary.

Here's the Prince of Pagliacci, Nashville's unsoul Blue-eyed Soul Brother **Ray Stevens**. First, the funny one, unless you're Arabic. Then, the Pagliacci tune:

"Ahab, the Arab" – Ray Stevens, #5, 7-62; #9, 7-62 R & B. Precursor of Weird Al Yankovic and the Demento Sound of wild comedy, **Ray Stevens** (b. '39) fired off this stereotype Rap extravaganza. "Ahab" (for *Moby Dick*'s crazed whaling captain) tippytoes an iffy Comedy Chan-

nel tightrope between ethnic comedy and political limbo via hot escapades of cool dude Ahab and his lovely main squeeze Fatima. Fatima is Concubine the First in some sultan's harem on the midnight oasis.

Crafty Ahab and trusty camel 'Clyde' sneak by the dark tent for the speedy getaway. Inside, vivacious voluptuous Fatima reposes on this hotcha zebra-skin rug, wearing a bone in her nose. She munches out on a pomegranate, some chitterlings, and several Hershey bars. Ahab and Fatima slink off for a hot little rendezvous. Although some of the stuff is tune, slashing with serpentine flutes and Mideastern minor chords, much of "Ahab" is performed in a RAP manner – it previews **Eminem**'s #1, 5-2000 "Real Slim Shady," Snoop Doggy Dog ("What's My Name?" #8, 12-93), Dr. Dre ("Nothing' but a 'G' Thang" #2, 1-93) or Tone Loc ("A Funky Cold Medina" #3, 3-89). Or **Notorious B.I.G.** ("One More Chance"/"Stay With Me" #2(3), 6-95) or **Tu-Pac** ("How Do You Want It,"#1[2], 6-96). Or Kid Rock's #4, 3-2000 Al. *Devil Without a Cause*. Ray Stevens is best, however, when clumped into his one Great Singer Pagliacci song:

"Funny Man' – Ray Stevens, #81, 3-63. Flirting with ribbony melismas, yodel-yelp falsettos, and key modulations, Ray packs a powerful punch with this Pagliacci primrose. His raggedy relationship tatters, as the girl he loves turns him down – and laughs. In the Motown tradition, Stevens' biggest hit is a Stevie Wonder-full "Everything Is Beautiful" (#1, 4-70) to promote racial harmony. His #28, 8-68 "Mr. Business Man" zaps workplace hypocrisy.

"The Streak" – Ray Stevens, #1(3), 4-74; #3 C. Too much skin! 'Interviewer' (Ray) solicits a news response from hokey couple, about just getting "streaked" by a clothesless man at the supermarket, who is NOT PG-13 loincloth swinger #8, 4-69 "Gitarzan." Clown prince Ray sings 3 parts to a 12-bar Blues groove: a ginchy bass line from some orangutang or gorilla; Jane's sky-high screech "BABY": and wild falsetto yodel-yell of Tarzan. Born in Clarksdale, Georgia, Ray [Ragsdale] Stevens enjoys a Country Soul sound (both the R & B and Country charts).

"Spiders and Snakes" – Jim Stafford, #3, 11-73; #66, 3-74 C. Eloise, Florida singer songwriter Stafford woos the lass (in their 10-year-old phases) by nabbing wiggly spiders and squiggly snakes. She is unimpressed. She wants to kiss him. He is unimpressed – but marks the concept down for later exploration. Stafford also roused up a #7 "Wildwood Weed" (7-74), which seemed strangely like marijuana.

Now we've wiped out the sad-clown Pagliacci Theme from Motown to Miami, let's visit the mountains.

"(You've Got to) Move Two Mountains" – Marv Johnson, #20, 9-60; #12 R & B. Marv has to move two mountains, steal a star from the sky, drain a river dry, swim across the widest deepest ocean. Why? To prove his lasting love to his lady fair. No problem. Detroit 'mountain'? "Garbage Hill" in Hines Park, where we used to toboggan on crisp icy-blue zero nights. Or 'Mt.' Elliott, a very, very flat street in Polish-American Hamtramck, next door to Bill Haley's Highland Park, a pancake-flat town with no highlands whatsoever. Great tenor, great song, great Motown groove, no topography.

"Over the Mountain: Across the Sea" – Johnnie & Joe, #8, 5-57 and #89, 9060; #3, 5-57 R & B. Joe Rivers and Johnnie Louise Richardson, original mountain climbing duo, spin this sweet R & B Bronx mountain sound. One of great 'Streetcorner' anthems of all time.

"The Mountain's High" – Dick (St. John Gosting) and Deedee (Sperling), #2(2), 7-61. Santa Monica has real California mountains, swooping thousands of feet into the celestial firmament. Dick and Santa Monica High School girlfriend Deedee formed the first of the big male-female duos from Marvin/Tammi to Elton/ Kiki to Linda/Aaron to Mariah/Trey Lorenz. Dick and DeeDee did "Blue-Eyed Soul" before **Phil Spector** and **Righteous Brothers** defined it. Remarkable team: Deedee sang among the highest of all soprano rockers (lyric soprano). Dick could top her high notes with a mountain-smashing falsetto that taught **Frankie Valli** just about everything he knows. Dick and Deedee cruise the alpine timberline, with crisp Swiss harmonies that float and yodel their way through only two chords – until they modulate half a step to the next half-key up. Long-lost lovers conquer crags and reunite. Dick's tag-eng WOO HOO, like **Buddy Holly**'s on "That'll Be the Day," is great falsetto Classic Rock exonified. Smoothie #17 ballad 3-63 "Young and in Love" followed.

"Thou Shalt Not Steal" – Dick and Deedee, #13, 11-64. After theatrical ballad (#22 "Tell Me" 3-62) and life-cycle song "Turn Around" #27, 11-63), then they romped back with #89 "All My Trials" (see Elvis's American Trilogy), and this Heartland Rocker named after a Commandment on Moses' mountain. [NOT from the Church of the Perpetually Wishy-Washy, with Seven Commandments and Three Suggestions.]

"Ain't No Mountain High Enough" – Marvin Gaye and Tammi Terrell, #19, 5-67; #3, 6-67 R & B. Marvin and Tammi's tune represents the high heyday of the Motown family. Marvin (1939-84) and Tammi (1946-70) utilize the suavest of the suave. Tacets rule here, with Marvin and Tammi almost stopping, then harmonizing sweetly, or just tossing in a little cool finger-popping. Their duo debut tune. Other smooth offerings for their Motown success story? "Your Precious Love" (#5, 9-67); "Ain't Nothin' Like the Real Thing Baby," (#8, 4-68) and "You're All I Need to Get By" (#7, 7-68).

Diana and the Supremes drifted philosophically apart. It is no surprise that two of her biggest songs were Marvin Gaye-inspired: "Ain't No Mountain High Enough" #1(3), 8-70; #1(1) R & B and "Missing You" #10, 12-84; #1(3), 12-84 R & B.

In the Top Ten Artists of all time in Joel Whitburn's 1999 7th edition of *Top Pop Singles* from *Billboard* magazine, the incredibly comprehensive Top Ten Tabulator found **Marvin Gaye** at #11:

1) Elvis Presley – 9,641 pts.
2) The Beatles – 5,360
3) Elton John – 5,176
4) Stevie Wonder – 4,455
5) James Brown – 4, 182
6) Madonna – 4,071
7) Rolling Stones – 3,819
8) Aretha Franklin – 3,782
9) Michael Jackson – 2,775
10) Pat Boone – 3,692
11) MARVIN GAYE – 3,475

C/O Joel Whitburn, Kim Bloxdorf, *Top Pop Singles*. Totally computerized, their system grants 100 points for 1st week at #1 song, plus 10 points, for each week at #1; also, they give 90 points for #2, 70 points for #3 and 5 points for #51-60, and 10 points for #91-100.

How could one jimmy a cold, loveless world into a monster hit? Take tremendous talent, and have one's sister go out with **Paul McCartney**:

"A World Without Love" – Peter and Gordon, #1(1), 5-64. Chart topper by **Gordon Waller** (b. '45 Braemar, Scotland) and orange-haired **Peter Asher** (b. '44 London). Jane Asher happened to be Paul McCartney's girlfriend, in the pre-**Linda Eastman McCartney** days. Peter and Gordon did an Everlys-type unplugged Soft Rock duo in 1963, with baritone tenor harmonies resounding mellowly, three or four notes south of the Everly Brothers.

Their Paul-penned tune conquered America, and they soon picked the very best of American singer/songwriters for hit material: #9 "I Go to Pieces" 1-65 (Del Shannon), and "True Love Ways" #14, 4-65 (Buddy Holly).

The **Temptations, Peter & Gordon,** and **Del Shannon** plod onwards between Michigan or English sloppy soggy gloomdrops of drizzle, seeking that ideal girlfriend who is sunshine on all the cloudy days. They seek warm May in the damp and drizzly lost Novembers of the solitary soul. That's what it's all about, really. LOVE. When you study Biology, you might get a dead frog. When you study Criminal Justice, you might have to fight crime. When you study Macroeconomics, you might fall asleep. When you study Popular Music, you must study the main ingredient – LOVE.

Ask the Beatles: "All You Need Is Love!"

Rock & Roll Thunder
Over the Mersey, the Thames,
and the Galaxy

18

Not too long after the Beatles conquered American charts, a new crew hustled their riverbend Delta Blues repertoire into action. [On Britain's River Thames Delta.] Raised on **Jimmy Reed, John Lee Hooker**, Buddy Holly and Chuck Berry, they called themselves quasi-modestly THE WORLD'S GREATEST ROCK & ROLL BAND.

As Mick and Keith gazed out into the ruddy mud flats over the lazy, languid Thames, gurgling like molasses in the rare noonday sun, they regarded **Jimmy Reed** – supreme Bluesman. The Thames stretches wide here, fanning to a slowly swishing half mile across. Flotsam and jetsam bob with the backrushing tide. Crew teams row and little boats dodge bottles and mudflats and London haze. Hot catfish day (73°) on the Thames.

Jim Cook and I pedaled bikes in 1961 through their London megalopolitan suburb of Dartford on the sloshing Thames Delta, about 15 miles (24K) from Buckingham Palace.

Back in Memphis and New Orleans and Clarksdale, by the Mississippi Delta – birthplace of the Blues and maybe Rock and Roll – it sizzled to 95°. **Chuck Berry** and **B.B. King** set up to play the Blues. Mick's dad was a Professor of Gymnastic Science (College Coach), highly regarded in his profession; the money, too, was not bad. Mick was a bright and successful student at LSE – the London School of Economics. Britain doesn't mollycoddle starry-eyed students. They dump average kids into the workaday world at 15-16. Mick moved up the scholastic totem pole and prepared for a Captain of Industry post. Somehow, he got run over by the Blues Train which zapped his suit and tie ambitions. It's all Chicago Blues star **Muddy Waters**' fault. ("I'm Your Hoochie Coochie Man" NC, '54; #3, 3-54 R & B). Muddy recorded "Rollin' Stone" in 1950 (see "Mannish Boy" too).

Mick Jagger's first mistake was to call his first group "Little Boy Blue and the Blue Boys." Fortunately, his talent was unsquashable. Flunking a solo singing debut at Blues Incorporated's Earling Club, he got his first job as a July 1962 intermission band. **Keith Richard[s]** played guitar, and **Brian Jones** played guitar, and piano, and clarinet. [Legally, Richard(s) has actually changed his name six times from singular to plural]. Jones emulated pioneer Blues slide guitarist, **Elmore James**, who did **Robert Johnson**'s 1938 "Dust My Broom," NC, '52, but #9, 4-52 R & B. **James** used **Sonny Boy Williamson** on harmonica. Ian Stewart, Mike Avory, and Dick Taylor were in the early Stones lineup, but they got downsized. **Bill Wyman** (b. Bill Parks, 1936) took over Taylor's bass job. **Charlie Watts** was a local Jazz drummer.

Most teenage idols hid behind a guitar. Or something. Buddy Holly, Ricky Nelson, Elvis Presley, Eddie Cochran, Chuck Berry, Del Shannon, Roy Orbison, Tommy Roe – they all paid their Fender or Gibson or Gretsch dues. What did **Mick Jagger** play? The **Beatles** – like the Crickets – had two guitars, bass, and drums. All singers singing. What did Mick play? Maybe the odd tambourine or harmonica. Mick just sang and pranced.

Buddy Holly's Crickets and the Beatles wanted to wear their scruffy goof-off clothes. However, due to natty dress codes from managers Norman Petty and Brian Epstein, they donned establishment suits. Pioneering INDIVIDUAL casual outfits, the Stones began to Roll.

Beecher Stevens, Decca exec, let the Beatles slip away. Another superbotcher, according to A & R legend, was Decca's **Dick Rowe**. He had a choice between signing the Beatles or **Brian Poole and the Tremeloes** (#97, 9-64, "Someone, Someone" but #2, U.K.) It was an honest mistake. You or I might have muffed the same call. Why? The Poole-less Tremeloes (Alan Blakely, Dave Munden, Chip Hawkies, Ricky West) from Dagenham, Essex, went on to many huge hits of their own. When **Chip Hawkes** wangled Brian Poole's job, the Tremeloes became a major British group in America, nearly vindicating Rowe.

"Silence is Golden" – Tremeloes, #11, 6-67; #1, 5-67 U.K. Shy Poole retired to family's butcher business, Chip Hawkes launched this ex-Four Seasons flipside. "Silence" may have the greatest vocal range in any R & R ballad. It tremulously trembles at top falsetto, and booms along on baritone. Like the "Star Spangled Banner's" tough high notes, this is not a karaoke song for just any squawky voice. Only Orbisons need apply.

"Here Comes My Baby" – Tremeloes, #13, 4-67; #4, 2-67 U.K. Chip Hawkes's son is Chesney Hawkes (#10, 8-91, "The One and Only"). Dad Hawkes's "wo-uh-ho" line is so ghostly a Holly echo that a true fan-addict might mistake it. Dick Rowe chose one when he should have GRABBED THEM BOTH.

Comes the atonement. Dick Rowe was looking to sign a new British group. **Andrew Loog Oldham** was just 19, yet his managerial moxie netted him nearly as key a role as that of **Brian Epstein** for the Liverpudlian Fab Four. Oldham worked for NEMS, like Epstein, and saw a drab future in his current situation. So Oldham signed with the Stones a cushy management deal.

Keith Richard corroborated: "Mick had been singing with some rock bands . . . he was doing Buddy Holly," which Rowe admired. Richard recalls, woozily, that Holly was just as big in England as Elvis. "Everything that came out was a record smash number one. By about 1958," Richards said, "it was either Elvis or Buddy Holly."

The "Mods versus Rockers" scene stalked England. At 15 or 16, many youths just hit the dole, or roamed around in street gangs of Rockers: Teddy Boy types, black leather and tight black levis, pointed 'roach-stabber' boots, greasy pompadours and sunglasses (see the Beatles in movie *Backbeat*). Mods? (Modernists) Italian continental look, snappy suits, pressed shirts (with *Saturday Night Fever* foppery, they blow a week's pay on sharp threads to dazzle the ladies).

The Stones sought the image of ANTI-BEATLE. The Stones debuted in Britain's *Melody Maker* with #26 Chuck Berry tune "Come On," and Lennon/McCartney Starr-sung tune "I Wanna Be Your Man" to #12 in '63. Their second tune was released in America. Its flipside – of Holly's #10, '57 "Oh Boy" – was the first Stones item to crease the charts:

"Not Fade Away" – Rolling Stones, #48, 5-64; #3, 3-64 U.K. The Stones' snowballing success story is littered with ironic turns: a hitless Chuck Berry song and a flipside Holly that didn't sound like Holly; upper-middle British youths assuming a shaggier unkempt look to emulate

their Bluesmen heroes, who, despite staggering poverty, often wore . . . rumpled suits and ties. **Keith Richards**: "We wanted to sell records for Jimmy Reed, Muddy [Waters], John Lee Hooker .. We were disciples."

Fashion? The Stones blasted a fashion free-for all. Their hair was longer, scragglier, scruffier, and they cultivated an image James Dean could dig – Rebels without a cause. To many Americans, the Rolling Stones represented the next diabolical incarnation of **Jerry Lee Lewis** – brash, brazen, and way too bold.

Unlike Brian Poole, Tommy Roe, Bobby Vee, Chip Hawkes, Adam Faith, Cliff Richard, or George Harrison, the Stones' raspily baritonic Mick Jagger sounded very LITTLE like Buddy Holly. "Not Fade Away," then, was their perfect spaceship to the stars. Buddy Holly himself was trying to sound like Bo Diddley on "Not Fade Away." (Diddley cut Buddy's "Not Fade Away" in '75.) Great original acts are not afraid to borrow the musical greatness of others. Like Elvis before him, Buddy in 1956 and early 1957 was merely trying to do what a handful of great white acts were doing in Rock's infancy – emulate great Rhythm and Blues stars. "Not Fade Away" packs a vintage Bo Diddley wallop. You can also hear a scorchy echo of Big Joe Turner:

"Shake, Rattle, and Roll" – Big Joe Turner, #22, 8-54; #1(3), 5-54 R & B. Big Joe Turner's (6'3", 260#, 1911-85) song and his style were first covered by **Bill Haley** (#7, 8-54). This twelve-bar Blues rocker was the absolute favorite of Blues expert **Charles Scheef** (1945-98, WUSB radio). Stones would agree. This benchmark for Rock and Blues won't win too many points among ardent feminists. Man tells woman to rattle pots, shake pans, and roll his Insta-Breakfast. Unique lyric, ginchy hooks, torrid tacets. Ralph and Alice Kramden's *Honeymooners* song? Archie and Edith Bunker? Leroy and Loretta Lockhorn? These are not the serene Cosbys or Seavers or *Father Knows Best*.

Turner burst on the R & B scene in 1945 with "S.K.'s Blues – Part I" (NC, 1945; #3, 3-45 R & B). "Chains of Love" hit #30 in 9-51 and #2(4), 6-51 R & B [(#10, 9-56) Pat Boone]. Joe's "Honey Hush" flattened the R & B competition for two glorious months – #1(8), 9-53, and #23, 12-53 Top 30. Joe's best?

"Corrina, Corrina" – Ray Peterson, #9, 11-60. This tender Chalypso version of Big Joe's #2(2), 4-56 R & B (NC HOT 100) Blues Holler melted a multitude of throbbing teenage hearts. It followed Ray's Death Rock #7, 60 "Tell Laura I Love Her." Before super #29, 7-61 "Missing You."

"Tell Me" – Rolling Stones, #24, 7-64. The song prances on the Mediant minor chord (**Em** in Key of 'C'), and it surges to a basic rock beat on the Watts-thump tomtom:

Tomtom:

Cymbal or snare:

       1   2   3   4

Each verse hangs fire. As the bibulous beat bubbles with ripply champagne splendor underneath, Jagger squeezes each word dry. Jagger waits . . . hanging fire . . . as the loveless days stagger by. You can visualize the shaggy, rail-thin singer, caressing his mike – his large mouth fondling each booming baritone word. The song prowls, stalks, corners, pounces.

Remember the squeaky clean Folk movement? Well-scrubbed young exec-looking groups (Serendipity Singers, New Christy Minstrels), with mild social action songs, were giving way to a new force in their midst:

"Subterranean Homesick Blues" – Bob Dylan, #39, 5-65. Is this the iconoclastic 16-bar blues that launched the Folk Rock movement? Bobby Zimmerman of icy Hibbing, Minnesota, drifted down a dusty road, and adopted the craggy delivery of folk poet-guru **Woody Guthrie** of dustbowl Depression Oklahoma.

Dylan apprenticed on Buddy Holly tunes, watching the Lubbock legend's 5th-to-last performance in the January 1959 Duluth Auditorium. Dylan signed on briefly with **Bobby Vee**'s North Dakotan garage band the Shadows. Dylan's audition as keyboard Shadow was but a prelude to his forthcoming personal Folk Rock Revolution, but Dylan had to flee Eastward to New York.

Pledging ZBT fraternity at University of Minnesota, and digesting the Beat Generation *On the Road* wanderlust of **Jack Kerouac**, and Whitmanesque poet **Allen Ginsberg**, Dylan dropped out of school and headed to Kerouac's 'Center of Saturday Night in America', the Lower East Side/ NYU/Bowery of New York's Greenwich Village. In the famous Bleeker Street coffeehouse the Bitter End and its 4 a.m. atmosphere of balmy New York (25°) winter, he discovered a subterranean world of expresso coffee, candleglow poetry, midnight madness, bearded bards, mellow 12-string acoustic guitars, and java jags. Strangely, so strangely, it was just across Washington Square from Buddy and Maria Elena Holly's Fifth Avenue apartment. [Sit tight. All this stuff comes together] .

Like Mick Jagger and the Rolling Stones, Bob Dylan had gotten scruffy, and craggy, and no one but no one was going to tell sage Bob what to do. His chubby Columbia Folk contract gained him success. Mixin' up basement medicine contains no subtle reference to recreational substances. The subterranean Beat Generation, through Bob Dylan and the Beatles and Stones, metamorphosed from a few thousand urban 1959 Bohemians to a full-scale 1965 Counterculture as the War heated up and tolerance simmered down.

Bob Dylan played the 1965 Newport Folk Festival with Weaver **Pete Seeger** in the wings to shepherd the new protégé of Pure Folk. When Bob plugged in his guitar, it is dimly reported, the venerable guru of the Folk movement put his fingers in his ears. Folk Rock music, they claim, was born that day in 1965, as Folk Purists groaned. Rock and Roll and the world would never be the same. Actually, the Animals' #1(3), 8-64 "House of the Rising

Sun" [Joan Baez, '60] far precedes it.

Dylan, in turn, altered the consciousness of **John Lennon**'s lyric writing (esoteric Al. #1 '62 *Sgt. Pepper*) and Mick Jagger's unruly social protest (#1 "Satisfaction" 6-65). "Subterranean Homesick Blues" title was inspired by Jack Kerouac's fastest book, *The Subterraneans* (1959), which the Beat guru slashed through in just three frenetic days and wild nights blitzed on Benzedrine. Dylan's lyric, too, flows with the Kerouackian flavor of wild spontaneous bop prosody – a motley collage of disjointed images, loosely related to outfoxing the 9-to-5 system. Even his 16-Bar Blues (begone, 12) outfoxed the R & R establishment with its seemingly endless banter between chord clusters. Like Beat mentor **Allen Ginsberg** (1926-97), Dylan rhapsodizes his lurching lyric with bouquets of surrealistic phrases: moxie metaphors, street-savvy scenarios, and neon midnight glory. Midnight oasis.

"The Last Time" – Rolling Stones, #9, 3-65. Stones' 2nd hard rocker. Their first top ten U.S. tune, #6 "Time Is on My Side," dribbled molassesly up the charts, as the Beatle Year faded into a new colossal era of Rock and Roll. Into the Golden Years, R & R packed it all into the vortex. Everything began to come together – Folk Rock, Soul, Blues, British Invasion, and Surf music. The Rolling Stones, In 1965, hit the cutting edge with "Last Time," a threat, not a promise.

"Last Time" projects throbbing rhythmic power from the Blues-based BIG THREE – **A**, **E**, and **D**. Keith Richard[s] crashes and smashes and flashes these same three chords, but he dips to chromatics. His **E** is the I tonic chord, rendering the **D** into a flatted seventh major (bVII). Still, he just blasts the same three chords.

"Satisfaction" – Rolling Stones, #1(4), 6-65; #19, 7-65 R & B. Note date. This Rolling Stones' signature song postdates Dylan's "Subterranean" blues by only one month. A good argument could be made for "Satisfaction" as Folk Rock. It is certainly a Protest Anthem, yes? Jagger blasts every English institution, beaming up a 'Generation X' chronicle of annoyed frustration, consternation, and thunderation. Mostly, he goes for the jugular: corporate advertising (dude preaches gospel of whiter-than-white shirts – Fluffo detergent); cigarette addiction and manliness (gotta smoke the identical cig to really be a rugged man): global confusion (he must drive all over the globe in quest for truth, and romantic buzz). "Satisfaction" grapples with no ghastly villains; it cites the entire system as hazardous to your serenity.

"Satisfaction" glows with internal fire. Mick and Keith express that unseen adolescent yearning and ultimate resignation: man, you just can't do it all. But, hey – let's give it a try!

Keith Richard[s] wrote THE RIFF! You know that 'E' to 'G' bottom bass thunder. The ol' BOM-BOMMMM-BA-BA-BOMMMMM . . . The one that sparks "Satisfaction." How so? Seems the laid-back Stone was slumbering away some wild adventure from the night before. In fitful sleep, this incredible bass riff – duplicated on rhythm and/or lead guitar – came to him in a DREAM. Keith woke up, grabbed his guitar, and twirled the tape dials. Legend has it Keith recorded ONLY THAT STERLING RIFF – and waited till later to add the rebel-tone lyrics with Mick Jagger. (See Glossary – Chord Theory and Mideastern Chord Change.)

Many a great half-song has been written while half-sleeping in the wee blotto hours. After composing the most famous guitar/bass lick in Rock and Roll history, Keith drifted back to catch a few more Z's. In countless TOP SONG SURVEYS SINCE 1968 (I remember WKNR, Detroit's 1968 Top 500 songs, with "Peggy Sue' #3), "Satisfaction" has been voted the #1 Rock and Roll song of all time. [Despite the fact that I dropped all those 'yay, 'Peggy Sue'" postcards in the mail all over the Greater Motor City Detroit Metro Area]. And Keith's riff stands, a bulwark, a fortress, a citadel of Rock and Roll thundertone splendor. Music for the ages.

In the Stones' "Satisfaction," Mick Jagger uses a crafty ticked-off tone. And isn't that what Rock and Roll is all about? It's about ticking off the older generation, eh?

IF ROCK AND ROLL ISN'T AT LEAST A LITTLE BIT DANGEROUS, CAN IT REALLY BE ROCK AND ROLL?

Heavy Metal? Steppenwolf? Iggy? The MC5? Bob Seger and the Silver Bullet Band? Bruce Springsteen? John Cougar Mellencamp? Aerosmith? Van Morrison? They were all listening, as kids, to Mick and Keith and their Dissatisfaction Ditty.

"Time is On My Side" – Rolling Stones, #6, 10-64. And HOW! Dubbed the World's Greatest Rock and Roll Band" by Jann Wenner's emerging R & R press – which named its rock-mag *Rolling Stone* in 1967 – the Rolling Stones have become the most enduring marathon band in Rock history. Yep, forty years in the limelight. This first American Top Ten tune used the musical style the Stones do best – Vintage American Delta Blues, with echoes of Muddy Waters, Willie Dixon, Jimmy Reed, or Howlin' Wolf. **Mick Jagger**'s raspy baritone surges through romantic escapades. He uses Del Shannon Revenge Rock lyrics. He struts an amalgam of harsh gutsy Talking Blues, and something from 1964 that sounds like current Rap. No doubt the Rolling Stones have Soul.

The Rolling Stones had time on their side to score some huge hits: #2(3), 2-66 "19th Nervous Breakdown," with Mideastern craggy sound; interracially-hot romance #1(2), 5-71 "Brown Sugar"; #1(2), 1-67 melodic ballad "Ruby Tuesday" (which later named an American restaurant chain); #2(3), 8-81 "Start Me up," about desire even after death (yep); #3, 7-80 "emotional Rescue"; #5, '86 "Harlem Shuffle"; #5, 9-89 "Mixed Emotions"; and #60, 10-94 "Out of Tears" – an amazing marathon of range of timeless R & R tunes.

"I Love You" – Volume's, #22, 4-62; NC, R & B. The Volume's "I Love You" is the best of only six songs in the Rock Era which have ever charted bearing the most obvious of probable titles. (Whitburn – *Top Pop Singles*). Ed Union of Detroit's non-Motown (Chex 1002) Past Blast floats around on a lot of fluffly falsetto.

Stafford, England's **Climax Blues Band** (NOT #3, 1-72 "Precious and Few" by Climax) had the topmost chart hit named "I Love You," with saxman/singer Colin Cooper at #12, 2-81. **Nine Days** revived their sweet love song for the Summer 2002 *The New Guy***½ sound track.

"Mother's Little Helper" – Rolling Stones, #8, 7-66. This Mideastern tune championed Dylan's wry quip that everyone must become stoned, from his #2, 1966 "Rainy Day Women #12 and 35." What was stoning the haggard mothers of Britain and America and Australia? Oddly, prescription drugs. Sleeping pills. Dexadrine to stay awake. Hormones. This darting Dartford rocker is a veiled prognostication of the King Elvis's 1977 demise – with 14 prescription drugs from Dr. 'Feelgood' Nick riddling his tired ancient 42-year-old body.

What rendered Mom uptight with snarling kids and Supermarket nightmares was . . .? Drowsy downers? Cloud Ten tranquilizers, a/k/a 'mother's little helpers?' Prehistoric Prozac? Or Ritalin's groggy antecedents? Sleek suavity serums of questionable medical malpractice. Hey, even Twinkies, greenies, Doritos, coke/Cokes, feelgoods, Yoohoos, uppers, coffee, whatever. Not even booze. Or cigs. Are ALL the yummy goodies really dastardly drugs? "Mother's Little Helper" portrays hypocrisy in legislating health and morality with homespun drugs in the spacey mid-60s. Jumpin' java, for instance.

The Stones hop a magic carpet of Richard's driving guitar, Wyman's fast-flashing bass, and Watts's incredibly punchy drums. Watt corners the 2/4 market on each beat of his 4/4 measures, driving the downbeat 1, 2, 3, & 4 with thunderous volume, and the in-betweens 1½, 2½, 3½, and 4½ beats at an echo volume maybe half the big beats. The Rolling Stones thunder Mom's helper.

"Ruby Tuesday" – Rolling Stones, #1(1), 2-67. Sweet harmonious melody. Their first stateside hit was the multi-layered string extravaganza (#49, 1-64) "That Girl Belongs to Yesterday" for great singer **Gene Pitney**. One mysterious girl, "Ruby Tuesday," flashes a chameleon-like changeability. She re-invents herself (see **Madonna**) in kaleidoscopic splendor. Does she typify for Mick the mystifying feminine mystique? She's an enigma, a paradox, a puzzle. Jagger twirls this tune in regal Madrigal style, with strings slicing the hang-fire gloom. Minor chords dance in Tinker Bell efflorescence. Jagger wonders and wonders. He can't figure her out! This both magnetizes and repels him. He'll have to let her go. He cannot own her. She is a free spirit. The bad-lad image of the funky, craggy Rolling Stones changed like 'Ruby' in this song. Here they cop the best of the **Everlys** or **Simon and Garfunkel** in beautiful melodies and harmonies. Other Stones' melody champs? #6, 12-65 "As Tears Go By"; #24, 7-66 madrigal "Lady Jane"; #14, 9-67 "Dandellon"; #25, 12-67 "She's a Rainbow"; and #1(1), 9 73 "Angie" [**David Bowie**'s 1970-80 wife"].

"Paint It, Black" – Rolling Stones, #1(2), 5-66. Sheik chic. The tune is flyaway, the beat is armed and dangerous. Jagger drags his jagged song beyond the desert quietudes in a rampage of rhythmic Mega-Watts fury. Gangbusters are powerless to halt this Stones' seizure of the sounds of silence. The Arabic musical-scale melody batters the battlements in a *jihad* crusade to rock with crackling thunder and lyrical lightning. And into its dotage, "Paint It, Black" may prove a Viagra Niagara of passion and power.

"Paint It, Black" defines the Stones' musical mutability. Like the Who, Led Zeppelin, or Beatles, the Stones' strength rests on the byword VERSATILITY. Let's begin with the dark mood of "Paint It, Black," and compare it to the Stones' biggest smash Un-hit that never made the charts – their notorious, brilliant, and terrifying "Sympathy for the Devil," where Mick plays 'devil's advocate' briefly.

Our demonbeat black-brushed song revels in its blue funk. Arabian traders follow the Demon Star Algol (El Ghoul) across the indigo skies over the Rub Al Khali Desert. "Paint It, Black" sinks into the Tartarean black quicksand of a vast spiritual wasteland. With the coal-black darkness of the River Styx in the midst of some vast desert, Mick Jagger booms baritone with macho intensity. You hear the haunted echoes of Hieronymus Bosch's lost souls hanging over the Pit of Dante's *Inferno*. Mick Jagger paints one gloomy dark abyss of chaos and despair. Black. Ebony. Desolate.

Like the Temps' #4, 1-58 "I Wish It Would Rain," this English Delta Mideast Blues number celebrates the groaning stratus fog drizzle that staggers the British Isles and Detroit in dark December. Watts cranks up his voltage on "Mother's Little Helper's" downbeat LOUDER on "Paint It, Black." Fighting the incessant drum BAM BOOM, Mick groans and moans that he wants all the sprightly shiny colors of his soul now draped in funeral black. No happy "Oh Boy" jubilant verse aloft, "Paint It, Black" drags joy beyond the Dark DOOR to Jim Morrison's grisly funeral pyre. Watts strikes a lone match of matchless rhythm in the underbeat tattoo. He flickers a glimmer of hope that if the heart still loudly beats, life shimmers within.

Out of the Stones' #5 Al.. *Beggars' Banquet* slithers their most controversial song (which failed to chart), "Sympathy for the Devil." You can't do "Paint It, Black" without this ode to satanic terrors.

"Sympathy for the Devil" – Rolling Stones, NC, 12-68. Somehow eluded the #1 spot on the Christian Contemporary Charts. So far, Contemporary Satanic Charts keep a lower profile. This item portrays the Devil's devious, raging fury and humor at the height of horror. Flash back to when John Lennon splashed the Beatles into Yankee hot water with his idle quip that "the Beatles were getting bigger than Jesus" – he meant the media thought so, anyhow, right or wringingly wrong. Suddenly here pranced Mick Jagger. His 5-minute diabolical persona? Lucifer. Readers of Milton recall the Devil's arch-fiend Beelzebub (**Queen**, "Bohemian Rhapsody", #9, 1-76, 'resurrected' to #2, 3-92), and the Lucifer connection. In "Sympathy," Jagger merely borrows the persona. His real-life Rock and Roll role has always been more imp than demon. They say he's truly a great guy, with no diabolical pretense whatsoever. Jagger's "Sympathy" takes on this crafty, cunning persona. Jagger had no pretense of being any devil, but he did devilishly prance

about on stage, like a Roman/Greek satyr with horny goat horns and cloven hooves, playing his pan-pipe in the lusty Arcadian meadows of American/British screaming groupies galore.

"Sympathy for the Devil" is a cakewalk over the hot springs of Hell. With a Jack Nicholson snicker and panther growl, Jagger plies the persona of diabolical Lucifer, prancing throughout history. Lucifer mentions he was there at the time of Jesus. Fabulously rich, he prides himself in sporting the best in taste. He commands the poor soul to whom he is speaking to treat him with courtesy and respect. Or else. Many a fire-and-brimstone preacher of the Old Evangelical Order has hollered to exorcise the Devil from our midst [Arthur Miller's play *The Crucible*, or Nathaniel Hawthorne's "Young Goodman Brown"]. When Mick Jagger paints it blacker than coal, it is not the *Run, Devil Run* of Paul McCartney's 9-99 eponymous #26 album; it is the Devil who has all of us on the run.

In the words of immortal cartoon possum **Pogo**: "We have met the enemy and he is US!" Jagger himself slides into the smarmy smock of Lucifer, playing his character with masterfully mocking demonic genius. He begins his No-Chart Rock classic in the nadir year for the U.S.A., 1968, in the aftermath of the Kennedy assassination and the roiling firestorm of Vietnam with its strident divided generations. After Jagger's Lucifer does his bit for evil, two faraway millenniums ago at desolate Golgotha and Calvary, he diabolically travels to all the scenes of 20th century 'action' [read: carnage, mayhem, and megadeath].

Lucifer stands smirking in the Bolshevik bloodbath, as the Russian czar and his family were butchered to usher in an un-Beatle, [Vladimir] **Lenin**, and his co-conspirator Josef Stalin. Called by many Americans a demonic duo, they presided over the deaths of 20 million Soviet countrymen as an infernal overture to Hitler's ghastly *blitzkrieg* [translated 'lightning warfare']. Ah, yes, Jagger's Lucifer made the scene here, too, at the *Saving Private Ryan* battlefields. Lucifer gleefully gushes about how the bodies all stank. Jagger paints it bleak, and black, for the forces of Good – in this bloodiest of all centuries (that good ol' one that brought us Rock and Roll).

Even "Sympathy for the Devil's" intro is a snarl, a piercing wildcat scream in the intense blackness. Hot, throbbing drums cast a sensuous overtone on Charlie Watts's frenzied beat. As the rhythmic tattoo pulsates and thrusts, the worldly Lucifer (in Milton's *Paradise Lost* a fallen angel) sneakily shuffles into the song. Lucifer snickers about the grisly death of Russia's Princess Anastasia in the mad-monk Rasputin czarist court, and chuckles over the odor of carnage as bulldozers dump body parts into hellish firepits. Jagger playing Lucifer twirls the twisting lyric into logical convolutions of devilishly tricky catastrophes. Keith Richard's machine-gun lead guitar spits crossfire.

Richards' guitar gushes out volcanic bombs of trebletone fireworks. Like a nuclear boom, Keith's lead hammers the stony silence – as the wildcat wails a wild "woo woo" on one ghoulish thirds note, up in the musical rafters. A thumping conga tattoo drives the crafty rhythm, and Mick's next logical gambit splashes at the unwary listener.

All so-called saints are truly sinners, chortles Lucifer,

and there's no cop who's not also a criminal. The leanest Stone then hops the Big Pond and asks 'who slew the Kennedys?' His answer is a classic of doling out sins of democratic fashion: we ALL are guilty of their murder (he snarls out jubilantly). All along, Jagger/Richard, "Sympathy" songwriters, have not painted an ebony pall over their Lucifer character. Lake Pallid Count Dracula in his best burgundy smoking jacket, Lucifer shimmers and coruscates with the iridescent crimson sheen of deepest night. Deepest passion. All along, Lucifer seems civil, courteous, sharp.

As the historical panorama promenades past us, we glimpse a more desperate undertone in Satan's archangel. He employs the best logic of Teddy Roosevelt (who was never, ever a Devil worshiper) – 'speak softly, and carry a big stick.' After he equivocates the criminal/cop Yin-Yang duality, and the sinner/saint dichotomy, he makes a request for respect. Respect. You know, Aretha Franklin/Otis Redding's opus ("Respect," #35, 9-65 [#4 R & B] for Otis; #1(2), 4-67 [#1(8) R & B] for Aretha). Everybody craves respect, even Lucifer, fallen archangel of Milton's *Paradise Lost*.

Lucifer, however, hides the massive mallet behind his back. You'd best conjure up some sympathy for me, Lucifer snarls, or I'm gonna LAY WASTE to your eternal soul!

After bouncing blithely along, with Jimi Hendrix/Bob Dylan's "Watchtower" wildcat growling in tenor harmony, Lucifer shucks off this burgundy cloak of gentility – and he is seen as the shaggy lusty fiend rampaging through primordial firelit caves of skulls, and 1000 Arabian nights of terror, passion, and intrigue. Lucifer will, indeed, paint it black!

The Christian mission, of course, is to repudiate the snares of the Devil and his luciferous lot. Many well-meaning grace-seeking pilgrims, however, fail to read Lucifer's small print, and instead of ascending **Led Zeppelin**'s Celtic Renaissance classic "Stairway to Heaven," they cruise the road's wrong fork, and end up on [#47, 1979] AC/DC's fast-lane "Highway to Hell." One disclaimer: we must not confuse either Mick or Keith with Lucifer; they were merely assuming his role to show that ghastly carnage that can lay a century to waste, when the just and noble and kind human spirit ignores the evil lurking out there, beyond the Love Fence. We gotta move on.

"Sugar and Spice" – Searchers, #44, 5-64; #2, 11-63 U.K. Sweet antidote to Devil Rock? Remember how Buddy Holly named his blockbuster "That'll Be the Day" after John Wayne's famous line in the 1955 film classic *The Searchers*? Beatles' Merseybeat pals the Searchers took it even closer than that to the Duke – they named their group. "Sugar and Spice" follows the Holly banner. The tune reconstructs Tommy Roe's "Sheila" chord pattern. Searchers' Everlyish trio is **Tony Jackson, Mike Pender**, plus **John McNally** (only drummer **Chris Curtis** rarely sang) – The Jackson Four?

"Needles and Pins" – Searchers, #13, 3-64; #1, 1-64 U.K. Hot on the Beatles' heels, and well before the Stones, the Searchers stormed America, with a song penned by 1) Cher's spouse; and 2) U.S. Representative to California: **Sonny Bono**. They look like they could be Bobby Rydell's back-up-group – with trimmed 50s Elvis-Rydell pompadours and sharp Mod two-button deep blue suits, choked with thin black ties and white shirts. The album cover reports their heights and weights, like sports/fan mags: bassman Tony Jackson, singer, age 23, height 5'9", weight 11 stone 2 (or, for quizzical Americans, 1 stone = 14 lbs, ergo 156 lbs.), hair brown, eyes grey. We don't share their fave ice cream, car model, or Dream Date. Young **Cher** does a nice "Needles and Pins" reprise on rare *Cher's Golden Greats* (Al. #195, 11-68).

Searchers' "Love Potion #9" (#3, 11-64) is a cool **Clovers**' cover [#23, 9-59] for the British **Jackson Four** (well, TONY Jackson). The Searchers' shifty repertoire and retinue took them down to America's 34th and Vine to see a gypsy about an aphrodisiac (1959's answer to Viagra) with zany repercussions. Dig it. (See Glossary – Chord Theory.)

"Bus Stop" – Hollies, #5, 7-66. In this one, and the next Hollies hit (#7, 10-68 "Stop, Stop, Stop"), the word STOP appears in 80% of all the title words. This delightful 'Bus' song wafts cherubic harmonies around a weird spot for lovers to meet – a sodden, soggy, gray British bus stop. The bright lad, however, totes an umbrella to shelter his lady love from the bedraggling onslaught of the gloomy mist. In a punchy narrative of two-word sentences (she's staying, bus leaves, love ripens, etc.) the Hollies build the sweetest of romances in this bus-stop queue (American – 'line'), plus a pew (American – 'sheltered bus stop'). So the British rain makes their love grow. Anyhow, he woos the blithe and bonny lass from June to August, and they live happily ever after. In many similar recent American bus stops, the lad and lass might by lucky not to be mugged.

"Love Potion #9" – Clovers, #23, 9-59;; #23, 12-59 R & B. **Buddy Bailey**'s R & B Clovers (NOT Coasters) from Washington D.C. stuffed a regal ring (13) of R & B hits into rock jocks' ballot boxes. First stereo hit R & R record, it covers a whole crystal ball world of spells, spiels, fortunes, and mumbo-jumbo. A Leiber-Stoller bonanza.

Armageddon section. **Armageddon**, we all know, is the biblical term for the Last Days, the fiery consummation of all that is earthly as written in *Revelations*. (See Religious Rock chapter.) Pray for surf.

"What Have They Done to the Rain?" – Searchers, #29, 1-65. FIRST FOLK ROCK SONG? Maybe. Early in 1965, the **Searchers**, before Dylan or the Stones, took a **Malvina Reynolds** song about nuclear fallout, and created one of the most beautiful harmonic Soft Rock ballads of all time.

The song floats in royal three-part majesty, building like Peter, Paul, and Mary's "Blowin' in the Wind" with three big crescendoes. The message? Stop above-ground nuclear testing NOW or kids will die (and all the 'Homer Simpsons' in all the world's nuke plants won't save us – because we're poisoning our only earth). It's never spelled out, though, and record buyers couldn't figure the message – but just loved the melody. This Searchers' Folk Rock Protest anthem was so beautiful it floundered at #29 (like the radioactive fish). Also, it BEAT BOB DYLAN to the Folk Rock arena – from England. The world had to wait, and learn the hard way, until somebody could brawnily stuff the Demon Atomic Genie back into the magic lamp. And he still keeps popping out.

The Searchers' Folk Rock Early Warning Siren did not fall on deaf ears. A young folk-singer lad, who gruffly gushed gravelly "Green Green" (#14, 6-63) for the New Christy Minstrels, fired off his own Armageddon salvo:

"Eve of Destruction" – Barry McGuire, #1(1), 8-65. Furious firestorm of debate. Breathing, groaning incarnation of the Angry Young Man. Barry's (b. '37, Oklahoma City) opening sortie blasts a bazooka at sleepy conformity; the Eastern World was now exploding.

It was. President Johnson ratcheted up the ante with the Gulf of Tonkin Incident (American ship shelled). Suddenly, a folksy Camelot world marching for peace and freedom found itself, in WWII-vet Pete Seeger's words, 'waist deep in the big muddy.' While tackling the Eastern blaze, McGuire and his booming baritone flattened all outposts of Hypocrites Anonymous, too.

Ponder all the collective hate they've got in Red China, blasted Barry, in **'D' major.** Then check out Selma, Alabama [On March 5, 2000, Dr. Martin Luther King's widow Coretta marched with Rev. Jesse Jackson and President Bill Clinton to remember the Selma violence.] "Eve of Destruction" was fierce, loud, and bold. It hit us all where it hurts – right in the heart of our hypocrisy.

Teetering tomtoms bellowed the war drum cannonade. McGuire loaded and fired. His one line about how kids [18] are old enough to be able to kill – but not yet vote – possibly earned today's 18-year-olds that precious voting right. He zaps the hypocrites who disbelieve in the concept of war, but are currently toting guns. He cites bodies now floating in the River Jordan in the Holy Land (could be 1965 – or 2002 Israel vs. Palestinian Yassir Arafat). McGuire shudders in disbelief that people miss the certain signs that Armageddon is nearly here. [Remember the Y2K frenzy before the turn of the Millennium?] McGuire's whole message darts to us, right on target, with the message of the *Bible*'s final book – *the Book of Revelations*. After Barry's monster hit, he settled down to performing Christian Contemporary Rock, an extremely important part of the total R & R panorama.

Nothing like a GREETINGS Draft Notice to wake a lad from a couch potato sleepy slumber. America was suddenly galvanized to curb the Communist menace, which Defense Secretary Robert McNamara perceived was right at our doorstep. President Lyndon Johnson, of longhorn Texan stock, did not believe in backing down. From the Sands of Iwo Jima to the shores of Tripoli, America stood at the ready to defend our cause of freedom. We ran into a crucial shortage of Allies in Vietnam among our WWII brothers in arms. France abandoned their French Indo-China colony at Dien Bien Phu in 1954, setting up a cleaved and bisected North Vietnam in Hanoi (Communist Ho Chi Minh – ruler). Down in Saigon, South Vietnam, Michigan State professor Wesley Fishel helped set up a U.S.-friendly government with Ngo Dinh Diem (1901-63) at the helm plus General Nguyen Cao Ky (b. 1930) and President Nguyen Van Thieu (b. 1923). Mid-60s America plunged into a tropical military quagmire from which it has not yet quite arisen, despite majestic tribute monuments in Washington, D.C. and Long Island.

We slid into a war involving half a million brave American men, boys, and a few women in the combat zone: 50,000 of them came home under a folded flag.

In the midst of this agonizing *Born on the 4th of July* firestorm (Tom Cruise, 1989***), the 'British Invasion' suddenly seemed a frivolous playful little wave on a schmoozy, snoozy little pond. So did bad-butt Gangsta Rap after the World Trade Center attack.

"Little Boxes" – Pete Seeger, #70, 1-64. Native New Yorker. Seeger's (b. 5-3-19) grandson toured with him in 1997. With a #2(8) "On Top of Old Smokey" big hit in the Weavers' days, and universal esteem from millions, Pete Seeger recently said to me: "I began to get along well with Rock and Roll after I got used to it, and after it blended with more socially committed lyrics like Bob Dylan and Malvina Reynolds were writing." Despite discouraging Dylan from Rock and Roll, Pete was welcomed Into the Rock Hall in 1996.

This Malvina Reynolds song crunches conformity. It's a verbal jab at Levittowns, where each little house in 1947 looked a lot like the next. (See John Cougar Mellencamp's #8, 1983 "Pink Houses"). Pete had a good point, though I still love my suburb regardless of architectural blanditude. If we're to enjoy the FREEDOM that comes with being Americans, we must shine and polish that freedom – and not look, talk, and think like zombie automatons.

The **Seekers'** lead singer is a lovely soprano, **Judith Durham** (b. 7-43), and they were originally from Australia before their England homecoming.

"I'll Never Find Another You" – Seekers, #4, 3-65. Judith's background singers, like many British stars, looked like a lean cross-country team, spattering mud and spikes to win the Wembly or Kent or Sussex Counties' Cup: Athol Guy (string bass, aha – vestiges of Old Folk), Keith Potger, and Bruce Woodley (guitars, acoustic). This three-guy baritone background soothes and smooths a band track plump with chubby bass violin notes. Seekers' insistent rocking drums (blasting the 1, the 2½, and the 3 beats) flare and flash a supersonic sound.

The message is simple, yet profound. The title says it all. They kiss off a fortune – and say they could lose or dump it, and it wouldn't really matter at all. LOVE is truly all that matters. If he loses her, or she him, though, it's instant romantic Armageddon. Tough love. Their #44 (2-67) lullaby "Morningtown Ride" is equally gorgeous and melodic.

"19th Nervous Breakdown" – Rolling Stones, #2(3), 3-66; #32, 4-66 R & B. Goofing on everything, regardless of race, color, or creed, the Stones womp emotional instability – no laughing matter. Mick's songgirl's deep-end frazzled plunge hovers in midair. Why? It's her 19th breakdown. Girl Who Cried Wolf Syndrome. Seems she's had so many death-defying leaps into the abyss that he's ready to abyss her goodbye.

With mocking and unsympathetic derision, Mick lets his feelings all hang out on "Toxic Parenting." Mom who neglected her has decided to get her million bucks back? Poor little rich girl. She blames everyone but herself.

Good Mideastern beat again, with devilish hooks. Mick tells her to stop whining, and get back to work. Blunt sells. (Don Henley/Eagles 10-94, #31 "Get Over It" tells the same message).

*The Rolling Stones (l-r: drummer **Charlie Watts**,lead singer **Mick Jagger**, lead guitarist **Keith Richard[s]**, Brian Jones's replacement **Ronnie Wood**, bassist **Bill Wyman**)*

In 1964, the Rolling Stones embarked on their first American tour. Our **Night Shift**'s venue was Lake Lansing. The cavernous old wooden resort was the Dells. A Phil Frank cartoon had piano man Bob Baldori, drummer Tom Helderman, and me decked out like *Mad* magazine characters. We'd been playing ΣAE parties and fraternities in Ann Arbor, plus seedy bar gigs and Northern Michigan dance halls. Our record simmered on the brink of release.

Our roadie Jim Whitney set up a steamy Summer Lake Lansing concert in June 1964 at this brontosaurus of an old lakeside roadhouse that held maybe 700 people [I used to hire super-tekkie Jim to plug in my guitar]. Expecting a sellout crowd, we got 'air support' from jock Gene Healy and Gentleman Jim Chase at Lansing's two rock stations, WILS and Big Jim WJIM, with spots about the Night Shift swamping the Mid-Michigan skies.

Something was happening in Detroit.

Some unheard-of British band was coming to Olympia Stadium, where #1 hockey legend **Gordie Howe** skated on thin ice for 25 years.

The **Stones**' booking baron got them a shot on **Dean Martin**'s primetime "Hollywood Palace," but they weren't exactly the Beatles yet. Nor Billy J. Kramer and the Dakotas. Nor the Searchers. They were the **Rolling Stones**, whose Buddy Holly song "Not Fade Away" was now cresting on the U.K. charts at #3 but the U.S. at #48. In America in 1964, a #3 hit in Great Britain and a dime might get you a cup of coffee. Luke- warm.

Tom Helderman: "I can't believe it. Same night! I wanted to go see THE STONES! But we gotta play the Dells gig."

Bob Baldori and I: "Don't even consider a trip to Detroit! You've got the biggest show of your life!"

Not quite. Signed as a pitcher by the Chicago White Sox, our wiry southpaw drummer (6'1", 165#) had pitched in the lower minors with crowds in the hundreds.

When the Rolling Stones arrived in Omaha during their first American tour in June 1964, the only people who met the Stones at the airport were two disgruntled six-packs of motorcycle cops, unlike the mobbed Fab Four.

The Stones shuffled into the giant Detroit, 10,000+ Olympia Stadium Hockey Arena. All their lives they'd played the Detroit/Chicago Blues of **Jimmy Reed**, John Lee Hooker, Elmore James, Howlin' Wolf, and their spiritual mentor, **Muddy Waters** – seminal Blues guitar guru who never had a Top 100 hit single or album. They expected a few Bluesmen at Olympia.

How many Rolling Stones ticketbuyers showed up at Olympia for the British group which would go down in history as the "World's Greatest Rock and Roll Band?"

Three hundred! Yep, 300!

We cranked up our own version of "Not Fade Away." The Stones' raunchier version – just out – mixed its bluesy sound into our old Holly version. Tom's tomtoms teeter-tottered between the speed of light and the speed of sound on "Wipeout."

The place went ape-kazinga. People just kept flooding in the door, with homemade I.D. and boppin' shoes. A cool breeze wafted over the little lake, and the parking lot bulged. We rocked the rafters and the surrounding area, and when the tally was over, they counted well over 500 rockin' rollickers at the Dells, Lake Lansing. 500 to 300!

Just a few miles down the pike from Olympia Stadium!

It was a magic night in Night Shift history. We'll never forget The Night the Night Shift Outrocked the ROLLING STONES!

It's been downhill ever since ... until NINE DAYS in May 2000!

* * * * * * *

What's for CUTE? In the Teddy-Bear Teen Idol years, CUTE sold billions. An inoffensive smile, fuzzy cuddlesome sweater, and a curlicue waterfall over boyish faces with dimples. **Peter Blair Noone** of Manchester, England named his fledgling teen-idol troupe after a CARTOON: Super squirrel Rocky and his moose Bullwinkle cavorted with Sherman, who metamorphosed to **'Herman'**:

"I'm Henry the VIII, I Am" – Herman's Hermits, **#1(1), 7-65.** Huge 1911, U.K. hit for Harry Champion. Peter's grandfather remembered it. The song batters the same driving verse, over and over and over!

HENRY THE VIII

The bass powers the song, as the drum sprays the R & R classic backbeat: bass drum does regular quarter notes, while snare snaps the 1½, 2 and 4 beats (Barry Whitwam). Guitarists **Derek Leckenby** (d. '94) and **Keith Hopwood** duel glitzy riffs, and Herman's happy tune hobbles along apace.

Other 1910-20s tunes to launch their **C-B-Bb-A7-D7-G7-C** chord shift or some variation are the "Charleston" (Arthur Gibbs, #1[1], 1-24) and "Ja-Da (Ja-Da Jing Jing Jing)" (Arthur Fields #4, 3-1919). Among 1890-1900s giant hit songs

---

with this same Ragtime/Jazz Age chordal flavor – in the very dawn of chord structure theory – are "Sidewalks of New York" (Dan Quinn, #1[9], 2-1895); "The Man on the Flying Trapeze" (Walter O'Keefe, #6, 1-34); "Daisy Bell," a/k/a "Bicycle Built for Two" (Dan Quinn, #1[9], 9-1893); "The Band Played On" (Dan Quinn, #1[10], 8-1895); and "After the Ball" (George J. Gaskin, #1[10], 4, 1893).

Many of these, of course, are waltzes (3/4 – see our Waltz King section), a rare time signature in Rock and Roll; Seal, however, uses it quite well in his #1(1), 6-96 "Kiss from a Rose," harnessing an ethereally-haunting minor-key melody in his Afro-British classic. Or check out Wings' Denny Laine and early Moody Blues' #1 U.K., 1-65 (#10 U.S.) "Go Now."

Herman's lyric is properly ludicrous. Girl marries eight guys, all named Henry. So he's – you guessed it – Henry the EIGHTH! Spoof on horrid king, who had Wife II beheaded (the six-fingered Anne Boleyn) for failing to produce children. [Or something. Maybe she forgot to take out the garbage.] Noone pronounces 'Henry' with three syllables and a Cockney missing 'H': "EN-ER-EE.

"Just a Little Bit Better?" – Herman's Hermits, **#7, 9-65.** Baritone Herman cornered the market on **Buddy Holly** echoes when the Beatles discovered Dylan, who bypassed Holly via Vee to NYC. Hermits feature a mountain of Holly hiccups even the Lubbock lad would envy. This is the #1 Hiccup song of the Rock Era, with more Holly hiccups per line than anything, ever. Bounces off drooly Manchester fog with happy electric optimism.

"There's a Kind of Hush" – Herman's Hermits, **#4, 2-67.** This Stephens-Reed concoction is the ultimate Audial Voyeur song of all time? The singer envisions the sweet-nothin' sounds of lovers in love. Millions of them Worldwide. Smooching. Playing kissyface. Grabbing each others' inner elbows (this is getting too steamy to go on). Nibbling earlobes.

"Wonderful World" – Herman's Hermits, **#4, 5-65.** This Sam Cooke classic goofs on the perpetual C-student syndrome [not Louis 'Satchmo' Armstrong's "(What a) Wonderful World."]. The kid grouses that he can't fathom history, biology, or other confusing school lore – but that his love for HER is crystal clear. Like **Sam Cooke**'s voice:

"Wonderful World" – Sam Cooke, **#12, 5-60; #2(2), 6-60 R & B.** Sam Cooke of Mississippi Delta town Clarksdale was a Gospel-oriented R & B Bluesman like **Ray Charles** – not like Jimmy Reed or Muddy Waters. Cooke's decade heyday (1957-66) placed 43 songs on the HOT 100. ("Wonderful World" 8th-biggest). Sam dynamically influenced the British Invasion. Cooke's tragic motel gunshot death, at the mysterious hands of a jealous husband in L.A., underscores the weltering tension which would erupt on the mean streets of Detroit (1967) and Saigon (1961-Present). "Wonderful World" is a peaceful fantasy oasis of love and hope. Snappy, punchy, profound.

"You Send Me" – Sam Cooke, #1(3), 10-57; #1(6) R & B. Epitome of smooth Gospel Soul. Toledo's Teresa Brewer's #8, 11-57 cover version couldn't supercede the original. Other Cooke-in hits? "Chain Gang" (#2, 8-60); his posthumous "Shake" (#7, 1-65); and big dance tune "Twistin' the Night Away" (#9, 2-62, with Rod Stewart double-chart cover versions: #59, 8-73 and #80, 7-87).

"Bring It on Home to Me" – Sam Cooke, #13, 6-62; #2(4) R & B. Sam's most plaintive Gospel weeper. He begs the lovely lass for her sweet affection. He promises money and jewelry. He begs for her to bring her lovin' back to him. This wonderful song is a listening adventure, well mirrored by thunderous Yorkshire 5'1" baritone Eric Burdon to Sam's Afro 'Irish' tenor: #32, 5-65, for Animals, a large charge of the British Invasion.

"Having a Party" – Sam Cooke, #17, 5-62; #4, 6-62 R & B. Sam's groovy party-animal WHAZZUP rocker padded the 'R & R Doldrums' era between Buddy and the Beatles. London-Glasgow superstar **Rod Stewart** sandpapered his super vocal way through "Having a Party" (#36, 1-94) and Sam's #9 mega-hit "Twistin' the Night Away" of 2-62. Sam's twistin' parties shadow the Good Ol' Fun Dance Days. Soul/Jazz baritone **Lou Rawls** in background. Like all archetypal Rock Hall first inductees, Cooke is still very big in Great Britain.

"Cupid" – Sam Cooke, #17, 6-61; #20 R & B. Valentine's Day Carol. Cute melody about flying Greek imp with arrows of love. Compare to **Connie Francis**' #14, 7-58 "Stupid Cupid." It's a great Sam Cooke tune about love and naivete and disillusionment, like #28, 6-59 "Only Sixteen." At 16, he's miserable. The dramatic irony? At 17, now he knows ALL about love.

"A Change is Gonna Come" – Sam Cooke, #31, 1-65; #9 R & B. Among the most heartfelt of responses to Bob Dylan's prophetic "Blowin' in the Wind," posthumous "Change" describes his humble Mississippi beginnings: born by the river, in this little shack, he meets hardships and forges a life from his upwardly-mobile Johnny B. Goode dreams. Like Elvis's searing spotlight, Cooke's fame and charisma proved no boost to his longevity. Both **Jackie Wilson** and Nolan Strong had been shot (and recovered) from jealous girlfriend/groupies' irksome ire and fury. Cooke's untimely death snapped short the career of one of Rock & Soul's greatest all-time singers. Check the original Class of 1986 in the Rock Hall of Fame:

Chuck Berry	Everly Brothers (Don & Phil)
James Brown	Buddy Holly
Ray Charles	Jerry Lee Lewis
Sam Cooke Little Richard	
Fats Domino	Elvis Presley

If there's one area in America where Afro-American people have not suffered widespread discriminiaton, it's the R & R Hall of Fame first class (54.6% Afro, 5x national average).

So far, the hermetically sealed Rock Hall envelope has not selected Herman's Hermits. Like Bobby Rydell, Frankie Avalon, Johnny Tillotson, and other teen idols, the Rock Hall has not been too kind to good-looking guys not deemed Blues legends, quintessential Rockabiliies, or major movers and shakers in songwriting and unique recording techniques. The Hall prides itself on merit (Holly, Orbison) over hype (Fabian). Only recently have women been selected. The early years of R & R were skimpy with female chart action, but the list is still embarrassingly short, starring first Queen of Soul **Aretha Franklin** (1987). The First Real Heavy Metal Group, Ray and Dave Davies and their **Kinks**, attained the Hall in 1990!

"All Day and All of the Night" – Kinks, #7, 12-64; #2, 11-64 U.K. It's a big backbeat brew of chromatic-chord cotton candy, incisive social protest, R & R comedy ('Lola'), and musical profundity. Bassman **Peter Quaife** blasted blotto bass leads of dynamic intensity. Former Rolling Stone drummer **Mike Avory** fired complex drum tacets into riffs at cheetah speed. The Kinks smacked a thudding new beat and cutting-edge chord pattern into a coolly casual song. With Ray (lead vocals, rhythm guitar) and Dave (lead guitar, vocals) Davies powering vocals, they do chromatic runs to the bIII chords. With brilliant treble thunder and amps up to 11, the Kinks fire off something fantastic that could just as easily be termed Heavy Metal, four years early.

"All Day and All of the Night" flaunts this new stop and go rhythm. It darts. Floats. Dribbles. It pivots. With their innovative zeal like the Beatles, the Kinks never stagnated. Ray (b. '44) and Dave (b. '47) Davies hail from north of London. They panned the rhythmic gold of this "Louie, Louie" type beat for three top ten tunes. Other Proto-Metal chartbusters? "You Really Got Me" #7, 9-64 and "Tired of Waiting for You" – #6, 3-65, which was tied for their biggest hit. Is the next one a Folk protest song?

"A Well-Respected Man" – Kinks, #13, 12-65. Hatchet job on hidebound British drab conformity. Like Pete Seeger and Malvina Reynolds' "Little Boxes," this satirical masterpiece balloons the bloated Babbitt stereotype of the British hierarchal class system. The Kinks mock the patrician lad's fragrant undershirt, his snobbish airs, and his carnal satyr-lusts beneath a cloak of respectability. The Kinks paint a portrait of a self-indulgent, dull, dim grey bureaucrat with no soul, no life, nothing real. The song simmers in deliberately mediocre minor-key drabness. Kinks kinkily sing in their intentionally dullest, banalest, blandest monotone to pictorialize this dumpy chump. Nifty song – reminds you of –

"It's Good News Week" – Hedgehoppers Anonymous, #48, 12-65. Certain Yankees didn't get this dark-humored one by perplexing producer **Jonathan King** ("Everyone's Gone to the Moon", #17, 9-65). With happy sicko glee, the lyric mentions how science has now discovered a way to give the 'rotting-dead' this obsession to live. Despite its preppy bounce, it foreshadows both Punk and Gothic Rock, plus Thrash Metal (Megadeth and some Metallica) in its grisly lyrical feeding frenzy. Cool tune. Later, anti-hypocrisy songs swept America.

"Games People Play" – Joe South, #12, 1-69. South-erner South (nee Souter) swamps hypocrisy, complaining about folks who don't mean what they say or say what they mean. Comic tune, in a hip *Seinfeld* sense. Joe South's major lyrical theme? RURAL EXPATRIATION. Economically, many farm folks are forced into the factory smokescapes for desperate cash.

"Don't It Make You Want to Go Home?" – Joe South, #41, 8-69; #27, 10-69 C. Perhaps one of the Top 100 R & R songs ever written. South invokes pungent imagery – some of which is now outdated, like his strawberry fields. Today, perhaps they've ripped down the old 'Passion Pit' megascreen and put up . . . a strawberry field" [See Talking Heads' "Nothing but Flowers" later]. In our town, they blew up the old Patchogue Drive-In (sweet *Star Wars* and *King Kong* and mosquitoey-brew memories) to build up some UA Monsterplex with 13 screens. South's other images bring home nostalgic Country reverie, like Les Paul's "Mockin' Bird Hill." We'll check out the connection between **Joe South** (who primed his tunesmith pump via Kinks, Dylan, and Johnny Cash) and the later **Kinks**, who much later used his sentimental style for their biggest and most anachronistic hit. In this song, South laments the riverside drag strip, former dairy farm of Grandma South. Joe's bird savvy invokes Country saint Hank Williams "I'm So Lonesome I Could Cry" (#8, 2-66, B.J. Thomas) and his lonely whippoorwill. Then he scarfs up a Greyhound ticket (one way!) to return back home, 'freaking out' over the mini-mall monstrosity. Just when he goes down to the ol' fishin' hole, figuratively, BOP, a dead carp smacks him across the nose. **John Denver**, 1943-97, does the same thing on his #2, '71 South-inspired classic "Take me Home, Country Roads", but at least the country is still there. Besides penning Dakotan country star **Lynn Anderson**'s #3, 11-70 "Rose Garden," South did this one for **Gene Pitney**'s greatest imitator:

"Down in the Boondocks" – Billy Joe Royal, #9, 7-65. Frankie Valli's "Dawn" Theme: Rich girl. Daddy owns the Georgian town mill. Lover Billy toils in the mill. Aspires to big-buck riches. Move from shack? Mansion and happily-ever after? Echoes **Joey Powers**' #10, '63 "Midnight Mary" plot. Stunning Irish tenor. Chalypso flavor.

"Come Dancing" – Kinks, #6, 5-83. Ray Davies' sentimental masterpiece. He recalls his big sister going to dances at the 'Pally' (probably Palladium, BIG dance-hall yesteryear name). With Joe South's gripping heart-zinging images, Davies paints his canvas on a tableau of **"Ab major"**, one of the prettiest keys you can use. He lavishes a lush, velveteen organ sound over the whole merry-go-round dash back in time. Lyric? The little guy watches his sister in the moonlight, as she kisses some anonymous date good night. She comes into the house and has a row (Amer. 'argument') with their 'Mum' about being out after (good grief, Charlie Brown) midnight.

Kid grows up. Memory lingers. The old Pally. The old glorious dances. The old deep purple garden wall. His big sister smooching some penguin-suited guy in the misty mystic moonlight. He dreams of meeting gorgeous girls, and carrying on with them. It's a slice of pubescent longing, a tapestry of stardust, etched with golden dreams, of moonlit arbors and long lost kisses in dreamy shadows.

BAM – they knock down the Pally. He grows up, plays in a band, and WOOMP, there it is. The wrecking ball. CRASH. Pile of old bricks and gruff cop on the corner. Song pulls no punches. On the day the ravenous bull-dozers smash the old Pally, all of his childhood perishes. Besides losing his old pal the Pally, "Come Dancing" strikes a somber personal chord, at the real-life loss of their sister. For the world, however, it symbolizes even more grief about bygone and nevermore teenage dreams.

"Come Dancing" is a danse macabre on a magic carpet to Limbo. That Palladium symbolizes for Ray Davies all of the youthful passions now gone to seed in the wake of long long years gone by, and wretched silence and finality. Elegant **Glenn Miller** twilights of romance and adventure get superceded by the clamor and clangor of raunchy Heavy Metal, git-down-and-dirty Disco, discordant Grunge, and in-yer-face Rap. Actually, Ray was no stranger himself to sensational song:

"Lola" – Kinks, #9, 9-70. Ingenue lad sallies forth, lookin' for love in bizarre bar. A taste-tempting treat of broad-sided guitar chords beckons the greenhorn kid to a place down in London's Old Soho (red light district, like "House of Rising Sun"). Here, wrote Davies, you guzzle 'champagne' which sneakily resembles Coca Cola; (London strip clubs water drinks and substitute cheapo soda pop for zingier spirits). The Coca Cola folks of Atlanta were not amused, and made Ray re-press the master and reprint the record as "CHERRY cola," adding another risqué dimension to an already strange song. With double entendre zingers, the bubbling straight chap (oozing with hilarious naivete) picks up the husky-voiced 'LOLA.'

Buoyed by boozy honeylust, the lad is taken aback by Lola's forwardness. "She" flumps her mitt on his knees. "She" invites him home. Something is very fishy here. Though the straight-arrow kid has no beef against those of alternate lifestyle orientation, and through the tragic scourge of A.I.D.S. hadn't yet walloped the do-it-if-it-feels-good Disco 70s, something about Lola tells the lad "she" is not his type. For a first encounter of the sensual kind, he is looking for a girl more, well, feminine. Naturally, we all discover to his mortified surprise that the 'girl' he attracts turns out to be a drag queen. Drunk and bamboozled in a 'muddled-up' world (but still chaste), the lad bumbles home, chugs Alka-Seltzer, and sobers up. "Lola," however, could never have eluded them and been a hit in the drowsy 50s era of Frisbees, hula hoops, and cherry malts. The Kinks' "Lola" is a great reason for Rock and Roll and the rest of the universe not to take itself too seriously. In 2-93, transvestite entertainer **RuPaul** enjoyed a #45 hit, "Supermodel."

Let's bounce back to 'Girls' Group' Soul:

A soulful NYC singer/songwriter, **Doris Troy** (nee Higginson), who sang with **Pink Floyd** on their all-time longest album (*Dark Side of the Moon*, 741 weeks), got the **Hollies'** American career off to a rocky start on the Beatles' heels in late 1964. All this music interconnects. About the Hollies . . . let's do two here:

"Just One Look" – Doris Troy, #10, 6-63; #3, 6-63 R & B. Doris had the marvelous ability to do a double voice – easy and smooth on the low notes, and Hard-Rock hard and tough and gutsy and intense on the high ones. **Hollies** took "Just One Look" to #98, 5-64 (#2, 3-64 U.K.).

"Look Through Any Window" – Hollies, #32, 12-65; #4, 9-65. U.K. Maxed-out treble guitar. Ever been drifting along on the road, wondering who all those people are in other cars? Why are they going wherever they're going? What empassions and empowers them? Who do they love? Why are they tailgating you? The answers to similar questions may not be found in this remarkable song. It just glows with a 'groovy beat' and melody and harmony vocal.

HOLLYCHORDS, for FUN & PROFIT:

Here's the chord connection: the **Beatles** and **Hollies** like the chromatic bVII chord and Polynesian bVI. If you happen to be a Rolling Stone or Kink, however, you'll probably choose the Mideastern chromatic shift: blast the bIII chord, as the Davieses do in "All Day and All of the Night."

Polynesian Shift	C – Ab – Bb – C
(Beatles/DCV/Hollies)	I – bVI – bVII – I
Mideastern Shift	C – Eb – C
(Rolling Stones/Kinks)	I – bIII – I

"Stop, Stop, Stop" – Hollies, #7, 10-66. This one is the Hollies' straight Lola song. With an exotic effect of a bizarre trilling instrument (like Beach Boys theremin on "Good Vibrations"), the naïve Hollie attends a strip joint. Obviously , the gal he's ogling IS a fully-formed female, and it is plain for the swooning lad to decipher that she is, indeed, a mammal. He gets dizzy, swooning woozily as her sexy serpentine body coils and twirls. "Stop3" has

him imploring the bar to cease the sensuous music, for it's driving him up a tree of desire. Or a Tree of Knowledge. Hints of Eden and apples and serpents run rife here. Great song. A study in titillating, tantalizing temptation.

Hollies' original line-up featured **Allan Clarke** (b. '42) lead vocals; lead guitar, **Tony Hicks**; **Eric Haydock**, bass (b. '43); **Dan Rathbone**, drums. The key name that sprang out of the amorphous early Hollies is **Graham Nash** of Blackpool (b. '42), later of (David) **Crosby**, (Stephen) **Stills**, and later (Neil) **Young** in 1968 to "make records that say something." In 1966-68, the Hollies took the bronze medal for British popularity, outsizing the hits of everyone but the Beatles and Stones:

"Jennifer Eccles" – Hollies, #41, 3-68. Sweet music-box tune, as Morrison/Joplin/Hendrix strutted in the wings. Atlantan **Tommy Roe** kept on keepin' up with the upbeat ungloomy tunes:

"Hooray for Hazel" – Tommy Roe, #6, 9-66. Roe headlined for the Beatles, #4 act on his 1963 British tour. "Hazel" hammered snappy snare, and Tommy's tremendous tenor on jealousy theme.

"Dottie, I Like It" – Tommy Roe, #114, 2-68. "Dottie" and her Jerry Allison-style drum blur couldn't hit the heights, due to a lackluster hype and a fickle public to whom "Peggy Sue" was a distant memory of nevermore 50s dreams. Roe had early luck with **Robin Luke** cover "Susie Darlin'" (#35, 10-62), his gruffer bluesy "Everybody" (#3, 10-63), and debutante doll "Sweet Pea" (#8, 6-66). I spoke with Tommy in some 1990 smoky chic Techno nightclub in the West Village, Little Darlings. Over sneering smoky faces practicing their SUPERBAD STARE, the smiling Atlantan towered (at 5'11"). His happy R & R goodtime tunes cascade down the corridors of time as he gracefully ages. Very, very slowly.

"Long Cool Woman (in a Black Dress)" – Hollies, #2(2), 6-72. The Hollies' biggest hit starred a new constellation of Hollies with **Mikael Rickfors'** lead vocal in a Swamp Rock Creedence Clearwater vein. Brit Gangsta Rock.

Here is a list of groups, via the Modean R & R Research and Wombat Arranging and Fribble Association, which have never ever – not even once – had a Top #1 song on the U.S. HOT 100 charts, during the Rock Era from 1955 to 1999. First the group you thought had 5 #1 songs from 1955-93. Second, their highest hit and top peak position on Joel Whitburn's *Billboard* tabulations:

MAJOR ARTISTS WHO NEVER HIT #1 THROUGH 1999

Allman Brothers, "Ramblin' Man," #2, 8-73.
Backstreet Boys, "Quit Playin' Games," #2(2), 6-97.
Baha Men, "Who Let the Dogs Out?" #40, 7-2000.
Hank Ballard & Midnighters, "Let's Go³," #6, 9-60.
Pat Benatar, "We Belong," #5, 10-84.
Big Bopper (J.P. Richardson), "Chantilly Lace," #6, 8-58.
Black Crowes, "Hard to Handle," #26, 6-91.
Black Sabbath, "Iron Man," #52, 1-72.
Blues Traveler, "Run-Around," #8, 3-95.
Laura Branigan, "Gloria," #2(3), 7-82.
James Brown – [that's right!] "I Got You (I Feel Good)," #3, 11-65.
Jimmy Buffett, "Margaritaville," #8, 4-77.
Jerry Butler, "Only the Strong Survive," #4, 3-69.
Freddy 'Boom Boom' Cannon, "Palisades Park," #3, 5-62.
Mariah Carey, Ha ha, I was spoofin' – 8 of her first 10 went to #1. Just checking to see if you were reading the small print.

Eric Carmen, "All by Myself," #2(3), 8-84.
The Cars, "Drive," #3, 8-84.
Johnny Cash, "A Boy Named Sue," #2(3), 7-69.
Chad & Jeremy, "A Summer Song," #7, 8-64.
Jimmy Clanton, "Just a Dream," #4, 7-58.
Classics IV, "Traces," #2, 2-69.
Patsy Cline, "Crazy," #9, 10-61, [#2(2) Country].
Nat King Cole (after '55), "Ramblin' Rose," #2(2), 8-62.
Alice Cooper, "School is Out," #7, 6-72.
Elvis Costello, "Veronica," #19, 4-89.

Creedence Clearwater Revival, "Proud Mary," #2(3), 1-69; "Bad Moon Rising," #2(1), 5-69; "Travelin' Band" #2(2), 1-70; and "Lookin' Out My Back Door," #2(1), 8-70.

Crosby, Stills, and Nash, "Just a Song Before I Go," #7, 5-77.

Cyrkle, "Red Rubber Ball," #2(1), 5-66.
Deep Purple, "Hush," #4, 8-68.
Depeche Mode, "Enjoy the Silence," #8, 4-90.
Diamonds, "Little Darlin'," #2(8), 3-57.

Dion & the Belmonts, "Where Or When," #3, 12-59; Dion DiMucci cut "Runaround Sue" with the **Del-Satins** and listed it as "Dion," #1(2), 9-61.

D.J. Jazzy Jeff & the Fresh Prince, "Summertime," #4, 6-91.
DMX, "Money, Power, and Respect," #17, 4-98.
Dr. Hook, "Sexy Eyes," #5, 2-80.
Antoine 'Fats' Domino, "Blueberry Hill," #2(3), 10-56, stuck

behind Elvis's "Love Me Tender," #1(5), 10-56, President Bill 'Elvis' Clinton's favorite song.

Bob Dylan (yep), "Like a Rolling Stone," #2(2), 7-65.
Duane Eddy & His Twangy Guitar, "Because They're Young," #4, 5-60.
Dave Edmunds, "I Hear You Knocking," #4, 12-70.
Electric Light Orchestra (ELO), "Don't Bring Me Down," #4, 8-79.
Emerson, Lake, & Palmer, "From the Beginning," #39, 8-72.
En Vogue, "My Lovin' (You're Never Gonna Get It)," #2(3), 3-92. "Don't Let Go (Love)," 11-96.
Fabian (Forte), "Tiger," #3, 6-59.
Fabulous Thunderbirds, "Tuff Enough," #10, 4-86.
Jose Feliciano, "Light My Fire," #3, 7-68 (#1, Doors, 6-67).
Flamingos, "I Only Have Eyes for You," #11, 6-59.
Eddie Floyd, "Bring It on Home to Me," #17, 10-68.
Dan Fogelberg, "Longer," #2(2), 12-79.
Foghat, "Slow Ride," #20, 12-75.
Foreigner, "Waiting for a Girl Like You," #2(10), 10-81. All-time record for #2 song. ("I Want to Know What Love Is" LATER hit #1).
Fortunes, "You've Got Your Troubles," #7, 8-65.
Foundations, "Build Me Up, Buttercup," #3, 1-69 (hardly ever confused with Fortunes, Falcons, and Fiestas).
Samantha Fox, "Naughty Girls (Need Love Too)," #3, 2-88.
Fugees, "Killing Me Softly," #2(3A), 3-96.
Glenn Frey (solo), "The Heat is On," #2, 12-84.
Art Garfunkel (solo), "All I Know," #9, 9-73.
Gerry & the Pacemakers, "Don't Let the Sun Catch You Crying," #4, 5-64.

Johnny Gill, "Rub You the Right Way," #3, 5-90.
Go-Gos, "We Got the Beat," #2(3), 1-82.
Grass Roots, "Midnight Confessions," #5, 8-68.
Grateful Dead, "A Touch of Grey," #9, 7-87.
Great White, "Once Bitten Twice Shy," #5, 5-89.
Sammy Hagar (solo, pre Van Halen), "Your Love is Driving Me Crazy," #13, 12-82.
M.C. Hammer, "Have You Seen Her," #2(2), 9-90.
Corey Hart, "Never Surrender," #3, 6-85.
Jimi Hendrix (alas, true), "All Along the Watchtower," #20, 9-68.
Don Henley (solo), "Sometimes Love Just Ain't Enough," with Patty Smyth, and vice versa, #2(6), 8-92.

Faith Hill, "Breathe," #2(5+), 11-99.

Hollies, "Long Cool Woman (in a Black Dress)," #2(2), 6-72.

Buddy Holly, well, not really. *Billboard* rerouted some old tabulations (Jukebox, Airplay, Record Sales), where "That'll Be the Day" was listed #3, 8-57, on ancient *Top 100* which preceded HOT 100. It was always a

Best-Seller #1. When the smoke had cleared, Buddy Holly finally got his official #1, over 25 years after 'The Day the Music Died' 2-3-59.

Hootie and the Blowfish, "Only Wanna Be with You," #6, 8-95.

Englebert Humperdinck II, "Release Me," #4, 4-67. (EH the First was a German opera composer in the 19th century.)

Impressions, with Curtis Mayfield, "It's All Right," #4, 9-63.

Isley Brothers, "It's Your Thing," #2, 3-69 ("Shout" only #47, 3-59 and #94, 3-62).

Jermaine Jackson, "Let's Get Serious," #9, 3-80.

Etta James, "Tell Mama," #23, 11-67.

Jay and the Americans, "Come a Little Bit Closer," #3, 9-64.

Jethro Tull, "Living in the Past," #11, 11-72.

Jewel, "You Were Meant for Me," #2(2), 11-96.

Howard Jones, "No One Is to Blame," #4, 4-86.

Tom Jones, "She's a Lady," #2, 2-71.

Journey, "Open Arms," #2(6), 1-82.

Kansas, "Dust in the Wind," #6, 1-78.

Kenny G., "Songbird," #4, 8-87.

Chaka Khan, "I Fell for You," #3, 9-84.

B.B. King, "The Thrill is Gone," #15, 12-69.

Ben E. King, "Stand By Me," #4, 5-61.

King Curtis, "Soul Twist," #17, 2-62. Great sax player who played on Buddy Holly's last records.

Kingsmen, "Louie, Louie," #2(6), 11-63.

Kinks, "Tired of Waiting for You," #6, 3-65; "Come Dancing," #6, 5-83.

Kiss, "Beth," #7, 9-76.

Lenny Kravitz, "It Ain't Over Till It's Over," #2, 6-91.

Frankie Laine, "Moonlight Gambler," #3, 12-56 (Pre-1955 biggees).

Led Zeppelin, "Whole Lotta Love," #4, 11-69. Wow.

Lettermen, "When I Fall in Love," #7, 11-61.

Donna Lewis, "I Love You Always Forever," #2(9), 6-96.

Jerry Lee Lewis, "Great Balls of Fire," #2(4), 11-57. Not the 'Killer' of HOT 100 charts, with Elvis's "Jailhouse Rock" (#1[7]) in the way.

Little Anthony & the Imperials, "Tears on My Pillow," #4, 8-58.

Little Richard (Penniman), HUH? "Long Tall Sally," #6, 4 57.

Little River Band, "Reminiscing," #3, 7-78.

LL Cool J, "Hey Lover" #3, 11-96.

Lobo, "I'd Love You to Want Me," #2(2), 9-72.

Loggins & Messina, "Your Mama Don't Dance," #4, 11-72.

Trini Lopez, "If I Had a Hammer," #3, 7-63.

Frankie Lymon & Teenagers, "Why Do Fools Fall in Love?" #6, 2-56.

Lynyrd Skynyrd, "Sweet Home Alabama," #8, 7-64.

Melissa Manchester, "You Should Hear How She Talks About You," #5, 5-82.

Martha & the Vandellas, "Dancing in the Street," #2(2), 8-64.

Dave Matthews Band, "Crash into Me," #19A, 1-97; "Crush," #75, 2-99.

Clyde McPhatter, "A Lover's Question," #6, 10-58.

Brian McKnight, "Back at One," #2(6), 8-99.

Sarah McLachlan, "Adia"/"Angel," #3, 5-98.

Megadeth, "Symphony of Destruction," #71, 10-92.

Metallica, "Enter Sandman," #16, 8-91.

Roger Miller, "King of the Road," #4, 1-65.

Joni Mitchell, "Help Me," #7, 3-74.

Eddie Money, "Take Me Home Tonight," with Ronnie Spector of Ronettes, who never had a #1 either, #4, 8-86.

Moody Blues, "Nights in White Satin," #2(2), 8-72.

Van Morrison, "Domino," #9, 11-70.

Mötley Crüe, "Dr. Feelgood," #6, 9-89.

Willie Nelson, "Always on My Mind," #5, 3-82.

Aaron Neville, "Tell It Like It is," #2, 12-66; "Don't Know Much," #2(2), 9-89, 23 years later – bizarre.

Night Ranger, "Sister Christian," #5, 3-84.

Stevie Nicks (solo), "Stop Draggin My Heart Around," #3, 7-81, with Tom Petty and Heartbreakers.

Nine Days, "Absolutely (Story of a Girl)," #6, 4-2000 (but #1 on Casey Kasem's *American Top 40* and #1A, 4-2000).

Nirvana, "Smells Like Teen Spirit," #6, 12-91.

Tom Petty and the Heartbreakers, "Stop Draggin' My Heart Around," with Stevie Nicks, #3, 7-81.

Pearl Jam, "Last Kiss," #2(1), 5-99.

Wilson Pickett, "Land of 1000 Dances," #6, 7-66.

Pink Floyd, (OK, OK, they had only one): "Another Brick in the Wall," #1(1), 80 (next biggest: #13, 5-73 "Money").

Gene Pitney, "Only Love Can Break a Heart," #2(1), 9-62.

PM Dawn, "I'd Die Without You," #3, 9-92.

Pointer Sisters, "Slow Hand," #2(3), 5-81.

Elvis Presley. Are you kidding? Just checking to see if you're still reading this nifty list. 18 #1's, second only to Beatles' 20.

Pretenders, "Back on the Chain Gang," #5, 12-82.

Gary Puckett and the Union Gap, "Young Girl," #2(3), 3-68; "Lady Willpower," #2(2), 6-68.

Quarterflash, "Harden My Heart," #3, 10-81.

Queensryche, "Silent Lucidity," #9, 3-91.

Bonnie Raitt, "Something to Talk About," #4, 7-91.

Ramones, "Rockaway Beach," #66, 12-77.

Rare Earth, "Get Ready," #4, 3-70.

Jimmy Reed, "Honest I Do," #32, 9-57.

Della Reese, "Don't You Know," #2(1), 9-59.

R.E.M., "Losing My Religion," #4, 4-91.

LeAnn Rimes, "How Do I Live?" #2(4), 6-97.

Smokey Robinson (solo), "Being with You," #2(3), 2-81.

Ronettes, "Be My Baby," #2(3), 8-63.

Rush, "New World Man," #21, 9-82.

Bobby Rydell, "Wild One," #2, 2-60.

Mitch Ryder/Detroit Wheels, "Devil with a Blue Dress On/Good Golly Miss Molly," #4, 10-66.

Salt-N-Pepa, "Shoop," #4, 10-93.

Sam & Dave, "Soul Man," #2(3), 9-67.

Sam the Sham and the Pharaohs, "Wooly Bully," #2(2), 4-65; and "Little Red Riding Hood," #2(2), 6-66.

Carlos Santana, "Black Magic Woman," #4, 11-70. [Until 1999. Then the 53-year-old guitarist cut loose with two mega-monsters: #1(12), 7-99 "Smooth" and "Maria, Maria," #1(11+), 2000].

Boz Scaggs, "Lowdown," #3, 7-76.

Jack Scott, "My True Love," #3, 6-58; "Burning Bridges," #3, 4-60.

Seals and Crofts, "Summer Breeze, #6, 9-72; "Get Closer," #6, 4-76.

Shai, "If I Ever Fall in Love," #2(8), 10-92.

DeeDee Sharp, "Mashed Potato Time," #2(2), 3-62.

Skyliners, "Since I Don't Have You," #12, 2-59.

Dusty Springfield, "What Have I Done to Deserve This?" #2(2), 12-87.

Snoop Doggy Dog, "Nuthin 'But a 'G' Thang," #2(1), 1-93.

Bruce Springsteen, "Dancin' in the Dark," #2(4), 5-84.

Steely Dan, "Rikki Don't Lose That Number," #4, 5-74.

Steppenwolf, "Born to Be Wild," #2(3), 7-68.

Cat Stevens, "Morning Has Broken," #6, 4-72.

Stylistics, "You Make Me Feel Brand New," #2(2), 3-74.

Sweet, "Little Willie," #3, 1-73.

Talking Heads, "Burning Down the House," #9, 7-83.

Joe Tex, "I Gotcha," #2(2), 1-72.

Thompson Twins, "Hold Me Now," #3, 2-84.

Johnny Tillotson, "Poetry in Motion," #2, 10-60.

Ike & Tina Turner (not Tina solo), "Proud Mary," #4, 1-71.

Shania Twain, "You're Still the One," #2(9), 2-98 (ties record for 2nd for weeks at #2).

Luther Vandross, "Power of Love/Love Power," #4, 4-91.

Sarah Vaughan, "Make Yourself Comfortable," #6, 11-54.

Billy Vaughn, "Melody of Love," #2(1), 12-54.

Ventures, "Walk – Don't Run," #2, 7-60.

Village People, "Y.M.C.A.," #2(2), 10-78.

Gene Vincent & His Blue Caps, "Be-Bop-A-Lula," #7, 6-56.

Junior Walker & the All-Stars, "Shotgun," #4, 2-13-65; "What Does It Take to Win Your Love?" #4, 5-69.

War, "The Cisco Kid," #2(2), 3-73.

Warrant, "Heaven," #2(2), 7-89.

Jody Watley, "Looking for a New Love," #2(4), 3-87.

Who, "I Can See for Miles," #9, 10-67.

Jackie Wilson, "Night," #4, 3-60.

Weird Al Yankovic, "Eat It," #12, 3-84.

Xscape, "Just Kickin' It," #2(1), 9-93.

Yardbirds, "For Your Love," #6, 5-65.

Timi Yuro, "Hurt," #4, 7-61.

Frank Zappa, "Valley Girl," #32, 7-82, with daughter Moon Zappa.

Zombies, "She's Not There," #2, 10-64.

ZZ Top, "Legs," #8, 5-84; "Sleeping Bag," #8, 10-85.

Thus endeth the list of non-#1 artists. A lot of them surprised me. How about you? The record for the longest time at #2 without hitting #1 goes to **Lou Gramm**'s Anglo-American **Foreigner**, and their "Waiting for a Girl Like You" #2(10), 10-81. For #2 at 9 weeks see Donna Lewis/Shania Twain.

Let us return again to the Mikael & Hollies' wailing about this 'Long Cool Woman.' I can't figure out all the words in "Long Cool Woman," but I still love the song with its Creedence overdrive. Here are other lyrics I can't decipher (These are what they sound like to me, nonsense or no nonsense):

"Please don't get my gate be undersea," –
"Come Go with Me," Dell Vikings, #4, 2-57.

"Lucille, you know too your cuckold's wheel," –
"Lucille," Little Richard, #21, 3-57;
#1(2) R & B.

"I felt her nose, ahh, in her ear," –
"Louie, Louie," Kingsmen, #2(6), 11-63.

"Stompin' ack the lower catfish Snarf," –
"Green River," Creedence Clearwater Revial,
#2, 8-69.

"A Hound Dog," CROCKING' alla dime." –
"Hound Dog," Elvis Presley, #1(11), 5-56.

"I'm real good aaaiiiee Ed, I'm fakin' real cool Fred." –
"I Get Around," Beach Boys, #1(2), 5-64.

Jimi excuses himself to "kiss this guy." –
"Purple Haze", Jimi Hendrix, #65, 8-67.

Since Jimi Hendrix's tastes in romance ran exclusively to female smoochers, the last one is most absurd. You can play "Purple Haze," the World's Most Popular Ever #65 song, over and over and over, and the great guitar wizard is still seems to be inadvertently smacking a kiss on some stunned, amazed kazoo player's noggin.

"The Air That I Breathe" – Hollies, #6, 4-74. "The Air That I Breathe" is this breathtaking seraphic harmonic super song. The Hollies regard the sweet lulling afterglow of love. He needs no cigarettes, or lights, or sound. Just the air he breathes – and to love her. **Hollies** named themselves after **Buddy Holly**.

Ever have a hassle naming your band? Creative combos for years have grouched and scrapped over band names. Among great names our band the Night Shift rejected were:

Genghis & the Tartars – for the Wayne State football team I briefly played on, until the coach insisted I get a crewcut, so I huffily quit, figuring it was time to Rock and Roll.

Lenny & the Thundertones – only two problems: A) There was already a local band by that name, led by Lenny Drake, who could have taught Eric Clapton Speed Lead Guitar; and B) We didn't have a guy named 'Lenny,' and the only thunder from our dinky amps came when Danny Beaubien dropped it on my toe.

The Beetles – in 1962, I was looking for a name something like my heroes the Crickets, and as an early geology major, I had too many rocks (and Rock and Roll) in my head to think up a really clever English major pun like "Beatles."

Four Guys with Towels Around Their Necks – Larry Glazer and I loved that one. The rest of the band was aghast, trembling for our dignity. Besides, it created a sartorial dilemma: how do you keep the stupid towels around your neck on a screaming solo?

Wayne Fontana and the Mindbenders got their name from the name of a horror film. **Eric Burdon** and the **Animals** sang a very depressing song about industrial life after "House of the Rising Sun":

"We Gotta Get Out of This Place" – Animals, #13, 8-65. Number thirteen. Burdon checks out his father's premature gray hair and his 9 o'clock exhausted bedtime from slavin' in the sordid sweatshop. Rock and Roll is a liberator? Many bands have used it to slide suavely out of slavish drudgery. Anyhow, the 5'1" Burdon blasts a deep jangling sepulchral bass line with his ultramacho voice. Rising into gruff baritone range, he excoriates the abominable conditions people must suffer in order to get a little bread on the grubby table. In the grim gaslight glow. Generation X? It began here. Despair, anger? Existential nihilism? Burdon vamps minor chords to bloat his misery, rising to the hopeful major on his stinging cry of desperation: "WE GOTTA GET OUT OF THIS PLACE"! He desperately seeks a better life for his girl and himself.

"San Franciscan Nights" – Animals, #9, 8-67. So Burdon defects. He joins the love-in flower power generation of the Grateful Dead. He thinks the nights in San Francisco are warm. He is inspired by **Mamas and Papas'** pal **Scott McKenzie** (Philip Blondheim) of Jacksonville, Florida, where the nights are really steamy.

"San Francisco (Be Sure to Wear a Flower in Your Hair)" – Scott McKenzie, #4, 5-67. Psychedelic anthem. Counterculture consciousness was coming to fruition, with peace, love, harmony, and a little dope. This 'Flower Power' anthem contains one of the prettiest melodies ever written. Idyllic harmonic flow. Angel-food chords.

"I Left My Heart in San Francisco" – Tony Bennett, #19, 8-62. Bennett's incredible Jazz timing and enunciation loft this marvelous ballad to Tony's mezzanine to Heaven. Tiny cable cars vault part way to the twinkling stars. Bennett never disdained R & R, like some hoity-toity unemployed ex-crooners. "In the Middle of an Island," #9, 8-57, his biggest Rock Era hit, thumps a nice easy-rock Chalypso beat. When Bennett's superb Italian Jazz cabaret tenor hit the blue and the windy sea, it's a musical masterpiece moment, whether or not we're writing a book on Rock and Roll.

Donovan Leitch (b. 1946, Maryhill, Scotland) tossed out a few Flower Power tunes:

"Sunshine Superman" – Donovan, #1(1), 7-66. Donovan describes in 12-Bar Blues the rare sunshine which o'erleaped his window today. Donovan skirts chord-progression boredom routine with well-placed expectant sevenths and slides. Whuzza slide? Well, say you're rocking along on a 'D' major, avoiding your bottom low "E" string: suddenly you slide down to a quick 'C#' on your top three strings, slurring swiftly back to your root tonic chord **D** (I).

"Sunshine Superman" is powered by the lead guitar pyrotechnics of **Jimmy Page**, previewing his **Led Zeppelin** guitar guru phase. Donovan's initial releases on Hickory yielded some Folk-Rock artsy tunes, like the antiwar "Universal Soldier" (#53, 9-65 and #45 for **Glen Campbell**, temporary **Beach Boy**). Donovan's follow-up, "Mellow Yellow" #2(3) in 11-66, features **Paul McCartney** in the whispered response; Donovan's "Hurdy Gurdy Man" experiments with internal vocal punctuation through phasers, tremolo, and mixing magic. "Jennifer

Juniper" #26, 3-68 is an "Everyday" Hollyecho music box classic. His last top ten trip chauffeured him, like Ringo in the *Yellow Submarine* "Octopus's Garden", to the bottom of the ocean to "Atlantis" (#7, 4-69). Donovan still dabbles in R & R, and is the father of actress Ione Skye.

Psst – meet Aussie Stephen Wright, guitarist George Young of Scotland, and drummer 'Snowy' Fleet – the **Easybeats.**

"Friday on My Mind" – Easybeats, #16, 3-67. Dutch bass player and guitarist (Dick Diamonde and Harry Vanda). One unique smash hit. The rhythm guitar twangs the bass line, doubling the kicky beat; meanwhile, no drum at all intercedes – it just hangs fire, waiting in the wings for its ultimate snare smash-up on the raucous 2 & 4 backbeats. Wright haggles the hassle of WORK. Weeklong drudgery. He grumps and grouses about the 9-to-5 struggle. You get the idea he's in an office, not a coal mine. The Easybeats' perfect panacea for bureaucratic bullbarf? A romantic rendezvous. To build their climax, the Easybeats spare the background voices like We Five's "You Were on My Mind." When they all finally dart into the song, after a few Bee Gees' style chipper chirps, Snowy Fleet rips the rhythm on drums of fire.

"Downtown" – Petula Clark, 1(2), 12-64. Pet's (b. 1932) biggest hit. Pulses with electric inner-city optimism. Like the Easybeats' ecstatic cityscape, Downtown London for perky Petula symbolizes a colorful winking neon glow, a rich toasty cozy homeland of friendly people, shimmering shopping sprees, yummy restaurant delights, and a bottomless purse quaking with quivering quid. MONEY, LOVE and LAUGHTER. Downtown. One ecstatic song, like her very caring #5, 6-67 "Don't Sleep in the Subway!"

A tale of two towns – Toronto and Detroit. Toronto's rep is clean and cosmopolitan. Sophisticated. A cultural mecca of civilized Canadian charm. Detroit, four hours down Highway 401, is a big factory town. Martin Luther King's 50s Dream WAS Detroit, with the greatest financial 1966 opportunities for Afro-Americans in the U.S.A. Smoky, steely, tough, and brawling, Detroit was nevertheless one of those Blues meccas (see John Lee Hooker) and Chuck Berry "Promised Lands." Until Vietnam split our nation in half:

"Black Day in July" – Gordon Lightfoot, NC, 1967. Remember Lightfoot's marvelous tale of the grisly demise of a lake freighter on stormy Lake Superior ("The Wreck of the Edmund Fitzgerald," #2[2], 8-76)? Lightfoot, Folk/Rock troubadour from Orillia, Ontario, seems the logical dispassionate guy to sing a song about the burning of Detroit in the ghastly 1967 riots. Windsor, south of the Motor City, got the best Canadian view (and whiff) of the fiery catastrophe. With no air play in Detroit, "Black Day in July" is a not-too-subtle Canadian's bewilderment at his volatile Yankee cousin's racial melting pot – boiling over.

We were living in our 85% Afro neighborhood on Detroit's Near West Side, and endured the blazing inferno of the worst civil insurrection ever seen in the United States. Strolling with my dog Snarf, I heard an assault rifle shatter my neighbor's window in the glow of sporadic gunfire and flames. Snarf and I dove into the dinky shrubbery, shivering in the 90° heat till the assassins slithered away.

Beginning July 26, 1967, the Motor City suffered blasting and firebombing and shrill sirens and bullet barrages. An eerie orange horizon glowed with dancing tiger claws of flame. Motown Records, home of an Afro dream of harmony and integration, just groaned. The "Motown Years" were 1962-66. This is why. National Guard tanks, with scared kids just like me riding shotgun, rumbled down our backstreets. Afro-owned businesses smeared "SOUL BROTHER" on their windows, to avoid the ubiquitous TORCH. (We pondered painting "Soul Dog" on our black dog we'd gotten from our African-American 11-year-old puppy-peddling neighbor and friend Keith). Looting ran rampant. Color TV's appeared in every home for only 50 mysterious dollars per new set. **Gordon Lightfoot**, from his lofty Canadian perch, watched in baffled sympathy as the old American Dream torched itself. Scores officially perished. Hundreds unofficially. The entire commercial enterprise of inner-city Detroit erupted on the funeral pyre of masochistic madness.

That new group, the **Doors**, resonated their own Ray Manzarek-driven funeral-pyre danse macabre: "Light My Fire" (#1[3], 6-67). As **Jim Morrison** rock-crooned about funeral pyres, I watched my friendly idealism go up in smoke and down in flames. This Day They Drove Old Detroit Down marked the catastrophic end to Lyndon Johnson's Great Society. The cataclysm sundered forever Dr. Martin Luther King's Dream of a peaceful and harmonious racial Shangri-La or Bali Ha'i (this side of Hawaii, where it still works). Musically, Gord delivers a swashbuckling rocker with a lilt of Chalypso. Lightfoot sums up the city's Armageddon, and the befuddled white suburban dweller's reaction – he sits there calmly over his cup of tea. This song runs totally counter to **Pet Clark**'s ingenue debutante "Downtown," and takes a harder dimmer view of these mean flaming streets. By 1967, Motown's harmonic dreams of a crimeless town were in shambles. Woodward Avenue was no longer the boulevard of golden dreams. From harmonic to SARDONIC spells the gruesome urban nightmare of Motown 1967; listen to Lightfoot, and hear the genesis of an entire Gangsta Rap mean-streets subculture. It's a tough culture, where, as Jerry Butler eerily predicted, "Only the Strong Survive" (#4, 3-69; #1 R & B).

One area which might have an understanding of the utter horrors of deep racial strife is South Africa. Everybody hollers along with our next blockbuster entry, but few are aware that lead singer Michael Lubowitz (Manfred), like college icon **Dave Matthews** comes from Johannesburg:

"Do Wah Diddy Diddy" – Manfred Mann, #1(2), 9-64. Right. You recall its thunderous chorus. Lubowitz booms the *tacet a cappella*. His honey was suddenly there, simply strolling down the street. THEN WE ALL HOLLER THE TITLE!!!

"Mighty Quinn (Quinn the Eskimo)" – Manfred Mann, #10, 3-68. With Quinns for in-laws from Motown to Tokyo to Texas, I was impressed with Mann's macho tale of this Eskimo or Inuit not named Ootek of Aklavik, but after some Irish guy. **Bob Dylan**'s quixotic and cryptic lyric describes an Eskimo, who magnetizes friendly pigeons. Folk Rock in both Britain and America meant the infusion of profound lyrics by the Hibbing Bard. Pigeons, too.

"The Pied Piper" – Crispian St. Peters, #4, 6-66. Real name? Peter Smith. "I'm going to be bigger than Elvis," Crispian bragged. Born in Swanley, Kent, England, Peter/Crispian also traveled to South Africa. First this song made it. Nice quavering baritone, with trembles of Elvis's tremulous Super Mumble-Murmur. One great line tells of folks' quests after heaven – and it turns out it's right there at home. **Ruth Etting** sang happiness can lie under your own eyes . . . "Back in Your Own Back Yard." Crispian St. Peters, on dueling octaves, erupted for one BIG ELVIS song, squirming the HOT SPOT. Then, in supernova fashion, he vanished back into the big starry sky.

Like Andy Warhol put it, another one with his "fifteen minutes in the spotlight." Bigger than Elvis, Crispian? For one brief shining moment, maybe he was Elvis. Sort of.

"I'm Telling You Now" – Freddie and the Dreamers, #1(2), 3-65; #2, 8-63 U.K. Rock and Roll offers a great excuse to quit your job as a milkman. Besides, if you already look like Buddy Holly (or Elvis Costello), how can you lose? **Freddie Garrity** of Metropolitan Manchester Milk Associates found the mighty [**Derek**] **Quinn** to play lead guitar. They did great cover songs and a dance. Their #36, 3-65 "I Understand" is a counterpoint (2 tunes at once) cover of doo-whop **G-Clefs'** #9, 1961, cover of crooners **Four Tunes'** 1954 #6 song. They did their own silly dance, "Do the Freddie" (#18, 4,65), cavorting around like jumping jacks or puppets. With Holly echo and vibes and looks, Freddie played the Pagliacci spectacled clown to Buddy's image, with mixed reviews. He was a lot more dignified then **Tiny Tim**. A beautiful song – "I'm Telling You Now." A brisk and frisky cache of golden guitars plunges along the melodic IV and bVII chords. Love. The reason for the song.

"Tip Toe Through the Tulips" – Tiny Tim, #17, 5-68. In the zany *Laugh-In* glow, New York's unusual looking Herbert Khaury (1930-96) twittered with his teeny-tiny ukulele on this #1(10), 9-29 Nick Lucas song. Tongue-in-cheek, both Tiny and Freddie wept all the way to the bank.

"She's Not There" – Zombies, #2(1), 10-64. Filed toward the alphabet's finale, Rock's Jazz keyboard wizard of way-out beats, **Rod Argent**, teamed up with singer **Colin Blumstone**. Guitar man Peter Atkinson, drummer Hugh Grundy, and bassman Chris White spin with Argent some convoluted syncopated polyrhythms which suggest 70s Jazz Rock. "Tell Her No" #6, 1-65, turns the beat around, and "Time of the Season" (#3, 2-69) blurts out the understated romantic disaster between the sexes: men often crave women for their shapely figures and gorgeous faces, whereas, quip the cynics, women often chase men for the size of the wallets. During the "Time of the Season," the Zombies jazzily brag about their riches and sugardaddy expertise.

The **Yardbirds** organized in Surrey, England in 1963. They balked at mediocrity, going for the Blues Gold with scorching lead guitar wildfire. Despite guitar incursions by **Duane Eddy**'s Twangy Guitar, the **Ventures**, the **Fireballs**, **Johnny and the Hurricanes**, and Long Island's #1, 1959 guitar instrumental "Sleepwalk" with **Santo and Johnny**, the guitar functioned as a very upfront background instrument in Rock's formative toddlerhood, to the HUMAN VOICE. Singer **Keith Relf** was tragically electrocuted in 1976. Sam Samwell-Smith played a fine bass-keyboards role. Jim McCarty is the drummer. Here is a list of the Yardbirds' lead guitarists:

1) **Anthony Topham**, replaced in 1963.
2) **Eric Clapton**, 1963-65, who later gravitated to Cream and glory. Some say his is the World's Greatest Lead Guitarist.
3) **Jeff Beck**, 1965. Two teeny-tiny hits, "Goo Goo Barabajagal [Love is Hot]" #38, 8-69 and "People Get Ready," #48, 6-85, are no measure of Beck's amazing axe rep. Stunning soloist.
4) **Jimmy Page**, 1966 and beyond. Virtuoso guitar maestro for the unquenchably versatile Led Zeppelin. Page dominated the 70s with his fast-fret fire and dedication to Rock and Roll.

We must not forget, too, that via 'Jimmy James and His Blue Flames,' America too had gone guitar mad, with **Jimi Hendrix** taking lead guitar to a new dimension. **Johnny Rivers** slung his Chuck Berry song "Memphis" at California's Whiskey A-Go-Go to stem the British Wave (#2, 5-64), and played his own guitar as well as Chuck Berry did aeons before. The voice never really left the music scene.

"For Your Love" – Yardbirds, 5-65. Powered by a R & R cavalcade of **Jeff Beck** and **Eric Clapton**, the Yardbirds stormed out of the blocks with a new BLUES center to British Rock and Roll. Their follow-up was "Heart Full of Soul," nabbing number nine three months later. For a third hit, they risked Blues echoes of **Muddy Waters**' #5 (R & B only) '55 "Mannish Boy," also revered as Bo Diddley classic "I'm a Man" (#17, 10-65).

When the Yardbirds finished their act, the vocalist would never again have ELVIS'S center SPOTLIGHT in the old way. Elvis's guitarist **Scotty Moore** might chuckle, because now the gorgeous golden groupies were watching the lead guitarist – often ignoring the singer.

"Detroit City" – Tom Jones, #27, 3-67. After his debut "It's Not Unusual" (#10, 4-65; #26, 5-65 R & B), the leather-lunged Rock balladeer popped this nostalgia piece into the soulful soup. Pontypridd, South Wales, is a tough coal-mining area where Vegas opera-voiced Welsh tenor rockers are few and far between. Two of the top ten names in America and Britain are distinctively Welsh – Williams and Jones. **Tom Jones Woodward**, (b. '40, Pontypridd, Wales), was a husky, middle-sized muscular kid who got his first 'nose jobs' in a brawl or two, Tom brandishes the King's similar studly appeal. He has played the venues from Vegas to Venus. Though noted for his too-tight pants almost exploding on Vegas stages, to the delight of slot-machine matrons, Jones deserves credit for his Operatic Rock tenor, and soulful power vocals.

Jones spins this Mel Tillis-penned Country dynasty yarn about Rural Expatriation. White Soul. "Detroit City" laments the assembly line worker's killer quandary – making cars and bars in a blur of remorse and regret (see Mellencamp or [Joe] South). Hopping a hobo freight train to the Motor City, this white auto worker, too, feels disenfranchised. Isolated. Yearning for cotton fields and balmy breezes. A Rappish spoken soliloquy cites his desperation. Having left Detroit (and forgotten to turn out the lights), we often feel a reverse twinge of homesickness for the brawly factories, smoke-stained streets, and the hapless Detroit Tigers . . . when we lie on this Long Island beach, smiling at sailboats, the twinge disappears.

"Without Love" – Tom Jones, #5, 12-69; #41, 2-70 R & B. Like his prior "I'll Never Fall in Love Again" (not Dionne Warwick's song), of course this Jones weeper lavishes too many tears. Kneeling in televangelistic paroxysm, Jones writhes in tight-trousered sorrow as he sings of long lost love, while lades' hotel-room keys spatter the stage around him. **Tom Jones** has a helluva voice, up there with Opera Rockers Elvis, Jackie Wilson, or Roy Orbison. His biggest hit? "She's a Lady" (#2, 2-71; #42, 3-71 R & B). Most importantly, this blue-eyed Welsh Britrock Soul boomer crossed over into both R & B and Country charts with his inimitable Country Soul style: "Say You'll Stay Until Tomorrow" (#15, 1-77 and #1[1], 12-76 C).

"A Summer Song" – Chad & Jeremy, #7, 8-64. Chad Stuart and **Jeremy Clyde** (b. '43 & '44) met at London's Central School of Speech and Drama. Chad mostly sings and writes; Jeremy sings and plays guitar, sitar, and banjo. Baritone harmonies interweave a tapestry of fleeting summery images, like lead-in #21 "Yesterday's Gone." "Willow Weep for Me" treads on tricky standards chord pattern of #2, 1932 Paul Whiteman hit(#15, 11-64). The

Mersey River does not drain a Mississippi's worth of worldwaters. It just slurps up the sopping drizzle that overhangs the English industrial corridor, below old seaside strands at Blackpool. The Ferry Across the Mersey runs from Birkenhead to Liverpool.

"Ferry Cross the Mersey" – Gerry & the Pacemakers, #6, 2-65; #8, 1-65 U.K. **Gerry Marsden**'s big smile brought sunshine to Liverpool. One great chunk of Chamber of Commerce FUNTIME, this frolicsome ferry ride. Gerry Marsden and his intrepid Pacemakers deliver the song sincerely. Sure, the 51° status drizzle dampens your summer outing a tad, but with this kind of smiling camaraderie, who cares? Gerry is one of the nicest guys in showbiz, taking his jovial, jocular Oldies Caravan on the road for four decades and beyond. Lester Bangs was a brilliant writer, but his mammoth vocabulary must have been in a bad mood (see 2000 rock flick *Almost Famous****) when he blindsided poor undeserving Gerry: *"[The Pacemakers] looked . . . as twerpy as humanly possible. You hear Mersey-sound garbage at its pinnacle: innocuous but raucous, a clatter."* Too many brilliant words are wasted, in rock criticism, tearing down good and imaginative musicians who deserve a pat on the back – not petty insults. Then Bangs, trying to say something nasty, proves he's not so cuttingly critical as he thinks – with this curmudgeonly compliment: *"Like many (perhaps most) of the Liverpool groups, the Pacemakers had no funk, no soul, no danger, and talent that could be measured in dollops, but they were having the time of their lives, and it was infectious and that was all that mattered anyway."*

Like Freddy Boom Boom Cannon, Gerry and the Pacemakers exemplify what Rock and Roll is all about – HAVING FUN! Gerry did. Never did he say, "Look at ME, I am the Great Gerry Marsden." With humility, he simply went out and delivered his delightful enthusiastic hits.

This sloshing ferry careens over a friendly harbor to a cozy destination – chums at the grog shop, dinner at Mum's, a date with one groovy chick. These Merseybeaters and ferry flotilla shipmates are native Liverpudlians: piano man **Les Maguire** (b. 1941); **Les Chadwick** (b. '43) bass; and older bro **Freddie Marsden** (b. '40) on drums. **Gerry** (b. 24 September '42) **Marsden** strummed guitar, and did a lot of solo vocalizing, from resonant baritone to first tenor ("How Do You Do It?" #9, 7-64). Wallasey's Maguire actually had to ferry cross the Mersey to make gigs.

This minor-key tune swoops and rolls along, making the world safe for democracy. Gerry sings it with a hopeful and happy lilt and fine voice. It's people like Gerry Marsden that make Anglo-America great today. Sorry, Bangs.

"How Do You Do It?" – Gerry & the Pacemakers, #9, 7-64; #1, 3-63 U.K. Big bouncy intro tune, with U.S. year time lag? "How Do You Do It" is vintage Holly. Impish with its risque double entendre title, "How Do You Do It" escalated Gerry's Pacemakers from Liverpool obscurity to instant fame. For a short time in the U.K., they eclipsed their townmates the Beatles.

"How Do You Do It" is 100% FUN Rock and Roll. His

sprightly major triad chords bounce like Bobby Vee's "Rubber Ball." His happy crisp tenor zings off swirling blue stars. "How Do You Do It" sparkles with simplicity and danceable electric rhythm. The Pacemakers make Rock and Roll fun again, like "I Like It" (#17, 10-64; #1, 6-63, U.K.).

"Don't Let the Sun Catch You Crying" – Gerry & the Pacemakers, #4, 5-64; #6, 4-64 U.K. also #112, 12-70 U.S.A. Gerry's first, and biggest U.S. hit. Catching the Lonnie Donegan skiffle fever, brother **Freddie Marsden** and Gerry skipped around to skiffle groups (the **Mars Bars**). They honed their fast rhythm riffs and even banjo trills. After building expertise at fast skiffly strokes, it turned out weirdly that their first Stateside hit, this one, was a minor key romantic ballad at a molasses tempo. Gerry offers advice to the lovelorn in "Don't Let the Sun Catch You Crying," ignoring all the British meteorology cynics who quip, "WHAT SUN?"

Scarfing a little tremolo from Brian Poole and the Tremeloes, Gerry offers some hope and glory and a winsome smile to his friend. She is presumably a girl who may be bouncing her beleaguered affections his sympathetic way.

When this high-north seaport hunkers down in its tunnel of darkness, in the gloomy-weather Christmas/Chanukah season of Winter Solstice, sometimes the only sunshine for weeks in December was . . . **Gerry**.

"You'll Never Walk Alone" – Gerry & the Pacemakers, #48, 6-65; Also #1, 10-63 and 1985 U.K. In the wake of the tragic Bradford Stadium collapse, generous Gerry donated all his 1985 profits to victims' families. Yep, the one from *Carousel*. Gerry and Crew placed their first three British releases at #1 U.K.: "How Do You Do It?"; "I Like It" (#17, 9-64), and this reflective crescendo song. This one has become a famous soccer anthem today in Britain.

"I'll Be There" – Gerry & the Pacemakers, #14, 12-64. After their first two #1's were penned by Mitch Murray, Gerry discovered Big Apple master songsmith **Bobby Darin** for "I'll Be There." Gerry follows a different melody entirely from the other sweetly melodic "I'll Be There" (Michael Jackson & Other Four of Jackson Five, #1[5], 9-70 plus Mariah Carey #1[2], 5-92).

VOCAL CHORDS

"I'll Be There" builds its lovely empathetic mood through Gerry's liberal use of the III mediant major chord, a **B** major in Key of 'G', rising to sweet sub-dominant IV **C** chord. It's these little tricks of the songwriter's trade that make for song favorites. We take the smooth Chalypso-type mood, the singing strings, and the soaring chord leaps, and the total sound is profound.

"I'll Be There" is a friend of mine. Not a bosom buddy or anything, because only people (and dogs, and some cats, and an aardvark in the London Battersea Park Zoo) can be true friends, but "I'll Be There" is an old pal of mine. You can retire to your solitary room, flip the old needle onto "I'll Be There," and think back to super tender moments and bygone romance. Or current romance. Those zingy III chords enchant me, and Gerry's curling voice reminds us all that music is a place in our hearts.

Gerry Marsden made it as just one of the guys. The Gerry & the Pacemakers' *Greatest Hits* album wasn't huge [#44, 5-65]. Two other albums trucked on up to #29 & #13. For this fifth one, Gerry showed his humility. Gerry's groovy *Greatest Hits* aggregation shows his face at about the actual size of a dime, on the far left of a 12"x12" album, smiling very, very humbly. Though the Beatles are friends and neighbors of Gerry in Liverpool, we can learn a lot from their divergent approaches. Each worked. The **Beatles** went on to become the biggest band in the history of the world. Gerry went on to spearhead oldies galas. Indeed, his 1985 collaboration of showbiz compadres on "You'll Never Walk Alone," made #1 in the U.K. billed anonymously as the 'Crowd'. It's in the mode of selfless Long Island troubadour **Harry Chapin** [#1, 7-74 "Cat's in the Cradle," about absentee fatherism]. Selfless Marsden did it as a benefit for disaster victims at the Bradford City Football Club, donating ALL the songs' proceeds to victims' families (and the taxman, who gobbled too much of it). Gerry is that kinda guy.

If you can be like Gerry, loving your music in the best Holly tradition, you can be a star. It does not matter how many records you sell! Like American **Freddy Cannon**, who with the Belmonts did a spectacular #81, 1981 revival "Let's Put the Fun Back in Rock and Roll," Gerry and the Pacemakers love their music and share that love with their loyal lifetime fans.

Their songs become our friends. They sing about the most important thing in the world – LOVE.

In 1776, Great Britain temporarily lost the middle part of North America. In 1964, they gained it back.

America's Golden Age of Rock

19

The rush of Beatlemania took America by surprise. April 15, 1964: the Beatles had fourteen singles in the American Hot 100. All at once [Elvis had nine]. All-Beatle top 5: 1) "Can't Buy Me Love," 2) "Twist and Shout" [#17, 6-62, Isley Brothers], 3) "She Loves You," 4) "I Want to Hold Your Hand," and 5) "Please, Please Me." Astounding record(s)! Never before equaled. Or since. After such a surprise British Invasion, some of the American counterattack came from **Phil Spector** who first earned top honors as a Record PRODUCER, with his Before and After Beatle hits:

"Be My Baby" – Ronettes, #2(2), 9-63; #4 R & B. Epitomizes Spector's Wall of Sound. Other producers tossed out song after song, whipping session guitar twangers in and out of the studio like butterbeans on Piggly Wiggly shelves. Master of OVERDUBBING, Spector sculpted multi-layered productions for months, spinning dials with the precision of a neurosurgeon. **Ronnie Spector** (Veronica Bennett, b. 1945) sings a petulant lead. She purrs, sensuously. Her come-hither style floats wooingly above sister Estelle Bennett Vann and cousin Nedra Ross. Later Ronnie would marry Phil (1968-74).

In classic oldie "Be My Baby," what you don't hear is what you get. The music stops. No sound – save a fingerpop or two. Suddenly, swoopingly, the whole kit and kaboodle EXPLODES. Everyone gushes "BE MY BABY!" A Rock and Soul masterpiece. It's the super silence, though, that sells. The GHOST notes – that aren't there. Did Phil find this chord cache of gold anywhere? Maybe. First, the **Orlons**. Perhaps back further **Joe Jones**.

"South Street" – Orlons, #3, 2-63; #4, 3-63 R & B. Philly R & B quartet fronted by **Rosetta Hightower**. "South Street" follows 2nd hit #4, 10-62 "Don't Hang Up" and debut "Wah Watusi," #23, 8-62, for tall debs. Gender-integrated crew with bass Steve Caldwell.

"Down at Papa Joe's" – Dixiebelles, #9, 9-63; #9 R & B. Shirley Thomas and her Memphis Dixieland Soul trio harmonize princessly about his neon night spot in New Orleans' French Quarter. Dixieland chords:
C – B – Bb – A^7 – D^7 – G^7 – C
Perhaps they got it from Joe Jones:

"California Sun" – Joe Jones, #89, 4-61; NC, R & B. Remember Joe's (b. 1926) gravelly baritone comic tune "You Talk Too Much" (#3, 9-60)? The New Orleans archetypal piano player loved this ancient chord shift. Valet for Blues legend **B.B. King**, Jones also first wrote the only Soul Semi-Surf Song, "California Sun." Jones did it in 'F' originally, blasting dual dueling saxes (alto and tenor) before he ran down the **F – E – Eb – D7 – G7 – C7 – F** corridor. Nice hotcha pizzazz Crescent City R & B. Differs from:

"California Sun" – Rivieras, #5, 1-64. These South Bend, Indiana, yearners jam on this every-guy grass-skirt fantasy. After recording this perennial spring Surf Rock hit, **Marty Fortson** joined the Marines; Manager **Billy Lee Dobslaw** toured with the group and sang lead. A super 'Eb' organ powers the rump-kicking rhythmic wail. Buddy Holly's last gig? The SURF BALLROOM, of Clear Lake, Iowa, a block from choppy Clear Lake (1mile or so across). Surfboards are nil and zilch.

Before retuning once more to the Wall of Sound of yesteryore, another key California Sound tune is this one. Massive, rhino-rampaging speed machines, milled in Motown, screamed to high Heaven on the grease-groaning drag strips of the San Fernando Valley. This tune hails from NASCAR nexus Nashville, Tennessee. It stars lead singer **Bucky Wilkin** (b. '46, Tulsa, OK), one of **Bobby 'Boris' Pickett**'s ghoulish Crypt-Kickers from our family favorite Halloween carol "The Monster Mash" (#1, 1962):

"G.T.O." – Ronny and the Daytonas, #4, 8-64. Stars the Pontiac G.T.O. Gran Turisimo Obbligato, (of European touring/racing circuit and the Grand Prix). Three 'deuces' (3 double-barrel carburetors). The WA-WAH part chimes shrill falsetto. Recoils on the High 'A' note. In the braggadocio era, this macho talk suited the gridiron, the dragstrip, or the dance. The Ronettes, Marvelettes, and Velvelettes (#45, 10-64 "Needle in a Haystack") joined Johnnie Richardson ("Over the Mountain")'s **Jaynetts**:

"Sally, Go 'Round the Roses" – Jaynetts, #2(2), 8-63; #4, 9-63 R & B. Eerie Ring Around the Rosie R & B twinge;

like the mediaeval nursery rhyme, the ashes-ashes-all-fall-down part implied that the Black Plague (killed ¼ of Europe) could be staved off by some whirligig-ring of danse macabre dervishes with roses in their hair (previews of flower children to come).

Phil Spector loosened his monopoly on Girls' Group action. Spector righteously electrified these blue-eyed Soul brothers:

"You've Lost That Lovin' Feeling" – Righteous Brothers [once the Paramours], #1(2), 12-64; #3, 1-65 R & B. Bobby Hatfield (b. '40, Beaver Dam, Wisconsin) is the blond guy with the swooning Irish tenor. **Bill Medley** (b. '40, Santa Ana, California) sings baritone. "Lovin' Feelin'" laments good love gone bad. Blue-eyed Soul 'Brother' belongs in that shadowy Shannon-Orbison-Jackie Wilson domain of Greatest Singers Ever.

"You've Lost That Lovin' Feelin'" dissects a broken romance. She no longer feels the same towards him, and he can pick up the bad vibes in her body language. Playing off opposing octaves, Hatfield and Medley deliver a one-two punch of passion and power, as they implore the lass to return the lovin' feelin'. Their spiraling-away "Gone . . ." leaves the lulled listener in the same blue funk the Brothers Righteous portray. Spiraling down the long years, "Lovin' Feelin'" at one point became the most-played oldie of all time (1977). Their #1(3), 3-66 "(You're My) Soul and Inspiration" uses the same Spector stardust and flexed vocals of "Lovin' Feelin'," the legendary Spector Sound-Wall. Just what is a WALL OF SOUND?

Phil's recording career began with a #1(3) **Teddy Bears** song named for his father's tombstone epitaph: "To Know Him Is to Love Him" (9-58). Phil sang his own baritone, below Carol Connors and Marshall Leib. Soon Phil busted out into production from his teenage (b. 1940, too) beginner's luck. He fired off Swedish-tenor **Ray Peterson**'s wonderama of spectacular sound: #25, 5-59 "The Wonder of You." "Graveyard Rock" balladeer Ray, of "Tell Laura I Love Her" (#7, 6-60), debuted on this song of romantic sorrow. How did Spector do it? Spector nursed his full sound with overwhelming precision. He'd add horns. Dump horns. Drag in cellos, oboes, cowbells, harps, gourds. He'd mix a flügelhorn. He'd overdub, overdub, overdub. With magic legerdemain, he'd avoid the 'overmodulation' bugaboos in the studio, where records came out way too fuzzy. He'd use the best new 8 or 16-track machines and wring every precious note.

"Little Latin Lupe Lu" – Righteous Brothers, #49, 5-63; NC, R & B. Booming along with toasty a cappella tacets, the upbeat debut describes a sweet little señorita of Latino heritage who knows every 60 Fun-Dance Era song in the book: Watusi, Mashed Potato, Twist, whatever. Dynamite harmonies. Outstanding beat.

"(I've Had) the Time of My Life" – Bill Medley and Jennifer Warnes, #1(1), 9-87. The movie *Dirty Dancing**** didn't hurt record sales. Super duet, anchored by Medley's mellifluous soulful savvy.

"Unchained Melody" – [Bobby Hatfield of] Righteous Brothers, #4, 7-56; #13, 8-90, also cassette-only #19, 10-90; #6, 8-65 R & B. This bewitching song lavishes power and glory. **Al Hibbler** (1915-2001) took "Unchained Melody" to #3, in 1955, and was trumped by bandleader **Les Baxter** [#1(2), 4-55]. In 1955, Alex North/Hyzarek penned the tune for the obscure Elroy 'Crazylegs' Hirsch flick *Unchained*. **Duke Ellington** (celebrated in Stevie Wonder's "Sir Duke" #1, '77) featured a fine baritone singer, **Al Hibbler,** whose blindness the legendary bandleader shielded from the audience through elaborate stage machinations. Bobby Hatfield's "Unchained Melody" ticks at 69 rock-steady beats a minute, but we can't keep the **Eb** chord a secret any longer.

As we float down this enchanted river, on the strength of **Bobby Hatfield**'s towering tenor, we drop from the big Sub-Dominant IV **F** chord one step down to a very ethereal, very striking **Eb Major** chord. For this Vocal **BRIDGE**, we stray from the song's regular **Streetcorner [C–Am–F–G7]** chord pattern, where we switch chords every measure. Though most music fans don't know just WHY they love this love song more than all the other love songs, I'd be willing to bet it's that stunning **THREE MAJOR MEDIANT (III) chord**. It pounces like a snow leopard upon Bobby's shimmering *melismas* and tremulous tenor tones. As all those lonesome rivers flow into the mighty sea, these semi-sacred chords embrace the airwaves where they angelically float. The result? Music is just a purple twilight curtain or two away from Heaven. (See Glossary/Chord Theory).

When you glide up to the bridge, the song floats with the angels. I picture lonely rivers flowing to some sub-arctic sea vividly, an almost-sensual combining of all the flowing world-waters. A mystic vision. I visualize some majestic moonlit mountain mystique, with wilderness rivers like Canada's MacKenzie or the Yukon-Klondike, on their gushing silversplash westward trek to Kuskokwim and the mighty Pacific in a wild Alaskan torrent of glory – 'peopled' only by grizzly bears and salmon the size of Gramps's Winnebago.

Where do you visualize this unchained river? One of the great glories of music is that you can furnish your own mental images of rivers and thunderbolts and meadows and sweet kisses in stardust gazebos or rickety rowboats. Rock and Roll and its cousin, the big-beat ballad, give each of us a unique vision for each of the songs we love (unless re-fashioned by *MTV*'s video images).

You may remember "Unchained Melody" as the theme song from the spooky romance/thriller *Ghost* (1990***), starring Patrick Swayze, Demi Moore, and Whoopi Goldberg. Great songs take on new meanings for generations through movies. To each listener, each memorable song has a slightly different and very unique meaning. For a half century, this gorgeous love song has anchored the Top Ten Tunes of millions – it may be starring on your own marquee. The Righteous Brothers were eleccted to Rock's Hall of Fame in 2003.

Nowhere in the star-spangled lyric do the actual words 'Unchained Melody' appear.

UNCHAINED II

Now about that pregnant **Eb** chord we lost.

F – G – F – Eb

[Here, the 'lonely river' goes to the sea, the sea.]
This one solitary chord shift (into the jazzy chromatics [bIII] realm of the musical scale), probably sold about 20% of the records. This Mideastern bIII shift mocks a Polynesian bVI one. How? The **Eb**, is in the Key of 'C' off the sub-dominant IV **F**.

We love many other items in Bobby's "Unchained Melody": His crescendo genius; his 16th-note melisma hooks on the top notes, his gruffer dramatic treatment the second time around. Righteous Brothers followed with biggest hit, #1(3), 3-66 "(You're My) Soul and Inspiration," and "He" (#18, 6-66; NC, R & B). Plus a gonzo #5, 12-65 "Unchained Melody" echo "Ebb Tide," (Frank Chacksfield, #2, '53), and N.C. "You'll Never Walk Alone." Splitting from 1968-74, they reunited for their tour of "Rock and Roll Heaven" (#3, 5-74), a tribute to bygone 60s superstars like **Jim Morrison** and **Bobby Darin.**

"Devil with a Blue Dress On & Good Golly Miss Molly" – Mitch Ryder and the Detroit Wheels, #4, 10-66. 100% Pure Rock and Roll. Ryder's Polish Hamtramck is a clean but sooty smokestack enclave town next to Bill Haley/Jackie Wilson's Highland Park (population 30,000 each). The two little towns nestle in the underbelly of Detroit. By Hamtramck, Blessed Sacrament Cathedral oversees a conservative Slavic Catholic neighborhood. Heart-of-gold Edith Bunker ladies scrub nicotine-yellow smoked sidewalks. Beefy men guzzle duck soup (blood soup) in shot and beer softball-team sports bars. Squat kids, choking in the shrill sodium-light glow of the Ford Highland Park and Chrysler plants, grow up with Johnny B. Goode dreams to become rock stars – and get outta this smoky place. To a hi-ranch in Roseville, Warren, or St. Clair Shores. Maybe someday, Union Lake. Or Eminem's **Slim Shady** Sterling Heights. **Mitch Ryder** is part of the white Pre-Heavy Metal R & R Detroit Explosion of the mid 60s.

Raised on Soul music, white **Mitch Ryder** (William Levise, b. '45) sang in a black quartet until dubbed 'Billy Lee & the **Rivieras**,' Mitch had a #17 hit on the Righteous Brothers' soulful "Little Latin Lupe Lu" himself in 1966, proving again that Soul was not related to pigmentation. In the 1966 *Rock Revolution*, I wrote "As **Ray Charles** and **Stevie Wonder** would agree, true Soul involves a careful use of 16th-notes, syncopation, and volume control . . . but the essence of Soul lies in the sincere musical expression."

Mitch's dynamic 2-song medley combines classic Blues with a raucous lyric about this character's ultra-passionate proclivities. Mitch bellows and yells and screams. Some sad day, I fear, I will hear this one on an elevator, c/o the mavens of Muzak.

"Molly" hit #10, 2-58 for **Little Richard**. "Devil," more obscure, hit #125 in 1964 on **Shorty Long**'s original (he did #8, 6-68 "Here Comes the Judge" and #97, 9-66 "Function at the Junction."

"Sock It to Me, Baby" – Mitch Ryder and the Detroit Wheels, #6, 2-67. Who was that last major leaguer to win 30 games in a season? Mitch Ryder's Detroit Wheels, and his spiffy New Year's paper whistle provided THIS theme song for the "SOCK IT TO 'EM, TIGERS" World Champ Tigers of 1968. Swaggering Tiger pitcher Denny McLain won 31 glorious games the only time in the last 65+ years (with help from Al Kaline and Willie Horton on an integrated champ team). Soulsmiths like Mitch and the Righteous Brothers took their style from obvious R & B legends.

"Tell It Like It Is" – Aaron Neville, #2(1), 12-66. Original Mr. Grace Note. Neville nudges notes. His lofty Irish tenor skirts syllables. He's a symphony of speed work (#2[2], 9-89, "Don't Know Much," with lovely **Linda Ronstadt**).

Three very important women in R & R bolstered the American backlash – **Lesley Gore, Cher,** and **Mama Cass.**

"It's My Party" – Lesley Gore, #1(2), 5-63; #1(3) R & B. Lesley Gore pioneered the Cool Teen sound so popular in the 2000+ **Britney Spears/Christina Aguilera/Jessica Simpson** Era. The NYC strawberry blonde (b. '46) celebrated her 17th with this debut blockbuster. With her everybody's-pal voice and perky poodle, she sold millions. Teen disaster scenario? Boyfriend Johnny ducks out of the party with best-friend Judy. Lesley bounces back from the jilt and the bank. Her follow-up? [It's] "Judy's Turn to Cry" – #5, 7-63; #10, 8-63 R & B. In this repentant retort, humble Johnny returns. Then he punches out some other ogre. Everyone, except the ogre, lives happily ever after. Lesley's crisp soprano uses very sophisticated Jazz progressions.

Life magazine lamented the day in 1965, when Joan Baez and seven folk singers at the Big Sur Festival tried to embrace rock music [finally] with a Beatle number, they failed. Why? "Musicologists marvel . . . that they had to abandon their efforts because it was too complicated melodically and harmonically to be learned." Lesley Gore, however, championed Women's Rock far beyond crying at teenage parties. She set out to revamp the whole male-female role concept on her #2(3), 1-64 "You Don't Own Me." Gore declared the guy she dated shouldn't think of her as a possession, a trophy, a shiny bauble to dangle at friends' parties.

"I Got You Babe" – Sonny & Cher, #1(3), 7-65; #19, 8-65 R & B. Rockin' couple? **Sonny Bono** (1935-1998) and **Cher Lapierre** (b. '46, California). Sonny's #10, 8-65 "Laugh at Me" defends against snickers from boring tweed execs who sneered at his bearskin vest, orange and purple gondolier shirt, wide-wail corduroy Kelly green pants, Dutch Boy haircut, and blue fur shoes. Sonny hit big in music, TV variety shows, city government

(Mayor, Palm Springs) and the halls of Congress (U.S. Representative, California). "I Got You Babe" runs rife through **Bill Murray**'s hilarious flick *Ground Hog Day*. Sonny rode an OK baritone, a bad marriage, and a lack of respect to superstardom. Zingy wing-it tune. "I Got You Babe" covers tough love, and spending all the money before it's earned. Sonny met an untimely death at 62 in 1998 when he hit a tree in a Lake Tahoe ski accident. At age 19, I lived just below his mountain on the Lake Tahoe beach with fraternity brothers, and we washed his dishes in a gambling casino. [I hitchhiked back to Detroit with 16¢ in my pocket]. The big message of "I Got You Babe" is this: only LOVE really matters? Love will conquer all.

"The Beat Goes On" – Sonny & Cher, #6, 1-67. Were more prophetic words ever sung? Sonny's rumbling bass drums cascade that eternal Rock and Roll rhythm beyond the sunset, over flamingo California palms, and blue lonely surf.

"Dark Lady" – Cher, #1(1), 1-74. Born with a Gypsy, an Armenian, and a French connection ('46, El Centro, California), Cher became a media magnet. Movie star (*Mask****; Moonstruck*****); talk-show personality; international informercial star. She hawks diet drinks, and busts her abs on various mediaeval torture exercise devices. She trolls along on huff and puff treadmills at 55+ with the energy of a 25-year-old dashing desperately to beat the hourglass to the railroad crossing.

"Dark Lady" monster-mashes fortuneteller mumbo-jumbo ("Love Potion #9"), and dark intrigue of **Paul McCartney**'s uncharacteristic cutthroat carol [James Bond flick], "Live and Let Die," #2(3), 7-73. Seems Cher and the fortune-teller have a mutual man. One is very peeved off at the other, and glowers with murderous intent. A heinous crime erupts. The music, marvelously, follows the dastardly plot line. Guitars chop. Tympani thunder. The bass bubbles its tense, intermittent machine-gun blasts. **Lesley Gore**'s party violence, like **Bobby Vee**'s in #33, '61 "Stayin' In," involved a punch in the nose, not capital punishment. "Dark Lady" reverberates with icy terror. Cher's multifold career has spanned four decades in a flurry of timeless tunes.

"If I Could Turn Back Time" – Cher, #3, 7-89. Ringing trombonish alto, lusty contralto. Cher laments the mirror mirror on the wall – as we all do, in Dorian Gray fashion, if we're fortunate enough to age . . . Cher scored with "Love and Understanding" #17, 6-91. One of the true divas of rock, Cher LaPierre shines on her own musically, far beyond the glare of the tempestuous tabloids she graces. Cher's predictable return to Hot Dance Tracks and Neo-Disco found Cher pleasantly surprised with "Believe" #1(4), December 1998. Cher's biggest hit ever.

Supergroup time. First there was this groovy group called the Mugwumps. **Zal Yanovsky**, later of the Lovin' Spoonful, joined with Halifax, Nova Scotia, lead tenor **Denny Doherty** (b. '41, Nova

Scotia) and **Mama Cass Elliot**. They all shacked in "Creeque Alley" (#5, 4-67), a palmfrond getaway in the Virgin Islands.

"California Dreamin'" – Mama and the Papas, #4, 1-66. Closest I ever personally got to the Top Five national hit record. Howzat? You see, I took Sherry Pilafian to the 1959 Dearborn High Sophomore Hop (triple date). Sherry who? Pilafian. Like Cher LaPierre (Sarkasian), a nice Armenian name. This green-eyed lady is the twin sister of **Peter Pilafian**, who played the electric viola solo for "California Dreamin'". The Bridge's Mideastern tonal scale differs from the one we're used to. Strange, exotic, entangled with kismet and karma and Cher's sound on "Dark Lady." His voodoo viola bewitches the song.

The lyric is more predictable. Leaves go brown. Our lone pedestrian muses the drab spittle-smeared curbs and the dank, raw drudgery of impending gray Eastern winter. Dapper Canadian 'snowbird' **Denny Doherty** ponders ditching his main squeeze and hotfooting it to warm, safe Los Angeles. With a Call-and-Response pattern, Mama Cass's crystalline voice booms in. At 5'2" and 275#, **Cass Elliot** was full-figured and zaftig. Her sprightly muu-muus swirled joyously as she pealed her folksy anthems to the ringing rafters. Elliot brought visionary hope to many singers to come: Barry White, Blues Traveler's John Popper, Bachman-Turner Overdrive. Songwriter and leader **John Phillips** (1936-2001) wrote, harmonized, and arranged most of their great hits.

"California Dreamin'" flirts with key gloom, resolving to a few rainbow majors. A slow-rock ballad, it shows what you can do with a good lead singer and three harmonizers with great voices. John's wife **Michelle Phillips** (b. '45, California), is remarkably beautiful and has a perfect airy soprano, like these very first British Invaders – the **Caravelles**, and their #3, 11-63 "You Don't Have to Be a Baby to Cry." Two months before the Beatles' rocked New York shores, whispery Londoners Andrea Simpson and Lois Wilkinson conquered bronze in America.

"I Love How You Love Me" – Paris Sisters, #5, 9-61. Priscilla, Sherrell, and Albeth Paris. Nice. Wispiest, breathiest Top Ten tune I've ever heard. Violins caress trembling melody. Coos, woos, purrs, murmurs, whispers, cajoles. Wow.

Like chugging maple syrup straight? **Patience and Prudence**'s #4, 8-56 "Tonight You Belong to Me" features 11 and 14-year old **McIntyre** sisters reviving Gene Austin's #1, 1927 hit. Ultracute kids with perfect pitch, cherubic melody and harmony. Ever take 11 lumps of sugar for your coffee? Or 12?

"Dedicated to the One I Love" – Mamas and Papas, #2(3), 2-67. Their second biggest hit? I'd do their BIGGEST #1(3), '67 "Monday, Monday" here, but you heard it 17 times yesterday at the pizzeria, Cat Grooming Emporium, Fabric Bonanza, Burger Bag, Grab-Yer-Cash Machine, tree house, Milk-0-Mania Mart, Six-Pack-A-Rama, Jiffy Lube, Motor Vehicle Monster, Sinova Beach and the

Dew Drop Out. Papas/Mamas hailed from the Big Apple (Mama Cass); South Carolina (John Phillips); Long Beach, California (Michelle Phillips); and Nova Scotia, Canada (Denny Doherty).

Good friends with **Scott McKenzie**, of flower-in-hair #4, 5-67 "San Francisco" fame, Phillps and McKenzie worked together in the Folk group the Journeymen. McKenzie later penned Beach Boys' "Kokomo" (#1, 9-88).

"Dream a Little Dream of Me' – Mama Cass, #12, 7-68. #1, 1931 Wayne King Standard. Cass's solo tour triumph skipped to a tragic stop at her untimely death at 32 of heart disease. John and Michelle's daughter Chynna Phillips starred in **Wilson Phillips**:

"Release Me" – Wilson Phillips, #1(2), 6-90. Chynna, a kid of Mamas/Papas, teams with **Carnie** and **Wendy Wilson**, kids of Beach Boys' genius Brian Wilson. Two other #1's ("Hold On" #1, 3-90, and #1, 2-91, "You're in Love") anchored their careers. Nice flowing harmonic blend . . . just like their Mamas and Papas.

Jug-Band Music was one of those groovy little byroads off the Rock and Roll superhighway. Woolies' drummer **Bill "Bee" Metros** assembled an odd amalgam of thimbles, dragged out a washboard, and cranked out perennial Jug-Band anthem "San Francisco Bay Blues" (catch Clapton's Al. #1[3], 9-92 *Unplugged* rendition).

It rolled down the tonic to the Dixieland six – G – F# – F – E – chord change. Jug-Band Music was a) Acoustic, b) A folk offshoot, and c) Grandfather of the Unplugged Generation. [**Extreme**'s "More Than Words" (#1, 3-91), Clapton's elegiac lament "Tears in Heaven" (#2[4], 2-92)]. Jug Band superstars included a Soft Rock crew from New York City starring lead singer **John Sebastian** (guitar, zither, harmonica) and ex-Mugwump lead guitarist **Zal Yanovsky**. Sebastian one-man banded it, almost, with his 12-string, harmonica, jugs, and kazoos. Joe Butler buzzed and thrummed and chonked and titillated the drums, only crashing and smashing and bashing them for one song:

"Summer in the City" – Lovin' Spoonful, #1(3), 7-66. 'Twas the steamy sensuous Summer of '66, and Motor City scorched in sizzling sidewalk steam. Hot engines hissed hot oil on hot pavements with rainbow oil slicks drooling down hot gutters. They brought a drag strip full of 409's, Little G.T.O.'s, AC Cobras, Jaguar XKE's, and voluptuous 'Vettes into the recording studio to peel off rubber all over the tape. John gazes at cool chicks suffering in the shadowless high noon. **Spoonful** (Rock Hall 2000) expresses all the prowling libido that rocks young summer nights with forbidden roaring desires for hot easy love and one-night impasse affairs. The song blasts a grinding, creaking, clanging, jangling pandemonium crescendo that bursts with raw hot summer passion. Long before Bruce Springsteen's asphalt anthems, the Spoonful revved his restless mood. High summer beckoned stormy 60s America. In their #2(2), 5-66 "Did You Ever Have to Make Up Your Mind?" this Spoonful dude digs both sisters. Their father insists he choose one. Juggish, laid-back, groovy little zowie number.

"Rain on the Roof" – Lovin' Spoonful, #10, 10-66. Simply one of the sweetest Soft Rock 12-string melodies ever woven. Nifty vignette: lovers caught under tin roof in summersplash thunderstorm splendor. Pitter-patter. Hugs, kisses, and all that good innocent stuff. At first. "Nashville Cats" (#8, 2-66) is a spoof, with bassist **Steve Boone**, on1966 Country guitar-pickers.

"Hanky Panky" – Tommy James and the Shondells, #1(2), 6-66; #39, 7-66 R & B. Basic Rock. Dayton's Tommy James (nee Jackson) played the ukulele at three, sez Fred Bronson. Moved to Niles, Michigan, in Chicago's skyscraper shadow. Cut first record at 12. Glommed "Hanky Panky" from Brill Tin Pan Alley writers Jeff Barry and Ellie Greenwich (who wrote it as goof). Recorded the song as a 'who cares' B-side in 1963. Standard 12-bar blues progression. Couple of tacets. Totally unrelated to scrappy #10 '90 Madonna "Hanky Panky." Luck? Bad.

Suddenly, some Pittsburgh rock jock rode "Hanky Panky" incessantly on his show. The legend claims the record got bootlegged (sold counterfeit with no artist royalties). Tommy to rescue. He asked his ex-Shondells to fly to Pittsburgh. Nah, they said. Tommy did solo shots on Pittsburgh TV, trying to recoup his losses of royalties on 80,000 copies. Naturally, new Shondells stormed in to help. So yep. Rest is history. Three years after fizzling, "Hanky Panky" clutched the #1 huge *Gold Rush* nugget. Patience, a virtue.

"I Think We're Alone Now" – Tiffany, #1(2), 8-87. Sixteen-year-old cutie **Tiffany Darwisch**, Oklahoman/ Californian pop prodigy, lavished techno drum vibes, phasers, and reverb units. She won a #1 hit on her first try, plus follow-up #1(2), 11-87 "Could've Been." Like Lesley Gore, pert Tif is dynamic and resourceful in her princess-style soprano. Or catch her bouncy Beatle reprise – #7, 2-88 "I Saw Him Standing There."

"I Think We're Alone Now" – Tommy James and the Shondells, #4, 2-67. Clandestine cutie. Plot: guy sneaks girl into bushes for fondling fun. Their odyssey is a frantic search for solitude and action. Since Caveman Ugblook, guys have been trying to drag girls off into bushes in gentlemanly fashion. Tiffany's song-character dragging him into the bushes, too, is a new tack. The Shirelles' #1, '60 "Will You Love Me Tomorrow?" lingers on, a generation later; in the history of the world, despite computerized perfection, still no boy has ever gotten pregnant. Wild song, this. Whoopee.

"Mony, Mony" – Tommy James and the Shondells, #3, 4-69. This puzzling Hard Rock Party Animal Anthem dates back to writer's block. Tommy stood outside the studio on a clanging New York neon night. He gazed up at a blinking sign for Mutual of New York (M-O-N-Y). So yes, "Mony Mony" has a meaningless meaning – just like much of life. **Billy Idol** took this wedding/jamboree/bacchanalia monster hit to #1(1), 9-87 as "Mony Mony 'Live'," after a lukeward #107 studio version in 1981.

The British Invasion created a Yankee Backlash of American Bands. **Len Barry** and his **Dovells** resisted, and the Barbarians bad-mouthed British haircuts, but there was no stopping the English tidal wave:

"1-2-3" – Len Barry, #2, 9-65. Philly Leonard Borisoff's Macedonian-American R & R background is unique. With his Dovells ("You Can't Sit Down," #3, 4-63, "The Bristol Stomp" #2, 9-61), he enjoyed several big doo-whop hits with a machine-gun beat. Barry chided his European R & R colleagues about their ample hair. He said American "man's haircut" acts should get a lot more record buyers – and that Beatle buyers were unpatriotic. His last hit was "I Struck it Rich" (#98, 9-66) . . .

"Are You a Boy Or Are You a Girl" – Barbarians, #55, 9-65. Provincetown, Mass., band from the local garage? If Punk Rock was not yet a musical genre, the Barbarians gave it hope and glimmer. This one taunts long-haired rock musicians for androgynous qualities. Weirdly, no buzz or baldy or crew-cut Barbarians existed. One had Tiny Tim-type shoulder-length hair – with the other three hovering between early Mick Jagger and later Creedence Clearwater Revival. Song mocks itself.

The British Bandwagon didn't look half bad to the **Beau Brummels**: lead singer **Sal Valentino** (Sal Spaminato); lead guitar guy Ron Elliott; bassman Ron Meagher; and John Peterson.

"Don't Talk to Strangers" – Beau Brummels, #52, 10-65. Heart of Rock and Roll! With Shannon's raging chord patterns, and dynamic harmonies, this song carries an instrumental bridge second to none in punch and pulsing power. Why a ho-hum #52? A botched bungle of bad hype and iffy distribution (their LABEL collapsed belly-up in the middle of their would-be smash). Their biggest hit? #8 "Just a Little" of April 1965. The Beau Brummels of San Francisco are the first Yankee Backlash group to successfully capture and market the big booming British beat and bounce it back. Big debut? #15, 1-65 "Laugh, Laugh," plus #8 "Just a Little."

"Just Like Me" – Paul Revere and the Raiders, #11, 12-65. With Revolutionary War uniforms for TV's *Where the Action Is*, these guys were crucial to the American rebound. **Mark Lindsay** sang lead. **Paul Revere** (b.

'42, Boise, Idaho) assembled the group originally as an instrumental act ("Like, Long Hair" #38, 3-61), a piano classic. Paul Revere fired two speedo lead guitars into the instrumental epicenter of "Just Like Me", creating an earthquake and an explosion heard from Jimi Hendrix to the Who's Pete Townshend. If you're tracing the rise of Heavy Metal or the loss of the vocalist's charisma to the lead guitarist's, start here:

"Kicks" – Paul Revere and the Raiders, #4, 3-66. Recreational drugs drooled across America into the later sixties. Greenwich Village provided some. Jazz and Blues had not furnished R & R with role models who were entirely sober, abstemious, or drug-free. One HUGE reason for heavier drug involvement was the Vietnam War. Guys in foxholes don't figure, "Gosh whillikers, me O my, this funny cigarette might shorten my 66-year life span." **Kicks** champions instant drug rehab – and friendship. It's the most vehement anti-drug hit of the 60s.

"Crying in the Chapel" – Elvis Presley, #3, 4-65. King's only top ten tune for four years (**Sonny Til and the Orioles**' original #11, 8-53, #1[5], R & B). Devotional motif rebounded in **Kitty Kallen**'s #4, 7-54 "In the Chapel in the Moonlight" and **Frank Pizani**'s marvelous Highlights' "City of Angels" (#19, 10-59). Streetcorner perfection. Elvis sang in a deep baritone with the Soul of Sonny Til. His next song is more prophetic.

"In the Ghetto" – Elvis Presley, #3, 5-69; #60, 6-69 C. Elvis, who had every inkling of tough times on mean streets in housing projects (Memphis, age 13) sings a sad song about a poor ghetto kid who dies in the hail of gunfire . . . and on the same day, another little poor lost waif is born, destined to the same fate. Sad cyclic disaster.

America's answer to the British Invasion might not erupt with earthquake fury from 48-track Recording Emporiums, with carpets of gold, and genius Dial-Twirlers with diamonds in their starry eyes. Like **Bobby Vee's Shadows** in their frozen garage, many rock and rollers used homey basement Do-It-Yourself Recording Studios. There's a great scene in the *Buddy Holly Story***** (1978). **Gary Busey** (Buddy), Don Stroud (Jerry Allison), and Charles Martin Smith (Joe B. Mauldin) fool around with a bunch of garage sound-baffle feathers. They try to discover the mystical origin of some chirping. Rat-a-tatting the garage's silent feathers (which fly all over) with his swift sticks, the drummer discovers it – a cricket. Spuriously, they gain a name for their group – as the record simultaneously breaks nationally due to Buffalo's 'Mad Man Mancuso's' 24-hour "That'll Be the Day"-playing marathon binge. [A fun but inaccurate story]. Many great records bloomed in a 'girdle-clothesline' basement or a rainbow oil-glop puddle in the GARAGE.

"Gloria" – Shadows of Knight, #10, 3-66. Chicago's **Jim Sohns**, amid the grease and glitter of half a '55 Chevy and two Lambretta 175 motor scooters, concocted this cover classic with his old Wollensak tape recorder. Three head-banging chords batter your quietude – **E-D-A**, throughout the song. Sohns growls passionately about this 5'4" super chick who, around midnight, comes up to his room, knocks on his feverish door, and apparently bedazzles his senses all night long.

"Gloria" – Them, #71, 5-65. Belfast Northern Ireland's Irish baritone superstar **Van Morrison** (b. '45) hit with this debut ditty. Dubliners Declan and Con Clusky and John Stokes (the **Bachelors**) mellowed the Invasion via their sweet "Diane" (#10, 4-64) and "Marie" (#15, #1 for Tommy Dorsey in 1937).

"96 Tears" — ? and the Mysterians, #1(1), 9-66. Rudy Martinez of Saginaw, Michigan cloned **Mick Jagger**'s style, 100 miles north of the last factory and farmland before your roll into the great gray glooms of the Northern Boreal Forest of Hiawatha. And sparkling stars.

Saginaw's "96 Tears" **Rudy Martinez**, son of a migrant worker, worked the sugar beet plantations of Sebewaing and Zilwaukee. Rudy's Mexican folks journeyed north on tangerine dreams and golden freeways, questing after a name-in-lights Johnny B. Goode vision. Rudy's garage-band sound is tantalizing. Like Del Shannon, and the Beau Brummels, he jaggers his Latino/Chicano revenge-tinged vocal about this lass's 96 tears of remorse for him. The big Farfisa or Hammond organ undulates between a **G** and **G** minor chord shift, until the vocal bridge plunges to a sassy somber **Em**. Rudy tells her it's time for her to roll down there (down to the minor six chord?) lookin' up. Finally, he resolves to a **C** major and his own blue mood, spangled with forlorn falsetto "woo-hoos." **Question Mark (Rudy)** may never know about a scruffy alley cat who roamed our backyard we named "Mysterian" (1980-91). Rudy avoided One-Hit Wonderdom with #22, 11-66 "I Need Somebody" before blasting off with the rest of us into gossamer oblivion. **Madonna** country:

"This Used to Be My Playground" – Madonna (Ciccone), #1(2), 7-92. Madonna was born (8-16-58) in Bay City, just north of Saginaw. (Or perhaps Detroit or Pontiac, if you believe other bios). Cheerleader at North Adams High School, near Pontiac, Madonna's girlhood home was bulldozed to make way for the Detroit (football) Lions' Silverdome. Her plaintive ballad eulogizes all our collective dreams and shattered childhoods scrunched in the name of progress.

* * * * * * *

Forefronting the Yankee backlash, **Brian Wilson** took on a defensive posture (via his over-competitive pop Murry Wilson) against the British Invasion. Many emotional problems bedeviled the gentle California football star, who did everything right and still couldn't please his demanding dad. Perhaps the greatest genius in American Rock and Roll (I wrote in a *New York Times* column in 1995), Brian Wilson suffered like **Karen Carpenter** – he tried to be too perfect. The **Beatles** launched their *Sgt. Pepper* Concept Album #1(15), 6-67; Brian Wilson stewed himself into his lonely room to create their own competitive Psychedelic *Wild Honey* (Al. #24, 1-68), a compromise package which emerged from his "Smiley Smile" concept album idea that fizzled. Via Murry Wilson's prodding, and mom Audree's nurturing, they evolved into maybe our most complex mid-60s rockers. Brian steered silently from his bedroom – with a Beach Boy tour package fronted by Mike Love and Al Jardine and even **Glen Campbell** and Toni Tennille:

"Surfer Girl" – Beach Boys, #7, 8-63; #20, 4-63 R & B. Quinessential beach bunny fantasy. She honors her chaste polka-dot bikini, with Sally Field *Gidget* sweetness, Annette's [or Britney Spears'?] Mouseketeer innocence, and Sandra Dee's glorious bod. Brian's Scottish tenor fashions his male-equivalent of a girl's Prince Charming in the fluff and feathery foam of the eternal royal blue swirling sea. Barbie Baby, his dream doll in nearly-buff bikini, watches his surfing escapades by the roaring ocean, in 100% genuine love with him. It doesn't get any better than that . . . You hear echoes of Chuck Berry and the Letterman (#17, 2-62 "Come Back Silly Girl"). Brian dreams far beyond the mystical, iridescent, Pacific Ocean. Every guy's greatest *Baywatch* fantasy comes true.

"Help Me, Rhonda" – Beach Boys, #1(2), 5-65. Beach Guys featured FIVE great lead singers. **Al Jardine** once quit the young surf group for dental school, a "$afer bet" than teenage idoling. Beach Boys' chart action sent the 5'5" Hawthorne High football teammate splashing back, bumping temp replacement 15-year-old David Marks. Al's supercool tenor commandeers "Help Me, Rhonda" (or our kid Rambha's version "Help Me, Rambha"). Jardine skims his French tenor off the lofty notes, and **Mike Love** (both baritone and tenor) bounces to the deep bottom notes, chiming in with perhaps the most famous R & R vocal bass line of all time. In an Orbison lyrical motif, Al convinces girl-pal to help HIM disconnect with ex – and "Rhonda" rises romantically with a primrose promise of new love.

Mike Love's barrelroll baritone seethes with rhythmic thunder on "Rhonda's" low notes. Their #1 hit features the Jardine-Love duo in the lead, cavorting with their **Kingston Trio** shirts, **Chuck Berry** riffs, and **Lettermen** harmonies to synthesize great American Rock and Roll.

"Good Vibrations" were on deck for the Littoral Lads from Hawthorne, California. The flowering of American Rock never could have blossomed without their Surf Rock and Car Classic songs. Their "Kokomo" (#1, 9-88) beckons us to punt the humdrum and surf the sky.

"Blue Moon" – Marcels, #1(3), 3-61. Marcels womp the bass line with verve, vitality, and punch. Rodgers and Hart first cashed in on this Streetcorner chord classic (**C— Am – F – G7**) in 1934. **Cornelius Harp** wafted the fine tenor lead, but the craftiest vocal riffs go to the integrated baritone/bass combo duo of **Dick Knauss** and **Fred Johnson**, who carry the song to its frolicsome comic peak. Hip multicultural crew – like the Dell-Vikings and Hootie and the Blowfish. The Pittsburgh doo-whop R & B Soul stars also scored with "Heartaches" (#7, 10-61) perennial platter smash: #1 Ted Weems, 1947, and #12 Guy Lombardo in 1931. All Rock and Roll is interconnected. Often to the semi-ancient past.

"Corrina, Corrina" – Bob Dylan, NC, 1963. The Bard of Greenwich Village and Hibbing, Minnesota (b. 5-24-41), chose this **Big Joe Turner** (#41, '56) and Ray Peterson (#9, '60) anthem to plug in his guitar. Though many Folk Rock fans count Bob's "Subterranean Homesick Blues" as the benchmark for the birth of Folk Rock, Bob had become 'plugged' on his #22, 9-63 *Freewheelin' Bob Dylan* album. Technically, his "Baby, Let Me Follow You Down" electrically predates even "Corinna." With Leonard Gaskin on bass guitar, Herb Lovelle on drums, Dick Wellstood on piano, and Howie Collins and Bruce Langhorne on guitar, Dylan and "Corinna²" chucked the Unplugged Generation and the Acoustic Fetish in two fell swoops. A little later, Bob put the hammer down.

"Positively 4th Street" – Bob Dylan, #7, 10-65. After socking it to the censors with his #2(2), 7-65 "Like a Rolling Stone," Bob sauntered on over to my daughter Lauri and her husband Larry Barnes' turf in the East Village by the *NYPD Blue* Police Station at 5th Street and Second Avenue. "Little Ricky's" is an Elvis-paraphernalia store on the corner of 3rd Street and 1st Avenue. Benny's Burritos adorns the nearby block, and the Hell's Angels Headquarters guards the corner; no one has ever even remotely considered motorcycle kleptomania there.

Lauri and Larry (and ultra-young lad Maxwell – our first grandchild) go to a gym called Crunch, and the whole shebang of this India Indian/Ukranian/New Age neighborhood is just down the street from Buddy and Maria Elena Holly's apartment on Fifth Avenue by NYU.

This is Bob Dylan's adopted world [replete with 1961 blue VW Microbus on *Freewheelin'* album cover]. It's a world which later skated over to the Bowery, and CBGB's, to launch our Punk and New Wave chapters down the road. When Dylan arrived in the East Village *Bitter End* coffee house milieu from tundra Minnesota, he was spellbound by the ambience. With his preference for *On the Road* prose of Jack Kerouac and the music of Buddy

Holly, Bob helped Folk purists to violate their Old Adage: THOU SHALT NOT PLUG IN THY GUITAR!

Just down the block from Bill Graham's vaunted Second Avenue Fillmore East, and the cold-water flat of young **George** and **Ira Gershwin** – Bob Dylan, like Buddy Holly, synthesized the best of a whole diverse hodge-podge of musical styles. And he added a new poetic dimension.

Dylan digested the Beat-Generation poetry of **Gary Snyder**, Gregory Corso and Lawrence Ferlinghetti. He assumed the brawling, gushing, firebrand cadence of his friend and poetic hero, America's unquenchable poetic genius **Allen Ginsberg** (1926-97). Ginsberg's wild idiosyncratic lifestyle gave Bob material for his own explorations of the American spirit. Dylan brought the Dust Bowl craggy vocal style of **Woody Guthrie**, and the profound melodies of Lubbock's Crickets. By the time he positively got to 4th Street, Bob Dylan – in true American self-reliance – had his own musical agenda. He went from darling of the Folk Movement to brash young iconoclast, igniting millions in a firestorm of musical debate.

Dylan's "Positively 4th Street" lyric concerns false friendship. The Judas Factor is nothing new, dating back to the New Testament. With the pied piper sound of a catchy organ, Dylan excoriates this nervy lying Judas in his midst. The guy claims he's Bob's friend, but gabs behind his back and grins to see him in the gutter. In a dim omen of Dylan's near-fatal motorcycle crash (7-29-66), Dylan looks at this insincere, shallow sycophant – who would rather see him paralyzed (which Bob almost was in the accident). Dylan actually broke his neck, and suffered long and painfully. His Del Shannon Rain-Walking Revenge Motif cranks up the tachometer, and Dylan doles out bitterness, disillusionment, anger, and resentment. Naturally, critics loved it.

Musically, "4th Street" saunters. Promenades. The organ drives the surging bass and right-on guitar, and the slow backbeat pulses on the insistent 2 & 4 beats. The range is Dylanesque – not Orbisonic. The Hibbing Bard is in full command. As **Al Kooper** of **Blood Sweat & Tears** played organ on #2, '65 "Like a Rolling Stone," so rolls the organ atop Bob's 4th Street opus. His message rocks with his battlefield beat. It's a simmering answer to Folk purists who dissed Dylan for 'selling out' to the wily siren song of the electric guitar. As Dylan's mighty message strides through the 4 a.m. snaggletooth streets, of dog-waste gutters and divine hallelujah visions, he hammers away at gatekeepers and handlers trying to change him into something he'd rather not be.

Commerciality. Many Folk singers disdained 'selling out to the establishment,' preferring instead a small coterie of devoted esoteric fans. [See hilarious deodorant-shtick album cover of #48, 1-68 *The Who Sell Out*]. In a sense, that meant – no money coming in. Very skimpy royalties. Starving in sincere garrets. Not so Dylan. HE HAD A MAJOR MESSAGE. HE WANTED TO REACH A MAJOR AUDIENCE. He wasn't selling alibis. He wasn't selling any cutesy Cheshire-cat smile, wrinkle-free khaki blandness, or hoop-de-doo hoopla of Teen Idol hype. Very positively, on 4th Street and anywhere else, Bob Dylan broadcast his message to a much wider audience than the Folk family. Brandishing his poetic vision and his hammering-on guitar, Bob knocked down the Jericho walls of narrow musical categories. He almost solitarily created a new musical art form.

And once they met Bob Dylan, **John Lennon** and the Beatles would never be the same. For one thing, sez Joe Leodato, the whole *Sergeant Pepper* (#1, '67) DOUBLE-album concept was taken from Bob's Al. #9, 7-66 *Blonde on Blonde*. Only Dylan, too, would have the audacity in his lyrical 50s afterglow phase to say to **John Lennon**: "You guys do great melodies and songs . . . why don't you ever write about ANYTHING IMPORTANT?" [Paraphrase].

"A Hard Rain's Gonna Fall" – Bob Dylan, NC, 1963. Off *Freewheelin.'* Ultimate Armageddon. With messianic splendor, Bob whips off prophetic gems of cryptic wisdom: deserted highways made of diamonds; newborn babes in the woods, surrounded by wolves; girls who hand him rainbows, fountains of blood and thunder; people wounded by love – and hatred; a white man parading with a black dog.

Bob's "Hard Rain" is nuclear fallout. Strontium 90, a radioactive isotope that mimicked calcium, fell out of swirling clouds from above-ground atomic bomb testing. Slithering into the grass, the cows, and eventually mother's milk, it could easily kill children. Remember, we touched upon this disgusting theme in **Malvina Reynolds**/Searchers' "What Have They Done to the Rain?" (#29, 1-65). Dylan sings with Psalmic passion of a Sephardic bard in Israel. King David, and **Miriam** are the first cited singers of their gender. Dylan describes Noah's Deluge and a 40-day cloudburst. "Hard Rain" updates the Nuclear Genie and its monstrous potential to inflict human suffering and death.

Structurally, nothing like "Hard Rain" ever was. His verses just kept tacking on lines – like the children's nursery rhyme about the poor old lady who swallowed a spider (that wriggled inside of her). "Hard Rain" is prophetic, disturbing, scary. Redone in the 90s by **Paul Simon**'s wife Edie Brickell ("What I Am" #7, 11-88) and the New Bohemians, "Hard Rain" bellows "BEWARE!"

"Baby, Let Me Follow You Down" – Bob Dylan, NC, 1963. Spoken Blues credited to pal Ric Von Schmidt [rarity if Dylan doesn't write his own]. Dylan borrows the very best harmonica/guitar simultaneous techniques he learned from Bluesmaster **Jimmy Reed**. His tremendous tune, with just a hint of taboo/Folkie electronic amplification, froths its bubbly way along swirling seashores of time, on a rainbow ribbon of Blues exotic. On the same first album, the 20-year-old wunderkind sang: "Fixin' to Die" (which he wasn't, as he glides past 60ishly); the yodelful "Freight Train Blues"; and the classic Joan Baez fallenmaiden tune that steered Eric Burdon's **Animal**-istic baritone boomer, "The House of the Rising Sun."

"I Want You" – Bob Dylan, #20, 7-66. Dylan had only six songs ever in the HOT 100 Top 20? Yep. This upfront tomcat tune is among them. Dylan rocks!

"Love Minus Zero/No Limit" – Bob Dylan, NC, 1965. Riding his own subterranean wild waves from Al. #6, 5-65 *Bringing It All Back Home*, Dylan revs his melodic genius into the Holly, or Everlys' style. With poetic profundity, Dylan scampers all over the English language to describe his love. On the album cover he flashes quick photo-pix of new movers and shakers jiggling the old R & R and Folk establishments: Ginsberg, Joan Baez, and "Puff (The Magic Dragon)'s" (#2, 3-63) pal, **Peter Yarrow**.

"Like a Rolling Stone" – Bob Dylan, #2(2), 7-65. Derisive ditty in the Del Shannon mode of self-improvement (he wants her to improve). Her hang-ups? She went to the poshest school but just got totally juiced and wasted. He snubs her sniffles, calls her Miss Lonely, and tells her she'll have to learn to live out on the solitary streets and sidewalks of the Manhattan milieu. Her toasty home is long gone. 'Rolling Stone' rained American stardom for Bob, as the **Rolling Stones**' nasty-as-they-wanna-be "Last Time" (#9) and "Satisfaction" (#1) surged them to international superstardom in Spring 1965. In the later 90s, the Rolling Stones (apropos, yes?) cut their version of this Dylan classic. Between this song and London's Rolling Stones, a great Rock and Roll magazine was about to be created in San Francisco via Jann Wenner and crew.

"Lay Lady Lay" – Bob Dylan, #7, 7-69. A not-so-private song for his wife Sarah Lowndes, to whom Bob was married for twelve years from 1965. His fear of bringing kids into this nuclear nightmare world line, from his bitter "Masters of War," was truncated a tad when he and Sara brought five of them to this fizzing world. Large brass bed. Perhaps as Vietnam, the H-bomb, and Bowery squalor subsided to a cheerier 70s outlook, Bob and Sarah reconsidered. Bob's gravelly baritone here thunders the velvet tune along. We kiss Kerouac's sad woebleak gloomgleak night farewell via Bob's sweet horizontal love song.

"Hurricane" – Bob Dylan, #33, 11-75. Though a cello rides this upbeat song like a bucking bronc, it's one of Dylan's top three rockers. My Rock History student Lisa Dalba's favorite song, "Hurricane (Part I)" is a feisty Dylan tribute to iffy ghetto justice in the imprisoning system. The song leads with a jab. Boxer Rubin 'Hurricane' Carter, on a fast fist track to his weight-class championship (middleweight? cruiserweight?) gets mixed up in a smoky midnight barroom shootout, and the bartender bleeds to death on the peanut-shell/spittoon floor. Carter takes the rap and serves the time for murder. 'Was he framed?' Dylan asks. The shrieking pulse of the low-tone cruiserweight fiddle smacks off the purple Jersey skies. A long song (see Marty Robbins' glorious gunfighter western waltz #1, '59 "El Paso"). Dylan's defense of the downtrodden, and willingness to stand up for unpopular causes, brands him a contender for the #1 lyricist shot.

Beyond his mid-60s heyday, Dylan delivered: his masterful duo "Knockin' on Heaven's Door," with Christian-Contemporary Byrd **Roger McGuinn** and Roger's heavenly Rickenbacker 12-string electric – #12, 9-73 (from Dylan's flick *Pat Garrett & Billy the Kid*); his **Dire Straits/**

Mark Knopfler duo when Jewish Dylan entered his Born-Again Christian pilgrimage – #24, 9-79 "Gotta Serve Somebody," with a hard-edged Zionist verve; and his incredible melodic masterpiece of symphonic Light Metal, #31, 3-75 "Tangled Up in Blue." **Bob Dylan** (Rock Hall 1988) is usually tangled up in genius – from his surrealistic bop prosody (Ginsberg's phrase) to his full-throttle street-savvy baritone "Hurricane."

Folk Rock arrived when Bob plugged his guitar in at the Newport Folk Festival. Suddenly (thanks Bob), it was OK to use big words in lyrics. You could still be cool.

"It Ain't Me, Babe" – Turtles, #8, 8-65. Westchester High School in Los Angeles spawned **Mark Volman**'s and **Howard Kaylan**'s group. Among other handles they shed like a locust's skin were the Nightriders, **Phosphorescent Leech**, and good ol' Flo & Eddie. The Turtles hacked away at Dylanesque Rock and Roll, harmonizing mellifluously in a variety of with-it and campy styles. They had incredible success in the Golden Age of Rock and Roll. "It's Ain't Me, Babe" opens on a throbbing minor riff:

Abm – F#m – Abm – F#m – E

Quavering quaking tremolo guitar makes the song. Seems this guy's girl expects him to be a cowboy hero, dying for her in chivalrous fashion. "It Ain't Me, Babe," is his caustic reply. Through Bob Dylan's lyrical vision here, sex roles changed. Guys no longer opened every door. Folk Rock/Country icon **Johnny Cash** concurred:

"It Ain't Me, Babe" – Johnny Cash, #58, 10-64; NC, C. With sweet harmonies from future wife June Carter Cash of Country dynasty Carter Family, Johnny Cash belts out his rough and tumble version of Bob Dylan. The more conservative Country establishment embraced Dylan's works before the more politically active Rock establishment: perhaps thinking Dylan was Folk, not Rock. Cash's version is a watershed pioneering venture for CROSS-OVER cooperation in music and Hit Chart Integration. When Johnny Cash sang or spoke, people gazed in awe.

"Happy Together" – Turtles, #1(3), 2-67. Turtletop triumph. One of the happiest titles since Buddy Holly's #10, 12-57 "Oh Boy" – not the 4-2002 "Oh Boy" by Cameron/Juelz Santana. Nice muted Kaylan-Volman blend on tiger chords at intro. As second tenors or high baritones, they use the roughest piano key: – F# major. Finally, a chipper song not raging at the world. Not miserable (and trying to share that morose malevolent misery with innocent us)! They mute their rhythm guitars on the tacet tiptoe verse, and boom into heavier thrashing chords like Tommy James' "Alone Now" on the resounding chorus. The Turtles also flip a "fab" bass run onto "You Baby" (#20, 2-66). "She'd Rather Be with Me" involves (#3, 5-67) a touchy little showdown; ebullient "Elenore" (#6, 9-68) rhymes ETCETERA, with BETTER (ah, Brooklyn goes

to L.A. again). Their last hit offering is the poky-paced "You Showed Me" (#6, 1-69). Of course, they are **Turtles**, so who expects fast R & R songs?

"Black Crow Blues" – Woolies, NC, 1966. Big air play in Chicago. My band, the Night Shift/Woolies, also knew Dylan songs were cool... Rare 12-Bar Blues for Dylan. Piano man **Bob Baldori** wailed an unforgettable harmonica lead. Spotty, sporadic national uncharted action.

"Who Do You Love?" – Woolies, #95, 3-67. This luckier old Bo Diddley Blues tune stars brother **Bob** and **Jeff Baldori** (keyboards and guitar), **Stormy Rice** on lead vocal, plus **Bill Metros** on drums, with kudos for 6'8" Gene Jewitt, 'Zocko' Groendal, Kris B. Bacon or Spyder Snyder (bass), and a juggled bar band roster of lead singer/guitarist Johnny B. Goode dreamers like me. Woolies later backed and recorded an album with **Chuck Berry** (*San Francisco Dues*, NC, 1971). The Woolies' "Who Do You Love?" was #3 in Detroit, #2 in Miami, but shunned in the Big Apple. Woolies' version was covered by **Jim Morrison and the Doors, George Thorogood & the Destroyers.** Woolies covered Bo's great original plus **Ronnie Hawkins and the Hawks/ the Band** [yes, Bob Dylan's The Band, with Robbie Robertson, Levon Helm, and Rick Danko].

"Don't Think Twice, It's All Right" – Peter, Paul, and Mary, #9, 9-63. Mary Travers' long, straight blonde hair shimmered and flipped in the August 1963 sunshine. The six-foot Kentucky folk diva and her two celestial baritones, Peter Yarrow and Paul Stookey, sang out Bob Dylan's Civil Rights anthem "Blowin' in the Wind" (#2, 6-63 for them). The occasion featured the largest all-time American crowd, Dr. **Martin Luther King**'s 800,000-strong March on the hot Washington Mall. Ironically, they were but the opening act for the "I Have a Dream" speech, by Rev. King (tragically, only #88, 5-68, Motown).

Peter, Paul, and Mary and their songwriting wunderkind Bob Dylan were now Folk Phenomenons. Instant legends, even. College girls ironed their hair, emulating Mary's golden tresses. Whole fraternities (mine, anyhow) scarfed up acoustic guitars, and ragtag folk trios warbled the Kingston Trio, Brothers Four, Peter Paul, and Mary, or Bob Dylan. The trio also scored with #21, 4-69 gorgeous melody "Day is Done," Gordon Lightfoot's "For Lovin' Me" to #30, 1-65, and antiwar ballad #52, 4-66 "The Cruel War" – about a girl so heartbroken when her man goes to war, that she threatens to dress in men's clothes and join him at the front. **John Denver** started with folk stars the Chad Mitchell Trio [#43, 11-63 "The Marvelous Toy"], and ponned PPM's LAST charted hit, #1[1], 12-69 "Leaving on a Jet Plane"; few groups' LAST songs go to #1.

"Don't Think Twice" is Dylan exonified: incisive, steely, stoical, and wayfaring on the Kerouackian American road at the aftermath of a rusty relationship. The legendary Folk trio pretties the harmonies into eager emotion, but Dylan's sad sayonara sends him slogging down the lonesome trail.

Dylan's lyrical legacy surged in '65 with two schoolmates at P.S. 164 in Forest Hills, Queens, New York. **Paul Simon** (b. Newark, New Jersey 11-5-42) and **Art Garfunkel** (b. Queens, NY 10-13-41) met in a 6th grade production of *Alice in Wonderland*. Paul hopped and bopped as THE WHITE RABBIT, and Art grinned groovily as THE CHESHIRE CAT [Fred Bronson's great *Billboard Book of Number One Hits*]. Soon their careers took off on Garfunkel's sparkling Irish tenor and Paul's with-it 2nd tenor and first-rate guitar riffs. In a mirror echo of the **Everly Brothers**, they stormed the Top 50 with their *Bandstand* teen hit "Hey Schoolgirl" as Tom & Jerry (#49, 12-57). **Paul Simon**, with Howie Beck and Mickey Borack from Queens, 'soloed' on this vroooooming little ditty:

"Motorcycle" – **Tico and the Triumphs, #99, 1-62. Paul Simon**, thinly disguised as an audial Hell's-Angel motorcycle gang, hit the top 20 in my motorland mecca on **Del Shannon**'s AMY label. **Art Garfunkel** (taller one, blonde Afro-style hair, though Caucasian) and Simon signed with Columbia on the new Folk wave. Their Al. #30, 1-66 *Wednesday Morning, 4 a.m.,* released in 1964, simmered until 1965's Folk Rock Explosion. Producer **Tom Wilson** created their destiny via an overdubbed bass and guitar:

"The Sounds of Silence" – **Simon & Garfunkel, #1(2), 11-65.** Simon and Gar lead off their Folk Rock anthem by saluting their old pal darkness. Darkness kept mum. A watermark in rock and roll history! It's the first time such a deep and powerful poem also happened to nab #1 on the charts. "The Sounds of Silence" resurrected the clean, cherubic crystalline sound of the Everly Brothers for a new generation: Paul Simon = **Don Everly**'s second tenor: Art Garfunkel = belltone **Phil Everly**. The Everlys were Scotch-Irish Appalachian singers; Paul and Art were Jewish kids from the Big Apple. Garfunkel was among the first Jewish performers to use his real name on records, their mid-60s incarnation; (Simon did too, but 'Simon' is a little more ethnically ambiguous). Rock and Roll is a multicultural manifesto meshing with the message of Dr. King. Major Jewish Rock pioneer icons included Folk Rock guru Bob (Zimmerman) Dylan; producers Phil Spector and Shirelles Florence Greenberg; Chuck Berry's Leonard Chess; pre-Motown Fortune Records' Jack and Devora Brown; Brill Building songwriters Carole (Klein) King, Cynthia Weil, Ellie Greenwich, Jerry Leiber and Mike Stoller, singers Lesley Gore, the Shangri-Las (#1, '64 "Leader of the Pack" motorcycle Graveyard Rock song), the Turtles, Simon & Garfunkel, and aspiring songsmith/baritone **Neil Diamond**.

The alienated "Sounds of Silence" isolato staggers alone, along tight cobblestones avenues or alleys. In the drizzly, streetlight halo, he zips up his coat. BINGO – a giant neon light. Cinema noire, grotesquerie.

His wild dream touts the taboo term NAKED, referring to (safely enough) the eerie light where he beholds a comatose 10,000 myriad crowd who pray to this neon god. They hear, but do not heed. They talk, and they do not listen. It is one vast necropolis, one dead city of neon nightscape zombies. Saddest of all, people scribble songs harmonic voices will never share. Why? Nobody dares disrupt these malignant 'sounds of silence.' Angst and alienation slither on smoky East Village streets, by 'deli'/drug dens and paper bag guzzler guys with red and yellow eyes. Scarred seedy sleazo subways make denizens wish for the neutral scent of cow manure. Prophets' words adorn subway walls, prognosticating a gloomy gray future of silence, alienation, and loneliness. The cold Big City's hustle-bustle is hoi polloi staring off into space. Ghouls step over bodies in the gutter. Postmodern Wasteland. Simon and Garfunkel lament this loss of humanity.

"Sound of Silence" begins on a minor. The first verse looms in the original 1964 acoustic. Tom Wilson dubs the drum/bass rhythm track into verse two and the puzzle fits together. This low throbbing subway band track asserts the power of the gloomy message. "Sounds of Silence" presages a grim future in an impassioned lonely city full of robot-reject zombies from *Night of the Living Dead*. If the song paints such a gruesome nihilistic (belief in nothing) picture, why, then, is it so beautiful?

Their Everly sound shmoozes with brooding existentialism. In simmering Vietnam-glutted 1965, the "Sounds of Silence" was like Punxatawney Phil the Woodchuck; it looked at the bleak wintry future, and crawled back to nestle in its grubby subway hole. If I can just snuggle, snurfles the Pooh-Bear groundhog, maybe reality will go away. And leave me alone. And comfy.

A 1982 Simon and Gar Central Park Reunion Concert proves their harmonic gusto is nearly 100% Everly, brother . . .

"Wake Up, Little Susie" – **Simon & Garfunkel, #27, 4-82.** Snoozy Susie, a little woozy – her dad still mad at bad cad lad. Cool. "Sounds of Silence" hops from Susie's snurfly drive-in show to existential despair. Simon & Garfunkel's singer/songwriter masterpiece speaks of subway or tenement-hall graffiti as prophecy.

"Homeward Bound" – **Simon & Garfunkel, #5, 2-66.** One of the best-crafted heart-wrenching studies of band tour roadweary homesickness ever done. True story? (Catch Bob Seger's "Turn The Page" – NC, from #34 Al. 5-76 *Live Bullet*). "Homeward Bound" spells out the sheer boredom of city-hop gigging. Fans think it's all roses for these reluctant superstars, not prickling thorns. Simon & Gar gripe about stupid flicks, smokestack despair, endless nicotine dream of scruffy magazines. It's probably a kickback to Simon's solo coffeehouse tour of England before Simon & Gar won fame. Why? The song came out just two months after "Sounds of Silence." It's unlikely they'd have had TIME to get that world-weary or lonely amidst a sweet swarm of young groupies.

On a nomadic tour of one-night stands, they shuffle suitcases, and guitars. No word about amps, roadies, groupies, or (like the later Who) trashing hotels. Nope, Simon & Gar were a little too dignified and quiet for such cockamamie shenanigans. A swirling sea of strangers' faces produces nomadic regrets. Dreamy thoughts recede back HOME. For each, home means some NYC *Seinfeld* cozy apartment with hi-fi music whirling, and a girlfriend lying (not overly clad) with open arms on a waiting couch. This NYC romantic dream rebuffs the palm tree, the hammock, and the grass skirt for urban cliff-dwelling apartment bliss. HOMEWARD BOUND! All the lonely one-night stands in the world can't make up for a lasting relationship in a cozy homey apartment overlooking Washington Square.

In bleak snow-swirling January 1959, financially frustrated Buddy Holly kissed his pregnant wife Maria Elena Santiago Holly goodbye. He left on a frozen BUS tour of lonesome one-night stands in the arctic northern gut-basket of the U.S.A. Girls from Bob Dylan's Dave Van Ronk's 'North Country' twinkled sparkling come-hither eyes at the newlywed Lubbock lad, but he kept his reverie eyes on the prize – Maria. He was on a "Homeward Bound" tour of one-night lonely stands, scruffy suitcase and Fender Stratocaster guitar in hand. On February 3, 1959, the day Don McLean's Music Died, Buddy's Homeward Bound odyssey pulled up short . . .

"I Am a Rock" – Simon & Garfunkel, **#3, 5-76.** In English class at Queens College, they encountered John Donne's breathtaking conceptual poem: "No man is an island, entire of itself." "I Am A Rock" is a steely stoic manifesto. "Can't hurt me," boasts the lad. Rationalizing, he tells himself he logically doesn't care about love. He will not perish in love's fire; he refuses to light a match. Intricate, profound harmonies. They don't spare the chromatics. They sing Everly echoes angelically (Simon the seraph, Garfunkel the cherub?) and perch on the prettiest chord shifts, IV sub-dominants and the bVII seven chord. The drum beat and throbbing bass are big and deep and powerful. Trickly guitars interweave a tapestry of spun-gold arpeggio splendor. Synthesizing the lyric power of Kerouac and Dylan and Ginsberg with the sweet sounds of the Everly Brothers or Peter, Paul, and Mary, Simon and Garfunkel are two of the most important reasons for the Rock Revolution.

Rocks feel no pain? Islands never weep? In declaring himself to be a rock or an island, our porcupinish narrator rationalizes, with dramatic irony, that he can steel himself against pain, anger, despair. Eventually love and hope, too. A chilling way to cope in Rotten Gotham A crusty exterior is often necessary to survive in a tough world. If you declare your love, you're OUT THERE and VULNERABLE.

Look at the rock in the gutter. Maybe it sat there for a million years, while fleshy loving humans can't stretch to a century without luck and perfect constitutions. For those who make it, there's one sobering thought: your second century is guaranteed to be much tougher than your first! Humans grow old, if fortunate, and die too soon. The life

of loving can be a pretty sad scenario. There's only one thing worse – the life without love [Tom Jones's "Without Love" #5, 12-69]. Simon and Gar's stubbly cobble reminds us, in brilliant dramatic irony, that if we try to reject love, we are simply fooling ourselves. Their snow-smothered December day is dark and deep. They gaze from their 150-year-old brownstone window, overlooking Bleeker Street, on a rare moment of Currier & Ives silence in Melville's Old Manhattan. Greenwich Village reverie. Simon and Gar wield their poetic tools carefully. The morose morbid word SHROUD is a pallid Melvillean symbol, like the malevolent whale *Moby Dick*, of the evil which can lurk in the supposedly pure whiteness of white. A shroud blankets the dead from sight [i.e. the singer's capacity to love has, sadly, croaked]. He staggers around in a loveless world, lost and alone. And smug. He thinks he's well-adjusted. He's fooling himself. Aren't we all? We all bumblingly believe we can make it alone. Tough, steely, black belt in stoic strength. Are we ripping ourselves off? Somehow, love busts on through and melts the most titanic iceberg. Ice is, geologically, a rock. Shielded with his books and poetry and alienation, the singer retreats into himself. Will he, come certain spring, doff the armor, spy a new lady friend, and stroll through Central Park to fall in love again? Yep, if he's lucky.

"The Dangling Conversation" – Simon & Garfunkel, **#25, 8-66.** Clobbered as "overwordy" by *Times* critic, this duet Is a pastel Interior adventure. The day is a watercolor still-life. Their dark apartment hosts a vapid, nowhere kibbutz of idle chit-chat. She reads Emily Dickinson and he Robert Frost. Great melody. Sad song of hopeless autumn in their New York relationship.

"A Hazy Shade of Winter" – Simon & Garfunkel, **#13, 11-66.** Same weather as "Homeward Bound" only with much melted snow gone gray, grubby, and oozy. Same sparkling bVII chords. Twirling harmonies. From woe-bleak gray stratus sky they pop out of existential gloom: it's the sunshine of his life. Down the pike:

"Hazy Shade of Winter" – Bangles, **#2(1), 11-87. Susanna Hoffs** (lead singer and guitar) and sisters **Vicki** (lead guitar) and **Debbi Petersen** took Simon and Garfunkel's existential song to new distaff heights. Their new generation bopped to Hip-Hop or 120 beats/minute Techno Dance Rock in the multifarious clubs lining the East Village in Manhattan and the world beyond. Great beat. Great harmonies. For a pixieish delight of a tune about the horrors, hassles, and hang-ups of Dreaded Monday Back at the Office/Factory/Dungeon, sample the **Bangles'** ultracute spiffy Item (one of our favorites): "Manic Monday, #2(1), 1-86.

"At the Zoo" – Simon & Garfunkel, **#16, 3-67.** Fun in NYC? Bronx, Prospect Park, Staten Island, Central Park Zoos! With kidlike exuberance, they bob and bop and plod zanily through the zooming zoo. They meet kindly elephants, insincere giraffes, skeptical orangoutangs. Cotton candy confection, this one. Real Rock and Roll.

Flip side is their groovy original "The 59th Street Bridge Song (Feelin' Groovy)":

"The 59th Street Bridge Song (Feelin' Groovy)" – Harper's Bizarre, #13, 2-67. Like the California Bangles, **Ted Templeman**'s Cal crew sing the spontaneous groovies of contemplating the nifty "59th Street Bridge Song." When you crawl gridlockishly over this toll-less freebie, a/k/a Queensboro Bridge, you are enchanted with the sheer majestic power of the Big Apple skyline.

"Scarborough Fair/(Canticle)" – Simon & Garfunkel, #11, 3-68. This breathtakingly gorgeous double tune ('Round') takes you back to Guinevere, King Arthur, Merlin the magician, Sir Lancelot, and a motley troupe of troubadours and jesters in Robin Hood's Sherwood Forest street turf. It's a blithe combo of parsley, sage, rosemary, thyme (so-named #4 album a year earlier – 11-66). The original song was first published in 1673 in England (Whitburn's info).

Two musicologists' terms spark the tune(s) – counterpoint or polyphony. In its simplest form, you get the ol' "Row, row, row your boat, gently down the stream," which dips into Taoist mysticism in its punch line – "life is but a dream." Other common Rounds? "Frere Jacques," "Little Tom Tinker," "Three Blind Mice." Or the **G-Clefs**' #9, 9-61 " I Understand/Auld Lang Syne."

"Mrs. Robinson" – Simon & Garfunkel, #1(3), 5-68. Simon and Gar ROCK to a 100% pure Everly melody. From 1967 movie *The Graduate*****; Dustin Hoffman debuts as naïve college grad seduced by older Anne Bancroft, before falling wildly in love with her daughter. Buoyant melody. People in song are smarmy patronizing wardens in institution, speaking to "Mrs. Robinson" as a lower form of life. Everybody's favorite Simon & Gar singalong rocker.

Dianne Lancaster's favorite, "Cecilia" (#4, 4-70), is about a promiscuous and unfaithful girl. Their #18, ,9-70 Simonlyric 18th century folk tune from Bolivia/Peru is "El Condor Pasa" [the condor passes, or 'condor pass']. All profound stuff. Like the Peruvian troubadours **Sisal**, of 1999, "El Condor Pasa" throbs with haunting flutes, lilting harmonies, and high-altitude polyrhythms which cast a heavenly airy aura.

"The Boxer" – Simon & Garfunkel, #7, 4-69. Flashback – after *Wednesday Morning 3 A.M.*, their acoustic Columbia album, schmoozed in moribund mediocrity, Simon did solo gigs in London as an American acoustic folk singer of the Dylan ilk. When Tom Wilson added bass and drums, "Sounds of Silence" THUNDERED to #1. Simon, soloing half a world away, had to be tracked down.

Sadly, like the Beatles, Simon and Garfunkel didn't last long enough together, with their last album the all-time favorite *Bridge Over Troubled Water* (#1[10], 2-70). *Sgt. Pepper* set the precedent for printed lyrics. Simon's dour "Boxer"? An ex-pug, of working-class stock, confronts the lonely glum midnight subways, the dank fetid squalid stench seeping into his lonely soul.

The boxer contemplates his ugly scenario. He drifts. In his everyday way, like Huck Finn on the Mississippi, he comes up with great big ideas in small-word blurts. One of the greatest lines ever written? Remember? It's about how a guy hears whatever he chooses to hear, and punts the remainder.

"The Boxer" was banned in Motown, April 1969. DETROIT – not Podunk. Well, a chunk of it was K/O-ed. The Seventh Avenue part, with the hookers. [In 1957 the wholesome Everly Brothers' "Wake Up, Little Susie" was banned in Boston because of drive-in movie smooching.] One hustler line? And one hooker word (found in the *Bible,* in Babylon)? The "Boxer" was dumped in Detroit, of all places, where they eat nails for breakfast and munch murder for lunch. Purveyors of public prurience duked it out with prunes of proper prudence. The lyric battle waged its wanton way into the Heartland. Rap-steeled spicylanguage fans of 2000+ might snicker at all the 1969 censorship hoopla. The whole language issue misses the focal point.

The song sings of a sad and lonely man. Battered into punch-drunk woozy oblivion, he staggers the icy streets. Woebegone. Alienated. Like the reeling dreamer in "Sounds of Silence." Totally solitary. Like Melville's wild-eyed isolatoes shuffling the Moby docks, he gazes balefully out to the gray sea. He is a living ghost. The shell of a man once in shape. Now very far out.

The boxer yearns for "The Human Touch" (Bruce Springsteen #16, 3-92). He craves a street girl's warmth to shield him from the utter desolation he feels in his old cold soul. No posh pension awaits him. His ring winner's share? Gouged by sharks and goons and thugs. He wanders alone and friendless. Bereft of health insurance.

The song floats along in the Key of 'B', hanging a long moody time on the **G-minor** chord that pedal-points the boxer's absolute desperation. As the fadeout waltzes off into the sunset, whole symphonies join the ringing guitar's sonorous **G-minor** extravaganza. It builds to a New York Philharmonic Bernstein-style crushing climax, with the G-minor blaring to the intergalactic Milky Way and the Andromeda Nebula. Finally, FINALLY, it struts simply back to the big **B major** chord, and then flutters away in an acoustic swirl of beautiful *arpeggios* in butterfly formation.

Under LONELY in the dictionary, look for a haggard boxer and two FOLK ROCK troubadours.

"Lonely Man" –Elvis Presley, #32, 3-62. Eeriest song the King ever sang, bar none (not even #55, 9-56 "Blue Moon" banshee wail comes close). In this heart-tugging dirge, you envision a late-life Elvis lumbering to his lady's door, disheveled and downtrodden. [Though he was but 26]. Alone – even ghostly. A sad organ skims the soprano notes, with death-march tonic and sub-dominant I and IV chords to ferry him across the river Styx or wherever to a happier Limbo of lost love.

Simon and **Garfunkel** wrote their own, while other new Folk Rock stars clambered up the Dylan lyrical bandwagon.

"Mr. Tambourine Man" – Byrds, #1(1), 5-65. First Folk Rock #1 smash hit. The Byrds meld timely Dylan lyrics, ethereal harmonies, and thumping thunderbeat. Byrds' main voice is **Roger McGuinn**, whose 12-string mellow Rickenbacker guitar is further enhanced by the harmonics of **David Crosby** (later of **Crosby, Stills, Nash and/or Young**). **Chris Hillman** manned the D-tuned loudest bass in 42 countries, with **Mike Clarke** (d. '93) on drums. Like the Yardbirds of Britain, these Byrds' impeccable credentials doomed them to success.

McGuinn ['Jim' at first], apprenticed with talented **Bobby Darin**. Also the Chad Mitchell Trio – folk group genesis of **John Denver**. Percussionist **Gene Clark** toured with the New Christy Minstrels.

Remember – the **4-string Electric Bass is simply the bottom four strings of a Guitar** – the '**E,**' '**A,**' '**D,**' and '**G**' – **tuned down one octave**. This necessitates chunkier strings. The D-tuned bass of Chris HIllman is the most revolutionary thing in this Dylan jingle-jangle tambourine song. You ignore the low 'E' as your bass note, and you tune down one more note to 'D.' Today electric basses often sport 5 or 6 strings, to nail the very LOWEST bottom notes. On his 11-99 album *Zooma*, Led Zeppelin's John Paul Jones played 10 and even 12-sting basses.

The tambourine man in the song may be a thinly-disguised dope peddler lavishing greenies, pot-stuffed brownies, sky-high hashish, or an L.S.D. 'trip' to the moons of Uranus. Dylan's amazing melody conjoins the Byrds' high-flying harmonies. "Mr. Tambourine Man" salutes troubadours down the ages with songs of joy. A tambourine is a great excuse for a lead singer with no other instrument (Mick Jagger and Jim Morrison used them, too). Its jingle-jangle underscore with grand accent the big 2 and 4 beats on your R & R song. "Mr. Tambourine Man" never pokes or plods or meanders – it DRIVES, with the ringing, singing tambourine packing the percussive power and punch. In "I'll Feel a Whole Lot Better" [#103, 7-65], their total sound is a magic blur of dynamic close harmonies and great big mastodon-sized rhythm guitar by Crosby and McGuinn.

"All I Really Want to Do" – Byrds, #40, 8-65. McGuinn compared the crossover musical revolution as a kind of halvah: "Latin and blues and jazz flavors, Anglo-Saxon and Black church music." The Byrds' new Rock Fusion album touched off a metamorphosis from single to album. Their musical highs and lows were brilliant and booming; the treble stormed. Bottom tones anchored. Somewhere in the magic middle of their songs, they found a groove, caught a celestial wavelength, and joined Dylan's lyrics with the Everly Brothers' harmonies. Folk Music and Rock Music would never be the same. They would both be new and improved. It's too bad the Byrds' flight was so short. **Cher**'s first solo hit (#15, 7-65), this song is about friendship only. No romantic interludes or exploitation. Just be my pal. Clever internal rhyme scheme. When Gene Clark split in 1966, McGuinn and Crosby had full lead vocal responsibility. **Gram Parsons** arrived, succumbing to an OD in 1973.

"Chimes of Freedom" – Bruce Springsteen, NC, recorded 7-3-88, live. Stockholm, Sweden. Perhaps Springsteen's best song? Written by Dylan. Song of peace, patriotism, empathy, freedom, caring and sharing. Powered by the big Heartland Rock convocation of Bruce's E-Street Band: Miami Steve Van Zandt, Clarence Clemons, Max Weinberg, and the rest.

Dylan's "Chimes of Freedom" was also by Byrds (NC, '65). Dylan fires off opaque oxymoronic metaphors here, in a flash flood of gushing genius gone amok: The Byrds' "Chimes" cruises the music like a riverboat paddling the Mississippi surf. With big block tonic **G** chords (Key? 'G'), "Chimes" rolls, caressing its mystical lyrical kingdom. Dylan singles out mute, aching souls with non-nursable psychic wounds. He salutes strung-out, bummed-out, bad-trip sufferers. He sings out gustily in his coda to every last hung-up soul all over our universe. As we all gaze together at those enchanted, mystical chimes, they flash bright freedom in the aftermath of Kennedy's Camelot, and the plain of Vietnam's long, long war. The Byrds topped the charts again with Pete Seeger's *Ecclesiastes* biblical adaptation #1(3), 10-65 "Turn, Turn, Turn." In "My Back Pages" #30, 4-67, the Byrds sing how they grow YOUNGER. "So You Want to Be a Rock and Roll Star" (#29, 1-67) gave us wannabe air-guitarists a cool blueprint. How can a great song fail to fly high for three great artists/groups? Here's how:

"Today's Teardrops" – Rick Nelson, #54, 11-63. Began as 'B'-side. Penned by **Gene Pitney** and sung by (NC) **Roy Orbison**, this can't-miss throbbing melodic masterpiece withered in Program Directors' circular files. After reprising Glenn Miller's #3, 1940 "Fools Rush In" to a nice #12, Rick's teardrops of today flowed for this great song doomed to the Dew Drop Inn 3:33 a.m. night-owl slot in East Bezuzus, Oblivion. It's still a cosmic mystery why so many truly great songs end up in the Dastardly Dumps of Obscurity. Ten teardrops per tune . . .

John Lennon was stunned when **Bob Dylan** mentioned to him that the Beatles' melodies were great, but why didn't they write about something important? Paul got pensive and in the Beatles' transitional period from popular to esoterically psychedelic, they hit this middle ground. For clarity, profundity, and timeless elegance; we must go back to yesterday.

"Yesterday" – Beatles, #1(4), 9-65. With 2500 recorded versions, Paul's theme song was first to log over 5 million performances, with 25,000+ hours of American TV and radio airplay (Whitburn's tabulational masterwork, *Top Pop Singles 1955-93*). Paul reflects. All his life, once splendid, now shimmers before him in tatters. He shrugs. His stoic philosophy befits John Wayne, Gary Cooper. Yesterday, all Paul's worldly troubles seemed so remote, distant. Today they've returned, a wrenching emotional burden on his tired shoulders. He now believes in the inevitable reality of yesterday. A dignified string chorus of mellow cellos overlays his sere and floundering soul, in the aftermath of his lady's departure. The lost and lonely Beatle fidgets with second-guessing – perhaps he said something wrong? In a tidal wave of pain and remorse, he longs for yesterday. All Paul, 100% McCartney. In beautiful 'F' major, Paul stalks from 'E' bass note into **D-minor** in an acoustic spin that echoes Johann Sebastian Bach. Needling their somber way into Verse II, the blue-velvet cellos arrive – brusque and commanding. "Yesterday" is a pensive masterpiece for the ages.

"Paperback Writer" – Beatles, #1(2), 6-66. They quibble over an emerging manuscript. The would-be literary superstar tells the publisher how he can snap it 'round for instant fame and fortune, chopping chapters, gushing 1000-page extravaganzas in a week or two. No real writer cannot empathize. Fame and success? Great. In the meantime, "a steady job' will be nice, too.

Rollicking music ping-ponged the Atlantic. With a bulbous turban bejeweled above his goatee, Sam acquired a back-up group with the hardest word in English/Egyptian to spell . . . pharaohs!

"Wooly Bully" – Sam the Sham and the Pharaohs, #2(2), 4-65; #31, 6-65 R & B. With his SPANGLISH countdown ('Juan-two-tree-quatro'), **Sam Samudio** (b. '40) of Dallas told a spicy story about a dog, a girl, and a bull of the wooly variety. A 12-Bar Blues, "Bully" plumps along, oozing sweat in the 100° July Dallas heat. The wheezy organ pumps passion from the iffy lyric inspired by some Tijuana or Juarez go-go skin show of questionable virtue. Sam became a streetside *Bible* gospel preacher.

His "Little Red Riding Hood" [#2(2), 6-66] croons of wolfish desire. Evil wolf lures lovely little lass into deep dark woods, peddling a protection racket. This sneaky wolf is about as successful as the old *Looney Tunes* comics' hopeful beau of grown-up Red Riding Hood – Elmer Fudd. By 1950, Little Red Miss Hood stumbled out of Looney Tunes, leaving stumblebum Fudd a sad stooge solo act. Sam the Sham's wily wolf hits an equal impasse by knotted, gnarly oaks. In the frantic fadeout, Sam the Sham desperately attempts his masquerade in his absurd sheep suit. Sam the Sham's street-savvy bass voice, soaring to spooky baritone, inspired the persona of Wolfman Jack, legendary *American Graffiti***** (1973) DJ and R & R legend.

America's TV moguls, begging for a Beatle to replicate *Help*, used American ingenuity. Result? Manchester, England's **Davy Jones**, (b. '45) teen idol second tenor, offered a leadoff line-up: bassman **Peter Tork**, (b. '44) of Washington DC; drummer **Mickey Dolenz** (b. '45); and later *creator* of Music Television (*MTV*), Houston's **Michael Nesmith** (b. '42). Call them the **Monkees**.

"Pleasant Valley Sunday" – Monkees, #3, 7-67. With 500 hopefuls at NBC casting call, Columbia execs rejected the **Lovin' Spoonful** ('more trouble than they're worth') and **Stephen Stills** of **Buffalo Springfield** (imperfect teeth). Only Nesmith had been a true working musician, Jones and Dolenz were Ricky Nelsonish kid actors.

Bubblegum king **Don Kirshner** shepherded Colgems songwriters, crackerjack studio axemen, and candy land princes of percussion. With oodles of hype, and marshmallow mountains of promotion, the first Semi-American Quasi-Beatles womped the #1 spot with their great debut "Last Train to Clarksville" (#1, 9-66). Heather Murphy says they grew into their instruments, and were such nice guys everybody liked them in the process. The Monkees' worst critics couldn't help but love them because of their hilarious gift of self-parody. Contestant John Capalongo, on **Regis Philbin**'s 11-21-99 *Who Wants to Be a Millionaire*, referred to the Beatles as the FAB Four. He called the casting call Monkees the PREFAB FOUR.

With the Beatles' *Help***** and *A Hard Day's Night*****, Rock and Roll rampaged over Hollywood via London, and the Monkees' appeal was cinematic. Lampooning Chaplin pantomimes and Burns and Durante vaudeville shtick, they yokked it up with cartoonery buffoonery.

"Pleasant Valley Sunday" zaps suburban conformity. They nip suburban status-seeking squires and blowhard Babbitts at the height of their bluster of smoky barbeques. One great reason for the Monkees' smashing success here and in the UK? The Beatles stopped touring forever in 1966. Their last gig was atop their studio roof, playing for startled lunch-munchers outdoors. It was not unlike Joe Zilch's (or yours or my garage band) playing a new gas station opening or a Sweet Sixteen Soiree. Also, the Monkees had a great Rock and Roll sound.

"I'm a Believer" – Monkees, #1(7), 12-66; #1 U.K. Seven weeks? You can't really fake success. With hyper hype and TV exposure, you can pad the profits. You can't, however, take a bad song and make it command the #1 American spot for seven weeks. The Monkees also scored silver and bronze with a #2 "Alternate Title" in the UK, and "Valleri" (#3, 3-68) in America. "I'm a Believer" is by the King of Adult Contemporary, **Neil Diamond** of Brooklyn, from the Brill Building factory of post-Tin Pan Alley hits. The song swaggers blithely with jolly enthusiasm. Plot? Kid thought genuine true love only pertained to fairy tales. Sees dream R & R queen. Insta-Love. Poof.

Speedy conversion. He sees her face, and suddenly, eureka, he's a believer. No more gnawing doubting-Thomas. 100% converted. Bouncy, catchy Diamond-studded tune. The hit maker? Idol **Davy Jones** was named after a locker ('Davy Jones' Locker' = sailors' euphemism for drowned, reposing at bottom of sea). Nice song, fun singer. Ballooned us away from exploding jungles, as did Monkees' ultracute "Daydream Believer" [#1(4), 11-67], by the Kingston Trio's John Stewart. A six a.m. alarm, a cold, stinging shaving razor, and a very sleepy girl named Jean surround our intrepid hero. Coach to the rescue:

"Daydream Believer"– Anne Murray, #12, 12-79; #3, 1-80 C. Nova Scotia's favorite snowbird Anne Murray zinged this thing back up the Disco Decade charts. Fine resonant contralto, Anne. She started in Springhill, NS, Canada, and taught gym a year before busting out big with her mellow "Snowbird" (#8, 7-70). "Snowbird" anchored the Michigan-to-Florida word 'Snowbird' for a pensioner who keeps an established summer home in Ontario or Grand Rapids, and hotfoots for sunny climes come the first ghastly snowflake. Her style? Was it Canadian Folk Rock Contemporary British Soul Blues Country? R & R mellowed, and the *Adult Contemporary Billboard* lists fanned teenage fans' fandom out to a big, rich new audience, thirtysomethings.

Neil Diamond (b. Noah Kaminsky, Brooklyn, 1-24-41) sent his deep baritone way into the R & R Idol ELVIS SPOTLIGHT for awhile, but he wanted MOR! [M.O.R. Middle of the Road].

"Brooklyn Roads" – Neil Diamond, #58, 5-68. Young Neil fades back to his walk-up Brooklyn flat-solid brownstones; 4" x 4"'s hold up five-story scaffoldish porches full of tricycles, billowing clothesline shirts, and old lost aromas of gefilte fish, sauerkraut, and peach pie. Neil learned the power of popular music from **Pete Seeger and the Weavers**. But Neil secretly wanted to be like Elvis. Few realized (not even the young self-assured songsmith/singer) how close Diamond would come. At Manhattan's hepcat haven, the Brill Building, Neil rubbed shoulders with **Carole King**, Cynthia Weil, Ellie Greenwich, and a constellation of Classic Rock tunesmiths. Neil had one advantage over other good singers there – he's a great one. Neil Diamond is classified at #1 Adult Contemporary position from 1964-Present ahead of Billy Joel as TOP MALE VOCALIST. Neil is listed at 19th Artist overall, with 3177 points in Joel Whitburn's Top 500 Artists/Groups of All Time, just behind **Chicago** (3181).

"Come Back When You Grow Up" – Bobby Vee, #3, 7-67. Neil's vocal appeal mirrors the rich baritone vitality of Buddy Holly's #1 protégé – **Bobby Vee**, who started Bob Dylan's musical career via his garage band the Shadows of 1959. Bobby watched the Psychedelic pandemonium unfold before his North Dakotan eyes.

Unlike Neil Diamond, Bobby Vee had few Elvis pretensions. Like many of us 60s forlorn Bopper/Valens/Holly mourners, we were all too busy trying to be BUDDY. After a time of teen-idoldom, autographing for goggle-eyed groupies, Bobby settled down with his childhood sweetheart, and raised a fine family of boys who would later become his back-up band – the Vees. His spirited advice rebounds down the long years to nouveaux [single] rock stars with lusty libidos; before dancing and romancing, check her I.D. In the Groovy Groupie Sweepstakes, Bobby Vee took the Gentleman's Boulevard instead of the Sleazo Back Alley. He saw his R & R colleagues drag groupies off into closets, fracture bodies and souls on heroin and cocaine, and chugalug six-packs of Jack Daniels:

"Chug-A-Lug" – Roger Miller, #9, 9-64; #3 C. Country kid guzzles cheap wine outside subteen barn with hoodlum friends. Follow-up to "King of the Road" (#4, 1-65). Song hero and pal run ten long miles in blitzed glee, and barf in the fadeout. Weird Al Yankovic fans will dig it. Not for the weak of tummy.

Back to the Brooklyn Bridge – still damaged by improvements.

"Girl, You'll Be a Woman Soon" – Neil Diamond, #10, 4-67. Diamond shines on this teenybopper lyrical theme three months before B. Vee. Slow rolling ballad, reverberating with strings and rumbly blur of deep blue guitar. Let's go to **Pickett & Puckett:**

"Young Girl" – Union Gap, featuring Gary Puckett, #2(3), 3-68; #1, 1968 U.K. Or, for that matter, follow-up "This Girl Is a Woman Now", #9, 8-69. Yep, **Gary Puckett** (b. '42), is from Dylan's arctic hometown Hibbing, Minnesota. YOUNG GIRL! You hear this breathtaking Italian tenor perched alone on this shimmering note. Then BAM. The Union Gap rushes in, muskets ready, bedecked in crisp blue Yankee Civil War uniforms – suddenly you wonder which 60s you're in [Paul Revere & the Raiders wore Revolutionary War uniforms]. Puckett has one of the top 20 Dramatic/Operatic tenors in the Rock Revolution. He admonishes the young lusty teen queen who obsesses him to flee from his fevered mind. Why? He knows his insta-love for her is far 'outa-line.'

"I Thank the Lord for the Night Time" – Neil Diamond, #13, 7-67. Mixed-bag piety but a groovy tune. The 9-to-5 routine, he grouses, isn't sending him anywhere super. Neil's simple solution? The 5 o'clock bell, and his swingin' girlfriend to cap off his homeward-bound commute.

"Five O'Clock World" – Vogues, #4, 11-65. Bill Burkette's Turtle Creek, Pennsylvania, Vogues love After Five. The factory whistle blows, and the Vogues cheer that nobody owns any piece of their precious fun time. Echoing the **Lettermen**, they celebrate long-haired girls who wait to zap their workaday blahs.

"Kentucky Woman" – Neil Diamond, #22, 10-67. Neil's splash of Southern sunshine. Diamond suddenly discovered down-home mountain roots, and re-slung this song in Brooklyn Country album *Tennessee Moon*, (#14, 3-96; #12 U.K.). Neil does an intriguing duet with former Cricket **Waylon Jennings**. Neil's sweet Kentucky woman seems to shine via her own personal aura. Whatever goes wrong, she instantly makes right for him.

Simon & Garfunkel
(left, Art Garfunkel, right, Paul Simon)

"Red Red Wine" – Neil Diamond, #62, 4-68. Diamond bade farewell to Brill buddies and Bang Records producers Ellie Greenwich and Jeff Barry with this ode to a cheap date – wine! Rock and Roll, however, disappears into obscurity, resurfaces, and is resurrected as THAT SUPER NEW SONG by UB40. "Red Red Wine" (#34, 1-84; then #1[1], 8-88, NC, R & B.) Like Chubby Checker's "Twist," twice #1 (1960 & 1961), "**U**nemployment **B**enefits (form) **Forty**" [UB40] had two hits with this one. The punchy Reggae beat suggests Jamaica – not smoky, red-brick, Birmingham, England. After UB40's **Temps**' (#6, 9-90) "The Way You Do the Things You Do,' Neil arrives. The bottle of Red is the anesthesia from life's baleful realities. The rotgut is his friend, his warm jacket of courage. In the homeless shanties of the gutter nightscape wasteland, UB40 serenades in counterpoint (see Lightfoot).

"Cracklin' Rosie" – Neil Diamond, #1(1), 8-70. This Rosie song has nothing to do with a girl named Rosie. (Nor does Neil worship Buddy Holly in #6, 11-69 "Holly Holy"). "Rosie" too is a sad hymn to a bottle. This semi-rosy ode follows the old hobo jungles, Skid Rows, Bowery buccaneers, underpass trolls, huddled-up homeless men with nowhere to run. No place to hide.

Buttressed by solid bottom on bass and horn section, Neil's big baritone booms down to a **Johnny Cash** bass. Diamond's down and out hobo croons woozy praise for his bubbly Rosé wine which lulls him to fitful sleep. Pathetically, the bottle is his baby. He tenderly loves his "Rosie, Child," the way to happiness. He mutters that she's a 'store-bought' sweetheart. The poor old sot loves (hopefully not literally) his bottle of Rosé wine. Neil began with "Solitary Man," about Melinda and Sue and his triangular love trials and tribulations [resurrected: first #55, 5-66, then #21, 7-70]. His follow-up? #6, 8-66 "Cherry, Cherry."

Other Diamond gems? "Longfellow Serenade" (#5, 10-74), about "Hiawatha's" **Henry Wadsworth Longfellow**, the ELVIS of the 19th century; #1(1), 5-72 "Song Sung Blue," previews Neil's #1(2), 10-78 **Barbra Streisand** collaboration "You Don't Bring Me Flowers." Neil's #24, 2-70 "Shilo," like America's *Calvin & Hobbes* comic strip (1980-95), concerns an imaginary playmate. No tiger, just a pal. Neil reminisces about his faded childhood, and the adult world that left him vulnerable and hurt and bitter. As a kid, he could conjure 'SHILO,' his imaginary pal. Why would Neil (or Noah) name an imaginary pal after a Civil War battlefield – Shiloh? Who knows? **Shilo**, perhaps, was just a magical mystical word to him, like WOMBAT.

Like most Neil Diamond productions, he begins on a low gravelly baritone murmur. Wisp of instrumentation, too. He crescendos to a swashbuckling musical climax. In a puff of hope, Neil says he wishes his old pal SHILO could come back and console him today. Super song, and hook. Sad.

"America" – Neil Diamond, #8, 4-81. Neil's Greatest Hit? Check her if you're an immigrant: ☐ or here if you're the son of an immigrant: ☐. If not, this tune might lose a few percentage points. Diamond delivers with the frenetic fervor of a young man seeing the Statue of Liberty for the first time in New York Harbor. A stunning anthem of freedom. Since the Osama bin Laden/WTC tragedy of September 2001, "America's" oldies airplay has soared. Diamond underscores the frantic flights of millions of refugees, seeking a hopeful lamp of liberty, and a golden door of opportunity.

Neil starred in the umpteenth remake of *The Jazz Singer*, 1980. The original stars rich megaphone-style baritone **Al Jolson** in the first semi-talking movie (1927**½). The son of Cantor Oland tries to please his Russian father, who looks down on pop singing. Movies then, like now, had many of the era's top hits, like Jolie's "Rockabye Your Baby with a Dixie Melody" (#1[8], 8-1918); "April Showers" (#1[11], 1-22); "Swanee" (#1[9], 5-20); "California Here I Come" (#1[6], 5-24); "Toot, Toot Tootsie Goodbye" (#1[4], 12-22); and "My Mammy" (#2[2], 6-28 and rerun #18, 2-47). The **Happenings** also did "My Mammy" (#13, 7-67). **Bob Miranda** sang lead. Great tribute to Mom. Tremendous Happenings' version previous of George Gershwin's 1930 "I Got Rhythm" (#3, 4-67) from musical *Girl Crazy* [Whitburn].

Diamond's three-decade domination of the *Billboard* charts sparkled with his "America" anthem – sometimes mistakenly called "[Comin' to] America."

Johnny B. Goode immigrant odyssey. **Chuck Berry**'s little dude twangs his guitar by the railroad track, dreaming of his name in lights – JOHNNY B. GOODE – TONIGHT. For the immigrant kid, the gold-paved streets point up a neon stairway to the stars which glitter like diamonds over Neil Diamond's gold-paved "America." Or Led Zeppelin's – a Stairway to Heaven.

"Indiana Wants Me" – R. Dean Taylor, #5, 9-70, NC, R & B. First white Motown artist to hit Top Five. R. Dean Taylor (b. '39, Toronto) was mesmerized by "Shilo" and the genius of Neil Diamond. When we worked in the 1966 Motown songwriters' basement, he told me "I'd love to discover that kind of tremendous hook." Soon, he did. A shoot-'em-up number. The song-guy killed a man, apparently for saying something really bad about his girl-friend (or perhaps wife, because they have a kid). The song shrieks with screaming sirens like TV show *Cops*; fugitive flees, darts into the abyss (until they chase him back into Indiana). "Indiana Wants Me" reprises Del Shannon's "So Long Baby" revenge motif. Taylor presages Gangsta Rap in its violent siren roar. Drum thunder. Screaming code-red guitars. Trapped fugitive's last stand. White Motown balladeer. Soon we'll cover the Blues:

"Green Onions" – Booker T. & the MG's, #3, 8-62; #1(4) R & B. Named after horticulturalist **Booker T. Wahington**, the Memphis Stax/Volt rhythmic session superstars consisted of Afro **Booker T. Jones** on keyboards; **Al Jackson** (1935-75), drums; Caucasian guitar wizard **Steve Cropper**, guitar; and the most famous bass man of the era, (white, like Disney namesake) **Donald 'Duck' Dunn**. These guys starred with John Belushi and Dan Aykroyd in the *Blues Brothers* (1980****). "Green Onions" is a catchy instrumental with a lead organ sound of MULTICULTURAL Booker T and the funky Soul bottom pulse of Dunn and Jackson and Crooper.

"When a Man Loves a Woman" – Percy Sledge, #1(2), 4-66; #1(4) R & B. Sledge (b. '40), working as an orderly in hometown Leighton, Alabama, sang faithfully at Galilee Baptist Church. Nights he sang with the Esquires combo. Covering Smokey Robinson and Beatles tunes at a gig, he drifted down into the dumps about a lost girlfriend. Stopping the music, Percy commanded his band to play a gutsy slow ballad beat. Percy Sledge simultaneously created this song in practically one inspirational fell swoop! They quickly cut the master at Muscle Shoals, Alabama, with the most famous Soul session guys in the U.S.A. not employed by Motown, the famous integrated Soulsters **Booker T. and the MG's**. With the storied record production of Quin Ivy and the MG's nucleus, they released Sledge's master locally. It soon hopped to the Aretha label, Atlantic, and the rest is obviously history.

When love is good, it's the best thing in the world. To love is to flaunt one's vulnerability. To wear one's heart on one's sleeve. Contrast to Simon and Garfunkel's "I Am a Rock," its polar opposite. The ivory-tower academic steels himself from human feeling in an armor suit of books and studies and work; he is immune, he hopes, to love. He builds a mighty fortress made of steely self-sufficiency. He has no friends, because friendship can create pain. He is a rock. A rock 'lives' for millions of years, and feels nothing. Perhaps the poor intellectual has rocks in his head.

Most of us cheer the **Percy Sledges** who agonize for love. "The Rock of Gibraltar" hit #20 [Frankie Laine, 7-52], but it's the living, loving Percy Sledges who make it to Number One. Yet, as Tennyson mused in "Locksley Hall," "'Tis better to have loved and lost, than never to have loved at all." It is LOVE that raises us all above the slugs and clods and pebbles of this earthy Earth.

And here is the unhidden Glory of Rock and Roll. To study Rock and Roll is to look beyond the mysterious veil which love coquettishly promises. When you pore over algebra and macroeconomics, you study cold numbers and hard money. To study biology, you cut up dead frogs. To study the popular song, however, you study living love. Vital love. Love throbs its booming backbeat – with surging amps and coruscating rainbow lights. Here lies the glory of Rock and Roll. The glory of love.

A man loves a woman.

"When a Man Loves a Woman" – Michael Bolton, #1(1), 10-91, NC, R & B. New Haven, Connecticut's softball semipro 'Soul Provider' (#17, 7-98), Michael (b. Michael Bolotin, 1954) dusts the grace notes. He hammers the Sledge song with Blue-Eyed Soul. Skillful cover of Sledge.

Bob Dylan promised us all that "The Times They Are A-Changin'." There was a nasty little war firing up over in Vietnam. The war altered forms of Rock and Roll in strange ways never perceived possible. The impact of the up-front singer retiring to the back of the band – only to be overwhelmed by the fiery pyrotechnics of the flaming guitar – this impact has never been measured. When **Jimi Hendrix** kicked off the Monterey Pop Festival on June 16, 1967, with his smoking guitar flashing frantic feedback to "The Star-Spangled Banner," no one could ever go home again.

Bill Medley and Bobby Hatfield – Righteous Bros.

Rock & Rockets' Red Glare: Cannonade Serenade

While we weren't looking, a little war sneaked up, pounced on us, and took over the world. Flashback Dien Bien Phu, French Indo-China 1954. The French got tired of defending their besieged jungle fort. Locals took over their ancestral property. Somehow, normally-mellow Brigadier General **Dwight David Eisenhower** (1890-1969), President and Commander-in-Chief of Allied Forces in World War II, decided we Americans would straighten out the insurrection in Southeast Asia. Ike sent over a few advisers. Result? EQUATORIAL SNOWBALL. Snowball? A few token Kennedy troops were sent to newly-bisected South Vietnam and Ho Chi Minh's North Vietnam. Flare-up? Each flickering ember in the Vietnam fire got doused by kerosene – not water.

"Ballad of the Green Berets" – Staff Sgt. Barry Sadler, #1(5), 2-66; #2(2) C. Green Berets were the vanguard of the U.S. Army Special Forces in Vietnam, flunking 97 of 100 aspirants. Vietnam war policy was congressionally undeclared. Big military guns advised against an Asian military quagmire: General **George F. Kennan**, who formulated our "Contain Communism" policy, and Commander-in-Chief, General/President **Dwight Eisenhower**, warned of military catastrophe befalling any American land war in Asia. We could bomb and defoliate the whole place, and still the Vietnamese people would not be conquered.

Sgt. Barry Sadler and all the brave American soldiers didn't debate the military policy of their Pentagon leaders. They did their duty. They tried to stop communism in Southeast Asia, no matter who blundered at the Pentagon. The foot soldier does not fabricate policy. He just enforces it. Barry Sadler (1940-89) took the risks, got a snare-drum leftfield hit song, and sold a million records to people confused about policy – but 100% behind any kid who had to go over there.

Things got worse. President **Lyndon Johnson** (1908-73) did a *déjà vu* scenario with the 1898 Spanish American War's "Remember the Maine" incident in the nearby Battle of Manila, Philippines. Our 60s warship had been ostensibly fired upon, creating the Gulf of Tonkin Incident Resolution. Its immediate repercussion? From a mere handful of advisors, suddenly we zoomed from 25,000 American soldiers to 184,000 [540,000, America's darkest year – 1968]. Pallid light flickered in our national tunnel of darkness. Campus militancy, flaming cities, the drug/booze epidemic, and an escalating war all exploded *en masse* – just like the 2001 surprise attack of 9-11.

Drifting into Vietnam, our war music was rah-rah whoop-it-up. As we limped out on prostheses, or wheeled away in Ron Kovic's paraplegic despair, or returned to flag-draped Montana cemeteries, the war got bigger. We Americans are a noble nation that believes in happy endings. Our TV godlet tells us so. We can resolve any ugly situation, no matter how gruesome or grotesque, in a one-hour drama.

The Vietnam War was always fought with HOPE. **Ike**'s father ran a general store in HOPE, Kansas. President **Bill Clinton** (b. '46) was born in HOPE, Arkansas. Beloved singer/comedian **Bob Hope** (b. 1904) entertained our troops in the longest war in American history (c. 1963-75).

In 1965, only one American senator, **J. William Fulbright** of Arkansas (1908-95), was against the congressionally undeclared War in Vietnam's policy of sending troops to Southeast Asia. Teenaged **Bill Clinton** was moved by this maverick senator who defied his colleagues' military unanimity. Finally, Fulbright was joined by Wayne Morse and Mark Hatfield of Oregon. By 1968 the tide had altered forever. Young Al Gore, Senator's son from Tennessee, didn't agree with the war, but decided to serve in Vietnam anyhow (though he could have stayed stateside). Our military quest underwent the deepest scrutiny by the American people; 98% of America favored the war effort in 1964-65, but by 1968 (Dr. King, Robert Kennedy, streets burning, millions protesting) only 49% favored continuing the limited-strategy war effort. Declare a victory, murmured the masses, and bring our sons home, alive. When Dr. Martin Luther King reluctantly spoke up against Civil Rights President **Lyndon Johnson** in 1966 – and opposed the war – American military unity tattered. Working people began to question tactical rationale, self-determination, and religious values. Though a few seedy Communist radicals infused the protest marches, the overwhelming majority of political activists were the kids next door.

The Rock Era wheeled along to military marches of all kinds. **John Philip Sousa** roused up the Spanish-American war effort [#1(8), 7-1897 "Stars and Stripes Forever"].

Recall World War I's instant mobilization for "the Great War to End All Wars"? This war-torn battle-scarred planet has never seen such wholesale carnage, destruction, and death as Hitler, Josef Stalin, and Pol Pot brought us within most vicious century in human history, Century Number Twenty. No wonder Generation X saw a gloomy future. The rest have high hopes for the titanic new millennium, and hope it doesn't go down in flames . . . or icy seas.

"Over There" – American Quartet, #1(9), 9-1917. Lead tenor **Billy Murray** sang this and **George M. Cohan**'s (1873-1942) OTHER big patriotic #1(8), 2-1905 "Yankee Doodle Boy." Legendary flag-waving songsmith **Irving Berlin** (1888-1989), wrote **Kate Smith**'s "God Bless America" (#10, 4-39; #5, 7-40). Our 1917 Yankee "doughboy soldiers" entered the giant war ravaging the European continent, in a hail of gunfire, poison gas, and massive exploding shells. Murray's American Quartet shared its "Over There" limelight with: the Peerless Quartet, #1(2), 10-1917; Nora Bayes #1(3), 11-1917; Murray solo #5, 12-1917; Prince's Orchestra #6, 1-1918, and legendary tenor **Enrico Caruso** #1(3), 10-1918. "Over There" is a rallying cry. Rousing songs inspire patriotic attention to the most arduous and terrifying of all tasks – shooting at people you don't know to preserve your own freedom, home and family. War is hell, but Hitler is worse.

"Snoopy vs. the Red Baron" – Royal Guardsmen, #2(4), 12-66. America's beloved beagle saves the world for democracy, yay. In 1966, there were still so few Americans in Vietnam that a war song might still be funny. *Peanuts* (1950-2000), #1 60s comic strip, features beloved dog Snoopy blasting through the blue sky above Germany. Snoopy dueled aerial skirmishes with German air ace Baron von Richthofen – actual World War I biplane whiz, who shot scores of Allied pilots out of the European sky. Their 'dog' fight in battling biplanes flaunts all the swashbuckling bravado. Ultimate macho. Or canine. Snoopy fantasizes his heroic machine-gun aerial firefights, bopping the Baron's parachute back to flak fields of Flanders. American TV highlighted cowboy sanitized violence. In these *Father Knows Best* years, the bloodreel never really showed some poor soldier with half his head blown off. This ghastly stuff had to await ghoulish 'snuff' movies or Larry Flynt. Or *Faces of Death*. Or Steven Spielberg and Tom Hanks' 1999 *Saving Private Ryan*. Snoopy's cartoon war was a fun football game.

How so? Listen to "Snoopy's Christmas" #1(5), 12-67 (*Billboard* Special Christmas chart). The rascally Red Baron, and American beagle air ace Snoopy, dream of quaffing root beers with lovely French maidens in the Argonne, and they quit their shootout for Christmas. The bloody revival of death, destruction, and doom would have to wait till December 26th . . .

America's most beloved cartoonist, **Charles Schulz** (1922-2000), realized the demonic rigors and horrors of real war from his service during World War II. Most 'comics,' cartoons, and VIDEO games of today feature World Wrestling Federation hulks and robot monsters gleefully smashing each other to rest-in-pieces smithereens.

Schulz and his beloved *Peanuts* gang rarely resorted to violence. The modest cartoonist represented bedrock America. Schulz explained that his characters symbolized parts of his personality; **Schroeder** the musical side; **Linus** the innocent kid seeking security in a chaotic world via his security blanket; **Lucy** the fussbudget occasionally zapped by selfish crabbitude. **Charlie Brown**, of course, represents all of us – losing the big game, too shy to ask the pretty red-haired girl out, and never able to kick the blasted football. But Charlie Brown never gives up Hope – and neither does Rock and Roll. Or America.

Fifties rock fans may recall the **Coasters**' 2nd-biggest smash – #2(3), 2-59 "Charlie Brown." The name was coincidental. The Leiber-Stoller comic classic involved a class clown who tossed spitwads, twirled dice for 7-11 in the gym, and had the audacity in that well-behaved era to call the English teacher "Daddy-O." "Good ol' Charlie Brown," of *Peanuts* fame, glory, and legend, would never dream of upending the establishment. In his calm and kind way, *Peanuts*' Charlie Brown and all the millions of Americans like him are what keeps this nation strong and powerful and sympathetic to the struggles of a world bludgeoned by poverty and despair.

The Coasters' cut-up Charlie is always good for a chuckle with his applied tomfoolery. However, Charles Schulz's good ol' Charlie Brown is the essence of the All-American dream, tempered with a tone of existential reality in the post-modern era. A dedicated Christian, Charles Schulz works out Biblical parables (see Robert Short's *The Gospel According to Peanuts*, 1966) through the adventures and misadventures of Charlie, Lucy, Patty, Shermy, Franklin, Pigpen, Marcie, and Sally. Millions of 90s baseball fan-addicts were overjoyed to finally see Charlie hit the home run which won the game. Finally. Maybe best of all, Charlie Brown finally got kissed by the pretty girl. Perhaps it is no coincidence his camp romance is a girl named PEGGY JEAN. **Buddy Holly**, we recall, sang the golden charms of "Peggy Sue" (#3, 10-57). "Jean" (#2, 1969) is the breathtaking ballad done by "Good Morning Starshine" star **Oliver** (Swofford, 1945-2000), who passed away the same week as the beloved cartoonist. Indeed, Schulz's last cartoon was scheduled for Valentine's Day 2000. Remember poor ol' Charlie Brown standing forlornly at the mailbox for valentines that never came? A few hours before his last scheduled Sunday comic, Schulz lost his epic battle with a long, arduous illness.

Snoopy, however, will continue to keep up the good Rock and Roll dogfight in those halcyon blue skies above Germany. Schulz's alter ego of adventure and courage, Charlie's beagle Snoopy soars resolutely aloft on the wings of America's plucky hopes and dogged bravery.

The melody for "Snoopy vs. the Red Baron?" Pure Power Rock. Throbbing with booming tonic major chords, the sprightly tune cascades through flying fusillades of fortissimo notes. Each ringing note is accented, like a Disco song. In harmony, and hell-bent-for-leather whoosh, the hit tune could well be classified as Surf Rock, though Snoopy surfs the sizzling skies.

Yes, Schulz saw enough of the horrors of World War II

in that dismal smokescape beyond his father's homespun barber shop in Minnesota. Schulz was part of Tom Brokaw's *The Greatest Generation* (1998). Where would we all be today without German-American Schulz's adolescent bravery? Schulz extracted, from a terrible war with 300,000 American battle deaths (Vietnam, 50,000 . . . bad enough), a positive vision of his American homeland that coalesced into the most important cartoon kid in the Rock Era, GOOD OL' CHARLIE BROWN. And the most important cartoon dog – SNOOPY.

When 1966 Snoopy battled the Red Baron, no one protested. The war in Vietnam had not yet escalated to full troop strength. In 1968 – our national nadir year – Robert Kennedy was gunned down in the aftermath of the tragic death of Martin Luther King, Jr. During the first half of the 60s, "protest" was a non-word. By 1968 Mayor Daley's Chicago Police Riot at the Democratic Convention, an entire generation became disenfranchised, bitter, rebellious, and rootless.

It's hard to tell which generation it was . . .

There wasn't anyone, however, who didn't feel like Charlie Brown now and then. And there wasn't anyone – even John Wayne – who didn't secretly admire America's bravest beagle, bopping about in his glory-bound biplane – defending his home and freedom.

"There's a Star-Spangled Banner Waving Somewhere" **– Elton Britt, #7, 9-42.** Country blockbuster with electric guitar and sad story. Young man with a bad leg tries to enlist, but gets classified 4-F (Physical Disability). Britt's Irish tenor sparks a wave of sympathy. Very few Vietnam Era folks tried desperately to join up! Disabled lad figures a flag waves somewhere, and there's a job he can do to help. Vietnam was not World War II. The stakes were Armageddon. Had Hitler won . . . well, we don't even want to think about it. Britt toyed with Rock and Roll on "Blacksmith Blues', NC, 1952 (Ella Mae Morse, #3, 2-52). Blacksmiths served the cavalry, and Morse dabbled in a Jazz Rock Blues blend far, far ahead of her time. Song features a clangy ANVIL hammering Rock 2 & 4 beats.

"White Cliffs of Dover" – Righteous Brothers, #118, 10-66; #21, 11-66 U.K. WWII hit (#1[1], '42) for **Kay Kyser Orchestra** looked forward optimistically to a peaceful future of bluebirds over the white chalk ($CaCo_3$) cliffs of Dover, England, eighty miles from London. Ferryboat terminus from LaHavre, France. Righteous Brother **Bobby Hatfield**'s performance on this and "Ebb Tide" match his "Unchained Melody." A song of hope and inspiration.

"Der Fuehrer's Face" – Spike Jones & His City Slickers, #3, 10-42. You think Gangsta Rap skateboards on controversial language and impossible risqué acts? Wait'll you catch what Spike Jones and his off-the-wall Dixieland/Big Band blasters did to Chancellor Adolf Hitler's face. Jousting for #1 Gross-Out Song of the Century, Jones's madcap musical marauders salute the psychopath Chancellor of Germany with what can only be described in 'PG-13' as a four-letter "F" word for a 'rectal belch.' World War II blazed on the darkling continent.

Whole civilizations clashed by fiery night and sulfurous hellfire. The fiery forges of Pittsburgh and Detroit cranked out tanks and planes and technology to help the Allies – until we were invited into the worldwide holocaust and catastrophic genocide by Emperor Hirohito of Japan on December 7, 1941, as gentle Hawaiian breezes tried to blow.

Jones mocks Hitler's 'Master Race' idiocy, in goofy German dialect, and brandishes a couple of America's greatest weapons: unlimited courage in the face of grave danger; and frontier desperado humor. Like comic icon Charlie Chaplin in *The Great Dictator* (1940****), Spike Jones pulverizes terror with moxie and in-yer-face humor. I am not being facetious when I say this: Hitler should have known better than to go up against the American one-two punch of Bugs Bunny and Mickey Mouse. Fearless in the face of danger, they knew that they were backed by **John Wayne** and **Jimmy Stewart** and **Babe Ruth** and **Joe Louis**. Via satire, Jones's contribution to the American and worldwide war effort was staggering. If you thought the Rolling Stones' #3, '68, "Jumpin' Jack Flash" was a real GAS, you may be Spike-Jonesless.

Jones's Dixieland dudes' biggest smash was #1(3), 11-48 "All I Want for Christmas (Is My Two Front Teeth)." He armed his band with standard trombones and tubas and stuff, but also toy pistols, toy whistles, bullwhips, sirens, and Clarabellle-the-Clown horns (from *Howdy Doody* TV kiddie show). Jones pioneered drums' cowbells for Ringo Starr and Charlie Watts. Typically, Jones's comic routine was to first sing the pretty song straight, and then rip it to shreds via a comic infusion of harmonic saboteurs. Long before the **Who**, Spike would often destroy his own drums. [Check out hilarious #4, 1-45 "Cocktails for Two," #8, 7-46 "Hawaiian War Chant," or boffo yokko gonzo #19, 6-43 "The Sheik of Araby"]. King of parody, Jones (1912-64) let a lot of gas out of Adolf Hitler's monomaniacal balloon. On his ghastly flight, Hitler went over like a lead zeppelin. Fortunately, great R & R crews like **Led Zeppelin** and the **Beach Boys** and the American **Eagles** were created to stuff the bloody War Genie back into the bottle.

"Rose, Rose, I Love You" – Frankie Laine, #3, 5-51. Flipside of Frankie's #2 "Jezebel," this war-fling romance is an old Chinese melody – "Mei Kui". American soldier must leave his "flower from Malaya." His ship chomps at the bit on the jetty. He must return home. Most GI's had only Betty Grable's rear-view pinup, and 12 grubby guys snoring in bunks three feet away. Privacy zilch.

"The Last Farewell" – Roger Whittaker, #19, 4-75. British sailor stands atop the deck of his rigged ship, waiting to cast off from this palm-tree battlefield to his drizzly England and the folks he left behind. He laments his sad parting with his tropical sweetheart. A stoical sense of DUTY magnetizes him to a fateful battlefield.

"Distant Drums" – Jim Reeves, #45, 4-66; #1, C & U.K. Along with **Patsy Cline**, Reeves (1924-64) was the first major Country Crossover star in both America and the U.K. Like **Conway Twitty**, and Country Charley Pride (#21 "Kiss an Angel Good Mornin'," first Afro-American Country star), Reeves's minor-league baseball career was scratched woefully early by a bum ankle.

Had the U.S.A. really listened deeply to "Distant Drums," they might have reconsidered the war. Jim Reeves? No fiery-eyed radical. He was a beloved and conservative Country star – steady, strong, and trusted. Drums plod military triplets. He sings of a wide gray sea. He implores his precious Mary the war might alter forever their potential wedding. Love me here and now, he begs, as soldiers have done since Helen of Troy or Julius Caesar, because NOW might be all the time there will ever be. At least Gentleman Jim asks her to MARRY him. Like one billion soldiers have bamboozled their babes, he wants one golden romantic night with her – to take to the lonely battlefield. Will she submit? The obscure song knows.

Sadly for Reeves, it was already too late. His private Beechcraft, nearly a carbon copy of Buddy Holly's fateful Beechcraft Bonanza in 1959, crashed into a rainy dark mountain (7-31-64). **Patsy Cline** (1932-63) was killed with **Cowboy Copas** and **Hawkshaw Hawkins** in a May 1963 plane crash. America's #1 novelist (2001 Almanac poll) **John Steinbeck**'s (*Grapes of Wrath*) last words on 12-20-68 quoted Reeves unforgettable "Distant Drums."

"Johnny Reb" – Johnny Horton, #54, 8-59; #10, 9-59 C. Texan Horton salutes fallen Confederate soldiers. Tribute to feisty Southern side in 1861-65 Civil War that ripped the U.S.A. in two. It's a requiem for those who gave their lives in a hard-fought campaign for dubious principles – but never lost their honor on the way to their glory. His kind references to "Honest Abe" Lincoln and the North show mutual respect. Song slams along on sheer snare-power, buttressed by all-American instrument – the BANJO. Army Rock, like #69, 7-60 "Johnny Freedom."

"Sink the Bismarck" – Johnny Horton, #3, 3-60; #6, 3-60 C. Horton celebrates brave British tars of ill-fated North Sea battle between H.M.S. Hood and gigantic German battleship Bismarck. After big guns boom on gray iceberg ocean, the plucky smaller Hood goes down to a titanic watery grave (see Kingston Trio's WWII sea battle "Reuben James" or Bogart/Hepburn's 1951 *African Queen*****). In the final assault on Bismarck, British sailors hurl behemoth battleship, too, to Davy Jones' Locker.

Johnny Horton is the most important military R & R singer in American history. Married to **Hank Williams'** widow Billie Jean Jones, Horton started on Wanda Jackson's and Elvis's *Louisiana Hayride*. Johnny plugged pluckily through five obscure years of obscurity on "low-shelf" major labels like Dot and Mercury before blockbustering with his war sagas. Born on two different dates: [4-30-25 (Whitburn) and 4-3-29 (Clarke)] – Johnny died on November 5, 1960, in a terrible Texas car crash. With Horton sadly out of the picture like General Patton, military adventurism would never be the same again.

"Mr. Custer" – Larry Verne, #1(1), 8-9-60; NC, C; #9, 10-60 R & B. Comic role of 1876 cavalry soldier in the employ of one General George Armstrong Custer of Monroe, Michigan. He signed for a tourist cruise to Montana's scenic Little Big Horn River area. War whoops pierce the stillness. Classified 5-Z (Conscientious Coward), Verne's hilarious sniveling character whines and wheedles to skip out on big upcoming shindig at the Little Big Horn. Valor-Impaired, nobody ever called him dumb.

In the last 3,467 years, there have been only 43 supposed years of peace (because some tiny skirmish went unreported). A sarcastic bumpersticker from the Vietnam Era read: "War is good business. Invest your son."

"Billy and Sue" – B.J. Thomas, #34, 6-66. Remember Thomas's incessant elevator upbeat anthem "Raindrops Keep Fallin' on My Head" (#1[4], 11-69)? "Billy and Sue" came from a very unlikely antiwar writer. No **Phil Ochs**, anti-militantly anti-marching. He is no **Bob Dylan**, frying war-machine "Masters of War" moguls on skewers of invective. Nope, B.J. Thomas wrote about the biggest reason of all for foxhole carnage – lost love. Who is most likely to join the military? The jilted.

At the dorm at Michigan State, my friend Larry lost his girlfriend to a rival. The super-jock student joined up at mid-term. When asked at the recruiter's where he wished to serve his country, he wrote down VIETNAM, VIETNAM, VIETNAM. We never saw him again. The War ate up friends and history.

"Billy and Sue" begins with a twangy little Duane Eddy riff zooming up and down from the tonic bottom-note 'B' down to the six minor **Abm** – and all notes in between: B—Bb—A—Ab and back. Tangy little twangy riff. Underpins the pretty song. Billy's dramatic Country tenor reverberates off his 4" sideburns. His droopy tale? Billy and Sue are two American Heartland teens (see John Cougar Mellencamp's #1[4], 7-82 "Jack & Diane"). They fall in love, pledge their troth, vow to marry. Billy gets shanghaied into the service. Many guys, searching for the essence of machismo, discover it in the Army, The Marines, the Navy, or the Air Force. But there are risks.

Billy ends up in the soupy slop of foxhole Hell. He hides well, waiting for his daily dose of sunshine from Sweet Sue. One dark and dismal day – you guessed it – the bad letter finally arrives, after a haunting hiatus. Sure enough, it reads, "Dear John . . ." Billy, of course, shrieks in a raging fury to the top of the battle-storm hill. He is cut down in a thick shrapnel volley, and dies a hero for his country. Thomas's last-verse moral? Broken hearts kill many soldiers, soldiers brought to desperado battlefields by the fatal literary criticism of a "Dear John" killer letter. The bullet is merely an accomplice.

"Billy, Don't Be a Hero" – Bo Donaldson & the Heywoods, #1(2), 4-74. Seven guys from Cincinnati, Ohio, near Mark Bourdeau, fronted by keyboardist Donaldson (b. '54) and singer MICHAEL GIBBONS. Billy is here. He busts up with the girl back home, we figure, and his mother tells him to keep down. It's like **Ernest Tubb**'s #16, 8-44 (#1 C) "Soldier's Last Letter." The doomed lad asks Mom not to chide him for muddy boots (Merle Haggard; #90, 3-71 [#3 C]), when he returns to the home he'll never see again. The commander calls for volunteers for a dangerous mission, and daredevil Billy's hand is the first one up, reflecting the rebel's reaction to much maternal advice.

His girlfriend receives a State Department form letter. It tells her Billy died a hero for his country. The letter claims she should be proud. Bo and Michael's punch line? He hears she tossed the letter into the gutter or something. In the 50s **Johnny Horton** brought us American Cold War peace-timers military glory. In the 60s President Johnson brought us military reality in Vietnam. By the 70s many grew weary of too much reality and glory. Too much was enough, the American people voted.

This song came out when my daughter Lauri was seven. She liked the snappity snare, rollicking fife, and the pounding beat, and never became a big war fan. Can a nation's music affect its whole attitude toward war?

So when were America's big wars?

Revolution: 1774-1783, or so.

War of 1812: [Obviously] 1812-15.

Mexican War: 1848-50.

Civil War: 1861-65.

Spanish-American War: 1898.

World War I a/k/a 'The Great War': 1917-18
(1914-18 for most of Europe).

World War II: 1941-45
(1939-45 for most of Europe and Canada).

Korea: 1950-53.

Vietnam: approximately 1964-73, or '75.

Gulf War: 1991.

Afghanistan War: (unnamed after one year) 2001-

Bobby Vinton (b. '35, Canonsburg, Pennsylvania) doled out poignant war tunes in #1(1) "Mr. Lonely" 10-64 and "Comin' Home Soldier" #11, 11-66. The first was sculpted in relative peacetime, before the tip of the tropical Titanic iceberg Vietnam squashed our national pride to humble horror. Vinton's songs offer a boy-next-door view of loneliness on the far outposts of freedom. No letter today . . .

Simon and Garfunkel played a counterpoint trump card, to contrast war's miseries and domestic turmoil with the sweet melodic splendor of Austrian Franz Gruber's beloved Christmas carol *"Stille Nacht, Heilige Nacht"* of 1820 – first performed not on Beethoven/Bach's clavichord/pianoforte, but on the 'Spanish' GUITAR: In German, stille [still] means SILENT. Nacht means NIGHT. Heilige means HOLY. Hitler's henchmen said "HEIL Hitler."

"7 O'Clock News/Silent Night" – **Simon & Garfunkel, NC, 1966.** Early Vietnam warning from NYC troubadours. Chilling counterpoint aura. First, they perform Gruber's guitar carol so celestially that only the Everly Brothers could have approached such star-twinkling Christmas harmony. From *Parsley, Sage, Rosemary & Thyme* Al. #4, 11-66.

Season of peace. Slowly, clandestinely, a serpentine radio station slithers into their song. Barely audible. Then a bloodreel newscast cranks up in volume, nearly drowning their peaceful carol. The newscaster simply mouths the teleprompter's feed. Cameo 1966 news items: Village comedian Lenny Bruce dies at 42 of substance O.D.; Dr. Martin Luther King disagrees with LBJ's hawkish Vietnam War policy and plans to march; Chicago Mayor Daley was ready to call out the National Guard; arch-fiend Richard Speck attacked, mutilated, and strangled nine nurses in Chicago; the House Un-American Activities Committee investigated rising anti-war demonstrators; and Former Veep **Richard Nixon** (1913-94, our later deposed Prez) predicted five more years of war. Nixon condemned anti-war activity. All the while, the angelic voices of Simon and Garfunkel struggled with their silent song about snow and Christmas and the promise of the Virgin Mary and peace on earth, good will to men. And women.

And little children, who grow up to be soldiers.

"Where Have All the Flowers Gone? – Kingston Trio, #21, 1-62. 1996 Rock Hall of Fame Inductee [and Weavers'] **Pete Seeger** penned these prophetic lyrics. Seeger soldiered in World War II. Senator Joseph McCarthy's House Un-American Activities Committee in 1952 censured the Weavers for their ultra-liberal politics, temporarily destroying their careers. Apolitical, upscale, and patriotic, the **Kingston Trio** sang a Chalypso forgotten-soldier song. He arrives home from the war, and no one is at the railroad station to greet him: "Two-Ten, Six-Eighteen."

Seeger's "Flowers" carol asks the musical question about the flowers' destination. Seems young girls picked them. He asks where the girls have gone: to meet young men. Throbbing acoustic guitars reel the Chalypso beat and Streetcorner chord pattern, intermixing soft baritone harmonies with masterfully enunciated lyrics. The young men, they tell us, have gone to soldier [an obtuse verb]. Where do the soldiers go? Graveyards! Where have the world's graveyards gone? Changed to flowers. And the flowers, of course, return to the pretty ladies whose men go to prove their gaucho glory and cowboy honor on the *Sands of Iwo Jima* **** (1949, John Wayne). A cyclic mandala. And the song goes round and round.

"2 + 2 = ?" – Bob Seger System, NC; #19, Detroit only, 1969. #17, 12-68 "Ramblin' Gamblin' Man" established **BOB** Seger as Detroit's premier rock and roller. "2 + 2 = ?" comes off Bob's obscure album by the same name (Al. #62, 2-69). We're treated to an angry young Seger (b. 1945 Dearborn, Michigan), screaming at generals, politicos, and bureaucrats about the death of his drinkin' buddy over in Southeast Asia. Bob demands to know WHY.

"Universal Soldier" – Donovan, #53, 9-65. [Also #45, 9-65, Glen Campbell.] **Buffy Ste. Marie**, Native American/

French-American folk singer, doesn't blame big corporations, policy makers, political hacks, lobbyists, or the Man in the Moon. Buffy declares, via Dylanesque Scottish flower-power bard **Donovan**, that the one who does the killing is the soldier. Himself. No longer do the soldier's orders come from afar, says peaceful Buffy. The Stones' "Sympathy for the Devil" who-slew-the-Kennedys question is answered by blaming us ALL! Buffy says the Universal Soldier's orders come from first HIM, then 'YOU,' then 'ME." With earth-nurturing maternal flair, Buffy asks how the current belligerent system is any way to stamp out the scourge of worldwide war. Too much logic here. If folks stop shooting at each other, we can't have a war. Reflects this flower-spangled bumper sticker: What if they gave a war and no one came?" NOT this one: "Work is for people who don't know how to fish!" [Rob Pace]

"For What It's Worth" – Buffalo Springfield, #7, 1-67.
Somehow the war invaded America, too, seething the streets of Watts, California. Canadian-American Buffalo Springfield (named for farm equipment) reported on it. Toronto's **Neil Young** and **Stephen Stills** found Steven Furay, bassman Bruce Palmer, and Ontario drummer Dewey Martin. The paranoia syndrome begins when you're constantly afraid. It suggests Bolsheviks or KGB or Gestapo police. If you step beyond the line, some paramilitary force will shackle you and drag you away in screaming chains of tyranny. Racially charged song, ambiguous enough in puns to skirt the issue. It could just mean Mayor Daley's Chicago cops will take you away if you're black or have long 'hippie' hair.

Some vague protest march plods along. A thousand placard bearers march the hot streets. Gunfire erupts. The song is a masterpiece of urban tension, reflecting the L.A. riots of 1966 preceding urban explosions in Detroit and Gary and Newark in 1967. Or the little town of Bethlehem in 2002.

Make no mistake about it. There were two wars. One on the streets of Saigon, South Vietnam. Another on the streets of Detroit (see "Black Day in July").

"Ohio" – Crosby, Stills, Nash, and Young, #14, 6-70.
Toronto's **Neil Young** (b. 11-12-45) wrote this elegy to four students killed at Kent State University in National Guard overreaction to some rock-throwing demonstrators. Innocent bystanders were killed in the crossfire. By this time, the Nixon Administration's 'incursion'/expansion of the war into fascist Pol Pot's Cambodia next door was not met with overwhelming support in America's heartland. Pol Pot was responsible for killing a larger percentage of his countrymen than anyone in the bloody 20th century – even Hitler and Stalin. When 18-year-old Guardsmen's bullets cut the heart out of the American dream, support for the Vietnam war veered down to the 20% range.

"Lay Down (Candles in the Rain)" – Melanie, #6, 4-70.
Sounds like a cast of millions, thousands, maybe even hundreds and scores and dozens. All chant peace (79-part harmony?) **Melanie Safka** came from Queens and wore long floral-print granny dresses. She wore granny

glasses like those festively donned by **John Lennon**. Melanie's sweetly sincere quest-for-peace now song reverberated through all the black-light head shops and New Age palaces in the U.S.A. She reached peace-loving kids whose own quests took them into eclectic spiritual territory like – Yin-Yang [Taoists for Jesus]. They all got together with their peaceful candles in the drizzle, and prayed for peace on earth, good will to men. Melanie brought the gospel **Edwin Hawkins Singers** (#4, "Oh Happy Day" 1969, **Paul Anka** production) to sing behind her, a *pace en terra* peace chant that sounds like multitudes.

"Battle of the Alamo" – Marty Robbins, #34, 10-60; NC, C. Marty (1925-82) delivers one of the most stirring war songs in history. He makes Davy Crockett and Jim Bowie and Colonel Travis seem as heroic and gigantic as John Wayne's 1960 *Remember the Alamo* ***½ could portray them. San Antonio Texican patriotism. For the ages.

"Abdul Abulbul Amir" – Hank Thompson, NC, 2000 [and NC, Liz Dean, 1947]. My mom Liz Dean (1908-97) wrote scathing editorials against Hitler from her "Women's Clubs" column in the *Detroit Free Press*. She lullabyed this saga to 4-year-old me with her unfiltered Old Golds contralto. She got the song from her brother, banjo player Reuben Maury (1899-1980) and Pulitzer Prize winning newspaperman (1941, editorials). "Abdul etc." is a wickedly ironic waltz. Seems two guys, puffed with pride and braggadocio, crashed into a duel. One was Abdul Abulbul Amir. A Goliath of a warrior, he'd storm redoubts, shout 'hullaloo' to encourage the men on the battlefield, and swashbuckle with his Braveheart troops. Abdul was the big cheese. Then he ran into **Ivan Skavitsky Skivar**. Ivan hailed from Russia (Moscow). Those Muscovite Russians who turned back Hitler [*Enemy at the* Gates 2001***] were never ever regarded as wimps by us Americans suffering a Cold War (1946-90). Skivar had a gorgeous girlfriend, played Spanish guitar (huh? A 1910-or-so ROCK star?), was a whiz at euchre, and a swordsman who glittered gold [it's not a safe sport for Silver Medallists.]

One fine day, the Russian strapped on his gun and his #1 'cynical sneer,' and swaggered uptown. Skivar made the fatal mistake of tromping on Abdul's toe. In a fray that would later figuratively play out in the abortive Russian conquest of **Afghanistan** and/or Chechnya, the Cossack northland Russians grappled with the Muslim might of centuries and this macho lifestyle. So tough Turk Abdul and murderous Muscovite Ivan gouge and claw and rip and punch and bash and smash all night long into the Ultimate Free-for-All fight. Naturally, they both kill each other very dead! Girlfriends and admirers hover over their star-crossed double grave, wondering why. Moral? Deadly force over trivial toe-tromping can ruin your day – and all the rest of 'em.

Macho Country baritone **Hank Thompson** (b. '25, Waco, Texas) cut this song at age 74. I've got to believe that a) Hank is a very manly singer like **Johnny Cash**; and b) If he accidentally stepped on somebody's toe, he'd have the common survival sense to say "Excuse me."

"What Is Truth?" – **Johnny Cash, #19, 4-70; #3 C.** Check the date. By 1970, even Johnny Cash (b. '32) of Kingsland, Arkansas, voiced his powerful bass views about the War's continuing chaos. He empathizes with the Voice of Youth. President Nixon, seeing four kids killed at Kent State, and listening to conservative charismatic Country legend Cash questioning the war effort, began a steady process of "winding down" the war. Nixon brought the 500,000+ troops slowly back home. In World War II during four ghastly years of fiery combat, the U.S. lost over 300,000 men (Russia lost 20,000,000 citizens). Vietnam's 10+ years saw the scythe harvest 50,000+ American fighting men; there's no consolation at all in that smaller number if just one of those boys is your cousin, your friend, or your boy. "When Johnny Comes Marching Home" was the #1 hit, then. "What Is Truth?" asks Big John Cash. When Johnny Cash spoke, America listened.

"War" – **Bruce Springsteen, #8, 12-86.** Freehold, New Jersey's 80s bard rumbles his incredible **Edwin Starr** cover of classic Motown. This is the only major song an entire 80s generation, steeled to Punk Rock and Heavy Metal and Hip-Hop and Industrial and Post-Disco and Dance Music, ever really knew about the general topic of War. The 80s didn't really have one (OK, Granada).

"War" – **Edwin Starr, #1(3), 7-70; #3 R & B.** The original. After Kent State, after Johnny Cash, businessman Berry Gordy realized it was now safe enough to express his bubbling dissent against the eternal disproportionate flow of African-American soldiers to Vietnam. Gordy picked Motown's most rumbling voice – it's very hard to out-boom the Four Tops' **Levi Stubbs**, or the **Contours**. Starr asks what war is good for? He answers his own question with a disgusted and absolute "NUTHIN'!"

War music is drum music. Don't spare the mammoth snare. War's only good buddy, besides the Grim Reaper, Starr says, is the undertaker. Starr's follow-up, #26, 12-70 "Stop the War Now" (#5 R & B) didn't pussyfoot around with subtle suggestions either. Finally, the seven-year-old war was catching some inner-city flak and Motown thunder. Rock's first big war was Vietnam. Rice paddies blared **Creedence Clearwater**. **Jimi Hendrix**'s fuzztone southpaw guitar solos blasted sampans floating the Mekong River Delta.

Before he even disengaged his Beatlehood, John Lennon fell in love with **Yoko Ono**, NYC peace activist and artist ☮ :

"Give Peace a Chance" – **John Lennon and the Plastic Ono Band, #14, 7-69.** Repetitious chant recorded in Lennon/Ono's hotel suite in neutral Montreal. John married Yoko on March 20, 1969. They invited reporters into their honeymoon suite, fostering peace on earth or wherever. For a background chorus of thousands, variety show host Folk singer Tommy Smothers was recruited, plus the local Hare Khrishna scholars of the Bhagavad-Gita from Swami Bhaktivedanta Prabhupada. [c/o Bob Roberts, Union Lake, Michigan 7-2001.]

"Give Peace a Chance" – **Peace Choir, #54, 3-91.** Among champion chanters: **Tom Petty, Iggy Pop, M.C. Hammer, Lenny Kravitz** ("Again" #6, 11-2000), **Little Richard, Rascals' Felix Cavaliere, Adam Ant, Bruce Hornsby, Alannah Myles** (#1, 1-90 Elvis tribute "Black Velvet"), and young **Sean Lennon**. John's assassination on December 8, 1980 never dimmed the quest for peace that his life symbolized.

Lennon's arrival in America was met with less than pure joy with the State Department and F.B.I. President Nixon and his surveillance team trailed the popular Beatle with unrelenting snoop savvy, watching his nearly every move with his artistic Asian bride. Lennon was inducted into the Rock and Roll Hall of Fame – early-on with the Beatles, and in 1991 as a solo artist. A 2000 VH-1 poll voted him the greatest songwriter of all time. As John Lennon and Yoko Ono chanted from Montreal, and the war widened into Laos and Cambodia, a strong 'whiskey baritone' sound emerged from America's Dust Bowl:

"Okie from Muskogee" – **Merle Haggard, #41, 11-69; #1(4), 10-69 C.** The Country icon (b. '37, Bakerfield, California) razzed longhair student protestors. The chorus is bedrock American pride. Haggard champions the small-town values of Muskogee, Oklahoma, where well-behaved students still respect their college dean. The most rough-neck pastime on the campus is still football, and guys wear leather boots (not beads and Roman sandals). Pumping mainstream sentiment, "Okie" croons a strong stand for small-town America. Merle's Country crossover song smacked counterculture rebels. Merle boasts that folks don't smoke demon-reefer marijuana is Muskogee. (Merle, however, inhaled a constant cigarette, currently blamed for 400,000 American deaths per year). The basic two-chord song, with a half-tone modulation on the last verse, also stands for musical simplicity like "Give Peace a Chance." To get the democracy message through to the people, you don't need a 47-chord cantata symphony or a fugue that counterpoints 15 melodies at once in a hodge-podge of puzzling profundity. Haggard and Lennon-Ono state their opposing cases eloquently.

As in the horrific Civil War, we were a nation divided unto itself. In 1968, one strong voice pierced the 98° muggy jungles with raw power and rip-roaring Rock and Roll – **John Fogerty** (b. 5-28-45, Berkeley, California). As the Golliwogs, he and **brother Tom** assembled drummer **Doug Clifford** and bass guy **Stu Cook**. For at least a stormy year, they may have comprised the Greatest Rock and Roll Band on Earth – **Creedence Clearwater Revival**. As their paddlewheel steamer "Proud Mary" chugged from California's Gold Rush country down the muddy mighty Mississippi, Rock and Roll would never be the same again: Swamp Rock had begun.

Berkeley, California, combines a view and promise. San Francisco Bay glows goldenly beyond the silent cats'-paw fog, and swirls on seven hills around a town of cable cars and stars. When John Fogerty and brother Tom looked out their **El Cerrito** and Berkeley windows, they could see halfway to Vietnam. Creedence didn't party like the **Grateful Dead**, or turn on like Timothy Leary (1921-96) to LSD, or wreak wildly sarcastic antiwar music on sleepy small-town America like:

"Fixin' to Die Rag" – Country Joe (McDonald) & the Fish, NC, 1967+. Ragtime roast? Guy figures he's been sentenced to military death by the Democrats/Republicans Johnson & Nixon. In sardonic gloom and glee, Joe hollers for St. Peter to prop open those Pearly Gates. His #106, 7-69 "Here I Go Again" bounces the message off the Pentagon that the war is a toll-free highway to Hell. With a banjo at batty speed, jabbing at serenity, Joe slurs and slides down the scale, as the troop train chugs off to the ship, the plane, the snaky jungle, and the grave.

John Fogerty was actually in the Army before all Vietnam hell broke loose in 1967 (unlikely to serve a second tour). Furthermore, Creedence's Vietnam songs weren't really Protest Music. They were gut-busting anthems for 'poor grunts' consigned to jungle rot, c-rations, snake and spider sleeping bags, and the deadly drone of 'friendly fire,' wasting the foliage in white-hot flak and fly-by.

Here's one:

"Run Through the Jungle" – Creedence Clearwater Revival, #4 [simultaneously with flip side "Up Around the Bend"], **4-70.** Plunges along at 66.6 steady beats per minute, like a Mekong River sampan cresting the chop. It dodges crocs snapping up feet, in the hot Nam noonday haze of smoke and terror. Creedence's jungle songs dig deep into the *Heart of Darkness* or *Apocalypse Now* (1979 ***½) Armageddon music. Few American soldiers knew any Vietnamese languages. You couldn't tell the deadly Vietcong from friendly South Vietnamese soldiers. "Run Through the Jungle" thunders this booming hot reign of terror in religious terms: Fogerty says the Devil's on the loose. The cry of Satan is heard, as 200,000,000 guns are loaded in the catastrophic rumbling of inky jungle night. The mountain thunders its wrath, and a voice of doom snarls and fills the land with smoke.

This Arch-Fiend reputedly is cryptically blessed with a high IQ – placing in the Gifted and Talented group of Archangels. According to scriptural scholars and John Milton (*Paradise Lost*), the Devil was banished to the nether regions for his challenge to God, not high intelligence. Creedence advises the terrified inmate of the Army or Marines in Vietnam he'd better run through the jungle. Or

in Tennyson's throttling 19th-century tones: "Theirs is not to reason why – theirs is but to do or die."

"Run Through the Jungle" staggers blunderingly along in 'D', like a terrified foot soldier leapfrogging from snakes to crocodiles, over punji-stick traps and shoebox bombs and past razor-brandishing 'ladies.' He darts from the fricassee frying pan into the final fire. Bassist **Stu Cook** hugs his bottom note. Drummer **Doug Clifford** smashes snare and bass drum in ceaseless thumping thunder. Fogerty's flying-fret fingers dance on the high riffs, adding eerie syncopated quirks to the intro helicopter's chop of the 4th-of-July midnight skies, ablaze in red fire and green terror.

"Fortunate Son" – Creedence Clearwater Revival, #14, 11-69. Flip of #3, "Down on the Corner," about streetcorner pals Willie and the Poor Boys, not yet invited from their studly streetcorner maneuvers for an all-expense paid tropical vacation to South Vietnam. My friend Lt. Jim Cook led and lost half a Marine platoon on the North Vietnam border (Jim now sells pacemakers in Atlanta). Jim's daughter married one of the Black Crowes' rock group. One of my wife's cousins, however, had a more somber homecoming, with a serious brain injury and full pension. His disability U.S. Marine pension allowed him and his attack dog to dabble in questionable anesthesias for their permanent pain. In 1999, before his 50th birthday, he died of old age. My wife and I attended his funeral and 21-gun salute with honors at Arlington Military Cemetery, where President Kennedy is buried. Who, then, is the fortunate son?

John Fogerty answers. He cites the senator's son. He lambasts the system. He impales the Selective Service and their quixotic new 1970 draft lottery. Who shall go? Who shall stay? He cites grueling inequities in the Selective Service draft system – tantamount to the Death Penalty in an era that didn't believe in it. If you could debate your way out, you stayed. Inarticulate? So long, pal. **Phil Ochs**'s "Draft Dodger Rag" slings a comedy list of deferment possibilities, some lacking humor: he supports an invalid aunt, has bat-like eyes, flat feet, a taped-up back, and a dislocated brain. His moribund excuses roll from the pathetic to the sublime to the absurd, and he keeps piling on ANYTHING to keep him Stateside (piling with a Golden Shovel). He claims epileptic fits, ONLY when a bombshell hits (kitschy rhyme, right). He moans he's addicted to over 1000 big-league drugs.

Popular Music, however, is a powerful agent for change. With the new DRAFT LOTTERY, every guy could take that tropical vacation for Uncle Sam. When the silver-spoon tycoons discovered their sons hustling off to troop trains, the war wound down, fast. In January, 1973, the quietest war truce celebration in history whispered across the United States.

"Run Through the Jungle" and "Fortunate Son" are musically Screaming Blues, laced with drum-riff thunderboomers and rhythm-axe lightning. No stodgy easy plod. Fogerty captures the same magic sound on 1997 *Blue Moon Swamp* super-tracks "Walking in a Hurricane" or "Rambunctious Boy." As in all wars, Fogerty says, the privileged get to push pencils on the home front, while the unfortunate sons (yes, some poor Mom's kid) must shiver and bleed in gully-wash Gettysburg trenches. In the 1863 Civil War, you could buy your way out of the draft for something like three hundred bucks, as medieval believers bought indulgences for so much time in Purgatory.

The United States of America has a pretty good track record on winning wars, if anyone really wins. Our Vietnam experience, like mighty Russia's own disastrous Afghanistan and Chechnya adventures, proves that a dogged and determined native people can possess superhuman energies to resist. SUPERPOWER can be a very iffy role to play in international geopolitics. Since the Vietnam War ground to a halt in 1975, with a last whimper, America in the long run has won, sort of. Saigon today, though called Ho Chi Minh City (population 4 million), blooms with Coca Cola and Rock and Roll. The rich ride Chevies to the Mekong levee where the bombs bled it dry. The good ol' boys, via rye whiskey and Maui Wowie, sang "That'll be the day we die.' Rock and Roll now rules Old Saigon.

"The Americans (A Canadian's Opinion)" – Gordon Sinclair, #24, 1-74. 74-year-old Toronto broadcaster Gordon Sinclair lists all the good things Americans have done to help those in need around the world. How we're heart-of-gold people. With a bulging symphonic concert band, he 'Raps' to the rest of the world to learn how to appreciate their Yankee allies and protectors.

"One Tin Soldier – Legend of Billy Jack" (Jeff-less **Coven** #26, 9-71+) exhorts us about the futility of totally preparing for peace. Theodore Roosevelt of Sagamore Hill, Oyster Bay, Long Island, brought us a bully war in 1898. He led the charge up San Juan Hill in firebrand splendor, a soldier's soldier who proffered a little chunk of advice that American Pentagon policymakers never forgot: "SPEAK softly, BUT CARRY A BIG STICK." Teddy, among the bravest of America's brave, died at 60 – partially of a broken heart when his beloved son Quentin Roosevelt was shot down and killed on a Snoopy vs. Red Baron-type bombing mission in World War I in Europe.

"Who'll Stop the Rain?" – Creedence Clearwater Revival, #2(2), 2-70. John Fogerty's "Rain" is a loose euphemism for "War." Fogerty's title is a prayer. He implores whatever Deity he can conjure to cease the Rain of Fire and Reign of Terror over Vietnam and America. The genius of Creedence is in their no-gimmicks Rock and Roll. Pure, straightforward THUNDER ROCK. Fogerty may be one of the top seven rock vocalists of all time. Brother Tom (1941-90, respiratory failure) wrings awesome rhythm guitar hellfire. No sound characterized Vietnam better than CCR's John Fogerty and his Swamp Rock sound – not even this Hendrix one:

"Star-Spangled Banner" – Jimi Hendrix, NC. From June 1967 Monterey Pop Festival and beyond [on Al. #15, 10-71 *Rainbow Bridge*], Jimi's piercing fuzztone feedback instrumental stirred battle boomers, as bagpipes stirred in *Brave Heart* (Mel Gibson's 1996**** Scots' nationhood

epic). Jimi bends, slurs, and quavers **Francis Scott Key**'s anthem written in the rockets' red glare at Baltimore's Fort McHenry in the War of 1812. The stars and stripes survived the night. The "Star Spangled Banner" was adopted as our official national anthem as late as 1930, beating out Katherine Ann Bates's "America the Beautiful." Lyricist's Key's melody partner was some anonymous German who wrote it as the old drinking song "To Anacreon in Heaven". Hendrix's iconoclastic version of the anthem brought cheers and jeers. Jimi the Legend could turn "The Star Spangled Banner" into Rock and Roll. He was ready to launch his own University of Rock Lead Guitar, with himself as founder and president.

"The Star-Spangled Banner" – John McCormack, #1(3), 5-1917. Yes, Number One! Has a more stirring patriotic song ever been recorded? **John McCormack** (1883-1945) of Athlone, Ireland, simply sang "The Star Spangled Banner" in his belltone Irish tenor style. Not even yet selected as our national anthem by Congress, Francis Scott Key's vivid sea battle lyric portrays the pyrotechnic panorama which raged all night long. By dawn's early light, Key could discern a floating motion from a ragged and battered wisp of tricolor. Red, white, and blue caught the first sunbeams, and the brave Americans held Fort McHenry. The melody is a froggy baseball fan's nightmare; "The Star Spangled Banner" has a towering vocal range that only **Roy Orbison** or **Elvis** or **Michael Bolton** or **Mariah Carey** – or Ireland's U2 **Paul Hewson** [Bono] – might find comfortable. For the average ho-hum sing-along guy flubbing its notes, our second-string national anthem "America" might be a lot more comfortable:

"America the Beautiful" – Louise Homer, #8, 7-25. Acclaimed New York Metropolitan Opera contralto (1870-47) hit the vaunted top ten at age 55. **Ray Charles** has a breathtaking version, too, of this more peaceful patriotic hymn (NC, c.1980, and live at Super Bowl XXXV, 2001). It's in Rock's 4/4 time, too, unlike the "Star Spangled" 3/4 waltz.

In 1917, McCormack was rendering a wonderful Golden Oldie even more wonderful. His stunning crystal countertenor would make a bulldog cry. The guy who first hit the infant charts at #2(2), 7-1892 with "The Star Spangled Banner" wrote another war song:

"When Johnny Comes Marching Home Again" – Patrick S. Gilmore, #1, 1863. Next to the North's "Battle Hymn of the Republic" and the South's "Dixie," this may be the biggest song of the Civil War. Since Southern soldiers were called 'Johnny Reb,' the tune had universal American appeal in both the United States and Confederate States of America. The bloodiest battle ever fought on the soil of the entire Western Hemisphere [50,000+ died in 3 days] was fought on the 4th of July of 1863 in Gettsyburg, Pennsylvania. Like the American optimists we'd always been, we gobbled up Gilmore's happy homecoming. Compare Tony Orlando's #1(4), 2-72 "Tie a Yellow Ribbon (Round the Old Oak Tree)" from our 1991 Gulf War experience. In the real Civil War, however, brothers killed brothers on green, green hills of home. When World War I began to fester in the tragic Sarajevo, Yugoslavian Archduke's assassination, we tried to stay out of it as long as possible. Early on, we got a stark message from an unusual source:

"The Star-Spangled Banner" – Margaret Woodrow Wilson, #7, 5-1915. Can you imagine Chelsea Clinton or Tricia Bush with a hit record? After all, Chelsea's father [nicknamed 'Elvis"] is the first Rock and Roll generation president. The second one – George W. Bush (b. '47), lists Buddy Holly as his favorite singer. President Woodrow Wilson's daughter Margaret sort of sabotaged his campaign promise to "keep us out of war" with her gung-ho resurrection of Gilmore's golden oldie. After Wilson and before McCormack, our future National Anthem got its first crack at the #1 record position. Piano and celeste virtuoso **Charles Adams Prince**, whose relative, President John Adams, predated the anthem, cranked up his super session band. [No relation to #1 "When Doves Cry" 1984 **Prince** of Minneapolis – of course.] Director of Columbia Records, Prince and **Prince's Orchestra** accompanied almost all Columbia artists. As a band they hit #1(2), 7-1916 for the "Star Spangled Banner's" first shot at the pop pinnacle. *Jeopardy* of April 1997 should have done their homework. They said there's been only one charted version. They also completely forgot Jose Feliciano's #51, 1968 version. The one they recalled was a fine and passionate version by Whitney Houston:

"The Star-Spangled Banner" – Whitney Houston, #20, 3-91 & #6, 9-2001. Thomas Edison (1847-1931), a teenager at the Civil War's advent, was too young to invent the record player. (**Emile Berliner** invented the record in 1874.) Whitney's live Superbowl XXV version on January 27, 1991 galvanized 80,000 patriots. President George Bush's (b. 1924) short war was the polar opposite of Vietnam; rather than 20-80% of the American people against it at any given time, it stayed short enough (less than a month) so that 98% of the American people favored it. His son, Texas governor George W. Bush, became President in 2000, and 92% of the American people favored his handling of the Afghan War.

"Ruby – Don't Take Your Love to Town" – Kenny Rogers and the First Edition, #6, 7-69; #39 C. Elton Britt, in his "Star Spangled Banner Waving Somewhere" 1944 hit, gamely tried to go off to war. His injury forbade it. "Ruby" stars a paraplegic returnee from combat, like Ron Kovic in *Born on the Fourth of July* (Tom Cruise, 1989***½). The insistent bass skates (placid Key of 'C') with an acoustic guitar hammering on the root tonic and dominant notes (pluck pick on bottom G; for a split second, play the low E string open – suddenly hammering on to the 3rd fret "G" note with your speedy finger).

Kenny's band track is muted. His lyrical style is so matter-of-fact that gnawing desperation bubbles up slowly and dangerously. The snare fires on the 2 & 4 beats. Kenny solos the lyric – fondled by the "RUBY" female chorus. He says he didn't start the endless Asian war. He

confesses he was proud to accomplish his patriotic duty. We see at once he is no rabble-rouser, no bomb-chucking anarchist counter-terrorist. Just a simple soldier. Ruby, he loved. Once. He has almost given his life for his beloved U.S.A. His enthusiasm is dying. So is he.

He broods now, his will to live paralyzed. **Kenny Rogers** (b. '38 Houston) is the ultimate crossover hit maker. Kenny played bass with Columbia Records' Bobby Doyle Trio (Jazz); he worked with the JAZZ-STANDARDS-SOFT ROCK group the **Kirby Stone Four** ("Baubles, Bangles, and Beads" #25, 7-58). Kenny crossed to FOLK with the **New Christy Minstrels** (gorgeous #17, 4-64 "Today"), among first to do FOLK ROCK: Barry McGuire's #14, 1963 "Green Green" already *Gold Rush*ed.

Kenny also belonged to STREETCORNER group the Lively Ones, flirted with SOUL music, and finally settled on a straight ROCK style on the PSYCHEDELIC ROCK side when he and Mike Settle formed the **First Edition**: #5 "Just Dropped in (to See What Condition My Condition Was In)" in 2-68 & "But You Know I Love You" – #19, 1-69.

With raspy baritone sting, Rogers relates the tragic wheelchair story which helped bring down a big war. Sprouting a few silver strands in his bushy beard, the 31-year-old ahem-ed his doleful story about his character's star-crossed war effort. Seems he got gravely wounded. Paralyzed. Desperation slathers into the dark lyric like black butter into an innocent artery.

We now realize that his girl (wife, maybe) Ruby needs a man. He admits it is difficult for this lusty young lass to love a guy with 'bent,' paralyzed legs. He mutters about the carnal needs and desires of girls her age. He knows the tragic truth. The war has emblazoned his manhood, but stolen his potency. He is angered, he is embittered, he is scarred. Unlike the ultra-brave wheelchair racers I know (Nick Katsounis [1942-94], Peter Hawkins, Rob Loughlin, George Lindeman, Jesse Walsh), who made the best of a paraplegic catastrophe, Ruby's guy is all out of gumption. His sad wheelchair has locked into Cruise Control and Automatic Pilot for the Pearly Gates.

Suddenly Kenny's shuffling guitar and bass halt. Sudden stop. Ruby is fixin' to slither off to the Honkytonk Stardust Suburban Cowboy joint to find a Viagra Niagara stud to take care of her earthy desires. Just the skitching, snickering drum keeps on keepin' on. In a hissing rage of desperate futility, he declares that if he could get to this gun, he'd put the lusty lass into the ground. Monstrous murderous thoughts occlude his former logic. He writhes. Again he implores, begs, beseeches, whimpers: "Ruby, Don't Take Your Love to Town." It gets even more lurid. He madly mumbles and murmurs that he's heard whispers that his earthly time is almost up. He wishes she'd have the simple decency to wait for his natural death before grabbing another guy to service her carnal craving.

This song really hit America whre it hurts. This war, which seemed eternally long, ripped off a part of the very manhood the loyal soldier had fought to find. The bloody battlefield hurtled him too far beyond Viagra. Not blessed with my pal Jim's six thumb stitches for his war heroism, this sad paralyzed man is just a couple steps from the ultimate military horror show written about Dalton Trumbo, in his banned antiwar WWI novel *Johnny Got His Gun*. This catastrophic war casualty is well portrayed by major Heavy Metal band **Metallica**'s first chart hit:

"One" – Metallica, #35, 2-89. In an ultra-tragic war hospital, a paralyzed war hero yearns for euthanasia. All his limbs are gone. Machine-gun staccato notes thunder from **Lars Ulrich**'s snare drums, **Kirk Hammett**'s firebomb guitar, and **Jason Newsted**'s bass – as **James Hetfield** hammers the grisly vocal with a World Wrestling Federation leather baritone. The soldier's face is an amorphic protoplasmic blob of scar tissue (see Heavy Metal chapter). He cannot see, hear, or feel. Bassist **Cliff Burton** was killed when their tour bus skidded and rolled over on him in Sweden (9-27-86). Our unknown soldier is seemingly trapped forever in this neutral throbbing hunk of flesh, praying for death. Finally after aeons of agony, soldier "Johnny" manages to communicate the morbid message in Morse Code ("LET ME OUT OF HERE!") to astounded medical personnel, who thought him to be brain-dead (in the 1918 pre-electroencephalographic days). In the 13th concentric circle of his own living Hell, he craves death. It's far creepier than their metal anthems "Enter Sandman" or "Fade to Black." The "Ruby" soldier might have felt a little luckier than the poor tragic soul trapped in Metallica's "One." But not much. Bleak, forlorn, and hopeless situation. Kenny Rogers' sad song shows both one man's desperation and a great nation's collective military agony. He yearns for a quick violent surcease of pain and horrific helplessness.

"Galveston" – Glen Campbell, #4, 3-69; #1(3) C. Never underestimate the power of a popular song to wage, postpone, or end a war. **George M. Cohan**'s "Over There" marshalled yippie yahoos from Yanks on their first European adventure. (#1, 1917, American Quartet). **Glen Campbell**'s "Galveston" struck a bitter minor chord. A great nation downsized a war that split our country in half as certainly as the Civil War: Longhair vs. Shorthair, Dad vs. Son, Vet vs. Student, Black Draftee vs. White Deferee, Older Generation Policymakers vs. Poor Guys Who Had to Go Actually Fight the War. Written by **Jimmy Webb**, Campbell's "Galveston" hit #1(6) Adult Contemporary. Unless you lived in a guru cave atop Mt. McKinley, you could not miss hearing this monumental torch tune.

Like President Clinton, Glen Campbell is a Scottish tenor from a small town in Arkansas who impressed the girls with his handsome boyish looks. Snazzy jazzy rumors about Campbell's torrid relationship with Country star Tanya Tucker never got anywhere near the press the Prez got for his 1996 alliance, but the somewhat moral public forgives singers easier for passion than Presidents. America glorifies the workaday Gospel of Work, and the stable rock-ribbed family relationships which made America strong and powerful. President **Franklin Delano Roosevelt** sent teenagers **Bob Dole** and **George Bush** into battle against Hitler. Senator Dole returned a decorated, injured war hero. Bush escaped a doomed plane in WWII. Senator Dole was silver medallist for the 1996 Presidency against sax-wielding Bill "Elvis" Clinton. Dole's

favorite song is Campbell's #3, 11-68 "Wichita Lineman."

Bill Clinton of Hope, Arkansas, lived the Johnny B. Goode dream, too. He used to gig around with his sax by the railroad tracks, and play air guitar. Like 2001+ President **George W. Bush**, he admired the life and legend of Buddy Holly, and how a nice friendly guy with some new ideas can hit the top in his field. Young Bill lived through his stepfather's alcoholism and wife abuse, finally standing up to his stepfather at age 14 and commanding him never to hit his mother again; the bamboozled bruiser stopped and decided the big strong kid was right. Both Clinton and Dole grew up in modest middle-class homes, sharing traditional American values. Bill Clinton's teenage years were highlighted by a class trip handshaking with PT-109 U-boat WWII hero/captain and President **John F. Kennedy** (1917-63, and Jimmy Dean's hit, #8, 3-62 "PT 109").

Al Gore didn't believe in the Vietnam War, but went anyhow so someone else wouldn't have to in his place. **George W. Bush** served at home in the National Guard. President George W. Bush's (b. 6-7-46, Connecticut) turf "Galveston" is a sub-tropical port for Houston on the Gulf of Mexico. Toni and I loved the seagull boardwalk, combo surfer/shark sculpture, hot friendly breezes, and cozy neon night. Two things brought Galveston to national prominence – a wretched 1900 hurricane (see 1999 **Isaac's Storm**), and this hit song. Like patriot Paul Revere, this song warned us and the world that even a superpower could not conduct an open-ended war in a napalm jungle, without formulating a unified front and timetable policy.

"Galveston" surfed the crest of American popular opinion as the Southeast Asian option dragged on towards 50,000 American lives – plus hundreds of Aussies and Kiwi soldiers loyal to our way of life. It is very hard to believe that superstar singer Campbell actually dropped out of school at 14 (Kids – don't try this at home) in Delight, Arkansas. He spent a lot of time in major American rock groups after their first success, and scored early with 9-65 Folk Rock anthem "The Universal Soldier." Revered for his uncanny lead guitar wizardry and fine Scots tenor voice, Glen played guitar for 50s **Champs** in 1960.

"Tequila" #1[5], 2-58 by the **Champs** was the #1 instrumental of the 50s R & R Holly Days with **Danny Flores/Chuck Rio**'s super sax sounds. Also featured **Seals (Jimmy)** and **Crofts (Dash)**, of #6, "Summer Breeze" 1972 fame. "Tequila" celebrated a fiery drink (that bites you) of Baja Californian Mexican origin, with a dinky little worm at the bottom. Drifting to California, Campbell became a star studio guitarist, backing the **Beach Boys** and the **Hondells** (#9 "Little Honda", motorbike ad/hit combo).

Campbell hit with Kerouac road-pilgrim #39 "Gentle on My Mind" (by John Hammond) of 7-67. Glen's 6'1" howdy-pal demeanor earned him friends galore in showbiz, and soon he acquired his own *Glen Campbell Goodtime Hour* from 1968-72. He mirrored the style of the *Laugh-In* or *The Smothers Brothers*, and pulled in young upscale kids on track to Wall Street dazzling success. Glen Campbell looks like my Canadian cousin Darrell Amlin now lawyering in Grosse Pointe, Michigan. Darrell was a well-liked kid and he has carried it over into his adult life with wife

Marty Hair and daughter Katie. Sort of like Glen. When people trust you and your ideas, they'll listen to you. Or your song.

Glen Campbell was no radical. Glen was a good ol' American boy. Symphonic songwriter **Jimmy Webb** wove a wistful web of Eddy-ing guitars, silky strings, and romantic cotton-candy in earlier songs like **Donna Summer's** #1(3), 9-78 "MacArthur Park". It was #2(2), 5-68 by *Camelot's* King – **Richard Harris**. Also #38, Four Tops '71 and **Waylon Jennings** #93 (his 1st post-Buddy Holly HOT 100 hit). Donna's Disco dervishes do a twirly whirling strobe light stomp to this Webb song about cakes left out in the rainstorm in MacArthur Park.

General Douglas MacArthur was our commander of the Pacific Theatre in World War II who said old soldiers never die; they just fade away. "Galveston" zeroes in. It's a tiny little web-sight of terror. The lyric concerns a soldier cleaning his gun in some seemingly godforsaken War Zone. A shrill sense of suspense marches with the sagging violins. In the pleasant melodic Key of 'F' major, Campbell's clan spends a lot of time parading down the three-two run of **Am** and **Gm** ominous chords. The soldier dreams of strolling the golden sunset Gulf with his beautiful girl. Webb's chord progressions are never boringly normal. In his mind's eye, he recalls the great swooping waves of Galveston crashing, and he dreams of his Surfboy Texan home and his adorable girlfriend.

Into the roaring vocal bridge, Webb and Campbell soar up to the **Ab major** (bIII Mid-eastern chord), rushing through a myriad of majestic new changes, before decrescendoing back to the slim, tight verse. The bridge, naturally, is about their love. He sees her in his mind's eye still standing astride the water. She gazes pensively out into the mystic sea. Somehow, our haggard thoughts drift back to **Jody Reynolds'** #5, 1958 Graveyard Rock song "Endless Sleep" and the Islanders' 1959 "Enchanted Sea." Glen's final stanza is as prayerful as John Fogerty's "Who'll Stop the Rain?" He nearly whispers, wondering whether she still faithfully waits there on the beach at Galveston -- the beach where they once ran together. He is not talking about track-star quarter-mile repeats or marathon grit. He is pondering survival. Glen explained to me (July 2000, Patchogue, New York) that "Galveston" actually covers the Spanish-American War of 1898 (a rankling offshoot of the Texan War of Independence and the Mexican War). As a Vietnam song, though, "Galveston" thunders with truth and power and love and glory.

Will he return to his love? Or will he perish in some woebegone firefight or Ho Chi Minh Hanoi prison that candidate John McCain escaped? He is but a soldier, cut from the common Scottish stock that rolled off Albion's Isle, to the skirl of bagpipes, with *Braveheart* courage on the clanging fields of history. In the final coda verse, Glen confesses, he is scared of dying, before he can dry her lonely tears, before they can watch the shimmering white sea-birds dancing in the sunshine – on their beach at Galveston.

Like a flash or flare in the hot, sweaty, snaky jungle night, "Galveston" rocketed into the HOT 100 Royal Five. The booster rocket for its successful orbit, in the Year America Walked on the Moon, was **Glen Campbell's** trusty All-American smile. This powerful vignette of Glen and his girl burned into the hot heart of war-torn America. Suddenly, for just a loving moment, the big war stood still.

9-11-2001

President Roosevelt labeled December 7, 1941 as "a day that shall live in infamy." When Pearl Harbor was attacked, Hawaii was not yet a state. The attack on September 11, 2001 by the secret terrorist minions of Osama Bin Laden is by far the worst warlike event on American soil since the Civil War. At both the Battle of Gettysburg (July 2-3, 1863) and during the Vietnam War (1963-75+) we lost 50,000 brave American soldiers. When the World Trade Towers fell, the toll was in brave civilians, firemen, policemen, and children. The slimy evil that is terrorism knows no 'honor among thieves,' no code of righteous conduct, no Robert's Rules of Military Order. From Day One, it was obvious the Afghan War was no Vietnam; all they shared was an elusive enemy, and a demonic proliferation of kamikaze desperadoes, to whom the sanctity of human life has no meaning.

Terrorism is neither Christian nor Jewish nor Muslim nor Hindu nor Shinto nor Buddhist. It is **anti-love** and **anti-human**. Terrorism is the polar opposite of religion. Jews, Christians, and Muslims share their progenitor father-figure **Abraham** – who helped sire all three of these great religions, and half the world's people in 2002: 15 million Jews, two billion Christians, 1.2 billion Muslims (*National Geographic*, December 2001). The Muslim people had no more to do with blowing up the World Trade Center than the Christians did (Timothy McVeigh) in the Oklahoma City bombing. People of good will everywhere abhor and detest the evil spirit that wreaks violence from innocence, death from life, despair from hope. These three great religions share the concept of an evil spirit called the Devil. Men and women since the dawn of time have strived to resist evil, to counter hate with love.

Sometimes you have to go to war. As I write this, my nephew Tyler Harris, former Punk Rock drummer, and marathon runner, is serving his country in Afghanistan with the U.S. Marines. He is a great lad. Whether the instigator be Adolf Hitler, Osama Bin Laden, or any hometown crackpot with a spare A-bomb in his basement arsenal, Americans have stepped in to defuse the smoldering terror. Among the lost lines of the other "Star-Spangled Banner" verses, you'll find "Then conquer we must, when our cause is just." Americans are friendly and helpful and selfless when it comes to helping the oppressed. We don't really start wars – but sometimes we finish them.

Crossing the Great Divide - 1970

Jack Kerouac faded away the decade after the 2-3-59 'Day the Music Died.' In Kerouac's Beat Generation classic *On the Road* (1955) finale: "The evening star must be drooping and shedding her sparkler dims on the prairie . . . before the coming of complete night that blesses the earth, darkens all rivers, cups the peaks, and folds the final shore in."

Jack Kerouac

Jack's inadvertent flower children had no idea that Psychedelia might bring them the lifespan of a mayfly. San Francisco debuted a counterculture of Heavy Rock, Sizzling Substances, and existential New Age philosophy. Led by the 50s Beat Genera-

tion novelist **Kerouac** (1922-69) and poets **Allen Ginsberg** (1926-97), **Gary Snyder** (1930-) and **Lawrence Ferlinghetti** (1919-), they lyrically created the wild new frenzy of Folk Rock. Their poetic genius focused on **Bob Dylan** and **Jim Morrison**. Jack Kerouac, football star, short-haired Republican French-Canadian, wrote the greatest most famous book in history about traveling the American road, yet he never owned a driver's license. Nor did he speak English till he went to school, though he was 'Born in the U.S.A.' (#9, 11-84, by Kerouac fan Bruce Springsteen). Father of the Beat Generation, Kerouac never really even cared much for Rock and Roll – maintaining his serious Charlie 'Bird' Parker Jazz fandom until the bitter end.

"If Jack Kerouac had never written *On the Road*," writes **Doors**' keyboard [and faux bass] virtuoso **Ray Manzarek** (b. 2-12-39), "the Doors would never have existed." Ray's super autobiography *Light My Fire*, 1998, printed on acid-free paper, is among the premier rock bios ever. You realize without Ray there might have been no superstar **Jim Morrison**, who wrote Kerouackian lyrics. Quebeçois Kerouac's Columbia University football scholarship ended with a stress fracture. He retired to the fraternity fireside, his pipe, a beer or seven, and quested after the Great American Novel. He joined the Marines and the Navy the same day (few beers), and ended up in the Merchant Marine. His sister ship got torpedoed in the North Sea.

After a harrowing hell-bent-for-leather cross-country odyssey in 1949 Hudsons, Cadillacs, and streamlined chariots of fire with Grateful Dead Merry Prankster Dean Moriarty (Neal Cassady), Kerouac wrote about his midnight neon highway experience. He was buoyed by Benzedrine, beers, Jazz sax records, cigarettes, Ritz crackers, Popsicles and his loving mom Memere. Jack Kerouac cranked out his 125,000 word *On the Road* in just three frantic frazzled weeks, scribbling his whole book on 20-foot scrolls of art paper. Viking Penguin took a chance, and Signet grabbed the paperback edition.

All over the U.S. kids snuck Kerouac's *On the Road* inside the stuff we were supposed to read. Some of the kids were **Bob Dylan, Jim Morrison, Janis Joplin, Jerry Garcia, Bruce Springsteen** (and for what it's worth – me.) Kerouac's only book-turned-movie, *The Subterraneans* (1960*¼, Dearborn's George Peppard, and Leslie Caron too) hit the stands in 1959, the Year the Music Died; it inspired Bob Dylan's #39, 4-65 "Subterranean Homesick Blues." The *Subterraneans* he wrote in three days about his love affair with an Afro girl that the MGM movie moguls mangled to FRENCH to avoid "Happy Days" 50s controversy. During the next couple of years, JK suffered from the ELVIS SPOTLIGHT. Brilliant, hyper, and glib, he swooned through William Buckley's *Firing Line* or the *Steve Allen Tonight Show*. Kerouac cut a record. Rap, maybe. Talking Blues?

"October in the Railroad Earth" – Jack Kerouac & Steve Allen, 1959, NC. The first Rap record? To stave off terminal shyness, the blue-eyed, black-haired halfback tugged at a bottle of cheap Thunderbird wine. He read his woozily romantic poem about neon Jazz nights, railroad brakeman jobs, wild wine parties, and furtive satori affairs. **Steve Allen** (1922-2000) played Cool Jazz piano like Dave Brubeck. *On the Road* seethed through wild hobo travels across this purple-mountain and amber grainwave land.

"Watching the River Flow" – Bob Dylan, #41, 6-71. Dylan and Kerouac loved watching the break-up of their high northern snows (Minnesota and Massachusetts) in March or April. The crackling river was a Taoist thing, an ever-surging tributary to all the earth's mysterious interconnected waters. Dylan's Blues-powered sound cascades here like clumps of flotsam and jetsam, as his weariest river winds somewhere safe to the sea.

"(Sittin' on) the Dock of the Bay" – Otis Redding, #1(4), 1-68; #1(3), 2-68 R & B. Sadly, Otis's shining R & B future vocal power was snuffed out just three days after he recorded this biggest hit about the mile-long Oakland pier jutting toward San Francisco. Blue-star Blues Star Otis's pensive and dejected dock-plopping tune is entirely unlike him. Redding was Mr. Energy. When he took the time to cruise his thoughts, the gray Frisco Bay water brought him down. Otis and guitarist **Steve Cropper**'s tune bespeaks an aimless, isolated loneliness, like Kerouac looking out the bottom of a head-busting hangover over the fishy and sullen East River. Fingers squeak

on Otis's frets. A III major (**G** to **B**) mediant chord portends his wayfaring woe. Nowhere to run [Martha & the Vandellas, #8, 2-65]. Nowhere to hide. Dumping his usual staccato style, Otis gets weirdly remembered for this slow musing song about a woebegone dock-squatter far out into end-of-America San Francisco Bay. And the high "E" and "B" strings squeak their mousy goodbye.

"Backstreets" – Bruce Springsteen, NC, 1975. Off Al. #3, 9-75 *Born to Run*. The Boss echoes Kerouac's run-all-night dream visions; he slow-dances in the dark on Stockton's Beach, grinning off moonlight lake ripples. He heads headlong down the breathtaking boulevard of countless jukebox joints with his girl. *On the Road*'s Sal Paradise (Jack K) has just had one meaningful affair (with Mexican migrant young-mom Terry) in a swirling quickie blast. *Born to Run* glows and throbs with the epitome of Kerouac and Allen Ginsberg's 'Junkyard Poetry.' The screaming sax of 'E Street Band's **Clarence Clemons** is the living embodiment of Kerouac's Beat Generation Jazz Rock, roaring in the midnight coffeehouses.

"Midnight Confessions" – Grass Roots, #8, 8-68. Bassman **Rob Grill** pulls off a dynamite lead here, with drummer Rick Coonce. Chordal curve ball? You blast from **G** to **D7**, but suddenly you hit the bVII **F major**, which turns out to be the Sub-Dominant IV, because then you're into the Key of 'C' by surprise. In 1968, a simple 12-Bar Blues or Streetcorner Progression would be like finding a cat at a dog show. Great memory: sliding home from work, pedal to metal, to Union Lake new cottage of Summer '68, after midnight Detroit Tiger game with pal Jim Bremer [retired to Galveston] and Tigers on pace for World Championship 1968. The power of great music? Personal evocation. A one million-seller can symbolize one million different yesteryear memories to one million listeners.

*Jerry Garcia of the **Grateful Dead***

"Truckin'" – **Grateful Dead, #64, 11-71.** The Dead performed tunes differently every time, refusing to be a cover band for their OWN songs ... "Truckin'" trucks along, cruising in smooth mode, with Everly-ish thirds Appalachian harmonies weaving the tangled skein of Jerry's pristine melody. It's a Road Song for the Ages. Inducted into the Rock Hall of Fame in 1994, **Jerry Garcia**'s stunning on-the-road rep was vindicated in his suitcase lifetime, with rhythm guitar wizard **Bob Weir**; bassman **Phil Lesh, Bill Kreutzman,** and **Mickey Hart** on drums. Keyboarder **Brett Mydland** died in 1990 (37), while **Ron 'Pigpen' McKernan** (organ and harmonica) died in 1973 (liver). Dead sent 13 albums into orbit, like Al. #63, 1-70 *Live Dead* [Oxymoron Dept.]. Their highest? 1975, #12 *Blues for Allah* and renaissance #6, 7-87 *In the Dark*. In many ways, the Dead live. "Truckin'" alludes to their "long, strange trip."

One "Bubble Gum" song by **Ron Dante** and a studio cartoon group outsold everything by two Morrisons, Hendrix, and Joplin put together in the singles category in 1969. Bubble Gum music was simple and danceable. Teenybop kids without a Juilliard Music degree could understand what was going on. Happy, frisky major chords. Carrot-topped Archie plunked guitar and sang. The beat boomed loudly on the big two and four.

"Sugar, Sugar" – **Archies, #1(4), 8-69; #1 U.K.** #1 song of Bubble Gum genre. **Toni Wine,** background vocal. 'Reggie Mantle' played bass and 'Jughead' thumped the drums. Wielding micro-skirts and tambourines, go-go talents of the lithe, limber, and lovely brunette Veronica and her blonde clone Betty were extra-musical. Regardless of carping critics, Ron Dante's Archies' "Sugar2" was on target for four million record buyers, clobbering anything else in 1969. **Dante**'s musical career began at age 11 when he fell out of a tree, broke his arm, and the doc recommended some easy wrist exercises. Dad Dante bought the kid a guitar. At twelve, Kid Dante formed a band, the Persuaders. "Sugar2" multi-tracks Dante's boyish Staten Island tenor. The Archies' third hit (#10, 11-69 "Jingle Jangle") soon followed. Wearing many hats, Ron Dante scored: a #19 Detergents' parody of Shangri-las Death Rock #1, 1-64 "Leader of the Pack" ("Leader of the Laundromat"); simultaneously, the dashing Dante hammered out a huge top tenner, fronting the **Cuff Links** – "Tracy" at #9, 9-69. Despite dimmed visibility, Dante dominated the 1969 charts.

"Yummy, Yummy, Yummy" – **Ohio Express, #4, 5-68.** "Yummy3" nabs a goofy sugar high, and a tricky lyric so naughty that Little Richard or Notorious B.I.G. could never sneak it by. Sounds innocent enough, but spiked with double entendre pun. Great melody, deliberately nasalized by **Joey Levine,** produced by **Kasenetz and Katz.** The eager vocal chugs along with the choo-choo express-train beat. Candy-apple guitars and cotton-candy rhythms spike this bubbly song.

"Simon Says" – **1910 Fruitgum Company, #4, 1-68.** New Jersey **Mark Gutkowski, Steve Mortkowicz,** and other Polish-Americans chortle fun music. A festering organ plies choppy big beat waves. Major three and four-part harmonies swoon. 'Simple Simon' goes back to a medieval nursery rhyme (which needles slow learners). Fruitgum Company racked up three melodic harmonic gold records. "1, 2, 3 Red Light" (#5, 7-68) concerns a chaste young maiden stopping an affectionate octopus of a lusty lad. "Indian Giver" #5, 1-69 stereotypes returned presents.

"Indian Lake" – **Cowsills, #10, 6-68.** SMILE – YOU'RE IN BRADY BUNCH AND PARTRIDGE FAMILY TERRITORY! Aha, Family Values music. **Barbara Cowsill** (1934-85) and her five boys and their sister Sue are known for wispy "The Rain, The Park & Other Things" (#2, 9-67). In #2, 3-69 "Hair" (theme from *Hair*), a lot of shaggy people wandered around looking for their clothes. The **Cowsills** became the prototype for the immensely successful TV family show *The Brady Bunch*.

"Indian Lake," among best of the Bubble Gum genre, is glutted with war whoops, eager cresecendoes, and flyin'-high harmonies. Delightful day-tripper picnic, swim in the cove. Dig:

"I Think I Love You" – **David Cassidy & the Partridge Family, #1(3), 10-70.** Mom Partridge, **Shirley Jones,** delighted us in her 'Laurie' *Oklahoma* heroine portrayal as sweet blonde marriageable soprano. Cassidy's tenor clicks vocally in the first of many mass-media Teen Idol hits with real-life stepmother Jones (b. '34). Remember #6, 2-71 "Doesn't Somebody Want to Be Wanted?'

"Ragtime Cowboy Joe" – **Chipmunks, #16, 7-59.** Yep, the first bubble-gummers are these toothy little dudes led by their irascible leader chipmunk **Alvin,** and his snazzy harmonica. Rest of the chipmunk roster? **Simon & Theodore.** They hold down a Christmas record for Squirrel-type Critters with their perennial "The Chipmunk Song (Christmas Don't Be Late)," gnawing away at the HOT 100; #1(4), 12-58. "Ragtime Cowboy Joe" is **Bob Roberts'** big #1 hit in 1912. David Seville (**Ross Bogdasarian** 1919-72) puppeteered the little dickenses through speed-up studio magic tricks, and pioneered their supercute Chip N' Dale chipmunky style. Bubble Gum's infancy.

"Sweet Pea" – **Tommy Roe, #8, 6-66.** Roe's crisp Irish tenor complements Bobby Vee's reverberating baritone in their early years of carrying Buddy Holly's torch to the Beatles (see Tommy's #1, '62 "Sheila"). Tommy asks coquettish Belle-of-the-Ball to dance. "Sweet Pea" is also the name of a questionable infant with Popeye and Olive Oyl in the cartoons. Tommy and Sweet go out on the moonlit terrace to swoon and spoon and smooch. They fall in love. They ride off to his white castle on his white horse. They live happily ever after. The butler did it.

"Dizzy" – **Tommy Roe, #1(4), 2-69.** Tommy Roe's double-gold record chord pattern ploofs around, stopping, stalling, starting up dizzily again. His head spins. He's in a maelstrom, a whirlpool of love. Fiddles crunch away the BIG 2 & 4 backbeat. Drives you dizzy. Rock songs since time immemorial have doted on love's illnesses. Martha Reeves' Vandellas talked of a (#4, '63) "Heat Wave" (fever, high blood pressure?), Little Willie John and Peggy Lee did "Fever" (#24, 7-56, and #8, 7-58; also #7, 11-65 by "Hang on Sloopy's" McCoys). Here's a sick song that launched a very well career:

"Good Lovin'" – The [Young] Rascals, #1, 3-66. Debuting with Joey Dee's Starlighters, the Young Rascals are bona fide practitioners of Blue-Eyed Soul (despite some brown eyes). "Good Lovin'" interweaves Call & Response Gospel Blues with Rock and Roll. Kid feels bad. [Dizzy?] Family doctor assures him he's O.K. Prescription? Love.

"The Peppermint Twist" – Joey Dee & the Starlighters, #1(3), 11-61. Passaic, New Jersey's **Joey DiNicola** anchored the house band at the Peppermint Lounge, and this supersonic-tempo song advertised the place. Manhattan night club attracted **Jackie Kennedy**, socially sanctioning R & R to adult contemporary horde. Dee's band also helped launch career of **Jimi Hendrix**.

"All Shook Up" – Elvis Presley, #1(9), 4-57; #1(4) R & B; #1(1) C. Either America dug feelin' ungroovy, or perhaps dug Elvis. He begins by itching like this man atop some tree bussing with fuzz. What is a fuzzy tree? 'Smoke Tree' or 'Venetian Sumac': Cotinus Coggyria. Brimming with fuzzy, downy stuff, the poor fuzzy tree often suffers from local pyros whose lighters make it go POOF. Ah – the eternal mysteries of our pop and rock favorites.

"Burning Love" – Elvis Presley, #2(1), 8-72. The King's Top Ten finale. Fever and flame. You can see the poor King's sphygmomanometer blood pressure reading in orbit off the charts as his ebbing life winds down. Or maybe it's just his libido or mojo rising. The ELVIS SPOTLIGHT sent him to Vegas in a one-piece squirmy leather jumpsuit. Despite 2 a.m. racquetball marathons, Elvis "inhaled whole cakes." Sad song, cousin of Graveyard Rock.

"Bad Case of Lovin' You (Doctor, Doctor)" – Robert Palmer, #14, 7-79. Blue-eyed Soul singer sees doctor with problem of lovesickness. Palmer leaps into his Little Richard gusto here. Unlike his #2(1), 8-86 plodding "I Didn't Mean to Turn You On," the song swings, it grooves, it flies off on frantic tangents. His razzing, rangy tenor strides the high-note tightrope. The Maltese/English rocker pitches **Mitch Ryder** dynamism with #16, 3-78 "Every Kinda People". His other goodies? Calypsoish debut "Man Smart, Woman Smarter," #63 in the Bicentennial afterglow 12-76; and "Early in the Morning" #19, 10-88; plus #2 "Simply Irresistible" 7-88.

"People Got to Be Free" – Rascals, #1(5), 7-68; #14, 8-68 R & B. Very serious tribute. **Felix Cavaliere** and the Rascals made the Rock Hall of Fame in 1997 for their starbright dedication to super Blue-Eyed Soul. So affected by the tragic death of Dr. Martin Luther King, they composed this elegy. Long Island and NYC's **Felix Cavaliere, Dino Danelli, Gene Cornish,** and **Eddie Brigati** formed a Rock brigade for peace, love, and racial understanding. Like the Righteous Brothers, they got early airplay on Soulful R & B stations who had never checked out their rascally photo. "People Got to Be Free" delivers a stunning message. It's written in hyperbolic Afro Gospel style. This overwhelming idea? ALL people need freedom. One more echo of Dylan's "Blowin' in the Wind"?

We could classify this one under hymns. Dr. Martin Luther King (1929-68) died that we might all be free. Toni and I visited the bleak garish Lorraine Motel in Memphis where a bullet struck down the civil rights leader. Cavaliere's gospel-supercharged song rocks, but its impact is stone sober. After the deaths of Dr. King in April, and presidential hopeful Robert Kennedy (42) in early June, a dark chapter descended upon America. Urban streets turned uglier with sporadic shots. Pistol-packing perverts and angry anarchists blew up the system and themselves in splattering little holocausts of terror and hate. In 1968, President Johnson stepped down. A bloody 'police riot' trashed the Chicago Democratic Convention that nominated Minnesota Veep Hubert Humphrey. Hot August Chicago. Led by David Dellinger, Jerry Rubin, and Abbie Hoffman, the 'Yippie' party mobilized young starry-eyed peaceful idealists for their Festival of Life. Mayor Richard Daley's 24,000 paramilitary enforcers – cops, National Guardsmen, and federal troops – brandished tanks, bazookas, and righteous zeal. Daley's confrontational strategy (says David Szatmary's *Rockin' in Time*), created a police riot, and injured 198 protestors armed with flowers.

After President Nixon emerged victorious, on a plurality instead of Peace candidate Eugene McCarthy, many former flower children switched to the Blues and their new badboy offshoots, Punk or Heavy Metal.

Songs of religious belief in harmony and tolerance, however, continue to rule in America. We are an idealistic and good-hearted people. The Rascals scored big with #1(3), 4-67 "Groovin'," a let-it-all-hang-out Sunday song of funtime splendor. Their #4, 9-67 "How Can I Be Sure?" highlights Jazz tacets of Four Freshman power and Beach Boy expertise.

"Black and White" – Three Dog Night, #1(1), 8-72. Three Dog Night's multiracial classic Jazz Rock. **Danny Hutton** (b. '42 Buncrana, Ireland) joined **Cory Wells** (b. '42 Buffalo, New York) and **Chuck Negron** (b. '42 NY, NY). All three share lead vocals and imaginative harmonies. In 1954, the old 1896 Plessy vs. Ferguson 'separate-but-equal' doctrine of segregated education was overturned. **Rosa Parks** took any seat she wanted in Dr. King's Montgomery Bus Boycott. **Governor George Wallace** (Presidential victor, Michigan, 1968) stood in the schoolhouse door in Alabama to keep Afro students out. Four martyrs died for the cause of equality: Jewish kids Schwerner and Goodman, African-American Chaney, and Italian **Viola Liuzzo** of Detroit's First Unitarian Church, where the MC5 launched Punk Rock music in 1969.

In 1954 Kansas, the Brown vs. Board of Education Supreme Court decision ruled public school segregation unconstitutional. President **Dwight "Ike" Eisenhower** sent the National Guard to perform its awesome interrational duty. "Black and White," 3 Dog Night's 2nd-biggest hit, speaks to this issue. Named either for an Australian Aborigine or Native American custom of bringing in more dogs to sleep on your cold feet the frostier the wigwam/tent gets, a '3 dog night' is the coldest of all. The song was originally in Reggae style. Chuck Negron and the other Two Dog Night render it into Jazz Rock splendor.

David Arkin and Earl Robinson wrote "Black and White" in 1955 to celebrate the overturning of the 'Jim Crow' laws. Black ink and white paper symbolize complementary racial groups in our American multicultural melting pot. Three Dog Night cites the beauty of little kids not old enough to understand the mucky nuances of discrimination and prejudice. Stop and go tacets lurch a multiracial brotherhood theme.

"Ebony and Ivory" – Paul McCartney and Stevie Wonder, #1(7), 4-82; #8 R & B. Biggest hit for either post-Beatle Paul, or Stevie. They expand the 'black and white' metaphor to a keyboard – be it piano, organ, or accordion – that has both black and white keys. The world is blessed, contend Caucasian Paul and Afro-American Wonder, with people of similar hues. Why can't we all live together in harmony, they contend, like the black (ebony) and white (ivory) piano keys?

Stevie Wonder devoted his life to racial understanding, along with **John Conyers** (b. 1921) Congressman from Detroit. They developed legislation to help YOU celebrate the birthday of Dr. Martin Luther King.

"Green Tambourine" – Lemon Pipers, #1(1), 12-67. Lead singer **Ivan Browne**, bass player Steve Walmsley, Ram Jam guitar guy Bill Bartlett, and Reg G. Nave – keyboards, fog horn, toys, and yep, a green tambourine. Lemon Pipers piped from Oxford, Ohio. Wayne Jancik's One-Hit Wonders story: Buddah Records nearly dropped Lemon Pipers, just as they cut a Paul Leka/Shelley Pinz song they didn't want to record. Of course, it hit #1!. This Bubble Gum Folk-Rock song tells a true story about an English one-man street troubadour; some people use a guitar case for donations. This guy used? A green tambourine.

"Love Grows (Where My Rosemary Goes)" – Edison Lighthouse, #5, 2-70. Upbeat uplifting Flower Power rocker. **Tony Burrows** of West Country, England, probably doesn't know that our Monroe, Michigan, has an Edison Lighthouse for Detroit Edison with a smokestack 600+ feet high. Tony headlined the Kestrels, the Ivy League, psychedelic **Flowerpot Men** and White Plains: "My Baby Loves Lovin'" (#13, 6-70).

"Ride Captain Ride" – Blues Image, #4, 5-70. North to Alaska. Whenever this song [Tampa (singer Mike Pinera) and Alaska (Frank Knonte)] bopped onto our 59 Olds's AM radio, our 1st-grader Lauri would bounce up and down wildly on Konte's effervescent organ solo.

"Traces" – Classics IV, #2(1), 2-69. Dennis Yost and the Classics IV paint a whole misty-mood drizzle world in their minor-key excursion of lost-love sulk. "Traces" spins a cascading organ, as Yost's blue mood wriggles into our sad sodden soul. Faded photos, defunct love letters, pieces of yesterlove. With dark burgundy melodic beauty, "Traces" jabs the unexpected Jazz chord at every turn. Also catch #5, 11-68 "Stormy." **Yost** is a master of gray days gone astray in lonely loveless fogs – and wispy muted Jazz soundscapes. Melancholy solitude.

"Brown-Eyed Girl" – Van Morrison, #10, 8-67. Among R & R's enduring musical jewels! Belfast baritone **Van Morrison**, last seen with 'Gloria' and 'Them,' ((#93, 5-65) is the other major Morrison [JIM!] to slam the sixties with lung-lasting power. With a BASS guitar lead, yet . . . Morrison's bass banger blasts the same low note. Wherever you expect the note to come in, it either hesitates, or syncopates, or hangs fire. Then it implodes. Or implodes

Naturally, everybody loves Morrison's (b. George Ivan Morrison '45) voice too, with its gruff evening swagger. Three-generation Rock Classic. Morrison pumps up the hot pair's secret hideaways – some lowdown drizzly hollow, vacant stadium, or clandestine waterfall where they can tryst again, like last summer. They skip blithely down to the soccer stadium. Two versions on their activities on the grass are rated "G" and "PG-13."

"Make Love to Me" – Jo Stafford, #1(7), 1-54. Back in not-so-naïve '54, Jo crooned this title ("runnin'" and "laughin'" substitute in his lyric). Censors zapped "making love" in Van's 1967 lyric. Weird, eh?

"Wild Night" – Van Morrison, #28, 10-71. Girls stand around, muses Van, all dolled up to look at each other. Guys boogie down on the corner. All wait, impatiently, for something COSMIC to happen in their microcosmic lives. "Wild Night" salutes that first magic night when the new luscious warm spring busts out a fine fury of raging hormones and sweet summer love dreams. A hazy moon with a rainbow ring around it peeks through the french-fried fog. Lusty love bristles. The wild night is alive with love – down the road. Come out and join the jamboree.

"Wild Night" – John Cougar Mellencamp, #3, 5-94. Mellencamp Americanizes the old Irish song. Faxed from the Derry Dawn Owen land of green 1971 fields and stone cottages, hunching into the sheep-strewn road, Morrison laterals the ball to Hoosier cornfield Heartland rocker John – who'd seen a few wild nights of his own (b. '51). Several zinger hooks throttle this classic. One is the finale of "Wi-yi-yi-yi-yild night" that obsesses him. The sizzly night itself is the turn-on. *Grind* headlined 1997 MTV; it featured poolsful of shapely dancers and hulks bumping and grinding in orgiastic rhythms to Hip-Hop and Rap and Rap/Salsa. Girls swayed in thongs (**Sisqo**, #3, 2-2000, "The Thong Song"). In the 50s, *Grind* would have been called a "burlesque show."

Rock enjoys its role as rebel rouser. Each young generation freely believes in the abolition of all censorship. Censorship Abolitionists have a baby daughter . . . and a subtle change occurs. Out in the Wild Night, Van and John may be looking for a –

"Wild Thing" – Troggs, #1(2), 6-66. Or Wild Thong. The PRESLEY SPOTLIGHT. Reggie Ball changed his surname to Elvis's, so **Reg Presley** sings about this lovely Wild Thing. Tromping on three big major chords, the song lurches forward. The most *insincere* "I Love You" ever recorded darts from Cupid's arrow to the poor besieged lassie. He says he THINKS he loves her (see David Cassidy, #1, '70), but must know for certain. He demands she prove her love and hug him fiercely. [Remember **Wild Thing**, the MUPPET? And their mammothly spectacular **Dr. Teeth and the Electric Mayhem Band?**]

The demure damsel ponders his middling ardor, and "Will He Love Me Tomorrow"? Tomorrow he will find a new Wild Thing to do the Wild Thing with. [also see **Madonna**'s (#1, 6-98), "Papa Don't Preach" – you can pay for the baby.] The old story: GUY craves Insta-Love – GIRL demands commitment.

"In Your Eyes" – Peter Gabriel, #26, 8-86; #41, 5-89. **Phil Collins** isn't the only **Genesis** superstar. London's Gabriel worships the glimmering heat and light in her eyes (the light from 1000 churches). A kicky with-it chorus thumps a near-Reggae beat. Others charted better: #1(1), 5-86 "Sledgehammer"; #8, 11-86 "Big Time."

"Disco Duck" – Rick Dees and His Cast of Idiots, #1(1), 8-76; #15, 10-76 R & B. Young WMPS Memphis DJ **Dees** (b. '50) ingratiated himself to Disco Rock lovers/haters with this tune. Catch **Ernie & *Sesame Street***'s #16, 8-70 "Rubber Duckie." Disco haters deplored automatic drum machines and the steady double-heartbeat pulse of 110-130 beats per minute. Dees milked the glitzy mirror-ball dance fever trend. It never left. **Madonna**'s early NYC career blossomed in the 80s in pixilated underground palaces. Now it's called DANCE music, House Music, or Techno. But it's still good ol' Neo-Disco to us. He starts off with a Wolfman-Jackish Rap line, surrounded by all the Disco regalia; funky bass, faux drums. **Steve Cropper** chops on axe. Lyrically, Dees begins as Disco klutz, not duck. Magically, he begins to metamorphose into a weird duck, flapping his wings and quaking in joyous pandemonium. He could be Donald Duck's cousin, with **Donald 'Duck' Dunn** fondling bass guitar.

It's a rare moment in music. If Dees fowled out on a medical degree with the ducky tune, would have be accused of quackery?

Meanwhile, afterburners fired up. Squelched rumors of a **Beatle** break-up spurred the **Rolling Stones** onward and upward. The Stones suffered the loss of original leader **Brian Jones** in a swimming pool drinking-diving fatal combo incident, on our 4th wedding anniversary (July 3, 1969), which I am absolutely certain he was not celebrating. The year 1967 brought us the official concept of the CONCEPT ALBUM. Take twelve songs. Tie them together with some theme or motif. The Beatles got the Old Mac band together, resurrecting Paul's Pa's ancient combo as *SERGEANT PEPPER'S LONELY HEARTS CLUB BAND* #1(15), 6-67. A plethora of pop profs passionately adores *Sgt. Pepper*. It's a nice album, but **Marty Robbins** beat them to the CONCEPT punch by almost eight years with his super #6 Al. *Gunfighter Ballads and Trail Songs* ('59) for pioneering the CONCEPT concept.

Brian Wilson, resident Beach Boy genius, painstakingly tried to counter the Beatles' blockbuster. He compiled symphonies in his head full of esoteric Jazz-laden tracks for an enormous concept album tentatively called "Smiley Smile." After years of frustration, "Smiley Smile" erupted simply as consolation-prize *Wild Honey* (Al. #24, 12-67). Their champ album, *Surf's Up* (#29, 10-71), was a long time comin'. The intentionally ghastly cover featured an emaciated stick-figure **Don Quixote**. Slyly sarcastic surf. The California passion of Surf Music springs (summers?) to life every golden June.

Simon and Garfunkel's *Bookends* (#1[7], 5-68) lavished the lyrics on the vinyl records' big 12"x12" back cover [cutting-edge *Sgt. Pepper* pioneered (try reading a CD liner).] *Bookends* features "America" (#92, weirdly , in 11-72) and "Old Friends" which asks about how weird it would be to be 70 .. [60 is close . . .].

So, how can you put out a tricky concept album, have it hang onto #2 for six weeks, and see it called a flop? Only the **Rolling Stones** know for sure, thanks to a few ice-veined critics betsotted on the vinegar of human unkindness. Their *Satanic Majesties Request* (12-77) featured a snazzy 3-D cover. More gimmicks? An octagon of an album called *Through the Past, Darkly* #2(2), 9-69; and *Sticky Fingers*, #1(4), 5-71, featuring, er, a zipper.

"She's a Rainbow" – Rolling Stones, #25, 12-67. Delightful melodic ditty, supercharged with phasers and echoes. Flaunts Mick's resonant ballad baritone. Stones' "Brown Sugar" (#1[2], 5-71 stars Mick and a sweet bronze lass; "Brown Sugar" suggests the 2nd incarnation of "Louie, Louie" #2(6), 11-63.

"Jumpin' Jack Flash" – Rolling Stones, #3, 6-68.
A gas. In Don McLean's R & R panorama "American Pie" dedicated to Buddy Holly [#1(4), 12-71], he couches his rock stars in names like 'King' (Elvis) or 'Jester' (Dylan). Mick Jagger is 'Jack Flash.' For years the Stones have bandied about diabolical images for fun and profit. [see Stones' "Sympathy for the Devil"] "Jack Flash" is a Devil alias name [see write-up in "Paint It Black" section]. Halting staccato rhythms, slashy passions, rhythmic thunder. As McLean mentioned, "Fire" is the only pal the Devil has:

"Fire" – The Crazy World of Arthur Brown, #2(1), 9-68; NC R & B. Whitby, England's Arthur Wilton (b. '44) was Rock's 2nd major theatrical singer, after **Screaming Jay Hawkins** (1929-2000). Jay got wheeled onto the stage in a coffin. Arthur Brown had a wild stage show, long before the MTV video portion or Kiss and Alice Cooper – descended from Arthur Brown's topsy-turvy world. Brown featured a fiery thrill show, his turbaned head and Caped Crusader costume rampaging through the smoke and mirrors and flames (mentioned in "American Pie").

"Honky Tonk Women" – Rolling Stones, #1(4), 7-69.
NOT Girl Scouts!

ROLLING HONKY-TONK RHYTHM

Clops in on a cowbell. Disjointed in outer space, a bass drum reels in, followed by Keith doing something else on rhythm guitar. Bill Wyman thrusts whatever note he can into silent areas. The cowbell by Charlie Watts?

♪   ♪   ♪   ♪   ♪
1   2   3   4

By 1969, just about every note you could fill in a R & R song had been filled. Greener pastures meant exotic new beats.

Galumphing along in the Key of 'G', "Honky Tonk Women" sings about upstairs shenanigans with slim shady ladies at the Sagebrush Saloon. Graphic goodie. When she blurts she wants to take him upstairs for some ride, she didn't have a Stairmobile.

He makes it with some easy Memphis queen of the ballroom, and subdues a Big Apple babe in a wrestling match. A third verse sprinkled with androgynous sailor musings was X'd out. On the chorus, everyone chimes in with "HONKY TONK WOMEN" in a holler sing-along.

"Lady Marmalade" – La Belle, #1 1-75. Soul diva **Patti LaBelle** celebrated two #1 records. With her echoey melismas and gospel-glow style, "Lady Marmalade" touts an integrated encounter with street hustlers in New Orleans. Patti began with Blues Belles and #15, 4-62 "I Sold My Heart to he Junkman." She rolled into Rap with NC,'91 **Big Daddy Kane** duo in "Feels Like Another One" (#3, 9-

91 R & B). Into her fifth hit decade, the Philly Soul belter bedazzles with her incredible powerful voice. With Michael McDonald (#4, 8-82 "I Keep Forgettin'"), she lofted her other hit monster, "On My Own" (#1[3], 3-86). Song hit #1, 5-2001 with **Christina Aguilera**, **L'il Kim** and **Pink**.

In the 1970 Beatles' aftermath, the Stones hit their marathon stride. Straddling a new Disco decade, they were not afraid to change with the times. They co-opted the funky **Funkadelics'** ("One Nation Under a Groove," #28, 9-78) sound, and the mammoth rhythm track of **James Brown and His Famous Flames:**

"Say It Loud – I'm Black and I'm Proud" – James Brown, #10, 9-68; #1(6) R & B. Ranked 5th of all time by Whitburn's *1999 Top Pop Singles* number compilation system. **James Brown** also has the second highest number of charted hits.

1.	Elvis Presley	151	12.	Beach Boys	59
2.	**James Brown**	99	13.	Rolling Stones	57
3.	Ray Charles	76	14.	Marvin Gaye	56
4.	Aretha Franklin	76	15.	Neil Diamond	56
5.	The Beatles	72	16.	Connie Francis	56
6.	Elton John	69	17.	Dionne Warwick	55
7.	Frank Sinatra	68	18.	Temptations	55
8.	Fats Domino	66	19.	Brenda Lee	55
9.	Stevie Wonder	65	20.	Ricky Nelson	54
10.	Pat Boone	60	21.	Rod Stewart	54
11.	Nat 'King' Cole	60	22.	Jackie Wilson	54

Of these 22 artists, only 18 made the Rock Hall of Fame by 2002+. **James Brown** and Famous Flames always deliver incredible energy: Nat Jones and PeeWee Ellis on alto sax; **Maceo Parker**, tenor sax; Jabbo Starks, drums; Bootsy and Phelps Collins, bass and guitar. Brown was inducted into the 1st R & R Hall Class in 1986. "Say It Loud" reaches out to disenfranchised urban youth whose self-images skirmish with disaster. He assures them no mistakes were made by God. With the fiery invective of a *Bible*-thumping gospel preacher, Brown reassures all ghetto youth that they too could rise like Johnny B. Goode and become stars someday in their own galaxy. *The Commitments* **** stars a galaxy, too, of Irish kids who live and breathe Soul (see Rockflix, and 2000 Rap fans). They chant, "SAY IT LOUD – I'M BLACK AND I'M PROUD!!!" They are not, of course "Black." Yet, they are, in spirit. When it comes to the enjoyment of Rock and Soul, we are all Black, all White, all Asian.

The Rolling Stones' 70s incarnation took them away on "Wild Horses" (#28, 6-71), with "Tumbling Dice" (#7, 4-72) musical gambles. They sang of Glam Rock baritone **David Bowie**'s wife "Angie" [Barnet] (#1, 9-73). This relationship oddity is one of the strangest inter-band connections ever. Other Stones' chartbusters? "Fool to Cry" (#10, 4-76), #1 "Miss You" in 5-78 (#33, 6-78 R & B), and #8 "Beast of Burden" in 9-78. "Emotional Rescue" glommed #3 bronze in 1980. It flirted with the tabooest item of all – reverse necrophilia – in "Start Me Up" #2(3), 8-81 (we're PG-13 here, check the fadeout words). The Stones spread-eagled decades: "Undercover of the Night" #9, 11-83; and "Harlem Shuffle" #5, 3-86, they fishtailed into the 90s with "Mixed Emotions" at #5, 9-89. Two 90s blockbuster albums cinched the marathon World's Greatest Rock and Roll Band audial destiny: #2(1) Al. *Voodoo Lounge*, of Summer 1994; and their Amsterdam Paradiso Club and Paris Olympia Theatre live album *Stripped* (#9, 12-95). The eternal image of Jagger flailing and darting across the stage, pouty lips disgorging gutsy lyrics, changed the direction of Rock and Roll.

About album art. Vinyl Rembrandts reached a pinnacle in the Psychedelic Era (see L.S.D., Leary, and legal and magic mushrooms or psyllocybin). Psychedelic Rock and Roll fluttered with streaky strobe lights, black-light posters of iridescent purple and chartreuse and hot pink, simultaneous snippets of old movies flashed on ceilings – no screens – pulsing blobs of motley wavy colors dribbling and drooling along raggedy walls of old 40s ballrooms (see Kinks' #6, '83 "Come Dancing") – or the old Grande ("gran-dee") Ballroom on the Grand River in Detroit. Psychedelia merged with emerging Punk Rock. The ear-shattering **Motor City Five (MC5)** of **Rob Tyner** blasted dissonant angry chords, and rebellious amps-to-11 volume. Thanks to the Grateful Dead's sound system pioneering, R & R no longer involved just a Dinko Plinko Amplifier and the school's rotten staticky P.A. system. Now your nine-foot amps could bust glass in Idaho. With Detroit's MC5, the Psychedelic Light Show and R & R Pandemonium involved the **Southbound Freeway**, Ann Arbor's **Rationals**, the **Underdogs**, **Woolies**, **Iggy and Stooges**, and young **Bob Seger**.

On mildewy peeling Grande walls, movies pulsed, swirling rainbows drooled, amps spit fire, Rock and Roll thunder boomed, and miniskirted girls shimmied up against shaggy guys in ripped Levis and flower shirts. Teeny tiny tapes and dainty eentsy CD's require eagle eyes to read them. Big foot-square albums, however, blared vocal and visual messages in cardboard glory.

Sergeant Pepper was critically worshiped and deified by the newly emerging R & R press (*Creem*, *Crawdaddy*, and Jann Wenner's citadel of the True

Rock and Roll Press, *Rolling Stone*). Albums and music AND art! Wild floral colors lit up what used to be drab photopix. Album art of 1967 Psychedelia rivalled the Uffizi Gallery, Paris's Louvre, New York's MOMA (NYC Museum of Modern Art) or Metropolitan Museum of Art. **Creedence**'s Al. #1(4), 9-69 *Green River* shimmies a green silken textured cover, like money. After the Stones' dreamy-Oz emerald 3-D *Satanic Mysteries Request* Psychedelic album (#2, '67), album art blossomed into elaborate fantasias which glowed rococo with voluptuous vitality. **Janis Joplin**'s Big Brother album, by cartoonist R. Crumb, is a masterpiece of PG-13 cartoonery (*Cheap Thrills*, #1[8], '68). **Carlos Santana**, a Hall of Fame shoo-in with eight Grammies in 2000 for his amazing *Supernatural* (Al. #1, '99 & 2 #1/2 singles) was in the forefront of Psychedelic art [a tiny CD, but still showcases a new millennium of Psychedelic art]. Very shapely female figures with wings adorn his classic album *Abraxis* which boasts a surrealistic dream sequence – Al. #1(6), 10-70. **Billy Joel**'s debut *Attila* shows him standing with duo drummer Jon Small, in a bloody slaughterhouse, like in *Rocky*****(1976) with Sylvester Stallone bashing inert globs of beef on the hood. Woozy oozy blood seeps from the hacked sides of extinct beeves.

Album art. Some cutesy. Some drooling with Death Rock grotesquerie. Careening album art paused at the top of the multi-colored mountain, wheezed, and slowly slid back down.

The 70s deluged us with tapes, 8 track and regular cassettes. CD's and DAT's were still just a marketer's dream. RECORDS felt the bite. A technology revolution ground on, as 90s RAPPERS in the 90s saved vinyl from a brontosaurus fate.

"Tremor Chri--" – Pearl Jam, #18, 11-94, b/w **"Spin the Black Circle"** #58, 11-94. **Eddie Vedder**'s Seattle-based Grunge Rock crew debuted with gusto: Stone Gossard and Mike McCready, guitar; Jeff Ament, bass guy, Dave Abbruzzese percussion. Their sound spearheads much of the 90s R & R mood. Other hits (higher on Modern Rock Tracks) include #31, 8-96 "Who You Are" and droning dark dirge "Daugther" at #97, 2-96, backed with an un-cheery ode to Blues guru (and convicted murderer) **Huddie Ledbetter** called "Yellow Ledbetter" [a/k/a 'Leadbelly']. On their Al. #1(1), 12-94 *Vitalogy*, Pearl Jam's craggy baritone Vedder serves song stylings. Vedder insisted the vinyl album be first released.

One – Beatles, Al. #1(10), 11-2000. *One*, yep. What other group that split up 30 years before could not only lavish 27 former #1 Anglo-American songs, but snag the #1 spot into double-figure weeks? Only the FABBEST four!

The Beatles Anthology – Beatles, Al. #1(3), 12-95. Good stuff: Ben Bernie's #1(4), 4-27 "Ain't She Sweet," their first Decca-audition disc; John and Paul's Holly "That'll Be the Day" (former bootleg); Gerry and Pacemakers' old #9 "How Do You Do It" (former Beatle reject); #1(8), 3-1912 American Quartet hit "Moonlight Bay" in comic glee; and "Free as a Bird" (#6, 12-95).

Amazingly, before Mid-80s CDs, TAPES once ruled the world. Like the Autobahn/Interstate system, tapes are a [Nazi] German invention (1945, perfected 1947). TAPES changed the recording industry. Half a century of one-track tapeless recording (1897-1947) produced disgruntled musicians. When one poor schlump missed one note, everybody grumblingly retreated to Square One. Or TAKE TWO. Or TAKE 57! Tapes altered the old aluminum acetate style of literally 'cutting' a record (the sharp needle wobbled and gouged the disc via vibrations). Now it became technologically possible to overdub. Remember? Les Paul perfected overdubbing. He'd blend many layers of his guitar in fragile mix-downs with the alto purity of wife Mary Ford's silken voice.

It was not immediately planned, though, that they replace records. In the 60s, home tape recorders became economically possible – which created Garage Rock bands like ours and yours. You could cut your own Billion-Seller and be your own Johnny B. Goode hero, dancing in the ELVIS SPOTLIGHT.

Drawbacks? Tapes [instead of records] would rip, snap, or unravel, littering the landscape with snaggy loopy yards of spaghetti tape skeins. Soon tapes cleaned up their act. We got 4-track tapes (didn't work). Then 8-tracks (did, almost). Cute eight-track tapes were stuffed into big *Brady Bunch* 70s Olds Toronado radios.

Tape cassettes gradually took over the 80s record industry, displacing venerable vinyl. Just as this mediary technology was horning in on records' turf, tapes too were tekked-out by shimmering new hologram CDs. Tapes' big hang-up is the WHIRR problem. Huh? You want your pal to hear a favorite goodie on your #5, 5-86 Billy Ocean *Love Zone* album? Tracing his Trinidad treasures all over creation on tape, it's WHIRR WHIRR WHIRR WHIRR! Oops, too far. REWIND REWIND REWIND! Oops again. FAST FORWARD FAST FORWARD FAST FORWARD FAST FORWARD! Tapes over records? An improvement is supposed to be an improvement! CDs select certain cuts, but can you easily cut into the middle of a song? RAP saved vinyl. DJ's need the feel of turntables, so they can groove and jump and scratch and manhandle records to achieve their desired effect. By 2001 little silver pancakes conquered the music world.

CD (Compact Disc) purveyors boasted they'd last forever – like the 'unbreakable' 45s and 33 1/3s

THE MP3 GENIE IN THE BOTTLE

"Genie in a Bottle" [#1(5), 7-99] is lusciously lovely Mouseketeer **Christina Aguilera**'s sultry siren song about her romantic capabilities for the lucky owner of the bottle; it precedes her #3+, 1-2000 "What a Girl Wants." What most guys (and girls) really want is free music – as MP3 assaulted this millennial recording industry. NAPSTER/ MP3 also wreaked unholy havoc among recording tycoons trying to squirrel away every royalty for their artists, and best of all, for themselves. The March 8, 2000 Stephen Williams *Newsday* article cites this cyberspace genie, swirling sensuously in the bottle/computer, waiting to lavish the free love of Free Music to a generation squashed by debt and desire. NAPSTER is a service bandied about as the most obvious villain. Hard-working recording artists see the whole shebang as just another bootleg way to rip off their royalties (a moxie mogul stunt since the dawn of recorded time).

The Motion Picture Experts Group (MPEG) recently developed a new downloading system: 50 megabytes only, of disk space (previously, the regular CD nabbed 600 megabytes). Williams explains how you can first copy, via a computer hard drive. Then you "slice, dice, database, and dupe" like other files. You can download it to portable players, he says, or just swap it with pals. Too good to be true?

But of course. As we speak, lawyers galore are marshalling, positing a computer hardware tax to assure artists' royalties. Lawyers seek legislation to forbid downloading – as they do the pirate, or bootleg records of the past. It looks like another cosmic checker game. Prediction? Record companies will soon tap NAPSTER for big fees. Royally, the rocking royalties roll on, regardless of technology. The beat goes on. Everybody plays, and everybody pays. In February 2001, NAPSTER was (temporarily) zapped in court. Their viability remains to be seen in appellate courts.

of mid-century. [But silver pancakes can scratch like 'unbreakable' albums.] With DAT's (Digital Audio Tapes) waiting in the wings, which are even smaller, we'll all need electron microscopes to read the furshlugginer liner notes. The supposed death of VINYL RECORDS was ignored by millions of us REAL record lovers, loyal to our brontosaurus technology. Loving our psychedelic album art. Blessing our licorice-pizza Beatle platters. True vinyl fans would not let their beloved black wax croak. Records are a musical tapestry, a colorful quilt of nostalgic music that keeps the world cozy and happy. Records are a distant mirror to our past. They are windows to a world of make-believe: a stardust honkytonk ballroom, a boulevard of broken dreams, a land of enchantment.

"The Long and Winding Road" – Beatles, #1(2), 5-70. Conductor Leonard Bernstein (1918-90) of the New York Philharmonic said this might be the greatest song ever written. Musicologists snapped to attention. For years, the Lennon-McCartney team turned out the Beatles' classic canon. McCartney's poignant curvy road odyssey is a wayfarer's cup of tea and love, beyond the madding crowd of hurly-burly wanderlust. It's a fireside, and a kiss from his lifetime lovemate Linda at the end of the tough trail. As the Beatles faded into their late era, the world's greatest third singer (via Paul and John) discovered similar symphonic sounds:

"Here Comes the Sun" – Beatles, NC, 2-70. George Harrison solos his lead vocal on this incredible Hollyesque sunshine song of promise and spring and resurrection [catch **Richie Havens**' atomic right-hand blazing strum on his cover – #16, 3-71]. Major chords parade a carpet of daffodils and hyacinths and tulips beneath a rare halcyon robin's-egg British sky. "Winter is passed. The sound of the turtle is heard in the land" [the great Ernie Harwell, Detroit Tiger Hall of Fame broadcaster, quoting the *Bible* and opening each fresh new season]. **George Harrison** invites his "little darlin'" to celebrate the melting ice and glorious future. **Richie Havens** opened at Woodstock, but his biggest hit was yet to come. In the meantime, John and Paul let George do it.

"Something" – Beatles, #3, 10-69. With the Beatles' evening star sinking low, and a new decade dawning on a Yoko future, the third Beatle crafted a masterwork. Its delicate chord shifts and zesty curling vocal rank "Something" among the Beatles' Best. George hangs on the tonic seventh for an eternity. He murmurs about her enchanting movements. The woman? Probably wife Patti Boyd Harrison. Patti, later tied the knot with guitar wizard **Eric Clapton**. Studying the sitar in India (guitar-type instrument) added an exotic sound; Harrison studied Hin-

duism/Trancendental Meditation on the Subcontinent with **Maharishi Mahesh Yogi** (as did Beach Boy Mike Love and many other stressed-out rockers). "Something" is the song which leads up to Lennon & McCartney's "Long and Winding Road."

"Bonnie Came Back" – Duane Eddy & His Twangy Guitar, #26, 12-59. Without Eddy's Rebels war-whooping it up with his Phoenix phalanx of snarly sizzling saxes, would the Beatles have ever clicked? Eddy's rockin' "Bonnie" instrumental squeals tires and girls. Modulating up a few keys, it drifts into the Beatles' first record "My Bonnie" (#26, too, in 1964). Like the Scottish Folk-song lassie, Bonnie returns from the Long and Winding Road of her destiny.

Let's flip back again to Paul's "Yesterday" and check out the music patterns. If CHORD THEORY isn't your thing, hurdle this burly sidebar.

YESTERDAY'S CHORD THEORY

"Yesterday" is in F major, we recall. Paul hits the expected **Dm** (6 minor) of the Streetcorner **F-Dm-Bb-C**[7].

"Yesterday" proceeds slowly and pensively. Paul's signature song sometimes shifts chords every syllable for 2500 "Yesterday" versions recorded. One power shift goes – **Em**[7] – **A**[7] – **Dm** – **C** – **Bb** – **Dm** – **Gm**. With fleeting and gossamer changes like that, "Yesterday" floats. Spins. Broods. The three notes we play in a chord are a TRIAD. Our I tonic chord is **C**, and it contains the root MIDDLE C as we build our song – or Paul's. In the Key of 'F' Paul is using, we have a different set of chords; compare these:

Keys:

I	IIm	IIIm	IV	V	VIm	VIIdim	I or VIII
C	Dm	Em	F	G	Am	Bdim	C
F	Gm	Am	Bb	C	Dm	Edim	F
G	Am	Bm	C	D	Em	F#dim	G
D	Em	F#m	G	A	Bm	C#dim	D
E	F#m	G#m (Abm)	A	B	C#m	D#dim (Ebdim)	E
A	Bm	C#m	D	E	F#m	G#dim (Abdim)	A

This table covers many popular PIANO or ORGAN (C, F, or G) keys, or keys for GUITAR or BASS (E, A. G, or D). Woodwinds transpose down to Bb. To get from "Yesterday" to "The Long and Winding Road," we must pass this fragrant poppy field of Enchanted Chord Theory.

Anonymous chord inventors, becloaked in Igor black hoods, and shuffling about the drafty dank castles in scraggly sandals, discovered the II super-tonics (Viola!), the III mediants (Eureka!), and the IV sub-mediants (Zowie!). Whole generations of lead guitar whizzes with speedo speed can't name a mediant or a super-tonic, but can knock your socks off with finger-fret lighting.

To get to that tricky diminished chord (**Bdim** or **Edim**), we must back up to MINOR. Simple concept. To change any MAJOR TRIAD to a MINOR TRIAD, just flat the third note. In other words, you lower the middle note a half step. Here's your **C** minor chord: C-Eb-G.

To make the tricky DIMINISHED chord, in Key of C, flat both the 3rd and 5th notes of the C major triad (C-D#-F#, with D# same as Eb). This concept can be applied to any other key too. If you're doing "Brown-Eyed Girl" in 'G' and you want to hit the dominant V chord, it will be **D major**. Your IV sub-dominant is, simply, four steps up, or **C**. If you play guitar or bass, and your song is an 'E' major blues like "Kansas City," the **B** chord will be your V dominant chord, and the **A** is sub-dominant and IV. For sax buffs, **Bb** may be your tonic with an **F** dominant V chord, and an **Eb** IV sub-dominant. Jazz hovers around sixth chords, as does Blues. To make a **C6** chord, just add the sixth note in your scale C – E – G – A (A is 6 notes up from root C note). To make a seventh chord, almost always used with your dominant V chord (V7), just go up another half step beyond the sixth chord. Out of this, you'll get a nice Blues run, too. Blues and rhythm guitar thrive on rambling along from the fifth to the sixth to the seventh and back down. The **C7** chord can be built like so: C – E – G – Bb. Ninths? Just add your second note one up from your octave eighth note. In Key of 'C', add a D just above the octave. So, you get C – E – G – D: **C9**.

Elevenths, you want elevenths? Another Jazz favorite. Ride up another four beyond your octave to the sub-dominant root note. In Key of 'C', it's F. Nobody has hands stretchy enough for C-E-G-F, so they wing it: **C11**.

Now that we've figured out Paul's "Yesterday" manifesto, we too can write and sing our own megahit like "Yesterday," "Today," or "Tomorrow."

"Yesterday" – Beatles, #1(4), 9-65. Super song already listed. Worth listing twice. Thrice. Fice.

"Today" – New Christy Minstrels, #14, 4-64. Streetcorner-chorded Folk song. Guy volunteers to taste girl's wine and devour her strawberries. He says he'll remember today beyond 1,000,000 tomorrows. Good line, eh? Write your new hit. Send 10%.

"Tomorrow" – Kingston Trio, NC, 1959. Hilarious item about guy with ticket on train to place called Morrow and hassled about when and where. (You want to go to Morrow tomorrow?) Pun fun.

Paul's "Long and Winding Road" masterwork alludes to the wild, windy night. Our world-weary traveler spans the teeming globe. He seeks inspiration, meaning, inner peace, paradise, gold, love, or a bagel with lox. The prodigal son returns. Finally, after a nightmarish long, long trip, he comes back to her door.

TIME FOR JAZZ

Besides imaginative chord patterns, the Beatles caught a pass from **Dave Brubeck**'s Jazz quartet and experimented with nonconformist time signatures. In "Strawberry Fields Forever" (#8 flipside of #1, 3-67 "Penny Lane"), John and Paul juggle the perplexed tempo from 4/4 to 9/8 to 4/4 to 2/4 to 6/8, and then to 9/8 to 4/4 to 9/8. The strawberries don't drift along; they lurch. The Beatles broach Jazz chords like **Dmaj7** and **C#dim**, or **Eb11** and **F#9** or **C#6**. No wimp chords. Where did the Beatles learn this stuff? **Chuck Berry**, for one. As early as his 1955 first hit #5 "Maybellene," Berry employed a slew of Jazz ninths: **Bb9, Db9, C9**. Smooth sixths and sevenths bounce up and down the Blues riff scale. These ninths, though, are a sweet chunk of Chuck's early real true love (from **Benny Goodman**'s guitarist **Charlie Christian**), JAZZ.

Ironically, Chuck Berry desired to become a crooner like his hero **Nat King Cole**; listen to "Maybellene's" flip "Wee Wee Hours," late night bluesy reverie. Chuck's "Thirty Days" hit #45 for Rockabilly super singer Ronnie Hawkins and his

Hawks, who later became Bob Dylan's legendary band the **Band**:

"Up on Cripple Creek" – **Band, #25, 11-69.** Arkansas leader **Levon Helm** belts Blues, with star-studded cast of Canadians. Great bassist **Rick Danko** (1942-99) anchored sound. **Robbie Robertson** handled lead guitar and many vocals. Robertson inducted solo **Eric Clapton** into Rock Hall in 2000, only artist ever to enter THRICE (with Cream '93 and Yardbirds '92). Cripple Creek is in tip-top Colorado. Lyric is vintage WOODSTOCK about hearty partying and loving.

Though the Hawks/Band expanded Chuck's title to "40 Days," **Chuck Berry** wrote it with a snazzy Jazzy **C9+5**. You do the **C9** but raise your G to Ab in the chord. He also kicks in an **Fdim** and a **C9** before slogging back to this tonic **F**. It fades on a hanging **F6** . . .

The Fab Four also learned polychordal Jazz from the **Crickets** – Buddy Holly, Joe B. Mauldin, superdrummer Jerry Allison. Producer **Norman Petty** steered the Blues/Rockabilly/Rock Crickets to Jazz chords and arrangements. Petty's Pop Standards Trio's monster hit was **Duke Ellington**'s #3, 2-32 "Mood Indigo" at #14, 8-54 for Norm, wife Vi, and guitarist Jack Vaughn, while "On the Alamo" zoomed to #29, 12-54.

Can we find a better pipeline to Pure Jazz for Buddy (via Norman Petty) than the ultimate Jazz royalty – **DUKE ELLINGTON** (1899-1974), #1[3], 10-30, "Three Little Words," #2[1], or 10-31 "Solitude"? Crickets' "Maybe Baby" stomps from **F** to **G#dim**. Buddy's #58, 8-58 "Fool's Paradise" (covered by "American Pie's" guy Don McLean, #107, 2-74) uses zingers, too: **Bdim**, **Cdim**, plus grace-note melismas and curly tones to wow even Aaron Neville or Mariah Carey or Whitney Houston.

Petty and Holly's two final symphonic songs were recorded with **Dick Jacobs**. Buddy collaborated with great R & B sax wizard **King Curtis** for one brief shining moment on *Reminiscing* (Al. #40, 1963). Curtis (1934-71, stabbed in NYC as innocent bystander) scored big instrumentals like "Soul Twist" (#17, 2-62), and "Ode to Billie Joe" (#28, 9-67, and #1, 8-67 for Mississippi's sultry alto Bobbie Gentry). He's best noted for his playful sax on Carl Gardner/Bobby Nunn **Coasters**' smashes like #1(1), 6-58, "Yakety Yak" and #2(3), 2-59 "Charlie Brown." The Holly/Jacobs "Moondreams," cut at NYC's Knights of Pythias Hall, sails on cirrus cotton-candy chords.

"True Love Ways" – **Buddy Holly, NC, cut January 1959**, three weeks before fatal crash. Buddy's sweet song for Maria. Never performed live. Polynesian and Mideastern chord changes. Amazing combo of Classical, Soft Rock, and Jazz balladry. Strings spangle dignity, charm, and pure newlywed love. King Curtis saves his most ethereal gorgeous sax lead for this one. Buddy left on his Winter Dance Party tour into frozen North Dakota and Dylan territory. First rocker to experiment with strings, Buddy puttered with *pizzicato* (plucked) violins on "Rainin' in My Heart,' (#88, 3-59); it flabbergasted NY Philharmonic session folk, unused to Classical crossover.

TRUE LOVE CHORD WAYS SIDEBAR

Holly loaded this idosyncratic melody with major plunges to the Polynesian bVI chord (like **C** to **Ab**) and the Mideastern bIII chord (like **C** to **Eb**). The song shifts uncannily from its melodic Key of 'Bb' into subterranean surrealistic chord changes: **F9, Gm, Ebm, Adim, Eb6**, and then a stunning rise to the **Db** major (bIII).

"True Love Ways" – **Peter and Gordon, #14, 4-65; #2 U.K. Peter Asher** wasn't just a red-haired brother to Paul McCartney's girlfriend Jane; he was a Buddy Holly fan. Through this Britwave Invasion anthem, and through his 70s producing of Linda Ronstadt's Holly hits, Asher maintained a direct link to Lubbock. Asher (b. 1944) and **Gordon Weller**'s (b. 1945) harmonic tapestry suggests Everly Brothers. Jerry Lee Lewis's PG rated cousin, **Mickey Gilley**, scored with "True Love Ways" in the *Urban Cowboy* era: #66, 8-80, #1(1), 6-80 C.

So John, Paul, George, and Ringo, hypnotized by the Holly aura, learned their Jazz from Holly and Petty. Their closest R & R link to breathtaking Jazz chords of esoteric complexity? *The Buddy Holly Story Volume II*: "That's What They Say," "What to Do," "True Love Way," "Moondreams," and "Peggy Sue Got Married." "Crying, Waiting, Hoping" (done by **George**) influenced "Something," which in turn influenced Paul and John to do Bernstein's Greatest Song Ever written, "The Long and Winding Road."

"Nowhere Man" – **Beatles, #3, 3-66.** Bereft of a point of view, our Nowhere Hero suffers from DYNAMIC WISHY-WASHYISM. Lives in Nowhereland. Sort of a Babbitt character, waiting for peer group to make up his mind for him on what to believe. Great lead/rhythm guitar chord surge in bridge. On their #4, 3-68 "Lady Madonna," Catholic Paul gets warmed up for his massively meaningful hymn "Let It Be." "Lady Madonna," too, is about mother nurturing throughout history. The song is powered by hammering bass-clef keyboard. Rolls along like a speedy stampede. **Fats Domino** took "Lady Madonna" to #100, 9-68, NC,R & B. New Orleans piano sage's last charted hit.

"Hey Jude" – **Beatles, #1(9), 9-68.** Biggest Beatle hit. Jude, Patron Saint of Lost Causes. "Jude" uses enormous commitment and belief; also, it symbolizes utter futility. International geopolitics were getting uglier and uglier. Riots flared in America, and wars crushed flaming Southeast Asia. Never fear, "Jude" reassures. In a Gregorian-chant style horde of pilgrims, "Jude" shuffles off heavenward, following humanity across the ages. It mashes major chords with ringing keyboards and harmonic choruses (backing Paul, who leads the pilgrim caravan.) On a more humdrum but homey note, JUDE is also a nickname of John [and Cynthia Powell's] kid **Julian**

Lennon. "Get Back" (#1[5], 5-69 touts Linda Ronstadt's Tucson, Arizona.

"Ob-La-Di, Ob-La-Da" – Beatles, #49, 11-76. Refugee from *The White Album*. Super song, shoulda been at least #4. Wonderful melody. Paul sings a cryptic Dylanish lyric about a guy named Desmond and his girl Molly. Desmond buys her a big diamond (20 kt.) ring. The powerful message after the nonsense-syllable title is LIFE ROLLS ON. The world will continue twirling and swirling and whirling, whether each person is having a blast or not. In their own little world, Paul's Desmond and Molly have carved out their private chunk of happiness – singing and caring little about consequences. Life will go on around us even if we're not living much of it.

*The **Beatles**: l-r **Paul, Ringo, George & John***

"Sgt. Pepper's Lonely Hearts Club Band"/"With a Little Help from My Friends" – Beatles, #71, 9-78. The #1(15) *Sgt. Pepper* album made a big hit: revolutionary printed lyrics, cast of thousands on cover, #1 umpteen weeks. Oddly, this eponymous song had highest (#71, 9 years later) chart #'s for the concept album's single sides. It had cohesion. For instance, Paul's homespun Jug Band-style "When I'm 64", (NC, '67). I love his fuse-mending, Isle of Wight-swimming grandkid future vision of domestic bliss with his lifemate **Linda Eastman McCartney** (married 3-69). As he and Linda lived their early 50s, working on causes of peace, and animal welfare, things looked good for hitting 64 together. Tragically, Linda took ill and passed away in April 1998, shattering Paul's life, as well as his cottage retirement dream. I feel very sad for Paul when I hear my 174th-favorite song "When I'm 64." No matter how wealthy we are, long-term planning is iffy. Rock and Roll is not now, and never has been, conducive to longevity. Like Gerry and the Pacemakers' Camelot hymn from *Carousel* "You'll Never Walk Alone" (#48, 6-65, but #1, 1985 U.K.), Rock and Roll allows us to DREAM OUR DREAMS AND LIVE OUR VISIONS. *Sgt. Pepper* printed the lyrics (a boon indeed to hummers and strummers), and produced a great allusive sideline song:

"Summer Rain" – Johnny Rivers, #14, 2-67. Couple makes out while listening to *Sgt. Pepper*. I love the Beatles, but aside from "When I'm 64" or maybe Lennon's opus "A Day in the Life," I'd swap the whole album for just one of these under-hyped cameo gems (which didn't overwhelm the HOT 100): "All My Loving" #45, 3-64; "Roll Over Beethoven" #68, 3-64 [George Harrison']; "Thank You Girl""#35, 4-64; "Words of Love," or "I'll Follow the Sun" NC [Buddy Holly sound]; "If I Fell" #53, 8-64; or "Rain" #23, 6-66 with simulated bagpipe skirls.

***Magical Mystery Tour* – Beatles, Al. #1(8), 12-67.** *Sergeant Pepper* isn't even the Beatles' best concept album of the year 1967. This is. The cover rivals Pepper: Beatles in goofy bunny, walrus, and cat-thing outfits, plus some other indeterminate animals. Album has 2½ bona fide Beatle biggees: "Penny Lane" (#1, 2-67), "Strawberry Fields Forever" #8, 2-67, and "I Am the Walrus" #56, 12-67, snorfling in the background. "Penny Lane," like "Louie, Louie," was scoured for racy lyrics; they finally discovered most of these cryptic places were just local Liverpool parks and streets. "The Fool on the Hill" is a timeless tune of mellow cellos, and compassion for the clairvoyant slow learner (check Five Keys' streetcorner classic "The Wisdom of a Fool" #35, 12-56).

Straight surrealism in their Salvador Dali "Walrus." Baudelaire. Burroughs. Freak-out mudpie jellyroll free association stuff that Bob Dylan, through Kerouac-Ginsberg, told Lennon he should be writing. And write Lennon did – *In His Own Write* (1965, prose, not poetry/music): "Puffing and globbering they drugged theyselves rampling or dancing with wild abdomen, stabbing in wild posthumes."

Turn on to Beatles' (#96, 3-68 "The Inner Light"), implode into splendor. In 1968, #1(9), 12-68 the *White Album* crested, blank except for the cover serial number of the individual album. Their Beach Boy tribute echo "Back in the U.S.S.R." made the stodgy Communist block laugh at itself; John's 12-Bar Blues questions ALL authority (and common sense) with bonkers "Why Don't We Do It in the Road?" John echoes Paul in his breathtaking MOM tribute to his well-meaning mother "Julia" (who turned him over to Aunt Mimi, and then was killed by a bus in Liverpool). They mock Westerns with sorry-ending "Rocky Raccoon." Soon John met Japanese-American artist Yoko Ono in the big city; three Beatles were suddenly jilted of their fraternal band relationship. Cool album cover.

Letterman Reverse Top Ten of other Psychedelic-Era Album Covers of artistic fascination:

10. ***Their Satanic Majesties Request* – Rolling Stones, Al. #2, 1967.** 3-D Mick with nifty wizard's dunce cap. Fuzzy spinning red Saturn (planet, not car) in Taj Mahal background.

9. ***Jimi Hendrix Experience Axis: Bold As Love* – Jimi Hendrix, Al. #3, 2-68.** Jimi's persona is a part of Hindu Ganesh elephant god of many arms and trunks.

8. *I Feel Like I'm Fixin' to Die* – **Country Joe & the Fish, Al. #67, 2-68.** Psychedelia. Storm Thorgerson.

7. *Grateful Dead* – **Grateful Dead, NC, 1967; Al. #25, 10-71.** Jerry, the Creature from the Black Lagoon, an Uncle Sam top hat, and floating fire on the far horizon.

6. *Disraeli Gears* – **Cream, Al. #4, 12-67.** Blues gurus fry flames. Red. Pink. Magenta. Orange-Red. Loudest album cover on block. Dig it.

5. *Inner Mystique* – **Chocolate Watch Band, Al. NC, 1968.** Angels in white on noggin of blue bathing-capped gal, flanked by paratrooper angel; 1901 Soroptimists; sunray-headdress Indian; red and blue chrysanthemums.

4. *West Coast Love-In* – **Peanut Butter Conspiracy/ Chambers Brothers, Al. NC, 1968.** A Love-In is a Peace and Love Celebration in some park where everyone expresses inner feelings of brotherhood. A few take off some clothes and smoke some stuff. LSD was legal then. Long-haired maiden has hair marbled brown like gnarly tree trunk nearby. She wears fringed Indian leather pants; blue swirls of blueberry/raspberry syrup cascade above chunky mushrooms and pear-shaped leaves of sweet poison ivy.

3. *In-A-Gadda-Da-Vida* – **Iron Butterfly, Al. #4, 9-68.** Single of same name #30, 8-68. Two spherical globules of amoeba-like monstrosities collide and maybe do it in the road. Band plays guitars. Oxymoron, like Led Zep. You know how can a butterfly be heavy iron or a balloon of lead?

2. *Anthem of the Sun* – **Grateful Dead, Al. #87, 8-68.** Fiery, crinkly, curlicue mandala wheel of life spins in Hindu splendor. Faces of major godlets are blue. Many-eyed Argus monsters stare blankly. By **Bill Walker**, Michaelangelo of album art.

1. *In Search of the Lost Chord* – **Moody Blues, Al. #23, 10-68.** On the left, a skull; on the right, a baby in a womb; an old decrepit man squats in meditation. Fire sprouts out of his multi-headed bony face – the fire spells MOODY BLUES. The death's-head left skull needs a little dental work.

Great album art is part of the majesty of vintage vinyl. Big foot-square canvasses of multicolored album art accompanied your favorite songs – not some dinky CD or tape or DAT micro-item in a blur of cryptic figures and a barrage of teeny tiny 4-point type no one bothers to read. Mainstream rockers like **Bobby Vee** and **Paul Revere's Raiders** also jumped on the Psychedelic art bandwagon. Great pop artists from Peter Max (*Yellow Submarine*) to R. Crumb (Janis Joplin's album) to Andy Warhol to **Jerry Garcia** – an amazing artist himself – furnished mini-Michaelangelo foot-square classics of Pop-Rock art for the ages.

THE LOST CHORD

The lost chord? It's in **Buddy Holly**'s rare and profound orchestral song "Moondreams." First the spiffy lyric dances over **A7**, **G9**, and **Cmaj7**. In Rock and Roll, you can count the major seventh chords in a thousand hit songs on one hand. Then "Moondreams" bounces down to a melodic **Bb7**. The coda is spellbinding. On the last fleeting line Holly's moonbeams vanish. Then what happens? The LOST CHORD! The violet velvet violins float the song from **G9** to **G7b9** to (Good grief, Charlie Brown) the big one: **G7#5b9**.

George Harrison and John Lennon and Paul McCartney never forgot Buddy Holly. A very long and winding road of lost-chord 'Moondreams' led them to this beautiful song.

The long, winding road led them all to HER door. They trudged through wildfog or windswept British nights, through the American Storm, into all their consciousness-raising and Psychedelia. The raw, windy road led them through incredible musical experimentation, through symphonic synthesis, through chaotic "Walrus" glops of metaphorical wildswoops. The Fab Four's American odyssey winged them through the archetypal music of Buddy Holly, Chuck Berry, and Little Richard. They sloshed in Del Shannon's "runaway" rain. Never satisfied with being #1, they changed from four similar guys to four wild-ranging individuals, with free-thinking independent ideas. They synthesized. Invented.

"Those Were the Days" – Mary Hopkin, #2(3), 9-68. In the blindsided aftermath of manager Brian Epstein's mysterious (accidental?) O.D. death, the Beatles took the reins of their own careening carriage. They recorded Pontardawe, Wales's sweetest soprano cutie, Mary Hopkin. At tender age 18 she sings this nostalgia song about her former pub pals, now gone to seed. So many great songs are a quick "Hello Goodbye" (Beatles #1[3], 12-67), as wayfaring strangers trudge alone in this wild world of woe and wonder. The Beatles produced Mary's own 'Yesterday' song at their own enterprise – Apple Records.

The Beatles emerged as not just the most popular band in the world, but as a way of life.

John McCormack, (1883-1945)
THE "Irish Tenor"

Frankie Laine (L) and **Mitch Miller**

Duke Ellington

Annette [Funicello] and **Frankie Avalon,** 1976

Buddy Holly [middle, without glasses] and the **Crickets:**
drummer **Jerry Allison** and bassman **Joe B. Mauldin**.
1–1

The Platters–
(L-R): Herb Reed (bass),
David Lynch (tenor),
Tony Williams
(lead, high vocal),
Zola Taylor,
Paul Robi (baritone).

Antione 'Fats' Domino,
of New Orleans

Teen idol **Pat Boone**
Who outsold everyone but Elvis,
1955-57.

Jerry Lee Lewis, 1957

Paul Anka

Johnny Cash

1-2

Elvis Presley, (1935-1977)

Connie Francis,
America's #1 female singer of the late 50s.

Jiles P. Richardson -- the **Big Bopper**, 1958. During 2000, the Big Bopper's son toured as the Big Bopper, and autographed this for Buddy Holly Memorial Society President Bill Griggs.

Ritchie Valens' (on record) girl-friend **Donna** [Ludwig] with his manager Bob Keane, 1959.

Little Richard

Johnnie Ray

Patti Page, #1 female singer 1950-1957.

Eddie Cochran, 1958

Gene Vincent (middle) and his **Blue Caps**, 1956.

Wilson Pickett

American Bandstand's ageless (OK, 44 in '73 here) **Dick Clark.**

Cab Calloway

Sam Cooke, among 10 other original Rock and Roll Hall of Fame Inductees, in 1986.

Two avid golfers: **Alice Cooper** (w/out make-up) and bal-ladeer sensation **Johnny Mathis** [#4 *ever* in album sales].

Carole King, outstand-ing Brill Building song-writer (60s), and 70s record-ing star.

John Lee Hooker, bluesman

Johnny Horton ←

Buddy Holly (any resem-blance to Clark Kent is *not* coin-cidental), 1959.

1–5

Crickets: Top to bottom; Jerry Allison, Buddy Holly, Joe B. Mauldin.

The Crystals

Jerry Lee Lewis, when he's 64.

Bo Diddley

Neil Sedaka, 1975

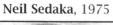

Corner across from South **Philadelphia** High School, alma mater of Chubby Checker, Frankie Avalon, Bobby Rydell, Dee Dee Sharp, Little Eva, and Fabian--of *Bandstand* Fame.

Annette [Funicello], *Beach Blanket Bingo* Surf Star.

Jan [Berry] and Dean [Torrence], Surf Rock silver medalists, 1964.

The **Beach Boys:**
(L-R): Bruce Johnstone, Dennis Wilson, Mike Love, Brian Wilson,
Al Jardine, Carl Wilson.

Roger Miller

California Teen Idol
Ricky Nelson.

The **Four Seasons** -- East Coast stars.
(L-R): **Frankie Valli**, Tommy DeVito,
Bob Gaudio, Joe Long.

1-7

Del Shannon

Gene Pitney

Shannon and Bill Griggs

Gene Pitney, Rock Hall 2002

Singer's singer **Roy Orbison**

(L-R): **Roy Orbison, Bruce Springsteen, Tom Waits, Elvis Costello,** and guitar player/producer T-Bone Burnett, 1987.

1–8

Motown headliners the **Supremes:** L-R: Diana Ross, Mary Wilson, Flo Ballard, 1964

Otis Redding, Volt Soul Star, 1966.

Aretha Franklin, 1st female Rock and Roll Hall of Fame Inductee (25 males), 1987.

Motown's **Temptations.** Clockwise from top left: Eddie Kendricks, Melvin Franklin, Otis Williams, Paul Williams, David Ruffin, 1965.

Marvin Gaye, Motown, 1965

Tina Turner and **Mick Jagger**

Tommy Roe

Motown's **'Little' Stevie Wonder**, Age 14.

Teen Idol **Ricky Nelson**

SUN Studios, 706 Union Ave., Memphis, Tennessee. Where Elvis began.

Bob Dylan, 20-year-old superstar (and **Bobby Vee's** former keyboard man).

Country Rock legend **Johnny Cash**

Beatles John Lennon, Paul McCartney,
George Harrison, Ringo Starr.

Beatles in directors' chairs

The Searchers:
Top L-R: John McNally, Tony Jackson,
Mike Pender. Seated: Chris Curtis.

Herman [Peter Blair Noone] of **Herman's
Hermits**, and Gary Lewis, singing star and son
of Dean Martin's comedy partner Jerry Lewis.

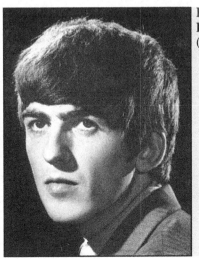

Beatle **George
Harrison**
(1943-2001)

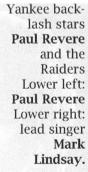

Yankee back-
lash stars
Paul Revere
and the
Raiders
Lower left:
Paul Revere
Lower right:
lead singer
**Mark
Lindsay.**

1-11

The Byrds-- Folk Rock stars, 1966. Standing-- Roger McGuinn, and lowest in Byrds' tree, David Crosby (later anchor voice of Crosby, Stills, Nash, [and Young]).

1990s Grunge superstars **Pearl Jam**'s biggest single hit was Graveyard Rock cover "Last Kiss" [#2, 1999]. Jeff Ament, bass, on left, and Eddie Vedder, vocals, on right.

The Flipside of **Beach Boys'** Surf Rock was racing Detroit's fastest cars. (L-R): Bruce Johnstone, Carl Wilson, Mike Love (hat), Brian Wilson (driving), Al Jardine, Dennis Wilson.

Jimi Hendrix-- Extreme Sports star. Paratrooper, --101st Airborne Division.

Marty Robbins, NASCAR driver, Country Rock singer-songwriter, and accidental *inventor* of Heavy Metal in 1961.

Jan and Dean, pioneering Extreme Sports as a preview for their hit "Deadman's Curve."

Jim Morrison, Doors' baritone Rock legend, 1968.

Surviving **Doors'** keyboard guru **Ray Manzarek**, 1998.

Jimi Hendrix (center) and the Experience

Sly and the Family Stone

Young **Janis Joplin**, and doll, on a rare cold day in Gulf port Port Arthur, TX.

Janis Joplin, starry-eyed rock diva.

Linda Ronstadt

Former Beach Boy **Glen Campbell**, great Scottish-American tenor (2000).

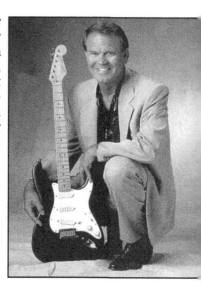

Gerry and the Pacemakers
[Gerry Marsden, w/hat]

AC/DC--Rock Hall 2003
(L-R): Malcolm Young, Brian Johnson, Phil Rudd (drums), Angus Young, Cliff Williams

Michael Jackson--
King of Pop

Dionne Warwick

1-14

John Lennon and **Mick Jagger**-- convocation of perhaps the top two lead [or co-lead] singers of the Rock Revolution.

Ray Charles-- 'The Genius' was among the first 11 artists (1986) ever voted into the Rock and Roll Hall of Fame.

Singer-songwriter **Paul Simon**

Singer-songwriter soprano **Joni Mitchell**

The Mamas and the Papas.
Clockwise: from 6'5" John Phillips (tallest Rock Hall inductee?): John Phillips, Spanky McFarlane, Phillips' daughter Mackenzie Phillips, lead singer Denny Doherty. Mama Cass Elliot and Michelle Phillips fill out the original M&P roster.

'Blue-Eyed Soul' stars the **Righteous Brothers:** (L) Bobby Hatfield, (R) Bill Medley [tenor Hatfield sings "Unchained Melody"]. Rock Hall, 2003.

1-15

Rod Stewart: marathon singer-songwriter.

Brill Building songwriter and Light Metal star **Neil Diamond.**

Jazz Rock star **Van Morrison**

Double decade superstars, **The Bee Gees, (L-R): Robin Gibb** (lead singer 1967-1972 British Invasion Era); **Barry Gibb** (lead singer, 197-80s Disco Era); **Maurice Gibb**.

Troubadour **James Taylor**

Cher and Sonny Bono

You're Welcome in the Home of the Blues

Nestled into the flickering neon nightscape, the midnight pastel Memphis glow of **W.C. Handy**'s 2-room shotgun shack leaps out at you. Blues purists jigsawed Blues-founder Handy's boyhood home, dragged it across town, and clumped it back together under a mellow Memphis moon. It's just two blocks down fabled Beale Street, from Handy's protégé **B.B. King**'s swingin' razzmatazz Blues emporium:

"St. Louis Blues" [by W.C. Handy] – Prince's Orchestra, #4, 5-1916. Down in sultry midtown Memphis, W.C. Handy primed his bluesfather genius – and out came "Yellow Dog Blues" in 1914. "Yellow Dog Blues" didn't bite until Joseph C. Smith's Orchestra doggedly hit #4 in February 1920. **Bessie Smith**'s #3, 1925 version of Handy's "St. Louis Blues" stars **Louis 'Satchmo' Armstrong** on trumpet. **Fats Waller** (1904-43) played organ, and **Alberta Hunter** sang #16, 10-27 "Beale Street Blues."

"Nobody Knows You When You're Down and Out" – Bessie Smith, #15, 8-29. Greatest Blues singer ever? Some say so. Smith (1894-1937) belts this classic down the long corridor of faraway years – and defines the BLUES. Larry Glazer fondled this million-chord manifesto on guitar. Larry's fingers squeaked on tall frets. Camel smoke and a nub of flame glowed by his guitar pegs: The Glaze sang the pregnant line about when the dude gets ahold of a dollar bill again someday, he's gonna squeeze it until the dollar's eagle grins. An amazing metaphor. One amazing song. It's about TRUE friendship – beyond status-seeking grubbing for money. Will anyone befriend the poor guy?

Born in Chattanooga, Tennessee, Bessie ("Empress of the Blues") was orphaned at seven. Starting with **Ma Rainey**, Bessie sang for pennies in the streets. Plucky Smith went right to the top, nailing a Columbia contract like **Bob Dylan** or **Simon and Garfunkel**. Smith's formative years glow with mystique and intrigue. Did she record as "Rosa Henderson" at Swan/Emerson before her 1923-33 Columbia heyday? Did she do an Okeh demo in 1923? Could she really have saved the mighty Columbia Records (and CBS) from bankruptcy in the Depression with her 160 Blues sides (they could pay her NO ROYALTIES and a flat $250 per side). When she died in a shattering car crash in Mississippi Delta Blues epicenter Clarksdale, MS,

home of **John Lee Hooker** (b. 1917) and *Crossroads* of Robert Johnson, did she bleed to death because EMS and medical personnel rejected her for the color of her skin? Bessie Smith mysteries abound. As time recedes, they deepen.

"Nobody Knows You When You're Down and Out," like Holly/Beatle polychordal extravaganzas, is tricky. The 12-Bar Blues form is the comfy one, remember?

Bessie's "Nobody" shuffles jauntily along, a fingerpicker's delight. Lyrically, the song prophesied the Depression. Paper millionaires played Superman from Empire State cliffs when their self-worth – measured in money alone – plummeted to the bottom of dark despair. In the Depression, one-fourth to one-third of the adult male bread-winning work force was frustratingly out of work. By 1939, Bessie Smith wasn't the only one who sang the Blues.

Somehow, whole outa-work families, grubbing along on beans and spuds and Quaker Oatmeal, managed to catch two flicks per week at the local Bijou (with a new summer miracle in 1929-35: Air Conditioning). You need to hear this song. All America loved and somehow bought Bessie's records in the dirt-poor Depression. For the best modern "Nobody" version, check out the ONLY GUY INDUCTED INTO THE ROCK HALL OF FAME THREE TIMES BY 2000: **Eric Clapton**! Via the Yardbirds ('92), Cream ('93), and solo ('00), **Eric Clapton** made it into the Cleveland Hall thrice. Not even a Beatle or Elvis or Buddy ever hit the Rock and Roll Triple Crown.

On Eric's #1(3) Al. *Unplugged* (9-92), the British Blues Virtuoso – of Ripley, England (b. 3-30-45) – renders a faithful and fantastic version of the Bessie Smith 'Down and Out' Blues classic. Her classic nuances are there. Eric's vocal is top-notch, spiked with both Ghost Notes he doesn't quite play, plus Great Notes he does. After stints in the 1963-65 Yardbirds, 1966-68 Cream, 1968 Blind Faith, plus the 1963 Roosters, 1966 Ginger Baker, and John Lennon's Plastic Ono Band (1969), Eric formed his own **Derek and the Dominoes** in 1970. Eponymous *Eric Clapton* [Al. #13, 7-70] collects friends and mentors. Singing background for Eric on this album are Buddy Holly's **Crickets: Jerry (J.I.) Allison** (drums) and **Sonny Curtis** (guitar). Clapton singles trickled into the high charts: #18, 10-70 "After Midnight"; "Let it Rain" (#48, 9-72); various "Layla" singles (1st #51, 3-71, then long "geriatric" version #10, 5-72). "Layla," like Eric, charted three times (also #12, 10-92). During 1971-72, Clapton went into a reclusive wrestling match with his beloved guitar and a few un-beloved demons. He emerged 1-0 in the standings. Buoyed by the stunning guitar fire of **Jimi Hendrix**, Clapton's stardom whomped his demons. Eric didn't want to lose it ALL at 27 as Jimi did – or **Janis Joplin** (1943-70), one of the great Blues divas of all time.

When Eric was 'down and out' everybody knew him, and was rooting for him. At the 2000 Rock Hall Induction, his smile showed the calendar was his long-lost friend: thick hair still brown (and there), slim physique and springy step, unlined face and indomitable spirit – despite living the True Blues for over half a century. Eric Clapton stood on the shoulders of many unforgettable Blues pioneers. They changed the world with their bittersweet songs of love and glory and splendor and mud and sorrow and beans and rice.

Among Eric's diverse Blues-legend mentors: **Huddie Ledbetter/Leadbelly, Woody Guthrie, Billie Holiday, Bessie Smith, Ma Rainey, the Weavers, Lightnin' Sam Hopkins, Howlin' Wolf, Muddy Waters, Jimmy Reed, B.B. King, Ella Fitzgerald** 2000 Rock Hall Inductee, **Nat 'King' Cole, Sarah Vaughan, Lloyd Price, Robert Johnson, Fats Domino, Elvis Presley, Buddy Holly, Chuck Berry, LaVern Baker, Charlie Christian, Blind Lemon Jefferson, Eric Burdon (Animals), John Lee Hooker, Roy Brown, Elmore James, Louis Jordan, Willie Dixon, Duke Ellington, Count Basie, Memphis Slim, Jimmie Rodgers I, Clarence'Frogman' Henry, Paul Robeson, Marian Anderson**, and **Willie Mae 'Big Mama'Thornton**. The absolute culmination of Clapton's Blues art may be his Al. #3, 6-2000 *Riding with the King* – on the cover, Eric is chauffeuring the Memphis Bluesmaster **B.B. King** in a '62 Caddy convertible.

Gold Rush avoids easy classification. Just because one star has been in a Blues or Country or Polka or Heavy Metal or Bluegrass 'bag,' it doesn't mean we're going to always label them in that narrowed classification. *Gold Rush* tries not to stuff any artists into RACIAL zones of segregation. Your favorite Britpop, Gospel, Easy Listening or Country singers may be deep in the heart of the Blues chapter. Great R & B artists sing among the Country stars. Swedes and Hawaiians headline the Latino Explosion. Long Island cowboys yodel to lonesome shopping malls, deep in the heart of our Psychedelic, Disco, or Surf Rock chapters. One Long Islander's great 1980 (#1) viewpoint we champion:

"IT'S STILL ROCK AND ROLL TO ME." – Billy Joel.

Exclusionary *Gold Rush* isn't.

Back to the Blues – a "Mood Indigo" [**Duke Ellington**] of love and triumph and suffering and soul.

"Layla" – Eric Clapton (& Duane Allman, guitar), #51, 3-71; #10, 3-72, and #12, 10-92. LAYLA, like Peggy Sue, is a musician's wife, **Patti Boyd Harrison Clapton**. She was Eric's bride from 1979-88, and a Beatle's (George before that [1966-74]). "Layla" lambasts Blues in a chord-splash explosion – with intertwining arpeggios. Rich Guilfoyle calls the slow-version "Geriatric Layla."

The Blues are a mutual expression of a less than perfect universe. We all pay the rent/mortgage; we all have to eat and sleep and pay semi-beloved taxes. We win and lose at romance and life. No one can be swaggeringly, bubblingly happy all the time. I hope. Our troubadours of the Blues have brought us their own pain, frustration, poverty, and unrequited love. They have shared their innermost souls. The Blues, as early Rock and Roll, marches down an entire century of Anglo-American music. Unlike Surf Music's 1962-65 heyday, the Blues surf and skateboard the whole musical spectrum. Bessie's sentiments in the Rock Era?

"When I'm Back on My Feet Again" – Michael Bolton, #7, 5-90; NC, R & B. Modern-day Blue-Eyed Blues Soulster Bolton (b. Bolotin '53, New Haven, Connecticut) bolts back into Bessie Smith's bailwick. Bolton cruises through a litany of groans, hoping friends will congregate again – when he gets back up. Bolton has the gravel, the guts, the grace notes for Soul/Blues. Only those into Pigmentation Discrimination can deny him his Blues roots.

"Sad Songs (Say So Much)" – Elton John, #5, 6-84, NC, R & B. Elton John of Pinner, Middlesex, knows sad songs bring people together. Misery loves company. Elton (b. **Reginald Kenneth Dwight**, '47) has impeccable Blues credentials, fronting Bluesology in 1966 in the first British Wave – and backing Brit Bluesman **Long John Baldry** (#88, "Let the Heartaches Begin" 1-68). Steampacket's Baldry also started **Rod Stewart**'s career. "Sad Songs" rumbles and rocks along with Elton's pumping piano. As a kid, Elton suffered with **Del Shannon**'s rain hike in #1, '61 "Runaway," and emulated his Coopersville, Michigan idol's falsetto "Cry Myself to Sleep" (#99, 6-62) via #1 (3), 12-72 "Crocodile Rock."

You don't have to be an authentic Mississippi Delta dwelling, $12-guitar-fingerpicking, Afro octogenarian like Mississippi John Hurt or guitar guru like Sam 'Lightnin' Hopkins to sing the Blues. The Blues blankets our spiraling Rock and Soul century, with a multiracial big-beat bridge of empathy and caring. Elton (#3 ever) teamed up with **Stevie Wonder** (#4 ever Artist of Rock Era) on #4, 1-83 NC, R & B, "I Guess That's Why They Call It the Blues."

(**Stevie Wonder**, harmonica). Precedes "Sad Songs". Super mid-beat funky-harp riff. Elton hangs on bluesy 7ths. Good combo of 'Ebony-Ivory' Soul. When you almost abandon hope, Elton John advises, just tune into the sound of the Blues. Others feel your pain. His jolly "Club at the End of the Street" (#28, 4-90) features friends in the same pulsating pub. They party/commiserate together. Sad songs. Not so sad when you share with a friend. Carole King's super song "You've Got a Friend" delivers the same message for **James Taylor** (#1, 6-71), inducted into the Rock Hall in 2000.

Earlier chapters already covered the illustrious Blues Yodeling of **Jimmie Rodgers I**, and meteoric careers of **Leadbelly (Huddie Ledbetter)** and **Crossroads** legend **Robert Johnson**.

"**Midnight Special**" – **Johnny Rivers, #20, 2-65, NC, R & B.** Rocked the Los Angeles Sunset Strip Whiskey A-Go-Go Yankee Backlash crowd. Born **John Ramistella** (11-7-42) in New York. Lived in Baton Rouge, Louisiana. Johnny's Delta Blues style highlights his Italian Streetcorner savvy and Chuck Berry driving guitar wizardry. Rivers' cool Southern Big Apple tenor voice resonates with American melting pot *chutzpah* and dynamo drive, like Blues guitarist **Albert King** (1923-92, NC, '61 but #14 R & B "Don't Throw Your Love on Me So Strong").

On Leadbelly's "Midnight Special," Rivers suavely portrays the poor jailbird's plight: terrible food, but don't gripe or you'll get in big trouble with some goon (who sprinkles nails on his raw tiger burgers). **Leadbelly** would know. Married at 15, the Louisiana cotton plantation refugee played Cajun accordion, then guitar. He got nailed for murder in 1916, serving 6½ years of a 30-year sentence. Southern justice being what it was, some framing may have occurred, but murder is murder. When media hawks lambast Rapjammer **Snoop Doggy Dogg** (#8, 12-93, "What's My Name?") for a drive-by shooting in California, or **Puffy Combs** (with Jennifer Lopez) for gunplay in 2000, he is not the first Rock/Blues/Rap/Whatever musician to get nabbed for high crimes.

"Midnight Special's" unique musical hook? Two jagged tempos. The verse slides with dotted eighths and sixteenths forging the trail. On the chorus, Rivers hammers eighth notes at full rockin' power and volume. Other Rivers' Blues? #2(2), 5-64 **Chuck Berry** absentee-father tune "Memphis." Also, Rivers wrote his #1(1), 9-66 "Poor Side of Town."

Willie Dixon wrote Johnny's #7, 6-65 "Seventh Son" Blues anthem. Echo of **Count Basie**'s guitar guy **Jimmy Rushing** (1903-72). The late Willie produced, and played bass, on nearly every vintage Chicago Blues Chess record ever cut – like Berry's biggees. Rivers also coolly reprised **Huey 'Piano' Smith**'s New Orleans classic (#52, 8-57 & #5, 7-57 R & B) "Rockin' Pneumonia and the Boogie-Woogie Flu" (#6, 7-72). Smith's title alludes to Blues/Rock legend **Chuck Berry**'s classic rocker:

"**Roll Over Beethoven**" – **Beatles, #68, 3-64.** Wow! Among Chuck and the Beatles' greatest squelched hits (#29, 5-56 Chuck). One of **George Harrison**'s greatest vocals ever – he echoes both Beatle Paul, and Chuck Berry, and just for once trumps them both? As a goof on Chuck's classically trained piano-plunking sisters, Chuck penned this anti-authoritarian R & R anthem. Raw Rock and Roll energy, untamed, with droll digs at Beethoven and Tchaikovsky. Chuck paints a new R & R canvas of fuse-busting jukeboxes, and rhythm reviews.

Chuck and George Harrison/Fab Three fire off a basic 12-Bar Blues, with a simple 2nd measure IV chord variation. The frantic lyric gouges the gone quietude. George breathlessly sings and swoons over Chuck's new R & R world: sock hops, teen passions, Cokes and fries and the promise of sweet evermore lovin' in the smash-beat afterglow. George's protégé lead guitar is vintage Chuck Berry. 50s R & R anthem settles down to the finale with golden Boogie Woogie Blues repetition: "ROLL OVER BEETHOVEN, ROLL OVER BEETHOVEN" (you can guess the rest).

Besides Rivers' "Midnight Special," **Leadbelly**'s other hits were reprised by Folk and Blues belters. "Boll Weevil" is a Talking Blues/Semi-Rap. Leadbelly's saga of a pesky cotton-chomping bug was redone by husky velvet-bass baritone **Brook Benton** (#2[3], 5-61). He echoes Paul Robeson's basso profundo "Ol' Man River" (#7, 6-28). Folksters the **Highwaymen** took Leadbelly's 1851 trad-folk "Cotton Fields" to harmonic highs. Leadbelly's echo? **Sonny Boy Williamson** (a/k/a Aleck Ford, 1899-65). Sonny played guitar and harmonica like Jimmy Reed, and cut loose with his amazing (NC, '55) #3, R & B, 10-55 "Don't Start Me Talkin'" hit at age 56.

"**So Long, It's Been Good to Know Ya**" – **Weavers, with Gordon Jenkins, #4, 1-51.** Rare Woody Guthrie waltz like Leadbelly's "Goodnight Irene" (#1[13], Weavers, '51). In So Long," the Oklahoma dust storm blows people out of their church, nearly zaps a wedding there, and the dust cloud blots out the sun. In the midst of this swirling apocalyptic Armageddon, unruffled victims cordially mumble: "So long, it's been good to know ya." Woody's "This Land Is Your Land" (New Christy Minstrels, #93, '62). Sprawling purple mountain majesty anthem for America. Woody highlights our New York Island of Long, plus endless skyways, golden valleys, rolling wheat fields, west-forever highway ribbons, sparkly sands beyond the rolling dust clouds. Breathtaking American panorama.

Dylan's mentor **Woody Guthrie** (1912-67) of Dust-Bowl Oklahoma played Folk Blues. Guthrie's son **Arlo** high-jumped to hitdom with his 25-minute hit Rap Thanksgiving Carol about "Alice's Rock and Roll Restaurant" #97, 12-69 and "The City of New Orleans" #18, 7-72. Guthrie wrote over a thousand songs in his abbreviated life – craggy voice and shaggy hair and baggy pants. Despite poverty and Depression and *Grapes of Wrath* hoboing like John Steinbeck's Tom Joad, Guthrie wrote the music of the people of America:

Blues legends here: **W.C. Handy, Robert Johnson, Leadbelly, Bessie Smith, Billie Holiday.** We also integrate the traditional with the modern, the innovative, the eclectic, the great Blues artists of all eras and genres and R & R styles:

"Mendocino" – Sir Douglas Quintet, #27, 3-69. Doug Sahm (1943-99) rocked! Like Duke Ellington and Duke of Earl Gene Chandler, **Doug Sahm** and Four Other Guys from San Antonio, Texas declared themselves royalty! Knights anyhow. Douggie became SIR Douggie. Add a big Yankee backlash Farfisa organ and you've got your big hit — #13, 4-65 "She's About a Mover." "Mendocino" celebrates the groovy life on a lonely promontory coast cape on the most desolate of Northern California coastline (20 miles south of Eureka, in the drizzle belt). Another Sir? Or Big Sur?

"Sir Duke" – Stevie Wonder, #1(3), 4-77; #1(1) R & B. Ranked #4 Recording Artist of all time, Stevie salutes his mentor 'Sir Duke' ("Take the A Train," #11,7-41), **Ellington**, Jazz bandleader of multiple big band hits. Duke Ellington won the hearts of color-blind Americans everywhere. Jazz royalty, Duke from Washington, D.C. performed the best of Berlin and Gershwin and Top-of-the-Pop Standards and Jazz. Ellington was rooted in the Blues: #19, 3-31 "Rockin' in Rhythm," or #16, 7-32 "Blue Ramble."

"(We Ain't Got) Nothin' Yet," by the **Blues Magoos**, (#5, 12-66) is Tiger bleacher pal Randy McGill's favorite song. Actual HAPPY blues, like Buddy Holly's 12-Bar Blues anthem "Oh Boy" (#10, 12-57). Buddy also did 12-Bar-Blues (NC, '57) "Mailman, Bring Me No More Blues." Very early cut. Covered on Beatle bootleg. Buddy's trademark 'hiccups' stem from 'Mississippi Blue Yodeler' Jimmie Rodgers [1987-1933, a/k/a the Singing Brakeman].

"They Can't Take That Away from Me" – Billie Holiday, with Count Basie Band, #12, 5-37. Ken Burns (PBS, 2001) says she might be the best Jazz and Blues singer of all time. Donald Clarke: Billie ("Lady," 1915-59) "sang behind the beat . . . she transmuted these leftover rejected songs into gold, sometimes turning a melody line inside out."

On March 8, 2000, Supreme diva **Diana Ross** reprised her 1972 film *Lady Sings the Blues* by performing this sultry torch tune at Billie Holiday's Induction into the Rock and Roll Hall of Fame. In her 1935-39 heyday, Holiday scored 36 Top 30 hits, led by #1(3) "Carelessly." Bonanzas include #2(1), 8-38 "I'm Gonna Lock My Heart," #6, 11-35 "24 Hours a Day"; #3 "The Way You Look Tonight"; taboo lyric "Strange Fruit," #16, 7-39; and "God Bless the Child." Miss Ross sang the soul-searing "Strange Fruit" *a cappella*, to a ghastly hush from the Rock Hall tux and gown crew; the 'strange fruit' she described, in eerie Jazz-phrasing, was the terrible phenomenon of lynching, with the most grotesque images of shame and horror. Radio stations, aghast at Holiday's 1939 subject matter, zapped it from play lists, and the strange song sold in an underground style.

The essence of Billie's Midnight Blues style, with piano bar profundity and curly Jazz chords, is behind-the-beat, in sensuous slurred reverberation. Felled by opium, heroin, and alcohol addiction, Billie's cold turkey efforts to quit were sadly smashed by backsliding. Her gorgeous vocals curled and flowed and drifted in pre-psychedelic swirls and whirls, like fancy silver.

"Built for Comfort" – Howlin' Wolf [Chester Burnett], NC, 1970. With his gruff macho baritone, Wolf chuckles that his physique is a tad padded; this Blues morsel is a tremendous rhythmic adventure. Named for wolf howls in his prowling Blues. From Chicago Blues Chess collaboration with his proteges, **Keith Richard**(s) and the **Rolling Stones**. Traditional Bluesmen often name themselves after their sounds – like fast-fingered **Lightnin' Sam Hopkins**, Texas Blues Man.

"Slow Down" – Beatles, #25, 9-64. Beatles rock out on **Larry Williams'** Screaming Blues salute to Little Richard. John at helm, rampaging Revenge Rock lyric with fervor and passion; Paul (covering Williams' "Dizzy Miss Lizzie") and George ("Roll Over, Beethoven") show that the Four were just as Fab covering the best of American Screaming Blues. Williams (1935-80) was a cousin (and chauffeur) to Blues star **Lloyd Price**.

"Rhapsody in Blue" – George Martin and Larry Adler, NC, 1994 on *Glory of Gershwin Anthology* instrumental album #111, 9-94. Martin is England's most famous producer (Beatles). **Larry Adler** is a harmonica virtuoso. Marking his 80th birthday, Adler assembled R & R royalty: Elton John, Sting, Meat Loaf, Cher, Jon Bon Jovi, Carly Simon, Sinead O'Connor and Elvis Costello. The occasion? Honor the memory of his piano genius friend **George Gershwin** (1898-1937) (#3, 10-24 & #7, 9-27 "Rhapsody in Blue"), who grew up with his brother Ira in a redstone flat over Second Avenue at 4th Street in the Village. Their first hit as songwriters? The #1(9), 5-20 classic by vaudeville star **Al Jolson**, "Swanee (How I Love You)". The Happenings hit with Gershwin's "I Got Rhythm" (#3, 4-67). The Streetcorner/Blues/R & R/Pop Standard group featured Paterson, New Jersey's **Al Miranda**. His #2(2), 6-28 Jolson follow-up "My Mammy" (#13, 7-67) is a Mother's Day classic. Dynamic chord changes and rush of heavy harmonies [George, music, Ira, lyrics].

"Love Walked in" – Flamingos, #88, 10-59, NC, R & B. By Gershwin. Breathtaking hushes, pauses. Romance exonified. You can feel every delicious curve of her beautiful body as she presses close in the ebb and flow dance floor afterglow. Rivals "Lovers Never Say Goodbye" (#50, 4-59; #25, 3-59 R & B).

Gershwin gems? "Embraceable You" (Johnny Mathis) and "I've Got a Crush on You" (Linda Ronstadt/Nelson Riddle *What's New*, Al. #3, 10-83). When Gershwin died in 1937, in the grim shadow of the Nazi Holocaust half a world away, the normally low-key *Penguin Encyclopedia of Popular Music* unabashedly blurted: His "early death from brain-tumor was the single greatest loss to USA music this century." A bold statement.

Classically-trained Gershwin owed his greatest inspiration to America's people's music – The Blues. His great orchestral masterwork is anchored in the Bessie Smith/Ma Rainey/W.C. Handy/Leadbelly tradition:

"I Only Have Eyes for You" – Flamingos, #11, 6-59; #3, R & B. Sadly, this magic tune is all most folks recall of the Flamingos' Soulfire Jazz/Blues/R & B vocals. Awash in a smoky scenario of rose-colored love, "I Only Have Eyes for You" features the in-sync interweaving harmonies of brothers **Jake** and **Zeke Carey** of Baltimore, and lead singer **Nate Nelson.** Even on Heavy-Rotation Oldies Overkill, this smooth song takes on a majesty of its own. With only one take, the early Flamingos melded lush full harmonies of breathtaking chordal complexity. In the lyric, the love-swooning guy can't tell whether the night sky has stars, or the ruddy day is sunshiny or cloud-blanketed; the only thing he really SEES is his girl. He can't tell the fragrant garden from the gridlock thoroughfare, and he doesn't care. He's hopelessly, blissfully, and totally in love. Can you mix Ethereal Orchestral Jazz with the Blues? Yep: Flamingo Power Rules!

Their "Mio Amore" (my love) hit only #74, 7-60 (#27, R & B), but you couldn't tell the stargazers on the long-lost long-ago Lake Michigan sundown sands that it wasn't #1 in the universe. The quintessence of shimmering Duke Ellington-style ethereal romance? See the Flamingos. "I Only Have Eyes for You" was #2(1), 7-34 for violinist/bandleader **Ben Selvin. Art Garfunkel** did a great Blue-Eyed Soul blond-Afro-haircut #18, 8-75 version. (Rock Hall 2001).

"Whatever Lola Wants" – Sarah Vaughan, #6, 4-55; NC, R & B. Sarah bent the notes like Billie Holiday, with ballerina precision. Blues thirds abound. [No relation to Kinks' #9, 8-70 drag queen 'Lola'; this one is truly 100% female.] Seductive, sensuous, sassy. Between Sarah and Ella Fitzgerald, and Billie Holiday, the Blues [with a side of Jazz] are defined.

"Workin' at the Car Wash Blues" – Jim Croce, #32, 6-74; NC, R & B. Jim Croce (1943-73) began as a Folk singer at Temple University, **Bill Cosby's** Philly alma mater. Like John and Yoko, Jim and wife Ingrid were a devoted duo, inking with Capitol Records. **Croce** had an amazingly resonant baritone, similar to Canadian Gordon Lightfoot's. Croce delivers throbbing Blues and soulful ballads in his inimitable clear style.

"Operator" – Jim Croce, #17, 10-72; NC, R & B. Croce too has a tough time with nasty phone. Wryly, he murmurs, his ex-girl now dwells in L.A. with his ex-friend, the ignoble Ray. Floating around the rancorous love triangle is a melody pure and delicious. Masterful 12-string work by **Maury Meuhleisen.**

Jim Croce (pronounced 'Crow-chee') thrives on comic urban Blues or breathtaking ballads. The Italian-American Philadelphia troubadour's use of Ebonics (a/k/a 'Black English') is uncanny. His characters like Bad Leroy Brown are Leiber-Stoller-types, like "Yakety Yak" Coasters comedy legend. Another Philly success story, Croce toured the college coffeehouse scene. Croce drove a truck, like Elvis, till stardom stole him. "Leroy Brown" mirrors the legend of:

"Big Boy Pete" – Olympics, #50, 5-60; #10, 6-60 R & B. Huge in Detroit. Brown vs. Pete. THIS Brown, unlike Leroy Brown, wins – cutting black cigar from Pete's mouth. This barroom brawl features the baritone duo of Charles Fizer and Walter Hammond. Stetson hats fly in surly knife duel. "Big Boy Pete" in turn harks back to an older barroom brawl/crime:

"Stagger Lee" – Lloyd Price, #1(4), 12-58. Rare old 8-Bar Blues, by one of Rock/Blues/Soul's true pioneers. New Orleans' **Lloyd Price's** (b. '33) "Lawdy Miss Clawdy" NC, '52, but #1[7], 5-52 R & B, is one of the first true Rock hits, appearing on an early Elvis album. Stagger Lee and Billy get into fatal saloon dice argument. Billy gets mad because Stagger won all his money and the Stetson hat. Finally Stagger Lee shoots Billy (despite his 3-kids-and-sickly-wife desperate plea). Is Rap violent? Hmmm. Atlantan Bubble Gum King Tommy Roe took Stagger Lee to #25 in 5-71, too. Lloyd, Rock Hall 1998. Lloyd's hits? "Personality" #2(3), 4-59; "I'm Gonna Get Married" #3, 8-59; and #14, 2-60 "Lady Luck." **Dick Clark** made Price re-record Blues Standard to be less violent (from murder to a punch in the nose?).

"Bad, Bad Leroy Brown" – Jim Croce, #1(2), 6-73. Stagger Lee ilk. Barroom brawl songs ('Stack-O-Lee' rivals Ragtime in age) drift beyond "Frankie and Johnnie," over 100 years ago. With custom Lincoln Continental and 500-cu-in Caddie El Dorado, Leroy guzzles gas and chutzpah, and loses. Croce's Blues Rock wedding classic hangs fire on the supertonic II chord. "Leroy" has a solid Blues foundation, chord-structurally and rhythmically. Lyrics, too, expand Croce's high comedy and Brown-Eyed Soul dialect technique: Leroy, like Stagger Lee, shoots dice. Leroy ogles this cool chick 'Doris.' Somehow, despite being the baddest dude in the place, and packing an arsenal, 6'4" Leroy gets royally whupped. Leroy Brown learns a nasty lesson about fooling around with the wife of a psychopathically jealous guy – a guy who batters bullies for fun and profit. "Leroy" proves the adage: "No matter how tough you think you are . . ."

"Workin' at the Car Wash Blues" is Croce's last Top Forty hit. He's a would-be tycoon wearing a rubber suit and washing cars. He envisions an air-conditioned office, grandiose swivel chair, and a vivacious voluptuous secretary on his knee. Instead, we find him with the droopy car wash blues. Poor guy: Win-the-Lotto champagne dreams on a beer wallet. Long before **Eminem's** 2000 #1 "Real Slim Shady" or **Vanilla Ice's** African-American Ebonics – **Jim Croce** mastered the dialect. Croce delivered some of the most street-savvy "tales from the 'Hood'" ever concocted, and he did it without the hostile racial terminology that sparks much Rap of the Gangsta Variety. Was Jim Croce 30 years ahead of his time?

"Rainin' in my CAR"?

"Rainin' in My Heart" – Slim Harpo, #34, 5-61; #17 R & B. Mississippi Delta Slim Harpo (James Moore, 1924-70) had an unquenchable Blues sound. Harp (a/k/a 'Harpo' or 'Harmonica Slim') player confesses he was wrong. Begs woman to come home. Apparently she did. Second hit? Rakish raffish rappish 1966, #16 (#1 R & B) "Baby Scratch My Back." The first song features Blues guitar wizard **Lightnin' Slim** a/k/a Otis Hicks. Harpo's smoldering baritone combines with the audial-dynamite throb of the bottom-tone bass, which hammers like a solo by Jazz bassist **Charlie Mingus** (1922-79).

All too often Blues is considered an African-American man's genre. Dangerous stereotyping indeed:

"Runaway" – Bonnie Raitt, #57, 5-77. Carrot-tressed daughter of Broadway star (John Raitt) begins chart quest with **Del Shannon**'s blue-funk rain-slosh song. Riding a razor-sharp lead guitar with her own lightning riffs, Bonnie Raitt lavishes a cutting-edge alto to cream the competition. Bonnie's mentor could belt Blues himself, though he's best known for straight Heart of Rock and Roll material: (see Connie and Bonnie B. Goode chapters).

"Two Kinds of Teardrops" – Del Shannon, #50, 4-63; #5, 5-63 U.K. Great lyrical hook: happy and sad tears with his own crosses to bear. Del Shannon rose out of small-town Michigan Coopersville to briefly wrench away the squiggly spotlight from Elvis. For one month in eerily early 1961, #1(4) "Runaway" ruled the runway to the world. There's a 50% probability **Ronettes** back him on "Teardrops." Del dries her tears and makes her smile. Strong Blues kick. Unique. Inventive. Heart of Rock/Soul/Blues, like 1st Rock/Soul/Blues diva **LaVern Baker**, on her #76, 5-57 (But #5 R & B) "Jim Dandy Got Married." One of Baker's ultimate Rockers. Snarling saxes assist semisenior superman James Dandy, groom.

"I Hate Myself for Lovin' You" – Joan Jett & the Blackhearts, #8, 6-88. Speaking of "Runaway," Philly-born Joan (b. '60) named her debut group the **Runaways** – an all-female rock band. Ever feel that love is a self-stomping barefoot walk on nails and glass shards? JJ berates herself, with jett-engine amps, for getting mixed up with this nowhere loser. Blues belter 80s Power Rock – like the best of **Springsteen** and **Seger**. Straight-up Rock, roots in rough Blues. Barrels all the way back to **Leadbelly**. Or **Blind Lemon Jefferson**:

"See That My Grave Is Kept Clean" – Blind Lemon Jefferson, NC, 1921. Dylan recorded Lemon's (1897-1929) morose and sour Jeffersonian ode to himself. Jefferson codified the Blues. Recorded 100 songs. Died of hypothermia in Chicago blizzard. Proved to **Ray Charles** and **Stevie Wonder** that vision impairment is not impairment to Blues stardom, as **Ronnie Milsap** proved (#5, 6-81 [#1 C]) on "There's No Getting Over Me." Country Soul ballad. Also "Any Day Now," #14, 5-82 reprise for

keyboard Milsap of **Chuck Jackson** #23, 4-62 Soul standard. Or **Jose Feliciano** on his #3, 7-68 (#29 R & B) 'Doors' tribute "Light My Fire."

In Step – Stevie Ray Vaughan, Al. #33, 8-89. His virtuosity shines also on *Texas Flood*, Al. #38. Or catch Stevie's *Couldn't Stand the Weather*, Al. #31, 7-84. One of the greatest pure Blues guitarists of all time. Vaughan (1954-90) was killed en route. Helicopter crash.

"Black Velvet" – Alannah Myles, #1(2), 1-90. Tribute to King Elvis, deified as 'Black Velvet' throughout sultry Mississippi moon song. You expect Alannah to ooze out in that hot purring murmuring alto voice her true Mississippi Delta Queen nature, but she turns out to be from off-the-atlas "Buckhorn, Canada." Sometime Torontonian Myles captured the Elvis essence of Deep South hot nights, with passions and desires and steam. Heart of Slow Blues, Myles suggests legendary **Mildred Bailey** (1907-51), whose Slow Blues serenades include "Georgia on My Mind" to #19, 1-32 (see **Ray Charles**), #10, 3-37 "My Last Affair," **Satchmo**'s "Rocking' Chair" (#13, 6-37), and her biggest – #2(2), 8-38 "So Help Me."

"Stumblin' In" – Suzy Quatro, #4, 2-79. Quatro (b. '50) made it in England before strutting her Detroit-born talents back home as bonafide star Blues belter. Just like **John Travolta** was 'Vinnie Barbarino' on *Welcome Back, Kotter*, 'Leather Tuscadero' was Suzy Quatro on 50s nostalgia show *Happy Days*. **Chris Norman** sings 5th harmony for Suzy. The tumbling, bumbling, stumbling idea lumbers up against our fast-paced computerized continuum. We used to have careers. Now we have 2½ jobs. No benefits. Corporate greed culled millions of good folks in a tornado of downsizing. When we stumbled in to our third job and $4.25 per week or whatever at Hamburger Heaven, we got replaced by Robbie the Robot.

Rock and Roll and the Blues let us forget about our hard work for awhile. Music is an escape vent for those who stumble in to the stuffy Dagwood office, and have to wear squeezy ties and fermented fake smiles. In the 'real world' of 9 to 5, some sell their souls to marry a corporation or computer that enslaves them. No wonder we ALL sing the Blues. Can you beat the groaning noisy steel-mill cauldron of wage slavery? Can you unravel the endless office paper-clip chain?

John Travolta stumbled in – to *Saturday Night Fever* (1977****). His **Bee Gees** Disco sound track hit #1 for 27 glorious weeks. His big reason? ESCAPE! On magic Saturday night, the hapless working drone comes ebulliently alive. In the strobe light glow, he can be someone.

At the job? Don't ask. **Van Morrison** and **John Cougar Mellencamp**'s "Wild Night" pumps passionate feelings: into the mild golden gloaming. A promise of jiffy romance is underlain with a red-hot guitar manifesto. In the Wild Night, LOVE is the Main Event? Leadbelly and Slim Harpo and Eric Clapton also sing about love. Once in awhile their Blues anthems gripe about paying the rent, but mostly it's about satisfying some lovely lady. No computer whizbang can calculate that he'll become in love. It just happens. Like Suzy and Chris, you stumble bumblingly and Bumsteadly (Dagwood); you fumble your way into love. And we wouldn't have it any other way, would we?

There's a real glory here. It transcends logic. Science. Or the cold lab. Peter Cetera, bassman for Jazz Rock experts Chicago, found the "Glory of Love" #1(2), 6-86.

Suzy Quatro compares love to firelight, Shakespeare to a summer's day. In Rock and Roll, you can't always make out the words. But you can always make out.

"Somebody to Love" – Jefferson Airplane, with Grace Slick, #5, 4-67. R & R Blues' first major diva **Gracie Slick**. When hope slinks out and despair slithers in, it's time to find 'somebody to love.' In this pill-popping venue of Haight-Ashbury San Francisco, in the 'freaky' 60s, this breed of LOVE is fast and frantic and furious. Gracie is the powerhouse of "Somebody to Love." Her thrusty alto crackles. She plays Demon Rocker Blues Diva. Soaring into soprano, Slick slides the rundown chord shift from her odd silken Key of 'F#' down to the bVII chromatic **E** major. She booms out her hopped-up sense of the immediate NOW. Guitars of **Paul Kantner** and **Jorma Kaukonen** thunder duel wizardry. Grace notes (and Grace) fly over the mountain of love. With staggering Blues thirds and blackpool eyes of charismatic Rock and Roll enchantment, Gracie Slick and Jefferson Airplane (slang for 'split paper match used as a marijuana cigarette holder') sing the Blues with punch and power.

Bonnie Raitt, Odetta [Holmes], Joan Jett, Melissa Etheridge, Heart's Ann Wilson, LaVern Baker, and Gracie Slick are among the greatest Blues singers ever, just like Bessie Smith or Billie Holiday. The FIRST FEMALE inductee into the Rock Hall of Fame (1987), **Aretha Franklin**, anchors our Soul chapter. On her #2(2), 12-67 "Chain of Fools" (#1[4] R & B), **Joe South** sessionizes on guitar, above a spitfire R & B funky bass. Aretha unloads a frantic Gospel soprano – the essence of Soul Blues. **Melissa Etheridge**'s #94, 4-89 "Similar Features" has the same drive – about her lover's fantasy about another girl who looks a lot like her. American Bluesmasters inspired the British and beyond.

"Boom Boom" – Animals, #43, 12-64. With Chas Chandler's bottomtone bass cranking out soulful licks in the song's deep nadir, baritone **Eric Burdon** grabs the gruff, gravelly sound of #60, 5-62; #16 R & B "Boom Boom" of the master bluesman of Clarksdale, Mississippi, the incomparable **John Lee Hooker** (born 1917). In Burdon's coal-mining Newcastle, England, Real Blues are a way of life. He sings the Blues like he means it.

"Hobo Blues" – John Lee Hooker, NC, 1949; #5, 5-49 R & B. Genuine 100% Delta Blues baritone describes Depression poverty. See Hooker sidewalk cameo in *The Blues Brothers* (1980****). John Lee Hooker is well-known to Detroiters and urban America. Hooker played a 1962 concert at the Traffic Jam, on the Wayne State University campus in inner-city Detroit. Delta legend Hooker was panned by some egg-headed *Daily Collegian* music critic, with ritzy symphonic tastes. This great retort appeared by 19-year-old Blues expert **Larry Glazer**, my good friend, bandmate, and current Judge of Lansing Circuit Court:

"You are obviously misinformed as to what constitutes great music. Your narrow highbrow opinion will soon go the way of the dinosaur. America is changing, and you will grow to realize that John Lee Hooker is one of our greatest national treasures. Long after your snippity words are forgotten, John Lee Hooker will someday be in the Rock and Roll Hall of Fame." [1962!!]

Larry was always a visionary. I humbly mentioned a Rock Hall of Fame in my *Rock Revolution* (1966), rebounding my friend's super concept. In 1991, John Lee Hooker was inducted into the Rock Hall of Fame. The snippity critic was not.

"One Bourbon, One Scotch, [and] One Beer" is on Hooker's Al. *The Real Folk Blues*, (NC, 1987). Like Martin Luther King, Hooker didn't avoid controversy: "I Don't Want to Go to Vietnam" (NC). Hooker was also revered by 60s Blues Revival Folk for his "Peace Lovin' Man," "I'm in the Mood" (#30, 11-51; #1[4], 10-51 R & B), "Boogie with the Hook," "Boogie Chillun" (NC, '49; #1[1], 1-49 R & B) and "House Rent Boogie." Hooker's #62, 10-89 Al. *The Healer* features **Carlos** Santana, plus **Bonnie Raitt**, Los Lobos, Canned Heat and **George Thorogood**. Hooker died June 21, 2001, aged 83; the legendary Bluesman played his last gig just three days before . . .

"Them Changes" – Buddy Miles, #81, 5-70; #36, 4-70 R & B and #62, 7-71. Following his supernatural "Memphis Train" (#100, '69) drummer and singer Miles logged many Boogie Blues miles. Buddy **GUY** did 1966 legendary *Hoodoo Man* (NC), album. Also with Clapton's Al. #136, 10-91 *Damn Right I've Got the Blues*. Other stars in our multicultural Blues smorgasbord include: #105, 5-73 "Blues Band Opus 51, part I," by the Siegel-Schwall Band; **Tommy Chong**'s [Cheech & Chong comedy stars] Motown band **Bobby Taylor & the Vancouvers** #29, 4-68 (#5 R & B) "Does Your Mama Know about Me" [Asian-American Soul/Blues]; **Etta James** (#23, 11-67 "Tell Mama" and Elmo James (#9 R & B only, 4-52) "Dust My Broom"; **Sonny Boy Williamson** (NC. '47 but #4 R & B only 2-47 "Shake the Boogie" – murdered in Chicago 1948); **Chuck Willis** & "C.C. Crossing Blues" (NC, '50; #1[9] R & B); **Amos Milburn** "Chicken Shack Boogie" (NC, '49; #1[5] R & B); **Harvey Fuqua**'s Moonglows ("Sincerely", #20, 3-55 and #1[2] R & B – covered by **McGuire Sisters** #1[10]); Brownie McGhee (#2 R & B only, 10-48 "My Fault") and brother 'Stick" McGhee & His Buddies — #26, 8-49 and #2(4) "Drinkin' Wine Spo-Dee-O-Dee" and #2(1) R & B only "Tennessee Waltz Blues"; **Ivory Joe Hunter** (#1[5] R & B only, 1-50) "I Almost Lost My Mind", covered #1(4), 6-56 by Contemporary Christian Pat Boone; Afro/American Indian Roy Milton [& His Solid Senders] — #20, 8-46 "R.M. Blues" and #2(2) R & B; **Otis Redding, James**

Brown and **Wilson Pickett** (see SOUL); Detroit's Sugar Chile Robinson (#4, 10-49 R & B only), 9-year-old piano prodigy; Johnnie Taylor (1938-2000) – #5 "Who's Makin' Love? – #1(3) R & B; **Big Joe Turner** (#30, 9-51 "Chains of Love" [#2(4), 6-52 R & B – #10 for Pat Boone 9-56]; **Dinah Washington** – #8, 4-44, R & B "Salty Papa Blues" and R & B #9, 4-44 "Evil Gal Blues"; and "Prince of the Blues" Billy Wright, #3 R & B, 10-49 "Blues for My Baby." You'll find these stars in the usual Blues sources. Now let's tap some Blues crews from different ethnic backgrounds who groove to Blues variations:

"Johnny B. Goode" – Johnny Winter, #90, 1-70. A true Johnny B. Goode – situation with super guitar solos. Brother Edgar vanquished charts with the Monster Mash's cousin, "Frankenstein" (#1, 3-73), on a "Free Ride" (#14, 8-73). "Whitest" Blues of all with twin albino guitar guys smoking lead-guitar bazookas. Caucasian brothers of Leland, Mississippi, mastered Delta Blues sound. Johnny lavishes axe expertise on his sound-barrier solo.

"(When She Wants Good Lovin') My Baby Comes to Me" – Chicago Loop, #37, 11-66. Powered by guitarist **Stefan Grossman**, **Loop** rampages groove on just one steady chord. New Year's Eve party horde: shrill keening whistles, rip-roaring shouters, 18-wheeler Mac trucks rampaging over your simmering psyche.

Here are a few Blues-based songs by Rock artists many people think are a long way from Delta Blues. Surprise:

"A Wonderful Time Up There" – Pat Boone, #4, 2-58. Boogie Woogie piano/bass runs are the heart of the Blues, speaking of hearts. The melody is just the Walking Bass line. In Key of "C," C - E - G - A- Bb - A - G - E.

Lyrically, "A Wonderful Time Up There" speaks to believers and second-class sinners. The Revelations lyric metes out the pearly gates for good believers. Boone's booming baritone is straight Boogie-Woogie, first cousin to the Blues. No 12-Bar pattern here. It sports sixteen. Mostly the Big Three major Chords I, IV, and V. Sprightly Gospel sound. And yes, Blues. The melody, as Joe Stuessy points out in his excellent Rock History text *Rock and Roll*, is a Direct Walking Blues arpeggio riff.

"Let Me Be There" – Olivia Newton-John, #6, 11-73. Granddaughter, indeed, of Nobel Prize physicist Max Born. In chord structure this song's 16-bar structure parallels "Wonderful Time Up There," complete with bass guy oom-pahing in background. "Let Me Be There" is structured like Basic Blues, though Newton-John's debutant diva voice and Barbie-Doll smile typecast her otherwise.

"I Saw Him Standing There" – Tiffany (Darwisch), #7, 2-88. Norwalk, California, girl's answer to **Beatles**, who could boogie Blues with the Best: #1, '64 "Can't Buy Me Love," and #12, 9-68 "Revolution," John's wackyish "Why Don't We Do It in the Road," and Ringo's Carl Perkins' Rockabilly "Matchbox." On Beatleclone tunes, Tiffany, 16, rocks.

Now let's do some Blues most people think of as traditional Blues:

"Polk Salad Annie" – Tony Joe White, #8, 7-69; NC, R & B. White Bayou Bluesman's lyric creeps among pieroghs, bayou hummocks, alligator dens. Under cypress knees and knobs he unearths this one tasty Polk salad green. For every 1,000,000 songs about love there's one about weird vegetables [Kingsmen, #4, 1-65] "The Jolly Green Giant," "Rutabaga Rock?"

"Summertime Blues" – Who, #27, 9-70; NC, R & B. London's rockers' dynamite live version of the #8, '58 Eddie Cochran Blues Rock classic. Heavy Metal power and thrust. Perennial Rock and Roll, with Who's thunder-metal flair.

"Good Rocking Tonight" – Roy Brown, NC, 1948; #11, 6-48 R & B. "Rock Around the Clock's" grandfather. A slew of serious R & R profs proffer "Good Rocking Tonight" as the first R & R song. Covered by **Elvis** and **Buddy Holly**, only **Pat Boone**'s #49, 1-59 charted. **Roy Brown** is part of a whole kit and kaboodle of Blues legend names: **Wynonie Harris, Big Bill Broonzy, Charlie Christian,** and **T-Bone Walker.** Christian (1921-42) is crucial to electric guitar evolution.

Like Chuck Berry with Jewish Leonard Chess of Chess Records, Charlie Christian played electric Jazz guitar for Jewish bandleader **Berry Goodman** (1909-86).

B. B. King. circa 1948

"When Love Comes to Town" – B.B. King with US, #68, 4-89; NC, R & B. B.B. King leads ALL Blues Artists in CHARTED HITS. Crackling lead guitar fusillade. Zesty sandpaper tenor vocal. Band track maxed in masterpiece mode. King has inspired and revolutionized Rock and

Blues since his *Beale Street Blues Boy* show hit the Memphis Radio waves in 1949. B.B. calls all his guitars "Lucille" after a girl who accidentally burned the place down where his early guitar was staying. Four #1 R & B hits: "3 O'Clock Blues" at #1(5), 12-51; "You Know I Love You" #1(2), 9-52; "Please Love Me" #1(3), 6-53; and #1(2), 11-54 "You Upset Me Baby" (NC Top 30).

"The Thrill Is Gone" – B.B. King, #15, 2-69: #3 R & B. King doesn't waste notes. He's no frenzied speed-metal freak, grubbing for flashy fiery fretwork. He seeks the right note, lingering on minor thirds and bending old notes in shiny new ways. "Thrill" is his highest HOT 100 hit. #15? The top rungs are reserved for pop princes like Shaun or David Cassidy, Bobby Sherman, Menudo, the New Kids on the Block, N' Sync, or Donny Osmond. In general, the great Blues legends have been by-and-large ripped off in the HOT 100 chart-topping category. Why? Thirteen-year-old girls buy the lion's share of records. The Blues, like B.B.'s guitar-engorged "Thrill is Gone," are the seedbed of Rock and Roll. Had there been no B.B. King, Eric Clapton might have played "Itsy Bitsy Teeny Weenie Yellow Polka Dot Bikini" (Brian Hyland, #1, 7-60). Or simply CHASED the bikini.

B.B. King conquered the world. After the 1962 Moscow mavens of Cultural Music let in a few Jazz maestros (Benny Goodman and Dave Brubeck), **B.B. King** was the first real Bluesman to capture the Soviet Union (OK, maybe Louie Armstrong . . .). Blues riffs can win the hearts and minds of the people better than bombs. The millennium brought the inevitable collaboration; *Riding With the King* (Al. 7-2000) hit instant #3 and soon went platinum, besting his previous topper #25, 2-71 *Live in Cook County Jail* by 22 notches. Reason? An Anglo-American Blues miracle: B.B. King's chauffeur in the video, and partner on lead guitar, is **Eric Clapton**.

"Got My Mojo Workin'" – Muddy Waters, NC, 1948. Muddy (b. McKinley Morganfield, Rolling Fork, MS) did a 1950 R & B number called "Rolling Stone," (NC) thereby naming a ubiquitous British band. Muddy's stage name constitutes the molasses-slow flow of the big wide Delta River. Muddy started on slide guitar (see his "Mannish Boy"). When I talked to Muddy at a 1966 gig on Hamilton Avenue in Detroit, his lead guitar expertise would make 99% of would-be axehandlers mothball their Gibsons. Waters astoundingly never attained the HOT 100 charts. His R & B-only hits include #10, 7-51 "Honey Bee," #7, 5-56 "Forty Days & Forty Nights" and #9, 11-51 "Still A Fool." Like John Lee Hooker, Muddy Waters's music appealed to the rough blue-collar ghetto guys who nomadded it North to the hot forge and dark cool bar. A Mojo can be a good-luck charm, a talisman, or even a voodoo doll. Or it can have rawer, coarser connotations for mid-century bar hoppers.

Muddy Waters (1915, Rolling Fork, Mississippi, died 1983, Chicago) traveled the Northern Blues road to Chicago, marshalling at the Blues Shrine with Leonard Chess in the Windy City. Muddy's peerless guitar attack won some trusty fans: "I'm Your Hoochie Coochie Man" NC,

1954; #3, 3-54 R & B. Waters spanks the high frets on this classic Blues triumph. His highest R & B chart song "Hoochie Coochie Man" found a strong string of followers over in **Jeff Beck** and Eric Clapton and Keith Richards' England. My old band the Night Shift/Woolies did a wildfire tune called "The Hoochie Coochie Man Is Back" (NC, in 1974). Muddy Waters delivered a stinging guitar barrage. He'd pounce like a princely panther upon the hapless notes before they could defend themselves. Like Sassy Sarah Vaughan or Ella Fitzgerald, he'd sneak up on his note, surround and then nab it with full treble fury. Muddy Waters was a great singer, too. His chugging baritone swooped into top tomcat tenor. He taught Chuck Berry (via Charlie Christian) the best way to lay your hotshot axe licks in between your suave vocal lines. First Muddy would shoot off a supercool line, and then he would jam back at it with some sterling riff. Check this technique out on protégé **Chuck Berry**'s Rock anthem "Johnny B. Goode" (#8, 5-58; #2[2] R & B).

Muddy's other R & B Blues monsters? He first hit the R & B chart with #11, 9-48 "I Feel Like Going Home," and followed up with #10, 1-51 "Louisiana Blues" and #8, 4-51 "Long Distance Call," featuring Blues legend **Walter Horton** on harmonica. Other Waters classic R & B legends? Yep, many: #6, 11-53 "Mad Love"; **Foghat**'s #33, 9-77 "I Just Want to Make Love to You" as #34 "Just Make Love to Me" in 6-54; #4, 10-54 "I'm Ready" (last two written by Willie Dixon); and "Trouble, No More" at #7, 1-56.

Via Muddy at Leonard Chess's label in Chicago, somewhere in this mid-century vicinity, the concept of real CHICAGO BLUES emerged.

Muddy Waters epitomizes the feeling and genius and pure power of Chicago Blues. His assumed name is a mirror of his Delta Blues home. Down where the slow, sluggish, meandering Mississippi twists and seethes to the sullen sea, **McKinley Morganfield** strutted his turf – fomenting a big brassy guitar sound that would revolutionize the world. Muddy Waters, Bluesman. Sophomore class, 1987 – Rock and Roll Hall of Fame. Cleveland, Ohio. Muddy's kid **Big Bill Morganfield** plays the 2000+ Bluesfests. His 1999 *Rising Son* album has some daddish tunes: "Champagne & Reefer," "Screamin' & Cryin'," and "Diamonds at Your Feet."

"Walking the Blues" – Willie Dixon, NC, 1955; #6, 9-55 R & B. Chess Records (and Checker) also got blessed with the Walking Bass style of **Willie Dixon** and his All-Stars. Dixon (1916-92) was the Golden Gloves Heavyweight Champ of Chicago in 1936. He wrote hundreds of classic Blues tunes, and played a firebrand walking bass on zillions of sessions for Waters, Chuck Berry, and Chess stars (usually an upright double bass). Dixon also produced the whole Chess shebang in the 50s. No wonder Waters owes nearly half his sound to the virtuoso bass guy. Bizarrely, this is Dixon's only top ten R & B hit – but bass stars stand off in the second shadow beyond the ELVIS SPOTLIGHT.

"Ain't That Lovin' You Baby" – Jimmy Reed, NC, 1956; #3, 2-56 R & B. Blues legend **Jimmy Reed**'s biggest hit ever on the R & B charts. Tightroping along with his cool harmonica and his downstroke rhythm riff on his rumbling guitar, Jimmy Reed sparks this ode to an anonymous lover. Jimmy Reed rides a groove of COOLTH, teaching Bob Dylan all about the harmonica/guitar at the same time. Reed's streetwise tenor sings the sad-dive Blues of a hundred backstreet pubs, neon ebbing, in the garbage-can stunned Alka-Seltzer morning of lost time and nevermore romance. One great song.

"Hush Hush" – Jimmy Reed, #75, 10-60: #18 R & B. Jimmy chides his woman on believing sorry scuttlebutt. His 12-Bar Blues jumps along in his one-man band guitar/harp solo. Jimmy's spunkly little triplet riff in 'E' on the last measure is always beguiling and fantastic.

"Soul Man" – Blues Brothers, #14, 12-78. *Saturday Night Live* comic genius **John Belushi** (1949-82) and great straight man Dan Aykroyd reprise Sam & Dave – #2(3), 5-67. **Steve Cropper** and **Duck Dunn** star in band of same name in cult classic movie. **Ray Charles** plays cameo part – blind piano genius runs pawn shop and shoots just above punk trying to rip off a bass. Before Blues Brothers, they unleashed **John Belushi**'s '75 dynamite **Joe Cocker** imitation. Comic **Steve Martin** hit #17, 5-78 "King Tut" via *SNL*. David Letterman's bandleader **Paul Shaffer** worked at *SNL*, 1975-80. **Ray Charles**'s #9, 11-61 (#1 R & B) "Unchain My Heart" followed other Blues classic #1 "Hit the Road, Jack" for Ray, consummate Blues/Soul/R & B/Jazz/Country superstar. Ray belongs in nearly any chapter about Rock and Roll.

* * * * * * *

Big Three Time. **Jim Morrison, Jimi Hendrix**, and **Janis Joplin** are three of the most important names in Rock and Roll. Their youthful martyrdom is a lodestar from which R & R stratosphere seekers must gauge their own meteoric careers. They LIVED the Blues. Why not start with Jim?"

"HE'S YOUNG, HE'S SEXY, AND HE'S DEAD . . ." — *Rolling Stone*

So goes the sensational blurb. They categorize Jim Morrison (12-8-43 – 7-3-71) as forever young. The Byronic brooding genius, stoned on Kerouac and self, invaded the innocent hearts of young girls the world over with his Greek-god chiseled face and drop-dead baritone voice. A mixture of Oedipal id, theatrical satyr, and teenage idol, Jim Morrison stormed the R & R stage like there was no tomorrow. Pretty soon, there wasn't.

And 62% of the magic **Morrison** sound was keyboarder/bassist **Ray Manzarek** (b. '39, Chicago).

"Light My Fire" – Doors, #1(3), 6-67; NC, R & B. Star of the eight-minute eternity version is **Manzarek**. We can't dismiss the thumping tattoo of drummer **John Densmore** either, or **Robbie Krieger**'s rockin' riffs on lead guitar. Bass man is . . . no one. Hah? Yep, Manzarek is so good he fudges the bass line on his faux-bass keyboards [though **Lonnie Mack** (#5, '63 "Memphis") and others did rare Doors bass sessions].

Ray Manzarek, like the Crickets' Jerry Allison, is the Second Superstar of the group. Now, about this fiery epic . . . Poet James Douglas Morrison was deeply attuned to Rimbaud, Baudelaire, Ginsberg, and Jack Kerouac's 1959 *Mexico City Blues* (esp. the poem about being free of 'the slaving meat-wheel of life' and being safe in Heaven dead). The DOUGLAS in his name was provided by his admiral father – for General Douglas MacArthur, Commander of the Pacific Theatre in World War II.

So Morrison uses the term pyre to rhyme with fire. In India, the ghastly 18th-century custom of suttee sprang malevolently in outback villages: when the man died, 'social security' for the widow meant she had to jump onto the funeral pyre, and be consumed in the flames when her dead husband was cremated. Though gonzo guitarist **Robby Kreiger** actually wrote "Light My Fire," Ray supplied the eerie organ aura – and Morrison penned the Poe-esque funereal pyre verse.

PYRE? A month after this song got very, very big, gargantuan fires consumed many American cities in bitter rioting. Detroit, for one. This fiery metaphor I recall was first used in Jody Reynolds' Graveyard Rock follow-up: "Fire of Love," (#66, 8-58) with same stunning tremolo as "Endless Sleep." Reynolds, and Al Casey's ghostly guitar, are progenitors of Death Rock, Death Metal, and Gothic. Love's white-hot fiery fever burns, consumes. "Light My Fire" is minor-key, nearly all the way through. The Doors' debut and signature song resonates with ominous foreboding.

Ray Manzarek, in his outstanding autobiography *Light My Fire* (1988), says basically Robby wrote the #1 tune in the 'fabled Summer of Love.' The song would stun the Beatles' chart domination. When Robby first sang it, ostensibly in Dylanesque voice, drummer John Densmore said it sounded like a Sonny & Cher Folk Rock song. Robby's parents supplied a place for them to practice, and Ray began to fool around with the mesmerizing **A minor** to F# minor progression on the organ. From this central slide, Manzarek fashioned Blues/Jazz polychordal profundity that had the local Garage Band stumped, puzzled, and terminally befuddled:

"All my piano lessons paid off. All my Classical studies came to fruition . . . A simple circle of fifths was the answer. The chords were **G** to **D**, **F** to **Bb**, **Eb** to **Ab** (two beats on each chord) and then an **A** for two measures. Run some Bach filigrees over the top in a kind of turning-in-on-itself Fibonacci spiral – like a nautilus shell – and you've got it. 'Eureka!' An illuminati moment. . . . Cartwheeling into 'Light My Fire.' Leaping into history."

The Doors rehearsed and cut their demo. Ray laments that despite the cutting-edge sound, they were rejected by Capitol (Beach Boys' label), RCA (Elvis' label),

Liberty (Bobby Vee/Crickets' label), Dunhill (Woolies' label), Decca (Buddy Holly's original label), and Reprise (Sinatra's homegrown label). Ray mentions the absurd Kafkaesque or Eugene Ionesco flavor of their getting rejected by Capitol; he called the cylindrical Capitol Records palace on Vine Street in Hollywood a 'true temple of Mammon.' His encounter with the Woolies' producer **Lou Adler** was infuriating. Adler listened to each Doors' classic for maybe ten seconds: "I wanted to rage at him . . . 'How dare you! We're the Doors! This is (expletive) Jim Morrison! He's going to be a (expletive) star!' . . . My brain was a boiling, lava-filled Jello mold of rage." Adler listened to their future #1 "Hello, I Love You" for maybe 20 seconds before fleeing to lunch or whatever.

Anybody who's ever believed in a song will understand perfectly how the Doors' musical genius felt. In the Woolies' case, winning the Michigan State Fair Battle of the Bands got a bonus one-way ticket to Hollywood. Dunhill picked up "Who Do You Love" (#95, 3-67) – but their A & R commandos lavished zillions more millions on the **Mamas & Papas** and other Dunhill superstars – not a Baldori-powered Rock band from Lansing, Michigan.

"Light My Fire" has far transcended its month-long siege of Summer 1967, firing up the midnight American urban underbelly with seething flames of passion and apocalyptic vision. **Jim Morrison** (1942-97), with his James Dean stare, Byronic charisma, and magnetizing eyes, has become the symbol for anyone, anywhere, anytime, whoever rebelled against anything. Sheathed in Manzarek's harmonic blanket of tempestuous Post-Classical polychordal vision, Morrison commands center stage. Sacrificed upon the altar of Rock and Roll, Morrison in death takes on a dimension only comparable to Buddy Holly or Elvis himself.

As my Motor City flashed and flared with tongues of terrible flame, sporadic gunfire, and the death of dreams in the bloody Detroit Riot of July 1967, this somber pyro anthem lit up our flickering smokescape.

Anticipating the rapid rise of FM radio, the Doors and their eventual Elektra label pressed both an AM three-minute Insta-"Light-My-Fire" and an eight-minute Album-Style-Giganto- "Light-My-Fire". The Doors show a similar style of long-song intensity on their version of our Woolies' **Bo Diddley** cover "Who Do You Love" – on Al. #8, 8-70 *Absolutely Live*. It's a dynamic version that suggests the later work of Buddy Holly fan **John Prine** (b. '46, Illinois): Al. #66, 4-75 *Common Sense*, and (on his Holly-named) Oh Boy label, #159, 4-95 *Lost Dogs and Mixed Blessings*. Though Prine has a Country and Folk background, the Doors and Prine share some tricky allusions and musical stylistics. On the eight-minute superside of "Light My Fire," Morrison's coffee break features a rolling, sloshing, tidal wave of crescendo rising power by Manzarek and his minions. Densmore's drums dance the hypnotic pulse, and Krieger lays back, waiting for the Manzarek opus to subside. Then Robby begins the refurbished intro. After his shimmering slide guitar enters the ethereal sway of the cresting Doors, Manzarek and Krieger play off each others' Stromboli-volcano energy – and Densmore clobbers half-tacets into pulverized silence.

Jim Morrison

To disregard "Light My Fire" is to disregard Rock and Roll. It is one of the most powerful and commanding songs in the history of music. "Light My Fire" has cast its wild and enchanting spell on several generations of rock fans. No doubt it will carry many more down their own roads of rebellion. Three out of four Doors were still alive beyond the Millennium.

"Roadhouse Blues" – Doors, #50, 4-70; NC, R & B. This Doors' triumph shows their Blues explosion. Fooling impishly around with the 12-Bar Blues pattern, "Roadhouse Blues" conjures the Wasteland imagery of Post-Modern Blue Funk that surges into extreme sadness in the vast hangover of sunrise regret.

Students seem to chuckle at Jim's wake-up health regimen. He drones disconsolately how he struggles up out of bed, and selects his breakfast. Wheaties? Oatmeal? Nah. He selects the 'hair of the dog cure' – he gets a BEER for himself. Then, with utter hopeless desperation, he surveys the prospects for the cosmos: all our futures are totally uncertain, and to make matters worse, THE END always lurks near. Disney it ain't. The bleak new day staggers along, guaranteeing nothing. Love and life evaporate into an existential swamp of potential doom. In a backwash of 'misery loves company,' Doors fans can understand Jim's down-in-the-dumps resignation to his chemical fate. Buttressed by iffy substances, and untethered by any limits whatsoever, Jim Morrison finds a bleary-eyed Limbo reality in the wailing Kerouackian midnight Wurlitzer roadhouse – a place of castaway dreams and characters.

Surfing the night.

"Roadhouse Blues" is one rockin' song! Jim's raspily ribald "Roll-baby" command invokes a party-animal virility of King Solomon proportions. Buoyed by the keyboard fantasia of Manzarek, the slide-guitar thrust of Krieger, and the jangling jungle thumps of Densmore, "Roadhouse Blues" crests the #4 Al., 3-70 *Morrison Hotel/Soft Parade*. The biggest album for the Scottish-American baritone's Doors was Al. #1(4), 8-68 *Waiting for the Sun*. As a living example of their undying popularity, **The Doors** checked in at #8 in March 1991. The Doors made the Rock Hall of Fame in 1993.

The driving impulse for "Roadhouse Blues" is Manzarek's pedal-point bottom-tonic BASS note on his keyboard's low echelons. Cowboy star **John Wayne**'s (1907-79) actual given name was **Marion Morrison**, and "Roadhouse Blues" shuffles like one of his noble horses into the golden California sunset. "Roadhouse Blues" has an earthy, punch-drunk, swaggering sound. Good Blues tune for Jim & Doors (who cryptically named themselves after mystic poet William Blake's passage through to another dimension).

"L.A. Woman" – Doors, NC,1968. Morrison's haunted nightscape epic. Rock's "Lizard King" booms in a romantic reprise of the glitzy midnight world of downtown Los Angeles. It's a garish *Pulp-Fiction* world of screaming sirens, torrid passion, and cold French fries. The L.A. doll is street smart, suffused with savvy in a world of topless bars, electric pills, coke and smoke and toke (and hopefully not croak).

Morrison's rise and fall were uncannily predictable. **Paul Anka** once borrowed my belt for a TV show we were on in Windsor, Ontario. The teen idol hit #1, too, on his first tune "Diana" in 1957, and wrote "My Way" for Elvis and for Frank Sinatra (#22, 11-77 for the King; #27, 3-69 for Chairman of the Board). Anka philosophized: "Many entertainers find their biggest enemies are themselves, and that they're prone to self-destruction. If you take care of yourself and don't self-destruct, this is a great life!" Anka never lacked self-assurance.

Morrison read deeply into Beat literature. He rebelled against his emotionally cool military father, and set up a weird alliance with his mother that psychologists termed "Oedipally pathogenic." With Kerouac's Catholic-Buddhist sense of cosmic dread, Morrison visualized no Las Vegan happily-ever-afters in the mode of Paul Anka or Wayne Newton (#4, 4-72 "Daddy Don't You Walk So Fast"). And Morrison was certainly no Pat Boone. Heaven did not seem to be his goal.

The gritty gutter-glutted night world of the Doors' "L.A. Woman" reflects a central scenario in Kerouac's *On the Road* (hardcover 1955, Viking). 'Sal Paradise,' Jack's alter-ego, strolls down a lively street in 40s Denver. "At lilac evening I walked with every muscle aching among the lights at 27th and Wilton in the Denver colored section, wishing I were a Negro, feeling that the best the white world had offered was not enough ecstasy for me, not

enough life, joy, kicks, darkness, not enough night."

This passionate sense of longing in Jim Morrison is a vital part of his everlasting popularity. Heaven knows he was no saint. Nor moral paragon. In the words of Billy Joel:

"Only the Good Die Young" – Billy Joel, #24, 5-78. Joel staunchly states his preference; he'd prefer to laugh among sinners than cry in the company of saints. Why? Sinners have a lot more fun, he says. He chides a chaste maiden named, ahem, 'Virginia', to fracture her innocence for a moment's passion. Joel's clarion call to let-it-all-hang-out hedonism in this song put it on the Catholic Church's CONDEMNED list. [See Madonna's #1(8), 11-84 "Like a Virgin" or #1(3), 3-89 "Like a Prayer"]. Jim Morrison and Mick Jagger are both studies in the live-it-up lifestyle; Keith Richard(s) is no president of any Temperance or Anti-Drug Crusade either. Jagger, however, parceled out his long wild party with some regard for Aristotle's Golden Mean. So did Ray Manzarek. Therefore, they somehow lived long lives in the Rock Star category – far beyond half a century. The lights of Los Angeles blinded Jim Morrison like a deer on the midnight highway. Morrison was a supernova blazing in the wee hours just before dawn – a dying star with a big bang before the last ebb and the evermore ashes. Morrison soared skyward. Look out below.

"Riders on the Storm" – Doors, #14, 7-71. The day gloomy "Riders" entered the *Billboard* charts (7-3-71) was a much better day for me (6th anniversary) than Jim (died). His early demise was not entirely unpredictable, and maybe due to alcohol more than drugs – though apparently he had been trying to cut down on his self-destructive habits in Paris. "Riders" is eerily aglow with creepo Death Rock images. A psycho killer stalks a demon road that squirms like a slimy toad [poor toads, they deserve better press]. If one picks up this ghastly Hitchhiker, his family might just perish. "Riders on the Storm" vamps a basic Blues in a minor key. It mocks a standard 12-Bar Blues major progression in the Key of 'E'. It never resolves into something very pretty. Why should it? Morrison died in its wake. He was [probably . . .] found dead of a heart attack in a Paris hotel bathtub. His Parisian tomb has become a macabre cult shrine, with many midnight movers apparently indulging in romantic interludes upon his grave. "Riders on the Storm" rides out the stormy life of Jim Morrison to, as the Traveling Wilburys put it (#63, 2-89), "The End of the Line." One of the few near-totally minor Blues anthems ever recorded, "Riders" swoops us away to a *Mad Max* (Australian 1979****) desolation wasteland.

To this day, students of my Rock Music History elect Handsome Hunk **Jim Morrison** – despite a semi-paltry 16 charted hits and only 3 Top Ten tunes – one of the TOP THREE stars in Rock history. No surprise.

"Hello, I Love You" – Doors, #1(2), 6-68. One of Doors' only two #1's. In America's gloomiest month ever, "Hello" sparked a wildfire fury of one-night-stands. Though Jim

Morrison's casual "Hello, I Love You" is an invitation to quick intimacy, it belies the fact that the sweet music that burbles deep within your soul can have a lifetime commitment. Many Woodstock pilgrims might sooner dump a favorite girlfriend or boyfriend than a favorite song. Or a commitment to a rakish rogue rebel singer, with a rapscallion twinkle in his eye. Like Jim.

An amazing letter adorns the Rock Hall of Fame basement. It's from Jim's dad **Admiral Morrison** to the Miami Police Department. Its gist? Basically, please give my son Jim a break; you arrested him on stage for showing a little too much of himself – but he's basically a good kid who accidentally let the alcohol supervise his unfortunate actions. A wistful plea from a remorseful – but kind – absentee dad, locked into his military career stoicism . . . What went wrong in America in 1968?

"Abraham, Martin, & John" – Dion, #4, 11-68. Bronx Dion's bio sketch cites four fallen leaders: **Abraham Lincoln, Dr. Martin Luther King, John** and brother **Bobby Kennedy**. That April, America lost Dr. King in a hail of gunfire at Memphis's Lorraine Motel. In early June, Bobby Kennedy died by California assassin on his ill-fated campaign to right the wrongs of a war endlessly ensnaring our well-meaning country. In 1993 the Brady Bill passed Congress, banning assault rifles to psychopaths. An ancient adage appeared – "lock the barn door after the horse has been stolen." Later in the song, Dion sees a vision: all four charismatic American leaders walking on some faraway heavenly hill in the mystic mist. Stirring elegy. Flipside NC, '68 "Daddy Rollin': is dynamite Blues. So the Doors sang "Hello, I Love You." They mocked the old system where you had to get to know her a little first before blurting such endearments. Jim's Insta-Love is hot, ringed by no wedding rings, no TRUE "I-love-yous," no commitments, no hassle. The **Shirelles**' #1, '60 "Will You Love Me Tomorrow" message vaporized, as the go-go later 60s guillotined the Guilt Monster.

"I love you" has been whispered billions of times, in varying degrees of sincerity. Remember the Troggs' #1 sarcastic "Wild Thing" – where the waffling woo-er claims he thinks he loves her? Well, Morrison gets the silver medal for semi-sincerity here. The Woodstock Generation spawned a new morality, a new mobility, a new reluctance to the long-term commitments. When **Joni Mitchell** and Ritchie Havens and 500,000 Woodstock R & R pilgrims assembled at Yasgur's Farm in 1969, they desperately sought freedom, enlightenment, camaraderie, fulfillment, edification, consciousness-raising, a few rays, great Rock and Roll, and in Joe Sikorik's words, some tried "To get high" and get some action. Jim Morrison's Insta-Love song spawned new kids on the block named Rainbow and Dweezel and Zak and Cigartha and Sun Bear and Jimi.

"Woodstock" – Crosby, Stills, Nash, and Young, #11, 3-70. Canadian-American songstress **Joni Mitchell** wrote this song for a very temporary Woodstock weekend 'nation' of peace, love, and harmony in the foothills of the Catskill Mountains where Rip Van Winkle 'slept twenty years.'

The **Devotions** hit #36, 2-64 with latter-day Streetcorner comic tune "Rip Van Winkle." It's among only songs with BASS lead singer (check it out), **Ray Sanchez**. Latino-Jewish-Czech-Italian quartet (Weisbrod, Hovorka, Pardo). Hooray for the American Johnny B. Goode melting pot of multicultural Rock and Roll! Woodstock featured an idealistic generation of counterculture pilgrims – out to change the world. Later teenagers have been accused of apathy and sleepiness. So were 60s kids – until they got their draft notices. The 1999 Woodstock Reunion Concert cost a lot more, drew many multitudes (fewer bacchanalians) and helped cause the Spring 2000 at-long-last Reunion Tour of **Crosby, Still, Nash, AND Young.**

"Love the One You're With" – Stephen Stills, #14, 12-70. Love-'em-leave-'em anthem. Free love. Ode to Altamont and Monterey and Woodstock and Goose Lake, Michigan. Love pilgrims craved quick pleasure. Despite the Woodstock erotic experimentation, shunning 'traditional family values,' one reporter was so moved by Stills' fellow singer David Crosby's liver transplant at age 53 that he reported donated a pint of blood to help fulfill Crosby's overwhelming 110-pint requirement.

A lot of selfless quiet people bravely donate blood. What's the big deal? "Why Crosby?" they queried the news-hawk. As a boy, he explained, he was drawn to the mystical musical magic of the Everly-style harmonies of Crosby, Stills, and Nash. "They circumscribed my boyhood," he confessed. "They gave their blood, through their music, to me." Besides, mused the hard-bitten streetbeat reporter, "the idea of my blood coursing through their veins is an incredible trip. Maybe I could be a small part of one of Crosby's concerts, though personally I have no musical talent."

Like, wow. That's heavy! Music is in your blood. Sangre vida.

* * * * * * *

The Blues are never far from death. Blues singers, as a rule, do not live a long time. They got shot, stabbed, choke in their own vomit, have heart attacks at 27, commit suicide, crash cars, lose Russian Roulette games, disappear, or die of weird diseases like Leadbelly with Lou Gehrig's disease. Throughout his Blues-Rock pilgrimage, Morrison diligently read his hero Jack Kerouac's *On the Road* for inspiration. In 1969, Jack Kerouac was wasting away watching *The Galloping Gourmet* on TV. His mother Memere and third wife Stella Sampas huddled around him as he inhaled Jack Daniels boozily and chomped cigarettes. After 47 years, his friends, modest fortune, and big heart gave out. Like many severe alcoholics, Kerouac died of internal bleeding on the operating table in Florida. Track and football star, his strong constitution steeled his body to thirty years of hard drinking and drug-glutted abuse. At 47, he was too old to die young, too young to die old. Kerouac was NOT 27. Jack Kerouac's death was a grim prognosticator of the untimely demises of three of his greatest protégés: **Morrison, Hendrix, Joplin**. On October 21, 1969, when Kerouac died beyond lost friends, alone in surfy Florida, the Quasimodo bell tolled for the sixties party. There were many bills to pay.

"Break on Through" – Doors, #126, 4-67. Jim surfs River Styx. This secret debut record (#1 "Light My Fire" followed in Summer '67) was an evil omen to Jim's iffy longevity – he breaks through to the sinister, dark "OTHER-SIDE," an unveiled death euphemism. Jim Morrison, like everyone treading water on the sea of life, had this thing about death. In his mid-twenties, he had little longing, though, to see his mid-forties. What took Kerouac 47 years to do to his beleaguered body took Jim Morrison just 27. His band, all survivors, watched him fade away in sloshed donnybrooks, embarrassing arrests and haggard hangovers. Keyboard genius **Ray Manzarek**, guitar whiz **Robby Krieger**, and soft-pedal drummer **John Densmore**, continue to write, groove, and spark new sounds beyond the millennium.

Jim joins a caravan of musicians who died young of overindulgence or world-weariness or inept pilots or redeye roadhouse food or too much or not enough love: Blues greats Jimmie Rodgers I, Billie Holiday, Slim Harpo, Alberta Hunter, Blind Lemon Jefferson; Rockers Gene Vincent, Ritchie Valens, Buddy Holly, Brian Jones, Johnny Ace, Dennis Wilson, Stevie Ray Vaughan, the Allman-Skynyrd contingent; Soul stars Otis Redding, Clyde McPhatter, three Temptations and most of the Platters; Jazz greats Charlie Parker, Wes Montgomery. Even Elvis. Jim Morrison had to deal with a self-induced self-inflicted blue funk from the same military-father syndrome that eventually led Folk Protest guru **Phil Ochs** to squander his own life in his sad hopeless Brooklyn flat. The saddest thing for music people is "What could he have contributed to the Rock/Blues panorama had he survived?" Morrison wasn't around long. During his supernova career, he lofted a handsome James Dean face, and a great Byronic baritone to the fickle stars above.

Twinkly lights of Seattle's Skid Road shone down into misty Seattle. Slush seeping into grizzly gutters framed the backdrop for this big town where winter can't figure whether to rain or snow. Lumberjacks of old skidded the logs down the hill to Puget Sound, and Skid Road became Skid Row, catch-all name for any slum anywhere. We mentioned Motown's omnipresent gloom – its draped and hanging stratus cloud that sloshes the slush in November nastiness and mourns the death of the sun. Detroit

is only Bronze Medalist for cloudiness. Seattle gloms the gold. Or grey medal.

Seattle bands of the 90s got called GRUNGE. Many are into GOTHIC or DEATH METAL. Some, like **Kurt Cobain**, were into death itself. Others, like **Eddie Vedder** and **Pearl Jam**, epitomize the raunchy sound of Seattle and its frizzy cloudlet that stalks the sky. Pearl Jam mirrored the raw cacophonic majesty of Seattle's Greatest Lost Spirits:

On a slushy stratus-drizzle day in Seattle, November 27, 1942, **Jimi Hendrix** was born. The southpaw lad flipped a right-handed guitar over backwards to learn a quaintly mirror-image grid of frets and chords. Hendrix scooted around a lot. In truth, Jimi's resume is a candidate for Weight Watchers. He played such hot Blues for **Little Richard**, and wore such flamboyant outfits, that Richard fired him – Richard doesn't like to be upstaged. Jimi also handled the frantic guitar upswoops of **Joey Dee** [nee Joseph DiNicola] on "Shout" by Joey Dee & Starlighters, #6, 3-62. Then he cavorted over to Motown's Soul crew from Canada – Bobby Taylor and the Vancouvers. Hendrix bounced amok, forming **Jimmy James and the Blue Flames**. Somewhere along the way Jimi Hendrix may have become the most important guitar innovator of all time. He could sing well too. At one point, he starred on stage with Pro Wrestling's grossest guru, **Gorgeous George**, who infuriated the macho men in the audience by taking his bleached hair out of curlers in the ring. Hendrix, always ahead of his time, just might have anticipated the wild fan-addict power of the 2002+ World Wrestling Federation. The **Animals'** bass player Chas Chandler was enough of a virtuoso on bass to know Hendrix was a genius on guitar. By 1967, Hendrix's fame in England built a nice comfy purple haze around him to conquer America:

"Purple Haze" – Jimi Hendrix, #65, 8-67, NC, R & B. Guitar champ and mellow whiskey baritone. In 1966, he formed the **Jimi Hendrix Experience**. His integrated Experience featured **Mitch Mitchell**, drums, and bassist **Noel Redding**. Album superstar: #5, 8-67 *Are You Experienced*, #1(2), 10-68 *Electric Ladyland* (featuring topless troupe), and #3, 2-68 *Axis: Bold As Love*. All went platinum. Mysteriously, lukewarm singles action on charts. Like Buddy's Crickets, Hendrix shone in United Kingdom; his 'haze' hit #3, 4-67. Shockingly, Jimi's *Greatest Hits* NEVER perforated the Rhythm and Blues charts here.

"All Along the Watchtower" – Jimi Hendrix, #20, 9-68; #5, U.K. Hendrix + Dylan = Unique Musical Enlightenment. Jimi mumbles and growls in the best of Dylan's craggy style, murmuring the saga of the wildcat on the watchtower. The ferocious feline is an ominous portent of impending doom. Armageddon strikes again. Hendrix was a visionary. Like the **Del-Vikings**, **Bruce Springsteen's E-Street Band, Hootie & the Blowfish**, the **Dave Matthews Band**, the **Marcels, All 4 One**, and **Bobby Taylor's Vancouvers**, Jimi had an integrated band. He needed only three musicians (Noel Redding, bass; Mitch Mitchell, drums). Lighting his guitar on fire in London didn't hurt, either, in the publicity department.

"Foxey Lady" – Jimi Hendrix, #67, 12-67. Hendrix's second hit after that violet haze item. How pervasive is Jimi's influence? For years I've scooped kids into car to our FREE Kiddie Zoo, two miles away. No $10 Bronx Zoo fees. A few buffalo, two mountain lions, couple bald eagles, wildcats, barnyard stuff. Naturally, what have they named the coppery burnished fox at the Zoo? FOXEY LADY. Even a lettuce company has assumed the vulpine adjective: FOXEY LADY.

The power of Jimi's music goes far beyond some sweet 60s chick. It goes far beyond music, even. Jimi Hendrix is an integral part of our national consciousness. He is simply the most innovative rock guitarist of his era. He single-handedly shifted the focus away from the lead singer and over to the active axe-man cranking like-wow riffs to goggle-eyed girls. Influenced by **Sam 'Lightnin' Hopkins** (b. 1912), **Chuck Berry, Robert Johnson**, and **B.B. King**, Jimi blurred the old Rock genres. Listen to bassist extraordinaire **Noel Redding** on this and other Hendrix cuts; Jimi's guitar genius is amply complemented by stuttering, staggering, streaky bottom lines on bass – exactly the Jazz Rock Fusion sound Hendrix wanted in his integrated band. All the old stars had put the old notes into the old places. Jimi, Noel, and Mitch put them all somewhere new. And glorious.

Like Chuck Berry, Jimi wasn't just a great guitarist, he was an acrobat. Berry had his patented 'duck walk,' and he could play guitar behind his back. With bedazzling showmanship, Hendrix fired the guitar over his head, played it with his teeth, and took Marty Robbins's #1, 1-61 "Don't Worry" broken-amp feedback liability and turned it into a Heavy Metal asset. A looming physical presence, Hendrix's movements emitted a catlike sensuality last seen somewhere in the sizzling ELVIS SPOTLIGHT. Jimmy's debut was "Hey Joe" (NC, '67, but #6, 1-67 U.K.). We lived briefly in Victoria, British Columbia, on my academic scholarship the same year. Midway between Seattle, where I never met Hendrix, and Vancouver on the B.C. Canadian mainland, we tried to do "Hey Joe" with my band, but I frankly didn't like the lyrics about some guy going to shoot his 'old lady' because he caught her fooling around. Why the clueless guy would ask him where he's going with a smokin' gun, I have no clue. Most folks just run off via Nike Express when a friend or fiend brandishes a weapon. But WOW, Jimi's smokin' GUITAR! His unearthly supernatural bends and slurs and slides and double-note riffs were something miraculous that we mid-rank guitarists couldn't fathom. Hendrix was just too com-

plex. Like Del Shannon and Buddy Holly, Hendrix's U.K. fame eclipsed his U.S.A. singles action, like "And the Wind Cries Mary" #0 here and #6, 5-67 U.K.

Jimi's "Star Spangled Banner," spiked with far-out feedback, opened the Monterey Festival in 1967, erupting into the whole Love-In Rock Festival Happening of the late 60s. By 1969, the Hendrix Experience petered out, hassled by haggling, squabbling, squawking, and the usual testosterone hostility that band-brothers get into. Although Mitch Mitchell remained loyal, bass-champ Noel Redding joined Fat Mattress, leaving Jimi to party alone on the high red-glare rocket frets and bursting-bomb riffs at the 1969 Woodstock Festival. Miraculously, in a swath of guitar fireworks, which stole the breath from a half million strong, Hendrix landed like a cat – back on its feet directly on the melody line. A paratrooper in 1961, Hendrix had served Uncle Sam. He had no particular non-guitar 'axe' to grind (except against American strategists' stalemate policy). His anthem jabbed a bolt of Rock lightning from the cumulonimbus green skies, thrusting a tornado of molten fire into fans' hearts – and supercharging 500,000 souls in the largest temporary nation in the history of the world: Yasgur's Farm, Bethel, New York, U.S.A., Earth, Solar System, Milky Way, Universe . . . Big Bang.

On the 18th of September, 1970, Hendrix was gone. Blues and Rock kingpin, Hendrix changed the way the world looked at the guitar. No longer was it for accompaniment; the Eddie Van Halens and Richie Samboras (Bon Jovi) could soon rejoice – the guitar often became the song. Always a party lover, Jimi and girlfriend Monika Danneman returned to her apartment in London after a triumphant tour of the European continent. His death, by asphyxiation, was ruled an accident – smothered by a lethal combo of drugs and alcohol in his fitful sleep.

Our Rock and Roll Tour took us in 1994 from the **Big Bopper**'s grave in Beaumont, Texas (Jiles P. Richardson, 1930-59) to oil boom town Port Arthur, Texas, population 58,724 in 1990. When you whisk up beyond off the Louisiana Gulf, and the purple dusk deepens behind the flamingo sunset over cobalt blue breakers, you suddenly jolt north. In the twilight gloaming, a hundred million lights command your eyes. You just know Port Arthur is twice the size of New York City.

It better be. It's the birthplace of the Greatest Blues Singer of all time. [Ignore subjective comments like this. Feel free to insert the '2nd, 14th, 38th, or 428th-best Blues Singer of All Time,' depending on your own musical conditioning. We music fans thrive on our differences as well as our similar opinions].

"Piece of My Heart" – Big Brother and the Holding Company, lead by Janis Joplin, #12, 8-68; NC, R & B. Janis Joplin (January 19, 1943 – October 4, 1970) was born just off the Gulf of Mexico in the Texan scorching subtropics. We visited the Lamar College Library where 'Beatnik Janis' worked as a page. Can you imagine the Southern Comfort-swilling double-voiced coke and smoke Blues belter, shelving books about macroeconomics or gardening or solid waste disposal? At 14, Janis kissed her junior high school goodbye. It's a big brick edifice across the hot cement from the college library where Janis toiled stacking books. Kitty-corner from a fine cathedral. Just down the block is the bright baby-blue frieze and tablature of the new Buddhist Temple. Since the War ended in Vietnam, thousands of temple 'Boat People' enriched the economy of Port Arthur by shrimping, sampan-style, off the Coast. In Janis's 1958, Texans rejoiced at barbecues, barber shops, and beefy boys bashing themselves and a football in slam-bam glee. **Janis** loved Folk music: the Kingston Trio and especially (says critic Lauren Gregory) the contralto husky stylistics of **Odetta** [Holmes, b. 1930], Al. #75 *Odetta Sings Folk Songs*, 9-63. Janis read books, dreamed of L.A. and New York, and couldn't wait to get the hell out of town. In 1960, she fled to Venice, California, then returned to Outlaw Blues/Country bars in Texan academic Alamo Austin, and boomtown Houston. By 1966, she lassoed Sam Andrew (b. 1941) on guitar, Peter Albin on bass and back-up vocals (b. 1944), Jim Gurley on guitar, and David Getz on drums, piano, and vocals.

This R & R classic Joplin rouser spearheads #1(8), 9-68 *Cheap Thrills* album. If America was hitting its "Abraham, Martin, and John" morale doldrums, at least we had a new Blues singer to circumscribe our collective misery with the boldest new sound in years. The last time a voice like Janis's was heard was, well . . . never. She ran her life at FULL-TILT BOOGIE pace. In the marathon running community we call it red-lining; you do not hold back. You do not break your frantic stride. You do not let up. You race as fast as you can as far as you can and you never, never look back. It makes HYPERACTIVITY look like TRANSCENDENTAL MEDITATION.

Jack Kerouac's 1957 *On the Road* yielded the name of Janis's top album: *Pearl*. "Somewhere along the line I knew there'd be . . . visions; somewhere along the line the pearl would be handed to me" (*Pearl*, Al. #1[9], 1-71). One of Kerouac's protégés too, Janis dug his lonesome midnight bars. Her life and haunted voice raced ahead at top end, speedometer buried in the center of the Red Line.

"Piece of My Heart" glowers like a smoldering ember, ranging from her tender purring alto to a wild winging whiskey soprano that scatters the stars from the sky. First recorded by Aretha Franklin's sister **Erma Franklin** (#62, 11-67, #10 R & B), Erma's Soul hit became Big Brother's Blues MONSTER DASH.

As this anonymous guy cuts away little chunks of her heart, she wails out her banshee misery on the staggered downbeat, calling back in time to **Billie Holiday** and **Bessie Smith** and **Blind Lemon Jefferson**. With the Blues, you need not be Afro or male to apply. No prude, Janis's multifarious affairs and exotic relationships caused a lot of press rancor. It was OK, they bellowed, for a

Bluesman to go out tomcattin' with golden groupies galore – but a woman? Janis did what she wanted, when she wanted to. A far cry from the goody-goody junior high kid, the high school loner, and the Folk Singer who loved the Kingston Trio, Janis emerged in the late 60s as the major Blues force in Rock and Roll music. There has never been anything like her. Perhaps there never will.

Janis Joplin

"Cry Baby" – Janis Joplin, #42, 5-71; NC, R & B. Original was by **Garnet Mimms and the** Enchanters (#4, 8-63, #1 R & B). Great Screaming Blues with mountainous range and passion. An "A" performance trumped by Janis's "A+." A gut-wretching experience to listen to this song. Imagine having to sing it. No one ever gave more than Janis at a performance. Guzzling her swig of liquid courage (Southern Comfort), the plucky little girl from Port Arthur first drained the bottle and then emotionally and physically drained herself. Have you ever been to a great bar, loved the band, and noticed that everybody around had their own agenda? No one was listening, guys were grabbing girls or barfing on amps, and no one was listening to the singer? Well, Janis Joplin gave all her fans everything she had. And this great singer was never ever rewarded with a well-deserved place on the R & B charts like Blue-Eyed Soul artists like Righteous Brothers. Oddly, neither was **Jimi Hendrix**. She gave 111% each concert. Not like the poor band who had to play Lodi:

"Lodi" – Creedence Clearwater Revival, #52, 5-69. "Lodi" floats, like a wagon train trekking the long dusty desert. "Lodi" lumbers onto the shifting whispering sands in a plodding caravan. Destination? The Promised Land. But it never arrives. "Lodi" is "Johnny B. Goode" gone bad. Johnny B. Badde. If #2 flipside "Bad Moon Risin'" isn't scary enough, CCR's grim rolling rock dirge drips with Coulda-Been, Shoulda-Been, but Never Was.

"Lodi" aims at Anywhere U.S.A. "Lodi" paints a bar band's furtive dreams of the illusory BIG TIME. Janis

Joplin, at least, had a #1 album and rep. When people listened to her, they'd shelled out mucho dinero so they'd better shut up and listen. Not in Lodi. Splattered amps and Monday Night Football. Nobody listening. Fanzine guy said we'll make it, though. Won't be long . . .

It wasn't long. It was never. They are stuck here in Lodi again. Lodi is the name of typical towns in California, New Jersey, Ohio, Mississippi, or Alaska. Though bereft of *Billboard* HOT 100 honors, the guys and girls in this hopeful band are working musicians. They are one step up from gig-less basement bands – chiming their lightning riffs and clever chords to a creaky tape machine. And hooking their dreams to a lost blue star. Our stuck-in-Lodi guys may have day jobs that pay. The Holiday Inn or Best Western or Howard Johnson gig may pay them $200 a night. Plus all the beer they can keep down.

"Lodi" is a great song by a premier Rock and Roll group. CCR and *Gold* Rush dedicate "Lodi" to all the bands who fudged that their record was #13 in Japan, or all the bands who warbled Morris Albert's "Feelings" (#6, 8-75) to an unfeeling Dew Drop Dip lounge-lizard clientele. "Lodi" salutes all the bass guitarists who chortled with lukewarm groupies in romantic rendezvous in naugahyde booths. "Lodi" goes out to all the great Blues/Rock bands since the dawn of time whose records only hit #77 in Kalamazoo. Or all the bands who sang their guts out to a blasé bland bunch of tin-ear brawlers who never heard a note.

"Lodi" corrals the has-beens, the never wuzzes, the maybe-someday bands. "Lodi" is for all the bands who long to get their name in little lights for "Johnny B. Not-Bad." Or, MEDIOCRITY RULES! In the real world, these prisoners of Lodi will never see their name in lights. If they're lucky, somebody's sister Sue will paint a dinky wavy sign for their bass drum. You hear the rolling Fogertys' guitars wail. Their bleak lonesome chords bemoan the Lodi sentence. No fancy frills. Just honest, throbbing, rhythm-guitar Rock and Roll. Dash of the Blues. **Janis** never worked in Lodi. She streaked across the starry sky, a blazing comet of Bold Brash Blues.

Lodi is neither heaven or hell for working musicians. Lodi is limbo. Starting up as the Golliwogs and Blue Velvets, **Creedence** must have started here in some fame-forsaken Lodi. It is rumored they played an early Golliwog gig to nine people. Lodi is the outback apotheosis of musical humdrum. Say you want a hit record so bad you can taste it. What do you do? What unleashes the superstar or star from the Lizard Lounge Band, the Krumke Garage Band, or Bobby Freako's Basement Band? Who knows? *¿Quien sabe?*

Luck. Talent. Breaks. Who-you-know. What-you-know. Money. Timing. Pizzazz.

Sometimes, Lodi Limbo isn't so doggoned bad. With your day job and a dream, the weekend gig may still cash your big ticket. Your name in lights. Be good, Johnny.

Janis Joplin ran the vocal gamut. And gauntlet. At times in "Cry Baby" – she seemingly has two voices at the same time. Two actual voices singing a two-note chord in raspy simultaneous splendor. The most malleable instrument in Rock and Roll, Janis Joplin's shredded voice near the end could do it all: explode, jingle, roar, yelp, buzz, hurrah, hullabaloo, and thunder. Try her "Cry Baby." It is not a song. It is an adventure.

"Me and Bobby McGee" – Janis Joplin, #1(2), 1-71; NC, R & B. Flat broke in a seedy Baton Rouge train station, Janis glumly waits for a train that never makes the scene. She feels faded. Bobby, this guy she loves, flags down a truck. They head down the mighty Mississippi down by New Orleans in this Kris Kristofferson classic tune. In the big hot rig, she blows a homey lonesome tune on her harmonica. Bobby sings. Blues. They travel the road of life. Together. For awhile.

They hold hands. The metronome windshield wipers slap time as they sing. People who can't commit one lousy school poem to memory can often sing 1000 different songs – memorized by osmosis in some sidelong back closet of the mysterious brain. Bobby and she groove to the wheeling road-quest adventure of life itself. Poverty, yep. Love? We got that, too.

Kristofferson went to Oxford after a football career, and then janitorialized Nashville recording studios till his own big break came, culminating in his Country hymn "Why Me?" – #16, 4-73; #1 C. He knew the David Houston-Tammy Wynette classic "My Elusive Dreams" (#89 HOT 100, '67, and #49, '75 for great Rockabilly Charlie Rich. The vagabond lover drags his significant-other from a little Nebraska farm up to a possible gold strike in Alaska. His dreams never pan out. When Kris wrote "Me and Bobby McGee," he already had a good start. Country music, in so many ways, is just another home for the Blues.

So Janis follows Bobby from coal mines in Kentucky and out to the California sun. They're shopping for summertime.

Off to California's Promised Land, things are peachy-keen between her and Bobby. Through ramshackle nights of sleety desolation, he shields her from the burning cold. Then – the inevitable break-up. . . In the heart of the Promised Land, *Grapes of Wrath* author John Steinbeck's own heavenly Salinas, near San Francisco. Then she sadly feels him slip-sliding away, like so many road-fever nomads since the dawn of time, and the sunset of commitment. He's a wayfarer, a seeker, a groper, a pilgrim on the road to destiny. An all-man Allman-style RAMBLIN' MAN.

Aren't we all? Aren't we all wayfaring strangers, reeling through this woe-besotted world, as **Burl Ives** ("A Little Bitty Tear" #9, 12-61) so folksily sang in the traditional "Wayfaring Stranger"? Bobby disappears, she wishes him well, they go on alone.

This song is a bitter end to Woodstock. It prophesied a new Throwaway Era of relationships. You hang your love out to dry, and buy new clothes when the old ones aren't looking. Though Janis's dream gets busted way back in Baton Rouge, she rides the aftermath all the way to the Beach Boys' California sun. Or as Ada Jones and **Billy Murray** sang to #1 in 1909, "Shine On, Harvest Moon."

"Summertime" – Janis Joplin, NC, 1969. Genesis' lead singer **Peter Gabriel** had a nice (NC) 1994 version, but Joplin's rendition has a left-field shot [with Flamingos' "Love Walked In"] at being the BEST GERSHWIN ever recorded. Listen to it, and see if YOU don't think Janis performs the impossible – singing two notes at the same time. A honeysuckle vignette of Southern summertime splendor: fish jump, cotton rises high, the sun beams, and Momma hushes her fretful wee babe in the summer glow. "Me and Bobby McGee" first hit Nashville in 1969 via **Roger Miller** (#12 C). By the time Janis's posthumous swan song was released, we hardly had time to find out just what we'd lost. In the best Orbisonic crescendo tradition, Janis builds her beautiful song. The first verse takes off on the Folk Key of 'G,' but by the second verse we power shift into the Rock and Roll/Blues favorite – 'A' major. Then the riffs begin.

From Big Brother to the Kozmic Blues Band to her last band, Full Tilt Boogie, Janis gave everybody everything she had. Shuffling among her last-ditch memories was a wish to return to her high school class reunion, where the in-group had taunted her as a tomboy. She wanted to arrive as PEARL, shrouded in furs and glory.

She was finally shrouded by an overdose of heroin, complicated by alcohol and other drugs. She staggered alone back to her hotel room at the time. Her friend had forgotten to show up. She had a new boyfriend. Life was looking up for her. She was trying to kick all her self-destructive habits. It was too late. **Don McLean** met a Blues-singing girl who looked a lot like **Janis**. Smiling, she turned away.

"American Pie" – Madonna [Rupert Everett, backing vocals], #29, 2-2000. #1, rest of the world. The Pontiac Michigan ex-cheerleader reprised the second most popular song ever on a 1999 VH-1 poll vote (see next chapter). Madonna's melodic version stalled at #29, because some dense mogul decided kids would no longer get the opportunity to buy American single records – and must buy the whole album (soundtrack to Madonna's movie *The Next Best Thing*), or score freebie singles downloads on Napster. **Rupert Everett** joins Madonna on low fifths harmony, and adds a cushy blend to her sweet version. Madonna's "American Pie" is a Blues byway.

R & R purists may disagree, but I think Madonna's rendition of the Hudson troubadour's rock saga is pretty good. Rupert and Madonna's lighthearted promenade is a sprightly weekend in the park, not a decade's American odyssey of bittersweet R & R tragicomedy. To Madonna's credit, she credits the girl that sang Blues – the great **Janis Joplin**. Here is the unforgivable sin of the millennial edition of the Chevy/levee/dry Rock capsule history – Madonna's 2000 handlers forgot to include the most important line about the superstar the song salutes in the first place (the widowed-bride reference to Rock primary pioneer **BUDDY HOLLY**). Aside from the torn lyric darting like a headless chicken after the best part was chopped away, Madonna's vocal is beautifully enunciated, cozy with sweet major chords, and abuzz with talented versatility.

Indeed, Madonna shares with the great Buddy Holly this gift to reinvent one's musical style to the song. Madonna's "American Pie" is not a travesty – it's an oversight. The sin of omission? The cut-up version basically ignores the mysterious **Morrison/Hendrix/Joplin** aura that interfaced the dying decade – into the shrieking strobelight pandemonium of Madonna's 70s Disco and 80s Dance phases. In her sweet purling voice, and giddy girlish glee in "American Pie," you know that Buddy's spirit still reigns over Rock & Roll like Santa over Christmas. . .

Jimi Hendrix

Stax of Soul

BLUES and SOUL sound a lot alike. Our former chapter "Stax of Soul" is excerpted briefly here to make room for some photos of your favorite artists. This is what we featured: First, Motown never had a monopoly on Soul Music. The great stuff came, too, from **Ahmet Ertegun** and **Jerry Wexler** at Atco/Atlantic Records. Or form Stax/Volt and the Muscle Shoals, Alabama, studio that featured great white Soul session artists like bassist **Donald 'Duck' Dunn** and guitar guru **Steve Cropper,** who began with #3, 8-62 **Booker T. & the MG's** "Green Onions." We gave **Ray Charles** credit for leading off Soul music with #1(1) R&B, 1-55 "I Got a Woman," and we touted Jerry Lee 'SMOOCHIE' Smith's #3, 7-61 Mar-Keys' instrumental "Last Night." They became the MG's – and went on to show great backup respect for the man who wrote Aretha's #1, '67 "Respect" – the great **Otis Redding** (1941-67). Otis's frantic "Respect" version hit #35, 10-65 (#4 R&B). We followed **James Brown**'s unsubtle pure

Soul sound on #8, 4-66 "It's a Man's Man's Man's World" and #15, 7-70 (#2 R&B) "Get Up (I Feel Like Being a Sex Machine (Part I)." **Little Richard**'s #44, 7-56 "Reddy Teddy" (#8 R&B), Eddie Floyd's #28, 9-66 "Knock on Wood," and **Wilson Pickett**'s Falcons' #17, 4-59 "You're So Fine" (#2 R&B) orbited **Aretha Franklin**'s blockbuster #1(2), 4-67 "Respect" (#1 for 8 weeks R&B). We featured Otis Redding's "Try a Little Tenderness" – #25, 12-66, #4 R&B.

Sly & the Family Stone's #1(4), 1-69 "Everyday People" is a great plea for Rock and Soul multicultural understanding, and **Bobby 'Blue' Bland**'s #28, 12-61 "Turn on Your Lovelight" (#2 R & B) shone the way. We contrasted the disparity between HOT 100 chart numbers and R & B numbers (somehow, **Jimi Hendrix** never hit the R & B charts). We saluted pioneer **Nappy Brown** and the Zippers' #57, 1-57 "Little by Little" (NC R & B), and his #25, 4-55 "Don't Be Angry" (#2 R&B); his sax-powered scorchers predated Elvis and even Little Richard. We did Arthur Conley's #2, 3-67 "Sweet Soul Music," **Johnny Taylor**'s #5, 10-68 "Who's Makin' Love" switcheroo, and White Soulster Roy Head's #2(2), 9-65 (#2 R & B) "Treat Her Right." **Joe Tex**'s #10, 10-67 "Skinny Legs and All" and Frankie Ford's #14, 2-59 "Sea Cruise" doubled up with British semi-Soul **Fortunes**' #7, 8-65 "You've Got Your Troubles" and mixed Jamaica/British **Foundations**' #3, 1-69 eternal oldie, "Build Me Up, Buttercup." Vintage Soul is supplied by Jessie Hill's #28, 3-60 "Ooh Poo Pah Doo."

We chased the Philly Soul sounds of the #2(2), 3-75 **Stylistics** on "You Make Me Feel Brand New" and #10, 10-72 "I'm Stone in Love with You." Or Ferndale, Michigan's **Spinners** on **Sam Cooke**'s "Cupid"/"I've Loved You for a Long Time." We did **Smokey Robinson**'s post-Miraculous #2(3), 2-81 [#1(5) R&B] "Being With You," and Scottish-American falsetto Michigan **David Lasley**'s #36, 3-82 "If I Had My Wish Tonight." David's brother Dean told a story about this fearless NYC cabbie (#1 dangerous job) getting kicked out of a car in pitch-black Northern Michigan. Terrified of bears, he spent the night in a tall tree, shuddering and trembling, as giant 30-pound raccoons circled below in ambush (nary a bear).

The **Gladys Knight and Pips** section surveyed her #1(2), 9-73 "Midnight Train to Georgia" (originally PLANE), and "I Heard it Through the Grapevine." This segues to **Marvin Gaye**'s #1-ever Motown "Grapevine" of #1(7), 1-68, plus raucous #8, 3-65 "I'll Be Doggone" (#1 R&B). **Al Wilson**'s parable from Genesis "The Snake" hit #27, 8-68, and covers a tenderhearted chick who revives some venomous snake that bites her when she hugs the slithery monstrosity. Moral: GIRLS – some guys are snakes – ditch the abusers early-on, and pick the gentler guys for romance.

In keeping with *Gold Rush* policy to integrate sounds, tans, and genders, we mentioned R & R band Creedence Clearwater's #43 "Grapevine" (NC, R &B) version, and moved on to Soul legend **Curtis Mayfield**'s (1942-99) tremendous #20, 10-61 "Gypsy Woman" (#2 R&B). Thematically, we covered Cher's #1(2), 5-71 "Gypsys, Tramps, and Thieves," and blond teen idol Brian Hyland's #3, 9-70 "Gypsy Woman" cover. We applauded Curtis Mayfield's **Impressions** on #4, 9-63 "It's All Right" and #14, 12-67 "We're a Winner" (both #1 R&B).

Philly Soul again marked "STOP (The Sound of Philadelphia)' at #1(2), 3-74 by Three Degrees, **Harold Melvin & Blue Notes**' #3, 9-72 "If You Don't Know Me by Now," and the un-Irish Ohio **O'Jays**' sensational upbeat #1(1), 1-73 "Love Train." Sam Cooke's nephew **R. B. Greaves** inherited his crystal tenor for #1(2), 10-60 "Take a Letter, Maria," about guy's cheating wife (and his instant sweet secretary solution). Original Philly Soul was from Anthony Gourdine's BROOKLYN (5'9" **'Little' Anthony & the Imperials**') – astounding #4, 8-58 "Tears on My Pillow" and #16, 6-65 "Take Me Back," a paragon of emotion and unrequited love.

We surveyed the fledgling **Jackson Five**: #2(3), 4-71 "Never Can Say Goodbye"; Michael Jackson/Other Four's #1(1), 8-72 sentimental song "Ben" to an actual RAT, and Bobby Day's original on #2(1), 8-58, "Rockin' Robin" (#7, 3-72, J5), plus #1, 3-70 "ABC" by J5. We did younger sister **Janet Jackson**'s debut #64, 12-82 "Young Love" (#6 R&B). We followed the white **Osmonds**, with a J5 Soul echo ("One Bad Apple", #1[5], 2-71, NC R&B) and similar gorgeous sister (Marie, #5, 9-73, #1 C, "Paper Roses"). **Rare Earth**'s life-celebrating #7, 7-71 "I Just Want to Celebrate" (#30, 9-71 R&B) is a rare Motown Caucasian crew, like Toronto star I worked with at Motown writing songs (1966), **R. Dean Taylor** (#66, 2-71 "Ain't It a Sad Thing," and

#5, 9-70 "Indiana Wants Me," about a fugitive on the lam). British Soul/Disco/Rock star Leo Sayer's #2(5), 9-80 "More Than I Can Say" we traced to **Bobby Vee** roots, as penned by Crickets Jerry Allison and Sonny Curtis – #61, Bobby, 2-61, but #3, 4-61 in Sayer's U.K. (also we did Vee's #33, 4-61 flipside "Stayin' In," banned for violence because of a schoolroom punch in the nose [see Tu-Pac]).

Major Lance was 6'6" – a foot and an inch for each UM: #5, 1-64 "Um, Um, Um, Um, Um, Um." **Bobby Lewis** had #1 song of 1961 – insomniac's lament (over lost love), "Tossin' and Turnin'," followed by #9, 8-61 "One Track Mind." Lance (1942-94) was a great guy who sent me umpteen pix for the *Rock Revolution* (1966). Britsoul gushes forth from iron-pipes **Joe Cocker** in #1(3), 10-82 "Up Where I Belong." Beginning with Mike Berry, and gravitating to Union Lake's Elle Ortwein, Cocker thrived (#68, 11-68, #1 U.K.) "With a Little Help from My Friends" (Beatle tune). His #69, 10-69 "Delta Lady," and Boxtops' cover (#1, '67) "The Letter" (#7, 4-70, Joe C), took him to "Up Where We Belong" partner Jennifer Warnes's "Right Time of the Night" (#6, 1-77). His #5, 1-75 "You Are So Beautiful" is the Soul of White Blues balladry.

We dug **Tom Waits**'s amazing NC, '76 "I Wish I Was in New Orleans." His froggy baritone and firebomb lyrics are filtered through five packs of Old Golds daily – and his Blues-giant imitation of Louis Satchmo Armstrong is impeccable. In a booze fog, Tom's song-guy rhapsodizes his jaded Mardi Gras glories and catastrophes. Under a Dixie moon, with raggedy shards of a life once full, and now bloated with beer and regret, Waits etches his romantic reverie in gold Soul. We include Tom's "Downtown Train" (#3, 11-89, **Rod Stewart**). We do Scotsman Stewart's Soul salutes: #48, 6-85 "People Get Ready" (**Impressions**, #14, 2-6), about a fast train to the Promised Land; #24, 11-71 "(I Know) I'm Losing You," **Temptations**' #8, 11-66 (#1 R&B) tune; and **Sam Cooke**'s classic #9, 2-62 (#1 R&B) "Twistin' the Night Away" (#59, 8-73, and #80, 7-87); Rod's #83, 1-76 and #10, 3-90 "This Old Heart of Mine" shows you can't keep a great **Isley Brothers** song (#12, 2-66, #6 R&B) down.

Great Soul tunes by **Sam & Dave**' Sam Moore (b. Miami, '35) and Dave Prater (1937-88, car accident) stomped the competition: #21, 4-66 Ed McCoy favorite (#1 R&B) "Hold On! I'm A Comin'"; #9, 1-68 (#4 R&B) "I Thank You," and Billy Joel's #112 debut cover with Hassles, **Sam & Dave**'s #7 R&B, 12-66 "You Got Me Hummin'." The Cornelius Brothers and Sister Rose did #3, 4-71 (only #20 R&B) "Treat Her Like a Lady" and gorgeous #2(2), 5-72 "Too Late to Turn Back Now." We cameoed the **Fantastic Johnny C**'s #7, 10-67 "Boogaloo Down Broadway," 2002 Rock Hall inductee **Isaac Hayes**'s #1(2), 10-71 "Theme from Shaft," and Wild Cherry's #1(3), 6-76 "Play That Funky Music."

We covered **Wilson Pickett**'s (b. '41, Prattville, Alabama) #1(1), 6-65 R&B "In the Midnight Hour" #21 HOT 100); his #23, 11-66 (#6 R&B) energetic "Mustang Sally"; "Funky Broadway," at #8, 8-67, #1 R&B, with trad Pickett rump-kickin' beat; and Pickett's #32, 4-67 (#6 R&B) "I Found a Love." We explored **Otis Redding**'s nifty cover of Jagger/Stones' "Satisfaction" to #31, 3-66 (#4 R&B).

We celebrated **Aretha Franklin**'s coming of age as the Queen of soul – beyond the ho-hum ballads she began with; we checked out her #100(1), 9-62 "Try a Little Tenderness," and jumped to : #7, 5-68 (#1 R&B) "Think"; #2(2), 7-71 "Spanish Harlem"; and her Beatle #17, 11-69 "Eleanor Rigby" with its tremulous cello and ghostly counterpoint that remembers this lonely lady (now memorialized as a cherished statue on a Liverpool park bench). Then we did Aretha's street-savy #7, 9-85 "Who's Zoomin' Who." Aretha was born in Elvis's Memphis (3-25-42), and raised at the New Bethel Baptist Church in Detroit by her preacher dad. Like Tina Turner's wayward mother, Aretha too, was abandoned by her MOTHER. Dad splitting is bad enough, but MOM? You could ask John Lennon, if he were here. Singers often find superstardom as a consolation prize for childhood miseries.

Answering the misery problem, Aretha found religion to segue into our Religious Rock chapter, after our upcoming Timeless Troubadors. From her #10, 8-68 "I Say a Little Prayer" [Dionne Warwick, #4, 10-67], Aretha traveled over a "Bridge Over Troubled Water" (#6, 4-71, #1 R&B) – finding that bond of friendship so well described in Simon and Garfunkel's #1(5), 2-70 original. Rock and Soul share deep commitment, great friendship, precious love.

After a hearty slice of "American Pie," we'll journey over "A Bridge Over Troubled Water" to discover the deeper meanings of our musical pilgrimage.

Timeless Troubadours

23

Gold Rush veers off into a new direction here. Like the Yukon and Klondike Rivers split at Dawson City, in the Yukon, *Gold Rush* splits in two as well. The first part, remember, was a chronological survey. The next part of *Gold Rush* is thematic. We follow various musical, lyrical, and historical ideas. Even a few fashion fads. We'll roughly follow timelines of many different Rock styles: Soul, Religious Rock, Disco, Jazz Rock, Heartland Rock, Heavy Metal, Punk Rock, Glitz Rock, Singer/Songwriters, Latino Rock and Salsa, Sports Rock, Light Metal or Easy Listening, Country Rock, Women in Rock (though they're obviously everywhere else in *Gold Rush*), MTV and Rock Flicks, plus some New Directions from Hip Hop to Grunge, Celtic Renaissance, and the New Folk and Disco and Latino sounds. Your favorites? They're here. Check them out.

So long, Miss American Pie. **Don McLean** (b. 10-2-45), bard of New York's Hudson River Valley, was the first major Rock and Roller to truly realize that Rock already had a long and noble history. Unlike the stubbier and fluffier version by **Madonna**, Don McLean's "American Pie" is eight minutes long, like "Light My Fire." McLean's panorama was voted the #2 most important hit of all time to distill the whole (VH-1, 2000) Rock canon.

Don McLean joins a group of major singer/songwriters dominating the industry for over a generation. Instead of a horizontal Rock history, our 1971 watershed year will now cause us to shift to vertical contributions. Many artists in the Singer/Songwriter crew – like **Elton John, Billy Joel, Rod Stewart**, or **James Taylor** – have scored hits for 30+ ultra-marathon years.

"Killing Me Softly" – Roberta Flack, #1(5), 1-73; #2(4), 2-73 R &B. Teacher **Roberta Flack** (b. '39) starred on piano at neighborhood recitals, and prestigious Howard University in Washington. Teaching music in North Carolina, she scored on three classics (before venturing into her own sterling compositions): "You've Got a Friend" #29, 6-71, "You've Lost That Lovin' Feeling" #71, 10-71, and the Shirelles/Carole King's timeless admonition to innocence – Roberta's #76, 1-72 "Will You Still Love Me Tomorrow?" Then the big one hit. Earthquake. A-Bomb. Anyhow, Number One. Seventies' solo songwriters (and beyond) underscore two tenets of New Easy Rock and Roll: 1) Get a little bit softer and don't bust their eardrums; and 2) Write it yourself:

Fugees hit #2(3)A [Airplay], 3-96 with a Reggae beat on this Flack hit. Roberta scored #1(6), 3-72 (#4, R & B) with "The First Time Ever I Saw Your Face." About "Face." It's a first-time lesson in enunciation. Flack's powerful alto ascends into soprano range, with quavering tremolo. After "Face" fired Flack into the singer/songwriter 6-week spotlight, she scored again – "Where Is the Love?" (#5, 6-72) with former classmate **Donny Hathaway**, prodigious producer-songwriter-singer-arranger-piano player (b. 1945, Chicago; d. 1979 jumping off 15th floor of Essex House, by NYC Central Park). Soft Soul star Hathaway also scored with #2, 2-78 "The Closer I Get to You."

Lori Lieberman wrote "Killing Me Softly" after watching New Rochelle troubadour **Don McLean** sing his enchanting Rock and Roll historical panorama. It all connects.

"American Pie" – Don McLean, #1(4), 12-71. Don dedicated this song and album (*American Pie*, #1[7], 12-71) to **Buddy Holly**. The Fugee-Flack-Lieberman-McLean-Holly connection? These interlocking directorates conjoin musical generations, far beyond old loves and misty memories. McLean (pronounced MacLane) reflects my grandmother Rachel MacLean's (Nana's) Scottish MacLean clan. Don's American roots go deep into the fertile green Rip Van Winkle Catskill bluffs, foothills of the Mohawk Vale ("Bonnie Eloise," #1, 1838), and Hudson River Valley above mammoth Manhattan.

Buddy Holly? Don sings that he's not sure he cried after reading about Buddy's widowed bride, Maria, of five months. It affected him as a teenager deeply. In pure crystal Scots tenor, via his signature song's unofficial title – he cites The Day that the great Music Died. Holly. The Day this Music Died? – FEBRUARY 3, 1959. Half of the universe can also name **Ritchie Valens** (Rock Hall, 2001, "Donna"/"LaBamba", #'s 2 & 22, 1-59) and the Big Bopper ("Chantilly Lace," #6, 8-58). Rock History quiz whizzes may recall semi-skilled pilot Roger Peterson, and his rickety Beechcraft Bonanza, 18° 35-mph blizzard. Or the three stars' last concert – Surf Ballroom, Iowa, 1313 miles from any ocean's surf, on the wintry tundra of Clear Lake, just a snowy meadow south of Minnesota. *The Buddy Holly Story* (1978****) and *La Bamba* (1987****) stir students today to gaze into the distant mirror of Winter 1959. **Gary Busey** sang the sound track and became Buddy, shedding 40 beefy pounds and dyeing his strawberry-blond hair black and curly. Maria Elena Holly watched the film 19 years later, of Busey's portrayal in horn-rimmed glasses and supercharged Fender Stratocaster. Through his little combo – Allison, Mauldin, and Nicki Sullivan – **Buddy Holly** moved the world.

How many 50-year-old execs can sing or Rap these? "The Crossroads" (Bone Thugs-N-Harmony) #1, '98; or #2, 10-2000, "Ms. Jackson" (Outkast)? Many aged-out retired teenagers forget to listen to the music which fires up the following generation. "American Pie," however, would not go away, for all generations.

In the aftermath of the untimely departure of Hendrix, Joplin, Morrison, Gene Vincent, Otis Redding, and Rolling Stone Brian Jones, Don McLean was impelled to write a song which panoramically zoomed the whole glorious Age of Rock and Roll. Why didn't Don begin with **Johnny Ace** (1929-54, Russian roulette, rock pioneer of "Pledging My Love," #17, 2-55)? Or **Chuck Willis** (1928-58, peritonitis, bluesmaster of "C.C. Rider" #12, 4-57, later #10, '85 by Mitch Ryder)? Somehow, McLean realized they hadn't the universal appeal of guy-next-door Buddy Holly. What about **Ritchie Valens**? Or **Eddie Cochran** (1938-60), Minnesotan "Summertime Blues" #8, 8-58 star killed in a 70 mph taxi smash-up in London? Buddy was the true legend with the biggest sound of all; he became a major compartment in Don McLean's soul.

"American Pie" defines the soul of America. Popular music is a mirror of our culture. Entire wars have been dusted into fragile peace with the impact of a song like Glen Campbell's "Galveston." "American Pie" rings a decade in a rainbow of nevermore oblivion. "American Pie" chronicles the rise of rock music, its golden heyday, and its backslide from sweet innocence and simplicity to acid-glutted jaded overcomplexity and strident cacophony. Don McLean: "I liked Buddy Holly because he spoke to me." Buddy spoke to me, too. I was just 16 and too old for my *Detroit News* paper route in shivery February. When that flimsy Bonanza fell out of a starless sky, it chucked my tottering childhood into the dumpster. Our folks couldn't figure out our fuss. Every kid in America (and the U.K.) had the rug pulled out from underneath. No more wistful world of "Peggy Sue" castles in Spain. The lemon-meringue menu for our wispy chiffon bouttonniere prom was instantly downsized to moldy bread and water.

Remember Buddy's incredible contributions to Rock and Roll? Don did. Check out a few cameos:

1. American Holly proteges appeared from every hamlet and garage: Bobby Vee, Tommy Roe, Gene Pitney, the Bobby Fuller Four, and the post-Holly Crickets themselves.

2. Holly's stunning sound leapfrogged the Big Pond. His U.K. aura eclipsed Buddy's Stateside rep: the **Hollies**, Herman's Hermits, the Stones' ["Not Fade Away"], Gerry & the Pacemakers, Billy J. Kramer, the Tremelos, the Beatles, and Eric Clapton.

3. Buddy first fronted the now-regular band set-up: lead singer plays lead guitar; drummer, bass, and rhythm guitar do back-up band track and vocals. Look at Beatles, Beach Boys, Eagles.

4. Holly shared record production, spotting Norm and Vi Petty at controls.

5. Buddy left-handedly created the Motown Soul Empire for Berry Gordy, via brother Robert Gordy's "Everyone Was There" #96, 11-58.

6. Holly provided a role model for us all: humble, friendly, unassuming, inventive, pioneering, and fun-loving.

7. As Keith Richard(s) said, "Buddy was one of us. He was a real troubadour, man. He paid his dues, and without Buddy there'd really be no Rock and Roll as we know it or any kind of Beatles or Rolling Stones."

8. Buddy Holly popularized the troubadour motif that sparked the 70s and beyond – singer/songwriters. Holly typifies the Softer Rock sound of Don McLean, James Taylor, or Paul Simon. Soft Rock Singer/Songwriters like Elton John echoed Buddy.

Inspiring Motown, "American Pie's" Buddy got everybody 'Dancing in the Street.' He spoke to Don McLean, and he spoke to me, and he speaks to you today from "That'll Be the Day" or Madonna's "American Pie." Or **Shania Twain**'s "Man! I Feel Like a Woman," of #34, 5-99 Holly hiccup fame. When that plane went down in surfless Iowa, Rock and Roll grew up.

"American Pie" is an appreciation of the 50s, and an elegy to the 60s. McLean sets up his panoramic 8-minute cast of thousands: the "King" is **Elvis**, the 'Jester' is **Bob Dylan**. Jumpin' Jack Flash is **Mick Jagger**. As the King of Rock looked down, the Jester usurped his hard-earned Crown of Thorns. Wow, profound theology here. The Rock and Roll diorama almost flips fabulously into a medieval morality play – with Dylan's thorny crown a bold allusion to Jesus wearing the Crown of Thorns on His miserable trek from Golgotha (the 'place of skulls') to Calvary and the Cross. No one was ever foolish enough to say that KING was an easy job. Elvis, of course, bore the crown of thorns, figuratively, as a SIZZLING ELVIS SPOTLIGHT bore down upon his fevered brow atop a wriggling jumpsuit of lost youth. Obviously, we can't compare Elvis too closely to Jesus, as Elvis's Rock and Roll quest was simply a materialistic vocal enterprise – buttressed by a lot of soulful striving. Jesus' mission, obviously, was to save mankind from the oppression of sin. Elvis, like the rest of us, was one of those part-time sinners who could use a little saving.

When McLean refers to the Jester, hobbled on sidelines wearing a cast, he covers **Bob Dylan**'s own near-fatal 1966 motorcycle accident. At the heart of his R & R deification by pop pundits, Bob donned the Disabled List cloak with a nasty fractured neck. It took him out of the garish public eye for a year. It also deepened some of his morose fixin'-to-die lyrics:

Then Don lumps our whole dizzying 60s generation under one intergalactic banner; we are the 'lost-in-space' generation. Drifting. Spinning. Oscillating in orbit. Perplexed kids of the infant 70s didn't know whether to protest the vanishing war or publicize the seven-eyed fish snagged near Homer Simpson's glowingly-reviewed Nuclear Power Plant.

The lost generation in inner space didn't know whether to smoke dope or Camels or nothing, whether to believe in organized religion or mysticism. Or nothing. Or worship alfalfa sprouts. Do we have to, they implored, strangle in a fancy-schmancy suit and tie in front of some 1000-brained computer about to be invented, that'll downsize us all to 2¼ hamburger jobs and clinical depression with no affordable clinics?

Since more suit and tie folks exist in Millennium III, staring at the Cathode Cyclops of their glowering computer monitors, than there are tie-dyed Deadhead geodesic dome dwellers in granny dresses and broccoli-raising glee, let's assume that Don's Lost in Space Generation has been found. Let us not assume that they are all over-joyed about it. Not all of Pearl Jam or Smashing Pump-kins or Creed or Nirvana's chords are happy, fun-time tonic major chords, plink-plunking in euphoric joy and Dairy Queen-slurping ecstasy.

When Don's Jack Flash sits on a hot seat candlestick, the 60s generation, groping along, begins to lose direction. It's an allusion to **Mick Jagger**, plus the Crazy World of Arthur Brown's mega-hit, "Fire" (#2[1], 9-68). Positive vibes and free-love energy that went into a committed and idealistic generation were symbolically shattered. At the late-60s Altamont California Festival Rolling Stones concert, promoters stupidly hired only Hell's Angels as "rent-a-cop" security. Unfortunately, head-busting went with the territory. Stoned and rowdy revellers partied on amok into the grapy leather-fringe flamingo dusk. Jack Flash, a/k/a Mick Jagger, tried a "Start Me Up" (#2[3], 8-81) rou-tine with the Stones. On the downbeat, an overzealous Hell's Angel manhanded a front-row fan. When the acrid smoke had cleared, the fan died. This rotten incident did more to halt all humungoid Rock Festivals in the late sixties than any other regular bummers or downers: O.D.'s, naked frolickers, sanitary nightmares, gridlock catastro-phes, starvation, sunstroke, or temporary deafness from the Grateful Dead's 23 miles of roaring amps turned up to a zillion.

Don says everybody rose to dance, but nobody got a chance. A vagabond generation, with two left feet apiece – dangled in outer space. The band? Beatles' *Sergeant Pepper*, #1(15) '67 of course, the most influential album of the decade. Sergeants, he says, furnished a melody, but no one could dance, because the band wouldn't get off the field. Beatle Blues, however, were beaten back by the thumping nightsticks of Mayor Daley's Chicago gen-darmes in their gung-ho crusade for law, order, and cur-few. Then he met up with a Blues-belting lass, echoing Janis Joplin. She sparked a grim coda. After the Febru-

ary 3, 1959 'Death-of-the-Music' interlude into our opti-mistic consciousness, we witnessed the British Invasion (Beatles' "Helter Skelter" about grisly Charles Manson murders, and 'Jack Flash' watching a fan die in utter hor-ror) against a backdrop of California terror. The Byrds flew "Eight Miles High" (#14, 4-66), plummeting fast. Like many ill-fated planes and dreams.

"American Pie" employs really two songs, musically. The first one is the floating verse. It shuffles around VI and III minor chords, building a foreshadowing aura of impend-ing doom. Don's voice is so innocent and pure and friendly, though, that when you blast back to the happy-tune Buddy Holly chorus, it beguiles you bewitchingly into believing that all is well and fair and fun in 50s America – forever-more. As McLean strums the groovy **G major** tonic chord for his zippy chorus, we know our revelry is just tempo-rary. Beyond the neon dazzle lurks darkness. McLean tantalizes us with both frisky and funereal tempos. Be-ginning with an unplugged-generation acoustic flourish, he lets his fine voice do the painting of this breathtaking canvas. After he mentions Buddy's expectant wife, Maria, then the tempo glides into a slow, deliberate chorus. Vir-tuosos ply the throbbing bass and swirling piano. Into Verse Two, he jacks up the pace to Rock and Roll rhythm, and the song takes off for two shimmering sides and eight simmering minutes.

"American Pie" is a masterpiece of crescendo and de-crescendo, shuddering to a gloomy halt, at the somber revelations of **Janis Joplin** at her own Armageddon battle-field. His mystery girl socks it to the Blues. How appro-priate. Janis's message bodes no pie in the sky. No pink bunny and canary-yellow Tweety and smiley purple Barney the dinosaur, or pretty "Peggy Sue." Janis, with no happy news, smiles and turns away. The music is gone from the holy store.

Our favorite songs carry nearly religious overtones. We chant them, as we would the litany. We memorize them, as *Bible/Torah* passages. We love them, as precious parts of our struggling family of man. They are as deep as belief. "American Pie" is not Pat Boone's "Wonderful Time Up There" Boogie to Heaven. If Rock and Roll represents a secular religion, then Holly's songs are sacred to Don McLean. Is Buddy Holly, then, killing us softly with his song? NO. Holly's song uplifts McLean's poetic spirit, and inspires one of the top melodies in the history of Rock and Roll.

Like many religious saints, Holly's career is crucified on a cross of modern technology; a tiny plane, facing the gigantic cosmic terror of snow-swept arctic skies, plunges into the nevermore abyss. All is lost. When Don and I, and maybe you, lose our faith in nice guys like Buddy Holly finishing first, a bit of our own religious tapestry unravels.

One earthquake song. "American Pie" shepherds Rock and Roll's birth and starry-eyed innocence. Then it low-ers the boom. Don's sweet chorus is a cotton-candy con-fection of a pleasant Hollytone 'Oh Boy' melody. As his beautiful *Brigadoon* tenor lollygags over the Mount Everest notes, dark storm clouds clump on the far gray horizon.

At least the good ol' boys supposedly chugging rye and whisky survived. Their tippling feats were a tad exaggerated by Don McLean, but RYE is a good rhyme for die. "American Pie" makes everyone consider his own mortality. Some happy news? Buddy's Crickets are alive and well, and into their seventh decade. [Holly Memorial Societ Veep George Nettleton tells me the 2001+ rumor about Peterson's Beechcraft Bonanza being named the "American Pie" is totally false.]

More than ten major stars have participated in tales about giving their own Beechcraft Bonanza ticket and seat to feverish **Ritchie Valens**; among this crew left to mourn are **Paul Anka**, guitarist **Tommy Allsup**, **Dion**, Belmont **Carlo Mastrangelo**, and Country baritone star and 1959 Cricket '2nd-bass' man **Waylon Jennings**. Allsup has the best claim. His wallet was found in the wreckage, which did not burn. Allsup was a survivor, gleaning a 2000 Grammy – first regular Cricket to do so (Glen Hardin earned one years ago, but never appeared with Buddy Holly). Reports of his death, says Allsup in 1985 PBS interview, were exaggerated. Some laundry problem caused Buddy to take Tommy's wallet to show I.D. in Fargo, North Dakota. Land of **Bobby Vee** and **Bob Dylan**.

When my Gibson and I sang "American Pie" in Dr. Felheim's 1972 bemused University of Michigan class, Rock and Roll was finally bashing down the castle door of the academic ivory tower. Rock and Roll history has been snowballing ever since, with thousands of other Rock Lit pioneers like Dave Marsh and Peter Guralnick and Fred Bronson and Kim Bloxdorf and John Jackson and Tim White and Wayne Jancik. Academia is a bit sluggish. No matter. Buddy Holly lives, sez Sonny Curtis, every time we play Rock and Roll.

The rest of the McLean's Rock and Roll gospel? [Thanks to McLean's foresight, musicologists now study Rock as a new cousin of America's other just-admitted genres of music – Folk and Jazz].

On his last hit "Castles in the Air" (#36, 10-81) Don overshines his #105 remake of Buddy Holly's "Fool's Paradise" (#58, 8-58). Fluff stuff of love. Don's "Crying" (#5, 1-81; #6 C) shows only great singers like him need apply to this quintessential Roy Orbison classic Orbisong (#2, 8-61). Great versions too by Jay and the Americans (#25), Del Shannon, and Glen Campbell. Don's silver-medal song over his career, "Crying." Among his most interesting songs is peppy #21, 12-72 "Dreidel," about a little Jewish spinning top. In "Vincent" (#12, 3-72), Don poeticizes the career of Vincent Van Gogh, empathically painting a starry night vision of the tortured painter's fated life, and suicidal death. Don's sweet tune and verbal agility match the classic painter's whirling, swirling technique.

James Taylor (Boston '48) and wife **Carly Simon** (b. '45, NYC) are troubadour spouses. Her father owned Simon & Schuster Publishing Company; Taylor's dad was Dean of University of North Carolina, Medical School. As singers, songwriters, and lyric sculptors, they are a peerless duo of Easy Rock and Meaningful Roll. Taylor started off in a group called the Flying Machine in 1967. Paul

McCartney inducted Taylor, the first Beatles' Apple recording signee, into the Rock Hall of Fame in March 2000. "Smile a Little Smile for Me" hit #5, 10-69 for a different **Flying Machine**.

"Fire and Rain" – James Taylor, #3, 9-70. Recall his line about shattered flying machines? "Fire and Rain" is profound. Taylor scoops powerful innuendoes from quavering syllables. James hung out at Martha's Vineyard, Massachusetts, played the Bleeker Street, NYC coffeehouse panorama like the Bitter End, and underwent a bout with depression. Taylor's appeal? His easygoing light drawl, and his self-penned lyrics. Laced with universal problems and vulnerability they make us all not only sympathize, but empathize. We hear what he's singing, we feel it in our hearts, and maybe we, too, have been in somewhat similar emotional turmoil.

"Handy Man" – James Taylor, #4, 6-77. [#2, 12-59 for Jimmy Jones; #22, 7-64 for Del Shannon.] Taylor, Jones and Shannon have a Broken Heart Repair Shop. Pleasant new audial mirror of original singers' yestergenius. Taylor reprises: **Marvin Gaye**'s #6, 11-64 "How Sweet It Is to Be Loved by You" (#5, 6-75); #5, 11-62 Drifters' "Up on the Roof" (#28, 6-79); and a mellow #10, 8-58 Everly extravaganza "Devoted to You" with wife Carly in 1978 (#36). Taylor's signature hit?

"You've Got a Friend" – James Taylor, #1(1), 6-71. Follows haunting ballad debut "Carolina in My Mind," (#67, '70 and #118, '69). The early 70s witnessed the emergence of eight major new male rock stars: **James Taylor, Elton John, Jim Croce, Joe Cocker, John Denver, Rod Stewart, Don McLean** and **Billy Joel**. Though singer/songwriter Taylor borrowed "Friend" from friend **Carole King**, it's still a magnificent chunk of music, maybe Taylor's greatest hit. Peter Asher produced "You've Got a Friend." It surveys the boundaries of friendship, and discovers there are none. "Friend" is no gargantually gigantic symphonic production, like "Bridge Over Troubled Water," "Nights in White Satin," or "A Day in the Life." Taylor rides roughshod over fancy stuff in "Friend." He canters along in a minimalist folkish style, sprinkled with star-spangled sincerity. The song won two Grammys, one for Taylor and one for songwriter King. Friendship, yes, really matters. Why is it such a perennial favorite? Universality. We all know the POWER of its heartfelt message. The song slides along, burgeoning from minor to major to reflect a sympathetic mood for a friend in emotional need. The listener hears a spareness of instrumentation, a profundity of lyric power. The song breathes. When you're troubled, it promises, I will help you. What more could we ask?

Taylor's career drifts over an eclectic variety of Soft Rock styles and genres, like his **Sam Cooke** reprise (#12, 5-60) of "Wonderful World" (#17, 1-78). Unlike fellow baritone crooner and cover artist **Pat Boone**, whose right-on baritone floods each note, Taylor dances each tricky trapeze of melody with breathtaking Soul melismas, slurs, round-offs, and soaring glides through the wild blue yonder.

Other Taylor hits: #11, 3-81 "Her Town Too"; "Your Smiling Face" (#20, 10-77); "Don't Let Me Be Lonely Tonight" (#14, 12-72); and "Shower the People" (#22, 7-76). Whether skillfully rendering smooth Soul, or skimming the magic notes of his own hits, **James Taylor** is the consummate charismatic performer. His compassionate lyrics frame a way of life for his fans. His 6'4" basketball build adds a Lincolnesque tone of celestial height and authority to his song-weaving. Rock Hall Inductee 2000.

"You're So Vain" – Carly Simon, #1(3), 12-72. Taylor's former spouse Carly startles listeners by her lyrical hook about conceited listener. The vain guy, so they claim, is a composite combo of hubby James and Mick Jagger. Quite a compendium of complaints here in Carly's biggest hit. Her with-it alto strides right into the guy's bloated ego – his stomach is 'apricot,' and he has a yacht, and a Lear jet to chase eclipses. Musically, a battering bass line and throbbing drums keep the even-tempo tune rockin' at a steady roll.

"Nobody Does It Better" – Carly Simon, #2(3), 7-77. Ever get a little embarrassed with these full intimacy singer/songwriter manifestoes like this? I mean, like, I'm very happy that they're compatible in bed, and hey, it's no problem because they're even married and all that jazz. Why are they telling us the details of their bedded bliss? Nice song, but I prefer her non-personal #11, 8-80 "Jesse," where the dude just pours wine. As they seek the birds and bees to tell the world, maybe we'd prefer the birds: (James and Carly were married from 1972-83.)

"Mockingbird" – Carly Simon with James Taylor, #5, 2-74. Frantic Blues revision, with a great harmonic Simon-Taylor blend. The original was by **Inez and Charles Foxx** (#17, 6-63; #1[1], R & B). A brother-sister team, with hard-driving counterpoint harmony.

Anne Murray (b. '45) of Springhill, Nova Scotia fires down the Wimp Weather gauntlet:

"Wintery Feeling" – Anne Murray, NC, 11-79; #73, 2-80 C. Anne taught gym on Canada's smallest province, Prince Edward Island, an *Anne of Green Gables* misty wonderland of red clay, red potatoes, and hardy folk who don't wince at winter. Anne chides her California ex, who deserted "beautiful" Montreal, that Quebec's December sky shimmers with glimmering silver. Silver, not gloomy grey. With her Patti Page-style murmuring contralto, she makes the sun-seeking dude look like a weather wimp. She says if he never get cold, how can she keep him warm? In an easy climate, the sun gets taken for granted by those who run from storms. She says these snowflakes and she have seen countless drifters, who couldn't take the tough wintry weather, and fled to Florida. Her sweet Nova Scotia alto is as alluring as 2000+ Sarah McLachlan's soprano on her #4, 11-98 "Angel." California, she intones, is too plasticized, too flamingoey, too

warm, snowless, and too easy. If you don't suffer a bit, she stoically says, echoing her stern Scottish forebears, how can you revel in the sunshine when it finally arrives? This harmonic duo with her brother is spellbinding in its Everly-style Appalachian interweaving. "Wintery Feeling" appeals to any of the million-plus people in North America who have ever completed a marathon [26.2 miles (41K)]. It says you have to earn your sunshine.

"Cotton Jenny" – Anne Murray, #71, 4-71. Anne beautifies a masterpiece melody by Ontario troubadour **Gordon Lightfoot**. Its lyrical upshot? – who needs money? Jenny's spinning wheel twirls out circles and mandalas of everlasting love. A super song.

"You Needed Me" was Anne Murray's biggest hit at #1(1), 7-78 (#4 C). This winsome waltz promises empathy – beyond love. "Danny's Song" hit #7, 1-73 and #10, 12-72 C. This pristine Danny melody by singer/songwriter **Kenny Loggins** is about his nephew. Musical diamond, like Anne's "Shadows in the Moonlight" (#25, 5-79; #1(1) C. Anne cavorts with moonlight lover under purple Milky Way romantic blanket.

"Snowbird" – Anne Murray, #8, 8-70; #20, 7-70 C. Anne's mellow contralto floats like a Michigan or Ontario snowbird winging its warming way south to the palm fronds of Florida. Her "Snowbird" Express ditches that grand ol' wintery feeling for two or three weeks; enough is enough. For those braving Canada's boreal blasts, Anne's sprightly frostbite antidote lofts us to eternal-summer land. Melodious tune. Tall range of notes, as Anne shifts to breezy easy soprano. Anne tapped musical gold with this snow critter. Zapped winter too – to Anne's gentle-breeze land of peaceful waters murmuring in the balmy sunwave glow. Anne began as a Folk singer on local *Singalong Jubilee* from Halifax, Nova Scotia, until she glided into orbit on stateside **Glen Campbell**'s *Goodtime Hour*.

Other great Canadian singers?

"Home from the Forest" – Gordon Lightfoot, NC, 1967. A down and out lonely old vagabond soldier, not quite homeless, possesses a dim grubby stairway and a cot. Once a girl loved him back in the eternal springtime of some glorious forgotten year. It's sentimental – never mawkish or maudlin. Lightfoot hammers his finger-picked Folk Rock guitar. The dark drizzle deteriorates to icy snow. There is no way out, just liquid solace, from the filthy "Cracklin' Rosie" pop-wine bottle he cherishes as his friend. He is obviously doomed. For one brief shining moment, we share his dismal plight and realize he's a precious human being who needs help. Gordon Lightfoot's marvelous melody, haggard derelict tale, and stinging beat point the way to our enlightenment.

"The Wreck of the Edmund Fitzgerald" – Gordon Lightfoot, #2(2), 8-76. No song like this ever was. Maybe one movie – *Titanic*. Beset by screaming siren sounds, Lightfoot's (b. '38) song tells of the near-instant break-up and disappearance below icy Lake Superior waves of the ore ship Edmund Fitzgerald. A true story. The titanic Great Lakes freighter toted a 26,000-ton heavy load of hematite – iron ore – toward the later home of the Rock Hall of Fame – Cleveland, Ohio. Big Canadian-American lakes are truly inland seas, Lake Superior is the deepest and darkest, with icy water that never warms below roiling blustery waves. They almost made Whitefish Bay, close to the Soo boat locks at Sault Ste. Marie, in the isthmus between Lake Superior and Lake Huron. A sudden gust? The narrow Edmund Fitzgerald snapped and plunged downward, killing all 29 crew members in minutes. Toothpick-shaped lake freighters can be 800 feet long. [Nearly as long as the biggest ocean liners in their 1945-60 heyday: the Queen Elizabeth or S.S. United States.] Diving expeditions proved the big ship snapped mysteriously in half. Instantaneous plunge. No hope. Great song. The last eerie unforgettable verse is at the Mariner's Church ceremony in Detroit. You can tour the over-500-foot ore freighter William S. Mather next to the Rock Hall in Cleveland.

"Sundown" is Gordon Lightfoot's big #1 song [#1(1), 4-74]. Grisly macho showdown with Sundown, his romantic rival. Lightfoot's breezy #10 follow-up is "Carefree Highway." His first chart hit? "If You Could Read My Mind" (#5, 12-70).

From her lofty office in the Brill Building off Manhattan's Tin Pan Alley, **Carole King** (b. Brooklyn, Carole Klein, 2-9-42) dotted the decades with her song stylistics. Her fame started with teenage-crush ode by **Neil Sedaka** – "Oh Carol" #9, 10-59. Carole's Brill Building songwriting adventures produced "Will You Love Me Tomorrow," "Take Good Care of My Baby," and "You've Got a Friend." **Jerry Seinfeld**'s June 1, 1996 comment: If you do one good thing, you can always say, like Olympic athletes, "It's only one thing, but at least I did one great thing in life." The early 70s unleashed a profound plethora of moderate-tempo, phosphorescent, philosophical songs fitting Jerry's "GREAT-THING" concept. They shimmered like fireflies on the charts, as the Big Beat downsized:

"**It's Too Late**" **– Carole King, #1(5), 5-71.** From *Tapestry* Al. #1(15), 4-71 – *Sgt. Pepper* of the 70s. "It's Too Late" gazes through the broken shards of a busted relationship. With minor-key sorrow, Carole explains to 'baby' that it's all over, kaput, finito. *Tapestry* sold zillions. *Billboard* and Whitburn/Bloxdorf list it as #3 for the 70s, womped by **Fleetwood Mac**'s incredible Al. *Rumours* with #1(31) and the Bee Gees' *Saturday Night Fever* at #1(24). [Michael Jackson's 80s *Thriller* hit #1(37).] Carole's cover art is understated and muted, a reaction to a Psychedelic half-decade of excess and splashy splotches of garish skullduggery. New Yorkers are among more conservative dressers in the U.S.A. [Subway glop won't zap dark outfits like it stains frilly whites.] Carole

wore *Seinfeld* chic for the era. *Tapestry* is pure Manhattan. On one of **Paul Simon's** "Hazy Shade of Winter" (#13, 11-66) afternoons, Carole muses comfortably on a Greenwich Village windowsill. Up front is a hazy gray tomcat, gazing defiantly into the camera's glum corner. Wistful Carole ponders the finality of the too-late relationship. Barefoot, and wearing understated gray sweater and Levis, she regards her fate confidently. She leads off a long successful era of confident women in Rock and Roll: King scored sidelong superstar hits with #9, 1-72 "Sweet Seasons," #2(1), 8-74 "Jazzman," #9, 1-75 "Nightingale," and #14, 8-71 with James Taylor on "So Far Away." Revamping her Brill Building songstress youth, she hoisted the Chiffons' 60s Rock and Soul anthem "One Fine Day" to #12, 5-80. The 70s were a major decade for Carole King.

"**I Am Woman**" **– Barbra Streisand, #114, 3-64.** [Also blockbuster by **Helen Reddy**, #1, 6-72.] Out of Melbourne, Australia, Reddy tossed the gauntlet and roared her distaff anthem. Streisand launched the song. The Equal Rights Amendment thundered throughout state legislatures. The Roe vs. Wade abortion issue flared. This is the Brooklyn diva's solo [low] chart debut – and was followed by her breakthrough (#5, 4-64) ballad "People." With 9207 Whitburn points in *Top Pop Albums; 1955-96*, Barbra is listed fifth in album sales of all time behind Elvis (15,538), Sinatra (12,766), Beatles (10,918), and Johnny Mathis (10,072).

"Delta Dawn" by **Helen Reddy** hit #1(1), 6-73. She enjoyed three #1's, like "Angie Baby" of 10-74. "I Am Woman" chronicles the rise of women in a new enlightened age – plus all their seven-league strides in zapping the good-ol'-boy 'glass ceiling.' "Delta Dawn" tells sorry tale of an aging Southern Belle, fading with dignity.

Disco Era? A bonanza for **Donna Summer** and **Maxine Nightingale** and **Olivia Newton-John** and **Gloria Gaynor**. Crooning baritones were suddenly replaced by saucy sopranos and confident contraltos. In 1996, no solo male enjoyed a #1 hit for months. The distaff revolution found its demure, multi-talented spokesperson in the persona of **Carole King**, with her hazy cat, blah sweater, and standard Levis.

A Blues-singing girl with no happy news? "American Pie" eulogized superstar **Janis Joplin**. Singing more Suburban Blues, far from the muddy Mississippi, was **Karen Carpenter** (1950-83). Brother **Richard** (b. '46) shepherded her Soft Rock musical arrangements. Karen's muted stylistics caressed her songs with spirit and deep feeling. Karen Carpenter had one of the most melancholy and hauntingly beautiful voices of all time.

"**We've Only Just Begun**" **– Carpenters, #2(4), 10-70; NC, R & B or C.** Slides into your soul like a golden sunrise, with pink flamingo cirrus clouds over a tropical lagoon of sky-blue. New horizons. Day to day bliss. Ebony shadow and burnished gold bounce back at the rising sunshine. Song of deep promise. A song for new beginnings – maybe your wedding.

"Rainy Days and Mondays" – Carpenters, #2(2), 5-71. From Karen and Richard's upbringing in New Haven, Connecticut, before sunny Downey, California. The song charts the woe-is-me bleak drip-drop of steady rain on the gloomy windowpane. It adds a soggy twist to Fats Domino's "Blue Monday" (#5, 1-57) or the Mamas and Papas' "Monday, Monday" (#1, 4-66). **Richard Carpenter** (b. 46) masterminds the keyboards and sings harmonic vocal fifths that anchor the lower range beneath Karen's stunning English-American (and Italian) alto.

As teenagers, Karen and Richard made the pilgrimage to Johnny B. Goode's 'Promised Land' – Downey, California. In school, Karen played drums like Madonna (in Greenwich Village). Karen and Richard placed ten singles in the top three; like "For All We Know," #3, 2-71; "Hurting Each Other" #2(2), 9-72, and "Superstar" #2(2), 9-71. They scored a Wonder Bread chart-topper of the Motown **Marvelettes'** soul-studded "Please, Mr. Postman" #1(1), 11-73. Karen endeared herself to Ernie, Bert, and the Muppet multitude by singing "Sing" from *Sesame Street* to its #3, 2-73 perch.

Karen had a one-in-a-billion voice. Her sweet pure alto murmurs, purrs, and soothes down through the generations, tinged with a tone of eternal melancholy. No matter how happy the song, she can make it sound blue and sad. And that's truly a COMPLIMENT. Bittersweet, happy-that-hurts angst. [It's tough enough for a W.A.S.P. of over-privileged wealth to sing the "I've Got the Maxed-Out Credit Card, Scuffed Tennis Racquet, Cruddy Croissant Blues."] Karen's vocal genius never required screaming. The only other yin-yang happy and sad blend I've encountered like this is Barbra Streisand's death-knell dirge (1963) of (ulp) "Happy Days Are Here Again." (#1, 1930, Ben Selvin Benny Meroff's Orchestra). Listen to Karen's blue-funk Beatles' "Ticket to Ride" rendition (#54, 2-70). A gracious gift of grief sums up her midnight blue songs.

Sadly, Karen Carpenter's life was curtailed by too much love, too much affection, too much trying to please everyone but herself. Someone once said, 'you can't be too rich or too slim.'

"Top of the World" – Carpenters, #1(2), 10-73. Sandwiched in center of three #1 triumphs, "Top" in 'Bb' is the semi-sunniest. A high-hat marks the steady drum beat. A happy bass kicks in, bubbling the bottom like a perky percolator on wake-up duty. Karen sweetly coos minor keys to mute the mood a mite. She wends her winsome way into the sweet chorus off deep contralto notes. Richard chimes in, underscoring her blithe globe-climbing sojourn with easygoing fifth notes at half volume. Harmony (i.e. Everlys & Simon-Garfunkel) builds Appalachian thirds – the second voice hits the third note of the tonic chord, and it's mixed in a bit quieter. Richard croons lower fifths and sevenths at less volume. The effect is extraordinary.

Among the prettiest melodies ever constructed, this plushly soft Soft Rock tune is a big friendly teddy bear song.

"Close to You" – Carpenters, #1(4), 6-70. A Disneyesque flight of sprightly birds flutters when her lover arrives. Stars shoot out of the sky as he strolls by. "Close to You" is a clever confection about angels and moondust and shooting stars penned by "Stardust"-style songwriters **Bert Bacharach** and **Hal David**. "Close to You" drifts, spins, enchants. Film fans recall Rick Moranis (*Parenthood****½) singing "Close to You" *a cappella* to his wife in her elementary-school classroom.

"Do You Know the Way to San Jose?" – Dionne Warwick, #10, 4-68; #23, 5-68 R & B. Un-stars who never hit stardom now pump gas or park cars? Born 12-12-40 in East Orange, New Jersey, Warwick[e] was the #1 Adult Contemporary female singer of all time. Getting their start on **Del Shannon's** flipside "The Answer to Everything," Bacharach/David honed their suave skills with this lament about the Expressway to Oblivion. Silver screen pilgrims and teenage idol wannabes mark time in Limbo Lodi, or Purgatory Pasadena. Listen to bass drum thump in bandbreak tacets. Dionne's velvet voice sings their plight.

"I Say a Little Prayer" – Dionne Warwick, #4, 10-67; #8, 11-67 R & B. She tosses out a jiffy velvet-voiced prayer for her lover, while pondering which dress to choose that day. Hmmm: 1) Most women still wore dresses daily, and 2) He gets to think about what she looks like standing there looking for a dress in her lingerie. The Bacharach/David team isn't into embarrassing confessional eroticism – just a tantalizing, tempting hint. And a prayer. Crafty combo, like cleavage adorned by a gold cross.

"That's What Friends Are For" – Dionne Warwick, #1(4), 11-85; #1(3) R & B. Other big hits: "Walk on By" (#6, 4-64); "Message to Michael" (#8, 4-66); "Then Came You" #1(1), 7-74; "(Theme From) the Valley of the Dolls" #2(4), 1-68; #6, 12-69 "I'll Never Love This Way Again"; #10 "Heartbreaker" of 1982; and the vocal of **Herb Alpert** (#1, '68) "This Guy [Girl]'s in Love with You" – (#7, 2-69). Dionne's soulful precision, phrasing, and classy dignified style are the best in the Pop Rock business. Her aunt Cissy Houston, and her niece (or cousin) – **Whitney Houston**, prove that genetics can play a factor in superstardom. At 30th on Joel Whitburn's all-time Artist List 1995-99, 7th Female act, 5'5," 110# Dionne Warwick[e] scored 56 singles in the HOT 100 for 15th place ever, and 3rd Female in number of top singles. Can't miss roster: **Elton John, Gladys Knight**, and **Stevie Wonder**. She marshals a harmony brigade for brooding buddies: they tell each other to keep smiling. Like James Taylor's "You've Got a Friend," the song imparts awesomely sage advice on – Friendship. Also, it demonstrates that hit records are rarely do-it-yourself girl and guitar solos.

"Yesterday Once More" – Carpenters, #2(1), 6-73. Richard is the tunesmith of the duo, penning "Yesterday Once More" and "Top of the World" with collaborators. As the darkling decade dipped down into the Disco Deluge, the Carpenters' rainbow shimmered, spindrifted, swirled, and faded. "Yesterday Once More" casts a flashback shadow on the Carpenters' enchanting Soft Rock career.

"Please Mr. Postman" – Carpenters, #1(1), 11-74.
Richard and Karen's last #1 hit was Motown's first: "Please Mr. Postman" (Marvelettes #1[1], 9-61), starring Wanda Young and Gladys Horton. **Beatles**, too, cut "Please Mr. Postman." "Postman" is a slightly hopeful song. When mail was cheaper than non-existent e-mail or long-distance phone, people wrote letters. "Postman's" singer hopes twitchingly by the naked mailbox. She craves just one card. Just one letter. From that globe-hopping faraway beau. Instant pick-me-up. To repair her downer mood. She stands, forlornly, at the empty mailbox – like Good ol' Charlie Brown, painfully awaiting that precious Valentine from the little red-haired girl. Will it ever arrive? Unlikely.

Symptoms, for Karen Carpenter, begin here. Even her last '911' hit – by phone, the Marvelettes' "BEechwood 4-5789" (#74, 4-82) – couldn't save her. Waiting for a letter, stasis and inaction burn her psyche. Standing in the HOT SPOTLIGHT of FADING ELVIS, Karen's own fading career posed for downswoop. Elvis's problem was bulimia, hers the flip side – starvation in a land of culinary plenty. So many last songs are ironic like that: **Buddy Holly**'s pensive "It Doesn't Matter Anymore"/"Raining in My Heart" (#1 U.K., 3-59); **Jim Croce**'s "Time in a Bottle" (#1, 12-73); and **Elvis**'s grim symptom-overload "Way Down" last lifetime hit (#18, 7-77), which the King followed by the (#22, posthumous 11-77) ironic Anka-Sinatra success tune:

"My Way" – Frank Sinatra, #27, 3-69.
Somehow, you know the Chairman of the Board is in control. He never gained weight, he kicked the cig habit when his friends got lung cancer, he had two drinks and stopped, he rollicked on past 80. **Paul Anka** (b. '41, Ottawa, Canada) and **Frank Sinatra** (12-12-15 to 5-14-98) have a lot in common. Sinatra did it his way. Frank sidestepped the Rock Revolution. Number two on Whitburn's Album Artist rankings, he never stopped selling: #7 ever in charted hits in the Age of Rock (1955-Now), and #2 in Albums. Anka's song proves it; Frank did it his way, selling out Vegas and vanquishing Hollywood.

Frank's hits? "Somethin' Stupid" #1[4] with daughter Nancy in 3-67; "Strangers in the Night" #1(1), 5-66; and #2, '57 "All the Way." His irrepressible #4, 11-66 "That's Life" inspired us all to keep on keepin' on when the going gets tough – just pick yourself up, dust yourself off – and charge back into the race. His "New York, New York" was #32, 5-80. "My Way" shows Sinatra's tenacious grit and pluck and staying power. Unlike Karen or Elvis, the Chairman of the Board ran HIS marathon, HIS way, for 82 years. When the marathon ended on May 14, 1998, Frank's full life was a testament to his scrappy self-reliance.

"These Boots Are Made for Walkin'" – Nancy Sinatra, #1(1), 1-66.
The Chairman's kid from Jersey City was married to singer (#2, 2-57 "Teenage Crush")

Tommy Sands (1960-65), who dumped her. Perhaps the gruffest revenge song of all time – she stomps all over him. They say Frank was so mad, he vowed Sands would never work in showbiz again. Hey, a #2 record – and when was the last time you heard "Teenage Crush" on the Oldies Overkill elevator or dentist's office? Somehow, Tommy's little monster hit was crushed by Demon Oblivion. Tommy who?

"Superstar" – Carpenters, #2(2), 9-71.
Karen sings this **Leon Russell** Elvis Spotlight anthem with deep melancholy and California soul. Nope, Elvis and Karen were not far apart in true self-image, unlike truly confident 82-year-old Frank Sinatra. Elvis tried to punt 82 pounds from 250# via speedo yo-yo diets. Karen tried to hover dangerously below 82 pounds. In 1967, svelte Karen began dieting from a nice 5'6", 111# shapely figure. With Dr. Nick-style prescription medication (uppers), Karen fought her perceived Battle of the Bulge. Lest we gloat, none of us can ever see ourselves as we truly are. This football nation has a gender double-standard on weight. If you're a guy, ten or twenty pounds are no big deal. Not for Karen.

Squirming in the Elvis Spotlight and out of it, Karen's success mode and obsession to please took on a dangerous and deadly downward spiral. Imperially slim, she uffered in silence. She starved herself more. Her final pre-storm success, "Touch Me When We're Dancing" (#16, 8-81), parallels "We've Only Just Begun." This pretty face, those sparkly eyes, that sweet All-American smile. You wince when you consider how Karen was destined to suffer the deep agonizing prolonged pain inflicted upon Auschwitz and Dachau and Biafra and Bangladesh. But hers was self-inflicted.

Critic Jen Schwarz and I agree – **Karen Carpenter**, for different reasons, sang a classic style of heartfelt Blues with all the zest and pain of **Janis Joplin** (or **Billie Holiday** or **Bessie Smith**). On February 4, 1983, at 105# and nearly beating her anorexia, she died of cardiac irregularity (as Elvis did). When their #1 "Please Mr. Postman" floated the tiptop charts, the #2 song was **Neil Sedaka**'s comeback "Laughter in the Rain"; Karen's life was like that. Her happy-sad songs rollicked with upbeat Rock and Roll, and droned with sad Jazz Blue chords: ninths, major sevenths, mediant minors. Rainy laughter.

"American Pie" met a girl that sang deep Blues. Her tale is just as tragic as Jim, Jimi, or Janis's. Maybe more so. She was only looking for approval . . . not capital punishment . . .

"I'll Have to Say I Love You in a Song" – Jim Croce, #9, 3-74.
Reflecting Karen Carpenter's wily reserve about expressing emotions, Croce's shy victim stews with reserve over unexpressed love and affection. **Maury Muehleisen**, on spellbinding 12-string guitar, accompanies Jim's rhythm guitar, surrounding Croce's smooth and sincere baritone. "I LOVE YOU" is the subject of most songs. This one commiserates with the poor guy who balks at saying it. He's nervous. Or scared. Or unsure of commitment (like us all). Three little words: so easy . . . and so hard to say. An angelic melody drives this

gorgeous hit for the Philly singer/songwriter troubadour.

Jim Croce (1943-73) was a distinctive-looking Rock star. Check out Jim's *I Got a Name* album (Al. #2[2], 12-73). Tall, slender. His smiling cigar-studded face is crowned with an enormous Fu Manchu moustache. Mixed messages: chubby cigar AND something totally new in '73 – running shoes. (American Frank Shorter won the 1972 Olympic Marathon, starting the fitness boom.) Like the new breed of R & R songwriters with great voices, who would dominate the next generation (Rod Stewart, James Taylor, Elton John) – Jim Croce had a message and a mission. Unfortunately, he wasn't blessed with time.

"Thursday" – Jim Croce, NC, 1973 [from *I Got a Name*]. "Thursday"? Simply one of the prettiest songs of all time. He seeks a lifetime of love; she shops only for a friend. Jim skips skillfully from major to minor on folksy frets, joined by Maury's unplugged 12-string majesty, whizbang bass guy Joe Macho, and Rick Marotta drumming. Background vocals breeze in like summer surf at Waikiki.

"I Got a Name" – Jim Croce, #10, 10-73. Philosophical twin of #1(2), 11-73 "Time in a Bottle." With his spellbinding baritone, Jim ponders the phenomenon of spiraling time. Like the hourglass, the swiftly eroding calendar thumps us all. Particularly Jim and Buddy. Croce wishes to spend his precious time with this precious girl (Ingrid) in a sweet soiree for three – girl, guy, and guitar. They say the song also spins for Jim and Ingrid's unborn child, as a fervent dedication to the loneliness of life on the road, and the homeward-bound promise of cozy family life. Croce's pensive pen creates these magnificent, museworthy tunes. He skirts Kerouac's lonesome road.

Jim carried his name along life's highway like his dad had done before, adventuring and roadhouse roughhousing in summer storms and winter chill. His nomadic wanderlust is sparked by an accelerated sense of time. It was as if he knew something about destiny. On September 29, 1973, Croce performed his final concert, with his faithful guitar man Maury, at Northwestern Louisiana University. The small chartered plane (70 miles – to Natchitoches) never really cleared the runway, smashing into a tree. Jim and Maury were instantly killed. Odd stat: "Time in a Bottle" was only the 3rd posthumous #1 U.S. song in the Rock Era (Janis Joplin, Otis Redding, [Buddy Holly if you count United Kingdom]). Four unforgettable entertainers.

"Lean on Me" – Bill Withers, #1(3), 4-72; #1(1) R & B. FRIENDSHIP again. After #3 bronze-meal 7-71 "Ain't No Sunshine" [when she is gone], Withers (b. '38, Slab Fork, Virginia) catapulted to #1 on the strength of this heartfelt baritone tribute to a friend in need. Helping others, he offers, is one of the great reasons we're all here. #2(2), 8-72 "Use Me." Selfless Withers missed the Me-First Generation Bus.

A thriving 70s green Back to the Land movement, was a backlash against smoke and steel and drudgery. One Army kid, **John Deutschendorf**, got dragged all over the earth by his career-soldier dad. Looking for roots he never had, he found Colorado. After a short paisley-tie and Princeton haircut stint in the mid-60s, he replaced Chad Mitchell with the **Chad Mitchell Trio**, joining Joe Frazier (not the heavyweight champ) and Mike Kobluk at Gonzaga University: (#43, 11-60 "The Marvelous Toy"). Then he drifted into songwriting, Levis, granny glasses, a blond Dutch Boy haircut, and a winning smile:

"Take Me Home, Country Roads" – John Denver [Deutschendorf], #2(1), 6-71; #50 C. John's (1943-97) first #1, as a songwriter, was ironically Peter, Paul, and Mary's last charted hit – #1, 11-69 "Leaving on a Jet Plane." John's first semi-solo hit blasted to #2 backed by Bill and Tammy Danoff's Fat City, who later launched a festive bombshell; their "Afternoon Delight" (#1[2], 5-76 with Starland Vocal Band) is a sizzling ditty about not waiting till 10:38 p.m. for a tantalizing tete-a-tete. Somewhere along the dusty road, Denver acquired Grape Nuts, cornsilk hair, and Colorado. Or heavenly West Virginia. "Take Me Home, Country Roads" is a vital vignette of a bygone, simpler time and place. It's a heart-of-America lost land of whistlestops and general stores and Burma Shave and cracker barrels. Denver spins his "Hickory Holler" tale (#40, 2-68 O.C. Smith) in the guitar key of 'A' major, with his Country Folk Rock Danoff Trio resonating a homespun optimistic Everly echo. Denver spangles his rural byway with buoyant imagery: mountains of faraway, sparkly blue waters, dusky painted sky, glow of misty moonshine. **Bob Dylan**'s poetic lyrics in #6, 5-65 album *Bringing It All Back Home* influenced John. Buddy Holly inspired Denver to learn to sing (Denver's #81, 3-72 Hollytune "Everyday"). [Weirdly, Charleston, West Virginia, led Detroit in 1970 industrial pollution to #1 U.S. most-polluted smog status – due to hard-rock coal mining smelters and a valley that trapped the seething smoke. Sometimes "almost-heaven" can be a place in your own mind.]

"Rocky Mountain High" – John Denver, #9, 11-72, NC, C. Two miles above sea level, John rolls the Key back to Bluesmen's 'E' major. The song reverberates with cryptic messages: In a sense, these majestic peaks hint at born-again Christian conversion. Always pro-environment, John Deutschendorf changed his name to the capital of Colorado, his adopted state [Denver]. John's 1998 reprise of "It's a Sin to Tell a Lie" (#1, '36, Fats Waller; #7, '55, Somethin' Smith & Redheads) shows John's prodigious Jazz/Country/Folk comic expertise – and friendly boy-next-door charisma.

We all depend on our favorite music to help us along. Turning inside, like Taoists and Buddhists and some New Age pilgrims, Denver scopes in the mountain scene and he marvels. This secular-worship song hit is almost a hymn. Good friends serenade and salute a star-splashed sky. Chugging gusto around a cozy Colorado campfire, Denver celebrates life.

"Back Home Again" – John Denver, #5, 9-74; #1(1) C. Denver enjoyed four #1's and two #2 tunes, and starred in the 1977 *Oh, God* movie with timeless troubadour George Burns (1896-1996). Denver did not play the Lord; he was the secular pilgrim. Denver's #1 "Sunshine on My Shoulders" of 1-74 inspired a great Vancouver TV show; it was so good they cancelled it. Denver's environmental commitments reached their peak with #2(4), 10-75 "Calypso," dedicated to his hero, Calypso skipper Jacques Cousteau (1910-97). Cousteau's Calypso studied and saved the world's oceans. [**Harry Belafonte**'s #1(31), 1956 *Calypso* tied for 3rd place album of all time.] Denver's vocal range is prodigious, Belafonte's, too.

Back Home Again, album AND single, captured #1 at Mid-Disco-Decade (7-74). Fab floral gold handwriting frames a 7"x7" homey vignette of John, wife Annie, and friends in a snowy Colorado winter scene. A cheery cluster of folks in bell-bottom Levis, mountaintop smiles, and denim 50° jackets [at 20°] greets record buyers. Flanked by a motley menagerie of fluffy Persian cats, Malemutes, Cocker Spaniels, and Abyssinian Lionhounds, they're a pastel palette of happy kids and tomorrow dreams. Easy Rock Currier & Ives/Norman Rockwell portfolio. His wife is expecting, and new joy is on the way. Tragically, in 1997 Denver joined Buddy Holly and Ricky Nelson and Jim Croce in their skyward attempts (more later). After breaking up with his Annie, his silver sundown tarnished a bit. John's last big hit was "Shanghai Breezes," #31, 3-82. His Soft and Hard Rock and Country and Blues were softening the ice and melting the stern cold stares of the Communist world.

In 1969, John Sinclair of Ann Arbor, Michigan's White Panther Party wrote *Guitar Army*. Not all wars are won with bazookas and blunderbusses and Big Bertha cannons. Perhaps Freddy Boom Boom Cannon was our secret weapon. Or that sincere blond Colorado Kid with the boyish smile, and sunny American Dream.

"Rhinestone Cowboy" – Glen Campbell, #1(2), 5-75; #1(3), 6-75 C. Razzed by Johnny Carson for his high Scottish tenor, Campbell jocularly fired back this deep-tone tune about a neon rodeo cowboy, a Don Quixote figure like Robert Redford/Jane Fonda's *Electric Horseman**** (1979). Like Buddy Holly's low 'A' on "Peggy Sue," versatile guitar star Campbell showed 1st tenor wasn't his only range.

You can't get much further south than Brownsville, Texas. Texan **Kris Kristofferson** (b. 1936) zigzagged from Oxford University to the Army to a janitor's job in Nashville, building his songwriting retinue. Kris scored major hits on "Loving Her Was Easier (Than Anything I'll Ever Do Again)" #26, 5-71, (NC, C), repentant hymn "Why Me?" #16, 4-73 (#1 Country), and NC, '85 (#1[1] C, 5-85) "Highwayman." Having talked at length with Kristofferson in a Detroit Forest Avenue bar gig he

was playing in 1969, I knew he could write about an awful "morning after." When he discovered Christianity, like Dion's born-again experience, it changed his life and hung the bygone thirst out to dry.

"Sunday Mornin' Comin' Down" – Johnny Cash, NC, 1970; #1(2), 9-70 C. As the strung-out, hung-up, burnt-out 60s sloshed over into the discoid seventies, this Kristofferson-penned masterpiece highlights the ugliest agonies of the BIG HANGOVER. Cash had recently seen the light through the ministrations of his new wife **June Carter Cash**.

Stark sad song. Cash's dark sincere bass vocal verifies this aftermath saga. Those who've suffered the twerpy hangover (three beers plus all the sidestream Marlboro smoke you can eat) may also know the real doozy disaster. This may be the realest hangover song ever written, rife with gallows humor.

Our hung-over hero wakes up eerily early, Sunday. He can't find anywhere in his head that doesn't hurt. Kristofferson sardonically grumbles that the beer he guzzled for breakfast wasn't half bad – so he decides upon a second brew 'for dessert.' He searches the spinning closet for his least-dirty shirt. John Cash sings with sympathy and pain. No funster romp, like **Jimmy Buffett**'s Key West anthem about dillying around and getting jocularly wasted: "Margaritaville."

Cash's Catastrophic Sunday? Up at the crack of Noon. Whereas **Buffett**'s boozy spiral of wild margaritas and floppy flip-flops, and a chummy bygone affair gone awry are taken as one big YOK and GUFFAW, Cash's deathly hangover goes much deeper. No shrimp-on-the-barbie with pals and gals. Cash is woefully, ghastlily alone.

His "Sunday Mornin' Comin' Down" might be the loneliest song ever written. It snakes along from major to minor. Cash's hardpan bass nails the listener with his persuasive raspy timbre and woebegone tone. The Hangover Victim gets no sympathy, no mommy with ginger ale and a plumped-up pillow, no *Scooby Doo* on TV. Our victim wakes up with half his head on one side of the room. Half on the closet floor. He has to crawl over and slowly screw them back together. He stumbles into the cigarette-butt and dog-dung gutter in the obscene blaze of blue day.

Cash's song-guy staggers past the Dispy-Doodle Slide Playground. Family togetherness abounds. He sniffs frying chicken some family is about to share – and he doesn't own three beans. A happy dad is pushing his darling little girl on a zippy swing. Gazing alone, at this family tableau, it makes him feel worse. Ever more isolated. Ever more alienated. In abject despair, Cash wrings out the rags and tatters of his broken heart, almost rising to low tenor. Staggering the lonely garish avenue, Cash prays to be stoned – because of the horrible isolation of his huge Sunday hangover. **Jack Kerouac** suffered the D.T.'s in 1962 at Ferlinghetti's country cabin, and lived to write about it in *Big Sur* ('62). Only this can trump Cash/Kristofferson's bad trip. We can imagine drugs are a part of this package from the buzz word stoned, obviously, but we can only imagine this poor alcoholic's last night's gobble and guzzle jamboree: one quart Boone's Farm apple wine, three chugs Southern Comfort, two snorts Jack Daniels, seven pickled pigs' feet, one bag marshmallows, one can mushroooms (magic), three raw eggs, some anonymous Royal Blue booze, three martinis, Old Barfbreath, a six-pack of Milwaukee's Best Compost Beer, three tentacles of Kentucky Fried Octopus, and an entire school of Bag O' Fish Deluxe.

Kerouac was searching for the "CENTER OF SATURDAY NIGHT IN AMERICA. Kristofferson describes the DEAD center of Sunday morning. Shards of lost faith dazzle the grubby gutter. The hangover victim ingloriously ambles past a Sunday School. Just as the dark chords funereally retro-shift from the pretty sub-dominant IV through glum minor III and II chords, you hear a faraway lonely bell toll. Maybe he can return to his past religion of yesterday. Maybe he can't. Without the song's dark grim sense of humor, the guy might not have made it. Could be worse. Now he could be homeless. At least his cleanest dirty hamper shirt has a closet.

As an Alka-Seltzer perk-up to this ugly Sunday of the Big Queasy Headache and burbling, gurgling gut, Kris Kristofferson got born again. Cash 'saw him one.' Cash got both born again and soulmate June Carter Cash.

"Margaritaville" – Jimmy Buffett, #8, 4-77; #13 C. Buffett (b. '46) partied New Orleans' Vieux Carre and strummed his 6-string on his Key West front -porch swing with his summertime Conch buddies and "Parrothead" pals. If ever Surf Music kicked back in for an East-Coast resurgence, it's here permanently in Margaritaville, just down the surfboard-rental boulevard from the **Beach Boys'** #1(1), 9-88 "Kokomo" (not #2[3], 2-55 Perry Como "Ko Ko Mo"). Written by Flower-Power star Scott McKenzie (#4, 5-67 "San Francisco"), "Kokomo" reverberates with good times and surf's-up glory. This friendly Florida Keys local pub is the launch pad for every jet set palm breeze paradise of everybody's dreams. Like Chuck Berry and the original Beach Boys, the song pumps up our American love affair with Rand McNally's Road Atlas – and grass skirts: Jamaica, Bahama, Key Largo, Montego, and Montserrat's mystique. Buffett's buffet of big-ticket hits? "Changes in Latitudes, Changes in Attitudes" (#37, 9-77), "Cheeseburger in Paradise" #32, 4-78, #84, 12-78 "Mañana" ['Tomorrow'], and #35, 9-79 "Fins." They distill the day-glo fiesta best of Jimmy's sunny world view. In the burger tune, he gently chides vegetarians about the splendor of juicy junk food. A great comedy nutritional spoof which hit #9, 1-76 for **Larry Groce** is "Junk Food Junkie." Disney jingle writer's live coffeehouse recording. Cute flap about sham health-nut; by day, he's 'Mr. Natural' at organic foods emporium. By night, aha, the Teenage Werewolf stalks! Groce gorges on Twinkies, Ding-Dongs, and Old Moon Pies (see Al Yankovic's "Eat It").

In 1984-85, the Rock and Roll world stunned the Me-First Generation by doing charity concerts for Band-Aid and Live-Aid – pledging 85 million dollars for humane charities. Most of it trickled into the 'Taxman's' fulsome coffers. In 1979, **Stephen Stills** and **Jackson Browne** demonstrated with thousands in a free concert against nuclear power, after the wretchedly disastrous Three-Mile Island 'event' ('nukespeak' for 'accident'), Amish Pennsylvania.

"Running on Empty" – Jackson Browne, #11, 2-78. Incisive singer/songwriter. Armed with guitar and an irreverent twist of phrase, German born Browne's (b. '48) tenor story sees the whole world as one big energy junkie, groaning for another petrochemical fix. As he runs toward the sun, he feels he's losing time. And ENERGY. The Earth, they said, was getting thirsty. The Carter administration pushed Solar Energy, but all of us Petro Junkies kept on cruisin' our SUV's. Saddam Hussein's Iraq and Saudi Arabia controlled 40% of the world's oil in 2002, providing another American incentive to search for other energy sources. Some sources, like a nuclean plant meltdown after a terrorist attack like 9-11-01, could be potentially more hazardous than Sadam Hussein.

Browne headlined the Al. #19, 10-79 *No Nukes* benefit (Asylum 801), which included stars on the rise (**Bruce Springsteen, Tom Petty, Bonnie Raitt**) plus big current stars rising against radioactive power down at Homer Simpson's nuclear power plant: **Graham Nash, Jesse Colin Young, James Taylor, Doobie Brothers.** Despite technical strides, nuclear power is still an iffy genie. Browne also spoofed attorneys in #13, 8-83 "Lawyers in Love." As we rolled into the Me Generation, Browne satirized those of us lusting after the Almighty Buck. Fun song, though 1,000,000 honest lawyers may wonder about its tone.

Browne was not the lone ranger of meaningful lyrics. Long Island produced two fine poets beyond Walt Whitman: **Billy Joel** (next chapter); and his neighbor from Huntington, **Harry Chapin**, who started the charity ball rolling, doing benefit concerts a decade before they becam fashionable. Chapin (1942-81) wrote some of the most meaningful Folk Rock of the century. His use of chromatic chords (he loved the bVII) and his commanding distinctive baritone and shrill falsetto make you hear a Chapin song once and never forget it. Chapin was killed by a monster truck in his small, fuel-efficient economy car on the Long Island Expressway in 1981. His social consciousness and senseless death caused me to join an informational group called C.R.A.S.H., which advocates plunking these behemoth 3-trailer 'Monster Trucks' back onto railroads where they belong to save 10,000+ lives per year.

"Cat's in the Cradle" – Harry Chapin, #1(1), 10-74. A cat's cradle is a kiddie game. Strings get looped tightly around fingers. They're passed on to the next players, and it ends up a tangled web. Wife Sandy Chapin wrote these words to chide Harry about being away so much on tour or benefits. Song is about kid whose dad never has time. Bleak horns horn in on mood in jiffy instrumental bridges. As kid grows, he has no time for his retired father. Tables turn. Oops, gotta hurry, no time . . .

"Taxi" – Harry Chapin, #24, 3-72. Harry debuts his tune on a quavering minor key. He runs into a girl he used to date. She's a big-time actress now, he's a taxi hack. They discuss old times. She over-tips him. Shameless, he squishes the $20 bill into his second-string shirt. Like most of us, he never quite gets what he wants in life, like U2's famous #1, '87 "I Still Haven't Found What I'm Looking For." Life's a trade-off, he discovers. He'd rather pilot a big silver jet than a stubby Yellow Cab – but hey, at least when you run out of gas you can pull over and hoof it home. You don't crash.

My old taxi-driving friend Denny Jaggers' favorite song? Glad you asked. It's **Lee Andrews and the Hearts'** #45, 8-57 (#11 R & B) "Long Lonely Nights." Great R & B tenor and Streetcorner R & B ballad. Heart of mellow. SOUL chapter follows this . . . Lee's #45 hit also defines the next DeeJay's age plus the speed in rpms of a single record:

"W.O.L.D." – Harry Chapin, #36, 1-74. On a station with the AARP *Modern Maturity* call letters "'OLD,' the fading Rock Jock plays Rock and Roll, but is aging out of the market. Bittersweet. Poignant. Chapin was a tireless, selfless crusader for helping unfortunate lost souls, stumbling in the void. Or the deli.

Joni Mitchell is from Saskatchewan's Saskatoon (b. 11-7-43, Fort McLeod, Alberta, no tropic isle itself). Way out there, Dylan's wild Yukon north winds 'hang' heavily along the Canada-U.S.A. borderline. Actual temperatures in Saskatoon often plunge to –50° Fahrenheit, and don't ask about the Wind Chill in Detroit Red Wing hockey icon Gordie Howe's hometown (b. 1929).

Joni Mitchell [Roberta Anderson] began troubadouring with husband Chuck Mitchell, working with our band (on, well, separate nights) at the Wayne State University (Detroit) watering hole on Woodward Avenue – the ALCOVE. [I was 19, the place got raided for under-21 fake-I.D.-less kids, and I galumphed out the back door (in mid-song), tripping over upteen garbage cans and my pride].

Rock transformation spun Joni to stardom, and Chuck to divorce court. Joni's unique cold-weather genius mirrors Dylan's. They both dazzle with hardscrabble and spindrift imagery that overwhelms the purveyors of dinky-vocabulary tunes. Her hip stratospheric soprano is among the highest of the Rock Revolution this side of **Mariah Carey**'s dog-whistle-pitch Mt. Everest notes. With a cigarette

ember tucked into the faraway end of her Martin guitar, Joni dangles wry quips and hip Motor City smokestack jive. By 1997, her Saskatoon Soul won her a semi-free trip to the Rock Hall of Fame in semi-tropical Cleveland (hey, it's all relative). She fiddled with irony and raggedy Kerouac Neo-Beat imagery even before Bob Dylan:

"Big Yellow Taxi" – Joni Mitchell, #67, 7-70, and #24, 12-74. Amy Grant (#67, 6-95) reprised Joni's song – pave over yesterday's paradise, for some new grubby parking lot. Joni's song rails against farmers declaring pesticide war against the planet. Joni juggles trees, causes, and ideals, and focuses the title – a big yellow taxi has taken away her 'old-man.' Then Joni giggles a groovy girlish giggle, and her sword-straight flaxen blonde hair wriggles, framed by her Icelandic blue eyes and her wispy wiry body. Her forte is ALBUM Folk Rock, Fronted by this outstanding creative cavalcade: Al. #2(4), 2-74 *Court and Spark*; #2(1), 12-72 *Miles of Ashes* and her magnificently evocative #4, 12-74 *The Hissing of Summer Lawns.*

"Help Me" – Joni Mitchell, #7, 3-74. She thinks she's falling into love. Joni also wrote "Woodstock" #11, 3-70, for Crosby, Stills, Nash, and Young – where she played at the monstrously mammoth Rock Festival. Her lyrics are surreal, turning into butterflies above the 1st Woodstock fiesta. All the Woodstock Nation people are 'stardust' and golden. Idealistic youth found a savvy spokesperson in Joni Mitchell. Her trend-setting visionary music cascades down to the present day. To Canada.

***Jagged Little Pill* – Alanis Morissette, Al. #1(12), 7-95.** Alanis, brunette French-Canadian lyricist and singer, combined the Canadian surrealism and streetwise savvy of Joni with the craggy, jagged vocal delivery of **Bob Dylan** – packaged in 90s grunge-glutted nihilism and wry cynicism which sold mega-million albums. "Ironic" (#4, 3-96) and "Hand in My Pocket" (#15A, 6-95) dusted the topmost singles rungs. Her #6, 7-96 "You Oughta Know" reverberates Alanis' no-holds barred sincerity. Or catch #3A, 8-96 "Head Over Feet" or #4A, 3-98 "Uninvited" ["A" stands for "Airplay Chart"]. Or her #23, 2002 "Hands Clean." Alanis dumps stardust for an inside-out sweater or recycled chicken-feed. The echo of **Joni Mitchell** and **Gordon Lightfoot** shines in Morissette's [and Sarah McLachlan's] sincere styles. In his "Early Mornin' Rain," Lightfoot ponders the technological monster – airports – which forbid him to hitchhike or hobo the rails: he gets stuck on the cold soggy ground. The 1966 line frames the attitude of Alanis. She is no Goody Two-Shoes ingénue, no dippy-bippy ditzy debutante. No buxom bimbo. No airhead with the IQ of a grape. Alanis Morissette is her own person. Isn't that what all these Timeless Troubadours were singing about in the first place? Freedom. The American/Canadian way. Tell it like it is. Don't let the system get you down.

Rock and Roll has never let anyone kick it around. It takes care of its own.

A Joyful Noise Unto the Lord: Rock, Roll & Religion

Faith is a bridge to life. There's Faith Music here for all you Believers and Doubting Thomases (and those into Anarchistic Polkas and Agnostic Chalypsos). In "Joyful Noise," we'll show how religion intermingles with the Big Beat, and how some of the biggest songs have a religious message. Our 'Spirit' is interdenominational, with a flair for inclusion. We're not narrow-minded or xenophobic or exclusive here. This pantheistic world deserves a basic respect for everybody's religion, whether he/she be devout disciple, or part-time pilgrim. You may be surprised at some of our picks. Yes, we'll include the good ol' hymns which have fortified the American spirit, but we'll toss in a few bizarre tunes, too. All these important songs address the basic questions: What is the meaning of my life? What is my mission? In this cosmic dilemma, Who cares? What about sin and guilt, or do we have a blast and let it all hang out? What are my personal responsibilities toward others' happiness? How can I find my own?

"Bridge Over Troubled Water" – Simon & Garfunkel, #1(6), 2-70. Didn't we say the **Everly Brothers** sounded like a couple of angels? And that Simon and Gar sounded like the Everly Brothers? So be it. Vocal mostly by **Art Garfunkel; Paul Simon**, third-verse harmony.

"Bridge" is among the great secular hymns of all time. It is a profound statement upon the true meaning of friendship and empathy. Just when you think you are truly alone, a friend comes out of the blue to help you through your travail. Whether that friend is Jesus or just ol' Ernie or Stella from down the block, you are consoled and comforted in your time of despair and desolation. Remember we just covered **James Taylor/Carole King**'s #1, 6-71 "You've Got a Friend." Garfunkel's "Bridge" goes a step beyond James Taylor's wistful "You've Got a Friend" – it carries you over the river of despair to the Promised Land (*Revelations* 21:1-2) of hope and purpose and love.

So many great hymns begin with a simple piano. Art Garfunkel has one of the purest crystal tenors of all time. His first four golden notes emote his friend's weariness. You feel every little note of agony that drifts past the glum gray window of his friend's desperation. "Bridge" is certainly no teenage lament about somebody dumping her date because she had to wash her hair or feed the hamster. "Bridge" spans the deep river of bereavement. There is nothing secular anyone can do to bring back a lost loved one. It is very nice to know, however, that a good friend is standing by, ready to listen and not judge – to comfort and console at the crucial moment of deepest need.

The pretty melody drones dolefully. Strings float on high. Deep sadness pervades the song, echoing bewitching *Ecclesiastes* 9:11: "The race is not to the swift or the battle to the strong." Often the strongest people we depend upon die, and we just can't figure it out.

Like literature, rock and ballad lyrics pulsate with throbbing metaphors. I will be a bridge, declares the metaphorical sincere singer (defiantly challenging a seemingly impossible civil engineering feat). In the second verse, the singer's friend is down by the cold sidewalk, awash with chilly brooding gloom. Maybe homeless. "Blessed are the poor in spirit, for theirs is the kingdom of heaven' (*Matthew* 5:3). "Bridge's" second verse builds, each silver note ringing with Art's most powerful lyrical, musical, and religious statement. Verse three brings in Paul Simon. They whisper to this evanescent "silver-girl" as she sails along. The hymn vaults heaven-bound through the stratosphere in a wispy cirrus-cloud swirl of thunderous strings and tympani. His sailing silver angel shines her healing light. An orchestral climax throbs and thunders.

Friendship shies like a white dove catching the morning's first golden sunbeam. "Bridge Over Troubled Water" is not just a song. It is a monumental religious experience. **Boyz II Men** and **Mariah Carey**'s sweet elegy, #1(16), 12-95 "One Sweet Day," shares this deep, pensive feeling of empathy and friendship. It is also the #1 song of the Rock Era from 1955-2002.

"I Still Haven't Found What I'm Looking For" – U2, #1(2), 6-87. Religion searches for meaning in the cosmos, and Rock and Roll is a bully pulpit. Besides the fact that you can meet girls and travel to faraway paradises, you can also get everyone to hear your ideas. It is lucky that when we finally locate an authentic Irish tenor actually from Ireland, he is an excellent Irish tenor.

Born **Paul Hewson** in Dublin, he switched his moniker to **Bono**, pronounced "bah-no" – not like Sonny Bono. **David Evans** of Wales, bandmate, metamorphosed into 'The Edge.' A band congregated at Dublin's Mt. Temple

High School. One pre-U2 name was, ulp, **Virgin Prunes**.

In 1960, U.S. pilot **Gary Powers** flew high over the Soviet Union on a 'reconnaissance mission' (military euphemism for spy flight). When his "U-2" plane was shot down and his puffy parachute ballooned to Soviet soil, he delivered his best "WHO ME?" to the unamused grumpy Soviet authorities. [My son's band Nine Days tours with SR-71 ("Right Now", #24 Modern Rock Tracks, 12-2000); they're named for the fastest airplane ever made]. Premier Nikita Khrushchev's crew reprimanded the plucky lad Powers and sent him home. "The U2 Incident" rocked the sleepy Eisenhower and Nixon Era of 1952-60. In April 2001, the U.S. had a similar spy-plane catastrophe over China. Suddenly for Hewson, it was Prunes Begone and a new name (U2) with pizzazz.

This song/quest queries the Cosmic Question: what is the meaning of my life? Cymbals crash. Drums and boss guitars blur into a thunderthrob. Bono/Hewson's tall tenor parades the parapets of Bewilderment.

"Still" begins with a pizzicato guitar flipping a couple of strings, replicating the sound of bongo drums. Odd R & R Key of "C#". The boomer bass nabs a note and hangs on. U2's spiritual desert is dotted with *Joshua Trees* [U2 Al. #1(9), 4-87] and gila monsters: "At once the Spirit sent Him out into the desert, and he was in the desert forty days, being tempted by Satan" (*Mark* 1:12-13). Bono implores the heavens in his lonely pilgrimage: he has ascended the highest mountains, dashed through fields, crawled up city walls (Jericho?), grappled with soul-searing desires, clutched the Devil's hand and STILL – he can't find what he's looking for.

Late in the *Bible*, a line occurs – "Be merciful to those who doubt" (*Jude* :22). In the Atomic Age, unquestioning belief is a rare commodity. All devout Christians and Jews who think must occasionally wear the itchy cloak of Doubting Thomas. We grope along, together.

Bono's final verse sows seeds of atonement, redemption, hope: he confesses his belief in "Kingdom Come," and how all various colors eventually bleed into some combo color (usually the crimson/brown of earth or dried blood). Bleed is paramount. As the mocking soldiers fashion a Crown of Thorns which caused Jesus to bleed as he carried the Cross to Calvary, Jesus suffered immensely. In His last moments, he called out "Eloi, Eloi, lama sabachthani." ("My God, my God, why have you forsaken me?").

Despite his doubts, Bono carries on through the wilderness with the Cross. Is he addressing Jesus? He uses the amorphous 2nd-person "YOU." Or is he simply addressing some friend or girlfriend? Is this song a prayer? Our earthly lives are pilgrimages, yes. Mundanely, they're often just pilgrimages to the 7-11 for Snapple fruit punch, Kleenex, and the *TV Guide*.

"Still" rumbles along, a jaunty coagulation of his bass punching the C#, guitar flitting on jumpy riffs, cymbal and snare skooshing and snarling in the Arizonan wilderness. The guys stand as far from the Emerald isle as possible in their mammoth album *Joshua Tree*. It miraculously entered the UK charts at #1, and went platinum in just 48 hours. Nothing before, Beatle or Stone, ever swooped to glory so fast.

It scored the big ▲[10] in Whitburn's *Top Pop Albums*, which stands for a DECA-MILLION sales (10 million). A cosmic WOW.

The stark B & W cover, fuzzied with indistinct daguerrotype frowns, shows four pilgrims deliberately looking scraggly. The hardscrabble moonscape on the front is barren of life, swirling with erosion channels, alluvial fans, and dry, arid lifelessness. The Joshua tree is native to Arizona. It looks supernatural. Otherworldly. Surreal . . . Imagine a giant cactus with a trunk and branches. At branch end, great spiky yucca-type clumps stab the sky. Not a fun tree. Dark, stark. Hopeless. On the back cover, the band stands solitarily, far away and at right angles to each other. Communication is nil.

Bono and U2 opened up a triumphant tour of the USA, beginning (naturally) in Arizona. If you don't own this album, try to picture *Peanuts* cartoonist Charles Schulz's beagle Snoopy's cousin Spike, a moustachioed pooch who lives alone in the Joshua-strewn American desert. A cartoon vulture hangs out on the local saguaro cactus. An ends-of-the-earth prop. Generation X didn't wish to see the pleasant green hills of the Emerald Isle. Jockeying across a spiritual desert, they wished the landscape could reflect their crisis. U2's desert sports steamy salt flats, slithering sidewinders, and one grotesque Joshua tree spearing the hopeless leaden sky. This bleak *Mad Max* (1979***) landscape pleads with us: don't come here . . . we're too ugly. The land of the Joshua tree is a land of desolation. An absolute wilderness.

Jesus did 40 days in just such a wilderness. **Barry McGuire** (Contemporary Christian singer) sang that the Jordan River was full of floating bodies in his apocalyptic Armageddon song (*Revelations* 16:16) "Eve of Destruction" (#1, 8-65). Barry refers to the lifeless desert seven miles northeast of Jericho where Jesus was 'tempted in the wilderness by the dark spirit of Satan.' [Or see Rolling Stones' "Sympathy for the Devil".] Not unlike Joshua, Arizona. Bono and the **Edge** (guitarist) and **Adam Clayton** (bass) and **Larry Mullen** (drums) boom out their spiritual quest into the ragtag void? They crave answers. Some answers arrived in the form of big time success. The throbbing drums, skittering bass heartbeat, groaning guitar, and piercing tenor vocals all came together in a passionate frenzy of the pilgrims' quest to discover the meaning of life. Lagging a tad in the USA, U2's #21, 10-01 "Beautiful Day" hit #1 worldwide with a sunny spiritual forecast. Sixties troubadour **Bob Lind** knew their feeling. Lind says he called out his girl's name, while desperately seeking something – anything – to believe in.

"Elusive Butterfly" – Bob Lind, #5, 2-66. One tremendous song and poem. Lind sees love metaphorically, a fleeting butterfly you chase like a leprechaun to the end of the rainbow over Galway Bay. Via 'mind canyons' and abandoned forgotten dreams. Lind relentlessly pursues this flittering-flash butterfly which represents love. In Lind's quest, he brandishes a net made of wonder, as he trails the elusive critter all his seeking life. **David Gray** (#57+ "Babylon" 12-2000) echoes Bob's '66 aural aura. Bob Lind traveled, in vagabond pursuit of love's precious butterfly, far, far beyond his native Baltimore to coffeehouse Denver, San Diego, and the stars. The butterfly is a key Taoist symbol. Taoist leader Chaung Tzu of China dreamed he was a butterfly – then couldn't figure whether he was Chuang Tzu dreaming of a butterfly – or a butterfly dreaming he was Chuang Tzu. As Thomas Carlyle put it, why not turn DOUBT into WONDER? Strings breeze this "Butterfly" along. A swift sunbeam on a panoramic musical canvas.

"Slip Slidin' Away" – Paul Simon, #5, 10-77. Frothy with wit, Simon's solo Soft Rock hit describes the raggedy family breakup epidemic of the 70s. Hypnotized by the Disco strobe light, families went POOF in a lusty, dusty era of passion. Simon descends to the vocal bridge. Coyly, with Socratic curmudgeonry, Simon sez: The Lord's information is unavailable to us mere mortal pilgrims. Good line. U2's quest to discover the meaning of life was blindsided by success. Thud.

"Deep River" – Paul Robeson, #19, 10-27. Robeson (1899-1976) perhaps had the most commanding and memorable bass voice of all time. African-American reformer, law school graduate, All-American football player, and Metropolitan Opera star, he is best noted for what were once termed "Negro Spirituals." – like *Show Boat* theme "Ol' Man River" (#7, 6-28), and #13, 11-25 "Steal Away." Robeson's father was a minister (Whitburn says) who escaped slavery. "Deep River" involves a metaphorical trip across the River Jordan in the Holy Land. It's an African-American trip not only 'up from slavery,' but into the eternal glory of the Promised Land. "Deep River" is among the FIRST great musical Bridges over Troubled Water to achieve deliverance from earthly toil and woe. "Wayfaring Strangers" have ascended "Stairways to Heaven" long before Rock and Roll [which also brings us AC/DC's metal manifesto and polar opposite: "Highway to Hell" #47, 79]. "Deep River" has sung the honored funeral guest of many generations to great rewards in the hopeful Beyond. When Paul Robeson hits the deep low note in this breathtaking song, the world pauses. The jangling clamor of the world drifts away into Simon and Gar's #1 SOUNDS OF SILENCE.

Two "Deep River" versions deserve silver and gold acclamation for their beauty and abiding faith: contralto **Marian Anderson**'s (1897-1993) riveting "River" – where she gets down to male baritone range; and **Johnny Mathis** (b. 9-30-35), from #10, 4-58 Al. of gospel songs: *Good Night, Dear Lord* (orchestra **Percy Faith**). Each one is an illuminating, electrifying experience – three deep rushing minutes of heavenly communion with Whoever or Whatever you believe in.

Over the years, gossipmongers blamed the Beatle break-up on **Yoko Ono**, Mrs. John Lennon. John met and married Yoko (Asian-American artist and rock-and-roller) in a New York City rendezvous.

Bands like the **Beatles** experience serious rifts (and riffs) over long years of playing and touring and bickering and squabbling, like Cain and Abel (*Genesis* 4). Let's check out a few religious Beatle tunes, and see their fundamental differences: Paul is a Catholic, John a Unitarian utopian, George a Hindu with swaddling clothes of Christianity, Ringo a secular lad with a Christian background. Manager Brian Epstein was Jewish, like Simon and Garfunkel.

"Hey Jude" – Beatles, #1(9), 9-68. Beatles' all-time #1 hit. Paul McCartney knew Jude was patron Saint of Lost Causes, among the obscure prophets [see Thomas Hardy's *Jude the Obscure*]. Jude is not Judas, the apostle who betrayed Christ. This Jude wrote the last book before *Revelations*, and Jude is a 2-page mini-book by Jude to tell Christians how to beware of false teachers and false prophets. This Jude does not claim to be an apostle (*Concordia Self-Study Bible*), and he may cryptically be "the brother of the Lord" (*Matthew* 13:5 and *Mark* 6:3). Brother of the Lord? This brings up all kinds of sticky questions about Jesus' mortal siblings.

"Hey Jude" opens to Paul's ponderous piano, like "Bridge Over Troubled Waters," or "Let It Be." Paul McCartney, while not southpaw-slinging his electric bass, is a fine keyboard guy; John Lennon tickles ivories in "Imagine." "Jude" drones its elephantine first verse. You feel the tension build. Paul in control, melodic key of 'F.' Ringo joins the 2nd verse, cymballically. Halfway through it, George plays Frankie Valli on the falsetto, with John in harmony. The song builds to its ultimate pandemonium. Jude, we wrest from the lyric, takes the sad song, and in his Heavenly Fix-it-Shop he makes them all better with the Band-Aid of love. On a more literal note, JUDE was the Beatle nickname for John and Cynthia's son **Julian Lennon** (#9, 10-84 "Valotte").

Then cometh the gushing waterfall. Crescendoing the song, Paul and crew cascade the chromatic (bVII), jumping from comfy **F** to the stunning **Eb major** chord, then sub-dominant IV chord, **Bb**, and back home to tonic **F**.

As the weary caravan of human misery plods along a dusty earth dotted with Joshua trees and despair, St. Jude intercedes to put us back on the right road [toward the Deep River]. Paul, with his smiley hopeful vegetarianism and ecological awareness and save-the-whales zeal, has tried to play his part in improving the human condition – yet realizing too well it's a long trek and many of us will not make it. Have a nice trip.

"Let It Be" – Beatles, #1(2), 3-70. Is "Let It Be" the most popular hymn of the Rock Revolution? Some say so. "Let It Be" is all **Paul**. The song debuted on the HOT 100 at number six, highest first entry ever. It's a Mom song, celebrating the nurturing and sanctity of motherhood. Paul's Catholic reverence invokes the Virgin Mary. In times of emotional turmoil or trouble, he calls out not to a friend like Simon and Gar, but to the pristine image of the Blessed Virgin to comfort him and assuage his grief.

He also calls to the spirit of his departed and beloved mother, who shared the name "Mary." Let us zoom back to the Beatles' reason for being – grief about mothers. The song is written about Paul's own mother who died of a 'long illness' when he was a young teenager. John Lennon, you recall, had been cast away by mother "Julia" to his Aunt Mimi's (*White Album*, Al. #1[9], 12-68). As Paul's mother Mary slowly succumbed to her agonizing illness, John's free-spirited mother Julia was struck and killed by a bus. Misery loves company? The two lads met, slashed their mutual agonies through a stubby amp, and the rest is Rock and Roll.

Paul's Catholic background cased him to invoke Mother Mary for the loss of his mother, Mary McCartney. Jesus' mother interceded in his dark times of personal distress. Paul pondered whether he would indeed notch that lofty plateau in "When I'm 64" (*Sgt. Pepper*), and a cottage on the Isle of Wight with his helpmeet wife Linda Eastman McCartney. The sad events of 1998 consigned Paul to a second emotional nightmare, when he lost his beloved Linda to the same virulent scourge.

Christianity concerns death and resurrection. "Let It Be" is a song of inborn hope and faith and love and purpose. A beacon in the dark night of earthly despair. "Let It Be" is a deeply Christian 'bridge over troubled water.' Invoking a simpler age, its mediaeval leap of faith is astounding in the smoky grey Liverpudlian cloud bank. McCartney has a simple answer to cut through all the stress and agony of daily life. [Cynics call it "The Jesus and Mary Pill."] Paul simply meditates – or prays – with Mary's spirit on his mind. This formula, plus a rosary, has worked for countless millions of pilgrims on dusty thirsty cobblestrewn highways of tribulation and despair.

Musically, "Let It Be" is no complex Beatle frenzy, no esoteric hodge-podge of quarter-tones, steam calliopes, 13/16 time signatures, MIDI lost-in-space music, Techno-Synth popcorn, or dissonant cacophony. "Let It Be" presents a simple, beautiful melody. It transcends complexity. "Bridge Over Troubled Water", in grand Orbisonic Spiral, rushes to a breathtaking crescendo. "Let It Be," on the other hand, just keeps on keepin' on, a human caravan of aspiration and inspiration. It states its musical case, hammers the lead line for dramatic effect, and fades away on the Catholic mantra "Let It Be". Let what be? Let the universe unfold. Let God handle the master plan. Bumper sticker stuff again: LET GO: LET GOD. He echoes the philosophy of croon star Doris Day:

"Whatever Will Be, Will Be" – Doris Day, #2(3), 6-56. [Spanish "Que Sera, Sera"]. Her cute melody offers a formula for romantic and wedded bliss. As the moppet frets her way up the rungs of life's ladder, various calm relatives/teachers reassure her with the title and its profound ramifications. Just sit back, relax, and let the universe happen.

"Baby Hold on to Me" – Gerald Levert, #27, 2-92; #1, 1-92 R & B. Star of #5, 8-87 "Casanova," Gerald brought brother Sean and ex-O'Jay dad Eddie for this multigenerational LET IT BE song. The future really isn't ours, to actually see, so 'whatever will be, will we.' Levert joins Paul McCartney's jet stream, and echoes Doris Day's lyric verbatim.

Morose undertones? The **Beatles** were about to break up. Obvious reason besides religion? **Yoko Ono** captivated John in a way Cynthia (1st wife and mother of Julian) could never do. She lassoed John and corralled his globetrotting soul. She offered a one-woman alternative to smooth and direct and sculpt her own Beatle. Rejoice! It's understatement time: Paul, George, and Ringo were less than enchanted with Yoko. If the Beatles were breaking up, was it time to let it be?

"Imagine" – John Lennon and the Plastic Ono Band, #3, 10-71. Unitarian Utopianism has never hit #1 on the charts. **John Lennon**'s (1940-80) ode to harmony and pacifism and secular cooperation won him billions of friends and enemies. Lovers of peace cheered his powerful statements. Some ultra-conservative Christians and Jews and Muslims saw his 'imagine no Heaven exists, and there's no Hell down in some fiery pit below either' line as blasphemous banter, more worthy of Marxist **Vladimir Lenin**, who founded the Soviet Union. Lennon's flippant line to the press about "We Beatles are more popular than Jesus" torched their tunes all over down-home America. Ralph Waldo Emerson said "to be great is to be misunderstood." Quoted out of context, Lennon meant that the media uproar, which made his band commandeer the front pages, was not necessarily good – it just happened. Mostly, he meant they were getting more PRESS at that time. Lennon's wry Brit wit didn't play well in Paducah, Kentucky. When he explained, the world forgave, but his ex-comment still rankles [like Jane Fonda's ill-advised trip to Hanoi].

Like "Let It Be," "Imagine" fires its opening salvos off a lulling piano intro. Unlike "Let It be," however, Lennon insists that we CAN change the world. That people will finally "Come Together" (Beatles #1, 1-69) and rally for peace. In **Friend and Lover's** "Reach Out of the Darkness" (#10, 5-68), Jim and wife **Cathy Post** sing how 'groovy' it was for divergent people to be rallying together in "Love-Ins" and peace rallies to change the world, save the planet, and harmonize ethereally. Lennon was listening. John and Yoko insist we can solve mankind's agonies: hunger, damnation, materialism, war. McCartney's anthem is more nebulous, hedging by generalizing about troubled times rather than precise problems. Lennon imagines there is no religion, and no concept of country. He tackles world hunger, 15 years before Harry Chapin, Band-Aid, and Michael Jackson. He posits a social contract, international brotherhood, and a global economy of peace and prosperity. Why didn't it work?

Medieval philosophy, maybe. The divinity-bestiality quandary. We're a little lower than the angels, so they say. And a little higher than the slugs and slithering slime of the earth.

We are all brothers and sisters, according to zealous John Lennon. We'll share the wealth. Beatles' "Taxman" is a more pithy, sarcastic Harrison look at the British land-sharing system – 'one shilling for you,' grubs the taxman, nineteen for us. John and Yoko believed wars would end and we could be 'Happy Together' (Turtles, #1, '67).

Christianity takes a gloomier view about this muddy Limbo Earth: "Do not suppose that I have come to bring peace to the earth. I did not come to bring peace, but a sword" (*Matthew* 10:34). Conventional Christian theology gazes beyond the blue horizon. It overrides secular suffering with a promised land of heavenly bliss – via a 'long and winding road' of faith and/or good works. And a DEEP RIVER. We earthy earthly humans cannot create utopia; Fundamentalist Evangelical Protestant sects, Muslims, and the Catholic Church generally look beyond utopia – it is past the grasp of most Christians except, perhaps, Unitarian optimists who believe in the perfectability of mankind and the upward spiral via science, technology and progress. Or jackpotting the $20 million lottery. Most Christians, like Paul, prefer to let it be.

This last bloody century granted Generation X too much cynicism and despair to believe in the Peaceable Kingdom (*Philippians* 4:7). A future teeming with starving overpopulated hordes like futuristic *Soylent Green* (1973***) dismisses a shining utopian golden city of total love and cooperation as an air-castle pipe dream. Most millennium people would agree with the Medium Beatle that we'd better let it be. It's too big to control by ourselves. But imagine if we could . . .

Lennon, via Ono, generates the overweening optimism. We can build a more utopian state. We can share the land?

"Share the Land" – Guess Who, #10, 10-70. Yankees had no corner on the land-division market. Winnipeg, Manitoba's superstar singer **Burton Cummings** and his Guess Who (later splintered to **Bachman-Turner Overdrive**) shoveled up a communal agrarian reform scheme that makes "Imagine" sound like Wall Street and Coca Cola. With starry-eyed assurance, and Gospel tacets, Cummings says they'll soon be equally apportioning all the land. We'll all shake hands and learn to live and love together. Some say that's been tried before, and that equal-land 'barons' soon become grumpy listless communists. Who knows? Good song, through, musically. [Guess Who's biggest is #1(3), 3-70 "American Woman," redone in 2000 by Lenny Kravitz]. Cummings' tenor throttles the high notes with the soulful spirit of **Ray Charles** chastising the Raelettes.

Other songs of the era shared Lennon's optimism of a secular paradise.

"Shambala" – Three Dog Night, #3, 5-73. The Three Tenors of Jazz Rock – **Chuck Negron, Danny Hutton, Cory Wells**, sing with gusto about the dazzling lights of Shangri-la-style 'Shambala' (thanks, Fred Friedberg). A celestial glow o'ershines this lovely land of Shambala, and its marbled halls of New Age demi-paradise. This mystic utopia washes away troubles and earthly cares.

Back in the mid-70s, our family would go to *Shambala* restaurant in Port Jefferson, Long Island, New York, to eat the groovy bran muffins and purple cabbage and tofu and odd ice cream that came from a goat, [Alas – kids wanted McDonalds]. Nifty gospel feel. Earthly paradise song ("All men's efforts are for his mouth, yet his appetite is never satisfied" – *Ecclesiastes* 6:7).

"My Sweet Lord" – George Harrison, #1(4), 12-70. The Third Beatle rejected both McCartney's maternal nurturing view and Lennon's utopian optimism. **George Harrison** (1942-2001) turned inward and eastward to sculpt a personal pantheistic philosophy. He traveled to India for Transcendental Meditation with Swami Maharishi Mahesh Yogi. "My Sweet Lord" is a marvelous rock tune. So marvelous, indeed, that Harrison embarrassingly had to pay out mega-royalties for inadvertently lifting his hymn's tune from the Girls' Group Era: "He's So Fine" (Chiffons, #1[4], 2-63). With millions of people and millions of potential melodies, it is a miracle they don't crash accidentally/coincidentally more often.

"My Sweet Lord" involves a mantra, Hindu for a simple prayer repeated over and over, like "OM". The Transcendental Meditation group fashioned a series of semi-personal mantras based on the age of the devotees. Harrison travels back a lot farther in time than the Maharishi. He consults Hindu sacred books the *Vedas* and the *Bhagavad-Gita*. My friend Bob Roberts in Michigan – a wedding photographer and tri-athlete – follows the Hare Khrishna movement and has one of those double Rock and Roll sideman names like **James Jamerson, Mitch Mitchell, Robyn Robbins**' (I saw Dick Richards at my class reunion the other day, too). Anyhow, Bob supplied a copy of *Bhagavad-Gita* by His Divine Grace A.C. Swami Prabhupada. *Bhagavad-Gita* was written in India in Sanskrit millennia before the *New Testament*. Despite a pantheon of millions of gods, godlets, and demi-gods, the Hindus rely on three major deities: **Vishnu, Shiva**, and **Khrishna**. Hindus believe that the soul transmigrates or passes from one body to another until nirvana is reached. [And **Kurt Cobain** of rock group **Nirvana** missed the connection.] Once a state of nirvana consciousness is attained, generally among the Brahmin (intellectual or contemplative) caste, the soul no longer undergoes this upward metamorphosis from body to body. [Buddhists rebelled from Hinduism, as Protestants protested Catholicism.]

Hindus feel you can be Christian and Hindu at the same time. George toyed with that concept in "My Sweet Lord." Chanters chant "Alleluia," sliding into "Hare Khrishna" (pronounced Ha-Ray-Chrish-na, meaning "Hail the god Khrishna" [with a slight similarity to 'Hail Mary']). Christians and Jews take a more exclusionary view of being Jewish, Christian, and Hindu simultaneously. The Jewish *Torah* intertwines the *Bible*'s first five books: "Do not worship any other God, for the Lord . . . is a jealous God" (*Exodus* 34:14).

Harrison says he really wants to see his Lord, here and now, an impossible dream. Who wouldn't wish a mystic glimpse of their Lord while they are still upon the earth? **Dishwalla**'s #15, 4-96 "Counting Blue Cars" asks a friend to share his innermost thought about God, because the singer really yearns to get a chance to meet with HER. Zen gender switcheroo? Or legit prayer? We certainly have Mother Nature. Longing for cosmic insight is a universal desire. It darts from salt miners on Spitsbergen to Tahitian belles on bikini beaches. It floats from New York freeway car-phone commuters to vanquishers clawing at world's-ceiling Mt. Everest. It thunders from Arabian caravans to Indian bazaars, from Aborigine boomerangers to smoke-smeared gauchos to Toledo topless go-go patrons. The quest for knowledge of God is as old as the Garden of Eden (*Genesis* 3:4-5 "You will not die," the serpent said to the woman. "For God knows that when you eat of it your eyes will be opened, and you will be like God, knowing good and evil"). "Sneaky Snaky" line, eh? [Tom T. Hall, #55, '75]. Dust to dust.

"Act Naturally" – Beatles, #47, 9-65. [Buck Owens' #1(4), 4-63 Country.] Politically and religiously, **Ringo** shared the sounds of silence of Harpo Marx. He never said a thing. With a cosmic wishy-washyism not even attributable to Charles Schulz's beloved pilgrim, good ol' Charlie Brown, Ringo maintains his sphinx-like silence on politics and religion – and just grooves to good ol' Rock and Roll, like Snoopy doing his happy hedonistic Dance of Life. Ringo rock rolls on.

"Arms of Mary" – Chilliwack, #67, 8-78. Named after their town by Vancouver, British Columbia, Chilliwack sings with angelic Everly harmony about a young man's first torrid affair (see *David* or *St. Augustine*). Granted, the lusts of the flesh are hardly grounds for religion, but he worships (alas, idolatry) his first girl: "Mary" takes away his boyhood "naivete." He wishes he were in her loving arms right now. Divinity? Blasphemy? Or just a great song?

"Put Your Hand in the Hand" – Ocean, #2(1), 3-71. Back up to the Beatles' hand-y item, #1(7), '64 "I Want to Hold Your Hand." Classy conjunct? Hand-clapping percussion. It's sparked by a unique heavenly handclap:

The Beatles didn't revolutionize Rock and Roll. They just flung out a few crucial changes. Like this:

The backbeat is key here. Ringo amplifies his second beat, echoing it. Then he implodes the fourth beat with his eighth-note shot on the 3½ – handclappers double up his snazzy sound.

Ocean, and most rock and rollers, ignores the subtle 3½ shot. The bass drum booms its bullfrog backbeat at 2, 2½, and 4. Beyond the basic beat, handclapping amplifies Ocean's wide popularity. Since 72% of the world's surface is already ocean, they skyrocketed for the sky.

For Ocean's **Janice Morgan** (b. London, Ontario), this tune was stardom. It's harder to get much closer to #1. Morgan's cool-breeze soprano sang the Bandwagon Approach to Christianity. **Ocean** invokes its teeniest cousin, the pint-size little Sea of Galilee; "Tell my brothers to go to Galilee," Jesus said at the Resurrection, "and there they will see Me" (*Matthew* 28:10). Just 20 miles long and 12 miles wide, the salty little sea resembles our Great Salt Lake in Utah [shrine of the MORMONS]. **Morgan**'s mission and pilgrimage shine through her bouncy song, and handclappers help out with verve and zeal. They 'Make a joyful noise unto the Lord.'

"When the Saints Go Marching In" – Louie 'Satchmo' Armstrong, #10, 4-59. I really can't believe this song wasn't #1 somewhere, somehow, somewhen. "The Saints" was an oldie when Louis scratched the top ten with his heavenly gold trumpet – as a world of weary wayfaring strangers and pilgrims approached their personal World War II Armageddons. One of the Seven Churches in Armageddon's *Revelations* alludes to #2-biggest English-speaking city in the world in George Washington's day – Philadelphia (Rock and Roll's secular Dick Clark/*American Bandstand* semi-shrine). See *Rev* 1:11. "When the Saints Go Marching In" was a Dixieland Jazz favorite during World War I (1914-18), when teenage Louie's fomenting "Wonderful World" was but a bedazzling chunk of hot scorchy New Orleans night life, outside a hundred Houses of the Rising Sun. With French-Afro-American joie de vivre joy-of-living, Louie, and his Sousa-style hot marching Jazz bands, decorated sultry Southern nights with their 'joyful noise unto the Lord!' "The Saints'" Judgment Day hallelujah anthem filled America with Satchmo's sizzling Jericho trumpet.

America loves "The Saints" because it celebrates two lives – this one AND the next. The song is a promise of celestial glory beyond the Deep River [Mississippi? Jordan?] of day-to-day doldrums, or despair. The song seeks divine inspiration. "Saints," showed Louie (and **Weavers** #27, 8-51), is a joyous affirmation of life on this bittersweet tragicomic earth. It also forecasts a land of glory which (paraphrasing similar Happy Hymn "Do Lord") outshines our sun in splendor but not our Son.

You want a DIRECT tie-in to Rock and Roll destiny? **Tony Sheridan** (Jerry Lee Lewis-echo voice) sang LEAD on the **Beatles**' first record. The flipside was "My Bonnie" (later #26, 2-64, but released by Decca in 1962). The single on Decca (Tony Sheridan & the 'Beat Brothers') was worth $15,000 in 2001 (sez Whitburn). Tony's A-side? Yep, Satchmo's song, entitled "The Saints."

Some say Louie's "Saints" may be #1 somewhere, faraway, someday . . .

"On the Wings of a Dove" – Ferlin Husky, #12, 11-60; #1(10), 9-60 C. Fall River, Missouri's **Ferlin Husky** ["Gone," #4, 3-57] details the Gospel/Bluegrass/ Country testimonial to the Noah situation. After 40 days of cloudburst rain and 150 days at landless sea (*Exodus* 7:24) the two-by-two ark animals got a little waterlogged. Finally atop Mt. Ararat, as the world waters receded, Noah sent out a dove to search for land (*Genesis* 8:6-11). Covered on **Loretta Lynn**'s *All-Time Gospel* Favorites (Heartland, 1997), Husky's lickety-split waltz OOM-PAAAHED like a German band in lederhosen. Or a steamy tent revival:

"Brother Love's Travelling Salvation Show" – Neil Diamond, #22, 2-69. Brooklyn pilgrim Diamond, of Brill Building boogiemeisters, served a great crescendo. Under a glorious Mississippi moon, frenzied preacher Brother Love fishes for wayward souls. The passion and the power and the glory. Southern salvation and sweet-potato pie. With a gospel-gusto voice that suggests sandpaper on fire, Diamond hollers to the ringing, rip-roaring gospel tent on a demonically hot sultry August night.

"One Toke Over the Line (Sweet Jesus)" – Brewer and Shipley, #10, 4-71. Mike Brewer to One-Hit Wonders' Wayne Jancik: "It's about ANY drugs, or anything you push too far. A toke [obviously a puff of pot, weed, marijuana] seemed apropos at that time . . . I'd had one too many hamburgers, one too many Holiday Inns, one too many nights on the road: toots, tokes, everything." Down the Bummer Road of bleary hangovers, SUNDAY MORNIN' COMING DOWN [see Johnny Cash].

Noah himself sampled a tad more of the grape than the Lord was pleased with (*Genesis* 9-20:24). Noah got 'bombed' and his sons had to cover his immodest sunburned form as he writhed, wishing someone would invent the Alka-Seltzer. *Genesis* says Noah repented and lived 950 years. If you throw away your demon rum, slick sickie cigs, and beer today, the best you can hope for is another 90 years. Sorry. "One Toke over the Line" highlights the old line: "there are no atheists in foxholes."

Suffering songsters invoke Jesus and Mary here. You hear a faint cry of Yale's "Whiffenpoof Song" of 1909 and #19, 6-46 by **Tex Beneke**. Tipsy collegiate songsters warble into the tavern afterglow at Mory's Pub, and they say they will be doomed from this place until eternity [**Bing Crosby**, #7, 11-47]. One line caused a book/movie, *From Here to Eternity* (1952****), and the resurrection of **Frank Sinatra**'s incredible singing career. Whiffenpoofs puff on. Over kegs of prayerful brewskis, they bargain with God to take MERCY upon them and their sinful scoundrels. They compare themselves to God's little sheep, gone astray. Looking perhaps, for a buxom Bo Peep show.

Just a stinky, sleazy railroad station stands between Brewer and Shipley's trendy tokers, redemption, and salvation. They are pie-eyed and pickled. Wasted. Wounded. They bob and weave their woozy boozy way home to the most painful illness for which sympathy is measured in thimbleful – the wretched hangover. When the party is over, say Johnny Cash, Paul McCartney, Tom Shipley, the Whiftenpoofs, and Ocean, Jesus can forgive you: Call to Him.

"Why Me?" – Kris Kristofferson, #16, 4-73; #1(1) C. A <u>bass</u> lead singer? In 1971, Kris was looking up from inside a bottle of doubt and despair. Emaciated, strung-out, punch-drunk, K.O.ed by demons. Shortly thereafter he found Jesus and hits. Jesus, of course, had never been lost. "Why Me?" takes the astonishing view. The penitent asks the Lord basically "What did I do, after spending these last years studying for the derelictcy, and leading the life of a wretched dirt bag, to DESERVE Your Grace?" The sinner doesn't quibble; he marvels. With the patience of Job, the singer absorbs his fate, and prays with gratitude and comprehension for the Amazing Grace he has received – despite his miserable station in life (*Job* 42:1-71). This is the bulwark and essence of the Judeo-Christian faith. The repentant sinner bears his cross, his sackcloth, his dust and ashes, and his humility. He repents and atones. He receives Grace he never dreamed of in the old lost days. A slow song. Funereal pace. Serious. Sombering.

"Morning Has Broken" – Cat Stevens, #6, 4-72. #1 in many Protestant and Catholic hymnals. Goes back a couple hundred years. "Morning Has Broken" has one of the prettiest pure melodies ever written, rippling with dancing arpeggios. Cat's chords swirl in harmonic ecstasy. The singer of this precious Christian/Jewish hymn converted to Islam in 1979.

Cat Stevens (b. '47 **Steven Georgiou**, London, Greek-British parentage) troubadoured the coffeehouses of Hammersmith College as a Folk singer. Shackled a year ('68) to ghastly tuberculosis, Stevens then recuperated for a year. Then his singing career took off. His concordant canon is landmarked by mystical symbols:

Nothing about this song is discordant or jangled. In rock-steady 3/4 time, the devotional hymn leads us through the dewy sunrise in the Garden of Eden. You ponder the first mystical bird. Dewy green grass. Golden shafts of sunlight. The innocent age. Long ago. Yesteryear Eden.

"Oh Very Young" – Cat Stevens, #10, 3-74. What are you going to leave us as your legacy, Cat asks the very young. Emerson or Shakespeare could envy Cat's next niblet of oracular wisdom: WE ARE JUST DANCING UPON THE WEARY EARTH A VERY SHORT TIME. Sounds like *Psalms* or *Ecclesiastes* or this gem from *Proverbs* 24:26: "An honest answer is like a kiss on the lips."

Stevens philosophizes in "Wild World," (#11, 2-71), that it's well-nigh impossible to make it just on a smile alone. His lyrics flash and flare with fiery language, like Japanese haiku poetry dancing with the wisdom of Confucian or Shinto or Zen Buddhist philosophy.

At some point the Christian peace pilgrim, Cat, became disenchanted with peace, or Christianity. His "Moon Shadow" (#30, 6-71) lurches with intense passion, hinting at an exotic world of Arabian Nights and Midnight-at-the-oasis intrigue. In late 1979, Cat's conversion to Islam garnered a third name: Yusef Islam. When Salman

Rushdie's *Satanic Verses* black comedy was deemed blasphemous to the Muslim religion in 1990, the Mohammedan proselyte lowered the boom. Like those who cast the first stone at Mary Magdalene, Georgiou-Stevens-Islam joined with his new Islamic Fundamentalist Shi-ite brethren in denouncing the book. Some of these starkly-literal zealots (not Cat), like Osama bin Laden, called for the painful torture and death for the author who, in England and America, believed in certain freedom of the press to satirize anything – even religion. Freedom of Speech wasn't a big deal in their hard-baked sect; they forbade it under pain of death. Rushdie figured he was just writing black comedy like Voltaire or Rabelais. Here in America via the *Comedy Channel* or *Saturday Night Live*, nothing is sacrosanct; no sacred cows avoid McBurgerism. 'Humorists' blast everybody, regardless of race, color, or creed. Hopefully, Millennium III will see some peace. Morning has broken on a wild world.

"City of New Orleans" – Arlo Guthrie, #18, 9-72. Remember dust-bowl vagabond troubadour **Woody Guthrie**, **Bob Dylan**'s hero and mentor? Woody's kid Arlo escaped from #97, 12-60 "Alice's Rock and Roll Restaurant" to sing this rhapsody in blue about the odyssey of a southbound train. It throttles the mystical deep Delta, chugging its way down from Kankakee, Illinois, to New Orleans. **Steve Goodman** (c. 1946-84) wrote this rockin' rail reverie, and took it to #113, 2-72 first himself. The train, romanticized in myth and legend, was a dying breed of 1972 transportation. General Motors cannibalized city streetcar lines to sell autos. The trucking lobby made chickenfeed out of the once-powerful octopus of America's rail network. The hip kid narrator treks down the Mississippi rails to New Orleans. **Louie Armstrong** took virtually the same train to trek North to Chicago – to help create Jazz, prelude to Rock and Roll. Wistful, nostalgic, powerful Guthrie celebrates a bygone era:

Pullman porters, card games, paper-bag bottles and nearly-empty passenger cars. Also, Madonna moms with nursing babes, smokescape ramshackle freight yards, romantic whistle stops. Sons of porters and engineers ride along on their father's incredible whooshing magic-carpet locomotion sculpted from steel and bygone glory. **Cat Stevens** did a hopeful #7, 9-71 song called the "Peace Train" (see **O'Jays'** "Love Train"). Whereas the communal train brought folks together, the solitary automobile fragmented them into little insular dots of light – streaking alone down the lonely highway. A passenger train, no matter how motley, is a congregation. At age 5, I rode a train with my mother and father and sister Blair to Butte, Montana, and we blasted through the purple Dakota twilight into the lost American night. I will never forget. **Willie Nelson** took "City of New Orleans" to #1(1) C in 8-84.

"Amen" – Impressions, #7, 11-64; #110, 12-69; #17, 1-65 R & B. Christian mantra. Curtis Mayfield's Impressions' "Amen" dances with the Big Three I-IV-V chords, and floats like an angelic choir on the easiest lyric ever to remember. Second easiest?

"Dust in the Wind" – Kansas, #6, 2-78. Just when you think your world is ginchy and groovin', and that your spiffy girlfriend is peachy-keen, here comes Kansas to really ruin your day. If you want despair, meaninglessness, and spiritual desolation, turn to your *Bible*. Huh? Wait a doggoned minute. I don't really mean that. The *Bible* is truly a treasure-trove of tremendous hope and inspiration. Most of it. But . . . Beware of *Ecclesiastes*. *Ecclesiastes* takes on the voice of the "Philosopher," son of David of Jerusalem. He is no Pollyanna, no cheery happy-go-lucky huckleberry:

"Someone who is always thinking about happiness is a fool. A wise person thinks about death." (*Ecclesiastes* 3:8) Not fun, this. Nor Kansas's gut-wrenching song – "Dust in the Wind." Rock and Roll is primarily about LOVE. Once in a blue moon it broods over untimely death:

"As long as people live,
Their minds are full of evil and Madness,
And suddenly they die." (*Ecclesiastes* 9:3)

Drac Rock? Take Mark Dinning's sorrowful "Teen Angel" (#1, 1-60), squashed by a train while seeking a lost high school ring. Take non-nirvanic **Nirvana**'s **Kurt Cobain**. Rock and Roll can still hover a bit too close to the Alternative graveyard (see Marilyn Manson). Sarah McLachlan's #4, 11-98 "Angel" (Jonathan Mulvoin, Smashing Pumpkins' keyboardist,) O.D.-ing in a lonely hotel room. The Old Testament Philosopher is even gloomier about all our futures. Just 'dust in the wind':

"A human being is not better off than an animal,
Because life has no meaning for either.
They are both going to the same place –
The dust." (*Ecclesiastes* 3:19-20)

In panic and consternation, you flip to another book for comfort, solace, contentment. You grab *Lamentations* by mistake:

"The Lord is like an enemy,
He has swallowed up Israel . . .
He has multiplied mourning and lamentation . . .
He has laid waste his dwelling like a garden; . . .
The Lord has rejected his altar
And abandoned His sanctuary."
(*Lamentations* 2:5-7)

"Laid waste," like Lucifer in Rolling Stones' "Sympathy for the Devil." Aaaargh, you groan. You gnash teeth. You flub and flounder for a real biblical pick-me-up. You find this woeful scrap: "It is all useless. It is like chasing the wind." (*Ecclesiastes* 2:26)

Even Jesus (*Matthew* 10:34) said He did not come to lavish peace but a sword. He gave warning that Christianity never purported to be an easy religion to follow. Punt the hammock, the Doritos, the root beer, and the Sofa-Spud pigskin TV.

Keep reading. It gets better in the *Bible*'s other books. Just remember – Christianity: Wimps need not apply. "Who ever loses his life for my sake shall gain it." (*Matthew* 10:39)

"So I say to you: Ask and it shall be given to you;
Seek, and ye shall find. Knock, and the door shall be
open to you." (*Luke* 11:9).

Faith, then, is crucial to the Christian concept of salvation: "Everyone who asks receives; he who seeks finds; and to him who knocks, the door shall be opened" (*Luke* 11:10). Strong song, "Dust."

Kansas is located in the very heart of the United States of America. In Kansas, Surf's Down. Kansas is just a cloud or two below the Land of Oz. The Emerald City. The Wizard. Dorothy and Toto. And the Man of Straw. All he is is 'dust in the wind.' The wimpy Wizard, too. Follow the yellow brick road to the dust. Dust and Death Rock – all the way back to rocky *Ecclesiastes*.

Steve Walsh of Topeka, Kansas, founded his rock group **Kansas** in 1970. **Kerry Livgren**, keyboards/guitar; **Phil Ehart**, drums; **Dave Hope**, bass; **Rich Williams**, second guitar, and **Robby Steinhardt**, first (and only) violin (see Dave Matthews Band). Lead singer Walsh split in 1981, and was replaced by **John Elefante**, later a major Christian Contemporary Rock producer [Whitburn]; Livgren, too, became a Christian Rock star.

Kansas is filled with dust beyond the wheat. About the 30s Dust Bowl, **Woody Guthrie** sang "So Long (It's Been Good to Know Ya)" when the dust covered the fledgling farms with despair, starvation, and bankruptcy [#4, 1-51, by the **Weavers** of Pete Seeger fame, see Mellencamp]. The American Johnny B. Goode Dream descended nightmarishly into the vortex of the terrible tornado (see Allen Ginsberg's long poem *Wichita Vortex Sutra*, 1969, a Kansan/Hindu/Jewish/East Greenwich Village extravaganza rated RX for adult language).

"Dust" swirls along in a folksy minor key. The harmony is haunting. The dust-choked pale blue sky whirls. Cirrus clouds of cotton-candy roll around the heavens all day. Beeves lumber placidly around in their squishy feed lots, thinking they will live forever, never whopperizing into McBurger. The 1971 Kansas Turnpike speed limit was 80 mph. Many Americans blast through Kansas's cornfield panorama as an impediment to California or the Big Apple. "Dust in the Wind" makes you stop in Kansas. And hover there.

The song discusses life's quizzical and puzzling meaning. In the 50s, songs talked of malt shops, sock hops, the big smooch. The windy dust discloses: If you close your eyes briefly, the precious moment disappears. We're all dinky drops of water in this endless ocean. All that we build will crumble. We are just wispy wind dust . . . Not fun music. Makes you think. Cosmic gloom.

Kansas had many other hits: "Carry On, Wayward Son" (#11, 2-77). Or "All I Wanted (#19, 11-86). They sandwiched oddly-spelled "Point of Know Return" (#28, 11-77), intriguing "People of the South Wind" (#23, 6-79), and "Play the Game Tonight" (#17, 5-82). From the Prodigal Son parable to their Mystic Quest for Spiritual Contentment, or OZ, **Kansas** straddles gut-basket America. The teeming Heartland. Suddenly, our ATM's and Olds Delta 88 Royale and geraniums and Mars Bars and Apple computers and static cling and squirrels bopping acorns off our noggins aren't that important anymore. In the big, LONG picture, we're already history. In late Pastor Milt Heitzman's terms, "We're outta here."

Huh? Check out that wimpy pebble on the path. Geologists tell us it's been around for millions of years. De-spite yogurt and marathons and good lovin' we can't hack 100.

As morose Taoist poet **Tu Fu** remarked in his 1000+-year-old poem "Jade Flower Palace":

"Among these lanes of life

Disappearing in the distance,

Who can make himself eternal?"

Good question. Christianity has some answers. All your hoarded money can't buy another minute, sez Kansas. And Jesus: "Do not store up for yourselves treasure on earth, where moth and rust destroy, and where thieves break in and steal. But store up for yourselves treasures in heaven." – *Matthew* 6:19-20

Dust in the wind.

"Exodus" – Ferrante and Teicher, #2(1), 11-60 and amazingly #6, 12-60, R & B. *Exodus* (1960***). Theme booms *Torah*'s action-packed story of the founding of Israel in 1947 after a double-millennia hiatus. Stars Paul Newman. Not a Rock song. Italian-and-Jewish-American Juilliard grads. Classical pianists. Innovative chord progressions. Supersonic arpeggios. Stunning crescendos. Instrumental. Vocal? [NOT **Bob Marley** song] –

"Exodus" – Pat Boone, #64, 1-61. Also titled "The Exodus Song (This Land Is Mine)." As a Born-Again Evangelical Christian, **Pat Boone** feels a major kinship with his Jewish brethren. He journeyed to the Holy Land on several pilgrimages. Boone mirrors *Exodus* 15:1-2:

"I will sing to the Lord,

For He is highly exalted . . .

The Lord is my strength and my song;

He has become my salvation.

He is my God, and I will praise Him,

My father's God, and I will exalt him."

Pat wrote the words to "Exodus." Not noted as a songwriter/lyricist, Pat was so moved by the melody and movie that he sculpted the story of a Jewish pilgrim returning to the long-lost Holy Land of Zion, of Palestine, and now Israel. As #1 Christmas carol was written by Jewish **Irving Berlin**, "White Christmas," one of the most powerful popular Jewish songs of all-time was half-written [lyric] by one of America's premier Contemporary Christian singers, Pat Boone. This #64 song presages Pat's first Top Tenner since 1958: "Moody River" (#1[1], 5-61). In this bizarre Graveyard Rock ballad, a girl commits suicide because of her agonizing guilt over cheating on her Mr. Nice Guy. He's left with a glove of his lost love (see Cobain, Shannon, and "Angel").

Boone's #4, 2-58 "A Wonderful Time Up There" slipped into our Blues Department, but it's a tremendous example, though, of Religious Rock and Roll. As Pat surfs the Boogie Woogie melody arpeggios, he also warns his spiritual brother to prepare for a glorious or gruesome reckoning arriving the next fateful morning. [Yes, it's a wonderful time up there, but yes, pal, you better 'straighten up and fly right' if you wanna get there.] Or as **Barretta** once said, if you do the crime, you have to pay the time.

"Ebony Eyes" – Everly Brothers, #8, 1-61; #25, 3-61 R & B; #25, 3-61 C. Flip of Cricket Sonny Curtis's #7 "Walk Right Back." Airplane disaster Rap item too real in Holly-Valens plane aftermath: 2-3-59. His gal, 'Ebony Eyes,' takes Flight 1203. Our hero soldier, on leave, awaits his love's arrival. Squawky loudspeaker tells relatives to report to a chapel across the street. Light Metal and Grave-yard Rock.

"You Light Up My Life" – Debby Boone, #1(10), 9-77; #4, 10-77 C. Coming off his biggest smash hit, a #1(4) cover reprise of Ivory Joe Hunter's #1(5) R & B 1950 "I Almost Lost My Mind," Pat celebrated his third daughter Debby's birth (9-22-56). The super croon genes came from Papa Pat and Grandpa **Red Foley** (#5, '51 C. "Peace in the Valley"). First tri-generational top ten star. Debby cashed in all her hit record chips (except #50, 2-78 "California") for "You Light Up My Life." It's slow and melodic and plodding. Glowingly she marches from ingénue alto to powerful diva soprano. It's a song of interdominational faith and hope and inspiration. Never quite mentioning God or Jesus (or Khrishna or Buddha or Moses or Zoroaster), the song nevertheless takes on the golden tones of celestial glory. Enwreathing you in spiritual wonder, it bounces from Cloud Nine to Cloud Eleven with her sweet innocent pure soulful commitment.

Debby's song offers a gorgeous melody, with a celestial crescendo. Whoever her mystical inspiration is, she floats over sweet IV sub-dominant chord shifts and subtle stirring strings. The song seems buoyed heavenward upon angels' wings. It, ahem, lights up your life. (*John* 8:12 "Jesus spoke . . . I am the light of the world. Whoever follows me will never walk in darkness, but will have the light of life").

"Place in This World" – Michael W. Smith, #6, 5-91. Christian Contemporary Rock is a form of 'Lite Rock' with a Christian theme. It has its own charts. Out of over 10,000 myriad radio stations (Campbell's *Media & Culture*, 2000), there were 509 Christian stations, 559 Gospel, and 968 "Religious," so nearly 20% in 1998 pursued Salvation with a Beat. Smith is a virtual legend among devotees of Contemporary Christian music. In this cavalcade of religious stations, **Michael W. Smith** is usually somewhere near the top of the ROCK-OF-AGES ROCK charts. Smith's Contemporary Christian hits are Legion. From his pilgrimage to Country/Gospel capital Nashville in 1978, Smith challenged and dominated his devotional Rock style. During this iffy era searching for commitment and certainty and faith, Michael shone his light: "Come, let us walk in the light of the Lord? (*Isaiah* 2:5). Smith penned #29, 5-86 "Find a Way" for **Amy Grant**.

Showing the dilemma of human existence in a materialistic world, Smith skillfully handles the theme, and his burgeoning international fame. His follow-up follows his Christian orientation of service (with a smile): #60, 9-91 "For You," and #27, 9-92 " I Will Be Here for You." That last lyrical hook dovetails into the Rembrandts' *Friends* sitcom theme, #17, 9-95 "I'll Be There for You," bespangled with British Invasion verve and vitality last seen in Gerry and the Pacemakers' selfless #14, 12-64 "I'll Be There" and spirited #23, 4-65 "It's Gonna Be Alright." Smith. Common name, Smith. Uncommonly powerful voice. And message. And mission. Friendship may be a temporal and worldly extension of the human bond of religion.

> "The first time I heard Elvis, it was like busting out of jail." – *Bob Dylan*

"(There'll Be) Peace in the Valley (For Me)" – Elvis Presley, with especially, the Jordanaires, #25, 4-57; NC C or R & B. Power and the Glory. In 1-2001, Elvis's eponymous album hit #13 on the Contemporary Christian charts. Elvis, like St. Augustine, St. Paul, St. John, Mohammed, Buddha, Moses, and King David, lived a life of the flesh. Augustine and Mohammed and Buddha tasted the forbidden fruits of many exotic courtier ladies. Moses killed a man in a fight. The *Bible*'s second-best-known person, King David, is best known for killing the blustering giant Goliath who might have recently blocked **Michael Jordan**'s basketball flights.

Elvis was torn between lusty love and fervent belief. Of catlike grace and great passions, Elvis toted the turbulence of the Red Sea ("the Lord drove the sea back with a strong east wind and turned it into dry land" *Exodus* 14:21) into his fiery stage performances. Elvis knew fire and brimstone. His Baptist upbringing caused him to grasp the deep guilt that Rock Idoldom brought forth. With groupies galore bashing down the door to get their bosoms autographed, what could a poor Southern boy do? He could pray?

Elvis lived his blazing life in second gear. Someday, he believed, he would find peace. The **Jordanaires** helped. After all, weren't they a Gospel group? Neal Matthews, Duane West, Ray Walker, and Louis Nunley. The beat staggers, then flows. Coming off his tenor tacet, Elvis emotes sincere resignation.

Elvis took time out from his legendary Rock and Roll idoldom in 1957 to speak to a cynical kid. Me. My bone-white AM radio glowered from the midnight bedroom dresser. I'd been puffing a pack a day of Camels, courting zits and teenage wasteland, and getting bored with nearly everything but Rock and Roll. I was too big and strong (5'5" 120# at 14) for God.

When I heard Elvis sing a hymn, I recognized the future 'King' as a credible source. Since I was an apprentice 'Hood,' Pat Boone's testimony was a little too preppy for me. As a junior-high scrapper, I turned out 2-2 in boxing bouts: ("They will beat their swords into plowshares" *Isaiah* 1:4). My pugilistic rewards were a black eye, a crooked nose, and an ego in critical condition.

Huston Smith's *The Religions of Man* shows the Islamic *Koran* as it sees itself – like the Mormon Church of the Latter-Day Saints – an extension of the Judeo-Christian *Bible*. The Koran says: "By the noonday brightness, and by the night when it darkeneth, the Lord hath not forsaken thee, neither hath He been displeased. Surely the future shall be better for thee than the past; and in the end He shall be bounteous to thee, and thou shalt be satisfied."

Like wow, man. Isn't that the essence of most religions? If you follow the rules, you will get your heavenly reward, with minor sins forgiven. From a pantheistic viewpoint, aren't many religious squabbles a waste of time? Shouldn't we all be living together in peace and prosperity? Peace, in the valley? A peaceful valley. Disney, sheep, green grass, friendly folks. When Elvis sang that song, I guess I knew there was something out there beyond the street. I discovered, via Elvis and my own boxing mediocrity, that black eyes and busted lips were highly overrated by the blood-and-guts cowboy entertainment media. Popular music is a lever. With it, you can move the world. Or, alleluia, the universe.

"Take My Hand, Precious Lord" – Elvis Presley, NC, 1957. Salvation Army writer Henry Gariepy tells how Gospel-Blues star **Thomas A. Dorsey** (b. 1899, and not big bandleader Tommy D.) got a tragic telegram: his beloved wife had died in childbirth. A few hours later his baby boy joined his mother, and his little family was buried in the same casket. Despondent and utterly devastated, he talked to an empathetic friend. God seemed to direct him to his piano. His grief poured out upon the keys. Fragile and stunning and soul-searing, Dorsey's anthem of staggering FAITH thunders through the rich baritone and tenor top notes of Elvis and his echoing posse the **Jordanaires**: Tired, weak, worn, the pilgrim asks the Lord to protect him with his "Lord is My Shepherd" staff – and to take his little hand in his frightful trek through the Valley of the Shadow of Death Elvis's manly Gospel fervor overarches the stinging plight of this wayfaring pilgrim. The song leads him home.

Elvis would soon need his own balm of consolation. His precious mother, **Gladys Presley**, would soon leave this world. Their graves lie next to one another in the Memory Garden of Graceland. To the side is the tiny infant grave of **Jesse Garon Presley**, Elvis's twin brother, stillborn. With public health care and guaranteed hospitalization, back in 1935, Jesse might today be playing Vegas – singing "Take My Hand, Precious Lord" for the memory of his mother, his father, and his brother Elvis.

"I Heard the Bells on Christmas Day" – Henry Wadsworth Longfellow, 1864. Lyricist/poet Longfellow was the Elvis of the 19th century. Revered in America and England, the Boston Brahmin poet doubled as lyricist. In his own very dark night, and America's bloody Civil War, **Longfellow** fashioned the greatest Christmas carol of all? His Yankee soldier son was wounded, and Henry knew well how many brave Southern lads had fallen in battle defending a states-rights system they believed in. In the poet's despair, he mirrors Dorsey's passage via *Isaiah* (41:12-13):

Those who wage war against you
　Will be as nothing at all.
For I am the Lord, your God,
　Who takes hold of your right hand
And says to you, Do not fear;
　I will help you.

Believer Longfellow wrestled with the Generation X de-spair of **Kurt Cobain**'s group Nirvana (#6 "Smells Like Teen Spirit" 12-91 and "Come As You Are" #32, 3-92), which whispered various 'God-Is-Dead' rumors that have been popping up by cynics since the dawn of time. In the 19th century, the philosopher **Friedrich Nietzsche** [1844-1900, 56] propounded the "God is dead" theory in his *Man and Superman* and *Thus Spake Zarathustra*. I recall an old graffito on the bathroom wall at Wayne State University's Old Main Building:

"God is Dead." – Nietzsche
"Nietzsche is Dead" – God . . .

Longfellow thunders to unbelievers. At the war's bottom, he creates a verse that caresses fervent belief. When Longfellow's bells peal, the poet thunders that God is NOT dead nor asleep. He says that the spirit of WRONG will fail. RIGHT will prevail. He wishes us all 'Peace on Earth and Good Will to Men.'

It was covered by **Johnny Cash**, on NC, '88 *Christmas Album*. Anyone more straightforward and believable? Many Christmas carols I love, like "It Came Upon a Midnight Clear" [My mother, Liz Dean's (1908-97) favorite carol. Born in Butte, Montana, she reported for the *Detroit Free Press* and once interviewed Eleanor Roosevelt. She taught me to appreciate the richness of our language. And to hang onto my dreams . . .] Also "Silent Night"; "O Holy Night"; "O Little Town of Bethlehem"; and "O Come All Ye Faithful." Pop-Rock format tunes?

"Jingle Bell Rock" – Bobby Helms, #6, 12-57; #13, 12-57 C; #35, 12-58; #36, 12-60; #41, 12-61; #58, 12-8-62. Also # 1(2), 12-63 *Billboard's* Special Christmas Singles. Nifty Country Rock item for Bloomington's (Indiana) perennial Christmas guy Helms (1935-97). Other biggie had quasi-religious theme: "My Special Angel" #7, 10-47; #1(4) C. Bobby's best? First hit? "Fraulein" — #36, 7-57: #1(4), 4-57 C. Hillbilly classic, about a U.S. soldier stationed in Deutschland, and his German girlfriend.

"Rockin' Around the Christmas Tree" – Brenda Lee, #14, 12-60; #50, 12-61; #59, 12-62. Festive funster frolic. In radio play, Brenda's Christmas class is #4 ever. Mistletoe, caroling, cheer. Rock Hall 2002 for Brenda.

"A Holly Jolly Christmas" – Burl Ives, #13, 12-64, Christmas List. Troubadour triumph from Big Daddy (1908-95). Totally secular and politically correct song. Just fun. No angels or crèches.

The Christmas season has brought us many beautiful carols beyond 1942's #1(12)+ "White Christmas" – most popular song of all time (till '97 Irving Berlin/Bing Crosby). Joel Whitburn's amazing *Top Pop Singles* listed Special Christmas Singles up to 1993. Samples? OK, *Billboard* did 3 to 38 from 1963-74, and rebounded in 1983 and 1985; number are 'Christmas List' Rankings: **Beach Boys**' #3's of '63 and '64 – "Little Saint Nick" and "The Man with All the Toys"; Bryan Adams' '85, #4 "Christmas Time"; **Stevie Wonder**'s inspirational #24, '66 "Someday at Christmas Time"; Andy Williams' Bing cover, #1(5), '63 "White Christmas"; Al Martino's classic "Silver Bells" of '64; **John Lennon**'s #3 hopeful antiwar "Happy Xmas (War is Over)," '71; **Paul McCartney**'s #10, '84 "Wonderful Christmastime"; Elvis's surging Blues-belter "Blue Christmas" at #1(2), '64 (yep, Beatlemania-time); the Temptations' "Rudolph, the Red-Nosed Reindeer" at #3, ,'68; Barbra Streisand's #1, '66 "Sleep in Heavenly Peace (Silent Night)" – [see Simon & Garfunkel]; **Bruce Springsteen**'s rockin' "Santa Claus Is Coming to Town" #1, '85; the Drifters' streetcorner classic "White Christmas" #4, 12-63; the irreverent and naughty anti-carol (though melodic), "Grandma Got Run Over by a Reindeer" by Elmo and Patsy, #1(4), '83; Elton John's #3, '73 "Step into Christmas"; the Kinks' bleak NC "Father Christmas"; **James Brown**'s #2, '65 "Santa Claus Go Straight to the Ghetto"; the Carpenters' wispy ethereal #1(3), '70 "Merry Christmas Darling"; Joan Baez's #16, '66 "Little Drummer Boy"; Cheech and Chong's #3, '71 "Santa Claus and His Old Lady"; Gospel icon Mahalia Jackson's #5, ,'64 "Silent Night, Holy Night"; B.B. King's #17, '64 "Christmas Celebration"; Roger Miller's heartwarming #13, '67 "Old Toy Trains"; **Roy Orbison**'s stunning #27, '64 "Pretty Paper"; Prince and the Revolution's #5, 12-84 "Another Lonely Christmas"; and Stan & Doug's Yiddish Anne Murray "Snowbird" parody, #7, 12-70 "Christmas Goose."

Green trees and red roses nearly qualify our next secular hymn as a carol:

"What a Wonderful World" – **Louis 'Satchmo' Armstrong with Kenny G.**, **#53S** ["S"=Sales, in stores], **8-99.** This may not be the most wonderful song in the history of music, but then again it may. It's a hymn of amazing faith. You'll see it again at the end of *Gold Rush*, without Kenny. Louie Armstrong reigned over a century of American popular music. This hymn celebrates his love of life. This is actually the prettiest version – but Louie gets a solo shot at our finale. **Kenny G**[orelick, b. '56, Seattle] is a fine golden-toned Jazz Fusion saxophonist. He specializes in the high, mellow ones – soprano and alto. He regally enwreathes Louie's most sacred sandpaper baritone. The two Jazz giants bring us a magnificent ballad. It celebrates everything the Lord has put here on the earth for us to enjoy. Like a Celtic troubadour, Kenny G. and his enchanted saxophone surround Louie's sylvan green and marshmallow cloud domain; their musical harmonies sprout wings and soar aloft on hope and faith and dreams and love. It's yours for a song.

"Mary's Boy Child" – **Harry Belafonte, #12, 12-56.** Belafonte's 2nd hit single ever (despite megamillion albums). One stunning Irish tenor Calypso Rock performance. Forerunner of **Bob Marley and the Wailers**. In Jamaican dialect, the Harlem Folk singer focuses on both Mary's nurturing and the infant Jesus. A Rembrandt Madonna & Child vignette, in the days before **Madonna**, Rock star. Gorgeous, crystalline melody. We could easily do a 40-page chapter on Christmas songs with a big beat. We'll save that theme for our follow-up, *Platinum Rush*.

Back to the land of Un-Christmas, a 364-day per year expanse of work and coffee and flat tires and mumbo-jumbo. And grinches.

"I Will Follow Him" – **Little Peggy March, #1(3), 3-63; #1(1), 4-63 R & B.** If you checked out Whoopi Goldberg's *Sister Act*, you'll recall the on-the-lam lass teaching her sister nuns the elements of Rock and Roll. As the winsome comedienne Whoopi hit her teenage years, this quasi-religious diamond glistened on her airwaves. **Margaret Batavio** hailed from Lansdale, Pennsylvania. She was just about 14 and about Whoopi's age for her first and last #1 song. This HIM part makes it a HYMN.

Time for dad. The Lord is noticeably paternal in most theological history, so let's cover songs related to Dad: Patriarchal role model? Worshipful icon? Or a wretched bum who skedaddled outta town on a Midnight Train to Nowhere:

"Ships" – **Barry Manilow, #9, 10-79.** Brooklyn's **Barry Alan Pincus** (b. 6-7-46) went to Juilliard and wowed the moms of America with this theatrical Lite Rock. In "SHIPS," Manilow metaphorically describes a strained relationship with dad. Walking the forlorn beach, he is reminded of two alienated ships which pass each other during the deep, dark night. Communication? Zilch. Rancor? Nah. A dad and son relationship stuck in neutral. Spinning gears. Don't we all demand more than that of our dads? Or of (in Native American terms) the Great Father?

"Papa Was a Rolling Stone" – **Temptations, #1(1), 10-72; #5, 10-72 R & B.** One of the greatest Barber-Shop harmonic adventures in Rock and Soul. Dad? A bad cad lad. How so? He punted his responsibilities, as 50s 'family values' dissolved to a Disco Inferno of hot pumping libido. The lyrics ooze with irony. Vagabond 'Dad' calls home wherever his hat gets laid, or whatever. The drifty-dude plays 'Dad' with whomever he can sweet-talk into a night's rest, or the rest of the night. They lavish a cryptic line, sparkling like a Zen Buddhist koan (cosmic question or puzzle). When the galloping gallivanting gal-chaser finally kisses the highway hello, and his temp family goodbye, all he leaves them, says the temp Temps, is ALONE!

Deadbeat Dad. Neon nomad. Voodoo vagabond. **Ricky Owens** soars tenor lead. **Melvin Franklin** scours deep bass. **David Ruffin** anchors 2nd tenor. "Big Daddy" is nowhere to be seen. Caustic chuckle.

In this most fatherless of all societies in history, how are the young children to perceive God the Father?

"Hi, Mom. I'm home." If Mom is home . .

The gender concept of God has undergone more re-working in the last generation than in two previous millennia. Catholics in the U.S.A. now salute one another with Jesus' greeting to His disciples: "Peace be with you." Is the concept of God Him/(Her)self undergoing a radical shift into a more nurturing Mother Nature omnipotence and omnipresence?

"That Silver-Haired Daddy of Mine" – Gene Autry, #7, 8-35. Owned California Angels! First big hit for 'Singing Cowboy' Autry (1907-98), who learned his cowboy yodeling from **Jimmie Rodgers I**. In this teary tune about dear old dad, Dad rocks out on the porch rocker. His old porch-rocking-chair dad grapples with Father Time on the vine-caressed porch of his Appalachian cabin. Losing the battle, by degree, he doggedly fights onward. Mysteriously, the kid is remorseful. He opines, he'd sacrifice everything he owned if he could only ATONE! One of those five-letter oddities that seems to have escaped our feel-good language. Atone means to not only say we're sorry – but to pay back for the hurt we caused. This silver song is a slice of another century, really.

Slim Whitman, too, yodels it well. Pinnacle? The Everly Brothers (NC, '58-'59). Off the *Songs Our Daddy Taught Us* album [NC]. Dedicated to their peripatetic but loving dad **Ike Everly**. Sounds like two cherubic angels. When the elder Everly passed away in the 80s, the feuding brothers reunited at Albert Hall in London in his honor: [Al. #162, 3-84 *The Everly Brothers' Reunion Concert*].

"The Living Years" – Mike and the Mechanics, #1(1), 1-89. "Mike," ostensible lead singer, is really two Pauls: **Paul Young** (1947-2000) and **Paul Carrack**. They sing for bassist **Mike Rutherford** (Genesis, the group, not the *Bible* intro). Song dotes on loss when dad passes away. Like the atoner in "Silver-Haired Daddy," the singer is perplexed at why his dad had to die when they were still feuding. It's common throughout history – a father dies just as the son reaches manhood. Not the ideal Pop and kid relationship from **Eddie Fisher**'s #1 "Oh! My Papa." The heartbeat of Rutherford's bass stings. The kid grieves alone. Pizzicato guitar riffs ride this molten melody. How many of us wish we'd said something more loving to someone whose death arrived quite unexpectedly? A song of remorse. Regret. For a similar theme, catch "The Old Man," by Celtic tenor **John McDermott** [*The Irish Tenors*, Al. 1998], a teary tune about father/son relationships cut off suddenly by death – without last words.

Renewal? In his own newborn son, 'Mike' sails through a generational exchange with his own little boy. He is trying to make up for the stuff he and his departed dad missed. In 2000, Paul Young departed. Did he and son have unanswered issues? It goes even deeper than just a biological relationship to a bygone dad. How deep? Some say it this way . . .

> "Our father, who art in Heaven,
> Hallowed be they name . . ."
> *Matthew 6:9-13*

"Heal the World" – Michael Jackson, #27, 12-92: #62, R & B. In the spirit of Band-Aid and **Stevie Wonder**, Michael Jackson provides this secular hymn for school choirs (church and state separation). (80 beats/minute) In melodic key of 'Eb', it hangs onto the I-IIm-IIIm chords endlessly; a place in your heart, he says, is love.

"Wind Beneath My Wings" – Lou Rawls, #65, 3-83; #60 R & B. Jazz-Gospel-Soul Rawls's powerful Chicago baritone took a breathtaking gratitude anthem from Country star **Gary Morris** (NC, '83, but #4, 8-83 C). Sweeping metaphor. People are powered by people. It hit #1, 3-89 for **Bette Midler**. The Paterson, New Jersey singer/actress defined the HERO concept in a new way with her sterling theatrical rendition.

"From a Distance" – Bette Midler, #2(1), 10-90. Our Gulf War hymn. While Bette sang this powerful song of peace, President George Bush the First had to unleash the American aeronautical juggernaut on the minions of Saddam Hussein, who was invading Kuwait. Her final observation? The Lord watches us, from afar. Song is a Deist hymn. **Ben Franklin** believed in this mechanical Watchmaker Theory of God: God is like a cosmic clockmaker who winds up the universe and watches the Gargantuan Watch tick onwards – [not interceding much, if at all, in human affairs]. Ben's 18th century Deism doesn't grab a lot of converts in Millennium tent revivals nowadays. Hard to cuddle a clock.

On Midler's #3, 3-80 "The Rose," an Indian legend mystically sing that the earth itself is a living, breathing organism called Gaia in other cosmologies. The dormant seed snuggles under winter snows.

"Just As I Am" – George Beverly Shea for Billy Graham, late 1940s (not #19, '85 Air Supply tune). **Reverend Billy Graham** (b. 11-7-1918) of North Carolina has brought more people to receive Jesus Christ into their lives than anyone in history. Except Jesus Himself. This hymn accompanies us as we walk forward if we got to see him in some pavilioin. In the twilight of a majestic mission, Reverend Graham continues to preach.

Charlotte Elliot (1789-1871) wrote this classic in 1836. Its five excellent verses are universally drowned out in the murmur and hubbub of the myriad marchers to communion with Reverend Graham. In "Just As I Am," lambs return to the fold (theme of **Bing Crosby/Fred Waring**'s #7, '46 "Wiffenpoof Song").

"How Great Thou Art" – George Beverly Shea for Billy Graham, 1948+. Although neither this nor the last one 'charted' with *Billboard*, they are #1 in millions of Christian hearts. The majestic melody was inspired for Swede **Carl Boberg** in 1886 by a rare monster thunderstorm in Scandinavia. Missionary **Stuart K. Hine** made the song a truly international affair, says Gariepy. The song was translated into German. Then Russian. Hine heard it in Czechoslovakia, and whipped up four out of five English verses in 1930. *Christian Herald* pollsters found "How Great Thou Art" to be American's favorite hymn in 1974. We've already covered Rock standards and/or secular hymns like "Amazing Grace," "Blowin' in the Wind," "Promised Land," "The Twelfth of Never," "Unchained Melody," "Earth Angel," "My Sweet Lord," "A Place in the Sun," "Thou Shalt Not Steal," "Eve of Destruction," "Devil or Angel," "He Ain't Heavy . . .," "You'll Never Walk Alone," "Devil with a Blue Dress," "Crying in the Chapel," "Where Have All the Flowers Gone," "Lady Madonna," "Hey Jude," "Abraham, Martin, and John," and "The Snake." Now how about a few swift items?

"Levon" – Elton John, #24, 12-71. Levon has a kid named Jesus who wants to go to Venus. Street preachers will always be with ye. Good EJ tune, lyrical oddity. Kid born on Christmas Day.

"Superstition" – Stevie Wonder, #1(1), 11-72; #1(3) R & B. Triskaidekaphobia anthem (fear of the Number '13'). A 13-month-old baby gets into some shenanigans. Wicked, kicky bass cavorts on devilish riff. Soul of Funk. Dredges up medieval superstitions of cats, witches, plague, and thirteen.

"Highway to Hell" – AC/DC, #47, 10-79. Among first Metalmongers to chart. AC/DC originally meant electrical current. Despite its diabolical premise, this electrifying song is really an imp – not a full-fledged demon. The Australian group was formed by Easybeats' kid brothers Angus and Malcolm Young and lead singer **Bon Scott**. Scott dies of fast-lane alcohol at age 33 in 1980. Heart of Rock and Roll. Stormy Hard Rock.

"When the Roll is Called Up Yonder" – Statler Brothers, NC, 1992. In June 1906, the **Haydn Quartet** hit #6 on the infant charts with this beloved old hymn. **Harold Reid** booms his big basic bass voice into the voluminous verse as the Lord's trumpets blast and blare the Statlers' revelation. Reid rumbles, anchoring the heavenly harmonies of the higher three Stats: **Phil Balsley, Jimmy Fortune**, and **Don Reid**.

"The Roll" rocks. Professor **Jimmy Black** penned the popular hymn in mourning for his student, Bessie, who succumbed to pneumonia in 1893. Piano player and poet, Black (1856-1938) wrote the song in a half hour of (perhaps Divine) inspiration.

"Just a Little Talk with Jesus" – Bluegrass Cardinals, NC, 1980. In 1981, **Ernie Sykes** and I cut demos. First tenor for the Bluegrass Cardinals, Ernie played the Grand Ol' Opry and the Cardinals made a fine name for themselves in the Gospel/Bluegrass realm. The joy of harmony. Down through the ages. From David's lute. Even Pan's flute. "I will sing of the Lord's great love forever" (*Psalms* 89:1).

"You've Got Another Thing Comin'" – Judas Priest, #67, 11-82. Only one HOT 100 hit. Judas Priest shows up on a lot of Favorite Band rosters. Heavy Metallurgists from Birmingham, England, Priest's chief priest is singer **Rob Halford**, with Thrash Metal axe-handlers K.K. Downing and Glenn Tipton, Ian Hill (bass), and drummers Dave Holland and Scott Travis. Big album successes, starting with #128, 3-79 *Hell Bent for Leather* plus *Screaming for Vengeance* and #17, 4-86 *Turbo*. Judas Iscariot betrayed Jesus. **Pat Boone** (yes) cut this in 1997.

"Back Stabbers" – O'Jays, #3, 7-72; #1(1) R & B. Refers to nasty business slugs who smile right in your face, while scheming to take your place. Hmmm, biblical *déjà vu*. "I tell you the very truth, this very night, before the rooster crows, you will disown me three times" (*Matthew*

26:34). Is this Jesus talking to the sly, wily Judas, the turncoat who gave any of us with some red hair a bad name?

No way. Jesus here chides his trusted friend Peter. Peter, we all know, founded the Christian Church upon a Rock. We are all aware of the cunning and deceit of the bitterly avaricious Judas. Judas sold out Jesus for a wretched thirty pieces of silver and paid the ultimate price of remorse. Judas returned the silver to the chief priest who mocked him. He threw the money into the temple in disgust. In ultimate extreme atonement, Judas took the samurai way out – he committed suicide (not *hari-kiri*, but hanging). To this day, Western civilization has looked upon suicide and euthanasia as the Curse of Judas Iscariot, one of the few Julius Caesar-era people with a last name (besides Julius himself).

The suicide solution never appealed to Peter. He knew he had to take the high road and face his sin, his guilt, and his sorrow at denying and disowning the Man he had followed as the Messiah. He denied Jesus three times and sold Him to the executioners. Remember how **Dr. Martin Luther King** (and others) put it? How 'an eye for an eye' leaves everybody blind?

Capital punishment is once again on the rise – and as we all hang "Tom Dooley" from the white oak tree, we must remember, who is hanging on the next tree?

Barrabas, a thief, was crucified next to Jesus. Jesus said to his fellow sufferers: "Today you will be with me in paradise." (*Luke* 23:42)

The world was full of backstabbers in the days of Caesar Augustus and Pointius Pilate. Julius Caesar had been mercilessly stabbed in the back by his 'friends,' and from the front by his 'best friend' Brutus (rationalization? The 'good of Rome'). **Mahatma Gandhi**, a Hindu man of peace, was assassinated in India in 1947. Dr. King, peace pilgrim, was cravenly gunned down while organizing a garbagemen's strike two miles from Elvis's Sun Records.

Helen and daughter Trace Reddy sang "You and Me Against the World" (#9, 6-74). After her feminist anthem "I Am Woman" (#1, 6-72), Melbourne, Australia's **Reddy** offered this uplifting #9 secular song, like Anne Murray's "You Needed Me" #1, '78. Moral? UNITED WE STAND.

And Judas Iscariot, who betrayed Jesus, was the only apostle who kept his last name. You can't help but wonder how history would have changed, had Judas chosen one name like Madonna, Fabian, Cher, Eminem, Brandy, Derek, Sisqo, Annette, Janet, Santana, or **Prince**. Indeed, it's very interesting to note that the only other apostle to temporarily betray Jesus (three times), had a temporary last name – which was changed by Jesus, with Divine Providence. When the apostle totally repented his sins, he spent the rest of his life founding and organizing the most popular religious movement in the history of the world. In *Matthew* 16, Verses 13-19:

Now when Jesus came into the district of Caesare's Philippi, he asked his disciples, "Who do men say that the Son of man is? And they said some say John the Baptist, others say Elijah, and others Jeremiah or one of the prophets. He said to them, "But who do you say that I am?" Simon Peter replied, "You are the living

Christ, the Son of the living God." And Jesus answered him, "Blessed are you, Simon Bar-Jona! For flesh and blood has not revealed this to you, but my Father who is in heaven. And I tell you, you are Peter, and on this rock I build my church, and the powers of death shall not prevail against it. I will give you the keys of the kingdom of heaven . . ."

Last name? Yes, Simon Bar-Jona. When Jesus changed Simon's name to Peter, he built his church upon the rock. And he spent the rest of his life – and worldly pilgrimage – ATONING for forsaking the trust of Jesus. Judas Iscariot never had the chance to turn his life around. He sold his soul for thirty pieces of filthy silver. Now, I'm not saying two names create sin and downfall, and I'm certainly not saying that Peter created Rock music by building the church upon a rock, but, I'm just pointing out a very weird coincidence. If nothing else, changing two iffy names to one great one can give one a blank slate, a fresh start, and maybe a little 'amazing grace.' Or steadiness, like the Rock of Gibraltar.

Blinded for a time by remorse, Peter, too, dealt with cosmic questions about the worth of his own life. Finally, Simon Bar-Jona began to act. As Peter, he decided to help build the most powerful church in the history of the world. In the 20th century, with the help of their interfaith brethren the Hindus and Buddhists and Muslims and others, Christian churches have been instrumental in changing the world from spreading communist materialism to a more spiritual and democratic planet. It was Peter who started the Rock rolling. [Christian Contemporary hit by **Chuck Girard**, '83 "Blessed Be that Name of My Rock"].

"Ask Me" – Amy Grant, NC, 1991. Off 1991 *Heart in Motion* Al. #10, 3-91. **Amy Grant** (b. 1960) married **Vince Gill** in 2000. This tune concerns her friend, a victim of sexual abuse. The victim asks where God went during this vulgar violation of her girlhood. And how does she then wrestle with the shame? The fourth line of the quatrain is the kicker: she says the Lord's mercy is restoring her life once again. The kid wobbles under a terrible personal burden. Her only release is prayer. She bears her emotional burden alone. Almost. She turns to God, and the deep shame slowly lifts. One of the peculiar dastardly byproducts of child abuse it that the abuser rarely feels the same shame as the innocent victim. On very rare occasions, even the trusted priest/minister may be the abuser (2002 Church scandals). Amy Grant shows that God's mercy brings life. Grant's world-view differs greatly from Madonna's, but their sounds dovetail into demi-disco synthesizers, 48-track mega-productions, and audial gold. Among Contemporary Christian albums of 1-27-2001, you'll find #2 **Anne Murray**'s Louie Armstrong echo *What a Wonderful World*; #3 and #4 **Yolanda Adams**' [*"Mountain High – Valley Low"*]; #6 **Tommy Walker**'s *"Never Gonna Stop"* **Michael J. Smith**'s #11 *Freedom*; #22 **Third Day**'s *Offerings*; and #38 **CeCe Winens**' *Alabaster Box.*

"Put a Little Love in Your Heart" – Jackie DeShannon, #4, 6-69. A sweet, melodic, plodding pleas for tolerance and love. Cute blonde Sharon Myers of Hazel, Kentucky, debuted on radio at age 6, and fronted the British Invasion by cutting **Sonny Bono**'s song "Needles and Pins" (#84, 6-63) before blockbuster **Searchers** #13, 3-64 smash. Jackie toured with Fab Four and penned **Kim Carnes**'s #1(9) "Bette Davis Eyes." A three-minute sermon – like **Michael W. Smith**'s Amy Grant song "Place in This World," or Ray Stevens' #1(2), 4-70 "Everything is Beautiful."

"Alone Again, Naturally" – Gilbert O'Sullivan, #1(6), 6-72. Agnostics' Anthem: For those wafflers and wobblers about the existence of God, we have Waterford, Ireland's Irish baritone, **Gilbert Raymond O'Sullivan**. His Catholic sensibilities demand at least the husks of faith. He cries out about the mysterious ways of God, and the loss of both his parents. If the Lord really exists, then how come he has now abandoned me, he beseeches the cold star-blanket. The tone is familiar. Two of four gospels bring us widely different messages. In *Luke*, Jesus appeals to His Heavenly Father: "Father, forgive them, for they know not what they do." Despite His apostles' betrayal, and His agonizing crucifixion, Jesus still utters that upbeat comment to His fellow sufferers after his prayer (*Luke* 23:34), about them joining him "in paradise" (23:42). Then, in resolute faith and trust, He says "Father, into Your Hands I commit my spirit." (23:46). The Gospel of St. Mark, however, takes an opposing view. You can see where Gilbert O'Sullivan is coming from: "My God, why have You forsaken Me?" (*Mark* 15:34).

O'Sullivan's quizzical torch song clutched the hit pinnacle for one-ninth of 1972. All our old beliefs were shredding: U.S. military invincibility, forever-marriage, Mom stays home, steak and eggs are good for you, America is always right. Church attendance lurched ominously. Worship picked up at the golf course.

A slow beat wafts O'Sullivan along. His cloyingly powerful melody plods and dips and swoons. Like a Pied Piper caravan, "Alone Again, Naturally" reminds us all of our terrifying human dilemma. We live and die completely alone. The song is nowhere near atheistic. It is hopeful of God's presence, still. It is not even lapsed Catholic. It stumbles along, like Creedence's "Lodi," in that sticky Lost Limbo of Agnosticism. Agnosticism, you know, is that neutral nowhere position where most thinking Christians occasionally suffer and squirm; "Is there a God or not? I don't know for sure . . ." When your parents die, yours is the next generation on Death Row. The Front Lines. It is a sobering thought.

For an answer, Christians look to the cross – and back to "Hey Jude" ("Be merciful to those who doubt" *Jude* :22). All things work together for good, so they say, and we can't always see the Big Picture as we're scrounging and clawing around down here on earth. O'Sullivan's #1 song is honest, challenging, and powerful. Just before the death of New York Archbishop John Cardinal O'Connor (1920-2000), he blessed the "Doubting Thomases" along with the steadfast believers. O' Sullivan's subsequent offerings aren't so cosmic: "Claire" #2(2), 10-72, and (yep) "Get Down" #7, 6-73.

"Hold On! I'm Comin'" – **B.B. King and Eric Clapton, NC, 2000** [on Al. #3, 6-2000, *Riding with the King*]. Super Anglo-American Blues collaboration of multicultural Gospel Soul. Covering Hall of Famers **Sam** [Moore, 1935-88] and **Dave** [Prater], and their Stax-dynamo sound (#21, 3-66; #1[1] R & B) from revival-tent Georgia, King and Clapton deliver a masterpiece of double-barrelled atomic Soul. Prater's engorged lyric measures the depths of a commitment of friendship or love. Never be sad, he says, just HOLD ON, I'll be there soon . . . "Lean on Me" became Bill Withers' (#1, '72) signature song, plucked from their "Hold On!" litany of rescue rhetoric. At the height of their slower-tempo bridge, Clapton and King implore their suffering friend to hang on a little longer. They'll be there to save the day. Have faith. To call out their NAMES for a great reaction [not unlike calling upon the Lord in times of tribulations], Their laid-back combo millennial version avoids the hot Soulfire and supercharged rhythmic thump of the original – but the timeless message keeps rollin' on – and it rocks, really rocks. Upon this rock . . .

"One of Us" – **Joan Osborne, #4, 12-95.** MTV video tune. Like O'Sullivan's, Osborne asks unasked questions about the nature of God. She wears the current stigmata of body-piercing (nose) in her video quest to discover God's ultimate nature. "One of Us" pans the garish midway of Old Coney Island, South Brooklyn. Carny grotesques loom. We see the Michaelangelo Sistine Chapel scenario on the rickety salt-water taffy boardwalk. The Lord gives life to Adam; the head is cut out, and anyone can play 'God' in the two-dimensional picture, simply by sticking his or her head through the oval hole.

Osborne asks whether we might see God and not recognize Him. She skateboards with her impish come-hither smile and long curly blonde hair, into what was once called blasphemy. Like Botticelli's Venus on the half-shell painting, Joan Osborne coquettishly queries whether God could be one of us. She semi-sacrilegiously posits His persona as a regular 'slob' riding the grubby bus with the rest of us rapscallions. Slob. Ouch. She questions whether God could be commuting home on the bus after a hard day at the Unfolding Creation. Bizarre but honest question. Jesus DID grow up among carpenters. Fortunately, she did not plunk Him onto the subway, the El, or some speed-of-light messenger's bicycle barreling down Fifth Avenue (flattening Cadillacs in His cycling wake). Slow. Musing. Religious? "Then the Lord rained down burning sulfur on Sodom and Gomorrah . . . but Lot's wife looked back, and she became a pillar of salt." (*Genesis* 19:26, 26).

Bible passages like that have kept folks through the ages from flippantly describing God. In the VIdeo Age, however, reading takes a back seat to swiftly swirling phosphors, dancing in computer-generated profusion on a Cathode Cyclops TV. Should the new world order be merciful to "One of Us?" To some little kid trying to sort out the theological meaning of life, Joan's unreal video is a toughie. If God's Son can walk among men and suffer on a cross, whey can't God take the bus? No lyrical oatmeal here. Squirmy stuff.

"What a Friend We Have in Jesus" – **Anybody and Everybody, #5 most popular hymn, 1990 newspaper poll.** Penned by **Joseph Scriven** (1819-86) for his ailing mother, this Irish hymn answers O'Sullivan's wrenching doubts. Scriven emigrated to Canada at 25, overcoming the appalling grief of losing two fiancées before marriage (the first drowned the night before their marriage, and the second underwent a brief fatal illness). Scriven created the spellbinding melody long after his rich words cheered up his ailing mother.

His title thunders out the essential message of comfort and consolation that Christianity burns for: What a friend we have in Jesus [who will personally bear all our griefs and sins]. He then carries all his burdens, tribulations, bills, and hassles, back in prayer.

THE SACRED FOUR CHORD AND ITS HARMONY OF BELIEVERS

Most of the world's best-loved hymns live by three basic chords: I, IV, and V. The most important chord shift is always to the sub-dominant IV chord. Chiming the Big Four chord is often a religious revelation. The IV chord is the one that makes coal miners and boxers cry. When your hymn hits the BIG 4 chord, you can resolve back to your Tonic I by shifting through a IVm to your I. If your hymn rolls in the Key of 'C', you loft to the very pretty IV chord **F major**. Hang there on your last harmonic triad (F-A-C): slide back your middle note to **Fm** (F-Ab-C), then slowly, lovingly cascade back to your root I chord **C** (C-E-G). Best-loved hymns, like big Rock and Roll anthems, use just three big chords to get their inspirational message across. With a few exceptions, you'll find the Three-Chord I-IV-V Rule spanning the star-spangled Best-Loved Hymns: "What a Friend We Have in Jesus," "I Love to Tell the Story," "Church in the Wildwood," "How Great Thou Art," "Amazing Grace," "Rock of Ages," and "The Old Rugged Cross."

"Oh Happy Day" – **Edwin Hawkins Singers, #4, 4-69; #2(2), 5-69 R & B.** Gospel group wIth all-powerful pipes. Jesus washes all their sins away. From an R & B stance, Hawkins' gospel groovers champion Christian faith and fellowship to conquer twin glooms of sin and doubt.

"What's Love Got to Do With It?" – **Tina Turner, #1(3), 5-84; #2(5), 6-85 R & B.** The last tune by the Hawkins multitude was about Baptism: "They were baptized by Him in the [River] Jordan" (*Matthew* 3:6 and, verbatim,

Mark 1:5). This one is about sex, a topic not ignored by the Holy Scriptures: "See that no one is sexually immoral" (*Hebrews* 12:15). What's sex got to do with it? Ours is an era of MTV shows like *Grind*. Bikini-bippy babes swivel hot hips in burlesque ardor. The heat goes on. Men's animalistic passions power a billion bogus "I-love-you's" [See "Wild Thing"]. Tina's gams have long attracted men to her speed-shimmying performances, and to her ageless bronze body. (OK, 60+, but check her I.D. anyway.) From volatile Ike Turner to satirical Mick Jagger, Tina magnetizes desire.

"Jezebel" – Frankie Laine, #2(2), 5-51. Laine lavished Biggest of 1951 Big Beats (Latin Rock) on this Rhumba-Mambo-Jumbo queen of temptation. With chromatic chord runs and modulations galore (bII, bIII), he storms the spirit of Demonic Desire. Magnificent climax. Operatic finale even **Meat Loaf** could envy. The girl is the Temptress, personified (see Marty Stuart's "Tempted" #5, 8-91 C). Macho Welsh Soul belter **Tom Jones** sang the biblical siren, allure of Samson's nemesis, "Delilah," to #15, 3-68.

Buddha once loosely declared, "If there's been another human drive as strong as sex, I'd never have become the Buddha" (Siddhartha Gautama [Buddha], who overcame the lusty world of the flesh to become the ultimate Buddhist guru). **Tina Turner** became a Buddhist. She is among the few American Rock and Soul stars (and African Americans) to practice this Asian religion. Just down the Boulevard from Janis Joplin's Lamar College of Port Arthur, Texas, a massive Buddhist Temple yawns placidly aloft, like Buddha himself smiling over the high Himalayas. Vietnamese refugees ('Boat People') found freedom, democracy, happiness, religious temples, and shrimping waters off the Gulf Coast. They settled down, like a hundred million American pioneers before, in the red-gold Promised Land of Rock and Roll.

"Onward Christian Soldiers" – Salvation Army Bands eternal, 1880+. Words? Rev. Sabine Baring-Gould. Music? Arthur Sullivan (Gilbert & Sullivan, not Gilbert O' Sullivan). Rousing rocking hymn brings heathens to Jesus like no Alka-Seltzer ever could. Lyrics shout: Jesus is our Master, and He leads us bravely versus the cunning foe. Confuses, perhaps, King David with Jesus. Rousing spirit of Christian warriors. For a second opinion, try:

"Turn, Turn, Turn" – Byrds, #1(3), 10-65. *Ecclesiates* 3:1. **Pete Seeger** adapted it. The song is one of the first of the modern R & R and Folk-Rock tunes to shun rhyme. Common in Rap and Heavy Metal today, non-rhyming songs go back a lot farther than 1965. B.C., actually. Seeger modifies the original words to sculpt a more pacifistic message: "A time for war and a time of peace" (3:8) becomes "time for peace," and he swears it won't be too late.

Pete ruggedly fought his way through apocalyptic *Saving-Private Ryan's* World War II.

"The Lord will judge between the nations
 And will settle disputes for many peoples.
 They will beat their swords into plowshares

And their spears into pruning hooks.
Nation will not take up
 Sword against nation,
 Nor will they train for war anymore."
 Issiah 2:4

The **Byrds'** searing guitars burn like trumpets of Zion. Their instrumental bridge blasted 666,666,666 '66 car radio speakers to Kingdom Come. With the harmonic power of the **Everly Brothers**, the swooping crashing hard Rock of their own invention, and the best Folk-Rock Seeger sentiments aligned to *Ecclesiastes* and beyond, the Byrds bellowed their celestial message.

Their flagrant message of unconditionally declared PEACE finds one key New Testament echo:

Jesus said: "Blessed are the peacemakers, for they shall be called sons of God." – *Matthew* 5:9

I talked with Pete Seeger and his bassist grandson at Southampton College, Long Island, in Fall 1994. He said "I can't believe they're still giving me credit for *Ecclesiastes*; all I did was interpret this mysterious book of the *Bible*." Modest guy, Pete. In Seeger's happy hoontenanny audience, everybody sings along. There's a Byrd (**McGuinn, Clark[e], Hillman, Crosby**) to match your favorite note in their audial rainbow:

There is a time for everything,
And a season for every activity under heaven;
a time to be born and a time to die,
a time to plant and a time to uproot,
a time to kill and a time to heal,
a time to tear down and a time to build,
a time to weep and a time to laugh,
a time to mourn and a time to dance,
a time to scatter stones and a time to gather them,
a time to embrace and a time to refrain,
a time to search and a time to give up,
a time to keep and a time to throw away,
a time to tear and a time to mend,
a time to be silent and a time to speak,
a time to love and a time to hate,
a time for war and a time for peace.
Concordia Bible version

Pete Seeger believes that everybody can be part of a hit record. Check out what his unique lyrical adaptation chucked OUT: 1) the time to be silent; 2) the time to keep and throw away (I once had a book on *Eliminating Clutter* on my grubby basement desk, but I lost it under a pile of clutter); 3) a lot of stuff about building and dancing and searching; and 4) the part about giving up; it is simply not a part of the classy package that is Pete Seeger.

A song can take on many magnificent variations. Seeger shared his personal conceptions of the *Ecclesiastes* philosophy with the Byrds. Seeger swallowed his Folk Purist pride and finally embraced the new youthful spirit of Rock and Roll. As the Vietnam War heated up, Seeger stuck in a more strident reminder of what he'd subtly murmured via the Kingston Trio in "Where Have All the Flowers Gone?"; Seeger had the *chutzpah* to flip the final line into a concocted coda where he and his flock of Byrds swear peace won't be too late. It wasn't. It still isn't.

Byrds' lead singer **Roger McGuinn** (a/k/a Jim) believed we could effect changes on earth – despite *Ecclesiastes*. On his magnificent #44 Al. 1-91 *Back from Rio* – starring Rock superstars **Tom Petty** and **Eagles' Timothy B. Schmit**, he takes on catastrophes like the Shrinking Ozone Layer, Polar icecaps drowning coastlands, and chopping down rainforests the size of Nebraska, EVERY YEAR, to make cheap hamburgers for meat-seeking billions of earth's eaters. **McGuinn** has long been involved in Christian mission concerns and saving his only planet – like *Ecclesiastes* and Pete Seeger warned . . .

Not every generation expressed the buoyant optimism of Pete Seeger or Roger McGuinn. After all, the 80s business climate was into downsizing and job switches. Croissants oozed fat. Grunge-drizzle 90s gloom festered during the most prosperous economic era in American history. All Pete had to deal with in his 'easy life' were the Depression, World War II, Korea, and Vietnam. Also a sneaky Cold War snaked *Father Knows Best* families into mausoleum-crypt fallout shelters – waiting for some idiot to fire up the nuclear spark so that all of us lost limbo souls may get blown away – Poof! (Kingston Trio's sarcastic "Merry Minuet").

"Dear God" – **XTC, NC, c 1990.** This British New Wave crew (bouncy "Mayor of Simpleton" #72, 4-89) scorched the FM air waves with this apotheosis to God, or no God, or perhaps a god. Or godlet. In spots, the singer is a True Believer. In spots, he is among the Faith-Challenged. **DePeche Mode**'s (#28, 12-89) "Personal Jesus" is an all-synthesized offering by Basildon, England's **David Gahan**, his backing bandsmen, and a robot or two. "Blasphemous Rumours" too, chased the religious butterfly.

"The Devil Went Down to Georgia" – **Charlie Daniels, # 3, 6-79; #1(1) C.** Country Soul item about Devil vs. Fab Fiddler from Peach State (Daniels) in a contest. In Faustian Crossroads Fiddle Duel, Devil gets his due. Daniels is famous for cross-cultural clash Country Rap comic tune "Un-easy Rider," #9, 1973.

"He" – **Al Hibbler, #4, 10-55; #13 R & B.** Blind African-American piano player, (1915-2001) inspiration to **Ray Charles** and **Stevie Wonder**, sings song of great faith. **Righteous Brothers** reprised Hibbler's "He" to #18, 6-66 to ward off Sign-of-the-Beast 6-66 date. Though the Lord sees the wretched, selfish way we all live, He will always forgive. When Peter asked Jesus how many times to forgive his brother when he sins against him, and suggests a mere seven times, Jesus replies:

"I tell you, not seven times, but seventy-seven times [seven.]" – *Matthew* 18.22

Hmm, math fans, 539 times. A little more patient than most of us hothead humans. That's why He's Jesus, and we're not!

"I Believe" – **Frankie Laine, #2(3), 2-53.** Perfectly non-sectarian hymn. Positive and inspirational. Mulligatawny mish-mosh of metaphors. All work well. Inspiring words get us through our muckamuck days: Each

drop of falling rain brings a beautiful new flower. Somewhere out THERE, a candle is glowing – like a Thomas Kincaid painting. It's nice. No $100/hour 'shrink' fee to figure out the cosmos. With a nice strong tapestry of belief, we can weave our own happiness and tranquility.

Sometimes it matters whether we listen to (and absorb) gloomy tunes or hopeful ones.

"Plastic Jesus" – **Carl Koenig, NC, 1961.** In his basic-black '57 Chevy on our way to geology class in 1961 (rocks, Rock, etc.) my good ol' fraternity brother Carl Koenig would squawk this little semi-blasphemous ditty in his comedy-style baritone: He chortled the words about he didn't care whether it'll rain or freeze, so long as he has this plastic Jesus adorning his quivering dashboard. It bubbled up recently like a midnight mushroom, onto the impishly irreverent *Imus in the Morning Show* in New York City and beyond. For years, Christians have made 'heh heh' bargains with God. If I become more pious, will you get me richer or healthier, Lord? In Abe Lincoln's day our '59 Starfires toted dashboard St. Christopher Medallions (patron Saint of Travelers, now desanctified). The local priest at Sacred Heart said the medallion was good only to 40 mph, so Joe Buczynski (1942-62) went out and bought three of them (let's see, 40 x 3 = 120 mph, not bad), and briefly had the fastest 1957 Ford in town. Devilishly dastardly little ditty, "Plastic Jesus." It has precious little place in the religious chapter. Let us move one.

"Losing My Religion" – **R.E.M., #4, 4-91.** Some of the wry pious will question whether R.E.M. had any to begin with. Is this Athens, Georgia, group as symbolic of a world at risk, a world losing its moral compass and ethical order? The line where the singer confesses he's blabbed way too much is the key to the song. People lose (or temporarily misplace) their religion.

Glib **Michael Stipe** aw-shucks-es us. He says gosh, I'm up there in that hot garish [Elvis] Spotlight. Then the shadowy corner. The song jingles and jangles, a pleasant tune that smacks of the breezy easy "Touch of Grey" teddy-bear genius of **Jerry Garcia** and the **Grateful Dead**. Though we all enjoy Stipe's (b. '60) tune of "Losing My Religion," and the bass and drum expertise of **Mike Mills**, and **Bill Berry**, it's hard to decipher just which religion or belief system got the boot here – Confucianism, Zoroastrianism, Jainism, Vedanta, Methodism, Unitarianism, Episcopalianism, Greek Orhodoxy, communism, Holy Eggplantism, or the First Church of Rock and Roll. This song befuddles. It makes us think. Fortify our own beliefs, maybe. R.E.M.

Anyhow, I love the melody. It echoes Tex-Mex Rockabilly floating on a squirmy rubber raft on the Agnostic Ocean. Makes you think.

"We Are the World" – **USA for Africa, #1(40, 3-85; #1(2) R & B.** The Big Beat stopped amassing golden mountains of cash – and took **Harry Chapin**'s Long Island example and made a record for those less fortunate. Isn't this what religion is all about? Helping? Who starred here? The VARSITY. In order of soloists: songwriters

Lionel Richie, and Stevie Wonder, plus Rock and Soul stars Paul Simon, Kenny Rogers, James Ingram, Tina Turner, Billy Joel, Michael Jackson, Diana Ross, Dionne Warwick, Willie Nelson, Al Jarreau ("We're in This Love Together" #15, 8-81 Soul-Jazz-Rock singer), Bruce Springsteen, Kenny Loggins, Steve Perry, Daryl Hall, Huey Lewis, Cyndi Lauper, Kim Carnes, Bob Dylan, and Ray Charles. Money from the song was supposed to go to the needy in Africa and parts of the U.S.A. Some of it did (if the taxman and unscrupulous tycoon didn't grab it). A great humanitarian gesture. Buzzword? Caring. Good ballad too. Inspired by –

"Do They Know It's Christmas?" – Band Aid, #13, 12-84. The British inspiration of **Bob Geldof** of the Boomtown Rats, this one featured George Michael, Boy George, Paul Young, Sting, Phil Collins, Duran Duran, Kool and the Gang, and Bananarama. Soon the whole altruistic enterprise spanned the globe via satellite, and Rock and Roll became a religious mission.

"America the Beautiful" – Ray Charles, NC, 1985 or so. When the lyric was written in 1893 by **Katherine Bates**, it was inspired by her trips to breathtaking Pikes Peak, Colorado. [#8, 7-25 by Louise Homer, revered contralto of the New York Metropolitan Opera]. Samuel Ward's old hymn "O Mother Dear, Jerusalem" supplies the tune, while Bates sculpted the psalmic lyric. Church and state merge in melodic purple mountainous majesties. Almost *a cappella*, Soulmaster Ray is joined first by a few crucial piano notes. His melismas and vocal improvisations are stupendous in scope, like the amber waves of golden grain, cathedral peaks, and Shangri-La valleys. Ray performed it (again) at Super Bowl XXXV, 2001. If Ray's version doesn't stir patriotism in the iciest heart, try this:

"The Power and the Glory" – Phil Ochs, NC, 1974. Phil Ochs spent half his adult life dodging FBI microphones hidden in his soup. Joining the Rock and Roll bandwagon long after Dylan, America's major political 60s cynic Ochs wrote this rare blockbuster patriotic American hymn. Snapping with snarly snare, and hot-footing it like a hundred Sousa marchers, "The Power and the Glory" is Johnny B. Goode on the 4th of July. It is the small-town square's band shell in the Congregational steeple shadow, and Norman Rockwall and Currier-Ives and sweet blonde Peggy Sue and Chevys by the levee. Ochs barely scratched the *Billboard* 200: Al. #168 *Pleasures of the Harbor*, 12-67 – and never charted a single. His impact, however, is profound.

"The Power and the Glory" promotes a way of life that America still symbolizes to the world. Land of hope, land of freedom. All that good down-home stuff. Most incredible of all, it came from the man deemed the harshest critic of the American military and industrial establishment! Ochs wrests the tag end of the Protestant paternoster ("Our father, who art in Heaven . . ."), and wrestles with the separation of church and state. Of all the American patriotic hymns, "The Power and the Glory" best combines the American dream to the selfless Christian ideal,

and marches those Christian soldiers in a never-ending panorama down the long ages of humankind. "The Power and the Glory" is Phil's final offering. Peace be with you.

"Rock of Ages" – Statler Brothers, NC., 1992. Staunton, Virginia's **Statler Brothers** got so rich after their first few hits like #4, 11-65 "Flowers on the Wall," they actually bought their boyhood schoolhouse to record their Barber-Shop Quartet Country classic. "Rock of Ages" and the U.S.A. were born the same year – 1776, **Rev. August Toplady** started the first British Invasion of 'Rock' music. In 1776 on a windswept green English moor, he was suddenly swamped by a fierce and furious cloud-burst. By some miracle, he found a large rock with a major sheltering gash in it. The lyrics were literally inspired: Rock of ages, they sing – cleft for them (meaning, obviously, split). Then they beseech the stone to let them hide themselves "in thee." Whether it was the Rock of St. Peter's Church (or St. Paul's of London), or just the sheltering stone that dashed his dour dreams of getting drenched, "Rock of Ages" has become one of the best loved Anglo-American hymns of the Christian experience. "Rock of Ages" was a Top Ten hit in those golden days when Gospel was not segregated from mainstream Pop music. Hitmakers: Two: Louise Homer again, and Alma Gluck in a divine duo: #10, 10-1914. At both ends of the Barber-Shop/Gospel Quartet spectrum, the Statlers showcase magnificent solos: deep bass **Harold Reid** and ethereal countertenor **Jimmy Fortune**, plus the usual **Don Reid** magnificence, with Phil Balsley's great sound.

"The Old Rugged Cross" – Statler Brothers, NC, 1992. #1 song of all in sales, 1913-43. This one waltz outsold every other song – opera, classical, or popular. It is the most frequently requested hymn of all time. Armed with three chords and a dream, **George Bennard** (1872-1956) set out from his birthplace, Tim Bazzett's Reed City, Michigan, and was converted to Christianity at a Salvation Army Revival in Lucas, Iowa.

Reed City is rugged turf. My father-in-law, Tony Piazza, (1906-96) farmed the logged-over stumplands, piney hills, and Michigan outback, where the state bird (the mosquito) is so ferocious that three of them can carry you away. With 160 acres and two mules (Jack and Jenny) Tony and my mom-in-law Leota Quinn Piazza set up a burgeoning dairy farm. From cutover stumpland totally wasted by 'hero' Paul Bunyan and his executioner's axe, Michigan was sold down the river to provide mammoth Victorian mansions and 'cottages' for Boston and Newport and New York lumber barons in the 1880s. George Bennard watched the crucifixion of the helpless pines of Michigan, pines which once rose 175-200 feet high. At some point in Bennard's life, he underwent some mysterious moment of trial. His life and destiny hung in the balance. No Bennard biographer can actually pinpoint it.

At Camp Dearborn, I attended a Vesper Service with future Reverend Jerry Crick presiding (our counselor, seeking a divinity degree at Ohio Wesleyan). We sat on tree-trunk benches, watching the sunset flare and flash in flamingo and baby blue and charcoal gray over the deep indigo-blue lake water rippling the Hiawatha shores. It was one of those great moments as I ran searching for something to fervently believe in (Camel cigarettes, motor scooters, and Sheila M? All left something to be desired in my 13 or 14-year-old Lost Limbo). At the edge of the vespers outdoor chapel stood an Old Rugged Cross. It was strong. It was resolute. It was the symbol of a way of life. Beyond the dark street shone an everlasting light. Beyond the sunset.

On a faraway hill stands the "Old Rugged Cross," symbol of shame and suffering, the lyric leads. The repentant singer says he loves the old timeworn cross, where our best and dearest was slain to absorb our collective sin and guilt. He'll cherish that old rugged cross, he vows – rejecting worldly trophies and other less important baubles. Someday, he vows, he'll exchange the rustic cross for a heavenly crown.

Line two in the chorus packs a personal wallop. They played this noble hymn at my friend Lance Hugelmeyer's funeral in June 1996; Lance was the top 40+ runner on Long Island for 10 years, running well till the finale. He was felled at 56 by a fatal heart attack. Lance and I won the "Buddy Run," a 3.1 mile 5K race our Bohemia Track Club hosts [16:59, 5:28/mile] outright – 300 runners, when he was 50 and I 47. When they played "The Old Rugged Cross" at my good friend's funeral, the song's trophy line stung like a swarm of bees. Lance always put wife Lorraine and family and friends first, and heeded *Ecclesiastes'* admonition about stockpiling earthy treasures.

Dion DiMucci, however, in his Christian Contemporary Rock song "I Put Away My Idols," (NC, 1989) said it quite well: Cadillacs croak in junkyards. Hopefully, we can all see our trophies for what they truly are – just glitzy pyrite fool's gold from some game. [And whether gold beats silver or bronze is a moot point. In the LONG run, they are all just mile markers – on that road, as Banjo Jack Williams puts it, where you "get promoted to glory."]

A whole 'heavenly host' of hitmakers stormed the Jericho walls of the Top Ten citadel. It's a behemoth of a bulwark. Very few artists are ever privileged enough to view the fleecy cloudlets from atop its pearly gates of fame and glory and gold. But many bear the cross that U2's **Bono** alludes to in his "I Still Haven't Found What I'm Looking For." Just like Dion's Cadillacs ending up in a junkyard, so goes the quixotic quest for personal glory in the iffy arena of Rock and Roll.

"The Old Rugged Cross" was once a major hit for a long-forgotten yesteryear superstar. He sang for the biggest-name evangelist in the early 20th century – former baseball player and boxer **Billy Sunday**:

"The Old Rugged Cross" – Homer Rodeheaver, **#5, 3-21. Homer Rodeheaver**? Though the name ELVIS is spattered amongst the blue and silver stars of the celestial firmament, who really remembers Homer Rodeheaver? [Maybe only Homer Simpson]. Sometimes, when you put enough history behind you, all the generations are pretty well forgotten. So often, a precious loved one will live on in our memories as long as we live. But when we are all gone, these memories become a blur, an interstellar blip in the frosty night of the Great Beyond. It is not a pleasant thought. [Equally sadly, this happens to old relic renditions of favorite songs too. *Gold Rush* seeks to reclaim this musical Old Gold bonanza for you]. Christianity promises salvation not only from the inevitabililty of death, but the bleak desolation of obscurity. As God keeps his eyes on the little sparrow, or the lilies of the field, so shall He watch over us all. That is the promise of the *Bible*.

Whither **Homer Rodeheaver**? In Homer's life (1880-1955), he also shared another sunny thought under **Billy Sunday**'s swooning salvation mega-tents: "Brighten the Corner Where You Are" (#6, 9-1915). Though Homer is long gone – and no one under the age of 99 really remembers much about him – his friendly sentiments continue to steer the human race. GLORY is always transient. As long as we can whisk the dust out of our grubby little corners, and make the world sparkle like the warm new grass in #6, '72 Cat Stevens' "Morning Has Broken," Homer Rodenheaver did not sing in vain. Or **George Beverly Shea**, Rev. Billy Graham's faithful bass/baritone hymnmaster of "How Great Thou Art" fame.

We don't recall Homer Rodeheaver as we do Elvis, or Buddy, or Chuck or John Travolta, or N'Sync, or Mariah Carey. **Homer Rodeheaver** sang just too long ago. Nary a Goldy Oldies station features his hymns. Yet billions of us worldwide lost pilgrims cling to his "Old Rugged Cross." Much of this weary world still harbors the hope that it will exchange that splintery Cross for a Crown. We needn't ask: "Where have you gone, Homer Rodeheaver?" It's a good bet, saith the Prophet, that Homer is feeling no pain.

And we, still dancing upon **Cat Stevens'** old earth for a short time, must ponder our own destinies. Are we a Rock and Roll Rogues' Gallery of sinners – like Steve Miller's Band's #1, '73 "Joker[s]"? Or are we little lost Whiffenpoof sheep bleating our bumbling way through the cold cosmos for want of a Good Shepherd? Imagine – are we Cheshire-grinning utopians wrestling lightning bolts into perfect Shangri-Las? Are we seekers on a trail of confusion, Gropers Anonymous muddling through life? "Let It Be," the heavens cry out, and we struggle to understand. Ob-La-Di, Ob-La-Da – life goes right on.

Lord have mercy , warble the Wiffenpoofs, on imperfect strivers like we are. We are the world.

"Music is well said to be the speech of angels. It brings us near to the Infinite; we look for moments across the cloudy elements into the eternal light, when songs lead and inspire us. Serious nations . . . have prized song and music as a vehicle for worship, for prophecy, and for whatsoever in them was Divine."

— Thomas Carlyle (1795-1881)
from *The Light*, 10-15-2000,
Congregational Church of
Patchogue, New York
[Rev. Diane Prosser – Pastor]

Disco Inferno . . .
The Dancing Queen

Dance music energizes the Club Scene, and the Neo-Disco strobe light swirls a new hot Millennium with Dance Fever. Like **Madonna**, the **Bee Gees** had the good sense to re-invent themselves to capture the new mirror-ball market, and blast the rhythm rampage sky-high. So does *Gold Rush*. In order to bring you a generous collection of photos of your favorite stars, we're downsizing the Disco chapter by half, with the essentials intact:

"Jive Talkin'" – Bee Gees, #1(2), 5-75; #5, 8-75 U.K.
Though the top-rank 60s Bee Gees played their own instruments like the Beatles, and twin **Robin Gibb** (b. 12-22-49) sang lead, they re-invented their style to crest the Disco Wave. Surfing the *Saturday Night Fever* dance pavilions of Discomania, with older brother **Barry Gibb** (b. 9-1-47) singing piercing falsetto, the British Australian Bee Gees stormed the citadel of great Italian-American and Afro-American R & B Disco stars. From a Brit Invasion guitar-slinging combo, producer Robert Stigwood (RSO Records) transformed them into essentially a Philly Soul trio – and arguably the premier 'BOY BAND', vanguard of **N'Sync** or the **Backstreet Boys**. They traced a line from **Little Anthony and the Imperials**, or Philly Soulsters the **Stylistics**. Robin's twin brother **Maurice Gibb** married (#1, '67) "To Sir with Love") **Lulu**. The Bee Gees swapped drummer Colin Peterson for Dennis Bryon, guitar guy, and Vince Meluney for funk, slash, and chop guitarist Olan Kendall. They picked up new key player Blue Weaver.

Robin cruised tremendous tenor leads on debut #14, 6-67 "New York Mining Disaster 1941," fictitious catastrophe but very real huge hit. He also lofted #6, 1-69 "I Started a Joke" and #8, 9-68 "I've Gotta Get a Message to You." Soon their middle-years career celebrated #1(4), 6-71 "How Do You Mend a Broken Heart," and their ballad legend grew. Monster hits like #15, 1-68 "Words" pulsed with vocal percussion and top-line tenor expertise, but the Bee Gees hit the chart skids in the 1972-74 zone (#94, #93). We'll return to the Barry Bee Gees, but let's tap their vocal fountainhead – the great falsetto singers of the early 60s: Jimmy Jones, **Roy Orbison**, **Del Shannon**, **Frankie Valli**, and Lou Christie. Lou?

"Rhapsody in the Rain" – Lou Christie, #16, 3-66. Born Lugee Sacco (2-19-43) at Glen Willard, Pennsylvania, Lou Christie began in 1961 as Lugee and the Lions. Only star besides Elvis to get his bottom half banned on TV (*Joey Bishop Show*, 1969), Christie shook his ample leonine mane and cut loose with falsetto adventures to vibrate coliseum rafters. Possible Father of Disco Music, Lou blasted falsetto and the new Disco beat ten years early on #24, 1-63 "The Gypsy Cried" – co-written with his gypsy-dabbling fortyish songwriter Twyla Herbert.

After quasi-naughty #1, '65 "Lightning Strikes," Christie crunched this frothy rain rhapsody with a little help from Twyla and Tchaikovsky's *Romeo and Juliet*. The lyric celebrated the lovers' hot-make-out binge in his car, with steamy fogged windows and windshield wipers flopping frantically. Mock morality play. Lou visualized ANGELS crying at their panting passion, but it always sounded to me like EGGSHELLS crying. I would visualize these dinky eggy critters weeping and wailing and humpty-dumptying and gnashing their gnarled little gnasty gnon-teeth. How did we know these bawling EGGSHELLS were pioneering a new 1-2-3-4 rhythm – DISCO? Or that they were setting up a glittery glitzy gala of strobe lights and polyester, for their hot Saturday Night Omelet?

Big Bands of the 30s and 40s hammered the Downbeat, accenting the One & Three beats. Rock and Roll of the 50s, 60s, and all points to the Big Now, accents the Two & Four beats. Disco hammers every one of the four big beats with equal intensity. Early Disco-beat songs before its 70s heyday include **Supremes**' #1, '64 "Baby Love," **Chiffons**' #1, '63 "He's So Fine," and **Aretha Franklin**'s #1, '67 "Respect." Bee Gees' "Jive Talkin'" pads a variation on the trad Disco beat, by crunching eighth notes at equal intensity:

Christie nailed notes hitherto reserved for songbird Bobbettes or Chantels or moppet sopranos. Surfing the **Four Seasons**' tenor rainbow, Christie's "Mr. Tenor Man" says BASS/BARITONE is nice, but the TENOR man gets all the girls. His #10, 8-68 (#2 U.K.) "I'm Gonna Make You Mine" features Lou's roller-coaster falsetto, streaming from this 60s Italian pompadoured teen idol with catlike green eyes, muscular burly bod, and white suits later parleyed into alter-ego **John Travolta**'s *Saturday Night Fever*. Though a Disco Dude Emeritus by the 70s, Christie's amazing #80, 2-74 "Beyond the Blue Horizon" is a crescendo masterpiece (#9, 9-30 Jeanette MacDonald). **Lou Christie** furnished the Cool Disco dude prototype.

Besides "Jive Talkin's" eighth notes, many older Rock ballads did Triple Subdivision (12th notes). For each beat, you hit 3 notes (4 x 3 = 12, of course): Fats Domino's "Blueberry Hill," Platters' "Only You" or "Great Pretender," or Bobby Darin's "Queen of the Hop." Quadruple Subdivision (16th notes) is found in many Buddy Holly-style songs: "Peggy Sue," Tommy Roe's "Sheila," Lou Gramm's "True Blue Love," and the American Breed's #5, 12-67 "Bend Me, Shape Me":

Triple Subdivision (12th notes)

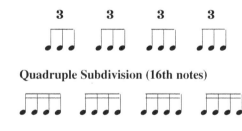

Quadruple Subdivision (16th notes)

In Disco, EVERY beat of the BIG FOUR slams. The tempo chugs from 108 to 130 beats/minute. No leeway. 108 to 130. Drilled rhythm.

"**Disco Inferno**" – Trammps, #53, 3-77; #9, R & B; #11, 2-78. Lead singer **Jimmy Ellis** steers tenor brothers Harold and Stan Wade, plus baritone Robert Upchurch. Philly's Trammps also feature their bass man, **Earl Young**, singing a rare lead. Like "Rock Around the Clock," the 2nd go-round for their song hit the heights, and the tune set longevity records for its gossamer record-lifespan era. Trammps, welding smooth Philly Soul to a jackhammer fire-forge beat, ratcheted the thermometer up to broil in sizzling basement Disco Infernos. The Club Scene flickered into full flower, engorging the hot midnight world with passion-pumping paradiddles (16th notes) and Insta-Romance.

"Boogie Oogie Oogie" hit #1(3), 6-78 for **A Taste of Honey** – named after Martin Denny's #50, '62 instrumental (and NC **Beatles**' – Paul's – remake). "Boogie" drags out accoutrements of Discomania: high-hat coolly muted, prowling funky bass riffs, incessant and loud; suave *pizzicato* treble guitar, stabbing *staccato* minor key chords at mid range – 124 beats/minute. Hazel Payne plucked bass and sang. Some cool kazoo-style item *glissandos* all over the scale like a canary that just inhaled a six-pack of Boone's Farm apple wine.

"**Le Freak**" – Chic, #1(6), 1-78; $1(5), R & B. Norma Jean Wright spun vocals. Luci Martin drummed, as **Madonna** did, in her early Village Disco phase as the new 80s bloomed. Disco Rock is an offshoot of Soul, and many of its stars are female and/or African-American. Chic's heyday was orchestrated by whiz-bang lead guitarist **Nile Rodgers**. Chic's "Good Times" hit #1, 6-79. Chic's "Le Freak" defines the 70s Disco Age. Swathed in celestial moon glow, Norma Jean calls out to the dancing-queen throng. Silky strings soar in silver splendor. "Le Freak" promises escape. The Disco guarantee! As **John Travolta** stepped onto the golden stage, swaddled in a pure white Mark Twain suit, he was no longer just a humdrum, ho-hum clerk from the grocery warehouse – he was the Emperor of Saturday Night's frantic fever.

He was the Ultimate King of Midnight. Travolta strode the strobe kingdom in panther slinkiness, and his 31-inch abs-glutted waist garnered all the gaga glances once reserved for the first King of Midnight – **ELVIS**. And Disco never disappeared, as some non-dancers might have wished. Metamorphosing into Hip-Hop and Dance Music and Techno-Funk and Eurobeat or whatever, Disco stormed the Millennium, conquering the night and taking no prisoners.

Disco is multicultural and gender-friendly. Some may not adore the same solitary chord or insistent beat hammered for seven inglorious incessant minutes – but they've got to love the way Disco brought people together. "Le Freak" fires funky muted minors and Jazzy sixths to mute your glee. It's not quite paradise – just a weekend fiesta escape from paper clips, molten steel vats, or bosses' battleaxe badgering.

"**Summer Sand**" – Dawn, #33, 6-71. Greek/Puerto-Rican singer **Tony Orlando**, and Afro super back-up singers **Telma Hopkins** and **Joyce Vincent**, plump up an old theme about callous waves zapping lovers' sand castles – see Pat Boone's #1(7), '57 "Love Letters in the Sand" or Stevie Wonder's #52, '64 "Castles in the Sand." Dawn's dynamic innovation is rhythmic. This is 100% Disco, five years before the Big Impact. Other Disco pioneers?

Reverend **Al Green** (b. '46, Forest City, Arkansas, Rock Hall '95) took the *Soul Train* north to Detroit City, missed the bus, and ended up in Michigan's #2 town Grand Rapids. With his **Sam Cooke**-style Soul crooning charisma, Al helped launch Discomania:

"Let's Stay Together" – Al Green, #1(1), 12-71; #1(9) R & B. With the ease and consummate coolth of **Smokey Robinson** – even **Nat King Cole** – Green's commanding tenor rides a *Soul Train*-style rhythm track that chugs to endless romantic destiny. The pitty-pat pulse of his Soul/Disco anthem dates back to Honolulu's teen idol **Robin Luke**, and his monumental #5, 8-58 "Susie Darlin'" rhythm:

Sue Luke's Pitty-Pat Rhythm:

1   2   3   4

Al coaxes and chides and sweet-talks his lady to stick by him – an odd prelude to a Dance Fever Era where lifetime relationships went POOF in a puff of Cinderella midnights and vanished yesterdreams. In the Disco Era, penicillin would cure ANYTHING, and the "One-Night Stand" highlighted the hell-bent-for-leather midnight masquerade.

Meanwhile, back at Al Green, "Let's Stay Together" floats like a wispy cirrus cloud in the strawberry-marshmallow Key of 'F'. Green gravitates up to Sub-Dominant **Bb** on his sweet-slurry flurry of vocal escalators. His don't-rush-me 95 beats/minute previewed a punchier pace. Green followed with #3, 10-72 "You Ought to Be with Me" (#1 R & B), and hit with #3, 7-72,, "I'm Still in Love with You."

Al Green is among great artists with colors for their names – Bobby 'BLUE' Bland, James BROWN, Panama RED, Deep PURPLE, YELLO (#51, 8-87, Swiss, "Oh Yeah"), ONYX (#4, 5-93 "Slam," a rare gem), King CRIMSON, Clint BLACK, BLACQUE (#5, 10-99 "Bring It All to Me'), BLACKstreet (#3, 5-98 "I Get Lonely"), INDIGO Girls, RED Hot Chili Peppers (#9, 6-99 "Scar Tissue"), REDman (#3, 10-98, non-Bee Gee "How Deep Is Your Love"), BLUE Oyster Cult, BLUE Magic (#8, 5-74 "Sideshow"), GREEN Day, Dobie GRAY (#5, 2-73 "Drift Away"), or GOLDEN Earring (#10, 11-82 "Twilight Zone"). The guy named for the ABSENCE OF COLOR?

"Can't Get Enough of Your Love, Babe" – Barry White, #1(1), 8-74; #1(1) R& B. Barry White's titanic titles dwarf the *Gettysburg Address*. Clarke's *Popular Music* says White's voice "sounds like chocolate cake tastes." The Galveston (b. '44) bass/baritone singer soars nearly to tenor in his beefy-titled #2(2) "You're the First, the Last, My Everything." Big strong voice, big strong guy. Elvis's "It's Now or Never" (#1, '60) jolted Barry into a positive-direction singing career, when in his youth he majored in Applied Tomfoolery. From #18, 10-94 "Practice What You Preach," the big Disco Dude shows he certainly has #40S (Spoken Rap, 10-99) "Staying Power."

George McCrae's #1(2), 6-74 "Rock Your Baby" is also vanguard Disco. The Floridian tenor's wife Gwen shared his stardom, with #9, 5-75 (#1 R & B) "Rockin' Chair." Houston's **Billy Preston**, who backed the Beatles AND Gospel legend Mahalia Jackson (#21, 1-48 "Move Up a Little Higher"), scored big #1(1), 7-74 (#10 R & B) "Nothin' from Nothin'"). Keyboard star of 60s *Shindig*, the smiling star with 7" Afro hairdo has a googol showbiz pals – and hit #1(2), 3-73 "Will It Go Round in Circles."

"Who Loves You" – Four Seasons, #3, 8-75. Of all 60s groups, perhaps the Frankie Valli 4 Seasons translated best into the Disco Deluge. Valli also crunched #6, 5-75 (#31 R& B) "Swearin' to God," with Disco fever like his signature song #1(2), 5-78 "Grease" (#40 R & B). Their biggest Disco chartbuster is "December 1963," at #1, 1975 AND #14, 1994, a bi-generational Dance Trax blockbuster.

The **Rolling Stones** hit #31, 12-78 with "Shattered." Check out Charlie Watts's strong 1-2-3-4 beat at double-heartbeat tempo (120). The **Jackson Five** also did Disco, with #2(2), 3-74 (#1 R & B) "Dancing Machine."

David Lasley's #36, 3-82 "If I Had My Wish Tonight" is among many Disco-era hits to sing nearly ALL *falsetto*. Others? But, of course. Pioneers – among the earliest, we have the prototypical **Frankie Lymon and the Teen-agers**' #13, 4-56 "I Want You to Be My Girl" (#3 R & B). Of course, being 13 helped. **Little Joe & Thrillers** were a bit older – with their R & B falsetto hi-jinx thriller about a tiny chick named "Peanuts" (#22, 9-57; oddly, no R & B #). Leslie Martin led R & B 'Boy Band' the Schoolboys from New York City to #15, R & B (#91, 2-57 HOT 100) with "Shirley," which trumped Top Ten in my town Detroit. The prettiest girl in my 7th grade class was Shirley Gonda, and Shirley Werner likes **Shirley Ellis**'s nifty novelty "The Name Game" at #3, 12-64.

Ian Whitcomb of Wicking, England, not only wrote an early R & R autobiography, but hit #8, 5-65 on a Brit Invasion 100% Disco falsetto song – "You Turn Me On (Turn On Song)," at a time when the make-out expression 'Turn-On' was invented (see Tim Tam & Turn-Ons).

"Bread and Butter" – Newbeats, #2(2), 8-64. Larry Hanley of ARP, Texas (not A.A.R.P.) is probably the first Disco King who had no idea that he was. Perhaps, though, it's Lou Christie or Frankie Valli. The Newbeats concocted a New Beat of slapping 1-2-3-4 Disco energy with Hanley and siblings Mark and Dean Mathis. Unlike Valli, Christie, or falsetto icon **Del Shannon**, the whole "Bread and Butter" song is falsetto, like previous #8, '65 Whitcomb tune.

Dastardly plot. Bad-luck guy returns home early. His sweetie is eating bread and butter with Dude #2, who says so-long to strawberry-jam guzzling gal. Jilted guy, sad and forlorn, scrams. The Newbeats hit #12, 10-65 with even-better rocker "Run Baby Run (Back into My Arms)." The super sax snarls, the organ does backflips and easy squeezy cushiony wheezes, and a kick-rump xylophone chimes the odd note on the chunky Disco jackhammer beat. Henley's unheralded falsetto wafts in the baby-blue azure sky above Mt. Everest.

"Everlasting Love" – Robert Knight, #13, 9-67; #14, 10-67 R & B. Three-time winner. Now and then a song floats along that's so positive and melodic that it can't help but triumph, thrice. Disco quadruple 16th-note beat for this Tennessee Soulster Knight. **(Little) Carl Carlton** (B. '52, Detroit) hit #6, 9-74 (#11 R & B); Carlton moved on to #22, 8-81 and #2(8), 6-81 R & B monster "She's a Bad Mama Jama (She's Built, She's Stacked)." Nearly three decades later, the adorable **Gloria Estefan** skimmed the Disco Dance Latin zone with her #27, 1-95 HOT 100 version of "Everlasting Love."

Neo-Disco? Catch #2(1), 5-90 (#1 R & B) "Hold On," by **En Vogue.** Dawn Robinson's R & B quartet from San Francisco also scored with two more silver medal-songs: #2(3), 3-92 "My Lovin' (You're Never Gonna Get It)," and #2(4), 11-96 "Don't Let Go (Love)."

"Super Trouper" – ABBA, #45, 4-81. On Stockholm, Sweden's Al. #17, 12-80 *Abba*, this two-guy, two-girl Europop crew salutes the epitome of Disco glory. They're adorned in the requisite Travoltan pure white outfits, amidst a multitude of gung-ho fans arrayed in everything from cowboy chic to Arabian Knight. Everybody gazes agog at one Travoltish dancer who hogs the blinding blitzkrieg beams of the squirmy ELVIS SPOTLIGHT. A few chapters ago, the Hendrix guitarists stole the spotlight. Now Discomania took it full circle. Our "Super Trouper" is a DANCER, an anonymous athletic Swede in an American Western shirt. Key shift is focus! No longer was it Stage-Front Zoom on the lead singer. The DANCER her/himself gobbled up the glory (see *MTV* and *VH-1*, and singer/dancer/superstars **Janet** [Jackson], **Britney Spears**, and **Ricky Martin**).

Stockholm's finest? **Anni-Frid (Frida) Lyngstad, Agnetha Faltskog** (lead alto/soprano vocals), **Bjorn Ulvaeus** (axe) and **Benny Anderson** (88s). They began with #6, 6-74 "Waterloo," named for Napoleon's last stand (1815); to meet one's 'Waterloo' means to lose, perhaps to die. Country boomer **Stonewall Jackson** took another "Waterloo" song to #4, 5-59 (#1[5], C). Its big booming bass drum cannon beat was 100% pure 1-2-3-4 Disco (a rare intersection of Country and Disco). If you want to make it in Rock and Roll, it's a good idea to speak English – and many Scandinavians speak it better than many of us.

"Super Trouper" begins as a madrigal, sporting new rhymeless free-verse lyrics. "Trouper" concerns groggy Glasgow nights, blinding spotlight beams, and the Lone-liness of the Long-Distance Superstar in the Key of 'F#.' Angst leaps out of the woodwork. The album peddles *Weltschmerz* (world-pain) in #8, 11-80 "The Winner Takes All." With drummer Ola Brunkert and bass Rutger Gunnarsson controlling the song, darkness at noon pervades Lapland twilight, as Santa Claus readies his sleigh to hike back the long blonde Snow Queen Trail to perfect age seventeen:

"Dancing Queen" – ABBA, #1(1), 12-76. We all remember these Dancing Queens. Sweet, young, seventeen? Like **Britney Spears, Debbie Gibson, Christina Aguilera, Tiffany, Jessica Simpson** – the eternal ingenue. Dewy-eyed debutante. Perfect blonde cheerleader, bubbly and bosomy and perky and pristine. The chaste maiden with the winsome evermore smile.

The Dancing Queen. ABBA scored also with #3, 9-78 "Take a Chance on Me" and #14, 5-77 "Knowing Me, Knowing You." Their #1 U.K. and #13, 9-76 "Fernando," Spanish Civil War saga, recounts melodically long-ago cannon fire as Europe marshaled for World War II. This #1 Adult Contemporary hit record cornered the market on Swedish-Spanish Soft Rock.

"Disco Queen" – Hot Chocolate, #28, 5-75; #40 R & B. Kissin' cousin of Dancing Queen above. British integrated group did lively Disco, like #3, 11-75 "You Sexy Thing" and #8, 2-75 "Emma." Roster from England, Grenada, and the Bahamas.

Soft Cell's #8, 1-82 "Tainted Love" was steered by Marc Almond from Britain – and song set old-era longevity record on charts.

Otis Redding's surviving **Bar-Kays** hit #5 R & B, 8-76 (#23, 10-76) with "Shake Your Rump to the Funk." Let-It-All-Hang-Out laisssez faire FCC regulations brought us **Mystical**'s #15, 9-2000 "Shake Ya A—." And **Nelly**'s teapot tempest at #7, 4-2000 "(Hot S—) Country Grammar."

The **Silver Connection** took Disco airborne with #1(3), 10-75 "Fly, Robin, Fly," and followed up with #2(3), 3-76 "Get Up and Boogie." Disco taught hordes of secretaries, accountants, and cops to do the Hustle at the Disco Dervish in Peoria. Or maybe Studio 54, Xenon, Xanadu, or Zanzibar.

"Get Down Tonight" – KC & the Sunshine Band, #1(1), 7-75; #1(1), 4-75 R & B. Like the Dell Vikings or Marcels of old, or Hootie's Blowfish and the **Dave Matthews Band** of new, KC's Floridian Sunshiners are an integrated band. They first skyrocketed in England. Seven to eleven bandsmen cavort in uniform white bell-bottomed leather Elvis jumpsuits – tiptoeing the Disco Soul tightrope. **Harry Wayne Casey** (b. '51, K.C.) of Hialeah Opalocka-Boca Chica Key, Florida, and **Richard Finch** (b. '54) of Indianapolis, Indiana, got together to study Junkanoo music – a Key West conch blend of booming steel drums, kazoo-flavored flutes, and klonking cowbells [see **Baha Men**'s #10, 8-2000 Al. *Who Let the Dogs Out?*].

With conga guy Fermin Goytisolo, guitar man Jerome Smith flutters a few speed whiz 2nd notes. The bass sputters in, on one basic note. Disco bass is always funky.

The jury is still out on whether to play with or without PICKS. At some point, the low-level star of the band became the THUMB.

Disco/Dance DJ's require VINYL and the song's LONG version – maybe seven minutes instead of 2¼. Despite a cup of coffee for eight-track tapes, vinyl persevered. Jocks blasted small snippets into the mix. And that's the way ("uh huh uh huh") we like it.

Casey [KC] at the Bat grand-slammed five homers, like #1(2), 10-75 "That's the Way (I Like It)." Weirdly, of 18 HOT 100 hits, the KC Krew either hit the TOP TWO or #35 and below, except maverick #18, 12-83 "Give It Up." Examples – #35, 2-78 "Boogie Shoes," and #88, 9-77 "Shotgun Shuffle." "That's the Way," we remember for its caveman holler "UH HUH UH HUH."

"(Shake, Shake, Shake) Shake Your Booty" – KC & the Sunshine Band, #1(1), 7-76; #1(4) R & B. This earthquake of a booty-shaking song sparked America's Bicentennial Year. In the Hudson River, a flotilla of tall old ships cruised the skyline shadow. Union Lake, Michigan, was a star-spangled 4th of July barrage of red-white-and-blue Roman candles and shimmery Happy Birthday America blasts. In the next 15 years, the old communist scheme of drone work and gray hopeless drudgery would give way to the rebirth (or birth) of international democracy. A Presidential line of resolute leaders oversaw the collapse of totalitarian governments who forbade Western culture like Rock and Roll: Ford, Carter, Reagan, Clinton, and two Bushes. The Sound Track for the crumbling of the old socialist order was American Rock and Roll. The Afghan **Taliban** forbade Rock and Roll – or any music – while Osama Bin Laden sat in silence in his 2001-02 cave.

From Ragtime to Dixieland to Sousa's U.S. Marine Band Marches, American big-beat music wriggled its inventive way through Mississippi Delta Blues, Boogie-Woogie, Swing Jazz, and the Rock Revolution. A peaceful, but NOT silent, *coup d'etat* had taken over the world. It tossed no bombs, drew no blood. It simply symbolized a joyous way of life. Hail, hail to Rock and Roll!

The electric guitar is mightier than the sword.

KC's #1(1), 8-79 "Please Don't Go" somehow eluded R & B chart action, but Disco dancers with the energy of the Tasmanian Devil shook their booties (or whatever) into the garish sunrise. In the afterglow, grubby cigarette butts and coke stash floated in gutters rippling with sweet lost rainbows in the evermore oil slick.

"Celebration" – Kool and the Gang, #1(2), 10-80; #1(6) R & B. Before KC and Krew shuffled off, Kool and his Kats kommanded the Klub Scene. Buttressed by bass boomer **Robert 'Kool' Bell**, this Jersey City, New Jersey, band impressed Rock pressman Joe McEwan: "Like a messy, ketchup-laden cheese steak plopped down at a staid dinner party, funk was rude, greasy, and unwanted . . . Kool and the Gang made nasty silly. There was the guy

who ate raw hamburger and chocolate buttermilk for lunch." Kool's Krew jumped to dance destiny with debut blaster "Jungle Boogie" (#14, 12-83). Hybrid between Old Soul, New Funk, and Rising Disco, it quavers in joyous pandemonium – powered by Kool's craggy bass runs, grand slam saxes (Ron Bell), and Cuban congas.

"Celebration" never lost its appeal. A perennial favorite at weddings and wild parties, it shares the Disco aura with #8, 11-79 (#1[3], 9-79 R & B) "Ladies Night." On "Cherish," at #2(3), 8-75 (#1 R & B), Kool took the **Bee Gees'** magical mutability into Lionel Richie's arena of sweet sincere balladry. Beyond funk and bluster, they ride ballad expertise with #2(1), 11-83 "Joanna." The **Association** did a different "Cherish" to #1(3), 8-66.

"Come and Get Your Love" – Real McCoy, #19, 6-95. NEO-DISCO is also called Dance music. **Redbone** had the original to #5, 1-74 and #75 R & B, with Native American Leon Redbone and singers Lolly and Pat Vegas. Pete DePoe thumped war drums, as they did 67.89% Disco, and 22.11% Swamp Rock. This hit's 2nd go-round features Swedish O'Jay (Olaf Jeglitza), plus two serious-looking Afro singers – Vanessa Mason and Lisa Cork. Like **Janet Jackson**, they hit #3 in 90s with a non-Del Shannon "Run Away" (It's not Janet's, either).

"Love Will Lead You Back" – Taylor Dayne, #1(1), 1-90. Long Island's Leslie Wonderman – 'Taylor' – sparked the charts with this #1 HOT 100 and Adult Contemporary blockbuster. Her others that skirt Disco include #2(1), 11-88 "Don't Rush Me," and #3, 6-88 "I'll Always Love You" (#21 R & B).

"Forever" – Mariah Carey, #9A, 6-96 [A = Airplay]. **Mariah** sings "Forever" so passionately she could bring tears to a cabbage. Forty years before her mellifluous coloratura soprano coalesced, **Little Richard** piloted her graceful *melisma* style – try his #54, 4-57 "Send Me Some Lovin'" (#3 R & B). Mariah's debut #1(4), 6-90 "Vision of Love" pays homage to the Disco tradition.

"Dim All the Lights" – Donna Summer, #2(2), 8-79; #113 R & B. Donna stuffed three #1's, a penultimate silver #2, and a #4 into 1979. Born Adrian Donna Gaines (New Year's Eve, 1948), Summer sang Gospel in church, and won the lead role in musical *Hair*, noted for its *Genesis* outfits (birthday suits). She married German actor Helmut Sommer ('Summer' in German), and cut sizzling #2(2), 7-75 "Love to Love You Baby." Her #6, 8-77 (#9 R & B) "I Feel Love" features bass-rumbling waterfalls, and hammering hi-hats pulsating to infinity. On "Love to Love You Baby," Donna rocks and sways and shimmies and swoons. Her slinky soprano floats off to some perfumed boudoir. She feasts her lusciously lovely tigress eyes upon him and then poof . . . the alarm clock, aargh.

No surprise she hit #1(3), 4-79 with "Hot Stuff." "Dim All the Lights" is the Heart of Disco. [Bill Haley rocked around the alarm clock to his own #11, 11-54 double dimmer "Dim, Dim the Lights"].

After the lights were dimmed, the "Bad Girls" came out, to the tune of #1(5), 5-79 (#1 R & B). With BEEP BEEPS and TOOT TOOTS, hornish horns salute the 2 a.m. street girls, out getting a little pedestrian exercise in fishnet spandex. Girls from near and far ply their public-utility trade, as a caravan of action-seeking black sedans cruises chicks in rotten Gotham. Donna magnetizes listeners (mostly male) with her scorching siren song. Wonder why the good people are always interested in the bad ones – or are they often the same?

The title track for her Al. #1(1), 11-79 *On the Radio* hit #5, 1-80 (#9 R & B). Wearing a Scottish coal-miner's cap, and her bright-full-lipped smile with a puffy skirt, she wiggles a 'shame shame' index finger. Her pink and blue tropical paradise décolletage robe sparks record buyers to buy her deep purple star-strewn skyline. Summer dreams. Disco queens.

Songs may have been sizzlier in the 70s, but dancers forgot to touch each other any more. The dance floor often clotted with a writhing, pogo-sticking, mosh-bashing horde of dancers alone together.

The Solo Swinger Battalion.

"Mony Mony 'Live'" – Billy Idol, #1(1), 9-87. Billy salutes 60s star **Tommy James & His Shondells**' #3, 4-68 rockin' hit named for the **M**utual **o**f **N**ew **Y**ork ad sign by the recording studio. Idol's U.K. always had a tradition of meet your pals at the pub. As the Pig N' Whistle metamorphosed into Argon Club 34¼, guys didn't have to pay girls' admission, liberating guys from Weight Watchers' Wallets. Basic beer gave way to the Secret Parking Lot Caper, with some coke, a quick toke, and/or fast hot action up in smoke. Saturday Night Oz Fever.

Donna Summer

"She Works Hard for the Money" – Donna Summer, #3, 5-83; #1(3), 6-83 R & B. A whole world of

newly single women now worked hard to make ends meet. Many had been "The Wanderer," like **Dion**'s #2, '61 song, or Donna's different "Wanderer" to #3, 9-80 (#13 R & B). Donna advised this dip-twit brute, who is mentally and maybe physically abusing Donna's friend, to treat her right. Donna begins her Disco Crusade: her #79, 7-99 "I Will Go with You (Con Te Partiro)" was recorded in Italian with **Andrea Bocelli** (Al. #23, 11-2000 *Verdi*). In Fall 1999 Donna had the #1 Hot Dance Track Single in Europe. Disco will survive:

"I Will Survive" – Gloria Gaynor, #1(3), 12-78; #4, 1-79 R & B. A song about Women's EMPOWERMENT. In the words of droll feminist Flo Kennedy, "A woman without a man is like a fish without a bicycle!" No longer does a woman have to be an appendage of some useless man. Gloria's song-girl is at first unceremoniously dumped. She's frozen at first, stunned, petrified.

"I Will Survive" shifts from a rhythmless intro to a kickstomp 117 beats a minute; the hi-hat spins with the big 1-2-3-4 beats of the commanding bass drum. The bassist plants himself at the root of the minor chord (**Am**). The minor chord mirrors her early sadness and indecision. When we're absolutely certain she's made it emotionally and financially, we'd probably hear a major chord (**A**).

Dance floors from Maine to Mexico are ablaze with female sing-a-longers when Gloria's timeless Empowerment Anthem hits the DJ's big speakers. With whirligig gusto, newly liberated lasses peal out thunderous choruses to make the Mormon Tabernacle Choir sound like a whispery duet. A choppy guitar blanket sails the trebly strings. The odd violin lurks in the background. Her beatless coda intensifies her uncertainty. But Gloria's song-girl is feisty, plucky, resilient, and above all newly self-sufficient.

Paradise it ain't. With pals and courage, she will bear up, smile, and seek a hopeful rosy future. Newark, New Jersey's (b.'49) **Gloria Gaynor** stuffs the American Dream into a nutshell here. Not quite "Johnny B. Goode's" rags to riches dream. Gloria's is the "I'm gonna make it anyhow on my own, you jerk" motif. She picks up the broken pieces of her sad life, gets on with it, and ricochets her grief into new streetwise awareness and maturity.

It's a SELF-POWERED SUCCESS STORY . . . like America. She takes charge. She empowers herself. Big Daddy is no more. Who needs the clod anyhow? Out of ex-bitterness and regret, she restores hope and faith. Maybe love will come around again, too, but on HER terms. Then Gloria can shift that gloomy **D-minor** to a sunnyside **D-major**.

"Never Can Say Goodbye" – Gloria Gaynor, #9, 11-74; #34, 12-74 R & B. Great artists often have trailaway second-best tunes we nearly forget. This one is a daisy, or a forget-me-not. This one contains a breezy forever flavor, and a rhythm track that just won't quit. Any prettier G.G. tunes? Maybe one: #75, 11-75 **Les Paul/Mary Ford** flashback "How High the Moon" [#1(9), 3-51].

Gaynor reflects the mellow sound of **Gino Vanelli**, and his #4, 9-78 (#21 R & B) "I Just Wanna Stop." Canadian Gino's brother Ross produced **Earth, Wind & Fire.**

"September" – **Earth, Wind, and Fire, #8, 11-78; #1(1) R & B.** L.A. Funky Jazz/Disco/Soul combo sported 33 HOT 100 hits, 46 R & B. Leader **Maurice White** drummed for **Ramsey Lewis Trio**, and plays everything, especially the exotic karimba. Hugest hit was a real "Shining Star" (#1[1], 2-75), with 1-2-3 punch: #2(2), 7-79 "After the Love Has Gone" and #3, 10-81 "Let's Groove." Rock Hall of Fame 1999.

Johnnie Taylor's (1938-2000) "Disco Lady" stormed to #1(4), 2-75 and #1(6) R & B. The "Who's Makin' Love?" #5, 10-68 Soulster dazzled the Disco dance floor.

"Love Child" – **Supremes, #1(2), 10-68; #2(3) R & B.** Supremes pioneered Disco. Catch the big 1-2-3-4 beats in #1, '64 "Baby Love" and '68 "Love Child." The title is a euphemism for an illegitimate kid. Diana Ross tells turned-on guy to simmer down; she's saving her total passion for marriage, because she doesn't want her song-girl's kid to follow the pattern she did of fatherless families. Touching tune. Musical masterpiece. 88% Disco beat that didn't even know it WAS Disco yet. Maybe the first Soul Disco tune was **Fontella Bass**'s #4, 10-65 "Rescue Me."

"The Legend of Xanadu" – **Dave Dee, Dozy, Beaky, Mick and Tich, #1, 2-68 U.K.; #123, 4-68 U.S.A.** Super song, with sound of **Monkees** to the max. It's about a mythical romantic place, with the name of a movie starring the lovely **Olivia Newton-John**; her other song "Xanadu" scorched the charts to #8, 8-80. Movie was named after long poem by British Romantic poet Sam Coleridge. Dave Dee, etc., are no relation to Romantic poet Sam Coleridge. Dave Dee, etc., are no relation to **Dicky Doo & the Don'ts**, of #28, 2-58 "Click Clack" fame.

"Physical" – **Olivia Newton-John, #1(10), 10-81; #28, 1-82 R & B.** With 10 chartbusting weeks at #1, was "Physical" the biggest Rock and Roll song of all time? Though pigeonholing purists might label it solid "Disco," Olivia's workout tune splattered the 80s with double-figure domination of the #1 apex. Recently, the #1(14) "Macarena" is among the few big-beat songs to challenge. Elvis's #1(11), '56 "Hound Dog"/"Don't Be Cruel" extended to eleven weeks, but it was really two songs trading tiptop positions via the cool-flipside route. By 2001, **Destiny's Child**'s #1(11+) "Independent Women – Part I" spanked the high charts with a catchy blend of Soul/R&B/Hip-Hop/Reggae/Rap. To top Olivia, you've got to cover all the bases.

Nearly pure Disco, the rambunctious "Physical" previewed TV infomercial workout tapes which cajole, goad, and coax a world of sofa spuds to de-rump and get their acts in gear. When the Cockney dude declared, "Olivia, Oi luvv-a-ya," he realized "Physical" reverberates with double-entendre naughtiness. Olivia Newton-John is an Anglo-Aussie-American princess. With "sparkling blue country eyes" (Kerouac term), and her zoom-in Pepsodent debutante smile, Olivia (Sandy from Grease) was the world's 70s sweetheart. Even into 2000, the only tunes with a pretense of Rock and Roll to surpass "Physical"

are: the aforementioned "Macarena"; Rock and Soul tug-of-war "The Boy Is Mine," #1(13), '98, by Brandy & Monica; #1(12) **Santana/Rob Thomas/Feat**'s "Smooth"; and **Puff Daddy**'s Rap Elegy for Notorious B.I.G. – #1(11), '97 "I'll Be Missing You."

Puff Daddy's elegy at #1(11) samples the tune for **Sting and the Police**'s #1(8), '83 "Every Breath You Take." Therefore, with 8 + 11 weeks at #1 under different lyrical cloaks, **Police/Puff Daddy**'s combo tune "Every Breath You Take – I'll Be Missing You" is the #1 song of all time, in weeks commanding the #1 slot! 19 weeks!

"Physical" shows a steamier, more sensuous side to Olivia's Barbie-Doll chaste image. In Grease, remember, she metamorphoses from innocent ingénue as Sandy to hotshot leather lass, to attract the rapscallionish Danny Zucco (John Travolta). "Physical" bashes thunder drums in even-volumed big 1-2-3-4 cadence. Olivia kicks loose with a marathon vocal that downpedals her normal dreamy melodies to cash in on the Big Beat.

"You're the One That I Want" – **John Travolta and Olivia Newton-John, #1(1), 4-78.** 'Vinnie Barbarino,' ya know? Like young Ricky Nelson on the Ozzie and Harriet Show, Travolta grew up on TV. That **Fonzie**-type kid on Welcome Back, Kotter parleyed his cool TV rep into bigger Teen Idol fame. His intense tenor whirled upwards into Irish leprechaun rainbow range. With 'Sandy' (Olivia Newton-John) in Grease, John dueled a duo and assumed the Elvis position. With catlike green eyes and jet black hair, Travolta had the Italian-stallion moves, the with-it wisecracks, and the torrid teenage following. His #10, 5-76 "Let Her In" and #47, 9-78 "Greased Lightning" liberated him from flash-in-pan status – and his continuing R & R presence shines in #25A [Airplay], 11-96 "The Grease Megamix." On their #5, 8-78 "Summer Nights," Olivia and John spin a romantic ballad. Its last theatrical note is a major Rock resolution, swirling a hanging minor, and finally grasping the last melodic major-chord note in a tonic togetherness finale.

"My Thang" – **James Brown, #29, 6-74; #1(2) R & B.** If you ego is the size of a lone Cheerio, you shouldn't go into Rock and Roll anyhow. Without Brown's supremely confident Godfather of Soul stylistics, Disco and Funk and Rap might never have Hip-Hopped out of the R & B/Soul Apollo Theatre. Brown's heyday was 1958-76, but he still spins the high charts with his all-pervasive influence.

Brick's "Dazz" zoomed to #3 (#1[4] R & B) as Jazz/Disco Fusion. It's unrelated to **Dazz Band**'s #5, 4-82 (#1[5] R & B) "Let It Whip." **Van McCoy** hustled to #1(1) on "The Hustle," a gargantuan group dance of sober-impaired complexity. It spins at 90° angles in a complex foot-stompin' style. Strings ride fluffy clouds on high, and get-downers Boogie in Disco's first gleaming.

Meco's #1(2), 9-77 (#8 R & B) "Star Wars Theme/Cantina Band" is West Point trombonist bandleader Meco Monardo's intergalactic saga song – pulsing again with the 2002 Star Wars resurgence. Remember Luke Skywalker and Jedi Knights and fussy frumpy robot C3PO? And Darth Vader's green fire-wand?

"Y.M.C.A." – Village People, #2(3), 11-78; #32 R & B. This Jock Rock Glam/Glitz Rock and Soul anthem has been boisterously blaring over your baseball stadium for a generation. The song is simply a lot of fun for everyone. People comically attempt to contort their inflexible bods into letters Y – M – C – A. Their hilarious limb-flapping wave looks like macaroni trying to do the Macarena. Who are these [Greenwich] Village People anyway? **Victor Willis** (cop), Felipe Rose (Indian Chief), Glenn Hughes (motorcyclist), Alexander Briley (Army guy), David Hodo (construction worker), and cowboy Randy Jones.

The actual Y.M.C.A. they celebrate is the 34th Street 'Y,' by Penn Station, just a mile south of peep show Times Square. With spoofy fervor and theatrical wizardry, they strut their wild routine – engaging in various macho jobs (#24, 6-78 "Macho Man"); "Macho Man" plies the huff-puff theme of working out with aerobic glee. With #45, 5-79 "Go West," the one-year Village People phenomenon is best remembered for their second biggest hit to "YMCA," #3, 3-79 "In the Navy." They previewed the Rock Video 1981+ *MTV* Era. A mecca to New York's alternative lifestyle community, this wide-open YMCA catered to the *joie-de-vivre* atmosphere of the whoop-it-up late 70s, before the ball dropped on the 80s. With a colorful array of costumery often seen in the Greenwich Village Outrageous Hallowe'en Parade, the Village People zapped gray-suit conformity in a whirlaway wonderland of grand/grotesque garb.

"Little Darlin'" – Diamonds, #2(8), 3-57; #2(2) R & B. These Toronto white Diamonds had SOUL. Fronted by tremendous **Dave Somerville** at lead tenor, they did G-Clefs' #24, 7-56 "Ka-Ding-Dong" to #35, 9-56 (#8 R & B). Diamonds gleamed on many R & B covers of Frankie Lymon, the Rays, and even Buddy Holly's first songwriter hit BEFORE he hit as a singer, Diamonds' #13, 6-57 "Words of Love" (re-covered' by Beatles). Ted Kowalski and Somerville pioneered falsetto before Lou Christie or Del Shannon. Diamonds' gems? #29, 10-58 "Walking Along" and #18, 1-59 "She Say." They added the big line dance craze "The Stroll" (#4, 10-57). "Little Darlin'" has Chalypso/nearly Reggae beat, fab falsetto, and even Bill Reed's BASS Rap vocal on bridge.

"Right Back Where We Started From" – Maxine Nightingale, #2(2), 2-76; #46, 4-76 R & B. London's Nightingale dusted off the moon with this Disco triumph, and "Lead Me On" hit #5, 5-79. Monster Disco rhythmic thump "Good Vibrations" hit #1 twice (Beach Boys '66 and different song by **Marky Mark & Funky Bunch** in 7-91, at #64 R & B). The 2nd one is Disco.

Walter Murphy gave us #1(1), 5-76 "A Fifth of Beethoven," mixing Disco, Classical/Orchestral, and Irish seltzer.

Discotheque downsized in 70s to 'Disco,' from Johnny Rivers' 1965 Go-Go Discotheque Club era. The music establishment often panned Disco because it put working musicians out of business. Club owners hired Disc Jockeys, not Live Bands. Nothing new – piano rolls and Talkie movies put Ragtime piano players out of showbiz.

Records put live Vaudeville on the unemployment lines.

From the 60s Fillmore East Pop Palace profusion, the NYC and San Francisco 'Underground Scene' demanded 24-7-365 nonstop Rock. Merging with Psychedelia, the Scene offered streaming strobe ceiling lights, rotating mirror-ball chandeliers, and pulsating rainbow rays. Skimpy dancers swooned and swooped to twin turntables. Even the Old Stars, who bypassed Rock and Roll itself, scrambled to the Disco Dervish bandwagon: **Ethel Merman, Percy Faith,** the **Boston Pops Orchestra,** and **Barbra Streisand.**

Somewhere into the hodge-podge mix, the automatic drum machine arrived, to the cussing consternation of drummers. With the P.C. (Personal Computer), M.I.D.I. technology crafted whole complex rhythm sections by pre-programmed sequencing. Suddenly, who needed **Gene Krupa, John Bonham,** or **Neal Peart** (**Rush,** #44, 6-81 "Tom Sawyer")? Or **Keith Moon,** or **Ringo**? The difference between Disco and plain Rock, besides the 1-2-3-4 beat, is the focus upon the DANCER, sometimes even beyond the BAND:

"Flashdance . . . What a Feeling" – Irene Cara, #1(6), 4-83. Irene Cara (b. '59, New York City) said goodnight to no-beat music. "Flashdance" not only spearheads a major dance movie, but also features one of the Top 25 driving rhythms in all R & R history (of course she has a nice voice too). Her fervent dance fever gusto sparks her sledgehammer 1-2-3-4 Disco pulse in this inspirational teen dream anthem. More than a hit record, this song is a way of life for every girl taking Jazz or Tap dancing (possibly from Kristen Cahill Dean). Dreams of dancing glory ride along with these pirouetting 'Janie B. Goode' visions. Smitten by the allure of Broadway or ballerina halls of splendor, gazillions of starry-eyed girls put on their dancing shoes and get the 'Flashdance' feeling. Hollywood beckons on a pirouette and a prayer.

Cara's cool sound dazzled the high charts with debut #4, 6-80 "Fame," #13, 10-83 "Why Me," and #8, 3-84 "Breakdance." Carrot-topped early female Rock pioneer **Lesley Gore** wrote Irene's sophomore hit, #19, 8-80 "Out Here on My Own." [Jennifer Beals is the *Flashdance* actress, Cara the great singer].

On "You Make Me Feel Like Dancing," #1(1), 10-76 (#43 R & B), **Leo Sayer** joins the Disco bandwagon. His Blue-Eyed British Soul thrives on un-Disco #1, 2-77 "When I Need You" (#2[5] R & B). **Yvonne Elliman's** #1(1), 2-78 (#60 R & B) "If I Can't Have You" furnishes Honolulu Disco sunshine on **Bee Gees'** song. Its inclusion on #1(24), 11-77 *Saturday Night Fever* album soundtrack didn't hurt sales. She apprenticed for a Top One song with #14, 10-76 "Love Me" (not Elvis's #2, '56, or 112's #17, '98 different two "Love Me's"), Yvonne triumphed, too, with #15, 3-77 "Hello Stranger," which IS related to **Barbara Lewis's** gorgeous #3, '63 Soul song. Lewis's cool voice could take you away to Venus:

"Venus" – Shocking Blue, #1(1), 12-69. Early Disco tune makes us figure Disco began either 1) On Venus; or 2) In the Netherlands, with Mariska Veres' saucy alto lead

– with spicy soprano hooks. She sirenly sings she's the Greek goddess Venus – the fire of his desire. "Venus" – as two different songs – hit #1 three times:

Bananarama blasted the same kicky tune to #1(1), 6-86. London's Siobhan Fahey, Keren Woodward, and Sarah Dallin weave wild harmony for their Venus (Roman goddess Aphrodite, too) escapade.

No song belongs to any absolute category. Let's Quantitatively Analyze "Venus II' here. Grab your beaker, compass, tongs, and frog:

"Venus II": A Quasi-Scienterrific Analysis:

52%	Proto-Archaeo Disco
14%	Hard Rock
3%	Euro-Dance Rhythm
11%	Science Fiction
4%	Dutch Invasion
2%	Pure Rock and Roll
1%	Wheaties
4%	Heavy Metal
1%	Lite Metal
1%	Girl-Group
2%	Pepsi-Cola
2%	Kats' Pajamas
100%	

We could also re-name it "New Wave."

"Venus" – Frankie Avalon, #1(5), 2-59; #10, 3-59 R & B; and this Disco version #46, 1-76; Adult Contemporary #1, 1-76. Philly *Bandstand* teen idol singer/trumpeter Avalon (B. '39, Philly) invokes Greek goddess of Love to bring him a sweet pedestal princess for happy-ever-after homemaking. Frankie's 2nd "Venus" hit go-round features a snappier Disco thump. Teen Idols spring eternal, as long as Venus wafts her perfumed blossoms:

"I Just Want to Be Your Everything" – Andy Gibb, #1(4), 4-77; #19, 8-77 R & B. Bee Gees' kid brother Andy (1958-88) dominated the Disco Era, as three of his songs wrested #1 for one-fourth of Disco Zone 1977-78. Three of the best R & R histories are astounding in their NON-mention of Andy: Joe Steussy's *Rock and Roll*, Rolling Stone's *Illustrated Rock History*, and Donald Clarke's *Penguin History of Popular Music*. With Andy's pure falsetto choruses, kick stomp rhythm tracks, chick-a-booming guitars, and flashing hi-hats, Andy's 1st three records snagged #1. With his pleasant teenage smile, great British teeth, blond hair and almond-hazel eyes, Andy G. guided his silver Smokey Robinson tenor into a Blue-Eyed Soul sound as suave as Vintage Motown.

The Manchester lad rides high notes like an unsinkable cork on a charcoal-gray Icelandic titanic ocean. His bassist chuffs quarter-notes, clutching the Tonic root note A (Key of 'A'). Laying on the expectant **B-minor** (IIm) chord awhile, the expected Dominant Seventh (**E7**) never happens. Andy's cool tenor stalks the mix, overriding his screaming audience with charisma. Muted guitar riffs sporadically blister the treble zone, playing off swirly velvet strings into the hot chorus. "I Just Want to Be Your Everything" reels at 102 beats a minute, slow Disco in fast molasses gear. Drum riffs crunch and sparkle. Whenever Andy grabs a breath, or on iffy tacets, the snare lambasts a tempestuous tattoo. Like Jazz impressionist **Sarah Vaughan**, Gibb surrounds the crashing beat. Nothing slipshod or tatterdemalion wrecks this champ Disco hit.

*Andy Gibb, younger brother of **Barry, Robin,** and **Maurice Gibb: The Bee Gees***

"Shadow Dancing" – Andy Gibb, #1(7), 4-78; #11, 5-78 R & B. As of 2001, tied for 39th-most popular song of all time (7 weeks). Andy's #1(2) "(Love Is) Thicker Than Water" flashes the afterglow of the first, and he did non-Knight/Estefan "An Everlasting Love" to #5, 7-78. Andy hosted TV show *Solid Gold* (Lori Ghiringhelli), and then married Dallas's ultra-gorgeous **Victoria Principal**; they coalesced on the Everly Brothers #1, '58 Rock Ballad/Hymn "All I Have to Do Is Dream" to #51, 8-81. Andy's downhill spiral lasted longer than his meteoric rise to superstardom at 19. Just five days before his 30th birthday, and on the road to beating some nasty substance situation, Andy died of a heart virus – not unlike the one which stalked hardier **Bob Dylan** (#12, 9-73 "Knockin' on Heaven's Door") in 1997.

"Oh! Darlin" – **Robin Gibb, #14, 8-78.** Robin's solo Beatle reprise from their Peter Frampton movie *Sergeant Pepper's Lonely Hearts Club Band.* Robin does Paul McCartney proud. At some magic point, the **Bee Gees'** lead vocals shifted from one great tenor to another, but the 2nd one cranked it up a notch to fizzing falsetto high above the 'Valli' zone. Brother **Barry Gibb** hit #3, 11-80 with "Guilty," and #10, 1-81 in **Barbra Steisand** duo. Bee Gees did best as a full set.

The Bee Gees - Clockwise from top:
Barry, Maurice, & Robin Gibb

"Stayin' Alive" – **Bee Gees, #1(4), 12-77; #4, 1-78 R & B.** The Bee Gees' Brisbane, Queensland, Australian aspirations launched a local TV show and record deal. Soon it was time to conquer the world. North to England. The falsetto/tenor fantasia of Barry and Robin meshed with bass guitar odysseys of Robin's twin Maurice. Trouncing their 'A'-grade 1967-71 British Invasion phase, they zoomed to 'A+' plateaus – with six successive songs at chart zenith (see Elvis, Beatles, Supremes, Four Seasons, Mariah Carey, Dan Quinn). **Barry's** #7, 10-75 "Nights on Broadway" was the #1(2) "Jive Talkin'" that launched his formidable falsetto. Not only do the Bee Gees feature the most famous twins in showbiz/Rock, but they represent the first-case scenario where a major band, past their heyday hit prime, simply flipsided the LEAD SINGER in the band to create a higher new heyday than before.

"Stayin' Alive" reverberates with joy and sorrow. On one hand, Barry's high-wire escapade is a joyous dance of life, a rainbow of sights and sounds and sensations. On the other hand, a lot of great artists were currently careening toward **Jim Morrison's**/**Red Hot Chili Peppers'** "Other Side." Beatles' aging **John Lennon** hunkered down into his Dakota Hotel househusband abode, while 40s and 50s giants **Bing Crosby** and **Elvis Presley** headed for the Last Round-Up. Brother Andy's swoon started in his early 20s.

"Stayin' Alive" was the second of six chart toppers: #1(3), 9-77 "How Deep Is Your Love"; "Too Much Heaven" at #1(2), 11-78; "Tragedy," #1(2), 2-79; and #1(2), 4-79 "Love You Inside and Out." Their 43 HOT 100 hits didn't halt at the Disco border of the amorphous 80s. In the aftermath, Bee Gees buzzed onwards with #45, 11-81 "Living Eyes," #75, 9-87 "You Win Again," and their 5th and 6th rebounds — #7, 7-89 "One" (Not Metallica's song), and #74, 10-93 "Paying the Price of Love." "Alone" hit #28, 6-97, proving that "STILL Waters (Run Deep)" (#57, 12-97).

Bee Gees' "Night Fever," at #1(8), 2-78 (#8 R & B) was the 2nd biggest Disco hit of all time ("Physical," #1[10]). And the big brother band boogies on, millennially.

Alicia Bridges' "I Love the Nightlife (Disco Round)" at #5, 7-78 (#31 R & B) was the ultimate Disco monster hit in the Bee Gees' aftershine and Night Fever carousel. Bridges' vocal is streetwise and solid – she celebrates a perpetual rave-up party.

"Too Much Heaven" – **Bee Gees, #1(2), 11-78; #10, 12-78 R & B.** This wistful wannabe rush to paradise leaps and twirls and flips with windswept curlicue strings, and sweet meadows of happy huckleberry lovers in pastel-bouquet gardens of romantic glee. Whoopee, Heaven.

On this earth, we have a lot of earth. Grubby dirt. Suddenly the up-front lyrics smacked the starstruck romantic in the face – and the pristine white suits got smeared with barnyard mud and slime and non-fragrant fertilizer. Disco dreams were dashed by junk bond hawkers, carnivorous computers, dead-end jobs, Me-First mania, and the quick coke croak. Some ghastly new disease began to interlope down at the steamy Village bath scene – and a giant chunk of one of the most artistic and creative and theatrical communities in history would suffer a plague to rival the Middle Ages' Black Death. By 1983, the party was over, and the sad hangover began.

But the hits just kept on rockin', blasting past any tragedy in their way. "Tragedy"? **Thomas Wayne** (1940-71), brother of **Johnny Cash**'s guitarist Luther Perkins, hit #5, 1-59 with "Tragedy" during **Buddy Holly, Ritchie Valens,** and the Big Bopper's last month before the Day (2-3-59) that the 'music died.' In the song, his last note is a Major Seventh chord [In Key of 'C,' it would be C—E—G—B]. Morose note. Wayne was killed in a car smash-up tragedy (see Seattle Grunge gurus **Pearl Jam**'s #2, '98 "Last Kiss," a cover of **J. Frank Wilson**'s #2, '64 original).

"Tragedy" – **Fleetwoods, #10, 5-61.** NOT Fleetwood Mac. Or Big Mac. Seattle's Soft Rock troubadours bring us a lovers' sad saga of downtrodden drizzle and forever goodbyes. The old sun set into a cloud-bank, and simplicity and Rock drifted apart on that Major Seventh chord. Long before Seattle set up shop as Grunge Capital, and long before **Jimi Hendrix** erupted guitar-fire odysseys, the capital of America's Great Northwest interwove sullen, muted harmonies to droop moods. Long before "Alternative' gloom-tunes volleyed with discordant tonal slurs and harsh strident sounds of nihilistic despair, the Olympia, Washington **Fleetwoods** (**Gary Troxel**, b. '40, Barbara Ellis, and Gretchen Christopher) cradled their tragic tears in wistful wisps of #1(1), 9-59 "Mr. Blue" harmony. Jazz Rock flickered on the horizon.

"Tragedy" – Bee Gees, #1(2), 2-79; #44 R & B. We bid fond adieu to the midnight movers' fading Party-On Decade. With chirps of alarm and dismay, the Bee Gees eulogize a sad sayonara to romance, a Disco decade, and the Fleetwoods and Thomas Wayne, whose song "Tragedy" is a totally different tune. The Bee Gees' "Tragedy" has a unique spiraling Barry Gibb falsetto melody, and a wafting balloon of enchanting brotherly harmonies.

As the exhausted calendar swooped swiftly to the molten millennium, Disco would be back again and again: Dance Music never dies.

* * * * *

Space Cowboy on the Yukon Delta

"Space Cowboy on the Yukon Delta" is a former chapter now streamlined for your quick perusal (and photographic pleasure). *Gold Rush* covered pretty extensively the **Steve Miller Band**, highlighting their greatest hits like #1(1), 11-73 "The Joker" (that touts him as 'space cowboy'). We did #8, 5-77 "Jet Airliner," #1(2), 5-82 "Abracadabra," and his Bonnie & Clyde tale #11, 5-76 "Take the Money and Run" Steve kept his gold records mounted over the WASHING MACHINE, to keep Rock and Roll glory in its proper perspective. We celebrated his signature song #1(1), 8-76 "Rock 'n Me," with its Tacoma (WA), Atlanta, Phoenix, L.A., and Philly Rock tour. Miller, of Madison, Wisconsin, is a pathologist's son, whose 1968-69 San Francisco band featured **Boz Scaggs** (#3, 7-76 "Lowdown").

We also showcased **Grand Funk Railroad** of Owosso, Michigan, on #1(1), 7-73 "We're an American Band"; the Scottish "Saturday Night" (#1, 10-

75) Bay City Rollers; **Daddy Dewdrop**'s #9, 3-71 "Chick-A-Boom (Don't You Jes' Love It?)"; CCR's supersonic tourin' tune #2(2), 1-70 "Travelin' Band"; **Lobo**'s (Florida's Roland Kent Lavoie) #5, 4-71 "Me and You and a Dog Named Boo"; Bobby Rydell's #2(1), 2-60 "Wild One"; and #1(4), 4-75 "Love Will Keep Us Together," by the **Captain and Tennille** (Toni Tennille was only Beach Boys' Beach GIRL singer).

CASEY KASEM (b. Detroit, '32) we celebrated as super disc jockey. His American Top Forty spans the continent with his friendly, week-by-week survey, and his helpful and friendly and kind comments about rock stars. If Superstar X bites the dog, stomps on anthills, snorts Sterno/Kerosene on his Count Chocula, and belongs to the Attila the Hun Fan Club, Casey will mention the time Superstar X rescued a fluffy kitty cat from a mulberry bush. Casey ignores the razzmatazz pizzazz, and just plays the song. At *Gold Rush*, we revere Casey's example and enjoy his show.

Casey Kasem, world-class DJ, and host of weekly international radio show "American Top 40."

We also cameoed the #5, 7-72 **Raspberries'** "Go All the Way"; Buddy Randall's similarly Fab Four echo sound of the **Knickerbockers** and #20, 12-65 "Lies"; ill-fated Beatle proteges **Badfinger** (of Fab Four Apple label) and #7, 2-70 "Come and Get It"; "Bang a Gong" at #10, 1-72, by Glam Rockers **T. Rex** (vocal background by the Turtles); also

Glen Campbell's #1(1), 2-77 "Southern Nights" and #39, 7-77 "Sunflower."

Then we did SOUTHERN ROCK: the **Allman Brothers'** amazing #2(1), 8-73 "Ramblin' Man"and the later Gregg Allman's Band's #49, 4-87 "I'm No Angel"; **Lynyrd Skynyrd**'s "Free Bird" at #19, 1-75 and #8, 7-74 "Sweet Home Alabama"; **Pure Prairie League**'s #27, 5-75 "Amie"; Dutch Rockers the George Baker Selection and #26, 11-75 delightful melody "Paloma Blanca" [Sp. 'white bird']; **Orleans**' #6, 7-75 "Dance With Me"; the Buoys' grisly #17, 1-71 "Timothy," where a mine collapse forces them to (yecch) eat their dog; and the **Marshall Tucker Band –** #14, 3-77 "Heard It in a Love Song."

The YUKON? We did Great Canadian Rockers, too: **Bachman-Turner Overdrive**'s #12, 5-74 slacker anthem "Takin' Care of Business," #14 Thunder Rocker 1-75 "Roll on Down the Highway," and #1(1), 9-74 "You Ain't Seen Nothin' Yet"; **Ronnie Hawkins** and the Hawks' (later Dylan's THE BAND) super Rockabilly #45, 6-59 Chuck Berry Tune "Forty Days" and minor-key Blues tune #26, 8-59 "Mary Lou." We celebrated BTO's Randy Bachman till 1970, and did original #1(3), 3-70 "American Woman" (#49, 2-99 by Lenny Kravitz -- we did Lenny's version, and mentioned #4, 11-2000 Kravitz smash "Again"). Other **Guess Who** hits? #6, 4-69 "These Eyes," #5, 12-69 "No Time," and #6, 7-74 "Clap for the Wolfman," featuring one of America's Big Three DJ's: **Dick Clark, Casey Kasem**, and **Wolfman Jack** (b. Bob Smith). We did the Band's #53, 8-68 pilgrimage "The Weight" (Levon Helm, Robbie Robertson). We did **Neil Young**'s #1(1), 2-72 "Heart of Gold" and fellow Ontario troubadour Gordon Lightfoot's NC, '76 "Summertime Dream."

America is a group of three Americans who met in London (Dan Peek, Gerry Buckley, Dewey Bunnell). Big hits? #1(3), 2-72 "A Horse with No Name," #8, 10-72 "Ventura Highway," #5, 1-75 "Lonely People," and Holly'/Beach Boy echo super-song #1(1), 4-75 "Sister Golden Hair." **Rolling Stones**' #1, 9-73 "Angie" and #1(1), 5-78 "Miss You" stormed the Disco Decade. Songwriter of Archies' mega-million #1 "Sugar Sugar" **Andy Kim** hit big with #1(1), 6-74 "Rock Me Gently." The **Doobie Brothers** rocked out on #1(1), 1-75 "Black Water," #15, 8-73 "China Grove," and #1(1), 1-79 "What a

Fool Believes." **Seals and Crofts**' pensive #21, 9-73 "We May Never Pass This Way Again" got #1 treatment at #21, and we chuckled at Paul Simon's slip-slidin' #1(3), 12-75 "50 Ways to Leave Your Lover." **Tony Orlando**'s #15, 8-61 sneeze ode "Bless You" led to his multicultural **DAWN** threesome, with Afro stars Telma Hopkins and Joyce Vincent. Orlando (b NYC, '44, Latino/Greek Anthony Cassavitis) and Dawn scored #1(3), 11-70 "Knock Three Times," and Gulf War (1991) anthem #1(4) "Tie a Yellow Ribbon Round the Old Oak Tree." We jumped to **Jerry Butler**'s #7, 10-60 "He Will Break Your Heart" [#1(3) for Dawn in 3-75 as "He Don't Love You"]. We saluted Butler's #11, 6-58 "For Your Precious Love" (Fred Friedberg song), #4, 3-69 "Only the Strong Survive," and favorite #11, 10-61 "Moon River."

We covered **Nat King Cole**'s #3, 11-46 Mel Torme classic "The Christmas Song," and Dad's favorite, Cole's #1(5), 4-51 "Too Young." We did **Barbra Streisand**'s actual ROCK song, #6, 10-70 "Stoney End," her "Memory" from *Cats* (NC '81), and #1(3), 12-76 "Evergreen" theme. **Loggins & Messina**'s Hard Rock #4, 11-72 "Your Mama Don't Dance" and **Gallery**'s #4, 2-72 "Nice to Be With You" preceded **Mac Davis**'s Lubbock Texas #1(3), 7-72 "Baby Don't Get Hooked on Me." Blue Swede's #1(1), 2-74 "Hooked on a Feeling" took B.J. Thomas's #5, 11-68 hit all the way to the top. Danish star Jorgen Ingmann took his overdubbed guitar tune "Apache" to the penultimate #2(2), 1-61 position. **Styx** showed up for #6, 12-74 "Lady," and #8, 9-77 "Come Sail Away." **Creedence** returned for #4, 4-71 "Up Around the Bend," and #8, 1-71 "Have You Ever Seen the Rain?" Then we sailed on to the Disco Zone by reprising the ROBIN Gibb **Bee Gees** in their first Pre-Disco phase of the 2nd British Invasion: #15, 1-68 "Words" (with VOCAL PERCUSSION) and "To Love Somebody" at #17, 7-67 (Michael Bolton, #11, 10-92). Finally, our Yukon Space Cowboy rode along "Blinded by the Light" -- #1(1), 11-76 **Manfred Mann**'s Earth Band. They're a Manchester England and Johannesburg South Africa bunch who used **Bruce Springsteen** at #1 songwriter's credit for this outstanding Dylan-influenced lyric.

Rockin' Jazz Razz-Mo-Tazz: Art, Orchestral, and Jazz Rock Fusion

26

Without Jazz icons **Duke Ellington** (1899-74, '31 "Rockin' in Rhythm"), **Louie 'Satchmo' Armstrong** (1900-71, '56 "Mack the Knife"), or **Louis Jordan** (1908-75, '45 "Caldonia Boogie"), Rock and Roll might have vanished before it began. Without the Jazz stylistics of Ella Fitzgerald, Billie Holiday, Clarence 'Pinetop' Smith, or Charlie Christian, Rock and Rollers might be plunking acoustic guitars and singing with 0% gusto. Rock and Roll owes a tremendous debt to Jazz – and its cousins Blues/Boogie-Woogie, Country, and Folk. When Rock and Roll first blasted everything else off the musical scene, some understandable resentment bubbled. As the upstart art form – powered by three chords and a dream – grew into itself, it branched out to literally embrace ALL of these kindred musical spirits. Jazz, home of the most technical and esoteric music (along with Classical), took awhile to cozy up to the Big Beat. When the Psychedelic 60s swirled into the 70s, Jazz Rock Fusion stormed the stage – offering the best of both worlds.

Rock and Roll. Like the Polka, Best-Loved Hymns, and half the world's Folk Songs, Rock thrives on three chords and a cloud of dust. In basic 4/4 time, Rock thumps the blistering backbeat on the 2 and 4 beats (or 2, 2½, and 4 beats). Rare ballads will take you to a waltz 3/4 rhythm. The Streetcorner chord pattern might mix in a fourth chord, the VIm chord and maybe, just maybe, a II or II7 on the bridge to volley you to your big V7 dominant. Then you crunch on back to your tonic I, and resolve the sweetness of your melody. Most of recorded history? You keep it simple. You keep it basic. You keep the music close to the people who love it. If it gets too far out and esoteric, you ditch it and get back to basics.

Until Jazz rolls in. In the Ragtime era, Jazz and Blues and Boogie Woogie had a few pat chord for-mulae of their own: 12-Bar Blues or Dixieland Jazz jumps through the I down to the VI, to the II, to the V7, and bops on back home. Nothing far out. Nothing esoteric. Nothing which only appealed to a certain elite coterie of aficionados with musical pedigrees. Through the Louie 'Satchmo' Armstrong band and **Paul Whiteman** orchestral years, Jazz played campy venues: 'hooch' palaces, speakeasies, blind pigs, bordellos, underground after-hours clubs. Jazz, like Rock and Roll, started out as a synonym for the act of love.

In the **Benny Goodman** Swing Jazz years, the 'licorice-stick' clarinet wizard snowed the world. Big Bands featured virtuoso soloists of every instrument. Soon Pop music wobbled off the standard groove. Into the wondrous midnight world of the extraordinary. Before long, the world just bubbling under the HOT 100 was swinging to magnificent improvised solos of **Charlie 'Bird' Parker, Ornette Coleman, Maynard Ferguson, Dizzy Gillespie, Miles Davis, Thelonius Monk, Mose Allison, John Coltrane, Stan Kenton, Dave Brubeck, George Shearing, Charlie Mingus** or **Gene Krupa**. Earlier great Jazz bands toured the world, headed by Jazz legends **Louis Armstrong, Count Basie, Duke Ellington**. Jazz singers like **Al Jolson, Bing Crosby, Sarah Vaughan, Billy Eckstine, Frank Sinatra,** and **Ella Fitzgerald** took center stage. The world of musical respectability opened up to the Jazz greats. Being the 'new kid on the block,' it took awhile to integrate Carnegie Hall (Benny Goodman) and for Jazz courses to penetrate the hallowed halls of ivy. Just like Rock History today. Into the New Millennium, over 70 colleges in New York State alone offered courses in Rock History, and its peripheral disciplines: Rhythm & Blues, Country Music, Jazz Rock, Sound Recording, Ethnomusicology. Courses in Rock and Roll history are obviously among the most popular college courses in America and beyond, and Kendall-Hunt is among the pioneers in this new publishing field.

We've chronicled the innovate careers of **Buddy Holly, Del Shannon, the Beatles, Gene Putney**, and **Ray Charles**, and how they worked complexity into their songs. As Jazz musicians assimilated into the Rock and Roll fray, they were grudgingly joined by members of big urban Classical symphonies. All these more traditional musicians were hired by rich R & R studios to overdub and sweeten gruff, rough and tough rock tracks. Early on, Jazz inroads to Rock occurred in the artful antics of such Jazz virtuosos as **Stan Getz, Wes Montgomery**, the **Buckinghams**, the **Fifth Dimension, Big Al Hirt, Ramsey Lewis, Herb Alpert**, the **Happenings, Kenny Ball & His Jazzmen, Lou Rawls**, the **Lettermen, Nino Tempo** and **April Stevens.**

"25 or 5 Till 4" – Chicago, #4, 7-70, #4, 7-70; #48, 9-86. Piercing the technical veil of Jazz via Rock and Roll, this acclaimed crew from (surprise) Chicago plunked 48 tunes into the HOT 100 over a generation. A cornucopia of top-notch talent, horning in on a woodwind whirlwind of profound sound: **James Pankow** on trombone, **Lee Loughnane** on trumpet, **Walt Parazaider** on reeds. Debuting as **Chicago Transit Authority**, their introductory song "Introduction" (surprise) contains a cryptic time signature shift. They picked up on Brubeck's 9-61, #25 "Take Five," and the piano legend's 5/4 time signature – plus Brubeck's **7/4** "Unsquare Dance" (ironically #74, 12-61) from his *Time Further Out* album (Al. #8, 1-62 – remember, 1962 kids bought 99¢ singles, and adults $4.99 albums).

Chicago's unique time signatures? WINDY CITY TIME:

$$\frac{4}{4} \frac{6}{8} \frac{7}{8} \frac{6}{8} \frac{7}{8} \frac{6}{8} \frac{7}{8} \frac{6}{8} \frac{3}{4}$$ In just one song . . .

Jazz had been creating this esoteric hard stuff for years. Musicians impressing musicians. In music, nothing is right or wrong. It's just what is. Or what's popular. If you love the music, that's what matters. We can all appreciate the great technique of the virtuoso Orbison, Brubeck, or Chicago's **Peter Cetera**, lead singer until 1985, whose split with Chicago produced #1(2), 6-86 "Glory of Love." Cetera's glide-glazed vocal rides the note – then glides off. The chord pattern favors Blues sixths and Jazz ninths. Peter's follow-up, #1(1), 9-86 "The Next Time I Fall," boosted the big-time career of the 'First Lady of Contemporary Christian Music, **Amy Grant**, on her #29, 5-85 "Find a Way." Amy takes the Michael P. Smith hit to her first HOT 100 and top 30 hit.

Rock and Roll was new to eclectic time signatures. Not so Jazz. Jazz created them. The prestigious bailiwick of musically literate sight-reading experts, Jazz crunches the best efforts of the three-chord band down the block. Chi-

cago didn't start the Jazz revolution in Rock and Roll – they just spearheaded it. Among their top-notch musical colleagues? **David Clayton-Thomas's Blood, Sweat, and Tears**, the **Paul Butterfield Blues Band, Cream, Genesis, Yes, Sugarloaf**, plus **Emerson, Lake and Palmer**. Chicago's "25 or 6 till 4" kicks off with a hammering rhythm track. Bass and drums blast staccato flourishes; the horns scramble to fill the dead air, and Cetera sings a fine second tenor vocal. He chafes at the clock. Chicago has two tunes that clobber the calendar, following up with #7, 11-70 "Does Anybody Really Know What Time It Is?" Time is immaterial, philosophizes the Zen lyric, but the song's guy just wants to love the girl overtime. At the time, the **Guess Who**'s "No Time" (#5, 12-69) chomped the charts, so Chicago's clock-musing music must have been influenced by them, probably not US:

Chicago, 1986. Top: l-r, James Pankow, Danny Seraphine, Bill Champlin, Jason Scheff. Bottom: l-r, Lee Loughnane, Walt Parazaider, and Robert Lamm

"Time Drags Me Down" – Strum, NC, 2-70. Fred Peacock on background vocals; **Matt Clark** lead guitar, **Joe Marra** drums. Paul Simon-style song. Despite 17 chords Jazzfully rendered, it still had a Mama & Papas flair. I played bass and guitar and sang lead. Great **Julie Tkach** harmonies. Hit #1 in hometown Monroe, Michigan, plus it sizzled the Top #5 Up North.

"Green-Eyed Lady" – Sugarloaf, #3, 8-70. Jerry Corbetta played a mean keyboard bridge after his own leapin' lead vocal. This lovely lady with sea-green eyes enchants with sensuous mystique. Listen to the eclectic electric interplay on the incredibly complex bridge between Corbetta and bassman **Bob Raymond** – who darts in with a 16th-note cadenza that surrounds the beat but doesn't blast it. Corbetta's fine Jazz Fusion vocal spins off the mystical complexity of this amazing midsection. Other breadwinners for Sugarloaf? "Don't Call Us, We'll Call You" (#9, 12-74), which arguably started the Rap concept of including tiny chunks of other records, Sugarloaf uses Beatles' #1 "I Feel Fine" sample.

"Tell Her No" – Zombies, #6, 1-65. Rod Argent on keyboards empowers this Jazz Fusion vision. **Colin Blumstone** sings epitome-of-coolth vocal. Pal's advice-to-lovelorn lyric is incidental to the fits-and-starts lurch and blurt technique of this excellent song. Full five years before the Jazz Fusion movement took off, the Zombies of Hertfordshire (north of London) rampaged Jazz polyrhythms. The breathy Blumstone baritone connects to the Argent keyboard. Paul Atkinson's quick-chop guitar melds with the burbling beatific electric bass impressions of Chris White.

"A Taste of Honey" – Herb Alpert and the Tijuana Brass, #7, 9-65. Best known for a Mexican-flavored trumpeter style, like #6, 10-62 "The Lonely Bull (El Solo Toro)." With a chromatic grace-note riff to the bVII chord, Alpert spun off his multiple talents as bandleader, producer, instrumentalist, and finally easygoing singer: #1(4), 5-68 "This Guy's In Love With You."

Herb Alpert doubled as a composer, orchestra leader, and record company owner in Los Angeles, starting up A & M Records with Jerry Moss. Master of album art as well, Alpert blasted off five #1 albums like *Whipped Cream and Other Delights* (#1[8], 6-65). It stars an irresistible lass with a whipped cream outfit (only?) on an emerald green backdrop. After multi-tracking the bullfight arena sounds on the "Bull" item, Alpert swayed away from Mexicano "Ameriachi" style to straddle the Easy Listening market. Alpert also steered Surf Rock – producing sessions for **Jan and Dean**. As **Mitch Miller** is to family singalongs, Alpert is to Light Jazz. He offers a friendly, non-threatening alternative to anything gross or grubby or garish or ghastly. Suave, mellow, cool.

Alpert's aces? #11, 12-65 "Zorba the Greek"; #18, 7-66 "Mame"; #1[3x], 12-68 "The Christmas Song" [x = Christmas Singles chart]; #1(2), 7-79 "Rise"; and his **Janet Jackson**-vocalized #5, 4-87 "Diamonds." Alpert's popular Light Jazz preludes deeper Jazz Rock.

"Deep Purple" – Nino Tempo and April Stevens, #1(1), 9-63; #4, 10-63 R & B. Larry Clinton's #1, '39 evocative classic portrays sleepy walled gardens, twinkly stars, mists of longlost memory, and love thriving on moonlight beams. The song loves the big swoosh to the mediant III chord, and glides on starbeams of smooth, embraceable harmony. Also #2, '39 **Jimmy Dorsey**.

A waterfall of jazzy Chalypso bliss? No wonder. This brother-sister team, prognosticating the **Jackson II** or **Donny & Marie Osmond**, hails from Niagara Falls, on the unCanadian side. Following the rhythmic motif of **Louis Prima** and **Keely Smith**, (#18, 11-58 "That Old Black Magic"), Nino and April do Half Rap. Nino jazzfully sings. April 'Raps,' and coos the spoken lyrics. Brother Nino wafts a wild vocal that veers along – as just the winsome melody. Her whispery style previewed Standards reprise — #11, 12-63 rehash of **Paul Whiteman** & Orchestra's #1[11], 10-20) debut, "Whispering." "Deep Purple" skirts Jazz Rock.

"A Lover's Concerto" – Toys, #2(3), 9-65; #4, 10-65 R & B. Since we're scrunching Orchestral and Classical Rock along with Jazz and Art Rock, " A Lover's Concerto" is apropos. Remember Richard Dreyfuss in *Mr. Holland's Opus* (1996****)? This plucky music teacher bucks the system and teaches his R & R opus – his mission rests on teaching terminally-bored adolescents that the 'groovy' new hit by the Toys is really Johann Sebastian Bach's famous Minuet from his Anna Magdalena notebook. Bach wasn't totally into discovering 20th-century chord theory yet; it was only arpeggios, then officially, or playing each note of the triad individually. Of all the famous people you know, Bach had the most kids by one (hard-toiling) wife – 20. [Wow]. Can you imagine her yelling at him in the middle of his gung-ho composing: "JOHANN – TAKE OUT THE GARBAGE!" **Barbara Harris**, lyric soprano, and the Toys zoomed from Woodrow Wilson High in Queens, NYC, to dust off the stars with their Classical Rock opus. Their fame couldn't survive #18, 12-65 follow-up "Attack," so Bach's talented Toys shuffled off to a new playground with diminishing fame: #76, 9-66 "Baby Toys."

"Java" – Al Hirt, #4, 1-64. Al (1922-99) pingponged into the 1964 Beatle Invasion's hoopla. New Orleans' trumpet maestro and Jimmy and Tommy Dorsey Big Band vet, Big Al stormed out of New Orleans and cut a few sides with **Pete Fountain** in 1950s. In the roostertail wake of London trumpeter **Kenny Ball**'s #2(1), 2-62 "Midnight in Moscow," in the FIRST British Invasion, many American Trad Jazz ['traditional Jazz'] artists tasted chart success, like **Village Stompers**' #2, '63 "Washington Square." Hirt toiled and amassed big 300# rep on vibrant Vieux Carre in Crescent City. Bandleader of extraordinary charisma, the big bearded boomer of Hot Jazz/Dixieland tunes energized America and beyond. This peppery instrumental trumpet lead is dedicated to our national legal drug for all ages – good ol' expresso hypermania – caffeine. This Coca Cola's for you. Al's hits got even sweeter: #15, 4-64 "Cotton Candy," and #30, 7-64 "Sugar Lips."

"Along Comes Mary" – Association, #7, 6-66. "Mary" got a bad rap and rep for touting a not-so-innocent drug: 'Reefer Madness.' 'Mary' here is couched reference to marijuana, the Wicked Weed. Machine-gun speed lyrics whipped by so fast few could put them all together – shadowing Dylan's word bath #34, 5-65 "Subterranean Homesick Blues." "Along Comes Mary" flirts with major sevenths, diminished chords, and other accoutrements of the lofty Jazz musical package. Russ Giguere pounds out paradiddles (16th-note rolls) on percussion part way into the complex song. Influenced by the **Lettermen** . . .

"Mary's" street poetry wafts a Beat Generation aura into the Jazz-Rock: Ginsberg, Corso, Ferlinghetti, **Wes Montgomery**, Beat guru **David Amram**, **Billy Taylor**, or **Chick Corea**. The boffo bass blur of Brian Cole (d. '72) far outduels nearly anything attempted in Rock and Roll.

"Never My Love" – Association, #2(2), 8-67. Rainbow ripples of tremolo guitar surround their interweaving harmonies. Penned by the Pop-Rock Addrisi Brothers ("Cherrystone" #62, 6-59), "Never My Love" was among the first round of Rock Era wedding songs: #9, '57 "The Twelfth of Never" (J. Mathis); #4, '65 "Unchained Melody" (Al Hibbler and/or Righteous Brothers); #10, '58 "Devoted to You" (Everly Brothers), and other pillowy Soft Rock anthems of wonderful wedded bliss. [Few realize that the biggest version of "Unchained Melody" is neither by the Brothers Righteous nor Al Hibbler (1915-2001). It is by Big Band/Jazz bandleader **Les Baxter**, his Chorus and Orchestra – #1(2), 4-55. It is the theme for the movie *Unchained*. (c/o Don Howard, Russell Stevenson, Frank Monastero, Bill Ryan and Manny Berrard)].

On "Windy" (#1[4], 5-67), songwriter Ruthann Friedman's breezy smiling lass strolls avenues, trailed by wind-whipped red and golden leaves, dreams of love, and stardust. She's like her British/Australian cousin:

"Georgy Girl" – Seekers, #2(1), 12-66. Back in the same time zone, "Georgy" related (via **Seekers'** soprano **Judith Durham**) to half a world of romantic escapade and intrigue. **Seeker** Keith Potger (guitar) hails from Sri Lanka (nee Ceylon). The Seekers and the Association sought a New Woman persona here. She's free, down-to-earth, and takes charge of her own life. She finds a Jazz/Soft Rock "A World of Our Own" (#19, 5-65). Stooping blithely, Windy hands her guy a rainbow. Like, wow . . .

"Everything That Touches You" – Association, #10, 2-68. Upper song for a downer American year (M.L. King, Robert Kennedy, Chicago Convention police riot). In the Key of 'G', it features Jim Yester's and Jules Alexander's guitars. Bandleader **Terry Kirkman** blasts full speed ahead on a crescendo crush. It leads to one of the most complex harmonic counterpoint finales in Lite Rock music. If you liked Simon-Gar's #11, 3-68 "Scarborough Fair (/Canticle)," you'll love this. The final verse attains symphonic proportions, closing in on the bombasto volcanic cannonade at Tchaikovsky's *1812 Overture* finale. Whitburn cites Kirkman for playing 23 instruments. Orchestral Rock?

In June, 1961 (age 18), I slept in a scruffy red phone booth in a sooty old brick barrio of Birmingham, England (see "She Loves You" Beatle entry), and it felt like my old buddy Detroit. Silver-medalist to London in size, drizzly Birmingham stokes the Stoke-on-Trent, Wolverhampton, Coventry, and Warley-Walsall industrial corridor. Their tanks and planes sent Hitler high-tailing it into history – along with a little help from the Motor City in Michigan, and a few million brave Anglo-American soldiers who laid their lives on the line. Birmingham's **Moody Blues** featured first lead singer **Denny Laine**, on their debut gold grabber #10, 2-65 "Go

Now." Later **Laine** took off on the WINGS of song with ex-Beatle Paul with Linda McCartney's **Wings**.

"Go Now" – Moody Blues, #10, 2-65; #1, 1-65 U.K. Laine's Love-in with American Blues took him back to Bessie Banks' obscure and obtuse version of the song. The Jazz background of "Go Now" wobbles along in 3/4 waltz time, hammering a plinky honkytonk electric piano (**Mike Pinder**, also vocals). Graham Edge furnishes a flashy percussive patter to complement Clint Warwick's deep insistent bass hikes. Zapped by success, early Moody Blues swapped personnel after their temporary Medley of Big Hit ground down to a sudden "Stop!" (#98, 4-66). Bass, **John Lodge**. (Detroit expressway coincidentally has same name). Lead guitarist and vocalist **Justin Hayward**. He later soloed with Lodge on a great titled tune: "Blue Guitar" (#94, 12-75). It's Orchestral Rock and Blues, off Justin's *Blue Jays* album (Al. #16, 4-75).

"Nights in White Satin" – Moody Blues, #103, 2-68 and #2(2), 8-72. ORCHESTRAL ROCK is an extension of everything that came before – not an offshoot or aberration. Here's a song everybody recognizes. My Aunt Lydia Skeels said: "There are three kinds of classical music: music I recognize, music I don't recognize, and the *William Tell Overture*." "Satin" theme suggests the great **Duke Ellington**'s classic, #27, 6-53 "Satin Doll." Songs are vastly different, and magnificent for different reasons.

A cult Classic Rock/Symphony record, the Moody Blues' *Days of Future Passed* (Al. #3, 9-68) went platinum when few did. The Side Two symphony is a Concept Album extraordinaire. Like *The Grand Canyon Suite*, the Moody Blues chop their day into chunks – three traditional movements of contrasting mood and power. They hired classical heavyweights: The London Festival Orchestra conducted by Peter Knight. In 1999, Heavy Metal legends **Metallica** performed with a big orchestra too. The 2nd Movement, "Evening: The Sun Set: Twilight Time," features vibrato violas, presiding over the sweet golden sunset of our romantic seashore fantasies. Then the satin nights roll in. Armed with a MELLOTRON to bolster the gargantuan orchestra, they shimmy from Mideastern bIII chromatic chord changes to the ol' Del Shannon "Greensleeves" **Am-G-F-E7** run pattern. On the bridge, a shrill flute seethes as lovers cavort on their billowy davenport of dreamy desire. Hot stuff.

Need a cure for **Fats Domino**'s "Blue Monday" [#5, 1-57]?

"Tuesday Afternoon (Forever Afternoon)" – Moody Blues, #24, 7-68. At least one big single escaped the album immediately. This Rock and Jazz and Orchestral opus waffles in with syncopated bass, muted guitar, and a hovering whoosh of violins. On the verse, Hayward plies minor-key waters, shuffling over shoals of deep blue melancholy. In the beefier chorus, he rises to a major-minor mix that swamps the pensive journey with passion and resolve. Ever had a semi-productive Tuesday afternoon where your job/school just lingered on forever?

Hayward's wayward Tuesday odyssey brings you home. Their #12, 2-73 "I'm Just a Singer in a Rock and Roll Band" follow-up combined a **Byrds** or **Neil Young** flavor with Jazz vocalics (complex chords) and a kicky, jiffy beat. They also hit big with amazing "Gemini Dream" (#12, 6-81). Expanding upon the rococo symphonic productions of Tony Clarke and Knight's palatial arrangements, they succeeded on their inventive conceptual classics like : #62, 11-83 "Blue World," #27, 9-83 "Sitting at the Wheel," and 6-88 #30 "I Know You're Out There Somewhere."

"Your Wildest Dreams" – Moody Blues, #9, 4-86. So I'm barrelling down Nichols Road out of Ronkonkoma, Long Island, and I catch this live 1986 interview with Justin Hayward and buddies on WBAB Babylon: "Where do you get your inspiration?" asked the Rock Jock, a mere lad of 29 or so.

"BOODY AW-LEE" chimed Hayward, without a breath.

Texan Holly tossed a little Cockney accent ("bai-by" and "gaow") into his own last song, "It Doesn't Matter Anymore," #13 in U.S.A. and #1(3) in U.K. The blokes down at the 'Dog & Mug' really recognized Holly's genius. While searching the globe for the heart of gorgeous melody, the Moody Blues had only to dart back three decades to the melodic magnificence of Holly's legendary Lubbock song book. Buddy's own mentors, **Norm** and **Vi Petty**, sweetened Buddy's more strident Bluesy/Bluegrass high school creations. Likewise, NYC producer **Dick Jacobs** (1918-88) brought his symphonic studio moxie to Buddy's timeless "True Love Ways" (#25, UK, Zilch U.S.A. '59). Forward-thinking Jacobs (#16, 10-56 "Petticoats of Portugal" and #17, 9-57 waltz "Fascination") first engineered orchestral strings into Rock music via Buddy Holly. His concept expanded to the **Drifters, Skyliners,** and **Phil Spector.** It's a current ivory-tower fiction that Orchestral Rock started with the Moody Blues.

The Moodies' 1986 "Wildest Dreams" opens to a huff-puff bass line wiggling around a bump-thump bass drum. "Wildest" flirts with a snurfling organ and silky strings. Angelic harps, even. By the time Hayward's skyward Holly-tenor vocal chimes in, Hollies whisk over a swirling seascape of fleecy cloud-puffs. Enchanted forests by the seashore reach up toward the turret-twirling castles in the baby blue sky.

Lyrically, all is not totally rosy. Does the singer's lamented runaway princess still remember his tender love? Pale blue hazy skies rush back to him in a bittersweet reverie. Misty yesteryear memory. To her, he's a momentary flashback. A quick cameo. To him, she's the vision of all that is holy and precious. Can she ever return? A five-part harmonic chorus, echoing the Jazz-vocal **Beach Boys** at high tide, blankets Hayward's heartfelt lead vocal. The song's Magic Kingdom is sweet major chords. Wisps of wistful minors. "Your Wildest Dreams" could easily have notched #1 for **Bobby Vee** or **Tommy Roe** in Hollyshadow 1962. Even as **Springsteen's** Heartland Rock Era rolled into Middle-of-the-Road (MOR) mishmosh, or into Rap and Hip Hop or Grunge or New Wave, there was still room at the top for the good-natured

Lubbock progenitor of the whole R & R panorama – with his Moody Blues echo. No easy feat for a song thirty years too old and forty years too pretty to make it. But "Your Wildest Dreams'" #9 rating was beyond the wildest Hollie/Holly dreams, in an 80s soundscape of Michael Jackson, Madonna, and the Boss. Music fans know – greatness hurdles the decade barriers. The Moody Blues' greatest hit, unencumbered by esoteric mind-blowing complexity, is a simple song that people can love. "Your Wildest Dreams" is a pied piper song. You tag along trying to hug it. Then it snags you in its net of enchantment.

"Boody Aw-lee . . ." From Birmingham, England? The big forge. Soot and smoke to rival Pittsburgh or Akron. Old red phone booths – for vagabond voyagers to hunker down out of the endless gray 55° drizzle. Hard to believe such a beautiful angelic melody of ethereal Everly ecstasy can come from a buncha blokes from Birmingham? [See *Led Zep IV* #2(4) untitled 11-71 album for brick-row land of soot and blue-collar glory skyline scenario – sold 16M]. A million strong working folks in redbrick row houses. Surrounded by bleak oozing smokestacks, swirling stratus clouds, and limitless romantic dreams, they share the wilder dream of lasting love.

'Boody Aw-lee.'

Escape to happily ever after. Rock and Roll, hint of Chalypso. Bali Ha'i island wildest dreams.

"Moondreams" – Buddy Holly, NC, 1959. Absolute FIRST Orchestral Rock item ever. Perhaps Soul star **Jackie Wilson** (also on Brunswick, like Buddy's Crickets) preceded Holly with operatic tenor and silvery strings (#22 "To Be Loved" 4-58 with Milton DeLugg Orchestra), but Holly is the FIRST mainstream R & R star to thwart the 'guitars-only' barrier and bridge over into the Classical music sound. BUDDY HOLLY DID JUST ABOUT EVERYTHING MUSICAL IN ONLY 1½ FATEFUL YEARS. Holly is the source. With Buddy Holly captaining the destiny of Rock and Roll, Rock met Symphony for the first time anywhere.

"Your Wildest Dreams" mirrors the enchanted and progressive Rock chord patterns, melodic twists, and harmonic rainbows of three unheralded masterpieces off his *Buddy Holly Story, Volume II*: "What to Do," "Crying, Waiting, Hoping," and "That's What They Say."

"Peggy Sue Got Married" – Buddy Holly and the Hollies, NC, 1996. The Hollies' #119, 2-96 *Not Fade Away* album (including Crosby, Stills, and Nash vet **Graham Nash**), consisted of Nash, **Allen Clarke, Bobby Elliott,** and **Tony Hicks.** They jumped at the chance to vocally 'accompany Buddy' on his "Peggy Sue" follow-up. Buddy laid down the vocal and guitar on his Greenwich Village tape recorder, with bride Maria Elena doting over bagels and bliss. After the plane crash, Petty sweetened tapes via George Tomsco's group the Fireballs (Jimmy Gilmer's #1, '63 "Sugar Shack") and 2000 Grammy-Award Cricket guitarist **Tommy Allsup** (info. John Goldrosen). **David Box** covered song later, with original Crickets – which included Peggy Sue's actual husband **Jerry Allison** doing his classic accented paradiddle 16th-note roll:

JERRY & PEGGY SUE ALLISON'S
16TH-NOTE ROLL FOR BUDDY HOLLY:

The Hollies' respectful version, for the guy whose name they needed to thrive, includes all the original Hollies' plus Hicks's guitar, Elliott's drums, and **Ian Parker**'s vocals, orchestral arrangement at London's Pelican studios. Buddy and the Hollies. Nice ring to it. Combo from 'your wildest dreams.'

Suddenly the Back-to-School Monster pounced: swimming, fishing – begone. Productivity was King. Forget about kisses and cherry lips of strawberry love:

"See You in September" – Happenings, #3, 7-66. Remember their Jazz-Rock classics already? Gershwin's dynamic #3, 4-67 "I Got Rhythm," and the Jolson Dixieland-flavored #13, 7-67 "My Mammy." The backbeat cavorts. Harmonizers volley. Lead **Tom Giuliano** lofts on omnipresent tenor, The Big Band booms. Electrifying debut.

Lyrical tension: she's taking off for summer with parents. He's alone and gloomy. He wishes her a good time. But not too good. Danger lurks in the romantic summer moon. One magic musical moment! When the Happenings happen onto the last syllable of 'a-BOVE,' they sound like the entire Mormon Tabernacle Choir. Euphoric moment. Halo of Streetcorner Italian Soul.

"Sealed With a Kiss" – Brian Hyland, #3, 6-62. Hyland promises everlasting love sealed with a kiss on envelope (see "Please Mr. Postman" #1, '61). Beautiful melody. Gorgeous harmony. Summer love. Three unbeatables for a bronze-medal #3 hit. Throbbing with a **Bobby Vee**-style overdub, Hyland's summer escapade (see Chad & Jeremy's #8, 7-64 "Summer Song") bursts a few Jazz chordal oddities. Moody **Em** shifts to **Am**. In the bridge, Hyland sails to the **A major** IV chord (sub-dominant). "Sealed" often jumps to the bizarre chromatic VII chord – **D major**. At lipstick letter finale, he's waffling between the morose **Em** and the more harmonious **A major**. Just before you think he'll settle for a tender tremolo, and fade away on the irresolved minor, he finishes up on a big strong **E major**. It would take Simon and Garfunkel seven magic years (#7, 4-69 "The Boxer") to find a similar sayonara. "Sealed with a Kiss" seems a regular Teen Idol ballad. It is not. Its chord variations give it a true Jazz structure. **Beach Boys** did Jazz Rock, too, in 'Four Guys' quartet/quintet style:

"Graduation Day" – Four Freshman, #17, 5-56. Esoteric Jazz harmonies of **Ross** and brother **Don Barbour**, plus two other freshmen. Sniffly graduation song from their Indianapolis Jordan Conservatory ponders evermore summer; astounding tag-end major sevenths, diminished, augmented. Lyric? Senior prom, out till three. Blue blazers, penny loafers, Princeton haircuts.

"Moments to Remember" – Four Lads, #2(6), 9-55. Pals rip goalposts down, party on beyond New Year's Eve; lovers entwine by drive-in movie glow. **Bernie Toorish**, super tenor, leads Toronto guys "Standing on the Corner" watching girls pass by (#3, 4-56). Do they want to punt happy college days of honey-toned harmonies and hot honeys? "No, Not Much" [#2(4), 1-56]. Previewing Beach Boy Surf fantasias, lads and lassies escaped to Bali Ha'i "Enchanted Island" (#12, 6-58). Or **Four Coins**' #11, 5-57 "Shangri-La."

"Love Is a Many-Splendored Thing" – Four Aces, #1(6), 8-55. Jazz riffs too. Two steamy lovers. Earth stands still. Two happy lovers smooch atop a windy, lofty hill. Despite cinema-powered lyric, Four Aces ace the vocalization with 'A+' grade. Ultra romantic. Dreamy. As 'Pop Standards' cruised into the 1955-New Rock Era, this splendid thing is among the best cruisers. One weird line: Her fingers somehow clutch his throbbing heart, and somehow teach the organ to sing. (She's a cardiologist?)

"Don't Worry Baby" – Beach Boys, #24, 5-64. Brian Wilson salutes three foursomes' tight harmonics. **Brian Wilson** and the **Beach Men**? "Don't Worry Baby" Is FOUR GUYS' JAZZ vocalizing. Lads? Freshmen? Aces? Or Hi-Los' Al. #19, 10-57 *Now Hear* This? Whatever. From a three-chord R & R Surf Blues band, Pa **Murry Wilson** whipped his three sons' harmonies into shape. The three Hawthorne High overachievers (Brian was quarterback football hero) and their cuz **Mike Love** found a fifth voice in **Al Jardine**. Just add Chuck Berry. Beach Boys spliced the Berry guitar magic to hot Jazz harmonics – and this ultimate Drag Race Graveyard Rock song emerged.

Brian's 'Irish' tenor/falsetto lyric rolls around his next race. He tells his girlfriend he's afraid he'll crash the car, because he can't back down from his drag race duel. Like many resigned women watching their soldiers strap armor for battle, she tells him he'll be OK. Not to worry. Take her love along, she implores him, figuring it'll act like a St. Christopher's medallion and save him from a fiery crash. Love heals all – it didn't save 'Tommy' in #7, '60 **Ray Peterson**'s Graveyard Rock anthem "Tell Laura I Love Her." Tommy crashed. Smoochy love . . . who needs seatbelts or speed limits? Love, Rock and Roll, Religion, and Drag Racing often spin entirely on Faith. Great Rock and Roll is often great compromise. Brian combined the Four Lads, Chuck Berry, and his own drag racing lyric. Bassist/keyboarder **Carol Ray**, according to singer/songwriter Teddy Kalivas, played on many of the Beach Boys' hits, representing another gender dimension of their great sound.

"A Whiter Shade of Pale" – Procul Harum, #5, 6-67. Orchestral groove goes gonzo. Surreal fandango light-tripping, a lyrical adventure. The fandango is a speedy

Spanish dance, mentioned in **Queen**'s #9, 1-76 "Bohemian Rhapsody," the epitome of Art/Glam/Opera/Pomp/Jazz Rock (whew). After the 1st line, Procul Harum (Latin: procul means 'beyond these things') gets a little weedier and murkier. The big Orchestral Rock hit lumbers along on the tintinnabulalating vibrations of Gary Brooker's massive Farfisa organ, and **Robin Trower**'s guitar. Their "Whiter" purplish fandango, lyrically pulsating with a surreal bop motif, echoes the classical melody of J.S. Bach's *Sleepers Awake*. Their #5, 5-72 *Procul Harum Live* album with the Canadian Edmonton Symphony chases a classical melodic rainbow.

"Windy" – Wes Montgomery, #44, 11-67; #48, 12-67 R & B. Guitar whiz's Montgomery's ultra cool rendition of Association's #1 hit. Wes surrounds the actual note, blanketing his musical mood in mystique and sophistication.

"(You Don't Know) How Glad I Am" – Nancy Wilson, #11, 6-64; #11, R & B. Chillocothe, Ohio, Soul Jazz diva. Classic Diana Ross beauty and a sweet smile. Behind-the-Beat Sarah Vaughan alto stylistics. Recorded with **Cannonball Adderly** and **Ramsey Lewis**. Soul-chart Jazz hits like #10 R & B only 12-74 "You're as Right as Rain" and **Bonnie Raitt**'s #18, 11-91 "I Can't Make You Love Me" to #87 R & B.

Dave Brubeck

"The 'In' Crowd" – Ramsey Lewis, #5, 7-65; #2(3), 6-65 R & B. Prolific Jazz Rock interpreter. Lewis scored 17 HOT 100 hits. This one features a funky Boogie piano (Lewis's forte) to the **Dobie Gray** classic (#13, 1-65; #11 R & B) "The 'In' Crowd." Catchy tune about status-seeking clique. 'In' crowd walks and talks a certain way. "Cool group" scenario never leaves us. Check out your local high school reunion. Soulster Gray (a/k/a Leonard Victor Ainsworth) cut #82, '87 Country-only "Take It Real Easy."

Piano man **Ramsey Lewis** (b. '35, Chicago) clobbered charts with hearty handclap Boogie on McCoys' reprise "Hang on Sloopy" #11, 11-65 with his Trio: **Eldee Young** on bass, and **Isaac 'Red' Holt** thumping drums. Cameos? "Wade in the Water" #19, 7-66 (#3 R & B); #44 "Sun Goddess" 3-75, non-vegetarian "Hot Dawgit" #50, 1-75 and "7-11" #67, 6-87 R & B).

"You and Your Baby Blues" – Solomon Burke, #96, 3-75; #19, 1-75. CROSSOVER stardom. Basically a Soul artist Preacher [and Mortician], Burke dovetails into the Blues here, and segues into Jazz Rock. Blessed with 26 HOT 100 hits, Burke's booming soulful Jazz style peaked with 3-65 smash #22 "Got to Get You Off My Mind" (#1[3] R & B).

"Kind of a Drag" – Buckinghams, #1(2), 12-66. **Dennis Tufano** and Chicagoans shun drag racing (or nonstandard gender apparel) in lyric, and powershift into organ-paced Jazz harmonies. Buckinghams preview Jazz chords, progressions, and Progressive Rock movement: "Hey, Baby" (#12, 9-67), "Don't You Care" (#6, 3-67), and "Mercy3" (#5, 6-67). Shifting with sidewinder minor chords, "Drag" is empowered by the same whooshy overriding organ sound which sparks:

"Time Won't Let Me" – Outsiders, #5, 2-66. Cleveland's equally-Italian lead singer **Sonny Geraci** steers super Classic Rock groove. Kid can't wait for undecided girl to make up mind. Nifty beat. Floater Rock classic, with overarching order. Same groove as #5, 12-67 "Bend Me Shape Me" (with "Peggy Sue" 16th-note paradiddle) by the American Breed.

***Bitches Brew* – Miles Davis, Al. #35, 6-70.** Nary a HOT 100 single. Jazz trumpet legend Davis (1926-91) was born in Alton, Illinois – home of Robert Pershing Wadlow, tallest man in history (8' 11½"). **Sly & the Family Stone** (#8, 2-68 "Dance to the Music') influenced Davis to seek a wider audience, and a bigger beat via Rock and Soul. Davis dishes out a Goliath of a trumpet sound. Record sales never kept pace with music industry in influencing Jazz Rock movement. How so? Davis and entourage earned 23 Grammy Awards. Miles Davis is a giant among Jazz artists, and a talented artist whose paintings we visited in an Ann Arbor Art Show [U. of Michigan], along with great stuff by Grateful Dead's **Jerry Garcia**, and **John Lennon** (1998).

"Three O'Clock in the Morning" – Lou Rawls, #83, 6-65; NC, R & B. Rawls's epitome-of-cool bari-bass voice commands a song. He doesn't just sing it. It was an old favorite of Liz Maury Dean – my mom – at #1(8), 11-22, by bandleader **Paul Whiteman**.

"Dead End Street" – Lou Rawls, #29, 3-67; #3, 4-67 R & B. Rawls monologues the first minute with a Rap-preview heady harangue about how cold Chicago can be. It's WET cold, too, chilled to the bone by the big inland sea (Lake Michigan). Lou talks of 'The Hawk,' making up his own personal Afro-American mythology about the North Wind (Borealis?). Detroit and Minneapolis (much worse) and Chicago are the coldest big metropoli in the U.S.A. In this uplifting song of the civil rights era, Rawls rises by bootstraps from bitter cold and poverty to realize (via pluck, guts, Soul) the American Dream: Johnny B. Goode. Other Rawls Jazz Soul triumphs? "Your Good Thing is About to End," #18, 7-69 (#3, R & B); "A Natural Man", #17, 8-71; #2(2), 6-76 "You'll Never Find Another Love Like Mine"; and his Mr. Mellow baritone swan song, "Love Is a Hurtin' Thing" (#13, 9-66; #1 R & B).

"Mack the Knife" – Ella Fitzgerald, #27, 5-60; #6 R & B. Considered the greatest of all Jazz singers by devoted fans, **Ella Fitzgerald** (1918-96) enjoyed her only Top Thirty Rock Era hit with this **Bobby Darin** afterglow reprise of **Louis Armstrong** classic. Ella's "A Tisket, A-Tasket" (#1[10], 6-38) vamps a nursery rhyme, while she also commandeered Jazz/Pop vocalics with #1(2) twin 11-44 hits "I'm Making Believe" and "Into Each Life Some Rain Must Fall." Cameo chart chompers? #6, 6-48 "My Happiness" (#2, '58 **Connie Francis**); Ella's Inkspots' collaboration #5, 4-45 "I'm Beginning to See the Light"; #9, 11-40 "Five O'Clock Whistle"; and oft-cited **Louis Jordan** duo at #9, 6-49 "It's Cold Outside." Ella's last chart (#75, 4-63), is a Jazz/Ragtime classic. The original?

"Bill Bailey, Won't You Please Come Home" – Arthur Collins, #1(8), 7-1902. Hot Ragtime Jazz and it's Almost Rock and Roll! The miffed, ticked, raging gal once tossed Bill out with nothin' – only this fine tooth comb. In a fit of sorry atonement, she begs steady Mr. Bailey to return; no rapscallion, rounder, or blunt bluggard, HE's a good-hearted MAN in love with a good-timin' WOMAN. (Listen to **Willie Nelson** and **Buddy Holly**'s bassman **Waylon Jennings** on gender flip side, "Goodhearted Woman," #25, 2-76, and #1[3], 12-75 C. Ella's tie-in to Rock and Roll? How about her #19, 2-38 (or year 16 B.H. [before Bill] Haley]): "Rock It for Me"? Ella Fitzgerald was a Jazz legend and her musical memory is a national treasure.

"White Room" – Cream, #6, 10-68. "White Room" you hear everywhere, like their debut Pre-Metal Basher #5, 1-68 "Sunshine of Your Love." For interior decorating fans, this white room drapes black curtains. Cream flashes a whole phalanx of flamboyant firepower out of the guitar section. On lead guitar (Class of '92, '93, and '99 Rock Hall Inductee) **ERIC CLAPTON**. On bass, **Jack Bruce**. Drums? **Ginger Baker**. Cream, due to its instrumental

virtuosity, downpedaled the excellent vocals, improvising their 'Power Trio' format into long guitar explorations. Without Clapton's guitar-solo cadenzas, Rock and Roll might have continued its blatant domination by egomaniac singers. Clapton also masterminded a Crossover approach to Rock genres, excelling in Blues, Jazz, and Mainstream Rock and Roll.

To many Rock aficionados, rock idols are prophets. Lead guitarists' twangy cadenzas can serve as secular sermons to a world thirsting for inspiration. Super axe soloists get worshipped. Maybe even in the manner of ancient gods. Bad sign? Witness the London Underground graffiti groupies gravitating to apotheosize Eric: ERIC CLAPTON IS GOD!!!

In the ensuing years, the planet has discovered that Eric is not, indeed, God, but that he's a magnificent virtuoso guitarist. He's a very frail human being, like the rest of us, who tragically lost his little son, Conner, 4, to a fall from a skyscraper in Manhattan. Jazz greats know that heartfelt music improvisation can assuage great pain and suffering. Brokenhearted, Clapton composed this moving elegy:

"Tears in Heaven" – Eric Clapton, #2(4), 2-92. In this *Unplugged* album tribute (Al. #1[3], 9-92) to his son, and having just gone to the circus with him the day before, Clapton asks the dark, brooding question of whether his boy would even recognize him in Heaven were the two to meet. Would he know his frequently-absent road-weary dad, not married to his mom? Awesome cosmic questions aside, it's a fine song. Ringing with Folk-style chords in the guitar-friendly Key of 'A', Clapton walks the low 'E' string down from A to Ab to his **F#m** VIm chord. Plummeting from his sonorant tonic major to a gloomy minor, we can feel his resigned remorse. Eric's "Tears" bridge ascends the scale to the bIII chromatic chord '**C major**'.

Time can bring the proud man onto his knees, he warns. Cascading from foreboding minor to cheerful major chords, the lyric spins in the opposite direction; Eric warns of the coming apocalypse. He offers a Taoist yin-yang solution: His emotional landscape has been stripped bare. His will to carry on burned over and salted. He was not there to help her. He cannot atone.

British poet Algernon Charles Swinburne took an 1880's agnostic vision of death:

> "From too much love of living,
> From hope and fear set free,
> We thank with brief thanksgiving
> Whatever Gods may be –
> Thtn no man lives forever,
> That dead men rise up never,
> And even the weariest river,
> Winds somewhere safe to sea."

Swinburne, *Hymn to Proserpine*

Flighty Greek goddess Prosperpine visited the Underworld for magic pomegranates (no Twinkies?). Swinburne's cosmic tenet offers no hope, no resurrection, no reason for profound faith. Only blessed REST from lifelong agonies of guilt-scarred souls. It is NOT, however, **Loretta Lynn**'s comforting 1997 Christian vision "In the Sweet Bye and Bye," when parted parents meet departed kids in a resurrective happy homecoming on that beautiful faraway shore. Clapton's cosmic gloom is not unusual. The terrible loss of a child has scarred many a grieving parent for the rest of his earthly years.

SUNNYSIDE PROPHETS vs. GLOOM AND DOOMERS

Most of English literature has been written by people who are predominantly gloomy: Hemingway, Steinbeck, Carlyle, Joyce, Faulkner, Kerouac, Sinclair Lewis, H.L. Mencken, Joseph Conrad, Poe, Ibsen, Arthur Miller, Joyce Carol Oates, Frank Norris, T.S. Eliot, Sylvia Plath, F. Scott Fitzgerald, Nathaniel Hawthorne, and Herman Melville.

Shakespeare you might put in the middle. This leaves us with Charles Dickens and William Wordsworth and James Michener and Ralph Waldo Emerson to hype the sunny side. It is hard for them to carry the optimism of the Anglo-American people on their shoulders.

Many writers of gloomy tunes were English majors in college. **Dylan** and **Paul Simon** do not splash sprightly Pollyanna ecstatic giggles. Some parents who were not English or music majors wonder why their kids love depressing Grunge or Heavy Metal or Life's-a-Bite, Barf-on-Your Shoe Alternative Angst Rock.

Eric Clapton returns to HOPE. He offers up his total unworthiness. Clapton purges chunks of guilt and remorse. He quizzes the Cosmos, that "When the Roll Is Called Up Yonder," Conner and he might reunite. He expresses hope that he will see his boy a long, long ways down the road of life. And over the Great Divide. Got to be strong, he resolutely tells himself, just to carry on. To work on amassing worthiness. Sorrowful and contrite, he muses destinies. Maybe, just maybe, the guru 'god' guitarist fervently meditates – almost prays – someday he'll see Conner Clapton again, and he can somehow make up for the time that was lost. **Clapton** is not now and never has been **God**. Nor is **Hendrix**. Not even **Pat Boone**. And **Elvis**, despite "Take My Hand, Precious Lord" in 1957, is no direct cousin of JESUS. Little Johnny B. Goode is just a plucky kid by the old railroad track with a guitar and a dream. Never, ever a god.

Rock and Roll stars aren't even saints. Our Rock and Roll heroes are like our sports heroes. Sometimes we are very disappointed to discover they have died of booze, or gotten caught with some shady lady, or man, or both – in some Transylvania tryst. Nope, Rock and Soul singers are not gods or saints. For all rock history, some rock stars have been rakes and rapscallions and ribald rounders. Ant those are the good ones.

"Roll Over Beethoven" – Chuck Berry, #29, 6-56; #2(1) R & B. One Rock and Roll anthem that changed the world. With this one big tune, the St. Louis Rock star tweaked and piqued Classical complacency, expanded the 12-Bar Blues format, dynamically promoted Rock and Roll in its infancy, and laid the foundation for all the Rock lead guitarists who ever were, are today, and evermore shall be.

Phoneless, Chuck bugs the DJ to spin a song. Which? His own, "Roll Over Beethoven." For nearly half a century, rock bands have been disguising their voices, and calling stations to request their own songs! HYPE SPRINGS ETERNAL.

Berry's sisters, buoyed by Chuck's mother and teacher, copiously studied Classical music, deigning to regard Popular music worthy of their time. Chuck chides them with "Roll Over Beethoven" – and to let Tchaikovsky in on 'the news.' He's not really slamming **Ludwig Von Beethoven** (1770-1827), but just using our impish American iconoclastic sense of humor. American Rock and Rollers, he's saying, are at least as important as highbrow musicians.

With **Johnnie Johnson** blurring the 88's in machine-gun swooping *glissandos* and *arpeggios* and jackhammer trills, Chuck was free to unleash the whizbang *cadenzas* he'd heard from **Charlie Christian, T-Bone Walker**, and **Muddy Waters** – and add a few of his own hot licks. Unencumbered by basic 12-Bar Blues form, he shifted into a Rockabilly mode. The R & B Rock legend revamped a musical fraternity generally composed of poor white kids from Southern shotgun shacks.

Berry's lyrics were hip, All-American, and geographically profound. He offered an exciting teenage paradise – eternal *Happy Days* malt shops; jiggling, jangling juke boxes; and whirling poodle-skirt Peggy Sue cuties becoming blonde *Bandstand* bombshells. Barry's vibrant neon 50s America rocked all night long!

Chuck is the Poet Laureate of 50s Rock and Roll. And far, far beyond. Jazz Rock and "Johnny B. Goode"? If it weren't for that kid plunking his pawn-shop gunnysack guitar down by some long lost railroad track, we may as well have kissed Jazz Rock good night. With **Les Paul**'s overdubbing, and solid-body guitar invention, he can take credit for shaping Chuck's career (Les at 84+ still played a regular Monday gig in the Village). After the human voice, the electric guitar is the most important ingredient in the Rock and Roll recipe. Berry owes a major debt to Delta Blues gurus **Son House** and **Charlie Patton**, points out Larry Epstein – and to Jewish American entrepreneur Leon Chess (Chess Records Prez).

Remember **Bob Seger**'s jukebox standard, "Rock and Roll Never Forgets" [#41, 7-77]? Bob says that all of the musical children of Chuck Berry now hammer away at Chuck's guitar riffs and hooks.

Not just Poet Laureate, Chuck and his alter ego 'Johnny B. Goode' pioneered the hot-licks electric guitar catechism for flying speedmetal maestros of the future. With chords crunching from majors and sixths and bluesy sevenths, plus minor thirds and diminished ninths with just a tiny tremolo touch and bend on the pinkie, Berry opened up a frontier of Jazz Rock Riff Mania.

Blues guru **B.B. King** swoons on one-note stands. He bends and caresses his slowly slurring notes from his guitar 'Lucille.' **Eric Clapton** is a dizzying combo of slow ribbony bends and speedo guitar fire, echoing his mentors Chuck and B.B. in a Brit combo of blazing digits. (Catch King & Clapton's Al. #3, 7-2000 *Riding with the King*).

JAZZ-ROCK ODYSSEY: CHUCK BERRY'S ESOTERIC BLUES

A myth says that Rock and Roll was very simple to begin with. Don't search for elementary three-chord offerings in Chuck's first smash "Maybellene." Early on, Chuck's admiration for the poignant styles of **Nat King Cole** and **Charlie Christian** led to a glitzy array of jazz ninths and augmented fifths. The flip side, "Wee Wee Hours" on Chess Records, is a somnambulent sleepwalk of melancholy mood.

"Maybellene," far from a kiddie '3 chords and a cloud of dust,' begins on a Jazz-Rock **C9+5** chord, and fires off an **F6, F7**, and **Bb9** before it zooms out of the blocks (on the part about why can't she be true . . .). That **C9+5** chord which launches "Maybellene" off the dominant chord is no wimp. No simple big three I-IV-V⁷ here. Chuck's "Brown-Eyed Handsome Man" flaunts a Mel Bay guitar-chart **Am7b5** to befuddle its normal sweet melodic key of 'Eb.' "No Particular Place to Go" (#10, 5-64, CB's first comeback) jolts from its easy one-flat 'F' major key to a Polynesian progression bVI chromatic **Db7**. Chuck's "Promised Land" (#41, 12-64) sported diminished chords, flatting both the third and fifth notes of the root tonic (in Key of 'C', a **Cdim** is C-Eb-F#[Gb]). Chuck's riffs and Jazz Rock chords weren't necessarily intended to blitz Jazz guitar virtuosos – just R & R fans.

With snortfire lyrics and virtuoso hot Jazz riffs, Chuck spreads the R & R gospel far and wide, from Rockingham roller rinks in Detroit, dance pavilions in St. Louis, or Liverpool live bands careening off subterranean Cavern walls. The Beatles' #68 George Harrison vocal version of the Berry hit we've already covered, so let's squeeze a big Orchestral Rock group in here, and bounce back to Berry and Beethoven:

"Roll Over Beethoven" – ELO (Electric Light Orchestra), #42, 4-73. Few songs we do THRICE – Just the unforgettable . . . Booming out of redbrick Birmingham, England, with **Jeff Lynne** on vocals and guitar, **Roy Wood** from the Move, and **Bev Bevan** on drums, ELO set a precedent for theatrics and Orchestral Rock. "Roll Over Beethoven" is a multi-layered audial adventure, fraught with flash and flair. They duel each other on an electric power trip extraordinaire. When the Move split up by 1971, Lynne and Wood looked for Rock French Horn players and CELLISTS (Szatmary). ELO'S "Roll Over Beethoven" engorges Chuck's "Roll Over Beethoven" with the classical symphonic instruments he spoofed in his original lyric. Dramatic irony, like déjà vu, strikes again and again.

"Don't Bring Me Down" – ELO, #4, 8-79. Progressive Rock zooms to a zenith here. ELO also scored with #9, 12-74 "Can't Get You Out of My Mind," #8, 5-79 "Shine a Little Love," and yet another conception of Coleridge's "Xanadu" (#8, 8-80) in their Olivia Newton-John collaboration. Their "Hold on Tight" (#10, 7-81) and #10, 11-75 "Evil Woman" scratch the Top Ten in double figures. Among ELO Orchestral nuggets, try #13, 10-76 "Livin' Thing," #18, 2-86 "Calling America," or non-phone-y "Telephone Line" (#7, 6-77). Richard Tandy now did keyboards and guitar, while Lynne moonlighted with Bob Dylan, George Harrison, Tom Petty, and Roy Orbison – with the **Traveling Wilburys** (Al. *Vol. I* #3, 11-88).

Chuck Berry challenged a whole generation of guitarists to pump up technique. From his 'Chuckabilly' trademark sound, we see roots of Heavy Metal, Orchestral Rock, and Jazz Rock. Even the Glam Rock theatrics of Chuck's duckwalk and behind-the-neck strumming suddenly mushroomed into make-up and iffy stories about biting heads off live chickens.

A recent TV *History of Rock* features guru guitarists **Eddie Van Halen, Les Paul, B.B. King,** and the Who's **Pete Townshend**. All rave about **Jimi Hendrix**. In Hendrix's own day, his genius was misunderstood, while his Top 100 single hits burbled and blipped: #65 "Purple Haze," #67 "Foxey Lady," #82 "Up from the Skies," and #74 "Dolly Dagger." Anyone who heard him play at Woodstock or Monterey, however, realized Jimi Hendrix was no esoteric egghead – he was a living, firebreathing southpaw virtuoso, with key knowledge of Jazz progressions and techniques.

"Pinball Wizard" – Who, #19, 4-69. Banner tune from Rock opera *Tommy*. "Pinball Wizard" paints the poignant picture of a teenage kid unable to see, hear, or speak. On the pinball machine, however, a sixth sense impels him to perfection. Before the 80s Pac-Man craze, old pinball machines ate your nickels in sarcastic glee:

the 'silver ball' eluded the vainly-flapping flapper flapping furiously at it.

I recall a 1969 Detroit inner-city chicken shack, where a relic turquoise juke box rehashed "Pinball Wizard." Chicken shackers cheered me as I flapped the flippers furiously – razzmatazzing me as I proved it was no Tommy. No Tommy at all. Townshend (b. '45), singer **Roger Daltrey** (b.'44), drummer **Keith Moon** (1947-78), and bass maestro **John Entwistle** (b. '44) comprised the group many great Jazz/Orchestral/Punk/Glam/Alternative/Blues Rock musicians call THE WORLD'S GREATEST ROCK AND ROLL BAND – to the chagrin of 10,000 other good bands (Stones in particular) claiming the crown. The Who easily fit into Blues, or Heavy Metal, or Hard Rock. Their experimental Jazz chord progressions, plus Keith Moon's otherworldly percussion prowess (in the Gene Krupa-Buddy Rich-Joe Morello Jazz tradition), award them this chapter.

"Boris the Spider" – Who, NC, 1967. Creepy-crawly little ditty about this tiny tenant with a Russian name. Features **John Entwistle**'s mastery of the electric bass. In mock seriousness, Entwistle flutters a garland of grace notes on his very, very rare BASS LEAD on the bridge. The DEEP DEEP bass vocal hits nether notes never nailed in regular Rock and Roll, like a LOW 'F' note – full 2½ octaves below Middle 'C'. Just too super and entomologically dynamic to crest the tenor-glutted charts. Nice arachnid arrangement.

"The Kids Are All Right" – Who, #106, 8-66. The Who frisbeed this brassy, metallic screamer into the British Invasion. Early on, the Who fired salvos of Progressive Rock power: the melodic and harmonic tune reels rollickingly along in the sweet Key of 'D'. Matt Clark's favorite, "Kids," bounces blithely into orange soda-pop major **G** and **A** chords, the Big Three pillowy I, IV, V7 chords. Then ZAP, out of the blue(s), Pete and John powershift into a bVII **'C' major** chromatic. The Who are even more spellbinding because they are a 3-instrument band – like the **Doors**. Daltrey handles the odd harmonica, but like **Mick Jagger**, he's primarily a singer. Entwistle doubles on French horn (answering ELO's want-ad), of all things.

"My Generation" – Who, #74, 1-66; #2, 11-65 U.K. Armed with one of the best musical bands of anybody's generation, London's Who fired off two gimmicks: 1) They used a speech impediment (aarrgh, the cruelty of humor), stuttering, to define their generation's inarticulate passion (good ol' Porky Pig, the genuinely nicest of the Looney Tuners, has the same disability); and 2) They invented GLAM ROCK, after a fashion, with their DESTROY-THE BAND gimmick, which skipped a generation since **Jimmy Durante**'s similar "STOP DA MUSIC!" or Spike Jones's rampages. "My Generation" tells the next generation to listen up. Under the guise of a minimalist vocabulary and halting, uncertain speech, the "Kids [who were] All Right" (#106, 8-66) told their elders to bug off, because they were steering the new world order.

Musically, "My" is an exercise in complex simplicity. Each verse sits on just one bluesy chord. Townshend walks the Blues standard **G, G6, G7, G6** pattern. "My Generation" also serves up an incredible bass lead from Entwistle, a fluttering, plectrum-plucked glob of low speed-metal notes that commands the whole bridge. Outside of **Marty Robbins**' watershed #3 "Don't Worry" in 1961, which accidentally invented fuzztone bass and distortion, or Jazz bass fiddle maestro **Charlie Mingus**, how many BASS leads can you think of on songs' bridges? [OK, OK, **Van Morrison**'s #10, 7-67 "Brown-Eyed Girl"]. Starting in Key of 'G', Daltrey's dudes modulate to 'A', then to 'Bb,' and storm off sunsetward in the Key of "C". Meanwhile, drummer Keith Moon, crushes the skins with a twirling tattoo of triplets, twelve to the bar with lusty gusto:

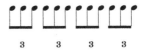

Moon's Lunar Triplets showcase the Who's Jazz-based technique.

The Who
Left to right: Roger Daltrey, John Entwistle, Keith Moon, and Pete Townshend

"Baba O'Reilly" – Who, NC, 1971. From Al. #4, 8-71 *Who's Next*. Never does this Irish colleen Baba's name spark the song.The unforgettable lead-off suggests a zither, banjo, or dulcimer.You do remember their cry: IT IS ONLY A TEENAGE WASTELAND! Captures spirit of adolescent enmired in choices, pizzas, passions, zits and bewilderment. So does "Won't Get Fooled Again" (#15, 7-71). "Behind Blue Eyes" (#34, 11-71) shows jazzfully that pretty blue smiley eyes hide blue-funk sadness. It's an audial mirror of **Crosby, Stills'** M.O.R. anthem for sweet blue-eyed **Judy Collins**, "Suite: Judy Blue Eyes" #21, 10-69. [Collins' "Chelsea Morning" (#78, 8-69) is the inspiration for President Bill and Hillary Clinton to name their child Chelsea.] The Who's #18, 3-81 "You Better You Bet" shows their talent survived the stunning loss of **Keith Moon**, who O.D.-ed after viewing opening night of *The Buddy Holly Story* on Buddy's birthday, September 7, 1978. Small Faces' **Kenny Jones** replaced the irreplaceable Moon.

"Who Are You" – Who, #14, 8-78. Clever way to sneak your group's moniker into song title, eh, what? Falsetto flourishes on this flamingo fandango. In the wake of the "#1 Rock Drummer of All Time"'s untimely passing (*Rolling Stone* poll), the Who brought their fancy fireworks back to Wembley, Wight, and the World. From **Sophie Tucker**, "Last of the Red Hot Mamas," to the Who with amps at 11, the "show must always go on." The unsinkable Sophie brandished a hot #7, 9-24 "Red Hot Mama," and followed up with her immortal #15, 9-29 "I'm the Last of the Red Hot Mamas."

When I was 18, I got nearly crushed waiting for a **Del Shannon** concert at the Lightguard Armory on Detroit's Eight Mile, as 8000 fried fans smashed breathlessly into each other by the door. Understaffed security chuckled. No joke. In 1979, 11 fervent Who fans were killed in such a ghastly crush at Cincinnati's Riverfront Stadium (see Gerry & Pacemakers). It was the worst similar tragedy in Rock history. Like Clapton, the Who brushed off their grief over time, and got back on stage. Many touring bands put 70-hour-week factory workers to shame, with their blood, sweat, and tears commitment to their fans and their musical careers.

"Spinning Wheel" – Blood, Sweat, & Tears, #2(3), 5-69; #45, 8-69 R & B. Canadian tenor **David Clayton-Thomas** prowls Jazz Fusion with this classic. Blood, Sweat, and Tears ran the table for two glorious years with three silver-medal records: "Spinning Wheel," their debut cabaret command performance "You've Made Me So Very Happy" (#2[3], 3-69), and songscribe **Laura Nyro**'s pensive cosmic "And When I Die." Early B.S.T. guy **AL** [NOT Alice] **Kooper** (#96, 4-67 "No Time Like the Right Time") has a checkered history. After their #3, 1-58 novelty romp "Short Shorts," Al joined Four Seasons' **Bob Gaudio**'s **Royal Teens** of Brooklyn. Keyboarder Kooper did Folk/Rock/Psychedelic studio work with **Dylan, Paul Butterfield's Blues Band, Tom Rush**, one-third of **Crosby, Stills, and Nash [Stills]**, and **Moby Grape** (#88, 7-67, "Omaha").

Blood, Sweat, and Tears horned in on the hits. Main sax man was Berklee College of Music's **Fred Lipsius**, bolstered by **Jerry Weiss** and **Randy Brecker** on trumpets; Dixieland splice featured **Dick Halligan** on trombone. It's the closest thing to a Big Band Comeback since University of Michigan's **Si Zentner** (Jimmy Dorsey Band vet) hit #41 with "Up a Lazy River" (#19, 6-32 Hoagy Carmichael "Lazy River" Standard Pop hit). More standard accoutrements: guitar by **Steve Katz; Jim Fielder** on bass, from **Frank Zappa**'s iconoclastic Mothers of Invention. Jazz-swathed **Bobby Colomby** on drums.

An early photo of B,S, & T shows nine sideburned guys – a nontet? – out standing in their field. Actually, it's a drooly puddle in dankest, dreariest November. Their de-

meanor, though, shows that their combined Music Theory courses were poised to launch Progressive Rock Fusion extraordinaire. So, naturally, they broke up. Squabbling, carping, grappling for leadership. This usual quarrel stuff murders great bands' aspirations of grandeur.

Lo and behold, as leader Kooper dragged off the Weiss and Brecker faction, they were replaced by Juilliard's **Chuck Winfield** and **Lou Soloff** on trumpet. Most of all, they struck gold with **David Clayton-Thomas**, vocalist nonpareil. Clayton-Thomas, on the cusp of the Hyphen connection, already enjoyed five #1 hits in the second biggest country in the world, Canada, with his Bossmen. Clayton-Thomas's smoky blue tenor spearheaded a rush of R & R Jazz Fusion never before seen, or heard. With a supercool **Joe Cocker** sandpaper sound, he looked a bit like my 6'2" 260# pal Dave 'Big Bopper' Brady who, at 200#+ could leap and hurdle four-foot cyclone 1961 wire-mesh fences. This stuff hustles back to the Big Band Era:

"I'll Get By (As Long As I Have You)" – Harry James, #1(6), 4-44. State-of-the-art trumpeter **James** (1916-83) launched #2 album star ever – **Frank Sinatra**. James' chartbusters include "I Don't Want to Walk Without You" #1(2), 2-42; gigantic #1(13) "I've Heard That Song Before" of 1-43; "I'm Beginning to See the Light" #1(2), 1-45, or his barely-50s #14 "Mona Lisa," featuring **Juan Tizol** on trombone, with equal rampages of quivering notes high up in the azure stratosphere. James and **Louie Armstrong** set the mark for Jazz trumpeters. Harry got his start with **Benny Goodman** (#1, 6-34 "Moonglow," #11, 7-36 "Stompin's at the Savoy"); Benny romped similar flights of stratospheric fancy on the clarinet. Time-surfing?

"Beautiful Ohio" – Henry Burr, #1(9), 5-1919. Ever wonder who set the world's record for recording sessions? The New Brunswick Canadian tenor is said to have recorded over 12,000 different records. Balladeer Burr (1882-1941) enjoyed 24 #1 records such as: #1(8), 9-1909 "I Wonder Who's Kissing Her Now'; #1(4), 11-1910 "Meet Me Tonight in Dreamland"; "M-O-T-H-E-R (A Word That Means the World to Me)" at #1(6), 2-1916; and two World War I heart-tuggers – #1(11) "Just a Baby's Prayer at Twilight (For Her Daddy Over There)" of 4-1918, and #1(2), 11-22 "My Buddy."

"The Trail of the Lonesome Pine" – Henry Burr and Albert Campbell, #1(3), 6-1913. Yesteryear moonlight memory. Nostalgic long lost classic from my maternal grandparents' Virginia's breathtaking Blue Ridge Mountains. Flood of happy/sad memories of my smoggy boyhood on Atkinson Street in Detroit – with my mother lullabying in her dear old Old Gold and Lucky Strike husky contralto.

"Hi-De-Ho" – Blood, Sweat, & Tears, #14, 8-70. This tune plays with tempo. They rock the beat from molasses-slow to bouncy Blues chugging. His voice gravelizes into baritone on the finale, with revved-up fervor. "Lucretia MacEvil" hit #29, 10-70, and "Go Down Gamblin'" #32, 7-71.

"And When I Die" – Blood, Sweat & Tears, #2(1), 10-69. Should you do a whole theological cosmology in one 3-minute fell swoop? This **Laura Nyro**-penned classic doubles as Religious Rock. "And When I Die" leads off with a lonesome Arizona campfire harmonica. It hovers over the sunburnt slabs of golden stone, brandished by harmonikatz Steve Katz. Handclaps punctuate the tempo-deprived scene:

At first our singer rationalizes he's not afraid of dyin',' or doesn't really care. He figures that when he leaves this bittersweet tragicomic life, there will be one little child born somewhere, somehow, to carry the message of his yestersoul which has been promoted to glory. A staggering new concept in immortality! He's not pushing any Pearly Gates or Wash & Wear wings. Nor any Golden Cobblestone Promenades through sunset seashore mango groves, with grass-skirt houri maidens adorned in sweet smiles. Does he actually talk of transmuting the soul into a living, breathing child – somewhere far away on this tired old overpopulated planet? Or is he speaking of a sympathetic soul mate somewhere?

Deep stuff. Some little kid somewhere in India, Siberia, Uruguay, or Mozambique IS you, after you're gone. Of course, it could be symbolic. Some kid, maybe your own, will carry the torch of your existence. [Talented **Laura Nyro** (1947-97) wrote this classic and passed away; out of six billion worldwide inhabitants, you wonder WHO she might be now . . . it's really eerie. Try not to think about it!]

After the first verse – spare and laconic – a brash blast of horns horns in. The song begins in the Key of 'A'. The bass hurdles from the root to the fifth note and back. The long version of the song unleashes some twirly solo resembling a clavichord or harpsichord: (not credited, like Lipsius' harmonica intro). Ever wonder what happens when somebody's extraneous noise actually gets on your record? [We had a fire engine on the fadeout of "It's So Easy," 1967]. **Blood, Sweat, & Tears** treat the album credits with *Seinfeld* humor: "B,S, & T also thanks Miss Lucy Angle (in her Poll Parrot shoes) whose footsteps can be heard at the close of this selection. She is also very attractive."

New CD technology has great audial quality, but where can you squeeze that king of info on your dinky, eeny-meeny, spud-size CD? My boy Jeremy's 2nd homegrown CD (**Nine Days**' '97 *Monday Songs*) has pix and info so small that manager Andy Mendelsohn had to find his own mini-photo via a magnifying glass.

BST's lyric doesn't quite swear there isn't a Heaven, but then PRAYS that no Hell exists. Weird. Kind of like the perplexed would-be atheist who scrawls on the subway wall:: "There is no God, and Mary is His Mother." He says, only his death will reveal the true reality of these cosmic quandaries. It's like Robert Burns's stunning epitaph: "If there's another world, he lives in bliss/If not, he made the best of this."

"We'll Sing in the Sunshine" – Gale Garnett, #4, 8-64. Kiwi Gale (b. '42 Auckland, new Zealand) promises her guy one year (only) of a blithe and torrid affair –- then see ya later, alligator. Fine melody, but Autumnal Equinox turns them both into pumpkins of nevermore.

"Bungle in the Jungle" – Jethro Tull, #12, 11-74. Ian **Anderson**, Progressive Rock's premier flutist, discovered 'Jethro Tull' as actual 18th century farm-machine inventor. Many groups lavish literary allusions: **Uriah Heep** (#39, 7-72 "Easy Livin'"), smarmy character in Charles Dickens' *Dombey and Son*; "Romeo and Juliet," #6, 4-64 Johnny Dean and Detroit's **Reflections**; *Moby Grape*, after Melville's white whale *Moby Dick* (1851); and **Toto**, named after Dorothy's little black dog in *The Wizard of Oz* [#1(1), 10-82 Toto tune, "Africa"]. **Nine Days** named their SONY album after novelist Thomas Hardy's *Far from the Madding Crowd* (*The Madding Crowd*, 5-2000).

Jethro Tull glibly lambasts their jump-up-and-boogie "Bungle" enterprise in a gleeful expression of Jazz Rock fever. Album wise, Tull Rules! #1(2), 5-72 *Thick as a Brick*; #3, 11-72 *Living in the Past*; #1(1), 7-73 *A Passion Play*; and #8, 3-77 *Druidic Songs from the Wood*. Tull's #7 Al. 5-71 breakthrough, *Aqualung*, is best known for a song which never even charted: also "Aqualung." It stars a creepy flasher-type character on a park bench who ogles little girls.

Tull's Celtic Renaissance music is akin to Scottish (Al. #143 *All Around My Hat*, 12-75) band **Steeleye Span**'s madrigal style of Rock. **Jethro Tull**, like **Donovan**, helped pioneer the 1997-2000+ Celtic Renaissance of Celine Dion's *Titanic* #1 "My Heart Will Go On," plus Sarah McLachlan's "Angel."

In 1961, Jim Cook and I searched vainly for the British Surf's-Up scene at Blackpool near the Fab Four: All we found in the June 52° icy rain was a squashed shelter under some forlorn cement abutment that jutted grubbily toward the stony beach. As the steely sky drooled over Tull's Blackpool abode, cool-looking freckled English girls were covered up (with disgusting raincoats under umbrellas)! Jazz Rock stars **Steely Dan** (#19, 4-78 "Deacon Blues") weren't invented yet. Finally, we hitchhiked lorry-laden byways to Bonnie Scotland, and met a couple girls in a youth hostel along the scenic Bonnie Bonnie Banks of "Loch Lomond" – immortalized in Scottish song by Welsh-American tenor Evan Williams (#10, 3-12); Irish Maxine Sullivan (#9, 12-37, Claude Thornhill's Orchestra); and Jewish clarinet genius, 'Mr. Swing Jazz' **Benny Goodman** (#12, 12-37). He actually had 26 songs in the Top 20 in the year 1938 alone!Among them #7, 6-38 "The Flat Foot Floogee." Loch means lake in Scottish dialect.

"A Scottish Soldier" – Andy Stewart, #69, 4-61. Stewart's commanding baritone eulogizes a Scots' soldier losing his life in the green hills of Austria's Tyrol. A bagpiper pierogh plays the soldier back home to even greener hills (like Tom Jones's Welsh elegy, to himself, #11, 12-66 "The Green, Green Grass of Home") and eternal rest. The flip side bends the mood. "The Muckin O' Geordie's Byre" is about a bunch of guys who try to clean out a cow barn and get so drunk you can hear their pandemonium five miles away. My Great-Auntie Bella Lumsden (1898-1992) loved it. Featuring an accordion, "Muckin"" is a Reel.

"In a Big Country" – Big Country, #17, 10-83. Stuart Adamson (d. 2002) played a mean Dumferline, Scotland bagpipe-guitar. Or keyboard synthesizer Faux-Bag-pipe. With technology to simulate Scotland's national instrument, Stu joined Mark Brzezicki (drums), Bruce Watson (rhythm guitar), and bassman Tony Butler, to bring a big wide sound of BAGPIPE ROCK AND ROLL. Ah, the simulation age. Actual bagpipes may be shrill and commanding and riveting, but they don't change chords or keys or centuries very well. The bagpipe/synthesizer/combo guitar did. In 1966, Afro-American **Rufus Harley** played Jazz Bagpipes on Al. NC '66 *Bagpipe Blues* (Michael Ochs' *1,000 Album Covers*).

"Quiet Village" – Martin Denny, #4, 4-59; #11, 5-59 R & B. Lucian Moga ('Luch') the cool priest's kid (Roumanian Orthodox) in my 10th-grade class, gently got up and walked out of class when our history teacher Ms. W—— went berserk? Why did the poor gal go ape kazinga? And chase Luch around the room? It's all Martin Denny's fault! Julius Wechter's, too. Progressive Non-Native Hawaiian Jazz. *Gold Rush* and Jazz celebrate multiculturalism.

Native New Yorkers, Denny and Wechter (marimba and vibraphone) skimmed across the Big Pacific Pond to Hawaii, for a territory destined for everybody's paradise and 1959 statehood. Later with the Baja Marimba Band (easy exotic Progressive Jazz), Wechter womped the welkin with #41, 12-63 "Comin' in the Back Door." He played on the Vaughn Monroe classic "(Ghost) Riders in the Sky" #1(12), 4-49 – longer at #1 than anything in the Rock Era 1955 until the "End of the Road" #1(13) by **Boyz II Men** in 1992.

Film legend **James Dean** cut a record playing bongos, (no vocal). Denny's August Colon bopped bongos; Harvey Ragsdale handled bass and the exotic marimbula. Armed with this line-up, Denny added an exotic palm-tree aviary array of birdcalls – macaws, parrots, tawny frogmouths, ostriches, emus, and Birds of Paradise. With these *Exotica* #1(5), 5-59 special BIRD effects, Martin Denny struck it rich. We all imagined tromping through sultry jungles of voluptuous verdure and romantic intrigue. Actually, we were all at the Holler-Dollar Car Wash, the U-Pull-'Em-Self-Service-Dental-Emporium, or the Fried-Fritters-Fill-'er-Up, Eat and Get Gas Roadhouse. Or in the back of Ms. W—-'s class, creating Martin **Denny**, via **Denny** Jaggers and the Bear.

Denny Jaggers sat on one side of class; the Bear (my big redheaded hockey star pal Jack 'the Bear' Berry) sat on the other. Ms. W— jiggled in consternation and despair, not looking directly at them. The Bear, Luch, Jags, and the rest of us would do our Martin Denny impressions: CAW-CAWS to lead off, followed by ear-piercing AAAIIIEEE, GAAAAWWWRRRK, BAG-A-DA-GAGGAK, YIYIYIYIYIYIYI, and the ever-lovely SCROOOOO BEEEEE DOO! Ms. W—-'s daily lesson plan cowered in Limbo. An ugly chorus of adolescent aviary squawkers and earthbound aardvarks, and amorous rhinos and hippos and elephants, wailed and caterwauled and yelled and screamed. Only a few dutiful and beautiful girls (Sue Davis, Lenore Swan, Sherry Waltensberger, Diane Vollmer, Shirley Gonda) imitated giraffes and sat silently, smirking. When the poor teacher finally went bonkers, Luch coolly ambled out the door, unwilling to be whipped with the ugly stick (pointer) she dangerously brandished. "One of your teachers, I'm sorry to say," confessed Luch to the Principal's office battalion, "one of your teachers is goin' nuts."

It was all Martin Denny's fault. We all got off scot free. Luch, too. Denny's Exotic Jazz and jungle jive delivered Tarzanland to us Midwestern Rockabilly Rompers. How? Bongoes, Denny's passionate piano, and birds, birds, birds, BIRDS!!!

"Night Train" – Buddy Morrow, #27, 8-52. This song goes out to the memory of MICKEY SHORR! For all you Detroit dudes and dudettes, it's the Bewitching Hour, and by a Sawbuck to a Deuce you'll hear Buddy's "Night Train" for all the Cool Babes cruisin' Woodward, Eight Mile, or Telegraph in Dig-It Dearborn, Rampaging Roseville, Frantic Ferndale, and Blasting Bloomfield Hills!

Mickey Shorr was the BIG D's **Alan Freed, Dick Clark, Casey Kasem, Dick Biondi,** and **Wolfman Jack** all rolled into one. He prime-timed WXYZ radio, the coolest call letters in the USA, and then shifted to evenings to squeeze in his *Bandstand*-style TV show. Big, bespectacled, bombastic, Shorr was major Teddy Bear DJ guru for the town that created Hitler's defeat from our smoke and soot and steel factories. The **Big D**, riding high in 1957 to swagger and swoon and groove-a-tune, was mesmerized by the swingin' sway of Shorr and his DJ and early VJ thrall. Shorr had his own language. Via his TV dance show like *American Bandstand*, we eager tennyboppers got to tell time ("A Dime past Lucky Seven") in Shorr's cryptic jargon after we danced on his show: my cousin Darrell Amlin, my pal Janie Zimmerman, coolest of the cool Don Dunlop and Sheila Mervak.

Shorr (1921-88) had a few platter irons in the fire that almost panned out, when he wasn't hammering his Jazz theme, Morrow's "Night Train": #60, 6-62 Shorr's *Ben Casey* spoof "Dr. Ben Basey," and Dickie Goodman duo, pie-facing the Cold War (#91, "Russian Band Stand," 5-59, as Spencer & Spencer). Shorr was the ultimate AM jock. His lingo scudded like a shooting star; he breezed alliterative gems ('kool kruising kats wailing along on wonderful Woodward Avenue under soft summer skies . . .") To be a disc jockey in the big 50s metro sprawl meant unbridled power – you might say, a big DJ's hypnotizing power over the teenage world was much much more dynamic than the influence of the President of the United States. Power and glory.

We were all saddened when Mickey Shorr was mysteriously demoted to Car Speaker tycoon. In the Payola aftermath of 1959, our pal Mickey somehow got banished from his beloved air waves, Ritchie and the Bopper's plane crashed, and Rock and Roll had been stolen by a "bunch of Bobbys" with perfect waterfall haircuts, dimples, and fairly good songs. For the rest of his life, Shorr sloshed around his Auto Speaker car radio franchises, stuffing long green into National Bank of Detroit. We missed his booming friendly baritone and his mystic vision at the 'Bewitching Hour' (midnight).

The chugging "Night Train," bleary with smoke and steam and time's ravages, finally caught up with me: Yaphank, Long Island. In 1988, my wife and I went to Alphonso's Midnight Palladium – and bandleader **Buddy Morrow** showed up. Morrow could have been Tommy Dorsey, Harry James, or Benny Goodman, but he was a tad out of sync. Morrow started a fine Big Band in 1952 (like Brian Setzer in 1996), just two years before a sideburned Memphis truck driver swamped the Big Band Era in a tidal wave of Rock and Roll. Morrow apprenticed with **Artie Shaw, Tommy Dorsey, Bunny Berigan** (trumpet, 1909-42, #4, "Honeysuckle Rose") and venerable **Paul Whiteman**, establishing himself as one of the top Jazz trombone players in the world. Buddy won bandleader stardom with an unsung band cover of **Frankie Laine's** "Jezebel" #2(2), 5-51 flipside, Laine's #3 "Rose, Rose, I Love you," (#8 Morrow). In the Pre-Rock Era, one good song might have seven big hit versions.

We shared the same nickname, 'Mo.' Buddy was born (1919) Muni "Mo" Zudekoff, smoothing his trombone tone with the Yale Collegians. The Jazz Rock ambassador gestured at his new Big Band. "Look at these guys, Mo, just look at 'em. Big bands never really fade away. We always did Jazz. We did Jazz Rock before anybody named it. I've always believed in the big beat!"

Then the energetic young septuagenarian bounced energetically back to his magic bandstand, stuffed with twenty-something trumpeters, peach-fuzz sax jockeys, and oboe hoboes. He kicked his power percussion sound off with a tremendous trombone tacet. They flew away on hot, throbbing wings of golden sound to Stardustland.

"Grazing in the Grass" – Friends of Distinction, #3, 4-69; #5, 4-69 R & B. What? English class? Verb declensions in Jazz Rock and Soul? He digs it, she digs it, whatever . . . Two L.A. guys, Floyd Butler and Harry Elston, harmonized with two L.A. girls, Jessica Cleaves and Barbara Love. Buttressed by modified a Streetcorner pattern, "Grazing" is a great funky Jazz Soul groove. Hit rebound? #6, 3-70 "Love Me or Let Me Be Lonely."

"New York State of Mind" – Billy Joel, NC, 1976. From Al. #122, 6-76 *Turnstiles.* Proving that William Martin Joel (b. 5-9-49 Hicksville, Long Island) is deeply steeped in Jazz, one need only access this critically-unacclaimed masterpiece third charted album. Joel opens with a Sinatran piano treble flourish. Gathering momentum, he adds some of the best: **Liberty DeVito**, his faithful long-time drummer; Doug Stegmeyer on bass; and midnight-halo saxman Richard Cannata. Billy's loving lyric describes a city's mood and ambience the way other lesser lyricists might simply describe a pretty girl. Rejecting Hollywood and Miami and glitzy escapes, Billy makes the pilgrimage from his middle-class suburb Hicksville to the Hudson River line-up of skyscrapers and Broadway and untold glory. He spins a tale of smoke and sorrow and ecstasy and after-hours adventure, and oilslick rainbows in the drizzly dawn.

On the same album, Joel jumps from a similar jazz intro, where Broadway lights dim in an Energy Crisis power failure – but then he wrests the power, surges the big amps, and cuts footloose and fancy-free over the Rock and Roll dominion he commandeers. Billy Joel is grounded in utter respect for the John Coltranes and Charlie Minguses and Dave Brubecks and Quincy Joneses (b. '33, Chicago, #14, 12-81 "One Hundred Ways"). Rather than keep up with the Joneses, however (or Jerry Lee Lewises), Joel fashions his own Jazz Rock statement – albeit it one with a 'New York State of Mind.' He somehow melds a century of great American popular music into his smoky tenor and goldfaring keyboard expeditions.

"The Boy from New York City" – Manhattan Transfer, #7, 5-81. Take a basic Blues hook, in, say, Key of 'E' – do an **E-E6-E7-E6-E** up and down run. Tim Hauser, Janice Siegel, and crew offer this vignette of a cool Playboy pad New York 60s 'Seinfeld'-style guy – mohair suits, spending loot, dynamite apartment, cool car, stacked and stocked bar; Jerry Seinfeld, in the fitness fandango 90s, canned the bar for an eighteen-volume cereal cupboard to feed Cosmo Kramer, or *Friends* like Rachel or Ross. Original by **Ad-Libs**, led by lead **Mary Ann Thomas** of Newark (#8, 1-65). "Kool Kitty" purrs to pals about a superhunk from Big Apple. Don't confuse Manhattan Transfer with the **Manhattans** ("Kiss and Say Goodbye", #1, 4-76) and Philly Soul Thompkins'-style tenor **Gerald Alston**. Each is ultra cool. Ultra soulful and Jazz-tinged.

"Tight Rope" – Leon Russell, #11, 8-72. With a leathery vibrato voice just as beautiful as Joe Cocker's, Russell walks a Jazz-Rock-Ballad tightrope. He uses a stubbly bass. He tightropes between life and some macabre funereal pyre. Silver-haired Russell strolls through his song on tiptoe kool-kat feet.

"Moonlight Feels Right" – Starbuck, #3, 4-76. Bo Wagner plays perhaps the fastest, most 'totally awesome' marimba/vibes solo in Rock history. For vibes, also catch Be-Bop sound of #2, 2-50 "Rag Mop" with vibe maestro **Lionel Hampton**. Starbuck stars offer romantic rendezvous song about the dazzling lights of Baltimore and steamy summery Chesapeake Bay. Bruce Blackman doubles lead vocal/keyboards in this Atlanta septet's only top ten tune. Name? After Starbuck – Ahab's first mate, second in command of fated Pequod in *Moby Dick.* Starbuck was the only one with any brains to survive

Ahab's mad monomaniac quest to pursue the malevolent whale around the globe. Sadly, Melville's Starbuck went down with the ship. Sadder, so did fleeting fame.

"More Than a Feeling" – Boston, #5, 9-76. **Brad Delp**, lead singer from Boston, Massachusetts, wakes up to gush of cloud, and croaked sun. (Boston, or Blackpool – a sad weather forecast). The song begins on the straight dominant **D** chord. A herd of flangers, distortion, and digital delay murmurs in the keyboardist **Tom Scholz**'s background, waiting to pounce on the unsuspecting chorus. When Delp hits the elusive word 'sun,' he's flinging a triplet melisma – not Mickey Mouse music.

Delp says he loses himself inside a familiar old song. Great universal line, eh? Village Jazz aficionados got literally stoned, bobbing and weaving in a Buddha crouch, 'swinging in' druglessly to favorite Jazz albums by Miles Davis, Maynard Ferguson (Al. #22, 4-77 *Conquistador*), and the immortal **Charlie Bird Parker** (1921-55, Bebop sax guru). Rock fans now took their escapism music that seriously. As Delp tunes into the cosmic vibes, Boston slips away too – brandishing a tonic **G** chord with **Barry Goudreau**'s guitar flashing flangers. And bassman Fran Sheehan sat, not on the expected low 'G' note, but on the thirds note 'B'. This is Jazz.

Armenian-American Sib Hashian pounds the percussion. "More" doesn't sport way-out 2 a.m. Jazz chords like **Eb9+5** or anything, but it does fire off the odd oddity: a chromatic modulation of **F#m** a half tone below the tonic; and a **Bm** mediant third minor grabs the dominant **D** major, with a thirds F# bass note. The whooshing of the "Effects Box" of wah-wah wizardry makes a dynamic audio panorama out of Goudreau's brassy axe. By 1975, guitar amps went from ON and OFF to many mystic new moods.

"Amanda" – Boston, #1(2), 9-86. Goudreau always sought the stars; his other group was Orion the Hunter in Boston's interim. Orion? #58, 6-84 "So you Ran" – Orion is the most bright constellation in the winter sky, sparked by stars Rigel and Betelgeuse. "Amanda" preceded #9 "We're Ready" 12-86 and #20, 3-87 "Can't-cha Say (You Still Believe in Me)/Still in Love." Back to basics (#51, 6-94) with "I Need Your Love."

Jazz Rock was also spurred onwards by the spontaneous Beat poetry of Allen Ginsberg (1926-97). Touring with **John Lennon** and **Yoko Ono**, Ginsberg played an accordion-type squeeze box, chanted his Hindu mantra OM, and sang Blake's "Little Lamb" in the quavering bass boom of a cantor. Sporting a Moses-style massive beard embracing his kindly owlish eyes, Ginsberg was **Jack Kerouac**'s best friend (and character 'Carlo Marx' in *On the Road*). In *On the Road*, semi hero Dean Moriarty (actually **Neal Cassady**, who later toured with the **Grateful Dead** on their Ken Kesey magic

Bus excursion) goes absolutely wild listening to far-out piano Jazz improvisations of white English piano maestro **George Shearing** – who inspired three major Soul pianists who were also blind like Shearing – **Al Hibbler** (1915-2001, Al. #20, 8-56 *Starring Al Hibbler*), **Ray Charles**, and **Stevie Wonder**. Shearing's big hit? #25, 5-49 international million-seller "September in the Rain" with his Shearing Quintet. Shearing toured with "Velvet Fog" (1925-99) **Mel Torme** (#1 "Careless Hands" 3-49).

Fans make or break musical careers. The Beats were the essential jazz fans. When Allen Ginsberg gravitated to Rock and Roll – Kerouac never did – he took a world of Folk-Rock fandom along with them. And he spoon-fed them Jazz Rock. His poetry rocks!

"Against the Bourgeois!
You raise your hip and dandy costume
Against the Money Establishment,
You pogo to garage bands."

– Allen Ginsberg, "To the Punks of Dawlish," 11-18-79, in *Collected Poems 1947-80*. New York: Harper & Row, 1988.

Be they rich or ragtag, Rock fans can move the universe. I sat with **Allen Ginsberg** after he played his accordion for 10,000 screaming Ann Arbor, Michigan, fans waiting for **John Lennon** and Yoko to show up. If you dig out their obscure *Sometime in New York City* (Al. #48, 7-72), you'll unearth song "John Sinclair." John, leader of the White Panther Party, was busted and swiftly tossed into jail for ten years for possession of two pot joints. Two. Smoking anything is a community event for all who breathe nearby. After 10,000 'Free John Sinclair' pilgrims showed up at the Arena with candles and prayers and weed, the Ann Arbor City Council tossed out the Old Guard. The new 3-2 majority of Ann Arbor People's Party members voted in a new marijuana law in 1971. Those nailed for one joint had to pay a $5 fine. They could mail it in . . .

Revolutions are peculiar. The Rock Revolution changed the planet. Many ragamuffin guerrilla armies have rampaged roughshod over bigger, stronger military juggernauts. Witness the Chechnyans and the Afghanistanis versus the Russians.

Sinclair dashed off a sparkly book called *Guitar Army* (see Punk Rock **MC5**). Long forgotten, the book presents a revolution of guitar-slinging, peace-loving, pot-puffing pilgrims on the road to the Lennon/Ginsberg utopia in "Imagine" (#3, 10-71). The Yoko-John song about Sinclair is long defunct and extinct, a dinosaur of yesteryore. "Imagine" thrives, though, and Sinclair's *Guitar Army*'s big beat goes marching on. With three chords and a dream, any band could now rule the upper atmosphere . . . in a domain once reserved for angels.

"Bad, Bad, Leroy Brown" – Frank Sinatra, #83, 4-74. Sinatra? No angel. Neither was I. Neither are you. Leroy is 'badder' than super-ape Old King Kong, and meaner than any junkyard mutt that is 50% teeth. Indeed, Brown is an icon of sorts – the bad ghetto dude; his first name buzzes the multitude that Leroy is probably either Black or French, where his name means (LeRoi) the KING. **Jim Croce** (#1[2], 4-73) and his original "Leroy" hit toyed with Ebonics [Afro-American English] a full generation before white Rappers like **Eminem**. Croce follows the royal theme and calls him 42nd Street's King (a less than pious NYC address). After years of not being the World's Biggest Rock and Roll fan, legendary croonmaster **Frank Sinatra** (1915-98) finally joined the bandwagon with his Cool Jazz (or Easy Listening Adult Contemporary Jazz Rock) version of Croce's #1 story, a gamblers' showdown in "Stagger Lee" & "Frankie and Johnny" tradition. Though #2-Ever Album Artist Sinatra might not be super gung-ho to admit it, Jazz icon Sinatra rocked a bit on past blasts: #1(4), 8-46 "Five Minutes More"; and #3, 10-56 "Hey! Jealous Lover" of 10-56. Sinatra, of course was a national treasure for his Un-Rock slow Jazz 2 a.m. melancholy sound like #27, 1-49 masterpiece "Autumn in New York." Frank's "Leroy" is nowhere near his first interlude with a Jazz-Rock pairing. Try his #75 "Everybody's Twistin'" of the Kennedy Era (4-62), when Sinatra and the Prez were good friends. Sinatra's 'Rat Pack' pal Peter Lawford married into the American 'royal' Kennedy family. Frank swings on "Leroy Brown." Nice Big Band rendition. *Gold Rush* finale features a Jazz-icon Sinatra section.

"Smoke on the Water" – Deep Purple, #4, 6-73. Heavy Metal? Hard Rock, Acid Rock, or Mainstream Rock and Roll? It's an actual story about a burnt-out concert in Switzerland (Montreux Casino) over the water of a breathtakingly beautiful Swiss mountain lake (with a Heavy Metal tale by Coverdale). "Smoke" brings back a lot of lakeside memories to the lakester Deans, too.

"Smoke on the Water" uses the same chord chain as "Wake Up Little Susie" (Everlys) or "Money" (Barrett Strong), and shadows the Stones' "Satisfaction." You shoot from tonic **G** (I) up to a chromatic flatted three major **Bb** (bIII) and to the sub-dominant **C** (IV). And back. "Smoke" is powered by a thundering fuzz bass and a deep throbbing rhythm guitar covering octaves just above on the same patterns with bar chords. Then it kicks in a JAZZ newie – the **C#** chord (bV or #IV). You run the riff once. The second swing by, you fly up a half tone:

G—Bb—C,   G—Bb—C#—C,   G—Bb—C—Bb—G

That's it. The magic run. Whenever you hear that big golden oldie, they're pounding that riff into hyperspace.

"Smoke" is no simple Heavy Metal rock song. Its bashing bonanza of Deep Purple chords sheathes a savvy musical sophistication. Deep Purple commands the center of the Art Rock or Heavy Metal movements. Vocalist **David Coverdale** formed **Whitesnake**, with bass guy **Glenn Hughes** gravitating to Ozzy's **Black Sabbath**. Jazz Rock here. Many hats they wore.

As Art Rockers, too, Deep Purple joins the **Moody Blues, Procul Harum**, and **ELO**, plus "Smoke on the Water's" headlining act **Frank Zappa**. Now and then they tacked on some 101-piece orchestra [whoever afforded these session costs must have been a maestro of macroeconomics her/himself].

Despite its blood-and-thunder rhythm rampage, "Smoke on the Water" and "Amie" remind me of sweet 70s summertime on Long Lake, Oakland County, Michigan. On these halcyon water-ski weekends of high July, blue shimmering lakes ripple; puffy cumulus clouds float over dippy dragonflies and blonde beach bombshells. We celebrated summer at the drive-in movie with our beloved state bird (the mosquito), and dashed to the Dairy Queen for a brisk Breeze, whirling in strawberry raspberry marshmallow glee over sweet frozen yogurt glaciers of Antarctic glory.

The 4th of July brings our slightly-illegal Fireworks-aroma to Long Lake. Neighbors horde everything from cherry bombs to dynamite until America's birthday blastoff. At pearly flamingo sundown over the deep-blue lake, a flash and a flare, and rockets' red glare, bombard the sleepy shore. Swirling streamers of gold and green and PURPLE and red-white-and-blue cascade out of the smoky 10:00 p.m. gloaming midsummer Michigan skies. It's a hot rush of golden America and purple twilight glory.

And the fireworks? What happens to a clear Michigan night, bludgeoned by the powerhouse pandemonium of Deep Purple's guitar man **Ritchie Blackmore**, and keyboard whiz **Jon Lord**? After the fireworks, it gets very smoky. Green and blue and red smoke rain down on the darkling lake. Dazed ducks, astounded bluegills and incredulous largemouth bass gaze, bulgy eyes agog, at the audiovisual assault. You get . . . you guessed,

SMOKE ON THE WATER – FIRE INTO THE SKY.

Heralded as the UK Heavy Metal anthem, "Smoke on the Water" is also a prelude to R & R sophistication through Jazz Rock chordal experimentation. Ex-Searchers ("Needles and Pins" '64) drummer **Chris Curtis, Ian Gillian**, and **Rod Evans** sang, and the hot purple band coalesced. **Joe South**'s "Hush" (#52, 9-67 Billy Joe Royal) hit beginners' luck for Purple's worthy cause (#4, 8-68). So did **Neil Diamond**'s #22, 10-67 "Kentucky Woman." (Purple hit #38, 11-68). **David Coverdale** heisted the lead singer spot late in 1973.

Not bad for a Jazz Rock outfit that fired off *cadenzas* of smoky improvisations into three symphonic movements. Their 1969 *Concerto* album (NC) is an Orchestral Rock pinnacle, with Malcolm Arnold conducting the **Royal Philharmonic**. Deep Purple crested with Al. #7 *Machine Head* of 4-72; Al. #6, 4-73 *Made in Japan*; and Al. #9, 3-74 *Burn*. Cadenzas are solos by excellent individual musicians.

Deep Purple fires off some incredible guitar speedwork from **Blackmore** and keyboard expert **Lord**.

The song's background has to do with a fire at a 12-3-71 Montreux concert over Lake Geneva, Switzerland, a fan riot of overexuberance. In songs, our OWN memories of the tune are, symbolically, maybe more important to US than the actual occurence in the hit song's genesis. [Like, who cares what went down at the recording session, if the song reminds us of some magic night of love somewhere else]. Deep Purple opened for Frank Zappa at the feted fated concert (info Whitburn).

"Hush" – Billy Joe Royal, #52, 9-67. All this stuff interconnects. Billy Joe Royal was **Gene Pitney**'s greatest vocal protégé. Joe South wrote Royal's thought-provoking material like "Down in the Boondocks," #9, 7-65. Royal had the first "Hush." Irish tenor Royal injects deep feeling and punchy Southern Rock rhythm track. Should have been #7 or so. When "Smoke" screen subsided, Deep Purple never did.

"Runaround" – Blues Traveler, #8, 3-95. #1 harmonica player, NYC's **John Popper**, wheezes out starry clusters, entire Andromeda or Milky Way nebulas of notes, in the small span of a quick solo on the song's bridge. Lyrics are surreal, via Blues Traveler's Jazz genius.

"This Masquerade" – George Benson, #10, 6-76; #3, 5-76 R & B. Following in the fret steps of guitar guru **Wes Montgomery**, Pittsburgh's Benson adds his precise intriguing vocals to this **Leon Russell** song. Minor-key mood suggests Martin Denny's *Exotica*. As an R & B/Jazz guitarist, Benson rates among the top. Soul Jazz cameos? The Muhammad Ali movie song "The Greatest Love of All" – #24, 7-77; a reprise of the Drifters' "On Broadway" (Benson #7, 3-78); and his largest chart goodie, #4, 7-80 "Give Me the Night." All Benson's songs quiver with polychordal discoveries in a mellow mood.

"Can't Take My Eyes Off You" – Frankie Valli, #2(1), 5-67. Frankie Valli apprenticed his falsetto by studying Pop Standards, assimilating their timing and delivery. This song slides through a sheaf of suave minor keys. An ethereal organ floats on high. Valli gently fondles the mood as succinctly as Sinatra swoons his enchanting #6, 1-58 "Witchcraft." Catch Valli's wistful "My Eyes Adored You" – #1(1), 12-74; ode to a fantasy, he's never touched and caressed the girl of his dreams. Only dreamed.

"Lovin' You" – Minnie Riperton, #1(1), 1-75; #3 R& B. Her lyric soprano flits to high coloratura like **Mariah Carey**, and flirts there awhile with notes of celestial fire. Riperton's potential was tragically curtailed (1947-79). Her only other hit? The modest #76, 8-75 "Inside My Love."

"Honky Tonk (Parts I & II)" – Bill Doggett, #2(3), 8-56; #1(13) R & B. Long Island's Rock and Soul pioneer Doggett (1916-96) fired up his scorchy horn section and his own mesmerizing Hammond B-3 organ. Doggett was also blessed with a #26 hit, "Slow Walk," in 11-56.

Doggett's "Honky Tonk" instrumental got stuck at #2 behind an Elvis monster tune. Essence of Slow Boogie-Woogie 12-Bar Blues. Double-sided unforgettable rhythm guitar, a first-rate growly sax, and snappy counterbeat to warm the stormiest winter night.

"Muskrat Love" – Captain & Tennille, #4, 9-76. Toni and Capt. Daryl Dragon whuffle a whispery and wildly weird Jazz ballad about the amorous muskrats Susie and Sam. They snuggle up together in a minor-key profusion of wiggly, squiggly smooches down in the reedy old swamp. Hot stuff. Freddy 'Boom Boom' Cannon did "Muskrat Ramble" (#54, 1-61), reprising Jazz icon **Louis** 'Satchmo' **Armstrong**'s #8, 7-26 debut "Muskrat Ramble."

"Like Long Hair" – Paul Revere & the Raiders, #38, 3-61. Long before British Invasion backlash, Paul did Orchestral Rock. Actually "Rach", pronounced Rock, via **Sergei Rachmaninoff**'s "Prelude in C-Sharp Minor." Armed with a new electric piano (see **Ray Charles**'s #6, 6-59 "What'd I Say"), Portland, Oregon's Raiders raided the classics for one of R & R's premier early instrumentals.

"Bumble Boogie" – B. Bumble & The Stingers, #21, 3-61. R.C. Gamble, L.A. electric piano session guy, and friends wailed out on Rimsky-Korsakov's classic "Flight of the Bumble Bee" (Freddy Martin, too, #7, 5-46, on alto sax; **Jack Fina** on unplugged piano). Gamble split for 2nd big instrumental hit for Bumble, #23 "Nut Rocker," lightly lifted from also-Russian Peter I. Tchaikovsky's (1840-93) *Nutcracker* ballet (3-62). Russian Rock and Roll?

"Alone at Last" – Jackie Wilson, #8, 10-60; #20, 11-60 R & B. From our Great Singers chapter. Wilson's Brunswick producers conveniently 'found' this everlasting melody in Tchaikovsky's "Piano Concerto in B Flat" opus. Hmm – any Russian Musical Invasions in 1960-61? Orchestral Rock is an oddly Russian-American phenomenon, launched like Sputnik at the height of the Cold War (1960 pilot Gary Powers U-2 spy plane incident). One cheesy chunk of dramatic irony, for your pleasure: the old Malenkov/Bulganin and Stalinist Soviet Union forbade Rock and Roll; a whole generation missed Chuck Berry, Buddy Holly, Elvis – even the Beatles. (They did allow Jazz stars Louis 'Satchmo' Armstrong, Benny Goodman, Dave Brubeck). Finally **Blood, Sweat, and Tears** was allowed to tour and later **Billy Joel**, because they incorporated more sophisticated Jazz Rock into their act.

Old Russian tunes came trickling into America, devoid of copyright protection through ASCAP and BMI. We scarfed them up as freebies.

Is Orchestral Rock a communist conspiracy, one might query? Nah. No way. It's a Czarists' (or pre-1917 Tsarist) conspiracy. Conversely, Rock was seen as decadent Anglo-American music that would rot young Soviet minds:

"Back in the U.S.S.R." – Beatles, NC, 1968. Super spoof, Beatles take off on B.O.A.C. British Airways. Beach Boy echo. Surf Romp Rock? Balaiaikas substitute for guitars in Soviet Georgian S.S.R. down near firestrom Chechnya.

Orchestral Rock, then, started with Buddy Holly's "True Love Ways" and "Moondreams," 1960 instrumentals, and **Jackie Wilson** – not, as some bouncy bandwagon R & R texts now claim, by BS&T, Zappa, or Chicago (excellent outfits all). Or the Moody Blues or Procul Harum.

***Cruising with Ruben and the Jets* – Frank Zappa and the Mothers of Invention, Al. #110, 12-68.** Zappa's esoteric breed of Rock and Roll lampooned his Garage Band brethren, plus some 50s Rockabillies that Zappa visualized as having the brains of a spaghetti squash. Frank and Mothers become 'Ruben & Jets,' a garage-band rabble of rockers. One cut concerns a Pterodactyl. The big dinosaur bird is dying. Why? 'For her love.' Or to ooze into our Mobiloil, umpteen years later.

"Valley Girl" – Frank Zappa, with daughter Moon Unit Zappa, #32, 7-82. Frank and Progeny sling Valley Girl satire. Incorporates jargon of Overprivileged *Beverly Hills 90210* California Mall Buffs . . . stuff like 'gnarly' and like 'like'. Wildfire success for a cult hero and his kid. Other provocative titles? Yup, one — #86, 10-74 "Don't Eat the Yellow Snow." Zappa zapped all institutions, even Disco Rock in #105, 3-77 "Disco Boy" or #45 jibe 4-79 "Dancin' Fool." Frank wasn't a real fan of the draft either: #103, 5-80 "I Don't Wanna Get Drafted."

Zappa (1940-93) was of Sicilian ancestry and sported a special tuft of jazzman hirsutitude – a thick black clump of hair on his lower lip south of his mouth, a 'Soul Patch.' Not quite a goatee. Born in Baltimore, he traded coasts for California at 10, and apprenticed himself on Russian composers (Stravinsky) and Soul music (1st band, the Soul Giants, became the Mothers). Their 1st album *Freak Out* (Al. #130, 2-67), joins **Marty Robbins'** #6, 12-59 earliest concept albums *Gunfighter Ballads and Trail Songs*, in beating Beatles' [*Sgt.*] *Pepper* Power to the CONCEPT ALBUM. *Freak Out!* patterns **Ruben**, with one cut "Wowie Zowie," an excellent example of Zappa's iconoclastic ability to zap everybody, regardless of race, color, or greed.

Zappa's album career, much rosier than his singles slump, included nine top 40's. Highlights? *Apostrophe(')* — #10, 5-74, and an album named after cartoonist Roger Price's 1953 *Droodle* fad, Zappa's #23, 7-82 *Ship Arriving too Late to Save Drowning Witch*. His daughter Moon Unit became a famous Vee-Jay – as the *MTV* and *VH-1* monolith expanded.

Zappa dabbles in classical forms, like the rondo, the atonal unmetered experiment, the arch (A B C B A [Stuessy]). He also explores classical composers beyond **Bach-Beethoven-Brahms** (or the Beatles) – **Cage, Varese, Stockhausen, Strindberg**.

Up on US-10 near Reed City, compositional home of "The Old Rugged Cross," there's a delightful log-cabin lodge, the Emerson Lake Inn. It overlooks a Royal Blue pristine Michigan lake, and little rustic cabins that waft aromas of woodsy yesterday. You murmur . . . "Hmm, Emerson Lake, where is Palmer?"

"Nutrocker" – Emerson, Lake, and Palmer, #70, 3-72. EL & P establish their own unique groove on the B. Bumble & Stingers 1962 "Nut Rocker" Tchaikovsky sleight-of hand. **Keith Emerson** (no relation to Ralph Waldo) became the most important person in the ART ROCK movement. The band's NC, 1969 *Five Bridges Suite* somehow hired the Sinfonia of London Orchestra for their Jean Sibelius (wrote *Finlandia*) "Intermezzo." Their starburst symphony spliced snitches of Dylan's "Country Pie" with Bach's *Brandenburg Concerto IV*. Then they tucked in **Leonard Bernstein**'s (NY Philharmonic conductor) *West Side Story* (#1 [54], 10-61), and its classic Latin Rock song "America." The E, L, P & P album was so technically magnificent that naturally it flopped commercially.

"Karn Evil 9" – Emerson, Lake, and Palmer, NC, 1973. The MOST COMPLEX ROCK AND ROLL SONG ever recorded – (Stuessy). Emerson combined with **King Crimson** (*In the Wake of Poseidon* Al. #31, 9-70; top single #80, 1-70 "The Court of the Crimson King"). Singer/guitarist **Greg Lake** and snare drummer **Carl Palmer** came from Atomic Rooster and the Crazy World of Arthur Brown ("Fire" #2, 9-68). Armed with heavy artillery of musical talent, they launched Al. #11, 12-73 *Brain Salad Surgery*.

No three-chord rippy bippy garage-band song, "Karn Evil 9" ensnares a half hour of your life. It embraces three 'Impressions' or movements, like a concerto. The first is a dreary woebegone landscape (like Poe's "Ulalume" or "Usher" or his midnight-dreary "Raven") with a somber intro, three grim verses, and a short coda or codetta to space the movements. Palmer's percussion pans the lyrical mood, creating a complex web of unrelated beats, with Lake's bass patterns in tow. Part II zings a zestier tempo, and dovetails into seven verses; they run the Rock and Roll gamut, flashing back to Ragtime, surfing the vortex, and dredging up a happy/sad carnival with the AAB pattern verses. They pounce upon a pedal point (Stuessy), a constant note that keeps on playing, despite the complex kit-and-kaboodle of chords and arpeggios twirling above and beyond.

Remember, "Karn Evil 9" is just three British Midlands guys. No London Philharmonic. Forecasting the Rap 'sampling' craze, Emerson's multiple-keyboard swoon takes him to an ancient oldie samples on the upright: "Alexander's Ragtime Band," which ran away with the Rock Toddler Era honors: #1(10), 9-1911 by **Arthur Collins** (baritone) and Byron Harlan (tenor). Also #2(1) on 11-11-11 for **Billy Murray** (1877-1954), the MOST POPULAR RECORD SELLER OF THE PRE-1920 era.

From the frolicking fun stuff of Movement Two, 'Karn' fans descend into the slurpy maelstrom. No super carny of 2/4 Ragtime/Dixieland/Baby Rock and Roll here. Back to Armageddon, *Apocalypse Now****, the frying pan, and the fire. The hero grapples with a Computer Monster, achieving a Pyrrhic victory. The organ duels the tympani, and the whole thing lurches off into a state-of-the-art sequencer. Sequencers, like juke boxes of yore, carved the future out of musicians' souls. The machine, like folk song "John Henry (Steel-Drivin' Man)": of #20, 1927 **Gil Tan-**

ner fame, pits noble John Henry, sledge-hammerer, versus the wicked steam drill. The exhausted muscleman Henry beat the drill. He won the battle, then collapsed. You can plug in a whole brainy sequence of fancy rhythms, reverberant timbres, multiple pitches, and cavernous volumes into your synthesizer. Then you can walk away and it becomes your creation. In a sense, it becomes you. Emerson, Lake, and Palmer foretold the futuristic direction of 80s and 90s Techno-Synth Rock and Roll. In a way, it's miraculous. In a way, it's creepy. Technology can be an improvement, or it can rip the heart out of a living, breathing musician – and then track down his soul.

"Lucky Man" – Emerson, Lake, and Palmer, #48, 3-71; #51, 12-72. It's the sarcastic EL & P tune everybody hears at US-1 Auto Parts Emporium, the Taystee Freeze Slurperama, or Piggly-Wiggly's Liver-Land aisle. With Everly harmony, this supposed 'lucky man' takes his lumps on the chin. Fate punts "Lucky."

"Soul Inspiration" – Anita Baker, #72, 9-90; #16 R & B. Nifty Soul-Jazz twinge to Toledo and Detroit's star on Elektra. Not all Jazz-Rock songs are as complicated as "Karn Evil 9?"

"Puttin' on the Ritz" – Taco, #4, 6-83. Thirties flashback. Indonesia has over a hundred million people now, spread out on an archipelago of 50,000 islands in the tropical surf. Indonesia's biggest hit (next to Fil and Hari Goeltom)? **Taco Okerses** (Indonesian-Dutch rock star from capital Jakarta) mirrors 1930s celluloid Art Deco America. We rap a lot about R & R's connection to older forms of music; this one flips the format. Though Irving Berlin was among the World's Oldest (101) and MOST SUCCESSFUL (in number of hits) SONGWRITERS in history, he had only one top ten tune that he himself performed: #10, 6-1910 "Oh, How That German Could Love!" "Puttin' on the Ritz" is among Berlin's string of classic song pearls, and it made a rich man richer (Harry Richman & Orchestra, #1, 2-30). Richman never got smug about his #1 champ song. The vaudeville pianist and Broadway star became an aviator. In 1935 he set the world altitude record – and in 1936 he did Charles Lindbergh one-step better – the first trans-oceanic round-trip flight. Taco artfully renders this period piece, bolstered only by a snappy electric bass.

You hear a big theatre organ (Fox in Detroit or Radio City in Manhattan?) swooping *glissando* rushes after the second verse. Taco fades a phaser in on the clever internal rhyme of 1920 movie-mag lyric: when he mentions cowboy star 'Gary Cooper', two Betty Boop-time girls chime in "SUPER-DUPER" echo rhyme. "Ritz" describes NYC Big Rich folk who promenade Park Avenue adorned in spats, furs, high hats, tiaras, (and their 'snoots' in the 1930 air). The long song hits the bridge three times, with heavy vocal echo.

"Ritz" samples the big Byron Harlan-Billy Collins #1 and Billy Murray #2, 1911 hit "Alexander's Ragtime Band," too, like "Karn Evil 9," and soon clomps off on the Broadway skyway with conceited feet.

"Boogie Blues" – Gene Krupa, #9, 7-46. With **Buddy Rich**, among most respected drummers of Jazz/Big Band Era. Krupa could rock. We saw him once on Times Square (1962) playing one of his speedskins solos. Steamy, sultry 90° summersweat night. They opened the doors. Financially challenged at age 19, we watched the legendary **Gene Krupa** expand everybody's rhythmic consciousness, while we craftily ambled along the sidewalk outside, treasuring every booming beat. Krupa (1909-73) tattooed his sterling drum collection, smacking snares and tearing up tom-toms. He bashed the bass drum like a middleweight flurrying a volley of killer punches. "Boogie Blues" shows that R & R rhythm goes back a lot farther than "Rock Around the Clock." Even **Bill Haley**'s Rock and Roll far outdates his clock: #12, 5-53 "Crazy Man Crazy." Krupa created a lot of Rock drumming techniques. And hits: #2(1), 2-41 "High on a Windy Hill"; #7, 10-45 "Along the Navajo Trail"; and #9, 6-50 "Bonaparte's Retreat."

"Rag Mop" – Lionel Hampton, the Hamptones, and Orchestra, #7, 2-50; #4 R & B. When Hampton's dad was killed in WWI, the lad learned snare drum from a nun in Kenosha, Wisconsin. The beloved lad (b. 1913) went on to become the foremost vibraphone player of all time.

With his virtuoso drum and piano skills, Hampton apprenticed with **Benny Goodman** in the 1930s. Lionel & Orchestra's hits? #6, 11-37 "After You're Gone"; Be-Bop Jazz #9, 3-46 "Hey! Ba-Be-Re-Bop"; and "Wizzin' the Wiz" – at #10, 5-39.

Music, unlike some parts of 1930s America, was comparatively color-blind. A particular bond existed at that time between Jewish stars like Benny Goodman of Chicago and great Afro-American stars like Hampton. It was like the friendship between Detroit Tiger slugger **Hank Greenberg** (58 home runs in 1930s) and his 1947 rookie friend **Jackie Robinson**. Via his own orchestra and first hit with Gene Krupa on drums (Krupa white and Polish), Hampton took "The Mood That I'm In" to #20 in 1937; afterwards, he introduced some greats: stand-up bass player **Charlie Mingus**, who lavished 16th and 32nd and 24th-note runs like confetti; Tuscaloosa's great Jazz, Rock, and Soul star **Dinah Washington** (1924-63), who teamed with Brook Benton to a #7, 5-60 "A Rockin' Good Way (To Mess Around and Fall in Love)"; and the ever-cool **Quincy Jones** (b. '33, Chicago), producer-arranger-trumpet-star still kickin' out the jams: #9 platinum *Back on the Block*, of Christmas 1989, and #68, 4-96 "Slow Jams."

"Tonight" – Jay (Traynor) and the Americans, #120, 11-61. When Jay Traynor of Brooklyn and upstate Greenville, NY, split after their monster hit "She Cried" (#5, 3-62, chromatic bVII chord to glory), the Americans just found a new JAY. Jay and crew were signed by **Jerry Leiber** and **Mike Stoller** (*Smokey Joe's Café*, 1994+ Broadway Show and #79, '55 song for the Robins). Someone's cockamamie idea nearly named them 'BINKY JONES and the Americans.' Serious singer John Traynor, traumatized, settled for his first initial "J" instead of BINKY, leaving the yoks and guffaws to the Leiber-Stoller **Coast-**

ers. Traynor's "Tonight" highlights *West Side Story*. It blends classic Latin Chalypso, Rock and Roll, and Balladry.

When **David Black** showed up for their other American theme tune, #25, 8-63 "Only in America," he reluctantly became the new 'Jay,' scoffing uproariously at the BINKY BOMB of an idea. Traynor becam the BLUE Jay. "**Jay**" **Black**'s operatic Italian territone (low tenor-baritone combo) soared to nearly unrockable heights on their flurry of Classic Gold. One in particular:

"Cara, Mia" – Jay (Black) and the Americans, #4, 6-65. Reprise item by #8-album-sales giant **Mantovani** and vocal by David Whitfield #10, 8-54. **Jay and the Americans**' "Cara, Mia" has a smooth Chalypso rhythm and Streetcorner I-Vim-IV-V7 chord pattern that wafts through more complex progressions. Jay, in command of L ——— ——O———N———G note on word "die," shadowed the Carusos and Pavarottis and Placido Domingoes. Black reminisces: "When you had a hit song, songwriters would come to you with 'The Son of Cara Mia' or "Come Little Bit Closer Rides Again." "Closer" hit the #3, 9-64 pinnacle for the guys. Producers **Tommy Boyce** and **Bobby Hart** (#8, 12-67 "I Wonder What She's Doin' Tonight") only had one 'take' for Jay's vocal. Jay wasn't overjoyed: "How dare you release this?" he yelled at them from the Vince Lombardi Plaza on an I-80 New Jersey pay phone; he'd heard it on the radio. When the voice told him "Cara, Mia" was already on the charts, and zooming up fast, he snickered, and blurted, "Then disregard this call!" Other Jay and American Rock or Jazz Rock hits? Traynor debut #5, 3-62 "She Cried"; #25, 8-63 "Only in America"; #18, 11-65 "Sunday and Me"; #19, 11-69 "Walkin' in the Rain"; also Drifters' #16, 2-60 "This Magic Moment" at #6 for Jay, 12-68; the Orbison-Melson classic "Crying" #35, 5-66 (#2, 8-61 Big O). Jay(s) sang Jazz/Opera/Rock.

"Some Enchanted Evening" – Ezio Pinza, #7, 9-49. THE romantic ballad from *South Pacific*, by great BASS lead singer Pinza. His low notes shook rafters like **Paul Robeson**: #7, 6-28 "Ol' Man River" or "Negro Spiritual" (50s term) #19, 10-27 "Deep River." Jay's rendition (#13, 9-65) maintains the operatic girth, but shifts to high baritone/Italian tenor range; Jay's Chalypso beat ricochets a little R & R splendor into the mix.

"Stranger on the Shore" – Mr. Acker Bilk, #1(1), 3-62; #7 R & B. The peaceful haze-blue skies of placid Somerset shine warmly down on the beach; my wife and I spent one of our grandest days in plush Cornwall winding around Mr. Acker Bilk's A39 shores with our toddler Lauri in 1970. We marveled at peach-colored sands, jutting crags, lonesome gulls, and a California 72° peach of a day. You know this song. 'Mr.' Bilk's swirling clarinet fritters around the pretty notes. He swoops and swoons like a nightingale over the little lavender's-blue mountains that smooch the shore. His feathery song floats his joy to you, as you fondle the sunset over Bideford and Bridgewater Bay. If you never get anywhere else on this Rock and Roll Rainbow, someday see Ilfracombe,

Somerset. Some enchanted evening, its shore may swirl like Acker's golden clarinet for you. **Benny Goodman** was the #1 clarinetist: #5, 9-35 "Body and Soul"; #4, 10-36 "Love Me or Leave Me"; #4, 1-37 "Smoke Dreams"; and #1(3), 1-37 "This Year's Kisses." Goodman popularized SWING Jazz.

"Wonderland by Night" ("*Wonderland bei Nacht***") – Bert Kaempfert & Orchestra, #1(3), 11-60; #5, 12-60 R & B.** I only remember a January 1961 night of blue stars, icy snowbanks, and warm blue summer eyes. The sound track of my life resurges with memories of Bert Kaempfert's majestic love song – with **Charly Tabor** on the starboard trumpet solo. Bert Kaempfert produced the very first REAL Beatles recording. "Wonderland by Night" does for starlight and sleigh-bell moondreams what "Stranger on the Shore" does for a mellow easy summer mood, doing your very favorite nothing.

"Baker Street" – Gerry Rafferty (Raphael Ravenscroft sax solo**), #2(6), 4-78.** Ravenscroft coaxes a kick-rump soaring sax out of Baker's controlled savvy tenor vocal. Jumps with punchy Jazz riffs. Where does Rafferty hotfoot it to after Baker Street? "Right Down the Line" #12, 8-78, #1(4) Adult Contemporary. Jazz-Rock tune with a tricky chord progression.

"Year of the Cat" – Al Stewart, #8, 12-76. Kaleidoscope song. Stewart's slinky tenor pussyfoots into his song about comedian Tony Hancock. Stewart's wayfaring vocal slides around in the Key of 'G' – mostly in a murmuring '**E minor**.' Flashback Black and White Bogart & Peter Lorre moves – *Casablanca***** 1942. Stewart tomcats around, ogling this shimmering doll swathed in silk, swirling like watercolor paints. The pastel pastiche of her Monet garb gleams in a spritz of summer shower. After a hotcha tete-a-tete rendezvous – and swimming sensuously into the mediant major chord '**B**' or III or 'watercolor,' Stewart soars aloft to the bridge; the girl's eyes shine like a Honolulu moon hugging the iridescent sea. The quivering lass sports patchouli perfume. Incense cozies the boudoir. Voluptuous vignette of purple passion.

By garish dawn, the bus gobbles up the tourists and skedaddles. Stewart's Dylan & Garfunkel pen teems again with denouement, shattering the sharp sunshine in a strobe whirl of yesternight reverie. He still hears the drum pulse to a new rhythm of a new throbbing day. A magnificent confraternity of musicians: **Andrew Powell**'s string ensemble leads off to mellow cellos and **Bobby Bruce**'s ringing violin. Three guitars lateral the musical pigskin aloft, each climbing above the other to an EXCELSIOR mountaintop of guitar glee: Stewart, Tim Renwick, Peter White. A guitar climax shrieks shrilly. Just as it trails off, suddenly **Phil Kenzie**'s lofty alto sax comes screaming with rampaging power. Once on the mountaintop, it takes the whole band a long time to return to the kitty-kat in the valley below. A great moment in a great song.

JOHN COLTRANE (1926-67)

How can a guy be such a Jazz innovator and esoteric superstar – and never have a HOT 100 or R & B 100 hit? It happened to **Muddy Waters** on the HOT 100, but his R & B hits are legion. Such greats as **Bruce Springsteen, Creedence Clearwater Revival, Little Richard, Fats Domino**, and even **Bob Dylan** never had a #1 HOT 100 hit, but this is ridiculous. The greatest tenor sax man of all time, say Jazz fans, was **John Coltrane**. Sadly, *Gold Rush* follows the charts, so many of the greatest musicians get sidetracked into faint praise. Coltrane did place two of his excellent albums on *Billboard*'s charts: #194, 11-67 Al. *Expression*, and #186, 11-71 Al. *Sun Ship*. By the same token, we must flee from another great sax man, **Charlie 'Bird' Parker**, revered by even the *World Almanac* as the GREATEST JAZZ IMPROVISER OF ALL TIME in JAZZ (not Rock). Parker (1920-55) wove his musical magic on alto sax. His only charted hit – single OR album – was #15 R & B (only) 12-48 "Barbados."

Here's a list of some great Jazz superstars whose chart non-adventures or under-appreciated adventures are a sad commentary on the ignoring of genius by the garish popular arena: **Big Bill Broonzy** (Blues singer, guitarist), **Billy Taylor** (piano), **Al Cohn** (tenor sax), **Zoot Sims** (sax, clarinet), **Dizzy Gillespie** (trumpet, #22, 11-45 "Salt Peanuts"), **Sun Ra** (piano), **John McLaughlin** (Al. #15, 2-73 *Birds of Fire*, Jazz Fusion guitar), **Gerry Mulligan** (bari sax), **Red Nichols** (cornet/trumpet), **Kid Ory** (trombone), **Percy Heath** (Bass, Modern Jazz Quartet/MJQ), **Thelonius Monk** (piano), **Stan Kenton** (OK, many hits like #5, 9-50 "Orange Colored Sky"), **Lightnin' Sam Hopkins** (Blues singer/guitarist, NC Top 30, but #6, 3-52 R & B "Coffee Blues"), **Chuck Mangione** (Al. #2[2], 10-77 *Feels So Good*, flugelhorn), **Herbie Mann** (Al. #20, 5-69 *Memphis Underground*, flute), **Van Morrison** (Al. #29, 6-93 *Too Long in Exile*, vocals/songwriting in Jazz, in addition to R & R fame), **Jelly Roll Morton** (piano, singer), **Eubie Blake** (Ragtime piano), **Ray Brown** (bass). Hundreds of others probably also deserve more press. Maybe thousands have toiled in obscurity like Thomas Gray's unknown stars in "Gray's Elegy in a Country Churchyard." Playing their ever-lovin' hearts out to stifle their pain (and some midnight jukebox), they wailed and flowed and ebbed and soared and sang and passed. Geniuses ALL!

"Caldonia Boogie" – Louis Jordan, #6, 6-454; #1(7), 8-45 R & B. Alto sax master architect of Rhythm and Blues, Rap, and Jazz Rock. Also comedic yodel-kick falsetto. Catch this one; it's 1945 true Rock and Roll with a funky jazzy beat.

"Open the Door, Richard" – Count Basie, #1(1), 2-47; #2(1) R & B. Sophisticated Soul Big Bandsmen Basie took Louis Jordan's first-ever Rap song. **Basie** (1904-84) boogied piano with Pre-Rock expertise, and showcased sax star **Lester Young**. Basie? Held up as a Big Band standard for superstardom. Great guy, too, the scuttlebutt whispered.

"Boogie Woogie" – Tommy Dorsey & Orchestra, #3, 10-38; #5, 1-43; #21, 8-44; #4, 9-45. You pick it: 12-BAR BLUES, BOOGIE-WOOGIE, ROCK AND ROLL, JAZZ ROCK, or LITE ROCK. This is where it all begins for this perennial favorite. Almost. "Pine Top's Boogie Woogie" [same song] hit #20, 2-29 for **Clarence 'Pine Top' Smith**. Think only **INXS** and **Nirvana** and **Smashing Pumpkins** have grim tragedies? It goes with the musicians' zigzag on-the-road lifestyle. As Smith's Rock and Roll Boogie, from the 20s, zoomed up the fickle charts, he was shot to death in a bar brawl.

"Boogie Woogie on the St. Louis Blues" – Earl 'Fatha' Hines, #11, 5-40. Papa of Jazz piano. Great Boogie blaster, too. Hence, Rock and Roll.

"Rockin' in Rhythm" – Duke Ellington and his Famous Orchestra, #19, 3-31. YES! Check out that title. Rock and Roll, 1954? Pine Top Smith and Duke Ellington were rockin' at the 1929 Stock Market Crash, almost. Master Song Tabulator **Joel Whitburn**, attached to understatement, waxes into rare P.T. Barnum rhetoric for Duke: "Perhaps the single most creative talent in American popular music history." Wow. No ifs, ands, buts, maybes. "Rockin' in Rhythm" followed up his majestic song "Mood Indigo" (#3, 2-31), maybe one of the top ten most perfect melodies ever recorded; "Mood" features **Barney Bigard** on clarinet and **Arthur Whetsol** on trumpet. The follow-up cruises the cool corridors of VERY VINTAGE Rock and Roll. Sonny Greer's drums don't make up for the lack of electric guitar and bass of Duke's "Rockin'," but the pace, the mood, and the spirit are there. The Duke (1899-1974, of Washington, D.C.) was deified in Rock and Roll/Jazz Heaven by similar genius **Stevie Wonder** on #1(3), 4-77 "Sir Duke" (Blues Chapter). Perhaps Ellington's 2nd-greatest exotic melody, rife with deep Jazz chords and technique? "Flamingo" #11, 6-41. Tropical euphoria and eternal summer romance. Other Classic Jazz by Duke? #3, 5-33 "Sophisticated Lady"; #4, 5-33 "Stormy Weather"; #4, 10-35 "Cotton"; #9, 6-37 "Scattin' at the Kit-Kat"; and #4, 7-37 "Caravan." "Mood Indigo" was originally titled "Dreamy Blues." **Paul McCartney** first called his master-work "Yesterday" . . . "Scrambled Eggs."

"Rikki Don't Lose That Number" – Steely Dan, #4, 5-74. Passaic, New Jersey's piano man/singer **Donald Fagen** teamed up with **Chevy Chase**, *Saturday Night Live* comedian emeritus, on the drums. With **Walter Becker** on voice and bass, the Jazz/Rock compendium did what they said couldn't be done: 1) Name your group after an erotic toy from Beat guru William Burroughs' banned 1959 N*aked Lunch*; and 2) Dump touring, and ignore the singles market. Just hang out in the studio and hope for album royalties, which arrived with five golds and three platinums spearheaded by #3, 10-77 *Aja*. Jazz/Rock Fusion. Incredible technique. Blasting into the 80s, they scored their bronze-medal chart rung on #10, 11-80 "Hey, Nineteen" (not #19 "Hey, Ten"). Unique Jazz vision, with Bob and Betty Starr's cuz Fagen's keyboard leads and unbridled surreal lyric. Fagen apprenticed vocals/keyboards with **Jay and Americans**, and soloed successfully with #26, 10-82 "IGY (What a Beautiful World)."

"Reeling in the Years" at #11, 3-73 is a frequent rotation Steely Dan hit. It's a breezy Loggins & Messina or Seals & Crofts type tune, and reminds us that killing time is hazardous to life. P.S. Don't look now, but storming out of Santana's (Al. #1, '99) *Supernatural* wake, Steely Dan's *Two Against Nature* assaulted the album charts in March 2000, and hit #6 nationally and #3 bronze-medal in New York City. Old great bands never die, and maybe don't fade away, either. Super sounds always open the door... Roy Still points out their 2001 Rock Hall Induction.

"I Can't Dance" – Genesis, #7, 2-92. Phil Collins, Jazz/ Progressive Rock superstar, claims (but we all know better) he can't dance, but he can sing and dance with the best, when he's not drumming. Phil yodels admirable falsetto in this fun Jazz/Rock romp, pitting his rhythmic mastery against the mediocre horde.

Phil's #3, 4-87 "In Too Deep" gets a shallow review. Nice **Genesis** song. Though Phil has seven personal #1 songs, the only one he shares with Genesis is #1(1), 5-86 "Invisible Touch." It wafts Jazz. Phil's Phills are Phantastic. Epitome of Jazz Rock. Super drummer.

"Cantaloop" – US3, #9, 11-93; #21, 12-93 R & B. This is "ACID JAZZ," according to Nine Days' keyboardist Jeremy Dean, winner of 1990 **Louis Armstrong** Jazz Award at Patchogue-Medford High School. Hip-Hop, Rap, Soul and Rock. Dates back to tireless Progressive Jazz keyboard troubadour **Herbie Hancock**:

"Rockit" – Herbie Hancock, #71, 9-83; #6, 7-83 R & B. Hancock's forte is midnight Jazz piano solos, intermeshing with his soulful bandleader **Miles Davis**. Hancock's biggee? #42, 3-74 "Chameleon."

"Eye in the Sky" – Alan Parsons Project, #3, 7-82. Alan jump-started Orchestral Art Rock in 1982, and produced for **Pink Floyd** the longest-running album on the charts in history – Pink Floyd's *Dark Side of the Moon* (741 weeks, #1 just one week, 3-73).

"See Emily Play" – Pink Floyd, #134, 9-67. Floyd's debut hit. Humungous Pink Floyd section later. David Gilmour (guitar), Roger Waters (bass), Nick Mason (drums) and Rick Wright (keys) made up the bulwark of Pink Floyd. So named for two Georgia bluesmen, Floyd Council and Pink Anderson. Band Name Etymology Freebie – when my son Jeremy (Nine Days) was 16, he and Andrew Cassese and Brian Costello and Jim Harrison started a band called ANDERSON COUNCIL. Jeremy played drums at the Village's CBGB's, where Punk and New Wave began. You may have seen Andrew Cassese as 'Wormser,' boy genius, in 1984***¼ *Revenge of the Nerds*. **Brian Costello**, actor, appeared on *Third Rock from the Sun* TV show and in Nine Days' "Absolutely" video [#2, VH-1, 7-2000].

"Up-Up and Away" – Fifth Dimension, #7, 6-67; NC, R & B. Producer **Johnny Rivers** produced one of Jazz Rock's greatest groups for his Soul City label. These Soul sensations hopped in their lead-less zeppelin and soared up and away from easy chords and wimp harmonies. Lavishing five-part harmonic extravaganzas, New Jersey's gorgeous **Marilyn McCoo** teamed with St. Louis's **Billy Davis**. They nabbed three friends (Florence La Rue, LaMont McLemore, and Ron Townson) and vanquished stratospheric Jazz chords like conquistadors conquering small Central American republics on their lunch hour.

"Aquarius/Let the Sunshine In (The Flesh Failures)" – Fifth Dimension, #1(6), 3-69; #6 R & B. The Fifth Dimension sings a song from the 60s musical *Hair*, about folks with a lot of hair and not very many clothes. **McCoo**'s sweet voice coos in soprano splendor. The guys chime in with gusto and power. The lyrical theme is very New Age, digging the 12 signs of the Zodiac and steering the stars via astrology. *Hair* was condemned by the strict Christian Church as blasphemy and heresy ("Hi, **Pat Boone** – what's your sign?" "My sign is not the Zodiac – it's the CROSS!") "Aquarius" talks of the dawn of a glorious New Age of the astrological sign of Aquarius [the Water Bearer], brimming with peace, joy, love, understanding, and an extra large strawberry shake and Big Fries.

Then the double-song shifts gears. The tempo pulses slower, stronger, sexier. Hidden Soul kicks in. McCoo married Davis, and they lived happily ever after until the 80s. McCoo hosted TV's *Solid Gold* (1981-84). Four Dimensions sing and harmonize on the hook line and title. The soulful leader carries them vocally aloft. The good news? Peace will prevail on the placid planets. And yes, LOVE, 100% bonafide genuine love, will now re-direct the stars through the intergalactic cotton-candy nebular fluff. Nifty forecast, eh? 5-D Jazz Rock.

"Owner of a Lonely Heart" – Yes, #1(2), 11-83. **Jon Anderson** sings, Steve Hoe twangs guitar. Drummer Bill Bruford was replaced by Alan White. By 1991 Yes was an octet, also showcasing Alan White, Trevor Rabin, Tony Kaye on keys, bassist Chris Squire, keyboard virtuoso **Rick Wakeman**, and other stars. Yes, **Yes** can make Garage Bands unplug their hopeful Gibsons, and slink back to the beerful Karaoke Klub in tearful despair.

"Roundabout" – Yes, #13, 2-12-72. Starburst. This song is much more than your average British traffic roundabout, where cars whirl to different destinies together. It's an unreal audial happening. **Tony Kaye** on keyboards is greased lightning. Ivory maestros sit there in awesome awe. One incredible song. In math genius precision, the song fits into tight jigsaw patterns, and all fits together nicely at the finale.

Quiz Time. True or true? The question?

Is **Yes** one of the most technically excellent bands in the history of Rock and Roll?

☐ YES   ☐ YES

I don't know why. I just can't seem to flunk anybody on this one.

* * * * * * *

It's Windy City time again:

"Saturday in the Park" – Chicago, #3, 8-72. Joyous painting of the good life. It rings with the harmony of the human spirit. Besides a groovy collection of cool Jazz chords, and a flamboyant flash of blazing horns, you have a very pretty tableau of park life. Count the fleeting images, just for fun. A man sells ice cream. Italian songs hover in the air. The band surrounds Cetera with Pankow's trombone and Loughnane's trumpet. Little kids and puppies dance on green grass. Balloons and Frisbees. Big city. American melting pot. People of all races and nationalities and languages thrive and revel. There is no status situation, with folks putting on the ritz. **Peter Cetera** sings, enwreathed with the enchanting aura of Pankow's trombone and Loughnane's trumpet. In the big city park, with balloons and oranges and laughter and hope and love, Saturday is the center of the world.

"Feelin' Stronger Every Day" – Chicago, #10, 6-73. Motivational tune. Superstars never overlook the value of repetition and repetition. Songs with a billion words like Springsteen and Manfred Mann's "Blinded by the Light," Dylan's "Subterranean Homesick Blues," and Blues Traveler's "Runaround" are Rock and Roll rarities. Most songs hammer a hook line again. And again. And again. (See 2000+ Neo-Techno-Synth-Discoid-Dance Music).

"Stronger" hypes the fitness boom of the early 1970s. **Frank Shorter** won gold in the 1972 Marathon. Suddenly America discovered it could do a lot more with its couch potato lifestyle than just run to first base or send for oxygen when legging out a triple. Chicago's "Feelin' Stron-

ger" echoes and resounds and clamors for the listener's attention, like #7, 6-71 "Beginnings."

"Harry Truman" – Chicago, #13, 2-75. After the Nixon Watergate scandal, America tried to bop on back to a golden era of truth, justice and the American Way. President Truman's desk sign announced: THE BUCK STOPS HERE. His "bribers beware" credo didn't always apply to R & R hypers and A & R folks. Good Jazz bass. Topnotch harmonies. A man of the people, armed with only a high school education and his blunt honesty, Truman pinch-hit for President Roosevelt and delivered the Allied coup de grace to Hitler and Hirohito in World War II. "Harry" is a musical quest for lost integrity. In "Baby, What a Big Surprise" (#4, 9-77) Chicago shifts into the Adult Contemporary mode. On #1(2), 6-82 "Hard to Say I'm Sorry," Chicago finally zoomed to their zenith with this one with a universal sentiment – how do we apologize to the one (or three) we love? Our pride keeps getting in the way. In their melodic #3, 11-84 "You're the Inspiration," she's the meaning in his life. The chorus serves a rare Chicago I-VIm-IV-V7 Streetcorner pattern. Chicago, unused to such R & R ballad simplicity, shows that they can compete with the best Doo-whop groups on their own turf. New lyrical theme? Nope:

"(You're My) Soul and Inspiration" – Righteous Brothers, #1(3), 3-66; #13, 4-66 R & B. White Soul power. **Bobby Hatfield** flags down high-flyin' falsetto notes, with **Bill Medley** bringing up the bass. **Phil Spector's** WALL OF SOUND toys with majestic crescendos and decrescendos. In snazzy Continental suits and ties ¾-inch wide, the slender Brothers Righteous were the epitome of mid-60s coolth. The lyric looks at the girl as a sweet drug, or love addiction. He absolutely NEEDS her to get by . . .

Chicago blends many more voices. **Phil Spector** used a smattering of horns in his Wall of Sound impact. Chicago followed suit with #1(2), 9-88 "Look Away." Chicago's full-race Jazz orchestration spun other songs into the soundscape firmament: #3, 11-86 "Will You Still Love Me"; #3, 6-88 "I Don't Wanna Live Without Your Love"; #5, 12-89 "What Kind of Man Would I Be?"; and an *Ecclesiastes*-echoing "Chasin' the Wind" #39, 1-91. Quality proves it's rarely flash in the pan. Chicago zooms on.

"Mercedes Benz" – Janis Joplin, NC, 1971. Off Al. #1(9) *Pearl*. Not quite Jazz. Not quite Rock. Sort of a sardonic prayer. Janis, quivering in her twilight Elvis spotlight – belts this Mammon Anthem in full-tilt boogie intensity. I THINK it's a clever slam against hypocrisy and materialism. If it's meant straight, sorry, Janis. Anyhow, first she implores the Lord to send her the best car Germany can dole out – Mercedes Benz – as if she's won some cosmic lottery. Next, in solo *a cappella* all along, she asks for a color TV (posh in 1970), because quiz show 'Dialing for Dollars' might be calling her. Her third verse tightropes religious frivolity; she asks for one glorious night on the town. She says she's counting on the Lord, and prays He won't let her down. Then in the ultimate absurdity, she scarfs up something that can only be described as gutsy on Non-*Chutzpah*-Impaired: she begs for the Lord to BUY HER THE NEXT ROUND of drinks.

Audiences, sipping Southern Comfort and Woodstock Way-Out Rebellion, didn't know whether to gasp aghast – or LAUGH at Janis's irreverent daring crossing to the Danger Zone of sacreligious humor. Finally, the most pathetic near-hootennanny ever doesn't quite erupt. Requesting a vocal background from the crowd, Janis calls out: "EVERYBODY!" NOBODY sings. Nobody. Just Janis, boogieing solitarily on a deserted stage full of solo despair. Of all the jokes in lyrics, this has a shot at being the #1 saddest: the album was posthumous (she'd died 10-4-70, O.D.-ing on life).

"You Must Have Been a Beautiful Baby" – **Bobby Darin, #5, 9-61. Bobby Darin** (1936-73), consummate Jazz performer. For that matter, Bobby was the consummate Rock performer. Or Folk performer. Or interpreter of Pop Standards. This one salutes Dixieland Jazz via the #1 tune of 1938 for **Bing Crosby** (#8 Tommy Dorsey). Like his equally (#14, 2-61) super version of Mills Brothers' #22, '52 or Hoagy Carmichael's #19, '32 "[Up a] Lazy River," Darin hits all the vocal inflections. Some say he out-Sinatra-izes Sinatra. This uptempo "Baby" melody romps magnolia Dixieland chords. Darin's sweet-talk really swings. Jazz Razz-mo-tazz, nestled in Big Band Rock and Roll. Bobby put all the jigsaw music styles back together . . .

"Songbird" – **Kenny G, #4, 4-87; #23 R & B.** The #1 90s instrumentalist of **Acker Bilk** Cool Easy Jazz started playing soprano sax at 17 with **Barry White**'s Disco dudes. "G" fondles, caresses, and hugs a note with precision and passion combined. "G" (b. '56 Kenny Gorelick, Seattle, Washington), unrelated to NYC weatherman "Mr. G," graduated University of Washington in accounting (Phi Beta Kappa and Magna Cum Laude, sez Whitburn). **Johnny MATHIS** was the vocal Mr. Romantic Kenny G of two other decades, a ballad crooner in a Jazz class by himself:

"Misty" – **Johnny Mathis, #12, 10-59; #10, 11-59 R & B.** Mathis smoothly cradles the gossamer melody of this timeless love song, from Erroll Garner's #30, 10-54 piano instrumental. Virtuoso Jazz pianist **Garner** (b. '21, Pittsburgh; d. '77) also hit #8, 10-49 R & B as "Errol" with movie theme "I Cover the Waterfront." As we come off the string lead on the bridge, Mathis's silvery falsetto slinks in, sounding just like the instrument itself on the same high note. Johnny's jazzy ending fondles a major seventh. "Misty" got a lot of air play, until Clint Eastwood's *Play Misty for Me* about a homicidal DJ stalker in gun-guzzling California (1971**). Flick stars Jazz alto sax Soul rocker Cannonball Adderley.

"Mercy, Mercy, Mercy" – **Cannonball Adderley, #11, 1-67; #2(2) R & B.** Alto sax guru Adderley (1928-75) pioneered Jazz Fusion. Nifty tacets. Cameos? #41, 4-61 "African Waltz" and #66, 2-63 "Jive Samba." Like **Dave Brubeck**, Adderley loved to mix up unrelated genres for fun and profit.

"What Will Mary Say?" – **Johnny Mathis, #9, 1-63; #21, 3-63 R & B.** Johnny's long string of hits postponed forever an Olympic berth, via his high-jumping skills in San Francisco. A track phenom in hurdles and world-class high jumper, Mathis excelled at basketball, too. Singing coach Helen Noga smoothed whatever rough edges Johnny's world-class voice might have suffered at the high school level, and she created a Gold Medal Singer. Mathis, along with Frank Sinatra and the Kingston Trio, helped create the album. *Johnny's Greatest Hits* #1(3), 4-58, spent an unprecedented 178 weeks, or 3½ years, on the charts, smashing records galore (in the 'beforemath' of Pink Floyd's 741-week astonishment). Again, Johnny is behind only **Elvis** (15,538), **Sinatra** (12,766), and the **Beatles** (10,918). Johnny ranks 4th of all time in Joel Whitburn's Top 500 Album Artists (10,072 points) in his acclaimed *Top Pop Albums 1955-96*.

"Mary" is one of the sweetest songs ever written and tenderly sung. Forsaking his innocent angel Mary, the song's protagonist tries to elude the *femme fatale* clutches of some titillating temptress. He's doing a lousy job of pushing her away. Hanging on the hook of "What will my Mary say?" – Johnny wheedles and wrestles, to no avail. One "Wonderful, Wonderful" (Johnny's #14 debut, 2-57) melody, "Mary."

Johnny's ballads like #22, 12-57 "Wild Is the Wind" changed the world (and doubled the population). Johnny and Helen, and Armenian-American Columbia mentor and executive George Avakian, created Mathis's own genre of popular music. Out of audacious poetic license, we'll call it JOHNNY MATHIS'S LULLING "MIDNIGHT MAKE-OUT COOL JAZZ." "Wild" fits this description. It glimmers and gleams with muted Jazz chords, splashing sixths and ninths and major sevenths and augmented or diminished chords into the I-IV-V7 usual Chord Soup. Johnny's unique vocals cruise old notes like fresh new blue surf caressing his golden California shore. "Wild Is the Wind" bursts from the Anthony Quinn film of the same name (1957**½), a tender and graceful love ballad. Johnny's unlimited vocal range glides from ringing baritone to gentle falsetto with nary a pop. In Roy Orbison's Great Singer class, Mathis squeezes a multitude of moods out of each ripe purple-grape cluster of dewy notes. Mathis is a master builder of crescendo ("Begin the Beguine") in his painstakingly sculpted songs. He is, of course, on a different wave length from two other singers of the Metal variety with the same amazing range: **Robert Plant (Led Zep)** and **Steven Tyler (Aerosmith)**.

We realize and appreciate Johnny's giant stature in popular music (and Olympian leaps). Johnny enjoyed 45 singles on the HOT 100, including his #1 Everywhere Anytime Classic Oldie 9-57 "Chances Are," but only 12 in R & B list, which frowns on Pop Standards. His #1 duo tune is "Too Much, Too Little, Too Late" at #1(1), 4-78 & #1(4), 3-78 R & B with **DeNiece Williams**. Also #1 Adult Contemporary (its 'proper slot.') Johnny Mathis is a musical institution. He bridges all the gaps between Big

Bands, Jazz-Orchestral, Show Tunes, Soul or R & B, and (very) Soft Rock.

"An Old Fashioned Love Song" – Three Dog Night, #4, 11-71; #1 Adult Contemporary. That's what Rock and Roll and Jazz are all about! This catchy Three Dog Night song blends Rock, Jazz, and Love in a great symphony of harmonic, polyrhythmic sound.

Remember Three Dog Night's #1(1), 8-72 "Black and White?" **David Arkin** and **Earl Robinson**'s 1955 monumental song, lyrically, championed and celebrated the legal end to segregation in the United States via *Plessy vs. Ferguson* Supreme Court 1954 decision. **Rosa Parks** now rode in the front of the bus, and **Dr. Martin Luther King** spread his message of brotherhood and equality throughout the land in his martyrical pilgrimage. Musically, "Black and White" was a REGGAE song, an advance scout for Rock & Roll, or Rhythm & Blues, forecasting a whole genre of hot Jamaican-British and Caribbean-American music – related to our Latin chapter. "Old Fashioned Love Song" celebrates life and love in NEW rhythm patterns.

Beyond Britain's own racial harmonies, various similar situations to the American segregation experience have plagued the Commonwealth as well, first in India, and then the Australian Aborigine or New Zealand Maori or South Africa Zulu indigenous peoples. My wife Toni and I visited the 'First Nation' Slavé-Dené conclave in Fort Simpson, by the Arctic Circle in Canada's enormous Northwest Territories (5x Texas's size). That day they were holding their first-ever high school graduation (1994) for the community's kids. Canada avoided many of the problems the USA had, with 'Indians' (now Native Americans). Surging strains of 11-71 Three Dog Night's #4 "An Old Fashioned Love Song" drifted over the Lake Erie-sized Great Slave Lake out of Yellowknife. On the Liard Highway, we drove 240 miles (400km) on a long gravel road without seeing one other car or human being (ten big black bears, though) – but a THREE-DOG DAY (no midsummer Arctic NIGHT) serenaded us with old-fashioned LOVE MUSIC. A nutshell? Three Dog Night, named for the coziness of 1,2, or 3 dogs sleeping on your feet on cold Native American wigwam nights (perhaps Australian, too), shattered any racial complacency with their forthright anthems. And Three Dog Night is STILL a hit in Santa Claus Land.

Three Dog Night employs the best of Jazz Fusion into their Rock and Roll gusto: soulful R & R delivery, choppy Jazz chords, kicky improvs, and excellent band.

The explosion of Rock and Roll in 1955 stifled much of the great emerging Hot and Cool Jazz, on the rebound with Charlie Parker/Lionel Hampton Be-Bop Jazz. Dixieland Jazz, however, gave Rock and Roll an impetus for its insistent heavy RHYTHM. Swing Jazz gave it the magnificent lead cadenzas (via Benny Goodman, or Duke Ellington, later modified into Guitarese by Jimi Hendrix or Eric Clapton – who followed Goodman's guitarist Charlie Christian's lead style. From Christian's style to Les Paul's solid-body Jazz guitar, and Chuck Berry's pyrotechnic fretfire on the upper strings – it's a short trip. From Louie Armstrong's New Orleans to Elvis's Memphis, or Hendrix's Seattle to Clapton's England is just minor sojourn on the Jazzful golden-brick road to Rock and Roll.

By 1970, via Jazz Fusion, the two great disparate musical genres sang ONE great song, and played one super solo.

*Steely Dan - Walter Becker (l) and
Donald Fagen (r)*

Frank Zappa

Heart of Rock & Roll

"Joy to the World" – Three Dog Night, #1(6), 3-71; #46, 4-71 R & B. One of Rock's big 70s launch pads was a LILY pad. Three Dog Night's ode to "Joy" bellows the triumph of mankind over despair, frustration, boredom, and meaninglessness. "Joy" is a song for joy for the ages. And the frogs. How many times have you been haggling or struggling or bumbling or slogging through the murky muddy muck, when suddenly, from on high, you hear the golden-throated tones of this Chuck Negron/ Danny Hutton song rasping their Call of the Wild: JEREMIAH, they holler gleefully, is a BULLFROG!

Certainly all-inclusive. **Chuck Negron** (b. 6-8-42), **Danny Hutton** (b. 9-10-42) and the other One Dog Night crew feel so wildly, unbridledly happy with the entire universe – for a golden moment – that they wish the greatest of joy to a bunch of bluefish, pilot fish, angelfish, groupers, groupies and guppies. And especially this pond-hopping amphibian.

Nobody sleeps when "Joy" hits the airwaves. Three Dog Night is primarily a singing group of Danny and Chuck plus **Cory Wells** (b. 2-5-42). They swap lead vocals. Their band? Joe Schirmie, on bass; Mike Allsup, guitar; Floyd Chester Sneed, drums. Organmeister Jim Greenspoon leads off with an inauspicious little double measure on the electric piano. Schirmie and Allsup waft in, and the chimy little song sounds like it's just warming up. It isn't. Suddenly – PANDEMONIUM BUSTS LOOSE!

The vocal roars in with Jeremiah with one the Top Ten Tacets of All (Rockin') Time. Look out!

Here it comes:

JEREMIAH! A BULLFROG!!!!

This froggy Rainbow Connection is the stuff of legend. Our daughter Lauri's apartment is a Kelly green Frog Preserve, adorned with hundreds of statue frogs, stuffed frogs, pictures of frogs. Our son Jeremy was born in 1972; Toni and I insist his name has nothing to do with this Jeremiah Bullfrog or the Brit Invader duo 'Chad and Jeremy' – but, hey, the power of the subconscious. You never know. Then there's this 'Kermie' thing. Remember the *Muppets*? If you were lucky enough to see the 4-star *Muppet Movie* and (*Muppets Take Manhattan* or *Christmas Carol*), you may have noticed **Jim Henson**'s alter-ego KERMIT the FROG's "Rainbow Connection" (#25, 9-79). Henson (1936-90) also scored with "Ernie's" bathtub anthem – #16, 8-70 "Rubber Duckie." With a plucky pink Stage Pig Girlfriend like Miss Piggy behind his stairway to the stars, friendly green Kermit (a/k/a "Kermie") leapfrogged the Top 25 during Discomania – before *The Simpsons* or *Spongebob Squarepants*. Three Dog Night's rainbow rescues us from boring, humdrum stumblebums who wreck our day.

Three Dog Night was a generation ahead of their time: The third time around on the chorus, they power-shift to the macho Blues key of 'E' and offer a syncopated inter-beat "Joy to the World" chorus. On the last fadeout chorus, Three Dog Night returns to the 'D', blasting at 84 passionate beats per minute. As they trail off into the sunset, they hammer a majestic mountaintop of a giant falsetto note. They nail the big 'A' just south of High C. "Joy to the World" is a fine Christmas carol, too. **Mariah Carey** on #3, 11-94 Al. *Merry Christmas*, COMBINES the Carol and the 'Tri-Canine' chart-topper, two different melodies. Three Dog Night's hot lyric promises joy, peace, love, and romance. Who could ask for more? (See Glossary/Chord Theory.)

"Easy to Be Hard" – Three Dog Night, #4, 8-69. From the Rock musical *Hair*, this catchy tune gushes the theme of CHARITY. The song champions causes of social justice, and scolds nay-sayers who refuse to help the less fortunate. The song prowls first on a dreamy melody, intensifying in rasp and rhythm. The Jazz Rock energy of Three Dog Night a full power shows their third hit to be among their best.

Astoundingly, the Rock Hall of Fame hadn't located them by 2003. They also scored big with #7, 7-71 "Liar," #12, 3-72 "The Family Man," #4, 3-74 "The Show Music Go On" [an Old Broadway litany], and their utopian, 8-70 "Out in the Country."

"One" – Three Dog Night, #5, 5-69. First big original hit. Their debut? Soulful #29, 2-69 cover of Otis Redding's classic "Try a Little Tenderness" (original Ted Lewis #6, 2-33). "One" fires off puzzling phrases. Both NO and YES, he says, are very sad experiences. Greenspoon's electric piano sneaks in. The chorus intercepts his wayfaring pilgrimage. They bash the starry skies, yelling 'NUMBER' at mega-decibels. **Harry Nilsson** (1941-94) wrote "One" (no relation to **Metallica**'s antiwar anthem). Their theme? SOLITARY is overrated.

"Everybody's Talkin'" – **Nilsson, #113, 8-68, and #6, 8-69.** From *Midnight Cowboy* (1969***). Harry's forté is soaring Chalypso Rock. You swoop and glide with Nilsson's airy tenor, on cotton-candy curls of notes that stream from deep in his soul. However, *Midnight Cowboy* punts cotton candy for New York's sleaziest, seamiest underbelly. Pathetic Ratso Rizzo (Dustin Hoffman) and greenhorn stud Joe Buck (Jon Voight) seek destiny. Gets it. Nilsson followed with the buoyantly poignant "I Guess the Lord Must Be in New York City" (#34, 11-69). Like all Nilsson, it bears a tinge, a twinge, or a binge of melancholy. Nilsson's biggest hit is "Without You" (#1[4], 12-71), penned by badluck Badfinger's Pete Ham and Tom Evans. Like Orbison in "Blue Bayou" (#29, 9-63) or **Carl Perkins** in "Blue Suede Shoes" (#2[4], 3-56), Nilsson incorporates a technique that good Rockabilly singers had been doing for years – high-jumping octaves (Billy Joel, too, on "Piano Man").

"**Without You**" – **Mariah Carey, #3, 1-94.** Nilsson echo. Eight of 10 of her first releases nabbed the coveted #1 *Billboard* HOT 100 spot. Like Three Dog Night and Nilsson, Mariah leads off with a bare, spare plinky piano plunking. Choosing tough Key of 'F#', along with the production ideas of hubby/Sony President Tommy Mottola, Mariah flashes back to the old Streetcorner Chord Pattern from the 50s 'Still of the Nite': **F# – Ebm(D#m) – Abm(G#m) – C#7**, or the minor streetcorner **I – VIm – IIm – V7** patterns. A little more somber than a IV major third chord.

Mariah flexes her passionate Irish-Venezuelan-Afro-American vocal chords. **Johnny Tillotson** hit #7 with totally different "Without You" in 8-61.

Mariah Carey

"Eli's Comin'" – **Three Dog Night, #10, 10-69.** Bronx White Soul/Gospel/Rock star **Laura Nyro** ("Up on the Roof" #92, 10-70 Drifters' echo) penned this energetic rouser. Rapscallion Eli is coming to town. A churning chorus chomps down on the counterpoint. It all comes together in one climactic outburst. Their sole British hit (#3) is #1(2), 5-70 wild-party "Mama Told Me Not to Come." The lad's mum warns him of the funny cigs at this potful party; it may be the same bash that Joe Cocker went to for #30 Lennon-McCartney's "She Came in Through the Bathroom Window." No matter what you do, the nurturing figure of Mom always hovers in the background. Your conscience. If Mom has not now or never been around for you, her voice will be echoed, perhaps, by your aunt, your sister, Mother Teresa, or for gender equality, Jiminy Cricket.

On #5, 12-71 "Never Been to Spain," Floyd Sneed clicks in on the castanets. Apropos. An occasional guitar skirts the melody. By the second verse, more stuff intrudes. Though our song leader's not been to Spain, he's caught the cool glories of Oklahoma. Blues number in gutsy Key of 'E'. Soon he flips from Oklahoma to Oz, Shangri-La, and Heaven. Soaring crescendo Jazz-Rock Fusion.

"**Rock and Roll Fantasy**" – **Bad Company, #13, 3-79.** Named after U.S. Western flick (1972***). Like Badfinger, British Bad Company relied at first on a throbbing, heavy R & R beat, rife with macho tunes like #5, 8-74 "Can't Get Enough." King Crimson's lead singer (b. '46, Lancashire) **Boz Burrell** played bass and sang harmony for Middlesbrough's **Paul Rodgers** – piano-man vocalist. From **Mott the Hoople** (love these R & R names), Hereford's Mick Ralph did guitar, with Simon Kirke on drums. Hoople? Glitz Rock #96, 6-74 "The Golden Age of Rock and Roll."

The hook line burgeons the rest of the song, and carries it along. Like many R & R fantasies, it concerns some vivacious Venus. Or, from a girl's viewpoint, "Johnny Angel" (Shelley Fabares, #1, 3-62). Bad Company never left the scene: #16 "If You Needed Somebody" (11-90) and #38, 9-92 "How About That."

"**Mississippi Queen**" – **Mountain, #21, 4-70.** 'Power Rock' NYC group of Leslie West and **Felix Pappalardi** (1939-83, shot). Early Metalmongers? Hard Rock heroes? Mainstream Rock with interchangeable Hard Rock and Heavy Metal power.

"**Baby Let's Play House**" – **Elvis Presley, NC, 1955; #5, 7-55 C.** This one really boogies. **Scotty Moore** (1999 Rock Hall of Fame Inductee [March 2000]) wails on his guitar. **Bill Black** prods old stand-up bass with slap sound. New drummer **DJ Fontana** books it at supersonic speed. ELVIS'S FIRST-EVER CHARTED HIT ANYWHERE . . . Rockabilly classic. Masterpiece melding of Sam Phillips' slap bass/echo chamber effects. Flat-out Thunder Rock, like Ritchie Valens' hangover lament, "Ooh, My Head." Lyric rated "V" for Violence. Otherwise, super song by King waiting for coronation. Heart of Rock and Roll.

"Promised Land" – Elvis Presley, #14, 10-74. (Flipside, "It's Midnight," hit #9, 10-74 C.) Elvis's careening career spawned several comebacks, like a satellite show from Hawaii. Elvis, in steamy leather, dieted down to 170# to simulate the lean look he once enjoyed. Elvis's star dimmed to Final "Way Down" in #18, 6-77. The King was aging ungracefully. In a mystical pact with his mother Gladys to live her exact life span (ostensibly about 42 years, 5 months, and a few days), Elvis geared his last tragic tailspin. Elvis didn't know, of course, Gladys had fudged her age by three years – she was actually 45 when she succumbed to a heart attack after years of liver and kidney problems. Elvis? Three extra years. Think about it.

How important was Elvis to the history of popular music? Consider this. Joel Whitburn's 'Rock Era' dates from 1955. The old Pop Memories Era lasted from 1890-54. Those who inadvertently deify Elvis in the pantheon of Rock Heaven might consider – we date the Christian Era from Jesus' approximate birth date. On a lesser scale, but similarly, we date the Rock Era from August 1954: Sun Records released Elvis's debut "That's All Right." In a 1994 poll, 11% of the American people astoundingly believed Elvis was still alive. Wild world . . .

"An American Trilogy" – Elvis Presley, #66, 5-72. When the King launched #2(1), 8-72 "Burning Love," the world rejoiced at his Rock rocket. Too long, critics carped, he'd been Las Vegasizing – doing weepy lounge ballads and thin Jazz arrangements. "Burning Love" described the flames licking his body and his temperature soaring – (leather jumpsuit and 100° muggy stage is its own steamy sauna). The lyrics pointed to heart issues. Gorging on full cakes and 1500-calorie sandwiches, Elvis's appestat veered way out of control. His personal physician Dr. Nick rationalized pumping him full of 14 kinds of prescription drugs: "He's ELVIS! How do you tell him he can't have a pill to help him sleep or something?" Good question.

The best songs often miss the top 40. Check out fab flip side of the 'first protest song' "MTA". The Folk-based **Kingston Trio** 'invented' the album in popularity terms; "MTA"'s flip is "All My Sorrows." later redone by White Soul duo **Dick & DeeDee** (falsetto-baritone, she a lyric soprano "The Mountain's High" #2, 7-61). The California couple's "All My Sorrows" metamorphosed (#89) into "All My Trials." "All" is a parent's lament. The father regrets to his little child that parents don't live forever, and that his earthly trials will very soon be finished.

Peter, Paul, and Mary say it succinctly in "Puff the Magic Dragon" #2(1), 3-63. Parent tells bedtime super story about Little Jackie Paper and pal Puff, a brontosaurus-style sea dragon. A giant 2-D Puff picture hangs on NYC's 81st Street P.S. #6, where NYC Road Runners have winter hot-chocolate awards ceremonies – Peter Yarrow went to school there. The father explains that the kid would grow up and leave the imaginary dragon playmate alone. Great euphemism for death (some critics saw 'Puff' as marijuana, too). I like to think of it as a golden mellow lullaby.

"American Trilogy" (meaning three songs or stories) is a three-way combo of "All My Trials," and the two opposing Civil War anthems: The "Battle Hymn of the Republic" and the South's "Dixie" (ironically penned by Long Islander Dan Emmett as "Dixie's Land"). "An American Trilogy" is a classic **Roy Orbison**-style crescendo song. An entire symphony (Orchestral Rock) rises to Elvis's staggering summit, in his soaring *fortissimo* finale from massive baritone to Caruso Italian tenor.

Elvis had five years left. We all could feel it. At this precarious point in late life, he wheedled into marriage and fatherhood – nine months to the day after wedding Priscilla Beaulieu, a girl he had courted since she was an innocent 13 in Germany. Unlike **Jerry Lee Lewis**, Elvis waited in Southern Gentlemanly manner, for his bride to come of age. By the 70s, Elvis was retrogressing into uncomfy late middle age. The ELVIS SPOTLIGHT kept him burning – a hunk of volcanic burnin' burnt-out love. Even ELVIS HIMSELF reeled under the awesome production of trying to still BE ELVIS.

"The mass of men lead lives of quiet desperation," said Henry David Thoreau. Everybody grumbles and groans about working 40-55-70 hours/week – we envy Elvises who work a scanty 12 days a YEAR in Vegas (with 50x our lifetime incomes annually). But wait. Elvis only had to show up for a few shows. All Elvis had to do was go out there and BE ELVIS. It was too much. All his trials came to court. Elvis was convicted. Of being Elvis? Of abusing his beleaguered body and soul? Of having a genetic predisposition to heart disease? In **Dion**'s words from "Abraham, Martin, and John" (#4, '68), it seemed good people die young. 'Good'? Elvis was at heart a good kid. He loved his mom and his Grandma Minnie and his Daddy Vernon. Though he was a little too early for the charity **Band-Aid** bandwagon of the mid-80s, Elvis was generous to a fault. He gave away Cadillacs and his time and good will to help others less fortunate.

To Elvis expert **Steve Roullier** (husband of lyric soprano Alice Maupin), our international fascination with the King's incredible career is his "undiluted authenticity in performing great Soul/R & B to a larger mixed racial audience. With a physicality not seen in the standard White crooner, and learned from **Wynonie Harris** [#1 R & B 5-48 "Good Rockin' Tonight"] – but in Elvis's own style – Elvis became the greatest singing sensation of all time." CATLIKE is the way Elvis asked members of his Memphis retinue to call his stage style – and Elvis strutted with panther power in full command of his destiny. And his century.

The aging monster stalks us all. If we're lucky! Elvis speeded up the process during his obsessive final years. Unable to truly relax, he tried New Age formulas, meditation, Eastern philosophy, and deeper Christianity. When gray strands pierced his trademark sideburns, Elvis just ebonized them. Our universal human Battle of the Bulge caused the burgeoning King to blast away at his bulbous belt-buckle fast – he'd play midnight racquetball in his Graceland private court with Red West and pals. Red West and Sonny West wrote the Brutus-style book, *Elvis: What Happened*, three weeks before Elvis died at 42 on 8-16-77. "Yo-yo" dieting joined the list of suspects.

Elvis would work up a sweat hacking away at karate chops. The Lion in Winter at ancient 42 could look back over many heydays from the Hound Dog Years: #2 "Burning Love," is his last top ten tune ever. Though one critic describes the song as overly erotic, it also grotesquely describes Elvis's high blood pressure, his fevered fatal super-stress, and his tortured headlong plunge into the swirling vortex. "An American Trilogy" came from Houston's **Mickey Newbury**'s (#21 in 11-71, #93, 10-88 C). You can feel Elvis sweating half an auditorium away. You can feel the perspiration beads cascading down his lost Lion King brow. His burly body wheezes goodbye.

He is fading away, this old Rock and Roll soldier – and you know it. A major part of your life – your own Rock and Roll Rainbow – is hovering over the dark charcoal somber sea. You can almost hear **Jody Reynolds**' Graveyard Rock Prelude, #5, 5-58 "Endless Sleep." Big surf bashing on cold midnight winds; "Endless Sleep" gnashes its gargantuan vibrato death knell. Or El's #11, 12-55 C. dark, brooding "Mystery Train." As Elvis totters.

"My Way" – Elvis Presley, #22, 12-77; #2(1), 11-77 C. We all know the haunted guitar in #1(8), 3-56 "Heartbreak Hotel." Elvis's debut HOT 100 #1 song has nothing on his gloomy **Paul Anka** song "My Way" – in dredging up a chilly undercurrent of hopeless despair. Despite desk clerks dolled up in funereal ebony, heartstruck lovers caterwauling in the gloppy dank gloom, and bawling bellhops, "Heartbreak Hotel" is a posh, pretty-posy Ritzy Romper Room compared to the Generation X utter bleakness of Anka's Me-First manifesto, "My Way." For Anka and **Sinatra**, they truly did it their way. Not Elvis.

When you get to 80 like the Chairman of the Board (or 60 like Anka in 7-2001), you can smile smugly back at the doting crowd. And wave victory. Elvis was in a death-grapple with bulimia. He oscillated his weight in a snapped yo-yo ride to nowhere. To understand Elvis's free fall, the specter of **Karen Carpenter**'s anorexia battle looms. Always aiming to please the audience, Karen lived and died by the motto: "You can't be too rich or too thin."

At their singing trade, both Karen and Elvis were the best. Each suffered from the HORRORS OF INCUMBENCY. Sometimes you do something spectacularly well – sing, sell, run, dance, share, love, or dream. Suddenly, you are called back to do that precious thing again and again and again. Suddenly, you are very tired of singing or running or writing or whatever you're extremely good at . . . where do you flee? Look at **Michael Jordan**, World's greatest jumping man. When Jordan's dad died (as Elvis's beloved mom did), Jordan typically looked for a way to please his father's memory. Pop Jordan was a baseball fan, so Michael became a temporary pro baseball player.

Horrors of Incumbency. You're good. Your fans expect you to be the best. Forever. The reeling King commanded himself to do live shows a few days a year (12 or so). On "My Way," did Elvis miss the boat? Did he perform Manager 'Colonel' **Tom Parker**'s way? Elvis's crafty manager (1910 to 1-22-97) masterminded Elvis's meteoric rise. The Dutch-born 300-pound carnival barker steered

Elvis to stardom, taking only his modest 50% of the King's earnings (some managers get 10%). When Elvis died, Tom showed up in shorts, Hawaiian shirt, and his most formal baseball cap at the royal funeral. Did Elvis sing it the way Mama Gladys and Daddy Vernon wanted it? Did he sing twice as great to make up for the loss of his tiny twin brother **Jesse Garon Presley** on that bleak 1935 Birth Day when Jesse wasn't quite born? Was he trying to please his loyal fans? Elvis never, like fellow Teen idol **Rick Nelson**, grew into a mature "Garden Party" stance (1971): don't obsess trying to please everybody. To truly love others, Ricky opines, mustn't you truly respect yourself first? And Elvis, supposedly 'self-centered,' perhaps really wasn't. Was he so 'other-directed' in letting them shape his image that he forgot how to be himself? Whichever self was he trying to become? All of who ever tried on Elvis's face as teenagers (but it didn't fit) can empathize with the King's limelight agonies.

Remember, surrounded by sugary strings, honeyed horns, and posh pastel Vegas retinue, is this 'King' just a small lad grown up? As the huge full orchestra pumps up the skyward volume, you feel the fire of the early Gospel songs Elvis sang in the little white church in Tupelo, Mississippi, where we also nurtured our own American "Johnny B. Goode."

Elvis was born in a two-room shotgun shack off the Mississippi Delta in Eastern Mississippi. Daddy Vernon actually did hard time for a fudged signature on a nickel-dime $4 check. Elvis first won a prize for singing sad songs at age 10 about a terrible Dog Euthanasia experience, "Old Shep" (#47, 12-56). A kid has to actually shoot his faithful pooch for lack of money to pay vet.

Trying to live up, in a very human way, to the superhuman persona deemed the GREAT ELVIS – can be a killer experience. The pressure and stress could topple a King.

"My Way" – Paul Anka, NC, first a demo. Wizard songsmith Anka cut the vocal demo for Sinatra and Elvis; then he cut his AI. #188, 1-72 *Paul Anka*. Like a fiery fighter plane shot out of the sky, Elvis's career exploded and fizzled back to Earth in tatters, in the ghastly wake of his untimely death.

Paul Anka handled his own success much better, like his hero **Frank Sinatra**. Anka invested his mountains of millionaire-at-15 money from #1(1), 7-57 "Diana" (about a crush on his BABYSITTER Diana Abood). No 2nd-string singer/songwriter, the Lebanese-Canadian Teen Idol charted 53 HOT 100 hits, like: #7, 1-58 "You Are My Destiny"; #16, 4-58 "Let the Bells Keep Ringing"; #15, 12-58 "(All of a Sudden) My Heart Sings"; his biggest hit #1(4) "Lonely Boy" of 6-59; empathetic/romantic #2(3), 8-59 "Put Your Head on My Shoulder"; #2(2), 2-60 "Puppy Love"; #8, 5-60 "My Home Town"; #10, 5-61 "Dance On Little Girl." The Ottawa, Canada songwriter penned **Buddy Holly**'s last song – the pensive, nearly existential #13, 3-59 "It Doesn't Matter Anymore." Anka had only 15 fewer Rock Era hits than Frank Sinatra, and one-third as many as Elvis himself. After his #7, 11-75 Disco Era rebound of ballad "Times of Your Life," Paul showcased the suavest halls of Vegas and Reno and Branson, Missouri. The plucky Canadian Teen Idol now makes a very good buck. In a recent interview (not the time Paul Anka borrowed my belt on the 1966 *Robin Seymour Swing' Time* TV show), Anka said:

"This singing life can be tremendous; great hours, great people, great money. Royalties and Oldies keep your name on the neon marquee, and life is very, very good. With a normal family situation, you can thrive. Too many singers self-destruct. Their fascination in the seamy side, and the tragic O.D. stories make the news."

Anka jimmied his R & R "You Are My Destiny" (#7, 1-58) into a comfy life. Early on, Paul bought his own master tapes and became an entrepreneurial tycoon. By the 70s Anka engineered a full-force comeback: he helped headline the swingin' seventies' Disco daze: "You're Havin' My Baby," #1(3), 7-74, and album *Anka* at #9, 8-74. The Ontario lad directed a bonanza R & R career on his own, before assuming the business suit and haircut and Easy Listening tag.

Paul commences his "My Way" on the standard conformist **'C' major** chord. Anka's classic tune is loosely based on French song *"Comme L'Habitude."*

"My Way" seethes with confidence. Lifetime of achievement in song. "My Way" is no song for Johnny One-Note monotone wimps. It flees from G below Middle 'C' to the E ten full steps above. Is there too much pride in "My Way"? Who knows? In the Middle Ages (and gruesome flick *Seven* 1996***), Pride is one of the Seven Deadly Sins – and #1 on the Top Seven Sin Hit Parade. But Elvis is no *Macbeth*, swamped with 'overweening pride.' No more so than Anka or Sinatra, who were rarely Confidence-Impaired.

Elvis's old pal the Country chart was a tad kinder to the Anka-Elvis compendium song: [#22, 12-77; #2(1) C]. Also, the King's "Unchained Melody" hit #6 C. in 3-78, and "Guitar Man" hit #1 C. on 1-81 (only #28 HOT 100). The semi-streetcorner "I Was the One," flipside to "Heartbreak Hotel" (19, 3-56), CHARTED as Elvis's FIRST RECORD (TOP 100) AS WELL AS HIS LAST (Country Chart ONLY). As Dream Weaver Walt Disney (and songwriters Washington-Harline) put it so well, "When You Wish Upon a Star" (#1, '40 Glenn Miller), your dreams will really come true.

"Where the Blue of the Night Meets the Gold of the Day" – **Bing Crosby, #4, 1-32; #27, 11-40.** Joel Whitburn, THE expert musical chartman ever, calls **Bing Crosby the most popular entertainer of the first 50 years of the 20th century.** This BLUE-GOLD ballad is Bing's theme song. His most famous song is what *Guinness* called the biggest-selling hit of all time (till 1997) – Irving Berlin's immortal "White Christmas" #1(11), 10-42+. Bing's color imagery sets up Elvis's own with this University of Michigan maize and blue two-tone tribute. A treasure trove of Bing's swift 16th-note melismas later metamorphosed to **Mariah Carey**'s inimitable style. Crosby mellowly caresses the deep purple stardust sundowns of lost long-ago Radioland with his beloved bassoon baritone. **Harry Lillis** "Bing" **Crosby** was [probably] born

3-4-1903 in Tacoma, Washington. Crosby had one Easy Listening Pop Standard in the Rock Era:

"True Love" – **Bing Crosby and (Princess) Grace Kelly, #3, 9-56.** A classic harmonic love song, "True Love" represents what Rock and Roll was rebelling against in the first place – easy, pretty songs. Rock? Rife with youth and fire and thunder. What goes around comes around:

"True Love" – **Elton John & Kiki Dee, #56, 11-93; #2 U.K.** Even if **Elton** and **Kiki** were ready for this sweet ballad of plighted troth and musical marmalade, American Rap, Hip-Hop, and Punk Denizens of Alternative Angst were not. Elton and Kiki croon a breathtaking reprise of Bing's Older Mr. Entertainment style with Grace Kelly (viola-voiced soprano and Princess of Monaco).

So did Bing have any hits that might be remotely classified as Rock and Roll? Nope, not a one. But he did Swing it a bit. Hint of rhythm. When I was three, my folks had this 78 rpm cowboy tune of his – #2(4), 8-36 "I'm An Old Cowhand" (from that Rio Grande). The "Susanna"-style confusing lyrics went on about how he was a cowboy who never actually viewed a cow. Bing be-bopped the un-lyrics "yippie-yi-yo" and "kai-yay." Bing nearly rocked a bit on his first hit, #12, 3-31 "Just a Gigolo":

"Just a Gigolo/I Ain't Got Nobody" – **David Lee Roth, #12, 3-85.** Van Halen lead singer Roth does Dixieland. Also "Gigolo" #1(2), 1-31 hit for **Ted Lewis** and His Band, so Bing, crooner like **Pat Boone**, started as a 'Cover Artist.' Roth fliptune "Nobody" scorched 6-21 (#3) charts for Marion Harris. Roth took "I Ain't Got Nobody" from 1944 **Louis Prima** tune (NC) Vegas legend Prima's "Civilization [Bongo, Bongo, Bongo]" (#8, 10-47) actually ROCKED, eight years early.

"That Old Black Magic" – **Louis Prima and Keely Smith, #18, 11-58; #26, 12-58 R & B.** Premier Hallowe'en carol! HALLOWE'EN CAROLS? But, of course: Naturally, **Bobby 'Boris' Pickett's** #1(2), 9-62 "Monster Mash"; **Santana**'s #4, 11-70 "Black Magic Woman"; **Eagles'** #9, 9-72 "Witchy Woman"; the Z-SECTION, John Zacherle's #6, 3-56 "Dinner with Drac" and **Warren Zevon**'s #21, 3-79 "Werewolves of London"(cited by Larry Barnes); **Michael Jackson**'s #4, 2-84 "Thriller"; **Gene Simmons'** (not-the-one-from-**Kiss**) #11, '64 "Haunted House," and belfries of others.

Louis Prima (1911-78) is a major Rock and Roll pioneer, who created a genre of his own with his Jazz-singing wife **Keely Smith** (b. '32). [My niece is Keely Harris, no connection?]. Talented Smith also played a comedy foil to Prima, like great 50s comics **Sid Caesar** (b. 1922, see *Grease*) and **Imogene Coca** (11-18-1908-6-2-2001). Barnstorming with Red Nichols in 1932, New Orleans' singer/trumpeter Prima combined cabaret Jazz-scat singing and a Latin thunderbeat (a la **Tito Puente**). "That Old Black Magic" instrumentalized to #1(1), 2-43 for **Glenn Miller**, weaving a tender trap of siren-song infatuation. With a multicultural Big Band/Jazz/Latino/Rock style, Louis whooped it up in Vegas. His ebullient personality and cool raspy baritone took the stage by storm. Keely deadpanned Louie's best routines (like **Cher** later did to **Sonny Bono**). She first sang with him at age 18 for #12, 11-50 "Oh Babe." His primo Prima orchestra's hits include: #8, 7-35 "The Lady in Red," #4, 7-35 "In a Little Gypsy Tea Room," and trad sea shanty #6, 5-45 "Bell-Bottom Trousers." Critic Michelle Aquino's favorite, Louie Prima covered to #15, 11-60 the Beatles' FIRST producer **Bert Kaempfert**'s blue-star blockbuster, #1(3), 10-60 "Wonderland by Night" ["*Wunderland bei Nacht*"]. **Prima** was a friend of **Bing Crosby**, and ambassadored **Elvis** onto the palatial stages of the voluptuous Vegas nightscape. Louis Prima is a major link between Big Band Jazz and the Rock Revolution.

"Pennies from Heaven" – Bing Crosby, #1(10), 12-36. In the Depression, people actually picked up pennies from the gutter. This cheery Crosby tunes encourages sufferers with hope and faith. And money, raining from the friendly skies. **Crosby** also foretold the advent of Elvis with his Hawaiian Jazz ballads; the King's movie career was bolstered by his most popular album ever, #1(20), 10-61, *Blue Hawaii*. Bing's Hawaiian "Sweet Leilani" was also #1[10] in 4-37. The Big Kahuna? His most monstrous #1 hit ever was "White Christmas," perennially reaching #1(11), 10-42, #6, 12-43, #5, 12-44, #1(2), 12-45, #1(1), 12-46, etc. Other Crosby Hawaiian songs, with dreamy electric guitars of the slide-steel variety? "Now Is the Hour" #1(3), 1-48; and "My Isle of Golden Dreams" #18, 11-39. Other beat-buffetted Bing blockbusters? "Zing a Little Zong" (#18, 8-52); "Pistol Packin' Mama" (#2[4] with **Andrews Sisters** 11-43); "In the Cool, Cool, Cool of the Evening," with Present Reagan's 1st wife Jane Wyman at #11, 8-51; Gospel tune with son Gary Crosby "Down by the Riverside" #28, 1-54; Latin-flavor "Baia" #6, 6-45 with Xavier Cugat; #3, 7-45 "On the Atchison, Topeka, and the Santa Fe." Bing's brother **Bob Crosby** was a semi-superstar, with highlighted hits like #1(3), 6-35 "In a Little Gypsy Tea Room," #1(4), 8-37 "Whispers in the Dark," and #22, 7-51 "Shanghai."

Bing Crosby was the heart of 1930-55 American popular music. After his last #97, 12-57, "How Lovely is Christmas," Bing retired to the golf course. Almost two months to the day after Elvis died, Crosby (74, maybe 77) died on the 18th green (10-14-77) of a heart attack.

THE TWO GIANTS OF EACH HALF OF THE TWENTIETH CENTURY DIED JUST 59 DAYS APART. The 70s were tough on Princes of Pop Music: Morrison-Joplin-Hendrix. Then **Elvis**, perhaps the biggest entertainer of all time. Slipping away, almost in silence. **Bing Crosby** too vanished into the dark mood-indigo Western sundown.

And Bicentennial 1976 Disco dervishes danced on. Mad-dash macabre rock-it-up. Yok it up. The party would go on forever. Would no one ever die?

"When My Blue Moon Turns to Gold Again" – Elvis Presley, #19, 12-56. This one ties the Crooner and Rock Eras in a strong knot, color-coded to the blue-gold theme. Check out the similar title to Bing's #4, 1932 "When the Blue of the Night Meets the Gold of the Day." Elvis and Bing sang their separate super songs of astronomical power. Love, we all knew, was somewhere out there in the stardust inter-galactic lilac fluff out there beyond the Milky Way. We just had to reach out and grab it.

Elvis had long admired the Blue Moon stuff. His #55, 9-56 "Blue Moon" – with its otherworldly falsetto wail – powered the **Marcels**' #1, 10-61 hit [Glen Gray and His Casa Loma Orchestra (#1[3], 1-35)]. Elvis's first release? Bill Monroe and the Bluegrass Boys' NC "Blue Moon of Kentucky." A Blue Moon just means you get two full moons in the 28-day lunar cycle in just one-month. The second moon is astronomically called the BLUE MOON. My first-ever album, *Elvis* (#1[5], 11-56), spun incessantly in our knotty-pine Dearborn basement (with fellow 13-year-old pal George Gliga bumping his 6'6" head in our basement ping-pong marathons, as we discussed Elvis's cool blue-gold moon). Despite a chord shortage (2, 3 if you stretch), song has one of the greatest pure melodies in music history. We all have an Elvis song in our hearts that for each one of us is special. It holds the best tune, the best memories, or reminds us most of our lost youth and innocence. [Or lost ping-pong marathons]. The following may be yours:

"Can't Help Falling in Love" – Elvis Presley, #2(1), 12-61. Bob and Kathy Emerick's favorite. They chose this song to bless their wedding. My friend Bob is a retired teacher,and lifeguard on the Great South Bay in Patchogue, NY. Zillions of fans, worldwide, along with the Emericks, believe this is the most romantic song of all time. Elvis slides from his tenor Rockabilly in the last tune to resonant Italian baritone. Elvis shows the utter reality of love. You don't invest in it. You don't measure and decipher or computerize and program it. You just FALL. Kerplunk. Nothing rational at all. You can't help falling in love. Whomp! There you are.

Why is this Elvis song voted his BEST in a worldwide poll? Musically, it packs all the prettiest chord progressions you can fondle. In the mellow Key of 'D', "Falling" begins on a soft sweet arpeggio tonic major D, with bristly brushes petting the snare. At a metromonic 72 beats a minute, "Falling" features a pittypat of trickling triplets. They wash away your weariness like a warm summery shower. Elvis croons into his first two verses, with a commanding macho baritone that even **Bing** would envy.

Both Elvis's river here and the Righteous Brothers' "Unchained Melody" river flow somewhere safely to the nestling arms of the open sea. Elvis breaks the bank on SINCERITY in this Love Ballad. He pours out his truest feelings of lasting love and cherished fidelity. If the verses are magnificent earthly treasures, his vocal BRIDGE soars skyward, like Simon & Garfunkel's #1, 70 "Bridge over Troubled Water." Elvis's beautiful melody is the musical wellspring from which flows this eternal river of eternal love he serenades a weary world with. It is no coincidence – is it – that his back-up quartet/quintet is the **JORDANaires**? As romantic rivers flow, "Can't Help Falling in Love" is – for Elvis's ardent fans worldwide – the River Jordan of secular Love Balladry. It's a sweet invitation to some kind of promised land . . . Elvis's modified Streetcorner chord pattern climbs foothills of chordal destiny – messing around with mediant minors, while seeking the II chord and the eventual dominant and return.

Gordon Stoker and his **Jordanaires** crystallize Elvis's magic, mesmerizing harmonies of this ultimate slow dance favorite. The most magic moment in a momentous song is often the climax of the Vocal Bridge. In this Elvis swan song, it's a moment of lyrical kismet. Karma. The dangling of fate – and the sweet afterglow of resigning yourself to the fact that you're deeply in love.

Unlike his earlier passion-powered "One Night" #4, 11-58, Gerri Clements' favorite King song, this Elvis Anthem perks promises of Forever Love. Of the hundreds of millions of women who adored the King, and the thousands who shared his love, only one did he ever actually marry – **Priscilla Beaulieu Presley**. Though this Rock and Roll Rainbow tries to gouge the gossip, we must say that a lot of Elvis's deep despair in the final years was romantic. His overtaxed heart was not that of a digital computer. When Elvis continued romantically roving after his marriage, due to temptation and just being Elvis, he was totally shattered when his innocent bride Priscilla took a similar retaliation with a romantic rendezvous with the karate instructor. This completely broke Elvis's will.

For the King, Life did not begin at forty. It meant hospital stays, pills and despair, a yo-yo Armageddon with his weight monster, puffy Las Vegas exhaustion, inconsequential affairs, and his final solitary night: racquetball till the wee hours, the usual insomnia, and his last tragic episode with his big, sad, lonely heart. On August 16, 1977, Elvis Presley, biggest entertainer in the history of the world, felt his heart ebb away as his 'Blue Moon Turned to Gold Again.'

America's first famous nonconformist talked about marching to a different drummer. We cannot, **Henry David Thoreau** (1817-62) insisted, be all the same. In the 60s, Thoreau RULED! Monkees' **Mike Nesmith**, who designed MTV (1981), wrote a nifty little tune about a girl who is trying to tell her boyfriend that the two of them march to the beat of a different drummer. The girl was **Linda Ronstadt**, her guitarist Bobby Kimmel, and the song was listed as the **Stone Poneys, featuring Linda Ronstadt** #13, 11-67 "Different Drum." With the **Lesley Gore** #2(3), 12-63 "You Don't Own Me" theme, Linda sang she favored casual dating – not POSSESSION.

"It's So Easy" – Linda Ronstadt, #5, 10-77; #81, 11-77 C. BUDDY HOLLY'S BIGGEST HIT that never hit? In the U.S.A., Buddy's split with early Crickets **Jerry Allison** and **Joe B. Mauldin** coincided with this release. "It's So Easy" starred 1999 Grammy winner **Tommy Allsup** on lead

guitar. Though Buddy's loyal U.K. fan folks lofted him to #17 on the Melody Maker charts, the rocker was Buddy's last Down-Under lifetime hit (#8, 1-59, Australia). Let's now tout the Tucson lass with dark sweet eyes of love fire. **Linda Ronstadt** soon scored with poignant mournful ballad "Long, Long Time" (#25, 8-70). Linda's new producer **Peter Asher**, orange-haired Brit Invasion half of **Peter & Gordon** (#1, '64 "World Without Love") duo, found her a studio back-up band. They would emblazon their #1 American 70s Rock Band status all over the Soundscape of our lives: **Glenn Frey, Don Henley, Randy Meisner,** and **Bernie Leadon** – the **Eagles**. By March 2000, *Eagles/Their Greatest Hits* (#1[5], 3-76, became the biggest-selling album in history – with over 25 million sold. Their next one, *Hotel California* (#1[8], 12-76) wimpily sold a measly 14 million or so. Linda launched two terrific unheralded hits as the seventies snuggled into discodom: #51, 12-73 "Love Has No Pride," and a #67 song made famous by a rare BRITISH Country/Folk combo of **Dusty** and brother Tom Springfield, the #20, 8-62 Pre-Beatle "Silver Threads and Golden Needles." Enter **Peter Asher**. This English-Arizona connection clicked in summery Los Angeles. Asher took Linda through her commercial zenith. Linda hit her Rock and Roll Mainstream heyday with Asher's Rock resurrections by **Buddy Holly, Chuck Berry, Roy Orbison, the Everly Brothers,** Motown **Smokey Robinson, Martha Reeves,** and Soul stars **Doris Troy, Little Anthony**, and others. The Lovely Linda's crowning achievement?

Linda boogies "It's So Easy," with her come-hither rasp scorching the craggy guitars. She hammers Buddy's double-voice downbeat; Holly's airy Irish tenor on the first "It's So Easy" ricochets into his gruff, growly macho rasp. Linda xeroxes Buddy's masterful double-tone dynamism. One of the great things an artist can do is make a great bygone artist live again with a fresh new sound. The judgmental term 'cover version' has a phlegmy undertone. 'Cover versions' are not inferior and obsequious Grubbo-Crummo-Mart prints of the real Michaelangelo painting. They are personalized interpretations. Linda's soulful and respectful "It's So Easy" proves her Holly expertise. She added her own Arizonan (Mexican, German, and Irish) polycultural sound-mix to Holly's Tex-Mex Rockabilly rocker. Like **Mariah Carey**, a blend extraordinaire.

Her *a cappella* verse wiggles its sultry 111° Tucson July Soul into the penultimate finale. After two lines of whispery "It's so easy" with ringing echo and jasmine of tambourine, Asher crashes the whole kit and kaboddle for Linda's last *coup de grace*. You may recall that our band cut this tune in 1967 with **Ed McCoy** at Detroit's Big Mack Records. Somehow, our "It's So Easy" had enough 'White Soul' to snag airplay at both WCHB and WJLB, Detroit's two big Soul stations. I don't believe Linda knew my version of "It's So Easy." However, Eagle **Glenn Frey** was born in Detroit and skedaddled to the suburbs (Royal Oak) like we did (Dearborn) in the shifty fifties. We were kids. Who knows? Three chords and a cloud of dust. All this stuff interconnects.

"That'll Be the Day" – Linda Ronstadt, #11, 9-76; #27, 9-76 C. She echoes Holly's masterpiece, down to the cut-time backbeat, the muted *pizzicato* guitar plunging from the IV to the I major in the instrumental bridge, and the impish Dennis-the-Menace vocal style. A swash of treble metal blankets her "That'll Be the Day" in the Fender Stratocaster guitar glow that Buddy pioneered. For a Mr. Sincere guy, Holly's creation "That'll Be the Day" lathers sarcasm and dramatic irony: girl threatens to leave guy, he chuckles 'yeah, sure, that'll be the day, uh huh.' All is not rosy in this relationship; it may relate to Buddy's stormy high school amours (see *Buddy Holly Story* 1978****.) Buddy (Gary Busey) refuses to kiss her Barbie-blonde face goodbye as she boards the bye-bye bus for college; he's had enough of her yakky run-your-life style. The actual girl of his dreams, with whom he "Can't Help Falling in Love," is his later bride Maria Elena Santiago [Holly] (b. '32). Holly's monumental song headlined the Rock Revolution. Metamorphosing into McLean's "American Pie," the Smithsonian Institution's #5 greatest song ever (1901-2000), "That'll Be the Day" became a secular icon. Good ol' boys chugged rye whiskey, revved levee Chevies, and lamented that this might be their final day on the planet.

"It Doesn't Matter Anymore" – Linda Ronstadt, #47, 7-75; #54, 9-75 C. Ronstadt does Holly's last hit first. This song groans the Grunge, remember? Buddy Holly does Eddie Vedder or Kurt Cobain or Smashing Pumpkins? Not exactly. **Paul Anka**'s nihilistic song for Buddy, however, fondles futility. This 1975 Ronstadt rendition, like 1959 #1(3), U.K. original, spindrifts a groggy Generation X grimness that drizzles with gloom-doom doubt and bewilderment and despair. Fun, it ain't.

Philosophically, "It Doesn't Matter Anymore" presages a glum world view. Musically, it's cutting-edge for 1959. Remember, Petty-Jacobs-Holly first wafted strings into Rock and Roll. Enchanting violin-viola counterpoint buttresses the melody, rivaling Holly's "Everyday" in its ability to play something as simple, yet profound, as a music box minuet.

RUFF RIFF? NOPE.

"It Doesn't Matter Anymore" offers a voluptuous variation of the old Blues riff where you root the tonic note, and slide sensuously through the sixth and seventh notes; in C, that's two notes, the root C and the shuffling G-A-Bb-A-G pyramid. "It" offers a slide guitar that glides a half-tone upwards at the top of the pyramid – to an unheard-of (in the R & R 50s) major seventh. Your notes read a root C, plus a blues glide of G-A-B-A-G. No big deal. It's just that stuff, however, which can un-blur the difference between a good song and a great one.

Peter Asher plays drums on this winsome song, which debuted Linda's #1(1), 12-74 *Heart Like a Wheel*, first of three #1 albums tailgated by #1[5], 10-77 *Simple Dreams* and #1(1), 10-77 Al. *Living in the USA*. Linda's vocal 'sidemen' here are women – Wendy Waldmen and Linda herself.

There's a ghastly irony to plane-crash posthumous hits. We all recall **Otis Redding**'s #1(4), 1-68 "Sittin' on the Dock of the Bay." It covers end-of-the-lonesome-road Frisco futility. We still hear the echo of **Jim Croce**'s quavering baritone from #1(2), 11-73 "Time in a Bottle." Never enough time, is there? "It Doesn't Matter Anymore" was the first in a long ominous series of hits by doomed superstars who might be here today if they'd had polyester or a bus ticket. These magnificent heart-wrenching ballads sweetly mask the terror of the tarmac. Or the immortality of soaring to the stars.

Linda Ronstadt

"Blue Bayou" – Linda Ronstadt, #3, 9-77; #2(2) C. First you hear a bass. It plunks only the 1, 2½, and 4 beats. Then Linda's belltone soprano swoops to alto. After mastering the Holly legend, she echoes "Bayou" writer **Roy Orbison**. This song seems droopily slow, but isn't tempo deceptive? At 90 beats a minute, "Blue Bayou" is a lot faster than her **Chuck Berry** R & R song "Back in the U.S.A." #16, 8-78. Linda and Peter don't put much stuff between the beats. It's lean, spare, laconic, sparse. A steel guitar surrounds Verse Two, with normal bass player Kenny Edwards on mandolin.

Rick Marotta plays ancient cowbell plus a 'Syn-drum.' Rock and Roll was going Techno! To try to stop it would be like lassoing a tornado. With a M.I.D.I. sequencer, you could now punch out your drum thunder on a keyboard, and program the breaks, fills, and rockin' riffs with a snare set-up or a big drum set. In the monumental chorus, Linda jumps up an octave. Long, long into the song, when we're dazzled by her alluring alto and her soul-searing soprano, a vocal background chimes in dramatically. One of her sidemen is one of the Top Twenty sluggers in R & R history – the **Eagles' Don Henley**. It's a swamp lyric in the Blues-booming Key of 'B'. A bayou is a hummock higher than the surrounding swamp; i.e., a four-foot mountain. It's a New Orleans blue funk song, where she and Roy dreamily hope to return – for solace, comfort, friendship, and consolation. Or for Jambalaya, with Linda and Kermit. I recall a colorful galaxy of cherry Muppets doing "Blue Bayou" tune, with Linda and Kermit the Frog.

Linda hit #10, 2-80 with "How Do I Make You." It's Thunder Rock. Mark Goldenberg hammers lead guitar, while Linda does a rare falsetto soprano in a yodelly high jump to 'B' below High C, just for fun. Linda sings Soul on #44, 2-79 "Just One Look," **Doris Troy**'s #10, 6-63 tune. She also covers the **Rolling Stones**' #7, 4-72 "Tumbling Dice" hall party sound to #32, 4-78. Stones proved in the marketplace, and their Steel Wheels touring agorae, that they still kicked butt. Rock and Roll, from the Fountainhead.

"When Will I Be Loved?" – Linda Ronstadt, #2(2), 4-75; #1(1) C. For **Don** and **Phil Everly**, it was their second hit off their new singer/songwriter million-dollar Warner Brothers contract. For Linda, it was also her second monster hit beyond her first and only HOT 100 #1, the 12-74 "You're No Good" (#51, '64 Betty Everett of SHOOP SHOOP fame). Also, "When Will I Be Loved?" was Linda's biggest Country hit and only Country #1 song. Producer Peter Asher plays cowbell. **Andrew Gold** does guitars/tambourine/backing vocals; Linda didn't forget his help, and sang background for Andrew on his lone Top Tenner – #7, 3-77 "Lonely Boy." Here's the way Kenny Edwards' bass works, like Rindy Ross's bassman prowls the root note on their **Quarterflash** #3, 1-81 mammoth "Harden My Heart."

THE RAMPAGING RHYTHM: LINDA'S BASS

♫. ♫. ♫. ♫. ♪

A simple splotch of dotted eighths.

"Blue Money" – Van Morrison, #23, 2-71. Belfast's **Van Morrison** visited Big Bopper turf and the ol' **Lefty Frizzell** line: "If You've Got the Money [Honey], I've Got the Time"

(#1, 50, Frizzell, and #1C, '76 **Willie Nelson**). **Jeff Baldori** [Woolies] and **Cub Koda** [Brownsville Station, #3, 10-73 "Smokin' in the Boy's Room"] toured in 1980 as the **Blue Money Band**. Rapscallion promises gal they'll paint the town with HER Blue Money. "Domino" (#9, 11-70) edged out Van's 1967, #10 "Brown-Eyed Girl." Snarly, snappy sounds accompany Morrison's jazzy baritone.

"Jambalaya (on the Bayou)" – Hank Williams, #20, 9-52; #1(14), 8-52 C. Hank Williams' bizarre story of a love affair starring a cigar-store 'Indian.' "Kaw-liga" hit #1(13) Country in 2-53; "Jambalaya" hit #1(14) C; it's flat-out Country Rock, with molten mid-tempo Cajun Soul. Big shindig on the bayou: "hog-wild" style guitar pluckers serenade the swingin' swamp with moonshine, music, and mirth. **John Fogerty** and the Blue Ridge Rangers hit #16, 12-72 (#66, 2-73 C) with this Cajun classic. Fogerty recreates the original sound. John returned with #10, 12-84 "The Man Down the Road." The Old Fogerty magic was still there – with his trebletone guitar leads crackling and sparkling alongside his dynamic bullwhip tenor.

"A Fool Such As I" – Bob Dylan, #55, 12-73. What's Dylan doing with somebody else's material, at mid-70s? Bob Dylan apprenticed to the best: Woody Guthrie, Jack Kerouac, Buddy Holly, Elvis (#2, '59), and **Hank Snow** of LIVERPOOL (Nova Scotia, Canada).

"A Fool Such As I" – Hank Snow, NC, 1952; #3, 12-52 C. With a cut time Western Swing sound and an immortal guitar and fiddle duo on the instrumental, Hank at 38 tries to sound 83. Dylan picked up on this Old Wise Sage Sound at 20, with Woody's help. Snow (1914-99) pioneered R & R with #27, 7-50 "I'm Movin' On" and especially "The Rhumba Boogie" of 3-51 (NC, #1[8], C). Hank's version sweetly sways in the sweet beauteous Key of 'Ab.' He pounces upon **C-major**, the mediant major, an unprecedented Country innovation, before topping off on the sub-dominant IV chord **Eb** and returning. The effect is profound.

Remember, too, Dylan takes life pretty seriously, wrestling with Born-Again Christianity in the 70s (#12, 9-73 "Knockin' on Heaven's Door," #24, 9-79 "Gotta Serve Somebody"). Bio guy Anthony Scaduto cites folk singer **Theodore Bikel** on Dylan's 30th birthday trip to Jerusalem's Wailing Wall: "Dylan has told me that Israel appears to be one of the few places left in the world where life has any meaning." In June 1997, Dylan was hospitalized for pericarditis, a serious heart inflammation: "I thought I was about to see Elvis," he wryly quipped – just before they sprang the Hibbing bard from the secret hospital. Later in '97, the rockin' rebounder scored with Grammy album *Time Out of Mind*, writer **Larry Epstein**'s favorite.

"Drift Away" – Dobie Gray, #5, 2-73; #42, 5-73 R & B. Lassoing the beat, Gray presages Reggae. The song is one of many tuneful tunes about getting 'high' on music. Star-spangled melody, via Kelly Booth.

"Gimme Gimme Good Lovin'" – **Crazy Elephant, #12, 3-69.** Crazy Elephant's lone hit? A studio-cool gazpacho by Ohio Express's **Joey Levine**. The Cadillacs' **Robert Spencer** bellows the macho lead. Vintage Katz-Kasenetz Wall of Sound. Classic rocker. Hammering hook (the title, plus "Everyday . . ."). Sad the circus left town. We could have used a few more elephantine Thunder Rockers.

"Centerfold" – **J. Geils Band, #1(6), 11-81.** Hmm, centerfold 'angel'. THUNDER ROCK – here we go. The poor Hard Rock dude suffers this dastardly dichotomy. Just when he falls in love with this apparent angel, he discovers she's been posing in her best buff Lady Godiva birthday outfit for some Cheapo Creepo Layout Stag Mag. He's torn between his own anger and lust. Every girl, no matter how seamily sensuous, is still somebody's ex-little kid. Geils brings a sense of humor to their Power Macho Rock style. Whoopee – fantasy surprise.

"Love Stinks" – **J. Geils Band, #38, 5-80.** Geils' crew smashed the door down with a ponderous Power Metal intro. The rhythm guitar blares in the cozy piano Key of 'C'. Lead singer **Peter Wolf** married movie star Faye Dunaway. In this romantic go-round lyric, love now stinks. Our hero's amour with amorous lasses has obviously abated in the amusingly grumpy lyric. Wolf snarls amid a 'YEAH YEAH' chorus of Heavy Metal glee. Wolf lavishes his gutsy baritone among fire-breathing guitars. On wild waves of flame, the band bashes the chorus: guitar man Geils, lanky Boston DJ Wolf, keyboardist/writer Seth Justman, harmonica player Richard Salwitz, and bassman Danny Klein.

Geils' #1(4), 11-81 *Freeze-Frame* album followed. Their #18, 2-80 equally-niftoid Al. *Love Stinks* cover shows Joe College and his Barbie Baby Sweetie, cheek to cheek, with love wafting between their innocent eyes. The title *Love Stinks* clutches their halo. Flip it. In some utterly uninteresting urban project, Wolf grimaces his best super-sullen James Dean. Geils followed their "Centerfold" triumph of NA-NA-NA-NA-NA-NA with #4, 2-82 "Freeze-Frame."

"Bad to the Bone" – **George Thorogood and the (Delaware) Destroyers, NC, 1982.** A large-case comment trumpets the album's inner cover:

"TO BE FULLY ENJOYED THIS RECORD
SHOULD BE PLAYED AT MAXIMUM VOLUME"

Heed the advice. Lonesome George is just not Thorogood without a whole lot of his steely slide DECI-BELS (Gibson ES 335 TD, white) in your ears. Of his #43, 8-82 Al. *Bad to the Bone*, this goodtimes Boogie song never charted, despite constant airplay. On the HOT 100, the only Thorogood single in his reprise of #9, '58 Johnny Otis Show's "Willie and the Hand Jive" (#63, 5-85). Thorogood is one of the great Bluesmen of two centuries, despite fickle, iffy charts. Delaware Delta Vintage Blues.

"Who Do You Love" – **George Thorogood and the Destroyers, NC, 1986.** Off #33, 9-86 *Live* album, this is the "Who Do You Love" that keeps the memory of this Bo Diddley hit alive – long after other great versions by Ronnie Hawkins, Jim Morrison, and our Woolies/Night Shift have receded into Hit Heaven. George's chartless boogie-down version gets all the Oldies airplay.

Destroyers' roster? George; sax/vocal back-up Hank Carter; bass boss Billy Blough; piano pounder Ian Stewart; and Jeff Simon. Despite massive airplay, Thorogood cultists galore, full 16,000 fan concerts like the one at Nassau Coliseum son Jeremy and I went to see, these Thorogood giant hits never ever even bubbled under to #132½. None of us will ever truly understand all the foibles and did methods and logic of the Hit Charts. Example: how did *Break the Cycle* hit #1 their 1st week (6-9-2001) with Al. *Staind*, with no previous high-chart experience?

"Come on Eileen" – **Dexys Midnight Runners, #1(1), 1-83.** Video looks like the Irish capital of Dublin. Their follow-up inspired *The Commitments* (#86, 5-83 "The Celtic Soul Brothers"). These guys, however, are from the heart of Birmingham, England. "Eileen" flashes blasts of falsetto in banshee splendor. Their hook "Too-Ra-Loo-Ral" is obvious to those whose Scottish grandmothers lullabyed them to Bing's biggee:

"Too-Ra-loo-Ra-Loo-Ral" – **Bing Crosby, #4, 10-44.** You may also know it as "An Irish Lullaby." Bing was quite Irish, but he was not a tenor. His molten baritone – even bass – voice sang a nation to "True Love" (#3, '56), and sometimes to sleep. Now and then, to tears. Think Bing had the original? Nah.

"Too-Ra-Loo-Ra-Loo Ral (That's an Irish Lullaby)" was by **Chauncey Olcott** (#1[4], 12-1913). Internationally famous 'Irish tenor,' Olcott was American born. He pumped the demands of Broadway/Tin Pan Alley, and created some of the most beloved 'Irish' quasi-hymns. Oddly, all four of Olcott's four monstrous Irish hits were in 1913; the original #1(7) "When Irish Eyes Are Smiling" (**John McCormack** #4, 5-1917); wonderfully weepy "Mother Machree" (#7 Olcutt 8-1913); and #5 "My Wild Irish Rose" 7-1913, from his rave-review 1899 Broadway musical, *The Romance of Athlone*. "My Wild Irish Rose's" chartbusting career had already been usurped by great SCOTTISH tenor **Albert Campbell** to #1(6), 6-1899.

"Eye of the Tiger" – **Survivor, #1(6), 6-82.** The big orange/black cat rampages on a hammering Rock and Roll rhythm with crunching cadence and shimmering guitars. The lyric is intense, bodacious, and ultra-brave. Chicago Blues & White Soul's singer **David Bickler** teamed with keyboards/singer **Jim Peterik**:

"Vehicle" – **Ides of March, #2(1), 3-70.** Shakespeare's *Julius Caesar* furnished band name. With dapper don's 1969 black Coupe DeVille, **Peterik** cruises for chicks. He's the 'friendly' stranger lurking in a jet-black sedan (the one everybody's mother warned them about). He's selling speedo love, candy, and a horn-swoggled Jazz-

Rock **Blood, Sweat and Tears** sound. The girl? She ran screaming, and her 6'5" 250# powerlifter boyfriend ate the Cadillac for lunch. This Peterik/Bickler tiger-eye sparked *Rocky III* with Sylvester Stallone (1982**½).

"The Search Is Over" – **Survivor, #4, 4-85.** As electrifying as their torrid tiger tune is, "The Search is Over" is spellbinding. With the echo of **Journey**, Bickler blasts his wish-fulfillment odyssey. He searches worldwide amid star-spangled loneliness, finally finding the girl of his dreams on a lofty pedestal – and they live happily ever after. In the mid-80s, **Survivor** was as hot as any band. Though this is their most beauteous tune, and "Tiger" tromps their Biggest-Hit category, the silver success medal goes to *Rocky IV* theme "Burning Heart" (#2[2], 11-85), with #9, 10-86 "Is This Love" in the ascendant.

Freehold, New Jersey, is good country for budding superstars. Born on September 23, 1949, **Bruce Frederick Joseph Springsteen** is the only son of a Heartland 'working-class' (hey, aren't we all?) family. With just a few infant months in **Bing Crosby**'s Crooner Decade, Springsteen was among the first generation to grow up on a diet of Wheaties and Rock and Roll. His heroes were **Elvis, Buddy Holly, and Roy Orbison**. Later **Bob Dylan**. By 1972, Springsteen's redbrick smoke and steel style coalesced into the nucleus of the **E STREET BAND**. At decent-paying gigs on the Jersey Shore, Bruce and Company dreamed dreams of "Johnny B. Goode." After the 'Castiles,' **Steel Mill**, and Earth and Child, Springsteen rocked out with the new '72 lineup: the amazing **Clarence Clemons** (sax), **Danny Federici** on keys, **Gary Tallent** on bass, **Max Weinberg** on drums, and **Miami Steve Van Zandt** on guitar.

"Glory Days" had not yet arrived, but a lot of good A & R men were trying to turn the New Jersey lad (who looks like my dad, especially at age 38) into the next Reconstituted Dylan. **Dylan** is a spectacular Rocker/poet, but Bruce's boundless Rock and Roll energy re-created the gusto of Holly and Elvis with the lyrical genius of Dylan. He drank in just enough Kerouac and Dylan to spark this song which dominated a major phase of my life. And probably yours.

"Born to Run" – **Bruce Springsteen, #23, 9-75.** After guzzling a quick shot of fame on this road-warrior anthem, rock star Bruce settled down and became what everybody said he could be – a superstar. Bruce's *Born to Run* Al. #3, 1975, bested his singles effort by twenty notches.

More importantly, "Born to Run" paints a "runaway" dream. Springsteen squeezes out all the Graveyard Rock drag-race angst of the Beach Boys and **Jan & Dean** with **Del Shannon**'s "Runaway" blue funk. "The Boss" hops up the tempo with a guitar riff whose Saracen blade could slice through all the gold at Fort Knox. Naturally, it's in 'E'. What else? Nothing but that Macho Blues Key could ever work for Springsteen's triumphant **James Dean** tenor.

Dean? Springsteen radiates that sulky, sullen, Presley-Dean aura of the guy who mumbles a bit – and it's cool, real cool. Thanks to the Lennon-McCartney brainstorm on *Sgt. Pepper* to feature lyrics on albums, we're treated to Springsteen's surrealistic landscape. Springsteen experts know his Highway 1 & 9 litany where we were all born to run. In the deep night, we glide astride Powerglide blasters past glorious mansions. Throbbing, thrill-gorging zillion-horsepower cars streak far beyond the modest speedburning hot rods of Jan, Dean and the Beach Boys. For Bruce, shuffling 'E' Street with his band, Detroit doled out some legendary cars. This midnight monster landscape deepens and darkens. Busting out on the shrieking Jersey frontiers with Highway Dusters, shrieking Chevys, and supersonic Vettes, the **Boss** celebrates in a day-glo 1969-72 rainbow of Killer Orange, Slime Green, Bopper Blue, or Midnight Royal Purple.

Then Springsteen turns his dreamy visions to the girl 'Wendy' in his ultimate romantic Rock and Roll song. Bruce tells her, with the same woebleak existential despair we feel in his gloomily marvelous "My Hometown," they've gotta flee the scene, like the **Animals**' #13, 8-65 wasteland "We Gotta Get Out of This Place," or Del Shannon's fugitive young couple fleeing some amorphous goggle-eyed goon, in #30, 2-65 "Stranger in Town." In the eerie asphalt showdown glow, Bruce tells Wendy it's their destiny, their karma to RUN. From what? To what? [Marathon running dominated at least 20 years of my life from 1983 till now; I searched for local 5K and 10K racing gold in Bruce's Freehold, New Jersey. No chrome wheels, Mickey Mouse mags, headers, triple carbs, Positraction, or modifieds. Just Nike racing shoes, hell bent for leather.] Bruce's album shows him bearded and smiling. The flip side features his Afro-American friend Clemons and a tempestuous tenor sax. On "Born to Run," he is joined by Dave Sancious on keys and Boom Carter on drums.

"Born to Run" is 4½ minutes of American nightscape adventure. The frenzied pace keeps your life in the fast lane just winding out gears, lashing steel against steel, and murdering boredom in the frenzied firestorm of Springsteen's vision.

Rolling Stone editor Jon Landau punched up the classic remark in 1974: "I saw Rock & Roll's future and its name is Bruce Springsteen." Anthony DeCurtis of *Rolling Stone's History of R & R* calls "Born to Run" Springsteen's first masterpiece. He raves on:

"Inspired by the spine-tingling emotionalism of Phil Spector and Roy Orbison, Springsteen crafted openended songs rife with operatic reach and symphonic power, songs like "Thunder Road," "Backstreets," Born to Run," and "Jungleland" that took the everyday triumphs and failures of his beach town losers and shakers and raised them to an epic scale."

Such is the magic of America. We all live the Johnny B. Goode dream. Bereft of Kings and Princes, we make our own. We champion Springsteen's universality. He writes about us all on a grand, universal, epic scale. [With a little screaming midnight asphalt on a quest for neon Saturday night paradise].

In the wake of superstardom, you'll sometimes find a phalanx of lawyers. The release of a second album was stymied by a tight court injunction. Many artists have done solo-hit sayonaras by lack of a great product on Album or Single II. Not Bruce. Nearly three years later, Columbia's epic *Darkness on the Edge of Town* (#5, 6-78) finally hit the streets. Evocative title. A wealth of symbolism pulsates within. You can imagine, that outside the Last Roadhouse neon dazzle, there broods a silent desert of lost tumbleweeds and broken dreams.

Only two singles arose: #33, 6-78 frenzied "Prove It All Night" and frantic #42, 8-78 "Badlands." If you've ever seen the Badlands of South Dakota, you know the barren landscape he's dealing with. In 1994, we visited the Little Prairie on the House there. A sod and log house, built in 1908 and bermed right into the rattlesnake and prairie-dog earth, served as home and castle to a pioneer family – complete with outhouse, potato cellar, and chicken coop. Badlands.

Bruce Springsteen, like **Jerry Garcia** in the **Grateful Dead**, built his superstar pyramid on his exceedingly generous live concert marathons. The E Street Band didn't just follow the opening troupers with a 30-minute fazz-bazz set – and then WHOOSH, off on the Lear Jet. Nope, the Boss and his mighty musical family pumped up their rep with three and four-hour exhausting live shows. Bruce gave every last ounce of energy as his versatile voice plummeted to baritone and soared into tiptop tenor. A magnificent wordsmith like Dylan, Springsteen added a new dimension in showmanship. Besides his own material, Bruce regales his grateful audiences with snippets of **Buddy Holly, Mitch Ryder, Chuck Berry, Roy Orbison, Elvis**, and his British Invasion heroes the **Searchers**. Springsteen pulled a lot of his pals into his concert limelight, too, sharing the Elvis Spotlight and its burden; Bruce resurrected the career of one of America's greatest varsity Rock and Soul stars:

"This Little Girl" – **Gary U.S. Bonds, #11, 4-81.** Into the 80s, Gary U.S. Bonds had Springsteen to thank for his resurrection back to fame and fortune. This super song, produced by Bruce and guitar man **Miami Steve Van Zandt**, features **Clarence Clemons** and Gary's 'new Daddy G.' saxman. Springsteen's own Clarence Clemons owes his sprightly yet gruff sax leads to the roaring sax of **DADDY G**, Bonds's sax guru on his Norfork hits. Greil Marcus credited (or slammed) Bonds as radiating 'ab-

surd enthusiasm.' Isn't exuberance what Rock and Roll is all about? **Holly** and the **Beatles** and **Springsteen** had it, too, thankfully. Very few rockers became superstars – if they fell asleep during their own performances.

"New Orleans" – **Gary U.S. Bonds, 36, 10-60; #5 R & B.** Your quintessential Bonds bombshell. "New Orleans" touts the cradle town of Rock heritage. Dynamic Frank Guida production. On a royal purple LeGrand label, this lyric flamboyantly flashes live oaks and Spanish moss and Southern Belles. Daddy G sax drives this one at top end, screaming down the I-10 Delta from the Crescent City to Baton Rouge. Bonds's tremendous magnolia blossoms waft wondrously. Sultry with summer romance.

Bonds's second career also included the old Waylon Jennings classic (produced by Buddy Holly) "Jole Blon (Gorgeous Blonde)" at #65, 7-81. Bonds's last HOT 100 hit #21 in 6-82: "Out of Work." Hopefully he isn't, because he is a Rock and Soul icon. And Bruce knew it all along.

Springsteen aided others, too. The Punk Rock career of **Patti Smith** zoomed to insta-zenith #13 in 4-78 with "Because the Night". Bruce wrote the **Pointer Sisters'** #2(2) "Fire" – which he'd penned for **Elvis**, who faded away too fast to ever record it. More than just a great writer, Bruce primed his rep as consummate performer. Into the 80s, he ditched his New Balance running shoes for iron, pumping up biceps and record sales.

Bruce's breakthrough into singles superstar status needed very slow dudes to back him up. Matter of fact, a couple of **Turtles**; **Mark Volman** and **Howard Kaylan** had seen their #1, 1967 "Happy Together" heyday go kaput in the #100 "Eve of Destruction" 6-70 finale of the Turtles' recording career. Now, as Superstars Emeritus, they boogied into the studio background: producing, sessionizing, and doing harmony vocals. For Bruce's first top tenner, he added a Turtle or two and an odd metaphor . . . how do hearts eat, anyhow?

"Hungry Heart" – **Bruce Springsteen and the Turtles** (vocal background), **#5, 11-80.** Like **Turtles**, "Hungry Heart" emerged out of *The River* — #1(4), 11-80. This two-disc set spawned primordial Rock and Roll goodies like "I'm a Rocker" and philosophical Goliaths (which would become 1996 movie titles) like *"Independence Day."* All *The River* songs make you think – the watermark of a good Dylan or Simon & Garfunkel album. DeCurtis says "Stolen Car" suggests the "Inevitability of loss and life of terrible freedom on the endless nightlit highway." Excellent observation. When you feel a constant need to tear up the fiery-asphalt midnight pavement, it means you're less than comfy at home. As Springsteen read his way deeper and deeper into the *Apocalypse Now* (1979****) *Heart of Darkness* (Joseph Conrad's seminal apocalypse novel), Springsteen began to feel an uneasy existential angst. Early uncertain Springsteen-via-Dylan songs are a bridge over bubbly water (the Simon & Garfunkel River of Darkness) in Bruce's philosophical progression. As early as his touted debut album, 1973s postcard-splashed *Greetings from Asbury Park*, Al. #60, 6-75, Springsteen sowed the seeds of existential despair – paving the way for a whole Alternative

Scene of Generation X gloom. This earth has never been fully rosy – without thorns. Misery-mongers stalk our besieged psyches on all sides. Life evolves as a Yin & Yang whirligig wheel of good and bad, beauty and grotesquerie, love and hate, happy and sad. To every thing, there is a season.

"Hungry Heart" reads like a Blues tune. It stomps around on hungry hardscrabble IIm chords, always trying to find its elusive melodious tonic or dominant chord. The mode is universality. The fire of desire heats up the world to fever pitch – in the smoking wake of Springsteen's unforgettable giant ♥ of Rock and Roll vision.

"Dancing in the Dark" – Bruce Springsteen, #2(4), 5-84. Bruce blasted his highest hit, backed with a solid rhythm track and volcanic vocal. Dark dancing cinches his rising Rock and Roll rep as THE BOSS. *Nebraska* [#3, 10-82] is Bruce's darkly brooding interim album. Not the OZ of Kansas, this is the Ooze of Tornado Alley next door. Maybe not. Maybe it's the barren emotional landscape of Bruce's "song-guy" persona – a New Jersey factory escapee. He's a refugee from responsibility, blasting through 90 mph Nebraska on a swirl-slosh rainswept March highway of dead dreams and dormant hopes. No doubt *Nebraska* influenced the bleak B & W album vision of *U2*'s #1(9), 4-87 *The Joshua Tree*.

With due respect to Bruce, and the great state of Nebraska, Bruce's concept album fixates upon refugees and desperados. Bruce's great lyrics paint the drooling skies, the windshield-wiper metronome blue funk, and the seedy Bonnie & Clyde characters whose ghastly fight and flight contrasts to the real American heartland: Fourth of July balloons, church spires taller than grain-elevator skyscrapers, golden retrievers cavorting with Frisbee kids, and the ball game blasting beyond the Pepsi and potato salad and Levi cutoffs and "Peggy Sue" smiles.

Nebraska showcases low-life grotesques: In his Lincoln lyric "Reason to Believe," some sicko pokes a dead dog with a sharp stick, while "Johnny 99" waves his gun spasmodically. Let's face it. These are not the normal folk we encounter daily at the Bagel Oasis, the Jiffy Lube & Boob-Tube Repair, the K-Mart Hamburgerarium, or the Prairie Powderama and Blow-Dry Hair Place. *Nebraska* stings with frontier violence, a *Pulp Ficition* (1994½*) or *Selma & Louise* (1994*¼) tragidrama of blood-spattered rage. Nevertheless, *Nebraska* pioneered the UNPLUGGED sound. *Nebraska* is a masterpiece of musical minimalism. Like Punk Rock's **Ramones** in their NC, 1977+ "I Wanna Be Sedated," and like the whole Punk movement, Springsteen's *Nebraska* pares down to simplicity and the roots of Rock and Roll. *Nebraska* needs no fancy over-instrumentation. It stands, alone and strong. It's a fresh, honest prairie panorama of music that confronts the howling void. *Nebraska* reverberates beyond the confusing spaghetti swirls of Techno-Synth wires, Robbie-the-Robot 'musicians,' MIDI-mangled Unsoul faux rhythms, and money-grubbing moguls who release anything mildly commercial, no matter how bad.

"Hungry Heart" has rugged simplicity. More than anyone in Rock and Roll, **Bruce Springsteen** suggested the halo of bygone Elvis – he had the baritone echo, the magnificent sullen mumble, and the raw catlike energy. *Nebraska* was decimated by the loss of one outtake, a bare-bones rocker and mixed bag of American pain and glory – "Born in the U.S.A." The torch was passed.

"Born in the U.S.A." – Bruce Springsteen, #9, 11-84. The album of the same name was #1(7) for seven weeks, and generated #2(4) "Dancing in the Dark," #7 "Cover Me," #6 "I'm on Fire," #9 "I'm Goin' Down," and a few others we'll touch upon. *Born in the U.S.A.* is a firestorm of Springsteen stardom. "Born in the U.S.A." is also Springsteen's best-known song. Even President Reagan saw it as a pinch-hit national anthem. "Born in the U.S.A." has darkness on the jagged edge of its swaggering gonzo refrain – BORN IN THE U.S.A.! It is a dark-side ode to the "Johnny B. Goode" dream. The song begins with the bashing thunderous drums of Max Weinberg (of 1993+ *Conan O'Brien Late Show*); he smashes the unsuspecting snare on the 2 and 4 backbeat at volcanic volume. A bizarre glockenspiel tinkles in with high echoey treble. Gary's talented bass line fortifies the soulfire – with steady slurred one-note and half step slides. Blues sixths and sevenths belie the awesome reality that this is essentially just a two-chord song – darting from its home plate Key of 'B' out to the warning track IV chord **E**. Much of the charm of "Born in the U.S.A." rides not just on Bruce's spirited vocal, but the piano-organ-glockenspiel unique ubiquity of Danny Federici's keyboard/xylophone.

"Born in the U.S.A." was sculpted as a doleful ballad for *Nebraska* – and rejected as an outtake for future stardom among the Greatest-Ever Hits of the Rock Revolution. Today's outtakes may just become tomorrow's meteoric hits. "That'll Be the Day" was a 1956 Decca flop, until producer **Norman Petty** gave **Buddy Holly** artistic license to sculpt the future #1 according to Holly's own audial vision. The #1 record of all time, **Francis Craig**'s #1(17), 1947 "Near You" was originally a B-side.

Now, about those perplexing lyrics. "Born in the U.S.A.," despite what many rock fans (and Springsteen devotees) think, is actually a stunning indictment of the old American Dream. This is Ron Kovic's *Born on the Fourth of July* (Tom Cruise, 1989***½) – not Joe Rah-Rah's "Hooray, Hooray, USA, Right or Wrong, but Never Wrong!" Springsteen's lyrics lurk.

Bruce begins on a depressing note. From there it's all downhill. The song guy's first line gets him born somewhere in "dead man's" burg. Next he hits the ground, comparing himself to a grubby fleabag dog. Not a sunnyside-up intro. A hometown scrape escalates into a GREETINGS from his dreaded local Draft Board. He gets shipped screaming to Vietnam. In the grim lyric, his own brother batted around from Da Nang to Quang Tri to Khe Sanh – and had a woman (he semi-loved) in Saigon ('Ho Chi Minh City'). The result of all this tenderness and heroism? His brother gets shipped back to the U.S.A. in a body bag. When Cruise and Tom Berenger cinematized Ron Kovic's own patriotic disillusionment and firefight paralysis, it was a wake-up call and a re-opening of an old national war wound [*Born on the 4th of July*].

A very serious question – who REALLY LISTENS to Rock and Roll Music? Everyone, some might say. Not quite so. Many of us listen to the rhythm track only. We never decipher certain lyrics, which range from crystal clear to garbled gibberish. Many of us hear little chunks of the lyric we like. Or, in Simonized style (Simon and Gar, "The Boxer" 1969) we hear just what they wish to hear – then 'disregard' the remainder. Many of us don't really care what the singer is saying; we hear it a hundred times at the Toothodontist's Office, and we can't parrot back 1¼ lines of the song.

We are all rock critics. Yes. Good ones. No 'Air-heads' or 'Bimbos.' We all consider ourselves far superior to those *American Bandstand* floppitty ingenues and teenyboppers who rated records. Remember? Ever-sunny host **Dick Clark** would present the life's work of some tremendous band busting their rhythms to make #77 on the charts. Clark would air 30 crucial seconds of their musical pride and joy, their 'Be-Bop Baby.' Then the Samurai Record Flayer, Filleter, and Be-Bop Butchers on the Teen Record Review panel would slice their dreams to smithereens with a piddling, belittling crack: "It's too weird. Can't dance too good to it, I give it a 65." The poor band's Moon-launch got blown out of the sky. Dreams dashed. Johnny B. Goode hopes torpedoed. No Glory Days for this reject band, just the odd gig at Lulu's LaRitz Dog Grooming Saloon. Billy and the Nice Guys' best effort got raked over the coals by some non-musician who never really heard what they were trying to say.

"Born in the U.S.A." is a riddle in a conundrum in an enigma. Everybody listened. Few really heard. Long ago, some tunes glided to the top via payola. Some by honest heavy hype. Some by don't-rock-the-boat conformity to old musical grooves. Many music outfits have talent – but never go anywhere.

"Born in the U.S.A." didn't just hit the Top Ten because of its mucho macho Springsteen hook line 'BORN IN THE U.S.A.': IT SUCCEEDED BECAUSE OF WHAT THE HALF-LISTENERS WANTED TO HEAR. Few jumpin' jingo Americans wanted to hear the bad parts about the war, the hometown scrape, the fleabag cur in the dead man's lost town. Somehow, we all saw in Bruce's American anthem of fomenting Generation X that – hey, nothin's perfect, we all get a few bad breaks, buy we love the good ol' U.S.A. anyhow!

The American people, among the most optimistic visionaries in this tired old Western Civilization, have a funny way of seeing the rosy side of the picture. This has been long reflected in our popular music. **Ben Selvin** hit #1 in 1927 with Irving Berlin's "Blue Skies"; the blues were gone, and the bluebird of happiness sang his song. Number One in the dastardly trenches of Armageddon Death Row World War I was a chirpy sweetie from the **Knickerbocker Quartet:** #1(5) "Pack Up Your Troubles in Your Old Kit Bag (And Smile, Smile, Smile)." Rodgers and Hammerstein's *South Pacific* album was #1(31) in 1957, and anchors the bronze medal #3 album of all time position with 262 charted weeks (5 years). Among its hit songs is one that describes our zesty national rainbow consciousness: we're "Cockeyed Optimists." In a triumph

of irony, and a legacy of rampant optimism, most Americans still believe "Born in the U.S.A." is a rollicking happy vindication of the entire American way of life. The whole shebang. Bruce tells the bittersweet story – good and bad – and it still comes out YAY U.S.A. Born in the U.S.A. Ambassador to the world.

"Glory Days" – Bruce Springsteen, #5, 6-85. The old gold tarnishes to 'GLORY DAYS!' A day in the sun. Then the cloudburst, forevermore. Bruce and the E Street Band boom the sad truth – our moments of transcendent glory are very short and fleeting. They're quick rays of golden sunshine, zapped by that dark ugly gush of dismal dank slobbery rain. Bygone glories live on, in our re-run memories.

"Glory Days" opens with a fastball down the middle. This hotshot speedball pitcher cinched his varsity glory back in high school. When the Big Game balks its sad finale, and the diamond's glitter fades, so fades the hurler's glory into a boozy haze of bar buddies swapping old revamped stories of beer blotto lost midnights. Verse Two greets us with a faded Prom Queen, her withered corsage and girlish figure fumbling into dumpy gloom and jaded cynicism and cellulite. She, too, reminisces on the bygone sporting scene. She wistfully ponders the disappearance of hubby Bobby two long years ago. If she ever gets the urge to cry, Bruce says, she tries laughing instead.

Life's like that. You get the bitter, the sweet. You cling to the hope and the afterglow. A rainbow shimmers in the sunny South beyond Brooklyn's Gravesend Bay, far over Far Rockaway, far far away into the surging Atlantic. You try to catch the rainbow.

"Glory Days" is Basic Rock. Down the middle. Over the plate. Fortified with the Hammondish organ of **Danny Federici**, "Glory Days" is a three-chord major manifesto. **Miami Steve Van Zandt** rides the rock and roll waves. The beat is steady, insistent, even heroic.

It's a song, of course, about heroes. It's a song about disillusionment. Heroes are notoriously romantic figures. Fans can make them. Break them. Crush them. Springsteen built himself into an Elvis. He is a hero made – not just born. After a rocky-road Freehold upbringing, and the usual generational hassles with his dad, Bruce hammered the 6-night gigs with his Heartland Rock-evolving band.

"Glory Days" and "Born in the U.S.A." energize Springsteen's 1984-87 heyday. They're a pumped-up power pinnacle for a Dutch-American Jersey kid who sings Heartland Rock with the best of the Midwest – factory-town **Bob Seger** and Hoosier **John 'Cougar' Mellencamp**. Before globbing his E Street Band together from a smoky suburban assembly line, Springsteen's early band incarnations included an obtuse coagulation of teenage idols: 'Castiles'; 'Earth'; 'Child'; 'Steel Mill'; and (hey, wow) 'Dr. Zoom & the Sonic Boom.' By 1971, Springsteen assembled a multitudinous 10-piece band, hopped up with horn section and go-go-boots back-up singers. Bruce Springsteen was ready to Rock and Roll. As 70s Boy Wonder, Bruce was declared the 'Future of Rock.' Fulfillment of that Insta-Stardom took ten years. Three chords and a cloud of dust. Tough road. In "Born to Run," Bruce barreled down "Thunder Road" and a "Tenth Avenue Freeze-Out" (#83, 1-76), before hightailing it for the "Badlands" of *Nebraska* (or South Dakota), where his "Hungry Heart" led him to Rock idol destiny.

Springsteen's Freehold teenage years were pockmarked by athletic mediocrity, so he invested his second chance and built a body. Born in the USA is a workingman's rock romp. Springsteen enhances a T-shirt. His famous Levis are strangled by a rhinestone spangled black belt – and a cool red baseball cap stuffed into the pocket.

With a national #1 album, he'd come a long way from the 1973 *Asbury Park* era of fair-to-middlin' 25,000 albums sold – and opening for Jazz-Rock giants **Chicago**. By the 80s, he rose to #3 artist of the decade. For a few golden 'Glory Days,' nothing the Boss cut missed the top ten. When you bought a Springsteen song or twelve, you knew you were purchasing a 111% performance. Gusto, glory, and the heart of Rock and Roll. Thunder Rock!

Even Bruce, however, could sling a ballad. We are a nation of jocks, ex-jocks, and sports fans (see Sports Rock). The macho quest for gridiron, diamond, ring, track, and hoop stardom permeates our rampaging lifestyle – just a generation or so from the frontier pioneers. Now and then, we like to sing the Blues. Sad songs, yes:

"My Hometown" – Bruce Springsteen, #6, 12-85. Precious few songs bring tears to the eyes of smoke and steel stoics and inmates of 70 hour/week noisy factories. This item does. It makes S.W.A.T.-team vet cops cry. It's about dreams. Dreams that don't quite come true. It's about a kid growing up in a dim factory town. It covers his racially tense high school years. "My Hometown" is about this guy's Promised-land dream to pack up and head South, leaving his smoky scraggly town of steel and stone. California dreamin' – Jersey home plate. He needs to revamp his career and find a tuft or two of green grass for his little guy. Like his own dad, he doesn't quite make it.

He props up the kid behind the behemoth old Buick's steering wheel and sez to his boy – take a real good look all around – THIS, he waves – is your own hometown. It's a grim note of futility. Finality.

One rainbow: The father, resigned to his economic fate, obviously loves his little boy. He will do all in his limited power to vent his own frustration, and raise his son the best he can. Despite the loss of his upward economic mobility, something far more important is at work here – DAD. Dad is at perhaps his most important job; he is sculpting the greatest work of art the world has ever known: A little boy or girl . . .

The E Street echo is never far behind. Nothing unplugged about "My Hometown." **Danny Federici** caresses the mood on second synthesizer (which sounds strangely human) on the vocal bridge. **Max Weinberg** supplies the muted bass-drum thump and the little high-hat tap on beats two and four. Bass notes surround the maxed-out father's mood with swooping grace-note strength and deep low power with **Miami Steve** to the axefire max. The big guy, **Clarence Clemons**, finds his super sax stun-

ningly backgrounded in this lonesome ballad for the ages. The big Four and Five chords swoop and spindrift, caressing the sweet melody in a slow surge of weary resignation and lukewarm reality.

When discussing the racial strife (a backseat gun in times of trouble), Springsteen is a world away from Peter, Paul, and Dylan's #2, 1963 "Blowin' in the Wind" optimism. In the sunny Camelot Era of JFK and Dr. King's Freedom Marches in 1963, we all just had to crunch the big cosmic jigsaw puzzle together. The what? Yahoo! Utopian harmony glittered the Yellow Brick Road to the Emerald Hills and City of Oz. Or Shangri-La. Or Paradise Alley. No Vietnam thorn, yet, in the American rosy balloon hovering in HyperSpace.

Just when you think "My Hometown" is an exercise in smoky futility because he can't ever get out, he contradicts himself and the glory and power reappear. He does something. He stays with his faithful Kate. He grins and bears the smoke, steel, and cosmic weariness. He raises his little boy. He makes consolation-prize plans. Maybe the palm-tree visions will vanish, but the man and his family are still there. He's coping. Like a man.

Somehow, his family is pretty happy in their hometown. God bless them.

"Workin' on the Highway" – Bruce Springsteen, NC, 1984. The fifties gracefully ignored great album cuts – because most record collectors couldn't afford the $5 for an album. Think that's bad? A one-side scratchy old #1(7), 8-1907 or #2(1), 5-1904 copy of Enrico Caruso's "*I Pagliacci – Vesti La Giubba*" (On with the Play)" would also set you back five bucks. In 1904! For many people, this was a WEEK'S PAY! My niece Gail Warde came to one party at Aunt Jo's – Alan Warde and crew were hardly astounded she had 40 CD albums, for this year alone.

"Workin'" slings an A-1 Elvis echo. Bruce pits a disgruntled papa and a Casanova kid (Bruce) after his daughter. The total sound? With the big bold bashing beat and the organ blasting full tilt boogie for **C** (I) to **F** (IV), Springsteen gives us one of the best Rock and Roll songs to come down the pike since **Eddie Cochran**'s legendary "Summertime Blues," redone in Heavily Metallic splendor by **Blue Cheer** (#14, '68) and the **Who** (#27, '70). The lusty lads snarf up a beefy rhythm on their rockin' rollickin' highway to Heaven. Or Limbo. Busts a snooze.

"Cover Me" – Bruce Springsteen, #7, 8-84. Springsteen's third chartbusting Top Tenner stalks Bruce's best Elvis-style baritone vocal, with sizzling shudders of Rockabilly passion. On a whirlwind of rhythmic fire, "Cover Me" covers Bruce's 1984 pinnacle of rock-idol power. "Cover Me" calls out to cover a few more Springsteen R & R triumphs: "Tenth Avenue Freeze-Out" #83, 1-76 is vintage Springsteen at its screamingest – heart-of-rock-and-roll gold. When Bruce wrote "Fire" (#2, 11-78) for the **Pointer Sisters**, wasn't it inevitable he'd score later with hot-blooded #6, 2-85, "I'm on Fire"? He combines a smoldering slurry desire-fire that shades the hottest moods of **Elvis**'s "Burning Love," #2, '72, or Graveyard Rock legend Jody Reynolds' "Fire of Love." We cover Bruce's #8

"War" and #9 "Streets of Philadelphia" elsewhere, but two #9's also stand out: "I'm Goin' Down" of 9-85 echoes Bruce's spiraling nightscape mood, purring with murmuring of promised passion; "Tunnel of Love" (12-87) casts the same enchanting mood with eerie carnival overtones of funhouse fright. In 1984, I tried to take my two kids Lauri, 17, and Jeremy, 12, on Disneyland's Matterhorn ride. After a half-hour of line grumbling, 200 folks like us were told the alpine tram was closed for the day. We three took the tunnel-of-love "Small, Small World" ride, obviously for much younger kids. Later we found out a lady was killed on the Matterhorn ride we were fifth in line for (Disneyland's 9th death in 30 years). Somehow, Tunnels of Love bear eerie overtones. One of the great things about a Springsteen song, like those of **Bob Seger**, is that the singers are great charismatic stars – but their MUSIC is always just a little bit dangerous.

Springsteen albums blazed: #1(4), 11-80 *The River*; #1(7) *Bruce Springsteen & the E Street Band 1975-85* of 11-86; #1(1), 10-87 *Tunnel of Love*; #2(2), 3-95 *Human Touch*. With the dark brooding spirit of *Nebraska*, Bruce salutes **John Steinbeck's** *Grapes of Wrath* (1939) in Al. #11, 12-95 *The Ghost of Tom Joad* (alluding to *Grapes'* hero/victim). The *2001 World Almanac* picked **John Steinbeck** (1902-68) as favorite author of all time (Shakespeare won the Silver Medal). The Springsteen legacy continues to unfold.

"Darlington County" – **Bruce Springsteen, NC, 1984.** This and "Workin'" stem from *Born in the U.S.A.* Each follows the Rock and Roll Rounders, Rogues, and Rapscallions category. These two 'wild and crazy guys' in the song named 'Me and Wayne' go cruising. The boys try to impress the Jersey jewels that they're big spenders and high rollers, from New York City. Flashing 200 bucks and swaggering, crude catcalls, they promise the girls they're gonna rock all night long. The song does. The ribald rolling beat thunders along in everybody's favorite key – good ol' 'G'. As we mentioned before, the great sound of a great musician is underpinned by a great rhythm track. Check out **Garry Tallent**'s insistent bass. In the Disco Era, and with the rise of Motown and high-quality stereos and even quadraphonic (4 speakers with different parts of the song), the BASS emerged from the Boss's song's bottomtone range.

Springsteen's drifters, renegades, and rebels on the fried midnight neon midnight roads show us the power of an image (**James Dean**), the power of a singer (**Bruce Springsteen**), and the throbbing Heart of Rock and Roll.

"We Got the Beat" – **Go-Gos, #2(3), 1-82.** In the mid-60s, the guitar-brandishing **Debutantes** scorched the Detroit Rock scene. Masterminded by **Eddie Cowling**, they did a dynamite re-make of the Five DuTones' #51, '63 "Shake a Tail Feather." The female-of-course Debs dabbled with the HOT 100, but ditched the dream after a good fight, a little airplay, and a bit of hype. More importantly, the Debutantes played their own guitars. They became the forerunners of the **Go-Gos, Joan Jett, Bonnie Raitt** (1999 Rock Hall Inductee), and **Melissa Etheridge**. They were

way too early. The 'Girls Group' era was sparked with great female singers who often just stood prettily and swayed their chiffon-swaddled bods in rocking rhythm to the male whizbang guitar groovers behind them. Though **Sylvia Vanderpool** of Mickey and Sylvia ("Love is Strange" #11, 1-57) actually played her guitar, she was a rarity. Fifties female guitar-slingers were few and far between. **Les Paul** played; **Mary Ford** sang.

Suddenly arrived the **Go-Gos**. [Not the **Goo Goo Dolls**, of #9, 12-98 "Iris" fame]. Their debut "Our Lips Are Sealed" (#20, 8-81) debutanted the colorful career of singer **Belinda Carlisle**, ace guitarist **Charlotte Caffey**, and rhythm axe-handlers Jane Wiedlin and Kathy Valentine. Valentine, who also thumps bass, looks a bit Asian (their L.A. connection) on their #1(6) *Beauty and the Beat* super-pun album of 9-81; if she is Asian (and she is very obviously female on the bubble-bath cover) she covers two more links in the multicultural chain of American Rock and Roll: the female Asian-American rocker.

The BEAT (We've Got) is basically thundered by **Gina Schock**, drums and percussion. The Go-Gos are a talented batch of singer/songwriters (who just happen to be very attractive, rarely a liability). In the hoopla wake of their big album, they took a "Vacation" (38, 7-82) and went "Head Over Heels" [#11, 3-84]. On *Beauty and the Beat* romantic harmonies highlight "Fading Fast." Check out their metaphorical wit on "Skidmarks on My Heart," or Gina's layered drum fills and power-packed paradiddles. Listen to the soprano sweetness of Belinda. The name 'Go-Gos' emphasizes energy and spunk and perky cuteness. On the saucier side, it implies a kind of spicy unadorned dance style. The Go-Gos go-goed for three glorious years, picking up where the early Beatles left off – pure harmonic Rock and Roll that was FUN again.

"Lido Shuffle" – **Boz Scaggs, #11, 3-77.** You know, "LIDO, WO-OH-OH-OH-OH-OH..." **Boz** (b. '44, Ohio) and **Steve Miller** hooked up at University of Wisconsin in the 60s (Scaggs was Steve's singer with the Marksmen). Later the Ardells. Scaggs was raised in Texas, returning for madcap Madison years as a White Soul turbulent tenor. Scaggs Folk-sang in Stockholm, Sweden, and cut *Boz*, a big Swedish Folk album on Karusel Records. Then he did sideman stuff with Muscle Shoals' famous Stax/Volt studio, rejoining Miller's Mainstream Rock & Soul fraternity band. After a major R & R career with six top 20 hits, he retired from music to open a 1983-87 San Francisco restaurant. It's intriguing. Besides Miller, who shaped Boz's career?

Managers are often media dynamos. 'Colonel' **Tom Parker**, circus barker, jump-started Elvis's career from Hillbilly Cat to World-Class Superstar. Buddy Holly's **Norman Petty** smoothed his rough Texan edges, and helped him sculpt the most versatile, talented musicianship among the Fab Fifties phenoms. Ritchie Valens's **Bob Keane**, Beatles' **Brian Epstein**, and Stones' publicist/manager **Andrew Loog Oldham** created R & R destiny. **Irving Azoff** steered the careers of **Boz Scaggs** and the **Eagles**, PLUS masterpiece melodist **Dan Fogelberg**, Jazz-Rocker **Steely Dan**, and conch Rocker **Jimmy**

Buffett.

Scaggs kicked off with clever tunes: BOZ punned along with ancient Buick transmission 'Dyna-Flow' on his semi-hit "Dinah Flo" to #86 on 9-72. VIOLA! Bicentennial Year 1976. Just when Boz was considering Kirby Vacuum sales, or ostrich farming, suddenly "It's' Over" zoomed to #38 on the HOT 100. Boz Scaggs' "Lowdown" high-jumped to a #3 booster skyrocket for July 4, 1976 – his biggest hit. Other chart champs? #15, 3-80 "Breakdown Dead Ahead," the Ray-Parker-on-guitar #17, 6-80 "Jo-Jo," and #14, 11-80's "Miss Sun." When his restaurateur kahuna phase faded away, he blipped back to Hitsville with #35 "Heart of Mine" at age 44 in 1988.

"Radar Love" – Golden Earring, #13, 5-74. Dutch Invasion Power Rock. One of greatest Rock songs of all time is by two-hit Golden Earring. Dutch, you know, is English's closest cousin (unless you count Frisian, a Dutch Islands rare language spoken by a few thousand). Almost all Dutch (and Swedish and Danish) kids speak fluent English. Golden Earring's lead baritone blues singer is **Barry Hay**. **Peter Rudge**, managing both the Stones and the Who, smoothed a contract deal with MCA's corollary crew Track Records. They toured with Joe Cocker and Led Zeppelin. Golden Earring's guitar guru is **George Kooymans**, with Cesar Zuiderwijk on drums and Magnus Gerritsen on bass. The "Radar Love" beat jackhammers ... "Radar Love" lavishes a speeding bass, driving drums, a Mississippi-Deltaish Dutch lead vocal, and a Led Zep intensity. Super Rock and Roll song. In 1982, Golden Earring reemerged with their biggest #10, 11-82 "Twilight Zone." Shades of 'Killer' Jerry Lee Lewis's frantic Ferriday, LA, and Rock and Roll Fever.

"Paradise by the Dashboard Light" – Meatloaf, #39, 9-78. With **Ellen Foley** and "Rapper" **Phil Rizzuto**, NY Yankee announcer. Too good for 1978 alone, Meat Loaf re-arrived in 1993 and galumphed to the top spot, along with #1(5), 9-93 "I'd Do Anything for Love (But I Won't Do That)" with **Patti Russo**. No wispy featherweight, Mr. Loaf, as the *New York Times* chucklily calls the former **Marvin Aday** (b. '51, Dallas), got his start singing with Detroit rock legend **Ted Nugent**: "Paradise by the Dashboard Light" concerns a Casanova embroiled in a Kissyface Countdown. Armed with the eight arms of an octopus, and with 'Russian hands and Roman fingers,' Loaf's trying to get to second base with this lass who smooches to first base and stops him.

Though many rockers have landed in the Cleveland Hall of Fame, New York Yankee announcer **Phil Rizzuto** ('Scooter' at 5'6", 150#) was the only one on the HOT 100 top 40 to make the OTHER Hall of Fame. The first one? Cooperstown, NY's Baseball Hall of Fame, est. 1939. Phil calls out the play-by-play in some amorphous baseball game on the car radio. The whole game charade is a big metaphor for Meat Loaf grabbing in the back seat at his unconvinced date, acted in song by singer Ellen Foley. When the batter in the radio game gets to first base, so does the suave Mr. Loaf. You could serve Meat Loaf into the Great Singers chapter with his Caruso Italian Dra-

matic tenor: **Jackie Wilson,** 1960 **Elvis, Del Shannon, Roy Orbison, Jay Black, Gary Puckett**. Playing Eddie in the *Rocky Horror Picture Show* in L.A., Loaf's voice could Samsonize an opera venue – and bring down the house.

Meanwhile, back at the petting zoo: Phil raps on about a ballplayer rounding second base and headed for third, and poor confused Ellen asks the horniferous lad whether he really loves her or just craves her bod. In 1978, wedding rings were often discarded like hula-hoops. She demands he says he'll love her till the end of time. At the finale, he twists her words into a bizarre pun; he prays for the final curtain of time itself. Why? So he can end his time with her.

Back seat Boogie. Loaf stormed the HOT 100 citadel on a wispy cliché: #71, 5-71 "What You See Is What You Get." His breakthrough biggee (#11, 3-78) is theatrical silvertoned ballad "Two Out of Three Ain't Bad." After twin #39ers, 11-78 "You Took the Words Right Out of My Mouth," and this dashboard paradise saga, he virtually vanished. When *Beauty and the Beast* (1993****) chalked up another Disney triumph, Loaf coattailed its fame and fortune into a voluptuous video.

Millions of kids, buoyed by Rock and Roll and magnetic libidos, seek paradise by the dashboard light. As teeny Toyotas get squeezier and squishier than the cruising Continentals and El Dorados of old, kids still fire up the passion superchargers. Vans and SUV's can become mobile motels of fertility.

The human race proliferates. We are not presently an endangered species. In my lifetime, the world population has more than doubled to 6,000,000,000+. Stern prognosticator Benjamin Zuckerman says that by 3400 A.D., our ten sextillion [10,000,000,000,000,000,000,000] squished grumpy earthlings will EACH get one square foot of land. MTV is not dressing up its curvaceous cuties in ankle-length cloth swaths to push abstinence.

"Journey to the Center of the Mind" – Amboy Dukes, #16, 6-68. Full-volume Psychedelic Rock sparkled with **Ted Nugent** on Heavily Metallizing lead guitar. Recently Nugent (b. '48, Detroit) hosts Detroit-area radio talk show as self-titled *Motor City Madman*. He champions bow-hunting adventures, stalking species throughout the frozen planet. **Ted Nugent** creates safaris in music and life, journeying to the center of the Macho Bull's-eye. Other solo shots at stardom include his Darwinian/Spencerian Survivalist "Dog Eat Dog" #91, 11-76, Nugent, too, named his biggest hit after a weird but serious disease – #30, 8-77 "Cat Scratch Fever." With his own 2000+ ultra-macho Michigan radio show and hunting column in Michigan, the Motor City wild man rocks on, druglessly, into his virile 50s. Don't miss his sayonara song "Wango Tango" at #86, 7-80.

"Footloose" – Kenny Loggins, #1(3), 1-84. Logged into the AOR Adult Contemporary Rock format, Messina's Loggins (b. '47) cut loose. He inherited the Easy Listening gene, perhaps from cuz Dave Loggins of Mountain City, Tennessee – whose "Please Come to Boston" hit #5 in 6-74, a very pretty ditty. Kenny warmed up with #4, 11-

72 "Your Mama Don't Dance" with **Jim Messina**, plus their 11-73, #15 "My Music." In the solo arena? #7, 12-80s "I'm Alright." "Footloose" crunches quietude, and joyously zaps the sounds of silence. Great drums, super speedo vocal, nice total package. Movie theme flat-out ROCKS!

Kenny didn't shake loose the "Danger Zone" (#2, 5-86) of Elvis's spotlight. Kenny's "Nobody's Fool" (#8, 7-88), and he's kept this Heart-Rock style as a "Conviction of the Heart" (#65, 10-91).

"The Boys Are Back in Town" – Thin Lizzy, #12, 5-76. R & R romp. Named after the Model T Ford (Tin Lizzy), this band is Multi-Anglo-Irish-American. Lead singer/poet **Phil Lynott** was born in Dublin of Afro-Irish parents. **Samantha Mumba** parleyed the same ethnic combo into her #4, 9-2000 "Gotta Tell You." Resembling **Jimi Hendrix**, Lynott clicked first in U.K. with Irish pub sing-along "Whiskey in the Jar" (NC, '73; #6, 2-73 U.K.) later covered by **Metallica**. With a rising Euro-Rep, Thin Lizzy's Brian Robertson added Scotland to the ethnic mix. Also American Scott Gorham, lead guitar. In the USA, *Jailbreak* hit Al. #18, 6-76. They're stamped Heavy Metal, but "The Boys Are Back in Town" is just good ol' Rock and Roll. Bassist Lynott commanded center stage with charisma and fancy fretwork. By the height of their heyday, Thin Lizzy's Lynott developed hepatitis, beat it, but died in 1986. Like Hendrix before him, Lynott's excursion into skull and crossbones substances caused his untimely death at 35.

After the **Beatles** split up, four very different brilliant musical careers headed in four very different directions. **John** and **Ono** bedded down, publicly, for a Bed-In and art exhibition of his droodly sketches. **Paul** and wife **Linda** coattailed Denny Laine and they flew away on **WINGS** of song. **George Harrison** melded his Transcendental Meditation and Hare Khrishna Consciousness to his Religious Rock songs already covered. **Ringo** discovered he had a lot of friends in the world of music. Solo Beatles. Let's flip the order, eh?

"You're Sixteen" – Ringo Starr, #1(1), 12-73. Ringo's drums thump the medium-pace beat with the accuracy demanded of the drummer in the World's Greatest Rock and Roll Band. At 33, Ringo was a tad elderly to sing this ogly ode to a teen dream queen. Matter of fact, at 27, so was Johnny Burnette. Or **Chuck Berry** (32) with #2 "Sweet Little Sixteen."

"You're Sixteen – You're Beautiful" – Johnny Burnette, #8, 10-60. Memphis Rockabilly. The album photo is unforgettable. Burnette stands looking at you from a swash of buff light. One white buck loafer on the spacey floor, and one on tiptoe, Burnette has his preacher-style hands raised at 10 and 2 o'clock. He wears tight black pants and a black, buttoned long-sleeve dress shirt. His white tie matches his shoes. Black and white. His princely

Elvis pompadour crowns his serious, lookin'-for-trouble face. The massive Vaseline haircut towers four inches above his brow. The Great Singers Chapter would fire a WELCOME mat Johnny's way. Mirroring **Buddy Holly**, Johnny logged 4 Top 20 tunes into a tiny 15-month career. A natural baritone like Elvis, Burnette's low notes match **Conway Twitty**'s jaguar rasps; into the high tenor zone, Burnette rides the burnished melismas of 30 years hence on the timbre of Buddy Holly. It is one GREAT Rockabilly voice, bouncing off the long faraway years. Johnny Burnette's early seminal Rockabilly trio with brother **Dorsey** (#23, 2-60 "Tall Oak Tree") caused covers by the **Yardbirds** ("Train Kept A-Rollin'") and **Rod Stewart**. Ribbons, curls, peachy strawberry-wine lips. Ideal 50s girl. Most of all, he's powered by STRINGS.

"God, Country, and My Baby" – Johnny Burnette, #18, 10-61. A philharmonic phalanx of flying strings sears the high notes with violin fire and brimstone. Johnny delivers an old patriotic sentiment in a song you will never hear anywhere, anytime, on anyone's favorite Oldies Ozone Overkill station. Basically, the pretentious title comprises the main three reasons he feels justified in fighting – unquestioningly – for his country. It's been effectively blacklisted by the Sentimental Censor Police.

He crosses the German Rhine, so it's a rehashed World War song. A snappy snare hits a weird Chalypso beat. Johnny and strings rattle off the most well-sung war-martyr song you will never hear. Grab this rarity before it disappears into the twinkling twilight of time. Despite my punchy review, it's a beautiful piece of music and melody, fronted by a tremendous singer singing his last HOT 100 hit.

"Little Boy Sad" – Johnny Burnette, #17, 2-61. Flexing his Twitty rasp, his Jack Scott muscles, and his Mariah Carey grace-note melismas, Johnny Burnette offered album gems: twangy-guitar reprise of #5, 10-61 Leroy Van Dyke's "Walk on By"; and Elvis-reject "Girl of My Best Friend," that garnered the #19, 4-61 honors for **Ral Donner** and the **Starfires**. Best of all is Johnny's "Dreamin'," #11, 7-60. Brother **Dorsey Burnette** rumbled baritone to Johnny's golden tenor, and enjoyed a classic of his own on the stunning #48, 6-60 "Hey Little One" (also #54, 1-68 and #13, 2-68 by Glen Campbell).

Johnny's career was cut tragically short. As eerily as **Buddy Holly**'s last gig at the Surf Ballroom in Clear Lake, Iowa, Johnny went on a fated vacation to CLEAR LAKE, California. He met a tragic death at age 30 when struck by a speedboat and hit by the propeller. Son **Rocky Burnette** scored #8, 5-80 with "Tired of Toein' the Line," blooming with yodel-kicks. Johnny's 1960 "You're 16" lofted a gaggle of violins into the azure heavens. Ringo Starr fires off **Paul McCartney**'s kazoo in his #1, 1973 song. Great song, wild kazoo gimmick. Some devotees say they still see Elvis and Johnny Burnette at the Dairy Queen Maltomania in Kazoo, Kansas. Or was it Kalamazoo, Michigan?

"Back Off Boogaloo" – Ringo Starr, #9, 4-72. Produced by George Harrison. Title via Fantastic Johnny C and #7,

10-67 "Boogaloo Down Broadway." Slaphappy song. I thought it was "BLACK DOG, BOOGALOO." Whenever Ringo's puppy-friendly baritone graced the Miami air waves, by the alligatorish slough at our old Golf Lake Apartments, I'd grab my 25-lb. Snoopy-style ebony dog Snarf, and dance amok, like 1½ jack-in-the-boxes pogoing. I'd sing along with Ringo's ostensible "BLACK DOG BOOGALOO." Snarf would look up at me with very understanding brown eyes, jet-black fur, and squishy footpads. Our daughter Lauri, five, would dance along singing 'BLACK DOG BOOGALOO.'

Ringo and you may have a different impression of the song.

"It Don't Come Easy" – Ringo Starr, #4, 5-71. Produced by George Harrison, this first Ringo hit followed Ringo's first solo salvo, #87, 11-70 "Beaucoups of Blues." Ringo was always drawn to Blues and Country music (remember his Buck Owens' #47, 9-65 Beatle tune 'Act Naturally'?). Believe it or not, Ringo walked out on the Beatles' first – back in 1968. Why? The other three lay down separate tracks for the *White Album* so Ringo quit for NINE DAYS! Ringo was ticked off because 75% of the Beatles were not treating him like an integral 25% part of the Beatles. Shortly thereafter, Harrison split for the same reason. Lennon and McCartney had long lived different lives – Paul was swinging back to a more conservative farm-ranch domestic life style with **Linda**, not unlike **John Denver** and Annie's Colorado experience: kids, sheep, and soon off to the fateful Mull of Kintyre in Scotland. John and **Yoko** yoked a cushier midnight cityscape of New York Village coffeehouse clamor and clatter.

It's hard to pinpoint why and when the Fab Four split, but the Fab Three all rallied around pal Ringo after the bust-up. To help his fledgling solo career skyrocket to the summit, they chimed in on his album *Ringo* (Al. #2, 11-73). Paul played kazoo. Ringo's first #1 song, "Photograph," (10-73) was penned by pal George Harrison, who also produced, and arranged **Badfinger** to sing back-up on "It Don't Come Easy."

Patchogue, NY singer/keyboardist Teddy Kalivas interviewed the big **Beatles/Eagles** secret combo concert. The #1 band of all time combined with the band with the #1 album of all time. Eagles' guitarist **Joe Walsh** played guitar and sang John and Paul harmonies for the solo **Ringo Starr** on his concert tour. In the 70s, Ringo's career almost matched the Beatle chart dominance. In 3-74, he did a credible version of Tony Williams and the Platters' leadoff Rock Ballad, "Only You," #6, 11-74. Earlier that year, he put together a group, with Vandella vanguard **Martha Reeves** on vocal background with Merry Clayton – 'Fifth Beatle' **Billy Preston** pumped keys and Tom Scott blasted sax; the successful result? The grooviferous #5, 3-75 "Oh My My."

Boogieing, Ringo concludes in the leapfrog lyric, is a great cure for death (keeps you very much alive). Hoyt Axton's (1937-99) mom Mae wrote Elvis's debut #1(8) 3-56 "Heartbreak Hotel." She also doled out Mom-style health advice here:

"No No Song" – Ringo Starr, #3, 2-75. Axton plunked a kicky Reggae beat into this New Eschew Brew tune – it's about giving up drugs, alcohol, tobacco, whatever. "No No" uses Ringo's baritone range. It's a nifty thrifty melody. Dots of block major chords spangle the melody with color and charm. You spend a lot of time dancing on the dominant seventh chord, waiting to buzz back to your harmonic tonic. Ringo's skittish snare duels his pulsing tom-tom.

The wonderful world of the Giant Alka-Seltzer Cure beckoned him. In 1925, the kindly press (no tell-all tabloids then) claimed Babe Ruth had a 'bellyache from too many hot dogs and strawberry soda pops.' Actually, the big slugger was whooping up whoopee with wild ditzy Red Hot Mamas, while wifey sat home and stewed. In the "No No Song," Ringo sings of moonshine in Nashville, plus pot and coke. Despite the party-on years, the new Ringo looks surprisingly youthful. His 1989 All-Starr Tour conquered the known universe, so he returned for a second swoop in 1992, fortified with his NC, 1991 *Time Takes Time* album. In June 1997, Ringo teamed with Paul McCartney for the first time anywhere on songwriting credits for Paul's wildly successful *Flaming Pie* album. And Ringo rocks on.

George Harrison's monumental Hindu/Christian "My Sweet Lord" (#1[4], 11-70) spawned a philosophical follow-up:

"What is Life?" – George Harrison, #10, 2-71. From George's *All Things Must Pass*, Al. #1(7), 12-71. In our Religious Rock chapter, we juggled John's Unitarian #3, '71 "Imagine" with Paul's Catholic #1(2), '70 "Let It Be"; George, however, is the only one to somehow glue two major faiths together in #1(4), 11-70 "My Sweet Lord." Harrison combines faith, hope, charity, and Khrishna Consciousness. "What Is Life?" parades chromatic bVII chords into star-spangled harmonies. George ponders the bombshell question. His staggering topics rarely coalesce into everyday songs like "My Sweet Cadbury's Caramellow Candy Bar," "What is Her Bikini Size?", "Give Me a Lincoln – Give Me Gold Chains and Croissants on Earth," or "All Those Bud Beers Ago." Nope, George's songs belie his Buddha smile – they are serious philosophical interior monologues.

"What is Life?" may not be quite as deep as first imagined. He's after a girl. Most songs in *All Things Must Pass* revolve around the mystical music of the spheres: Hindu reincarnation, realization of the nature of God, quest for spirituality. Intriguing ambiguity. "What?" is certainly not the obvious prayer that "My Sweet Lord" is. Whatever level this #10 song generates for you the listener, you'll probably agree it's a beautiful, melodic, harmonic Harrisong. **John Hampson** of **Nine Days** penned a super tune in 1996, "Things We Said," with the memorable line "without you, it's so hard to be me." Deep commitment. Harrison follows same theme – his life is meaningless without this girl.

"Bangla Desh/Deep Blue" – George Harrison, #23, 8-71. George chased the GIMME GIMME Monster out of the musical arena. He sponsored a song with a totally SELFLESS and other-directed attitude, at the groaning gateway of the "Me Decade." A prelude to the Charity Rock of **Harry Chapin** and USA for Africa.

Bangla Desh is the former East Pakistan, over past India's Mother Teresa Calcutta side; Bangla Desh is a very poor country, whose rich three-crop soils can't feed its overburgeoned hordes, reeling under floods, monsoons, and plagues. Like the R & R birthplace on our Mississippi Delta, the Bangla Desh Delta is the confluence between Burma's Brahmaputra River and the 'Mother Ganges' of the Subcontinent of India's billion pilgrims.

What would it take to lure reclusive super-producer **Phil Spector** and his Wall of Sound out of cloistered seclusion? The powerful Harrison sound. And magical mystique. With the sitar wizardry of **Ravi Shankar**, and the Transcendental Meditation of **Maharishi Mahesh Yogi**, George Harrison concocted a world health consciousness that overspread any personal financial tycoonery he might be enjoying.

Long before Band-Aid or USA for Africa – even long before **Harry Chapin** – the introspective Beatle George devised the BENEFIT CONCERT idea. He'd showcase a cavalcade of superstars. Like Woodstock Festival, George's Madison Square Garden Benefits (2) for Bangla Desh included a hefty honor roll of superstars: **Ringo** (super)**Starr, Eric Clapton, Billy Preston, Leon Russell**, and others. Harrison's "My Sweet Lord" was consciously inspired by the **Edwin Hawkins Singers'** #4, 4-60 "Oh, Happy Day" ([#2, 5-60 R & B], and unconsciously by the **Chiffons'** #1(4), 2-63 "He's So Fine"). The world was inspired to help the starving millions in Bangla Desh, through George's selfless act of charity. All the money, of course, was hacked away at and grubbed by triplicate tax bureaucrats, as in George's Beatle song "Taxman." Sharp red pens slashed George's altruistic dreams to shreds of liens and snags and snares. At this writing, some of the charity money for the little kids who died a generation ago is still cubbyholed in a Washington or London drawer marked "GIMME!" If joining the GIMME generation, maybe it's best to join George on #1(1), 5-73 "Give Me Love (Give Me Peace on Earth)." Melodic, friendly, fun.

"All Those Years Ago" – George Harrison, #2(3), 5-81. In the aftermath of America's 9-11-2001 terror attack, the world lost another Beatle. The everyday terror of George's passing? He died not of assassins' bullets – but of an old age that isn't very old: 58. The cause was that proverbial 'long illness' which insidiously conquers a third of the human race. George, like Paul, experimented with vegetarianism to stay healthy. His major vice was nicotine (400,000 lives/year in U.S.A.). On November 29, 2001, half of the magic Beatle sound was forever stilled.

George wrote "All Those Years Ago" as a tribute to his fallen bandmate **John Lennon**. It is no strawberry-shortcake sweetly sentimental sayonara song. No, indeed, "All Those Years" tells the story of enduring friendship amidst a backdrop of bandmate semi-sibling rivalry. His elegiac song for John augments John's feisty genius, but George calls his martyred pal 'weird' in one quixotic spot. It showed how stunned George and Paul were on December 8, 1980. Truly Ringo was the only Beatle with a regular show of instant emotional sympathy. Something in the dreary way of grey Liverpool upbringings caused a particularly worldly Stoicism to permeate the treble-Beatle reaction – but only Ringo reacted. After all, there was the personal terror aspect. George, himself, was nearly assassinated at Christmas-tide 1999 by a wayward prowler. Was it a botched robbery at George's 100-room mansion? Or a more sinister plot? Fortunately, the berserk intruder was not brandishing an American bazooka or Saturday Night Special. Though security totally muddled the invasion, George and his wife actually clobbered the guy over the head with a lamp, and sat on him until the bobbies finally arrived with the straitjacket and rescue. "All Those Years Ago" is a cryptic tribute somewhere in the twilight zone of reverence. George played in the **Monty Python** movie *The Life of Brian* (1979). In it, his view of God represents the Hindu concepts of maya and lila – the cosmic mystery and mysterious wiles or amusing ways of God. It suggests **Topol**'s "If I Were a Rich Man" from *Fiddler on the Roof* (Al. #30, 1-72); the character Tevye bargains – even jokes – with God, a sometimes dangerous laugh track to seek.

George's "Got My Mind Set on You" was the last #1 Beatle song (10-87). His biggest song with the Beatles (Arnita Mason's favorite) was his unforgettable "Something." "All Those Years" comes from *Somewhere in England* (Al. #11, 6-81), rife with George's gutsy honesty; he zaps the record industry's trendy, glitzy Disco dazzle, quibbling with Paul about his #1(3), 4-80 "Coming Up (Live at Glasgow)," with Disco accoutrements. After **Brian Jones** died in a drinking and diving accident, the **Rolling Stones** turned squabbles into baubles, and lesions into cohesion. Into 1970, the Beatles were attached by centrifugal force. Enter ELO's Orchestral Rock singer/producer **Jeff Lynne**. Lynne used Classical/Pop variations since his first *Swingle Singers* album, the #15, 11-63 *Bach's Greatest Hits* with **Ward Swingle**, Alabama sax man. Lynne fired up #1(1), 10-87 "Got My Mind Set on You" for George. Lynne, producer. This blockbuster hit reheated is an obscure item by Blues Guru James Ray (no relation to M.L. King assassin) of Washington:

"If You Gotta Make a Fool of Somebody" – James Ray, #22, 11-61; #10, 1-62 R & B. Great Blues song in **James Brown** tradition – only more tuneful. Ray was a homeless street person when discovered. Died mysteriously soon after success, age c. 24. His "Got My Mind Set on You" never charted nationally tallied (#38 on WKNR, Motor City, in ragtag summer 1962). Super Soul Sound. Could he have become James Brown II? Death snags potential, a timeworn R & R tale.

Harrison's seedbed is his #8, 11-87 Al. *Cloud Nine* – "Real songs!" George said, "played on real instruments by real people." Needless to say, the Techno-Synth-Industrial-Dance-Hip-Hop-Robbie-the-Robot Boogie was not George's bag. Harrison traveled on the Wilburys with Orbison, Lynne, Tom Petty, and another shy guy with the midnight stage shades – **Bob Dylan**.

Paul McCartney's checkered career Winged its way to superstardom again. Paul's 25% of the Beatles kept pounding out the hits, while dragging home and family up on stage for the ride (**Linda Eastman McCartney** on keyboards/backing vocals). Paul, Linda, and **Denny Laine**'s **Wings** soared to 19 BIG chart hits in America before they perched upon their biggest UK hit of all time. You may faintly recall **Wings**' 20th hit, a nice #33 item called "Girls' School" from 11-77. The flip side is a slow droning hymn to the Scots' peninsula (mull) of Kintyre. For all of our Anglo-American kinship and camaraderie, this McCartney anthem to "Home, Sweet Home" shows that in some aspects of music, culture, and clouds, we Yanks and British are worlds apart:

"Mull of Kintyre" – Paul McCartney and Wings, NC, 12-77 U.S.; #1 U.K. "Mull of Kintyre" features an Anglo-American rift of sensibility. Plodding, purposeful, and beautifully bestrewn with bagpipes. "Mull" epitomizes the soft grey-green misty meaning of life in a cool, verdant, living land of rocky seashores and purple moonscapes over castle battlements and lost dreams.

When I first heard "Mull of Kintyre," it reminded me of my dear old grandpa, coal and salt miner Joe Dean, off to meet his cronies at the Chippewa Bar in Windsor, Ontario, in 1950. My dad was born in Kilwinning, Scotland, in 1910. Country Ayrshire, fifteen miles from Robert Burns's cottage and the treasured Brig O'Doon (bridge over the River Doon). It later changed into *Brigadoon*, marvelous Scottish musical (1947) by Lerner and Loewe. The film (1954), starring Gene Kelly and Van Johnson ****, is among the top musicals. Though my dad came to Windsor in 1923 and the Motor City to work the factories in 1932, my ancestral Scottish home is just 25 miles from McCartney's Mull of Kintyre. Maybe that's why it hit me so hard the first time I heard it: a song from 'The Auld Neighborhood.' "Mull" is a big hit. How big? "MULL OF KINTYRE" WAS THE BIGGEST-SELLING HIT SINGLE IN THE HISTORY OF THE U.K. UNTIL 1985.

Harry Lauder, possibly the only knighted Scottish tenor on *Billboard*'s 1890-Present charts, sang "Roamin' in the Gloamin'" to #5 in 1912. His "My Bonny Bonny Jean" (#9, 7-16) sparked the Bonnie Jean song from *Brigadoon*, plus the beautiful song that sure sounds like a Scottish tenor's work but isn't – **Oliver** (Swofford's) #2(3) "Jean" is the 8-69 follow-up to his chummy Chalypso "Good Morning Starshine" (#3, 5-69). Good Scottish and Irish Music, from the Celtic Crescent, has always been among the aural delights of the British soundscape.

Enter the Mull. Mull that over. A mull is a peninsula. The

Mull of Kintyre dangles down off the Firth of Clyde and Loch Fyne like a quivering uvula tickling the thick throat of some coloratura soprano fishing for 'Bb' above High 'C'.

Wings waltzed "Mull," a Key-of-'A' extravaganza at 89 plodding, 3/4 beats per minute. McCartney mulls his happy homebody stance: he's traveled to distant mountains, valleys of green, painted deserts with fiery sunsets. All these scenic wonders just give him a nostalgic homing-pigeon urge to beeline back to his lovely **Linda**. Just before John's New York Last Stand, Paul and Linda retreated, as many weary entertainers do (John Denver, Steve Miller, George Harrison) to a rural W.B. Yeats-style 'Lake Isle of Innisfree'. Paul and Linda ponder nature and sunsets, and punt gridlock and leeches and vampires trying to sink their talons and teeth into the princely power brokers of Rock and Roll. Sadly, their untimely parting due to her last illness is among the greatest tragedies in our Rock and Roll family.

Paul and Linda's villa on the Mull of Kintyre was accessible: ferry from Saltcoats by Kilwinning to the storied Isle of Arran: or summer boat to Claonaig on the Mull; Scots Gaelic is spoken in fringe villages like Rhunahaorine and Macharioch. The Mull's big city is Campbelltown, near actually, 'New Orleans,' Scotland.

With crescendo welling up, Denny Laine undergirds Paul's tenor with a fifths-lower baritone harmony on the second chorus. We're treated to a swirling skirling BAGPIPE chorus (actually synthesized over **Linda**'s deft keyboards). **Linda Eastman** obviously married Paul for love. She had almost as much money as he did, via her U.S.A. Eastman/Kodak photo fortune. After the hubbub and hurly-burly of touring clipped Wings' wings, Paul and Linda returned to their ideal family situation on Mull: organic farming, shepherding, and 'don't eat anything with a face' vegetarian causes. Together they found some 20th-century peace of mind in a chaotic world of bombs bursting in air. Rockets' red glare.

When you think PAUL McCARTNEY you visualize instantly BEATLES, which only occupied nine years of Paul's life; **Wings** flew for nigh three times that. Spasmodically. Wings is like an extended family. Paul and Linda recruited Moody Blues' lead singer (#10, 2-65 "Go Now") **Denny Laine** to handle guitar and background vocals. A funereal procession of fated drummers joined Wings. Guitarists, too: drummer Denny Seiwell (split 1973), guitarist James McCulloch (d. heart failure, age 26). Other personnel 1970-81: drum major Joe English, and guitar guy Henry McCullough. **Billy Joel**'s most-admired mentor? "McCartney, of course."

The Scots' trek continues in Verse II: Sweet *Brigadoon* heather dapples in the bonnie glen. Linda's soprano blends angelically with the Laine high baritone and Paul's tenor. Funereal bagpipes again. In April 1998, the light of Paul's life was snuffed out. His beloved Linda passed away to the same scourge that took the life of his mother Mary. It took Paul until 11-99 to get back to recording (Al. #26+ *Run Devil Run*). Theirs was a love song for the ages.

McCartney is a man for all continents. Britishly, Paul

radiates the American ideal of the 'melting pot.' Born of Irish immigrants in English Liverpool, McCartney's vocal power base includes Screaming Little Richard Soul/R & R/Blues, Motown Suave Coolth; Buddy Holly Tex-Mex Rockabilly; Bouncy Bubble Gum; Sinatran Yesterday & 'Eleanor Rigby' Orchestral Ballads; and Classical Long, Winding Road Standards, that carry him back to his moonmist Scottish castle and deep purple stardust sanctuary. Some call **Paul McCartney** the #1 Entertainer of All Time.

"Mull of Kintyre" strides slowly through a kaleidoscope of reflective moods. It's a groggy, foggy 55° dim British cloudscape, with jagged crags and shimmering fishing sloops bobbing on a silver sea. The Scots' Mull is a soggy enchanted land, looming just an Irish Sea away from the magic mushrooms of kelly-green leprechauns perched on pots of gold in the great Rainbow West. "Mull" plays the sea and sky interface splendidly, shifting between soothing beauty and homesick uncertainty. The message is essentially Tennyson's "Home is the sailor, home from the sea . . ." The Mull is just a wailing banshee's breath away from the Emerald Isle. A similar grey-green foggy tune of enchantment to come from America is Don McLean's NC Scots-Irish "The Mountains of Mourne." **Reba McEntire**, Country star, obviously traces her Scottish clan back to the Mull of KINTYRE [Kintyre = Entire with Mc attached].

Kintyre – shadowy greenish-gray immensity of long ago. Scottish clans clashed on mossy battlements. **William Wallace** and Robert the Bruce and the Campbells (*Braveheart*, 1995***½, Mel Gibson) ripped lightning bolts from the sky in titanic struggles. Lion-hearted clansmen of Old Mull. Flashy red-green tartan kilts and silver swords. Kintyre – lost in time and space. Paul McCartney's "Mull" takes two more steps up **Led Zep**'s "Stairway to Heaven" in the evolution of Celtic Renaissance music – previewing **Celine Dion** or **Sarah McLachlan** via **Linda McCartney**'s enchanting style. Kintyre is Paul's plateau. In the song, he touts the happy hearthside. He sings of home and family and passionate longings for a sacred place. The green, green hills o' home. Paul touts the rolling mists off the stormy Irish Sea. SANCTUARY from the hot pressurized klieg glow of the ELVIS SPOTLIGHT.

"Mull" is an enchanting come-hither call from the sensuous sires of the Scottish gray-green mists, skirted by scudding dragons of cloud over silvery lost bays. Scotland the Brave. How, then, did Paul's "Johnny B. Goode" dream come true? How did he overleap crass class-consciousness? How did he become the British Knight in 1996, with the Order of the British Empire from Her Majesty, Queen Elizabeth II? How did a poor kid, from the shipbuilding nexus of smogstrewn Liverpool, catapult to superstardom? Rock and Roll. For years, British noblemen have resided on some lofty gold-green crag, astride the stormy swirling cold Irish Sea. Swordplay often determined who owned what – and for how long. In 1964, a new musical path to British nobility arose.

Paul earned his Mull of Kintyre mansion the American Way. Like Johnny B. Goode. He carried the guitar in this gunnysack. Deep down. Down into the labyrinthine cave of the Beatles' Liverpool Cavern. Down into the neon Nether-Never Land of Hamburg's tuff-enuff Reeperbahn Sin City. After blasting **Buddy Holly** and **Smokey Robinson** and **Del Shannon** tunes as an apprentice cover band, Paul and **John Lennon** penned their musical destiny. They are now the most famous and best-loved songwriting duo of all time.

Until the Band Aid 1985 multi-superstar extravaganza, or **Elton John**/Bernie Taupin's tribute to Princess Di, 1997's #1 "Candle in the Wind II," "Mull of Kintyre" was the BIGGEST RECORD in the history of Great Britain. Mull that over. And try to find it on American radio . . .

"Band on the Run" – Paul McCartney and Wings, #1(1), 4-74. Paul punches up his Little Richard high tenor intensity. He juggles the frenzy of roadweary touring bands with amazing electric and explosive excitement. You hear the big bold THUMP of the mammoth bass drum in tandem with Paul's insistent bass guitar. Wings mashes the beat like a cannon blasting 120 cannonballs per minute in Disco Drive (though this one is straight-ahead R & R, not Disco). Their interplanetary sound took them to the "Venus and Mars Rock Show" (#12, 11-75). By 1975 Rock and Roll was a Triplanetary Phenomenon. Decent song. On #10, 7-82 "Take It Away" the song comes in slices. One part easy ballad. One part muted chorus with embellishments. One part with strings n' things. Then Wings swoop(s) in with a flamboyant "Peggy Sue" paradiddle on drums. The majestic melody you'd swear was concocted by Buddy Holly at the 1957 Lubbock, Texas, Cotton Club.

"Give Ireland Back to the Irish" – Paul McCartney and Wings, #21, 3-72. Political hot potato. Despite an intro of how tremendous Great Britain is, the BBC was aghast. The song thrived as an underground cameo with virtually no airplay. The song did quite well in Ireland, Canada, (and yes, Scotland). Transplanted Brits gird the globe with mixed loyalties to the Crown. McCartney knew a lot about fragmentation. The 1970s Beatle documentary *Let It Be* features many strained directions the 'cutest Beatle' was manhandled into. After active in-fighting, conciliatory dialogue, and painful negotiations took place, all Fab Four echoed their fragmentary futility. Together, they were the #1 band in history. Solo, their individual superstardom shone through. Four dimming superstars, on their long and winding roads.

"My Love" – Paul McCartney and Wings, #1(4), 4-73; #9 U.K. After a little fun fluff stuff, #10, 12-72 "Hi Hi Hi," Paul and Linda offered this tuneful bedtime smoochfest triumph. Like Carly Simon's #2(3), 7-77 "Nobody Does It Better," there are some overly intimate songs that just make the listener nervous. He/she feels he/she is a Peeping Tom/Pam. Their great follow-up rocker to "Band on the Run" is #3, 1-74 "Junior's Farm." Paul lassos a tonic bass note, and hangs on for dear life. With firm hold on the tornado bronc, Paul thunders and stomps along, with hiss towering tenor high in the silver saddle. The Rock and Roll rhythm overlays Paul's bronze-medal hit that scatters and spatters the stars like ghost riders in the sky:

"(Ghost) Riders in the Sky" – Outlaws, #31, 12-80. Dawning the new decade came a phantasmagoric stampede out of Rock and Roll's stormy Country-Western origins. #2(1), 5-79 C. for Johnny Cash and #27, 7-73 C for banjo/guitar virtuoso Roy Clark. Cowboy Rock classic goes back to #21, 4-49 (#8 C) **Burl Ives**. On mainstream charts, it helped chart Rock and Roll. Also a huge hit for Connecticut's Duane-Eddy-echo instrumental crew, guitarist Vincent Bell Lee's **Ramrods** (#30, 1-61).

"Riders in the Sky (A Cowboy Legend)" – Vaughn Monroe, #1(12), 4-49. This bari-bass Vaughn Monroe (1911-73) cowboy ghost anthem commanded #1 center stage longer than ANY SINGLE SONG IN THE ENTIRE ROCK ERA FROM 1955-92 [**Boyz II Men**, 1992 "End of the Road," #1(13)]. Big Stampede in the Sky. Though Vaughn sounded like a resonant booming bass crooner, he hog-tied a Rock and Roll song about five years before its pals bucked out of the chutes. "Ghost" chords are slightly revolutionary. It starts on the sub-mediant minor (VIm). If you're in 'G', begin with **Em** chord. Rise sporadically to tonic **G** and sub-dominant **C**. It's about a ghost herd up in the sky – a thunderous stampede of red-eyed devil steers, stomping anything in their hell-bent-for leather path. The cowboy's nightmare stampede ends on an iffy moment of happiness, atonement, or salvation. "Repent," sez the sky-ghost, or you'll ride along with us ghost-wranglers lassoing the Devil's herd way up in the raggedy sky. Reborn, the Rock and Roll cowboy of 1949 returns to the rootin-tootin' range. A better man.

ROBIN & SUSIE LUKE'S NIFTY PARADIDDLE ENCORE . . .

In Rock and Roll, the beat is everything. "(Ghost)' has the Robin Luke "Susie Darlin'" modified paradiddle; you lose one of your sixteenth notes in an accented eighth. It comes out here . . .

The R. Luke Modified Pitti-Pat Ghost Paradiddle

Paul McCartney's #3, 11-74 "Junior's Farm" has a nice booming Tex-Mex beat too. More Inter-Beatle interludes? OK:

"She's the One" – Chartbusters, #33, 7-64. Our Night Shift drummer **Tom Helderman**'s favorite faux Britrockers anthem. Washington D.C.'s gung-ho rockers' #92, 11-64 "Why (Dontcha Be My Girl)," essentially imitates the Beatles' fresh sound. Should have hit #7 or so. They were among the 1st Yankee groups to capture the British Invasion style, even before **Beau Brummels**' great Revenge Rocker, #15, 1-65 "Laugh, Laugh."

"Denise" – Randy and the Rainbows, #10, 6-63; #18, 9-63 R& B. This White Streetcorner crew from Queens NYC starred lead singer **Dom 'Randy' Safuto** and his brother Frank, Ken Arcipowski, and a couple of (great) real zeroes: brothers Mike and Sal **Zero**. Four Seasonish entire FALSETTO chorus. The skittish snare and thumping tom-tom provide a rhythmic blanket that fortifies their super five-part harmonies.

When Paul's Wings flew over their huge #1(5), 4-76 "Silly Love Songs," they knew that LOVE is the premier song topic – it beats nuclear physics, quasars-pulsars astronomy, washing machine repair, floor wax technology, or cat grooming. Randy's Rainbows find the pot of gold. This one delightful song is their stamp of audial immortality. Back to Fab One:

"Let 'Em In" – Paul McCartney and Wings, #3, 7-76. Martin Luther? Phil and Don? A wealth of allusion to "American Pie." Who arrives at their unplanned wild party? Sister Susie, Uncle Ernie, Brother John, and other assorted doorknockers and bellringers. Many songs have been written about after-hours nightclubs. Or Risin' Sun Houses of Blue Lights. For Johnnie Ray in 1954 (and Archie Bleyer at #2), it was this secret bootleg joint –

"Hernando's Hideaway" – Johnnie Ray, #14, 6-54. Clack of castanets. Shadowy silhouettes. Hernando's secret blind pig or house of blue lights is a chic after-hours bistro, turning the wee hours into glory time. It's a clandestine cabaret, and who cares what time it is? You've got to say you were sent by 'Joe.' Secret rendezvous. Smokey Joe's Café. Ray serves up a lurching tango of romantic espionage. Catch his total melodic echo in #8, 8-2000 "Dance with Me" – by **Debelah Morgan** (with Neo-Disco Dance thunderbeat, and interweaving harmony vocals).

"The Green Door" – Jim Lowe, #1(3), 9-56. Hey, I had no idea Tony Martone's friend Jim Lowe was a big WINS and WNEW DJ in the Big Apple when he cut his nifty tune. It sounded like an upright piano echo out of New Orleans and Eubie Blake in 1899 or whatever. Story line? Dude outside after-hours shaky 'club' claims he knows somebody, or the password, or the secret knock. They just 'dis' him. Behind the mysterious green door, a smoky eyeball peeps suspiciously out at him. He groans – but still nobody wants him in. They think he's a vice cop? A narc? All the while, this super rolling Boogie piano keeps on plinking, like **Teresa Brewer**'s Ragtimeglow #1(3), 2-50 "Music3." "Green Door" was my 1956 favorite song – until the **Dell-Vikings** and **Buddy Holly** were invented.

Paul McCartney's "Let 'Em In" mention of 'Phil and Don' is obviously the **Everly Brothers**. What Lutheran Church founder Martin Luther is doing there, I haven't a clue . . .

"Maybe I'm Amazed" – Paul McCartney and Wings, #10, 2-77. This 'live' version is very closely related to the 1970 rendition rumored to be cut on Paul's 4-track home recording gizmo. I'm personally amazed at this great song. As it cascades over our midnight airwaves, it just keeps getting better. Paul's dramatic intensity radiates a volcanic vocal power, almost as if his VOICE itself is a brilliant metallic Heavy Metal instrument. On *McCartney* (#1[3], 5-70) Paul sounds like all the Fab Four, not just the #1 bassist in history. Every year "Maybe I'm Amazed" gets better, and next year it might become his best. Wings' biggest hit was #1(5), 4-76 "Silly Love Songs." There aren't any.

"The Girl is Mine" – Paul McCartney and Michael Jackson, #2(3), 11-82; #1(3) R & B; #1 Adult Contemporary. In the superstar heyday of the Gloved One, he took time out to do a duo with the quadragenarian (40-year-old) Beatle. Follow-up to Paul's biggest hit – a multi-racial excursion with **Stevie Wonder** – "Ebony and Ivory" at #1(7) in 4-82. Paul's collaborations with Jackson and Wonder produced Paul's two biggest solo hits – like Michael/Paul's #1(6), 10-83 "Say Say Say".

In June 1997, Paul and **Ringo Starr** launched a fiery #2 *Flaming Pie* album, showing that Liverpool lives! On #7, 11-85 title song "Spies Like Us," (Dan Aykroyd and Chevy Chase), Paul goes with the pop flow. It's Paul's last charted Top Ten tune. His last 80s HOT100 hit? This one. Which one? "This One" (#94, 9-89).

In the home and hearth 80s, Paul and Linda retreated back to their comfy Mull of Kintyre. Grey-green gloaming. Sunsets of fire. Paul McCartney sailed pensively beyond the millennium.

John Lennon's career swooned in the aftermath of the Beatle break-up. Unlike **George Harrison**, he had no central vision, or Phil Spector to steer his stars and align his smoking sitar. Unlike **Ringo**, he had no posse of pals who paraded his good-natured R & R songs into "Let's win one for the drummer Beatle!" Unlike **Paul**, he acquired no full touring band to embellish his ideas and power his potent package of kaleidoscopic music. With his assertive bride **Yoko Ono**, John (1940-80) fought a four-year-long agonizing battle with J. Edgar Hoover, the FBI, and the State Department for his politics. No big Rah-Rah war fan, John gave the best years of his life in a furtive quest for world peace. As early as 1966, his movie *How I Won the War* cast the fated Beatle as ghostly victim of a grim battlefield finale. As a trapped soldier, his character entreats the enemy with the bayonet about to take his life: "Have a heart, man," he says. The opposing soldier stabs him in the heart.

In a dramatic and fateful quandary, men of peace have so often fallen victim to the pathological craziness of this seething swarming planet. **Dion DiMucci** (b. 7-18-39), before his Christian Born-Again conversion, was deeply into a trembling addiction. Dion put it best in #4, 10-68 "Abraham, Martin, and John" – it seems to him that many really good people die young. Dion, of course, snapped out of his addiction (see autobiography *The Wanderer*) and rocked the oldies.

Martin Luther King was gunned down by the crazed James Earl Ray. **President Kennedy** was assassinated by the embittered Lee Harvey Oswald. Presidents Lincoln and Garfield and McKinley, too, were assassinated; critics of President Clinton's Vietnam War ideas, influenced by John Lennon, might do well to consider that the American President's job involves a higher likelihood of being shot and possibly killed than almost any battlefield soldier. At least those not in constant firefights. It is not just an American thing, this senseless violence. Perhaps the major 20th-century man of peace was **Mahatma Gandhi** of India, also killed by a wanton assassin.

The reason the Christian Church exists is due to just one unjust execution.

When Senator **Bobby Kennedy** was killed, a candidate that American youths believed was the secular messiah for 1968 peace, it cut the heart out of our innocence and naivete. A range of cynicism gripped the land. This ugly war, that no bureaucrat dared equip his military juggernaut to WIN, was strangling the American John Wayne pilgrim spirit. We continued shooting into the eerie jungle with half-loaded guns at half-loaded Vietcong. Scottish philosopher Thomas Carlyle (1795-1881) said "Gunpowder makes all men tall." British gun laws, though favoring rich sportsmen, at least keep a lot of loyal British subjects alive. Like **George Harrison**. Detroit, with a city population of 1.3 million (4+ Metro, 1968), had more murders than all of Sweden, Norway, Denmark, the Netherlands, Belgium, Luxembourg, France, England, Scotland, and Wales combined. "Guns do not kill people," loomed the bumpersticker, but then again, it said, people rarely kill guns.

Anyone who doubts the mortal danger of the President's job might just have asked President Reagan (#21, 4-60 "Mr. Lucky," Henry Mancini). Reagan beat the odds. With the Duke-like Scottish luck of **John Wayne**, whose 1955 *Searchers* ironically titled Buddy Holly's "That'll Be the Day" [to die] for Buddy, Ronald Reagan did not die. The bullet hit just the right chest cartilage, and the President fully recovered. Press Secretary James Brady was paralyzed, creating the Brady Bill of 1993 – too late to save a Beatle, but on time to stop 600,000 felons from obtaining guns from 1993-2001. Law-abiding hunters had no trouble obtaining firearms.

As Beatle **John Lennon** sang songs of peace and summertime in his new American home at Central Park's Dakota Hotel, a young 'bipolar' John Lennon 'fan' from Colorado named Mark David Chapman was sharpening his three names . . .

"Instant Karma (We All Shine On)" – John Ono Lennon, #3, 2-70. As interior Beatle squabbles burned to fever pitch, John juggled names with **Yoko Ono**. George played lead guitar and music whiz **Billy Preston** manned the keys to karma, kismet, and destiny. In the Hindu world the Beatles sought with Ravi Shankar (sitar) and Maharishi Mahesh Yogi (Transcendental Meditation), John Lennon came to believe in the reincarnation of souls. Then he ditched the idea in a swampy Big Apple blur of life in the fast lane. Mick Jagger said, "If a little is good, too much is better." John grappled with every cause from gender slavery to reincarnation to freeing John Sinclair of Ann Arbor on a pot bust. The magnificent melodies of the Beatle past took a few lumps, as chanting became the order of the day – and the chant trend continues full force in this latter-day Age of Rap and Beyond. Much mean-streets music is a mirror and a reflection of John & Yoko's newspaper style album cover on their ill-fated #48, 7-72 *Sometime in New York City.* "Instant Karma" contains a reverb echo beat. Lennon urges the people (via their newfound power) to keep on shining, like the sun, the moon, or the stars.

Lennon's 'Karma' anthem implies regenerative reincarnation. It foretells long, happy life spans. Like John's #3, 10-71 secular hymn "Imagine," "Instant Karma" delivers a mystical message of world peace and cooperation. What is this gonna-getcha *bete noire* 'karma'? Some Godzilla or Creature from the Black Lagoon? Nope. Just the Hindu term for fate. We're back to Doris Day (#2, '56) and Eddie Money's ("Baby Hold On" #11, 1-78) concept of "Whatever Will Be, Will Be." Instant Karma, it turns out, like Instant Ovaltine or Instant Cash or Instant Jiffy-Lube, does not have to be too terrifying.

"Power to the People" – John Lennon/Plastic Ono Band, Yoko Ono/Plastic Ono Band, #11, 4-71. Lennon/Ono sing a laundry list of good folks who need empowerment in the coming revolution (see "I Am Woman" – Helen Reddy, #1, '72). In divvying up the good life, they mention the names of seemingly billions of disenfranchised down-trodden minority groups. Their chant of POWER TO THE

PEOPLE boomed raucously over an America still surging with dissent over Vietnam, and disenchantment over noxious pollution. Lennon, a street-savvy lad from Liverpool, and Ono, a NYC artist who'd seen rampant discrimination against Japanese-Americans (strangely minimal for blond German-Americans) as a child in WWII, combined to package this potent message of instant change. It was time, they said in revolutionary style, to share the goodies in a new way. The FBI remained glum. The Lennon/Ono combo was likely to find a microphone in their car, their biff, their soup. Though **Gerry**'s [Marsden, of Liverpool's Brit-Invasion Pacemakers] biographical sketch describes himself (#6, 2-65 "Ferry Cross the Mersey"), it could also describe his Liverpool chum **John Lennon**:

"He was the cocky Liverpudlian with the infectious grin, some hearty and hummable pop songs, and a wacky sense of humor. He could be cutting but not malicious, and always had that endearing Merseyside characteristic of smiling through any adversity. He also possessed iron determination."

Ghosted by Ray Coleman of *Melody Maker*, the book touts Gerry's early days as an eight-stone six (112#) juvenile boxer at Our Lady of Mount Carmel. After garnering a feisty rep as a Liverpool "Street Fighting Man" (#48, 9-68, the Stones), Gerry's Pacemakers hit the big time. **John Lennon** hit the BIGGER time. Suddenly, via Yoko and the American anti-war movement, he shifted his old ideas about bopping the bad guy – and became a Gandhian man of peace. Quite a transformation.

'Sometime in New York City,' old Lennon feistiness took hold. Unlike Marsden, whose politicking consisted of a #1 reprise of "You'll Never Walk Alone" to aid Bradford stadium collapse victims' families (6-85), John Lennon took on the whole juggernaut of the world's power structure. With the frantic fervor of Burton Cummings and the **Guess Who**'s "Share the Land," and **Three Dog Night**'s Shangri-La "Shambala" utopian dream, John tried to change the world to his Peaceable Kingdom vision.

Two kids from Liverpool, **Gerry Marsden** and **John Lennon**. One with a smile, a left jab, and a charity record Oldie. The other – the first kid on his block to rule the world.

"Stand by Me" – Ben E. King, #4, 5-61; #9, 10-86; #1(4), 1-61 R & B; N.C. '86 R & B. John Lennon took "Stand by me" to #20, 3-75, on #6, '75 Al. *Rock and Roll*. King's Gospel/Soul fervor stems from his namesake, Dr. Martin Luther King, to whom he is not related. Originally "Lord, Stand by Me," this song proved a box-office bonanza for the Drifters' ex-lead singer Ben (nee Ben Nelson, b. '38, Henderson, North Carolina). Bolstered by a loud WHISK brush-style snare drum and a unique syncopation of finger popping, Ben lofts his suave tenor into the mountainous range. He implores his ladylove to stand by him at all costs, and he fears not tumbling skies and crumbling peaks crashing into the sea. The song could as easily be sung to the Lord as to the girl. This very 196l-ish song was admirably revived for 1986**½ River Phoenix and Kiefer Sutherland film, *Stand by Me.*

On this classic R & R album, Lennon rocks on in the basic Blues Rock Keys of 'E' and 'A'. He does: first Punker **Gene Vincent**'s classic #7, '56 "Be-Bop-A-Lula," with a dynamite guitar lead echoing **Cliff Gallup** from the original; **Chuck Berry**'s #2, '58 "Sweet Little Sixteen," awash with wailing saxes; a snazzy groove on **Little Richard**'s "Slippin' & Slidin'." Two terrific tunes merge with a thematic motif: **Sam Cooke**'s "Bring It On Home to Me" (#13, 6-62), and incomparable Richard's #54, 4-57 but #3 R & B, "Send Me Some Lovin'". Lennon's last living album, *Shaved Fish* Al. #12, 11-75, doesn't feature Rebel Rocker roots, so *Rock and Roll* is his sayonara triumph featuring Buddy Holly's breathtaking echo with "Peggy Sue."

A small Beechcraft Bonanza lumbered up into the icy blizzard night from Mason City Airport carrying three stars heading into the sky. February 3, 1959 – a day that shall live in infamy.

The little plane was flying the wintry Ghost Rider in the Sky Express Lane to snow-swirling Dakota.

Deep in December, a scraggly cadre of ragtag losers mixed it up with dedicated sincere John Lennon fans outside the Dakota Hotel in New York's Tavern on the Green – our marathon finish line in Southwest Central Park. One troubled desperado from Colorado, brandishing the three names of an assassin – Mark David Chapman – was heard to cry out "Mr. Lennon!" The poor wayfaring stranger Beatle, Peace Pilgrim in this woeful world, was struck several times by a volley of any-kid-can-buy-'em bullets from a $29 Saturday night pistol. He died from profuse bleeding on the way to the hospital from the Dakota. Dakota.

"Just Like Starting Over" – John Lennon, #1(5), 11-80. John joined the precious few (not even Elvis) whose first posthumous release hit No. 1 – naturally no consolation prize. But their fans remembered: **Buddy Holly** #1(3) U.K., "It Doesn't Matter Anymore" 3-59; **Otis Redding** #1(4), "Sittin' on the Dock of the Bay" 1-68; **Jim Croce** #1(2), "Time in a Bottle" 11-73, and **John Lennon**, with this one. [Gangsta Rapper Notorious B.I.G.'s posthumous "Hypnotize" (#1, 4-97) entered the charts at #1 after he was cut down in a hail of bullets]. John's song pulsates with dramatic irony. He begins with *a cappella* musing about life being so precious. He's joined by Benny Cummings' Singers' ringing "OOOOOOOO's:" The lyric, a fly-me-to-the-moon adventure, talks about soaring and gliding aloft. Lyrical lovers fly away. John never realizes the mystical, otherworldly element. Eight guys anchor the horn section, led by faux restaurateur Howard Johnson. Tony Levin's note-surrounding deep bass anchors a great optimistic song. Irony strikes again.

"Woman" – John Lennon, #2(3), 1-81. John contributed seven songs to #1(8), 12-80 finale Al. *Double Fantasy* with seven from Yoko (whose songs, somehow, did not chart). John's ballad expresses deepest emotions and thankfulness for showing him "meaning" to his success. Does that mean that this Beatle, who controlled billions of the world's greatest R & R fans, never really realized how super he was all along? SHE shows HIM success? Remember John's abandonment by his mother Julia (her namesake song on the *White Album*)? Remember how he was farmed out to dutiful, dear old Aunt Mimi, who raised him? Thankful to Mimi. Jittery about Julia's love. Yoko was much older than John. His first wife Cynthia Powell, mother of son **Julian Lennon** (not Sean), was pretty and sweet, but proved unchallenging to John's teeming mind. Part intellectual and part Philistine street dude, John bore the brunt, psychologically, of guys everywhere who want to be both smart – and one of the guys.

With Yoko, John received physical affection, nurturing, and encouragement. In his 5-year Dakota househusband phase, John mellowed. For the first time in his life, he felt serene and personally satisfied. One of the hardest things about his senseless murder is the fact that he beat back his personal demons, his eclectic substances, and his tawdry escapades. He underwent a spiritual cleansing and a rebirth of sincere dedication to his Rock and Roll craft. He was "Just Like Starting Over". The world mourned, flags at half-staff, for the assassinated Beatle. We mourned for ourselves, too. And our lost youth. We mourned not just for the John Lennon we lost, but for the newly emerging John Lennon – Superstar II – who was never to be.

"Watching the Wheels" – John Lennon, #10, 3-81. JL's 3rd hit from his last album of his lifetime. This is John's deep philosophical cosmic equilibrium song. It echoes Redding's dock-sitting "Dock of the Bay" or Holly's Anka finale, "It Doesn't Matter Anymore," where he tells himself nothing matters. John mentions how he's bombarded by advice from people he didn't ask for advice. John's echo chamber echoes early Elvis expertise. John's satisfied song says he's de-carouselled the merry-go-round; he's sitting tranquilly watching the entire universe's deistic wheels spinning smoothly in space. "Wheels" is a whirling mandala of dark fate. So what really matters in life? Yoko, for one. Yup. And toddler Sean.

"Beautiful Boy (Darling Boy)" – John Lennon, NC, 1980 When my little guy was four years old, seems he was nervous about a ferocious BUP in his closet. Maybe a BOOP. Something like that. Since the BUP/BOOP (pronounce OO as in WOOL) was fearsome, and my little dude couldn't sleep, I would often have a BUP encounter. I would grab the amorphous BUP by its polka-dotted invisible tail, grapple its gargantuan girth to the top of the stairs, and get it into a World Wrestling Federation 'Airplane Spin.' Twirling it over my head (its three purple eyes squinting), I'd fire it down the stairs. I'd kick it to the landing, toss it out the front door, and stuff its thirteen legs and 138 claws into the grubby snowbank in the gutter. By this time, our lad was giggling and chortling with glee. Then he could catch mucho zzz's. And sleep soundly.

"Beautiful Boy" . . . saddest song a Beatle ever did? The front album cover shows a John-loves-Yoko sweet smooch. The album's backside shows a stark street scene at about 69th and Central Park West. Why they picked a B & W photo of them frowning by the curb by a vivid wire mesh trash can I'll never know – but it's wryly appropriate. In their posh warehouse-wide apartment in the tony spiffy Dakota, John and Yoko had a safe sanctuary against the world's evil. A haven of safety. John could raise his little boy in peace and prosperity. Richer than Croesus, he and Yoko had the luxury of his full-time househusbanding and fathering. [In the liberated 2000s, not many mothers are financially able to stay home with Little Latchkey Louie, who darts the sticky streets selling snake toenails and skyhooks].

John opens his song with a "BUP" warning: He tells little Sean (4) that the monster's gone. It's running away, says John, and daddy is here. In the wonderful movie *Mr. Holland's Opus* (1995****), Richard Dreyfuss plays a music teacher whose relationship with his teenage boy Cole is strained due to the lad's deafness and the father's seeming indifference. In order to repair their emotional rift, Dreyfuss conducts a performance of "Beautiful Boy," using a system of flashing colored lights to simulate sounds. Father and son reunite. Lennon's song has never stopped reverberating, for all of us. How many billions of poor kids have had to fend for themselves in this chaotic demanding world, because Daddy's shield has been smashed into yesterday's tragedy? Or they suffer from psychic distance like Dreyfuss and son. John Lennon, remember, never had his dad around him (until he got Beatle-rich, when ol' Mr. Lennon arrived looking for a handout from his rich Rock and Roll abandoned boy).

Despite the agnostic stance of Lennon's #3, 10-71 "Imagine" anthem, he about-faces for the deliverance of his little loved lad. He says to say a small prayer . . . Each day, he unbelievably utters in 1920s sunnyside Dale Carnegie mantra, that things get better and even better. The chorus thunders the BEAUTIFUL BOY motif; he's a proud and happy father watching his innocent lad all tucked in with his teddy bear and his cubbling blanket. Before turning out the proverbial light, Lennon muses: LIFE is actually what's happening to a person when he thinks he's too busy with different plans.

His plans were riddled with destiny. John Lennon's legacy of peace, freedom, individuality, and Rock and Roll will live on as long as music brings us its homespun heartbeat. And yes, Virginia, John Lennon didn't quite begin that way, but he left us with something we can only call "Family Values" for the 21st Century.

All he was saying? Give peace a chance. And one more. All you need is love.

"Too Late for Goodbyes" – Julian Lennon, #5, 1-85. Lo and behold, John's first child sounds a lot like John – particularly on John's #1(1), 9-74 "Whatever Gets You Through the Night." Zak Starkey beat Julian to the pro touring circuit, but Julian's #9, 10-84 "Valotte" 10-84 championed the HOT 100 charts first, followed by #32, 3-86 "Stick Around." "Too Late" knocked off double gold (2M sales) worldwide.

But now, what about Rock and Roll and RE-BELLION?

"Smokin' in the Boys' Room" – Brownsville Station, #3, 10-73. Michigan's **Cub Koda** (d. 2000) plays lead guitar, and did an album with my pal Jeff Baldori's **Blue Money Band** in 1981. Cub also wrote for the ultimate old record-finders magazine, *Goldmine*. With the gruff raspy baritone of **Michael Lutz** rocking out pro-nicotine camaraderie, and Henry Weck bashing skins on the Stomp-It Speedway, "Smokin' in the Boys' Room" sizzled its butt to the top (cig butt, but of course). Age-old cosmodrama of kids-finding-limits. This Hard Rock anthem helped lead off the eventual rise of Metalmania:

"Smokin' in the Boys' Room" – Mötley Crüe, #16, 7-85. Heavy Metal, they say, best symbolizes R & R Rebellion. **'Vince Neil' Wharton**'s first top thirty tune, with **'Nikki Sixx'** (Frank Ferranno) blasting bass, has **'Mick Mars'** (Bob Deal) wailing Thrash Metal axe. True to original Ann Arbor, Michigan, sound. All the Beatles smoked, with George suffering a bad scare recently. Over 3,000+ 13-year-olds started smoking today in America. Anyhow, it's a great rock song. And with candy cigarettes, it's not even too hazardous to your precious health (say, man – you can always get new teeth).

"You Shook Me All Night Long" – AC/DC, #35, 9-80. AC/DC's Aussie/Scot HARD ROCK is Mainstream or Heartland or Thunder Rock, or the more janglingly metallic Heavy Metal. Led off by *bon vivant* **Bon Scott**, their first juggernaut hit was #47, 10-79 "Highway to Hell" (From our, uh-huh, Religious Rock chapter). Scott hailed from gloomy Glamis *Macbeth* country, up in Kirriemuir, Scotland. Scott died of liquid substances in 1980 London. Glaswegian brother guitarists **Angus** and **Malcolm Young** kept on truckin' for Newcastle's Brian Johnson. Many met in Melbourne, Australia, and were sibling-connected to the **Easybeats**. You could easily classify Aussie Hard Rockers AC/DC in the METAL chapter, but they're also the down-the-middle epitome of Rock and Roll, i.e. Thunder or Heartland Rock, despite a different continent/island. "You Shook Me All Night Long" is one great rockin' rasp of affirmation that – yep, the ol' folks back at home DO have something to fear with Rock and Roll. Coming down on one of the greatest choruses in the history of the Big Beat, AC/DC rampages. *Back in Black* album hit #1 in U.K., #4, 8-80 U.S.A.

Among other AC/DC unforgettables are biggest chart hit #23, 12-90 "Moneytalks," uninhibited #44, 1-82 "Let's Get It Up," #37 eponymous 12-80 "Back in Black," and their Freeway Faustian Flamethrower – "Highway to Hell" (a #47 song you thought, as I did, was at least #7). AC/DC measures electrical current, among other preferences. They're a stethoscope for the Heart of Rock and Roll.

"River Deep – Mountain High" – Supremes & Four Tops, #14, 11-70; #7, 12-70 R & B. Finally! Someone (Ross and Stubbs) got a big Top 20 hit out of this excellent unappreciated tremendous song. Deep Purple hit #53 in 1-69, but the song was the reason producer **Phil Spector** quit show biz in utter despair:

"River Deep – Mountain High" – Ike & Tina Turner, #88, 5-66. Also #112, 10-69; NC, R & B. 'FLOP?' Gonzo producer **Phil Spector** saw his Wall of Sound career screech to a standstill. Stressed out. The public, he said, wouldn't know a great song if it came up and bit them on the rump. This Tina crescendo is a fabulous song. The Wall of Sound thunders triumphantly in the swirling swoosh of raw guitars buzzing and crackling and zinging and screaming . . . very, very passionately. They hit #3, 6-66 in the U.K. with this American Un-Hit. Unleashed Rock and Soul firestorm.

"Saturday Night's Alright for Fighting" – Elton John, #12, 8-73. Bar brawls from tough working-class neighborhoods in Belfast, York, Glasgow, Stoke-on-Trent, or London were commonplace with the bellyful of bad beer. Elton John's (b. 3-25-47 as Reggie Dwight, Pinner, Middlesex, England) Pinner hugs the Harrow Road north of Hillingdon. People work hard during the week. Sometimes the smoke and steel and snarl get to them. Weary weeklong workers cave into the Terrier & Harrier, inhale a few brews, and then go a fast three rounds in the alley garbage-can ring. Beer muscles.

Britain is more conducive to bar brawling than America. Many fights in Pinner or Wolverhampton or Tom Jones's Pontypridd (10 miles north of Cardiff, Wales) end up the next morning with two Alka-Seltzers and a black eye. Maybe some dental ballet. In Detroit or Miami or Chicago, that same fight might end up with the instant fire-blazing death penalty; you never know what weapon that 'weak' stranger's packing. One of Elton's top rockers of all time. Jammin' guitar, sizzling bass line, drums of Montana thunder. In Elton's quaint Pinner pub.

"Movin' Out (Anthony's Song)" – Billy Joel, #17, 3-78. This song concerns a typical family quarrel about the meaning of life. Materialism thumps many of our arduous labors. Joel tells the folks the fancy house in Hackensack [NJ] isn't worth wage-slavery or early death. If that is "moving on up" on the status escalator, Billy says he's moving out.

"Allentown" – Billy Joel, #17, 1-82. OK, now it's time – HEARTLAND ROCK, says Toni Celeste, IS NEARLY THE SAME AS HARD ROCK! Heartland Rock, like "Allentown," is Mainstream Hard Rock and it plays well in America's 'Rust Belt.' It easily translates to the British Midlands, or Canada's Hamilton, Ontario, forge of smoke and steel and rust dust and destiny. Heartland Rock, though, can easily shift its smoky rustbelt habitat to encompass the cornfield Indiana epics of **John Cougar Mellencamp**, or the Jersey Shore musical moods of **Bruce Springsteen**. Or in the case of "Allentown" or "You May Be Right," **Billy Joel** of Oyster Bay, Long Island.

Allentown, Pennsylvania, sits on the eastern edge of America's 'Arsenal of Democracy.' The Arsenal's fiery-red heart still beats in the throbbing Ford Rouge factory in Dearborn, Michigan, that has more workers than my suburb – Dearborn – had people – 100,000. Motor City Detroit, remember, is just an overgrown Allentown. From its fiery forges rolled out red-hot Rock and Roll. First **Jackie Wilson** boxed his way out, and helped Ford Rouge worker **Berry Gordy** set up the Motown Empire. They both boogied to the smokin' steel urban Blues of **John Lee Hooker** (b. 1917, Clarksdale, MS), whose molten tones were molded in Fortune Recording Studios of **Devora** and **Jack Brown** at Alexandrine and Third. **Nolan Strong** recorded there and refused a reputed million-dollar Motown offer. His cousin **Barrett** launched Motown on his seed "Money" (#23, 3-60). **Smokey Robinson** idolized Nolan, and his style follows the Strong lead; though Smokey's eyes created his nickname, they reflect the gray smoky skies of the biggest industrial behemoth in the history of the world.

Just living in our Motown neighborhood meant we kids inhaled the equivalent of half a pack of Old Gold unfiltered longs every day – even if we didn't smoke! Heartland Rock pioneers **Mitch Ryder and the Detroit Wheels** roared out of Hamtramck, a little Polish-American town literally swallowed up by Detroit. While **Martha and the Vandellas** danced in the madcap Motown streets, Heartland Rock legend **Bob Seger**, and the **Eagles' Glenn Frey**, floated on the factory fringe of fiery forges. **Kid Rock** and **Uncle Kracker** (#5, 3-2001 "Follow Me") took Metro Motown beyond the millennium. In **Bruce Springsteen**'s 11-95 "Youngstown" factory song, an old worker actually yearns for the flames of Hell just to keep warm and toasty for eternity.

One way Detroit and Allentown cleaned up their act was by going out of business. "Blue Collar Blues" of 1972 chronicles the worker's Generation X despair, and shoddy production results. Old Detroit dinosaurs loved one war – the 1971 16.9¢/gallon GAS WAR on Terrible Telegraph Road, spine of Detroit's Western suburbs. In 1973, gas tripled to over 50¢/gallon. Disco dudes checked out their eight-track tape players in rusty behemoths – and started shrinking into dinkier cars.

So how does GAS affect record sales in the midst of smoky, steely Allentown, and Heartland Rock? The price of gas regulates album sales very closely via would-be spending cash. Auto designers and the all-powerful Washington EPA, bamboozled by the OPEC vise of international oligopoly, dumped SUV dreams and dealt people kiddie cars with 50 miles per gallon, about the size of a coffin.

Billy's "Allentown" drags the air hammers and anvils and hissing forge into the recording studio. His song's hero is depressed, disillusioned. All the promises of his teachers fell through – if kids worked hard and behaved. Factories shut down. "Allentown" inspired Springsteen's "My Hometown." Joel lives on an island (Long). Springsteen hugs the Industrial Eastern fringe almost in sight of the saltwater-taffy Jersey shore. Spending summer weekends on the gorgeous Jersey Shore, Billy recalls, World War II vet dads came home to a good-wage American promise. All these promises of industrial job stability and benefits fudged the final truth. America is the only civilized nation in the world without universal health care coverage.

Joel champions many causes. His #57, 5-90 song about the boat named for his daughter (and Christie Brinkley's), "The Downeaster 'Alexa'," publicizes the plight of clammers and deep-sea fisherman floundering on the shoals of weakfish economic depression. In "Allentown," Joel goes to bat for steelworkers. Integral to the defense and auto industries, the steel industry was a bulwark of American might and the thick, friendly fist of democracy. Waiting workers stewed in unrequited dreams: Summer cottages, snowmobiles, and Harleys, strong American union wages. Beer and shot afterglow. The wafting snowflake promenade – down friendly smoky neon streets to that Gibraltar oak-solid colonial. Home to steak-and-spuds dinnertime. Sweetly chortling Edith Bunker wives, and 3.2 grinny Leave-it-to-Beaver kids. A floppy Snoopy beagle. Some grumpy orange Garfield tomcat, too. One that owns the whole Allentown block. With smashing metallic clanks, and shrieky air whistles, Joel plods through his steady song. A hymn to disillusionment. Allentown kids scramble for a better future. No coal mine. No hot forge. Maybe shirtsleeve hands-on executive entry level. Maybe nothin'. Grad certificates adorn aging wallpaper. America's golden streets still glitter.

Maybe we can varnish the tarnish.

Billy Joel is still a raging success into the 21st century, because he can articulate the seething frustration of a generation anesthetized on promises. Stoned on the gasps of the Hard Work Gospel, "Allentown" perches on Punk Rock malaise, an unnamed trepidation that burgeoned in Britain in 1977 Punk anger. Suddenly, we all got thrust into this urban inferno of groaning homeless cardboard castles, or dragged-out, drugged-out lost innocence. And three lousy hamburger jobs to make payments on the amp. No cradle-to-grave security anymore. Maybe there never was. [No wonder the **Ramones'** (#81, 7-77 "Sheena Is a Punk Rocker") sang their chuck-it-all anthem "I Wanna Be Sedated"].

In Allentown or Attila's Outer Mongolia, on a clam boat in the Great South Bay, or rocking and rolling with his Uptown Girl ex, Joel just may be the most versatile Rock and Roll genius of his generation.

Billy Joel 'didn't start the fire.' But he fans the forge.

There is no Lotto. There is no Oz. Maybe some day, as Shel Silverstein put it, "You can go to Detroit."

"Brandy" – Looking Glass, #1(1), 6-72. Let's face it, Rock and Roll isn't big on Sea Shanties. Despite the rollicking Kingston Trio's "(What Do We Do with) A Drunken Sailor" or even mammoth Shanty "Sloop John B," (#3, 4-66 Beach Boys) our waterborne wonders have been few and fishy. Here's one. Brandy works in a seaside pub. She sloshes wine and whiskey to sailors who probably would prefer a frothy brew after a frothy sea voyage. All the sailors love Brandy. She's a fine girl, they chorus. She'd make a very fine wife. Then, they add the collective

kicker: his true lover, and his lady, is really THE SEA. These aqueous nomads prefer their roustabout life to a tidy seashore cottage in the lee of the hurricane. Many a lass, alas, has fallen victim to such a wave-wandering cowboy ramblin' man. Looking Glass's other biggee? #33, 7-73 "Jimmy Loves Mary-Anne," with New Jersey lead singer **Elliott Lurie.**

"Both Sides Now" – Judy Collins, #8, 11-68. Judy Collins's haunting voice and summersky blue eyes make this an unforgettable song. So does its super songwriter **Joni Mitchell** (Rock Hall '97). It took till 1802 to actually name clouds Cirrus, Cumulus, or Stratus; casual listeners think this tune's title is "Clouds," which she dauntingly admits she doesn't understand. Then she muses on carnivals, fairy-tales, and finally love and life itself. In an ebullient confession, she says she doesn't know much about ANYTHING (though we can all tell she's truly bright). Her Light-Metal Folk song spins into cirrus clouds of cotton-candy wonder and unknown infinity. Deep stuff. Not really fluff. Too many people on this weary old planet claim to know it all. The whole enchilada. So many imponderables exist in the universe. Those who believe they have it totally figured out may be living in a 'Fool's Paradise.' How important can popular music be in determining the course of a nation's destiny?

"Chelsea Morning" – Judy Collins, #78, 8-69. When young **Bill Clinton** (b. '46) was at Oxford University in England, he and his future bride **Hillary Rodham** were bedazzled by the bright optimistic promise of this song. "Chelsea Morning" is wispy and pastel. Chelsea is a London neighborhood where **Thomas Carlyle** sculpted the Gospel of Work concept that today powers the American Dream. Somewhere between Oxford and Carlyle and Lite Rock, Governor and Mrs. Clinton decided that SOCKS was a great name for a cat. For a kid, they needed something a lot classier. Chelsea Clinton arrived and thrived, thanks to the all-pervasive influence of American music.

"Hot Blooded" – Foreigner, #3, 7-78. One of the Greatest Rock and Roll Groups of All Time. Named for Anglo-American line-up. New Yorker **Lou Gramm** fronts line-up with vocals, tambourine, guitar, and harmonica. **Mick Jones** of Britain plays guitar like **Eric Clapton**; Mick is among foremost axeslingers of the Rock Revolution. Ed Gagliardi booms bass. Foreigner's Power Rock anchors a generation. "Hot Blooded" features a gaggle of groupies searching for sweet sensations. Lou Gramm's craggy tenor spins around the note, rocking dynamite rhythms (Dennis Elliott, drums) in note-bending ecstasy. Lou is a consummate Rock singer, brandishing an arsenal of White Soul, Orbisonic crescendo, Operatic Dynamism, Heavy-Metal Screaming Blues, or Tender Balladry. Naturally, his repertoire can echo **Buddy Holly**:

"True Blue Love" – Lou Gramm [solo], #40, 2-90. Crickets could dig it. Tom-toms tattoo "Peggy Sue" tempo. Gramm spindrifts stars above. Gramm's collage of rhythmic Blue-Eyed Soulfire includes #5, 1-87 "Midnight Blue" and #6, 10-89 "Just Between You and Me."

"Double Vision" – Foreigner, #2(2), 9-78. Mick Jones played Speed-Lead axe for album band (NC HOT 100) Spooky Tooth in early 70s – (Al. *You Broke My Heart When I Busted Your Jaw* #84, 5-73). "Double Vision" sparks double whammy of singer/songwriter Jones's steamy guitar salvos and Lou Gramm's White Soul volcanic vocalics. Foreigner scored seven platinums, and two #4 albums – #4, 3-77, eponymous *Foreigner* and 1-85 *Agent Provocateur*. Their biggest bombshell is ironically entitled *4* (yep, numeral 4 [four], (see Beatles' Al.. #1(10), 12-2000 *1*). Their *4* soared sextuple platinum (six million). Foreigner also hammered the #1 spot for ten weeks. No such luck with the number one number two song of all time:

"Waiting for a Girl Like You" – Foreigner, #2(10), 10-81. In Whitburn's *Top 1000 Singles 1955-93*, this breezy song is gloriously listed as the #833 biggest single hit ever. Every song that ever nailed #1 for even one dinky week hits the Top 832. Due to the charttopping power of Olivia Newton-John's Discoid Jock Rock jumper "Physical," Foreigner's procrastinatory silver "Girl" is probably still waiting. This slow, sensuous, White Soul anthem toys with fantasy and falsetto. Dream girl comes true.

"I Want to Know What Love Is" – Foreigner, #1(2), 12-84. Whoopee! The #376 biggest song of all time (Whitburn), thanks to one week fondling the top rung. Both this one and "Waiting" sift sinuous Soul into Gramm's gravelly tenor triumphs. Prowling the stage with electric energy rivaling mentor Mick & the Stones, Lou Gramm's blond Afro overtops shattering notes that command the band and arena with punchy Thunder Rock power. Like Freehold, New Jersey's boss Bruce Springsteen, Foreigner easily fits the Heartland Rock, Torchbearers, or Thunder Rock category. On this one, though, and "Waiting," Lou and Mick and All Greenwood's keyboards weave a silky swash of yearning burning romance that Smokey Robinson and the Miracles could groove to; Gramm's pipes trapeze from gutsy Rock to smooth Soul. Swathed by Jones's Spooky Tooth leads, which crest in fifty musical directions, Lou Gramm is one great reason the Gramophone/Victrola was invented by Thomas Edison [and the flat-disc record in the 1880s by Emile Berliner].

After a squirmy wait at #2 on the quirky HOT 100 charts, Foreigner hunkered back and grooved to album art and sales. My favorite, #10, 12-82 *Foreigner Records*, a greatest-hits extravaganza, actually looks like a JUKE BOX for "Juke Box Hero" – one of those windowsill naugahyde-boxes hooked to the big diner juke box in the corner. You slip out the sleeve, and bingo, their hit cavalcade arrives too. I'm not so artistically overjoyed about their provocative *Head Games* (#5, 9-79) with a sweet ingenue in a music-notes-print miniskirt, looking terrified next to the #1 plumbing device found in this grungy Men's Room. Gramm's great Blue-Eyed Soul voice, Jones's virtuoso leads, and drummer Dennis Elliot's rockin' rhythms make them Rock Hall candidates.

"Juke Box Hero" – Foreigner, #26, 3-82. Outside the Patchogue, NY Theatre for the Performing Arts (August 2000), I asked Lou Gramm (on his gutsy-performance comeback from a serious illness) if he'd heard my son Jeremy's Nine Days #6, 4-2000 hit "Absolutely." I sang him a song snippet about how sad the girl looks in pix, and the river she wept that might drown the entire world. Gramm grinned, a tad burlier than in his 80s phase, and exclaimed, "Hey, Maury, I've got a young family, and your son's song is #1 AT MY HOUSE." With proper paternal respect and semi-humility, I must admit it was one of my greatest moments in Rock and Roll. You always love musical praise, but it's ten times better coming from someone in showbiz you really respect and admire for THEIR musical expertise. "Juke Box Hero," yep. It's like Kid Rock's echo of Bob Seger's roadweary-band classic "Turn the Page" – "Only God Knows Why" (#21, 2000). Or Dollar's Graveyard Rock #74, '80 ill-fated "Shooting Star." "Juke Box Hero" pans the scene. It lavishes squirmy groupies, all-night bus marathons, flirtations with quixotic substances, industry rip-offs. It features the glitz of midnight romps, fan-mag pix, and the roller-coaster whirl of jiffy fame and cotton-candy glory. You catch a little longing in Gramm's beseeching tenor, for some home comforts a la Paul Simon/Art Garfunkel's #4, '66 "Homeward Bound." The musical key to "Juke Box Hero" is doubling the bass's note on low rhythm guitar – a dynamic macho crackle undergirds the power polyrhythms. Foreigner is currently anchored nearby in Bellport, Long Island. In R & R destiny, however, they span the faddish years, spinning the best of White Soul vocals (Gramm) with the best throbbing Speed Metal fireworks in the fast lane (Jones). Heart of Rock and Roll, Foreigner.

Second-string Foreigner smashes, juke-box pan-flashes, and songs of love, laughter, and luck: #4, 3-77 "Feels Like the First Time"; #4, 7-81 "Urgent," with sax solo by Motown's Junior Walker; frigidity ode #6, 7-77 "Cold As Ice,"; #12, 9-79 "Dirty White Boy"; my fave "Blue Morning, Blue Day" [#15, 12-78]; and their 80s star-spangled spate: #12, 3-85 "That Was Yesterday"; #6, 12-87 "Say You Will," echoing Jackie Wilson; and #5, 3-88 "I Don't Want to Live Without You." Fifties guitar legend Duane Eddy played lead guitar on Foreigner's #42, 3-95 "Until the End of Time." It is totally unrelated to Perry Como's great-for-different-reasons Crooner anthem #1(1), 8-45 "Till the End of Time." Anyhow, Foreigner's brand of Rock and Roll is equally timeless, universally appealing, and still brings down the house!

"Don't Look Back" – Boston, #4, 8-78. "More Than a Feeling" (#5, 9-76), Boston is one of the great Rock groups of two heydays, 1976-78 and 1986-87. Tom Scholz (guitars and keyboards) had an engineering masters from prestigious M.I.T., but really wanted a #1 song: #1(2), 9-86 "Amanda." Brad Delp sang lead, and the duo also scored on #9, 12-87 "We're Ready." In 9-76, their #5 "More Than a Feeling" debut featured Barry Goudreau's guitar, Sib Hashian's drums, and Fran Sheehan's bass. Oddly, Boston is from Boston.

"Show Me the Way" – Peter Frampton, #6, 2-76.
For an old Pepsi ad in China ("Come alive with Pepsi"), somebody translated it quite literally: COME OUT OF THE GRAVE WITH PEPSI! Needless to say, that 70s marketing ploy wallowed in absurdity and cautious sales. On Peter Frampton's *Peter Frampton* debut album, he nabbed #32, 5-75, with nary a blockbuster single. This American ad expression translated a lot better just 5 miles south of London Bridge and Anne Boleyn's ghastly Tower. Bechenham's Frampton was the hottest rocker around with his #1(1), 2-76 *FRAMPTON COMES ALIVE*.

We have not said too much about hair. We zero in on the music of these fab singles. Clothes and HAIR make the Rocker. It was always somewhat so. It is more so today. Hair, yes. Or, in 2002+, lack thereof. Frampton had shoulder-length hair. No sweat. Here's the biggee: Frampton also had PINK hair. Well, not really. Look inside the album. Unearth the middle of the album. You'll catch Britrockers John Simons (drums), Bob Mayo (guitar), and bassman Stanley Sheldon – all with rather normal-looking long British bandsmen hair. You then figure you've been bamboozled. Frampton is a fake, you figure, and the pink-magenta hair gimmick was just there to vacuum you $7.99 plus tax. Then you tote this live Frampton double album home and discover his outstanding music. Tricky stage lights turn his hair (the ordinary brown color, of perhaps, mine or yours) into some otherworldly glowing flamboyant phenomenon – DAYGLOW PINK. Here's the Frampton/Foreigner connection. They stem from humble [pie] beginnings:

"I Don't Need No Doctor" – Peter Frampton, #73, 9-71.
The word SUPERGROUP dates back to the Archaeozoic mid-60s: the **Yardbirds** reeled off gunslinger guitarists galore (Beck, Page, Clapton). Heavy Metal guys Humble Pie rolled out of Essex in 1971. **Peter Frampton** and **Steve Marriott** of Small Faces duoed on vocals, with **Spooky Tooth**'s Greg Ridley on bass. Foreigner's **Mick Jones** also gigged with Spooky Tooth! Frampton came alive to his 1977 "I'm in You" #2(3) in 5-77; his second-most played song is "Baby, I Love Your Way" (#12, 6-76), and Frampton scored with #10 "Do You Feel Like We Do" 9-76. After a terrible car crash, Frampton's career bounced back with #74, 2-86 "Lying." For two years, Frampton bore the "next Elvis" cross as well as anyone could.

"Fools Fall in Love" – Jacky Ward, NC, 1977; #9, 9-77 C.
Why in the world would I include a song that's neither fast Mainstream Rock here, nor even on the HOT 100 charts? Three good reasons: JERRY LEIBER - MIKE STOLLER - HARRIET COSTELLO

The **Drifters**' #69, 3-57 version (#10 R & B) launched their illustrious careers – via the Brill-Building-arena songwriting genius of **Jerry Leiber** and **Mike Stoller** (both born 1933). Popular music in America unfurled around the magic pianos on Broadway of **Bobby Darin, Carole King, Barry Mann, Gerry Goffin, Ellie Greenwich** and these two guys. Super R & B crossover hit. Texan Jacky Ward's excellent tenor weaves into silky strings and mellow electric-piano fleecy *arpeggios*. Jerry and Mike describe, clinically, the foolish romantic, comparing him to flighty young girls in school: simply play for them two bars from "Stardust," Ward croons. Or hang a zany lover's moon in the purple sky. Wow. Metaphorical magnificence. Lieber-Stoller connected to the Tin Pan Alley New York songwriting tradition of 1890s-1920s **Harry Von Tilzer** and **Irving Berlin**, or early recording icons like **Dan Quinn, Billy Murray**, or **John McCormack**.

As their lyrical songcraft Tin Pan Alley world receded into Garage Bands' sub-literary Hot Hormone Hits, Lieber and Stoller kept the faith. Shakespeare and Melville and Emerson were as real to them as Elvis – whose career was paved on their cool allusions (like Detroit's PURPLE GANG) in their [#1, '57 "Jailhouse Rock"). "Fools Fall in Love," too, is a lyrical masterpiece and excellent tune.

Hoodwinked by rosy dreams, lovers swoon. Blinded by the light. Love-blind air castles they build have a foundation of 'wishes,' and they use beams made of RAINBOWS. Wow! If that isn't one of the most unique thoughts in all popular music, what is? Visualize that. A Sleeping Beauty castle in the air – thick tree-trunk-style beams are made of RAINBOWS. Profound, majestic lyric.

Comes the Leiber-Stoller dramatic irony. Just when we're feeling they're kind of detached brilliant Shakespeareans, unaffected by the naïve schoolgirl's teenage crush, suddenly they zap us with a dose of reality. The former cynic about LOVE now gets hooked. He laments HE'S a BRAND-NEW lovin' FOOL. Zowie.

Jerry Leiber and **Mike Stoller** are the Lennon-McCartney or Simon-Garfunkel of the 50s. But who is HARRIET COSTELLO? Read on.

Clovers	"Love Potion #9" #9, #23, 9-59
	(also Searchers, #3, 11-64)
Coasters	"Charlie Brown" #2(3), 2-59
	"Little Egypt" #23, 4-61
	"Poison Ivy" #7, 8-59
	"Searchin'" #3, 5-57
	"Yakety Yak" #1(1), 6-58
	"Young Blood" #8, 5-57
Dion DiMucci	"Ruby Baby" #2(3), 1-63
Drifters	"Dance With Me" #15, 10-59
	"There Goes My Baby" #2(1), 6-59
Wilbert Harrison	"Kansas City" #1(2), 4-59
Ben E. King	"Spanish Harlem" #10, 12-60
	"Stand by Me" #4, 5-61
Maria Muldaur	"I'm A Woman" #12, 12-74
Elvis Presley	"Don't" #1(5), 1-58
	"Hound Dog" (arr.) #1(11), 8-56
	"Jailhouse Rock" #1(7), 10-57
	"Love Me" #2(2), 11-56
	"Loving You" #20, 6-57
	"Treat Me Nice" #18, 10-57
Robins	"Smokey Joe's Café" #79, 12-55
	(also by Buddy Holly)

"Smokey" here is your tip-off. The Harriet Costello connection? These 50s songwriting gurus had a new glory heyday in the 90s Broadway revival of their song cavalcade – *Smokey Joe's Café*. Harriet is a librarian, who works with my wife Toni. She and her husband Jeff saw the Manhattan play, and she gave me the Lieber-Stoller *Playbill* for your cataloguing glee.

"I Write the Songs" – Barry Manilow, #1(1), 11-75. Brooklyn Pop star Manilow's (b. '46) biggest hit is a salute to all the super songwriters illuminating our lives. His song here is no egomaniacal trip; Barry's concept of "I" is actually every songwriter of the Rock (and June-Moon-Croon-Lagoon) Revolution. Manilow rode his mellow Light Jazz style to success. Sophisticated demeanor. Tenement past. Poor neighborhood punching bag for street toughs. Barry started on accordion. Juilliard dropout. CBS mail clerk. Barry made big bucks, hyping commercial JINGLES. Manilow's success horizon neared after accompanying **Bette Midler** at '72 Continental Nightclub/Bathhouse gig. Manilow's chart gems include: #1, 5-77 "Looks Like We Made It" and "Can't Smile Without You," at #3, 2-78. He joins a rare few with a #1 debut: "Mandy" 11-74. His smoothly Sinatran "Somewhere in the Night," rose to #9, 12-78. Manilow/Sinatra spin-off? Harry Connick, Jr. hit big on albums like #16, 7-94 Al. *She,* that had one single: #67, 10-94 "(I Could Only) Whisper Your Name." Back to the big Boogie beat:

"Gloria" – Laura Branigan, #2(3), 9-82. Our heroine 'Gloria' carves out her own cosmic destiny. Once shivering on the brink of disaster, like personality-flipping "Georgy Girl" (Seekers, #2, 12-66), 'Gloria' is now master of her fate, captain of her soul. Using an Italian melody sung and composed by Umberto Tozzi in 1979 [Whitburn], Branigan shucks classifications like corn husks. Our local CD store stuffs Laura into R & B category. Joel Whitburn lists Gloria as a pop artist. Tony Jasper's *International Encyclopedia of Hard Rock and Heavy Metal* says she just squeezes in, a "poppy version of Pat Benatar." Clarke's landmark Penguin pop *Encyclopedia* safely calls her a 'singer.' We simply call Laura Branigan a terrific Rock and Roll star.

The Brewster, New York, ingenue accompanied songwriter/surrealist **Leonard Cohen**: [Al. #63, 4-69 *Songs from a Room*]. Noel Harrison's Cohen classic "Suzanne" (#56, 10-67) presents images of kids in seaweed, and of Chinese oranges floating past Suzanne's *David-Copperfield* shanty beside the river. **Donna Summer** and the **Village People** hit phenomenal success in roaring Greenwich Village. Branigan's "Gloria" became a Greenwich Village icon with chutzpah and feisty determination – much like 'Donna' or 'Peggy Sue' in the 50s represented the blonde cheerleader pedestal Pocoima (CA) or Prairie Princess. Laura Branigan scored with #7, 4-83 "Solitaire," "Self Control" (#4, 5-84), and "Power of Love" (#26, 11-87). "Gloria" shares the same soulful Atlantic record label as Queen of Soul **Aretha Franklin** ("Freeway of Love" #3, 7-85). Laura Branigan's TOTAL SOUND is pure SOUL, regardless of her rosy Irish pigmentation. Rock and Roll is multicultural and multiracial. "Gloria" is one of the greatest songs ever, in anybody's category.

Irish-American Branigan is no Soul singer by birth – just by gusto, like Northern Ireland's **Van Morrison**. Her Giant Beat nails the listener to the wall in its bashing crashing intensity. Like **Melissa Etheridge** or **Janis Joplin** or **Joan Jett** or **Kim Carnes**, Branigan brims with vocal power. Laura apprenticed with modest debut #69, 3-82

"All Night With Me." Laura's 4th hit slogs slowly and soulfully through her downtrodden midnight malaise: 1983's #12 "How Am I Supposed to Live Without You." Redone:

"How Am I Supposed to Live Without You?" – Michael Bolton, #1(3), 10-89. Michael's Greatest Hit? Bolton romped for a touchdown. Michael Bolton actually wrote the song for Laura's first popularization of it. In the razzmatazz pop world, a singer with a #62 hit often defers status to the #2 hitmaker. Russian-American soulsmith Bolton [nee BOLOTIN, b. '53, Connecticut] fronted Heavy Metal group **Blackjack**, grappling with modest success: #62, 7-79 "Love Me Tonight." Bolton sings lead. As a Blue-Eyed Soul solo, Michael (no one ever calls him, or the 'Gloved One,' Mike or Mick) hit with #82 "Fool's Game" In 5-83. He took baby steps up the success mountain until his #19, '87 "That's What Love Is All About." His incredible Soul anthem, Otis Redding's "Sittin' on the Dock of the Baby," splashed to #11, 1-88.

"New Year's Day" – U2, #53, 4-83. Happy New Year! We'll get to these R & R superstars [Grammy 2000 Best Song, #21, 9-2000 "Beautiful Day"], with a real Irish tenor from Ireland, very soon. It laments the Northern Ireland 'troubles' (euphemism – read: Violence with English Army). Their first chart hit in America.

"Keep On Lovin' You" – REO Speedwagon, #1(1), 11-80. **Kevin Cronin** of Champaign, Illinois, lead singer, rhythm guitar; Gary Richrath mans the lead. Not many groups name themselves after an Oldsmobile offshoot (R.E.O. is Ransom E. Olds, who began making the 100+-year-old line in Lansing, Michigan – 'Speedwagon' is their 1911 fire truck). So far, there are no rock band Toyotans, Isuzu Speedrockers, or Mitsubishi Marauders. Nice song. Complex harmonies and sophisticated bass lines by Bruce Hall. This huge #1 catapulted them from ho-hum #94-58-56-77 run at 'Where's the fire?' speed.

"I Love Rock and Roll" – Joan Jett & the Blackhearts, #1(7), 2-82. Remember **LaVern Baker**'s gutsy "Jim Dandy" (#17, 12-56)? It took 25 years for Joan Jett to pick up LaVern's Rock and Roll torch. Sure we had **Gracie Slick** and **Linda Ronstadt** and **Aretha Franklin** and a hundred great female Rock singers in the interim, but **Joan Jett** struck the pose. Adorned in chic sleek leather, a guitar slinging like the *Rifleman* at High Noon, Jett blasted out her crispy alto vocal atop a rockin' rhythm-track. Arguably, she came up with the BIGGEST ROCK AND ROLL HIT OF ALL TIME TO 1982 BY A FEMALE LEAD SINGER. Olivia Newton-John's "Physical" was #1(10), and Kim Carnes's "Bette Davis Eyes" hit #1(9), but some sidetrack them into Disco or Adult Contemporary sub-genres. No one will ever tab "I Love Rock and Roll" with any tag other than straight-down-the pike ROCK AND ROLL!

The **Runaways**, suggested by **Del Shannon**'s classic song, were the Philly girl Jett's (b. '60) first band. Rock Hall '99 inductee **Bonnie Raitt**, another real guitar-playing rocker, had HER first chart hit [#57, 5-77] with Del Shannon's "Runaway." Like the **Go-Gos**, the Runaways played their own instruments. Working out of L.A., Joan's Runaways volleyed: #106, 8-76 "Cherry Bomb," and #110, 3-77 "Heartbeat." Enter Kenny Laguna, refugee from the Big Apple's Brill Building. Also Richie Cordell, who penned "I Think We're Alone Now" for **Tommy James**'s Shondells (#4, '66) and later **Tiffany** (Darwisch — #1, '87). Add the rising-Punk Sex Pistols' influence and Hard Rock London Experience. When Joan's Blackhearts finally arrived on the scene, the stage was set for the biggest female R & R anthem of all time.

Joan Jett played a recent concert for Olympians. She was joyously flabbergasted when a superstar 10K (6.2 miles) runner greeted her on the street with the only words of English he knew – "I LOVE ROCK AND ROLL!" An international Rock and Roll anthem, yes? The lyric? Some guy meets a girl, they get instantly amorous, and then sleep it off in a love-tornado of bittersweet goodbye?

Her tumultuous, tempestuous tune bashes around in bluesy 'E'. Rhythm guitar doubles the bass line. Drums echo Power Rock thunder. Joan mentions the cute guy in the bar looks about 17 [isn't anyone checking ID's anymore?] Whatever the outcome, JJ emerged with the Biggest R & R anthem ever (even to date) for a female, guitar-slinging star. Encore? Their #7, 5-82 "Crimson and Clover," vibrating volcanically with eerie tremolo and phasers.

"Crimson and Clover" – Tommy James and the Shondells, #1(2), 12-68. Surreal lyrics, vibrato pulse. Their biggest hit. Mystical otherworldly Space Mountain experiments with distortion, digital delay, flangers, and flashy reverb. Like Bee Gees' "Words," lead vocal tremolo actually simulates beat. Unique searing music. In March 2000, Metallica's "NO Leaf Clover" (2-2000) was at #74.

"Cover of the *Rolling Stone*" – Dr. Hook, #6, 12-72. Ray Sawyer (Dr. Hook) of New Jersey fantasizes his own beloved mug on cover of music mag *Rolling Stone*. He savors the idea of saving copies to give to Mom and pals. *Rolling Stone*, R & R journal extraordinaire, granted his fervent request shortly afterwards. **Dr. Hook/Sawyer** debuted with ardent "Sylvia's Mother" (#5, 4-72). Hook's hit "6"-pack? Sam Cooke's naivete ballad – "Only Sixteen" (#28, 6-59, Cooke) to Dr. Hook's #6, 1-76 hit hook; #6 "Sharing the Night Together" in 9-78; the huskily titled #6, 4-79 "When You're In Love with a Beautiful Woman," and his biggest hit ever (equally quintational to 'Sylvia's Mom') – "Sexy Eyes" at #5, 2-80. Hook's greatest un-hit title among his Rock-Comedy gems? "Roland the Roadie and Gertrude the Groupie," #83, 7-73.

SWOOP! Back to the Heartland. And Heartland Rock and Roll. Two Torchbearers here. One from **James Dean**'s rural Indiana turf. The other fondles the smoke and steel Motor City megalopolis from the ragged winter cornfields where winds and metal get heavy. [All from the backseat of his old '60 Chevy.]

"Small Paradise" – John Cougar Mellencamp, #87, 2-80. A Dutch-American farm boy from Seymour, Indiana (b. 10-7-51) struggled under the tigerskin disguise ('Cougar') dubbed him by **David Bowie**'s manager Tony DeFries. Indianapolis, Indiana (731,000) is the only U.S. big town with no major lake, river, or ocean. It fans out like a wheel. Bedrock Americana. **James Dean** (1930-55) grew up nearby in Fairmount. **John Cougar Mellencamp** was raised in Seymour. Seymour lies a fast half-hour away from the Southern home of the man that *Der Spiegel* called the Greatest Athlete in the World – **Muhammad Ali**. Mellencamp grew up on Heartland Rock turf surrounded by Rock and Roll radio. Mellencamp could hear his Hard Rock idol **Mitch Ryder and His Detroit Wheels**, pioneer patriarchs of Heartland Rock.

With cougar moves of James Dean, welterweight fortitude of his heavyweight hero, and unbridled dedication to Rock and Roll – Pure Rock – of Mitch Ryder and the Detroit Wheels, 'Cougar' carved out a career. Mellencamp strafed the Top 30 with #28, 10-79 "I Need a Lover." Between 1980 and 1988, Cougar celebrated 16 straight top 30 tunes, with nine cracking the coveted top ten.

"Hurts So Good" – John Cougar Mellencamp, #2(4), 4-82. Both **Bruce Springsteen** and **John Mellencamp** are unblond Dutch-American rockers. Each sported a jet-black haircut much shorter than the Frampton pink look. Looking a little bit dangerous, Mellencamp celebrates Vintage Rock PURITY. You'll find nary a flügelhorn or zither or Techno-Robotic MIDI. Upon rare occasion, a sax or trumpet may intrude his guitar-drum-bass corral. Mellencamp is big on Basic Rock and Roll. He hammers Heartland Rock.

His Keys are guitar-friendly, Blues-suffused macho Rock and Roll Keys. "Hurts" plus biggest hit "Jack and Diane" are in Buddy Holly's 'A', with "Small Town" in 'B' and "R.O.C.K. in the U.S.A." in 'E'. "Hurts So Good" serves loud metallic guitar chords, backed by a crashing smashing beat. Handclapping doubles the drum on the basic rock beat. In premier Heartland Rock fashion, the bass drum slices through all the beats, while they bash the snare or cymbal's 2, the 2½, and the 4 beats very hard. It's a standard variation of the old backbeat theory of hitting the two and four beats quite hard.

Love 'hurts so good'? Discussing the 'love bite' of passion, he confides she's a lot younger than she is innocent. John offers a cool gravel growl, plus yodel-kicks and a Holly hiccup or two. Cougar/Mellencamp was jolted by its adoption as an S-M anthem in the Village on the 'Wild Side' (see Lou Reed).

"Jack and Diane" – John Cougar Mellencamp, #1(4), 7-82. No innocent caper, this Jack-Diane rendezvous. He writes about 16-year-old pigskin studs wooing pink-kneed cheerleaders. Jack's very straight intent is not of the choirboy ilk. Jack starts out this little ditty by calling it one. "Ditty" leaps out of Middle English and means a simple song. In some ways, "Jack and Diane" isn't too complex – the Big Beat on the R & R 2, 2½, and 4 again, plus handclapping. A monster Metal rhythm guitar crackles chords like bullwhips. The "love-me-now" male libido isn't too hard to explain either.

In a more complex manner, "Jack and Diane" represents the life and death of the American way. Check the yummy prop – the Taystee Freeze, ice-cream mecca to the Bible Belt and beyond. Mother Nurture – A Milky Way of sweet delights: innocent, ultra-white, billowy, pillowy, bosomy splendor. Diane is polishing off a chili dog. Kids know they will live forever, so who needs to watch fat grams, cholesterol, or even onion breath with dapper jock Jack? The lyric glows with promise: Jack's an incipient football star, Diane's a dairy-queen debutante. She adorns Jackie's backseat. [Did **Cougar** drive a Mercury 'Cougar' for panther passion?]

Part of the eternal mystery of **James Dean**'s timeless halo is that he was at one time, macho, vulnerable, cool, funny, shy, outgoing, handsome, lonely, brilliant, and athletic (see **Jim Morrison**/Doors). But Dean mumbled a bit. This ultra-cool-mumbling Method Acting technique is not Dean's alone; he got if from Marlon Brando via Elia Kazan. In the Who's "My Generation" (#74, 1-66), they stutter and push the inarticulate aspect of their confused, existential age. **Elton John** coolly stutters in #1, '74 "Bennie and the Jets." This cosmic brooding started with James Dean. Maybe even Ernest Hemingway. Or Melville, Hawthorne, Shakespeare, and Chinese Poet Tu Fu.

The life and death of America has to do with how the society keeps on keepin' on. How Diane rebuffs Jack's offer of instant intimacy. An echo of #1, '60 **Shirelles**' "Will You Love Me Tomorrow" plays in the sound track of all our lives. Jack conjures his best #1 James Dean look in the lyric. To Mellencamp that means his most come-hither gaze. He asks her to doff those chic Bobbi Brook slacks behind some shaky shady tree. Whether she, and all the Dianes of America, submit to all the Jacks' desires will tell America's future. If a few girls out of a hundred get pregnant at 16 and abort or have their babies, the society will go on. If 99 out of 100 choose single motherhood at 15 or so, nothing we do here will ever be the same again. There is absolutely no didactic message here. Just the facts, Ma'am. Like rural kids since time immemorial, they rap about running off to the city where it's all happening. Maybe.

John sings of the Bible Belt. Yep. Church attendance in the American Heartland far outweighs church attendance almost anywhere in Europe or Asia or Africa. In the rave-up vocal bridge, with star-spangled bass drums crashing like Independence Day fireworks, Mellencamp rolls from his beloved "Bible Belt" to a phrase that cuts right through to the mystic midnight throbbing heart of America – HANG ONTO AGE 16 JUST AS ECSTATICALLY LONG AS YOU POSSIBLY CAN! He warns how changes come crashing in very, very, fast, and we have to bear the brunt of responsibility as women and as men. [Boom! Aaarrgh, the HOUSE payment].

Sixteen, then, is a very precious Holding Pattern. We see the airport of adult responsibility, but we keep on gliding and soaring and floating in the funtime blue azure skies like young free eagles on high. Then, like fated Greek demi-god Icarus, our feathery wings' wax melts

too close to the sun, and we plunge back to earth. Free falling [in Tom Petty's #7, '89 'heartbreaking words'].

Jack and Diane are like Johnny B. Goode plunking his gunny-sack guitar and dreaming of fame. They give us the whole American experience in miniature. Just two country kids with, perhaps, a future. They are a microcosm of every eager young couple in America.

As Jack and Diane go, so goes America. Maybe the world.

"Pink Houses" – John Cougar Mellencamp, #7, 12-83. Here's JCM's dig at conformity and tackiness. It echoes the spirit of **Pete Seeger**'s Malvina Reynolds song "Little Boxes" (#70, 1-64) of 'ticky-tacky' plywood and boring similarity. Mellencamp returns to his small town. This time we get a more jaded, world-weary approach. 'PINK' is crucial. Symbol searchers and sifters will notice that pink isn't quite the pure white of innocence, nor is it the scarlet of hot sensuality. Like gray between black and white, pink is Miss In-Between. (Nathaniel Hawthorne's "Young Goodman Brown"). John celebrates and laments simultaneously our little mutual pastel pink houses we share in suburbia. With his rich smoky tenor, he sounds very sincere.

"R.O.C.K. in the U.S.A." – John Cougar Mellencamp, #2(1), 2-86. John's *Scarecrow* album #2(3), 9-85 is among the best ever. Great albums fire off hit singles like fireworks. First is "Small Town" (#6, 11-85). "Small Town" is utter resignation; he was born, raised, and will probably die in a small town – he speculates morosely that's where they'll bury him. His tiny town, though, allows him the romantic persona he wishes to symbolize. It's convoluted, moody, and resigned to Kankakee or Kalamazoon karma.

"R.O.C.K." is the second hit off *Scarecrow*. John rolls out a litany of his R & R heroes: The **Shangri-Las** (#6, 11-65, "I Can Never Go Home Anymore"); **Martha** of the Vandellas; White Soul singers **Mitch Ryder** and **Felix Cavaliere**'s **Young Rascals**. Also great Soul icons **Jackie Wilson, James Brown, Frankie Lymon**. His most intriguing choice? The **Bobby Fuller IV**. Fuller's Holly-esque Tex-Mex wrangler anthem "I Fought the Law" nabbed #9 in '66. Bobby died tragically in a carbon monoxide accident while parked with his girlfriend. They were an All-American couple like "Jack and Diane." "R.O.C.K." really does! Grooving in macho 'E,' it spurts its Basic Blues message in an Old Faithful geyser of Goodtime Rock and Roll. This song is a celebration of all the good things that came out of the USA. Like Rock and Roll.

"Rain on the Scarecrow" – John Cougar Mellencamp, #21, 5-86. Bitter message. Hint of future economic misery. Under the guise of prosperity, a huge chunk of the American work force has been enslaved in a dragging drudgery of three hamburger jobs at minimum wage. No benefits. Off-the-books wages. No Social Security. No future. Sick a day? See you later, alligator.

It started generations ago. People had to leave their farm homes for the city. RURAL EXPATRIATION – where the bloated robber barons bit the [farm] hands that fed them. Promises or poverty? The American Dream or desperation? Grim "Scarecrow" stalks the answer. Things will get better, say the pundits. We just need more education and computers. If education were the whole answer, why was Hitler's Germany the most educated nation in history? Perhaps we must skewer our educational system to be more kind and humane. Once the system runs too ME FIRST amok, the good people get stomped. Like the poor victims – good Indiana farm folks – in "Scarecrow." Should we educate by dry algebraic formulas, by stuffy parameters of accountability feasibility? Or should we look to the living, breathing kid whose life we're shaping?

"Scarecrow" probes the dark heart of Heartland economics. Apocalypse NOW Heart of Darkness. The soulless, octopus-tentacled First Tycoon Bank strangles the poor dirt farmer and his family. Seymour, Indiana cradled **John Cougar Mellencamp.** Like Fairmount's **James Dean.** A bright kid, John graduated from local Vincennes University. His manager named the kid after a big tawny cat. Like **Steve Miller, Bob Seger**, and other Heartland and Rustbelt Rockers, Mellencamp played his share of fraternity parties with splotches of beer spilled on his amp.

Love those early band names. Don't you? Like the Mamas & Papas' were MUGWUMPS. Or CCR was GOLLIWOGS. Mellencamp was in 'Crepe Soul.' Crepe Soul? Plus (wowie zowie) SNAKEPIT BANANA BARN. One more time, for the road – SNAKEPIT BANANA BARN.

To understand "Scarecrow," you check the B & W concept album cover photo. John broods pensively over a sere fuzzy scarecrow and rusty tractor. He gazes mystically into a sharp dark barb of the barbed-wire fence. His thick tousled black hair glows in the gray bleak dead fields of icy November. He ponders the dissolution of rural America – Dust Bowls, Depressions, and greedy banks. Does John sell out to the big city? Nah. His gonzo success with "Scarecrow" rocks all the world's small-town pilgrims – trying to hold on tenaciously to a little bit of land and a little bit of respect. JCM is no greenhorn. He cut his album in Belmont, Indiana, but he had it mastered in New York City. Somehow, he keeps his integrity in a cutthroat world of fast deals, fast lanes, and big lies.

Would you put your grandmother on your album? That's how strong his family values are. One cut, "Grandma's Theme" [NC, '85], is a one-minute ballad by Grandma Laura Mellencamp about a baby on a long-ago train. Good grandkid, JCM.

"Rain on the Scarecrow" makes no pretense of HOPE. In the spirit of Generation X and existential despair – this song wallows in utter desolation. 'Desolation Row,' as Kerouac and Dylan called it. "Scarecrow" too wallows, with dignity.

In the darkly haunting refrain, a father apologizes to his son. The boy was to have inherited their family farm, but some strangling second-mortgage lien lost it to the bank. A tangled skein of choking debt, and overwork, and backbusting competition stole the father's youth, will, and purpose (compare Springsteen's "My Hometown").

The 'Farmers' Bank' – note their name's bitter irony – foreclosed on their old family farm. Like Brutus (*et tu Brute*) stabbing his 'friend' Caesar, the failing farmer has to face his old 'friend' . . . the bank – to profane and blaspheme his Life's Work at some awful bankruptcy auction. [Up in Custer, Michigan, I have seen this phenomenon too many times among fellow dairy farmers who didn't save as my father-in-law Tony Piazza did].

As the rocking-chair grandma murmurs of the Promised Land, the young father cites 97 graveyard crosses in the courthouse year; coincidentally, 97 families lost their farms. In an outburst of wild wailing uncontrollable despair, the lost father confesses – he feels like the sopping, waterlogged scarecrow out in the cold November rain. Pondering his grandpa, his name, and his lifetime neighbors, he thinks of his lost farm and considers dying, like some lifeless scarecrow out in the rain. Death Rock. Graveyard Rock. John suggests **Pearl Jam's** #2, 1999 revival of J. Frank Wilson and the Cavaliers' car accident song "Last Kiss." Mellencamp lofts a stinging 80s indictment of sugary claptrap schemes, forked-tongue tycoon promises, and failed farms. And families.

"Scarecrow" is out of tune with lap-tops and modems and fax and e-mail. The song shuns Techno-Synth. It uses real, live, breathing musicians: Larry Crane, acoustic guitar; Mike Wanchic, backing vocals; bassist Toby Myers. Kenny Arnhoff? Drums, tambourine, vibes, and vocals. Thrash boom bam. Beyond the crunchy funk and heavy thrash, however, the deep meaning of "Scarecrow" looms like the Riptide in the hurricane afterglow. As in *Gone With the Wind*, Scarlett O'Hara's land is nearly sacred to her. It was her father's land. In "Scarecrow," it was his father's land. And his father's father's land. All the way back to the Native American consciousness. To return the land to the faceless heartless corporation is like a small death. The pain will continue to burn . . .

In Springsteen's "My Hometown" and JCM's "Scarecrow," we see the bitter dregs of the Johnny B. Goode Dream. Work hard, practice, and you'll make it big. Here, as in Upton Sinclair's 1900 Chicago novel *The Jungle* or Frank Norris's naturalistic *The Octopus*, hard work just gets you suffering and grief. "Scarecrow" offers dim shades of the mocking bumpersticker:

LIFE'S A BITE – AND THEN YOU DIE.

Mellencamp, rural nostalgiac, teaches American history by electric guitar. "The only time my education was interrupted was the time I spent in the classroom." – George Bernard Shaw (1854-1950).

Out East, rustlings from the Rust belt ripple in the sad lonesome sax of **Springsteen's Clarence Clemons.**

An entire canvas of country America in the post-Industrial Age is lovingly stroked by the craggy second tenor of the Hoosier's "Scarecrow" vignette. John sings Norman Rockwell or Currier & Ives gone to seed. JCM scratches rural reality like crows scratching the frozen night-the-music-died cornfields of Clear Lake, Iowa. Or a million other lonely locations. In lost America.

"Cherry Bomb" – John Cougar Mellencamp, #8, 10-87. The long electric slide from heyday to humdrum that stalks superstars was marked by two '87 hits – this one and #9, 8-87 "Paper in Fire." "Check It Out" (#14, 2-88), "Pop Singer" (#15, 4-89), and "Get a Leg Up" (#14, 10-91) assure the stature of Mellencamp. With his monster-smash #3, 5-94 "Wild Night," in 10-94 (#1), he challenged the 43-week all-time HOT 100 record of "Whoomp – There It Is". As a hopeful follow-up, he released the embarrassing "Dance Naked" (#41, 10-94), which proved that #8 "Cherry Bomb" was no bomb. Like Chuck Berry's #1, '72 "Ding-A-Ling" thing, John's "Key West Intermezzo" (#14, 8-96) shows his Heartland Rock staying power in a millennium era of Techno-Synth and Rap and Hard Core and pantomiming 'Boy Band' **T**rack **A**cts. At age 43, Mellencamp suffered a heart attack; his doc blamed it on 3-4 packs of cigarettes per day (some say they enhanced his smoky sound). By 1999, he was working out, but hadn't quite dumped his cig habit – maybe it surrounds his Marlboro tenor, and it's part of his ambience.

"Just Another Day" (#46, 2-97) arrived for John, singing his upbeat message in "Your Life is Now" (#62A, 12-98). And John Mellencamp rocks Millennium III.

Bob Seger was born (5-8-45) in my hometown Dearborn, Michigan, and we went to different schools together. Dad Stewart Seger ran a Big Band in Detroit. Bob roamed the suburban Metro Motown area, perching upon Royal Oak and Ann Arbor. When we moved out to Oakland County's Union Lake, Bob's girlfriend sold us a humongoid tomato plant from her job there at Thompson's Greenhouse by middlebrow Bogie Lake ('Boogie Lake,' Oakland County inspiration for Bob's #6, 2-80 "Fire Lake"). Now Bob lives at posh Upper Straits Lake, where he joins a few Detroit Tigers/Lions/Pistons in a Preserve for Motor City Moguls with Too Much Money. But he's still the same good ol' Bob. Just **Bob Seger** – biggest Heartland Rock star in Michigan. Bob grew up in Ann Arbor, by the University of Michigan. Hotbed of ideas.

Flashback 1965. Our band the Night Shift was playing the Sig Ep house, University of Michigan. Wailing wildly on our Beatle set, we fractured silence with screaming Rock and Roll. Swirling suds and coeds basked in the midnight aura. Outside? Five below zero, of course. Our Night Shift scampered out on our break into the ice-blue Michigan midnight. A silver globe hung in the frozen inky sky. We tried to take our usual Non-Cigarette Break, like garage-band pals the Greasytones (Paul May, Dave Gordon, Cass Koziara, Gary 'Huckleberry' Hildebrandt, Toba Kuta, Doug Warren.)

"What's the thunder?" drummer Tom asked. "Real loud band at the ATΩ House next door." We wandered over, mushing like Uglook's Iditarod sled dogs racing the frozen –30° Alaska moon to Nome. When we finally met them, we knew we'd met our match. And more. Young Bob Seger shook the stage, his guitar on fire. Bob turned out to be one of us – a hard-driving Michigan Garage-Supercharged songwriter with a fondness for genuine Rock and Roll. Someday, a decade later, Bob would outshine his hero too, **Mitch Ryder**. Seger's R & R anthems would soon power the whole world. From a little Boogie Lake in Michigan.

"Persecution Smith" – Bob Seger, NC, 1967 or so. Seger does Dylan. He tightropes between this psychological study of a paranoid gun buff, and a comic Hard Rock song. Bob Seger debuts with a song too good for the charts. This combat-fatigue survivalist waits with itchy trigger finger for the poor hapless mailman. Seger does a Screamin' Blues with a side of Dylan, and a COMEDY shtick about this psychopath cocooned in his Jiffy Home Arsenal. (In the Michigan Militia **Timothy McVeigh** Oklahoma City bombing aftermath, or WTC tragedy, "Persecution Smith" is a ghastly art-imitates-life scenario). Seger's regional charisma mesmerized everyone within a 300-mile radius of the Motor City. Most records go national if they hit the Heartland and have any kind of distribution. Somehow, Seger stayed stuck in the middle. Like **Marty Robbins**, Bob Seger ["Heavy Music' '67] helped invent Heavy Metal – but nobody noticed (see "Smash Thrash" Heavy Metal chapter). Seger was actually a big national star, once. Then twice. But everybody outside Michigan tragically forgot for ten years.

"Ramblin' Gamblin' Man" – Bob Seger and the Last Heard, #17, 12-68. Top Twenty isn't exactly Anonymous City. Somehow, folks forget Bob was ALREADY a star. They envisioned him surging full fire from Al. *Live at Cobo Arena (Live Bullet)*, [#34, 6-76] into the Elvis Spotlight. "Ramblin' Gamblin' Man" is the lyrical seedbed for the **Allmans'** R & R classic, #2(1), 8-73 "Ramblin' Man." Forerunner of the Allmans' #2, "Ramblin' Man," this is their lyrical seedbed. Bob's ramblin' dude gets born by a lonely riverside. His school is a wheel of fortune and a pair of snake-eye dice. Like many a vagabond urchin, Seger's song-persona left home at 13. The lyric is a line, of course. He's trying to roust some amorous action out of a sweet little chickadee that he's sweet-talking. After this #17 bonanza, Seger then plodded eight years, with only one record trumping the #69 slot until his career's Bicentennial Surge. Bob "Bubbled Under" with Metal anthem #103, "Heavy Music" in 9-67. Seger's follow-up was #97 "Ivory" (5-69), followed by #103, 8-69 "Noah." That strange nowhere number – **103** – shows up again in his magnificent 5-75 "Beautiful Loser." Just when it appeared that Seger's career was doomed to the Lodi Holiday Inn, some wild Night Moves appeared on the purple fireworks horizon. No loser, Super Seger. But first, the struggle.

"Lookin' Back" – Bob Seger System, #96, 11-71. You can't live your life in some Nowhere Land 50s malt shop, he preaches. You must move on. Many early Seger songs feature Rock and Roll sermons; he makes us think, he makes us dance. His message was often a little too controversial for the radio; in 1971s "2+2=?" he asks why his friend must die in an eternal war. Seger's music, during this 1968-75 period, is simply some of the HOTTEST AND BEST ROCK MUSIC EVER RECORDED. One song is notable in Bob's mid-career ascension to Superstardom:

"If I Were a Carpenter" – Bob Seger, #76, 7-72. First ballad. Noted for years as a consummate concert screamer, Bob soft-pedaled his sound, and showed he was blessed with a fine Folk-style baritone (and a tiptop tenor, too, on rockers). This Tim Hardin-**Bobby Darin** classic Folk ballad shows a fine lady, like Billy Joel's #3, 9-83 "Uptown Girl," a thing or two about class status.

"If I Were a Carpenter" – Bobby Darin, #8, 9-66. Like Seger and Holly, Brill Building **Bobby Darin** had one of the most malleable voices in the history of Rock and Roll. The ballad spins a "What if . . ." theme; would the Lovely Lady still love him, he asks (amid a spinning swirl of bVII chromatic major chords) . . . Would she still love him if he were a poor tinker with pots and pans, a miller with his grinding mill wheel, or a carpenter? Now a carpenter was not a bad job in 1972 Detroit at all, what with chunky union wages and benefits. [Biblical scholars say Jesus did a little carpentry work Himself during the other thirty years of His life.] In Darin's New York City, carpentry didn't hold quite the prestige. Musically magnificent Folk Rock classic. Seger stormed two mountains.

"Get Out of Denver" – Bob Seger, #80, 7-74. Like the Beach Boys' #3, '63 "Surfin' U.S.A.," mile-above-sea-level "Denver" is a screaming rocker – 99% vintage Chuck Berry, with Bob's great voice and Chuck's chops, riffs, and dynamic din. Roadweary hell-bent-for-leather wanderlust.

"Katmandu" – Bob Seger, #43, 8-75. AHA! Top of the world trip places world-wanderer Bob in the middle of the sky. Katmandu, Nepal, is about as far away and HIGH as anyplace an expatriate can explore. In 1975, it was renowned for its intrigue, like the #28, 7-69 "Marrakesh Express" in Morocco of Crosby, Stills, Nash. Also easy substances, to abuse. In June 2001, the Nepalese Crown Prince shot and killed all of the Royal Family – and said it was an accident. Nepal is north of Bangladesh and India. Its green/purple foothills strut up into the sky.

"One Bourbon, One Scotch, One Beer" – George Thorogood and the Destroyers, NC, 1986. Essence of **John Lee Hooker** Talking Blues. Poor schlump with job and girl problems orders 3-fers. George's superbad (meaning great) baritone vocals and sizzling slide guitar

are the essence of Blues Rock. Nearly Heartland Rock. Sloshed theme powers George's own "I Drink Alone." *Live* album [#33, 8-86] features Chuck Berry's "Reelin' and Rockin'," and Muddy Waters' "Bottom of the Sea." Thorogood's "B-B-B-B-B Bad" rattles down through the corridors of time with swizzle sizzle.

Four Thorogood albums hit the #32 to #33 range in nine years (1979-88) of chart action, culminating in his #32, 2-88 *Born to Be Bad* success. Part of GT's charm, you know, is that despite the macho Harley outfits, swagger, B-A-D Blues riffs, and athletic look, the good kid from Delaware with the smokin' slide guitar has all the meanness of a teddy bear.

"Night Moves" – Bob Seger, #4, 12-76. Throbbing adventure about yesteryear make-out moves in a cornfield backseat of a '60 Chevy. Among the most monumental Slow Rock Ballads of all time. Why, then, did one of the greatest Pure Rock and Rollers of all time have to slow his torrid tempo in order to storm the bastions of New York and Los Angeles, the two keys to international stardom? In a 1972 [Detroit] **Creem** article, gonzo rock critic **Dave Marsh** cites the Seger Enigma: 1) Seger had ten top 10ers in Detroit (7 years), and three sold 50,000+ in Motown Metro Area; 2) #103 "Heavy Music" did 66,000, but its record company croaked as the song surged (and faded) nationally; 3) Bob's "2+2=?" found 'disc jockeys playing one of the most powerful antiwar songs ever recorded,' but Seger's inept record company botched the hype and distribution, and blew off the hit: and 4) 'No one ever played a Seger single in the Big Apple, San Francisco, or L.A.' Then Marsh ('72) asks the inevitable to his national fan base – "If Bob Seger is so good, why haven't you heard of him?"

Hideout Records, with Punch Andrews at the helm, is the culprit, hints Marsh. Seger's first record was "East Side Story." **Glenn Frey, Suzy Quatro**, and other big stars cut their first tunes at Hideout. Our Night Shift/Woolies recall them pretty well, too. "Persecution Smith" came second, and showed the "Collective Alienation" that Marsh sees as a corollary of the Detroit experience (see **Del Shannon** and #30, 2-66 "Stranger in Town"). I see this 2nd Seger tune as much funnier than Dave does. Seger is obviously steeped in Dylan at this time (weren't we all?). Seger's magnificent HONESTY is best portrayed in his comment: "Fantastic lyrics. I never really understood any of [Dylan's] lyrics." Universal truth. Dylan was Rock and Roll filtered through Kerouac-Ginsburg-Salvador Dali glasses. Hello, Dali. The mysterious essence of Dylan is his surreal imagery.

"Heavy Music" happened, and Bob Seger invented **Led Zeppelin, Steppenwolf**, and **Iron Maiden**. Cameo/Parkway, (Philly Chubby Checker/Bobby Rydell label) released "Ramblin' Gamblin' Man." It went national to #17. According to Seger, they took the money and ran, too. The big song hit #17, DESPITE ZILCH AIR PLAY in monstrous markets New York and Los Angeles. For records to break nationally, unknown acts must blanket the hinterlands and volatile 'Break-Out Areas' like Detroit, Seattle, Miami, Dallas, or Baltimore. In a crush on Detroit superstars, Cameo traded Bob. In a rush on Detroit White Soulsters, Bog Seger got swapped to biggee Capitol Records (Beatles, Beach Boys) for a banjo-hitting-second-bass-man, a warm Stroh's beer, and half an order of fries (extra ketchup). Or, a washed-up relief pitcher, 14 soggy Fritos, a case of Old Frothingslosh Brew, and a flügelhorn player to be named later. **Punch Andrews** atoned for Bob's national obscurity, sez Marsh, by linking Seger's destiny with an old fraternity brother at Capitol Records. Seger clicked back into overdrive with "Katmandu." Number 43 isn't #1, but it's back into the marathon. Bob and I ran cross-country in high school. We both knew about the need for stamina in what our fellow Detroiter and cross-country runner **Glenn Frey** calls "The Long Run" (#8, 12-79). Seger knew a lot about pacing. Though his Springsteen-style sets and chops and riffs and vocal marathons exhausted his audience, Bob was also in it for the long run. Seger is among our premier R & R marathoners.

In 1976, Bob Seger, like Johnny B. Goode, became the Superstar that he was all along. How? Night moves . . .. ah, yes. "Night Moves" surveys passion and power trips out in the grasser 'boonies.' Windswept snow cornfields squeeze Michigan's low, rolling Irish Hills. As Buddy Holly's life ended in just such a frozen cornfield, so Seger's superstardom began there? His song is a PG-13 erotic confession. At times, like any guy battling a binding bra, he bumbles, fumbles, and grumbles.

He confesses his frustrations. He says he's a little bit too tall (rarely a problem for guys), needed a couple of pounds (not for cross-country speed). "Night Moves" spoke to every Yesterday kid on the planet. Ego sprains. Frazzled teenage lost loves. Squashed pink carnations and totaled pick-up trucks. There is no easy time of life. Not even "Jack and Diane"'s Taystee-Freeze idyll or romp in the passionate grass.

Bob's bassman **Chris Campbell** came over one summer (1973?) to see about renting our cottage over the winter – we rent it over the years to a variety of temporary souls on a nine-month lease. Bob never forgot his roots. Bob's dad Stewart Seger's Orchestra played the old Walled Lake Casino (it wasn't – it was really just a dance pavilion). Jack Berry and I saved some guy's life there once on their roller-coaster; safety bar wouldn't catch.

Even at age 16, Bob was slamming down would-be hits. Dafydd Rees tells of Seger's other first recording session. With Max Crook and the **Del Shannon** musitron. In Crook's basement. It was no "Runaway" hit, however. When Seger was with the 1966 **Omens**, he dared cut a parody of **Sgt. Barry Sadler**'s gung-ho #1 hit "Ballad of the Green Berets" – like **Phil Ochs**'s brazenly antiwar "Draft Dodger Rag." Naturally, Bob's breakthrough bridge to "Night Moves" was the #34, 5-76 *Live Bullet* Cobo Hall album. Recorded on stage, Seger praises the Motor City fans as the world's best. Bob's passion-paced live show slingshots Rock and Roll at 111% effort. Whether you were an animal keeper at the Detroit Zoo (Randy McGill) or a Vietnam vet back from DaNang (Jim Pavlinak), a factory hand or a canutin' valve salesman, you felt like you were an integral part of Bob's piston-pounding Metro Motown Sound.

Bob Seger is Rock and Roll. When you're mixed up in watching Bob's fevered concerts, you, too, are a piece of that glory. By the time Seger got to "Night Moves," he acquired Joe Miquelon, guitar, Doug Riley, keys and also double-name regular keywhiz – **Robyn Robbins**. Or guitar guy Drew Abbott, and drummer Charlie Allen Martin. "Night Moves" flows with folksy ease through Bob's intro. It doesn't yet have a lot of beat. By the time he gets to the THUNDER part (wiping out winter in a meteorological dilemma), Bob grinds out his high tenor gravel. He scratchily hits the crescendo with an intensity matching the masters: **Orbison, Pitney, Jackie Wilson, Del Shannon**.

About this weird thundersnow weather report. Recently at an April 5K I ran in Bob's Ann Arbor's Briarwood Mall. In 18 minutes it snowed, sleeted, iced over, rained, hailed, and thundered. At one point, rhinoceros-sized flakes clobbered us. So that's how you can have winter and summer in Michigan at the same time. "Night Moves" knows. Bob's bicentennial Rock Classic tuned our aging nation into the silent terrors of the snowy windswept cornfield, and the swift passage of demon time. Henry Fonda in *On Golden Pond* is asked about the impact of his 80th birthday: "I can't believe it got here so fast!" That wild WHOOSH of time makes us all yearn with nostalgia for our awkward teenage years of groping, moping, and splendor.

Seger is among the greatest Hard Rock artists of the Rock Era – yet his big successes in the sales arena are laid-back, understated ballads. No flashy fire-boomers. Till "American Storm", perhaps.

"Hollywood Nights" – Bob Seger and the Silver Bullet Band, #12, 8-78. Named for the Lone Ranger's special silver bullets (and maybe for the Motor City's "Murder City" image), the Silver Bullet Band finally gets Bob back on track of his real destiny: as a Power Rocker. **Chris Campbell** on bass. **Alto Reed** on sax. Lyric zings. Michigan kid discovers Hollywood Hills, more statuesque and sensuous than Ann Arbor's Irish Hills. Endless summer, too. Surf's up. A kid from Detroit, Seger shouts, can make it anywhere. After 12-hour shifts on the assembly line or forge or rolling mill, anything else is quasi-retirement? Seger's nearly Heavy Metal tune blasts a sledgehammer steel mill beat. He cavorts over the playmate pleasure palaces of the rolling-hill rolling mill that is shimmering Tinsel Town. [Compare to super song "Say Goodbye to Hollywood," by Long Island Rock marathoner **Billy Joel**, who uses the thunderous throb of Phil Spector's Wall of Sound – like the pulsing rhythm track of the **Ronettes** #2, 1963 smash "Be My Baby."] Nothing understated about "Hollywood Nights." Seger galvanized, with shrieking guitar fire and Screaming Blues sandpaper vocal, a whole generation of serious rockers. Their motto approximated this message: 'DISCO IS SORTA LIKE A VACUUM CLEANER!' Or stronger lampreyesque terms to that effect. True 70s Hard Rockers from the Heartland rebelled against Disco's simulated Techno sounds, and synthesizers, like John Henry rebelled against the steam drill. Zack de la Rocha **Rage[d] Against the Machine** named themselves for this anti-mechanistic Luddite fervor (#69, 10-99 "Guerrilla Radio"). "Hollywood Nights" is about a passionate rendezvous with some red-hot girl atop the little Hollywood Mountain of Love:

"Mountain of Love" – Harold Dorman, #21, 2-60. Sledge, Mississippi's Dorman had no mountains at all. Just a sad memory atop whatever molehill lovers' lane they used to park at. Then she married some other guy. Only HOT 100 for Dorman. Established musical immortality (good thing, he passed on, 1988, at 61).

"Mountain of Love" – Johnny Rivers, #9, 10-64. Johnny's groovy harmonica swooped from Baton Rouge and the Big Apple. Rivers' rendition of Dorman's Rock classic is a masterpiece of finding cool sounds and putting them all together. Rivers was on a hot streak. Many Rivers rockers charted in the Beatle and Go-Go craze aftermath. From the Frug and the Watusi and the Mashed Potato and the Hully Gully and the Madison, suddenly a battalion of Go-Go girls strutted the stage – as the hip band frothed nearby. On Rivers' "Mountain of Love," we were no longer in Schlumpsville – we were pulsating in the molten heart of the Whisky A-Go Go on electric Sunset Strip in Los Angeles. Hot flashy tambourines on the big 2 & 4 beats shake the world. Johnny's vibrant harmonica and vocal were half chic Manhattan and half sultry Delta Blues. Who cared whether he was COVERING Dorman's hit? Rivers was rocking and rolling to superstardom. Dorman? Dormant. Johnny's 2nd verse features squealy soprano Call & Response oohs and aahhs. A glib chorus of silken starlets enchants the rising song. Formula for a hit? Take a great song, have a couple other hits under your svelte belt, and sculpt a dynamite arrangement. Like Blues star **Bo Diddley**, Rivers hammered Rockin' Blues:

Bob Seger and the Silver Bullet Band:
(l-r Chris Campbell, Craig Frost, Bob Seger, and Alto Reed)

"Mountain of Love" – Charley Pride, NC, 1981; #1(1), 12-81 C. Charley Pride started his baseball career with the Butte, Montana Pioneers, but a slight lack of great talent kept him out of the major leagues. He went the entertainment world one better. Pride became the first major African-American Country star. Yet Charley's "Mountain" sounds just as R & R-oriented as Dorman's. Each came from Sledge, Mississippi, 20 miles from Robert Johnson's Clarksdale and the fateful Crossroads. Though Sledge they both knew might have been world apart in the segregated 50s, Charley helped change our national race consciousness. [Ray Charles did big Country hits – but in his R & B style; Pride's baritone hillbilly twang has to be heard to be believed.]

Sledge has 577 people (formerly 579, but Dorman died and Pride split because of too much money). It's a rich commentary on American race relations' improvement, though. An Afro-American from Mississippi now hits the height of the Grand Ol' Opry today. Since his debut #9, C & W, 12-66 "Just Between You and Me," the amiable Pride collected 29 #1 Country hits. Biggest HOT 100? The gorgeously melodic #1(5), 10-71 C. "Kiss an Angel Good Mornin'" (loving the lass devilishly when he returns home).

Back to Detroit lad Bob Seger on Hollywood's mountain. Since the closest topography to Sledge, MS, is 623-ft. Thacker 'Mountain' 50 miles away by Oxford, and since Seger's Laurel Canyon foothills rise to 9000-ft Mt. Baldy, we may assume that purple mountain majesties are in the mind of the beholder. Bob Seger holds her, feverishly, in the Hollywood Hills.

"Fire Lake" – Bob Seger, #6, 2-80. 4th of July fireworks over Boogie Lake (Commerce, MI). Ominous ballad. Is "Fire" figurative? [One oozy Heartland River in Cleveland – Cuyahoga – caught fire (oil slick) in 1970 environmental disaster.] Nifty minors in this song. Super Seger vocal. Hammers big 2 & 4 beats. Crushing intensity. Something a little scary about "Fire Lake."

"Against the Wind" – Bob Seger, #5, 5-80. Like "Night Moves," a song about aging. Like your parents told you, it doesn't get any easier. He talks of still haggardly running into the wind. Bob's cross-country experience gives him a figurative AND literal rationale here. In a larger sense, it covers all the burdens we'll ever have to face. Though not a religious song, "Wind" certainly brooks theological overtones. This one carried me through the winter of '83. It kept playing in my head, while I was bashing half-mile repeats into the 12° frozen gale. Bob Seger knows about stamina. No matter how hard our lives get, we have to (in Sinatra's words from #4, 11-66 "That's Life") haul ourselves back up and re-enter the Big Race of Life.

"Rock and Roll Never Forgets" – Bob Seger, #41, 7-77. When your 'sweet 16' party disintegrates into confetti and confession, and you hit a weary 31 years, it's time to don your party duds and return to the Rock and Roll from whence you came. Play the old vinyl records you love, he advises. Real Rock and Roll. Tribute to fire-breathing lead guitar and flamboyant showmanship of **Chuck Berry.** Seger says to a whole world of axemen/women, plugged to a guitar (not a computer), that all of Chuck Berry's musical protégés are groovin' to the fiery rock gospel of his lead guitar wizardry. If you're weary, and no 'Bridge over Troubled Water' friend is available in the flesh (or the phone), drag out your favorite little audio pals. Your music will soothe (or energize) the savage beast (or listless couch potato). Get into those kicks. Getting high on music is healthy, legal, and fun. Rock and Roll never regrets!

"Old Time Rock and Roll" – Bob Seger and the Silver Bullet Band, #28, 4-79; #48, 9-83. This Seger anthem is the #2 song of all time in all the jukeboxes in the Milky Way Galaxy (behind Patsy Cline's #9, 11-61 "Crazy"); the road to glory is a long 'Stairway to Heaven' – not a jiffy trip. Bob hunkers down with the Anti-Disco rockers, allying with Old Funky Soul via Stax/Volt or Motown. If pre-programmed Disco zaps his R & R eardrums, he'll jump out the main door, looking for genuine Delta Blues and fastball Rock and Roll. Celluloid cinema fans often recall **Tom Cruise** dancing with a faux microphone in his boxer skivvies in *Risky Business****, '83 – acting out this Seger classic; by the chart numbers, you see how movies can punch up record/tape/CD sales for second chart appearances. All Rock and Roll darts back to the cottonpickin' Delta and **Bing Crosby/Paul Whiteman**'s "Mississippi Mud." ["Mississippi Mud" – Paul Whiteman Orchestra, Bing Crosby vocal, #6, 5-28. Whiteman enjoyed thirty Top 20 tunes that year.] Bob Seger bears the torrid torch with this Retro Rock anthem.

The song with the Silver Medal for Most Juke Box Plays, EVER, is this simple Seger Rock and Roll anthem. Since **Patsy**'s steel-swathed Country classic is a ballad, that makes the Seger song the MOST POPULAR ROCK AND ROLL SONG OF ALL TIME!! In one arena, anyhow. The Jukebox Jungle.

It came out of earlier Seger classic: #41 "Rock and Roll Never Forgets."

"Old Time Rock and Roll" sings, with stargazy reverence, the glories of a bygone day. Real music for real people. The heady mesh of guitars, cymbal crash of drums, the echoey eerie vocals of rock stars gone but never forgotten.

Seger shows an old American trait here – rugged individualism. He doesn't care what a lot of other cronies are listening to: He'll sit and spin his old FINAL VINYL platters in solitary if he has to! His dock will not collapse (pier pressure). His peers can like whatever they want. His music sensibilities are self-reliant. How many of us can say we are never affected by our friends' musical tastes? The raw edge of ribald Rock, Bob said, and gutsy Soul, had been steamrolled by Easy Listening, mangled by Robbie the Robot faux drummers, and wasted to Wimp Rock. If it meant retro-rocking it back to the old masters,

so be it. Bob would risk one of the worst comments you could ever call an American in our postmodern futuristic flyaway society – "He's OLD-FASHIONED!"

You pick it. How does a song that flumps to a mere #28 on *Billboard*'s gonzo HOT 100 turn out to outshine the whole Oldies-Overkill collection of great Rock classic hits in the long run? Cross-country. Marathon stamina.

Remember "In the Still of the Nite," by Fred Parris and the **Five Satins**? Voted #1 on the WCBS-FM "Doo-Whop Shop" as the greatest 50s song of all time, it hit #24, 9-56. Its follow-up (Bill Baker lead) almost beat it out (#25, 7-57) via a mellow sax riff, but you hear the "To the Aisle" about 1/100 as much as this Monster Hit. Time will tell.

"Like a Rock" – Bob Seger, and, yes, the Silver Bullet Band, again, #12, 5-86. To most contemporary Rock fans, "Like a Rock" is no longer a song. It's a line. A line co-opted in a hot Chevy truck commercial. Like Pavlov's salivating dogs in his experiment, every guy in America hears Bob boom 'LIKE A ROCK!' And what do we do? Our fantasies forget about the grass-skirt bikini babes or *Victoria's Secret*. Our real diabolical fantasies arrive; we want to go out RIGHT NOW and buy an ENORMOUS CHEVY TRUCK, HOT RED, and drive macho-ly over submissive giant boulders somewhere in Colorado or Montana or Wyoming or Alaska. We all want to utter the most macho line this side of John Wayne: "Like, Man, I'm really not INTO 'gas mileage . . .'" [And roar away in our Battleship Behemoths, flattening K-Marts and airplane hangars in the wild wakes of our forty-foot-high tires!] "Like a Rock" never plays through in the commercial. It's just an itty-bitty chunk of the great Seger charisma. The soundbite Chevy song slides slowly and reverently. It describes his own youth. His biceps were hard, like a rock. His gaze was steel and iron. When you're a kid, you can do anything. When you're old enough to get the red truck and smash the Wyoming mountains, it may already be too late.

"American Storm" – Bob Seger and the Silver Bullet Band, #13, 3-86. One of the Top 38 Rock and Roll Songs of All Time. Coming off a crunch of Streetcorner chords, Seger pumps up the Power Rock Fusion between Heavy Metal and Hard Rock and Vintage American Thunder Music. In this one song, Bob Seger lofts his vocal power right up there with the Springsteens, Orbisons, McCartneys, Holly(s) and Elvises in the Pyramid Panorama of All the Greatest Rock Stars who ever were. Throbbing heart of Rock and Roll.

The 60s, with drug double-entendres and cutesy puns, sang blissful messages about getting high. Journeying to the center of mind. Or 1999's hullabaloo about 'Heroin chic,' with pasty, pallid models with the energy crisis of Dracula's dames. Wasted. Gaga swirling ships. People have been getting stoned on something or other since the dawn of time (see Noah, Religious chapter). Some societies staunchly forbid alcohol – and go off in a smoky cloud of opium. Or cannabis sativa. Or cigarettes. Some O.D. on the legal drug caffeine. Then there's the real nasty stuff: heroin, crack, angel dust, and old standby cocaine – early ingredient of Coca-Cola (snafued by the Fuddy Duddy Drug Czars, and Czardines, so Coke switched caffeine for cocaine). What's Seger got to say about 'coke'?

Watch out, America, Another song on Seger's big #3 *Like a Rock* 4-86 album is "Tightrope." "American Storm" storms along such a tightrope. Why? As you may know, once in a blue moon an occasional musician may stray from the primrose path and (gasp!) use a controlled substance. Seger, of course, doesn't want to alienate his friends and A & R men and musicmates who have sniffed or snorted or smoked or chugged. "American Storm" will lose its heavy message if it drowns in its own storm of heavy, didactic, preachy lyrics. Seger skims a deft lithe lyrical tightrope here. He sings an anthem for MODERATION in the vices. Go easy. He sings the snowstorm of coke in America, also the can't-get-warm snowy COLD [January average Detroit 22°]. The swirling snowstorm of cocaine is from Colombia, Venezuela, and Ringo Starr's #3, 2-75 "No No Song" (where the virtuous Beatle eschews the demon snow). Seger brings in the funhouse terror – the victim crashes into the mirror, and shards of splintered glass shatter. But he never bleeds. By then, it is far too late. He's hooked. It's like falling asleep in a snowbank, and never waking up. Seger fires off a burning plea for moderation, maybe abstention, from the vices. And he couches it in a super song.

NATURALLY, Bob plays his own guitar (well). Key personnel figures: **Craig Frost** keys, **Chris Campbell** bass, **Bill Payne** ivories, **Pete Carr** on guitar, and **Russ Kunkel** percussion. And sax? It's **Alto Reed**! **Eagles**' super sandpaper tenor **Don Henley**, and crystalline lofty Irish tenor **Timothy B. Schmit**, handle back-up vocals on "Storm."

Kunkel and Seger kick off "American Storm's" beat, hammering the 2 & 4 for a little too much intro. Tension builds. "Storm's" in 'E', of course. No other key has the testosterone. Major chords sail like flares, doubling the power with flaming rhythm guitar chords on the backbeat. Seger mutes his instruments on Verse I. Tension impacts the chorus with broiling brimstone.

Once he hits the chorus, Bob's Streetcorner vintage R & R chord pattern (**E–C#m–A–B7**) swamps your entire being. Only at the fadeout finale does Seger alter the pattern. He blindsides your chordal expectation with a bVI Polynesian chromatic special – **C major** to bVII **D major** and back to the expected tonic **E major** (see Bryan Adams' "Everything I Do"). The effect? Incredible. Seger fans' credo? NO WIMP ROCK! Bob and Punch and Chris and Alto never disappoint. No wimp rock. Heart of Rock and Roll. Bob's 1st #1 ever didn't arrive until movie theme "Shakedown" in 1987 – but he was #1 with Michiganders and Michigeese for over a generation.

"Gimme Some Lovin'" – **Blues Brothers, #18, 5-80.** Can two comics from *Saturday Night Live* make the transition from the laff track to Pure Chicago Blues? In the case of life-gorging **John Belushi** (b. '49, Wheaton, Illinois – died '82) and **Dan Aykroyd** (b. '52, Ottawa, Ontario), and HOW! Their hilarious video featured black gangster suits, sunglasses, froggy fedoras, workadaddy white shirts and thin bad-lad black ties. First they stood silent and unmoving on stage. Sizzling Sam & Dave "Soul Man" Stax-style saxes streamed in, followed by **Steve Cropper**'s Muscle Shoals guitar, and the most famous bass on the Hurricane Coast – **Donald 'Duck' Dunn. Matt 'Guitar' Murphy** integrated their White Soul sound. Suddenly, the two comics marionetted into speed-of-light action: flying, leaping, tappy-toeing, flailing arms and feet in a bust-'em-up Snoopy strut – a supersonic kangaroo pogo-stick-jumping celebration of life.

All the while, their faces remained serene and expressionless. Imagine the whirling tornado of the Tasmanian Devil mixed with the placid stone face of the Sphinx. They zoomed into "Soul Man." "Jake Blues" (John, tenor) and "Elwood Blues" (Dan, bass and baritone) covered their beloved Hot Soul with consummate high style. Their duo spawned a very funny movie, *The Blues Brothers* 1980**** (see review). Belushi tragically O.D.'.d, but Aykroyd set up a House of Blues chain centering in Chicago. His love for 'Chicago Blues,' 'Stax/Volt Memphis Blues,' and 'Delta Blues' took Delta expatriates and made them stars again. It's a triumph of Jewish record entrepreneur **Leonard Chess** and his brother, plus a battalion of Afro-American Blues stars. With James Brown, ZZ Top, and Mary Chapin Carpenter, the Blues Brothers rocked out at the 1-16-97 Super Bowl XXI in the Big Easy. As Cleveland highlights the Heart of Rock and Roll, Jake and Elwood and the New Blues Brothers take us back to its real conception.

"The Power of Love" – **Huey Lewis & the News, #1(2), 6-85; #81, 9-85 R & B.** Of all the 'Blondie' comic strips I ever read (14,365), the two songs I remember most from Dagwood singing in the bathtub are Buddy Holly's immortal "That'll Be the Day" and Huey Lewis's 'Power of Love.' When you listen to New Yorker Lewis's good NEWS, you sample the meaning of Rock and Roll. Huey Lewis (b. '50, NYC) began in a Country Rock band in the 70s, gravitating to San Francisco by 1980.

Singer John Cipolina (Quicksilver Messenger Service), who died in 1989 of emphysema at 45, had a brother **Mario Cipolina** who became Huey's bass man. Rock and Roll may seem like it has a million different stars, but sometimes, it's more of an interlocking directorate. All this stuff interconnects.

Chris Hayes lambasts funky fills and quirky guitar chops. Bill Gibson cymballized A-1 percussion, while Sean Hopper tickled keyboards. Johnny Colla doubled on rhythm guitar and sax – The NEWS is simply a great band. With 12 top ten tunes in six years (1982-88) Huey Lewis joins a bunch of other unrelated Lewises in the rock-a-beatin' boogie ranks: Jerry Lee & His Pumping Piano, Gary & the Playboys, Barbara, "Tossin' & Turnin'"'s Bobby, Jazz-Rock Ramsey, and maybe Meriwether. [Had Huey been triplets, would he be *Ducktales'* Huey, Louie, & Dewey Lewis and the News (and Unca Donald and Scrooge McDuck Lewis)?] Catch Colla's snarly bari rasp. Huey's hurly-burly "Power of Love" drove nine other songs to the lower 90% of the Top Ten.

HEY KIDS!
HOW NOT TO WRITE A #1 HIT SONG!

Isn't that what popular music is usually about? The Power of Love. Love power usually fires most of the music we enjoy into the winner's circle. You want topics that REALLY need a little hype, a little push? Try writing a #1 song about:

Eggbeaters	Nail Polish
Cat Food	Kohlrabi
Floor Mats	Tennis Racquets
3-in-1 Oil	Static Cling
Anti-Perspirant	Rottweilers
Earwigs	Slugs
Garbage Cans	Toenail Clippers

No wonder most songs are about love, eh? It takes a real super songwriter to nail #1 with "Baby, the Cat's Nail Polish Got Static Cling by the Slugs' Toenail Clipper!"

Huey's 1st #1 compares love to a train, chugging with the power of love. One #1 can breed another. An oddity in upfront Rock and Roll lyrics? Genuine (but good-natured) sarcasm. Did it work?

"Stuck with You" – Huey Lewis and the News, #1(3), 8-86. Lovers grow accustomed to each others' faces. And bods. But lovelight still flickers. Passion plods. Huey exclaims how overjoyed he is to be stuck with her. Weird, at first. Then we ponder. Don't familiar things often take on an undertone of the friendly, the comfy, the cozy? (#70, '56 Rosemary Clooney, "I've Grown Accustomed to Your Face," from *My Fair Lady*). Lewis toys with (hey, here's an oxymoron) Romantic Realism. This tepid relationship offers a lukewarm program of 3-in-1 Oil, floor-mat vacuuming, Friskies' Gourmet Cat Dinner, and Lug the Tuesday Trash Cans to the Curb. Love, minus fluff. After the red-hot big flames of passion flop down to little filigree flickers and flares and flashes, the power of lukewarm love conquers all. He is very, very glad to be 'stuck' with her. This is the kind of love that keeps the whole world spinning round and round.

"I Want a New Drug" – Huey Lewis and the News, #6, 1-84. Huey wants a drug without backlash hangovers. Is a 'positive drug' getting stoned on R & R success? From #7, 2-82 debut "Do You Believe in Love," the News scorched a high-life of big-beat bombshells: their #8, 9-83 revamp of Exile's #102, 1981 "Heart and Soul"; #6, 7-84 "If This Is It"; the ultra cool #3, 10-86 "Hip to Be Square"; **Bruce Hornsby**'s song "Jacob's Ladder" to their third #1 (#1[1], 1-87); #6, 7-87 "Doing It All for My Baby"; #3 "Perfect World" of 7-88; and #44, 5-94 "(She's) Some Kind of

Wonderful." In late '79, **Smokey Robinson** took "Cruisin'" to #4. In December, 2000 **Huey Lewis** and actress **Gwyneth Paltrow** hit #3 on *Billboard*'s Adult Contemporary chart (despite a paltry #0 for their "Cruisin'" hit on the HOT 100).

With muscular Muscle Shoals Soul rhythm, too, "I Want a New Drug" turns out to be no drug at all – just positive relationships, garnished with a slam-bam rhythmic pulse. As the dual sax lead reels along with the organ fill, we begin to discover that this wonderful new safe drug is great Rock and Roll. Like this:

"The Heart of Rock and Roll" – Huey Lewis and the News, #6, 4-84. Lafayette, we are here. Cradled in the Vieux Carre French Quarter of New Orleans, and raised in Memphis, Chicago, and Detroit, Rock and Roll zoomed into the biggest center cities in the 50s – the City of Angels and Huey's Big Apple. Surging the 60s with a British/Motown flair, it Discoed through the 70s. By the 80s, Huey focuses on R & R epicenters New York and L.A.

I drive down to Greenwich Village by my kid Lauri's place. It's 2 a.m. Frenzied rock 'em sock 'em madcap street. At two a.m. KIDS ARE PLAYING, AGE NINE, dribbling hoops by the steamy stoops of Huey's New York City birthplace. Electric energy carouses the pizzeria promenade. Huey Lewis digs back in time to **Gary U.S. Bonds**'s (b.' 39, Jacksonville, Florida) #1, 5-61 screamer, "Quarter to Three," for rhythmic inspiration.

New York, he chortles. Where else can you do 500,000 things at 2:45 a.m.?

What's a great way to send your album to #1, 11-83? Pick a catchy title that'll attract guys, too, not just 13-year-old girls. How about Al. #1(1), 9-86 *Sports*? *Sports* features a classic working-guy bar. Shot and beer place. You know it's gotta be **Mitch Ryder**'s Hamtramck, Michigan. Or **Springsteen**'s smog-strewn New Jersey. Or blue-collar Blue Island, Illinois. No preppy yuppie suburban sports bar here. *Sports*' bar is a place where they smoked big demon cigars over the last generation whether it ever became cool again (like 2000+) or not. Over the old oak bar, under the basketball, next to the egg-shaped hanging hybrid guitar, you see the Blues Brother bartender shadowed by a sign:

> HANGOVERS INSTALLED AND SERVICED

The softball team type band is decked out in Levis and varsity jackets. All their hair is sport short like 2002, the shortest hair for guys in a half-century cycle: Teddy Roosevelt's 1905; the Kingston Trio's 1959, and Gangsta Rap's golden edge of NOW. Huey himself looks like a relief pitcher for the Mets. Huey's coarse sandy hair, cleft chin, Aberdeen blue eyes suggest **Kirk Douglas** in *Spartacus* (1960***). Maybe **Mel Gibson** in *Braveheart*. Huey flashes a cross between a Mona Lisa maybe smile and a steely stare. And a loosened Dean Martin tie. When Huey and the News utter this line about the rump-kicking backbeat, you know they're the jock band (see Sports Rock chapter) for the job.

"The Heart of Rock and Roll" fades in on a lub-dub heartbeat. For 20 eternal seconds. If you're buttering up

Program Directors with such interminable intros, you'd better have a few incumbent hits, a big rep, or beauteous Britney Spears, for leverage. To Huey, Dewey, Scrooge, and the News – with hits galore – no problem! As the heart throbs louder and louder, Gibson storms in on a cymbal crescendo. Then he pulses the passionate rhythmic extravaganza, helped out by a little handclapping. Think **Beatles**, when they discovered the heart of Rock and Roll on #1, '64 "I Want to Hold Your Hand."

All Rock and Roll ties together. Like a family, it sputters and squawks and guffaws and cries and laughs. Most of all, it loves. It's energized (thanks, Huey and News Staff) by the POWER OF LOVE. No sleepytime ballad, the "Heart of Rock and Roll" bombardier beat bashes along at 140 beats a minute. It's enough to dizzy the Disco dancing queen out of her glitzy go-go boots. After the lub-dub intro and Gibson's cymbal swoosh, the rhythm track redlines with NYC marathon fever.

Spindrift a second. Flashback Huey and "Johnny B. Goode." No guitar, gunny sack, or railroad track for the harmonica Kid Huey. Huey started out a hopeful yogurt baron. A mogul of gooey milk curd. By night, he had a secret rendezvous with Rock and Roll: Huey would escape the cow culture of daylight drudgery; he'd don his Kat duds, and watch the crimson clouds cascade into the blue horizon (behind the Flatiron Building). Lewis's early band Clover almost hit the 70s big time, backing Elvis (Costello, a fine singer/songwriter of the Punk New Wave Dylanesque ilk). Lewis helped bring back a key component to Rock and Roll. Johnny Colla played SAX like **Bruce Springsteen**'s Clarence Clemons or **Gary U.S. Bonds**'s R & R sax patriarch, the mysterious **Daddy G**. With Lewis's News in action by 1980, it didn't take too long to go top ten: "Do You Believe in Love" (#7, 2-82); #41 "Workin' for a Livin'," 8-82; plus #8, 9-83 "Heart and Soul" on their new San Francisco Chrysalis label.

Lewis laments the technolization of rock music in "Heart of Rock and Roll." Real Live Ringos and Gibsons were getting replaced by Darth Vader thump machines, synthesizers, and MIDI mastermind machines. At Huey's advent, so rose the mixed blessing Music Television *MTV*. *MTV* brought us incredible new videos to augment or obfuscate our music pleasure. At best, it could enhance a song onto a new pretty purple visual plateau. At worst, it could stifle artists, substitute bump-grind eroticism for true music, lavish listless "track acts," and spit out half a song. Half a song? When you're watching MTV, you're no longer just a music fan; video choreography components give you at least half of your entertainment experience. Images you fantasized, now become spoon-fed by the TV set. Monkee **Mike Nesmith**'s 1981 'invention' *MTV* also adds an excellent new dimension to old rock: you can finally be SURE whether John or Paul – or Brian Wilson or Mike Love – sang Beatle or Beach Boy lead vocals – via the video proof.

Like vintage **Chuck Berry**, "Heart" zooms around the Rand McNally Road Atlas of America. Lewis touts the sparkly nightscape of the Sunset Strip, with dazzling starlets, clad scantily. In a Chuck Berry blur, he swoops into a bonanza of big towns: Boston, Baton Rouge, Tulsa,

Austin, Oklahoma City, Seattle (Hendrix's **Nirvana**), and San Francisco. Huey extols actual LIVE MUSIC! In the universal Key of 'C' major. Music for real people, people who laugh and cry and love. Not Muzak. Not elevator stuff. Not automatic bands. Not lip-sync wimp junk. Not lounge-lizard concerts. Not just DJ shticks. Piano bars and DJ's are OK, but Huey touts the whole band – five alive guys. NOT MUSIC IN THE CAN.

Huey's "Heart of Rock and Roll" fades in on a lub-dub heartbeat. As he fades out, on that throbbing pulse, we too will fade from Rock's heart to its extremities. Fringe rock music comes and goes. Sometimes it's New Alternative Funkpunk Glamglitz GoGo Industrial Reggae or something; green-haired adherents must wear fishheads on their feet and upchuck on the chicken-suited mosh pit. Whatever it is, it's welcomed as a part of the Rock Panorama. No matter how bad a day we have, don't forget one thing – ROCK AND ROLL LOVES YOU!

Lewis fades into the blue horizon. He recedes into his song's spoken fadeaway. Horns blare, drums pump, and the immortal Cipolina bass pulses to their 140-beat commando groove. Huey belts out two real homes of Rock and Roll.

First he shouts Cleveland, where the Moondog Show of **Alan Freed** coined the term 'Rock and Roll' semi-officially in 1952 (see John Jackson's Freed biography *Big Beat Heat*). A white DJ who played 'Negro Rhythm and Blues, he sold prep white America the power of Rock and Roll. It paved the way for Elvis and Buddy and Chuck. Especially Chuck. Freed coyly slid his moniker onto Chuck's songwriting credits on "Maybellene" (#5, '55) – in exchange for some welcome air play. **Chuck Berry** opened the Rock and Roll Hall of Fame on Labor Day, 1995, in Cleveland.

Just before "The Heart of Rock and Roll" fades into history, Huey Lewis bellows with his loudest leather-lung baritone blast to reach Planet Earth's 11 billion ears. He shouts: DETROIT!

And the rest is Rock and Roll.

Snippets

These **Snippets** are a former chapter that bit the dust to bring you more great photos: **Dan Hill**'s fine ballad #3, #11-77 "Sometimes When We Touch"; **Morris Albert**'s #6, 6-75 cabaret "Feelings"; **Fats Waller**'s #17, 11-29 "Ain't Misbehavin'" (#1 C, '86 Hank Williams Jr.); **Bobby McFerrin**'s giddy #1(2), 7-88 (#11 R & B) "Don't Worry – Be Happy"; the **Shangri-Las**' motorcycle elegy #1, 10-64 "Leader of the Pack"; Walter Brennan's 'rap' #5, 4-62 "Old Rivers"; Joanie Sommers' #7, 5-62 WWF "Johnny Get Angry"; **Johnny Cymbal**'s #16, 2-63 "Mr. Bass Man"; and 11-year-old **Gayla Peevey**'s #24, 12-53 "I Want a Hippopotamus for Christmas" (what would she do if she GOT one?).

We reluctantly zapped **Rick Springfield**'s #1(2), 3-81 "Jessie's Girl"; **ZZ Top**'s #103, 12-81 "Tube Snake Boogie" (Billy Gibbons' vocals); Johnny Mathis's premier romantic ballad #30, 5-63 "Every Step of the Way"; **Sue Thompson**'s campy #3, 12-61 "Norman"; Gene Austin's #74, 5-57 "Too Late" – and #1(7), 8-25 "Yes Sir, That's My Baby"; **Gene Autry**'s #1, 12-49 "Rudolph, the Red Nosed Reindeer"; **Human League**'s #1(3), 3-82 "Don't You Want Me" and **Human Beinz**' #8, 12-67 "Nobody But Me"; Jimmie Rodgers' Aussie rouser #41, 1-60 "Waltzing Matilda"; Ray Parker's #1(3), 6-84 "Ghostbusters." Also stereo pioneer **Roy Hamilton**'s #13, 1-58 (#2 R & B) "Don't Let Go";

THE Irish tenor **John McCormack**'s #1(5), 7-1911 "Mother Machree"; **Paul Robeson**'s #7, 6-26 "Old Man River"; South Africa Xhosa-tribe Miriam Makeba's #12, "Pata Pata"; **Stories**' #1(2), 6-73 "Brother Louie" (Sam Ligon, Mark Bourdeau); Marvin Rainwater's Native American #18, 5-57 "Gonna Find Me a Bluebird"; Dale Hawkins' #27, 6-57 "Susie Q," Rockabilly SOUL item, or Carl Mann's #25, 6-59 "Mona Lisa"; **David Lee Roth**'s #3, 1-85 "California Girls"; Kim Wilde's #1(1), 3-87 "You Keep Me Hangin' On"; Hollywood Argyles' #1, 5-60 "Alley Oop" cartoon tune; **George Hamilton IV**'s teen-love #6, 11-56 "Rose and a Baby Ruth"; the Playmates' #4, 11-58 car-tune "Beep Beep"; **Mario Lanza**'s #97, 5-58 "Arrividerci Roma"; **Little Willie John**'s #13, 9-60 "Sleep"; **Willie Nelson**'s #20, 5-80 (#1C) "On the Road Again"; **Canned Heat**'s #11, 12-68 "Goin' Up the Country," and the Pyramids' instrumental Surf classic, #18, 2-64 "Penetration."

Guy Mitchell's "Singing the Blues," #1(10), 10-56, may be the longest Rock song at #1 for an entire millennium. Longer songs are ballads. Guy's Soft Rock Columbia tune was produced by Mitch Miller, who said he'd never do Rock and Roll. Sure, it's Lite Metal indeed, but it rocks – like Guy's #2(1), 6-51 "My Truly, Truly Fair"; this silver-medal song says maybe you can't live upon LOVE ALONE, but still he and his girl are 'gonna' try. *Gold Rush* loves these songs, speedily.

John Cougar Mellencamp

Bruce Springsteen

Smash, Thrash, and Crash - Rip-Roaring Rise of Metalmania

28

Heavy Metal Rock has always been armed and a little bit dangerous. Brandishing flaming axes, a battalion of mega-amp blasters scorches the ex-sounds of silence. METAL, of all genres, is most HEAVILY a 'guy thing,' with sparse female fan-addiction. Heavy Metal loves women, though. Ul-tra-macho head-banging Monster Metal roared out of **Mitch Ryder** and **Bob Seger's** Metro Motown in the late 60s. Urban Gangsta anger (see Rap, or #1 '59 "Mack the Knife") can lead to riots, fires, and desolation. Heavy Metal often sublimates anger into a crashing catharsis, a voluminous vent, a productive pipeline to friendship, and good times.

Heavy Metal never dug sleepy conformity. When suburban petunias got too pretty, Metallurgists just might rip them out by the roots, stomp on them, and peel off hot rubber from big red '67 Deuce-and-a-Quarter Buicks that screamed up the spine of wild midnight Woodward Avenue in the warm strung-out beery American night. Just plug in.

"Heavy Music" – Bob Seger & the Last Heard, #103, 9-67. Starts serenely. A little finger-popping. Some heavy breathing. Fender barroom bass of Chris Campbell, prowling and growling. A muted rhythm axe chops its way into the fray. Seger's raspy street high baritone busts in, headed for his frantic tenor. Real Rock and Roll. Like **Mitch Ryder's** frantic **Detroit Wheels** – only slower, more ominous. Bob makes unmistakable erotic sounds to some girl. She returns the compliment. Drums hammer. Guitars crackle. Campbell's soupy bass attaches itself to the tonic chord root note like a hangman's noose.

Eager Seger builds. Manly Key of Blues – 'E' major. Passion seethes. Bob and chorus of "HEAVY MUSIC" swoop upwards. They grab chromatic modulations, rising and sweating and rasping in unglued orgiastic pandemonium. Into shrieking Robert Plant-falsetto, Bob lofts his molten sound above the redhot factory glow. With bombastic White Soul, the song's climax gushes, a geyser of volcanic metallic Rock and Roll. You know you're not in Kansas anymore . . .

Bob Seger invented Heavy Metal music. As Alan Freed coined the term ROCK and Roll in 1952 Cleveland, not-yet-superstar **Seger** coined the phrase HEAVY MUSIC, starting a R & R trend to capture adolescent male macho musical tastes in a sweltering swoosh of amps-to-11 mammoth metal. Just five months later, a gruff baritone from East Germany and Canada welded the weighty music to hot biker iron.

"Born to Be Wild" – Steppenwolf, #2(3), 2-68. John Kay's [Joachim Krauledat] lusty phrase about Heavy-Metal [style] Thunder sideswiped the serene, waked the dead, and drove a strident stake into the vampire heart of boredom. Rev that big motor, he called. Seek the highway. Troll for adventure. He paved the way for **Bruce Springsteen**'s "Born to Run" [#23, 9-75] Highway 9 odyssey, and celebrated the Motown Screamin' Mochines. Ghosts of the Old Road stalked blustery night winds on freeways of destiny. With your car and your girl and your night you could have it ALL. Steppenwolf (Hermann Hesse 1927 novel) sang out a Thrash Metal barrage of Harleys' screeching tires and guitarfire. Heavy Metal vagabonds screamed down the 100-mph James Dean Memorial Highway.

Heavy Metal arose for a lot of reasons. There is a natural testosterone tendency for every guy in the band to keep turning his OWN AMP UP HIGHER than the guitarist next to him (over there by the furnace). When amps ranged from Wimpy to Super-Wimpy to Dinky to Eensty-meentsy, it didn't matter who was louder. Nobody was. One acoustic BANJO could blast your Micro-Mini Amp to Kingdom Come. When I first heard "Tremolo" off **Jody Reynolds** Death Rock debut "Endless Sleep" (Al Casey, guitar – #5, '58), it fractured my quiet world. I HAD to have that wobbly foghorn cascading from a big black box full of tubes in my basement (by where I wrote girls' numbers on the wall). My drawback at 15? Larry Glazer had taught me only two chords. In 1962 Ed Braun's new AM and FM radio had REVERB(ERATION), and I was hooked. Somewhere out there lurked enough amps and foot-pedal accessories for my faux-Fender Supro Sahara ($60) to RULE the ENTIRE UNIVERSE.

Muscle guitar gives you Amp Enchantment: the more AMPS, the MORE POWER. Tragically, though growly volcanic eruptions from your ardent axe may be the sweetest thing to your ears, some old sourpuss four miles away always sends Officer Aardvark over to your basement.

He snatches the plug from your Basement Blasters band to zap your Maxi-Metallic Joy. They'll be sorry. When your band goes multi-platinum, the old dude (with green Batman ears like 3 Doors Down's[#1, 2000] "Kryptonite") will beg for forgiveness – and grovel for your autograph for his flawless va-va-voom 19-year-old granddaughter.

John Kay's Steppenwolf had a lot of people to thank besides Bob Seger or the Doors. A whole battalion of thunderers: Mr. Beaubien of Detroit, for helping invent the electric guitar; **Les Paul,** for devising the solid-body; Leo Fender, for buying Les's idea; **Thomas Edison,** for amp and microphone technology; Ma Rainey, for singin' the blues; Elvis for "Hound Dog"; Little Richard, for murdelizing quietude in "Tutti Frutti"; Eddie Cochran, for toying with major metal in his '58 "Summertime Blues"; and mostly **Marty Robbins,** whose accidental invention (#3, '61 "Don't Worry") of FUZZTONE and fried FEED-BACK caused Twist-Era twangers like the Ventures to fool around with new WAH-WAH Pedals, EFFECTS boxes, REVERB/TREMOLO, and planet-conquering volume.

"Born to Be Wild" is the eternal Speed-Trap Song. Cops behind billboards should blare this to Mach One Ferraris (and 1978 Gremlins). This speedo ditty hammers metallic thunder in a hot love world of honeys on Harleys. "Born" presages **Ozzy** and **Megadeth** and **Metallica,** and a slew of axe-slammers' exploding music over the oilslick-rainbow highways of the warm American neon midnight glow. The beat hammers. The drums pound. It's a clarion call to ditch the office cubicle, the lathe, the salt mines. It's a thrill ride to the sweet oblivion of unlimited freedom and magic empowerment on the road. It's a magic carpet ride aloft. Who needs a STAIRWAY to Heaven!

Their "Magic Carpet Ride" stormed to #3, 10-68, via the insta intro and Arabian silent cushion of amour. Other Steppenwolf hits include #10, 3-69 "Rock Me," #29, 9-74 "Straight-Shootin' Woman," and Hoyt Axton's song #60, 3-71 "Snow Blind Friend."

"Touch Me" – Doors, #3, 12-68. The Doors aren't usually mentioned as Metalmongers – but should be. "Light My Fire" hit #1(3), 6-67, peaking its eerie flaming aura over Detroit's smoldering torso in the terrible July riots of 1967. Long before "Born to Be Wild," **Robby Krieger's** mesmerizing lead slide guitar rollercoasters on flying high-fret fantasias – to help shape **Jimmy Page's** later **Led Zeppelin** magic. Most of all, great musician **Ray Manzarek** (b. '39, keyboards & keyboard **bass**) sculpted the Doors' early Metal magic as much as the hypnotizing surreal baritone of Rock icon **Jim Morrison** (1942-70). In Ray's 1998 Putnam autobiography *Light My Fire,* outstanding writer Ray mentions the natural tension between too-loud guitarists and the keyboard hordes. Playing both keyboards and bass simultaneously for the Doors, Ray describes his big new Rhodes Keyboard Bass. Playing bass with his left hand, he used Jazz-great **John Coltrane's** Jazz sax ideas, on BASS: "The old Coltrane solo [for "Light My Fire"] was hypnotic and ecstatic! The repetitive **A-minor** to **B-minor** triad pattern on a deep, gut-rumbling, chest-cavity-massaging, lower-two-chakras-stimulating bass instrument was

incredible." On boosting his amps to guitar level, he hits a common gripe against us sneaky volume-twiddling guitarists. His red/black Vox Continental Organ was "sleek and loud. You plugged it into a guitar amp and cranked the sucker. A keyboard player could then compete with those maniacs of loud . . . the guitar players. Volume to equal Robby [Krieger]. And Super-Beatle amps" (p. 163).

"Tell Me How" – Buddy Holly & the Crickets, NC, '58. Flip of #17 "Maybe Baby" is a head-banger. Buddy's Crickets had the loudest band in the 50s. Buddy first popularized the Fender Stratocaster long before Metal guru Jimi Hendrix. Check out drummer Jerry Allison's incredible drum LEAD on "Tell Me How." On "Peggy Sue," Holly needed a spare rhythm guitarist, Niki Sullivan, just to flip his treble-bar 'gearshift,' as Buddy spun into his supersonic golden guitar blur in his 16th-note downstroke lead.

Enter the ROADIE. Roadies lug stuff. Now they doubled as amp whizzes, guitar tuners, equipment stevedores, electronic Einsteins, groupie scouts, and coffee/stronger stuff 'gofers.' Once Holly set the pattern and Seger/Doors/Steppenwolf coalesced it, **Jimmy Page** and **Eric Clapton** fired up the **Yardbirds'** fuzztone and feedback fusillade across the Atlantic. **Heavy Metal** juggles a screaming vocal and throbbing backbeat, offset by amps turned to the Moon with dazzling distortion. The **Animals' Eric Burdon** toyed with metal music for years: Blues guru John Lee Hooker's #60, 5-62 "Boom Boom" to #43, 12-64; Animals' own #15, 2-65 "Don't Let Me Be Misunderstood," or #13, 8-65 smog-buster "We Gotta Get Out of This Place." When early Metal man **Mitch Ryder & the Detroit Wheels** took a combo of Little Richard's **#10,** 6-57 "Jenny, Jenny" and Animals' #10, 9-66 "See See Rider," he hit #10, 12-65 with "Jenny Take a Ride." Metal roots?

"See See Rider Blues" – Ma Rainey, #14, 1-25. When Gertrude Malissa-Pridgett (1886-1939) got hitched to Vaudeville hoofer Bill 'Pa' Rainey, 'Ma' launched the first major Blues song actually tabbed Rock and Roll. Before the electric guitar was invented she set up the rockin' style for **Bessie Smith** and Soul star (#12, 4-57) Chuck Willis. Burdon's transformation of the Blues classic to metal is amazing.

Eminem and the Beastie Boys owe a debt to Burdon in #15, 12-67 "Monterey" (about its Rock Festival), follow-up to #9-87 "San Franciscan Nights." "Monterey" not only previews Metal with Burdon's English Yorkshire White Soul – it previews Rap. **Jimi Hendrix's** smoking guitar screamed out to a sizzling orange sky, and Burdon screamed out for a myriad 10,000 guitars to groove at a billion decibels and CONQUER the World.

"Kick Out the Jams" – MC5, #82, 3-69. Rob Tyner (1945-91) and his Motor City Five straddle Punk and Heavy Metal genres. On the cusp of the Underground/Alternative FM horn of 1968, their strident sound surged its wild way out of the smoky quagmire of midtown Motown. Like RAGE AGAINST the MACHINE [Al. #4+, '99 *The Battle of Los Angeles*], their iconoclastic Luddite spirit saluted the Arsenel of Democracy's troubled torn times. Furious with smoky blue funk and rage, against a lifetime of perceived wage slavery in some hellish demon-forge cauldron, the MC5 screamed out their cosmic woes into the dark blue winds and Michigan snowswirl skies. With amps half as big as Cadillacs. To the max. They lived at my alma mater Wayne State University (**Casey Kasem's**, too). When the student paper the *Collegian* was commandeered by black-activist revolutionary John Watson and re-dubbed *The South End,* the White Panther-affiliate MC5 moved into the newspaper office. After 1967's bloody Motown riots, a 1968 fiery convulsion might have consumed the Motor City, but a calming miracle occurred. The black and white Detroit Tigers, striped orange and black, won baseball's World Championship with efforts by Afro Willie Horton and white Al Kaline and Denny McLain, only pitcher in 65 years to win 30 games in a year [31-6].

Rising rage in Detroit spurred White Panther Prez John Sinclair's book *Guitar Army.* In Detroit and University of Michigan's Ann Arbor nearby, Sinclair and Jack Forrest and Pun Plumonden visualized a rising guitar consciousness to blot out the world's bombs that rained from the smoky skies. Nervous local Draft Boards and the business community fought to squelch the voluminous voice of youth, trying, as usual, to overturn the old world order. Soon Sinclair was busted for possession of two joints; new draconian drug laws sent him to jail for ten years. The MC5, the White Panthers, and Heavy Metal poised to take over the world – by GUITAR.

Almost did it, too. **John Lennon** & Yoko filled a 10,000-seat Ann Arbor arena to free John (see Lennon-song "John Sinclair" on Al. #41, 7-72 *Sometime in New York City).* Using the system to CHANGE the SYSTEM, the Panthers movement elected two new members to the Ann Arbor City Council from their party, resulting in a 3-2 majority with some liberal democrat. Result? Pot possession became only a $5 fine, mailed in like a parking ticket, in Ann Arbor.

"Kick Out the Jams" bellowed out of the Grande Ballroom on Grand River Avenue, just a mile from Motown Records and Aretha Franklin's preacher-dad's church with 7000 devotees. The MC5 screamed this number in 1967 concerts with **Bob Seger,** the Southbound Freeway, and our Woolies. Singer **Rob Tyner** (1945-91) boomed the strident MC5 message. The MC5's other ultra-loud guy, Fred 'Sonic' Smith (1949-94), married Patti Smith (Punk Rock chapter). The MC5 opened up lyrical floodgates recently tantamount to Rap vocals. Their title's vanished fifth word was, naturally, bleeped [to HALF a word, referring to the maternal parental unit].

Did both Punk Rock and Heavy Metal get their start in the cavernous basement gym of the FIRST UNITARIAN CHURCH at Detroit's Cass and Forest Aveunes? In 1969, the MC5 cut a live album (rare PINK disc) there in their benevolent subterranean sanctuary – and the MC5 spat out brash, raw, basic tri-chordal Metal, rampaging fire and brimstone with amps at 11. Tyner and Fred 'Sonic' Smith died of adjacent heart attacks (46 and 45), too old to die young, and too young to die old. But their Metallic spirit lives on.

"Dolly Dagger" – Jimi Hendrix, #74, 10-71. Jimi's last charted hit after his tragic 9-18-70 O.D. Jimi was voted the #3 Heavy Metal Artist of all time in a 2000 VH-1 poll, behind **Ozzy Osbourne/Black Sabbath** and **Led Zeppelin.** Seattle's Metal magician is the lead guitarist to lead all lead guitarists. A Psychedelic Blues artist during the dawn of Metal (see Blues), Hendrix's southpaw axe spews frantic fuzztone and feedback and frenzied hard-core Metalmania. Later the pollsters recanted, and simply called Jimi the #1 guitarist of all time. His legend looms and engorges with time.

"Candy" – Iggy Pop, #28, 11-90. Another Ann Arborite (b. '47, James Jewel Osterberg) like Seger, rail-thin Pop performed with the MC5 at the Grande Ballroom, straddling the Punk/Heavy Metal emerging genres. One of his classics is "Real Wild Child," from #75, 10-86 Al. *Blah Blah Blah;* his thunderous baritone smokes the bass clef. 'Ivan's' "Real Wild Child" hit #68, 9-58; 'Ivan' is the middle name of lead vocalist Jerry 'IVAN' Allison, Buddy Holly's drummer. Lead guitarist Buddy Holly's Crickets got the song from Australian idol Johnny O'Keefe. All this stuff interconnects.

Iggy was Iggy Stooge for awhile, for 'The Stooges.' Iggy stands for debut band the Iguanas (info Kim Bloxdorf/Joel Whitburn). "Candy" rampages into the 90s, and features **B-52's'** (#3, '89 "Roam") Kate Pierson on vocals, too. A Punk-Rock icon, Muskegon and Ann Arbor Iggy hit with Al. #90, 7-90 *Brick by Brick,* #120, 9-77 *Lust for Life,* #106, 8-69 *The Stooges,* #72, 4-77 *The Idiot,* and #110, 7-88 *Instinct.*

Rock and Roll thrives on irony. Like R & R's early years, the births of Punk and Heavy Metal spawned preachy, up-in-arms rhetoric and bombastic barbs. Quoth the *London Times:* "Punk Rock is a generic term for the latest musical garbage . . . It features sceaming, venemous, threatening rock sounds." What's new?

"Detroit Rock City" – Kiss, NC '76 [flip side of #7, 9-76 "Beth."] Kiss changed Rock and Roll – and Heavy Metal – by becoming superstars BOTH through their musical expertise AND their theatrical stage show. Rampaging out of another R & R cradle – New York City – Kiss features four virtuosos: **Paul Stanley** ['Star Child,' guitar], **Gene Simmons** [b. '49, Haifa, **Israel,** 'Bat Lizard,' bass], **Peter Criss** ['The Cat', drums], and **Ace Frehley** ['Space Man,' lead guitar]. Frehley's speed-metal splendor overtops rhythm riffs by Stanley. Simmons' bass blasts the bottom for Criss's polyrhythmic thunder. With war paint on their faces, Cat and Star Child's smoochy band sets up the visuals of Rock Theatre pioneered by the Beatles' *Help & Hard Day's Night****.* Kiss's whole theatrical commotion paved the way for video-blasting *MTV* and *VH-1.*

"Detroit Rock City" hits **Del Shannon's** good ol' "Runaway" (#1, '61) chord configuration – Am – G – F – E7. Scored in the common Key of 'C,' for awhile, "DRC" plunges the Polynesian bVI and the chromatic bVII chords

– the melodic **Ab & Bb** – into their strident mixed bag of distortion and sonic booms.

Though all sing sensationally, Simmons' voice in particular is a Heavy Metal instrument. Big Kiss hits? Right: #7, 9-76 ballad "Beth," #11, 5-79 "I Was Made for Lovin' You," and #8, 2-90 "Forever." Vintage HARD ROCK/ HEAVY METAL. *Gold Rush* does Hard Rock and Heavy Metal interchangeably. They are one and the same (though Hard Rock shades a bit more into our Heartland Rock chapter as well). "Christine Sixteen" at #25, 7-77, is a rapscallion rocker in the make-out Key of Ab. Kiss's monster R & R anthem was so great it hit twice in one year:

Kiss

"Rock and Roll All Nite" – Kiss, #68, 5-75; #12, 11-75. Bisecting the Disco Decade with frothing, volcanic, Hot Rock, Kiss booms their theatrical thunder with this celebration of 100% pure Rock and Roll. Born in Israel, Gene Simmons is among the few Israeli Rock icons, but the Land Of Zion (Pat Boone, #64, 1-61 "The Exodus Song") certainly helped create Rock and Roll with its Jewish theatrical expertise and talent. This song smashes and thrashes the huge 2, 2½, and 4 beats. It's the perfect

Party-Animal anthem for generations of unsleepy promenaders on the Boulevard of Rock and Roll Dreams. One of greatest Rock songs of all time.

"I Can See for Miles and Miles" – Who, #9, 10-67. Who's only single-digit single features Daltrey/Townshend's vocal echoes of Simon & Garfunkel or Everly Brothers: gentle harmonic swoops, ironic raspy hooks. Most of all, Heavy Metal guitar busts the silence, via Townshend's windmill knockout strum and Jon Entwistle's supersonic bass. The song hero has X-Ray Vision. He sees through deceit and hoopla. Keith Moon's drum-fills smash and crash bashingly , and the Who define the meaning of Metal – 100% virtuoso expertise on the strings and skins. Unforgettable song.

"River Deep – Mountain High" – Deep Purple, #53, 1-69. Catwalking between Orchestral/Art Rock and Heavy Metal, these "Smoke on the Water" (#4, 5-73) Metal classicists also reprised Neil Diamond's Easy Rock "Kentucky Woman" to #38, 1-68. With hits like #81, 4-73 "Woman from Tokyo," **David Coverdale** went on to lead **Whitesnake** (#2, 10-87 "Is This Love?"). This deep-river hit stars the Phil Spector-style Wall of Sound. An ambitious production, this song only got the kudos it deserved, chart-wise, in the UK with Tina Turner. Monumental chunk of Rock and Soul adventure. Purple's early hit "Hush" (#4, 8-68), is a hard-driving cover of Georgia's **Billy Joe Royal's** (#52, 9-67). Deep Purple didn't just carve out Jazz Rock – they also embraced the stormy metallic twang of screaming guitar-fire Heavy Metal.

"Wonder Woman" – Billy Joel, NC, '70. From Al NC. '70 *Attila*. Jon Small on drums. The garish album cover shows Billy and Small dressed in French Three Musketeers cavalier armor. Standing in a bloody *abattoir/*butcher shop, they contemplate raw gory carcasses of meat on tenderhooks. Billy Joel fondles the keys of his big Hammond B-3 organ, warbling a foot-pedal wah-wah. Though Heavy Metal ATTILA sounds like eight hundred Mongols swooping out of Outer Mongolia's Gobi Desert in the Dark Ages, their entire band is just TWO guys. Like some current Metal or Rap motifs in lyrics, "Wonder Woman" snarls sarcastically about this hated ex-girlfriend. Del Shannon (1935-90) founded **Revenge Rock** with his molten-Metal #28, 10-61 "So Long Baby." Shannon's bitterness falls far short of Attila's dangerous munsters (RAGE Rock often counts Limp Bizkit, Korn, or Rage Against the Machine in its orbit). Joel's Attila ditty "Revenge Is Sweet" contains raunchy nastyisms that show Billy was going through a bad stretch in his trek toward the mellow, with-it superstar he became. Revenge Rock unlocks the primitive ID (see Freud), going back to man's beast-spurred primordial consciousness – seeking instant sensual gratification and brutal violence. The earliest HEADBANGER, Attila the HUN (406-53 a.d.), attired in Heavy Metal (armor), was no Mr. Manners himself. He pulled the plug on Europe's Easy Listening Era: pillaging, ravishing, and doing disgusting things too horrible to mention in a civilized comic strip like *Hagar the Horrible.*

"The House of the Rising Sun" – Everly Brothers, NC, '68. Don Everly growls an Eric Burdon baritone on the sinister verse – buttressed by a Ray Manzarek-style [unlabeled] Hammond B-3 organ that could scorch the solar corolla on the surface of the sun. Like Eric's #1(3), 8-64 foray into Brit Folk Rock, "House of the Rising Sun," Don uses a "Piano Man" jump-the-octaves mode to loft from molasses-slow low stalking verses to Robert Plant/Steven Tyler shrill high verses. These are followed by an organ attack of Heavy Metal wildness to shake the thunder down from the skies. That's right – the **Everly Brothers.** Obscure NC, '68 Warner Brothers *The Hit Sound of the Everly Brothers.* ORIGINAL '86 Rock Hall inductees, with a true Heavy Metal sound you'd have to hear to believe.

Paranoid – **Black Sabbath, Al. #12, 2-71.** My Dearborn High School pal [Dr.] Bob Sigler treated fast-lane **Ozzy Osbourne** for a throat infection. The way many Heavy Metallurgists sing (like World Wrestling Federation growl merchants), it's a wonder they're not treated more often. Black Sabbath is often mentioned as Heavy Metal Founders. *Black Sabbath* debuted at #23, 8-70. *Paranoid* is the second step to their top hit and only top ten album – #8, 9-71 *Master of Reality.* Six platinum albums included #11, 1-74 *Sabbath Bloody Sabbath* (inspiring U2's "Sunday, Bloody Sunday"), #28, 6-80 *Heaven and Hell,* and #48, 2-76 *We Sold Our Soul for Rock and Roll.*

A 'Black Sabbath' involved a witches' sabbath medieval gathering. Ozzy's Birmingham, England, smokescape cohorts chose the name more for shock value than satanic legerdemain. Their magically bedazzling albums, however, thrash with head-banging guitar magic. Newer albums bore their quasi-religious style: #39 Christian-echo 10-83 *Born Again,* and #122 Post-Modern 2-94 *Cross Purposes.* Black Sabbath's smoggy industrial Midlands colossus – like Detroit's – shook up flower-in-hair San Franciscans stoned on love and brotherhood. With dungeons/dragons/gorgons' dark side, Ozzy sparked a generation of Metal – like Metallica and beyond. Singer Ozzy worked with Tommy Iommi on guitar, William Ward on drums, and Terry 'Geezer' Butler on bass; in the late 70s, he acquired the 'Blizzard of Ozz' moniker.

Again, HARD ROCK and HEAVY METAL are fairly interchangeable here. Ozzy Osbourne was voted the #2 Hard Rock artist (VH-1, 2000) of all time. The 2002 MTV show *The Osbournes*, a reality sandwich of Ozzy's home life, hit the top 10 of the Neilsen Ratings. Ozzy's Heavy Metal is an answer and a catharsis to raging hormones. Pundits proclaimed Metal gone in the late 70s – and they were also wrong about the demise of Disco (see Techno/Dance/'House' music), the passing of Punk (see Green Day/Blink 182), and the Last Tango of Latino Rock (see Ricky Martin, Christina Aguilera).

"Some Kind of Wonderful" – Grand Funk Railroad, #3, 12-74. White Soul barrage with metallic flares – from Soul Brothers Six's #91 '67 song. **Mark Farner** (guitar) jammed with bassist Mel Schacher and drummer Don Brewer in Flint, Michigan. Many Metal blockbusters: #1(1), 7-73 "We're an American Band" of party-time tour-bus celebration; #4, 5-75 "Bad Time," and their biggest hit – a remake of **Little Eva** Boyd's 'Girls Group' classic #1, 6-62 "The Loco-Motion." Perky Melbourne, Australian soap star **Kylie Minogue** locomoted to #3, 8-88, with her Neo-Disco, Techno-Synth, Dance style "Locomotion." The Grand **Trunk** Railroad crisscrossed Michigan back when the world was a kid – through 'Buick-town Flint.' Grand Funk also hit on breakthrough #22, 8-70 "Closer to Home," and #29, 1-72 "Footstompin' Music." Tthe Michigan marauders kept "Shinin' On" (#11, 7-74, produced by Todd Rundgren).

"Eighteen" – Alice Cooper, #21, 2-71. Super Hard Rock statement of life's crossroads. Indecision. Glitz glam slam bam. 'Alice Cooper' began as good ol' French-American **Vincent Fournier** (b. '48 Detroit), emerging as the semilovely Shock Rocker Alice. Glen Buxton rode guitar, Michael Bruce rampaged keyboards, Neal Smith bopped drums, and Dennis Dunaway tweaked bass. For all those worldwide gropers groping, and crying out "I'm 49, and I don't know what I want to be if I grow up," "Eighteen" offers answers. But mostly more questions. Strident, loud, brash, great. Angst of 18, yay.

"School Is Out" – Gary U.S. Bonds, #5, 7-61; #12, 8-61 R & B. You crave REAL early Metal Mania mixed with Soul? NO ONE rocked it with a heavier, louder sound than Gary. Frank Guida raced the LeGrand VU meter high beyond the breakneck overmodulated line of +3. Springsteen's saxman Clarence Clemons' own mentor, 'Daddy G,' played legendary sax for Bonds. A wild streetscene crowd clapped pandemonium on Bonds's bombastic background. Gary's happy rasps are hallelujah jubilant. He celebrates his upcoming carefree summer of Yankee bleacher fandom, and hi-jinx with wild pals.

Alice Cooper did a different "School Is Out" (#7, 6-72). It, too, celebrates oppression's deliverance. Coop ditches Old Devil Rhyme. Carping about principles and principals, he grumbles that HE CAN'T FIND ANY WORDS THAT RHYME. Both stars' sandy voices jolt into jolly jubilation gear for school's sayonara. Summer sunshine, hooray. Girls, girls, girls.

"Poison" – Alice Cooper, #7, 8-89. Named for some 16th-century witch, Cooper's renaissance surged when *Wayne's World* glorified the vet Metal guru. Paparazzi shot some pix of Alice, without make-up, playing good ol' bourgeois GOLF, and ruined his Gothic stage image. Glam Rock crew **Poison (Al. #2[1], 7-90 *Flesh and Blood*)** of Harrisburg, PA, does Metal. See Glam Rock chapter.

"New World Man" – Rush, #21, 9-82. Neal Peart, Rush drummer, was often voted #4-ever R & R drum star of all time: 1) **Keith Moon,** Who; #2) **John 'Bonzo' Bonham,** Led Zeppelin; 3) **Jerry Allison** of Buddy Holly/Crickets. With only Jerry alive into 2001, could Peart be toying with the Silver Medal? **Alex Lifeson** handles guitar for the singing expertise of bassist **Geddy Lee** (no relation to *Brenda Lee, Dickey Lee, Peggy Lee, or* **Curtis Lee** [Phil Spector-produced #7, 7-61 "Pretty Little Angel Eyes"]). On throat, Geddy handles most of the details. His Robert-Plant malleability soars above Peart's wildfire rhythmic core. Rush's #44, 6-81 Mark-Twain-inspired "Tom Sawyer" gloms silver, with #45 "The Big Money" at bronze. Their album resume is impressive, including #2(1), 11-93 *Counterparts*, and double #3's of 3-81 *Moving Pictures* and 9-91 *Roll the Bones*. They hit four #10's in a row on *Billboard's* 200, too – 11-81 *Exit . . . Stage Left*; 10-82 *Signals*; 5-84 *Grace Under Pressure*; and 11-85 *Power*. They are so expert at guitar wizardry, as are many Metal guitarists, that they use TABLATURE, instead of just notes written for piano on scales with bass and treble clefs.

Banjo star/Folk singer **Pete Seeger** says tablature dates back to the 16th century – for LUTES. Forerunner of the guitar, cousin of the harp, the LUTE had strings, too. TABLATURE varies from instrument to instrument by the NUMBER of STRINGS. Guitar tablature has SIX strings. You'll also find vibratos, trills, and slides. **Eddie Van Halen** punctuates his riffs with single-note rhythm slashes, palm mutes, hammer-ons, bends, pre-bends, and pull-offs.

"Don't Stop Believin'" – Journey, #9, 9-81. Santana's #1, 2000 *Supernatural* album shows the power of this Chicano superstar to keep the hits coming. Both guitarist **Neal Schon** and keyboard wizard **Greg Rolle** began with Santana in the early 70s. **Aynsley Dunbar,** well-traveled drummer of John Mayall and Frank Zappa/Mothers of Invention fame, joined Journey. The line-up was set with the acquisition of Operatic Rocker **Steve Perry.** Other Journey personnel include Jonathan Cain, replacing Rolle in 1981 (Whitburn info); when Dunbar fled for Jefferson Starship and Metalmongers **Whitesnake,** Steve Smith took over. **Ross Valory** anchored bass for aeons. Perry is a throwback to the Great Singer Era of Del Shannon, Roy Orbison, Jay Black, Gary Puckett. This beautiful ballad strides confidently into the top ten as an example of True Love Power, the fired-up fuel of vital Rock and Roll.

Schon's tommy-gun chords throb a baleful echo on the verse. The story lyrically? Small-town girl. Meets hardscrabble Detroit lad, also on train [a real oddity in the MOTOR City, but Journey's from San Francisco]. Smoky perfume, cheap wine, hot rendezvous. Poetry intensifies in the bridge and beyond: strangers on the Boulevard [West Grand Boulevard? Dilapidated by '81, bygone jaded ghost glories], with hot spunky metaphor – "STREETLIGHT-PEOPLE" reverie. Then the sweet refrain. Life is viewed as a continuous movie.

Journey eliminated what Joe Stuessy points out as **Alice Cooper's** stage props: mutilating a toy doll by stomping, stabbing, sensually abusing, and cutting off its head [Cooper's #1, 3-73 Al. *Billion Dollar Babies*]. Cooper is perhaps the touchstone for Gothic Rock.

"Separate Ways (Worlds Apart)" – Journey, #8, 2-83. Rebounds Journey's magnificent band track against the celestial sphere. It bounces off planetoids, asteroids, and the Milky Way in a simmering hot-wax jacuzzi of Power

Metal. Lyrically, it lingers over regular love expressions. No problem. Who wants a song with unenchanted lyrics like "I just now called you to say take out the garbage," "Scrubbing my clunker's vinyl top reminds me of your lovely ankle," or "The ATM machine ate my card and barfed back an I.O.U. that broke my toe"?

An amazing hit song. Any portion of the Top Ten you scrape means success. Both the Eagles and Journey took a little flak for being too good, too successful. Their majestic melding of styles drew that echo of Folk Purists who lambasted electric music for its sales achievements. Journey is among the greatest artists of all time (Dylan, Creedence, Jimi, Bruce) without a #1 HOT 100 song. Their plaintive super ballad, "Open Arms," logged a #2(6), 1-82 slot. They also soared with #4, 7-81 "Who's Crying Now" and double #9's 1-85 "Only the Young" and 4-86 "Be Good to Yourself." With Journey, you're not talking Oldies – hardly even Classic Rock, with big #12, 10-96 (#1 Adult Contemporary) "When You Love a Woman."

"Lights" – Journey, #68, 8-78; #74, 1-93. Spare, laconic lyric. Companion volume to Hemingway's pint-sized 120-page masterpiece *The Old Man and the Sea*. This Journey melody is so gorgeous, you believe you've unearthed a new Shakespeare's Greatest Hit.

Longing song. Early morning nostalgia. He longs to watch the sunrise over the bay. It's not a 'flamingo' or 'violet' or 'sun-spattered' or 'jagged craggy seashore' bay. He packs up all his spare adjectives and fires them like skipping stones into the froth breaking on the hopeful morning shore. You the fan can furnish your own do-it-yourself adjectives (or *Gold Rush* is having a special this week – Adjectives, 11 for a dollar).

The sparkling tune to "Lights" will light up your life. Perry's dramatic tenor wafts to 'Irish tenor' range. You almost feel you're watching the great gray breakers bashing the headlands in the green, green, golden morning over Galway Bay.

"Faithfully" – Journey, #12, 4-83. Sung by Matt Searing of Funky in the Middle, at our son Jeremy's wedding to Kristen, "Faithfully" is #1 in the hearts of many millions. It covers the romantic saga of a music man, and his avowed promise to remain faithful in the wake of the road's gaudy temptations. As **Steve Perry's** hovercraft voice hurdles to the high rafters, the girl can't help but believe him. Love is powered by faith. Though many a rapscallion, rogue, or rascal has reniged on "Promises, Promises" (Dionne Warwick, #19, 11-68), this song is very convincing that love will bind this song's two lifetime lovers for a lifetime plus an eternity.

Penned by 1981+ keyboard guy **Jonathan Cain,** it is one of the most magnificent road songs ever done. "Faithfully" takes us all on a trip to Alaska's midnight-sun – keeping the crowd aglow. Freed from rhyme via Led Zep's "Stairway to Heaven," "Faithfully" ascends the heights of eternal love. No matter how far away, as midnight bus wheels roll to uncertain destinies, love will prevail.

"Barracuda" – Heart, #11, 5-77. **Ann Wilson** has one of the greatest Hard Rock/Heavy Metal altos of the Rock

Revolution. Lead singer to Heart, this early Seattle screamer fronted a superstar female Metal band (a rarity) that almost became a war casualty. In '75, manager Mike Fisher's Draft Lottery # came up at the Vietnam finale. He fled north to Vancouver, British Columbia, and signed Heart, who is full of Soul.

"Barracuda" features a machine-gun attack of spitting rhythm guitar and bass. Ann's sister **Nancy Wilson** (not same-named Jazz chanteuse) plays keyboards and guitar, with Howard Leese and Fisher's brother Roger on guitar. Drummer Mike DeRosier and bassist Steve Fossen pack the rhythm track with metallic flame.

Their #9, 7-76 "Magic Man" set the standard. Along with Gracie Slick, Ann soared into Janis Joplin turf in gutsy, fire-breathing female vocals. She inspired Joan Jett and Suzi Quatro and Pat Benatar with their own Hard Rock/ Heavy Metal sounds. Heart's "What About Love?" hit #10, 6-85. "Never" grabbed #4, 4-85. "These Dreams" smoked the charts to first #1 in 1-86. Their heaviest hit is #1(3), 5-87 "Alone." The girl-wants-guy-only-for-HIS-body theme is rare, but hit #2(2), 3-90 in a piercing pomp power "All I Wanna Do Is Make Love to You."

"Cum on Feel the Noise" – Quiet Riot, #5, 9-83. Their natural Speed Metal follow-up is #31, 1-84 "Bang Your Head (Metal Health)," via album #1(1) 4-83 *Metal Health*. Carlos Cavaso, guitar, sparks Kevin DuBrow's L.A.-style gravelpit vocal.

Blue Öyster Cult is one of the few Long Island bands to reach this high in a generation: #12, 7-76 "(Don't Fear) the Reaper." Philosophy is 99% Jack Kerouac & *On the Road's* follow-up 1958 *The Dharma Bums* (like spinoff Kerouac sitcom *Dharma & Greg*). **Donald 'Buck Dharma' Roeser** strokes a monstermetal guitar, with a wild tenor vocal by **Eric Bloom.** Follow-up? #40, 8-81 even-better "Burnin' for You." Blue Point, Long Island, on the Great South Bay, once furnished 75% of the U.S. oyster crop.

"Get Off of My Cloud" – Rolling Stones, #1(2), 10-65. Heavy Metal to the max. Keith Richard[s] rampages on Metallic Hard Rock. Wyman's supersonic bass blasts. Watts's power-punching drums preview Peart. Mick Jagger hollers at sleepy guy asking him to punt loud 3 a.m. party. Their high life needs no flak. Also catch "Paint It Black" or "The Last Time." On quasi-Metal #2(3), 8-81 "Start Me Up," Mick gets down & dirtier (catch fadeout locker-room line about an erotic dead man buzzed by a live babe). The Stones, Kinks, Who, Animals, and even the Beatles helped pioneer Heavy Metal (catch feedback in #1[2], 7-84 "A Hard Day's Night").

"Whole Lotta Love" – Led Zeppelin, #4, 11-69. Zep – supergroup. From unhumble 'New Yardbirds' beginnings, **Jimmy Page (**b. 1-9-44, Heston, England) of Jeff Beck's group and Donovan sessions (#1 '66 "Sunshine Superman") created the band with the #1-voted song of all time – "Stairway to Heaven," NC, of 16M monster album *[Untitled] Led Zeppelin IV.* All it took was a magic voice: **Robert Plant (**b. 8-20-48 West Bromwich). No voice like Plant's ever was. Stalking a rich full baritone, Plant swoops

upwards on a long Jerry Lee Lewis slur-glide. With no perceptible vocal shift or hurdle, he dances a falsetto-pitch tightrope; it might give Frankie Valli or Lou Christie a run for their money. His sizzling Call & Response tacets inflame the crowds. **John Paul Jones** handles bass and keyboards; named for an American Naval commander (perhaps inadvertently), Jones is the dominant bassist of a generation with the Who's John Entwistle, was born five miles from Mick Jagger at Sidcup. Drummer **John 'Bonzo' Bonham (1948-80)** of Coventry is the driving force behind "Whole Lotta Love." Somehow, you know he's not that fifth-chair squirrelly kid fooling with flams and paradiddles and ratamacues on his dinky drum pad. Bonham is the rhythmic hallmark.

Led Zep was the best at what they did. They practiced a versatility/virtuosity not seen before or since. They bounce from basic Blues to wildly experimental Jazz Rock solos. They wander from mysterious Xanadu in Lauri's "Ramble On" (weirdly NC, '69), and dabble in Folk Fusion/Celtic Renaissance in *IV's* runic "Battle of Evermore."

"Whole Lotta Love," their biggest chart single, showcases Plant's otherworldly tenor talents. Nothing artificial or boring or wimpy gets anywhere near this song. With this frantic single as a booster rocket, their Album Armada steered the stars. After #10 eponymous *Led Zeppelin* of 2-69, six of their next eight albums hit #1, selling around **50 million albums** in the USA alone. So long to the 'single' record. Kids too rich for 45's snorted whole albums in a rush to grab it all at the speed of NOW.

"Moby Dick" – Led Zeppelin, NC, '69. From *LZ II, Al. #1(7),* 11-69. Boffo Bonzo number. Zep's trademark is splashing Blues riffs off the deep curlicues of Jones's bass or keyboards. Page fondles the fuzztone freedom of his supercharged treble swirl. Like **Foreigner** (with Heavy Metal credentials), they often double the riff an octave apart on bass and guitar. Then Page crisply surges up to the top tall notes, spraying speed at hyper-treble overdrive – as Jones continues the basic riff. "Moby" mangles the ex-silence with complex *cadenzas* in 'D'. Then the hot band sneaks off for coffee & what-not. Bonzo is left alone to outfox the Big Band Jazz drum sharpshooters like **Buddy Rich** or **Gene Krupa** in his massive mammoth million-drum marathon. Like the sinister white whale that dismasted Captain Ahab in Melville's whaling tale, "Moby Dick" is an action-filled adventure with peril, promise, and glory.

"Stairway to Heaven" – Led Zeppelin, NC, 11-71. #1 R & R song of zillions.. Voted #1 ever in the 2000 VH-1 awards, it mysteriously never CHARTED on the HOT 100. Atlantic (and later their own label Swan Song) didn't want a single to cannibalize album sales, so they anchored it to *LZ-IV.* For 7:55 of your life, you listen to Jimmy Page flirting with the **A-minor** chord. You can actually hear his nimble fingers squeak on the strings in his beefy instrumental intro. Like the madrigal "Greensleeves" (#25, 3-52 Mantovani), or Del Shannon's ubiquitous #1 '61 "Runaway," "Stairway" jogs between **A-minor** and more melodic **G-major.** Here Plant's tenor sounds as gossamer and wispy as **Donovan**'s #23, 11-67 "Wear Your Love Like Heaven," or #33 puffy fluffy 10-68 "Laleña." As Plant climbs his crescendo "Stairway," he starts to put the hammer down. His tone becomes gravelly, wry, feted, fated.

Led Zeppelin -- out standing in their field.
l-r: ***John Paul Jones***, *bass;* ***Robert Plant**,*
singer; ***Jimmy Page**, guitarist; and*
***John 'Bonzo' Bonham**,drummer.*

The Zep anthem makes you WONDER. Plant's grand cosmic bewilderment shines a wan glow. The *Untitled IV* album cover, haunted by its ZOSO logo, flashes an old man trudging under a pile of sticks he carries. The rear cover gives us old redbrick smoketown tenements – you'd think it Baltimore or Detroit, were it not for fancy English chimneys and thrusting lavender lupines stabbing the floral foreground. The backdrop looms with a sterile high-rise. Its 20-story soulless bulk pierces a hazy sky.

Open the album. Inside, a Druid-style lantern bearer in an ancient cloak perches like a vulture atop a craggy mountain. This Merlin the Magician necromancer gazes to the dark black and white citadel village below. Crenelated ramparts reflect an eerie dim glow from a faraway mountain. A scraggly skeletal female person climbs frantically to the old man's ghastly summit.

This is not the Stairway to Heaven we all had in mind. It is a Druidic Hymn to Disillusionment. Plant gapes, in awe and ardent WONDER. One reason we all love this climactic song is because we all feel this way from time to time. We amble through our lives, bamboozled by Snoopy's hedonistic happiness. Then BOOM – you hear a song with an undertone of nervous uncertainty. You get zapped by a glop of gloom.

She'll be BUYING, purchasing, Plant murmurs, this rickety "Stairway to Heaven." You know, like she's shopping at the Smith Haven Mall. Once you put a price on salvation (Judas + 30 pieces/silver), it adds a medieval stench of indulgences paid to unscrupulous church charlatans for a few years' free time in the lobby of Purgatory. Beyond the ironic Zen lyric, you'll find a beautiful melody. In its gloaming glimmerings of magic Sherwood Forest, "Stairway" previews the Celtic Renaissance. On the way

to **Sarah McLachlan**, you'll pass **Stevie Nicks/Fleetwood Mac's** #11, 3-76 "Rhiannon," or dark broodings like **Metallica's** #16, 8-91 "Enter Sandman" or #10, 6-96 "Until It Sleeps." [Also see Jethro Tull, Loreena McKennitt, and Celine Dion]. On the mezzanine of "Stairway to Heaven," John Bonham returns from tea break to offer a grand crescendo in the Roy Orbison tradition. "**Stairway to Heaven**," everybody's favorite song, never charted, eh? Let's not bet the ranch:

"**Stairway to Heaven**" – **Neil Sedaka, #9, 3-60; #16, R & B.** Master melodist Sedaka teamed with ace lyricist Howie Greenfield at Lincoln High School in Brooklyn. His smooth Irish tenor blossoms with self-harmonized overdubs, sweet major chords, and Greenfield's potent metaphor. TOTALLY different song. Teddy-bear cute, blithe, fun. The title was inspired by TV show *Stairway to the Stars* – itself inspired by the #1, '39 **Glenn Miller** hit (#4 Kay Kyser) of the same name. Sedaka's bouncy, peppy song bops and grooves from Lincoln High to the Pearly Gates . . . what a wild strange trek it's been.

"**Stairway of Love**" – **Marty Robbins, #68, 4-58; #2(2) C.** Marty Robbins, who furnished the 'pink-carnation' phrase for Don McLean's "American Pie," was an American treasure (1925-81). Without this #2 Robbins' song, no Led Zeppelin could have accrued. Huh? Remember, Marty accidentally INVENTED HEAVY METAL back on #3, '61 "Don't Worry" (#1[10] C)? His bassman's old tube amp blew up, and weird fuzztone feedback cascaded out of the crippled amp in demonic low tones. Most Country conservatives would have junked the session. Marty just said "Cool! Leave it in."

So, yep, "Stairway to Heaven's" cousin hit #2 somewhere important. And Marty invented Heavy Metal. And yessir, without Marty this history chapter would be history. Or NO history. So yes, Virginia, Marty Robbins invented Led Zeppelin.

"**Fool in the Rain**" – **Led Zeppelin, #21, 1-80.** Marginally computerized, much of *Gold Rush* was typed on my picnic table on a $99 Brother electric – not acoustic – typewriter. This current review looks up at dingy skies about to splash a gusher. The song title, ulp, is ominous.

Good song, though. Oddball key for Zep – standard 'C'. Mostly ghostly. Blues duel with Jones and Page. Like a symphony, it rises to a jiffy middle Movement. Then it returns to the old retro riff.

On "Kashmir," **Led Zeppelin** finds a wonderful and exotic beat – almost a bolero crescendo. At NC, on #1(6) Al. 3-75 *Physical Graffiti,* the British Hard Rock quartet rides up to the top of the world. Wedged into the Karakoram Range of the High Himalayas, beyond the gun-thug cadres and cabals of Osama Bin Laden, the Taliban, and the contraband camps beyond Katmandu, the breathtaking Veil of Kashmir avoids arctic blasts in its bracing blue-green land of eternal springtime. Bonham's polyrhythmic pulse makes you feel you're lumbering atop an elephant on a howdah, on a mystery expedition to this perfumed exotic land of steamy nights and passionate pleasures.

"All My Love" – Led Zeppelin, NC, '79. From Al. #1(7), 9-79 *In Through the Out Door.* Despite Zep's penchant for complex music, they use an oft-repeated hook in this fave classic. As in #65, 3-70 "Living, Loving Maid (She's Just a Woman)," they bleed a bold Blues; it's the heart of emerging Metal, like "All My Love" is a guidepost. Again, bass and guitar riffs double an octave apart. Their oddly-apostrophe'd double entendre "D'yer Mak'er" scraped the top 20 (#20, 10-73). "Trampled Under Foot" blasted to #38, 4-75.

"Black Dog" – Led Zeppelin, #15, 12-71. You won't hear much about a black dog, like my dear pal Snarf [Snarfi Sue, Abyssinian Lionhound, 1966-84]. You will hear a great Blues groove in 'A', with Page's guitar gorging on his lofty-fret expertise. Zep's #16, 11-70 "Immigrant Song" hit their bronze-medal HOT 100 rung – Number Sixteen. A band who helped ALBUM DOMINATION of the old SINGLES market, Led Zeppelin ran the table on the competition. Their first ten albums hit the following heights in their tensome hit string, 1970-82:

Peak Positions? **10 – 1 – 1 – 2 – 1 – 1 – 1 – 2 – 1 – 6.**

They were named for an unfunny joke reaction: "Like, wow – man. Your stupid joke went over like a lead balloon." Somehow, it metamorphosed from balloon to dirigible to blimp to zeppelin. Could they have made it as LED BLIMP? Why LED – not the HEAVY METAL, LEAD? Homonym hang-up. Soundalikes. Some fans rhymed it with BLEED – not FRED. LED is only pronounced LED.

Like the eclectic virtuosity of the **Dave Matthews Band** (Al. #1, 3-2001, *Everyday*), a Led Zep concert didn't just PLAY a stage act. They marauded. Jones's mandolin, and Page bowing his guitar strings as if playing a fiddle like Matthews' **Boyd Tinsley**, created an eclectic mix, fortified with the multi-drum polyrhythmic thunder of Bonham. Plant would crest over the audial fray, splitting stadiums with pandemonium. With his lion's mane whooshing around at stage epicenter, Plant's voice soared, crested, rumbled, cajoled , coaxed, pleaded. Over something labeled the Disco Decade, Led Zeppelin presided as British Kings of Rock and Roll. John Bonham died tragically in the Morrison/Joplin/Hendrix/Moon manner on September 25, 1980, of 'asphyxiation,' just 2½ months before John Lennon was assassinated in New York City. Three Zep members adrift, Plant scrounged a Supergroup.

As the **Honeydrippers**, Plant, Page, guitar icon **Jeff Beck**, and Chic's Nile Rodgers reprised Phil Phillips's #2 '59 Soul ballad "Sea of Love" to #3, 10-84. In a [half]way, that #3 is Led Half-Zep's highest charted single. They have a '99 Rock Hall invitee to thank:

"Sea of Love" – Del Shannon, #33, 12-81. Little Richard hit #42, '86 on "Great Gosh A' Mighty," and the Everlys scored #50 '84 "On the Wings of a Nightingale." Via the fandom of **Tom Petty,** who like *Elton John* idolized Del, this stunning new release of Phil's phantastic phabulous love song was produced by Tom. Cradle of Heavy Metal? Check out the modulational electric rampage of Del's pedal-to-the-metal #95, 5-65 "Break Up" or phaser/feedback frenzy #94, 5-66 "The Big Hurt." As early as 9-64,

Del's hot cover of Bobby Freeman's #5, 5-58 "Do You Wanna Dance" (also #12 '65 Beach Boys) showed Del's devotion to great Classic Rock/Soul, and YES, Heavy Metal, before it was even defined.

"Sea of Love" – Phil Phillips, #2(2), 7-59; #1(1), 8-59 R & B. Nothing whatsoever to do w/ Heavy Metal. Just a beautiful song. If fondles a III major Mediant chord, and soars romantically heavenward. Born John Phillip Batiste, the 'Irish' tenor shared his French Afro (b. '31 Lake Charles, LA) heritage with Classic Soul rockers like **Chuck Berry, Antoine 'Fats' Domino,** and **Allen Toussaint** ('98 Rock Hall inductee as non-performer). Phil's breezy serenade suggests a romantic, bygone magnolia age.

"We're Not Gonna Take It" – Twisted Sister, #21, 7-84. Rock, Roll, and Rebellion. Long Island's **Dee Snider's** mammoth Metal anthem. From Jerry Seinfeld's Massapequa, Snider's hyper explosion is complemented by the smashing percussive thunder of A. J. Pero. Part of this song's Jock Rock charm is Dee's hulking sandy baritone. He packs in anti-establishment groans galore, in rebellious glee. He sounds like he's flipped a lasso around a tornado, and won't let go. Twisted Sister's Glam Metal goodies also include #68, 12-84 "I Wanna Rock" and #53 Shangri-Las' torch throwback "Leader of the Pack" at #53, 11-85.

"Bang the Drum All Day" – Todd Rundgren, #63, 5-83. One reason people cut records, like BTO's #12 '74 "Takin' Care of Business," is to dump the 9-to-5 hassle. Everybody wants jackpot instant millionairedom. For bonus points, they often crave hit records to tick off the ex-girlfriend. "Bang the Drum" doesn't focus upon a girl. The Upper Darby, PA (b. '48) Rundgren's Swedish-American Rock savvy produced Meat Loaf's #14, 10-77 *Bat Out Of Hell* album; fourteen is an OK number, but its slow, lolling, rolling sales pattern took it to over 12 million sales.

'Bang the Drum' is Todd's odd ode – with a super rhythm track – to sublimation of violent energies into musical outlets. This is the Hedonists' International Anthem: Party, Party, Party, and party on. From his melodic debut #20 '70 "We Gotta Get You a Woman," Rundgren cruised Metal and other venues: #5, 10-73 ballad "Hello, It's Me," and #16, 4-72 "I Saw the Light."

Revenge agenda? He wants to bang the drum all day, pretend it's his boss's HEAD, and punt the workaday conspiracy. No matter how much freedom our democracy serves, it's tempered and tethered by BOSSISM. Old Dithers kicks poor Dagwood; Dagwood TAKES it, because he won't rock the boat – or because he's married to gorgeous bombshell **Blondie** (see Punk and/or New Wave). This Rundgren romp wants to have 100% pure 'FUN FUN FUN' (Beach Boys, #3 '64) till Big Daddy confiscates the joyride T-Bird. 'Big Daddy' can symbolize a lot of authority figures for us: the boss, the police, the system, the computer, literal dear ol' Dad, or even the Lord. Sooner or later, no matter how much frolicking and having a blast we do, Dad arrives to repossess that T-Bird. Then it's back to mush soup.

Personally, I knew Todd's feelings back in 1958; I was a teen cruiser of Malt Malls and Sip N' Nip roller-skate waitress drive-ins. I used to love to ride shotgun with my pals, a la Wayne & Garth. I'd bang dashboards in rockin' ratamacues and razz-mo-tazz jazz rat-a-tat-tats. My buddies would scream along with the AM rock classic in the Metro Motown glow of swooping used-car spotlights and red blinking radio towers and swirling snow.

"Bang" is basically a good-time song, although it's a tad sadistic. It drives workaholics bananas. Todd tattoos the tomtoms. The fluffy Farfisa organ rhythmizes the flow, and sails on the sweet major triad. Getting warmed up, Todd's raspy baritone blasts onto the band track. He cuts it so HOT and overmodulated he sounds like he's in Mammoth Cave. The song makes his teacher grab his/her boogie board and hit the heavies off Westhampton Beach – realizing three of the greatest reasons for teaching – June, July, and August (psst – educators' secret). Nice blend, "Bang." Committed to the drumming passion, Rundgren's drummer-hero starts out as a flub-a-dub kid with a stick and coffee can and a dream. From his school desk, he ambles into the Thunder Pumpkins Garage Band. He bypasses the Work Gospel workadaddy format. He shoots through to the RICH & FAMOUS plateau in one fell swoop. Who needs 9-to-5? Isn't it better to be Bugs Bunny, free and cool and funny, than fussy fop Elmer Fudd? Next stop: ELVIS Spotlight.

"Gold" – John Stewart, #5, 6-79. Folk stars the KINGSTON TRIO – inventors of the album – did a Heavy Metal tune? **John Stewart,** anyway. In the aftermath of Dave Guard bolting for the Whiskey Hill Singers, Stewart arrived to write and sing frequent lead, with his resonant baritone and Hollywood looks. Wooing comely lass **Stevie Nicks** (Fleetwood Mac) to bewitchingly harmonize on his self-penned showbiz expose, Stewart pinch-hit Lindsey Buckingham's guitar and harmony fills – and a big airy rocking Fender Rhodes keyboard (see Doors). With the Trio ('61-'67), his vibrant vocals bounced off **Bob Shane's** deeper, raspier baritone, and **Nick Reynolds'** high baritone in the tenorless troubadours' troupe. Stewart's only previous solo solo thwacked #74, 9-69 "Armstrong" to the moon (our intrepid astronaut hero).

Since Mac's AI. *Rumours* clutched #1 for 31 unreal weeks, commandeering 1977, GOLD struck John Stewart. John already penned Monkees' monster #1(4) 11-67 "Daydream Believer" (#12, '79 Anne Murray). Back in '65, 21,000 singles were released per year by companies big enough to show up on lists. Today, many hotshot artists don't even bother with mini-profit SINGLES – they leap to gonzo ALBUMS. Of 21,000 singles, only 15 or 20 sit atop the #1 peak annually. If your band is with MCA or Columbia or Polygram or RSO, like Stewart (b. '39 San Diego), you've got at least a snowball's chance in Hell. If you're with Warthog Records or Ernie's Dad's Basement, or Joe Potatoes' Garage Studio label, good luck . . . Unlike myriads of rags-to-rags stumblebums, who fumbled with out-of-key voices and fuzzbuster crackly amps, Stewart metamorphosed R & R dreams into gold. Sliding minor keys, "Gold" struts keyboards and suggests the wavy Beach Boys' "California Girls" mood. Stewart's macho arena voice is powerful and commanding. He returned on the "Midnight Wind" (#28, 9-79), but the San Diegan "Lost Her in the Sun" (#34, 1-80). Gold dust in the wind.

"All Right Now" – Free, #4, 8-70. Tetsu Yamauchi played bass for this Heavy Metal/Hard Rock British crew in the afterglow of this monster hit (1972, replaced Andy Fraser). One of the greatest R & R rampagers of all time. Free scored on effervescent vocals of Paul Rodgers (with the Firm & Jimmy Page, #28, 2-85 "Radioactive"). Hmm, missing . . . lots of Asian or Asian-American R & R stars. No good reason.

"Black Star Oblivion" – Loudness, NC, '86. Japan's **Loudness** is powered by the lightning flashpoint fingers of **Akira Takasaki** (AI. #64, 5-86 *Lightning Strikes*). **Minoru Niiharu** booms the banshee-style lead vocal in universal Rock language English (how many Americans speak Japanese?). Masters of their instruments? Bassist Masayoshi Yamashita and drummer Munetaka Higuchi. From Gretsch in Brooklyn, Fender in NYC, and Gibson in Michigan's Kalamazoo, Japan's Yamaha or Sony wrested the action away from American bankers' shores. Without Japanese genius at electronics, the world might be hacking at ersatz amps of crackly old tubes and staticky terminal feedback. Berry Gordy's engineers recorded the whole canon of 1959-65 Motown hits on a simple 4-track recording machine. "Black Star Oblivion" will never be "Elevator Muzak." It begins on a Mt. Fujiyama explosion and gets louder and LOUDER and LOUDER!!! Earmuffs optional. Higuchi's supersonic bass scubas the toasty bottom. Niihara's gonzo Ginza tenor trades heavenly stairways with Robert Plant.

"Runnin' with the Devil" – Van Halen, #84, 5-78. Remember Blues guru **Robert Johnson's** spurious pact with the Devil, at "Crossroads" Highway 61 in Delta-land Clarksdale, Mississippi? Or Charlie Daniels' #3, 6-79 "Devil Went Down to Georgia"? Or the Stones' "Sympathy for the Devil"? **Eddie Van Halen** (b. Nijmegen, Netherlands, 1-26-57) toys with the ultimate underworld speed merchant and outruns him on the high frets of his smoking guitar. Heavy Metal often focuses on the lead guitarist [like Jimmy Page] as much or more than the lead singer (Van Halen's **David Lee Roth,** b. 10-10-55, Indiana). Van Halen metallically covered Classic Rock's #1 '64 Roy Orbison "(Oh) Pretty Woman" to #12, 2-82, and Martha/Vandellas/Motown #2, '63 "Dancin in the Street" to #38, 5-82. Their steamy video "Hot for Teacher" hit #56 HOT 100, 5-84. A classroom of lusty libidos leers upon the charms of their young teacher. They hit with #15, 4-79 "Dance the Night Away" and #13's '84 "Panama" and "I'll Wait."

Van Halen (left to right)
Alex Van Halen, David Lee Roth,
Eddie Van Halen and Michael Anthony

"Jump" – Van Halen, #1(5), 1-84. Wow. First Eddie married lovely actress Valerie Bertinelli in 1981, and then he and Roth and bassist Michael Anthony and drummer brother Alex Van Halen jumped to #1. Then Roth jumped ship: #3, 1-85 "California Girls" [Beach Boy Carl Wilson, harmonizer]; and #1 Album Rock solo song "Just Like Paradise" at #6, 1-88. **Sammy Hagar (**b. 10-13-47, Monterey, CA) took over on lead throat. "Jump" is one of the first Heavy Metal songs to crunch the chart apex. The TITLE "Jump"went to #1(8) again with **Kris Kross**'s 4-92 tune (#2 R & B); they're a JUNIOR HIGH Rap crew (b. '78, '79) of Chris 'Mack Daddy' Kelly and Chris 'Daddy Mack' Smith.

Brothers Eddie and Alex bizarrely flipped early from drums to guitar. The real action, in Van Halen, is in the fulminating volcanic rush of Eddie's fire & brimstone leads.

"Why Can't This Be Love?" – Van Halen, #3, 3-86. Hagar's bronze here presaged #5, 7-88 "When It's Love." His 1985-96 stint included #13, 10-88 "Finish What You Started," #27, 10-91 "Top of the World," and double 22's of '86, "Dreams" and "Love Walks In." "Can't Stop Lovin' You" hit #30 in 8-95. Van Halen's album chart numbers reflect their Led Zep NUMBERING system for albums. Unlike simpler Beatles"#1(8+) Al, 12-2000 titled *1* [One], they swooped to #1(3) and #1(4) in '86 and '88 with names like Al. *7550* and Al. *OU812*. This Dutch double-whammy brother crew, and singers? MAJOR Metal guys. In May 2001, Eddie was sidetracked with big health problems.

***To Hell with the Devil* – Stryper, Al. #32, 11-86.** Christian-oriented California Metal group – brother Michael (singer) and Robert (drums) Sweet. Guitar guy? **OX**

FOX (Rich Martinez). Tim Gaines, bass (Whitburn). They hit #23 in 11-87 with "Honestly," and won't be "Runnin' with the Devil." Their **Amy Grant/Michael W. Smith** type titles include #88, 11-88 "I Believe in You" and #71, 7-88 "Always There for You." Christian Rock? Also see Pat Boone, Zao, Religious Chapter, or **Creed**. Creed's #5+, 2002 "My Sacrifice" uses the same haunting and bizarre beat as Led Zeppelin's "Kashmir."

"Dr. Feelgood" – Mötley Crüe, #6, 9-89. One of America's premier Metal bands, Crüe's **Mick Mars** and **Vince Neil Wharton** and **Nikki Sixx** and **Tommy Lee Bass** found some gorgeous girlfriends. Bass married Heather Locklear, and Sixx married *Playboy* Playmate Brandi Brandt. Neil then married mud wrestler Sharisse Rudell. "Home Sweet Home" is the title of a 19th-century blockbuster by peripatetic Long Island John Howard Payne, but the same title hit #89, 10-85. Revamp "Home Sweet Home '91" rose to #37, 11-91.

Their other top tenner "Without You" of 2-90 marched to number eight, followed by girlwatching #12, 5-87 "Girls, Girls, Girls." Crüe's album exploits are legion: Al. #1(2), 9-89 *Dr. Feelgood*; Al. #2(1), 6-87 *Girls, Girls, Girls*; #2(1), 10-91 *Decade of Decadence;* and their eponymous #7, 4-94 *Mötley Crüe.*

"Love Bites" – Def Leppard, #1(1), 8-88. Remember J. Geils' #38, 4-80 "Love Stinks"? Sheffield's Midlands Metallurgists Def Leppard stroked the cynicism on love gone bad. Unlike Mellencamp's Heartland Rock #2, 4-82 "Hurts So Good," offering a bonus 'love bite' between handclaps, Leppard's bite is feistier. Astounding wounded drummer **Rick Allen** had a slightly better New Year's Eve (12-31-84) than teen idol **Ricky Nelson** (12-31-85, killed in plane crash) or **Hank Williams Sr.** (1-1-53, died at 29 in back of Cadillac, substances); Allen tragically lost his left arm in a car accident, and never gave up hope he'd anchor Def Leppard's rhythm section. With grim fortitude, he returned to his drum gizmo. He re-learned and compensated for his lost arm with new fancy footwork and flabbergasting practice sessions. He is a profile in courage for every rock musician, and anyone with a disability.

Three top tunes sparked their debut year, 1983: #12 "Photograph," #16 "Rock of Ages," and #28 "Foolin'." **Joe Elliott** sang lead, with Steve Clark (d. '91, substances) and Phil Collen on guitars. Rick Savage on bass. Elliott's elan blasted hits like #10, 1-88 "Hysteria," #2(1) 4-88 "Pour Some Sugar on Me," #12, 3-89 "Rocket," and #15, 4-92 "Let's Get Rocked." Their "Animal" crested at #19, 10-87, and "Two Steps Behind" at #12, 9-93. Albums are the big story: #1(6) Al 8-87 *Hysteria* hit sextuple platinum (6M), with #1(5), 4-92 *Adrenalize* quintuplinizing five million fans; *Slang* hit #14, 6-96, and *Pyromania* #2(2), 2-83.

"Here I Go Again" – Whitesnake, #1(1), 7-87. Supergroup defines a collection of stars from different great bands. With Deep Purple's **David Coverdale** and keyboarder **Jon Lord**, Whitesnake added **Aynsley Dunbar** on drums. Their metallic Rock and Roll mission nearly accomplished, they glommed one of the top guitarists anywhere – **Steve Vai**. This Anglo-American Metal crew's guitarist (b. Carle Place, Long Island) studied under the tutelage of **Joe Satriani** (Al. #23, 11-89 *Flying in a Blue Dream,* and nifty-titled Al. #29, 11-87 ***Surfing with the Alien).*** Satriani also taught **Metallica's** Kirk Hammett. Both Vai and Hammett made great speeches in Guitarese. Listen to the Guitarese eloquence of Hendrix or Clapton or Townshend or Page or Slash or Van Halen. Or the Ventures' Bob Bogle, or **Duane Eddy** or Ricky Nelson's James Burton, or Gene Vincent's Cliff Gallup

Some moneyless Johnny B. Goode kid in Mongolia or Tierra del Fuego or Novaya Zemlya or Kenya snags a transistor and a grubby guitar. Maybe he'll become the next Ricky Martin or Bruce Springsteen (or Janie B. Goode may become Destiny's Child). Rock and Roll is a groundswell guerrilla army of passion, pyrotechnics, and power. International Heavy Metal is so strong it bashes the shackles, melts the prison bars, unleashes the lost hope, and frees the enslaved mind to the swooning glories of freedom. In 1990, the leaden St. Petersburg skies (formerly Leningrad) of Vladimir LENIN fell to the musical swath of JOHN Lennon. Russian and Chinese kids now frazzle their folks' leaden state muzak with frantic Rap and Thrash. No longer must they drone a humdrum cheerless dirge. The Rebel Rouser ?

"Forty Miles of Bad Road" – Duane Eddy and His Twangy Guitar, #9, 6-59; #17, 7-79 R & B. Whereas most lead-guitar stars now play their rockin' riffs on the high-fret strings, Eddy crushed the LOW ones. He nailed that deep BASS note, and his growly twang punctured the silence like thunder. Surrounded by the scruffy-sax-sound trio of stars Johnson, Douglas, and, of course, HORN, Eddy pulverized the blotchy pavement. This Construction Zone Instrumental reminds us all of one thing; Metal may have superior guitarists to those of the 50s, but they still haven't figured out a method to get the singer to stay silent for maybe 3 ½ minutes out of four so their hot guitars can scorch the sky. Duane's twangy guitar nabs the 'Leppard's' share of the song – with wild Rebel whoops and yips dotting the quiet airtime.

In the early 60's and beyond, **Bob Bogle's Ventures** featured a Surf Rock instrumental sound for his guitar wizardry on songs like the #4, 3-69 theme from "Hawaii Five-O." First Seattle 'Metal' band. After **Eddy**'s modest success #72, 3-58 "Movin' N' Groovin," he cut loose with the spitfire #6, 6-58 "Rebel Rouser" and the cannonade serenade #27, 8-58 "Ramrod" and #15, 11-58 "Cannonball." "Bonnie Came Back" at #26 launched the Beatles' first release "My Bonnie," a Scots' Folk Waltz we sang as kindergarteners in 1949. Eddy cashed in on the Go-Go fad before Johnny Rivers with #12, 10-62 "(Dance with the) Guitar Man." Eddy's #23, 1-59 "The Lonely One" presages by three days 'The Day the Music Died," and became the BBC theme song for their 1961 R & R Show via Radio Luxembourg, which EVERY British rock hopeful listened to as the 60s dawned. Heavy Metal? Maybe Eddy invented it . . .

"Once Bitten Twice Shy" – Great White, #5, 5-89. Great dog cliche for singer whose name IS a scrappy breed of 15# British terrier – **Jack Russell.** Off 5-89 Al. . . .

Twice Shy at #9, they combine two critters unbeatable at potential ferocity, pound for pound – this mini-dog and the marauding Great White Shark. This L.A. Hard Rock crew delivers a straight-ahead Rock and Roll song. Their "Angel Song" hit #30, 9-89. The bassman's name is equally Hollywood: TONY MONTANA .

"Wind of Change" – Scorpions, #4, 6-91. Rarely do you find a Heavy Metal coagulation named the PRETTY BUNNIES, the CUTESY KITTIES, the HONEYTONE HAMSTERS, or the TWIRLY BURPY NERDY BIRDIES. Maybe the burp. Heavy Metal volume merchants are named for anything very hard to cuddle. Among the most international of R & R success storied, Hanover, Germany's **Scorpions** produced the Euro metallic fury of twin brothers Michael and Rudolf Schenker (b. '52). Their #5, 5-88 Al. *Savage Amusement* and #6, 3-84 *Love at First Sting* spiked the charts, and #25, 3-82 "Rock You Like a Hurricane" is their penultimate single success.

TWINS time. Probably the most famous R & R twins are Maurice and Robin Gibb (b. 12-22-49) of the **Bee Gees.** ROBIN sang most of their Pre-Disco leads in their 1st British Invasion heyday (1967-72), like #11, 11-11-67's "Massachusetts."

"Hold Me Now" – Thompson Twins, #3, 2-84. Not only are these Techno-Synth Rockers not Heavy Metal guys – they're not even TWINS (see Statler 'Brothers'). Britrock trio. NEW ZEALANDER (a R & R Kiwi rarity) Alannah Currie does XYLOPHONE (another R & R rarity) and percussion; **Tom Bailey** does synthesizer and lead throat; Conga drum and twin synthesizer guy is Joe Leeway. Bouncy, in-control sound: #6, 9-85 "Lay Your Hands on Me," #8, 1-86 "King for a Day," and #11, 5-84 "Doctor! Doctor!" Twins?

"Twins" – Pete Mervenne & Kingtones, NC, 1963. [#20, WKNR Keener Countdown, Detroit; #1, Lansing, MI]. Before fertility drugs, twins occurred once every 100 births. "Twins" is possibly the greatest TWINS song of all time. When our Night Shift/Woolies had the Thursday gig at Okemos' Coral Gables Bar, the Friday regular Kingtones mashed the Michigan market, but got squashed by national distribution. With a sensational voice melding the best of **Ritchie Valens'** "La Bamba" trills, **Buddy Holly**'s "Peggy Sue" glottal stops, and **Del Shannon/ Roy Orbison**'s dramatic crescendo power, French-American Pete Mervenne plunked this tableau about his doozy TWINS snafu.

Seems he's in love with this one identical twin – but can't figure out *which,* because they're uncannily identical. A kick-bun spitfire rhythm guitar crackles and doubles the bass riff. "Twins" throbs with ultra Heavy Metal thundertones. Pete's lilting '63 lyric boasts a comic macho conclusion. He scrambles his amorous urges, and makes out with BOTH twins. His conclusion? Whatever's great fun with *one* is – you guessed it – twice as much study fun with TWO beauties. Mervenne cut this in an old abandoned movie theatre in Sparta, Michigan, in Shannon's shadow (our Night Shift cut the Lost Tapes here: "Hitchhikin'", "Whispering Winds"). Pete's flip side, "Have Good Faith," is a breathtaking early salvo of Blue-Eyed Soul, before Eric Burdon, Mitch Ryder, or the Righteous Brothers. When Mervenne begins into his masterful 16th-note *melisma* fusillade, the monster-reverb Hammond B-3 organ cruises atop the sound. Due to defunct rack jobbers, weak promo, and a small label (Derry), **Mervenne & Kingtones** (not Kingsmen), and thousands of other great bands, never became the stars they so richly deserved to become. Sometimes fate, kismet, karma, etc., is like a vacuum cleaner or lamprey.

The biggest early-rock actual twin act was the **Kalin Twins**, Harold and Herb, of Port Jervis, NY (b. '34). With amazing Everly echoes (see Simon & Gar/'Tom & Jerry'), they blasted "When" to #5, 6-58, and "Forget Me Not" to #12, 9-52. Non-twin **Travis & Bob** hit #8, 3-59 with Everlyish "Tell Him No." Twins again?

"(Can't Live Without Your) Love and Affection" – Nelson, #1(1), 7-90. In the doleful aftermath of Dad **Ricky Nelson's** (Rock Hall '87) New Year's Eve '85 plane crash, his Norwegian-American twin sons carried on his superstardom. Like Debbie Boone/Pat Boone/Red Foley, it's a rare tri-generational fame. Ricky's boys hammered the top 20 thrice with bassist **Gunnar** and rhythm-axe slinger **Matthew** (b. '67): #6, 11-90 "After the Rain" and moderately-metallic #14, 3-91 "More Than Ever." The handsome Nordic-blond lads favor Ricky's TV-star *"Ozzie & Harriet"* folks, **Harriet Hilliard Nelson**, Big Band vocalist, and **Ozzie Nelson** (1907-75). All three generations were major stars. "White Sails (Beneath a Yellow Moon)" hit #2(2), 7-39 with Ozzie's easygoing baritone; Harriet chips in vocals on #15, 12-39 "Who Told You That I Cared" (hmmm – *Beverly Hills 90210* sarcastic attitude, Pre-War). Teaneck, NY, and Hollywood Ozzie's amazing band scored 38 Top 20 tunes in Ozzie's 1930-40 FIRST [Pre-Ozzy Osbourne/Black Sabbath] **Blizzard of Ozz** decade.

Any TRIPLET triumphs? No quadruplets/quintuplets/sextuplets. In 1986, triplets Diana, Sylvia, and Vicky Villegas of Mexico, says Whitburn, won an *MTV Basement Tapes* contest. A scanty five years later, their threefold romance blossomed into the **Triplets'** #14, 3-91, "You Don't Have to Go Home Tonight." Psst – what's the 1st Britrock R & R record to smack the American Heartland at the #1 spot? Nope – not the Fab Four, but their Scottish vanguard.

"Telstar" – Tornadoes, #1(3), 11-62; #1, 9-62, U.K. Keyboard wonder Roger LaVern soared aloft on a hypnotic *musitron*-sounding organ, like the American reaction to Russia's satellite Sputnik – satellite **Telstar.** Norman Hale also keyboarded their Scottish Surf Rock otherworldly wheezy, breezy #1 hit. Heinz Burt on bass. "Ridin' the Wind" hit #63, 2-63. Beatle preludes. In the U.K., 'tornado' is almost untranslatable.

Marc Storace sang lead on "School's Out" (#67, 6-86) and #25 Al. 4-83 *Headhunter* for **Krokus** of Zurich, Switzerland, with **Freddy Steady** bashing drums and the

Van Arb/Kiefer guitarslinger team trading off with the roaring bass of Chris Von **Rohr.** It's the same flower in German/Swiss, where K = C. Crocuses jump out of the March snow like gangbusters. Rock and Roll dreamers are like crocuses. We risk it all to burst forth out of the snow to reach the sunshine – a resurrection of hope, beauty, and good ol' Rock and Roll.

"Smoke on the Water" – Pat Boone, NC, '97. Huh? **Boone** (b. Charles Boone, '34, FL, Christian Soft Rock crooner) doing Heavy Metal? You kidding? Sort of. It's actually his own wild hybrid genre – JAZZ METAL. "My wife hates Heavy Metal," Boone says, "so I just cruise around with my car speakers up high." Clad in leather, and astride a burly Harley bike, Pat's 1997 phase sported fake dimestore tattoos, but REAL biceps (yep, 62 years old). With an eclectic bunch of Jazz greats, Boone's '97 *In a Metal Mood* features **Elvis's** straight-laced rival Boone in hot leather, with a four-pointed star shining fiercely out of his hazel right eye.

Boone's Deep Purple "Smoke on the Water" tribute sounds nothing like Jazz, nothing like Metal. It's a wild new Cabaret Biker-Bar Be-Bop Soft Metal synthesis only Pat could concoct. He fashions a Jazz WALTZ out of Zep's "Stairway to Heaven," a haunted Hendrix "Wind Cries Mary," and a swingin' version of his golf pard Alice Cooper's "No More Mr. Nice Guy." With *chutzpah* (for a Crooner), Pat shakes up Contemporary Christians and Satan worshippers alike. The shock value flashpoint of his amazing album dumbfounded music critics in all areas. Nobody ever told them what to believe about Jazz Metal, so they clammed up, treading quagmire in the blobbo kiddie pool of Dynamic Wishy-Washyism. Boone scorches chart segregation, and I admire his vision and enjoy his new sound, though it's certainly unique. His "Enter Sandman" echoes both the #1(7), 10-54 Chordettes' "Mr. Sandman" and Metal icons **Metallica:**

"Enter Sandman" – Metallica, #16, 8-91. Gloomy nightmare lullaby from incredible singer **James Hetfield.** Drummer **Lars Ulrich** and Speed Metal guitar legend **Kirk Hammett** relay the ominous message with Grim[m] Fairy-Tale monsters lurking in closets of terror. Metallica's dark theme of UNEASE pervades their Greatest Hits. As we illustrated in the War Rock chapter, their classic #35, 2-89 "One" tells the grisly tale of a poor wounded soldier. An exploding shell metamorphosed him into a faceless chunk of pulsing protoplasm, praying for his own release and death from his limbless, sightless, hellish limbo. "One" is from Dalton Trumbo's banned antiwar novel of 1917 WWI, *Johnny Got His Gun.* The hapless victim of World War 'One' dreams that the cosmic 'Sandman' will spell surcease of his death-purgatory agonies. Metallica's top 20- follow-up "Enter Sandman" arrives beyond their Zazula early stage, and paints a nightmarish dreamscape of nothingness in the abyss. Bassman **Cliff Burton** was killed (24, icy Swedish road, '86) when the bus flipped, and landed atop the thrown-out Burton, who was sent reeling from slumber to eternity down the tragic embankment. The band had played cards to determine who would sleep in Cliff's upper bunk . [Ritchie Valens 'won' the coin toss to ride in Buddy Holly's ill-fated plane in '59]. Burton drew the **Ace of Spades** [Paul Lengyel story]. For Burton, the advent of the entering sandman coincided with the unwelcome entrance of the Grim Reaper. Or, via another Metallica title – "Fade to Black."

Metallica rules – this is the Power Rock litany of millions. Burton died before Metallica careened into platinum superstar status. Replacement **Jason Newsted** fills in admirably. Metallica appeals to everybody, but especially to a world of young men raised on hamburger jobs (2 ½ at a time), dwindling economic opportunity, and the computerization of a techno world flaring amok. Their other hits include #34, 3-92 "Nothing Else Matters," #35, 12-91 "The Unforgiven" [#59, 4-98 too], highest-hit #10, 6-96 "Until It Sleeps," and Brit-Invasion flashback with **Marianne Faithfull**, #28, 4-98 "The Memory Remains," followed by Zen-titled #96, 3-2000 "No Leaf Clover." Beyond the choppy singles success, Metallica's forte is ALBUMS, beginning with Al. #28, 8-87 *The $5.98 E.P.: Garage Days Revisited.* [An E.P., or Extended Play, was a four-song hybrid between a single and an album in the 50s – singles 99 cents, E.P.s $1.49, albums $4.99]. Their monster breakthrough album? #9, 9-88 Al. *And Justice for All.*

The title cut, " . . . And Justice for All," echoes the Pledge of Allegiance. In literate angst, they match the erudite Simon & Garfunkel in an allusion contest. Metallica's *Webster's* firebomb vocabulary features 'animosity, overpower, premonition, expiration, schizophrenia,' and Britishly spelled 'smouldering.' Not your dime-a-dozen Bubble Gum Bopper words. They quote Emerson, and ply the Stygian waters of Lethe and the River of Death. Metallica here surfs black broiling tidal waves of despair, destruction, and doom. It's a fun promenade through gardens of darkfall gloom. "Blackened" laments the "Death of Mother Earth." "Harvester of Sorrow" features a suffocated life smothered by hate-seeds (A+ metaphor). In "The Frayed Ends of Sanity," he wobbles over twisted schizophrenia.

" . . . And Justice for All" hobbles on a morose 'E' note that splatters happiness like a mosquito. Now and then they alight on an F#, as Hammett hammers guitar, and Newsted's bass spews similar splotches of speed-demon notes. Ulrich's snarly snare jars any listeners' ex-relaxation with his slashes of slam-dunk rhythmic power. Hetfield, aloft on his craggy Hulk Hogan baritone bonanza, commits mayhem on Muzak-mongers. He decries our lack of true justice anywhere. Metallica's volcanic fulminations show their strident, atonal, deliberately cacophonic side. Hetfield rails against society's unjust power base. "One" concerns a legless, armless soldier, lolling in hospital, praying amorphously for Dr. Kevorkian's euthanasia release. Birdy, chirpy, sweet arpeggios fly away. Hammett's grim Rock symphony is a thunderous barrage of staccato guitars that simulate the machine-gun terror of the victim's last adventure. Ulrich doubles paradiddles. Newsted's bass staggers, at Speed Metal rapid fire. Hammett's guitar bleeds the horror of the victim's personal

Apocalypse, Now. Metallica's album success is legion: #1(4), 8-91 *Metallica;* and #1(4), 6-96 *Load,* with 12M+ Metallica fans plunking down their ex-cash.

In their zeal to rescue youth and the planet from oppression, they make a lot of money on the side. How MUCH? A 1995-96 1½ year survey discovered they made 28 Million Bucks. **Kiss** actually topped the Metal Department with 35 mil. **Oprah Winfrey** (b. Mississippi, '54), beloved entertainer, topped the richest entertainer-of-the-survey-years with $171M. Other R & R stars? Beatles, $130M; Michael Jackson, $90M; Stones $77M; Eagles $75M; Garth Brooks 51M; John Travolta (movies too, $33M), Mariah Carey 32M.

Buddy Holly, Ritchie Valens, and the Big Bopper died because they had to hop a plane to do their LAUNDRY when the grubby unheated bus broke down in arctic Iowa. Many 1959 stars got ripped off by duck-and-run profiteers, palladium plug-uglies, sleight-of-hand sharks, and their best friends. In the current Rock and Roll world, second-line stars have many of Buddy's financial woes, owing monster companies for recording time and bus gas . . .

"Enter Sandman." **Chuck Berry** avoided the nightmare by dumping all the entourage, flying light with guitar (no amp), and thriftily paying local back-up bands. Millionaire singer R & B singer **Toni Braxton** (#1[11], 10-96 "Un-Break My Heart") declared bankruptcy, prompting a draconian 2001 new law lobbied by the banking industry, to make it very hard for any of us to follow her suit in catastrophic financial circumstances. *Gold Rush* avoids most money issues. We do music here.

"Symphony of Destruction" – Megadeth, #71, 10-92. Metallica's Dave Mustaine (singer, guitarist) bolted the band in '82 to form Megadeth. Named for the 50-megaton A-bombs designed by Albert Einstein and Werner Von Braun in WWII to kill mega-millions, Megadeth rampaged the *Billboard* 200 album chart: #2(1), Al. 8-92 *Countdown to Extinction*; #4 stun-pun 11-94 *Youthanasia.*

Queensryche's #9, 3-91 "Silent Lucidity" features Scott ROCKenfeld, Geoff Tate, and Eddie Jackson from Bellevue,Washington; #3, 11-94 Al. *Promised Land* echoes the *Bible,* and **Chuck Berry.**

***Screaming for Vengeance* – Judas Priest, Al. #17, 8-82.** Named for savvy euphemism for taking Jesus's full name in vain (defying Judeo-Christian First Commandment). Singer Rob Halford and guitar whizzes Glenn Tipton and K.K. Downing rode to fame on *British Steel* (Al. #34, 7-80 debut). Judas Iscariot, we recall, won few fans for his betrayal of Jesus for 30 silver coins; Judas hanged himself.

Cut-loose head-banging hordes thrill to the screaming electric Power Metal of myriad bands. Among these pioneers and princes of power? Swedish speedish Metalman **Yngwie Malmsteen.** Or **Rod Argent** of **Zombies** and Argent to Al. #23, 9-72 *All Together Now.* Or Lemmy Kilmister's 1977 (#174, 5-82 Al. *Iron Fist)* **&** **Motorhead.** **Werewolves,** maybe, those 1978 groovy ghoulies howling hairily to the spooky moon. Or the Curt Rotterdam/ Jim Harrison concoction **Iron Eggplant.** Can anyone forget Jim Lea (bass, violin, vocals) and Noddy Holder's **Slade**, and #33 Al. 6-84 *Keep Your Hands off My Power Supply?* Or Japan's Kyoji Yamamoto's **Bow Wow** [not Bow Wow Wow]? Or Dave Wall's Kerouac-inspired **Desolation Angels?**

How about Canadian Metal guys? Kurt Smith's **Alpha Centauri** [nearest star to Sun, 4+ light years away]. Miles Goodwin's Montreal **April Wine** (Al. #26, '81, *The Nature of the Beast*).

Recall **Jorma Kaukonen's** archaeozoic **Hot Tuna (Al. #30, 8-70)?** Or **Black Oak Arkansas** (#25, 12-73 "Jim Dandy"), who combined Southern Rock/Heavy Metal? Before Van Halen, **Sammy Hagar** already mangled Metal anonymity with Al. #17, 1-83 *Three Lock Box.* Remember Steve Marriott's incredible **Humble Pie,** with Metal album #6, 4-72 *Smokin'*? Or **Dave Peverett's** (d. 2000) album-bonanza **Foghat** with #11, 9-77 Al. *Foghat Live?*

"Sweet Child O' Mine" – Guns N' Roses, #1(2), 6-88.
Between Irish tenor Axl Rose and tightrope guitar maestro Saul 'SLASH' Hudson, Guns N' Roses challenged for the Prettiest Metal Melody of All Time (if that's a compliment). Choir boy nor moral paragon is Axl (B. '62, IN). He sizzles the banshee high notes, accompanied by shimmering arpeggios from Slash's flashy guitar. "Sweet Child" dances on Slash's music-box octaves. No beat intrudes until 2nd-string guitar Izzy Stradlin plays off the high bass runs of Michael 'Duff' McKagan. Then . . . a hint of beat. Stephen Adler whispers a sniggling snare into the fray, then bashes the Slash solo with his eighth-note jubilee. In "C#," McKagan duels Adler. By the time Axl's verdant tenor notes hit Killarney's emerald hills and Galway Bay, you already love the song. **David Bowie** had to change his 'David Jones' name to avoid getting mixed-up with Monkee Davy Jones. Axl Rose's REAL name William Bailey led off the 20th century Hit Parade:

"Bill Bailey, Won't You Please Come Home" – Dan Quinn, #2(2), 2-1902. Arthur Collins' #1 hit, "Bill Bailey" nabbed #2 for Waltz King **Dan Quinn** (1859-1938). Quinn and **George Gaskin** and Len Spencer had all those HITS on those 'Great 1890s Songs We Love to Sing' [& forget who sang them]. Remember Dan's East Side and West Side odyssey, all over town on the #1(9), 2-1895 "Sidewalks of New York"?

Dan's #1(7), 12-1896 "A Hot Time in the Old Town" – or the marches of John Philip Sousa – were about the Heaviest Metal of the 19th century (often the bass player's 'metal' was a TUBA or Sousaphone). Steamy and spluttering with spunk and pizzazz, "Hot Time" celebrates life in NYC's Old Bowery, where poverty was no excuse for a down-in-the-dumps mood (see Rap chap.).

"Sweet Rosie O' Grady" – George J. Gaskin, #1(8), 4-1897. Yep, the original spare Irish anthem on the GRAPHOPHONE. Records were metal cylinders, and GRAMOPHONE grooves gouged deep. Beloved hits scratchily played, over and over and over. Piano-oriented. Key of 'C' – down to **A7, D7, G7,** back to **C.** Gaskin's greatest goodies? #1(3) "My Wild Irish Rose"; wedding mainstay #1(8), 3-1893 "O Promise Me"; and sentimental

#1(6), 1-1896 "The Sunshine of Paradise Alley."

Len Spencer's "Ta Ra Ra Boom Der E" of #1(8), 1-1892 also may be the first Rock and Roll song. A German-American OOM-PAH item. Len's mom was a top suffragist and his dad invented a penmanship system ['Spencerian Method'] and got rich. Spencer's reprise of Stephen Foster's 1850 "OLDIE" "Old Folks at Home" hit #1(6), 8-1892. He also did racially-insensitive ditties called 'Coon Songs' that I won't dignify by reprinting titles.

Who had the longest consecutive streak of #1 hits on the MAIN Pop Charts? **Dan Quinn.** He debuted in 1892 – his five-year streak gave him TWELVE (12) all-#1 hits in a row. Three R & R centuries, Dan's record still stands.

"Welcome to the Jungle" – Guns N' Roses, #7, 10-88.
After his short-lived marriage to Erin Everly, Axl hit the news with antics that hit the press, the fans, and the charts. Sales-wise, no problem. Axl knew about sweet chromatic chords on "Sweet Child" (bVII), and he uses the distortion pedal. At the song's end, when Slash's super solo simmers, they trail off into a lurching baritone. They all ask where they're all going . . . the question is almost cosmic. Like Gaskin's skid-row torch tune about Paradise Alley above, Guns goes to #5, 1-89 "Paradise City." Other G & R? #10, 9-91 "Don't Cry"; Jimmy Beaumont/Skyliners reprise (#12, '59) "Since I Don't Have You" to #69, 3-94; McCartney Death Rock #33, 12-91 "Live and Let Die" (#2, '73 Wings).

"November Rain" – Guns N' Roses—#3, 6-92. Breathtaking Metal balladry. Echoes Elvis's #16, 2-70 "Kentucky Rain" or Del Shannon's #1 '61 "Runaway" drizzle hike. You know all three of these solo R & R pilgrims are on the same lonely road going nowhere. Elvis frantically asks old Kentucky general-store crackerbarrel philosophers, older than the hills, as to where the fugitive girl went. In their dotage, they stare at him befuddledly. Metal pioneer Del Shannon watches bright headlights stab streetlight shadows. Icy sleet asks the midnight hiker why the girl ran away, and where she'll stay – Del's little lost 'Runaway.' Axl married Don Everly's daughter Erin, but she filed for divorce 21 days later.

"November Rain" is a great song about loss and grief and desolation. On this ballad, no one gets squished in the mosh pit. Slash's fiery axe cross-cuts the beat, in a crossfire of ethereal Metal splendor, counterpointing Axl's vocal flight. Axl hits the Merge onto the High Lonesome Hank Williams Freeway.

"November Rain" renders a personal moment of grief for Axl Rose into one of the best elegiac tributes in Rock since "American Pie." I have taught Rock History at the college level into my fourth decade. My favorite assignment takes students' Hit Parades. They select their top ten tunes ever, give me 30-second taped excerpts, and 50-100 words per tune on why they love them. "November Rain" was selected by my students for your Rock UnCyclopedia here. I knew the song was very good; gazillions of them showed me it was great. "November Rain" is dreary and uplifting all at once. A Metal masterpiece. [Voted #5 video of all time, *VH-1*].

"Hard to Handle" – Black Crowes, #45, 10-90, and #26, 6-91. My old friend Lt. Jim Cook, of Atlanta and Vietnam, and wife DeeEllen, are proud parents of a daughter who married one of the Black Crowes. Unfortunately, I copied down the names of Jim's horses (Mari Legs and Perk Up) by mistake, and lost which Crowe the kid married. One of these: Chris or brother Rich 'Guitar' Robinson, Jeff Cease, Steve Gorman, Marc Ford, or Johnny Colt. The Black Crowes' #30 "She Talks to Angels" hit big, as did Al. #1(1), 5-92 *The Southern Harmony and Musical Companion.* Named after a Dixie hymnbook, there are not hymnists nor 'black,' but a Southern Rock/Hard Rock Atlanta crew whose Al. *Shake Your Money Maker* nailed #4, '90.

"Dream On" – Aerosmith, #59, 10-73, & #6, 1-76. Can you picture lanky **Steven Tyler** (b. Steven Tallarico, 3-25-48) coming from Sunapee, New Hampshire? It's a Currier & Ives town of 975 happy souls, hard by the indigo shores of five-mile-long Lake Sunapee in the Sunapee Mountains. Morning mists burnish red-gold autumn maple splendor. I see Aerosmith's Tyler crashing the R & R ramparts from South Detroit, or East St. Louis, or East Brooklyn, or stockyard Chicago. OK, there is some Back Bay Boston in his background. A voice that can writhe and rumble and cry with anguish and agony and joy like that has got to have eaten Smoke and Steel Flakes for breakfast. With nails for raisins.

If you seek prudish passionless lyrics, ditch your Aerosmith CDs now. "Dream On" is the cutting edge of frantic Heavy Metal, with guitar gurus **Joe Perry** and Brad Whitford on guitars. Tom Hamilton anchors bass, Joey Kramer drums. Aside from Perry's five-year sabbatical in the 1979-84 zone, Aerosmith remained reasonably intact for a generation. Discovered in the Bostonian Fenway fens, playing local *Cheers* pubs, Aerosmith split for NYC's Kansas City Club. Columbia Records' jackpot fell onto their destiny-bound doorstep. From a sonorous baritone, Tyler's timbre swells into a frantic banshee tenor like Robert Plant – power-shifting into falsetto with nary a twinge of speed bump. Like a savvy surfer, Tyler's not satisfied with one wild wave. With crescendo intensity, he bashes wave after tsunami monster tidal wave off those greased-lightning vocal cords. Though he snagged 53 in 2001, by some miracle of chemistry he still looks about 34.999 (says Lori Ghiringhelli).

"Walk This Way" – Aerosmith, #10, 11-76. Great R & R lyrics get often smushed by screeching guitars, smash-crash drum thunder, whooshing keyboards, and keening guitar phasers. Then the bass uppercuts the overwhelmed singer off an amp the size of a Rolls-Royce. **Run D.M.C.** took "Walk This Way" to #4, 7-86 (#8 R & B), rejuvenating Aerosmith's moribund heyday slide. RUN is Queens, NY's **Joseph Simmons**, while 'DMC' is **Darryl McDaniels**. Rock jock Jason Mizell mixed up the mishmosh, with 'samples' of Aerosmith's Bicentennial smash. Comeback?

"Dude (Looks Like a Lady)" – Aerosmith, #14, 10-87. Remember we did the Barbarians' #55, 9-65 "Are You a Boy or Are You a Girl?" "Dude" tackles androgyny (char-acteristics of both sexes). Since 20s *Sheik of Araby* matinee idol **Rudolph Valentino** sported eye make-up, certain handsome males were taunted as TOO good-looking by beefier bruisers. Elvis got ribbed for his Valentino cat-like grace and swivel-hip moves. Mick Jagger caused a sensation with his wispy build, painted-on pants, and pouting lips. Rock and Rollers are infrequent bodybuilders (Jack Scott, Billy Ray Cyrus), and have long put up with verbal abuse from football guys whose girlfriends have stormed the stage, not the gridiron.

"Dude" blasts the macho key of 'A'. Decibels galore swamp the silence, as Aerosmith dances off the sub-dominant **'D'** chord. Joe Perry's lead replicates the "Louie, Louie" #2, '63 Kingsmen feel, or the Rick Derringer machine-gun guitarfire explosion

The McCoys (Rick Derringer, lead guitar) stormed to #1(1), 8-65 with eternal singalong "Hang On, Sloopy." Union City, Indiana, Heartland Rock. Despite her bad neighborhood, the noble guy loves Sloopy, this poor but sweet chick. Derringer's bridge explodes into a Pre-Metal outburst of guitar flame and volcanic White Soul. Todean's fave from '65. Sloopy hangs on. Rick & Sloopy live happily ever after.

Aerosmith's non-Sarah McLachlan "Angel" crested at #3, 1-88, and "Love in an Elevator" scored #5, 9-89. They celebrate apple-pie American violence in #4, 11-89 "Janie's Got a Gun," and hit #9, 3-90 with "What It Takes." Their "Crazy" (not Patsy Cline/Willie Nelson's) blasted to #17 in 5-94, while naughty "Pink" nailed #27, 2-98. Tyler's biggest hit – at age 50 – may be his most plaintively beauteous: #1(4), 9-58 "I Don't Want to Miss a Thing." Like "November Rain," this #1 tune has been voted the band's prettiest tune. Sure, his un-Orbison "Cryin'" vaulted to #12, 7-93, showing their Power Rock prowess. It rose like an Unleaded Zeppelin over the American ionospheric airwaves. The 1998 song, though, may be their signature song, for this marathon Metal band. Not counting rock icons like Duane Eddy (Rock Hall '94), the Doors, Cream (Hall '93), or Led Zeppelin ('95), **Aerosmith** has some claim as the first American Heavy Metal band to attain the Hall of Fame (2001).

At age 53, Tyler rampaged again. In March 2001, Al. *Just Push Play* zoomed to #2 its first release week. In just three weeks, their "Jaded" (#9+, 1-2001) soared to #28 on the HOT 100. Remember Archimedes' Mathematical leverage motto: "Give me enough AMPS, and I can MOVE the WORLD." Or something like that . . .

The surge of Power Metal blasts the quiet out of the skies with a monstrously magic carpet ride into the frontiers of sound. Earmuffs optional. Guarded by an army of guitars at full tilt boogie, Metal is still strong and vital and sometimes ticked off at the world.

Lop the RYCHE from Queensryche, and you're boppin' with Wayne & Garth's *Wayne's World* ***½ Rock and Roll fantasy. Our next odyssey is into the wild outrageous uninhibited frenzy of Glam or Glitter or Glitz or Thrillingly Theatrical Rock and Roll.

Does fashion – even costumery – affect sales and musical destiny? Or **Destiny's Child** (Twiggy, 1967, the miniskirt)? Let's check out the wild after-hours neon gala:

All That Glitters Is Glitz?
Or Gold?

Rock and Roll was always Theatre. Watch Elvis swagger in *Jailhouse Rock*. Check out Chuck Berry duckwalking to "Johnny G. Goode." Catch hauntingly-still Roy Orbison – emoting each terror-trembling note – garbed in funereal black. The Beatles romanced, Jagger pranced, Jimi's guitar entranced. We've already done Kiss, Alice Cooper, Iggy Pop. Many stars flirt with Metal, Punk, Glam. Or Rococo Rock. "The Age of Excess," David Szatmary (*Rockin' in Time, '97*) calls this flamboyant style.

From age eight, Brixton's David Jones swore he'd be the #1 Rock star from England, but **Monkee Davy Jones** hit fame first with his natural moniker. Jones II shifted gears, swapped surnames with a Texan Alamo martyr, and became **DAVID BOWIE**:

"Rebel Rebel" – David Bowie, #64, 6-74. Bowie was born 1-8-47, 13 years to the day after Elvis. He blurts to this messy-faced lover who has a torn dress, tears of regret, and a hot-tramp rep. Szatmary connects Heavy Metal and Glam/Glitz Rock: "A theatrical, glittery, sometimes androgynous Heavy Metal, exemplified by David Bowie, epitomized rock and roll excess." He mentions Bowie's R & R apprenticeship with **T. Rex** (Mark Bolan), of "Bang a Gong (Get It On)" fame [#10, 1-72 & #1, 7-71 U.K.]. "Bowie began appearing in a dress publicly as well as on the album cover of *The Man Who Sold the World*."

Rock and Roll is inclusive. It welcomes rockers of all races, religions, ages, ethnic backgrounds, alternative lifestyles. Some Glam Rockers have same-gender flings or long-term relationships. This chapter is also inclusive of those artists with opposite-sex preferences. This is a book about love as well as music, and everyone is welcome in the Home of Rock and Roll. This Glitz chapter relates more to costumery than lifestyle, and *Gold Rush* wishes all artists happiness with whatever lifestyle they choose.

"Rebel 2" is a basic Rock and Roll song. Mainstream Rock. Bowie is a master mime – an odd theatrical gift for a singer. He metamorphosed into a new persona – *Ziggy Stardust and the Spiders from Mars* (Al. #75, 6-72). Clad in a form-fitting spangled leotard outfit, the slim entertainer entranced his audience with flaming orange hair, spideresque movements, and deep baritone macho vocals. Bowie spearheads Glam. Debut ditties include #66, 4-72 "Changes" (stutters like Who's "My Generation") and #6, 7-72 "Starman." He married Angie Barnett, actual subject of Rolling Stones' #1(1), 9-73 "Angie."

"Rock and Roll Part II" – Gary Glitter, #7, 7-72; #4, 9-72 U.K. Paul Gadd changed his name into a whole new Rock category for this Glitter Rush chapter. DRAB was out. Glitz and glitter were in. Glitter's R & R manifesto booms a burly macho vocal, with a Mainstream or Thunder Rock feel, into the arena of iridescent spandex, silver sheen, and gold-dust dreams. Glitter recharged to R & R Part III with #35, 11-72 "I Didn't Know I Loved You (Till I Saw You Rock and Roll)."

"Space Oddity" – David Bowie, #124, 1969 and #15, 1-73; #5, 10-69 U.K. Beating the American astronauts to the Moon, Bowie actually recorded his Al. #16, 3-**73** *Space Oddity* back in '68 – but it was a slow roller that rocked. Title? A pun on Stanley Kubrick's futuristic phantasmagoria *2001: A Space Odyssey* (1968****). What started as a bad trip for 'Major Tom' ended up as Bowie's stairway to the stars.

Listening to the Village People's "Macho Man" of #25, 6-78 fame, we discover 'macho' is tough to define. Much of Bowie's Glam Rock stance comes from *Iggy Pop and the Stooges*, who erupted with the MC5 and out of Detroit's Grande Ballroom. Both **Iggy** and Bowie are rail-thin, sometimes sing 'topless,' and sport thunderous resonant BARITONE voices that dive deep down into non-Glam Johnny Cash range.

"Space Oddity" is one very sad tale. Astronaut 'Major Tom' floats in space, previewing the ill-fated U.S. 1986 Challenger explosion tragedy (or see Tom Hanks in 1995*** ½ *Apollo 13*). Tom keeps signaling back to Earth, and to his wife. In plaintive ballad style, Bowie murmurs the cockpit is unraveling, dials are haywire, gauges are kaput. As hopes to safely return to home-plate Earth recede into peril and tragedy, the control tower whines to doomed Major Tom about static. Poor Tom is swallowed up by the immensity of space.

"Fame" – David Bowie, #1(2), 6-75. Bowie's #1 FAME certainly surged via this tune's co-writer and vocal backgrounder. Never hurts to have JOHN LENNON on your record. The mid-70s were #10, 2-75 "Golden Years" for Bowie. Rambling down the murky corridor of time, Bowie's rhythm track hammers in a hopscotch style, smushing the insistent beat with a hint of Jamaican sunshine.

David Bowie

"China Girl" – David Bowie, #10, 6-83. Bowie's double heydays (1973-75 and 1983-85) produced this multicultural stormy and steamy ballad, and a few other biggies, like #8, 9-84 "Blue Jean." Or catch Bowie's hookup with Glam stars Queen to #29, 11-81 "Under Pressure." Or Bowie's excellent Rock and Roll rampager, and maybe his best rocker – #14, 9-83 "Modern Love."

"China Girl" suggests two Easy Squeezy Oldies: **Ames Brothers'** #38, 2-60 "China Doll," and **Mills Brothers'** huge wartime "Paper Doll ," #1(12), 7-43. Bowie murmurs hoochie-coochie with dainty Asian dame, and flirts with abusive relationship, telling her to 'hush' up. Rhythm track prowls in on little cat feet. Feisty lyric. 70s Modern Love. Bowie grooved with **Mick Jagger** in 8-85 (#7) to vintage Motown on their #2, 8-64 Martha/Vandellas' classic "Dancing in the Street." Pitching the growly baritone power of Motown anchors Edwin Starr or 4 Tops' Levi Stubbs, both Bowie and Jagger remind us not to forget that Motor City. Who can? [This is the only charted Bowie tune of 27 that he didn't write].

Bowie's ominous North American nervousness came out in his #66, 11-97 tune produced by **Nine-Inch Nails:** "I'm Afraid of Americans." Logging in to millennial reality (Whitburn info), Bowie launched Internet Bowienet in 1998. Many current groups promenade the Internet for fun & profit.

"Every Rose Has Its Thorn" – Poison, #1(3), 10-88. 'Major Tom' Dept.: this Harrisburg, PA, Hard Rock/ Heavy Metal/Glam quartet wins coolest-name drummer contest: RIKKI ROCKETT. Also guitarist **CC DeVille**, bassguy Bobby Dall, and **Bret Michaels** on vocals. Their non-choirboy success debuted with #9, 3-87 "Talk Dirty to Me." "Nothin' but a Good Time" flim-flammed #6, 4-88. They echoed Loggins-Messina's "Your Mama Don't Dance" to #10, 2-89. High-voltage #3, 7-90 "Unskinny Bop" and #4 , 10-90 "Something to Believe In" aced decade's debut.

"The Bitch Is Back" – Elton John, #4, 9-74. Reggie Dwight (Elton, b. 3-25-47) is the single most important artist of the Rock Revolution in 2002 (Whitburn's Artist Top 500 – since Elvis is gone, and the Beatles split up, #3 Elton climbs to the pinnacle). Growing up in semi-staid surroundings in Pinner, Middlesex, near London, Elton achieved early stardom without excess in style, costumes, or music. His early #92, 8-70 "Border Song" and breakthrough #8, 11-70 "Your Song" show the breezy Folkish style of James Taylor or mellow Jim Croce. First perceived as an Easy-Listening swami with super phrasing and 16th-note melisma grace notes, Elton unloaded his arsenal of fastball Rock and Roll. Gradually. Soon #24, 12-71 "Levon" sported a kid 'Jesus' who wanted to go to Venus amid a backdrop of street-vendor balloons. Elton's #6, 5-72 "Rocket Man" pumps up Bowie's astronaut theme from "Space Oddity." Soon jumbo specs (begun modestly as a tribute to Buddy Holly) dwarfed Elton's face, and he reeled under a haberdashery of hot hats. With mink capes, boulder-size rings, fire-engine red suits of Santa hue, and platform stilt-shoes, Elton jovially mocked the British penchant for charcoal grey.

This big hit stars a witch with a capital 'B.' Splashing the hit lyrics of songwriting pard **Bernie Taupin,** Elton struts the neon pub-scape in his bluesy 2nd-tenor style. He mashes the 88's with the gusto of Jerry Lee Lewis, one of the first to throttle theatrics (and piano-pouncing) into his R & R act. **Dusty Springfield** (1998 Rock Hall) does background vocals.

"Island Girl" – Elton John, #1(3), 10-75. Whether Elton wore a space cowboy outfit with a cape and jeweled turban, or just a T-shirt and Levis, his MUSIC cast him as a top-notch songwriter/performer and superstar. **Elton** composes the MUSIC, **Bernie** the lyrics. Hence, Elton wrote one blockbuster "Candle in the Wind," while Bernie wrote TWO ["Candle in the Wind I & II]. Joel Whitburn's Top Artists (500) of 1993 and 1999 include:

1993		1999	
Elvis Presley	9486 pts.	Elvis Presley	9641 pts.
Beatles	5177	Beatles	5360
Stevie Wonder	4362	ELTON JOHN	5176
ELTON JOHN	4310	Stevie Wonder	4455
James Brown	3992	James Brown	4152
Rolling Stones	3736	Madonna	4071
Pat Boone	3677	Rolling Stones	3819
Aretha Franklin	3569	Aretha Franklin	3782
Marvin Gaye	3454	Michael Jackson	3775
Michael Jackson	3431	Pat Boone	3672

Madonna's meteoric rise in three years, from 23rd-place and 2931 pts., stems from her Glam Rock intro in NYC's Greenwich Village playing DRUMS. She shows the recent power of women in Rock.

This 'Island Girl' rocker mangled the #1 spot for three weeks in Discomania. New York has a Caribbean population rivaling London's. Is this one large 6'3" island lass, who likes to boogie on the 'Disco 'Round,' really a *girl* at all? Or perhaps more of the Esquerita or RuPaul (#45, '93 "Supermodel") dress-up variety? Whatever her situation, this girl-person from the Islands commits the world's oldest profession – meeting several guys during her midnight misadventures. As a Rocker with Glam overtones, "Island Girl" sails with a great beat, great melodic chords, and Elton's tremendous voice.

"Don't Tell Me" – Madonna, #4, 11-2000. Madonna (b. 8-16-58, ostensibly Bay City, MI) began her career like Bob Dylan – in the Village. Like Karen Carpenter, she played drums. Like Elton John, her formidable musical arsenal includes a breathtaking variety of styles and genres. The word RE-INVENT seems to have been re-invented to describe the Michigan blonde, who challenged the Beatles for Most Top Ten Songs by 2002. Some of Madonna's fan base consists of people on the fringes of the regular 2.3 kids/3 bedroom Suburban lifestyle – such as after-hours high-lifers of the neon nocturne Village. So far, there hasn't been a millennium big enough to tame Madonna down. Her musical versatility keeps her vamping the Glam Rock, bouncing off fashion frenzies, mastering musical profusion, and glomming hit after hit after hit – despite two kids, a hubby (Guy Ritchie), and a quadragenarian (40) birthday bash. Glam, Madonna, and Re-Invent go together like Rock . . . and Roll.

"All the Young Dudes" – Mott the Hoople, #37, 9-72; #3, 8-72 UK. Singer **Ian Hunter**'s Hoople crew pioneered theatrical aspects of Glitter Rock, via a macho Hard Rock style produced by **David Bowie** (who claps and plays guitar). **Gary Glitter**'s cooking-foil outfits masqueraded the new sound, and mainstream artists like Rod Stewart appeared as 'Python Lee Jackson' in #3 UK-only "In a Broken Dream." It's no surprise Glitz emerged in the mirror-ball strobe light 70s, a freewheeling era unencumbered by anything much more virulent than the herpes virus. Another Brit crew postured their Pomp Rock orchestrations, waiting to erupt:

"Killer Queen" – Queen, #12, 3-75; #2 UK. Freddie Mercury (b. Zanzibar, 1946-91) started life 30 miles from Tanzania, East Africa moving to Hampton, Middlesex, by bass boomer **John Deacon** of Leicester. **Roger Taylor** drummed the complex Queen beat to teen beat triumph on this debut. Their first Rococo Rock record lofts this vocal phantasmagoria into the ethereal firmament. With this dynamic debut, they poise on the happy brink of creating their own genre. "Killer Queen" is like Gene Chandler's #1 '62 "Duke of Earl" or Clarence 'Frogman' Henry's #20 '56 "Ain't Got No Home." Their first hit cinched the group's NAME. "Killer Queen" may be even more intense, convoluted, and frothy with innovations than their

operatic opus and sophomore hit "Bohemian Rhapsody." For sheer musicianship and gonzo musicological theory, Queen is nowhere near the same page as Joe Zilch's No-Frills Garage Guys.

Example: Steely Dan's Non-Glam album *Two Against Nature* garnered the Best Album Grammy, 2001. Interviewed by *Newsday's* Letta Tayler, Dan's **Donald Fagen** (b. '47), kidded her back about being out of the spotlight for 20 years: "Our narcissism never waned." He calls his own controversial lyrics (after the flap about **Eminem's** "Real Slim Shady") "stealth trash." When Tayler asked their secret technique, Bob Starr's colleague said "good music." She asked whether Eminem's music [like #6+, 4-2002 "Without Me"] was no good – baiting Fagen: "Well, rap music doesn't have any music, does it," he astoundingly replied. Jazz Rock and Rococo Rock people might applaud Fagen's candor, Rappers decry it.

Rock Hall 2001 Inductees Fagen (keyboards, vocals) and Walter Becker (bass, vocals) did many hot studio tunes like "Peg" (#11, 11-77) and #19, 4-78 "Deacon Blues," with a tone of respect for Queen's own bassman John Deacon. ZANZIBAR? Freddie M. from ZANZIBAR?

"Zanzibar" – Billy Joel, NC, '78. From #1(8) Al. 11-78 *52nd Street*. Hicksville, Long Island's Billy is among the World's Greatest Keyboardists – like Fagen. ZANZIBAR in this song is an exotic JAZZ FUSION club. Album cover tableau: Billy in white shirt, black tie worn open-collared (like Dean Martin), blue small-checked sport coat, Levis, and running shoes. The atmosphere/ambience, as Joel cradles a trumpet, in the pale blue NYC alley, suggests Frank Sinatra's #2(18), Al. '55 *In the Wee Small Hours of the Morning*. Though Joel dressed as Attila the Hun's sidekick in a charnel-house butchery (Al. *Attila*, NC, '71), he never did Glitz or Glam. In this polyrhythmic Latin-flecked Jazz tune, he's loving a waitress from shantytown, lamenting the Yankees' misfortunes, bragging about copping his pop's car, and revving a cushy tab (credit, yay) at Club Zanzibar.

"Bohemian Rhapsody" – Queen, #9, 1-76, & #2(1), 3-92. *Wayne's World* (1992***+), goofaroo *Saturday Night Live* flick, rejuvenated Queen's opus to a roaring rebirth. "Rhapsody" is the essence of Rococo Rock. It pumps the ornate, the ostentatious. Rambling through a mosaic of Mozart styles, it skirts Classical forms like the rondo, minuet, aria, and the fugue. Not the Froog, a 60s dance. It also skirts, and pants, Jazz Rock. Queen signed with the Doors' Elektra Records, via *showcasing* demo gigs and big press, avoiding the drag of teensy club jobs. **Creedence Clearwater** once played to a crowd of nine people.

"Bohemian Rhapsody" you don't slap down in one jiffy spiffy take. The **Beach Boys**' production of #1 '66 "Good Vibrations" cost Brian Wilson a relative $25,000 fortune. The most expensive album produced in the UK was #1(15) '67 *Sergeant Pepper* with the Fab Four. As the Glam Rock Era dawned, Queen's Al. #4, 12-75 *A Night at the Opera* snagged the UK production-expense silver medal. When the smoke and mirrors cleared, Queen dispatched the old #1 champ, **Slim Whitman**'s #1(11) UK "Rose Marie," though this rhapsodic opus crunched #9 first in the USA before its U.K. #1 streak. "Bohemian Rhapsody," a title gently borrowed from Classical composer **Franz Liszt** (1811-96), jolts the jiggly genres of Rock and Roll: Opera Rock, Classical Rock, Folk Rock, Hard Rock, Glam Rock, Heavy Metal, Soft-Rock Balladry, Handel's *Messiah* Oratorio Rock, and Orangoutang Go-Ape Wild Rock.

They fire off Italian Grand Opera terms: Figaro, Magnifico. They harmonize tight tacets and cascade mile-a-minute melismas. They dribble hot *arpeggios* off the rhythmic backboard. Queen's musical chain has no weak link. The Rock Hall rewards quality musicianship, like Steely Dan and Queen, Class of 2001. Deacon's bass blasts bends, slurs, and clusters atop Taylor's tantalizing tattoo of drum fire. May spatters 4th-of-July guitar fireworks. Mercury's mammoth voice rises like Mt. Kilimanjaro atop the hubbub crowd below. [We belong to Bohemia Track Club, Bohemia, NY, and commit 5K races that really rock]. If Queen stopped with only these two big hits, they'd have a shot at the Rock Hall and posterity.

"Crazy Little Thing Called Love" – Queen, #1(4), 12-79. Redone by authentic Rockabilly/Country star **Dwight Yoakum** in 1999, this classic darts along with Blues/Jazz/Be-Bop/Rockabilly energy. You even hear Swing Jazz of the 30s.

Cab Calloway (1907-94) of *The Blues Brothers (1980****)* is best noted for #1, '31 "Minnie the Moocher" and #8, 6-32 "Minnie the Moocher's Wedding Day." Via his #2(4), 7-39 "(Hep-Hep!) The Jumpin' Jive," Cab paved the way for Rockabilly, and a crazy little thing called love. Jock Rock, anyone?

"We Are the Champions" – Queen, #4, 10-77; also #52, 7-92. This Jock Rock fight song is no joyful paean of humility and modesty. The grisly film *Seven* (1996* ½) shows the ancient medieval orders of the Year 1313's Top Seven Deadliest Sins Hit Parade. Weirdly, PRIDE is the #1 TOP Deadly Sin. Up and comers include Lust, Gluttony, Sloth, Avarice. In sports-gorging Anglo-America, we don't sweat deadly sins much. You often hear: "Be proud of your school, flag, and home."

Freddie Mercury's rise and fall is the stuff of legend, and tragedy. Queen exploded onto the scene in '75, but began in '71. The entire band held together until Freddie's passing in 1991 from a grim scourge disease. "Bohemian Rhapsody," remember, flutters on a Classical motif, intermingling tight *a cappella* harmonies with slashing machine-gun staccato bolts of treble lightning. It churns and skips and sighs. They juxtapose Hard Rock riffs against bombastic buffoonery. Eel-like tendrils of tenor and falsetto twist the shrill Miltonian lyrics. Building upon the cosmology of the Stones' "Sympathy for the Devil," they invoke Beelzebub from his hot-tub hellish jacuzzi in some coalsmoke cavern of Hades and *Paradise Lost.* They leap brazenly into the mystic windswept hallelujah night. Mercury's vivid vocal vaults to the vicinity of Bb beyond the High 'C' zone, among the highest male vocal notes ever. He soars to Mock Opera grandeur. "Bohemian Rhapsody" darts in and out of life's rosy awakening, its ruddy prime time, and its tawny afterglow. OK – what

does Queen do for an encore?

Well, they also did #16, 5-76 "You're My Best Friend," and #13, 11-76 "Somebody to Love." Their #49, 3-77 "Tie Your Mother Down" never became a Mother's Day anthem. Their #24, 11-78 "Bicycle Race"/"Fat Bottomed Girls" never scored gold records at Weight Watchers. "Champions," however, gets broadcast anywhere, anytime, at any athletic struggle. It's a Victor's Hymn, of sorts. PRIDE is the byword of the sizzling Self-Image Generation. Back at Michigan State in '65, we read about those creepy medieval gloomsayers and their anti-pride rhetoric. Our MSU football team was #1 in the national college polls week after week. With barnstorming 6'8" 300# Charles BUBBA Smith at defensive end, Spartan Stadium rocked with frantic win-crazed cries of "KILL, BUBBA, KILL" and "WE'RE NUMBER ONE!" Mournfully, we drove 6000 miles to watch our unbeatable behemoth football team crush the weak PAC-10 West Coast challenger in the Rose Bowl in Pasadena, California. When everybody's New Year's Day smoke/hangover had cleared, our biggest grid-iron juggernaut in football history was humbled at the hands of a team I will convince NO one was inferior:

SCORE?   UCLA 14, MICHIGAN STATE 12

Loving a team is like loving a woman. It can break your heart. Unless, joy of joys, you win the big one.

So what is the basic appeal of "We Are the Champions"? Many things. First, at least they shifted the narcissistic "I-I-I-I-Me-Me-Me" focus to the healthier WE! Then they launch their bazooka lyric. It plods at first: remorse, regrets. Early on, the song stalks its message in metronomic 6/8 precision. Odd rocker tempo, toying with *triplets.* At a cross-country well-conditioned 62 heartbeats/minute, Freddie chronicles his list of human frailties and mistakes.

CHAMPS' CHORD PROGRESSION

Debuting in **Eb-major**, he leads with the **C-minor** sub-mediant. He jumps to the straight Dominant V chord (**Bb7**) off the VI minor, with Deacon's bass on a C note. Queen perches on the **Bb** for a pregnant moment, and suddenly Freddie whips into a new key – resonant **F-major** with this chord march: **F–Am7–Dm7–Bb–C.** Just when you think you're circling a simple 12-Bar Blues Progression, or elementary Streetcorner pattern, songwriter Mercury mercurially storms to a new dimension. Bouncing off dominant V **'C'** (with Jazz Theory 501 expertise), he squeezes in a **Bb-dim** (IV diminished) and a quick-fix six diminished (VI-diminished.) Then BOOM, you're zapped with a super-tonic ninth minor: IIm9 or a **G-min9.** Then an **Ab6**, a sub-dominant **Bb7**, to a mezzoforte dominant seventh sustained (contains a fourth, not F) of his **C7-sus.** Perched on that precarious technical precipice, like Wile E. Coyote above the Grand Canyon on a wobbly rock, Freddie and Champs plummet melodically back to good ol' key 'Eb' on the word WORLD at their finale. This complexity makes some novices throw guitars out the window.

Rock and Roll began with three merciful Blues chords: I, IV, and V7. Via Jazz Rock and Art Rock and Queen, simplicity gave way to flamboyant baroque embellishments, careening with diffuse, obtuse, and caboose ideas. The upshot of their "Champs" song? "We made it, Baby." Won the trophy. Glommed the gonfalon. Swooped to victory. Hooray. Lyrical moral? If we just all try our best and work *together, we can be the CHAMPS.* Simple as that. Forget the *furshlugginer Mezzoforte* sustained chord. Just sing the song. It's OUR victory – together.

"We Will Rock You" – Queen, [#4, 10-77 with "Champions" flip side] #52, 11-92. From Al. #3, 12-77 *News of the World.* Earthquake Rock! Brian May penned this classic chant-rock anthem. For 1½ minutes, Queen previews RAP. It's a no-chord, no-holds-barred CHANT. For these 1½ minutes, technically this song isn't, chord-wise. Via the big throaty booming bass drum and tom-toms of Roger Taylor, "We Will Rock You" fires down the gauntlet. Direct challenge to rival's pride. Starts in kidhood. Mud on face. King of the hill. Disgraced today, he eventually plans to rebound. To conquer the world. Five times the big chorus chant thunders: "WE WILL," they say, "WE WILL ROCK YOU!" Primary notes they hit (making this a TUNE) are G, F#, E, D, and two E's. Simple, yet profound. So far. No real chord yet. It looms on the horizon. Staggering bullishly along, the chant picks up a lost and lonesome **C** chord. Pivoting on a *pedal point,* burbling low and rising, five repeats of the title skim by. Tension builds. The pressure to change chords rises (you know what I mean – EXPERIENCE this part of the song). An upswelling of notes slouches toward a zenith. Finally, BOOM! A huge A-BOMB CHORD CHANGE!

"Rock You" tumbles to a surprise **A-major.** Lumbering to the super-tonic major triad **D,** it whirls to an **A-sus,** sustaining a 4th note. Twisting and whisking, "Rock You" hammers. Squeegeed in between beats, Mercury's narration/vocal/tune taunts and jeers. In-yer-face trash talk arose via this macho challenge song and later in the Rap arena.

Catch the same flavor in their #1(3), 8-80 "Another One Bites the Dust." This dustbiter ditty was their second platinum platter. Stormy, strident, super song. At #1(3), Queen's 2nd-biggest hit.

"Radio Ga-Ga" – Queen, #16, 2-84. Queen's last Top 20 tune as an intact band before Freddie's tragic fadeaway in '91 to an intimately transmitted disease. "Ga-Ga"? An airy combo chant, roaring rhythmic montage, and harmonic spectacular.

"Somebody to Love" – Queen and George Michael, #30, 5-93. After risque album sleeve for #11, 5-82 "Body Language," Queen's remaining Glam rockers joined ali-kazam Wham Glam **George Michael** (#1[3], 12-84 "Careless Whisper").

"Man on the Moon" – R.E.M., #30, 2-93. Lead singer **Michael Stipe** eulogizes comedian Andy Kaufman in a lunar tribute. "Man on the Moon" has ALT ROCK (Alternative Rock) 90s ties to Glitter Rocker **David Bowie**'s #15, 1-73 "Space Oddity." Stipes matter-of-fact belltone tenor also stands up well on #6, 1-89 "Stand" and #9, 9-97 haunting refrain "The One I Love." The latter title echoes Glitter pioneer Neil Sedaka's #1(1), 10-74 "Laughter in the Rain." This dreamy ballad is unlike his Hard Rock monster hit duet, "31(3), 9-75 "Bad Blood," which starred the #1 living singer of all time (in 2002) on backing vocal – **Elton John.** Elton hyped and engineered Sedaka's comeback. R.E.M. featured none of the outrageous fashions of the 70s Glitter Rock era, but championed the lyrical themes (like #19, 1-95) which feature no timidity. Like **Fred Schneider/Cindy Wilson**'s campy convocation the **B-52's,** and their 80s Surf/Glitter extravaganza, #3, 9-89 "Love Shack," R.E.M. keeps the pulse of Rock and Roll glittering with power and passion.

"Hot, Hot, Hot" – Buster Poindexter & His Banshees of Blue, #45, 12-87. David Johansen (Buster) founded the **New York Dolls.** Here is a list of the NY Dolls' HOT 100 Singles and all their Top 40 albums:
1) _____; 2) _____; and 3) _____. Their eponymous Al. 9-73 *The New York Dolls* hit #116. **Johnny Thunders** began the Dolls [no relation to Johnny THUNDER (singular), who soulfully rocked kiddie nursery rhyme to #4, 12-62 on here-we-go "Loop de Loop"]. Thunders' Dolls appeared in cellophane tutus, six-inch spiked heels, and ruby lipstick. OUTRAGEOUS was their byword. Chutzpah and costumery were their forte (see MTV 'Fashion Awards'). The Dolls were an event. Ardent critics fuddy-duddied that they blew up too many amps, had to be scraped off the ceiling from excessive wild partying, and carried nonconformity from the sublime to the ridiculous. Worse, some said they lacked tight musical technique. Unlike Glam stars **Freddie Mercury/Queen, David Bowie,** or **Elton John,** they failed, critics said, to start with great songs and record them flawlessly.

"I Put a Spell on You" – Screaming Jay Hawkins, NC, 1956. Screaming Jay (1929-2000) really invented Glam and Glitz Rock. When the women he chased (exclusively) saw his Dracula costume, they set speed records and esCAPEd. In 1956, Jay was wheeled on stage in his traditional coffin, waving a skull, named Henry . . . or Clarence. After smoke and brimstone and weird voodoo incantations, Hawkins performed with his Draculine Death Rock/Soul tenor. He was 'Gothic' when gothic wasn't cool. Jay never quailed at song-topic conventions: "Feast of the Mau-Mau" (cannibalism), and "Constipation Blues" (never mind) demonstrate fearless songwriter's wit. Via his volcanic visuals, Hawkins paved the way for MTV and VH-1. Screamin' was followed by the **Crazy World of Arthur Brown** and his #2, '68 "Fire."

"Rough Boys" – Pete Townshend, #89, 11-80. The Who's Pete Townshend hit with #9, 8-80 "Let My Love Open the Door," brushing the top ten. "Rough Boys" played well in the countercultural East Village & San Francisco. Musically, the song is super. The lyric? Controversial.

"Beth" – Kiss, #7, 9-76. Kiss nabbed its highest chart height not with a head-banging smash-metal wailer – but a tender ballad. Maybe an alibi. Pretty and ultramelodic slow number. Excuse song. Tells his girl 'Beth' he'll be home a little later. Then a lot later. Much, much later. Finally, the truth squirms out – he's ostensibly staying out all night with 'the Boys' in the band. Nothing new!

"Sparrow in the Tree Top" – Guy Mitchell, #8, 3-51. Poor sad sack, still at tavern, calls wife. Like a sparrow, he really loves his forsaken mate – but fears it's too late for him to duck back into the house. The shifty sparrow claims that, yep, he was at the Jaybird Jumpin' Jive Lounge, but he was thinking only of HER [Yeah, right]. Also #8, 3-51 by **Bing Crosby** and **Andrews Sisters.** Glam, it isn't.

Kiss's **Gene Simmons** (b. Israel) started life as Gene Klein. His name change? Maybe he forgot there already was a guy with the middle & last names 'Gene Simmons.' His 1st name? "Jumpin." Huh?

"Haunted House" – Jumpin' Gene Simmons, #11, 8-64. Gene (the First) makes a real bad real estate investment. Buys haunted house. From Elvis's Tupelo, Mississippi, Jumpin' Gene hears chains rattling in decrepit 'Handyman's Special.' Wacko ghost drinks hot grease from scalding pan. Ghost tries to run him out of haunted house. Nope, says Gene. He booms he BOUGHT the place, so ghosts (and squirrels) better realize HE's the BOSS. Not Glam Rock. Super Graveyard Rockabilly tune, though. Qualifies for this chapter under Screaming Jay Hawkins Grotesquerie Clause. Gene's other charted hit, alas, is deader than a dodo bird: #83, 11-64 "The Dodo."

"I Was Made for Lovin' You" – Kiss, #11, 5-79. Hmm, same chart number as other Gene Simmons extravaganza. THIS Gene is called BAT LIZARD. Ace Frehley? SPACE MAN. Peter Criss? THE CAT. Paul Stanley? STAR CHILD. Kiss assumed the wild look to outdo the less musically-gifted New York Dolls. Therefore, a band who never made it big (except for Buster Poindexter's later #45 '87 "Hot, Hot, Hot) crucially influenced a whole aura of Glam Rock. And Kiss became the best-paid Glam or Heavy Metal band in history, trumping Metallica. Much of Kiss's theatrical *raison d'etre* relates to TV producer Bill Aucion's bizarre prop shop: snow machines, Roman candles, smokescreens, monster lights, sirens, drum assemblies hanging in the air. With spandex, glittery jew-els, and stilt shoes, Kiss loomed large over their stage, strutting pure Metal Rock with Glam accoutrements. Other Kiss singles smashes? #16, 3-77 "Calling Dr. Love"; #15, 12-76 "Hard Luck Woman"; #25, 7-77 "Christine Sixteen"; and #49, 10-84 "Heaven's on Fire" [ponder THAT title]. Sometimes the Wheel of Fortune turns Kiss's way, seemingly "Forever" (#8, 2-90):

"Wheel of Fortune" – Kay Starr, #1(10), 2-52. Throbbing triplet notes bolster a big hit about kismet, karma, and Romance Roulette. Born Kathy Starks on Oklahoma Indian reservation, the torch-singing sultry alto tromped the top spot ten weeks, provoking **Vanna White** TV quiz show "Jeopardy." Glamorous but Non-Glam Starr, unrelated to the ever-cool **Ringo,** also scored on #2(1), 5-50 **Perry Como** hit "Hoop-De-Doo," semi-rocker #4, 5-50 "Bonaparte's Retreat," #3, 8-50 "I'll Never Be Free," Rock Era #9, 9-57 "My Heart Reminds Me," and self-harmonized hobo swan song "Side by Side" (#3, 1-53, see Roger Miller).

"Rock and Roll Waltz" – Kay Starr, #1(6), 12-55. This Russ Steinke-favorite hit contains a quaint old couple with a wind-up Victrola. In the 1950s, their hearts promenade the 1910s or so – they try to waltz to a rock tune. Chic gal arrives home from date. She peeks at them waltzing to new Rock and Roll, and she giggles. Tempo jogs back and forth from 3/4 waltz to 4/4 rocker.

"Walking the Dog" – Rufus Thomas, #10, 10-63; #5, R & B. King of Memphis Blues. Big Daddy (1917-2002, b. Cayce, MS) was the opposite of understated. Among oldest active Rockers. Daughter Carla scored big with #10, 1-61 (#5 R & B) "Gee Whiz." Dad Rufus surprised 60s with his own big hit at age 46.

Thomas gloated in the Theatre of the Absurd. A genuinely happy man, you can tell. Despite a penchant for pulchritudinous females only, Rufus bombarded the Rock and Soul world with fashion cannonballs: pink Bermuda shorts, spats, purple frilly shirt, cape, plaid Tam O'Shanter topping hair-impaired pate. The most important thing that he wore was his electric smile. Rufus Thomas: Feel-good Doc of Happy Soul. "Walking the Dog" lurches eloquently on little stutter steps. First Rocker to use stuttering in the vocal, too, paving the way for the Who's "My G-g-generation" affectation of a speech impediment.

"No More Mr. Nice Guy" – Alice Cooper, #25, 4-73. Detroit's 'Alice' (b. Vincent Fournier, 2-4-48) jumped from his Phoenix AZ high school track team to a theatrical bombshell here: boa constrictor necktie, china-doll guillotine, electric chairs (and guitars). Glam Rock goodie with banshee falsetto.

Though NY Giants' manager Leo Durocher claimed 'nice guys finish last,' the world spins on amiable leaders' social friendliness – Bill Clinton, both George Bushes I & II, Mikhail Gorbachev. Hopefully, we packed away the Hitlers and Stalins on the scrap heap of dumpster history. Alice Cooper, counter to his image, is a nice guy (with a boa tie) who plays golf, when nobody's looking.

Raw Power – **Iggy & the Stooges, Al. #182, 4-73. Iggy Pop** [Iggy Stooge, too] pioneered Glam from debut on Chicago's Rush St., DRUMMING for Jazz star **Buddy Guy** and Bluesbuster 'Blind Limey' Catterson. Somewhere in a screaming blue funk, Iggy got teed off, fled to Florida, and retired (at 21). After a failed tycoonery at a lawn mowing enterprise, he did Glam, influenced Bowie and the Punk Ramones, and eventually skyrocketed to #28, 11-90 "Candy," an overnight sensation 25 years later.

"Walk on the Wild Side" – Lou Reed, #16, 2-73. South Shore blue-collar Freeport, Long Island's Lou (b. '42) and **John Cale** genre-jumping Punk/Glam/Metal/ Art Rock crew the **Velvet Underground.** From Psychedelic opening volleys like Al. #171 *The Velvet Underground and Nico* of '67, they never plunked a single into the HOT 135. "Wild Side" is Lou's solo charter, and it's a doozy. Swaggering through the squalid afterglow Bowery, "Wild Side" shatters lyrical taboos with its same-sex intimacy blurted up-front to all the backwater hamlets of the U.S.A. Censorship took a hike in '73, and Rap freedom prevailed. "Wild Side's" instrumental background is nearly as furtively naked as the quickeroo passion encounters in this raw urban nocturne travelogue. A stand-up bass rollicks down Bleecker Street alongside his let-it-all-hang-out vocal. Reed's album appeal? Fondled top ten with Al. #10, 10-74 *Sally Can't Dance,* and hometown Al. #40, 1-89 *New York.* His #89, 4-78 Al. *Street Hassle* quivers a quagmire of surreal NYC street tableaus. His literary 6-79, Al. #130 *The Bells* preens a parabola of Edgar Allen Poe. Early on, David Bowie helped Reed's solo adventures, producing his penultimate peach – Al. #29, 12-72 *Transformer.* Reed's roundup of influences lassoed Andy Warhol, Cale, Bowie, and apocalyptic spontaneous superpoet Allen Ginsberg.

From Lou's unheralded Al. *Loaded,* he says the '*girl's life got saved by Rock and Roll.*' For those of us jogging in vintage Nikes over here on the TAME SIDE, that's one great chunk of Lou's oracular wisdom. His Bowery mystique goes back to a magic instrumental.

"Harlem Nocturne" – Viscounts, #52, 12-59 & #39, 10-65; #17, 3-60 R & B. Wonderful adventure in tremolo blasting power from Jersey's Polish-American brothers Joe Spievak (planet-vibrating Fender bass) and Bobby Spievak (spitfire lead-guitar arpeggio odyssey). Tenor saxman **Henry Haller** soars celestially into the Clark Smith cymbal & snare flutter fantasia. Larry Vecchio's ethereal organ wheezes breezily – floating atop the whole heavenly musical firestorm. You can feel these REAL MUSICIANS' sweet sunrise serenade of home fries and coffee, beyond lofty Harlem's **Apollo Theatre** on 125th Street.

"Girl, You Know It's True" – [It wasn't], 'Milli Vanilli', #2(1), 1-89; #3 R & B. Hoaxmasters Fabrice Morvan of France and Rob Pilatus of Germany snagged a Turkish term for 'positive energy,' and lip-sank this #2 hit. Yep – lip-**SANK.** Those of us who lip-SYNC our songs are truly singing songs we truly sang and recorded, somewhere. The puppet cover of **N'Sync's** melodic 2000 album gives

us what these two Milli Vanilli handsome singers did – they choreographed the song – but didn't actually sing it. A hoax. A fake. Doubly tragic, after they were stripped of their 1989 Best New Artist Grammy, they mulled their questionable place in rock history as Glam MIMES – masquerading as singers. Sadly, Pilatus OD-ed on a substance, and some tagged it to guilt. "All or Nothing" (#4, 1-90) zoomed topward with three names: John Davis, Brad Howe, and Charles Shaw. They're the REAL Milli Vanilli voices. More press they'd get here, but weren't they involved in this fakery and Charlatan Ghost Rock? *Gold Rush* admits to rare sugar-coating. The musicians we celebrate have given their souls to Rock and Roll. We try to eliminate their hangnails, booze benders, woozy drug buzzes, zits, and be-bop bed checkers. Heaven knows we musicians aren't saints. But we ARE MUSICIANS.

"Great Gosh A'Mighty! It's a Matter of Time" – Little Richard, #42, 3-86; NC, R & B. Glam Rock **founder.** Richard (b. '32, GA) rocked from his sexagenarian phase toward his septuagenarian phase, hurdling toward the FOURTH millennium (1000 years ahead of time). If anybody else had the nerve to do a song called "I'm the King of Rock and Roll," we might loft a verbal barb; in Richard's case, so be it. If he says he is, we believe it. Who else was a major-league influence on **Buddy Holly, Elvis, Bill Haley,** and **Paul McCartney?** Richard's 50s sax platoon swayed in a wave of yellow Bermuda shorts and knee socks. Richard fired **Jimi Hendrix** because HENDRIX was too flashy, and stole Richard's Glam spotlight.

"I Want Candy" – Bow Wow Wow, #62, 5-82; #8 UK. Assembled by Sex Pistols' guru Malcolm McLaren, and powered by Adam & Ants, they straddled Punk/Glam/Metal with their 15-year-old Rangoon (Burma/Myanmar) lead singer, Annabella Lwin a/k/a Myant Myant Aye. She posed in her birthday suit for their record cover. "I Want Candy"? Orig. by **#11, 6-65 Strangeloves.** Bo Diddley/Johnny Otis Show "Hand Jive" beat (see #1[14], 9-95 "Macarena"). Named after zany movie, Strangeloves had 2 drummers, plus #100, 6-66 "Hand Jive."

"A Boy Named Sue" – Johnny Cash, #2(3), 7-69; #1(5) C. Glam? NAH. Though Country (and Punk) icon Johnny Cash chose drab black garb (that Lou Reed shadowed), Cash is the opposite of Glitz and Glitter. This COUNTRY RAP hybrid hit was a comedy bombshell. The story? Absentee rapscallion names son "SUE" and then hightails it west of the Pecos. Kid grows up. Bullies taunt him about name. He punches them out and gets very tough. Fully grown, he stalks the sadistic Paternal Parental Unit who sired him, split the scene, and saddled him with that anvil of a name: Sue. At long last, he finds dear ol' Dad dealing stud poker in some beerfroth dive.

Nasty barroom brawl. Surprise. Gray old man, scrappy, is still in fighting trim. Big, ugly, fierce. He mashes the old man – but spitfire sire lurches up, and slashes a chunk of ' Sue's' ear. Finally, oldster at bay, he confesses WHY he named him SUE. Seems he knew he was a ramblin' man. He wouldn't be there to toughen the spunky lad. The

NAME, he claimed, made the KID STRONG. Lo and behold. Eureka. His brawling boy grins a Hulk Hogan grin. The two beefy bi-generational battlers slap each other with manly howdy thumps to the shoulder – and go back to chug a 6-pack of Reunited Joy. Songwriter? Kiddie lit superstar **Shel Silverstein**. Cash also did #29, 4-76 (#1 C) "One Piece at a Time." His song-guy rips off car parts, assembles hybrid monstrosity Caddie over several years. When his wacky contraption finally sputters down Wide Track Drive in Pontiac, Michigan, everybody LAUGHS at him (rather than envies him).

At the end of "A Boy Named Sue," the names he considers for HIS future son are BILL and GEORGE . . .

Boy George of Culture Club

"Do You Really Want to Hurt Me?" – Culture Club, #2(3), 12-82; #39, 2-83 R & B. If my diary of our 1961 European adventure is accurate, I think Lt. Jim Cook and I biked through Bexleyheath, East London, on the day that Georgie O'Dowd [**BOY GEORGE**] was born – American Flag Day, June 14, 1961. [Jim went to Vietnam, lost half his platoon in a Viet Cong firefight, returned Stateside safely (6 shrapnel stitches), and his daughter married one of Atlanta's Heavy Metal **Black Crowes**]. **Boy George** apprenticed as a make-up artist with the Royal Shakespeare Company, and stormed a ragtag relationship with glitzmongers Bow Wow Wow. Boy George changed gender stereotyping forever. O'Dowd uses Glam gimmickry. You can't fake, however, his fine tenor voice. Whatever some caustic Glamophobic critic said about George's outrageous outfits, lipstick, or dress, the fact remains – first and foremost, George is an excellent musician. 'Milli Vanilli's' Pilatus and Morgan may have been fine dancers, good midfielders, nice kids. They, too, were duped by the zoom-to-the-Elvis-Spotlight system. This George song is a fine Slow Rock ballad, murmuring minor chords and iffy blue funk in a sweet musical swirl.

Culture Club has also been Ron Hay (keyboards AND guitars), bassman Michael Craig, drummer Jon Moss, and clothing designer Sue Clowes. Their well-deserved Best New Artists 1983 Grammy showed their melodic style. Their second-prettiest group tune may be #10, 10-83 "Church of the Poison Mind." The montage of White Reggae on "Hurt Me" subsides in the religiously-toxic tune. Boy George charmed America his omni-pop package of wild behavior, and amiable, bubbly personality.

"The Crying Game" – Boy George, #15, 3-93. One super strawberry swirl of melody. Zigzags keys and lost chords. Movie theme about hermaphroditism *The Crying Game* ('93**½). He was picked to sing this beautiful song. With a name like GEORGE (not Tony/Toni, Bobby/Bobbi, or CHRIS), why even cite gender? George dragged out all the stops in his eclectic Glitz costumery, fashionizing the wit and wisdom of Clowes' colorful ensembles.

"The Crying Game" power-shifts chords, wrings out honeyed harmonics, and spoofs love's arrows. George's boy-choir tenor voice is an ultimate malleable instrument – like Robert Plant's, for he never snags the falsetto speed-bump. From a chordal perspective, "The Crying Game" is a great adventure, and one of the most melodic songs to come out of the 90s, an era often known for darker, atonal Grunge angst.

"Karma Chameleon" – Culture Club, #1(3), 12-83; #67, 2-84 R & B. Finally, a group's Greatest Song coincides with its biggest hit. "Karma Chameleon" is simply an audial delight. It has the flavor of the tunes of Tommy Roe in the Irish tenor glow of Buddy Holly's high range. [Compare to #1 '62 "Sheila" or #108, 11-62 "Piddle de Pat"] Roe, an Atlanta football star who didn't do Glam Rock, was also master of melody, like #1(4), 2-69 "Dizzy" (#2 tune in 1969). "Karma Chameleon" has just such a pleasant tune.

A chameleon, of course, is a lizard, which changes color for protective coloration, and Roe didn't sing lizards. *Karma,* of course, is Hindu for fate. Boy George shows we can change our costumes, our minds, our way of life. In Rock and Roll, entertainers vault to the stage and shuck their inhibitions like frumpy old clothes. Stars must steel themselves against the busted string, the squeak-squawk vocal note, the paralyzing stage fright, and the dreaded ghostly BOO from the audience. Stage nervousness has caused many an entertainer to assuage his fear with Cloud Ten greenie pills, boozy back-room bouts, sly quickeroo affairs. Secret ulcers. Glam-less U2 says to wear the Heavenly Crown you first must carry the cross. No one ever had it easy. The "Karma Chameleon" melody, however, rings with just enough harptone splendor – it's a pure, rollicking tune that burns brightly with its own winsome Rock and Roll fire.

Many Mainstream Rockers have added a splash of Glitz, Glam, or other Gimmickry to sell records. Chuck Berry played the guitar behind his head. Jerry Lee Lewis jumped on his piano. Elvis swiveled hips to begin the Rock and Roll marathon . . .

Rock & Roll - Marathoners and 38-Hit Wonders

Many artists enjoy a splashy success of "38-hit Wonder" superstardom. Their beat goes on. And on. *Gold Rush* salutes a few superstars with long marathon credentials. Many of them have been clobbered by personal problems, health catastrophes, and sneaky knockout calendars, but bravely strode back to that magnetic limelight. **Rod Stewart** steps up to the plate first (b. 1-10-45); OK, maybe the Cricket plate. Many of our marathon stars are ENGLISH, and were influenced more by Buddy Holly's **Crickets** than American baseball. Rod's 2000 sore throat, like **George Harrison**'s in 1997 and 2001, or **Van Halen**'s in 2001, turned out to be worse than expected – but each marathoner rallied and thrived:

"Maggie May" – Rod Stewart, #1(5), 8-71. Superstar Stewart launched a dynamic, explosive career. Many of our Marathon Rock superstars – the Eagles, Elton John, Billy Joel, Fleetwood Mac – achieved lofty rankings on their hot hit trails and musical treks. The world first knew Rod's moonlaunch monster "Maggie May" as ostensible debut. It fades in with a guitar strut. A 12-string echoes the FOLK tinge – as does his folksy Key of D. A fluttering mandolin duels a plunging bass.

"Maggie" is Rod's 2nd hit, after #126, 7-70 "It's All Over Now." Rod wrests the filigree phrases of **Bob Dylan's** mood in classic #6 '65 album *Bringing It All Back Home*. Dylan could make a potato cry on his lonesome harmonica solo on "Baby Blue's" bridge. Rod's #42, 2-72 "Handbags and Gladrags" uses another Dylan line – a tattered vagabond stands outside the door. For Dylan's squiggling Dust Bowl **Woody Guthrie** troubadour echo, or for **Mick Jagger**'s street-swagger baritone, Stewart plugged in his raspy 'whiskey tenor' [a term unrelated to whiskey/booze]. Had that halfway-decent #126 number been his chart peak, he might have joined us as cops, teachers, vacuum cleaner salesmen, or assistant wombats. He kept working with the **Faces** (a/k/a **Small Faces**), featuring one later Rolling Stone, **Ronnie Wood.** Their #17, 1-72 "Stay with Me" is 90% Stewart and his 3rd major hit. The Faces led off with a catchy local midnight haunt – #16, 11-67 "Itchykoo Park." Its lyrics say they became high to touch the sky. Lyrics like that joined hula hoops and bell bottoms in a 60s-70s time warp. With songwriter

Martin Quittenton, "Maggie May" sets up romantic escapades mirroring Dustin Hoffman in *The Graduate* ('67***½).

American poet **Carl Sandburg** (1878-1967) gave Rod the line about wishing he hadn't ever seen her face in his well-known anthologized poem "Mag." The Galesburg, IL, poet described Chicago as the 'City of the Big Shoulders.' He also defined Folk Rock (see "Sloop John B"), and inadvertently launched the British Invasion's Third Wave – **Rod Stewart** and **Elton John. James Taylor** also semi-fits this marathon chapter, but he's overwhelmingly over there in the Easy Squeezy Listening/American chapter.

Lyrically, the "Maggie May" song-guy knows he should head back to school. The late September calendar says so. Old enough to be his mother, Maggie's got him by the romantic bootstraps. He even cites this Oedipal parallel: he wanted just advice & friendship, but she offered everything – totally exhausting him (see Jerry Lee Lewis, #7, '58, "Breathless"). Blockbuster "Maggie May" justifies every uncertain lad's bittersweet lament: he may not know where he's going in life – but on the road to destiny it's nice to have great loving along the way. "Maggie" is a hymn to uncertainty.

A flippitty organ sails the top treble domain. The purling bass throttles the bottom tones with rolling seaworthy splendor. Guitar magic doles molten golden notes. After his passionate dalliance with a lady he thinks needs wrinkle cream on sunny days (in London?), he ponders escaping to romantic freedom. Does he borrow his old man's pool cue? Does he hook up with a barnstorming Rock band? Listen . . .

"You're in My Heart (The Final Acclaim)" – Rod Stewart, #4, 10-77. Echoes his #13, 8-72 hit "You Wear It Well." Touch of finality, though. With dramatic irony, Stewart wonders whether he'll be around to shoot shuffleboard at Methusaleh's Alligator Acres. Ballad "You're in My Heart's" catchy chorus contains one of the prettiest PURE melodies ever fondled. The lass is his combo lover and best friend.

"Tonight's the Night (Gonna Be Alright)" – Rod Stewart, #1(8), 10-76. Stewart's biggest hit. The follow-up, #1(4), 12-78 "Do Ya Think I'm Sexy?" – hit the R & B charts at #5, 1-79. It's a cool Disco come-on, but not so nifty for mini-moppets who catch this hyper-hormone Stewart rocker (dynamite rhythm track). "Tonight's" passion prelude whispers to chaste chick to just let her inhibitions run amok. He proffers wine, song, and cuddly comforts. Naturally, the innocent lass forgot to take her dose of **Carole King**'s #1, '60 "Will You Love Me Tomorrow?" Stewart's torrid squeeze of that blistering Bicentennial era was no ingenue – Swedish bombshell blonde Britt Eklund (b. '42). Britt coos as Rod woos. She makes sweetly seductive sounds. As Rod & the Cute Kid plod woozily to boudoir, his drumbeat hops along on little pittypat 'simple drags.' Whatever the tempo, his ancient Roman Epicurean message is clear: live it up, now (it might be later than you think).

"Young Turks" – Rod Stewart, #5, 11-80. The London lad with the Glaswegian ancestry advises young hearts to free passion like Pop Standard "The Old Lamplighter," by [Swing & Sway with] **Sammy Kaye** to #1(7), 11-46. Aside from #1(8), 5-41 schmaltzy "Daddy," this was clarinetist/saxman/bandleader Kaye's (1910-87) biggest hit. First streetlights were 19th-century GAS lamps, lit & snuffed by lamplighter. This noble old dude courteously left some lamps dark for park-bench lovers. He recalled his own lost love of long ago, gone to her 'great reward.' Kaye scored on #1(4), 9-50 "Harbor Lights" (see #8, 1-60 **Platters**). The Browns' Rock-Era "Old Lamplighter" (#1[4], 7-59) was reprised by the instrumental **Greasytones** (N.C., '62, Doug Warren, Toby Kuta, Dave Gorden).

Turks. Rod avoids the words TURKS, but he plumps up his regular theme – the Demon Aging Process. Rod enjoyed tunes of glory: his **Bryan Adams/Sting** trio of #1(3), 11-93 "All for Love"; his #36, 1-94 "Having a Party" (Ronnie Wood, guitar, on Sam Cooke #17, 5-62 reprise); and Top 40 marathon return in **7-98** to "Ooh La La" (a phrase dipping back to **Everly Brothers'** amazing #1 '57 "Wake Up Little Susie"). Flipside of Rod's #54, 11-96 "If We Fall in Love Tonight," is **Tom Waits**'s wonderful beery & teary "Tom Traubert's Blues"/(Waltzing Matilda)."

"Forever Young" – Rod Stewart, #12, 8-88. Rod reaches out beyond the lure of self to his friend with Ponce de Leon promises. He toasts that their sparkling zest for life will vaccinate them against infirmities of aging and knockout calendars. Again, Rod's hammering theme: ROCK PERPETUATES YOUTH AND VIGOR. One thing about singers lost in their prime – **Jim Croce, Otis Redding, Kurt Cobain, Notorious B.I.G., Buddy Holly** – they all will remain forever young in our spiraling memories. We never see them in deepening sad decline, as Elvis bloated and faded away. Even Michael Jackson's hyperbaric oxygen chamber, however, can't protect us from a cruel and unusual full-frontal calendar attack.

"In the Year 2525 (Exordium & Terminus)" – Zager & Evans, #1(6), 6-69. Were Rod to make it to this ghastly futuristic year, he'd likely discover atrophied human monstrosities on a *Mad Max* moonscape planet. It might be bad enough to make him yearn for a recommendation from **Norman Greenbaum**'s "Spirit in the Sky" (#3, 2-70, Nina tune). Immortality is an impossible commodity on earth – especially for us rockers. And Soul legends, like:

"The Motown Song" – Rod Stewart and the Temptations, #10, 7-91; NC, R & B. Party theme. This do-it-yourself shindig depends upon bringing some ancient Motown records, and wrestling with window sashes and old musty-dusty hi-fi speakers. Flashback – Vernor's Ginger Ale, Martha/Vandellas, and some splendor and glory with someone you love. **Melvin Franklin** (1942-95), big chummy bassman, anchors "The Motown Song" an octave below Rod's melody. Like lead countertenor **Eddie Kendricks** (d. '92,) and "My Girl" 2nd tenor and lead **David Ruffin** (d. '91, substances), Melvin is too-soon gone. Rod's own scare in 2000 makes him a survivor of the Valley of the Shadow, for now. When your musical contemporaries and old friends die of old age, at your age, you realize your worries about acne or athlete's foot may be a little overdramatized. [Providentially, so far no major Rock and Roll star has died of athlete's foot. Desenex and Micatin sales, however, are up].

"Reason to Believe" – Rod Stewart, #62, 7-71, and #19, 8-93. Rock and Roll gives you a reason to believe? Folk singer/songwriter **Tim Hardin**'s 1971 & 1993 hit spangles a generation with starstruck significance. In many of our endeavors, we rationalize ANY possible reason to believe that whatever we do is right. Stewart pitches into the wild aerospace night of rolling-home midnight romantics, maybe stopping at the 7-11, pizzeria, Gal & Pal Pub, or the Moon of Manakoora:

"The Moon of Manakoora" – Ray Noble Orchestra, #15, 3-38. Among the most haunting melodies ever written. Wispy waltz. Chromatic chord shifts. Tropical moonmists, romantic escapades, slosh of silver surf. London pianist Noble, among first British Invaders, had a song sell a million, never climbing above #12. **Eddie Peabody**'s "Moon of Manakoora" is most melodic – played on his BANJOLINE, which resembles a mandolin,a softly-plucked banjo,a Hawaiian or Spanish guitar, or a percussion instrument ('68, NC).

"By the Light of the Silvery Moon" – Snooky Lanson, with Ray Noble Orchestra, #12, 4-42 and #23, 7-44. Hit #1(9) for Billy Murray/Haydn Quartet in 4-1910. **Roy 'Snooky' Lanson** (b. Tennessee) starred on Lucky Strike's smoky *Your Hit Parade (1950-58),* prototype for *MTV* which played the week's top seven hits. He's one of three reasons to believe I could bring you such a book. Thanks, Snooky, Mom, and Dad, wherever you are – for showing a Motown small kid that popular music had so much glory and splendor. Rock and Roll's reasons to believe don't have to be perched on the Silvery Moon of Manakoora. Sometimes finding another kindred person with your hopes and fears and dreams . . . is really what matters. Rod Stewart sings that love is what counts. Love hovers like the Moon of Manakoora above all the haggling hassles of life. It sure beats daily hang-ups like changing her car's oil, emptying wastebaskets, taking her cat to the vet, or picking wildflowers for HER. Wait a minute – maybe that's what love is all about. Service? With a smile? And with the golden bulbous Moon of Manakoora nodding on high – aloft beyond the fading flamingo sunset.

"Rhythm of My Heart" – Rod Stewart, #5, 3-91. Stewart swashbuckles in – 98/beats/minute. Trebled keyboards simulate the Bay City Rollers or Big Country's Scottish bagpiper sound. Skittering triplet rhythms (12/measure). "Rhythm" lets you know it's no wimply fleaweight #345 Pick to Click in Zinga-Zulaland. Rod tossed out an international Scots' Expatriate Anthem for the entire terraqueous globe. His haunting chorus hangs our fears out to dry. "Rhythm" resounds in the tough Key of 'C#'. He feels the wild romantic rhythm of his heart pound like some unhumdrum drum. He murmurs 'I Love You' to his cherished Scottish seascape beyond the Firth of Forth. He's found his precious homeland, somewhere in the heathery hills of Scotland – where the silver sea meets the robin's-egg blue sky (see McCartney's "Mull of Kintyre"). "Rhythm" jives its songwriters' cosmology with some mystical magical land far away over Oz's Rainbow. Also, it's got a great melody and beat. Give it a 98.

"Beyond the Sea" – Bobby Darin, #6, 1-60; #15, 2-60, R & B. Darin (1936-73, b. NYC), not gifted with perfect heart rhythms (rheumatic fever, childhood), knew he had to make his musical destiny early. "Beyond the Sea" is a mysterious cosmic bridge between Bobby and his lovely *Gidget* bride, actress Sandra Dee (the real one – not the one in *Grease*). Bobby's Soft Rock ballad, cushy with Jazz embellishments, floats above his Streetcorner chord pattern (with Jazz ninths), high above the rainbow drizzle-glare streetlights of his Joe DiMaggio Bronx. Someday, Bobby promises, they'll kiss the way they did here. On some far shore beyond this world they know and love, he promises eternal happiness. Nevermore, he sighs, will they have to sail over perilous reefs and shoals of this bittersweet and tragicomic world. Bobby's melody is Charles Trenet's "La Mer" [The Sea], and his seashore vision is a *Castaway* (2001***1/2) Bali Ha'i, fraught with astronomical hyperbole – it's around the Sun and beyond the Moon. Without heavy vices, versatile Bobby Darin lived the Musician's-Curse lifespan (37), succumbing to a failed heart-valve operation (like George Maury at 71). But "Beyond the Sea" lives – a strawberry cotton-candy cirrus cloud of Pop Oz beyond the yellow-brick rainbow. A happy, restful land beyond the churning sea. The BIG SONG can somewhat immortalize the Big Singers whose Big Time in the Elvis Spotlight was way too small . . .

For Rod Stewart, tropic seas are languid and placid and warm and sensual and peaceful. No sharks. In "The Moon of Manakoora," the song spearheads 1937 Dorothy Lamour film *Hurricane*****, whose wild and windy special effects have never been equaled. One reason "Moon of Manakoora" means so much to me is that you and I and Bobby Darin know/kenw that a lolling, lulling calm is a wonderful thing. It exudes tropical languor. Maybe passion. Zephyrs of love waft in sheltering palm trees. Rod's Scottish tribute makes Scots the world over – on castaway far shores beyond the sea – proud of their tartan heritage.

"Your Song" – Rod Stewart, #48, 4-92. Rod's fine tribute echoes the equally-tremendous career of another superstar singer-songwriter for the ages – marathoner **Elton John.** Crustier, whisperier vocal, but nearly xeroxed band track.

"Your Song" – Elton John, #8, 11-70. Unlike "Maggie May," Elton's (b. 3-25-47, b. Pinner, near London) first blockbuster hit plunked him into the Easy Listening zone. He'd soon leap out. Elton's #92, 8-70 "Border Song" is a secret prelude on Congress label, before this Uni smash. Elton and Anglo-French songwriting partner **Bernie Taupin** buzz-sawed a lot of labels: MCA, Rocket, Geffen, Arista, Columbia, and Epic. "Your Song" hunkers down into Elton's comfy ballad range. With swirling grace-note *melismas* and minors, "Your Song" pirouettes around words like 'anyway,' which, anyway, show a tender tentative intimacy that's all Elton. This pal-Elton mood twinkles again in his friendly follow-up, later a title for a sensational American sitcom – "Friends" (#34, 3-71). Just when everybody thought Elton was a nice quiet kid from Pinner, with crafty curlicue arpeggios on his acoustic piano, the hits got hotter. "Rocket Man" started to rock, softly.

"Rocket Man" – Elton John, #6, 5-72. President Kennedy's space race of 1960-63 put a man on the moon in 1969 ahead of Soviets (see David Bowie's 'Major Tom'). Elton metaphorically cites the Hyper-Man of the Rocket Age – burning on both front afterburners, and raging across the iridescent sky at breakneck speed. Listen to Elton slur and slide through notes. Seeking one note, he pulses along on an even parabola of sound. Like Jazz divas **Sarah Vaughan** or **Ella Fitzgerald, Elton** first pauses – then poises – before nailing the note.

Bernie Taupin's lyrics to #8, 8-72 "Honky Cat" involve controversy ('honky' to *American Heritage* is anti-white'offensive slang'). Elton/Bernie's ultimate meaning, though, involves racial understanding. Elton addresses early discord and current improvement. The roaring rocker swings the afterbeat, jumping with quick *arpeggios* and Blues sevenths. Elton plays his best piano riffs by ear. Though he reads music well, his real forte (see Jazz) is improvisation. In Jen Ruestow's cited #41, 3-72 "Tiny Dancer," Elton offers a minimalist masterpiece. His next 37 songs over 14 years hit the Top 40, with a high-numbers run from "Rocket Man" at #'s 6, 8, 1, 2, 12, 2, 1, 1, 2, 4, 1, 1, 4, 14, and 1. Stardom eluded him, due to superstardom.

His big reason was nostalgia:

"Crocodile Rock" – Elton John, #1(3), 12-72. Breakthrough signature song. Elton celebrates hoppin' boppin' American Holly Rock in a swooning blanket of Streetcorner harmonic chords. With this rockin' reptile, Elton put Old Rock and Roll permanently on the map as a beloved HISTORICAL commodity. It's a K.O. one-two punch, along with **Don McLean**'s happy-tune, gloomy canvas #1(4), 11-71 "American Pie." Responding to **Bill Haley**'s #6, 1-56 "See You Later Alligator," **Elton**'s Nostalgia Rock anthem rings with allusions like "American Pie." "Crocodile Rock" dazzles all the living generations on the planet with its Rock reverence, torrid dance-fever chords, and bouncy beat. One generation (24+ years) separates this first John/Taupin #1 from their #1(14) 10-97 "Candle in the Wind II" (simply the biggest hit of all time). "Crocodile Rock" stars quintessential 50s cutie Susie, jitterbugging with Elton at some super yesteryear sock hop. It is fun, it is innocent, it's a Londoners' tribute to delightful Americana.

"Crocodile Rock" features **Dee Murray**, bass; **Nigel Olsson**, drums; **Davey Johnstone**, guitar. The tune gets downright beauteous when he slides off the dominant seventh (V7 or **D7**) back to the swirling sub-dominant four chord (IV or **C**), before gliding back to his tonic (I or **G** chord). This sweet basic rhythmic Maytag wash rocks you with a steady roll. This one-two punch with "American Pie" made the Rock and Roll world discover that it had a history. Back at its original moorings, Rock was a lot of fun to dance to, again. Uncluttered by heavy orchestral razzmatazz and esoteric gobbledygook, "Crocodile Rock" just features a beautiful melody and an easy, fun, nostalgic lyric. The first major hit to celebrate OLDIES was "Those Oldies But Goodies (Remind Me of You)" (#9, 5-61, Little Caesar & the Romans). Carl Burnett 'Little Caesar' named himself after Gangsta Movie Star George Raft, and splashed the 1st OLDIE-ECHO top ten tune.

Elton tightropes from tenor to baritone, always with the right amount of gruff/tender Soul, mixed perfectly. On his gator groover here, he pole-vaults tenor to shrill falsetto, reprising the lost "Cry Myself to Sleep" (#99, 6-62, #29, UK) of his early hero, 1999 Rock Hall inductee **Del Shannon** (1935-90). In the very same June 1962 (which came 1st – chicken or egg?), another falsetto swoop, from the guy 10th of all time in top 40 hits (38) to Elton's 2nd (57), echoed for Elton's #1 song eleven years later:

"Speedy Gonzales" – Pat Boone, #6, 6-62. Like the Hollywood Argyles' #1 '60 "Alley Oop," the Royal Guardsmen's #2(4) '66 "Snoopy vs. the Red Baron," Archies' (#1, '68) "Sugar, Sugar," or **Blondie**'s (#1[6], 2-80) "Call Me," Pat Boone celebrates a popular cartoon character in song. "Speedy Gonzales," last top tenner for Elvis's #1 1955-56 rival, covers a Mexican mouse's shenanigans. Speedy's discontinuance may relate to political incorrectness, for his stereotype didn't typify the ideal. Ethnic overtones aside, the song rang out with a piercing soprano with a little la-la ya-ya routine, woven around Elton's Streetcorner chord pattern. Essentially, Pat & Del supplied this Elton John falsetto. Elton's derivative style is a TRIBUTE, not just an echo. Boone's chart goodbye? #100, 4-69, "July, You're a Woman."

Elton's bouncy "Crocodile Rock" reminisces on when R & R was very young, plus the blast he had with his songchick 'Susie.' Born in 1947, it'd be tough for 9-year-old Elton to have a car and his own place in the 50s, as described – unless it was the dump occupied by Speedy/Snoopy/Archies' fellow cartoon character **Sluggo**, this 8-year-old pal in comic-strip *Nancy*. Sluggo dwelt in a holey-wall, tincan-yard, ramshackle solitary shack, with latchkey I-don't-caregivers permanently Out to Lunch. Anyhow, Elton elevates his 50s flashback dreams into *Happy Days* Wonderlands of Malt Shop paradise. When Elton's 1st #1 commandeered Christmas 1972, he and Susie cavorted in his levee Chevy (see "American Pie"). In 1961

Europe the only American cars were a few '53 Pontiacs in rich Kiruna, Sweden. England bloated with cool Jags, silly Citroens, the odd Rolls, and a slew of Mickey Mouse Morris Minors the size of a sofa or an MG. Elton's Chalypso beat, with Darin #2, '59 "Dream Lover" *pizzicato* guitars, rolls along in friendly Folk Key of 'G'. He fondles both his piano and big Farfisa organ. Elton delivers a 50s we wish really could have been there for all of us who lived through these bittersweet years. "Crocodile Rock," however, brings us a semantic snafu and clarity catastrophe spinning us back to a mid-century marathon singing star:

"Tennessee Waltz" – Patti Page, #1(13), 11-50; #2(3), 2-51, C. Thirteen weeks. #1 Waltz of all time. Patti Page was born Clara Fowler in Merle Haggard's Muskogee, Oklahoma, November 8, 1927, in a family of 11 kids. She is probably the most important female singer of the fifties. A Marathon is a 26.2-mile race, and our Marathon singers often have a recording career over 26 years. When you do your first marathon, you often 'hit the wall' at 20 miles, and drop out. Patti's last charted hit was #80, Country, 5-82 "My Man Friday," culminating an amazing 30+ year career. Patti Page had four HUGE songs that commanded the #1 spot for 36 total weeks, or 75% of an entire YEAR in the 50s. Since Patti's primary platters spun during 1950-55, she's rarely mentioned by Rock Revolutionists. She purred and murmured and over-dubbed her beautiful velvet contralto ballads. Via **Les Paul** multi-tracking technology, she harmonized one, two, three, and even FOUR Pattis. Indeed, Whitburn lists her #11, 1-50 major hit "With My Eyes Wide Open I'm Dreaming" as the '**Patti Page Quartet**.'

What semantic disaster? OK, Patti lullabies her lyric. She's also dancing, as she sings, to the gorgeous 'Tennessee Waltz.' Yeah, right. OK, OK, if she's dancing to the 'Tennessee Waltz,' how can THIS song she's SINGING possibly BE the "Tennessee Waltz"? Which of the two tunes is, ulp, imposterizing? This tangled verbal conundrum really thumped my 7-year-old mind, and yes, I love "The Tennessee Waltz," I think, if I can just figure out which one it is . . .

Elton John's "Crocodile Rock" has the same semantic buzz-saw, or Tasmanian Devil tornado. How can the Elton/Susie team be croc-rocking, if they're referring to some OTHER ancient 50s song about this Croc-Rock dance sensation? Somewhere in the misty galaxies far away, a crocodile (from DUNDEE?) is waltzing with an alligator (cartoon *Pogo's* pal Albert?). See ya later, alligator. Sometimes overly analytical song analysis can be a crock, so it's best to sit back and just enjoy the music (now, if I can just find the "Tennessee Crocodile Rockin' Waltz.")

Patti Page's dreamy ballads explored midcentury sentimentality:

"The Doggie in the Window" – Patti Page, #1(8), 1-53. Among cutest songs of all time. Of course, I was ten, wanted a DOG, and had only my sister Blair's cat, Woomp, and 11 guppies that were mine, all mine. Perky Patti gazes longingly into the pet shop window. In a sweet swoon of nurturing affection, she ponders purchasing the mixed-breed puppy for gazillions of rationalized reasons: protection, companionship, exercise, and good ol' love. In 1953, the Snoopy-style Beagle was our cuddly #1 breed. By the new millennium, cute or fluffy breeds were replaced by the new favorite breeds: Bull Mastiffs, Rottweilers, and Tyrannosauruses (often named 'Rex').

"Who Let the Dogs Out?" – Baha Man, #40+, 7-2000. [Al., #10, 7-2000]. Song sensation swept the Jock Rock nation. Rick Carey sang lead vocal, with Anthony Flowers thumping goat-skin drums. Chorus? Herschel/Pat/Marvin/Chea/Monks/Isaiah/Moe/Monty Taylor/Steve Greenberg. The name Baha Men comes from Bahamas (BAHAmians). This Bahamian/Jewish Jock Rock crew sings a frantic Rap/Rock/Soul/Hip-Hop extravaganza about mongrel dogs' bones, and about a snappy horde of Junkanoo-music Junkyard dogs (see Jim Croce's #1 '73 "Bad, Bad Leroy Brown"). These mangy mutts you WISH were trapped in a doggie-window, or maybe a tiger cage. Spirited rockin' song.

"Mockin' Bird Hill" – Patti Page, #2(1), 2-51. Duetting with Patti, PATTI wings a sweet pastoral melody. Her summery song blooms with twittery, chirpy mocking birds and rural tranquility. Despite hardscrabble shacks, creaky rusty bygone mills, and her ten-dollar mule that plows the sweaty furrows, Patti glosses over poverty and finds inner peace. Her waltz melody wafts this cozy countryside paradise down the long decades (see Les Paul's version). My wife grew up on a Michigan farm (160 acres, dairy) without the poverty. I grew up in smoke & steel motorhub Detroit. She was seven and I eight, but this was our mutual 1951 favorite song. Patti's mockin' bird influenced her vocal protégé, **Anne Murray**'s #8, '70 "Snowbird." Maybe her windowpane Doggie influenced Elton's torrid two-step Crocodile.

Patti Page is a major-league singer. Debuting with #27, 4-49 "Money, Marbles, and Chalk" (see "Rose & a Baby Ruth"), Patti first hit #1[5] with 8-50 "All My Love," a prelude to her monumental "Tennessee Waltz" triumph, which outlasted anything in the Rock Era from 1955-92 at #1. Patti's weepiest torch tune follows her lockstep Waltz meter – #1(10), 8-52 "I Went to Your Wedding." Gonzo satirist **Spike Jones [& His City Slickers]** featured a crocodile-tears 5-handkerchief bawler named 'Sir Frederick Gas' to howl out Weird-Al lyrics to #20, 1-53 as a hilarious spoof [Patti, at the bank, took it very well]. Patti's #8, 5-51 "Mister & Mississippi" is a double-tempo nostalgic ballad (see CCR's "Proud Mary" or Henry Mancini's "Moon River"). She grows up on the Mississippi River, falling head over heels for a nomadic gambler who reflects her own vagabond heritage. Patti's #3, 11-53 "Changing Partners" reviews "The Tennessee Waltz's" waltz tempo and dance angst. She also scored: #5, 8-51 "Detour"; #4, 8-52 "You Belong to Me" (#7, 6-62, Duprees, and #1[12] '52 Jo Stafford); and haunting #2(2), 6-56 Rock Era smash "Allegheny Moon." Her closest tune to Rock and Roll is another double-tempo tune – #2(4), 2-54 "Cross Over the Bridge." It previews Rock, pitching redemption to this ribald scoundrel on reckless rip-roaring sprees. Her

weirdest song was Gothic Death Rock theme song to whodunnit Bette Davis flick, #8, 4-65 "Hush, Hush Sweet Charlotte."

"Daniel" – Elton John, #2(1), 4-73. Inspired by a blind person, "Daniel's" mystical message says we're sometimes impaired in one area of vision – but clairvoyant in others. How so? Daniel flies from Heathrow to Spain. Short hop. Elton and lyricist Bernie Taupin watch red taillights recede into ebony skies. Right away, your R & R-tragedy-reeling mind is dreading AAAARRRRRGH, not another ghastly plane crash. Thank you, E & B. No crash. As Daniel soars aloft, so does the convoluted chord pattern in piano-friendly Key of 'C'. Elton's mediant seventh (III7, or **E7**) tailgates his flutish Mellotron and electric piano. "Daniel" simulates the appeal of hero Del Shannon's keyboardist Max Crook's musitron sound. Drummer Olsson uses Spanish maraccas. Davey Johnstone's American BANJO sparks the song (trombone supports "Honky Cat," via Jacques Boulognesi.). **George Michael** duetted with Elton on #1(1), 12-91 "Don't Let the Sun Go Down on Me," a live-audience echo of John's unforgettable original:

"Don't Let the Sun Go Down on Me" – Elton John, #2(2), 7-74. And the Beach Boys? Elton features vocal backings by Beach Personnel **Bruce Johnstone** (unrelated to Davey), **Carl Wilson,** and only female-ever Beach 'Boy' – **Toni Tennille.** Recorded in Caribou Ranch, Colorado, Elton relishes one of his most convoluted, complex orchestral arrangements (the Beach Boys pioneered this stuff). Herein lies the genius of Elton John. He takes the best of the past, hews together the best of the present, and always has an eye on the future. A passionate longing song. Soul and Desperation. Great life-force sunset song.

"Philadelphia Freedom" – Elton John, #1(2), 3-75; #32, 4-75, R & B. Elton commands respect for his selfless humanitarian benefits, his musical versatility and universality, and his friendly unconceited manner. He is also decent and courageous, plus modest. There's no reason to brag; his NUMBERS brag for him! Next to Elvis's 104, remember Elton is 2nd in Top 40 hits (57); he ties for 5th in Top Ten hits (27, with Stevie Wonder 28, Madonna 33+, Beatles 34, and Elvis 38). Elton's 6th in most charted hits in 2000. He's rated #3 Top Artist of All time by Joel Whitburn's Top 500 Artist Rankings: Elvis 9641 pts, Beatles 5360, and Elton 5176 and gaining.

"Philadelphia Freedom," yes. **Billie Jean King** beat Bobby Riggs, 53, in a heavy-hoopla national TV male-female tennis showdown. Billie used the purse as seed money to launch a tennis enterprise to bring equality in sports to women. The 70s Philadelphia Freedom was a [now-defunct] women's tennis team. Billie Jean has a pleasant smile, glasses, bobbed short haircut, and massively muscular quadriceps for pouncing upon the day-glo chartreuse ball as it whurfles over the net. Killer forehand smash, too. It seems Elton had one of those from-afar crushes on Ms. King (b. '43). He penned his Philly classic in Key of 'F'.

PHILLY CHORD ADVENTURE

Serving on an **F-major** on the lobbing lyric, he shifts to easy super-tonic seventh (II7 or **G7**), and then unruly **Fm6/Ab.** His chorus trumps the melodic sub-dominant (IV or **Bb**), and spin-drifts the knee-high line on **Eb, D7, Gm7, and Eb7.** His supertonic bluesy seventh drifts brazenly through a chromatic slur off the mediant III seventh (**A7**), down to the Polynesian bVI (**Db**). Then back to the Big Four Chord (**Bb**). Simplicity strikes out. This tennis-team triumph smashes polychordal oddities over the net at you; you dodge and feint and slice and smash. When he gets to the light-shining part, you're racquetting through a Chord Wonderland: **Bb, Gm7, Bb, Bdim** [diminished], **C7, Bb, Am7, Gm7, F.** He just walks down to the I chord via the IV, IIIm, IIm, and I. So as not to leave the **Mideastern bIII chromatic** chord behind (**Ab**), Elton stuffs it into the guitar 'tacet.'

Lyrically, he looks for inspiration to Billie Jean King, captain of the Philadelphia Freedom (1974-76 heyday). One of the most complex chordal odysseys in R & R, this big #1 hit is vintage Elton.

"Sorry Seems to Be the Hardest Word" – Elton John, #6, 11-76. His lyrical message is crystal clear: when it comes to apologizing, the whole human race (particularly guys) is Sorry-Impaired. His title says it all. How often, bulbous in our pride and balloooooooning self-image, do we fail to make amends for the hurt and pain and sins of omission related to others? Tender ballad. Excellent emotional exploration.

"You Gotta Love Someone" – Elton John, #43, 11-90. Surreal lyrics: slice off a chunk of the sun. Cheat the Devil. Burn up the highway. Rip off the moon's face and halt the world in its cosmic course. All before high noon. Casual listeners just hear a pleasant hook & chorus, a sweet Elton John melody. This is why I prefer FOREGROUND MUSIC. It helps to catch the wild words tossed out with the serene, placid mood of some great songs we half-hear.

"Gotta Serve Somebody" – Bob Dylan, #24, 9-79. Ultramarathoner/ hitmaker Bob was raised in the Lower 48's icebox – Hibbing, Minnesota – among few towns with a MINUS January average low temp. His Jewish dad sold washing machines in a largely Christian community. With a firebrand Sephardic bard style, Dylan took his 70s conversion seriously, warning backsliders of the deadly yin-yang that fundamental Christianity poses: either you must

serve God or the devil. Either-or. The Duality reality.

Elton ran with Dylan's theme, casting his musical vision "You Gotta Love Someone" into the melodic keyboard toughie Key of Eb. Among Elton's bizarro chordal concoctions, he frequently doubles the **Fm/Eb,** and fires off a **Bb** sustained. The big refrain blazes boldly through this chord outwash: YOU'VE GOTTA LOVE SOMEONE. Popular music is about love, and service.

Since Elvis is gone, and the surviving half of the Beatles aren't performing together anymore, does that make Elton John our #1 Artist into Millennium III?

"Goodbye Yellow Brick Road" – Elton John, #2(3), 10-73. Off same-named album, which nabbed 6 million buyers (Al. #1[6], 10-73). Elton addresses disillusionment theme. Oz? For real? Or for make-believe? The albums are real: Al. #1(10), 11-74 *Greatest Hits;* #1(7), 6-75 *Captain Fantastic and the Brown Dirt Cowboy;* #1(4), 7-74 *Caribou;* #6, 7-92 *The One*; or #13, 4-95 *Made in England.* Elton romps through Symbol Forests in his gold-paved Oz curtain call. OZ must have looked pretty good to British kids born just before Elton – as the *Wehrmacht, Luftwaffe,* and *Blitzkrieg* strafed English gardens with monster bombs in Hitler's tragic tornado of mega-death. As our 30s Depression brightened a bit, dark clouds gathered over Europe. American geography buffs, of course, know 'Oz' floats over breadbasket Kansas. Dorothy told us all about it, when the world first came into color.

One of my students' kids, 6, believed (via ancient films) that at some cinematic point, the world (Oz, anyhow) actually did blossom into vivid technicolor from dark creepy black and white. I'd be willing to wager MILLIONS of other 'Baby Boomer' kids had the same weird notion.

Elton says goodbye to the yellow-brick road to Oz. Smart move. Even the actual movie *Wizard of Oz* ('39****) was littered with mortal peril. One of the 'munchkin' dwarfs actually hanged himself (it's IN the movie). Oz proved no Oz. The Wicked Witch clawed, the munchkins guffawed, and Dorothy got stoned in the poppy field (#11, '67 "Ding Dong! The Witch Is Dead," Fifth Estate). When Dorothy, the Scarecrow, the Tin Woodman, and the Cowardly Lion finally got to the Emerald City, Mighty Oz himself turned out to be a fake, a charlatan, a Humbug. "Goodbye Yellow Brick Road" is another great hymn to disillusionment. Want an Oz ANTIDOTE? Try **Dr. Seuss**'s *I Had Trouble in Getting to Solla Sollew* ('65). Like Dorothy's character, Seuss's little critter-hero meets grisly obstacles to his own imagined Emerald City ['on the banks of the beautiful river Wahoo/where they never have troubles, at least very few']. Zapped by toothy obstacles at every turn, our *Solla Sollew* pilgrim finally gets tough, brandishes a big bat, and takes care of business.

Elton shows us that yellow-brick roads, supposedly paved with gold or glory, often turn out as muddy quagmires into dismal swamps. From the snazzy fool's gold yellow-brick road to Elton/Bernie's #18, 8-94 "Circle of Life" in *The Lion King* ***½, their message is strong. Growing up, you shuck the naivete. You dump the kiddie attitudes. You become an adult, albeit grudgingly. You go to work. You pay the bills. Most of all, you gotta love someone.

"The Winner" – Bobby Bare, NC, 1976; #13, 3-76 C. Shel Silverstein (1934-99) penned **Johnny Cash**'s #2, '69 "A Boy Named Sue" and this hilarious Anti-Brawl Anthem. Another bar scene: feisty lad challenges vet bar scrapper to fight. Old roustabout says OK. Vet first explains all the trophies you get from winning bar fights: cauliflower ears, migraines, and a nose busted so much a sneeze might explode it. His ex-teeth rolled away like Chiclets on a San Antonio avenue. He busted three ribs in a fight he 'won' (the loser had seven). Via hyperbole and grotesque logic about 'winning,' challenger begins to realize winning looks suspiciously like LOSING. Our hero reconsiders fight. They make up, sip beer. Ends up hunky-dory. Peachy keen. Peace, love, brotherhood, male bonding, Miller Time, and the Big Bonus – longevity.

In his amazing *Uncle Shelby's ABZ Book,* Shel's crafty book alter-ego tells some disconsolate kid: THERE IS NO OZ AND THERE IS NO EASTER BUNNY . . . MAYBE SOME DAY YOU CAN GO TO DETROIT! (1961). Why not Oz?

"Over the Rainbow" – Judy Garland, #5, 9-39. At age five, when I first saw a color movie (pre-TV 1948), I had a crush on Judy/Dorothy (but it never worked out). Accompanied by the Victor Young Orchestra (#1[4], 6-35 "She's a Latin from Manhattan"), Judy sang one of the most enduring ballads of all time. Voted #1 ever in a 2001 Library of Congress/Smithsonian poll, "Over the Rainbow" adds a new dimension to every kid's pre-fab conception of Heaven. The classic film shows a sad tableau of free-flying bluebirds and earthbound melancholy – uplifted by glowing gleams of HOPE. Tony Martone sees its leprechaun celestial vision as a celebration of the PROMISE of a Great Beyond, but a realistic adventure that proves there's nothing perfect on earth (and Heaven's Mezzanine, Oz). Basically, we have to chart our own destinies with pluck, determination, and courage. No Wizard can give us what we yearn for. It must come from within us.

Jazz diva **Peggy Lee**'s #11, 9-69 "Is That All There Is" takes the world-weary *Weltschmerz* way out, zapping wonder and awe and hope and faith. Her glum song determines that this world (and the NEXT) are terminally BORING. Joel Whitburn calls the sparkling-eyed princess **Judy Garland** "as electrifying a performer as ever sang on an American concert stage." Sadly, growing up was child star Judy's biggest problem. Her talented daughter **Liza Minnelli** (Al. #19, 10-72 *Liza with a 'Z'* – b. '46, LA) sought the same star-studded stairway to heaven. Liza proves, with her torchy Streisand voice, that rising into the Judy Garland-Frank Sinatra-Dean Martin-Sammy Davis showbiz family can be genetic.

Judy's "Rainbow" signature song wasn't even her top chart hit: #4, 11-44 "The Trolley Song" and #3, 7-40 "I'm Nobody's Baby" both stomped the rainbow's chart rung, as did her #3, 1-42 **Gene Kelly** duo "For Me and My Gal." In Judy's Oz Carol, the Rainbow and the Leprechaun chase our dreams around the universe. Fighting bulemia with diet pills, she downpedalled her rainbow in war-torn winter 12-44 (#27) to a carol that borders on the (ulp, Grinch) sarcastic: "Have Yourself a Merry Little Christ-mas." When Judy Garland, America's darling, died of old age in lonely London, another tornado slammed down onto the rolling Kansas prairie below Heaven's Mezzanine – Oz. Old age? Judy was 47.

"Candle in the Wind I" –Elton John, #6, 11-87. Marilyn Monroe (b. Norma Jean Baker, 1927-62) was the most beautiful actress in the world. A tad zaftig by today's svelte standards, the 5'5" blone bombshell sported the size 14, 143#, 38-26-36 luscious bosomy ideal that discombobulated men on five continents (plus a few 6th-continent Antarctic penguins). Like "Rock Around the Clock," "Candle in the Wind's" hitdom involved TWO hey-days. The second one clobbered the competition. Marilyn's blondeened hair magnetized males to her flagrantly feminine figure. Goggle-eyed men and boys from 9 to 99+ ogled this cinema icon. Even your semi-innocent scribe was once thrust into the wicked well of demon temptation via her va-va-voom calendar. You see, in 1953 the only way a young lad (10, me) could see what the top or bottom half of an adult female really looked like was to gaze gaga with a cracked magnifying glass at the pages of the *National Geographic*. Far off on an eentsy-meentsy palm frond, tee-heeing, you might find a winsome lass in [only] a grass skirt. She was always a football field away.

So here I am, attached to this silly radiator, my hands clutching for dear life, and two oversized monsters grabbing me. Huh? Oh, yeah, Marilyn Monroe . . . you see, at age ten I blundered into a little log-cabin Mobilgas station. THERE SHE WAS! On a back-room curvaceous calendar, for the first time in my little life, I saw what a woman really looked like, ahem, upstairs, anyhow (her shapely legs folded pretty demurely). Hoping to re-join my folks back at the Chevy, I was thwarted by my feet, which decided to attach themselves to the floor. I stared, transfixed. It was just Marilyn, and, wow, me.

Suddenly, I was interrupted by these two 6'2", 222# old men about 22 years old. "GET OUTA THERE, WISE GUY. YOU CAN'T LOOK AT THAT CALENDAR!" They had another think comin'. My hands somehow grabbed the radiator, and these two bruisers couldn't pry them off. So that's MY seedy, sleazy, tawdry tale of how I first encountered Marilyn Monroe, and the fab female form, in the flesh. I don't know whether or not we want to know about yours. So Elton John and Bernie Taupin wrote us all a very, tender, empathetic tale Candle in the Wind. **Marilyn Monroe** never really knew who to be. Bandied about on casting couches, she offered her favors to father figures who lusted after her sweet body. When she tragically lost her life in 1962 at prime-time 35, nobody ever figured out whether it was suicide or an accidental sleeping-pill O.D. She married a great intellectual (playwright **Arthur Miller**) and a great baseball star (Joltin' **Joe DiMaggio**, the Yankee Clipper). She flirted [and what-not] with the President of the United States AND his kid brother. She was beautiful, rich, and unhappy. Like a zephyr snuffing a candle, Marilyn's weak will condemned her to half a life. Two billion men worldwide would have loved the opportunity to take her in, give her love and coziness and NURTURING on their bus-driver paychecks. It was not to be.

Her candle extinguished itself long, long before her legend. Like Elvis, James Dean and Buddy Holly, she will always be larger than life. Gone, never forgotten?

A fine elegiac hit, "Candle" flamed anew in 10-97 to perpetuate the royal memory of Great Britain's beloved **Princess Di.** Taupin's new lyric glorified Elton's top-notch melody in a splash of Universality. **Puff Daddy's** elegiac #1(11), 6-97 "I'll Be Missing You" had a short life as the biggest tribute of the Rock Era (for **Notorious B.I.G.,** shot to death in a Rap turf war). Elton/Bernie trumped it immediately with a requiem for a beautiful princess, whose Oz dreams were shattered in one terrible Parisian moment. According to James Mitchell, "Candle" also burned in a THIRD version – the mysterious unrecorded version – for brave young Ryan White, who succumbed to Acquired Immune Deficiency Syndrome. Now let's move to the song that sent **Bing Crosby** and **Irving Berlin's** immortal Christmas Carol "White Christmas" out of the #1-ever spot, after 65 years wearing the champ's heavyweight belt:

"Candle in the Wind II"/"Something About the Way You Look Tonight" – Elton John, #1(14), 10-97; #1(17+), U.K. Two of the world's most beloved women passed away during the same fateful week near Labor Day '97 – **Princess Diana of Wales,** and **Mother Teresa** of India. Elton's "Candle II" was sung at the largest funeral in British history. Taupin revised the Marilyn Monroe melody to England's own 'rose.' Loftier in tone and lyrical power, Bernie's new words nostalgically drift back to the Romantic Era when 'Brittania ruled the High Seas and the 'sun never set on the British Empire.' He conjures cascading visions of English glories and bygone Camelot. Never-ever fading beyond sunset, the spirited footsteps of England's Rose will eternally wander along the greenest English hills. Elton mourns loveliness lost, the empty days without the beautiful 'golden-child,' whose strawberry-blonde hair was a benchmark for regal beauty. We Americans old enough to recall the shock and aftermath of President Kennedy's tragic death (at 47, 11-22-63), can turn to our English brethren with compassion and somber respect. Our youthful leader too represented the best of national hope and destiny. We too were crestfallen at the unexpected loss.

Princess Diana changed the character of British royalty forever. Her tragic and senseless death in a Paris tunnel at 100 miles per hour ('escaping paparazzi photographers') marked a moment of stark disbelief for Anglo-Americans the world over. Beyond a rapacious tabloid maze of shorn steel, unemployed seatbelts, and a titanic mangled Mercedes, there lay the broken shards of all of our dreams. A hive of hornets stabbed away at the fleeting fragments of Britain's thunderstruck Crown.

She was a beautiful Princess, a devoted mother. She was imbued with an American-style optimism that made her OF the people. **Diana Spencer** was the living antithesis of the word 'stuffy." Indeed, she reached out to victims of starvation, of love diseases, or land mines, with equal bravery and compassion. Selfless tributes to downtrodden, woebegone people made Diana revered internationally. She had every right to hunker down with Prince Charles and hide away at lofty Balmoral Castle. But she chose to go to the people who also loved her – on Poverty Row.

That's where she met **Mother Teresa** of Calcutta, India. A monumental crossroads occurred when the 4'10" Saint of Calcutta reached up to cinematic Diana's statuesque shoulders to present the pretty Princess with a Rosary. The beloved nun started life quite well-to-do in Albania. At her fullness-of-life passing at 87, she owned only a pair of sandals, a couple of knick-knacks, and a robe not unlike the one Jesus took to the green spring hills of Calvary. Two of the most spectacular women in world history died the same week. The one given half a life was buried with the Rosary given by **Mother Teresa.** Each lady was among the richest in the history of the world for what really matters – LOVE. The powerful phenomenon of Popular Music helps us all remember the noble lives of so many fallen martyrs, and does it for a song (see "American Pie").

Elton also helped our worldwide memories of **John Lennon** (1940-80), with his #13, 3-82 "Empty Garden (Hey Hey Johnny)." It's the best ELEGIAC song done for the martyred Beatle, a tribute showing Elton's power of friendship, like Diana Ross's **Marvin Gaye** #10, 12-84 tribute "Missing You." Elton never missed a note. His fine #6 Marilyn Monroe elegiac classic underwent a masterpiece of Taupin lyrical recycling, vaulting heavenward into a rainbow of international tears. Indeed – perhaps more simultaneous tears were shed on Bernie's refurbished lyric "Candle in the Wind II" than at any other moment in human history (via Diana's funeral broadcast to five billion people). The lad from Pinner, with the cute "Crocodile Rock" debut #1 song, came a long way to show the world something about the real meaning of Crowns and Thorns and gold.

Elton's flipside of his #1(14) hit, "Something About the Way You Look Tonight," was actually listed as the 'A' side for the last eleven of the fourteen weeks in America. Anticlimactically, it's technically the big side, or 11/14 of the huge hit. It's a great ballad, too, but because of the power and impact of the "Candle II" song, I'm agreeing with super-chronicler Joel Whitburn, and subordinating this fine big hit to this semi-fine little paragraph. [See Elvis's #1(11) '56 "Hound Dog"/"Don't Be Cruel"]. Helping the candle-power of its platter partner, "Something" helped "Candle II" not only become the world's largest-selling record, but the #2 record at #1 – 14 weeks – in history (see "One Sweet Day," another elegiac song, but without a specific subject).

"I Don't Wanna Go on with You Like That" – Elton John, #2(1), 6-88. Elton's 2nd-string hits and lesser luminaries are great compositions, too. His #9, 6-92 "The One" rides the Polynesian chord and the whirlwind to glory; #18, 1-90 "Sacrifice" hovers hauntingly over the concept of love and service; #3, 5-80 "Little Jeannie" reminds me of the whole Jeannie-Blair-Joey-Joan-Madelyn Dean crew, and you of something else; Aretha duo #16, 4-89 "Through the Storm" (#17 R&B) shows Elton's Pinner Soul; Beatle flashback #1(2), 11-74 "Lucy in the Sky with Diamonds" rehashes *Sgt. Pepper;* #7, 1-86 "Nikita" lessens Anglo-

Soviet tensions.

Elton wore 1975 Goliath glasses and multi-hued glitzy outfits of outrageous fun and festivity. Just to have a good time. There's a bit of Pagliacci in Elton, though. His sad clown persona erupted in many personal problems for his health and concerning his life style. Many downer doldrums dragged him into a blue funk and iffy substances. Elton was sidelined with potential life-threatening scares. For a time he was like Marilyn Monroe's vulnerable Candle in the Wind. As the 70s Decade of Excess simmered down, Elton and the world breathed a sigh of relief. All his dedicated fans were overjoyed to see him on the comeback trail.

Elton John

"I'm Still Standing" – Elton John, #12, 5-83. This great Rock and Roll song symbolizes Elton's courageous comeback. Or anybody's great comeback. Like Sinatra's #4, 11-66 "That's Life," Elton picks himself back up, dusts himself right off, and jumps back into the marathon race. As others tumble around him, he bravely stands up for the musical destiny he achieved – and his dedication to his loyal fans. With pluck, courage, and resolute musical genius, he dukes it out with various monsters. He's a little like Boppo the Clown, every kid's holiday present. Remember your vinyl punching bag with sand in the bottom? Whenever he's punched, he totters back up with a big plucky smile. The resiliency of these marathon troopers, in bringing us our favorite songs in far-flung venues of this rockin' planet, is a testimonial to the power and glory that is Rock and Roll.

TODEAN'S DAY-TO-DAY SAMPLER:

"Sunday Morning Coming Down,"
   Johnny Cash, #46, 8-70.
"Sunday Will Never Be the Same,"
   Spanky & Our Gang, #9, 5-67.
"Monday, Monday," Mamas & Papas, #1(3), 4-66.
"Manic Monday," Bangles, #2(1), 1-86.
"Blue Monday," Fats Domino, #5, 1-57.
"Tuesday Morning," Nine Days, NC, 1998.
"Tuesday Afternoon," Moody Blues, #24, 7-68.
"Ruby Tuesday," Rolling Stones, #1(1), 2-67.
"Wednesday," Royal Guardsmen, #97, 9-67.
Wednesday Morning, 3 AM,
   Simon & Garfunkel, Al. #30, 1-66.
"Thursday," Jim Croce, NC, '73
   [Al. #2(2), 12-73 *I Got a Name*].
"Black Friday," Steely Dan, #37, 5-75.
"Friday on My Mind," Easybeats, #16, 3-67.
"Friday I'm in Love," Cure, #18, 6-92.
"Saturday Night," Bay City Rollers, #1(1), 10-75.
"Saturday in the Park," Chicago, #3, 8-72.
"Saturday Night's Alright for Fighting,"
   Elton John, #12, 8-73.

"Club at the End of the Street" – Elton John, #28, 4-90. Cheers. For years, many Americans felt guilty about going to bars. We make them dark, like German Rathskellers. In Great Britain, the Dog & Whistle or Knave & Skittles or Coachman at Arms is often bright and cheery, despite WARM beer. Unwimpy British pubs often sport the local rugby, soccer, or Cross-Country Hotfoot Harriers, sipping a brew or two. In America a lot of folks religiously don't drink, a hangover of the Prohibition Era. Perhaps we've never quite formed the clubby bar-pals image, like comic-strip Hagar the Horrible and Lucky Eddie. Or have we? *Cheers* and *Friends* give us a second opinion. Elton's end-of-street club hosts a delightful roster of denizens. He spices his life with the best idea from Jimmy Stewart's 1946**** *It's a Wonderful Life* – that FRIENDS are of paramount importance to all man/womankind. Like Rod Stewart, Elton's bar-stormers also listen to old Motown Records, citing the magic moods of Marvin Gaye's monumental music.

With **Dionne Warwick, Gladys Knight,** and **Stevie Wonder, Elton** sang soulfully on #1(4), 11-85 "That's What Friends Are For" (which showboats a Stewart intro). As Elton's half-century mark sped by (3-25-97), he mellowed out on the vices, and started to enjoy all his accolades for one of history's greatest ambassadors of great popular music. **Elton John** has become an icon, in the same league as **Elvis,** the **Beatles, Buddy Holly, Frank Sinatra,** or **Louis Armstrong.** The Pinner Piano Man strikes again, and makes everybody happy.

"Piano Man" – Billy Joel, #25, 2-74. Everybody's favorite Rock and Roll Waltz. In Soft Rock splendor, **Billy Joel** (b. 5-9-49, Hicksville, Long Island, NY) seesaws baritone/tenor octaves, and captures the microcosmic Pub Soul of 1974 America. Billy sings his credo – music is a refuge for the lonely, but it's also a wellspring of joy. The Piano Man's musical magic smothers despair at lonely outposts of solitude.

Twilight bonanza. Flatland Hicksville is suburban sprawl. Solid middle-class upbringing. Megalopolis suburbia. Mall Rock or Sprawl Rock is what excellent *Newsday* rock critic Glenn Gamboa calls it. Comfy town Hicksville ain't the Ritz. It nearly abuts Levittown. Billy's folks squabbled a little. Some drinking battered his family bliss, so he ducked the academic life at 15 to seek the musician's Promised Oz. We already hassled the Hassles of Hicksville – and Attila – Billy's two prior metamorphoses before he became THE ENTERTAINER. Forty percent of the Hassles (Billy, drummer Jon Small) became Heavy Metal/Thrash bashers Attila. Billy used his whole name – William Martin Joel – to co-opt the handle of Yankee 2B star/manager Billy Martin. Then he used that Piano-man stage moniker for his Sunset Strip gigs in piano-bar 'Tinseltown' LA/Hollywood. Billy's lounge-lizard characters at the piano bar are real. "Piano Man" chronicles his smoky-haze adventures in this martini milieu. Like **Sheryl Crow**'s #2(6), 8-94 mid-afternoon "All I Wanna Do" bar buddies, Billy's night-club grotesques become a little microcosmic universe. This isn't **Elton John**'s bonhomme "Club at the End of the Street." Nor was it downtrodden or terminally gloomy, like #1 '56 "Heartbreak Hotel" or #4, '58 "Lonesome Town." More like CCR, it was stuck in middle-earth yuppie pub #52, '69 "Lodi" again.

"I wanted to write and sing like my idol, Paul McCartney," Billy told Five Towns College students (Jeremy Dean's school, like the great Suffolk County Community College). Billy's success thrust him from Hicksville to Mike & Sue Polansky & GLIRC's Oyster Bay. It was a long way from the Echoes at age 15 in Beatlemania '64 to a solo contract with Columbia Records [catch his NC '71 debut Al. *Cold Spring Harbor*, re-issued #158, 1-84]. "Piano Man" is Billy's first big hit, after Hassles' #112, 11-67 Sam & Dave reprise "You've Got Me Hummin'." Also, his *Cold Spring Harbor* non-hit "She's Got a Way" was finally re-mixed and slowed down by top-notch tekkies at Columbia – hitting a belated #23, 11-81. Billy felt his debut album was zapped by some speed-demon tape mixer, who twirled his tenor tones to sound like Alvin of the Chipmunks. After "Piano Man's" eponymous album *Piano Man* hit a snazzy #27 in 1-74, Columbia doled out two more quality Joel statements: Al. #35, 11-74 *Streetlife Serenade* and super-sleeper Al. *Turnstiles* at #122, 6-76. *Turnstiles* glowed with an almost Sinatran Rock hybrid sound that celebrated the turnstile Subway Series, and a "New York State of Mind," its equally-sleepy super song that a fickle public first ignored (NC, '76). Then suddenly the floodgates busted loose with the ubiquitous sound of **Billy Joel**.

Who had the largest-selling album at #1 Columbia Records of all time – beating out Simon & Gar's legendary *Bridge over Troubled Water*? Yep, you guessed it.

Billy Joel, with his album *The Stranger* of 11-77. Here's the snickery kicker. Billy's monster album sold over five million, yet peaked for six weeks in a row at silver-medal #2 ["Johnny B. Goode" hit #8, "Old Time Rock and Roll" #28]. After *The Stranger* established his superstar rep, he aced the album arena forever: Al. #1(8), 10-78 *52nd Street;* Al. #1(6), 3-80 *Glass Houses;* Al. #7, 10-82 *The Nylon Curtain;* Al. #7, 8-86 *The Bridge;* Al. #1(1), 11-89 *Storm Front;* and #1(3), 8-93 *River of Dreams.* The Piano Man's Rock and Roll marathon dominates three decades and promises chunks of a millennium or two.

"Piano Man" is a rare WALTZ. Alternating verses trade baritone/tenor octave leaps. At Billy's piano bar, a common urban fixture in the 1895-1975 zone, the smoky ambience and chattery chuckles belie a frazzled undertone of sadness. Paste-on smiles – inner tears. Fading fake optimism. These revelers, feigning laughter and good cheer, are dynamos of desperation. Pagliacci the Sad Clown strikes (out) again. Beyond the neon dazzle? Brooding darkness.

Billy's signature song milks this mood. His wickedly winsome waltz cuts in on the common 4/4 hit dance crop. "Piano Man" brushes the Saturday Night Disco Fever's overture. On his smoky baritone first-volley verse, Joel seems calm, cool, collected. Suddenly, his keening tenor verse, an octave above, hollers the bar's denizens' pain and agony and despair. He sings an anthem for the Alka-Seltzer Disabled. [His ironic follow-up is #80, 6-74 "Worse Comes to Worst," with free bonus cosmic gloom, but buoyed by a #77, 8-74 "Travelin' Prayer"].

Naturally, his next tune is the electrifying "The Entertainer" (#34, 11-74), which froze his stardom for three years by telling too much strident truth. [not #31, 3-65 (#10 R&B) Tony Clarke's "The Entertainer"]. Billy's 'Entertainer' is a muckraking industry expose. An everyman piano-bar 'serenader' fronts a long-haired combo. Today they champion the high charts, win girls' hearts. Off the charts? Gold-digging groupies forget them forever. On his Hard Rock rhythmic rampage, Joel laments entertainers' terror of the demon charts. Rock-idol dreams are impaled on the 'Discount Album' racks like ANY OLD CAN of BEANS!

One super simile. Popularity is one jiffy fickle process. In the back of his second Top 40 hit, however, lurks the Ultimate Consolation Prize: IT'S BETTER TO BE A HAS-BEEN THAN A NEVER-WAS! Billy's song-guy juggles instant fame. Instant obscurity. The HOT 100 sizzles souls as well as hearts. Billy gripes about a song that took him years to write, but he had to squash it to 3:05's worth of orphic wisdom. He takes the cynic's quip about Rock fame. Remember how **Steve Miller** put it all in perspective by displaying his GOLD RECORDS over his washing machine? Compare Billy's discount-rack display of the dusty, grubby can of old beans. "Piano Man," however, is an unforgettable signature song.

"Just the Way You Are" – Billy Joel, #3, 11-77. Billy's 3953 Wilshire Blvd, LA, "Piano Man" gig at the Executive Room underscores this next smash. Same ambience, posh restaurant. Billy's first Top 3 hit tells the pretty lady, over rose wine and fancy tablecloths, everything she always wanted to hear. She's been trying on new shoes and personalities. Billy Sinatracizes his mellow sax-spangled song, telling her just to be herself. Don't change your personality for me, he explains. Discover your essence. Who wouldn't want to hear this – if handled right? Sweet velvet minor chords swoosh into Billy's philosophical premise – be happy with who you really are. Unlike poor pathetic "Eleanor Rigby" (Beatles, #11, '66), we don't have to put on some face scrunched into some jar next to the door . . . and we never know whom the fake face is for. Quintessence of sincerity – just be yourself (Jiminy Cricket's advice from Disney's *Pinocchio*****).

"My Life" – Billy Joel, #3, 11-78. Same theme? Don't put on the faces of "The Stranger" or unreal personas to be somebody you're not. "My Life" isn't of the naughty seductive ilk like #24, 5-78 "Only the Good Die Young" (banned by Catholic Board). Nor is it the hard-work-will-kill-you motif in #17, 3-78 "Movin' Out (Anthony's Song)," which zaps our crazy-quilt rush to seek serene suburbs while pumping adrenaline at hummingbird speed. "My Life" twists the focus back to the self-analytical singer. Yeah, sure, it has a little NYC feistiness, reflecting a jumpy, wired, hyper style and a defensive in-yer-face stoop-sitting posture. Unfindable parking places and subway-token muggings on the Paradise Line cause that edginess.

Billy's brand of Rock and Roll is New York City, like Dion & the Belmonts, Carole King, Bobby Darin. "My Life" concerns hassles. Its bristly porcupine stance is delivered without malice. It's a Rock song. No Piano-Bar Blues. You hear the big crashing 2 & 4 **Liberty DeVito** drum beat, as Billy lambasts serenity. In the folk-friendly Key of 'D', Billy bops chords on big hammering changes. Cymbals crash BETWEEN his lyrical breaths. "My Life" is a celebration of independence and self-worth.

"Theme from New York, New York" – Frank Sinatra, #32, 5-80. Frank sang Big Apple praises. If he can make it big in New York, he can make it basically anywhere. He touts his tempestuous and titillating town for its sleepless buzz, street-savvy chutzpah, its Old Boroughs of urbane lost splendor. His Apple Anthem rebounds off the eagle-high concrete stanchions of Yankee Stadium after each victory (and, ulp, loss) of the 1998-2000 'threepeat' World Champs. Pulsating with civic pride, Sinatra's "NY2" reflects his enchanted midnight smoky Jazz ballad, #27, 1-49 "Autumn in New York." It's nearly as majestic a musical moment as his cover of Billy Butterfield/Margaret Whiting's #15, 2-45 (& HER solo #29, 2-54) "Moonlight in Vermont," a Christmas-card sleigh ride into Jazz excellence. Sinatra (#2 ever, album artist rankings) and Joel describe this mystique of the "New York State of Mind." This chic gotham flashback is Joel's kaleidoscopic vision of New York City from the suburban afterglow (see Jazz Rock). Sinatra's New York reflects his penultimate metropolis ode #84, 10-57 "Chicago."

"Chicago" – Ben Selvin Orchestra, #5, 11-22. No other bandleader made more recordings (2000+) than violinist Ben (Whitburn info). Selvin celebrates some Prohibition brazen wild man who actually danced with his own WIFE (not the usual 'Flapper' floozy expected of high-roller sugardaddies). In the dismal throes of our failed boozeless experiment, an Al Capone underworld of blind pig 'teacup bars' and 'speakeasies' sprang up in a seedbed of crime and sensuous sin. Selvin & Sinatra juggled urban loyalties, too, eschewing the West Coast. Bi-urban Selvin's 10-25 "Manhattan" hit #1(4).

"You May Be Right" – Billy Joel, #7, 3-80. Any song beginning with tinkly crashing glass shards on hot asphalt might make you feel you took the bad turn into the sleazo 'Flats Fixed' neighborhood under the Old El. Billy shot to the top with #1(8) Grammy-grabbing 10-78 Al. *52nd Street,* first of four #1 albums. *Glass Houses* hit #1(6), Al. 3-80, with impish Billy chucking a rock at a window; "You May Be Right" leads it off. The bass thumps big steady 2 & 4 beats, with a gossamer grace-note fluttering behind the backbeat – on the root note of Billy's chord. His Delta Blues Key of 'A' unlocks the Masters-of-Rock cabinet: Paul McCartney, Buddy Holly. Billy spices his polychordal adventure by slamming the **'G'** chromatic shift or bVII major. Billy's **David Ruffin-**of-the-Temps' vocal range scoops out a dynamite rhythm track.

His lyric paints his song-guy as a 'lunatic' Saturday-night Casanova. On Friday he crashes her party. His girl thinks he's daft for strolling solo through tough Bedford-Stuyvesant ['Bed-Sty'], or racing his motorcycle in the oilslick rainy rainbow. As he cruises the dead-end alley-ways with a desperado devotion to adventure and kicks, he tells her she must be looking for a daredevil. Whenever Billy downbeats the chorus off a pregnant Screaming Blues tacet, he unleashes his Rock and Roll Tornado.

Billy Joel, jousting and jabbing his welterweight wizardry, watched the Friday Night Fights between Disco vs. Rock, Country vs. Soul, Metal vs. Croony Tunes. Suddenly he jumped into the skirmish epicenter – and declared PEACE.

"It's Still Rock and Roll to Me" – Billy Joel, #1(2), 5-80. As long as you hit the big 2 & 4 backbeats, or kissin' cousins the 2, 2 ½, and 4 beats, it's Basic Rock. Long before the MTV Fashion Awards, Billy had a few salient remarks on style. **Thomas Carlyle**'s 1837 *Sartor Resartus* hinged the meaning of life and the universe on outward symbols like fashion. Billy cites pink sidewinders, orange pants, and Beau Brummell (a 19th-century fop/dandy dresser). Most dance-fever dudes could care less about the obtuse allusions. They just love the beat and hope to meet girls. The bass prowls. Billy rides the ginchy bass lead on a pizzicato beat, which accents EVERY beat Disco-style – but he plays the grace note off the main beat:

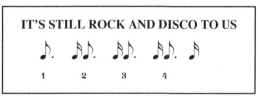

IT'S STILL ROCK AND DISCO TO US

♪. ♪♪. ♪♪. ♪♪. ♪

1   2   3   4

Billy's jumping lyric is star-spangled with internal rhymes and slick era slang – like 2002+ Rap hot punk, cool junk, old funk. Scrambled internal rhyme emblazons Billy's title mantras. "It's Still Rock and Roll" now highlights the repertoire of high school marching bands and junior-high choruses. Mainstream America. The song is a lot of fun. Billy dawdles on the echoing bass in the first half of his verses. Then he brings in the handclappers and rock-a-beatin' drums to bash the backbeat 2 & 4. The skittery bass thumps all four beats. In the inter-verse hollow, it scampers into triplets, chopping the measure into an even dozen crunches.

His lyric gripes that you can't really hear the **true sound** of a great band in some **fanzine** (fan magazine) with a 'teenybopper' target market. Example? See 2001 N'Sync 42-page photo riot. Many dancing queens don't have to dissect paradiddles and hammer-ons and sax timbre. They just love the song. It has a great beat. You can dance to it. Working musicians may be loathe to consult *Teen* for advice on how to play a hit song, but *Guitar Player* and *Modern Drummer*, like Jazz *Downbeat*, offer tips. Lyric mags like *Song Hits* or *Hit Parader* offer word structure to budding singers/artists/stars. Also, *Spin, Goldmine*, or *Rolling Stone* cover the rock scene expertly. "Still Rock & Roll" has its share of chord jogs. In the Key of 'C', the bass perches on Lower Mezzanine note 'B' on the way to chromatic bVII **Bb**. It jumps quickly to sub-dominant IV or **F**. Again, just Alphabet Soup to a jumping frivoler at the Midnight Flame Day-Glo Dance-atorium – what counts is the BIG BEAT and lockstep thunder R & R magic. Billy carries on his fashion observations in #18, 1-85 "Keeping the Faith," from Lucky Strikes, chino pants, and Sen-Sen, to his dad's aftershave and X-rated items. So Billy juggles baby-blue Lincoln Continentals, the Jive Age, Zocko orange trousers, and the Beautiful People. He spoofs peer-group pressure, and defines what's currently COOL on the razor's-edge of NOW. Basically, Billy Joel totally dismisses R & R fragmentation, integrating it all into a mulligatawny mish-mosh of styles that ALL become ONE type of 'E Pluribus Unum' grand music – good ol' Rock and Roll.

"Sometimes a Fantasy" – **Billy Joel, #36, 10-80.** Billy Joel and Holly hiccups. Unbeatable combo? Billy here deciphers real from unreal, genuine from sham, bona fide from fake. Joel enjoyed five #1 Adult Contemporary #1 songs. Billy's lower-echelon chart tiptoppers are all great: #92, 8-92 dare-to-cover-Elvis "All Shook Up"; #77, 8-90 "That's Not Her Style," with **Richard Marx** (#1, '89 "Satisfied') vocal background. Billy's #10, 6-86 "Modern Woman" and #18, 11-86 "This Is the Time" demonstrate his consummate versatility. Other Classic Rock tracks include #10, 8-86 "A Matter of Trust"; #6, 1-90 salute to bi-polar happy/sad moodiness, "I Go to Extremes"; chide-your-roaring-yesternight-pal #17, 2-79 "Big Shot"; Carioca/Salsa #19, 8-80 "Don't Ask Me Why"; #3, 9-83 Four Seasons'-inspired "Uptown Girl," about ex-wife Christie Brinkley; and sledgehammer rocker #20, 9-82 "Pressure." These are ALL #1-quality songs that incredulously eluded top gold. Among his finest sleepers is his super duo "Baby

Grand" with Original Rock Hall Inductee ('86) **Ray Charles**, #75, 4-87 (NC R&B), a hymn to two of their most faithful friends – their pianos. Blues legend **B. B. King** calls his beloved guitar "Lucille," and the keyboard duo fondles their respective ivory companions.

"We Didn't Start the Fire" – **Billy Joel, #1(2), 10-89.** Billy's 2nd-biggest hit is an auctioneer's timeline of U.S. Post-WWII history. Billy was challenged by some students who said history was boring. His smoldering Rap chant, spattered spasmodically with melodic choruses, scattershoots familiar and esoteric names plus historical firestorms. He swoops from baldly brutal JFK getting 'blown away' to tender Music-Appreciation thank-yous: "Wo-uh-ho Buddy Holly." He emblazons two important New Yorkers (orig. from Commerce, OK, and Lowell, MA), slugger **Mickey Mantle** and Beat writer **Jack Kerouac.** Billy's Un-Pyromaniac chant relives the burgeoning panorama of the Rock Era's historical backdrop. He pulls few punches, grappling with world leaders who threatened everybody's way of life in the testy fallout-shelter Cold War 50s. Billy's song is welcome in Music, or English, or History classes – wherever there are with-it teachers and non-stodgy administrations. Billy cites South Korean Prez Singman Rhee, British politicians' boudoir scandals, Russians suffering Afghanistan, U.S. Moonshot astronauts, Give-'Em-Hell Prez Harry S. Truman, and even Pepsi wars. This panorama sent wheelbarrows of Joel money back to the bank, with Presidents Washington, Lincoln, and Jackson on the $1, $5, and $20 smiling all the way.

"Goodnight Saigon" – **Billy Joel , #56, 3-83.** *Platoon* (1986***½) plundered our deepest national Vietnam conflicting attitudes as the vanguard of a cinematic trend. Billy beat the fad to the foxhole. His tribute to the American foot soldier is uncanny. A chopper volleys his tense intro. You can smell the acrid smoke and terror. The song lumbers slowly at first. Billy ascends a bushwhack Irish tenor sound, slinking stealthily through the fire flash *Apocalypse Now* (1979*** ½) jungle. Billy punts his mellow midrange for a shrill wail of fear and loathing.

"Tell Her About It" –**Billy Joel, #1(1), 7-83.** As in rock-infancy "Runaround Sue" or "Little Town Flirt," Billy proffers advice to pal squatting in blue funk of jilted despair. Buck up, buddy, sez Billy. Rising on trickly streamers of flashy falsetto, Billy bubbles along in 'Bb', the pretty key – then swaggers into all-purpose 'F' in the chorus. Much of Billy's building blocks of Rock come from his forebears on Brooklyn gas lamp corners, serenading lost halos:

"The Longest Time" – **Billy Joel, #14, 3-84.** Like the 'Patti Page Quartet' or Studio Adventures of **Prince**, Billy commandeers ALL the voices in this faux a cappella hit. He masquerades as the Four Seasons or Dion/Belmonts. In melodious 'Eb', Billy, Billy, Billy, and Billy (see Patti/ Patti/Patti/Patti Page) sing falsetto, lead tenor, baritone, and bass. He sounds like all the **Backstreet Boys & N'Sync** (#1, 1-2000 "Bye Bye Bye") in sync. His quasi-quartet in middle mode (Quasi-mode? Oh!) delivers one great Rock song in the Streetcorner style of the Five Satins or Danleers. All that intrudes is a little finger-poppin', and yes, one very dramatic bass guitar that steers the song. That lean spare bass provides Billy's entire instrumental rhythm track. As Elton John's "Candle in the Wind" eulogizes Marilyn Monroe or Princess Diana, Billy's "Longest Time" and "Uptown Girl" celebrate the celestial beauty of mate Christie Brinkley (b. '54, Malibu, CA [where else?]). Their blissful decade was shattered by a helicopter crash she survived. From #2(6) AI. *The Stranger,* Billy features a 'New York State of Mind' in his inimitable "Scenes from an Italian Restaurant." Juggling red, rose, and white wines to set a romantic mood, Billy schmoozes from sweet-talk to Dixieland Jazz (yep, check his TUBA on the bottom of his Mach One instrumental bridge). It's a true "Manhattan Spiritual"(big hit by British Reg Owens, #10, '58)

"You're Only Human (Second Wind)" – Billy Joel, #9, 7-85. Billy delves darkly into his own adolescent bouts with steamy depression, desperation, and despair. Unlike the **Red Hot Chili Peppers'** #1, 2000 "Otherside" that uglily describes throat-slitting suicide, Billy handles the taboo topic with kid gloves. Billy mentions his own experience with less-horrible depression in his Attila phase (what Sir Winston Churchill called 'the Black Dog' of deep depression). Billy advises the young Generation X nihilist (belief in NOTHING) to get positive. To endure. To pace her/himself. To take life as a brave marathoner – when you "Hit the Wall" exhausted at the 20-mile mark, you push on to the faraway finish line. With pluck and perseverance, Billy suggests, that terrible dark period may recede into a bright, shiny future. Never let it be said that Rock and Roll is no therapist.

"The Downeaster 'Alexa'" – Billy Joel, #57, 5-90. Billy named his boat after his and Christie's daughter Alexa Joel – and turned it in the song into a fishing boat plying the choppy breakers off Long Island Sound, or the open Atlantic Ocean. It's a tough seafaring life, with maybe Moby. Maybe bankruptcy. Billy donated his proceeds from this modest hit to helping the struggling fisherfolk: clammers, baymen, and fishermen off the Long Island seacoast. Never let it be said that Rock and Rollers are selfish.

"The River of Dreams" – Billy Joel, #3, 7-93. Billy plunges deeply into mystical convolutions of consciousness. He discovers his metaphorical deep River Jordan, perhaps a River Styx (see Paul Robeson's "Deep River"). In black/white video, with Gospel chorus, Billy violates all stereotypes you have of this intense pulsing river in your OWN Song Fantasies. Joel, more a pragmatist than a mystic, churns us all into a labyrinth of doubt and bewilderment. He brings the blessed blank slate of Doubting Thomas into his religious pilgrimage. Like Paul Simon at Graceland, Billy spangles his soulful Gospel chorus with Jordanaires' harmony and vintage Soul. Joel, once accused of fripperary sidelights like fashion, fast cars, and fine wine, now confronts silverbeard middle age, and the long hard descent down the ladder of success. Never let it be said that Rock and Rollers are shallow.

"To Make You Feel My Love" – Billy Joel, #50, 8-97. It's not the **Bob Dylan** flavor here that's scary. Marathoner Dylan's magnificent comebacker album *Time Out of Mind* [Sony, '97] won three Grammy nominations, including Album of the Year. What's scary is the echo of another master NYC songsmith of long, long ago – **Bobby Darin** (1936-73). Billy rides a whistling organ stripe of sensational sound to destiny on this undying love song.

If you're looking for Billy's Greatest Hit Sleeper, you may have come to the right audial place. [It's dynamite by songsmith Dylan, too]. Can you really beat the lyrical majesty of Dylan combined with the keyboard sophistication and vocal versatility of Billy Joel? Props are there: a rainy wind blowing in his face at the start; rollin' seas, memories, and even CRAWLING down a windswept desolate avenue. It's a minimalist masterpiece of crescendo blending. Bare and spare at first, "To Make You Feel My Love" bops the syncopated bass in on Billy's first Dust Bowl verse. Into the bridge, the surging snare drums careen into lockstep cadence. A grand mammoth roller-rink Hammond B-3 organ floats ethereally on high like the Moon of Manakoora. Far beyond Billy's heyday charttoppers, this amazing song trudges ponderously along, the weight of half a century vying with its desperado passion.

After a seven-course meal of *Billy Joel's Greatest Hits, Vol. III,* try this bittersweet dessert. Only BOBBY DARIN ever did anything like Billy's cameo Dylan classic (aside from, of course, Dylan). Darin's love songs like this one include #3, 1-63 "You're the Reason I'm Living," plus heartwarming #10, 5-63 "18 Yellow Roses," and #6 Folk classic of 12-66 "If I Were a Carpenter." The best songs don't always ensnare the highest chart rungs on the ladder of madding-crowd worldly success. Billy Joel's Darin-echo Dylan song, with its sodden sleet-slashing dedication, builds a Stairway to Heaven under a Crown of Thorns.

Two major California groups had a similar impact to Billy Joel, Elton John, or Rod Stewart – one from San Francisco's Haight-Ashbury, the other from Everywhere, USA. The second gathered and coalesced and hung out in Los Angeles, debuting as background singers/instrumentalists for Linda Ronstadt:

"Touch of Grey" – Grateful Dead, #9, 8-87; #1, Album Rock Charts. Jerry Garcia (1942-95, b. CA) and his faithful Grateful Dead, revered denizens of 710 Ashbury St., San Francisco, dragged bag and baggage around with them for 30 years. Ambassadors of good will and partyanimal zest for life, they finally scored a top ten singles hit in the aftermath of an eclectic R & R blend of genius, stardust, and celebration of life. Loyal 'Deadhead' fans everywhere will never forget their freewheeling odyssey, their plucky funtime marathon concerts, and their magnificent 'long strange trip.' For a touring band that seemingly reveled in Bugs Bunny's anti-work ethic, no band ever worked harder on stage to bring their slaphappy fan-addicts a great spirited show. Their exhausting four-hour sets were the stuff of counterculture tie-dyed legend.

Anybody in Rock and Roll who gets flags lowered to half-mast at his passing has obviously become an American legend. In the Book of Luke, Jesus speaks to loyal followers from Tyre, Phoenicia, Jerusalem, and all over the Middle East. Jerry's 'Deadheads' followed him on his secular mission/pilgrimage of enlightenment. Jerry was never a Messiah, but always a Teddy Bear. Sometimes that's the next best thing to comfort the afflicted. In the Psychedelic Era of peace, love, brotherhood, and legal L.S.D., the Dead eagerly glopped together a Folk/Country/Blues/Psychedelic Rock hybrid sound. From their Folkie origins at Mother McCree's and their sleepy commune, they sang the rising Psychedelic consciousness of the Golden City by the Bay. In the words of their mentor **Jack Kerouac** in *On the Road:*

"When the sun goes down and I sit on the broken-down river pier watching the long long skies . . . over the West Coast, and all that long road going, all the people dreaming . . . . in the land where . . . the stars'll be out, and don't you know that God is Pooh Bear? "

Kerouac reveled in 'potato-patch San Francisco fogs.' His West Coast enclave of Beat Generation poets, writers, mystic environmentalists, and beautiful girls surrounded his coffeehouse spotlight hoopla.

Jerry Garcia's father drowned on a fishing trip when Jerry was very young. Sharing the pain of Lennon & McCartney losing their mothers in their early adolescence, Jerry's agonies somehow smoothed into a smiling transcendental Pooh Bear persona. Rambling his hot licks and improvising with Jazz savvy into the wee hours, Garcia galvanized American revelers into his unique moveable-feast confetti soundscape. Everybody loved Jerry Garcia. Peace and love pumped through his charismatic veins.

Irish tenor **John McCormack** hit #1 with "Mother Machree" in 1910; Jerry and the neophytic Dead started as MOTHER McCREE'S UPTOWN JUG CHAMPIONS. Beatlemania Year 1964. Jerry joined with keyboard/harmonica/vocal guru **Pigpen McKernan**, named after Snoopy's "Peanuts" pal, and with gonzo guitar guys **John 'Marmaduke' Dawson** (unrelated to Kym & Jim Dawson), and ageless **Bob Weir**. The Dead traded for bassist **Phil Lesh** and drummer **Bill Kreutzman** (for a shortstop to be named later, a pack of R & R bubble-gum cards, and an order of onion rings). As once-jollier Kerouac faded behind his 1965 liquid armor, the Dead rallied behind new literary lion **Ken Kesey**. Kesey's rainbow-splattered 'Magic Bus' filled with real-life *On the Road* heroes like **Neal Cassady** ('Dean Moriarty'), and a goggle-eyed gaga grinny group of legal LSD experimentees. Trip? Timothy Leary's 'tune in, turn on, drop out' spree. Tom Wolfe's *Electric Kool-Aid Acid Test* tells the zany episodes of their wacked-out sojourn across America, the Andromeda Galaxy, the Psychedelic fringe, and the frontiers of R & R consciousness.

Somewhere in the 1966 Ozone Zone, Jerry and the Dead began their gung-ho concerts. Jerry cut his teeth on Bluegrass and Folk, while Lesh dug eclectic Charlie

Mingus-powered Jazz bass. Sadly, no one in the entire universe will ever commandeer the Complete Dead Collection. They are the most bootlegged band anywhere. And don't care! An unwritten (and written) law zaps your jiffy tape recorder at common rock concerts. With the Dead, your dinky 'taper' sound item was always welcome. Other Dead rosterites? Singer Donna Godchaux joined spasmodically with hubby Keith (until he was killed in '80 motorcycle crash). Mickey Hart played 2nd drummer. Jerry's own fantastically amazing guitar expertise is even more astounding when you realize his brother accidentally cut off a grisly chunk of Jerry's middle finger when they were kids, in a woodchopping catastrophe.

The Dead extinguished the need for a mini-amp the size of a Chihuahua doghouse. ROADIE became a necessary multitude. Stevedore roadie hordes ferried the Dead's 24 TONS of amp equipment with 6-foot speakers to be piled like Egyptian pyramids. The Dead, out of karmic kindness, unravelled a tangled skein of freebie benefit concerts for every sorry group from Cowboys Who Can't Yodel to Cat Burglars with Bulldogs Gnawing Their Butts. Jerry's lead guitar improvisations fantail out of the coffeehouse Beat scene of poets **Philip Whalen, Gary Snyder, Lawrence Ferlinghetti,** and peripatetic **Allen Ginsberg** sailing in from the Bowery, Soho, or Cloud Ten. Jazz buffs, mostly.

The Dead fired back Rock and Roll splendor and glory to its most unheralded cog in the great **Mandala** or **Yin-Yang** cosmic wheel – the AUDIENCE. Without dedicated listeners, a singer sings to a frog bog. To the Dead, a concert was a PARTICIPATORY EXPERIENCE. They were goodtime pilgrims on a mission of monumental music. Money was no object. Check under empathy or compassion in *Webster's,* and there's Jerry smiling. Their sets were a heavenly hodge-podge. They even covered people who put them down, like **Merle Haggard** ("Mama Tried"), whose "Okie from Muskogee" zaps 'California hippies.' Jerry and Dead celebrated Rock classics: Chuck's "Johnny B. Goode," Buddy's "Not Fade Away," Marty Robbins' "El Paso," Jimmy Reed's "Big Boss Man." They played Woodstock. They played Altamont when the Hell's Angels poured gasoline on the flames of rage seething the hot crowd. The Dead deplored head-busting tactics, and pushed peace with John Lennon's vigor and spirit. Many Dead members died in untimely fashion, like hard-drinking 'Pigpen' who passed away unmysteriously in '73, and keyboarder **Brett Mydland** in '90. The Dead's vagabond odyssey lavished a few hits, before a touch of grey speckled their sideburns with the calendar's nasty uppercut.

Yes, "A Touch of Grey." Jerry skitters along like a tumblin' tumbleweed. His song dips and spins and surges. "Tumblin' Tumbleweeds" was #13, 12-34 by King of the Cowboys **Roy Rogers** and Bob Nolan's Sons of the Pioneers. Great instrumental, too, by Roger Williams (#60, 8-56), who charted 23 hits like #1(4), 8-55 "Autumn Leaves" and #7, 8-66 lion-king flick theme "Born Free." "Touch of Grey" is an ironic ode to moderation and kindness and tumbleweed troubadours, Jerry chides pollution tycoons who blast the world with virulent toxins. He indicts evil alchemists for cows that give KEROSENE. He even zaps many of his fellow rebels; he says kids fail to read by 17 – and their only laconic utterances are a boring litany of hostile obscenities. Though his song arrived in 1987, it well describes the steroid steers with Mad Cow or Hoof & Mouth Disease in 2001+, or the Strontium 90 radioactive grass that cows ate in the 1963 Ban-the-Bomb era. The cow's milk killed thousands of children with genetic-mutation diseases. Ironically, Jerry's generation, struggling to free America from uptight anti-freedom forces, ended up baffled. Allen Bloom's *Closing of the American Mind* fumes against the 'satanic forces of androgyny' which pervade 'Jumpin' Jack Flash.' Bloom blames the Rolling Stones for the end of High Culture, and Decline of Western Civilization. Rock and Roll, of course, has never sought sainthood, despite Madonna's "Like a Prayer" or Van Halen's "Livin' on a Prayer." We can't blame ALL Rock and Roll, though, because some Thrash/ Smash kid writes a kill-the-police and puke-on-his-grandmother song.

The Grateful Dead are guilty of no mean-spirited rancor. Jerry & Crew always championed peace and love and freedom, man. Like Jesus' loyal followers at Galilee, Deadheads pilgrim thousands of miles to see their favorite band.

The recording industry takes care of its own. Bemused by the plucky band's perseverance, program directors (PD's) en masse shifted the Dead's melodic "Touch of Grey" to Rock Jocks and Drive-Time gurus in the midst of the Big-Hair Junk Bond Era. The Grateful Dead grew up with *Rolling Stone* magazine, which started rent-free on October 18, 1967 at 748 Brennan Street, San Francisco, above Garrett Press. Its first edition contained a review by founder **Jann** (pronounced 'Yon') **Wenner,** a Donovan interview, and a muckraking piece on the Monterey Pop Festival. At Bill Graham's Fillmore West at 1805 Geary St., the Dead evolved Psychedelia. "I was sort of a beatnik guitar player," Jerry whispered hoarsely after a 3½-hour stage stint, "We could get into coffeehouse poetry readings as kids. No I.D. needed. After three-four tiny cups of expresso, we'd be whirling around on the ceiling fans."

Now, zowie, the Dead finally stormed the sacrosanct SINGLES Top Ten for the FIRST TIME, a generation later. In the midst of second mortgages, third-rail commuter frenzy, and four-flusher cutthroat bull markets, the smiling Dead were still out there orbiting the Earth at fifteen miles an hour, with their left turn-signal permanently ON. Now & then they'd light upon the yellow-brick road, seeking the Emerald City and the Wonderful Wizard of Whoopee.

Comes Jerry's rollicking chorus, riddled with tragic dramatic irony. Jerry & Dead chime in harmonically about how they'll all GET BY, and how they will all SURVIVE. Ouch. We see the ugly reality that starry-eyed Jerry never did. On the gloomy side, civilization is collapsing. Creeks choke toxically in the gullywash wasteland by Homer Simpson's nuke plant (with 7-eyed monsterfish). The prolific human race explodes like lemmings dashing suicidally into Norway's fjordland seas and maelstroms. .Mean-

while, Jerry grins his big friendly Pooh Bear grin, and fires off three golden chords and a cloud of gold dust. His wonderful wheezy chords bob and weave in the warm California sunshine.

"Touch of Grey" interweaves a wobbly world. Jerry & His Least Dangerous Band fade in with ragged optimism. A cowbell coruscates off a church-bell xylophone. Snurfling along on bottomtone bass runs, **Phil Lesh** undergirds "Touch of Grey's" fervent message with strength and solidity. Orbiting the Key of 'B', "Touch of Grey" stunningly bounces from dominant V7 **F#** to subdominant IV **E,** flashing through the chromatic bV-major – a shimmery interplay of F#—F – E – F – F#. The mutability of their constantly shifting chords mirrors the uncertain path of the world itself. Like a champ prizefighter, Jerry bobs and weaves and ducks the roundhouse haymaker of the mammoth champ. With Muhammad Ali's 'Rope-A-Dope' skill, fancy Bugs Bunny footwork, and American true grit, Jerry counters the fist-clenched Angry Young Man firebrand with low-key, laid-back friendliness and kind understanding. A profound prophet on a long, strange trip (from #64, 4-71 "Truckin'").

When the Dead cascade into their joyous life-loving chorus about how they'll all survive, Lesh lashes a bullwhip bass run. "Touch of Grey" is the chart culmination for Jerry & noble followers – from his Mother McCree's Jug Band to Thunder Mountain Tub Thumpers and Warlocks. "A Touch of Grey" zaps the establishment, of course. So does the whole Dead canon of Classic Rock.

"Casey Jones" – Grateful Dead, NC, 1970. Off Al. #27, 6-70 *Workingman's Dead*. Radio wouldn't play it. Old train wreck song had new cocaine rationale. Icon **Johnny Cash** echoed the original "The Wreck of the Old 97," by Vernon Dalhart (#4, 5-25). Dalhart's #1(5), 3-25 AND #1(7), 12-25 [go figure] "The Prisoner's Song" sold SEVEN MILLION, and was the #1 non-holiday record of the Pre-Rock Era (Whitburn). Reckless engineer in original slams steep three-mile grade on Lynchburg-Danville Virginia line at 90 miles per hour. Train jumps track. Daddy of all Graveyard Rock. Song became Kingston Trio's new-lyric #15, '59 "M.T.A." Dead's "Casey Jones" is a milder admonition, not quite a catastrophe – as stoned engineer sniffs and SNORTS more than locomotive. Try similar theme by British Blues guru:

"Cocaine" – Eric Clapton, #30, 6-80 [as double-sided hit with "Tulsa Time"]. With Chicago Blues John Lee Hooker-type baritone, Clapton warns, but says cocaine is O.K .In Jerry's 1910 San Francisco, it WAS O.K., legally. Sigmund Freud, father of psychiatry, used it constantly, as open opium dens spilled out onto lavender-lilac evening porches in the earthquake afterglow. Relic drug ditties? **Cab Calloway** scorched the 7-32 charts with #11 hot pot smash "Reefer Man." Nobody said it was healthy.

"The Music Never Stopped" – Grateful Dead, #81, 10-75. Jerry's squiggly melody threads like the blue highways of Amerizona. Monument to a band on the run, roadweary, roadworthy revellers high on life. You can hear the echoes of Everly careening down the corridors of their Appalachian thirds harmony. They gallivanted across the planet spreading joy and laughter, coming blissfully to your burg to help you guys party it down. Like Grand Funk Railroad, an American band . . .

"Sugar Magnolia" – Grateful Dead, #91, #91, 2-73. "Sugar Magnolia" takes a Deadhead "Alabama Getaway" (#88, 6-80), seeking some sweet Southern sunshine with a party-on lilt that would find way to **Jimmy Buffett**'s 'Parrothead' dominions and capital "Margaritaville" (#8, 4-77).

"Don't Let Go (Love) (From 'Set It Off')" – En Vogue, #2(3), 11-96. Jerry Garcia appreciated ALL kinds of music. This is 100% opposite to Grateful Dead, who rampaged to their own different drummer . . . in the FIRST Disco Age. **Neo-Disco** Techno 'Dance' music like R & B Terri Ellis's En Vogue provides a great beat, a rockin' vitality, and a punctuational nightmare. Big mid-90s bonanza. Back to Dead:

In the Dark –Grateful Dead, Al., #6, 8-87. This launchpad album, of course, couches their HUGE HIT. "Grey." We orbit it as we speak here. Both album and single zapped the old Dead taboo against boogieing into the Top Ten. Their previous mega-monster was Al. #12, 9-75 *Blues for Allah.* They'd also chortled in glee with #18 Al., 11-73 *Wake of the Flood,* and #16, 7-74 Al., *Grateful Dead from the Mars Hotel.* Also an ACTUAL 'Live' unpilfered album – Al. #29, 10-81 *Dead Set.* Or catch #28, 9-77 Al. *Terrapin Station, and* Al. #23, 5-80 *Go to Heaven.* Also unbeatable combo #37 Al. 2-89 *Dylan & the Dead,* plus Al. #26, 10-95 *Hundred Year Hail.* Great Dead albums (29+ charted) run the gamut, from clustery concept albums to continuous spaceman far-out lead-guitar frenzies of bold fiery-fret frazzles of sky-high splendor and road-hopping barnstorming love odysseys without punctuation or pause like this chunky Kerouackian sentence here I keep trying to end [Whew]. Anyhow, the Dead are a great album band.

In her "Look for the Silver Lining," **Marion Harris** (#1[3], 4-21) launched a big Jazz Age blockbuster. Her torchy meteorological Pre-Weather Channel song tells us all to ignore the "Touch of GRAY" cloud, check the silvery lining, and maybe a groovy new dance will arrive. And the "Charleston" did – via **Arthur Gibbs & His Gang** (#1[1], 1-24). Two-hit wonder, Gibbs (#7, 8-23 "Louisville Lou"). Proto-Rock Dance of 20s featured standing on one leg, like flamingo, while twirling other below knee. Prelude to Rock (via the Twist). For first time, dancers separated, and danced solo.

As his hero **Buddy Holly**, symbol of Rock's innocent youth, sang his debut #1 "That'll Be the Day" [when he may die], so Jerry Garcia similarly named his group after the Grim Reaper (see Blue Oyster Cult's "Don't Fear the Reaper"]. Somehow, we starry-eyed lost innocents, groping through this Wayfaring Stranger's world of woebegone sorrow, never actually believed it could happen to Jerry Garcia. Jerry died at 53 of old age (heart attack, officially). His zest for his music still flamed, though the smoldering embers of his ex-health slowly slipped away.

We will never forget them. Good ol' Grateful Dead. When you heard "Touch of Grey," did it remind you of your own old neighborhood gang? Or of the 'touch of gray' sneaking up on your 'World's Oldest Teenager' pals at the last class reunion? Jerry's song makes me sad and happy. Even with that weary touch of gray, Jerry tells us, we'll make it to the restful destination at the end of our long, hard roads. We have long-gone friends we'll never see again in this world. Like Elton said, "(we're) still standing." "Touch of Grey" is a wonderful anthem about HOPE. We are here, for now. We have our music.

God bless us, every one. And Jerry, wherever he may be.

Glenn Frey, like Bob Seger, stormed the Motor City ramparts, hot-shotting Woodward Avenue with aimless wild dreams. In 1965, we all quested after Kerouac's Center of Saturday Night in America. We drag-raced the lost ghosts of the old road. Hanging out at Hideout Records in Dearborn, Glenn sharpened his sound in the sodium glow under the marshmallow Motown moon. **Dave Marsh**, premier rock critic of a generation, founded now-defunct *Creem* magazine in Fortune Records' Cass Corridor. He describes Frey's White Soul milieu via James Taylor's premier background singer David Lasley (b. '47, my wife's cousin). Marsh's vignette about risque Third Street, abuzz on the periphery of reality, highlights the electric neon night we Metro Motown expatriates shared: "Detroit . . . returns to haunt all it's touched." He cites Lasley's liner notes in Al. *Missing Twenty Grand.* Marsh says Lasley was COMPELLED to mention Detroit roots (I tipped Lasley off to Fortune, from his Sault-Ste. Marie/ Manistee Upstate roots). Marsh cites other Detroit Rock pilgrims: "George Clinton, Iggy Pop, David & Donald Was, Bob Seger, Mitch Ryder . . . all those who escaped." All those of us – Marsh and Frey and Bob and I – who escaped Detroit as it torched itself to the ground that ghastly week of July 26, 1967, all of us carry a heartful of precious broken memories. No matter how stamped in cynicism we may get, we all return to the semi-sacred shrine at Michigan and Trumbull, dear old bygone [Detroit] Tiger Stadium, to worship the tatters of our so-long-pal youth. The Eagle flies home to Frey's home.

Our Night Shift/Woolies "Who Do You Love"

was ripped off onto NYC bootleg Al. *Michigan Brand Nuggets,* and a pink-vinyl Punk afterglow of the MC5. Dave Marsh: "Forgotten talents scattered across the two discs, from the goofy one-shot doo-wop of Tim-Tam and the Turn-Ons' "Wait a Minute" to the incipient folk rock of Southbound Freeway's "Psychedelic Used-Car Lot Blues" to the full-throttle growl of the Woolies' "Who Do You Love. . . . the Woolies emerged as Chuck Berry's favorite backing band." [Freeway's Larry Miller became an ultra-hip FM rock jock in Detroit and San Francisco].

"Wait a Minute" – Tim Tam & the Turn-Ons, #76, 3-66. These Allen Park lads fractured the WKNR Keener Countdown with their #5-locally hit. Ricky 'Tim Tim" Weisand & brother Dan's band sculpted this super R & R song with night-club legend Nick Butsicaris. It throbs with drum thunder like Frankie Valli's Four Seasons meeting the Bobby Fuller Four on Mitch Ryder's screaming Detroit Wheels.

Like the rest of us denizens of Detroit's smoke and steel and dark scabby snow, Glenn Frey flew to a warmer clime. There he formed the Eagles, who sang background for **Linda Ronstadt.**

"Take It Easy" – Eagles, #12, 6-72. The Eagles are the Beatles of the sizzling 70s. Like Rod Stewart, Elton John, Bob Dylan, Billy Joel, and the Grateful Dead, the Eagles loom larger than life in shaping the Rock Revolution. Their greatness hinges upon this simple, yet profound, observation:

THEIR SONGS SOUND A BIT EASY TO PLAY. THEY ARE NOT. Out in the glimmery L.A. sunshine, by fast-lane Hotel California, Glenn finagled self and pal **Don Henley** into the greatest one-two vocal punch since **Lennon-McCartney.**

As you groove to the molten rolling 12-string chords of Glenn's "Take It Easy," his Holly-echo rolling thunder reverberates in peaceful easy feelings of romantic reverie. Eagle lyrics are old friends, rippling in the folksy ubiquitous Key of 'G'. Love fugitive on the run, Glenn romanticizes the flat-bed Ford pick-up, the SEVEN women tangling his mind, and that Winslow, Arizona forlorn corner. [In 1962, I hitchhiked that route with $15 guitar, faithful sleeping bag, and 16 cents on the way back to Glenn's Motor City with a Rock and Roll dream]. As Frey was born in Bob Seger's Royal Oak, Michigan (11-6-48), **Don Henley** comes from Gilmer, Texas (7-22-47). Glenn's fastball-down-the-middle tenor plays off the jagged, craggy 'whiskey-style' tenor of Henley. Eagles' flight highlights top-notch musicians: **Randy Meisner** (till '77) and Irish Tenor **Timothy B. Schmit** on bass; Flying Burrito Brothers' **Bernie Leadon** and **Don Felder,** guitar; and virtuoso singer/guitarist **Joe Walsh** of Cleveland's James Gang (#51, '71 "Walk Away"). Eagles assembled in airy aerie/eyrie from America afar: Frey Metro Motown, Henley Lone Star State, Meisner Nebraska, etc. When their All-American band finally assembled, they flew to England

to record.

Auspicious debut, #12 "Take It Easy." Penned by lyricist **Jackson Browne** (#8, 3-72 "Doctor My Eyes" & #11, 2-78 "Running on Empty"), "Easy" swindles boredom and erupts in excitement. Juggling seven scrappy women in his passion-powered mind, he ponders four who wish to possess him, two who want to toss rocks at him, and one cool lady who claims to be his bosom buddy. Critic Harry Sumrall says they co-opted Jackson Browne: "Dressed in Western gear, with guns and bandeleros, their long hair and mustaches drooping, they look dangerous. They weren't." He zaps their "sleek, flaccid" style. I disagree. "Easy" is neither snakeskin-sleek nor cellulite flaccid; it's a rip-roaring desert-flower YAY song of Rock splendor (sorry, Harry). Its rolling bridge cuts loose in Duane-Eddy twangy euphoria. The throbbing chorus echoes the harmonic precision of America's OTHER California band – the **Beach Boys.** On the trailaway fadeout, amidst a dark desert black sky of light-speed notes like blue stars, Henley's harmonizers swoop eaglefully beyond the far moon-shimmer peaks of lost Arizona. Heart of Rock and Roll.

FREEDOM rings. When Buddy Holly (1936-59) bellowed his yippee yahoo #10, '57 "Oh Boy," his sun-spangled West Texan smile melted a touch-of-grey world – a dark worldscape awash in nuclear fallout, monster arsenals, and grim gray colossus the Soviet Union. Elvis may have been great, but BUDDY HOLLY taught the snarling world to sing. "Take It Easy," the Eagles implore. Vietnam is winding down. Penicillin will cure ANYTHING lusty lovers might suffer. Gas is still 25 cents/gallon. We beat the Russians to the moon. Let's glide down the Freedom Highway and have a blast.

Not to worry. Even the chords are friendly: Big I, IV, and V whooshes of twelve-string turbulence, with a minimum of morose minors. Renegade riffs dust the tall notes like tumbleweeds and popcorn, blowing briskly below the booming blue Western skies. Do not fret, the soaring Eagles coax and goad and chide. The war will end soon. Glenn Frey pounces to our emotional rescue. We will save the earth. And the stately California redwoods. [On 9-16-96, Don Henley & Bonnie Raitt were arrested for protesting clear-cutting a Redwood virgin stand of tall timber]. In 1972, Frey sang to take it easy. You will get rich anyhow, and nobody needs to wear a tie.

"Witchy Woman" – Eagles, #9, 9-72. The Eagles' second hit unleashes the unique Marlboro tenor of **Don Henley.** He cruises this Hallowe'en carol with a sound sticky as a cat's tongue. The eerie melody oozes with midnight prowling stealth. Frey's and Henley's voices, alike in RANGE, are day vs. night in timbre and style. A ghostly chorus of scary OOOOOOHHHHHs casts a nighthawk shadow. This witchy midnight lady has ruby-tinted lips and raven-black hair. Sparks coruscate from her clingy claws. Like, wow. No more "I love you, baby/climb in the back seat" regular blarney. He cites the coke-buzzed fuzziness of this bewitching ditzy dame who's "Stuck in the Middle with You" (Gerry Rafferty's Scottish Stealers Wheel, #6, '73). Eagles chronicle the Age of Excess. This silken Vampira smacks a lusty man's ability to push her away. The enchanted lass drove herself up the wall with an easy-to-figure-out silver spoon (and coke sure ISN'T Coca Cola here). Or even rum:

"Rum and Coca Cola" – Andrews Sisters, #1(10), 1-45; #3, R & B. Our folks thought OUR songs about boozing and cruising were overdone. There was an Armageddon war on. Foxhole WWII foot soldiers enmired in muck and terror didn't think, "Hey, maybe these Camel cigarettes might kill me . . . in 40 years." In wartime, traditional take-it-slow morality gets jackbooted. **Patty, Maxene**, and **LaVerne Andrews** grew up in **Prince's** Minneapolis, MN. Scottish-American tripletone trio became the most popular female vocal group (Whitburn) of the entire Pre-Rock 1890-1954 era. They celebrate getting tipsy on Jamaica's Pre-Reggae export, and the #1 soft drink in the world (see Kinks' cross-dressing "Lola"). Andrews Sisters debuted with Yiddish #1(5), 1-38 "Bei Mir Bist Du Schön" ['To Me, You Are Beautiful']. Also? #1(3), 10-40 "Ferryboat Serenade"; early Boogie Rocker #2(3), 11-40 "Beat Me, Daddy, Eight to the Bar"; Swing/Jazz/Featherweight Rock #1(9), 12-43 "Shoo-Shoo Baby"; #1(5), 9-49 "I Can Dream, Can't I" – and Little Richard's "Good Golly Miss Molly" inspiration, their #15, 9-46 "The House of Blue Lights." The **Kingston Trio** took a more coy and punny approach to love & booze:

"Scotch and Soda" –Kingston Trio, #81, 4-62. Bob Shane's commanding baritone on Dave Guard's song highlighted *Animal House* fraternity shady soirees. Shane sings lovin' makes him HIGH – a term which applied first to alcohol, not just 60s drugs. Mellifluous murmurs, polychordal profundity. Cool.

"Peaceful Easy Feeling" – Eagles, #22, 12-72. Glenn, again, on 3rd hit. Frey's EASY theme sparkles this squeezy rendezvous in bluesy Key of 'E'. His tete-a-tete with a Latino or Afro-American girl shows the Eagles didn't do Dynamic Wishy-Washyism. They set the smooth tone for Jiffy Love Encounters in a Disco Era whose Disco music they never offered. The mellow 12-string sets the gorgeous sound of the 1999 Rock Hall Inductees' mammoth major chords, swirling harmonies, and dusty Roadrunner rhythmscape. You hear this song? You get a peaceful, easy feeling.

"Already Gone" – Eagles, #32, 5-74. Celebrating a wide-open decade of ghost-town relationships, Frey guffaws his rockin' farewell, echoing fellow Michigander **Del Shannon**'s blunt Revenge Rock. Twangy in Key of 'G', Glenn dumps the lass, rampaging into his wahoo song of freedom and victory. Followed by a Rebel Yell. Prowling the low tones, Randy Meisner slaloms around Henley's thrashing snare and tom-toms. Another goodbye song – red-hot, never blue. Kiss-off relationships symbolized the swaggering 70s. The Eagles offer their closest entry (tied with "James Dean") to Mainstream Thunder Rock – slashing with molten metal, A-bomb roundhouse rhythm, and sunburnt slabs of Screaming Blues. They roar across the Casanova landscape, seeking to make four people happy instead of two sad.

"James Dean" – Eagles, #77, 9-74. Rock and Roll! Dynamic **James Dean** (1931-55) was the quintessential brooding movie star, forever frozen into that 9-30-55 moment just before he took off in a Porsche Spyder on a grim date with destiny. After just doing a public service plug on the dangers of speeding, race-car aficionado Dean and mechanic Rolf Wunderlich raced down the California highway at 85 mph, Dean driving. By the time Don Turnipseed sleepily pulled out onto the highway from a country crossroad, Dean never had a chance. Turnipseed (and Wunderlich), to the relief of Turnipseeds everywhere, survived. If bongo-drum thumper Dean had sung, he'd have made a million on Rock records. His sidekick 'Plato' in *Rebel Without a Cause* ('55****) had a Teen Idol at-bat: **Sal Mineo** hit #9, 5-57 with "Start Movin'" and #45, 1-58 with "Little Pigeon" on his rough-hewn baritone. Unlike smooth-glide #64, 6-73 "Tequila Sunrise," "James Dean" and "Already Gone" are the closest the Eagles swooped to Hard Rock/Heavy Metal. "Dean" kicks in with a thunderous "Peggy Sue" paradiddle. Wild high-strung guitar riffs jitterbug the lofty frets. The fearless lyric twists frantically, like the hell-bent-for-life of the Indiana silver screen idol – whose meteoric life emblazoned his legend across a purple sky.

A committee of Frey, Jackson Browne, and J. D. Souther wrote "James Dean." Amarillo's Souther (#9, 7-79 "You're Only Lonely") wafts a Timothy B. Schmit belltone Irish tenor. Crystal-toned Souther scored a hit with Byrds of another feather: Byrd Chris Hillman's Souther, Furay, and Hillman's #27, 8-74 "Fallin' in Love," and Souther's **James Taylor** duo at #11, 3-81 "Her Town Too." "James Dean" trails away on boughs of Holly. Dean's abrupt life was summed up "Too fast to live, too young to die."

"Suite: Judy Blue Eyes" – Crosby, Stills, and Nash, #21, 10-69. With angelic Everly harmonies, the tremendous Folk Rock trio dedicated their rollicking ode to Judy Collins' blue eyes. The Woodstock Generation picked up the CS & N harmonic vibes and ran with them. Soon they quartetted with **Neil Young**, joining Stephen Stills from their Buffalo Springfield sojourn. Great road code song.

"Best of My Love" – Eagles, #1(1), 11-74. "Dean" was the end of the Eagles' stardom – a prelude to superstardom. With this "Dean" follow-up, they strung together 4 #1's, a #2, and a ho-hum #4. "Best" is first. Henley to the fore. They were blessed with a modest 22 HOT 100 singles from 1972-2001, and just 3 other top-ten tunes. The Eagles, however, became all-time champs with their #1(5), 3-76 album – *The Eagles/Their Greatest Hits 1971-75,* was the first platinum album ever certified (one million sales), and it went on over 25 years to become the BIGGEST-SELLING ALBUM of ALL TIME (25+ million by 2002+).

"Best of My Love" surveys a stormy, tattered relationship. Henley's sound sails on a slurred burrowing of a Meisner bass line. The Eagle Chorus swoops after. Eager R.I.P. for a burnt-out romance. The melody echoes the tender Jazz/Light Rock balladry of the **Classics IV** – #3, 12-67 "Spooky," #19, 5-69 "Everyday with You, Girl." Or **David Gates** and **Bread**: #10, 9-70 "It Don't Matter to Me"; #11, 7-72 "The Guitar Man"; or #9, 11-76 "Lost Without Your Love." In the dim twilight of gaslight gloaming, the Eagles lament the faded beauty of an ex-good love gone bad. They sang to a world awash in uncertainty.

"One of These Nights" – Eagles, #1(1), 5-75. Weird. The Eagles' five #1's perched precariously, all for one week only. This Henley Hallowe'en haunt huddles in the "Spooky" Range (Classics IV). Don wails ghostly falsetto and invokes werewolves beyond the garlic zone. The bulbous full moon calls him. Night fever makes him borderline hyper. The wicked whooshing wind moans over her demonic desires. Romping through a gauntlet of spirited banshee minors and sixths and ninths in 'G', Henley storms the jouncing chorus.

"Lyin' Eyes" – Eagles, #2(2), 9-75; #8, 10-75, C. Frey at bat. Deception and intrigue tune. "Eyes" idles along smoothly, seemingly forever, before hitting its big harmonic everybody-jumps-in chorus. Is it a ballad, with two verses and a bridge? Is it a rolling Rocker, with a couple of 12-Bar Blues verses? Nope, a hybrid. On the 2nd verse, Frey's finesse vocal gets harmonically tailgated. When they womp the gingery chorus, they resemble the Phoenix Tabernacle Royal Eagles' Choir, dancing from the 4th to the 5th dimension of sound-surround splendor. Most listeners could give 2½ owly hoots about their peregrinations and flapping polychordal flights – from sub-mediant VI-minor **Eb** to **D7** and **G**. Fans just groove to the BASIC SOUND! With a beautiful song like this, though, the poor couple's relationship has maybe ten minutes to live. The Eagles, however, soared high over the prevailing Disco Carousel.

Frey's frazzled funk over her untruth spelled Splitsville. This uptown girl, adorned in lace, is a mean mistreater. So long, baby. Like **George Harrison**'s unheralded Beatle classics, consummate pinch-hitter **Joe Walsh**'s "Take It to the Limit" scorched #4, 12-75. Walsh soloed DURING the Eagles' heyday on #23, 8-73 "Rocky Mountain Way," #12, 6-78 "Life's Been Good," and #19, 5-80 "All Night Long." Post-Eagle #34, 5-81 "A Life of Illusion" ran parallel to **Randy Meisner**'s #19, 1-81 "Hearts on Fire"(Meisner from Rick Nelson's Stone Canyon Band). Eagles' amazing 1974-80 flight had no limits, glomming #1, 12-76 (#43 C) with Johnny-Come-Lately "New Kid in Town." "New Kid" is Heather Apple/Tom Giordano fave tune. "Heartbreak Hotel" moved WEST:

"Hotel California" – Eagles, #1(1), 2-77. Time Warp 1994. Video, VH-1. Original Eagles, perching. Dim stage. Small auditorium. A wiry 12-string shimmies. Older, still-hawkeyed Eagles add instruments, one by one. Whiteline fever California. **Don Felder** wipes out guitar gremmies with his audial tidal wave. A sinister "Mission Bell" signals the building tension. Their inspiration? **Donnie Brooks**'s super multi-layered #7, 6-60 classic

"Mission Bell." [It recalls my cool classmate Denny Mancuso, whose song "Summer Skies" hit in Japan after working with Brooks]. If ANY song delivers the meaningless-of-money theme, "Hotel California" churns with zeal and grotesque symbolism. Sanity and health beat riches.

"Hotel California" is a rogue's gallery wax museum of spiritual horrors. In its spare time, it's also a great song. The effete and decadent and jaded are the HAPPY inmates. Henley's reporter-style third-person vocal hisses serpentine lyrical lines to convey the oxymoronic garish AND eerie mood. He paints a macabre vignette of snaky denizens whose burnt-out lives are hollow shells [watch your back, you might step on a slimy metaphor]. "Hotel California" is a last-gasp asylum, a coke-stroked pleasure dome of despair. It's a hellish Purgatory of Hieronymus Bosch sufferers over Dante's fiery pit. Stabbing at flickering reality with jagged, serrated steel knives, they can't kill this beast of California wild-party excess – with 100% stoned midnights and no welcome dawn. Like Punk icon (Sex Pistols) **Sid Vicious**'s violent scenario in Manhattan's Carlyle Hotel, "Hotel California" makes Elvis's "Heartbreak Hotel" vacation seem like fun-fun-fun Disneyland.

Fun? Henley staggers a funhouse maze in muted Key of 'D' and all its miasmic quagmire minors. In "Hotel California's" second incarnation on MTV/VH-1, the song is even more terrifying than ever. These lost souls have no redemption, no atonement, no remorse, no hope. The song finds a hallowed spot in my Top Ten Terror Tunes. I keep them all in a spiritual cobwebby catacomb cave – like Stephen King's 'high-shelf' films too scary for his 3 and 8-year-olds. When these spooky songs drool and ooze onto the radio, I snap the button to "Oh Boy" or "Glad All Over" or "She Loves You, Yeah3" on the Mr. Fun-Stuff Oldie-Goldies Good Cheer Show.

Henley's final Purgatory scene says inmates may 'check out' (death euphemism) upon their own free will, but are NEVER allowed to truly LEAVE. Once you're HOOKED, Cloud Seven is never as good as Cloud NINE. The fix is mandatory. They can never gain total freedom from their obsession or addiction. Henley knows he's toying with their deepest DT (delerium tremens) nightmares of whatever ADDICTIONS these Hotel California prisoners are strapped to. Does Hotel California symbolize junkies? Retirement communities? Life itself? Drug abuse experts point out hard drugs kill 50,000+ per year, alcohol over 200,000, and semi-innocuous legal cigarettes kill 400,000+. Here at the hotel, ALL these may be indulged at once (with a side of sensuality). Whether the actual Hotel California is a 1910 opium den, 1929 speakeasy/blind pig, 1970s shooting gallery for heroin needlemania, 1990s crack house, Neo-Goth Neo-Heroin chic 2001 dive – or even a friendly deli doling Marlboros to 12-year-olds like I was and maybe you too – the 'Hotel California' speaks to us all with messianic evangelical fire. It crows at us: curb your killer appetites, get in shape, go to work, help your family.

We're ditching the Hotel California now, fast. The creepo limbo lodge is startin' to scare me. Maybe you, too. WE can check out anytime we want, and yep, leave. Just a disclaimer before we go. The Eagles never intended this horror-show tableau to represent the 32,000,000 great people of California, like my cousins Liz & Dave, Ann & Jim, Alice & Steve, and my sister Blair and family Bob, John Maury, Bo, Joe, and Michelle. This is one SUPERBAD hotel. And if you've never deeply listened to its sinister message, simply sit back and enjoy the pretty music. It's a fine song with amazing surreal chord changes and harmonies. The melody is as magnificent as the fore-boding lyric is brilliantly creepy. [Next time you book me in "Lonesome Town" on "Lonely Street," I'll take the fleabag couch in "Heartbreak Hotel." I wouldn't send a rattlesnake to the "Hotel California"]. Gorgeous melody, though.

"Life in the Fast Lane" – **Eagles, #11, 5-77.** Much safer place. Good ol' Graveyard Drag-Race Death Rock. Surges into frantic-freeway Jan & Dean 'Deadman's Curve' overdrive. Type-A wacked out frazzled flight to despair. Don sings to slow down. Mellow out. Make sure those pills are Vitamin C. Lyric in Key of Blues 'E' squiggles along funky Jazz sixths. Bikini odyssey fires up two lov-ers in lyric. Don pushes lost quest for serenity. Gaze at a cloud. Feed a bunny rabbit. Tootle down flowery byways to fragrant orange groves. Snooze.

Avoid a "Heartache Tonight" (#1[1], 10-79). Get off Andy Williams (#5, 9-59) "Lonely Street." Save your adrenaline for the true rocker's marathon – "The Long Run" (#8, 12-79). Both the **Beatles** and the **Eagles** celebrated a Magic Seven-Year Heyday, before brotherly squabbling sent them sadly on solo trails: **Beatles** – 1963-70. **Eagles** – 1973-80, give or take a year. Henley's marathon ham-mers to the finish line, thumping ALL the 1-2-3-4 beats like a Disco song. Guitar riffs splatter spitfire wildcat Blues.

"I Can't Tell You Why" – **Eagles, #8, 2-80.** Just as silvertone tenor **Timothy B. Schmit** established his Art Garfunkel/Phil Everly vocal magic, the Eagles bagged it and scattered. Nary a Yoko. On the Eagles' mid-90s comeback, Irish tenor Schmit stormed the HOT 22 Air-play citadel on #22A 12-94 "Love Will Keep Us Alive" – #1 Adult Contemporary. We saw Don Henley bust out into his rouser against mollycoddled whiners – #31, 12-94 "Get Over It." Instead of blaming toxic relatives, bad breaks, unfair colleagues, and awful luck, Henley says the whiner should bench-press his courage, pull himself up by the bootstraps, and get back into the Race of Life. In post-Eagle times, Henley and Frey rebounded into admirable solo acts like Lennon & McCartney.

"The Boys of Summer" – **Don Henley, #5, 11-84.** Don kicked it off with #6, '81 "Leather and Lace" with lovely golden-eyed **Stevie Nicks** – a song rejected by Crickets' 2nd-bass-man **Waylon Jennings** and wife Jessi Colter. In a huge bronze-medal hit that previewed the press feed-ing frenzy about President Clinton's dalliances, Don hung out the charts to dry with #3, 10-82 "Dirty Laundry." "The Boys of Summer" is a magnificent Rock and Roll song. Sparkling with vitality and enthusiasm, Henley intros his anthem with major Metal and never lets up. Naturally, it's a love song. The lyric plunges along with summer beachside romance, Coppertone passion, and the prom-ise of lasting love after these annoying 'Boys of Summer' vanish from the landscape of their lives. Naturally, the green-eyed Jealousy Monster seethes through many a steamy lyric. Hasn't Rock and Roll and Pop and Soul ALWAYS sung of lost loves and reunited glories? If pop music ever strayed into humdrum topics – lawn-fertiliz-ing, dog grooming, bill-paying, or toenail-clipping – it would lose its power, its romance, and its everlasting glory.

"The Boys of Summer" doesn't wallow in self-pity. Henley's fleeting images dash in kaleidoscopic energy: Deadhead bumper stickers, surfland cruising convertibles, the endless splash of worldwater waves, and her golden sunbeam hair shimmering in the endless California sun-shine glow. Henley revels in Rock and Roll. His cutting-edge vocal flirts with Screaming Blues. "The Boys of Sum-mer" is a 100% R & R soul-searing fastball down the middle. Three chords and a cloud of dust.

After the 80s rolled away with a whimper, Henley's an-nulment anthem "The End of the Innocence" (#8, 6-89) crafted a Coda to Forever Love. This boys-II-men tale paints lawyers frittering away big details, as an old ITEM drifts into TWO, and California houses and lives are hacked in half. Rock and Roll was no longer corralled in Teenaged Wasteland.

"Sometimes Love Just Ain't Enough" – **Patti Smith with Don Henley, #2(6), 8-92; #1(1) Adult Contempo-rary.** When Patti Smith, married to Punk Rocker Richard Hell, gloms the EASY LISTENING #1 hit, you know that some weird generational flip-flop just happened, and noth-ing is the same as it was. As Mick Jagger once mused – the future ain't what it used to be, and furthermore, it never was (maybe it was Yogi Berra).

"The Heat Is On" – **Glenn Frey, #2(1), 12-84.** Three fried Frey flyers scurried around the Top 20 before Glenn bolted back to silver-medal status – thanks to comic Eddie Murphy's *Beverly Hills Cop ('84***)*. Theme song involves Jazz/Blues/Rock funky sixths and sevenths. The rhythm track simply kicks butt. This is a cop show song to lead all cop show songs. In his #12, 4-85 "Smuggler's Blues," Glenn taps a vein of cool street-savvy tunes with a TV panorama of moxie cops from Sgt. Joe Friday to Kojak to Barretta to Rockford to Murphy. Some of the Detroit scenes on the runaway cig-smuggling truck dart through my old neighborhood of old brick Victorians, graffiti, and hopelessness, plus busted bottles and dreams. In the **Purple Gang** Prohibition Era in Detroit (immortalized in Elvis's "Jailhouse Rock"), 85% of illegal booze ('hooch') crossed the Detroit River from Windsor, Ontario. "Smuggler's Blues" is a commonplace occurrence on the Ambassador Bridge and Windsor Tunnel. Today, Metro Motown lads besiege the Windsor Canadian topless girlie shows, and even good folks smuggle "Cigarettes, Whusky, and Wild, Wild Women" (#15, 3-48, Red Ingle).

"You Belong to the City" – **Glenn Frey, #2(2), 9-85.** Thanks to unIrish Murphy, Frey contributed this clas-sic for *Miami Vice,* 80s TV sensation with Don Johnson in pastel cotton sport coats and a 3-day 5-o'clock shadow. It suggests **Nick Gilder**'s #1(1), 6-78 "Hot Child in the City," a smoky night scenario where waif flees authority. Runaway child runs wild. London lad Gilder fled to Vancouver & notched #1 hit. **John Cougar Mellencamp**'s #15, 3-84 "The Authority Song" flips the **Bobby Fuller Four's** Cricket blockbuster by **Sonny Curtis**, #9, '66 "I Fought the Law." "The Authority Song" is Rock and Roll for the ages. It celebrates the *Rebel Without a Cause* label that often symbolizes America's culture, America's intuitive genius, and America's crime dilemma all at once. **Marlon Brando**'s answer in ('54***½) *The Wild One* – "What're ya rebelling against?" "Whaddya GOT, man?"

Frey hit with #13, 8-88 "True Love." Like the solo Beatles, the solo Eagles thrived.

"White Rabbit" – Jefferson Airplane, #8, 6-67. The most amazing thing about "White Rabbit" is neither superstar diva **Gracie Slick**, nor excellent bassist Jack Casady, nor **Marty Balin**'s great harmonies, nor **Jorma Kaukonen**'s spellbinding guitar. Nope. It's that little girl from Lewis Carroll, ALICE (middle name IN, last name WONDER-LAND), chastely usurped by Walt Disney's princess-producing minions, could actually get stoned out of her everlovin' blue-eyed mind, long, long before this song . . .

One impetuous critic called Gracie (b. 10-30-39, Chicago), the FIRST Rock diva, forgetting all about LaVern Baker, Wanda Jackson, Brenda Lee, Darlene Love, Ronnie Spector, Dusty Springfield, Jackie DeShannon, Connie Francis, Aretha Franklin, Tina Turner, Martha Reeves, Ruth Brown, Etta James, Teresa Brewer, Timi Yuro, Shirley Alston, Gladys Knight, Mama Cass, Dee Dee Sperling (of Dick & Dee Dee), Petula Clark, Arlene Smith/Chantels, or Dee Dee Sharp. Slick was certainly great at Rock and Roll, and very good at what she did, but no way was she FIRST.

"White Rabbit" is a wake-up call. Though her San Franciscans did not lobby for drug ABSTENTION, they certainly did hint that drug binges might indeed kill you. One little pill, she sings, makes you huge. One, teeny-tiny. Mom's wimpy pills don't do anything, so ignore them. Prognosticating a great novel title, *Go Ask Alice,* she brings to life the Dormouse, the White Rabbit, and especially the Magic Mushrooms of Alice's adventure in Wonderland. The whole zany Zen odyssey, and its jolly jabberwocky, rave on.

"Miracles" – Jefferson Starship, #3, 8-75. By the time their name flipped from just airborne to extraterrestrial, Starship's 'enterprise' star-trekked to a melodic harmonious song. Gracie joined Jefferson Airplane/Starship in 1966. When they cut #5, 4-67 "Somebody to Love" on the obtuse North Beach label in 1966, the band coalesced. Marty (b. Martyn Buchwald, Cincinnati '43) was the catalyst, along with Finnish-American Jorma Kaukonen and his fast-fret theatrics. Their first album? #17, 1-67 RCA *After Bathing at Baxter's.* Splashing into the Psychedelic Rock milieu with gonzo album art was everlasting Al. #3, 5-67 *Surrealistic Pillow.* Their next seven albums creased the top 20, averaging (for you math lovers) #12.857 on the charts [Mathman strikes again]. It took a rosy cepha-

lopod to bust the #3 moorings of their Slick surrealistic space odyssey: Al. #1(4), 7-75 *Red Octopus.* Did it eclipse their Psychedelic trip?

AIRPLANE ALBUM ANGST

#17, 3-69 Al.	*Bless Its Pointed Little Head*	
#12, 12-70 Al.	*The Worst of Jefferson Airplane*	
#11, 9-71 Al.	*Bark*	
#3, 7-76 Al.	*Spitfire*	
#28, 7-84 Al.	*Nuclear Furniture*	
#7, 10-85 Al.	*Knee Deep in the Hoopla*	

Any hack A & R stumblebum can think up a title like the BEST of the Sugar Wombats, but it takes a real tricky trooper to come up with a "The WORST of . . ." collection. Such zany Zen titles and liner-note surrealism blasted ho-hum Schlock Rock dreams to smithereens. Airplane's singles? Not too shabby, either, along the way-out off-the-wall Symbolism line:

SLICK SEMI-SUPER SINGLES

#42, 9-67	"Ballad of You & Me & Pooneil"
#98, 4-68	"Greasy Heart"
#64, 11-68	"Crown of Creation"
#60, 11-71	"Pretty As You Feel"
#66, 12-78	"Light the Sky on Fire"
#26, 4-86	"Tomorrow Doesn't Matter Tonight"
#73, 12-88	"Wild Again"

"Pretty As You Feel" tells the young moppet to upgrade her self-image into a more positive mind-set. TELL yourself you look just fine, sez Starship. All the hair goo, fingernail glop, and transformation myth hooey in all the fan mags can't change you, or grub your cash. Or "Tomorrow Doesn't Matter Tonight": Passion doesn't use a compass/protractor, and plot a graph of where a French kiss can lead to Russian hands and Roman fingers. Or an unwanted new kid on the block. Slick slings wisdom in her strong and resolute take-charge alto. By 1975, Starship absorbed ancient Afro-American fiddler **Papa John Creach** (d. '94). They were the first band to feature TWO bass players: David Freiberg and Pete Sears. Craig Chaquico replaced Kaukonen, who had his own agenda with Jack Casady's band – their Al. #30, 8-70 *Hot Tuna* was semi-unamazingly named for their band Hot Tuna.

Jefferson Airplane/Starship is like Times Square. Stand there long enough, and everybody in the known universe will pass by. With their shuffly revolving-door roster, if you wait long enough, everybody in San Francisco will have done a stint as Third Bassman or Second Senior Stevedore Roadie Apprentice.

Major singer Marty Balin split in 1979. Slick's coffee break hit the 1978-81 zone. Well-traveled **Aynsley Dunbar**, drum-guru for everyone (Zappa, Bluesbreakers, Journey), is the drummer for 17.336789% of all the bands in *Gold Rush,* a conservative underestimate. Aynsley joined in 1982. Ancient mariner **Paul Kantner** said goodbye in 1984, taking 'Jefferson' with him and his lawyers. The wriggling remainder was left with the moniker 'Starship.' By 1989, by some Miracle like this song here we're dodging, the whole 1966 marathon roster reunited – Slick, Balin, Kantner, Kaukonen, and Casady. "Miracles" is an interweaving harmony champ, and captures the aura of **Fleetwood Mac** with its interwoven mystique.

"We Built This City" – Starship, #1(2), 9-85. For building blocks, these urban masons used ROCK and ROLL. This hook reverberates. Hammers. Gracie's powerful pipes echoed 1967 Psychedelic magic to new 3-piece generations snagged in junk bonds. "We Built This City" throbs with nearly the same frantic intensity of "Somebody to Love." Like any good marathoner, Gracie knew that when your fast-twitch muscle fibers in your quads start to fade, you increase your mileage and stamina, and cut your weight. "Nothing's Gonna Stop Us Now" went to biggest-ever #1(2), 9-87 as flick *Mannequin's* theme. Somewhere into her grueling marathon, Gracie fired away some things that weighted her down, and tromped the accelerator to the max. Their "Sara" hit #1(1), 12-85, with the bewitching birthday-cake spell of **Stevie Nicks** or **Christine McVie** of another myriad-rostered supergroup:

"Oh, Well – Pt. I" – Fleetwood Mac, #55, 1-70. How could such a great band begin with such a ho-hum, insipid Nowheresville title? And an INSTRUMENTAL? Looking for a big hit, they chanced upon the song **Buddy Holly**'s mother's wrote, a melodic collage of his song titles: "Buddy's Song" (via Randy, Ann, and Nyna McGill), in their Al. #69 *Kiln House,* their first perforation of the Top 100 albums. Peter Green and Jeremy Spencer left the group after this teaser. Key player was John Mayall's Bluesbreaker (oh, no, not Aynsley Dunbar again) bass man **John McVie.** Drummer **Mick Fleetwood** soon arrived, and a nucleus congealed. All they needed were a couple of great female singers. Like the Eagles and Jefferson Airplane/Blimp/Helicopter/Starship's rocketty rockers, this UK/USA supergroup flourished with a big crew of versatile stars. Mayall?

"Don't Waste My Time" – John Mayall, #81, 1-69. John Mayall (b. '33, Cheshire) brought together a mini-multitude of budding rock stars with his Delta purist Bluesbreakers. Steeped in the canon and credo of **Robert Johnson, Jimmy Reed, and Howlin' Wolf,** Mayall manufactured success stories galore. Harmonica/keyboard bluesman Mayall also launched **ERIC CLAPTON,** future Rolling Stone Mick Taylor, **Fleetwood Mac,** and (lo and behold), the ubiquitous **Aynsley Dunbar.** Mayall gravitated to New Orleans Blues. His son Gary Mayall hosted GAZ S ROCKIN BLUES, a DJ show about Reggae and Jamaica and **Bob Marley and the Wailers.**

"Rhiannon (Will You Ever Win)" – Fleetwood Mac, #11, 3-76. Just beyond Led Zep and Jethro Tull, Stevie Nicks rocked into the smoldering new Celtic Renaissance with "Rhiannon." White magic, Druids, gloomy forest groves, Yule logs – you name it. Stevie was born in Phoenix, Arizona (8-26-48), in the hottest city in the Western hemisphere (July av. high – 105 degrees). Her cool blue soprano burrows into your reverie like a cuddlesome woodchuck into your favorite flowerbed. Her pesky thrilling voice hunkers down four notes, and drives you bonkers. As an alto/soprano or 'sopralto,' she's no toothy

woodchuck, but a tigress of stunning beauty. Her enormous evening eyes surround you as she passionately purrs her sensual siren song. Stevie fiddled around with the occult before drifting off to a New Age conclave in California. She previews the Celtic Renaissance of Sarah McLachlan or Celine Dion.

"Rhiannon" blossoms like the night-blooming Cereus in the morose key of A-minor. Singer/songwriter Stevie rousts this tantalizing song-lady temptress. Meanwhile, guys are checking out the alluring Stevie's own buxom beauty, with her swirling blondish tresses adorning her flawless Clearasil face and dynamite figure. Unattached to steam calliope, flugelhorn, or tuba, Nicks just sings. Sometimes the vocal pipes can be the toughest instrument of all. She's surrounded by expert musicians/background singers. Mick FLEETWOOD donated half the band name. John & Christine McVie furnished the MAC part, John hurdles bass riffs, and Christine does jill-of-all-trades stuff – lead and background vocals, keyboards, and even futuristic Techno-Synth programming concoctions. **Lindsey Buckingham** plays guitar and sings tenor. Rockabilly idol **Johnny Burnette**'s (#8, 10-60, "You're 16") son **Rocky** hit with #8, 5-80 "Tired of Toein' the Line," but Johnny's nephew **Billy** (#68, 11-80, "Don't Say No") joined Mac in 1987. "Rhiannon" revved up the Druidic supercharged 455-hp Broom, sweeping from London through the Beatles' Liverpool, over Reykjavik, Iceland, Santa's Father Christmas pad at the North Pole; swooping down the Gold Rush Yukon River, and over Vancouver to the warm Santa Monica Freeway of California. "Rhiannon" is an Anglo-American phenomenon, conquering BOTH the U.S. and U.K. They came a long way on the Top 200 albums chart, from #198, 8-69 eponymous *Fleetwood Mac,* to its quintuple platinum reincarnation *Fleetwood Mac* at Al. #1(1), 8-75 – with a lot of semi-sensational stuff in the middle, like #49, 4-73 Al. *Penguin.* Their monster album heyday, 1975-90, produced eight fab foothills and one Mt. Everest. *Tusk* hit Al. #4, 11-79, and featured a marching band, while *Tango in the Night* (Al. #7, 5-87) and wildly successful Al. #1(5) *Mirage* would have been a major statement for any regular band. **Fleetwood Mac**'s Al. #1(31) 2-77 *Rumors* (17 million+) was the biggest Rock and Roll album of all time in weeks at the top (or second now, if you figure Michael Jackson's #[37] SOUL album 12-82 *Thriller*).

"Say You Love Me" – Fleetwood Mac, #11, 7-76. Like Lennon/McCartney or Henley/Frey, Nicks is sensationally complemented by the husky Blues vocals of a bandmate – this time Christine McVie. When lights simmer down, McVie coos, the guy woos her until sunrise. Mick's drums mash the big 2 & 4 beats with a splash of cymbal crash. John's bass bomps along on the root note of his tonic chord. The bridge shifts between the supertonic II **B-minor** and the dominant V7 **E7** toward the booming crescendo at the Bridge finale. Love steers the mystical wheel of life. Although Christine here is assured of no promises, no certainty, no commitment, no future, and no ring, she insists on the one absolute. Through all the roamin'-in-the-gloamin' ages, HE SAYS HE LOVES HER. Key item.

"Roamin' in the Gloamin'" –Harry Lauder, #5, 2-1912. Kindly Scottish tenor/comedian (knighted like SIR Paul McCartney) strolls with his bonnie lass along the banks and braes o' Glasgow's River Clyde. Even long before Rock and Roll, canny Harry knew that night time was the right time.

"Dreams" –Fleetwood Mac, #1(1), 4-77. The miracle of Mac is not the bewitching murmuring purring of lusciously lovely Stevie Nicks. Nor the gargantuan flams & paradiddles of lanky Mick Fleetwood. Not the multi-faceted spousal duo John & Christine McVie. It's not even equally talented Lindsey Buckingham, whose call & response vocal plays off the winsome harmonies of Stevie & Christine in #10, 1-77 rocker "Go Your Own Way." The miracle is not their switcheroo roster, which brought Delaney & Bonnie's (#13, 5-71 "Never Ending Song of Love") 2nd-generation rock-star kid **Bonnie Bramlett** into the mix in 1993. The miracle is NOT that a full generation of quibbles, squabbles, and mumbled mutterings has not blasted them apart. The miracle is that their whole melodic/rhythmic package works so beautifully for such an ultra-marathon third of a century plus.

Their breakthrough album is #34, 11-74 *Heroes Are Hard to Find*. From #55 debut "Oh Well-Pt. I," their hit drought lasted six years to 11-75, #20 "Over My Head." Then their 'DREAMS" came true. Never afraid to experiment, they actually ensnared the entire University of Southern California Marching Band on #7, 10-79 "Tusk." It shimmies with crowd noise, hyperactive drum flourishes, a weird eternal **Dm** chord, and hornswoggling bass rasps. Elephantine tune, "Tusk." "Dreams," though, floats along on a dreamier minor-key wave. Nicks purrs and rhapsodizes about the romantic rendezvous freedom concept, in a freewheeling era of unhitched musical partners. All the while, John's massive bass simply STALKS, luring you back to a couple of other dream-tunes.

"In Dreams" – Roy Orbison, #7, 2-63. Roy starts on a beatless swirly intro, like Gloria Gaynor's #1(3) '78 "I Will Survive." Roy shuts his eyes, swathed in a mellow Chalypso beat and big friendly chords. In regal Orbisonic fashion, he crescendos his peak summit, disdaining falsetto for his own towering *bel canto* Texan tenor. When he tromps that mystical tall note, you sit transfixed, saying WOW – like the biggest Roman candle just exploded in star-shimmer whorls and whirls of Life Saver green-purple-white-red-gold-blue. Roy's wish-fulfillment song is a dreamy crescendo masterpiece. Fantasy girl.

"All I Have to Do Is Dream" – Glen Campbell and Bobbie Gentry, #27, 2-70; #6, C. We measure the beauty of a melody against this #1(5) '58 Everly Brothers classic. Flash back to your grubby old school gym. Dismiss all the seedy images of odoriferous ancient sneakers, and limburger gym clothes that slithered away to the Maytag ALONE – after neglect by old Unwashed Arnold. Friday night the old gym was transformed into a romantic wonderland. "All I Have to Do Is Dream" is the living embodiment of longing and tender love.

Under the goofy gonfalons of crepe hanging around, swaying with the fake palm tree and Bali Ha'i mural, there you were with SUZIE. This monumental song came on. Suzie smiled, her sweet chiffon dress swishing. Maybe granddad had a jumble of actually-innocent thoughts about this beautiful girl he magically held in his arms for 2 ½ wonderland minutes. It wasn't even hot smoldering passion when the angelic Everlys held sway over itchy suits and shmeared make-up. Or Campbell/Gentry reprised memories for a dawning Disco deluge. With Suzie in that magical world of prom and paradise, prom promenaders could think only of tender kisses and forever.

Oops, let's dissect the chordal magic. Hopefully, it won't turn a romantic moment into a mutilated dead frog. The verse is anchored in a Streetcorner chord pattern in the Blues-guitar mainstay Key of 'E': **E – C#m – A – B7**. Naturally, the bridge lofts to super-dominant IV **A**, dances down to the super-tonic II **F#-major**, and perches on the dominant V7 **B7**. Their climactic moment occurs on the downslide to the need-her-so new verse: V7 – IV – IIIm – IIm – I. He DREAMS his entire LIFE totally AWAY with this cuddly chord collection: **F#m** up to **B7**, and slide **B7 – A – Abm – F#m – E**. Simple, profound.

Crooner/actor Richard Chamberlain hit #14, '63 with this classic, followed by Andy Gibb/wife Victoria Principal at #51, '81 and Nitty Gritty Dirt Band at #66, '75. This golden romantic song is truly an ode to wish-fulfillment; high on cotton-candy fluff of forever love, its carousel spins to sweet infinity.

When Don & Phil, or Glen and Bobbie, slid down the dreamin'-their-lives-all-away chute to reality, you realized that beyond those fleeting magic moments of romantic reverie, there'd be a steely slate gray tomorrow – take out the coal clinkers, scrub the sink, and slather your shoes with polish and gleaming hope. Life's drudgery is circumscribed and consecrated, and somehow made bearable – even glorious – by bouncing from these upbeat magical musical moments into the realization that it's all worthwhile. The Everlys and Fleetwood Mac know the ultimate truth – "Dreams" merge into reality, and reality emerges as a dream.

"Dreams" is the most popular single Fleetwood Mac ever had. Totally unrelated to Orbison's and the Everly's masterpiece, they are bonded into a musical trinity by a kindred romantic vision. **Aerosmith** (#6, 1-76) said? "Dream On."

Rumours – Fleetwood Mac, Al. #1(31), 2-77. MONSTER is too tiny a term to describe its unprecedented chart dominance. Thirty-one weeks. The Year 1977 signaled the final triumph of the album over the single record. Eight track-tape players and brittle tapes overwhelmed entire Oldsmobiles. Regular tapes sought to backdate vinyl in a wild whirr of REWIND-REWIND-REWIND and FAST FORWARD-FAST FORWARD. CD's were but a holographic gleam on the audial horizon. Christmas 1977 brought us the #1 movie sound track album of all time, #1(24) *Saturday Night Fever*.

Three other albums had equaled – even surpassed – *Rumours*. Linked to Broadway shows AND LATER movies, *West Side Story* snagged an entire YEAR with #1(54, yep, 54) from 11-61 to 12-62. *South Pacific* also hit #1(31), from 3-58, as did **Harry Belafonte**'s *Calypso*, which captured 1956 with its similar #1(31) chart domination at the very outset of Album Charts ('55). Nothing like *Rumours* ever was – before or since – in the Rock Era. Even now, millennially, only the Gloved One's #1(37) *Thriller* has surpassed this Major Mac Attack.

"Yesterday's Gone" – Chad and Jeremy, #21, 5-64. Mellow multi-talented **Jeremy Clyde** (b. '44) and **Chad Stuart** (b. '43) preview the smooth-vocal Mac sound from Britain. Clyde plays guitar, piano, banjo, sitar, and Indian bongo/congas from India, the *tablas*. Their Everly blend suggests Simon/Gar, too, but in a baritone/low tenor zone about five notes south. This morose will-o'-the-wisp autumnal farewell bids fond goodbye to a summer fling. The yester-lovers' gossamer future promises major-league memories.

"Don't Stop" – Fleetwood Mac, #3, 7-77. First Rock song ever to elect a President of the United States. Governor **Bill Clinton** won in '92. Victory revelers danced amok to this Mac anthem. "Don't Stop" swaggers – a HELLO song, not a muted goodbye. Christine McVie's lead vocal blends a reeling, rolling mix of nonstop amour: soft warm lips, seductive romantic cadence, and the ardent heat of purple passion.

Gazing at the *Rumours* brown & white album cover, you notice Stevie Nicks is no Godzilla. The honey-blonde winsome lass, amid whirling veils, strikes a voluptuous ballet pose. She looks bold, sensuous, sweetly enchanting. Hot, steamy songs like this, some argue, can create people – on grassy knolls [see Van Morrison's "Brown-Eyed Girl"] or on porch swings [see Brenda Lee's "Sweet Nothin's"]. People were making new people, however, long before Bill Haley rocked around the clock and told his main squeeze "See Ya Later, Alligator." "Don't Stop" bomps and romps along on the chugalug bass of **John McVie**:

THE YOU'VE-SEEN-THIS-BEFORE BASS LINE

♪.   ♪♪.   ♪♪.   ♪♪.   ♪

1   2   3   4

McVie's humpty-dumpty bass sound drives the chord's root note. If a **C** chord, it's the deep 'C' note, as a pedal point. He rhythmically salutes his wife's come-hither contralto. Along with Fleetwood cymbals, "Don't Stop" is undergirded in a rocking hammock of romantic harmony. Bass anchor is JOHN McVie. Many JOHNS buttress the bass guitar bulwark: Led Zep's JOHN Paul Jones; the Who's JOHN Entwistle (catch "Boris the Spider"); JOHN Illsley of Dire Straits; JON Bon Jovi's bassist JON Such; or JOHN Deacon of Queen. How many electric bass solos do you hear? The name John, too, is a little stan-

dard – often out of the Elvis Spotlight. Bassists are rarely Flash or Slash or Zocko or Rhamphorhynchus. STING, of course, plays bass. So does Kiss's GENE SIMMONS. The most famous bassist of all time – **Paul McCartney** – is a former guitarist who assumed bass duties in the Beatles by default; Stu Sutcliffe was a fine graphic artist who hit the right notes, but got the rhythm in the wrong places. Most bass men fade into the darkling penumbra beyond the searing Elvis Spotlight. Bass? Often just a hop, skip, and jump away from the burning rays of big fame. Want the spot with least pressure in the band? Play bass.

In "Sara" (#7, 12-79), the ebullient Nicks clicked again (in melodic 'F'). Her purling purr murmurs coquettishly, "C'mere." Confused with Starship song of same name. Stevie pussyfoots around this mystic poet 'Sara," while John huddles up to the root note. Sayonara, Sara.

"Little Lies" – Fleetwood Mac, #4, 8-87. "Hold Me" bounced Mac back from their #86, 6-80 "Sisters of the Moon" and #60, 2-81 "Fireflies" doldrums – followed by #5, 3-87 "Hold Me" and #19, 6-87 "Seven Wonders." "Little Lies" is the ultimate McVie vehicle. She coos, with Nicks' echo wafting sweetly. Christine's frisky keyboard nails a bagpipe sound that wheezes wondrously up yonder. New Big Mac attacks? Yep. "Save Me" hit #33, 4-90. The B-side (Whitburn) of their #10, 1-77 Fleetwood drum rampage, "Go Your Own Way," clambered the AIRPLAY charts to #41A in 9-97 – "Silver Springs." "Landslide" takes them all the way back to the beginning – a live version off 1975 album *Fleetwood Mac,* to #51 in the Summer of 1998.

We built this generation upon Rock and Roll. Ultramarathoners all: **Rod Stewart, Elton John, Bob Dylan, Billy Joel, the Grateful Dead, the Eagles, Jefferson Airplane/Starship, Fleetwood Mac,** and countless others scattered all over *Gold Rush.* Due to their amazing musicianship, vocal and songwriting abilities, and Divine Providence, most of them have been blessed with amazing marathon hit making and touring endurance in –

THE LONG RUN.

The Eagles: L-R: Bernie Leadon, Glenn Frey, Don Henley, Randy Meisner and Don Felder

Tango Fandango - Latino Rock: Chalypso To Reggae To Salsa

31

Before some English language purist claims Rock and Roll is strictly from the U.S.A. (*norteamericanos*) and that English is the only proper Mother tongue, ask the dapper dude, "Who invented the guitar (*la Guitarra*)?"

The advancement of Rock music as we know it would have been pretty silly with the following co-agulation of instrumentation:

ROCK WITHOUT LATINO INFLUENCE

1 lead singer, and throat.

1 drummer, thumping big bass drum only.

1 clavichord, (developed from lute and Spanish guitar).

1 bagpiper, piping the poor song into an early grave.

1 tuba to play bass (which is bottom 4 strings of guitar, wound to lower octave).

1 piccolo, for squeaky bridge.

1 poor caterwauling cat (*el gato grito*), with tail stepped on, to simulate high treble guitar lead.

1 bullfrog, to get Bud beer for disgusted producers and sound mixers.

1 trombone, to play "When the Saints Go Marching In" for the record's funeral.

1 Alka-Seltzer – the FRANTIC FIZZING is the best part of the whole song.

Of course it's absurd. Without the Spanish guitar, a R & R record would be denuded of its soul, stripped of its passion. How important is the Spanish culture in the nurturing of Rock and Roll? We can only answer by mentioning a few important cities where Rock grew and flourished: San Francisco, Los Angeles, San Diego, San Antonio, Las Vegas, Amarillo or El Paso. The millennial Latino Explosion of Ricky Martin, Marc Anthony, Enrique Iglesias

(#2, 2001 "Hero"), Christina Aguilera, Jennifer Lopez, and Selena comes from a long tradition of great Latino performers.

Spanish influence on American popular music tangos back a lot farther than the Rock Era. While great classical guitarists like **Carlos Montoya, Ernesto Lecuona,** and **Andres Segovia** generated international fame and reverence into this century, Spanish popular music darted into the American pop mainstream. A quixotic ban on North American and British music in World War II created our South American and Caribbean musical infusion. We'll roll and rock on to the *puertorequeño* hits of **Ricky Martin** or the Salsa spectaculars of **Gloria Estefan**, the Mexican timeless guitar fire (*guitarra fuego*) of **Santana**, and the Rastarfarian French/Spanish British universe of **Bob Marley** or even UB40. First let's backtrack to a few musical conquistadores who beamed their booming beat to the frozen northland.

"Begin the Beguine" – Xavier Cugat, #13, 11-35. For Latino Big Beat aficionados during the Depression: XAVIER CUGAT RULED! **Xavier Cugat** (b. Barcelona, Spain 1-1-1900) studied classical violin in Berlin for the Havana Opera of Cuba. *I Love Lucy*'s Cubano hubby Desi Arnaz ['Ricky Ricardo'] is best known for Cugat's classic "Babalu" [#27, 4-44, vocal Miguelito Valdes]. Arnaz never hit the Top 30, but 90% of 50s America associated "Babalu" and Ricky. Don Reid [not too Latino] sang #13, 11-35 "Begin the Beguine" in Cugat's Big Band. Cugat, though authentically Spanish, borrowed from Franco-Americans. The BEGUINE is a dance rhythm of French Caribbean origin (Martinique and Guadeloupe) journey-ing to Paris in 20s Jazz Age. Triplets and a Rhumba Boogie beat forecast later Calypso. Without heavy elec-tric guitars by 1935, Cugat's Beguine pranced on lico-rice-stick clarinets, splashing surging melismas into the thin reedy melody.

Cugat clones copied. In 1935, COVER VERSIONS were normal flattery. Legendary songsmith **Cole Porter** (1893-1964) glommed the royalties from them all: clarinet icon **Artie Shaw**'s big band who began the beguine (#1[8], 9-

38 and #20, 2-42); African-American piano maestro **Eddie Heywood** (#16, 1945); and incomparable **Frank Sinatra** (#23, 1946).

"Begin the Beguine" – Johnny Mathis, NC, 1979. On Al. #122, 2-79 *The Best Days of My Life*, [$1.00 at 1999 Patchogue, L.I., Salvation Army bargain bin]. Mathis sings his absolute best on this song, which ROCKS! Swash-buckling Chalypso guitars build climactically like the cre-scendo *Bolero* of **Maurice Ravel**, another Spanish/French contribution to Beauty and the Beat. Johnny skateboards a hairsbreadth from Rock and Roll. Cole Porter, accord-ing to rumor, wrote it in Indonesia, south of Vietnam, from an island war dance, the KALABAHI. With one of the most melodic chord patterns of all time, "Beguine" rivals equally convoluted "Stardust" by melodist Hoagy Carmichael.

"Star Dust" – Louie 'Satchmo' Armstrong, #16, 12-31. Satchmo steered us to Rock and Roll. Satchmo was not Spanish; he was African-American (1901-71). His "Star Dust" version, nowhere near the biggest, only hints at Spanish influence. Others' chart achievements?

STARDUST STARS

Irving Mills	#20, '30
Isham Jones	#1, '31
Bing Crosby	#5, '31
Wayne King	#17, '31
Lee Sims	#20, '31
Jimmie Lunceford	#10, '35
Benny Goodman	#2, '36
Tommy Dorsey	#8, '36 & #7, '41
Sammy Kaye	#16, '39
Artie Shaw	#2, '41
Glenn Miller	#20, '40... among others

THE LOST STARDUST –
SUPER-NATURAL CHORD DOWNSHIFT

One chord change marks "Star Dust" for the ages – in the Key of 'C', it runs from the VI chord **A** to the V chord **G**, downshifting and modulating from VI to V via the Polynesian Chromatic route. Now? The bVI Polynesian chord: from **C** to **Ab** and back, via

F – A7 – Ab – G7, on his "Star Dust" word 'melody.'

Some Stardusters differ, choosing to plunk an **A-dim** chord (you flat the third and fifth notes off the root note A). Melodist extraordinaire Carmichael wrote it with the diminished chord; **Mitchell Parish** did the words. Few three-chord

---

garage bands applied. Especially here:

C – G – Am – C – B7 – B7b5 – E7 – E7+

Or the Einstein's Chord finale of the first time through:

G7 – A7b5 – D7– G7b5 – C

"Memories – loves" [sweet] refrain . . .

Algebra class? As Ragtime math teacher Ted Haiman says, Music is often math. A dotted eighth is just an alias for a 3/16 note. Rock and Roll is about LOVE, not math. Rock and Roll may be an ESCAPE from academic an-noyances. "Begin the Beguine," too, has wild chord math:

ALL THAT MATH JAZZ

Sadly, to world-class Math Avoiders, MUSIC IS MATH. Like math, we must measure frac-tions, like half and quarter notes. You must add nimble notes to sculpt a major triad, a dimin-ished seventh, a Jazz ninth. Or something eerily otherworldly, like this chord from the planet Neptune:

F#

CMA

This way-out polychord dwarfs other chunky nastyisms like these toughies: **C11** or a **Gm7/C** or even **Bbm7** (**b10**).

In this curious cluster, there are no wimpy chords.

In the complex math that is music (especially Jazz), we must solve very complex musical equations very fast – and not miss a note – or maybe get booted out of the band.

Most people aren't looking for math in music, though – they are looking for Star Dust. Or the sun-swoon sands of romantic Waikiki. They want sheltering palms, almond-eyed beach beauties, pink flamingo sunsets, indigo sea-shores – and titillating torrid rip-roaring tropical bikini mid-nights of purple passion.

"Oh How She Could Yacki Hacki Wicki Wacki Woo (That's in Honolulu)" — Arthur Collins and Byron Harlan, #1(2), 10-1916. We're a tri-lingual society here in the United States – English, Spanish and Hawai-ian. This gal must be the grass-skirt grandmother of Surf Rock's finest Hawaiian queen:

"Honolulu Lulu" – Jan and Dean, #11, 9-63. Surfer girl with stars in her eyes. Ideal Beach Blanket Bingo California *Baywatch* girl. Hawaiian guitar plays "Aloha Oe" before wiping out into hot "Honolulu Lulu" throbbing Surf Rock guitar lead.

"Aloha Oe" – Frank Ferera, #10, 2-24. The big Hawaiian music fad of 1916-21 produced music on the Hawaiian [slide] guitar. We mentioned its 1931 invention by **Joe Kekeku**, rigging electric pickups later. These steely acoustic 1916-21 guitars were EXTERNALLY miked. Ferera and wife Helen Louise played on these syrupy romantic instrumentals. This Hawaiian anthem was written by **Queen Liliokalani**, deposed in 1893 in a peaceful takeover of the old British Sandwich Islands (now Hawaii). "Aloha Oe" is a farewell song of magnificent melodic beauty, and an oldie in 1924. It first hit sheet music in 1878. The thumping drumbeats and rhythmic gusto of Hawaiian music crucially influenced Latino and Caribbean music in the next century and beyond.

At the millennium, some of the greatest Hawaiian artists not famous stateside, but superstars nevertheless (see later Hawaiian section): **Leabert Lindsey, the Ka'au Crater Boys, Dennis Pavao**, 1000-pound late star **Israel "Izzy" Kamakawiwo'ole, Gary Haleamau, Cyril Pahinui**, and **Keali'i Reichel.**

"Night and Day" – Fred Astaire, #1(10), 12-32. Some bumbling talent scout wrote about Fred Astaire: "Can't act, can't sing – can dance a little." Dapper Astaire proved his mettle as an excellent actor, a fine singer, and perhaps the greatest male dancer of all time [or tied with **Gene Kelly** who did "For Me and My Gal" with **Judy Garland** (#3, 1-42)]. Super dancer, fine tenor, fine song.

This Cole Porter Latin classic "Night and Day" is based on an Islamic religious chant from Morocco, the California-sized country of Bogart's #1, 1942 *Casablanca* ('white house,' in Spanish) and **Crosby, Stills, and Nash**'s "Marrakesh Express" (#28, 7-69). "Night and Day's" chordal interface gives us a hint of Chalypso, that Proto-Reggae combo of Rock and Calypso (see **Johnny Nash** and **Jimmy Cliff**, #1 "I Can See Clearly Now").

"Carmen: Toreador Song" – Emilio DeGogorza, #6, 2-1905. Brooklyn-born operatic baritone of Spanish parents. The poor aria got downpedalled to the Camp North Star (Banky Rubenstein) song of questionable culture vulturism; our impish counselor taught it to us 1949 6-year-olds as "Tor-ee-a-dor-ee, don't spit on the floor-ee!"

"Flying Down to Rio" – Fred Astaire, #6, 4-34. Brazil is Portuguese, not Spanish, but its magnificent music of **João Gilberto** certainly has a Jazz Latin flavor. **Morris Albert** ("Feelings") represents Brazil's large English-speaking population. Astaire hypes early air travel – and iffy adventure.

"Amapola" – Jimmy Dorsey, #1(10), 3-41. It's about a pretty poppy, a unique term of endearment. Not Rock. Certainly Latin. Big Band icon **Jimmy Dorsey** (1904-57, alto sax) sadly faded away just as his #2(4), 2-57 "So Rare" sax masterpiece duked it out with Elvis and new

Rock and Roll. The Dorsey Brothers' combo added up to the #2 top artists of the entire 1890-1954 era. One catch – brother **Tommy** (1905-56) was 4th in Joel Whitburn's authoritative *Pop Memories 1890-1954*, with 20,439 points, and **Jimmy** 17th, with 10,552. Combined, only #1 **Bing Crosby** topped the two. In swing and sway 1941, Dorseys ruled – and lavished Latino rhythms.

"Temptation" – Bing Crosby, #3, 12-33. Irish baritone sings Latino classic. Nice job for #1 U.S. singer 1900-50. "Temptation," like Lecuona's "Malaguena," revels in chromatic chord shifts (say, from **E** to **F**, or **C** to **C#**, half-steps). The real HAWAIIAN-SPANISH MISSING LINK was #15 in 2-34 Ted Fio Rito, who covered Crosby. A gorgeous Rock "Temptation" rendition? #27, 5-61 by the **Everly Brothers**. Very Un-Bing. First top-30 Rock hit to blast phasers, or at least flangers, in the recording studio. Anyhow, it sure sounds like a jet plane hurtling across the studio ceiling at Mach One. Everly harmonics? Standard impeccable angelic sound. Flawless Latino Rock n' Roll. In 1961, Hendrix was apprenticing . . .

Ted Fio Rito's Hawaiian-Latino connection involves his #15, 2-34 "Temptation" plus his yearning for returning to #1, 1-34 "My Little Grass Shack in Kealakekua, Hawaii." Our frozen Depression reminded America that if you had to live in a tarpaper shack or a hobo jungle up in the snow-swirl arctic tundra (Green Bay?), you might as well hitchhike to Hawaii (good luck) and hang out at your 81° poverty palace down among those sheltering palms.

"Delicado" – Percy Faith, #1(1), 4-52. Torontonian bandleader Faith's (1908-76) dreamy #1(9) "Theme from a Summer Place" (1-60) unfolded the 60s. Magnificent ROCKER on a HARPSICHORD (sparked the 17th and 18th centuries) played by **Stan Freeman**. Faith furnishes background orchestra (hey, sometimes we all run on FAITH, don't we?) for scores of important singers: **Tony Bennett, Johnny Mathis, Burl Ives**. Faith's hugest hit is the mysterious #1(1), 4-53 "Song from Moulin Rouge."

Faith scorched this rocking Un-Rocker instrumental of monstrous Rockitude.

Delicado means delicate. It is not! The harpsichord blasts, congas thump, guitars twang, horns blat. "Delicado" ascends to roaring crescendos of rhythmic fire. Chord changes are extraterrestrial. If you seek a super song, the Canadian guy with the English name, the Latin beat, the 250-year-old instrument, and the passion-pulsing summer cottage will offer you un-delicate "Delicado," among the LOUDEST songs of the Almost-Rock Era!

"Blue Tango" – Leroy Anderson and his Boston Pops Concert Orchestra, #1(5), 12-51. Combines Orchestral/Latino sound. Sold two million copies. "Blue Tango" had the longest run ever on TV's *Your Hit Parade* – 23 weeks in the Top Seven, according to stat master Joel Whitburn (38 weeks overall). "Blue Tango" also hit #6, 3-52 for Hugo Winterhalter. After #9, 12-49 "Blue Christmas," #18, 1-52 "Blue December," and before 11-52, #19 "Blue Violins," Hugo wedged in Leroy's monster hit. [Oddly, this orchestrator never actually played the true Blues.] We've taken

Whitburn's exceedingly accurate charts and found the longest-charting singles. With never a 'HOT 100' from 1930-54. Whitburn combined a variety of sources for his tabulation expertise: ASCAP lists, sheet music sales, Record-label publications, *Billboard* 1913-Present, *Talking Machine World* mag, *Your Hit Parade* 1935-54, and radio airplay. Plus a few other sundry chroniclers. Chart size was miniscule. Like so: 1890-1899, only 1-3 songs; 1927-33, 20; 1940-54, 15-30 best-selling records; and last and even more intoxicatingly confusing – 15-30 1945-54 disc jockey charts. Here 'tis, via Whitburn's skillful interpolations.

OK, it's our rather official list of Very Oldies' Chart-Hugging records:

FORMERLY YOUNG
OLDIES OF LONGEVITY

Weeks

38   "Blue Tango" – Leroy Anderson and Boston Pops Orchestra, #1(5), 12-51.

36   "Paper Doll" – Mills Brothers, #1(12), 7-43.

34   "Be My Love" – Mario Lanza, #1(1), 12-50.

34   "The Loveliest Night of the Year" – Mario Lanza, #3, 4-51.

33   "You Always Hurt the One You Love" – Mills Brothers, #1(5), 6-44.

31   "Vaya Con Dios" – Les Paul and Mary Ford, #1(11), 6-53.

30   "Boogie Woogie" – Tommy Dorsey, #5, 1-43. (Re-entered charts, but we count only consecutive weeks).

30   "Any Time" – Eddie Fisher, #2(2), 12-51.

30   "Maybe You'll Be There" – Gordon Jenkins Orchestra, #3, 6-48.

30   "I Get Ideas" – Tony Martin, #3, 6-51. (His 'ideas' got the audio banned from the very first *MTV* show, *Your Hit Parade*. Snooky Lanson and Dorothy Collins just mimed).

30   "In the Mood" – Glen Miller, #1(12), 10-39 (whatever they were in the mood for couldn't be banned, because there were no lyrics).

30   "Frenesi" – Artie Shaw, #1(13), 7-40.

Both "Vaya Con Dios" (the 'Lord be with you') and "Frenesi" are upcoming *Gold Rush* Latin songs: *Canciones d'Oro*. "Blue Tango" holds the Methuselah Old-timers' Record for longevity. Until 1993, however, only seven Rock Era 1955-93 songs beat "Blue Tango's" long run, and three of them hit just 39 weeks.

Oddly, today songs stick around longer. Of course it's comparing apples and oranges. They tabulate 100 hits more accurately now, since 1991 Sound Scan [*Billboard*].

NOT FADE AWAY

From Singles of Longevity (Source: Joel Whitburn's *Top Pop Singles, 1955-99*):

The Biggest 1990-99 songs top all other songs in Rock Era.

Weeks on HOT 100 (not TOP 10)

[70]   ["One Headlight" ("Air"-only) – Wallflowers, #2(5)A, 1-97].

69   "How Do I Live?" – LeAnn Rimes, #2(4), 6-97.

65   "You Were Meant for Me" – Jewel, #2(2), 11-96.

[63]   ["Don't Speak" ("Air"-only) – No Doubt, #1(16)A, 10-96].

[63]   ["If You Could Only See" ("Air"-only) – Tonic, #11A, 5-97].

60   "Macarena (Bayside Boys Mix)" – Los Del Rio, #1(14), 9-95.

[60]   ["Walkin' on the Sun" ("Air"-only) – Smash Mouth, #2(1)A, 7-97].

[59]   ["Fly" ("Air"-only) – Sugar Ray, #1(6)A, 7-97].

Amazingly, only ONE of these ever hit #1 on the main HOT 100 chart ("Macarena"). The longest chart run for the 1955-89 crew sneaks in via a 2nd popularity in 90s: Four Seasons' 54-week "December 1963 (Oh, What a Night)": #1(3), 12-75, and #14, 8-94. Otherwise, it's "Tainted Love" by Soft Cell #8, 1-82, with 43 weeks.

"Frenesi" – Artie Shaw, #1(13), 7-40. *La cancion de Mexico*. Born Arthur Arshawsky (5-23-1910), all-American clarinetist/bandleader Shaw had the big version of "Stardust" (also spelled "Star Dust") – voted #1 ever in a *Billboard* 1956 poll of disc jockeys. Artie's #1(6), 9-39 "Begin the Beguine" version was voted #3 ever. If ever anyone challenged **Benny Goodman** for #1 clarinetist ever, it is Shaw. Shaw launched this Mexican song to a quarter of a year at #1. He followed it with the sweet Mexicano follow-up, "Adios, Marquita Linda" (#18, 9-40). Artie's chartbusters? #2(1), 2-38 "Goodnight, Angel"; #1(2), 12-38 "They Say"; #9 Jazz classic 9-39 "Traffic Jam," and #9, 3-41 "Dancing in the Dark" (see Bruce Springsteen). Shaw wasn't Latino, but he fired off a sweet version of "Temptation" (#21, 1-44). Bob Swezey says when Shaw retired, Shaw never played his clarinet again.

"Vaya Con Dios (May God Be With You)" – Les Paul and Mary Ford, #1(11), 6-53. Mary's sweet murmuring contralto voice leads Les's guitar magic through a wondrous melodic masterpiece. Look in the dictionary under *Canciones Lindos* (Beautiful Songs). A whirly blur of melody will swoop its celestial swath onto the page of your *diccionario*. In the midst of that misty whirr of super songsters, you'll find Les and Mary up front. From a dark *hacienda* (home) to a perilous journey, the song bids a loving *adios* for a safe return – with a tolling mission-bell to mark his way. Her contralto could stop the thunder. His smooth murmuring guitar could stop *el toro rapido* in his tracks – to go sniff the flowers (*flores por toro*) like peace-loving *Ferdinand the Bull* (*El Toro Fernando*, Munro Leaf).

"Perfidia (Tonight)" – Xavier Cugat, #3, 1-41. Classic Latin-American hit, recorded 1½ years earlier. The word *perfidia* also gets translated as perfidious, or devious and tricky: tricky chords, nice Caribbean beat. It also hit #15, 10-60 for the **Ventures**. Smooth Surf Rock guitarist Bob Bogle played lead guitar like Chet Atkins:

"Moon Over Miami" – Chet Atkins, NC, 1962. From *Caribbean Guitar*, Al. #33, 10-62. Our 1972-73 hometown Miami is among the most important Latino cities in the world with 3.5 million people. Chet's nimble fingers feather the frets on this #1(3), 1-36 Latin favorite by piano legend **Eddy Duchin**. Chet Atkins (1924-2001, Rock Hall of Fame 2002) ruled in Nashville. Chet played rhythm guitar on Elvis's "Heartbreak Hotel," and some flashy riffs on the Everly Brothers' "Wake Up Little Susie."

"Brazil" ["Aquerelo do Brasil]" – Xavier Cugat and His Waldorf-Astoria Orchestra, #2(7), 1-43. Cugat and Walt Disney (1900-65) introduced a with-it cartoon parrot named Jose Carioca to serenade the questionable-singing superstar Donald Duck. Vibrant splashes of color (swirling multi-hued sidewalks, shimmery blue surf) lullabyed a world at war – and dreaming in grim Tele-News black and white. The *Samba* is one of Rock's earliest Latin beats. Flashy maracas chuff. A deft counterpoint fans dancers. The song mirrors memories of **Carmen Miranda** (1913-55) dancing dervishly, an entire fruit basket atop her smiling face:

"Mama Euquero" – Carmen Miranda, #25, 5-41. It translates from Portuguese (Brazilian) as "I Want My Mama." She matches Cugat's 3-40, #17 similar song *en Español* – "Quiero A Mi Mama," with vocal by Carmen Castillo.

"Quiero Mucho (Yours)" – Xavier Cugat, vocal Dinah Shore, #16, 9-41. Without Cugat, could Rock have begun? Cugat launched the rhythmic counterpoint to ward off the no-beat trend among formal orchestras. Rock and Xavier attracted gorgeous women. He married Abbe Lane, not to mention bombshell **Charo**.

"Dance A Little Bit Closer" – Charo and the Salsoul Orchestra, #104, 1-78. Her "Cuchi Cuchi" Salsa style keeps her perpetually on some TV talk show somewhere. A sprightly personality indeed.

Other Cugat Latin Rock progenitors? The Cubano "Acuellos Ojos Verdes" became #16, 9-41 "Green Eyes." **Dinah Shore** (1917-94) did a Rumba too with Xavier: #19, 12-40 "The Rumba-Cardi," plus her own #1(4), 7-44 "I'll Walk Alone." In sum-

mer 1944? Cugat sent "Amor (love)" to #10 and "Cuanto Le Gusta" to #27, 1-49.

"Amor" – Ben E. King, #18, 7-61; #10, 8-61 R & B. Follow-up to Ben's two post-**Drifters** bombshells: "Spanish Harlem" (#10, 12-60) and the immortal "Stand by Me" (#4, 5-61 and #9, 10-86). Cugat reprise, in **Billy Eckstine** baritone style.

"Kiss of Fire" – Billy Eckstine, #16, 4-52; #8, 6-52 R & B. Baribass Billy, of velvet Soul legend, performed this Argentine tango "El Choclo" with his usual commanding easy tiger splendor. In 7-59, Eckstine dynamically sang "Temptation" to #7 R & B (NC, Top 30).

"Kiss of Fire" – Georgia Gibbs, #1(7), 4-52. Gibbs's pale #1(3), '55 "Dance with Me Henry" covered Hank Ballard's more risqué "Work with Me Annie" [#1(7), 4-54 R & B, NC HOT 100]. Gibbs's first #1 song, this fiery-kiss Tango, is a lot steamier, too, and got banned on the 'PG' *Your Hit Parade* TV show . . .

"Jamaica Farewell" – Harry Belafonte, #14, 10-56. Born in the throbbing heart of Harlem, Belafonte (b. '27) began his career as a pop African-American singer with an air-castle Irish tenor voice. Catch Harry's beloved St. Patrick's Day anthem "Danny Boy" on his #2(2) Al. *An Evening with Belafonte* in 3-57. Belafonte's mother came from Jamaica, his father from the West Indies. Poignant lament, "Jamaica Farewell." Pure melody. Dubbed a Folk or Calypso singer, Harry nevertheless championed music with a BIG BEAT. Remember, Belafonte's Latin/Caribbean album *Calypso* only relinquished its 31-week reign to two other albums: #1(54) *West Side Story* of 1962, #1(37, '82) *Thriller* of Michael Jackson, and tied #1(31), 1957 *South Pacific* ad 1977 Fleetwood Mac #1(31) *Rumours*.

"Jamaica Farewell's" Harry laments leaving his lass in Kingston – Jamaican capital (see Bob Marley). BONGOS follow Calypso and its R & R hybrid, Chalypso, like fame followed the Beatles. This #14 song inspired Nick Reynolds, Bob Shane, and Dave Guard to form the Folk **Kingston Trio**. We combine Caribbean music, streaming with Reggae, with Latin-American/Spanish music. Though Rock and Roll champions informal styles of fashion, it was Belafonte and the Kingston Trio who pioneered sport shirts (no tie, no suit) on stage – looking a bit like the later **Beach Boys**. Indeed, the Surf legends' father/manager Murry Wilson, deliberately had them dress like the Kingston Trio. Rockers still wore suits. "Jamaica Farewell" highlights an old island paradise, with sonorous dancing girls, a colorful marketplace, and his long lost ladylove.

"Island in the Sun" – Harry Belafonte, #30, 6-57. Almost a prayer. Essence of pure melody. Both Belafonte and the Kingston Trio's careers began with the lovely lullaby a father sings to his daughter – "Scarlet Ribbons" (#30 for H.B. in 12-52). "Island in the Sun" gave workaholic Americans some place to dream about on the Winter Fantasy circuit. [After a week in palmetoo-bug, shark-ey paradise, many ran screaming back to their beloved paper clips and time clocks and Xerox pandemonium.]

"Deportee" – Kingston Trio, NC, 1959. After the **Beatles** (123 weeks), no band spent more time at the #1 top of the album heap than this gung-ho Folk and Folk-Rock Trio (46 weeks). **Elvis** (64 weeks) and **Michael Jackson** (49) put the Trio in the #4 All-Time-at-#1 position. Despite a little iffy 50s ethnic humor, you could see their fervent empathy for the plight of Mexicano laborers in "Deportee" California. This melodic album song blurts a tragic tale of indignity and suffering. With fluttering flamenco-style *guitarras*, the Trio weaves troubadour **Woody Guthrie**'s (1912-67) story of illegal immigration, capture, and deportation in a plane the **Big Bopper** would have guffawed at flying. The rickety crate, bedeviled by virulent gremlins, catches fire over Los Gatos Cañon (Canyon of the Cats or Pumas). It crashes. No one is saved. The ugly irony ricochets off the newsflash – that these lost souls, someone comments, were ONLY deportees. Without heavy-handed didacticism, the Trio sang that you're never too important for compassion and sympathy.

"Lady of Spain" – Eddie Fisher, #6, 9-52. Fine dramatic tenor Eddie's "Lady of Spain" fan-dances. Last Big Crooner Fisher was often hobbled by an out-to-lunch rhythm section. Eddie (b. '28, Philadelphia) updates this **Ray Noble** classic (#5, 9-31, and revamp #19, 2-49) with sporty blasting harmonic horns. The '49 version sports a new trio, after Noble's noble lead singer had been killed [yes] by a bomb.

"[Oh] Holy One" – Freddy Fender, #107, 5-60. I was in a fake-I.D. bar in Toledo about a thousand years old named the NEW BAR with Denny Jaggers, Dave Brady, Larry Glazer, Jack 'Bear' Berry, and Don 'Zorro' Zabinski. We were 16, prowling by the burlesque show. **Ritchie Valens** was killed the year before, and we thought his Irish tenor *Mexicano* voice could never be replaced. Suddenly, out of the beery pigs'-knuckle midnight howl of the Frankie Avalon jukebox, I was serenaded by a Valens-vibrant voice. He sang about a beautiful, sweet señorita. Pedestal princess. Fame took awhile, *quince años*:

"Before the Next Teardrop Falls" – Freddy Fender, #1(1), 2-75; #1(2), 1-75 C. Baldemar Huerta (b. '37, San Benito, Texas) named himself after a Fender guitar. Recording in Spanish from 1956-59, Fender spent the next 15 years in obscurity (and worse). Bilingual "Teardrop" is a melody marshmallow. Like Valens, Fender's voice sounds tender and gentle. By looking at them both, you'd think they played defensive tackle for the New York Giants. A rare Rock Era bilingual hit. Freddy took "Wasted Days and Wasted Nights" (NC, '60) to #8, 6-75 (#1 C). Third? Huerta astoundingly picked **Doris Day**'s 1954 #1 ballad "Secret Love" to #20, 10-75. Mexican-American Freddy took Polish-American **Les Paul**'s "Vaya Con Dios" ot #59, 5-76 (#5 C).

"I Can See Clearly Now" – Johnny Nash, (with Bob Marley's Wailers as backing band), #1(4), 9-72; #38, 100-72 R & B. I taught a 1972-73 Rock and Roll class at Miami-Dade Junior College to about 60% *Cubano* students who loved this rambler Nash smash. **Jimmy Cliff** took "I Can See Clearly Now" to #18, 11-93; #98, 1-94 R & B. Ironically, CLIFF is the authentic Reggae guru, Nash the fine Houston tenor. Cliff did authentic early Reggae with his "Wonderful World, Beautiful People" to #25, 12-69; NC R & B. Reggae movie star. Nash's Niftiest Hit, revamped for comedian John Candy's *Cool Runnings* (1993****), highlights wild Olympic bobsled ride of climatologically impossible Jamaican bobsled team. In 1969, Jimmy Cliff hyped Reggae. Mountainous Jamaica has 2½ million people – 75% Afro-Jamaican, 15% Afro-European, 10% Asian, Caucasian. English? Official language. Patois? Creole. Creole features French origins. The intermixing of Franco-Spanish-American music exploded from this island tinier than Connecticut: JAMAICA.

Rock and Roll, we recall, was mostly born on the Mississippi Delta between Memphis and New Orleans. Louisiana runs on French law. Musical tradition is very French. Jamaicans' Creole is a kissin' cousin of our Cajun, which comes to us from ACADIAN, the Canadian Nova Scotian French settlement written up in Longfellow's long poem *Evangeline*. **Harry Belafonte**'s adopted spot KINGSTON (600,000) is the capital, and **Kingston Trio** namesake. In his "Banana Boat Song" (#5, 1-57), stevedores work all night long with just a rum drink – a Jamaican export. Jamaica and Haiti practice ancient Voodoo-style religions in combination with Christianity. **Bob Marley** (1945-81) and the Wailers, **Nash**'s back-up band, were Rastafarians. They worship Ethiopian emperor Haile Selassie (now departed). They often wear dreadlocks (curly long Afro hair) and smoke ganja (pot, weed, marijuana) as part of their religion. Johnny Nash ended up with the legendary Bob Marley and the Wailers on his record, long before their #1(1), 7-74 "I Shot the Sheriff" became an Eric Clapton (#1, 7-74) classic.

"Caribbean" – Mitchell Torok & Louisiana Hayride Band, #26, 8-53 and #27, 8-59; #26, 9-59 R & B. CAJUN "Caribbean" features a conga-line monkey. Lurching with a hybrid beat, Torok's tantalizing tune involves one of the most poly-ethnic and polyrhythmic blends ever to characterize the emerging Rock Revolution. First, Torok headlined the **Louisiana Hayride** before the young 1954-55 Hillbilly Cat of Tupelo (Elvis). "Caribbean" foreshadows R & R in the CAJUN frenzy of the early fifties. CAJUN bashed all the four beats [1-2-3-4] like Disco later. Case in point?

"Big Mamou" – Pete Hanley, #19, 4-53. When I heard "Big Mamou" (and Delores Gray's #21, 5-53 revamp) I though it was the loudest song in the world. Little did I know the Rock and Roll was waiting in the wings, to rampage the rafters in raucous rhythm. Like Jo Stafford's "Shrimp Boats" #2(2), 10-51, "Big" gave a French Caribbean Connection: soft Louisiana moon floating on high, pirogues on the crawfish-pie bayou, wheezing accordions, snatches of patois or Cajun French. Most of all, a MONSTER beat!

"Jole Blon" – **Roy Acuff, NC, 1947; #4, 4-47 C.**
Also "(Our Own) Jole Blon," a French-Cajun expression meaning 'beautiful blonde.' Roy sang and fiddled. Also cut by **Waylon Jennings** and produced by Buddy Holly to NC, 1-59, before Waylon became a Country star.

The hot new beat meandered down to the Gulf of Mexico. It bobbed and weaved and loped to Jamaica, and became several new types of music: Calypso, Chalypso, Ska, and Reggae. Each one of them is closely related to Rock and Roll.

All of them have as much a Franco-American Connection as they do Latin American. [I am ½ Franco-American, but 1/16 of that is Hispanic.] To further confound this ethnic mulligatawny stew, both French and Italian (Romanian, too) are Romance languages derived from LATIN. Shouldn't we call some of these sub-genre sounds LATIN-American? "I Can See Clearly Now" is essentially a Chalypso song hybridizing into the newer Bob Marley-style Reggae beat. Cliff, not Nash, first commandeered the cutting edge of early Reggae. **Johnny Nash** (b. '40, Houston) began as **Johnny Mathis**'s only major pop imitator: Nash's #23, 12-57 "A Very Special Love" garnered the 17-year-old lad's continued success. He did a classic early Rap inspirational and multicultural sermon, with **Paul Anka** and George Hamilton IV, called "The Teen Commandments" (#29, 12-58).

Before we can truly understand Reggae or Ska, let's shift gears from Belafonte's pure Calypso to its popular 1958 R & R relative hybrid – Chalypso.

"Susie Darlin'" – **Robin Luke, #5, 8-58.** "Susie," however is the quintessential Chalypso song [and the writer's favorite song for 20 years, so he shamelessly stuffed it in here twice]. Producer Bob Bertram, you recall, thrummed the pittypat beat with sticks while hitting his pants pocket in the basement studio, and farmed the bust-loose hit song to Dot Records after it hit #1 in Honolulu, Hawaii. "Susie" sold a million. The song's great charm rolls off the Holly 'wo-uh-ho' hiccup tacet:

THE WORLD'S GREATEST CHORD CHANGE			
A	E7	C#	D
"Wo-uh-ho Su-sie Dar-lin'"			
I	V7	bIII	IV
Tonic	Dominant	Mediant	Sub-Dominant

Robin's gimmick to catapult Honolulu's "Susie" to #12 Record of Year 1958? A Hawaiian ukulele.

Luke was the only star to imitate the Holly hiccup successfully (magnificently, on "Won't You Please Be Mine"), during Buddy's own lifetime. Chalypso Rock hits: **Paul Anka**'s #1, '57 "Diana"; **Neil Sedaka**'s #9, 10-59 "Oh! Carol", about Carole King; the **Everly Brothers**' sensational slow Chalypso "Love of My Life" (#40, 11-58); Pat Boone's #6, 6-62 "Speedy Gonzales"; Frankie Avalon's #1(5), 2-59 "Venus." Among the LAST of the genre is **Stevie Wonder**'s great #1(3), '84 "I Just Called to Say I Love You" (replete with final cha-cha-cha finale flourish).

"Love Is Strange" – **Mickey and Sylvia, #11, 1-57; #1(2), 12-56 R & B.** Super duo of Afro guitar-strumming stars **Mickey Baker** – and one of first women to play guitar, **Sylvia VanderPool**. Small romantic Rap dialogue session between her and "Loverboy," with metallic guitars blazing. Buddy Holly echoed this tune on an obscure tape (#105, 1969, Buddy's last charted Single hit in U.S.A.). The song became the basis for his first hit as a songwriter. **Mickey** and **Sylvia**'s follow-up was #46, 12-60s "What Would I Do." Sylvia later recorded solo as, oddly enough, "Sylvia." Out of the blue in March 1973, Sylvia's "Pillow Talk" jumped to #3, eclipsing "Love Is Strange." Scores of other Chalypso hits, like Bobby Darin's #2(1), 4-59 "Dream Lover," were often marked by a swift *pizzicato* muted guitar.

"Words of Love" – **Buddy Holly, NC, 9-57.** Solo release on Coral label minus Crickets. Buddy's Chalypso features first R & R vocal overdubbing. He sounds like two Holly Brothers [Everly echo]. Commercially unheralded, Buddy's "Words of Love" scored two big commercial repercussions: 1) **Dave Somerville**'s Diamonds followed up their monster smash "Little Darlin'" #2(8) with songwriter Buddy's "Words of Love" (#13, 5-57) two months later, [before Buddy's Crickets' "That'll Be the Day" zoomed to #1 in Cash Box]; and 2) The **Beatles**, who named themselves after Buddy's Crickets, recorded "Words of Love."

"Heartbeat," Buddy's last lifetime hit, only snagged #82 in 12-58. 1999 Grammy winner **Tommy Allsup**'s feathery lead guitar touch, and Holly's incredible voice, sculpted a great Chalypso sound. Donald Clarke can't believe Buddy's "It's So Easy" didn't chart here (#8, 1-59 Australia, though) and that "Heartbeat" hit only #82. Donald Clarke raves on that with Elvis in Germany in the Army, Buddy was poised for #1. Clarke says he had more talent than Elvis, and might have survived without compromising his personality. [Elvis's getting drafted was crafted, some say, by a few jealous draft-board dragoons and military higher-ups who didn't like his swagger and haircut.]

Several Holly tunes nudge his "Tex-Mex" Latino beat. No one in Texas is ever very far from Latino culture. **Buddy Holly** couldn't have done much more in an uptight social climate to show he loved Latino culture: he married Maria Elena Santiago. Holly Latino-flavored songs? "Crying, Waiting, Hoping," "What to Do," "That's What They Say," "Wait Till the Sun Shines, Nellie," "Peggy

Sue," "Peggy Sue Got Married," and "Everyday." And, of course, "Love Is Strange." Which it is? As a topic for a book, however, you can't beat it – love is so tied in to Rock and Roll.

Long before the deluge of Reggae and Ska, we had a pixieish Jamaican soprano (b. 1946) who started out as Millicent Smith:

"My Boy Lollipop" – Millie Small, #2(1), 5-64; #2(1) R & B. Within the tornado of Beatlemania, this Caribbean cutie launched a "Blue Beat" bombshell. Remember the sugary Chordettes' "Lollipop" awhile back? Millie's cute Islands soprano twang overarched a profusion of hot horns. She rocks it in folksy melody, and bubbly "D" major. The drum hammers its big 2 & 4 beats. The insistent bass runs up and down its Boogie-Woogie arpeggio course. Into the center of the song, she fires off a harmonica like Delbert McClinton's masterpiece on this:

"Hey Baby" – Bruce Channel, #1(3), 1-62; #2(1), 2-62 R & B. Louisiana Hayride vet Channel (pronounced Sha-Néll, as in Chanel #5) rode to #1 glory in this savvy vocal, trading off with **Delbert McClinton**'s best-known harmonica of the era. Del's harmonica idea, on **Roy Orbison**'s #25, 8-61 "Candy Man" Blues number, powered the Beatles' first hit (#17 U.K. '62) "Love Me Do." Delbert taught his technique to harpslinger **John Lennon** when they were both 4th-or-5th billing on a British tour. Del also sparked Millie's "Lollipop." He hit #8, 12-80 with his "Giving It Up for Your Love." [Countryish Blues, rife with harmonica whizbang stylistics.] Millie's follow-up? #40, 8-64 "Sweet William." She made her modest mark, however, on destiny, by shaping the sound of Ska and the sound of Reggae – with her fired-up schoolgirl gusto, and her steamy chugging horn section. A blast of brass.

"The Israelites" – Desmond Dekker & the Aces, #9, 5-69; #1, 4-69 U.K. In the fledgling 70s, Psychedelia faded, Heavy Metal thundered, Singer/Songwriters warbled, Glam-Glitz Rock pranced, Disco pulsed, Religious Rock preached, Soul got Funky, Ska skipped, and Reggae roared. **Desmond Dacris**, (b. Kingston, Jamaica) advanced the "Blue Beat" of Millie Small to new heights and convoluted Rock N' Reggae rhythms. British fame fanned out from their one U.S. hit to #2 U.K., 9-70 "You Can Get It if You Really Want It." This evolved into Rap somewhat. The Rock Jock would murmur his DJ patter over the record or its B-side. "The Ten Commandments," by **Prince Buster** [#81, 2-67; #17 R & B] is an early Rap preview. Buster, a record-store mogul (Buster Campbell) of Jamaica, recorded this missing link between earlier SKA, and later Reggae. From Buster, Reggae evolved via DJ's King Stitt and Sir Collins. The coining of the term Reggae probably follows **Frederick 'Toots' Herbert**'s and the **Maytals**' prototypical record, "Do the Reggay."

It came out of something called RYDIM, a dialect offshoot of the term rhythm. Ward expostulates: "Reggae brought the bass to the forefront, emphasizing a complex interrelationship between it, the trap drums, and the percussion instruments. The rydim was shot through with silences, and to this day few non-Jamaicans can play it. The pulse is divided as finely as 64 times, and cross-rhythms abound. The bass seems to be the lead instrument, and the guitar is reduced to playing *changa*, mere scratching at a chord." [That chord-scratch is also part of Funk R & B.]

"Day After Day (It's Slippin' Away)" – Shango, #57, 5-69. Tied with Dekker (5-69) for early Reggae hits is Anglo **Tommy Reynolds** of T-Bones (#3 instrumental 12-65 "No Matter What Shape Your Stomach's In") and of **Hamilton Joe Frank and Reynolds**: #4, 5-71 harmonic "Don't Pull Your Love" and #1(1), 6-75 "Fallin' in Love." As **Shango**, Reynolds Reggae-ed the Ring of Fire earthquake fear of Californians. He ponders the shaking demise of L.A. and San Francisco in a mega-quake – and envisions rowing little Noah's arks to lofty altitudinous IDAHO. **Shango**'s cute/sad novelty song helped **Bob Marley** by jump-starting REGGAE.

Before we can tackle the Magic of Marley, let's do SKA. Ska is a midpoint between Chalypso and Reggae. Millie Small's "Lollipop" is often accorded the 'First Ska Song' credits.

Antoine 'Fats' Domino (b. '28, New Orleans) was nearly worshipped in Jamaica. The New Orleans Afro-Franco-American (**Chuck Berry** too is Afro-French) reeled his careening beat over the Delta air waves and out to Jamaica. Fats rocked to a Rock-Steady easy beat, whereas these early Ska tunes rampaged (like 2000+ Punk) at mile-a-minute rhythms: Prince Buster's "Al Capone," "Confucius" by Don Drummond, and the Maytals' "Broadway Jungle." The Ram Jam club in Brixton in Britain's Cornwall/Devonshire 'tropics' featured Alton Ellis's "Rock Steady" and the Jamaicans' "Ba Baa Boom." Steady beat rallied from the torrid Torquay tropics of Plymouth in Southern England to the Plymouth/Dodge/Chrysler plant in Detroit, and back to the Atlantic via the voice of Lady Soul's "Rock Steady" [Aretha Franklin, #9, 10-71; #2(2), 11-71 R & B.]

Previewing RAP, voice-over DJ's like Sir Coxsone at the Ram Jam became an integral part of early Reggae records. They added their own patter, and double-tracked to make a complete new product (the term "overdubbing" has a risqué Jamaican meaning). Raunchy? [These are the PG-13 titles]: "Fire in Your Wire" by Laurel Aitken, and "Bang Bang Lulu" by Lloyd Terrell.

Did "Gangsta Rap" begin with **Dennis Al Capone**, (named for Chicago Prohibition gangster)? Capone celebrated Black Pride with his 1970 "Cassius Clay," pumping up **Muhammad Ali**'s win over white Joe Bugner. Let's unite three wildly divergent strains on the Fringe: Ska, Skiffle, and Reggae. Remember white **Lonnie Donegan**'s #8 U.S. & U.K. 1956 "Rock Island Line"? Glasgow, Scotland's **Skiffle King Donegan** had only two stateside hits, this and #5, 6-61 "Does Your Chewing Gum Lose Its Flavor (on the Bedpost Overnight)" (#3, 2-59 U.K.). Donegan enjoyed 26 UK Top 20 tunes, as tabulated by British mainstays for UK chart action: *Melody*

Maker, New Musical Express, Record Mirror, and *Music Week*. Among Donegan tunes with a Skiffly-iferous beat are (all UK chart #'s): #7, 4-61 "Have a Drink on Me," #1, 6-57 "Puttin' on the Style," #18, 1-59 "Skiffle Party," #1, 3-60 "My Old Man's a Dustman," and #2, 4-56 "Lost John," (#58, 6-56 USA). The white Scotsman's influence on the Island rhythm of the Wailers and Bob Marley is intriguingly profound. Country Rock star **Marty Robbins** sent Ska/Reggae style hits into the early years HOT 100 – twin #16, 1962s "Ruby Ann" and his torrid temptress tune "Devil Woman."

"In the Summertime" – Mungo Jerry, #3, 7-70; NC, R & B. Filtered through Jamaican rhythms, **Ray Dorset** of Ashford, Kent (b. Spring Solstice 3-21-46) hefts the cheery lead vocals. Mungo Jerry pioneered the unplugged generation, with Paul King on American BANJO and Colin Earl on piano. Aside from their terrible advice on motoring to guzzle a drink, then drive, this is one fun and frolicsome song.

It is Skiffle. It is Ska. It is Reggae. Back to Nash? Before Cliff and Marley, the Houstonian dealt Ska:

"Hold Me Tight" – Johnny Nash, #5, 9-68; #21 R & B. A rock-steady rydim binds Nash's sterling Irish-tenor tune together. He strings along the bubbly bomp-pa-bomps (or, "Bop-pa-bow-ba-bow-ba-bow pow's) in this fleecy love lyric. Syncopated Ska shuffle rhythm floats the groove sky high.

Music never dies. Though Disco headlined the 70s, you hear it today at full blast as 'House' or 'Industrial' or 'Dance' or 'Techno-Synth' music at the club down the block. Rockabilly recedes, but gets bolstered by the Neo-Rockabilly surge of the **Stray Cats** in 1980, or Paul McCartney's #26, 10-99 album *Run Devil Run*. Ska then drifts, bubbles and sizzles the Millennium on the Ska-loped East Coast of the U.S.A. via Brendan and Shelley Tween's **Mephi-Ska-Pheles**, or the **Scofflaws** or **Edna's Goldfish**.

"Roots, Rock, Reggae" – Bob Marley and the Wailers, #51, 7-76; #37, 6-76 R & B. Legendary **Bob Marley** (Rock Hall '94) is the main Founding Father of Reggae, despite iffy respect from the fickle singles HOT 100 chart. His duo albums fared better: #8, 5-76 *Rastaman Vibration* and #20, 7-77 *Exodus*. In a triumph of posthumous power, Marley resurfaced to Al. #60 *Chant Down Babylon* in 1-2000. Marley is very relevant in Millennium III. In all of Ska and Skiffle and Reggae, there were many fine stars: Cliff, Nash, Donegan, Mungo Jerry. Only one, however, has earned the daunting title of SUPERSTAR – **Bob Marley** (1945-81). His sailor father (50) English and teenage mother Jamaican, Marley battled childhood on the tough 'island paradise' streets of Trench Town, Kingston. Four hundred years of British colonial rule produced some of time-on-hands anarchy. Somehow, the belltone tenor prowled the Trench Town streets respected, revered, and nonviolent. Street thugs knew Bob was a champion soccer player (son Rohan recently played roving football linebacker for University of Miami Hurricanes).

Marley's musical favorites? **Elvis, Jim Reeves, Fats Domino, Sam Cooke**, and **Drifters' Ben E. King**. King's 'smoky tenor' sound grew smokier as Marley's voice deepened into teenage Ganja, the marijuana part of his Rastafarian religion. Rastafarianism was thrown into desperate turmoil when worshipped Ethiopian emperor Haile Selassie died in 1975. By 1960, Marley garnered a band nucleus: **Bunny (Neville) Livingston** and **Peter (McIntosh) Tosh**; with Marley on guitar, the three vocalists spread-eagled the scale – Bunny falsetto/tenor and Tosh a volcanic baritone.

Marley's manifestos electrified the Kingston and Jamaican Top Ten. In the U.S. and Britain and Canada and Australia he championed Reggae buffs; back home his music RULED, like his first in 1963, "Simmer Down." After a downer factory-job trip to America's 2nd-smallest state, Delaware (staying with mom as 'Robert Nesta'), Marley returned home. He entered politics. Rock and Roll often fuels politics: the **MC5** and **John Lennon/Yoko Ono** changed marijuana laws in Ann Arbor, Michigan. The Mike Curb Cengregation's (#1, '72 "Candy Man") **Mike Curb** became Lieutenant Governor of California. Now Marley's actual religion decreed that smoking POT was part of a religious ritual – and that their right to smoke pot should not be tampered with by meddlesome legislators.

Sadly, after influencing diverse artists like Stevie Wonder and Eric Clapton and Paul Simon, Bob Marley passed at only 36, from a long illness. Universally mourned as a gentle yet powerful figure, Bob Marley headlined a whole new form of music. Don't confuse Bob's **Wailers** with:

"Tall Cool One" – Wailers, #36, 5-59 and #38, 4-64. John Greek's Tacoma Washington Wailers were one of a billion Ventures-style instrumental groups in 1960+ with pluck and savvy and good luck on the fickle Top 40 charts.

"Tomorrow People" – Ziggy Marley, #39, 5-88; NC, R & B. Marley's children rallied around the Reggae beat. Like Ska, Reggae never died. When Buddy Holly was killed, Rock and Roll endured. 'Ziggy' Marley is son David, backed by a whole Cowsill-Partridge/Wilson/Phillips/ Nelson extravaganza of ganja genetics and the kaleidoscopically complex Jamaican beat: sisters Sharon and Cedella, and brother Stephen too.

"Montego Bay" – Bobby Bloom, #8, 9-70; #3 U.K.; NC, R & B. Like Harlem's Harry Belafonte launching the Calypso craze, Big Apple Bobby Bloom bandwagoned the Reggae beat with this Jeff Barry tune from the Brill Building. Amid splashes of bongos, swooping white seagulls, flamingo-pink sunsets and shimmering sands, Bloom/ Barry battled the bummer NYC drizzle and rank skank slushy gray snow. They won this trip to Jamaica's northwest coast Eden (Kingston is SE Jamaica).

Sometimes, if you "wish on a star," your big dreams may come true: [#1, #5, #10, #12 in 1940 for Glenn Miller, Guy Lombardo, Cliff "Jiminy Cricket" Edwards, Horace Heidt. Best "When You Wish Upon a Star"? Sorry, I'm partial by a calendar accident (I was born 12-28-42) to **Dion and the Belmonts'** #30, 4-60 version. In a Latin style, Belmonts also do in 7-60 a majestically magnifique #38

"In the Still of the Night" (#3, 10-37 Tommy Dorsey Orchestra, Jack Leonard vocal).

"Raindrops" – Dee Clark, #2(1), 5-61; #3 R & B. "Montego Bay" had such a sweet island that I didn't have the urge to tell you Bloom was accidentally shot to death in 1974, a very young man. At least **Dee Clark** made it to a heart attack at 52 in 1990. With a rafters-high Irish tenor like **Clyde McPhatter** or **Sam Cooke**, Clark mixed into his drizzly ditty in the Key of 'A' some mellifluous Chalypso, wafting zaftig strings, and a very early twinge of Ska/ Reggae. During his riding fadeout, he hits the High 'C' of Lyric or Coloratura Soprano. Clark also tickled the SKA and REGGAE genres with his #20 "Hey Little Girl" (in this va-va-voom high-school sweater) of 8-59, and #18, 5-59 "Just Keep It Up."

"Mother and Child Reunion" – Paul Simon, #4, 2-75. Paul's Latin Manhattan beat is all Reggae. The band is authentic, with commanding polyrhythms and skirling guitar. Simon, perhaps, had not suffered the Trench Town deprivation of Marley or the agonies of Tosh and Bunny, either of whom's lives were just as tragic as Marley's. **Paul Simon** and **Bob Marley** both sing with Soul.

Simon's estranged-family song says he would not give (her) false (glowing) hopes. The old Mom and Dad and 2.7-smiley-kids world had ballooned away into a fallout shelter. Simon sings to his daughter. He's the steady parent, reassuring her that the missing mom will soon return. In the naïve malt shop 50s, teenage topics in tunes stretched to proms and smooches and love, love, love. But "Bye, Bye Love" cranked up the amps, and Daddy (or Mommy) was long gone, leaving a world of Quasi-Parent, Semi-Senior, Junior Assistant Step-Grandfathers and Portable Cousins. Like the political realism of Reggae in Kingston, Simon sings the drab downslide of good love gone bad.

Marley and **Simon**. Two super visionaries. (Marley Rock Hall '94, Simon & Garfunkel '90, Simon SOLO, 2001).

"Bicycle Race" – Queen, #24, 11-78. India has over one billion people, and nary a monster hit on our charts. They also speak English (and Hindu, Maharati, Urdu, Punjabi, and others). **Queen** is a sneaky way for me to pay tribute to music of India, which fits sideways into this Latino chapter. People from Bombay, Calcutta, and New Delhi, have major populations in central and South America, particularly Guiana, Trinidad, and Brazil. Anurag Purwar, Santanu Chaudhuri, and Srimvas Pendurti told me all about Queen's **Freddie Mercury**'s time in India, so I selected this bike-race salute to a favorite form of Indian transportation. Big Indi Pop artists are Alisha Chinoy, Suneeta Rao, Sukhwinder, Garry Lawer, and the late Naazai Hassan. Misha Chinoy's hit "Made in India" dominated the 90s. Other big billion-fan songs – often from their thriving MOVIE industry, include 60s "Aawara Hoon" by Mukesh from movie *Aawara*, and 80s hit "Aap Jaisa Koi," from *Qurbani* by Naazia Hassan. Sufi Pop from Pakistan is also popular, including the group Junoon, and

the later Nusvat Fateh Ali Khal. Indian Rappers include **Baba Sahgal**.

Now let's get away from the Jamaican/Indian/ New Orleans/Haitian French Connection. Remember, French too is a language derived from Latin, as is Italian, Portuguese, or Romanian (but not Indian Sanskrit/Hindi). Let's dart back to the more standard Spanish selections. You think Latin Rock? Spanish blooms.

"La Bamba" – Los Lobos, #1(3), 6-87. Most popular all-Spanish U.S. hit in two decades. In 1959 **Ritchie Valens**'s (Rock Hall 2001) #22 flip of #2 "Donna" sported a clicking wood block sound echoing *caliente* Spanish rhythms:

LIVIN' LA VIDA LOBO

Los Lobos' ('The Wolves') tremendous version accompanied actor Lou Diamond Phillips' portrayal of young Ritchie in one of R & R's greatest flicks: *La Bamba* (1987****). **Ritchie Valens** is the wellspring of the 2000+ Latino Explosion. Without Ritchie, we might not have **Ricky Martin, Gloria Estefan, Enrique Inglesias,** or **Marc Anthony**. **David Hidalgo** is the fine Valenzuelish 'Irish' tenor from East Los Angeles. Flanked by top-notch musicians Cesar Rosas, Conrad Lozano, Louie Perez, (and un-Chicano saxman Steve Berlin), Los Lobos' Ritchie follow-up scored too: "Come On, Let's Go" to #21, 9-87 (#42, 9-58 debut for Valens). This song drives the macho bravado. "Come On, Let's Go" he says, "AGAIN", may signify a simple second dance. Even Bubble Gum music is not quite innocent.

"La Bamba" – Crickets, NC, 1964. Jerry Allison and Sonny Curtis Anglicize it in English into a Surf Rock tune. In England and beyond, their post-Holly career featured two Top 20 tunes: **Carole King**'s U.K. #5 "Don't Ever Change," and Jerry's tremendous "My Little Girl," #134, 3-63; #17, 2-63 U.K.

"La Bamba" – Trini Lopez, #86, 6-66. Dallas's Trinidad Lopez sings Ritchie's Spanish folk song about a non-sailor, a captain: not a "*marinero, pero el capitan!*" Trini's (b. '37, Texas) go-go beat blasted out a cymbal-powered rhythm track of *muy rapido* pace and electric energy galore. **Buddy Holly** fronted the **Crickets** until 2-3-59, and married **Maria Elena Santiago**.

Lopez became 1st Latino Rock superstar after Valens, and perhaps 1st Folk Rock star with #3, 7-63 "If I Had a Hammer." The animated, ultra cool Texan also scored with #23, 11-63 "Kansas City," and #20, 1-65 "Lemon Tree."

Trini Lopez

"Black is Black" – Los Bravos, #4, 8-66. **Mike Kogel** from Germany took his three Spanish friends to Britain in search of El Dorado record gold. Once 'Mike & the Runaways,' (odd moniker from Del Shannon's '61 blockbuster), Los Bravos' Kogel's German tenor over-topped Antonio Martinez' guitar, Manuel Fernandez' haunting keyboards, Miguel Danus's power-bass, and Pablo Sanilehi's rockin' percussion. One yodel-kick screech, "EEEEEEYEOWWWWW," is one of the defining moments of Euro Rock and Roll.

"The Wah Watusi" – Orlons, #2(2), 6-62; #5 R & B. **Rosetta Hightower** sang lead, with her very appropriate name for tall Watusi tune. Cameo/Parkway was looking for a nice group of girls who could dance, to whisk them away from snoopy legal beagles snurfling around from smoldering Payola. The Orlons fit the bill: fun-loving great dancers. Tragedy lurked: (after prophetic #19, 9-63 "Cross Fire," in a ghastly case of life imitating art, Orlons' singer Shirley Brickley died of a gunshot wound (1977).

"Wah Watusi" inspired early Rap "El Watusi," #17 in 5-63 for Afro-Latino **Ray Barretto** (see Rap). **Sam the Sham** hit #82, 2-66 with **Billy Lee Riley**'s classic "Red Hot."

"Some Kinda Fun" – Chris Montez, #43, 12-62. Montez fans probably expected to see his *mucho grande* biggie here — #4, 8-62 "Let's Dance" (#15, 9-62 R & B). This follow-up is superior. Born Ezekiel Christopher Montez in 1943 L.A., CM was **Ritchie Valens'** more

easygoing echo. With a silvery shivering organ following his vocal, Chris smilingly saluted various popular dances. By 1966, he'd mellowed into a string of easy Latino hits: #22, 1-66 "Call Me," #16, 4-66 "The More I See You," and Frank Sinatra's (not Cyndi Lauper's) #17 hit in 1947, "Time After Time" (#36, 10-66).

"Come Dance with Me" – Eddie Quinteros, #101, 3-60. After 35 lost years, I dug this Quinteros gem out of a Bay Shore garage sale (25 *centavos*). REAL Ritchie Valens imitation? This is it. You can't get much closer to the HOT 100 than this tune [numbered #101 for a loopy switchback highway that ribbons its scenic way along the breathtaking Pacific coastline]. Eddie combined Valens and Holly magic into one sizzling Rock and Roll tune. Too bad the Mammoth Moguls of Hot Hit Hypeland never looked him up. Eddie Quinteros underscores what everyone knew all along; the wellspring of Great Latino Rock and Roll went down on that plane with Buddy Holly. **Ritchie Valens'** (Valenzuela's) music – via **Santana** or **Ricky Martin** – refuses to ever fade away.

Just a great kid with a great song. "La Bamba"/"Donna." Or maybe **Eddie Quinteros**, too. Three chords and a cloud of dust. At #101, Eddie was ALMOST FAMOUS. Aren't we all?

"Boogie on Reggae Woman" – Stevie Wonder, #3, 11-74; #1(2) R & B. Stevie glides through music genres with consummate ease and expertise. The complex beat strides right out of Jamaica. Stevie's jamming keyboards pioneer cutting-edge technology in Rhythm, Blues, Rock and Soul. Now Reggae, too. Wonder hit bronze on #3, 6-70 (#1[6] R & B) "Signed, Sealed, Delivered I'm Yours." "Signed" is vintage Soul, with incredible drums and bomp-ba-bomp bass that surge out of the Caribbean, like his #5, 8-80 "Master Blaster (Jammin')" [#1(7) R & B].

"The Star-Spangled Banner" – José Feliciano, #50, 11-68. **José Feliciano** and **Stevie Wonder** share with **Ray Charles** a sightless situation. Tremendous triumvirate. When José first sang this anthem, his heartfelt 16th-note vocal melismas tickled the fancy of the press. The Old Guard believed you had to sing the anthem totally straight. No fancy stuff. No quivering notes, no flashy guitar speed riffs (Feliciano is simply one of the World's Greatest Rock or Flamenco/Spanish Guitarists). José sang it for the Tigers/Cardinals World Series. The Detroit Tigers' star pitcher Denny McLain won 31 games that year – only 30+ winner in 70 years; Tigers won the Series, 4-3. Feliciano's biggest hit was a ginchy cover of the Doors' "Light My Fire" (#3, 7-68), followed by Tommy Tucker's Blues tune "Hi-Heel Sneakers" at #25, 10-68.

"Flamingo" – Duke Ellington, #11, 6-41. Glows with Spanish tinge. "Sir Duke" reigned over Jazz and Latino expertise in the 88s. Muted 2 a.m.-style Jazz master-piece. Nice instrumental. Reprised to #28, 9-66 by **Herb Alpert and the Tijuana Brass**.

"Patricia" – Perez Prado, #1(1), 6-58; #1(2), 7-58 R & B. Matanzas, Cuba's orchestra leader wasn't scared of compromising big bari sax with driving drums and pizzicato, to forge Rock and Roll sound to successful big band. Wrote the tune to Lou Bega's #3, '99 "Mambo #5." His driftier pastel opus, "Cherry Pink and Apple Blossom White," held down #1 for 10 weeks in 3-55.

"To All the Girls I've Loved Before" – Julio Iglesias & Willie Nelson, #5, 3-84. Enriqué Iglesias' father doubles with stardust Texas Outlaw Willie to sing true everlasting love (for hundreds of girls). Melodic. Catch rare **Kenny Ball**'s Dixieland English classic – "I Still Love You All," #18, 5-61 U.K. Check out Afro/Cuban/German **Lou Bega**'s "Mambo #5."

"Bimini Bay" hit #4, 1-22, and the Benson Orchestra forsook Hawaiian music for Spanish.

"Fernando" – ABBA, #13, 9-76; #1(2) Adult Contemporary. A flute crests the melody like Simon and Gar's "El Condor Pasa," or Peruvian/Ecuadoran minstrel stars **Sisal** (Al. *Viento* '99, which means 'WIND'). "Fernando" honors those who died to defeat fascism in the pre-WWII Spanish Civil War.

"El Condor Pasa" – Simon & Garfunkel, #18, 9-70. Breathtaking melody. Why? At 23,000 feet on Mt. Aconcagua in the High Andes, the rare condor has been known to pass by the "Pass of the Condor." Simon penned the lyrics to this 18th-century Peruvian tune.

"You Can Call Me Al" – Paul Simon, #23, 8-86. Impish groovy tune about deceit. Subterfuge sells. "Al" fractures composure. This lad's alias 'Al' is for his girlfriend 'Betty.' They go sneaking around on a chuckly crafty affair. Middle-aged sneaker 'Al' ponders deep cosmological questions to Latin/African beat from his giant renaissance album *Graceland* (#3, 9-86, platinum Grammy). Simon's "Al" anthem extracts the perfect metaphor for a fitness era of $199 washboard ABS machines, a stomach muscle not invented until 1986. He grumbles about a soft midriff, when his life is hard. As snappity pooches gnaw his ankle, he is being dogged by demons of consternation and chaos. Who isn't? 'Al' ducks back in alley with a "roly-poly" girl with a face like a bat.

'Al' descends into lower rings of his hellish destiny. He feels utterly alone. Estranged. Isolated. 'Al' suffers from existential despair, with a South African polyrhythmic Latino beat. Everybody's laughing at him. He finds himself in a neighborhood (maybe Spanish Harlem?) where he doesn't speak the language (unlike Simon, who is fluent in Spanish). He sees angels flitting about the high-rafter architecture. They spin infinitely. Unwilling to ignore any blessing from On High, he mumbles "Amen!" and "Hallelujah!" We chuckle in his plight. Even in the Age of Einstein, there are no atheists in foxholes. Pat and Meredith Glazer's favorite "The Obvious Child" (#92, 12-90) Simon-ized a cast of millions, and a frenzied Latin Beat. Meantime, "Al" thunders on, a caravan of clustery

drums thrumming the heartbeat of humanity. Paul's South African integrated group **JULUKA** played a complex polybeat style from Soweto, South Africa. They do a form of street music called "Township Jive" or MBAQUANGA. On "All Around the World," also NC, '86, Simon introduces to the big time **David Hidalgo** and **Los Lobos**, generating their name at the top of the cinematic list to power Lou Diamond Phillips' voice in *La Bamba* the following year – and combining Mexican/South African Rock and Roll music.

Paul's rich instrumentation lavishes many bizarre new exciting ideas, particularly for sax fans. Simon himself sparks a new six-string electric bass, doubling **Baghiti Khumalo**'s bass line Simon also adds a deep sax I've only seen once – a BASS SAX. All this stuff interconnects.

"Al" and "Betty" dance their Cheaters' Waltz among orange peels, egg creams, and garbage pails. We move on.

"Graceland" – Paul Simon & Everly Brothers, #81, 12-86. Tease of Spanish rhythm, this ode to the Elvis-epicenter Memphis home is a magnificent hybrid. Pedal steel Nigerian guitarist **Demola Adepoju** fires up "Graceland." Simon's *Graceland* concept album (Al. #3, 9-86) is the *Sgt. Pepper* of the 80s. The title song says a lot of things we perhaps don't want to hear about Elvis worship. His first line is a poetic masterpiece. He describes the magic sheen of the Mississippi Delta. It shone scintillatingly, resembling some National-style guitar. Poorboys and Pilgrims, he says, all make the trip – like some mystical collage of *Canterbury Tales* on Jack Kerouac's holyboy road back in 1399 a.d.

Back to earth. Our hero travels with his nine-year-old boy, child of Marriage #1. The singer has some reason to think that they will get 'received' at the semi-religious pilgrimage/shrine Graceland. The idea of being received at Graceland is paramount here. You visit Elvis's inner shrines: his tiger-skin den and pool table room. I was personally most struck by the swing set for baby Lisa Marie Presley. Somehow, I couldn't visualize Elvis, in blue-black leather jumpsuit, with blue-black coiffed pompadour, out in the backyard with a tragic schematic diagram, a hammer, and those three little words that have driven us daddies bonkers since the dawn of time: SOME ASSEMBLY REQUIRED. In my wildest dreams, I love to think of Elvis fighting with those dismal directions, as I did for Lauri and Jeremy's rinky-dink swing set. I can see Simon, too, with his 9-year-old in tow, chuckling over it. Or **Don** and **Phil Everly**. They sing background for Paul's tremendous trio.

Simon also did #86, 3-87 "The Boy in the Bubble." This poor kid, affected by every known germ in the universe, has to live his entire life in this claustrophobic germless bubble. Despite all the miracles of long-distance calling, cameras, and jungle lasers, Simon ponders the poor little lad's irrevocable medical horror show. He empathizes. Paul's 2000 Al. *You're the One* was nominated for a Grammy.

"Spanish Eyes" – Al Martino, #15, 12-65. Baritone Italian-American crooner **Al Martino** (Al Cini, 1927, Philly) grew up a few stoops away from #1 mid-century Opera tenor **Mario Lanza**. Martino's latter-day Crooner Era blockbuster was #1(3), 5-52's "Here in My Heart." "Spanish Eyes" concerns a ravishingly beautiful Mexican girl whose eyes are blue. Nice crescendo in the Orbison tradition, by one of the few crooners to hurdle the 1955 Rock and Roll monster. Hits: Melodious #3, 4-63 "I Love You Because" – #1 C for 1950s Leon Payne and cut by early Elvis; #9, 2-64 "I Love You More and More Every Day"; and the gorgeous tune #27, 5-67 "Mary in the Morning." **Vic Damone**, who married the girl **James Dean** loved, Pier Angeli, hit #4, 4-56 with "On the Street Where You Live" – similar Italian dramatic balladeer.

"Don't Let the Stars Get in Your Eyes" – Perry Como, #1(5), 12-52. Charismatic Perry (1912-2000) helped launch Rock and Roll with this offbeat big-beat frenzy item. With red, white and blue streamers and balloons and a booming oom-pah on the 1½, 2½, 3½, and 4½ beats, this "Stars" extravaganza swings from stars and planets and the heartbreaking summer lakeshore moon. The rhythm rolls. Como did a lot of Latin-beat songs, mostly in the "Italian Craze" (see Rosemary Clooney) of the early 50s; Nancy Kupersmith cites Perry's hit – "Papa Loves Mambo" [#4, 10-54]. When Perry Como serenaded with Caribbean flavor, you knew some big, brash, bold beat was hiding just around the corner.

"That's Amore" – Dean Martin, #2(5), 11-53. You know, when that moon smacks your eye just like this/ huge pizza pie . . . [Theme from *Moonstruck* (Cher, Olympia Dukakis, 1987****)]. Martin is another Italian mellow baritone to spearhead the Italian Era of Sub-Rock 1953. Born 6-7-17 as Dino Crocetti, Steubenville, Ohio. Half of Martin-Jerry Lewis comedy team. Martin the straight man. TV variety host in 60s. Loose collar, drink in had, ubiquitous cigarette. The Italian word AMORE (love) is a kissin' cousin to the Spanish word AMOR. Beyond heavenly pizza, Dino sings stars that make one drool like good 'ol pasta-fazool (*pasta fagioli* or pasta and beans). On a Neapolitan odyssey, Dean falls in love in the shadow of the ultra-blue isle of Capri and rumbling Mt. Vesuvius. His winsome waltz steals the hearts of lovers everywhere – Italians, and those who wish they were.

America's #1 food, PIZZA, sprinted past HAMBURGERS in a 1992 popularity poll (Italy usurps Germany). The first pizza oven in the U.S.A. (coal-fired, 1906) is at Lombardi's on Spring Street in NYC's Village.

I was culturally deprived as a kid. My Scottish father believed Italian food was canned Franco-American spaghetti. I never had pizza till I was 13. Really. Now, it is possible to fall in love if one – alas! – has no PIZZA, but it is very, VERY difficult. Without love and tomato sauce, life can get bleak and nasty real fast. Toby Kuta and Glenn O'Kray and Louis Baldori and I went to Angelo's new pizzeria on Michigan Avenue in Dearborn. I gazed at the first up-close pizza pie I'd ever seen, lurking on the next table. It looked all bloody and drooly and slimy and disgusting. I wanted to flee, and just bowl at the Maples Bowling Alley. When the pizza arrived, it quivered there on the plate. OD-ing on *Mad* magazines, I half-expected a tentacle to slither upwards from the Hallowe'en-orange blob of oscillating ex-flesh. How can I ever eat this monstrosity, I thought? Peer pressure pounded me, so I dove right in. After a bout with "Pizzamouth" ['scalded tongue'] I discovered something about pizza (pie) I will never, ever forget: Pizza is one of the most delicious delights in the universe. Whew.

Thanks, **Dean Martin**, for showing a Scottish-Canadian American kid the glories of first-line pizza. "That's Amore" did more to sell PIZZA, America's favorite food, in that first spectacular line, than all the Domino's/Little Caesar/Papa John's/Pizza Huts' ads put together. Indeed, via the Power of Popular Music, it may have created them. A great OOM-PAH waltz, too, from the guy Elvis idolized – DINO. Since the advent of Rock and Roll and Pizza, how many lovers have spoken semi-sacred vows on their dates? Listening to R & R and munching mushrooms and peppers and eternity. Isn't it ironic that Rock and Roll, Civil Rights, *Playboy* bunnies, TV, and pizza all arrived at the same time?

"Innamorata" – Jerry Vale, #30, 3-56. Born Genaro Vitaliano ('22, Bronx), the velvet-voiced Vale is a love-song legend among great Italian Crooners. Relax, every pizzeria in the universe will regale you with Jerry Vale's Greatest Hits. Biggest hit? #14, 7-56, "You Don't Know Me," redone soulfully by Ray Charles (32, 7-62).

"Even Now" – Nana Mouskouri, NC, 1979. Gorgeous song. Greek Nana Mouskouri is an international superstar who sings fluently and without accent in nine languages, including English and Spanish; Greek is neither a Latin-derived language like Spanish, nor a Teutonic-structured language like English. Greek stands alone. Among Greek rockers, and rock fans: **Tony Orlando**, **George Michael**, Mike Fountis, and Bill Metros.

Nana Mouskouri's majestic song orbits around producer Andre Chappelle's vision on *Only Love – The Very Best of Nana Mouskouri*, Al. #141, 10-91. A sweetly sculpted blend of slurring bass surrounds the root note – and the mesmerizing mezzo-soprano's astonishing voice. As she hits the phrase about December's chilly gray days, the song shags through glum snowbanks of loneliness and isolation. Like Walter Huston's "September Song" by Kurt Weill (#12, 1-39), "Even Now" spans the dark lyrical desolation of ebbing life and romantic afterglow. "Even Now" has a breathtaking melody. **Nana Mouskouri** has that one voice in a billion.

"Love Is in the Air" – John Paul Young, #7, 7-78. Born Glasgow, Scotland. Raised Australia. Unlikely candidate for Latino stardom. With Disco gusto, this '78 classic bubbles and jumps to a near-Reggae beat of supercharged Salsa power. Only hit. One wonders why. Young scored with #42, 12-75 "Yesterday's Hero."

Bob Marley

"Oye Como Va" – Santana, #13, 2-71. Axemaster **Carlos Santana** (b. 7-20-47, 12 Grammy nominations, 2000) spikes San Francisco Psychedelia with Autlan de Navarro, Mexican Salsa sounds. He traveled north to the Bay with his dad, who anchored a *mariachi* band. "Oye Como Va" ('see how it goes') was his most direct early link to Latino Rock (until #2[1], 2-2000 "Maria Maria" off #1 Al. *Supernatural*).

"Oye Como Va" – Tito Puente, NC, 1964. Santana mirrors the Native New Yorker magic of Tito, also known like Elvis as the King (*El Rey*) in his Manhattan mambo King milieu. Puente was among the most versatile of musicians (1923-2000) majoring in percussion: vibes, congas, bongos, sax, drums, keyboards, and his maestro machine the *timbalés*. Puente's WWII service got him a free trip to Juilliard. Uncharted Spanish-language hits abounded in L.A. *barrio* as well as Miami and New York City: "Abaniquito," "Pare Cochero," and "La Leyenda." Puente was a superstar in nearly all phases of big-beat Latino music: Mambo, Rhumba, Cha-Cha, Tango, and Meringue. Santana's "Oye Como Va" skips along with a lot of '**A minor.**' Riffs twist the top notes between the Spanish lyrics. In #1(6), 10-70 Psychedelic album *Abraxas*, Santana conceptually comes right off his last length epic, into the same key, of "Oye" and beyond.

"Black Magic Woman" – Santana, #4, 11-70. Santana's skilled bandmates are **Gregg Rolie**, keyboards, **Neil Schon** guitarist (later formed **Journey**). Carlos Santana's own gonzo guitar blossoms with bends and turns and single-string swoops and slides. Santana's solos transfix his audience with shimmering enchantment (*encantada*). His airy tenor floats over the meandering melody. Carlos also scored big on #9, 1-70 "Evil Ways" and #17, 4-81 "Winning." **David Brown** cushions the low rhythms on Jazz-riff bass; he circles the beat like **Ella Fitzgerald**, rather than pounce on it.

Santana weaves a magic spell with this winsome lass. Dormant off the top 20 for 17 years ["Hold On" – #15, 8-82], Santana splattered "Where Are They Now" pundits

with his super-monster *Supernatural*, Al. #1 in November 1999, featuring **Dave Matthews**, Everlast, and **Rob Thomas** of **Matchbox 20** – the "Smooth" combination single "Smooth" by Thomas and Santana hit #1(12), 7-99.

"Maria Maria" – Santana, #1(10), 2-2000. Biggest 'Spanglish' hit of all time. Buoyed by his overarching throbbing guitar, "Maria2" tells the woebegotten but hopeful story (*canto de esperanza*, song of hope) of this girl who grew up in Spanish Harlem (see **Ben E. King** and/ or **Aretha Franklin**). It's produced by **Wyclef Jean** ("911" #48, 10-2000, and Al. #9, 9-2000 *The Ecleftic: Two Sides II a Book* – no relation to **Erykah Badu**'s #6 "Bag Lady" 8-2000). Santana's splashes of high guitar fire curl around the story of 'Maria,' growing up in NYC North, and migrating to East L.A./Hollywood. Maria is half Spanish/ Latino (*chola*). The guy in the song ponders his own rootless restlessness (see Detroit riot "Black Day in July"). Demon streets get hotter and hotter (*mucho caliente*), and the song's singer gets a nasty eviction letter. He gazes up at the sky (*el cielo*) and dreams of paradise – and the song trails off on his musing about the hopeful Maria as his lover. Naturally, we never know the outcome – like a good Hemingway novel.

"Caribbean Queen (No More Love on the Run)" – Billy Ocean, #1(2), 8-84; #1(6), 6-84 R & B. Billy Ocean globetrotted from Trinidad in the Caribbean to London. He debuted with #22, 4-76 (#3 U.K.) "Love Really Hurts Without You." Isn't that unique title a wild new way of looking at an old bad-love situation? The British Soul star was steeped in the suave **Sam Cooke** sound. Billy Ocean moved to the U.S., and apprenticed this #1 giant Grammy hit. Ocean's Latino beat also throbs passionately in his third #1 song, with abrupt title: #1(2), 2-88 "Get Outta My Dreams, Get Into My Car."

"Those Were the Days" – Carroll O'Connor and Jean Stapleton, #43, 12-71. No Latin connection at all. We just had to include it somewhere, because what's an American pop music study without the Archie Bunker *All in the Family* theme song? Dublin, Ireland's Carroll O'Connor (1924-2000) was songwriter and piano player in his spare glory, and was a tremendous actor.

"Rhythm of the Night" – DeBarge, #3, 2-85; #1(1), R & B. Snowy Grand Rapids, Michigan makes no cars. It's largely Dutch, conservative, as cloudy as Great Britain. R & B singer **El DeBarge**, of the Glam Soul DeBarge family, sings of a wild trip under stars that are electric. Keyboard El and brother Mark (trumpet and/or sax) spur the DeBarge Charge via electric excitement in the **Michael Jackson** mode. Brother James was married abruptly to **Janet Jackson** ["Doesn't Really Matter, #1, 6-2000]. El shimmied back to the Top 6 with follow-up #6, 6-85 "Who's Holding Donna Now" and #3, 4-86 "Who's Johnny?"

Norwegian-Latino Connection? It's (zowie) time for Nelson and Nilsson [Norwegian for "Son of Nils"]:

"Coconut" – Nilsson, #8, 6-72. Un-Latino Norwegian-American **Harry Nilsson** (1941-94) often sang sad songs like the evermore #1(4), '71 "Without You." Here's a fun-stuff Calypso/Reggae number (see Shango and "Marianne"). Except for a bellyache of the lime and coconut variety, this Calypso Latino hit (by way of Hagar the Horrible's Oslo), is the cutting edge of Midnight Sun Latino Rock.

Ricky Nelson's #1, '61 "Travelin' Man" is a masterful Chalypso stunner about his sweet señorita down in Old scenic Mexico (plus the Alaskan Eskimo and a few dozen other bona fide true loves). Another flashback rerun is the Kingston Trio's #21, '62 perfect Chalypso Latino roundabout: "Where Have All the Flowers Gone?" Or catch the Carpenters' *pizzicato* Chalypso of Herman's Hermits' "There's a Kind of Hush" (#4, 2-67, HH; #12, 2-76, Carpenters).

"I Shot the Sheriff" – Eric Clapton, #1(1), 7-74; #33, 9-74 R & B. **Bob Marley** wrote it, and Honolulu's Yvonne Elliman sang back-up. This gunslinger Reggae anthem plumps the old self-defense plea. Clapton's savvy tenor and hot guitar produce a classic Reggae Rock rock track.

"Some Enchanted Evening" – Jay and the Americans, #13, 9-65. Bronze medalist **Jay Black** and his Operatic Rock waft this *South Pacific* classic. "Evening" predates the Rock Era, and adds a schmoozy tone of schmaltzy South Sea enchanted romance. In 1949, six versions graced the top ten. Perry Como's was #1, and among the best, like Bing Crosby's #3. The genuine article: **Ezio Pinza**'s #7, 9-49 version. Like Paul Robeson, Pinza (1957) was one of very precious few BASS Opera singers (New York Metropolitan Opera 1926-48). I was perhaps the only loyal groupie who watched his TV sitcom *Bonino*. **Jay Traynor**'s Americans' "Tonight" from *West Side Story* is also Latin Rock.

"Rico Suave" – Gerardo, #7, 2-91; NC, R & B. Rap. Like upcoming **Santana** and **Gloria Estefan**, Gerardo uses Spanglish (half- &-half Spanish & English); Gloria sings, he raps. Guayaquil, Equator, named for the Equator, was his home until age 12 when he became a *norteamericano* in L.A.

"Bad Boys" is by **Inner Circle** (#8, 5-93; #58 R & B). Theme song to shoot-'em'up TV docudrama *Cops*. Reggae flavor. **Calton Coffie** handles quintet vocals for Kingston, Jamaica, 90s group.

"Just Another Day" – Jon Secada, #5, 4-92. Jon was smuggled out of Fidel Castro's restrictive Cuba at age eight. The talented singer volleyed a lofty string of hits: #13, 9-92 "Do You Believe in Us," #18, 1-93 "Angel," #27, 6-93 "I'm Free." **Barry Manilow** hit #8, 8-68, with "Copacabana," a Cuban tribute with a hot salsa beat.

"Informer" – Snow, #1(7), 1-93; #10, 12-92 R & B. White Torontonian **Darrin O'Brien** (Snow) crushed the competition of Reggaemongers over the entire calendar with this blockbuster that hugged #1 for nearly two months. His follow-up wasn't too shabby, either, hitting #19, 5-93 for "Girl, I've Been Hurt."

"Conga" – Miami Sound Machine, #10, 12-85; #60 R & B. Born **Gloria Fajardo** (12-1-57) in Cuba, tiny tot Gloria fled to Miami and Floridian freedom in the wake of the Castro takeover. Her father had been bodyguard for former Cuban President Juan Batista. Her husband **Emilio Estefan** arrived in 1965. Like **Carlos Santana** and **Ritchie Valens** (Valenzuela) before him, Emilio was destined for stardom. In 1973, he worked days for Bacardi Rum, and by night he played accordion in local *restaurantes* for tips and smiles.

Then the standard Johnny B. Goode story unfolded. At a private party, Emilio had to scare up some musicians: he found Juan Marcos Avila, 15, bass; and Enrique 'Kiki' Garcia, 17, percussion. Soon their little band bumped into an unusual Miami combo fronted by (amazingly for Cubano combos) a FEMALE singer (a gorgeous one at that). Emilio took two steps forward:

He hired and married her. Oh, and, of course, he loved her too.

Actually, it wasn't all that whirlwindish, like Buddy Holly and Maria Elena Santiago. In 1978, business unfolded into love. CBS International initially recorded them only in Spanish. After bilingual albums and a circuitous route to Epic Records, they recorded one side English and one *en Español*. With their first success "Conga," here at home, they were frequently releasing tunes for three distinct markets, sort of: all-English, all-Spanish, and combo Spanglish, as they called it. Whatever they called it, it worked. It's a wonder so few market moguls had tried such a hybrid sound before.

Before we return to the Sound of Spanglish Rock, Let's get really far out. What's the 'farthest-out' place you've ever heard of? My brother-in-law Bob Cooter has been there; he confirms my suspicion – no place on the planet is insulated from Rock and Roll.

"The Ring of the Bell" – Hongk, NC, #1, Ulan Bator, Outer Mongolia, 2-90. OUTER MONGOLIA? It really exists. Hongk was the #1 1990 Rock and Roll group in icy Outer Mongolia, stuffed as a Russia/China buffer country way out in the Gobi Desert, by China's end-of-the-world Zhin-kiang Province.

Don't look now – but OUTER MONGOLIA NOW TREMBLES WITH THE THUNDERTONES OF AMERICAN ROCK AND ROLL. No place on the planet is Rockless (OK, well maybe one Antarctic glacier, when the -100° blizzard whups the ionosphere into a frothy frenzy). A 3-26-90 New York Times article by Nicholas Kristof puffs Hongk; it says "The Ring of the Bell" resounds with Simon-Gar's theme of disillusionment. They also reverberate with sidelong influences of **Pink Floyd, Elton John**, and **Deep Purple** (whose #4, 5-73 "Smoke on the Water" reflects some polluted ex-communist regimes, with smoke swirling their nuclear waters and with two-headed seven-eyed fish glaring eerily).

Mr. Kristof raves on about Rock and Roll on Attila the

Hun's Gobi Desert in the 1990s. Citing the Mongolian penchant for single names only (hmm, Elvis, Madonna, Prince, Selena, Joe, Shaggy), he writes Mr. Tsogsaikhan wears an orange tie and dark suit, and sports long hair. He reminds the *Times* scribe of a Young Democrat. The bandsmen studied journalism at Irkutsk University. This Soviet icebox features cold waves of actual -75° that are chillingly common.

Some might quip: WHO CARES about Rock and Roll in OUTER MONGOLIA? Maybe we all ought to. My sister Blair says Ulan Bator, Outer Mongolia, has three channels: one with Russian PBS-style "talking heads," and the OTHER TWO are *MTV*.

HONGK represents the triumph of democracy over communism in the world's most faraway outpost from the New York, London, and Los Angeles Rock and Roll epicenters: Democratic protests began in late December, Kristoff notes. HONGK's greatest hits were latched onto as rallying anthems. After the protests became major league, Outer Mongolia's Community Party threw out their whole Politburu – and agreed to finally hold FREE ELECTIONS.

Rock and Roll – SECRET WEAPON! The big beat took a long time to defeat stifling Stalinist propaganda in the well-sealed communist world. In Outer Mongolia, in 1990, the GUITAR/BALALAIKA CURTAIN CAME TUMBLING DOWN. Remember the Beatles' droll Beach Boy imitation in "Back in the U.S.S.R."? Sensuous balalaikas ring resonantly, and Georgian S.S.S.R. girls keep comrades cozy [Paul McCartney plays DRUMS on this salute].

As stern Cold Warriors glared at each other in grim gray gloom, the splash of Psychedelic vibra-color showed that Rock and Roll was a lot more fun than slaving away on the GROAN DRONE EXPRESS. In 2001, NYC was pleasantly invaded by Hongk's Arctic neighbors, SIBERIA's Red Elvises. [Suffolk College student Malachy Gately watched Hongk's neighbors, the **Red Elvis**, on February 10, 2001, in New York City. His T-shirt announced: "Kick-(Butt) Rock and Roll from Siberia." This Ukranian-Siberian SURF ROCK band also does sensational Rockabilly.]

While the Beatles played, the forces of surf's-up democracy were tilting and sparring and feinting and jabbing in the glum world arena. CocaCola, Rock and Roll, and Hollywood.

It took thirty-two years to bring out the gunnysack guitar Yankee Kid into the international tag team. The Old Champion had seen his name in lights for a new fourth decade. The Old Afro-Rockabilly Champion in R & R vs. Communism just smiled that sly St. Louie smile of 1958, back when he traded in his gunny-sack guitar for the big guys' axe . . .

JOHNNY B. GOODE – YOU WIN!!! Or, perhaps in the particularly American language of Bumperstickerism, this might get the message through, too:

> ## HONK IF YOU LOVE HONGK!!!

And now, for those music-hating terrorists holed up in Afghanistani Taliban caves, Rock and Roll will not be ignored. If Tyler Harris and the U.S. Marines don't get

there first . . . Rhythm is gonna get you . . .

"Rhythm is Gonna Get You" – Gloria Estefan and the Miami Sound Machine, #5, 6-87. By 1987, Gloria was no longer a one-shot hit maker: "Words Get in the Way", by this Miami Sound Machine, hit #5, 6-86. How often do we wreck the romantic mood by letting our silly mediocre words foresake us? "Rhythm" pulls out all the rhythmic stops. The echoes of **Tito Puente** and **Xavier Cugat** are heard in the passionate polyrhythms of the Miami mariachi marauders' musical groove. Gloria is also a peerless choreographer, and dances up a storm.

By 1987, Gloria Estefan had emerged as the first Hispanic-American female Rock and Roll star. Their marriage survived grabby groupies, creepo A & R crooks, and a tragic bus accident. To get to the gig, many entertainers do Lear Jets. Traveling is always risky business. Private cars are among the unsafest of all ways to go (Eddie Cochran, Johnny Horton), so Gloria took a big safe TOUR BUS. Metallica's bassist **Cliff Burton**, you recall, was killed in Sweden – thrown out of bus that landed on top of him off an icy highway.

On March 20, 1990, Gloria's bus crashed into a similar-sized vehicle. Gloria suffered a broken back, an injury which has taken the lives of many people. For a time, her life hung in the balance. There was a question of survival, not just getting back to singing, and dancing – her choreographic mainstay. Gloria Estefan is no quitter. After slow painful recuperation, she first returned to the mike, and finally the dance-fever limelight. The feisty Miami girl lunged back into dynamic choreographic routines.

With darting ebony eyes and an impish smile, the diminutive dynamo glows with the kind of charisma once reserved for media superstars of the early years: **Bob Hope, Bing Crosby, Jimmy Durante, Louie Armstrong**. Or **Judy Garland**. Her name is G-L-O-R-I-A. Salsa Rock legend.

"Rhythm" fries the dull status quo. It shows that the BIG BEAT itself can be a Temptress, a fickle lover you swoon for and she eludes you. Like many Latino dance songs, the lead singer calls out how to dance the dance. This goes back to Motown or even Cameo's Chubby Checker:

"Limbo Rock" – Chubby Checker, #2(2), 9-62; #3, 11-62 R & B. With a Welsh name (Ernest Evans) and an Afro-American Philly *Bandstand* background, Checker is an unlikely Salsa candidate. But did Chubby help spearhead the sound? The Limbo, every party animal knows by now, is a dance where people try to squiggle knees first under an ever-lowering bar. The skirts of 1962 made the Limbo an athletic contest for guys, a daring adventure for game girls (and leering rapscallions).

Chubby's checkered career included these Cameo/[Parkway] cameos: #1(3), 1-61 "Pony Time," #8 "Let's Twist Again" 6-61, 9-61's #7 "The Fly," #3 Slow Twistin'" of 3-62, 9-62's #10 "Popeye the Hitchhiker," the risqué Frat/Folk #12, 11-63 "Loddy Lo," the ever-mysterious #17, 12-63 "Hooka Tooka." After being bounced by the Beatles, Chubby returned with his amazing June 1988 #16 "The Twist (Yo Twist)" with the **Fat Boys**.

Gloria Estefan, of Miami Sound Machine

"Live for Loving You" – Gloria Estefan, #22, 10-91. The way the DJ's and VJ's play this shake-it-up supersong, you'd think it was #1 for 72 weeks in a row. Not so. A fine statement of faithful and physical love. Tremendous beat. You can dance to it. Hot guitars lash treble frets. A crackling bass commands the frenzied foundation. Gloria's "Anything for You" leaped to #1(2), 3-88, their biggest chart hit. Three platinum albums bizarrely just missed Top 5: 3-86 #21 *Primitive Love*, #6, 7-87 *Let it Loose*, and #8, 8-89 *Cuts Both Ways*. Other #1 singles? "Don't Wanna Lose You" 7-89, and #1(2), 1-91 "Coming Out of the Dark" (#60, 2-91 R & B). The last one is more than metaphorical. Her long-term healing process was buoyed by the fine background vocals of **Jon Secada** and **Betty Wright** (#6, 11-71, "The Clean-Up Woman" and #8, 3-78 "Dance with Me").

"Heaven's What I Feel" – Gloria Estefan, #27, 5-98. This big hit highlights Gloria's tireless feisty energy, spunky streetwise Salsa Soul, and her one-of-the-girls beauty that keeps her fans feeling she's their friend, not just a faraway superstar. She also scored with #8 "Bad Boy" (3-86 and #74, 4-86 R & B) and "Can't Stay Away from You" (#6, 1-88). Gloria glommed the bronze medal with a #3 "1-2-3" 3-88 tune unrelated to Len Barry (#2, 9-

65) of the Dovells' namesake hit: "1-2-3." Among her best are #27, 1-95 Robert Knight's "Everlasting Love," plus #42, 4-96 "Reach," and big #2(1) N'Sync combo hit 9-99 "Music of My Heart."

An Estefan tune always erupts with rocking rhythm. You'll hear rumba and conga and tango and mambo and mango tones. Her Caribbean combo sound explodes into the flamingo Florida night. And all points north. Nice girl finishes first. A Rock and Roll career is no sprint. It's a marathon. With strong family ties, they will rock (and salsa) on and on. Whoosh.

Los Canciones de mi Padre – **Linda Ronstadt, Al. #42, 12-87.** After capturing the Mainstream HOT 100 and the Country and Adult Contemporary charts, Linda shifted gears back to her Mexican heritage with this Spanish-only album. Nice mellow sounds, Title means 'Songs of My Father.'

"Willie and the Hand Jive" – **Johnny Otis Show, #9, 6-58.** Multicultural Macarena of the 50s. Born John Veliotes, the Greek-American R & R grandstander amassed the top era R & B acts. Voted into the Rock Hall in 1994, Otis's big hit is this Bo Diddley-beat bombshell. "Willie's Hand Jive" is also a hands and arms dance like the "Macarena."

'Willie' of hand-jive fame is a contemporary cousin of 'Johnny B. Goode.' He, too, gets famous, and his name in lights. Not by guitar. Willie flashes this speedo Hand Jive hand-dance, electrifies the world, and hits Johnny B. Goode's big Name-in-Lights phase. He hand-jives on TV to zillions of rapt fans, but Berry beat Otis to this starbound-kid concept by two months.

"Macarena" – **Los Del Rio, #1(14), 9-95 and #23, 7-96.** [1995 as "Bayside Boys mix"; 1996 as "nonstop"] As the MACARENA craze screeched into overkill, its international popularity exploded into Oldies Never-Never Land like Bobby McFerrin's 1988 #1 disappearing act "Don't Worry – Be Happy."

The "Macarena" is the "Hand Jive" of 1996-97. With 60 weeks on the *Billboard* charts, some say its it the "Bunny Hop" of NOW (Ray Anthony, #13, 11-52). Or the "Hokey Pokey." Whatever it is, it's a lot of fun to try. Rock and Roll is a participation sport. After a while, you get tired of spectating.

The Macarena should be around for awhile (like #52, 12-96 "Macarena Christmas"), despite its temporary demise, due to Program Directors and Rock Jocks who smashed it in a fit of pique, after just hearing for the 1,234,567th time. And Rambha taught it to a bunch of folks (John and Alan Warde's kids) at Aunt Jo Warde's wedding celebration for cousin Anne.

For the record, the "Macarena", with 14 weeks at #1, is tied for 2nd-ever in the Rock Era behind #1(16) "One Sweet Day" (Mariah Carey and Boyz II Men) and two other 14-weekers: Boyz's '94 "I'll Make Love to You" and Whitney Houston's Dolly Parton-penned "I Will Always Love You." The "Macarena," however, was not only a prelude to the Latino Invasion, but it may also have been the Most Popular Rock and Roll Record of all time, at #1 siege. Or is it Salsa and Roll? IT is far and away the #1 foreign-language item ever. And it was Rambha's Rose Maria's favorite song, for a week anyhow. Bravo, Macarena.

Latino music has ALWAYS been a major force in American popular music. It's both one of the direct rhythmic ancestors of Rock and Roll and one of its SPIN-OFFS. After all, when all those Big Band silent drummers were either out on coffee break (or temporarily croaked, because NO BEAT could be found), **Xavier Cugat** and **Tito Puente** were out there tattooing hot Mambos and Rumbas and Cha-Cha-Chas and Meringues and Beguines and Boleros. South of the Border, the *salsa caliente* throb never stopped pulsing passionately at the *Cinco de Maio Fiesta* and beyond (see Rosemary Clooney's "Mambo Italiano").

The new Latino Explosion stormed the ramparts of the HOT 100. *Billboard*'s HOT 100 on November 21, 1999: **Santana**'s "Smooth" #1; and #3 Latino **Marc Anthony**'s "I Need to Know." "Be With You" was #9, with Marc Anthony's "You Sang to Me" at lucky thirteen. In October 2000, **Christina Aguilera**'s "Come on Over Baby (All I Want is You) hit #1 in its 11th HOT 100 week; **Ricky Martin**'s risqué "She Bangs" was #28 in only its 2nd week.

So, as the new century glimmered on the *bello horizonte*, the Latino presence was felt on charts recently dominated by singles-oriented rappers. **Puff Daddy**'s friend **Jennifer Lopez**'s "Love Don't Cost a Thing" hit #12, (from 11-2000); Lopez's "i'm Gonna Be Alright" with **Nas** hit #1, 2002. **Ricky Martin**/Christina Aguliera's "Nobody Wants to be Lonely" was #13, on 2-24-01, just FIVE weeks into its chart run. "The Macarena" and Gloria Estefan represent the beginning of the beginning in the Nifty Nineties, as 2000+ should produce about 2000+ more Latino stars on the *Ciento Caliente* [HOT 100].

The Latin people have always known one thing – music is hardly music, without a BEAT! Or, as lovely Gloria Estefan put it so well – 'Rhythm Is Gonna Get You.' Macarena on.

Johnny Mathis, *who began the Beguine in our Latino Rock chapter. Johnny is the #4 album artist of all time.*

Tommy (trombone) and *Jimmy (sax)* *Dorsey -- Jimmy's Latin-flavored "Amapola" was #1 for ten weeks in the WWII era.*

Chubby Checker -- *King of the Twist and the Latino-beat Limbo.*

JOCK ROCK -
Sports Rock Meets the
Gold Rush '90s Waltz Kings

Rock and Roll spurs cellar-dweller teams to win pennants and glory. An old saying claims every pro athlete would like to be a rock star – and that every rock star really wants to be a pro athlete. Either way, you hopefully end up with girls galore. Hopefully. We've done Sport Rock already. Most "Sports Rock" tunes we already covered on other musical-motif turf. **Huey Lewis**'s Al. #1, '83 *Sports* we covered. We saluted Heartland Rockers' sports: **Bob Seger**'s (runnin') "Against the Wind," **Bruce Springsteen**'s ex-fastball pitcher's "Glory Days," cheerleader **Toni Basil**'s "Mickey," and gridiron gonzo star 'Jack' of **John Cougar Mellencamp**'s Midwest "Jack and Diane." Plus Britrock **Queen**'s Glam "We Will Rock You"/"We Are the Champions." Or Glam Disco's Village People's "YMCA."

Sometimes, when coach cuts you from the team you really wanted to make, you pick up a loose guitar. Maybe your school has 5,000 students, and you got lost in the semi-jock shuffle.

Heavy metal music has long rated high on the MACHO-METER. So has real genuine Blues and Heartland Hard Rock. Recently, Rap music has shouldered the Macho burden. Some say Rap sanctions ugly violence on the football field as you get smeared by a six-pack of surly defensive linemen who sprinkle nails on their raw Sharkflesh Flakes breakfast:

"The Stars and Stripes Forever" – Sousa's Band, #1(8), 7-1897, and #1(3), 2-1901. A CENTURY OF (sort of) ROCK AND ROLL. Sousa's Band had the most macho sound around. Most famous march of all time! BIG BEAT, anyhow, on the 2/4 rhythm. (With a TUBA for a gridiron BASS). Military marches rally troops. Can you just see Teddy Roosevelt and His Rough Riders rampaging over San Juan Hill in the Spanish-American War (with their Walkman head sets?). If you don't have a war, and too often we do, sports can sublimate and channel your bone-crunching, teeth-gnashing macho spirit.

All the way through the glory and exhaustion of the World's Greatest Pedestrian Tour – the 26.2 mile New York City Marathon – I heard the next song blasting out in international neighborhoods, and over the feelin'-groovy 59th Street Bridge into Midtown and *Seinfeld* country:

"Gonna Fly Now" – Bill Conti, #1(1), 4-77. Gala THEME FROM *ROCKY* spearheaded aerobics from treadmills to step dance to five-borough 26.2-mile marathons. Sylvester Stallone's four-star 1976-77 *Rocky* showed a lot of us we loved to rock, run, and roll. *Rocky* triumphantly jogged the streets of Philadelphia, questing after a Heavyweight title. As he ran up the steps of the museum in the ruddy gray dawn half-light, it spurred a million of us sofa spuds to hit the Nike marathon roads.

Beach Boy **Brian Wilson** (b. 6-20-42) had it all. Football captain at Hawthorne High and part-time track star, he and his athletic brother **Dennis** (1944-83) surfed the glory net.

Beach Boys: (left to right), Bruce Johnstone, Dennis Wilson, Mike Love, Brian Wilson, Al Jardine, and Carl Wilson

"Be True to Your School" – Beach Boys, #6, 11-63; #27, R & B. On the cusp of Beatlemania and the American Surf Rock tidal wave, the Beach Boys of Summer rocket-launched this Rah-Rah loyalty song. It's a Big 10 fight song, too (weird selection for Pac-10 guys).

The Beach Boys' "Be True to Your School" is as rousing and inspiring and patriotic as **George M. Cohan**'s WWI anthem "Over There", at #1 in 1917 for the American Quartet, and in 1918 for Enrico Caruso. Military music rouses us, as the War Rock chapter showed. Football, no wimp sport, is still a lot safer than war. "Be True" pumps up pom-pom pomp. Brother Carl surfs his **Chuck Berry** lead guitar flourish. Brian tells everybody to be true to your school, like you might be true to your girlfriend. Moot point. For the recording session, Brian brings in cheerleaders **Marilyn and the Honeys** – he would soon marry Marilyn.

Brian cruises other schools' neighborhoods. Wear your varsity jacket, he advises. He mentions his letterman sweater, and his letters in football and track. He's proud to wear it, and gets his identity from his quarterback career, as well as his Surf Rock band.

"On Wisconsin" – Prince's Orchestra, #5, 8-1915. Celeste player **Charles Adams Prince** was related to 2nd President John Adams and son John Quincy Adams. He was the **Mitch Miller** of the OUGHTS and TEENs (1900-29), directing the Columbia Records Orchestra (biggest record company of all – EVER). "On Wisconsin" fires up a mashing big beat, and fires the Hail Mary bomb to the end zone when the forward pass was first invented. How's this for hype and hyperbole? They vow to carry the pigskin all around Chicago (tough touchdown). Other great college fight songs of old? Any Rock and Roll?

"Notre Dame Medley" – Guy Lombardo and His Royal Canadians, #28, 11-40. This one drags down all the thunder out from rainy skies in the booming lyric. When you get to loyal marching songs, swooping ever onward to the victory, you're hooked. **Michigan State**'s "Spartan Fight Song" caused us to drive 6000 miles to watch our team lose the Rose Bowl (UCLA 14 – MSU 12), but the rousing music was fantastic. The **University of Michigan**'s "The Victors" touts my other alma mater. Same saga every year! My Big Ten team pushes close to a national title with the same game plan – three yards and a cloud of dust. They play some #33 PAC-10 outfit (or the University of Southeastern Yukon) and lose 25-24, because some surfy galoot lobs another Hail Mary pass snagged in the last second by some schlump with super-glue velcro fingers in the Michigan end zone.

"Take Me Out to the Ball Game" – Harvey Hindermyer, #3, 11-1908. And radio "Gold Dust Twin" **Harvey** didn't even get the BIG HIT here. It was the **Haydn Quartet**. Tenor **Billy Murray** (singing lead for Haydn Quartet) was the ELVIS of the entire pre-1920 recording industry. With 116 charted singles, he's 8th in the whole 1890-1954 zone and hit #1(7), 10-1908 with this immortal diamond classic. But, how about those peanuts and Crackerjacks? **Albert Von Tilzer** wrote this 3/4 waltz as an ad, somewhat, for a new popcorn bonanza with caramel – CRACKERJACK. What's even worse, Sports Fans, is that Albert never went to a major league baseball game until 25 years after this song hit the top of the charts. Almost every fan in America knows this song. During the moss-cov-

ered 7th-inning stretch, we all burble along with the fun lyric [though after the 2001 WTC tragedy it was often replaced with "God Bless America"]. Baseball, like Rock and Roll, is an escape from the humdrum workaday world.

Billy Murray (1877-54) and **Harvey Hindermyer** (1882-57), however, have pretty well been lost by obscurity. The Rock Hall of Fame doesn't go back far enough to immortalize these lost waltz kings. This is a start. Generation X had no monopoly on the meaninglessness of some sweatshop jobs. Remember, "Take Me Out to the Ball Game" fast-pitches the ULTIMATE ESCAPE. He says he doesn't CARE whether he ever comves back. Nihilism Express.

"Na Na Hey Hey Kiss Him Goodbye" – Steam, #1(2), 10-69; #20, 11-69 R & B. JOCK ROCK sing-along melody bids funny farewell to relieved relief pitchers, shuffling to grumpy showers after a grand-slam "gopher ball." Sledgehammer beat. Macho Big Apple chorus fades in and out to crescendo. Unforgettable words: "Na, na, na, na, na, na," torrid taunt. One of Jock Rock's best-loved refrains, unless you're the scowling ex-relief pitcher.

"Mr. Touchdown, U.S.A." – Hugo Winterhalter, #9, 10-50. How can I ever forget the sterling line-smashing gridiron gallop of my hero "Mr. Touchdown, US.A."? I was seven years old, and my dad had just brought home our first-ever TV set (Sears Silvertone, 10") so he could watch football. Like every other bright-eyed bushy-tailed lad who worshipped Bobby Layne and Doak Walker's world-champ Detroit Lions in the 50s, I wanted to grow up to BE Mr. Touchdown. Hero extraordinaire. Alas, I found my goal never materialized due to a cruel fate. I suffered from a slight lack of size (165#), strength, speed, and talent, so I became an Elvis-haired bench jockey. With a clean uniform, I could wave at the girls better anyhow, and didn't get crunched as much.

The **Baha Men**'s #40+ "Who Let the Dogs Out" 7-2000 is a thunder of canine consternation. They woof their way into decibel levels to blow out the sound of the **Who** at Wembley, amps cranked to eleven. "Dogs" is a hilarious Jock Rock standard, like **Los Del Rio**'s #1(14), 7-96 "Macarena" (with myriad fans smacking elbows and shoulder and rumps in gung-ho gusto). Vangelis's #1(1), 12-81 "Chariots of Fire" theme floats like a willowy marathoner (Grete Waitz?), but sparked British sprinters in the long-ago Olympics.

"Daisy Bell" (a/k/a "A Bicycle Built for Two") – Dan Quinn, #1(9), 9-1893. In the 1890s, "Century Clubs" of strapping Irish lads like **Dan Quinn** mounted their one-speeds on Sunday and hit the dirt roads for Patchogue, 50 miles from Brooklyn, returning after the exhausting hundred-mile day. Mile-a-Minute Murphy, behind a special Long Island Railroad train, and wooden planks on the rails, tucked and drafted, and cranked his one-speed bike up to sixty miles an hour. Wow.

"Daisy Bell" is about a Sunday romp between lovers in Central Park on a newly invented bike built for two. Love and sports and a waltz. What more did a guy need? WALTZ: A SONG IN 3/4 TIME. Very few rock and roll songs use 3/4 time (see "Piano Man"). We womp the 4/4 beat with a drum-abuse smack on the big two and four beats. We rarely kick into the 2/4 march time either. Rock and Roll is nearly a monopoly of 4/4 time.

In the 1890s and 'Nineteen-Oughts', the WALTZ was the name of the game. It rallied the SPORTS to bike, to box, or to Boogie. Ragtime piano players ran a swing bass, playing octaves with their left hands on the ONE beat, and hitting the TWO-THREE on the triad chord.

"The Sidewalks of New York" – Dan Quinn, #1(9), 2-1895. All around the big town, tiny-tot scramblers played "ring-a-rosy," or London Bridge as it was falling down. Sweet on a 23-skidoo gal named Mamie O'Rourke, Quinn raves about hotcha hot-time 1890s Broadway night life. The oompah Waltz hammered the tuba's bottom notes, Dan and Mamie "Trip that fantastic light, upon the sidewalks of New York" (echoed in Procul Harum's #5, 6-67 surrealistic fandango in "A Whiter Shade of Pale").

"The Band Played On" – Dan Quinn, #1(1), 8-95. Looking for big 90s superstars? No one of the 20th century (except maybe Santana, 2000) has ever had a follow-up of a #1(9) song eclipse that song and hit the Big Ten weeks at #1! Guy Lombardo waltzed this classic to #1 in 1941. The "Band Played On" just tells about Casey and his 1895 strawberry-blonde girlfriend. Some folks got terribly loaded and almost "exploded." Drinking in the 1890s was over twice per capita it is today. Fortunately, the horse was often smart enough to waddle home, bestrewn with the queasy rider.

"Slide, Kelly, Slide" – George J. Gaskin, #1(3), 1-1892. Among our most ancient Sports "Rock" selections, we have the "Silver-Voiced Irish Tenor's" song about 1880s greatest base thief, baseball star **Michael 'King' Kelly.** Gaskin also sang "After the Ball" (#1[10], 4-1893). This weepy waltz waddles through the heartbreak of Prince Charmings sneaking off with Suzy Floozies, and a few other romantic disasters. Remember Gaskin's "Sweet Rosie O' Grady" (#1[8], 4-1897)? Or #1(10), 11-1897 "On the Banks of the Wabash"? Nope? How about [of course] his #1(3), 5-1899 "My Wild Irish Rose"? Though all George J. Gaskin's Irish classics are gone, you'll find them all in old *Sing-Along with Mitch* albums – or on a Kelly-green sheet of lyrics down at the parish on St. Patrick's Day.

"In the Good Old Summertime" – John W. Myers, #1(7), 10-1902. Waltz. Our most popular baritone Waltz King sparked a bygone era of Sunday picnic baseball games, strolls down shady lanes, and extinct terms of endearment like "TOOTSIE-WOOTSIE." Electric guitar pioneer **Les Paul** and wife Mary Ford took a swingin'er "Good Old Summertime" to #15, 6-52. Since we did "The Rock and Roll Waltz," Sonny & Cher's I Got You, Babe," and Jack Scott's #3 "My True Love," it behooves us to find other 1890s-tempo waltzes in the Rock Era. Scott followed with #28, 9-58 "With Your Love," plunging to the baritone Rockabilly vocal basement.

"Kiss from a Rose" – Seal, #1(1), 6-95; #52, 9-95 R & B. Even fewer waltzes crack the #1 barriers. One wonders at the paltry R & B chart number from the Afro-English singer. **Sealhenry Samuel** (b. '63, London) is Nigerian and Brazilian, and sings a melodic triumph in an era cussed for strident cacophony. Seal debuted with #7, 6-91 "Crazy."

Billy Joel's "Piano Man" is also a waltz, dueling octaves with the tension of the California bar scene.

The Waltz form is pretty much a lost art, however. So let's return to Jock Rock baseball in 4/4 time.

"Brown-Eyed Handsome Man" – Buddy Holly, #113, 10-63; #10, '63 Australia; #3, 3-63 U.K. OK, OK, so what's a BASEBALL SONG doing smashing the Top 10 in the U.K. and Down Under? And why #113 in U.S.A.? Differential distribution. Bad hype. In Britain, Buddy WAS Elvis (Elvis never toured there, or Australia, as Buddy did). CRICKET is also a game there – the forerunner of BASEBALL.

"Brown-Eyed Handsome Man" is the only spectacular collaboration between two of Rock's biggest 50s legends, singer **Buddy** and songwriter **Chuck Berry.** Chuck thought so much of this ditty about the Venus de Milo, 30-mile desert hikes, and dashing around third base for homeplate (on this high fly), that he recorded it in 1956. Then he cut it again unsuccessfully (7-29-61). Not only is this the only Holly-Berry collaboration ever, but it's a dynamite Hard Rock track for Holly. Sports link? Holly (and **Johnny Cash**) were favorites on my high school and college (Wayne State U.) football teams.

Check the Holly numbers here: (c/o John Goldrosen, *Remembering Buddy*, and Nigel Smith, Prez Australian Buddy Holly Appreciation Society):

Song	Peak Position U.S.A.	U.K.	Australia
"That'll Be the Day"	#1(1), 8-57	#3	#2
"Peggy Sue"	#3, 11-57	#6	#2
"Oh Boy"	#10, 12-57	#3	#2
"Listen to Me"	—	#16, 3-58	—
"I'm Gonna Love You Too"	—	—	#38, 3-58
"Maybe Baby"	#17, 3-58	#4	—
"Think It Over"	#27, 7-58	#11	—
"Early in the Morning"	#32, 7-58	#17	—
"It Doesn't Matter Anymore"	#13, 3-59	#1(3)	#1(8)
"It's So Easy"	—	—	#8, 1-59
"Peggy Sue Got Married"	—	#14, 9-59	#7 (off EP)
"Baby I Don't Care"	—	#13, 7-61	—
"Reminiscing"	—	#17, 10-62	—
"Well All Right"	—	—	Charted, 3-59
"Brown-Eyed Handsome Man"	#113, 10-63	#3, 3-63	#10
"Bo Diddley"	#116, 4-63	#4, 6-63	#5, '63
"Wait Till the Sun Shines, Nellie"	—	—	#26, '62
"Wishing"	—	#10, 9-63	—
"Love is Strange"	#105, 4-69	—	—

In the U.S., Holly also charted with #58, 8-58 "Fool's Paradise," #82, 12-58 "Heartbeat," and #88, 3-59 "Rainin' in My Heart." It's simple to see how hit patterns flow, isn't it?

"Centerfield" – John Fogerty, #44, 5-85. Al. *Centerfield* #1(1), 2-85. 'Born again," we celebrate new green grass on the old ball field. And once again, Chuck/Buddy/Paul McCartney's "Brown-Eyed Handsome Man" rounds 3rd and heads home. PASSION – that's what this Fogerty summertime anthem is all about. Passion for baseball. Passion for sport. Passion for competition.

For **Creedence Clearwater**'s John Fogerty, it's a renaissance of hope. A renaissance of a superstar's career. Fogerty rip-roars into his 'Centerfield' position with handclapping, most basic of all rhythms. Handclapping maybe started Rock and Soul thousands of years ago in the fields of Africa (Craig Boyd). Or in a sultry rainforest. "Centerfield" blooms with the magical aura of playing centerfield in the blossoming *Field of Dreams***** spring sunlight. To an American sports fan, it is almost a call to worship on high. To every baseball fan, St. Patrick's Day brings new green dreams and diamond visions.

Fogerty is a genius of seeming simplicity. With gusto, he combines the torrid handclapping, zowie lead and rhythm guitar riffs, and home run thunder beat of his crunching drums and prowling bass. His clapping pattern?

GUNG-HO GUSTO CLAPPING IN "CENTERFIELD"

Fogerty's burning tenor vocal rides the stomping drumbeat like a bucking bronco. He'll 'Bang on the Drums all Day' (see Jock Rock song by Todd Rundgren). Spring sunshine just arrived. "Centerfield" is President **George W. Bush**'s favorite song. He played college baseball at Yale, and made $17 million owning the Texas Rangers baseball team.

Baseball springs eternal. It's as American as apple pie. Whenever the snow slinks back to its arctic icebox, baseball erupts. Ordinary life is suspended on magic spring afternoons at Wrigley Field and Fenway Park – the REAL shrines of the Summer Pastime. In the Dark Ages of the 1995 baseball strike, the greedy battled the stupid into a stranglehold on America'$ game. Betrayed, jilted, and dumbfounded, lifetime fans deserted the wonderful game of their kidhoods. By 1996, the owners brought us the Bugs Bunny Ball, juicing it up a notch as they did after the Dead Ball Era of **Ty Cobb** – to make Babe Ruth into the slugger who revolutionized the game. Now Ruth's memory and stats are ripped off. Assistant utility second-benchwarmers now routinely hit 25 home runs (instead of the old 6 or 7) for $10 million/year of our ex-money.

Willie Mays could hit 100 home runs today (not a bad feat for a guy 70+ years old). We won't comment upon steroids.

Fogerty's song-guy is a grinny kid who begs Coach to put him in the game. Fogerty runs through a whole litany of all-time baseball legends: Shoeless "Say It Ain't So, Joe" Joe Jackson; 'Say Hey' Willie (Mays); the mighty Case ("Casey at the Bat" by E.L. Thayer and #2, 1893, for Russell Hunting); Joe DiMaggio (Where Has He Gone, Paul Simon?); and the greatest batter of them all (.367 or 367 hits/1000 at-bats), Ty Cobb. "Centerfield" is a baseball Boogie for the ages. Fogerty's summertime-dream album zoomed to #1 in that eager month of baseball hopes and dreams – February 1985 – when pitchers and catchers report to their hopeful homes in the palm-tree breezy Florida hamlets of the Grapefruit League.

***John Fogerty** (2nd from left) with **Creedence Clearwater Revival**, 1971. Left to right: **Stu Cook, John Fogerty, Doug Clifford**, and **Tom Fogerty**.*

After "Take Me Out to the Ball Game," "Centerfield" is the #1 ballpark song of all time. It's a little kid's song. We're all still kids. It's a fun song for the Littlest Leaguer in his/her Field of Dreams. "Centerfield" serenades the frumpy-cap kid in a blousy uniform sitting on the pine bench, dreaming of the game-winning grand slam on the sweet summertime emerald diamonds of lost America. Song of innocence. Butterflies and Charlie Brown and popcorn. Hope springs eternal on the green grass of Yankee-land. Or Sox-land. It celebrates Fogerty's golden moment of super sunshine – blasting the ball deep into the far stands. Baseball is the last game to vanquish the clock. Nor is it squashed by a computer. It's one of the last grassy bastions of Old America. "Centerfield" is guiltless and guileless. It hypes only a boyish love for the Grand Old Game.

Gene Pitney is the first Rock and Roll star to create a Do-It-Yourself hit record – and play all the instruments, while singing all vocals and backgrounds. In 1978, **Prince**

followed his lead. **Fogerty** here plays at least the lion's share of instruments. He is the band and the producer. Fogerty, quintessential Rock and Roll singer, sings the epic baseball song. How could he not pay homage to two of the biggest reasons for Rock and Roll – **Chuck Berry** and **Buddy Holly**? "Brown-Eyed Handsome Man" was Chuck's intended follow-up to "Maybellene." Chuck's re-recorded 1961 version, still uncharted, featured piano wizard **Johnnie Johnson**, Blues Brothers' pal **Matt 'Guitar' Murphy**, legendary **Willie Dixon** on bass, and unheralded Eddie Hardy on drums.

Holly never dragged out the Philharmonic for "Brown-Eyed Handsome Man." He cut the demo in Norm Petty's Clovis Studios c. Christmas 1956 – with **Jerry Allison** homering hammering drums, and second bass-man **Larry Welborn** blitzing bass runs. According to Holly's outstanding biographer **John Goldrosen**, an unknown guitarist ghosts the session (Aha! A Berry/Holly duo. Nah, that's ridiculous!). Anyhow, Buddy had a rendezvous with destiny. In the aftermath, Buddy's tapes were sweetened by producer Norman Petty, who worked with Jimmy Gilmer's Fireballs (#1, '63 "Sugar Shack" and #15, 12-63 "Daisy Petal Pickin'). Buddy's baseball song was released in the 1963 Buddy Holly Renaissance and big in the Commonwealth at #3, 3-63. In November 1999, **Paul McCartney** re-plucked "Brown-Eyed Handsome Man" for this *Run Devil Run* bonanza R & R album – and gave the venerable Berry tune a Cajun flavor.

When new grass grows on the field of hope and the *Field of Dreams* (1991****), Buddy Holly lives again. In one gargantuan home run swing, John Fogerty pays respectful homage to both the founding fathers of baseball and the proud papas of Rock and Roll.

"Centerfield" is a screaming line drive monster mashed to deep center. Spring rises, green and clear. The hammered horsehide is going, going, gone. Jock Rock rules!

Basketball was first hyped on a grand scale via the Harlem Globetrotters. Who can forget their theme song, almost lost in antiquity?

"Sweet Georgia Brown" – Ben Bernie, #1(5), 6-25. The original 'Yowsah, Yowsah' guy, vaudevillian Benjamin Anselwitz reminds us of the early Jewish and Afro-American connection to early pro basketball, as entrepreneurs and players. Or take the authentic early African-American rendition by **Ethel Waters** (#9, 9-25). Original Blues star Waters serves up a slaphappy slam-dunk. Nifty tune.

"Run for the Roses" – Dan Fogelberg, #18, 4-82. Kingdom for a horse? The Kentucky Derby blasts off the nation's biggest spectator sport – horse racing. Dan Fogelberg concocts a silvery ode to a glorious stallion (or mare). If you shook out all the player piano keys of Von Tilzer's Tin Pan Alley, and dragged handlebar-mustachioed Irish tenors out of the bygone calendar, you'd be hard pressed to unearth a sweeter melody than this Peoria kid's nifty tune about a horse. This sports classic joins the greats.

Fogelberg paid his dues. He drifted to L.A. and folk-sang. He played sessions in Nashville. He amassed an aviary of helpful birds (**Eagles**) to spring him up to hitdom: Joe Walsh on debut #31, 2-75 "Part of the Plan," and harmony-vocalizer **Don Henley** on #24, 10-78 "The Power of Gold."

Dan Fogelberg

Fogelberg's Heartland pure Irish tenor sparkles the squishy underside of the puffy clouds. He hails from Johnny B. Goode country. He studied painting at University of Illinois, but his crystal voice got in his way. He sessionized for **Roger McGuinn (Byrds)**, and **Jackson Browne**. From his first name ('Danny Boy') to his last, he's 100% American melting pot; you can't deduce whether 'Fogelberg' is Swedish, Jewish, Norwegian, German, or Dutch, though you've fairly safely wiped out Mongolian, Kenyan, or Cherokee. Who cares? Greatness is multicultural and all-inclusive. His ethnic background doesn't matter. That's the point. He is an American vocal treasure.

Why do we love "Run for the Roses"? Let us count the ways. OK, it's about his horse. Fast one … the horse is running in the Derby, the crowning glory of a thoroughbred's career. After a mere three years of flailing, hot-maned and thunder-hooved, around dinkier race tracks, a champion horse like Seattle Slew (1974-2002) gets his shot at the Big Show. It's the Major Leagues. Perhaps you are a lover of horses. Or cowboys. I, too, am a lover of races. In 1982, I was training 70 miles a week for the Boston Marathon. Thanks to Dan's #18 song spearheading my mental sound track in the race, I was able to shatter the qualifying barrier and succeed.

Songs are like that. It's not what they are – it's what you think of them. AND WHAT THEY CAN HELP MAKE YOU! Even if your blundering pal says your favorite song reminds him of a vacuum cleaner, you've got to consider him temporarily delirious. What really counts in music appreciation is your opinion alone. If you love CAR racing, try the Beach Boys/Jan & Dean's Drag Race Rock, like J & D's #3 "The Little Old Lady from Pasadena."

Take this WALTZ, please. I was saving it for the Sports Waltzes chapter [Odd combo? . . . Nope.] "Run for the Roses" is a frantic equestrian caper in the lilac-wafting bluegrass sunshine of Old Kentucky. A waltz? This 3/4 time gallop is an ungainly gait, isn't it? Only the 65-70 mph cheetah, or the 60 mph pronghorn antelope, may seem more speedily graceful than the champion stride of a Derby racehorse. With horses spinning away into dazzling space in the 40-45 mph sprint range, it's sobering to note that we fleetfoot humans have still not yet broken the 30 mph barrier.

In May 1935, Jesse Owens broke FIVE world track records in one day (Yost Field, University of Michigan). How? In 1928, Owens' track coach, feisty Irishman Charles Riley, told him to stop galumphing. His form was bonkers. He was a blur of flailing arms and piston-pumping legs. "Stop clumping like a penguin," Riley put it. "Stop flipping out your arms and legs all over the place. Watch the race horses," Coach Riley said. Their motion is smooth, silky, and speedy. No wasted motion. The quiet Owens lad 'listened up' to his surrogate father, 'Pop' Riley.

Five records in one day? Nope, not exactly. HE BROKE THEM IN 45 MINUTES! First, he tied the 100-yard dash at 9.4 seconds. Then he wiped out the 220, the 220 hurdles, the 200-meter by proxy, and he set a new record in the long jump – 26 feet, 8½ inches.

In 1936, Owens took his fast feet to the Berlin Olympics. Adolf Hitler, who refused to 'shake the hand of a Negro,' was made to look the utter fool (that he was) for espousing hits 'Aryan Physical Supremacy' doctrine – that 'blond-haired blue-eyed athletes were superior.' [Rock and Soul music has proven that NO one is superior, nor inferior, to anyone else; we can all rock!]

I love this song because I identify with all three: Jesse Owens, Dan Fogelberg, and even (this is, aarrgh, weird for a Boston marathoner), the racehorse in the Kentucky Derby. Moreover, I also love the song for its celestial Everly or Simon and Garfunkel melody. Musically, "Run for the Roses" tiptoes on its III chord mediants. Like "Sea of Love" (Phil Phillips, Del Shannon, Honeydrippers), the second chord rises to the III, but Fogelberg chooses the more muted minor. Fogelberg swoops down to the chromatic bVII chord **Eb**, if in Key of 'F') before resolving to his tonic **F**. Fogelberg is a maestro melodist. On his #9, 12-81 masterpiece "Leader of the Band," Debbie Haibon's wedding song, he acknowledges his debt to one of the first sports rockers of all time – **John Philip Sousa**, one of few band legends to offer an eponymous tuba-type instrument – the Sousaphone. If that isn't old enough, he goes back to the Hogmenay Greatest Hits Collection of Robert Burns in the late 18th century in #2, 12-80 "Same Auld Lang Syne."

Fogelberg distills the best from the best and creates the best. His name – Fogel Berg (or Vogel Berg) translates to 'Bird of the Mountain.' Apropos. You expect to hear this golden-toned angelic stuff when you attain the summit of your tiresome climb.

May you win the gold. If not, the bronze is pretty nice too. In the interest of keeping this book under seven quadrillion pages, our Sports Rock chapter must grab the trophy and hotfoot it down the road. Other JOCK ROCK anthems? For hockey's penalty box: **John Cougar Mellencamp**'s "The Authority Song" #15, 3-84, or the **Bobby Fuller IV**'s "I Fought the Law" #9, 1-66. For a new opposing-team's relief pitcher: the **Troggs**' "Wild Thing" #1(3), 6-66. For any hopeful victory? **Queen**'s eternal "We Are the Champions" [#4, 10-77] backed with the tumultuous "We Will Rock You." For mad scrambling dirt-bike, roller derby, or skateboard jockeys, **AC-DC**'s #35 "You Shook Me All Night Long" or #47, 10-79 "Highway to Hell." For track meets and cross country or road races or baseball: **Bruce Springsteen**'s amazing #5, 6-85 "Glory Days" or #23, 9-75 "Born to Run"; or **Bob Seger**'s #28 "Old Time Rock and Roll." Or for general gung-ho gusto gutsy sports fandom? **Joan Jett**'s "I Love Rock and Roll" #1(7), 2-82; **Toni Basil**'s "Mickey" #1(1), 9-82; **Buddy Holly**'s #38, 5-58 "Rave On"; **Jerry Lee Lewis**'s #2(4), 11-57 "Great Balls of Fire"; the **Routers**' "Peggy Sue"-rhythm instrumental #19, 11-62 "Let's Go"; or the **Cars**' vocal "Let's Go" reprise to #14, 8-79; the **Isley Brothers**' unquenchable #47, 9-59 "Shout"; **The Baha Men**'s #21, 2000 "Who Let the Dogs Out?"; **Chuck Berry**/the **Beach Boys** tune-combo "Sweet Little Sixteen"/ "Surfin' U.S.A." [#2(3), 2-58 and #3, 3-63], and the **Beatles**' ever-blastable 1-2-3-4-countdown rocker: #1, 2-64 "I Saw her Standing There." ROCK? Jock Rock ROCKS!

Casey
*(without **K.C.'s Sunshine Band**)*
at the Bat

Punk, Rockabilly, and New Wave Rebels in the Old Surf

Every new generation of rockers is a New Wave, and all Rock and Roll has ALWAYS been 'DANCE' music. Each generation has to shake up the one before with something a little more outrageous, a little bolder, a little wilder. Rock's ultimate focal point or nexus? Probably Louis Armstrong's New Orleans. The Motown Sound? Nexus at 2648 West Grand Boulevard in Detroit (by *Creem* magazine at 3729 Cass Avenue). The Rockabilly nexus was the Sun Recording Studio at 706 Union Avenue in Memphis, just a few miles from the center of Rock and Roll itself by 1957 – 3764 Elvis Presley Boulevard, Graceland. Could one Big Apple nexus produce both the American epicenter of NEW WAVE music and Punk Rock? The center of both is CBGB's at 315 Bowery in the East Village, Manhattan. This tough Bowery neighborhood has seen Rock and Roll flourish and wane. The apartment of **George** and **Ira Gershwin** hovers astride the old Fillmore East, **Bill Graham**'s East Coast mecca of Psychedelic wizardry languishing in bygone glory. In its hot-blooded heyday, the venerated venue hosted **Jimi Hendrix, Jeff Beck, the Dead, Led Zep, John & Yoko,** and the **Allman Brothers**. By 1980 or so, Punk rolled to New Wave. CBGB's heralded Bowery bar launched underground record legends, for stars unwilling to grub for the drag of commerciality.

Dave Walker (*American Rock and Roll Tour* R & R gonzo geographer) raves on about "long, dark, narrow, loud" CBGB's:

"Dump of dumps, CBGB-OMFUG was the mid-70s hatchery of the American punk (and later, new wave) movements. In previous lives it had been a wino bar . . . Owner Holly Kristal installed rock 'n roll in 1974 and then began booking such acts as the Ramones, Blondie, Television, Patti Smith, Talking Heads, the Dead Boys, Wayne County."

"Heart of Glass" – Blondie, #1(1), 2-79. Debbie Harry (b. '45, Miami) named her crew after the comic strips' most gorgeous, perfect housewife. The cartoon Blondie looks very good for her age [90+ – a debutante when strip began in 1930]. Harry found guitar guys **Chris Stein** and Frank Infante, bassman Nigel Harrison, keyguy Jimmy Destri, and drum-thumper Clem Burke. They blasted a throbbing staccato bass line with a drum driving triplets. 'Blondie' suffuses her sparkling street-savvy with a kick-butt stompin' beat. On a flying trapeze of Bluesy velvet, her ruffly voice purrs cute clichés. Her tangerine tambourine basks. Harry shares the Super Enunciation Gene with **Frank Sinatra**. Blondie's among few to hit #1 on first record. Blondie's quixotic chart numbers flash FOUR #1's, nothing at #2-10, and a wild collage of #24-39's: follow-up #24 "One Way or Another" 6-79; #39, 5-80 "Atomic"; and last hit #37, 3-82 "Island of Lost Souls." Let's crunch those big bopper #1's:

"The Tide Is High" – Blondie, #1(1), 11-80. In sputter bass profusion and ginchy guitars, Debbie's high-tide song is the essence, the flowering, of three big Rock and Roll genres: SKA, PUNK, and NEW WAVE. And for a six-pack of Soul, we'll throw into the INTRO to ALTERNATIVE. Bubbling along in a Key of 'B' mood at 99 Ska-copated beats a minute, Blondie's swirling "Tide" Follows the Rock-Steady Rydim of **Johnny Nash** or **Jimmy Cliff**. The "Tide" title mirrors red-gold Nassau sunrises over the Kingston Trio's "Sloop John B." The Trio's **Nick Reynolds** said (9-29-96), that people need simple and memorable tunes: "THEY CAN"T WHISTLE A SONG FROM METALLICA." "The Tide is High" represents Nick's adage; you can easily whistle Blondie's pleasant rolling romantic ramble about patience. All the other girls crave this hunk, but she's waiting patiently. She yearns and burns to become his #1 squeeze. She keeps the passion embers smoldering until the high tide brings her to a rendezvous.

How, does "Tide" mirror Ska, Punk, and New Wave trends? A syncopated Ska beat. Out of the Punk-Rock CBGB milieu, Debbie's roots lie with the Punks' credo of SHATTER CORPORATE ROCK! When music gets too chummy and comfy with Wall Street, Punk sets out to blast the status quo. Rebels rouse snoozers. As Punk shuffled off out of its embryonic oeuvre into 1978, Punk buffs darted into new directions.

Fashion has always been crucial to music. Take Elvis, perhaps the first Punk Rocker. In a grey-suited Mr. Average era, **Elvis** socked sartorial splendor into his act: turned-up collars on vibra-glow pink/silver/black sports shirts; *Seinfeld*'s Kramer's wardrobe of eclectic bombastic and bamboozling bombazine; blue fur shoes; and a princely pompadour tabbed by scimitar sideburns. Yes, fashion. **Debbie Harry** sideswiped Punk into New Wave pointed boots, thrift-shop chic, big spiky hair, and black lipstick. New Wave was not just music; it was a way of life.

What Punk Revolution? As you listen to Harry's Holly hiccups, or spiffy yodel-kick, you wonder what traditions might spawn Blondie's unique sound. Rumor says 1977 was the Punk Year, and many follow sheepishly. Punk is an ongoing phenomenon. Its HEYDAY was 1977, but it covers half a century. Punk's infancy? It's much more than fast-Thrash slash of supersonic drums.

"Trouble" – Elvis Presley, NC, 1957. You want surly? Burly? Ticked off? This album cut (Al. #2[1], 9-58 *King Creole*) throbs with combative fire. Elvis's black-leather growling snarl meshes with Scotty Moore's marauding rebel bazooka-fire guitar. **James Dean** might be the first punk rocker, if he sang. Elvis also crunched **Carl Perkins**' #2(4), '56 classic on El's 3rd HOT 100 hit – "Blue Suede Shoes" (#20, 4-56, Presley cover version). Tossing tough tacets, Elvis challenges the world not to cross the line of his precious blue suede shoes (some unwary oaf's Waterloo).

Is the first *MTV* shtick really Elvis's Punk-style "Jailhouse Rock" #1(7), 10-57? Maybe. Or check out **Jack Scott and the Chantones**' #11, '58 Punk prototype "Leroy" (tossed back in slammer again).

"Break Up" – Jerry Lee Lewis, #52, 9-58. Though mangled by the media for marrying his 13-year-old second cousin Myra (his bass player's kid), Jerry DEFINES Punk in this musical manifesto. In mid-snarl, Jerry assaults his smoking piano, gallops glissandos on the raging keys, and rampages over this **Charlie Rich** rocker. Without the press hatchet job on his career, this roaring R & R spitfire song would have gone top ten as a given. In his anti-establishment gusto and fiery Rock and Roll dedication, and the speed of today's Punk drummers on the piano keys, Rockabilly **Jerry Lee Lewis** (and **Gene Vincent**) are THE 50s Punk archetypes. "The Killer" always seemed just a bit dangerous – a main Punk Rock requirement. Jerry Lee Lewis was Mt. Vesuvius about to erupt on the quivering quietude. Prowling Proto-Punk Power, Jerry broke-up with superstardom.

"Race with the Devil" – Gene Vincent & His Blue Caps, #96, 10-56. Madcap combo of PUNK ROCK, DRAG RACE ROCK, and DEATH METAL. Lead guitar whiz-bang **Cliff Gallup** gallops the scorched frets. With waterfall pompadour, spasmodic contortions from a motorcycle acci-

dent, and garbed in a full black leather outfit, Gene preened his Mt. Vesuvius tenor to the heights of quivering, quavering desperation in blockbuster "Be-Bop-A-Lula" (#7, 6-56). "Devil" bounces shimmering vocal with redline fever on the lost ghost highway to James Dean/Robert Johnson's haunted Crossroads.

Vibrant boogieing chorus. In 1998, **Gene Vincent** (1935-71) finally made the Hall of Fame. In #26, 10-99 album *Run Devil Run*, **Paul McCartney** recorded Gene's CU (Coming Up Strong) 10-56 "Bluejean Bop." In Vincent's race, he's crankin' 99 miles an hour – but the Devil hits 101. We all wrestle our own demons, don't we? Cliff Gallup won '99 *Guitar Player* mag Lifetime Achievement Award.

Is Gene Vincent the first Punk Rocker? His name was legendary throughout battling beer bars of Britain. He survived a 70mph taxi crash that killed **Eddie Cochran**, and an awful motorcycle crash. In the Morrison-Hendrix-Joplin fadeaway, brooding Virginian Vincent, mourning the loss of his marriage, allegedly O.D.-ed on liquid courage. The fickle Rock press had already forgotten him, but his music and style will endure. Another Proto-Punk possibility is the legendary **Johnny Cash**. Check out his #88, 10-57 (#3 C) "Home of the Blues" or #17, 9-56 "I Walk the Line" (#1C). Or catch **Ritchie Valens**' #42, 9-58 Proto-Punk powered "Come On, Let's Go."

"The Way I Walk" – Jack Scott, #35, 6-59. Unlike the King, Scott wrote his songs. Italian-Canadian factory worker from Detroit, Scott/Scafone recorded this baddest of the bad Early Punk theme song: (redone in 1977 by Punk icon **Robert Gordon**). Washington, D.C.'s Gordon fronted Punk Scene. His album *Too Fast to Live, Too Young to Die* is a James Dean epitaph: Gordon hit us with Sun's **Billy Lee Riley**'s "Red Hot" (#83, 10-77). **Link Wray**, guitar.

"Rumble" – Link Wray and His Ray Men, #16, 4-58. Part Native American, Punk and Heavy Metal pioneer Link Wray and his throbbing *tremolo-vibrato* instrumental caused eight billion of us girl-watching guys to go out, buy a guitar, and plug it into a hefty hotbox of NEW vibrato sensation. A 12-Bar Blues, "Rumble" cranks along on the edgy minor, with a lightning high-fret tightrope act by Wray (1994 *Pulp Fiction* soundtrack).

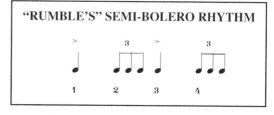

"RUMBLE'S" SEMI-BOLERO RHYTHM

Key Proto-Punk outfits? The **Shadows of Knight**, Britain's **Them**, **? and the Mysterians**', ("96 Tears"); and the **Who** cranking amps to blue stars. The **Who** were revered by even the angry Punk Rockers who hated all other members of the Rock Establishment. "You don't sing about love to people on the dole," mused **Sex Pistols'** (Al. #106, 12-77 *[Here's the Sex Pistols]*) Punk guru **Johnny Rotten**. Reggae sprouted into an Eden battered by hurricanes and unemployment. Rotten hated the musical complexity of bands like Emerson, Lake, and Palmer. Rotten attacked personal poverty with a smoking axe.

Eric Clapton (on Al. #1[3], 9-92 *Unplugged*) does **Bessie Smith**'s gut-wrenching song (#15, 8-29), "Nobody Knows You When You're Down and Out." The song stars a dollar with a grinning eagle, a friendless fellow once rich and now busted, and a wry Lost Generation X or Jazz Age Punk attitude.

British Punk Rock staggered out of the blocks in 1977, on the cusp of the Rockabilly Revival. Forlorn **Gene Vincent** struck a chord among 1977 British Punk Rockers and Rockabilly Revivalists. Forget frilly flügelhorns, slick sweet strings, or pretty angelic voices caroling lovey dovey ditties. They preferred **Joey Ramone**'s (1952-2001) Surf Rock basic Punk, like #81, 7-77 "Sheena Is a Punk Rocker."

Dirt-poor emerging punks were shackled to the dole in an old smoky urban core of despair (see the **Commitments**, with Andrew Strong on strong Soul vocal of #67, 10-91 Otis classic "Try A Little Tenderness"). Punk Rock doused the Disco and demanded Real Rock and Roll. Punk thrives upon REBELLION. Just as gray-suit execs wear their *Preppy Handbook* kelly-green pants on the GOLF COURSE, so Punk Rockers sport green hair, or purple hair, or lip rings and tattoos of dastardly dragons. Ex-journalist, teacher, and gonzo guitarist **Mark Knopfler** points out a whole subculture.

"Sultans of Swing" – Dire Straits, #4, 2-79; #8 U.K. Featured on Charlie Gillett's *Honky Tonk* radio show, the group thrived: Mark (b. '49); brother David, rhythm guitar; John Illsley, bass, and Pick Withers, drums. The 'Sultans of Swing,' mythical band in their tune, play the "down-South" London venue. The Sultans, like Punks, revere 'Creole' and Delta Roots of Rock. Creole could imply Kingston, Jamaica. It could be Elvis or Delta Blues from New Orleans. Dire Straits blasts moneygrubbers in "Money for Nothing" #1(3), 7-85. No teenybopper terror tune, it's just a bunch of young self-assured guys at a dance. Uplifted by Rock and Roll (and Disco-Era platform soles), they knock trumpet bands and Faux Rock. On the fadeout, Knopfler launches one of everybody's favorite guitar arpeggios into the foggy London night.

Much of the Punk movement missed this chartbusting stage in America. The 1977 U.K. scene was totally dominated by the **Sex Pistols**, with **Johnny Rotten** (John Lydon, b. '56, a month before Elvis's "Heartbreak Hotel"). Bassman **Sid Vi-**

cious (b. Jack Ritchie) grabbed a lot of media attention for killing himself (1957-79) with a heroin overdose. Pistols also featured bassist Glen Matlock, guitarist Steve Jones, and Paul Cook on drums. Survivors' 1996 comeback is legendary.

First – the Rockabilly Revival.

"My Girl Josephine" – Jerry Jaye, #29, 4-67. The 50s scarcely died ('50s – 1955-64) before Jaye (Gerald Hatley, Manila, Arkansas) started reviving them. Original hit #14, 10-60 (#7 R & B) for **Antoine 'Fats' Domino**. Pleasant jumpy tune. Flicker flashes again. Rambling rhythm carousel wheezes puffily along, bouncing a friendly 12-Bar Blues romantic romp. **Jerry Jaye** captures the skooshy sound of Domino's big beat. His tenor vocal blooms with Fats's friendly smiley style. Jaye needs only 66 more chart hits to top the Domino dynamo.

"I'm in Love Again" – Antoine 'Fats' Domino, #3, 4-56; #1(9) R & B. Punchy beat and horn section, and nifty New Orleans Afro-French accent. Fats showed us Rock and Roll could be funny and fun, too. Dude frets gal's mangy mutt poochily chomping his tender calf – and he's cowed by shaggy critter. "It's You I Love" #5, 5-67 is a cute item, too. Fats sold 25+ million with 66 charted hits. Unlike Chuck Berry, Fats is not classic Rockabilly. He is a New Orleans Soul giant. Fats covered the Beatles' "Lady Madonna" (#100, 9-68).

Trombonist/singer **Clarence 'Frogman' Henry** is Fats's main echo man. Besides his tenor/frog-bass/falsetto "Ain't Got No Home" (#20, 12-56; #3 R & B), the Algiers, Louisiana soulster (b. '37) also scored a huge success with "But I Do" [a/k/a "I Don't Know Why," #4, 2-61 (#9, 3-61 R & B)], and #12, 5-61 "You Always Hurt the One You Love."

"I Hear You Knocking" – Dave Edmunds, #4, 12-70. Wheezy sound rivals Mitch Ryder's New Year's favor in #6, 2-67 "Sock It To Me Baby." A 1955 #2 R & B hit for **Smiley Lewis**. Edmunds ended up with Rockpile (#51, 11-80, "Teacher2"). **David Essex** hit #5 with "Rock On" (11-73). Essex splices distant past into *American Graffiti* generation, inadvertently launching Punk. "Rock On" revives memories of Jimmy Dean, silver screen. Edmunds' bleeds a litany of Rock's cherished pioneers into his lyric and spoken bridge.

"Rock This Town" – Stray Cats, #9, 9-82. The Punk aftermath in Britain gave three Long Islanders a blaring success: **Slim Jim Phantom, Brian Setzer** (b. '60), and **Lee Rocker**. Rocker (Lee Drucher) twirled the old Bill Black string bass. Phantom's (b. Jim McDonell) drum set was thrifty: one solitary snare, and a cymbal you could hide under a pancake. With bleached blonde hair, and thin tattooed arms, Setzer suggested Bowzer of popular 70s Rock Revival Show *Sha-Na-Na* ("Top Forty", #84, 8-71). Led by bass-baritone **John 'Bowzer' Baumann** of Queens, Sha Na Na began in 1969 skipping classes together at Columbia University. Their Retro Rock TV show of 50s quips, skits, and hi-jinx jiggled Disco dudes into full-race nostalgia. **Sha-Na-Na** covered Reflections' #6, '69 "Romeo & Juliet" to #55, 4-75. Shadowing their sound were **Flash Cadillac** and "Did You Boogie (With Your Baby)" #29, 8-76 with **Wolfman Jack** mumbling.

The Stray Cats' battle cry "Rock This Town" throbs with adolescent juices. In the old Teddy Boy or Rocker spirit of Elton John's #12, 8-73 "Saturday Night's All Right for Fighting," "Rock This Town" blasts out scrappy macho challenge: some oaf gazes at him briefly. If he stares at him one more time, a free-for-all is gonna bust out on the startled dance floor. Short fuse. In Britain, where that fighting was slated, no recreational Saturday Nite Special handguns adorn pubs. Before Cats, Setzer played for Punk Rock 'Bloodless Pharaohs,' and did New Wave with **Blondie**'s own producer, Jimmy Destri. IT ALL CON-NECTS. The Stray Cats opened for the **Rolling Stones**, then hit the stardom freeway. "Rock This Town" pulsates with Rockabilly technology: Elvis, Gene Vincent, Carl Perkins and Sam Phillips' madcap marshmallow 50s props – real-gone echo chambers, slaphappy stand-up bass, and speed-of-light lead guitar. Via #3, 12-82 "Stray Cat Strut," Cats ruled the midnight airwaves.

"(She's) Sexy + 17" – Stray Cats, #5, 8-83. Slim Jim Phantom married **Britt Eklund.** This anti-school song echoes **Todd Rundgren**'s #63, 5-83 "Bang the Drum All Day." Our hero hatches a cabal of student inmates for a school 'jailbreak.' When he busts into the chorus, his Gene Vincent tenor nicks a power shift yodel-kick. He ponders the willowy curves of shapely 'Tina Marie.' He and Johnny and Eddie duck out of class, to mythic 25¢ beer empo-rium. Hoodwinking older generation? Who did Brian Setzer play in *La Bamba* (1987****)?

"C'mon Everybody" – Eddie Cochran, #35, 11-58. From make-out rocker #18, 3-57 "Sittin' in the Balcony" to swan song #8, 8-58 "Summertime Blues," Eddie pioneered Punk Rock and needled the establishment. He paved the way for **Tool**, the Jam, and **Green Day**. Oklahoma (later Minnesota) Hard Rocker Cochran does a wool-over-parents'-eyes party song. He thinks trashing the homestead will result in a week's grounding. Cockeyed optimist? Baritone Rockabilly Cochran is among our most dynamic Rockabilly rock stars, and Punk saint of sorts (Rock Hall'87).

After #35, 10-83 "I Won't Stand in Your Way," and finale #68, 1-84 "Look at That Cadillac," with **Dave Edmunds** spinning dials, the Stray Cats disbanded. [*Live Nude Guitars* indeed – Al. #140, 5-88]. By 1994, Setzer cashed in on another NEW nostalgia fad, the even-older BIG BAND revival: **The Brian Setzer Orchestra**, Al. #158, 4-94 – and Swing Jazz or Jump Music. In a career starkly the same length as Buddy Holly's (9-57 to 1-59), the **Stray Cats**' 9-82 to 1-84 reign halted. For a little over a year, though, you could say Meow Music Ruled!

Malcolm McLaren owned the sex boutique in London, where recent rises in the unemployment rate staggered the British economy (120% rise in three years to 1977). McLaren orbiters Paul Cook, Wally Nightingale, and Steve Jones's band was the Swankers; store clerk Glen Matlock joined the group. The Sex Pistols arrived with #106, 1977 *Here Come the Sex Pistols* 1977 album. Gung-ho fans loved the **Sex Pistols**. Now what kind of juvenile delin-quent would name themselves something like 'Sex Pistols'? Surfing with the Sextones: [In 1959, at church camp, we formed a little vocal quartet: Ross, 14, (Irish tenor), me, 16, (tenor), Larry G., 15, (bari-tone), Karl Perrin, 15, (bass). With two guitars among us, that made six. 'Sextones' (for 'sextet,' meaning six, or 4 singers plus 2 guitars). In no way will I be judgmental about the selection of the Sex Pistols' controversial name.]

Nightingale got fired. [Too clean-cut.] McLaren offered job to **New York Doll** Richard Hell, but Hell's skirt confounded the Sex Pistols' image. Lyndon shuffled in with an "I Hate Pink Floyd" T-shirt. After sneering and singing Alice Cooper's #7, '72 "School's Out," Johnny Lydon/Rotten was hired. Pink Floyd?

"Another Brick in the Wall (Part II)" – Pink Floyd, #1(4), 1-80. From Al. #1(15), 12-79 *The Wall*. Not Punk Rock. Pink Floyd Cockney growl headlines a chilling concept album about estrangement and despair in overcrowded British classrooms. Their bitterest enemy? The DARK SARCASM sadistic teachers lord over cashless Cockney charges – like Lulu's in "To Sir With Love" #1(5), 9-67. PINK FLOYD IS ITS OWN ROCK GENRE. Yes, Pink Floyd also plays Art Rock, Orchestral Rock, Rococo Rock, Heavy Metal, Punk and New Wave, Heartland Rock, Marathon Rock, A.O.R. (Album-Oriented Rock), or P.F.R. (Pink Floyd Rock).

Unique group, Floyd: singer-guitarist **David Gilmour**, bassist **Roger Waters**, percussionist **Nick Mason**, key-board maestro **Rick Wright**. Floyd took the Beatles' Con-cept Album concept and steered it to infinity with their #1(1), 3-73 *Dark Side of the Moon*. The Fab Four's #1(15) *Sergeant Pepper* grabbed 63 weeks on the charts (over a year) and the coveted Grammy. Floyd's *Dark Side of the Moon* battered all longevity records to a jellied pulp. *The Wall* stuck around 123 weeks, but went deca-platinum (10 million sales). *Dark Side* only eclipsed the competition at #1 for one week. By 1997, Pink Floyd had twelve certi-fied platinum albums of over a million sales. Bizarrely, they had only two top 40 singles, this and #13, 6-73 "Money." *Dark Side* sold over 13 million records since 1973. *Dark* has the all-time *Billboard* record for Top 200 status – the Methuselah Award for Longevity.

WEEKS CHARTED FOR *DARK SIDE* – **741**!

For 14¼ years (741 weeks), *Dark* dominated the top rungs of the hottest hits ladder. Their #1(2), 9-75 *Wish You Were Here* album actually out-championed *Dark* too, at the top. *Wish* hit #1 for TWO weeks back in 9-75. Other champs? **Johnny Mathis**'s *Johnny's Greatest Hits*, 490 weeks; *My Fair Lady* (480) (info c/o Joel Whitburn's great *Top Pop Albums 1955-96*). The 4th one, *Phantom of the Opera*'s soundtrack, 331 weeks, never rose above #46. Then *Oklahoma* soundtrack, 331; and **Carole King**'s *Tapestry* (#1[15], 302 weeks). Long before their American long chart run, Floyd scorched British charts with "See Emily Play" (#134, 9-67 U.S.A.; #6 U.K.) Syd Barrett/David Gilmour's Rococo Rock emanates from collegiate Cambridge, England.

"The Wall" is a Humpty Dumpty slam on utter boredom, resentment, and school hostility. Too many poor kids are stuffed into tiny old grey rooms with burnt-out wardens and boring textbooks. In a weird way, "Wall" dumps on the educational establishment. The total album, in full contest and concept, does not. Is it a cry for help? So is Rock and Roll.

Superficial Floyd critics perceived them as that 'anti-educational' rock group with a "Wall" of snarly snappy kids yelling they ain't needin' education. Many anti-Floyd cynics miss the startling rhythmic and melodic innovations: Gilmour's lightning staccato sixths and ninths; bass star **Roger Waters**' sloshing frontiers of low-note riff mania. Floyd concerts are still major sellouts. **Jeremy Dean, Nine Days**' keyboarder/singer: "People are still looking for and finding that place where only Pink Floyd can take them. As you round out the musical waterfall of their sound-surround swoon of audial frenzy, you can get, in a word, 'comfortably numb'."

Pink Floyd:
***Richard Wright** (left),* ***Roger Waters** (top),* ***David Gilmour** (right), and* ***Nick Mason** (bottom)*

"The Wall" tippy-toes. A funky guitar sets the table. A snare and bass drum ka-chick and flump. The big Waters bass snakes in, shadowing their sinister classroom. It's suffocating. A sliver of knowledge – a slither of hate. The tough classroom seethes with Cockney moppets in bouffant hair, and feisty Teddy Boys armed with frown and sneer and snarl.

Education has failed them. In America they'd be stereotyped BURNOUTS. In London, they're called victims of a system that kowtows to the overprivileged (like America's *Beverly Hills 90210*) and ignores the 'working class.' Working class? Hey, don't we all work? "The Wall" zaps the system, the establishment, the status quo. It's not the Monkees' gentle jab at suburban barbecue squires in #3, '67 "Pleasant Valley Sunday." It's a thin blue flame of Punk fire. Anger and bitterness seethe with hopeless future rage. The scapegoat? The threadbare villain and sarcastic intellectual snob at the classroom helm. The tough kids tell the teacher/automaton to leave all the kids alone. The songs jabs at uniformity.

"The Wall" dances its funky groove. This anti-grammatical chorus chimes in, with fiery fervor. "NO EDUCATION!," they chant. Waters steers his pulsing bass into ominous turf. Is the song a celebration of Philistinism and the Sex Pistols' 'Anarchy in the U.K.'? A celebration of ignorance? Or, in the ancient words of English philosopher **Thomas Hobbes**, prototype of *Calvin*'s cartoon tiger, "In our century, life is nasty, brutish, and short . . ."

Actually, the song is worse than that. And better.

The song celebrates the possibilities of education. What might be? The snarling student should understand that the teacher too is a victim of the system. Just as **Charles Dickens**' sorrowful *Hard Times* stereotypes, Mr. Gradgrind and (get this!) Mr. McCHOKEUMCHILD, had to be overseers in sardine-squished classrooms, teachers today suffer, too. Folks consigning their kids to Zilch Property Taxes must pay the consequences. Both teacher and child are victims. TAX-PAC local anti-tax groups, infuriated that teachers (who used to take the Vow of Poverty) are finally making respectable salaries, now try to paint them as moneygrubbers – pitting the community in America against its own children's quality education. Education is stodgy. We study algebra because the ancients did in their Quadrivia curricula at the University of Paris and Bologna, and yes, Cambridge and Oxford. Fairly recently American education punted Latin (60s) requirements. Colleges required Greek (30s).

This swamped teacher of tough London Cockney kids, stoned on Messianic fire, strokes his own bloated ego by putting down his poor students with "DARK SARCASM" within his "CLASSROOM." Bad way to teach. Floyd reflects these smoldering students. Waters' loud, sinister bass bellyflops in on the snarled word 'EDUCATION.' **Aretha Franklin** and **Otis Redding** said it well: what the haggard teacher and the surly students all need is simply RESPECT – not sarcasm. A KIND sense of humor works wonders.

In **George Bernard Shaw**'s immortal words – "The only time my education was interrupted . . . was the time I spent in the classroom." Super advice... so we see it twice.

What's the 'Wall'? What's this brick in the wall? Big metaphor. SYMBOL POWER! The WALL is everything that stifles and crushes your glowing future. This plug-ugly juggernaut, the Wall, squashes and squelches the very dreams that the poor have in rising through the choking smoky system. To money, fulfillment, maybe joy.

Grimly, a 1995 *Newsday* survey queried 6th graders on Long Island to choose between being rich and being happy: RICH   63%   HAPPY   37%

Ouch. What about LOVE? Here in America, streets are still paved with gold. I gabbed with a St. Petersburg, Russia, world-class runner at Paul Fetscher's party (Paul on 1979 *Runners' World* cover). She mentioned the old Johnny B. Goode dream: name in lights, gold freeways. Apparently, we're still the land of milk and money and gold records (even for Punk rockers who decry commerciality). Globetrotting raconteur, Paul recalls a marathon he ran in Russia. All the foot-stomping runners sang along with every word of **Neil Diamond**'s song (comin' to) "America" (#8, 5-81) in this Russian nightclub. Why? It seems after 60 years of smoky collectivism and lost dreams, they all wanted to come to America, Home of Rock and Roll.

The Wall – **Pink Floyd**, Al. #1(15), 12-79. Critics like Dave Marsh call **Floyd** one of the most important bands to spearhead the Rock Revolution. (Their rare first vinyl album was #131, 12-67 eponymous *Pink Floyd*. Their early album chart numbers were, like Britain, *Obscured by Clouds* (Al. #46, 6-72); #70, 11-71 *Meddle*; #55, 11-70 *Atom Heart Mother*; and tongue twister #74, 1-70 *Ummagumma*. Beyond the title song, *The Wall* pursues the pathetic plight of kids incarcerated in a choke-child school/jail of overcrowded poverty. Street denizens mutter amok in the orange-peel streets, under a wan ashen sky.

Once lassoed by the marathon lariat of *Dark Side*'s 14¼-year *Billboard* 200 incumbency, the poor charts never had a chance. Floyd's huge strength lies in the ALBUM – not the single. For instance, like album-superstars **Led Zeppelin**'s uncharted blockbuster "Stairway to Heaven" (NC, 11-71), Floyd's world-famous lead cut from Al. #1(2), 9-75 *Wish You Were Here* [named, surprise, "Wish You Were Here"], never hit the HOT 100 charts – despite constant Classic Rock airplay. Floyd's Greatest Album Hits? Quadruple-platinum (4 million) #3, 2-77 *Animals*; *The Wall*; 4-83, #6 *The Final Cut*; #3, 9-87 *A Momentary Lapse of Reason* (3+ mil) – and two 90s smashes of double-platinum sales splendor: #1(4), 4-94 *The Division Bell* and #1(1), 6-95 *Pulse*.

The British **Sex Pistols**? Much of their anti-Pink Floyd kids' attitudes were fomented a year or so before in the swirling controversy of **Johnny Rotten**'s fiery diatribes against the system (even against incumbent Rock stars). Rotten never claimed to be the Second Coming of Operatic Orbison or Elvis or anything.

Rotten's basic goal? To breathe dragon fire back into Rock and Roll – and make it dangerous once again (Clarke). They reflected the angst and strident sound unleashed at the Motor City's Grande Ballroom (#82, 3-69) by Rob Tyner, Wayne Kramer, and Fred 'Sonic' Smith in #82, 3-69 "Kick Out the Jams" by the **MC5** (**Motor City Five**).

ANARCHY implies a total lack of government. Riots in the streets. No law and order. Just chaos, consternation, and pandemonium. People throwing Twinkies and tomatoes.

"Anarchy in the U.K." – Sex Pistols, NC, 1976; hit in U.K., 11-76. The Sex Pistols signed a monster contract with international EMI, trashing hotel rooms. Then anarchy erupted. EMI fired them. American giant A & M (**Herb Alpert**'s outfit) hired them, and fired them in a week for alleged obnoxious behavior. Next contract? VIRGIN Records, naturally. Then they snagged Queen Elizabeth's 25-year Silver Jubilee bandwagon:

"God Save the Queen" – Sex Pistols, NC, 1977; #2, 7-77, U.K. Blasted as blasphemous and anti-monarchial, the Sex Pistols' sizzling song was up to its wax in MONSTER HITDOM. They stormed the Bastille, and iconoclastically brought down all the traditions. Their "My Way" (NC, 1978; Top Ten U.K., 1978) is nothing like Frank Sinatra's dreamy and dignified treatment of this Paul Anka classic. Nothing like Elvis. Spitfire version by Rotten's vocal replacement **Sid Vicious**. Vicious (1958-79, heroin O.D.) also cranked U.K. Top Ten with his reprise of Eddie Cochran's "C'mon Everybody."

The Pistols' agonized style of zap-the-establishment followed the New York Punk scene and Glam afterglow. Like heroes **Iggy Pop**'s **Stooges**, the **MC5**, and the **New York Dolls**, they spat at the audience and assumed the timely uniform: black boots that make your feet itch just thinking about wearing them; short straight spiked hair, often green, pink, purple; motorcycle jackets spangled with studs and spikes and mega-zippers; T-shirts glowering with grandmother-shocking words, ripped and shredded like the wearer was just 0-1 in a tiger fight. The byword of Punk Rock is **James Dean**'s REBELLION, be it in volume, hairstyle, clothing, tattoos or body piercings.

Flash back to early zealous preachers who smashed **Elvis** and **Jerry Lee Lewis** records. One Anglican vicar barred the door of a Sex Pistols' concert, shouting, "For the love of the Lord, Stay OUT! They're the Devil's children!" "God Save the Queen" did not endear the Sex Pistols to the British establishment. Like Russia's Revisionist Josef Stalin, the Sex Pistols suffered a media freeze – fan mags refused to run their ads; chambers of commerce and local organizations had midnight meetings to keep them out of their hamlet or burgh or shire. Monarchists attacked Sex Pistols' **Paul Cook** and **Johnny Rotten** with knives, pipes, razors, and cricket bats (since cold-steel/hot-lead pistols were only available to American children). The Sex Pistols' EMI firing was a result of factory workers in the record-pressing plant on a sit-down strike against handling their stuff. **Guns N' Roses'** later American TV tirade was ignited by Pistols' BBC outburst of motherblush obscenities.

"Pretty Vacant" – Sex Pistols, NC, 1977; #6, 10-77 U.K. The Pistols' furor cranked along fabulously, with this tune charging the British charts, followed by #8 "Holiday in the Sun." An album with a name related to male anatomy hit #1 in 11-77 (#106 here), their lucky month.

Suddenly the British Punk scenario ran out of steam. Sex Pistols' songs slid down the charts, despite upsurges by the new **Clash**, the rise of new INDIE LABELS (Independent Labels) concept, the Elvis Costello Rock Against Racism movement, and the CBGB revolution in New York.

Bumper sticker:

IF YOU CAN CATEGORIZE IT, IT'S OVER.

– Lisa Rinaldi, 1996

Lisa critiques Neo-Punks like Rancid (#8 Modern Rock Tracks Air Play "Time Bomb" 8-95) and the airwaves-to-smithereens phenomenon of Green Day – #2(2), 12-94 "When I Come Around" and #4, 10-2000 Al. *Warming.* [Besides the HOT 100, *Billboard* keeps other charts for Rock styles.]

BILLBOARD'S OTHER CHARTS

Billboard keeps many other charts. For *Gold Rush* listings past our usual HOT 100, R & B, and COUNTRY charts, here are acronyms for the rest:
A = Airplay (Most Played Songs by Disc/Video Jockeys)
J = Juke Boxes (Most Played)
S = Sales (Store's Best Sellers)
T = TOP 100 (Before Summer 1958 HOT 100 Began)
H = Honor Roll (for Hits)
C = Coming Up Strong
Some of these are current. Some long gone. Here are *Billboard's* Other Charts, as of February 17, 2001:
1) Top Pop Catalog Albums (Long-Running Favorites, like Pink Floyd's *Dark Side of the Moon* with 1244 weeks)
2) Heatseekers Albums (Best Sellers by New Artists)
3) Hot Rap Singles
4) Top R & B/Hip-Hop Albums (Notice interchangeable terms in 2001 – in early 1990s, known unfortunately as 'Black').
5) Hot R & B Singles and Tracks
6) Hot R & B/Hip-Hop Airplay (and Recurrent Airplay)
7) Hot R & B Singles Sales
8) Hot Dance Music (Techno, House, or Neo-Disco)
9) Hot Country Singles & Tracks & Top Country Singles Sales
10) Top Country Albums (& Catalog Albums)
11) Top Jazz Albums & Contemporary Jazz Albums
12) Top Classical and Classical Crossover Albums
13) Hot Latin Tracks

14) Hits of the World: Japan, Germany, U.K., France, Eurochart, Spain, Malaysia, Greece, Canada, Netherlands, Australia, Italy, Ireland, Belgium, Austria, Switzerland (formerly New Zealand charts recently disappeared, perhaps temporarily)
15) Top Independent Albums & Internet Album Sales [Napster zapped in federal court, 2-16-01]
16) Top Video Rentals and Sales, and Top DVD Sales
17) Top Kid Video
18) Adult Contemporary (often cited in *Gold Rush*)
19) Adult Top 40
20) Top 40 Tracks (Mainstream Top 40 Airplay on Radio)
21) Mainstream Rock Tracks
22) Modern Rock Tracks
23) *Billboard* Video Monitor: VH-1, MTV, CMT (Country Music Television), BET, Rockmusic, Disney Channel, MTV2, MTV Europe, JBTV, College Television Network, RAGE
24) HOT 100 Airplay and HOT 100 Recurrent Airplay
25) HOT 100 Single Sales

AND FINALLY – their two BIG CHARTS: HOT 100 Singles and *Billboard* 200 Albums. Whew.

The Sex Pistols did not classify themselves as 'Punk.' The Establishment did that. Musicians over the years have adopted many bizarre uniforms. At some point near the Punk Rock Era, however, may people stopped listening intently to the music – even the message – and began to concentrate overmuch on what the band folk were (or weren't) wearing. *MTV* arrived in 1981, shifting the focus from the song to the singers' sartorial splendor. Videos pulsed in Vibra-Color. The melody receded, some say, into Oldies Ozone Zone.

Remember the "Day the Music Died," back on 2-3-59? The Buddy Holly, Ritchie Valens, and Big Bopper plane crash put innocent teenage dreams on the endless spin cycle. Almost twenty years to the day later (Ground Hog Day, 2-2-79, my dog Snarf's 13th birthday), Sex Pistol Sid Vicious died of a heroin overdose. The Chelsea Hotel at 222 West 23rd Street, NYC, has housed many bohemian notables since 1905: writers O. Henry, Thomas Wolfe, Mark Twain; rockers Jimi Hendrix, the Grateful Dead, Jefferson Airplane, Janis Joplin, and Bob Moritz's kid. Arthur C. Clarke wrote his *2001: A Space Odyssey* here. Beat guru William Burroughs wrote the big erotic novel of the 50s here: *Naked Lunch*, banned by more city councils than the Sex Pistols.

In 1978, Vicious's girlfriend Nancy Spungen was murdered at the Chelsea. Sex Pistol **Sid Vicious** was charged with the grisly crime, though his alibi had some validity to many fans. Vicious died before trial. Somehow, Sid missed out on the national mourning for Holly, for Valens, for Cochran, for Otis Redding, Jim Croce, for Elvis, or for Jerry Garcia. Murder zaps Teddy-Bear Teen Idol images.

"Because the Night" – Patti Smith, #13, 4-78. Like Marshall Crenshaw, Mark Knopfler, and Chuck Berry (autobiography), Patti Smith of New Jersey (via Chicago) combined journalism with rock music. "Because the Night" achieved something the Sex Pistols never did in America – a top 20 hit. Patti Smith was a lot tamer than Sid Vicious. Instead of messing around with Murder One charges, Patti Smith's main press mess was her refusal to shave her underarms. She co-wrote "Night" with **Bruce Springsteen**, who dabbled in black-Levis Punk accoutrements, like fellow Heartland Mainstream superstars Bob Seger and John Cougar Mellencamp.

America's #1 Punk crew?

"Do You Wanna Dance?" – Ramones, #86, 4-78. Let's face it – this is not the most radical song in the universe. If you can call any rock songs Standards, "Dance" is one. Ramones loved Basic Oldies Rock, with a swoosh of Surf and a fusillade of guitarfire.

"Do You Wanna Dance?" – Del Shannon, #43, 9-64. Del Shannon, 1999 Rock Hall inductee, blasts this ruddy rocker sky-high to #22, '64.. **Bobby Freeman** (#5, 6-64 "C'mon and Swim") wrote it and took it to #5 in 1958. Forward-thinking Shannon, prolific singer/songwriter on his own, may just be the first Retro Rock Star. *Who Put the Bomp*'s Greg Shaw credits Shannon with: ". . . a charged, kinetic rampage, with irresistible chord changes, ringing rhythm guitar by Del, and those piercing falsetto flights . . . an ideal pairing with the Royaltones' raunchy, solid rock guitar and sax, providing a dynamic underpinning for Shannon's own super-charged vocals and rhythm guitar."

Royaltones did instrumentals "Poor Boy" (#17, 10-58) and "Flamingo Express" (#82, 1-61), with tenor sax guru George Katsakis and vintage supersonic-speed Punk drummer. Two chords on "Flamingo." "Do You Wanna Dance" also hit for **Beach Boys**' #12, '65; **Mamas & Papas** #76, '68; and torch singer **Bette Midler** #17, '73.

Patti Smith was among the first of the American punks (early 1975 CBGB's). The **Ramones** were the most infamous. Smith married the 1968 **MC5**'s **Punk Fred 'Sonic' Smith**, and explored the musical relationship between Heavy Metal, 'Hard Rock,' Glam Rock, and Punk. The Ramones blasted Oldies at a raunchier level.

Shannon cut "Do You Wanna Dance" with the studio VU Meter probably cruising far beyond the overmodulated +3 barrier, crashing headlong into sonic-boom nonexistent +4 range. In the Rock Screamer Key of 'A,' Shannon's keyboard 'Terminator' **Max Crook** ripped out all the stops.

Punk Rock dashes a hell-bent-for-leather sprint: drum for your life! The Royaltones' phalanx of spitting saxes, snarly speed-of-light snare, and crackling guitar chops and slashes, reverberated with zoom and pizzazz. When Dearborn's **Royaltones** hooked up with Coopersville's **Del Shannon** at Detroit's Alexandrine Street, Twirl Records, these Michigan Marauders slammed down a sound unheard-of in the Rock and Roll Era. It was 100% pure HARD ROCK – and it galvanized the Punk and Heavy Metal Eras to arrive.

"Oh, How Happy" – Shades of Blue, #12, 5-66; #16, 5-66 R & B. One of the sweetest tunes ever written. Cleancut. Three suburban Livonia guys and a very pretty girl, Linda Kerr, with enormous dark eyes. Mellow White Soul.

Mariah Carey-style melismatic 1966 grace notes. Their smooth love sound suggests **Smokey** at his smokin'est. Mellow chiming bells. Sweet combo of handclapping and finger popping, "Oh, How Happy" is a happy song about love, and more love, too happy for Punk. Del Shannon, however, was saddled with as much emotional burden as any Johnny (Rotten) Come Lately. Del's musitron ROARS! The **Ramones**' "Do You Wanna Dance" version is much more, ulp, sedate.

The Ramones

"I Wanna Be Sedated" – Ramones, NC, 1975+. The Ramones met at a party in 1974, and like fledgling bands since time immemorial, started playing parties first. RAMONE is not their real last name (see Righteous 'Brothers'). Lead singer Joey Ramone is really **Jeffrey Hyman** (1952-2001), and the other three Ramones are Johnny Ramone (nee Cummngs), DeeDee Ramone (Doug Colvin, d. 6-6-2002), and Tommy Ramone, whose real name would flunk the national spelling bee champ: Tom Erdelyi (see Erykah Badu).

The Ramones hurled lyrical energy: "Now I Wanna Sniff Some Glue," "Blitzkrieg Bop," and "Beat on the Brat." When the Ramones' 1976 first album played the U.K., on Bicentennial Day July 4, 1976, it helped begin a British revolution against old fogeys still mucking around in bygone frumpy and dowdy attitudes. "I Wanna Be Sedated" is the ultimate thumb-your-nose-at-society song (with a fast and furious fifties flavor). It says the hopeless modern world is rotten to the core, it's not worth going through the motions, and that it's best to curl up into a cocoon. Sedated.

Anaesthetized. Spaced-out. The Ramones' Punk Funk is often a facetious panorama of a bloated, flatulent society of automaton conformists. Letta Taylor (*Newsday* 4-22-01) calls the Ramones' music a *"blitzkrieg"* [German "lightning warfare"] of three chord, chain-saw riffs and comic book lyrics . . . the Ramones wanted to blowtorch corporate bloat, slick packaging, and big hair."

When we discuss drugs and rock music, we must also discuss sordid conditions that drive people to drugs and drink: racism, academic and athletic pressure, lost love, or blazing wars. "I Wanna Be Sedated" is a cry in the wilderness. It chops away the frills. Shakes up parents. [What more could you ask for in a Rock and Roll anthem?]

The Ramones' British tour launched Punk Rock in the U.K. The Ramones, however, had a lighter touch, and a nifty gift for self-parody, like **Alice Cooper**. The Sex Pistols took themselves much more seriously. The Ramones chugged along jovially on their three-chord continuous-concept symphony, and had the blast we're supposed to have with Rock and Roll. Lanky **Joey Ramone** blasted almost Leather Surf Rock sounds.

Back in the States, the Ramones' medley careened: "Cretin Hop," "Bop Till You Drop," the quasi-beauteous "Wart Hog," "The KKK Took My Baby Away," "Psycho Therapy," "Animal Boy," and surprisingly melodic/complex **Sonny Bono/Searchers**' hit "Needles and Pins." Their first charter puffs a comic book jungle-bimbo bombshell, **Sheena: Queen of the Jungle** – "Sheena Is a Punk Rocker" #81, 7-77. Ramones' album swath cut deeper: #49, 11-77 *Rocket to Russia*; Phil Spector-produced #44, 2-80 *End of the Century*, and #83, 3-83 *Subterranean Jungle*.

Besides their Shannon/Freeman/Beach Boy cover, they sandwiched their highest hit — #66, 12-77 "Rockaway Beach." Rockaway Beach furls the south shore of Brooklyn near Kennedy Airport. A mountainous landfill trash heap glows with whooshes of seagulls. Around the curl of the white sands, shimmery with shards of ex-beer bottles, you can almost see the shivery Parachute Jump at Old Coney Island. Rock and Roll has always mirrored a Coney Island Funhouse House of Mirrors. Splendor and glory and horror and hate co-mingle with LOVE, the main reason popular music exists. From its spawning ground at CBGB's, deep in the graybeard wino Bowery, Punk Rock slam-dunked its scary message to a sleepy America. WAKE UP, it thundered, and SMELL THE SLIME!

"Kill the Poor" – Dead Kennedys, NC, 1980; #49, 1980 U.K. SHOCK ROCK troopers of San Francisco. Our nation still sincerely mourned the death of youthful Camelot's Golden Age, in the wake of one beloved murdered President and his presidential-hopeful brother. Punk Rock delivers shock. The DEAD KENNEDYS is one group whose name alone might guarantee it an American airplay ban (see #4, '68 Kennedy elegy "Abraham, Martin, & John" by Dion). Not unlike the Sex Pistols' anti-Queen song(s).

The Dead Kennedys sprouted monikers like **Klaus Fluoride** (bass), **Easy Bay Ray** a/k/a **Ray Valium** (guitar), or

lead singer **Jello Biafra**, named after nervous dessert and a country with millions of starving kids. Some Punk aggregations, sopping in sardonic glee, named their bands Squashed Squirrel Puke or Toad Jam or Dead Janitor Earwax.

"California Über Alles" is a crafty satire of Hitler's "Deutschland Über Alles" (translated as 'Germany Over All!') and served up the Dead Kennedy's first single, an Un-Hit. Their *Sturm Und Schlag* (storm and smash) style resulted in titles unfit for this family Rock history.

The Dead Kennedys are equal-opportunity offenders. "Kill the Poor" staggered the establishment. Their 'final solution' / 'modest proposal' suggests **Jonathan Swift**'s dastardly tongue-in-cheek plan for starvation in Ireland in the 18th century; rich Englishmen and ladies could fry, fricassee, and roast the Irish babies. Swift got swift parliamentary action on quick wheat and potatoes for the Irish poor with this fiendish dark-comedy 'joke'. The Dead Kennedys get the selfsame reaction. Though they never ever charted on the Top 100 Singles or 200 Albums, their impact was felt in underground hideouts and John McManus's college-dorm stations throughout America. [The Dead **Milkmen**, a more conventional Philly R & R quartet, scored with esoteric Albums #101, 12-88 *Beelzebubba*, #163, 8-87 *Bucky Fellini*, and Al. #164, 6-90 *Metaphysical Graffiti*, but the Dead Kennedys kept mum of the heartless charts.]

Jello Biafra ran for mayor of San Francisco in 1979. He hit the Top Five (#4 of 10 candidates). Their album NC *Fresh Fruit for Rotting Vegetables* featured this "Kill the Poor" and "Deutschland" medley, plus "Let's Lynch the Landlord," "Stealing People's Mail," "Forward to Death," and unloveliest "I Kill Children." Album *Frankenchri--* – yields "MTV – Get Off the Air," "Goons of Corruption," and seriocomic chanty "At My Job," about mundane workaday life.

"Nothing But Flowers" – Talking Heads, NC, 4-88. Off Al. #19, 4-88 *Naked*. Armed with gonzo guitar, fine tenor, and a very weird message, head Head **David Byrne** dazzles us with his topsy-turvy world. Every 'tree-hugger' environmentalist laments lost lovely meadows vanishing by urban blight. Byrne and Jerry Harrison (guitar and keyboards), Tina Weymouth (rare female bass player) and her hubby Chris Frantz (drums) flip the old Rural Expatriation theme from the tear-jerky to the absurd.

"Nothing But Flowers" was simply too super a song to make it: Talking Heads (named by the counterculture after faceless 'suits' chatting on TV) lament the tragic loss of beautiful Pizza Huts, Dairy Queens, 7-11's, and honkytonks. Where'd they go? They were viciously swallowed up by killer grass, daisies, meadows, peaceful valleys. While these things fell apart, Byrne warns us – soothsayeringly – no one really 'paid much attention.'

Songs are usually about love, or dancing, not entropy. Byrne laments his lost Angry Young Man stage, when he falls in love with this gorgeous highway. Cars and real estate, he gushes, are sacrificed for cornfields and flowers. Byrne's Absurdist anti-environment goof wants to bring back scenic JUNKYARDS, (hey, *Gold Rush* was created on my pals Rob and Lori Ghiringhelli's $1.00 Garage Sale swivel chair). Starting on the Punk cusp, the Heads headed into the New Wave category.

"Psycho Killer" – Talking Heads, #92, 2-78. Byrne was born in Dumbarton (near Glasgow) Scotland. Weymouth came from Coronado, California. Of all Punk Rock groups, and most of the New Wave, they are possibly the most musically sophisticated and innovative. Check out the Talking Heads' smashing **Al Green** echo on #26 hit, 11-78 "Take Me to the River," their African echo in "I Zimbra," or their spin-off Tom Tom Club (Frantz & Weymouth) and #31, 1-82 "Genius of Love." Or harmonic Hollies/Searchers'-echo #25, 9-86 "Wild, Wild Life."

"Burning Down the House" – Talking Heads, #9, 7-83. PYROMANIA BOOGIE RAP prize. They electrified their esoteric Punk purist fans with (aaarrrgh) a Top Ten hit. Like bloodlusty cavemen gazing at charred oozing embers in some ghastly primordial fire, Heads celebrate trashing of one's own domicile. Change-of-pace monotonic vocal suggests Rap. Heads hammer chant of TITLE, over and over and over and over. Band disbanded 1991. Burnt out? Nah, reunited for 2002 Rock Hall induction.

"Wicked Ruby" – Danny Zella and the Zell Rocks, #71, 1-59. Like other 50s Punk Prototypes, Zella was the baddest of the bad! He stormed the North Detroit suburban fringe, milking his mad amp for adolescent angst **Eddie Cochran** and **Gene Vincent** missed. With a Detroit waterfall haircut (change 10-40W oil weekly), coal-black leather jacket, 14" pegged black Levis, and ebony engineer boots, frenzied Zella played the wildest Mobil station opening (Livernois and Eight Mile Road) in the history of the universe! "Ruby" was one bad dudette. She'd have to be, to handle the ultra-greaseworthy band's riotous attentions. 'Ruby' towers six foot two, and clobbers the poor lad with her high heel shoes. He's no Mr. Peaceful himself, but her apology defied explanation: You are lucky, hollers the big bad babe, that you didn't end up dead! Bad, bad lass deserves **Leroy Brown** (Jim Croce, #1, '73).

"Little Bit O'Soul" – Music Explosion, #2(2), 5-67. Punk Rock? A 1977-80 phenomenon? Now way! Mansfield Ohio sprouted **Jamie Lyons**' 100% pure Punk Rock. It lurches in footloose gear with full speed Screaming Blues tonsils and gravel-guts rasp.

"Should I Stay or Should I Go" – Clash, #45, 7-82; #50, 2-83. The Clash started by **Joe Strummer** dumped his 101'ers band at the 100 Club London bar gig. Perhaps the only Turkish-English major R & R star (b. John Mellors, '52), Strummer was born in Ankara, Turkey. He joined **Mick Jones** [not MICK JONES of Foreigner/Spooky Tooth] on guitar and vocals – plus bassman Paul Simonon and Nicky Headon. When they entered the plucky lollapalooza arena of Punk Rock, they bellowed 'out with the old.' "No Beatles, No Elvis, No Stones!" In 1976, controversial comments by big English stars angered many Punk Bands with fervent ideals about racism. The Clash followed

leader Tom Robinson (#10 U.K. "2-4-6-8 Motorway") in renouncing racism. They were joined by **Elvis Costello**, Buddy Holly look-alike, and 250,000 British Punk vanguard youths, in the forefront of both the zap-the-racists and save-the-melody movements to combat the National Front, often categorized as the neo-Nazi movement. The Clash were blatantly political, like many of their San Francisco 60s Psychedelic brethren, who lay down in front of troop trains in their End-the-Vietnam-War quest. *Combat Rock* (Al. #7, 6-82) and *London Calling* (Al. #27, 2-80) clattered Tex-Mex gold:

Cyndi Lauper

"I Fought the Law" – Clash, NC, 1979; U.K. hit. In these strange days of 8-track tapes in aircraft-carrier-size Oldsmobile Toronados, the Clash reprised the old **Sonny Curtis** song the **Bobby Fuller IV** thundered to #9 in '66. They frighteningly change Sonny's sunny mild line about leaving his girlfriend to killing her. Chilling switcheroo of Jock Rock anthem. Sonny's song-guy just robbed.

"I Fought the Law" – Crickets, NC, 5-59. Buddy Holly's replacement singer **Earl Sinks** had a nice thin country tenor, but Sonny's hit hung fire for six years. The Hollyless Crickets managed a NC, U.S.A., but #27, 2-60 U.K. "When You Ask about Love," on Sinks' lead vocal. They followed up with Sinks' & Crickets' #33, 5-60 U.K.-only "Baby, My Heart." Crickets' original **Jerry Allison** blasted drums, with **Joe B. Mauldin** bopping bass and **Sonny Curtis** on guitar. Buddy's producer's wife **Vi Petty** and Dudley Brooks play piano, with Buddy's Jordanaire-style troupe the **Picks** (John and Bill Pickering, Bob Lapham) handling background vocals. The Crickets weren't protesting a thing.

The Ultimate Holly Echo version is by the **Bobby Fuller IV** (#9, 1-66). Like Holly before him, Bobby's short season conjures cries of 'what might have been.' The El Paso Texan forged a booming blaster band of Tex-Mex rhythmic fire with splashes of Early Punk dynamism. Guitar guy Bobby's Holly-twang vocals merged with one of the most rampagin', rip-roarin' Thunderbeats of all time – provided by Chicano drumstick-blur thumpmaster **DeWayne Quinico**. The Fuller IV's drummer could teach a whole battalion of Punk or New Wave drummers about rockin' rhythm. Bobby's brother Randy Fuller complemented Quinico with his driving bass pulse. Jim Reese and Bobby Fuller furnished the speedburning rhythm/lead guitar riffs and fills. "I Fought the Law" tore like a torrid Texas tornado. (No Thunderbeat like Bobby Fuller's ever was, or may never be again). Sonny's antisocial message, and Fuller's roller-coaster rhythms are Vintage Punk flavored.

Not enough Fuller pix were taken of the Baytown, Texas lad, with his thick brown pompadour and Brian Wilson-style smile. The whole band was decked out in these fire-engine-red (almost vermilion) high button suits. They followed "I Fought the Law" with **Buddy Holly**'s "Love's Made a Fool of You" (#26, 4-66). *Billboard* did a mega-ad for third single, "The Magic Touch" (NC '66). Bobby died in a 'mysterious circumstance' (Whitburn) out in California. We prefer to think it was a Lover's Lane carbon monoxide, (though we've heard stories from Lee Harvey Oswald to Jack the Ripper). If the former, Bobby's youthful martyrdom is a stern warning to always crack open your window, no matter how icy the arctic gale, to admit fresh air if you've got the motor idling during some midnight rendezvous. Via his Chicano drummer, the Bobby Fuller IV provided a rhythmic link to the Latino Explosion of 1999-2001+: Ricky Martin, Christina Aguilera, and Santana's #1(6+), 2-2000 "Maria Maria". And why not? **Buddy Holly**, by marrying **Maria Elena Santiago** [Holly], and by co-starring with **Ritchie Valens**, may have helped bridge the W.A.S.P.-Chicano gap – VERY early on.

To think that Buddy Holly's music (and Sonny's) would be relevant in Disco-Era England, rankled by unemployment and cynicism and despair, is pure proof of his worldwide acclaim. The Clash and the Dead Kennedys may be changing the core-rotten system through Rock and Roll Power Politics – but they never forget to pay hiccup homage to tall smiley Texans as apolitical as tumbleweeds. Or check out the **Ramones**' combo Holly/Surf Rock audial glow on #81, 7-77 "Sheena Is a Punk Rocker" and #66, 12-77 "Rockaway Beach." The Clash captures the West Texas-New Mexico border fervor of Big Sky cattle country – in the midst of anarchy in the U.K. In the midst of their Cricket-chirp and Fuller-brush "I Fought the Law," and "Should I Stay or Should I Go," you can hear the long lost lonesome wail of Buddy Holly somewhere out there over Arizona on a spindrift moonshine stardust magic carpet.

"Rock the Casbah" – Clash, #8, 10-82. Into the 80s, the Clash picked up prodigious influences – Beat poet **Allen Ginsberg** (1926-97), Rap forefather **Grandmaster Flash**, and the only 'Old Wave' band the Clash really trusted – the **Who**. Soon the Clash were backing the Who, particularly at the New York Mets' Shea Stadium, where the Beatles had once conquered America. "Rock the Casbah" features some supersonic **Paul Simonon** bass runs, and hyper-speed Punk drum adventures by Nicky 'Topper' Headon. To me, "ROCK the Casbah" always sounded a little like something a little gamier and raunchier, but the

song pits the beat against the melody. The big beat wins. New Wave? Gothic Rock?

"Kiss Them for Me" – Siouxsie and the Banshees, #23, 8-91. Hey, hold it. **Siouxsie Sioux** (Susan Dallion) had the Sex Pistols' Sid Vicious for a drummer in the 70s, plus **Adam Ant**'s guitarist. Funny how long it takes to get the big break. They eluded commercial blockbusterdom – like the Sex Pistols in America. Siouxsie rocked with her #2 Modern Rock Tracks 2-95 (#126, 3-95) "O Baby" and Al. #127, 3-95 *The Rapture*. Like Joe Strummer, she debuted at the 100 Club in London. A banshee is a female spirit in Gaelic folklore that forecasts a family member's death by a long, eerie, wild wail, way out on the darkling windswept moors. Avant-garde Gothic Punk.

"Goody Two Shoes" – Adam Ant, #12, 11-82. Maybe Punk Rock and New Wave just metamorphosized into Alternative Music. Both names are etymologically intriguing. Hah? Siouxsie comes for the Sioux/Native American tribe of South Dakota, near Gene Autry's "Sioux City Sue," the Beatles' "Rocky Raccoon," and banshee-bewailed Gen. George Armstrong Custer. "Adam Ant" could be the first ant (with cohort Eve Ant), or perhaps the word adamant, meaning an ancient stone believed to be unyielding, or impenetrable. Adam (b. Stuart Leslie Goddard, 11-3-54, London) played and networked his act onto **Malcolm McLaren**'s turf. Ant coalesced a drum duo for a big rhythm section, catapulting to seven top tenners in the U.K. in the fledgling 80s, like Cinderella-spiked "Prince Charming" (NC 1981; #1, 9-81 U.K.). Ant pioneered British video scene with pirate/Highwayman get-up. Ant's act split into glam spin-off **Bow Wow Wow**, whose sugar jag ("I Want Candy" #62, '82) we already spun into a Kelly-blue sno-cone. Ant shuffled talent, for he had (#17, 3-90) "Room at the Top." Gothic Rock doesn't quite fit the neat tidy parameters of GRAVEYARD ROCK. Or DRAG RACE ROCK. Gothic Rock takes in Adam's work, plus gloomy tunes from Wake-Up-Little-Siouxsie's Banshees, plus die-hard ditties from groups/artists like **Bauhaus**, **Nick Cave**, or the **Cure**. Many rolled into Techno-Synth under the crafty lead vocal techniques of a former Banshee with the actual name of (not Jello Biafra or Lardmouth Rainbow Crackerjack) BOB SMITH:

"Love Song" – The Cure, #2(1), 8-89. "Friday I'm in Love" (#12, '92) is their best tune. With Lawrence Tolhurst on drums till 1990, tenor Smith's cure for anonymity was "Just Like Heaven" (#40, 10-87). Gothic Rock waffles between Punk and New Wave, waddling through lyrical gloom. "Love Song" moves beyond the earlier phase of draculine lipstick adorning pallid funereal skin. A full moon brings out Gothic Rockers with moonscreen (MPF Moon Protection Factor 13). Check out the bone-white pallor of Shock Rock **Marilyn Manson**, named for psycho killer Charles Manson and for Marilyn Monroe (though 'Marilyn,' like 'Alice Cooper." is male). Manson does *Letterman* and *Leno* more than he sings (Al. #31, 11-95 *Smells Like Children*). Because of his blasphemy-for-fun-and-profit sense of humor, few fundamentalist Christians are big

M.M. fans. To 2000, Manson's HOT 100 record page comes up ghostly white and blank.

Smith? Bob Smith? Nope, no problem. Just a cure. Cure's *Wild Mood Swings* (Al. #12, 5-96) made their *Wish* (Al. #2(1), 5-92) come true. The Smiths fell into this Gothic Rock bag, too – no relation to the **Smithereens** (#37, 2-92 "Too Much Passion") or **Smith** (#5, 9-69, Shirelles' Hard-Rock echo of "Baby, It's You"). All in all, the GOTHIC ROCK move is a Bates-Motel final-vinyl rest stop on the transcontinental Rock and Roll freeway.

"My Best Friend's Girl" – The Cars, #35, 10-78. Singer/ songwriter **Ric Ocasek** bounces along on a whole basketball court of **Buddy Holly** and **Bobby Vee** ("Rubber Ball" #6, '60) 'wo-uh-hos,' hammering hiccups, and glottal stops. Born in Baltimore, Ocasek's Boston trip collected the Cars: **Benjamin Orr** on bass and vocals; keyboarder Greg Hawkes of Baltimore; lead guitar Elliot Easton (nee Shapiro); David Robinson, drummer. "My Best Friend's Girl" is an ancient theme in pop music, first exemplified by **Vernon Dalhart**'s #4, 12-24 "The Pal That I Loved (Stole the Gal That I Loved)." Anyhow, Ric Ocasek juggles the dilemma – how did the girl get to be his best friend's girl, because she used to be his? [Or catch **Ral Donner/Starfires**' #19, 4-61 "Girl of My Best Friend"].

"Let's Go" – Cars, #14, 6-79. Sports or Jock Rock list, like **Ray Charles**'s #1(2), 9-61 bye-bye starting pitcher anthem – "Hit the Road, Jack." The first "Let's Go" is a boss instrumental. It's based, like Rick's hiccups on Cricket hiccups and paradiddles:

"Let's Go (Pony)" – Routers, #19, 11-62. Mike Gordon and Scott Engle's quintet. Engle later joined Righteous Brothers-ish group the **Walker Brothers** (#13, 4-66 "The Sun Ain't Gonna Shine Anymore" #1, 3-66, U.K.). Though you may not recollect this song's title, artists, and chart number, I know you know this song from football games. You'll also recognize it as **Toni Basil**'s rhythm track for her #1(1), '82 "Mickey."

The "Let's Go" beat doubles up a 16th-note drum roll with the following hand clapping pattern at bottom of page.

You can blast the **Dick Dale & the Del-Tones** 16th-note Surf Guitar blur on the guitar or bass to augment Routers' driving drums and Surf Rock flavor. Dick Dale's warp-speed right-hand riffs are a frantic forerunner of hyperactive Punk guitar speed blurs, and Speed Metal/Heavy Metal. The Cars' "Let's Go" has its own rock-steady flavor, with a hint of Reggae, but mostly, it's just a fun song.

"You Might Think" – Cars, #7, 3-84. Sometimes the best parts of songs are the invisible GHOST NOTES. Ghost notes, as in **Clapton**'s solos. Huh? Take **Phil Spector/ Ronettes**' pregnant finger-popping pause on Girls Group #2, '63 "Be My Baby." Or hang-fire silence and Bill Haley's tacets on #1(8), '55 "Rock Around the Clock." These small silences make the cool crashing of the full band more sensational. "You Might Think" has some of the best jiffy silences ever to grace Rock music. Ocasek's trapeze tenor leaps with rhythmic thunder.

"Tonight She Comes" – Cars, #7, 11-85. Greg Hawkes whooshes the organ; David Robinson slams the intro drums. "Tonight She Comes" and "You Might Think" float along on Ocasek's underplayed quickeroo vocal. He clips and snips syllables. Flagstone to flagstone, swirling stepping-stone salmon stream. **Orr**'s rippling bass bridges the frothing spillway.

Notice *pizzicato* plunking of the muted guitar strings. The Cars loaf along. Muffled plinks. Steam calliope wheezes. Neat, controlled sound. Out of the Punk Rock tradition, the Cars slalom into New Wave on water-skis. You don't hear *basso profundo* anger. No screeching agony. No scream of pure rage. You get the idea that nope, they're not too mad about anything. Few petty annoyances, maybe. Just a rocking little relationship. Ocasek handles 90% of the lead vocals.

Car-Tunes? Ironically, their biggest hit, #3, 3-84 "Drive" (#1 Adult Contemporary), features the tremendous lead vocal of bassman **Benjamin Orr** (1953-2000). Next in line is #4, 11-81 "Shake It Up," with debut #27, 6-78 "Just What I Needed" and "You Are the Girl" (#17, 8-87). Albums? Their sextuple-platinum *The Cars* (6 million) only hit #18, topping all the low-number TOP 200 triumphs. Also #3, 6-79 *Candy-O*, #3, 4-84 *Heartbeat City*, and #5, 9-80 *Panorama*.

Like **Mick Jagger**, or **Steven Tyler** of Aerosmith, Ric is regally thin. For Rock singers, wasp waistlines can be achieved through rigorous cross-country training. Or by the dreaded PUSHAWAY (push away from the dinner table). Mick Jagger jogs. Some unnamed rockers achieve this lean, mean look through the 'miracle of chemistry.' Greenies, ludes, club drugs, steroids, speed, bennies, dex, coke, crack, Ecstasy, pot, cigs, booze. [The Cars are INNOCENT of this overindulgence]. *Gold Rush* spends precious little time dissecting stars' coke and smoke diets, sordid affairs, and kinky habits. We've ignored an ugly fanzine downswoop to 'Heroin Chic,' starring fanmag cover ghouls with pasty pallid ennui faces, chicken-track

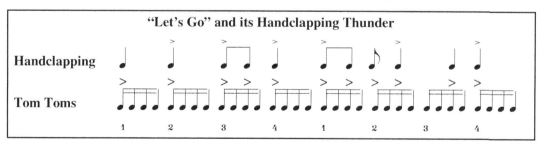

"Let's Go" and its Handclapping Thunder

Handclapping

Tom Toms

1   2   3   4   1   2   3   4

needly skinny arms, and Critical Condition stamped on their frowzy frowns.

Is it safe to say we're just in it for the MUSIC? Nah. If these personalities didn't lead such fascinating lives, this book might be reduced to a cup of quarter notes, a dollop of drum-thump, a twangy twist of twiddly guitars, and a supercharged hiccup on afterburners. If it weren't for the hot people that make the cool music, we'd have a lean tome indeed, with no punch and power.

Ocasek hit the solo charts with #15, 9-86 "Emotion in Motion," off Al. #31, 10-86 *This Side of Paradise*. The Cars roared from New Wave to Punk and back into their own Express Lane. For the Wishy-Washy record, let's call them a great ROCK Band.

"Girls Just Want to Have Fun" – Cyndi Lauper, #2, 12-83; #80, 4-84 R & B. Like **Madonna**, Cyndi (b. '53, Queens, New York) did her own thing. At age seventeen, she hitchhiked with her dog Sparkle to Canada, studying art in Vermont. Luke Crampton tells of her first bands like "Blue Angel" causing her bankruptcy (she lost the entire $232.16 fortune). When New Wave hit the U.S.A., Cyndi fashioned a ruffly-strip skirt of NEWSPAPER (like a *Mad* magazine 1955 paper eucalyptus tree). Cyndi brandished a new vivid rainbow of hair: Punk pink, orange, chartreuse, and passion purple.

Cyndi Lauper's debut album, *She's So Unusual* (34, 2-84), featured this quixotic title. Cyndi's multi-hued escape from the existential shadow of gray-slush despair signaled a New Wave of soprano swagger. No naïve born-yesterday ingénue, Cyndi has a streetwise swagger. She zaps gloom with frisky smile, sugary-chic Minnie Mouse blouse, and perky upbeat energy. Cyndi's #1 idol, like Ric Ocasek's, is Buddy Holly. In "Girls," Cyndi warbles a wonderland of Holly hiccups. She also squeals nifty yodel-kicks like **Johnny Horton, Eddie Cochran**, or New Orleans wunderkind **Frankie Ford** ("Sea Cruise" #14, 3-59). With her impish Goldie Hawn smile, she whirls her big blooming blousy poodle skirt of tattered newsprint. She whisks a rainbow of dazzling dervish hugga-bunny charm in the new *MTV* milieu. A funky guitar merges with a **Lawrence Welk** bubble machine (#1, 12-60 "Calcutta," North Dakota bandleader). Cyndi sings from the squashed streets of midnight Manhattan. Date with destiny. Behind the bubble machine, she bankrolls a squeaky, squealing organ that cradles her girlish Brooklynese lyric soprano.

Like Madonna in "Papa Don't Preach" (#1[2], 6-86), Cyndi has a 'discussion' with her dear ol' dad; Cyndi's real-life dad split when she was just five. A chattering fife helps counter her song-dad's fuddy-duddy arguments. She prates teenage liberation in her pearly soprano. She is up to no harm, she insists, with hiccups and bloops and whoops and chortles. Please, Daddy, just a good time with my friends . . . She is up to no shenanigans, she wheedles. A Macy's credit-card twinkle lights up her cute eyes. Just a good time . . .

A nice disco-thump 124 beats/minute, with yodel-kicks like **Little Richard**'s #17, 1-56 "Tutti Fruiti." "Girls" has Soul.

"FUN" GIRLS' BACKBEAT

Tempo: 124

Treble

Bass

1   2   3   4

"Good Rockin' Tonight" – Wynonie Harris, NC, 1948; #1(1), 5-48 R & B. Along with songwriter Roy Brown's R & B #11, 6-48 version, the Blues classic gets tagged often as the first true R & R song. Recorded by **Elvis** in 1954 on Sun, and by **Buddy Holly** on home tape recorder. Also Pat Boone's #49, 1-59. A little male kiss and tell braggadocio?

"Rockin' at Midnight" – Honeydrippers, #25, 1-85. Led Zep leftovers **Robert Plant** and **Jimmy Page** team with guitar guru **Jeff Beck** and Chic's **Nile Rodgers**. Roy Brown medley, with hints of his "Good Rockin' Tonight." Not that **Cyndi Lauper** hypes the Harris-Brown sound, nope. But some of her little vocal touches are reminiscent of their basic Boogie style. Cyndi's costume chic darts back to the original stage show Boogie blaster, **Louis Jordan**:

"Choo Choo Ch'Boogie" – Louis Jordan and His Tympani Five, #7, 8-46; #1(18), 8-46, R & B. EIGHTEEN WEEKS AT #1 for the neon sax man Jordan! Cited by Prof. Steve Marcuson as a bridge to Rock and Roll. In 1950, Jordan offered "You Dyed Your Hair Chartreuse." (Cyndi must have bought it). Bandleader Jordan slam-dunked 40s hits galore. Jordan's jumpin' jivey Big Band started the rock rolling. Way before *MTV*, maybe even universal TV itself, Jordan hyped the video aspect with neon saxophones swaying in formation. His "Caldonia [Boogie]" at #6, 6-45 and #1(7), 5-45 R& B features comedy yodel-kick falsetto. Jordan's #2(3), 7-44 "Is You Is Or Is You Ain't (My Baby)," despite only hitting #3 R & B, but incredibly #1(5) Country, practically defined the term Rhythm & Blues.

Jordan's initial Rock and Roll offerings include the #3, 10-42 R & B only "I'm Gonna Leave You on the Outskirts of Town." His blatantly politically incorrect follow up (#1, R & B, 11-42)? "What's the Use of Getting Sober (When You Gonna Get Drunk Again)?"

We can't ignore the video component of Cyndi Lauper, any more than we can ignore the video power of Elvis's "Jailhouse Rock" shtick, or Louis Jordan's #21, 9-47 "Boogie Woogie Blue Plate," which domineered the R & B charts at #1(14) in August 1947. Jordan's video act was meant to be watched on *MTV*, if they'd just had the futuristic foresight to invent it . . .

"Time After Time" – Cyndi Lauper, #1(2), 4-84; #78, 5-84 R & B. Change-of-pace second hit. Hard to trump a #2 song, but Cyndi did. Remember British Caravelles' airy, breathy "You Don't Have to Be a Baby to Cry" (#3, 11-63)? Few do? Lofts a fresh, sweet whispery melody like Cyndi's "Time" or Paris Sisters' #5, 9-61 "I Love How You Love Me." Pretty song.

"True Colors" – Cyndi Lauper, #1(2), 8-86. Echoes last whispery tune. Cyndi hurled many hot hits into the Rock Arena, like #3, 7-84 "She Bop" with the same 'self-awareness' theme as #3, 10-92 Madonna's "Erotica" or Christina Amphletl's Austrian Divinyls's #4, 3-91 "I Touch Myself." "All Through the Night" hit #5, 10-84; Cyndi's zany and madcap "The Goonies 'R' Good Enough" was #10, 5-85, and 11-86 "Change of Heart" hit #3. Or take her #6, 5-89 "I Drove All Night" (two seasons – winter and construction). Cyndi fractures labelmongers. Punk? New Wave? Good ol' Rock and Roll? Breathy Balladeer? Who cares? It's fun to have her in the R & R arena. She just wants to have fun. Who doesn't? Rock on . . .

"White Wedding" – Billy Idol, #108, 11-82; #35, 5-83. This Idol gesture scorches Billy's PUNK & ROCKER mode. Dangerous wedding. Billy asks the song's little sister – rhythm guitars and maxi-bass snarling – just what she has done. Billy's (b. '55, New London) early band name categorized estranged youths nurtured, as some said, on Gloomy Tunes and vinegar – GENERATION X. Billy Idol's "White Wedding" swaggers with a veiled threat. Skillful sarcasm powers this bitter sibling classic. Nice day, he prods, to throw a WHITE WEDDING! He snarls the title. Rattlesnakes have hissed up close, with less danger, than the way Idol pronounces "White Wedding." Showdown at Apache Gulch or Tombstone? "White Wedding" notoriety followed his debut #23, 7-82 "Hot in the City." Billy Idol never actually mentions unwanted pregnancy, but you have an inkling something hasty spurs Sis's marital experiment.

"Rebel Yell" – Billy Idol, #46, 1-84. Like many stars, Idol's best numbers often languish on the lower rungs. His easy-beat follow-up, "Eyes Without a Face" #4, 5-84, has a very surrealistic title of grotesquerie interfacing dreamy melody. "Yell" may not be rated PG, but it's got one of the kickiest beats and screamingest vocals in any Rock and Roll song anytime or anywhere. "Rebel" and "Wedding" both hit Top Ten U.K. In U.K., Idol puffed his image by Presley posing via his sensuous super sneer. Like vintage Early Elvis, Idol's earlier rockers are tremendous (also NC Euro-hit "Twistin' by the Pool"). In 1986 he reprised William Bell's old #45, 1969 "I Forgot to Be Your Lover" as his own #6 "To Be a Lover." His #1(1), 9-87 "Mony Mony 'Live'" monster captures Tommy James's #3, 4-68 electric energy. Idol cruised with the "Cradle of Love" to #2(1), 5-90. Big Bopper's Beaumont, Texas, neighbor Johnny Preston hit #7 with 3-60 "Cradle of Love," a different song, followed by super falsetto #14, 6-60 "Feel's So Fine." The ONLY 50s Teen Idol ACCORDIONIST? Tony Bellus – #25, 4-59 "Robbin' the Cradle."

"King for a Day" by Thompson Twins, hit #8, 1-86. Besides their biggee #3, 2-84 "Hold Me Now," these New Wave Anglo-Kiwi un-twins unfurled the regal banner. With new MIDI Techno-Synth keyboard technology and drum-programming, they hit #11, 5-84 with "Doctor! Doctor!". Also scored on #28, 9-89 "Sugar Daddy."

"Heartbreaker" – Pat Benatar, #23, 12-79. Born Pat Andrzjewski ('53, Long Island, New York). Semi-Punk Rocker Pat horrified the sounds of silence with her Rock and Roll fire. "Heartbreaker" suggests the gusto of Gracie Slick on #5, 4-67 "Somebody to Love" or Janis Joplin on "Piece of My Heart" #12, 8-68. Due to outfits and nail polish, Pat gets plunked into Punk. Twin #5's "Love Is a Battlefield" (9-83) and "We Belong" 10-84. Or Punkish anthem #9, 10-80 "Hit Me with Your Best Shot." OK, but she's a straight Rock and Roll star. More later. Pat pumps Polish-American Heartland Rock.

"People Are People" – DePeche Mode, #13, 5-85. All-Synth band from Basildon, Essex. David Gahan, vocals. French for 'fast fashion.' Signature songs? #8, 4-90 "Enjoy the Silence" and #28, 12-89 "Personal Jesus."

"Whip It" – Devo, #14, 8-80. Robbie-the-Robot Rock? Our car fortunately blew out a tire in Mogadore, suburb of Devo's Akron, Ohio, tire capital of the world (three for the price of 1¼ tires). Devo's philosophical premise? The first New Wave Robot group watched the "Gotta Get Outa This Place" mood of fleeing factories. Devo posited the idea that the world was devolving, or retrogressing, as in Dean R. Koontz's thriller Midnight. We are lurching backwards in surrendering comforts of civilization. Akron, once-grand tire town of hefty Victorian homes, is swathed in smoke and soot and steel. People work and drink hard. Shot and beer anesthesia 12-hour shifts, tiresome tires with toxic fumes. The Goodyear Blimp started here. Like the tragic fated 1937 Hindenburg zeppelin crash, Devo sees civilization collapsing (entropy) from within. Hence, Devo dons robot costumes, paints their faces gray, and sings ginchy songs like "Whip It."

Devo's song plugs their "Rustbelt" environment, like #59, 5-83 "Theme from Doctor Detroit." Akron straddles the great gritty coalmines of nearby Western Pennsylvania. Devo peddles Gothic Rock pessimism, imported from R & B coal-miner Lee Dorsey (#8, 7-66 "Working in the Coal Mine"). Devo met at Kent State, where Neil Young and Fred Peacock (plus Julie Tkach/Phil Hruska) dedicated songs to the four students killed at the All-American Ohio college by National Guardsmen with scared and hasty triggers in the antiwar protest of 1970: Neil's four dead at "Ohio" anthem and Fred's "KS Rebellion" (both NC). Devo was two brother combinations: Mark and Bob Motherbaugh and Jerry and Bob Casale, plus Alan Myers.

"I Ran (So Far Away)" – A Flock of Seagulls, #9, 7-82. Brothers Mike/Al Score scored with British New Wave classic, plus space age love song called "Space Age Love Song" (#30, 11-82). Anything in parentheses? Yep – #26, 5-83 "Wishing (If I Had a Photograph of You)."

"Hungry Like the Wolf" – Duran Duran, #3, 12-82. Speaking of odd family combos, Duran2 features the following re-tailored **Taylors**: guitar man **Andy**, bassman **John**, and drummer **Roger Taylor**. NONE OF THESE TAYLOR BANDMATES IS RELATED. **Nick Rhodes**, keyboards. From redbrick Birmingham, England, Duran Duran twanged their way to the lupine legends of Yellowknife, NWT Canada. Techno-Synth flair. Duran2 is among the first rock groups to tour Communist China.

"Werewolves of London" – Warren Zevon, #21, 3-78. If you ravenously crave real Gothic Rock, seek out Zevon's midnight haunt. He whoops up background banter of "How-oooo" wolfy wails. Session superstars include guitarist **Jackson Browne**, drummer **Mick Fleetwood**, and bassist **John McVie**. Eerie foggy echo of Three Dog (Wolf?) Night's utopian road to "Shambala" (#3, 5-73). Only furry beasties prowl the dank deserted streets. According to Zevon expert Larry Barnes, "Werewolves of London" inspired Michael Jackson's ultimate #1 "Thriller" million-dollar-production video. This **Barnes**-storm video was voted #1 EVER in 2001.

"Watching the Detectives" – Elvis Costello, #108, 3-78. Liverpool Buddy Holly lookalike and Elvis Presley namesake leaped Atlantic in vanguard of the first New Wave. Elvis C. was not exactly Punk. He loved cryptic Dylanesque lyrics, Gifted with a tony tenor and surreal lyrical expertise, the New [Elvis] Wave smacked the American shore.

Elvis Costello's popular upswing was flanked by three excellent sidemen – bassist Bruce Thomas, drummer Pete Thomas and **Steve Nason** on keyboards. Costello excels on far-out Rockabilly extravaganzas like "The Angels Want to Wear My Red Shoes." Costello, however, attached a crafty warning label onto his Al. #50, 11-81 *Almost Blue*:

ELVIS II's DISCLAIMER

This album contains Country and Western music and may produce radical reactions in narrow-minded people.

Elvis Costello favors all phases of Rock and Roll: Blues, Soul, Country, and Folk-Rock. His albums' success scorched his singles, topping out at #10 in 2-79 with *Armed Forces*, #11, 3-80 *Get Happy*, #24, 8-83 *Punch the Clock* and #32, 2-89 *Spike*. By 1986, album titles delightfully flaunted the absurd: #84, 10-86 *Blood and Chocolate* and #39, 4-86 *The Elvis Costello Show (Featuring Elvis Costello) – King of America*. [Sorry, but Rock traditionalists accept only ONE Elvis as King of America].

"Veronica" – Elvis Costello, #19, 4-89. Costello, master of melody, is buoyed by the addition of Rock and Roll's most famous bass guitarist (and coincidentally, co-writer) **Paul McCartney**. Rocking on, Elvis thrived on *All the Useless Beauty* (Al. #53, 6-96).

"Everyday I Write the Book" – Elvis Costello, #36, 8-83. [I have perhaps never felt personally closer to a song title.] Elvis Costello was born in two places: Whitburn says Liverpool, Clarke says Paddington in London, home of Michael Bond's kiddie-lit Winnie-the-Pooh-pal *Paddington Bear* and singer **Seal**. Costello (b. **Declan Patrick McManus**, '55), is often considered the main New Wave British Invader for a generation (like Al. #34, 3-94 *Brutal Youth*), and made the Rock Hall in 2003.

Elvis Costello was arrested for singing. Yes. At a CBS convention, he tried to get himself signed by serenading the record moguls and moxie millionaires. Busted for 'busking,' he went on to stardom anyhow. Wallflowers rarely show up at #1. Unless you're hiding the one-in-a-billion voice of an Orbison under a bushel, you must shine your own light when chasing stardom. Nobody's gonna make you a star!

Two exceptions: *Big Beat Heat* writer **John Jackson** told me the story of **Fabian** (Forte)'s meteoric rise. Entrepreneur **Bob Marcucci**'s brother lived in a Philly row house next door to handsome 16-year-old Fabian. Marcucci happened upon a Forte family tragedy – the EMS ambulance was hauling the elder Mr. Forte out on a stretcher (heart attack he survived -- kid's newfound income helped). Though Marcucci's cohort said Fabian 'couldn't carry a tune in a bucket,' the Cameo elves spliced chunks of the suave hunk's spoken-style baritone. With a few *American Bandstand* shots, hope turned to hype. Fabian became an Insta-Idol to a coterie of looks-oriented 'teenyboppers' who adored him. Exception #2 – released in May 1996, **Jakob Dylan and the Wallflowers**' album *Bringing Down the Horse* glommed Top 10 in March 1997. *Rolling Stone*'s Gerri Hirshey paints Bob Dylan's kid (6-12-97) with "sharp Armani shoulders, sterling Samoyed-blue eyes . . . [and] feisty as the old man." Hirshey laments that Jakob's revolutionary dad was just a guy back in her Social Studies book.

"Tiger" – Fabian, #3, 6-59. Right-place, right-time. Fabian Forte (b. '43, Philly) dazzled 50s girls with his Elvis waterfall haircut, hunk bod, and his big cat song. Also twin #9s, 3-59 "Turn Me Loose" and 11-59 Elvis-echo "Hound Dog Man."

"99 Luftballons" – Nena, #2(1), 12-83. Gabriele 'Nena' **Kerner** of Hagen, Germany, and her peace party of 'Greens' (Save-the-Earth, like Greenpeace) sent up 99 balloons to protest nuclear power. A 1979 nuclear accident (called 'event' or 'incident' by Nuclear Regulatory Commission) rocked Three Mile Island, Pennsylvania. An 'event' at Chernobyl stole thousands of lives in the Ukraine from this generation and the next. It was also before good ol' cartoon schlump 'Homer Simpson' took control of his local power plant.

"West End Girls" – Pet Shop Boys, #1(1), 3-86. **Neil Tennant**, British fan mag *Smash Hits* writer, joined keyboard man **Chris Lowe**. Their exotic blend of New Wave and Techno synthesizes an easygoing sound. In the spirit of Reagonomics: #10, 5-86 "Opportunities (Let's Make

Lots of Money)" has a real **Barrett Strong** Motown message echo. Pop-Rock triumphs: #9, 6-86 "It's a Sin"; Willie Nelson's #5, '82 hit "Always on My Mind" to #4, 3-88, #18, 10-88 "Domino Dancing."

"The Safety Dance" – Men Without Hats, #3, 6-83. Early Techno-New Wave brother-trio from Montreal, Quebec. First verse is maybe RAP, check it out. **Ivan Doroschuk** is singer-sogwriter. Brother **Stefan** plays violin and guitar, and brother **Colin** helped out. Like "Luftballons" the veiled message was anti-nuclear, like many songs of Jackson Browne. Hatless guys enjoyed #13, 8-83 Al. *Rhythm of Youth.* Infectious thrum. Catchy tune, impossible to get out of your head (good sign of a hit). Matter-of-fact vocal touts dancers as friends, non-dancers as outcasts. Guys had a second single based on #1, 1825 "Pop Goes the Weasel" – "Pop Goes the World" to #20, 10-87. From 'Up Over' to Down Under:

"Down Under" – Men at Work, #1(4), 11-82. These Australian Rockers picked up a New Wave of hammering bass and drums (**John Rees** and **Jerry Speilser**). With **Ron Strykert** on lead guitar, singer and rhythm guitarist **Colin James Hay** sprang to TWO #1's in a row. Following debut #1(1), 7-82 "Who Can It Be Now?" "Down Under" Australian travelogue touts a place everyone wants to go: kangaroos, wombats, and world-class surf! Men at Work squashed "Overkill" to #3, 4-83. "It's a Mistake" wasn't, at #6, 6-83. Switcheroo "Dr. Heckyll & Mr. Jive" hit #28, 9-83. Then they split. Politics?

Other Aussie goodtime tunes? **Charlie Drake**'s #21, 1-62 "My Boomerang Won't Come Back," and #3, 6-63 "Tie Me Kangaroo Down, Sport" (rhymes 'platypus'-duck with 'amok'), by **Rolf Harris**.

Australia's **AC/DC** (singer Bon Scott, guitar-guy brothers Angus and Malcolm Young) hit #37 with "Back in Black," and #23 in 12-90 with "Moneytalks." In September 1980 they hit big with #35 "You Shook Me All Night Long." AC/DC was elected to the Rock Hall for 2003.

"Call Me" – Blondie, #1(6), 2-80. Six different "Call Me" songs/melodies in Rock Era: #13, '70, Aretha Franklin; #21, '58 Johnny Mathis; #22, '66 Chris Montez; #26, '82 Skyy; #54, '85 and '86, Go West & Styx's Dennis DeYoung – all different songs called "Call Me." Blondie's "Call Me" leads the pack. **Go West** did bouncy #8, 5-90 "King of Wishful Thinking." Blondie's #24, 6-79 "One Way or Another" is a rock classic, like her #37, 5-82 "Island of Lost Souls," splashed by subterranean New Waves.

"She Blinded Me with Science" – Thomas Dolby, #5, 2-83. Dolby's sound graces movie *Howard the Duck.* Audio/video MIDI pioneer with synthesizer and techno state-of-the art innovations. As Punk often dovetailed into 'Alternative,' much Old New Wave metamorphosed into Middle-Aged Wave and then Techno-Synth. In the after-Math of his "Science" hit, Dolby's (b. '58, Cairo, Egypt) vivid imagination surged: #67, 6-83 "Europa and the Pirate Twins," and #62, 2-84 "Hyperactive." Dolby married *Dynasty* queen Kathleen Belle.

So long, Old New Wave section. Now we slosh to the Middle-Age Wave section. Thence to the Really New New Wave section. Their resurrective capabilities are miraculous.

"The Mayor of Simpleton" – XTC, #72, 4-89. Middle-Aged Wave bouncy melody, unique spindrift lyric. **Colin Moulding**, bass, **Andy Partridge**, guitar, **Dave Gregory** keyboards. Very much unlike Old Wave songs like Gary Numan's #9, 2-80 "Cars."

"No One Is To Blame" – Howard Jones, #4, 4-86. Whitburn calls Howard a synth wizard. Paul and Linda McCartney and Smith's Morrissey called him a noble fellow militant vegetarian. At Manchester University, Jones and his first synthesizer became a one-man band, and top-notch entertainment. At 15, Howard's family emigrated to Canada, but he returned to England and Manchester. His new song, "New Song," hit U.K. #3, followed by three more top ten U.K. singles, and a #1 U.K. album – *Human's Lib.* Jones's #10, 4-85 album *Dream into Action* nudged the Top Ten. "No One" features **Phil Collins** on drums. Jones stood up for political causes ('Meat is Murder' movement), and strove to liberate downtrodden. Other Jones' smashes? #5, 3-85 "Things Can Only Get Better"; "Everlasting Love" (#12, 3-89), plus #32, 4-92 "Lift Me Up."

"Sweet Dreams" – Eurythmics, #1(1), 5-83. The BIG VOICE of the Eurythmics is Aberdeen, Scotland's **Annie Lennox** (b. Christmas Day, 1954). Doubling on flute and keyboards, singer/songwriter Lennox lofted this haunting tune. Gimmick? Oh, yeah. Her short hair. The guy's suit. The dress-for-success guy tie with power print. The poker-face delivery. Annie and gimmicks? Well, it's easy not to hit #1. Munching her monotonic short range of notes, Annie's sugary dreams rampage the hot globe and seven swirling seas, beset by aerial pandemonium and strange squeaky squeals. Quite a quest. Soon they bop on back to the Scottish stratus cloud, and wan dusk grey. No relation to **Patsy Cline**'s #44, 3-63 (#5 C) Country classic "Sweet Dreams (Of You)." Patsy reprises #2(1), 6-56 Country **Faron Young** hit, later **Tommy McLain** smash (#15, 5-66). Weather Channel [Kristina Abernathy], anyone?

"Here Comes the Rain" – Eurythmics, #4, 1-84. David **Stewart** is the Eurythmics' other resident musical maestro. He composes, sings, synthesizes, and plays guitar. He harmonizes with Annie's smooth contralto effortlessly and Everlyishly. This rainy song flagged *Touch* as a top album (#7, 2-84) for Aberdeen's Annie, from the Scottish Highlands. Annie's duo with **Aretha Franklin** netted empowerment hit #18, 10-85 "Sisters Are Doin' It for Themselves"; also #21, 5-84 "Who's That Girl" (the Un-Madonna tune), and #23, 9-83 "Love Is a Stranger." Their #1 Album Rock "Missionary Man" was #14, 7-86. Annie's hot mellow-rock rep soared in 4-95 with her gorgon-glutted Al. #11 *Medusa.*

Soon Lennox doffed her austere garb, grew out her

hair, and displayed a very versatile and melodic voice: reprise of #4, 6-69 **Jackie DeShannon**'s "Put a Little Love in Your Heart" with **Al Green** (#39, 11-88, NC, R & B). Annie's #14, 9-92 "Walking on Broken Glass" features her rich throbbing vocal, great harmonizers, and session bass player's extravagant riffs. Annie's #23, 3-95 "No More 'I Love You's'" is a haunting and globally universal sentiment. Her punctuationally tragic title coruscates down the corridors of your memory. She's selling sincerity here – not hype or hypocrisy. Annie's integrity is a major part of her charm.

Techno can merge somewhat with new Wave, but Punk grades more into the Alternative banner. Green Day's **Billie Joe** (Armstrong), **Mike Dirnt** (nee Pritchard, guitar), and Tre Cool Neo-Punk (drums) conquered 1994 in Neo-Punk pandemonium.

"Basket Case" – Green Day, NC, '94; #26A, 8-94; #9, 8-94 Album Rock Tracks. The lyric leads off with this zinger: singer gives SELF creeps. Calibrating paranoia, Green Day blends a of frantic ranting joy with wry slashy lyrics. At blow-your-top tempo, the song races 111mph toward the brick wall of nihilism, or belief in nothing (with a side of futility). Green Day flashes back to old London, with sooty grey existential despair. Creaky wooden shacks flanked grimy redbrick high-rise warrens. Stodgy staid society took a peek at the Sex Pistols and the Clash, shuddered, and went back to sleep. America embraced them and the **Ramones**, in an afterglow of Iggy and the Dolls and Alice Cooper, and all the Zap-the-Establishment bands since Gene Vincent almost out-Elvised Elvis.

Rock and Roll has always been about rebellion. When actor (and bongo-drum basher) **James Dean** rebelled against the speed limit on that fateful September 30, 1955 California highway, and crashed into Don Turnipseed at 85mph, he set the pattern that would reverberate out of all the amps of all the ages with all the thunder of a hundred thousand tornadoes.

On *Dookie*, Al. #2(2), 2-94 Green Day brings Rock and Roll full circle to 9+ million buyers. First, American R & R icons influenced British Invasion rockers. American Folk Rockers and Psychedelia mushroomed. **Iggy** and the **MC5** ricocheted into Heavy Metal and Glam Rock. Glam birthed Disco via Soul. Robbie the Robot bopped into the Techno mix at the Disco. Punks were both purists (Rockabilly Roots) and radicals ('Anarchy in the U.K.'). Anger abated. New Wave bypassed Surf Rock, flirting with Graveyard or Gothic Rock, with doldrums of despair.

Berkeley California's Billie Joe jams his staccato chords. **Tre Cool** prods Prozac-droning folks to snap up and listen. **Mike Dirnt** brings bottom rhythms up to the top. Future Shock catapults dreams into a vortex. An abyssal void of confusion. Green Day offers no consolation. Just an invitation to rave-up thrash clash. While striving to embrace ourselves as our best friends, sometimes we wonder if we're good enough. Iffy era. Green Day says

it's a "basket case."

Beyond the surging, slashing guitars . . . beyond the gnarly robust baritone squawks of Neo-Punk defiance, there beats a spitfire hope and a passionate promise that this old blue-green living planet may just keep on keepin' on. California, here we come:

"Geek Stink Breath" – Green Day, NC, 1995; #27A, 10-95; #9, 10-95 Album Rock Tracks. No more Mr. Nice Title. Punk revels in the grotesque, slimy, absurd. Like 12-95 "Brain Stew/Jaded" [#35A], the Punk ethos can find equal boredom in the British barrios or Kingston carnivals or Motown busted-glass basketball projects. **Green Day**'s single-figure top tune is #6A, 12-94 "When I Come Around." Or #11A[Airplay], 12-97 "Good Riddance (Time of Your Life); or #3, 10-2000 Modern Rock Tracks – "Warning."

BORING is one of the catchwords and buzz signals of Neo-Punk style. It catches the ultra-new Wave of Alternative angst. Wobbling and waddling through an old, cold universe, Green Day and their Alternative compadres **Nirvana** and **Soundgarden** and **Pearl Jam** feel a **Mad Max** or **Soylent Green** energy which hurls them into a brownish grey future, a *Waterworld* of cheerless bewilderment. They have their good moods too, but much of the soft underbelly of the Boring Revolution explores glum gloom.

In "Basket Case," Billie Joe asks whether we all have time to heed his WHINE. WHINE is nothing new under the sun. Our generation whined too. In "Basket Case," life is a 500-piece jigsaw puzzle with 250 pieces missing. You might say – how can he moan and groan with a zillion seller? Remember, the spotlight for Elvis was always a bit squirmy – never comfy. 'Success' is a mixed bag. Like 2000s **Creed** taking us "Higher" [#1, 2000], Green Day shoots the moon. But it croaks.

Final Vinyl album buffs will be disappointed at **Dookie**'s deflated and elfin album art on the little CD. Tiny cartoon hodge-podge: mushroom cloud, soaring Sabre Jet, Dookie bombs falling, King Kongs and Neanderthal cavemen. Day's Tom Thumb cover glows with swaying palms and witches and muggers and aliens and nowhere nattering nabobs in a dance macabre of (Whee! What fun!) apocalyptic doom. Great album art never really died; it's just a victim of Weight Watchers. CD art got squashed to vignettes and miniatures (from zaftig 12" x 12" VINYL to 5 3/8" x 4¾" dinky CD). Teeny-tiny pix. Bite size.

"Basket Case" feeds all instruments in slowly. **Green Day**'s #2(1) Al. *Insomniac* of 10-95 kept critics up all night trying to decipher its creepily clandestine messages (and fun phrases). Fuming fulminations of fire and brimstone? Nah, just the good ol' band down the block. Segregated (NC, HOT 100) onto the #1 spot 10-2000 on the Modern Rock Tracks chart (FINALLY, #1 somewhere), **Green Day**'s "Minority" hammered sleepy ears with latter-day **Kinks** thunder.

"No Excuses" – Alice in Chains, #48A, 2-94. As with **Jimi Hendrix**, the Fleetwoods, and the Ventures, rainy Seattle is the home of many pioneers of the Rock Revolution. "No Excuses" surges from their #1(1), 2-94

Al. *Jar of Flies*. Alice in Chains' wildly successful album features a poor grotesque three-legged dog with a pathetic Mona Lisa smile on the stunning cover. Grunge often grooves to the macabre.

"Mr. Jones" – Counting Crows, #5A, 1-94. Adam Duritz powers Dylanesque vocals for this San Francisco Alternative band. Remember Dylan's emerging-counterculture song "Something is Happening Here, But You Don't Know What It Is, Do You, Mr. Jones?" Not be confused with the **Black Crowes**, or **Sheryl Crow**, Counting Crows make bold statements about the twisted nature of society with songs like their "Round Here" (#31A, 6-94) and #6A, 10-96 "A Long December." Counting Crows' San Francisco *August and Everything After* (#4, 1-94 Al.) gave 6 million CD buyers an opportunity to get to know "Mr. Jones" even better.

The **Black Crowes'** "She Talks to Angels" hit #30, 3-91. Alternative-to-Alternative – Black Crowes lambast Southern Hard Rock like a fastball down the middle.

"Superman's Song" – Crash Test Dummies, #56, 10-91. Winnipeg, Manitoba's Brad (singer) and Dan Roberts (bass) also marshaled the #4 1994 HOT 100 song with "Mmm Mmm Mmm Mmm" (seems we were just covering 6'6" Major Lance's magnifoop "Um Um Um Um Um Um").

"All I Want" – Toad the Wet Sprocket, #15, 6-92. Zany, obtuse, surrealistic, wild, and footloose name – TOAD THE WET SPROCKET. Sprocket? The band nabbed its name from the topsy-turvy British TV comedy *Monty Python's Flying Circus*; **Glen Phillips** handles vocals, with Dean Dinning on bass and Todd Nichols on guitar. In 1994, "Fall Down" [#1(6), 5-94 Modern Rock] fell up to #33 in June, with "Something's Always Wrong" at #41, 10-94. Not Punk, not Alternative. Just splish-splash amphibious fun on a bike. Their 10-94 Al. *Pisces Iscariot* won copper-medal #4. Toad's 1997 *Coil* features "Crazy Life" and "Little Buddha." [Muppet Kermit rides a bike].

"Free As a Bird" – Beatles, #6, 12-95. Newer Liverpool Grunge/Alternative sound. Powered by a long-gone Lennon lad with a 1977 demo vision. Also #11, 3-96 "Real Love." Lots of potential . . . like new crew the **Rolling Stones** (#94, 3-98 "Saint of Me"). Also catch Stones' Dylan #16 Album-Track-only 11-95 "Like a Rolling Stone."

"Bullet with Butterfly Wings" – Smashing Pumpkins, #22, 11-95; #2(6), Modern Rock Tracks. Seattle Grunge sound from windy Chicago: **Billy Corgan**, lead guitar, lead throat; **James Iha**, auxiliary lead guitar; D'Arcy Wretzky bass; Jimmy Chamberlin on drums. Keyboarder **Jonathan Melvoin** (1942-96) died after partying in a lonely 1996 hotel room, inspiring **Sarah McLachlan's** ballad hymn, "Angel."

Lull ('91) juggled wild titles and a slashing sound. "Rhinoceros," "Cherub Rock," and "Mayonnaise." Named for a bygone Hallowe'en spirit of outhouse tippers, window soapers, and rowdy rabble gangs up to no good, **Smashing Pumpkins'** soared to #12, 2-96 with "1979" In March

2000, Smashing Pumpkins Al. *Machina/The Machines of God* entered the charts at #3 (with Bone Thugs-N-Harmony debuting simultaneously with #2 – *Resurrection*. "Ava Adore" nailed #42, 7-98, better than "Perfect" [which hit #54, 10-98]. Their monster album? Al. #1(1) 11-95 *Mellon Collie and the Infinate Sadness*.

"Dancing Days" – Stone Temple Pilots, NC 1995; #63A, 4-95; #3, 3-95 Album Rock Tracks. Fragmented charts? Pilots' "Interstate Love Song" was #1 fifteen weeks on Album Rock Tracks – yet TOTALLY SHUT OUT on *Billboard* HOT 100 [8-94]! It hit #18A, 9-94. San Diego's **Scott Weiland** and Dean & Robert DeLeo reprise Led Zeppelin's lost cut from Al. #1(2), 3-73 *Houses of the Holy*. Previously they earned a major fan following with #1(3), 6-94 *Purple* album. By 1996, their semi-religious pilgrimage brought us Al. #4, 4-96, *Tiny Music . . . Songs from the Vatican Gift Shop*.

"March of the Pigs" – Nine Inch Nails, #59, 3-94. What's a nice Classically schooled pianist like Mercer, PA's **Trent Reznor** (b. '65) doing in a tuff-enuff outfit like 9-Inch Nails? Thrashing out contemporary consciousness. "March of Pigs" is off *The Downward Spiral* [follow-up 6-95 *Further Down the Spiral* hit #23]. With the omnipresent gray stratus cloud of Seattle floating woozily over Reznor's Pennsylvania, he ricochets a Transylvania atmosphere that forecasts Grunge. From their first album, *Pretty Hate Machine*, Al. #75, 2-90, it was obvious that Nine Inch Nails would be necessary to hammer the stake deeply into Dracula's ice-blooded heart. Their biggest is #17, 8-99 "The Day the World Went Away."

"Macarena" – Los De Mar, #102, 9-95. Like **Hank Ballard** and his #28, '60 "The Twist" covered by Chubby Checker to Insta-Fame, the biggest craze of the mid-90s actually stems from this group whose name MAR means ocean. The duo that clutched the #1(14) spot for most of late 1996 is called Los Del RIO, meaning river. Los Del RIO'S #1(14), 7-96 version may be the most popular Rock or Salsa song of all time.

"This Is a Call" – Foo Fighters, #35A, 7-95. After the sad suicide of Kurt Cobain of Nirvana, his drummer **Dave Grohl** assembled the Germs' guitarist **Pat Smear**, percussionist Bill Goldsmith, and bass guy Nate Mendel. Their name relates to a mirage or apparent flame seen by WWII fighter pilots. Album Rock Trax #6, 7-95 "This Is a Call" then #13A, 2-96 "Big Me" and 10-99 signature song "Learn to Fly," at HOT 100 #19.

"Kitty" – Presidents of the United States of America, NC, 1995; #13 Album Rock Tracks. Chris Ballew, vocals. Never President Ballew. Biggest tune? #29, 3-96 "Peaches." What 'Prez' Chris yells at a nasty cat would definitely sack his career as Sunday School teacher. Punk pokes and prods pentagons of power. Dave Dederer, Jason Finn.

"Pinch Me" – Barenaked Ladies, #15, 9-2000. What's in a NAME? Torontonian rockers **Steven Page** and **Ed**

Robertson labored for ten years to become overnight sensations. With bandmate Kevin Hearn, they fractured frenzied Barenaked Ladies' Ontario fans with impish lyrics. Not even ONE barenaked lady is in the group – just these typical guys running through garden sprinklers in gym shorts. Name gimmick. "Pinch Me" loops along, a whimsical trek through relationships. The funky bass flops the bass clef and the lyric blasts a beeline of suburban-sprawl happenings. An altogether pleasant musical experience, floating on their breezy easy laid-back lyric. Lyrical Punk overtones (with a side of Weird Al comic genius). Their Beach Boy tribute "Brian Wilson" hit #68, 11-97, and "One Week" spent one glorious week at #1[1], in 10-98. Hearn got seriously ill just when Barenaked Ladies really hit the big time (album *Maroon* DEBUTED at #5, 9-2000). Comedians **Charlie Chaplin** and **W.C. Fields** died on Christmas Day (comedy is always a bittersweet experience).

"Deja VooDoo" – Kenny Wayne Shepherd, NC 1995; #9, 10-95 Album Rock Tracks. Voodoo Blues guitar star, Kenny Wayne Shepherd (b. '77) grew up on the sultry Delta near Shreveport, Louisiana. Named for Blues legend **Leadbelly**, #108, 1-96 Al. *Ledbetter Heights* sends this Crossroads Scottish-American wunderkind soaring with Stevie Ray Vaughan expertise.

"Hooligan's Holiday" – Mötley Crüe, NC, 1994; #10, 2-94 Album Rock Tracks. **Vince Neil** flew the Crüe coop, so ex-Scream screamer **John Corabi** pinch-hit for Neil. Albums are Crüe's forte: #1(2), 9-89 *Dr. Feelgood*; #7, 4-94 *Mötley Crüe*, and #6, 7-85 *Theatre of Pain*. Mötley Crüe is not alone among Heavy Metallurgists in Metal Renaissance: ALL on the Album Rock Tracks category (only), we have #29, 11-94 "Train of Consequences" by **Megadeth**; and ½ Led Zep combo of Page and Plant to #2(3) "Gallows Pole" in 10-94; **Pantera** (Sp. 'panther') and #21, 9-94 "Planet Caravan"; solo **Ozzy Osbourne** #3, 10-95 "Perry Mason;" **Queensryche**'s #33, 5-95 "Disconnected." "Can't Stop Lovin' You" hit #2(4) Album Rock Tracks, 2-95 (only) for **Van Halen**, like their #6, 12-94 "Bridge." The Heart of Rock and Roll. Crüe bangs streetcorner chords in a waterfall of guitars and ecstasy.

"Time Bomb" – Rancid, #48, 9-95, HOT 100 Airplay; #8, 8-95 Modern Rock Tracks. Their Berkeley, California follow-up "Ruby Soho" hit #13, 12-95 on the Modern Rock Tracks Section. Strident. Singer and guitarist **Tim Armstrong**, Berkeley, California with **Lars Frederiksen**; Brett Reed handles drums and Matt Freeman bass.

"Down with Disease" – Phish, NC, 1994; #33, 5-94 Album Rock Tracks. With a fan entourage like the **Grateful Dead**, Phish pulled out *A Live One* (Al. #18, 7-95). Phish rocks with Jazz riffs and spiffy gifts. Three from Burlington, VT, sing: **Mike Gordon**, **Trey Anastasio**, **Page McConnell**. Phish encourages taping.

"Smells Like Teen Spirit" – Nirvana, #6, 12-91. **Kurt Cobain** dragged (screaming) the Alternative/Grunge Rock revolution into the American home. Song voted #1 Song of 90s in October 2000 *VH-1* poll! "Teen Spirit" comes full circle from the Beach Boys' also #6 [11-63] "Be True to Your School." Cobain, bassman Chris Novoselic, guitarist **Jason Everman** and drummers Chad Channing and **Dave Grohl** came from Aberdeen, Washington, the cloudiest place in the Lower 48 states. Their blockbuster album *Nevermind* #1(2), 10-91 scorched the decade.

On February 24, 1992, thin, blond, serious Cobain married **Courtney Love**. "With got 300 cloudy days a year and raining all the time, Aberdeen has the highest suicide rate in the United States" said Prof. Don Emerson, who fled Aberdeen to happier Monroe College, Michigan, where I first taught Rock History in 1969. Many fine well-adjusted and happy Aberdeenians might disagree with Don's assessment, but I remember the fact gloomily.

Nirvana is a Buddhist term that comes from Sanskrit Hindu and later Urdu Buddhist. NIRVANA means to EXTINGUISH DESIRE, NOT some kind of Hindu or Buddhist paradise. To zap all your worldly desires, and enter into a oneness with the cosmos (the individual soul or ATMAN conjoins with the universal soul or BRAHMAN): this is NIRVANA.

"Smells Like Teen Spirit" galvanized a 90s generation of X. Some CD buyers were fed up with smiles and sunny surfy songs of sweetness and light. Not enough songs covered the reality of life, with zits and bugs and guts and ghastly decisions to work five jobs and still starve.

Angry music was back on tap down at the Pokerface Pub. Nirvana followed up their big #6 hit with #32, 3-92 "Come As You Are." Like plane crash victim **Ritchie Valens** with one major hit, #2, 1-59 "Donna/LaBamba," Kurt Cobain spiked a legend through his tragic demise. Cobain was a young man with great promise, a charismatic personality, and a brilliant and ironic wit. After one suicide watch from a desperate incident, he finally took his own life at the home in Seattle he shared with his wife and baby – like Ernest Hemingway, it was a self-inflicted gunshot wound on 4-8-94. A whole musical movement mourned its leader and spokesman.

Kurt Cobain was the voice of the restless and intense "Generation X" era. With his strident, angst-glutted, and tormented vocal wail, he defied the comfy-yuppie establishment. Cobain challenged the tottering R & R to ditch its Big Hair Bands, plump comfy melodic chords, and Heartland twang. With his minor-key Cloud Coast dramatic dirges, he summons Roy Orbison's ghosts of the lonely, and Del Shannon's lost woe-bleak evermore drizzle. Craggy, scraggly, and haunting – the Cobain chorus endures in the millennial sounds of Staind and Creed.

Nirvana scorched the album charts, if not the HOT 100: #1(2) *Nevermind* 10-91 debut; #39 early-recordings/lost tapes/Indie stuff *Insecticide* (#39, 1-93), and their mammoth quadruple-platinum #1(1), 10-93 *In Utero*. **Kurt Cobain** grew up amidst the grey stratus gloom. He met and married a young singer with a slight physical resemblance to Blondie's Debbie Harry, a girl who fronted one of the few female Seattle Punk/Alternative/Grunge bands:

"Doll Parts" – Hole, #58, 12-94; #4, 10-94 Modern Rock Tracks. Ode to doll dismemberment. Hole escaped from Seattle scene to form L.A. band in 1989; returned. Love plays guitar, sings, and even acts. Hole functioned as a mixed gender band, starring Eric Erlandson, Patty Schamel, and Kristen Pfaff. Somberly, two years after the Cobain-Love merger, **Pfaff** was found dead in her bathtub.

"The Man Who Sold the World" – Nirvana, #39, 2-95; #6, 1-95 Modern Rock Tracks. This 'live' version arises from a David Bowie album reprise onto Nirvana's #1(1), 11-94 *MTV Unplugged in New York*. Nirvana also scored on the Album Rock Tracks list with #3, 10-94 "About a Girl." Seattle Alternative Rock (related to Grunge Rock) is mixed from gunpowder of Punk Rock and the leaden cannonballs of Heavy Metal. It's slushy lyrics bleed Dylanesque skepticism and dark imagary. The music is a minor-key barrellroll of **Doors'** angst, **Hendrix'** guitar thunder, and the **Who's** lightning-bolt 'teenage wasteland' ["Baba O'Reilly"]. Kurt Cobain's powerful cadences, minor vibrant Jazz chords, and beguiling baritone should keep his music played for a long, long, time. As his shrill, shrieking guitars trail away . . .

"Daughter" – Pearl Jam, NC, 1993; #33A, 11-93 on new HOT 100 Sales and Airplay Section. Nirvana neighbor Eddie Mueller became **Eddie Vedder**; guitarists **Mike McCready** and **Stone Gossard** joined bass boss **Jeff Ament**. **Dave Abbruzzese** switched with **Dave Krusen** as **Pearl Jam** drummer. The nucleus of Temple of the Dog crystallized into Pearl Jam. Into 1994 they assumed the princely crowns of Alternative royalty with their #1(1), 12-94 album *Vitalogy*. Four multiplatinum albums followed them to 1996. In October 2000, Vedder & Jam launched a fiery fusillade of *Live* albums from their conquests of Europe – ALL hitting the *Billboard* 200 at one time, an unprecedented gambit (two at once is rare): Poland [#103], Milan [#125] and Verona [#134], Italy; London [#137], and Hamburg, Germany [#175].

Vedder is a talented unique baritone, but doesn't deserve the rep as mouthpiece of Generation X with its full-race exploding angst and agony. His vocal swoops and glides and glissandos are the stuff of legend. They deliver an old sound in a new direction. Like their brethren **Hootie and the Blowfish** or **Creed**, Pearl Jam reflects a current world-view buzz of irony and reality and street-savvy wisdom. You can tell by their lyrics, powered by dim grim minor chords which rampage through roiling baritone passion.

Like much Protest Music in the Folk-Rock Age of Dylan, Nirvana's angst anthems seek truth. It may be ugly, but you want to hear it so you can deal with it. Alternative mode Rockers don't want sweet malted fluff. They write songs about murder and mayhem and mammoth problems that swamp psyches in an abysmal morass of despair. You can't chuckle your way out of their existential quagmire. Eddie Vedder's sound magnifies the power of the composite groan, the collective scream. Vedder's booming supercharged vocal cruises lower notes of des-

tiny. You know he's not dealing with Susie's zits – he's dealing with the decline and fall of Western Civilization, the bleakness of the cosmic void, and the cold blue stars in a lonely sky beyond love.

"I Got Id" – Pearl Jam, #7, 12-95 with Neil Young. It never hurts, when you're psyching out Freud, to Rock and Roll, with one of the few legends left – **Neil Young** (b. '45, Toronto). "I Got Id" shows the cerebral nature of Pearl Jam's deep material. The ID represents Freud's concept of the primordial caveman essence of the human psyche, challenged by his more modern EGO and counterbalancing Super-EGO. Pearl Jam naturally pun the 'I got it' expression into a new and incredible sound. **Neil Young** plays organ and guitar, too, in this double experience between the Seattle kings of alternative and rock icon.

"Corduroy" (NC '94) hit #59A, with minor keys and jangling Jazz riffs. In 1994, Eddie & PJ swamped Album Rock Tracks with hits like 12-94, #1(8) "Better Man." Their "Spin the Black Circle" also hit #16 in 11-94, while "Dissident" ranged to #3 in 3-94. After oldie "Last Kiss" hit #2, 5-99, Vedder and Pearl Jam launched their blockbuster #2 *Bi-Aural* album of 5-16-2000. Pearl Jam never shies from the controversial title: "Stupid Mop." STUPID MOP? Certainly no 50s tune this side of #6, '56 "A Rose and Baby Ruth" could have borne such a gonzo moniker. Pearl Jam does their share of protesting ugly scenarios.

Pearl Jam encourages Rock and Roll fans to roll on past pure nihilism. They challenge the inherent idea that such a "belief in nothing" entertains – 'why try to change anything anyhow, because nothing really matters in the long run.' Jam's four monster albums? *Vitalogy* – #1(1), 12-94, produced by Nick Didia/Brendan O'Brien, 5 million; *Ten* – #2(4), 1-92, 9 million, 248+ weeks on chart; *Vs.* – #1(5), 5M; and *No Code*, #1(2+), 9-96; to their credit, Pearl Jam still releases vinyl for us DJ's or vinyl traditionalists.

An undercurrent of caring and sympathy underpins the work of Pearl Jam. In the guise of rebellion, they bring up things the bland nowhere men should have thought of very long ago. When we got too complacent in the 60s, our younger generation straightened us out. They will do it again.

Remember **Johnny Cash**'s (#19, 4-70; #3 C) "What Is Truth?" When Punk icon Big **John Cash** spoke up to our jangling discordant generation, we shut up and listened. Johnny surveyed alternatives to war and pollution and despair. Johnny Cash rumbled eloquently about TRUTH in his street-wise throaty baritone blasting down to bass: just ask – boomed Johnny – the voices of our youth. Today, we suffer a déjà vu malaise. Among the voices of Alternative or Punk or Grunge or Thrash/Heavy Metal, some are strident, some are mute, and some are profound. Words of wisdom are also spoken by guitars, not just by words. Rock and Roll is a search – not a destination.

Hip Rap Soul

Whoomp? Here it is. Soul/R & B created Hip-Hop/ R & B. Rap took over the urban universe of the streets. Rough, roaring guys, but yeah – they could really harmonize. 'Hip Rap Soul' gets the people back together. We don't do music segregation in *Gold Rush*.

"When the Going Gets Tough, the Tough Get Going" **– Billy Ocean, #2(1), 11-85; #6, 12-85 R & B.** **Little Richard's** (b. '32 GA) Soul music joined with and created Rock and Roll. Like all popular music, Soul/Rap/Hip-Hop often leans on cliches or popular expressions to form titles from disconnected words. Billy Ocean (b. 50, Trinidad) grabs title expression from football. Mainstreaming Rock and Soul, this multicultural song weaves human endeavor, athletic achievement, and love. Nice hook, over & over.

"Living in America" – James Brown, #4, 12-85; #10, 12-85 R & B. If any catalyst sparked the hot rise of rhythms to create RAP, it is Godfather of Soul **James Brown**, born 5-3-33, in Barnwell, SC. Much victory credit in Rocky IV ('85***) flick goes not to Italian stallion Sylvester Stallone as 'Rocky,' but to James Brown for energizing America. Notes Rap expert **K. Maurice Jones**: "The beats singer James Brown and his band created during the late 60s became the most sampled thing in Rap" [like "Funky Drummer (#51 '70, #20 R&B) snare solo]. Jones cites Punk/New Wave Rockers outside the ghetto like **Blondie** (#1 '81 "Rapture") as among first to praise Rap – and use it. The show *Yo! MTV Raps* starred Fab Freddy, and rocked to the pioneering **Grandmaster Flash** beat.

Brown's "Living in America" might be his best song. Like **Neil Diamond**'s #8, 4-81 "Comin' to America," the immigrant experience permeates the message. In the Black Experience, the history of forced emigration and eventual freedom is as important as the Europeans' escaping poverty to a land where 'streets paved with gold' turned out to be cobblestones – so singers like Diamond and Brown had to manufacture their OWN diamonds and gold.

Muhammad Ali, (b. Louisville, Kentucky, '42 as 'Cassius Clay'), is a central figure in the evolution of Rap. The champ picked Jeff Forrest and me out of a thousand throng at 1967's Detroit Muhammad Speaks Temple (taking his name from the Black-only Islamic sect). He walked up to us, shook our hands, and made us two lone white strangers feel welcome in the Afro community. Starstruck by the Champ, I tried to later buy a *Muhammad Speaks* newspaper from a Malcolm X and Reverend Fard Muhammad news-vendor. The Black Supremacist yelled at me and called me a 'white devil' and didn't want my fifty cents. I grimaced and shuffled off, having some minor inkling of the downtrodden way my African-American brothers and sisters must have felt in the tense climate of rampant segregation which stalked the sizzling sixties. [What's a white Detroit kid know about Soul/R&B? Well, I marched with Dr. Martin Luther King in 1963, hence this integrated book. Also, I worked as a songwriter for Motown Records during their 1966 heyday]. My dad was a welterweight boxing champ in 1928 Windsor, Canada, and a heavyweight-champ **Joe Louis** fan. My father-in-law, Tony Piazza, had to do a little impromptu boxing of his own on the Roaring 20s South Side of Chicago. Dad and Pop believed top athletes should be humble.

Ali was stripped of his championship belt because of his antiwar stance. He followed his first spiritual leader, Dr. Martin Luther King, who parted company with old friend President Lyndon Baines Johnson on war and peace by 1965 (see **Will Smith** in *Ali*, 2001***). I liked the way Ali teamed up with sportscaster/hypemaster Howard Cosell for buoyant interviews. Rap-preview rhymes like this came out when brash Ali challenged musclebound champ Sonny Liston:

" I'm gonna contribute to Sonny's dismemberment,
I'm gonna hit him so hard he'll wonder where October and November went . . ."

Ali resembled a bronze Atlas. He floated like a butterfly, stung like a bee. One iron fist. One steel.

Jones cites his Rap-preview razzle-dazzle: "Clay was blessed with dashing good looks, a spectacular shuffle that left his opponents dizzy, and a knockout punch. Charisma was in his sweat." Ali fashioned the Rap style – and James Brown plugged in the hot locomotive rhythm track. With streetcorner sayings, bragging, and smooth style, Ali fomented the "pulpit phrases of black America." Ali's Hip-Hop relative, **L. L. Cool J** (#3, 11-95, "Hey Lover," #3, 7-96 w/ Total "Loungin'"), displays the same brash bold echo. To a confused suburbia, Jones explains Ali's urban appeal: "For many blacks, he was a symbol of pride and independence. He stood up to the system. Ali exposed America to the power of a strong black man and the wonderful tradition of his community. In this sense, he was one of Rap's forefathers."

James Brown's "Living in America" is a Rock and Soul testimonial to black pride, like his #10, 9-68 (#1[6] R & B) "Say It Loud – I'm Black and I'm Proud." Brown, like the Fab Four, the King, or Aretha the Queen of Soul, has gathered up many a title in his career, like Mr. Dynamite or Soul Brother Number One.

In his early-on "Please, Please, Please, " he hit #105 on the HOT105 in 11-60 – but #5, 4-56, R & B – over four years before. Soon his "Try Me" carved out a new Soul style: only #48, 12-58, despite a #1(1), 11-58 R & B pinnacle.

Aretha Franklin and James Brown

Brown's preacher-style call and response comes out of the thunderous mode of Aretha's father, Detroit's **Reverend C. L. Franklin,** of Grand River Avenue's New Bethel Church. African-American scholar **W. E. B. DuBois** (1868-1963) said the PREACHER is "a leader, a politician, an orator." Rev. Franklin rumbled slowly at first, like a tiny earthquake. With the spirit, he rose from rumbling baritone to countertenor into what Jones says his parishoners called his 'hoopin' voice.' James Brown led his musical community with a similar spirit through his music.

In **Chuck Berry**'s #37, 6-59 "Back in the U.S.A" (#16 R & B – and #16 by Linda Ronstadt, HOT 100, 8-78), Berry celebrates 24-hour burgers, frantic interstates, and jaunty skyscrapers. James Brown's postmodern U.S.A. hypes American free enterprise, entrepreneurship, and bootstrap economics. He also bought a chain of R & B radio stations, practicing his preaching.

Critics caterwaul that Rap lost the MELODY in a strident slam-bam pandemonium of the BIG BEAT ALONE, steering the rudderless, long-gone tune into a quagmire of chant and bellow and holler. Not so. Brown simply takes us farther back to African rhythmic roots.

Griot is the African term for singing storyteller. Like British brethren the bards and minstrels, who wandered country fairs, griots kept the oral tradition, K. Maurice Jones' 'exalted people.' The griot's job involved a first-rate memory – details, stories, facts, anecdotes, wisdom. Their fascinating tales, told with polyrhythmic complexity on the drums of Africa, may have been the rhythmic underpinning – maybe even the birthplace – of Rock and Roll. Jones: "The griot wore many hats: historian, storyteller, comedian, reporter, mediator, social commentator, and often performer of religious ceremonies and rites of passage." Shanghaied to America, Africans were dragged in chains in the dark of night on sardine-squeezed slave ships. With a Babel of a thousand different oral languages, and sparse weaponry, they couldn't communicate with each other to defend themselves. They became 'Africans' only, like calling Englishmen, Danes, Italians, Poles, French, Ukrainians, and Germans all "Europeans." Many well-meaning Americans of tan-disabled hue called them all 'Negro,' Spanish word for 'Black.' Their rich lost African cultures had a polyglot tapestry of oral tales and legends. Legends were often interwoven with conga or bongo drums.

Griot kingdoms? The Ibo, Benin, and the Niger (pronounced "nye-jur"), which today is the huge 111,000,000+ nation of Nigeria. The fountainhead of Rock and Soul rhythms may now be found on the fertile coasts of Ghana, Liberia, Senegal, or Gambia. In early pre-written-language civilizations there, oration was paramount in governing societies. Monotone drones were OUT. Embellished, colorful, poetic language was IN – not unlike Ireland.

Enter Rap. Not all of its smooth-to-noisy messages may be welcome in white-flight suburbia. Rap maximizes the stereotype of the Muhammad Ali-type male as proud, loud, strong, and capable of handling any situation. Rap music or Rap Rock, then, is a return to Pan-African polyrhythmic origins, says Jazz/R & B guitarman **Craig Boyd** ("Back on Track," 8-2001). Rap's strident message, however, is on the cutting edge of NOW.

"Papa's Got a Brand New Bag" – James Brown, #8, 7-65; #1(8) R & B. One of Brown's greatest vocalic treasures in his steamy Rock and Soul arsenal is his triumphant hallelujah scream (rivalling the Rebel Yell in gung-ho gusto): "OOOOUUUUAHHH!" (or something like that). Brown screams for joy, for life, for kicks, for the power and glory of the midnight hour in his beloved hot throbbing America.

Joel Whitburn's Top R & B 1942-95 lists Brown at #1 in charted hits, and #1 in Top 500 R & B artists .

TOP R & B ARTISTS - Whitburn Point System

Number of Charted Hits		Number of Points	
1) James Brown	118	1) James Brown	8495
2) Aretha Franklin	94	2) Aretha Franklin	7269
3) Ray Charles	85	3) Stevie Wonder	6378
4) Temptations	82	4) Temptations	6243
5) B. B. King	75	5) Louis Jordan	6234
6) Stevie Wonder	71	6) Ray Charles	5771
7) Isley Brothers	71	7) Marvin Gaye	5295
8) Gladys Knight/Pips	66	8) Gladys Knight/Pips	5056
9) Marvin Gaye	63	9) Isley Brothers	4898
10) Fats Domino	63	10) Fats Domino	4891

James Brown & His Famous Flames spar and parry with each other, with Muhammad Ali's butterfly grace and raging-bull power and strength. Brown writhes and footstomps and begs on his knees for the woman's sweet love. Big **Maceo Parker** creates a University of Saxophonia. **Fred Wesley** makes a unique R & S (Rock & Soul) instrument welcome – a TROMBONE, from Dixieland/Dorsey tradition. Brown and his Funky Rap Soul cronies have always been the hottest road show around. "Papa's Got a Brand New Bag" gets warmed up for his biggest-ever HOT 100 hit – #3, 11-65 [#1(6) R & B], "I Got You (I Feel Good)." With these blockbuster soul screamers, James Brown simply revolutionized music. While storming the beleaguered bastions of quietude, he also delivered a big message.

"King Heroin" – James Brown, #40, 3-72; #6 R & B. Brown counterattacks HARD drugs. Other community service projects in JB's brand-new bag of antidotes? "Don't Be a Drop-Out" at #50, 10-66 (#4 R & B); #53, 7-66 "Money Won't Change You" (#11 R & B); #33 R & B-only "Soul Pride"; and prelude to "Living in America" – #52, 5-68 and #13 R & B "America Is My Home." His last one commemorates Dr. King's life (see White Soul crew Rascals' #1, '68 "People Got to Be Free," and Dion's #4 "Abraham, Martin, and John," on similar theme).

"Teardrops from My Eyes" – Ruth Brown, NC, HOT 30; #1(11), 10-50 R & B. Ruth Brown's (b. '28, Virginia) '93 Rock Hall Induction is for her domination of the formative years of Rock and Soul. Ruth was like Fats Domino, Ray Charles, Lloyd Price (#1[7] R & B-only 5-52 "Lawdy Miss Clawdy"), and two Hanks – Williams and Snow. They were all doing real Rock and Roll before Alan Freed even coined the term. Among unrelated-to-James-Brown Ruth's pioneer Soul offerings, we have Ruth's mega-smash "(Mama) He Treats Your Daughter Mean" – NC, '53, but #1[5], 2-53 R & B [also #99, 9-62, HOT 100).

"Atomic Dog" – George Clinton, NC, '83; #1(4), 1-83 R & B. Kannapolis, NC (b. '40) George pilgrimmed to funky Motown, forming Parliaments in original Streetcorner mode back in 1955. He cut #20, 7-67 (#3 R & B) "I Wanna Testify" with the spirit of **Marvin Gaye**'s preacher-echo in #22, 11-63 (#15 R & B) "Can I Get a Witness" (with Supremes' backing vocals). Clinton's Glitz Soul involved Afro rainbow wigs and fire-engine red *Soul Train* suits, disdaining drab togs for multi-hued Soul/Jazz/Funk impact. Cubbiest-word Soul song? Maybe his #89, 2-79, but #1(4) R & B "Aqua Boogie (A Psychoalphadiscobetabioaquadoloop)." James Brown's Maceo Parker and Fred Wesley horn in with their horns, with Bootsy Collins on bass.

"The Message" – Grandmaster Flash, #62, 10-82; #4 R & B. Message? Not all sweetness and light. Until this Rap/Soul message, the *Soul Train* and Disco party-hearty mood frolicked and whooped it up to the great **Louie 'Satchmo' Armstrong**'s happy standard; Satchmo's smiling stage personalitiy and rainbow trumpet avoided gutter-slime. Jones, on Grandmaster Flash: "His Rap painted a dismal, graphic picture of life in America's slums." He says the Reagan/Bush 1980-92 era chose to ignore inner-city problems, but that modern griots told their sordid tales. 'Maury' Jones continues: "With amazing speed, Rap began to diversify and multiply. Before long listeners could choose between the party-down braggadocio of old-school rappers like Kurtis Blow; b-boys – rap terminology for macho men – like L.L. Cool J; the black nationalism of Public Enemy, the gangster rap of Ice-T, and others."

"The Breaks – Part I" – Kurtis Blow, #87, 9-80; #4, 6-80 R & B. By 1980, the 12" single evolved for the blossoming DJ world. Can one good DJ put a whole seven-piece band out of business? **Kurt Walker** (Kurtis Blow) DJ-ed NYC discotheques. Ramming DJ patter into his Rap, he synthesized his Sound-Check DJ art form around legendary Jamaican pioneer Rappers of early Ska or Reggae – like U Roy. Blow combines the swagger of James Brown or Muhammad Ali with his double-turntable scritch-scratch patter. Tunes were topical, like #71, 4-85 (#29 R & B) "Basketball." Also #37, 8-82 R & B-only "Tough" and R & B-only #16, 11-85 "If I Ruled the World."

"Big Ole Butt" – L. L. Cool J, NC, 1989; #57, 8-89 R & B. L(adies) L(ove) Cool J(ames) was born Jim Smith (8-68, Queens, NY). At 17 he clobbered silence with #15 R & B-only 11-85 "I Can't Live Without My Radio." His biggest blockbusters? #9, 12-90 "Around the Way Girl" (#5 R&B), #3, 11-95 "Hey Lover" (#3 R&B), and #6, 10-96 "This Is for the Lover in You." A big ol' butt? But, of course; **Queen**'s #24, 11-78 Glam Rock "Fat-Bottomed Girls" was the aerobics dancealong song in 2003, at the Village's Second Avenue gym *Crunch* (until the zaftig ladies murdered the CD). RAP, too, doesn't sell zillions on suave subtlety. All that hotcha lady-lovin' produced an inevitable L. L. Cool J condition: "Father" [#18, 1-98].

Rock pioneer **Jimmy Bowen** (see Buddy Knox/Rhythm Orchids), a millionaire Country record producer, mused from his retirement mansion in Ka'anapali, Maui, Hawaii: "Every night I get down on my knees and thank the Lord for Rap Music.

Why? It drives so many people to COUNTRY music." Many rappers feel as alienated from Country Rock as some 'honkytonk angels' and 'good ol' boys' (not HOMEboys) feel from Rap. Our mission in *Gold Rush* is to bring all music fans together.

Rap drums hammer the beat. The funky guitar chops – and even cross-cuts – major beats. Bass runs, organ riffs, or horns often drive the song. Despite lack of melody, sometimes almost extraterrestrial MIDI techniques slice off a chunk of beatworthy sound to wrap the Rap with rhythm.

"Can't Truss It" – Public Enemy, #50, 10-91; #9, R & B. OK, Rap is usually controversial. Very few Rap stars are hollering their grocery lists in Frantic Gear. A firestorm of angry reaction bazooka-ed when Enemy's 'Professor Grif' (Richard Griffin) made anti-Semitic remarks in 1989. Perhaps he forgot the two white Freedom Riders who gave their lives to register Afro-American voters in 1963 – see Gene Hackman's scary *Mississippi Burning* (1988***1/2); their names are SCHWERNER & GOODMAN [their Afro-American fellow Civil Rights martyr had nearly the same name as 2001-Vice President Cheney – CHANEY]. Folk singer *Pete Seeger,* too, a white freedom marcher, was a big part of Dr. King's process. Indeed, check the pix of Dr. King's 1963 800,000-strong March on Washington. Over 25% of the Civil Rights marchers were white. Public Enemy also hit with political #20, 7-89 "Fight the Power (NC, R&B). Enemy leaders Chuck D (Carlton Ridenhauer) and Terminator X (Norman Rogers) believe in the American right of free speech, lavishly practiced.

"Check Yo Self" – Ice Cube, #20, 7-93; #1(1), R & B. Not to be confused with **Ice-T** ("I'm Your Pusher," NC '88; #13, 10-88 R&B). **O'Shea Jackson** formerly led L.A. Rappers N. W. A. (which stands for Ni—— with Attitude): N. W. A. hit #45 R&B, 8-89 with "Express Yourself," an authentic Delta Blues melody to its roots: Charles Wright and the 103rd Street Rhythm Band (#12, 8-70 & #3 R&B), with **Bill Cosby**'s help. Ice Cube crunched #15, 3-93 (#7 R&B) with "It Was a Good Day." COUNTRY RAP?

"Big Bad John" – Jimmy Dean, #1(5), 10-61; #1(2) C. *Jimmy Dean* the tall Texan sausage man – NOT the legendary 50s icon/actor – laid down this sad Rap tale. Dean also clicked with bio sketch "P. T 109" at #8, 3-62, about President Kennedy's heroic WWII Navy career. "Big Bad John" is 90% pure Rap, aside from a few harmonizers on title. You've heard this sad saga on your local elevator. Big John is 6'6", 245#. Though he may have possibly killed a man in a long-ago fight, he is now a gentle giant. The mine caves in. Noble Big John perishes, saving the other miners, as he holds up the mine-shaft archway till his co-workers can flee to safety. Like Samson tearing down the temple, John goes out in a blaze of glory.

"If Ever You're in My Arms Again" – Peabo Bryson, #10, 5-84; #6 R&B. Smooth gorgeous melody, unrapped. South Carolinian Soulmaster Bryson reminds us all that pop music works best when it's about love, not hate. Remember his **Regina Belle** duo "A Whole New World (Aladdin's Theme)" [#1(1), 12-92, #21 R&B]? Like **Aaron Neville,** Peabo is a journeyman at grace-note melismas. With quivering and tremulous precision, Peabo scored early with #16, 7-83 (#5 R&B) "Tonight, I Celebrate My Love." Not Rap. Just very cool . He's often best recalled for his Disney adventure with French-Canadian chanteuse **Celine Dion** – #9, 1-92's melodic ballad theme, "Beauty and the Beast."

"Messin' Around" – Memphis Slim, NC '48; #1(2), 5-48 R & B. Memphis's **Peter Chatman** (1915-88), 6'6" piano-playing Blues singer, embellished his authentic Rock and Soul style with a buzzing hybrid hive of jazzy trombones and trumpets. Missing link between Be-Bop, Jazz, Big Band, Rock and Soul, and Vintage Delta Blues.

Nat 'King' Cole (1917-65), ultra-smooth supercrooner, was drafted into service by drunk at piano bar. Result? Huge #9, 4-44 and #1(10), NEW R&B chart, "Straighten Up and Fly Right." Voted into Rock Hall '99 (Early Influences, w/ Billie Holiday), Nat was no rocker or shocker, but his stature and stardom go unquestioned. Before Hip-Hop, Nat was essence of HIP. His style influenced a tremendous tenor from original R & R Hall Class of 1986:

Cole-ishly smooth **Sam Cooke** (b. '31, Delta's Clarksdale, MS, d. '64, gunshot) scored with the ultimate violence-in-music "Frankie and Johnny" (#14, 7-63, #4 R&B). Traditional Folk Blues (#9 and #18 in 1927 for Ted Lewis and Frank Crumit) it's a 1840s tragic tale of jealousy and rage. RAP zapped for violence? Each pistol-packin' lover in this barroom saga is furious (Frankie and Johnny ARE a guy & girl, despite masculine names). Va-va-voom 'Nelly Bly' sneaks upstairs with Johnny. Frankie blasts him to Kingdom Come. Cooke died in a similar motel jealousy rage. Is violence American as apple pie?

"Head to Toe" – Lisa Lisa and Cult Jam and Full Force, #1(1), 4-87; #1(2) R & B. **Lisa Velez** sings lead, backed by Alex 'Spanador' Moseley and Mike Hughes. Also #1 follow-up, 8-87 "Lost in Emotion," and #8, 7-86 "All Cried Out."

"Step Right Up" – Tom Waits, NC, 1976. On Al. #89, 11-76 *Small Change.* Hilarious graveltone Rap by Waits (b. '49) in Kerouac coffeehouse jive talk. Like a circus barker, Waits hypes some mysterious product here – a catch-all of late-nite TV trash ads.. He mystifies it in his marshmallow Marlboro cloud, trotting out every hackneyed cliché ever used to vacuum up suckers for this cryptic THING he's hawking. He promises stuff like 'goodies for the little lady,' 'cuts your lawn,' 'cures your denture breath,' 'it'll walk your dog,' and weird, wild 'doubles on a sax.' Sax? Lew Tabackin, tenor. This White Soul craggy Rap vocal by Waits echoes **Louie Armstrong**'s archetypal red beans & rice New Orleans charisma. Smoky Waits helped start Rap in Bicentennial '76. Like **John Prine**, Waits has always been ten years ahead of his time. Waits's Salvation Army-shiny suits and constant glowing cig – super-glued to lip – give us the impression he smokescreens reality. Don't we all? Finally, the world of commercialty caught up with Waits's bizarre genius; in May 2002, **Waits** launched two (2, count em, not 1 but 2) albums to his highest-ever positions the first week – #32, 5-2002 *Blood Money*, and #33, 5-2002 *Alice*.

BANG – time for **GANGSTA RAP**. With a blood & thunder tradition of Folk/Rock/Soul/Blues/Rap, we mull guts & gore sagas like "Frankie & Johnny," Lloyd Price's #1(4), 12-58 gunslinger "Stagger Lee," hitman #1(9), 8-59 "Mack the Knife" (Bobby Darin), or the Kingston Trio's #1(1), 9-58 passion-stabber/murderer [and hangee] "Tom Dooley." Was it any surprise that Rock and Rap and Roll/Soul might turn grisly and ghastly?

"Nuthin' but a 'G' Thang" – **Snoop Doggy Dogg, and Dr. Dre, NC, '93; #1(3), 1-93 R & B.** Snoop (b. surf's-up Long Beach, CA, '72) grew up in the 'hood' (neighbor-hood, of course) with **Dr. Dre** (#6, 6-96 "California Love," with **2-Pac**). "'G' Thang" is the essence of Gangsta Rap – a Rap sub-stratum that puffs the seedier side of back-alley life – with #19, 9-98 follow-up "Still a G Thang.' Much Rap music samples bite-size chunks of older records, driving everybody batty about royalties at BMI and ASCAP. Maybe Napster, too. "Nuthin'" freely borrows (rips off, some say) word for word from Leon Haywood's #15, 9-75 "I Want 'a Do Something Freaky to You," itself no choirboy hymn. Claims of innocence run rife in **Mystical's** #18, 3-99 "It Ain't My Fault 2." Snoop rebounded with dogged "Woof" to #62, 1-99, and #12, 10-98 "Come and Get with Me." He also scored triplet #8's produced by Dre – 5-93, "Dre Day," 12-93 "What's My Name," and 1-94 "Gin and Juice." In a firebrand firestorm of a 1996 trial, Snoop Doggy Dogg was acquitted of first-degree murder in an LA drive-by shooting. Life imitates art?

"Family Tradition" – **Hank Williams, Jr., NC, '79; #4, 6-79 C.** With **Johnny Cash**, Hank's pappy **Hank Williams** is possibly Country music's most revered and adored leg-end. Junior, no slouch, had 96 charted Country hits to 1994. Senior, everyone knows, died of old age (29) from a bottle of liquid courage to wash away an excruciatingly painful back injury after falling off a horse. Kid in song is grilled about own intemperate habits. He replies, hey, it's OK. It's simply a FAMILY TRADITION.

"I Get Around" – **2 Pac [Tu-Pac], #11, 7-93; #5, 6-93 R & B.** As our sons and daughters grow up and search for role models, many parents and religious leaders are fight-ing the desire to join the 2 Pac Shakur Fan Club. As role models go, he is gone. Rock and Roll has martyred many entertainers in a serious epidemic of plane crashes, car wrecks, drug/alcohol O.D.'s, or other natural untimely deaths. Very few entertainers come to the bench on mur-der charges. Remember **Leadbelly**'s 6-year jail term for a murder he MAY have committed? Or **Puff Daddy Combs**' 2001 acquittal, where a girl was shot in the face by a gun he might have had, or owned? Remember Punk Rock's Sid Vicious's suicide after a murder rap?

"I Get Around" is NOT the Beach Boys' fun-fun-fun surf romp (#1, 5-64). It's no pleasure promenade down Holly-wood Boulevard or Sunset Strip. Like 2-Pac's "Smile" with **Scarface** at #12, 6-97 or even #9, 3-95 "Dear Mama," "I Get Around" is a street-savvy manifesto of Gangsta Rap, which permeates potboiler cinema from 1972 *Blacula* (***) to 1994 *Pulp Fiction*(*). Into Millennium III, a plethora of blood-spattered Guts-O-Ramas like documentary *Faces of Death* splattered the screen (starless in acting, rating). Ex-precious human life is downsized to the squashed slug or scrunched snake category. In the flick *Juice* (1992*1/4), 2 Pac stars as a psychopathic trigger-happy youth on an armed-robbery rampage. If you want hooray Block-buster endings, rent a Disney flick.

Tu-Pac didn't seem too comfortable anywhere. Despite impressive rhythmic rhyming talents, he always seemed to be in the wrong place at the right time. He joined **Digi-tal Underground** (#11, 3-90 & #7 R&B "The Humpty Dance"), with Chopmaster J. Anyone who thinks this is about Mr. H. Dumpty, in the E.R., because of a tall wall fall, will end up with egg on his face. Shakur was not your ordinary window-soaping prankster. First he got nailed for beating up *Menace II Society* director Allen Hughes. He was then shot five times (11-11-94) in a Big Apple robbery, and survived. In 1995, 2 Pac was sent to jail for four years on a forcible sex conviction, but they let him out of the gunless-prisoners' jail that year for good be-havior. *Me Against the World* [Al. #1(4), 4-95] was headed for a double platinum, and Al. #1(2) *All Eyes on Me* was poised on the launch pad for 5M quintuple platinum.

On *Friday the 13th*, September 1996, Tu-pac was riding in an LA car. Someone shot him four more times. Five bullets weren't enough the first time, but the number NINE was no 7-11 lucky shot for 2 Pac. His number was up, like the plugged pug in Hemingway's "The Killers." In May 1997, fellow Rapper **Notorious B. I. G.** might have en-joyed an immortal #1 album – *Life After Death,* but he too died by a smoking gun. **Tu-Pac's** Rep and Rap live on: #1(2), 6-96 "How Do U Want It," and #21, 3-98 "Do for Love."

Director Robert Townsend starred Rappers Naughty by Nature and Cypress Hill in his 1993 (*½) *Meteor Man.* Here's his rationale for a casting call:

"I needed rappers in my movie, because they're the HEROES kids look up to these days . . . "

"Hip Hop Hooray" – **Naughty by Nature, #8, 1-93; #1(1) R & B.** Personnel? East Orange, NJ's Anthony 'Treach' Criss, Vincent Brown, and Kier 'dj KG' Gist. Rap stars. Movie stars. **Cypress Hill** ("Insane in the Brain," #19, 7-93 & #27 R&B), starring Cuban Rapper Sam Reyes and Mixmaster Muggs Muggerud, hit big at the same time. In 3-60 **Conway Twitty**, Country star with 40 #1 C. hits (plus Irish anthem #10, 11-59 "Danny Boy, #18 R & B) had a big philosophical hit about his dedication to a girl— "What Am I Living For?" In a violent interface of guns and Gucci, Gangsta Rap struggles to decipher the things that matter in life: possessions, people, honor, glory. The human panorama is a multi-millennial turf war. Nothing has changed. What matters? What are we living for?

And now – a word from a young lady who marched along with me with **Dr. Martin Luther King** in 1963 Detroit. It's Nepotism Time. Since Reyes is the older brother of Mellow Man Ace (#60 R&B '90 "Mentirosa), let me pull out the wisdom of one of my own role models, my sister Blair Dean [Cooter]. After our Detroit neighborhood seethed and burned and tumbled down in a devastating fireflash of July 1967 urban rioting, some of it racial, Blair (age 21) wrote this letter to the *Detroit News:*

"The outbreaks of racial and class strife in our cities merely reflect the increasing willingness among all segments of our population to resort to violence as an attractively packaged panacea for society's ills . . . Physical repression will curb the present activities of the Black Nationalists, but it will not weaken their appeal to future generations. In order to reinstate the rule of law in our own nation and throughout the world, we must close our gun cabinets and open our minds."

I recently unearthed this yellowed clipping. Blair's youthful compassionate zeal reflects her hero Dr. King's life. As if we haven't been editorializing all along, let me get more blatant. RAP is nobody's villain. It is a rhythmic form, a musical chant. It is a monologue about important issues. Positive Rappers like **Will Smith** or Hammer bear a powerful message, and James Brown rapped about finishing school, getting a job, loving a family. Like any other medium in America, Rap will become just as violent to women and majority/minority groups as good people will allow. Rap can be a productive forum for key controversies, or a 'bathroom-talk' cussfest. Or, perhaps, both at the same time. As we Hop to Hip Rap R & B Soul, let's check out what Brown calls "Get on the Good Foot – Part I" (#18, 8-72, #1[4] R&B). Brown believes the Rap music message should be used to CELEBRATE:

"Brother Rapp (Part I)" – James Brown, #32, 5-70; #2(2), R & B. Brown kicks off the Rap movement. Without this song, built upon the positive self-images of Muhammad Ali and the griots, today there might be no low-rider Toyotas with darkened windows blaring megabass sonic booms from trunk speakers to rooftops of destiny. We are all at the wheel of the Rapmobile. We can steer it safely, or into frontiers of libidinous anarchy, and over the cliff of rage and random violence and self-destruction. Or up to the golden meadows of love and justice and kindness. It's really a King thing.

"I'll Be Home" – Flamingos, NC, '56; #5, 2-56 R & B. Un-Rap masterpiece. Snuggling melody and fireside romance. Just you and her. Yummy beverage, munchos. Johnny Mathis album surfing decades. You smooch to the magic of the Righteous Brothers, Diana Ross, Luther Vandross, Peabo Bryson. Now you want some really intimate music. Pick the 2001 Rock Hall Inductee **Flamingos'** "I'll Be Home." With super lead tenor NATE NELSON (1932-84), Chicago Streetcorner Flamingos triple-teamed heavenly harmonies via brothers Jake and Zeke Carey. A song of love. Love as service. Spirit of Aretha Franklin's NC '94 #5, 4-94 R&B "Willing to Forgive." Pride destroys many relationships.

"Boogie Chillun" – John Lee Hooker, NC, '49; #1(1), 1-49 R & B. Hooker fled Delta bull's-eye, Clarksdale, Mississippi, to Detroit with a Blues dream. Hooker's (1917-2001, Rock Hall 1991) incredible Blues riffs energized a new Afro world of urbane urban Americans with factory financial power. At age 16, I saw a girl get shot not 20 feet away on the street Hooker describes – Hastings St., baddest avenue in the Motor City. "Boogie Chillun" is set among smoky midnight 'Paradise Alley' claptrap clapboard shacks. His cement-mixer baritone bellows his Blues legend and savvy. Pre-Rap.

"I'm in the Mood" (#30, 11-5, #1[4] R&B) is one of his best. Hooker is a master of the Talking Blues, a kissin' cousin and progenitor of RAP. He didn't invent the genre, but certainly boosted it, connecting his urban odysseys to Rock and Soul. Rock fans know him for **George Thorogood and Destroyers'** reprise "One Bourbon, One Scotch, and One Beer." Or catch his #5 R&B-only '49 "Hobo Blues," or #60, 5-62 "Boom Boom" (#16 R & B).

"We Are Family" – Sister Sledge, #2(2), 4-79; #1(1), 5-79 R & B. Simply one of greatest Soul tracks of all time. Sisters Sledge (Joni, Debra, Kathy, and Kim Sledge) share Rock and Soul world harmony. The bass spins off the kicky drum beat. The message is UNITY.

"Loser" – Beck, #10, 1-94. Beck Hansen (b. KC, raised LA) won Male Artist of '96 by *Rolling Stone* AND *Spin* magazines. "Loser" samples Dr. John's "I Walk on Guilded Splinters." Beck's #94, 11-96 "Devil's Haircut" and #78, 5-98 "The New Pollution" show his eclectic and innovative style. He spins off to Detroit White Rappers **Kid Rock** (Al. #4, 2-99 *Devil Without a Cause*) and **Eminem** (big hit "Stan," and #6+ 2-2000 "The Real Slim Shady"). Beck reprises Rap scratches of Grandmaster Flash, histrionic power of Bob Dylan, slide guitar fireworks of Stevie Ray Vaughan, and the bass ballistics of James Jamerson of Motown. Eclectic, like Wyclef Jean. Beck often gets associated in late-90s parlance as **Beck, Bush, and Björk**.

Bush (NOT the two presidents) is London's quadrangle of quality: Gavin Rossdale and Nigel Pulsford, guitar (Rossdale lead singer); Dave Parsons, bass, Robin Goodridge, drums. Hits? "Comedown" at #30, 9-95; #28, 1-96 "Glycerine," and 10-99, #67 (hmmm) "The Chemicals Between Us." In the closest election in American history, George W. Bush was quickly granted the victory in 2000 by 300 votes nationwide. Five months later, voters still wondered.

Björk (#88, 2-94 "Big Time Sensuality") is our only major Icelandic artist. In 1970, we drove a VW 'Beetle' all over Iceland's tundra. At one time, we watched a volcano erupt, a geyser blow off steam, and saw the Midnight Sun (typical R & R blast). Her #32 Al. *Post* put her arctic land on the musical map.

"No, No, No" – Wyclef Jean with Destiny's Child, #3, 11-97. Multi-talented Jean (b. '70) of the **Fugees** (Bob Marley's "No Woman, No Cry to #38A 6-96) told my student Dan Axelrod about his eclectic choices in music. Wyclef Jean simply said, "I like all kinds of music." Wyclef Jean is *Gold Rush's* kind of star. With **R. Kelly**, Jean scored on #7, 2-98 "Gone Till November" and Bee Gee sampling #45, 8-97 "We Trying to Stay Alive."

Any JACKSONS today? Back to the Jackson Seven? Or Jackson 33? **Michael**'s kid sister **Janet** (see MTV) became the 4th-biggest female artist of all time on Whitburn's '99 chart (Madonna, Aretha, Supremes). Five brothers are Michael (#9 Artist ever), plus **Jermaine, Tito, Marion**, and **Jackie Jackson**. In the Jacksonian arena, we have female Rockabilly queen Wanda Jackson, Country boomer Stonewall Jackson, Opera/Gospel chanteuse **Mahalia Jackson**, and Soulster star **Chuck Jackson**. The Shondells' lead singer Tommy JAMES is really Tommy Jackson. Beatle pal Tony Jackson of Searchers surfed British Invasion wave. Jackson Five's sis **LaToya Jackson** hit #56, 5-84 (#29 R&B) with "Heart Don't Lie," before foldout fantasias and a men's mag modeling career. **Reverend Jesse Jackson** does not sing, but ran for President after being Dr. King's right-hand man. In the Rap oddity arena, Rev. Martin Luther King's world-famous "I Have a Dream" speech actually charted (a cappella) at #88, 5-68 (editorial comment: 'shoulda' been #1[18]).

In the African-American community, JACKSON is a ubiquitous surname. **Freddie Jackson** hit #12, 9-85 (#1 R&B) "You Are My Lady" and #18 (#1[6] R & B) "Rock Me Tonight (For Old Times' Sake)." Freddie hit NINE #1 R&B 1985-95 tunes from NYC home base. Millie Jackson of "Hurts So Good" good fame at #24, 9-73 (#3 R&B) is unrelated to **"Bull Moose" Jackson**, with #21, 11-47 "I Love You So, Yes I Do" #1(3) R & B fame. **Walter Jackson** (1938-83), suffered from polio, performed on crutches, and hit #12, 9-85 (#1 R&B)

with "You Are My Lady." White Soul Joe Jackson (not SHOELESS Joe, ballplayer) hit #21, 6-79 with "Is She Really Goin' out with Him" and #6, 8-82 "Steppin' Out."

"Love Makes the World Go Round" – Deon Jackson, #11, 1-66; #3 R & B. Ypsilanti, Michigan's Deon had a Smokey Soul precision, and a double-edged **Janis Joplin** rasp to provide a mammothly memorable voice beyond the Motown orbit. See-saws in this song totter and teeter, like love – Earth's secret power source. Deon Jackson had a great voice – at Motown, he would have made superstar.

"Don't Stop 'Til You Get Enough" – Michael Jackson, #1(1), 7-79; #1(5) R & B. The Jackson Five were the mid-season Motown darlings – rising on the lost wings of **Frankie Lymon**'s Teenagers of the 50s, and **Stevie Wonder**'s deepening voice. Other J5 youthful blockbusters include #1(2), 5-70 "The Love You Save," #2(3), 4-71 "Never Can Say Goodbye," Disco sojourn #2(2), 3-74 "Dancing Machine," and #1(4), 11-79 "Rock with You." The 5'8" 120# tenor from steeltown Indiana wasn't just messing with a little nest egg or hyperbaric life-extension chamber on his solo flight. He was reaching for the shuddering Elvis Spotlight, that star-studded flash of shrieking fire that busted up the Beatles, crashed the little airplanes, and brought the proudest and greatest Rock stars of all time to their trembling knees in prayer and sorrow.

"Banned in the U.S.A." – Luke/2 Live Crew, #20, 7-90; #13, R & B. Nasty-as-they-wanna-be tensions from sooty snowpile caverns of Gary. Or the blasted busted-bottle Bronx, smoldering, an ember of anger, a page of rage. This is the one that spawned the record-rating Congressional controversy, which ended up shadowing the Movie Rating system of G, PG, PG-13, R. **Luther 'Luke Skyywalker' Campbell** plumped up his free speech cushion, and debated for the right to say ANYTHING he pleased. Follow-up to 1st hit, #26, 9-89 "Me So Horny." Luke still Raps: #26, 3-98, "Raise the Roof."

"Beat It" – Michael Jackson, #1(3), 2-83; #1(1), 4-83 R & B. Vintage King of Pop heyday. From 1983-88, eight of 13 MJ singles hit #1 on the HOT 100 (nine on R & B charts). In "Beat It," Michael Jackson reminds us that cornered, even a rabbit will fight to the death. "Beat It" is about defeat and courage. No one wants to be defeated, Jackson reminds us. You have to show strength. Right or wrong becomes meaningless. Is "Beat It" a sad commentary on animalistic human nature? No matter how much we listen to the calm voice of Jesus advising us to forswear violence, we have biblical silver-medalist David chiming in with his zingy slingshot, toppling Goliath. David, like Miriam, was the first noted singer of his gender.

"Beat It," like a biblical parable, asks puzzling questions. What are we beating? Inhibition? Addiction? A tough bully? Are people just squawking like battling bantam roosters in some dippy cock-of-the-walk shootout? WHAT in the world IS worth fighting for, anyhow? Honor? Glory? Cabfare? Segue back to the music. Like Jackson's #7, 11-88 (#2 R&B) "Smooth Criminal," "Beat It" skirts the iffy issue of COOLTH in the 'Hood.' If you must live there, you've got to walk the walk and talk the talk. Singer/songwriter Jackson's funky dynamism bounces in staccato style from major to minor key. He 'Moonwalks' from funky MTV grooves to choppy pregnant tacets. He bongos the drum case, complementing Bill Mahler's Synclavier and Steve Porcaro's Synthesizer and programming expertise in this integrated band-track effort. State-of-the-art MIDI computerized music oozed into 80s big hits – with CYBORG man/machine special effects.

When Jackson metamorphoses into a monster in million-dollar video MTV opus #4, 2-84 "Thriller," he confuses many of his youngest fans who once adored him. My daughter Lauri mentions, from her speech pathology post in Brooklyn, the direct correlation between Power Rangers' frenzied fans and kids solving problems by bloodlust bashing of nearby innocent victims. Barney the Purple Dinosaur, and Misterogers to the rescue? "Beat It" and Misterogers show us how to avoid conflict. Of course, 6'5" 250# powerlifter black belt bodyguards help mediate conflicts pretty well, too.

"Billie Jean" – Michael Jackson, #1(7), 1-83; #1(9) R & B. Problems – passion and paternity. Since Hank Ballard's amazing #1 R&B classic (11-54) "Annie Had a Baby," the Rock and Soul establishment has been strangely silent on possible parenthood. "Billie Jean," the accuser and the song, do not deal with urban stiletto violence. MACHO over many generations has been determined in arenas of sport, and bloodbaths of senseless wars. Another manly sport is womanizing. This is true in Afro-American, Asian, Caucasian, and ethnic Hispanic culture. Since the dawn of time, men have sought to vanquish enemies on the battlefield and swagger to bed with similar broad-based bravado.

Jackson hotfoots around impishly in the downer key of "F#-minor." Most EVERY huge Rock anthem is basically in some MAJOR key. Like Classical composers Haydn or Grieg or Beethoven or Rachmaninoff or Schumann, the Gloved One scoots along on one dismal chord of "F#m," setting an accusatory and somber mood. Splashes of strings pounce like Vincent Price into his bat-cape. In eerie futurama sound, "Billie Jean" features a Bat Cave of otherworldly synthesizers (Greg Smith, Bill Wolfer). As the indicted rogue dances till 3 a.m. with Billie Jean, she whips out a snapshot of [their?] kid with similar roguish eyes. Louis Johnson's bass surrounds moonwalking Jackson, who owlishly and "Urkel-ly" prances away. From responsibility? From DNA testing? African drummer Ndugu Chancler thunders. Michael leaves final doubt for all questioning his paternity potential. He says the androgynously-named 'Billie Jean' is not his lover, but just some mere girl. And he trails off in full denial. Is 'Billie Jean' about 'family values'? The modern trend has skirted the 'nuclear family.' In the 50s, America's percentage of children born outside of legal marriage mirrored England's

in the 1850 Industrial Revolution – about 5%. By 2001+, with a differently structured welfare system in both England and the U.S.A., it's now over 30%. Contrast Jackson's parenting denial with Rapper **Will Smith**'s shouldering of Dad-responsibilities in his #20, 1-98 "Just the Two of Us." [Or Shaggy's #1, 11-2000 Jacksonian "It Wasn't Me"].

As Jackson puffs through denial with Holly hiccups, glottal stops, and locomotive wheezes (which all sound pretty good), somebody raises the new kid in town. Who? **Madonna**'s "Papa Don't Preach" is an equal-opportunity song (#1, 6-86). 'Dad – don't preach,' she argues, she's keeping her baby. When Madonna was pregnant with her first child Lourdes in 1996, she handled her own maternal responsibilities with zillions of megabucks. In the real world of minimum wage, though, who pays for the baby? Easy answer. Proud new GRAMPS. Kids raised by grandparents usually end up doing quite well. Until somebody dies of old age. Life's like music, say the starry-eyed commentators. Preachers tell us we're a little above the hairy, snurfly, and slimy animals staggering or slithering around on this earthy earth – yet we're a long ways below the angels harmonizing on the fluffy golden clouds aloft. Lovelight sparkles by night in lovers' eyes. Many dewy-eyed damsels, stoned on the True-Love Smokescreen, have created many million sweet little new kids, because they never listened to **Carole King/Shirelles'** (#1, '60) "Will You Love Me TOMORROW." Guys, with eyes on the prize, will still say anything . . . just before they hotfoot it far, far away forever.

"Man in the Mirror" – Michael Jackson, #1(2), 2-88; #1(1) R & B. Holly hiccup champ song for Gloved One. This self-awareness pilgrimage talks about zapping bad habits, helping others. Great Gospel vocal help from Siedrah Garrett, and Winans and Crouch Choirs. Not a tale of self-indulgence, it's a pang of remorse and a vow of atonement. Between "Billie Jean" and "Man in the Mirror," Michael snared five #1 hits, like **Paul McCartney** duo "Say, Say, Say" to #1(6), 1-83 (#2[4] R&B).

"Mr. Ghost Goes to Town" – Mills Blue Rhythm Band, #15, 12-36. *Gold Rush* does MJ's "Thriller" in our MTV video section, so here's a 'Hallowe'en Carol' sneak preview. Lucky Millinder began here as singer, amassing an overriding orchestra with Gospel star **Sister Rosetta Tharpe** (1915-73), plus "Honky Tonk's" (#2, '56) **Bill Doggett**, and archetypal Rock song "Good Rockin' Tonight's" **Wynonie Harris**. Ghost stories are nothing new, and Thrillers thrill and chill.

Sister **Rosetta [Nubin] Tharpe** scored a #13, 8-42 hit with Lucky Millinder's band – "I Want a Tall, Skinny Papa." Trumpet and trombone legends **Dizzy Gillespie** and J. C. Higginbotham also worked with Millinder (1900-66). Tharpe also hit with R & B roaster #21, 7-42 "Shout, Sister, Shout."

Another great Soul & Roll Pre-Star was **Freddie Slack** and His Orchestra. Their amazing "Cow Cow Boogie" glommed #6, 10-42 (#9 R & B). Slack penned the "House of Blue Lights," where Little Richard's "Good Golly Miss

Molly" is still rockin' (last we heard). Millinder's biggest hit was #19, 7-51 "I'm Waiting Just for You" [#2[8] R&B], covered by crooner **Pat Boone** to smooth #27, 3-57 (#1 '56 "Don't Forbid Me" hit #10 R & B, 3-57, on flipside).

"Bad" – **Michael Jackson, #1(2), 9-87; #1(3) R & B.** Five years after Michael's triumphant #1(37) Al. *Thriller,* Jackson countered with huge album *Bad,* which debuted at #1(6), 9-87. Like **Madonna, Toni Basil,** or **Janet Jackson**, Michael's appeal is extra-dimensional and choreographic. Age of VIDEO. He represents the first age of MTV animation. His suave Moonwalk contrasts to his herky-jerky 'Thriller' or 'Bad' personae. Supernatural? In "Thriller," his naïve date, terrified, watches him metamorphose in Hallowe'en fantasy from Michael to monster in a ghetto graveyard purgatory of terror.

Bad set an ALL-TIME record for number of #1 hits – FIVE: 11-87 "The Way You Make Me Feel," 8-87 "I Just Can't Stop Loving You," "Bad," "Man in the Mirror," and 5-88 "Dirty Diana." Michael's otherworldly forays took him to the Wizard's turf – OZ – in his **Diana Ross** duo "Ease on Down the Road" (#41, 9-78, #17 R&B). He's minimally cast in this twilight-time tune, a career trough and gray Soul adaptation (*The Wiz* [1978** ½]) of *The Wizard of Oz* (1939****). Gray? Black & White?

"Black Or White" – **Michael Jackson, #1(7), 11-91; #3 R & B.** Jackson showcases Rock and Soul from his multicultural podium. For Heavy Metal fans, he features **Guns N' Roses'** guitar star Slash. For Rappers, Bill Bottrell. "Black Or White" is also Old Soul (like Nat King Cole), Rap, Punk or Heartland Rock, and has Adult Contemporary appeal. The Everly Brothers signed the first million-dollar recording contract (Warner Brothers, 1960), effectively CREATING their music empire. Jackson trumped them. Sony of Japan upped the ante on Michael's contract to a reported ONE BILLION DOLLARS. Sales tapered in the wake of career-threatening allegations and innuendoes. [See *Titillator Tabloid*]. Check out, too, Three Dog Night's great classic "Black AND White."

"You Are Not Alone" – **Michael Jackson, #1(1), 9-95; #1(4) R & B.** After #7, '93 "Will You Be There," friends and siblings helped him top the charts. Sister **Janet** and Michael preceded this hit with #5, 6-95 "Scream." SONY got some seed money back on their investment with #30, 6-96 "They Don't Care about Us"; #42, 5-97 "Blood on the Dance Floor"; and #91, 8-97 "Stranger in Moscow." Jackson translates small-group shyness (opposite from most of us) to becoming a stage dynamo.

In 1994, Jackson did the last thing in the world from everybody's mind – something well-nigh impossible in the segregated 50s of his new pop-in-law's superstardom. He married the Boss's daughter. Actually, the KING (Springsteen is exempt from this tale). On May 26, 1994, a week after my wife and I toured Graceland in Memphis, Michael Jackson married Lisa Marie Presley, only daughter of ELVIS and Priscilla Beaulieu Presley. Their conjugal connection quashed fertilizer rumors about 'Jacko's Other Life.' Michael and Lisa lived happily ever after, for a

year and a half – when Lisa Marie filed for divorce. About that divorce. *Gold Rush* will doff its ivory-tower dignity and ponder the eternal question—why, oh why, did they split up? We like to think – no, we prefer to fervently BELIEVE – that the problem WA$ NOT MONEY . . . .

"U Can't Touch This" – **M. C. Hammer, #8, 4-90; #1(1) R & B.** Hammer accentuates the positive aspects of the 'Black Experience.' He is one major step between James Brown's pep-rally politics and the evercool Cosby-esque Rap humor and wit of **Will Smith** in "Wild, Wild West" (#1[3], 2-98). Born in Oakland, CA, 3-30-63 as Stanley Kirk Burrell, Hammer got nicknamed Little Hammer for resembling slugger **Hank Aaron** (#1-ever 755 home runs). Melodic seedbed for this Hammer hit is dreadlocked **Rick James's "Super Freak"** (#16, 8-81, #3, 5-81 R & B). Funkmeister James's biggest R & B hit? #1(6) 7-83 "Cold Blooded" (#40 HOT 100).

"U Can't Touch This" is a macho-gruff tune. Hammer's bullish baritone anti-drug Rap cuffs the 'cowards' who slink into their fuzzy netherworld of anaesthetized stupor. He extols the virtue of nonviolence in the M. L. King style, but there's some **Teddy Roosevelt** in Hammer. Lauding and applauding nonviolent solutions, he nevertheless stands shirtless on stage, clad in 2-strap overalls, and flexing 'cut' muscles to start the 'AB FAD' (see TV contraptions for $299 to build 'abs,' a muscle not invented until 1966). Roosevelt charged San Juan Hill with silver sabre. He said "speak softly – but carry a big stick." Hammer borrows extensively: Jackson Five, Marvin Gaye, Prince, Chi-Lites [Philly Soul – #1(1) 4-72 "Oh, Girl" and #3, 10-71 "Have You Seen Her?"]. M. C. Hammer's HOT 100 champ is #2(2) 9-90 "Pray" (#4 R&B). Others – "2 Legit to Quit" at #5, 11-91 (#3 R&B) and *Addams Family* (1991***) movie theme "Addams Groove" (#7, 12-91 & #15 R&B). Hammer is a hit among churchgoers, who disdain darker, bloodier Gangsta Rap.

"Summertime" – **D. J. Jazzy Jeff & the Fresh Prince, #4, 6-91; #1(1) R & B. Will Smith** (b. '68, Philadelphia) is the rapper star of TV sitcom *Fresh Prince of Bel Aire.* The other 50% of the duo is Jeff Townes. Smith's emergence as Rap superstar is built upon his macho, hammering image as a good unwimpy guy. He has fun, gets along with everybody, and eschews the steely stare, posturing, and swagger of guys doomed to playing the constant tough role. Will's movie theme "Men in Black," #1(4)A, 6-97 [Airplay], and his "Getting' Jiggy With It" of 2-98 hit the Big HOT 100 #1 for three weeks. His #17, 12-98 "Miami" is a swashbuckling travelogue of all the gorgeous girls to meet along warm Miami shores (compare lyrics to Beach Boys' #3, 7-65 'California Girls' on the Pacific Coast). Will Smith is one reason Rap was the #1 hitmaking music in 2001, via his positive energy and gentle comic coolth. Koolth?

"Summer Madness" – **Kool & the Gang, NC, '75;** flipside of #35, 4-75 "Spirit of the People." Their uptempo "Madness" rode heavy airwave saturation, and Will Smith/Fresh Prince sampled much Kool. Disco/Funk/Soul/Rap Fusion. All this stuff interconnects.

"Bo Diddley" – **Bo Diddley, NC, '55; #1(2), 5-55 R&B.** We did Bo's [Elias McDaniel] prehistoric #20 '59 Rap song "Say Man" (#3 R&B). He scored 'dozens' on his sax man Jerome Green. In 1999, Rap inventor Bo said there's a lot of current Rap he'd be ashamed to have his mother hear . Bo had a great new beat (see 'Macarena'), a minimal-range pre-Rap tune, and a rectangular guitar.

"(You Gotta) Fight for Your Right (To Party)" – **Beastie Boys, #7, 12-86; NC, R&B.** The white Beastie Boys' Rap fight song conquered suburbia with its Rap and Roll message. Lead singer **Adam Horovitz**'s stepmom, Gillian Horovitz, was among the fastest female marathoners overall in the New York City 2000 Marathon in 2:45 (6:20 min,/ mile, 26.2 miles) – at an amazing 45 years old. The Beastie Boys formed in '91: Adam, 2nd **Adam Yauch** (MCA), and Michael Diamond (Mike D). Their DJ? **Dr. Dre,** whose famous #8, 5-93 "Dre Day" we cited. BEASTIE is an acronym for 'Boys Entering Anarchistic States Towards Internal Excellence.' Their Al. *Licensed to Ill* #1(7), 11-86 had the Rap sales record; they followed, not ill-advisedly, with *Ill Communication* and Al. #45, 4-96 *The In Sound from Way Out.* Jazz beckoned, with #28, 8-98 Al. Intergalactic.

"Private Dancer" – **Tina Turner, #7, 1-85; #3 R & B.** Ike Turner (b. '38) entered the Rock Hall with wife Tina in 1991. He helped discover Rock and Roll as piano player for singer/saxman **Jackie Brenston** (1930-79, b. Clarksdale, MS), with classic "Rocket 88" – #1(5), 5-52 R&B-only. A Rocket 88 is an Oldsmobile, perhaps. Everglamorous Tina (b. Anna Mae Bullock '38, Nutbush, TN) still danced at full-tilt boogie at 63+, and still does TV stocking ads. Her bio-pic *What's Love Got to Do with It* (1993***) pits Ike's troubled temper against the saintly Soul songstress's burgeoning superstardom.

Tina followed King-of-Rhythm Revue bandleader Ike Turner till he caught her. The scrappy couple carved out an entire aeon of Rock and Soul – from Pre-Bill Haley to Beyond Millennium. **Bob Seger** (#69, 6-76) cut her girl-hood hometown story "Nutbush City Limits" (#22, 9-73 for Tina). From tiny-town obscurity and a fractured farm family with MOM ditching the kids, precocious Anna Mae drifted into groupie-hood, doting on cool Ike Turner's rhythms. They became an item. Their debut "A Fool in Love" bopped the competition to #27 (#2 R&B) 8-60. "I Idolize You" tailgated at #82, 12-60, but #5 R&B. Then they launched #14, 7-61 "It's Gonna Work Out Fine" (#2[2] R&B).

Tina is the quintessence of raw stage energy. A nonstop dervish, she whirls amok with hot vocals and soulful passion. Biggest mutual hit? Cover of CCR's #2, 1-69 "Proud Mary" to #4, 1-71 (#5 R&B). As their tempestuous marriage disintegrated from lovers' spats into eight-round middleweight championship bouts (70s), Turner tussles stormed into nastier free-for-alls. It was time to punt Ike. She outgrew him. Into the 80s, Tina headlined in Rio de Janeiro with Whitesnake, Queen, AC/DC, and Rod Stewart. By 1985, she duetted with Mick Jagger. Ike drifted off into a blotto blue funk.

"Private Dancer" is a peep-show allusion to the seamier side of Times Square. Hot girls wriggle and wobble in tiny skin-show booths for snaggletoothed oglers to froth over, and stuff horny quarters into slots to keep bye-bye Miss American thigh curtains from clunking down. When the curtain drops, the popeyed ogler is out of quarters, out of luck. Tina purrs contralto, shmoozing her siren call.

In her "I Don't Wanna Fight" (#9, 5-93 & #51 R&B), a fighter gets weary. Punch-drunk (see Simon & Gar's #7 '69 "The Boxer"). At her 1991 Rock Hall Induction, Tina hit her career zenith – Ike his nadir, a quagmire of jail time for substance charges. After years of love/hate aggravation, Tina Turner turned her tribulations into triumphs.

"Wipeout" – **Fat Boys (with the Beach Boys), #12, 7-87; #10, 8-87 R&B.** Co-writer of this Surf Rock instrumental anthem (#2, '63, **Surfaris**) was talk show host Morton Downey, Jr. (d. 2001, 68). Besides this Surf Rap hybrid, Large Lads galumphed from Surf Soul to Philly Twisterama with **Chubby Checker** (b. '41, South Carolina) with #16, 6-88 "The Twist (Yo, Twist)" (#40 R&B).

"Shining Star" – **Earth, Wind, and Fire, #1(1), 2-75; #1(2), R & B.** Fuzzily fulminating out of the Ancient Greek Cosmology of the earth's four main elements (they missed the 4th, 'water'), this LA R & B crew is the brainchild of kalimba guru **Maurice White.** Rock Hall 2000 Inductees, they enjoyed 46 great R&B Top 100 hits spanning over 2 ½ decades. "Shining Star" is their SHINING STAR. .It has the Holy Grail of timeless hits – a super singable HOOK line you can't forget, because it's just too cool. They chomped the 10-81 charts with #3 "Let's Groove." Jazz Soul. Excellent melodies. Maurice White apprenticed with **Ramsey Lewis**, Jazz icon.

"Keep On Truckin'" – **Eddie Kendricks, #1(2), 8-73; #1(2), R&B. Kendricks** (1939-92) carried the countertenor high leads for the #4 most-popular Soul/R&B Artists of all time – the **Temptations**. This truckin' manifesto captures Dr. King's mood of positive strides ahead for his people (OK, all people). Eddie's "Boogie Down" hit penultimate #2(2), 1-74.

"Kiss" – **Tom Jones, #31, 12-88; NC, R & B.** Welsh White Soul belter of va-va-voom Vegas wrangles a hip Rap anthem. His thundertone baritone cruises low range like **Billy Eckstine** or **Bill Medley**. This song is a "Good Thing," like **Paul Revere & the Raiders'** song "Good Thing" (#4, 12-66). Other tan-impaired Soul? "Good Thing," at #1(1), 5-89 by the **Fine Young Cannibals**; Roland Gift's gifted/talented Birmingham, England, crew also hit with #1, 1-89 "She Drives Me Crazy" and #11, 8-89 "Don't Look Back." Kiss? See KISS (Heavy Metal/ Glam Rock).

"Pump Up the Jam" – **Technotronic, #2(2), 10-89.** International team – Belgian DJ/producer Thomas DeQuincey; female rapper Ya Kid K, non-singer Felly – Zaire model who videoed the chanty tune to international MTV fame. Two other top tens, like #6, 6-92 "Move This."

"Sixty-Minute Man" – Dominoes, #17, 8-51; #1(14), 5-51 R & B. 2nd-year Rock Hall inductee ('87) **Clyde McPhatter** (1932-72) did smooth tenor for bandleader Billy Ward (see #12 "Stardust" and #20 "Deep Purple" – '57). Vintage Un-Rapped R&B classic about guy with insatiable appetite for lovin'. Often called 'First R & R Record.'

Another #1(14) R&B hit of yesteryore was #23, 2-54 Top 30 – "The Things I Used to Do," by **Guitar Slim and His Band**. Band? It included 1st-year '86 inductee **Ray Charles**. In 11-89, Charles cut "I'll Be Good to You" with **Quincy Jones** and **Chaka Khan**, known for #3, 9-84 "I Feel for You." Consummate bandleader Jones, in turn, cut smooth song "One Hundred Ways" to #14, 12-81 (#10 R&B) with **James Ingram**, whose 12-86 #2(1) duet with lovely **Linda Ronstadt** "Don't Know Much" (NC, R&B) dusted off the far stars for romantic power.

"A Little Bit of Soap" – Jarmels, #12, 7-61; #7, 8-61 R & B. Richmond's Nathaniel Ruff's streetcorner serenaders divvy up one of the all-time top 300 Rock and Soul songs. Cool Chalypso beat. Echoes music power of Flamingos, Drifters, and Jay 'Bird' Uzzell's **Corsairs** (#12, 12-61 "Smoky Places" [#10 R&B]).

"At My Front Door" – El Dorados, #17, 10-55; #1(1), 9-55 R&B. Named after Cadillac's luxury car and the Gilded Man Legend of South America (see Scrooge McDuck *Ducktales*). **Pirkie Lee Moses**'s streetcorner kings presided over Chicago's Englewood High School. Glenn O'Kray's favorite song presaged other streetcorner Carusos: **Edsels'** (named for Ford flop car) #21, 5-61 "Rama Lama Ding Dong"; **Shep & the Limelites'** #2(1), 3-61 "Daddy's Home"; or Newark's tremendous **Fiestas'** "So Fine" (#11, 4-59, #3 R&B).

"Can't We Be Sweethearts?" – Cleftones, NC, 1955. **Herbie Cox**'s sparkling tenor spun off Warren Corbin's 'Bowzer' basement bass notes. "Sweethearts" was the 7th 45-rpm record I ever owned, and I love it to this day. An old pal, this song. Cleftones' chart action? #57, 5-56 "Little Girl of Mine" (#8 R&B); #18, 5-61 (#10 R&B) "Heart and Soul" – which uptempos Larry Clinton's #1 '38 version, and echoes Surf Rock gurus **Jan & Dean**'s #25, 6-61 "Heart and Soul." From Jamaica, Queens, NYC.

"Weak" – SWV (Sisters with Voices), #1(2), 4-93; #1(2) R & B. New York's **Cheryl 'Coko' Gamble, Tamara 'Taj' Johnson**, and **Leanne 'LeLee' Lyons**. They scored on Michael Jackson follow-up #2(3), 7-93 "Right Here/Human Nature" that hit #1(7) R & B. Power to spare.

Johnny Gill hit #3, 5-90 (#1 R&B) with "Rub You the Right Way." From a family gospel group in Washington, D.C. (Wings of Faith), Johnny monstered four big hits, like #1(2), 6-90 R&B "My My My" (#10, 8-90 HOT 100).

"Ice Ice Baby" – Vanilla Ice, #1(1), 9-90; #6 R & B. Floridian Dutch-American rapper helped boost Rap to #1 in suburbia. Ice (Bob Van Winkle) mainstreamed a music style in a new area.

"Devil Or Angel" – Bobby Vee, #6, 9-60; #22, 10-60 R & B. Finnish-American Vee sings good vs. evil about the confusion of love – with Teen Idol Green-Eyed Soul. Original? **Clovers** at #3, 1-56 R & B-only. Vee does a tremendous double-shot Soul song of **Temps/ Freddie Scott** on his #35, 4-68 "My Girl"/"Hey Girl."

"Gangsta's Paradise" – Coolio, #1(3), 8-95; #2(5), R & B. **Weird Al Yankovic**, Polish-American R & R comedian, strolled out onto the Awards stage with a Coolio hairstyle. Lest anyone chuckle at a white guy with straight-up electric dreadlocks, let's not forget two haircuts that revolutionized first music – then the world.

1) Elvis's Pompadour – with a vertical-line D.A. [Duck's 'aft'] in back, Elvis's full thick blue-black hair flashed a sheen of rockin' afterglow.
2) The Beatles' Prince Valiant or Dutch Boy haircuts – manager Brian Epstein prescribed the revolutionary hairstyle that up-ended the universe,

At the millennium, many Rappers zapped all hair – like Michael Jordan – popularizing the BALD look (or reality). One other guy's hairdo angered 50s factory workers more than anybody in the world except **Gorgeous George**, a pro wrestler who took his bleached-blonde leonine locks out of curlers before entering combat. The other guy?

"Easter Parade" – Liberace, #26, 4-54. Long before one-named stars like Madonna, Prince, and yes, Coolio, **Liberace** (b. Wladziu Valentino Liberace 1919-87, Milwaukee) and violinist brother George Liberace wowed the Edith Bunkers of brand-new Televisionland (#27, 5-52 "September Song"). Liberace (pron. 'libber-ah-chee') took a lot of flak from Al Bundy hubbies for his coiffed mane, fluttery ruffles, and natty tuxedos. Consummate Classical-pianist showman. Could have been 1st Glitz star – but played speed-key Classical piano. Liberace scoffed at snippy critics , 'I cried all the way to the bank.' Like MTV Fashion Awards 2001+, "Easter Parade" too is a sleek fashion show – an NYC Fifth Avenue promenade. Upscale ladies and gentlemen strode the glittery streets, topped with chic chapeaus or billowy bonnets for paparazzi snapshooters. "Easter Parade" slugged it out on the HIT Parade eight times from 1933 to Liberace – with **Bing Crosby** #22, '47, **Guy Lombardo** #11, '39, and **Leo Reisman's Orchestra** at #5, '33. In 2001, acquitted Rapper **Puff Daddy Combs** wears Easter Parade-type finery, but also commands the macho appeal of 'Dapper Don' John Gotti of Howard Beach.

"Stormy Weather" – Leo Reisman & Orchestra, #1(8), 3-33. Composer Harold Arlen sang the lead vocal. Also #1 for Soul songstress **Ethel Waters** in 1933. The BIG version everybody (especially **Redd Foxx** on *Sanford & Son*) recalls is Fred Sanford's fantasy girl (#21, 9-43 version) – **Lena Horne**. Reisman hardly gets any press today. This guy was very important, like Dr. Dre or Babyface or Will Smith. Reisman did #1(6), 1-32 "Paradise," covered by super Soul tenor **Sammy Turner** to #46, 2-60, after Turner's blockbuster #3, 6-59 nursery-rhyme hit "Lavender Blue." Leo Reisman sang #1(2) 10-34 "The Continental," spawning a 50s TV show and *Saturday Night Live* skit. Paradise?

Back to **Coolio**'s Paradise. He takes the theme from something ultra-positive in the Afro community – **Stevie Wonder**'s "Pastime Paradise" from his Al. #1(14) 10-76 *Songs in the Key of Life* (Grammy '76). Stevie's Jazz/Soul Ellington tribute "Sir Duke" is the album's flagship. Coolio followed this MCA Sound biggie with his **Kool & the Gang** reprise "Too Hot," to #24, 12-95 (#5, 1-80 by Kool). **Coolio** hit #3, 6-94 #12 R&B) with "Fantastic Voyage." It's originally by **Lakeside**, and hit #55, 1-81, but #1(2) much later (11-90) R & B. This 9-man nontet, from Dayton, Ohio, had 17 1978-90 charted R & B hits, including a funky Beatle cover – "I Want to Hold Your Hand, " to #5, 1-82 R&B-only.

Rappers like Artis Ivey (b.. '63, Compton, CA – **Coolio**) often take an older song and add Rap lyrics, handclapping, a pulsing bass, and 17 lawyers to avoid BMI lawsuits on sampling torts and tarts. Coolio's "1,2,3,4 (Sumpin' Now)" hit #5, 3-96, followed by #12, 7-97 "C U When You Get There" – employing the Rap idea for clever initials, and alphabet letters for words.

"Waterfalls" – TLC, #1(7), 6-95; #4 R & B. Lisa 'Left Eye' Lopez (1971-2002, car accident) of TLC burned down the house of boyfriend Andre Rison, wide receiver for the Atlanta Falcons ('94, 5 years probation). "Waterfalls" fractures the musicologist's gripe that Rap lacks melody. "Waterfalls" takes these three husky contraltos and shimmers rainbows of harmonic ecstasy. Catch Steve Cole's sax-driven 2001 Jazz version. In 11-94 TLC hit #1(4) with "Creep"; their tweener tune was #2(3), 3-95 "Red Light Special," followed by #5, 11-95 "Diggin' on You." A four-year hit hiatus stranded them in neutral, but 1999 yielded 2-99, #1(4) "No Scrubs" and #1(3), 6-99 "Creep."

Lopez's two friends are **Rozonda 'Chilli' Thomas** and **Tionne 'T-Boz' Watkins**. "Waterfalls'" gloomy verses warn of certain doom. A son ignores his mother's sharp warnings—see Merle Haggard's "Mama Tried" or Elvis's "In the Ghetto." The kid becomes a final statistic in a frozen gutter. Another obsessed by loving loves the wrong woman. Her shared disease cuts his lifespan by fifty years in the Doom Roulette of promiscuous lust. "Waterfalls" was the #3 biggest hit of '95. "Waterfalls" slashes good ol' chord swoops from Tonic I to Dominant Seventh V7. Suddenly, out of the rainbow rush of the fine spray at the bottom of the waterfall, TLD actually fires in a little religion, as Donna Summer did in the Glitz Blitz of her passionate Disco Inferno.

"Convoy" – C. W. McCall, #1(1), 12-75; #1(1), 11-75 C. McCall first did Country Rap with verse to #40, 2-75 (#12 C) "Wolf Creek Pass." Audobon, Iowa's William Fries [C.W.] got elected mayor of Ouray, CO, via this trucker-talk Rap song. C.B. radios preceded cell phones. Truckers try to foil the 'bears' (cops) with speed-trap radar, and roll their Convoy caravan in a frantic 98 mph speedburning frenzy. We already covered Country superstar **Johnny Cash**'s Rap extravaganza "A Boy Named Sue."

"Mind Playing Tricks on Me" – Geto Boys, #23, 10-91; #10, 8-91 R & B. Lead man **Richard 'Bushwick Bill' Shaw** first lost his eye in a shooting. The Jamaican dwarf then experienced this big hit as a minor consolation. Follow-up samples Marvin Gaye's #2, '71 "What's Goin' On," with an even more ominous portent: #40, 5-93 "Six Feet Deep." Or #82, 5-96 macrocosmic "The World Is a Ghetto."

"Kung Fu Fighting" – Carl Douglas, #1(2), 10-74; #1(1) R & B. With a barrage of Asian gongs, horns, and counterpunches, Jamaican-British engineering student Carl Douglas delivered his Rappish statement on martial arts, and also #48, 2-75 "Dance the Kung Fu."

Shaquille O'Neal, 7'2", 300# basketball All-Star center, trades off novelty glory with 'dat wascally wabbit' Bugs Bunny in "What's Up Doc? (Can We Rock?)" Shaq Raps in this preview for **Michael Jordan**'s 1996 blockbuster *Space Jam****.

"Can I Change My Mind?" – Tyrone Davis, #5, 12-68; #1(3) R & B. Greenville, MS, Soul tenor's Un-Rapped debut smash. Hugest HOT 100 tune? #3, 3-70 (#1 R&B) "Turn Back the Hands of Time." It's no relation to the wondrous waltz by crooner **Eddie Fisher** (#8, 9-51) "Turn Back the Hands of Time." Fisher married **Debbie Reynolds** and **Liz Taylor**, and is the father of Princess Leia (Carrie Fisher, *Star Wars*).

"U.N.I.T.Y." – Queen Latifah, #23, 11-93; #7 R & B. Dana Owens (Queen L) of Newark, NJ, hit stardom. Royalty? Duke Ellington, King Floyd, Count Basie, Duke of Earl, M.L. King, and Snoopy's Red Baron.

"Since I Met You Baby" – Ivory Joe Hunter, #12, 11-56; #1(3), 12-56, R & B. Crystal treble piano powers this slow love song in rainbow glory. Gorgeous melody, nice tenor. Hunter (1914-74) also helped Pat Boone's cover-tune career with his #1(5), 1-50 R&B-only "I Almost Lost My Mind" – #1(4), 6-56 for Boone.

"Whatta Man" – Salt-N-Papa (with En Vogue), #3, 1-94; #3, R & B. Cheryl 'Salt' James, Sandra 'Pepa' Denton of Kingston, Jamaica, and their DJ pal **DeeDee "DJ Spinderella LaToya' Roper**. It's taken from Linda Lindell's #50, 8-68 R&B-only "What a Man," sampled for their new sound. RAP samples chunks of other songs. This waffles between Rap and melody on the funky chorus. They conclude the guy is a good man. From #19, 11-87 "Push It" (#28 R&B), they rebounded to an **Isley Brothers**' echo on this classic (see #2[1], 3-69, and #1[4] R & B "It's Your Thing"). Salt-N-Pepa's Al. #4, 3-94 *Very Necessary* sold 5 Mil. Their MTV act includes them slinking about in some Victoria's Secret lingerie. They writhe as you sit by your TV with your preacher, your grandmother, and your date. Your dog ate the remote.

"Everybody Plays the Fool" – Aaron Neville, #8, 7-91; #1(5), R & B. Mr. Grace Note Aaron Neville (b. '41, New Orleans) reprises excellent song by Cuba Gooding (dad of actor C.G. Jr.) of the Philly-Soul **Main Ingredient** (#3, 7-72, #2[3] R&B). They also also top-tenned with #10, 2-74 "Just Don't Want to Be Lonely" (#8 R & B). Main Ingredient hit #15 R & B-only 10-89 "I Just Wanna Love You." Neville scored two #2's – 23 years apart: #2(1) 12-66 and #1(5) R&B "Tell It Like It Is" and #2(2) Linda Ronstadt duo 9-89 "Don't Know Much" (NC, R&B). His #56, 5-95 "Don't Take Away My Heaven" is among his best. Neville's quivering, quavering tenor belies his grizzly-bear powerlifting strength.

White Rappers 3rd Bass took #1 song of 1830s England, now nursery rhyme, "Pop Goes the Weasel" to #26, 7-91; #26 R&B. It was about wage-slaves on spinning machines with a spinning-jenny 'weasel.' Hip-Hop authentic sounds from Brooklyn & Queens.

"Power of Love/Love Power" – Luther Vandross, #4, 4-91; #1 R&B. Vandross's (b. '51, NYC) epic story on Epic Records is a testimonial to his suave style. With seven R&B #1's, Vandross, like Richard Marx and Barry Manilow, got his start in pop superstardom by penning commercial jingles. "Endless Love" is a duo with **Mariah Carey**. Among Vandross's 23 HOT 100 and 41 R&B chart successes are: #33, 10-81 "Never Too Much " (#1[2] R&B); #15, 11-86 "Stop to Love" (#1 R&B); "Here and Now" #6, 12-89 (#1 R&B); and   1st-line of Barrett Strong's #22, '59 classic "Money"—#10, 5-92 "The Best Things in Life Are Free." In 9-96, Vandross hit #52 with "Your Secret Love." Vandross is a major entertainment giant, a consummate artist, a superstar. His silky songcraftings hark back to a smooth musical dimension. His Soul stylistics are impeccably groomed, but 'Un-Rapped.'

"Why Can't We Be Friends?" – War, #6, 5-75; #9 R & B. **Eric Burdon**'s post-Animals' band was an integrated combo Among funky cameos are #2(2), 3-73 "Cisco Kid"; #8, 7-73 "Gypsy Man"; #3, 5-70 "Spill the Wine," and shackled-car fad #7, 9-75 "Low Rider" (#1 R&B).

Tōne Loc arrived with #2(1), 12-88 "Wild Thing" (#3 R&B), no relation to the **Troggs'** #1 '66 hit – or its cute parody at #20, '67 by "Senator Bobby," with a voice-over that sounded like the man who might have been president, Senator Robert Kennedy. In the June 1968 aftermath of Dr. King's assassination, so too was Senator Kennedy gunned down senselessly. Tōne Loc followed up different "Wild Thing" with #3, 3-89 "Funky Cold Medina." Tōne Loc is no relation to LA Rockers **Rhinoceros**, with John Finley via Steve O'Shaughnessy and Lynn, and their cool #46, 2-69 "Apricot Brandy." Tōne is from LA, too. Hispanic pals there called him Antonio Loco, which Rapper Anthony Smith snipped to Tone Loc.

Speaking of top Latino Rappers, check out **PM Dawn's** #1(1), 10-91 [#16 R&B] "Set Adrift on Memory Bliss," by brothers **Attrell** and **Jarrett Cordes (Prince Be & DJ Minutemix).** Their other gold grabbers? #3, 9-92 "I'd Die Without You," #6, 3-93 (#62 R&B) "Looking Through Patient Eyes," and #44, 9-98 "I Had No Right."

"Any Radio Show" – Frantic Ernie Durham, NC, '57. Overarching the great Soul stars I heard as a starry-eyed 13-year-old in Smokey's Motor City on WCHB or WJLB, the golden tones of Ernie cascaded over the midnight factory-glow moon – and the lullaby sirens of yestermorrow. Without cool dudes like Ernie, who zinged and zowied internal rhyme and nonstop alliteration, Rap today might be as exciting as the Gray Pages Phone Book. A genuinely happy man with the lovable demeanor of **Louie 'Satchmo' Armstrong**, Gentleman Ernie wasn't mad at anybody or anything. He rolled and rocked with the flow.

"My Adidas" – Run D.M.C., NC, '86; #5, 5-86 R & B. Rappers **Run D.M.C.** and rockers **Aerosmith's** careers collided on their #4, 7-86 "Walk This Way" (#8 R & B). This fast-sneakers ode slam-dunked Run's highest R & B chart hit. Queens, NYC, trio: RUN (Joe Simmons), DMC (Daryl McDaniels), and JAM MASTER JAY (Jason Mizell). They also skimmed stardom with #29, 10-86 "You Be Illin'" (#12 R&B), and #21, 3-93 (#9 R&B) "Down with the King." As Rock features wild fashions, so Rap sprouted the Adidas footwear of Run D. M. C. Soon came baggy pants, multi-pocketed jackets for stashing whatever, hooded sweatshirts of dusky hue, Gangsta wool hats at above 65 degrees, and a walk-that-walk walk. Rappers began with Disco, but chose trickier rhythms of frantic funkmongers to lambast their big sound.

"Fencewalk" – Mandrill, #52, 4-73; #19 R&B. This Jazz Funk Rock Latino septet (7) named themselves after a large baboon with a psychedelic baby-blue lavender rump, and a red and blue face (nope, not kidding, check Animal Planet channel). They're the only other well-known Rock combo besides the **Beach Boys** with three WILSON brothers. For Mandrill, Lou, Richard, and Carlos 'Mad Dog' Wilson.

The Rap message got enhanced by Fox's *In Living Color,* with choreographic 'Fly Girls' like Goldie Hawn on *Laugh-In* ('67****). *In Living Color* launched careers for many rappers who missed the *Arsenio Hall Show* or MTV's *Yo, MTV Raps* segment – as well as the incipient stardom of comic **Jim Carrey.** *Rap* got recognized as a polyrhythmic podium to get your message across. The Real McCoy?

"Run Away" – Real McCoy, #3, 3-95; NC, R&B. Unrelated to Janet Jackson's #3, 9-95 "Runaway," or Del Shannon's #1 '61 Rock Classic. I used to be Vice-President of **Ed McCoy's** Big Mack Records, a Detroit Soul studio on West Warren Avenue near Livernois in Detroit, totally unrelated to Germany's **Olaf 'O'Jay' Jeglitza** and **Patricia 'Patsy' Petersen.** Real McCoy also cranked cool #3, 8-94 "Another Night" and #27, 3-97 "One More Time."

"Free Your Mind" – En Vogue, #8, 9-92; #23, R & B. Confusing the issue, En Vogue sported a runaway hit called "Runaway Love" which snagged #51, 10-93 and #15 R&B WITHOUT **Run D.M.C.'s** Adidases. En Vogue teamed on #3, 1-94 "Whatta Man" (see Salt-N-Pepa). "Don't Let Go (Love)" snatched #2(4) in 11-96, bigger than #2(3), 3-92 "My Lovin' (You're Never Gonna Get It)." "Whatever" sparked #16, 7-97. San Francisco quartet features Dawn Robinson and Terry Ellis.

"My Prerogative" – Bobby Brown, #1(1), 10-88; #1(2), 8-88 R & B. Even before Bobby and Whitney Houston got hitched in '92, the Roxbury, MA (b. '69) R&B star had enviable huge hits: #3, 11-89 "Roni" (#2 R&B), #3 "Every Little Step" 3-89 (#1 R&B), #1(2) Glenn Medeiros duo "She Ain't Worth It" (only #43 R&B), and totally Un-Elvis #8, 7-88 "Don't Be Cruel" (#1 R&B). With lovely Whitney, #7, 1-92 "Good Enough" WAS, but Brown's tailspin trail of superstardom skidded in his quest to catch the OTHER huge-star Brown – JAMES.

"Baby" – Brandy, #4, 2-95; #1(4) R & B. Like first telegenic Rock or Soul star **Ricky Nelson** (1940-85), Brandy [Norwood] endured the hassle of instant music-biz success. Each was hampered by being good-looking, talented, famous, and already a TV star [**Thea**, '93, and main actress in '96 **Moesha**]. Blessed with enormous Keene-painting innocent eyes, beautiful bronze skin, and large, lovely lips, Mississippi-born Brandy's voice is a special bonus. "Baby" represents Brandy's cotton-candy sweet music.

With **Monica**, Brandy's bombshell blockbuster is their quarter-year-commanding #1(13), 5-98 "The Boy Is Mine," followed by overshadowed super hit #1(2), 12-98 "Have You Ever?" Other Brandy dandies? OK: Debut #6, 10-94 "I Wanna Be Down"; #9, 9-95 "Brokenhearted"; #2(2), 12-95 "Sittin' Up in My Room"; and vocal combo slugfest with stars **Gladys Knight** and **Chaka Khan** – #25, 8-96 "Missing You."

"Thong Song" – Sisqo, #3, 2-2000. Sisqo (b. '77, Baltimore) began with **Dru Hill** (of #4, 11-97 "In My Bed"), plus Redman duo #3, 10-98 "How Deep Is Your Love," and **Will Smith** duo on #1(1), 5-99 "Wild, Wild West." Sisqo loves tiny thong bikinis. One-piece Beach-Blanket-Bingo matron bathing suits shrank in '60 to Bryan Hyland's (#1, 7-60) "Itsy Bitsy Teeny Weeny Yellow Polka Dot Bikini." Millennial beaches featured these cover-nothing 'G'-string THONG bikinis of 1996+. Sisqo's popeyed ode to ogling takes the ebbing Beach Boy tidal wave down to Rap's real nitty-gritty. Sisqo's hit run wasn't "Incomplete: (follow-up #1, 8-2000). The 5'4", bottled-blond Sisqo found a lot of male record-buyers to share his "Thong Song" – young men with a real interest in swimwear.

In 4-2000, Jay-Z (featuring UGK) had a song called "Big Pimpin'" that hit #18, as Rap fare grew more risque with this epistle to hustlers' side men. Also, Nelly hit #7, 4-2000 with "(Hot S—) Country Grammar." Mystical chimed in with #14, 8-2000 "Shake Ya A—," in a censor-testing freewheeling era. "It's Over Now" hit #1 R & B and #6+ HOT 100 11-2000 for 112, and "Promise" by Jagged Edge hit #9+, 12-2000. Rap often ditches euphemisms, subtlety, and polite reserve to bring us mean-streets blunt reality, with a side of Barnyard Anglo-Saxon English. On the

slightly more reserved side, we have #7, 4-2000 "Wobble Wobble" by 504 Boyz, and "Party Up (Up in Here)" to #27, 2-2000 by DMX.

"Foolish" – Ashanti, #1(7+), 2002. The 2002 charts have been convincingly crushed by the total domination of Long Island newcomer **Ashanti**. Eight week sand beyond at #1 on the *Billboard* HOT 100 beats anything by the Rolling Stones, Celine Dion, Simon & Garfunkel, Ricky Martin or Jennifer Lopez, and it ties Madonna, the Monkees, and Marvin Gaye. Ashanti's soulful song stylistics are anything but foolish. She pulled off a chart coup that really hadn't been seen since the Beatles or Elvis, when his 1956 "Love Me Tender" at #1 trumped his "Love Me" at #2 – Ashanti scored BOTH #1 & #2; #2 is her "What's Luv?" 2-2002 collaboration with **Fat Joe**.

"It's So Hard to Say Goodbye to Yesterday" – Boyz II Men, #2(4), 9-91; #1(1), 8-91 R &B. One of most creative Barber-Shop Soul quartets fomented in Philly's High School of Performing Arts. In many ways, they ARE the 90s. Their Mariah Carey Soul/Elegy/Anthem hit #1(16), 12-95. Unstoppable? Untoppable.

"Whoomp! (There It Is)" – Tag Team, #2(7), 5-93; #1(1), R & B. Our cat Woomp (1952-70) had 58 kittens. Tag Team began in Denver, thrived in Atlanta. Cecil Glenn ('DC, the Brain Supreme') and Steve Gibson ('Steve Roll'n') made their song title a part of our language. For me, they brought back the fuzzy puffy memory of an orange & black tortoise-shell Hallowe'en cat with gold-green eyes. Good ol' Woomp. There she was. A great cat. May YOUR songs bring you such great memories. Yay, Woomp.

"I Wanna Know" – Joe, #4, 1-2000. This mellow Soul echo cruised like Smokey Robinson's smooth sound to #4. While other stars blast 'big pimpin','hot s— country grammar,' and funky oscillating rumps, Joe croons his silken romance epics. While slim shady characters spit in innocent folks' onion rings in small-change-nasty Burger Bonanzas, Joe and his fireside carried on the Johnny Mathis/Miracles/Philly Soul tradition of easy lovin'. In the audial aura of **Tony Williams/Platters**' eternal, ethereal love ballads, Joe reminds us that all is not frantic, furious, nor ugly, nor nasty, nor blunt. **Deon Jackson** told us love made the world spin. Paul McCartney philosophized that maybe "Silly Love Songs" (#1[5], 4-76) are maybe the marmalade, strawberry jam, or black cherry jelly on the Wonder Bread of life.

JOE [Thomas, b. '72, Cuthbert, Georgia] began his hot career with 2nd-hit #11, 2-96 "All the Things (Your Man Won't Do)," which is no Disney promenade itself. "I Wanna Know" is the one in the middle of a hit sandwich, too. After #10 "Faded Pictures" of 12-96, Joe hit the big time with #1(1), 12-99 "Thank God I Found You." Joe teamed with **Mystical** for 1-2001's huge hit "Stutter," which sailed at #1(4+) at the Ides of March.

Joe knows. Beatles too. "All You Need Is Love" (#1, Fab 4, '67). Yay, Joe. And maybe **Lobo.**

Lobo? See next Easy Squeezy Rock chapter . . .

Movie idol **James Dean**. Elvis memorized Dean's part in 1955's *Rebel Without a Cause*.

Rock and Roll's new generation is born--to Jefferson Airplane/ Starship's Gracie Slick, 1971.

Beat poet-singer **Allen Ginsberg**, major influence on John Lennon, Bob Dylan, Jim Morrison, and Janis Joplin.

The Cars (L-R) Benjamin Orr, Greg Hawkes, David Robinson, lead singer Ric Ocasek, and Eliot Easton.

Harry Belafonte of New York. His **Calypso** music of 1957 pioneered **Bob Marley's Reggae** rhythms.

Bewitching contralto **Stevie Nicks,** of **Fleetwood Mac.**

Christian Contemporary star **Amy Grant.**

Heartland Thunder Rocker **Bob Seger.**

Eric Clapton, 1972

Jim Croce

Colorado singer-song-writer **John Denver.**

The [Young] Rascals of New York City

Hall & Oates Darryl Hall (R) and **John Oates** (L) are the #1 duo in sales in R&R history.

Since Elvis is gone, **Elton John** is #1 in Top 40 hits, according to master chart chronicler Joel Whitburn: Elvis 104, Elton 57, Beatles 51.

Singer/song-writer **Carly Simon**

Tremendous tenor **Gary Puckett** (upper left) and the **Union Gap**

Jimmy Buffett of "Margarita-ville," minus his **Coral Reefer Band** and 'Parrotheads.'

Foreigner (L-R): Lead singer **Lou Gramm**, singer/keyboard maestro **Mick Jones**, Rick Wills, and Dennis Elliott.

The Who– (L-R from top): **Keith Moon**, drummer; **John Entwistle**, bassist; **Roger Daltrey**, singer; [bottom] **Pete Townshend**, guitarist.

Tina Turner

Metallica, (L-R): **Cliff Burton**, bassist; **Kirk Hammett**, guitarist; **Lars Ulrich**, drummer; **James Hetfield**, singer.

Journey, (L-R): Singer **Steve Perry**, Jonathan Cain, Neil Schor.

Iron Maiden, Heavy Metal album stars-- named after medieval torture device.

Ozzy Osbourne's pioneer Heavy Metal group **Black Sabbath.** [Ozzy A.W.O.L.].

The Police, (L-R): **Sting** [Gordon Sumner], Andy Summers, and Stewart Copeland.

Neil Young

Alice Cooper (L), Kaki Hunter, and **Meatloaf** (R) in 1980 UA movie *Roadie*.

Bon Jovi, (L-R): David Rashbaum, Alec John Such, **Jon Bon Jovi**, Tico Torres, **Richie Sambora**.

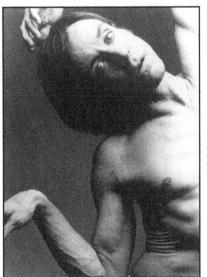

Iggy Pop a/k/a Iggy Stooge

Bruce Springsteen with his trademark Fender Telecaster guitar.

Elvis (1935-1977)

Tom Petty and the Heartbreakers
(L-R): Stan Lynch, drums; Mike Campbell, guitar; Ron Blair, bass; **Tom Petty**, vocals and guitar; Benmont Tench, keyboards

Patti Smith

Aerosmith, (L-R):
Guitarist **Joe Perry**, bassist Tom Hamilton, singer **Steven Tyler**, guitarist Brad Whitford, drummer Joey Kramer.

Carlos Santana, and his singing guitar.

Steve Miller, sans band

Billy Joel

Don
McLean

**Three Dog
Night**.
Lead singer
Chuck Negron
is on right,
with Cory
Wells and
Danny Hutton
to his right.

Olivia
Newton-John

**Rev. Al
Green**,
Disco Soul
performer.

Cliff Richard,
70s star in
America,
British super-
star since
1958.

The Eagles:
(L-R), **Glenn Frey**, vocals and guitar; **Don Felder**, guitar; **Don Henley**, vocals and drums; **Joe Walsh**, guitar and vocals; **Timothy B. Schmit** (high tenor vocals, low bass guitar).

Fleetwood Mac
(L-R) **John McVie**, bass; **Christine McVie**, keyboards; **Stevie Nic** vocals; **Mick Fleetwood**, drums; **Lindsey Buckingham**, guitar.

Queen:
(L-R): Singer **Freddie Mercury** [of Zanzibar], bassist John Deacon, drummer Roger Taylor, guitarist Brian May.

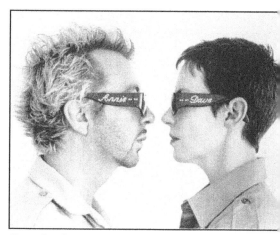

Eurythmics: David Stewart and **Annie Lenno**

Blue Oyster Cult, and their Brooklyn Bridge (from Manhattan). (L-R): singer **Eric Bloom**; keyboarder Tommy Zvonchek; guitarist **Donald 'Buck Dharma' Roeser**; drummer Jimmy Wilcox, bassist Joe Bouchard. Bloom is Howard Stern's cousin.

Debbie Harry, of NYC's **Blondie**

'Weird Al' Yankovic, and noisy friend.

Bob Dylan

KC and the Sunshine Band
Richard Finch is on left; **Harry Wayne Casey [KC]** is second from right.

Barry White

Mick Jagger, Stone

Tom Waits

Madonna
[Ciccone]

**Olivia
Newton-
John**

Dire Straits' multitude.
Lead singer and guitar guru **Mark Knopfler**
is in top row, third from left.

U2–(L-R): **Larry Mullen Jr.**, drummer; **Adam Clayton**, bassist;
the **Edge [Dave Evans]**, guitarist; **Bono [Paul Hewson]**, singer.
They met in home-port Dublin, Ireland, in 1976.

**Eric
Clapton**

**Freddy
Fender**

Gene Autry (1907-98)-- The Western Swing cowboy guitarist nearly lived long enough to see his beloved California/ Anaheim Angels (founded 1962) finally win the World Series (2002).

Garth Brooks' song "Friends in Low Places" is the biggest-selling [15M] Country song of all time.

Dixie Chicks (L-R): Emily Robison, Natalie Maines, Martie Seidel.

'Country' Charley Pride. Like Conway Twitty, Charley's major-league baseball aspirations were sidetracked, but Country stardom beckoned.

Tim McGraw-- Son of New York Mets' pitcher Tug 'Ya Gotta Believe' McGraw.

Faith Hill ↑

Rodeo Rider **Reba McEntire** →

Bryan Adams

R.E.M.

Punk Rock hitmakers and 2003 Rock Hall of Famers the **Clash** (1982).

Motown R&B Barber Shop Quartet **Boyz II Men**. They twice had the #1 song of the Rock Era, like #1 (16), 12-9 "One Sweet Day." (L-R): Shawn Stockman, Michael McCary, Wanya and Nathan Morris.

Paul and **Linda McCartney** of **Wings**

Dave Matthews

James Dean

Photo by my student Laura Oreste on December **6**, 1980. Yoko Ono with **John Lennon.** Lennon died on December 8, 1980, the day after Pearl Harbor's December 7th--a "Day which will live in infamy" (1941).

Surf Ballroom, Clear Lake, Iowa--**Buddy Holly's** 2-2-59 final performance on the Eve Before the Music Died.

Kurt Cobain of **Nirvana**

Clear Lake, Iowa, cornfield where Roger Peterson piloted a wayward-wind Beechcraft Bonanza to destiny, **2-3-59.** Monument by farmer at Gull Rd. and 315th Street.

Perhaps last photo of **Del Shannon,** January 1990.

Will Smith--"Fresh Prince" of family Rap.

Eminem a/k/a Marshall Mathers a/k/a Slim Shady.

TLC--featuring (L) Lisa 'Left-Eye' Lopes, T-Boz [Tionne Watkins] (M),and Chilli [Rozanda Thomas] (R).

2-Pac, star-crossed turf war Gangsta Rapper.

Whitney Houston

Shaggy ↑

Notorious B.I.G. Subject of Puff Daddy/P. Diddy's #1 (11) elegy "I'll Be Missing You." →

Shakira

Smashing Pumpkins (L-R): Jimmy Chamberlain, drummer; James Iha, guitar; **Billy Corgan**, vocals, guitar; D'Arcy, bass.

Rage Rockers **Rage Against the Machine** (L-R): Tom Morello, guitar; Timmy C., bass; Brad Wilk, drums; Zack De La Rocha, lead singer.

Justin Timberlake of N'Sync, and **Britney Spears**.

Nirvana (L-R) **Dave Grohl**, drums; **Kurt Cobain**, vocals, guitar; **Kris Novoselic**, bass.

Alanis Morissette

Blink-182

Gold Rush country's Alaskan **Jewel** [Kilcher].

Backstreet Boys

Buddy Holly's Crickets 1996:
(L-R): **Joe B. Mauldin**, bass, vocals; writer Maury Dean; and **Jerry Allison**, drums, vocals.

Nine Days
(L-R): Vince Tattanelli, drums; John Hampson, vocals, guitar; Jeremy Dean, keyboards; Brian Desveaux, vocals, guitar; Nick Dimichino, bass.

Nine Days

Creed
(L-R): Scott Philips, drums; **Scott Stapp**, vocals; Brian Marshall, bass; Mark Tremonti, guitar.

Light Metal --
The Easy Squeezy Stuff

We do Love Songs here. None of them are silly. Not even **Paul McCartney** & Wings' biggest hit:

"Silly Love Songs" – Paul McCartney & Wings, #1(5), 4-76. As Beatle brother **John Lennon** lent his name to multiple political agendas, Paul hunkered back into his unabashed arsenal of sweet love songs. With aw-shucks charm, Paul told the absolute truth about popular music: a light-hearted happy song about love can rescue the world from war and poverty and despair and hopelessness. Don't we all need a shot of music and mirth now and then? Yep. Aren't silly love songs a lot more fun than nuclear annihilation, the Plague, Jack the Ripper, and raccoons strewing your garbage over the garish avenue? Love is the lodestar that lights your weary way home from "The Long and Winding Road" (#1[2], '70, Paul & Beatles). A love song can almost get you through a war:

"Till the End of Time" – Perry Como, #1(10), 8-45. The great Perry Como (May 18, 1912 to May 13, 2001) could well have been the nicest man ever to wear the superstar singer crown. With 132 pop hits in the Top 100 from 1943 to 1974, the Canonsburg, Pennsylvania, ex-barber emerged as a giant among Crooner superstars. World War II cannons blasted away "Till the End of Time" dreams, but Perry's Lucky 13th charted hit – his 1st #1 – marked V-J Day (Victory over Japan), and the end of the bloodiest war in human history. Perry's melody comes from **Frederic Chopin**'s "Polonaise in A-Flat Major." Perry extracted something eternal and enduring from the aftermath of Hitler's *blitzkrieg* march through battered Poland, Chopin's homeland.

To hear Perry Como's calm, reassuring Italian-American baritone wafting over the postwar airwaves, it was an American lullaby. Perry told us it was OK to sleep. Everything would be all right. And he made it so. He was the kind of guy who just didn't care to say anything bad about anybody. Even his funtime travelogue, #38, 4-69 "Seattle" (at age 57), missed the stratus clouds of our cloudiest town; Perry brought us only the bluest skies and the greenest grass (Phoenix' eternal blue skies produce a golden, green-less desert). Perry's Saturday night prime-time TV show 1955-63 spanned the entire Rock Revolution. Perry began with **Ted Weems**' Chicago Big Band. Weems cut Elmo Tanner whistling on 8-3-33 song "Heartaches." It flopped. Fourteen years later, the breezy tune got re-launched to #1(13), 3-47 for Weems. This tune

and Perry's "Till the End of Time" were among very few 1900-50 songs to top two million sales. Perry and Weems enjoyed a dual late-bloomer. They cut it in 1939, but it didn't fly until 1947. Perry's chart debut was #18, 8-43, "Goodbye, Sue." Four years later, the Como/Weems #2(5), 8-47 "I Wonder Who's Kissing Her Now"; should-would-coulda glommed #1 (in August 1947) but, the most popular song of all time was in the way – **Francis Craig**'s #1(17), 8-47 "Near You."

Perry Como defined Easy Listening. Rockers' only gripe against Como songs was that his inaudible drummers were on eternal coffee breaks. Como also flirted with Rock and Roll: #3, 12-45 "Dig You Later (A-Hubba-Hubba-Hubba)." His #1(1), 3-56 "Hot Diggity" was a fun waltz that just happened to get stomped from its pinnacle perch by that new thrill-thrasher sensation in his debut #1(8) "Heartbreak Hotel" – **Elvis**, one of Perry's biggest fans.

The king of casual cardigan-sweater chic generated friendship among the 100 million people who bought his 27 gold records. Perry married high school sweetheart Roselle (d. '98). Everybody loved Perry.

Como also may have started Soul and Rap, inadvertently. His next #1 was #1(3), 3-46 "Prisoner of Love," **James Brown** used it in his 50s debut act, finally recording it to his first Top 20 HOT 100 tune (#18, 4-63, and #6, 5-63 R & B). Other Como cameos? His #1(1), 6-46 "Surrender," #1(3), 5-47 "Chi-Baba, Chi-Baba (My Bambino Go to Sleep)," #1(2), 4-49 "'A' – You're Adorable," *South Pacific*'s "Some Enchanted Evening," #1(2), 4-50 "Hoop-Dee-Doo," his sacred #22, 12-49 "Ave Maria," his *Victory at Sea* "Beneath the Southern Cross" melody as #1(4), 6-53 "Not Other Love," and his penultimate #1(8), 3-54 "Wanted."

The King of Easy Squeezy Listening lullabyed into the Rock Era. Of all the Crooners we rebelled against as teeny teen terrors, Perry Como was never among them. He was too cool: #5, 8-55 "Tina Marie," #10, 3-56 Soft Rocker "Juke Box Baby," #4, 6-56 "More," #8, 6-56 "Glendora," delightful melodious #1(2), 2-57 "Round and Round," Toni's fave #1(1), 1-58 "Catch a Falling Star," #4, 1-58 "Magic Moments," and his swan-song final top ten #10, 11-70 "It's Impossible." The 2nd favorite song of all time among Rock fans is **Don McLean**'s #1(5), '71 "American Pie." Perry took Don's unheralded masterpiece "And I Love You So" to #29, 4-73, his final Top 40 tune.

Perry Como serenaded the world with NON-Silly Love Songs. He traded panic for calm, rage for compassion, hate for love. Maybe General Douglas MacArthur, General George Patton and Commander in Chief (President) Dwight David Eisenhower won that big war with all of our help, but I kind of believe that **Perry Como** helped put a sad, smoldering world of terror and travail, and final triumph, back together into the kind of place we always wanted America to be. Thank you, Perry, for teaching my Rock and Roll generation and me the meaning of the word KINDNESS.

Billboard lists the Top 500 Album Artists 1955-1996 contains many pre-Rock Easy Listening icons:

1. Elvis Presley	15,538	pts.
2. Frank Sinatra	12,766	
3. Beatles	10,918	
4. Johnny Mathis	10,072	
5. Barbra Streisand	9,207	
6. Rolling Stones	8,982	
7. Elton John	7,290	
8. Mantovani	7,157	
9 Bob Dylan	7,061	
10. Ray Conniff	6,998	
30. Bee Gees	4,941	
93. Perry Como	3,139	

Mantovani? Annunzio Paola Mantovani (1905-80), orchestra leader, hit with Al. #12, 5-57 *Film Encores*. Plus #2(1), 11-35 "Red Sails in the Sunset." From Venice, Italy, he played classical violin in London. **Ray Conniff** was a trombonist with nary a #1 album or single – but sweet music like #34, 10-56 "I Miss You So." Other Easy Listening icons include Mathis, Sinatra, Streisand, #15 Lawrence Welk, #17 Andy Williams, #19, Henry Mancini, #31 bandleader Billy Vaughn, #42 Mitch Miller, #43 Nat 'King' Cole, #59 Barry Manilow, #61 Enoch Light (#48, 11-58 "I Want to Be Happy Cha Cha"), #65 Dean Martin, #82 Tony Bennett, #87 Ferrante & Teicher, and two we're about the feature: #45 the **Lettermen**, and #91 **Anne Murray**.

"When I Fall in Love" – Lettermen, #7, 11-61. Totally unrelated to the *Late Night with David Lettermen* show, L.A.'s Lettermen were the #1 Adult Contemporary group of the 60s. They had an amazing influence on the Association and Chicago. Their harmonic blend is so even, it's hard to discern which note is the melody and which is the harmony. Rock and Roll cherishes its Grunge Groovers, Thrash Kats, Funkys in the Middle, and Dancing Disco Dervishes – but Rock cherishes its silken, softer sounds, too – a prelude to love in bloom. "The Way You Look Tonight" (debut #13, 9-61) is an idyllic Prom moment of chiffon romance, a slow dance with a star-spangled destiny. Without these Lettermen harmonies, there might have been no America's band – the **Beach Boys**. The Lettermen's letter-sweaters were made possible in this formal wear-a-suit era by the casual cardigans of charismatic **Perry Como**, whose "Catch a Falling Star" earned the first gold record ever officially given by the Recording Industry Association of America. "When I Fall in Love" is the Lettermen's biggest hit (Doris Day #29, 1953, and #1 for Letterman, Adult Contemporary).

"Cherish" – Association, #1(3), 8-66. With muted Jazz and Soft Rock Lettermen harmonies, **Terry Kirkman**'s (plays 23 instruments) Association was the standard-bearer for melodious Southern California groups beyond the Beach Boys and Lettermen. Nice crescendos and finalé counterpoints. Debut tune #7, 6-66 "Along Comes Mary" tossed a street odyssey. Breezy #1(4) "Windy" puffed a romantic dream of this cute girl boppin' down the avenue like the **Seekers**' "Georgy Girl." Rod Harris's "Never My Love" touts a forevermore romance at #2(2), 8-67, while #10, 2-68's "Everything That Touches You" is a convoluted Soft Rock classic, with a crescendo counterpoint climax of stunning power and precision.

"You Won't See Me" – Anne Murray, #8, 4-74. Anne (b. Springhill, Nova Scotia, '45) is the essence of easy, breezy Lite Metal, winging her winsome way with her #8, '70 Canadian "Snowbird" to sweet sunny climes. I hope I never discover Springhill looks like the rolling mill for Detroit's smoky factory colossus, because I picture perfect pristine daisy-dotted slopes and Kelly-green Disney meadows and rainbow leprechauns and tartan towns for the Scottish-Canadian alto. Anne takes this Lennon-McCartney castoff song to melodic glory.

"Could I Have This Dance?" – Anne Murray, #33, 9-80; #1(1) C. An aural super shadow of **Patti Page**'s #1-ever #1(13), '50 "Tennessee Waltz," this velvety melodic Murray number spins off romantic rafters with a pastel golden glow. Anne's other Heart-of-Lite-Metal great hits include: "Love Song," at #12, 12-73; signature classic #1(1), 1-78 "You Needed Me"; and Cricket **Sonny Curtis**-penned Everly classic "Walk Right Back" (only #103, 4-78, #4 Country).

"Carolina in My Mind" – James Taylor, #118, 4-69; #67, 11-70. *Gold Rush* has two big criteria. We pick the big ones, and we pick the good ones. Taylor (b. '48, North Carolina) sings a homeward-bound ballad. Taylor's low-tenor Light Metal tunes? #31, 10-71 "Long Ago and Far Away" (#8, '44 **Perry Como**) is backed by **Joni Mitchell**, with **Carole King** on piano; #20, 10-77 "Your Smiling Face"; **Buddy Holly** flipside "Everyday" to #61, 11-85; and Everlys' #10, 8-58 "Devoted to You" – with Lite Metal partner **Carly Simon**. Rock Hall 2000, Taylor.

"Watching Scotty Grow" – Bobby Goldsboro, #11, 12-70; #7, 1-71 C. Most songs simply warble about desire (and therefore prospective fatherhood). This **Mac Davis** song actually cares what happens after the little tyke is actually born. The young dad dotes in Key of 'D' on his precious little son. Bobby scored #9 Pagliacci-theme 1-64 "See the Funny Little Clown." Beyond the honky-tonk afterglow, he prefers fatherhood. Dad and dude build a tumbledown castle from building blocks. He horseback-rides the Oshbosh B'Gosh kiddo off to bed, while his wife urges him to come warm her up. He halts for a pint-sized prayer. He plus God are watching Scotty grow.

In Bobby's #53, 12-65 "Broomstick Cowboy," Bobby (b. '41) ponders his kid prancing manfully on a hobbyhorse broomstick with six-guns snapping – he visualizes real-life death on some forlorn battlefield. In the fallout-shelter aftermath of Hiroshima's mushroom roar, and our Unhappy Daze Cold War posturing, he broods about the end of the postmodern world in a whispery whimper. Bobby practiced Graveyard Rock, with his #1(5), 3-68 terrifying "Honey," about his love's departure in her life's prime of natural causes; he plants a memorial tree, and hopes to see her in Heaven (see Clapton, "Tears in Heaven"). The upsurging Vietnam War provided lyrical fodder for Bobby's morose #19, 6-68 ballad "Autumn of My Life."

In "Broomstick Cowboy," guns boom in firestorm jungles. His growing boy shoots marbles and silver bullets, and collects halcyon days and Willie Mays bubble gum baseball cards. Though we all do long-distance worrying now and then, Bobby is disconsolate that his adored boy may someday be target practice on some faraway field of blood and honor.

"I Didn't Raise My Boy to Be a Soldier" – Peerless Quartet, #1(4), 4-1915. Europe exploded over a Yugoslavia/Bosnian archduke assassination, and America sang songs like this to avoid getting into the fray at first. Many precious young worldwide 'broomstick cowboys' found their final teenage resting-places in dank, sodden foxholes. Bass **Frank Stanley** led Peerless 'Boy Band' on bellflower crank-up Victrolas (relic record players of scratchy 78 rpm records). Though Woodrow Wilson was elected to the keep-us-out-of-war platform, pacifism receded in a geyser of rushing xenophobic war fever when the Germans sank the Lusitania. Their new song's stance?

"Over There" – Peerless Quartet, #1(2), 10-1917. Songwriter **George M. Cohan, John Wayne**, and Saddam Hussein knew the truth about the United States of America – we are a big friendly country that believes in individual freedom. We will do whatever we can with a big kind heart to help anybody in need. Nasty foreign governments know, however, they must not ever step upon our Blue Suede Shoes. "Over There" spun at #1(9), 9-1917 for the American Quartet. Though these rousing battle-cry anthems jolted 1918, they had no guitar firepower, and would be considered Easy Listening today.

"It's a Long, Long Way to Tipperary" – John McCormack, #1(8), 1-1915. Snoopy's Tipperary is an emerald green romantic chunk of the Southern Irish Auld Sod. THE great Irish tenor 'covered' the American Quartet's #1(7), 12-1914 rendition as the big ugly 'Great War' [WWI] began on the battlefields of Europe. McCormack's spellbinding tenor made cops cry. So did this immortal ditty:

"Danny Boy" – Dennis Day, NC, 1951. Unofficial Irish national anthem. It memorializes the spiritual bond between two soldiers – one fallen in battle, and one kneeling sentinel over his grave. Welsh tenor **Andy Williams** took it to #64, 10-61, while Afro Soul star **Jackie Wilson** hit #94, 2-65 (#76, 12-64 Patti LaBelle, too). Danny's Scottish brother?

"Loch Lomond" – Evan Williams, #10, 3-1912. Dying in some faraway war, Williams (1868-1918) sings to his tartan comrade – you take that 'high road' but I will take that 'low road,' but I'll return to Scotland before you do. . . He means his spirit will reach the bonnie shores and braes and burns o' Scotland after he dies – but before his friend shuffles back on the long march. He laments he'll never see his lady love again by the 'bonnie-banks' of Lake Lomond.

"Time in a Bottle" – Jim Croce, #1(2), 11-73. In a minor-key tapestry, Jim (1943-73, faulty airplane) muses the mysterious phenomenon of time – and how people squander it. 12-string compadre Maury Muehleisen floats this spindrift ballad into our souls and memories. It's tacitly dedicated to Jim's child his bride Ingrid carried.

"One Kiss for Old Time's Sake" – Ronnie Dove, #14, 4-65. Virginian Dove (b. '40) had 20 HOT 100 entries, like #14, 10-64 "Right Or Wrong" and #16, 6-65 "A Little Bit of Heaven." Tenor Lite Rock balladeer.

"Baby, I'm Yours" – Barbara Lewis, #11, 6-65; #5 R & B. Barbara (b. '43) is from Metro Motown's South Lyon, where I almost got killed in 1971. I was doing something unsafe, of course – driving a Lambretta 175cc bike legally with my light on at 45 mph. The ditzy van driver didn't see me when she lurched out from a gravel side road. To avoid a slight case of death, I slammed a 90° right turn at 30 mph. She clipped the bike. I flew off into a wonderful ditch, enjoying an Insta-Lunch of mud, cattails, algae, and relief.

Thanks to helmet, leather, and Levis, I got scratched up but escaped without broken bones. Why am I telling you this? If you read this far, you are a musician. We musicians aren't always that bright when it comes to self-preservation. The **Allman Brothers** lost two guys in separate bike disasters at nearly the same grim corner a year apart. Now I am a wimp. I drive tank Oldsmobiles with stuffy seatbelts. But I still surf . . .

Barbara hit biggest with #3, 5-63 "Hello Stranger" (#1 R & B). Her album-pix look sweet, light-skinned, debutantish. She sang make-out music extraordinaire: #11, 9-65 "Make Me Your Baby," #28, 7-66 "Make Me Belong to You," and #72, 4-67 "I'll Make Him Love Me." Soul Jazz.

"Rainy Night in Georgia" – Brook Benton, #4, 1-70; #1(1), R & B. South Carolinian Soul charmer (1931-88, meningitis) rattled baritone low tones in this soggy slosh of super song. 46th-biggest Rock Era Artist [Whitburn]. From Georgia gullywashers, drizzle seeps into his water-logged Soul. Bygone romance is a backdrop – a façade. His romantic loss oozes from blue gloom into a hobo vignette of boxcars, pawnshop guitars, and love on the rocks. His mellow hits? #3, 11-59 "It's Just a Matter of Time"; #2(3), 5-61 Rap-spiced Talking Blues "Boll Weevil Song"; Gospel Soul Rocker #19, 1-62 "Shadrack"; and **Dinah Washington** duo #5, 1-60 "Baby (You've Got What It Takes)."

On **Berlin**'s #1(1), 6-86 "Take My Breath Away," lead singer Terri Nunn's echoes Benton, says Keely Harris.

"I'll Follow the Sun" – Beatles. [On 31(9) Al. *Beatles '65*]. Paul salutes **Buddy Holly**'s sound. Other Hollytone Beatle song include #35, 4-64 "Thank You, Girl," NC, 2-64 "Little Child," and #10, 5-64 "P.S., I Love You" [P.S. for "Peggy Sue"]. Beatle Light Metal includes #12, 7-64 "And I Love Her," #53, 8-64 "If I Fell," #1(4), 9-65 "Yesterday," #3, 10-60 "Something," and the song New York Philharmonic Conductor **Leonard Bernstein** called the greatest song ever written, Paul's #1(2), 5-70 "The Long and Winding Road." **Rolling Stones** did beautiful (Lite Rock) #6, 12-65 "As Tears Go By."

"That's What They Say" – Buddy Holly, NC, 1959. Buddy's greatest unheralded song. Stunningly melodic, it bears a Generation X message of cosmic doom. Disillusioned kid frets elders who tell him true love will arrive – just be patient. Holly & Cricket committee serve a baroque brocade of far-flung polychord fantasies, celestial harmonies, and a rhythm track rolling like Texas tumbleweeds. Buddy's producers the Pettys (Norm & Vi) hit #14, 9-54 with **Duke Ellington**' #3, '31 Jazz classic "Mood Indigo."

I met my **Cricket** heroes, **Jerry Allison, Joe B. Mauldin,** and **Sonny Curtis** (b. 5-9-37) at 1962 Detroit Lakes, Minnesota. Hurtling aimlessly across On-the-Road North Dakota wheat field prairie, I saw a CRICKETS TONITE sign at a cows and cornfield crossroads. I yelled to Bill Baker and to Bob and Tommy we were going, as the Green Jet ('47 Buick) screeched around the corner. "NO, WE'RE NOT!" chorused three unenraptured pals. "Let's vote," I offered meekly. The vote was 3 to 1 against me. We went anyhow. That ol' jalopy with 285,000 miles, and ex-rear fender, and NO HOOD – was MY car. Sonny was impressed when we handed him a plump list of 38 Cricket-tunes. At the July lakeside dance hall 'concert,' I met this blue-eyed 'Peggy Sue' blonde. Between sets we sat on a lakeshore picnic table, gazing at the North Dakota balloon moon. The Crickets cranked up "Maybe Baby," and I dragged the astounded girl back inside to watch them.

Sonny wrote "Love is All Around," (#29, 7-80 C), better known as the *Mary Tyler Moore Show* theme song, plus #15, 4-81 C "Good Ol' Girls." The jury is still out on whether he did #28, 9-53 "The Best Way to Hold a Girl" when he would have been 16. Sonny told me once he considered another insect name for the Crickets – like the **Beetles.** Oddly, the Beatles named themselves after the Crickets.

"You're Having My Baby" – Paul Anka, #1(3), 7-74. A good one for Paul to croon to his wife, who had five girls. Paul's first career yielded Easy Squeezy #11, 9-60 "Summer's Gone," and biologically-impossible #14, 2-58 "All of a Sudden My Heart Sings." Like Elvis's eerie finale, Anka's "My Way," Buddy Holly's last hit (also by Anka) was #13, 3-59 "It Doesn't Matter Anymore" (#1 in U.K. and Australia).

"Escape (The Piña Colada Song)" – Rupert Holmes, #1(3), 10-79. Topnotch arranger, Holmes (Streisand, Drifters, Pitney). "Escape" lyric pumps up a stale-marriage 7-year itch. Sneakily writing a personal ad for a fling who

likes moonlit sand dune strolling, he ends up (surprise!) with the same ol' squeeze. SHE too felt the relationship was stale popcorn. They live happily ever after, with fresh new activities.

Unrelated **Clint Holmes** of Bournemouth, England hit #2(2), 3-73 with kidhood nostalgia "Playground in My Mind." **Bertie Higgins**' #8, 11-81 "Key Largo" (Bogart/ Bacall flick, 1948****) is a mythical Florida Keys spot with blue singing seas, flamingo sunsets, and smoochy couples strewn about golden shores. Only 7 mosquitoes.

Key West's **Jimmy Buffett**'s "Come Monday" hit #30, 7-74 (#58 C) on this Soft Rock debut. He croons his palm-frond 'Parrothead' Eden of flip-flops, Hawaiian shirts, cut-offs, and "Margeritaville" and "Kokomo" [#1, '88 Beach Boys] cuties. Buffett's lyrics zap the humdrum, the workaday.

"Exodus" – Bob Marley & the Wailers, NC, 1977; #19, 7-77 R & B. Marley's February 6th birthday is now a Jamaican national holiday – despite HOT 100 (even R & B) lack of big-ticket recognition. For other "Exodus," see **Pat Boone**, major Easy Listening guy of 50s: #1(6), 10-57 "April Love," and gorgeous #5, 5-58 "Sugar Moon," Quaker love song #5, 9-56 "Friendly Persuasion," and forgotten Top-Tenner #7, 7-58 "If Dreams Came True." Pat and Bob – no comparisons whatsoever. **Marley** = REGGAE.

"Tower of Strength" – Gene McDaniels, #5, 10-61; #5, 11-61 R & B. Afro-American Gene's full Croon Rock baritone sounds a lot like white **Pat Boone**, who doesn't sound at all like **Little Richard** he covers on #8, 4-56 "Long Tall Sally" (#6, Richard). But Gene's adventurous vocal arsenal also pulsates with growls, quavering high-altitude falsetto, and hot Jazz melismas: #21, 8-62 "Point of No Return" and #10, 1-62 "Chip, Chip." Great singer, suggesting the unlikely vocal combo of Pat Boone and **James Brown**.

"Lost in Love" – Air Supply, #3, 2-80. Australian/English duo, with 7 Top 5 hits, 1980-82. **Russell Hitchcock** (b. '49) and **Graham Russell** met in stage production of *Jesus Christ Superstar*. They RUSSELLed up #1(1), 5-81 "The One That You Love," and scored big time on #2(4), 6-80 "All Out of Love." My friend Kathy Cavanagh's son proposed to his girlfriend at an Air Supply concert. She accepted. There are no silly love songs, Paul McCartney hinted.

"A String of Pearls" – Glenn Miller Orchestra, #1(2), 1-42; #27, 2-44. Miller's (b. Clarinda, Iowa, 1904-44) silvery trombone winged a sweet sunshower of romance to a world awash in firestorm frenzy. Don't step on that tricky metaphor. In a World War II where the ominous sky rained hellfire, Glenn Miller was among the last-ditch rescuers of relaxation. **Tom Brokaw**'s *The Greatest Generation* (1998) included bombardier Bill Johnson of Dearborn, Michigan, who flew over the Himalayan hump to dispatch the Japanese juggernaut; Bill was my dad's best friend, and "String of Pearls" was his bride Jean's favorite song. Dancers were couples then. No one was marooned on the dance floor – shimmying solo in the strobe mirror-ball glow.

Miller hit #1(1), 8-40 on "Blueberry Hill" (yep, Fats's #2, '56 tune), a follow-up to #1(1), 9-39 "Blue Orchids." Glenn's megamonster was #1(12), 10-39 "In the Mood." Inspired by one-armed trumpet star **Wingy Manone** (#5, 2-36 "Please Believe Me"), "In the Mood" has a hot title we can't rate PG. In the mood for WHAT? Glenn's #1(9), 9-41 "Chattanooga Choo-Choo" included his famous band-stars: Hal McIntyre and Ernie Caceres, alto sax; **Ray Anthony** and **Bobby Hackett**, trumpets; Wilber Schwartz, clarinet; **Tex Beneke** and Al Klink on tenor sax; bass by Herman Alpert; and guitar – Jack Lathrop, though guitar and bass were still 2nd-string percussion instruments for his instrumental classics, whispering at Teeny-Tiny volume.

Miller hit #1(10), 2-42 with "Moonlight Cocktail," with Chummy McGregor's world-class piano (Glenn's theme song was legendary #3, 7-39 "Moonlight Serenade"). Glenn began with **Ray Noble**'s #7, 7-35 "Solo Hop," and his next masterpiece is best known (#5, 9-39) by **Judy Garland**:

"Over the Rainbow" – Glenn Miller Orchestra, #1(7), 8-39. Seven #1 records in ONE year ('39) isn't too shabby; Glenn's 'flops' that year included 18 OTHER HITS in the Top 20. "Over the Rainbow" whisks us away from scooping recycled dog food, vacuuming the garage, and taking out the garbage barefoot in the snow. Glenn and Judy float us away to Never-Never Land Oz of star-spangled splendor – with an iridescent glow of Emerald green. In the stardust ballrooms of romance and forever, you could hear the snappity snares of distant drums. For two years in the 'Army Air Force,' Glenn ambassadored like **Bob Hope** (b. 1903), entertaining the troops. Bad news hung in the air like atomic fallout.

On #1(8), "I've Got a Gal in Kalamazoo," 8-42, Glenn touts the Michigan town where 11% of Americans (1992) believed Elvis was living (15 years after he died). It's also near Del Shannon's Coopersville. In December 1944, Glenn boarded a plane over the darkling English Channel. The wreckage was never found. America's premier Big Band leader would be joined 15 years later by the 50s most beloved Rock and Roller in an icy Iowa cornfield – a few miles north of where *The Glenn Miller Story* began. Glenn's last #1? "That Old Black Magic" (2-43).

"You, You, You" – Ames Brothers, #1(8), 6-53. Quartet crooners like **Ed Ames** and three siblings clinched the lion's share of the 1948-54 Pop Standards Era. Ed hit #8, 1-67 solo with deep baritone "My Cup Runneth Over," while the quartet had 3 #1's. Their coolest hit? #3, 11-54 "The Naughty Lady of Shady Lane." So-called 'naughty' lass arrives in stodgy community, throwing hot come-hither glances at every-ineligible guy. Before pandemonium hits the sleepy, nosey, scandal-grubbing neighborhood, we discover the flirty lass is only NINE DAYS old.

"Paper Doll" – Mills Brothers, #1(12), 7-43; #2(5), 5-43 R & B. The Mills Brothers were perhaps the least dangerous band of all time. Piqua, Ohio's Herbert, Harry, and Donald (b. 1012-15) also included father and/or brother JOHN Mills. Under 'gentlemen' in the dictionary, the Mills Brothers should be pictured. From 1931's #1(4) "Tiger Rag" all the way to #23, 1-68 "Cab Driver", the mellow Millses crunched the big charts with their smooth Soul stylistics – #1(2), 1-32 "Dinah," #2(2) and #2(1), 6-34 "Swing It, Sister."

"Paper Doll" is an ostensibly innocent wish-fulfillment fantasy. Our hero's lass has bolted, so he'd now prefer a safer two-dimensional gal (hmmm). My folks loved the Mills Brothers' #7, 2-52 "Be My Life's Companion," and cute lightning bug ode to a firefly, #1(3), '52 "The Glow-Worm."

"Daisy a Day" – Jud Strunk, #14, 2-73; #33 C. Might be the saddest song in the world. I don't know. Born in Jamestown, New York, Jud gravitated to Down East Maine and did country-store Folk-Rock, with a 1968 *Laugh-In* role with **Goldie Hawn**. Gist of the stark tale: Jud's a kid. He recalls an old man in town who gave his adored wife one daisy per day. The song chugs along, overarched by Jud's pristine Irish tenor and the song's minimalist Country waltz band track. The lad is touched by their smooching as they totter along into their deep 80s (and also buy him candy). Surrogate grandparents. Here's the horror of it. Naturally, the poor old lady dies. It's not even untimely, so thereby it's more tragic. They made the best of their wedded bliss – but there wasn't enough time (like Jim Croce's "Time in a Bottle"). In the sad coda, the kid watches the forlorn old man wobble up the hillside every-day – to give her one daisy.

A succinct masterpiece. Strunk walks an iffy tightrope to avoid slush sentimentality. He keeps his worldly audience on a tear's brink. He never quite mentions death or graveyards (Jud's euphemism is 'hilltop'). Strunk accomplishes what many of those Graveyard Rockers failed to do. He takes a very real and genuine natural tragedy (not some misguided lass chasing a high school ring, and squashed by a speeding train). Jud wrings out the utmost in understated emotion.

Perhaps naturally, Jud Strunk (1936-81) had to be killed in a small plane crash beyond his beloved Farmington, Maine.

"Every Breath You Take" – The Police, #1(8), 6-83. Most popular song of all time in WEEKS at #1. Huh? Eight weeks is great, but . . . Hold on. If we tag on this Police Sting to **Puffy Daddy**'s elegy for **Notorious B.I.G.**, #1(11), 6-97 "I'll Be Missing You," We just do the math: 8 + 11 = 19. NINETEEN weeks at #1. That combo beats **Francis Craig**'s #1(17), '47 all-time champ "Near You," and modern-day elegy #1(16), 12-95 "One Sweet Day," by Mariah Carey & Boyz II Men. "Every Breath You Take" walks a short-range tightrope and **Sting**'s (Gordon Sumner, b. 19-2-51, Northumberland) plodding surveillance vocal to its Classic Soft Rock glory realm. We never forget his thudding, stalking bass, nor his hammering Streetcorner muted Chord Pattern. No matter how you cut it, it's a great classic melody and a creepy lyrical exercise in stalking. **Andy Summers** furnishes guitar, and **Stewart Copeland** the heavy, ominous drum throb. Copeland's father worked for the CIA, so this Anglo-American band's name – the **Police** – is apt and apropos.

Somehow, every time I hear Sting's booming and bludgeoning bass and the flat gray tenor he temporarily assumes to cast the darkling mood and spy tension, I'm reminded of an old *Mad* magazine gripe: "Waiter – there's a microphone in my soup!" Since **Puff Daddy** did more than 'sample' the rumbling melody (and much of the lyric) to "Every Breath You Take," we'll go all out here and say that It's the SAME furshlugginer SONG – and therefore its 19-week chart run is the winner and still Heavyweight Champ of the chopped-up chart-run #1 crown. Consecutive-week champ? **CRAIG**.

The **Police** began with Curved Air. Copeland doubled (like Dave Matthews' Band's Boyd Tinsley) on electric violin. Sting backed **Cherry Vanilla**, doing American Punk Rock. They debuted as the Police on #32, 2-79 "Roxanne," a red-light blue-plate special of a lass who reigns the boogie nights. Their sophomore offering (#74, 11-79) is "Message in a Bottle." Their Big Ten breakthrough boomed on #10, 10-80 "De Do Do Do, De Da Da Da."

"Every Breath You Take" follows you around worse than Santa Claus. It knows when you're sleepy or wide-awake (so be good for surveillance' sake, and watch out, poutlessly). Sting's song-guy is not Sting (**Gordon Sumner**). The song-guy will be watching. Nothing is funny about a disturbed guy stalking a girl. This annoying and perilous espionage phenomenon is a byproduct of a TV panorama glutted on the euphemism of 'ACTION' (meaning gratuitous violence, with a side of grisly horror). Sometimes it's hard to divorce the singer form the malevolent persona he plays in the song, eh? The song-guy persona is that of a messed-up moonhowler. Stalkerman watches her every step – every move she tries to make. The Police's high-energy Bridge posits the old ownership paradox – why can't she see she belongs exclusively to HIM?

"Every Breath You Take" slings the Ownership Fallacy – you can't own a girl or guy like a car or a cow. When **Puff Daddy** got hold of Sting's spy anthem, he transformed it into an elegy (see Elton John's "Candle[s] in the Wind I & II") for his gunned-down friend **Notorious B.I.G.**; the whole lyrical approach sidestepped Sting's original foreshadowing intent – and opened up a new #1(11) dimension of Light Rap/R & B/Soul tributes. Though the double-song missed the consecutive-weeks-at-#1 record, its combined 19 weeks tops anything on the Big Chart, anytime.

"**Fields of Gold**" – Sting, #23, 6-93. Sting's Police also enjoyed light-hearted Soft Rocker #3, 8-81 "Every Little Thing She Does Is Magic," and more standoffish #10, 2-81 "Don't Stand So Close to Me." Their parent album #1(17), '83 *Synchronicity*, hit bigger than *Sgt. Pepper* at #1(15), '67. In 1997, the Police got back together for #59, 12-97 "Roxanne Remix," with **Puff Daddy**'s Remix and Full Force. Puff Daddy's nightclub shoot-'em-up in New York gave the paparazzi and gossip mavens press fodder for 2000-01, and Puffy and Jennifer Lopez were acquitted of serious charges.

*Sting – of the **Police** (Rock Hall 2003)*

It took Sting awhile to find these "Fields of Gold." First, he had to split with the Police, and volley a foursome of top tenners into the solo arena: #3, 6-85 "If You Love Somebody, Set Them Free"; #8, 8-85 "Fortress Around Your Heart"; #7, 10-87 "We'll Be Together"; and #5, 1-91 "All This Time." Sting is no oldie; he's a continuous R & R phenomenon. Seems Sumner got his **STING** nickname from an old shirt. The athletic soccer star wore his yellow and black-striped rugby longsleeve shirt frequently, so his pals gave him a "BEE" nickname. Check out *Saturday Night Live*'s **John Belushi**'s killer-bee outfit. Sting's "Fields of Gold" is a romantic trek, with blanket, bread, wine, and girl, through fields of golden barley [sounds like 'bongly']. For non-barley buffs, barley is the big ingredient in BEER. The words themselves go back aeons together: barley and beer. This idyllic interlude stars Sting, his lusciously lovely lady, and some golden BEERfields.

In his #17, 2-92 "If I Ever Lose My Faith in You," Sting considers the yawning chasm, the almighty Void, the Last-Kiss Abyss, and all that gloomy stuff. He hinges his whole trust and faith in the cosmos not in God, but on his relationship with this girl. Sting teamed on #1(3), 11-93 "All for Love," with **Rod Stewart** and **Bryan Adams**. In 2001, Sting won a major award for #17, 4-2000 "Desert Rose." A sleeping giant for Big Beat music, the Muslim world praised his use of **Cheb Mami**, whose spirited chanting simulates, with melisma grace notes, the *muezzin*'s call to prayer. Long before microphone technology, the muezzin called out atop the high *mosque* (church/temple) for five-times-a-day prayers among devout Islamic men (see Cat Stevens). Mami's Arabian background is still rare in American pop music. Sting, however, is a bi-generational superstar.

"I Will Always Love You" – Dolly Parton, NC, 1974; #1(1), 4-74, and #1(1), 7-82 Country. Also #15, 9-95 C, with Vince Gill. Dolly Parton, (b. 1-19-46, Tennessee) penned this Country classic that mangled 99 other great songs for 14 weeks on the Big Charts for Whitney Houston. Some Parton critics were so snowed by Dolly's hyperbolic jumpsuits, girlish maple-syrup soprano, and stunning gifted hourglass figure that they forgot to check out her gifted and talented music. She began on a Knoxville radio station at age 11, replacing *Norma Jean* (#8, 10-64 "Go Cat Go," and #86, 7-65 "I Wouldn't Buy a Used Car from Him") as **Porter Wagoner**'s partner on 1967-74 TV show. Joining the Grand Ole Opry in 1969, Dolly enjoyed her first Country hit, smart #24, 10-67 "Dumb Blonde," and first HOT 100 (#60, 1-74), "Jolene."

"I Will Always Love You's" tempo would lose a drag race to blackstrap molasses. Dolly's #4, 10-71 "Coat of Many Colors" is music-box melodic, tracing its parable back to Joseph's Technicolor *Bible* dreamcoat. In this homespun ballad, she warms up for her giant hit by cherishing a bright ragtag coat her mom sewed, while K-Mart coat kids snickered in school. Despite Appalachian poverty, she says her mother sewed love into every stitch —and that's what really counts. Her #1(1), 8-74 C "Love Is Like a Butterfly" skims above her #14, 1073 C "My Tennessee Mountain Home." These sweet Easy Squeezy mockin' bird hill tunes of sunset splendor and wild whippoorwills paint Dolly's honeysuckle home as a pastoral paradise.

"I Will Always Love You," however, rises above these other fine hits like Mt. McKinley/Denali above Mt. Foraker and Mt. Silver Throne in Alaska. Her big song is among the most poignant and tender goodbye ballads ever lullabyed. Retreating in the going-going-gone afterglow of a stubbed-out affair, Dolly tells the guy she'll love him forever. Her sweet soprano slings a sad goodbye.

"I Will Always Love You" – Whitney Houston, #1(14), 11-92; #1(1), R & B. Besides being beautiful, Whitney (b. 8-9-63) grew up calling **Aretha Franklin** 'Auntie Ree.' Daughter of **Cissy Houston**, and cousin (some bios say 'aunt') of **Dionne Warwick**, Whitney was born into Easy Soul royalty. This is the song that hit #1 longer than any other tune in the Rock Era (1955-92). Boyz II Men had just toppled Elvis's #1(1) "Hound Dog"/"Don't Be Cruel" ('56) with their #1(13), 7-92 "End of the Road." Ironically Whitney K.O.-ed their record via this tender tune.

Whitney sings "I Will Always Love You" in savvy "A-major," where Blues champs play. Whitney nudges a hot Aretha-style Gospel tremolo, with melisma sprinkles, that twirl the stars in the far skies in blue whirls of zigzag spindrift. Then she drops from Dolly's Barbie-doll soprano to a huskier mezzo soprano (low-medium soprano) extravaganza of sound and fury, the heart of lost bygone love. The golden sax on the Bridge grows torrid. She ratchets the passion up a key. [Any tenderfoot ogler scoping in Whitney's #1(14) Al. *Whitney Houston* '85 will testify – her WOW one-piece bathing suit makes *Victoria's Secret*est catalog model look like she's wearing a burlap potato bag]. Whitney modulates up to 'B,' and dances off little

fadeaway notes with transcendent theatrical glory and splendor. After this production by **Jermaine Jackson**, pre-Soul Star supermodel Whitney went on to spiraling superduperstardom, via #1(11), 6-87 *Whitney* (9 million) and #1(20), 12-92 *The Bodyguard* (15 million). Whitney Houston enjoyed seven #1 records in a row – more than ELVIS or the BEATLES. Anybody ever top that?

"Lindley, Does You Love Me?" – Dan Quinn, #1(3), 8-1894. Better known for his bicycle-built-for-two sidewalks of New York and #1(7), 10-1899 "Curse of the Dreamer," brawny Quinn slung a slew of TWELVE #1 blockbusters to knock the bejabbers out of the 90s' HOT 100 (the 'HOT 10' in 1899). Sadly, most of the living Dan Quinn fans probably no longer are (see Jock Rock/Waltz Kings chapter). Top tunes? #1(4), 10-1894 "My Pearl Is a Bowery Girl"; #1(6), 11-1894 "And Her Golden Hair Was Hanging Down Her Back" and #1(4), 11-1898 "At a Georgia Camp Meeting."

"Desolation Row" – Bob Dylan, NC, 1965. Our right fielder Paul Agostino wouldn't put his favorite Dylan saga in the Light Metal chapter, but alas, here it is. Bob's outstanding melody skateboards with surreal spontaneous lyrics into a wondrous street-life epic worthy of the best of **Allen Ginsberg** or Lawrence Ferlinghetti. From #3, 10-65 Al. *Highway 61 Revisited*, it's named (like "Subterranean Homesick Blues)) after another **Jack Kerouac** novel – this time *Desolation Angels* (1960).

"I'll Never Fall in Love Again" – Dionne Warwick, #6, 12-69; #17, 1-70 R & B. Another dynamite Burt Bacharach/Hal David lyric. Dionne is 5th-female ever on Whitburn's list. This song is a cute self-spat about all the liabilities of love. After a horror show of jilting jerks, worthless clods, and unrequited love that yields its basic byproducts – sorrow and pain – Dionne vows to never fall in love again. Then she decides . . . at least not until tomorrow. She springs from flustered to new-love starry-eyed. Dionne clicked with openers #8, 12-63 "Anyone Who Had a Heart," and #6 brooding 4-64 "Walk on By." Lush string arrangements fortified Warwick, who has the Jazz Soul precision gift shared by **Sarah Vaughan** and **Ella Fitzgerald**. Whitney Houston's mom **Cissy Houston** hit #92, 4-71 (but #31 R & B) with **Ronettes**' reprise "Be My Baby." Lead singer of **Elvis**'s back-up **Sweet Inspirations**, Cissy previewed Whitney:

"Saving All My Love for You" – Whitney Houston, #1(10, 8-85; #1(1), 6-85 R & B. Carole King's husband/ songwriting-partner Gerry Goffin penned this tantalizing tease. King hit #2(1), 8-74 with her own Lite Metal "Jazzman," plus Brill Building classics #9, 1-72 "Sweet Seasons" and #9, 1-75 "Nightingale." On her #1(3), 3-86 "Greatest Love of All," Whitney launches into Star-of-Bethlehem Gospel gear on this theatrical torch tune. Her #1(2), 5-87 "I Wanna Dance with Somebody (Who Loves Me)" bops on back from the mountaintop to the Disco. Fantastic follow-up? Her #1(2), 8-87 "Didn't We Almost Have it All?" Theatrical classic.

"Exhale (Shoop Shoop)," [#1(1), 11-95; #1(7) R & B] floundered in June 1994, but finally rebounded and crunched the top spot in 1996. Other Whitney cameos? Yep: #1(2), 10-87 "Where Do Broken Hearts Go?"; #1(2), 12-90 "All the Man I Need"; #8, 3-96 "Count on Me"; #15, 12-98 "When You Believe" with **Mariah Carey**; #4, 9-99 "My Love is Your Love"; and UN-Elvis #2(3), 12-98 "Heartbreak Hotel" – a different song altogether.

"One Moment in Time" – Whitney Houston, #5, 9-88; #22 R & B. 1988 Summer Olympics theme song. She holds the Olympic torch of aspiration and achievement on every whirling grace note, every booming theatrical stanza of her musical tribute to athletic excellence. She crystallizes peak performance. Flesh and spirit strive to excel against all odds.

Whitney Houston

"I Don't Want to Cry" – Chuck Jackson, #36, 2-61; #5 R & B. Great singer Chuck toys with **Jackie Wilson** Orchestral Soul, as he duels with sawing violins and tripletongue triplets on trumpet. Unheralded Soul Power giant. Chuck's breathtaking Carole King song here may be superseded by his #23, 4-62 "Any Day Now" (see Ronnie Milsap) at #2(3) R & B.

Country Soul. **Ronnie Milsap** (b. '46, North Carolina) hit #14, 5-82 and #1(1) C with this Jackson classic – long before the Jackson Five – but not BULL MOOSE: **Bull Moose Jackson and His Buffalo Bearcats** notched #21, 12-47 and #1 R & B with "I Love You, Yes I Do." Any other major ungloved Jacksons?

"Let's Get Serious" – Jermaine Jackson, #9, 3-80; #1(6) R & B. Michael's brother Jermaine of Jackson Five was a top-notch producer, songwriter, and recording star in whatever spare time he could spare. He even big-brothered his backsliding sibling with advice in #78, 11-91 "Advice to the Badd." Bassist Jermaine (b. '54) also did #9, 12-72 cover of Streetcorner "Daddy's Home," and 17 HOT 100's and six Top 20s.

"Some Days Are Diamonds" – John Denver, #36, 6-81; #10 C. Denver (1943-97) brings his Greenpeace message on a submarine sandwich of sensational song stylistics. His bread of life is his optimistic lyrical poetry, pleasant boyish smile, and pure second tenor. The GREENS of his sandwich are his environmental crusades – saving eagles and owls and rainforests and oceans. The meat of his sandwich (or bean dip or tofu) is his skill at creating Currier & Ives melodies that waft Americana like billowy Independence Day clouds over a Pepsi picnic park. With Denver's impish grin, his Dutch-Boy corn-silk hair, and his good-natured song, you know that plucky American optimism is alive and well somewhere out on the Satellite Dish of Eternity.

"Some Days Are Diamonds" says each day has a solo shot at the big time, but usually the puny day strikes out. When a burly new day finally smacks its grand-slam home run, however, it makes up for all the gray glops of gritty gloom that whisk your way in triplicate terror. Denver's basic premise is that some days are diamonds and other days are just stones (not beatles). Among other multidimensional Denver hits on Easy speed: Lucky #13, 12-74 "Sweet Surrender," on a soaring eagle's odyssey aloft; double-sided ocean-journey "Calypso" at #2(4), 10-75; and flipside #1(1) c, 5-89 "And So It Goes," with Jeff Hanna's cool **Nitty Gritty Dirt Band**. Denver's farewell Al. '98 *Forever, John* features an eerie eyrie of mystical flight: NC "On the Winds of an Eagle." John Denver? Colorado sunshine, and fresh breath of endless blue sky.

"Sailing" – Christopher Cross, #1(1), 6-80. Texan Cross (b. '51) first approached this seafaring success like silversmith Paul Revere: #2(4), 2-80 "Ride Like the Wind." His "Never Be the Same" hit #15, 10-80. No Cross pix on pink-flamingo green album cover for 1980 Grammy-glommer Cross – but a great pastel seashore sky on flipside.

James Ingram hit #2(1), 12-86 with lovely **Linda Ronstadt** on "Somewhere Out There," in a multicultural panorama (he's a Soul star, she's German, Mexican, and Irish).

"Don't Cry Out Loud" – Melissa Manchester, #10, 11-78. Stoics' Anthem. British 'stiff upper lip' translated over the Big Pond to cowboy chic – John Wayne, Gary Cooper. Liberated women, too, must manfully swallow their pride and tears and agonies. Show must go on. Melissa rocks out on #5, 5-82 "You Should Hear How She Talks About You" and murmurs #6, 5-75 "Midnight Blue."

"I Love Me" is **Gray Gordon**'s #17, 3-40 hit (vocal Rita Ray). Bizarro self-image, eh?

Maureen McGovern hit #1(2), 6-73 with "The Morning After." Day of reckoning, Alka-Seltzer romantic hangover (see Shaggy and "Angel of the Morning") . . .

"To Sir With Love" – Lulu, #1(5), 9-67. Born Marie Lawrie ('48, Metro Glasgow, Scotland), Lulu's saucy Scottish Soul alto steers this sentimental movie theme from 1967 (***½). Afro-American Sidney Poitier thrives in tough Cockney London classroom, causing thousands of us 1967 kids to go into teaching (me, anyhow), as *Mr. Holland's Opus* **** did in late 90s. Check out the prowling bass that backs the copper-haired bonnie lass.

"Moon River" – Henry Mancini, #1, 10-61. Dreamy Mississippi River musical journey by Pennsylvanian composer (with 4 Oscars, 20 Grammys). It meanders like the lazy flow of twilight's last gleaming. Gorgeous melody. A rare format: first half – basic instrumental, with scattered ooh and aahs from chorus; second half, melodious vocal.

"Are You Sincere" – Andy Williams, #3, 2-58. Andy's (b. 12-3-28, Wall Lake, Iowa) silvertone voice serenaded the air waves with sleepytime Welsh tenor sincerity. Andy followed **Perry Como**'s modus operandi – cardigans, relaxed sincerity, and carrying the Crooners' torch into the Rock Era. With his Windex blue eyes, the Welsh-American tenor enjoyed #2(4), 3-63 "Can't Get Used to Losing You," #5, 9-59 "Lonely Street," and his paradisiacal pub in Spain – #37, 4-61 "The Bilbao Song" (It stars a balloon moon floating over some screen-porch shoreside tavern of ideal friends and camaraderie and sincerity. We never found the place on our '61 Riviera odyssey). Williams had 47 HOT 100 hits. His cutest Lite Rock tune was Peggy Powers duo, #8, 5-57 "I Like Your Kind of Love." Williams opened the first non-Country concert hall in 2nd-Nashville mecca Branson, Missouri, a town of 5000 people with 4 million visitors per year.

Johnny Mathis's gorgeous croon tunes include #78, 5-60 (#10 R & B somehow) "Maria," a melody of unearthly beauty. Johnny's world-class voice reverberates with all the tender love a man can handle in one song. When you murmur Maria's moniker softly, Johnny whispers, it's nearly like PRAYING. From #1 album ever: #1(54), '62 *West Side Story*.

"Popsicles and Icicles" – Murmaids, #3, 11-63. Yep, murmaids who murmur. Clever punny name, like Beatles. L.A. sisters trio from Swathmore College, Pennsylvania: **David Gates** of **Bread** wrote this clever melodic tune. Girls seek perfect Teen Dream who likes sparkling stars, gonzo guitars, and unthreatening pastimes like baseball. Dream dude. "Popsicles and Icicles" chugs along on pink chords. By the time Gates made it to Bread, the whole universe decided to croak:

"If" – Bread, #4, 3-71. **David Gates** goes starkly cosmic. Ultimate astronomical ballad. Quivering planetoids spin past Armageddon asteroids out in the far-off solar system. First the earth stops twirling. Stars wink out one at a time. Solution? They fly away from this annoying inter-galactic hassle. He'd spend the end with her, he romanticizes. Let's just fly away, he offers, from this cosmic catastrophe of exploding planets, crashing comets, and intergalactic fluff hissing and fizzing at 14 squashillion degrees.

Can love really conquer thermonuclear annihilation? Absurd? 'Fly away' from planetary collapse? The black hole Void and Abyss? Like Icarus and Daedalus, on Greek "Broken Wings" (#1[1], 9-85, Mr. Mister, followed by #1[2], "Kyrie,") the two lovers fly away to some new solar system, some new galaxy, some entirely new Creation. We, the audience, are dumbfounded. We are asked to project a willing suspension of disbelief. And WE DO. In a hundred thousand similar songs that play with stars and moons and setting suns, we irrationalize the cosmos.

Love will conquer all. Take a sweet breathtaking baby blue melody, add a wisp of wonder and a shred of faith, and Love will zap any obstacles in our way. Even to the end of the universe, 'love will keep us together.' Long live love. And, good luck . . .

"If" is also a great #1(8), 1-51 different lyric/melody **Perry Como** song. Written in 1934, the incipient blockbuster waited 17 years for the big time (also #8, '51 Jo Stafford, #10, '51 Billy Eckstine). With a BEAT, who knows how far it could have gone?

"Make It With You" – Bread, #1(1), 6-70. Debut and only #1. Bread is Jim Gordon on drums, and Robb Roger and James Griffin on guitar. Their minimalist presentations avoid nasty noises, bashing drums, fuzztone frenzy. Their #3, 10-71 "Baby, I'm-a Want You," spins on Gates's gentle countertenor in the Phil Everly, Art Garfunkel, Smokey Robinson mode. Other nifty slices of Bread? #11, 7-72 "The Guitar Man"; #14, 7-73 "Aubrey"; and #15, 4-72 "Diary." Their harmonic masterpiece, #10, 9-70 "It Don't Matter to Me," trails off into the wild blue cotton-candy whorls of the Andromeda Nebula of loneliness (and a few chromatic chord modulations [bVII] on Gates's galactic keyboards).

"Everything I Own" – Bread, #5, 1-72. The poor guy lost his girl and his hope for the future. He'd give EVERYTHING he owns to have her back again. How many millions of people, torn apart by bickering in their last doddering years, must now lament for an eternity the loss of their cherished fellow bickerer? Gates trails off into whispered tacets as the band track shushes. His song-guy's woeful whimper trembles with regret and remorse. And Gates's tremendous lonely voice trails off into the lost wind.

This is no simple 'come-hither baby' lounge lizard lollapalooza. It's the high-lonesome wail of keening banshee pain, far out on the gray moors of desolation and despair. None of us can ever know the true depths of another's grief. This haunting ballad gives us a shudder of an inkling.

"Lost Without Your Love" – Bread, #9, 11-76. I feel a lot better about this one. It's only 11.1% as desolate as the last. Here, we're talking, you know, like, the girl dumped him. Seems she had to wash her hair. Or give the beagle a bath. We get the feeling the pain of losing her love will soon be his gain.

"Make Me Lose Control" – Eric Carmen, #3, 5-88. Lead singer for **Raspberries**, Carmen (b.'49, Cleveland) scored #2(3), 12-75 "All by Myself" and #4, 11-87 "Hungry Eyes."

Lobo hit #8, 12-72 with "Don't Expect Me to Be Your Friend," flip of #2(3) "I'd Love You to Want Me."

"Raindrops Keep Fallin' on My Head" – B.J. Thomas, #1(4), 11-69. The Hugo, Oklahoma (b. '42) and Texan tenor parleyed his talent and curly hair into a string of Soft Rockers: the mellifluous #9, 6-70 "I Just Can't Help Believin'" with a **Duane Eddy** guitar interlude; and #15, 2-72 "Rock and Roll Lullaby," about a very young mother. "Raindrops" played instrumentally on our toddler Lauri's music-box in 1970 exactly 1,234,567 times until it was mysteriously broken.

"Eleanor Rigby" – Ray Charles, #35, 6-68; #30, 7-68 R & B. Ray did "Rock and Roll Shoes" to #14, 8-84 (NC, R & B) with B.J. Thomas. Here Ray reprises **Paul McCartney**'s sad elegy, with a side of weeping cellos. Both Soul giants, Ray and **Aretha Franklin** (#17, 11-69; # 5 R & B) eulogized Paul's internationally lonely martyr to solitude, 'Eleanor.' Perhaps it is because some African-Americans, who invented the Blues, have borne more than their share of human suffering. "Eleanor Rigby" was enslaved by her reticence to ever do or be anything. Everyone dreads no one will come to his/her funeral [though it's tough for the dear departed to count the house]. This grim thought reverberates around the sympathetic world as a poignant monument to repressed passion – or simply to human caring and sharing. No one wants to end up like Eleanor, or Father McKenzie, darning his grubby old socks in the lonely night – or writing sermons no one will ever hear (as parishioners nod off in Sunday zombie twilight sleep). Eleanor is someone no one wants to be.

"If I Didn't Care" – Ink Spots, #2(1), 4-39. The Ink Spots' "The Gypsy" hit #1(13), 5-46. Comic Redd Foxx serenaded junkyard-baron son Lamont in *Sanford & Son*, with **Jerry Daniels**'s countertenor sound of "If I Didn't Care." Afro-American Daniels also played electric guitar. Hoppy Jones (1903-44) did the low 'Rap' bass bridges. "Maybe" hit #2(6), 8-40. Some mainstream critics might classify the whole first half of the 20th century as VERY Light Metal.

"Wind Beneath My Wings" – Gary Morris, NC, 1983; #4, 8-83 C. Great metaphor – SHE's the wind underneath his heavenbound wings. First Soul star **Lou Rawls** #65, 3-83 (#60 R & B) scratched surface, then Morris sang Dramatic Tenor sound. Blockbuster followed by **Bette Midler** – #1(1), 3-89. Morris's Country biggee? #9 C, 5-85 "Lasso the Moon" (don't try this at home).

"Cool Change" – Little River Band, #10, 10-79. Easy Kiwi Rock from rare Rock spot New Zealand (bassman Roger MacLachlan). Singer Glenn Shorrock is from U.K. "Reminiscing" hit #3, 7-78, and "Lady" #10, 1-79.

"That Lucky Old Sun" – Frankie Laine, #1(8), 8-49. Chicago's Frankie LoVecchio (b. 1913) sang about backbreaking labor and factory drudgery. Pent-up shop inmate envies sun, rolling all over the heavens on its daily rounds. Boomer Crooner Laine is a super nice guy (we were on same TV show in 60s). He hit with cowboy theme song #1(6), 11-49 "Mule Train," #1(2), 2-50 "The Cry of the Wild Goose," and #5, 7-52 cowboy classic showdown – "High Noon (Do Not Forsake Me)."

"Three Times a Lady" – Commodores with Lionel Richie, #1(2), 6-78; #1(2) R & B. Suave singer/saxman Lionel formed his Commodores in Tuskegee, Alabama, in 1970. Their "Easy" hit #4, 6-77, and "Sail On" sailed the same to #4, 8-79. Richie split with Commodores to a fine solo career. Their name jumped out of a dictionary; though they were teased by pals with misname the 'Commodes,' Richie-less Commodores hit #3, 1-85 "Nightshift" – #1(4) R & B. New lead singer of Heatwave J.D. Nicholas (#2, 7-77 "Boogie Nights"_ sang night-shift elegiac tribute to both **Marvin Gaye** and **Jackie Wilson**, extraordinary Soul/R & B talents cut down in their primes. Wilson faded away in a nursing home for 9 years after a paralyzing stroke on horrified **Dick Clark**'s TV show. Like **Righteous Brothers**' #3, 5-74 "Rock and Roll Heaven" Commodores ponder faraway Soul Heaven, with Marvin and Jackie in the celestial limelight.

"Endless Love" – Lionel Richie and Diana Ross, #1(9), 7-81; #1(7) R & B. Motown monster beat Marvin's #1(7), '60s "I Heard it Through the Grapevine." Dynamic duo and Brooke Shields movie theme. Diana's silky soprano weaves magic harmonic finalé note. In #1(4), 9-83 "All Night Long," Richie simulates Harlem's **Harry Belafonte** on authentic Jamaican accent for his fiesta. He dazzles hot dancers from Martinique to Manistique (Michigan) with their broiling rhythm track.

Lionel said "Hi" to his 4th #1 with #1(2), 2-84 "Hello." Echo Chamber cranked up to '10,' Lionel fashions easy squeezy love song for "Dancing on the Ceiling" (#2[2], 7-86), title track for 3rd big album: #1(2), 8-86. Richie's #1(2), 10-82 "Truly" hit silver-medal record #2(9) R & B; he's as close to button-down Cosby as R & B gets. Lionel was voted #1 Artist of 1984 in *Billboard*, ahead of **Michael Jackson**, **Bob Seger**, and **Bruce Springsteen**. Richie is no Oldies act – #39, 4-96 "I Don't Wanna Lose You." Superstar Power.

"Lady" – Kenny Rogers, #1(6), 11-80; #1(1) C. Kenny is King of CROSSOVER. His silver mane, teddy-bear style, and fine gravelly baritone swamped the 80s with hits on the Pop Top 100, plus Country AND R & B. Written by **Lionel Richie**, "Lady" is an enchanting ballad. Houston's Rogers (b. '38) began rocking with the **First Edition**: #5, 2-68 parachute anthem "I Just Dropped in (To See What Condition My Condition Was In)."

On "What About Me?' Rogers duetted with **Kim Carnes** and **James Ingram** to #15, 9-84; #70, 11-84 C; and #57, 10-84 R & B. Kenny's Big Three ballads include #6, 6-69 "Ruby," plus these two:

Kenny Rogers

"Lucille" – Kenny Rogers, #5, 3-77; #1(2), 1-77 C. This cheatin' honky-tonk scenario is an actual circa-1890 Toledo, Ohio, bar next to the Amtrak Depot. Kenny's song-guy is making whoopee with this bar-flower when her mountainous husband lumbers into the bar. Kenny, no stranger to self-preservation, considers flying Supermannishly out the back window, and escaping to the relative comfort of trash cans bashing and crashing in the chicken-bone and rice-gravy-slime night (see **Jay & the Americans**' #3, 9-64 "Come A Little Bit Closer"). Then the rapscallion develops real sympathy for the poor big lug hubby. The elephantine farmer-husband tells his sad aggrieved tale. Seems she dumped him and her three ultra-hungry kids, and some (hmm) unidentified crop in his lonely fields. You feel sorry for the big stooge. Kenny's Casanova song-guy seethes with temporary GUILT.

Later he vanquishes his conscience, and still takes the unfaithful frowzy bar babe to the Cheap Shot No-Tell Motel. Then he stonewalls his former desire in a sonic boom of World-Class Remorse: He can't 'hold' the lady because of the husband's tragic story. Very few candlelight Casanovas admit to their inability to satisfy a woman's desire (most exaggerate their potency). All the while, the squirmy waltz wiggles on the deep, throbbing bass, buttressed by Rodgers' superb sandpaper echo.

"Coward of the County" – Kenny Rogers, #3, 11-79; #1(3) C. Tommy's father dies in prison. Among his last earthly advice to his sons is 'turn the other cheek – don't

be a fighter like I was.' Tommy listens and heeds. Dad's memory follows him into sweet romance with Becky. Never does Tommy develop a scrappy rep among the oafs and brawny bruisers in town. One day, three 'Gatlin Boys' call on his precious Becky. We can tell by her torn lip and dress that they had paid both Tommy and Becky the ultimate violent insult.

Mild Tommy returns to their old saloon. Naturally, three Gatlin Boys sit and snicker. Tommy recalls his pop's peaceful advice. He goes to the mantel. We all think he's grabbing a shotgun. Tommy has second thoughts. A Gatlin calls him 'Old Yeller' (a Disney dog movie and a frontier pun for cowardice). Tommy locks the door, unafraid of desperados. The saloon shuts up. Bystanders fade into woodwork. Tommy ferociously smashes all three Gatlin Boys to jellied protoplasmic pulp. He spares no punitive measure. We never discover whether he shoots them, a dim possibility, or just tears the terrible plug-ugly triumvirate apart with his bare hands. When the blood and beer and busted bones settle down into hushed silence, Tommy stands victorious. No Gatlin 'Boy' stirs. He gazes shamefully at his daddy's picture, and begs for forgiveness for the weakness of his strength. He admits that sometimes you must fight to really be a man.

Tommy sums up the entire spirit of America to boot. We stayed out of World Wars I and II until we couldn't stay out any longer. **John Wayne** never went out looking for fights. Like America, John Wayne, and Tommy, we didn't start fights. We finished them.

King David, the first reported musician in history, was the second-most recognizable figure in the *Bible*. Goliath was not.

"Islands in the Stream" – Kenny Rogers and Dolly Parton, #1(2), 8-83; #1(2), 9-83 C. Named for **Ernest Hemingway**'s posthumous novel. Kenny has 20+ #1 records (C.), like **Dottie West** duo #1(2), 2-78 C. "Every Time Two Fools Collide." Kenny's rhapsodic tete-a-tetes with **Sheena Easton**, Kim Carnes, and Dolly doubled everybody's pleasure and their revenue receipts. Kenny covered Vintage Heartland Rockers, too, capturing a rare **Bob Seger** Easy ballad, #13, 10-78 "We've Got Tonite" (as traditionally spelled "We've Got Tonight"), to #6, 1-83 (#1 C) with Sheena. In this follow-up to Bob's rampaging #4, 5-78 "Still the Same," this Epicurean Seger song says 'cancel tomorrow – tonite's all that matters, baby.'

"Bette Davis Eyes" – Kim Carnes, #1(9), 3-81. Kenny's bandmate shared scrubbed Folk multitude (14 singers), the **New Christy Minstrels** (#14, 6-63 Barry McGuire lead on "Green, Green"). All three singers had a sandpapery ultra-cool vocal sound. **Jackie DeShannon** wrote this giant Rock hit for Bette about silver-screen Grand Dame Davis, whose own raspy Lucky Strike contralto flipped Hollywood on its eager 30s ear. Though **Olivia Newton-John**'s Disco Rock "Physical" hit #1(10), Carnes's smokin' delivery and husky vocal gave her quite a few votes for #1 Biggest Female Rock Song of All Time. It's NOT really Easy Listening, but bounces off Kenny's tunes. You know by now that *Gold Rush* is not wild about Chart or Genre or

Music-Style Segregation. We integrate here. All this great stuff interconnects.

Kenny and Kim's #4, 3-80 (#3 C) "Don't Fall in Love with Dreamer" spearheaded Kim's rise to her giant #1(9) Bette Davis triumph.

The Irish Tenors – The Irish Tenors, #1 *Billboard* **Classical Charts, 4-2000** [which we don't feature]. The Three Tenors — **Luciano Pavarotti** and crew – fractured the Classical charts for #1(23) in 1994, prompting this Irish Tenor wave: **Anthony Kearns, John McDermott,** and **Ronan Tynan** (Finbar Wright replaced McDermott, 2001). They share the *bel-canto* (Italian, 'beautiful song') cirrus-cloud purity of THE Irish Tenor **John McCormack** (1883-1945). McDermott's "Danny Boy" is first-rate, but Kearns's voice is best-suited to the tune. Their trio version of **Chauncey Olcott**'s #1(4), 12-19-13 "Too-Ro-Loo-Ra-Loo-Ral" is a Kelly-green leprechaun pot-of-gold bonanza. Though we shy away from Grand Opera in *Gold Rush*, we salute the greats – **Mario Lanza, Enrico Caruso, Maria Callas, Paul Robeson,** and these three Auld Sod Tenors. They express the Bob Owen zeal of anti-crown gusto in "Only Our Rivers Run Free." Great music comes in many forms.

"Leader of the Band" – Dan Fogelberg, #9, 11-81. Ultimate Father's Day song, like McDermott above's "The Old Man." This Fogelberg Band leader is obviously a father. His own life, Dan sings, has been a pale shadow of his father's wanderlust and musical passion. The irony? Here's troubadour Dan, crashing the vaunted HOT 10 in *Billboard*, bucking the Disco/Funk/Punk tide. His noble Pop's potential music never came to fruition, via record chart success. But Dad had the dream and his enthusiasm and talent to pass it on to his son Dan. He says his Chicago and St. Paul brothers didn't hear the same musical CALL (compare the priesthood or ministry). Music is often a pilgrimage, a crusade. Not just a job. Maybe a Divine command. Lifeblood.

Bard Dan grows up solitarily, son of an ex-cabinetmaker and soldier. He eases in on his Tonic chord (I) in the sweet Key of "Ab-major," cruising up to the Mediant III chord **C**. Though his dad was no indulgent marshmallow and they disagreed somewhat, Fogelberg grieves the swift passage of time. His Everlyish ethereal chorus swoops impishly just below the cathedral dome. Peoria, Illinois' Fogelberg sees his dad's weariness, his tired eyes, and he worries about his dad's decline. The song slings an amazing metaphor: It's crucial to music, genetics, life, and destiny. His pop's blood actually runs right 'through' the instrument. His paternal song is indelibly painted upon the lad's very soul.

In his pensive conclusion, he forgives his dad's shortcomings and distance, but praises him for his inspiration and his blessing. Lamenting the macho father-son lack of 'I-love-you's,' "Leader of the Band" trails off into the vermilion/purple Western sunset – and we all stargaze at the forlorn cactus of despair. If your father is still living, you may not yet understand what his vision feels like.

"Part of the Plan" – Dan Fogelberg, #31, 2-75. Eagle Joe Walsh fondled lead guitar on this Fogelberg debut, showing Dan's harmonic connection to America's biggest band (26 million for *Eagles' Greatest Hits 1971-75* is #1 anywhere, anytime, as of 2001). **Don Henley** harmonizes on 2nd hit #24, 10-78 "The Power of Gold," with fellow-Eagle **Glenn Frey** on #7, 8-81 "Hard to Say." "The Language of Love" scored #13, 2-84 for solo Dan. His #9, 12-80 "Same Old Lang Syne" samples traditional Scottish songwriter/poet **Robert Burns**'s New Year Anthem (Scots Holiday *Hogmenay*). Burns (1759-96) also wrote the Greatest Hits of the 18th Century, like #1(11), 1784 "Flow Gently, Sweet Afton," a sweet lullaby waltz for his sleeping sweetheart Mary. Like many a road-warrior Rock troubadour, Burns loved too many women and too many pints of beer (often simultaneously). Providentially, his horse knew the way home from the Rabbit & Rooster Pub in Ayr, Ayrshire, Scotland – by the bonnie Brig O-Doon (Bridge over the River Doon, genesis of Broadway musical *Brigadoon* [1947****]). In Fogelberg's version, with his own tune and Burns's, he meets his old flame in a supermarket checkout line. They invest in a six-pack, and tip a few wee cups o' kindness. They guzzle yesterdays.

"Auld Lang Syne" – Guy Lombardo & His Royal Canadians, NC, 1927-77. Weird, isn't it? **Led Zep**'s "Stairway to Heaven" never hit charts. Neither did this best-known hit by dance bandleader who sold 100 million records. Guy (1902-77) first dusted the charts with #1(7), 9-27 "Charmaine." His Easy Listening cavalcade includes: #1(3), 5-31 "(There Ought to Be a) Moonlight Saving Time"; #1(3) cowboy so-long song of 10-33, "The Last Round-Up"; #1(4), 10-34 "Stars Fell on Alabama"; and genetically-astonishing #10, 3-48 "I'm My Own Grandpa." With featured guitarist Don Rodney, Lombardo smoked Pre-Rock charts with #1(11), 3-50 "The Third Man Theme." Every New Year's Eve, even before eternal *Dick Clark's Rockin' Eve*, Lombardo hosted the poshest and purplest Manhattan New Year's Eve gala. He played "Auld Lang Syne" to millions of huggers and kissers as the clock banged the New Year with hope and forevermore. After Guy faded away into his own Auld Lang Syne, Dan and his ex-girl, and their silky saxophone, spent a bittersweet Hogmenay rehashing auld times. The sax swirls atop their yesterdreams. And ours.

"Longer" – Dan Fogelberg, #2(2), 12-79; #85, 2-80 C. Still shopping for a gorgeous wedding melody? With Jerry Hey's golden flügelhorn solo, and Gail Levant skying heavenward on her honey-toned harp, Fogelberg caresses this celestial melody. Older than Old Ocean, beyond birds' highest flights, longer than stars stream around the Milky Way – he has been in love with her. The sheer POWER of this non-silly love song flips astronomical bodies about the galaxy like badminton birdies. His folk-style second verse (Key of mellow 'G') returns us to the green moss-bearded virgin rainforests of cool British Columbia. With the spirituality of **John Denver**'s #9, '72 "Rocky Mountain High," Dan compares his love to cathedrals in the mountains, or the deep green primeval forest itself, in its dewy splendor and Thomas Kinkade vibrant glow.

In an age of uncertainty, with relationships suffering the lifespan of a mayfly, Dan Fogelberg's "Longer" promises the closest thing to permanency our frail human condition can conjure. Years pass by too fast, Dan says, and the flickering fire mellows into embers of love and trust, lines will burn into the imaginary book about their lives – and he'll still love her forever. **Shakespeare** said that, in a sonnet that got the boot to bring you more Rock star pix.

Dan uses a few chordal tricks to achieve his song's stunning beauty. Much of it glides easily from tonic I **G** to sub-dominant IV **C**, with forays into sweet chromatic bVII **F-major**. Bobbing buoyantly, he cruises in his Bridge to the Polynesian Chord Shift (see Buddy Holly or DCV). As he trails off the harmonic **C** chord, he hits the startling bVI **Eb** Polynesian Chord, quickly rising into a Mideastern Chord bIII major **Bb**. Most folks who love a gorgeous song don't even want to hear all that deep Alphabet Soup Chord Theory. What they care about is that "Longer" is one of the greatest pure tunes ever written. **Richard Marx** was listening:

"This I Promise You" – N'Sync, #7+, 9-2000. Justin Timberlake's curling Irish tenor steers this magnificent melody into a new millennial dimension. It's living proof that strident Rap can peacefully and harmonically coexist with vintage world-class melody. Songwriter **Richard Marx**'s #7, 1-94 classic love song "Now and Forever" hit #1(11) Adult Contemporary. Timberlake's tune shuffles in at 78 romantic beats per minute, and drums somehow whisper. On the verse crescendo, a gentle tension wreathes his sighs and love-me-forever pledges of fidelity. When the other 80% of his 'Boy Band' (hey, the **Beatles** are a boy Band) whoosh in on **Lettermen** harmonics, "This I Promise You" hits the rainbow trail.

Like Fred Waring's Pennsylvanians' #3, 10-27 "Sweetheart of Sigma Chi," her sensational beauty does not fade in the afterglow. With 'Blue-Eyed Soul' 16th-note melismas to rival a **Righteous Brother** (Bobby Hatfield and #4, '65 "Unchained Melody"), Timberlake promises his ladylove the moon. He soars the tenor stratosphere. With nary a snap, crackle, or pop, he clambers up into the angelic falsetto realm dared only by angels and **Frankie Valli** (4 Seasons).

Beyond Timberlake (what a great Teen Idol NAME, Timberlake), N'Sync personnel include **Chris Kirkpatrick, Josh Chasez, Joey Fatone,** and **Lance Bass**. "This I Promise You" is top-notch pop music, serenading in the great tradition of **Perry Como, Tony Bennett** (#1[8], 9-53 "Rags to Riches"), **Buddy Holly, Elvis,** the **Everly Brothers, Dan Fogelberg,** and **Richard Marx.**

"Kiss Me" – Sixpence None the Richer, #2(1), 11-98. Like 'Sir' Doug Sahm's **Sir Douglas Quintet** [#13, 4-65 "She's About a Mover"], they present the audial illusion of Britishism. **Leigh Nash** wafts her sweet airy vocal. Guitars by Matt Slocum, Sean Kelly. Drums Dale Baker. Bassist Justin Cary. Austin, Texas crew delivers romantic invitation to blue-white stars, marshmallow moon, and

sleepy ivied garden walls, like **Perry Como**'s magnificent #18, 10-75 "Ivy Rose." Leigh's crew hit #32, 9-99 with "There She Goes." Just a Love Song? Six billion people, who probably owe some credit for their creation to some love song, will admit that Love Songs Rule!

"Believe in Me" – Dan Fogelberg, #48, 4-84; #1 Adult Contemporary. Maybe it all started with master Irish Tenor **John McCormack**'s #10, 9-1911 "Believe Me If All Those Endearing Young Charms." This lyric idea dashes all the way back to Shakespeare's contemporary Ben Jonson. Time cannot fade the couples' love. McCormack's follow-up was #6, 8-1912 "Silver Threads Among the Gold," 1912 answer to Grecian Formula (as her golden hair goes gray, he still adores her). Fogelberg's "Longer" promises their love will last forever. It's impossible, we all sadly realize. One must leave the earth first (usually). "Believe in Me," however, is the essence of timeless, endless love (see Marx, Fogelberg, Richie, N'Sync, Como, Holly, and Presley).

"Wait Til' My Bobby Gets Home" – Darlene Love, #26, 7-63; [oddly] N.C., R & B. Simply one of the most spirited super songs of all time! Since every guy in 1962 was named Bobby/Bob/Robert, **Darlene Love**'s Girl Group extravaganza boomed a one-size-fits-all Dance Trax wonderland of sweet sound. After singing lead with the **Crystals** (a/k/a Blossoms) on monster hit #1(2), '62 "He's a Rebel," Love proved that her name LOVE is the essence of what *Gold Rush* is all about.

"Playing for Keeps" – Elvis Presley, #21, 2-57. Even the King sang about permanency. This unheralded flip of #1(3) "Too Much" shows the King's sentimental vulnerability. Love is real, he promises. Our national favorite Elvis song isn't big #1 "Hound Dog" or "Jailhouse Rock," but his second-place #2(1), 12-61 "Can't Help Falling in Love." Elvis's playing-for-keeps baritone doffs his superhuman cloak, and he becomes one of us all. If Elvis himself is ensnared by the obsession that falling in love creates, it could happen to any of us. And it did.

Elvis conjures Hatfield/Hibbler's "Unchained Melody" river, that lonely old river that seeps and gurgles and dashes its weary way to the lonesome sea. He says we are all playing for keeps.

Paul McCartney and his bride Linda listened to the wisdom of Elvis. Maybe Burns and Jonson and Shakespeare. When they hit Wings' top chart pinnacle with #1(5), 4-76 "Silly Love Songs," Paul sang the song very drolly, very tongue in cheek. He knew that we knew that there is no such thing as a silly love song, just like there is no such thing as an ugly woman. Our lives are circumscribed by 'silly love songs.' We love and cherish them, and we use them to create new people. They are the glorious sound track of our inglorious working lives.

We can't help falling in love . . .

Lionel Richie *of the* **Commodores**

Bandleader **Glenn Miller**

Anne Murray

The Lettermen *(1967)*
L-R: **Jim Pike, Gary Pike,** *and* **Tony Butala**

36 Blue Star-Spangled Country And Roadhouse Rock

Over a CENTURY of Country Rock? In Tennessee mountain homes and Arkansas hollers, in South Carolina hamlets and Detroit factory-glow brewsloshers' baseball bars, Country music has streamed along with kissin' cousin Rock and Roll in the musical marathon of America. With the **Carter Family's** #3, 8-28 "Wildwood Flower," **Vernon Dalhart**'s #4, 2-25 "Wreck of the Old 97," and **Roy Acuff**'s #12, 12-38 "Wabash Cannonball," lullabyed by a steel guitar serenade, Country Music is the vanguard of Rock and Roll. Memphis, Tennessee, brought us Sun Records' Elvis, Carl Perkins, Roy Orbison, Johnny Cash, and Jerry Lee Lewis. Nashville, Tennessee, brought us the Grand Ole Opry. New Orleans brought us the whole Ragtime/ Dixieland/Jazz/Cajun collection, with some added hot sauce. Texas Western Swing added a cowboy dimension. But America was a nation on the move. Rural Southerners had to leave their Depression homes and flee to big industrial Northern smokescapes. Country Music, grounded in Rock and Roll, is the most popular music on the planet. **Karaoke** cowboys warble in Yokohama. Sequined yodelers flash honkytonk guitars in Thailand and Madagascar. Greenland Inuits rampage 4-wheel Jeeps over July icefields, with **Alan Jackson** (#28, 2-2002 & #1[C] "Drive [for Daddy Gene],") or **Shania Twain** or **Faith Hill** soothing hungry polar bears. The last guy you'd expect to stun America by sponsoring a Country Music Explosion is **Henry Ford.**

Both Bluegrass and Country Music were boosted with a firm Ford chassis. **Elvis** "Tony" Alderman played fiddle in a 1924 band acutally named the Hillbillies. The word HILLBILLY hails from Michigan's stumpy Porcupine Mountains of the Upper Peninsula – where January is colder than Anchorage, Alaska. The quartet of Elvis the First, fiddler Charlie

Bowman, banjo plucker John Hopkins (not Johns Hopkins), and brother Al Hopkins formed a string fearsome foursome. In toddler times for the USA, a PIANO cost as much as the moon, so many Country stars used portable GUITARS, BANJOS or FIDDLES. Electric pianos were a future fantasy. MANDOLINS, LUTES, and DULCIMERS fit well into early Country's 'Unplugged Generation.' SPEED METAL dominates Heavy Metal Rock and Hard Rock – but the banjo and guitar and fiddle speed of these obtuse Country/Bluegrass stars is truly awesome: Stars were the Hillbillies (a/k/a Hill Billies), Earl Johnson & Dixie Clodhoppers, the Fruit Jar Drinkers [Prohibition reference], the Possum Hunters, and the Skillet Lickers.

"Footprints in the Snow" – Bill Monroe & the Bluegrass Boys, NC, 1946; #5, 12-46 Country. One pioneer invented an entire category of Country music – BLUEGRASS – and wrote Elvis's first record, "Blue Moon of Kentucky." At age 83, **Bill Monroe** (1911-96) continued to perform, despite being wheeled center stage suffering from multiple infirmities – but buoyed by the everlasting youth of his spirit. *Rolling Stone* (1996, Hallowe'en) Editor Anthony DeCurtis calls the 'Father of Bluegrass' **Monroe** a "peer of such giants as Louis Armstrong, Duke Ellington, and Miles Davis." Bill's big brothers hogged the blockier instruments, leaving little Bill with the cute one with eight heavenly strings tuned somewhere between Italy, a Kentucky holler, and St.Peter's summer home – the mandolin. "I wanted a music of my own," Monroe opined, "It's a music that brings people together and makes friends." **Buddy Holly** later cut a Monroe-echo Lubbock High School school song. Holly's first record – the "Lost Tape" – is his pre-voice-change Monroe classic "Footprints in the Snow." Therefore, Monroe, via the **Crickets**, helped launch the **Beatles**.

"Kentucky Waltz" – Bill Monroe & the Bluegrass Boys, NC, 1946; #3, 3-46. When Carl Perkins met Elvis, the first thing the future King asked his blue-suede shoes Rockabilly pal was "Do you like Mr. Bill Monroe?" Perkins gushed, "I LOVE Mr. Bill Monroe!" Elvis said, "I do, too." The Everly Brothers Don & Phil, Johnny Cash, and

Cricket **Sonny Curtis** were also in awe of Monroe. Bluegrass is Kentucky's motto and ground cover ['Blue-grass State']. "Kentucky Waltz" prompted the #1 waltz of all time − #1(3), '50 "The Tennessee Waltz," from Patti Page. It was originally (#12 C, 11-48) a big hit for **Ray Acuff**).

"Polka on a Banjo" − **Flatt & Scruggs, NC, 1960; #12, 12-60 C.** If Bluegrass is the purest form of Country music, as Peter Guralnick calls Rockabilly the purest form of Rock, then **Lester Flatt** (1914-79, b. Overton County, TN) and **Earl Scruggs** (b. '24, Flintville, NC) are among the purest of the pure. Scruggs − banjo virtuoso. Flatt, amazing guitar star (mandolin, too). Despite Olympian world-class banjo/mandolin style, Flatt and Scruggs are best known for "Foggy Mountain Breakdown" at #55, 3-68 (#58 C). They did comedy like **Homer & Jethro's** #17, 5-53 parody of Mama Thornton/Elvis's "Hound Dog" and Patti Page's #1(8) 1-53 "Doggie in the Window" − ("That Hound Dog in the Window"). Flatt & Scruggs' signature song is TV sitcom theme #44, 12-62 "Ballad of Jed Clampett" (#1[2] C), inspired by Bill Hayes's Disney series #1(5) 2-55 "The Ballad of Davy Crockett."

Since Country Music uses electric guitars, basses, and drums and the big 2 & 4 Backbeat, *Gold Rush* treats Country music as a parallel universe to Rock and Roll. Since we've already discombobulated inflexible purists in Soul, Punk, Heavy Metal, Hip-Hop, Religious Rock, Latin and Jazz Rock, and Heavy Metal, it's time to wobble Country concepts. See **Billy Joel**'s #1(2), '80 "It's Still Rock and Roll to Me." Any Country Rap?

"Is You Is Or Is You Ain't (Ma Baby)?" − **Louis Jordan & His Tympani Five, #2(3), 7-44; #3, 6-44 R&B; #1(5), 7-44 C.** Soul/Jazz/Early Rock pioneer Jordan scored #1 Country-Western tune. An Afro-American gap existed in #1 C. tunes till #1, '69 "All I Have to Offer You Is Me," by RCA's **Charley Pride**. Country charts ['Hillbilly Hit Parade'] began in 1944 via Pee Wee King, following lead of 'Harlem Hit Parade's" [R&B charts] 1942 debut.

"San Antonio Rose" − **Bob Wills & His Texas Playboys, #15, 9-39. Bob Wills** (1905-75) sharecropped with ex-slaves on his dad's Kosse, Texas, farm. Bandleader Bob hosted four generations of world-class fiddlers and sculpted Rock's plaintive ancestor − Western Swing. Dumped brusquely from Jazz bands, fiddles faltered. Bob heard Blues and Jazz riffs as he and Playboys barn-stormed New Orleans, the Dixieland Delta, and Molly Altizer's San Antonio − home of Davy Crockett's/John Wayne's Alamo. Inspired by Jazz clarinetist Benny Goodman, whose Swing Jazz featured jivey cadenzas and improvisations, Wills became the King of Western (or Texas) Swing. Fiddle star Wills featured drummers − a Country rarity, previewing the BIG BEAT for Elvis's D.J. Fontana. His "New San Antonio Rose" trumped the original, twice (#3 C, 1-44, after #19, 3-43 Top 30). Wills made

the Rock Hall, Class of 1999 − Early Influence Category.
"New Spanish Two-Step" hit a modest #20, 7-46 − but it tied an all-time #1 record at #1(21) C, 5-46.

"Faded Love" − **Bob Wills & His Texas Playboys, NC, '50; #8, 11-50 C. Essence** of long lost lone windswept sorrow songs. **LeAnn Rimes'** 1999 same-named album wafts this sweet forlorn tune to the "Deep in the Heart of Texas" (#1, Alvino Rey, #3 Bing Crosby, '42) stardust skies. As steel guitars weep **Hank Williams's** Country laments, so Bob's fading fiddle cascades down the corridors of sad reverie. This so-long song of love's faded petals is a mid-century flowering of deep emotion . Never mawkish or maudlin, Faded Love" makes rodeo roustabouts cry into their frothy neon Pearl brews. "Faded Love" is the throbbing heart of true Country music.

Henry Ford again. Bizarrely, the incredible popularity of the Grand Ole Opry AND the automobile is due to a guy from MOTOWN (Dearborn, Michigan). Ford loved to camp with peanut-baron Luther Burbank and **Thomas Alva Edison** (1847-31). Without these World's Greatest Tinkerers, the world (working for peanuts) might discover the following things missing: the thrifty family car, the electric guitar, the vinyl record, the Grand Ole Opry, and Rock and Roll. Henry Ford believed in rural values of hard work, family gardens, and a good Country fiddle at sundown, like Bob Wills.

"If You're Gonna Play in Texas (You Gotta Have a Fiddle in the Band)" − **Alabama, NC, 1984; #1(1), 8-84 C.** Fort Payne, Alabama, nurtured four guys who loved a good fiddle and a Barber-Shop heavenly harmony: **Jeff Cook**, fiddle, keyboards; **Randy Owen**, guitar; **Teddy Gentry**, bass; and one of Country's few Armenian-American stars, **Bennett Vartanian**, drums. Naturally, all sing, admirably. In Bob Wills's grand tradition, they carry on the feeling and flavor of fiddle-powered hits. Alabama enjoyed 20 straight #1 Country hits. Edging Conway Twitty's 40 #1 C. hits, Alabama lavished 1998's *For the Record: Alabama 41 Number One Hits* package.

"Freight Train Boogie" − **Delmore Brothers, NC, '46; #2(1), 12-46 C.** Alton (1908-1964) and Rabon (1916-52) Delmore's Country Blues showcased their French-American Louisiana Delta roots on the Opry, attracting fans like the **Everly Brothers, Carl Perkins, Johnny/Dorsey Burnette, Roy Orbison,** and **Elvis Presley.** "Freight Train Boogie" is an uptempo blaster, with a favorite locomotive whistle motif. Delmores hit #1(1) C 9-49 "Blues Stay Away from Me," and #7, 2-50 C "Pan-American Boogie." Country Boogie (Boogie-Woogie) often uses a 12-Bar Blues chord progression, plus Walking Bass on the piano − plus a rampaging drum backbeat. It parallels **Elton Britt's** chugging #5, 4-46 C "Detour," about Elton's Arkansas bust-axle highways.

At Christmastide December 26, 1925, 77-year-old white-bearded Uncle Jimmy Thompson of Laguardo, Tennessee, who found his fiddle flair in the CIVIL WAR (1861-65), contested other fiddlers at **Nashville,** Tennessee's tiny new WSM 1000-watt radio station. Legendary announcer George Hay, 30, set up an 'hour or so' of old familiar tunes every Saturday Night. The Grand Ole Opry was born (via Ford's fiddling contests). First Opry stars? DeFord Bailey, Uncle Dave Macon, the Dixieliners, the Binkley Brothers, Dixie Clodhoppers, and the legendary **Minnie Pearl** [#10, 3-66, "Giddyup Go – Answer"]. With her straw-colored 40s upsweep hairdo, and cute hat (w/ tag dangling), Minnie sang out "HOW-DEE!" – sparking many a grumpy mood to bust out in a big smile.

'Amps' back then were just cordless large guitars called DOBROS. Dobros helped power the Opry among booming banjoes and shrill fiddlesticks. With a metal Resonator where the guitar's deep canyon looms, dobros and orchestral guitars doubled and tripled acoustic volume. Compare it to the bicycle.

In the 1890s, bikes jump-started man's speed of locomotion from 3-4 mph to 10-12 mph. Ford's Easy Payment Coupon "Model T" car dumped the bike for go-to-work transporation. Likewise, the Dobro destroyed the wimpy volume of ordinary guitars. Zapping the Dobro, in turn, was the Electric Guitar. We can't say Mr. Beaubien or Joe Kekeku or Les Paul or Leo Fender invented the electric guitar – any more than we can claim Ford invented the car. Anyhow, the electric guitar dumped the Dobro, and CREATED Rock music – and probably Country.

"Some Kinda Earthquake" – Duane Eddy & His Twangy Guitar (& the Rebels), #37, 10-59. Eddy also recorded "Detour" on Al. #5, 1-59 *Have Twangy Guitar – Will Travel.* The Arizonan/New York guitar guru, who played the melody on the low rhythm-guitar area notes, crunched the high charts with #6, 6-58 "Rebel Rouser" (#17, 8-58 C). Eddy's crackling sound rumbles snarly baritone notes. This shortest-song-ever-to-chart on the HOT 100 (1:17) shakes and quakes its metallic fervor and fired-up frenzy. Our summers are often doomed to roads damaged by improvements (Eddy's #9, 6-59 "40 Miles of Bad Road"). Jane Drake, Sally Ickes, and Danielle D'Amico tell of orange-cone extravaganza roads nearby with only two seasons – WINTER and CONSTRUCTION.

"The Brakeman's Blues" – Jimmie Rodgers [I], #7, 8-28. Railroad brakeman dubbed 'Father of Country Music." Rodgers did Folk and Blues, too. Meridian, MS, Country Blues star (1897-1933) cascaded Mach One Yodels off his swooping tenor, popularizing the art, like #2(1), 3-28 "'T' for Texas" [a/k/a "Blue Yodel"]. Singing glories of Road and Rail, Rodgers previewed Rock and Roll. His yodels got NUMBERED: #10, 11-28 "Blue Yodel #3," and #19, 1-30 "Anniversary Yodel (Blue Yodel #7)." **Janis Joplin**'s #1 '71 "Me & Bobby McGee" echoes his hit title #14, 4-29 "Waiting for a Train." Born in "Johnny B. Goode" yellow-pine evergreens, Rodgers busted out of home at 14, joined a snake-oil medicine show, juggled railroad jobs, and chased stardom. After fifteen years of chasing rain-

bows, Jimmie shuffled into Victor Talking Machine Company's (later RCA) sporty porta-studio, accompanied by his best pal – his guitar. Over five smoky feverish years, he launched a skyward flight to destiny, but was consumed by music and consumption. Rodgers is best known for melding the sounds of Blues to 'Hillbilly' music. This Rodgers synthesis, along with **Carter Family** Appalachian harmonies, created Country music. Rodgers' dreaded lung malady TB caught up with him in a lonely Manhattan hotel room May 26, 1933, age 35.

"Wildwood Flower" – Carter Family, #3, 8-28. Threesome legends: **Sarah Carter**, lead soprano, zither/autoharp; hubby **A.P. Carter**, harmonizer; cousin **Maybelle Carter,** alto. Her daughter June married Country treasure **Johnny Cash** (b. '32, Arkansas). Family togetherness trio contrasts to Rodgers' stark solo sessions at last-stand NYC Taft Hotel. Papa A.P. Carter paid factory dues in Detroit. Dumped smokescape. Grubbed jobs at Copper Creek and Clinch Mountain, Virginia, as carpenter, blacksmith, and songsmith. "Wildwood Flower" hails from Ford's camping chum **Thomas Edison**'s Camden, NJ studio. Their debut oozed with gloom (#10, 4-28 "Bury Me Under the Weeping Willow"), but they flipped moods on #9, 10-28 signature song "Keep on the Sunny Side." Smiling 'Mother Maybelle' sang on 1969 *Johnny Cash Show,* gamely harping at a zither (20+ strings, like horizontal mini-harp w/ guitar pick). Their poignant and wistful family-reunion among the clouds is #17, 8-35 gospel hymn "Can the Circle Be Unbroken."

"Praise the Lord and Pass the Soup" – Johnny Cash with the Carter Family and the Oak Ridge Boys, NC, '73; #57, 8-73 C. 3½ generations of Country stars – Cash at zenith, and new Oak Ridge Boys on way up. The **Oak Ridge Boys,** seemingly new in 70s with #3 C, 7-77 "Y'All Come Back Saloon," actually joined the Opry in 1945 – with 40+ revolving-door Barber-Shoppers Emeritus. Star line-up includes **Duane Allen** (b. '43), lead; **William Lee Golden** (b. '35, baritone, big beard); Richard Sterban (b. '43, bass); and Joe Bonsall (b. '48, tenor). Oak Ridge, Tennessee, won World War II for us, via nuclear rocketry experts we'd smuggled out of Germany (Einstein, Von Braun) to design the Hiroshima A-Bomb.

"Elvira" – Oak Ridge Boys, #5, 5-81; #1(1), 4-81 C. Everybody's favorite O.R.B. singalong. Borrows a raspy bass vocal riff from Rivingtons' #48, 8-62 "Papa-Oom-Mow-Mow" Like the New Yorkers they aren't, O.R.B. stretched cherry-wine lipped 'Elvira' to rhyme with 'FIRE.' "Bobbie Sue" arrived to #12, 1-82 fanfare (#1[1] C), bouncing her winsome way into our hearts. ORB also bonanza-ed with family-value NC '82 [#3, 11-82 C] "Thank God for Kids" and #72, 3-83 "American Made" [#1(1), 2-83 C].

"Gonna Take a Lot of River" – Oak Ridge Boys, NC, '88; #1(1), 7-88 C. **Steve Sanders** replaced Golden in '87 (Whitburn). This huge hit deals with the confluence of rivers, like Pittsburgh's Monongahela and Ohio. Bassman Sterban stirs and burbles the bottom of the song like a huge channel catfish prowling Mississippi Delta meander bends, looking for fishhooks not to bite. Great American music, from Gospel ["Deep River"] to Popular ["Proud Mary"] to Country ["Chattahoochee"], often finds a sacred river, down by **Stephen Foster**'s #1 1851 "Old Folks at Home" (Swanee). ORB's 17 #1 C.-only classics include 9-81 "Fancy Free," 4-80 "Trying to Love Two Women," 3-85 "Little Things," 6-87 "This Crazy Love," or debut #1, 4-78 "I'll Be True to You." "Lucky Moon" (#6 C.-only) spurred the 90s for these Tennessee titans.

"Lovesick Blues" – Hank Williams, #24, 5-49; #1(16), 3-49 C. Alabama's **Hank Williams** peppered the Country charts with his high lonesome baritone barely half a decade – but his echoes surpass half a century. "Move It on Over" shot up to debut #4, 8-47 C on the former 'Hillbilly Hit Parade' and 'Juke Box Folk Records' *Billboard* chart [officially Country chart in 1958]. "Lovesick Blues" is Hank's mainstream debut smash. "Lovesick Blues" goes way back to 1922. Singer/songwriter Hank's (1923-53, b. Mt. Olive, Alabama) meteoric career passed on some survival skills to his son:

"A Country Boy Can Survive" – Hank Williams, Jr., NC, '82; #2(3), 1-82, C. Urban survival kit. Remember Crocodile Dundee's famous "You call THAT a KNIFE?" line . . . when he unsheaths a monstrous Bowie knife at unlucky would-be muggers shaking a dinky blade? Hank Junior arrives at crime-showdown with an arsenal, and scares the stupid mugger off into the slimy alleyway night. Will the Williamses be a tri-generational onslaught? "I Don't Know" [**Hank Williams III**, #54, 1-2001 C]. Baritone/bass Hank Junior for openers hit #67, 2-64 on Hank's "Long Gone Lonesome Blues" (#5 C). Other Junior hits? All C: #1(2), 8-70 "All for the Love of Sunshine," #1(2), 4-72 "Eleven Roses," threepeat 1981s #1's "Texas Women," "Dixie on My Mind," and "All My Rowdy Friends (Have Settled Down)." He's best known for Monday Night Football theme.

"My Bucket's Got a Hole in It" – Hank Williams, NC, '49; #2(1), 11-49, C. Three chords and a cloud of dust. No mysterious metaphors here. When Hank laments a holey bucket, he's probably just grumbling about a holey bucket, with this checkered Folk epic. Born HIRAM Williams, his major influence was an 'old black man named Tee-Tot' [Rufe Payne, d. 1950 or so]. Hank forecasts Rockabilly with his rampaging steady rhythm. Song covered to #12, 3-58 (#6 R & B, #10 C) by TV Teen idol **Ricky Nelson**. From cornbread ramshackle boyhood to honkytonk paradise, Hank Williams broadcast his Country Soul all the way to Ricky's Hollywood Hills, and **James Burton**'s twangy lead guitar.

"Long Gone Lonesome Blues" – Hank Williams, NC, '50; #1(8), 3-50 C. Hank's lonesome yodeling echoes Jimmie Rodgers' style, and Hank in turn powered one of Rock's icons **Del Shannon** (1935-90), with his guitar and Williams yodeling techniques, Shannon impressed his Coopersville, MI, coach enough (as Charlie Westover) for

a starting fullback slot – and he became a "Runaway" success (#1, '61). **Tom Petty** and **Elton John**'s singing hero Del cut NC '65 Al. *Del Shannon Sings Hank Williams* in the heart of Motown, with Motown Records' session Soul guitarists on Country steel guitar. **Raul Malo and the Mavericks** covered Williams's #29, 5-51 "Hey Good Lookin'" [#1(8), 7-51 C] to #72 C in 1992, and rebounded to bigger 90s C. successes, like #22, 8-95 C "Here Comes the Rain."

"Kaw-Liga" – Hank Williams, NC, '53; #1(13), 2-53 C. Pronounced 'caw-lie-ja.' Morose ballad of unrequited love affair of cigar-store wooden 'Indian' in love with Indian maiden. Tragically, his heart is made of knotty pine. Tempestuous tom-tom rhythm – like **Johnny Preston**'s #1 '59 "Running Bear" and **Paul Revere**'s #1 '71 "Indian Reservation." Hank's "Kaw-Liga" womped Country charts a month after Hank's mysterious death after a gig on January 1, 1953 at age 29. **Moon Mullican** helped Hank sculpt Cajun lyrics for his biggest mainstream hit "Jambalaya" (#20, 9-52, #1[14] C, and #3, Pop star Jo Stafford). Into his old age (28), Hank dove deeper into his substance-induced lonesome blue funk. He was bedeviled by agonizing back disc pain after a toss from a horse. **Hank Jr**. took "Kaw-Liga" back to #12 C in 5-80.

"Kaw-Liga" – "Country" Charley Pride, NC, '69; #3, 2-69., C. RCA sent out no picture sleeve for Charley's debut. When he played for Memphis Red Sox in the old American Negro League in 1954-56, he didn't look a lot different from his teammates (as he did with Butte, Montana, Pioneers). His tried and true straight Country baritone is Hank Williams revisited. "Kaw-Liga" spins on an axis of controversy too. Its Native American cigar-store protagonist 'PINES away' for his lovely maiden in the antique store. Charley's (b. 3-38, Sledge, Mississippi) first three hits were labeled "COUNTRY" Charley Pride. **Paul McCartney** said about his idol **Buddy Holly**: "When we first heard his record, we didn't know if they [Crickets] were black or white. We just caught their great MYSTIC IMAGE and their great sound." Profound Beatle comment. In the days before MTV, with just a smidgeon of Bandstand, you could hear a singer's career and never SEE the singer.

With 29 #1 hits to 1994, Charley Pride HUMBLY amassed the #5 total in the history of Country Music, passing Eddy Arnold at 28. Pride's #1 C hits include #1(3) 2-71 "I'd Rather Love You," #1(1), 10-73 "Amazing Love," and #1(1), 12-82 "Why, Baby, Why," and Hank's #2[1], 3-52 "Honky Tonk Blues" to #1(1) C, 2-80.

"Mississippi Cotton Pickin' Delta Town" – Charley Pride, #70, 11-74; #3, 8-74 C. Charley's tableau paints his 500-souls hometown Sledge, Mississippi, like white Sledge Rockabilly **Harold Dorman** [1926-88] of Sledge. Each Sledge-hammer star stormed the charts on a "Mountain of Love" (#21, 2-60 Dorman; #1, 12-81 C, Pride; also #9, '64 Johnny Rivers). This burg? Under a blistering sun in muggy 100-degree High July, Charley's vignette vibrantly describes Sledge's four world-anchoring corners.

Sleepy noon silence. Cracker-barrel philosophers chewing batting averages. Old myriad-cloven live oaks of blessed lemonade shade. Gorgeous multiracial Mississippi belles. And one fleabag hound scratching all the world's evils right in the center of Mam'selle Hepzibah's Strawberry Social. Not just a song. It's a painting. And a way of life. Sledge, Mississippi.

"Kentucky Waltz" – Eddy Arnold, NC, '51; #1(3), 4-51.
Cover Versions again. **Pee Wee King**'s (1914-2000) "Tennessee Waltz" is a next-door neighbor's Answer Song to **Bill Monroe**'s #3, 3-46 "Kentucky Waltz." In R & B, it meant a crooner like Pat Boone taking a **Little Richard**'s Screaming Blues – and gently re-paving it for suburban sophisticates. With his smooth Country style, **Eddy Arnold** was considered a Cover Artist for more 'Hillbilly' authenticists. Arnold fits with **Bing Crosby, Perry Como, Frank Sinatra.** Arnold's "Bouquet of Roses" snagged #13, 6-48 on the big chart – but #1(19), 5-48 C. [One rose for each time she busted his heart – not his bank]. Eddy even bigger with mouthful-titled #22, 11-47 "I'll Hold You in My Heart (Until I Can Hold You in My Arms)." It clutched #1(21), 8-47 C. #1 – a shy HALF YEAR. Eddy's steady starstompers? #23, 3-49 "Don't Rob Another Man's Castle," at #1(12), 2-49 C; and #1(11) C "I Wanna Play House with You" of 6-52 for Eddy, the "Tennessee Ploughboy." His 1994 charted hit total stood at 145, behind only **George Jones.** [NOT **GRANDPA Jones**, of "'T' for Texas" fame at #5, C 12-62. Born 1913, star of *Buck Owens/*Roy Clark's *Hee-Haw* Country comedy show]. Superstardom? Let GEORGE do it:

"White Lightning" – George Jones, #73, 5-59; #1(5), 3-59 C. Moonshine hot-rod epic. J.P. Richardson – the **BIG BOPPER** (1930-59) – wrote this rum-running ode to backwoods stills. The Bopper had a fine booming baritone. Jones carries Bopper's charisma and fast action. The Bopper knew "Mountain Dew," cut by Willie Nelson (#23 C, 10-81) with our old camp campfire flavor. Starring Uncles Mort and Bill, "Mountain Dew" also inspired the bristly baritone of movie star **Robert Mitchum** (1917-97, elegy by Freddy Byrnes). Mitchum's movie sound track theme produced #62, 9-58 and #65, 2-62 "The Ballad of Thunder Road." It's a Boss Hogg switchback moonshine saga of booze cruising and cliff crashing. Jones's #4 C, 10-55 "Why Baby Why" signaled his Country charisma. It was covered by **Pat Boone** (b. 34, Jacksonville, Florida) who married Country royalty **Shirley Foley:**

"Smoke on the Water" – Red Foley, #7, 9-44; #1(13), 8-44 C. NO relation to Heavy Metal **Deep Purple**'s Montreux Rock Festival armageddon song. Blue Lick, Kentucky's Boone pop-in-law (1910-68) lit up the Country cavalcade with electrifying titles and tunes: #8, 8-49 C. "Two Cents, Three Eggs, and a Postcard'; "Cincinnati Dancing Pig" porker corker at #7, 9-50 (#2 C); "Milk Bucket Boogie" at #8, 3-52 C; and Rock-inspiring "Salty Dog Rag" #8, 3-52 C. When **Buddy Holly** and bandmate Bob Montgomery sang Foley's hot cornpone cutie – #5, 2-52 C "Too Old to Cut the Mustard" at a Lubbock High School assembly, they brashly targeted their less-than-overjoyed principal.

"Good Ol' Girls" – Sonny Curtis, NC, '81; #15, 4-81.
Among Nashville's most genuine stars, **Cricket** Sonny Curtis played lead guitar in Buddy Holly's early Nashville sessions at Owen Bradley's Barn. With 13 Country hits and #28, 9-53 HOT 100 "How to Hold a Girl" pre-Cricket smash, Sonny enjoyed – "My Way of Life" at #49 C, and #134 in 10-66; super #120 (#36 C, 2-68) "Atlanta Georgia Stray"; "The Straight Life" at #45 C., 7-68; and his eternally-syndicated classic Mary Tyler Moore sitcom theme, #29, 7-80 C "Love Is All Around." Sonny plays a fine fiddle. Sonny's best-known hit is "I Fought the Law" – as done by the **Bobby Fuller Four** (#9, '66), the **Clash** (NC) and **Hank Williams Jr.** (#15 C. '78). Great guy, Sonny. Class act. Cricket lead singer/bassist **Jerry Naylor** sparked the Country caravan with his #69, 3-70 "But for Love" (#54, nine years later, 3-79 C). Despite a heart attack at age 24 in 1964,Naylor fully recovered; 10 charted Country hits helped the process – like Buddy's "Rave On" to #80, 5-78 C, and #27 C. 1-75 "Is That All There Is to a Honky-Tonk?"

"(There'll Be) Peace in the Valley (For Me)" – Red Foley & the Sunshine Boys, NC, '51; #5, 7-51 C. With Christian Contemporary pioneer Pat Boone as his son-in-law, Red Foley shared this song with the only mid-50s singer to top Pat in record sales – **Elvis Presley** (#25, 4-57). Elvis and his Gospel-anchored **Jordanaires** sing "Peace in the Valley" so breathtakingly – in the sincere Red Foley tradition – that they could turn an old flea-hotel atheist hound dog into a true believer.

"Chantilly Lace" – Jerry Lee Lewis, #43, 3-72; #1(3) C. "Chantilly" sparked the Killer's resurrected R & R career in stardust honkytonks from Natchez to Motown to the Yukon to the Moon. Jerry's 100% Pure Rock and Roll #30, '61 "What'd I Say" is also **Ray Charles'** best tune of the era (#6, 6-59). Jerry's decade of 40 Days in his own wilderness abated with #94, 7-68's ode to lost beer: "What's Made Milwaukee Famous (Has Made a Loser out of Me)" – #2(2), 6-68 C. Jerry's follow-up to "What'd I Say?" shows his canny Country savvy, and maybe his best-ever Country song – **Hank Williams** #27, 4-51 "Cold, Cold Heart" (#1, 3-51 C). Jerry took it to #22 C. in 8-61. Jerry's beer tune salutes Milwaukee's sudsy export and his own personal remorse. Drinking is often a bleary attempt at anesthetizing from pain. Jerry named his boy after the famous Tonight Show host **Steve Allen** (1922-2000), who gave him his national TV break. The lad tragically drowned in Jerry's rock-star swimming pool.

I sort of talked to Jerry at a grubby sticky-floored hangdog honkytonk in 1966 Motown. Jerry's piano may have been drinking. After a cold-turkey vanishing act from the Top 20, due to a paparazzi feeding frenzy about his young bride Myra (13, yep, YOUNG), Jerry defiantly released #93, 1-59 "I'll Sail My Ship Alone" (#1 C, '50, Moon Mullican). Country Music's tight family shunned the reprobate rapscallion on three occasions ('58-'61, '61-'63, '65-'67), as Peter denied Jesus in the prelude to Golgotha. The Milwaukee song, however, seemed to be a first sign of Jerry's pride crumbling to the side of confession and atonement. This night was not so religious. The Killer bravely tried to negotiate a stairway sticky with beerbarf and hopelessness. He staggered with this golden groupie downward. I needed an interview. The grubby basement wreaked the Funeral of the Giant Onion. The Killer's lion mane was flyaway. One frilly shirttail fluttered flabbergastedly. We both somehow got stuck in the doorway like 'Meathead' and 'Archie Bunker," and I busted out laughing. I don't think he did. I got no interview, but I got an education. "Thanks anyhow, Killer," I farewelled. In June 2000 at Long Island's Canoe Place Inn, I once again confronted the Killer. At age 64, he no longer hurdled atop his piano at 5.8 on the Richter Earthquake Scale. I was glad to see he'd mellowed a bit. Jerry Lee Lewis's Contrarian Years danced on treble heaven-bound keys, while he blasted a devilish Boogie bass on the hot bottom. He embroiders late middle age with toys and chicks: #4, 10-77 C "Middle Age Crazy," #18, 4-79 C. "I Wish I Was Eighteen Again," and #4, 1-81 C "Thirty-Nine and Holding." Jerry Lee Lewis is barnstorming whatever millennium he can fondle his keys in. The Killer rocks on.

"Lawdy Miss Clawdy" – Mickey Gilley, NC, '76; #3, 10-76 C. Gilley's is **John Travolta's** quick-change venue from *Saturday Night Fever* into *Urban Cowboy*(***). Like televangelist **Jimmy Swaggart**, Gilley is Jerry Lee Lewis's cousin. Gilley sweated dinky-dive piano bars for 21 years to become this overnight sensation. Gilley's bar joined thousands of new couples to dance and guzzle and ride the mechanical bull. Gilley cloned cuz Jerry Lee's piano glissandos and Boogie beats and thumb-twiddling twitches. If we did a Country Soul chapter, Gilley would lead off. Gilley (b. '36, raised in Jerry Lee's Ferriday, LA) scored with Soul spinoffs like #22 "Stand by Me" (#1 C) 5-80, and #1 C sweet ballad 8-74 "I Overlooked an Orchid." Rife with Jerry's deliberately slurred vocalics, Gilley GLIDES up the scale in a parabolic curve of rising pitch – not pausing for each individual note. **Lloyd Price**'s original #1(7) R & B only, "Lawdy Miss Clawdy" has **Fats Domino** on piano. Also cut by Elvis. Less-known Gary Stites charted HOT 100 to #47, 2-60. "Clawdy" bludgeons the backbeat splendidly, throbbing with triplets (12 per measure), and hanging on the Tonic Seventh for an eternity. Song ripples with passion. A little bit dangerous – like all great Rock and Soul. Maybe Country, too, eh?

No More Mr. Nice Guy – Pat Boone, Al. 1997. Yep, Pat Boone did HEAVY METAL at age 62. *Rolling Stone*'s Jancee Dunne (5-96) interviewed Rock's Pop Standards pioneer, trying out a new blend of Heavy Metal/Jazz Rock. Dunn quizzes Boone about meeting Elvis:

RS: You knew Elvis back then. What was surprising about him?

Boone: His loneliness.

Clarke Heaton once experienced a religious ceremony in Pat Boone's swimming pool, Boone presiding. My life-long friend Janie Zimmerman/Richardson interviewed Pat for the Dearborn High Pioneer newspaper. Clarke and Janie came away starstruck. Since charting NC '80, #60, 11-80 C. "Colorado Country Morning," Pat bought a Camaro Z-28, and cruises Hollywood Boulevard with his

Heavy Metal CD's blasting. The Fountain of Youth is out looking for Pat to discover HIS secret.

"If Drinkin' Don't Kill Me (Her Memory Will)" – George Jones, NC, '81; #8, 1-81, C. Though Jones metamorphosed from crew-cut smiley kid to Country kingpin, with perfect silver-toned ultra-thick Reagan hair, he never forgot his roots. Many stars have slurped the suds, George's song-guy sings about hazy midnights and Alka-Seltzer afterglows. George's signature hit is #76, 7-61 "Tender Years." Also #1(6) C 4-62 "She Thinks I Still Care" and double whammy 1974 C. #1's "The Grand Tour" and "The Door." True Country marathoner Jones scored with #34, 1-92 C. "I Don't Need Your Rockin' Chair" and #24, 11-93 C. "High-Tech Redneck."

Jones's Graveyard Country songs are profound and spellbinding, like Hank Williams' last earthly release #1(1) C "I'll Never Get Out of This World Alive." Jones volleyed with #2(2), C 11-68 "When the Green Grass Grows over Me," and continued later with #60 C 4-94 "Honky Tonk Myself to Death":

"He Stopped Lovin' Her Today" – George Jones, NC, '80; #1(1), 4-80, C. CMA (Country Music Association) Record of the Year. In this heartbreaker, George intones in a funereally 3rd-person style, that he stopped loving her today for one and only one reason – today he died. No hidebound cynic can snicker at this one. It's too awful, too real. One reason love is so precious is because it is so fragile, so temporary. It really cannot last an eternity. Jones's awesome elegy to human frailty is a foreboding reminder of death's agonizing finality – and futility, if we squander time with loved ones on insignificant bickering and quarreling. Rock critic Dave Marsh says George Jones IS Country music. **Tammy Wynette** and George served up a #1(2) C, 12-76 harmonic "Near You." The cover version by Larry Green hit #3, 10-47. The original?

"Near You" – Francis Craig & His Orchestra, #1(17), 8-47; NC, C.

Nashville piano guy Craig (1900-66) was also 46 years old. He apprenticed alto sax with **Glen Gray & Casa Loma Orchestra** (#1[3], 1-35, original "Blue Moon," covered by **Benny Goodman** to #2[2], 1-35). On the new Bullet label of Jim Bulleit's, Craig cut the theme song "Red Rose."

Then he plunked down "Near You" as the FLIPSIDE [Buddy Holly's #1 "That'll Be the Day" was flipside]. Decca revamped Craig's master and distributed it. Wildfire hitdom, however, created superhuman demand, it caused the first Nashville record pressing/stamping plant. Thereby creating Nashville's coming Juggernaut of monster hits. Craig had one other hit—#3, 1-48 "Beg Your Pardon."

CRAIG'S "NEAR YOU" HELPED CREATE TELEVISION

It became the theme song for 'Mr. Television," comic **Milton Berle** (1908-2002). Into Millennium III, not a ripple worried "Near You's" lofty position, despite a few 1992-95 songs of longevity. Seventeen weeks. Started Nashville. Created TV. Not bad for a furshluggi= FLIPSIDE!

In *The Blues Brothers* (1980****), **John Belushi** and **Dan Aykroyd** sing Soul music in a rough Country honkytonk divided from bottle-throwing hooligans by flimsy chickenwire. Their integrated Blues band has to jiffily think up a Country song. With frilly falsetto voices, they squiggle and wiggle and lull the poopkickin' roughnecks into a sweet stupor with this classic **Tammy Wynette** anthem:

"Stand by Your Man" – Tammy Wynette, #19, 11-69; #1(3), 10-68 C. #1, UK, 1975. **Tammy Wynette** was born Virginia Wynette Pugh (5-5-42) in Itawamba County, Mississippi. "Stand by Your Man" symbolizes an entire way of life. She sings a plaintive tale of a goodtimin' man and a long-suffering woman who loves him. Tammy pumps up her sense of duty. Despite his ragtag rabble-rousing honkytonk lifestyle, SHE stands silently and lovingly, toting the patience of Job. She transcends his pretzel-scarfing, beer-inhaling shenanigans. On the sweet sainthood ladder, she's just 42 rungs below Mother Teresa.

Tammy's first two verses? Slow deliberate Country ballad: slim bass notes, unpretentious rhythm guitar, and Tammy's pleading voice. She carries the first two verses on her slim back. When three booming beats strike the amazing free-for-all chorus, a weeping steel guitar surrounds the song. On "STAND BY YOUR MAN," her smooth chord shift vaults from Tonic **'A'** to breathtaking mediant III chord **'C#' major.** Fans unencumbered by Music Theory just hear this upward swoon as "THAT SUPER VOCAL JUMP AND GREAT TWANGY GUITAR!" This shift simply sells the song.

"Stand by Your Man" is the glue that holds the world together. If every woman left every guy (or vice versa) because the sorry sap spilled his beer or cussed at the cat or forgot the kid's soccer game, our world would be a shaking, quaking, promiscuous horde of lounge lizard love leapers. And our kids would be raised by a ghostly glow on the Internet or the TV Cathode Cyclops. Tammy pleads passionately to give all the love you can give. She advises standing beside her man. **Waylon Jennings** and **Willie Nelson** would describe her as a "Good Hearted Woman" (#25, 2-76; #3, 1-72 C). Party-hearty guys' view.

Two partying buddies sing praises of one's long-suffering and saintly spouse – good-hearted lass who loves this goodtimin' guy. He flirts with atonement and contrition – but still returns to theY'all Come Back Saloon for next Saturday's stag rampage.'

"My Elusive Dreams" – Tammy Wynette and David Houston, #89, 7-67; #1(2), C. Like **Porter Wagoner with Dolly Parton,** Houston helped launch Tammy's career. Godson of 1920s pop star **Gene Austin,** Houston's pedigree ran back to Robert E. Lee and Sam Houston. Tammy and David share American odyssey dreams of wilderness and long hard roads. She bears his kid in Memphis, they vagabond it to Nashville. From a tiny farm in Nebraska, they seek a lost Gold Rush mine, up in Alaska. They stick it out together. Heartstring-zinging harmonies.

"Almost Persuaded" – David Houston, #24, 7-66; #1(9), 6-66 C. Reflection of own wedding band makes dancing wolf stop in mid-howl. NINE weeks at #1 C held the top spot **longer than any 1962-Present Country Song.** This emotionally wringing waltz/bolero surveys the deepest desires of rampaging id or caveman lust. He celebrates the Jiminy-Cricket return of conscience and faithfulness at the door of temptation. Houston (1938-93) uses **Johnny Horton** yodeling expertise with #75, 10-67 (#1[2], C) "You Mean the World to Me." It suggests Aussie/English yodel star **Frank Ifield** and his #5, 9-62 "I Remember You" (original hit by **Jimmy Dorsey Orchestra** #9, '42). Ifield hit #44, 12-62 on Hank Williams' "Lovesick Blues." Or yodelmeister **Slim Whitman's** (b. Tampa, Florida '24) #9, 7-52 "Indian Love Call" (#2C) from 1925 Paul Whiteman oldie.

"D-I-V-O-R-C-E" – Tammy Wynette, #63, 6-68; #1(3), 5-68 C. Little Joe's dad is splitting. Divorce? Final today. Tammy's divorce ode shuffles off like a little lost Beagle. In folksy Key of 'D,' Tammy is the victimized and aggrieved partner. Without doling blame, we realize the nasty cad is a rake, a rounder, a rambler. The kid will pay.

Popular music is a mirror and a reflection of our way of life. Tammy won 1968-70 CMA Female Vocalist of the Year. She cemented her queenly position by marrying **George Jones,** from 1969-75. With his tempestuous touring, irregular hours, and ultra-friendly honkytonk angels, Tammy's life began to imitate her art. Separate ways carved out separate, phenomenal, careers. The Elvis Spotlight stressed Tammy out. It often broke her frail health. Her similar-themed "I Don't Wanna Play House" hit #1(3), 6-67 C. A tuff little ditty. Steel guitar weeps. Little kids gab. The sad lyric? Daddy said goodbye, so why grow up to be mommies and daddies? Stark. Though Rock and Roll often surveys the happy prospects of getting married, Country music often laments getting divorced. [Doug Howard quipped that if you play Country music backwards, you get your dog, pick-up truck, beer, and girlfriend back!]

Tammy's Greatest Hits chugged up to Al. #37, 11-69. She outsold all other Country female artists with that achievement – even **Patsy Cline.** Among Tammy's 19 #1 Country hits? #1 C. "Bedtime Story" 1-72; #1(2) C.

"You and Me" 8-76; and Jones duo "Golden Ring," 6-76. Starting as a beautician, she snagged a TV show, and moved to Nashville in 1966, for good. Very good. Last big hit? "Justified & Ancient" – with the KLF, to #11 HOT 100, 2-92 (NC, C); Kopyright Liberation Front hit #5, 6-91 with "3 A.M. Eternal." Last hurrahs are always unpredictable. **Tammy Wynette** (1942-98) will stand by her awhile-ago man **George Jones** in the winner's circle of greatest and most beloved Country Artists of all time. In April, 1998, the Country music family mourned her loss at 55 to various health complications.

"Honky Tonk Man" – Johnny Horton, NC, '56, but #96, 3-62; #11, 4-62 C. Tyler, Texas' Johnny (1925-60) went to both Baylor and University of Seattle on athletic scholarships. Seattle piqued his Gold Rush curiosity, prompting an Alaskan odyssey. A LONG commute resulted in his marrying Billie Jean, widow of Hank Williams, from 1953 until his untimely death in a car crash. Few recall his amazing Country vocalic tricks that make him one of the greatest singers of all time. Rasps, yodel-kicks, falsetto swoops, and gruff flourishes spike the "Singing Fisherman's" adventurous tales with zingy lyrical and musical hooks and lines . . . but no sinkers.

This "Honky Tonk Man" prelude previews Country winners #7 C "I'm a One-Woman Man" (9-56) and first #1 C. "When It's Springtime in Alaska (It's Forty Below)." The Alaska tune is a gallows-humor escapade with 'Red-headed Lil' at the Red Dog Saloon. He mushes Iditarod-style to Point Barrow (off the true Gold Rush Trail, on the Arctic Ocean, but who sweats precise geography?). His snowflake caravan is an ominous portent to his untimely goodbye. Three months later, #1(6) 4-59 "Battle of New Orleans" forever etched the name **Johnny Horton** (#1[10] C) in our national consciousness. Johnny celebrated a war effort two weeks after the War of 1812 actually ended. Hurdling octaves with dazzling dexterity, and shmoozing from tender to tough in song stylistics, Horton landed two more whoppers: #3 (#6 C), 3-60 "Sink the Bismarck," and (naturally) #4 (#1[5] C) "North to Alaska."

"Honky-Tonk Man" – Dwight Yoakum, NC, '86; #3, 3-86. Why do we love Pikesville, Kentucky's Dwight's (b. '56) echo of **Johnny Horton** and **Hank Williams**? A groovy '53 Cadillac graces the back cover. He sings 'authentic 'Hillbilly music.' Dwight uses a mandolin and acoustic guitar/resonator dobro.

Dwight's "Guitars, Cadillacs" followed his honky-tonk hit to #4 C, 7-86. Roaring to #1, 11-88 C was "I Sang Dixie," and three consecutive #2 tunes C: 3-97 "Ain't That Lonely Yet?", 3-93; haunting 6-93 "A Thousand Miles from Nowhere"; and 7-93 "Fast as You." In March 2001, Dwight's 93-week siege of *Billboard's* Country Album Charts continued apace, with his 1999 compilation still at #58 and re-rising: *Last Chance for a Thousand Years: Greatest Hits.* Summer 1999 brought Dwight's fearless juggling of genres (Orchestral/Blues/Britrock/Glitz/Country) with his outstanding Rockabilly remake of **Queen**'s biggest hit— #1(4), 12-79 "Crazy Little Thing Called Love."

"The Tennessee Polka" – Pee Wee King, NC, '49; #3, 9-49 C. Accordionist King cornered the market on great Polish-American-Appalachian Country music. Born Julius Kuczynski (Wisconsin, 1914-2000), King hit big with #1 "Slow Poke" (Virginia Argo), sung by Redd Stewart [not Rod]. Pee Wee King rolled out the barrel, had a blast, and CREATED Country radio via his 'Hillbilly Hit Parade' in 1944 – to rival the new R&B 'Harlem Hit Parade.'

"She's Got You" – Patsy Cline, #14, 1-62; #1(5), 3-62 C. Patsy's biggest COUNTRY hit of all time. Patsy's "Crazy" (#2, 11-61 C, #9, 10-61) is still the most popular jukebox song of all time. Patsy's vivacious voice zings the heartstrings of nighthawks at America's forlornest diners and roadhouses and JiffyLube way stations on the oilslick Interstate of Life. "She's Got You"? If romantic jealousy didn't propel dastardly deeds, perhaps they'd give a war and no one would show up. Patsy's wispy image shimmies in a time warp. Rap and Punk and Neo-Disco and Grunge fans can't exactly place her time zone. She seems strung out there in lost time beyond the Big Band 40s, too trad for Rockabilly 50s, no 60s Psychedelia buff, no Disco 70s dervish, no 80s junk-bonder, or 90s Grunge or Gothic gal. Perhaps the best Patsy Cline song we haven't already nuggeted in Gold Rush is her Bob Wills tribute "Faded Love," at #96, 8-63 (#7, 9-63 C), a posthumous masterpiece reprised ('99) by Le Ann Rimes. Cline's rep soars with time. **Cowboy Copas** ("Alabam" – #63, '60, #1 C) and **Hawkshaw Hawkins** (#6, 8-48 C "Dog House Boogie") rode to destiny with Patsy in a small 3-5-63 Tennessee airplane.

"The Wild Side of Life" – Hank Thompson, #27, 6-52; #1(15), 3-52 C. Johnny Cash's mentor Hank (b. '25, Waco, Texas) captures the passions of the stardust **Honky Tonk Angels** down at the Dew Rock Inn. The Navy vet debuted with fragile #2(2) C, 1-48 "Humpty Dumpty Heart," and currently rocks his third half-century (1948-2001+). Terrific titled tunes? (ALL C-only): #3, 6-52 "Waiting in the Lobby of Your Heart," #1(2), 12-53 "Wake Up, Irene"; #4, 3-56 "The Blackboard of My Heart"; #8, 2-74 "The Older the Violin, the Sweeter the Music"; #10, 7-74 "Who Left the Door to Heaven Open?"; "Tony's Tank-Up, Drive-In Café" at #32, 2-80; and #82, 12-81 "Rockin' in the Congo." Hank's "Wild Side of Life" defines the **Honky Tonk** as meeting place, shrink's couch, watering hole, bonding barn, and dance frenzy. It's a mecca for all those wild cowpokes and semi-angels squandering their joy on an instant's reverie and a lifetime's regret. His commanding baritone cruises the beer bar venue, splashing down on canvas an American institution – the wild neon honkytonk, a stairway to Heaven, or coal chute to Hell. Or both.

"It Wasn't God Who Made Honky Tonk Angels" – Kitty Wells, #27, 8-52; #1(6), 7-52 C. Similar Cross-over Country-to-Pop star Kitty was actually BORN in Nashville (1919). With bobbed raven hair and a sweet wifely smile, Kitty debuted with this answer anthem. Her #2(15), 3-55 C, "Makin' Believe" holds many records for ALMOST hitting #1 (see Foreigner). She did "I Can't Stop Loving You" (#3, 3-58 C) four years before Ray Charles #1 Soul/Country crossover, and peppered 71 charted Country hits with #1(4) "Heartbreak U.S.A.", 5-61, and #1(1), 5-54 C, Red Foley duet "One by One." Odd, it is, to debut at #1 at age 33 – the age of Jesus at Golgotha, the place of skulls, en route to Calvary. If Kitty bears a dark cross in the song – and if it is an ANSWER song – what is the question?

"Squaws Along the Yukon" – Hank Thompson, NC, '58; #2(4), 8-58 C. Of Thompson's 79 charted Country hits (Wells 81), "Squaws" is his bronze medalist, though politically iffy. We traveled the Yukon River in 1994 in Alaska and Canada's Yukon. We drove 250 miles on a road without seeing another human being (10 bears). Thompson mushed on: #7, 12-58 C, "I've Run out of Tomorrows"; #72, 3-76 C, "Asphalt Cowboy"; #15, 3-71 "The Next Time I Fall in Love I Won't"; #10, 3-60 C, "A Six-Pack to Go," and its result "Hangover Tavern" (#12, C, 9-61); and its ursine warden "Smoky the Bar" (#5, 10-68, C). In his rapscallionish ramblings, his Northland neon nightscapes, and his voluptuous vagabonding, Hank hooks up with some sugary honkytonk angels.

Here's Kitty's basic question: how come married men masquerade as single dudes, and cause 'good girls' to go grievously wrong. In the early years, the macho field of Country music skidded along on the lusty libidos of Casanovas in cowboy boots. For awhile, women were victimized. By the time we got to Disco and **Loretta Lynn,** things changed.

Into his 75th year, Hank still cranked out songs in that hefty low baritone/high bass voice that taught Johnny Cash a thing or three about straight vocal delivery and storytelling expertise. Al. *Seven Decades* (2000). Thompson writes tumbleweed whimsy, like "Condo in Hondo," or "Sting in This Ole Bee." **Hank Thompson** is truly a giant in the history of Country music with his big, rumbling baritone. The honkytonk pioneer sings funny, punny thunderbeat-boogie lyrics of passion, pain, and lonesome six-packs. [Coincidentally, I walk my friends Ted and Diana Haiman's deerhound 'Thompson'].

"He'll Have to Go" – Jim Reeves, #2(3), 12-59; #1(14), C. Patsy Cline performed an ostensible eerie duet (#5, C, 11-81) with legend **Jim Reeves** (1924-64, b. Texas) on Ted Lewis's #8 '33 "Have You Ever Been Lonely?" Tekkie splicers captured the ghostly essence of each haunting voice. "He'll Have to Go" is the Texan baritone baseball star's signature song. Ultimate in easygoing macho coolth, Jim's on the phone with the girl. Obviously, some other guy is over at her place. Jim's somber waltz tells her it's decision time. The other dude will have to leave, pronto. No bluster. It's pure Gary Cooper at High Noon (1952****). We assume Jim's firm, steadfast command made the other guy slither out the window.

"Four Walls" – Jim Reeves, #11, 4-57; #1(8) C. Claustrophobes' hymn. Jim's brooding molasses-slow waltz blooms with dark violet melancholy melody. Four lonely walls squash his soul in the aftermath of a stubbed-out affair. Low tones of lonesome desolation. Not a fun song, just unforgettable. "Mexican Joe" #23, 4-53 (#1[9] C) is a fun fiesta song. Jim hit the 2nd-place silver-medal on the Country charts: #2(3), 7-58 C, "Snowflake" (#66, 1-66 – it was written by a 9-year-old girl, and first cut in 1952). On July 31, 1964, Jim Reeves was killed in a Nashville plane crash on an identical Beechcraft Bonanza to the Holly/Bopper/Valens 1959 tragedy.

"Girl on the Billboard" – Del Reeves, #96, 6-65; #1(2), 3-65 C. Franklin Delano Reeves (b. '33, North Carolina, no relation to Jim) parleyed his presidential handle into some punny hits: #9 C, 7-71 "The Philadelphia Fillies"; the phon-y #4 C, 8-65 "The Belles of Southern Bell"; and the good ol' guy bi-polar dichotomy, "Workin' Like the Devil (For the Lord)" at #33, 4-71 C. **Freddie Hart** (b. '26, Lochapoka, Alabama, U.S. Marine WWII vet) scored a bonanza with #17, 8-71 "Easy Loving" (#1[3], 7-71 C) and #1(6), 1-72 C, "My Hang-Up Is You."

Tex Ritter (1904-75, dad of *Three's Company*'s John Ritter) hit #10, 6-48 C with COUNTRY RAP "Deck of Cards," a religious parable. It was covered to #7, 9-59 (#11 C) by DJ **Wink Martindale**, who hosted *Tic Tac Dough*.

"Memphis" – Chuck Berry, NC, 1959. Was teenage R & R America really ready for songs about divorce, estrangement, and poor little Marie – juggled between two warring ex-spouses? Perhaps the first LATCHKEY-KID Rock song, Berry's Country/Jazz/Rockabilly music is unique. "B" side of Chuck's #37, 6-59 "Back in the U.S.A." Chuck also did a Country/Blues rocker called "Carol" – to #18, 8-58, and #9 R & B. Atlanta's **Tommy Roe** (b. '42) championed this chick to #61, 4-64, (saga of a guy trying clumsily to dance).

"Gone" – Ferlin Husky, #4, 3-57; #1(10), 2-57 C. Desolate desperado ballad. Move over, Grunge Rock of 90s. Gouging a glop of gloom out of a sunny day, "Gone's" gone girl makes guy lonely. Fats Domino-type triplets (12 beats/measure) drive the slow tempo and world-class melody. Husky's beseeching resonance tipped off **Roy Orbison** and **Conway Twitty** about crescendo power.

"I Ain't Never" – Webb Pierce, #24, 8-59; #2(9), 7-59 C. Louisiana 1921-91 star also scored with #22, 11-54 "More and More" (#1[10] C). Also #1(17) 2-54 C, "Slowly"; #1(12), 10-53, C, "There Stands the Glass"; and triple-shot #1(13) C, "Love, Love, Love" of 9-55. From the *Louisiana Hayride*, Webb created his careless existential ode to indecision and indifference – #1(12) C, "I Don't Care" in 6-55.

"In the Jailhouse Now" – Webb Pierce, NC, 1955; #1(21), 2-55 C. This whimsical chunk of crime and punishment boomed over Pierce's guitar-shaped swimming pool, tying Eddy Arnold and Hank Snow for longest

#1 hit on any major chart (HOT 100, R & B, Country) ever. **Willie Nelson** hit #72, 10-82 C, with it. Ninth in Country hits (96), Pierce is second to Eddy Arnold only with weeks at #1 (111), to bronze stars Buck Owens and Hank Williams (at 82) in Whitburn's 1994 tally. In 8-72, **Mel Tillis** took "I Ain't Never" to #1(2) C, beginning one of many great Country dynasties with his #24, 11-58 C. "The Violet and the Rose." Daughter Pam waited in the wings. Tillises (b. Tampa, Florida '32 and Plant City, Florida, '57), scored hits galore. After high school football and a Korean Air Force tour, Mel wrote controversial hits like **Kenny Rogers'** #6, 6-69 "Ruby, Don't Take Your Love to Town." Or **Bobby Bare**'s Rural Expatriation ode, "Detroit City" (#16, 6-63, #7 C); Welsh **Tom Jones** took it to #27, 3-67.

"Maybe It Was Memphis" – Pam Tillis, NC, '91; #3, 12-91 C. Her Country superstar dad **Mel Tillis** hit #1(1), 12-80 with "Southern Rains." Pam's uptempo rocker zeroes in on magic spell of Elvis's boomtown just down the pike from Nashville. Pam eased into stardom via #71, 11-84 C, "Goodbye Highway," and clicked in the 90s via #5 C, 12-90 "Don't Tell Me What to Do" and 1985 NC Warner release "One of Those Things," #6 C in 4-91. Title champ? #11, 5-93 C. "Cleopatra, Queen of Denial." A simpler "Please" echoed her top rep to #25+ C, 12-2000. Mel's nice kid spans eras. Her #2(1) C, 8-94 "When You Walk in the Room" was written by **Jackie DeShannon** (b. '44, Hazel, Kentucky, and #99, 1-64); Liverpool's **Searchers** (Tony Jackson, John McNally, Mike Pender, Chad Curtis) hefted it to #35, 10-64. "In Between Dances" (#3 C., 6-95) Pam pondered her gold-rush nugget of Latino/Salsa/Tex-Mex splendor:

"Mi Vida Loca (My Crazy Life)" – Pam Tillis, NC '94; #1(2), 11-94 C. Perky Pam scorched the pinnacle with this Cubano-beat Country extravaganza. She influenced the Latino Rock Explosion of 1999-2001+ via Ricky Martin's #1(5), 4-99 "Livin' La Vida Loca." Super Pam-song, this bouncy non-loco rococo Country Rocker.

"Tennessee Flat-Top Box" – Roseanne Cash, NC, '87; #1(1), 11-87 C. Dad **Johnny Cash** (b. 2-26-32, Dyess, Arkansas) lofted this one to #11 C, 11-61 (also #84 HOT 100), with a hot single-string lead on the low notes (a la Duane Eddy). It dovetails into a two-string riff, with bends and twangs and slides and glides. Johnny's Columbia Records launched her #1 2-81 C. "Seven Year Ache" to #22 on the big chart. Roseanne's 11th #1 is a humdinger hybrid of super Beatle echo on Lennon/McCartney's "I Don't Want to Spoil the Party" 3-89 [#39, 2-65, Fab Four]. The **Beatles** did top-notch Country via **Ringo Starr**, on **Buck Owens'** #1(4), 4-63 C, "Act Naturally" (#47, 9-65). **George Harrison** xeroxes **Chet Atkins'** guitar magic.

"Tennessee Flat-Top Box" is a mammoth metaphor for a smokin' guitar. Daughter of Johnny and first wife Vivian Loberto, Roseanne grew up in California with her mother, but skedaddled to Nashville after high school sprang her with a diploma and a dream. She married the hottest star in Nashville, **Rodney Crowell** (#1[1], 7-89 C "Above and Beyond").

"Cry, Cry, Cry" – Johnny Cash, NC, '55; #14, 11-55 C. Johnny Cash is an American National Treasure. So much for objectivity. Johnny rises ABOVE and BEYOND. Johnny Cash IS Country Music. Before we knew him on the big chart, Johnny's #4 C, 2-56 double-sided "Folsom Prison Blues" b/w "So Doggone Lonesome" actually outscrambled Elvis's "Heartbreak Hotel" to glory – on Elvis's Memphis label Sun. Pleading the plight of the forgotten prisoner yearning for freedom via the lonesome train whistle, "Folsom Prison Blues" scored on the HOT 100 for Now-Superstar Johnny in 5-68 (and #1[4] C).

Brother **Roy Cash** ran the Dixie Rhythm Ramblers in the late 40s. Johnny's kid brother **Tommy** (b. 40) cut "Six White Horses" to #79, 12-69 and #4, 11-69 C. Like Dion's #4 "Abraham, Martin, and John" of 10-68, Tommy's tune eulogizes John Kennedy's brother Bobby and Martin Luther King, Jr. on Roseanne's #1(1), 8-88 Crowell-produced "Runaway Train," she assures that in the Country field, no will will ever forget the name of CASH. After Johnny's 1950-54 Air Force tour, Johnny worked Detroit's auto factories as a sweeper on the assembly line. Johnny's Tennessee Two? **Luther Perkins**, guitar; **Marshall Grant**, slap bass fiddle. Sun Records in 1954 Memphis also featured a fiddle and a steel guitar – stock stuff for Opryland, but off the main beam for Rock and Roll. Johnny Cash is also revered by Punk Rockers, whose frequently-black outfits mirror his sartorial leadership. Johnny says he wears black in respect for the downtrodden, the poor in spirit, and the unfortunate sufferers of this hardscrabble earth. Like his hero Abe Lincoln (1809-65), he believes in plain speaking.

It dovetails into his vocal style. He doesn't need glides and grace-note melismas and doodads and embellishments. Johnny Cash sings his song straight. Like Western hero Gary Cooper, or **John Wayne**, American, Big John Cash (6'3", 210#) is big on trust. We look up at the big Arkansas traveler, and we say, yep, if Johnny says so, it must be right. In the era of the gimme-gimme antihero, Johnny Cash still plods his weary pilgrimage to Rock and Country destiny (Rock Hall '92).

"I Walk the Line" – Johnny Cash, #17, 9-56; #1(6), 5-56 C. INTEGRITY. It's not so much what Johnny says but how he says it: "Hello, I'm Johnny Cash." SUN Records sports a jumbo 50s Million-Dollar Quartet photo: Elvis, Carl Perkins, Jerry Lee Lewis, and this young guy with a winsome shrug and a howdy smile. You can scan the litany of 2001+ Country stars and starlets: Billy Gilman, Keith Urban, Joe Diffie, the **Dixie Chicks**, Chad Brock, Lee Ann Womack, Jamie O'Neal, Shedaisy, Kenny Chesney, Martina McBride, Terri Clark, Phil Vassar, Clay Davidson, Neal McCoy, Hal Ketchum, Collin Raye, Rascal Flatts – they all owe a major debt to Johnny Cash. In "I Walk the Line," Johnny sings of the life he must alter to nurture love. He thinks of her constantly. She is every breath he takes. He shuns the bad habits to be true. He hates not being with her. Johnny's signature song modulates from one key to another. He skids from high baritone to bass, anchoring at rock bottom on the word "MINE" – she's his, so he walks the line. LINE is a metaphor for control. John's road to superstardom was blessed with **June Carter Cash**, soulmate/wife since 1968. With June's inspiration, Johnny's line reverberates about how easy it is for him to stay true. Johnny Cash epitomizes truth.

Patsy Cline

"Don't Take Your Guns to Town" – **Johnny Cash, #32, 1-59; #1(6) C.** Johnny and **Marty Robbins**, like Roy Rogers and Gene Autry, are among the #1 interpreters of the Old West in Country-Western music. Kid 'Billy Joe' fails to heed his terrified gingham mom's dire warning wrapped in prophetic, ominous title. Nearly *a capella*, Cash carries the story from hotshot teen gunblazer to saloon swaggerer. This itchy trigger-finger kid, stoned on wanderlust, swaggers into a tough saloon, packing pistols for 'self-defense.' Cash says he meant no one harm. But hey – was the gun loaded? At the gunsmoke saloon, the greenhorn kid gets marooned in a sad showdown (see **2-Pac**). **Billy Joel** did a Long Island response: NC, '74 "Ballad of Billy the Kid."

"High Noon (Do Not Forsake Me)" – **Frankie Laine, #5, 7-52.** Cooper movie theme****. World-class Western tombstone showdown. Italian-American crooner Laine covered Hank Williams with dramatic operatic tenor to #21, 1-51 "Hey Good Lookin'," #21, 10-52 "[Tonight] We're Settin' the Woods on Fire" (NC Hank, and #2, 10-52 C), and "Your Cheatin' Heart" to #18, 3-53 (stunningly higher number than Hank's). Six years before the Beatles, Laine's gunfighter-ballad CONCEPT ALBUM arrived, #71, 10-61 *Hell Bent for Leather*. What sparked it?

"Big Iron" – **Marty Robbins, #26, 3-60; #5 C.** Gundown sundown rundown. FIRST CONCEPT ALBUM – Marty's #6 Al. '59 *Gunfighter Ballads and Trail Songs*. 'Big iron' meant simply a gun. The ultimate showdown song. It's the blaze of glory song about the dusty saloon road – a Texas Ranger with a lightning gun pits his trigger-speed against a desperado gunning for Victim #21.

"Singing the Blues" – **Marty Robbins, #17, 11-56; #1(13), 9-56 C. Guy Mitchell** hit #1(10) with Marty's big song. Earlier Marty snared #7, 2-55 C with Elvis's first [uncharted] hit "That's All Right." Buddy Holly used Marty's gonzo lead-guitar riff from Robbins' 2-57 #3 C. "Knee Deep in the Blues" for his supposed 'A'-side of #1 "That'll Be

the Day" – "I'm Lookin' for Someone to Love." Since Buddy was so devoted to wife Maria, here are 3 wife songs:

"My Woman, My Woman, My Wife" – **Marty Robbins, #42, 3-70; #1(1), 2-70 C.** Glendale, Arizona's **Marty** (1925-82) dedicates this touching and tender ballad to the one person who can tie a raggedy life back into a neat knot of happiness. With heartfelt love, he laments how the passage of time and too much Arizona sunshine have aged his adored wife. He prays that if HE'S earned a little space in Heaven, that the Lord should give it to HER. For a definition of love as SERVICE, "My Woman" is the benchmark, the fountainhead.

Sonny James (NC '74; #4, 4-74 C) sang similar devotion in "*A Mi Esposa Con Amor* (To My Wife with Love)." Their wife-as-saint theme appears in many songs, by both rogues and 'Country Gentlemen' (Sonny's nickname).

Frankie Laine (b. 1913) takes the Robbins song "You Gave Me a Mountain" (#7 C, 3-69, Johnny Bush) to new heights at #24, 2-69. All this world's disasters befall this poor guy. He's blindsided by a Book of Job array of horrible catastrophe. He questions why the Lord gave him a mountain he might never scale. Great crescendo.

"El Paso City" – **Marty Robbins, NC '76; #1(2), 4-76 C.** Marty's ethereal haunting tenor presides. He toys with **reincarnation** theme – dreaming that he (circling over burgeoning new El Paso CITY) might actually BE the dead cowboy in his #1 '59 earlier saga "El Paso." The Southwest Texas border town blooms beyond the eerie moonlight glow over jagged cliff El Capitan along the midnight road. Buzzing with his slide and slur vocal technique at its most profound, this ghost song echoes on. In 1982, the "Cigarettes and Coffee Blues" (#14, 3-63 C) ran him down, as well as his Arizonan love for steak and eggs (Sp. *Huevos*). His stock-car racing star Type-A personality, too, caught up. Robbins passed away at 57 on the operating table during coronary bypass surgery more routine today. Blessedly, Johnny Cash and Waylon Jennings, next-door neighbors and hospital roomates, survived similar simultaneous operations in the later 80s.

Marty Robbins

"I'm Moving On" – Hank Snow, #27, 7-50; #1(21), C. Remember his Pre-Rock #1(8), 3-51 C, "Rhumba Boogie"? Snow's song-guy rides the rails to opportunity, glory, and a fresh can of beans. Skirts 12-bar Blues pattern. This song is a major influence on Cash and Blue-Eyed Soulster Matt Lucas (#56, 5-63) of Memphis. "I'm Moving On" is tied for record in weeks at #1, ever, anywhere on big charts. No one beat Hank Snow for zenith-hugging #1 songs: "I Don't Hurt Anymore" hit #22, 7-54, and #1(20), 5-54 C. These Hank (1914-99) songs are the #1 and #4 Country songs of all time, for #1 time domination. Parallel charts? OK. Francis Craig had #1(17) on Top 100/Hot 100/Top 30, and #1(18) "Choo Choo Ch'Boogie" 8-46 by **Louis Jordan** topped the R & B/ Soul charts, tied by Joe Liggins' "The Honeydripper" at #1[18], 8-45).

"Crazy Arms" – Ray Price, NC '56; #1(20), 5-56 C. Dallas's PRICEless Ray's monumental ballad is rocker **Jerry Lee Lewis's first record.** The more laid-back Price and his Cherokee Cowboys celebrated #1(4), 7-57 C (and #63, 10-57) "My Shoes Keep Walkin' Back to You." Price's 109 charted Country hits rank him 5th ever. He doesn't lash or slash or blast. He smoothly murmurs and slyly slurs the silvery words: #1(13), 7-58 C (#71, 8-58) "City Lights"; #2(8) C, 4-60 "One More Time"; and #1(3) C and #93, 1-73 "She's Got to Be a Saint." Perryville, Texas' Ray (b. '26) trioed with **Willie Nelson** and **Roger Miller** on poignant #19 C, 6-82 "Old Friends," of Simon & Gar profundity. Ray's signature song? #11, 8-70, and #1, 6-70 C. "For the Good Times." I recall long-gone Jim Hilbert and his Roadrunners' viciously funny parody of this Price Countrypolitan classic – and the rowdy rip-roarers who echoed the lost green smoky Dixieglow moon.

"(Ghost) Riders in the Sky" – Johnny Cash, NC, '79; #2(1), 5-79 C. Essence of pure Cash. With due respect to booming bari crooner **Vaughn Monroe** (#1[12], 4-49), the **Outlaws** (#31, 12-80), or Connecticut's **Ramrods** (#30, 1-61 instrumental), no one on the planet can do "Ghost Riders" with the flair and gusto of Johnny Cash. On the same theme, Cash recorded with the semi-official 'Four Horsemen' – **Waylon Jennings, Kris Kristofferson**, and **Willie Nelson** – a tune called "Silver Stallion," to #25, 3-90 C. Also dubbed 'The Highwaymen,' after Kristofferson #1(1), 5-85 C song. Alfred Noyes' poem "The Highwayman" stalks the 18th-century stagecoach moonlight road, as Kris stalks deep bass notes along with Johnny and Waylon. High-baritone Willie SOUNDS comparatively tenorish, but truly blossoms in Crooner Cruiser Control.

"What Part of No" – Lorrie Morgan, NC, '92; #1(3), 12-92 C. Named by daddy George for **Loretta Lynn**, Lorrie (b. 49) mirrored dad/daughter triumph and tragedy. She scored on #1(1), 2-90 C, "Five Minutes," the pedestrian "We Both Walk" at #3, 3-91 C, and #2(2), 9-92 C. "Watch Me." Dad **George** (#1[3], 2-49 C) suffered a fatal heart attack at 51 in 1975. Her husband **Keith Whitley** (1955-89) reeled in a short lifeline of woe reminiscent of

Roy Orbison, Janis Joplin, or Hank Williams. For a moment in the Southern sun, Whitley was the ELVIS of the Opry Spotlight. His #1(2), 1-89 C, "I'm No Stranger to the Rain" held the middle of five consecutive #1 C. songs for the Kentucky "Hard Livin'" (#10, 3-87 C) singer, who died of too much life, awash in desperation. Whitley curves his baleful voice around clusters of sad nevermore notes, with a James Dean meteoric finality.

"Somewhere in My Broken Heart" – Billy Dean, NC, '91; #3, 5-91 C. Quincy, Florida's Billy's quest for a #1 hit was answered with his #1, C, 5-13-2000 Kenny Rogers duo "Buy Me a Rose." Basketball star Dean also hit #4 C with 5-92 "Billy the Kid." **Billy Ray Cyrus** (b. '61, KY), bodybuilder and dancer, hit #1(5) C. and #4, 5-92 HOT 100 with "Achy Breaky Heart." His millennial comeback was steered by 2000 # 11+ C. "You Won't Be Lonely Now" and fiery #43 C., 1-2001 "Burn Down the Trailer Park."

"I Love a Rainy Night" – Eddie Rabbitt, #1(2), 11-80; #1(1) C. Eddie Rabbitt (1944-97) was born in Brooklyn, but moved to the Wild West (East Orange, New Jersey). Penning Elvis's #16, 2-70 "Kentucky Rain" led to Eddie's fine career—tied for 17th with 17 #1 C. hits. Rabbitt rockers? #1, 2-76 "Drinkin' My Baby (Off My Mind)," pure R & R #1(1), 6-80 "Drivin' My Life Away," Clint Eastwood & orang-outang movie theme #1(3), 12-78 "Every Which Way but Loose" (#30 HOT 100), and **Crystal Gayle** duo #7,10-82 "You and I" (#1 C). Rabbitt forgets not Brooklyn/ NYC via his Dion tune "The Wanderer" at #1, 5-88 C.

"Jambalaya" – Fats Domino, #30, 12-61; NC, R & B, & C. R & B pioneer Fats wangled a spiffy rendition of Hank Williams' Louisiana lightning . Welcome to our Gold Rush CAJUN Country section. Since Fats is ¼ French, perhaps more than songsmith Williams, he can introduce this five-alarm Cajun hot sauce on his Rhythm & Rock repertoire. *C'est la vie*! Hank's Bayou blaster surveys family bon temps celebrants, whooping it up on swamp hummocks, with Jax beer and crawfish pie (yum?).

"Bayou Talk" – Jimmy Newman, NC, '62; #12, 12-62 C. Jimmy's "A Fallen Star" (#23, 6-57, #2 C) sang of his love for a girl, or a meteorite. Jimmy Yeve Newman (b. Big Mamou, LA, '27) serenaded #7, 7-55 C. "Blue Darlin'," and chased his Cajun Country dreams, returning to the cypress "Alligator Man" (#22, C, 12-61) swamps.

"Twist and Shout" – Isley Brothers, #17, 6-62; #2(2), R & B. When the **Beatles** carted off Hank Ballard's "Twist" and the Isleys' "Shout" to #2(4), 3-64 as "Twist and Shout," we realized the Isley Cincinnati genius: brothers O'Kelly, Ernie, Rudolph, Marvin, and main man Ronald. The sound of ZYDECO parallels CAJUN music, like **Jean Knight**'s (#2, 5-71 "Mr. Big Stuff") #50, 5-85 and #59 R & B "My Toot Toot." It's a wild wheezy New Orleans **Bessie Smith** Blues sound – and rides the accordion like Cajun via Cajun Soul.

"Down at the Twist and Shout" – Mary-Chapin Carpenter, NC, '91; #2(1), 6-91, C. Hey – any CAJUN hits about this famous song renamed as a bar? One.

From the Bayou-less wilds of Princeton, New Jersey, and Washington's Beltway suburban sprawl, Brown grad Carpenter represents a hip new *Friends/Frasier/Seinfeld* upscale chunk of the Country cavalcade. With her joyous jambalaya Cajun jamboree beat, the blonde 'Folkabilly' star returns a sidestream French-American genre to the top of the charts where it belongs:

CAJUN, like BLUEGRASS, is a lively part of the COUNTRY MUSIC FAMILY.

Cajun (Acadian) settlers came from Hank Snow's/Anne Murray's Nova Scotia, Canada. They were run out by British settlers who were run out of Britain. All these pilgrims sought better land and the good life for their families (Le Bonne Vie). The problem is, the world's never had quite enough good land, and never will. Mary's goodtime Cajun anthem whoops up deep Mississippi Delta bayou glory and foot-stompin' party-animal *bon vivant* music. Kissin' cousin' to Hank's "Jambalaya," and "Big Mamou," Mary's swamp scorcher seeks release from stress and paper-clip hassles and computer Beltway squabbles. Who was "Twist" inventor **Hank Ballard's** (Rock Hall '90) favorite singer? **Hank Williams,** a unique R & B star's choice. Jazz guru sax legend **Charlie 'Bird' Parker** also picked Hank. Music trickles deeply into your Soul. Time for the Swamp Serenade.

Cajun music combines Country with Rock and Roll, and frosts the confection with sweet French icing and Blues/R & B on the hot quaking cake. Washboards, maracas, and dobros blast Cajun music, spiced with accordion explorations in the Delta land of love. In the goodtime slaphappy key of 'A' major, Carpenter wafts a midnight Shangri-La vision: good times, good pals, frantic footstompin' beat (**Del Shannon's** last album ['91] features "Let's Dance," a Cajun similar musical adventure). Mary brings us no Honky-Tonk Horror Hole of sleazebag brigands and babes, snarly snapping turtles, and smashed dreams. It's a cozy family smile-suffused pub. Bayou mecca. Fun, games. Dance, dance, dance. From her snappy snare intro to the sweet fiddle and roller-rink accordion, you can tell somebody's having a lot of fun. Maybe you. Over the steamy swamp, a big marshmallow moon floats regally on high. Beyond the Spanish-moss squishy cypress bog, folks fry their worries in a jambalaya crawfish-pie bonanza. She dishes out alligator stew, too, but I'll pass. Everybody whoops it up. *Laissez le bon temps rouillez:* 'Let the Good Times Roll' (#20, 8-56, #1(3) R & B Shirley & Lee). Everyone is having a great time. No corner wallflowers weeping, no down-in-the-dumps dipsticks. No barfing snapping turtles.

In the wistful words of the winsome Washingtonian lass, they "Never Had It So Good" (#8, 9-89 C). There's no "Quittin' Time" (#7, 1-90, C). The sultry bayou seethes with "Passionate Kisses" (#4, 12-92 C). Her coolest title? #90, 10-94 and #1 C. "Shut Up and Kiss Me."

""Down at the Twist and Shout" is the quintessence of **Jack Kerouac's** lifetime quest, on the road and off it, from factory shot & beer bars of hometown Lowell, Mass., to the seacoast majesty of Northport/Cold Spring Harbor, Long Island, to purple mountain Colorado majesties, to wild East Village or San Francisco saloons, and finally to the pink/turquoise sunset strands of South Florida. As **Ponce de Leon** searched for the Fountain of Youth, Kerouac and his millions of R & R followers quested after the Center of Saturday Night in America. And so does Rock and Roll.

Riding atop Mary's spunky sound is the fiery fiddle, with its sensuous sawing squeak floating high over bottomtone rhythms – like a floppy cornsilk-yellow Delta moon. And maybe, sludged over alligator nests and Jax beer or Dr. Pepper rusty cans, you'll find an old steel hulk of the BIG Country #1 FIDDLE FAN of long ago – **Henry Ford's** ancient 'Tin Lizzie' Model T Ford. At 100 beats a minute, hammering each beat like a Disco syn-drum, her tune gamely salutes 'Hurricane parties,' where brave/foolhardy gonzo celebrants dare 100+ mph monster winds to dump their magnolia trees in their laps. Mary sings of a fiddly waltz from 1910 that serves Insta-Youth. She slams the Big Three **A** (I), **D** (IV), and **E7** (V7) chords. She plies her pilgrim path from Lafayette, LA, to equally French Cajun Baton Rouge ('Red Stick'), and down to the steamy bottomland Delta marsh – home of our Delta Blues chapter on B.B. King, Howlin' Wolf, and Jimmy Reed. Down to the red hot heart of Rock and Roll.

"Shrimp Boats" – Jo Stafford, #2(2), 11-51. Even Big Bands swirled the Cajun theme. Though hampered by the lack of an audible rhythm section, Stafford's steely soprano paints a vivid vignette of Gulf Coast shrimpers plying the high tides. This passionate waltz covers women who wait, their desire burgeoning, for their returning men out on the silvery sea. Pop crooner Stafford's "Feudin' and Fightin'" (#7, 8-47, #7 C) signaled this seacoast double-tempo jangly waltz. Jo covered **Delores Gray's** Cajun version (#16, 11-51), and Gray returned with #21, 5-53 "Big Mamou." **Jo-El Sonnier** hit #9, 7-88 C with Cajun Revenge rocker "Tear-Stained Letter."

"Bubba Shot the Jukebox" – Mark Chesnutt, NC, '92; #4, 6-92, C. Neo-Luddite rampage. Bubba engages in hot-blooded 'jukebox-icide.' From Big Bopper's Beaumont, Texas, Chesnutt, began with chummier relationship to glowing bar companion in #1 C, 11-90 "Brother Jukebox." This one celebrates an unsanctioned-by-N.R.A. love/hate relationship with American machines gone awry. One Michigan man murdered a soda-pop machine that ate his quarters at a gas station. The guy plugged it four times, as the gas station attendant ran the sub-four-minute mile AWAY from the gun-toter. When the pop machine killer was convicted ($1000 fine and/or 30 days) hundreds of similarly ripped-off folks paid tidbits of his fine or offered to serve a couple days of his sentence. Mark's big ones? #1 C, 9-93 "Almost Goodbye," #7, 12-95 C, "It Wouldn't Hurt to Have Wings," #1 C, 2-95 "Gonna Get a Life," and #1 C. 2-97 "It's a Little Too Late." Into the galumphing millennium, Chesnutt switched a bit with **Kenny Chesney** (#14+, 1-2001 C) "Don't Happen Twice."

"Touch Me (I'll Be Your Fool Once More)" – **Big Al Downing, NC, '79; #18, 4-79 C.** Big Al (b. 1940, Oklahoma) is an Afro-American Country singer who plays piano. He hit HOT 100 with #85, 2-75 "I'll Be Holding On." With 15 charted C. hits, #20, 7-80 C. "Bring It on Home" is his 2nd biggest.

"Still" – 'Whispering' Bill Anderson, #8, 4-63; #1(7), 2-63 C. Bill (b. '37, Columbia, SC) apprenticed as a sportswriter before his spellbinding lyric tenor was discovered when he DJ-ed in Florida. "Still" is simply **Country Rap.** Sincere verses shimmer like spoken vows. Bill's wispy cirrus-cloud tall notes glide like a Maui hang-glider over the deep blue sea. Other Anderson biggees include #82, 10-62 (#1[7] C); #10 C "Peanuts and Diamonds"; and #76 C, 12-81 "Whiskey Made Me Stumble (The Devil Made Me Fall)."

"Rose Garden" – Lynn Anderson, #3, 11-70; #1(5), C. Grand Forks, North Dakota's **Lynn** (b. '47) rides championship horses in shows. Relationships are not rose gardens, unless one digs thorns, too. Megahits? #1(3), C, 8-71 "How Can I Unlove You" (#63, HOT 100), and NC '88, #24, 7-88 C) "Under the Boardwalk." Lynn is no relation to Bill, or **John Anderson** (#2[2], 8-92, C-only "Seminole Wind").

"Under the Boardwalk" – Drifters, #4, 6-64; #4, R & B. Johnny Moore took over for lead singer Rudy Lewis (d. '64, heart). This Classic Rock and Soul charmer covers the smooching jamboree of this couple seeking coolth underneath the Coney Island/Long Beach boardwalk on Long Island. They sniff the fries, hear the tootling carousel, ponder Nathan's footlong hot dogs with mustard, and enjoy the sea breeze beyond the hot tar "Up on the Roof" (#5, 11-62). The off-the-beach couple finds an oasis below the hot summer sunshine. To frazzled Brooklynites, the Coney Island boardwalk IS 'The Country.'

"Wild and Blue" – John Anderson, NC, '82; #1(2), 9-82 C. John Anderson (b. '54, Orlando) fled Disney to Nashville at age 18, jolting Urban Cowboy Country's with back to roots #8, C. 8-81 "Chicken Truck"; #1, 12-91 C. "Straight Tequila Night" and #30C, 8-25 "Tokyo, Oklahoma."

"Don't It Make My Brown Eyes Blue" – Crystal Gayle, #2(3), 8-77; #1(4) C. This murmuring ballad crossed over to the entire planet, hitting #2 HOT 100 with Crystal's sultry alto. Crystal is **Loretta Lynn**'s sister (also "Peggy Sue" Webb's sister – "I'm Dynamite," NC '69; #28, 6-69 C). Crystal (nee Brenda Gail Webb, b. '51, Paintsville, KY) grew the longest, most breathtaking flowing dark hair.

Crystal is the first Country singer to tour (wow, what a billion-potential record market) China. Her Country behemoths include #84, 12-83 and #1 C. "The Sound of Goodbye"; and #1 C "Til I Gain Control Again" 11-82 (see Hawaiian star **Leabert Lindsay**). Crystal's 18 #1's paced the CMA 1977 & '78 Vocalist of the Year at FOURTH female ever in 1994 Country hits. Blue-eyed fixation?

"Blue Eyes Crying in the Rain" – Willie Nelson, #21, 8-75; #1(2), 7-75 C. Can't pigeonhole Wille into any comfy category. Born in 1933 Fort Worth, Texas, Willie strummed his first guitar at age nine – and wrote great songs like

Roy Orbison's #15, 12-63 "Pretty Paper," Joe Hinton's #13, 8-64 R & B "Funny," or Patsy Cline's #9, 10-61 "Crazy." Willie served in our 'forgotten war' Korea 1950-53, and landed a job plunking stand-up bass for **Ray Price**. Into 60s Hendrixmania and Psychedelia, Willie chucked his silver suit and 50s pompadour for jogging shoes, a singlet, and red bandanna to set off his salt-and-pepper beard. The outfit alone sent shock waves throughout conservative Country factions, so Willie settled into "Outlaw" territory in Austin, Texas (like Buck Owens or Merle Haggard in equally-renegade Bakersfield, California). Willie played BENEFITS. No angel, Willie partied amok with his hi-jinx entourage, yearning to get back "On the Road Again" (#20, 9-80, and #1 C, as a follow-up to **Bob Wills**'s masterpiece "Faded Love" at #3 C for Willie in earlier 8-80). Willie and former Buddy Holly Cricket **Waylon Jennings** paraded their Texas Outlaw spinoffs.

Buddy Holly Memorial Society President Bill Griggs says that Buddy actually began Outlaw movement for Waylon. He told his rookie 18-year-old 2nd bass-man Waylon to cut his OWN records – and not let anybody downpedal his natural sound. Finally, 15 years later at big RCA, Waylon hit #1 C. paydirt in 8-74 with "I'm a Ramblin' Man." Willie did "Blue Skies" (#1 C, '78, by **Irivng Berlin**) and "Blue Eyes." "Blue Eyes Crying" is not just a song; it's an adventure. Willie's twinkly blue Santa eyes sparkle. Slow and methodical, his tale of everlasting romance plods from this world into an otherworldly supernatural dimension. UP YONDER they'll someday meet, and amble timelessly along, holding hands in Heaven. It's one of the most hopeful, wistful, and spiritual lines ever written – yet one of the saddest. Willie's instrumental guitar lead on the bridge ripples with ghost notes that twirl and spin and vanish on the afterbeat and afterglow. Unforgettable haunting song of surreal parting. Don't miss it.

"If You've Got the Money, I've Got the Time" – Willie Nelson, NC, 76; #1(1), 7-76. Impish Lefty Frizzell tune. Rapscallion takes her Cadillac and her money to honkytonk. **Frizzell** (b. Corsicana, TX, boxer, 1928-75, stroke) hit #1(3) C, 10-50 with this ode to his jalopy and nerve. Frizzell scored with #29, 8-51 "I Want to Be with You Always" at #1(11) C and #1(4) C, 1-64 "Saginaw, Michigan."

"You're the Reason God Made Oklahoma" – David Frizzell and Dottie West, NC, '81; #1(1), 1-81 C. Polar opposite #1's for Lefty's kid brother (b. '41). West (b. '32) hit with #14, 3-81 (#1 C) "What Are We Doin' in Love" (duo with **Kenny Rogers**). Her Frizzell duo trades verses, then harmonizes on gorgeous chorus. Farm-flavored theme fashions the Good Life on green John Deere tractor. Frizzell's answer-back song of ultra-patient (but sarcastic) wife to hard-drinkin' hubby: #1(1), 5-82 C "I'm Gonna Hire a Wino to Decorate Our Home."

"Always on My Mind" – Willie Nelson, #5, 3-82; #1(2) C. Hindsight haunts us all. Little things we shoulda done. But didn't. Willie offers a kind rationalization. His #1-ever song looks back and laments the loss of wonderful things they never got to do. Universal sad story. We all get zapped by too many hours at office, typewriter, computer, flaming forge. Someone we love waits. When that precious someone is taken from us, forever, we mourn the loss not only of that person – but of the time we righteously squandered at more mundane occupations.

"Georgia on My Mind" – Ray Charles, #1(1), 6-60; #3 R & B; NC, C. The Genius of Soul lofted this out beyond the Chattahoochee sundown glow. His impeccable timing, immaculate phrasing, his dynamic vocal slurs and gravelly – almost gruff – tenderness all converge to create a musical masterpiece for the first-year ['86] Rock Hall of Famer. It's a prelude to revolutionary chartbuster Al #1(14), 5-62 *Modern Sounds in Country and Western Music.* Michael Bolton's #36, 8-90 NC R & B rendition isn't bad either. Great Country classic missed Country charts. Original at #10, 8-31 hit for **Frankie Trumbauer Orchestra**, featuring legend **Bix Beiderbecke** on cornet. Shmoozy and dreamy sweet-potato pie Georgian ode. Is 'Georgia' the name of the GIRL, we wonder, the STATE, or the STATE of MIND? Sleepytime Old South classic, mellifluous with magnolias and summertime dreams. Albany, Georgia's blind piano genius Ray, Little Richard, Otis Redding, and James Brown (SC too) are all from Georgia. Ray lavished "Ruby" to #28, 11-60 (#10 R & B) as follow-up, blurring music genres. Other Southern-fried Charles classics include Hank Snow's #1(21) C, '50 "I'm Movin On" to #40, 11-59 (#11 R & B), plus #8 semi-instrumental #8 "One Mint Julep" of 3-61 (#1 R & B). He hit #8 with Hank Williams' "Take These Chains from My Heart" (#7 R & B) and #29, 11-62 (#23 R & B) with Hank's "Your Cheatin' Heart."

"Mammas Don't Let Your Babies Grow Up to Be Cowboys" – Willie Nelson and Waylon Jennings, #42, 2-78; #1(4), 1-78 C. The two Texans had a different conception of freedom and bringing the music of the people to the people. Willie's bandanna and Nikes, and Waylon's cowboy macho dark garb, provided a good contrast. Willie's Jazz/Pop Standards style and virtuoso lead guitar meshed with Waylon's own Johnny Cash style stardom. When Buddy Holly split with first Crickets Jerry Allison (drums) and bassist Joe B. Mauldin, moving to New York (presaging the Yoko Ono Lennon crisis), Waylon became the Cricket bass player at age 18. Buddy produced Waylon's first record, the Cajun "Jole Blon" ['gorgeous blonde'] for the young Littlefield, TX, DJ (b. '37) soon touring with the ill-fated Winter Dance Party.

Offered **Ritchie Valens'** seat on the hapless Beechcraft Bonanza, Waylon turned down Buddy's airborne invitiation. In Waylon's autobiography, Holly apparently joked, "Hope your ol' rickety bus freezes up." Rowdy Waylon (to his later horror) supposedly answered in total jest – "I hope your ol' plane crashes." Forty years of repressing that ugly scenario couldn't shake it from Waylon's eerie and haunted reverie. He internalized his personal guilt, feeling he somehow caused that cosmic mechanical/pilot error tragedy. Forty years.

No wonder Waylon became an Outlaw. Everyone shrouds some terrible secret. Maybe the macho men suffer the most. Stoic stasis. They just can't whisper their secret to anyone. "Cowboys" touts a desperado philosophy. Mamas' lads oughta become docs or lawyers or whatever – NOT cowboys. Willie and Waylon are joined by Waylon's wife **Jessi Colter** (m. 1969), who hit big with #4, 4-75 (#1 C) "I'm Not Lisa." When Willie and Waylon and Jessi and **Tompall Glaser** (#7, C-only, 8-71 "Rings") released #10, 2-76 Bicentennial album *The Outlaws*, it was rumored to be the first All-Country album to ever sell a million.

"Luckenbach, Texas (Back to the Basics of Love)" – Waylon Jennings [coda by Willie Nelson], #25, 5-77; #1(6), 4-77 C. That six-week run is among the longest in the 'Modern Country Era.' Waylon/Willie portray a tiny Texas semi-ghost town – literally resurrected to tourist-trappitude by their record's massive popularity. Jennings is 11th-ever Country on Whitburn's complex Top Artist list (7277 pts, '94, to Willie's 9th-position 7660). Waylon's magic movers? Pensive waltz #54, 6-79 (#1[3] C) "Amanda"; rip-roaring #1(3) C, 7-78 "I've Always Been Crazy"; #21, 9, 80 world-famous "Theme from the Dukes of Hazzard (Good Old Boys)" at #1 C; and #10 C, 6-81 "Wild Side of Life"/"It Wasn't God Who Made Honky-Tonk Angels." At the height of heyday popularity (1968-87), marathoner Jennings toured with the remaining Crickets – **Jerry Allison, Joe B. Mauldin, Sonny Curtis,** and newer Gordon Payne – tossing in a big Buddy Holly medley (catch Al. #46, '76 *Waylon Live*). Waylon (1937-2002, diabetes) never forgot his old friends.

"Runaway" – Narvel Felts, NC, '78; #30, 3-78, C. Felts (b. '38, Arkansas), White Soul virtuoso covers Bonnie Raitt's first hit and **Del Shannon's** classic with classic glides and tenor swoops; his **Jackie Wilson** Country Soul on #7 '58 "Lonely Teardrops" (Felts #62, 5-76, #5 C) is outstanding. Unheralded superstar Felts's best may be magnificent #67, 5-75 (#2 C) "Reconsider Me" (#28, '69 Johnny Adams).

Jack Greene (b. '30, Alabama) drummed for **Ernest Tubb** before his own glory spotlight on #65, 1-67, and #1(7), 10-66 C. "There Goes My Everything" – covered by our only hitmaker ever from [Madras] INDIA, with one BILLION English-speaking [and singing] people, crooner **Englebert Humperdinck** (#20, 6-67).

Chet Atkins' "Yakety Axe" hit #98, 7-65 (#4 C), a jovial response to "Yakety Sax" – by Boots Randolph at #35, 3-63 (NC, C). An AXE is a GUITAR, of course, and Nashville session star and exec Atkins was among world's Top 25 guitar players.

"(Old Dogs – and Children And) Watermelon Wine" – Tom T. Hall, NC, '72; #1(1), 12-72 C. Business guy waiting for flight gets advice from woolly-haired janitor/sage in dark bar. Slow down, oldster opines . . . women waste you, money corrupts. Only three things really count (see title). Watermelon wine? Scarce stuff. Hall's "I Like Beer" (NC, '75, #4, 9-75 C) previewed **Garth Brooks'** beer chic in #1-ever Country "Friends in Low Places." Olive Hill, KY Hall (b. '36) previews current microbrewery fad, dismisses wine snobs as effete. His follow-up (NC '76, #1, 1-76 C), "Faster Horses (The Cowboy and the Poet)," pits a ditzy poet against a saddle-sore pragmatic cowboy. The cowpoke scoffs at poetic ideals of purity, beauty, truth: 'buffalo-chips," he calls them. The cowboy sage says life's answer is in faster-paced horses at the track, younger hotter women, older vintage whiskey, and more big money. Long before **Madonna**'s #2, 2-85 "Material Girl" quest, here was this money-mad wrangler doling out shot & beer truth from HI$ angle.

"Yesterday, When I Was Young" – Roy Clark, #19, 6-69; #9 C. Clark (b. '33, VA) anchored the *Hee-Haw* Country comedy/variety/music show with **Buck Owens and Grandpa Jones.** The banjo virtuoso's stunning tenor ballad broods French *ennui* and German angst and Weltschmerz over the dolorous passage of Demon Time. He wakes up to discover it got way too late way too early. Deep stuff. When I heard it first at 27, I felt 72. Sweet tender tightrope melody, swathed in silky strings. Lighter Side Dept.: Roy also did #9 C, 8-72 "The Lawrence Welk Hee-Haw Counter-Revolution Polka": No relation to North Dakota bandleader **Welk** (1903-92), who enjoyed #1 Country hit "Shame on You" (#13, 9-45, Top 30).

Steve Wariner (b. '54 Indiana) teamed with Glen Campbell on NC '87 #6, 5-87 "The Hand That Rocks the Cradle."

"Midnight Fire" – Steve Wariner, NC, '83; #5, 8-83 C. Wariner's Country star rose over 1985 along "Life's Highway" (#1 C, 3-86), after #1 C "You Can Dream of Me." The bass-playing star rose into HOT 100 fame, too, with Bill Anderson-penned #30, 4-99 "Two Teardrops" and #42, 9-99 "I'm Already Taken." Crossing over to R & R glory, Wariner's Beatles' "Get Back" hit #72 C. in 9-95. Wariner's **Bob Luman** (NC, '72; #4, 9-72 C) "Lonely Women Make Good Lovers" stormed to #4 C. 10-83 for Steve. Luman (TX, 1937-78) hit with anti-violence comic #7, 9-60 "Let's Think About Livin'," an ANTI Graveyard Rock counterpunch, so his own untimely death has a sad and puzzling ring. **Glen Campbell** and **Tanya Tucker** (b. '58, Seminole, TX, to Wilcox, AZ) duetted on Bobby Darin's Chalypso #2 '59 "Dream Lover" – to #59, 9-80 C, highlighting their close relationship.

"Blood Red and Goin' Down" – Tanya Tucker, #74, 8-73; #1(1), 7-73, C. Tanya/Glen kept supermarket checkout readers scanning gossip. Her clever-titled tunes carry her purry contralto to ringing heights of twangy ecstasy: "Two Sparrows in a Hurricane" #2(1), 9-92, C. Tracing a direct attractive/teen/contralto line from **Brenda Lee to Tanya Tucker to Le Ann Rimes,** Tanya lavished tiptop tunes: #1(1), 8-75 C. "San Antonio Stroll"; original "Delta Dawn" #72, 7-72 (#6, 5-72 C); Buddy Holly's #70 HOT 100-only "Not Fade Away" 1-79; and #2(2), 10-89 "My Arms Stay Open All Night." Her #72, 7-72 (#6 C) "Delta Dawn" stars an aging Southern Belle – #1 HOT 100 later by Australian **Helen Reddy**.

"I Meant Every Word He Said" – Ricky Van Shelton, NC, '90; #2(2), 6-90 c. Cowboy stetson askew, the Danville Virginia (b. '52) tenor hit 5 jackpot #1's in a row, like: #1(1), 1-89 "From a Jack to a King" (Ned Miller, #6, 12-62, & #2[4] C); and #1(1) 8-87 C "Somebody Lied." Into the 90s, he teamed with **Dolly Parton** on #1(1), 3-91 C. "Rockin' Years."

"The Harper Valley P.T.A." – Jeannie C. Riley, #1(1), 6-68; #1(3), 8-68 C. In "Harper Valley P.T.A.," the lady of the fling, in a miniskirt, swaggers into the P.T.A. lair and lambasts all of THEM for their own hypocrisy for accusing HER of impropriety. Jeannie socks it to whole frumpy P.T.A. throng. As miniskirts rose, so did community eyebrows. Lady is a widow – not even divorced or separated. Town grand-dames pant for scandal. Tom T. Hall's comic PTA tale is told from viewpoint of little girl whose mom has been slandered. Her mom blasts into the meeting, revealing townsfolks' closet skeletons. A Pandora's Box of Hallowe'en gossip is let out of the bag ('Shirley Johnson's' gin nip, principal's skirt-chasing, married deacons begging HER for a date). Jeannie alludes to 'America's first mass-market erotic novel best-seller – Grace Metalious' 1956 *Peyton Place* (10M copies), a tell-all about torrid affairs of this sneaky, once-prim New Hampshire burg. Riley concludes that Harper Valley, too, is a Peyton Place, and all the PTA mavens are hypocrites.

Steamy public aftermath of passion theme like **Sammi Smith**'s #8, 1-71 & #1(3) C "Help Me Make It Through the Night." Orange County, California's Sammi's romantic rendezvous leads to devil-may-care fling, previewing Disco.

"This Time" – Sawyer Brown, NC, '94; #2(2), 11-94 C. Mark Miller (b. '58) of Ohio sings lead, with Michigan's Bobby Randall on lead guitar. Sawyer Brown spun many hot hits into the Country stratosphere, plus #44, 2-99 HOT 100 "Drive Me Wild." "Thank God for You" hit #1(1) C, 7-93, and "Some Girls Do" #1(1), 3-92 C. "This Time" echoes the old **Troy Shondell** #6, 9-61 torch tune, overlain with a sprawling organ-driven blanket of sound tromping along on triplets, 12 per measure.

"(I'm Still Looking for Some) New Blue Jeans" – Troy Shondell, NC, 1988; #79, 2-88 C.). One-hit Teen Idol Shondell (b. '44, Indiana) produced masterpiece "This Time." Hope he finds his pants.

Restless Heart hit #11, 11-92 (#9, C) with majestic last-note on "When She Cries," plus six consecutive #1 C songs like 5-88 "Bluest Eyes in Texas." **Ed Bruce** has a long checkered baritone career, from #109, 11-63 "See the Big Man Cry' to #3, C for the Arkansas traveler (b. '40) to "You Turn Me On (Like a Radio)" of 11-84. Let's do controversy:

"Dropkick Me, Jesus" – Bobby Bare, NC, '76; #17, 10-76 C. Bare (b.'35, Ironton, Ohio), baritone balladeer, spirals a football metaphor that astounded, flabbergasted, and perplexed believers, atheists, agnostics, and football worshippers alike. In the most way-out religious analogy ever concocted in a Country waltz, Bare lays bare all lyrical inhibitions. Not totally irreverent, he compares HIM-SELF to the FOOTBALL (obviously, via title). He beseeches the Lord, in a flagellant order more devout than the hair-shirt monks who whipped themselves in the 12th century, to kick **him** beyond those 'righteous UPRIGHT goalposts of life. Bizarro premise. Or catch **Ray Stevens'** #41, 5-87 C "Would Jesus Wear a Rolex?"

"Singin' in the Kitchen" – Bobby Bare, NC, '74; #29, 11-74 C. Ultra-normal one. Nifty ditty. Bobby's wife Jeannie and Bobby Bare Jr., 6, whoop it up in kiddie kitchen singalong, using pots and pans as percussion. As unpretentious and fun as the pilgrim pigskin one is weird. Bobby hit with gorgeous Folk tune "Four Strong Winds" (#60, 10-64, #3 C, Canadian semi-hymn), plus #31, 4-80 C "Tequila Sheila." His biggees? #2(1), 12-58 "All-American Boy" (as 'Bill Parsons'), #10, 10-63 Folk tune "500 Miles Away from Home" at #3 C; #16 Mel Tillis-tune "Detroit City" 6-63 (#6 C), and #1(1) C 5-74 "Marie Laveau."

"Tempted" – Marty Stuart, NC, '91; #5, 8-91 C. Only big Philly star from Philadelphia, Mississippi (b. '58). "Peggy Sue" style tom-tom tattoos (16th-note paradiddles). Marty's rich electric Rockabilly tenor booms along with his Elvis smile and Rod Stewart flyaway thick hair. Touring at 13 with Lester Flatt, he married **Johnny Cash's** daughter Cindy for six years, after working for Johnny. How do you write a script for more leverage to future Country success? "Tempted's" lyrical theme suggests **Frankie Laine's** #2 '51 "Jezebel" (1 *Kings* 16:32-33), who nailed King Nebuchadnezzar with dastardly doom. Sometimes girls get just too beautiful for guys to ignore.

Country 'Johnny B. Goode' story: Kid with gunny sack guitar by railroad track? Marty? Despite being hampered by good looks, outstanding talent, a great voice, and great musicianship, the kid becomes a star anyhow ... Marty's hit cavalcade includes: #2(1) C, 11-91 "The Whiskey Ain't Workin'"; #8 C, 4-90 "Hillbilly Rock," and #7 C, 2-92 flaming "Burn Me Down."

"Foolish Pride" – Travis Tritt, #112, 5-94; #1(1), 4-94 C. Tritt's #10+, 12-2000 "It's a Great Day to Be Alive" is a three-minute reason for his crossover stardom; Travis (b. '63, Marietta, GA) joined in big HOT 100 with **Lonestar** and **Faith Hill/Tim McGraw** with #28+, 8-2000 (#2 C) "The Best of Intentions." Travis hit with #2(1) C, 9-91 "Here's a Quarter (Call Someone Who Cares); #1(2), C, 12-92 "Can I Trust You with My Heart," and #3 C, 2-91 "Drift Off to Dream."

"Sixteen Tons" – Tennessee Ernie Ford, #1(8), 11-55; #1(10), C. Bombardier bass singer Ford (1919-91) flew many missions in World War II. His "Sixteen Tons" portrays the dim, grim miseries of hard-coal miners. Is a man made of MUD? Of Blood & Muscle & Sinew & Skin? A strong back and an indomitable soul? He laments owing his meager earnings and earthly soul to the monopolistic 'company store,' when no one could afford a car to shop elsewhere. Burly minor-key ballad of steel-fisted miner getting tired and old in deep coal mine despair. Among deepest bass singers to ever sing lead. Ernie's hit list?

#6, C. 9-52 "Blackberry Wine"; #14, 12-50, but #1(14) C. "The Shot Gun Boogie"; and his #5, 3-55 & #4 C. "The Ballad of Davy Crockett." If anyone exuded the deep range, and hardscrabble balladry of ramshackle America like Bristol, Tennessee's Ernie, it's Randy:

"Hard Rock Bottom of Your Heart" – Randy Travis, NC, '90; #1(4), 1-90 C. Few Country tales clutch #1 for a month anymore. This Ford-style mining metaphor highlights Randy's spitfire-guitar talents. The 2001+ HOT 100 included high-chart Country stars, unlike chart-segregated Generation X era of lone Rappers, lone Grungers, and lonesome Country stars singing in claustrophobic vacuums of coteries of fans. It began for Randy with his double-wave "On the Other Hand," at both #67, 8-85 C, and #1(1), 4-86 C. He then cruised to 9 of 10 C. #1's like **Led Zeppelin's** album surge. Travis's top tunes? #1(3) C., 4-87 "Forever and Ever, Amen," #1 C, 11-88 "Deeper Than the Holler," #1(2), 11-92, "Look Heart, No Hands," and classic #1(1) C, 7-88 "Honky Tonk Man."

"Amarillo by Morning" – George Strait, NC, '83; #4, 2-83, C. Among prettiest Country ballads of all time. Straight Strait Country sound. Nothing fancy or frilly or gimmicky. George (b. 52) comes from Poteet, Texas, near San Antonio – a long way from Panhandle North Texas Amarillo. U.S. Army and SW Texas State agriculture degree. George "Unwound" (#6, 5-81 C) talents over high-prairie vermilion orange sundown Amarillo. Sunrise, too. George uses few slurs, glides, melismas, or hiccups, and avoids much yodeling. He sings his song straight. His title echoes Cliffie Stone's 1947, #4, 3-47 C "Silver Stars, Purple Sage, Eyes of Blue," which punches up memories of Old Route 66 roadhouses of Amarillo yesteryear.

There's nothing "Easy Come, Easy Go" (#71, 1-93 and #1[2], 8-93 C) about Strait's straight trail to success; with this 25th #1 C. tune he ranked 7th (with an up-zooming bullet) in # of #1 C hits, like star songs: #1 C, 9-86 "It Ain't Cool to Be Crazy About You"; ace in the hole "Ace in the Hole" (#1 C, 8-89), and Travis-answer tune, #1(5) C, 4-90 "Love Without End, Amen." George glommed #1(5), 9-95 C. "Check Yes or No," and 6-97 #1 Country album *Carrying Your Love with Me*, showing the Strait Path is no gullywashout road to Nowheresville. "The Fireman" hit #5, 6-85 C.

"All My Ex's Live in Texas" – George Strait, NC, '87; #1(1), 5-87 C. The spirit of **Bob Wills** lives on in this Western Swing lush litany of his old flames. George enjoys a curly steel guitar intro, joined by the jolting bash-smash-crash of the rock-ribbed big 2 & 4 backbeat. Soon the Texan Wills fiddle swoops in, marking out Texas Country turf. Tex ex's? 'Rosanna' in Texarkana, 'Alison' in Galveston, 'Dimples' [Dimples?] in Temple, and "Ilene" floating around the amorphous purple ether near the Moon. The rockin' rhythm swings Wills-style Western Swing, like an old shed door flapping red-gold hollyhocks in the summer sunshine. So where does Strait's "song-guy" live? Texas? Nope, he dwells in Tennessee, beyond ex-range and lawyer lassos.

"Does Fort Worth Ever Cross Your Mind?" – **George Strait, NC, '84; #1(1), 9-84, C.** Typical barroom lament? Twin cities Dallas/Fort Worth feature Strait's song-guy on bummer trip. Naturally, his girl's with the other dude , having a blast in Dallas, while he broods, fumes, and stews. [George himself, though will "Go On" – #40, 8-2000, and #2 C]. "The Best Day" hit #3 C in March 2000, and #41 HOT 100 – the big chart penetration Country stars have long deserved. His 10-2000 Al. *George Strait* DEBUTED at #1 on the Country album charts, and #7 on the Billboard 200 big album chart, an unprecedented Country album achievement. In 2001, George's "Don't Make Me Come over There and Love You" hit #1 C.

"She Got the Gold Mine (I Got the Shaft)" – **Jerry Reed, #57, 7-82; #1(2), C.** Country/RAP-scallion and actor. With the gravelly baritone gusto of the Big Bopper, Reed jabs at divorce lawyers who give him shaft in marital settlement. Reed (b. Jerry Reed Hubbard, Atlanta, '37) clicked Big Chart Gold Mine with #9, 5-71 and #1(5) C. "When You're Hot You're Hot." His Country-RAP style #8, 10-70 (only #16 C) "Amos Moses" is a gator-hunting gala along Alligator Alley – alligator-poachers, and bayou blasters.

"Cajun Moon" – **Ricky Skaggs, NC, '86, #1(1), 1-86 C.** Whizkid Skaggs (b. '54 Cordell, KY) manhandled mandolin at 4, maestroed it at 5. Bluegrass guru **Bill Monroe** watched, bedazzled, as tot Skaggs rocked out on Bluegrass cadenzas. Skaggs plays fiddle, banjo, steel guitar. Like **Ernie Sykes** and Long Island's Opry vet **Bluegrass Cardinals**, Skaggs lofts a tremulous Irish tenor. Of Ricky's 11 charttoppers, his signature is NC '83 #1(1) C. "Highway 40 Blues," plus #1C, 4-89 "Lovin' Only Me."

Modern Bluegrass music, triumphantly, has its own dedicated following who chase Bluegrass festivals all over the world. Countrypolitan music hurt Bluegrass for awhile, dampening airplay. Expert Lee Michael Demsey of *Bluegrass Unlimited* magazine publishes Un-*Billboard* Bluegrass charts. In late 1999, he mentions, Bluegrass champ's album Ancient Tones celebrated the Scotch-Irish Celtic link. On his charts, **Alison Krauss** had #25 from mainstream Country, but many other names are more familiar to Bluegrass aficionados especially: **Laurie Lewis & Her Bluegrass Pals, Blue Highway, Mountain Heart, Scottie Sparks, Del McCoury's Band, Longview**, and the **Kathy Kallick Band**. Bluegrass is about as vintage an American art form as you can find, and it still relies on acoustic MANDOLINS and BANJOS, even DOBRO guitars and DULCIMERS. Yet in its ancient Highland Scots and Irish emerald moor roots, Bluegrass hastens us back to Folk balladry like "Barbara Allen" or "Foggy Mountain Breakdown."

"Walk on By" – **Leroy Van Dyke, #5, 10-61; #1(19), 9-61 C.** 6th-longest #1 C. song ever tells midnight girl to wait on dark corner. He'll love her in the shadows, but they must act as strangers on the public street. Squeaky sneaky rendezvous. Van Dyke's amazing "Auctioneer" (#19, 11-56; #9, 1-57 C) is a fast RAP auction from his Spring Fork Missouri. He whomps words at 250+/minute.

"Walk on By" echo? His "If a Woman Answers (Hang up the Phone)" at #35, 10-62 (#3 C).

Carl Smith hit #1(8), 7-53 C with "Hey Joe!" – no relation to **Jimi Hendrix** classic. This Joe has zillions of hot girls snuggling somehow. Smith scorched charts with #1(7), 11-54 C. "Loose Talk." **Johnny Rodriquez** hit #70, 9-73 (#1 C) as 1st Latino Country star on "Ridin' My Thumb to Mexico." **Michael Martin Murphy** hit #19, 7-82 (#1 C) with "What's Forever For?" His huge hit is ghost-horse #3, 3-75 "Wildfire."

"Blue Kentucky Girl" – **Emmylou Harris, NC, '79; #6, 9-79 C.** Like Mary-Chapin Carpenter and Holly Dunn, Harris championed Folkabilly movement. Emmylou (b. Alabama, '47), hit #1(2) C. with Patsy Cline anthem "Sweet Dreams" to #1(2), C., 10-76. Her rich crystal soprano and silver hair took her to #1(1) C, 10-82 "(Lost His Love) On Our Last Date." With **Dolly Parton** and **Linda Ronstadt**, she rose to #6, 3-88 C with "Wildflowers."

Floyd Cramer (1933-97, session piano man, Nashville) was cutting his last recording date before giving up and returning to the day-job world. He called it "Last Date." Lo and behold, it skyrocketed to #2(4), 10-60 (#11 C, and #3 R & B). He rebounded his new-found fame with #4, 3-61 "On the Rebound."

Emmylou Harris's Al. *Red Dirt Girl* debuted the Country Album charts at #5, 9-2000, and #54 Billboard 200. Emmylou? Not BLUE

"Blue Christmas" – **Ernest Tubb, #21, 12-49; #1(1), C.** Yep, the ELVIS one. Tubb sings it straight. The King's #1(2), 12-64 Christmas-chart version (off Al. #1[4], 12-57 *Elvis's Christmas Album*) features a kingly snow flurry of cool grace notes and frosty mumbled murmurs. Tubb (1914-84) is best known for #23, 8-41 "Walking the Floor over You," which WOULD have been #1(20) or so, but Country charts were born four years later. Tubb's 82 Top 40 C. hits slot him 8th ever – and 58 top 10 tunes rank him fifth ('94 Whitburn rankings, the latest) behind only **Eddy Arnold** (92), **George Jones** (79), **Conway Twitty** (75), and **Merle Haggard** (71). Tubb sang #1(2) C, 11-46 "Rainbow at Midnight."

"Tumbling Tumbleweeds" – **Sons of the Pioneers [Roy Rogers], #13, 12-34.** Roy Rogers (1911-98), King of the Cowboys, and **Bob Nolan** formed this vintage Cowboy band. Go West – young man. Their close harmony blends the golden gloaming and purple sundown and sagebrush on Old Montana Trails. The song rolls on chromatic chord changes (drop or rise ½ step, like **C** to **C#** or **B**). Roy's yodelmaster tenor sang sunburnt slabs of the Golden West, before he was stolen by the silver screen to become the cowboy monarch – with his faithful wife **Dale Evans** (1912-2001) and horse Trigger. Roy also hit with #65, 12-74 (#15 C) on "Hoppy, Gene, and Me" – about fellow cinema wranglers Gene Autry and Hopalong Cassidy.

"The Fightin' Side of Me" – **Merle Haggard, #92, 2-70; #1(3), C. Bakersfield, California's** Haggard (b. 4-6-37) will always be remembered for his #41, 11-69 (#1[4] C)

"Okie from Muskogee," with bedrock small-town values and feisty pro-war lyrics. Merle's hard-luck dad died when he was nine, so Merle drifted the hobo rails at 14. His seven-year-itch of wrangling, rambling, and roaring sent him to the slammer for burglary (1957-60). Then-Governor **Ronald Reagan** (1911-) commuted the reformed rebel a pardon, and millionaires rarely revert to petty theft. He played bass with Wynn Stewart's (1934-85, #1 C. 2-67 "It's Such a Pretty World Today") band. Then he formed the Strangers, also **Bobby Vee**'s later band's name. "The Fightin' Side of Me" is a conservative backlash against Vietnam War protestors, and particularly those who bad-mouth America. Merle's prison stint zapped his draft eligibilty, and at 32 he wasn't so desirable to his Draft Board – like recent unmarried, kidless high school grads rated A-1, in my generation. Haggard sings Currier & Ives, and Norman Rockwell America, with Thanksgiving kids gnawing on turkey legs, surrounded by love and laughter.

Mostly, Merle sings the Blue-Collar Blues of the working man.. He sings the hard times, the honkytonk losers, the air-hammer gongs of the Liberty Bell. Songs of freedom. This backlash tune is a bumpersticker echo:

> AMERICA: LOVE IT OR LEAVE IT!

"Soldier's Last Letter" – Merle Haggard, #90, 3-71; #3, 2-71 C. #1(4), 5-44 C. for **Ernest Tubb**, #16, 8-44 Top 30. Like **Johnny Horton** marrying Hank Williams' widow Billie, Tubb called Jimmie Rodgers I's widow. A ghostly aura pervaded his rise to fame – with Rodgers' Martin guitar, and his TUXEDO GIVEN by his WIDOW, Tubb scored this macabre phosphorescent "Last Letter" song that dominated WWII. The death of a soldier boy, and his last letter to mom, do not relate to military strategy. They are basic and tragic truths. They hit home, like a bombshell.

Haggard hunkers down into his baritone bunker. The kid's last foxhole produces his last letter. He writes his mom not to scold him like he was still a kid, if he stomps into her house in muddy boots from the war. The missive sears with dramatic irony. Naturally, he will never finish his letter. When Tubb passed the torch (or cigarette) to Haggard, the ember of authenticity glowed down through the ages. **Johnny Cash** sponsored Merle's climb from darkness into the Elvis Spotlight. Oh, and the soldier's last line? He prays that God will keep America free.

"If We Make It Through December" – Merle Haggard – #28, 11-73; #1(4), 10-73 C. Bleak lament about financial and emotional desperation. Merle's biggest hit, ironically, Good bouncy melody for woeful situation. Merle's "Daddy Frank" (#1[2] C, 10-71) tells tearful tale of blind guitarist Frank, and hearing-impaired wife. Kids chime tambourines, but they're so poor they hobo to cold campfires.

"One More Town" – Kingston Trio, #97, 10-62; NC, C. **Nick Reynolds** takes a lead vocal here, playing his normal four-string guitar. The Folk Kingston Trio somehow got themselves ironically voted the #1 Country Band of 1958, without EVER hitting the Country charts (*Billboard*

has never had a Folk Chart). Nicky's ramblin' rainbow-chasing ballad takes a one-way ticket to destiny. "One More Town" champions Haggard's eternal nomad, looking for something tremendous that never shows up. Wanderlust Paradise Express. The Trio's #93, 5-62 "Jane, Jane, Jane" plies this "Daddy Frank" blind/deaf motif. The Kingston Trio ranks #3 of all time for most album weeks at #1 (46, behind Elvis's 64 and the Beatles' 119).

"Workin' Man Blues" – Merle Haggard, NC, '69; #1(1), 7-69 C. A snarly twangy guitar spits fire. The song crunches in in odd-unbluesy Key of 'Ab.' Merle's kids need new shoes. He muses on guys who toss their bills out the window, and slip away from home. Nope, he says. After a roughneck Saturday night, he's back on the roustabout crew. Merle's breakthrough was #5 C, 4-66 "Swingin' Doors." He cut "Barroom Buddies" to #1(1) 5-80 with **Clint Eastwood**. "Workin' Man Blues" touts these working folks and family men with self-reliance and self-sufficiency. His rustly eighth-note throb accents the R & R 2 & 4 backbeats. A ring jangles now and then, and a triangle. Other Haggard hit hits? **Willie Nelson** duet of federales and desperados, #1(1), 4-83 C "Pancho and Lefty"; #25 Country album *If Only I Could Fly* of 10-2000.

Haggard is 5th on Whitburn's all-time Country Artist list: 1) **Eddy Arnold**, 12,581 pts.; 2) **George Jones**, 11,161; 3) **Johnny Cash**, 9,545; 4) **Conway Twitty**, 9,545; 5) **Haggard**, 8,920; 6) **Webb Pierce**, 7,927; 7) **Ray Price**, 7,716; 8) **Dolly Parton** [#1 female artist], 7,711; 9) **Willie Nelson**, 7,660; and 10) **Buck Owens**, 7,459. An amazing marathon crew of troubadours.

"Coal Miner's Daughter" – Loretta Lynn, #83, 12-70; #1(1), 10-70 C. Loretta hit national prominence with this autobiographical song. Sissy Spacek is backed in the flick by the **Band** from Bob Dylan's Big Pink Woodstock adventure. **Lynn** (b. '34, Butcher Holler, Kentucky) started with #14 C, 6-60 "I'm a Honky Tonk Girl." Her "Success" [#6 C., 7-62] blossomed for this "Blue Kentucky Girl" [#7 C, 5-65] who became a grandmother at 32. Married at 13, Loretta Webb left her Webb site to marry Oliver 'Mooney' Lynn, bearing four kids in her teens in Washington State.

"Don't Come Home A'Drinkin' (With Lovin' on Your Mind)" – Loretta Lynn, NC, '66; #1(1), 11-66 C. Cryptic combo of submissiveness and assertiveness for sweet blue-eyed Loretta. On one hand, she's the dutiful homemaker of the era. She cooks, cleans, and nurtures kids on their highway to high school. On the other hand, she fidgets and fusses over her wayward man. The scoundrel is stupefied by the neon razzle-dazzle (plus seven Stroh's beers). Upfront, earthy lyric. Since they're married, their intimate amours are zilch via her STOP SIGN. She draws the line at his staggering stupor. Loretta, Queen of Country Music, was Nashville's darling.

"One's on the Way" – Loretta Lynn, NC, '71; #1(2), 12-71 C. Her recipe for domestic bliss? Her three-ring family circus circle of kids doing darnedest things: one needs a hug, she sings, and one a spanking. Anyhow, she mulls a new upcoming arrival and maternity bliss. At the time, America was too poor to be able to afford to have young mothers go out en masse, to have to work to make it on two incomes.

Loretta's "The Pill" (#70, 3-75 & #5 C) is her empowerment blockbuster. Here was Loretta pushing birth control via the airwaves. It was almost 'Women's Lib.' The pill gave couples, and women in particular, the power to limit their families to whatever they could afford. Empowerment blockbuster. Flabbergasted Nashville Establishment. Flying in the face of Catholic, Mormon, and Fundamentalist 1975 doctrine (also Muslim and Orthodox Judaism), her family-planning flap rocked the old breed of patriarch with a new non-generation of uncreated un-kids. Revolutionary lyric.

Sandy Posey's total Country "Born a Woman" (#12, 7-66, NC, C) took on the 'born-female curse,' which sentences sweet wives and dutiful sweethearts to lies, unfaithfulness, and abuse. Posey's (b. Arkansas) flowery sweet crystal soprano pleads and coaxes and coos in melodic splendor, but she carries her burden of world-class suffering, just being born a woman. Not Loretta's song person. Loretta's song-mom takes charge.

"After the Fire Is Gone" – Conway Twitty and Loretta Lynn, #56, 2-71; #1(2) C. Embers smolder. Conway and Loretta commiserate ashes of ex-love gone bad. In Country Blues wildfire Key of 'E,' "Fire" fires up Conway's craggy baritone. Big Bopperizing his blues, he hollers that love will be wherever you can find it! They harmonize on how chilly it gets, when the gray ashes cool. The Conway/Loretta tandem also scored on #1(1), 6-73 joyride on the Freeway of Love: "Louisiana Woman, Mississippi Man."

"Silver Threads and Golden Needles" – Loretta Lynn, Tammy Wynette, and Dolly Parton, NC, '93; #68, 12-93 C. Wow, what a triumphant triumvirate of Country royalty. This classic first spun (#20, '63) for 1999 Rock Hall then-Folk star **Dusty Springfield** (1939-99). #67, 4-74 for lovely **Linda Ronstadt**. A GREAT Country Folk song, with braided sweet Appalachian harmonies fluttering in delicate ecstasy – try to hear it! Loretta's big numbers? Yep. She was third-ever (1994, Whitburn) in hits for Country female artists: 77, with 81 for **Kitty Wells**, and 99 for **Dolly Parton.**

"Linda on My Mind" – Conway Twitty, #61, 2-75; #1(1), 1-75 C. Lucky 13th #1 Country hit for former baseball star **Harold Jenkins** (b. Friar's Point, Mississippi, 9-1-33, d. 6-5-93) Reposing with this other girl, his impish mind darts back to his fantasy LINDA. This furtive flesh fantasyland is nothing revolutionary. In the last week, exactly 3,567,219,769 lovers worldwide have channel-surfed the same demonic imbroglios of forbidden romance in their own X-rated minds. It's endemic to the species. Twitty muffles the first line with surging intensity. He explodes from hang-fire baritone to turgid tenor. You can feel the guilt he sings, and the taboo temptation of titillating 'Linda.'

Waylon Jennings, who debuted with Crickets

"Slow Hand" – Pointer Sisters, #2(3), 5-81; #7, 6-81, R & B, NC, C. Anita, Bonnie (lead), **June,** and **Ruth Pointer** are preacher's kids from Oakland, CA, whose #2(2), 11-78 **Bruce Springsteen** song "Fire" smoked the charts. This anthem to easygoing love chides the speedo lover, and praises the sensitive liberated lover who considers HER pleasure as much as his own. **Conway** nobly answers their clarion call (hmmm, what a self-sacrificing guy) to #1[2] C, 4-82. He offers a slow hand. He says he'll consider her passion, too. Good ol' Conway. As a Rockabilly rocker [#1 HOT 100, '58 "It's Only Make Believe"], Twitty counterbalances a lot of R & R genres. His #1(1), 2-81 C "Rest Your Love on Me" was written by the Britrock Disco icons the **Bee Gees.**

"Crazy in Love" – Conway Twitty, NC, '90; #2(2), 9-90 C. The Twitty Empire started with an old touring bus, and expanded into 'Twitty City,' a nine-acre theme park housing Conway's entire world. For a slight fee, fan-addicts could tromp Conway's trails, and peer into almost every aspect of his family's life. Like 'Dollywood,' Twitty City is a monument to a gregarious Country superstar. In the old days, Webb Pierce started this fishbowl fad with his guitar-shaped swimming pool and guided home tours. **Jerry Lee Lewis** followed suit. William Lee Golden of this Oak Ridge Boys preferred living in a Native American teepee. Twitty built his Twitty City Empire around bus touring, traveling a killer itinerary of zillions of weekly concerts. Always thinking about his fans. The fast-food regimen got to be too much, and Conway passed away on tour of an abdominal attack, a shade shy of 60. His total of 40 Number One hits was untopped anywhere – until Alabama's 41-#1-hit collection smacked the charts in 1998.

"Hooked on Music" – Mac Davis, NC, '81; #2(2), 2-81 C. Lubbock Texan Mac (b. '42) reflects on his Crickets memories on Texas's Panhandle Tornado Alley. Mac started in Easy Squeezy Listening with #1(3), 7-72 [HOT 100] "Baby, Don't Get Hooked on Me." Like Clown Princes of Country, Jerry Reed, Ray Stevens, Bobby Bare, and **Little Jimmy Dickens** (#15 '65 "May the Bird of Paradise Fly up Your Nose" #1 C), Davis tossed out dickenses like "It's Hard to Be Humble" (#43, 3-80, #10 C). Can't be humble when you're perfect, he chuckles.

"You Never Even Called Me by My Name" – **David Allen Coe, NC, '75; #8, 7-75 C.** Alanna Nash says Coe lived in a cave with his wife collection; we can't corroborate that theory. This jiffy parody ruminates on the 'Perfect Country Song.' A hotshot songsmith tells Coe he needs props, motifs, recurrent lyrical themes – a train, a honkytonk drinker, a pick-up truck, and good ol' Mom. So he concocts this hilarious ghastly Hallowe'en Carol – he's drunk the day they spring his MOM outa the slammer. He tromps his pick-up's pedal and spits gravel to pick her up at RR station. Alas, she gets squashed by 'danged' train. Humor in a jugular vein.

    Merle Haggard's "Mama Tried" NC '68, #1(4), 7-68 C features the REAL mama. Bad lad is slammed into slammer. Instead of blaming 'Toxic Parents,' Merle absolves Mom from any blame at all. She's's innocent, and tried to warn him of life's pitfalls – but life was the pits, and he fell in.

"The End of the World" – **Skeeter Davis, #2(1), 1-63; #2(3), 12-62 C.** Mrs. Ella Holley, Buddy's mom, sent me one of my prize possessions – Al. *Skeeter Davis Sings Buddy Holly* (NC, '66). Born Mary Frances Penick (Dry Ridge, KY, '31), Skeeter also fractured the HOT 10 with her Skeeter & Skeeter overdubbed super song "I Can't Stay Mad at You" (#7, 9-63; #14 C). When **Hank Locklin** (b. 1918, FL) created #8, 5-60 (#1[14] C) "Please Help Me I'm Falling," an ode to temptation, Skeeter's answer-backer "(I Can't Help You) I'm Falling Too" hit #39, 8-60 and #2(3) C. Her #26 (#5 C) vocal version of Floyd Cramer's #2 "Late Date" was "My Last Date (With You)." Skeeter recorded for our old band the Night Shift's SOUL label Fortune (Detroit) in 1952, and was seriously injured when her sister Betty Jack Davis was killed in a 1953 car crash. Their audial legacy is uncanny. The **Davis Sisters'** duo #18, 8-53 "I Forgot More Than You'll Ever Know" [#1(8) C] is one of the Top 25 Greatest authentic Country songs of all time. Their heavenly harmony is so closely-linked and intense, it sends literal chills down your spine.

"Six Days on the Road" – **Dave Dudley, #32, 6-63; #2(2) C.** Truckers' testimonial – to workaholic hours truckers must log on TWO sets of books to stay afloat on the concrete sea. A cannon guitar crackles on the beefy low strings. Dudley sings to his ramshackle rig. He rollercoasters the hills and byways of over-the-road America. He salutes a bleary world feeding off coffee, No-Doz, cigarettes, and Country music.

"Eighteen Wheels and a Dozen Roses" – **Kathy Mattea, NC, '88; #1(2), 3-88 C.** Spins out where Dave Dudley's six-day truckin' odyssey left off. Her guy, this trucker, is retiring immediately (so much for the teenybopper market – Country straddles the age zones). His lady plans ever-lasting good times for the two lovers. Heartwarming tune. World class harmonies. Fronting a Bluegrass band out of West Virginia '76 high school, Kathy toiled as a tour guide at the Nashville Country Music Hall of Fame. It's the prototype for the 1995 $100,000,000 **Rock and Roll Hall of Fame in Cleveland, Ohio.** Marvelous melody. Other Mattea melodies? #1(1), 8-89 C. "Burnin' Old Memories"; #2(1), 4-90 "She Came from Fort Worth" C; and #9, 7-90 "The Battle Hymn of Love." '18 Wheels/12 Roses' pumps one of the Top 100 SWEETEST Country choruses you'll ever feast your ears upon.

"Let Me Love You Tonight" – **Pure Prairie League [Vince Gill, lead], #10, 5-80; NC, C. #1(3), Adult Contemporary.** Only one PPL Country charter – their NC '76, #96, 6-76 Gill-less Holly tribute "That'll Be the Day." **Roseanne Cash's duo** with RCA's solo Vince, #10, 7-85 C.-only "If It Weren't for Him," took the *bel canto* lyric tenor out of the OK zone – #38 C. 5-84 "Oh Carolina," and into the stardom realm. Single digits ensued with #9, 11-85 C. "Oklahoma Borderline" and the 90s shuffled a smorgasbord of #1s.

"I Still Believe in You" –**Vince Gill, NC, '92; #1(2), 7-92 C.** The tall, dark-haired tenor with the Ricky Nelson good looks was vociferously declared the CMA Male Vocalist of the Year in 1991-93. Though his haunting #3 C, 9-90 "Never Knew Lonely" gave some promise of his spellbinding range, his **Reba McEntire duet** (President George Bush I's #1 singer) #2(2), 5-90 "When I Call Your Name" surveyed his superstardom future.

    Vince Gill, like great Irish countertenor **John McCormack (**#4, 1917 "When Irish Eyes Are Smiling" & #1 "Star-Spangled Banner"), sings with such a stunning range and high crystal vocal purity, that he makes cops cry. Example – his #4, 9-91 C. "Look at Us." .

"Look at Us" – **Vince Gill, NC, '91; #4, 9-91 C.** Like Jimmie Rodgers II's #3 classic "Kisses Sweeter Than Wine (#6, 12-57 C), "Look at Us" surveys a beautiful lifetime relationship. A couple grows old together, and their true love shines through all the ravages of time. It is a monumental Country favorite, and an amazing chunk of rich devotion and selfless love. A+ melody, too. Also catch ironic #7C "Pocket Full of Gold," or Irish-tenor #3, 9-90 "Never Knew Lonely."

"One More Last Chance" – **Vince Gill, NC, '93; #1(1), 7-93 C.** Country punsters spin dazzling ironic titles like cotton-candy. This uptempo rocker is the follow-up #3, 4-93 C "No Future in the Past." The Gill tenor halo presides over his first-rate lead guitar and songsmithery. Pioneers like Vince helped bust up early-90s Chart Segregation voodoo; his #1 C "Tryin' to Get Over You" scrunched to #88, 2-94 on the BIG Chart, shadowed by #2, 7-92 C "What the Cowgirls Do." His "You Better Think Twice" (#2, 5-95 C) missed the major mark, but #72, 5-64 "Whenever You Come Around" served notice. His #37 "House of Love," with Christian Contemporary legend **Amy Grant,** not only clobbered the Country competition, but it set up a new house of love for them both. In 2000 this photogenic couple tied the knot. "Shoot Straight from the Heart" roosted at #32 and zoomed in March 2001.

"Dang Me" – Roger Miller, #7, 6-64; #1(6) C. Goodtime Charlie wows 'em at Oasis. Six rounds get bought. He buys five. He blows his fortune ($14.27) – the week's groceries, half the rent. Wife has one-month infant. Swimming in suds, the ribald honkytonker toasts his near-future, beer-future bankruptcy. Fort Worth Texan Miller's (1936-92) offbeat Jazz scat-singing (like Louie Armstrong invented) was the most exciting extra-vocalic gimmick since the vaunted Holly hiccup. Miller served sunshine:

"Walkin' in the Sunshine" – Roger Miller, #37, 3-67; #7, 4-67. Roger's funtime walk chortles and whistles with bliss and joy and euphoria and delight. A merry, jolly tune. You can't NOT whistle it. Miller double-whammied both HOT 100 and Country charts: #7, 5-65 and #2 C. "Engine, Engine #9"; British travelogue "England Swings" at #8, 11-65 (#3 C); teenage guzzle saga "Chug-A-Lug" to #9, 9-64 (#3 C), and even Elvis cover "Heartbreak Hotel" at #84, 11-66 (#55 C). Miller's catchiest Zen-type title? The perfunctorily-weird idea "You Can't Roller Skate in a Buffalo Herd" at #40, 6-66 (#35 C). Miller buffaloed and out-skated **Janis Joplin** to debut her swan song doing a rare un-Miller tune, **Kris Kristofferson**'s "Me and Bobby McGee" (NC, '69; #12, 7-69 C). Miller launched Janis's Blues masterpiece into the hit arena, with his own Prairie Soul Troubadour version. Raised by an uncle and aunt in Erick, Oklahoma (Vince Gill turf), Miller served in Korea. Brandishing his charismatic dapper mild smile, Miller concocted comic Country poetry for the ages. Bard, sage, trainyard campfire king:

"King of the Road" – Roger Miller, #4, 1-65; #1(5), 2-65 C. Hobo tale of lonesome rails. Harmless homeless grizzly rail-riding vet. Wayfaring stranger. "King of the Road" was inspired by comic **Red Skelton**'s beloved hobo portrayals and 1927 **Nick Lucas** banjo song (#3, 27), "Side by Side," reprised admirably by #1(10), 2-52 "Wheel of Fortune" star Starr, **Kay Starr** to #3, 1-53. Kay spindrifted **Patti Page**'s #1(13) 10-50 "Tennessee Waltz" overdubbing style, and laid down two sultry alto/contralto twin tracks. On *Your Hit Parade*, **Snooky Lanson** and **Dorothy Collins** bopped about in "Side by Side" clown duds and hobo jungles, with recycled stogies (cigar butts) rummaged in downtown dumps. Miller's song-guy hobo heads to Bangor, Maine. The delightfully daffy dude sings of a trailer for rent or sale. He 'rents' questionable 'rooms' for 50 cents, a suspiciously low 'flophouse' price in nearly any era (1965 cheapo motel? We stayed in the "$4 Motel' in '65 Oklahoma City, but a mouse jumped on my foot when I was taking off my socks). With an old worn-out suit (Levi-Impaired, I guess) and holey shoes, he salutes passing engineers (see Berry's "Johnny B. Goode"), and even memorizes their kids' names. For this beloved song, and similar contributions to Country Rock and even Jazz, Miller received the astonishing grand total of 11 Grammy Awards in 1964-65.

"Working Man's Ph.D" – **Aaron Tippin, NC, '93; #7, 6-93 C.** No rags-to-riches story – Tippin was a commercial airline pilot [$100,000/year in '93] before a safe landing in songwriting showbiz. Aaron's Al. *People Like Us* hit #5 Country Album charts, 10-2000 (single "People Like Us," #31+ C, 1-2001), and #53 in 8-2000 on the big *Billboard* 200 Album chart. Tippin's feisty "Kiss This" smooched the HOT 100 to #47, 9-2000, and #3 C.

Among Tippin's chart compadres, millennially, **Billy Gilman** hit #2 C. Album 8-2000 *One Voice*; **Toby Keith** hit #4, 6-2000 C with "Country Comes to Town" and #1 C. 10-2000 "You Shouldn't Kiss Me Like This," #32+, 12-2000, followed by #1C and #26 HOT 100, 2-2002 "My List." **Keith Urban** launched #37, 12-2000, and #1 C. 9-2000 "But for the Grace of God" (#157 Al. 11-2000 *Keith Urban*). Others? **Phil Vassar**'s #14 "Just Another Day in Paradise" C., 7-2000 (see Phil Collins); **Lee Ann Womack**'s #45 "Ashes By Now" 12-2000 (#4 C); **Chad Brock**'s #1 C. 2-2000 "Yes!"; and **Jamie O'Neal**'s #1, 9-2000 C. #40, 12-2000 and #1 C. "There Is No Arizona." **Faron Young** hit #12, 4-61 and #1(9) C with "Hello Walls" – unlike **Jim Reeves**' silent claustrophobic #1(8) C "Four Walls" of 4-57.

"Young Love" – Sonny James, #1(1), 12-56; #1(9) C. With its strolling Streetcorner-style (C – Am – F – G7) chord progression, "Young Love" is as sweet as a Milky Way bar. Hackleburg, Alabama's (b. '29) 'Southern Gentleman' created a simple tale of young teenage true love. Though all love falls short of his ideal, Sonny sets the sweet standard. Reminds you of #6, 11-56 "Rose and a Baby Ruth," a similarly teenage ballad from North Carolina's **George Hamilton IV**. "Young Love" was covered by cover-boy actor Tab Hunter's #1(6), 1-57 decent version. Sonny's illustrious Country career posted the ninth-most #1's, and 6th-best (Whitburn '94) for most weeks at #1 – 66 total. In 1967-71, Sonny avenged Tab's purloined hit, covering every major Soft Rock song in the universe for 16 consecutive #1 C. hits. The 'James Gang' of Crossover Classics?

ORIGINAL	SONNY SIDE UP
"I'll Never Find Another You" **Seekers**, #4, 3-65	#97, 7-67; #1(4), 6-67 C
"Born to Be With You" **Chordettes**, #5, 6-56	#81, 11-68; #1(1), 10-68 C
"Only the Lonely" **Roy Orbison**, #2(1), 6-60	#92, 2-69; #1(3), 1-69 C
"Bright Lights, Big City" **Jimmy Reed**, #58, 9-61	#91, 7-71; #1(1), 6-71 C
"Only Love Can Break a Heart" **Gene Pitney**, #2(1), 9-62	NC, '72; #2(2), 1-72 C

"Lookin' Out My Back Door" – Creedence Clearwater Revival, #2(1), 8-70; NC, C. **John Fogerty**'s wild back-porch trip has mystical visions and surreal hallucinations. A whole herd of elephants (of polka-dot hue?), dinosaurs, and giants flipping cartwheels enchants this lad. The non-lyrical 'doot-doot-doo' is the skyhook of Fogerty's fandango fantasy. Though Country music bolted far away from Psychedelia, this song is the closest you'll come to Psychedelic Bluegrass. Like Ringo's Starr's #48, '64 "Act Naturally," this one salutes a Country hero – and "Back Door" calls him by name. During this pictorial splash of mammoths and other magnificent megafauna, Fogerty says he's listening to Buck Owens:

"Rollin' in My Sweet Baby's Arms" – Buck Owens and the Buckaroos, NC, '71; #2(2), 9-71 C. Born Alvis (not Elvis) Owens (Sherman, Texas '29), Buck drifted Arizonally to Mesa, and formed the semi-'Outlaw' Bakersfield Sound. Sax trumpet-player **Buck**'s "Love's Gonna Live Here" (NC, '63) hit #1(16), 9-63 C. Great session folks like Buck often become later big stars. He paid his studio dues for **Faron Young**, Rockabilly tornado **Wanda Jackson**, and **Sonny James**. Owens' likeable winning smile and self-deprecating cornpone humor teamed him with banjo maestro **Roy Clark**, on Country's foremost syndicated marathon show, *Hee-Haw*. Tenaciously clinging to his 1959 blond crew-cut in shaggy 1972, Buck hosted Country Vaudeville, supermodel back-up singers and dancers, and family Heartland humor.

From first monster hit #4 C "Under Your Spell Again" of 10-59, his #2(8) C, 1-61 "Foolin' Around" showed he wasn't – in hitting the chart pinnacle. **Ray Charles** covered two Buck-penned hits for R & B & HOT 100 Crossover smashes – #6, 12-65 "Crying Time" (#5, R & B), and Buck's #1(2) C, 4-64 "Together Again" to #19, 3-66 (#10 R & B). Buck's #25, 1-65 "I've Got a Tiger by the Tail" scratched cattily to #1(5) C., and Buck's own version of the **Beatles**' "Act Naturally" hit #1(3), in 4-63 (C), the year before Ringo.

Buck's ultra-marathon career jolts with Country Rock splendor: his **Chuck Berry** "Maybellene" hit #1(2), 5-69 C; his #9, 3-74 C "On the Cover of the Music City News," a parody of Dr. Hook's comic ego-trip #6, 12-72 "The Cover of 'Rolling Stone'"; and his any #6, 7-74 C. "(It's a) Monster's Holiday." Buck sang serious stuff, too, like #9, 2-71 "Bridge over Troubled Water," Simon/Gar's #1 '70 ballad/hymn (catch **Aretha Franklin's** Soul cover at #6, 4-71 & #1 R & B). Did Buck ever pique the City vs. Country family feud? Yup. He had the nerve to cut #9, 11-70 "I Wouldn't Live in New York (If They Gave Me the Whole Danged Town)" – #000 in the Big Apple.

"Streets of Bakersfield" – Dwight Yoakum and Buck Owens, NC, '88; #1(1), 7-88 C. The Country music family drifts from generation to generation – with the older stars helping out the new. Jimmie Rodgers I's widow sponsors Webb Pierce. Faron Young backs Pierce; Buck apprentices Faron Young session; Buck boosts Dwight's career to first #1 C. tune, after Dwight hits #7, 4-87 C. on Elvis's #5, 8-61 "Little Sister." All this stuff interconnects. It's a Harmonic Blanket, not a tangled skein of solo threads. Millennially, Dwight's approach to tekkie chic is his 7-2000 C. album *Dwightyoakumacoustic.net*. He synthesises the ACOUSTIC sound with the computer. Yoakum, Ol' Buck, and Johnny B. Goode. A kid, a guitar, and a dream. Three chords and a cloud of dust.

"One More Day" – Diamond Rio, #36+, 1-2001; #1, 10-2000 C. Diamond Rio's Marty Roe, singer, and Jimmy Olander, (not Marty Olander), guitar, sparked the group to a debut oddity – #1 C. "Meet in the Middle." They, too, swooped the HOT 100 charts as brightest Diamonds since "Little Darlin'," #2(8) '57 for the **Diamonds** – their #36, 12-98 "Unbelievable" was tied by "One More Day" on 3-10-2001. **Joe Diffie** almost became (#1 C, '95) "Bigger Than the Beatles." With 32 1990-99 Country hits, he got a start.

"The Girl from Yesterday" – Eagles, NC, '94; #58, 11-94 C. Motown Eagles' Glenn Frey never flew too far from Country Rock (#12, '72 "Take It Easy"). Stunningly pure ballad melody. America's 70's Beatles the Eagles also hit #8, 10-75 C, with #2(2), 9-75 "Lyin' Eyes."

"I Hate You" – Ronnie Milsap, NC, '73; #10, 6-73. Start off with a feisty, zingy, in-yer-face title the exact opposite of what you expect. Ronnie joined a select superstar coterie of unsighted superstar musicians: Ray Charles, Al Hibbler, George Shearing, Stevie Wonder, Jose Feliciano. Ronnie's #44, 7-2000 *Country Album 40 #1 Hits* puts him on Twitty turf. Among his souvenirs? #5, 6-81 Country Soul-style "There's No Getting' Over Me" (#1 C), #16, 6-77 "It Was Almost Like a Song" (#1 C); #20, 10-81 "I Wouldn't Have Missed It for the World" (#1 C), and Joe Henderson's #8, '62 R & B "Snap Your Fingers" to #1 C. 5-87. Perhaps Ronnie's (b. Robbinsville, NC, '46) sweetest images come from his superbly titled (and sung) #24, 11-80 "Smoky Mountain Rain" (#1 C).

"Crying" – Roy Orbison and k.d. lang, NC, '87; #42, 12-87 C. [#2, '61, Roy solo]. A year before his abrupt passing, Roy employed his supernatural voice for one more curtain call. His BIG VOICE never failed the man that ELVIS called the greatest singer of them all. Ms. Lang hung onto the Texan tornado for dear life. Her side of the song shows Roy's is not the only otherworldly voice to wing its wondrous way across the High Plains in lonesome snowswirl splendor. Roy's #9, 2-89 "You Got It" hit #7 Country, and "California Blue" (NC, '89) spun to #51 C, 6-89. In March 2001, Roy's Al. 16 Biggest Hits climbed to #17 Country Album Charts, half a year after its release; his appeal is unforgettable and timeless. Canadian **k.d. lang** hit #38, 9-92 with "Constant Craving." She hits a note, and chorus reverberates back an eighth note later.

"Uneasy Rider" – Charlie Daniels Band, #9, 6-73; #67, 8-73 C. COUNTRY RAP? Hilarious COUNTRY RAP tale of '73 longhaired kid in short-hair good ol' boy era. Kid tucks hair under baseball cap to phone for roadside help from roughhouse roadhouse. Local hotshots hostile to *Easy Rider* 'hippie' lifestyle hassle him. Culture clash. Tooth sandwich imminent, kid attacks first – kicks guy with green teeth in the knee, tells story about his victim's secret radical life to amazed cronies, and hotfoots it outa there with Dew Drop Inn exploding in pandemonium. With Waylon/Willie and fiddlemeister Charlie Daniels (b. '36, NC), Country troubadours grew long hair and beards in

70s. Southern fashions paved the way for Presidents Carter and Clinton – George W. Bush shares his dad's **Reba McEntire** fandom, but HIS favorite singer is **Buddy Holly**, whose Country Rock masterpieces like "Oh Boy" NEVER hit the Country charts.

"Rhythm of the Rain" – Cascades, #3, 1-63; #7, 2-63, R & B. Nothing is ever as it seems. **John Gummoe**'s seemingly Italian-American, seemingly Seattle-cloudy song comes from a San Diego, California, sunny crew of W.A.S.P. guys like David(s) Wilson and Snyder. On a scale of 1 to 10 for gorgeous melodies with V7-IV-IIIm-IIm-I chord shifts, this rainy one gets an 11.

"Rockin' with the Rhythm of the Rain" – Judds, NC, '84; #1(1), 4-84 C. Mom **Naomi** (b. '46, Ashland, Kentucky) and daughter **Wynonna** (b. Christina Ciminella, '64) dotted the Top One position, with 14 of 16 releases hitting #1. And Wynonna, in a W.A.S.P. and Scotch-Irish musical genre, really IS half-Italian-American, unlike the rainless San Diego Cascades. "Mama, He's Crazy" rocked the rain to #1(1), 4-84, followed by #1 C, 10-84 "Why Not Me," #1 C. "Girls Night Out," and #1, 1-88 C. "Turn It Loose." Their 4-2000 *Number One Hits* rode at #23 in March 2001 on the Country Album Chart, an enduring testimonial.

"Like the Rain" – Clint Black, NC, '96; #1(1), 11-96 C. With his own rugged Roy Rogers howdy smile (but a BLACK cowboy hat, for his NAME), Clint hails from the Far West (for Long Islanders, anyhow) – Long Branch, New Jersey. His Houston construction job rendered a more authentic Country star address. The 1990 CMA Vocalist of Year trumped his Wynonna hit with #31, 10-99 "When I Said I Do" with Lisa Hartman Black. Clint cruised with #1 C, 3-94 "A Good Run of Bad Luck"; #1(3), 4-95 C. "Summer's Comin'"; #1(2), 1-93 C. "When My Ship Comes In," and #1(2), 3-90 "Walkin' Away."

"Sleeping Single in a Double Bed" – Barbara Mandrell, NC, 1978; #1(3), 9-78 C. Despite her Barbie face and beautiful figure, Houston's Barbara (b. '48) is a virtuoso on everything – steel guitar, sax, banjo, bass, maybe Sousaphone and steam calliope. Her "Surfer Girl" beauty complemented her time in Oceanside, California. The Mandrells blossomed – kid sis **Louise** (b. '54, Corpus Christi, Texas), too: #5, 8-85 C. "I Wanna Say Yes." Barbara's biggest is #31, 3-79 (#1 C) reprise of Luther Ingram's Soul extravaganza, "If Loving You Is Wrong (I Don't Want to Be Right)" – at #3, 6-72 for Luther (#1[4] R & B). Also Barbara's #1 C. tunes lit up the charts: 12-79 "Years," and super-titled **George Jones** duo "I Was Country When Country Wasn't Cool." Bad 1984 accident – the Lord (and seatbelts) helped her brave bounce-back to #5, 8-88 "I Wish I Could Fall in Love Today."

"Daddy's Hands" – Holly Dunn, NC, '86; #7, 8-86 C. Notch this sentimental masterpiece under Songs That Could Make a Turnip Cry. San Antonio's (b. '57) Dunn peaked with #1, 9-90 C. "You Really Had Me Going," but "Daddy's Hands" sings respectfully of her aging dad's toilworn hands. She muses the bleakness of his far fu-

ture. Her heart swells with poignant love.

    Johnny Cash's #42, 12-68 "Daddy Sang Bass" (#1[6] C) is a reverie drifting back to family singalongs. He ponders the reunion of his dear old family circle somewhere over the rainbow in the faraway sky.

"Slow Motion" – Malchak and Rucker, NC, 1986; #64, 8-86 C. For Afro-Slavic-American Country fams, we include this dynamic duo. Caucasian half Tim Malchak's "Colorado Moon" hit #37 C. 3-87; Dwight Rucker of NY is probably not related to **Hootie & the Blowfish**'s lead singer **Darius Rucker.**

    Here are a few other Country stars well worth mentioning: **Sheb Wooley** (b. '21) of #1(6), 6-58 "Purple People Eater" novelty-song fame, hit #51, 1-61 #1 C "That's My Pa." **Razzy Bailey** hit 4 #1 C songs, like 3-81 "Friends." The **Wilburn Brothers** scored #3 C, 11-66 "Hurt Her Once for Me" and 30 other C. hits. **Randy Barlow** had four straight top tens and NEVER hit single digits – like #10, 4-79 "Sweet Melinda." **Freddy Weller**'s Country Rock [**Chuck Berry**'s "Promised Land," to #3, 12-70 C] even did Bubble Gum – #3, 6-71 C "Indian Lake" (Cowsills, #10). **Johnny Bond** sang #7 C., 8-51 "Sick, Sober, and Sorry." **Gene Watson's** #1(1) C. 10-81 "Fourteen Carat Mind" hit big, like **T. Graham Brown**'s #1, 1-87 C "Don't Go to Strangers." **Billy Walker** charted 65 C songs (b. '29, TX), like #1(2), 3-62 "Charlie's Shoes." The **Carlisles** had 6 top tens, like #1(4), C, 1-54 "No Help Wanted." **Lionel Cartwright**? #1, 7-91 C "Leap of Faith." **Joe Stampley**'s 62 C. hits include #1(1), 11-72 "Soul Song" and reprise of **Swingin' Medallions**' party-animal Frat Rock stud rouser, #17, 4-66 "Double Shot (Of My Baby's Love)" to #8 C, 10-83. LA trio **Dave & Sugar** stormed apex with #1(3), 1-79 "Golden Tears." **Red Sovine's** #9 C. "Phantom 309" (#47 C, '75 too) is a Graveyard Trucker Ghost Story from 7-67. **Al Dexter** smoked the debut 'Hillbilly Hit Parade' with #1(13) C, 3-44 "So Long Pal," #1(16), 2-46 "Guitar Polka," and #1(3), 1-44 "Pistol Packin' Mama." **Roy Drusky**'s (b. '30) #5, 5-70 C. "Long, Long Texas Road" typified his 42 strong Country hits; **Connie Smith**'s 48 C. hits include #1(8) '64 "Once a Day" and #2(2), 5-71 "Just One Time." **T.G. Sheppard** (b. '42, Alamo, TN) had eight straight #1's in 1980-82, like 4-82 "Finally" and 7-81 "Party Time." **Jean Shepard** (diff. spelling) is best known for her #1(6), 7-53 "Dear John Letter" (#4, 9-53 Top 30). **Johnny Duncan?** #1(1), 3-78 "She Can Put Her Shoes Under My Bed (Anytime)." **Shenandoah**'s #1(2), 1-89 "The Church on Cumberland Road" led off a big hit string.

    Anne Murray (b. '45 Nova Scotia) is a superstar in several venues from Easy Listening to Folk to Soft Rock to Country – where her charted hits continue – plus her March 2001 #8 Top Contemporary Christian album *What a Wonderful World*. Anne's big Country chart #'s include #1, 4-84 "Just Another Woman in Love" and #1(1) C. "Now and Forever (You and Me)" 1-86. Crossover crew **Exile** had 10 #1's in 1983-87 zone, like #1(1), 7-86 "It'll Be Me." From Lookout Mountain, Georgia, come the **Forester Sisters,** with 5 #1's like #1(1), 6-87 C. "You Again." Country Rocker **Janie Fricke** bounced a great Tex-Mex groove off her signature #1(1) C. 5-83 "He's a Heartache (Looking for a Place to Happen)." **Righteous Brother** baritone **Bill Medley** (b. '40, Santa Ana, California) has 6 C. hits, like #17, 4-84 "I Still Do." **Ronnie McDowell**'s 27 hits include #1(1) C. 6-83 "You're Gonna Ruin My Bad Reputation" and his Boomer market #1(1), 6-81 C. "Older Women." **The Gatlin Brothers** of Texas spanked the charts with 42 1973-90 hits like #65 C., 8-90 "Boogie and Beethoven" and #2(2), 4-78 C. "Night Time Magic." **Mel McDaniel** caps his successful career with #1(1) C, 11-84 "Baby's Got Her Blue Jeans On." **Vern Gosdin**'s (b. '34) "Set 'Em Up, Joe" hit #1, 4-88 (#1 C at 53 years old, w/ 1st #1 at 49). Famale star **Charly McClain**'s Lucky 13 Top Ten tunes include #1 C, 2-85 "Radio Heart." **Shelby Lynne** of Quantico, VA. hit the 2001 Grammy jackpot after ten years toiling to become an overnight sensation with Country torch tunes like "Things Are Tough All Over," #23, C., 10-90. **Claude King's** huge "Wolverton Mountain" hit #6, '62, and #1(9), 5-62: the true story concerns actual **Clifton Clowers**, writes Whitburn. Clowers, KING himself of this Arkansas mountain, was a sharpshooter who lived to age 102 (d. '94); King's second-string superest song was #6, 6-65 C. "Tiger Woman." Greenwich, New York's **Hal Ketchum** blasted 90s+ with microcosmic Country hits like #2(1), 5-91 C. "Small Town Saturday Night." **Bobby Helms's** "Jingle Bell Rock" is on the Oldies Overkill Saturation List, but his #1(4) C 3-57 and #36, 7-57 HOT 100 debut "Fraulein" paved the way for this and his melodic #1(4) C and #7, 10-57 "My Special Angel" for the SOUTHERN Indiana belltone tenor. **Billy Grammer**'s "Gotta Travel On" #4, 11-58, hit #5 C. **Earl Thomas Conley** hit #1(1) C, 2-86 with "Once in a Blue Moon." With 16 #1 C. songs, Portsmouth, Ohio's Conley first hit at age 34 in '75 – #1's C. 5-84 "Angel in Disguise"; and 9-83 "Holding Her Hand and Loving You."

"Drive South" – **Suzy Bogguss, NC, '92; #2(1), 12-92 C.** At Illinois State, Suzy earned a degree in metalsmithery, but swapped Heavy Metal fleeting thought for Country. **Steve Earle**'s "Guitar Town" (#7, 6-86 C) reflects Fort Monroe, VA (b. '55). He later hung out with **Nirvana**'s **Kurt Cobain**; Steve's penultimate hit is #8, 2-87 C "Goodbyes All We've Got Left."

"Have I Told You Lately That I Love You" – **Gene Autry, NC, '46; #3, 10-46 C.** **Gene Autry** (1907-98), a singin' cowboy who graced the silver screen, invested his sizable fortune in the California Angels baseball team. Not as gung-ho a yodeler as Roy Rogers, Autry is a tremendous ambassador of Western Swing, like Bob Wills. **Ricky Nelson** (1940-85, killed riding Jerry Lee Lewis's ex-plane) hit #3 C with '58 #1 "Poor Little Fool." His #29 (NC, C) "Have I Told You Lately That I Love You" I learned for my mom. It sports country flair for the Hollywood Rockabilly. Bing Crosby/Andrews Sisters hit #24, 1-50 with it, too. Pretty melody & reminder. **Everly Brothers** hit #50, 9-84 and #49 C with **Paul McCartney**-penned "On the Wings of a Nightingale." The Everlys BEGAN in Nashville with Columbia, before Cadence vaulted them to 1st-year Rock Hall 1986 Induction. No strangers to Country charts: #1(7) C. "Bye Bye Love" 5-57; #1(8) "Wake Up, Little Susie" 9-57' #1(6) C. 6-58 "Bird Dog."

"Kiss You All Over" – **Exile, #1(4), 7-78; NC, C.** Smooch study guide. Lead singer **J.P. Pennington** and Lexington, Kentucky, band shifted to Country with ten big #1 C. songs like 12-84 "Crazy for Your Love" and 8-84 "Give Me One More Chance." Paul Martin took over at lead throat in 1989 with #2, 4-90 C. "Nobody's Talking." **Razzy Bailey** (b. '39, Alabama) hit with #67 HOT 100-only "I Hate Hate," and lobbed 4 #1 hits into Life-Begins-at-40 Zone, a princely perk of Country Music, like #1C's 7-81 "Midnight Hauler" and 8-80 "Loving Up a Storm."

Moe Bandy (b. '44, Meridian, Mississippi) busted broncs in a rodeo: #7 C, 6-75 "Bandy, the Rodeo Clown." His baritone Hank Williamsish salute goes out to his mentor, and everyone else in Country: #2(2), C "Hank Williams, You Wrote My Life." Let's bandy about more hits: #9, 6-79 C "Barstool Mountain"; #1 C, 10-79 "I Cheated Me Right out of You," #10 C. 10-81 "Rodeo Romeo," and #6 profound title – 2-87 "Till I'm Too Old to Die Young."

"Little Rock" – **Reba McEntire, NC, '86; #1(1), 6-86 C.** Not only was Reba's the Prez's dad's favorite singer (Geo. Bush I), but she is actually a cowpoke rodeo rider, too. In local rodeos, she competed as a horseback barrel rider. Rodeo broncos lack seatbelts, and wimps and wimpettes need not apply. At age 43, brother Pake McEntire rode with #3 C, 5-86 "Savin' My Love for You." Born on a Chockie, Oklahoma ranch (3-38-54), Reba starred in the 2001 Broadway show *Annie Get Your Gun*, a rootin' tootin' Wild West lead part for the cowgirl with the spunky style.

Great Country classics hinge upon a deft turn of flamboyant phrase, a ginchy pun, a gonzo example. 'Little Rock," all gemologist geographers know, is both the capital of Arkansas (President Bill Clinton), and Reba's wedding ring. The song swashbuckles a stormy beat. Her thick luscious hair blazes the klieg light glow from bonfire orange to primrose persimmon.

"Why Haven't I Heard from You" – **Reba McEntire, #101, 5-94, and #50S [Sales]; #5 C.** Mid-decade spawned many Reba hits: #1(1) C, Carson McCullers novel allusion, 3-95, "The Heart Is a Lonely Hunter," #2, 5-95 C, "And Still," plus #9, 11-85 C, "Ring on Her Finger, Time on Her Hands." "Why Haven't" is Reba at her dynamo peak. She chides, she scolds, she teases, she coaxes, she pouts, she pleads. Her zillion fans need no hard sell. Her 1st #1 is 10-82 C. "Can't Even Get the Blues," bucking the system for 5 ½ years from her risque debut #88, C, 5-76 "I Don't Want to Be Just a One-Night Stand." Remakes she starred in— #13 C, 11-81 Platters' (#5, '55) "Only You," and the Everlys' #1(5) '60 "Cathy's Clown" to #1(1), 5-89. Or even Alien Country Rock—#1(2), 1-92 C. "Is There Life Out There?" Her #31, 10-99 (#1 C) "What Do You Say" is her hottest HOT 100 hit, like her Al. #28, 12-99 *So Good Together*.

"Walkin', Talkin', Cryin', Barely Beating Broken Heart" – **Highway 101, NC, '90; #4, 2-90 C.** Formed in L.A., near actual California Highway 101, which skirts the savage Pacific Ocean surf. Paulette Carlson sings lead and plays guitar, with son Curtis singing harmony. After 1988-89 CMA Vocal Group of Year Awards, they launched #1(1), C. 2-88 remake of Johnny Cash's #14 C. 11-55 "Cry, Cry, Cry." Plus #6 C, 6-89 "Honky Tonk Heart." They show the spirit of **Bob Gallion** (b. '31) and his upbeat "Wall to Wall Love" (#5, 11-62 C). Bashes ALL 1-2-3-4 beats, like Stonewall Jackson's #4, "9 "Waterloo" and much, much later, like DISCO.

"Alabama Getaway" – Grateful Dead, #68, 6-80; NC, C. Nomadic troupe's 3rd-biggest single uses a Southern theme. Also, Dead's #91 "Sugar Magnolia" sure doesn't grow too well in North Dakota. Check out **Jerry Garcia's** solo #94, 4-72 "Sugaree," too. Jerry tantalized his Deadhead throngs with surrealistic Bop-Rock solos, and basic Tex-Mex Buddy Holly vocals (#9, '87 "Touch of Grey"). Zingy Dixie Dead.

"All the Gold in California" – Gatlin Brothers, NC, '79; #1(2), 8-79 C. Like the Oak Ridge Boys, Alabama, or the Statler Brothers, the Gatlins toast the Barber-Shop Quartet tradition (see Backstreet Boys, Miracles, N'Sync). Born from 1948-52, Larry, Steve, and Rudy Gatlin started as a Gospel Trio and wrote songs for Elvis. In West Texas, they hit with "Houston (Means I'm One Day Closer to You)" at #1(2) C, in 9-83, so they took off for "Denver" – #7, 3-84 C. In 3-88, after #4 C, 12-86 "Talkin' to the Moon," they found the #4 C "Love of a Lifetime."

Janie Fricke hit #1(1), 5-83 with "He's a Heartache (Looking for a Place to Happen)." Country #1's? "It Ain't Always Been Easy," 9-82; 6-86 "Always Have, Always Will."

"High and Lonesome" – Jimmy Reed, NC, 1954. This title by the #2 Delta Bluesman after B.B. King symbolizes the masterworks of both Hank Williams and Bill Monroe. Embedded within their three divergent styles of genius is this mysterious mystique – a keening, throbbing wail that shimmers over Scots-Irish moors and African mountains. It's a sense of suffering and glory and splendor and sadness. Reed's harmonica soars the wild woebegone earthly fray, sad and shimmering and high and lonesome.

"Big Boss Man" – Jimmy Reed, #78, 5-61; #13 R & B; NC, C. Great Blues legend **James Mathis Reed** (1925-76), sings sultry Southern Soul with a Country twang. Raised in drowsy Dunleith, Mississippi, on the cottonly Delta bottomlands, Reed had more charted hits than any other Delta Blues star **except B.B. King**. His song's sentiments reflect the fires of resentment and revenge stoked by wage slavery. This plug-ugly boss, Jimmy rationalizes, isn't really that BIG (Jimmy was 5'9" or so), just tall. Catch the same anti-boss hostility in **Johnny Paycheck**'s "Take This Job and Shove It" (#1(2), 11-77 C). Or Tennessee Ernie Ford's lash-out reaction to the "16 Tons" straw-boss. "Big Boss Man" reflects **Johnny Cash's** wry #2(2) 8-72 (#101, HOT 101) – "Oney." Their message? If the boss gives you Respect, you'll absorb the small indignities. If he's a lowdown insensitive jerk, the worker may wallow in fury and anger and bitterness. Nobody wants to work for a slavedriver. **Elvis**'s version

of "Big Boss Man" hit #38, 10-67 C.

Jimmy Reed wasn't a bitter guy. Easygoing and friendly, he drifted from Dunleith to **Jackson V**'s Gary, Indiana. By day he stoked forges – by night he played guitar in jivin' juke joints to the neon halo south of the Chicago skyline. Reed fashioned a weird gizmo to hold his harmonica in place while he strummed . He hung out on streetcorners, and even got busted for busking (singing for money), when 'Chicago's Finest' were hard up for real crimes to prevent. For four inglorious years, 1949-53, Reed juggled street concerts, and toiled in hot factories. He worked nights with his little combo with Joe (Jody) Duncan, Eddie Taylor, and Morris Wilkerson (see Blues).

"Big Boss Man" – Charlie Rich, #108, 11-63. Called the 'Silver Fox' for his hair which was mostly white at 39, Rich of Colt, Arkansas (1932-95) was already a star in the same ball park as Elvis or Carl Perkins. One of the best Rockabilly SINGERS ever, Charlie's Jazz phrasing and slur-and-glide macho tenor triumphs matched his Jerry Lee Lewis' piano Boogie style. His first big hit was rollicking #22, 3-60 "Lonely Weekends." His internecine #21, 8-65 "Mohair Sam" kept up the Elvis aura. After an Air Force Jazz group in 1954, and Sam Phillips' Sun studios in 1958, the 'Silver Fox' showed his best chops with Jimmy Reed's anti-overseer anthem. Rich was a white man with the musical Soul of a vintage Delta Blues star. #1(2), 9-73 "The Most Beautiful Girl" (#1 C, too), followed by #18, 1-74 (#1 C) "There Won't Be Anymore."

His most pensive tune? #1(2) C "Rollin' with the Flow." This good-ol-boy apologia for his angel stokes the homefires while he's at the honkytonk. This testimonial to surviving to ancient age of 30 is buttressed by wifey on the Angel Pedestal. It chafes at current Daddying philosophy, but recollects the changing 70s vividly. The wife, like **Donna Fargo** (#11, 5-72; #1[3] C), may be "The Happiest Girl in the Whole U.S.A." She oughta be – if big homes are her bag. Donna (b. '49, NC), scuttlebutt tells us, has a home in Tennessee the size of a K-Mart.

Rock and Roll Rebounders and Country Crossover Stars from the dawn of Rock include **Charlie Rich**, **Johnny Cash**, **Marty Robbins**, and **Billy 'Crash' Craddock**, who covered the **Drifters/Dion**'s "Ruby Baby" to #1 C and #33, 11-74, plus #16, 6-74 "Rub It In" (#16). Many former Rock stars saw their spotlights fade off center stage – and rebounded into the older family of Country Music. Examples? **Jerry Lee Lewis, Ricky Nelson, Bill Medley, Tom Jones, Tommy Roe** ("Let's Be Fools like That Again," #38 C, 12-86), **Billy Joe Royal** (Aaron Neville's #2, '66 "Tell It Like it is" to #2[2] C., 2-89), **Mac Davis, Vince Gill/Pure Prairie League, Kenny Rogers, Conway Twitty, Johnny Tillotson, Leon Russell, Linda Ronstadt, Bob Luman, Glen Campbell,** and **Bobby Bare.**

"She's in Love with the Boy" – Trisha Yearwood, NC, '91; #1(2), 5-91 C. Grumbling papa says the boy his princess loves is a no-good galoot and good-time Charlie with no prospects whatever. The wise mama reminds her couch potato hubby that he, too, had a similar future when met HER papa, who felt HE was a shiftless brutish oaf, too. It all comes down to LOVE – main ingredient of most beautiful music. Trisha and **Eagle Don Henley** hit #2(1), C with "Walkaway Joe," and she hit #23 HOT 100 with 6-97 self-penned "How Do I Live" [#2(4) LeAnn Rimes]. Trisha's 1995 double-whammy? "XXX's and OOO's (An American Girl)," and "Thinkin' About You." She reprised **Patsy Cline**'s "I Fall to Pieces" to #72, 6-94 C, with Soul star **Aaron Neville**.

"Smoke! Smoke! Smoke (That Cigarette)" – Tex Williams, #1(6), 7-47; #1(16) C. Capitol Records' 1st million-seller of ANY genre. The 1947 Camel ad spawned dangerous mixed messages: "More doctors smoke Camels than any other cigarette." Before the 1964 Surgeon General's report, cigs were only suspected of lung cancer, heart disease, or emphysema. My dad quit a hundred times a year (lived to 60), and my 88-year-old mom still smoked until two weeks before she passed away. Tex lived a long smoker's life (1917-85, 72, b. Illinois), until felled by lung cancer. His hilarious lyric has hyper dude groaning for another cig. After he dies, he conjures the audacity to to suggest that St. Peter must WAIT for him at the Golden Gate – just so he can puff one more cigarette. Cig fans galore guffawed at Tex's celestial nerve. Tex also scored with #4 C, 11-46 "The California Polka."

"Flowers on the Wall" – Statler Brothers, #4, 11-65; #2(4), 9-65 C. Jilted guy fakes indifference to lost girlfriend. His funtime activities include counting wall flowers in wallpapers, puffing constant cigs, and watching kiddie show *Captain Kangaroo* (Bob Keeshan); **Eric Heatherly** hit #50, 3-2000 and #6 C. with his reprise of Stats' classic. Statler Brothers named themselves after the Statler Hotel in Detroit. The quartet has one set of brothers: bass and contra-bass **Harold Reid** (b. '39), countertenor **Jimmy Fortune**, who replaced **Lew DeWitt** (1938-90, Crohn's disease), lead singer **Don Reid** (b. '45), and **Phil Balsley**, (b. '39). Though Phil is listed as a baritone, which he is, both he and Don zigzag comfortably from high baritone to low tenor.

The Statlers got their big break backing up **Johnny Cash**, like Elvis's Jordanaires. Among the most enduring and beloved Barber-Shop Quartets in popular music history. Their TNN Saturday night variety showcases their heavenly harmony. The song's high point? When Don's trusty baritone pauses an insta-second between 'Captain' and 'Kangaroo,' big booming foghorn-strong bass **Harold** hits the big note first way down below, octavely, down in the bottom of the well. Lew DeWitt's whimsical "Flowers" is a big rationalization. The spurned lover alibis to himself that he'd have FUN twiddling his time – counting wallpaper flowers – while SHE grapples with her conscience in asking HIM how he's doing now they've split. Fun sad song.

"Class of '57" – Statler Brothers, NC, '72; #6, 8-72 C. In the 1890s and 1990s-2000s, Barber-Shop Quartets ruled the Sidewalks of New York. The Statlers and the in-sync **Backstreet Boys** (& N'Sync) ruled Virginia, Orlando, Florida, and the world. From flower-bell morning-glory Victrolas to portable CD players, high school classmates have seen a lot of dreams come and go. "Class of '57 is two songs. One, a bittersweet tale with one-liners about how everybody at the 25-year H.S. reunion turned out . . . Two, it's a cryptic and deep mysterious onrush into time's darkest mysteries (with a bonus Streetcorner chord pattern):

Peggy is organist in the Presbyterian church now. Others sell Tupperware, go on welfare, do lab research, squirm in deep debt, disappear, swap wives and identities, and fritter away their only lives. It's a sweet thunderclap of reality about the awesome swift passage of Demon Time. Heady chunk of heartfelt nostalgia. Cosmic comic tale. Currier & Ives America. Life becomes really complicated, they muse, when you dart past age 18 . . . . Amen.

Stats hit #37, 11-66 C on third release, **Buddy Holly**'s "That'll Be the Day."

"Whatever Happened to Randolph Scott?" – Statler Brothers, NC, 1974; #22, 1-74 C. Scott was a silver-screen cowboy hero. Stats lament loss of trad American family values, in aftermath of new cinematic explosion of erotic exploitation. Or grotesque Sam Peckinpah Quentin Tarantino *Pulp Fiction* bloodbaths. Don confesses his bewilderment about fancy sub-plots and symbolism. You must drag your analyst along, he chortles, to unravel demented plots at the multiplex flix. Song's super punch line? He remarks about **John Wayne**'s Oscar performance as Sheriff Rooster Cogburn: *True Grit* [****], he admits, is the only flick he's truly understood in many years. Everything got so convoluted, so surreal, so antiheroish, so wildly warped, that the good guy WAS the bad guy. The antihero didn't RESCUE the pretty blonde in the gingham dress – he STALKED her . . . (i.E. *The Shining*).

"I Get So Lonely (When I Dream About You)" – Four Knights, #2(1), 1-54. Bubbly Barber-Shop number, anchored by bass guy Oscar Broadway. Tailor-made for Stats. As "Oh Baby Mine (I Get So Lonely)," the **Statlers** took this selfsame song to #2(1) C, 4-83. Harold burbles the OH BABY MINE line with style and grace.

The Stats' stats rack up covers and originals: their #3 C, 4-85 "Hello Mary Lou" was written by **Gene Pitney** as **Ricky Nelson**'s fab flipside (#9, '61) to romeo rocker #1, 4-61 "Travelin' Man." As 1972-77 CMA Vocal Group of Year, Stats cashed in, later hitting with #3, 4-84 C. "Atlanta Blue," #1 C, 8-85 "Too Much on My Heart," and #6, 5-89 C "More Than a Name on a Wall." Biggest hit ? #1(2) C, 3-78 "Do You Know You Are My Sunshine." Original "You Are My Sunshine" is by Gov. **Jimmie Davis** [1899-2000!] for cowboy stars **Gene Autry** (#23, '41) and Wayne King (#20, '41), plus **Bing Crosby**'s Pop cover to #19. "Sunshine" is the name of the Statler game. Purveyors of prime-time family sunshine, their swaying silken songs shine the best of the Northern Sunny South. They literally bought their boyhood school when it went out of business in Staunton,Virginia, and sang #1 C., 12-83 "Elizabeth"(my mother Elizabeth Maury Dean's parents came from nearby Charlottesville, VA).

"Oh, Lonesome Me" – Don Gibson, #7, 3-58; #1(8), 2-58 C. Opry's Shelby, NC (b. '28) Gibson is among major Rockabilly superchargers of Country Rock – like #21, 6-61 (#2 C) "Sea of Heartbreak," with snarly bass and rockin' rim-shot drums. Or #20, 6-58 #1[2] C. "Blue Blue Day." Or #1(1) C, 6-72 hot-stuff "Woman (Sensuous Woman)," inspired by best-seller book. Or his **Ray Charles**-hit-genesis #81 (#7, 3-58 C) "I Can't Stop Loving You" [#1(5), Ray '62]. Joel Whitburn's favorite.

"God Bless the USA" – Lee Greenwood, #30S [Sales], 6-91; #16, 9-2002 & #7, 5-84 C. Lee's breathtaking patriotic hymn seeks the Anthem Silver Medal as we speak, or sing. Sacramento's Greenwood (b. '42) won CMA 1983-84 Male Vocalist of Year. Greenwood's belief in the divine mission of American democracy goes out to free peoples everywhere. And those who wish. Greenwood's "Dixie Road" [#15 C, 4-85] also includes #1 C's 11-86 "Mornin' Ride" and #1, 12-83 "Going, Going, Gone."

Speaking of 40s stardom, **K. T. Oslin** (b. '41 Kaye Toinette Oslin, Arkansas) won first #1 C at 46, 1-88 "I'll Always Come Back." "Come Next Monday" [#1(2) C, 9-90, Oslin], Country music could find new instant "Heroes," [#4 C, **Paul Overstreet** of Oklahoma, 3-91 – unrelated to #9, C, 12-74 "I'm a Believer" – **Tommy Overstreet**]. **Eddy Raven** (b. Ed Garvin Futch, '44, Lafayette, LA) hit #1 C at 39 with 3-84 "I Got Mexico" and five other #1's like 6-88 C. "Joe Knows How to Live" #1 C. 8-89 "Bayou Boys." Also #60+ 3-2001 C. "Cowboys Don't Cry." **John Conlee** (b. '46 KY) may be the only former mortician to dig the Country Rock scene: #1(1) C "As Long As I'm Rockin' with You," plus #2(2), 5-80 C. "Friday Night Blues" and #1 C. 3-83 "Common Man."

Byrds' Chris Hillman finally hit big with **Desert Rose Band** in late 80s: #1(1) "I Still Believe in You"; #2(1)'s "Summer Wind" C, 7-88 and 10-87 C "One Step Forward." Impeccable Appalachian thirds harmony from this band from the Deep South [Southern California, which often gets mixed Mason-Dixon Line reviews in Nashville.]

Tracy Lawrence's #1, C "Texas Tornado" thrashed the competition with comeback splendor. Shot four times (fully recovered) in a Nashville botched holdup, Atlanta, TEXAS'S Lawrence (b. '58) dragged out the heavy musical artillery for protection: "Sticks and Stones" #1 C, 11-91. Tracy scored #1 C "My Second Home," and #1 C. "If the Good Die Young" of 2-95. His "Renegades, Rebels, and Rogues" (#7 C, 5-94) wallows in this wayward woozy wellspring of way-out wild alliteration.

"Timber, I'm Falling in Love" – Patty Loveless, NC, '89; #1(1)C. At hunting camp up in Michigan, daredevil Uncle Mickey Quinn would climb a small pine tree, and have one of the guys chop it down. For kicks, he would fearlessly ride it to the ground(and he's survived to 75+).

Patty (b. Pikeville, Kentucky) rides a bronc-buster of a rockin' song here – with Everly harmonies and Holly counterpunch chord progressions and a smashing beat that eluded arrest for speeding. Her cute-theme #3 C, 7-94 "I Try to Think About Elvis" is about this guy whose romantic image prowls with panther stealth into her lovestruck thoughts. She tries to focus on ANYTHING else but this unforgettable guy. Beat throbs a spunky tattoo. Her 2 & 4 beats stomp in slam-bam R & R splendor. Harmony cascades on rainbow waterfalls via overdubbed vivacious vocalizers. Patty's Al. *Strong Heart* surged to #13, 10-2000 on the Country Album charts. "Chains""hit #1, 1-90 C. and #1(2) C. 4-93 "Blame It on Your Heart" hit big, too.

We left **John Berry** "Standin' on the Edge of Goodbye" (#2[1], 3-95 C. My pal Jack Berry (no relation) still plays hockey at 58, but THIS Berry laid down a hat-trick threepeat of top five C. tunes, topped by #1(1) C, 2-94 "Your Love Amazes Me."

"Bop" – Dan Seals, #42, 1-86; #1(1), 10-85 C. After #1 C, **Marie Osmond** duo '85 "Meet Me in Montana," Dan reeled off nine straight C. #1 songs, and 11 of 12. His zigzag path from McCamey, Texas (b. '48) had a lot of talented family: Brady Seals of Little Texas (#4, C., 7-93 "God Blessed Texas"; & brother **Jim Seals (**Seals & Crofts, #6, 9-72 "Summer Breeze"); and cuz **Johnny Duncan** – #4, 7-78 C. "Hello Mexico (And Adios Baby to You)." Duncan's other major hit is #1(2), C 10-76 "Thinkin' of a Rendezvous." Dan Seals run-the-table champ examples? Yep: #1 C, 6-87 "Three-Time Loser," #1 C. 6-88 "They Rage On," and road-warrior truckin' odyssey, #1 C 11-88 "Big Wheels in the Moonlight." Rocker **Bob Seger**'s #2(4), 12-82, and #15, 1-83 C "Shame on the Moon" is his only Country charted hit. It may be the only time anyone from my home town, fiddler-jubilee entrepreneur **Henry Ford**'s Dearborn, Michigan, hit the Country top 15.

"Devil in a Bottle" – T.G. Sheppard, #54, 1-75; #1(1), 11-74 C. The ol' "chicks get more gorgeous at closing time" story. Sheppard (b. Alamo, Tennessee, '42) scored 8 straight #1's (9 of 10), like 7-81 "Party Time," #1(2) C, 8-79 "The Last Cheater's Waltz," and finally "Finally" of 4-82. **Collin Raye** (b. Floyd Wray, '59, Arizona) hit #1(1), 12-94 C. with "My Kind of Girl," and #87, 7-95 (#2 C) "One Boy, One Girl." In March 2001, "You Still Take Me There" took him to #56 C. the first week.

"If Bubba Can Dance (I Can Too)" – Shenandoah, NC, '94; #1(1), 2-94 C. Marty Raybon's gutsy vocals spearheaded this Muscle Shoals, Alabama crew. Mega-hits? #1(3), 6-90 C rocker "Next to You, Next to Me," and #1(2) C "The Church on Cumberland Road" of 1-89, and #1(1) C. 5-89 "Sunday in the South."

Clay Walker zoomed to 2 insta #1's – 93's "What's It to You" and "Live Until I Die." His March 2001 "Say No More" hit rung #50 on its third week up the Country chart ladder. From Big Bopper's Beaumont, Texas, his #2(2), 9-95 "Who Needs You" and #1, 6-94 "Dreaming with My Eyes Open," paved the way to down-home hot lyrical champ tune "Rumor Has It, " #1 C, 6-97.

Oklahoma City's **Bryan White**'s #1(1), 5-95 "Someone Else's Star," and #1 C, 10-95 "Rebecca Lynn," show him to be a master of the grace-note. He represents the hip direction of Country music, as do Kevin Sharp, Trace Adkins, Kenny Chesney, Bill Engvall, Rascal Flatts, Tommy Shane Steiner (#2C, 1-2002), Brad Paisley (#4+C, 3-2002 "I'm Gonna Miss Her [The Fishin' Song]"), #40+ HOT 100, 4-2002 and **Deana Carter** (#1, 4-97 Al. *Did I Shave My Legs for This?*). The **Bellamy Brothers**, Howard and David, rocked up nine #1 C hits in bombshell aftermath of #1(1), 1-76 HOT 100 "Let Your Love Flow."

"Pop a Top" – **Jim Ed Brown**, NC; **#3, 5-67 C.** Sparkman, Arkansas, Jim Ed [NOT JAMES BROWN] Brown (b. '34) sings a simple song of beer and soda pop cans. In '67, they had these annoying aluminum rings folks would thoughtlessly toss on the beach to shred innocent kids' feet later (see "Margaraitaville").

At least aluminum had no rust or lockjaw. By 1970, a new beer can rendered this hit obsolete, maybe. Brown's #71 C., 4-70 "Lift Ring Pull Open" sold fewer, but was environmentally greenwashed and safer. **Alan Jackson**'s "Pop a Top" climbed the 1999 charts.

"The Three Bells" – The Browns, **#1(4), 7-59; #10, 8-59, R & B; #1(10), 8-59 C.** In the shock wave of the 2-3-59 Day the Music Died, elegiac tributes sprouted. Brown apprenticed on Graveyard ballads. Jim Ed sings the story of 'Jimmy Brown's" birth, his little church and congregation, his wedding day, and three verses later his speedy death. A haggard drooling stratus cloud drizzles its forlorn desolation over the whole cosmic parade. Like **Marty Robbins**' #1, 4-59 somber ballad but rapid waltz "El Paso," the song's hero/protagonist laments his OWN death. Creepy harbinger of Ultimate Graveyard Rock (see Mark Dinning, Ray Peterson, Dickey Lee, J. Frank Wilson/Pearl Jam/Puff Daddy). The Browns (including Sisters Bonnie and Ella Maxine) enjoyed many mainstream ballad hits after #8 Country debut back in 8-54, "Looking Back to See." Their woven harmonies embraced songs like Harry Belafonte's/Kingston Trio's first record, Folk Standard "Scarlet Ribbons (for Her Hair)" – Brown's #13, 11-59 (#7 C). Or Sammy Kaye's #1, '46 "The Old Lamplighter," #5 & #20 C, 3-60).

"Time" – Pozo Seco Singers [Don Williams], **#47, 2-66 C.** Big Don Williams' (b. '39 Texas) tragic line here concerns how some people treat him kindly, some badly – but most people just drift in their own direction, and refuse to pay him any mind at all. Ouch – too much truth here. One reason people sing, or play sports, or work hard, or love passionately, is so their lives will matter. The grisly ghost of anonymity stalks us all. "Time" is one of the most important overlooked ballads ever recorded. 'Pozo Seco' means 'dry gulch' in Spanish, like an arroyo.

Lead singer **Don Williams** hit big nationally with his #24, 9-80, #1 C "I Believe in You." He sifts painfully through bitter disbelief and unbelief and doubt, fighting to create his own life's philosophy. He discovers the thing he most believes in is this sweet young lady, probably from fore-

runner #1 C, 4-75 "You're My Best Friend." His 17 American Country #1's pale in comparison to his U.K. rep. Don was voted Country Star of the Decade (1980-1990) in England.

"All My Rowdy Friends Are Comin' Over Tonight" – **Hank Williams Jr**, NC '84; **#10, 10-84 C.** Male bonding rip-snorter. Son of Hank scored scores of super triumphs with his hobnobbing baritone/bass basement vocals. His classic #1 C. '81 "Dixie on My Mind" emotes a love of the land like *Gone with the Wind*'s Tara. Or catch #1 C 8-70 "All for the Love of Sunshine" or ironic #1(2), 4-72 C "Eleven Roses."

Or his Holly/Cricket/Bobby Fuller IV #15, 8-78 C "I Fought the Law"; or his tamer postlude to this bar-busting brouhaha – #1(1) C. 9-81 "All My Rowdy Friends Have Settled Down."

"What Would You Do (If Jesus Came to Your House)" – **Porter Wagoner**, NC, '56; **#8, 3-56 C.** West Plains, Missouri's Porter (b. '27) enjoyed Country champ #1(4) C, 5-55 "A Satisfied Mind." Porter's blond Elvis hairdo frizzed to instant Afro in the perm fad Discomania era. Razor-thin Wagoner offered rhetorical religious hits like this. Wagoner hosted his own Country TV show with star Norma Jean (#8 C, 10-64), who had no idea her replacement would become the undisputed Queen of Country Music. Norma Jean's protégé had the most recognizable set of curves since Marilyn Monroe.

"I Want to Hold You in My Dreams Tonight" – **Stella Parton**, NC, '75; **#9, 5-75 C.** Stella's (b. '49, Tennessee) kid brother Randy (b. '55) dusted the Country hit parade with #30 C, 8-81 "Shot Full of Love." The real dynamite sibling of the family, though, arrived January, 19, 1946:

"Rockin' Years" – **Dolly Parton**, NC, '91; **#1(1), 3-91 C. The most popular female Country artist of all time** has enjoyed many rockin' years. In Joel Whitburn's Top Country Singles 'Kings & Queens of Country' section, she's eighth ever. In a male-dominated galaxy of talent, she's in the clear: 1) Dolly Parton, 7711 points (8th overall); Loretta Lynn, 6253 (17th); Tammy Wynette, 5720 (23rd); Kitty Wells, 5083 (31st); Tanya Tucker, 4753 (36th); Reba McEntire, 4746 (37th) and Crystal Gayle,4523 (39th).

"Mule Skinner Blues (Blue Yodel No. 6)" – **Dolly Parton**, NC '70; **#3, 7-70 C.** Jimmie Rodgers I is the taproot of Country Blues. **Fendermen** (Surf Rock chapter) took it to #5, 5-60. Dolly hit Country top ten with this rocker, followed by #1(1) C, 12-70 "Joshua." On her gossamer ballad "Love is Like a Butterfly," (#1(1) C, 8-74) she echoes Buddy Holly's "Peggy Sue" flipside "Everyday," reprised by **James Taylor, John Denver, Don McLean,** and **Bobby Vee.** [Or Bob Lind's '66 "Elusive Butterfly]. Dolly sings of soft satin wings and flitting momentary beauty, across the canvas of our brittle lives. A sunray of hope. With her silvery soprano, she dusts the motes off the moonbeams, and sizzles the warm new April sunshine into romantic splendor. Dolly's been married, however, to a low-profile farmer named (no relation) Carl Dean. Dolly began by writing hits for Hank

Williams Jr.: NOTHING about **Hank Williams Jr.** is like a butterfly. Somehow, the butterfly song was made entirely for Dolly. Her entire aura pulsates to that "Sweet Summer Lovin'" (#77, 9-79; #9 C) mode, bespangled with cotton-candy and Old Moon Pies and 7-Up.

"I Will Always Love You" – Dolly Parton, with Vince Gill, NC, '95; #15, 9-95 C. After #1(14) HOT 100 (#1[11] R & B) with Whitney Houston, Dolly charted for a third time with her song here – #1 in '74 and '82. Dolly's other well-known blockbusters? "Here You Come Again" – at #3, 10-77 and #1(5) C; #1(2) 10-80 "9 to 5" (#1 C) from same-named movie; #1(2) **Kenny Rogers** duo and Hemingway novel-title "Islands in the Stream" of 8-83 (#1 C); #50, 3-93 "Romeo" (#27 C); and C-debut #24 "Dumb Blonde" of 1-67 CMA   (Brilliant Blonde is more like it). See other entry of Dolly solo.

The first total-format Country station was KDAV, Lubbock, Texas, with Buddy Holly's mentor Hi-Pockets Duncan. In 1961, only 75 AM stations had an exclusive Country format. By the 90s, over 1500 stations carried exclusive Country or Country Rock. With a throbbing bass, heavy twangy guitar crunch, and snappy 2 & 4 tattoo on drums, isn't Country a kissin'-cousin of Rock? Over HALF of all American music into 2001+ is recorded in Music City U.S.A – Nashville, Tennessee. For perspective, that's more than all the other stuff COMBINED from New York, Los Angeles, Chicago, Detroit, Philadelphia. Even nearby Memphis.

Garth Brooks's Al. *Ropin' the Wind* ENTERED the Billboard 200 at #1 in 1991. Shania Twain's *Come on Over* (Al #2) became the BIGGEST-selling album of all time by a female artist, with over 15 million by 2000. In 2002, **Alan Jackson**'s album *Drive* ENTERED the *Billboard 200* at #1!

"Sold (The Grundy County Auction Incident)" – John Michael Montgomery, NC, '95; #1(3), 5-95 C. Montgomery (b. '65, Danville, KY) lambasted the 90s with #60, 5-93 #1(3) C. "I Love the Way You Love Me," and #33 HOT 100, 12-98 "Hold on to Me" on Atlantic. Others? Sure: "Beer and Bones" of #21 C, 3-93, and his #1(4) C. "I Swear" at #42 '94 (and #1[11] 4-94 for **All-4-One**, California interracial Barber Shop Quartet). JMM has others, like #73, 8-94 #1 C "Be My Baby Tonight," and lassoing impossiblity – #4 C. "Rope the Moon." All 4 One covered him again on his #1 C, 3-95 "I Can Love You Like That" to #5, 6-95 (#40 R & B).

"Neon Moon" – Brooks & Dunn, NC, '92; #1(2), 2-92 C. Leon Eric Brooks – KIX Brooks (b. '55 Shreveport, Louisiana) – and Ronnie Dunn (b. '53, Coleman, Texas) blasted into 1992-93 Vocal Duo of Year Award, with items like #1(1), 2-95 C "Little Miss Honky Tonk" and #5 C.-only

"Whiskey Under the Bridge." "Boot-Scootin' Boogie" was a #1(4), 5-92 Country champ that manhandled the HOT 100 to hefty #50. The big chart welcomed them with #38, 12-98 Roger Miller bittersweet saga "Husbands and Wives," and #69, 3-2000 "You'll Always Be Loved by Me." With a month on the Country chart in March 2001, their "Ain't Nothin' 'Bout You" had the #19 'Airpower' 'bullet'.

"The Keeper of the Stars" – Tracy Byrd, #68, 4-95; #2(2), 1-95 C. Byrd's swooping flight to the mountaintop crags contains star-titled tunes like #4, 4-94 C "Lifestyles of the Not So Rich and Famous," and #4, 8-94 C. "Watermelon Crawl." Byrd's Al. #30, 6-94 *No Ordinary Man* was prelude to millennial crossovers. Byrd's compadres: **Jo Dee Messina** (#1 C., 4-2000 "That's the Way" and #2, 10-2000 "Burn" C); **Shedaisy** (#11+ C., 11-2000 "Lucky 4 You [Tonight I'm Just Me]); the **Dixie Chicks** (Al. #1, 9-1999, Billboard 200, "Fly"); **Kenny Chesney** ("Don't Happen Twice" #14+, C. 1-2001); **Joe Diffie** (#5 C, "It's Always Somethin'" 8-2000); **Chad Brock** (#1 C, 2-2000 "Yes!"); **Rascal Flatts** ("This Everyday Love" – #9, 9-2000 C); **Trace Adkins** (#21, 2-2002 "Help Me Understand"); **Neal McCoy** (2-2001 C. #43+ C, "Beatin' It In") **Andy Griggs; Mark Wills; Blackhawk**, and a newcomer, with #19 Country Album Chart, 8-2000, **Elvis Presley** (Tupelo, MS).

Wade Hayes hit #5, 10-95 with "What I Meant to Say." You can't grab words you just said, and stuff 'em back into your mouth, can you? Hayes hit #1 with 11-94 C. "Old Enough to Know Better." "How Do You Sleep at Night" hit #68, 12-98 on the HOT 100.

"It Matters to Me" – Faith Hill, #74, 12-95; #1(3), 11-95 C. Faith (b. 9-21-67, Jackson, Mississippi) led off her Country career with #1(4) C, 3-93 "Wild One", on her way to conquering the HOT 100. No wishy-washy career moves for the beautiful Mississippi girl. She had the audacity to cover (very well) **Janis Joplin**/Big Brother's #12 '67 (year she was born) "Piece of My Heart." Her Country smash "Someone Else's Dream" shows us all to live up to our own realistic expectations – not some pushy relative's ideas of who we should become. We are already SOMEBODY, and we must celebrate that person. Now. Besides Faith's singer/songwriter talents, she plays second fiddle to no one in the gorgeous department. Her #8+, 1-2001 C. "If My Heart Had Wings" and #5+ C. "The Way You Love Me" of 2000 show her marathon stamina and vocal power. "There You'll Be" debuted at #46, 5- 2001.

"Breathe" – Faith Hill, #2(5), 11-99; #1 C. After 51 weeks on the HOT 100, "Breathe" was still breathing at #49; five weeks it cavorted with #1. Mets' 'Ya Gotta Believe' pitcher Tug McGraw's daughter-in-law didn't just hurl a hit song – she launched a phenomenon. Faith's celestial double-white video swirls with white sheets, white walls, and her angelic smiling face murmuring mellifluously about the tender sighs of her lover. In this VIDEO ERA, the telegenic factor never hurts. As she ascends the chorus, pulling out stops of pulse, power, and passion, the listener is wider awake than he's been for a year. "Breathe" is a breakthrough Country ballad in the HOT 100 arena.

Faith's Crossover breakthroughs rolled two fortunate 7's: #7, 5-97 "It's Your Love," and #7, 3-98 "This Kiss." After her #33, 12-98 "Let Me Let Go" ricocheted the charts, something big was breathing in the chutes. Faith's Pop-in-Law Tug McGraw helped the Mets win the Miracle 1973 pennant with slogan "Ya Gotta Believe." In the world of aspiring hits (baseball and music), Tug McGraw knew that with FAITH, all things are possible. And he passed his pearls of wisdom down to the kid (more Tug, later).

"Swanee" – Al Jolson, #1(9), 5-20. America loves its sunny Southland. Though this Floridian river Swanee ['Suwanee'] wasn't even settled yet when **Stephen Foster** wrote his 1950 #1 Swanee-ode "Old Folks at Home," it's a focal point for zingy heartstrings – down along that Swanee River. Born Asa Yoelson (1886-1950) in St. Petersburg, Russia, Al was raised as close to the South as you can get – Washington, D.C. His cantor father felt popular music was demeaning. Jolson's other Southern-Fried song themes include: #1(3), 3-1918 "I'm All Bound Round with the Mason Dixon Line," and two R & R revamps: "My Mammy" at #2(2), 6-28 [#13, 7-67 the Happenings] and #1(8), 8-1918 "Rockabye Your Baby with a Dixie Melody," – covered by comedian/singer **Jerry Lewis** [NOT Jerry LEE Lewis] to #10, 11-56. Anyhow, Country Rock is often just SOUTH U.S.A. Rock. Any other Country Rock rivers of importance? Yep:

"Chattahoochee" – Alan Jackson, #46, 7-93; #1(4), 5-93 C. Alan Jackson boarded that neon rainbow to Nashville in 1985. The Newman, Georgia, singer/songwriter/guitarist's, 'Johnny B. Goode' railroad tracks were just 15 miles from Georgia's Chattahoochee River. Dragging his lonesome tapes from rejection to despair, Alan gave thanks for a flight-attendant wife – which perhaps says something about his own looks – tall, light, handsome. After months of slipshod shuffling, Jackson made only one real contact in the Music City showbiz scene, another frustrated kid who also believed in traditional Country-flavored Rockabilly Rock. The kid was a short-order cook who sang a bit at the Nashville Palace. His name was **Randy Travis** (c/o Ace Collins' info).

Alan landed a job in the mail-room at Cable's TNN (The Nashville Network), just as Kathy Mattea worked in the Country Hall of Fame. To get your foot in the door, it never hurts to already be inside. In 1989 Arista Records/Tim DuBois hired Jackson to write songs after **Vince Gill's** career took off. Jackson's first modest nugget was #45, 10-89 "Blue Blooded Woman" singing for Arista. Alan believed in trad Country – even firing off the little rooster-crow like **Bob Wills** & his Texas Playboys in "Chattahoochee," his seventh #1 C. tune,

"Chattahoochee" is more than a song – it is a way of life. It's also 78.2% Rock and Roll. "Chattahoochee" reflects a typical Southern adolescent lifestyle. Opening on a twangy Duane Eddy/Link Wray riff, with snappy snare cuffing Basic Rock's 2, 2 ½, and 4 accents, Jackson ditches the Blues with his piano-friendly Key of 'C' here. Few Rock songs, too, feature a FIDDLE solo.

Jackson is comfy with both baritone and tenor in

"Chattahoochee." Like **John Cougar Mellencamp's** #1(4), 7-82 "Jack and Diane," Jackson's river romp describes growing up in the U.S.A. Alan's opening salvo has SOUTH written all over it. Female Ragtime/Gospel Boogie-Woogie piano player **Del Wood** played a honkytonk spinoff of "Swanee" called "Down Yonder" to #4, 9-51 (#5 C). "Chattahoochee" covers a boy drifting through life in Georgia. And having no-frills scampish fun. He and his girlfriend fog up Lover's Lane windows. He gets to second base, but she tosses him out sneakin' into third. He settles for a burger and a 'grape sno-cone' consolation prize. He takes the Georgia Belle home to her squirmy folks. Does he go home? Of course not! He heads back out to his Saturday night pals and their pyramid of cans down by the Chattahoochee River gurgling in the moonlight. It's not a grape soda monument to King Tut. Nor even Coca Cola, headquarted in local Atlanta a half hour up I-85. He hangs out with the Good Ol' Chattahoochee Boys into the muggy wee hours. You can imagine the up-to-no-good cussin' and guzzlin' the night away. For recreation, they lay down rubber on that riverside asphalt, and they never get nabbed.

He loves the muddy Chattahoochee. He's not the first Georgia poet Chattahoochee fan. The river itself speaks in "Song of the Chattahoochee":

Out of the hills of Habersham
Down the valleys of Hall,
I hurry amain to reach the plain,
Run the rapid and leap the fall,
Split at the rock and together again,
– Sidney Lanier (1842-81, c/o Dorothy Wolfe
and Nick Pappas, inspirational
Dearborn High School English teachers)

Like King Tut's Egyptian Pyramid, the guys' brew-can pyramid symbolizes a fervent belief in friendship, camaraderie, and just plain hanging out and goofing off. At Charlottesville, Virginia's Big House, a blocky appurtenance stood 100 feet away. The purpose of this whitewashed antebellum mini-lodge was to house the rapscallion lads. When they came home beery and bloated and blotto, from their romancin' and ragtag rebellion, they could 'sleep it off' at this place called 'The Office.'

Came the Chattahoochee. In Georgia, the 1990s Office was asphalt, and the shrine was a Lone Star beercan pyramid by the wild midnight moon.

"Livin' On Love" – Alan Jackson, #56S [Sales], 10-94; #1(3), C. The perfect Country song. No cry-in-your-beer lament. No cheatin' honkytonk, or train squashing dreams. "Livin' on Love" takes two couples rich in happiness. Opposite to Madonna's "Material Girl," this young/old foursome strolls through life in serenity because they have love. Nothing else matters. **Guy Mitchell's** #2(1), 6-51 marvelous "My Truly, Truly Fair" has this great line about how you can't live on only LOVE – but still he's gonna give it a try! "Livin' on Love" tries it, they like it, and it works. Jackson's young couple marries for love [in sweet melodic Blues Key of 'B']. They don't have a nickel. They pay annoying bills, but it never fazes their true love. They live happily ever after. The second/final verse has an old couple. Kids are gone, bills are gone. He can't hear, she can't see too well. They totter out the door together. No regrets. Here are four lives well invested. Jackson's profound simplicity reverberates through his minimalist masterpiece. 'Nuff said.

"Don't Rock the Jukebox" – Alan Jackson, NC, '91; #1(3), 5-91 C. Jukebox spins solace in the swirling neon glow. A steel guitar accentuates his sad mood. He doesn't feel like rockin', because his girl ran off. Like **Elton John's** #5, 6-84 "Sad Songs (Say So Much)," Jackson's jukebox blares out comfort and consolation for a quarter. A huge hit was suddenly under construction when a bandmate selected a rock tune. From the SINGER to the DANCER, the ELVIS SPOTLIGHT now shifted to the JUKEBOX itself. It was a long trek from Chattahoochee carpenter to used car salesman to songwriter to superstar – but Jackson's Box of Juke became a Golden Chariot to destiny driven by vintage steel guitar.

"Midnight in Montgomery" – Alan Jackson, NC, '92; #3, 4-92 C. Hallowe'en Carol. Very few Country tunes park in the Minor-Key Towaway Zone for long. Country music spins on three major chords. Jazz ninths, diminisheds, and augmented progressions usually stay the hell out. SOME ghostly legends, though, require a matrix of minor-key gloom. This one . . .

Jackson meanders through a sleety, smoky New Year's Eve midnight in Montgomery, Alabama. He's confronted – maybe – by a schnockered guy in a cowboy hat. THE Country singer (b. 1923, d. 1-1-53) greets the young star. The haunted wind picks up, and the spectral figure vanishes, like the Ghost Trucker in Red Sovine's "Phantom 409" of '67. To build his eerie mood, Alan conjures **Del Shannon's** (1935-90) icy-drizzle gloom progression from #1 '61 "Runaway" [or medieval 'Greensleeves']:

Dm—C—Bb—A7

In Country music, this progression is rare as platinum Bluegrass [in Key of 'A', Del used **Am-G-F-E7**].

Jackson dredges up 'Luke the Drifter' haunted allusions in the quagmire deep night – stars lighting up this purple sky, whiskey aroma in the rain-lashing air, and the inevitable title line "I'm So Lonesome I Could Cry." Jackson, you, and I know he's obviously singing about **Hank Williams, Sr.** Misty midnights in Montgomery? HANK, Jackson explains, always sings there. What about **Del**?

"I'm So Lonesome I Could Cry" – Hank Williams, NC, '66; #43, 6-66 C. Eerily, this Senior classic never charted on its first go-round. It was an out-take. B.J. Thomas (b. '42, Oklahoma) took this 77%-Country tune to #8, 2-66 (NC, C). Hank sings his violet-sky lonesome whippoorwill ode to desolation.

"I'm So Lonesome I Could Cry" – Del Shannon, NC, '65; NC, C. Michigan's **Del** (1935-90) helped cause the first slight 'Hillbilly Revival' ripple as a way-station to his 1999 Rock Hall Induction. His posthumous 1991 "Let's Dance" is a Cajun masterpiece. He may have been the best-ever yodeler ('72, NC "Coopersville Yodel"). Del hit #56, 3-85 C "In My Arms Again." His NC '65 Al. *Del Shannon Sings Hank Williams* is a great Hank echo.

"Mercury Blues" – Alan Jackson, NC, '93; #2(1), 9-93 C. James Dean (1932-55) drove a vintage Merc. Country Rock w/ Texan Western Swing, including Bob Wills's rooster-sound again. Good stuff. His buddy steals his girl back, after he stole her first – because she lusted after a shiny new Ford-built Mercury.

"Chasin' That Neon Rainbow" hit #2(2), 10-90 C. "Love's Got a Hold on You" hit #1(2) C, for Alan, as did #1, 5-95 "I Don't Even Know Your Name," a wild lyric about how a wild night results in getting hitched to a waitress whose name he doesn't even know. His foot-stompin' "Tall, Tall Trees" scorched #1(2), 10-95. HOT 100 inroads? His Tom T.Hall tune "Little Bitty" hit #58, 11-96, and two #43s followed – all Country champs: 12-98's "Right on the Money," and 3-99's "Gone Crazy." His #39 "Little Man" points out the plight of the small shopkeeper zapped by large Maxi-Marts that overtake entire small towns. Teaming with George Strait at #45 C, 2-2000 for "Murder on Music Row," Jackson basked in the platinum glow of his #9 Al. *Under the Influence* of 11-99. As #1 C, 3-2000 "It Must Be Love" hit #39 HOT 100, his #28+-C. 10-2000 "WWW.Memory" chided the computer age, Alan's 3-2001 self-penned "When Somebody Loves You" snagged Rung #42 C. in its first charted week, a major-league leap.

Jackson's #104, 8-94 and #1(3), 6-94 "Summertime Blues" is absolute proof that Country and Rockabilly Rock are nearly interchangeable. Drums slam the big 2 & 4 beats, and a twangy guitar 'eddies' along. [Catch Eddie Cochran #8, 5-58 original for comparison, or Psychedelia's **Blue Cheer** #14, 3-68 rendition].

Alabama

"Mountain Music" – **Alabama, NC, '82; #1(1), 3-82 C.** Just about the time you get real smug about **Conway Twitty**'s 40 #1 songs being tops for all time, ALABAMA steps up and trumps them with #41. "Sad Lookin' Moon," followed "She Ain't Your Ordinary Girl". This Statleresque Barber Shop Quartet (see Dion/Belmonts & quintet N'Sync) has over 20 million albums, and sold more concert tickets than any Country band in history (liner notes, #1 C. Al. '98 *For the Record: Alabama #1 Hits*).

Mountain music? Let's face it. Alabama's topography isn't exactly Coloradan, Alaskan, or Tibetan. Three Fort Payne, ALABAMA, cousins turn their steamrollered state into a veritable Switzerland with their spirited sound on this record. No Rock, R & B, or Country group has ever come close to catching their 21 CONSECUTIVE #1 C. HITS. In the 1980-87 zone, despite noble efforts (16) by **Sonny James** in 1967-71 or **Earl Thomas Conley** (1983-89), Alabama became the champs. Beginning as 'Wild Country' in 1969, they stacked their line-up with talent: **Randy Owen, Jeff Cook, Teddy Gentry,** and **Bennett Vartanian**. The roster rotates a bit, and all sing, expertly. "Mountain Music" is their trademark tune. Its up-country harmonies interweave in dynamic profusion. The fiddle skims the booming rhythm with trembling treble power.

"Love in the First Degree" – **Alabama, #15, 11-81; #1(2), 10-81 C.** Among first Country superstars to surf HOT 100 in the Disco afterglow. From openers NC '77, #78, 7-77 "I Wanna Be with You Tonight," they launched a firestorm of atomic hits with Elvis's RCA label. Let's re-surf from the Chattahoochee to their "Tennessee River" – #1(1) C, 5-80. Alabama lavishes a big, full, polished sound. "The Closer You Get" hit #38, 5-83, and #1 C, and helped America fall in love with the rich positive sound of Alabama. With beards and long hair, they revamped the crewcut 60s look. RCA saw in Alabama a quadruple new ELVIS – to compete with Statlers and Oak Ridge Boys. Critic David Gates writes in *Country*,

> "It seems perverse to argue that Alabama is more directly in the main line of country music than a Neotraditionalist like Ricky Skaggs; but, in fact, there's a pretty good case to be made. The great innovators of the past – Charlie Poole, the Skillet Lickers, Jimmie Rodgers, Bob Wills, even Ernest Tubb – were enthusiastic contaminators of 'pure' country music . . . Drums, electric guitars, and hot improvised solos, were once controversial. So were the influences of ragtime, blues, Tin Pan Alley pop, big band jazz, and fifties rock and roll."

Precisely. We have water-skiied this wave length all along: THE ROCK REVOLUTION is a MAGNIFICENT COMBINATION of AMERICAN POPULAR MUSIC STYLES for the ENTIRE 20th CENTURY, and beyond . . . Gates says Alabama's just the quintessential Rock band which does COUNTRY. Cook's guitar is very inventive, and their onstage excitement mirrors that of the **Eagles, Rush, or Bob Seger,** who are all their favorites. Indeed, compare Seger's classic #4, 12-76 "Night Moves" to Randy Owen's sandpapery delivery. In 1987, Alabama recorded "Deep River Woman" with Easy Soul star **Lionel Richie,**

to #71, 1-87, #10 C. Knowing this one could topple them from their #1 hit streak, they released it with multicultural All-American courage.

"Song of the South" – **Alabama, NC, '88; #1(1), 11-88 C.** Vibrant vignette of Southern lifestyle. Whatever was gone with the wind comes floating back with the heavenly aroma of sweet potato pie, one of the 3,000 great reasons God made South Carolina. Other 'Bama bombshells: "#1(4) C, 7-90 "Jukebox in My Mind"; #1 C, 2-89 "Southern Star"; #1 C, 2-83 "Dixieland Delight"; and #1 C, 9-93 "Reckless," and #15 C, 11-2000 "When It All Goes South." They teamed with **N'Sync** on #29, 5-99 "God Must Have Spent a Little More Time on You." Their #2(1), 7-95 "She Ain't Your Ordinary Girl" sums it up – they're no ordinary Country band, just a juggernaut of eternal hits.

"If Tomorrow Never Comes" – **Garth Brooks, NC, '89; #1(1), 9-89 C.** Luba, Oklahoma's **Garth Brooks** (b. 2-7-62) is not just a superstar singer, songwriter, and stage acrobat. Voice of Country music, Garth Brooks is Everyman. He is the Boy Next Door. He is the fullback on your team blocking out for you. He is the guy next to you at work. He is the man you want on your side. He is a real nice guy – thoughtful and gentle. It would not be a good idea, though, to even think about stepping on his Blue Suede Shoes. Garth Brooks is America.

"If Tomorrow Never Comes" begins in acoustic 'G' major. The singer gazes at his lady while she sleeps. He wonders about the long-term or imminent reality of death intruding into his happy home. Maybe in 50 years. Maybe tonight. He questions whether he's truly let the people he loves KNOW how much he cares for them. He muses over the loss of key people in his past life. Garth swoops from bass to tenor. He'd give **Frank Sinatra** a run for his megabucks on clear pronunciation, and **George Jones** a contest on timing and nuance. He asks himself a ghastly question: if she ever has to face the world without me, will she think so much of our time together, that she'll NEVER have another romantic relationship? Good question. In the words of Gerry O'Connor, "Guilt makes the world go round." "If Tomorrow Never Comes" is a wake-up call. Enjoy yourself, it's later than you think.

"Friends in Low Places" – **Garth Brooks, NC, '90; #1(4), 8-90 C.** With 15 million-plus sales, this song made a lot of FRIENDS, in all places. After throwing the javelin on a scholarship to Oklahoma State, Garth sold boots in Nashville, trying for the third time to make it as a singer. His mom, Colleen Carroll, once recorded for Capitol, and worked with Red Foley in 1954 on the *Ozark Jubilee* show. Songwriting legend Harlan Howard [not Doug Howard], and DeWayne Blackwell (writer of Fleetwoods' #1(1), 9-59 "Mr. Blue") wandered into the boot store and were impressed with Brooks's politeness. Could you script a better 'Johnny B. Goode' story? Garth met the two guys who'd write the biggest country hit of all time in a boot store.

"Friends " is a pal song. It's radically reactionary. Huh? He radically puts down sniveling snobs in HIGH places –

stuffed shirts who worship suburban chic status. It's conservative, too. He champions the value that's threaded down the long panoramic fabric of human history – FRIENDSHIP (see Jimmy Stewart's 1946**** *It's a Wonderful Life* on the importance of friendship).

He's ticked off at his ex-girlfriend, a shallow status-seeker who twiddles her SAT scores and looks down her nose at real guys in the real world. He opts for a blast at the good ol' 'Oasis' with his rowdy barroom buddies. OASIS implies a watering hole in the dry parched midst of some spiritual desert. It also implies the major late-90s British group **Oasis**, whose Al. *Standing on the Shoulders of Giants* debuted at #24, 3-2000 on the *Billboard* 200. At Garth's song's outset, he swings like Tarzan up to the Mediant III major chord, a Country oddity. Garth growls into the chorus with his nifty bass amp. The song staggers like a fullback with five linemen trying to drag him down – at 105 thunderous beats per minute. Like **Roy Orbison** in dramatic bolero "Running Scared" (#1, 4-61), Garth describes an encounter with his snooty rival. In Roy's song, Roy astoundingly ends up with the girl he thought he'd lose. In Garth's, he figuratively flips her to the high-falutin' chump who gets stuck with her.

Garth either confesses or brags he really isn't into societal graces – a whole set of fancy European royalty values Americans tossed away centuries ago: fingerbowls, pompous royal titles, ritzy marmalade spoons. To blatantly disregard her dress-up games, he shows up at this black-tie gala in cowboy boots. He touts his bar pals. They speak their minds. Maybe their roughshod manners and blunt, beefy, brusque style of loud talk aren't refined and insincere – but they're REAL folks. Anyhow, the romantic pain he's pretending not to feel gets melted away in the magic golden beer bubbles. Maybe a lovely affair with an Alka-Seltzer looms, when the red eye of morning sun sizzles his ex-slumber. He will pull reality over his eyes somehow. Here's to friendship. Meanwhile, his gold-digging date is in solitary up in her ivory tower:

"Ivory Tower" – Cathy Carr, #2(1), 3-56. Angela Catherine Cordovano (1936-88) had a sweet soprano torch tune about her man imprisoned in her cold intellectual Ivory Tower. We Americans share a funny hot/cold attitude about the Ivory Towers of Academia. On one hand, we worship knowledge. On the other hand, pompous pedantic purveyors of polysyllabic gobbledygook (like THAT, maybe) often get sorely misunderstood. Plain folk would just as soon hear John Wayne or Gary Cooper tell them in plain unfussy talk – "Yep" or "Nope."

"American Honky-Tonk Bar Association" – Garth Brooks, NC, '93; #1(1), 9-93 C. **Garth** gathers all disenfranchised hard-hat roarers at the Oasis, who moan about taxes, and welfare slackers. Jerry Lee Lewis's biographer Nick Tosches tells us 'Honky-Tonk' comes to us from a 2-24-1894 report in an Oklahoma newspaper. Several honky-tonk tunes were cut by **Prince's Orchestra** in 1918. Poet **Carl Sandburg** wrote in his 1927 American Songbag: "Country music would take honky-tonk to the dark obverse

of that carousing spirit . . . remorse and guilt and world-weariness. Honky-tonk music would come to be a howl of abandon followed by a lament of anguish." [All that before **Jimmie Rodgers** really got Country music rolling].

"Rodeo" – Garth Brooks, NC, '91; #3, 8-91 C. Bulls & blood he sings. Dust & mud & spurs & chaps. A woman pines for her wayward man, who lusts after . . . the DUST – of the **rodeo.** With wry Western humor, Garth traces the rainbow glory that is rodeo. All the gold quester will win are battered broken bones and homes. Still, he follows the leprechaun's bull.

"We Shall Be Free" hit #12, 9-92 C for Garth. He echoes Dr. Martin Luther King over the California Rodney King beating racial incident. Brooks faces controversy, never shuns it.

"The River" – Garth Brooks, NC, #1(1), 5-92 C. "The River" has one of the prettiest melodies ever sculpted. "The River" sees the universe as a vast river in which to sail the solo vessel of one's dreams, aspirations, and loves. The chorus serves up sweet harmony by **Trisha Yearwood** (Al. #4, 3-2000 *Real Live Women*, Country charts), with Kenny Malone on percussion. It swoops from pleasant Key of 'D' tonic splendor into the dramatic sub-dominant IV chord '**G**' with stark power and glory.

Is "The River" a metaphor for life? Garth leads off with the dream. Life is like a river. The dreamer himself is a VESSEL. Odd word. Could mean a jug or a ship. Each day is a battle, he sings, to steer safely within the two shores without running aground or breaking up. Then he shifts from the river to the clear blue sky with a Taoist yin-yang mandala. Boats rarely fly [hovercraft turbos]. Somehow, borne by faith, his vessel floats airborne. His song's great reason for being? Noble attempts!

You can never reach your destination, he philosophizes, if you never try. This line, of course, swoops to the IV chord hallelujah. Garth concludes: he'll sail his mysterious vessel until his proverbial river disappears. His own spirited anchor, of course, holds the bridge. With the 'good Lord' as his captain, he musically prays, he can navigate ANYTHING.

Not all rivers are so user-friendly. The rock group **Styx** (#3, 12-90 "Show Me the Way") named themselves after the Greek River of Death (a/k/a 'Lethe'); the ghostly boatman Charon ferried lost souls to the next grim underworld Bat-Cave or whatever. We covered the intense river murder mystery in #8, 2-92 **Richard Marx**'s "Hazard." We did the double teenage suicide Romeo/Juliet theme of **Dickey Lee**'s Graveyard Rock ballad "Patches" (#6, 8-62), with the girl floating with her face down in the putrid river. Or remember #1 '61 **Pat Boone**'s similar "Moody River"? In Armageddonist **Barry McGuire**'s ominous #1 "Eve of Destruction, " even the holy Jordan River is profaned with grotesque floating bodies. Among the most sinister river-theme songs is from Chicksaw County, Mississippi:

"Ode to Billie Joe" – Bobbie Gentry, #1(4), 8-67, and #54, 7-76, and new version at #65, 8-76; #17, 9-67 C. What was that horrible bundle, the nation demanded, that

Billie Jo McAllister tossed off Tallahatchee Bridge into the muddy muck? After the song-girl pa's mysterious death by fever, amid small talk of black-eyed peas, an ugly bundle of mystery topples into the roiling rapids and the muddy ooze in the dark tepid pools of the eerie river. Most folks figured it was an unwanted kid. Somebody's tragic decision in the pre Roe v. Wade era.

Not all rivers are nasty, though. Garth's river is a sparkling blue highway to the fertile endless sea. The **Jordanaires** were named after the **Bible's** River Jordan (not a basketball player). At the Jordan, virtuous souls may embark on a happier pilgrimage than in Barry McGuire's blood-red stream. **Alabama's** "Tennessee River" isn't half bad, nor **Alan Jackson's** "Chattahoochee." Garth's river is a symbolic inspirational tale of joy and promise and faith and salvation.

In "The Beaches of Cheyenne" (#1[1], 12-95 C), Garth sings of a shore that doesn't exist. Ever been to Cheyenne? The nearest real beaches to that High Plains (5000+ feet above sea level) town might be nearly a thousand miles away. The wild and windswept Wyoming plain affords you a nice view of tumbleweed tumbling, and purple sage whistling up the wind. Brooks wrings poetic profundity out a Zen geographical absurdity. Garth's stage show must be witnessed to be believed. He swings from ropes to try to touch whatever up-front portion of his audience he can reach. His universal appeal is that he is one of all of us. We can all identify with a muscular guy who waffles between coolly serious and good-ol'-guy fun-loving. With steel-blue eyes, salt & pepper hair, and an athleticism that took him to the New York Mets' 2000 spring training camp, Brooks rocks the world.

His first hit was NC, '89; #8, 3-89 C "Much Too Young (To Feel This Damn Old)." "The Dance" at #1(3) C, 5-90 preceded "Low Places," and his wistful and wondrous hymn "Unanswered Prayers" hit #1(2) in 11-90. His #1 C, 5-93 "That Summer" was followed by #1(2) C. 8-93 "Ain't Goin' Down (Til the Sun Comes Up)." With over 15 big #1 songs, Garth's forte is ALBUMS; #1(18), 12-94 Al. *The Hits* highlight his platinum cavalcade. Those gun-metal blue eyes signal a heart of gold. And when Garth Brooks's blue moon turns to gold again, Country Rock might assume the crown of #1 Rock and Roll style in world popularity. If it hasn't already . . .

"Blue" – LeAnn Rimes, #26, 6-96; #1(7), 5-95 C. With a sultry wisp of **Patsy Cline's** high and lonesome yodel-kicks, and a sweet style of her own cradled in **Buddy Holly's** own studio, 14-year-old LeAnn Rimes smacked the top spot for SEVEN glorious weeks in a Country era where a two-week vacation at the top spot is becoming more and more a rarity. A cast of thousands backed her at **Norman Petty's** legendary studios at Clovis, New Mexico. LeAnn proved in her #1 album *Blue* (5-96) that she's a spectacular singer and prodigy. Her blonde hair cascades around her tan shoulders astride a blue Levi vest below her baby blue eyes. Her cherubic smile warms the days of millions of fans. Three good reasons for her supernova success: talent, talent, and talent. Her lusciously emotional smoky contralto hogties the Texas

skies. Born in 1982 in Jackson, Mississippi, LeAnn gets her early genius from two other stars, like **Tanya Tucker** and **Brenda Lee:**

"Rock On Baby" – Brenda Lee, NC, '74; #6, 11-74 C. Brenda Lee Tarpley (4'9" 'Little Miss Dynamite) was the 4th biggest single artist of the 60s, after the **Beatles, Elvis**, and **Ray Charles**. Brenda eliminated all the female competition. Her "Rockin' Around the Christmas Tree" is now the 4th-biggest Christmas carol ever. With six top tenners on the 1974-75 Country charts, Brenda cut her first record ever – at age 10½ – **Hank Williams'** dynamite (#1 C) "Jambalaya." Brenda's belated Induction to the Country Hall of Fame showed how spectacular her songs were in both fields – and she even hit #12 R & B for "Sweet Nothin's." FINALLY, Rock Hall of Fame gatekeepers recognized her superstardom in 2002.

LeAnn's precocious prodigy status was buoyed by parental and grandparental support. LeAnn also writes songs, like #3+ C. "Talk to Me" off the *Blue* album of '96-'97. Her "Blue" lofts a Patsy Cline sound, replete with yodel-kicks. At 68 steady beats a minute, and the bluesy key of 'A', LeAnn toys with mediant majors and sophisticated yodels usually only coaxed out of much older voices. Her "Blue" blossoms with fantastic clusters of Country Rock hits of the past. Bill Mack ostensibly wrote it directly for Patsy Cline, but mothballed it when Cline was killed. NEVER figuring to use it, he was overwhelmed by the then-11-year-old's "Star Spangled Banner" rendition, and submitted it to her. Mack also composed "Fade to Blue," gonzo Blues "My Baby," and "The Light in Your Eyes." By Summer 1997, LeAnn climbed the HOT 100 with her breakthrough #2(4) 6-97 (#1 C) "How Do I Live?" Her smoldering Country Soul sought markets of people with no idea the kid was already a Country star. "Looking Through Your Eyes" hit #18, 4-98, and "Big Deal" #23 in 10-99. After three weeks on the Country charts in March 2001, her "But I Do Love You" ricocheted up from #50 to #41, a quick leap.

"Cattle Call" – LeAnn Rimes and Eddy Arnold, NC, '96; on #1 Blue album. Fourteen-year-old **LeAnn** and 78-year-old **Eddy** sing an outstanding duet on this sweetly sentimental Country Waltz. Smooth crooner Eddy hits some falsetto, as he calls errant dogies (cattle). This is a WESTERN song, native to sagebrush Arizona. It's a beautiful yodeled melody of tawny cactus and turquoise/vermilion sunsets over the cotton-candy-cloud mesas and mountainsides. LeAnn's follow-up album, *Unchained Melody*, and its title song, each hit #1 C for the Country prodigy (4-97). Meanwhile, back at Eddy, he still sang as well at 78 as he did at 45, or 33 1/3, way back on his records of the original cattle call:

"Cattle Call" – Eddy Arnold, #69, 11-55; #1(2), 6-55 C. Arnold's telltale tenor, of Country's #1 Artist ever for charted hits, is garnished with unexpected falsetto glides. He warbles to his dashing dogies out on the lonesome cattle trail. Eddy got it from the Tampa yodelmeister himself, **Slim Whitman** (b. '24), master yodelist, who hit NC '55 with it, but #11, 1-55 C.

"Hold On Partner" – Roy Rogers and Clint Black, NC, '91; #42, 11-91 C. Roy stunned the 1949 Saturday Matinee at the Virginia Park Theatre on Hamilton Ave. (now John Lodge Expressway) in Detroit. For nine cents, you could watch the King of the Cowboys Roy Rogers sing to his beautiful wife Dale Evans and his beautiful horse Trigger. Roy never plugged the bad guys. Just tied 'em up, and hustled 'em off to grim ol' Deadwood Jail. Roy teamed up with Clint Black (#1 C, 11-96 "Like the Rain") on this tribute to the continuity of Country Music (53 years) through the ages. Roy Rogers has the longest chart career of any artist in Country music, not even counting his #13, 12-34 **Sons of the Pioneers'** "Tumbling Tumbleweeds." Bizarrely, Rogers' first solo hit sang praises of the OTHER cowboy star's horse: the **Lone Ranger's** classic stallion "Hi-Yo Silver" to #13, 7-38. I learned my first Country classics from Roy and Gene Autry as a little Calvin & Hobbes/Dennis the Menace buckaroo in the late 40s – in the smoky midnight heart of Motown. When I was a little kid in Detroit, Roy Rogers represented to me everything that was right about America. And he still does.

"How Do You Like Me Now?" – Toby Keith, #36, 1-2000; #1(2), 11-99 C. Country Revenge Rock classic. Keith's macho growl booms beyond a thousand football fields of unrequited cheerleader love fantasies. Keith the pigskin star yearns for affections of lass who unceremoniously dumped him (we know not why). Keith returns after a little petty graffiti revenge, and becomes a major Country star. His title is unique and intriguing. He's dreamed, he gloats, of LIVING WITHIN the girl's RADIO – so she can't escape his MESSAGE! The message thunders back to **Del Shannon's** #28, '61 "So Long Baby": In other words (paraphasing Del), she's got this one jump (checkers-wise) on him – but he takes two jumps. Toby's smirking sayonara struts the gung-ho stage spotlight of a brand-new superstar. He's a wayfaring stranger on the Glory Road from Nashville to Paradise in Johnny B. Goode's hot klieg lights.

Keith's career continues with #1 C, 10-2000 :"You Shouldn't Kiss Me Like This" (#34, 12-2000 HOT 100). Keith is the vanguard of the new Country superwave: #4+ C, "Who I Am" **Jessica Andrews,** and #3 C, 1-2001 "This Everyday Love" **Rascal Flatts.** Or the semi-Country Irish **Corrs,** #45+ HOT 100 "Breathless."

After the 9-11-01 NYC bombing raid, America was stunned. Anger came later, like Toby Keith's #73+ 1st-week HOT 100 entry, June 2002, "Courtesy of the Red, White, and Blue (The Angry American)" – #22+C, 5-2002.

"Any Man of Mine" – Shania Twain, #31, 5-95; #1(2) C. First hit. Shania (b. Eileen Edwards, 8-28-65) hails from South of the Border – Windsor, Ontario – over the Detroit River's Ambassador Bridge. **Shania (**Ojibway Indian for 'on my way") lived in icy Timmons, Ontario and in the Thousand Islands of the St. Lawrence Seaway between Upstate New York and Ontario/Quebec, Canada.

Besides her Canadian heritage, she's also substantially Native American. Supermodel glamorous, Shania hit a 7-million platinum #5 album – *The Woman in Me,* in 3-95. A MERE PRELUDE to the BIG ONE. Shania's #2, 1997 Al. *Come on Over* sold 15+ million plus in the long haul – the most ever sold by a female artist on one album. Page one of The *Woman in Me* struts her big-haired classic gorgeous pose. The little photo of Shania in cowboy hat in a hot spring, from the shoulders up, simply enhances America's idea that she's amazingly beautiful.

"Any Man of Mine" leads off with a quasi-RAP line with contralto surging to giggly soprano. She squeezes intimately between the acoustic guitar and the hovering fiddle. She inventories qualifications for this Mr. Right. In real life, Shania's been hitched to producer **John 'Mutt' Lange.** His versatile R & R resume includes mega-productions of the **Cars, Def Leppard,** and **Foreigner** (appropriately, #2[10] "Waiting for a Girl Like You"). Mutt also sings harmonies and provides a crucial Un-Instrument that powered the Beatles' #1(7), 1-64 "I Want to Hold Your Hand" – handclapping.

The Shania Twain sound, via Mutt's production expertise, is a tony amalgam of posh vocals, lush strings, kicky guitars, thumping tom-toms, and snappy snare. She followed with #1(2), 11-95 C [#74 HOT 100] "(If You're Not in Love) I'm Outa Here." Her lyric debuts with every burnt-out pick-up line ever muttered at the Oozy Boozy Snoozy Floozy Lizard Lounge. Shania takes the timeworn Carole King retort – will you still love me tomorrow? Her 2-1998 breakthrough "You're Still the One" tickled the #1 spot with #2(9), 2-98. Close – but no cigar. By Spring 1998, Shania was a Mainstream star, no longer the exclusive province of the Country Cavalcade. She hit stratosphere with #4, 12-98 "From This Moment On," Her #7, 1-99 "That Don't Impress Me Much" features a guy with a pocket mirror, who loves in the following order: 1) Himself; 2) His car; and 3) MAYBE her. She ponders "See you later, Alligator."

Shania was born less than ten miles from **Henry Ford** – who first sponsored fiddling contests to help begin Country Music. "The River"? The Detroit River – between two great countries. One of the most exciting trends in Rock and Roll has been the rise of women in limelight glory and power. Our next chapter is NOT just women only. Perhaps the pioneer **Brenda Lees** and **Wanda Jacksons** and **LaVern Bakers** are finally getting their rightful prominence within the world's #1 music of the American century. Rock and Roll.

37

Bonnie B. Goode:
Women (and a few Good Men) in Timeless Rock and Roll

On the *Billboard* All-time Top 500 Artists to 1999, only six female artists rank ahead of **Concetta Rosa Maria Franconero**, born 12-12-38 in Newark, New Jersey. Three of them are **Supremes** [see Aretha, Madonna and Janet Jackson]. Concetta WHO? Like Chuck Berry's famed gunnysack guitar whiz Johnny B. Goode, Concetta transformed into a star via her talent and bravado. She became **Connie Francis.**

"Stupid Cupid" – Connie Francis, #14, 7-58. Connie rocks this vintage St. Valentine's Day carol. Impish internal rhyme powers songmasters **Neil Sedaka** and **Howie Greenfield** – Brill Building's finest. Tin Pan Alley went poof. New kids on the songsmith block were **Bobby Darin, Carole King, Barry Mann**, and Sedaka.

"Bad Blood" – Neil Sedaka, #1(3), 9-75. Elton John handles the dynamo-backing vocal for Neil's career rebound. Sedaka's barrage of bubbly tunes skyrocketed on a dizzying "Stairway to Heaven" (#9, 3-60; #16, 5-60 R & B) despite flak from a bobbysoxer who was a "Little Devil" (#11, 5-61). His skyward swoop was buoyed by living "Next Door to an Angel" at #4, 10-62. Elton scooped Neil's career back into prominence with Neil's decade-later second #1 after "Breaking Up Is Hard to Do" of 6-62: #1 "Laughter in the Rain" of 10-74. Brooklyn Lincoln High School and Juilliard School of Music grad Sedaka painted the Brill Building a colorful palette of Monet & Manet & Cezanne Impressionistic colors. And the multi-hued result was the Rise of Women in Rock and Roll. Without Neil Sedaka's friendly influence, rock melodies might be dull, penguin-suited, colorless blah.

"Stupid Cupid" chides the little Valentine imp with the arrows of love. Connie's gushy yodel-kicks rival **Cyndi Lauper**. **Dick Clark** featured Connie frequently on *American Bandstand*. Connie had the same basic appeal as Annette Funicello – sweet, gorgeous, figureful, Italian girl. **Connie B. Goode.** And very, very good she was.

"I'm Sorry I Made You Cry" – Henry Burr, #1(2), 6-1918. Burr dominated entire 1890-1930 era with champ-ever 12,000 songs sung and recorded. Connie steered this tune to #36, 5-58. Connie's chart debut? She sang one

early multicultural hit, with R & R's American Indian 50s star, **Marvin Rainwater** (#93, 12-57 "The Majesty of Love"). Sedaka's splashy melodies turned Connie into a teen idol.

"Everybody's Somebody's Fool" – Connie Francis, #1(2), 5-60; #2(1), R & B; #24, 7-60, C. Somehow, Connie was bereft of an invite to Rock Hall of Fame by 2002+. It may have something to do with Lite Metal. Her golden voice often got cutely compared to the sound of a trombone. Connie rarely rocked the rafters with Thunder Rock. Instead, she simply sprinkled sunshine: #9 "Frankie" (for **Frankie Avalon**) 5-59; #8, 2-60 "Mama" (for papa); and "Many Tears Ago," 11-60 (for forlorn lovers everywhere).

All the first eleven R & R Hall of Fame freshman class of 1986 were male: Chuck Berry, James Brown, Ray Charles, Sam Cooke, Fats Domino, Everly Brothers, Buddy Holly, Jerry Lee Lewis, Little Richard, and Elvis Presley. Of the 15 acts named in 1987, only Aretha was female. Aretha, of course, is the obvious Queen of Soul. Connie's credentials? Connie was the 'Top Female Vocalist of Pop/Rock in the U.S. in the 50s and 60s. **Brenda Lee** (Rock Hall '02) won the silver medal. **Madonna** wins for 70s, 80s, and 90s, with **Mariah Carey** surging.

"Where the Boys Are" – Connie Francis, #4, 1-61. This movie theme ballad reminds me of a wild party at Kathy Hanlon's house as THE BOYS were about to graduate high school in January 1961. Perhaps your pals, along with 1,234,567 groups in American history, called themselves THE BOYS: **Bob Baldori, Eddie Cowling**, future front man lawyer of Presidents George Bush I and II; **Jim Cook**, later Vietnam Marine and gonzo Atlanta salesman. We were also Jan Radke, Denny Jaggers, Jack 'the Bear' Berry, Dick Shattuck, the Big Bopper Dave Brady, Don 'Zorro' Zabinski (wrestling champ), Pete Cooper (cross-country captain), John 'Beatle' Hayes, Ray Jackson, Manuel Turchan, Squeeners Quigley, Dave Konkel, and Bill Baker. As I watch all of these dear old pals of mine fade into time's wilderness at each class reunion – I think, God bless THE BOYS, I still love 'em all.

Anyhow, Kathy lived behind our mentor George Yousko's U-Drive-In off Ford Road where some of my rowdy friends would got to well, uh, sober up on gallons of coffee. Kathy had a group of cute 10th-grade girls we'd go out with who called themselves (you guessed it) THE GIRLS. One blustery one-degree night, Kathy had this monster party, and we slipped and slid on the icy alley as a Canadian blue norther swept down from Hudson's Bay. Ex-prize-fighter George (47, looked 67) ran the U-Drive-In. He tried to dole out fatherly advice on the benefits of sobriety, but my pie-eyed pals had just torn down half of Dearborn, Michigan, gouging a swath out of Detroit itself. Kathy thought Zorro looked like Elvis (he still does, with silver hair), and she kept getting 'Lipstick on his Collar' (Connie, #5, 5-59) as he guzzled Italian table wine with Southern Comfort. The Bopper had eluded some cops by ditching Bob Sigler's beer out of the sunroof of his subzero VW Beetle; Bob is now a Maine doctor who once treated **Ozzy Osbourne**'s sore throat. Just before we all went our separate ways to Europe and beyond, THE BOYS had this one rip-roaring *American Graffiti* night I will never forget. I was probably with Sheila Mervak and/or Lucy Archer again, but the memories fuzz nostalgically and are up for grabs.

So that's where the BOYS were when Connie's goldentones swamped every airwave for every teenager in America. "Where the Boys Are" was simply a ballroom torch ballad, celebrating Spring Break in a fluffy romantic teenage movie. And **Connie Francis** followed us all over our European odyssey.

We will never forget her, and her fadeaway silver song.

Here's this time-warp Modean Theory of Favorite Songs: THE SONGS THAT CAME OUT WHEN YOU WERE 11 to 19 MIGHT JUST BE THE SONGS YOU WILL LOVE THE MOST FOR THE REST OF YOUR LIFE.

In "Where the Boys Are," which turned out to be maybe Coral Gables, Florida on Spring Break Bacchanalia, Connie stands around looking hot and beautiful. She waits patiently for Mr. Right to arrive. While she was inactively waiting for Prince Charming, Esq., a few other nifty hits came hopping down the Easter Bunny trail: Her weepy #6, 6-61 farewell "Together"; #1, 2-62 "Don't Break the Heart That Loves You"; and plaintive #7, 4-61 "Breakin' in a Brand New Broken Heart." After much personal tragedy, Connie rebounded with NC, 1983; #84 C "There's Still a Few Good Love Songs Left in me." We all hope so. She has always been a class act. And a pioneer of Women's Rock. Connie B. Goode.

"Like a Virgin" – Madonna [Ciccone], #1(6), 11-84; #9, 12-84 R & B. Rochester, Michigan, hovers in the eastern shadow of the doomed Detroit Lions' Silverdome and the Detroit Pistons' glitzy Palace of Auburn Hills. Bay City, Michigan, non-home of the **Bay City Rollers** (#24, 10-77 "The Way I Feel Tonight"), huddles in the crook of Michigan's famed "Thumb", and the hot mouth of the Saginaw River. If you read enough Madonna info, you'll discover she was born in both places. They are 75 miles apart.

The Madonna confusion started early. Throughout the history of the Catholic Church, the association of 'Madonna' and 'Virgin' has been linked to the Holy Mother of Jesus. On August 16, 1958, Madonna (b. Madonna Louise Ciccone) arrived on the Michigan scene in a place shrouded in mystery.

Unlike Botticelli's famous Venus, rising from flamingo seas on the half shell, Madonna did not emerge a full-fledged woman from birth. Tragedy-flecked childhood, first. Like similar icon **James Dean**, whose mother died when he was nine, of a tragic female "long illness" like Madonna's mother, Madonna had to fend for herself. **TIna Turner** and **Aretha Franklin**'s mothers abandoned them. Paul McCartney and John Lennon were also brought together when their mothers died when the Fab Two were sub-teens. Her survival tactics often bordered on shock value. No coincidence, it was, for **Michael Jackson** and Madonna to be the big stars of the video *MTV* 80s. Madonna studied choreography at University of Michigan (good, ahem, school) after a high school cheerleading career marked by coy moves (see tabloids again) with her teasing twirling skirtlet. Like the Drifters, Madonna lit out for the Great White Way "On Broadway," and the usual Fame & Fortune contract. She got mixed up in a couple of movies that will (hopefully) never be seen on Sunday School Video Jubilee Day. "Like a Virgin" is one of the most evocative titles ever fondled. Madonna's self-promotion is a lesson in humility to lesser stars.

For a short time, Madonna played drums in a New Wave band, For a long time, she hammered away at re-inventing images and sounds. Her stunning variety of sounds made her the #1 female singer of all time in 1999 – 6th overall Artist, after **Elvis** (9641 pts.), **Beatles** (5360 pts.), **Elton John** (5176 pts.), **Stevie Wonder** (4450 pts.) and **James Brown** (4152 pts.). The Godfather of Soul better check his rearview mirror with Madonna's 4071 pts. in 1999 (Whitburn). When her old beau Steve Bray from the Big D showed up in the Village, he and she did a few demo tapes with the band Emmy. Madonna's rise is turned on by the Disco phenomenon, too. She's always been crucially attuned to what is now called Dance Music, despite the fact that ALL Rock music is Dance Music. And Dance Music turned to pre-Rap DJ shticks. And the Alternative Lifestyle community of the Village People.

In 1982, Madonna's first records missed the regular charts. In the Post-Industrial Neo-Disco setting, "House Music" songs with L——O——N——G versions have a life all their own. Rap and Dance/Industrial/House DJ's have played a major role in SAVING VINYL. Though their actual 'air play' may be only a squashy 50' x 100' labyrinthine 3 a.m. basement, of some leather 'rave-up' Village dive, many Disco and Hip-Hop and Punk tracks joined their New Wave and Middle Aged-Wave R & R cronies later at the top of the charts.

Madonna's semi-virginal career kicked off in steamy Manhattan, in strobeswirl Discos and New Wave Emporiums. The Italian-American cheerleader with Marilyn Monroe's curly blonde hair, Madonna, is one of the most malleable singers of all time. She re-invents far-ranging R & R styles from Disco to Latino to Dance to Punk to

New Wave to Classic American-Pie Rock. Though she has so far avoided the Country chart, never underestimate her wide-ranging multi-musical skills. Like Cyndi Lauper, and much earlier Connie Francis, Madonna fires those little vocal fireworks (yep, the yahoo yodel-kicks and semi-sensuous squeals) into "Like a Virgin." She is coquettish, she is coy, and she captured the fantasy passions of a billion young lads worldwide with her magnetic music. The birth of Madonna's daughter Lourdes Leone in October 1996, cast a pall on Madonna's potential innocence as hinted in this song. "Like a Virgin," however, was still Madonna's biggest hit until 1994.

"True Blue" – Madonna, #3, 10-86. "True Blue" is a 50s Streetcorner masterpiece plunked into the heart of 1986. With the basic four-chord progression (I, VIm, IV, V7) of the **Five Satins, Johnny Maestro's Crests**, the **Elegants**, or the **Capris, Madonna** bounces her lusciously lovely soprano into the tune with a "HEY!" that mimics the Surf Rock curvaceous Mouseketeer cutie from Utica, New York – who also had just one stage name – **Annette** (Funicello). Mouseketeers **Britney Spears** and **Christina Aguilera** followed. Heavy echo boosts Madonna's throbbing rhythm guitar sound. The beat thumps a booming bass drum that simulates the Grand Canyon echo at moonrise. "True Blue" is so sweetsy a song, Madonna even uses the archaic 1929 love word "Dear," long consigned to Great-Aunt Effie. The lead guitar rides the deep background like a chariot of blue fire. "True Blue" shows Madonna's personal and promotional savvy. With-it lyric? She's heard all the lines. Sweet nothings have been whispered in her ear. Two Madonnas cruise the melody early on, doubling the sugary power of this punchy little platter. Background singers segue in Supremely, hinting of Miracles. And Vandellas. Pips, too. "True Blue" doesn't just drift. Or waft. With cheery cheerleader crescendo, she bobs and weaves her flippy way up the pure melodic scale. As Madonna ascends, a tapestry of vocal background unfurls. Her top tune sails with a clever counterpoint, a polyphonous texture that unites "True Blue's" unique total sound into two soaring simultaneous bubbly melodies. It contains the main volatile ingredients: "True Blue" is a masterwork of simplicity interwoven with secret complexity. On one hand, it's just a basic Streetcorner ditty, with four basic chords. In another context, it's a counterpoint harmonic blanket, twirling with star-spangled timbre and dynamic drive.

"La Isla Bonita" – Madonna, #4, 3-87. Huh? Madonna Ciccone doing South Sea Island Paradise surfy-turfy Rock? Can an Italian-American icon from snowbird Michigan really rollick along on lilting Latina Rock and Roll? Why not? If you check the origin of 'Latin' language, which splintered into Spanish, Italian, French, Portuguese, (Rhaeto-Romanian, and so on), it started out pretty close to Rome. Spanish "La Isla Bonita" means the "beautiful island." Madonna coos a Spanish lullaby. Sizzly romance blooms among the cozy sheltering palms. Tough tune for most males to shrug off. Tropic-isle paradise:

"My Isle of Golden Dreams" – Ben Selvin and his Orchestra, #4, 2-20. The Hawaiian craze hula-ed 1910s with "Aloha Oe." The icy winter of 1920 re-invented the island paradise Herman Melville wrote about in his 1840s *Typee* (with an affair with the beautiful Fayaway); Daniel Defoe got stuck in 1719 *Robinson Crusoe* with only a guy named Friday on his paradise isle, but who knows – maybe Robinson had Friday on his mind (#16, 3-67 **Easybeats'** "Friday on My Mind"). Anyhow, dreamy isles and grass skirts will probably continue to occupy the American male's drowsy reverie (see **Marty Robbins**, and Hawaii).

Madonna

"Borderline" – Madonna, #10, 3-84. Though her #16, 10-83 intro "Holiday" was no slouch, Madonna first rocketed into the top ten with this echoey Boogie. Saucy style and come-hither magnetism. Madonna followed this one with #4 "Lucky Star" in 8-84 (#42, 9-84 R & B).

"Material Girl" – Madonna, #2(2), 2-85; #49, 3-85 R & B. Madonna got criticized for her hedonistic assessment of the meaning of life. Money, she said, was fun! Groans moaned from spiritualists. How crass, how money-grubbing, how . . . materialistic. With plucky Dow Jones sincerity, Madonna admits she enjoys making too much money. See Tom T. Hall's 70s "Faster Horses" old cowpoke/guru who equates spiritual world to buffalo chips.

"Money for Nothing" – Dire Straits, #1(3), 7-85. British ex-teacher **Mark Knopfler** raps about the high life of a Rock star. He mocks the glitzy world of Hype-mania. Echoing BTO'S #12, 5-74 "Takin' Care of Business," money earned in Rock and Roll is "Money for Nothing" plus 'free chicks.' He lampoons himself and his band. Every band guy in the world knows that laying down a dynamite sound in the limelight is tough work. Knopfler sings the glories of gaga golden groupies who huddle by the stage door for hugs and beyond. He mocks *MTV*, groupies, A & R marionettes, studio tekkies, lifestyle, his record-buying public, and (lo and behold) himself. When satirizing, he covers all the bases. He razzes everybody's band hi-jinx. *Mad* mag chic.

"Crazy for You" – Madonna, #1(1), 3-85; #80, 5-85 R & B. Thus beginneth a long string of Madonna Monster Hits: two #5's in 4 & 8-85 with "Angel" and "Dress You Up"; #1(1), 4-86 "Live to Tell." Madonna scored on very pretty #2(2), 8-89 "Cherish" and mega-hit #1(3), 4-90 "Vogue." Other intervening goodies include her pump-up-your-self-image "Express Yourself" at #2(2), 6-89 and her swirling slosh of melodic balladry "Rain." Madonna's #1(4) "Music" of 8-2000 shows that the Material Girl still gets great material to counter the #1 hit barrage of **Mariah Carey.**

"Papa Don't Preach" – Madonna, #1(2), 6-86. Young song-girl finds herself unexpectedly expecting a little bundle of joy. "Papa, don't preach," she advises her father, I'm gonna keep this baby. We have no idea how old she is supposed to be. If she's 20 or 22, she can make an excellent case for not preaching. If she is 13 or 14 or 15, she may actually be singing to the fiscally responsible man in the picture (papa), "Don't preach, Papa, you can pay for my baby, and raise it too." The grandfathering clause, and Grandpa Santa Clause, of parental duties are now facts of life. The young girl's noble sentiment not to terminate her pregnancy is slightly complicated by staggering economic and social responsibilities of raising a child. At the age of 38 Madonna had her first child, Lourdes, and her 2nd in 2000. At this age, Madonna realizes that she now has the money and time to devote to her awesome responsibility of motherhood. At 15, however, girls often just wanna have fun. Baby arrives. Oops.

"Take a Bow" – Madonna, #1(7), 12-94; #40, 2-95 R & B. Babyface, backing vocal (#4, 6-94 "When Can I See You"). Unless your name is **Mariah** or **Boyz II Men,** it's very hard to stick your tune in the #1 spot for two months. Madonna's still riding her Hit Parade wavecrest: #6, 12-95 "You'll See"; #2(1), 3-98 "Frozen"; #5, 7-98 "Ray of Light"; #19, 6-99 "Beautiful Stranger"; and #4, 11-2000 "Don't Tell Me." Madonna has spent a lot of time at #1, for good musical and visual reasons. Admittedly, she's attractive. Anyone who ogled Marilyn Monroe in the 50s can see Marilyn's body style, improved through toning and Bally's heavy workouts. Madonna's range rises from purry suave contralto to floating soprano with ease and grace. The #6 Artist of All Time (Whitburn), Madonna scored with albums, too: Al. #1(5), 7-86 *True Blue*; Al. #1(6), 4-89 *Like A Prayer*; Al. #2(3), 6-90 *The Immaculate Collection*; and Al. #2(1), 11-92, bedtime story *Erotica*. When "Vogue" hit #1, Madonna 'won' the 1990 *Rolling Stone* "Worst Female Singer" and "Worst Video of the Year" awards. Ah, the sweet smell of success. [Superstar Overplay and Concomitant Jealousy strike again].

"Like a Prayer" – Madonna, #1(3), 3-89; #20 R & B. Now wait a sec. When all of us were lads back in our Italian-Polish factory neighborhoods, the word MADONNA, yes, meant Jesus' Mother. Times change. One reason this glitzy singer with songs like #3, 10-92 "Erotica" has been gouged by the pundits for her morality is the name coincidence. Had Madonna called herself FiFi or Bubbles or Va-Va-Voom-Bazoom, no one would have expected saintly behavior from the perky pert Pontiac hoofer in the R & R spotlight. Since her starry-eyed folks saddled her with the moniker MADONNA, folks expect her to push piety and propriety. [No wonder many Hispanic men in the U.S.A. have changed their 'Jesus' (pronounced, of course, 'Hey-Zeus') name to 'Jesse.']

About Jesus. Jesus himself didn't always hang around with pious saints. Among his friends was Mary Magdalene, whose rep had been dragged through the quagmire. When the Powers That Were Came to Be – saying she should be stoned, Jesus brilliantly said the one without sin might cast the first stone . . . Didn't someone once say "The Good Lord loves a sinner"? Hasn't the bulwark of Christianity always been mercy? Forgiveness? Love?

The world loves Madonna's versatile music. In 1990, when her #1 "Vogue" was in vogue, she took up jogging. She starred with Warren Beatty in the ultra-colorful cartoonish *Dick Tracy**** and the 1997 blockbuster *Evita***½. Her early 90s "I'm Breathless" hit #2 U.K. and U.S.A., surviving and thriving in a profusion of Rap from tough smoky streets. The hanky-panky you see in Madonna's sensuous "Take a Bow" video erupted earlier into her "Hanky-Panky" #10, 6-90 hit. After "Justify My Love" hit #1(2) in January 1991, her "Rescue Me" popped up two months later at an immediate #15 – highest HOT 100 Singles debut slot for a female artist in Rock and Roll history. The old mark? An obscure platter by Joy Layne "Your Wild Heart" from 1957 which hit #20 and stuck there. Madonna, too, very weirdly, only saw "Rescue Me" ascend the rescue ladder to rung #9.

From dance-hall dandy to megastar, Madonna cranked out the most brazen of the new *MTV* three-minute morality plays. She piped the venue to the max, squirreling away Rock Shock in tiny erotic acorns, which exploded into steamy potpourris of passion, with strong oaken roots to anchor her top ten reign. By 10-98, Madonna had re-invented herself (a constant Madonna-press cliché) into her sweet-kid vocal persona. She tossed out a bitter tidbit for the poor dumped dude to chew on: "The Power of Goodbye" (#13, unluckier for the Dumpee than the Dumper). Gorgeous Celtic Renaissance musical score; sad, sad message of goodbye. The Madonna magnetism floats on a devious duality between her "Boy Toy" coy persona, and the massive cross bisecting her heaving chest. The average guy looks, lusts, and says "WHOOPS, there's that cross again, reminding me of my animalistic nature." Madonna milks *MTV* for all the passion she can squeeze from the limelight; milk and lime may have a sour taste, but the bright blonde of mammoth media just might cry all the way to the bank. Madonna Ciccone does a great job reminding all of us temporary earthlings of the old mediaeval dilemma. We are a little lower than the angels, but not much higher than the beasts of the earth. Saints be praised.

Those who trash the Bay City (and Pontiac/Rochester) roller might consider that they probably had their moms at home beyond their own seventh birthdays. Motherless Michigander Madonna fended for herself pretty well in the aftermath of inconsolable loss. As Madonna greeted the Millennium as a new [double] mother, she now steels her frenzied focus to motherhood.

"Baby, Baby" – Amy Grant, #1(2), 2-91. Amy (b. '60, Atlanta) criss-crossed (or cross-crossed) the River Jordan from her Christian Contemporary stardom to encounter the madcap Mardi Gras of party-animal fever. Amy's ode to motherhood "Baby, Baby" is about a beautiful kid, Amy's daughter Millie, whose cherubic six-week-old face inspired this bubbly anthem of mother love.

"Every Heartbeat" – Amy Grant, #2(1), 6-91. Every one of her heartbeats bears his name. Amy's throbbing alto squeezes into the second line, echoing Evangelical "Can I Get a Witness" (Marvin Gaye, #22, 10-63) fervor that empowers her Christian Rock and Roll Vision. In many pulpits in 1956, that phrase would be an oxymoron. Fire and brimstone preachers wrestled live rattlesnakes, declaring Rock and Roll the 'Devil's Music.' Somewhere in the last forty years, someone recalled that the *Bible* itself has no prohibitions against Rock and Roll. (see Religious Rock chapter). Yea, verily, it even encourageth it: "Make a joyful noise unto the Lord" (*Psalms* 100)!

"Every Heartbeat" confirms that love is the primary power in the universe. Passion, within bounds, is a consecrated sacrament. Amy's hit also hammers a great rhythm track. She carries her song along in musical profusion and power.

"That's What Love Is For" – Amy Grant, #7, 9-91. Mystical chord pattern. New directions. Amy's song isn't asking for perfection in love. Indeed, it strongly believes in loving despite human failing. This kind of true love, untarnished by Demon Time, echoes some of the greatest writers in history:

> Let me not to the marriage of true minds
> Admit impediments. Love is not love
> Which alters when it alteration finds,
> Or bends with the remover to remove:
> Oh, no! it is an ever-fixed mark,
> That looks on tempest and is never shaken;
> It is the star to every wandering bark,
> Whose worth unknown, although his height be taken.
>
> Love's not Time's fool, though rosy lips and cheeks
> Within his bending sickle's compass come;
> Love alters not with his brief hours and weeks,
> But bears it out even to the edge of doom.
> If this be error and upon me proved,
> I never writ, nor no man ever loved
> Sonnet 116 – William Shakespeare
> [Top Hits of the 1590-1620 zone.]

To truly love someone, you love them not just for their virtues – but in spite of their impediments. "That's What

Love Is For" zigs and zags through a mysterious chord spiral. Whatever chord you expect is the one you don't hear. Isn't love a little bit like that? We don't quite get what we expect, but we love anyway.

"House of Love" – Amy Grant and Vince Gill, #37, 11-94. Grant taps Country musical roots with the sparkling voice of Vince, another Irish tenor with a pure belltone style. Classic harmony duet; they fell in love and married on 3-10-2000.

***What A Wonderful World* – Anne Murray, Al. #14, 11-99.** #1 Contemporary Christian Album Chart. Many notable Rock stars like Anne (b. '45, Nova Scotia) have performed Christian music. Anne's title track is the essence of **Louis 'Satchmo' Armstrong**'s secular hymn (see *Gold Rush* finale). **Pat Boone, Roger McGuinn, Barry McGuire, Dion [DiMucci], Michael W. Smith, Jimmy Clanton, Little Richard, Elvis Presley, Johnny Cash, Al Green, Anita Bryant, the Osmonds,** and also many Rappers have taken up the musical cross. With 12 weeks at #1 on this chart with Anne's album, we have the incomparable Soul/Gospel star **Yolanda Adams** [#1 Christian Contemporary Album, 10-99]. Others on the lofty celestial top of the chart include **Mary Mary, Third Day, the Gaithers (Bill & Gloria), Rachael Lampa, Zoegirl,** and others; many simultaneously appear (Adams, Mary2) on the Top Gospel Albums chart – which also includes **Shirley Caesar, Cece Winans** (a VERY important Gospel family), the **God Squad,** and **Hezekiah Walker.** These artists combine their calling (Christian faith) with their talents (music) to provide us a harmonic swirl of heavenly sound. Christian Heavy Metal/Grunge/Punk ranges from **Zao** to **Stryper** to the Ultra-Mainstream #1 sounds ["Higher" and "With Arms Wide Open"] of Tallahassee's **Scott Stapp**'s crew **Creed** – but these are a good ways from the trad Gospel sound.

"I Will Remember You" – Amy Grant, #20, 4-92. Amy's pensive song of sad goodbye. With sweet repetition, and shimmering rhythm surrounding her song, she sings a tearful farewell to someone very dear.

My mother (1908-97) was born in Butte, Montana. While I was getting my Shakespeare, an old poem fell out that she loved. The name **Bliss Carman**, like foggier names in Rock and Roll (**Chilliwack, Slim Harpo,** or **Felix Papalardi**), may never surge beyond the popularity of Shakespeare – or Madonna. There are no minor poets, and there are no minor songs. Love is universal, never trivial:

> There is something in the autumn that is native to my
>   blood –
> Touch of manner, hint of mood;
> And my heart is like a rhyme,
> With the yellow and purple and the crimson keeping
>   time.
> The scarlet of the maples can shake me like a cry
> Of bugles going by.
> And my lonely spirit thrills

To see the frosty aster like a smoke upon the hills.
There is something in October sets the gypsy blood
astir;
We must rise and follow her,
When from every hill of flame
She calls and calls each vagabond by name.
- Bliss Carman
No minor artists.

I am not worried about anyone forgetting Elvis, or Buddy, or the Fab Four or Rolling Stones. I have no fear anyone will forget Aretha or Smokey, Garfunkel, and Garth. The names Madonna and Prince and Led Zep and the Bee Gees and Mariah may already be permanently etched into our minds. To Sarah McLachlan, it is a different song with a similar name, and another wonderful pensive musical experience. "I Will Remember You" means a lot of things to Amy Grant. To me, it also means mention for all of the wonderful supporting cast. All those #20 singers (hold it, Hendrix was one) with #1 Johnny B. Goode dreams ["Johnny B. Goode" only hit #8]. This oversized pamphlet is for them. And for my Mom. Thanks, Amy. That's what love is for.

"Only the Lonely" – Motels, #9, 4-82. Martha Davis formed her plaintive quintet in Berkeley, and their sophomore hit is #9, 9-83 "Suddenly Last Summer." Their "Only" is no relation to Roy Orbison's classic. It has an evanescent glory of its own, with a pleading ode to all those worldwide lonesome souls who commiserate their isolation.

"Mickey" – Toni Basil, #1(1), 6-82. Toni Basil was born at mid-century (1950), and she worked as a teenager on acclaimed 60s Rock and Folk-Rock shows *Shindig* and *Hullabaloo*. At around age thirteen (our most impressionable musical age, perhaps), Toni was bowled over by the school spirit of those of the first rock cheerleaders, the Honeys, whose 15-year-old cheerleader Marilyn Rovell cut a record with **Beach Boy** Brian Wilson based on **Stephen Foster**'s #1, 1850 classic melody "Old Folks at Home" a/k/a "Swanee River". Their "Surfin' Down the Swanee River" throbbed with the Phil Spector "Wall of Sound" via Brian's studio expertise. Marilyn eventually married Brian. Daughters Carnie and Wendy Wilson, along with Chynna Phillips (kid of Mama and Papa Michelle and John Phillips) became stars **Wilson Phillips** ["Release Me" #1, 6-90]. In dark November 1963 (President Kennedy assassination), the Beach Boys came up with the biggest cheerleading hit of all time, before Toni's "Mickey": #6 "Be True to Your School." Featuring the L.A. Honeys cheering in the background, and the Big Ten "On Wisconsin" fight song, this jock-rock classic was the standard bearer for enthusiasm for years (see Sports Rock).

Toni's L.A. cheerleading expertise paid off. She landed a part in the grim counterculture disaster movie *Easy Rider* (1969), with Dennis Hopper and Peter Fonda. Later Toni went on to be the chief choreographer for one of the greatest R & R flicks of all time: *American Graffiti* (1974), showcasing the incipient talents of young **Harrison Ford, Suzanne Somers, Richard Dreyfuss**, Charles Martin Smith, Paul LeMat, and child star **Ronnie Howard**. In-

deed, Toni Basil was already a major L.A. choreographer for years before her singing career skyrocketed like her enthusiasm. Lauri Dean Barnes points out Toni's contribution via "Mickey" to the speedy rise of *MTV* and later *VH-1* – not to mention cheerleading.

There is much to be said for school spirit and rampant enthusiasm. Toni's high-energy style, bubbly enthusiasm, and winning smile could sell proverbial refrigerators to Eskimos. In a way, her "Mickey" paved the way for the combo choreography and spicy salsa dance numbers and marvelous vocals of **Gloria Estefan** and maybe **Janet Jackson**. Gloria, in turn, paved the way for the huge Latino Explosion of 1999-2000+, starring **Ricky Martin, Enrique Iglesias**, revamped **Carlos Santana**, plus Latino-Yankee girl stars like **Jennifer Lopez** (#16, 4-2002 "I'm Gonna Be Alright"), **Christina Aguilera**, and even part-Venezuelan **Mariah Carey**, who is perhaps the #1 popular female singer of all time, if you count recent #1 chart and sales figures. **Britney Spears** is not Latino, but her cheery dance routines are vintage Toni Basil.

Coming on the cusp of **Monkee Michael Nesmith**'s *MTV* craze, **Toni Basil**'s appeal is not only musical but also choreographic. The electric energy and ebullient enthusiasm of Toni's video helped create for her a major group of fans like Joyce BLum, and from clubs.

Toni had two more hits on the Chrysalis label: #77, 2-83 "Shopping from A to Z," and #81, 1-84 "Over My Head" in the **Bruce Springsteen** Heartland Rock Era. Like cheerleader "Peggy Sue" Gerron Allison, Toni Basil represents much of the beauty and the energy that keeps America accomplishing great things in business, and more importantly, in love.

Toni Basil's "Mickey" wasn't quite the first prototype from a perky, pulchritudinous singer with more bounce to the ounce than Pepsi-Cola:

"I Love Mickey" – Teresa Brewer with Mickey Mantle, #87, 9-65. Toni's mentor [womentor?]. Carrot-topped Terrific Teresa from Toledo, Ohio zings her gung-ho way through this ultimate fan song for the beloved New York Yankee centerfielder headed for baseball's Triple Crown that magic Yankee year: a league-leading .353 batting average, 52 home runs, and 130 runs batted in – BEFORE Steroid Era. The blond, blue-eyed center fielder from Commerce, Oklahoma, chortled a few modest 'aw, shuckses' Rap jam into Teresa's cheery lyrics, but somehow Teresa's tornado of enthusiasm failed to grab all the gold and glory of Toni Basil's #1 tune.

"Lost in Your Eyes" – Debbie Gibson, #1(3), 1-89. Long Island looms as a musical prodigy's Paradise/Limbo. The 15 x 125 mile svelte isle is laden with overwhelming talent, questing to become the next **Billy Joel** (like Amazing Mustang Boy or Iridescence, 5-2001). Debbie (b. '70) DID, distaff-wise, for three glorious years, 1987-89. Debbie played twinkle, twinkle, little piano at five; by age six, she wiggled words around dinky little notes. This tiny L.I. prodigy wrote actual songs. Debbie vaulted to Insta-Stardom with #4, 5-87 "Only in My Dreams," and "Shake Your Love" at #4, 10-87. "Out of the Blue" (#3, 1-88), the pretty lass was a star. Her first #1, "Foolish Beat," served notice to Madonna and Mariah they had a winsome talent trailing just a ways back. Debbie, and every other good female singer, still trails them.

"After the Rain" – Nelson, #6, 11-90. Twins of Rock Hall of Famer (1987). Like father, like son(s). **Ricky Nelson**'s two blond teen idol songs carry on their father's family tradition of making breathless girls swoon. Norwegian-American Hollywood twins **Gunnar** (bass) and **Matthew** (guitar) show their family's tri-generational superstardom:

"She Belongs to Me" – Ricky Nelson, #33, 10-69. Despite many of Ricky's fellow idols' yearning to be frozen into the 50s Chapter, Ricky kept up with new trends, and launched this Dylan classic into a Psychedelic Rock world. Ricky grew his hair long and went Country Rock like the Byrds' Gram Parsons' project – Flying Burrito Brothers.

"You Leave Me Breathless" – Ozzie Nelson and his Orchestra, #11, 6-38. Ozzie and Harriet round out probably the only three-generation wave of #1-hit Chartbusters. ABSOLUTELY no relation to Jerry Lee Lewis's "Breathless," or the 2001 Corrs. **Ozzie** and lovely songstress/wife **Harriet Nelson**, before they became Gunnar grandparents, touched off a fusillade of fireworks like #1(1), 7-35 "And Them Some," and a L.A. horticultural phenomenon – "Roses in December" (#3, 7-37). Male Nelsons inhabit this chapter of mostly female stars because I don't believe in gender or racial segregation. *Gold Rush* integrates every kind of music. We weave songs and sunshine. We're a FABRIC BONANZA of divergent musics.

"Stay (I Missed You)" – Lisa Loeb and Nine Stories, #1(3), 5-94. Lisa began in Dallas, meandering to *MTV*. Behind her owlish glasses and Mona Lisa smile lurks a fine precise mind. Her #18 "Do You Sleep?" of 9-95 can't be answered yes. Her "I Do" hit #17, 11-97. Her vocal timing and unusual presentation suggests another outstanding Jewish-American songwriter/star **Janis Ian** (born Janis Eddy Fink) in New York City:

"At Seventeen" – Janis Ian, #3, 6-75. Ian's bitingly incisive bitter tale about a girl not deemed beautiful. She bandies about the phrase "ugly duckling." Editorial comment: real men know there are no ugly women. Or ducklings. [Maybe a few lizards.] Ian laments in sad minor key getting chosen last for basketball in those gym popularity contests. Ian also did #14, 5-67 "Society's Child" about interracial dating – and all the hypocrisy of those who mouthe pompous platitudes, yet whisper dastardly nastyisms of discrimination.

"You're in Love" – Wilson Phillips, #1(1), 2-91. Family Values Bandwagon includes Surf Rock sound of the **Beach Boys' Brian Wilson** and the California Dreamin' sound of one Mama and one Papa. **Chynna Phillips** is daughter of John (1939-2001) and Michelle Phillips; **Wendie** and **Carnie Wilson** are daughters of Beach Boy mastermind Brian Wilson. Eagle **Joe Walsh** played guitar on their #4, 10-90 "Impulsive."

"Monday, Monday" – Mamas and Papas, #1(3), 4-66. Their second hit was their biggest. They power-shifted seraphic harmonies (and bVII chromatic chords) into the biggest song ever to celebrate (aaaaaarrrrrgh!) the beginning of the maybe-boring workweek. **Fats Domino's** "Blue Monday" hit #5, 1-57, #1(8) R& B. He reflects upon his wild weekend – super Saturday night, woozy Sunday morn floating back to grubby earth.

"Our Lips Are Sealed" – Go-Go's, #20, 8-81. The Go-Gos pioneered female Rock bands, with women handling their own instruments – as well as dishing out melodies and harmonies as sweet and blithe as the Wilson-Phillips Post-Modern Surf surge. **Belinda Carlisle** and three other Go-Go-Go's also scored with #11, 3-84 "Head Over Heels."

"Heaven Is a Place on Earth" – Belinda Carlisle, #1(1), 9-87. Actor **James Mason** piloted a weird atomic-powered submarine around the world in a bizarre 19th-century science-fiction Disney thriller, Jules Verne's *20,000 Leagues Under the Sea* (1954****). His son, perhaps a bit smarter than his brilliant British father, piloted himself to Belinda Carlisle. Belinda (b. 1950, Hollywood) married **Morgan Mason**. When the Go-Gos broke up in 1984, her solo career blossomed. Belinda debuted her solo sound with the nifty Duran Duran guitar solo riffs of Andy Taylor on #3, 5-86 "Mad About You." After "Heaven," she didn't have too far to fall with #2(1), 1-88 "I Get Weak."

Remember "Castles in the Sand"? Or the Shangri-Las' #1 "Remember (Walkin' in the Sand).' Belinda's #7, 4-88 "Circle in the Sand" sparkles on the surfside strand.

"Half Breed" – Cher, #1(2), 8-73. Bombastic with native American tom-tom thunder, "Half Breed" struts Cher's massive vocal range and power. Sinister overlay to spooky #1(1), 1-74 "Dark Lady," about a creepy fortuneteller – not good ol' Madame Rue down at the harmless "Love Potion #9" kiosk. Both songs surround Cher's raspy contralto. She seethes with distaff punch and power, but Cher's song-girl digs the bizarrely exotic "Half Breed." Cher also grooves to more Mainstream stuff like Girl Group **Betty Everett** echo "The Shoop Shoop Song (It's in His Kiss)" #33, 11-90.

In the White Soul category, Cher's #10, 11-87 "I Found Someone" was produced by fellow Soul practitioner **Michael Bolton**. Other chart-clambers for Cher? #17, 6-91 "Love and Understanding"; #52, 6-96 "One by One"; #8, 1-89 "Just Like Jesse James," and her Peter Cetera duo #6, 3-89 "After All." Also #1, '99 "Believe" (later), and #57, 5-99 "Strong Enough." Cher hit #14, 4-88 with "We All Sleep Alone." Speaking of women, another artist many women like to look at, and buy records from, is Cher's co-writer and producer on this hit **Jon Bon Jovi**.

"Blaze of Glory" – Bon Jovi, #1(1), 7-90. Born with the Italian name **Bongiovi**, Jon Bon Jovi (b. '62, Sayreville, New Jersey) whipped up a little phonetic transcription, and a crossfire Hard Rock/Heavy Metal sound that rampaged into girls hearts. His eager electric mayhem bashed former quietude. Armed with gonzo guitar guru **Richie**

Sambora (#63, 9-91 "Ballad of Youth"), keyboarder **Dave Bryan**, drummer **Tico Torres**, and extraordinary bass flyer **Alec John Such**, Bon Jovi erupted with big hair in 2-84 with their Un-Shannon new tune "Runaway" to #39. Their next three tunes fluttered "In and Out of Love" #69, 8-85. Suddenly they were rollercoastered to the zowie zenith of the pop pantheon with their cleverly titled #1(1), 9-86 "You Give Love a Bad Name." Bon Jovi in Women's Chapter? Hey, women LOVE them, like they love Duran Duran.

"Blaze of Glory" is a great name for the Rock star's sudden surge to the wonderful/terrible Elvis Spotlight. For Bon Jovi, it's also a great song. It flashes with the fiery flame of Sambora's pyrotechnic guitar, and the magic of John's right-on Rock and Roll voice. No "Miracle" (#12, 10-90), Bon Jovi shone with a flash of Thrash and a Power Rock promenade: #14, 6-95 "This Ain't a Love Song"; #9, 10-89 "Living in Sin," and [ulp] #97 "I'll Sleep When I'm Dead" (wonder why this missed Top Ten bandwagon).

"Livin' On a Prayer" – Bon Jovi, #1(4), 12-86. Bon Jovi's biggest hit. Other mammoth movers on the Bon Jovi 1986-90 Heyday Bandwagon? Their run-the-table string of nine straight top ten tunes skirts that lofty territory between stardom and superstardom – a nice place to hover. Among other triumphs: #1(2) "Bad Medicine" of 9-88; #3, 11-88 "Born to Be My Baby"; "I'll Be There for You" at #1(1), 3-89; and their Western post-office poster "Wanted Dead or Alive" at #7, 4-87. No flash in the prospector's gold-rush pan, Bon Jovi hit top ten #10, 1-93 "Bed of Roses" and passionate ballad #4, 10-94 "Always" (one of their best). At mid-decade? Their beefy #14, 6-95 "This Ain't a Love Song."

"It's My Life" – Bon Jovi, #33+, 8-2000; #11 Adult Top 40. Bon Jovi's A-bomb chorus on "It's My Life" boosts the throbbing tune to the Top Five songs of the fledgling millennium. With guitar guy Richie Sambora frogging a gruff bass/baritone vocal rhythm, Jon Bon Jovi hefts a high-life 'My Life' to the Rock and Roll Heavens. He invokes New Jersey neighbor **Frank Sinatra** in the bulging-beat chorus lyric, and captures the true Spirit of Rock Music. Mystic aura of Frank's/Elvis's "My Way." None of their hidden rhythmic pulse. Bon Jovi BLASTS it, "It's My Life" cascades in audial waves of glory and splendor.

Bursts with seething power upon the sleeping suburban scene like gangbusters. At 38, the vibrant and vital Jon Bon Jovi practically grabs the world by its penguin-suited lapel and demands R & R respect. "It's My Life" almost screams, "We are NOT an Oldies act; we are still the CUTTING EDGE of Rock and Roll." Bon Jovi's rhythm swoon involves Tico Torres' thunder drum bash, the Surround-Sound guitar-fire of maestro Sambora, and the bass-pulse and keyboard blanket of Such and Bryan. "It's My Life" glows with the essence of hedonism. Thankfully, their follow-up climbed charts too, #57, 2-2001 "Thank You for Loving Me." 'In His Life,' Jon echoes Elvis's Italian Opera phase with his 'It's now or never' (#1, '60) frantic frenzied dash for the gold, the glory, and the gusto.

"These Dreams" – Heart, #1(1), 1-86. Heavy Metal Belter Ann Wilson takes the tempo down a peg, smoothing out a suave and mellow ballad. Surprise first #1 blockbuster. In a mixed message of ardent victory and staggering defeat, Heart won the ultimate Heavy Metal Rocker indignity/triumph, #1(3) on the Adult Contemporary chart. On the cusp of the new decade, Heart was vilified for the seedy theme of their #2(2), 3-90 "All I Wanna Do Is Make Love to You," a ragtag zigzag affair from a limbo marriage.

"Dreaming of You" – Selena, #22, 10-95. Cult following erupted after Corpus Christi Texas's **Selena Quintanilla Perez**'s (1971-95) tragic death. Posthumous airplay boosted her "I Could Fall in Love" to #8A, 7-95. In a bizarre scenario with overtones of Mark David Chapman's supposed fandom for John Lennon, Selena was murdered by the president of her fan club, Yolanda Saldivar. Selena's ascension to stardom also parallels **Ritchie Valens**. One of the freshman class of 1986's Rock Hall Inductees, **Sam Cooke**, was killed by gunfire. Glory is dangerous, often tragic. Selena had a unique and very popular voice among Latino fans, and Selena helped spearhead the 2000+ Latino/Tejano Explosion.

"Morning Train" – Sheena Easton, #1(2), 2-81. Glasgow songstress Sheena's (b. '59) big-time commuter frenzy ode. With nary a hint of Scots burr, Sheena salutes her dedicated man enduring the workaday world – and returning to her for a romantic rendezvous. Sheena followed up with her voyeurish #4, 7-81 "For Your Eyes Only"; #9, 8-83 "Telefone (Long Distance Love Affair)"; #9 sensuous 12-84 "Sugar Walls"; and her second-biggest hit, #2(1), 11-88 "The Lover in Me." "The Arms of Orion" (#36, 12-89) highlights the big January constellation that loops the zodiac with ice-blue stars like Rigel and flame-red Betelgeuse (Beetlejuice): Sheena duets with **Prince** on the *Batman* movie "Orion" tune:

"When Doves Cry" – Prince, #1(5), 6-84; #1(8) R & B. Prince plays 24 instruments like **Bobby Darin**. Like **Gene Pitney**'s pioneering total do-it-yourself hit record, #39, 1-61 "I Wanna Love My Life Away," Prince's records often feature the talented singer/songwriter fondling all the instruments in a talented miracle of harmonic sounds. Born 6-7-58 in Minneapolis, Minnesota, prodigy Prince first named himself after his father's trio – the Prince Rogers Trio. Bob Seger's father, too, was a bandleader, like Ricky Nelson's dad. Prince's (no relation) full name is Prince Roger Nelson. Prince prides himself on unleashing a musical masterpiece of electronic wizardry.

"Purple Rain" – Prince, #2(2), 10-84; #4 R & B. PURPLE is an appropriate color for the royal sound of Prince's productions. Like Pitney acquiring Phil Spector's Wall of Sound later in his career, Prince latched onto the Revolution: **Wendy Melvoin**, guitar; Bobby Z and/or **Sheila E**, drums; Andrew Cymone, bass; plus cast of thousands.

Prince's name returned officially (and legally) to "Prince" in 2000. Prince suffered emotional trauma as a teenager due to a common-problem tug-of-war between his father and stepfather. Between June and September 1993 (when Prince switched temporarily to the pseudonym 'Victor'), he abandoned his name 'Prince.' Prince's new 'name' was an unpronounceable splotch, with some mystical connection to a combo male and female symbol.

"Purple Rain" is a rambling rococo groundswell of off-beat rhythms and Jazz-riff complexity (see Queen and Glam Rock). Prince is a unique and eclectic performer, imbued with talent. Critic **Dave Marsh** says "When Doves Cry," might be the most influential single record of the 80s. "Unforgettably carnal imagery – a great one, virtually inexhaustible in its intricacies." Then Marsh takes on 5'2" Prince's coldness"; he compares it to Dylan in maintaining an emotional distance from your subject.

"Raspberry Beret" – Prince, #2(1), 5-85; #3 R & B. Prince steers a pretty melody, coming back to his intimate message. Prince donned the duds of a multidimensional 80s **Little Richard**; Prince's face brims with blush and mascara and lipstick. He out-glitzes the Glam groaners on their own turf. Shock Rock never sought a staid audience. Prince's first song oozed "Soft and Wet" (#92, 11-78, but #12, 7-78 R & B). Prince racked up the Top Artist of the Decade crown in Whitburn's tally for the 80s with 881 points (Michael Jackson 860, Bruce Springsteen 632, Whitney Houston 574, and Madonna's 566). Prince's Al. *Purple Rain* led the pack for 24 weeks – nearly half of 1984. Fans dug his vibes and his wavelength.

If Prince taps the baser urges, and bypasses love, it annoys some critics. It even precipitated the PARENTAL ADVISORY stickers on CD's and records, after a Senate hearing that featured key witnesses **John Denver, Frank Zappa,** and Twisted Sister's **Dee Snider**. The diminutive Rock/Soul icon Prince invokes a multiple Rock genre approach. He taps all pop music to gush their rush of lush hush-hush mush. In other words, 'PG' it ain't.

"Little Red Corvette" – Prince, #6, 2-83; #15, 3-83 R & B. Prince pogo-sticked to his first top ten tune four years after his #11, 11-79 "I Wanna Be Your Lover" and #12, 10-82 "1999" knocked on the steely door. Prince's "Let's Go Crazy" hit #1(2), 8-84 run in the zowie wake of his biggee "When Doves Cry." Prince battered away with #8, 9-83 "Delerious," #3, 7-87 "Sign of the Times," and #7, 7-85 "Pop Life." Prince paraded into Rap Shorthand with #2, 8-87 "U Got the Look," #23, 3-92 "Money Don't Matter 2 Night," #8, 12-84 "I Would Die 4 U" and his #25, 2-85 "Take Me with U." His #1(2), 2-86 offering has same name as **Gene Simmons'** Heavy Metal/Glam Rock – "Kiss." The Minnesotan musical marauder blasted his zany "Batdance" to #1(1) in 6-89, following unique #8, 4-88 "Alphabet St." "Thieves in the Temple" nabbed number six in 8-90, and Prince picked up the New Power Generation and surged with #1(2), 9-81 "Cream" and #3, 12-91 "Diamonds and Pearls." A numerical oddity zapped Prince's 11-92 smash. It's called "7," and hit #7. Destiny? Prince is one mega-artist important enough to waltz between Warner Brothers, his main squeeze, and Paisley Park, his own label. Prince's later stuff? #3, 3-94 "The Most Beautiful Girl in the World." Songs named "I Love You" you'd expect, yes?

But "I Hate You" (#12, 12-95)? For a generation, Prince has been shaping Rock and Roll destiny. Like **Jimi Hendrix**, Prince has expanded the boundaries of the R & B/Rock and Roll world, and his musical expertise and upfront sensuality have carved out a major career. In 1999, he hit the top 40 with a revamp of his #12, 12-82 "1999" – at #40, 1-99. Hmmm.

"Save the Best for Last" – Vanessa Williams, #1(5), 2-92; #1(3), R & B. If you want to make it as a Soft Rock star, it doesn't hurt to be very beautiful – like **Anita Bryant**, whose "In My Little Corner of the World" hit #10, 7-60. Barnsdale, Oklahoma's Anita was Miss Oklahoma, and bronze medal (1st runner-up) winner for Miss America. Anita went on to a long recording career in Christian Contemporary Music, and the Beatles covered her #30, 6-59 "Till There Was You."

Vanessa Williams was the first Afro-American Miss America, but was shorned of her thorny crown when her previous *Penthouse* foldout photo-op caught up with her. Vanessa's #8, 1-89 "Dreamin'" rebounded her megastar potential. Those hazy blue eyes, sweet deep-toned tan, and dynamite curves didn't set back her surging success. "Save the Best for Last" is a tender love ballad of timeless beauty. The lush orchestral score surrounds her excellent emotive voice with beauty and grace. Her fireside love song suggests snuggling and Santa Claus. "Love Is" sparked #3, 1-93, and rhapsodic-melodied "The Colors of the Wind" hit #4, 6-95 (Disney flick *Pocahontas* 1995**** theme).

"Linger" – Cranberries, #8, 10-93. Cranberries are among the few native American fruits, relics of Pocahontas's day and Thanksgivings galore. Delores O'Riordan and the Cranberries hail from emerald-green County Limerick, Ireland; #22, 11-96 "When You're Gone" celebrates their honeyed harmonies.

"Total Eclipse of the Heart" – Bonnie Tyler, #1(4), 8-83. Wales rises, a green-gray magic kingdom at the edge of Britain's Western Sea. Wales shares a Celtic Fringe intensity with the Highlands of Scotland, the misty Shetland Isles of the groaning North Sea, and the emerald shower-sprinkled cranberry bogs of Ireland's County Limerick. Wales was very early vanquished by overwhelming English might, but like the Scots and Irish, perhaps wasn't quite conquered.

Welsh folks with names like Evans and Barnes and Williams and Tyler and Jones have gone down into the black-lung coalmines, and have performed the dirtiest toughest job in the world. My grandfather Joe Dean was a lowland coal-mining Scot of long-ago Welsh ancestry. He worked the grim dark coalmines of Scotland so his son could make it to Canada and the U.S.A. So his son could see the light.

When you listen to the booming baritone of Wales's own Elvis, **Tom Jones**, you realize he's piling a lot of Heartland Rust Belt experience into his music – just like Springsteen or Seger. When he wails his stormy "Thunderball" (#25, 12-65) or "What's New, Pussycat?"

(#3, 6-95), you know he's lived the smokescape life. Tom's monster hit is "She's A Lady," at #2(1), 2-71; #42, 3-71 R & B. Welsh Soulster sings of a 'Trophy Gal' he'd flaunt over some pizzeria dinner. Jones socked it to the casinos of Las Vegas with seething polyester power.

And **Bonnie Tyler**? Like **Ann Wilson** of Heart and maybe **Kim Carnes**, Bonnie has one of those rare tigress voices that can bridge the chasm between **Janis Joplin** and **Melissa Etheridge**. Bonnie (b. '53, Swansea) scored big with Streetcorner-pattern weeper "It's a Heartache" (#3, '78). Her raspy contralto surges with plucky Welsh determination.

"Eclipse's" spare loose vocal glides in slowly. She cascades into minor thirds. She methodically outlines her weird metaphor (just try to picture a heart getting eclipsed). By the time she stalks the shimmering chorus, we're swerving into a crescendo climax of huge Wall of Sound proportions, via **Meat Loaf** producer **Jim Steinman**. Steinman uses some of Springsteen's famed E Street Band: **Roy Bittan** on keyboards, and *Late Night* Conan O'Brien percussion chief **Max Weinberg**. They also used McCoys' **Rick Derringer**, one of the first pioneer guitar geniuses of impending Heavy Metal, ("Hang On, Sloopy," #1, '65); **Derringer** ("Rock and Roll, Hoochie Coo" #23, 1-74) later teamed with **Johnny** and **Edgar Winter**. "Total Eclipse" totally eclipsed Bonnie's later contributions, like "Holding Out for a Hero" #34, 2-84. Bonnie T? Good! Nice Neo-Disco reprise version of "Total Eclipse" at #2(1), 4-95 via **Nicki French**. But Wales wails.

It's no surprise Bonnie's vocal hero was **Mike Smith** of the **Dave Clark Five**, for the #1 Raspiest Singer of perhaps the Rock Revolution! You could turn your vocal chords into raw hamburger on just one of Smith's macho rasp-grasp swooners:

"Bits and Pieces" – Dave Clark Five, #4, 4-64. Tottenham/London's Smith hammered his poor throat in into baritone bits and pieces, as **Dave Clark** romped the drums in a showcase of White Soul. Smith's rebound of the Contours' #3, 8-62 "Do You Love Me" spun them to #11, 5-64. Perhaps Smith's premier Pro-Wrestler-style Rapmaster rendition is his #7, 6-65 Blues anthem, "I Like It Like That," originally #2(3), 5-61, and #2 R & B for **Chris Kenner** (b. Kenner, L.A., 1929-76). While Smith bench-pressed his Heavyweight voice to hits like #7, 4-67 "You Got What It Takes" (Motown **Marv Johnson** #10, 11-59), Tyler blasted her husky whisky soprano into the smoky night. Don't sing, said this Welsh doc (see Rod Stewart). Later, said Bonnie. Life is always on the edge anyhow, eh? You take your chances. Sit down in your safe comfy armchair, and you might get hit by a meteorite.

"Luka" – Suzanne Vega, #3, 6-87. Big Apple's Suzanne gets earmarked 'Alternative,' one of those 90s buzzwords for what Rock and Roll has always been about anyhow. Aphorism: Rock and Roll is an Alternative to whatever else in out there. There's a little Janis Ian in Suzanne Vega. She's also been a major influence on **Tori Amos, Ani DiFranco, Lisa Loeb, Tracy Chapman**, and **Alanis Morrisette**. "Luka" paints a dim etching of a little girl's

agonies amid strong hints of child abuse and even worse. Vega's other hit is the more normally titled #5, 10-90 "Tom's Diner."

"Because the Night" – 10,000 Maniacs, #11, 11-93. Ribald return of Punk. Myriad of maniacs refurbish the **Bruce Springsteen** song by Punk Rock poet Patti Smith (#13, 4-78) and her Group. Maniacs' "Trouble Me" was #44, 6-89 for Upstate NY rockers led by talented **Natalie Merchant** on vocals.

"The Night Has a Thousand Eyes" – Bobby Vee, #3, 12-62; #8, 1-63 R & B. Teen Idol Bobby dredges up ancient Greek Argus – the 1,000-eyed monster. Purple passion pit? Then 499 creepy voyeurs, and two Cyclopses are peeking at their Smoocherama. Vital and versatile star, Vee. For more lore on bizarre eye combos, see #4, 9-97 **Third Eye Blind** mega-hit, "Semi-Charmed Life" (Vee had a #13 hit called "Charms" in 3-63). The EYES have it.

"Don't Rush Me" – Taylor Dayne, #2(1), 11-88. Dayne's Long Island Hot Dance adventures make for zingy Pop-Rock music. She placed seven straight top seven songs in her 1987-90 era. TD's Neo-Disco sound gets plunked into "Pop" category, which means either 1) opposite of Mom; or 2) a mishmosh of fluff/disco/lite-rock/easy-jazz razz-ma-tazz. Dayne's is better than that. Like Prince, however, Dayne synthesizes. She gleans the best of Neo-Disco, the midnight strobe tempo banging a gong at 120 thumps a minute.

Taylor Dayne simply boogies to the beat [#7, 10-87 "Tell It to My Heart"; #5, 10-89 "With Every Beat of My Heart"; or #7, 2-88 "Prove Your Love"]. Her princess persona is wholesome, yet magnetic. Soulful, yet shopping-malled. Passionate, yet controlled. For three years, Taylor had Madonna and Mariah on the ropes. **Tiffany** dominated Ingenue Rock. From Norwalk, California (b. '71), she hit with #6, 11-88 "All This Time."

"Real Love" – Jody Watley, #2(2), 3-89; #1(1) R & B. Great Singer **Jackie Wilson** (Rock Hall, 1987) was her godfather. R & B belter Jody (b. '59, Chicago) won 1987 Best New Artist Grammy for #2(4), 3-87 "Looking for a New Love." Watley wombats: #6, 10-87 "Don't You Want Me"; "Everything" #4, 10-89.

"Take Me Home Tonight" – Eddie Money, #4, 8-86. New York's Finest NYPD officer **Eddie Mahoney** (b. '49) cavorted to #11 in 2-78 with one of the most universally ubiquitous songs on the Oldies Overkill station, "Baby Hold On" – which echoes Doris Day's nifty fifties trip #2(3), 6-56 "Whatever Will Be, Will Be." Eddie's miraculous "Walk on Water" hit #9 in 10-88, and "Peace in Our Time" (WWII echo) hit #11, 12-89. **Ronnie Spector** of the **Ronettes** filters in 'Girl Group' sound bites of her #2, '63 classic "Be My Baby."

"Autobahn" – Kraftwerk, #25, 3-75. Pioneer futuristic band, powered by synthesizer and atomic guitar. Much Techno Post-Modern music is on a direct beam to this

Düsseldorf band whose title describe German freeways (autobahns). President **Dwight David Eisenhower** ("Ike"), German-American Commander who defeated Hitler, superimposed 1957 Autobahn system over America. He called them 'Interstates.'

"I Love You, Always Forever" – Donna Lewis, #2(9), 6-96. **Foreigner**'s #2(10) "Waiting for a Girl Like You" won GOLD for Silver-Medal longevity. The whispery soprano of Welsh **Donna Lewis** eclipsed the hearts of Silver-Medal Silver Medallists everywhere – for longest HOT 100-reign at #2. She passed Dave Somerville's **Diamonds** ("Little Darlin'" #2[8], 3-57) and these non-shy **Shai** guys from Howard University, whose Soul classic "If I Ever Fall in Love" hit #2(8), 10-92. Garfield Bright and Carl 'Groove' Martin's Shai (pronounce 'shy') also hit with two HOT 100 tunes – 1-93 "Comforter" and 6-93 "Baby I'm Yours." Smooth sound. **Shania Twain**'s "You're Still the One" tied Donna at #2(9), 2-98.

"What Have I Done to Deserve This?" – Dusty Springfield and the Pet Shop Boys, #2(2), 12-87. London's Folk/Rock/Country/Soul diva danced back into the Elvis Spotlight with her Pet Shop Boys Retinue. Dusty attained Rock Hall of Fame in 1998 – two weeks too late after she passed away from a long illness (1939-1998). This penultimate winner floated her back into her last hurrah hit circulation after seventeen years of chartless wilderness. Tina Turner (#2[3], 8-86; # 3 R & B), with "Typical Male," never left.

"Fire" – Pointer Sisters, #2(2), 11-78; #14, 1-79 R & B. Grassy Sargasso Sea of #2 songs? The Pointer Sisters are equal victims to the Record #2 and Never #1 Club. So was "Fire's" superstar songwriter BRUCE SPRINGSTEEN. Good company inhabits that club: **Bob Dylan, Creedence Clearwater, Backstreet Boys**, and a cast of jillions (see **Hollies** for list). The **Pointer Sisters** have raw magnetic power that makes us all consider the flesh and the spirit. Oakland's Ruth, Anita, June, and Bonnie Pointer create the same sizzling attraction tantamount to Tina Turner.

"I'm So Excited" – Pointer Sisters, #30, 9-82, then #9, 8-84; #46, 10-82 R & B. Wild midnight frenzy. The Pointers' electric song bedazzles and enchants with its steamy counterpoint. In a panting skein of interwoven, overlapping tunes, the Pointers drape the airwaves with hot fever pitch Rock and Soul. Pulsates, vibrates, and throbs with passion. Epitome of excitement. Torrid heart of Rock and Soul.

On #3, 4-84 (#3 R & B) "Jump (For My Love)," the poor dude must jump through hoops to an eventual rendezvous. **Bonnie Pointer** calls out many songs in ministerial bliss. Parishioner sisters respond with Call and Response pattern. Dynamic energy, excitement, and intimate frenzied tempo.

"Neutron Dance" – Pointer Sisters, #6, 11-84; #13, 12-84 R & B. From Eddie Murphy's hilarious *Beverly Hills*

Cop (1984***½), "Neutron Dance" slings atomic theory into your Dance Mix. [A neutron is that mostly-neutral atomic particle that doesn't mess around too much with the scruffy proton or the dashing electron]. Pointer Sister chic. Other Pointers: #11, 7-85 "Dare Me," iffy #13 "Should I Do It" of 1-82, "Yes, We Can Can" #11, 8-73, #5, 1-84 "Automatic"; #33, 11-86 "Goldmine"; and #16, 6-82 "American Music." This next song could have graced the 'Girl Group' glory days of **Ronnie Spector/Ronettes, Crystals, Angels, Pixies Three, Murmaids**, and the **Orlons**:

"He's So Shy" – Pointer Sisters, #3, 7-80; #10, 8-80 R & B. 'Girl Group' 60s whimsy mashed decade squeeze between Discomania and Button-down Safety Dances (#3, *Men Without Hats*, 6-83). Funky kick-rump rhythm. Sounds like Vintage Doo-Whop from Brooklyn. Like #60, 1-65 "Whenever a Teenager Cries," by Reparata and the Delrons: **Mary ('Reparata') Alese**, Carol Drobnicki, Sheila Reillie. Info by Barbara Coley, Sandra Sprows, and TIna Good.

"Don't Know Much" – Linda Ronstadt and Aaron Neville, #2(2), 9-89; N.C., R & B. Melting pot magic. Take one sparkly-eyed Mexican/Irish/German R & R diva. Add one iron-pumping New Orleans Afro-French singer who wafts grace-note melismas so beautiful they float forever. Result? Harmonic majesty. As the decade drifted away, wondering where it had gone, this dynamic duo brought the lost melody back home to America.

MELODY? HUH?

Since the Big Band 40s, the melody has faded away into the BEAT." Tony DiFranco, colleague, film director, friend, and winner of the prestigious O. Henry Award for Short Stories (and novel *The Streets of Paradise*).

Their song represents the highest chart achievements for a mixed-race and mixed-gender duo. It's no surprise that the dawn of rock also heralded the heyday of Dr. Martin Luther King. "Don't Know Much" shimmers with a heavenly melody. In our Techno Pop, fake-drum cyber-babble, an occasional real melody shines through, hefting heavenward in its breathtaking simplicity – and inspired power.

The song sifts all emotion into one ultimate truth. The singers flaunt **Sam Cooke**'s fun-loving anti-intellectual approach from his wondrous #12, 5-60 "Wonderful World": he's a dufus in biology or history, but knows he loves the girl. Linda began with #13, 11-67 **Stone Poneys** and "Different Drum". Linda's first hit, remember, is written by **Mike Nesmith** – often credited with inventing *MTV*. **Lesley Gore**'s #2(3), 1-64 "You Don't Own Me," carves out her free-spirit relationship. Lesley echoes Linda's Thoreau allusion about hearing the different drummer of romantic freedom. Fans recall **Aaron Neville**'s #2, '66 "Tell It Like It Is." The R & B community knew Aaron six years earlier, as his "Over You" zipped to #21 R & B in 9-60. Despite an R & B #1(5), 12-66 Neville missed the R & B charts until #93, 12-95 "Use Me." His 29-year absence is an absolute mystery. Aaron and Neville Brothers Cyril, Charles, and Art did #75, 4-89 R & B "Sister Rosa," a tribute to brave **Rosa Parks**, who refused to go to the back of the bus during America's 1955 nasty bout with segregation. Aaron swirls 16th-notes into 32nds, and hangs suspended like a swan diver over a mid-air dotted eighth. Ronstadt/Neville's precision with the supreme vocal instrument is uncanny, the result sublime. Aaron celebrated two silver medal songs – 23 years apart. "Don't Know Much" is a celebration of the melody line. If the Heart of a song is its rhythmic punch, its gorgeous melody is its Soul.

"I'm the Only One" – Melissa Etheridge, #8, 8-94. Fort Leavenworth, Kansas, is home to one of the grimmest federal prisons ever erected. Laughless lock-ups bode dark dead ends for glum thugs and framed innocents. Leavenworth shimmers like Oz nearby. The colorful German town of Dachau, next to the ghastly concentration camp, spent much of World War II with wheezy accordions and purple tulips and beer buddies down at the singalong Rathskeller. Leavenworth is a smiling blonde town of K-Marts and McDonalds and Pizza Huts and red-white-blue 4th of July confetti cloudbursts. Rosy-cheeked Peggy Sue cheerleaders twirl teasy miniskirts in the red-gold autumn leafsmoke air.

Melissa Etheridge (b. 5-29-61) grew up in Leavenworth. Middle America. Like **Roy Orbison**'s Wink, Texas. Or **Buddy Holly**'s Lubbock. Or **Elvis**'s Tupelo, Mississippi, a few hummocks and cotton fields off the Delta. Melissa and Dorothy [via Judy Garland] grew up in Kansas. Dorothy dodged tornadoes (quaintly called 'cyclones'). When one caught up with her and dog Toto ["Over the Rainbow," #5, 9-39] she took a quick rocket trip – in her sturdy house – to the land of Munchkins and Yellow Brick Roads.

Etheridge is no Dorothy. She is no ingenue. She is no naïve waif wailing in the screaming tornado.

Maybe she is the screaming tornado. The depths of Melissa's alto passion are still uncharted. With whiskey-rasp edge that can trump Kim Carnes or Bonnie Tyler at their own Smokey Joe's purry sound, Melissa invites comparisons – **Janis Joplin** of Port Arthur, Texas. And to contemporary **Bonnie Raitt**. We might throw in a few icons like **Bessie Smith** or **Billie Holiday** or **Sarah Vaughan** or **Ella Fitzgerald**; Etheridge belts the best of the Blues.

Not all Blues singers write. Melissa does. Her "Come to My Window" hit #25, 2-94. A few quintuple-platinum tracks of Melissa's *Yes I Am* Al. #15, 10-93, are splendid Blues material. "Window" is Melissa's bust-out song. It's hard to leap out of the prison of one's soul without worrying about shards of splintering broken glass. Etheridge had two simmerers, "No Souvenirs" (#95, 11-89) and "Similar Features," #94, 4-89.

"Window" struts a vampy Blues groove. The song is a cry from deep in the brooding Leavenworth prison of someone's tortured soul. Her melodies sidetrack the rumbling rhythm. The depth of her power and passion side-

swipes the sleepy status quo. Nothing ho-hum about that song. Desire seethes. In Melissa's vocal bridge, she blasts town gossips; all that matters is the lone searing love affair. Secret midnight rendezvous. Similar passion emotes from **Freddie Mercury** of Queen, when he hits Bb by High C, or the multi-talented **Elton John** on his ode to Billie Jean (King, #1, 3-75), "Philadelphia Freedom." Melissa shares the flamboyant Screaming Blues passion of **Little Richard**, the Constant Craving (#38, '92) of **k.d. lang**. Her American Dream is not necessarily fulfilled in the regular scenario of happy hubby, 2.3 kids, a beige station wagon and rust-hued Retriever. (One kid, as of 1998). Leavenworth, Kansas, has 64,000 souls, mostly excellent Americans. Nothing sinister about these good people. Nothing awful goes on under their noses like Dachau burghers ignorant of the Nazi *Stürm und Schlag* atrocities at the secret local concentration-camp crematorium. Kansas Senator **Bob Dole** was wounded defending democracy in World War II. Leavenworth Prison cannot be compared to Dachau. Though Americans have recently dragged the death penalty out of its sarcophagus, executions outside of Texas are still few and far between, and buttressed by phalanxes of defense lawyers in a tug of war with the hangman. We are the good guys; we do not do genocide. A genocide of attitudes, however, can prevail in certain towns from Peyton Place to Gobbler's Grove. And in sizeable burghs like Leavenworth, Kansas. Like **Bobby Vee**'s "Night Has a Thousand Eyes" up in icy Fargo, North Dakota (population 74,111), the eyes of Leavenworth can ice romance. They can strangle passion. They can turn the sizzle to cold stone.

"I'm the Only One" seethes with passion. It tears down walls of inhibition and standoffishness. Etheridge defends her community of soulmates. Melissa also slings a mean guitar. Her 1995 Rock and Roll offerings were #16 and #42 2-95 "If I Wanted To," backed by "Like the Way I Do." In 1996, Melissa lofted #22 "I Want to Come Over" into the pulsing Blues vision. In 9-99? #51 "Angels Would Fall." Melissa is at the forefront of a whole line of female stars who have admirably competed with the male onslaught of thrashing guitar slashers with axes on fire. Her 12-95 album *Your Little Secret* not only hit #6 – it established Melissa Etheridge as one of the top Blues singers in rock music. She has at least one peer in the guitar department, a bonnie lass with flaming hair and flashing riffs – who earned Rock Hall honors for 1999 in the 2000 gala. We also can't forget the one talented young lady with an Arabic-American surname who scorched the 1988-91 charts with six straight #1 songs:

"Rush, Rush" – Paula Abdul, #1(5), 5-91; #20 R & B. American Dream again. With Brazilian and French-Canadian parents, **Paula Abdul** (b. '62, L.A.) carried Rock and Roll deeper into the video dimension we're about to briefly explore. Paula excelled in cheerleading with the pro Los Angeles Lakers – back in the Magic Johnson and Kareem Abdul-Jabbar era. Jabbar changed his name from Lew Alcindor to reflect his new Muslim religion; Paula got the ABDUL naturally. Paula's an excellent singer, and her forte is choreography.

Janet Jackson

"Nasty" – Janet Jackson, #3, 5-86; #1(2), 4-86 R & B. Brother **Michael Jackson** choreographed his spiffy MOONWALK, trumping Chuck Berry's Duckwalk. By 2001, sister Janet would be listed 3rd Female Solo Artist of all time (Whitburn, see **Madonna, Aretha**). **Paula Abdul** choreographed Michael's kid sister (b. 5-66) in her *Control* [Al. #1(2), 3-86]. In his wildest dreams, Michael never imagined that the plucky junior Jackson might usurp his own superstar powers and rule the planet. Janet's career careened at choreographically supersonic pace with #1, 7-2000 "Doesn't Really Matter," and #1(4+), 4-2001 "All for You."

"Forever Your Girl" – Paula Abdul, #1(2), 3-89; #54, 4-89 R & B. Virgin Records assured for three years, Paula never lost her top ten perch. Other chart-toppers include: #1(3), 12-88 "Straight Up"; #1(1), 6-89 "Cold Hearted"; and #1(3), 12-89 "Opposites Attract." All four #1's spun off from her 7-million+ *Forever Your Girl* album (Al. #1[1], 1-89). Then #1, 7-91 "The Promise of New Day" and #6, 10-91 "Blowing Kisses in the Wind." Into 1992, **Stevie Wonder** played harmonica on her #19 "Will You Marry Me."

We began with the phenomenon of CONNIE B. GOODE. So which female artist has been thriving on Blues guitar and vocals for over a generation? She sparks those stars who sandbagged through laggard Lodi/bar circuits for twenty years, dreaming of Overnight Sensationalism. Lost "Lodi" Limbo. In 1961, the fledgling **Beatles** Scots' Folk song "My Bonnie" ['My Bonnie Lies Over the Ocean']" hit #26, 2-64 . . .

"Something to Talk About" – Bonnie Raitt, #5, 7-91. This hit tune echoes Melissa Etheridge's complaint about the snoopy community and wagging tongues. Village busybodies have no place squawking about their relationship. Daughter of **John Raitt** (operatic low tenor), Bonnie ingenued at Radcliffe College. Born in 1949 beautiful downtown Burbank, California, she Joan Baez-ed her way through songs of peace and justice and freedom. Bonnie was selected for the Rock Hall of Fame in March 2000. Her career trajectory is amazing. Buoyed by Del Shannon's #1, '61 "Runaway" gloomy drizzle (to #57, 5-77), the carrot-topped Blues crusader hefts a slide guitar. A 25-year career eligibility criterion usually means an artist becomes a superstar in a five-year Career Heyday.

John Sebastian and Zal Yanovsky's **Lovin' Spoonful** had just such a profile for their simultaneous 2000 induction: monster Rocker #1(3), 7-66 "Summer in the City," two silver-medal spectaculars at #1(2), 2-66 "Daydream" and slow-Blues #2(1), 5-66 "Did You Ever Have to Make Up Your Mind?"; and several 1965-68 classics, scoring eight Top Twenty tunes. Sebastian cranked up a solo triumph with this #1(1), 3-76 Disco Era "Welcome Back" [Kotter], which created the Disco phenomenon of **John Travolta** (as 'Vinnie Barbarino' in the big Gabe Kaplan sitcom). Travolta later became many 90s and current teenagers' living embodiment of either the 50s (*Grease****), the 70s Disco nexus (*Saturday Night Fever ***½*), or Country music (*Urban Cowboy****). Anyhow, when the Spoonful reunited at the 2000 ceremony, John thanked the usual people, said a prayer for his 'Jewish angel' **Mama Cass Elliot**, and they all sang. Though John was hoarser than in their halcyon heyday, the effect was fun and frolicky and fuzzy and warm. A great typical Rock Hall of Fame Induction.

Not so Bonnie Raitt. After troubadouring in obscurity beyond "Runaway," (no HOT 100 hits, just albums), she was rescued from media oblivion by her monster album #1(3), 4-89 *Nick of Time* (how prophetic!). Suddenly this spunky Burbank bombshell became a major Rock and Roll star for the first time at the age of nearly 40 [39¼]. *Luck of the Draw* (Al. #2[2], 7-91) rocket-launched her first Top Ten single – #5, 7-91 "Something to Talk About." Besides the fact that it was a great song by a great Blues singer who brandishes a great slide guitar, it didn't hurt her Hall eligibility that *Nick of Time* garnered her four Grammies.

Bonnie's traditional upbringing featured a lot of music. Destiny deluged her with near misses. Always respected and appreciated, Bonnie somehow eluded the fast lane to fame. By 1972, her album *Give it Up* hit #138, pretty well eclipsing **John Cage and the Velvet Underground** territory. *Home Plate* rose bluesfully to #43, 10-75, and *Sweet Forgiveness* hit. #25, 4-77.

In 1986, after recording with **Prince**, Bonnie did charity gigs for Amnesty International, the Fourth-of-July Disarmament Festival, and the homeless-awareness "Wake-Up America." It was not long before Bonnie herself answered her own 'wake-up call' from a near-homeless drift of her own.

In 1988, she attended the **Roy Orbison** Memorial Tribute, and in 2-95, her version of Roy's last hit "You Got It" climbed to #33 on the charts. Then April 1989 sent her tenth album *Nick of Time* out to two million homes. She finally became the star we should have recognized her as in the first place. In 1990, Bonnie Raitt won Best Rock Performance, Female, at the Grammy Awards. Her album, which charted for two whole years, hit #1 in April 1990. Other hits? #73, 11-95 "Rock Steady," #15 "I Can't Make You Love Me" in 11-91, and #49, 3-90 "Have a Heart." As opposed to **Melissa Etheridge**'s "I'm the Only One," Bonnie had a #34, 4-92 conversely entitled "Not the Only One." Albums soared: #1(3), 4-89 *Nick of Time*; #2(2), 7-91 *Luck of the Draw*, and #1(1), 4-94 *Longing in Their Hearts*. The carrot-topped charmer sings metallic Rock and Roll with the same blazing gusto her fiery-colored hair (with one white wisp) suggests Blues.

Melissa Ethridge

Bonnie Raitt plays dynamite Blues guitar. Like Melissa Etheridge. There have been a lot of fine female keyboard players of the **Linda Eastman McCartney** ilk, and many fine female acoustic strummers, but Bonnie Raitt spearheads great female ROCK guitarists, flashing fiery riffs on tall frets with the best male axemen. She even donates to a Guitars for Women charity to bring cheap electric guitars to poorer neighborhoods.

Raitt's nonpareil Blues style was saluted at her Rock Hall Induction by another one of her axe-wielding distaff contemporaries, **Melissa Etheridge.** Bonnie's all-star 2000 ceremony produced the greatest induction speech I have heard – after many superstars over many years. Bonnie began by announcing that on stage were three guitar-playing women. She chided her gender for being slow to wield guitars. "I not only carry this thing," Bonnie said with a wry Mona Lisa smile framed by her fiery long hair, "but I can ride it too." She spoke deeply about the passion and pleasure and pain of the Rock and Roll

Obsession. How the music burns and sears her soul – and maybe ours, too – with a determined drive to capture the music. It's a lifetime commitment, she said, and the passion and obsession of it can overwhelm you. It was a deeply moving moment in our music, rooted in **Ma Rainey, Bessie Smith**, and the throbbing heart of the Blues. Maybe it's a family thing. Call it karma or destiny, its other name is Rock and Roll. And we all love it – or we wouldn't be here.

And the beat goes on.

* * * * * * *

The Johnny B. Goode Dream still lives worldwide, but the names have been improved to double the population of superstar aspirants. Instead of Johnny and Ronnie and Lonnie B. Goode, we now have Connie B. Goode. And Janie B. Goode.

Graffiti gurus can now scrawl on the wall:

BONNIE B. GOODE RULES!

Bonnie Raitt, 1995

MTV and ROCKFLIX:
Nifty Mix or Jiffy Pix?

The **Monkees' Michael Nesmith** (b. 12-30-42) was the only working musician of the four TV Monkees, whose charisma clobbered the hopes of 500 other talented casting-call candidates. Mike hailed from a famous family. His mom invented 'White Out' Liquid Paper to zap typing errors. In the 1890s, a more distant relative, spelled [James] **Naismith**, invented basketball. Mike's posterity was assured with his Monkee years, and his later solo career wasn't too shabby:

"Joanne" – Michael Nesmith and the First National Band, #21, 8-70. Besides 58 1966-68 immortal Monkees TV episodes, Nesmith played for Stax/Volt Memphis sessions, and launched **Linda Ronstadt**'s career on "Different Drum." Singer/guitarist Nesmith split with singer/drummer Mickey Dolenz, bassist/singer Peter Tork, and singer Davy Jones to this new 70s Country Rock band – #42, 11-70 "Silver Moon" and #70, 4-71 "Nevada Fighter." "Joanne" is about a beautiful burn-out from a meadow near a park. Her time is wrong, the romance doesn't work, and he tries to cushion her loopy downward spiral. His best Del Shannon Swiss yodel fails to buoy her soggy spirits. Had critics been kinder to this fine song, Nesmith might still be hawking Vintage Rock, wowing 200-seat emporia in Peoria. Instead, he had to go and invent *MTV*!

"Video Killed the Radio Star" – Buggles, #40, 11-79. Almost as famous as the *Day the Music Died (Holly, Valens, Bopper, 2-3-59)* is August 1, 1981. MUSIC TELEVISION's Cable channel kicked off its on-air broadcast with the first video ever. How it was cut in '79 and languished in the Un-Oldies Ozone for nearly two years is a story so dire and dastardly I can't relate it to you in a family *Gold Rush*. Anyhow, this poofy spoof, lampooning the Beatles' career, was the Buggles' sole HOT 100 hit. Their Buddy Holly vocal echo is uncanny. MTV's official birthing was 1981. Remember, *Gold Rush* takes Rock back to 1897 Ragtime:

"You Made Me Love You, I Didn't Want to Do It" – Al Jolson, #1(7), 9-1913. The old *Nickelodeon* was not a prehistoric Cable channel. Nope, a nickelodeon was either a 1) Jukebox, or 2) Tiny movie theater, which showed five-minute mini-reels (PG-13 stuff, mostly, not Pornomania Peep Shows). It followed 'Jolie's' Ragtime rouser, #1(5), 7-1912 "Ragging the Baby to Sleep." For a nickel – big money then – Ragtime Rock-aholics could review a sprightly five minutes of Al, disconnected grotesquely from his song. A plinky piano roll pumped along, way off base. It took a lucky 13 more years to premiere the TALKIES. Jolson was the first to star in a true interweaving of pictures and sound in his 1926 *The Jazz Singer.* Technically, you could say his featured "Swanee" [#1(9), 5-1920] was the very first MTV song. By 1926, Russian-American **Vladimir Zworykin** of Princeton, NJ, already invented the primitive TV camera (Iconoscope, 1923). Vlad's rudimentary picture tube (Kinescope, 1929) was hatching in his RCA lab – RCA helped invent both TV and Elvis. You can't make this stuff up. Though Jolson's movie treads on racially-insensitive minstrelsy (white actors in 'blackface'), Jolson's songs paraded the Hit Parades with gusto and cinematic punch and power: #2(2), 6-28 "My Mammy" (also #18, 2-47) and #1(4), 12-22 "Toot Toot Tootsie (Goo'bye)."

Our first regular Videos? Jim Farber of the *Rolling Stone Illustrated History of Rock and Roll* says the technique was introduced by **Oskar Fischinger,** German filmmaker: "While music had been used to support film since the beginning (the pianos and orchestras that accompanied the early silents), it was Fischinger who, in the Twenties, reversed the process, constructing animated shorts to support music (specifically, jazz and classical records)." Farber cites Disney's phantasmagorical 1940**** *Fantasia* as the first unintentional long music video. He speaks of **SOUNDIES,** in the 40s – "jukebox-like contraptions that unspooled performance pieces" done by **Bing Crosby** and other stars. Soundies, then, were actually *MTV*-style Videos in 40s Video Jukeboxes. You plunked a nickel, and the **Andrews Sisters** or **Perry Como** crooned and swooned in B&W or iffy technicolor. Hamstrung by skimpy hoopla, these visionary videos bit the dust in the 50s.

The first real VH-1 show was *Your Hit Parade* (NBC, 1950-58), a radio carryover starring Snooky Lanson and Dorothy Collins. American Bandstand, with suave host **Dick Clark,** ran for 39 years. Biographer John Jackson credits Clark with 'putting a face on the music.' Teens could finally SEE the record stars who lived for them in their radios (see Toby Keith, 2000).

"Union of the Snake" – Duran Duran, #3, 11-83.
Like **Dexys Midnight Runners**' (#1[1], 1-83 "Come On Eileen"), the telegenic Duran Two Crew hailed from redbrick Birmingham, in England's Industrial Heartland.

Making a video can cost three to 25 times as much as a basic audio track. You must muscle your way through the machinations of cinematographers and gaffers and splicers and make-up mavens. Big labels put up big front money, but it always comes out of artists' would-be royalties. Big money is being made, but who makes it? Midline artists are forever in debt to giant conglomerates.

Double Duran scored many hits via MTV: #1(2), 4-84 "The Reflex"; "The Wild Boys" at #2(4), 11-84; "A View to Kill" at #1(2), 5-85, and their notorious big #2(1), 11-86 "Notorious."

"My Boy Flat-Top" – Dorothy Collins, #16, 11-55. I was gazing starstruck at MTV in 1950. Perky blonde Dorothy Collins was a crooner cast on NBC-TV's *Your Hit Parade* from Windsor, Ontario – and the first Video Queen. She shared the week's Top Seven videos with **Snooky Lanson, Russell Arms, June Valli** (#29, 5-55 "Unchained Melody"), and **Gisele MacKenzie** (#4, 6-55 "Hard to Get"). The show had an actual 'VeeJay' countdown in random order – but #1 was always last. Until swamped in a Rock tidal wave, the *Lucky Strike Hit Parade* (1950-58 on TV, long before on radio) was the smokiest show on earth – with Golden Oldies like **Paul Whiteman**'s #1(6), 12-33 "Smoke Gets in Your Eyes" and **Tex Williams**' #1 '47 "Smoke! Smoke! Smoke That Cigarette." Collins covers **Boyd Bennett and His Rockets**' #39, 11-55 version.'Dad' sings about teenage son and his short buzzy haircut. From my kidhood ivory tower by our Silvertone 10" TV set, Video Queen Collins seemed to be a very nice lady with a sweet soprano. And a cigarette.

The Jackson Five

"Thriller" – Michael Jackson, #4, 2-84; #3 R & B.
The Gloved One's album *Thriller* was #1 (12-82) for 37 weeks, second only to #1(54) 1962+ *West Side Story* soundtrack. After Michael Nesmith shepherded MTV's birth with *auteur* fanfare, Jackson became the first Video superstar. His #1(3), 2-83 "Beat It" is surrounded by key *cinema noire* night props. In 2001, "Thriller" was still voted #1.

For tots, however, "Thriller" is a mixed bag of Hallowe'en treats and tricks. Why? Our plucky graveyard-strolling hero, Michael, turns into the monster. Computer-generated graphics power his werewolf-style transformation. In front of our terrified kids' eyes, *MTV* is Mass Media. To those of us more elderly than 13, no problem. No such good-guy-to-monster lurked in the 50s. Maybe kids today are more jaded. Many 80s moppets just smirked as idols metamorphosed into monsters. When our 50s R & R heroes crashed in a little plane into a lonely Iowa frozen cornfield, all we could do was shudder.

"Puberty Love" – Rock Peace, NC, 1980. *Attack of the Killer Tomatoes'* Sound Track. Seems rampaging rolling tomatoes attack when they hear squealy Minnie Mouse strains of this Clearasil anthem, "Puberty Love," about how neat and cool love is. My cousin Liz Maury and Lloyd Becker clued me in on this spoof of monster flix. We'll return to videos after a jiffy rundown of Rockflix. We use the Leonard Maltin *Movie and Video Guide star system*. Four, super flick. Three, good stuff. Two, merit. One, the odd quality moment. Zero stars? You may prefer to watch the slug races Snailathon Speedo Derby on the slimy log.

Almost Famous **(2000****½**).** 15-year-old wunderkind stringer for *Rolling Stone* magazine jimmies behind-the-scenes look at Rock royalty, enroute to their glory road and groovy groupies. Some realism. Lester Bangs as acerbic, sarcastic Rock critic.

American Graffiti **(1973********).** First great Rock history flick. One magic night somewhere in California before you kiss adolescence goodbye. Brink-of-stardom cast: Richard Dreyfuss, Suzanne Somers, Ron Howard, Harrison Ford, Wolfman Jack, Charles Martin Smith, Cindy Williams. Best actor? Paul LeMat as 'John Milner.' Top of the line, despite wallet-squeezing filming budget. Super Rockflick. Don't miss it.

Backbeat **(1994*******).** British Rockudrama of Beatles' early rise on 1961 Hamburg, Germany's sleazo *Reeperbahn*. B&W saga of jilted ex-Beatles Pete Best, Stuart Sutcliffe. In a swashbuckling mulligatawny stew of glory and garbage, salty 1961 Fab Four chase destiny in a vinyl groove.

Beach Blanket Bingo **(1965*****½**).** Surf-ari fantasia, highlighted by Mouseketeer **Annette Funicello**'s curvy bathing suit. Her #11, '60 "Pineapple Princess" maybe started Surf Rock. BBB is fifth nifty flick of her Surf's Up ilk. Frankie Avalon looks good, and sings a bit. Also features hi-jinx with fogey-generation cynics Paul Lynde and Don Rickles. Long ago, but somehow very very cool. Especially her bathing suit.

Blue Hawaii (1961***½) . Elvis in classic teen-dream travelogue. Swaying palms and lovely *Beach Blanket Bingo* bathing-beauty gidgets. Elvis plays on-the-make tour guide, whose romantic overtures are thwarted by Angela Lansbury. *Blue Hawaii* represents a tamed and shorn King headed for Soft Rock Las Vegas. His #1(20), 10-61 *Blue Hawaii* album was his biggest ever, and contains fan favorite #2, 12-61 "Can't Help Falling in Love." Eighth-biggest album of all time. Colorful flick.

The Blues Brothers (1980****). John Belushi and Dan Aykroyd play Jake and Elwood Blues, two Chicago dudes with sunglasses and porkpie hats. Nifty cameos by Ray Charles, Aretha Franklin, James Brown. Also Steve Cropper, Donald 'Duck' Dunn, and Stax/Volt Rhythm section. On a semi-heavenly quest to put the band back together, they try to save their boyhood Catholic school from bulldozer. World's greatest car chase. *Laugh-In's* Henry Gibson stars as jerk Nazi.

The Buddy Holly Story (1978****). **Gary Busey** was nominated for an Academy Award for his amazing Holly portrayal. He shed 40#, dyed his strawberry blond hair black, and emoted the sincere essence of Holly. Stars Charles Martin Smith, Maria Richwine, Don Stroud, Fred Travalena. Busey masterfully emotes the Lubbock lad whose 'That'll Be the Day' came much too soon. Buddy's virtuoso drummer Jerry Allison (Stroud) married quintessential R & R queen, the actual 'Peggy Sue.' *The Buddy Holly Story* flashes the true glory of Rock and Roll. It emblazons the brotherly aspirations of Rockers who dared to nearly dethrone the King of Memphis. The Day the Music Died is tastefully and poignantly handled, without a smidgeon of sappy or grisly melodrama. A few deviations from true story of Buddy's life – for dramatic effect, and fan controversy. If you must see only one Rockflick, make it *The Buddy Holly Story*.

The Commitments (1991***¾). Were it not for the constant intrusion of the ultimate copulative verb, this might be the perfect movie about a rock band's rise and fall. It's a rags-to-semi-riches and back-to-rags tale of Irish Soul Brothers and Sisters. Andrew Strong plays leather-lunged White Soul singer. Johnny Murphy as globe-hopping vet trumpeter. Set in drizzling dank streets of down, out, and on-the-dole Dublin. Plot? Irish band wrestles with destiny. Squabbles like Cain & Abel. They idolize Wilson Pickett, Motown, and the 60s. Story line hinges on possible gig with Soul icon Pickett, plus band's own budding stardom. The grey sky drools on them, and comic-relief oaf 'Pop' worships at Elvis's Graceland shrine. They sculpt a butt-kicking sound that champions all the best of 'Blue-Eyed Soul.' With a burgeoning background of desirable women on steamy vocals, some iffy romantic inter-band interludes, and an ugly tooth-sandwich donneybrook in the alley, the Commitments deliver a tremendous tribute to their African-American heroes. Landfill language.

Crossroads (1986***¼). Ralph Macchio. Ry Cooder sound track. Young Eastern kid seeks mystic **Robert Johnson** 'Crossroads,' down Highway 61 on the Mississippi Delta – where Johnson ostensibly made a pact with the Devil, exchanging his soul for a few dizzying superstar guitar licks. It comes down to a pyrotechnic guitar shootout (see "The Devil Went Down to Georgia") between axe prodigy Macchio, 17, and guitar virtuoso Steve Vai, who rampaged for both David Lee Roth and Frank Zappa.

Don't Look Back (1967***¼). Rare insight into Dylan mystique. In his transformation from Buddy Holly groupie to Folk Rock guru, Dylan emerges as a very real and vulnerable star. Allen Ginsberg poetically presides.

The Doors (1991***¼). Val Kilmer vamps the 'Lizard King' legend of **Jim Morrison** and his classic Doors troupe. Kilmer is a dead ringer for the Byronic baritone. The morbid Morrison swaggers and staggers his fey way to Rock and Roll Heaven. The movie stars Doors who survived, and thrived: Robby Krieger, John Densmore, and Ray Manzarek.

Eddie and the Cruisers (1983***). Out of *Ghost Story* novel plot line, Eddie Wilson (Michael Pare) plays 60s leather-jacket lad. Tom Berenger is 'Word Man,' lyrical legerdemain guy in the rock group. Eddie vanishes for 20 years like Rip Van Winkle. **John Cafferty** and the **Beaver Brown Band** (#7, 8-84 "On the Dark Side") play for the score in their best **Bruce Springsteen** style.

Eight Mile (2002***). Rapper **Eminem** headlines shoutdown Rapfest in tough Detroit neighborhood, south of 8-Mile Road city limits. Eminem integrates Rap milieu, with legendary Motown Soul station WJLB (area code 313), where R & B Rock Jock **Frantic Ernie Durham** laid the internal-rhyme cornerstone for Rap in 1957. Durham predated James Brown, Muhammad Ali and Grandmaster Flash. *Cinema noire* neon-drizzle saga. Using what Steve Chennault calls "the Dozens," or verbally 'scoring' on friends, Eminem's Rap duels actually defuse violence. It's an echo of Detroit's raging red-light Soul & Blues district of the 40s – Hastings Street – in speedy Rap rhymes.

The Endless Summer (1965****). Ultimate Surf Rock international trip. Two surfers troop around planet searching for the Perfect Wave. Low-budget (50G) classic Rockflick travelogue. Surf guru **Dick Dale & Deltones** ride 16th-note tidal waves on sizzling guitars. Surfers Mike Henson and Robert August surf virgin seashores of South Africa, Australia, Tahiti, and Oahu's big surf at Waimea Bay. Surf guitars, too, skim international shorelines, with amp blast gusto.

Flashdance (1983**½). Welder-by-day, dancer-by-night plot oozes implausible. No problem. Singer Irene Cara pulls it off via actress Jennifer Beals. Crackling band track smacks booming beat. Choreography began to take over the audial portion of a song. If R & R music, to you, means DANCING, add a star. Corny plot and seedy props get crunched by Cara's determination to dance magnificently.

Grease (1978***¼). **John Travolta** ['Danny'] woos perky Australian **Olivia Newton-John** ['Sandy']. They swap personalities for teen social situations. Around guys, he's cool, tough. Around her, he's tender, romantic. When he meets her with his pals within earshot, she has no idea WHO he is – since he tries to be ultra-bad. Her goody two-shoes rep of smiles and saddle shoes changes from sweet to slinkily sensuous to attract the lusty lad. Great cameo by 50s comics Sid Caesar (coach) and Eve Arden (administrator). Musically, the supposed 'fifties' have a suspiciously Disco 70s-ish rhythmic overglow.

Great Balls of Fire (1989***). Dennis Quaid as Jerry Lee Lewis, of flaming piano-killer fame. Alex Baldwin plays his then-pious cuz, televangelist Jimmy Swaggart. Rise and fall of the 50s bad lad, who wed his bassist's 13-year-old kid Myra Brown, among five or six other wives.

Hail Hail Rock and Roll (1987***½). **Jerry Lee Lewis**'s mother called **Chuck Berry** the single most influential figure in Rock history. Rockumentary with Stones' Keith Richards celebrates Chuck's 60th birthday bash. Linda Ronstadt, Eric Clapton, Etta James, and Julian Lennon do cameos, along with Chuck and right-hand piano man Johnnie Johnson.

Hair (1979**½). Like *Oh, Calcutta, Hair* made no pretense of dewy-eyed innocence. Everybody just chucked off their clothes impishly. This Disco retread of the 1969 Age of Aquarius is a prudishly pleasant PG romp through fun Rock and Roll. What did they spray on all that hirsute shaggy hair?

Hairspray (1988***¼). Director John Waters plays nasty '63 psychiatrist. Can you imagine Sonny Bono and Debbie Harry as persnickety parents? How about Jerry Stiller and transvestite Divine as parents of Ricki Lake? The **Cars**' Ric Ocasek plays a 'beatnik' brandishing bongos on #4, 11-81 "Shake It Up."

Hard Day's Night (1965****). Four stars are theirs to lose. They didn't, despite B&W drab. The world expected a splashy Elvis exploitation movie, with huge sets, lush scenes, mammoth production numbers. Fab Four flouted convention, and gave moviegoers James Thurber-goes-Zen-Buddhist. In own hilarious self-effacing style, Liverpool lads make a harmless mockery of everything in the universe: TV, local cops, future Rockumentaries. Music? How could it be anything short of super?

Help (1965***½). Bizarre sect chases Ringo for his magic ring. Another great Beatle movie, dancing from euphoria to impertinence to Vaudeville. Technicolor. Blokes have blast, and run amok.

Jailhouse Rock (1957***¼). Like *King Creole* ('58***), this B&W Elvis adventure sparkles with primal Rock and Roll energy. Many call Elvis's jailhouse set and title dance tune the First Rock Video. Features the REAL Elvis, before media monsters bamboozled him into his more sedate Easy Listening mode.

Janis (1975***½). Rise and fall rockumentary, with her family's blessing, shows Janis Joplin's pedal-to-the-metal concert style. Also catch Bette Midler's 1979*** *The Rose.*

La Bamba (1987***¾). Great Ritchie Valens portrayal by Lou Diamond Phillips – no Valens lookalike. Esau Morales plays brother Bob, whose character means well but messes up. Los Lobos' soundtrack is spectacular, capturing Valens' musical echo. Ritchie's manager Bob Keane: "Ritchie could have been the next Elvis."

Mr. Holland's Opus (1996****). Based on real-life career of East Williston, New York music teacher David Hackendorn. Star Richard Dreyfuss shines in the major music-teacher appreciation film of all time. Dreyfuss 'discovers' Rock and Roll via Toys' Bach-induced hit "A Lover's Concerto" (#2, 9-65). As a newly-minted 60s teacher, 'Mr. Holland' strives to interest bored school inmates – while he dreams of personal musical glory. With principled principal Olympia Dukakis helping him forge a game plan, Dreyfuss uses classic rock tunes, and more traditional music, to emblazon his distinguished teaching and compositional methodology and career. The movie culminates as he's getting 'downsized' by anti-tax misers. A whole orchestra full of his faithful students over the past 30 YEARS – including the female state governor – assembles to perform his OPUS he's been pluckily sculpting for a generation. Heartwarming.

National Lampoon's Animal House (1978****). Madcap campus revelry. This John Belushi and Tom Hulce flick brought back fraternities, which nearly disappeared in the Psychedelia aftermath. Wild soundtrack. Who can forget chant of TO-GA, TO-GA? Ultimate wild party-animal Animal House.

Prince

Purple Rain (1984**½). Prince plays his Streets of Minneapolis music. A certain sandbox scenario keeps it from getting excerpted on *Sesame Street*. Probably not #1 at church, either. Prince, like Little Richard, both satirizes his own flamboyant style with good humor – and takes himself very seriously.

Quadrophenia (1979***). The **Who**'s 2nd rock opera after *Tommy* is not for the faint of heart. Bright-eyed and bushy-tailed Jimmy goes 'Mod,'and gropes and copes with a netherworld of violence. Or catch 1969*** *Tommy* (Al. #4, 6-69), about a blind kid who plays world-class pinball machines.

Rock and Roll High School (1979***). **Joey Ramone** (b. Jeff Hyman, 1952-2001) and the Ramones trash Vince Lombardi High School. They commit the one act every Algebra-12 anarchist outside the U.K. has ever fomented in his dastardly dreams – they blow up the high school (hopefully when no one's in it). Snazzy rip-and-run R&R by Punk idols the Ramones, and Rob Tyner's Punk papas the MC5 of Detroit. The **Ramones'** #81, 7-77 "Sheena Is a Punk Rocker" is a Punk delight – with a lilting Buddy Holly chord wave, and a name chosen from everybody's fave pulp comic. Tarzan's alter-ego was the blonde shapely *Sheena – Queen of the Jungle* (c. 1953)

Rockula (1990***). With Bo Diddley and Toni Basil, how can you lose? Yep, Rock and Roll vampire. Teenybop vampires run amok. Nifty Diddley video.

The Rocky Horror Picture Show (1975***¼). Creepy cult cutie. Stodgy folks may blanch at blatant transvestitism and risque gags, but we give *stars* here, not "R" ratings. Perhaps all Rock is rated 'R', for rockin' rhythm. Anyhow, it was a dark and stormy night . . .

Straight dude Brad Majors and his chummy chaste fiancee (Susan Sarandon) naturally suffer a flat tire by the grotesque castle of mad scientist Dr. Frank-N-Furter. Highlights include a semi-svelte **Meat Loaf** warbling "Hot Patootie" and "The Time Warp." Back before they mothballed the Patchogue Triplex – for a Frankensteinish Monster-Plex – every Saturday midnight they'd bamboozle the quietude with a *Rocky Horror* rockin' riot. Boys and ghouls together.

Saturday Night Fever (1977***½). **John Travolta** plays Tony, Disco King of Bay Ridge, Brooklyn. Weekend escapades include tightrope dancing on the breezy cables of the Verrazano Bridge to Staten Island. Tony preens in his spiffy Quiana shirt and flamingo bell-bottoms – King of the Disco Floor, and the Moment. No one has worn such a famous white suit since **Mark Twain**. By Monday's reality sandwich, Tony is clerking again. Rays of Saturday Night glory glimmer through the gloom. The **Bee Gees** dominated the film score, hitting Al. #1(24) in 1978. Sixth-biggest album of all time.

See My Music Talking (1969***½). Jimi Hendrix, live. In his own time. Live "Purple Haze." Mesmerizing

sequence of "Foxey Lady." Rare must-see for Hendrix connoisseurs and super-fans.

The Song Remains the Same (1976***). The grand effect of the film is stunning. John 'Bonzo' Bonham storms arenas with thundering pizzazz on his drums – and cowboys a tractor on his English farm. Bonzo whoops it up with his little boy at his drums at the local pub, before cutting loose on his mammoth "Moby Dick" solo.

That Thing You Do (1996***½). In this light-hearted romp, local fictitious Ohio band the "One-Ders" gets very big, suspiciously fast. The One-Ders (pron. 'Wonders') nab #7 on HOT 100 before their "Johnny B. Goode" dreams bite the dust ['Johnny' himself topped out at #8]. *That Thing You Do* carves this British Invasion Era band's entire career out of this same-name single. It scoots amazingly to the top, mocking reality. With the zest and zowie of maybe Herman's Hermits, or Gerry's sunny-side Merseybeat Pacemakers, the One-Ders' one-string hit has a fresh, enduring quality of early Beatlemania.

This Is Spinal Tap (1984***½). Good ol' JADED. *This Is Spinal Tap* zaps everyone, regardless of race, color, or musical orientation. This is a real musicians' movie. Gargantuan spoof of industry, and of overindulgence. Contrived Britpop band 'Spinal Tap' goes on tour. They get lost in bowels of labyrinthine backstage cave, looking for lost limelight. Drummers galore croak, one in a 'gardening accident.' Another guy dies in the most disgusting gross manner we've ever heard of (so we're sharing it, sorry about your lunch) – the guy dies choking on somebody *else's* puke.

A million laffs, but some are bloodcurdling. If your band has ever struggled for #95 in Dawson City, Yukon Territory, you know that reality slaps our dreams with the wet dishrag of truth. Half the time, this super lampoon/tribute film rambles on so straightforwardly that even real touring road warriors don't know it's a big cosmic joke. Super comic/producer **Rob Reiner** is recording the Spinal Tap American [comeback] Tour. Lead guitarist 'Nigel Tufnel,' in his quest to jack up the WORLD'S LOUDEST BAND, drags out his own special amp. All the other amps in the world only go up to Ten (10). His mega-amp, however, has a magic dial that rams the sound all the way up to eleven (11)! Pow.

To Sir, With Love (1967***½). **Sidney Poitier** plays unemployed 'Black' engineer with scanty job possibilities, embarking upon unwanted London East End teaching career. Cockney street kids use tough talk. He attempts to teach them respect, in an uphill battle against the stifling system. "Sir" [Poitier] prevails. His orphic wisdom, aimed at tawdry teenyboppers, is didactic and blunt: "No man likes a slut for long, and only the worst kind marries one." Ironically "Sir" learns to love teaching, and love these surly, plucky white kids he shepherds from crayolas to perfume. Beyond **Lulu**'s terrific title song (#1[5] '67), the movie has too little music. Her great #22, 12-69 "Oh Me Oh My (I'm a Fool for You Baby)" was still a glint in some hit-sculptor's starry eyes. *To Sir, With Love* probably caused a million Anglo-Americans to go into teaching. One anyhow, me. *Mr. Holland's Opus* might just regenerate another generation to fill the retirement chasm left by us *To Sir, With Love* teachers now (hopefully) pushing sixty, and not daisies.

Wayne's World (1992***½). Beginning as a *Saturday Night Live* skit down in 'Wayne & Garth's' basement, *Wayne's World* quests after the Holy Grail of Saturday Night in America – in an AMC Gremlin. Who can forget wise-guy chorus serenading passersby with weird diner owner. Merry pranksters and pals squash their town with raucous sound. Alice Cooper shares Dana Carvey and Mike Myers' limelight.

Yellow Submarine (1968****). The peak of Mount Psychedelia may be at the bottom of the sea. Beatles' surrealistic world of Psychedelic **Peter Max** art and lifestyle are often cryptic. Like a Zen Buddhist *satori*, moments of glory arrive in the oddest shapes and sizes. The Beatles picked their 4th-greatest singer to launch their title song – #2(1), 8-66. Baritone **Ringo Starr** sings jovially. In the cartoon, burbling bubbles bloop. The 'Blue Meanies' frolic. The sanitized cartoon gives kids a fun drugless romp through flipping, tripping Psychedelia. Naturally, the flick may be interpreted on two levels – high and underwater – and they often blend. It's a fun "Octopus's Garden" of undersea Beatle wit and charm. It's the most vivid COLOR trip this side of Madonna's *Dick Tracy*. Beatles rival Disney's Greatest Hits.

Thus endeth **Rockflix**. Hundreds more exist for your viewing pleasure. In the video world, we can only do smatterings. This is an audial *Gold Rush*. Let's do MTV again. Other great flix? *Your Cheatin' Heart* ('64***), *Woodstock* ('70***½), *Rebel Without a Cause* ('55****), *Let It Be* ('70***½), and *American Hot Wax* ('78***).

"Fly Like an Eagle" – Seal, #10, 12-96. Sealhenry Samuel is a Brazilian/Nigerian star from Paddington [London], England (b. 1963). His B & W video reprises the **Steve Miller Band**'s #2(2), 12-76 song, among first xerox echoes by an R&B artist of a White Soul song. Besides Seal's wildly successful #1(1), 6-95 waltz "Kiss from a Rose," Seal broke into showbiz big time with his #21, 6-94 "Prayer for the Dying." Seal's "Eagle" video debuts with speedily swirling cumulus clouds – like cauliflower doing the Twist.

His video promotes *Space Jam (1996***),* starring **Michael Jordan** and **Bugs Bunny**. Two megastars. It's a "Johnny B. Goode" basketball fantasy. Some Afro-American or Anglo-Brazilian-Nigerian kids are teetering and tottering, playing hoops. Leaves skitter in the autumn whoosh – and swoosh. We zoom to 'Air Jordan,' flying planeless in the clouds in his ultimate quest to conquer gravity. Vignettes sprout: an old lonesome house, a dusty road. Suddenly, like 1938 *Wizard of Oz***** or 1998 *Pleasantville***, the video vaults into a quick splotch of vivid technicolor. Jordan slam-dunks the ball. Back to B&W and a goaltending purple monster. As the video trails away, we get lightning hints of hero Bugs Bunny and good ol' Daffy Duck. In this *Space Jam* promo video, Seal's combo video/audio is an improvement over the audio, alone. Videos are always expensive. Somebody pays the toll.

Videos can do three things: 1) They can improve sagging audios; if the songstress is beautiful, it will obviously boost sales; 2) They can downsize audios; your mystical audio song vision may be destroyed by some cheesy video; and 3) They can rev in neutral; the ho-hum video is better than the humdrum audio, so the song sags to #356 in Zanzibar. Warner Sunset Records maybe could get away with paying Bugs Bunny a case of carrots. But what about pricey Michael Jordan? "Fly Like an Eagle" floats on Steve Miller/Seal's funky little chops and vibrato minor chords. It's a good video that improves a good song by a good singer. Videos are tragically expensive.

We've saved gorgeous **Janet Jackson**'s (b. 5-16-66, Gary, Indiana) biggest blockbusters for your Video Section. Janet Jackson IS Video.

***Christina Aguilera**, performing #1 hit "Genie in a Bottle" on TV show "Beverly Hills 90210"*

"Any Time, Any Place" – Janet Jackson, #2(1), 5-94; #1(10) R & B. Janet's tune steams along like a marital guide to intimate bliss. She suggests the mood of **Chris Isaak**'s steamy video for #6, 12-90 "Wicked Game." Or **Merril Bainbridge**'s #4, 9-96 "Mouth." Janet's man's knotted hairdo stands straight up about five inches atop his head. Janet's ex-dress cascades demurely off her shoulder. Scene shifts from a grubby urban scenario to a cozy fireplace. They spend a lot of time going in and out of doors. Surrealist shutterbugs come in and swirl around disjointed images. Obviously, the guy is after her bod.

In the video wake of **Madonna**, the Jackson Five's kid sister created a new world beyond SIMPLY the SONG – she added a Choreographic Vision to catapult to #3 Female Artist of All Time. Recently passing the **Supremes**, Janet now looks up only to **Madonna** and Queen of Soul **Aretha Franklin.** Janet's #3 "Nasty" (5-96) wasn't. Springboarding her to stardom, she rode a wavecrest of huge chart grabbers: first #1(2), 8-86 "When I Think of You"; #2(1), 1-87 "Let's Wait Awhile"; inspirational #2(2), 11-89 "Rhythm Nation"; #1(3), 1-90 "Escapade"; #2(2), 6-90 "Come Back to Me"; #1(1), 11-90 "Love Will Never Do (Without You)"; and biggest hit – #1(8), 5-93 "That's the Way Love Goes." Janet's "If" hit #4 in 7-93 with Diana Ross. Janet again? "Again" hit #1(2), 10-93, while non-Ray Charles' "Together Again" crunched #1(2), 12-97. The Indiana choreographic princess did dynamic duos and choral combos: #3, 3-99 "What's It Gonna Be" with **Busta Rhymes**, and #3, 5-98 "I Get Lonely" with BLACKstreet.

On her #1(4), 9-89 "Miss You Much," she shows her #1 power sound. At age 10 Janet, whose childhood was blunted by stardom, played Penny Gordon Woods in *Good Times* (1977-79), a video boost dating back to **Ricky Nelson** on 50s sitcom *Ozzie &Harriet.* Janet's starbound itinerary included 1981-82 *Different Strokes,* and soon *Fame* arrived ('84). Her Insta-Marriage to James DeBarge in 1984 was instantly annulled. **El DeBarge** sang countertenor lead on #6, 6-85 (#2 R&B) "Who's Holding Donna Now" for DeBarge, with James handling smooth keyboards. By 9-95, Janet was a "Runaway" (#3), globetrotting the planet. In 1990, her #1(1) "Black Cat" featured *Living Colour's* Vernon Reid on lead guitar. Her poshest video takes us on a whirlwind tour of 99% of the earth. She seems to FLY to exotic spots like Sydney, Australia's Opera House, or faraway Taj Mahals of romantic ardor and intrigue.

"The Angels Listened In" – Crests, #22, 8-59; #14, 10-59, R & B. Italian-American maestro **Johnny Maestro** (b. Mastrangelo, Brooklyn) joined this vintage Soul/R&B crew in 1956, adding Operatic Rock to great hits beyond signature song "Sixteen Candles" at #2(2), 11-58. Major hits include #28, 3-59 "Six Nights a Week," #20 angel-theme 10-60 "Trouble in Paradise," and sensational pizzicato #14, 2-60 "Step by Step." As the **Brooklyn Bridge**, Maestro created some of Rock's greatest Streetcorner hits ironically in the Psychedelic Era, like #45, 3-69 "Blessed Is the Rain." With this one angelic invocation, you could argue that Johnny is among greatest Doo-Whop maestros ever. Brooklyn Bridge's "Worst That Could Happen" hit bronze HOT 100, #3, 12-68. Videos? Only frequent *American Bandstand* appearances.

"Crazy" –Aerosmith, #17, 5-94. Steven Tyler's "Crazy" video flouts the transformation of some sweetsy schoolgirls in short skirts into strip-joint mavens. They lust after the open road, fly into their convertible, and run away from home. Pied piper rock and roll. Nothing new (Crispian St. Peters' #4, 6-66 "Pied Piper"). Aerosmith (Rock Hall 2001) plays naughty pied piper to divert the innocent attentions of these murmuring teenyboppers. The girls bounce into a gas station. Cut to Tyler/Aerosmith, wailing topless on stage (all, alas, male). Flash back to gas station. Girls cause the 55+ attendant's world-class Lolita Leer. He's so enthralled with their nubile gorgeous figures, he fails to notice their klepto spree. They stuff widgets and snigglets and goodies down their blouses and into their bags.

The getaway. Refugee lasses jump in car, and back over orange cones. Car spits gravel (see "Uneasy Rider"). Rollin' down the highway. Aerosmith fires it up. Tyler's intense vocal crests (the Crests' vocal does not aerosmith). Tyler's amazing deep-gut notes cry like a lost steel guitar on some honkytonk stardust highway to Mars. The girls dash into a topless strip joint. Clad dancers slither and writhe around poles. They unite with Aerosmith. We hook up the two pulsating plots. The band wails, and two wiggly waifs run away from home. Girls skedaddle beyond Pole Cats and Kittens. They take off down a country freedom road. They spy a handsome muscular farm lad atop his droning tractor, tilling the hot, fertile soil. They stop and entice him (easily) into their ragtop. The three skinny-dip in some cow-wallow mudhole. Then, of course, they steal his clothes and he shamefully chases after their giggle-glutted car at 14 mph. Car goes 15 mph. The laff-meter registers three yoks and a guffaw, as they flail away into the sunset, like *Thelma & Louise* on a spree. Jaded? Aerosmith's "Jaded" hit #8+, 1-2001, proving Top Tens still stalk the Jaggeresque nifty fifty New Hampshire Rock star.

"Un-Break My Heart" – Toni Braxton, #1(11), 10-96. Braxton (b. '68, Severn, MD) won Best New Artist '93 Grammy on strength of #3, 10-93 "Breathe Again." Without MTV, she would be just another fine voice on the radio. Braxton is a visual experience. Her hot chart fever began with Rap Spelling Lexicon: #29, 7-92 "Give U My Heart" with Babyface. Her monster breakthrough was #7, 7-93 "Another Sad Love Song." The "Un-Break My Heart" video shows Toni in a variety of magnetic outfits. She ends up in a dazzling white dress with auroras of shimmering stars revolving around her, on stage, at the finale. Toni's #1(1), 6-96 "You're Makin' Me High/Let It Flow" stars her clingy blue jiggling jumpsuit. Braxton reviews candidates for her ardent affection. Over 99 of 100 musicologists watching and analyzing her melody and beauty have absolutely no idea what she's singing about anyhow. From #7, 4-94 "You Mean the World to Me," the blue-eyed Afro R&B star blasted to the silver-medal #2 HOT 100 spot on 3-2000 "He Wasn't Man Enough."

"One More Minute" –'Weird Al' Yankovic, NC, 1985. In 1986, Cleveland, Ohio's Polka King **Frankie Yankovic & His Yanks** finally won a Grammy for Best Polka Recording – a new category. Good-time accordion guru Frankie hit #12, 3-49 with "Blue Skirt Waltz." **Weird Al** (b. 10-24-59, Lynwood, California) followed his relative's musical fun formula – and grooved to Laff-trax Rock: **Sheb Wooley**'s #1(6), 6-58 "Purple People Eater," **David Seville**'s #1, 4-58 "The Witch Doctor," and Seville's beloved **Chipmunks**, Alvin, Simon, and Theodore. In #3, 2-59 "Alvin's Harmonica," that little rapscallion (later TV cartoon star) Alvin whips out his annoying harmonica whenever his flustered leader Seville asks him to join the squeaky vocal group (via jacked-up speed studio overdubbing tricks). The curmudgeonly little critter does his own thing and blissfully wrecks the song. Chipmunks' biggest is #1(3), 12-58 "The Chipmunk Song." Has Rock and Roll gotten too serious? Vaudeville shuffled off into the sunset. Pie-in-the-face sight gags have been replaced by ugly huge weightlifting things that smash each other and bleed in the cartoons – once the home of humor.

Al's an accordion guy. This wheezy, breezy instrument of choice of 1955 Detroit dads made the GUITAR the instrument of choice to us Detroit kids. The squeezebox was resurrected by Al for his princely parodies of pop corn. Al's first chartfondler? His #104, 3-81 "Another One Rides the Bus," zapping **Queen**'s #1, '80 "Another One Bites the Dust." Al's #63, 4-83 HOT 100 debut "Ricky" (see #1, '82 **Toni Basil**'s #1 "Mickey") jolted the status quo, and gently chided America's comedienne Lucille Ball *(I Love Lucy)* and Desi Arnaz – 'Ricky Ricardo.'

"One More Minute" builds to a comic volcano of impossible grotesqueness. At first you think it's a cool 50s baritone ballad of lost malt shops and sad sock hops. Off *Dare to Be Stupid,* "Like a Surgeon" hit #47, 6-85, parodizing Madonna's "Like a Virgin." "One More Minute" is a masterpiece of lyrical crescendo folly – and puzzled suspense. Is it a love song? Or a gross-out song? Al comes on like some echo-chamber baritone clone of the King – maybe Ersel Hickey, Crash Craddock (#94, 11-59 "Don't Destroy Me," #16, 6-74 "Rub It In" [#1C]), and Ral Donner/Starfires all rolled into one. Al uses his mock-serious vibrato, griping about the old days, when the chick messed him up. Then, he giggles monsterfully, that he has burned down their old malt shop meeting-place..

Al skids from the burning ex-malt shop into the horror show of absurd self-mutilation. Nope, I'm not talking about Wimp Mutilations like ultra-marathons or tiny tattoos or tongue-piercings. This is real hara-kiri stuff. First the song-guy sticks his nostrils together with Crazy Glue. Then he says he'd prefer to get his blood sucked by leeches than see the girl again for one more moment. After some upchuck bathroom humor about cleaning Grand Central Station's facilities, Big Al launches into the ultimate self-smashing torture – even worse than hara-kiri disemboweling. It is very dis-HEART-ening: He chooses to literally tear his heart out of his rib cage barehandedly – rather than suffer another minute with this girl. His queasy band, too seasick to plunk along their raunchy rhythms, scoots out the back door with a cacophonic final chord. His ex-

listeners, groovily grossed out, leave on the midnight train to the next decade. Goofy spoof.

A lot of Yankovic's mirth goes back to the golden Leiber-Stoller days of the **Coasters** and **Clovers**. The Clovers, you recall, did spiffy #23, 9-59 "Love Potion #9." The Coasters riddled rockettyboppers with a slew of comedy stew: #1(1), 6-58 "Yakety Yak," #2(3), 2-59 "Charlie Brown" (unrelated to Snoopy/*Peanuts*), and fan-dancer #23, 4-61 "Little Egypt."

"Poison Ivy" – Coasters, #7, 8-59; #1(4), 6-59 R&B. Their act was 100% Video Visuals, but the only videos were cameos on *Ed Sullivan* or *American Bandstand.* It's the midnite hour, and you try to catch some ZZZ's. Tenor **Carl Gardner** and bass Dub Jones (1929-2000) warn that "Poison Ivy"creeps in stealthily, like *Saturday Night Live's* absurd Land Shark skit [actual shark invades apartments, devours unwary folks]. **Coasters** made Rock Hall 2nd-year, 1987. Also baritone Billy Guy, first-bass Bobby Nunn (1925-86), tenor Leon Hughes. Many Video style Hallowe'en carols involved these creepy motifs: **Bobby 'Boris' Pickett's** #1, '62 "Monster Mash," John Zacherle's #6, 3-58 moldy oldie goldie "Dinner with Drac," and the Grossfest Gold Medal R & B Groover, or **Screamin' Jay Hawkins'** (1929-2000) tasteful cannibal NC '69 song "Feast of the Mau-Mau."

"Pride (In the Name of Love)" – U2, #33, 10-84. Serious Irish tribute to the life of Dr. Martin Luther King. **Bono** (b. Paul Hewson, Dublin) and U2's leadoff #53, 4-83 "New Year's Day" outline the bloody strife in Northern Ireland plaguing the Emerald Isle for centuries – since the English ran Scots off their lands and put them in Ireland. "Pride" is a monumental MTV achievement. Concert footage comprises many MTV videos. "Pride" pumps up the powerful Bono charisma and star quality. Just as *Backbeat* flaunted black-and-white Hamburg mean streets for the neophytic Beatles – so U2 reflects the bleakness of the Owen's Derry's struggle. That B&W shows up in their superstar #1(9), 4-87 *Joshua Tree* album (10 million).

"The Streets of Philadelphia" – Bruce Springsteen, #9, 2-94. Spirit of bleakness goes technicolor. Bruce wanders raggedy streets of wintertime Philly, garbed in a somber and frayed 45-degree jacket at 28 degrees. BLEAK translates monochromatically for Bruce's street tableau into gray drab, muddy maroon, wimpy indigo, and broken-glass diamonds. The slurping gutter, spiky with little shards of desolation ice, begins to freeze hard. Both moviemaker **Tom Hanks**, and **Bruce Springsteen**, risked tongue-wagging gossips questioning their straight lifestyles. They courageously stood up for their alternative-lifestyle brethren who were wasting away from the scourge of Acquired Immune Deficiency Syndrome. Magnificent video. Springsteen strolls ghetto streets. He watches kids playing hoops, and ragtag denizens warming frozen hands by flickering rusty-trash-can fires.

As Bruce ambles the desperate avenues of poverty and drugs and despair, he catches a quick glimpse of movie star Hanks, who portrays a man in a sad fadeaway from his dreaded disease. The video is also a political cry for help and funding. It is a beacon of light to illuminate the way to better research to combat this viral terror that stalks everyone, regardless of romantic orientation.

"Summer of '69" – Bryan Adams, #5, 7-85. Cool, scraggly-tenored Adams (b. '59, Kingston, Ontario) grew up in this northerly resort of Canada's not-too-tropical South Coast. His video here shows Bryan and his kidhood band storming an abandoned warehouse. They goof off, pitching stuff at each other. A Keystone Kops chase ensues, with very civilized Canadian gendarmes. Fun tune. The music is a Screaming Blues metallic odyssey, a zany frolic, a hi-jinx serenade. Adams, like his singular biblical namesake Adam, chauffeurs us back to some sunny sensual Garden of Eden. He lobs his happy musical flares through a bleary blur of metallic major chords. His wild yahoo vocal is a hymn to lost youth. The Summer of '69 makes us believe we can play volleyball and surf all day. We can sing with the moon, dance under the blue stars, and get some romantic action with the evening Eve of our dreams underneath the sheltering palm trees. Until Temptation snakes its slithery way and poisons Paradise. "Summer of '69" is an idyllic flashback. Rock and Roll, in both audio and video forms, is a whole way of life.

"Black Hole Sun" – Soundgarden, NC, 1994. #1(7), 5-94, Album Rock Tracks; #2(1), 4-94, Modern Rock Tracks. One of the most fantastic futuristic videos ever concocted. A splatter of whirling galaxies, exploding stars, quivering quasars, and abyssal black holes turns this dark Alternative song into a multi-dimensional adventure. Emerging from the Seattle slew of Grunge groups, Soundgarden hammers the sidelong charts with hyperspace histrionics.

"Absolutely (Story of a Girl)" – Nine Days, #6, 4-2000; #1(2), 7-2000, Casey Kasem's "American Top 40"; #2(2), HOT 100 Recurrent Airplay, 11-2000; Also, #2 on VH-1, Summer 2000. The video must have been a success, for it won the bronze medal in VH-1's 2000 new "Song That Kicks [Rump]" awards. If you watched Summer 2000 videos, you know this one. I hope you like it, too. The plot?

Long Island's **Nine Days** is practicing on one floor of a seemingly Soho or East Village NYC apartment. On a different floor, a pretty PG-rated girl is taking a bath. On another floor, a chunky fortysomething in a T-shirt and shiny old pants is sitting on his grubby couch with erupting springs. He's guzzling a brewski or three. OK, the action. Girl's tub runs over. Guy gets up to change channel on prehistoric remote-less TV set. Bathing girl's bath causes flood. It drools down stairs toward Nine Days and this wild party going on above them. The chunky guy accidentally sets old couch on fire. Sprinklers detect smoke, and douse whole apartment building, saving everyone. Girl gets dressed to check out wild party, like NYC's **Bobby Darin**, in #3, 3-58 "Splish Splash."

John Hampson sings lead, with **Brian Desveaux** harmonizing high thirds into second verse, and playing lead guitar. They sing of this magical girl. She cries a river

(Julie London, #9, 11-55, "Cry Me a River"), and this amazing river drowns the ENTIRE world. Seems the girl looks very sad in photos, but John ABSOLUTELY LOVES the lass – when she's smiling. It may be the catchiest song of the millennium. **Jeremy Dean** plays keyboards, **Nick DiMichino** plays stalwart tremendous bass, and **Vinnie Tattanelli** wails away on supersonic drums. He's the one with the Frank Zappa bottom-lip beardlet 'Soul Patch,' and an impish Ringo Starr smile. They are on tour now, probably in your town (if your town, tonight, is Chicago).

Meanwhile, back at the smoldering apartment house. The sprinkler douses the flames. The gorgeous girl, not yet smiling, gets dolled up and strolls up to the party. A multicultural party-animal battalion of revelers arrives at Nine Days' "Absolutely" wild impromptu show. The gorgeous girl dances and SMILES. A frenzied mob bedsprings the rafters as they leap and dance. The beery beefy dude joins the conclave, giving up on his croaked TV and ashen couch. He hurtles joyously in the air like a pogo-stick – catching every pulse of the Hampson/ Desveaux/Tattanelli/DiMichino/Dean beat. Outside on the avenue, a fender-bender of fans causes a 20-car smash-up. Nobody gets hurt. Everybody yells at each other. One of those streetside trucks contains actor Brian Costello. When Hampson cascades down the last chorus like John Lennon's 40-second "A Day in the Life" finale on *Sgt. Pepper,* the final chord is carried by Jeremy's big Hammond B-3 organ from the Sony Atlanta Sound Studios. It's a stark and dramatic visual on a video laced with 100% Pure Rock and Roll, powered by working-class American dreams, and celebrating the triumph of love.

"One Sweet Day" – Mariah Carey and Boyz II Men, #1(16), 12-95; #2(8) R & B. They stuff this talent bonanza into a modest recording studio. The video is simply their session. Mariah adorns the place in shapely cutoffs and Alpine *coloratura* soprano ecstasies. Boyz II Men bring back 1890s Barber Shop Quartet magic. Mariah lofts 16th-note *melismas* throughout her repertoire, often on a direct beam to **Johann Sebastian Bach** [catch *"Grosser Herr, O Starker Konig"* – ('Great Lord, O Strong King')]. "One Sweet Day" is the most popular record of the Rock Era, with 16 weeks atop the *Billboard* zenith (see **Francis Craig**, #1[17], '47 "Near You"). Her four Philly singers? Wanya and Nathan Morris, Michael McCary, and Shawn Stockman. Their entire video experience makes recording look like a fun, low-key experience. It rarely is. They fondle their earphones, music stands, clumpy chairs and bland sets. No big deal. Cutting the #1 record in the universe – for A THIRD of an ENTIRE YEAR – looks as easy as wolfing down your bowl of Wheaties, with a chaser of Captain Crunch. It is an elegy consoling a recent tragic loss – and celebrating a reunification in Heaven. Carey crunched the numbers again: #1(2), 4-96 "Always Be My Baby"; #1(1), 5-98 "My All," and #1(1), 12-99 "Thank God I Found You." Boyz II Men hit big on #1(1), 9-97 "4 Seasons of Loneliness." "One Sweet Day," however, overarches all the lesser songs with its power, impact, and spirituality. Its sluggish beat believes its magnificent Prosser message: Friday is tough – but Sunday's comin'!

Teen idol **Bobby Rydell**,
actual namesake of high school in "Grease"

"Grease," starring
Olivia Newton John *and* **John Travolta**

The Monkees, *starring (l-r)* **Peter Tork,**
Mickey Dolenz, *MTV-inventor* **Michael Nesmith,**
and lead singer **Davy Jones**

Ozzy Osbourne *(of* **Black Sabbath***) star of*
2002+ TV Show "The Osbournes" and
movie – "The Decline of Western Civilization,
Part II: The Metal Years"

Led Zeppelin, *stars of bio-pic*
"The Song Remains the Same"
(l-r) **John Bonham, Jimmy Page, John Paul**
Jones *(top), and* **Robert Plant**

And On . . . On . . . ON, to Rock-Ville Centre!

Don McLean to the contrary, the levee never dried and the music never died. Rock and Roll contines unabated, with the "American Pie" legacy of **Buddy Holly** steering its destiny ad its promise. Many great hits paraded the intervening years. To bring you our gala pix-galore 'centerfold,' we're zooming over some tunes.

John [Cougar] Mellencamp's "Key West Intermezzo" (#14, 10-98) celebrated the contiguous U.S.A.'s own tropical island. Blues guru **Eric Clapton**'s #5, 7-96 "Change the World" changed it, as did his #16A, 2-98 "My Father's Eyes," and blockbuster album #3, 2000 with **B.B. King**, *Riding with the King*. **Stevie Winwood** began with 12-66 "Gimme Some Lovin'" at #7 with the **Spencer Davis Group**. Also #10, 3-67 "I'm a Man" and super #76, 3-66 unrecognized "Keep on Runnin'." In his solo career, he went on to "Higher Love" at #1(1), 6-86, after 'playing in *Traffic*' (Al. *John Barleycorn Must Die*, #5, 7-70). Also #1(4), 6-88 "Roll With It."

Former leader of **Spooky Tooth** with Foreigner's **Mick Jones** was **Gary Wright**, who scored silver success on #2(3), 1-76 "Dream Weaver." **Paul Simon**'s solo career blossomed with #2(2), 5-73 "Kodachrome," Gospel-powered Dixie Hummingbirds collaboration #2(1), 8-73 "Loves Me Like a Rock," and rascallish #22, 4-72 "Me and Julio Down by the Schoolyard." **Stevie Wonder**'s Chalypso charmer was #1(3), 8-84 "I Just Called to Say I Love You," followed by "Part-Time Lover" at #1(1), 9-85. **Cheap Trick** successfully imitated Elvis's biggest hit – #1(11), '56 "Don't Be Cruel" – to #4, 7-88, despite taboo on covering Elvis. They also soared to fiery chart apex with #1(2), 4-88 "The Flame." **Bruce Hornsby's Range** quenched the flames with #4, 1-87 with "Mandolin Rain," and vivacious **Rindy Ross's Quarterflash** zoomed to #3, 10-81 with the dynamic, though atherosclerotic, "Harden My Heart."

"Kiss on My List" – Hall & Oates, #1(3), 1-81. Darryl Hall (b. '48, Daryl Hohl, Philly) competed in a Temple University Battle of the Bands against the band of NYC's **John Oates** (b. '49). Neither knew they'd pass the **Righteous Brothers** and **Everly Brothers** as Top Singles Duo of All Time. Of Top 500 Artists, they're 38th, Everlys 45th. This catchy Kiss/List tune championed the charts, along with five other #1's like #1(2), 1-77 "Rich Girl" (#64, 2-77 R & B for the White Soul stars), and #1(4), 10-82 "Maneater." They even covered the Righteous Brothers' #1, 12-64 "You've Lost That Lovin' Feeling" – the #1 Airplay song of all time at one point (Hall & Oates hit #12, 9-80). They also hit big with #4, 1-76 "Sara Smile" (about Hall's girlfriend Sara Allen).

Bob Seger snagged #1(1), 5-87 with theme song to Eddie Murphy's *Beverly Hills Cop* sequel. "Love of the Common People" hit #45, 5-84 by Paul Young (also #114 Everly Brothers, 11-67 and #106, 10-67 Vegas hero **Wayne Newton**). Despite vanished bus fare, holey pockets, patchy dresses, and frozen toes, this poor family sticks together with a wonderful adhesion borne of love and respect. The **Proclaimers** of Scotland (brothers Craig and Charlie Reid) hit #3, 6-93 with "I'm Gonna Be (500 Miles)," from movie *Benny & Joon*. **Blackstreet** hit #1(4), 10-96 with "No Diggity," no relation whatsoever to **Perry Como**'s #1, 3-56 "Hot Diggity."

Ace of Base's #2(3), 9-93 "All That She Wants" touts a friendly welfare system in Scandinavia that encourages single mothers to raise kids. Hot gal is looking for a man for amorous services. Contrast to **Michael Jackson**'s parenthood denial in the-kid-ain't-my-kid #1(7), 1-83 hit "Billie Jean." Ace of Base rampaged to #1(6), 1-94 with "The Sign."

"Don't Want to Be a Fool"– Luther Vandross, #9, 8-91; #4 R & B. Major singer, arranger, and producer Vandross scored biggest with **Mariah Carey** duo #2(1), 9-94 "Endless Love." Vandross has seven #1 R & B hits.

"(Everything I Do) I Do It for You" – Bryan Adams, #1(7), 6-91; #1(16), U.K. Until "Candle in the Wind '97," longest-running U.K. single ever at #1. Theme from Kevin Costner's *Robin Hood*, this lumbering torch tune flares with passion. The big metallic beat blusters along, like a tornado two miles away, stalking a great big 'X' marked on Ernie Fnerp's new Snazzo Mobile Home. When Adams' anthem strikes the bombshell booming bridge, the chord shifts in a rush of A-bomb energy. Only **Queen**'s #4, '77 "We Will Rock You" contains a chord shift so dynamic.

In 11-85, Adams paired with **Tina Turner** to #15, "It's Only Love." His ultra-dramatic #1(5), 4-95 "Have You Ever Really Loved a Woman" also crested big for the Kingston, Ontario and Vancouver B.C. tenor, along with #1(2), 4-85 celestial "Heaven," and energetic #6, 11-84 "Run to You."

"Power of Love" – Celine Dion, #1(4), 11-93. Quebeçois **Celine Dion** held the top spot with #1(6), 3-96 "Because You Loved Me," and danced the high wire of success with her Celtic Renaissance classics, #4, 4-92 "If You Asked Me To," and #4, 12-90 "Where Does My Heart Beat Now?" Much French-influenced music dates back to the 'Little Sparrow,' **Edith Piaf**, and her #88, 3-61 "Milord" (#1 Europe). She possessed the fragile strength of **Judy Garland**, whose biggest hit (think 'Dorothy' & Oz) was NOT #5, 9-39 "Over the Rainbow," but #3, 7-40 "I'm Nobody's Baby." Celine Dion reflects the best of both. **Art** and **Dotty Todd** scored with #6, 4-58 "Chanson d'Amour (Song of Love)" from NEW JERSEY. The British **Chris Barber Jazz Band** hit #5, 1-59 with delicate instrumental "Petit Fleur (Little Flower)." French-Canadian novelist **Jack Kerouac** sculpted the world-views of **Bob Dylan, Jim Morrison**'s **Doors**, and the **Grateful Dead**. Quebec's **Alanis Morissette** achieved #4, 3-96 with "Ironic," about how the whole day is out to get you – or get her album *Jagged Little Pill*, which sold TWELVE million copies 12-95.

Celine Dion

"You're So Square (Baby I Don't Care)" – Joni Mitchell, #47, 11-82. When Bob Dylan or Joni cover a song, it must be good. This is. Both **Elvis** and **Buddy Holly** sang this Rockabilly boomer. Solid Rock milestone. Songwriter Joni gave us "Woodstock" – #11, 3-70 for **Crosby, Stills, and Nash**. In the song about Rock's biggest Festival, she calls everybody STARDUST and GOLDEN. "Stardust" was the #1 song of the first half of the 20th century – #1 **Isham Jones**' 9-30 tenor sax instrumental, and **Bing Crosby**'s soothing #5, 9-31 baritone vocal plus a cast of millions. Crosby, Stills, and Nash (no relation to Bing), did a great #7, 5-77 "Just a Song Before I Go."

"Wannabee" – Spice Girls, #1(4), 1-97. English Posh Spice (Vicki Adams), Baby Spice (Emma Bunton), Sporty Spice (Melanie Chisholm), and Ginger Spice (Gerry Halliwell) join Scary Spice (Melanie Brown). Photogenic quintet. Spicy hits? #3, 5-97 "Say You'll Be There," #4, 8-97 "2 Become 1," and #9, 2-298 "Too Much." Sweet belltone harmonies, like their Country compadres the **Dixie Chicks**: #27, 11-99 "Cowboy Take Me Away."

As Julius Caesar, Jim Mattimore, John Parbst or Don Gilzinger once said, the words of a nation's popular music can be used to change the world.

"All I Wanna Do" – Sheryl Crow, #2(6), 8-94. A covey of Crows lambasted the Hot Hits Line, led by **Sheryl** (b. '63, Rennett, Missouri), the **Black Crowes**, and **Counting Crows**. Sheryl glued a copy of Jack Kerouac's *On the Road* to her teeming mind. She pursued a (1994 Grammy) Dylanesque trail of lyrical/musical destiny. Crow graduated from University of Missouri and taught music before fleeing to the Promised Land, Los Angeles, in that hypnotic California sun.

Came the apprenticeship. Track star hurdler Sheryl picked up jobs backing **George Harrison, Don Henley, Michael Jackson**, and other luminaries. She dusted the HOT 100 with her #60, 4-94 "Leaving Las Vegas." All the while her humungoid album (Al. #3, 3-94) *Tuesday Night Music Club* wobbled along its piecemeal path to glory.

Sheryl and pals do rolling chromatics in "All I Wanna Do," gliding a half step up and back in key. It bounces off their millions of listeners' consciousness in a hip rave-up mosh pit of wild abandon. This bizarre chord progression not only anchors "All I Wanna Do," but powers her big beat "Can't Cry Anymore" (#36, 7-95).

"All I Wanna Do"? First off, they're drinking beer at noon on Tuesday. Some rumbum L.A. bar. She's met some guy named Bill, or maybe 'Billy,' 'Mac,' or 'Buddy.' In their soft bar gloom, they face a garish car wash. She and this other lunch chugger chuckle over the CEO 'wannabes' fondling their Buick fenders outside with chamois tenderness at High Noon. They squirt and scrub in the sunglow glare. Skirts and suits scuttle in the mild breeze. Stoned on the Work Ethic. She and 'Bill/Mac/Buddy' drink beer. Not working. They're like impish work-slacker Francis in Mel Lazarus' cartoon *Momma*. Or maybe *Garfield*. Or *Bugs Bunny*. The anti-work rabbit still delights with his friendly Brooklynese street savvy, his desperado bravado, and his carrot of plucky, punchy power. Good ol' Bugsy, star of stage, screen and 1997 postage stamp.

Sheryl coos that all she wants to do is enjoy some fun before everybody dies. A voice in the wilderness? **Jim Morrison** sang the END would always be near, in his bleaker Roadhouse full of dark Blues (see #50 "Roadhouse Blues"). Many women songwriters, too, avoid primroses and lollipops. Back to Billy's bar. Don't we all need some fun while we're (**Cat Stevens**' #10, 3-74 "Oh Very Young") dancing on this fragile planet for a tiny while? Isn't FUN what Rock and Roll is all about? We all have surplus humdrum in our lives. BORING.

Sometimes, on the sprightly wings of a song, a speedy movement of glory comes glopping through the gloom. We listen, transfixed. It bashes the boring. Busts the blue funk. We rise to meet the song's pure joy. The song emancipates us from the shaggy shroud of Uglitude. We boogie to the euphoric pulse of this music we love. We are 100% alive.

Now, what's so profound and important about Crow's "All I Wanna Do"? Is it just two lunch-guzzling L.A. lovers getting schnockered? Despite its patrician Santa Monica Boulevard setting, Sheryl's Slacker Anthem champions the working person's BEER. Bizarrely, they are not working. BEER – not champagne or vermouth or frozen daiquiris or dinosaur-elderly scotch. Billy/Mac peels labels off Budweiser bottles. He shreds and scrunches them. Hawaiian guitar half-steps slide as she breezes the vocal. Sheryl's jiving Jazz riffs slur the slow-train backbeat. She spotlights a deliberately imprecise rolling rhythm against the splotchy downbeat. Meanwhile, Billy/Mac puffs Pall-Malls , pell-mell, smirkily impervious to the 90s California Nicotine-Police sting.

She's looking for enlightenment. For meaning. For satori or epiphany. Some tremendous understanding of the meaning of life. Some transcendent big buzz. She and Billy/Mac aren't contemplating any hell-bent joyrides in some doomed teen-tiny Toyota, tussling with some sturdy oak tree (Score: Oak Tree 1, Toyota Zilch). Do they discover Ponce de Leon's Fountain of Youth? And life's true purpose? Not exactly. Mostly, they're in a cross between Paradise and **Billy Joel**'s Happy Hour Desperado bar from his #25, 2-74 "Piano Man" pub. Sheryl blends a breezy, blithe, and winsome Pollyanna mood here with a Grunge undertone. **Grateful Dead** critic Pete Kaczenski quoted Wavy Gravy: "The beauty of the Grateful Dead was their relationship with their fans; they just take this great big ball of love and bounce it back out to the fans, and the fans bounce it back and each time it gets bigger."

Or Pete himself: "The reason I look up to Jerry Garcia? Not only did he make me laugh and smile – he also made me cry." If you can't distill any real human emotion out of a song, it's high time to punch your radio button.

Back to the CROW BAR. The deserted dive contains only a bored bartender scanning want ads to escape this oasis Billy/Mac and Sheryl have fled to. Back to **Billy Joel**'s bar. Every solitary social drinker was trapped in his bar persona – agonizing to get out. Sheryl and 'Billy' are kinda happy to be IN there, avoiding the SPF2 killer rays of the noontime California sun, and sorting out the ultimate meaning of life.

Here comes the dizzying epiphany. It swamps her reeling earthquake soul: She says the bar is theirs, plus they own the night, the day, the Budweisers and matches, the car wash outside the window, plus the sun and MOON. Wow. People scrimp and save all their lives to buy the things Sheryl Crow already has right there and now – a "Free As a Bird" (**Beatles** #6, 12-95) vision. A happy vision of the universe wildly spinning around her. It may be momentary, sure. Her a.m. agonies may bode Alka-Seltzer. Sometimes we pay for too much light, love, and understanding.

Have you ever read Margaret Wise Brown's kiddie lit classic *Goodnight Moon* (pix by Clement Hurd)? The story unfolds of this little rabbitty-kid at sleepytime: "Goodnight clocks and goodnight socks, goodnight nobody, goodnight mush, goodnight stars, goodnight air, goodnight moon." Perhaps you saw the world's oldest heavyweight champ, **George Foreman** (45 on 1995 show), campily reading this funny funzy fuzzy classic on *Saturday Night Live*.

Somehow, Sheryl Crow's "All I Wanna Do," the rabbit-kid's *Goodnight Moon*, Pooh Bear guru Jerry Garcia, and Champ George Foreman manage to meld the whole spinning universe together. Like the Zen Buddhist satori, or Christian epiphany. A vision of love?

The hottest hits often deal with petty annoyances of life. They zap the hangnails, bad hair days, or the coffee machine that eats your money and upchucks the coffee down the cupless drain. Contrast to more somber **Doors**; drowning in Blakean cosmic visions:

"Love Her Madly" – Doors, #11, 4-71. Crow deals with hassles; Morrison deals with life and death. Jim Morrison shares Kerouac's sadder apocalyptic vision of the City of the Dead (Necropolis), "Love Her Madly" digs into and chides the armor of a friend whose girl is walking out the door. Agonizing unrequited love.

"Don't Cry for Me Argentina" – Madonna, #8, 1-97. Entering the charts at sky-high #17, 12-17-97, Madonna's thrashing Disco/Latino beat could lambada the blue stars from the silver sky. From long-running Broadway play *Evita*, Madonna sings the sad song of doomed 50s Eva Peron, Argentina's charismatic and beloved first lady (wife of dictator Juan Peron). The melody was always magnificent. Add a punchy beat and Madonna's terrific timing and precision – and you've got a monster hit to eclipse her jujube-sweet #3, 10-86 "True Blue" or tropic fantasy "La Isla Bonita" #4, 3-87. Madonna's malleable voice drives the seething tune with passionate urgency and vintage Argentinean Soul.

"If It Makes You Happy" – Sheryl Crow, #10, 10-96. Madonna's Argentinean tango-type tune rides roughshod over dead air time. At every audial nook and cranny, a fluttery masterpiece of Johnnie Johnson-style virtuoso piano fills in gaps. Conversely, Sheryl Crow lulls us at her outset. We loll and laze in her cushy lyric. The jiggly song wobbles along. Then BAM – Sheryl K.O.'s our tranquility with her bombshell chorus. If it makes you happy, she rhetorically booms, then why are you so very sad? Good question. Do 'Happy Hour' inmates fidget and quiver in Billy Joel's "Piano Man" bar? Are they deathly certain that they could be movie stars – if they could only escape the cigarette-stoned Naugahyde booths of Grubbo Blubbo Lounge? Do they wear the tragic mask of "Eleanor Rigby," that she stuffs into a jar near her grim door? Who will it be for? Sheryl's salient question is so darkly powerful, that she rams the line home over and over again. If Madonna and Sheryl Crow are really looking to the Heart of Darkness for sadness, they need only seek the Dark Star that exploded like some killer asteroid over the City of Lights. Sheryl reconnoitered with #11 winning tune "Everyday Is a Winding Road" (3-97) and #20, 12-98 "My Favorite Mistake."

Sheryl's happiness level drifted to the sunny Surf Rock strands, with her beach celebration of California's eternal summer mood – #28, 4-2002 "Soak Up the Sun."

"Love Me Two Times" – Doors, #25, 12-67. In 1967, **Jim Morrison**'s stardust horizon gleamed with promise. Elvisgirls chased his brawny Byronic bod all over creation. You see the same energy in **Creed**'s #7, 11-99 song (and video) "Higher," still #30 after 50 charted weeks in 10-2000. A blizzard of iffy substances iced Morrison in the midst of his flowering. Long before Punk Rock or Generation X ever blasted their Alternative flamethrowers over a bubbly Lawrence Welk world, Morrison's will to survive lost its iffy spark. Like #1, 2000 **Matchbox 20**'s Grunge-gorged song "Bent," **Jim Morrison**'s will to carry on was fractured and bent by his own real and perceived demons. He began to sing the glories of busting through to that mysterious "other side." Death to Morrison seemed but another swashbuckling adventure. All his good looks and money and baritone bravado couldn't save him.

"People Are Strange" – Doors, #12, 9-67. Ray Manzarek played bass on his keyboards and devised supernatural treble gushes of ghostly glee. On Ray's amazing solo album *Golden Scarab* (NC, 1974), his sound is so much an audial mirror of Morrison – even the voice – that you have to believe Ray actually supplies about 80% of the Doors' total magic sound. With Jazz minor key profundity, **Robby Krieger** and **John Densmore** were just tremendous guitar/drum guys who'd lassoed Jim's demons. They ended up getting dragged through the thorny chaparral of the "Shifting Whispering Sands" (#5, 9-55 Billy Vaughn) of Morrison's lost wild dreams of dark Nevermore. "Three **Doors** Down" . . .

Remember Jim Morrison's "Roadhouse Blues"? Both **Morrison** and **Hank Williams** tempted the Grim Reaper. Williams's last songs were sardonic: the last hit record of his short (29) life was his #1(1), 12-52 C "I'll Never Get Out of This World Alive." The **Doors**' charismatic baritone idol shared the Country legend's fixin'-to-die fey manner, but he took himself (and Elvis Spotlight) a bit more seriously. One of Morrison's greatest songs is his

stunning "Roadhouse Blues" (only #50, 4-70). Remember the sodden verse when reeling Morrison awakens and grabs a beer? Like the sad sot in Johnny Cash's mournful Kristofferson tune "Sunday Mornin' Comin' Down"?

Its resolution is even more fitfully ominous: in devil-may-care hedonistic glee, Morrison lets it roll the whole night long. He says our futures are uncertain, and the END will always be near. Disney it ain't. The song reels and swaggers, like a drunken headless horseman hurtling over a cliff beyond the nevermore Wile E. Coyote abyss of doom.

Deep in the dark nether sub-basement of Cleveland's Rock Hall of Fame, you'll find an amazing letter to the Miami Police Department from Jim's dad **Admiral Morrison**: – please have mercy on my son [arrested for lewd acts on stage while heavily drinking]; Jim is really a good boy. He must have been drunk, so please forgive him, officers. Then the military leader confessed his own laxity in seeing his boy's youthful milestones, and shameful neglect. It is a raw and bold and sincere and heartrending statement for such a tough military man to make.

As **Bobby Darin** put it in his #10, 5-63 "18 Yellow Roses," a dad's love just never fades away. Unlike old soldiers. And the Morrison myth and legend soldiers its way past the everlovin' millennium.

"And the Wind Cries Mary" – Jimi Hendrix, NC 1967; #6 U.K. Can you believe this great supernatural classic never even notched #130? This is Hendrix's glorious gloaming song, floating on high over a way of life, in the wind, on some lost eagle crag. "Mary" never fades away either.

"Give Me One Reason" – Tracy Chapman, #3, 4-96. Born in future Rock Hall's Cleveland, Tufts grad Chapman resettled in Boston. "Reason" is a pure celebration of the Blues in the best **Bessie Smith** tradition. From her hotfooted debut, #6, 6-88 "Fast Car," True Blue[s] Chapman refused to be categorized as another R & B star. "Reason" smokes sensuously along with the crafty cadence and harmonica wizardry of **Jimmy Reed**, the chutzpah Soul Blues of **Billie Holiday**, the riff-romping precision of **B.B. King**, gut-thump get-down **Muddy Waters**, and the contemporary flair of **Kenny Wayne Shepherd**. Or the Folk majesty of **Odetta**. The only thing Chapman needs to do to make hits is to cut them. Once you can get her to the studio, it's a lock.

"Nothing Compares 2 U" – Sinead O'Connor, #1(4), 3-90. Song penned by **Prince**. The Dublin insta-star's crewcut never ran aground musically in popularity polls. When she flashed a picture of the Pope, though, and named him as a villain to the women of the world, it didn't do too much to sell records.

"I'll Be There for You" – Rembrandts, #17, 9-95; #1(7) Adult Contemporary. Theme of #1 sitcom *Friends* shows the power of love and friendship. Like **Simon and Garfunkel's** breathtaking #1, 2-70 "Bridge over Troubled Water," Rembrandts' song ties the yoke of undemanding friendship into a divine and ethereal relationship. We conjure visions of Rachel and Ross and sitcom pals, like Monica, Chandler, Phoebe, or Joey – FRIENDS! **Danny Wilde** and **Phil Solem** fashion a flashy echo of **Gerry and the Pacemakers'** bubbly Brit Rock of 1964 – like #23, 4-65 "It's Gonna Be Alright," Even "One More Chance/Stay with Me" by the **Notorious B.I.G.** [#2(3), 6-95; #1(9), R & B] echoes Rembrandts. Despite Gangsta Rap's tough trappings, the bottom line resurfaces: love conquers all. The Rembrandts' #14, 2-91 "Just the Way It Is, Baby" started off their mellifluous Everly-ish harmonies. "I'll Be There For You" is not just a catchy song title. It's a Way of Life. It's the path of empathy and selflessness and hope and joy and love. It is the bulwark of Christianity and many other great religions of the world.

"Vision of Love" – Mariah Carey, #1(4), 6-90; #1(2) R & B. Mariah Carey (b. 3-27-70) was an undistinguished high school student from posh Dix Hills, Long Island. Couldn't get motivated. The ol' underachiever tag. You know the tune. Mariah sat at Anneliese Scheef's Harborfields High School. According to the lovely Kristen Lee Cahill Dean, Mariah moodily stared out the window.

"Mariah," murmured her well-meaning teacher, "You're so bright. If you just applied yourself."

"Sorry," Mariah explained, "You see, I can't keep my mind on any class, because I really want to be a Rock star. I daydream about it constantly . . ." Mariah's teacher smiled befuddledly, shook her head, and stuffed Mariah's dream into a mental box marked "One Zillion Kids with Silly ROCK STAR VISIONS," kids whose dogs chewed up their homework and their sense of reality.

Mariah's soaring stratospheric coloratura soprano was a genetic gift from her mom **Patricia Carey**, Opera singer with the New York Metropolitan Opera. Mariah never doubted her own talents:

"I Still Believe" – Brenda K. Starr, #13, 4-88. Named after comic strip Brenda Starr, **Brenda Kaplan** paved the stairway to the starrs for Mariah. This interlocking jigsaw puzzle of Rock and Roll Royalty goes back even farther than Starr's *puertoriqueño barrios* in Manhattan and Sacramento, California, to "More Today Than Yesterday," by **Spiral Starecase** (#12, 4-69) with **Harvey Kaplan**, Brenda's dad. Mariah sang Starr back-ups, until her "Vision of Love" breakout (1990 Grammy Best New Artist Award).

No artist in this country has ever begun a career with five #1 songs in a row. Mariah's #1 chartbusting string is tremendous. The 1890s **Dan Quinn** beat it.

"Nothing's Too Good for the Irish" – Dan Quinn, #4, 2-1900. Quinn recorded for inventor Thomas Edison's Edison label, on graphophone cylindrical records, or for new Columbia Records in 1900. A gramophone played standard, 1/4-inch thick, record platters. Quinn's 20th record was for him a bust. It was his first-ever tune to MISS in the Win or Place Derby. Indeed, he'd never suffered a record LOWER THAN #2 on the charts during the

LAST 90s:

No one, not Elvis, the Beatles, Supremes, Whitney, Mariah, or anybody – has ever even come close to this incredible string of hits. Here are the biggest hits of the "90s":

THE CHAMPION DAN QUINN COLLECTION

"Daddy Wouldn't Buy Me a Bow-Wow"	#1(4), 12-1892
"The Bowery"	#1(5), 1-1893
"Daisy Bell" a/k/a "A Bicycle Built for Two"	#1(9), 9-1893
"Lindley, Does You Love Me?"	#1(3), 8-1894
"My Pearl Is a Bowery Girl"	#1(4), 10-1894
"And Her Golden Hair Was Hanging Down Her Back"	#1(6), 11-1894
"The Sidewalks of New York"	#1(9), 2-1895
"The Band Played On"	#1(10), 8-1895
"The Little Lost Child"	#1(5), 11-1896
"In the Baggage Coach Ahead"	#1(5), 11-1896
"A Hot Time in the Old Town"	#1(7), 12-1896
"My Mother Was a Lady"	#1(5), 3-1897
"You're Not the Only Pebble on the Beach"	#2(2), 5-1897
"There's a Little Star Shining for You"	#1(4), 5-1897
"She Was Happy Till She Met You"	#1(4), 9-1897
"Soldiers in the Park"	#2(2), 10-1898
"At a Georgia Camp Meeting"	#1(4), 11-1898
"Poor O'Hoolihan"	#2(2), 11-1898
"Curse of the Dreamer"	#1(7), 10-1899
"Nothing's Too Good for the Irish"	#4, 2-1900

From the #1 charts, **Dan Quinn** was the biggest recording star of any decade.

"Ta-Ra-Ra-Boom Der E" – Len Spencer, #1(8), 1-1892. Leonard Garfield Spencer is certainly a runner-up. Len (1867-1914) had an even bigger string of #1 and #2 hits in a row – 21 to Quinn's 20 – in the 1890s. "Ta-Ra-Ra-Boom Der E" became a Big Beat hit for my fading generation, with Buffalo Bob Smith's NC '50 show *Howdy Doody Time*. Our TV-infancy progenitor of *Sesame Street* starred this freckled puppet, *Howdy Doody*, Mr. Bluster, and **Buffalo Bob**. Bob's kiddie theme nearly rocked. The big bombastic bass drum boomed blissfully.

Some of Spencer's songs (thank heavens) would never have a chance for Moldy Oldie airplay, like his disgustingly racist #2(3), 11-1896 "All Coons Look Alike to Me." It must be remembered however, that Spencer merely mirrored the minstrelsy of his era, which also flaunted anti-Irish and anti-German barbed ethnic humor. Personally, I can't defend Spencer's racism, but we have to understand him in his post-bellum historical context of rising Jim Crow fever. Many of Spencer's other songs are permanently etched in the American consciousness, however. Totals in the Quinn vs. Spencer Championship Bout for their 1890-99 hits:

1) Champ **Dan Quinn** – 16 #1 songs and 3 #2 songs (nothing lower)
2) Challenger **Len Spencer** – 13 #1 songs and 11 #2 songs (1 #3, 1 #4, 1#5)
3) 1990-99 Challenger **Mariah Carey** – 15 #1 songs, 2 #2 songs and 13 #3-53 songs.

Any inter-century comparisons? **Beatles** 1964-70 had 20 #1 songs, 44 #2-96 songs; **Elvis** 1956-62 had 17 #1 songs and 37 #2-99 songs.

Len's **Stephen Foster** classic #1(6), 8-1892 "The Old Folks at Home" has such a beautiful pure melody, that it's the first post "Twinkle, Twinkle Little Star" tune that most kids ever learn on their dinky little clavichordy toy pianos. [I will never forget its little play-by-number book when I was 6 or 7: dear old "Swanee River" – "3-2-1, 3-2-1, 8-6-8, 5-3-1-2", and so on in numberiferous glee]. Oddly Spencer also launched African-American songwriter **James Bland**'s classic nostalgia tune, "Carry Me Back to Old Virginny" to #2(3) in 10-1893. He also got into all the new technology:

"Hello, Ma Baby" – Len Spencer, #1(6), 4-1899. Previewing cell-phone boom, Spencer called his girlfriend on the telephone. This could have been the first Ragtime Rock Song of the New Century, but leaped a pregnancy too early. By 8-1904, Spencer anticipated Led Zeppelin (or the Wright or Wrong Brothers) with his wordy #5 "Reuben Haskins' Ride 'Round the World in His Air-Ship". Then he came up with the #1 record of pre-1905 era, according to Whitburn's fascinating *Pop Memories 1890-1954*: "Arkansas Traveler" (#2[3], 11-1900 and #1([11], 3-1902). 1851 song remake. #1 song of pre-1905 (Whitburn). During the Year of '95, however, Dan had two #1 hits of nine and ten weeks. **Mariah Carey** trumped his with her "Fantasy" of #1(8), 9-95 floating the zenith, a prelude to ultramonster #1(16), 12-95 "One Sweet Day." So the hitmakers of each '95 beat out everybody else for #1 longevity (see Santana, 2000).

Mariah's debut "Vision of Love" #1(4), 6-90 was a promissory note. Both **Quinn** and **Carey** are Irish names, too, though Carey best represents the American melting pot with her Venezuelan and Afro heritage as well. So Mariah realized her vision that she daydreamed back in some 1986-fantasy classroom. Her very first record stormed to #1, like Hall of Famers' good company; **Elvis** ('86 Inducted), **Del Shannon** ('99), the **Four Seasons** ('90), the **Beatles** ('88), the **Doors** ('93), and **Buddy Holly** ('86).

"Dreamlover" – Mariah Carey, #1(8), 8-93; #2(4) R & B. Just before his Gangsta Un-Rap "Mack the Knife" hit #1(9) in 8-59 as Jazz Rock legend, **Bobby Darin** lobbed a hot *pizzicato* song called "Dream Lover" to #2(1) in 4-59 (#4, 5-59 R & B). The 50s R & B charts included a higher proportion of Caucasian acts than today. Pat Boone's #10, 3-57 R & B "Don't Forbid Me" (#1, 12-56); Ricky Nelson's #5 R & B "Be-Bop Baby" in 10-57 (#3, 10-57); or Brenda Lee's #25, 5-61 R & B "You Can Depend on Me" at #6, 3-61. "You Can Depend on Me" hit #4, 1-32 for R & R fountainhead **Louis 'Satchmo' Armstrong**.

"Dreamlover" is Mariah's biggest hit until her supernatural year of 1995, when she obliterated all the old chart records. The video stars Mariah, cavorting in shapely cutoffs in a wildflower field of paradise and passion. Her long hair ruffling in the summer breeze, Mariah invites us all to leisure and laughter and love.

MARIAH CAREY – CHARTTOPPING FEMALE ENTERTAINER OF THE CENTURY

Song & Chart Entry Date	Number & Weeks
"Vision of Love," 6-90	#1(4)
"Love Takes Time," 9-90	#1(3)
"Someday," 1-91	#1(2)
"I Don't Wanna Cry," 4-91	#1(3)
"Emotions," 8-91	#1(3)
"Can't Let Go," 11-91	#2(1)
"Make It Happen," 2-92	#5
"I'll Be There," 5-92	#1(2)
"Dreamlover," 8-93	#1(8)
"Hero," 10-93	#1(4)
"Without You," 1-94	#3
"Fantasy," 9-95	#1(8)
"One Sweet Day," 12-95	#1(16)
"Always Be My Baby," 3-96	#1(1)
"Forever," 6-96	#9A [Air]
"Honey," 9-97	#1(3)
"My All," 5-98	#1(1)
"I Still Believe," 2-99	#4
"Heartbreaker" with **Jay-Z**, 9-99	#1(2)
"Thank God I Found You" with **Joe & 98°**, 12-99	#1(1)

Mariah married Tommy Mottola, Prez of the Sony Music Entertainment juggernaut (1993-98).

"Hero" – Mariah Carey, #1(4), 10-93; #5 R & B. *Gold Rush* is full of heroes. A hero need not be a role model. We admire them for the way they can sing or act, the way they look, the way they slug home runs and run like the wind, or sing or play supersonic harmonica:

"Hook" – Blues Traveler, #23, 10-95. No harp featherweight, **John Popper** sports a whimsical lyric, some auctioneer-speed vocal harmonies, and a harmonica challenging the speed of light. Heroic song, musically. "Hook" is simply about what the song means – the hook is the mainline main line. When we listen to the Beatles' song that conquered the world, "She Loves You" yeah, yeah, yeah, we all remember the "Yeah3" HOOK. Blues Traveler hooked the hit parade with their #8, 3-95 "Run-Around." Popper and Blues Traveler's auctioneer lines about King Henry VIII, wife Ann Boleyn, and 1950 hero dog Rin Tin Tin are R & R lyrical gems.

Mariah Carey's theatrical "Hero" helped a lot of teens, with flagging self-images in a broken world, to realize that they were loved and appreciated.

"Fantasy" – Mariah Carey, #1(8), 9-95; #1(6) R & B. In vocal range and precision, Mariah is one of the most amazing singers of all time. Awesome pinpoint control. Grace notes and melismas? Perfect. She coruscates between petulant contralto and mountaintop soprano. Whisking up, up, and away into the downside of dog-whistle range,

Mariah actually sings so high you can hardly hear her. Where doe she even find lofty notes like that? Named by her New York Met-vet opera-star mother Patricia Carey for the **Kingston Trio**'s windsong "They Call the Wind Maria" (pronounced 'Ma-rye-ah'), Mariah symbolizes the current cavalcade of Rock stars. **Mariah Carey** joins that caravan that hitched its wagon to a star.

Actually, a star-spangled banner. Mariah's major big break came when she sang "The Star-Spangled Banner" at the NBA finals – the "Bad Boy" Detroit Pistons of Afro **Isiah Thomas** and Caucasian Bill Laimbeer clobbered, multiculturally, **Michael Jordan**'s powerhouse Bulls of Chicago. Mariah's #1(2), 9-99 "Heartbreaker" mixes it up with Rapper **Jay-Z**. Columbia Records pitched her talents somewhere between megastars **Whitney Houston** and **Anita Baker**:

"Giving You the Best That I Got" – Anita Baker, #3, 9-88; #1(2) R & B. Toledo, Ohio's Anita zoomed up I-75 to Motown and somehow found Elecktra Records. Her sound is polished Jazz-Soul-Rock. She is smooth and suave and sweet and Nina Harris's favorite singer. WITHOUT FANS, THERE WOULD BE NO STARS – only shower-singers. Anita also scored with #8, 8-86 (#2[2], 6-86 R & B) "Sweet Love."

"How Do You Want It/California Love" – 2 Pac (Featuring KC and Jojo), #1(2), 6-96. Rapper and actor **Tupac Amaru Shakur** started with **Digital Underground** in 1991. His rise to #1 included #11, 7-93 "I Get Around" and #9, 3-95 "Dear Mama." Shakur's fiery lifestyle charged him with shooting two off-duty officers in 1993 (Whitburn). Tu-Pac and his entourage were charged a month later on a morals-abuse charge. Two months later 2 Pac was found guilty of assaulting and battering his **Menace II Society** co-director Allen Hughes. In a Turf War grudge song about bi-coastal gangs, Shakur taunts two rivals with graphic images about what he did to the wife of one. East Coast vs. West Coast Turf warlords toss bazooka bombshells of Rage Rap – nothing like the friendly **Four Seasons** vs. **Beach Boys** 1963 rivalry. No one was surprised when the archly combative rapper was gunned down September 7, 1996, Buddy Holly's 60th birthday.

"Reefer Man" – Cab Calloway, #11, 7-32. NOW has no monopoly on sex, drugs, and musical scandal. Mr. Hi-De-Ho Cab Calloway (1908-94) rambles on about marijuana long before the *Rolling Stone* N.O.R.M.L. Hempilation tour with Ziggy Marley, the **Black Crowes**, and Blues Traveler (singing "I Want to Take You Higher") on Capricorn. 'Reefer madness' ran rife in high-life Depressionland. [Detroit first passed a law outlawing pot in 1928].

"More Beer" hit #30, 1-59 for the **Andrews Sisters**, who never touted pleasures of sobriety in mega-hit #1(1), 1-45 "Rum and Coca-Cola." Their #4, 5-39 Czech folk song "Beer Barrel Polka (Roll out the Barrel)" sizzled sudsy froth fans from Milwaukee to the Moon.

2 Pac [Shakur]

Notorious B.I.G. [Biggie Smalls]

"Under the Anheuser Bush" – Arthur Collins & Byron Harlan, #2(3), 4-1904. You read it right, right here. A Bud beer ad became the #2 song in the U.S.A., touting another frosty brew. This all-comedy tipsy duo also guzzled "Down Where the Würzburger Flows", at #1(5), 12-1902. Our own "Star-Spangled Banner" began as a drinking song melody, "To Anacreon in Heaven." Baritone Collins and tenor Harlan rocked a bit, too: #9, 8-1914 "Eagle Rock" and W.C. Handy's "Memphis Blues" to #8, 9-1915. No strangers to double-entendre controversy (though no 2 Pacs), Collins and Harlan did #6, 3-1910 "Down Where the Big Bananas Grow," and "Under the Yum Yum Tree" #1(5), 2-1911. Yum-yum buffs cavorted and wooed and cooed with their tootsie-wootsies. #1 1900-50 artist, **Bing Crosby**, couched his amorous stuff in clichés like #8, 1-34 "We'll Make Hay While the Sun Shines." He dredged up a very spicy Cole Porter tune with the **Dorsey Brothers** orchestra. It chuckles over the mating mazurkas of birds and bees: "Let's Do It (Let's Fall in Love)," #9, 3-29.

"The Old Gang of Mine" – Billy Murray and Ed Small, #1(6), 9-23. **Billy Murray**'s (1877-1954) clear resonant tenor made him the biggest singing sensation of the pre-1920 era. His "Old Gang" is a reprise of the Barber Shop boppers who preluded our 'Boy Bands.' Billy's old 23-skidoo gang was jus' chillin' on the gas lamp streetcorners:

"Sweet Adeline (You're the Flower of My Heart)"
– Haydn Quartet, #1(10), 10-1904. Buddy Holly and Bob Montgomery penned a melodic 1954 new Lubbock High School school song; their "Flower of My Heart," highlighted the first full-time Country radio station in the world, Hi-Pockets Duncan's KDAV Lubbock. "Sweet Adeline" concerns a tough gang on the corner, barbershopping their way into the hearts of these winsome fantasy girls of their dreams. "Sweet Adeline" was so overwhelmingly popular, and so representative of the genre, that Barber Shop Quartets Association members throughout the U.S.A. today call themselves the **Sweet Adelines**. Yet, who recalls the poor Haydn Quartet? Mitch Miller's *Sing Along with Mitch* (Al. #1[8], 7-58) crew gave mid-century barbershop buffs some flavor of the **Haydn**, **Peerless**, and **American Quartets**. The passionate vocals of **Elvis** were nurtured in the vocalic cradle of great Gospel 'Barber-Shop Quartets' like the **Blackwood Brothers**, or his own **Jordanaires**.

Haydn Quartet's hits? "Take Me Out to the Ball Game" with **Billy Murray** (#1[7], 10-1908); golden wedding classic #1(11), 12-1909 "Put on Your Old Gray Bonnet"; 2-1903 wintertime blockbuster #1(6) "In the Good Old Summertime"; and their moonglow #1(9), 4-1910 "By the Light of the Silvery Moon."

How permanent, then, is a nation's popular music? Long after the Haydn Quartet's singers are forgotten by the general population, their immortal songs boom through loud and clear. Tenors **John Bieling** and **Harry Macdonough** blended beauteously with baritone **S.H. Dudley** and bass **William Hooley**. Without the Haydn Quartet exploring four-part harmonic range and chord theory, could we ever have had **Dion and the Belmonts**? The **Four Seasons**? The **Beatles**? The **Temptations**? The **Beach Boys**? Or **Boyz II Men**? Or **N'Sync**?

The **Beatles** didn't batter down the walls of Jericho with #96, 3-68 "The Inner Light" or #95, 8-64 "I'm Happy Just to Dance with You." The **Haydn Quartet**'s artistic immortality is obscured by lost hits #1(2), 1-1906 "Would You Like to Spoon with Me?", #6, 5-1909 "Meet Me in Rose-Time, Rosie," or #5, 7-1908 "When It's Moonlight on the Prairie." Many of these classic barber-shop quartet songs were revived by family-fun *Sing Along with Mitch* (Al. #1[8], 4-58) series, with two more #1 albums – and sixteen Top Ten albums in the next three years.

Billy Murray's "That Old Gang of Mine" fondly reminisces on his ancient gang – a once-young streetcorner quartet who sang 'Sweet Adeline.' You can picture the Irish caps, the itchy wool, the tough smirk of these young grandfathers wallowing in their streetcorner reverie, long, long ago in the gas lamp glow in lost redbrick yesteryear.

"Heart of My Heart" – Don Cornell, Alan Dale, and Johnny Desmond, #10, 12-53. Bopping back Memory Lane to a reminiscence of a gang of tough curbside guys, Crooners Cornell et al harmonize down the long forgotten years. That's it in a nutshell. In America, the streetcorner gas lamp halo has always been loaded with tough, gruff, rough and ready dudes (plus a few dolled-up dames) ready to fight or sing on a second's notice.

Gangsta Rap rampagers carry their torch. Only into the 1990s, however, did we allow the radio to play some of the animalistic things 2 Pac Shakur said he would do to his rival's wife. A nation censors what it wants to. Despite being 'ruff-n' ready' tough GUYS, boy, could Cornell's crew ever HAR-Mo-NIZE!

"Regulate" – Warren G, #2(3), 4-94; #7 R & B. Kidhood pal of Snoop Doggy Dog and half-brother of Dr. Dre. Gangsta Rap cruised the airwaves. Kids of all hues, with blasting trunk speakers, abbreviated haircuts, and bad-butt scowls, boom the Gangsta rebellion into the smoky midnight void: "NO GENERATION was ever as tough as we are!" Like all generations, their menacing faces declare the unregulated message on the Death Row label. You could say 1995 was a "Gangsta's Paradise" via **Coolio**'s #1(3), 8-95 venture into **Lisa 'Left-Eye' Lopez**'s turf. TLC's mega-monsters for the threesome? #2(6), 6-92 "Baby-Baby-Baby"; #1(3), 6-99 "Unpretty"; and #7, 9-92 "What About Your Friends?" Perhaps **R. Kelly**'s #1(4), 2-94 "Bump N' Grind" was not what the 'silver voiced' Irish tenor **George J. Gaskin** sang about in the less-blunt era of baseball's "Slide, Kelly, Slide" #1(3), 2-1892. [German-American Dance singers' **Real McCoy's** "Another Night" almost set the bronze-medal record of all time in 8-94, with a #3(11) run, but had to settle for two twin #3(5)'s, with one lousy #4 week stuck in between]. **Ini Kamoze**'s #1(2), 8-94 "Here Comes the Hot-Stepper" gangsta-gabbed. **Montell Jordan**'s rough-and-ready-guy "This Is How We Do It" splattered the competition to #1(7) in 2-95. Cooler and quieter **Boyz II Men** just warmed up for the most popular song of a half century with their 4-95 #2 "Water Runs Dry."

Many 1990s voices were nasty, strident, and grim. They painted a *New Jack City* (1991*) crack house veneer over the old hopeful ivy of the Bronx and Brooklyn and Motown. We grew to believe in some past 1890s Golden Age of peace, love, and big howdy grinning brotherhood in the happy street.

Those 'happy days' never happened. Big myth. Billy Murray's rough-and-ready 'Dear Old Gang' would just as soon bust some jerk in the teeth as look at him for insulting their sister. Or mom. The Bowery Boys of 1893 were among the toughest gangs in the history of the world's plug-ugly thugs. **2-Pac** and **Notorious B.I.G.** might only make Junior Varsity capos in the 1889 NYC Gangsta Armies.

Remember that pristine line of golden nostalgia from **John W. Myers**, handlebar-mustachioed Welsh baritone of #1(4), 4-1895 fame? In that winsome blue-sky waltz, "The Sidewalks of New York," he woozily and boozily cooed: "They tripped fantastic light on the yestergone Sidewalks of New York." When I was a little kid in Detroit, and heard this line for the first time, I thought wow – can't wait to see that Big Apple, with all its friendly folks tripping . . . having fun all over their sidewalks. True Tin Pan Alley rhetoric eliminated 'smelly sidewalks' reality. Though **Billy Murray** sang #10, 1-26 "Keep Your Skirts Down, Mary Ann," New York still seemed slightly innocent. But this tripping part was pretty obvious. Before 60s hallucinogenic drugs, 'tripping' was used (like 'feeling high' in the Kingston Trio's "Scotch and Soda") to describe reeling drunken benders. Some Irish lads of 1893, with Italian or Jewish pals in the Olde Dutch *Bouwerie* (Bowery), weren't always overly friendly after Sweet Rosie O'Shenanigan kissed them off. And they'd guzzled a few pints of liquid courage.

As Gangsta Rappers devise more and more sophisticated weapons to 'out' or 'hit' or 'off' their enemies or haggle Turf Wars, they might take a time trip to that nifty Never-never Land of New York's Bowery in the true dawn of Ragtime Rock and Roll:

"The Bowery Grenadiers" – 'Big Mike' Sullivan and the Sons of Erin, #1(7), 11-1889. The ultimate Gangsta quartet song. It's based on the true story of rival gangs bashing each other's brains out in a notorious gang war. This unbelievable bloodbath began with the usual rough and tumble Irish fists, and escalated to knives, razors, and guns. Then guns became too wimpy for this battleground free-for-all which stole many lives. Some basement-bomb anarchist crew devised a wild system of mammoth HAND GRENADES, and the Bowery Grenadiers stormed into action, LAYING WASTE TO MUCH OF GREENWICH VILLAGE.

No wimpy rumrunner rubout. No crack house chieftain cut down in a measly hail of machine-gun flak. No pantywaist candy-rump *West Side Story* Romeo and Juliet tearjerker – with snurfly streams of tears slithering into the Hudson River. Nope, the Bowery Grenadiers really did gang wars up big in 1888.

First World Gang War almost broke out. After they blew up much of the Bowery with these monster grenades, Gangsta Ragtime arrived. Mike Sullivan and the Sons of Erin did this turf-war tune with the same madcap desperado style you see in our roughest fringes of Rap and Country Honky-tonk kick-tail music. The 1880s NYC turf-war dudes were just living up to their Gotham forebears; around 1850, some idiot got mad at Cooper Union Academy and shot and killed nearly 50 students. Where have all the Columbines gone? So when Mariah Carey's slings a Rap fantasy into her 90s "Fantasy," it's a (grenade) toss-up about which 90s we mean.

Kinder, gentler 90s voices championed the life-celebrating charts: **Boyz II Men** teamed with Mariah on #1(16), 12-95 "One Sweet Day". **Hootie and the Blowfish**, an integrated group, stormed the deca-million barrier (10M) with their gonzo album *Cracked Rear View* (#3, 7-94).

Boyz II Men hit #1(14), 8-84 and #1(9) R & B with "I'll Make Love to You." **Wanya Morris, Michael McCary, Shawn Stockman**, and **Nathan Morris** spin a magic harmonic sound. They have both the #1-longest and #2-longest #1 songs of the Rock Era. The sound comes from predecessors the **Delfonics** who helped define Philly Soul with their #4, 2-68 "Some Kind of Wonderful" (#32, 3-61 and #6 R & B) sound of the **Drifters**. Trading harmonic Soul-fired hits with the Drifters were the **Platters**:

"My Prayer" – Platters, #1(5), 7-56; #1(2) R & B. The Platters' pristine harmonies hover in summer-sky splendor over mean streets bloody with lives nasty, brutish, and short. "My Prayer" is a religious romantic meditation, which bops carnal Rock back to the Stone Age. 'Irish' tenor **Tony Williams'** majestic voice floats like a hovercraft over troubled waters, and his crystalline devotional vision spans the skies. He prays for his angel to stay with him forevermore – far, far away from "Rip your sweater off now," or current blunt Hip-Hop lines.

Maurice Williams and the Zodiacs (#1[1], 10-60) wanted to "Stay" in on that romantic plateau forever. As his song played in that magic 1960 orange-and-black Dearborn High October, I was somehow driving seven of our cheerleaders somewhere, who cares where. Sadly, the moment ended.

"Stay" – Jackson Browne, #20, 6-78. Browne's "Stay" is a rehash of the Zodiacs' fateful tune. It's also his ode to the ELVIS SPOTLIGHT. He plays guitar like JOHNNY B. GOODE. The audience energizes, empowers, and nearly CREATES him. One very Mystical vision, indeed. He begs his loyal audience to STAY. The luster of the Glory Road is lost on the lolling lull of humdrum everyday life. His audience is the electric power in his amplifier. It amplifies his mission.

Think about that. It's pretty scary:

APPLAUSE JUNKIE: WILL WORK FOR A SONG

"Turn the Page" – Bob Seger, NC, 1975. The singer psyches himself out. He deals with the days' last stubby cigarette. Hostile 'townies' glower at his long bandsman hair. He considers the sad fading embers of a burnt-out affair. Mysterious song. Bob almost envisions himself on stage. He's the audience as well as the entertainer. Lofted onto the squirmy stage, he plays at stardom. Like **Steve Miller** hanging his gold records above his WASHING MACHINE, Seger takes a mature view of the snares of glory. 'PLAYING STAR' is his key phrase. It's all happened so fast, Bob figures, he doesn't know whether he can fill his own Rock and Roll Shoes. The desolate mood is echoed by fellow Metro Motown rocker **Kid Rock**:

"Only God Knows Why" – Kid Rock, #19, 2-2000. Trailer-chic Michigander (b. Bob Ritchie, '71, my hometown Dearborn, Michigan), clobbers trappings of fame via the Rock and Roll carousel of hard-travelin'. Pills to zap pain. Downers on the road of life. Expanding Seger's smoke and steel consciousness into **Eminem**'s slim-shady neighborhood (Sterling Heights, MI), Rocker and Hip-Hopper Kid Rock laments that he's too long gone from his home, he's too roadweary, and 'Only God Knows Why.' Check 'em out – it's nearly a spittin' audial image of Seger's "Turn the Page" mood of confrontation and resignation. Prowling from a controlled echo-chamber baritone up to a Screaming Blues tenor, Kid confronts the chaos and consternation that ambush the famed and fortunate on the Rock and Roll road. With the **Twisted Brown Trucker Band**, Kid Rock's persona emerges from mobile home North Detroit suburbia. He invokes icons Seger, Jerry Lee Lewis, and Johnny Cash in an in-yer-face adventure Blue-Eyed Rap soliloquy. His roadfever anthems dart from unprintable "[Bug] Off" to other off-road odysseys of angst and anger, gorging on furtive glory. With his trademark fedora, ten-dollar stogie, two-strap white singlet, shiny pants, and James Dean defiant look, Kid Rock is the voice of all that is ticked off in the world. [Somehow, you get the feeling he knows he's putting on some of this image, and actually he has a pretty wry street-savvy sense of humor].

On the top octave, when Kid's oozing fire of pent-up emotion comes roaring out, he's closing in on **Del Shannon**, the Righteous Brothers, and the Rascals, in doling out Blue-Eyed Soul Power. Shannon, remember, comes from outstate Cooperville, Michigan, and began Revenge Rock (#28, '61 "So Long, Baby"). Michigan's trailer-park world is tough turf – and tornado territory. One great HOWL of Slow Rock White Soul! Kudos to the Kid (and hey – it's really not so bad at lakeside Michigan).

"The Real Slim Shady" – Eminem, #4, 4-2000. Eminem (Marshall Mathers) comes from Kid Rock's North Detroit world. The brash White Rapper with a bottle-blond crewcut grew up in East Detroit, and gravitated to Sterling Heights. His current compound does not really have a moat with alligators (cure for alligators? Michigan November). With his Eminem AI. #1(7), 6-2000 *Marshall Mathers LP*, Eminem celebrates a *Beavis and Butthead* and *"Stan"* world raised on Bart Simpson's with-it worldview. It's a stark and blunt and strident Rap soundscape. Be cool, and don't be a victim. The shady character in the song spits into fast-food customers' onion rings, and chafes at a three-job future at minimum wage. A whole world of Fringe Detroiters like my old band the Woolies (#95, 3-67 "Who Do You Love?") rocked in the aura of Metro Motown – and joined the rebellion that is the industrial Heartland. With the **MC5**, Detroiters formed Punk Rock. With **Del Shannon**, we launched the Great Singer/Revenge Rock sound. With **Bob Seger** and **Glenn Frey/Eagles**, we commandeered the 70s and 80s in Detroit gusto that powered Michigan Rock and Roll. And out in those Seger-glow cornfields, in the heavy winter winds, rip-roarers like Bob or Eminem or Del pile up **Alan Jackson**'s beer can pyramids with pals. They conquer the cornfields that night, and the world tomorrow.

With molten music for our KID – ROCK!

Eminem began with #36, 2-99 "My Name Is," produced by **Dr. Dre**, **Warren G**'s half brother. **Eminem**'s 2001 appearance on the Grammy Awards with **Elton John**, whose peaceful lifestyle he offended, made *Real World* headlines beyond the glow of guitar and glory.

"Right Now" – SR71, NC, 2000; #6, 5-2000 Modern Rock Tracks. **Mitch Allen**'s crew named themselves after the U.S.'s fastest jet plane. This song salutes Del Shannon's Revenge Rock with a pile-driving beat. Their hammering super Screaming Blues vocal bellows a rebound rendezvous. He busts up with Girl #1, and Girl #2 will fill the romantic void Right Now. Sort of a Kelly Girl Temp Romance. Blunt lyrics mash propriety. Now-it's-over so-long-baby furor suggest the best of Rolling Stones' "Paint it Black" or "Mother's Little Helper." Maybe Bob Seger's supersonic "Katmandu." Tough WWF gruff Metal tenor by Allen mixes with great vocals by drummer **Dan Garvin** (with **Nine Days**, 2001), and bass guy, Jeff Reid. Scimitar-sideburned Mark Beauchemin blasts firebrand guitar. The lyric addresses getting kicked while high. Allen, like Jagger's "Mother Little Helper," also blasts prescription soma like Ritalin. At Nine Days' Irving Plaza NYC concert, opening band SR-71's Allen dedicated "Right Now" to the Ritalin Generation. It's for all students, he says, forced to be stoned by the Establishment on downer drugs to curb hyperactivity. He has a point. Hyperactivity is no crime. Many of us rockers eat Hyperactivity Flakes for breakfast, and we channel our energies into Rock and Roll. Thrash and crash and smash music is a part of the Rock panorama, like **Megadeth**'s #29 Album Rock Tracks, 11-94 "Train of Consequences."

"Lightning Crashes" – Live, NC, 1995; #12A [Air], 2-95; #1(1), 2-95 Album Rock Tracks. Sad theme. Ghost Rock Graveyard ditty. Voice like Chris Isaak or even early Elvis. Floats hauntingly. Live followed it up with another smash hit of HOT 100 invisibility – # 2, 6-95 Album Rock Tracks "All Over You." Live's messianic-pose "I Alone" hit #6 A.R.T., 9-94 for Polish-American rocker **Dave Kowalczyk** of York, Pennsylvania. #35A, 1-97 "Lakini's Juice."

"What Would You Say" – Dave Matthews Band, #22A, 4-95; #5, 2-95 Album Rock Tracks. Number One college band in U.S.A. got shunned by 1995-98 HOT 100, Why? Finally, "Crush" hit #75, 2-99 and "I Did It" #71, 1-2001. Biggest Dave Matthews hit? #19A, 1-97 "Crash into Me." CRUSH and CRASH. How in the world could the Rock SINGLES establishment ignore the **Dave Matthews Band**, for cryin' out loud? Stuffed off in some obscure cubbyhole, Dave scrambled from England to Johannesburg, South Africa, and moved to New York City's posh Manhattan Yorktown Heights. His dad died way too young, and Dave found himself in Charlottesville, Virginia, Miller's Bar (my grandpa H.L. Maury graduated University of Virginia in 1895 or so). Matthews gathered an integrated Hootie-style combo, featuring R & R oddity a VIOLIN (by maestro **Boyd Tinsley**). Rounding out the rock mini-multitude are sax virtuoso **Leroi Moore**, bassist

Stefan Lessard, percussionist **Carter Beauford**, and Dave on vocals and guitar.

Other Matthews songs labeled laconically are #21A, 3-95 "Ants Marching," #55A, 12-95 "Satellite," #39A, 4-96 "Too Much," and 7-96 "So Much to Say." [Their March 2001 album *Everyday* (NOT named for Buddy Holly song) DEBUTED at *Billboard* #1!] Dave recorded his electric guitar for the first time. Matthews' band "blended their disparate influences – Jazz, Fusion, Funk, and Rock – with the rhythmic, lilting folk music, that reflected Matthews' formative years in South Africa" – *Rolling Stone* writer John Calapinto (12-12-96) explains Matthews' R & R multiculturalism further: "His voice is, like his music, a weave of accents and influences, a laconic Southern drawl one moment, a precise British inflection the next . . . his oversize T-shirts and baggy shorts say Hip-Hop; the necklaces (beads, shells, fossils) shout hippie."

Dave Matthews' crew consists of a bunch of with-it Virginians who incorporate dynamite Jazz Fusion riffs into their reverberating Rock musical adventures. College students rarely love subteen Bubble-Gum Bopper music, and Dave Matthews fills the sophisticated, esoteric void which began in 1959 when the **Kingston Trio** almost solitarily created the album – (they're still #4 of all time with most weeks at #1 – 46). Dave's RCA debut [hey, Elvis' label], *Under the Table and Dreaming*, zoomed to #11 in 10-94. Super debut. Their 5-96 *Crash* crunched the numbers, too, hovering at the #2 position. Their self-produced albums made them richer than Uncle Scrooge, and they alienated many poorer struggling bands by endorsing Napster – which bypasses bands' hard-earned royalties. The real villain is CORPORATE BLOAT. By not creating singles, record companies forced thrifty students to download Napster freebies. DMB is truly on their fans' side, and cannot be blamed for their topsy turvy Robin Hood position.

"Mmmbop" – **Hanson, #1(3), 5-97.** Neo-Gum lives! Bubble Gum Rock, sticking together the best of T. Roe and T. Rex, is alive and well in three well-scrubbed blond Heartlander brothers – the Hansons. With the yummy Tastee-Freeze innocence of Preppy Power, the Hanson sensations throttled all the zipgun-toting Gangsta Rap battalions back to the Top 100 sub-basement. Buddy Holly's Irish tenor echo **Tommy Roe** is the father of the **Archies'** Bubble Gum rock 60s fad. These Partridge/Cowsill/Jackson/Osmond-style kids salute the blazing Millennium with an eclectic blend of Neo-Gum, Neo-Disco, Rap-Zap, fun Rock and Roll. Despite the bored-to-death groans of Hanson hammerers, they offer an Alternative alternative and a wild new direction. The harmonic Hansons sock it to gloom and doom, echoing the Girls Group Era and the British Invasion in a swoon of Power Chords and destiny. Hanson's "I Will Come to You" hit #9, 11-97. "This Time Around" zoomed to #20 for the Hansons III (4-2000).

"Otherside" – **Red Hot Chili Peppers, #14, 3-2000.** Off their #1, 6-99 *Californication* (title track #72, 7-2000), "Otherside" trumps all the 60s suicide songs in the grim Graveyard Rock cortege. With the Grunge drone of bad mausoleum vibes, **Anthony Kiedis's** sad song-guy threatens to slit his own throat. It's a pretty melody, but don't 7-year-olds also check out the top ten? The L.A. Peppers' zoomed to stardom with their #2(1), 4-92 big hit "Under the Bridge." This is a very talented band, despite the despair cloud. Then they trolled under the bridge for "Soul to Squeeze" (#22, 8-93). Though their "My Friends" hit #27A, 9-95, "Scar Tissue" hit the nines: #9, 6-99. Personnel? **John Frusciante**, guitar; **Chad Smith**, drums; **Michael 'Flea' Balzary**, bass. Even before they made it ('88), they were maimed by the curse of Morrison-Joplin-Hendrix – Chili Peppers' guitarist **Hillel Slovak** allegedly O.D.'d on hard-drive substances – ancient decimator of Jazz and Be-Bop musicians in the 40s and 50s. Recreational buzzes made a comeback in the 90s among people who had too much and thought they had nothing. **'Thelonius Monster'** (Zander Schloss), named after jazz pianist Thelonius Monk, also plays guitar.

"Ornithology" was by **Charlie 'Bird' Parker** (NC, 1952+), "Greatest sax player in history" (alto). Kansas City's Parker (1920-55) died of an O.D., and the coroner estimated his age at 60. The complexity of Parker's riffs and cadenzas and improvisations has never been equaled.

"Don't You (Forget About Me)" – **Simple Minds, #1(1), 2-85.** Unforgettable tune. Scot Jim Kerr sang lead for this hauntingly unforgettable song (see Tim McGraw's "Please Remember Me"). Simple Minds clicked again with #3, 10-84 "Alive and Kicking," plus thought provoking #14, 1-86 "Sanctify Yourself." After a hitless hiatus in Anonymityville, Simple Minds returned with #52, 2-95 "She's a River." Kerr also got hitched to **Chrissie Hynde** of the Pretenders:

"Back on the Chain Gang" – **Pretenders, #5, 12-82.** Equally haunting song by Akron's Chrissie, whose husky alto murmurs 1st caliber Rock and Roll. Pretenders' other top tenner, #10, 10-86 "Don't Get Me Wrong," was admirably flanked by #14, 2-80 "Brass in Pocket (I'm Special)," and #28, 3-84 "Show Me." "Chain Gang's" sledgehammer beat bashes against ringing golden chords, and Chrissie's enchanting alto.

"Beautiful Day" – **U2, 10-2000.** Grammy winner. International #1 virtually everywhere except U.S.A. **Bono** and U2 never really left, hitting #16, 9-95 (#1 Album Rock) with "Hold Me, Thrill Me, Kiss Me," #7, 5-96 "Theme from Mission Impossible," and #26, 4-97 "Staring at the Sun." "Hold Me" is a long way from #5, 1-52 **Karen Chandler** or #8, 6-65 Mel Carter song of the same name. "Eclectic Discotheque" (#10, 2-97) had the pop predictors puzzled and fidgety.

"Love Shack" – **B-52's, #3, 9-89.** Even newer New Wave guitarist **Cindy Wilson** and keyboardist **Fred Schneider** hit the big time ten years after, with this ginchy Techno-Synth cult classic. Jackhammer Disco beat. From their debut "Rock Lobster" (#56, 4-80) through "Love Shack's" follow-up "Roam" (#3, 12-89), the B-52's have specialized in the unusual, the grotesque, the weird, like "Deadbeat Club" (#30, 4-90) and #28, 6-92 "Good Stuff." Per-

|

haps their far-outest item is "(Meet) the Flintstones," a #33, 5-94 echo of the first (1960) prime-time cartoon TV show, forerunner of the mostly magnificent *Simpsons*.

Gwen Stefani and No Doubt hit Al. #2, 3-2000 with *Return of Saturn*. Their "Don't Speak" clobbered the AIR-PLAY charts to #1(16), 10-96. **Better Than Ezra** hit #1(5), 3-95 Modern Rock Tracks, but NC '95 HOT 100. The timeless **Ramones** hit #30, 7-95 with Peter Pan Fight Song "I Don't Want to Grow Up."

No Mercy (not NO Doubt) did crunch the Big Chart to #5, 7-96 with their bouncy "Where Do You Go?." It's Power Neo-Disco, with the Robbie-the-Robot synth-drum blasting at breakneck speed, as they repeat the title. And repeat the title. And repeat. **Tony Rich Project** got richer on #2(2), 12-95 "Nobody Knows." **Tony! Toni! Tone!** believe that #9, 9-90 "Feels Good." Key Hip-Hop stars include Adina Howard and #2(2), 2-95 "Freak Like Me," Dionne Farris (#4, 1-95 "I Know"), and **All-4-One** hit #1(11), 4-94 with Country star **John Michael Montgomery**'s super ballad (#42, 2-94, #1 C) "I Swear." All-4-One's Afro-Latino-Polish-American mulitcultural combo previewed the 'Boy Band' millennial phenomenon of the **Backstreet Boys** or **N'Sync**.

"Runaway Train" – Soul Asylum, #5, 6-93. Even **Tom Petty** echo singer **Dave Pirner** was in the movie *Reality Bites*. Soul Asylum salutes the **Searchers** or **Byrds** in their harmonic tapestry, like in #20, 7-95 "Misery,"

Sponge hit #3 Modern Rock Tracks (#55, 8-95 HOT 100) with "Molly (Sixteen Candles)"; tragically, they are not related to the hip hot hit cartoon of the '00s – **Spongebob Squarepants**. Sponge's **Vinnie Dombrowski**'s spirited lead vocal proves Polish-American Rock and Roll is alive and well in the former 2nd-biggest Polish city on the planet – Detroit. Sponge missed the KEY HOT 100 chart on other songs, but "Plowed" hit #5, 2-95 on the A.R.T. charts. Their abnormal record label? ROTTING PIÑATA. Ah, youthful humor.

"Hot Rod Lincoln" – Commander Cody and his Lost Planet Airmen, #9, 3-72. Raffish rapscallion Rap item. Charting for **Tiny Hill** (350#) as "Hot Rod Race" at #29 in 1-51, this tune is the daddy of all Drag Race Rock songs in the entire Beach Boy-Jan & Dean canon! Cannon-speed cars thunder down snaky canyon hills of California's Highway 101, on the edge of Western Ocean destiny. Funny tune. Drag race kid drives father bananas in speed-burning 50s Lincoln. In the real 50s, no kid in the world had a Lincoln, and was lucky to pilot a rusty supercharged Ford or motor scooter. Or unlucky.

"Wake Me Up Before you Go-Go" – Wham, featuring George Michael, #1(3), 9-84. **Andrew Ridgely** (b. '63, NW London) was gonzo guitar guy for Wham. He split in 1986 to join the ranks of racecar demons blasting the tracks. Ridgely left his friend and neighbor **George Michael** (b. Georgios Kyriacos Panayiotou, 6-26-63, England) to snare the Elvis Spotlight. Beginning as Wham, they helped whisk away the "Rice Curtain" to recast communism in a new capitalistic robe with their trip to China. Wham was the first Western group ever to visit Elvis-less, Beatle-less, BeeGee-less China.

"Faith" – George Michael, #1(4), 10-87. Michael's solo hit track list got massive: #1(3) "Careless Whisper" 12-84; #1(2), 3-85 "Everything She Wants"; two #3,s in 7 & 11-85 – "Freedom" and "I'm Your Man." His 2-87 **Aretha Franklin** duet "I Knew You Were Waiting (For Me)" snagged the #1 spot a fortnight (#5 R & B). His pre-"Faith" prelude was blunt-as-you-wanna-be "I Want Your Sex," at #1(1), 6-87. "Faith" jumps and skitters on a lot of quick monosyllables that burst forth in rockety-bop glee. It's a nearly uninhibited song, and shines with the R & R aura of his mentor Elton John, or Deborah Voulgaris.

Michael hit #1(1), 9-90 with "Praying for Time" Also #1(2), 1-88 "Father Figure"; #1(3) "One More Try" of 4-88, and #8, 5-96 "Fastlove." Michael duetted with **Elton John** on #1(1), 12-91 "Don't Let the Sun Go Down on Me" (#2, '74, solo Elton).

George Michael

"Believe" – Elton John, #13, 3-95. Into his fifth decade of charted hits, 53-year-old Elton passed **Stevie Wonder** for *Billboard* all-time bronze medallist – at #3 behind **Elvis** and the **Beatles**. Elton's "Believe" is no relation to **Cher**'s #1, 1999 Dance/Neo-Disco rocker of the same name. Elton's "Believe" goes far beyond George Michael's "Faith" is embracing all of the aspirations of humankind. Elton's "Someday Out of the Blue" debuted at #56 in April 2000. And in 1999, Elton finally had a HOT 100 hit in an unconquered music field – COUNTRY – with lovely **LeAnn Rimes**, #29, 3-99 "Written in the Stars."

"It's the End of the World As We Know It (And I Feel Fine)" – R.E.M., #69, 1-88. Deserved a much higher number. Speed Demon Song. Chaotic lyric line spins at speed of light. Armageddon Rock. World is ending, but Stipe stays somewhat composed. Form pioneered by **LeRoy Van Dyke**'s Country Rock "Auctioneer" (#19, 11-56), and mastered by magnificent **Blues Traveler** musician **John Popper.** Their #23, 10-95 "Hook" not only features Popper's supersonic harmonic solo, but a harmonized vocal that may be the fastest R & R verse ever slammed down onto the poor bewildered blank tape. R.E.M.'s Armageddon tune posits a smug smirk for the end of the world (as we know it). Despite dire prognostications of caterwauling catastrophe, the guys are just grooving to the vibes: "Like, wow, party down." R.E.M. scored with #19, 1-95 "Bang and Blame," #10, 7-91 "Shiny Happy People," and #57, 12-99 "The Great Beyond," and #9, 9-87 "The One I Love." **Michael Stipe** is lead singer.

Chant – **Benedictine Monks of Santo Domingos de Silos, Al. #3, 4-94.** Talk about going way back in time, you never know what'll hit big, like 9th-century Gregorian CHANTS. **Tony Bennett**'s *MTV Unplugged* album hit #48, 7-95, still quite a way from #1:

"Everybody Wants to Rule the World" – Tears for Fears, #1(2), 3-85. These video stars surfed success with #1(3), 6-85 "Shout" [#56, 8-85 R & B], #3 "Head over Heels" of 9-85, and #2(1) "Sowing in the Seeds of Love" in 9-89. **Roland Orzabal** & **Curt Smith** kept their British Easy Rock rolling with #79 Al. 10-95 *Raoul and the Kings of Spain.*

Jar of Flies – **Alice in Chains, Al. #1(1), 2-94.** Though we hover around Super Singles, albums are their launch pad. **The Beastie Boys** hit #1(1) in 2-94 *Ill Communi-*

cation, keeping up with *Alice in Chains* (#1, 11-95). The Beatles' *Anthology* glommed #1(3) for Christmas 1995. **Blind Melon**'s *Soup* of 9-95 held down #28 – after their video of the little burly girl in her yellow dance school costume. **Bob Marley and the Wailers** returned to 6-95 *Natural Mystic,* proving Bob's Reggaeful immortality: #67.

"Wonderwall" – Oasis, #8, 1-96. Brothers **Liam** and **Noel Gallagher** of Manchester conquered U.K. with their Beatle echo classics. Paul McGuigan, bass; Tony McCarroll and Alan White, drums; Paul Arthurs, guitar; Joel Whitburn, information. Oasis pumped up an old cliché to the max – #4, 10-95 Al. *(What's the Story) Morning Glory?* Oasis was Britain's biggest hit band of the ebbing 90s.

Pulse – **Pink Floyd, Al. #1(1), 6-95.** Floyd proved superstars never fade away. Mid-90s superstar comebacks? **Bruce Springsteen**'s stark *The Ghost of Tom Joad* floated to #11 in 12-95. His *Greatest Hits* double-platinumed to #1(2) in 3-95. **Bob Seger** returned from an "American Storm" to Al. #27, 11-95 *It's a Mystery.* **Michael Jackson**'s *HIStory: Past, Present, and Future* overcame its pretentious buildup with a #1(2) clocking in 7-95. Country superstar **Alan Jackson** pierced the mainstream monopoly with his #5 *Greatest Hits Collection* in 11-95.

Van Halen's *Balance* #1(1) Al. 2-95 blitzed the lower 1999 on the Top 200. You want gabbiest mid-90s album? Here 'tis – **White Zombie**'s #6, 4-95 *Astro-Creep: 2000-Songs of Love, Destruction And Other Synthetic Delusions of the Electric Head.* **Tu-Pac**'s grim epitaph: Al. #1(4), 4-94

WHITHER SINGLES? MILLENNIAL DILEMMA

Are we TOO RICH to buy singles anymore? Annoyingly by 2000, many of the World's Greatest Hit Singles weren't even AVAILABLE as singles. You had to wait for an album you couldn't afford, and never bought, while record execs wept over slumping sales.

Madonna's "American Pie" remake (2-2000) debuted on the *Billboard* HOT 100 at #29 in February 2000, but failed to move up, because no SINGLE was available in stores. Then it flubbed back notch by notch into Oblivion, U.S.A. Her remake of **Don McLean**'s #1(5), 12-71 ode to **Buddy Holly** actually debuted on the BRITISH charts at #1 and it conquered Europe at #1. What happened?

Fred Bronson, in *Billboard*'s 3-18-2000 "Chart Beat," mentions that the demise of the single song in the CD ALBUM avalanche has disoriented American would-be buyers away from the main reason we have Rock and Roll – to celebrate the triumph of the INDIVIDUAL SINGLE SONG. In "A Single As British As 'American Pie'," Bronson says "How many kids with two or three dollars to spend on a single are not being trained to purchase records [italics mine] because the product they want is not available? And because they couldn't buy the song they wanted, how many have found a way to download it for free?" SCARCE SINGLES helped CREATE NAPSTER. R & R fans would love the opportunity to buy more like **Matchbox 20**'s #1(3), 3-2000 "Bent," **Vertical Horizon**'s #1(1), 1-2000 "Everything You Want," Savage Garden's $1.99 "I Knew I Loved You" [#1, 2000], since they were among the few available back in 2000.

Albums are tremendous. But the SINGLE glowing ember that fires up Rock and Roll is the SINGLE SOLITARY SONG. Long may it rule . . . for your budget and mine (and yes, it's true – I AM a Scottish-American).

Me Against the World. **Notorious B.I.G.** was fatally gunned down and his posthumous single "Mo Money Mo Problems," and album hit #1, 8-97. He joins the Holly-Redding-Joplin-Lennon brigade of stars struck down in their prime, who hit #1 posthumously.

"Step by Step" – New Kids on the Block, #1(3), 5-90. Teen idols. The Boston Proto-Boy-Band New Kids spearheaded Columbia's White Soul movement. It forecast the soulful song stylistics of the Backstreet Boys/N'Sync/or 98 Degrees ("Give Me Just One Night [*Una Nocha*]" #2, 8-2000). FORMULA – take 4-5 cute hunks who can sing. New Kids had a hit machine in the early 90s, with #1(1), 4-89 "I'll Be Loving You (Forever)" and #2(1), 9-89 "Cover Girl." Nine top tenners in a row began in double figures (#10, 6-88 "Please Don't Go Girl") and zoomed to the apex #1(1), 7-89 "Hangin' Tough."

Like many teen idols, the VANISH problem arrived in a year, but in that short year they showed a lot more talent than certain caustic critics gave them credit for, with their punchy amalgam of white-hot White Soul. Other Semi-New Kids hits? Yep: #7 (sensing target market of 9-year-old girls) "This One's for the Children" 11-89, and #7, 8-90 "Tonight." Then poof – in a career as short as Buddy Holly's, they departed for Destiny.

"When You Love a Woman" – Journey, #12, 10-96. Journey never left. Neal Schon, Steve Perry, Ross Valory, and Steve Smith. Now here's the problem with great comebacks: if every great band didn't stop recording great stuff, there'd be no place to stuff the stuff on the stuffed HOT 100. The HOT 100 has room for only 100, and great new bands are always out there.

The moral? Ask not why it's so hard to get your record on the HOT 100. If you do, it's a minor miracle. But good luck to you and your garage band. Let me know when you hit the big time, because *Gold Rush* is saving a spot for your upcoming BLOCKBUSTER hit:

> **[YOUR HIT HERE], #1(52) . . .**

"Hey Lover" – LL Cool J, #3, 11-95; #3 R & B. LL Cool J hits the bronze medal with this #3 with twinges of super Soul. **Russell Simmons** of NYC's Queens (yep, *Archie Bunker* turf) founded **Def Jam** Records, and turned the hammer-beat juggernaut into a dynasty with Queens-based talent: **Public Enemy** (#50, 10-91 "Can't Truss It," [#9 R & B]) with Terminator X and Professor Grif; and **Run D.M.C.** (#4, 7-86 Rap-Rock "Walk This Way" with **Aerosmith**). The **C & C Music Factory**'s "Gonna Make You Sweat" nailed #1(2), 11-90, followed by #3, 3-91 "Here We Go."

"The Look" – Roxette, #1(1), 2-89. Ultra-suave Swedish Pop-Rock duo (girl, Marie Frederiksson; guy, Per Gessle) dusted the charts with this first debut song at #1; they followed up with #1(1), 8-89 "Listen to Your Heart," #2(2) "Dangerous," of 12-89, and #1(2), 4-90 "It Must Have Been Love." *Pretty Woman* (1990**) theme song, "Joy-

ride" steamed to #1(1) in 3-91, and by 6-93 their almost real joyride at the top plummeted to #94, 6-93 "Almost Unreal."

"Counting Blue Cars" – Dishwalla, #15, 4-96. Shakes up the cosmos with a very interesting conception of either A) The Lord, or B) Mother Nature. Or both. After they spend time counting blue cars, comes the cosmic karma kicker – Guy asks pal to share all his personal thoughts about God, because someday the lad would very much love to meet with HER. Like Joan Osborne's 1996 Coney Island vision, "One of Us" – Dishwalla's song shakes up the religious status quo that anthropomorphizes God as white male, and all that trad jazz.

Blue – **LeAnn Rimes, Al. #3, 7-96.** At 14, LeAnn Rimes started at the top. Bill Mack wrote the song for **Patsy Cline**, whose "Crazy" (#9, '61) is the most played song – even now – on all the jukeboxes in America. Before Cline could hear the song, she was killed in a plane crash. Mack canned the song for 30 years. He dug it out when he heard a tape of this incredible 11-year-old singing "The Star Spangled Banner" at a horse show in Fort Worth, Texas. "Blue" zoomed to #26 on a *Billboard* HOT 100 (#1 C) list packed with Rap and Grunge. The 2000+ HOT 100 suddenly began to burgeon with Country stars: **Lee Ann Womack**'s #14 "I Hope You Dance" of 9-2000; Jo Dee Messina's "Burn" #42, 10-2000; Tim McGraw's #27, 10-2000 "My Next Thirty Years"; **Faith Hill**'s #2, 2000 "Breathe"; **Reba McIntyre**'s 11-96 "Fear of Bein' Alone," about isolation; **Alan Jackson**'s catchy little ditty "Little Bitty" #1, C in 1-97; and **Deana Carter**'s #1 Country 1-97 "Strawberry Wine."

"Who Will Save Your Soul?" – Jewel, #11, 5-96. Yodeling purringly like LeAnn, Jewel delivers a haunting song that flashes with soulful fire. Jewel's from Homer, Alaska.

"Now and Forever" – Richard Marx, #7, 1-94; #1(11), 1994 Adult Contemporary. Let no one claim melodic beauty has been lost forever. "Now and Forever" disproves any such glum theory. It is the very essence of melody. It murmurs and floats with the harmonic precision and beauty of **Felice** and **Boudleaux Bryant, Norman Petty** and **Buddy Holly, Simon and Garfunkel**. Or maybe the aural ambience of **Lennon-McCartney** – in gorgeous songs like "Michelle" or "Things We Said Today." Richard Marx wrote N'Sync's #6+, 8-2000 "This I Promise You," another angelic melody.

"Just Kickin' It" – Xscape, #2(1), 9-93; #1(4) R & B. Female R & B crew fronted by sisters LaTocha and Tamike Scott from Atlanta. Their #8, 12-93 "Understanding" is one more good reason to X-pand my sparsely populated 'X' section of the humungoid index. Sort of a soprano Boyz II Men crew. Hits? #9, 10-98 "My Little Secret," and #7, 5-98 "The Arms of the One Who Loves You."

"Signs" – Tesla, #8, 1-91. The Rock and Roll Continuum. Or, Rock bounces back. Originally by Lee Emmerson's Ontario **Five Man Electrical Band** (#3, 5-71), the song conjures Psychedelia. It's a jolt against the entire property-owning system, like Winnipeg Manitoba's **Guess Who** in their "Share the Land" (#10, 10-70). The five-man band and Tesla scoff at nasty TRESPASSERS WILL GET SHOT signs, and they defy tyrannical authority in the form of sign makers. Rock and Roll never harbored any love for the establishment.

"B**ch" – Meredith Brooks, #2(4), 4-97. This purry song by Miss Brooks does a quantitative analysis of a woman: a b**ch, a lover, a mother, etc; all the while she attracts the male of the species with her curly contralto – the befuddled dude wants her, he needs her, he loves her. He just can't figure her out. Of course guys too can be just as bipolar and unpredictable.

"Till I Hear It from You"/"Follow You Down" – Gin Blossoms, #9, 2-96. Like Soul Asylum, the Gin Blossoms echo the trebletone **Tom Petty** sound. It's a harking back to the **Honeycombs** and **Hullaballoos**: "I'm Gonna Love You Too," by the British Hullaballos (#56, 11-64) has seven Holly Hiccups per unsquare measure. **Ricky Knight**'s hep Hullaballoos were among the most colorful of Hollytone troubadours. Buddy's "Learning the Game" also made it to a modest Yankee #121, 5-65 for the bleached-blond band.

The clanging chords of the **Gin Blossoms** throb with steely echo. Their tenors wrangle the Tempe, Arizona 111° July heat with scorching sounds. Named after comic W.C. Fields' unfortunate alcoholic nose from drinking too much gin ('Gin Blossoms') **Robin Wilson**'s crew lobbed two quarters into the hit ring: #25 and #25 (7 and 11-93) "Hey, Jealousy" and "Found Out About You." With the sparkle of the 1965 **Byrds**' sound, the Blossoms' album *Congratulations I'm Sorry* pierced the Top Ten (#10, 3-96). By 2001, they split, and opened for **Nine Days** in Cleveland as **Gas Giant**.

"Breakfast at Tiffany's" – Deep Blue Something, #5, 8-95. Rumbling back to a venerable Audrey Hepburn and George Peppard flick of the identical name (***½, 1961), this preppy rock crew surveys Manhattan ambience in their chic video. The song talks about what people have in common. At least they both saw this movie *Breakfast at Tiffany's*. When I visit the graves of my relatives in Dearborn, Michigan, I pass by Joe Buczynski's grave (100 mph crash, eluding cops at age 20). Joe was my high school friend, the physically toughest guy I ever met, who made the mistake of too many beers and too fast a stick-eight '57 Ford Interceptor. A few yards over from Joe's plot is the grave of "George Peppard, actor, 1928-94."

I never met Audrey Hepburn and I never met James Dean and I never met Jack Kerouac and I never met Buddy Holly (though I've been friends with his parents and with his band the Crickets). Peppard is the only actor to ever portray the elusive Kerouac, in the only movie of Kerouac's books ever successfully scripted (1959**), *The Subterraneans*. George Peppard went to my high school and became a movie star. In 1948, that was bigger than becoming a rock star. Now, who knows? Deep Blue Something, perhaps.

Life is pretty simple, out there beyond the silly complexities and harrowing details we fritter our time with. All we have to do after we're born is to die. Sometimes along the way, we like to bask in a little love and groove to a sound track of super song. It's a long journey, and it deserves a jolt of joy now and then. Love keeps the human world spinning around, hokey as it may sound.

"End of the Road" – Boyz II Men, #1(13), 7-92; #1(4) R & B. Death March pace. Sad farewell. From the lead tenor's imploring plea, this glacier-slow song unravels. Frayed ends weave mystical 11th chords and diminished triads. The bari Barry swoops in. He Raps like **Barry White** on his begging saga of lost love. His spoken lines are so convincing that he almost pastes the torn relationship back together.

In the Motown-Philly voices of four young men from the City of Brotherly Love, the Barber Pole twirls red, white, and blue. The end of the road? The Road never ends.

"If I Can Dream" – Elvis Presley, #12, 11-68. Out of America's Darkest Hour, Elvis emerged with a magnificent song of hope and faith. We were mired in a military quagmire of seemingly eternal proportions – with little hope of decisive victory. Our nation lost both **Dr. Martin Luther King** and **Senator Robert Kennedy**, candidate and political savior for the Rock generation, in a fusillade of firestorm violence. The U.S.A. was reeling on the ropes, and communism kept getting redder.

Elvis himself was on the ropes. His hits flubbed along to forgotten #92, 5-67 "That's Someone You Never Forget." Elvis peeled away the years, dumped the slick 'B' movies, re-grew his sideburns, and headed for his Hawaiian international satellite comeback concert. "If I Can Dream" surged forth, a Rock and Roll Renaissance for a King deposed by the Fab Four and other five dynasties. A very hopeful song, "If I Can Dream" sees a utopian vision of imaginary worldwide bliss, years before John Lennon's "Imagine" ('71).

So what's new? Nothing. Umpteen non-utopian songs have been written about boy-meets-girl, boy-loses-girl, boy-and-girl reunite. Elvis pushes big dreams. Boyz II Men coax and implore and beg and reassess relationships. Nothing has changed since **Harry Von Tilzer** sat down at the bawdyhouse piano in the Ragtime long ago, and wrote his song of hope:

"Wait Till the Sun Shines, Nellie" – Byron Harlan, #1(9), 2-1906. The old song of bittersweet promise rolls around again (**Harry Tally** also tallied a #1). In the glow of a thousand Yukons and Klondikes and Tin Pan Alley cities of lights and kicks and night and love and Jazz and Blues, "Nellie" shines. And shines on.

"End of the Line" – Traveling Wilburys, #63, 2-89. Album *Volume One*, #3, 11-88. Supergroups? Hard to get much superer than the Barber-Shop Quintet Traveling Wilburys: **Jeff Lynne**, (of E.L.O.), **Tom Petty, Bob Dylan, Beatle George Harrison** and THE VOICE **Roy Orbison**. After a minor hit with "Handle with Care" (#45, 10-88), the Wilburys seemed headed to destiny. No one was aware that it would be the actual end of the line for the great Orbison (heart attack, age 52). With their incredible array of legendary vocal talent, they looked for someone to replace Orbison. As if anyone could. There was only one singer with the starry voice still around, and **Tom Petty** sought him out. **Del Shannon**.

"The Waiting" – Tom Petty, #19, 5-81. Like many American superstars, Gainesville, Florida's Tom Petty (b. '53) scored first in England, and then his rep zoomed to the moon here. Like unrelated Buddy Holly's manager Norman Petty encouraged, BE VERSATILE.

Would you believe?1) Petty's first album with the **Heartbreakers** sold 6500 copies and was hastily deemed a 'flop' by moxie moguls who wrote the kid off; 2) His third band after the Sundowners and Epi was named MUDCRUTCH. It starred Eagle Bernie Leadon's brother Tommy; and 3) Tom Petty filed for Chapter 11 bankruptcy in 1979, despite three little hits under his belt – the first (11-77, #40), got appropriately slapped with title "Breakdown."

Many bands, and Tom's hero and mentor **Del Shannon**, got royally ripped off somewhere between the box office, the Glory Road, and the bank. In Petty's cash case, it wasn't just petty cash. Their record company, Shelter, got sold as a tax shelter and vacuumed by a larger conglomerate, MCA. The company actually sued Tom for half a million bucks. When Tom's total assets peaked out at only fifty grand, the suit was dropped. Why? The ol' blood from a turnip analogy.

We could waste a lot of time crabbing about which shady manager ripped off which performer, and vice versa. We'll leave that to the accountants. Rock fans don't get too excited, anyhow, about the boring business penumbra off to the right of the limelight. The music excites.

Soon Tom Petty began to hammer the HOT 100. "The Waiting" was, perhaps, Tom's hardest part. Perhaps not. First Petty stormed the citadel of the vaunted Top Ten. Backstreet Records (see B. Boys) propelled his salable sound to destiny (#10) with their 11-79 "Don't Do Me Like That." Among his most-played big hits, Petty followed with #15, 1-80 "Refugee." "Here Comes My Girl" lurched to #59, 4-80 before all "The Waiting" paid off with #3 song with **Stevie Nicks**: "Stop Draggin' My Heart Around" in 7-81.

"Needles and Pins" – Tom Petty and the Heartbreakers with Stevie Nicks, #37, 2-86. Penned by Yank **Sonny Bono** (Congressman from California, 1997), "Needles" sparked the Liverpool **Searchers'** coup of 3-64 #13 hitdom. Petty's Heartbreakers include **Mike Campbell**, guitar; **Stan Lynch**, drums; **Ron Blair**, bass, and **Benmont Tench**, keyboards. Blair split in 1982, and was covered by **Howie Epstein**. Petty joined the Jackson Browne and James Taylor 1979 No Nukes Tour (Al. #19), and roared into the mid-80s with the blue-collar chutzpah of Heartland Rock-

ers **Bob Seger** and **Bruce Springsteen**. We might have included Tom Petty back there, but he's perhaps more of an ongoing phenomenon: in his showbiz song #92, 11-91 "Into the Great Wide Open," Petty charts the wobbly course of a jukebox hero, with roadies, hit records, and movie stars and Jim Morrison leather jackets. Petty later scored big on #13, 12-94 "You Don't Know How It Feels." Latter-day tunes include #68, 4-95 "It's Good to Be King" and #69, 9-96 "Walls.'

ROCK BIZ

The trend of Rock and Roll over the years has been to join the expensive establishment. RCA stole Elvis from Memphis's Sun label for #35,000. In the Bargain Bonanza Department, this is roughly equivalent to commandeering Manhattan Island for that famous $24 worth of wampum. Tiny Independent labels tackled the big brontosauruses. **Francis Craig**'s longest-#1 song of all time, 1947 #1(17) "Near You," was also the first 'Indie' hit to shatter the charts. Nimble Indies out-maneuvered giant companies, cranking out hits galore from garages and basement studios (see Rap, recently). The stuff sold, big. The cheesy establishment, of course, bought them out. Some little Indies grew into giants themselves: Atlantic/Atco, Chess, Motown, "Napster" . . .

MTV added a new dimension to solidifying the Rock Establishment, and Rock stars' Secret Poverty. Getting a new promising band on *MTV* was suddenly well nigh impossible. Some song, that a kid band might have cut with somebody's $10,000 nest egg, might now vault into video at a cinematographic minimum of $100,000. No problem – just gouge the ARTISTS' Royalties. Little 'Johnny B. Goode' wouldn't have a chance today. He'd have to pawn the gunnysack for his beat-up guitar. Then he might sell half a million albums (gold) and STILL lose money, paying back the $300,000 videographer bill for his *MTV* stardom and the almighty promo budget.

In the 2000+ 'Boy Band Era,' telegenic odds favored the really handsome blokes like Elvis or Ricky Nelson or Andy Gibb or George Michael – or some of N'Sync or the Backstreet Boys. Indies again ruled the 90s, with the rise of Seattle Grunge, and spurt of Gangsta Rap.

"Running Down a Dream" – Tom Petty and the Heartbreakers, #23, 7-89. Like many a would-be teenage idol, Tom had his big dream deferred. In 1973 he alighted in L.A., gathering seven decent offers. Consider, if you will, the unlucky seven tycoons who once turned down the **Beatles'** American or British audition tapes! Besides Elvis and Roy Orbison, Petty's two greatest Rock idols were **Del Shannon** and the Byrds' **Roger McGuinn**. Listen to "Mr. Tambourine Man" or "Turn, Turn, Turn." You'll detect the awesome similarity.

"Running Down a Dream" alludes to Del Shannon, not only Petty's main mentor but also **Elton John**'s. Petty sings of riding the high road, alone in his car: "Me-and-Del" are duetting on little Runaway . . . *Gold Rush* started that way. We must all spend some portion of our adult time commuting somewhere to work. Thanks to Tom and Del and Ringo and Buddy and Madonna and Otis and Mick and the nirvana of Rock and Roll, we are not alone.

"Walk Away" – Del Shannon and the Heartbreakers, NC, 1991. One of Del Shannon's finest records ever. Off his posthumous *Rock On* album, produced by **Tom Petty**. This song combines Del's old "Runaway" 60s style with a new dynamic Petty presence. Shannon shines on his self-penned **Peter & Gordon** classic (#9, 1-65), "I Go to Pieces." Two other great cuts are "Who Left Who," pitching Del's old revenge motif, plus fantastic Cajun "Let's Dance." Petty also produced Del's last charted hit – #33, 12-81 "Sea of Love." Ironically, Del's cover photo makes the 55-year-old look about thirty-three and thriving. Had not Del lost his life early in the year, this album might have launched his latest renaissance career. The Rock Hall of Fame finally paid tribute in 1999 to one of the top ten singers in the history of Rock and Roll. Del made the cut. Tom Petty's turn? Yep, Class of 2002. Here is the essence of Rock and Roll:

In our ultimate Cruisemobiles, we can bop around the byways and sing along with our idols. In a sense, we can live their dream vicariously. We don't have to confront 10,000 blazing eyes from our squirmy Elvis Spotlight. We don't even have to play air guitar. Give us a dashboard, like Tom Petty sings about, and we can chase Alan Jackson's "Neon Rainbow" into the golden future.

It all reinforces **Chuck Berry**'s footloose Johnny B. Goode dream. Yes, this is America, and yes, you can be a star. Petty, like **Darius Rucker** of Hootie and the Blowfish, has that quality of Everyman. A certain universality. He's a big chunk of our American multicultural panorama. Thin, and with long blond hair, Petty is also part Native American. Petty seems to have a lot of friends. Videos give us the impression he hangs out with a fun crowd. He has marathon staying power, like Billy Joel or Elton John or Rod Stewart or Bruce Springsteen. "Mary Jane's Last Dance" hit #14, 12-93. Tom Petty, like the rest of us, keeps plugging. Like Norman Petty, Tom shows an incredible musical versatility.

"King of the Hill" – Roger McGuinn, with Tom Petty, NC, 1991. On #44 Al, 1-91 *Back from Rio*. Also starring fellow ex-Byrd **David Crosby**, plus Elvis Costello, and

Timothy B. Schmit. Petty and McGuinn trade off lead vocals. McGuinn fondles his trademark Rickenbacker guitar – with Mike Campbell on 'baritone guitar' in Key of 'A'. Song revives entire echo/aura of Byrds' magical #1, '65 "Mr. Tambourine Man." "King of the Hill" stabs at weekend euphoria, hinting at a blotto and bleary-eyed maze of urban-underbelly L.A. coke highs and Gucci jewels. McGuinn's peculiar "Hotel California" motif oozes fried-egg tequila sunrises, castles of cracked crystal, and bombardier splendor of NO TOMORROW. Angelic melody. World-class vocal blend. Sinister lyrical claws.

"Free Fallin'" – Tom Petty and the Heartbreakers, #7, 11-89. Petty brought mentors back to the limelight – like this Byrds-style "Free Fallin'" shows. Or catch **Bob Dylan**'s #18-for-Tom 4-87 "Jammin' Me"; #12 feisty anthem "I Won't Back Down" in 4-89, and 3-85, #13 "Don't' Come Round Here No More." He also sang with his hero **Roy Orbison** in the Traveling Wilburys. Just before **Del Shannon**'s tragic and untimely death, Petty recruited Del for the Traveling Wilburys. It was never to be. Petty, however, keeps on rolling down the rockin' road. He's one of us all in the booming caravan – as we head for the Western stars.

"Hold My Hand" – Hootie and the Blowfish, #10, 10-94; and starkly, NC, R & B. Darius Rucker, one of Rock's great baritones, met the Blowfish on campus at the University of South Carolina. Their deca-million *Cracked Rear View* (10M) #3, '94 album soon included **Mark Bryan, Dean Felber**, and **Jim 'Soni' Sonefeld**. Crashing chords surround the heavy bass sound. A hint of thrash blasts the tune ahead. Darius lumbers his big friendly baritone. The group happens to be integrated, with one Blowfish looking a lot like Detroit Tiger 70s sensation **Mark 'The Bird' Fidrych**. Rucker is African-American, and the other three are Caucasian. Like the **Dave Matthews Band** or **Elvis** and his Sweet Inspirations, integration was a foregone conclusion. In so many ways, Rock and Roll has come a long way, baby.

"Only Wanna Be with You" – Hootie and the Blowfish, #6, 8-95; NC, R & B. Darius and the guys found their name via creative daydreaming. While dozing in classes, they'd occasionally look up and see some odd-looking student who resembled some animal. One favored a chubby owl (hence, 'Hootie'). Another suggested a blowfish because of his mumpsy puffy cheeks and spiny stubble. *Voila* – a name was born. This baritone boomer is NOT 1999 Rock Hall inductee **Dusty Springfield**'s debut, #12, 1-64 "I Only Want to Be with You."

"Time" – Hootie and the Blowfish, #14, 11-95. Hootie and his band symbolize the fun aspects of college. Touch football, zany golf, easygoing cutoffs, and spacey T-shirts. They represent the CAREFREE life that most fans believe Rock and Roll stars always enjoy. Hootie and crew spiked the charts with #13, 4-96 "Old Man and Me (When I Get to Heaven)," which offered fans a good ol' 45 rpm record. "I Will Wait" hit #18A on 8-98. Self-made zillionaires like **Dave Matthews' Band**, Hootie's crew wowed campus Americans.

Though Hootie ponders the grim phenomenon of "Time," as his ruff baritone slurs the gravelly notes, you know he's really having a blast anyhow. And so is the rest of the band. They don't flaunt the bleak stuff, like the **Goo Goo Dolls**' amazing #42, 4-2000 "Broadway." This video casts a grim gray factory smokescape, with young men nursing brews in the 'old-man bar,' waiting their morose turns to die. Though Hootie is a long way from Ragtime in the Yukon, or the booming bistros of New Orleans in the Louie Armstrong Dixieland Era, Hootie carries with him the noble legacy of the ages. He is a famous interpreter of the Popular Song to America and the world –a millennial bridge to **Louis 'Satchmo' Armstrong**'s [What a] "Wonderful World."

Hootie is one of a long succession of Great Singers to dot the high-flying airwaves of the planet over the last hundred years. It's a long way from a crank-up Victrola to the 100,000-seat packed superstar rock-idol venue and 100 tons of amps to serenade the world.

> "There are strange things done,
>   In the Midnight Sun,
> By the men who moil for gold – "
>   "The Cremation of Sam McGee," poem by
>   Robert Service, Klondike 1899 Gold Rush

Among the strangest things done in those claimstake days in Dawson City, where the Yukon and Klondike River merge, was the intrusion of real fancy honky-tonk rinky-dink pianos. Pumping up the volume in Gravel Gertie's or Klondike Kate's Saloon would be the Ragtime Rock Romper. Amid coiffed and rouged hot-time gals, you'd find some guy with a jumpin' left hand on the low keys. One of them up there, stoned on eternal daylight at Midsummer, June 21, 1899, might just have invented Rock and Roll.

Up at Michigan State in 1964, Toni and I went to a club called the Peanut Cellar in Lansing, Michigan. An old trooper with an eyeshade, striped shirt, and supersonic fingers tickled the ivories. He treated us to sing-along oldies from the 1890s – way back through the long caverns of time. When I recall the Rocking Rolling storming backbeat that swooned that beer-sotted upright piano, I first started to realize that the actual birth of Rock and Roll might not even belong in the yester-gone twentieth century. The combo of a strong Barber Shop Quartet, and a smokin' honky-tonk stardust piano pumper, may yet prove to be another true cradle of Rock and Roll, like New Orleans. Under a bloodshot moon in a hot arctic burgundy sky, Rock and Roll reverberated from the 1899 Yukon into the Land of Forever.

"Buddy Holly" – Weezer, #18A, 11-94. Check Weezer video. The *Happy Days* show clip dotes on the 50s as some pie-in-the sky peak of joy and euphoria. With checked argyle sweaters and squiggly smiles, they fluff the innocence we lost, or perhaps never really had, back in the fabulous Fonzie 50s. [Every Rock fan knows Henry Winkler's COOL FONZ]. L.A.'s **Rivers Cuomo** does vocals. Last great Holly Hiccup wielder, **Ric Ocasek** of the **Cars**, produced "Buddy Holly." Weezer's video vagabonds back to the old malt shop. A bunch of smiley Ralph Malph and Potsie characters groove to the fun Fonz era of the fifties. Or what folks thought the fifties symbolized. [Both *Grease* and *Happy Days* offered the 50s from a 70s perspective]. Weezer straddles the technical 1950-99 fence. **Weezer** sets up a tense conflict, and escapes to the utter placidity of a bygone Golden Era that never quite was.

Their chugalong chorus is pure 50s schmaltz. Not malts: "Wo-uh-ho" he sings, and says he looks like Buddy Holly. She resembles *Mary Tyler Moore*. Suddenly Camelot. Flashback, the Perfect Age. Maybe. *Mary Tyler Moore* gives America a video reference for this Age of Innocence. Most Americans too young for the Day the Music Died (2-3-59) can still share the memory of the cute antics of adorable ingénue **Mary Tyler Moore** of the *Dick Van Dyke Show*, or the *Mary Tyler Moore Show* of the 70s, with classic cast Ed Asner, Ted Knight, Gavin MacLeod, Betty White, and even **David Letterman** in a cameo weatherman role. **Cricket** bandmate **Sonny Curtis** wrote the *Mary Tyler Moore* theme song (#29, C).

Weezer returns us to the land of Currier & Ives. Norman Rockwell. Disneyland. A vision of love. *Reader's Digest* humor. Yesterday once again. Yep – love! Malts. Checked sweaters. Smiles. Rock and Roll. Simple and sweet and pure. Surf's up. Three chords and a cloud of dust.

*   *   *

"Wait Till the Sun Shines, Nellie" – Buddy Holly, NC, 1959; #26, 4-62 Australia. Harry **Von Tilzer**'s brother Albert wrote "Take Me Out to the Ball Game" and never went to a major-league ball game for 25 years afterwards. Harry wrote "Nellie" in a house of blue lights on a booze-blasted upright piano, waiting for his pals to stop dallying with the 'ditzy dames' upstairs at the ramshackle establishment. Somehow, though, I really believe Buddy Holly meant this song from the bottom of his heart when he sang it to his bride Maria.

This 19th to 20th turn-of-the-century tune sums up our whole Rock and Roll *Gold Rush*. It's about dreams. It's about little Johnny strumming his old guitar by the railroad track – dreaming of someday seeing his name 'JOHNNY B. GOODE' in majestic lights.

The song, like life, is a bittersweet, tragicomic adventure. It is a song about looking for an old pot of gold at the end of the rainbow – and finding only a rainbow. Sometimes, rainbows are not so bad.

Buddy recorded this solo tape with Maria Elena watching him in his apartment on Fifth Avenue by Washington Square in Greenwich Village. I know it was a scanty three weeks before his fateful Winter Tour took him to his own fateful crossroads when a little plane sought the sky and the stars in a swirl of snow.

The world knows Buddy never really intended to release "Nellie" this way. Even then, the world considered it a sixty-plus-year-old song with no commercial potential. The little song, miserably short, was sweetened by Buddy's producer, Norman Petty, with a few superfluous choristers warbling at the outset – and a burbling bass bubbling "Bup-bup" frippery vocal riffs. The magic, though, is in Buddy Holly's heartfelt vocal, garnished with hiccups astride chordal mediants – and the sweet combo of Buddy's rolling guitar blur, and the ultracool **Jerry Allison**-style 16th-note paradiddle drum thunder. The only other Holly fan I know who really LOVES this song is **Nigel Smith** from Melbourne, Prez of the Australian Buddy Holly Appreciation Society. **Paul McCartney** belongs to our American Buddy Holly Memorial Society (President is our photo supplier **Bill Griggs**, Lubbock, Texas)].

Rock and Roll is a deep personal experience. It's also a tribal initiation into our multicultural American culture. You can listen to your fave tunes in your lonesome room, or you can cut up the dance floor with your rowdy pals howling at a Colorado moon. Alone or together. Or both.

"Wait Till the Sun Shines, Nellie" has couple of major musical hooks for me. Van Tilzer and Andrew Sterling's magnificent rockin' century song leaps right up to the III Major MEDIANT; if you're in the Key of 'C', it's an **E major** (in 'A', it's a **C# major**). No matter what song uses this dynamic chord shift, I love it. But Von Tilzer was really on the inventive cutting edge of this kind of chord theory. "Nellie" is the only Holly song besides "Peggy Sue" (#3, 10-57) to feature the heavenly Holly GUITAR BLUR.

As the pitter-patter of **Jerry Allison**'s tom-toms blasts their slamming 16th-note paradiddle roll, Buddy's Fender Stratocaster guitar fades back into a continuous wave of reverberating pure chordal shimmer. Buddy's chords float mysteriously, adding an ethereal surreal timbre to the haunting song.

In the Sterling lyric (Von Tilzer, too), Buddy implores Maria to hang on, to wait till the sun shines again. The clouds will drift along. We'll be happy the lyric wishfully states, "by-and-by." An aeon, perhaps? It implies 1906 Nellie is not so peachy-keen at the moment. Maybe some yester-lost Sweepstakes ticket on a Blotto Lotto dream will spin off into wild delirious fortune and happiness. Maybe not. Maybe the next day the seedy sleazo South Side will still reek with old stogie butts, recycled dog food, and despair.

Rock and Roll, remember, is long on promises of tomorrow's ecstasy.

As Buddy fondles his Fender Strat, he croons his mixed message to Maria: someday they'll be happy, and he pleads with her not to cry. They'll wander along Lover's Lane, and the future will shine – by-and-by.

It's one of the happiest songs I've ever heard. It's one of the saddest songs I've ever heard. I was sixteen and our world lost Buddy Holly. I hate to say it – when you're of a certain age you should possess some wisdom – but I still can't figure out the grand cosmic reason why Buddy Holly died. He had so much promise in sculpting the direction of Rock and Roll (plus his burgeoning family). Maria had been expecting Buddy's child when he left on the grim Winter Tour of 1959. When the word came of his death, she lost their baby. Maria knew his ominous premonition. Buddy himself didn't even watch TV, she said, because he believed there were too many adventures to have in our short lives without hanging around constantly in front of a little screen. **Maria Elena Santiago Holly** wrote over the Internet in December 1996: "While many of his fans will relive his music, I will always remember him as the man I fell in love with many years ago."

I was just a baffled 16-year-old kid with frozen toes on an ice-blue night of stars and dreams. Kids can pick a lot of weird rock idols in their formative years. I lucked out. Who knows what could have happened had Buddy lived? He planned an album of **Ray Charles** songs. He and Petty and Dick Jacobs were messing around with strings and Orchestral Rock. He was finding chord shifts ignored by the greatest Jazz experimenters. There is no doubt that, given more than 1¼ years to hit his heyday, Buddy had a good chance of being the most profound single innovator in the history of Rock and Roll. But his time was cut very short. Like **James Dean**, there'll never be a picture of Buddy with receding hairline, graying temples, or love handles. Buddy's image is frozen into that youthful idyllic yesteryear, when fewer angry voices snarled. Back when a lot of Rock and Roll was about love and joy. Maybe it still is.

We juxtapose our happy memories of Holly's meteoric rise against his ghastly fall back to the earth. We all recall the Day the Music Died – in that terrible cornfield by Clear Lake, Iowa, seven miles from the Surf Ballroom, 1313 miles from any swirling surf.

Dion shared my feelings. We spoke of the impact Buddy had upon the young Italian teen idol from Belmont Street in the Bronx: "Buddy was about the nicest guy I ever met. You know, I was about third in line for Ritchie Valens' ticket. Forty bucks, though – that was as much as my old man made in a month. So I decided to take the frozen rattletrap of a bus."

In May 2000, **Dion DeMucci** released on Al. *Déjà Vu* his Buddy Holly tribute tune "Everyday (That I'm with You)." The legend goes on. The Belmonts' Carlo Mastrangelo, you recall, burned newspapers in the aisle of the ancient bus, whose heater was history. Frostbite was very real. Buddy's new drummer Charlie Bunch luckily ended up in a Michigan hospital with frozen toes – not on a rattletrap Beechcraft Bonanza. If polyester had been invented, however, and the stars' suits hadn't been so wrinkled, they might not have chartered the fated flight for Fargo, North Dakota. Dion was very shaken when he and the Belmonts suddenly were the Winter Dance Party – with a little help from **Bobby Vee** – and what Bobby calls the "World's First Garage Band" – the Shadows.

For our terrible year 1968, Dion wrote his reflective "Abraham, Martin, and John" (#4, 10-68). It's about two Presidents and Martin Luther King, but the song was inspired, Dion told me, by the looming specter of Buddy's early death. The song was a kernel of hope, too, in Dion's conversion to born-again Christianity detailed in his autobiography *The Wanderer*. The hook his song hammers? It seems that the good will die young . . .

Don McLean's "American Pie" – #1(4), 11-71 – also shares our personal sense of loss – Don couldn't recall if he'd cried, reading about Buddy's widowed bride, but the plane crash shook him up permanently. Us too. Rock and Roll never tried to be wishy-washy. Like life itself, it brings joy and sorrow. "Wait Till the Sun Shines, Nellie" brings us love and laughter. It brings us tears and sadness. The clouds may never drift by: the sun may fade away into the gloomy gray of Nevermore. It is when we give up our childlike wistful HOPE, however, and forget to dream, that we have lost the spark that empowers and kindles our flickering lives.

By and by, the sun will shine.

By and by, Rock and Roll will bring us new joy, new love, new hope.

Let's turn to Buddy's bandmate **Sonny Curtis**. Sonny furnishes a fascinating answer to **McLean**'s mainstream quandary about Buddy's life. After hitting the charts in the Country Rock field, and writing "Love Is All Around" for Mary Tyler Moore's theme song (NC, 1980; #29, 7-80 C), Sonny broadcast his version of Buddy's career to a smaller Country venue:

"The Real Buddy Holly Story" – Sonny Curtis, NC, 1980; #38, 3-80 C. Sonny's gentle baritone lyric explains a few differences between the well-meaning Innervisions Hollywood movie version and Buddy's real life [Lyrics c/o Sonny Curtis, 2001]:

> "Well, the levee ain't dry,
> And the music didn't die,
> 'Cause Buddy Holly lives
> Everytime we play Rock and Roll."

Isn't that a fantastic answer to McLean's death-of-Rock scare way back in 1971? Since 1971, Rock and Roll rampaged its insistent way through many wild changes, new styles, spin-offs, and bizarre metamorphoses, but it keeps on keepin' on. "One little snowplane out of the storm – and the great Rock and Roll was born." [from "American Sky," Maury & **Nine Days**' Jeremy Dean, 2001.]

From the ragtag Ragtime ragamuffin shores of Nome, Alaska, and Dawson City in the Klondike, pianos pumped a driving left-hand swing bass. The beat and the rhythm and the pulse and passion and power of Rock and Roll were born. From New Orleans to Memphis, the Blues darted North to the Motor and Windy Cities. Alan Freed called it Rock and Roll in his 1951-52 *Moondog* show in Cleveland. **Elvis, Chuck Berry**, and **Buddy Holly** sculpted the big beat sounds that would reverberate back with Beatle power into the world of today and tomorrow.

Rock and Roll is simple. And profound. Take three big major power chords. Add a throbbing beat. Splash a dash of Soul and quivering twang. Bring in a few billion people who love to dance to the music. And the joy of life.

The levee isn't dry, the music didn't die.

"'That'll Be the Day' came much too soon for Buddy. He was a good ol' boy, and he had a good Christian Soul . . . Buddy Holly lives, every time we play Rock and Roll." – [bandmate **Sonny Curtis**].

Buddy Holly,
1940 or so

40 It's Still Rock and Roll to Us!

A recent *Rolling Stone* magazine decree voted the Beatles #1 in everything. In a stunning songwriting dissection, **John Lennon** was voted #1 songwriter, with **Paul McCartney** second. The Fab Four nabbed all the goodies in the popular music panorama – except one – Best Vocalist. It went to a guy who straddled mid-century, in the wee small hours of smoky romantic afterglow. Or aftermath. The velvet-voiced crooner (b. 12-12-1915, Hoboken, New Jersey) both predated and overarched the rise of Rock and Roll. Like Country icon **Hank Williams**, belting so-long lover brews in honkytonks, **Frank Sinatra** spanned the American Century with one drink for his sweetheart, and one more for the lonesome road. From Lana Turner to Ava Gardner to Mia Farrow, husky-baritone 'Ol' Blue Eyes' Sinatra surfed the crest of a screaming wave of bobby-soxers, who agonized for his attentions. In the lucrative ALBUM category on the periphery of *Gold Rush*, Frank Sinatra is the 2nd-leading artist of all time, behind only Elvis, ever (Joel Whitburn's *Top Pop 1955-96 Albums*). Though Sinatra sidestepped the Rock Revolution, he is among a handful of entertainers to create the word 'superstar.' Right up until the end on May 5, 1998, Sinatra sought the good life, announcing for every year that "It Was a Very Good Year" (#28, 12-65). And Frank did it his way.

"Love's Been Good to Me" – Frank Sinatra, #75, 9-69. Summing up his long swashbuckling life at the tender age of 53 here, Sinatra extracts the essence of *Gold Rush*: love's been good to us all – via our magnificent tapestry of music. This Sinatra anthem, penned by sentimental 60s poet Rod McKuen, assesses his life. Basically, life was good, very good, for song slugger Sinatra. He represented the newly-legendary Italian-American presence in Big Apple music. His sports analogs were Yankees' centerfielder Joe DiMaggio (star of Simon & Gar's #1, '68 "Mrs. Robinson"), and Joltin' Joe's charismatic teammates **Phil Rizzuto** (see singer Meat Loaf) and **Yogi Berra**

(#8, 6-60 Ivy Three's "Yogi" – Hanna-Barbera cartoon Yogi Bear inspired by Yankee catcher). 'Chairman of the Board' Sinatra can put up with the pettiness, boredom, and daily excruciating agonies of life – as long as he knows he's got love, back at some cozy spot at the end of his personal rainbows.

Jazz stars like Sinatra, Bing Crosby, Glenn Miller, Paul Whiteman, or Tommy/Jimmy Dorsey brought us this romantic stardust ballroom vision. Whatever was meager or petty in our lives, we could banish it for three fadeaway moments of glorious song. Choking in a smoggy smokescape, or walkin' in Del Shannon's frazzled "Runaway" rainstorm, lost and lovelorn, we might have the Tresspassers-Will-Be-Shot Junkyard Rottweiler attached toothily to our tender ankles. Somehow, Sinatra and Friends could whisk us away in splendor to "Moonlight in Vermont":

"Moonlight in Vermont" – Frank Sinatra, NC, 1945. [#15, 2-45, Margaret Whiting/Billy Butterfield Band]. This classic Smooth Jazz melody needs no swirling Hawaiian guitars, no throbbing Chalypso pulse, no seraphic harmonies. Just Frank and the band. Drummer, alas, out to lunch. The impeccable delivery of Sinatra's Lucky Strike baritone drops the listener to rapt attention, like finding Bigfoot/Sasquatch footprints on jazzy Vermont ski trails – while the sun swoops behind the mountain, and the silver-blue Vermont moon rises huge in the forlorn indigo east. One of Frank's minimalist masterpieces, like #27, 1-49 "Autumn in New York." "Moonlight in Vermont" has the same classy aura and ambience as **Bing Crosby**'s Jo Warde #1(4), 4-44 "I'll Be Seeing You" (#4 Tommy Dorsey).

"Summer Wind" – Frank Sinatra, #25, 9-66. On the *Billboard/Variety* charts, Sinatra had only seven #1 songs in his methusalehan career. "In my opinion," writes my 6'3", 220# student Bill Suchocky, 20, "anyone who does not like Sinatra must be crazy." Sinatra commandeered the charts with something for everyone – 170 hits (singles) can do that. Elvis charted 151 hits in the Rock Era, but Sinatra's streak stretches beyond (therefore not officially tabulating). Sinatra banked 102 hits from 1942 to 1954, and the other 68 in the Rock Era 1955 onwards. For the Rock Era alone, Frank's results are very impressive at 7th ever: 1) Elvis 151; 2) James Brown 99; 3) Aretha Franklin and 4) Ray Charles both 76; 5) The Beatles 72, and 6) Elton John 69 [Whitburn's *Top Pop Singles 1955-99*].

Sinatra's Greatest Hits? You win: #1(8), 2-46 "Oh! What It Seemed to Be"; #1(4), 8-46; #1(4), 3-67 "Somethin' Stupid" (with daughter Nancy); and #1(1), 5-66 "Strangers in the Night." When Frank switched from Alex Stordahl's Orchestra to the world-famous **Harry James and Tommy Dorsey** Big Bands, he zoomed from simply great to legendary.

"Summer Wind" is a non-surfin' sand-strolling song. It laments the fickle fortunes of summer romance, like: **Pat Boone**'s archetypal #1(7), '57 "Love Letters in the Sand" (#6, '31 Ted Black's Orchestra); the **Happenings**' #3, 7-66 "See You in September"; or Brian Hyland's sensational melodic ballad, #3, 6-62 "Sealed with a Kiss." Frank trolls this goodbye mood in his Kurt Weill masterpiece, #8, 12-46 "September Song." Though he was but 31 in 1946, Frank surveys the urgency of time running out, like Joseph Kozma and **Roger Williams**'s "Autumn Leaves," says Ivan Sanders (#1[4], 8-55, Williams).

Frank Sinatra's vocal delivery defines the genre. Like Bing Crosby or Perry Como, Sinatra raises the vocal bar to a level other crooners dream of attaining. To get to Rock and Roll, my generation had to rebel against Sinatra's perfect delivery. Who would have suspected his best friend?

"Sway" – Dean Martin, #15, 7-54. Dean (b. Ohio, 1917-95) saluted his silver-medal triumph #2(5), 11-53 "That's Amore" with this South-of-the-Border remake of Mexican melody "Quien Sera." Martin's vocal idiosyncrasy dreamily and calculatedly MUMBLES a bit. Now THAT'S anti-Sinatra, Mr. Super Enunciator. In his tie-loosened martini-smile style, Dean and his sleepy mumble were all the spark needed to set off a new terror from Tupelo. The Tupelo terror helped inspire THIS 13-year-old Rock Uncyclopedia Dean to fall passionately in love with Rock and Roll:

"I Forgot to Remember to Forget" – Elvis Presley, NC, 1955; #1(5), 9-55 C. Elvis's second hit was his first #1 song anywhere. It followed his dynamite Rockabilly debut (NC, TOP 100, but #5, 7-55 Country chart) "Baby, Let's Play House." Surfing Sam Phillips' state-of-the-art echo chamber, Elvis caressed the virgin Memphis air waves in a passionate paroxysm of gusto-gorging gasps. Suddenly, it was all over for quietude and serenity. In an instant and bloodless revolution, America was conquered by guitar.

Dean Martin threw out the first pitch. Elvis slugged the grand-slam homer. Elvis's syllable-chopping murmurs are directly related to the King's avowed idol, CROONER Dean Martin [yep, and **Chuck Berry** idolized CROONER **Nat King Cole**]. Yep, Un-Rocker Sinatra's best friend Dino. "I Forgot to Remember to Forget" is an eerie forecast of the shuddering impact that this Tupelo/Memphis Delta Blues White Rocker would have. The song lurches and blurts and hypnotizes and hugs and boogies in a sound swoon of unleashed guitarfire Rock and Roll – steered by the 20-year-old Entertainer of the Century. The TOTAL SOUND lofts young Elvis to destiny. Elvis and Dean – in musical cahoots.

Frank Sinatra

"Learnin' the Blues" – Frank Sinatra, #1(2), 5-55. Frank lists a litany of romantic jabs, double-crosses, and uppercuts that send the lightweight Hoboken Hammerer to the ropes for the woozy eight-count. Guy in a bar. Girl gone. The old sad story. Sinatra masterfully milks this mood. He makes it almost fun to cry in your beer. He tells forlorn friend about the blues – how he'll shuffle the floor, wear out his shoes. He tells how her image never leaves, and how she'll haunt his dreams. There's no cure for the lovelorn, he mopes. Barstool suds downpedal his misery. His deliverance is a bad buzz in a dark ashcan alley. In his blue funk mood, Frank swaggers down his dismal alley back to "Heartbreak Hotel' in the wee small hours of 3 a.m.

In the Wee Small Hours – **Frank Sinatra, Al. #2(18), 5-55.** Longest at #2, of anything, anywhere. I think this is the first album I ever really noticed. In my future bandmate Bob Baldori's knotty pine basement in Dearborn, Michigan, I was surrounded by Uncle Pete Baldori's stand-up bass, Bob's second-string accordion, and trumpeter John Baldori's musical paraphernalia. In 1955, we factory-town kids could afford the odd 99-cent single. Actual albums, few and far between, were usually the royal province of Parents Only. In my house, music was an occasional happening when Uncle Lou blasted through town. In the Baldori household, it was LIFE ITSELF for John Baldori and his charming and pretty wife Lucille. Though Bob and Jeff Baldori's dad worked in the

Ford Motor Administration 'Glass House' by day, his midnights took him and his trumpet away to enchanted ballrooms. Mr. Baldori was also the only man in the neighborhood who still could run (maybe the only one who didn't smoke). After touch football extravaganzas with his four boys, we'd end up in the Baldori basement for Vernor's Ginger Ale and New Era Potato Chips.

I'd stare at this Sinatra *Wee Small Hours* album, parked over by the grub and Faygo red pop. Bathed in aquamarine blue, the cover was otherwise a *cinema-noire* lament of closin'-time delightful dirges, like lead song "In the Wee Small Hours of the Morning" (NC, '55). Or **Duke Ellington**'s #3, 2-31 "Mood Indigo," and Rodgers-Hart's ironic "Glad to Be Unhappy." The artful foot-by-a-foot vinyl record cover presages the blue, blue mood. Sinatra stands alone, woebegone, and disconsolate, on a blue nightscape Lonely Avenue. He fondles his sparkling cigarette. His tie loosened, Frank's rumpled fedora is cocked atop his drooping face. He is the picture of solitude.

In the Wee Small Hours sat at #2 for EIGHTEEN (18) weeks. It never ascended the golden throne where Doris Day reigned with her album #1(17) , 6-55 *Love Me Or Leave Me*. Bob switched from gonzo high school trumpeter (and secondary accordion) to become 'Boogie Bob' on the piano. When Bob and I got the old band back together in July 1999, the composite Woolies, Night Shift, and Trade Winds with **Larry Glazer** and **Bill Metros,** Bob's dad was still playing gigs four nights a week. Sometimes he drove 100 miles home on I-96 from Lansing to Detroit in the 'Wee Small Hours' after Michigan's modest 2 a.m. bar closings. In his 80th year. Since it's too late to thank my own parents, let me thank trumpet maestro John Baldori and charming singer Lucille.

"The Mummers' Dance" Loreena McKennitt, #18, 3-98. Also, #1, rest of the world. CELTIC RENAISSANCE section. Unavailable, of course, as a single here. Recorded in Stratford, Ontario. Loreena's otherworldly Canadian sound coruscates with ancient Celtic instruments. She plies her astounding mystical trail, questing after some Druidic/Taoist Holy Grail. Her haunting soprano suggests the early years of **Joan Baez**. This Celtic Renaissance adventure also takes on New Age accoutrements – Oud, Viola, Tabla, and Cello. The magnificent chorus drives the story from a mossy glade of hobbits and Robin Hood gnarled giant oaks to glistening Thomas Kincade garden gates and magical potions. Hit #19 FIRST WEEK on HOT 100. Along the same Celtic lines, you'll find **Enya** (b. '81) of Ireland, and Al. #9, 12-95 *The Memory of Trees*, plus her haunting Top Ten triumph, #10, 6-2001 "Only Time."

"Hurdy Gurdy Man" – Donovan [Leitch], **#5, 6-68; #4 U.K.** Nigel Eaton plays a gurdy guy in McKennitt's enchanting chanson. Harbinger of the 1997-2000 Celtic Renaissance, 'flower-power' Donovan of Glasgow, Scotland, traces the organ grinder's [a/k/a 'hurdy-gurdy man'] pied-piper siren call. With or without a monkey or a dog (like **Nitty Gritty Dirt Band**'s #9, 11-70 "Mr. Bojangles"), Donovan's hurdy-gurdy man cranks the barrel organ and vagabonds the mediaeval towns – singing lilting love songs.

"Manic Monday" – Bangles, #2(1), 1-86. Far from any magic forest glade, "Manic Monday" written by **Prince** laments the hyper-paced office merry-go-round. **Susanna Hoffs** and sisters **Debbie** and **Vicki Peterson** begin with a blue crystal-fountain Valentino daydream fantasy. Suddenly they lurch back to reality. 'Dilbert' cubicles. Paper clips. Frazzled commuters in the real world, they cuss the bus and bad-mouth the annoying train, questing to beat the clock. The clock wins. Tremendous triplicate harmony – anchored by Michael Steele. Surging past the longest-workweek Japanese in 1999, Americans can empathize with the Bangles' dizzying plight. You know – three jobs, no time, no glory. Bangles skirt Celtic fringe on bizarre ode to donut-shop cops, #1(4), 9-86 "Walk Like an Egyptian." They also scored big with #1(1), 2-89 "Eternal Flame" and #5, 10-88 "In Your Room." The Bangles' basic rock and roll is just plain fun.

"My Heart Will Go On" – Celine Dion, #1(2), 2-98. Charlemagne, Quebec's, Celine Dion's (b. 3-30-68) timeless song elegizes the furtive love affair of two star-crossed *Titanic* lovers. During their fateful Night to Remember [novel, Walter Lord, '55], the 'unsinkable' H.M.S. Titanic, on its maiden voyage, plunges to a watery grave. It collides with a giant iceberg 'calving' off the Greenland icecap. Two lovers embrace on the prow of the careening megaliner. They allude to current #1 hit "Come, Josephine, in My Flying Machine," by **Ada Jones**, the **American Quartet**, and **Billy Murray** – #1(3), 3-1911. These [RCA] Victor superstars of the un-teenage century were entertainment giants of their faraway vaudeville era. Who today has ever heard ANY of them? Sad, but true.

As the imperiled and doomed Titanic slips into the slushy super-cooled North Atlantic, it's a clear, starry night. Slush survival time is ten minutes. Celine's surreal ballad, like **Bobby Darin's** "La Mer" sea hymn "Beyond the Sea" (#6, 1-60), attempts to transcend this tragicomic planet – and take their eternal love to a new plateau of faith, a new dimension of eternity.

Dion's Titanic tune suggests three other doomed-ship sagas. One is Scottish **Gordon Lightfoot**'s spectacular November grey-squall disaster song, #2(2), 8-76 "Wreck of the Edmund Fitzgerald." The huge Great Lakes freighter snapped in half in a monster Lake Superior storm off Michigan's Whitefish Bay – killing 29 crewmen who never had the Titanic luxury of an hour to prepare lifeboats. It split like a toothpick and sank immediately. A grim Detroit bell tolls the tragedy in a shrieking minor-key blanket of doom. His icy song makes us all shiver (in August) to the depths of our most sleety and gray November souls.

The **Kingston Trio** did Woody Guthrie's WWII adaptation "Reuben James," of Carter Family classic #3, 8-28 "Wildwood Flower." It's unrelated to Kenny Rogers' #26, 9-69 "Ruben James." Guthrie's saga tells of the first American ship sunk by a Nazi U-Boat in the Hallowe'en prelude to World War II. Like Guthrie's "This Land Is Your Land," "Reuben James" is among the foremost of patriotic songs. With Trio lead singer **Bob Shane**'s burly baritone, it laments the senseless loss of all our sailors off the frigid

Iceland shore. They seek to preserve the memory of those who served their country. In 1912, World War I ('The Great War') flickered on the horizon. As Jack Dawson wooed his Titanic lass, archdukes played with pistols. Blue-white icebergs shimmered off Reykjavik, Iceland, in the starry night.

Ernest Van (Pop) Stoneman hit #3, 2-25 with "The Titanic." This venerable early Country star (1893-1968) anchored the fledgling Grand Ole Opry. When I was a lad of 13 at summer camp, we sang an irascible song about the sinking of the big unsinkable ship. The WORDS were grim and dire, about cute little kids plunging beneath the icy waters – the TONE of the song was uproariously upbeat. With a big OOM-PAH 2/4 meter, the suspiciously-smiley song told of class differences aboard ship (see movie). It told how the ritzy rich wouldn't hang out with poor steerage folks like Dawson. The Lord, they sang, told the ship it'd never land. The refrain told how SAD it was when the big ship plunged down, but the tune's tone mirrored the mirth of "Jingle Bells" or Buddy Holly's "Oh Boy." There's a 98.76% probability these are the same two songs. Titanic's gone – never forgotten.

"When You Wish Upon a Star" – Dion & the Belmonts, #30, 4-60. Super Streetcorner harmonies by Bronx Belmonts. Song hit #10 for 'Ukulele Ike,' a/k/a Irish tenor **Cliff Edwards** in 2-40, and #1 for bandleader/trombonist **Glenn Miller**. Edwards is better known today as the voice of Jiminy Cricket in Disney classic *Pinocchio*. Dion DiMucci, no 'Wanderer' here (#2, '61), wrestles with lightning bolts from the blue, plus karma and kismet and fate. He extracts some cosmic whimsy and optimism from his star-wishing (how many stars can you SEE in the high-rise streetlight Bronx glow?). For years, lovers, fearful of praying to God, have wished upon sidelong stars for the consummation of their romantic reveries.

Boys for Pele –Tori Amos, Al. #2(1), 2-96. Born Myra Amos in Newton, NC, Tori Amos forged her deep songs of blunt delicacy on the rim of Hawaiian volcano Mt. Haleakala of Maui. We visited the intense *caldera* (volcanic vent or hole) at Maui sunrise. We saw the smoking brimstone rim of sulfur-hissing Mt. Kilauea on the Big Island of Hawaii in 1999. **Pele** is Hawaii's fiery volcano goddess, who craves the sacrifice of BOYS, not the standard vestal virgins that every other volcanic society murdered (Mexico, Peru). Mt. Haleakala is the host of the strange ghost-green silversword plant. The smoking caldera can explode in igneous fury at any moment, even the one where you blithely dance the rim, gazing at the fruit and flower offerings to Pelé. Tori Amos's first album *Little Earthquakes* (#54, 4-92) contained the incendiary "Me and a Gun." "Cornflake Girl" hit nary a blip here, but #4, 1-94 U.K. Second album *Under the Pink* hit #12, 2-94. The Baltimore Peabody Conservatory scholarship prodigy tiptoed uncomfy lyrical themes like molestation in "Baker, Baker." "Caught a Lite Sneeze" caught #60, 1-96.

Dilate – Ani DiFranco, Al. #87, 6-96. Ani (b. '71 Buffalo, NY) played her first coffeehouse gig at 11. A fiscal enigma, she zaps the corporate establishment. She disdains big record labels, and pockets all the profits (Creed, Hootie, Vertical Horizon, and Don McLean have similar arrangements). With tunes like "Juke Box Fire" and "Glass House," songwriter DiFranco packs venues with Feminist Folk charisma. Ani formed her own Righteous Babe label. In 1997 she got a Grammy nomination by the establishment she chides. She says, "We begin as our parents' rebels – and end up as our kids' ESTABLISHMENT." Ani has a spellbinding voice, mesmerizing stage presence, and passionate fan base.

"The Power of Goodbye" – Madonna, #11, 10-98. This Celtic Renaissance song captures the essence of **Loreena McKennitt, Celine Dion**, and **Sarah McLachlan**. Madonna's re-invented voice jumps so many genres that she is now the #6 Artist of All Time (Whitburn's 1955-99 survey). Madonna re-invents Sherwood Forest, and cruises on Robin Hood's cupidic arrow of song. "The Power of Goodbye" wafts on teetering melodic chords and harmonies. She purrs this song in her cotton-candy ingenue "True Blue" voice. Madonna offered #2, 3-98 "Frozen," #5, 7-98 "Ray of Light," #19, 6-99 "Beautiful Stranger," and #4, 11-2000 "Don't Tell Me."

In February 2000, her Don McLean reprise of "American Pie" (#1, '71) stalled at its #26 debut slot. *Billboard's* Fred Bronson (3-16-2000) hints that Americans suffer from too much money, buying exclusively ALBUMS and making SINGLES unavailable. NAPSTER is available for singles downloading, bypassing the album and artists' hard-earned royalties. Napster has been called a form of internet piracy, whereby record companies and artists are blocked out from financial participation in the records they created. Some say it's no big deal – like taping a record in the 70s. Others say it undermines the whole ASCAP-BMI royalty process, and makes starving musicians hungrier yet. At any rate, students are not dumb. They know that if companies refuse to release affordable singles, they will get them on the 'bootleg' black market via Napster. It is only laissez-faire economics. The people hurt by Napster do not include Madonna (she has enough money) or thrifty students (whee – what a bargain). People hurt by Napster are your local band with a modest hit record, second-line stars with a couple of hits, and newer groups into deep debt to their record companies. In 8-2000, Madonna pranced again to the top with #1(4) Rap-hybrid "Music," and 'copper medal' #4, 11-2000 "Don't Tell Me."

"I Will Remember You" – Sarah McLachlan, #65, 11-95; plus 'live' version #14, 5-99. You want haunting? Hallowe'en has a ghost shortage for out-of-work goblins to cover the haunting range of this Celtic Renaissance anthem by the Halifax, Nova Scotia (b. 1-28-68), Canadian balladeer. Sarah helped headline the **Lilith Fair**, an all-female tour of rockers and ballad belters, In their 1997-2000 heyday, more than half the top 20 songs were for the first time by female artists. "I Will Remember You" has the dubious distinction of being one of the most popular funeral songs of the millennial era.

"Angel"/"Adia" – Sarah McLachlan, #4, 5-98 'Angel' and #3, 11-98 'Adia.' In the angel's arms, McLachlan promises, you can find true comfort. Few songs since **Simon and Garfunkel**'s #1, '70 "Bridge over Troubled Water" evoke such reverence. Like their #5, '66 "Homeward Bound," "Angel" rumbles through dank hotel rooms, meaninglessness, and despair. Sarah's spellbinding elegy has been said to be for Smashing Pumpkins' keyboarder **Jonathan Mulvoin** (d. age 34 in '96, substances). McLachlan's minimalist acoustic piano curls around Floyd Cramer "Last Date" (#2, '60) grace notes. Without a Celtic collage of Druidic percussion and forest flutes, Sarah simply sings her soft, sad soprano song with tremolo and passion and empathy. No one since **Joan Baez** has hit such a spellbinding charismatic wavelength. Sarah's audience sits silently thunderstruck. Sarah warns of circling vultures, and the thief of truth that is lying to oneself (see Laertes/Polonius dialogue, *Hamlet*). Like **Odetta** or Barbara Hoffman, Sarah's style is charismatic. Her "Angel" may be a pallid promenade with death, but it's also a masterpiece monument to life. The Celtic Renaissance of McKennitt, Madonna, Celine Dion, and Sarah McLachlan is a major phase of late-90s popular music. "Adia," says Dan Axelrod, is about Sarah's grandmother.

"I Don't Want to Miss a Thing" – Aerosmith, #1(4), 9-98. **Steven Tyler's** amazing voice drifts into passionate balladry here. Far from gloom-sodden, this Tyler-Perry hit is Aerosmith's biggest ever – in a generation of gung-ho rock and roll. With the grace and range of his idol **Robert Plant**, and with **Mick Jagger**'s stage presence, Tyler vaults to the top of a very classy ballad. Too gorgeous for Heavy Metal melody. Aerosmith never missed a millennial step, surging "Jaded" to #7+ (1-2001).

"Believe" – Cher, #1(4), 12-98. CHERilyn LaPierre may be the 3rd-oldest winner of a #1 hit (see Louis 'Satchmo' Armstrong, 62, or Morris Stoloff, #1(3), 4-56 "Moonglow/ Theme from *Picnic*" at age 57). With hammering 'Dance Trax' rhythm, Cher's updated and contemporary sound blasted the 'baby bands' off the charts – a testimonial to her Armenian-American Soul and huff-puff exercise videos. They keep her marathon dancing at 53 at a 21-year-old fitness level.

"One Week" – Barenaked Ladies, #1(1), 10-98. Tragically for their would-be guy audience, Toronto's 'Ladies' are NOT gorgeous girls in birthday-buff suits. They are just singer **Steven Page**, guitar guy **Ed Robertson**, drummer **Tyler Stewart**, and bassist **Jim Creeggan**. No Glitz/ Glam costumery. Just ordinary guys. Nifty, but true: "One Week" was Number One for One Week. These clothed male Torontonians' second song, #68, 11-97 "Brian Wilson," is named after **Beach Boys**' leader. Ladies' #16+ 9-2000 "Pinch Me" soared up the charts on their Nice-Guy whimsy and low-key approach. Barenaked Ladies' lyrics are clothed in clever new ideas.

"Lost in You" – Garth Brooks as Chris Gaines, #5, 9-99. Stymied from the HOT 100 by Country chart border guards, the guy with the biggest Country hit (15 million – "Friends in Low Places") of all time had to become somebody else to hit the high HOT 100! Hurdling musical barriers, Garth donned a new alter-ego. The former Oklahoma State track star (javelin) challenges stodgy folks who typecast singers into one immovable genre. Did his risky move work? Check the chart number.

"Banned in the U.S.A." – 2 Live Crew, #20, 7-90; #13 R & B. Luther 'Luke Skyywalker' Campbell (2 y's in a row) and his Miami Rap trio started Luke Records – pioneering for 90s Rappers rebuffed by big labels. Their first salvo was #26, 9-89 "Me So Horny," pushing the parameters of free speech until April 2001 'FCC Decency Standards' guidelines. 'Second Lady' Tipper Gore (1992-2000) spearheaded parents' group to issue Objectionable Language labels on music – just as movies, and later TV shows, were rated. Luke's lampoon of **Bruce Springsteen**'s "Born in the U.S.A" (#9, '84) won notoriety (i.e. sales) to grab cash, not airwaves. Two Rapster roads diverged: **Will Smith**'s street-legal airwave Rap serenaded America, while doomed **2 Pac** and **Notorious B.I.G.** blanketed underground Rap turntables.

"Livin' La Vida Loca" – Ricky Martin, #1(5), 4-99. Born Christmas Eve 1971, Ricky bounced anonymity out the window with this blockbuster during his Elvis Year, 1999. Teenage-idoldom took awhile. Ricky began at 15 with **Menudo**, whose #62, 5-85 "Hold Me" projected a fledgling Puerto Rican 'Boy Band' fifteen years ahead of its time (see New Kids on the Block). Menudo means small, tiny, or minute (in its clockless meaning), and all the Menudo singers were always *quince anos* – or fifteen years old. When Ricky darted out their revolving door due to the agonies of 'ageism,' he landed on his feet. Stints in Broadway's *Les Miserables* and TV's beloved 'soap' *General Hospital* didn't hurt the 6'2" 'hunk's' career.

In #2(2), 8-99 "She's All I Ever Had," Martin expresses his hopelessly romantic side. Richard Torres said in *Newsday* (2-18-2001) that steady rotation of monster hits means "today's hit is tomorrow's annoyance." Martin surged back with #14, 10-2000 "She Bangs." Country star **Pam Tillis**'s #1 C, '94 launch pad for Ricky's monster hit is "Mi Vida Loca," meaning 'my crazy life.' Martin was already a big record star in Puerto Rico (and NYC's Puerto Rican community) before his huge hit exploded onto the scene. First Latino Rock Superstar was 2001 Rock hall Inductee **Ritchie Valens** and "Come On, Let's Go" (#41, 9-58; #27, 11-58 R & B).

"Love Don't Cost a Thing" – Jennifer Lopez, #3, 12-2000. Yep, a Latino theme here. Parleying a come-hither vivaciousness into a bronze-medal hit takes talent, looks, and great luck. The Bronx (b. '70) actress and singer hit #1(5), 5-99 "If You Had My Love Tonight," #8, 10-99 "Waiting for Tonight," and #18, 5-2002 "I'm Gonna Be Alright." Like **Mariah Carey**, Lopez has a special enchantment for adolescent boys from 13 to 93. Any handy Mouseketeers? Two.

"Genie in a Bottle" – Christina Aguilera, #1(5), 7-99. What does lithe Christina have in common with **Britney Spears** ("Oops – I Did It Again" – #9, 4-2000)? Both are ex-Disney Mouseketeers. Covering three bases (female, Hispanic, and svelte ingenue idol), Christina and her desirable genie hit a grand-slam home run. Her #1(2), 11-99 "What a Girl Wants" and #3, 4-2000 "I Turn to You" have probably caused many a lad to forego the potential priesthood. In 1-2001, the Staten Island singer teamed with **Ricky Martin** on #13+ "Nobody Wants to Be Lonely." Christina's team of Lil' Kim and MYA hoisted her to #1, 4-2001, on **Patti LaBelle**'s #1, 70's "Lady Marmalade." More Latino NYC stars? How about #3, 9-99 "I Need to Know" and **Marc Anthony**. **Paul Simon**'s musical *The Capeman* launched NYC's Anthony (b. '69), who sold $100 seats in 2000 when other top acts were getting $35. Anthony adds strings and congas to his hang-fire tacets, with powerful results. "Bailamos" hit #1(2), 7-99 for **Enrique Iglesias**, son of international idol **Julio** (#5, with Willie Nelson, "To All the Girls I've Loved Before").

"Mambo No. 5 (A Little Bit of . . .)" – Lou Bega, #3, 8-99. In a time-warp far, far away, Bronx **Dion's** peripatetic 'Wanderer' (#2, 12-61, #10 U.K.) hopped in his car, drove around the world, tore open his shirt, and found a tattoo of ROSIE on his chest. Finally full circle, Afro-German-American **Lou Bega** presents an Afro-Cuban all-girl extravaganza from the booming *bierhalles* of Munich, Germany. The theme? **Kenny Ball & His Jazzmen**'s "I Still Love You All" [#18, UK, 4-61]. Bega leans on revered tunesmith **Perez Prado**, whose Mambos #1(10) "Cherry Pink and Apple Blossom White" and #1(1), 6-58 "Patricia" chomped the charts. Bega's globetrotting toast celebrates beautiful women everywhere – especially Sandra, Mary, Rita, Erica, Angela, Pamela, Tina, and Jessica. Lou is having a blast. He even chases girls on the rest of the album to Beluga Bay, East L. A., and yep, the Milky Way. On his *A Little Bit of Mambo* cover, Bega wears a beachside Mark Twain snazzy white suit – with a 1949 Sinatra "Wee Small Hours of the Morning" Panama hat. Bega's happy mambo suggests **Sisqo**'s #4(4), 2-2000 beach-bunny-leering anthem "Thong Song," but Bega's is much more suave.

"Belle, Belle, My Liberty Belle" – Guy Mitchell, #9, 8-51. Guy (b. Al Cernik, Detroit, 1927-99) touts a wayward lass in #4, 12-50 "The Roving Kind." As a sailor in the WWII aftermath, this American Casanova pitches wild whoopee at sweet colleens of Ireland's emerald Killarney shores, Polynesian princesses astride blue lagoons, and lovely lasses of Singapore, Paris, and Holland.

Wow! Here I was only 8, and conjuring up these fried Bali-Bali fantasies, but I was too young to understand what I was craving. After his international smooching smorgasbord, he troops dutifully back to his American 'Belle.' Astoundingly, she BUYS his story that he only LOOKED at all those curvy babes.

"Whispering" –Paul Whiteman & Orchestra, #1(11), 10-1920. Like Lou Bega, Paul Whiteman began with "Ladies and Gentlemen." "Whispering" also hit #11, 12-63 for

brother/sister act **Nino Tempo/April Stevens** (#32, 2-64 "Stardust"). It's all "Stardust." The #1 song of 1900-49, whispering stardust, rambles affectionately down through the whole century of wish-fulfillment popular music. Looking for Heaven, the winsome wisher often dreams it to be by the magic beach at Waikiki, in the lee of the big pink Royal Hawaiian Hotel in happy Honolulu.

Do I hear HAWAIIAN SECTION?

"Till I Can Gain Control Again" – Leabert Lindsey, NC, 1996. The best recent unheralded voice I've heard belongs to 6'1" 200# *paniolo* cowboy Leabert Lindsey of the Big Island, Hawaii. Fearless rodeo rider of Argentinean, and Scottish heritage, the 5th-generation Hawaiian singer/rancher/ukulele-guitarist resembles a younger Chicago Bears coach **Mike Ditka**. Lindsay's haunting tremolo and falsetto flourishes resemble THE singer **Roy Orbison**. Lindsey was playing a one-man-band gig in 1999 at the Royal Waikaloan Hotel on the Big Island's West Shore, after I did some wimp-wave surfing at Waikiki. Leabert's **Hapalaka Band** cruised the Hawaiian 80s: bass guy Roy Bucks, percussionist Mathew Philips, and Hawaiian-style **Slack Key** guitarist Marcus Wong-Yen; they offer **Jimmy Buffett** tropical-tattoo tunes like "Nice Day in Kona" and "Hawaii Misses You" recorded live at the King Kamehameha Hotel, Hawaii. Jus' Press Records (P.O. Box 6584, Kamuela, Hawaii 96743) produced Al. *Leabert Lindsey,*NC, with "Till I Can Gain Control Again" (#1, 11-82 C, **Crystal Gayle**), an absolute masterpiece. Leabert rolls down to booming Italian dramatic tenor, juggling cowboy sunset trails and sailors' lighthouses.

A friend of **Willie Nelson**, Leabert and Willie may do an album. Willie led off "'Til I Gain Control Again" with slightly-different title on Al. #27 '81 *Greatest Hits*. Personable storyteller and fantastic singer, Leabert interweaves beautiful Native Hawaiian ballads, Talking Blues, Rock Standards and originals. The Lindsey family (father Steve of Maui, brothers Bruce & Stemo, son Leejay) harks back over five generations of cowboy/*gaucho/paniolo* (Hawaiian cowboy) on the massive 225,000-acre Parker Ranch. Lindsey's prodigious vocal range fondles vibrato baritone and goose-bump falsetto. He carries on the Hawaiian falsetto tradition in Native-language "Na Alli Pualani," "Sanoe," and "Puuanahulu." On "Ahe Nani Molokai," Lindsey toys with a Swiss yodeling mastery in the boomer ballpark of **Del Shannon** or cowboy star **Gene Autry**. The best voices don't always hit #1. Yet Leabert serenades the big bulbous Hawaiian moon. Iridescent blue waves offshore sparkle magic moonglow fantasies, as Margaritaville mavens and lovers sip umbrella drinks and yearn for total togetherness.

"Walk Right Back" – Ka'au Crater Boys, NC, 1993. The Hawaiian Hit Parade has its own charts, since it's 3000 miles off the Mainland Ka'au Crater Boys and Leabert and Izzy shine there. The **Everly Brothers**, with **Crickets Jerry Allison** and songwriter/guitarist **Sonny Curtis**, hit #1(4) U.K. with this great song (#7, 2-61 U.S.) The Latino/Hawaiian connection shines through Ka'au Crater Boys

Ernie Cruz and **Troy Fernandez**. Still recording Surf Rock ["Surf"], they do sensational oldies too – with Fernandez' speed-of-light ukulele leads, and Ernie's mellow guitar on Cruz Control or Frolic Rollick mood: "Brown-Eyed Girl," "Lay Down Sally," Doobies' "Black Water," or Cascades' melodic masterpiece "Rhythm of the Rain."

"Sweet Leilani" – Marty Robbins, NC, 1992. Robbins (1925-82) recorded this 4-37, #1(10) **Bing Crosby** classic on a lost-treasure Columbia album. The great Arizonan singer/songwriter/guitarist was only 11 when this gorgeous fantasy song came to him over magic airwaves. Robbins' masterful Old Hawaii falsetto buoys his steel guitar classics: "Now Is the Hour," "Beyond the Reef," "Aloha Oe," and title tune "My Isle of Golden Dreams." Leilani is the quintessential perfect Hawaiian smiling maiden. She liberates the hassled man from laptops, dead batteries, tooth decay, snowballs, catbarf, and tax deadlines. Robbins invented Heavy Metal accidentally, pioneered the long (4:30-min) song, and united Rock and Country via his most popular Soft Rock song of all time, "Singing the Blues" ('56). He is immortalized in **Don McLean**'s #1, '71 "American Pie" with Don's 'pink-carnation' reference to his #2(1), 4-57 "A White Sport Coat (And a Pink Carnation)." And McLean's Robbins flashback album. Marty Robbins' Country Rock stardom is highlighted by his mastery of the Hawaiian musical vision. Robbins is a synonym for greatness.

"Marianne" – Terry Gilkyson & the Easy Riders, #4, 2-57. Gilkyson (1916-99) sweet-talked lovely lass Marianne with this Old Bahamas' Folk melody. These funtime Folk singers strummed acoustic destiny, surfing in **Harry Belafonte**'s Calypso wave and afterglow. A beach peach, "Marianne." Despite some unthinking blunt humor about Marianne's 'large and lovely' mom, "Marianne" is a tropic frolic and the mommy of all Surf, Parrothead, and Adult Contemporary fun & fantasy tunes.

"Living in a Sovereign Land" – Israel Kamakawiwo'ole, NC, 1996. Biggest pop singer of all time – approximately 1000+ pounds (c. 1958-97). 'Izzy' sings the Hawaiian independence rallying song, echoing vintage Jamaican Reggae with Ukulele Soul overtones. Wonderful talent: "In Dis Life" and "Starting All Over Again" are the essence of surf and sunshine. The U.S. 'appropriated' Hawaii in 1893 from Queen Liliuokalani, who WROTE Hawaiian National Anthem "Aloha Oe." The 2001 flick *Chocolat*****—with 5 Best Picture nominations, features Izzy's sensational sound. Other great Hawaiian talents include: **Amy**, Keali'l Reichel, Gary Halemau, Dennis Pavao, or Cyril Pahuinui.

Honolulu's **Robin Luke**'s #5, 8-58 "Susie Darlin'" is still the Hawaiian hit champ (see earlier entries), cresting a million records before Statehood.

"I Want It That Way" – Backstreet Boys, #6, 5-99. This Floridian fivesome spins a timeless harmonic sound, washed by worldwater waves, and woven by Barber Shop magic from the **Beach Boys**' shores to **Temptation** streetcorners of Motown or **Dion**'s Bronx Belmont Avenue. The Backstreet Boys continue a tradition of harmony that goes back to **Stephen Foster**, the American and Peerless Quartets, the **Mills Brothers**, the **Diamonds**, the Dovells, the **Miracles**. Even the **Beatles**, the **Eagles**, or the **Bee Gees**. In millennial parlance, they're a 'Boy Band.' More accurately, they're a vocal group – and no one ever faulted Motown's **Four Tops** for not playing instruments – in order to know harmony, you've GOT to have some familiarity with instrumental music.

Beware the Backstreet Backlash. Remember the 'boy-band' **New Kids on the Block**, of Donnie Wahlberg/Joey McIntyre fame (#1 '89 "Hangin' Tough")? One of the big problems of good-looking Teen Idols is their female fans' boyfriends often can't stand them. Hence, the Backstreet Boyfriend Backlash. Idols from Ricky Nelson to Bobby Sherman (#5, 8-70 "Julie, Do Ya Love Me?"), David Cassidy, Ricky Martin, and N'Sync have suffered the same bad-mouthing boyfriend rancor. The resentment has nothing to do with their music, so they put down their music anyway.

The Backstreet Boys named themselves for hometown Orlando's Backstreet Market. Personnel include **Brian Littrell, A. J. McLean, Kevin Richardson, Howie Donough,** and **Nick Carter.** "I Want It That Way" slides smoothly along on their silky harmonies, which combine dream-weaver styles of the Lettermen, the Philly-Soul Stylistics, the Association, and Lionel Richie's Commodores.

"Quit Playin' Games with My Heart" – Backstreet Boys, #2(2), 6-97. Nice interplay of hammerbeat Rap rhythms and unforgettable sweet melodies for any generation to hum. Catch their insistent 2 & 4 beats, hallmark of the Rock Revolution. Their blend murmurs an easy finger-poppin' style . By May 2000, their #4 Al. 11-99 *Millennium* hurdled the decamillion (10M) mountain (who NEEDS #1?) If you're searching for a pleasant melody, with a smoky Smokey Motown-flavored beat, catch their most-beauteous melody, #4A [Airplay] 11-97 "As Long As You Love Me." They also hammered the Top Ten with #4, 4-98 "Everybody (Backstreet's Back)," #5, 1-99 "All I Have to Give," and #6, 11-99 "Show Me the Meaning of Being Lonely." Their cardiovascular "Shape of My Heart" debuted at #39 (truly a big deal) in 10-2000 to hit #12 in four weeks. Thanks to the Backstreet Boys.

"Truly Madly Deeply" – Savage Garden, #1(2), 12-97. So here's this white Australian lad singing about bathing with this lass off the Great Barrier Reef – and sounding like the Miracles' Smokey Robinson. Maybe DeBarge. **Darren Hayes**'s hovering Irish countertenor plays off the **Ray Manzarek** style virtuoso keyboard magic of **Daniel Jones**. For Power of Melody, Savage Garden is among the most profound duos in the history of Light Metal. The Brisbane 'Blue-Eyed Soul' duo enjoyed the most popular record in Australian history. The phrase 'truly, madly, deeply' shuffles through the 1st-verse 6th line, but fans recall the song for Darren's catchy confectionery chorus – he fantasizes mountain climbing, seabathing, and lying around lovingly. Their #4, 2-97 "I Want You" debut flirts with Dylanisms of spontaneous bop prosody.

Savage Garden's album #6, 11-99 *Affirmation*, affirms their silky style. They were named for an Anne Rice vampire extravaganza novel set in Rock's other birthplace, New Orleans. Savage Garden's hit cavalcade includes #1(4), 10-99 gonzo follow-up "I Knew I Loved You," plus animalistic #19, 3-99 "The Animal Song." Somewhere in their fame and fortune, they stuffed in two trips "To the Moon and Back" [#37, 7-97, and #24, 7-98]. Essence of MELODY.

"Absolutely (Story of a Girl)" – Nine Days, #6, 4-2000; #1(1), TOP 40 Tracks, *Billboard;* #2, Adult Top 40; #2(2), HOT 100 Recurrent Airplay [11-2000]. Also #1(2), Casey Kasem's American Top 40, July/ August 2000; #2, VH-1 Video Chart, July 2000. This may not be the catchiest song of the entire infant millennium, but then again it MAY! [Please forgive a doting dad for this hoopla]. Personally, I never discovered how to hit the high charts, but my kid did – and maybe that's what America is all about. Dreams.

It all started in the freezing bleachers on a raw 1999 December day in Blue Point, Long Island. Nine Days' lead singer **John Hampson** strode to the plate. Bases jammed. Nine Days' softball team was named for a bar named for **Wilson Pickett**'s classic #23, 11-66 "Mustang Sally" [#6 R&B]. Mustang Sally's was playing for the League Championship. Game on the line. Down 11-9, last inning. A blue wind flicked snow flurries over the suffering December diamond grass. "Casey at the Bat" revisited. With his Mickey Mantle grin, 6'1", 175# Hampson cracked a monster grand-slam home run that sent the hapless centerfielder to swim Long Island Sound to Connecticut pursuing the flyaway softball. As I sat there with his teammates Tom Ozorow, George Murray, Andy Williams, John's brother Keith Solomito, and my left-fielder son **Jeremy Dean**, the snappy snow squall wafted me back to the soft sweetheart surf of Old Honolulu. I always knew theirs was a great band, but I never knew the sky was the limit to their victory.

Before Jeremy arrived as sax/keyboard pinch-hitter at their Monday night Village Pub gig in 1995, they already coalesced a bonanza of musical talent. Singer/co-lead guitarist **Brian Desveaux** plays in the same vocal ballpark as Don Henley or Bryan Adams. He writes savvy Dylanesque lyrics, and provides the hard-edged John Lennon complement to John's wow-'em-all Paul McCartney tenor and boyish smile. Then there's **Vinnie [Vince] Tattanelli,** master of rhythmic pulse – plus fill-in percussionist Dan Garvin, of SR-71, 2001. Vinnie's impish Italian smile and Zappa upper-lip mini-goatee are a fan magnet. Steady bassist **Nick DiMichino** resembles a suave young Dean Martin or Baldori. Nine Days busted the Long Island jinx – no L.I. band had a big HOT 100 hit since Dee Snider's **Twisted Sister** (Glam Heavy Metal) rampaged to angst flight song #21, 7-84 "We're Not Gonna Take It." No top ten in over two decades. The knock was a lack of original material in this 5-million-people Cover Band Land of bungalows, hi-ranches, maxi-malls, and Rambha's Wendy's cuisine. Even Nine Days, while pur-

suing their originals, had an Omnipop cover band called **Wonderama**, starring figureful blonde lead singer **Jill Paisano** (a//k/a **Jill Gioia**). Wonderama traveled the Tri-State circuit into a make-a-living profitable enterprise, gigging five nights a week. Indeed, Wonderama appeared on national TV (1998, "The View") as back-ups for Partridge Family teen idol **David Cassidy** [1(3), '70 "I Think I Love You"]. Our son Jeremy took the modest fee and bought cat food for our (now) two grandcats Ikey and Homey, since Jeremy married Kristen Cahill in 2000.

Jeremy's mom and I spent many a late weeknight at the Bitter End on Bleecker Street in the Village. We clapped vociferously as record exec moguls from Arista, EMI, Virgin, Columbia, or Reprise eased in for Nine Days' showcasing – showcasing means playing a few good tunes and hopefully impressing moguls to whip up the c'mere-kid-gonna-make-you-a-star contract. **Bob Dylan** and myriad later stars played the Bitter End. One night I was overjoyed they'd been wooed by Arista and RCA. Somebody offered them $250,000 to sign. When my band the Night Shift/Woolies serenaded the frozen 1963 Michigan hall-party nights, that would have been a king's ransom. "GREAT, Jeremy," I hollered with hallelujah happiness for him – "Congratulations on signing!" "We didn't sign, Dad. We turned it down . . ." It took us three weeks of absolutely puzzled befuddlement to realize they were right. When the offer came from Sony, now a part of the Columbia/Epic system, it was bigger and stronger. One strong part included **Pearl Jam**'s 10-million-seller Al. #1(1), 5-94 *Vitalogy* producers – Brendan O'Brien and Nick DiDia. Many good bands sign big contracts, but Nine Days' contract was accompanied by a miracle.

Just before this final showcase (of maybe 7-10 showcases), Jeremy was blindsided by a drunk driver as he tried to return home at 4 a.m. from a Woodbury gig. His '86 Chevy Blazer flipped in the crash. When we nervously arrived at the hospital as the doc stitched up a minor wound, Jeremy whispered, "Thanks, Dad – the seatbelt you made me wear as a kid maybe saved my life, the officer said." The hit-run bombed driver sputtered homeward, but his perforated radiator geysered him into a long, wobbly hike. The crash scene turned up his calling card – his license plate fell off. A week later insurance folks wangled Jeremy a HUGE new Blazer. Now a week later, noble Jeremy in great pain did yeoman service with sax and stormy keyboards – to showcase and sign. Walking Wounded Dept: drummer Vinnie's ankle was badly sprained from tripping on a slosh of beer in some pub. That Bitter End bitter night, Nine Days was only about 6.75 Days. They played their hearts out though, and Tricia I. and the loyal Nine Days roving fan contingent supported them with screaming and jumping after every number. I never found out whom the head honchos and gonzo kahunas were, but somebody saw something and Nine Days signed with Sony 550.

Their new song "Absolutely" was sneak-previewed to Modern Rock Tracks stations first, off their Sony album *The Madding Crowd* (named after Thomas Hardy novel). "Absolutely" won Best New Song at some major DJ/Program Director (PD) convention. It hit so fast they couldn't hold it down on the Modern Rock Tracks chart alone. The big HOT 100 sang its super siren song. John sang lead, Brian on thirds harmony up top in the 2nd verse. "Absolutely" debuted the big chart at #87 in April 2000. For your numerical pleasure, here is its trajectory to the peak position: #87, #71, #59, #52, #39, #34, #26, #18, #14, #11, and then a big leap to apex #6. I think if Sony would have released a cheap $2.99 single like **Vertical Horizon**'s or Savage Garden's, Nine Days might have won #1 on the HOT 100. As is, it hit #1 on *Billboard's Top 40 Tracks* [#1, Airplay]. For one glorious week in August 2000, "Absolutely" was #1 in America in Airplay, and held #1(2) on Casey Kasem's "American Top 40" radio show that blankets the world. This is the same band, like Everyband, that played the smoky pub scene for years to "Lodi" crowds of fifty friends and fifty other midnight ramblers who wandered into the bar and stayed for the great sound. The guys worked as forklift driver, machinist, pizza delivery-person, or student by day, rockers by night.

Jeremy is the only piano player I've seen whose feet fly higher than his hands while he plays, and he HITS the RIGHT notes (see video "If I Am"). He also designed *The Madding Crowd* CD surrealistic blue-green cover. Granted, it didn't hurt for Sony to choose Nine Days. In 1998, Richard Campbell sliced up the record corporate pie: 1) MCA/Universal/Polygram/A&M/Geffen—22.7%; 2) Sony/Columbia/Epic – 18.3%; 3) Time-Warner/Atlantic/Elektra – 17.9%; 4) Independents (combined) – 15.9%; 5) EMI/Capitol/Virgin – 13.3%; 6) Bertelsmann/Arista/BMG/RCA – 11.9%. With all the recent mergers and acquisitions, the sad-but-true adage may be: "Get big or get out." So hey, this girl looks very sad in photographs.

"Absolutely" has instant appeal to any girl who ever had a mood. It's ostensibly about John's girlfriend Teresa. At Nine Days concerts, it's sometimes hilarious. The Smiley Smile Phenomenon. Some kids, with mugs surly and gothic, suddenly become transformed into grinning bobbysoxers as John sings about when this girl SMILES. When he hits the SMILE tacet, suddenly nearly every girl in the place busts out in a big happy howdy smile.

As "Absolutely" crested, they were featured in *People, Seventeen, Rolling Stone, Billboard, Teen,* and scores of other fanzines and rockmags. They toured *Regis, Craig Kilborn,* and *VH-1's The List* with **John Travolta**. They were actually asked to sit down with **Jay Leno** on the *Jay Leno Tonight Show.* Leno features the greatest band talent on earth, as **Johnny Carson** or **Steve Allen** did before him. Very few bands are invited to sit down with America's host and kibbutz with bandleader Paul Shaffer. Nine Days shared the stage with Britney Spears, the Backstreet Boys, Bon Jovi, the Baha Men, Vertical Horizon, Metallica, and other groups. They played **President George W. Bush**'s Jan. 2001 Inauguration and met the Presidential family. It's a fast-lane jolt from the Mustang Sally's to the Village's Bitter End to the Big Apple's Madison Square Garden (and it couldn't happen to a nicer band).

Every band on Long Island won a major victory when Nine Days busted the jinx. It's not simply our kid's hit record. It is YOUR hit record, too. You chose it to brush the #1 spot for your magic millennial summer. From the bottom of our hearts, thank you.

This is America. John Hampson's stepdad Mike Solomito has been just as kind and supportive as Beach Boys' dad Murry Wilson was overbearing, ultra-competitive, and yet well-meaning in helping them to stardom. Brian and Vinnie's folks, and Nick's wife Gina have also helped immeasurably. Personally, my own "Johnny B. Goode" dream got sidetracked. However, the magic of America still shines: YOU might miss the big time, but your KID has a chance. My kid is famous on stage and website, though he's still working on 'rich' [recording/video costs, entourage fees, bus gas, studio time, blah blah]. Jeremy is very rich in one thing besides just globetrotting adventure – he is a great kid with a great mate and everybody loves him anyhow, whether his record is #6 or #606 or #0-Zilch. You are happy to see the good kids succeed. It means somebody did something right. Maybe we all did.

"Smooth" – **Santana, #1(12), 7-99.** Comeback 'kid' **Carlos** (53) tossed a torrid toro tune into the arena of longest Rock and Roll hits of all time: Maybe this is #1. Maybe it's Salsa Rock or Lite Rock. Matchbox 20's **Rob Thomas** spins his baritone vocal magic – on this clever #1 Al. *Supernatural,* which features many great guest artists for Santana's guitar magic to perform with. Matchbox 20 hit #3A [Airplay] on 10-97 "3 AM" and #5A 6-97 on "Push." Not-too-shabby album slate features superstars like **Dave Matthews, Eric Clapton, Lauryn Hill, Wyclef Jean, Eagle-Eye Cherry,** and **Rob.** Carlos Santana was born 7-20-47 in Autlan de Navarro, Mexico. In his July '99 *Rolling Stone* interviews he said "You validate your existence with sound."

Pop Staples (1917-2000, Rock Hall '99) and the **Staple Singers** hit #1(1), 4-72 and #1(4) R & B with "I'll Take You There." Staple Singers hit with #1(1), 10-75 "Let's Do It Again," a double-entendre title for this family Gospel R & B crew. Pop played the guitar. Everybody sang.

"If You Knew Susie" – **Eddie Cantor, #1(5), 7-25.** This Susie rocked Vaudeville venues of yesteryear with Eddie (1892-1964) until his Beatlemania sunset. Charismatic singer/comic Cantor starred on *Jimmy Durante Show,* rolling his big eyes and high-stepping with top hat and tails like Fred Astaire/Gene Kelly. Forerunner of all those Susie Darlin's and Suzie Babies and Peggy Sue's, Eddie's swashbuckling Charleston beat really did ROCK! All it needed was Les Paul's solid-body axe to bring down the house. Cantor's chart toppers included girls' names: #1(5), 2-1921 "Margie," and "No, No, Nora," of #1(2), 11-23.

"Silver Thunderbird" –**Marc Cohn, #63, 8-91.** Cohn's (b. Cleveland) ode to his favorite American car portrays a steely T-Bird. He's better known for full-throttled growl of #13, 3-91 "Walking in Memphis," which chases the spirit of Elvis strolling down midnight avenues (see Alan Jackson).

In the Vintage Blues department, how about **Bo Diddley**'s NC '75 Reverse Cover Version of **Buddy Holly's** "Not Fade Away"? Hall of Famer Bo ('87, Buddy '86) actually cut the song that Buddy wrote to celebrate Bo's own "Bo Diddley Beat." The **Grateful Dead** recorded "Not Fade Away" as early as 1965. On "Heart Full of Soul" (#9, 7-65, #2 U.K.), **Yardbirds** flaunt the Bo Diddley/Muddy Waters Delta Blues tradition. Keith Relf sings lead, with a triumvirate of firebrand guitarslingers never equaled: **Eric Clapton, Jimmy Page, Jeff Beck.**

The biggest hit (#1[15] or so of 1850) was "Oh, Susanna" – by **Stephen Foster**. It sparked the FIRST Gold Rush, at Sutter's Mill, California, in 1949 or so. As with many magnificent musicians, he was dragged by the bottom of a bottle away from the 40th birthday cake he never got to enjoy. **David Small** illustrates that President U.S. Grant (1869-77) said he knew only two tunes—"One is 'Yankee Doodle,' and the other isn't."

"You'll Be in My Heart" – Phil Collins, #21, 7-99; #1(9), Adult Contemporary. Melodic triumph for this Collins Disney movie theme. Pure tune scorches the azure skies with harmonic majesty. It's doomed, I hope, to become a timeless classic. What more could a beautiful melodious song want? A Grammy Award, maybe: 2000 Best Song in Cinema Award. Chorus cascades. Just one really cool song. Bravo, Phil. Nice guys finish first.

***Wide Open Spaces* – Dixie Chicks, Al. #4, 1-98.** Ten million buyers. Like the Bangles before them in pop-rock panorama, Dixie Chicks womped platinum album barriers with sweet tunes. **Natalie Maines** and sisters **Martie Seidel & Emily Robison** carried blonde cheerleader sound worldwide – blurring once-insurmountable barrier between HOT 100 and Country music. Natalie's pop Lloyd Maines is a Lubbock Texas bassist who gigged with Jerry Lee Lewis, Conway Twitty (#28, 1-59 "The Story of My Love"), and Lubbock's **Joe Ely**'s Flatlanders (info Bill Griggs). **Chicks**' checks came from singles (mostly #1 C): #27, 11-99 "Cowboy Take Me Away," eponymous #41, 9-98 "Wide Open Spaces," and #60 3rd-week 3-2001 "If I Fall You're Going Down with Me."

"You Make Me Wanna" – Usher, #2(7), 8-97. With Jagged Edge, Usher ushered in a rare 2 – 1 – 2 run of chart stardom with #1(2), 11-98 "Nice and Slow." Chattanooga's Babyface protégé Usher Raymond (b. '78) followed with #2(3) "My Way" to three-way triumph.

Chumbawamba's #6, 9-97 "Tubthumping" nudges pinnacle with this combo Rap/Rock rampager. Lax on church-approved language, it sings of dusting yourself off after a muddy pitfall. Plucky, feisty, resilient. A 98% fun Brit bar band song, marred by hangovers.

"Last Kiss" – Pearl Jam, #2(1), 5-99. Ironic. Pearl Jam's biggest hit. After "Given to Fly's" #21, 1-98 chart hike, **Eddie Vedder** and crew dredged up #2, too, 1964 Graveyard Rock classic for Texan **J. Frank Wilson and his Cavaliers**. In the dark mode of **Mark Dinning**'s "Teen Angel" (#1, '60), Vedder soars to Wilson's tenor. He etches a bleak pre-seatbelt car crash scenario. Wilson's #54, 11-64 Al. *Last Kiss* album cover was ridiculously sanitized – poor doomed girl was thrown out, hits tree, no

blood. She looks sweetly asleep with hair not even mussed. In today's *Pulp Fiction* bloodreel, one can only imagine some *Creepshow* abattoir of grisly meat-rack monstrosities scraped off the shrieking pavement with a spoon.

Even today the highway is still the monster. The sorrowful singer ponders living a good life from now on – to join his martyred girlfriend in Heaven. With Vedder's slightly altered lyrics, the tragedy still stuns us. **Edgar Allen Poe** believed the most poetic lyrical topic was the death of a beautiful young woman. Poe, like Jerry Lee Lewis, married his 13-year-old cousin. Poe's child bride soon died of a fever, as poetically vignetted in his "Annabel Lee," melodized by Harry Belafonte in 1958. It is amazing a sentimental 1964 melodrama such as "Last Kiss" could affect 1999. Maybe we're not so hardboiled as some surmise.

"Won't Get Fooled Again" – Who, #15, 7-71. Colleague Joe Baldesarre of Boise State says, "For subject matter, power, composition, prowess, and vocal harmony, topped off with a modulation of the fourth, no other rock song compares." **Pete Townshend**'s staccato guitar attack batters serenity into oblivion.

Professor Alan Black of Midwestern State in Wichita Falls, Kansas, finds similar excitement in #1(1), 12-74 instrumental "Pick Up the Pieces" (#5 R&B) by the AWB (**Average White Band**). The Scottish Soul group's Funk sound features Alan Gorrie and saxman Malcolm Duncan. I recall watching Seth Meidenman and Candace King & the Soul Shakers. Hot rain spattered the big outdoor tent, and hot licks serenaded frenzied dancers underneath the summer storm. Our great memories often stem from great songs.

Though **Percy Heath** played stand-up bass for the **Modern Jazz Quartet** (MJQ), I remember him best, though, talking deep-sea fishing, via my friend John Conner (fastest age 60+ indoor mile in world, 5:17). Heath is Jazz royalty, but fishing is his other great love.

"How Do I Live?" – LeAnn Rimes, #2(4), 6-97. 55+ weeks on HOT 100. Young Country diva crosses over to passionate ballad. She also reprised **Debby Boone**'s #1(10) 70s "You Light up My Life" to #34, 9-97. In 10-99, her "Big Deal" hit #23, followed by #71+, 9-2000 "You Can't Fight the Moonlight."

Sade's (pron. 'SHAH-DAY') "Never As Good As the First Time" hit #20, 3-86 (#8 R&B). Her best may be #5, 3-85 "Smooth Operator," according to Ariel Oringer. Sade is an Afro-English Jazz Soul singer from London and Ibadan, Nigeria. Born Helen Adu, she also scored #5, 11-85 on "The Sweetest Taboo."

***My Own Prison* – Creed, Al. #1, 1998.** Lead singer **Scott Stapp** carved musical destiny out of a shoestring budget. It's rumored this album cost them a mere $5000, and sold four million copies by late 1999. Their Wind-Up label wound them all up to pocket the profits and stamp out tycoons. Not bad for a Christian-oriented rock band. Their first album single "One" hit #70, 2-99. With a big baritone that beelines into your consciousness, Stapp steals the show. Adorned in leather pants, he simulates the charisma of Eddie Vedder, or the Pogues' Shane McGowan (1986 NC "Lorelei"), and even of the rock icon Scott admires – Doors'**Jim Morrison.** Creed hails from Florida's arctic (-2° once) capital Tallahassee (Freddy Cannon's #3 '59 "Tallahassee Lassie"). Stapp's bandmates are guitarist **Mark Tremonti,** bassist **Brian Marshall,** and drummer Scott Phillips. Their dark deep-toned R & R fireworks spangle the West Florida sundown afterglow. Creed offers spiritual quests, romantic barricades. He wrestles with meaninglessness toward some epiphany of realization and faith. Their future is bright. Their Al. #1(2+), 9-99 *Human Clay* (G&M) brought us noble spiritual sagas with multiple symbolic interpretations. "Higher" took us higher:

"Higher" – Creed, #7, 9-99. "Higher" is among the most universally-spun, heavy-rotation hit records in the history of popular music. Essentially a 1993 Seattle Grunge sound, its nimble spokesman **Scott Stapp** named his Creed Christianity and his son Jagger. When Don McLean asked whether we believed in Rock and Roll, Scott took the higher ground. He rolled the stones of righteousness for his first-born. Buddy Holly gave one-tenth of his R & R revenue to his Baptist church in Lubbock, Texas. Stapp comes by his zeal honestly in his pursuit of Rock icons, despite a little teenage rebellion against his minister father's message.

Donning black-and-white leather chic, with a two-strap t-shirt, Stapp offers a world-view hurdling back to the best musical moods of maestro **Ray Manzarek** of the **Doors. Stapp** even echoes the bullwhip baritone groan of classic **Jim Morrison.** His invitation to take the girl HIGHER is blatantly reminiscent of the flaming forges of urban pandemonium that stalked the 60s home front – in the wake of Vietnam and the Doors' eerie and smoldering #1(3), 6-67 "Light My Fire." With America and Southeast Asia awash in purging flames, it's no wonder pilgrims climbed 'higher' on woozy quasi-legal 'trips.' Maybe it's only love that gets Jagger's dad tuned into the cosmic wavelength toward the mountaintop. Creed's "With Arms Wide Open" shoulders the same uplifting theme. It set a record recently claimed by **Vertical Horizon**'s "Everything You Want" (2-2000) – longest-ever on charts before climbing to #1. It took Creed over half a year. Creed's inspirational "With Arms Wide Open" video shows a quixotic combo of Jim Morrison/Doors' tonality – and a resurrection of faith. Hot band.

Though Metalmongers **Stryper** (#23, 11-87 "Honestly") combined Christianity with Metal, and Evangelical Christian Crooner **Pat Boone** made a 1997 Metal album for kicks, Florida's Creed went out on a Seattle limb into the grey Grunge gloom, to resurrect fervent hope in their cloudy minor-key motif.

"Bent" – Matchbox 20, #1, 3-2000. Rob Thomas endures a litany of abuse on his VH-1 hike. This questionable neighborhood zaps him with the slings and arrows of outrageous reality. He tells the world how scared he is, but faces up to his trouble. "Bent" too crested six months later on his silky sandpaper sound. Matchbox 20? Kyle Cook and Adam Gaynor play guitars, with Paul Doucette drumming and Brian Yale bassing. "If You're Gone" clambered up from debut #52 (10-21-2000), rose to #5, and still held #8 in March 2001.

Kid A **– Radiohead, Al. #1, 10-2000.** Assembled at England's prestigious Oxford University, Radiohead features singer **Thom Yorke** and brothers Colin on bass and Jon on guitar (he has no brother named 'New'). Eddie O'Brien puncutates silence with his guitar, while Phil Selway punches drums (Whitburn info). Their major American hit is #34, 6-93 "Creep." Erica Wagner wishes they'd ditch this **Kid A** Techno-MIDI phase, and return to R & B guitar-powered roots.

The Miseducation of Lauryn Hill **– Lauryn Hill, Al. #1, 1998.** She began as a Jersey girl. Lauryn's experience with **Fugees** launched supernova songs like "Superstar" or #1(2), 11-98 off the album as single "Doo Wop (That Thing)." "Ex Factor" hit #21, 1-99.

Her friend **Mary J. Blige** hit #2(2), 1-96 with "Not Gon' Cry." Yonkers' Soul diva reached hottest highest heights with this *Waiting to Exhale* Whitney Houston flick song. Mary scored #3, 5-95 with Method Man on #7 '68 Marvin Gaye classic, "You're All I Need to Get By." Mary's #12, 3-2002 "Rainy Dayz's" weather forecast, for hometown Yonkers, NY, differs from Sheryl Crow's surf's-up California #28+, 4-2002 "Soak Up the Sun."

Undertow **– Tool, Al. #50, 7-93.** Hollywood Punk band, Tyler Harris fave. Supersonic drums via Danny Caney, vocals. French-American Paul D'Amour, bass; Maynard James Keenan, and Adam Jones, guitar.

"Why Don't You Get a Job?" is by **Offspring (#74, 4-99).** Singer Brian 'Dexter' Holland, guitar-slasher 'Noodles' Wasserman, and crew obliterate the sounds of silence. Beyond Speed Metal, Punk Rock is the logical destiny of protest music.

"Crush" – Dave Matthews Band, #75, 2-99. Dave made it to Charlottesville, Virginia, by way of New York City and South Africa [hmm, a white Afro-American?]. Protesting the apartheid segregation system in South Africa, he gravitated to University of Virginia and a fiddle-sax-bass-drums-guitar Fusion Profusion band. From #2(1), 5-96 *Crash* album, Dave scrunched to "Crush." No other band sounds quite like they do. Matthew's eclectic magic reflects the musical expertise of his great integrated Anglo-American band. Matthews' baritone murmurings tread upon topics profound, unique, and passionate. In "So Much to Say," he ponders the conception of Hell as being his closet, and Heaven being up in the sky, and offering central heat (isn't Hell supposed to provide free heat, too?). Harps, anyone?

"Unchained Melody" – Gary Garritan, NC, 1994. From Al. *Heavenly Love Songs,* NC, 1994. New Age soothing harp music. Transcendental Easy Rock style. Born Gary Garritano ('55, Patchogue, New York), Gary is among the foremost ELECTRIC harpists, with over 25 harps – many of which he either invented or constructed. Another famous New Age guru of sweet calming music is *Entertainment Tonight's* host, 6'5" marathon runner **John Tesh**. Born '52 on Long Island, Tesh joined Colorado Symphony Orchestra for sandstone tribute of 3-95, #54 *Live at Red Rocks. Unchained Melody* contains heavenly versions of "Love Me Tender," "Wind Beneath My Wings," and "Always on My Mind." Hyping his homegrown album from P.O. Box 400, Orcas Island, WA 98280, on late-night Seattle-area TV, Gary has sold over 100,000 of these gorgeous CDs. New Age music often dabbles in Taoism, Zen Buddhism, Baha'i, the occult, astrology, Druidic/Celtic magic (see Enya w/ Loreena McKennitt), or Transcendental Meditation. Gary credits wife Marianne, plus mom and kids for inspiration. If you like John Denver's cathedral Colorado mountains, Maui waterfalls, and majestic sunrises, catch these melodies Unchained.

"Four Strong Winds" – Ian and Sylvia, NC, 1963. How their magnificent Folk ballad never hit the charts eludes us. One of the prettiest harmonic-duo tunes ever written, eh? **Ian** (b. '33, Victoria, B.C.) and **Sylvia** (b. '40, Chatham, Ontario) **Tyson** stormed Canadian charts, and hit #115 Al. 9-63 *Four Strong Winds*. Gorgeous album cut of tune by **Searchers** (Al. #149, *The Searchers* #4) on cusp of Folk Rock. Song sings of the cold blue winds of high Alberta. Fearful of those killer winds, I put my wife and infant on the plane from Vancouver to Detroit, and took our mini-lab dog Snarf (a/k/a Snarfi Sue, 1966-84). The Rock Jock from Calgary said the temp was minus 32 degrees Fahrenheit, and the 40 mph NW gale brought us a wind chill of -111 degrees. I'll never forget the look on my noble, trusting, and sympathetic dog's woebegone face. She glowered at me as if to say, "I can't believe this. . . why don't you drive south to North Dakota, where it's a subtropical twenty below?" But sarcasm was never Snarf's forte. She'd agree with Ian that winds, yes, do blow very cold far out there on the December subarctic prairies. Where were the HOT 100 charts when the poor song froze its tail off? Other great versions are by Toronto's **Neil Young** (#61, 9-79), and **John Denver** (album cut on last album, '98 *Forever*).

"When You and I Were Young, Maggie" –Frank Stanley & Corinne Morgan, #4, 9-1905. Oldie back THEN, dating to at least 1863, maybe before. An old mossy mill signals nostalgia. Seeing silver threads among her golden hairs, and lamenting their lost precious time, the semi-young guy declares his fading sweet older lady is just as 'fair' to him this day as when they enjoyed youth's bloom. Whether he's myopic, a sweet-talkin' guy (Chiffons' #16, 5-66), or simply sincere about the love of his life, he sure makes her happy. Isn't that what music should do? Nice '75 reprise by locally popular Scottish tenor **Sydney Devine** (*Live, at Glasgow*) delivered with power, passion, and schmaltz.

Deep bass **Frank Stanley** (1869-1910) and tenor **Henry Burr** (1882-1941), leaders of **Peerless Quartet**, also scored with #2(4), 8-1907 "Red Wing (An Indian Fable)." It suggests the **Big Bopper**'s #1 song for **Johnny Preston**

of 10-59, Graveyard Rock's "Running Bear" (two Indian lovers drown in raging stream), without the goshawful tragedy. Hockey fans of the **Detroit Red Wings** will be semi-overjoyed to know this original-6 franchise took its name from THIS popular song – an oldie way back when the NHL was formed, long before the 1946-80 heyday of Mr. Hockey, **Gordie Howe**.

"(God Must Have Spent) A Little More Time on You" – N'Sync, #8, 12-98. Also #29, 5-99 on same-song duo with **Alabama**. Sampling suave Boyz II Men Motown magic, and champ rep of townmates the Backstreet Boys of Orlando, Florida, N'Sync presents an irresistible 'Boy Band' sound. Their interweaving harmonies suggest the Temptations or Beach Boys. N'Sync blitzed the #1 bugaboo with #1, 1-2000 "Bye, Bye, Bye." They silver-medaled on #2, 9-99 "Music of My Heart." **Justin Timberlake** is the lead singer with the thick curly hair, and he's flanked by melodic pals **Josh Chasez, Lance Bass, Joey Fatone**, and **Chris Kirkpatrick**. N'Sync's Blue-Eyed Soul is among smoothest, most popular sounds of the 2001 era. Their #1 Al. *Master of Puppets,* 3-2000 nabbed 10 million fan-buyers. They add a tight musical blend to their fanmag Teen Idol smiles. CUTE still works. Singer/songwriter Timberlake's "Pop" with N'Sync debuted at #29, 6-2001.

"Independent Women – Part I" – Destiny's Child, #1(11), 9-2000. Speaking of cute, how about really, really glamorous? Twiggy's 1967 miniskirts never really shone like Destiny's Children: **Beyonce Knowles, Michelle Williams,** and **Kelly Rowland** of Houston. Specializing in a sound-surround of tight counterpoint harmonies, this curvaceous rotating crew of Soul singers keeps the guys awake with their rainbow melodic swirl and hip Rap chat intertwined. Hip-Hop hip hep hopping hits. Triptych of tremendous talent. Their first #1 was #1(1), 6-99 "Bills, Bills, Bills" (fan's lament about Buffalo's NFL football team). Destiny's Child's passionate pitter-patter is a double-whammy audial and visual delight. They lambasted the quietude with #1(3), 11-99 "Say My Name," and #3 follow-up "Jumpin' Jumpin" of 4-2000. Destiny's Kid, courting Rock and Soul destiny, grooves to double/triple-word titles: like their double-"Jumpin'" and triple-"Bills" hits, plus #3, 11-97 "No No No (Part II)." See **Beach Boys**' #8, 11-64 "Dance, Dance, Dance" and #5, 2-64 "Fun, Fun, Fun." Named for a dog-eat-dog wilderness TV show, Destiny's "Survivor" #2(3+), 3-2001. Destiny Emeritus singers? **LaTavia Roberston** and **LaToya Luckett**.

Destiny's Child is like **Whitney Houston** triplets, (#4, 9-99 "My Love Is Your Love"). Her #2(3), 12-98 "Heartbreak Hotel," with **Faith Evans**, and Kelly Prince, mixes Rap with a twiny, twisty melody. The first "Heartbreak Hotel" doled out cobwebs and ghastly despair, and it was a lot of fun – thanks to the jolly-roger crew who punted no-beat music back to the Happy Snoozing Ground:

"Heartbreak Hotel" – Elvis Presley, the Jordanaires, Bill Black, Scotty Moore, D. J. Fontana, and Hoyt Axton's mom Mae Axton, #1(8), 3-56; #3 R & B; #1(17), C; #2, 5-56 U.K. We're on a cooperative kick here. So often the solitary moniker **ELVIS PRESLEY** masquerades as a solo production of a teenage ultra-idol. It was really a COMMITTEE of stars who created this blockbuster hit. To make the Memphis Sun studio vet feel at home in the Big Apple RCA studios, first they furnished the franchise lad with an A-1 Gospel group – the **Jordanaires: Neal Matthews** (d. 2000), **Louis Nunley, Duane West, Ray Walker,** and main man **Gordon Stoker.** Then **Bill Black** comically plunked bull-fiddle bass, and **Scotty Moore,** Lucky Strike sparking his guitar pegs, flashed flaming rockabilly riffs. D. J. Fontana thumped the drums. To perk up the Lonely Street scenario, Hoyt's mom **Mae Axton** penned this super sad song. The main happiness at Mae's dark wayside inn is that it created the international career of the most popular entertainer of the 20th century – **Elvis Presley** (1935-77). The **Jordanaires'** 1992 Gospel album contains a spirited version of **John Newton**'s #1, 1803 hit "Amazing Grace." **Floyd Cramer**'s piano is another highlight.

"Up Above My Head" – Frankie Laine and Johnnie Ray, NC, c. 1956. Both booming belters bellowed their best on this **Rosetta Tharpe** Gospel classic (NC '48; #6, 12-48 R&B). Full title? "Up Above My Head, I Hear Music in the Air." Laine and Ray, though unsuccessful, started a duet trend with a Gospel feel.

"Just Walkin' in the Rain" – Johnnie Ray, #2(1), 9-56. Big Ray Rock Era blockbuster was no washout. This one inspired **Del Shannon**'s *Gold Rush* extravaganza, #1(4), 3-61 "Runaway." J. Ray splashed morosely down the boulevard of his broken dreams , with no fun Gene Kelly 'Singin' in the Rain" (#1, '29 'Ukulele Ike' – Cliff Edwards) to paint a happy face. When Shannon drifts off his **Am – G – F – E7** downward chord spirals, he bellows that he's 'walkin' in the rain,' so Ray's TITLE becomes Del's lyric. All along Del's lonesome hike in the Grand Rapids ghost-gloom, the drizzle dapples his face. His lyric honors Johnnie Ray's song verbatim. For Del and all of us, though, it's not the RAIN that stings; it's what we THINK and FEEL about the RAIN! Del plods the solitary highway, impervious to others' stares. He is lost in memories. Ray frets what people think as they draw their drapes and stare at the soggy solo rainwalker.

Del's classic is one of the top ten Rock songs of all time. Ray's has been sadly forgotten. Del's "Runaway"? Regrets fly fast and free down the nevermore highway. "Runaway" is the International Anthem of All Lovers Who Have Been Unceremoniously Dumped (see Gloria Gaynor's "I Will Survive").

"Runaway" never will run away. This ode to brooding and worrying will spin on. It won't escape our timeless airwaves. There have been too many everyman/everywoman Del Shannons, sharing their romantic lost tears with the eternal drizzle. In Johnnie's silver-medal song, people gaze at the drenched dude, shake their heads and ask the musical question: "Who IS that romantic fool?" Despite wearing a hearing aid, Ray bridged the Crooner-to-Rock no-man's land. If regret is the flipside of love, we sure have a lot of great songs to celebrate our misery and gloom. Brood on.

"Get Together" – Jesse Colin Young & the Youngbloods, #62, 9-67, and #5, 6-69. During the darkest dregs of the Vietnam War, countertenor Jesse and Youngbloods admonished us from their Boston pulpit to get together and to smile on all our brothers. It became the official song of the National Council of Christians and Jews. Young's terrific tenor begged a warring world to pick up Jesus' amazing-grace message of peace on earth, good will to men. **Lowell 'Banana' Levinger** and **Jerry Corbitt** interwove haunting guitars to Youngblood's deep bass guitar pulse. **Joe Bauer** skillfully drummed. Merged with his Youngblood troupe, Young's young message is dynamic and profound. Love, he says, is just a song that we all sing. Fear, he warns, is the way people die. Can a song stop a holocaust?

Our entire parade of popular music recognizes the GENIUS of the INDIVIDUAL SPIRIT to write and perform the greatest all-time classics. Without COOPERATION of millions of great musicians, without artistic compromise and nifty networking, none of these great songs would have materialized. When we drift back to the sacrosanct Rock Hall Class of '86, we realize no one on their list is not great:

"Together Again" – Ray Charles, #19, 3-66; #19, 4-66, R & B; NC, C. Jazz documentarian Ken Burns (PBS 2001) says Ray helped invent SOUL. Ironically, Charles and **Stevie Wonder** didn't see color barriers, due to the disability of blindness. Charles helped reconstruct one of America's great treasures: Country music. "Together Again" hit #1(2) C (NC, HOT 100) in 4-64 For Texan **Buck Owens**. It chronicles the joy felt when lovers are reunited.

"Play Together Again Again" – Buck Owens and Emmylou Harris, NC, 1979; #11, 5-79 C. When I buy *USA Today* I often say, "I'd like this *USA Today* today." Sometimes someone laughs. Great song title, anyhow. Buck's #25, 1-65 and #1(5) C "I've Got a Tiger by the Tail" is a great plug for Detroit Tiger fandom. Let's put this stuff back together again. In the wise words of Mr. William Joel of Long Island, "It's Still Rock and Roll to Me."[All this stuff interconnects].

"Give Me Just One More Night (Una Noche)" – 98 Degrees, #2, 8-2000. Hit formula? Take a handsome, marketable Boy Band with Latino salsa connections. Add fiesta fanfare. Take a Spanish title that translates into Elvis's most dangerous song (#4, 11-58 "One Night" [*Una Noche*]). Mix in the ever-popular NUMBERS name, like 3 Doors Down, Matchbox 20, Blink 182, 112 (#6, 11-2000 "It's Over Now"). The main ingredient? A super melodic tune. Result? The penultimate #2 prize, the eternal Next Best Thing.

"Cotton Fields" – Odetta, NC, 1963. Spike Lee's dad Bill Lee plays lone bass. We had a whole century of American popular music before *Gold Rush* even began – from 1776 "Yankee Doodle" to 1890's "Sidewalks of New York." "Cotton Fields" had a COPYRIGHT back in 1850. Odetta [Holmes, b. '30, Birmingham, AL] also features **Leadbelly**'s "Midnight Special (NC, '41) on her NC '63 Al. *One Grain of Sand.* Much of our great Folk or Blues or Gospel music was once dubbed 'Negro Spirituals.' Many evoke a brave Louis 'Satchmo' Armstrong-style grin out of almost hopeless situations like slave life and death. A grin and bear it grin. Better times ahead. A Promised Land, even. From this sweet little kid in "Cotton Fields" who rocked her elemental cradle in that long-ago faraway cotton field way back home, the steeltown 20th century exploded. We suddenly sang spirited Soul, raucous R&B, hopped up Neo-Disco Hip-Hop and 'Dance' Trax, Gospel gusto, and strident, angry Gangsta Rap. The legacy flowed from the calm Moses-style deliverance messages of **Dr. Martin Luther King, Jackie Robinson, Stevie Wonder**, and **Odetta**.

Odetta never enjoyed a HOT 100 record, nor a Top 74 album [#75 Al. 9-63 *Odetta Sings Folk Songs*]. She shunned BOTH Rock and Soul for her minimalist Gospel Blues and Folk music, using either NO accompaniment, or just bassist Bill Lee, and perhaps her acoustic guitar. Her husky, commanding contralto mesmerized a generation of Folk purists, and galvanized America's traditional music to its people. She commandeered hushed concert halls to rapt, hypnotized awe and adoration. Eminent musicologist **Samuel Charters** gets votes himself for #1 Musicologist: "Odetta made us feel that it was a privilege if we hum the melody along with her under our breaths" [liner notes, 1999, Odetta's *Best of the Vanguard Years*]. Speaking of her dominating and riveting PRESENCE, Charters chuckles that if SHE'd been captain of the Titanic, it wouldn't have sunk. [Catch her breathtaking "Battle Hymn of the Republic"]. Charters: songs we identify with Odetta "are the chants and cries that have risen out of the long travail of African Americans in the United States." Calypso icon **Harry Belafonte** wrote: "The sensitivity and belief she brings to her performances surpass even her vocal gift." Does Odetta ROCK? She does NOW (1999+). Odetta was **Janis Joplin**'s main inspiration. On Odetta's previously-unreleased gospel boomer "Make Me a Pallet on Your Floor," she thumps the underclouds of Heaven with her gusto and vocal firepower. Hall of Fame Early Influence?

"Blue Jean Bop" –Paul McCartney, NC, 1999. Off #27, 11-99 *Run Devil Run* album. This vintage **Gene Vincent** flip of his #96, 10-56 "Race with the Devil" echoes **John Lennon**'s last great album before his finale – Al. #6, 3-75 *Rock and Roll*. Rockabilly is one fountainhead of Rock. Lennon also does Vincent's #7, '56 "Be-Bop-A-Lula" and Buddy Holly's "Peggy Sue." Paul's album brings his amazing **Fats Domino** echo on "Coquette" and many other Oldies tracks of quarter-Beatle splendor.

"People" – Barbra Streisand, #5, 4-64. Diva debut. 100 miles from Rock and Roll. Great message: people who really need other folks are among the most fortunate persons on earth. How many one-man bands hit #1? Case closed. Music, almost invariably, is a group activity. Streisand sings with Sinatran phrasing, casting her fate as eventual **#5 Album Artist of all time** (Whitburn): Elvis, 15,538 pts.; Sinatra, 12,766; Beatles, 10,918; Johnny Mathis, 10,072, Barbra, 9207. Yep, she leads the Rolling Stones: 8982. On 11-11-99, unforgettable Streisand's Al. *A Love Like Ours* hugged the #21 position.

Significant Other – Limp Bizkit, Al. #1, 7-99. **Fred Durst** and Limp Bizkit shot to stardom covering George Michael's "Faith." Supposedly carrying the Rage Rock banner, they hit the high charts with Durst's raspy baritone and Rappish monologue. They tour with **Korn,** whose album *Issues* of 11-99 hit #1 with the same style. No band could be totally enraged, however, with a comedian in the crew to think up L.B.'s #1 album 11-2000 entitled *Chocolate Starfish and the Hot Dog Flavored Water.*

The Battle of Los Angeles – Rage Against the Machine, Al. #1, 11-99. Lead singer **Zack de la Rocha** combines Hard Rock, Molten Metal, and Hip-Hop into a genre their band was granted by the rock press – RAGE Rock, an offshoot of Del Shannon and the Rolling Stones' "Under My Thumb" Revenge Rock. The Irvine, CA, Chicano 'Rage Rock' perpetrator wraps the gauze of sweet love around the wild wounds of political revolution. This huge #1 album dwarfs Rage's singles salvo, like #69, 10-99 "Guerrilla Radio." By October 2000, the rage abated after raging against itself, and the band split up.

"Please Remember Me" – Tim McGraw, #10, 4-99; #1 C. We should. Son of NY Mets' pitcher Tug McGraw ('Ya gotta believe!'), Tim is also the real-life husband of American beauty **Faith Hill,** of #7, 3-98 "This Kiss" fame. Like her #6, 5-2000 "The Way You Love Me," "This Kiss" is downright adorable. When **Lonestar**'s "Amazed" hit HOT 100 #1 in March 2000, the Country coup was bolstered by Faith's #2 HOT 100 silver medalist "Breathe" – an unheard-of one-two chart punch in a field dominated by Rap scrappers and rockers.

Tim's magnificent melody and poignant lyric speak to a lover, a fan, or a friend. He simply seeks that the person he's singing to will remember him. He seeks the Singers' Holy Grail: To enchant millions with a fine song, a song that will not be forgotten.

"Save Tonight" – Eagle-Eye Cherry, #5, 12-98. Tenor Crooner and trumpeter Don Cherry, later a pro golfer, had big ballad hits like "Wild Cherry" (#29, 4-56) and #4, 12-55 "Band of Gold." Don named his 1970 Sweden-born kid EAGLE-EYE. A long generation later, Eagle-Eye invokes Kahlil Gibran's passionate wilderness combo of guy, girl, loaf of bread, and jug of wine. Tromping on tacets and asides, this tambourine-spiked tune throbs with NOW passion. An ode to 'HEDONISM LIVES!'

On her #19, 9-97 "I Do," **Lisa Loeb** dons Buddy Holly

glasses, ponders rhythmic fantasies, and she still rocks. Videos are classics. Her monstering marauder hit is #1(3), 5-94 "Stay (I Missed You)."

"All the Small Things" – Blink 182, #6, 12-99. Neo-Punk, with a side of *Mad* magazine, Blink 182's style is fast-paced, off the wall, and unique. Suggesting the **Barenaked Ladies'** off-the-cuff humor, or the Big Apple **Beastie Boys**, this San Diego un-Surf crew debuted with semi-lovely #61A, 1-98 "Dammit." Their bust-out litany of annoying dinky things is a rockin' rebel's delight in the mock seriousness that masquerades for a world. Their album title for Al. #18+, 11-99 is *Enema of the State.* Blink 182 capsizes the boat somebody told them not to rock. Roster: **Mark Hoppus,** supercharged singer/bassist; **Tom DeLonge,** guitar soloist and executioner of quietude; and **Scott Raynor,** drummer. Blink 182 simply compares their jobs to a vacuum cleaner or a lamprey, while **Eminem's** firebrand spits green gobs into folks' onion rings. Blink 182 doesn't brandish the anger. Their cosmic grudge lasts maybe seven seconds – breaking out like a sunray of San Diego surfcrest destiny.

No. 4 – **Stone Temple Pilots, Al. #3, 11-99.** San Diego also launched the elliptical Stone Temple Pilots' orbit: **Scott Weiland,** vocals; Eric Kretz, drums; Robert DeLeo, bass. STP was NOT named for your favorite gasoline additive, but as the namesake of King Kong's gorilla follow-up – *Mighty Joe Young* (flix 1949, 1997). *Album No. 4* debuted at No. 3 (yep) in 11-99. Many great new albums start with a flourish near the top – then taper off. STP singles include #59A, 1-94 "Creep," and #36A, 5-96 "Trippin' on a Hole in a Paper Heart." Another stunning 11-99 week, STP was trumped by **Dr. Dre's** *Dr. Dre—2001* at #2, **Celine Dion's** #3, 11-99 Al. *All the Way,* and champ **Korn's** instant #1.

"I'll Be Missing You" – Puff Daddy, with Faith Evans, #1(11), 6-97. Combined with its melody – the **Police/Sting's** #1(8) '83 "Every Breath You Take" – Puff Daddy's song is the longest song in history at #1, for 19 NON-simultaneous weeks. Singles just don't debut at #1. This one did. Sean 'Puffy' Combs (b. NYC, '70) does a tribute to fallen rapper **Notorious B. I. G** (and thereby rapper 2 Pac Shakur). Wrapped around **Sting** and the **Police's** melody for #1(8), '83 "Every Breath You Take," "I'll Be Missing You" was temporarily the biggest elegiac hit of all time, until **Elton John's** #1(14), 10-97 "Candle in the Wind II" became the biggest hit of ANY kind of all time. During the millennial nightclub hoopla, Puffy was hassled by John Law. Leaving a NYC hot spot with shapely **Jennifer Lopez** (#3, 12-2000, "Love Don't Cost a Thing"), Puffy was toting a pistol after someone at the club was murdered – they escaped in his white suit and white Lincoln Navigator into Manhattan's gridlock, surrounded by 10,000 cops. In the Feb. 2001 trial, Puffy was absolved of the main blame, but took a weapons rap.

"Puffy" debuted in 11-96 with prophetic (for B.I.G.) "No Time" at #18. Then to two hits that strangled the oppositon for a total of 17 weeks: #1(6), 1-97 "Can't Nobody Hold Me Down" and this elegy. "Mo Money Mo Problems" hit

#1(2), 8-97, granting him over 35% of the Year 1997 at #1 on the Big chart. Puff pulls no punches, with guitar guru **Eric Clapton** on #4, 6-98 "Come with Me" Silver-medal stuff? "It's All about the Benjamins," with **Dave Grohl, Lil' Kim, Rob Zombie,** and **Notorious B.I.G;** also #2(3), 9-99 "Satisfy You" (duo **R. Kelly**). With Mase, Puffy hit #8, 7-98 "Lookin' at Me," and with Faith Evans in 3-99, they wailed "All Night Long" to #9. A thoroughly MAJOR Rap figure, Combs also sculpts songs and produces sessions. As P. Diddy, his "I Need a Girl (Part One)" Rap/Soul song hit #2, 3-2002.

"I'll Be Missing You" shares the grand tradition of Dion's magnificent Folk-Rock "Abraham, Martin, and John" (#4, 10-68). It salutes two Kennedys, Abe Lincoln, and the most famous Afro-American of the 20th century, Dr. Martin Luther King. Puff Daddy's big tribute is for Gangsta Rapper Notorious B.I.G.:

"Hypnotize" – Notorious B.I.G., #1(3), 4-97; #1 R&B. Christopher **Wallace** (1972-97, a/k/a 'Biggy Smalls') stormed the charts with his bullhorn shoutdown style. His 'live by the sword' credo shines throughout history among other Wallaces: **William Wallace** of Scotland [see Mel Gibson in *Braveheart* ('95***½)]; and Governor **George Wallace** of Alabama, avid one-time segregationist 1968 Presidential third-party candidate – who won Motown's Michigan. During his ill-fated 1972 campaign, George Wallace was gunned down, Kennedy-style, in a garish mall, and paralyzed for life. As William Wallace died on the torture rack during the tyrannical English king's reign, so **Notorious B.I.G. WALLACE** was slain defending some amorphous Rapper turf. 'Biggy' was arrested earlier for weapons charges, robbery, and assault. On the brighter side, he married Faith Evans. When he died at 24, he left a lot of orphan hits, too: debut #27, 8-94 "Juicy," #6, 1-95 "Big Poppa," #4, 1-98 "Been Around the World," and #19 ironic *Rocky*-echo "Victory" at #19, 3-98.

Puff Daddy's elegy outsold all the fond tributes for milder martyrs who gave their lives to achieve peace and brotherhood. Indeed, in the strength of Puff Daddy's eulogy to dominate the charts over 20% of 1997, it becomes apparent that perhaps only one Man has EVER had a stronger collection of hit songs to commemorate HIS untimely passing. They are called Hymns.

"Forget Him" – Bobby Rydell, #4, 11-63. Apparently the 20th-century Rock Hall of Fame DID! Ask any kid the high school's name in *Grease,* a fab 50s fluff film with suspiciously 70s props. It is RYDELL High. **Bobby Rydell** (b. Ridarelli '42, Philly) was among the most talented of **Dick Clark's** *American Bandstand* South Philadelphia High students: **Chubby Checker, Dee Dee Sharp, Frankie Avalon,** and **Fabian** [Forte]. This gargantuan secondary school challenges the Pentagon in size. Local un-rich Italo-American or Afro-American kids zoomed to Rock and Soul stardom on combo good looks, talent, who-ya-know, and hype. The Rock press vilified and excoriated them as second-stringers. Though **Clark** made the Rock Hall in 1993, not a single one of his Teen Idol troupe has yet made the cut. It's a tough toss-up with

Chubby Checker, but if I had to take any one of these South Philly fanzine faves and teenybopper idols, I guess I'd cast my vote for Bobby Rydell. Why?

Blondest of Clark's contingent (OK, medium-brown perfect pompadour), Bobby was, like fellow BOBBY Bobby Vee, a teen idol superstar who just happened to be a nice guy who finished first. If this cool hair thing seems trivial, don't forget that **Elvis** dyed HIS medium-brown hair **BLACK – to look Italian.** Talented drummer Bobby starred on breakout venue *Ted Mack's Amateur Hour* from ages 9-12. He sang and drummed for streetcorner crew **Rocco & the Saints,** with trumpeter **Frankie Avalon** (#1[5] '59+ "Venus"). Handsome Avalon stars in Annette's *Beach Blanket Bingo* flix, and sings "Beauty School Drop-out" in movie *Grease* [whither Rocco?]. Actor Rydell starred as good kid next door (not vain teen idol 'Conrad Birdie') in film *Bye Bye Birdie* (1962***). Rydell was a major league actor, drummer, and high baritone/low tenor Rock crooner. "Forget Him" bobs between vintage Sinatra, Bobby Darin, Elvis, and Orbison. This Tango Rock tune consoles a dumped damsel. Bobby's sympathy wedge pays romantic dividends. Hmm. Sly shy guy. And in flick, Boy-Next-Door becomes Elvis. Can't beat that storybook plot. Bobby's best include: #5, 5-60 "Swingin' School," #11, 6-59 "Kissin' Time," #4, 7-60 "Volare" (#1. '58 Dominico Modugno), and Dean Martin's "Sway" to #14, 11-60. Bobby duoed with Checker on #21, 12-61 Christmas classic "Jingle Bell Rock" (Bobby Helms, #6, 12-57 et al). Bobby – don't forget him.

"To Love You More" – Celine Dion, #11A [Airplay], 5-98. This one is 18.4768% prettier than her #1(2), 2-98 "My Heart Will Go On" opus. Lush strings here flirt with pizzicato pluckings to produce an ethereal symphony. "To Love You More" twirls its gossamer harmonies around her torch-bearing soprano, with the slimmest flicker of Irene Cara's "Flashdance" melodic mood. With less roaring percussion than Cara's theme, Celine's drummer still bashes away the silence on the big 2 & 4 beats. Celine also hit gold and silver with #1(6), 3-96 "Because You Loved Me"; #1(6), 12-98 "I'm Your Angel" (w/ R&B's R. Kelly); and unique Gangsta Rap and Quebeçois Chanteuse blend with Puff Daddy – "Satisfy You" (#2(3), 9-99. Celine married manager Rene Angelil, and despite his serious illness, they had a baby in 2001.

"Little Man" – Alan Jackson, #39, 7-99; #1 C. Country Rock protest song harbors a Populist sentiment for small towns and small-store businessfolks – before the Lard-Mart, Mega-Shop, Humungo-Barn, or, (going to the dogs), Bark-It-Flea-Market vanquished the 'little man's' commercial dreams. Alan sings the cause of each outa-business grocery, gas station, hardware, and general store. All that's left of an ex-town may be the forlorn Dairy Queen, closed for winter in a snowswirl of yesterdreams.

"Sunny Came Home" – Shawn Colvin, #7, 7-97. Poor 'Sunny's' story is so dismal that even her name is sarcastic. Maybe the Song of the Year '97 Award is a slight consolation prize. It begins as an acoustic lament for the break-up of Sunny's ex-romantic situation. The melancholy melody hovers over Jazz-Rock minors and diminisheds. 'Sunny,' enveloped in shady gloom, arrives back home to her old favorite room. She lights a match, grabs a few tools, and seeks to repair her metaphorical monstrosity of a life. The listener can only imagine that Sunny toys with desperation and possible self-destruction over her lost love. With her semi-sunny brave new attitude, Sunny hikes up her courage, slings a few tools, and starts fixing up her torn life. A song that wrests hope from abject despair sings its own fine praises.

"Jersey Girl" – Bruce Springsteen, NC, 1984. Live, 7-9-81 Jersey Meadowlands concert. Super singer/songwriter Bruce turns to **Tom Waits** (b. Pomona, CA, '49, backseat of taxi) for this lyrical triumph. Flipside of #7, 8-84 "Cover Me" single. "Jersey Girl" is no regular Waits promenade through some woozy New Orleans neon fiesta, with *Folies Bergere* temptresses and red beans and rice 5-alarm dinners. First two verses stake out a tender love ballad. He forsakes the old corner gang, and hotshot avenue girls, just to share carnival Saturday night with his Jersey Girl. Down by that shore, Bruce sings. The Meadowlands explode with homeboy razzmatazz when he hits the magic word JERSEY. In this greasepaint nocturne, Bruce says nothing else matters in the wide world when you're in love with this perfect Jersey girl. The third verse shifts tone. Knocking an uninspiring job, with a morphemic backwash of 'sha-la-las' backpedaling, Bruce trolls Highways One and Nine. Life rolls out before him. Relationships dangle in quivering uncertainty. Furtive love plays out its passions in cosmic insta-dramas – a flood of laughter and tears. Despite a downer line about the Grandma Babysitting Service, and the fact we're not dealing with Cinderella and Prince Charming here, an epiphany arises above the roadhouses, peep parlors, auto parts marts, and squashed squirrels: two people madly in love transcend the mud and smoke and desolation. Their love forges a romantic order out of the chaos of toilsome labor, nowhere junkyards, dead-end dreams. She's a Jersey girl, he loves her, and nothing else really matters.

"Farmer John" – Neatbeats, NC, 11-99. At haggard Millennium Eve, a Tokyo oldies group electrified the Manhattan Skyline with their frantic good ol' Anglo-American Surfin' Rockabilly Garage-Band Soul. It's embarrassing how few Asian-American groups we've welcomed to our Black & White HOT 100 charts. At the Village's Mercury Lounge near CBGB's, the red-eye act was the **Neatbeats.** Four Tokyo rockers clad in Beatle suitcoats and burgundy trousers hit the stage in roaring applause – and its teardown-the-amps aftermath. Armed with ¾-size blazing red/gold Gretsches and vintage Gibsons (American guitars), they stormed the little stage like gangbusters. They fractured the silence with the #14 Premiers' Garage Hymn "Farmer John." They pounced with pandemonium power with an unabashed array of R & R classics on the edge of *Gold Rush*. Is American Rock and Roll one of our greatest international exports? It's nice to see the Japanese, who invented much recording technology, bouncing the big beat back with gusto and glee. Rock on, Neatbeats.

"Annie's Song" – John Denver, #1(2), 6-74; #9 C. Signature song for Folk Rock legend and wife Annie Martell. When their 16-year marriage dissolved in 1983, Denver's unravelling life began to spin and spiral toward the skies. Emulating his Army pilot father, Denver (b. John Deutschendorf, 1943-97), sought the eagle's domain. John's last big HOT 100 hit, #31, 3-82 "Shanghai Breezes," topped the Adult Contemporary chart. His friendly howdy smile, Dutch-boy golden blond hair, and warm wildwood tenor gave all of us nature fans something to believe in – up there on his pristine Colorado 'Rocky Mountain High' peaks. His 1998 afterglow album *Forever, John,* lofts "On the Wings of an Eagle" and champions his passionate urge to fly – and to reach the forever skies . . .

Denver began as a fraternity folk singer with a burgundy sport coat and paramecium/amoeba tie. He eased into his Colorado Freedom persona with grace and good nature and vital energy. From skier to runner to softball teammate to hiker to the clouds, Denver celebrated America's top floor with good-natured singalong songs. "Annie's Song" glides through tender lyrics with muted passion. She fills all his senses, he sings, like nights deep in enchanted forests. He compares her homey charms to sleepy indigo rolling oceans, storms out on the starry desert, or his beloved Rockies erupting with wildflower springtime. Dazzled by fadeaway blue-white snowfields trickling past quaking aspens and Bambi fawns, Colorado spreads out its Alpine glory. Kelly-green emerald highlands smile.

So the rest of us are down here juggling mortgages, root canals, and kamikaze mosquitoes the size of ostriches. Meanwhile, John and sweet Annie lived up on this wholly Heidi mountainside, in a *Sound of Music* idyllic lodge, above the backfiring smoky fray and fumes below. When John and Annie split up, a part of American innocence and environmental consciousness went down with their titanic romantic adventure. I cannot think of his "Take Me Home, Country Roads" (#2, 4-71) without a backward nostalgic glance at my in-laws' Tony and Leota Piazza's Fountain, Michigan, farm ("Back Home Again" [#5, 9-74]). Believing we could save the forests and rivers, we faced the mountain stars and sunsets with boyish smiles. The good times might just ramble on forever . .

On a bright Fall 1997 day, 53-year-old Denver made the mistake of selecting an experimental plane. The gossamer-albatross type aircraft was somewhere between an 'ultralight' and the Buddy Holly Beechcraft Bonanza. Soaring into the ever-summer California skies, John's doomed plane fell to the ground like Icarus and Daedalus of Greek myth. Seeking eagle crags and sunshine, Denver's quest careened tragically back to earth on a solo flight to destiny. Musical immortality joined John to the mysterious airborne cavalcade of Buddy Holly, Ritchie Valens, Patsy Cline, Otis Redding, Jim Croce, the Lynyrd Skynyrd troupe, Stevie Ray Vaughan, and Ricky Nelson.

"The Impossible Dream (The Quest)" – Jack Jones, #35, 6-66. Don Quixote saga *The Man of La Mancha* stars Robert Goulet in an Orbisonic crescendo of Grand Opera baritone. Red West said, **Elvis** hated the handsome self-assured Goulet so much [*Elvis: What Happened?*] that it's claimed the King would literally shoot the TV screen with his pearl-handled pistol when Goulet came on the set. Hopefully Elvis liked this milder version. With the nightclub cabaret aura of **Frank Sinatra**, Jones notched 20 charted hits, even covering unrelated **George Jones**'s Rockabilly standard "The Race Is On" (#15, 2-65 J. Jones).

"The Impossible Dream" is a symbol for whatever we're trying to do that's just too big – but we do it anyhow. Some emotional mountain to hurdle. We bravely challenge unbeatable foes of the Goliath ilk. We right those 'unrightable' wrongs. Like Rough Rider **Teddy Roosevelt** (1858-1919), we charge up the hills of San Juan, and Denver mountains – because they are THERE. We know we can very well lose it all, but there is a nobility in our attempts. It is better, to roughly paraphrase Roosevelt and follow "Impossible Dream" lyric, to experience defeat in the arena, scorned and blanketted with scars (see crucifixion), than to sit blandly among those insipid noncommittal shlumps who never try anything, never say anything, never DO anything. "If he fails, he fails while daring greatly – so that his place shall never be with those cold and timid souls who tasted neither victory nor defeat." TR shuns those who simply fail to CARE. The Jones/Williams/Goulet/Denver impossible dream is this: one very tattered and tottering man, sapped of strength in his noble attempt, sought to reach those glimmering, 'unreachable' faraway stars.

"If I Am" – Nine Days, #68, 10-2000. #20, Adult Top 40; #35 Top Forty Tracks; #18, VH-1, 11-2000. Simultaneously, and unknown to each other, my son Jeremy and I clipped that Teddy Roosevelt wisdom and hung it up somewhere. He worked over five years so Nine Days could become 'overnight sensations.' I am humbly proud of the way our boy and his band have played the game. He has done his best. We, who believe in the power of Rock and Roll, zap the mundane, and go for the glory. Sometimes we lose, but life has a lot of consolation prizes to fluff up the real world, which isn't so bad either.

After the dizzying surge of their #6, 4-2000 "Absolutely (Story of a Girl)," the guys nabbed their own bus, and two roadies named Charlie (Drannbauer, plus 'Big Charlie') to heft stuff to stages all over America. In early 1999 they opened for a band (now defunct) called **Edna's Goldfish**. During Midsummer 2000 they shared the big stages with #1-record guys **Vertical Horizon** (11-99, "Everything You Want"), played the 2001 Presidential Inauguration, and hobnobbed with John Travolta, Britney Spears, and Destiny's Child. In this Rock and Roll epic of American history, aren't we all destiny's children? We often go where our songs take us.

Most of the VH-1 video is lead singer **John Hampson** pursuing some petulant star-crossed lass. You can't fake this stuff. The warehouse Nine Days plays in looks like Prez **Ed McCoy**'s Big Mack Studios on Detroit's West Warren, where I started this rock and roll fantasy in 1967 with our local hit "I Can't Wait." Nine Days in 2001 holed up in a Long Island studio, searching for another "Absolutely" to revamp the Top Ten on their second Sony album – and playing lucrative weekend gigs nationwide. "If I Am" is more pensive than their blockbuster "Absolutely." The song is a sweet coming-together of melody, an oasis of harmonic blend, in a desert often riddled with cacophony and strident discord. Cool tune.

"Getting' Jiggy with It" – Will Smith, #1(3), 2-98. Power of Positive Rapping. Launched like **Ricky Nelson** from a successful TV show and cinema career, **Will Smith** (b. 9-25-68, Philly) needed little record hype to hit big. Sparking the PG-13 Rap scene, with melodic garnishes, Will duets here with some scritch-scratch semi-automated electronic bird. The chirpy little critter storms along at Will, with Will. Whippoorwill? Smith's Rap patter plays to family convocations, with a hint of impish fun. His "Miami" (#17, 12-98) is a tourist travelogue of all the nightlife and bikini-clad daylife of multicultural beach babes. Smith's #20, 10-98 "Just the Two of Us" takes a proud papa's role in caring for his weekend son – like the #2(3), 2-81 Grover Washington (w/ Bill Withers) hit. It shows a close dad/son relationship can ease rocky roads into smooth boulevards. Will and pals **Dru Hill**, Feat, and Kool McDee dust off tumbleweeds and saddles in 5-99 with #1(1), 5-99 "Wild, Wild West."

"Baby, One More Time" – Britney Spears, #1(2), 11-98. With her cheerleader smile, her Disney Mouseketeer experience, and adorable figure, she could sound like the Chipmunks and still sell records. She's actually a good singer – if any guy is really listening. Born 12-2-81 in Kentwood, LA, Southern Belle Britney lofted her tune to the top on the first Jive-label try. Despite a rather revealing concert, where moms wondered whether their 7-year-old's role model was a bit underdressed for the occasion, Britney spins her enchanting spell over boys from 10 to 111. Presidential silver-medalist in 1996, Bob Dole (pushing 80), does a cute 2001 commercial where his DOG gets flustered watching the beauteous Louisiana lass on TV. In the case of severe beauty, music often gets downsized, even barely noticed. She scraped the top ten with 9-99 #10 "(You Drive Me) Crazy." Her 1-2000 "From the Bottom of My Broken Heart" topped out at #14. With Tiffany, Annette, Debbie Gibson, or Lesley Gore Cuteness attached to her stunning beauty, she blossomed on a song whose title sounds more like *I Love Lucy* than current jaded hot-stuff fare: #9, 6-2000 "Oops! I Did It Again" (ah, those sneaky little coy double entendres strike again). Hits stayed strong, and "Stronger" (#11, 11-2000).

"The First Night" – Monica, #1(3), 8-98. In Spice Girls/Britney Spears tradition, Monica [Arnold, b. Atlanta '80] coos sultry and seamless audio adventures. Her first dynamite disc was #2(3), 4-95 "Don't Take It Personal (just one of dem days)." Her hit skein is a yarn of success: #7, 10-95 "Before You Walk out of My Life"; #4, 3-97 "For You I Will"; and three peak performances – #1(5), 8-98 "The First Night," #1(4) "Angel of Mine," and the next *Gold Rush* item. Her #64 "Just Another Girl" of 2-2001 proves even superstars have ho-hum chart adventures – that most bands would enjoy.

"The Boy Is Mine" – Monica and Brandy. Or, perhaps, Brandy and Monica, #1(13), 5-98. Chased #1(14) "Macarena" (9-95) as all-time dynamic duo #1 record. For those of you getting annoyed by current and past profusion of one-name singers, here is a quickeroo list:

MONICA Arnold
SMOKEY the Bear
TWEETY and LARRY Bird
JAY-Z Jason Carter
MADONNA Ciccone
ELVIS Costello, or the other one,
    but Kings often avoid last names
DEREK [actually Johnny 'Mr. Bass Man' Cymbal]
TAZ Devil
FABIAN Forte
KERMIT the Frog [observe same middle name as
    Smokey The Bear]
ANNETTE Funicello
ODETTA Holmes
JANET Jackson
REBA McEntire
PRINCE Roger Nelson
BRANDY Norwood
LITTLE RICHARD Penniman
USHER Raymond
JOE Thomas
QUEEN ELIZABETH Windsor II [maybe her middle name is II. Don't mean to be disrespectful, but no one really knows the order of Her Royal Highness's name].

Brandy Norwood (b. '79, McComb, Mississippi) was born near Jimmy Reed & Muddy Waters' Mississippi Delta. Like Ricky Nelson, she never let good looks get in the way of her prodigious talents. She landed a regular role on *Thea* in '93, and starred in '96's *Moesha.* Brandy's hit resume is impressive: #4, 2-95 "Baby," and #6, 10-94 "I Wanna Be Down" (both #1 R&B). Her #9, 9-95 "Brokenhearted" teamed with **Boyz II Men**'s Wanya Morris, and she nearly won gold for #2(2), 12-95 "Sittin' up in My Room." Her first solo #1[2] is 12-98 "Have You Ever?" Teen idols with TV shows already? Here's the fountainhead.

"Poor Little Fool" – Ricky Nelson, #1(2), 7-58; #3, 6-58 R&B; #3, 7-58 C; #4, 8-58 U.K. First #1 hit EVER on new *Billboard* HOT 100 format – zapping obsolete jukebox/DJ-favorites 'Top 100.' Today's cryptic forays into trade mumbo-jumbo have sprouted nearly 50 new charts from diverse genres that segregate R&B/Hip-Hop from Dance Music, and fragment artists. Positively, they open up new areas of success. Ricky is unrelated to Nelson wrestlers 'Half' and 'Full' Nelson. Or Prince Nelson.

With four sweet Streetcorner chords and a Milky Way cloud of stardust, the first big RICKY (pre-Martin) had his first #1 with this lovely lament. After messing around with various girls' hearts, roving song-guy gets his own broken. Nyaah nyaah theme? Nah. Despite its predictable four-chord pattern and NO bridge, the simple tune would not be downloaded to mediocrity. It was no match for Ricky's 'dreamboat' next-door charisma and **James**

Burton's golden guitar. A big guy now, the Hollywood High tennis champ could dish it out and take it. Ricky's resonant, no-frills super baritone assured us all we'd make it through the teen terrors of lost love. After Elvis ('86), Ricky had the strongest Teen Idol credential for immediate access to the Rock Hall of Fame. Looking as good as ELVIS sure didn't hurt sales, either (see Britney Spears, N'Sync). Ricky convinced us we could all do California in our dreams – as a tri-Wilson brother team shuffled through Hawthorne High, surveying the rolling 60s Beach-Boy-Band surf.

"Red Sails in the Sunset" – Platters, #36, 8-60; NC, R&B. Guy Lombardo and **Bing Crosby** snagged #1 in this seashore sundown melody. My memory of it differs from yours: fishing w/ my cuz Darrell Amlin (13) and Grandpa Joe Dean (67) on Lake Erie. Red rented rowboat. Spluttery three-horse mini-outboard motor. "Pappy" singing this song to us, to his Molson's Ale, and to the big fish he was unsuccessfully stalking. . . Results? One 9-inch perch. As the sunset glowed deep red on the U.S.A.'s North Coast (and Colchester, Ontario's sunny Canadian Southland), Pappy fondled the Lucky Strikes we smuggled for him.
    Tony Williams (d. '92 at 64), cakewalks his sugarfest tenor on this sweet Platters disc. It's a lot like their #1(3), 11-58 "Smoke Gets in Your Eyes." "Smoke" has wafted its dizzying smoke rings into the many a Manhattan cabaret – where a new generation discovers the nicotine buzz. In 1946, **82%** of British men (like my grandpa of Scotland) smoked. Rationed freebies by kindly WWII tobacco hawkers, few British soldiers in foxholes worried – "hey, if I inhale this thing, maybe I'll only live to be 67, not 74." They were just trying to make it through the night. In my American 50s, the smoking rate neared 50%-60%, despite a few fuddy-duddy docs griping about emphysema, which took Tony Williams' life. This vintage Paul Whiteman Smoke Song of Depression-riddled 1934 is an ode to the smokescreen of true love.
    Smoke, as in Detroit's great massive cloud of Arsenal-of-Democracy factory pollution, gave us Lake Erie fisherfolk some of the prettiest, reddest sunsets on earth, and the old red sails glowed in the Western skies. Like a fake-out fogbank, LOVE manufactures smitten fools. The fools, who include you and me and Uncle Ernie and Aunt Gloria, get lost in the veil of tears. Leo Reisman hit #3 with "Smoke Gets in Your Eyes" in 1934. Tony Williams' perfect smoky tenor highlights both red-gold sailboat sundowns and "Smokey Joe's Café." It's a melodic puff of passion, doting over the smoldering embers of love's longlost flame. And a great family afternoon that produced one dinky nine-inch perch.

"Goodnight Irene" –Weavers, #1(13), 7-50. How in the everlovin' blue-eyed world can **Pete Seeger**'s Weavers whoop it up with a Folk song that skates over boozing, cheating, estrangement, homelessness, hopelessness, and even suicide – and still pull it off as light comedy? To top it off, this unlikely lass 'Irene' nailed the top spot for an entire quarter of a 20th-century midriff year

– longer than any Rock Era 1955-92 song? Only the Weavers, with gritty desperado humor from Woody Guthrie's windswept prairies, could pull off such a lyrical/musical coup. Oh, and one more thing. Lead low tenor **Pete Seeger**, alto Ronnie Gilbert, tenor Fred Hellerman, and bass Lee Hays did "Goodnight Irene" as a WALTZ. Until Patti Page tied it that year (not Lloyd Becker) at #1(13), it was the most popular waltz of all time. With joyous banjos plunking, *bierhalle* glorious Folk harmonies, and an overarching ¾ rhythmic thunderbeat, the acoustic purist Weavers nearly cinched that Big Beat music (4/4) would soon be blasting.

"Until You Come Back to Me" – Aretha Franklin & Stevie Wonder, #3, 11-73; #1(1), R&B. She grew up a mile from Motown's West Grand Boulevard, bypassing Motown. With Jerry Wexler of Atlantic Records, she got a tremendous performance from Stevie in this megasoul merger. Wonder, on loan from Motown, may just have made this combo disc the most significant Soul [temporary] duo in history, if you steer by charted hits – Joel Whitburn lists Top 14 in charted HOT 100 Hits, 1955-99:

1. Elvis Presley	151		8. Fats Domino	66
2. James Brown	99		9. **Stevie Wonder**	65
3 **Aretha Franklin**	76		10. Pat Boone	60
3. Ray Charles	76		10. Nat 'King' Cole	60
5. Beatles	72		12. Beach Boys	59
6. Elton John	69		13. Rolling Stones	57
7. Frank Sinatra	68		14. Marvin Gaye	56

    Aretha's 3-98 "A Rose Is a Rose" hit #26. For the unquenchable Soul diva, everything is still coming up roses.

"Slide" – Goo Goo Dolls, #8, 12-98. Multicultural milieu? Yep. Czech-American, Hungarian-American, and Finnish-American R & R crew. Perched on edge of Canada (Buffalo), they cover many bases in their Johnny B. Goode success story. **Johnny Rzenzik** handles guitar, with **Mike Malanin** on drums, and **Robby Takac** on bass. Their Johnny-Cash-derived album title, Al. #27, 9-95 *A Boy Named Goo,* chomped the charts, squishily. In order to BE a 3-man band, you've got to blanket your instrument with notes. Somebody must pack the white space with vital vocal/instrumental fills. All three share vocals (like 3 Dog Night). The Goo Goo Dolls' bombastic thunder rhythms turn the raucous hiss of nearby Niagara Falls into a little Baby Bop whisper. Their #24, 4-2000 "Broadway" is an amazing song, with video clips from a Rustbelt factory. Their tiny-name tunes score highest: #5, 10-95 "Name," #9, 12-98 "Iris," "Slide," and #16, 9-99 "Black Balloon" (sort of like the black jellybean, weird but cool).
    Verve Pipe arose from Michigan State University, our Night Shift venue in East Lansing. Holland-American line-up includes lead singer Brian Vander Ark. Their #5, 2-97 "The Freshman" appeals to the **Dave Matthews** college crowd, as Eddie Van Halen's Dutch-American guitar appeals to everybody.

"The Way" – Fastball, #5A [Airplay], 3-98. An Austin, Texas, Fastball pitcher. **Tony Scalzo**'s lyric relates to that All-American search for kicks, glory, love, midnight, joy, destiny. Destination? To be slackers in eternal summer. Sounds like **James Dean**, movie idol, on bongos. Can't be. These jolly rapscallions sip the summer wine amid a profusion of ultra-melodic chords. They split the scene as the sun scuttles over the morning horizon, and blithely seek the American Dream. Streets of gold. Scalzo plays bass/keyboards (see Doors' Ray Manzarek) and Tony sings lead. He trades off with guitar/keyboarder/co-lead singer **Miles Zuniga**. **Jerry Sheffield** plays drums. "The Way's" melody unfurls, gliding in a fantastic *arpeggio* profusion of delightful proportions. A Duane Eddy-style low guitar crackles and crunches deep notes, darting around the scrambling melody.

Scalzo marvels at the troupe of eternal slackers. Their car breaks down, and they walk and walk, without truly knowing the way. Taoist parable here. THE WAY is the essence of Taoism (Tao Te Ching), ancient Chinese religion symbolized by this round symbol of a dark and light fish scrambling eternally around and around, chasing in vain each others' tails. "The Way" also conjures Judeo-Christian pilgrimages on strange shores. Party-on wayfarers in "The Way" aren't big on family responsibility. Rather than cozy fireside, they yearn for the adventurous highway. They grope along together, living the grand illusion that it'll always be summer (see Beach Boys) – and that they will never fade to old and gray. A very optimistic, rose-colored glasses philosophy. These road pilgrims don't shun danger and adventure. They celebrated their next hit (#88, 12-98) on a "Fire Escape," careening back to the Top 20 with #20, 7-99 "Out of My Head." A Fastball down the middle. Rock and Roll.

"You Were Meant for Me" – Jewel, #2(2), 11-96. Angel-faced Jewel Kilcher (b. 5-23-74) of Homer, Alaska, grants us a haunting reverie in this enchanted Folk Rock disc. She comes down to the Lower 48 from a rugged Gold Rush land of Northern Lights and backyard grizzlies – and maybe 1897 Rock and Roll. Haunting? After 60 weeks, "You Were Meant for Me" still hugged the #29 *Billboard* position. Her wispy soprano swoops a flurry of gorgeous notes. She juggles eggs, cats, and alluring pajamas in her all-encompassing lyric – it spells out that Alaskan nights are for snuggling. Her follow-up "Foolish Games" glommed #7, 9-97, with "Hands" across the waters (#6, 12-98) and #51S [Spoken, i.e., her poetry] 9-99 "Jupiter (Swallow the Moon)" showing another facet of her lyricism.

Jewel grew up in hardscrabble Homer, Alaska, attending Michigan's famous Interlochen Music Camp, later living out of a van in the California surfglow. Her star ascendancy suggests similar careers from songsmith **Joni Mitchell** (Rock Hall '97) and **Linda Ronstadt** (pending). We actually saw a moose and mooselet munching some guy's front-yard white birch in DOWNTOWN Homer, in the eerie summer midnight twilight. Her home abuts a sandspit off the Kenai Peninsula south of Anchorage, Alaska's only skyscraper burg (300,000 to Homer's 3000 people). The stoney sandspit lavishes, for fishermen and fisherwomen, King Salmon the size of Winnebagos. Homer was the *Northern Exposure* prototype town – a TV show cancelled for being too good. From Homer, Jewel set out for the Hollywood lights, carting her guitar, her poems, and her songs. These supercharged ballads fire-powered her Janie B. Goode Dream.

"Laugh, Laugh" – Beau Brummels, #15, 1-65. San Francisco's **Sal Valentino**, and his group offered the first great major challenge to the British Invasion with this heavenly melodic revenge rocker. A doleful harmonica rides a rolling bronco guitar, spindrifting the blue Lake Tahoe starlight. With the dynamic chord profusion of **Del Shannon**, the harmony of the **Byrds** or **Everlys**, and a Thunder Rock beat presaging **Springsteen** and **Seger**, California answered their namesake 19th-century British dandy with a sweet swirl of outstanding Rock and Roll. Beau Brummel biggees? #8, 4-65 "Just a Little," and amazing #52, 10-65 "Don't Talk to Strangers." Were it not for the bottom-line downsizing of their belly-up record company Autumn, they might have been the greatest of them all. "Laugh, Laugh" is no laughing matter. It's one of the top 75 greatest Rock hits of all time.

"Semi-Charmed Life" – Third-Eye Blind, #4, 9-97. **Stephen Jenkins**, son of a University of California-Berkeley professor fronts Third-Eye Blind. He commands his audience with Jeffersonian splendor. Jenkins' hits include this jumping rock odyssey, plus #5, 12-98 "Jumper" and #9, 12-97 "How's It Going to Be?" Roster includes drummer Brad Hargreaves, guitar guy Kevin Cadogan, and Portuguese-American Arion Salazar on bass. Their Al. *Tattoo of the Sun* won tri-platinum (3M) laurels.

Rock rolls on: **Janet** [Jackson] hit #1(7+), 3-2001 with "All for You." Her *Billboard* ad was, in a word, amazing, and the song debuted at #14, after the PD/DJ horde put their eyes back in their sockets. **Dido**'s #6, 1-2001 thankful "Thank You" thankfully hit #1 Adult Contemporary. LFO's "Summer Girls" of #3, 7-99 hit big, along with the **Mighty Mighty Bosstones** and Brian Setzer's flashback-1940s Orchestra. Alanis Morissette's mid-90s afterglow flickered at #17, 9-98 "Thank U" (spelling Rappishly), far brighter than the uncharted ghostly pallor of moontan man Marilyn Manson. Notorious B.I.G.'s posthumous #1(3) "Hypnotize" mesmerized America, *Grease's* sweet 'Sandy,' **Olivia Newton-John**, on the mend, re-released #1(2), 8-74 "I Honestly Love You" for its unprecedented third chart adventure (#48, 11-77, and #67, 5-98). The Anglo-Aussie beauty cut her last version with **Babyface,** who scored multiple R & B hits (b. Ken Edmonds, '59): #7, 8-89 "It's No Crime" debut; #4, 6-94 "When Can I See You"; and #6, 10-96 "This Is for the Lover in You." **Sonique** cut #8, 2-2000 "It Feels So Good." **Pink**'s #7, 2-2000 "There You Go" and #5, 8-2000 "Most Girls," and Montell Jordan's #1, 11-99 "Get It on Tonite" cinched success. Grammy winner **Macy Gray**'s #6, 2-2000 "I Try" and **Jagged Edge**'s #9, 12-2000 "Promise" hit big. Gung-ho Detroit crew **Uncle**

Kracker hit #6+, 3-2001, with Eden's Crush – out of left field – hitting #8, 3-2001 the FIRST HOT 100 week! K-Cl and JoJo hit #11, 12-2000 with "Crazy," with **Outkast**'s "Ms. Jackson" nailing #1 from 11-2000. **Aaliyah** (#9, 2-2002 "Try Again" and #14, 1-2002 "Rock the Boat") was killed in a tragic Caribbean plane crash. **Alicia Keys** earned several 2002 Grammies on songs like her #1, 11-2001 "Fallin'" and #8, 2002 "A Woman's Worth." **Ruff Endz** leaped to #5 with 5-2000 "No More." Afro-Irish **Samantha Mumba** crunched #6, 8-2000 with "Gotta Tell You." **Joe** and **Mystikal**'s "Stutter" hit #1(1), 1-2001, with Dream's "He Loves U Not" picking the #10 daisy in 9-2000. **Crazy Town**'s "Butterfly" fluttered to #1(1), 1-2001 on the fickle charts.

"Angel" – Shaggy featuring Rayvon, #1(1), 1-2001. Rock and Soul thrive on combining the best of everything in a synthesis of smooth sound. Shaggy's Kingston-style tenor (b. '68 Jamaica as Orville Burrell) weaves around **Merilee Rush**'s original torchy ballad, #5, 7-68 "Angel of the Morning." A Countrypolitan smash by **Juice Newton** renewed the tune to #4, 2-81 (only #22 C). Juice also did sensational #7, 10-81 "The Sweetest Thing I've Ever Known" and #2, 5-81 "Queen of Hearts." **Shaggy**'s Valley Stream, Long Island Reggae Rap R&B features a singer named after **Buddy Holly**'s #37 '58 [#5 UK] hit "Rave On" – Rayvon.

With a **Steve Miller** bass line like "The Joker," and Rap counterpoint, Shaggy and Rayvon spout out one of the sweetest melodies ever cloaked in the mantle of Rap music. Rock music gets assimilated into itself after each genre's blazing heyday: Surf, Rockabilly, Brit Invasion, Psychedelia, Disco. Now maybe Rap is melding melody and moving back to the mainstream. Time will tell.

With two tunes in the top five at the same time, Shaggy's domination of 2001 was assured. His #1(2), 10-2000 "It Wasn't Me" – featuring Ricardo 'Rikrok' Ducent – is a raucous ditty with a hint of COUNTRY Soul twang. It covers superstud shenanigans (see **Dion**'s #2 '61 "The Wanderer"). The Don Juan's amours end up all over the house, including the cold-tile bathroom floor – as he introduced the taboo word 'buck-naked' into our allowed-words feeding frenzy on mainstream radio. In 1997 Shaggy bypassed **Janis Joplin** on his #72, 8-97 "Piece of My Heart," sampling the ORIGINAL by Aretha's sister **Erma Franklin** (#62, 11-67). Shaggy's "Boombastic" hit #3, 5-95, and "That Girl" #20, 6-96. **TLC**'s "Unpretty" joined Toni Braxton's #1(11), '96 "Un-Break My Heart" in the Number UN category, with #1(3), 6-99. Their catchy Rap/Melody "Waterfalls" hit #1(7), 6-95, and Melita Jason fave #1(4), 2-99 "No Scrubs" tied #1(4), 11-94 "Creep" for pinnacle chart success.

"All Star" – Smash Mouth, #4, 5-99. Despite Kindness-Impaired name, good rock group: San Jose's singer Steve Harwell, bassist Paul DeLisle, drummer Kevin Coleman, guitarist Greg Camp (Whitburn info). This hit weaves Rap-style cheerleading lines with smashmouth rhythms and a quirky, offbeat melody. Basic message? Hey, you are ALREADY an All-Star, so get your basic game on, and play the contest with power and courage. Same musical

groove and hot trip as big #2[1A], 7-97 "Walking on the Sun." "Till the Morning Comes," of #11, 10-99 fame, kept Smashmouth spinning.

"Everything You Want" –Vertical Horizon, #1, 11-99. One of top 2000 hits, fronted by resonant Boston tenor **Matt Scannell**. Steely psychodrama. Clever convoluted lyric. Pulsing with a metallic cascade of guitars, "Everything You Want" surveys the iffy stance of a girl who has no idea where she's going. Scanell forges a love lyric with the desolate and surreal intensity of **Roy Orbison**, the harmonic majesty of **Simon and Garfunkel**, the potent word power of **Bob Dylan**, and enough firepower to dislodge a battalion of Boy Bands from their strutting stage.

Vertical Horizon is a true class act. **Nine Days'** frequent tourmates, Matt is backed by Keith on guitar, Sean on bass, and Ed on drums. Skid marks blister the lost streets of Vertical Horizon's skidding song-guy's romance. Though rooted in balladry, the song throbs with an almost Heavy Metal flair as the crashing chorus unfurls its drama. The girl is thoroughly mixed up. She hears the forlorn echoes of lost angels. Then the lead singer's reverie muses on the romantic rival. Seems he says all the proper things. He does everything right. She still grills this guy on a slow burn of indecision. He tells her to sit tight and wait out her eureka moment when she sorts out her iffy romantic mind.

Del Shannon – Rock Hall '99 – wrote this song's theme way back in '65. On his obscure flipside "Why Don't You Tell Him," of #95, 5-65 "Break Up," Del asks girl why she won't tell the OTHER GUY it's all over between the two of them. Songwriter Shannon asks her why she won't let the yester-dude off the hook. Soon Del descends into the dramatic irony mode. A full tragic realization. The fickle lass, he comes to discover, isn't totally over Boyfriend #1. Shannon's last punch-line verse is like Vertical Horizon's. Del asks the waffling, wobbling girl why she can't tell HIM it's over, and that Del's song-guy is just a fling. Then the song trails away onto Del's lonesome #1 '61 "Runaway" road in the blustery Grand Rapids rainshower.

Matt Scannell's vertical skid marks screech down Del's passing lane to the rainy Boston chaos beyond. On the million-selling single CD, you see leather-jacketed Vertical Horizon with steel blue/gray eyes gazing at the lost horizontal horizon beyond the captivating music. Scannell's shaven head tops his serious-looking black goatee. The focal point fades to a hint of iridescent Royal Blue open-collared shirt. The pitter-patter of Shannon's icy drizzle powers Vertical Horizon's last O. Henry-style jolt of a verse. Ringed by the harmonic chorus, Matt screams into mystic Boston Harbor that HE is truly everything she needs. He is EVERYTHING she wishes she could somehow become. Cryptically, he then laments that HE TOO means an equal NOTHING in her eyes to the last boyfriend who also meant nothing. She is stranded in dismal romantic limbo. No one knows why.

Rock tragedy of Emo Rock proportions, without a solution? "Everything You Want" marches stoically at a slugabed 91 beats/minute beyond the battleship-gray horizon. The group's follow-up "You're a God" (#26, 8-2000), follows same stratus-cloud weather pattern of #58+, 2-2001 "Best I Ever Had (Grey Sky Morning)." Their big song didn't hit #1 for over five months, setting a record. Perhaps in that time, the wobbly woman can figure out her agonizing romantic dilemma. Maybe one of these two patient suitors will wait for her. Until Hell freezes over. But she'd best not bet the ranch.

"Good Old Rock and Roll" – Cat Mother and the All Night News, #21, 6-69. Produced by R & R guitar icon **Jimi Hendrix.** This compendium of Larry Packer (guitar), Bob [what's-his-real-name] Smith (piano), Mike Equine (drums) and Roy Michaels (bass) performed one of the first R & R nostalgia compilations (see Little Caesar, Don McLean). Bolstered by All-American BANJO of Charlie Chin, Cat Mother's newsy crew [FIVE singers] did a pop panorama: **Chuck Berry**'s #2(3), 2-58 "Sweet Little 16," Buddy Knox's #1, 2-57 "Party Doll," Big Bopper's #6, 8-58 "Chantilly Lace," **Little Richard**'s #6, 4-56 "Long Tall Sally," **Jerry Lee Lewis**' #3, 6-57 "Whole Lot of Shakin' Going On," and **Carl Perkins**' #2, 4-56 "Blue Suede Shoes." **Jimi Hendrix,** in his heyday, recognized even before Don McLean's "American Pie" rock history, that this great stuff was making a bid for immortality, like Bach, Beethoven, or Mozart.

"The One on the Right Is on the Left" – Johnny Cash, #46, 2-66; #2(2) C. Cash (b. '32, AR) understands Rock and Roll from the beginning. From Elvis's *Louisiana Hayride* and Sun Records in Memphis, Johnny saw and did it all. From boisterous, brawling U.S. Army and Detroit factory days to Country and Rock Halls of Fame, Cash thundered his honest baritone across myriad windswept prairie nights below lost blue stars. An American treasure, Cash battled many setbacks, from a heart bypass at 55 to a recent tissue malady and 2001 pneumonia. His Tennessee Two featured Luther Perkins on guitar and Marshall Grant on slap bass.

This tune features the Shel Silverstein-style whimsy of his biggest HOT 100, #2, 7-69 "A Boy Named Sue." In 1966, few Americans yet griped about the Vietnam War. Cash took a political hot potato. Why doesn't every band have the cohesion and longevity of the Rolling Stones (back when they first rolled)? Bands squabble and grumble and split up, because they're like quarreling brothers. Sibling Rivalry Syndrome. In this chuckly J. H. Clement lyric, Cash paints the Folk group's sorry plight. With political lyrics, the band emerges as one right-wing conservative, another a left-wing liberal. The whole jolly refrain chugs with that Cash thumping beat. Bickering descends to carping. Carping to name-calling. Name-calling to a big onstage fistfight. Johnny, standing outside the free-for-all, roars his big good-natured guffaw. The ex-band's fortunes disintegrate from solidarity to chaos (and black eyes).

SADLY, A ROCK & ROLL BAND IS AT BEST A TEMPORARY PHENOMENON.

Its spinoffs suffer in kind: Country, Hip-Hop, Cajun, Big Band, Folk, Skiffle, or Ska. The **Beatles** had only six big years on American charts. **Buddy Holly/Crickets** had only a year and a half.

"You're Still the One" – Shania Twain, #2(9), 2-98. Shania's first big HOT 100 Crossover breakout. Canadian Country diva follows lead of young **LeAnn Rimes**, who clobbered HOT 100 to #2(4), 6-97 "How Do I Live?" Shania, like Mariah, suffers from the cool problem of too much beauty (see Britney Spears). Adorned in bare midriff tops and seemingly spandex levis, Shania sways and sings, the essence of wholesome fitness and musical expertise. She was born 8-28-65 in my grandparents' Canadian town that my folks drove SOUTH to visit – Windsor, Ontario (see Country chapter). "You're Still the One" points out the guy's endearing charms, and how much he still loves him. It's unrelated to great #5, '76 same-titled Orleans' song. "Man! I Feel Like a Woman" (#23, 4-99) fires off Holly hiccups galore, tying two millennia with one beat and spirit. In 2001, it all started to come together. All this stuff interconnects.

"Heartbreaker" – Mariah Carey, with Jay-Z, #1(2), 9-99. Like we said about Shania, it helps to look good. The Shania/Mariah Video Component functions as a Secret Hype rally. Chasing **Madonna**'s string of hits, Mariah's candidacy wasn't stumped by #1(16), 12-95 hit "One Sweet Day" with **Boyz II Men**. Mariah's November 1999 Al. #1 *Rainbow* debuted at #1. The life-size 2-D record-store promo statue is cardboard. Her angel-white bikini attracts men and boys like Antz-2-Honey. She could sound like Jabba the Hut (*Stars Wars* monster) and still sell a gazillion.

Mariah's hits star-spangle the competition: #1(2), 9-97 "Honey" attracted boys and bees, "I Still Believe" crunched #4, 2-99. "My All" nailed #1(1), 5-98, and "Always Be My Baby" hit #1(2), 4-96. Though "When You Believe" skidded at #15, 12-98, Mariah volleyed with two big ones: #1(1), 12-99 "Thank God I Found You" and this "Heartbreaker" that only broke no hearts on her way to the bank. Though her millennial offerings are modest, she is destined to break out into song. You recall her mother Patricia Carey sang with the New York Metropolitan Opera, and named her after Broadway play *Hitch Your Wagon to a Star* song "They Call the Wind Maria" [pron. 'ma-rye-ah,' see Kingston Trio]. She hitched her wagon to a star, actually singing backup for Brenda K STARR (not Ringo). Mariah, embodiment of the American multicultural melting pot, would become a major SUPERstar.

If you run a 10K race (6.2 miles), you'll find two winners, male and female. It would never be fair to give the gold only to the guy who crossed the line first – or in the case of Southampton's Barbara Gubbins, to the woman who beat 150+ local runners in a five-miler, including all the guys (29:20 8K, or 5:53/mi). Is it time to determine the two big winners of the century in #1 songs? The **Beatles** scored 20 HOT 100 #1's, but who won the INDIVIDUAL honors? Elvis has 18 and Mariah 15 (Madonna 11) in the American Rock and Roll Century. So here are the winners: ELVIS PRESLEY and MARIAH CAREY.

Or, oops, perhaps that should read:
MARIAH CAREY AND **ELVIS PRESLEY!**
You pick.

Rockin' Always -
And Even Forevermore?

Remember back when you were fourteen? I have this theory, that we will love and never forget the big hits when we were all semi-innocent 14-year-olds. I have tried to make *Gold Rush* as objective as possible – but it's impossible. My musical life was circumscribed by the angelic harmonies of the Everly Brothers, the dynamic thunder of Elvis Presley, the cool hip lyrics of Chuck Berry, and the most believable pal-next-door rock superstar of all time – Buddy Holly. Had I been born into this surging millennium of cell-phones and Internet harried highways, perhaps *Gold Rush* would pay more homage to the monumental strident growls of Puddle of Mudd, Linkin Park, P.O.D., Eminem, or Scott Stapp's full-throated baritone – booming out the lyrics of limbo and the Creed of soul-searching. I don't know. I can only tell you about the songs that most matter to me. During my search to get to the center of these classic songs, I had to go far beyond my own musical loves. I had to discover yours. I have tried to be as enthusiastic about the songs I know YOU love as I am about the songs I love. Sometimes they are the same song. In searching for the greatest of popular songs in a rockin' century – or three – I tried to pick the songs I know *YOU* would pick to be played. Here they are in *Gold Rush*.

Over a "Long and Winding Road" of this musical odyssey, I must admit I learned a great deal about the music that matters in Anglo-America – and therefore the world. [Poor Frank Sinatra, regretfully, would not be happy at all to hear that in 2002, he was Iraq's Saddam Hussein's favorite singer]. In this penultimate chapter, I will try to bridge the songs that illuminated my life with the ones that spark yours.

When I was 15 years old, my parents paid me a generous allowance – but I had to do the dishes three nights a week to earn it. To assuage the mini-hassles of mashed potato bits, drooling off sticky plates into scalding water, I brought two friends – Don and Phil Everly. Though they didn't know me from Adam, I knew them, and loved their cherubic Appalachian tenor harmonies. They assured me that being a teenager had "Problems" (#2, 11-58), and "Bird Dog[s]" (#1, 8-58) might try to steal your girl, but that "All I Have to Do Is Dream" (#1[5], 4-58) and soon I'd find the "Love of My Life" (#40, 11-58).

Then Larry Glazer taught me how to strum an acoustic folk guitar – like the Everlys played. Someday, I believed, "Johnny B. Goode's" Rock and Roll dream might unfold. Though *our* band the Night Shift/Woolies made a few Michigan marks in the 60s, I had no idea that the Johnny B. Goode dream would be put on ice for a generation (see Nine Days' #6, 4-2000 "Absolutely [Story of a Girl]"). I have no idea how much of Nine Days' appearance on the *Jay Leno Show* is due to an old scratchy Everly Brothers album in 1958. I'm pretty sure it's very, very little. But this is America. If a lot of people put a lot of dreams together, sometimes a big one comes true.

"Temptation" – The Everly Brothers, #27, 5-61. This is one of the greatest songs in history, and that's an understatement. The #1 singer of the first half of the 20th century, **Bing Crosby,** lofted this ode to the figureful temptress up to #3 in 1934. Then the Everlys blasted it into orbit, with their otherworldly harmony presiding over one of the Top 200 band tracks in recorded history. An Afro-Cuban "Peggy Sue" beat, of 16th note rhythmic blur, powers this fantasy of *chromatic* chord shifts and hard-driving passion.

Everything I ever learned about harmony, I learned from the Everly Brothers. Producer Archie Bleyer of Nashville's Cadence Records streamlined their dual voices at EQUAL VOLUME, so you never knew WHICH voice was the MELODY, and which was the harmony. After media giant Columbia Records didn't know what to do with them, plunking them into a straight Country style in 1956, Nashville pruned and preened their sound. They are the only *group* to attain the Rock Hall of

Fame on the first ballot (1986). **Paul Simon and Art Garfunkel** took the pristine tenor harmonies of the Everlys, and smoothed the sweetest Folk Rock sound of their era.

The Everlys' "Temptation" is the first song to flirt with phasers and flangers in the studio – opening up a whole basket of wah-wah pedals and special effects to bolster the superstardom of Jimi Hendrix, Led Zeppelin, Bruce Springsteen, Pearl Jam, Creed, and every Heavy Metal band in the universe.

The song centers around this sweet siren who attaches her beauty, like Scotch Tape, to this lusty lad's libido. This was HOT STUFF for 1961, or 1934. The Everlys' angelic harmonies cascade in waterfall splendor, sparkling with rainbow guitar riffs from studio guitar whizzes like **Chet Atkins,** who backed Scotty Moore on Elvis's original "Heartbreak Hotel" (#1[8], 3-56). Atkins (1924-2001, Rock Hall of Fame 2002) ruled in Nashville. After firing off his flashy riffs on Don & Phil's first #1 – 11-57's "Wake Up Little Susie," Chet popularized the guitar for his "Nashville Sound." This unique Nashville Sound became the band-track bulwark of modern Country music. Chet worked at RCA as Music Director, and sold millions of instrumental albums like #7 Al. 2-61 *Chet Atkins' Workshop.* Chet crossed the Crossover Bridge from Pop to Rock to Country to Easy Listening. His distinctive finger-picking style played both the melody and the bass line simultaneously. Beatle lead guitarist George Harrison, who passed away also in 2001, wrote liner notes for his mentor Atkins. With virtuoso speed-of-light fret expertise, and aw-shucks humility, Chet Atkins was among the greatest guitarists of all time, on par with the legendary **Les Paul**.

Maybe more important than the magnificent rhythm throb, or the masterful melding of their Scotch-Irish extraordinary tenors, the Everlys' song tells the truth: love, and life, are all about temptation. **If Rock and Roll wasn't at least a bit dangerous, it wouldn't be half as much fun.** As the Everlys surf the flangers, the phasers, and all the jet-trails of new special effects, they ponder the bumpy roller-coaster ride of a jittery love affair. Love, they say, involves temptation. Awash in adolescent tidal waves of desire and despair, they surf the great joy at the heart of both love and Rock and Roll.

It doesn't get any better than this.

"Things We Said Today" – Beatles, NC, 1965. Like Foreigner's #1 #2 song, #2(10) "Waiting for a Girl Like You," the Beatles' Al. #2(9), 8-64 *Something New* makes mincemeat of the other lesser also-rans in the race to #1. It's hard to think of the Beatles as ever coming in second anywhere, but their #1-Band-of-All-Time rep is built upon a solid foundation of some of the greatest songs that never charted big. This little masterpiece never charted at ALL, yet it's a tremendous tribute to the harmonic magic of the Everly Brothers. Paul McCartney penned it. In Barry Miles' outstanding 1997 star-bio *Many Years from Now,* Paul says: "The song projects into the future, and then is nostalgic about the moment we're living in now, which is quite a good trick. It has interesting chords. It goes **C,F,** which is quite normal, then the normal thing might be to go to **F-minor,** but to go to the **Bb** was quite good." The Beatles got these chord shifts from Buddy Holly (via producer Norman Petty), and from the **Everly Brothers,** in their monumental "Temptation," a 27-year-old song in 1961 that was *still years ahead of its time.*

"Things We Said Today" is hard to beat for Beatle harmony. With Paul doing Phil Everly's 1st tenor, and John doing Don Everly's standard 2nd tenor, the bridge takes on the same surreal goosebump harmonic power of "Temptation." *Something New* also coruscates with other unheralded Beatle gems, which stud the lower decks of the Hot 100 like sparklers and bonfires around a summer 4th of July lake. Ringo Starr, a good singer relegated to #4 by the other fab Fab Three vocalists, pierced the top 20 with his Carl 'Blue Suede Shoes' Perkins tribute, #17, 9-64 "Matchbox." Everlyesque harmony spins and dips and weaves through #53, 8-64 "If I Fell" and #12, 7-65 "And I Love Her"; each demonstrates the Beatle contribution to melodic balladry — not just 3-chords-and-a-cloud-of-dust Rock and Roll. Why **Something New's** "Tell Me Why" never charted is a bizarre mystery. It's 100% Beatle enthusiasm, packed with Holly harmonies and Beatle gung-ho gusto.

"Lady Willpower" – Gary Puckett/Union Gap, #2(2), 6-68. Just when Bobby Kennedy was gunned down, in the aftermath of Dr. Martin Luther King's assassination, American morale dragged itself through the ashes of some slimy sub-basement. A war blazed in South Vietnam, and suddenly here came these guys from Bob Dylan's arctic Hibbing, Minnesota, dressed up as Civil War soldiers. **Paul Revere's Raiders** monopolized the Revolutionary War motif, so Gary Puckett donned the togs of General Pickett, and Puckett charged into battle on the fickle charts. The Union Gap snagged two silver medals. In his other #2 tune "Young Girl" of 3-68, Gary checked the groovy groupie's I.D.; he decided that "This Girl Is a Woman Now" (#9, 8-69). The Gap was founded in San Diego, where Minnesotan winters are just an icy memory. With Gary's soaring Dramatic Tenor, the Gap floated to Rock Hall-candidacy stardom with debut "Woman, Woman" (#4, 11-67). Their other top ten tune, #7, 9-68 "Over You," pretty well hurdles Gary Puckett into our Great Singers chapter, with Roy Orbison, Del Shannon, and Gene Pitney – except the Gap's career came about seven years too late to make the cut. But wow, what a great voice!

"Ain't It Funny" – Jennifer Lopez, Featuring Ja Rule, #1(4), 12-2001. Since we've already featured this blithe Bronx lass and her humungous hit-string, it's time we took notice of how **Ja Rule** commandeered the high charts. In the Rap milieu of the early 21st century, many big hits credit a whole crowd of singers. The word FEATURING has almost become a superstar itself, with star collaborations no longer a one-liner in *Billboard.* Indeed, a whole cavalcade of Rap royalty often struts the stage, making a joyful noise. Indeed, the big name in

Rap Royalty is now 'KING **FEATURING.**' Without a whole lot of fanfare, Ja Rule also spun their sound to the pop pinnacle (#1, 10-2000), with 2002's big star **Ashanti,** on "Always on Time." Ja Rule always seems to be on time to take it to the top – and take a few friends along for the ride.

"Youth of the Nation" – P.O.D., #28, 2-2002. Sporting one of the most thunderous choruses in Rock and Rap history, this song packs a wallop. It is a mystery why it didn't go top five. Not intended to be a pretty song, "Youth of the Nation" is a wake-up call. It's saying 'don't forget us.' It's saying that growing up now is as tough as it's ever been. Some kids skate through adolescence with few traumas. One poor kid, though, in this urban drama, takes his own life in a cauldron of despair (see Elvis's "In the Ghetto"). Much of the tough talking in strident street chants simply involves the survival instinct.

In the words of Curtis Sliwa, leader of the neighborhood-patrol Guardian Angels in the toughest streets of the Big Apple, the would-be mugger is "looking for a *victim* – not an opponent." My Detroit neighborhood, with a 1½ times higher violent crime rate than the South Bronx, taught us there was a way you walked. An unwimpy swagger, maybe. There was a leer, too. You didn't want anyone to think you weren't streetwise. Elvis pranced like a panther. So did Nathaniel Mayer (#22 '62 "Village of Love, #16 R&B, #1 in Detroit). When we suburban kids walked Nathaniel's rough & tumble inner-city blocks, before Motown burnt itself into a smoldering cinder in the deadly 1967 riots, we all swaggered and pranced and leered. It may have looked a tad silly, but as I recall, bad escapades were few and far between.

When I hear my students screeching through pale suburbs, trunk speakers afire in hot decibels of mad-as-hell rhetoric, I never chuckle. I've been there. Sometimes we cloak ourselves in courage to face the mean streets.

When the booming, bashing chorus of "Youth of the Nation" rattles freeway abutments, brick warehouses, and hot corners crawling with neon dazzle and passion, we must all shut up and listen. No matter how we padlock ourselves into compounds of supposed safety, the din and throb and pulse of hot city nights always arouses adventurous youth. The youth of the nation are to be nurtured and prized and helped in their quest just to grow up. They are never, ever to be ignored.

"Down Yonder" – Lawrence (Piano Roll) Cook, #22, 9-51. Piano Roll Cook was an old-time Ragtime Boogie-Woogie piano player. Although female Grand Ole Opry star **Del Wood** launched this rollicking Mississippi riverboat boogie to #4 the same month, Cook's version gets the nod. Why? Because COOK ironically named himself after the very contraption intended to replace him. He womped the piano-roll machine at its own game.

Machines have been wiping out real musicians' live gigs for a lot longer than the rise of some Disco drum machine under a 1975 *Saturday Night Fever* mirror ball. Oh, and by the way, "Down Yonder" was my favorite song when I was eight years old, and I still love that rinky-tink

plinkety-plink sound of an old bouncing upright piano. Toledo's **Johnny** [Paris] **& the Hurricanes** revived this smokin' oldie to #48 in 1960, brandishing wildfire guitars, a whooshing organ, and a hyper drum solo of cosmic decibel proportions. I fondly remember it blasting out Mr. Nelson's low-key lectures in Auto Shop. The road machines we studied would later dominate the Beach Boys' non-surfin' side, like drag-race anthem "Shut Down" (#23, 4-63). Jan & Dean's Graveyard/Surf/R&R "Dead Man's Curve" would have gone a lot higher than #8, 3-64, if there weren't so doggoned many Beatle songs clogging up the high charts.

"Down Yonder" echoed **Al Jolson**'s #1(9), 5-1920 "Swanee." The rare lyric in this usually-instrumental pre-Rock tune concerned a Mark Twain-type steamboat race on the Mississippi – starring the Natchez and the Robert E. Lee. Its sunny Southern sentiments of 1951 hark all the way back a hundred years beyond, to the masterpiece melodies of THE songwriter **Stephen Foster.** My mom showed me how to play Foster's original Suwanee River saga, 1850's "Old Folks at Home," when I was about seven years old. So when "Down Yonder" sprang to #2 on *Your Hit Parade*, I was overjoyed. My mom actually drew little numbers on the keys, figuring I liked numbers better than letters. I'll never forget that super tune: 3-2-1-3-2-1-8-6-8-5-3-1-2 [E-D-C-E-D-C-C(octave)-A-C(octave)-G-E-C-D]. That way, one of the World's Greatest Melodies looks like alphabet soup.

The **Player Piano was the first karaoke machine.** You pumped the piano pedal – like an old non-electric Singer Sewing Machine – and super Ragtime music came out. Just like **Jukeboxes** and **Drum Machines** and **Synthesizers** and **Napster,** the **Player Piano put working musicians out of work.** The perforated old holes in the **Piano Roll** (which looked like a cylindrical relic 1965 computer card) actually hit the right notes. You could buy piano rolls to mimic the best Ragtime/Boogie-Woogie/Jazz/Swing Bass piano guys – guys who actually breathed.

With *piano rolls,* all the musician 'wannabes' had to do was keep pumping that piano pedal. It wouldn't be long before the **Telegenic Component** also put some average-looking rockers out of business. **Once a band had to spend the price of a house to make a 'Video' that MIGHT get MTV or VH-1 Spin Rotation, it put 99% of the hopeful 'Garage Bands' permanently out of business.**

In this enlightened age, it is now possible for a band to get a gold record album (500,000+ copies sold), and still not make a cent — due to studio VIDEO DEBTS. During the stock market slide/crash year of 2002, some big studios were actually dumping big name bands with hit records on the charts – because they couldn't afford a lukewarm hit. "Down Yonder" was a lot of fun, but the piano roll was a bad omen for real-life piano players like my uncle Lou Maury.

In "Down Yonder," the lyric drags out a whole litany of family and assorted kissin' cousins – like Sammy, Ephraim, and Daddy. It reminds you of Paul McCartney & Wings' "Let 'Em In," starring Sister Suzie and Paul's actual Aunt

Gin {Ginny}.

After years of pensive wandering, following the untimely passing of his soulmate Linda in 1997, Paul met and eventually fell in love with a girl named Heather (see "Mull of Kintyre"). Like many Scottish chieftains of old, Paul's Heather showed her 'brave heart' when she fearlessly attempted to save innocent children from land mines in Princess Di's crusade. The equally-attractive young Heather fell victim to a terrible accident with her leg. Her name symbolizes the harsh beauty and blooming pastel colors of Scottish spring. We are the world – and we wish Paul and Heather all the very best.

The piano roll, however, may have been a bitter harbinger for showbiz – go technical, and get big or get out. Fortunately, all the Johnny B. Goodes and Paul McCartneys don't believe a word of that gloom. In Rock and Roll, you've got to follow the GLEAM – not the gloom.

"Hit the Road, Jack" – Ray Charles, #1(2), 9-61. Ray's 'Jock Rock' anthem often serenades disgruntled opposing relief pitchers, as they slink and shuffle off to the showers after blowing a nine-run lead. "Hit the Road, Jack" features Ray versus his coy Raelettes in a Gospel-inspired Call & Response of batter banter. Mocking his #6 '59 hit "What'd I Say," Charles keeps retorting with a 'what-did-**YOU**-say' comeback – implying that he didn't hear a word of their nagging. All true sports fans know the hideous truth, as prated by some anonymous male chauvinist of long, long ago: "Loving a sports team is like loving a woman – it can break your heart." In a minor-key chordal dive, the less-than-perfect guy fades away at full-tilt-boogie, mumbling and grumbling with hotdog energy.

Ray Charles' "Hit the Road Jack" is one of the great comedy songs of all time in Rock and Soul. Charles, we recall, is a charter member of the FIRST class of the Rock Hall of Fame in 1986. So who – Ray or the Raelettes – hits the road? Catch the song and check it out.

"Danny Boy" – Conway Twitty, #10, 9-59; #18, 11-59 R&B. How could the guy with the most #1 songs of all time (Country chart hits, mostly) come out with a Rock and Roll "Danny Boy"? And how could he take this unofficial Irish national anthem – almost a hymn – and jump from his solemn intro, and slow graveside pace, into a rip-'em-up rhythmic roarer in the Little Richard Screaming Blues motif? And how could a Scottish-American baritone (1933-93) from Mississippi, who scotched a budding professional baseball career, end up with the most popular "Danny Boy" of all time on the American charts?

With its spitfire, crackling, rip-roaring beat, THIS "Danny Boy" is the *only* one ever to hit the Top Ten. Few will forget Mayor Rudy Giuliani standing guard over the smoldering shrine to America's third-millennium 'Day of Infamy' – **9-11-2001.** As the New York City mayor, and Governor George Pataki, saluted the thousands of heroes – New York's bravest and finest firemen and policemen, and courageous civilians, the sad strains of "Danny Boy" wailed a multitude of forlorn farewells. The noble song was trying to put the nightmare to bed.

But the nightmare will never go to sleep. As long as men face each other on battlefields of honor and patriotism, there will always be boys named Danny headed for surprise graves sixty years early. "Danny Boy," according to master song chronicler Joel Whitburn, goes back to 1855 County Derry (which Bob Owen says the English stamped 'Londonderry'). "Danny Boy" is the ultimate male bonding tribute. Armed with just a III *mediant* major chord transition, to shepherd a world-class melody home to the emerald fields of glory, "Danny Boy" is the sweet sad song that makes hardbitten cops cry. It celebrates a manly friendship between brothers in arms. At first, the casual listener believes that one living soldier visits Danny's fresh grave. The soldier hears the [bag]pipes calling his friend home (see #69, '61 "A Scottish Soldier," Andy Stewart). Between the glens, and along the side of the mountain, the soldier feels the passing of summer and roses and Danny's young life. He kneels at the grave and prays a Catholic 'Ave Maria' for Danny's soul. He feels that Danny can hear him softly tread above him. Then it begins to get really deep and stark. The perceptive listener comes to realize that the singer of the song is actually the *dead soldier,* and that his comrade-in-arms Danny is paying graveside tribute – not unlike the bullet-riddled unfortunate cowboy in Marty Robbins' #1 '59 "El Paso."

The listener's suspicions are confirmed. Through pronoun-switching double lyrics, *Danny is actually* the living soldier who can leave, and the singer of the sad song must 'bide,' or abide. Unlike "Loch Lomond," we don't know which of the parted friends takes the high road or the low road. In "Danny Boy's" 2nd verse – as done at the same time by Harlem Calypso king Harry Belafonte, the dead soldier will lie peacefully at his gravesite, until his friend Danny comes to honor that grave. As all the flowers are now dying, the soldier somehow returns to life – an act of faith plucked out of *Brigadoon,* an act of faith as great as any in the Middle Ages. In any crusade.

Armed with one of the most otherworldly lyrics of all time, and one of the greatest folk melodies ever caressed, "Danny Boy" crosses over into Twitty rhythm to become – perhaps – the ultimate Graveyard Rock song of all time. Weirdly, Twitty's R&R version would be a great Rock tune – if it didn't carry so much emotional baggage. Some shocked 1959 critics called it blasphemy (they had yet to hear **Jimi Hendrix's** Woodstock guitar version of "The Star-Spangled Banner" or the Ramones' "What a Wonderful World"). If you can separate the former funerals from your reverie while pondering Conway's electrifying "Danny Boy," you'll swear it's the essence of great melody melded to Vintage Rockabilly firepower. But the non-Rock song will not sleep. Like the spirit of Danny and/or his friend, the friendship and the memories and the nobility of the sacrifice will transcend life and death itself. "Danny Boy," whether slow and leaden as the soft-rain Irish skies, or blasting a bombastic Twitty beat, will always be a great song for the ages.

"Where Were You (When the World Stopped Turning?)" – Alan Jackson, #28, 11-2001; #1(3+), C. Country star Alan Jackson's heartfelt memorial to the 2001 New York World Trade Center disaster is among the most spirited songs commemorating the victims of the Osama bin Laden terror attacks. Over five minutes of hushed balladry, Jackson conjures every American's somber reaction. Jackson cites the working person – police officer, teacher, or mother – and he ponders the hateful kamikaze act of suicide pilots. Like most blindsided Americans, he takes the "why do they hate us?" approach, and confesses he's not sure he can tell Iran from Iraq despite watching CNN. Like most Americans, he's stunned, because most of us can't figure out why anybody would hate us. We're upbeat, hard-working, humorous, neighborly people. We're all just trying to do the right thing. Never loftily poetic or obfuscatingly overdramatic, Alan Jackson's universal patriotic hymn covers American national heritage over 200 years – back to President ANDREW Jackson and beyond. His pristine melody and sincere sentiments are powerful, his message firm and resolute and indomitable.

The Al Qaeda Terrorists who toppled the World Trade Towers were motivated by fires of fanaticism fanned by Osama bin Laden. They inadvertently cast many of their Islamic brethren into unfortunate conflict. Like most Christians, most Muslims believe in peace, coexistence, and the Golden Rule. The God of Abraham in the *Torah, Bible, or Koran (Qu'ran)* is the same monotheistic God. We like to think we've outgrown the so-called 'Holy War' Crusades, which slaughtered millions of innocent Christian, Jewish, and Muslim children in a feeble attempt to force another religion down some true believer's throat. True believers in the *Qu'ran* do NOT see murder as the answer, or as a ticket to some warrior's *Walhalla* – the Old Norse/Viking combination Heaven, hunting lodge, and harem. Most true Muslims, like their Christian and Jewish brethren, believe that peace and love are the answer to hate and savagery. [During the Crusades, however, we weren't even spurred by the world's current lust for petrochemical power, for oil was then an anointment, not a power curse]. As **Dr. Martin Luther King** put it: "Let no man drag you so low as to make you hate him." Dr. King also countered the Old Testament with the New: "An 'eye for an eye' leaves everybody blind." The United States is slow to anger. By October 2001, Osama faded, and Saddam Hussein of Iraq glowed on the horizon in nuclear chartreuse. Determining his guilt was tricky business, and the prophetic words of Key's "Star-Spangled Banner" loomed on the horizon: "Then conquer we must, if our cause it is just." A year later, President Bush [II] was still collecting a coalition to tear apart Hussein's secret palaces, in search of small nuclear devices hidden under pillows and alibis.

Lee Greenwood's "God Bless the U.S.A" hit a 9-11-01 resurgence, and leaped to #16, 9-2000 (#7 C). Before we were even attacked, **Brooks and Dunn** enjoyed a #1 C-only hit "Only in America," unrelated to Jay/Americans' #25 '63 hit. **Aaron Tippin's** #37, 10-2001 "Where the Stars and Stripes and the Eagle Fly" also defined the American spirit.

Whitney Houston's "Star-Spangled Banner," which hit #20 in 3-91 in the wake of the 1991 (1st) Gulf War, rose again to glory, and hit #6 on the HOT 100 in 11-2001. It's

the highest position for the National Anthem – since it was officially DECLARED the National Anthem by Congressional decree in 1930. Previously, it was #1 in 1916 and 1917 (WWI) for **Prince's Orchestra** and **John McCormack,** respectively.

Expressing the frustration of many Americans in not finding the elusive Osama bin Laden in any of his regular caves, Country star Toby Keith (6'4", 235#, no featherweight) lambasted the terrorists with his #25, 5-2002 (#1C) "Courtesy of the Red, White, and Blue." It features a rump-kicking showdown, with America punting the sneaky attackers.

Alan Jackson's album *Drive* drove to **#1 in its first week,** a feat nearly unprecedented. The title track, #28, 3-2002 and #1C "Drive (for Daddy Gene)," forever etches Jackson's own father into the American consciousness. Like Springsteen's dad in pensive #6, 12-85 "My Hometown," propping the kid behind the Buick's big wheel, Mr. Jackson teaches the kid Alan to drive his car – but he also adds piloting an 18-foot plywood boat with a 75-hp Johnson outboard. In the song's finale, Alan teaches his own daughter to steer the Jeep and gallivant through a green daisy-dotted meadow.

"Rio" – Duran Duran, #14, 4-83. Duran Duran's sophomore hit has one of the most haunting melodies ever spun. This darling dervish 'Rio' dances temptingly along the Rio Grande in Texas. Texas is a long way from Duran 2's telegenic MTV triple Taylors: Andy Taylor, John Taylor, and Roger Taylor. All, amazingly, are unrelated. The Duran crew comes from England's #2 city, the hardscrabble industrial colossus of Birmingham.

Whether it's Techno-Synth or New Wave or Dance or Pop music, it's still Rock and Roll to us – and the melody sounds just simply great. Their best song cascades in pulsating ripples of melody and harmony. Their enviable hit string included #4, 6-83 follow-up "Is There Something I Should Know?" They also scored with #10, 1-84 "New Moon on Monday" and their 90s blockbusters – #3, 1-93 "Ordinary World," and #7, 4-93 "Come Un-Dun" (not Guess Who's jazzy rock tune #22, 10-69 "Undun"). Their millennial-era postscript is their ginchy-titled #52, 10-97 "Electric Barbarella."

"The Roving Kind" – Weavers, #11, 12-50. Though **Guy Mitchell** took this tune to #4, the Weavers' version epitomizes their hootenanny singalong style. Besides the biggest-hit waltz of all time – #1(13), 7-50 "Goodnight Irene," the Weavers also hit pay dirt with #2(1), 7-50 flipside "Tzena, Tzena," a Folk song of the fledgling country Israel. The Weavers' "Midnite Special" (#30, 9-52) prompted Paul Evans (#16, 1-60) and Johnny Rivers (#20, 2-65) to re-do this famous Leadbelly jailhouse rock tune. "The Roving Kind" stars a blithe lass with hair in ringlets and a come-hither smile. Seems her faithfulness leaps into question, but they sing her good spirits nevertheless. The Weavers' 1955 Carnegie Hall triumph actually began the Folk and Folk Rock boom.

The year 1956 saw **Harry Belafonte's** Caribbean Folk-style album *Calypso* hit #1 for 31 astounding weeks.

The Weavers' version of "The Roving Kind" was an adaptation of the English Folk tune "The Pirate Ship." The flipside, "Wreck of the John B"(attributed to poet Carl Sandburg in the 20s), caromed to the Kingston Trio – and from there became a party-album smash hit as the "Sloop John B" (#3, 4-66) for the **Beach Boys,** starting, hmmmm, a new Surf Folk Rock genre.

The Weavers' **Pete Seeger**, acoustic Folk purist, was voted into the Rock Hall of Fame ('96) despite disdaining Dylan's electric guitar at the Newport Folk Festival. **Pete Seeger** and the Weavers coalesced from the 1941 **Almanac Singers**, also starring **Woody Guthrie**. The early 50s Weavers, however, were a springboard to Rock and Roll with their rollicking beat and everybody-gets-into-the-act style. The Weavers brought music back to the people. Their hits thrived on audience participation and the simple joy of their music. They didn't do fancy. Just great songs. They were all excellent musicians, and they interwove friendly comedy, resolute political convictions, and the spirit of freedom into their classic Folk repertoire.

"Don't Speak" – No Doubt, #1(16A), 10-96. Into the late 90s, *Billboard* charts took a turn for the weird. You could top the Airplay charts for 16 weeks, and never make a dent in the HOT 100. Oh, well, Led Zep's "Stairway to Heaven" never even charted. At least now songs can be ripped out of albums, and plunked into the HOT 100 – without a single. Who really understands the current method? Anyhow, lead singer **Gwen Stefani,** guitar guy Tom Dumont, bassist Tony Kanal, and drummer Adrian Jones light up California's Orange County with their Monster hit record – with a mysterious little 'A' attached to their awesome number *16.*

"A Thousand Miles" – Vanessa Carlton, #5, 3-2002. In the grand tradition of singer-songwriters like James Taylor, Jim Croce, Joni Mitchell, or Carole King, young Vanessa Carlton creates her fervent ballad style through talent and musical quality. Her song is unrelated to Heartbeats' classic "A Thousand Miles Away" (#53, 12-56, #5 R&B). It is, however, twice as long-distance as Proclaimers' famous Scottish walking marathon – #3 '93 "(I'm Gonna Be) 500 Miles," or **Bobby Bare's** plaintive Folk/Country classic, #10 '63 "500 Miles Away from Home." You see, great music often begins in the Math Department, and somehow, all this stuff interconnects.

"A Moment like This" – Kelly Clarkson, #1(1), 9-2002. Speaking of ingénues, Kelly Clarkson parleyed her songsmithery expertise, by winning a famous *American Idol* star-search TV contest in 2002. Her new-found 'American Idol' status catapulted her RCA release from #52 to#1 in just one glorious week – an unheard-of jump. If anyone tells you the 'Teenage Idol' is a bygone memory from the 50s – don't bet the ranch. Teen idols are alive and well. Kelly has the talent – and telegenic pleasant looks – to back-up her new-found stardom.

"The Ketchup Song (Hey Hah)" – Las Ketchup, #76+, 10-2002. Don't let that meek first-week debut number fool you. This hip novelty number scorched the European charts at #1 for weeks, before peacefully invading the U.S.A., birthplace of Rock and Roll.

"Can't Get You out of My Head" – Kylie Minogue, #7, 1-2002. With the spunk and spice and Disco afterglow of equally-Australian Olivia Newton-John, Kylie Minogue rebounded to #7 with this Neo-Disco 'Dance track' tune. Her original heyday involved covering Little Eva's (#1, 6-62) "The Loco-motion" and its **Grand Funk Railroad** #1, 3-73 reprise; Kylie locomoted to #3 bronze medaldom in 8-88. Before rising to star status, Kylie was already a soap opera star (*Neighbors)* Down Under.

Nearly half of the top 20 during 2002 were female artists. Among other top-notch performers are: **Pink**, caucasian R & B star with two eight-ball 2002 hits – #8 "Don't Let Me Get Me" of 3-2002, and #8, 6-2002 "Just Like a Pill"; **Michelle Branch**, with #6, 2-2002 "All You Wanted" and #27+ up-and-comer 8-2002 "Goodbye to You"; **Avril Lavigne,** with her big "Complicated" hit at #2, 6-2002; **Mary J. Blige** at #1, 7-2001 "Family Affair"; international superstar **Shakira**, with #6, 9-2001 "Wherever, Whatever"; and **Nelly Furtado,** #5, 7-2001, "Turn off the Light." This Nelly is no relation to THIS next Nelly:

"Hot in Herre" – Nelly, #1(5+), 3-2002. This song here (herre?) might be light on spelling bees, but it buzzes heavyweight gold honors on the HOT 100. Nelly shot out of the blocks with his risqué Rap-rockin' #7, 4-2000 "(Hot S- - -) Country Grammar." In the same torrid zone, "Hot in Herre" blistered the #1 spot for a giddy chunk of 2002. Nelly also enjoyed another wonderful "Dilemma" in his career, perched on the horns of another #1(10+) song, "Dilemma," which debuted in 6-2000 as a take-charge follow-up; also starring Kelly Rowland. Its own #1 run was sidetracked by another Kelly – Kelly Clarkson's "A Moment Like This," in October 2002. As sage Soul superstar Stevie Wonder put it so aptly, in a song fading gracefully into the auld-lang-syne category – there will be "A Place in the Sun" (#9, 11-66) and a lot of hope.

"You Rock My World" – Michael Jackson, #10, 8-2001. Michael Jackson's millennial comeback snagged the top ten, but rumblings and grumblings of dissatisfaction from the 'King of Pop' shook the Sony/Columbia/Epic superstructure foundations. "Not enough promo," griped the 1984 superstar. Similar waves of consternation accompanied **Mariah Carey's** Columbia tenure, in the wake of her post-Tommy Mottola phase. Into the early millennial years, Sony and Columbia suffered from a jittery stock market downswoop, and dropped great name bands in the midst of their fledgling hit records. The bottom line may have been panic. Nevertheless, a top ten record is a top ten record – and the Jackson Five protégé proved he still had the superstar magnetism, despite a few new "Butterflies" (his #14, 11-2001 follow-up). Showbiz anger is nothing new. Before it became a big Rage Rock genre, the foresighted Everly Brothers were already mocking it:

"I'm Not Angry" – Everly Brothers NC, 1962. Off their #35, 9-62 *Golden Hits of the Everly Brothers,* one nugget-worthy gem is their tongue-in-cheek "I'm Not Angry." A rotten relationship encourages this jilted dude to stuff a voodoo doll with bats and owls. He rattles chains, and he wishes his ex a phone that never rings, a car that never starts, and a dress that rips at the big social moment. Then he fires the unltimate killer insult – he wishes her shoes will be too tight and will squash and scrunch her feet. The Everlys were perhaps reacting to the papa of the whole Rage Rock/Revenge Rock genre – **Del Shannon,** and his archetypal #28 1961 "So Long Baby."

"If You're Gone" – Matchbox 20, #5, 10-2001. In the tradition of their huge tune "Bent," "If You're Gone" may not be exactly Revenge Rock, but it's certainly aggrieved about its kaput romantic relationship. Rob Thomas's commanding baritone skirts the stars and surfs the asteroids, while seeking certainty where there is none. In the semi-Grunge tradition, the bottom of the band track is stuffed with a phalanx of baritone guitars (Kyle Cook, Adam Gaynor) to complement their lead singer. The song marches in lockstep cadence to some lost limbo between loves. Good tune.

"Drops of Jupiter (Tell Me)" – Train, #5, 3-2001. Speaking of astronomy, are you ready for a long trip? This cosmic odyssey may have spiked at #5, but its marathon run still had it listed at #46 on the HOT 100 **a full year** (OK, OK, 51 weeks) after its inauspicious debut. Rock and Roll has long dwelt among starry skies, throbbing planets, and the silvery moon; you might check out another interplanetary #5, Billy Vaughn's '57 "Sail Along Silvery Moon," or Ragtime Era "By the Light of the Silvery Moon," #1(9), 4-1910, by **Billy Murray & the Haydn Quartet.** Train's runaway hit has among the most clever lyrics of the Rock Revolution. It takes the video-game vet and rock fan on a splendid dash across the Milky Way, as does Sixpence None the Richer in #2 '98 "Kiss Me." Train's sound, however, rumbles like the mad-dash locomotive back in the evergreens by young "Johnny B. Goode." With a hint of Grunge, and a lofty melodic range, "Drops of Jupiter" salutes the big red planet, an astronomical love affair, and the best of millennial Rock and Roll.

Singer **Pat Monahan's** San Francisco Alternative Rock crew (Alt Rock) booms Dylanesque lyrics and galaxy-hopping – looking for, of course, love. From their #20, 10-99 "Meet Virginia," Train was on the right track. Rob Hotchkiss and Jimmy Stafford play guitars, with Scott Underwood on drums and Charlie Colin on bass. On Oct. 5, 2002, a planetoid named (wow – sounds like a refugee from a vowel factory) **Quaoar** was discovered out beyond Pluto (or Goofy, or Scrooge McDuck) in the Kuiper Belt. At 800 miles in diameter, it's unclear whether it's a mini-planet or a gigundo asteroid. Or both. Train and the Mauna Loa Observatory will keep us posted.

"Blurry" – Puddle of Mudd, #5, 12-2001. In love and war and Alt Rock baritone-guitar distortion, all is Blurry. Puddle of Mudd did not choose their name for intrinsic beauty. They go down in history among the greatest of Rock groups with nearly Zen Buddhist conundrum names: **Toad the Wet Sprocket** and **Jimmy Eat World.** The sound of the Mudd Puddle may be "Blurry," but their success is clear. In well over half a year, "Blurry" cleared up the fickle charts, riding the bucking bronco of the top ten for months. Their "She Hates Me" #20+, 9-2002 doesn't revel in lovey-dovey (or G-rated) lyrics.

"Hanging by a Moment" – Lifehouse, #2, 3-2002. Lifehouse stars talented **Jason Wade,** whose spirited vocals caused his silver-medal song to blanket most of the year in *Billboard's* vaunted HOT 100. Wade is also a talented lead guitarist, playing lead instrumental bridge in **Nine Days'** "Good Friend." The Sony label-mates showed that Rock and Roll success is often a fraternity (or sorority) of helping out other talented groups. Lifehouse's **Wade** pilots the lone guitar, with **Diff** on the drums and **Sergio Anrade** on the bottomtone bass.

"It's Been Awhile" – Staind, #5, 4-2001. Here's another song that wins a tug of war to bring the Grunge sound of the 90s beyond the millennium. Sometimes Rock and Roll veers off into deeper anger:

"In the End" – Linkin Park, #2, 10-2001. Armageddon Rock with strident voices is part of the package. When your biggest city is bombed, you rarely feel like chirping happy Bubble-Gum syrupy ditties. **Lincoln Park** is the name of two major suburbs of two big tough towns: Chicago and Detroit. The hip spelling of our sixteenth president, who adorns our penny, also previews the strident sound of Linkin Park. In the 9-11-2002 fallout, the percentage of young men blasting noisy trunk speakers of angry Rap/Rage/Revenge Rock has gone up substantially. One word in particular, scrupulously avoided over the aeons of Rock, seems to show up in some songs about three times per sentence. Are they simply blowing off adolescent steam? Or is it a deeper, gnawing rage about an Armageddon future with Middle-East soldiery – or three dead-end jobs w/ no benefits, while terrorist assassins stalk third-world Post-Modern wastelands? Or is it an attempt to turn the rest of the world into a permanent Battle Zone? Will everyplace become the new Ground Zero [a one-time term for the point of nuclear impact]?

On 10-30-2002, **Jam Master Jay** (Jay Mizell) of pioneer Rap group **Run DMC** was gunned down in gangland fashion at his Queens recording studio ["Walk This Way," with **Aerosmith**]. Turf wars rage on. No one wins.

Angry songs have always been with us. Linkin Park is nowhere near as angry as some. The percentage of furious, flailing Rage Rock and Nasty-As-They-Wanna-Be Rap songs is a mirror and a reflection of corporate crushing of small-business dreams. The individual gets crushed by the mindless corporation. Toilers toil, while soft CEOs buy $19,000 shower curtains and $5000 toilet-throne seats. It gets a little bleak, pondering the Internet pornomaniacs who troll for toddlers. It gets a little bleak, pondering a Mideast exploding with chaos and consternation – in the name of religion. It gets a little bleak, pondering the exit agonies of stubbed-out true love, good love gone bad. Where are we headed? Happiness or Armageddon? Where will it all take us, Linkin Park hints, "In the End"? Grisly mix-and-match future? Or a lost lorn cry in the wilderness?. Take your pick. Meanwhile, the trunk speakers get bigger, the growling gets nastier, and the wailing intensifies.

"Foolish" – Ashanti, #1(8+), 2-2002; #1 R&B. The 2002 charts herald the crushing domination at #1 by Long Island newcomer Ashanti, whose Soulful blend shows that there's always room for one more superstar. Eight weeks atop the *Billboard* HOT 100 beats anything ever by the Rolling Stones, Celine Dion, Simon & Garfunkel, Chuck Berry, Little Richard, James Brown, Led Zeppelin, Jimi Hendrix, Bruce Springsteen, or Pearl Jam, Dave Matthews, or Nirvana. Even Elvis only had a single-sided hit at #1 a week longer, as did the Beatles. Indeed, Ashanti pulled off a chart coup that hadn't been seen since Elvis's #1 "Love Me Tender" topped his own #2 "Love Me" the same week. Ashanti's "What's Luv?" collaboration with **Fat Joe** held down the #2 spot the same week as "Foolish" was #1. This newcomer is talented, promising, and her career is already big business.

"I Need a Girl (Part One)" – P. Diddy, Featuring Usher and Loon, #2, 3-2002. Also "I Need a Girl (Part Two)" – P. Diddy & Ginuine, Featuring Loon, Mario Winans, and Tommy Ruggeri, #4, 5-2002. This whole Part One & Part Two thing was started by the First Rapper – **James Brown.** As far as multimillion *Gold Rush* archivists can determine, this is the first two-part extravaganza in which BOTH SIDES zoomed to the Top Ten. Despite a name that changes faster than Keith Richard's/Richards', Puff Daddy/P. Diddy packs a power roster to buoy up sales. "Part One" features a heady mix of Rap banter with a tuneful chorus. The Half Rap/Half Rock & Soul hybrid began to emerge hugely in the early years of the 21st century.

"Cleanin' out My Closet" – Eminem, #4, 7-2002. This Graveyard Rap manifesto by Marshall Mathers of Metro Motown is a smidgeon scary. In the video, he's burying something in a gloomy and slimy cemetery. After legal squabbles with his mother, we see Eminem getting into shape by shoveling dirt. We don't know quite what he's doing, and we hope he's not burying his mom, symbolically. His Rap-lash style, at hip auctioneer speed, makes us realize his street-smart humor is often in a jugular vein, like *Mad* magazine. He revels in the Hallowe'en spirit of Applied Tomfoolery. America loves a long line of *imps* – not quite *demons* – from Dennis the Menace to Calvin [Hobbes] and Garfield the cat. At times, Eminem echoes Bugs Bunny rattling and goading and "dissing" and heckling world-class stooge Elmer Fudd. Eminem knows the way to multi-platinum lies in perfecting the art of ticking off the older generation. Since Elvis and the Rolling Stones and Barry White and John Cougar Mellencamp and Kurt Cobain, what has really changed?

Eminem's 9-2002 "Lose Yourself" hit #1(8+) in *Billboard's* Hot 100.

Among streetwise Rap & Soul performers, few were wiser than **Lisa 'Left-Eye' Lopez** of TLC. In 2002, her #1(7), 6-95 mega-hit "Waterfalls" prophesized her untimely farewell. Driving her car in Central America, Lisa spun off the road in a single-car tragedy and was killed. You may recall, she burned down boyfriend Andre Rison's house (he played pro football). Her song "Waterfalls" warned of a kid who didn't listen to his mother – dying in a frozen gutter. The road is a harsh mistress. The very talented Lisa Lopez (1971-2002) will be missed.

"U Remind Me" – Usher [Raymond],**#1(2+), 6-2001.** Usher's Soul/Rap/Hip-Hop hit streak rolled on apace into 2001, and never looked back with his follow-up #1, 9-2001 "U Got It Bad." Very few items in the *Gold Rush* index begin with '**U**,' though it womps '**X**.' Both Usher's name and #1 songs begin with '**U**,' and though it's a Rap spelling shorthand affectation, Usher makes a great point. A song may be BY me or us, but it's actually **4 U!** Do fans ever get mixed up on similar titles? Yep.

"How You Remind Me" – Nickelback, #1, 9-2001. With a Grungetone bass-clef passion, Nickelback's mega-monster song revels in intensity. Coming off a Scott Stapp/Creed-echo gravelly baritone vocal, and a surging baritone guitar and bass blur, "How You Remind Me" scuds along on the thudding bass drum. Like a crimson rose, the big sound of Nickelback blossomed to the *Billboard* pinnacle. Call it Grunge/Angst/Alt/Emo Rock, or whatever, "How You Remind Me" reminds me in its youthful turmoil of the **Doors.** Without the keyboard intensity of Ray Manzarek, Nickelback spins on its Jim Morrison/Chad Kroeger-style bellow of macho energy.

Though Neo-Gum bouncy tunes of the Britney Spears or Hanson ilk are peppy and sugary, and pulsing with big juicy major chords, this is not a Bubble-Gum world. *Gold Rush* celebrates only three kinds of songs: the happy, the sad, and those in between.

"Roam" – B-52's, #3, 12-89. It's hard to subdivide this upbeat tune. "Roam's" lead singer **Kate Pierson** jackhammers the New Wave beat. She convinces everybody that Rock and Roll can still be 100% fun with her sweet longing purr. The B-52's use Parrothead-style Hawaiian shirts, and a semi-Rap baritone chant from **Fred Schneider,** as in **Men Without Hats'** #3, '83 "Safety Dance." With their peppy, campy, bouncy style of pogoing all over the Dance Track Fever stage, the goodtime B-52's are a way of life. Since 1977, this Atlanta crew has bopped and grooved to rock and roll rhythms on stage. Singer/guitarist **Cindy Wilson** lost her guitar-playing brother Ricky in 1985, but with a show-must-go-on showbiz smile, the group re-grouped and thrived on the big charts and in the huge arenas of

America. On the 4th of July they co-headlined at Bald Hill, Long Island with **Nine Days,** and some B-52 beehive hairdos survived a gullywasher that brought down their curtain. It was the first fireworks show I've never seen, due to an obnoxious cloud of cloudburst.

Named for Kate and Cindy's beehive hairdos, which in turn were named after a WWII bomber (see SR-71), the B-52's roam to the eternal party of their ginchy "Love Shack" (#3, 9-89). It's somewhere between Gilligan's Island, Bali Ha'i, Shangri-La, and La-La Land. Kate skirts the majestic marshmallow melody into **Bangles or Go-Gos'** musical turf. Fred Schneider is the usual lead singer, but Kate glommed the *Billboard* bronze with "Roam." From their #56, 4-80 "Rock Lobster" debut, the B-52's scored into the 90s with some good stuff – #28, 6, 92 "Good Stuff," and *The Flintstones'* movie theme song, #33, 5-94 "Meet the Flintstones."

B-52's (l-r): Fred Schneider, Kate Pierson, Cindy Wilson, and Keith Strickland

"Fallin'" – Alicia Keys, #1, 6-2001. From out of nowhere, talented singer/songwriter Alicia bombarded the *Billboard* charts, nabbing a handful of Grammys for 2001 with her all-encompassing talents. She scored a #7, 10-2001 with the ironic "A Woman's Worth," and proved her collaborative skills on the FEATURING side of Eve's #2, 7-2001 "Gangsta Lovin'" ['Eve Featuring Alicia Keys']. 'FEATURING' was 2002's big Rap star.

"The Little Shoemaker" – Gaylords, #2(1), 7-54. First, Ronnie Gaylord and his Motor City trio scored a gigundo hit triumph in both English and Italian in the mid-50s **Italian song craze.** Similar Italian hits were Rosemary Clooney's #10, 11-54 "Mambo Italiano," or Dean Martin's first celebration of America's NEW favorite food

that sent the HAMBURGER to second-string status – his PIZZA ode of #2(5), 11-53 "That's Amore." You know, the moon zaps your eye, it's like this huge pizza pie – that's *amore.* Anyhow, "The Little Shoemaker" makes these magic dancing shoes, and some Flashdance kid whirls away to glory and paradise on the enchanted shoes. Somehow, this cute ditty became the theme song in Detroit for Roy O'Brien [he's got 'em buyin' and buyin'] Ford out at Gratiot Blvd. and Nine Mile Road.

How many of our favorite songs can become too precious – and even annoying – as jingles and plugs and spots and commercials? One 2002 example – Buddy Holly/Linda Ronstadt's hit "It's So Easy" – is Buddy's unintentional spokesong for Ziploc bags. Now, rather than ponder the big, brown eyes of Linda R. singing "It's So Easy" in sultry soprano, I picture dinky little carrot and celery sticks. Aaaarrrrgh, the aging process. You may also recall the May 2002 General Motors campaign to hype Pontiacs – and my favorite car, the glorious old Oldsmobile. Their ageless R&R theme song? Mexicano Barber-Shop streetcorner quartet Cannibal & the Headhunters: lead singer Freddie 'Cannibal' Garcia bellows their eternal 'Na-Na-Na-Na-Na' #30, 2-65 (NC R&B) "Land of 1000 Dances." Holly's "Oh Boy" once turned into "Oh Buick." By 2002, Chevrolet *finally* decided to play a little more of Bob Seger's classic, "Like a Rock" (#12, 5-86), except just the title, over and over and over and over. If the commercial is supersaturated, this is a form of Oldies Overkill.

One REVERSE jingle comes to mind. First, they had a Coca-Cola commercial. Then, the New Seekers turned it into a harmonic hit record with (seemingly) a cast of thousands: #7, 12-71 "I'd Like to Teach the World to Sing (in Perfect Harmony)."

A song-jingle commercial can either 1) Cast an ebony pall upon your ex-enjoyment of some great lost hit, or 2) Sell soap. It 3) Rarely improves the song.

"No Such Thing" – John Mayer, #13, 5-2001. Riddled with lyrical talent and Jazz Rock profundity, newcomer Mayer's astounding thesis is that reality isn't real. Musing over the 'real world,' he decides it doesn't exist. He wishes to scamper through the old stifling halls of his former high school, and declare that fact. All the hangups, all the social slights and cliques and grade-grubbing – all that was just for show. There is no such thing, Mayer declares, as the REAL World. It's basically a fig-newton of everybody's imagination. A fusion of Cool Jazz, funky bass guitar, and hip lyrics, "No Such Thing" shatters the old high school stereotypes. In the words of Mick Jagger, "Too much is never enough." Or, to be even more jaggerly cryptic, "The future isn't what it used to be. And what's more, it never was." On the one hand, Mayer is deep and philosophical. On the other hand, he is droll and wry and prophetic. In "Strawberry Fields," the Lennon wisdom is that *nothing* is truly real. Thirty-five years later, Mayer tacks on an existential extension of the Beatles' madcap Strawberry Fields philosophy – it's a topsy-turvy, Hobbes & Hobbit, zany kind of Easter Bunny landscape. Most of us are too busy working to really stop, along with

John Mayer and John Lennon, and ask this frazzled freeway world, "What's up, Doc?"

John Mayer is only the second Mayer ever to stomp to the *Billboard* HOT 100:

"Village of Love" – Nathaniel Mayer, #22, 4-62; #16, R&B. Nathaniel Mayer was the wildest, most uninhibited Soul commando ever to dart out the door of Third Avenue's legendary Fortune Records. Detroiter Nathaniel had towering tenor pipes, pipes which would make James Brown sound like a quiet choirboy. A processed 'do' four inches high made black-belt karate Nathaniel six feet tall, but he had an eight-foot voice. "Village of Love" is a streetcorner Soul anthem celebrating a long-gone Detroit Soul venue called "The Village" on Woodward Avenue. With his groups the Fabulous Twilights and the Dynamics, and knockabout gonzo drummer Butch Vaden, Nathaniel Mayer for one glorious summer had the #1 song in Michigan, and a national distributor. Nate Mayer ruled the Soul Empire with his pounding piano and his tornado-siren-volume voice. He was a wild guy to work with, at various sessions with my high-school girls back-up group, the Marteens [I was the first white Rock artist to be signed to Fortune]. Nathaniel brandished his Dracula-style red & black cape, some weaponry, and a larger-than-life bad-Leroy-Brown type rep.

Somehow, I mistakenly thought he died twenty years ago, like so many great Rock and Soul performers in permanent Hyper-Drive. I was happily astounded to discover that Nathaniel was co-headlining a Detroit Vintage Soul Festival with **Gino Washington** in Summer 2002. Gino's #121, 7-64 cult classic "Gino Is a Coward" was snuffed by Detroit-only distribution (where it was Top Ten). He recorded for Motown's biggest Detroit rival in the mid-60s, Golden World/Ric-Tic; they started the career of **Edwin Starr** (#1, '70 "War"), and featured the white Reflections' #6, 4-64 "(Just Like) Romeo & Juliet" in their integrated enterprise. Motown 'Funk Brothers' session men reportedly moonlighted at Golden World, up on Oakman Blvd. just three miles from the Motown studios on West Grand Boulevard at 14th St. The up-and-coming Ric-Tic studio was so upwardly mobile that – naturally – Motown bought them out. But Motown never, ever, bought out Devora Brown's Jewish and African-American Fortune Records – though it was reported she turned down a million dollars for Nolan Strong's contract offered by Motown (when a million was worth a small kingdom). Nolan's #1 Detroit hit "Mind over Matter" was squashed to national #112 in 1962, due to Devora's lack of national distribution. In Summer 2002, Nathaniel and **Gino Washington** reunited at a Detroit Vintage Soul festival. Some old Rock and Roll may perish in the onslaught of Demon Time, but its Soul lives on forever.

Only 40 years apart, two major Mayers mopped up the charts with their bold new ideas and unforgettable sounds.

'What I Like About You" – Romantics, #49, 2-80. What I like about "What I Like About You" is that you really can't place it anywhere in time. It's a quintessential Rock and Roll anthem. **Wally Palmer** sings lead and plays

guitar in this Caucasian-Persuasion Detroit Soul Rock crew, which features Coz Carter, too, on guitar, plus drummer Jimmy Merinos and bassguy Mike Skill. Though their biggee was #3, 10-83 "Talking in Your Sleep," this #49 gem gets the eternal airplay. It's fierce and fun Rock and Roll, like the Music Explosion's #2(2) 5-67 "Little Bit O' Soul," or #4, 9-67 Blue-Eyed Soul crew the Soul Survivors' Hard Rock "Expressway (to Your Heart)." Good songs like these are what Rock and Roll is all about.

"Soak Up the Sun" – Sheryl Crow, #17, 3-2002; #1 Adult Contemporary. Somewhere along the line, the cutting-edge Surf Rock gurus – the Beach Boys – became Beach Grandfathers and 'Adult Contemporary.' The Arkansas/California Girl shows that Surf Rock need not be an all-male campground looking for silent surfer girls to play Beach Blanket Bingo. Belltone Dixie Chick harmonies alight on Sheryl's sweet summer sunshine beach. Her volleyball bikini tableau features in-shape guys & girls chugging Perrier and driving Land Rovers for 'Woodies' (old surfboard-toting station wagons, with wooden sides, c. 1946, for 1962-65 Surf Era songs). Sheryl's bywords in this honey-toned melodic tune are FUN and FROLIC and FANTASTIC. She differs from 1962's no-oil, no-sunscreen era by cautioning she's wearing her "45." This means SPF45 sunscreen, since beach blondes have always been discriminated against by the burning sunrays (she could be nostalgizing for 45**rpm records,** too, but that's a long shot). With big ballooning Tonic and Sub-Dominant chords (I and IV), her sun-soaking song wafts blithely like a Beauteous Blimp of good years to come in the super sharkless surf. Surf's up. Let's Rock.

"Just Like Me" – Paul Revere/Raiders, #11, 12-65. Grunge Rock seems appropriate, with its minor-key marches, to follow the battlefield. In early Vietnam, like early Iraq II, dirges dragged along the spirits of reluctant soldiers. Not Paul Revere. Dressing up in Revolutionary War uniforms, they delivered a wild war-whoop here that just could be the dawn of the slashy Heavy Metal era. Keyboardist Revere of Boise, Idaho, was actually named after the American Revolutionary silversmith patriot. With Portland, Oregon's **Mark Lindsay** singing gusto-glutted lead tenor, the Raiders powered themselves to (eternal) Rock Hall candidacy with 15 Top 40 hits, like six-pack #6, 6-66 "Hungry" and #5, 4-67 "Him Or Me – What's It Gonna Be." Their straight anti-drug anthem, #4, 3-66 "Kicks," delivered a message to teenyboppers of all ages who watched them cavorting on their fired-up afternoon TV show *Where the Action Is.* The title tune "Action" was #13, 8-65 for Freddy 'Boom Boom' Cannon.

"Just Like Me" rampages into a guitar interlude that features TWO counterpoint leads, dancing atop the skinniest strings, and bending with interplanetary speed. The rhythm chugs along on a "Louie, Louie" beat (Raiders actually cut "Louie" a day before the Kingsmen, who hit #2, 11-63, but the Raiders only 'bubbled under' at #103). The Raiders' breakthrough, "Just Like Me," clamored for the top ten, and stunned an America giddy with the Brit

Invasion. Paul Revere's only #1 was the Native American lament, "Indian Reservation (The Lament of the Cherokee Reservation Indian)," of 4-71 – beyond their 1965-67 heyday. They also scored big with #17, 8-67 "I Had a Dream," #18, 2-69 "Mr. Sun, Mr. Moon," and #23, 9-71 "Birds of a Feather." Revolutionary American group. **HALL** candidates –

"Rich Girl" – Hall & Oates, #1(2), 1-77. You need 25 years of eligibility to qualify for the Rock Hall of Fame. "Rich Girl" is seemingly the ticket. This Temple University (Philadelphia) dynamic duo **passed** the revered **Everly Brothers as the top charting duo of the Rock Era.** Darryl Hall and John Oates enjoyed a six-pack of #1 hits, and explored the TOP Ten 16 times, nailing at least 34 Top 100 tunes. One wonders what one has to do to get a call from Cleveland? [Our garage band is still pining away, too, at last count, for the tail-end of a #95 song in 1967 – but these guys, what gives?] Hall & Oates furnish a slinky sound with a jackhammer funky beat and a rhythm track that won't quit. The 'Blue-Eyed Soul" brothers (OK, Hall has brown eyes) get pigeonholed into the Disco or R&B or Funk categories, and their hits are always cool, suave, and edgy..

For a barrage of Hall/Oates mega-hits, consult this list: #7 '76 "She's Gone"; #5 rocker of 5-81 "You Make My Dreams"; double #1's of 1981 – "Private Eyes" and "I Can't Go for That (No Can Do)"; #7, 1-83 "One on One"; #1(2), 9-84 "Out of Touch"; #4, 4-88 "Everything Your Heart Desires"; and 90s #11 "So Close" (9-90). Besides their originals, Hall & Oates hit #20 with a spiffy cover of the Temps' two Soul classics – "The Way You Do the Things You Do" and "My Girl" [#20, 8-85, "A Night at the Apollo," Hall & Oates]. Meanwhile, back at the Hall of Fame phone . . . in the words of the beloved bleacher bums of Brooklyn – "Wait'll next year."

"Release Me" – Englebert Humperdinck, #4, 4-67. What's a singer got to do to get noticed around here? **Arnold George Dorsey** was born in 1936 in Madras, INDIA. Despite a great Crooner voice (15 years too late), and a handsome telegenic face, Dorsey decided to change his ordinary name – so he picked some long-gone German Opera composer (a suggestion by similar nightclub star **Tom Jones's** manager [says Whitburn]). The result was a landmark trademark hit, the plaintive low-tenor "Release Me." Over the years, Englebert tore up the Adult Contemporary charts and the pleasure palaces of vibrant Vegas and beyond. His string of Pop pearls? OK: #20, 6-67 "There Goes My Everything"; #25, 9-67 "The Last Waltz"; #19, 5-68 "A Man Without Love," and his eternal post-passion "After the Lovin'" (#8, 10-76). Perhaps most importantly, EH is the only major star from the biggest English-speaking country in the world (900,000,000) – INDIA. "Namaste!"

"Ramblin' Man" – Allman Brothers, #2(1), 8-73. With Lynyrd Skyrnrd, the Allmans – Gregg and Duane – headlined **Southern Rock.** This Macon, Georgia crew fired up the afterburners for this road anthem. It puffs up

the persona of this guy who just can't settle down. Amazingly, they never charted on the Country charts (which, at the time, seemed to have an aversion to long hair and beards). When I have to go, baby, he explains, I really hope you're gonna understand. It's his destiny, yep, because he was born this rambling man. Lead guitar man Duane was killed in a motorcycle crash in 1971 at 24, while bassman Berry Oakley met a similar fate just a year later at a nearby intersection. **Dickey Betts** highlighted the Allmans' guitar squadron, and rocked out. Other hits? #19, 12-73 "Midnight Rider," #49, 4-87 "I'm No Angel," and #29, 3-79 "Crazy Love."

Allman Brothers (l-r): Marc Quinones, Allen Woody, Butch Trucks, Jaimoe, Gregg Allman seated: Warren Haynes, Dickey Betts

"Free Bird" – Lynyrd Skynyrd, #19, 11-74. This tribute to the martyred Allman brother soars like a free bird into the stratosphere, on the lead-guitar pyrotechnics of **Gary Rossington,** and the gutsy vocals of **Ronnie Van Zant.** Van Zant and much of the band perished in a 1977 plane crash. Among Toni's Top Ten Tunes, "Free Bird" Is the Epitome of Rock and Roll.

"What's Your Name?" – Lynyrd Skynyrd, #13, 12-77, and #38, 12-76. The band name came from the gym coach (Leonard Skinner), whose Jacksonville [FL] junior high school class they were kicked out of, for attitude and long hair. "What's Your Name" tells the riots of the road. It covers one of the two main non-aesthetic reasons guys often join R&R bands on tour: 1) Money, and 2) Girls. It's a hilarious tune. Grounded in Southern Blues, Skynyrd paints the rosy pictures of rock stars pretending one-night stands with golden groupies might be more than that. It's the ol' 'see-ya-next-year, honey' line. Girls unfamiliar with the Shirelles #1 '60 "Will You Love Me Tomorrow" song often end up pining away and pregnant, because of footloose dudes on the run in a super-charged tour bus.

Skynyrd also rocked out with big #8 "Sweet Home Alabama" of 7-74. It answers Torontonian **Neil Young's** two tunes which scorched the formerly segregated South – "Alabama" and "Southern Man." Skynyrd's only top ten tune here does *not* offer a welcome mat to Neil. Other hits? Yep: #27, 6-75 "Saturday Night Special" and #69, 4-78 "You Got That Right."

Ronnie Van Zant of Lynyrd Skynyrd

"What to Do" – Buddy Holly, NC '59; #29, 2-61 UK, and #27, 12-63 UK. Life promises us all a whole lot of uncertainty. This is one of the greatest songs of the Rock Revolution, bar none. In the numbers game, it got trounced by Buddy's biggees like 1957's #10 "Oh Boy," #3 "Peggy Sue," or big #1 "That'll Be the Day." Sometimes the numbers just don't tell the tale. This minimalist masterpiece belongs up with the best of Buddy's R&R triumphs. It's an acoustic tune that Buddy wrote and taped in his Fifth Avenue Apartment, with Maria looking on and smiling. It's a lot like the #1, 1980 *Double Fantasy* album hatching in John and Yoko Lennon's NYC **Dakota** apartment.

In just two months to the day after recording this "What to Do" hymn to uncertainty, Buddy would be flying to North **Dakota.** Arctic winter had checked in to R&R's Heartbreak Hotel. "What to Do" is a tale of lost love, rejection, and Grunge-lyric disillusionment.

Awash in a silvery tropical sea of lovely III mediant major chords, it's a bouncy tune that belies Buddy's downer mood. "What to Do" became a stark reminder in the UK of the grim grey stratus cloud that stalks the winter of our despair. Despite the courageous chords, the sweet Everly/Bryant style melody, and Buddy's good-pal tenor, the gloomy lyric perches like Snoopy's vulture in Charlie Brown's *Peanuts* saga. He asks 'what can I do?' The girl has deserted him. He says it haunts him. Then he cranks up a litany of nostalgic memories of happy days together: record hops, soda shops, walks to school. He tries to wrap his gloom behind a smile, but he knows he's fooling nobody at all. We all sympathize with the modest R&R legend. There is no one in the game of love – not even *Elvis* – who has not been unceremoniously dumped, while smitten.

This rare gloomy Holly lyric was great grist to the Beatle

mill of Top Ten Lennon-McCartney tunes. Or Don McLean's great Golgotha of Rock masterpiece – #1 '71 "American Pie." McLean's butterfly melody swoops along on marvelous fluffy chords of joy – and a leaden lyric of a musical nation spiraling to the brink of the dark abyss. Somehow, somewhere, we lost our generation in space, he said. Buddy's "What to Do" melody is not dissimilar to two of Buddy's other great songs – "That's What They Say" and "Crying, Waiting, Hoping," and parleys the popular Chalypso beat into Light Metal destiny. And Buddy Holly was the undisputed King of Light Metal. Though he could slam Hard Rock/Heavy Metal with the best ("Ready Teddy," "Rave On," "Tell Me How"), Holly truly created a whole Light Metal/Adult Contemporary/Lite Rock genre.

Though "What to Do" was never heavily promoted in America, it rose to popularity in the UK in the Holly afterglow. Though Holly was a superstar at home, in Great Britain he actually transcended superstardom. One group showed him the respect of naming themselves the Hollies (#3 group in England, 1964-68); one group had, as its first hit (#48) in America, Buddy's "Not Fade Away" (the Rolling Stones – and neither they nor Buddy ever faded); one other British group named themselves after a similar insect. The Beatles thought it excellent that Holly's crew was the CRICKETS, the name of England's closest game to American baseball.

Buddy took the uncertainty, ran with it, and soared to his own destiny. In Cricket Sonny Curtis's words, "Buddy Holly lives every time they play rock and roll."

"Good Friend" – Nine Days, #24, 8-2002 on Hot AC *Billboard* Charts, and #9, WLIR, New York City. Like Buddy's "What to Do," Nine Days' pensive and powerful ballad "Good Friend" leaped into the market, but then the promo bandwagon got a flat tire. Somebody at the top of Sony balked, and in a belt-tightening 'bottom-line' fiasco, they chose to put this great record on ice, while promoting angrier, more aggressive voices. Nice guys, however, do not really finish last. Since keyboardist Jeremy Dean is my son and the designer of your *Gold Rush* cover, I cannot admit to objectivity on this *Gold Rush* nugget. Let me predict that Nine Days will land on their feet.

Their long-awaited album is called *So Happily Unsatisfied* (how true, in the recording industry – what to do?). Their tune "Emily" sounds to me as powerful as the Beatles' "Eleanor Rigby," complete with Jeremy's strings-attached arrangement with violas and what-not. You can hear Brian on 3rds harmony on the #1(2)-in-Airplay song of August 2000, the #6 "Absolutely (Story of a Girl)," and great harmony on "Good Friend." Lifehouse's Jason Wade plays the lead on "Good Friend." It's a powerful statement about leaving someone you love – whether the guy and girl are splitting up, or whether it's about other good friends parting (see "Danny Boy"). Rock and Roll is about hope. We all hope "Good Friend" will find its niche on the high charts someday, but the competition is fierce. Among other great tunes on the album? "The Great Divide," "I Feel Fine," "Favorite Song," and the dynamic "The Joneses."

Almost any song in *Gold Rush* can become YOUR good friend. Maybe they already are. My kid Jeremy was once in a garage/basement band in our basement (at 16, Anderson Council). May you and you hopeful R & R band also rise to #6 – or close to it – and live the dream you're dreaming now. Cheers.

"Hero" – Enrique Iglesias, #3, 9-2001. Two bronze-medal #3 songs named "Hero" followed the 9-11-2002 terrorist NYC attack. The first is this Iglesias version, which coincidentally had been released before the planes hit the World Trade Center. Enrique and his international-superstar father **Julio Iglesias** (#5, 3-84 "To All the Girls I've Loved Before") have a Latino last name which translates to 'CHURCH' in English. The 9-11 catastrophe caused a lot of agnostics to suddenly pray a lot. The young idol Enrique's song casts a majestic, Orbisonic range into his fervent and powerful song. He even yodels – a Swiss technique rare in Latino vocals (Ritchie Valens hits falsetto in #22 '59 "La Bamba.")"

Chad Kroeger (Nickelback) and **Josey Scott** rode with another "Hero" to the #3 spot beginning in 5-2002. When **Mariah Carey** hit #1(4) with a similar title in 1993, she sang of finding the hero within oneself. Millennial heroic songs are perhaps less self-actualizing and more other-directed.

I have a hero. She is our daughter Lauri. On 9-11-2002, she and her husband Larry lived 1½ miles from Ground Zero. When Lauri was born, we had Martial Law in the streets of Detroit (1967) for the ghastly fiery rampage of an ugly urban riot. And now, when her baby was about to be born, Lauri's city was once again under siege. Lauri's mother and I fled Detroit, for our baby's sake. Larry (who worked one BLOCK from the World Trade Center) and Lauri decided not to flee. They stayed. On October 23, 2001, our first grandchild was born (they named him Maxwell Maury). Lauri is also a Speech Pathologist, and she spends her life helping people adjust their speech patterns to this wonderful place, America. Here everyone's religion is welcome, and every Old Country immigrant has a chance to begin seeking the glory of this land.

And as a footnote, without America there would not have been Rock and Roll. And could America really have been what it is today, without Rock and Roll?

"My Sacrifice" – Creed, #4, 10-2001. Scott **Stapp's** bullhorn vocal takes on the lofty crusade of some religious pilgrimage. As Pearl Jam's **Eddie Vedder** picked up the Grunge torch from doomed **Kurt Cobain** of Nirvana, so did Scott Stapp commandeer the "Higher" (#7, 9-99) ground for Rock idols into Millennium III. His lyrics are deep, his stage presence is profound, his fans are legion.

Scott Stapp of Creed mirrors Jim Morrison's end-can-be-always-near sense of urgency. We have no time to fritter away. All of this life matters. Unlike Morrison, Stapp is better grounded in faith and hope. With Christian charity, he shares his deeply-felt message via the mass medium of world-class Rock and Roll. Like **U2's** Bono, he carries that cross – that sacrifice – for what he believes.

"My Sacrifice" even gets political – maybe not even realizing its geographical meaning. In the aftermath of the WTC tragedy, and in the brief American-Afghanistani War, our unrequited search for Osama bin Laden took us to the High Hindu Kush and the Veil Of Kashmir in Pakistan/India. "Kashmir" is among **Led Zeppelin's** most haunting songs. Beyond Robert Plant's mesmerizing vocal we have the caravan of Bonzo Bonham's insistent drums, and the pulsating throb of John Paul Jones's ubiquitous bass, and the guitar mystique of Jimmy Page.

Kashmir has been the disputed province between two nuclear powers – Pakistan and India – for over 50 years. It is next door to Osama's cave in Afghanistan. Scott Stapp's baritone bears the cross of his pilgrimage, the sacrifice he must make in life. It is a magnificent and commanding vocal, and the crescendo fadeout (yep, an oxymoron, like 'Led Zeppelin' or 'Hot Ice') stalks the Himalaya Mountains, in a haunting torrent of tempestuous and turbulent sound. Of all the big R&R hits of all time, only Led Zeppelin's "Kashmir" and Creed's "My Sacrifice" have featured this hypnotizing siren beat. Listen for it. You'll know it at once.

Creed's follow-up, #6, 2002 "One Last Breath," also shows the seriousness of his Rock and Roll mission. Though Creed comes in a Neo-Grunge package, they do not sow the seeds of existential despair. Buddy Holly gave one-tenth of his earnings to his local Lubbock [TX] Baptist Church. Scott Stapp's father is a minister, and he too is not shy about Christianity in his life. Neither one was preachy, but their commitment transcended the lofty stages and arenas of their earthly triumphs in Rock and Roll. Like their forerunners **U2** of Ireland, Creed features a strong blend of mission and commitment. Their other mentors, **Eddie Vedder & Pearl Jam,** debuted at #72 (then #43) in 10-2002 with "I Am Mine." When all the older idols come back, the HOT 100 will need a HOT 1000.

"The Middle" – Jimmy Eat World, #5, 2-2002. Rank this one with the Glad Rock bonanzas of Buddy Holly's "Oh Boy," the Dave Clark V's "Glad All Over," or the Beatles' "She Loves You." This song is 100% Joy set to a rat-a-tat rhythm pattern and a hammering chorus. Besides proffering one of the great rock band names of all time, Jimmy Eat World features some dynamite vocals: lead singer **Jim Adkins** brandishes guitar, too, but once in the studio also handles keyboards and percussion. Rachel Haden harmonizes on other album tunes, with Tom Linton on guitar, Zack Lind on drums/percussion, and Rick Burch booming bass guitar in staccato style. Mark Trombino does technical stuff like sequencers, updating the sound. Rock and Roll has been erupting for over fifty years, but no one except Jimmy Eat World has ever found THIS sound. Way to go, Jimmy.

"Somewhere Over the Rainbow"/"What a Wonderful World" – Israel Kamakawiwo'ole, NC 1993. Judy Garland's "Over the Rainbow" was voted the #1 song of the 20th century in 2001. Not bad, for a song which only hit #5 in 1939, on its way to see the wonderful

Wizard of Oz. **Izzy** spins his own big rainbow tenor over **Louis Armstrong's** swan song "What a Wonderful World," and Garland's trademark tune. With a plinky ukulele and a minimal band track, Izzy's voice soars heavenward. It's on his 1993 *Facing Future* album in the Hawaiian section of your local record store, Borders, Barnes/ Noble, K-Mart, or Wal-Mart. Fly to Hawaii with Izzy, or hear him here.

Norah Jones ("Don't Know Why") copped Grammys in profusion in March 2003. She's the daughter of Beatles' sitar guru **Ravi Shankar** of India.

"Teach Your Children" – Crosby, Stills, Nash, and Young, #16, 6-70. It's only a song that symbolizes an entire generation. It's only gorgeous Everly Brothers-style harmonies doubled for our listening pleasure. It's only a supergroup of the **Byrds' David Crosby, Buffalo Springfield's Neil Young** and **Stephen Stills**, plus the **Hollies' Graham Nash** (plus bonus superstar steel guitarist **Jerry Garcia**, the big voice of the **Grateful Dead**). It's only the signature song of the "Woodstock" (#11, 3-70 C, C, S, N, & Y) generation, marshalling a half-million believers' pilgrimage to Yasgur's Farm in upstate New York – with stardust gold-rush dreams of peace, love, and in their case, especially harmony. "Teach Your Children" is simply a wonderful song that, fortunately, just doesn't ever go away.

Though Stills doubled on piano, this fabulous foursome is essentially a troubadour troupe of ex-Folk singers, and guitarists, amalgamated under the glorious festival banner of Rock and Roll. As the Woodstock theme song, "Teach Your Children" combines angelic Everlyesque harmonies with magnificent idealistic – yet realistic – Simon and Garfunkel echoes. C, S, N,& Y arrived (7-69, #29) on the "Marrakesh Express," and traveled musically to the ghastly scenario of Kent State, "Ohio" (#14, 6-70), where four students were gunned down by overzealous National Guardsmen. They discovered the top ten with #7, 5-77 "Just a Song Before I Go," eight years later. With angelic harmonies, they reflected a bleary-eyed Rock Hall of Fame bumpersticker with their magnificent 12th-comeback theme, #9 "Wasted on the Way" of Summer 1982:

> **IF YOU REMEMBER THE 60's,**
> **YOU WEREN'T REALLY THERE**

Then they split south for the "Southern Cross" (#18, 9-82), garnering millions of fans on their Rock odyssey.

Rock and Roll Gold Rush teaches of the sadness of artists' frantic lives. One fan donated a kidney to David Crosby in the 90s – because he loved their music so much. Also, he loved the idea of his own kidney filtering the lifeblood of Crosby's magnificent music. It made him feel he was truly a part of the Rock and Roll panorama, though the donor himself had no musical talent. It doesn't get any more dedicated than that.

Personally, I have attempted to reach your favorite song, and to treat it with the same awe and respect I would treat my own. Your music is among the most important things in the world. *Gold Rush* would not exist were it not for the music you picked to be played. As many of these grand old songs plod off into the proverbial sunset – and off the "Oldies Overkill" bandwagon – I have tried my very best to bring them back to you. Beyond the few artists privileged to enter the Cleveland portals of the Rock and Roll Hall of Fame – like **C,S, & N** and the **Buffalo Springfield** in 1997 – I have tried to bring you the best of the rest.

"Teach Your Children" is a plea for understanding between generations of rock fans. Parents' and childrens' health is precarious. Time kinda drags us all down. Bad things happen to good people. Their music, however, may just go on forever. The music, remember, has just one major ingredient. According to the Beatles, it may be the only thing we really need: "All you need is **LOVE**."

Elvis 30 #1 Hits – **Elvis Presley, Al #1, 10-2002.** Don't look now, but there's this great singer on the way up. In the entire **20**th century he never ever debuted an album at **#1.** His #1(5), 11-56 album *Elvis* was the first album I ever owned; my folks bought it for me for Christmas when I was 13. In that album, Elvis Presley emoted through a sad ballad called "First in Line." It never charted. But he did. The last line of the song explains that he was not only the first in line (for this love affair) but also the last. Some silly Internet blurb I got the other day was a little light on Rock history. The young historian claimed that 'Roots of Rock' meant Rod Stewart and David Bowie. Fine Rock stars both. The young Internet guru, alas, could use a few more decades in his critical repertoire. To some very, very young critics, 'Oldies' means the Thunder Rock of the 80s.

So who was the first in line? *Gold Rush* has come to see you, to put this whole pop panorama in perspective. Stewart and Bowie are fine talented singer/songwriters, but they were 11 and 9 when Elvis first clobbered the HOT 100 with #1(8) "Heartbreak Hotel." Indeed, Bowie was born in London on Elvis's 12th birthday. If you REALLY want to discover the roots of Rock, you can BEGIN with Elvis, and work your way backwards. Buddy Holly Memorial Society President **Bill Griggs** publishes the outstanding *Rockin' 50s* quarterly (P.O. Box 6123, Lubbock, TX 79493); Bill and Alan Robb cite in the Nov. 2002 issue some sheet music from 1934 (and the movie *Transatlantic Merry-Go-Round*) as having a song few of us have ever heard – it's called **"Rock and Roll."** If you're looking for Rock and Roll roots, please be prepared to go back a long, long way. I like to think *Gold Rush* gives you a few tremendous happy trails to follow while searching for audial gold. Maybe they will take you all the way back to a silvery Klondike moon, a long-silent saloon, and a few songs of nevermore – springing back to life. Remember, all this stuff interconnects – and it just might carry us back on faraway Klondike trails to the 1897 Alaska/Yukon Gold Rush.

When it comes to Rock and Roll, **Elvis Presley** (1935-77) will always be the first – and the very last – in line.

42 Take Good Care of Our Baby

Somewhere at the tail end of July 1999, our yard fell down. We Deans got pretty well smacked by a tornado. Maybe. Maybe it was just an instant hurricane. The storm front turned the sky green and slammed through Union Lake, Michigan. We were at the Ann Arbor Art Fair with friends Tom and Lee Plum, and missed the catastrophic cataclysm. I was planning to attend the Novi 50s Fair to see the main man for **Buddy Holly**'s rock and roll legacy. When we got home, it looked like our woeforsaken acre had been kissed by a small nuclear device. We lost seven 100-ft. champion black locust trees, and another piece of my heart. Miraculously, our summer home was grazed by a few small branches and brush. Fortunately for you, Tom Plum's favorite song anchors *Gold Rush*.

After one of the hardest days of my life, my wife and I got a handle on the ten cords of woods I'd been chain-sawing, bucksawing, and stacking. I had no time for the concert, so I went anyway. I had to go. Rock and Roll sings its siren song. We true rock fans are drawn like moths to a flame. I zoomed south to finally meet the singer who carried the R & R torch in the aftermath of the Day that Don McLean said the Music Died.

Tornado, shmornado.

* * * * * * *

One of the main reasons the Lubbock, Texas, Chamber of Commerce was able to obtain land for the **Buddy Holly** statue is that a terrible Texan twister had gouged a half-mile swath out of the center of town. Buddy's legacy rose again, like the Greek-legend bird the Phoenix from the ashes of defeat. The state with the greatest number of tornado deaths? Expectedly, big Texas. The silver medal, surprisingly, goes to Michigan.

February 3, 1959: The Fargo Kid got a call. Seems they needed a band to fill in for three big rock and roll stars who had just been killed in a plane crash. **Bobby Velline** was not quite sixteen. Stunned at the loss of his R & R hero and role model Buddy Holly, the kid took his 'show must go on' fortitude and called his big brother Bill, lead guitarist for their 'first Garage Band anywhere,' the Shadows. On and off, Velline was the occasional bandmate (no gigs, just band practice) of **Bobby Zimmerman** of nearby Hibbing, Minnesota. Zimmerman would later ramble on to the greener balmier non-pastures of Greenwich Village. Zimmerman, stymied on piano, changed his act to be more portable. He picked up a guitar and harmonica like Delta Blues icon **Jimmy Reed** – and became **Bob Dylan.**

From arctic Fargo, North Dakota, in the ice-blue prairie night of shrieking winds, Bobby Velline underwent a similar Clark Kent to Superman transformation. He has more of a baritone than Holly's 2nd tenor, but more people associate his sound with Buddy's than any other singer, any time, any place. In 1999 **Paul McCartney** came to honor Bobby at the Buddy Holly Rock n' Roller Dance Party. Paul performed "Rave On" on stage with him and the Crickets at the Roseland, saying "I'm here because Buddy Holly was a profound influence in my music." Blessed in 1961 with a HOT 100 #1 of his own to match his idol Buddy, Carole King's composition "Take Good Care of My Baby" [#1(3), 8-61], the Fargo Teen Idol, who finished first, went on to become **Bobby Vee.**

Weird I never met Bobby before. I missed his Shiawassee County Fair gig with Buddy's OTHER great protégé, countertenor **Tommy Roe** (b. 5-9-42, Atlanta, #1, 2-69 "Dizzy"). At the Novi 50s Fest, I slalomed between head honchos to the side of the stage for this big tent that held maybe 1000 fans.

Suddenly, there he was, in casual pre-show cutoffs and polo shirt:

"Bobby Vee?"

"Yep, pleased to meet you." He offered a sincere Dakotan handshake and his million-dollar Rock and Roll smile. He had 20 minutes to chat about showbiz and the Buddy Holly legacy. Holly's Beechcraft Bonanza was headed for Fargo and Moorhead Armory in Minnesota across the river. Bobby mentioned how contrary to popular belief, Bobby & his Shadows didn't do just Buddy Holly tunes at the fateful gig. Out of respect, they did mostly other material, knowing too that only Holly could do Holly at 100%. I finally blurted "Bobby, YOU did what every other musical guy in America wanted to do – you filled in for Buddy Holly."

*Teen Idol, **Bobby Vee**, 1961*

He said something that I know wasn't "Aw, shucks," but it could have been. Bobby is modest, sincere, and hasn't lost a step in wooing a crowd. Bobby Vee is just as nice a guy as I always figured he would be. I only regret I never got to meet him before. Basically, like me, and probably you, he's a family guy.

Like a "Rubber Ball" (#6, 11-60), Bobby Vee's hit records bounce on back to all of us. First his sons the **Vees** storm the stage. Son **Robby Vee** leads

off with an audial xerox of baritone Rockabilly **Jack Scott**'s #35, 6-59 classic "The Way I Walk," and plays dynamite lead guitar. Son **Tommy Vee** grapples the big electric bull fiddle bass – size of a cello – and plays it atop his head in Chuck Berry or Jimi Hendrix fashion. Other son **Jeff Vee** commands the rhythm battalion. Bobby launches a small sweet slice of his huge hit cavalcade. From #77 "Suzie Baby" of 8-59, Bobby took Clovers' "Devil Or Angel" to #6, 8-60, with Finnish-American Dakota Soul. His #61, 2-61 "More Than I Can Say" conquered England to #4, 3-61, prompting **Leo Sayer**'s blastoff #2(5), '80 version. Bobby's ballad "Run to Him" captured #2(1), 11-61, and his #3, 12-62 "The Night Has a Thousand Eyes" snagged bronze for his easy-as-1-2-3 HOT 100 coup. Gold? "Take Good Care of My Baby." In Carole King's lyric, the song-guy Bobby represents may be a nice guy, but he's no pushover. Sure, he messed up. She broke up with him. He tells the new guy, though, not to get too comfy in the relationship. Once he slips, Bobby's waiting in the wings with remorse, regret, and renewed commitment to make it work the next time.

Let's get real metaphorical here. Rock and Roll is our baby. It's a distinctively American art form, swathed in Delta Blues and Soul. It's serenaded by long-ago cowboys and barn-dance barnstormers. It's nurtured by half a century of rockin'-rebel refinements. Rock reaches from Rockabilly to Folk Rock to Emo Rock to Funk to Punk to Bubble Gum to Jazz Rock to Art and Orchestral Rock. It booms from Chalypso to Reggae to Zydeco to Cajun, from Motown to Philly Soul and from Rhythm and Blues to Hip-Hop and Gospel. With some Beatle modifications, Rock and Roll is still our baby. Though one snowplane fell out of the 1959 skies, the music will go on, like the lovers' mystic bond when the *Titanic* slipped away. Buddy Holly's music (Ritchie & Bopper too) forms a living legacy that steers Rock and Roll into new dimensions of harmony and glory.

So I'm standing there under a Novi tent after a tree-toppling tiny tornado, gabbing with Bobby Vee. Your instant impression is this – Bobby is the kind of guy you'd like your kid to be someday. Bobby's "Johnny B. Goode" story involves friends and bandmates: bassman Jim Stillman, drummer Bob Korum, fellow singer/lead guitarist Bill Velline (Korum is a Montana TV exec, and Stillman does a floating flea market extravaganza from Fargo to Phoenix).

Like many teen idols, Bobby has made a happy and prosperous complementary income out of yesterday. Bobby is now doing some of his best work (ERA Records via Capitol at 1750 Vine, Hollywood, CA 90028) both in his own studio and for bigger outfits. *The Early Rockin' Years* is a lost-tapes bonanza, with echoes of his wildly successful Al. #42, 7-62 *Bobby Vee Meets the Crickets*. Bobby's recent *Down the Line* is a 1998 concept album from Bobby's Roadhouse Studio [P.O. Box 757, St. Joseph, (Minnesota) MN]. His concept is 15 of Buddy's second-string hits plus obscure B-sides: "Tell Me How," counterpoint "Words of Love"/"Listen to Me" at the same time, and "It Doesn't Matter Anymore." "Words of Love" is on Al. #1(6) '65 *Beatles VI*. We all recall how the **Beatles** got their name from the **Crickets**. Bobby's *Down the Line* is family entertainment. Wife Karen worked on exec activities, and daughter Karen designed their cover.

*Bobby Vee (with guitar) and the **VEES**, 1999.*

Bobby's homegrown album encouraged my son Jeremy and me to do one, too: *Far from Every Day*, Al. 2002. We wrote a Holly tribute, too, "American Sky," that mentions Bobby [tonidean1@aol.com]. If you ever hear this album, remember that my **Nine Days** son Jeremy is the one doing the great musical stuff in there, and I'm just strumming and warbling.

Back to praise of Bobby Vee and what's right with America and Rock and Roll. Bobby has one of the greatest voices of all time. You respect him as a family man and role model (not a saint). Bobby charted 39 HOT 100 hits – all 'A' sides. Looking about 38 of his 56 years, Bobby still radiates that boyish enthusiasm. Bobby is the closest living legacy to Buddy Holly. Besides his OBVIOUS HALL of FAME credentials, what's the greatest thing about that Novi concert?

Bobby Vee and his boys the Vees seem to have more fun on stage than I've seen in decades. Like Buddy, Bobby loves his music and it is obvious. He carries on Holly's tradition. The music didn't die. Maybe, it never will.

As long as singers like Bobby Vee keep the tradition alive, the world will rock. Out of faraway 1960, Bobby's "Rubber Ball" bounces on back for you.

"What a Wonderful World" – Louis 'Satchmo' Armstrong, #116, 7-68, but #1 U.K. '68; then #32, 2-88. If you can find a song that celebrates the human spirit any better than Louie Armstrong's amazing "What a Wonderful World," let me know. He was born when the century opened, and he cleared all the major catastrophes of the bloodiest century in world history. Through two world wars and a Depression, Louis kept playing his trumpet, and singing his gravelly upbeat whimsy that made us forget our troubles – and he kept on smiling.

In the twilight of his life, he recorded a song that would not become a hit in his homeland until seventeen years after he passed away. Louie's song, however, lives on. And that is what we all want from our music. His green trees and red roses sparkle down the long years to our weddings and fiestas and sunrise reveries. His blessed nights and days are sacred with music and love. Tragically, his song is not Rock and Roll. However, his music of New Orleans cushioned the Big Beat, so it could be delivered to us by Chuck Berry and Elvis Presley and Buddy Holly. Despite Satchmo's age and infirmity and the bitterness he had to feel from racial injustice, he never stopped smiling. And neither did this wonderful, universal, adorable song that makes Louie's spirit follow us beyond our most precious dreams.

Epilogue

Long ago and far, far to the North, the Northern Lights shimmered blue-green and pink and spun-gold over the old saloons of the Klondike Trail to Dawson, up in the high aurora borealis Yukon just east of Alaska. Let us go there, you and I.

Jewel Kilcher zoomed south from the Land of the Midnight Sun. Tacitly named for her grandfather Yule Kilcher, who floated down the Yukon River on a raft after leaving Switzerland, Jewel grew up in Homer, Alaska, with one of the most breathtaking sights on the planet. Raised on 800 acres in an actual log cabin (1980s), she grew up with no TV, no running water, and only a coal stove to stave off Alaska's two seasons, winter and July. Like Swiss-American tenor **Del Shannon**, Jewel's upbringing was a 'Runaway' from rinkydink comfort and convenience. The angel-faced blonde lass was blessed with a super set of vocal pipes, and sang duos with daddy Atz Kilcher.

My wife and I batted around Homer in 1994 in our creaky '79 Chevy Malibu wagon. Flanked by the rugged gray Kenai Mountains to the south, and the majestic Valley of the Ten Thousand Smokes Mountains to the West atop the Aleutian Island chain, Homer is an artsy-fishy town ringed with icy titanic seas, breathtaking peaks, and constant challenges to basic survival. Yes, grizzly bears do occasionally lope along the high school track, causing human speed records. Roaring campfires dot the bracing and brisk June stony beaches, where brave shirtless surfers dare not go. A few short years ago, Jewel floated over this rock-ribbled fisher-paradise, sipping Alaskan beer, and celebrating in the sweet summer solstice where there is NO true night. We watched Homer Bay orca whales cavorting in the chilly surf, and grizzlies guarding the high hills from too much human complacency on lone gold trails. Midnight moose crunch baby birch leaves when June 4th lilacs bloom in barbecue backyards.

An Arctic Jewel was raised in a high Northern land where you can still pioneer. She chased the ghosts of thousands of Gold Rush prospectors mushing over the fabled Dawson Trail to the bonanza Yukon – where the sun never sleeps in high arctic summer.

A hundred years ago, peanut shells dotted the floor of the beery caverns of booming Dawson.

Roulette wheels spiraled. Roaring-camp girls danced their honkytonk stardust shimmy to the bounce and bulge of hot nuggets and racing hearts. In the center of the smoke and destiny, some piano puncher wore an eyeshade, a pin-striped shirt with cuff-garters, and a howdy smile. As the mad dizzy clock spun toward sunny arctic midnight, the lanky ivory tickler gushed forth a geyser of one waltz too many.

His left hand clutched the deep keys. His thumb pounded a baby Boogie. His soul grabbed a Swing Bass. His right hand rolled into Ragtime. His gold-studded Soul hammered together a basic Rhythm and Blues. With a ragamuffin lurch, an "Oh Boy" smile, and a hot Backbeat Jewel of a rhythm jag, some paradise honkytonk piano guy or gal struck the REAL Bonanza Gold.

And the name of this glory was Rock and Roll.

Just a Thought:

Gold.
There's a perfect
Melody out there somewhere –
And a perfect lyric, just waiting to unite
With this glorious tune. It hasn't quite been
Discovered yet. Someone will find it, perhaps soon.

I'm
Hoping
It
Might
Be
You.

NINERS' NUGGETS

This PIX-MIX spans the panorama of Rock and Roll music. You'll find favorites, superstars, and new artists you'll want to discover...

Aretha Franklin

Earth, Wind, and Fire

George Jones and
Tammy Wynette

Ashanti

Fleetwood Mac

Donovan

Carlos Santana

Creed--lead singer **Scott Stapp,** seated left

Janis Ian

Huey Lewis

Merle Haggard and **Willie Nelson**

Loggins and Messina

Patti LaBelle

The Oak Ridge Boys

Melissa Manchester

Live

Spice Girls

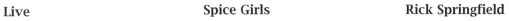

Rick Springfield

Slash of Guns 'n Roses

Yardbirds

Stray Cats--
Brian Setzer, (middle).

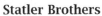

Statler Brothers

Gwen Stefani (ND hat) and No Doubt

Staples Singers (Left, Pop)

↑ **Chuck Berry** ↘

Elvis Costello

John Kay of **Steppenwolf**

Ed Cowling, Maury Dean, and **Chuck Berry's** piano man, **'Boogie' Bob Baldori**.

Ted Nugent

Rod Stewart

Shania Twain

Reba McEntire

Gary Garritan

Buddy Morrow

The Hollies and gold records

John Popper
of **Blues Traveler**

Dick and **Dee Dee**

James Brown and **Rod Stewart**

Beyoncé Knowles of
Destiny's Child

Sarah McLachlan

Jefferson Starship

Jason Wade of **Lifehouse**

Billy Joel

Bobby Vee (center) and **Sha Na Na**

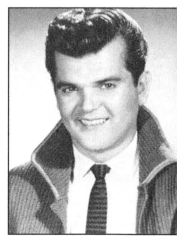

Conway Twitty

Ka'au Crater Boys

Buddy Holly and the **Crickets**
(L-R): Niki Sullivan, Joe B. Mauldin,
Buddy Holly, Jerry Allison

Jimmie Rodgers [II], 1998

Johnny Nash

Keith Richard[s] and **Mick Jagger**

Buddy Holly Statue, Lubbock, TX

Elvis and chili

Johnny Rivers

Sonny Curtis of the **Crickets**

Eddie Money

Carter Family, (L) Mother Maybelle Carter, (2nd from left) June Carter Cash [Johnny Cash's wife].

Graphophone-- 1906 cylindrical-record player

Bill Monroe

Aaron Copland and **Benny Goodman**

Paul McCartney

B.B. King

Everly Brothers
(L) **Phil**, (R) **Don**

Bob Dylan

Dion

Willie Nelson

Ritchie Valens

Ramsey Lewis

Stevie Wonder

Stonewall Jackson

Barry Manilow

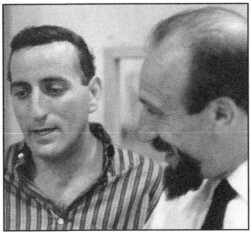

Tony Bennett and Mitch Miller

Engelbert Humperdinck,
Star of India (Britain, and America)

Little Richard and
Tanya Tucker

Def Leppard

Julio Iglesias, father of
Enrique Iglesias

Ricky Nelson (R) with Terry Bazzett

Dr. Dre

Blues Traveler

Adam Duritz
of **Counting Crows**

Guns 'n Roses,
Slash (2nd from left), **W. Axl Rose** (middle)

Goo Goo Dolls,
Johnny Rzeznik (center)

Kid Rock

Barenaked Ladies [some guys may be disappointed that this picture is correctly labeled].

Black Crowes

Pink

N'Sync

Stone Temple Pilots

Chapter Questions

Chapter One

1) Who was the 1955 movie idol who helped create both Rock and Roll and the **teenager** concept?
2) Who are the big three Rock and Roll stars of the 50s, who best shaped Rock music for the last half of the 20th century?
3) How are songs chosen for *Gold Rush?*

1) James Dean.
2) **Elvis Presley, Buddy Holly, and Chuck Berry.** Others nearly as significant include Antoine 'Fats' Domino, Little Richard, Jerry Lee Lewis, and the Everly Brothers. Other first-year Rock Hall of Fame Inductees impacted later as superstars: Ray Charles, Sam Cooke, James Brown.
3) **Merit.** We use **SINGLE RECORDS' success** as our major barometer. Most of our statistics come from **Joel Whitburn's** system of tabulating *Billboard's* singles lists on the **HOT 100, Country (C), and Rhythm & Blues (R & B)** charts. We also choose great songs from the lower charts, plus some albums, for qualities like critical acclaim, musical genius, or dominating the Oldies or Classic Rock playlists. *Gold Rush* is a comprehensive **playlist** of the top tunes of all time – and the best-loved songs.

Chapter Two

1) Who was the major songwriter of the 19th century who "wrote the book on [gorgeous] melody"?
2) During the 1890s era of the 'Waltz Kings,' who was the Irish-American singer with one of the greatest streaks of #1 songs of all time?
3) What were some 1880-1910 styles of music with a 'big beat,' that later shaped and coalesced into Rock and Roll?

1) Stephen Foster.
2) Dan Quinn. Other 'Waltz Kings' included Len Spencer and George Gaskin.
3) **Ragtime,** with new *chords, swing bass,* and *syncopation.* Experts included Eubie Blake and Scott Joplin. **Marches** included John Philip Sousa's big booming 2/4 beats and crashing rhythm. **Waltzes** often used Barber-Shop Quartet four-part harmonies that evolved into 50s **Streetcorner** music. Frankie Lymon's Teenagers became the prototype for 'Boy Bands' like N'Sync or the Backstreet Boys. The 1910s and 1920s introduced the **Blues, Dixieland Jazz,** and Louis 'Satchmo' Armstrong, all direct antecedents of Rock and Roll.

Chapter Three

1) Which revered performer best covers most of the 20th century, linking Dixieland Jazz, Blues, Soul, Ballads, and Light Rock?
2) Name a few stars of the early 20th century who paved the way for Rock and Roll.
3) "Rock and Roll is not conducive to longevity." Who were the three century-spanning songwriters who disproved this gloomy adage in the songwriting arena? They were NOT Rock and Rollers, being born too early.

1) Louie 'Satchmo' Armstrong (1900-71),
2) W.C. Handy, Al Jolson, Paul Whiteman, Gene Austin, Rudy Vallee, or Isham Jones. Later stars (1920-50) include Duke Ellington, Ella Fitzgerald, Cab Calloway, Count Basie, 'Fats' Waller, George Gershwin, Bessie Smith, Ma Rainey, the Mills Brothers, Bing Crosby, the Dorsey Brothers Tommy & Jimmy, Harry James, Glenn Miller, and Frank Sinatra.
3) Irving Berlin (1888-1989) composed the #1 song of the 20th century (until overtaken in 1997) – "White Christmas." Eubie Blake (1883-1993) wrote timeless Ragtime classics. Governor Jimmie Davis (1899-2000), whose long life straddled THREE centuries, wrote the campfire/cowboy anthem "You Are My Sunshine."

Chapter Four

1) According to tiny Chapter Four, what is the most important instrument in a Rock band?
2) Who are the three inventors/modifiers of the electric guitar?
3) **Vocal Range** is crucial to Rock stardom. Draw a chart of the male and female vocal ranges. Give examples of singers in these categories (see detailed chart on p. 34). Add your own examples of great singers omitted.

1) The human voice [the guitar wins the silver medal].
2) Mr. Beaubien, Detroit musician/electrician in the mid-1920s, possibly invented the electric guitar (his first name was probably BILL, for my piano player Danny Beaubien's older brother was named Bill Beaubien). I called Dan's electrician/guitarsmith dad "MISTER Beaubien" out of respect of his kindly nature, and his 66 years, back in 1962. Joe Kekeku of Hawaii invented Hawaiian or Slide Guitar in 1931, using a bottleneck to cascade a blurry GLISSANDO of sliding sounds. **Les Paul** invented the solid-body guitar in the 40s, AND played a job in the Iridium Room in Manhattan to mark his 2001 86th birthday.

3)   MALE   FEMALE
                          Soprano: Joan Baez,
                          Belinda Carlisle (Go-Gos),
                          Jewel, Diana Ross

Falsetto: **Mezzo (middle) Soprano:**
Lou Christie   Linda Ronstadt,
                          Madonna, Aretha Franklin

1ˢᵗ or 'Irish'Tenor: **Alto:** Vanessa Carlton,
Tommy Roe,   Reba McEntire,
Darrin Hayes/Savage Garden,   Sheryl Crow,
Paul McCartney   Melissa Etheridge

2ⁿᵈ or Dramatic Tenor:
John Lennon, Bob Seger,
David Ruffin (Temptations),   **Contralto:**
Brian Desveaux (Nine Days),   Toni Braxton,
Elvis Presley, Billy Joel,   Mahalia Jackson
Elton John   Stevie Nicks

Baritone: Frank Sinatra,
Eddie Vedder, Scott Stapp,
Notorious B.I.G., Toby Keith,
David Bowie, Bing Crosby,
Mick Jagger. Johnny Cash bounces
between Baritone and Bass (Bari-bass?)

Bass:
Tennessee Ernie Ford,
Paul Robeson (Very few, if any,
   R&R lead bass singers)

Chapter Five

1) Boogie-Woogie, Blues, and Rock and Roll often share one basic chord pattern. Name it.

2) Tell the names of major pre-Rock Crooners:

3) What rhythmic problem kept much Crooner Pop music off the Rock Oldies charts and playlists for over 50 years?

1) The **12-Bar Blues Progression.** The standard progression for ballads is the **Streetcorner** progression of four basic chords. Example:
   C — Am — F — G7
   See CHORD THEORY in Glossary for deeper 12-Bar Blues diagrams, but basically it follows this arrangement in Key of "C" for PIANO or the Key of "E" for GUITAR:

	C — F – C – G – F – C – G
	E — A – E – B – A – E – B
# of Bars:	4 — 2 – 2 – 1 – 1 – 1 – 1

2) Perry Como, Bing Crosby, Tony Bennett, Dean Martin, Frank Sinatra.

3) The drummer seemed to be on eternal coffee break, A.W.O.L., or temporarily dead.

Chapter Six

1) What did Louis Jordan do, to literally SPARK Rock and Roll (and perhaps MTV, too)?

2) How did Little Richard and Pat Boone sell records for each other? How did they sell the hot new idea of Rock and Roll to teens and parents alike?

3) Point out the pioneering contributions of any of these 50s legends: Elvis Presley, the Platters, Hank Ballard, Antoine 'Fats' Domino, Bill Haley, or LaVern Baker.

1) Jordan's Jazz/R&B Pre-Rock & Soul band of the 40s featured neon saxophones.

2) Richard cut Rock [Screaming Blues] songs with a rampaging soulful beat. Parent-approved, G-rated Pat Boone sold friendly family-oriented respectability with every Little Richard 'platter' he covered.

3) **Elvis** – voted #1 Entertainer of All Time. **Platters** – balladeer smooth Soul quintet of throbbing Rock standards. **Ballard** – Detroiter who launched raunchy guitar-powered style – he invented the TWIST in his spare time, liberating ADULTS to embrace Rock music for the first time ('60). **Domino** – beloved ambassador of non-threatening Rock and Soul, from R & R's cradle, New Orleans. **Haley** – his bombshell "Rock Around the Clock" defined Rock and Roll, and may have sold 33+ million copies by now. **Baker** – first Rock and Soul Diva, back when Janis Joplin and Gracie Slick were 13 years old.

Chapter Seven

1) Name some early **Streetcorner** groups, who relied on the piano-driven **C — Am — F — G7** four-chord pattern, with a **Bridge** to vary the pattern in the middle of the song.

2) Who singlehandedly created **Calypso,** forerunner of Reggae, Ska, Chalypso, Junkanoo, and Caribbean music?

3) Name a few **DJs (Disc Jockeys)** of the early Rock Era, and tell their importance to the Rock Revolution.

1) Danny & the Juniors, Dell-Vikings, Impalas, Cadillacs, Coasters.

2) Harry Belafonte, of "Day O/Banana Boat Song" fame. His album *Calypso* was #1 for 31 weeks, an unprecedented chart reign on *Billboard's* brand-new Album Charts.

3) **Dick Clark** – DJ and first major Vee-Jay (Video Jockey = VJ). Clark hosted daily dance-party TV show *American Bandstand* (1957 – late 80s). **Wolfman Jack** (Bob Smith) – Airwave institution, with friendly teddy-bear growly baritone (60s-90s). **Casey Kasem** – Hosts national radio weekly countdown "American Top 40," #1 show for 1/3 century (60s- Now). Other

stars included Bob Horn, Bill Lowery, Joel Sebastian, Jack Cooper, Jocko Henderson, Tom Clay, Dick Biondi, Mickey Shorr, Dewey Phillips, Frantic Ernie Durham, and Martha Jean – the Queen.

Chapter Eight

1) Name some of Buddy Holly's key Crickets, and musical colleagues.
2) Why was Buddy the most versatile Rock star of them all?
3) What happened on February 3, 1959?

1) Drummers **Jerry [J.I.] Allison** and Charlie Bunch; bassmen **Joe B. Mauldin** and Larry Welborn and later country star **Waylon Jennings;** guitarists Niki Sullivan, **Sonny Curtis,** and Tommy Allsup; also later Crickets like David Box, Glen Hardin, Jerry Naylor, Gordon Payne, or Buddy's junior-high songsmith duet partner – Bob Montgomery. Producers **Norman Petty and his wife Vi,** plus Dick Jacobs in New York, steered his musical career.
2) Buddy fronted the first major modern Rock and Roll band. He wrote his own songs. He sang lead, and played lead guitar. Buddy arranged and helped produce his sessions with the Pettys and Jacobs. Buddy's melodic and polychord adventures previewed Jazz Rock. Indeed, **Buddy Holly's R & R sound was at least five years ahead of its time, perhaps ten.** Holly introduced strings and orchestras to Rock and Roll, plus *overdubbing.* He was among the first of the significant *singer-songwriters.* Through enthusiastic musical vision, he was instrumental in naming the **Beatles.**
3) The music did not die, contrary to Don McLean's grand and gloomy "American Pie." Buddy Holly, the Big Bopper (J.P. Richardson), and Chicano-Rock sensation Ritchie Valens were killed in a blizzard plane crash, after their Ground Hog Day gig at Clear Lake, Iowa's Surf Ballroom. Buddy's legacy included the British Invasion and half a century of unquenchable Rock and Roll. As role models go, Holly was the kind of decent guy that parents would like their kids to grow up to be.

Chapter Nine

1) Which Folk group nearly created the record ALBUM?
2) What was the Weavers' role in shaping Folk music?
3) How did Phil Ochs and Bob Dylan change the direction of Folk music?

1) The **Kingston Trio** in 1958: Bob Shane, Nick Reynolds, and Dave Guard.
2) Rock Hall Inductee Pete Seeger, with Ronnie Gilbert, Fred Hellerman, and Lee Hays, sang *hoote-*

nanny sing-along huge hits at mid-century – like #1(13), 1950s "Goodnight Irene." They influenced the Kingston Trio with their Folk Standards, and Bob Dylan with their feisty political convictions.
3) Ochs's acoustic political agenda was edgy, rebellious, and questioning. Dylan's lyrical canvas was influenced by the profound 'spontaneous bop prosody' of Jack Kerouac's novel *On the Road,* and by the Beat Generation. Dylan challenged acoustic Folk purists by simply plugging in his guitar.

Chapter Ten

1) "Johnny B. Goode" is an archetypal song about the American Dream. How did Chuck Berry get the name for his song?
2) How did Jerry Lee Lewis fluster parents to ban his records?
3) How did Chuck Berry begin Surf Rock?

1) Berry named his rock anthem after his boyhood home on **Goode** Street in St. Louis, Missouri.
2) "The Killer" stomped on his grand piano, sang five-alarm suggestive lyrics, married his 13-year-old cousin (his bass player's daughter), and squabbled with fellow musicians. His music is the heart of Rock and Roll.
3) Chuck's "Sweet Little Sixteen" metamorphosed into the Beach Boys' "Surfin' U.S.A." Except for some octave-surfing by the beach guys, in waves of *falsetto,* each hit has an identical melody. The Beach Boys also shared Chuck's love of geography, and applied it to great surf beaches along the Pacific coastline. Chuck's exuberance about Rock and Roll morphed into the affluent Southern California cruising/surfing/drag racing subculture.

Chapter Eleven

1 Who was the only **duo** selected to the first class (1986) of the Rock and Roll Hall of Fame?
2) What do Jimmy Clanton and Ricky Nelson represent among 50s Rock stars?
3) How did Bobby Darin span all the categories of popular music?

1) Don & Phil, the Everly Brothers.
2) They are **Teen Idols,** whose recording success was bolstered by both talent and good looks. Teen Idols were often considered more 'boy-next-door' than 'super-bad.' Into the 21st century, Teen Idols crossed genders, like Britney Spears and Kelly Clarkson (as well as Justin Timberlake). In September 2002, after the perky and talented Kelly Clarkson won the "American Idol" TV show talent contest, her RCA release "A Moment Like This" broke all records for zooming to the top of the *Billboard* HOT 100 chart.

After its debut week at #52, it **skyrocketed to #1 in just ONE week.**

3) Singer/songwriter Bobby Darin began with a hard rocker (#3 "Splish Splash"), followed with a beautiful Chalypso (#2 "Dream Lover"), and trumped Sinatra at his own game with #1(9) classic "Mack the Knife." Darin also scored with Folk ballads ("If I Were a Carpenter"), 'White Soul' balladry (#3 "You're the Reason I'm Living"), or Streetcorner-style musical magic: #5 "You Must Have Been a Beautiful Baby," a cool cover of Bing Crosby's 1938 #1 hit.

Chapter Twelve

1) Pick the 2nd-biggest Surf Rock group of all time (with possibly the best Surf anthem).

2) Where did the Beach Boys' Jazz-infused harmonies begin?

3) How might supposedly carefree, sunny Surf/ Cruising music be riskily associated with "Death Rock"?

1) Jan & Dean – **Jan** Berry and **Dean** Torrence. The song is #16, 9-64 movie-title theme "Ride the Wild Surf," about the 30-foot storm waves on Waimea Bay, Oahu, Hawaii.

2) The Lettermen sculpted a jazz-powered vocal blend that mentored the Beach Boys' Surf Rock enchantment. The Beach Boys' rhythmic underpinning is Carl Wilson playing Chuck Berry-style guitar, plus brother Dennis Wilson driving the energetic drums.

3) Ever watched 'Extreme Sports' on cable TV? Fearless skateboarders and dirt-bike demons hurl themselves into spleen-splitting crack-ups. Neither surfing nor skiing ever classified as Wimp Sports. 'Fun' involves risk: sharks, 'deadman's curves,' killer sunburns, or maybe just a punch in the nose, from the 6'5" palooka whose bikini babe's belly button magnetizes the unwary amorous adventurer, on 'Paradise' Beach. Jan's & Dean's #25, 10-64 "Sidewalk Surfin'" **started the skateboarding craze,** which now keeps emergency room cash registers ringing all over this flippin', somersaultin', airborne planet.

Chapter Thirteen

1) What is the one song Elvis wished he'd recorded first?

2) Which singer became Elvis's favorite after Buddy Holly was gone?

3) Who are the "A-" singers in this Great Singers chapter?

1) **Del Shannon's** #1(4), 3-61 classic "Runaway."

2) Roy Orbison, of oiltown Wink, Texas. Orbison's range, tone, and timbre have never been duplicated.

3) There ARE none. They're all "A+" or straight "A" (of

course, Johnny & the Hurricanes are an INSTRUMENTAL group). The Penguins were great Antarctic-American songbird superstars. Shannon, Orbison, the Beatles, Jackie Wilson, Jimmy Beaumont, and the others are 'singer's singers,' appreciated for their technique, range, and audience charisma.

Chapter Fourteen

1) How important to the evolution of Rock music is Marty Robbins?

2) Describe the *Brill Building versus Garage Band* rivalry.

3) Classify the Four Seasons.

1) Marty accidentally invented Heavy Metal. His "Singing the Blues," covered by Guy Mitchell, may have been the longest #1 Rock and Roll song of all time for 30+ years. Marty's pink carnation in his #2 "White Sport Coat" made it to Don McLean's "American Pie" lyric. Marty also pioneered the L – O – N – G Song (#1 '61 "El Paso"), and anticipated great Afro-Cuban Reggae Rock via his "Devil Woman."

2) The NYC Brill Building relied upon pianos in the Key of "C", and star songwriters like Bobby Darin, Carole King, or two Neils – Sedaka and Diamond. Garage Bands used Key of "E" guitars and singer-songwriters who sculpted their songs from scratch.

3) They're an Italian-American Streetcorner-style Barber Shop Quartet. The Four Seasons defined the East Coast Sound of 1961-65 Rock. Producer Bob Crewe's snare-drum snapping rhythm track complements Frankie Valli's soaring falsetto flourishes. Their lyrics involve normal kids with bittersweet romantic adventures and busted wallets. The flip side of #3, 2-64 "Dawn (Go Away)" is actually Jazz-infused

Chapter Fifteen

1) Name some important early women Rock and Soul stars.

2) How does the Shirelles' "Will You Love Me Tomorrow" present a female viewpoint about intimacy?

3) How shocking were the Kingsmen's lyrics in "Louie, Louie"?

1) Wanda Jackson, Etta James, Ruth Brown, Brenda Lee, the Chordettes, Shirelles, Connie Francis, Cookies, Angels, Chantels, and the Crystals.

2) In the history of the world, no man has ever gotten pregnant. If they did, they might be a little less 'hot to trot' with some 'Wild Thing' they think they love.

3) Nobody knows. The U.S. Congress couldn't figure them out, nor could the snoopiest of FCC lyric-unscramblers. "Louie" remains an Extreme Party-Animal Song, with suspicions (only) of wild risqué lyrics.

Chapter Sixteen

1) How did February 9, 1964 get into the running for #1 Rock History date of all time? What happened then?

2) How did the Beatles combine the best American Rock and Roll to capture their own unique sound?

3) "Someday, the Beatles will be bigger than Elvis!" Who said that? Was it prophetic?

1) The Beatles invaded America on 2-9-64 on the *Ed Sullivan Show*. It mesmerized over 1/3 of all Americans alive at that time to watch the show, transfixed, at the Rebirth of Great Rock and Roll.

2) Buddy Holly's enthusiasm, sound, and band name; Little Richard's 'Screaming Blues'; Jimmy Reed's hot harmonica; Dion & the Belmonts Barber Shop harmonies; Del Shannon and Johnny & the Hurricanes' dynamic Thunder Rock sound.

3) Manager Brian Epstein was rebuffed by Dick Rowe and British Decca Records; Decca also botched Buddy Holly's stateside career. Rowe laughed at Epstein's nerve and chutzpah. With dramatic irony, Epstein never realized how prophetic his words would someday become.

Chapter Seventeen

1) When Berry Gordy Senior literally 'cashed in his chips,' what northern empire did his family begin?

2) What was the Twenty Grand?

3) Who was the direct 50s link to Motown's biggest star Michael Jackson?

1) The Motown Empire, via Berry Gordy, Jr., was housed in three four-square homes on Detroit's West Grand Boulevard, after the elder Gordy sold wood chips to help finance his move to the Motor City.

2) Detroit's major Soul venue in the 60s, on 14th Street near Warren. The Twenty Grand (i.e., 20,000 bucks) was the Motor City equivalent of Harlem's storied Apollo Theatre.

3) Frankie Lymon and his Teenagers of the Bronx. Lymon at 13 charted a dynasty of soulful Barber-Shop Streetcorner groups. See Dion & Belmonts, the Beach Boys and Beatles, Bee Gees, Duprees, Spinners & Stylistics, N'Sync & the Backstreet Boys.

Chapter Eighteen

1) Name some key British Invasion artists.

2) Name some famous performers never blessed with a #1 *Billboard* HOT 100 single in the 1955+ Rock Era.

3) Explain persona, or the Song-Guy Concept, in the Rolling Stones' "Sympathy for the Devil."

1) Beatles, Rolling Stones, Hollies, Yardbirds, Who, Kinks, Herman's Hermits, Searchers, Seekers, Gerry & the Pacemakers, Billy J. Kramer & the Dakotas, Donovan, Tom Jones, Petula Clark, Zombies, Chad & Jeremy, Peter & Gordon, later Led Zeppelin.

2) Bob Dylan, the Hollies, Creedence Clearwater Revival, Led Zeppelin, Jimi Hendrix, Bruce Springsteen, the Cars, Fats Domino, En Vogue, M.C. Hammer, Faith Hill, Little Richard, Jerry Lee Lewis, Dave Matthews Band, Metallica, and the Who.

3) Every singer assumes the lyrical role of a 'song-guy' or 'song-girl' – a persona – through the words of the song. Therefore, Mick Jagger is obviously NOT the Devil in the Stones' satanic-themed Rock classic that never hit the HOT 100. Mick merely assumes the horns and red-spade tail for the song's 5-minute duration. It is crucial to separate the song-guy persona from the ACTUAL SINGER when we listen to music.

Chapter Nineteen

1) When did Rock lyrics grow much more sophisticated? Who's responsible?

2) The Mamas and Papas featured three lead singers. Who dominated?

3) Dylan/Ginsberg/Kerouac's influence was lyrically revolutionary. Who did they influence, as Folk Rock dovetailed into Psychedelia?

1) Bob Dylan united Folk and Rock. His lyrics suggest poet Allen Ginsberg, and novelist Jack Kerouac [*On the Road*], with their bohemian Beat Generation influence. Simon and Garfunkel expanded this trend.

2) Canadian Denny Doherty, followed by Mama Cass Elliott, and Michelle Phillips. 'Papa John' Phillips mostly wrote, arranged, and harmonized.

3) Jim Morrison and Ray Manzarek's Doors, John Lennon, Simon & Garfunkel, Donovan, Bruce Springsteen, Tom Waits, Ricky Nelson, Neil Diamond. Via the Monkees, they influenced MTV. Dylan's literary masterworks upgraded teen lyrics into anthems of commitment and social change.

Chapter Twenty

1) Was the American National Anthem ever #1 in the United States?

2) Name a few songs which urged soldiers to battle. Name some taking a more peaceful stance.

3) Which songs show best the duality of war, presenting both sides with poignant power?

1) Yes and no. John McCormack took it to #1(3) during World War I in 1917. "The Star-Spangled Banner," however, wasn't chosen to BE our national anthem until 1930. Previously, we had none. Whitney Houston took it highest in the Rock Era, at #6 HOT 100 in 11-2001.

2) Battle Songs – Sgt. Barry Sadler's "Ballad of the Green Berets"; Royal Guardsmen's "Snoopy vs. the Red Baron"; Elton Britt's "There's a Star-Spangled Banner Waving Somewhere"; Johnny Horton's "Sink the Bismarck," "Johnny Reb," and "Johnny Freedom"; Merle Haggard's "Okie from Muskogee"; Toby Keith's Osama bin Laden Era "Courtesy of the Red, White, and Blue." More Peaceful Songs – Kingston Trio's Pete Seeger song "Where Have All the Flowers Gone?" Also Bo Donaldson's "Billy, Don't Be a Hero"; John Lennon's "Give Peace a Chance"; Hank Thompson's "Abdul Abulbul Amir"; and Edwin Starr's "War," later covered by Bruce Springsteen.

3) Kenny Rogers' "Ruby"; Glen Campbell's "Galveston"; Kay Kyser/Righteous Brothers' "The White Cliffs of Dover"; or Creedence Clearwater's "Who'll Stop the Rain?" During World War II – and not necessarily Vietnam – 99% of Americans figured "War is hell – but it sure beats Hitler."

Chapter Twenty-One

1) Name some 'Bubble Gum' Rock stars:
2) Spot the so-called 'easy' **tonic major** chords: **C, F#-dim, F, A-maj7, Bb+, G, G7#5b9, C#-aug** (see also Glossary and Chord Theory).
3) Why is Otis Redding's #1(4), 1-1968 signature song "(Sittin' on) the Dock of the Bay" out of character?

1) The Archies, 1910 Fruitgum Company, Chipmunks, David Cassidy/Partridge Family, Cowsills, Ohio Express, later Tommy Roe, Hanson.
2) **C, F, G.**
3) Redding was the epitome of exciting enthusiasm and Soul energy. His dynamic stage act offered a Soul explosion. This mystical brooding ballad was cut just three days before his untimely death, in a plane crash on frozen Lake Monona in Madison, Wisconsin. The pensive ballad takes place on a Berkeley/Oakland California dock, jutting out onto mild San Francisco Bay. His sad swan song, replete with finger-squeaks on the guitar strings, is the polar opposite of his dynamic whirlwind stage performances.

Chapter Twenty-Two

1) Who had more Rock Era HOT 100 hits than any other Bluesman?
2) Who is credited with evolving the Rolling Stones' name?
3) *Gold Rush* includes Jimi Hendrix, Janis Joplin, and Jim Morrison/Doors to anchor a Blues chapter. You might expect Sonny Boy Williamson, Elmore James, Robert Johnson, or Mose Allison. How do Rock's Big Three 27-year-old martyrs fit in here with more traditional Blues stars?

1) B.B. King. Jimmy Reed is second.
2) Muddy Waters.
3) Ray Manzarek of the Doors is grounded in Deep Blues as well as Classical music (see "Roadhouse Blues"). Hendrix's spitfire guitar emanated from the archetypal genius of Charlie Christian, Robert Johnson, and Chuck Berry; Hendrix also apprenticed with Screaming Blues legend Little Richard, and with Italian Bluesblasters Joey Dee & the Starlighters (#1, '61 "The Peppermint Twist"). For Janis Joplin, just listen to the Gospel Folk **Blues** influence on Janis by Ma Rainey, Bessie Smith, or by 50s Folk & Blues diva Odetta [Holmes]. Via Odetta, you can hear why Joplin's "Summertime" or "Cry Baby" are the quintessence of the soulful Blues tradition.

Chapter Twenty-Three

1) Which Folk Rock troubadour took us mountaineering through Colorado and West Virginia?
2) Compare and contrast Jimmy Buffett's "Margaritaville" with Johnny Cash's "Sunday Mornin' Comin' Down."
3) Why is Don McLean's Buddy Holly tribute "American Pie" among the most treasured songs of the Rock Revolution?

1) John Denver.
2) "Margaritaville" is a Key West surf's-up fantasy of fun, good times, and Happy Hour drinks with friends. Cash's doleful Kris Kristofferson ditty hits the dregs of a disgusting hangover, with desperado humor, lonesome remorse, and real pain.
3) Don salutes and laments the entire Rock Revolution to 1971, when "American Pie" stood alone a month at #1. McLean paints the panorama of Rock's promise and disillusionment, from his paper-route boyhood 50s to the battle-scarred blue mood of the reeling new 70s. Don's eight-minute epic saga shifts tempos and tightropes. He waltzes over the abyss of the future with desperado bravado. Despite his gloomy previews, he lofts a super summer-sky melody that skirts the stars in scope and grandeur.

Chapter Twenty-Four

1) What is the lyrical theme of Art Garfunkel and Paul Simon's "Bridge over Troubled Water"?
2) How do Paul McCartney's religious views in "Let It Be" differ from John Lennon's in "Imagine," or George Harrison's in "My Sweet Lord"?
3) Are hymns sometimes bigger than their singers and popularizers? In other words, just WHO was **Homer Rodeheaver?**

1) Friendship and faith in times of trouble.

2) McCartney's "Let It Be" hinges upon a Catholic-style faith of cosmic acceptance. His invocation of "Mary" has a double meaning. Lennon's idealistic and secular "Imagine" appeals to John's Unitarian-style concept of Utopianism. George's "My Sweet Lord" appeals to an interdenominational Lord. George invokes Khrishna, one of the three main gods of the Hindu pantheon.

3) Yes. Homer Rodeheaver had a #5, 1921 hit with "The Old Rugged Cross." It's an inspirational waltz powered by three big major chords (**I, IV, & V** chords). It's attributed to George Bennard of Reed City, Michigan. This beloved hymn is among the pillars and bulwarks of the Christian faith.

Chapter Twenty-Five

1) Which falsetto singer of the early 60s sang about weeping eggshells, and also previewed Discomania with his thumping all-accented 1 — 2 — 3 — 4 beat?

2) How did KC and the Sunshine Band epitomize the multicultural aspects of Rock and Soul?

3) Describe the international flavor of Disco by citing its #1 hallmark group.

1) Lou Christie. The Newbeats and Ian Whitcomb sang 100% falsetto (Whitcomb's #8, 5-65 "You Turn Me On"). The Newbeats sang about toast, butter, and jam in #2(2) 8-64 "Bread and Butter," but not crying eggshells or, perhaps, angels.

2) The Miami rockers featured KC (Harry Wayne *Casey)*, a White Soul artist, with a fully integrated big band and a dynamite sound.

3) The **Bee Gees** rocked from Australia to the Isle of Man in the Irish Sea. The Bee Gee twins had twin careers with alternating lead singers. In their star British Invasion phase (1967-71), twin Robin Gibb sang tremendous quaking tenor leads. Older brother Barry Gibb vaulted them to superstardom, with fantastic falsetto flourishes and high-wire vocals – in the late 70s *Saturday Night Fever* era.

Chapter Twenty-Six

1) Match performers and instruments: Herb Alpert, Miles Davis, Al Hirt, Charlie 'Bird' Parker, Thelonius Monk, Eric Clapton, Johnnie Johnson, Buddy Morrow, Ramsey Lewis.

2) Why is Jazz Rock often more musically sophisticated than ordinary Rock?

3) According to musicologist Joe Stuessy, which is the most complex Rock song of all time?

1) Davis, Hirt, Alpert – trumpet. Lewis, Monk, Johnson – piano. Clapton – guitar. Parker – sax. Morrow – trombone.

2) Jazz artists are often trained musicians with speed, technique, complex chord theory, impressionistic *arpeggios* and *cadenzas*, plus hot riffs, hooks, and virtuoso leads.

3) Emerson, Lake, & Palmer's "Karn Evil 9," from their #11, 1973 album *Brain Salad Surgery*. The keyboard's supersonic lead powers three 'impressions' or movements, like a concerto. "Karn Evil 9" tells the story of a diabolical carnival, like the evil "Hotel California" of the later Eagles. E,L, & P use a somber intro, three grim verses, and a codetta (small coda) to space the movements. Their infinitely complex and speed-lead tune rotates on a pedal point. "Karn Evil 9" reels under the satanic and sardonic big top for a half hour. It's a major musical listening adventure.

Chapter Twenty-Seven

1) Two of the entire 20th century's biggest stars died within two months of each other. Who were they, and what was their musical connection?

2) On which song does Billy Joel salute smoky Heartland Rock with a factory theme?

3) How does Bruce Springsteen symbolize Chuck Berry's "Johnny B. Goode"?

1) Bing Crosby's (1903-77) theme song was "Where the Blue of the Night Meets the Gold of the Day." Among Elvis Presley's (1935-77) earliest album hits was "When My Blue Moon Turns to Gold Again," after a series of two other 'Blue Moon' hits. [Don Gilzinger says Bing had the FIRST tape recorder in the United States, after the U.S. victors captured the Ampex/ Ampeg technology from the Nazis who invented it].

2) "Allentown" is about bygone Pennsylvania 'rust belt' jobs. It charts the despair and disillusionment of factory-shadow kids raised on industrial promises of good jobs with benefits – kids who are fed Smoke Flakes for breakfast, lunch, and forevermore.

3) Bruce Springsteen grew up in Freehold, New Jersey. He hitched his dreams to a guitar. With the lyrical power of Bob Dylan, the crackling bazooka guitarfire rhythms of Bob Seger, and the onstage charisma of early Elvis, "The Boss" dominated two decades with his booming barrage of gung-ho Thunder Rock.

Chapter Twenty-Eight

1) Which Heartland Rocker may well be the 'Father of Heavy Metal'?

2) Did the Most Popular [voted] Song of All Time — "Stairway to Heaven" — ever chart on the *Billboard* HOT 100?

3) What are some international examples of Hard Rock and Heavy Metal stars?

1) Metro Motown's Bob Seger, with his 9-67 "Heavy Music."
2) Yes and no. Led Zeppelin's Celtic Renaissance epic never did. It was embedded in an album, and unlike today with album cuts, could not technically chart. Neil Sedaka's totally different lyric and melody "Stairway to Heaven" made it up to #9 in 1960.
3) American Rock and Roll had a globetrotting adventure with England's Led Zeppelin, East Germany's Steppenwolf, Holland's Van Halen, Britain's Ozzy Osbourne/Black Sabbath, Australia's AC/DC (Scotland's, too), Japan's Loudness, or England's Def Leppard.

Chapter Thirty

1) What is the Monkees' connection with Glam star David Bowie?
2) Which 80s star had a melodic tenor, and soared to the top with "Karma Chameleon," "Church of the Poison Mind," and "Do You Really Want to Hurt Me?"
3) Why Is Queen above and beyond ordinary 'Garage Band' Rock?

1) Each English singer was named 'David Jones.' The Monkees' lead singer used his moniker 'Davy Jones' (sailor's euphemism for buried at the bottom of the high seas). Brixton's David Jones changed his handle to David **Bowie,** after a Texan Alamo hero.
2) Boy George – Georgie O'Dowd was born in Bexleyheath, East London, in 1961. He sang lead for Culture Club.
3) With their full pedal-to-the-metal style of Rococo Rock, they combine Grand Opera, Orchestral, and Art Rock – plus musical genius. Freddie Mercury's masterpiece "Bohemian Rhapsody" (title from composer Franz Liszt) runs rife with Mozart touches – the **rondo, fugue, minuet,** and **aria.**

Chapter Thirty

1) Which favorite Waltz defined a whole world of 'lounge-lizard' saloon inmates, centered around the popular song stylistics of a piano bar star who helps them escape reality?
2) What is the most popular song in the history of the world (until 2003, anyhow?)
3) Like Elvis in "Heartbreak Hotel," the group with the biggest-selling album of all time sang of an eerie and creepy and weird world. Where and what is it?

1) Billy Joel's "Piano Man," based on his actual experience in a Sunset Strip L.A. bar (see also Sheryl Crow's "All I Wanna Do").

2) Elton John/Bernie Taupin's "Candle in the Wind '97." It bested Bing Crosby's "White Christmas" in late 1997, with well over 30 million copies sold. This tribute replaced their #6, 11-87 belated tribute to Marilyn Monroe, with the same melody and different words.
3) California. The 'Hotel California' is a bizarre pleasure asylum of inmates stoned and broken. Prisoners of their kinky desires, they party on into mad midnights of furtive delights, perched for the frantic freefall of regret and retribution. The **Eagles'** 1971-75 *Greatest Hits sold 26+ million* **Albums.**

Chapter Thirty-One

1) Name some pre-1980 Latino influences on Rock and Roll.
2) How did the Miami Sound Machine change Latino/Latina Rock?
3) Besides Latino music, what else does Chapter 31 cover in international sounds?

1) Xavier Cugat, Ritchie Valens, Trini Lopez, Jose Feliciano, Tito Puente, Freddy Fender.
2) With Gloria Estefan singing lead, they presented a new female dimension to classic Salsa music, combining Rock with older Afro-Cuban, and Spanish-influenced polyrhythms.
3) Dean Martin/Al Martino's Italian-American music; Harry Belafonte/Johnny Nash's Caribbean music; Waylon Jennings/Mitchell Torok's Cajun music; Bob Marley/Shango/Mungo Jerry's Ska and Reggae; and Outer Mongolia's Revolutionary Rock by Hongk.

Chapter Thirty-Two

1) Name the Beach Boys' 'Jock Rock' anthem.
2) Who were the 'Waltz Kings'?
3) Why is Creedence star John Fogerty's song "Centerfield" so pivotal in Sports Rock music?

1) "Be True to Your School." Combining cheerleaders (the Honeys) and the University of Wisconsin Fight Song, "Centerfield" touts the rah-rah school spirit of Brian Wilson for sports in general, and football and track in particular.
2) These long-forgotten 1890s pop superstars (with unforgettable names) include the mighty Dan Quinn ("Sidewalks of New York"), George J. Gaskin (baseball blockbuster hit "Slide, Kelly, Slide"), and John M. Myers ("In the Good Old Summertime").
3) It not only defines the Kelly-green-grass baseball mystique of eternal spring and hope, but it alludes to the only shared song of two 50s musical giants – **Chuck Berry's** classic "Brown-Eyed Handsome Man," also recorded by **Buddy Holly.** It became a big hit for Holly in England four years after his untimely death, where the only quasi-baseball pastime is the

sport Cricket, also the name of Buddy's group the Crickets. Later rock giant **Sir Paul McCartney** recorded this song on his #26 Al. of 10-99, *Run, Devil, Run.*

Chapter Thirty-Three

1) Both Punk Rock and New Wave share one nexus or point of origin. Where is it?
2) How long was Pink Floyd's *Dark Side of the Moon* on the Album Charts in *Billboard?*
3) Was Punk a temporary phenomenon? Why or why not?

1) CBGBs on the Bowery, Greenwich Village, Manhattan.
2) **741 Weeks!** "The Wall," their later #1 (and only #1) single, was an indictment of mental and physical cruelty as perceived in the British educational system
3) **No.** Though Punk peaked in 1977 with the Ramones and Sex Pistols, it began with Gene Vincent and Johnny Cash in 1956, and thrived beyond the Millennium with Green Day, Blink 182, and Tool. Though Punk often thrashes angrily at authority, the happy sound of #5, 2002 "The Middle," by **Jimmy Eat World** [Ed. Note – I love that name], shows that Punk-style rhythms don't always take a ticked-off theme. Indeed, you could draw a direct line to the Punkish-power drum-driven sound of **Buddy Holly & the Crickets' frantic and deliriously happy song "Oh Boy"** (#10, 11-57) as possibly the very **first top ten Punk Rock hit.**

Chapter Thirty-Four

1) Which athlete is a central figure — via James Brown — in the evolution of Rap music (hint: his daughter boxed Smokin' Joe Frazier's daughter in June 2001)?
2) Besides Michael and Janet Jackson, who are some other important **Jacksons** in the Rap & Soul, or R&B field?
3) Gangsta Rap's 2-Pac Shakur is a key figure. Tell a little bit about his abbreviated life.

1) Three-time heavyweight champ Muhammad Ali.
2) Jermaine, Tito, Marion, Jackie, Chuck, LaToya, Freddie, Walter, "Bull Moose" [a/k/a Benjamin], Deon, and Gospel diva Mahalia.
3) 2-Pac joined Digital Underground. He beat up his director in Gangsta Rap flick *Menace II Society* (Allen Hughes). Due to a turf grudge, 2-Pac was shot five times in a Big Apple robbery, and was jailed for a sex crime. In gangland fashion, he was murdered while riding in a car in Los Angeles.

Chapter Thirty-Five

1) Paul McCartney's biggest hit with Wings was #1(5), 4-76 "Silly Love Songs." Are there any?
2) What song reigned at #1 longer than any other song?
3) Who are some important 'Light Metal' artists?

1) No.
2) Though Francis Craig's #1(17) 1947 "Near You" tops Mariah Carey/Boyz II Men's #1(16) 1995 "One Sweet Day," atop the longevity pinnacle, the combo crown goes to another collaboration whose double-whammy might not even quite be the same *song.* The tune, however, is the same. Though the weeks at peak were NOT consecutive, and even the title and lyrics are different, mostly, the sidelong winner may be this #1(19) megamonster smash – the Police and Sting's #1(8) 1983 "Every Breath You Take," plus the Rap elegy which samples it – **Puff Daddy**/P. Diddy's #1(11) 1997 "I'll Be Missing You." It commemorates the life and fatally-brief career of slain Rap guru Notorious B.I.G.
3) Kenny Rogers, a Rock/Country/Folk/Easy Listening star. Bread, with rich belltone melodies crafted by countertenor David Gates. Perry Como, beloved Crooner into the Rock Era. Whitney Houston and Dionne Warwick, a genetic one-two punch as well. Or the Police/Sting, though they slammed great Hard Rock (catch #10, 10-80 "De Do Do Do, De Da Da Da"), Or Dan Fogelberg, Richard Marx, Bobby Vee, N'Sync, or Vanessa Carlton (#5, 2-2002 "A Thousand Miles"). All of these performers never forgot the MELODY, in a backwash of rampaging rhythms. Still NOT honored in the Rock Hall of Fame into 2003, **Neil Diamond** epitomizes the Light Metal genre, and delivers some great, hall-worthy performances.

Chapter Thirty-Six

1) Which Northern industrialist was responsible for underwriting the evolution of Country music — by showcasing great fiddlers and fiddling contests?
2) What is the biggest-selling Country song of all time?
3) What Country movement do occasional duo Willie Nelson and Waylon Jennings represent?

1) Henry Ford.
2) Garth Brooks's "Friends in Low Places." It sold 15+ million copies. The song mysteriously NEVER charted (see Led Zep's "Stairway to Heaven") on the *Billboard* HOT 100. The lyric shows a clash of cultures in a fading romantic relationship.
3) The Austin, Texas, Outlaw movement. Rebelling against the more conservative Nashville Country music 'establishment,' Willie and Waylon created a whole new sound.

Chapter Thirty-Seven

1) Concetta Rosa Maria Franconero was the #1 female singer of the late 50s/early 60s in America. Who is she?

2) What are some of the reasons Madonna [Ciccone] has become the #1 female singer ever, and the #6 Artist on Joel Whitburn's Top Artist charts?

3) How does Bonnie Raitt represent the best of both traditional and cutting-edge Rock and Roll?

1) **Connie Francis**, still locked out of the Rock Hall of Fame into 2003.

2) Her versatility with music, and ability to 're-invent' herself in her ever-changing MTV video persona. From Streetcorner "True Blue" to Latina "La Isla Bonita" to New Wave "Material Girl," Madonna proffers a with-it smorgasbord of talented musical styles.

3) Bonnie's career began with Del Shannon's #1 '61 "Runaway" (#57 for Bonnie in '77). Bonnie brandishes her own lead guitar, like Melissa Etheridge. Bonnie sings with power and conviction, and she delivers punchy platinum albums to highlight her 2000 Hall of Fame induction.

Chapter Thirty-Eight

1) The 'inventor' of MTV in 1981 comes from an inventive family. Who? What? How?

2) How did the Beatles revolutionize movies about Rock and Roll?

3) Which musician's movie is a salient satire of the entire R&B industry?

1) The Monkees' **Michael Nesmith** (the one who also pioneered the wool winter hat, for Rappers galore), set up the MTV concept, with the Buggles' #40, 11-79 video on August 1, 1981. Mike's mom invented "White Out" Liquid Paper. His distant relative James *Naismith* invented basketball, about the time Rock and Roll started – 1896 or so.

2) They dumped cheesy plot lines for a zany, Thurberian approach to frantic cinematography. Besides great songs, they provided a topsy-turvy, fast-paced story line. Since it was impractical for the overbooked Beatles to create a spoofy TV series in America, the casting-call went out for the Beatlish Monkees – who lived and played the *Help*-style antics and hi-jinx to the hilt.

3) Rob Reiner's comedy *This Is Spinal Tap*. This imaginary touring group has a supersonic laff-trak. Their amp booms up to '11' (not just '10'). They keep losing drummers in ghastly gardening accidents, and other improbable disasters. They get lost in backstage labyrinthine mazes, on the way to the elusive lime-light. Super spoof. No band is complete without watching this fab flick.

Chapter Thirty-Nine

1) Who finds mystic enlightenment in a Los Angeles noontime bar across from a 1994 car wash?

2) For #1 records, who is the Entertainer of the Century — besides Elvis?

3) With this Gangsta Rap milieu of 2-Pac and Notorious B.I.G., where and when did we have the truly **toughest** urban turf wars in popular-music recorded history?

1) Sheryl Crow in "All I Wanna Do." In 3-2002, she left the dark bar to ride the Surf Rock rainbow to #1 Adult Contemporary glory with "Soak Up the Sun" (#17, HOT 100).

2) **Mariah Carey.** Check out her 15 #1 songs on p. 550. They include the Number One #1 song of the Rock Era officially, #1(16), 12-95 "One Sweet Day."

3) In 1888, Big Mike Sullivan and his Sons of Erin hit #1 with "The Bowery Grenadiers" (via sheet music in the dawn of recorded music and Top Ten charts). It told the sensational grisly tale of bloody war-zone turf wars among bellicose Lower East Side ethnic gangs. They made small potatoes out of Turn-of-the-Millennium shoot-'em-up arsenals, ghetto cowboy showdowns, and maybe Gangsta Rap. Flinging GRE-NADES, they battled to reign over redbrick flats, apple pushcarts, and all the free horse manure they could command. Scores of innocent people were killed in their urban riots.

Chapter Forty

1) Who is the #2 Artist of all time in album sales?

2) Describe Celtic Renaissance music.

3) What is the charm of Vertical Horizon's #1 hit?

1) **Frank Sinatra,** whose career straddles the Big Band/Crooner/Rock Eras.

2) Theatrical ballads, often using flutes. Though it trails back to Jethro Tull or Led Zep's "Stairway to Heaven," Celtic Renaissance music is a late-90s phenomenon: Celine Dion's titanic tune "My Heart Will Go On," Sarah McLachlan's "Angel," or Loreena McKennitt's "The Mummers' Dance."

3) "Everything You Want," #1, 11-99, combines a top-notch musical background with Matt Scanell's tale that reflects Del Shannon's theme in "Why Don't You Tell Him?" Vertical Horizon's musical package is profound. Also amazingly, much of their self-promotion paid off in glomming the lion's share of recording royalties – avoiding the bloated big-corporate rake-off which plagues and pauperizes so many top-grade bands we all think are rich.

Chapter Forty-One

1) Name one of the Gold Rush saloon-era gadgets to first put live working musicians out of business (hint: it's related to the music box, even the Jack-in-the-box).

2) Tell a little bit about Southern Rock.

3) What are some songs related to the 9-11-2001 World Trade Center tragedy in New York City?

1) The **Piano Roll,** one of the first **Karaoke-**type inventions from the Gold Rush days of upright saloon pianos, and sawdust & peanut-shell floors. It swirled in the upright's innards, while nubs struck the hammer which sounded the inner strings of the piano.

2) Two major groups headlining Southern Rock were the Georgian Allman Brothers, and the Floridian Lynyrd Skynyrd. Their flair for Country Rock somehow escaped notice at all on the Country charts, due to their long hair and firebrand style. Southern Rock is famous for great guitar leads (Dickey Betts, Gary Rossington, Duane Allman), and sadly for motorcycle and plane crashes that stole some talented lives way too early in the 70s.

3) "Where Were You (When the World Stopped Turning)? – by Alan Jackson. "Courtesy of the Red, White, and Blue" – Toby Keith. "Hero" – Enrique Iglesias. Re-releases of Lee Greenwood's "God Bless the U.S.A" and Whitney Houston's "Star-Spangled Banner." [Ray Charles' "America – The Beautiful" also enjoyed a lot of air play, but you might have to read these Chapter Questions to know that].

Chapter Forty-Two

1) Who took over for Buddy Holly on fateful February 3, 1959.

2) Why does *Gold Rush* choose Louie Armstrong's "What a Wonderful World" to anchor our book — first in Ch. 41, and last of all in Ch. 42?

3) What's the connection between the 1897 Klondike/Yukon/Alaskan gold rush — and Rock and Roll?

1) Bobby Vee and his Shadows. Bobby's public musical career actually BEGAN, says Bill Griggs, with their Moorhead, Minnesota gig that Buddy Holly was trying unsuccessfully to get to. Despite impossible shoes to fill, 15-year-old Bobby grew into his role, and became the #1 interpreter of Buddy Holly's sound in the next few years – branching out into his own style and superstar success.

2) This non-Rock ballad is simply a great song. It celebrates the triumph of the human spirit over pain and meaninglessness and despair.

3) Jewel [Kilcher] comes from Homer, Alaska. In the Ragtime honkytonks of the Midnight Sun, the first Boogie-Woogie bass patterns, Blues progressions, and Rock rudiments were hammered out of the keys of the old upright acoustic piano – echoing their Boogie/Blues brethren down in New Orleans. In the land of Gold and Glory, Rock and Roll coalesced, in the Center of Saturday Night in young America.

Glossary

Gold Rush features a Glossary with page numbers, for your easy reference.
The Index probably has explanations for you that aren't in here.

A

A & R (Artists and Repertoire)
Record promotion people who hype songs to radio stations. By the number of weekly spins, a song 'makes it or breaks it' for a high number of the 'charts'—and high sales.

A cappella
Without instrumental accompaniment. Generally just voices. 227, 328.

Acoustic
Non-amplified instrument, usually guitar. Not electrified.

Adult Contemporary
'*Light* Metal,' Easy Listening music. 319, 344, 443, 471-83, 528, 558, 581.

Advertising Jingles from Popular Songs
Hit commercials. 300, 595

African-American Music
(see R & B or Soul, too)
Primary source of Rock and Roll 7-15, 35-43, 157-66, 231-51, 283-94, 413-30, 457-70, 498.

Agnostic
Doubter who questions, but does not necessarily deny, existence of God. 277, 280, 302.

Air Play
On-air spins a record receives. The more spins, probably the more sales.

Album
Generally 12" x 12" foot-square 33 1/3 rpm vinyl record, featured throughout *Gold Rush*. **Album Art** peaked in the late 60s Psychedelic Era. 101, 224, 374.

Allusion
Reference to previous work of music, art, or literature. 343.

Alternative Rock/Alt Rock
(see Grunge, too) A 90s and 00s musical phenomenon, often with raspy dark baritone lyrics and minor-key interludes. 303, 332, 447, 452-56, 530, 548.

Alto
Lower female vocal range. 272, 328, 370-71, 472.

American Bandstand/Bandstand
50s to 80s TV show, starring DJ/Vee-Jay Dick Clark. 291, 308, 334, 451, 535.

Arpeggios
To play the notes of a chord one at a time. 149, 188, 198, 297, 326, 439.

Artists Who Never Hit #1 on the *Billboard* HOT 100
like Bruce Springsteen, the Who, Bob Dylan, or Led Zeppelin . . . 179-81.

ASCAP (American Society of Composers, Authors, and Publishers)
One of two major copyright clearing houses. 53, 312, 568.

A-Side
Hopeful HIT side of a 45 rpm record, hyped for radio air play. The flip-side is called the 'B-side.' 582.

Atheism
Refuting the existence of God. 307, 489.

B

Backbeat
Rock music accents the **2 & 4** beats, and soft-pedals the downbeat 1, and the 3 beat, in common-time 4/4 music. 283, 333, 547, 562, 590.

'Backstreet Backlash'
Resentment by female fans' boyfriends of handsome Teen Idols (like the Backstreet Boys) for their looks. Because of their looks, their music gets irrationally criticized. 571.

Back-Up Singers
Singers who harmonize with lead singer.

Bandstand (see American Bandstand)
291, 535+.

Banjo
Fretted instrument with long guitar-type neck. A round modified drum head of parchment covers its acoustic sound box. 390, 421, 485, 586.

Bar
1) one measure of a song; 2) a place where music fans watch musicians measure musical bars, and where thirsty fans and musicians measure beers.

Barber Shop Quartet
Four-part harmonic foursome, with 1st & 2nd tenors, baritone, and bass. 51, 105-06, 161, 274, 486-89, 510-12.

Baritone
Lower mid-range male voice, between high tenor and low bass. 102, 259, 302.

Bass
1) lowest regular male range (*basso profundo* is absolute lowest). 2) short for bass fiddle, or *bass guitar*. 102, 243, 260, 265, 269, 315, 427, 501.

Bass Guitar
Fretted electric instrument, usually with bottom four strings of guitar— tuned an octave below (therefore, much thicker strings). 32, 221, 239, 276, 286-87, 305, 371, 412.

BBC (British Broadcasting Corporation)
U.K. national radio and TV. 342.

Beat
Measuring unit of time in music, which segments the rhythm.

Beat Generation
50s Jazz stars like David Amram, plus poet/lyricist Allen Ginsberg and novelist Jack Kerouac (Bob Dylan's mentor). 401-03.

Be-Bop
Fast hot Jazz style of Beat Generation, with speedy cadenzas and improvisations. 314.

Big Bands
Generally, 1920s to 1940s Jazz bands with brass, woodwinds, and percussion for dancing. 306, 309, 497.

Billboard & *Billboard's* Hit Charts
Weekly magazine, whose hit charts are charted by Joel Whitburn. 341, 429, 443, 456, 577.

'Blue-Eyed Soul'
Great Soul or R&B-style music, by members of the 'Caucasian Persuasion,' who may actually feature hazel, green, or brown eyes, too (see Righteous Brothers, Rascals). 166, 220, 576.

Bluegrass
Southern Appalachian music coalesced by Bill Monroe, featuring high harmonies and fast picking on guitar, banjo, and mandolin. 125, 276, 402, 485, 502.

Blues
Also see Delta Blues. Musical style that mirrors melancholy mood by flatting the 3rd and 7th notes. Often in 12-Bar progression, with shuffle beat. 231-51, 302, 366, 480.

BMI (Broadcast Music, Inc.)
2nd major copyright clearing house. 53, 312, 468, 568.

Boogie-Woogie
Blues (often 12-Bar) on piano, with a frequent shuffle bass line. 30, 590.

Bootleg/Pirate Recordings
(see Napster, MP3) Counterfeit recordings, with NO artists' royalties. 191, 225.

Bossism vs. Freedom
Freedom is often amended, even in America, by unreasonable bosses' workplace demands (see Blondie/Dagwood/Dithers, or Todd Rundgren). 373.

Brass
Wind instruments like trumpet, trombone, Flügelhorn, tuba.

Bridge
Middle portion of song, with altered chord progression from verses or chorus. 101.

Brill Building, on Broadway [Ave.], New York
50s-60s hit factory, with songwriters like Bobby Darin, Carole King, and Neil(s) Diamond and Sedaka. 135, 351, 357, 421, 477.

Bubble-Gum Music
Happy major-chord, bouncy Rock music aimed at 9-14-year-old audience. 219, 555.

Bunny Hop
Dance craze; also, a big hit by Ray Anthony, #13, 11-52. 429.

C

Cacophony
Loud, harsh, jangling sound of discord. Opposite of harmony.

Cadenza
Short instrumental solo. 302, 371.

Cajun Music
Louisiana French-style Country Rock. Combines with R & B and Jamaican rhythms, often using fiddle and accordion with guitars. 418-19, 488, 496-98, 502, 516, 561.

Call & Response
From Gospel/Spiritual music, and applied to R & B (see "What'd I Say" or "Can I Get a Witness?"). 87, 158, 190, 359.

Calypso
Originally a Trinidad ballad style. Accents the 1, the 2½, and the 4th beats. Popular via Harry Belafonte in 1956-57. 56, 419.

Catholicism
Original faith of Christianity. 265-66, 339.

CBGBs (Bowery, Greenwich Village, NYC)
Original birthplace of both American Punk and New Wave music in late 70s. 437.

CDs vs. Vinyl, Tapes, and DATs
Merits of each. 225, 411, 453.

Celtic Renaissance
Ballad-style esoteric music of 70s, then 90s & 00s. 307, 342, 371-72, 410, 524, 546, 567-69.

Chalypso
Like Calypso, with a more polyrhythmic inner beat and R&R drum style. 56, 128, 299, 315, 392, 415, 419.

Cheerleaders of Rock
(see Sports Rock, 431-37).

Chicago Blues
Style derived by Chess Records' Leonard Chess, an off-shoot of Mississippi Delta Blues (see Muddy Waters, Jimmy Reed). 101, 239.

Chord Theory
A few technical Chord Theory Sidebars were relocated here, to bring you punchier information in the text. First, let's do chord theory.

It all begins with the **Major Triad**. A chord has three or more notes (two notes are called a **duad**, a term 9999 out of a myriad 10,000 have never heard of); we call a chord by the name of its **root note**. For instance, our basic C chord, in the Key of C, has its root at the 'C' note. It also features the third note upwards, the 'E' note, plus the fifth note 'G'. Therefore, a **C chord** might be played **C – E – G.** We call this the **'I'** or **Tonic Chord.**

Most of Rock and Roll lives and dies on only **three major chords**. The Key of C, for instance, features two chords which build upwards from the 4th and 5th **notes of the diatonic major scale in the Key of C.** The first of these chords is the **FIVE Chord**, building from the root fifth note in the Key of C – **G.** We call this the **Dominant Chord of G,** represented by three notes: **G – B – D.** The **Four Chord** fills out our Chord Trio. The fourth note in the scale of C is **F, also called the Sub-Dominant Chord. We build the IV Chord F through three notes – F – A – C.** These three basic chords also comprise most of Blues and Boogie-Woogie, too.

Much of Rock and Roll works via the **12-Bar Blues Progression.** In the Key of C for pianos, or the Key of E for guitars and basses, we do 4 bars of the Tonic 'I' chord, 2 bars of the Sub-Dominant 'IV' chord, 2 more bars of the Tonic 'I' chord, then 1 bar each of the Dominant 'V' chord, the Sub-Dominant 'IV', the Tonic 'I,' and then the **'turn-around'** Dominant 'V' chord:

Key of C:	C	— F —	C —	G —	F —	C —	G
Key of E:	E	— A —	E —	B —	A —	E —	B
# of Bars:	4	— 2 —	2 —	1 —	1 —	1 —	1

The **'A' chord is four notes up from E in the Key of E** (like 'F' chord in C).

In the Streetcorner Chord Progression ('Doo-Whop'

music), we add a **Six Minor chord to our big three I, IV, and V chords: A-minor – we play A – C – E.** These four chords comprise most of the ballad verses of early Rock and Roll in this pattern:

Key of C	C — —	Am —	F — G
Chord #	I	VIm	IV V

Jazz gets trickier: we also build chords off the 2nd, 3rd, 7th, and other notes in between on the black keys. In the Key of C, chords built off the two chord – **D** – we would call the **SUPER-TONIC chord.** In the Key of E, the II chord, a step up, would be F#. Chords built off the third note or three chord III, in the Key of C, we call the **MEDIANT** chord. In the Key of C, the III three chord is **E.** Chords built from the 6th note are called **SUB-MEDIANT chords.** That **A-minor (Am)** chord from the Streetcorner Progression is a Sub-Mediant Minor chord; its Sub-Mediant MAJOR chord would be **A major.**

Jazz brings us minor chords, frequently. To make a minor chord of a major one, simply flat the third note of your triad; instead of C-major with C – E – G, you'd lower the middle note a half-step to C – Eb – G. An **AUGMENTED chord** is when you sharp the fifth note, or raise it a half-step, thusly – **C-aug = C – E – G# (also known as Ab). A DIMINISHED chord** is when you flat BOTH the third and fifth notes, i.e., a **C-dim (or C+) is simply C – Eb – Gb (also known as F#).**

Sevenths are constantly used in Rock and Roll. The DOMINANT SEVENTH is our most important seventh chord. In the Key of C, it's the **G7, or the V7 chord, written as G – B – D – F.** Our seventh note is a full step down from the octave above the root note (Bb is two half-steps below C). A MAJOR SEVENTH uses one ONE half-step, so the chord **G-maj7 is written G – B – D – F#.** When Buddy Holly and Paul Anka used a major seventh on Holly's farewell song, "It Doesn't Matter Any More," it was revolutionary in the Rock and Roll realm.

Sixths add the 6th note to the major triad. In C, it's **C6 = C – E – G – A. Ninths** add the note just above the octave, the same note as the second note, only an octave higher. In Key of C, it's the second **D note, or C – E – G – D. Elevenths** go four notes above the octave, so **C11 = C – E – G – F.**

Chord Theory developed in the Ragtime/Jazz Era, but sheet music didn't universally feature chords above the musical notation until well into the 30s and 40s.

Now, let's do some of those relocated Chord Theory Sidebars that got bounced from the main text to our Glossary. We'll begin with p. 93 – Buddy Holly's "Everyday": **"Everyday" Chords, from p. 93**

Buddy Holly jumps to the Sub-Dominant (IV) chord as he ascends the glowing bridge. Then he niftily leaps to ITS respective IV chord, seemingly modulating (changing keys) up four keys. It's a **Circle of Fourths,** as **Doors'** keyboardist **Ray Manzarek** calls it in his autobiography *Light My Fire* (1998). Holly nabs the NEW IV chord and vaults to ITS IV chord, darts back a half-step, catapulting from the Key of 'E' to *its* Dominant Seventh (B7):

"Everyday" Bridge **E — A — D — G — C — B7**

Just a little alphabet soup. Holly concocts a mathematical masterpiece here, by dashing up the scale four times to the lofty, loftier, and loftiest Relative Sub-Dominant Four chords. When he chugs into that Dominant Seventy **B7**, he slides down the major-minor scale into the verse with the **Everly Brothers'** famous transition from their #1(5), 4-58 "All I Have to Do Is Dream." Ritchie Valens' #2, 12-58 "Donna" features the same dramatic downswoop:

     V — IV — III-minor — II-minor — I

In the Key of E for guitar, it's—

     B7 — A — Ab-minor — F#-minor — E

Beatles & Gene Pitney's Chord Ideas, pp. 154-55

Chord theory, hooray. The DIATONIC scale has major and minor chords. When the Beatles pounce down to the **SEVEN chord** (say, in Key of C down to a **Bb Major**), they're dealing with Chromatics. Often these Chromatic major chords are written with the flat in *front* of the chord name. Using the 'black keys,' our scale involves the following notes: **C, C#(Db), D, Eb(D#), E, F, F#(Gb), G, Ab(G#), A, Bb(A#), B, and octave C.** Notice that many of these may be written two different ways; they are the 'black keys' of your piano. This is how we number and letter these chords:

I	#I	II	bIII	III	IV	#IV	V	bVI	VI	bVIII	VII	I
C	C#	D	Eb	E	F	F#	G	Ab	A	Bb	B	C
G	Ab	A	Bb	B	C	C#	D	Eb	E	F	F#	G

That was for the Key of C, OR the Key of G. You can find these Chromatic intermediary chords in ANY KEY, just a half-step at a time.

Gene Pitney, 2002 Rock Hall of Fame member, pioneered the **Polynesian & Mideastern Chord** changes in Rock and Roll and Rock ballads. Though it goes back to Hawaiian guitar opuses in Jazz, Pitney popularized it. The **Polynesian chord shift** moves from the Tonic major I chord to the **bVI major**. Or: **C – Ab – C.** Pitney's breathtaking *crescendo* ballad "Half Heaven – Half Heartache" uses this extraordinary shift. The **Dave Clark V** of London, on the First British Invasion Wave, picked up the Pitney power, and cannonballed from their rocking verse on #6, 2-64 "Glad All Over" into the bombastic bridge. In the Key of D, they pounce Polynesianly from:

     D——Bb——D

Their foray into exotic chord swoops would be followed by an avalanche of **Rolling Stones:**

Go East, Young Man, p. 170

Musically, Mick Jagger and Keith Richard shift to the East. If the Polynesian chord shift is the lovely bVI major (C—Ab—C, or I—bVI—I), then the **Mideastern Chord Shift** rampages up to the **bIII major, or C – Eb – C, or I – bIII – I.**

The most famous guitar riff in history, Keith Richard's famous intro to #1, '65 "Satisfaction," is the Mideastern chordal shift. Perhaps getting this chord shift from Barrett Strong's 1959 Motown debut hit, "Money," Keith Richard (roaring) and bassist Bill Wyman (sparingly and funkily) take a mad dash from the bottomtone **E major to G major (bIII).** You hear the same Arabian-Nights Mideastern tones on their #1 "Paint It, Black," powered by a demon-dash rhythm jag.

Searchers' Sound Sounds Simple. It Isn't, p. 172

Sonny Bono wrote their hit "Needles and Pins," and he needles the three-chords-and-a-cloud-of-dust R & R establishment. It revolves around a key-change *modulation* and an astounding *riff*. The riff is easier. Begin in the Key of A. Make the regular A chord – not the bar chord. Float from the C# note to the D and down to the B. The song uses a modified *Streetcorner* chord pattern in A: (A – C#m – D – E7).

Into the Bridge, the Searchers borrow the Del Shannon "Runaway" chord slide. First they mount to the Mideastern Three Major chord (bIII, or **C#**) on the can't-stop line, rolling back the Shannon/"Greensleeves"/"Runaway" progression: **C# to B to A to G#7{Ab7}.** Mysteriously, they kiss the old Key of A goodbye, and ride home on their new toughie Key of C#. Fans don't dissect it. They just think it's cool.

British Invasion Key Shifts, p. 178

Basically, the Beatles, Hollies, and the Dave Clark IV seem to favor the Polynesian shift (C – Ab – C); the Rolling Stones, Yardbirds, and Kinks prefer the Mideastern (C – Eb – C). In "Shut Down," the Beach Boys also pioneer the Mideastern shift, before the British Invasion.

Unchained Eb Chords, p. 189

The Righteous Brothers' lost chord is a **bIII Chromatic.** For those wondering where that **Eb** chord escaped to, here it is:

     F—————————G———F———————Eb

[Here the 'lonely river' goes to that sea, that sea]

To the untrained ear, it SOUNDS like a bVII Chromatic. It's actually a **bIII** jazzy Chromatic . From a financial standpoint, most people have no idea just what chord that is, but this famous shift probably sold about 20% of the copies of "Unchained Melody." This off-the-wall Mideastern bIII shift *mocks* a Polynesian bVI one, or a Chromatic bVII one. This Eb chord is in the Key of C, but it seems like the Key of F. All the while, some lonely lost river promenades and burbles its mysterious romantic way to the world-water sea. And love throbs on and on . . .

Chorus

Main refrain of song, interspersed by verses and perhaps a bridge.

Christian Contemporary

'Light Metal' Easy Rock music with a spiritual, evangelical message (see Amy Grant, Pat Boone, Michael W. Smith). 260, 263-83, 344, 375, 525-29, 564, 574-77.

Chromatic Chords (see Chord Theory)

98, 102, 119, 148, 154, 261, 302, 436, 546.

Chromatic Scale

The 12 half-steps comprising an octave.

Clarinet
Single-reed woodwind. Popular in 30s (see Benny Goodman or 60s Mr. Acker Bilk). 315.

Classic Rock
By 2000+, "Classic Rock" comprised largely late 60s to mid-80s Rock Standards. 370+.

Classical Music
Although yoked by the 1750-1820 era, Classical music is often described as more 'serious' music than popular music (see "Roll Over, Beethoven, by Chuck Berry or the Beatles). 233, 303-04, 443, 482.

Coda
Final section of a musical piece, with differing melody and chordal structure. 230, 313.

Common Time
Regular 4/4 meter.

Concept Album
An album covering one thematic or musical idea or *concept* (see Beatles' *Sgt. Pepper* or Marty Robbins' *Gunfighter Ballads*). 134, 222, 229, 313, 333, 495, 517.

Contralto
Lowest female voice. 417, 519.

Counterpoint
Polyphony, or two harmonic melodies—interweaving simultaneously (see Simon & Garfunkel's "Scarborough Fair"). 165, 184, 199, 209, 298, 322, 523, 531, 589.

Countertenor
1st tenor, "Irish" tenor, or highest natural-range tenor. 390.

Country/Country & Western/Country Rock (C, or C&W)
American popular music with 'down-home' realistic lyrics and harmonious melodies (see Alan Jackson, Johnny Cash, Buddy Holly/Crickets). 247, 349, 443, 460, 485-521, 552, 578.

Country Rap/Country Soul
Country music, with a dash of Soul/R&B. 498, 502, 507, 519.

Creem
Detroit R&R magazine from the 70s, starring Dave Marsh. 357, 404, 437.

Crescendo
Music gets steadily louder in volume and pitch to climactic flourish at finale. 108, 127, 162, 319, 323, 341.

Crooner
Singer of sweet, resonant, orchestral ballad style, popular 30s to mid-50s. 326, 471, 479, 497, 565-66, 577.

Crossover Music
Popular in more than one market. 196, 214, 302, 480.

Cymbal
Round metal percussion plate with ringing sound.

D

"Dance" Music
[Ed. Note—it's **ALL** Dance Music]. 222, 283-93, 359, 437, 443, 522.

DAT (Digital Audio Tape)
The supposed technological wave of the future, beyond vinyl, tapes, and CDs. Though predicted in 1995 to revolutionize music, the DAT's tiny size makes artist information even more impossible to read than on the smallest 4-point-type CDs.

Day That the Music Died—February 3, 1959
Plane crash with Buddy Holly, Ritchie Valens, and the Big Bopper. 251, 292, 443, 562.

Deadheads
Followers of Jerry Garcia/Grateful Dead. 212, 219, 280, 310, 332, 402-04, 510.

Death Metal (also see 'Graveyard Rock')
Rock music with a memorial theme, focusing upon death. 240, 355, 379, 438.

Delta Blues/Mississippi Delta Blues
Vintage Blues (see Muddy Waters). 60, 96, 157, 167, 238, 587.

Diatonic Scale
Seven distinct pitches on the regular scale. Three types are major, minor, and modal. 154.

Diminished Chords
Flatten the 2nd and 3rd notes of a major triad. In Key of C, **C-dim** would be **C – Eb – F#**. In Key of G, **G-dim = G – Ab – B**. 102, 227.

Disc Jockey (DJ)
Radio personalities who play records. 58, 265, 308, 367, 459.

Disco
Upbeat Rock Dance music with 70s heyday. A Discotheque was a 60s dance club. 159, 202, 283-93, 326, 411, 468.

Dobro
Resonating acoustic guitar, sometimes played horizontally, like a steel/Hawaiian guitar. 487, 492, 502.

Dominant Chord (V chord)
In Key of C, it would be **G**, or **G–B–D**. 188, 227, 339, 384.

'Doo-Whop'/Streetcorner Music

Often Barber-Shop Quartets of early R & R, dominated by great Italian-American and African-American voices. [Ed. Note – Why hasn't anybody else amended the traditional 'Doo-Wop' spelling, seeing it as ethnically offensive?]

Downbeat

In 4/4 time, Big Bands accented the **1** beat – the down-beat – while Rock music accents the backbeat on the **2 & 4** beats. 547.

Drums

Usually a pedal bass drum, a snare, 2-3 tom-toms, a hi-hat pedal cymbal, and 2+ drumsticks or drum brushes or mallets. 522+.

Dutch Rock and Roll

331-37, 353-56.

E

Easy Listening/'Light Metal'/M.O.R.

Middle-of-the-Road Light Rock. 297, 391, 408, 471.

Echo Chamber

Pioneered by Sun Records' Sam Phillips for Elvis. 322, 346, 566.

8-Beat Rhythm

Core of R&R rhythm. Divides 4-beat 4/4 measure into eight parts.

Electric Guitar, Bass, Piano

To use a pick-up, an electrical cord, and a jack plugged into an amplifier to make the sound LOUDER.

Elegiac Songs

Songs for those who have died. Usually, they are slower, more serious songs (like Sarah McLachlan's "Angel" or Mariah Carey/Boyz II Men's "One Sweet Day") than traditional 'Graveyard Rock' or 'Death Metal' tunes. 543, 569, 579, 585. See "Danny Boy," 590.

'Elvis Spotlight'

Pressure of the limelight in vulnerable star performers. 50, 163, 202, 220, 252, 286, 323, 342, 388, 391, 463, 516, 553, 561.

F

Falsetto

Male singers' voices rise beyond normal range to soar to ['false] soprano (see Del Shannon or Four Seasons). 102, 122-25, 187, 283-84, 292-93, 388, 483.

Fanzine

Fan magazine, like *Teen* or *Teen Beat.* 400.

Feedback

Overwhelming distortion or drone of sounds back into amplifier's input, for echo effect. Often happens by mistake, by trying to turn amp up to '11' (see Rockflick *This Is Spinal Tap).*

Fender (guitars/basses)

Usually solid-body guitars/basses invented by Les Paul and developed by Leo Fender. (Buddy Holly and Jimi Hendrix used Fender Stratocasters). 328, 418, 563.

Fifth

Interval between first note and fifth note. In Key of C, fifth note is G, on a major diatonic scale.

Fingerpicking

Folk-style guitar or banjo plucking with all or most of the fingers as well as the thumb. Some performers uses fingerpicks.

Flat

To lower a note one-half step. Symbol = [b].

Folk Music

Traditionally, music of the people handed down from generation to generation. Preceding recorded music, old Folk songs depend on the Oral Tradition. Some subdivide Folk into Traditional and Urban Folk; the latter (see Kingston Trio, Bob Dylan) often is recently written, and contains social or political themes. 75-83, 195-98, 214, 402, 576.

Folkabilly

Combination of Folk with traditional Country ['Hillbilly'] music. 497, 502.

Folk Rock

Combination of Folk and Rock (see Byrds). 75-83, 195-98, 214, 261, 279, 310, 357, 383, 402, 475, 576, 581, 584.

Fortissimmo

Very loud, like the Who at Wembley. 323.

4-Beat Rhythm

Basic Jazz beat, or pulse, of a song.

Fret

Thin wooden wedges, straddling the fingerboard of many stringed instruments, like guitars, electric basses, banjos, and mandolins.

Funk

70s R&B style (see Funkadelics/George Clinton) characterized by complex percussion and speedy bass runs – often in 16th-note patterns. Funky rhythm guitars basically mute and chop. 459.

Fusion/Jazz Fusion

R&R with high technical competency, elaborate cadenzas, and harmonic fever-pitch style. 295-320.

G

Gangsta Rap

Loud Rap music with forceful lyrical agenda. "No More Mr. Nice Guy" Rap/R&B/Rock.

Garage Bands (also see Punk Rock)

Local new bands learning the Rock and Roll game through impromptu practice sessions – often in somebody's garage. Some catch a break, ride the lightning, and emerge with a gold record, to everyone's surprise. 72, 136, 193, 225, 310.

Generation X

80s-90s Rock (term coined by name of Billy Idol's first band). Restless generation, which spawned Grunge and developed Punk and Heavy Metal, to rebel against their Junk-Bond Era predecessors. 182, 206, 264, 328, 355, 400, 432, 450, 455, 474.

Ghost Notes

Notes that aren't there. Function of Eric Clapton or B.B. King's Blues guitar style, where the audience waits for notes that 'hang fire' in anticipation. 187, 231, 448, 498.

Gig

One particular band job.

Glam/Glitter Rock

70s phenomenon characterized by ostentatious, outrageous colorful outfits like feather boas, ocelot-print spandex pants, or towering tiaras (see Mott the Hoople, early Elton John, David Bowie). 290, 305.

Glissando

When 'The Killer' Jerry Lee Lewis rapidly skims his thumbnail down the piano's treble keys, it's the rapid pitch-blur or slide known as a glissando. Synthesizers like Max Crook's Musitron (see Del Shannon), the trombones of Big Bands and Stax/Volt Soul music, and the human voice (Marty Robbins) do continuous pitch-changing glissandos. 314, 438, 490.

Glitter Rock (see Glam)

290, 305, 381-82. Also called **Glitz**.

Glottal Stop

Linguistic term for the world-famous 'Holly Hiccup.' This vocal technique was pioneered by Buddy Holly (who perfected it from early inroads by Jimmie Rodgers I, Elvis on "Don't Be Cruel," and Gene Vincent). Other Holly hiccupers: Bobby Vee, Tommy Roe, Herman's Hermits, Ric Ocasek/Cars, Blondie, Cyndi Lauper. 50, 448, 464.

Goldmine

Collectors' R&R magazine with articles and classifieds. 347, 400.

Gospel & Gospel Rock (also see outdated 50s term 'Negro Spirituals')

Hymns, often Protestant or evangelical, with spirited delivery, frequently use Call & Response method of preacher to congregation. 265, 276, 525, 577-78.

Gothic Rock

Moon-tan mavens of midnight stalk Rock. 244, 270, 370, 393, 450-51.

Grace Note

A small note rendered before the beat – often part of a melisma.

Graceland

Elvis Presley's Memphis, Tennessee, large home. 424.

Grammy Awards

Recording industry awards given by pop music establishment. Slow to warm to R&R singers. Since 1959, Grammy Awards are somewhat related to a song's actual popularity. 329, 383, 401, 506.

Gramophone, Graphophone

Relic record players (c. 1905), using cylindrical records and needles nearly the size and heft of daggers. 549.

Grand Ole Opry (Nashville, TN)

Home of Country music since 1925 radio show began. 477, 485-87.

Graveyard Rock (also see Death Metal and Elegiac music)

Rock songs with a morbid story line. See Pearl Jam or J. Frank Wilson's "Last Kiss" or Dickey Lee's "Patches." 56, 76-77, 114-15, 188, 216, 240-42, 272, 300, 324, 331, 447, 473, 475, 490, 513, 518, 576.

Great Singers

Arbitrary *Gold Rush* term for 1960-68 group of Rock stars with powerful voices with great range (see Roy Orbison, Del Shannon, Gene Pitney, Jackie Wilson). 121-32, 337-38, 343-44, 358, 370, 570.

Griot

African tribal storyteller. 458, 462.

Grunge Rock

Heavy Metal, minor-key Hard Rock, popularized in the 90s. Often is melancholy in lyrics, gloomy in tone (see Nirvana, Pearl Jam). 92, 126, 224, 244, 328, 452-56, 493, 543, 547-48.

Guitar

6-stringed instrument with a narrow fretted neck and a resonance chamber. 30-32, 357, 332, 413-16+.

H

Hall of Fame (see Rock and Roll Hall of Fame) 237, 256, 337, 406+, finale of book.

Hammering On
Guitar technique. Play the 1ˢᵗ note, and tap the 2ⁿᵈ with your finger, using the 1ˢᵗ-note echo. 214, 370.

Handclapping (as major percussion instrument)
Since African field hands began handclapping for rhythm, it was a natural percussive style just waiting for the advent of Rock and Soul. 147, 268, 434, 520.

Hard Rock/Heavy Metal
One and the same in *Gold Rush,* characterized by macho baritone voices with a booming message, and flashy lead-guitar pyrotechnics. 322, 329, 347-48.

Hare Khrishna
Offshoot of Hinduism (see devotees like George Harrison in "My Sweet Lord"). 267, 338.

Harmonica
Small reed instrument, a/k/a 'mouth organ,' often used in Blues (see Jimmy Reed). 60, 236-240.

Harmony
How chords meld together. The 3-part harmony of a tonic major 'C' chord uses three basic notes: **C—E—G**.

Hawaiian, Slide, or Steel Guitar
Horizontal guitar played with slide or bottleneck, and devised by Joe Kekeku of Hawaii in 1931. 31, 357, 415, 570-71.

Heartland Rock/Thunder Rock
Basic guitar-powered Rock from 80s. See Bob Seger, Bruce Springsteen, John Cougar Mellencamp. 200, 299, 331-36, 347, 353-60, 431.

Heavy Metal/Hard Rock
High volume, strident message, speed-metal lead guitar. 71, 134, 177, 238, 311, 330, 338, 347, 356, 365-80, 431, 444, 490, 530.

Hillbilly Music/*Hillbilly Hit Parade*
Vintage Country music. Oddly, the 'hills' are NOT from Tennessee or Kentucky, they're originally the Porcupine Mountains of Upper-Peninsula Michigan. 485, 487, 492.

Hinduism
Primary religion of India (see George Harrison and Transcendental Meditation). 267, 339, 345.

Hip-Hop
Amorphous 90s term for combination of R&B, 'Dance', Rap, and Techno music. 284, 457-70, 554, 576.

Hit Parade/*Your Hit Parade*
TV show, 1950-58, which performed Top 7 songs of the week, starring Snooky Lanson & Dorothy Collins. 390, 416, 506.

Hit Parader
Magazine like *Song Hits* offering articles about performers, plus a few selected song lyrics (with no music). 400.

Honky-Tonk
Country term for roadhouse, jukebox music, with neon tears in many beers over lost loves. Term actually from 1890s (says Carl Sandburg), but became popular with Hank Williams, Hank Thompson, and Kitty Wells in 1951. 518.

Hootenanny
Folk-style sing-a-long. 279.

Horns
Saxes, trumpets, trombones, and other wind instruments. See Big Band, Stax/Volt Soul, and Funk.

Hype
Gung-ho record promotion by A&R people. 67, 303, 334.

I

Improvisation
To make up music and/or lyrics as one creates them. Instant songwriting.

Independent Labels/'Indies'
Small to medium recording companies, popularized in the early R&R 50s, and in the Rap-roaring 90s. 443, 560.

"Irish" Tenor
1st Tenor or Countertenor, highest natural male vocal range. 405.

Islam (Muslim Religion)
266, 269, 415.

Italian-American Contributions to Rock, and Italian-Language Music Craze of 1950-56
300, 425, 579-80, 595.

J

Jack
Hole in an amplifier or guitar that receives the guitar cord.

Jam
A Rock or Jazz group's improvisation.

Jamaican Music/Reggae/Calypso
(see Bob Marley, Harry Belafonte) 143.

Jazz, Jazz Rock, Jazz Metal, Jazz Fusion
American music from 20th century on, using good technique, improvisation, and syncopated beats. 207, 221, 227, 295-320, 368, 377, 383, 391, 414, 443. 555.

Jesus, and Religious Rock or Christian Contemporary Music
262-83+, 524.

Jewish Rock and Roll Contributions/Judaism
197, 265+.

Jingles
Ads. 300, 595.

Jock Rock/Sports Rock
R&R with a sports lyric theme. 133, 431-37.

"Johnny B. Goode"
Quintessential theme of starry-eyed kid with R&R dream (see Chuck Berry). 85, 157, 193, 203, 238, 288, 301, 324, 331, 342, 427-29, 487, 501, 515, 534, 553, 560-64, 573.

Juke Boxes
Coin-operated machine that plays selected popular records.

Junkanoo Music
Bahamian-style Rock and Soul. 393.

K

Karaoke
Japanese creation. Singer sings along with a lyric sheet and a pre-recorded band track. 164, 168, 485, 535.

Keyboards
Piano/Organ/Synthesizer. Throughout book.

L

Latino Rock
Rock music featuring a Latin beat. 413-30, 494, 523, 550.

Lead Sheet
Sheet music score, with lyrics, melody line, and chords only. Used often by studio musicians. A 'fake book' might be a book of 1000 such songs. Like Napster, it avoids paying royalties to artists.

Lip-Syncing
Artist pantomimes his/her own record (see Milli Vanilli). 163, 387.

Loud
Normal volume of Rock and Roll. As Ted Nugent said, "If it's too loud, you're too old."

Louisiana Hayride
Elvis's early barnstorming showcase. Unlike the Grand Ole Opry, it was a traveling revue. 493, 586.

Lyrics
Words to songs. Page 202, and throughout Gold Rush. Due to copyright laws, entire lines may not be quoted, so we tell the gist of the songs.

M

Major Chords (also see Chord Theory)
A major 3-note chord involves the root note, the major third note, plus the perfect fifth. In Key of C, it's **C – E – G.**

Major Seventh Chords
Sophisticated Jazz chord. You begin with the root major chord and add a major seventh; it's one half-step above a regular seventh note. In the Key of C, the **Cmaj7** chord features **C – E – G – B.**

Mambo
Latino dance craze sparking the late 40s and early 50s. Like Rock, it was torrid and passionate, and the beat throbbed. Their Afro-Cuban rhythms previewed Rock, and the horn sections previewed Funk.

Mandolin
Small stringed instrument, like early lute. A mandolin features 4 sets of doubled strings. 485, 502.

Marathon
26.2-mile foot race (and l—o—n—g performing career). 389-412.

March
Marching music (see Sousa), often in highly percussive 2/4 time.

Math & Music
To raise one octave means the octave note vibrates in a ratio of 2:1 to the lower note. Music is full of math, though mathophobes ignore this fact. 411.

Measure
A measure of a group of rhythmic beats. Rock music often has 4 (4/4 time); a *waltz* has 3 (3/4 time), and a *march* generally has 2 (2/4).

Mediant Chord (III chord major)
Third degree of diatonic scale. The Mediant chord in the Key of C is **E-major: E – Ab – B.** The Mediant Minor In Key of C is **E – G – B.** 186, 227, 315, 482, 491.

Melismas

16th-note 'grace' notes. In early Elvis, Little Richard, and Gospel music, melismas were key. Mariah Carey and Boyz II Men continued the tradition. 50, 88, 100, 132, 223, 384, 423, 460, 466, 508-09.

Melody Maker

British equivalent of *Billboard*. We feature many of *Melody Maker's* chart numbers of hits from the United Kingdom (listed under U.K.). 6, 327, 345.

Mezzo Soprano

Female singer with range hovering between high soprano and alto.

Mideastern Chord Change

To shift 1½ steps above the tonic major chord. A chromatic chord change is we call the Mideastern chord **bIII**. In the Key of C, the change goes this way: **C — Eb — C.** Keith Richard's famous intro riff in the Rolling Stones' #1 '65 "Satisfaction" employs this Mideastern chord change for dynamic effect. 155, 170, 178, 189, 394.

M.I.D.I Sequencers

Stands for Musical Instrument Digital Interface. Synthesizers, computers, and sequencers are digitally connected. This technology helped cause Techno Rock and New Wave. 329, 363, 450, 452.

Minor Chords

A minor triad involves a root note, a MINOR third note, and a perfect fifth. Instead of a **Major Triad** in the Key of C, like this: **C — E — G,** a **Minor Triad flats the third note: C — Eb — G.** The Doors and Grunge music revel in minor chords (see minor Blues "Riders on the Storm" by Doors). 302+.

Minor Scale

#1 diatonic scale in 18th and 19th-century music. Again, see Doors' "Riders on the Storm" for its rare appearance in Rock and Roll.

Mixing

Combining individual tracks from a multi-tracked record into a final mixed sound. Sometimes, the right blend can be nearly as important as recording the song itself.

Modulate

To change keys (usually one-half step upwards).

Mongolian Rock and Roll

Yep, it's finally come to Outer Mongolia. 427-28.

M.O.R./Easy Listening

299+

Motown Sound

Berry Gordy's 1960s Detroit Sound—a smooth R&B mix, powered by James Jamerson (bass), Benny Benjamin (drums), and the 'Funk Brothers' Motown backing band. The combination of Pop Orchestrations, Hot R&B, Gospel energy, and silky balladry featured such legends as Stevie Wonder, Marvin Gaye, the Temptations, Smokey Robinson and the Miracles, the Supremes, and the Four Tops. 157-66, 390, 457, 488, 530.

MTV (Music Television), and VH1

'Invented' by ex-Monkee Michael Nesmith, MTV added the video dimension to the good old sounds. A mixed blessing, MTV has many merits and demerits for the aspiring musician and Rock Star 'Wannabe.' 278, 313, 390, 443, 449, 522-24, 535-42.

Multitracking

Recording separate instruments or voices on different tracks (**overdubbing),** and then mixing them down to a polished sound.

Musitron

Early synthesizer used by keyboardist Max Crook on Del Shannon's #1, '61 "Runaway." Early 'Solovox' gizmos sounded like an organ more than a piano, with wild trailing pitch slurs. "Telstar," a #1 American instrumental by the Scottish band the Tornadoes, uses this early 'techno' technology. 121-25, 358.

Muzak

Light Easy Listening 'Elevator Music,' to encourage shoppers to buy things they don't need—with money they don't have. 363, 378.

N

Napster

System that allows free 'downloading' of music into 'CD burners,' thereby 'sharing' artists' blood, sweat, and tears – without paying them any royalties. Similar to old 'Bootleg' records, and other piracy. Big record companies refused to release **singles,** the *Gold Rush* benchmark, into the millennium. Unable to afford whole albums, many poor music-loving teens simply took the easiest way out – the 'freebie.' In late 2002, a major ruling ruled that price-fixing had occurred within the Huge-Company Recording Oligopoly – and that atonement must be financial. 225, 443, 461, 555-57, 568.

'Negro' Spirituals

50s term for African-American music with Gospel roots. 265, 578.

Neo-Disco/"Dance" Music

Dance music, 1988—Present. 343, 404.

New Age Music

Combining the easy orchestral afterglow of Mantovani with Celtic Renaissance and Classical overtones, New Age music has a loyal following (see Enya). 567, 575.

New Orleans
Cradle of Rock and Roll and Jazz (also see Memphis' contributions—Elvis, B.B. King).

New Wave
80s phenomenon from CBGB's, Manhattan. 194, 280, 437-56, 522.

Nihilism
Belief in nothing, as opposed to formal religion. Nihilism's belief in nothing is an offshoot of Nietzsche and Hemingway's Lost Generation and existentialism. Nihilism filled a void in the Seattle Grunge 90s scene. 197, 262, 453, 456.

Nirvana
Hindu/Buddhist state of temporal bliss and heavenly contemplative state (also, see group Nirvana's Kurt Cobain, who never found that bliss). 270.

Nuclear Power
And the Rock movement. 253, 261, 403, 451-52.

Number One, and Important Artists Who Never Hit Number One on the Billboard HOT 100 List
179-81.

O

Octave
An interval of eight notes on the major diatonic scale. Beyond the seventh white note on the piano in the Key of C, the note **B,** you hit the octave note. Mathematically, an octave is the interval between two pitches which will vibrate in a ratio of **2:1.** As Campbell and Brody explain in their excellent 2001 *Rock and Roll: An Introduction,* if pitches vibrate at this ratio to each other, they share the same letter name. Also, they're an OCTAVE apart.

"Oldies Overkill"
The theory that if a great song is overplayed on standard Oldies or Classic Rock stations, it loses its appeal. Sometimes, even the great ones can become annoying with supersaturation. 98, 130, 258, 338, 530.

Opera, and Opera-Style Rock Vocals
121-33, 314-15, 482, 541.

Orchestral Rock
Often uses strings, woodwinds, brass, and percussion, too, like a full orchestra. 298-99, 312-14, 323, 563.

Outlaw Movement
Country and Country-Rock faction, hailing from Austin, Texas, and starring Willie Nelson and Buddy Holly's ex-Cricket—Waylon Jennings. 498.

Overdubbing
Recording another track (multi-tracking) onto a record.

P

Pagliacci Theme
The sad clown motif in a song lyric. Smokey Robinson/ Miracles' #1 '70 "Tears of a Clown" is among the best with this prevalent romantic theme. 105, 397-98, 472.

Palm Mute
To muffle a guitar with the palm for a pizzicato effect.

Paradiddles
16th-note drum rudiments.

Parrotheads
Followers of Jimmy Buffett & the Coral Reefer Band – like Deadheads followed the Grateful Dead. 260-61, 336, 403.

Payola
Overzealous hype. The 1959 Payola scandal in the recording industry relates to paying under the table to play a record, regardless of its merit or mediocrity. 309, 334.

Pedal Point
A long sustained bass note, ranging over harmonic treble changes and melodic movements. 412.

Peg
Adjusts tension of guitar/bass/banjo strings.

Pentatonic Scale
A scale with only 5 notes (basically, the black keys on the piano).

Percussion
Instruments which are struck or shook. Ex., drums, tambourine, cymbals, bells, triangle. Technically, a piano qualifies as percussion.

Phasers
Special effects of guitar/amp sound modification. 314.

Philly Soul
Soulful Sound of Philadelphia. Heyday? 1969-74. 284, 309, 465, 468.

Piano
Hammers strike the inner strings of this ubiquitous descendant of clavichords, harpsichords, and distant cousin of the lute.

Pickup
1) Connector of an acoustic guitar, or other instrument, to microphonic amplifier; 2) Some 70s romantic rendezvous—an affair that often never lived to be an hour old.

Pizzicato
Plucked strings, usually on violin.

Player Piano

Among first contraptions to displace live musicians. A scroll of music, with perforations like Braille, rotated inside old upright pianos, as far back as 1910 and beyond. By simply pumping the pedals like an old sewing machine or foot-powered organ, the person 'playing' the piano would be treated to a whole Ragtime piano track (just waiting for karaoke to be invented). 535.

Polynesian Chord Change

Shift from the tonic chord to the 5 ½ chord, or the **bVI** [flatted sixth]. It's a chromatic chord change. In the Key of C, the change goes this way:

C —— Ab —— C

Buddy Holly uses this dramatic chord shift for the first time in Rock on the "pretty, pretty" line in his #3, 11-57 "Peggy Sue." 102, 148, 154, 170, 178, 189, 361, 414, 483.

Polyphony

Counterpoint. Two harmonic melodies at the same time. 199.

Pop/Pop-Rock/Pop Standards

Gold Rush covers all popular music ['pop']. We rarely use the term 'pop,' because so often it seems that the 'pop' artist is being put down – by the term 'POP,' by the critic. When in doubt, we leave it out. [Ed. Note – I like Pop music of all kinds. Only Bobby Vee, one of the greatest talents in R&R, ever admitted to doing Pop music, and I think his music is outstanding].

Power Chord

3 notes: The note itself, its octave above, and the 5th note in the middle (eliminating the 3rd note).

Power Rock/Hard Rock/Heavy Metal

353+

Progressive Rock

Often Jazz Rock. Sometimes with a dash of Heavy Metal or Hard Rock. 301, 304,

Psychedelic Rock

60s-era Rock with flamboyant props and stage shows: black lights, strobe lights, swirling kaleidoscopic whirling walls, incense (perhaps) aromas, outrageous outfits. In 1966, LSD was a LEGAL drug given out to students for psych department experiments. 'Turning on' to drugs was partially a reaction against a burgeoning war in Vietnam, and the ever-possible draft notice. 217, 229-30, 337, 402-03, 409, 437, 446.

Punk Rock

Rock, harking back to its 3-chord roots (see Gene Vincent, MC5, Ramones). 52, 65, 192, 220, 349, 437-56, 494, 554, 579.

Q

Quarter-Note

Standard length of a note, and, for fraction fans, half the length of a half note. In 4/4 time, we have 4 quarter notes per measure.

R

Rage Rock/Revenge Rock (see Revenge Rock)

368, 554, 578.

Ragtime

Syncopated piano music, 1897-1920. Forerunner of Rock and Roll, Boogie-Woogie, Blues, and Jazz. 219, 313, 433, 550, 553, 562, 590.

Rap

R&B spinoff from 1980 zone, with previews in 60s James Brown, and street poetry of the Champ Muhammad Ali. Heavy rhythmic accompaniment, and often minimal melody. Rhyming lyrics are halfway shouted, halfway sung. 1st #1 Rap song? Bobby 'Boris' Picket's 1962 "Monster Mash." 218. 224, 345, 457-70, 502, 582-85.

R&B (Rhythm & Blues)

Often African-American Rock & Soul. 157-67, 231-50, 278, 420-29, 433, 443, 449, 578+

Records

Vinyl, versus Tapes, CDs, DATs. 225, 411.

Refrain

Main repetitive chorus of song. The refrain differs from the storytelling verses or the intermediary bridge.

Reggae

Jamaican beat from 1960s on, influenced by Afro-Cuban rhythms. 320, 339, 388, 418, 421-22, 426-27, 459.

Revenge Rock

R&R with revengeful lyrics about good love gone bad. 121-25, 368, 554, 578.

Reverb[eration]

An electronic amp gizmo which manufactures an echo 1/30th of a second later.

Rhythm & Blues (R&B)

This term from the 40s (which fortunately replaced 'Race Music') is a catch-all term for mostly African-American music with a big beat. 157-67, 231-50, 283-94, 320, 449, 457-71, 528, 590.

Riff

Brief melodic instrumental interlude, shorter than a cadenza.

Ritalin
A drug given freely to children who fidget. Some of them, when they kick the drug habit, become Rock stars.

Roadies
Touring stevedores and equipment movers who also set up and tune up bands on the road. 386, 402.

Rock and Roll
Why we're here. In the Beatle Era, the term Rock and Roll was shortened to Rock. [Ed. Note – I first majored in geology, so to keep the rocks straight here, we're riding with the original term Rock and Roll]. Rock and Roll is powered by heavy drums and bass, and a fired-up guitar or two. Spirited vocals and dynamic lyrics keep Rock rolling into its second half century at the top. Pages 1-590.

Rock and Roll Hall of Fame, Cleveland, Ohio
Founded 1986. Selects greatest performers of all time (see list at *Gold Rush* finale). 237, 242, 256, 262, 337, 373, 383, 406, 432, 438, 460, 505, 533, Hall of Fame Section.

Rockabilly
Early Country Rock, like Carl Perkins' #2 '56 "Blue Suede Shoes." 52, 322, 326, 384, 439, 510, 578.

Rock Steady & 'Rydim'
Related to Reggae. 437.

Rococo Rock
David Szatmary's term for Glam or Glitter 'Art Rock,' and the "Age of Excess" in Rock and Roll. 381-83, 441.

Rolling Stone Magazine
Major R&R magazine since Jann Wenner founded it in 1967 in San Francisco. THE authority. 195, 224, 353, 403, 451, 490, 555.

Rural Expatriation
Recurrent theme in song lyrics: bankrupt farmers MUST move to smoky city, with bittersweet results. 177, 185, 354, 445, 494.

S

Salsa
Latin-American combo of Rock music with Spanish flavor (salsa means salty). 425-30.

Samba
Brazilian Folk dance, in 2/4 time. Cousin of the **Rhumba** or Rumba, but not Rambha.

Sampling
Rap technique from 80s. Vinyl is scratched. Chunks and phrases and riffs from older hits are 'sampled' or borrowed (as copyright lawyers perk up).

Saxophone/Sax
Single-reed brass woodwind invented in 1840 by Adolphe Sax. 33, 218, 315-16, 424.

Sequencers, M.I.D.I.
MIDI unit which first records, and then plays back by means of a synthesizer. 313.

Seventh Chords
Contains a root note, third, perfect fifth, and a seventh [NOT a *major seventh*]. In the Key of C, a **C7** chord features **C – E – G – Bb.** 227.

Sharp
Raising a pitch one-half step, indicated by 'Pound Sign' **[#]**.

Sheet Music
Before recording became popular in the 1890s, songs were available only in sheet music. Sheet music has musical notes transcribed into the treble and bass clefs on paper.

Shuffle
4-beat rhythm with a long and short eighth-note pattern. In other words, a dotted eighth note (actually, a 3/16th note) is followed by a 1/16th note in each of the four beats per measure. Buddy Holly/Crickets' #1 '57 "That'll Be the Day" has a shuffle beat, as does Bill Doggett's classic instrumental, #2 '56 "Honky Tonk Part II."

Singer-Songwriters
Although the term was launched via Elton John, James Taylor, Jim Croce, or Don McLean around 1970, the *singer-songwriter concept* was around at the birth of Rock: Little Richard, Fats Domino, Carl Perkins, Buddy Holly. 262-82.

Singles (single songs) **versus Albums**
555-57.

Sixth Chords
Add 6th note to tonic triad. In Key of C, it's **C – E – G – A.** In its first Inversion, if you flip the 'A' down to the bass area, it becomes an **A-minor** by ditching the 'G' note: **A – C – E.** [We can 'ACE' Chord Theory this way]. 227.

Ska
Early forerunner of Reggae, and still popular into millennium, via Scofflaws. 420-22, 437, 459.

Slack Key Guitar
Hawaiian tuning technique, to make open strings play melodic major chords. 570-71.

Slap Bass
Electric bassists slap with the thumb, rather than use a pick (plectrum). Crafted by Elvis's bassman Bill Black, the Slap Bass technique also flowered in the Funk explosion of the 70s. 322.

Slide Guitar

It smoothly moves from one octave to another in a *glissando* blur of sound. Slide guitars use a metal or bottleneck glass slide to slur and glide notes. Same as Hawaiian guitar. 31, 357.

Snare Drum

Top cylindrical drum, with two drum heads. Drummer strikes top head, while bottom head with metal snares resonates.

Soft Rock (see Easy Listening).

Solo

A key performer sings or plays alone or with softer accompaniment.

Song-Guy/Song-Girl Concept

The song-guy is the character or persona that the singer plays in the song. The lyric is often far different from the actual singer's personality. 250, 389, 398, 479, 490, 524, 582, 588.

Soprano

Highest female vocal range. From lowest to highest: mezzo soprano, lyric soprano, coloratura soprano [Opera terms]. 166, 282, 518, 549.

Soul/R&B

Characterized by heart of Motown or Stax/Volt Sounds of the mid-60s. 278, 327, 352, 457-70, 531, 577.

Southern Rock

Southern-style 70s Rock, with energetic guitar leads (see Allman Bros., Lynyrd Skynyrd). 312, 380.

Soundies

(40s jukebox videos). 535.

Spin Magazine

Rockmag of millennium. 400, 462.

Spins

Number of plays per week. The more spins, the higher the chart number.

Spiritual

Gospel music.

Standards, Pop

A lasting hit from the Big Band or Crooner Era, ranging all the way back to Tin Pan Alley (1890-1920) or the early Jazz Age (1920s).

Steel Guitar/Hawaiian/Slide Guitar

Invented by Hawaiian Joe Kekeku in 1931. Played horizontally, and big in 50s & 60s Country music.

Streetcorner Chord Pattern and Music Style

In Key of C, it's **C – Am – F – G7,** a four-chord progression. This long-ago enchanted music style ('Doo-Whop') serenaded many a 'cool chick' on some neon-dazzle Bronx streetlight midnight corner. Mostly crooned by Barber-Shop style Italian-American or African-American Rock stars, Streetcorner music wafts nostalgically along lost airwaves of nevermore. And evermore. 54, 101, 105, 134, 194, 322, 360, 411, 475, 506, 523, 582.

String Bass

Big 'bull fiddle,' largest of violin family. Evolved via Crickets' Joe B. Mauldin into the **electric bass.**

Studio

Place where most records are recorded. Live show recordings lose sound quality.

Sub-Dominant Chord

The IV Chord (or Four Chord) on the diatonic major scale. In the Key of C, the Sub-Dominant IV chord is **F,** or **F – A – C.** 188, 199, 227, 483.

Sub-Mediant Chord

The VI chord (or Six Chord) on the diatonic major scale. In the Key of C, the Sub-Mediant VI major and minor chords are **A and A-minor:**

    A =   A – C# – E;
    A-minor = A – C – E.

188, 199, 227, 483.

Super-Tonic Chord

The II Chord (or Two Chord) on the diatonic major scale. In the Key of C, the Super-Tonic II major and minor chords are **D and D-minor.**

    D =   D – F# – A;
    D-minor = D – F – A.

Surf Rock

Early 60s Thunder Rock, typified by Beach Boys. 87, 113-21, 206, 216, 222, 261, 422, 428, 432, 438, 526-27, 536, 570-71.

Swing Bass

Ragtime piano bass line, and foundation of Rock and Roll. 433.

Swing/Swing Jazz

30s & 40s Big Band Jazz. 320.

Syncopation

Playing off the main beat.

Synthesizers

They electronically create and change sounds.

T

Tablature

Notation system, often using numbers or letters, rather than musical notes. For use on string instruments like guitar. 370.

Tacet
Literally, to 'be silent.' Short *a cappella* phrase. Usually means in R & R that a singer hollers something, while the instruments are quiet for a bar or so. Then they all come crashing back. 90, 96, 166, 448.

Talking Blues
Early Rap-style acoustic Blues, mixed with regular Blues (see John Lee Hooker). 462, 570.

Tambourine
Small drum with one head. Held in one hand and slapped by the other.

Tango
Argentinian Latin dance, popular in early 50s. Passionate and throbbing like Rock and Roll.

Techno/Techno-Synth
Rock with heavy use of sequenced, programmed music, with drum machine. 328, 410, 443, 447, 450, 452.

Teen Idols
Handsome, and highly hyped, singers. 84, 87, 102, 110, 135-36, 558, 579.

Tempo
Speed of a song, usually consistent. In a *bolero*, the tempo or speed gradually increases in pitch and speed in a crescendo to a climax.

Tenor
Highest male voice, usually carrying melody. Most common range for Teen Idols. Highest tenor is 1st or 'Irish' or Countertenor; lower tenor is 2nd, or 'Italian', or Dramatic Tenor. 102, 260, 263, 284, 300, 389.

Thunder Rock
Powerful Rock music which avoids the drag of quietude. 122, 130, 213, 322, 330, 335, 584.

Timbre
Tone quality or color of voice. 280.

Tin Pan Alley
Lower East Side songwriters' headquarters. Birthplace of recording industry in 1890.

Tom-Tom
Small booming drums, played with sticks, hands, or mallets.

Tonic Chord
The basic triad in a diatonic major scale. The **'I' or One Chord.** In the Key of C, it's the root note, the third, and the perfect fifth: **C chord = C – E – G.** 163, 199, 339, 491.

Track
One part of a record to be mixed (perhaps the bass track).

Triad
Three-note chord of root, third, and fifth. Can be major or minor, diminished or augmented.

Trio
Three performers in an act.

Triplets
Divide 4/4 beat into three parts (so, 12 beats/measure). 377.

Trombone
Baritone brass with slides/glissandos, first used in Jazz and marching bands. 459, 472-75.

Troubador
Originally, a 12th or 13th-century French traveling musician. Used for current Folk performers.

Trumpet
Tenor brass instrument, with flaring bell, valves, and mouthpiece. Related to cornet and bugle. Key lead instrument of Big Band Era. 475, 478, 499,

Tuba
Bass brass instrument, with big booming bell, like Sousaphone. The tuba carried early bass sounds for rhythm section until c. 1930, when the string bass replaced it (and was, in turn, replaced by the electric bass around 1958).

12-Bar Blues Progression
#1 chord structure in Rock and Roll (and Blues, and Boogie-Woogie). In Key of C, it's—

	C	F	C		G	F	C	G
# of bars =	4	2	2		1	1	1	1

See pages 53, 60, 90, 100-01, 155, 201, 232-34, 394, 438 for 12-Bar Blues.

12-String Guitar
Paired strings, with lower four tuned in octaves. It has a fuller sound than the ordinary 6-string guitar.

U

Ukulele
Fretted Hawaiian 4-string guitar, tuned to a guitar's top 4 strings.

Unplugged
Fad, 1990-92—Rock stars, like Eric Clapton, played acoustically, in Folk fashion. 333

Upright Piano
Not a low and wide grand piano, but a taller, thinner instrument. Strings are arranged vertically on a sound board. The upright was the key Ragtime piano.

V

Vaudeville
1890-1920 live local variety show.

Verse
Story line of song, preceding chorus or refrain.

Vibrato
Quick pitch fluctuation, slightly beyond the regular pitch. Used in vocals, guitars, and amps, but not pianos.

Videos (see MTV, VH-1)
Songs with a video track for TV. 465, 514, 522.

Vinyl Records versus Taps, CDs, DATs
A comparison of quality. 225, 411, 453, 456.

Violin
Most treble instrument in violin family. Has four strings and no frets. Introduced into R&R by Buddy Holly, Dick Jacobs, and Norman Petty.

Voice
The #1 instrument in a Rock and Roll song.

W

Wah-Wah Pedal
Special-effect foot pedal for electric guitarist or bassist. It simulates a low whine.

Wall of Sound
Phil Spector's trademark record production method, using soaring crescendos, many unusual instruments, and powerful sounds. 188, 340.

Waltz
3/4 time song, most popular by Johann Strauss in 19th century. Also #1 for half of year 1950, with "The Tennessee Waltz" and "Goodnight Irene." 398, 404-08, 435, 475, 583, 590.

War
Songs of war, patriotism, nationalism. 205-16, 472-73.

Western Swing (see Bob Wills & Texas Playboys)
40s Texan Country music with fiddles and a big beat. 329, 486, 501, 509.

Whammy Bar
Gearshift on a guitar, altering pitch.

'Whiskey Tenor' (or baritone)
Gravelly, rough, sandpapery voice, unrelated to whiskey consumption. Sometimes nicotine, however, relates (see Tom Waits). 389, 405.

Whole Note
Long note running for a full measure in 4/4 time songs.

Women in Rock and Roll
Throughout *Gold Rush*: 139-47, 336, 521-35+.

Woodwinds
Sax, clarinet, flute, bassoon, recorder.

X

Xylophone
Because 'X' is always for xylophone. It's a percussion instrument, like the marimba or vibraphone (see Lionel Hampton). Xylophones have a piano 'keyboard' and are officially percussion instruments.

Y

Yodel
Swiss-style instant vocal shift between normal tenor or baritone range and falsetto. See Del Shannon or Roy Rogers. 100, 122, 125-26, 142, 316, 338, 438, 440, 449, 487, 491-92, 502, 516, 521, 580.

Yodel-Kick
Instant quick yodel or squeal at the end of vocal lines. See Cyndi Lauper, Little Richard, Frankie Ford. See same pages listed under 'Yodel.'

Your Hit Parade/Hit Parade (see Hit Parade).
390, 416, 506, 535.

Yukon
Canadian territory in far North, next to Alaska, where Dawson City GOLD RUSH took place in 1897-98. 559, 562, 590.

Z

Zen Buddhism
Eastern religion. 547.

Zither
Harp-style, hand-held stringed instrument (see Lovin' Spoonful or Carter Family).

Zydeco
Cajun music covering R&R, R&B, Country, and Caribbean music.

Bibliography

Since *Gold Rush*, the World's Largest Pamphlet, is mostly DISCOGRAPHY [TAPE-OGRAPHY, or C.D.-OGRAPHY], we offer this bonus excursion into the printed page. Here is a lean list of classic and current Rock Lit. Basically, it's *some* of the popular and academic background we used for *Gold Rush*.

Aaron, Michael. *Piano Course*. New York: Mills, 1945.

Aquila, Richard. *That Old Time Rock and Roll, 1954-63*. New York: Schirmer-MacMillan, 1989.

Amburn, Ellis. *Dark Star (The Roy Orbison Story)*. New York: St. Martin's Press, 1993.

Anthony, Dean. *The Beach Boys*. New York: Crescent Books, 1985.

Bacon, Tony. *Electric Guitars: The Illustrated Encyclopedia*. San Diego, CA: Thunder Bay Press, 2000.

Bass Player.

Bay, Mel. *Mel Bay Guitar Method Chord Book*. New York: Bay, 1958.

Berry, Chuck. *Chuck Berry: The Autobiography*. New York: Harmony Books, 1987.

Bible [*Holy Bible*, Concordia Self-Study, for Religious Rock Chapter; also used *Koran, Bhagavad-Gita, Upanishads* for world's religions].

Billboard. Our primary chart reference -- often via Joel Whitburn's *Record Research*.

Blesh, Rudi, and Harriet Janis. *They All Played Ragtime*. New York: Alfred Knopf, 1950.

Blue Suede News.

Book of 1000 Songs. New York: [Publisher lost in space], 1917.

Bronson, Fred. *Billboard Book of Number One Hits*. New York: Billboard Books, 1988.

Brown, Charles. *The Rock and Roll Story*. Englewood Cliffs, New Jersey: Prentice-Hall, 1983.

Brown, Peter & Steven Gaines. *The Love You Make* [Beatles]. New York: McGraw-Hill, 1983.

Burns, Ken. *Jazz*. PBS TV Series, 1-2001.

Cain, Robert. *Whole Lotta Shakin' Goin' On*. New York: Dial Press, 1981.

Campbell, Michael and James Brody. *Rock and Roll: An Introduction*. Belmont, CA: Wadsworth, 1999.

Carson, David. *Rockin' Down the Dial*. Troy, MI: Momentum Books, Ltd., 2000.

Cash Box – in the 50s, almost as influential for R & R charts as *Billboard*.

Circus.

Clarke, Donald. *Penguin Encyclopedia of Popular Music*. London and New York: Penguin and Viking Penguin, 1985.

Cole, Richard. *Stairway to Heaven*. New York: Harper Collins, 1992.

Collins, Ace. *The Story Behind Country Music's All-Time Greatest 100 Songs*. New York: Boulevard, 1991.

Comprehensive Country Music Encyclopedia. Editors of *Country Music* magazine. New York: Random House, 1994.

Country: The Music and Its Musicians. New York: Abbeville Press, 1988.

Country Weekly.

Crawdaddy.

Creem.

Crenshaw, Marshall. *Hollywood Rock*. New York: Harper Perennial, 1994.

Dalton, David. *James Dean: American Icon*. New York: St. Martin's Press, 1984.

Davies, Hunter. *The Beatles*. New York: McGraw Hill, 1968.

Dean, Maury. *The Rock Revolution*. Detroit, Michigan: Edmore, 1966.

DeCurtis, Anthony. "Bill Monroe." *Rolling Stone*, October 31, 1996.

DeCurtis, Anthony, and James Hanke, et al, eds. *The Rolling Stone Illustrated History of Rock and Roll*. New York: Straight Arrow-Random House, 1992.

DiMucci, Dion. *The Wanderer: Dion's Story*. New York: Beech Tree Books/William Morrow, 1988.

Downbeat.

Drum.

Eddy, Chuck. *The Accidental Evolution of Rock and Roll: A Misguided Tour Through Popular Music*. New York: DaCapo-Plenum Publishers, 1997.

Edwards, Gavin. *He's Got the Whole World in His Pants. .. And More Misheard Lyrics*. New York, Fireside, 1996.

Electronic Musician.

Favorite Songs of the Nineties. Ed. Robert Fremont. New York: Dover, 1973.

Fernando, S.H. Jr. *The New Beats: Exploring the Music, Culture, and Attitude of Hip-Hop.* New York: Doubleday/Bantam/Dell, 1994.

Ferris, WIlliam. *Blues from the Delta.* Garden City, New York: Anchor, 1984.

Francis, Connie. *Who's Sorry Now?* Introduction by Dick Clark. New York: St. Martin's, 1984.

Friedman, Myra. *Buried Alive: The Biography of Janis Joplin.* New York: William Morrow, 1973.

Frith, Simon. *Performing Rites: On the Value of Popular Music.* Cambridge, Massachusetts: Harvard University Press, 1996.

Gaar, Gillian. *She's A Rebel.* Preface by Yoko Ono. Seattle, Washington: Seal Press, 1992.

Gaines, Steven. *Heroes & Villains: The Beach Boys.* New York: Signet, 1987.

Garcia. Editors of *Rolling Stone.* Boston, Massachusetts: Little, Brown, and Company, 1995.

Garcia, Jerry. *Garcia.* New York: Straight Arrow. 1972.

Gariepy, Henry. *Songs in the Night.* Grand Rapids, Michigan and Cambridge, England: Eerdmans, 1996.

Garafalo, Reebee. *Rockin' Out – Popular Music in the U.S.A..* Boston, Massachusetts: Allyn & Bacon, 1997.

George, Nelson. *Where Did Our Love Go?* New York: St. Martin's, 1985.

Giddins, Gary. *Riding on a Blue Note: Jazz and American Pop.* New York: Oxford University Press, 1981.

Gillett, Charlie. *The Sound of the City.* New York: Dell, 1970.

Ginsberg, Allen. "To the Punks of Dawlish." 11-18-79, in *Collected Poems 1947-80.* New York: Harper & Row, 1984.

Goldmine.

Goldrosen, John. *The Buddy Holly Story.* Bowling Green, Ohio: Bowling Green University Press, 1975. New York: Quick Fox, 1979.

Goldrosen, John. *Remembering Buddy.* New York: Viking Penguin, 1987. DeCapo, 1995.

Gregory, Hugh. *Soul Music A-Z.* DaCapo Press, 1995.

Guitar. Other guitar mags? *Guitar Legends, Guitar Player, Guitar World, Guitar One,* and *Guitar & Bass.*

Guralnick, Peter. *Lost Highway.* New York: Perennial Library, 1989.

Guralnick, Peter. *Last Train to Memphis: The Rise of Elvis Presley.* Boston, Massachusetts: Back Bay Books & Little, Brown, and Company, 1994.

Guralnick, Peter. *Sweet Soul Music.* New York: HarperCollins, 1986.

Hagen, Chet. *Grand Ole Opry.* New York: Henry Holt, 1989.

Hardy, Phil and Dave Laing. *The DaCapo Companion to 20th Century Popular Music.* New York: DaCapo, 1995.

Hit Parader.

Hopkins, Jerry. *Elvis.* New York: Warner, 1972.

Horstman, Dorothy. *Sing Your Heart Out, Country Boy.* New York: Pocket Books, 1976.

Jackson, John. *Big Beat Heat.* [Alan Freed bio]. New York: Macmillan, 1991.

Jackson, John. *American Bandstand.* New York: Oxford, 1997.

Jackson, Richard. *Popular Songs of Nineteenth-Century America.* New York: Dover, 1976.

Jancik, Wayne. *One-Hit Wonders.* New York: Billboard/Watson-Guptill Publications, 1990.

Jasen, David. *Tin Pan Alley.* New York: Donald Fine, 1988.

Jasper, Tony and Derek Oliver. *The International Encyclopedia of Hard Rock and Heavy Metal.* New York and Oxford: Facts on File Publications, 1983.

Jazz.

Jazz Times.

John, Elton. *To Be Continued.* Milwaukee, Wisconsin: Hal Leonard, 1991.

Jones, K. Maurice. *Say It Loud: The Story of Rap Music.* Brookfield, Connecticut: Millbrook Press, 1994.

Kerouac, Jack and Steve Allen. "October in the Railroad Earth," poem from album *Poetry for the Beat Generation.* Hanover Records, 1959.

Kerouac, Jack. *On the Road.* New York: Viking Press, 1955.

Keyboard.

King, B.B. *Blues All Around Me*, with David Ritz. New York: Avon, 1996.

Kristof, Nicholas. "Hongk." New York *Times*, 3-26-90.

Laing, Dave. *Buddy Holly.* New York: Collier, 1972.

Maltin, Leonard. *Movie and Video Guide 2003.* New York: Penguin, 2002.

Mann, Alan. *The A-Z of Buddy Holly.* London: Aurum Press, 1996.

Manzarek, Ray. *Light My Fire: My Life with the Doors.* New York: Putnam, 1998.

Marsden, Gerry. *I'll Never Walk Alone*, with Ray Coleman. London: Bloomsbury, 1993.

Marsh, Dave. *Elvis.* New York: Dell, 1981.

Marsh, Dave. *Fortunate Son.* New York: Random House, 1985.

Marsh, Dave. *The Heart of Rock and Soul*. New York: New American Library, 1989.

Marsh, Dave. *The New Book of Rock Lists*. New York: Fireside, 1994.

Melody Maker.

Metal Edge.

Miles, Barry. *Paul McCartney: Many Years from Now*. New York: Henry Holt, 1997.

Millard, Bob. *Amy Grant: The Life of a Pop Star*. New York: St. Martin's, 1986.

Modern Drummer.

Morrow, Bruce. *Cousin Brucie: My Life in Rock and Roll Radio*. With Laura Bando. New York: Beach Tree-Morrow, 1987.

Murrells, Joseph. *Million Selling Records*. New York: Arco, 1984.

Musician.

Nelson, Willie. *Willie*. With Bud Shrake. New York: Pocket, 1988.

New Musical Express.

Newsday, especially R & R critics Wayne Robins and Glenn Gamboa.

Nite, Norm N. *Rock On, Volume One*. New York: Popular Library, 1974.

Nite, Norm N. *Rock On, Volume Two*. New York: Crowell, 1978.

Nite, Norm. N. *Rock On, Volume Three*. New York: Harper & Row, 1985.

Norman, Philip. *Shout: The Beatles in Their Generation*. New York: Warner, 1982.

Nugent, Steven and Charlie Gillett. *Rock Almanac*. Garden City, New York: Anchor, 1978.

O'Brien, Lucy. *She Bop: The Definitive History of Women in Rock, Pop, and Soul*. New York: Penguin, 1995.

Ochs, Michael. *1000 Record Covers*. Cologne, Germany: Taschen, 1996.

Ochs, Michael. *Rock Archives*. New York: Doubleday, 1984.

100 Best Songs of the 20s and 30s. Intro by Richard Rodgers. New York: Bonanza, 1973.

Orbison, Roy. *Only the Lonely*. With Alan Clayson. New York: St. Martin's, 1989.

Palmer, Robert. *Rock and Roll: An Unlikely History*. New York: Harmony, 1995.

Paredes, Jon, and Patricia Romanowski. *Rolling Stone Encyclopedia of Rock and Roll*. New York: Rolling Stone Press, 1983.

Partridge, Elizabeth. *This Land Was Made for You and Me: Woody Guthrie*. New York: Viking, 2002

Peer, Elizabeth and Ralph. *Buddy Holly*. New York: Peer International, 1972.

Penguin Encyclopedia of Popular Music. Edited by Donald Clarke [Contributors include John Child, Ronnie Graham, Ken Hunt, Robin Katz, Sue Steward, and John Tobler]. London and New York: Penguin and Viking Penguin, 1985.

Perkins, Carl. *Go Cat Go*. With David McGee. New York, Hyperion, 1996.

Peters, Richard. *The Legend That Is Buddy Holly*. London: Pop Universal/Souvenir Press, 1990.

Philllips, John. *Papa John*. New York: Dell, 1987.

Preiss, Byron. *The Beach Boys*. New York: Ballantine, 1979.

Rand McNally Road Atlas. 1997.

Rand McNally Road Atlas of Britain. 1993.

Record Collector.

Record World.

Rees, Dafydd and Luke Crampton. *Encyclopedia of Rock Stars*. London & New York: DK [Dorling-Kindersley], 1996.

Rees, Dafydd and Luke Crampton. *Rock Movers and Shakers*. London and New York: Banson and Billboard, 1991.

Riley, Tim. *Tell Me Why*. New York: Vintage, 1989.

Riordan, James and Jerry Prochoricky. *Break on Through: The Life of Jim Morrison*. New York: William Morrow, 1995.

Rockin' 50s. Publisher Bill Griggs.

Robinson, David. *Pop, Rock, and Soul*. New York: Pyramid, 1972.

Rolling Stone.

Roxon, Lillian. *Rock Encyclopedia*. New York: Workman, 1969.

Ryan, Thomas. *American Hit Radio: A History of Popular Singles from 1955-Present*. Rocklin, California: Prima, 1996.

Sandburg, Carl. *The American Songbag*. New York: Lomax, 1935.

Savage, Steve. *The Billboard Book of Rhythm*. New York: Billboard Books, 1989.

Scaduto, Anthony. *The Real Bob Dylan*. New York: Signet, 1971.

Seeger, Pete. *The Incompleat Folk Singer*. Lincoln, Nebraska: University of Nebraska, 1979.

Shapiro, Harry and Caesar Glebbeek. *Jimi Hendrix: Electric Gypsy*. New York: 1990.

Shirley, Kay. *The Book of the Blues*. New York: MCA Music, 1963.

Smith, Huston. *The Religions of Man*. New York: Harper & Row, 1958.

Smith, Joe. *Off the Record*. New York: Warner, 1988.

Smith, Wes. *The Pied Pipers of Rock and Roll: Radio DeeJays of the 50s and 60s*. Marietta, Georgia: Longstreet Press, 1989.

Smokey Joe's Cafe, Playbill, June 1997, Vol. 97, #6.

Song Hits.

Spin.

Springsteen. Editors of *Rolling Stone*. New York: Hyperion, 1996.

Strong, M.C. *The Great Rock Discography*, 3rd Edition. Edinburgh, Scotland, and New York: Canongate, 1994.

Stuessy, Joe. *Rock and Roll*. Englewood Cliffs, New Jersey: Prentice-Hall, 1994.

Sumrall, Harry. *Pioneers of Rock and Roll*. New York: Watson-Guptill, 1994.

Szatmary, David. *Rockin' in Time*. Upper Saddle River, NJ: Prentice Hall, 1996.

Teen.

Teen Beat.

Tosches, Nick. *Country: The Twisted Roots of Rock and Roll*. New York: Scribners, 1977 [DaCapo 1996].

Variety.

Village Voice.

Walker, Dave. *American Rock and Roll Tour*. New York: Thunder's Mouth Press, 1992.

Ward, Ed, Geoffrey Stokes, and Ken Tucker. *Rock of Ages: The Rolling Stone History of Rock and Roll*. New York: Rolling Stones Press/Summit Books, 1986.

Warner, Jay. *American Singing Groups*. New York: Billboard Books, 1992.

"What A Long Strange Trip." *People* [Jerry Garcia obit]. August 21, 1995, 64.

Wheeler, Opal. *Stephen Foster*. New York: Dutton, 1941.

Whitburn, Joel. *Billboard: Top 1000 Singles*. Milwaukee, Wisconsin: Hall Leonard, 1993.

Whitburn, Joel. *Bubbling Under the Hot 100. 1959-81*. Menomonee Falls, Wisconsin: Record Research, Inc., 1982.

Whitburn, Joel. *Billboard Book of Top 40 Hits*. New York: Billboard Publications, 1989,

Whitburn, Joel. *Billboard Book of Top 40 Albums*. New York: Watson-Guptill, 1991.

Whitburn, Joel. *Billboard 1994, 1995, 1996 Yearbooks*. Menomonee Falls, Wisconsin: Record Research, 1994-97.

Whitburn, Joel. *Pop Memories 1890-1954*. Menomonee Falls, Wisconsin: Record Research, 1986.

Whitburn, Joel. *Top Country Singles 1944-93*. Menomonee Falls, Wisconsin: Record Research, 1994.

Whitburn, Joel. *Top Pop Albums 1955-96*. Menomonee Falls, Wisconsin: Record Research, 1996.

Whitburn, Joel. *Top Pop Singles 1955-99*. Menomonee Falls, Wisconsin, Record Research, 2000.

Whitburn, Joel. *Top R & B Singles 1942-95*. Menomonee Falls, Wisconsin, Record Research, 1996.

BILLBOARD magazine chart data is c/o **Joel Whitburn**'s Record Research Books. These music reference books document the artists and their records that hit *Billboard*'s singles and albums charts – Pop, R & B, Country, Adult Contemporary, & Rock Tracks – and provide essential data for entertainment professionals as well as music worldwide.

JOEL WHITBURN'S Record Research Center is a thriving family-run industry. Joel's daughter KIM BLOXDORF has been very helpful to us in evolving our *Gold Rush*. You can order their books via their handy brochure. Or call direct:

RECORD RESEARCH INC.
PO Box 200
Menomonee Falls, Wisconsin 53052-0200
Phone: (268) 251-5408
Fax: (268) 251-9452
E-Mail: record@execpc.com
Home Page: http://www.recordresearch .com

White, Timothy. *Catch a Fire: The Life of Bob Marley*. New York: Henry Holt, 1983 [undated ed. 1996].

Wielick, Han. *Elvis Presley: Koning van d' Rock N' Roll*. Maastricht, Netherlands, 1960. [Dutch].

Wilson, Mary. *Dreamgirl & Supreme Faith: My Life As a Supreme*. New York: Cooper Square Press, 1996.

Yogi, Maharishi Mahesh. *Transcendental Meditation*, with Jack Forem. New York: Dutton, 1974.

Zollo, Paul. *Songwriters and Songwriting*. Cincinnati, Ohio: Writer's Digest Books, 1989.

Photo Credits

Book: **2:** Photofest, c/o Howard Mandelbaum; **4:** Photofest, c/o Eric Spilker; **6:** Photofest; **7:** Photofest, c/o Eric Spilker; **12:** Bill Griggs Collection; **14 (right):** Photofest; **14 (bottom):** Photofest; **20 (left):** Photofest; **20 (right):** Photofest; **25:** Photofest; **39:** Photofest; **40:** Bill Griggs Collection; **42:** Photofest, c/o Pierre Montel; **44:** Photofest; **46:** c/o Bill Haley & Jolly Joyce; **49:** Photofest; **55:** Photofest; **56:** Photofest; **71:** c/o Bob Keane & Bryan Thomas, 2000; **74:** c/o Mrs. Ella Holley; **75:** Photofest, c/o Howard Mandelbaum; **79:** Columbia, Phuong Baum & Don Hunstein; **80:** Photofest, c/o Ron Mandelbaum; **82:** Photofest; **85:** Photofest, c/o Eric Spilker; **90:** Bill Griggs Collection; **103:** Photofest, c/o Ed McGuire; **105:** Bill Griggs Collection; **109:** Bill Griggs Collection; **111:** Photofest, c/o Eric Spilker; **112:** Photofest; **116:** Photofest; **118:** c/o Derek Taylor & Beach Boys' Fan Club; **120:** c/o MD Photo Archives, 1989; **123:** Photofest, c/o Eric Spilker; **130:** Bill Griggs Collection; **138:** Photofest; **140:** Photofest; **143:** MD Photo Archives, c/o Scandore/Shayne; **144:** Photofest; **148:** Photofest; **156:** Photofest; **174:** Photofest, c/o Eric Spilker; **203:** Photofest, c/o Howard Mandelbaum; **204:** MD Photo Archives, c/o Perenchio/Merrick; **217:** Photofest; **218:** Photofest; **229:** Photofest; **238:** Photofest; **241:** Photofest; **246:** Photofest; **248:** Photofest; **288:** Photofest; **291:** Photofest; **292:** Photofest, c/o Howard Manelbaum; **293:** Photofest; **296:** Photofest; **301:** Photofest; **305:** MCA, c/o Art Kane; **320 (left):** Photofest; **320 (right):** Photofest; **322:** Photofest, c/o Ron Mandelbaum; **328:** Photofest, c/o Ed McGuire; **359:** Photofest; **364 (left):** Photofest; **364 (right):** Photofest; **368:** Photofest; **372:** Photofest; **375:** Photofest; **382:** Photofest; **388:** Photofest; **397:** Photofest; **412:** Photofest; **423:** Photofest; **426:** Photofest; **429:** Photofest; **430 (left):** Photofest; **430 (top right):** Photofest; **430 (bottom right):** Photofest; **431:** MD Photo Archives, c/o Derek Taylor & Beach Boys' Fan Club; **434:** Photofest; **435:** Columbia, c/o Lo-Anne Rios Kong & Ray Perlmutter; **441:** Photofest, c/o Ron Mandelbaum; **444:** Photofest; **446:** Photofest; **458:** Photofest; **476:** Photofest; **478:** Photofest; **481:** Photofest; **484 (top left):** Photofest; **484 (bottom left):** Photofest; **484 (top right):** Photofest; **484: (bottom right):** Photofest; **495 (left):** Photofest; **495 (right):** Photofest; **504:** Photofest; **516:** Photofest; **523:** Photofest; **533:** Photofest; **534 (left):** Photofest; **534 (right):** Photofest; **536:** Photofest; **538:** Photofest; **540:** Photofest; **544 (top left):** Photofest; **544 (bottom left):** Photofest; **544 (top right):** Photofest; **544 (center right):** Photofest; **544 (bottom right):** Photofest; **546:** Photofest; **551 (top left):** Photofest; **551 (center left):** Arista, c/o Sandie Smith and Michael Lavine; **556:** Photofest; **564:** Photofest; **566:** Photofest; **595:** Photofest; **597:** Photofest; **598:** Photofest; **602:** Photofest; **603:** MD Photo Archives, c/o Bobby Vee & the Vees. **654:** Photofest; **657:** Photofest; **659:** Photofest; **660:** Photofest; **667:** Photofest; **668:** Photofest; **676:** Photofest; **682:** Jeremy Dean.

Niner Nuggets: **605:** Ashanti: Photofest; Bennett & Miller: Columbia, c/o Don Hunstein; Fleetwood Mac: Photofest; Aretha Franklin: Photofest; Earth, Wind, & Fire: Columbia, c/o Roy Perlmutter; Slash: Photofest; Donovan: Columbia, c/o Don Hunstein and Sandy Speiser; Jones & Wynette: Photofest; Janis Ian: Columbia, c/o Art Maillet. **606:** Dave Matthews: MD Photo Archives; Creed: Photofest; Patti LaBelle: MCA, c/o Howie & Randee St. Nicholas; Huey Lewis: Photofest; Loggins & Messina: Columbia, c/o Art Maillet; Melissa Manchester: Arista, c/o Sandie Smith & Randee St. Nicholas; Haggard & Nelson: Photofest; Oak Ridge Boys: Photofest; Santana: Photofest. **607:** Live: c/o Radioactive & Paul Harris; Gwen Stefani: Photofest; Spice Girls: Photofest; Rick Springfield: Columbia, c/o Don Hunstein; Staples Singers: Columbia, c/o Don Hunstein; Statler Brothers: Columbia, c/o Don Hunstein; Stray Cats: Photofest; Yardbirds: Columbia, c/o Hank Parker; Ritchie Valens: Bob Keane. **608:** Shania Twain: Photofest; Rod Stewart: Photofest; Reba McEntire: Photofest; Elvis Costello: Columbia, c/o Art Maillet; Buddy Morrow, Columbia, c/o Don Hunstein; Gary Garritan: c/o Gary Garritan; Ed Cowling, Maury Dean & Bob Baldori: 'Big Bopper' Brady & Jack 'Bear' Berry; Ted Nugent: Columbia, c/o Roy Perlmutter; John Kay: Photofest. **609:** Dick & Dee Dee: Photofest; Chuck Berry: Photofest; Sara McLachlan: Arista, c/o Sandie Smith; Hollies: Columbia, c/o CRPS; Statue, Louis 'Satchmo' Armstrong Park, New Orleans: Todean Photo; Janis Joplin's Junior High School: MD Photo Archives; Nine Days: MD Photo Archives; Jefferson Starship: Photofest; James Brown and Rod Stewart: Photofest. **610:** Buddy Holly Statue: MD Photo Archives; Johnny Nash: Columbia, c/o Don Hunstein; Buddy Holly/Crickets: Photofest; Ka'au Crater Boys: c/o Roy Sakuma; Billy Joel: Photofest; Jimmie Rodgers II: c/o Tony Gallagher; Bobby Vee/Sha Na Na: Photofest; Conway Twitty: Photofest; Keith Richard and Mick Jagger: Photofest. **611:** Crickets: Photofest; Gramophone/Graphophone: MD Photo Archives; Paul McCartney: Photofest; Aaron Copland & Benny Goodman: Columbia, c/o Don Hunstein; Bill Monroe: Photofest; Elvis Presley: Bill Griggs Collection; Eddie Money: Columbia, c/o Art Maillet; Sonny Curtis & Jerry Allison: MD Photo Archives; Carter Family: Columbia, c/o Don Hunstein. **612:** Bob Dylan: Columbia, c/o LoAnne Rios Kong & Don Hunstein; Dion: Columbia, c/o Don Hunstein; Ritchie Valens: c/o Bob Keane; Stevie Wonder: Photofest; Ramsey Lewis: Columbia, c/o Don Hunstein; Carlos Santana & Keith Richard: Columbia, c/o Art Maillet; B. B. King: Photofest, c/o Howard Mandelbaum; Stonewall Jackson: Columbia, c/o Don Hunstein; Willie Nelson: Columbia. c/o Art Maillet. **613:** Keith Richard & Mick Jagger: Photofest; Whitney Houston: Arista, c/o Diana Lixenberg & Sandie Smith; Little Richard & Tanya Tucker: Photofest; Randy Starr: c/o Randy Starr and George Nettleton; Bobby Fuller IV: c/o Bill Griggs; Barry Manilow: Arista, c/o Carl Studna & Sandie Smith; Def Leppard: Photofest; Blues Traveler: Photofest; Dr. Dre: Photofest; Rick Nelson: c/o Tim Bazzett. **614:** Guns N' Roses: Photofest; N'Sync: Photofest; Pink: Photofest; Kid Rock: Photofest; Stone Temple Pilots: Photofest; Barenaked Ladies: Photofest; Black Crowes: Photofest; Counting Crows: Photofest; Goo Goo Dolls: Photofest.

Insert One: **1-1:** John McCormack: Photofest; Frankie Laine & Mitch Miller: Columbia, c/o Don Hunstein; Duke Ellington: Photofest; Annette [Funicello] & Frankie Avalon: Photofest, c/o Howard Mandelbaum; Buddy Holly and the Crickets: Photofest. **1-2:** The Platters: c/o Bill Griggs Collection; 'Fats' Domino: Photofest; Johnny Cash: Columbia, c/o Lo-Anne Rios Kong and Don Hunstein; Jerry Lee Lewis: c/o Bill Griggs Collection; Paul Anka: Photofest; Pat Boone: c/o Bill Griggs Collection. **1-3:** Elvis Presley: Photofest; Little Richard: Photofest; Johnnie Ray: Columbia, c/o Don Hunstein; Connie Francis: c/o Bill Griggs Collection; Ritchie Valens & Donna: c/o Bob Keane & Bryan Thomas; The Big Bopper: c/o Bill Griggs Collection. **1-4:** Patti Page: Photofest; Eddie Cochran: Photofest; Gene Vincent: Photofest; Wilson Pickett: Photofest; Cab Calloway: Columbia, c/o Sandy Speiser; Dick Clark: Photofest. **1-5:** Sam Cooke: Photofest; Alice Cooper & Johnny Mathis: Photofest; Carole King: Photofest; John Lee Hooker: Photofest; Johnny Horton: Columbia, c/o LoAnne Rios Kong & Don Hunstein; Buddy Holly: Photofest. **1-6:** Crickets: c/o Mrs. Ella Holley; The Crystals: Photofest; Bo Diddley: Photofest; Jerry Lee Lewis: MD Photo Archives; Neil Sedaka: Photofest; Philadelphia street: MD Photo Archives. **1-7:** Annette: Photofest, c/o Eric Spilker; Jan & Dean: Photofest; Beach Boys: c/o Derek Taylor & Beach Boys' Fan Club; Roger Miller: Photofest; Ricky Nelson: Photofest, c/o Maury Foladare; The Four Seasons: Photofest. **1-8:** Del Shannon, c/o Bill Griggs Collection; Roy Orbison, Bruce Springsteen, Tom Waits & Elvis Costello: Photofest; Roy Orbison: Photofest; Gene Pitney (top right): Photofest; Gene Pitney: c/o Bill Griggs Collection. **1-9:** Supremes: Photofest; Temptations: Photofest; Otis Redding: c/o Phil Walden Managment; Marvin Gaye: Photofest; Tina Turner & Mick Jagger: Photofest; Aretha Franklin: Arista, c/o Sandie Smith. **1-10:** Tommy Roe: Photofest; Sun Recording Studio: MD Photo Archives; Stevie Wonder: Photofest; Ricky Nelson: Photofest; Bob Dylan: Photofest; Johnny Cash: Photofest. **1-11:** Beatles: Photofest; Beatles: Photofest; Searchers: Photofest; Herman & Gary Lewis: Photofest; George Harrison: Photofest; Paul Revere: Photofest. **1-12:** Beach Boys: c/o Derek Taylor & the Beach Boys' Fan Club; Pearl Jam: Photofest; Marty Robbins: Photofest; Jan & Dean: Photofest; Jimi Hendrix: Photofest; The Byrds: c/o Perenchio Publicity. **1-13:** Jim Morrison: Photofest; Ray Manzarek: Photofest; Sly & the Family Stone: Columbia, c/o Sandy Speiser; Jimi Hendrix: Photofest; Janis Joplin (as child): Photofest; Janis Joplin: Photofest. **1-14:** Linda Ronstadt: Photofest; Glen Campbell: c/o Glen Campbell & International Fan Club; Gerry & the Pacemakers: Photofest, c/o Eric Spilker; Bobby Fuller IV: c/o Bill Griggs Collection; Dionne Warwick: Arista, c/o Sandie Smith. **1-15:** John Lennon & Mick Jagger: Photofest; Ray Charles: Photofest; Mamas & Papas: Photofest; Joni Mitchell: Photofest, c/o Eric Spilker; Paul Simon: Photofest; Righteous Brothers: c/o Perenchio. **1-16:** Rod Stewart: Photofest; Neil Diamond: Photofest; Van Morrison: Photofest; James Taylor: Photofest; Bee Gees: Photofest; Sonny & Cher: Photofest.

Insert Two: **2-1:** James Dean: Photofest; Gracie Slick: Photofest; Harry Belafonte: Photofest; The Cars: Photofest; Allen Ginsberg: Columbia, c/o Don Hunstein; Stevie Nicks: Photofest, c/o Howard Mandelbaum. **2-2:** Amy Grant: Photofest; Bob Seger: Photofest; Eric Clapton: Photofest; The [Young] Rascals: Photofest; John Denver: Photofest; Jim Croce: Photofest. **2-3:** Hall & Oates: Photofest; Elton John: Photofest; Carly Simon: Photofest; Gary Puckett and the Union Gap: Photofest; Jimmy Buffett: Photofest; Foreigner: Photofest. **2-4:** The Who: MCA, c/o Art Kane & Howie; Tina Turner: Photofest; Metallica: Photofest; Black Sabbath: Photofest; Journey: Photofest; Iron Maiden: Photofest. **2-5:** The Police: Photofest; Alice Cooper & Meat Loaf: Photofest; Iggy Pop: Photofest; Neil Young: Photofest; Bruce Springsteen: Photofest; Bon Jovi: Photofest. **2-6:** Aerosmith: Photofest; Elvis Presley: Photofest; Tom Petty and the Heartbreakers: Photofest; Patti Smith: Arista, c/o Sandie Smith; Steve Miller: Photofest; Carlos Santana: Photofest. **2-7:** Billy Joel: Photofest; Don McLean: Photofest; Three Dog Night: Photofest; Olivia Newton-John: Photofest; Rev. Al Green: Photofest; Cliff Richard: Columbia, c/o Phuong Baum & Don Hunstein. **2-8:** Debbie Harry: Photofest; Eurythmics: Arista, c/o Sandie Smith & Anoushka Fisz; Fleetwood Mac: Photofest; Eagles: Photofest; Blue Oyster Cult: Photofest; Queen: Photofest. **2-9:** 'Weird Al' Yankovic:

Cover and Glossy Insert Credits: **Jeremy Dean**

Lyric Permission Credits

Sonny Curtis - "The Real Buddy Holly Story"

John Hampson & Brian Desveaux/Nine Days - "Absolutely (Story of a Girl)"

Index

Your *Gold Rush* Index is easy to use. Look up the song titles and the artists/performers alphabetically. Naturally, we generally eliminate articles "a," "an," and "the" from song titles. In a very few cases, when the title looks awkward, we include it, alphabetically, in the order of the first word after the article. Examples? "The Way," by Fastball (not "Way"), is under the letter W. "The Long and Winding Road" is under L, because "Long and Winding Road" seems a little strange. Index items in italics are probably *album titles* or *movie titles* in our *Rockflix* chapter. A slash [/] often indicates more artist information. Due to a publisher's deadline for this improved and revamped Index, once in a blue moon an occasional oversight may occur. Under the 'Wailers,' Bob Marley's famous Jamaican Reggae group, we list the lead singer's name for easy reference — Wailers/Bob Marley 421 (for instance). Numbers after the names correspond to the page numbers which feature them. Speaking of numbers, let's begin — even before the letter **A,** with a few selected song titles which start with numerals. (Many of these you'll also see in the "A to Z" index.) Page numbers in *italics* indicate photograph. Photos in the two 16-page glossy inserts are indicated by '1-4' (1st insert, 4th page) or '2-16' (2nd insert, 16th page), and so forth.

Please note: for songs ending in a numeral, like "1-2-3," — these words get a dash to set them off from the page numbers. We often also list other groups that artists have performed with, and we feature multiple artist references. *Gold Rush* is faithfully cross-indexed, for your pleasure in looking up your favorite songs and artists.

Happy [Maxwell] Hunting in your search to find 38 of your all-time Top 40. If we missed any, just contact us at maxwellhunter.aol.com for the next edition (who knows, if you wish, *your* name just might end up as a reference, in our next new Index). Rock on.

Symbols

"1-2-3" — 192
"100 Pounds of Clay" 138
10,000 Maniacs 530
"18 Yellow Roses" 105
1910 Fruitgum Company 219
"19th Nervous Breakdown" 174
"2 = 2 = ?" 209
2 Live Crew 569
2 Pac [Tu-Pac Shakur] 461, 551
"25 or 6 Till 4" — 296
"26 Miles" 133
"59th Street Bridge Song" 199
"7 O'Clock News/Silent Night" 209
"96 Tears" 193
98 Degrees 577
"99 Luftballons" 451

A

Aaliyah [Haughton] 585
ABBA 286, 424
"ABC" 161
"Abdul Abulbul Amir" 210
Abdul, Paula 532
"Abraham, Martin, & John" 243
"Absolutely (Story of a Girl)" 543, 572
AC/DC 276, 347, 436, 466
Ace, Johnny 252

Ace of Base 545
"Act Naturally" 268
Acuff, Roy 26, 419, 485
Adam Ant 447
Adams, Bryan 390, 476, 543, 546, *2-12*
Adams, Yolanda 525
Adkins, Jim 599
Adkins, Trace 514
Adderley, Cannonball 301, 319
Addrisi Brothers 29
"Adia" 569
Adler, Larry 234
Ad-Libs 309
Aerosmith 145, 380, 448, 469, 541, 569, 593, *2-6*
"After the Fire Is Gone" 504
"After the Rain" 527
"Against the Wind" 359
Aguilera, Christina 223-25, 430, 447, 523, *540*, 570
"Ahab, the Arab" 165
"Ain't Gonna Kiss Ya" 142
"Ain't Got No Home" 57
"Ain't No Mountain High Enough" 166
"Ain't It Funny" 588
"Ain't That Lovin' You Baby" 239
Air Supply 474
"Air That I Breathe" 182
Alabama 486, 504, *516*, 517, 576
"Alabama Getaway" 510
Alan Parsons Project 317
Albert, Morris 364, 415
Album Art 101, 224, 453
Alderman, Elvis 'Tony' 485
Ali, Muhammad 353, 403, 420, 457.
Alice Cooper 369, 386
Alice in Chains/Layne Staley 453-54, 557
"All Alone Am I" 140
"All Along the Watchtower" 244
"All American Boy" 59
"All Day and All of the Night" 176
All-4-One 514, 556.
"All I Could Do Was Cry" 139
"All I Have to Do Is Dream" 98, 411

"All I Really Want to Do" 200
"All I Wanna Do" 546
"All I Want" 454
"All My Ex's Live in Texas" 501
"All My Love" 373
"All My Rowdy Friends Are Comin' Over Tonight" 513
"All Right Now" 374
"All Shook Up" 220
"All Star" 585
"All the Gold in California" 510
"All the Small Things" 579
"All the Young Dudes" 383
"All Those Years Ago" 340
Allen, Duane/Oak Ridge Boys 487-88
Allen, Mitch/SR-71 — 554
Allen, Rick/Def Leppard 375
Allen, Steve 89, 218, 489
"Allentown" 348
Allison, Jerry/Crickets 62, 231, 299, 327, 366-67, 422, 435, 446, 474, 499, 563, 570, *1-1, 1-6, 2-16*
Allison, Mose 295
Allman Brothers 294, 356, 437, 472, 597, *597*
Allsup, Tommy/Crickets 299, 327, 419
Almost Famous 536
"Almost Persuaded" 491
"Aloha Oe" 114, 415
"Alone Again, Naturally" 277
"Alone At Last" 312
"Along Came Jones" 55
"Along Comes Mary" 297
Alpert, Herb/Tijuana Brass 257, 297, 423, 442
"Already Gone" 406
"Always on My Mind" 498
"Amanda" 310
"Amapola" 415
"Amarillo by Morning" 501
"Amazing Grace" 10-11
The Amazing Mustang Boy
"Amen" 270
America 294
"America" 203
"America the Beautiful" 213, 281

***Doors*:** *(l-r) Jim Morrison, John Densmore, seated Ray Manzarek and Robby Krieger*

D

Dick Clark and Ella Fitzgerald

G

The Crickets l-r: Jerry Allison, Buddy Holly and Joe B. Mauldin

I

Elvis Presley

P

The Who

ROCK & ROLL HALL OF FAME INDUCTEES

To be selected for the Rock and Roll Hall of Fame, an artist must wait 25 years from the date of his/her first recording efforts. Technically, many 'Non-Performers' actually sang hits, like Carole King or Eddie Holland - but their major contribution has been in other areas, like, in their cases, songwriting.

1986 (Debut Year)

Artists:
Chuck Berry
Everly Brothers
James Brown
Ray Charles
Sam Cooke
Antoine 'Fats' Domino
Buddy Holly
Jerry Lee Lewis
Little Richard
Elvis Presley
Early Influences:
Robert Johnson, Jimmie
Rodgers [I], & Jimmy Yancey
Non-Performers:
Alan Freed & Sam Phillips

1987

Artists:
The Coasters
Eddie Cochran
Bo Diddley
Aretha Franklin
Marvin Gaye
Bill Haley
B.B. King
Clyde McPhatter
Ricky Nelson
Roy Orbison
Carl Perkins
William 'Smokey'
   Robinson
Big Joe Turner
Muddy Waters
Jackie Wilson
Early Influences:
Louis Jordan, T-Bone Walker,
& Hank Williams, Sr.
Non-Performers:
Leonard Chess, Ahmet
Ertegun, Jerry Lieber/
Mike Stoller, & Jerry Wexler

1988

Artists:
The Beach Boys
The Beatles
The Drifters
Bob Dylan
The Supremes
Early Influences:
Woody Guthrie & Huddie
Ledbetter ['Leadbelly']
Non-Performers:
Berry Gordy, Jr.

1989

Artists:
Dion [DiMucci]
Otis Redding
The Rolling Stones
The Temptations
Stevie Wonder
Early Influences:
The Ink Spots, Bessie
Smith, & The Soul Stirrers
Non-Performers:
Phil Spector

1990

Artists:
Hank Ballard
Bobby Darin
The Four Seasons
Four Tops
The Kinks
The Platters
Simon & Garfunkel
The Who
Early Influences:
Louis 'Satchmo'
Armstrong, Charlie
Christian, & Ma Rainey
Non-Performers:
Gerry Goffin/Carole King,
Lamont Dozier, Brian &
Eddie Holland

1991

Artists:
LaVern Baker
The Byrds
John Lee Hooker
The Impressions
Wilson Pickett
Jimmy Reed
Ike & Tina Turner
Early Influences:
Howlin' Wolf
Non-Performers:
Dave Bartholomew &
Ralph Bass

1992

Artists:
Bobby 'Blue' Bland
Booker T. & the MG's
Johnny Cash
Jimi Hendrix Experience
The Isley Brothers
Sam & Dave
The Yardbirds
Early Influences:
Elmore James &
Professor Longhair
Non-Performers:
Leo Fender, Doc Pomus, &
Bill Graham

1993

Artists:
Ruth Brown
Cream
Creedence Clearwater
   Revival
The Doors
Etta James
Frankie Lymon & Teenagers
Van Morrison
Sly & the Family Stone
Early Influences:
Dinah Washington
Non-Performers:
Dick Clark & Milt Gabler

1994

Artists:
The Animals
The Band
Duane Eddy
Grateful Dead
Elton John
John Lennon
Bob Marley
Rod Stewart
Early Influences:
Willie Dixon
Non-Performers:
Johnny Otis

1995

Artists:
Allman Brothers Band
Al Green
Janis Joplin
Martha & the Vandellas
Neil Young
Frank Zappa
Led Zeppelin
Early Influences:
The Orioles
Non-Performers:
Paul Ackerman

1996

Artists:
David Bowie
Jefferson Airplane
Little Willie John
Gladys Knight & the Pips
Pink Floyd
The Shirelles
The Velvet Underground
Early Influences:
Pete Seeger
Non-Performers:
Tom Donohue

1997

Artists:
Bee Gees
Buffalo Springfield
Crosby, Stills & Nash
The Jackson Five
Joni Mitchell
Parliament/Funkadelic
The [Young] Rascals

Early Influences:
Mahalia Jackson &
Bill Monroe
Non-Performers:
Syd Nathan

1998

Artists:
Eagles
Fleetwood Mac
The Mamas & Papas
Lloyd Price
[Carlos] Santana
Gene Vincent
Early Influences:
Jelly Roll Morton
Non-Performers:
Allen Toussaint

1999

Artists:
Billy Joel
Curtis Mayfield
Paul McCartney
Dusty Springfield
Bruce Springsteen
Staple Singers
Del Shannon
Early Influences:
Bob Wills & Texas Playboys
& Charles Brown
Non-Performers:
George Martin

*For Millennium III, a new
category was added -
Sidemen - for musicians who
backed the great stars.*

2000

Artists:
Eric Clapton
Earth, Wind & Fire
The Lovin' Spoonful
The Moonglows
Bonnie Raitt
James Taylor
Sidemen:
Hal Blaine, James Jamerson,
Scotty Moore, & Earl Parker
Early Influences:
Nat 'King' Cole &
Billie Holiday

Non-Performers:
Clive Davis

2001

Artists:
Aerosmith
Solomon Burke
The Flamingos
Michael Jackson
Queen
Paul Simon
Steely Dan
Ritchie Valens
Sidemen:
James Burton &
Johnnie Johnson
Early Influences:
None selected

2002

Artists:
Isaac Hayes
Brenda Lee
Tom Petty & the
Heartbreakers
Gene Pitney
The Ramones
The Talking Heads
Sidemen:
Chet Atkins
Early Influences:
None selected
Non-Performers:
Jim Stewart

2003

Artists:
AC/DC
Clash
Elvis Costello &
Attractions
Police
Righteous Brothers
Sidemen:
Floyd Cramer, Benny
Benjamin, and Steve Douglas
Non-Performers:
Mo Ostin

Made in the USA
Monee, IL
27 April 2022